STRANGE AMAZING AND MYSTERIOUS PLACES

First published 1993 by Collins Publishers San Francisco
1160 Battery Street, San Francisco, California 94111

Copyright © 1993 Collins Publishers San Francisco
Introduction copyright © 1993 William S. Burroughs

Library of Congress Cataloging-in-Publication Data
Marshall, Richard
Strange, amazing and mysterious places/introduction by William S. Burroughs;
essays by Richard Marshall
p.   cm.
Includes bibliographical reference.
ISBN 0-00-255109-8

STRANGE AMAZING AND MYSTERIOUS PLACES

Introduction by William S. Burroughs
Essays by Richard Marshall

CollinsPublishersSanFrancisco
A Division of HarperCollins*Publishers*

TABLE OF CONTENTS

Page 1:
Meteora, Greece. *Photo by Geoffrey C. Clifford*

Pages 2–3:
Easter Island, Chile. *Photo by Bob Sacha*

Left:
Swayambhunath, Nepal. *Photo by William Neill/Swanstock*

INTRODUCTION

Every place has a spirit: it may be good, it may be bad, it can be restful as eternity, or it can be jarring and hideous as a vicious brawl. The place spirit can inhabit a block, a house, a town, a valley; but the nature of these spirits is that they *remain*, while we petty human travellers come and go.

There is a block in New York City, on Prince Street between Mulberry and Elizabeth Streets, in the heart of Little Italy, just around the corner from where I used to live on the Bowery. A red brick parochial school from the turn of the century stands on one side, and on the other side there is an ancient stone wall, twelve feet high, enclosing the grounds of an old Catholic cathedral and running the full length of the block. I have rarely traversed this block without witnessing some jarring, discordant occurrence, a shabby bum screaming demented

Peter Menzel

curses at passersby: *"Don't looka me!"* Something unspeakably nasty lives there, some spirit from New York's earliest days—centuries old, older than the cathedral, perhaps older than Christ. You can feel it as soon as you set foot there, and you can feel it drop away as you leave.

India . . . pilgrims getting ready to dunk themselves into the Ganges. The pilgrims, naked and shameless, pose an insouciant affront to all the dreary Gods of Hygiene, who will scream out as the pilgrims wade into the living waters, "Oh, what a rash and unsanitary deed is this!" But the Ganges pilgrims are protected by purity of spirit, by a faith that can move mountains and protect them from the insidious attack of germs, bacteria, virus. Sickness cannot enter without chinks, and faith can seal the chinks, like God's own medicine.

The Kumbha Mela festival . . . a Saddu long-hair, up to his knees in the irridescent river. We see only his outline, the sunset across the river, city lights. Boats, tethered to stakes driven into the river bottom, show how shallow the water is, and how timeless the scene. Benares, India . . . raft in a gray milky light, where water and air smudge to delineate the detritus that litters the ghostly raft, the shockingly headless mannequin, the poised figure that has risen from the mist to animate a stylized posture.

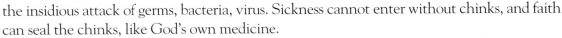

Jose Azel/Aurora

Mali . . . sand symbols. Beautifully balanced and potentious. The sand is like gold dust. You can see the meaning flicker and shift, from one symbol to another, moving towards a pattern of which we possess only the smallest fragment. Finger in the sand . . . don't ask questions. The finger knows, moving in the sand. Two men, one old and wrinkled, the other doing something with his hands; he is bent over, his back melting into a slab of rock. A bloodstained altar—like a side of beef on a shelf, dripping blood—is ready to receive the heart of a black sheep so the old man can read the steaming entrails. A withered old hag nearby, bent over, in darkness palpable as black paint.

Ice Floes, Antarctica . . . the ice cut clear and sharp as marble, and as permanent. Like the rock of Gibraltar in the Prudential Insurance ad, or was it the Bank of England? Tiny figures, people, penguins . . . the picture does have an advertising look, and it doesn't feel cold. . . . I recall some account of hot springs in the Antarctic, with strange, degenerate, diseased people living around the waters.

Tui De Roy

Galen Rowell/Mountain Light

Mount Kailas . . . rock-strewn prayer-cloths in bright colors under a blue sky, so intense it aches. The rocks are alive with scattered colors, red and blue, and the cloth is woven from rock; thin mountain air, like death in the throat, cold and blue as liquid air. Tibet . . . ghost traps of twigs and bright painted bits of cloth, little ghost whips flapping in the winds.

Easter Island . . . when I took ayahuasca in Pucallpa, Peru, the first effect was a number of South Pacific scenes and a clear picture of the Easter Island sculptures. The color blue shading from purple to light blue. Easter Island has been described as the loneliest place in the world —

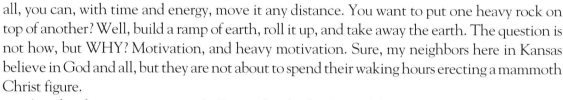

not only for its remote location, but for the absence that left these huge statues, and the unknown motivations that put them there.

The present population of Easter Island is about 2,000 people, a good percentage of them living off the tourists. At one time, the population was about 7,000 . . . what happened? War. And what were they fighting about? Why were the statues erected? The history of Easter Island is mostly questions. Carved wooden ancestor-sculptures show subjects suffering terminal starvations, so one assumes they arrived in that state.

As to how they moved the statues about, one does not need to evoke anti-gravity: pry . . . wedge . . . pry. . . . If you can move it at

Bob Sacha

all, you can, with time and energy, move it any distance. You want to put one heavy rock on top of another? Well, build a ramp of earth, roll it up, and take away the earth. The question is not how, but WHY? Motivation, and heavy motivation. Sure, my neighbors here in Kansas believe in God and all, but they are not about to spend their waking hours erecting a mammoth Christ figure.

Another factor is manpower. In Egypt, they had unlimited slave labor, but on Easter Island there was a limited population, and when the slaves outnumber the masters. . . . So it must have been a community project, and the spirit that animated the statuary is gone, leaving an enigmatic and specific absence. Something very definite and ominous happened here. One can see the huge statues' eyes go blank and meaningless.

There is a river in Egyptian mythology called the Duad; it is fed by all the filth of man's sojourn on the planet. All pilgrims must traverse the Duad to reach the Western Lands, a rather precarious Egyptian paradise (one can be evicted at any time, if one's mummy falls into disrepair).

P. Maitre & Y. Gellie - Odyssey/Matrix

Jordan . . . this is the most sinister and mysterious picture of them all: a temple—for what creature?—built into a living rock, that looks like some cloyingly sweet confection for giants. The streets are dry stream beds, cut by time and wind and dust. The temple is tilting under the weight of the oozing rock, and the street leads down into darkness. Above the ancient street, a final blaze of light that concentrates darkness without illuminating. Look, how this caustic darkness undercuts the rock.

These are Dead Roads: empty and sad as the graves of dying people. The last Patagonians and the hairy Ainu mark their males' graves with an erect phallus, crudely carved from wood and painted with ocher . . . wind and dust . . . the markers are broken and scattered . . .

Flute music, squeaky, off-key, fades out in one last distant false note.

A youth looks out over a desert. On his t-shirt is ETERNITY in rainbow letters. He yawns: *Eternity yawning on the sands.*

—William S. Burroughs

But after all, who knows, and who can say whence it all came,
and how creation happened?   —*The Rig Veda'*

At the root of the word "mystery" is the Greek verb muein, *which means "to*
close the mouth." As if to suggest a mystery is something that can be seen, or
experienced, but never completely explained. Certainly this is true in trying to
understand the nature of a place. But mysteries often reveal their clues through
association and their links with other mysteries. The pyramids built by Egyptians
and Mayans are obviously connected, while the Western Wall and the Black
Hills disclose their sameness only after a subtle reading of the underlying role of
each place for its people. This book has its origins in the attempt to illuminate the
connections, in mythology and ecology, between many places.

The places in Origins are the landscapes that exist before stories. They are
the sources of myths and the rivers of becoming. They are the places where people
and gods find their beginning. Photo of Antarctica by Tui De Roy

Namib Desert, Namibia. Photo by Jim Brandenburg/Minden Pictures

THE GREAT EMPTINESS: NAMIB DESERT AND ANTARCTICA

Certain Christian mystics believed that God could only be properly described by negatives, for to assert anything positive about him was to imply a limitation. For those men and women, the void that represented God was fullness. For Buddhist mystics, emptiness is the supreme mark of all phenomena, and they name space as the fifth element, after earth, fire, air, and water. Space is the primary condition which allows the expression of the other four.

Antarctica. Photo by Tui De Roy

At the desolate ends of the earth there are places where seeming emptiness contains great splendor.
Where fire and water flood the element of space in landscapes of unimaginable extremes. In Antarctica,
ice is the supreme excess; in the Namib Desert, appalling heat and dryness. And though everything
in these places seems to conspire by cold or heat to make life barren of its great variety, they contain in
the arch of dune and drift, in the myriad forms of ice crystals and grains of sand as much wonder
as the mystic's luminous and overflowing void.

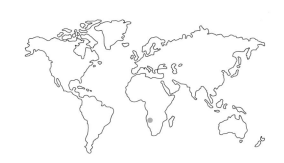

NAMIB DESERT, NAMIBIA

A cold sea current, turning north from the Antarctic, brushes the Namibian coast with a chilly hand. But for this Benguela current, summer temperatures in the Namib Desert might exceed even the 120°F they normally reach, and in winter the current can send temperatures plummeting to less than 60°F. Though it moderates the desert temperature, the ocean brings little moisture to Namibia's coastal plain, and the desert stretches for 1,200 miles from the north of the country to the south, an empty desolation of sand, shifting dunes, salt pans, and rocky outcrops that continues for a distance of about 100 miles from the shore to the edge of the Great Escarpment.

The northern part of the Namib, known as the Skeleton Coast, has recently been declared a national park. Here, lions sometimes prowl the beach to feed on stranded whales, as if to symbolize a meeting of wet and dry, heat and cold, like an image from some alchemical text. Herds of elephants and gazelle negotiate towering sand dunes, which, by a harmonic property of their shift-ing grains, sometimes seem to sing and roar, as if the earth had found a haunting voice here. The sound and light of the dunes dominate the Namib.

The desert sand is finer than snow and its curves and arches . . . are as graceful as the lines of running water. The dunes are always rhyth-mical and flowing in their forms; and for color the desert has nothing that surpasses them. In the early morning they are air-blue, reflecting the sky overhead; at noon they are pale lines of dazzling orange-colored light. From The Desert, *John C. Van Dyke.*

Despite the smooth exterior, there is treasure buried in the desert. In the Sperrgebiet (Ger-man for restricted area), a region lying along the coast north of the Orange River, vast numbers of gemstone-quality diamonds lie buried in the alluvial gravel, often beneath 50 feet of sand. They were first discovered in 1908, and at one time the Sperrgebiet accounted for 20% of the world's gem diamond production. Stories were once told here of people finding diamonds lying on the beach, stones washed out from the river's mouth.

The other treasures of the Namib are of a more modest nature. Of practical use is the narras plant, *Acanthosicyos horridus*. It sends 12-foot roots into the dry sand, searching for whatever molecules of water the Namib's 2-inch-per-year rainfall may have left behind, and manages to produce—miraculously—an edible gourd from this scant resource. Still more curious is the equally unattractive century plant, *Welwitschia mirabilis*, which survives solely on the moisture borne by the sea fogs that sometimes cover the desert. Its worn and straggling leaves stretch for yards across the desert, and some specimens are believed to be over a thousand years old.

Like the lichens of the Antarctic, the narras and century plants have found a way to express the delicate intricacy of a life in an environment stripped bare of almost everything that life normally requires. They are the true jewels of the desert, emblems of life's tenacity, and even more precious in their own way than the diamonds time has buried beneath the Namib waste.

Left:
Dunes imagined by the wind flow from shape to shape in the land of No One. The Namib, a 1,235-square-mile ocean of sand in the Tropic of Capricorn, is part of a vast landscape—and a country—rich in gold, nationalism, and ancient culture.
Photo by Nicolas DeVore III/Photographers/Aspen

Above:
Wall paintings found on the Skeleton Coast are believed to be over 25,000 years old. A stretch along the Northern Namib, the Skeleton Coast contains several archeological wonders. The people pictured here may be related to the Bantu or the San Bushmen—peoples who have long made Namibia their home.
Photo by Jim Brandenburg/Minden Pictures

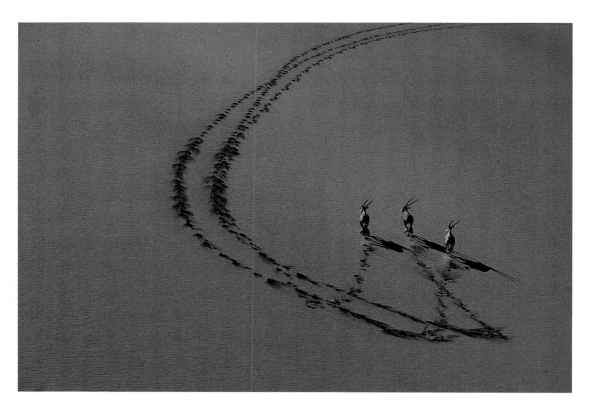

Above and right:

The Namib is a desert base for seabirds that flourish in places along the Namibian coast, particularly at Sandwich Harbor. Here pink flamingos with rose-colored wings fringed with black feathers feed in the shallows. Any moment they are likely to startle and take wing, wheeling off en masse. And when they do, in the words of the photographer Jim Brandenburg, "It's like fragments of a dream that scatter in the morning."

Oryx double back across a dune in the Namib. It is the ebb and flow of the desert heat that orchestrates the brown and orange colors in the sand, as well as the mostly pale colors of animals. It is also the heat that encourages a process of natural selection, or refinement, for animals that could not otherwise live in such a climate. The oryx of the Namib have an unusual circulatory system and a way of panting that cools the blood as it flows through the head. Lizards here raise themselves off the sand and run along on two legs, using one front and one back pad at a time.

Animal tracks in the dunes appear as a desert tapestry. The emptiness of the coast here was undisturbed until the 19th century, when the southwest coast of Africa became a target of European hegemony. The British, coming from Cape Colony, established a strategic harbor at Walvis Bay for their navy. Meanwhile, the Germans worked to control the interior of the country, attracted by an extraordinary wealth of minerals. *Photos by Jim Brandenburg/Minden Pictures*

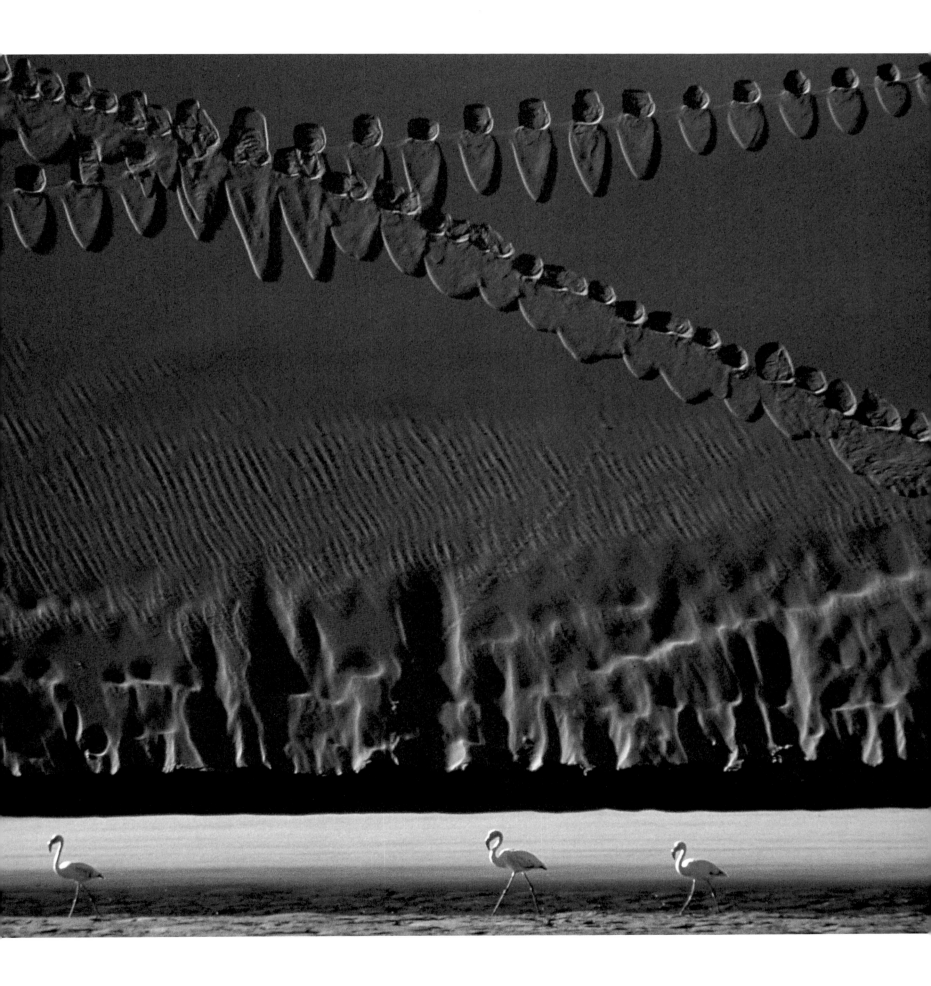

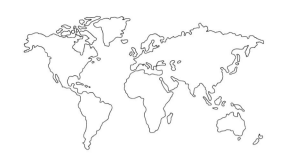

ANTARCTICA

The Antarctic continent is a profusion of simplicities. In the stark, year-dividing seasons of light and darkness the color of the continent is a simple abundant whiteness, a full-spectrum monochrome occasionally shot through with brilliant ice blues and greens, blindingly bright in sunlight or ghostly in the auroral dimness of the polar night. According to Admiral Richard E. Byrd, who spent five months in a hut under the Ross Ice Barrier in 1934, it was also a very quiet place.

The silence of this place is as real and solid as sound. . . . It seems to merge in and become part of the indescribable evenness, as do the cold and the dark and the relentless ticking of the clocks. This evenness fills the air with its mood of

unchangeableness; me at the table, bunk with me at ness in its ultimate

The substance 5.5 million square singular. Basically into various states and accounts for the world's fresh simplicity, this emental continent the farfetched and

it sits across from and gets into the night. This is timeless-meaning.

of the continent's miles is equally water, it is frozen of ice and snow, more than 60% of supply. Despite its stripped-down, el-has called forth elaborate exploits

of some of the world's great adventurers. By immersing himself alone in the polar absence, Byrd discovered "an exalted sense of identification—of oneness with the outer world which is partly mystical but also certainty."

This observation is similar to what Tantric Buddhists describe as the Great Emptiness—the union of emptiness and appearance. To those who attain such heightened states, Antarctica offers spectacular rewards. For above the white-on-white landscape, the sky can display a gorgeous, supernatural variety seen nowhere else. Admiral Byrd describes both the hallucinatory and transcendent qualities of the polar atmosphere.

On such a day I could swear that the instrument shelter was as big as an ocean liner. On one such day I saw the blank northeastern sky become filled with the most magnificent Barrier Coast I have ever seen, true in every line and faced with cliffs several thousand feet tall. A mirage of course. Yet a man who had never seen such things would have taken oath that it was real. The afternoon may be so clear that you dare not make a sound lest it fall in pieces. And on such a day I have seen the sky shatter like a broken goblet, and dissolve into iridescent tipsy fragments—ice-crystals falling across the face of the sun. And once in the golden downpour a slender column of platinum leaped up from the horizon, clean through the sun's core. A second luminous shadow formed horizontally through the sun making a perfect cross. Presently two miniature suns, one green and one yellow in color, flipped simultaneously to the ends of each arm. These are parhelia, the most dramatic of all refraction phenomena; nothing is lovelier. Quotes from **Alone** by Admiral Richard E. Byrd.

While the beauty of Antarctica's sky is unparalleled, the visible effects of the continent's weather are of immense importance to the world at large. At the Pole of Inaccessibility, Antarctic weather is a simple bitterness: the average annual temperature is -70°F, and ice-eroding winds regularly blow at 200 miles an hour. From the South Pole, glaciers and pack ice, vast mountains of fresh water, flotillas of icebergs venture into the south Atlantic, where they help to spawn the life-giving rains that bathe the globe. Thus the monochrome emptiness of this netherworld helps to nurture the color and variety of our local landscape.

Left and above:
All is quiet in the Bransfield Strait, which flows between the South Shetland Islands and the Antarctic Peninsula. The strait is named for a British captain, Edward Bransfield, who claimed the Shetlands for England in 1820. The islands' enormous commercial value lay in sealskin, and it was the seal trade that first led to scientific and commercial explorations of the region.

An iceberg disintegrates near Elephant Island, off the Antarctic Peninsula. In an echo of human life, icebergs begin to die as soon as they are born. Melting begins while the ice mass remains within an ice shelf, then accelerates as wind, salt, and mechanical stress come into play. To the trained eye, the changing shapes of each iceberg reveal much about its origins and about its journey. Though most of Antarctica is now clearly mapped and catalogued, it remains forever remote in the imagination. Its colors and shapes drift outside normal conceptions of landscape toward an abstract realm of warped scale and shattered perspectives. *Photos by Tui De Roy*

Left:
The cycle of the ice pack is one of nature's most extraordinary rituals and the major influence on the earth's climate. In late January in the Weddell Sea, the diminished ice pack is at the end of its annual cycle. At its height in September, the pack extends as far as 20 million square kilometers, then, slowly, "retrogradation" reduces it to as little as 4 million square kilometers. Thus, in an average cycle, nearly 16 million square kilometers of sea ice freeze, then melt. *Photo by Chris Rainier/Photographers/Aspen*

Top:
In between the half year of only darkness and the half year of only daylight there is the polar twilight, forbidding yet inviting, here giving an iceberg a ghostly outline. In the background, one can just make out the Antarctic Peninsula, which stretches north toward the South Shetland Islands, Drake Passage, and Cape Horn. Although Saudi Arabia gave up on the idea of towing icebergs north to provide fresh water to desert regions, the possibility lingers and its implementation hinges more on politics than mechanics. *Photo by Tui De Roy*

Bottom:
Chinstrap penguins go on holiday at a breeding colony on Deception Island. The Chinstraps, close cousins to the Adélie penguins, are the only breed of penguins in Antarctica still increasing—by more than tenfold in the last 25 years. Of the 17 species of penguin, 11 are found in Antarctica, and all those live on the ice pack. *Photo by Mark Jones*

Okavango River, Botswana. Photo by Frans Lanting/Minden Pictures

Waters of Life: Okavango River and Ganges River

Even before there was form or light, before the heavens were made, there was water. In the biblical Genesis account, water is the primordial substance. The Hindu tradition also accords primacy to water. Because water takes on the form of whatever contains it, it is an element in which form is potential but not realized. Thus, in a metaphysical sense, water is the protean mother of forms, just as, in a physical sense, it acts as mother by bringing things to life. The Ganges River—Mata Ganga, Mother Ganges—is seen by her followers as both spiritually and physically nurturing.

Ganges River, India. Photo by Chris Rainier/Photographers/Aspen

Botswana's Okavango River also inspires thoughts about the fundamental importance of water. It is the nation's principal river, and water has supreme importance for Botswana: in the nation's dominant language rain is called pula, and the word is used as both greeting and blessing, as the name of Botswana's currency, and on the national seal. The Okavango bestows life in a curious way: upon sand that is void of life, its waters deposit the soil they also nourish. Like the waters of Genesis, the waters of Okavango precede the land's formation.

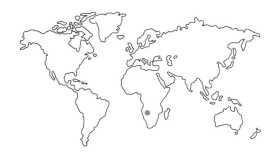

Okavango River, Botswana

Long-hoofed aquatic antelopes—sitatungas—tread floating beds of papyrus reeds; hippos wallow, crocodiles cruise, snake birds dart, and fish eagles swoop; night blooming water lilies gleam pale white by star light; and just a few feet below all this are the sands of the Kalahari Desert.

From the deepest part of the ocean to the highest peaks of the Himalayas, the earth's life-support zone is microscopically thin—even more shallow, relative to the body of the planet, than a pore in the skin of an orange. The rich abundance and variety of living things obscures how frail life's hold is, but in the Okavango Delta in northern Botswana the miracle is obvious. Here the river flows into the Kalahari and brings a bloom of life to a fan-shaped area larger than the state of Massachusetts.

The Okavango River originates a thousand miles from the delta in Angola's central mountains. Flowing southeast, it crosses a narrow strip of Namibia as it enters Botswana and winds its way through a fertile pan-handle for nearly sixty miles before it reaches a shallow de-pression cre-ated by the Gomare fault, where the river begins to braid into many shifting channels, creating the world's big-

gest inland delta before it disappears, 95% lost to erosion and the rest to the arid sands of the Great Thirst Land, the Kalahari. On its way to extinction, the river seasonally transports 350 billion cubic feet of water and 727,000 tons of salt, creating a thin organic carpet over the lifeless sand.

Along with streams, swamplike lakes, and lagoons, the delta supports seasonal savannah, forests of mopani trees and acacias, and clay pans that catch seasonal rainfall to provide waterholes for abundant wildlife. Africa's biggest herd of elephants and numerous predators—lions, wild dogs, hyenas—make this one of the richest and most primordial big game countries in Africa. Birds flock to the Okavango wetlands, too: pelicans, flamingos, egrets, and the endangered wattled crane all thrive here.

Although most of the Okavango Delta is protected by Botswana's enlight-ened conservation policies (a full 17% of the nation is preserved in national parks or game reserves), the life-giving waters are in demand elsewhere in the nation. One plan would dredge one of the delta's main channels, the Boro, to improve the flow of water to the diamond fields at Orapa and Lethakane, which currently depend on limited local water supplies. Advocates of the scheme point out that it would make use of the Okavango's water only after it had passed through the delta, but environmentalists fear that deepening the Boro channel would steal water from the adjoining seasonal wetlands.

With less than 5% of its land suitable for farming, Botswana's economic life's blood is the revenue from diamond and mineral exports. And diamond extraction demands water, just as the survival of the delta's birds, animals, fish, and plants demands it. Here, as elsewhere, water supports life in all its infinite refinements. From the thirst of a lion to the gleam of a diamond to the aspirations of the spirit, the river connects the realms of life into one continuous stream.

Inset:
Red lechwe prick up their ears in the delta, which provides fresh water and abundant food for a robust metropolis of animals and plants. Within the wetlands and woodlands that border the delta are some of Africa's last great free-roaming herds of cape buffalo, antelope, zebra, and approximately 60,000 elephants. *Photo by Nicholas DeVore III/Photographers/Aspen*

Above:
The Okavango River meanders in ever-widening coils. Fueled by mountain rains in March and April, the Okavango Delta extends for 60 miles and could contain Rhode Island, but only briefly; most of the river water and the water from local rainfall quickly evaporate, leaving life in the delta a seasonal proposition. *Photo by Nicholas DeVore III/Photographers/Aspen*

Following pages:
An elephant drinks from the Okavango in a scene that suggests a mythical era when gods and demigods first appeared out of stones and trees. Ironically, it was the tsetse fly—which carries sleeping sickness—that long protected the delta from humans. Modern insecticides have banished the fly, and now this place of beginnings may be coming to the end of its life cycle. *Photo by Frans Lanting/Minden Pictures*

Above:

In Benares, a Hindu offers his late afternoon prayers from a ghat at the edge of the Ganges. A river of names also flows around Benares: it is the legendary city of Kashi "the Luminous," "the City of Light along the River of Heaven." A British missionary called the city "grotesque, unnatural, forbidding," while another European found it to be the "heart of the world." The 108 Hindi names for the Ganges include "Carrying away fear," "Flowing like a stairway to heaven," "Purifier of the Three Worlds," and "Stimulator." *Photo by Raghu Rai*

GANGES RIVER, INDIA

The Ganges is a mother, and no child, they say, is too dirty to be embraced by its mother. Directly or indirectly, some 300 million people in India's northern plains owe their lives and their living to the water the Ganges brings down from the Himalayas.

At dusk the faithful launch little boats made of leaves onto the river, each carrying a cargo of rose petals and a burning candle. Pushed off from the steps of the ghat, the boats soon turn downstream, carrying with them prayers to Mother Ganges. As dawn breaks over Benares, and the riverside temples, palaces, and steps catch the first tints of pink and gold, the motley faithful gather by the river. Holy saddhus and fakirs, grandmothers and children wade waist deep into the water, scoop a handful and offer it back to the river that flows in heaven, on earth, and through the underworld for their ancestors and to the gods. Wrestlers in training stretch and test their muscles, slap their bellies, and go to it as the waterside steps begin to heat. White cows drink their morning fill in peace. The beggars are already here, the first funeral parties have come to the burning ghats, the naked devotees of Shiva have smeared themselves ghostly gray from head to toe in ashes, and the goddess river slides by. Over 6 million people gather, usually at Allahabad on the Ganges, to take part in the Kumbha Mela celebrations. Probably the world's largest religious festival, the month-long Kumbha takes place every twelve years at the cities of Hardwar, Allahabad, Nasik-Panchavati, or Ujjain. Pilgrims celebrate the river as an elixir of life and immortality, the equivalent for humans of the divine nectar upon which the gods feed.

Once there was a bad man, a man named Vahika, who gambled, who had killed a sacred cow, who never honored the gods, and who did not even honor his own mother. When he died and appeared before Yama, the Lord of Death, a long list of his misdeeds was read out. Not a single virtuous act could be found to balance them. There was no doubt Vahika was going to hell. But as he was standing there before Yama, something was happening in the land of the living. A vulture, which had been feeding on his body, had seized his foot bone for a morsel and flown off with it. In midair over the Ganges, another vulture fought with this bird for the bone. Just as Yama was about to condemn Vahika to the underworld, the vultures dropped his foot bone into the Ganges. Before Yama could open his mouth, a chariot entered the Halls of Death and carried Vahika to heaven; the immersion of a single bone of his body in the sacred river had purged his sins.

Originally, the goddess Ganga, after whom the river is named, had her home in the heavens, somewhere between the Big Dipper and the polestar, where Vishnu lives. In response to prayers, the god Shiva commanded Ganga to come down to Earth. She was angry and plunged down on the god to sweep him away, but Shiva, standing on Mount Kailas, caught and imprisoned her in the locks of his hair. He released her into Lake Manasarovar, whence she flowed in seven streams to the far ends of the earth. The great descent of the goddess is described in India's national epic, the *Ramayana: Devas, rishis, yakshas, and all celestial beings . . . hastened there to witness the marvelous and auspicious descent of the Ganges to the world. And the Gods, as they alighted from the sky, irradiated that cloudless canopy of heaven with the splendor of their divine ornaments, so that it seemed a thousand suns had risen there.*

Such a splendor is in the minds of pilgrims when they bathe in the formless form of the goddess or take her in their hands to make an offering to the gods.

Above:
Women immerse themselves in the Ganges, bathing and offering a morning prayer. The water they drink and offer praises to flows from the heights of the Himalayas, 400 miles away. For Indians, water is an essential part of every ritual, from birth, to marriage, to death. Every day bodies of the dead are brought to be burned at the river's edge in Benares. But the Ganges is also the source of life: according to the Katha Upanishad, "Right from the Waters, the Soul drew forth and shaped a person." During droughts, the river is often the only reliable supply of water. *Photo by Corwin Fergus*

Above, right:
Abandoned effigies lie strewn on a platform by the river. The figures include Ganesha, the elephant-headed son of Shiva and Parvati. Ganesha as the "Remover of Obstacles" has an enormous cult following in India: his image may appear anywhere, here or in the middle of a mustard field. In Hindu practice it is not the symbols themselves that are precious; they are simply tools in the relentless construction of the spiritual universe. These effigies have been left—Ganesha beheaded—their ritual use completed. *Photo by Linda Connor/Swanstock*

Right:
In Hardwar, more than 6 million people gather for the Kumbha Mela, the great religious festival that takes place every 12 years. It is a festival of cleansing and long life, based on the belief that some precious drops of *amrita*, or nectar of celestial life, were dropped here from the cup of Dhanvantari, the divine healer. It is believed that since then celestial waters have flowed into the Ganges at this spot. The quest for long life draws an extraordinary crowd of yogis, bureaucrats, peasants, sages, and the ailing, all equal in the embrace of Mata Ganga. *Photo by Peter Menzel*

Lake Titicaca, Peru. Photo by Eric Lawton/The Stock Market

FIRST PLACES: LAKE TITICACA AND WUPATKI AND SAN FRANCISCO PEAKS

In the seed is contained the flower. In myths of origins the beliefs of a people are first given voice and color. Among the most telling stories in every culture are those accounts that detail where people came from, how the world was made, and the roots of human destiny. People may trace their world's beginnings to darkness, to a void, to the mind of the Creator, or to a mountain. The Inca of Peru trace their civilization to the startling blue, reed-fringed waters of Lake Titicaca.

The Island of the Sun lies off Lake Titicaca's Copacabana Peninsula. Here the son and daughter of the Sun came to earth, sent by their father with a mission to civilize mankind. The Children of the Sun were to teach people the arts of agriculture, including irrigation, and the weaving of cloth.

Wupatki and San Francisco Peaks, Arizona, USA. Photo by Jack W. Dykinga

The migration legends of the Hopi people describe the wandering which brought them from the south, perhaps beyond Mexico, to their present homeland in Northern Arizona. One of their last stopping places was Wupatki, the Tall House, now a ruin in view of the San Francisco Peaks. It was in the shadow of these sacred peaks that the Hopi first encountered and established good relations with the spirit kachinas. In response to Hopi prayers, these beings brought and still bring rain clouds and fertility to the region.

The true Incas, descendants of the Sun's son and daughter, are said to have abandoned their people shortly before the white invaders arrived and destroyed the culture they had established. The Hopi also fear that a popular ski-resort in the sacred San Francisco mountains, the kachina homeland, will drive away these necessary spirits and bring an end to the Hopi way of life.

Above:

Two Uro women ride a reed canoe among the reed islands at the mouth of the Rio Huili, which flows into Lake Titicaca. Among the many legends woven around the lakeshore is one about two mermaids, Quesintuu and Umantuu, who in ancient times rose from the lake to make love to Tunupa, the Aymara god of fire and lightning. Women held a special place in ancient Peruvian religion: priestesses or *nustas* were in charge of religious ceremonies, and others, referred to as "daughters of the sun," were chosen to live apart in guarded houses, forbidden to marry or have relationships with men. *Photo by Victor Englebert/Photo Researchers*

LAKE TITICACA, PERU

Lake Titicaca lies on the border between Peru and Bolivia, at an altitude of 12,507 feet. It covers more than 3,000 square miles, and is about 700 feet deep. In the lake there is an island called the Island of the Sun. It is here where the Inca people began, and here where everything came to an end for them. It was here that the son and daughter of the Sun came down to earth and taught humans what they needed to know.

In the beginning, human beings just lived like animals, but the Sun, the Father of all things, saw this and felt sorry for them. So he told his son and daughter they had to go down to earth to help mankind. He gave them a golden rod, about as long as a man's forearm, and told them to go to the Island of the Sun in Lake Titicaca. From there, he said, they could go wherever they wanted, but anywhere they stopped to sleep or to eat, they had to shove the golden rod into the ground. If it disappeared, they would know they had come to the place where they should build their city. They must love their people as a father loves his children and teach them how to be civilized.

So the son and daughter went down to earth. From Lake Titicaca they went north, but they could never shove the golden rod all the way into the ground. At last they came to Rainbow Hill, in the Cuzco Valley. When they shoved the rod into the ground there, it disappeared immediately. This was where they were to build their city.

The son, who was called the Inca, went north to tell the people, and his sister, who was called the Coya, went south. Everywhere they went the people knew they were the children of the Sun and followed them to Cuzco. The Inca, whose name was Manco Capac, taught the men how to grow crops and water their fields while the Coya, whose name was Mama Ocllo, taught the women how to weave cloth and make clothes. After a few years they had enough followers to make an army, and the Inca taught them how to use weapons.

And so the empire of the Incas grew, and it was always ruled by the descendants of the first Inca and the Coya. Then one day the god Viracocha came to the Inca, who was called Huayna Capac, and said they must both go to Lake Titicaca. When they got there, Viracocha told the Inca to call all his magicians, because they had to be sent off to the Underworld. The magicians came and said to Viracocha's father: "Your son has sent me. Give me one of his sisters."

The first magician to get to the Underworld was one who had been made by the swallow. He was given a small chest. "Don't open it," he was told. "It must only be opened by Huayna Capac." But the magician could not resist. On the way back he opened the chest and saw that inside it was a very pretty woman with golden hair. But as soon as he saw her she vanished. When he got back, Viracocha was angry. If the magician had not been made by the swallow, he would have been killed. As it was, Viracocha sent him back to the Underworld.

This time the magician brought the chest back safely. When Huayna Capac opened it, it was as if all the world was lit up, and when he saw his new Sun Queen, he swore he would never leave her, would never go back to Cuzco. He called to one of his people: "Go back to Cuzco", he said, "and tell them that you are Huayna Capac!" Then he, his wife, and Viracocha, all disappeared.

Later, after the man who had been pretending to be Huayna Capac was dead, everyone started quarreling about who should be the next Inca. And that was when the white men arrived and destroyed everything.

Above:

Nearly 400 Uro live on the Bolivian side of the lake among the 40 islands known for the totora reed which provides the main material support for the entire lake civilization. The Uro fish and hunt birds with sling shots, and sell their wares to land dwellers for other goods. According to legend, the blood of the Uro is black, which enables them to endure bitter-cold nights and also to be saved from drowning. *Photo by Victor Englebert/Photo Researchers*

Right:

Lake Titicaca lies high in the Andes, stretching for 110 miles between Bolivia and Peru. At 12,507 feet above sea level it is the highest navigable body of water in the world. *Titi Qaqa* means "Rock of the Cat," and is the name given to the lake and to an island on which there is a sandstone cliff 25 feet high and 200 feet long. This was the most sacred place on earth for the Inca people, their Place of Dawning. Later peoples refer to this place as Island of the Sun, and ruins there support a myth of origins in which Inti, Father Sun, directed Manco Capac and his sister-consort, Mama Ocllo, to set out from there to build the human world. The Uro Indians live here now on islands big enough for a single family, and are known for their embroidery and tapestries. They rarely leave their islands. *Photo by Thomas Ives/Swanstock*

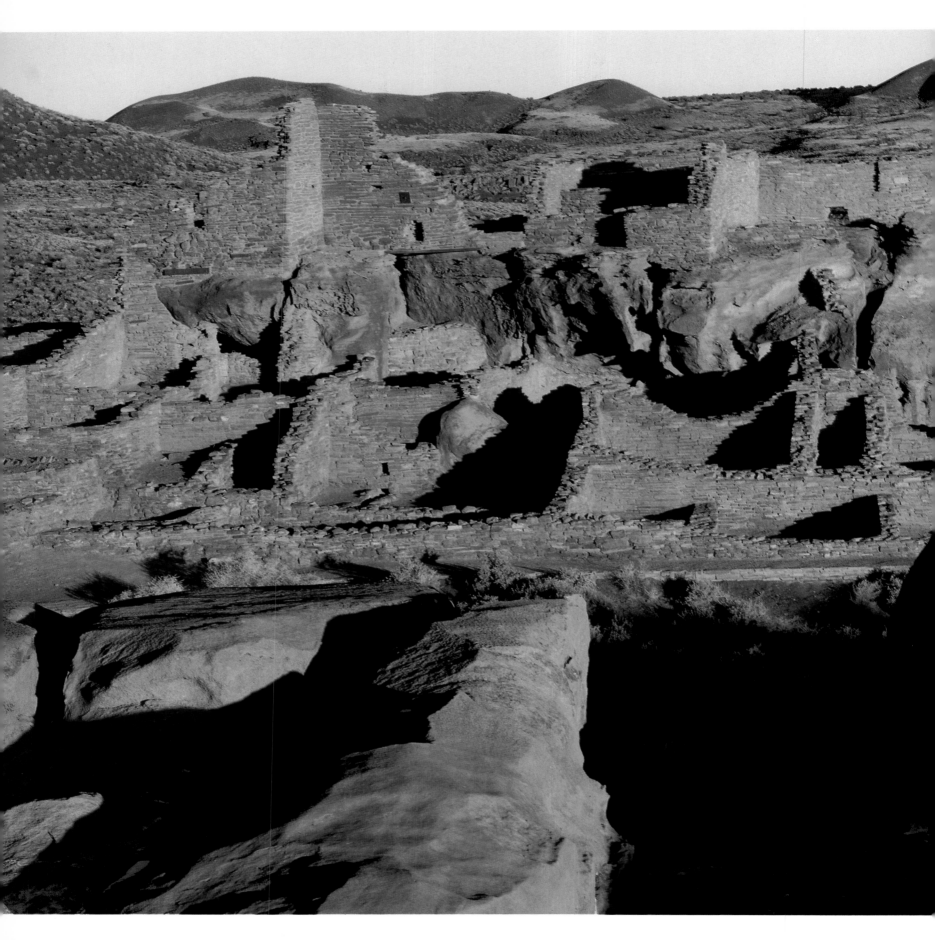

Above:
Among the elaborate migration stories of the Hopi people is the story of the Bird Clan, or Mother People, who lived in Wupatki on the way to their current home further east. Now an extensive ruin which lies in view of the San Francisco Peaks, northeast of Flagstaff *(see photo on page 31)*, this multi-story building had over 100 rooms. *Photo by Jack W. Dykinga*

Inset:
The Anasazi people or "those who came before" marked their totems on the walls of canyons near the San Francisco Peaks. *Photo by Debra Bloomfield/ Courtesy of Robert Koch Gallery, San Francisco*

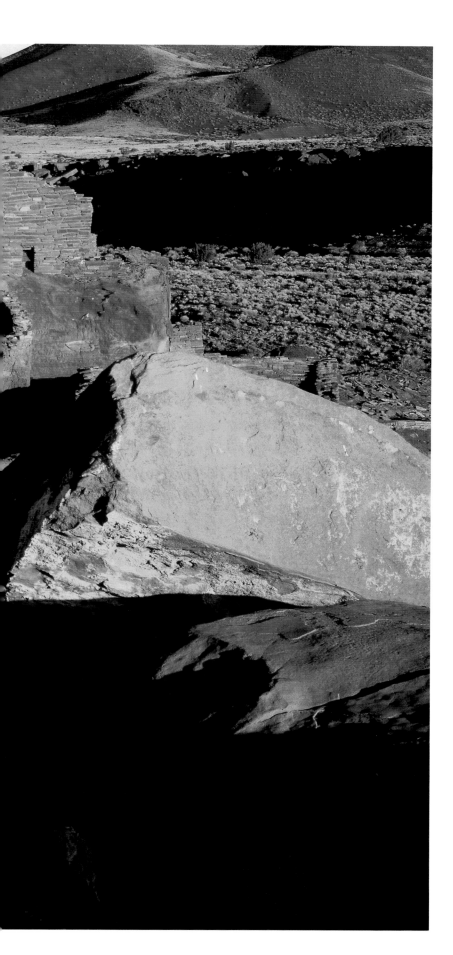

WUPATKI AND SAN FRANCISCO PEAKS, USA

When the Hopi people first moved into the southwest they stayed for some time in the region of Wupatki, which in their language means "tall house." This was perhaps in the 12th century AD. The Wupatki settlement lies in the shadow of the San Francisco Peaks: a sacred creation-place for both the Hopi and Navajo people, but for different reasons.

When the Hopi first began to live in the area, people reported seeing strange beings wandering around their villages near the foot of the San Francisco Peaks. The priests were puzzled, so they sent a warrior to find out who these beings were. He gathered together some prayer sticks, the kind with feathers that are called *paahos*, and climbed the mountain. When he got near the top, he heard a voice calling him from a kiva, an underground room where the Hopi hold religious ceremonies. He climbed down into the kiva and was greeted by a being who looked like a man, but was a spirit who lived in the depths of the mountain. Suddenly, an ugly creature with a black face, shining teeth, and a pointed nose joined them in the kiva. The mountain spirit told the warrior that this was Cheveyo and that he was a kachina, one of the beings that the Hopi people had been seeing around their villages. Al- though the kachina was

frightening, the warrior offered him the feathered prayer sticks. The kachina was pleased and said that in future he and other kachinas would make rain clouds over the mountains whenever the Hopi offered prayer sticks.

In time the Hopi moved away from the Wupatki area and settled some 80 miles east, in the Three Mesa region around Oraibi. But every year, when the sun marks the Winter Solstice by setting in a notch near the San Francisco Peaks, the kachinas leave their mountain home and move to the mesas. They stay with the Hopi all of the summer, creating rain clouds and bringing blessings, and then at the Summer Solstice, when the corn is grown, they return to the peaks with messages the Hopi give them for their ancestors.

As the Navajo tell it, the San Francisco Peaks were created by First Man and First Woman (along with other mountains marking the four directions) with pinches of earth they brought from the sacred mountains of the Underworld. They went about it like this: *The mountain of the west, they fastened to the earth with a sunbeam. They adorned it with abalone shell, with black clouds, he-rain, yellow corn, and all sorts of wild animals. They laced a dish of abalone shell on top, and laid in this two eggs of the Yellow Warbler, covering them with sacred buckskins. Over all they spread a blanket of yellow evening light, and they sent White Corn Boy and Yellow Corn Girl to dwell there.*

The Hopi say that sometimes the kachinas still appear around the peaks. But they don't regard it as a good sign; today kachinas only appear to those who lack faith, those who tread carelessly on the sacred peaks, or linger too late near the dark ruins of Wupatki.

Above:
A rainstorm sweeps off the San Francisco Peaks toward
Wupatki. The Hopi Road of Life extends far beyond the visible
landscape into the country, the solar system, and further into
the universe. When Hopis who have lived in accordance with
the Creator die, they become kachinas and pass without pause
into the next universe. Kachinas are the inner manifestations
of physical life; they are messengers of the life forces, of clouds,
minerals, plants, animals, and birds. At different times of the
year they are called to descend from their home in the San
Francisco Peaks. Like the rainstorms of August in the desert,
the kachinas fly from the heights to the aid of the people,
bringing life, the fullness of crops, and the continuation of an
ever-emerging world. *Photo by Macduff Everton/Swanstock*

The Serpent Mound, Ohio, USA. Photo by Courtney Milne

EARTH WORKS: THE SERPENT MOUND AND AVEBURY COMPLEX

While the snake slithers through the Christian and Jewish imagination, forever the symbol of evil, it enjoys quite another status in the beliefs of old Europe and the Americas. The snake is also the symbol of renewal, death and rebirth, fertility, and the life force itself.

Yet the snake's appearance in archeology is always enigmatic. As much as the Avebury Henge has been studied, no one knows the significance of the serpent-like pattern that the standing stones followed during the Bronze Age, when they wound among the hills and barrows of Wiltshire, England. Silbury Hill, south of the henge, is probably not the tomb of King Sil as was once thought, but more likely a fertility symbol in the shape of a womb, built by an advanced agrarian society. If so, the stone

Avebury Henge, England. Photo by Macduff Everton/Swanstock

serpent at Avebury is a complementary symbol of fertility. Which is perhaps a key to the Serpent Mound near Chillicothe, Ohio. This famous effigy mound was also once thought to be a burial site, but the Serpent is not built on burial grounds and may not be related in time or intent to the burial mounds close by.

  Whatever its purpose, the Serpent Mound, like Silbury Hill and Avebury Henge, was built with great planning and care and enormous outputs of labor and time. Throughout history, humans have erected monumental works marking the passages to the next world. With new examinations of these ancient earthworks, it may become clear that equal care was once used to build monuments to the origins of life.

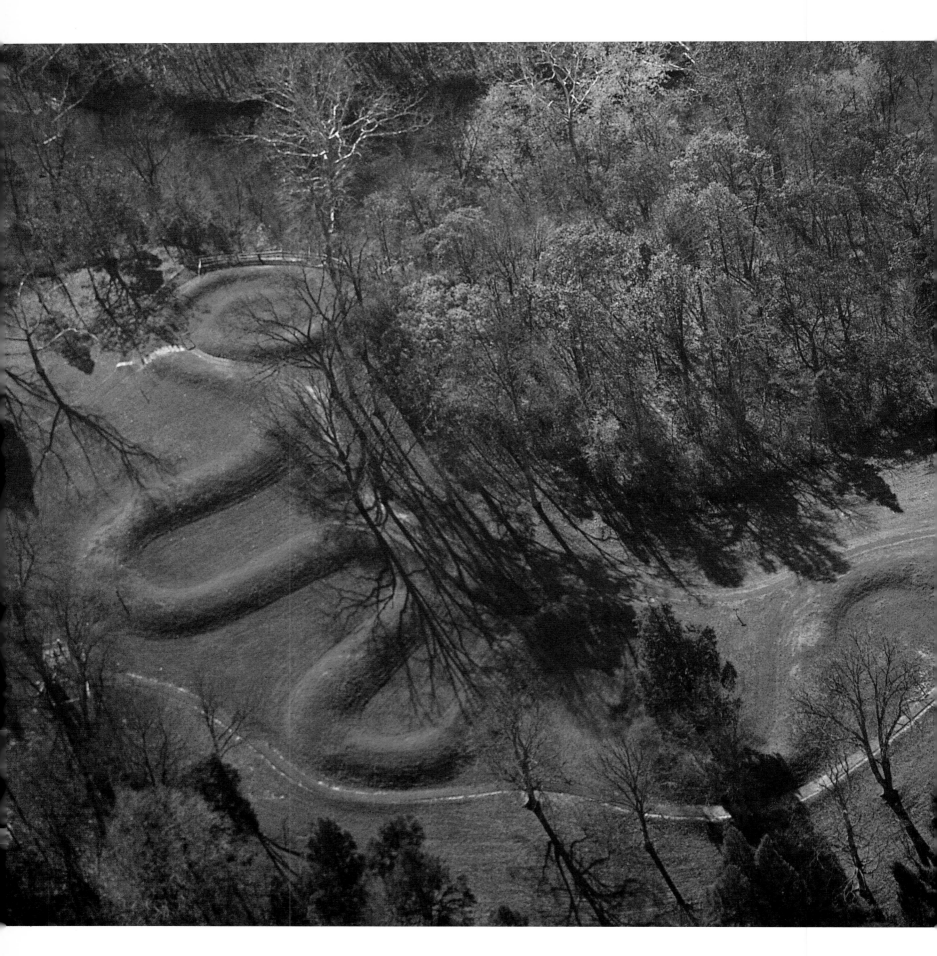

Above:

Imagine the Serpent Mound as it must have appeared originally, without the pathways and explanation plaques. To the frontierpeople, whose cultural roots were European and whose spiritual symbols— the spire and the cross—were cause to look up, the quarter-mile mound must certainly have seemed enigmatic and primitive. But to a culture whose spiritual territory and symbols were earth and sky, the Serpent Mound was an elegant expression of a mature world vision. Until 1991, the Serpent Mound was thought to be a product of the Adena people, who flourished around 500 BC and who had built a 10-foot-high mound a hundred yards to the south. But sophisticated carbon dating has revealed that the Serpent was more likely created early in the 8th century AD. The Hopi of Arizona, who believed the serpent was made by their ancestors, interpreted the oval mound near the snake's jaws as a village under the protection of the snake. The snake faced west because the people who made it were traveling west, and Tokchi'i, the guardian of the east, would protect them until they reached the wall of mountains separating east from west. *Photos by Courtney Milne*

42

THE SERPENT MOUND, USA

Imagine you are walking on top of a nondescript hill in the middle of Ohio. Your path follows the scrolling curves of a grass-covered embankment that slopes up from the ground to about shoulder level. The twisting body of the bank follows the curve of a nearby creek, its shape pressed close to the contours of the hill. The creek seems to crawl through the deep green grass like a living thing. At one end of the embankment a broad oval mound rises, enigmatic and final.

Suddenly, your attention is captured by a bright red cardinal that flies out of the nearby  woods, and for a mo- ment you soar with the bird, ascending. Just then, the Serpent reveals it- self. Look- ing down, you realize that you have been walking alongside the image of a huge, carefully sculpted snake, its 30-foot-wide body stretching over the land for a quarter of a mile, from the triple coil of its tail to the huge oval stuck in its gaping jaws.

What led the makers of the Ohio Serpent Mound (perhaps the Middle Woodland people), over a thousand years ago, to expend thousands of hours of work carrying earth and shaping a monument that can only be seen in its entirety from high above the ground? The Serpent Mound is just one of many animal earthworks, or effigy mounds, scattered through the interior of America. They include the bears and birds of Iowa, constructed around 500 AD on a bluff overlooking the Mississippi. The largest of the figures in this group, a bear, is 137 feet long and 70 feet wide. The Ohio Serpent Mound dwarfs even this impressive figure. Indeed, serpent effigies have been found in many lands, evidence of the important and varied role snakes have enjoyed in the mythology and religious literature of the world. The fact that snakes shed their entire skin and thus emerge into new life makes them a ready symbol for the feminine capacity to give birth, a capacity which extended to the new life of crops and green things. Minoan figures from around 1500 BC show the goddess of fertility holding a writhing snake in each outstretched hand. Too little is known about the people who built the Serpent Mound to accurately guess its true significance. They were farmers, and among the first people in North America to grow corn.

Often, the serpent as a symbol of earthly life is shown in conjunction with a bird, a symbol of divine inspiration. In ancient Egypt, the intertwined figures of cobra and vulture tended to the lower and upper realms. Hindu yoga uses a serpent to describe the life energy or *kundalini* that lies coiled at the base of the spine. Through spiritual exercise, this energy can ascend the spinal column to be transformed into visionary consciousness. Mesoamerica has the great figure of the Quetzalcoatl: the Plumed Serpent or the Precious Twin, the one who separated earth from heaven, whose scales were transformed into the bright feathers of a bird. It was he who rose from the ashes of carnal existence to shine above as the Morning Star.

Above:
One hundred standing stones once encircled the Avebury complex; only 27 remain today, restored to their places after centuries of neglect. Many of the standing stones were intentionally removed by Christian officials who feared the pagan power of the circle. *Photo by Macduff Everton/Swanstock*

Inset:
It is the Avebury complex taken as whole that has made it one of the most important Neolithic centers in the British Isles. Originally, the henge included two concentric circles that were bordered by a 50-foot-deep ditch and two stone avenues over a mile long. Silbury Hill is visible in the upper left. *Photo by Marilyn Bridges*

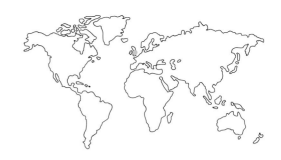

AVEBURY COMPLEX, ENGLAND

If you come by mist or moonlight to the giant circle at Avebury, the stones loom upon you and above you like cloaked giants or massive sentinels, likely at any moment to challenge your presence there. In full daylight, though, the stones have a different message: plunged deep into the earth, they seem charged with the same profound energies that drive the seasons of growth and cycles of life. For unlike the shaped trilithons of Stonehenge, Avebury's more famous but smaller neighbor to the south, these megaliths are natural and unshaped; their energy is raw and lively, and they look as if they had grown where they stand, each one as different from its neighbor as in any gathering of natural things.

But, of course, the 450-yard-wide circle, the biggest in Europe (and probably in the world), is anything but natural. It was care-  fully built by Bronze Age farmers over a number of years, they began their task around 1800 BC, a full two cen- turies before any work at Stonehenge had begun.

In the words of a 17th-century archeologist, John Aubrey, Avebury "did as much excell Stonehenge as a cathedral does a parish church." It almost certainly served as a great open-air temple, with two smaller and perhaps older circles lying within the great circle, and a 50-foot-wide avenue of megaliths leading from it to a site known as the Sanctuary, one-and-a-half miles away on Overton Down.

Almost due south of Avebury lies Silbury Hill, the tallest prehistoric mound in Europe. Its construction began around 2660 BC, and when complete it rose to its present height of 130 feet and covered five-and-one-half acres. A theory currently gaining wide appeal is that the mound itself represents the pregnant womb of the Earth Goddess, her body outlined by a water-filled moat at the mound's base. This theory describes the surrounding countryside, the henges of Avebury, the streams and ponds of Wiltshire, as part of a sacred landscape on which was enacted a yearlong series of rituals connected to the planting, maturing, and harvesting of grain. Traces of the pagan ritual calendar continue into the present era in the form of May Day festivals, St. Bridget's day, and most notably the Sele or First Fruits festival of England. *Sele*, variously interpreted as "proper time" or "favorable season," is a variation on *sil*, which would make Silbury, in one interpretation, "the mound of the proper time." One can almost imagine the cloaked stone sentinels at Avebury as brave young men guarding the pregnant woman who lies sleeping in the shape of Silbury Hill.

More traditional thought supposes (but cannot prove) that the mound is a vast burial monument, perhaps the tomb of an ancient king named Sil. The controversy over the real nature of the Avebury-Silbury complex exemplifies the ongoing shifts in perspective, from patriarchy to matriarchy, from scientific to spiritual, which have colored our interpretations of history since time began.

Above:
Though less well known than Stonehenge, the
Avebury complex is far older and more subtle in
appearance. Constructed at about the same time as
the Giza pyramids, the Avebury stones were set
into place around 2600 BC, so long ago that locals
consider them part of the natural landscape. Indeed,
some of the stones of Avebury were used to build the
village's stone fences and barns. The orginal purpose
of Avebury Henge and its partner Silbury Hill will
never be known, though recent speculations suggest
this was an elaborate ceremonial center for a pre-
Bronze Age farming culture. On significant days of
the farming calendar there would be processions and
dances along the stone avenues and special events
at Silbury Hill, thought by some to resemble a womb.
Sexual activity and human sacrifice may also have
been part of these rituals, which were directed toward
ensuring the fertility of the land. *Photo by Macduff
Everton/Swanstock*

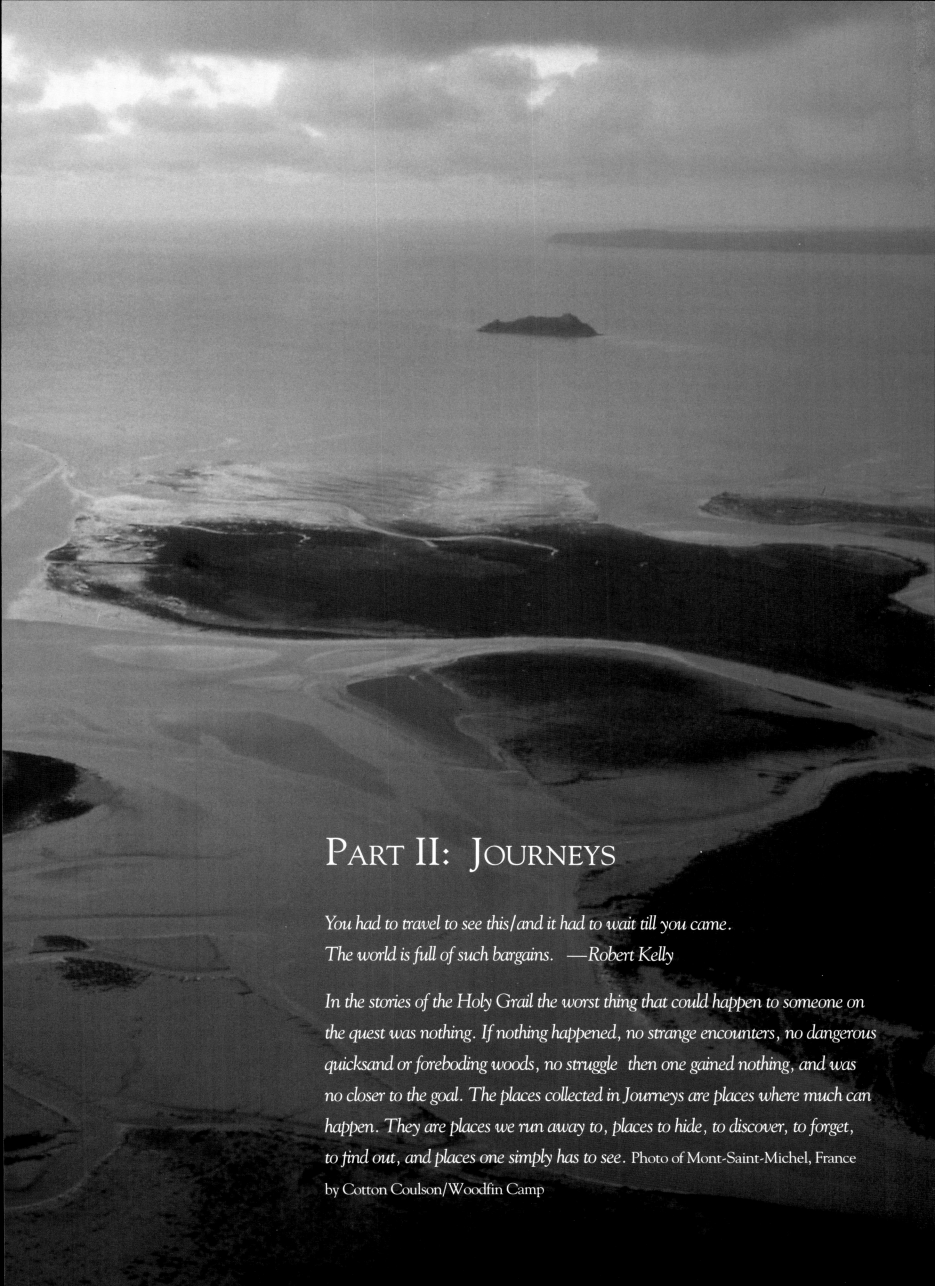

PART II: JOURNEYS

You had to travel to see this/and it had to wait till you came.
The world is full of such bargains. —Robert Kelly

In the stories of the Holy Grail the worst thing that could happen to someone on the quest was nothing. If nothing happened, no strange encounters, no dangerous quicksand or foreboding woods, no struggle then one gained nothing, and was no closer to the goal. The places collected in Journeys are places where much can happen. They are places we run away to, places to hide, to discover, to forget, to find out, and places one simply has to see. Photo of Mont-Saint-Michel, France by Cotton Coulson/Woodfin Camp

Uluru, Australia. Photo by David Burnett/Contact Press Images

MARKING THE PATH: ULURU AND THE NAZCA LINES

When men and women lived in closer harmony with the earth than they do today, the surface of the earth itself was the medium on which they drew the emblems of their society and beliefs. The Nazca people organized groups of surveyors who picked away a dark rubble of stones from the desert floor to create the outlines of trapezoids and avenues, birds, animals, and plants. This was the method by which the vast designs on the Nazca Plateau in Peru were created.

The resulting geoglyphs are among the most ambitious and enduring of human works. They are also among the most mysterious, not only because what they signify is often unknown, but because many of them, constructed long before people could fly, can only be seen from the air.

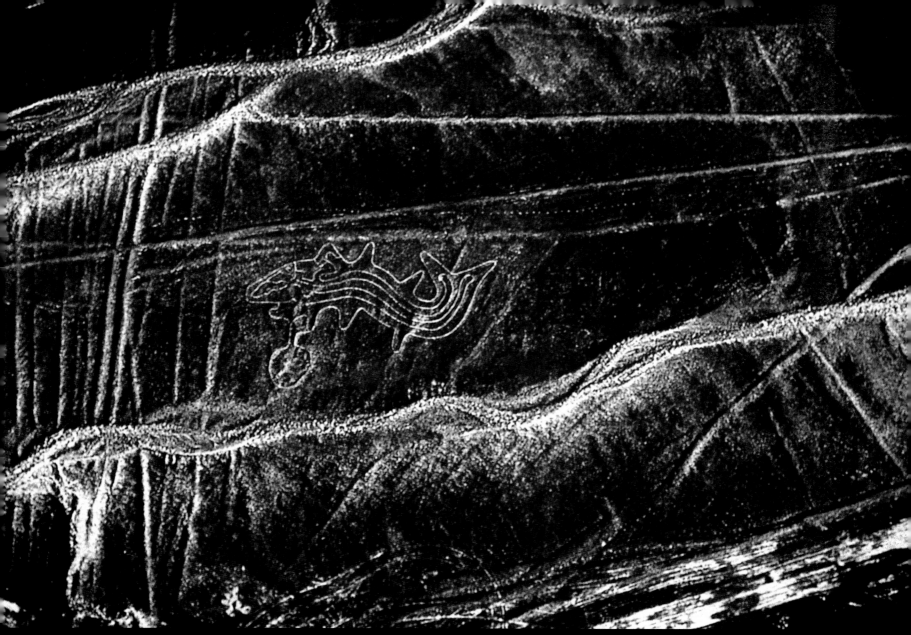

The Nazca Lines, Peru. Photo by Marilyn Bridges

Other ways of marking the ground cannot be seen at all. The Australian Aborigines celebrate their close relationship with earth by committing to memory the existing marks of the landscape. Their "song lines"—the stories and geographical accounts by which they remember how and where ancestral beings traveled in the prehuman Dreamtime—create a living geography that gives meaning to their lives. The songs telling these extraordinary stories are clan-specific, and to fulfill their promise demands a high degree of social cooperation. They are collaborative imaginative constructions of vast size and complexity, easily rivaling the great literary epics of Eastern and Western civilization.

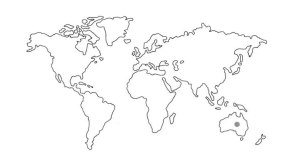

Uluru, Australia

This story happened in the Dreamtime. By telling and always telling these stories, the Aborigines of Australia remember how Uluru and all the land, its shape and color, describe the actions of their ancestor spirits.

Where the great rock Uluru now rears up out of the Australian desert there was once just a big waterhole. It too was named Uluru, and there was a spring there named Mutitjilda. On the dark side of the waterhole lived the tribe called the Kunia, the Carpet Snake people. On the other, sunny side lived the Mala, or Hare-wallaby people. The two tribes lived in peace.

One day, each tribe got an invitation from the Windulka, the Mulga Seed people who lived in the far west, in the Petermann Range. They wanted the Kunia and the Mala to come help them perform some important Windulka rituals.

The Kunia decided to go. When darkness fell on their first night out, they made their camp by Uluru. They were greatly surprised to find some very beautiful Sleepy Lizard women already there. They stayed with each other that night, and who knows what happened. But by morning the Kunia had decided they liked it at Uluru very much. The Kunia wanted to stay for a long time there with the Sleepy Lizard women. They forgot about their journey to visit the Windulka. On the sunny side of Uluru, the Mala people were busy with their own initiations.

They asked, "Who wants to walk and walk all the way to the Petermann Range?" No one did. So they did not go either.

Meanwhile, the Windulka were waiting. They waited and waited, but nobody came. Finally, they sent the bell bird, Panpanpalana, to find out what was going on. When Panpanpalana came back, he explained how the Kunia had just gotten married—they could not come; the Mala were too busy—they could not come either. To the Windulka, these sounded like petty excuses. They became angry. They decided to punish the Kunia and Mala. They took mud and sticks and made an evil-spirit dingo called Kulpunya. They sang evil into him. First they sent Kulpunya to punish the Mala. He killed most of them. Some escaped to the southwest, but were never heard of again.

Now something terrible was about to happen to the Kunia. The Windulka sent the Liru, the Poisonous Snake people, to fight them. They met at Mutitjilda Spring. They fought with spears, and before long Kulikitjeri, the leader of the Liru, wounded Ungata, the Kunia leader. Ungata's mother, Ingridi, was a very powerful woman. When she saw her son wounded she flew into a rage. She took her digging stick and spat a mystical substance known as *arukunita* onto it. It became an invincible weapon. First she knocked off Kulikitjeri's nose with it and then she killed him.

As the Liru were beginning to retreat, one of them set fire to the camp where the Sleepy Lizard women were staying. When the camp burned down, the battle ended. The Kunia picked up Ungata, but he was dead. They gathered around his body in great anguish. They sang until they sang themselves to death. It was a mass suicide.

Then the earth itself rose up against all the death and grief and fighting and became the great rock we call Uluru.

The Uluru summit is where water gathers, and every other part of the rock is a detail of the Sky Heroes' battle. Wanambi Pool is the blood of Ungata; Kulikitjeri's smitten nose is a 70-foot boulder; the bodies of the Kunia are scattered cylindrical stones; the evil-spirit dingo, Kulpunya, is a series of stones, each showing him in a different attack pose; and some of the Liru, those who became desert oaks, can still be seen making their way to the great battle at Uluru. When the Aborigines tell this Dreamtime story, they are not just telling what happened here in the Dreamtime, they are telling what happened here.

Left:
For the Pitjantjatjara Aborigines who inhabit the territory around Uluru, the stone is a living text of events that happened in the Dreamtime. Every shadow, crevice, pool, and indentation on Uluru is a hieroglyphic in the ancient text of stories that connect the Aborigines to their relatives, to their ancestors, and to their land. *Photo by Claude Coirault*

Inset:
Aboriginal rock art further illustrates the borders and paths of the Dreamtime. *Photo by Len Jenshel/Swanstock*

Above:
Uluru blazes like a distant fire on the vast expanse of
the Australian outback. It is the world's largest freestanding rock, a monolith rising an abrupt 1,000 feet
above the shimmering desert. It covers more than
three square miles, and around its base is a necklace
of waterholes that sustains a fringe of vegetation and
an abundance of wildlife. Geologists chart the face of
the rock in terms of sediment and layers, calculating
the ancient origin of the 3-billion-year-old continent
that was once linked to Antarctica. One Aborigine
describes Australia not as a land mass but as a story
mass, and charts the paths of dreams and songs that
connect the scattered inhabitants of the 2,500-mile-
wide land. Only the vast scale of Australia can support the infinite complexity of stories that comprise
the Aboriginal Dreamtime. Uluru stands as a story
intersection: a landmark that rises to show the way
through the wide and shifting territory of the dream-
ing mind. *Photo by Ken Duncan/Australia Wide*

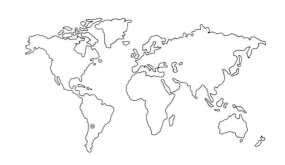

THE NAZCA LINES, PERU

On a desert plateau in southern Peru a killer whale trolls a human head through an arid sea of stones and a hummingbird sips with its 100-foot beak at the edge of the Pan-American Highway. A giant flower opens its four symmetrical petals to the blazing sky, and nearby a 300-foot, nine-fingered monkey is up to no good. And all across the plain is a parade of still stranger figures and geometries—huge spirals, highways enclosed by low walls, dead-straight tracks, and giant trapezoids.

But unless you fly over the plateau or climb the metal observation tower built where the Pan-American Highway bisects a delicate 600-foot lizard and the fronds of a 200-foot seaweed waving idly on the sand, you will never see these great geoglyphs. Traced by a total of some 620 miles of lines on the Nazca plateau, the figures are too vast to be comprehended at ground level, and for more than 2,000 years they were exposed only to the gaze of sky gods and soaring condors. So why did the Nazcas do it? Why did they spend more than 1,000 years, from about 500 BC to 500 AD, construct-ing figures they could never see in their entirety? They were already ancient when the Spanish came to Peru and recorded, in the 1580s, that the people of the region recalled the time, when a strange and saintly people had come to the land. In honor of those beings, they said, their ancestors had built "roads," as wide as a street and enclosed by low walls, which can be seen to this day.

At the city of Cuzco, the ancient Incan capital, the Spanish recorded something else. Radiating from the Temple of the Sun at Cuzco, there was a system of 41 straight lines, called *seques*, and upon these were marked 328 sacred points called *waqas*. These points were symbolic of social structures, cosmology, agriculture, and history, and were the focus of rituals. At Nazca, too, many of the lines radiate from small hills or elevations, often marked with cairns and strewn with fragments of pottery.

So perhaps the Nazca lines were predecessors of the Incan system, and were used to guide the feet of priests and others on ritual processions to points of power, magic, and memory. The figures of plants, reptiles, fish, birds, and mammals there may have served a slightly different purpose. They may perhaps have been clan and kinship emblems. Their outlines could also have been walked in ritual observations, and to absorb the power of the animal figures. Still other lines may have marked points on the horizon where the sun rose and set at times of solstice.

Whatever the truth may be, it seems certain that the Nazca markings had not one but many uses, and that by them the Nazca peoples regulated their lives and aspirations, and made the land itself their sacred partner.

Left and above:
Huge triangles march across the Andean foothills near Nazca. They often follow the course of waterways.

A 200-foot hummingbird stretches its beak toward an invisible flower. Hummingbirds were held to be messengers to the gods among the Nazca as well as other Peruvian peoples. The Nazca lines were made by removing the pebbles that cover the outer crust of the pampa surface to expose a much lighter colored ground below. The shapes of the animals are made of one continuous line that never crosses itself and is never broken.

A grid of double spirals spreads for a thousand feet across a low plateau near the Ingenio Valley. Over 200 spirals and several dozen animals are visible among the Nazca markings.
Photos by Marilyn Bridges

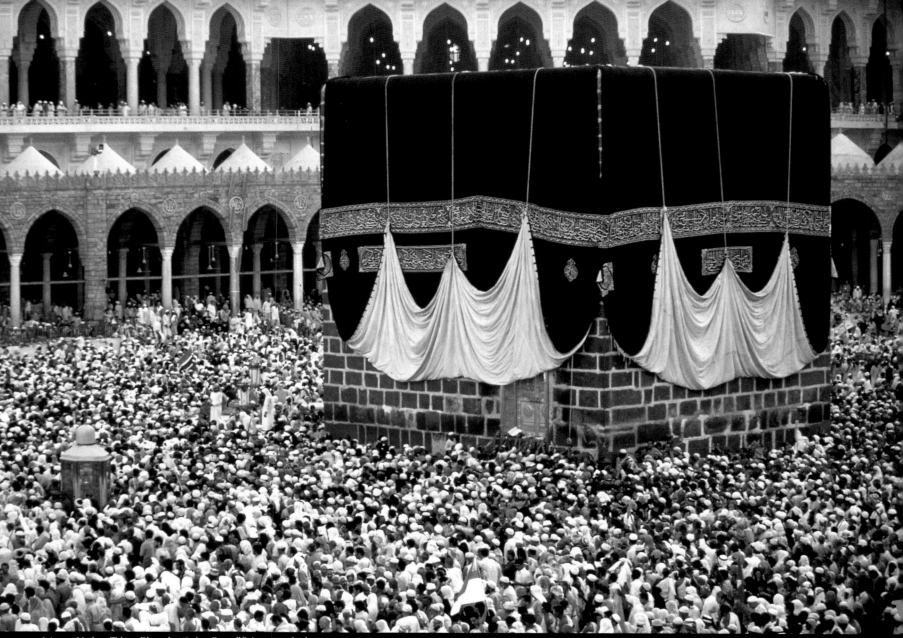

Mount Kailas, Tibet. Photo by Galen Rowell/Mountain Light

PILGRIMAGE: MOUNT KAILAS AND THE KA'BA OF MECCA

For every great religion there is a special place in the world where the divine and the mundane are connected: a central point that embraces the sacred possibility of revelation. For the faithful, such a place is the axis upon which the whole world turns, and from which it gains its meaning. Pilgrimage to such a place is an opportunity for ordinary men and women to experience the divine.

The Ka'ba of Mecca, Saudi Arabia. Photo by Mehmet Biber/Photo Researchers

At the Ka'ba in Mecca, the most holy place for all Muslims, and at Mount Kailas in Tibet, a place
equally sacred to Hindus and Buddhists, the act of pilgrimage is expressed by a circular path. As the
pilgrims circle the holy place, the force of their devotions seems to illuminate the gross matter of the
shapely mountain, the black meteorite in the silk-draped shrine, until the light cast by these sacred objects
is transformed into a more brilliant light that enters into the pilgrim's soul. From object to believer,
radiating from the center outward and from the perimeter inward, the circle continues.

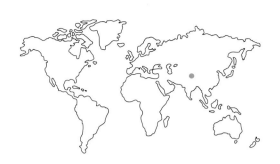

MOUNT KAILAS, TIBET

Sacred to Hindus and Buddhists alike, Tibet's Mount Kailas rises in snow-clad isolation from a 15,000-foot plateau some 600 miles west of Lhasa. At 22,156 feet, Kailas (in Tibetan, Kang Rimpoche; in Chinese, Kang-ti-ssu Shan) is not one of the highest Himalayan peaks, but its position and unusual symmetry make it one of the most beautiful. The Indus and the Brahmaputra rivers rise in the vicinity, and not far away is the source of the Ganges.

For Hindus, Kailas is the abode of Shiva, the Lord of Destruction, the Lord of the Dance, creator and preserver of the universe. Originally, he lived alone on the peak, meditating. But lesser gods sent Parvati, the beautiful daughter of the god Himalaya, to seduce him, because they knew that from such union a son would be born, one well able to defeat the demons of the world. For thousands of years Parvati practiced meditation at the feet of Shiva. One day he finally noticed her, and at that moment Kama, the God of Love, pierced him with one of his arrows. Shiva fell deeply in love with Parvati, and eventually their demon-headed son, Karttikeya, was born. He was followed by their elephant-headed son, Ganesha. This eccentric family of gods still lives atop the summit of Mount Kailas.

For Buddhists, this mountain is the abode of the Supremely Blissful One called Khorlo Demchong, a sky-blue Buddha clad in a tiger-skin skirt and a garland of skulls, and always found in sexual union with his consort, the red-skinned female Buddha Dorje Phagmo. The male represents compassion, the female, wisdom.

The Buddhist yogin Milarepa was perhaps the most famous pilgrim to visit Mount Kailas. Soon after he arrived, a local priest of the Bon religion named Naro Bhun Chon challenged him to a contest: whichever man could reach the peak of the mountain first would demonstrate the superiority of his religion, and the other would have to leave. Milarepa accepted the challenge. But while Naro Bhun Chon was making energetic spiritual preparations for the test, Mila merely took his ease. At last Naro's preparations were complete. He wrapped himself in his green cloak and, sitting on his ritual drum, set off flying through the air to the mountain peak. Milarepa, meantime, seemed to be soundly asleep. When Naro was halfway up the mountain, Mila's anxious disciples woke him up. Milarepa was unperturbed. First he waved his hand, and the Bon priest found himself flying round and round the mountain in circles, unable to rise any higher. Then Mila put on his cloak, snapped his fingers, and as the sun rose, flew instantly to the very peak of Kailas. When Naro Bhun Chon saw him sitting there he was so amazed he fell off his drum. It tumbled down the mountain, and you can still see the steplike marks it left as it fell. Naro acknowledged defeat, but Milarepa let him live on a nearby mountain and continue practicing his religion.

For earthbound mortals the circumambulation of the mountain usually takes three days, including crossing a narrow pass at an altitude of 19,000 feet. Hindus often increase the merit of their journey by first bathing in the ice-cold waters of Lake Manasarovar, the Lake of the Mind, near the foot of Mount Kailas. Buddhists enrich their pilgrimage experience by prostrating themselves at full length at every step around the entire circumference of the mountain. Nothing less is fully suitable to such a sacred place.

Left:
As the dew is dried by the sun, so the sins of men are removed by the sight of the Himalayas, so goes an old Indian saying. Here the power of Mount Kailas shines through an obscuring mist to move this pilgrim to a gesture of praise. *Photo by Galen Rowell/ Mountain Light*

Above:
A Tibetan *tankha* shows Mount Kailas rising in the center of the universe, presided over by its most famous inhabitants. Milarepa, the poet, cups his ear to hear the melodies of the songs he is composing. Khorlo Demchong embracing Dorje Phagmo *(center)*, and Naro Bhun Chon, the native mountain shaman *(right)*, complete the trinity. *Photo by Edwin Bernbaum*

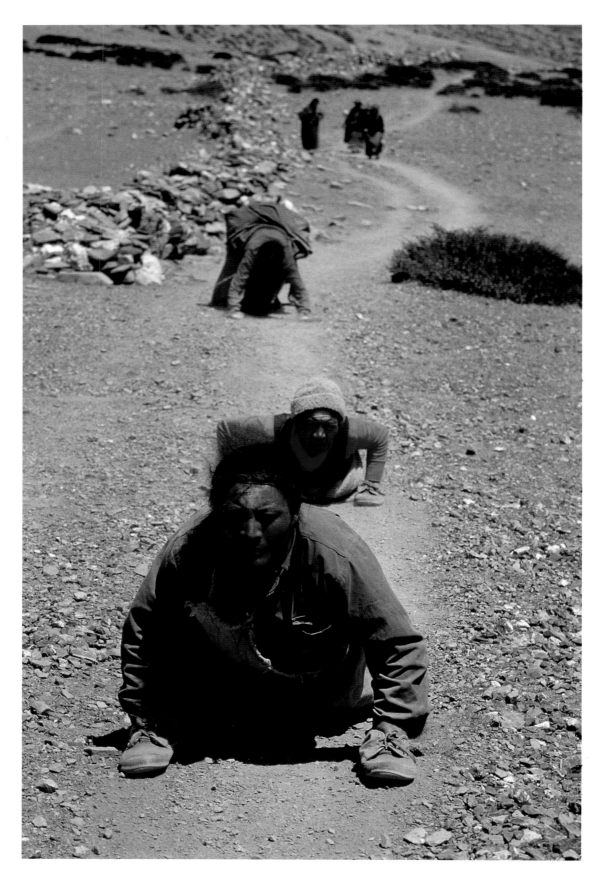

Above:
In Tibetan Buddhism, spiritual practice relies on the total engagement of the body, speech, and mind. Pilgrims circling Mount Kailas measure the distance with the lengths of their bodies. Mittens, shoes, and leather aprons protect the pilgrims from the rough gravel of the mountain. In these full body prostrations, the knees, chest, and forehead touch the ground in endless sequence. The route is about 32 miles, which translates to roughly 28,160 prostrations. Most of their clothes are abandoned near the summit (*see page 58*).

Right:
Tibetan letters spell out Om Mani Peme Hung, the great mantra of the compassionate Buddha Chenresig. The power of this mantra is said to be so great that even hearing it once in a lifetime can save a being from rebirth in the lower realms. The words are chanted, painted, and spelled out all across the Buddha's lands. The sacred route is clearly marked, though strewn with stony obstacles. *Photos by Galen Rowell/Mountain Light*

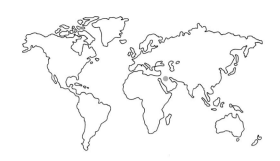

The Ka'ba of Mecca, Saudi Arabia

The Koran [22:26] says: *Keep my house clean for those who walk around it, and those who stand upright or kneel in worship. Exhort all men to make the pilgrimage. They will come to you on foot and on the backs of swift camels from every distant quarter; they will come to avail themselves of many a benefit, and to pronounce on the appointed days the name of God. . . .*

During the time of pilgrimage, or *hadj*, the first ten days of the last month of the lunar year, as many as two million pilgrims converge on Mecca. All wear the seamless white garment prescribed for the occasion, and are enjoined to remember the Koran's injunction: "Do not walk proudly on the earth." More of the world's Muslims make this pilgrimage every year, bringing politics as well as devotion. The two houses of Islam, Sunni and Shi'ite, have been increasingly at odds over the last 20 years, even here. It is written in the Koran [2:190]: *Fight for the sake of God those that fight against you, but do not attack them first . . . Do not fight them within the precincts of the Holy Mosque unless they attack you there; if they attack you put them to the sword. A sacred month for a sacred month: sacred things too are subject to retaliation.*

The only entrance to the Ka'ba is seven feet above ground. The English explorer, Richard Burton, dressed in the disguise of a Muslim pilgrim to get inside. He described walls and floors covered with colored slabs of marble, many of them engraved with quotations from the Koran; and above these quotes embroidered with gold were damask drapes. In one corner of the room there was a stone circled by a wide silver band. The faithful believe the stone was given to Abraham by the Archangel Gabriel, while skeptics call it a meteorite. It was originally white, but has been turned black over the years by the touches and kisses of innumerable pilgrims.

It is this stone in the Ka'ba in the courtyard of the Great Mosque at Mecca that powers the fervor of 650 million Muslims. They face toward it when they pray, and every Muslim must, if at all possible, make a journey to the holy place, the Navel of the World, and perform seven circumambulations there at least once in his or her lifetime.

After completing the circumambulations, the pilgrims journey to Mount Ararat (in Arabic, *Jabal ar Rhum*, Mountain of Mercy), some nine miles outside Mecca. The mountain is crowned by a minaret, from whose steps the pilgrimage address or *khutba* is preached. A sacrifice is made in remembrance of Abraham's willingness to obey God by sacrificing his son Isaac, and the pilgrims return to Mecca to complete their *hadj* by once again circling the Ka'ba. In this context, the Ka'ba is seen as containing the very essence of God, and each of the seven circuits symbolizes one of God's attributes: life, speech, power, will, knowledge, hearing, and sight.

In Arabic the word translated as "circumambulation" is *tawaf*. It derives from the word *tafa*, which has the meaning "to attain to the summit of a thing by spiraling around it." For the faithful, the summit approached at Mecca is the doorway to God himself.

Left:
Decorating the drab cinder-block walls of the Ka'ba are black-and gold-draperies, embroidered with verses from the Koran. Because human and animal figures are forbidden as decorative themes, Arab art focuses on three other motifs: plants, geometric shapes, and Arabic script. All reflect the Arab culture's love of ideal forms and, as one Arabist puts it, the "triumph of thought, idea, and imagination over the mundane reality of form observable in nature." *Photo by Mehmet Biber/Photo Researchers*

Above and following pages:
Under the stadium lights of the Great Mosque at Mecca, tens of thousands of pilgrims orbit the Ka'ba, walking in seven ever-widening circles as they complete the *tafa*. Muhammad was born about 570 AD, just a quarter mile away, not far from the main caravan road to the northeast. Before Muhammad's army conquered the city in 630 AD, there were hundreds of idols in the ancient shrine, several of them female. *Photos by Mehmet Biber/Photopress International*

The Dogon of Mali. Photo by Jose Azel/Aurora

ASKING THE WAY: THE DOGON OF MALI AND THE ORACLE AT DELPHI

Prophesy is knowledge that comes before its time; it cannot be guessed at from present circumstances. Sometimes it comes at random, in unbidden dreams or visions, and sometimes it is sought from an outside source, from a comet, a spirit, a deck of cards, or yarrow stalks. The classical world's most famous source of prophesy was the oracle at Delphi on the slopes of Mount Parnassus. According to the oldest legends, a priestess there inhaled the stupefying odor of decay arising from the body of a giant serpent, the offspring of the goddess earth; from these fumes she construed answers of a kind, for all who came with questions.

For Africa's great holders of anterior knowledge, the Dogon tribe of Mali, prophesy was a gift. But it was unsought by them, and where the Delphic oracle derived from the world's dark forces, the

Delphi, Greece. Photo by Courtney Milne

Dogon experience was celestial; its agents, the Nommo, came from outerspace. The information given to the Dogon by the Nommo was integrated into a sophisticated religious account, which located the navel of the universe as well as the soul's origin and destination in the Sirius star system.

History credits the Delphic oracle with many successful prophesies, but many more divinations were ambiguous and depended on seekers following the injunction carved at Delphi on Apollo's temple—KNOW THYSELF. For the Greeks, whom we think of as highly civilized and orderly, the oracle involved communion with darker, more irrational forces. For the Dogon, who were without the benefits of a written language, prophesy brought information that was at once more abstract and more elevating than that which Delphi provided. In both cases, the process of prophesy involved a kind of balancing, and perhaps this is always the case for those who seek, or experience, foreknowledge.

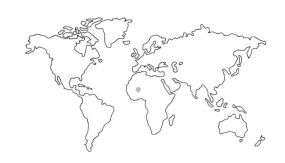

THE DOGON OF MALI

If beings from outer space wished to impart some knowledge to humans on earth, they might look for people who could keep a secret, people whose lives change slowly, who live far from the avenues of commerce and gossip. People not unlike the Dogon, who live in the remote Hombori Mountains of southern Mali. Their land is arid, their life is hard, and their farming methods are those of the Iron Age. Their myths, on the other hand, are entirely Space Age.

In their most secret religious teachings the Dogon record a curious story of visitors from another star system. The star people, called Nommos, and also the Instructors, came down to earth in a spinning ship. It made a great noise and wind and spurted blood when it landed. Something came out of the ship: it had four legs and dragged the ship to a hollow. The hollow filled with water and then the Nommos came out. They looked more like 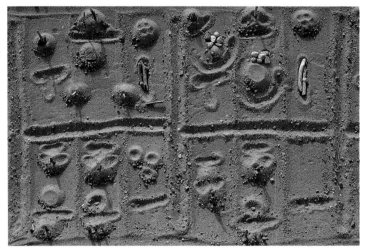 fish than humans, and they needed to stay in water. These Nommos were saviors and guardians for all of human kind. They gave advice. They gave their bodies for men to eat, and in the end they were crucified and will return to earth again one day with human bodies.

All this might be nothing more than one of the world's peculiar creation myths, which teem with beings visiting the earth from other worlds. But there is a difference: the Dogon's story is constructed around precise mathematical information about the star system the Nommos came from, near the bright star Sirius. The Nommos said that Sirius had a small companion star. It was white in color, very small, and immensely heavy. It rotated on its own axis and made an elliptical orbit of Sirius once every fifty earth years. All this is precisely true.

Until fairly recently, western astronomers knew nothing about a white dwarf star circling around Sirius. They first suspected that Sirius might have such a companion in 1844, when small disturbances in the star's movement were detected. Then, in 1928, astronomers understood that although Sirius' companion is very small (it is classed technically as a white dwarf and is called Sirius B), it is composed of extremely dense matter and therefore has enough mass to explain the effects. In 1970 the first photographs of the star were taken. The star's orbit, as the Dogon say, is elliptical and is completed in 50.04 years—a little more than two weeks longer than the Dogon predict.

Astronomers admit that the kind of knowledge the Dogon have about Sirius can only be obtained with advanced telescopes, which the Dogon have never possessed. They attempt to account for the Dogon's knowledge by a series of rationalizations. Sometime after 1928, a westerner with a compulsion to impart obscure knowledge must have visited the tribe and told them about the discovery of Sirius' satellite. Then, just for the pleasure of confusing the French anthropologist who collected the stories in 1934, the Dogon claimed they had had the information for centuries, and that it had been given to them by fish-like people from the stars. Even more ingeniously, the Dogon seem to have remembered a very ancient Babylonian story and modeled their ridiculous tale of the Nommos on it. This story, recorded in the 3rd century BC, tells how an egg-shaped vehicle landed in the Red Sea, and how out of it came an amphibious people called the Oannes. They looked terrible— half fish, half human—but they gave the people all the information needed to become more civilized.

Many astronomers now believe that among the vast number of stars and planets in the universe intelligent life may have evolved. The Dogon may be the last people on earth to preserve the record of an ancient contact between such extraterrestrials and members of our own species.

Left and above:
Nearly 250,000 Dogon people live around the cliffs of Bandiagara in the Hombori Mountains of Mali. The 900-foot-high cliffs are dotted with shamans' caves, burial grottoes, and granaries estimated to be over 500 years old. Many grottoes have become inaccessible: the long vines that once hung over the cliffs have withered and receded along with the forests that once produced them.

A diviner casts symbols in the sand in the Dogon village of Bongo. *Photos by Jose Azel/Aurora*

Left and above:

Banani, which means "I'm so tired I can't go on," is a typical Dogon village. The Dogon people originally trekked to Mali from the northeast, but their exact origin is not clear. They are millet farmers who depend on deep desert wells for their scant water supply, and when drought hit the sub-Saharan area in the 1980s, many starved.

A *hogon*, ruler priest, named Ansamba (*center*) oversees a ceremony commemorating the dead, in the cliffs near the village of Telli. He and his assistants have sacrificed three chickens and a sheep on the Amma Na, or rock altar, chanting as they work. In one Dogon story it is said that as the universe had drunk of his body the Nommo also made men drink.

Hogons are descendants of the eight original Dogon who were Nommos; they live apart from the rest of the tribe and no one is allowed to touch them.

Skulls of monkeys, birds, and other creatures peer from a fetish shrine at Kondu Guma. Before the Dogon people came, the Bandiagara cliffs were occupied by the Tellem people. (Tellem means "We found them.") According to Dogon legend, the Tellem were masters of the cliffs. They had horses that flew, or could fly themselves, and they used ropes that stood on end like staffs. They could also make their hands stick to the face of the cliff, which they climbed as easily as spiders. *Photos by Jose Azel/Aurora*

The Oracle at Delphi, Greece

Delphi, its white columns and plazas gleaming in the Mediterranean sun, seems a place of order and quiet. And so it is. But once it was a place of fear, and of prophecies that helped to shape the known world.

The history of Delphi, a drama in five acts, goes back to the Great Flood. After the waters had drained away, the earth was covered with a thick, fertile slime. Out of the ooze emerged a gigantic female serpent named Python, the daughter of the earth goddess Gaia. Python made her home in the caves of Mount Parnassus, and from there she sallied forth—vast, swollen and reeking of blood—to feast on the local people and their flocks. This is Act 1 of the drama: danger lurks and dark, female forces prevail. Delphi was then called Pytho, after the woman in charge. Gaia and another of her daughters, Themis, performed oracles there.

Act 2, enter the hero, Apollo, newly arrived at Parnassus from the island of Delphos. He is the sun god and the god of truth. He is the enemy of darkness and unreason. Taking his bow and arrow in hand, he kills the great serpent. Its body falls in a chasm, and from the huge, rotting bulk a miasmic stench rises through a cleft in the floor of a cave. The people rejoice at Python's death. They rename their village Delphi, after Apollo's homeland.

In Act 3 of the drama, Gaia too has been banished. A temple is built to Apollo, and the oracle moves in. Delphi continues to be a place of prophecy. A priestess named Pythia (the name now the only clue to the former owners), who will speak the words of Apollo, sits on a tripod inside. She inhales fumes that rise from a crack in the earth. Before beginning her oracular duties she has also inhaled the smoke of a potent mix of burning barley, marijuana, and chopped laurel leaves, the latter being sacred to Apollo.

Was the oracle accurate? It was renowned both for the ambiguity and the occasional plain accuracy of its answers, as a famous story demonstrates. Croesus, king of Lydia (560–46 BC), wanted to test the most highly regarded Greek oracles. He sent messengers to each one of them with instructions to ask, after exactly 100 days had passed, the following question: "What is the king of Lydia doing today?" Five of the oracles were wrong. A sixth was close. The oracle at Delphi replied as follows:

> Lo, in my sense there striketh the smell of a shell-covered tortoise,
> Boiling now in a fire, with the flesh of a lamb in a cauldron.
> Brass is the vessel below, and brass the cover above it.

As it happened, Croesus was, at that very moment, cooking a lamb-and-tortoise stew in a brass pot. Convinced of the oracle's accuracy, he questioned it about the more weighty question on his mind, namely the Persian Wars. The answer was that a great army would be defeated. Taking this for a good omen, Croesus sent his army into battle against Cyrus the Great. Again the oracle hit the mark, but it was Croesus' army that was defeated.

Act 4 of the Delphi drama. Time: 4th and 5th centuries BC. The oracle is well established. The cost of a private consultation has been set at a figure representing two days' wages for an average Athenian, not including the cost of goats to be sacrificed; state business (in keeping with current practice) is charged at ten times that rate. To satisfy all its customers, the oracle employs two priestesses working in shifts, with a third standing by in reserve. Those in urgent need of oracular help can obtain it by paying a special rush charge, the *promantoia*. But for matters of highest importance, full-scale consultations can only be had on the seventh day of the month, the day of Apollo's birth. In winter, the oracle is closed.

In the last act of the Delphi story, the oracle declines, as everything under the sun does. The Roman historian Plutarch (59–120 AD) was appointed high priest in an effort to restore its potency, but the gods wouldn't appear to him and the Pythia was uncooperative. Finally, in 362 AD, Delphi delivered its last oracle. The questioner was the Byzantine emperor Julian. He was trying to restore paganism in opposition to Christianity, and got the following depressing message: *Tell the king that the curiously built temple has fallen to the ground, that bright Apollo no longer has a roof over his head, or prophetic laurel, or babbling spring. Yes, even the murmuring water has dried up.*

Left:
The Sanctuary of Athena Pronaia, the foretemple, lies on the path to the site of Apollo's temple. Every Greek, and certainly every Athenian, would have stopped here to make some small gift to the patron of the city, and to ask for the goddess' help in his or her quest. Athena's temple is before Apollo's in other ways. The old temple columns (*foreground*), which have stood in place since the 5th century BC, were built over the ancient location of the oracle of Gaia. *Photo by Gary Braasch*

Above:

From the details of the ruins one can begin to construct the grandeur of the whole. Reordered on wooden shelves, the stone fragments of an entire civilization fill the 13 rooms of the Delphi Museum. Steles, entablatures, pediments, metopes, bronzes, marbles, friezes, statues of Athenian athletes, griffin heads, nymphs, all found on site, catalogue the comings and goings of several millenia. *Photo by Richard Ross*

Left:

The Doric columns of the Temple of Apollo rise out of the ages. Beyond them, the green hills of Parnassus flow to the sea. It is this conjunction of natural and constructed elements that contributes to Delphi's memorable power. Apollo's temple dominates the center of the sanctuary at Delphi. Built in the 4th century BC, the Doric structure once had 42 columns in its peristyle. On the seventh day of each month, the Pythia (the woman through whom Apollo spoke) took her seat behind these stately columns and prophesied. Apollo was above all the God of Truth, as verses from the era record: *(Photo by Hans Wiesenhofer/Anzenberger)*
O Phoebus [Apollo], *from your throne of truth, return*
from your dwelling place at the heart of the world,
you speak to men.
By Zeus's decree no lie comes there
no shadow to darken the word of truth
Zeus sealed by an everlasting rite.
Apollo's honor, that all may trust
with unshaken faith when he speaks.

Western Wall, Israel. Photo by David H. Wells/JB Pictures

TALKING TO GOD: WESTERN WALL AND BLACK HILLS AND BADLANDS

The point of contact between a people and their God varies according to their orbits. The Jews, a wandering people, have found contact by returning to a fixed point, the Western Wall. The Lakota are a centralized people who find God by scattering outward into the land of South Dakota.

For Jews, history's supreme moments occur when God is revealed in a personal relationship with mankind. Places that mark such revelations are holy, and so, by extension, are the lands around them. These places contain the physical evidence of God's appearance in the world. Jerusalem's Western Wall, a remnant of the Holy Temple, is such a place. It is a place chosen and watched over by God, a place where the Jewish people's cries and prayers to God are heard directly.

Badlands, South Dakota, USA. Photo by Jim Brandenburg/Minden Pictures

For many peoples, including the Lakota of North America, the divine does not abide at a singular fixed point but is revealed in a circle. The Lakota find the power of the universe interwoven and unending in everything they see, and trace the holy from plant to thundercloud, from sky to animal to man. They see the Black Hills and Badlands of South Dakota, and every animal, river, and cloud they contain, as the pure expression of a spiritual presence. It is into this land they go to speak with the spirits.

The paths of both peoples are found traced in a saying from the Christian mystics, who held that "God is a circle whose circumference is everywhere, and whose center is nowhere."

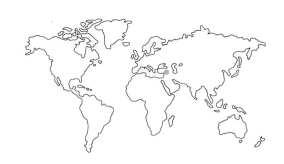

THE WESTERN WALL, ISRAEL

The *Kotel Maaravi*, or Western Wall, is the only remaining section of the massive wall that once surrounded the second temple. The first temple, built in the 10th century BC by King Solomon, was the sanctuary for Israel's holy of holies, the Ark of the Covenant. The Ark was a wooden box containing two stone tablets upon which God had inscribed his covenant with the Jewish people, and which he had given to Moses on Mount Sinai during the exodus from Egypt. As the Israelites traveled north from Egypt, they carried the Ark in a portable tabernacle. During the day God covered it with a pillar of cloud and by night with a column of fire. Once the Ark had been placed in the Temple's innermost sanctum, a cloud of unbearable glory, God's own presence, filled the room. Too bright for the priests to endure, it signified the sure homecoming of the Jewish people. The original temple was destroyed in 586 BC by the Babylonians. After the destruction of the second temple by the Romans in the first century and the later dispersal of the Jewish people, the surviving Western Wall became a focal point for the prayers and grief of the exiles, and thus gained its better-known name, the Wailing Wall.

In 1967, Golda Meir, Israel's future president, followed Israeli troops into Jerusalem's Old City, just captured in the Six Day War. As she stood before the Western Wall there, in the city that Jews had been forbidden to enter for the last nineteen years, she was filled with hope for the future of her people. Years later she recalled what she had seen on that fateful day: *There in that narrow alley—not the wide plaza that now stretches in front of the wall today—was a plain table, with a few Sten guns on it! Uniformed paratroopers wrapped in praying shawls were clinging so tightly to the wall that it seemed impossible to separate them from it—they and the Wall were one. These heroes, who only a few hours before had fought furiously for the liberation of Jerusalem, who had seen their comrades fall for Jerusalem's sake, went up to the Wall. They wept and wrapped themselves in praying shawls. . . . These were not Jews who had come to the wall to wail because they were not free and because we had not come home. These were men who had fought a bitter battle and who believed that this wall was now a symbol of the future and of the independence and dignity of Israel.*

But the Wall is not merely sacred for its past associations. For Jews, it is a place where God's divine presence remains and will always remain. This is because the Temple Mount, where God first directed Solomon to build his temple, is situated directly beneath God's own transcendent, heavenly Temple. The two sites, one worldly and the other celestial, are thus inseparably linked, and the Wall is continuously bathed in the divinity of God's presence. Moreover, to see the Wall is to be seen simultaneously by God, for (God says), ". . . mine eyes shall be open, and mine ears attend unto the prayer that is made in this place." At the Wall, God hears as well as sees the fervor of his people, and this is why prayers, supplications, and repentance are offered there more effectively than anywhere else. And even more: once the gift of God's direct presence has been obtained at the Wall, it is passed on to the children of those who have received it, and to their children's children, and so on, for all generations. Thus God's blessing spreads through history, traveling outward from its point of origin in ever-widening and infinitely embracing circles.

Left:
An aerial view of the Western Wall and the Dome of the Rock (*top center*), shows the multiple levels of civilization and faith that have shaped Jerusalem. The Dome of the Rock, a sacred site of Islam, stands on the foundation of the Temple of Solomon. The temple was built by the Jews around 950 BC, destroyed and rebuilt. A segment of the wall that surrounded the ancient temple survives as the Western Wall. *Photo by David H. Wells/Swanstock*

Above:
According to basic Jewish prayer "You shall love the Lord your God with all your heart, with all your soul, and with all your might." A reverent Jew bends in fervent supplication as he prays at the Wall. *Photo by David H. Wells/JB Pictures*

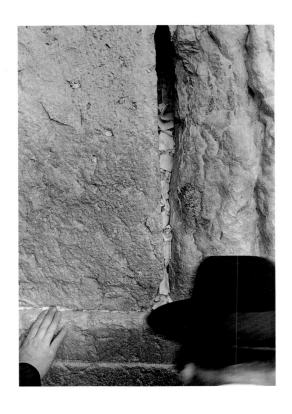

Above:

The paper prayers of thousands of pilgrims who visit the Western Wall fill the cracks between the stones. Periodically the prayers are cleaned out of the wall and disposed of. The Jewish idea of the covenant, a personal agreement between people and God, which is renewed and discussed on a regular basis, explains some of the correspondence. Prayers can now be faxed from all over the world to an agency which takes the actual paper and stuffs it into the wall. *Photo by David H. Wells/JB Pictures*

Right:

The Western Wall is divided by the *mehitzah* which delineates areas of prayer for men and for women. The wall is a contact point of shared history for all Jews, who as a people have few gathering places of ritual significance. It is the word of God that has been their central meeting place; it is around the word they gather. *Photo by David H. Wells/Swanstock*

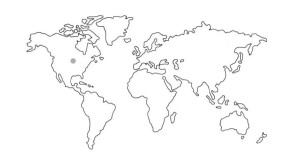

BADLANDS AND BLACK HILLS, USA

The young Lakota has been purified in the sweat lodge. He is preparing to enter the land and for the holiness of the land to enter him. He has heard the voice of the hot rocks hissing in steam as the water hits them, and the poisons that weaken his body and cloud his mind have been dispelled. He leaves the sweat lodge, wearing only a breechcloth and a buffalo-skin robe, his hair loose; the vision-seeker must be humble, as he indicates by his nakedness and his unbraided hair. He leaves his village and begins walking. He is beginning his vision quest; in his language it is called *hanble ceyapi*: "crying for a vision." He climbs until he comes to the high point where his quest will begin.

The young man has come here to find his power. He will find it only if a vision is granted. He cries out to the *Wakan Tanka*: the forces which animate the universe and appear in many forms. And he weeps, imploring the help of the sacred *wakan* beings, seeking their sympathy. Above all, he remains attentive to his own mind

and the visions that may stir in it. Whatever comes, whether heat, cold, hunger, thirst, or biting insects, he remains at his place. When the vision comes, it will empower him with the power of the mountains, animals, and plants, with the power of the special *wakan* that grant his vision. By studying and relating his vision, he will learn what shape his life should take, and what his special responsibilities should be.

Although the entire Black Hills region of South Dakota is sacred to the Lakota, some parts possess greater power. Black Elk, the Lakota sage, was transported to Harney Peak in his vision. From there he saw all mankind, and all the things that were both good and harmful in the great circle of the four directions. When he was an old man, he returned to the peak to pray for the life and welfare of his people, calling in sorrow to the *Wakan Tanka*. As a sign that his prayers were heard, rain fell from a previously clear sky and there was a sound of thunder.

Bear Butte, rising sharply from the rolling grassland, is a place sacred to both the Lakota and Cheyenne. General Custer demonstrated his contempt for Indian "superstition" by proudly riding his horse to the butte's summit. Before long, he and his men lay dead at the Little Bighorn, slain by the great Crazy Horse and his warriors.

Southeast of the Black Hills lie the Badlands. Here, more than one hundred years ago, was performed the Ghost Dance, the central ritual in a peaceful movement that prophesied the renewal of Indian peoples. Seen by the white authorities as a threat, the dance became a pretext for repressions that culminated in 1890 with the murder of more than 200 men, women, and children at a campsite on Wounded Knee Creek by the U.S. Army. With the massacre, the white barbarians sealed their possession of the sacred lands, and the Lakota dead were unceremoniously buried in a mass grave. Many of the children, "with their bodies shot to pieces, [were] thrown naked into the pit." Among the men, many were wearing Ghost Dance shirts, each decorated with emblems of the vision its owner had once found in the nearby hills.

Left:
Two buffalo roam the Badlands, on the edge of the Great Plains in South Dakota. The Lakota once followed enormous buffalo herds into the mazelike landscape, where the animals were easier to stalk and hunt. *Photo by Jim Brandenburg/Minden Pictures*

Above:
Bear Butte in the Black Hills. The Lakota call it Mato Paha, which means Bear Mountain, the Cheyenne call it Noahavose, the Good Mountain. It's here, according to legend, that the great Cheyenne prophet and leader, Sweet Medicine, met Maheo, the Creator of All. Maheo gave Sweet Medicine four arrows. Two arrows bestowed power over the buffalo, and the other two power over men. Both the Cheyenne and the Lakota still return to the mountain on vision quests. *Photo by Don Doll, S. J.*

Above:
In the Badlands it rains an average of 16 inches per year. Temperatures slide between –30°F and 115°F. The clay soil is eroding away by as much as six inches per year. In a few million years the Badlands will have disappeared. Despite their geological frailty and forbidding nature, the Badlands and the Black Hills have offered spiritual sanctuary of a durable kind. Black Elk, the Oglala prophet, relates a story from a Lakota man who *dreamed that the four leggeds (buffalo) were going back into the earth and that a strange race had woven a spider's web all around the Lakotas. And he said "When this happens, you shall live in square gray houses in a barren land."* Photo by Michael A. Smith/Swanstock

Angkor Wat, Cambodia. Photo by Marc Riboud

IMPERIAL REALMS: ANGKOR WAT AND KARNAK

We hunt through history like jackdaws for fragments of the looking glass which, if ever assembled, might show the full image of our human face. Often the records we seek are buried, sometimes in archives, often, like the ruins of Karnak, in desert sand or, like Angkor Wat, beneath tropical jungle. Major discoveries fill the gaps in human history, and can even reveal, as the discovery of Angkor Wat did, the face of an unknown empire.

Despite ourselves, we are surprised to find that people of ancient cultures were as intelligent, enterprising, and aesthetically advanced as we are. At other times we conclude that

Karnak, Egypt. Photo by Richard Misrach/Courtesy of Frankel Gallery, San Francisco

*the achievements we admire were built at social, political, and human costs that would now
be completely unacceptable.*

*At Karnak, for example, a dynasty of absolute monarchs claimed divine descent,
bolstered its power with the help of a state religion, and was able to dragoon the population
into building its monuments. At Angkor Wat the monarch also claimed sacred distinction.
Even to organize the hauling of stone for his capital, he must have controlled the Khmer
people rigidly. At both sites we experience something fascinating and magnificent, but also
grandiose and even oppressive.*

ANGKOR WAT, CAMBODIA

It is 1860, and a French botanist strikes out, by canoe and on foot, from the northern shores of Cambodia's Tonle Sap, the Great Lake. In front of him lies dense forest, and in the far distance a range of mountains. Henri Mouhot is in search of a rumored city, the monument of a lost civilization long since overwhelmed by the jungle. The French missionary priest who has told him stories of the city has joined him in the search. The jungle is quiet save for the soft call of tropical doves and the occasional howling of animals.

At length, the two Frenchmen find themselves at the edge of a moat. Beyond it a temple rises, hoary with vegetation; they have found the temple city of Angkor Wat, the ancient capital of the Khmer empire. They come at last to a ditch choked with the remains of a stone menagerie: fragments of lions and elephants lie jumbled among stone blocks and broken columns. Soon they reach a great arched gateway set in a crumbled wall of red stone enclosing some 24 square miles of jungle. Two miles beyond the gate, Mouhot and his companion find a gigantic pile of ruins: Beyond the temple of Angkor Wat they have reached the Bayon, the central complex of a second city, the walled confine of Angkor Thom. Here and there overgrown towers of monumental buildings reach the sky above the jungle roof.

On galleries and walls a profusion of carvings shows scenes from the life of a forgotten civilization: an army on the march, a naval battle, the dignities and pleasure of a royal court.

Mouhot saw and wondered. Later he wrote in his diary: "How many centuries and thousands of generations have passed away, of which history, probably, will never tell us anything: what riches and treasure of art will remain forever buried beneath these ruins." He had found, he believed, a site "grander than anything left to us by Greece and Rome," a site rivaling the temple of Solomon, and so glorious that it must have been erected by "some ancient Michelangelo."

By the end of the following year, Mouhot lay dead in the forests of Laos, far away from the ruins of Angkor. But his diary was brought back to Bangkok and eventually published. Eyebrows were raised, expeditions mounted, and by 1878 statues from Angkor were on display in French museums.

Now jump forward in time, 115 years from Mouhot's discovery of the ancient capital of the Khmer empire. Soldiers of the Khmer Rouge have possession of Angkor. They dream of creating an empire as vast as that of the Khmer from whom they take their name. They enslave the people of Cambodia, as the ancient Khmer must have enslaved the population for the completion of their projects. In the ruins, the soldiers decapitate Buddha figures, brood on the philosophy of their leader, Pol Pot, and use for target practice the languorous, divine bodies of the female *apsaras* decorating the temple walls.

But with some faint trace of respect for their Khmer forebears, they do not reduce Angkor to rubble. Within five years, the Khmer Rouge are ousted from power. The work of conservation begins again at the ruins. Roots are delicately pried from stone, fallen blocks are numbered for rebuilding, walls and arches are shored up and strengthened. Buddhist monks come back to the temples to resume their practice, and gradually the world's greatest religious monument emerges again from the jungle.

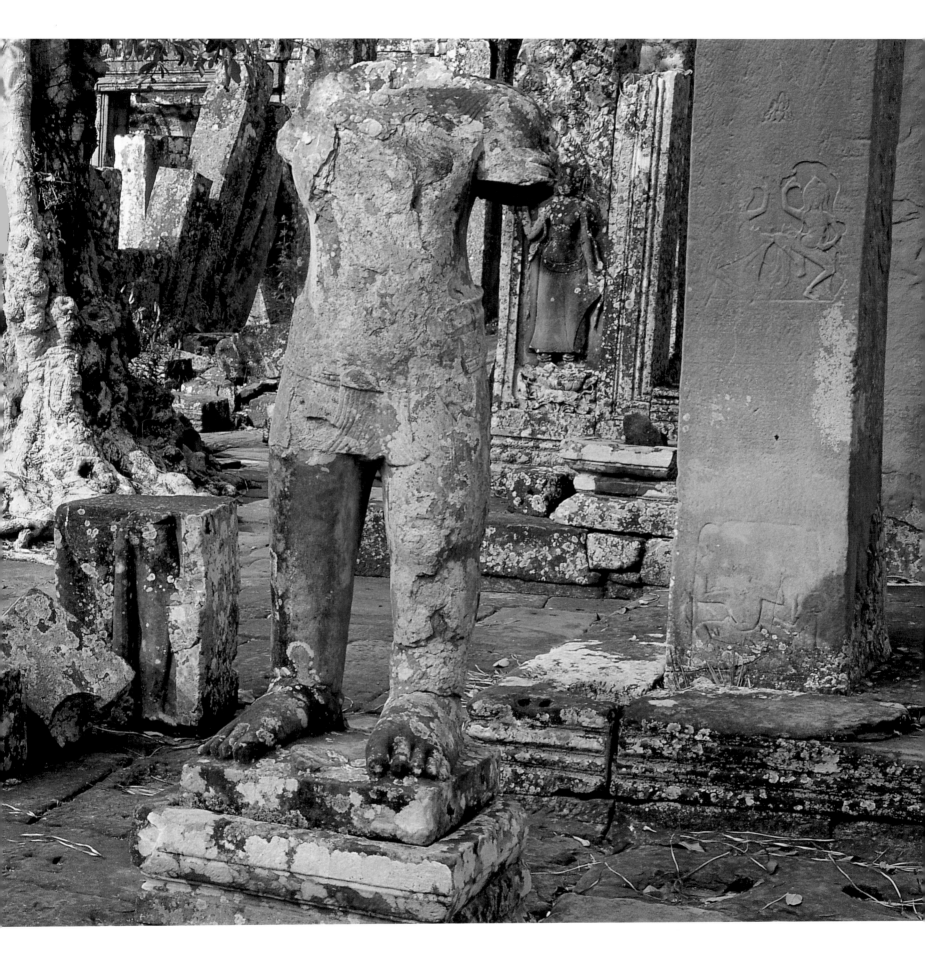

Above:
A headless statue wanders among the ruins of the Angkor Thom temple, just to the north of Angkor Wat. Together the 40-square-mile complex comprises the most extensive religious monument in the world. The French archeologists who saw Angkor Wat for the first time in the mid-19th century wondered what grand civilization had built it: the Romans or Alexander the Great, the Chinese perhaps? The Cambodians of the day were of little help; they said the temples were made by giants and angels. *Photo by Courtney Milne*

Left:
Crouching at the Banteay Srei temple is a stone Hanuman, the guardian monkey known for his courage and devotion as an ally of Rama in the *Ramayana*, the great Sanskrit epic that incorporates many of the legends and beliefs of Hinduism. Such is the vast legacy of Angkor Wat: it is a stone encyclopedia of Indian, Chinese, and Southeast Asian cultural and religious beliefs. *Photo by David Portnoy/Black Star*

Above:
Erected as protector deities along the temple's fringe, these stone figures have suffered the vandalism of centuries. In the time-honored tradition of cultural conquest, succesive occupants of Angkor Wat have tried to cut off the heads, the breasts, the hands, and the power of many of the figures. Those that remain seem to do so out of fierce loyalty to the Khmers, who flourished here from the 7th to the 15th century. *Photo by Ira Chaplain/Black Star*

Right:
What vandals have left intact the forces of nature threaten to swallow. The creeping figs that strangle Ta Prohm temple were probably there when Mouhot first came in 1860. Birds drop fig seeds, which sprout roots that wind their way down towers and trees on their way to earth, working through masonry and prying stones apart. Sitting atop Mount Bakheng, looking down at the complex of temples, walls, and moats that once housed half a million people, Mouhot wrote, "How many centuries and thousands of generations have passed away of which history, probably, will never tell us anything." *Photo by Roland and Sabrina Michaud/Woodfin Camp*

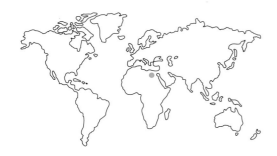

KARNAK, EGYPT

The ancient temple complex at Karnak on the east bank of the river Nile represents perhaps the most grandiose union of imperialism and metaphysics the world has ever seen. It was built, rebuilt, modified, and remodified over a period of more than 2,000 years, but was always at the service of the rulers of the Egyptian capital, Thebes, and the so-called Theban triad—the god Amun, his wife Mut, and his son Khonsu. It was a treasury into which flowed carnelian, turquoise, gold, rare marble building stones, and all the vast spoils of Egypt's expansive empire.

The first stage in the growth of Thebes occurred when its princes united Egypt under the Eleventh Dynasty (2133–1901 BC). Then, around 1560 BC, the rulers of the Eighteenth Dynasty expelled the Semitic Hyksos and formed the New Kingdom.

The 250 acres covered by the ruins at Karnak contain an extraordinary array of temples (dedicated to "guest" gods as well as to the Theban triad), obelisks, hypostyles (enormous halls whose roofs were supported by numerous pillars), and the massive ceremonial gateways known as pylons. The largest of these pylons is 370 feet wide and faces an avenue of ram-headed sphinxes leading to a landing stage on the Nile. Beyond the pylon is a huge courtyard containing temples dedicated to the triad and "way stations" at which the gods "rested" during their annual boat journey to Amun's second temple at Luxor when the Nile flooded. Beyond a massive statue of the pharaoh Rameses II is the great hypostyle court; it is considerably bigger than a football field and supported by 134 columns arranged in sixteen rows. The largest columns—12 of them, arranged in a central row—rise like massive tree trunks that are 70 feet high and 33 feet around. The placement of each was set by patterns inscribed in Egyptian religion, while the temple's use reflected Egyptian social structures. Laboring classes attended temple rituals by gathering under the sun in the open courtyard, straining to catch a glimpse of the priests passing by carrying the statues of a deity on their shoulders. Local officials and scribes were allowed into the second level, the twilight midsection, the hypostyle, while the dark inner chamber, where the statue of the deity resided, was reserved for priests and the highest dignitaries. The designs of the temples vary, but columns shaped like palms, lotus bundles, or papyrus stalks were popular. Ceilings were painted with the constellations of the zodiac, with vultures and stars recreating the Egyptian night in the clear blackness of the temple's interior.

This union of religion and warfare served Theban royalty well for some 500 years, but in 1085 BC the capital moved to Tanis in the Nile Delta, and subsequently Libyan and Nubian dynasties ruled Egypt. For more than 400 years after the decline of Theban royalty, the priests of Amun maintained a kind of theocracy, but in 661 BC, Amun-indifferent Assyrians, themselves no strangers to pillage, ripped through Egypt and dismembered the New Kingdom and its capital. The biblical prophet Nahum described the debacle with some relish:

Ethiopia and Egypt were her strength, and it was infinite; Put and Lubim were thy helpers . . .

Yet she was carried away, she went into captivity; her young children also were dashed in pieces at the top of all the streets; and they cast lots for her honorable men, and her great men were bound in chains. [3: 9–10]

The Assyrians were followed by Persian and Greek invaders, and in 29 BC, Thebes was sacked by the Romans. Most traces of the palaces and government buildings were obliterated, but the temples remained, the gargantuan and astonishing legacy of dead gods and an exhausted regime.

Above:
The identity of his face lost over time, a seated colossus presides over a portion of the extensive ruins of Karnak, the ancient city of Thebes. Since its beginnings in 2000 BC, pharaohs, queens, and princes of the ages have added their likeness or design to the great religious center. One inscription at Karnak reads:

It [the temple] *contains numerous royal statues . . . of every splendid costly stone, established as everlasting works. Their stature shines more than the heavens, their rays are in the faces of men like the sun, when he shines early in the morning. Photo by Richard Misrach/Courtesy of Frankel Gallery, San Francisco*

Left:
These capital-topped columns stand in the First
Courtyard of the Temple of Amun, a smaller court in
the vast complex of Thebes, the capital of Egypt from
2133 BC to 1085 BC. Amun, which means "hidden,"
was initially a local god conceived of as the breath
that gave life to all living things. *Photo by Markova/
Mexico/The Stock Market*

Above:
The temples at Karnak stand along a darkening Nile.
Priests once approached them from the river, disem-
barking at a small pier and following a ceremonial
path to the entrance. From its two main tributaries,
the Blue Nile out of Ethiopia and the White Nile
from Uganda, the river flows more than 4,000 miles
into the Mediterranean. The Nile is the secret of
Egypt, simultaneously spinal chord, artery, and
muscle. It allowed the Egyptians to move stones to
build pyramids to travel to the next world, and to
grow the grain and papyrus which fed and linked their
civilization with this world. *Photo by Richard Misrach/
Courtesy of Frankel Gallery, San Francisco*

Right:
A hieroglyph relief on a temple wall at Karnak depicts
a snake and an owl. The owl had the approximate
sound of an 'm,' one of the 24 single-consonant
sounds and an indeterminate number of two- and
three-consonant combinations that made up Egyptian
hieroglyphic language. There was no space between
words or punctuation to stop the stream of language.
Words could be read in any direction: up, down or
across. Animals usually faced the direction from
which the sentence began. *Photo by Wayne Eastep*

Swayambhunath, Nepal. Photo by William Thompson

HEIGHTS OF VISION: SWAYAMBHUNATH AND MONT-SAINT-MICHEL

Often when the sea-mist rolls across the Gulf of Saint Malo the roofs and spires of Mont-Saint-Michel seem to float in the sky, ethereal and otherworldly. This is the romantic essence and spirit of Abbot Hildebert's gothic tribute to the archangel Michael, the "captain of the heavenly host," who fought the dragon Lucifer and cast him out of heaven with his sword.

The golden disks atop the great Buddhist stupa at Swayambhunath shine like a burning flame surrounded by the peaks of the high Himalayas. Here the Bodhisattva Manjusri cast out the snake-like nagas who once inhabited a lake in the Kathmandu Valley. He, too, carried a sword, but when Manjusri banished the nagas he kindly used it to carve a small lake for their leader to live in.

Mont-Saint-Michel, France. Photo by Cotton Coulson/Comstock/SGC

Mont-Saint-Michel, in its soaring arches of granite and light, expresses a longing for freedom from repressive theology. It was built during the age of Abelard, who was castrated for his love of Heloise and became a monk. It was Abelard who wrote that motive and deed were critically important, and that reason should be the guiding force in the new world. Similarly, Swayambhunath was built during a kind of golden age in the Kathmandu Valley, when the Lichavis brought Sanskrit, poetry, and a love of art to the area.

Two major sites of pilgrimage: an 11th-century Roman Catholic church built on a mount of land that is now surrounded by the sea, and a 5th-century Buddhist stupa built on a hill in a valley that was once a lake. Though the waters around each place flow in or out, the original energy of the mounts remains, resplendent and ascendant, tributes to each culture's intense longing for an enlightened view.

Above:
Pausing in the heavy mist of a Himalayan morning, a reverent visitor prays to a small stupa at the foot of Swayambhunath. The shapes of these small stupas are a micro-version of the main stupa on the hilltop (*see page 98*); both encapsulate the sacred geometry of Buddhist architecture. By the arrangement of square, circle, triangle, crescent, and teardrop, Buddhists represent the nature of the elements, the nature of the senses, and the order of the process of the dissolution of the body after death. *Photo by Kevin Bubriski*

Swayambhunath, Nepal

The great Buddhist stupa at Swayambhunath in Nepal's Kathmandu Valley crowns a hill that rose miraculously from a lake that once filled the valley. Sacred lotus plants covered the surface of the lake; under their buoyant petals, the water lay deep and clear. But the waters were filled with swirling snake-like beings called nagas. One day a flame burst forth from one of the lotus flowers and its petals glowed with the colors of gold and jewels. The flower was recognized as the presence of the primordial Buddha, and its fame spread wide. Manjusri, an enlightened being, came to visit the famous site and took a walk around the lake. It would be a fine place for people to live, he thought, if it weren't for these troublesome reptiles. As the embodiment and protector of Wisdom, Manjusri carried a sword in order to cut through ignorance wherever he saw it. Now he raised it and cut a good-sized notch out of the Himalayas near Chobar. The waters of the lake emptied through the opening in the mountains and the snakes flowed out with it—all except the king of the nagas, and for him Manjusri thoughtfully carved out a small lake now known as Taudha. As the water drained away, the blazing lotus grew to become Swayambhu hill.

It is known for certain that the Kathmandu Valley was a lake, and the hill an island. It is known that there was an important Buddhist temple on this site more than 2,000 years ago. The first recorded work done on the stupa (a symbolic three-tiered Buddhist monument) was ordered by King Manadeva in 460 AD. By 1346 the great stupa at Swayambhunath was so well established as a place of pilgrimage that Bengali Muslims vandalized it in search of gold, not noticing that Swayambhunath's real treasure had always been in the teachings it embodies.

A great staircase ascends the hill from the east. It was built in the 17th century by King Pratap Malla, and at its base is a stone footprint made, according to the faithful, either by the historical Buddha, Sakyamuni, or by Manjusri. Halfway up this arduously climbed staircase are carved scenes of the Buddha's miraculous birth, and near the top stand pairs of the animals associated with the five families of Buddhas: elephants, horses, peacocks, lions, and the mythical birdlike creatures known as garudas. As you climb you will also notice some other animals: living, food snatching, here and now monkeys.

It seems that our images of perfection must always overlay some other image of imperfection by which ordinary humans can be embraced. In Gothic cathedrals, the role of the imperfect is filled by gargoyles; grotesque and demonic mannequins that give human frailty scale in the soaring context of the church. At Swayambhunath, these tribes of greedy, thieving monkeys guard the approach to this supreme model of cosmic wholeness and enlightenment.

The Swayambhunath stupa is a complete representation in stone of the purely formal universe. The geometry of the shapes from which the stupa is composed represents the five elements that comprise the cosmos: earth, the square platform on which the stupa is set; water, the round white dome of the stupa's base; fire, the triangular golden crown topped by two smaller ornaments; a crescent representing air; and a teardrop shape for the fifth element, space. Around the stupa, representations of the Buddhas of the five families oversee a long series of prayer wheels, which are turned as pilgrims circle the stupa's base.

From its founding to its location and design, the entire stupa represents the liberation of the cosmos in wisdom. And so, from the golden block surmounting its dome, the eyes of the Buddha gaze dispassionately and compassionately in all directions, comprehending at once the pilgrim and his close relations, the Swayambhunath monkeys.

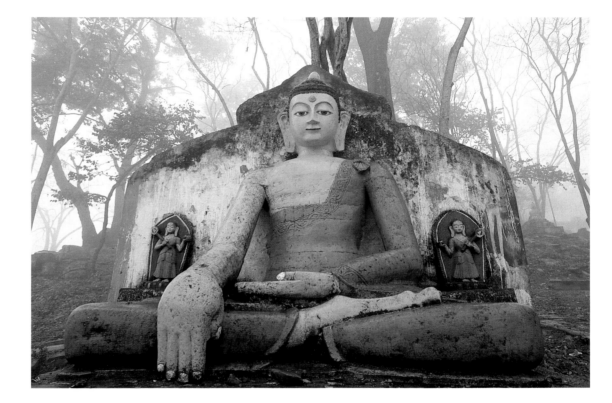

Left:

With eyes that shine from the depths of permanent meditation, the Buddha looks out in four directions over the Kathmandu Valley. The smaller third eye represents the ability to see into the future, as well as all around. The Buddha's face is of a unique Nepalese design: the coiled staff of his nose is also the Nepali numeral *ek* or one, and symbolizes unity. The 13 round golden disks that crown the stupa represent the successive steps along the path to Enlightenment. The monkey in the foreground represents the primates. The stupa is a common structure throughout the Buddhist world, though few rival the power of the stupa of Swayambhunath. *Photo by R. Ian Lloyd*

Top:

Draped like festive decorations for some impending celebration, thousands of prayer flags ascend the stupa. Printed with Buddhist prayers, the flags are hung outside where the wind can lift their messages from the thin cotton cloths and carry them throughout the countryside. *Photo by Kevin Bubriski*

Bottom:

The Buddha Shakyamuni touches the ground to call earth as his witness against the forces of evil and destruction. The "earth touching" pose of the Buddha is just one part of the complex gathering of statues, stupas, monuments, prayer wheels, and small shrines that cover the sacred wooded hillside of Swayambhunath. *Photo by Robert Holmes/Photo 20-20*

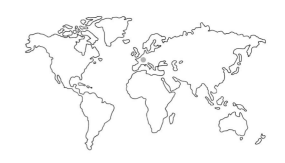

MONT-SAINT-MICHEL, FRANCE

Depending on the direction of your approach, the tiny island of Mont-Saint-Michel may seem irregular or cone-shaped; it may seem tree-covered, covered with houses, or girt with castle walls. Once you have explored the island, your sense of its multiple character will be confirmed, and it will seem that you have visited a place where church, castle, and village combine to form a microcosm of medieval society.

The island, now ringed by the sands of a wide bay in the Gulf of Saint Malo, also bears witness to the course of man's spiritual beliefs for more than 2,000 years. At the beginning of the 8th century, this rock, which was not then surrounded by the sea, was known as Mont Tombe, perhaps recalling a legend of its earlier history as a cemetery. Before that it was known as a site where Druids, and later Romans, worshipped a sun god. The first Christian constructions on the Mont were begun in 708, after Saint Auvert, then bishop of neighboring Avranches, had dreamed, no less than three times, that the Archangel Michael (destroyer of pagan shrines,

especially those on hilltops, his special provenance) had visited him and told him to build a place of prayer on the rock, reinforc- ing his instructions on his last visit by tapping the doubt- ful bishop smartly on the pate.

By the second half of the 10th century, a group of 50 Benedictine monks had settled on the island, along with a small lay community, and within a hundred years an abbey had been built on the crown of the rock. It was no coincidence, con- sidering its patron, that William the

Conqueror prayed at Mont-Saint-Michel before going off to conquer England. But the greater conquest of the 11th century was the First Crusade, when the inheritors of the traditions of Charlemagne and Constantine united against the East, where the source of Christianity's holy *light* was at stake. It was this crusade that powered the artistic expression embodied in Mont-Saint-Michel. In 1203 a great building program was begun by Abbot Jourdain. Within 25 years, and by dint of quarrying stones on the mainland, shipping them to the island, and hauling them sometimes more than 300 feet to the summit, a group of extraordinary Gothic buildings known as the Marvel had been built. Situated on the north side of the island, they include, to the east, the Almonry, where the monks cared for pilgrims and the poor, the Guest Room, and the Refectory, the monks' dining room. In the western part of the Marvel are the monastery's cellars, and above them is the Hall of Knights, originally a place where the monks copied manuscripts, but after 1496 the meeting place of the royal Knights of Saint Michael. Above this great hall are the cloisters, where the monks could walk in meditation or for exercise. The architecture of the cloister court has been thought to suggest the more feminine aspects of religion—love, poetry, and reflection—in contrast to the Great Hall below, with its demonstration of the masculine—will, construc- tion, and action. Soaring above everything is the church, built between the 11th and 16th centuries, its slender spire topped by a golden figure of the triumphant Archangel Michael.

Below the church buildings a wall fortifies the Mont. With its help the island withstood many attacks, principally from the English during the Hundred Years' War. Despite such difficulties, Mont-Saint-Michel has remained a major place of pilgrimage throughout most of its history, although it became a prison during the French Revolution and remained one until 1863. Restoration of the historic buildings began in 1874, and religious services were held there again for the first time in 1922. Today, a causeway links Mont-Saint-Michel with the shore, and pilgrims and tourists alike visit the lofty church and mingle, as they have done since the Middle Ages, in the cafés and shops of the main street, the winding Grande Rue.

Left:
The nave of Mont-Saint-Michel is barely visible in a heavy downpour of sunlight. Gothic architects sacrificed everything— even safety—for light, which symbolized not only a physical link between heaven and earth, but also the spirit and energy of the age. *Photo by Daniel Faure/Scope*

Above:
The cloister court of Mont-Saint-Michel is one of the most famous examples of early Gothic architecture. The style is expressed by this double row of pillars, which form a common border between court and outer range. *Photo by Jean Daniel Sudres/Scope*

Left:

Rising up from the coast of Normandy, the Abbey of Mont-Saint-Michel is named for Michael the Archangel, who appeared to Bishop Auvert in the 8th century and ordered him to build a monastery on this rock. Today Saint-Michel stands with Saint-Denis and Chartres as the third in the trinity of great French cathedrals of the Gothic transition. Henry Adams summed up the open-armed spirit of the place in his famous reflection, *Mont-Saint-Michel and Chartres: The priest and soldier were both at home here, in 1215 as in 1115 or in 1058; the politician was not outside of it; the sinner was welcome; the poet was made happy in his own spirit, with a sympathy . . . that suggests a habit of verse in the Abbot as well as in the architect. God reconciles all.* Photo by Charles Bowman/Scope

Above:

The original church built on the mount in 1020 by Abbot Hildebert was a modest 250 feet long. Succeeding abbots and architectural fashions demanded ever more arches and towers until it was all too much—by 1776 all but four arches of the original nave had collapsed or been torn down. In the early 15th century, Abbot Pierre le Roy plastered over the gate of the châtelet, and it was that change that most affected the nature of Mont-Saint-Michel. The celebration of light and the lyrical affinity of the mount with the poetry of *La Chanson de Roland* was hidden by this foreboding façade, erected under the spectre of religious wars and the corrosion of society. *Photo by Paul Spinelli/Profiles West*

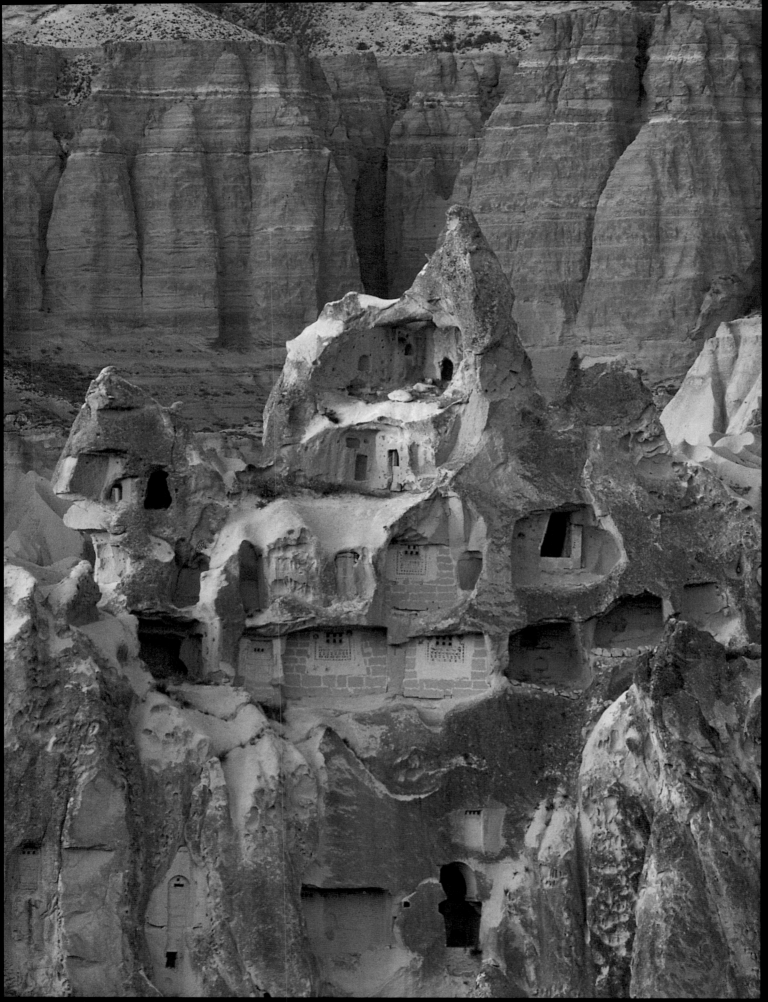

Cappadocia, Turkey. Photo by Hans-Jurgen Burkard/Bilderberg

SECRET CITIES: CAPPADOCIA AND PETRA

Hidden in the dry heat of Jordan, the city of Petra was undisturbed for 2,000 years. Buried from view in the canyons of an inhospitable plateau, the city's multicolored façades, reservoirs, and decorated tombs remained intact, and were no more vulnerable to time than the rock in which they were carved. On a plateau in the Cappadocian region of Turkey, houses, churches, and even whole underground cities were also carved into rock, a soft volcanic tufa. They too remained immune to weather, banditry, and the passage of time.

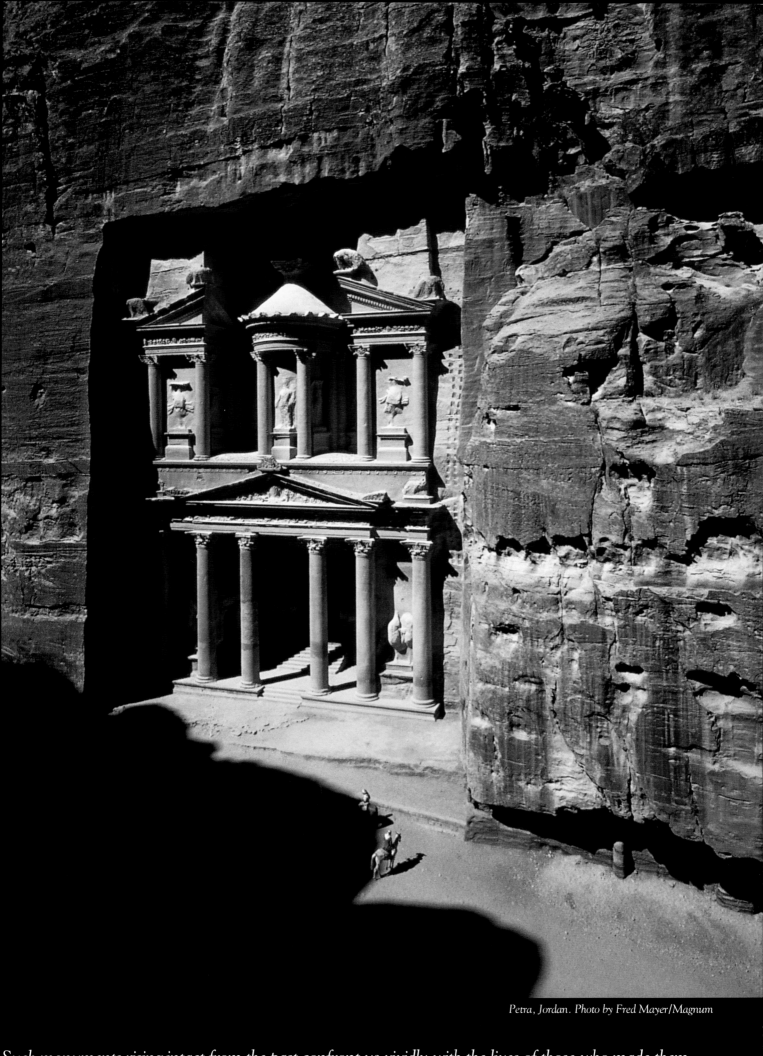

Petra, Jordan. Photo by Fred Mayer/Magnum

Such monuments rising intact from the past confront us vividly with the lives of those who made them, as if their desires and fears were somehow superimposed onto the rock along with the architect's plans. It is a strange thing about such hidden places: preserved by their remoteness, they affect us with a more immediate and greater sense of intimacy, and with more nostalgia, than those monuments that have always been the focus of the world's attention.

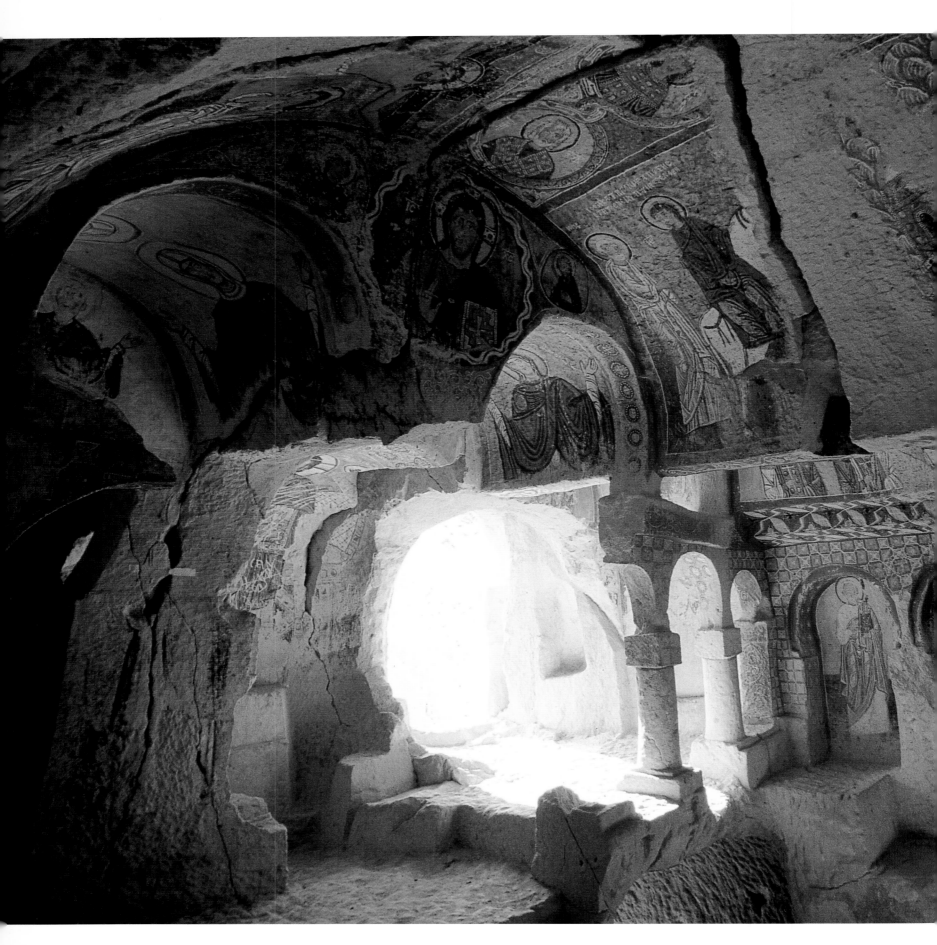

Above:
St. Mary's church, here hot with light, was built in the 13th century. The frescoes in Saint Mary's were painted by monks, and one can see in their work a reflection of the passion and simplicity of Saint Basil, their inspiration. His early vision of monastic life at Cappadocia resulted in some 400 small churches, characterized by arches, pillars, and small windows, being built into the rock. The frescoes' symbolic imagery includes the vine, representing Jesus; the lion, depicting victory and salvation; and the rabbit, conveying prophecy, sexuality, the devil, and magic.
Photo by Hans-Jurgen Burkard/Bilderberg

Inset:
A 9th century fresco of Judas betraying Jesus adorns the walls of Karanlik Kilise, the Dark Church. The real gift of Cappadocia to Christian theology was the Nicene Creed, developed by three Cappadocians.
Photo by John Elk III

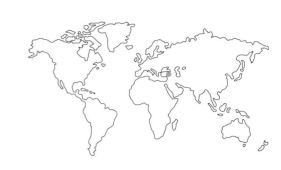

CAPPADOCIA, TURKEY

The area of east-central Turkey known as Cappadocia was one of the earliest regions to accept the Christian faith, and it was three Cappadocians—Gregory of Nazianzus, Basil of Caesarea, and Gregory of Nyssa—who successfully defended and refined the view of Christ expressed in the Nicene Creed against Arian heretics. The Trinity, they argued, is not one substance, but three *hypostases* (emanations); in other words, there is one god, not three, who is to be found *equally* in the Father, Son, and Holy Spirit. This is the view now common to the Roman, Protestant, and Orthodox Christian churches.

The famous rock-carved churches of Cappadocia's central plateau have proved to be as durable as the formulation of its church fathers. Eight million years ago, the central plateau was buried under the ash of repeated volcanic eruptions. In time this ash consolidated into beds of soft white rock called tufa. Interspersed between the tufa were layers of cindery breccia, basaltic lava, and beds of limestone deposited by the lakes that covered the area between eruptions. Where two ravines intersected, standing towers or columns were sometimes left; when such a column contained a mass of hard, crystallized tufa (ignimbrite), this protected the column below from erosion, creating mushroom-shaped pillars, which in Turkish are called *peribaca*—fairy chimneys— and which often reach heights of up to one hundred feet. The Göreme Valley contains one of the strangest and most spectacular collections of these curiosities.

Local people discovered that the soft tufa rock surrounding them could be easily carved out to form homes. Some were carved high up in the sides of *peribacas*, for security against bandits, but even more secure were elaborate underground cities and villages. One of the most impressive of these is Yeralti Sehri, which seems to have housed thousands of people, and even their animals. It is thought to be connected by underground tunnels to another city, Derinkuyu, two miles away.

When Christianity was established in Cappadocia, it was natural for the people of the central plateau to construct their churches as they did their homes. Some 2,300 churches have been found cut into the white tufa, and near the town of Nigde a rock-carved monastery, Eski Gümüsler, can still be seen, complete with churches, crypts, kitchen, refectory, reservoirs for oil and wine, and wall paintings dating from the 7th through the 11th centuries. There are also many rock-cut churches in the Göreme Valley. The Sandal Church has a painted fresco showing Christ's betrayal by Judas, which is also featured in the so-called Dark Church, where refectory tables and chairs are cut right out of the rock. In other churches frescoes show Saint Barbara and the Virgin, Saint George and the Dragon, and the Angel Gabriel. One of the most impressive (because low light levels have helped to preserve its colors) is a painting of Christ Pantocrator—Christ the Almighty—in the Dark Church. It is an image which, but for the success of the Cappadocian theologians in rescuing Christ from the inferior position ascribed to him by the Arian heretics, might never have been painted.

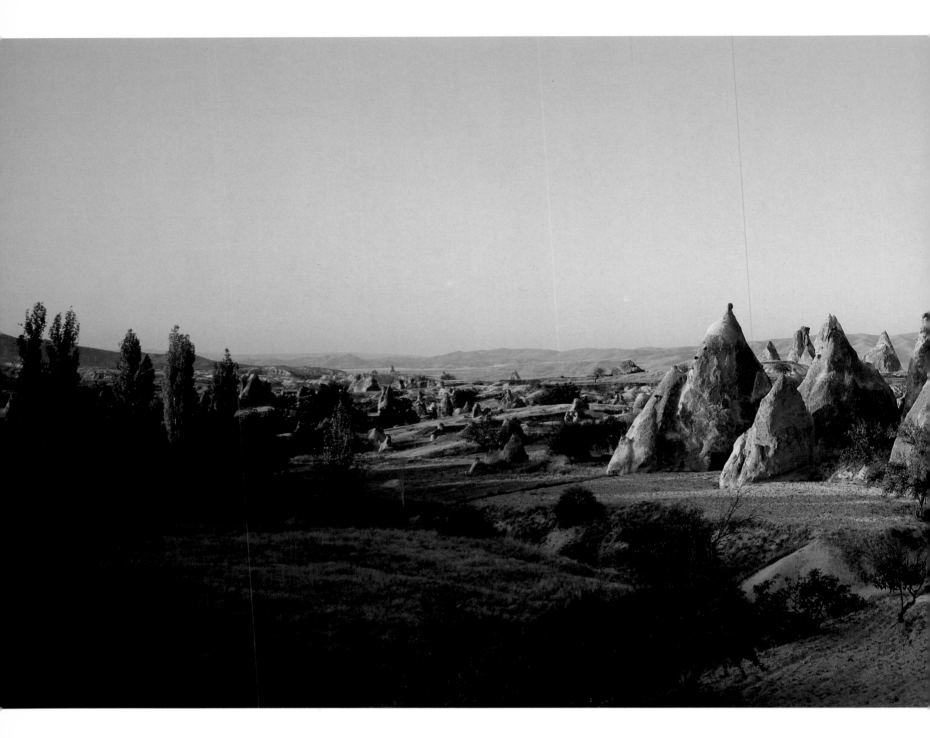

Above:
Stone beings, withered and macabre, stand massed in
the Goreme Valley. The landscape was created 30
million years ago, when Mount Erciyes Dagi erupted
and flooded 4,000 square kilometers with a white ash
that hardened into tufa (the same soft porous rock
used in the building of the Egyptian pyramids). In
Asia Minor the rock was sanded down by wind,
hence the fairy chimneys that dominate much of
the area. But there is something even stranger here,
hidden from sight. Far below the network of valleys
around Goreme, there are 37 underground cities,
some built to a depth of 18 to 20 stories, complete
with huge chambers and stairways, and connected by
tunnels nine miles long. It is estimated that a total
of 20,000 people lived in these cities. The cities were
probably built and protected by Hittites in order to
escape foreign cultures and armies. *Photo by Lee Day/
Black Star*

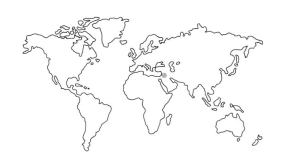

PETRA, JORDAN

Petra is something fabulous in the middle of nothing. A red-rock city hidden in the shadows of a vast beige desert. A desert strewn with sandstone mountains, it was once buried at the bottom of the sea.

Petra is forever a hidden place. You come to it through a deep, gloomy gorge, the Wadi Musa, no more than five feet wide in places, running for nearly a mile beneath 300-foot cliffs. You come to it today as camel trains from Africa and the Far East did in 500 BC, when Petra lay at the conjunction of several trade routes connecting modern-day Kuwait and Riyadh with Damascus and the Mediterranean ports of Gaza and Alexandria. The Nabateans of Petra believed that God (known to them as Dusares) was symbolized by stone; and at Petra, God's presence was glorious. The cliffs tower overhead in rainbow swirls of green and red; in banded blues, plums, mauves, and swathes of salmon and caramel, as if condensed all the into the durability

shades of gold; in pink, chocolate, God's hands had colors of creation of stone.

Like the swirling patterns on Petra's walls, the caravans flowed into the city from every direction. Lumbering camels laden with ivory, apes, silks, spices, pearls, slaves, and incense traveled through the marketplace of Petra. They replenished their water supplies from the aqueduct and the rock-cut channels that carried water into the city from its great reservoir, Al Birka, and from isolated springs. In time the cliffs became honeycombed with tombs cut into the living rock. Bathhouses, shops, colonnades, gymnasia, and galleries catered to traveling merchants and the city's 20,000 inhabitants; for entertainment, a Roman amphitheater with stone seats for some 4,000 spectators was cut directly into the cliffs. Petra became a cosmopolitan city whose architecture reflected Greek and Roman styles as well as the native Nabatean. The Natbateans like the Bedouin after them, were historically nomads. They didn't drink wine. They worshipped the spirits that lived in *wadis*, rocks and dunes. They were not easily provoked and flourished for nearly five hundred years.

When the power of the Roman empire began to fail in the third century AD, Petra was occupied by Arab tribes and later became part of the Byzantine empire. The development of seagoing routes to the East gradually reduced the caravan traffic, and Petra declined. Its death blow came in 747 AD, when a major earthquake seems to have shifted the local watertable while leaving most of Petra's buildings intact. Deprived of its lifeblood, the city died and was all but forgotten until 1817, when the Anglo-German traveler Johann Burckhardt made his way there in Bedouin disguise. Returning to Europe, he amazed the world with his tale of this astonishing city cut into rock. A lost treasure named for rock (Petra means "rock" in Greek), cut from rock, its God symbolized by rock, was, in the end, deprived of its survival by the rock's own violent upheaval.

T.E. Lawrence once said about the Bedouin, "They were a people of spasms, of upheavals, of ideas, the race of individual genius.... Their mind was strange and dark, full of depressions and exaltations, lacking in rule, but with more ardour and more fertile in belief than any other in the world."

Left:
Generations of travelers have ridden through the mile-long siq to remark on "the sudden apparition of the deep red mansion." The Pharaoh's Treasury or Khazneh façade includes sculptured figures, among them medusae, satyrs, male equestrian figures, dancing Amazons, eagles, and sphinxes. *Photo by Richard Steedman/The Stock Market*

Above:
The Wadi Ram desert lies in southern Jordan, a maze of mountains and desert, where various Bedu tribes still wander among hidden passes with their camels and sheep flocks. *Photos by P. Maitre & Y. Gellie - Odyssey/Matrix*

Following pages:
The interior of the Khazneh is designed as a monumental tomb that includes a central staircase, a portico, and various chambers. The main room is an almost perfect 12-meter cube, with framed doorways in the side and rear walls that lead to three smaller chambers. The building of the Khazneh has been dated from the middle of the 1st century BC to the 2nd century AD. *Photo by Fred Mayer/Magnum*

Part III: Arrivals

At last my soul explodes, and wisely cries out to me: No matter where!
No matter where! As long as its out of the world! —Charles Baudelaire

Astronomers talk of a place called "the surface of last scattering" and it is from
there that they begin to explain the creation of the universe. It is often difficult to
trace just where one journey ends and another one begins. The places collected
here are places at the end. They may have been the final destination for a culture,
a species, a city or a man. They are places that hold in their memory that which
has come before. Photo of Meteora, Greece by Geoffrey C. Clifford

Easter Island, Chile. Photo by George Holton/Photo Researchers

ANCESTRAL ZONES: EASTER ISLAND AND GALÁPAGOS ISLANDS

There are times when one arrives at a place just after something fantastic has happened. Things left behind are in strange disorder, or are slightly disconnected. One begins to collect the visible evidence of some invisible event, hoping, with these clues, to reconstruct the mysterious event in the past.

If the places where one arrived were the Galápagos Islands and Easter Island, the clues would be marine lizards and huge stone giants. On closer consideration, one would find them linked by mysteries of ancestry and isolation. Each is the unique product of an island environment (which is to say, of isolation); and in both cases, a shortage of food set off a certain chain of events.

On the Galápagos Islands, marine iguanas—the world's only sea-going lizards—evolved the ability to survive by eating seaweed growing just below the low water line. Their relatives, the land iguanas, continued meanwhile to live off land vegetation.

Galápagos Islands, Ecuador. Photo by Tui De Roy

When the Easter Islanders' food began to run out, alliances were formed along clan lines, and ancestral statues and carvings marked out and distinguished clan territories.

On Easter Island and on the Galápagos Islands, the zones claimed by different ancestral lines are still visible. The stone moai on Easter Island no longer function to claim specific territories, but they do stand witness to the evolution of a culture and claim the entire island as a territory of the past. The ancestral zones of the Galápagos Islands are still marked out by the foraging animals that evolved to inhabit the divergent environments of those islands. Such zones provide us with not only the secrets of these animals' ancestry, but with a most important clue to the origin of our own.

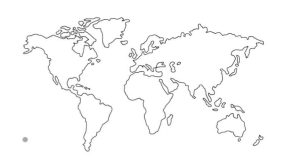

Easter Island, Chile

Little of what was once on Easter Island remains: a few of the faces, none of the trees. A forest of palm trees once covered the island's now grassy slopes, and for 1000 years the Easter Islanders used its wood for their canoes and houses, and for the rollers on which they transported their giant ancestral statues. Gradually the forests were cut for timber or burned to clear land for farming; at length, no trees were left, and the fertile land on which the islanders had grown their yams, bananas, and sweet potatoes began to erode. Without wood for canoes, fishing could only be done from the shore, and the only ready supply of protein now came from jealously guarded flocks of chickens. Stone henhouses were built and gardens were walled, but the food supplies continued to dwindle. As a last resort, the islanders took the only kind of population control available: they began to kill each other. In evidence of this, one third of the island's legends are about clan wars, and another third about cannibalism.

Carvings and rocks were used to delineate clan boundaries, and moai, the giant ancestral statues which made the islands famous, were erected to protect and guard clan territories. Carved from the soft rock of Ranu Raraku Volcano, the statues were empowered by the addition of white coral eyes. Their *mani*, the spiritual power, could only be disengaged if they were toppled off their platforms and broken. Clan chants were an-other source of ancestral power, recorded in a code of hieroglyphs on boards called *rongorongo;* the symbols are obscure, and only about one-tenth of the approximately 11,000 signs used have so far been deciphered.

When the power of a clan's statues, chants, and warriors failed, defeat came. Surviving clan members had no recourse but to take to caves in the island's volcanic hills, there to die or, for a time, to scrape together a subsistence living as best they could.

After a prolonged history of bloodshed and massacre, a kind of peace returned to the island in the form of a new religion, perhaps dedicated to the sky god Make Make. Petroglyphs depict this birdman cult, and it seems to have been established as an alternative to bloody war. During this time, a peaceful competition was held each year, in which contestants representing the clans dove into the sea from the cliffs at Orongo, and using reed floats, swam out to three small islands where the sooty tern nested. Whoever was first to return to the shore with a tern's egg thereby won for his clan chief the right to rule the island for the coming year.

Eventually the birdman cult failed and appears to have been replaced by more direct pleas to a primal source of fertility; this is one explanation for why many of the carved birdman symbols were later overdrawn with the universal symbol of female generation, the *yoni*. In 1862, Peruvian slavers raided the island and carried off men, women, and children to work in Peru's mines. Those who eventually returned to the island brought with them smallpox and leprosy, and within a few years only 110 Easter Islanders remained. Today, many of the ancient ancestral statues have been set upright again and gaze with blank but seeing eyes upon a peaceful island population of some 2,000 souls.

Left:
Faces of the ancestors stare with hollow eyes from the Nau Nau ahu (or temple) on Anakena Bay. Originally, the ancestors, or moai, had beautiful eyes made from white coral with red tufa irises, but they have since gone blind with age. These particular moai would have needed good vision. They were Polynesian sailors who volunteered for the island's first chief Hotu Matua, who came from somewhere near the Marquesas, to go in search of a wooded island. Easter Island was the place they found. *Photo by Courtney Milne*

Above:
Caves carved out of the island's volcanic hills provided tempo-rary shelter for factions of warring clans in the 17th century. In addition, the soft clay walls of the caves provided a permanent sketchpad. These images are thought to be from the birdman cult of the god Make Make. *Photo by Bob Sacha*

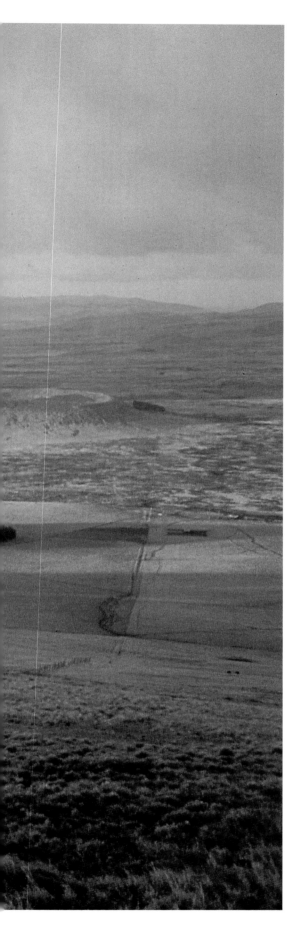

Left:
The isolation of Easter Island is tangible. It lies 2,500 miles to the west of Chile, and 1,190 miles from the nearest Polynesian island. This isolation seems to account for the enormous size of the moai on Easter Island. Other Pacific Islands, from Hawaii to Tahiti, had similar figures, but none were nearly so large. Building a culture far from any neighbors, the Easter Islanders had nothing with which to compare their work. *Photo by Bob Sacha*

Top:
Its body buried deep within the mountain, a giant face emerges from the slopes of Rano Raraku Volcano, one of three volcanoes on Easter Island. Most of the figures were carved from quarries in Rano Raraku, then moved to the foot of the mountain to await their final assignments. Local legend claims the moai "walked into place." *Photo by H. Gruyaert/Magnum*

Above and following pages:
Ancestors of the future, children at a grammar school in the island's main town of Hanga Roa celebrate Rapa Nui Week, a festival of songs, dances, and story-telling marathons which commemorates the age of the moai and preserves the traditional culture of the Easter Islanders.

Hundreds of moai occupy Easter Island; some are half buried, standing erect on temple platforms (such as those on the following pages), others are still embedded in the quarry stone from which they were carved. They average about 13–16 feet in height, though some are true giants over 50 feet tall. *Photos by Bob Sacha*

GALÁPAGOS ISLANDS, ECUADOR

On September 16, 1835, the British surveying and exploration ship *HMS Beagle* pulled into the Galápagos Islands, and from it disembarked the young Charles Darwin.

Among the first creatures he saw, sunning themselves on black lava rocks within a few feet of the pounding surf, were "large (2–3 feet) most disgusting clumsy Lizards. They are as black as the porous rocks over which they crawl. . . . Somebody called them 'imps of darkness'. —They assuredly well become the land they inhabit." (Darwin here uses the word "imp" in the sense of "Devil's children.") For the next 35 days, Darwin traveled from island to island, studying and collecting examples of plant and animal life.

On October 1, he reached Isabela, the largest of the Galápagos Islands, and confirmed his poor initial impression of the islands. He thought their volcanic landscapes were like "what we might imagine the cultivated parts of the infernal regions to be." After three days on Isabela, he wrote in his diary: *I should think it would be difficult to find in the inter* tropical latitudes a *piece of land 75* miles long, so entire *ly useless to man or* the larger animals. It was, of course, precisely this inter *hospitable charac-* ter that, by saving *them from human* interference, had *kept the islands* as a test bed for *the evolutionary* processes that 20 *years later Darwin* would explicate *in his revolution-* ary book *On the Origin of Species by* Natural Selection. On Isabela, Darwin saw the *landgoing coun-* terpart of the marine lizards whose appearance had troubled him: *We here have another large reptile in great numbers—it is a great Lizard, from 10–15 lb. in weight & 2–4 ft. in length, is in structure closely allied to those imps of darkness which frequent the seashore.—This one inhabits burrows to which it hurries when frightened with quick & clumsy gait. They are hideous animals; but are considered good food. . . .*

By October 9, Darwin had reached Santiago Island, where he found the terrestrial form of the lizard in uncomfortable numbers. He wrote, "The burrows of this animal are so very numerous; that we had difficulty in finding a spot to pitch the tents."

On Santiago Island, Darwin also saw great numbers of the giant tortoises, *galápagos*, for which explorer Tomás de Berlanga had named the islands. He found that they had worn roadways to the island's springs. "When they arrive at the Spring," he noted, "they bury their heads above the eyes in muddy water & greedily suck in great mouthfuls, quite regardless of lookers on." He also wrote that the islanders claimed to be able to distinguish tortoises from different islands on the basis of their shells. Tortoises living on islands with shrubby vegetation, for example, had long necks and a high arch in their shells that let them crane upward to browse; tortoises on islands with only ground-level vegetation had no such adaptations. Here were still more clues leading Darwin toward his theory of natural selection.

The bird life of the Galápagos confirmed Darwin's belief that species were not eternally fixed. In particular, he noted that the beaks of finches from the various islands showed every form, from thick, blunt beaks to "one so fine it may be compared to a warbler."

Such observations led Darwin to realize not only that "the several islands of the Galápagos Archipelago are tenanted . . . in a quite marvelous manner," but also that its birds, animals, and plants provide clues to the great mystery of how the diversity of living things has come about.

Left and above:
Booby trap or domestic bliss? The coastline of Isabela Island is home to many of the Galápagos' 8,000 human inhabitants, as well as these blue-footed boobies at Punta Vicente Roca. The blue-footed booby (*Sula nebouxii*) is truly a strange bird, even in this land of outrageous adaptation. It earned its popular name by landing on oceangoing ships and allowing itself to be caught and eaten.

A five-foot-long land iguana vacations near a lake in the bottom of a volcanic caldera on Fernandina Island. The Galápagos are one of the most active areas of volcanic activity on the planet. Herman Melville described the Galápagos, or as they were known in 1854, The Encantadas, as: *A group rather of extinct volcanos than of isles; looking much as the world at large might, after a penal conflagration. It is to be doubted whether any spot of earth can in desolateness, furnish a parallel to this group.*
Photos by Tui De Roy

Above:

Poised on the brink of eternity, the carcass of a dead land iguana emerges from recent volcanic debris on Fernandina Island. The firey origins of the Galápagos are still obvious on the four islands in the chain where active volcanoes continue to shape the landscape.

Galápagos hawks stalk the sulphuric mists of the fumaroles on Alcedo Volcano, on Isabela Island. Over 85 bird species are found on the harsh, windswept archipelago. Many species first landed when they were blown off their migration routes. Other species arrived in the hands of wayward pirates. *Photos by Tui De Roy*

Right:

In 1535 a Spanish explorer named Tomás de Berlanga stumbled on the islands which he named *Galápagos*, the Spanish word for the giant tortoises he found in abundance there. Centuries later, at the height of the Pacific whaling era, sailors feasted on many a meal of turtle stew. Contributions to nomenclature and culinary delight notwithstanding, it was the tortoises that helped steer Charles Darwin to one of the seminal theories of the modern age. The tortoises, like the iguanas, he noted, varied from island to island. Separated by miles of open water, the animals on each island must have refined their inherited characteristics as best suited their particular landscape; in short, they evolved. Six species of giant tortoises inhabit the islands. *Photo by Frans Lanting/Minden Pictures*

Machu Picchu, Peru. Photo by Bob Sacha

SANCTUARY: MACHU PICCHU AND METEORA

Prophets go to high places to receive the holy word, temples are built on hills, church spires strive for heaven. Heaven is above, we fall from grace, and hell is always below. In worldly things, we climb the social ladder, we aspire to live on Nob Hill, to consort with the high and mighty, and our corporate headquarters are towers that impose their height for miles around. In height there is distinction, isolation from the commonplace, and security.

The lure of high places has, consequently, given us some of our most extraordinary monuments, and of all none are more extraordinary than the monasteries of the Meteora in Greece and the

Meteora, Greece. Photo by Geoffrey C. Clifford

mountaintop city of Machu Picchu in Peru. Protected by lofty remoteness, each of these communities survived for hundreds of years as a sanctuary where a unique and ordered vision of the world was preserved.

At Meteora, monks sought to remove themselves physically, emotionally, and spiritually from the mundane and strove to suspend time in contemplation of the eternal. At Machu Picchu, too, the tide of history parted at the foot of the mountain. The invading Spanish conquistadores, bent on gold and dominion, passed by in the valley, leaving the Incan city undisturbed to continue in its yearly ritual of tethering the sun and, in its own way, holding back the flow of time.

Above:
"Stone within stone and man, where was he?/Air within air and man, where was he?/Time within time and man, where was he?" An empty doorway becomes a threshold to the city and conjures this verse from Pablo Neruda's poem "The Heights of Machu Picchu." The

Incan doorway narrows toward the top, a trapezoidal design that adds great strength to the structure. The Inca were masters of stonework, fitting irregularly shaped blocks together with such precision that to this day a knife cannot be inserted between the cracks. *Photo by Tui De Roy*

Following pages:
Between the summit of Huayna Picchu or Old Peak, *(center)*, and Machu Picchu or New Peak, on the other side, the terraced slopes of the city of Machu Picchu fan down the Vilcabamba ridge. *Photo by Brian Vikander/Westlight*

MACHU PICCHU, PERU

In 1572 Spanish conquistadores struggled up the Urubamba Valley from the ancient Inca capital of Cuzco, seeking the last Inca ruler, Tupac Amaru, to destroy him. North of Machu Picchu the Spaniards found Vilcabamba, the last Inca stronghold. They destroyed that city, and thus completed their conquest of the greatest empire of the ancient Americas.

But high above the conquistadores, unseen and remote, the city of Machu Picchu survived unharmed, and until 1911, no white man had ever walked through its plazas, climbed its stairways, or stood upon its high ramparts of fitted stone. Machu Picchu is a city above the clouds and—almost—beyond time.

Today a small train chugs daily up the valley, covering the 70 miles from Cuzco in about three and a half hours. From the station at the village of Machu Picchu a bus climbs laboriously, by way of innumerable hairpin bends, to the peak where the hidden city lies. In the rainy season, which lasts from December to March, you can look down from the city walls and see far below you flotillas of soft-topped clouds.

In an early example of environmental architecture, the Incas built their cities and fields into the contours and slopes of the Andes. They also built them in two parts, the *hanan-saya* or upper ward, and the *hurin-saya*, lower ward; such division was standard in Inca towns, as it encouraged competition on civic matters while also keeping political loyalties divided. Such strategies helped the Incan empire stretch its influence for 2,500 miles along the west coast of South America between 1250 and 1533.

A ritual timelessness—a temporary halting of time—was vital to Incan life. At Machu Picchu the buildings (in which no mortar was used, each stone of white granite carved to fit perfectly against its neighbors) seem not to be imposed upon the mountain but to be an organic part of it. And of all the constructions in this city none is more organically part of the place, or more poignant, than the great carved boulder known as the Intihuatana, The Tethering Place of the Sun. Each year at the Winter Solstice, when the shortening days had made it seem that the sun was fleeing northward from the sky and might never return, Inca priests performed a ceremony in which the sun was ritually tethered to the post carved from the great smoothed stone. Halted in its flight, the sun remained; days gradually lengthened, and life and harvests were assured for another year. To this day no one comes to this untouched city above the clouds without experiencing again that moment of timelessness that lay at the heart of Incan life.

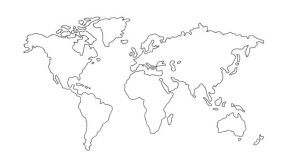

METEORA, GREECE

It is night, and a cold wind whips around the rock face. A young monk huddles against the wall of a shallow cave, his knees mere inches from an abyss. The stars are at eye level, and far away he hears a dog bark in the night. As dawn breaks, he peers out from his prison and sees, far below, the dull green of distant oaks, mulberries, and cypress trees, all dwarfed by the height and washing like a green tide at the base of the pinnacles that tower around him. An eagle sweeps past the entrance to his cave, and he starts back. He has broken one of the rules of his monastery and must remain here, crouching above the emptiness, until the term of his punishment is served.

The first to establish a monastery here was Athanasius, a monk from the monasteries of Athos. He sought peace and isolation from the world, and found it perched in midair atop one of Meteora's 1,000-foot columns of rock, perhaps the one where Ayion Pneuma, the Monastery of the Holy Ghost, now stands. As his holiness increased, he attracted the attention, as hermits will, of demons, who flew around in the air outside his cave. To thwart them, Athanasius moved to a still higher rock, the Great Meteoron. The discouraged demons gave up their pursuit. His reputation for true holiness spread and attracted disciples to the towering rock and there, by the middle of the 14th century, the Monastery of the Great Meteoron was established.

Athanasius' rule, the model for all subsequent monasteries, was strict. No woman was allowed even in the vicinity, and it was common for monks to mortify their flesh. Theophanes, who with his brother Nectarios founded the monastery of Varlaam (Barlaam), habitually wore an iron chain bound tightly around his waist and ate but once a day, consuming beans, bread, water, and nothing more. On the day the monastery was completed, Theophanes, foreseeing his imminent death, quietly composed his body into the shape of a cross, and died. As he did, the air was filled with a sweet scent, and an unknown star shone brightly and briefly on the monastery before disappearing.

To remind the Meteora monks of the world from which they had found sanctuary, many churches had murals depicting martyrdom in all its glorious and gory variety. Those in the Great Meteoron's Church of the Transfiguration are accompanied by gruesome illustrations of sin rewarded, in a grippingly vivid portrayal of the Last Judgment. The monasteries also had their talismans against evil: the bones, skulls, and other body parts of dead monks and saints. And with their help, the monasteries remained secure in their lofty fastness, even while armies crossed and recrossed the fertile plain below.

But not even sanctity and the haven of a towering pinnacle could hold time at bay, and today only six monasteries remain of the twenty-four that once made this the Stagi, the Place of Saints. Two of them, the Ayia Roussani (whose church is decorated with especially brutal scenes of martyrdom) and the Ayios Stephanos (which retains a silver reliquary containing the head of Saint Charalambos, a noted healer) now house nuns. Some monasteries and churches still cling, deserted, to their obelisks. Others are only tatters of wood and masonry, worn and plucked at by wind and rain. Whether you are of the faithful or not, they represent the austere truth at the heart of the vision of the Meteora monks: the vanity of all worldly aspirations.

Left and above:
Out of the way of worldly things, the monasteries of Meteora preserve the traditions of the Middle Ages as well as its art and architecture. The Monastery of Roussanou has held tightly to its rock foundations since 1380. Surrounded on three sides by a sheer empty drop *(photo on page 133)*, the monastery was accessible only by a wooden ladder until 1930, when the current bridge to the opposite hill and a concrete stairway were added.

In a crypt of the Monastery of the Transfiguration, the earthly remains of the monks make a grisly display of human mortality. *Photos by Geoffrey C. Clifford*

Above:
Hidden among the spires that rise from the plain of Thessaly in Greece are the monasteries of Meteora. The community came into its fullness in the 17th century, when over 24 monasteries found a foothold on the pinnacles here and exerted a spiritual hold on the lives of thousands of monks. Six of the original monasteries remain. *Photo by Geoffrey C. Clifford*

Herculaneum, near Pompeii, Italy. Photo by Enrico Ferorelli

MESSENGERS OF FIRE: POMPEII AND KILAUEA

In Pompeii and the surrounding area, the gods of fire did their spectacular work of destruction. Yet the inanimate things in the city, the houses, the streets, the goods for sale, were preserved as emblems of beauty and artistic finesse.

Vulcan, the Roman god of fire and blacksmithing, had his workshop in the red belly of Mount Etna, a volcano similar in type and temperament to Vesuvius. With his helpers, the cyclopes, Vulcan forged thunderbolts as weapons for his father Jupiter, the king of the gods. Although he was ugly and

Kilauea, Hawai'i, USA. Photo by Paul Chesley/Photographers/Aspen

lame, Vulcan was married to Venus, the goddess of love, beauty, and vegetation. On the other side of the world, the Hawai'ian fire goddess, Pele, makes her home in a crater on Mount Kilauea. She appears sometimes as a fearsome old hag and sometimes as a ravishingly beautiful young woman, a Hawai'ian Venus who demands amorous favors from the local demigods. In whatever form, it is Pele's actions that account for the exceptionally fertile soil of the lush Hawai'ian Islands, just as in the European myths Venus expresses the creative aspect of her husband Vulcan's fire.

POMPEII, ITALY

For almost two thousand years time has slept in the gray garden of ash and pumice which buried the Italian town of Pompeii in 79 AD. The victims of this eruption of Mount Vesuvius, their figures cast much later in plaster from molds left by their bodies in the ash, still lie as if they were sleeping. A gray child seems to slumber between the ash gray forms of his mother and father; a beggar, his bag of alms beside him and wearing good leather sandals, shields his face with an arm; a young girl clutches her bronze mirror. In bakeries carbonized loaves are preserved, and in bars the customers' graffiti is still legible. In a fresco a woman gathers flowers, still yellow as the sun, and on the slopes of a peaceful painted Vesuvius vines and olives grow, still green.

The tons of volcanic debris that fell that day buried Pompeii and all those who had been too slow  to escape the volcanic fury, sealing the streets, shops, bars, public baths, and private homes, temples, and broth- els in a thick gray preserving pall. There were warn- ing signs, but many ignored them. On August 20th, se- vere tremors had shaken Pompeii and caused great waves to rear up in the Bay of Naples. On the 23rd of August, the town began celebrating the Vulcanalia, the festival of Vulcan, fiery blacksmith of the gods. The next morning a ritual was performed that offered the inhab- itants of the un- derworld access to the upper, human world. Then the eruption began. Molten lava was flung a mile in the sky to descend as a rain of pumice, ash, and boulders. Clouds of poisonous gas killed birds on the wing and people in their homes.

As the eruptions flared, the inhabitants of Pompeii thought they discerned giant figures prowling in the shadows and plumes of smoke, as if their rites had indeed unleashed a vast subterranean violence. The historian Dio Cassius, writing 150 years after the eruption but drawing on contemporary accounts, described their visions: *Numbers of men quite surpassing any human stature—which creatures in fact, as the giants are pictured to have been, appeared, now on the mountain side, now in the surrounding country, and again in the cities, wandering over the earth day and night and also flitting through the air. . . there were frequent rumblings, some of them subterranean, that resembled thunder, and some on the surface, that sounded like bellowings; the sea also joined in the roar, and the sky re-echoed it. Then suddenly a portentous crash was heard, as if the mountains were tumbling in ruins. . . . Some thought that the giants were rising again in revolt (for at this time also many of their forms could be discerned in the smoke, and moreover, a sound as of trumpets was heard) while others believed the whole universe was being resolved into a chaos of fire.*

In Pompeii the gods of fire unleashed a destruction of the most spectacular dimensions; but out of this chaos a well-ordered city emerged, its streets, houses, and habits all preserved intact. Somehow the human population was preserved as well. From the depths of the earth, the fire gods transformed the populace of Pompeii into a kind of earthen people, holding them there as the ghostly gray, immobile bodies that still populate the town.

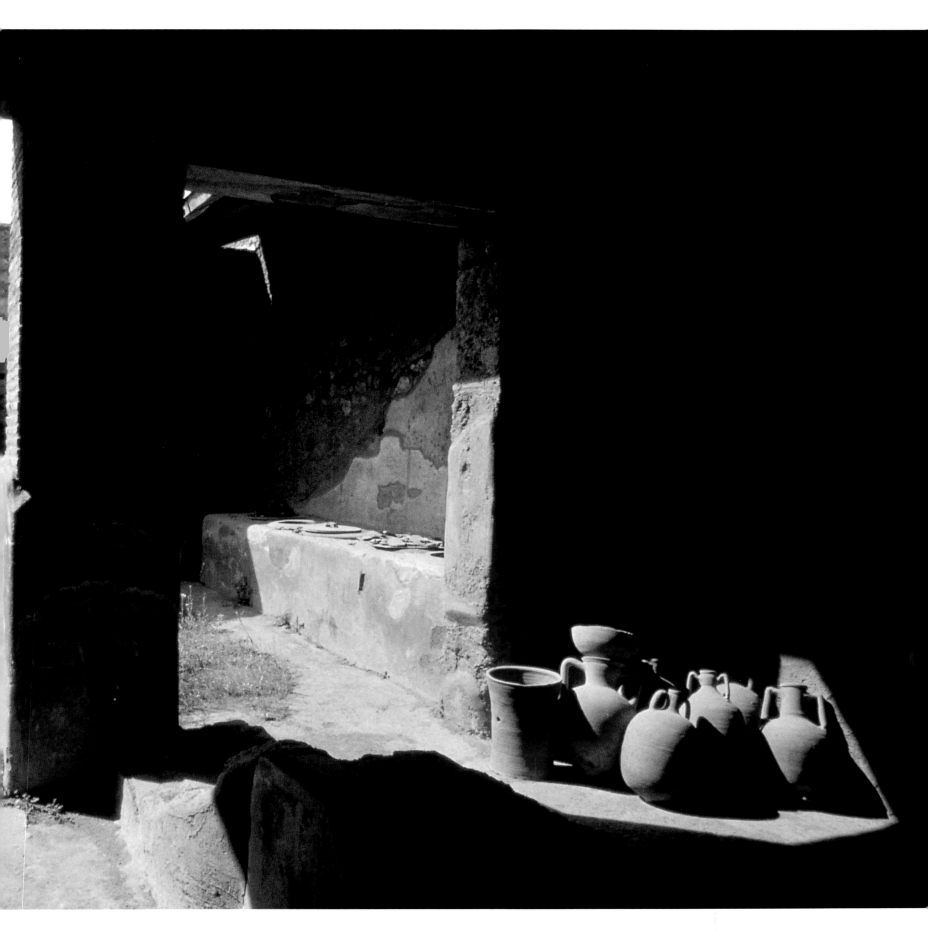

Inset:
When Giuseppe Fiorelli developed the technique for making body molds of the city's fallen inhabitants in 1864, a new wave of interest in Pompeii began. To know how people lived was interesting, but to see their bodies at the moment of death held a macabre fascination. *Photo by Enrico Ferorelli*

Above:
The courtyard of a villa in Pompeii closely resembles the backlots and garages of many a city past and present. The amphorae stored in the dark corner were probably used for carrying oil or wine. *Photo by Milan Horacek/Bilderberg*

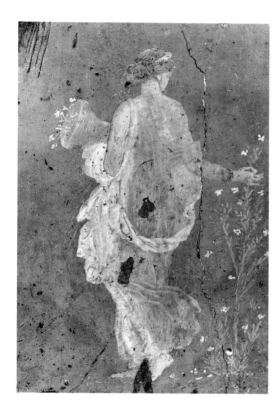

Left:
Frescoes of bulls and dogs, tigers and maidens, scenes from Mount Olympus, family portraits, laurel and ivy, jokes, bon mots, and obscene graffiti decorate the walls of Pompeii like pages in a fantastic book. The sense of color and design, the love of ornament and gesture tell as much about the minds of the ancient populace as the bread left in ovens tells about their diet. *Photo by Enrico Ferorelli*

Above:
The Via Stabiana, one of the main thoroughfares through Pompeii, runs along the left in the photo. The city streets were narrow by modern standards, around four meters wide, allowing the shade from the nearby buildings to cover and cool the road through the heat of the day; at night the avenues were lit with lanterns. When Mark Twain visited Pompeii he was outraged by the worn-out condition of the streets and bemoaned the ancient "generations of swindled tax-payers." *Photo by Milan Horacek/Bilderberg*

Right:
A wall fresco from the outskirts of Pompeii depicts Prima Vera, or Springtime, languorously plucking flowers. Venus in her gentle guise of Mistress of Nature was a close relative. Pompeii was under the special protection of Venus, and wall graffiti often refer to her in praise. *Photo by William Hubbell/ Woodfin Camp*

Above:
More than half a million years ago Mauna Loa rose from the bottom of the Pacific Ocean, and with its sister mountain, Mauna Kea, created the Big Island of Hawai'i. The goddess Pele lives in a caldera like the ones seen here, further down the slope of Mauna Loa on an attached volcano, Kilauea. *Photo by Jim Brandenburg/Minden Pictures*

Inset:
Visible from the small town of Volcano, the telltale smoke of Pele's displeasure rises above the coconut palms. Kilauea's lowland slopes are lush and green; the island's 1,800 kinds of flowering plants, and even the land itself, grow from the fertile soil of Pele's eruptions. *Photo by Debra Bloomfield/Courtesy of Robert Koch Gallery, San Francisco*

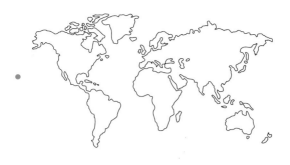

KILAUEA, USA

If you cannot find her by the smoke and fire of her restless movements, you might find her by the offerings left for her pleasure by faithful Hawai'ians. Hibiscus flowers, tequila, guavas, mangoes, and red wine, gifts for a passionate woman, left on the rim of a barren volcanic crater.

Other women get flowers on the doorstep, but the goddess Pele's home is the Halema'uma'u firepit in Mount Kilauea's huge caldera, a funnel-shaped chasm 3,500 feet in diameter and some 250 feet deep. To the west, looming above and beyond the cliffs of Kilauea's rim and rising nearly 14,000 feet above the sea, is the vast bulk of the world's biggest active volcano, Mauna Loa, the Long Mountain.

While Kilauea and Mauna Loa are among the world's most active volcanoes, they are also among the least harm- ful. For Pele, though fierce, is far less threatening to humans than Europe's fire god, more intimate in her habits. Many legends describe her outrageous passion for the demigod Maui, young trickster hero of the Pacific. Maui went fishing and snagged the Hawai'ian Islands out of the ocean and taught all the islanders how to make fire. He did not need to teach Pele,  however. Her heat is the heat of passion, curable only by the fun-loving Maui's vigorous and sustained attentions.

Like the earliest representations of Venus, whose appetites are not unlike her own, Pele is also associated with fertility and vegetation. The new lands that she created by volcanic action are among the most fertile and beautiful on earth, and possess, within a small area, an astonishing variety. On Hawai'i, the Big Island, landscapes range from the lunar calderas of volcano tops to upland groves of cedar, cypress, wild rose, and fuchsia, to enchanted forests of tree ferns and fragrant red-flowered ohia trees, where brilliantly colored birds sip nectar. All is as rich and new as the landscapes of Paradise.

Indeed, the Hawai'ian Islands are among the newest lands on earth, and Halema'uma'u is not Pele's first home. Legends tell how she first lived and found fire with her divining rod on Kaua'i, the northernmost island, but was chased away by her jealous sister Namakaokaha'i. From Kaua'i, Pele fled southeast, first to O'ahu, then to Maui, and finally to Hawai'i. In fact, these legends reflect the geological order in which the chain of islands was created. As the plates that form the Pacific floor drifted slowly northwest, they passed over a hot spot in the ocean bed. The heat caused eruptions that produced an island, and as this island was slowly carried away by tectonic drift, another was formed behind it. Even now a new underwater mountain called Lo'ihi is forming to the southeast of Hawai'i. In a few thousand years its peak will rise above the sea as the newest of the Hawai'ian Islands. By then Kilauea will be cool and Pele will have moved once more to a new home, to furnish it in time with the colors of fire and the softness of a living world.

Top:
The blood of the earth scabs over, is broken, and bleeds again. The landscape of an erupting volcano is a labyrinth of lava veins, foul vapors, lakes of red magma, fractures, smoke vents, rumbling orifices, and occasional fountains of fire. It is a living body, the earth made animate, the inside brought outside, the deepest nature of the planet revealed. *Photo by William Waterfall/The Stock Market*

Above and right:
2000°F streams of molten lava race down the slopes of Kilauea at up to 60 miles per hour, hitting the Pacific in an enormous explosion of steam. When the lava hardens the island will have grown 10 or 20 feet. The many names for lava in Hawai'i give testimony to volcanoes' mythic importance. Pahoehoe is the ropey twisted variety above; it moves into place slowly. Eventually, water will meet the lava again as rainfall, which erodes tiny cracks in the porous rock. Seeds buried under the crust will sprout in a few months, and in 50 years, the forest will have returned. For everything destroyed in Pele's realm something else is grown. *Photos by Len Jenshel/Swanstock*

Pyramid at Giza, Egypt. Photo by Benoît Pesle/Anzenberger

THE LIFE OF THE DEAD: PYRAMIDS AT GIZA AND PALENQUE

The great pyramid of Cheops at Giza in Egypt was once smoothly clad in white limestone, its geometry perfect and shining white under the desert sun. The New World pyramids of Mesoamerica never aimed for this perfect symmetry. Those at the Mayan city of Palenque in Mexico's Yucatán Peninsula are crowned with temples, like the Temple of the Inscriptions. Here, the Egyptian perfection of form was sacrificed for a kind of narrative, an articulation in carved glyphs of the pyramid's purpose.

Both pyramids enshrine dead leaders, the pharaoh Cheops and the Mayan ruler Shield Pacal, and both serve philosophies of the afterlife. For Cheops, who claimed divine ancestry, rebirth was assured and involved nothing more trying than being recognized by the gods and escorted to higher realms. As his pyramid rose inexorably to its perfect peak, so the dead pharaoh rose to heaven.

Palenque, Mexico. Photo by Macduff Everton/Swanstock

Shield Pacal, on the other hand, had to travel through strange lands and undergo a journey full of tests, challenges, and strange encounters; and the multi-level character of his pyramid reflects the give-and-take uncertainties of his journey.

In time, personal history entered the Egyptian account (as it does in the inscriptions of Palenque's temple), and the underworld described in later texts involves chance and change as in the Mayan realm of Xibalba. Since we know of no channel by which the earlier Egyptian view could have influenced the New World vision of the afterlife, it may be that the understanding of rebirth followed a similar course in both civilizations: evidence of something universal in our understanding of what lies on the other side of death.

Above:

"Look on my works, ye Mighty and despair!" cried Ozymandias in Shelley's poem. Yet despite the destruction and grafitti, the poverty and social upheaval around them, the pyramids of the Giza group have endured. The mystery of the pyramid's construction was perhaps partly solved in 1992, when a PBS film crew reconstructed a series of ramps along each side of a smaller-scale pyramid and discovered that individual stone blocks could have been moved by means of *tafla*, a local clay which, when watered down, allows blocks mounted on wooden sleds to be moved like bars of soap.
Photo by Richard Misrach/Courtesy of Frankel Gallery, San Francisco

154

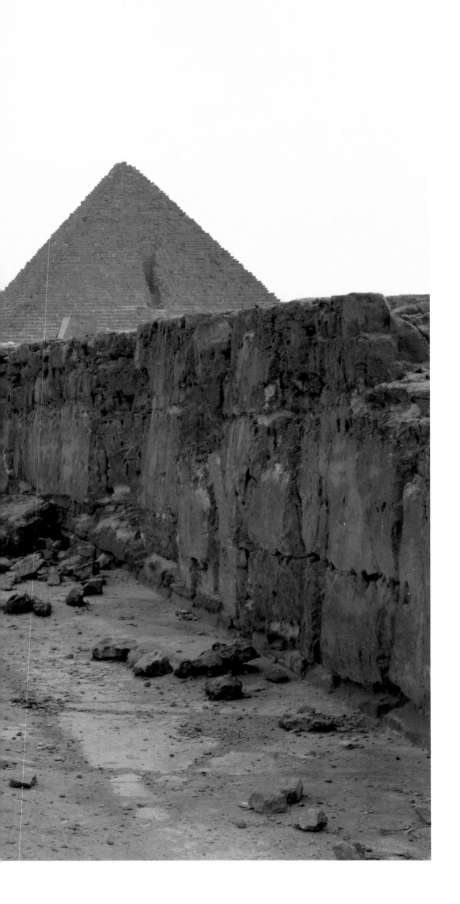

THE PYRAMIDS AT GIZA, EGYPT

At the end of the 20th century, scientists have so changed the concept of time, so compressed it, that all of human existence is reduced to no more than a passing moment of questionable significance. In a million years, some scientists say, there may be no signs that any civilization ever existed on this planet.

If human accomplishment seems transitory, one need only visit the Pyramids of Giza to be confronted with markers that rise out of the ambiguities of time to state clearly that "the pharaohs of Egypt lived here." And yet, it is part of the strange Möbius Strip of time that we know the pharaohs lived because we know they died. We know they died because the pyramids marked their deaths; and death marked the beginning of their new life.

The largest of the three pyramids at Giza, the Pyramid of Cheops (*see page 152*), is the centerpiece of the continuum of life into—and beyond—death. It is made of approximately 2.3 million blocks of white limestone from the nearby quarries across the Nile, each block averaging between 2.5 and 15 tons. All were set down over a period of about 60 years ending in approximately 2600 BC.

By the time of the construction of the pyramids the pharaoh Cheops had been reigning over Egypt for 50 years, and as he neared the end of his life he had made sure his tomb would be ready. A pharaoh, unlike ordinary people, could expect to enjoy a heavenly afterlife in the land of fertile fields that Osiris had prepared. But careful rituals had to be followed to arrive there, and Cheops spared no expense: his own or anyone else's.

There was no time off for the workers, the thousands of men hauling the stones, cutting them, and heaving them under ropes. No time for worship or sacrifice; he had closed the temples for 20 years while the work was going on. By the time the last workmen had left, Cheops complained that he had had to spend 1600 talents of silver just for their onions, their garlic, and their purges. But now his gleaming pyramid, a thing of supernatural size, stood waiting. And Cheops waited for the miracle that would launch him into the afterworld as one of the eternal gods. The priests had told him it would be as the Pyramid Texts now describe: *Re finds thee upon the shores of the sky in this lake that is in Nut* [the sky goddess]. *"The arriver comes!" say the gods. He* [the god Re] *gives thee his arm on the stairway to the sky.*

Not long after Cheops' death, the afterlife in Egyptian religion began to take a more democratic turn, and within 250 years, its doors had been opened to welcome anyone who could receive the proper funeral rites. So called "coffin texts," written on the inside of coffins from 2250–1580 BC, record the journey to the netherworld, wherein the Ba or spirit of the dead person transcends even the perfections of physical life.

Thy Ba shall not depart from thy corpse and thy Ba shall become divine with the blessed dead. . . . Thou shalt have power over water, shalt inhale air, and shalt be surfeited with the desires of thy heart. . . . Thy flesh shall be firm, thy muscles shall be easy and thou shalt exult in all thy limbs. . . . Thou shalt go up to the sky, and shalt penetrate the netherworld in all forms that thou likes.

The democratic idea that the afterlife was a grace available to everyone, not just royalty, was perhaps the great moral achievement of Egyptian religion, and of much greater influence than any engineering feat. It is this idea that has moved through the cultures of the world to become the ultimate mystery of human time. When intruders penetrated the innermost chamber of Cheops' pyramid in 820 AD, they found his granite sarcophagus still undisturbed after 3,000 years. They lifted the lid and found it empty.

PALENQUE, MEXICO

When Shield Pacal, the Great Lord of the Mayan city of Palenque, died in 683 AD, his body was buried deep within the pyramid known as the Temple of the Inscriptions. His casket was sealed by an intricately carved slab of rock, twelve feet long and weighing five tons. Its carving portrayed Shield Pacal at the moment of his death, tumbling backwards down the Tree of Life into the mouth of the Earth Monster into Xibalba, the Place of Fear, the Underworld. When the burial was complete and all the ceremonies had been performed, the staircase leading down to the tomb from the pyramid's upper temple was filled with rubble lest anyone enter until the lord was reborn.

The Temple of the Inscriptions and the tomb of Pacal at Palenque are perhaps the New World's most striking evidence of an ancient and profound belief in an afterlife. This concept of cosmic regeneration found its most vivid expression in Mesoamerica with the Classic Mayan civilization, which from 200 to 900 AD spread over the Yucatán into the highlands of Guatemala and Honduras. Closely linked to the afterlife, the invention

of very elaborate calender systems, one in particular, the Long Count calendar, allowed priests to reckon time back as far as 9 million years. Thus the Mayan concept of the afterlife was not of a place beyond living, but a short lapse of time in the immense flow of dates, an essen- tial passage in the many transits in the endless cycle of birth and death. During Pacal's nearly 70 years of rule (he took power in 615 AD), the city in the jungle had grown to dominate the southwestern part of Mexico's Yucatán Peninsula in the (present-day) state of Chiapas. The Palencanos had subdued their neighbors, and had used their blood for sacrifice to Chac, the long-nosed rain god. Under Pacal, they had made their city of pale stone elegant with pyramids, temples, and terraces, and told the story of their people and their rulers in intricate carvings and mysterious glyphs that can still be read on the stones of Palenque. When Pacal tumbled into Xibalba, he of all humans was thought certain to prove rebirth, to be reborn as a divine ancestor, a new god, able to guide the good fortunes of the city.

The Popul Vuh, the creation cycle of the Mayans, describes the fearful things Pacal must have encountered in Xibalba. Like the heroes of the story, Hunahpu and Xbalangue, he would have met the throng birds, and crossed the Blood and Pus rivers to the abode of One Death, Seven Death, Blood Gatherer, Skull Scepter, Bloody Claws, and Jaundice Master. He would have faced tests in the Dark House and the Razor House, in the Cold House and the Jaguar House. In the Bat House he would have confronted the monstrous snatch bats, with "snouts like knives" and adorned with eyes plucked from their victims.

After performing magical dances and a sacrifice without death, Pacal would finally have overcome Death itself, killing One Death, the first Lord of Xibalba, by trickery.

And perhaps he did. Today the pale stones of Pacal's city are ghostly against the jungle's dark trees and blood-red amapollo flowers, but they stand out clearly. Carefully excavated from the jungle that once swallowed it, Palenque has risen into the light of day. And perhaps in some other part of the world Pacal has also escaped from the Earth Monster and has risen into the light again.

Left:
Both tomb and library, the eight-tiered pyramid known as the Temple of the Inscriptions takes its name from three panels of glyphs in the temple on the summit. These inscriptions record the ancestral history of Palenque's rulers, Pacal among them. For many years the inscriptions remained a puzzle; but now the writing has been deciphered and much of the thinking of the ancient Maya has come to light. *Photo by Debra Bloomfield/ Courtesy of Robert Koch Gallery, San Francisco*

Above:
Proudly defiant, the face of a captured chief looks skyward. This life-sized figure is carved in the northeast corner of the palace complex (*see photo on page 153*) surrounded by other subservient chiefs and prisoners. The Maya were careful to record their victories and their wealth, as well as their myths and struggles. *Photo by Macduff Everton/Swanstock*

Above:

Great cities and green things have long flourished in the fertile jungle of the low-lying Yucatán Peninsula in Mexico and Guatemala. Cities like Tikal, Copán, and Chichén Itzá have ruins that rival Palenque's, and together with it, impart some of the glory that was Mayan culture. When Pacal and his descendants inhabited Palenque, from 600–800 AD, the city was a center of the surrounding region. They built this palace complex that extends over a city block and is

crowned with a unique tower. From here orders were given for the planting of crops, the construction of roads, and the waging of war. Doctors, accountants, astrologers, cooks, priests, scholars, and scribes lived and worked here. But all was not work. A ball game was played in a nearby court, whose ruined walls are still visible. It was a favorite pastime, and the fortunate winners of the game were ritually beheaded. *Photo by Macduff Everton/Swanstock*

BIBLIOGRAPHY

The writers and editors of *Strange Amazing and Mysterious Places* are indebted to the following sources:

Adams, Henry. *Mont-Saint-Michel and Chartres*. New York: Houghton Mifflin, 1933.

Bartlett, Des, and Jen Bartlett. Interview on National Public Radio: Forthcoming TV film on the Skeleton Coast; broadcast 10:50 AM, Eastern time, New York 4/11/93.

Baudelaire, Charles. *Twenty Prose Poems*. Translated by Michael Hamburger. San Francisco: City Lights, 1988.

Bernbaum, Edwin. *Sacred Mountains of the World*. San Francisco: Sierra Club Books, 1990.

Bierhorst, John. *Black Rainbow: Legends of the Incas and Myths of Ancient Peru*. New York: Farrar, Straus and Giroux, 1976.

Bridges, Marilyn. *Markings: Aerial Views of Sacred Landscapes*. Oxford, England: Phaidon, 1986.

Bridges, Marilyn. *Planet Peru*. New York: Kodak/Aperture, 1991.

Bridges, Thomas. "The Nazca Markings." In *Parabola: Myth And The Quest For Meaning*. Vol. III. #1, pp 48–53 (1978).

Brosnahan, Tom. *Turkey—A Survival Guide*. Hawthorn, Victoria, Australia: Lonely Planet Publications, 1990.

Budge, E.A. Wallis. *The Gods of the Egyptians, Volume I*. New York: Dover, 1969.

Byrd, Richard E. *Alone*. 1938. Reprint. Covelo, CA: Island Press, 1984.

Cassius, Dio, *Roman History*. Translated by E. Cary. London: Heinemann, 1925.

Casson, Lionel, and the Editors of Time-Life Books. *Ancient Egypt*. New York: Time Incorporated, 1965.

Corliss, William R. *Ancient Man: A Handbook of Puzzling Artifacts*. Glen Arm, MD: The Sourcebook Project, 1978.

Cottrell, Leonard. *Lost Cities*. New York: Rinehart & Co., 1957.

Courtland, Canby. *A Guide to the Archaeological Sites of Israel, Egypt and North Africa*. New York: Facts On File, 1990.

Cowan, James G. *The Aborigine Tradition*. Shaftesbury, England: Element Books, 1992.

Dames, Michael. *The Silbury Treasure: The Great Goddess Rediscovered*. London: Thames & Hudson, 1976.

Darian, Steven G. *The Ganges in Myth and History*. Honolulu: University of Hawaii Press, 1978.

Darwin, Charles. *Charles Darwin's Beagle Diary*. Edited by Richard Darwin Keynes. Cambridge: Cambridge University Press, 1988.

Darwin, Charles. *On the Origin of Species by Natural Selection*. London: Murray, 1859.

De Johngh, Brian. *The Companion Guide to Mainland Greece*. Englewood Cliffs, NJ: Prentice-Hall, 1991.

Earhart, Byron H., ed. *Religious Traditions of the World*. New York: HarperCollins, 1993.

Eck, Diana L. *Banaras: City of Light*. New York: Alfred A. Knopf, 1982.

Eliade, Mircea, ed. *Essential Sacred Writings from Around the World*. New York: Harper & Row, 1977.

Eliade, Mircea. *The Eliade Guide to World Religions*. Edited by Jan Couliano with Hilary S. Weisner. San Francisco: Harper Collins, 1991.

Ferguson, Wm. M., and Rohn, Arthur H. *Mesoamerica's Ancient Cities*. Boulder: University Press of Colorado, 1990.

Flaubert, Gustave. *Flaubert in Egypt*. Translated by Francis Steegmuller. Chicago: Academy Chicago Ltd., 1987.

Gibbons, Bob, and Bob Ashford. *The Himalayan Kingdoms*. New York: Hippocrene Books, 1987.

Gimbutas, Marija. *The Civilization of the Goddess*. SanFrancisco: HarperCollins, 1991.

Goldsberry, Steven. *Maui the Demigod: An Epic Tale of Mythical Hawaii*. Honolulu: University of Hawaii Press, 1989.

Grant, Michael. *Cities of Vesuvius: Pompeii and Herculaneum*. New York: Penguin, 1978.

Guiley, R.E., ed. *Harper's Encyclopedia of Mystical and Paranormal Experience*. San Francisco: HarperCollins, 1991.

Hadingham, Evan. *Lines to the Mountain Gods*. New York: Random House, 1987.

Haining, Peter. *Ancient Mysteries*. New York: Taplinger, 1977.

Hamilton, Edith. *Mythology*. Boston: Little Brown, 1942.

Harpur, James, and Jennifer Westwood. *The Atlas of Legendary Places*. New York: Weidenfeld, 1989.

Hemming, John. *Machu Picchu*. Wonders of Man Series. New York: Newsweek Book Division, 1981.

Herodotus. *History*. Edited by W.G. Waddell. Cambridge, MA: Blackwell, 1960.

Heyerdahl, Thor. *Easter Island: The Mystery Solved*. New York: Random House, 1989.

Hindu Myths. Translated by Betty Radice. London: Penguin, 1975.

Ingpen, Robert, and Philip Wilkinson. *Encyclopedia of Mysterious Places*. New York: Viking, 1990.

Johnson, Paul. *A History of the Jews*. New York: Harper & Row, 1987.

Kappan, L. "Response to the Extreme Environments." In *The Lichens*, Edited by V. Ahmadjian and M.E. Hale. New York: Academic Press, 1973.

Kasher, Menahem M. *The Western Wall: Its Meaning in the Thought of the Sages*. New York: Judaica Press, 1972.

Kelly, Robert. *Not this Island Music*. Santa Rosa, CA: Black Sparrow, 1987.

Latourette, Kenneth Scott. *A History of Christianity, Volume I: Beginnings to 1500*. New York: Harper & Row, 1953.

Lee, Douglas B. "Okavango Delta: Old Africa's Last Refuge."*National Geographic*, December 1990, pp. 38–69.

Lewis, Neville. *Delphi and the Sacred Way*. London: Michael Haag Ltd., 1987.

Macauley, Rose, and Constance Babington Smith. eds. *The Pleasure of Ruins*. London: Thames & Hudson, 1977.

Markman, Roberta H., and Peter T. Markman. *The Flayed God: The Mythology of Mesoamerica*. San Francisco: HarperCollins, 1992.

Meir, Golda. *A Land of Our Own: An Oral Autobiography*. Edited by Marie Syrkin. New York: Putnam, 1973.

Melville, Herman. *The Piazza Tales and Other Prose Pieces 1839-1860*. Chicago: Northwestern Press Newberry Library, 1987.

Michalowski, Kazimierz. *Karnak*. New York: Praeger, 1970.

Michell, John. *The New View Over Atlantis*. New York: Harper & Row, 1983.

Nabokov, Peter, ed. *Native American Testimony: A Chronicle of Indian-White Relations from Prophecy to the Present*. New York: Viking-Penguin, 1992.

Nagel, Georges. "The 'Mysteries' of Osiris In Ancient Egypt." In *The Mysteries*. Papers from the Eranos Yearbooks. Princeton, NJ: Princeton University Press, 1955.

Neihardt, John G. *The Sixth Grandfather: Black Elk's Teachings*. Edited by Raymond J. De Mallie. Lincoln, NE: University of Nebraska Press, 1984.

Nepal: A Travel Survival Kit. Australia: Lonely Planet, 1990.

Neruda, Pablo. *The Heights of Machu Picchu*. Translated by Nathaniel Tarn. London: Jonathan Cape, 1966.

Nightingale, Florence. *Letters from Egypt: A Journey on the Nile 1849-1850*. New York: Weidenfeld & Nicolson, 1987.

The Popul Vuh. Translated by Dennis Tedlock. New York: Simon & Schuster, 1986.

Pyne, Stephen J. *The Ice. A Journey to Antarctica*. Iowa City, IA: University of Iowa Press, 1986.

The Quest of the Holy Grail. Translated by P.M. Matarasso. London: Penguin, 1969.

Reader's Digest Association. *Folklore Myths and Legends of Britain*. London: Reader's Digest, 1973.

Reader's Digest Association. *Mysteries of the Unexplained*. New York: Reader's Digest, 1982.

Reader's Digest Association. *Quest for the Past*. New York: Reader's Digest, 1984.

Rufus, Anneli S., and Kristan Lawson. *Goddess Sites: Europe*. San Francisco: HarperCollins, 1990.

Sinclair, N.A., and J.L. Stokes. "Obligatively Psychrophillic Yeasts from the Polar Regions". *Microbiology* 11, pp. 259–69.

Van Dyke, John C. *The Desert*. 1901. Reprint. New York: Gibbs-Smith, 1980.

Von Hagen, Victor Wolfgang. *The Incas of Pedro De Cieza De Leon*. Norman, OK: University of Okalahoma Press, 1959.

Waddell. Austine, L. *Tibetan Buddhism*. New York: Dover, 1972.

Wallechensky, David, and Irving Wallace. *The Book of Predictions*. New York: Bantam, 1981.

Warner, Roger. *Angkor: The Hidden Glories*. Boston: Houghton Mifflin, 1990.

Waters, Frank. *The Book of the Hopi*. New York: Penguin Books, 1977.

Well, Steve, and Harvey Arden. *Wisdomkeepers*. Hillsboro, OR: Beyond Words, 1990.

Whitefield, Philip. ed. *Atlas of Earth Mysteries*. London: Rand McNally, 1990.

Wright, Ronald. *Cut Stones & Crossroads*. New York: Viking, 1984.

Credits:
Editor: Barbara Roether
Essays: Richard Marshall
Captions: Mark MacNamara
Director of Photography: Linda Ferrer
Design Director: Jennifer Barry
Design and Production Assistant: Kristen Wurz
Production Managers: Jonathan Mills and Lynne Noone
Photo Researchers: Anna Sever and Sarah Bendersky
Managing Editor: Maura Carey Damacion
Assistant Editor: Jenny Collins
Editorial Assistant: Sophie Deprez
Copyediting: Jonathon Schwartz
Special thanks to Edwin Bernbaum, Kevin Bubriski, and Miki Raver.

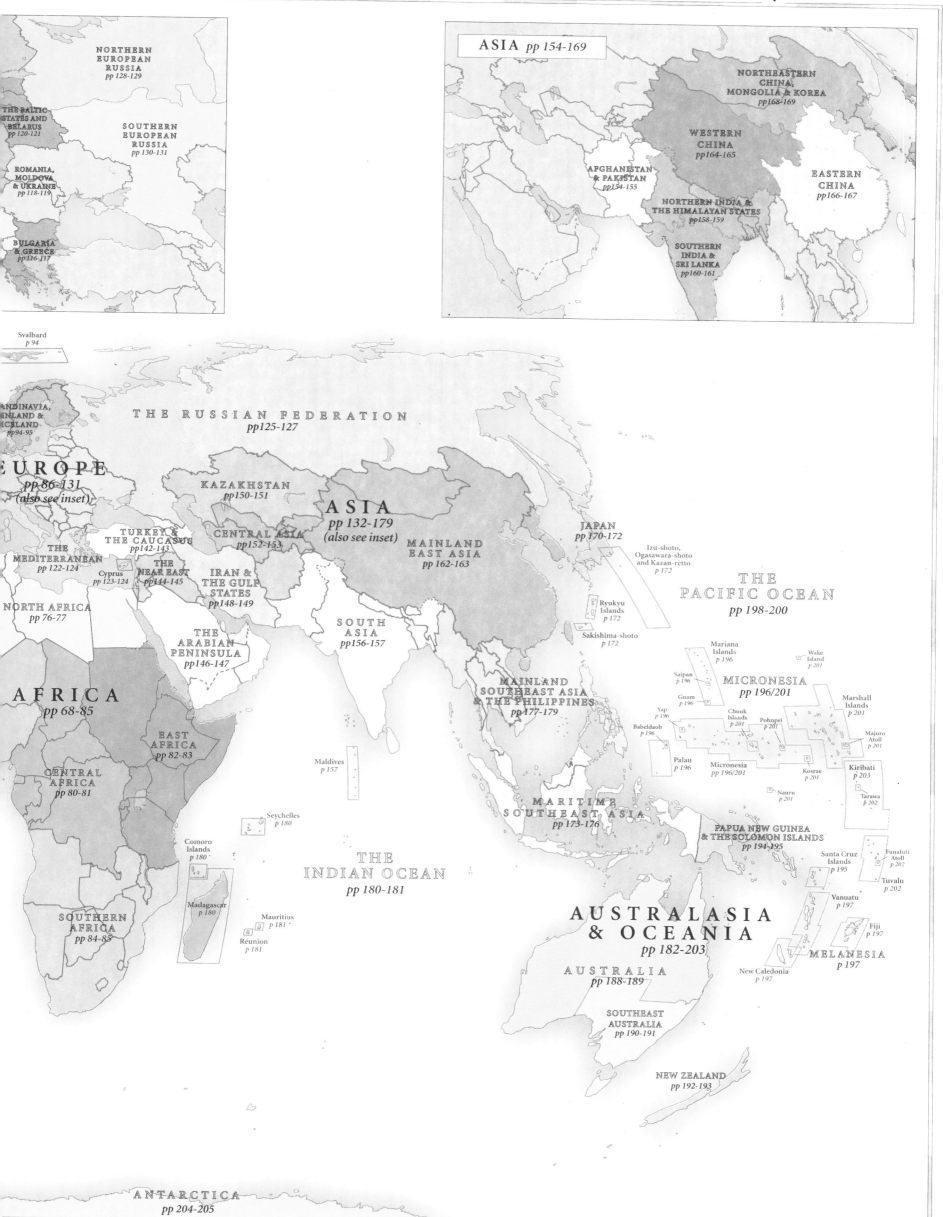

NORTHERN EUROPEAN RUSSIA pp 128-129
THE BALTIC STATES AND BELARUS pp 120-121
SOUTHERN EUROPEAN RUSSIA pp 130-131
ROMANIA, MOLDOVA & UKRAINE pp 118-119
BULGARIA & GREECE pp 116-117
ASIA pp 154-169
NORTHEASTERN CHINA, MONGOLIA & KOREA pp168-169
WESTERN CHINA pp164-165
AFGHANISTAN & PAKISTAN pp154-155
EASTERN CHINA pp166-167
NORTHERN INDIA & THE HIMALAYAN STATES pp158-159
SOUTHERN INDIA & SRI LANKA pp160-161
Svalbard p 94
SCANDINAVIA, FINLAND & ICELAND pp94-95
THE RUSSIAN FEDERATION pp125-127
EUROPE pp 86-131 (also see inset)
KAZAKHSTAN pp150-151
ASIA pp 132-179 (also see inset)
TURKEY & THE CAUCASUS pp142-143
CENTRAL ASIA pp152-153
MAINLAND EAST ASIA pp 162-163
JAPAN pp 170-172
Izu-shoto, Ogasawara-shoto and Kazan-retto p 172
THE MEDITERRANEAN pp 122-124
Cyprus pp 123-124
THE NEAR EAST pp144-145
IRAN & THE GULF STATES pp148-149
THE PACIFIC OCEAN pp 198-200
Ryukyu Islands p 172
NORTH AFRICA pp 76-77
SOUTH ASIA pp156-157
Sakishima-shoto p 172
THE ARABIAN PENINSULA pp146-147
Mariana Islands p 196
Wake Island p 201
Saipan p 196
MICRONESIA pp 196/201
AFRICA pp 68-85
MAINLAND SOUTHEAST ASIA & THE PHILIPPINES pp 177-179
Guam p 196
Marshall Islands p 201
Yap p 196
Chuuk Islands p 201
Pohnpei p 201
EAST AFRICA pp 82-83
Babeldaob p 196
Majuro Atoll p 201
Maldives p 157
Palau p 196
Micronesia pp 196/201
Kosrae p 201
CENTRAL AFRICA pp 80-81
Kiribati p 203
Nauru p 201
Tarawa p 202
MARITIME SOUTHEAST ASIA pp 173-176
Seychelles p 180
PAPUA NEW GUINEA & THE SOLOMON ISLANDS pp 194-195
Comoro Islands p 180
THE INDIAN OCEAN pp 180-181
Santa Cruz Islands p 195
Funafuti Atoll p 202
Tuvalu p 202
Madagascar p 180
Vanuatu p 197
SOUTHERN AFRICA pp 84-85
Mauritius p 181
AUSTRALASIA & OCEANIA pp 182-203
Fiji p 197
Réunion p 181
MELANESIA p 197
New Caledonia p 197
AUSTRALIA pp 188-189
SOUTHEAST AUSTRALIA pp 190-191
NEW ZEALAND pp 192-193
ANTARCTICA pp 204-205

FIREFLY
WORLD
ATLAS

FIREFLY

WORLD ATLAS

FIREFLY BOOKS

A DK PUBLISHING BOOK

GENERAL GEOGRAPHICAL CONSULTANTS

PHYSICAL GEOGRAPHY • Denys Brunsden, Emeritus Professor, Department of Geography, King's College, London, England
HUMAN GEOGRAPHY • Professor J. Malcolm Wagstaff, Department of Geography, University of Southampton, England
PLACE NAMES • Caroline Burgess, Permanent Committee on Geographical Names, London, England
BOUNDARIES • International Boundaries Research Unit, Mountjoy Research Centre, University of Durham, England

DIGITAL MAPPING CONSULTANTS

Cartopia developed by George Galfalvi and XMap Ltd., London, England

Professor Jan-Peter Muller, Department of Photogrammetry and Surveying, University College, London, England

Cover globes, planets, and information on the Solar System provided by Philip Eales and Kevin Tildsley, Planetary Visions Ltd., London, England

REGIONAL CONSULTANTS

NORTH AMERICA • Dr. David Green, Department of Geography, King's College, London • Jim Walsh, Head of Reference Services, Tisch Library, Tufts University, Medford, Massachussetts
SOUTH AMERICA • Dr. David Preston, School of Geography, University of Leeds, England
EUROPE • Dr. Edward M. Yates, formerly of the Department of Geography, King's College, London, England
AFRICA • Dr. Philip Amis, Development Administration Group, University of Birmingham, England • Dr. Ieuan Ll. Griffiths, Department of Geography, University of Sussex, England
Dr. Tony Binns, Department of Geography, University of Sussex, England
CENTRAL ASIA • Dr. David Turnock, Department of Geography, University of Leicester, England
SOUTH AND EAST ASIA • Dr. Jonathan Rigg, Department of Geography, University of Durham, England
AUSTRALASIA AND OCEANIA • Dr. Robert Allison, Department of Geography, University of Durham, England

ACKNOWLEDGMENTS

Digital terrain data created by Eros Data Center, Boulder, Colorado. Processed by GVS Images Inc., California, and Planetary Visions Ltd., London, England
CIRCA Research and Reference Information, Cambridge, England • Digitization by Robertson Research International, Swanley, England • Peter Clark

CARTOGRAPHY

EDITOR-IN-CHIEF • Andrew Heritage
MANAGING CARTOGRAPHER • David Roberts   SENIOR CARTOGRAPHIC EDITOR • Roger Bullen

Pamela Alford • James Anderson • Sarah Baker-Ede • Caroline Bowie • Dale Buckton • Tony Chambers • Jan Clark • Bob Croser • Martin Darlison • Claire Ellam
Sally Gable • Jeremy Hepworth • Geraldine Horner • Chris Jackson • Christine Johnston • Julia Lunn • Michael Martin • James Mills-Hicks • Simon Mumford • John Plumer
John Scott • Ann Stephenson • Julie Turner • Jane Voss • Scott Wallace • Iorwerth Watkins • Bryony Webb • Alan Whitaker • Peter Winfield

DATABASE MANAGER • Simon Lewis

DIGITAL MAPS CREATED BY | PLACE NAMES DATABASE TEAM
Tom Coulson • Thomas Robertshaw | Natalie Clarkson • Ruth Duxbury • Caroline Falce • John Featherstone • Dan Gardiner
Philip Rowles • Rob Stokes | Ciárán Hynes • Margaret Hynes • Helen Rudkin • Margaret Stevenson • Annie Wilson

MANAGING EDITOR | MANAGING ART EDITOR
Lisa Thomas | Philip Lord
EDITORS | DESIGNERS
Thomas Heath • Wim Jenkins • Jane Oliver | Scott David • Carol Ann Davis • David Douglas
Constance Novis (US) • Siobhán Ryan • Elizabeth Wyse | Rhonda Fisher • Karen Gregory • Nicola Liddiard • Paul Williams
EDITORIAL RESEARCH | ILLUSTRATIONS
Helen Dangerfield • Andrew Rebeiro-Hargrave | Ciárán Hughes • Advanced Illustration, Congleton, England
ADDITIONAL EDITORIAL ASSISTANCE | PICTURE RESEARCH
Debra Clapson • Robert Damon • Ailsa Heritage • Jayne Parsons • Chris Whitwell | Melissa Albany • James Clarke • Anna Lord • Christine Rista • Sarah Moule

EDITORIAL DIRECTION • Louise Cavanagh   ART DIRECTION • Chez Picthall

PRODUCTION
David Proffit • Hilary Stephens

Published in Canada in 1998
by Firefly Books Ltd.
3680 Victoria Park Avenue
Willowdale, Ontario, Canada
M2H 3KI

Canadian Cataloguing in Publication Data
Make entry under title:
World atlas
Includes index
ISBN 1-55209-201-1
1. Atlases
G1 121.W665 1998   912   C97-932525-0

INTRODUCTION

FOR MANY, THE OUTSTANDING LEGACY OF THE TWENTIETH CENTURY has been the way in which the Earth has shrunk. As we approach the end of this most dramatic of centuries, and the end of the second millennium, there is a greater need than ever for a clear vision of the world in which we live. The human population has increased fourfold since 1900. The last scraps of *terra incognita* – the polar regions and ocean depths – have been penetrated and mapped. New regions have been colonized, and previously hostile realms claimed for habitation. The advent of aviation technology and mass tourism has allowed many of us to travel farther, faster, and more frequently than ever before. In doing so we are given a bird's-eye view of the Earth's surface denied to our forebears.

AT THE SAME TIME, the amount of information about our world has grown enormously. Telecommunications can span the greatest distances in fractions of a second: our multimedia environment hurls uninterrupted streams of data at us, on the printed page, through the airwaves, and across our television and computer screens; events from all corners of the globe reach us instantaneously, and are witnessed as they unfold. Our sense of stability and certainty has been eroded; instead, we are aware that the world is in a constant state of flux and change. Natural disasters, man-made cataclysms, and conflicts between nations remind us daily of the enormity and fragility of our domain.

OUR CURRENT "GLOBAL" CULTURE has made the need greater than ever before for everyone to possess an atlas. The *Firefly World Atlas* has been conceived to meet this need. At its core, like all atlases, it seeks to define where places are, to describe their main characteristics, and to locate them in relation to other places. Every attempt has been made to make the information on the maps as clear and accessible as possible. In addition, each page of the atlas provides a wealth of further information, bringing the maps to life. Using "at-a-glance" photographs, diagrams, "at-a-glance" maps, introductory texts, and captions, the atlas builds up a detailed portait of those features – cultural, political, economic, and geomorphological – which make each region unique, and which are also the main agents of change.

A MAP PROVIDES ONLY A SNAPSHOT of the world at a given time. Drawing on the resources of a wide range of sciences and using the latest technology, the *Firefly World Atlas* is intended to equip the reader with the information needed to understand why the world today is the shape it is, and to recognize the processes of change that will determine its evolution in the next century.

PETER KINDERSLEY

CONTENTS

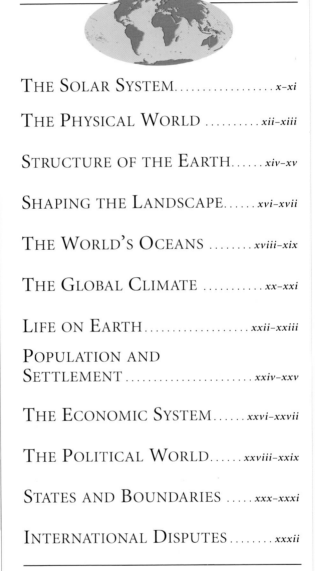
ATLAS OF THE WORLD

NORTH AMERICA

SOUTH AMERICA

AFRICA

KEY TO REGIONAL MAPS

PHYSICAL FEATURES

elevation

	6000m / 19,686ft
	4000m / 13,124ft
	3000m / 9843ft
	2000m / 6562ft
	1000m / 3281ft
	500m / 1640ft
	250m / 820ft
	100m / 328ft
	sea level
	below sea level

▲ elevation above sea level (mountain height)

▲ volcano

✕ pass

▼ elevation below sea level (depression depth)

sand desert

lava flow

coastline

reef

atoll

sea depth

	sea level
	-250m / -820ft
	-500m / -1640ft
	-1000m / -3281ft
	-2000m / -6562ft
	-3000m / -9843ft

▲ seamount / guyot symbol

▼ undersea spot depth

DRAINAGE FEATURES

main river

secondary river

tertiary river

minor river

main seasonal river

secondary seasonal river

canal

waterfall

rapids

dam

perennial lake

seasonal lake

perennial salt lake

seasonal salt lake

reservoir

salt flat / salt pan

marsh / salt marsh

mangrove

wadi

∘ spring / well / waterhole / oasis

ICE FEATURES

ice cap / sheet

ice shelf

glacier

summer pack ice limit

winter pack ice limit

COMMUNICATIONS

highway

highway (under construction)

major road

minor road

⊢···⊣ tunnel (road)

main line

minor line

⊢···⊣ tunnel (railroad)

✈ international airport

BORDERS

full international border

■ ■ ■ undefined international border

– – – disputed de facto border

▬ ▪ ▬ ▪ disputed territorial claim border

▬ ▬ ▬ indication of country extent (Pacific only)

▬ ▪ ▬ ▪ indication of dependent territory extent (Pacific only)

• • • • • demarcation / cease-fire line

autonomous / federal region border

2nd order internal administrative border

3rd order internal administrative border

SETTLEMENTS

built-up area

settlement population symbols

■ more than 5 million

◉ 1 million to 5 million

◉ 500,000 to 1 million

◎ 100,000 to 500,000

⊕ 50,000 to 100,000

∘ 10,000 to 50,000

∘ fewer than 10,000

■ ▪ • country/dependent territory capital city

■ ▪ • autonomous / federal region / 2nd order internal administrative center

■ ▪ • 3rd order internal administrative center

MISCELLANEOUS FEATURES

⚬⚬⚬⚬⚬ ancient wall

◇ site of interest

∘ scientific station

GRATICULE FEATURES

lines of latitude and longitude / Equator

Tropics / Polar circles

45° degrees of longitude / latitude

TYPOGRAPHIC KEY

PHYSICAL FEATURES

landscape features — *Namib Desert* / ***Massif Central*** / **ANDES**

headland — *Nordkapp*

elevation / volcano / pass — Mount Meru 4556 m

drainage features — *Lake Rudolf*

rivers / canals / spring / well / waterhole / oasis / waterfall / rapids / dam — *Mekong*

ice features — *Vatnajökull*

sea features — *Golfe de Lion* / *Andaman Sea* / INDIAN OCEAN

undersea features — *Barracuda Fracture Zone*

REGIONS

country — **ARMENIA**

dependent territory with parent state — **NIUE** (to NZ)

region outside feature area — ANGOLA

autonomous / federal region — MINAS GERAIS

2nd order internal administrative region — MINSKAYA VOBLASTS'

3rd order internal administrative region — Vaucluse

cultural region — New England

SETTLEMENTS

capital city — **BEIJING**

dependent territory capital city — FORT-DE-FRANCE

other settlements — Chicago / Adana / Tizi Ozou / Yonezawa / Farnham

MISCELLANEOUS

sites of interest / miscellaneous — Valley of the Kings

Tropics / Polar circles — *Antarctic Circle*

HOW TO USE THIS ATLAS

THE ATLAS IS ORGANIZED BY CONTINENT, moving eastward from the International Date Line. The opening section describes the world's structure, systems, and main features. It is followed by The Atlas of the World, a continent-by-continent guide to today's world, starting with a comprehensive insight into the physical, political, and economic structure of each continent, followed by integrated mapping and a description of each region or country.

THE WORLD

THE INTRODUCTORY SECTION of the Atlas deals with every aspect of the planet, from physical structure to human geography, providing an overall picture of the world we live in. Complex topics such as the landscape of the Earth, climate, oceans, population, and economic patterns are clearly explained with the aid of maps and diagrams drawn from the latest information.

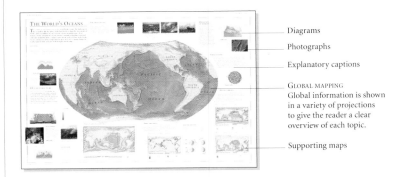

Diagrams

Photographs

Explanatory captions

GLOBAL MAPPING
Global information is shown in a variety of projections to give the reader a clear overview of each topic.

Supporting maps

THE POLITICAL CONTINENT

THE POLITICAL PORTRAIT of the continent is a vital reference point for every continental section, showing the position of countries relative to one another, and the relationship between human settlement and geographic location. The complex mosaic of languages spoken in each continent is mapped, along with the effect of communications networks on the pattern of settlement.

Locator map

Introductory text

Communications map

Population map

POLITICAL MAP
All of the countries in each continent are shown, with their political capitals and most populous cities.

Languages map

CONTINENTAL RESOURCES

THE EARTH'S RICH NATURAL RESOURCES, including oil, gas, minerals, and fertile land, have played a key role in the development of society. These pages show the location of minerals and agricultural resources on each continent, and how they have been instrumental in dictating industrial growth and the varieties of economic activity across the continent.

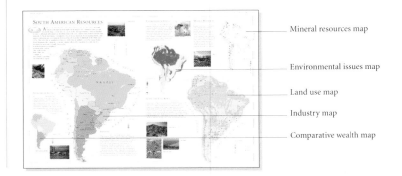

Mineral resources map

Environmental issues map

Land use map

Industry map

Comparative wealth map

THE PHYSICAL CONTINENT

THE ASTONISHING VARIETY of landforms, and the dramatic forces that created and continue to shape the landscape, are explained in the continental physical spread. Cross-sections, illustrations, and terrain maps highlight the different parts of the continent, showing how nature's forces have produced the landscapes we see today.

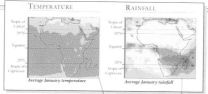

CLIMATE CHARTS
Rainfall and temperature charts clearly show the continental patterns of rainfall and temperature.

CLIMATE MAP
Climatic regions vary across each continent. The map displays the differing climatic regions, as well as daily hours of sunshine at selected weather stations.

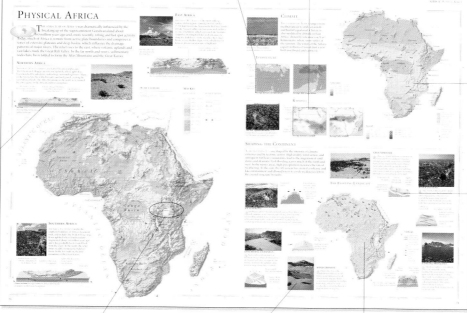

PHYSICAL AFRICA

CROSS-SECTIONS
Detailed cross-sections through selected parts of the continent show the underlying geomorphic structure.

LANDFORM DIAGRAMS
The complex formation of many typical landforms is summarized in these easy-to-understand illustrations.

MAIN PHYSICAL MAP
Detailed satellite data have been used to create an accurate and visually striking picture of the surface of the continent.

PHOTOGRAPHS
A wide range of beautiful photographs bring the world's regions to life.

LANDSCAPE EVOLUTION MAP
The physical shape of each continent is affected by a variety of forces that continually sculpt and modify the landscape. This map shows the major processes that affect different parts of the continent.

REGIONAL MAPPING

THE MAIN BODY of the Atlas is a unique regional map set, with detailed information on the terrain, the human geography of the region, and its infrastructure. Around the edge of the map, additional "at-a-glance" maps give an instant picture of regional industry, land use, and agriculture. The detailed terrain map (shown in perspective) focuses on the main physical features of the region, and is enhanced by annotated illustrations, and photographs of the physical structure.

REGIONAL LOCATOR
This small map shows the location of each country in relation to its continent.

TRANSPORTATION NETWORK

340,090 miles (544,144 km)	4,813 miles 7,700 km
12,872 miles (20,592 km)	2,108 miles (3,389 km)

New York's commercial success is tied historically to its transportation connections. The Erie Canal, completed in 1825, opened up the Great Lakes and the interior to New York's markets and carried a stream of immigrants into the Midwest.

TRANSPORTATION NETWORK
The differing extent of the transportation network for each region is shown here, along with key facts about the transportation system.

KEY TO MAIN MAP
A key to the population symbols and land heights accompanies the main map.

WORLD LOCATOR
This locates the continent in which the region is found on a small world map.

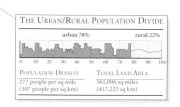

USA: NORTHEASTERN STATES

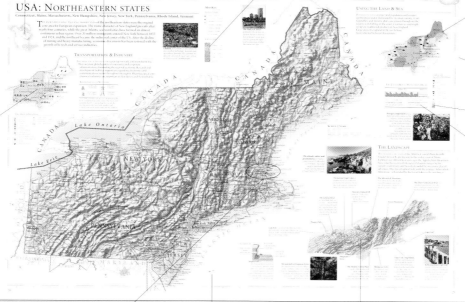

LAND USE MAP
This shows the different types of land use that characterize the region, as well as indicating the principal agricultural activities.

GRID REFERENCE
The framing grid provides a location reference for each place listed in the Index.

MAP KEYS
Each supporting map has its own key.

THE URBAN/RURAL POPULATION DIVIDE

urban 78%　　　rural 22%

0　10　20　30　40　50　60　70　80　90　100

POPULATION DENSITY	TOTAL LAND AREA
277 people per sq mile (107 people per sq km)	161,096 sq miles (417,222 sq km)

URBAN/RURAL POPULATION DIVIDE
The proportion of people in the region who live in urban and rural areas, as well as the overall population density and land area, are clearly shown in these simple graphics.

TRANSPORTATION AND INDUSTRY MAP
The main industrial areas are mapped, and the most important industrial and economic activities of the region are shown.

CONTINUATION SYMBOLS
These symbols indicate where adjacent maps can be found.

MAIN REGIONAL MAP
A wealth of information is displayed on the main map, building up a rich portrait of the interaction between the physical landscape and the human and political geography of each region. The key to the regional maps can be found on page viii.

LANDSCAPE MAP
The computer-generated terrain model accurately portrays an oblique view of the landscape. Annotations highlight the most important geographic features of the region.

JUPITER

- **Diameter:** 88,846 miles (142,984 km)
- **Mass:** 1,900,000 million million million tons
- **Temperature:** -153°C (extremes not available)
- **Distance from Sun:** 483 million miles (778 million km)
- **Length of day:** 9.84 Earth hours
- **Length of year:** 11.86 Earth years
- **Surface gravity:** 1 kg = 2.53 kg

MARS

- **Diameter:** 4,217 miles (6,786 km)
- **Mass:** 642 million million million tons
- **Temperature:** -137 to 37°C
- **Distance from Sun:** 142 million miles (228 million km)
- **Length of day:** 24.623 Earth hours
- **Length of year:** 1.88 Earth years
- **Surface gravity:** 1 kg = 0.38 kg

EARTH

- **Diameter:** 7,926 miles (12,756 km)
- **Mass:** 5,976 million million million tons
- **Temperature:** -13 to 37°C
- **Distance from Sun:** 93 million miles (150 million km)
- **Length of day:** 23.92 hours
- **Length of year:** 365.25 days
- **Surface gravity:** 1 kg = 1 kg

VENUS

- **Diameter:** 7,520 miles (12,102 km)
- **Mass:** 4,870 million million million tons
- **Temperature:** 457°C (extremes not available)
- **Distance from Sun:** 67 million miles (108 million km)
- **Length of day:** 243.01 Earth days
- **Length of year:** 224.7 Earth days
- **Surface gravity:** 1 kg = 0.38 kg

MERCURY

- **Diameter:** 3,031 miles (4,878 km)
- **Mass:** 330 million million tons
- **Temperature:** -173 to 427°C
- **Distance from Sun:** 36 million miles (58 million km)
- **Length of day:** 58.65 Earth days
- **Length of year:** 87.97 Earth days
- **Surface gravity:** 1 kg = 0.38 kg

THE SOLAR SYSTEM

NINE MAJOR PLANETS, their satellites, and countless minor planets (asteroids) orbit the Sun to form the Solar System. The Sun, our nearest star, creates energy from nuclear reactions deep within its interior, providing all the light and heat that make life on Earth possible. The Earth is unique in the solar system in that it supports life: its size, gravitational pull, and distance from the Sun have all created the optimum conditions for the evolution of life. The planetary images seen here are composites derived from actual spacecraft images (not shown to scale).

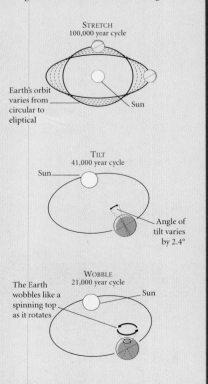

THE SUN

- **Diameter:** 864,948 miles (1,392,000 km)
- **Mass:** 1990 million million million million tons

THE SUN was formed when a swirling cloud of dust and gas contracted, pulling matter into its center. When the temperature at the center rose to 1,000,000°C, nuclear fusion – the fusing of hydrogen into helium, creating energy – occurred, releasing a constant stream of heat and light.

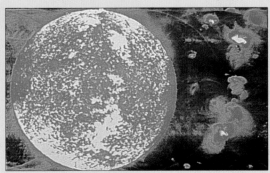

Solar flares are sudden bursts of energy from the Sun's surface. They can be 125,000 miles (200,000 km) long.

THE FORMATION OF THE SOLAR SYSTEM

The cloud of dust and gas emitted by the Sun during its formation cooled to form the Solar System. The smaller planets nearest the Sun are formed of minerals and metals. The outer planets were formed at lower temperatures, and mainly consist of swirling clouds of gases.

THE MILANKOVITCH CYCLE

The amount of radiation from the Sun which reaches the Earth is affected by variations in the Earth's orbit and the tilt of the Earth's axis, as well as by "wobbles" in the axis. These variations cause three separate cycles, corresponding with the durations of recent ice ages.

STRETCH
100,000 year cycle

Earth's orbit varies from circular to eliptical

Sun

TILT
41,000 year cycle

Sun

Angle of tilt varies by 2.4°

WOBBLE
21,000 year cycle

The Earth wobbles like a spinning top as it rotates

Sun

SATURN

- **Diameter:** 74,974 miles (120,660 km)
- **Mass:** 570,000 million million million tons
- **Temperature:** -185°C (extremes not available)
- **Distance from Sun:** 887 million miles (1,427 million km)
- **Length of day:** 10.23 Earth hours
- **Length of year:** 29.46 Earth years
- **Surface gravity:** 1 kg = 1.07 kg

URANUS

- **Diameter:** 31,763 miles (51,118 km)
- **Mass:** 86,800 million million million tons
- **Temperature:** -214°C (extremes not available)
- **Distance from Sun:** 1,783 million miles (2,870 million km)
- **Length of day:** 17.9 Earth hours
- **Length of year:** 84.01 Earth years
- **Surface gravity:** 1 kg = 0.92 kg

NEPTUNE

- **Diameter:** 30,775 miles (49,528 km)
- **Mass:** 10,200 million million million tons
- **Temperature:** -225°C (extremes not available)
- **Distance from Sun:** 2,794 million miles (4,497 million km)
- **Length of day:** 19.2 Earth hours
- **Length of year:** 164.79 Earth years
- **Surface gravity:** 1 kg = 1.18 kg

SPACE DEBRIS

MILLIONS OF OBJECTS, remnants of planetary formation, circle the Sun in a zone lying between Mars and Jupiter, known as the asteroid belt. Fragments of asteroids break off to form meteoroids, which can reach the Earth's surface. Comets, composed of ice and dust, originated outside our solar system. Their elliptical orbit brings them close to the Sun and into the inner solar system.

Meteor Crater in Arizona is 4,200 ft (1,300 m) wide and 660 ft (200 m) deep. It was formed over 10,000 years ago.

METEOROIDS

Meteoroids are fragments of asteroids that hurtle through space at great velocity. Although millions of meteoroids enter the Earth's atmosphere, the vast majority burn up on entry, and fall to the Earth as a meteor or shooting star. Large meteoroids traveling at speeds of 155,000 mph (250,000 kmh) can sometimes withstand the atmosphere and hit the Earth's surface with tremendous force, creating large craters on impact.

POSSIBLE AND ACTUAL METEORITE CRATERS

Map key
- ⊘ Possible impact craters
- ⊘ Meteorite impact craters

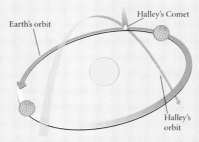

The orbit of Halley's Comet brings it past the Earth every 76 years. It last visited in 1986.

Earth's orbit — Halley's Comet — Halley's orbit

ORBIT OF HALLEY'S COMET AROUND THE SUN

THE EARTH'S ATMOSPHERE

DURING THE EARLY STAGES of the Earth's formation, ash, lava, carbon dioxide, and water vapor were discharged onto the surface of the planet by constant volcanic eruptions. The water formed the oceans, while carbon dioxide entered the atmosphere or was dissolved in the oceans. Clouds, formed of water droplets, reflected some of the Sun's radiation back into space. The Earth's temperature stabilized and early life forms began to emerge, converting carbon dioxide into life-giving oxygen.

It is thought that the gases that make up the Earth's atmosphere originated deep within the interior, and were released many millions of years ago during intense volcanic activity, similar to this eruption at Mount St. Helens.

PLUTO

- **Diameter:** 1,429 miles (2,300 km)
- **Mass:** 13 million million million tons
- **Temperature:** -236°C (extremes not available)
- **Distance from Sun:** 3,666 million miles (5,900 million km)
- **Length of day:** 6.39 Earth hours
- **Length of year:** 248.54 Earth years
- **Surface gravity:** 1 kg = 0.30 kg

ORDER AND RELATIVE DISTANCE FROM THE SUN OF PLANETS

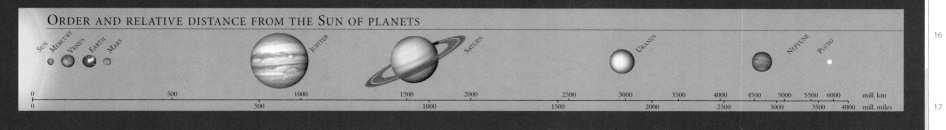

SUN MERCURY VENUS EARTH MARS JUPITER SATURN URANUS NEPTUNE PLUTO

500 1000 1500 2000 2500 3000 3500 4000 4500 5000 5500 6000 mill. km
0 500 1000 1500 2000 2500 3000 3500 4000 mill. miles

THE PHYSICAL WORLD

THE EARTH'S SURFACE is constantly being transformed: it is uplifted, folded, and faulted by tectonic forces; weathered and eroded by wind, water, and ice. Sometimes change is dramatic, the spectacular results of earthquakes or floods. More often it is a slow process over millions of years. A physical map of the world represents a snapshot of the ever-evolving architecture of the Earth. This terrain map shows the whole surface of the Earth, both above and below the sea.

THE WORLD IN SECTION

These cross-sections around the Earth, one in the northern hemisphere; one straddling the Equator, reveal the limited areas of land above sea level in comparison with the extent of the sea floor. The greater erosive effects of weathering by wind and water limit the upward elevation of land above sea level, while the deep oceans retain their dramatic mountain and trench profiles.

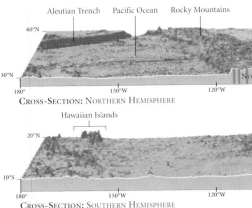

CROSS-SECTION: NORTHERN HEMISPHERE

CROSS-SECTION: SOUTHERN HEMISPHERE

MAP KEY

GEOGRAPHICAL REGIONS

- ice
- tundra
- needleleaf forest
- broadleaf forest
- cultivated land
- hot desert
- cold desert
- tropical grassland
- tropical rain forest
- mountain
- submarine regions

SCALE 1:66,000,000
(projection: Wagner VII)

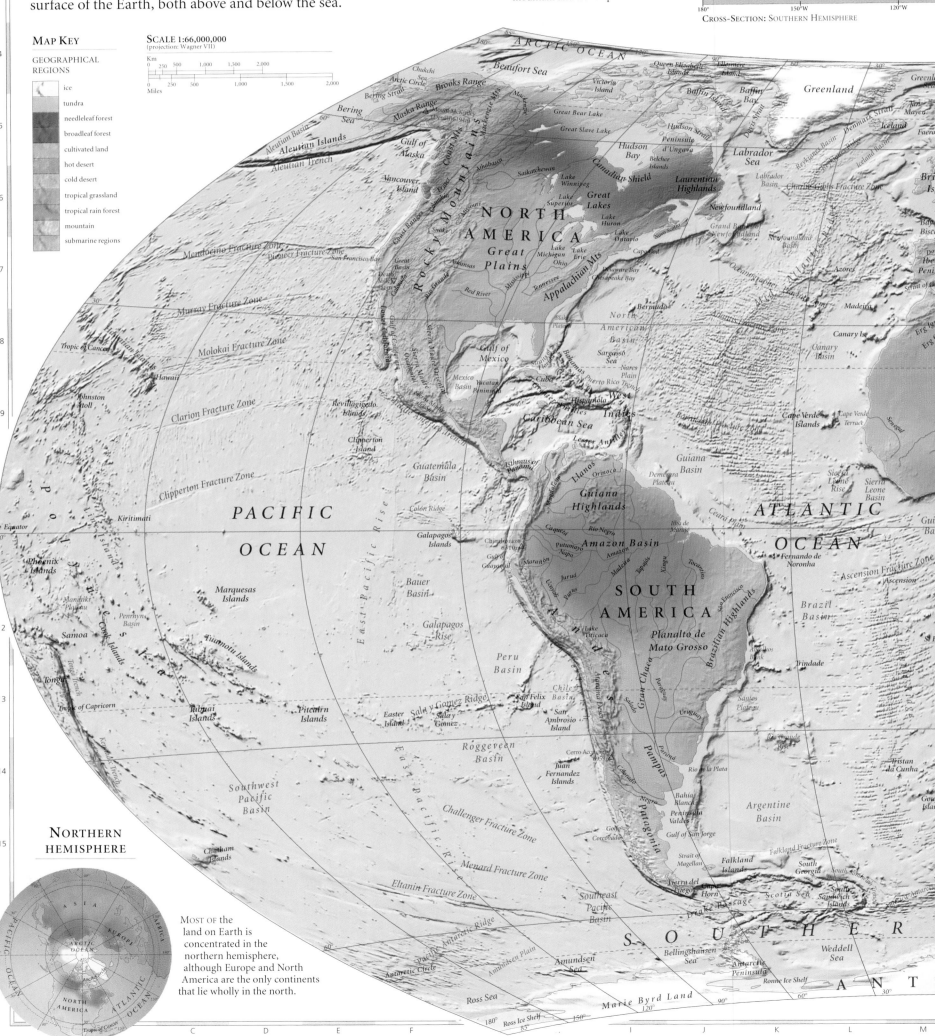

NORTHERN HEMISPHERE

MOST OF THE land on Earth is concentrated in the northern hemisphere, although Europe and North America are the only continents that lie wholly in the north.

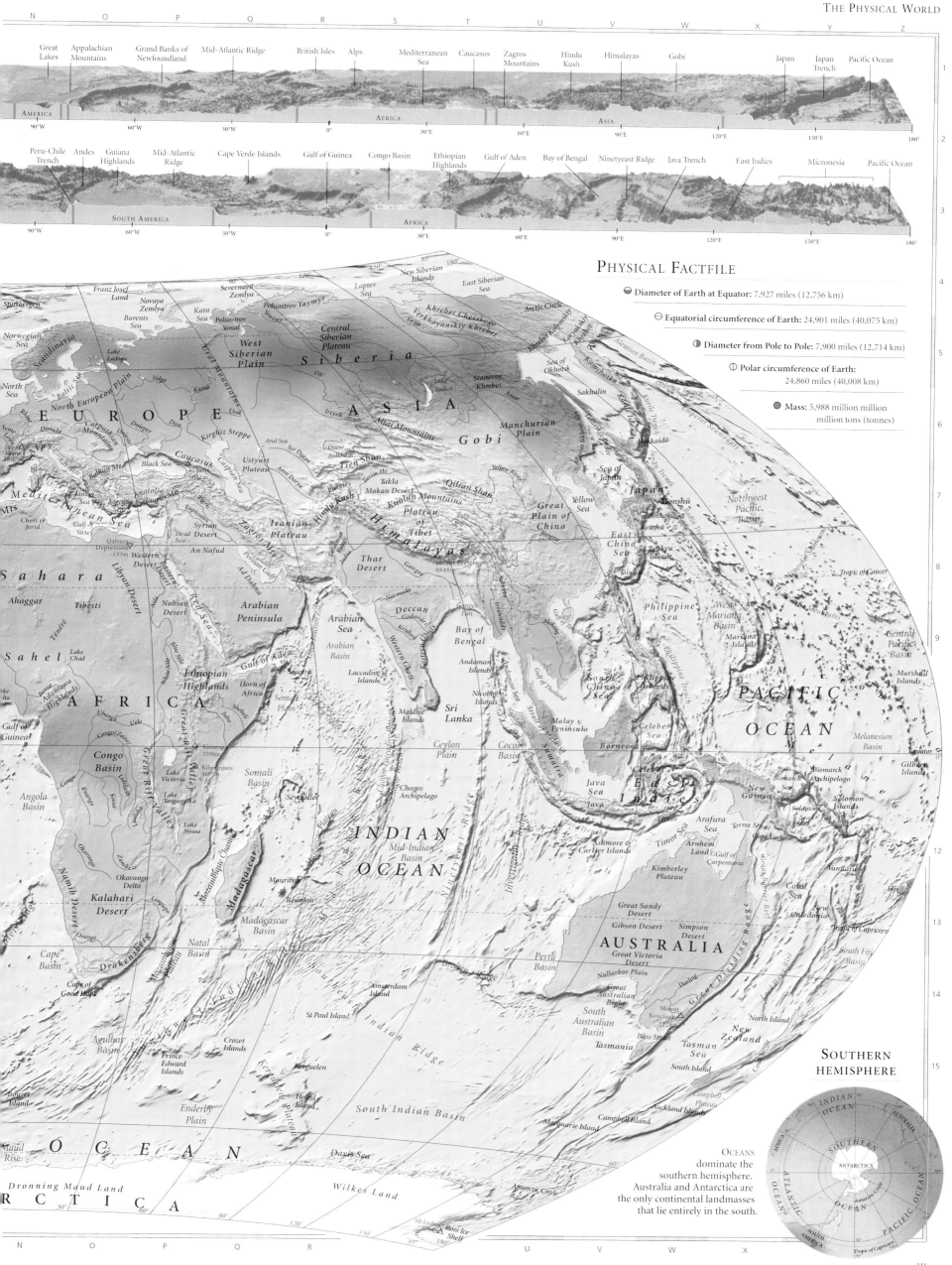

Great Lakes · Appalachian Mountains · Grand Banks of Newfoundland · Mid-Atlantic Ridge · British Isles · Alps · Mediterranean Sea · Caucasus · Zagros Mountains · Hindu Kush · Himalayas · Gobi · Japan · Japan Trench · Pacific Ocean

AMERICA 90°W · 60°W · 30°W · 0° · AFRICA · 30°E · ASIA · 60°E · 90°E · 120°E · 150°E · 180°

Peru-Chile Trench · Andes · Guiana Highlands · Mid-Atlantic Ridge · Cape Verde Islands · Gulf of Guinea · Congo Basin · Ethiopian Highlands · Gulf of Aden · Bay of Bengal · Ninetyeast Ridge · Java Trench · East Indies · Micronesia · Pacific Ocean

SOUTH AMERICA 90°W · 60°W · 30°W · 0° · AFRICA · 30°E · 60°E · 90°E · 120°E · 150°E · 180°

PHYSICAL FACTFILE

⊖ **Diameter of Earth at Equator:** 7,927 miles (12,756 km)

⊖ **Equatorial circumference of Earth:** 24,901 miles (40,075 km)

◑ **Diameter from Pole to Pole:** 7,900 miles (12,714 km)

◐ **Polar circumference of Earth:** 24,860 miles (40,008 km)

● **Mass:** 5,988 million million million tons (tonnes)

SOUTHERN HEMISPHERE

OCEANS dominate the southern hemisphere. Australia and Antarctica are the only continental landmasses that lie entirely in the south.

STRUCTURE OF THE EARTH

E ARTH TODAY IS JUST THE LATEST PHASE in a constant process of geological evolution that has occurred over the past 4.5 billion years. Earth's continents are neither fixed nor stable; over the course of Earth's history, propelled by currents rising from the intense heat at its center, the great plates on which they lie have moved, collided, joined together, and separated. These processes continue to mold and transform the surface of the Earth, causing earthquakes and volcanic eruptions and creating oceans, mountain ranges, deep ocean trenches, and island chains.

INSIDE THE EARTH

THE EARTH'S HOT INNER CORE is made up of solid iron, while the outer core is composed of liquid iron and nickel. The mantle nearest the core is viscous, while the rocky upper mantle is fairly rigid. The crust is the rocky outer shell of the Earth. Together, the upper mantle and the crust form the lithosphere.

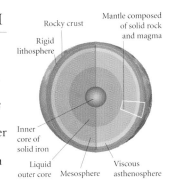

Rocky crust
Mantle composed of solid rock and magma
Rigid lithosphere
Inner core of solid iron
Liquid outer core
Mesosphere
Viscous asthenosphere

THE DYNAMIC EARTH

THE EARTH'S CRUST is made up of eight major (and several minor) rigid continental and oceanic tectonic plates, which fit closely together. The positions of the plates are not static. They are constantly moving relative to one another. The type of movement between plates affects how they alter the structure of the Earth. The oldest parts of the plates, known as shields, are the most stable parts of the Earth and little tectonic activity occurs here.

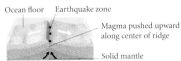

Continental plate
Oceanic plate
Plate boundary: most tectonic activity takes place here
Rigid tectonic plate
Shield area at center of plate: little tectonic activity occurs here

Inner core
Outer core
Subduction zone
Ocean crust
Movement of plate
Mid-ocean ridge
Lithosphere
Asthenosphere
Mesosphere
Continental crust

CONVECTION CURRENTS

DEEP WITHIN THE EARTH, at its inner core, temperatures may exceed 8,100°F (4,000°C). This heat warms rocks in the mesosphere. These rise through the partially molten mantle, displacing cooler rocks just below the solid crust, which sink, and are warmed again by the heat of the mantle. This process is continuous, creating convection currents, which form the moving force beneath the Earth's crust.

PLATE BOUNDARIES

THE BOUNDARIES BETWEEN THE PLATES are the areas where most tectonic activity takes place. Three types of movement occur at plate boundaries: the plates can either move toward each other, move apart, or slide past each other. The effect this has on the Earth's structure depends on whether the margin is between two continental plates, two oceanic plates, or an oceanic and continental plate.

MID-OCEAN RIDGES

Mid-ocean ridges are formed when two adjacent oceanic plates pull apart, forcing molten rocks onto the surface, which cool to form solid rock. Vast amounts of volcanic material are discharged at ocean ridges, and create the ocean floors. Submarine ocean ridges can reach heights of 10,000 ft (3,000 m).

Ocean floor
Earthquake zone
Magma pushed upward along center of ridge
Solid mantle

FORMATION OF A MID-OCEAN RIDGE

The Mid-Atlantic Ridge rises above sea level in Iceland, producing geysers and volcanoes.

OCEANIC PLATES MEETING

Oceanic crust is denser and thinner than continental crust; on average it is 3 miles (5 km) thick, while continental crust averages 18–24 miles (30–40 km). When oceanic plates of similar density meet, the crust is contorted as one plate overrides the other, forming deep sea trenches and volcanic island arcs above sea level.

Mount Pinatubo is an active volcano, lying on the Pacific "Ring of Fire."

Overriding plate
Chain of islands
Ocean trench
Diving plate
Volcanic activity

OCEANIC PLATES MEETING TO FORM AN ISLAND ARC

Tectonic Activity

- - - - - uncertain plate boundary
▲ volcanic zone
● earthquake zone
● hot spot
▼▼▼▼▼ rift valley

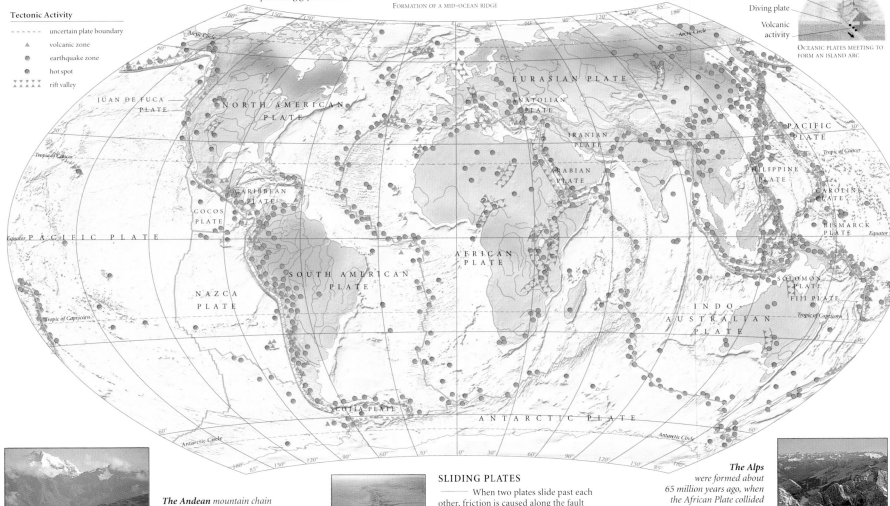

JUAN DE FUCA PLATE
NORTH AMERICAN PLATE
EURASIAN PLATE
ANATOLIAN PLATE
IRANIAN PLATE
PACIFIC PLATE
COCOS PLATE
CARIBBEAN PLATE
ARABIAN PLATE
PHILIPPINE PLATE
CAROLINE PLATE
PACIFIC PLATE
BISMARCK PLATE
SOUTH AMERICAN PLATE
AFRICAN PLATE
NAZCA PLATE
SOLOMON PLATE
FIJI PLATE
INDO AUSTRALIAN PLATE
SCOTIA PLATE
ANTARCTIC PLATE

Arctic Circle
Tropic of Cancer
Equator
Tropic of Capricorn
Antarctic Circle

DIVING PLATES

When an oceanic and a continental plate meet, the denser oceanic plate is driven underneath the continental plate, which is crumpled by the collision into mountain ranges. As the oceanic plate plunges downward, it heats up, and molten rock (magma) is forced up to the surface.

The Andean mountain chain is the typical result of the impact of a diving plate.

Oceanic plate dives under continental plate
Mountains thrust up by collision
Earthquake zone
Continental plate

DIVING PLATE

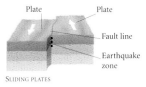

The deep fracture caused by the sliding plates of the San Andreas Fault can be clearly seen in parts of California.

SLIDING PLATES

When two plates slide past each other, friction is caused along the fault line that divides them. The plates do not move smoothly and the uneven movement causes earthquakes.

Plate
Plate
Fault line
Earthquake zone

SLIDING PLATES

The Alps were formed about 65 million years ago, when the African Plate collided with the Eurasian Plate.

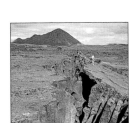

COLLIDING PLATES

When two continental plates collide, great mountain chains are thrust upward as the crust buckles and folds under the force of the impact.

Plate buckles as it collides
Mountains thrust upward
Earthquake zone
Crust thickens in response to the impact

CONTINENTAL PLATES COLLIDING TO FORM A MOUNTAIN RANGE

CONTINENTAL DRIFT

THE PLATES that make up the Earth's crust move only a few inches a year. Over the millions of years of Earth's history, however, its continents have moved many thousands of miles, creating new continents, oceans, and mountain chains.

1: CAMBRIAN PERIOD

570–510 million years ago. Most continents are in tropical latitudes. The supercontinent of Gondwanaland reaches the South Pole.

2: DEVONIAN PERIOD

408–362 million years ago. The continents of Gondwanaland and Laurentia/Baltica are drifting northward.

3: CARBONIFEROUS PERIOD

362–290 million years ago. Earth is dominated by three continents: Laurentia, Angaraland, and Gondwanaland.

4: TRIASSIC PERIOD

245–208 million years ago. All three major continents have joined to form the supercontinent of Pangea.

5: JURASSIC PERIOD

208–145 million years ago. The supercontinent of Pangea begins to break up, causing an overall rise in sea levels.

6: CRETACEOUS PERIOD

145–65 million years ago. Warm, shallow seas cover much of the land. Sea levels are about 80 ft (25 m) above present levels.

7: TERTIARY PERIOD

65–2 million years ago. Although the world's geography is becoming more recognizable, major events, such as the creation of the Himalayan mountain chain, are still to occur during this period.

CONTINENTAL SHIELDS

THE CENTERS OF THE EARTH'S CONTINENTS, known as shields, were established between 2,500 and 500 million years ago; some contain rocks more than two billion years old. They were formed by a series of turbulent events: plate movements, earthquakes, and volcanic eruptions. Since the Precambrian period, over 570 million years ago, the shields have experienced little tectonic activity. Today, these flat, low-lying slabs of solidified molten rock form the stable centers of the continents. They are bounded or covered by successive belts of younger sedimentary rock.

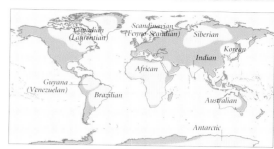

CREATION OF THE HIMALAYAS

BETWEEN 10 AND 20 MILLION YEARS AGO, the Indian subcontinent, part of the ancient continent of Gondwanaland, collided with the continent of Asia. The Indo-Australian Plate continued to move northward, displacing continental crust and uplifting the Himalayas, the world's highest mountain chain.

MOVEMENTS OF INDIA

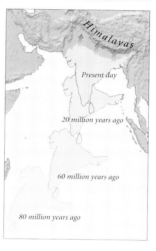

Present day

20 million years ago

60 million years ago

80 million years ago

Force of collision pushes up mountains

CROSS-SECTION THROUGH THE HIMALAYAS

The Himalayas *were uplifted when the Indian subcontinent collided with Asia.*

THE HAWAIIAN ISLAND CHAIN

A HOT SPOT lying deep beneath the Pacific Ocean pushes a plume of magma from the Earth's mantle up through the Pacific Plate to form volcanic islands. While the hot spot remains stationary, the plate on which the islands sit is moving slowly. A long chain of islands has been created as the plate passes over the hot spot.

Extinct volcano

Direction of plate movement over hot spot

Active volcano

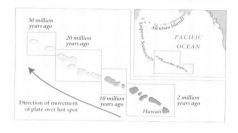

CROSS-SECTION THROUGH THE HAWAIIAN ISLANDS

EVOLUTION OF THE HAWAIIAN ISLANDS

30 million years ago

20 million years ago

PACIFIC OCEAN

Direction of movement of plate over hot spot

10 million years ago

2 million years ago

Hawaii

THE EARTH'S GEOLOGY

EARTH'S ROCKS ARE created in a continual cycle. Exposed rocks are weathered and eroded by wind, water, and chemicals and deposited as sediments. If they pass into the Earth's crust they will be transformed by high temperatures and pressures into metamorphic rocks or they will melt and solidify as igneous rocks.

GNEISS

[1] Gneiss is a metamorphic rock made at great depth during the formation of mountain chains, when intense heat and pressure transform sedimentary or igneous rocks.

Gneiss formations *in Norway's Jotunheimen Mountains.*

Basalt *columns at Giant's Causeway, Northern Ireland, UK.*

BASALT

[2] Basalt is an igneous rock, formed when small quantities of magma lying close to the Earth's surface cool rapidly.

LIMESTONE

[3] Limestone is a sedimentary rock, formed mainly from the calcite skeletons of marine animals that have been compressed into rock.

Limestone hills, *Guilin, China.*

CORAL

[4] Coral reefs are formed from the skeletons of millions of individual corals.

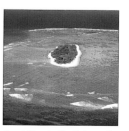

Great Barrier Reef, *Australia.*

SANDSTONE

[8] Sandstones are sedimentary rocks formed mainly in deserts, beaches, and deltas. Desert sandstones are formed of grains of quartz which have been well rounded by wind erosion.

Rock stacks *of desert sandstone, at Bryce Canyon National Park, Utah.*

THE WORLD'S MAJOR GEOLOGICAL REGIONS

Extrusive igneous rocks *are formed during volcanic eruptions, as here in Hawaii.*

ANDESITE

[7] Andesite is an extrusive igneous rock formed from magma that has solidified on the Earth's crust after a volcanic eruption.

Geological Regions

- continental shield
- sedimentary cover
- coral formation
- igneous rock types

Mountain Ranges

- Alpine (new)
- Hercynian (old)
- Caledonian (ancient)

SCHIST

[6] Schist is a metamorphic rock formed during mountain-building, when temperature and pressure are comparatively high. Both mudstones and shales reform into schist under these conditions.

Schist formations *in the Atlas Mountains, northwestern Africa.*

[5] Granite is an intrusive igneous rock formed from magma that has solidified deep within the Earth's crust. The magma cools slowly, producing a coarse-grained rock.

GRANITE

Namibia's *Namaqualand Plateau is formed of granite.*

SHAPING THE LANDSCAPE

THE BASIC SOLID MATERIAL OF THE EARTH'S SURFACE is rock: valleys, deserts, soil, and sand are all evidence of the powerful agents of weathering, erosion, and deposition, which constantly shape and transform the Earth's landscapes. Water, either flowing continually in rivers or seas, or frozen and compacted into solid sheets of ice, has the most clearly visible impact on the Earth's surface. But wind can transport fragments of rock over huge distances and strip away protective layers of vegetation, exposing rock surfaces to the impact of extreme heat and cold.

WATER

LESS THAN 2% of the world's water is on the land, but it is the most powerful agent of landscape change. Water, as rainfall, groundwater, and rivers, can transform landscapes through both erosion and deposition. Eroded material carried by rivers forms the world's most fertile soils.

Waterfalls such as the Iguaçu Falls on the border between Argentina and southern Brazil erode the underlying rock, causing the falls to retreat.

COASTAL WATER

THE WORLD'S COASTLINES are constantly changing; every day, tides deposit, sift, and sort sand and gravel on the shoreline. Over longer periods, powerful wave action erodes cliffs and headlands and carves out bays.

A low, wide sandy beach on South Africa's Cape Peninsula is continually reshaped by the action of the Atlantic waves.

The sheer chalk cliffs at Seven Sisters in southern England are constantly under attack from waves.

GROUNDWATER

IN REGIONS where there are porous rocks like chalk, water is stored underground in large quantities; these reservoirs of water are called aquifers. Rain percolates through topsoil into the underlying bedrock, creating an underground store of water. The upper limit of the saturated zone is called the water table.

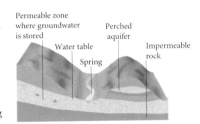

Permeable zone where groundwater is stored
Water table
Perched aquifer
Spring
Impermeable rock

STORAGE OF GROUNDWATER IN AN AQUIFER

World river systems: Sediment deposited annually per drainage basin

tons per sq mile per year
9120
6080
1520
760
2400
1600
400
200 and less
tonnes per sq km per year

World river systems

drainage basin

ARCTIC OCEAN

Mac-Yukon
Yukon
Mackenzie
Nelson
St. Lawrence
Columbia
Mississippi/Missouri
Colorado
Rio Grande

ATLANTIC OCEAN

Orinoco
Amazon
São Francisco
Paraná

ATLANTIC OCEAN

Rhine
Danube
Volga
Ob'
Yenisey
Lena
Amur
Tigris/Euphrates
Indus
Yellow River
Ganges/Brahmaputra
Yangtze
Mekong

Niger
Nile
Congo
Zambezi
Orange

INDIAN OCEAN

PACIFIC OCEAN

Murray/Darling

RIVERS

RIVERS ERODE THE LAND by grinding and dissolving rocks and stones. Most erosion occurs in the river's upper course as it flows through highland areas. Rock fragments move along the riverbed in fast-flowing water and are deposited in areas where the river slows down, such as flat plains, or where the river enters seas or lakes.

RIVER VALLEYS

Over long periods of time rivers erode uplands to form characteristic V-shaped valleys with smooth sides.

Resistant rock
River
Chemical erosion cuts valley in softer rock

RIVER VALLEY EROSION

DELTAS

When a river deposits its load of silt and sediment (alluvium) on entering the sea, it may form a delta. As this material accumulates, it chokes the mouth of the river, forcing it to create new channels to reach the sea.

The Nile forms a broad delta as it flows into the Mediterranean.

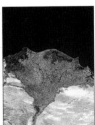

DRAINAGE BASINS

The drainage basin is the area of land drained by a major trunk river and its smaller branch rivers or tributaries. Drainage basins are separated from one another by natural boundaries, known as watersheds.

Watershed
Major trunk river
Alps
Apennines
Tributary river
Delta
River mouth
Po Valley
Dolomites

The drainage basin of the Po River, northern Italy.

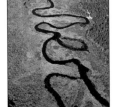

MEANDERS

In their lower courses, rivers flow slowly. As they flow across the lowlands, they form looping bends, called meanders *(left)*.

The Mississippi River forms meanders as it flows across the southern US.

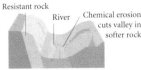

The meanders of Utah's San Juan River have become deeply incised.

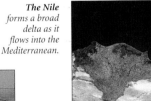

Mud is deposited by China's Yellow River in its lower course.

DEPOSITION

When rivers have deposited large quantities of fertile alluvium, they are forced to find new channels through the alluvium deposits, creating braided river systems.

LANDSLIDES

Heavy rain and associated flooding on slopes can loosen underlying rocks. These crumble, causing the top layers of rock and soil to slip.

A huge landslide in the Swiss Alps has left massive piles of rocks and pebbles, called scree.

GULLIES

In areas where soil is thin, rainwater is not effectively absorbed and can flow overland. The water runs downhill in channels, or gullies, and may lead to rapid erosion of soil.

A deep gully in the French Alps, caused by the scouring of upper layers of turf.

ICE

DURING ITS LONG HISTORY, the Earth has experienced a number of glacial episodes when temperatures were considerably lower than today. During the last Ice Age, 18,000 years ago, ice covered an area three times larger than it does today. Over these periods, the ice has left a remarkable legacy of transformed landscapes.

GLACIERS

GLACIERS ARE FORMED by the compaction of snow into "rivers" of ice. As they move over the landscape, glaciers pick up and carry a load of rocks and boulders; erode the landscape which they pass over and are eventually deposited at the end of the glacier.

A massive glacier advancing down a valley in southern Argentina.

POST-GLACIAL FEATURES

WHEN A GLACIAL EPISODE ENDS, the retreating ice leaves many features. These include depositional ridges, called moraines, which may be eroded into low hills, known as drumlins; sinuous ridges, called eskers; kames, which are rounded hummocks; depressions, known as kettle holes; and finely-ground loess deposits.

GLACIAL VALLEYS

GLACIERS CAN ERODE much more powerfully than rivers. They form steep-sided, flat-bottomed valleys with a typical U-shaped profile. Valleys created by tributary glaciers, whose floors have not been eroded to the same depth as the main glacial valley floor, are called hanging valleys.

The U-shaped profile and piles of morainic debris are characteristic of a valley once filled by a glacier.

A series of hanging valleys high up in the Chilean Andes.

The profile of the Matterhorn has been formed by three cirques lying "back-to-back."

PAST AND PRESENT WORLD ICE COVER AND GLACIAL FEATURES

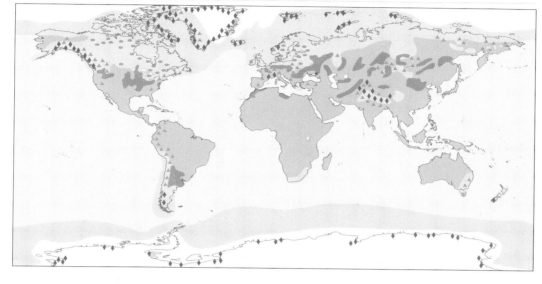

Past and present world ice cover and glacial features

extent of last Ice Age	present day ice cover
loess deposits	glacial field
post-glacial feature	
glacial feature	

ICE SHATTERING

Water drips into fissures in rocks and freezes, expanding as it does so. The pressure weakens the rock, causing it to crack and eventually shatter into polygonal patterns.

POST-GLACIAL LANDSCAPE FEATURES

Kame terrace
Kettle hole
Esker
Braided river
Windblown loess
Retreating glacier
Drumlin
Terminal moraine
Glacial till
Bedrock

CIRQUES

Cirques are basin-shaped hollows that mark the head of a glaciated valley. Where neighboring cirques meet, they are divided by sharp rock ridges, called arêtes. It is these arêtes which give the Matterhorn its characteristic profile.

FJORDS

Fjords are ancient glacial valleys flooded by the sea following the end of a period of glaciation. Beneath the water, the valley floor can be 4,000 ft (1,300 m) deep.

A fjord fills a former glacial valley in southern New Zealand.

PERIGLACIATION

Periglacial areas occur near to the edge of ice sheets. A layer of frozen ground lying just beneath the surface of the land is known as permafrost. When the surface melts in the summer, the water is unable to drain into the frozen ground, and so "creeps" downhill, a process known as solifluction.

Irregular polygons show through the sedge-grass tundra in the Yukon, Canada.

WIND

STRONG WINDS can transport rock fragments great distances, especially where there is little vegetation to protect the rock. In desert areas, wind picks up loose, unprotected sand particles, carrying them over great distances. This powerfully abrasive debris is blasted at the surface by the wind, "weathering" the landscape into dramatic shapes.

DEPOSITION

THE ROCKY, STONY FLOORS of the world's deserts are swept and scoured by strong winds. The smaller, finer particles of sand are shaped into surface ripples, dunes, or sand mountains, which rise to a height of 650 ft (200 m). Dunes usually form single lines, running perpendicular to the direction of the strongest wind. These long, straight ridges can extend for more than 100 miles (160 km).

DUNES

Dunes are shaped by wind direction and sand supply. Where sand supply is limited, crescent-shaped barchan dunes are formed.

PREVAILING WINDS AND DUST TRAJECTORIES

Prevailing winds

northeast trade	westerly
southeast trade	westerly
polar easterly	trajectory of aeolian dust
polar easterly	

Dust trajectories

Barchan dunes in the Arabian Desert.

Complex dune system in the Sahara.

TYPES OF DUNE

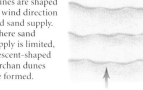

wind direction
Transverse dune
Barchan dune
Linear dune
Star dune

TEMPERATURE

HOT AND COLD DESERTS

Arctic Circle
Tropic of Cancer
Equator
Tropic of Capricorn
Antarctic Circle

Main desert types

hot arid	semi-arid	cold polar

MOST OF THE WORLD'S deserts are in the tropics. The cold deserts, which occur elsewhere, are arid because they are a long way from the rain-giving sea. Desert rocks are exposed because of lack of vegetation and are susceptible to changes in temperature. Extremes of heat and cold can cause both cracks and fissures to appear in the rock.

HEAT

FIERCE SUN can heat the surface of rock, causing it to expand more rapidly than the cooler, underlying layers. This creates tensions that force the rock to crack or break up. In arid regions, the evaporation of water from rock surfaces dissolves certain minerals within the water, causing salt crystals to form in small openings in the rock. The hard crystals force the openings to widen into cracks and fissures.

The cracked and parched floor of Death Valley, California, one of the hottest deserts on Earth.

DESERT ABRASION

Abrasion creates a wide range of desert landforms, from faceted pebbles and wind ripples in the sand, to large-scale features such as yardangs (low, streamlined ridges) and scoured desert pavements.

Wind abrasion
Faceted rock
Wind direction
Desert pavement
Gravel
Sand desert
Wind rippling
Thermal fracturing

DESERT FEATURES FORMED BY ABRASION

This dry valley at Ellesmere Island in the Canadian Arctic is an example of a cold desert. The cracked floor and scoured slopes are features also found in hot deserts.

THE WORLD'S OCEANS

TWO-THIRDS OF THE EARTH'S SURFACE is covered by the oceans. The landscape of the ocean floor, like the surface of the land, has been shaped by movements of Earth's crust over millions of years, to form volcanic mountain ranges, deep trenches, basins, and plateaus. Ocean currents constantly redistribute warm and cold water around the globe. A major warm current, such as El Niño in the Pacific Ocean, can increase surface temperature by up to 46°F (8°C), causing changes in weather patterns that can lead to both droughts and flooding.

SEA LEVEL

IF THE INFLUENCE of tides, winds, currents, and variations in gravity were ignored, the surface of the Earth's oceans would closely follow the topography of the ocean floor, with an underwater ridge 3,000 ft (915 m) high producing a rise of up to 3 ft (1 m) in the level of the surface water.

Elevated sea level over ridge in ocean floor

Depressed sea level over trough in ocean floor

Base level of the sea surface at 0 ft (0 m)

Actual relief of ocean floor

HOW SURFACE WATERS REFLECT THE RELIEF OF THE OCEAN FLOOR

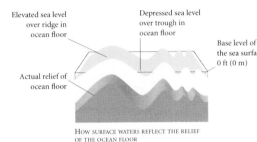

The low relief of many small Pacific islands, such as these atolls at Huahine in French Polynesia, makes them vulnerable to changes in sea level.

OCEAN STRUCTURE

THE CONTINENTAL SHELF is a shallow, flat seabed surrounding the Earth's continents. It extends to the continental slope, which falls to the ocean floor. Here, the flat abyssal plains are interrupted by vast, underwater mountain ranges, the mid-ocean ridges, and ocean trenches, which plunge to depths of 35,828 ft (10,920 m).

Abyssal plain
Trench
Volcanic island
Flat-topped guyot
Seamount
Oceanic ridge
Continental shelf

TYPICAL SEA-FLOOR FEATURES

BLACK SMOKERS

These vents in the ocean floor disgorge hot, sulfur-rich water from deep in the Earth's crust. Despite the great depths, a variety of lifeforms have adapted to the chemical-rich environment that surrounds black smokers.

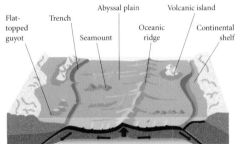

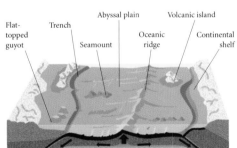

A black smoker in the Atlantic Ocean.

Surtsey, near Iceland, is a volcanic island lying directly over the Mid-Atlantic Ridge. The many active geysers and volcanoes reflect intense volcanic activity.

Chimney
Plume of hot mineral-laden water
Water heated by hot basalt
Water percolates into the sea floor
Ocean floor

FORMATION OF BLACK SMOKERS

OCEAN FLOORS

Mid-ocean ridges are formed by lava which erupts beneath the sea and cools to form solid rock. This process mirrors the creation of volcanoes from cooled lava on the land. The ages of sea-floor rocks increase in parallel bands outward from central ocean ridges.

THE GREAT OCEANS

THERE ARE FIVE OCEANS on Earth: the Pacific, Atlantic, Indian, and Southern oceans, and the much smaller Arctic Ocean. The ocean basins as they exist today are relatively young – only about 80 million years old. One of the most recent plate collisions, between the Eurasian and African plates, created the present day arrangement of continents and oceans.

The Indian Ocean accounts for approximately 20% of the total area of the world's oceans.

Ocean depth

Sea level
200m / 656ft
1000m / 3281ft
2000m / 6562ft
3000m / 9843ft
4000m / 13,124ft
5000m / 16,400ft
6000m / 19,686ft

AGES OF THE OCEAN FLOOR

Arctic Circle
Tropic of Cancer
Equator
Tropic of Capricorn
Antarctic Circle

Jurassic 208 million years old
Cretaceous 145
Tertiary 65
Quaternary 23 0 23
Tertiary 65
Cretaceous 145
Jurassic 208 million years old

Age uncertain
Continental shelf

Currents in the Southern Ocean are driven by some of the world's fiercest winds, including the Roaring Forties, Furious Fifties, and Shrieking Sixties.

The Pacific Ocean is the world's largest and deepest ocean, covering over one-third of the surface of the Earth.

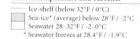

The Atlantic Ocean was formed when the landmasses of the eastern and western hemispheres began to drift apart 180 million years ago.

DEPOSITION OF SEDIMENT

STORMS, EARTHQUAKES, and volcanic activity trigger underwater currents, known as turbidity currents, which scour sand and gravel from the continental shelf, creating underwater canyons. These strong currents pick up material deposited at river mouths and deltas, and carry it across the continental shelf and through the underwater canyons, where it is eventually laid down on the ocean floor in the form of fans.

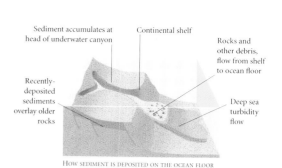

HOW SEDIMENT IS DEPOSITED ON THE OCEAN FLOOR

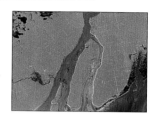

Satellite image of the Yangtze (Chang Jiang) Delta, in which the land appears red. The river deposits immense quantities of silt into the East China Sea, much of which will eventually reach the deep ocean floor.

SURFACE WATER

OCEAN CURRENTS move warm water away from the Equator toward the poles, while cold water, in turn, moves toward the Equator. This is the main way in which the Earth distributes surface heat and is a major climatic control. Approximately 4,000 million years ago, the Earth was dominated by oceans and there was no land to interrupt the flow of the currents, which would have flowed as straight lines, simply influenced by the Earth's rotation.

Imaginary globe showing the movement of water around a landless Earth.

OCEAN CURRENTS

SURFACE CURRENTS are driven by the prevailing winds and by the spinning motion of the Earth, which drives the currents into circulating whirlpools, or gyres. Deep sea currents, over 330 ft (100 m) below the surface, are driven by differences in water temperature and salinity, which have an impact on the density of deep water and on its movement.

SURFACE TEMPERATURE AND CURRENTS

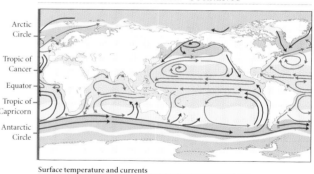

Surface temperature and currents

- ······· Ice-shelf (below 32°F / 0°C)
- Sea-ice* (average) below 28°F / -2°C
- Seawater 28–32°F / -2-0°C
- * Seawater freezes at 28.4°F / -1.9°C
- 32–50°F / 0–10°C
- 50–68°F / 10–20°C
- 68–86°F / 20–30°C
- → warm current
- → cold current

DEEP SEA TEMPERATURE AND CURRENTS

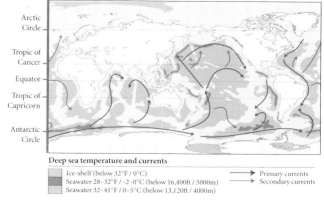

Deep sea temperature and currents

- Ice-shelf (below 32°F / 0°C)
- Seawater 28–32°F / -2-0°C (below 16,400ft / 5000m)
- Seawater 32–41°F / 0–5°C (below 13,120ft / 4000m)
- → Primary currents
- → Secondary currents

TIDES AND WAVES

TIDES ARE CREATED by the pull of the Sun and Moon's gravity on the surface of the oceans. The levels of high and low tides are influenced by the position of the Moon in relation to the Earth and Sun. Waves are formed by wind blowing over the surface of the water.

HIGH AND LOW TIDES

The highest tides occur when the Earth, the Moon, and the Sun are aligned *(below left)*.
The lowest tides are experienced when the Sun and Moon align at right angles to one another *(below right)*.

TIDAL RANGE AND WAVE ENVIRONMENTS

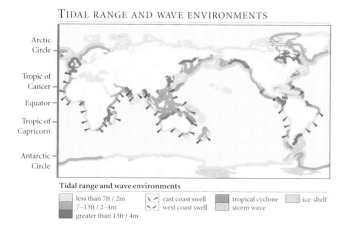

Tidal range and wave environments

- less than 7ft / 2m
- 7–13ft / 2–4m
- greater than 13ft / 4m
- east coast swell
- west coast swell
- tropical cyclone
- storm wave
- ice-shelf

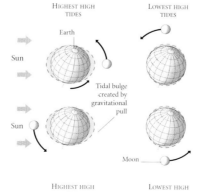

HIGHEST HIGH TIDES

LOWEST HIGH TIDES

Earth

Sun

Sun

Tidal bulge created by gravitational pull

Moon

HIGHEST HIGH TIDES

LOWEST HIGH TIDES

Map labels

OCEAN
Chukchi Sea
Beaufort Sea
Bering Sea
Aleutian Trench
Gulf of Alaska
Mendocino Fracture Zone
Murray Fracture Zone
Molokai Fracture Zone
Clarion Fracture Zone
Clipperton Fracture Zone
PACIFIC
Central Pacific Basin
OCEAN
Southwest Pacific Basin
Pacific-Antarctic Ridge
OCEAN
Amundsen Sea
Bellingshausen Sea
Southeast Pacific Basin
NORTH AMERICA
Baffin Bay
Davis Strait
Greenland Sea
Arctic Circle
Hudson Strait
Hudson Bay
Labrador Sea
Newfoundland Basin
North American Basin
Gulf of Mexico
Sargasso Sea
Yucatan Basin
Middle America Trench
Caribbean Sea
Guatemala Basin
SOUTH AMERICA
Perú Basin
Nazca Ridge
Sala y Gomez Ridge
Chile Basin
East Pacific Rise
Scotia Sea
Weddell Sea
Antarctic Circle
South Sandwich Trench
ATLANTIC
Mid-Atlantic Ridge
Canary Basin
Tropic of Cancer
Barracuda Fracture Zone
Brazil Basin
OCEAN
Equator
Rio Grande Rise
Tropic of Capricorn
Argentine Basin
Mid-Atlantic Ridge

THE GLOBAL CLIMATE

THE EARTH'S CLIMATIC TYPES CONSIST of stable patterns of weather conditions averaged out over a long period of time. Different climates are categorized according to particular combinations of temperature and humidity. By contrast, weather consists of short-term fluctuations in wind, temperature, and humidity conditions. Different climates are determined by latitude, altitude, the prevailing wind, and the circulation of ocean currents. Longer-term changes in climate, such as global warming or the onset of ice ages, are punctuated by shorter-term events, which make up the day-to-day weather of a region, such as frontal depressions, hurricanes, and blizzards.

THE ATMOSPHERE, WIND & WEATHER

THE EARTH'S ATMOSPHERE has been compared to a giant ocean of air that surrounds the planet. Its circulation patterns are similar to the currents in the oceans and are influenced by three factors; the Earth's orbit around the Sun; rotation around its axis, and variations in the amount of heat radiation received from the Sun. If both heat and moisture were not redistributed between the Equator and the poles, large areas of the Earth would be uninhabitable.

Heavy fogs, as here in southern England, form as moisture-laden air hovers over cold ground.

TEMPERATURE

THE WORLD CAN BE DIVIDED into three major climatic zones, stretching like large belts across the latitudes: the tropics which are warm; the cold polar regions; and the temperate zones, which lie between them. Temperatures across the Earth range from above 30°C (86°F) in the deserts to as low as -55°C (-70°F) at the poles. Temperature is also influenced by altitude; because air becomes cooler and less dense the higher it gets, mountainous regions are typically colder than those areas which are at, or close to, sea level.

AVERAGE JANUARY TEMPERATURES

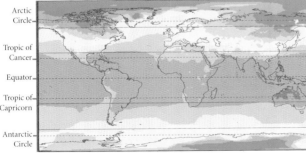

AVERAGE JULY TEMPERATURES

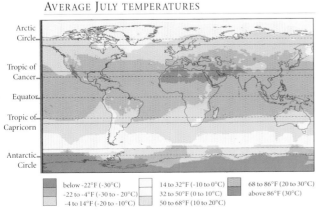

below -22°F (-30°C)
-22 to -4°F (-30 to -20°C)
-4 to 14°F (-20 to -10°C)
14 to 32°F (-10 to 0°C)
32 to 50°F (0 to 10°C)
50 to 68°F (10 to 20°C)
68 to 86°F (20 to 30°C)
above 86°F (30°C)

GLOBAL AIR CIRCULATION

AIR DOES NOT SIMPLY FLOW FROM THE EQUATOR TO THE POLES, it circulates in giant cells, known as Hadley and Ferrel cells. As air warms it expands, becoming less dense and rising; this creates areas of low pressure. As the air rises it cools and condenses, causing heavy rainfall over the tropics and slight snowfall over the poles. This cool air then sinks, forming high pressure belts. At surface level in the tropics these sinking currents are deflected poleward as the westerlies and toward the equator as the trade winds. At the poles they become the polar easterlies.

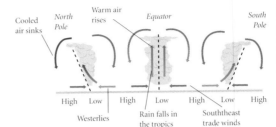

Cooled air sinks — North Pole — Warm air rises — Equator — South Pole

High — Low — High — Low — High — Low — High
Westerlies — Rain falls in the tropics — Souththeast trade winds

The Antarctic pack ice expands its area by almost seven times during the winter as temperatures drop and surrounding seas freeze.

CLIMATIC CHANGE

THE EARTH IS CURRENTLY IN A WARM PHASE between ice ages. Warmer temperatures result in higher sea levels as more of the polar ice caps melt. Most of the world's population lives near coasts, so any changes which might cause sea levels to rise could have a potentially disastrous impact.

This ice fair, painted by Pieter Brueghel the Younger in the 17th century, shows the Little Ice Age which peaked around 300 years ago.

THE GREENHOUSE EFFECT

Gases such as carbon dioxide are known as "greenhouse gases" because they allow shortwave solar radiation to enter the Earth's atmosphere, but help to stop longwave radiation from escaping. This traps heat, raising the Earth's temperature. An excess of these gases, such as that which results from the burning of fossil fuels, helps to trap more heat and can lead to global warming.

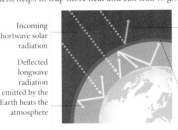

Incoming shortwave solar radiation

Deflected longwave radiation emitted by the Earth heats the atmosphere

Deflected shortwave solar radiation

Greenhouse gases prevent the escape of longwave radiation

 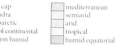 

The islands of the Caribbean, Mexico's Gulf coast, and the southeastern US are often hit by hurricanes formed far out in the Atlantic.

OCEANIC WATER CIRCULATION

IN GENERAL, OCEAN CURRENTS parallel the movement of winds across the Earth's surface. Incoming solar energy is greatest at the Equator and least at the poles. So, water in the oceans heats up most at the Equator and flows poleward, cooling as it moves north or south toward the Arctic or Antarctic. The flow is eventually reversed and cold water currents move back toward the equator. These ocean currents act as a vast system for moving heat from the Equator toward the poles and are a major influence on the distribution of the Earth's climates.

In marginal climatic zones years of drought can completely dry out the land and transform grassland to desert.

The wide range of environments found in the Andes is strongly related to their altitude, which modifies climatic influences. While the peaks are snowcapped, many protected interior valleys are semitropical.

TILT AND ROTATION

The tilt and rotation of the Earth during its annual orbit largely control the distribution of heat and moisture across its surface, which correspondingly controls its large-scale weather patterns. As the Earth annually rotates around the Sun, half its surface is receiving maximum radiation, creating summer and winter seasons. The angle of the Earth means that, on average, the tropics receive two and a half times as much heat from the Sun each day as the poles.

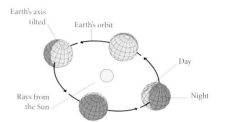

Earth's axis tilted · Earth's orbit · Day · Rays from the Sun · Night

THE CORIOLIS EFFECT

The rotation of the Earth influences atmospheric circulation by deflecting winds and ocean currents. Winds blowing in the northern hemisphere are deflected to the right and those in the southern hemisphere are deflected to the left, creating large-scale patterns of wind circulation, such as the northeast and southeast trade winds and the westerlies. This effect is greatest at the poles and least at the Equator.

Maximum deflection at North Pole · Westerlies · Deflection to right in northern hemisphere, creates northeast trade winds · No deflection at Equator · Deflection to left in southern hemisphere, creates southeast trade winds · Polar easterlies · Maximum deflection at South Pole

MAP KEY

Climate zones
- ice cap
- tundra
- subarctic
- cool continental
- warm humid
- mediterranean
- semiarid
- arid
- tropical
- humid equatorial

Ocean currents
- warm
- cold

Prevailing winds
- warm
- cold

Local winds
- warm
- cold
- seasonal *
- * (seasonal winds which can either be warm or cold)

PRECIPITATION

WHEN WARM AIR EXPANDS, it rises and cools, and the water vapor it carries condenses to form clouds. Heavy, regular rainfall is characteristic of the equatorial region, while the poles are cold and receive only slight snowfall. Tropical regions have marked dry and rainy seasons, while in the temperate regions rainfall is relatively unpredictable.

Monsoon rains, which affect southern Asia from May to September, are caused by sea winds blowing across the warm land.

Heavy tropical rainstorms occur frequently in Papua New Guinea, often causing soil erosion and landslides in cultivated areas.

AVERAGE JANUARY RAINFALL

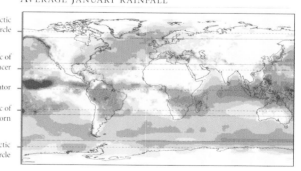

Arctic Circle · Tropic of Cancer · Equator · Tropic of Capricorn · Antarctic Circle

AVERAGE JULY RAINFALL

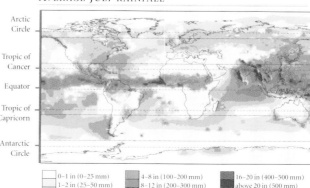

Arctic Circle · Tropic of Cancer · Equator · Tropic of Capricorn · Antarctic Circle

- 0–1 in (0–25 mm)
- 1–2 in (25–50 mm)
- 2–4 in (50–100 mm)
- 4–8 in (100–200 mm)
- 8–12 in (200–300 mm)
- 12–16 in (300–400 mm)
- 16–20 in (400–500 mm)
- above 20 in (500 mm)

The intensity of some blizzards in Canada and the northern US can give rise to snowdrifts higher than 10 ft (3 m).

The Atacama Desert in Chile is one of the driest places on Earth, with an average rainfall of less than 2 inches (50 mm) per year.

Violent thunderstorms occur along advancing cold fronts, when cold, dry air masses meet warm, moist air, which rises rapidly, its moisture condensing into thunderclouds. Rain and hail become electrically charged, causing lightning.

THE RAINSHADOW EFFECT

When moist air is forced to rise by mountains, it cools and the water vapor falls as precipitation, either as rain or snow. Only the dry, cold air continues over the mountains, leaving inland areas with little or no rain. This is called the rainshadow effect and is one reason for the existence of the Mojave Desert in California, which lies east of the Sierra Nevada.

Moist air travels inland from the sea · As air rises it cools and condenses leading to cloud · Dry air in "shadow" of mountain

THE RAINSHADOW EFFECT

LIFE ON EARTH

A UNIQUE COMBINATION of an oxygen-rich atmosphere and plentiful water is the key to life on Earth. Apart from the polar ice caps, there are few areas that have not been colonized by animals or plants over the course of the Earth's history. Plants process sunlight to provide them with their energy, and ultimately all of the Earth's animals rely on plants for survival. Because of this reliance, plants are known as primary producers, and the availability of nutrients and the temperature of an area are defined as its primary productivity, which affects the quantity and type of animals that are able to live there. This index is affected by climatic factors – cold and aridity restrict the quantity of life, while warmth and regular rainfall allow a greater diversity of species.

BIOGEOGRAPHICAL REGIONS

THE EARTH CAN BE DIVIDED into a series of biogeographical regions, or biomes, ecological communities where certain species of plant and animal coexist within particular climatic conditions. Within these broad classifications, other factors, including soil richness, altitude, and human activities, such as urbanization, intensive agriculture, and deforestation, affect the local distribution of living species within each biome.

POLAR REGIONS

A layer of permanent ice at the Earth's poles covers both seas and land. Very little plant and animal life can exist in these harsh regions.

TUNDRA

A desolate region, tundra has long, dark freezing winters and short, cold summers. With virtually no soil and large areas of permanently frozen ground known as permafrost, the tundra is largely treeless, though it is briefly clothed by small flowering plants in the summer months.

NEEDLELEAF FORESTS

With milder summers than the tundra and less wind, these areas are able to support large forests of coniferous trees.

BROADLEAF FORESTS

Much of the northern hemisphere was once covered by deciduous forests, which occurred in areas with marked seasonal variations. Most deciduous forests have been cleared for human settlement.

TEMPERATE RAIN FORESTS

In warmer, wetter areas, such as southern China, temperate deciduous forests are replaced by evergreen forest.

DESERTS

Deserts are areas with negligible rainfall. Most hot deserts lie within the Tropics; cold deserts are dry because of their distance from the moisture-providing sea.

MEDITERRANEAN

Hot, dry summers and short winters typify these areas, which were once covered by evergreen shrubs and woodland, but have now been cleared by humans for agriculture.

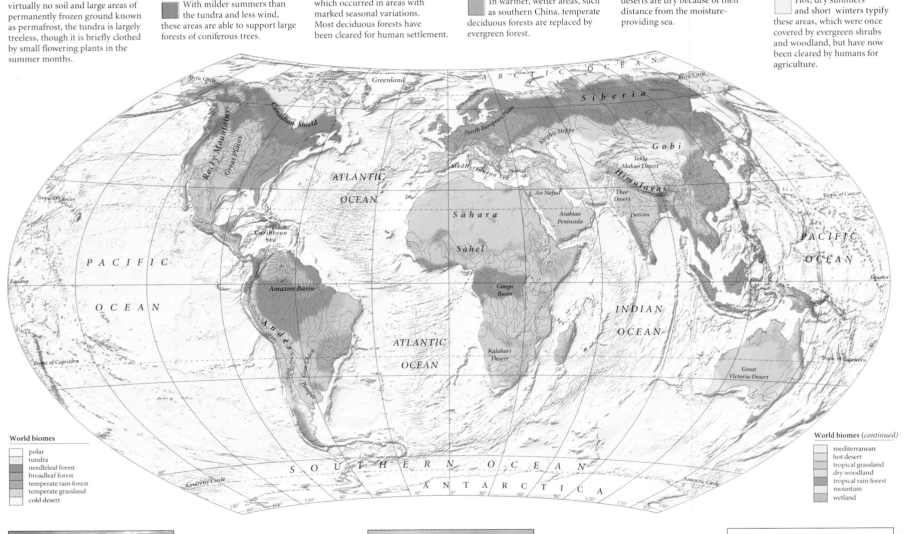

World biomes
- polar
- tundra
- needleleaf forest
- broadleaf forest
- temperate rain forest
- temperate grassland
- cold desert

World biomes (*continued*)
- mediterranean
- hot desert
- tropical grassland
- dry woodland
- tropical rain forest
- mountain
- wetland

TROPICAL AND TEMPERATE GRASSLANDS

The major grassland areas are found in the centers of the larger continental landmasses. In Africa's tropical savannah regions, seasonal rainfall alternates with drought. Temperate grasslands, also known as *steppes* and *prairies*, are found in the northern hemisphere and in South America, where they are known as the *pampas*.

DRY WOODLANDS

Trees and shrubs, adapted to dry conditions, grow widely spaced from one another, interspersed by savannah grasslands.

TROPICAL RAIN FORESTS

Characterized by year-round warmth and high rainfall, tropical rain forests contain the highest diversity of plant and animal species on Earth.

MOUNTAINS

Though the lower slopes of mountains may be thickly forested, only ground-hugging shrubs and other vegetation will grow above the tree line, which varies according to both altitude and latitude.

WETLANDS

Rarely lying above sea level, wetlands include marshes, swamps, and tidal flats. Some, with their moist, fertile soils, are rich feeding grounds for fish and breeding grounds for birds. Others have little soil structure and are too acidic to support much plant and animal life.

BIODIVERSITY

THE NUMBER OF PLANT AND ANIMAL SPECIES, and the range of genetic diversity within the populations of each species, make up the Earth's biodiversity. The plants and animals that are endemic to a region – that is, those that are found nowhere else in the world – are also important in determining levels of biodiversity. Human settlement and intervention have encroached on many areas of the world once rich in endemic plant and animal species. Increasing international efforts are being made to monitor and conserve the biodiversity of the Earth's remaining wild places.

ANIMAL ADAPTATION

THE DEGREE OF AN ANIMAL'S ADAPTABILITY to different climates and conditions is extremely important in ensuring its success as a species. Many animals, particularly the largest mammals, are becoming restricted to shrinking regions as human development and modern agricultural practices reduce their natural habitats. In contrast, humans have been responsible – both deliberately and accidentally – for the spread of some of the world's most successful species. Many of these introduced species are now more numerous than the indigenous animal populations.

POLAR ANIMALS

The frozen wastes of the polar regions are able to support only a small range of species, which derive their nutritional requirements from the sea. Animals such as the walrus (left) have developed insulating fat, stocky limbs, and double-layered coats to enable them to survive in the freezing conditions.

DIVERSITY OF ANIMAL SPECIES

DESERT ANIMALS

Many animals that live in the extreme heat and aridity of the deserts are able to survive for days and even months with very little food or water. Their bodies are adapted to lose heat quickly and to store fat and water. The Gila monster (above) stores fat in its tail.

AMAZON RAIN FOREST

The vast Amazon Basin is home to the world's greatest variety of animal species. Animals are adapted to live at many different levels from the treetops to the tangled undergrowth that lies beneath the canopy. The sloth (below) hangs upside down in the branches. Its fur grows from its stomach to its back to enable water to run off quickly.

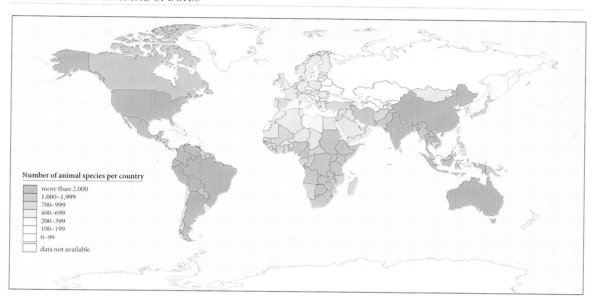

Number of animal species per country

- more than 2,000
- 1,000–1,999
- 700–999
- 400–699
- 200–399
- 100–199
- 0–99
- data not available

MARINE BIODIVERSITY

The oceans support a huge variety of different species, from the world's largest mammals, like whales and dolphins, down to the tiniest plankton. The greatest diversities occur in the warmer seas of continental shelves, where plants are easily able to photosynthesize, and around coral reefs, where complex ecosystems are found. On the ocean floor, nematodes can exist at a depth of more than 10,000 ft (3,000 m) below sea level.

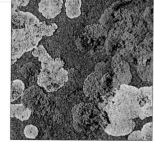

HIGH ALTITUDES

Few animals exist in the rarefied atmosphere of the highest mountains. However, birds of prey such as eagles and vultures (above), with their superb eyesight, can soar as high as 23,000 ft (7,000 m) to scan for prey below.

URBAN ANIMALS

The growth of cities has reduced the amount of habitat available to many species. A number of animals are now moving closer into urban areas to scavenge from the detritus of the modern city (left). Rodents, particularly rats and mice, have existed in cities for thousands of years, and many insects, especially moths, quickly develop new coloring to provide themselves with camouflage.

ENDEMIC SPECIES

Isolated areas, such as Australia and the island of Madagascar, have the greatest range of endemic species. In Australia, these include marsupials such as the kangaroo (below), which carry their young in pouches on their bodies. Destruction of habitat, pollution, hunting, and predators introduced by humans are threatening this unique biodiversity.

PLANT ADAPTATION

ENVIRONMENTAL CONDITIONS, particularly climate, soil type, and the extent of competition with other organisms, influence the development of plants into a number of distinctive forms. Similar conditions in very different parts of the world create similar adaptations in the plants, which may then be modified by other, local, factors specific to the region.

COLD CONDITIONS

In areas where temperatures rarely rise above freezing, plants such as lichens (left) and mosses grow densely, close to the ground.

RAIN FORESTS

Most of the world's largest and oldest plants are found in rain forests; warmth and heavy rainfall provide ideal conditions for vast plants like the world's largest flower, the rafflesia (left).

HOT, DRY CONDITIONS

Arid conditions lead to the development of plants whose surface area has been reduced to a minimum to reduce water loss. In cacti (above), which can survive without water for months, leaves are minimal or not present at all.

DIVERSITY OF PLANT SPECIES

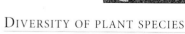

ANCIENT PLANTS

Some of the world's most primitive plants still exist today, including algae, cyclads, and many ferns (above), reflecting the success with which they have adapted to changing conditions.

RESISTING PREDATORS

A great variety of plants have developed devices including spines (above), poisons, stinging hairs, and an unpleasant taste or smell to deter animal predators.

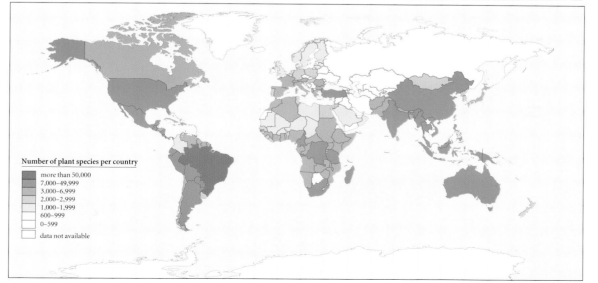

Number of plant species per country

- more than 50,000
- 7,000–49,999
- 3,000–6,999
- 2,000–2,999
- 1,000–1,999
- 600–999
- 0–599
- data not available

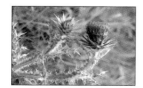

WEEDS

Weeds such as bindweed (above) are fast-growing, easily dispersed, and tolerant of a number of different environments, enabling them to quickly colonize suitable habitats. They are among the most adaptable of all plants.

POPULATION AND SETTLEMENT

THE EARTH'S POPULATION IS PROJECTED to rise from its current level of 5.7 billion to approximately 10 billion by 2025. The global distribution of this rapidly growing population is very uneven, and is dictated by climate, terrain, and natural and economic resources. The great majority of the Earth's peoples live in coastal zones and along river valleys. Deserts cover over 20% of the Earth's surface, but support fewer than 5% of the world's population. By the year 2000 it is estimated that over half of Earth's population will live in cities – most of them in Asia – as a result of mass migration from rural areas in search of jobs. Many of these people will live in the so-called "megacities," some with populations as great as 40 million.

PATTERNS OF SETTLEMENT

THE PAST 200 YEARS have seen the most radical shift in world population patterns in recorded history.

NOMADIC LIFE

ALL THE WORLD'S PEOPLES were hunter-gatherers 10,000 years ago. Today nomads, who live by following available food resources, account for less than 0.0001% of the world's population. They are mainly pastoral herders, moving their livestock from place to place in search of grazing land.

Nomadic population

Nomadic population area

THE GROWTH OF CITIES

IN 1900 there were only 13 cities in the world with populations of more than a million, mostly in the northern hemisphere. Today, as more and more people in the developing world migrate to towns and cities, there are 23 cities whose population exceeds 5 million, and over 284 "million-cities."

MILLION-CITIES IN 1900

Million-cities in 1900

● Cities over 1 million population

MILLION-CITIES IN 1995

Million-cities in 1995

● Cities over 1 million population

NORTH AMERICA

THE EASTERN AND WESTERN SEABOARDS of the US, with huge expanses of interconnected cities, towns, and suburbs, are vast, densely-populated megalopolises. Central America and the Caribbean also have high population densities. Yet, away from the coasts and in the wildernesses of northern Canada the land is very sparsely settled.

North America's central plains, the continent's agricultural heartland, are thinly populated and highly productive.

Vancouver on Canada's west coast, grew up as a port city. In recent years it has attracted many Asian immigrants, particularly from the Pacific Rim.

SOUTH AMERICA

MOST SETTLEMENT IN SOUTH AMERICA is clustered in a narrow belt in coastal zones and in the northern Andes. During the 20th century, cities such as São Paulo and Buenos Aires have grown enormously, acting as powerful economic magnets to the rural population. Shantytowns have grown up on the outskirts of many major cities to house these immigrants, and often lack basic amenities.

Venezuela is the most highly urbanized country in South America, with more than 90% of the population living in cities such as Caracas.

Many people in western South America live at high altitudes in the Andes, both in cities and in villages such as this one in Bolivia.

AFRICA

THE ARID CLIMATE of much of Africa means that settlement of the continent is sparse, focusing in coastal areas and fertile regions such as the Nile Valley. Africa still has a high proportion of nomadic agriculturalists, although many are now becoming settled, and the population is predominantly rural.

Cities such as Nairobi (above), Cairo, and Johannesburg have grown rapidly in recent years, although, on a global scale, only Cairo has a significant population.

Traditional lifestyles and homes persist across much of Africa, which has a higher proportion of rural or village-based population than any other continent.

EUROPE

WITH ITS TEMPERATE CLIMATE and rich mineral and natural resources, Europe is generally very densely settled. The continent acts as a magnet for economic migrants from the developing world, and immigration is now widely restricted. Birthrates in Europe are generally low, and in some countries, such as Germany, the populations have stabilized at zero growth, with a fast-growing elderly population.

Many European cities, like Siena, once reflected the "ideal" size for human settlements. Modern technological advances have enabled them to grow far beyond the original walls.

Within the densely populated Netherlands the reclamation of coastal wetlands is vital to provide much-needed land for agriculture and settlement.

ASIA

MOST ASIAN SETTLEMENT originally centered around the great river valleys such as the Indus, the Ganges, and the Yangtze. Today, almost 60% of the world's population lives in Asia, many in burgeoning cities, particularly in the economically buoyant Pacific Rim countries. Even rural population densities are high in many countries; farming practices such as terracing in southeastern Asia making the most of the available land.

Many of China's cities are now vast urban areas with populations of more than 5 million people.

This stilt village in Bangladesh is built to resist the regular flooding. Pressure on land, even in rural areas, forces many people to live in marginal areas.

Population density
(inhabitants per sq mile)

More than 520
260–519
130–259
55–129
28–54
15–27
1–15
Less than 1

NORTH AMERICA

Population 18.9%   World land area 17%

EUROPE

Population 7.5%   World land area 7.1%

AFRICA

Population 22.7%   World land area 20.2%

SOUTH AMERICA

Population 13.2%   World land area 11.8%

POPULATION STRUCTURES

POPULATION PYRAMIDS are an effective means of showing the age structures of different countries, and highlighting changing trends in population growth and decline. The typical pyramid for a country with a growing, youthful population, is broad-based *(left)*, reflecting a high birthrate and a far larger number of young rather than elderly people. In contrast, countries with populations whose numbers are stabilizing have a more balanced distribution of people in each age band, and may even have lower numbers of people in the youngest age ranges, indicating both a high life expectancy, and that the population is now barely replacing itself *(right)*. The Russian Federation *(center)* still bears the scars of the Second World War, reflected in the dramatically lower numbers of men than women in the 60–80+ age range.

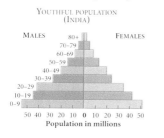

YOUTHFUL POPULATION
(INDIA)

MALES   FEMALES
Population in millions

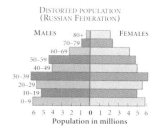

DISTORTED POPULATION
(RUSSIAN FEDERATION)

MALES   FEMALES
Population in millions

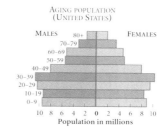

AGING POPULATION
(UNITED STATES)

MALES   FEMALES
Population in millions

POPULATION GROWTH

IMPROVEMENTS IN FOOD SUPPLY and advances in medicine have both played a major role in the remarkable growth in global population, which has increased five-fold over the last 150 years. Food supplies have risen with the mechanization of agriculture and improvements in crop yields. Better nutrition, together with higher standards of public health and sanitation, have led to increased longevity and higher birthrates.

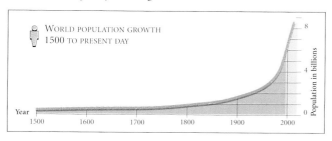

WORLD POPULATION GROWTH
1500 TO PRESENT DAY

Year
1500   1600   1700   1800   1900   2000

Population in billions

WORLD NUTRITION

TWO-THIRDS OF THE WORLD's food supply is consumed by the industrialized nations, many of which have a daily caloric intake far higher than is necessary for their populations to maintain a healthy body weight. In contrast, in the developing world, about 800 million people do not have enough food to meet their basic nutritional needs.

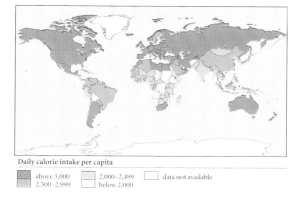

Daily calorie intake per capita

above 3,000   2,000–2,499   data not available
2,500–2,999   below 2,000

WORLD LIFE EXPECTANCY

IMPROVED PUBLIC HEALTH and living standards have greatly increased life expectancy in the developed world, where people can now expect to live twice as long as they did 100 years ago. In many of the world's poorest nations, disease and inadequate nutrition mean that the average life expectancy still does not exceed 45 years.

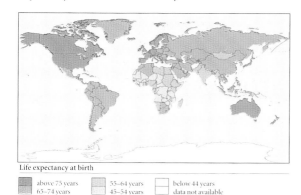

Life expectancy at birth

above 75 years   55–64 years   below 44 years
65–74 years   45–54 years   data not available

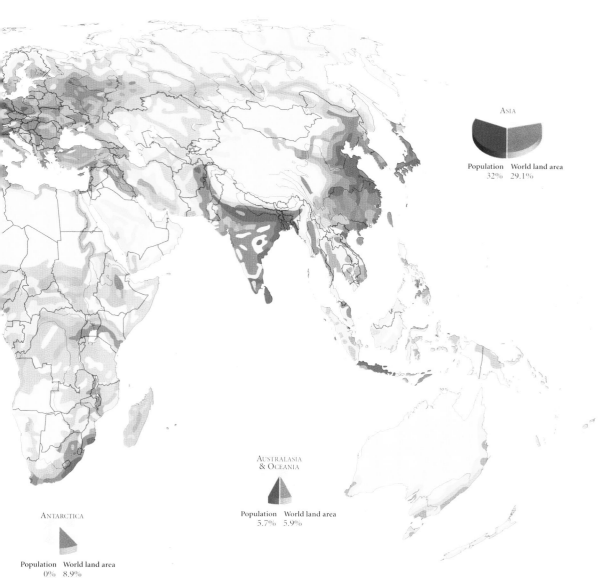

ASIA

Population   World land area
32%   29.1%

AUSTRALASIA
& OCEANIA

Population   World land area
5.7%   5.9%

ANTARCTICA

Population   World land area
0%   8.9%

AUSTRALASIA & OCEANIA

THIS IS THE WORLD's most sparsely settled region. The peoples of Australia and New Zealand live mainly in the coastal cities, with only scattered settlements in the arid interior. The Pacific islands can only support limited populations because of their remoteness and lack of resources.

Brisbane *on Australia's Gold Coast is the most rapidly expanding city in the country. The great majority of Australia's population lives in cities near the coasts.*

The remote highlands *of Papua New Guinea are home to a wide variety of peoples, many of whom still subsist by traditional hunting and gathering.*

AVERAGE WORLD BIRTHRATES

BIRTHRATES ARE MUCH HIGHER in Africa, Asia, and South America than in Europe and North America. Increased affluence and easy access to contraception are both factors which can lead to a significant decline in a country's birthrate.

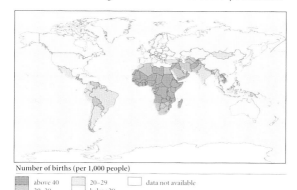

Number of births (per 1,000 people)

above 40   20–29   data not available
30–39   below 20

WORLD INFANT MORTALITY

IN PARTS OF THE DEVELOPING WORLD infant mortality rates are still high; access to medical services such as immunization, adequate nutrition, and the promotion of breast-feeding have been important in combating infant mortality.

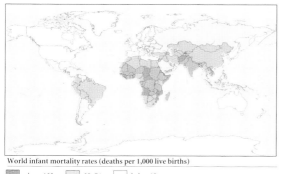

World infant mortality rates (deaths per 1,000 live births)

above 125   35–74   below 15
75–124   15–43   data not available

THE ECONOMIC SYSTEM

THE WEALTHY COUNTRIES OF THE DEVELOPED WORLD, with their aggressive, market-led economies and their access to productive new technologies and international markets, dominate the world economic system. At the other extreme, many of the countries of the developing world are locked in a cycle of national debt, rising populations, and unemployment. The state-managed economies of the former communist bloc began to be dismantled during the 1990s, and China is emerging as a major economic power following decades of isolation.

Trade blocs

	EU		NAFTA		ASEAN		LAIA
	CACM		SADC		ECOWAS		CEEAC

TRADE BLOCS

INTERNATIONAL TRADE BLOCS are formed when groups of countries, often already enjoying close military and political ties, join together to offer mutually preferential terms of trade for both imports and exports. Increasingly, global trade is dominated by three main blocs: the EU, NAFTA, and ASEAN. They are supplanting older trade blocs such as the Commonwealth, a legacy of colonialism.

INTERNATIONAL TRADE FLOWS

WORLD TRADE acts as a stimulus to national economies, encouraging growth. Over the last three decades, as heavy industries have declined, services – banking, insurance, tourism, airlines, and shipping – have taken an increasingly large share of world trade. Manufactured articles now account for nearly two-thirds of world trade; raw materials and food make up less than a quarter of the total.

SHIPPING
Ships carry 80% of international cargo. Extensive container ports, where cargo is stored, are vital links in the international transportation network.

MULTINATIONALS
Multinational companies are increasingly penetrating inaccessible markets. The reach of many American commodities is now global.

PRIMARY PRODUCTS
Many countries, particularly in the Caribbean and Africa, are still reliant on primary products such as rubber and coffee, which makes them vulnerable to fluctuating prices.

SERVICE INDUSTRIES
Service industries such as banking, tourism, and insurance have been the fastest-growing industrial sector in the latter half of the 20th century. Lloyds of London is the center of the world insurance market.

Countries reliant on a single export
- bananas
- coffee
- oil/petroleum
- copper

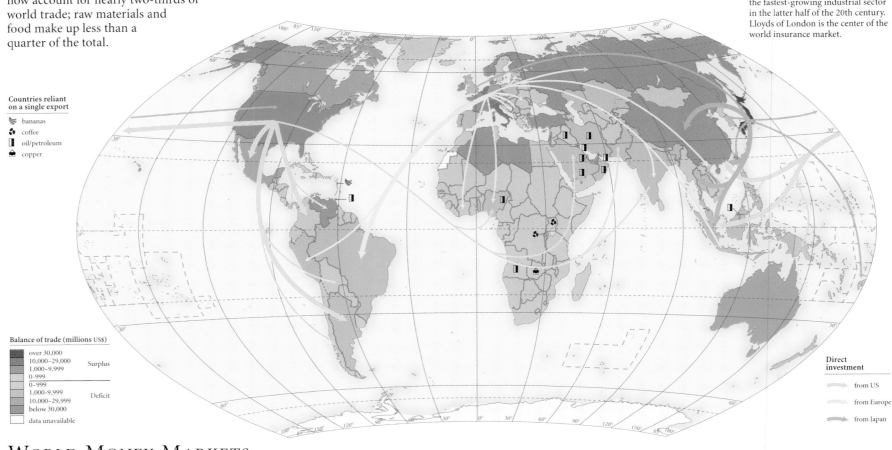

Balance of trade (millions US$)

over 30,000	
10,000–29,000	
1,000–9,999	Surplus
0–999	
0–999	
1,000–9,999	
10,000–29,999	Deficit
below 30,000	
data unavailable	

Direct investment
- from US
- from Europe
- from Japan

WORLD MONEY MARKETS

THE FINANCIAL WORLD has traditionally been dominated by three major centers – Tokyo, New York, and London – that house the headquarters of stock exchanges, multinational corporations, and international banks. Their geographical location means that, at any one time in a 24-hour day, one major market is open for trading in shares, currencies, and commodities. Since the late 1980s, technological advances have enabled transactions between financial centers to occur at ever-greater speed, and new markets have sprung up throughout the world.

NEW STOCK MARKETS

NEW STOCK MARKETS are now opening in many parts of the world, where economies have recently emerged from state controls. In Moscow and Beijing, and several countries in eastern Europe, newly opened stock exchanges reflect the transition to market-driven economies.

THE DEVELOPING WORLD

INTERNATIONAL TRADE in capital and currency is dominated by the rich nations of the northern hemisphere. In parts of Africa and Asia, where exports of any sort are extremely limited, home-produced commodities are simply sold in local markets.

MAJOR MONEY MARKETS

London
New York
Tokyo

Location of major stock markets
- Major stock markets

The Tokyo Stock Market crashed in 1990, leading to a slowdown in the growth of the world's most powerful economy, and a refocusing on economic policy away from export-led growth and toward the domestic market.

Dealers at the Calcutta Stock Market. The Indian economy has been opened up to foreign investment, and many multinationals now have bases there.

Markets have thrived in communist Vietnam since the introduction of a liberal economic policy.

WORLD WEALTH DISPARITY

A GLOBAL ASSESSMENT of Gross Domestic Product (GDP) by nation reveals great disparities. The developed world, with only 25% of the world's population, has 80% of the world's manufacturing income. Civil war, conflict, and political instability further undermine the economic self-sufficiency of many of the world's poorest nations.

Cities such as Detroit have been badly hit by the decline in heavy industry.

URBAN DECAY

ALTHOUGH THE US still dominates the global economy, it faces deficits in both the federal budget and the balance of trade. Vast discrepancies in personal wealth, high levels of unemployment, and the dismantling of welfare provisions throughout the 1980s have led to severe deprivation in several of the inner cities of North America's industrial heartland.

BOOMING CITIES

SINCE THE 1980s the Chinese government has set up special industrial zones, such as Shanghai, where foreign investment is encouraged through tax incentives. Migrants from rural China pour into these regions in search of work, creating "boomtown" economies.

Foreign investment has encouraged new infrastructure development in cities like Shanghai.

URBAN SPRAWL

CITIES ARE EXPANDING all over the developing world, attracting economic migrants in search of work and opportunities. In cities such as Rio de Janeiro, housing has not kept pace with the population explosion, and squalid shanty towns *(favelas)* rub shoulders with middle-class housing.

The **favelas** *of Rio de Janeiro sprawl over the hills surrounding the city.*

COMPARATIVE WORLD WEALTH

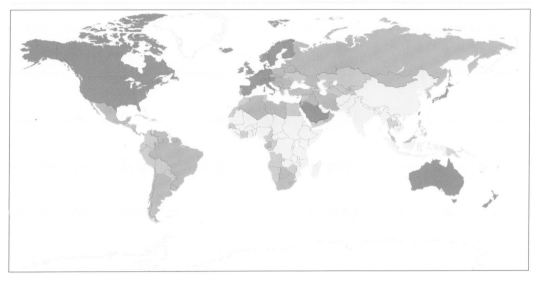

World economies
- high income
- upper-middle income
- lower-middle income
- low income
- data unavailable

ECONOMIC "TIGERS"

THE ECONOMIC "TIGERS" of the Pacific Rim – Taiwan, Singapore, and South Korea – have grown faster than Europe and the US over the last decade. Their export- and service-led economies have benefited from stable government, low labor costs, and foreign investment.

Hong Kong, with its fine natural harbor, is one of the most important ports in Asia.

AGRICULTURAL ECONOMIES

IN PARTS OF THE DEVELOPING WORLD, people survive by subsistence farming – growing enough food only for themselves and their families. With no surplus product, they are unable to exchange goods for currency, the only means of escaping the poverty trap. In other countries, farmers have been encouraged to concentrate on growing a single crop for the export market. This reliance on cash crops leaves farmers vulnerable to crop failure and to changes in the market price of the crop.

The **Ugandan uplands** *are fertile, but poor infrastructure hampers the export of cash crops.*

A **shopping arcade in Paris** *displays a great profusion of luxury goods.*

THE AFFLUENT WEST

THE CAPITAL CITIES of many countries in the developed world are showcases for consumer goods, reflecting the increasing importance of the service sector, and particularly the retail sector, in the world economy. The idea of shopping as a leisure activity is unique to the western world. Luxury goods and services attract visitors, who in turn generate tourist revenue.

TOURISM

IN 1990, THERE WERE 425 million tourists worldwide. Tourism is now the world's biggest single industry, employing 127 million people, though frequently in low-paid unskilled jobs. While tourists are increasingly exploring newly-accessible and less-developed regions of the world, the benefits of the industry are not always felt at a local level. There are also worries about the environmental impact of tourism, as the world's last wildernesses increasingly become tourist attractions.

Botswana's **Okavango Delta** *is an area rich in wildlife. Tourists go on safaris in the region, but the impact of tourism is controlled.*

MONEY FLOWS

FOREIGN INVESTMENT in the developing world during the 1970s led to a global financial crisis in the 1980s, when many countries were unable to meet their debt repayments. The International Monetary Fund (IMF) was forced to reschedule the debts and, in some cases, write them off completely. Within the developing world, austerity programs have been initiated to cope with the debt, leading in turn to high unemployment and galloping inflation. In many parts of Africa, stricken economies are now dependent on international aid.

In rural **Southeast Asia**, *babies are given medical checks by* UNICEF *as part of a global aid program sponsored by the* UN.

TOURIST ARRIVALS

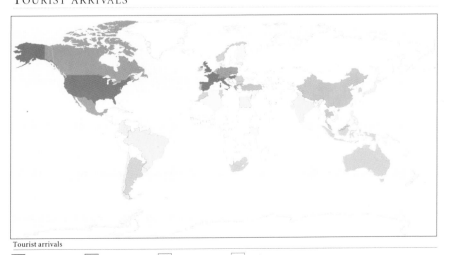

Tourist arrivals
- over 20 million
- 10–20 million
- 5–10 million
- 2.5–5 million
- 1–2.5 million
- 700,000–999,000
- under 700,000
- data unavailable

INTERNATIONAL DEBT: DONORS AND RECEIVERS

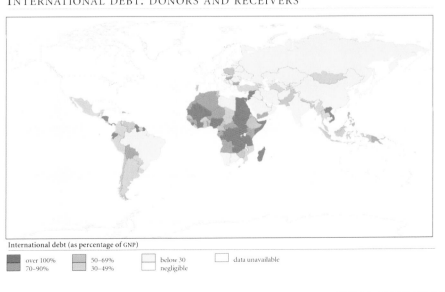

International debt (as percentage of GNP)
- over 100%
- 70–90%
- 50–69%
- 30–49%
- below 30
- negligible
- data unavailable

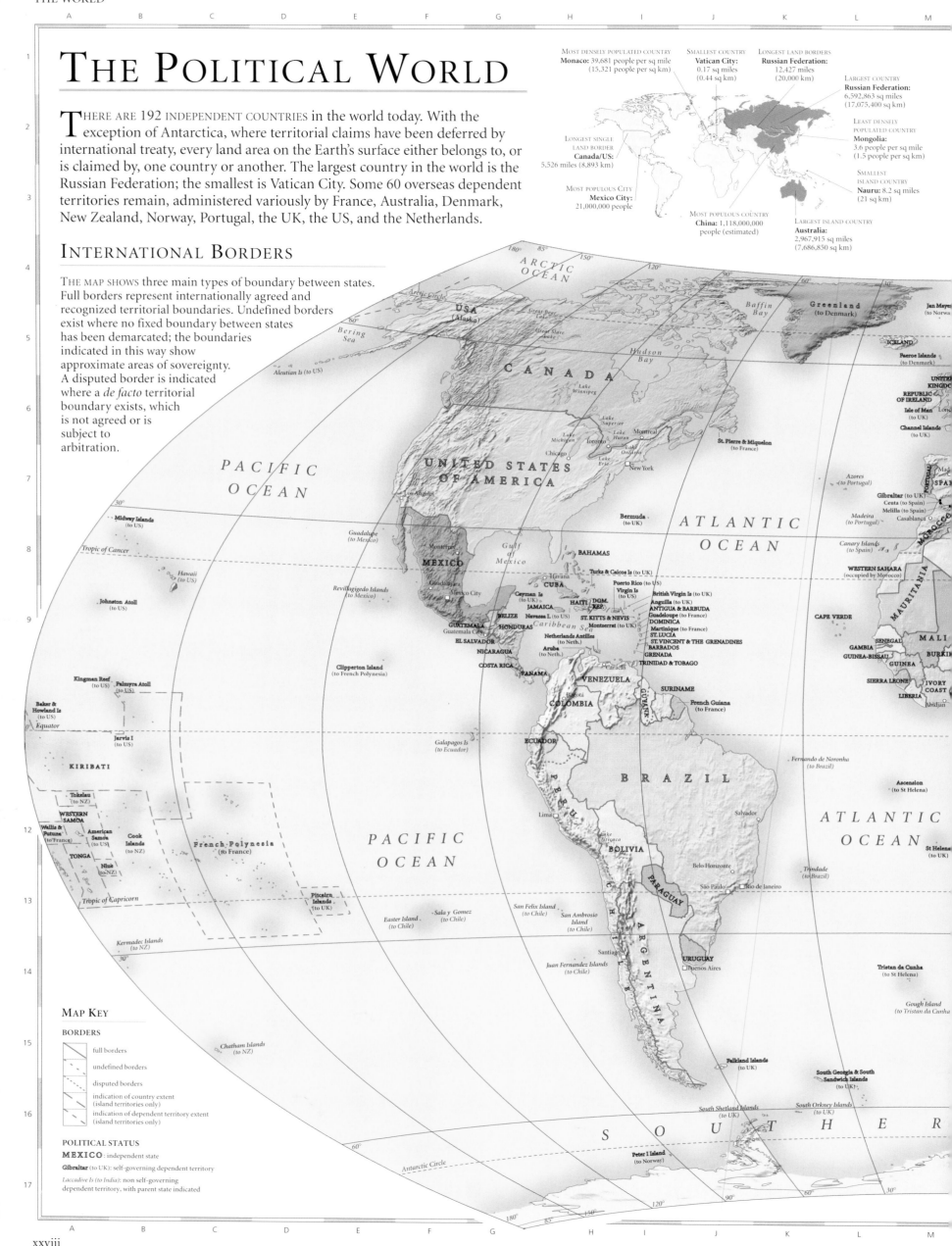

THE POLITICAL WORLD

THERE ARE 192 INDEPENDENT COUNTRIES in the world today. With the exception of Antarctica, where territorial claims have been deferred by international treaty, every land area on the Earth's surface either belongs to, or is claimed by, one country or another. The largest country in the world is the Russian Federation; the smallest is Vatican City. Some 60 overseas dependent territories remain, administered variously by France, Australia, Denmark, New Zealand, Norway, Portugal, the UK, the US, and the Netherlands.

INTERNATIONAL BORDERS

THE MAP SHOWS three main types of boundary between states. Full borders represent internationally agreed and recognized territorial boundaries. Undefined borders exist where no fixed boundary between states has been demarcated; the boundaries indicated in this way show approximate areas of sovereignty. A disputed border is indicated where a *de facto* territorial boundary exists, which is not agreed or is subject to arbitration.

MOST DENSELY POPULATED COUNTRY
Monaco: 39,681 people per sq mile (15,321 people per sq km)

SMALLEST COUNTRY
Vatican City: 0.17 sq miles (0.44 sq km)

LONGEST LAND BORDERS
Russian Federation: 12,427 miles (20,000 km)

LARGEST COUNTRY
Russian Federation: 6,592,863 sq miles (17,075,400 sq km)

LEAST DENSELY POPULATED COUNTRY
Mongolia: 3.6 people per sq mile (1.5 people per sq km)

LONGEST SINGLE LAND BORDER
Canada/US: 5,526 miles (8,893 km)

SMALLEST ISLAND COUNTRY
Nauru: 8.2 sq miles (21 sq km)

MOST POPULOUS CITY
Mexico City: 21,000,000 people

MOST POPULOUS COUNTRY
China: 1,118,000,000 people (estimated)

LARGEST ISLAND COUNTRY
Australia: 2,967,915 sq miles (7,686,850 sq km)

MAP KEY

BORDERS

- full borders
- undefined borders
- disputed borders
- indication of country extent (island territories only)
- indication of dependent territory extent (island territories only)

POLITICAL STATUS

MEXICO : independent state

Gibraltar (to UK): self-governing dependent territory

Laccadive Is (to India): non self-governing dependent territory, with parent state indicated

THE WORLD IN 1914

THE EARLY YEARS OF the 20th century saw the mainly European colonial empires reaching their greatest extents by 1914. Two world wars inaugurated their disintegration, but even in 1950 there were only 82 independent countries. Since then, over 100 have gained their independence, culminating in the breakup of the former Soviet Union after 1990.

PERCENTAGE OF EARTH'S LAND SURFACE
CONTROLLED BY COLONIAL EMPIRES IN 1914

- Independent: 29.8%
- Chinese: 6%
- Ottoman: 1.5%
- Russian: 15%
- Portuguese: 1%
- Spanish: 1%
- British: 21.5%
- Dutch: 1.4%
- Danish: 1.5%
- American: 7.6%
- Japanese: 0.4%
- German: 1.6%
- Italian: 1.8%
- Belgian: 1.6%
- French: 7.7%

COLONIAL EMPIRES IN 1914

Colonial Empires in 1914

- Belgian
- British
- Chinese
- Danish
- Dutch
- French
- German
- Italian
- Japanese
- Ottoman
- Portuguese
- Russian
- Spanish
- American
- Independent

RUSSIAN FEDERATION

Svalbard (to Norway)
Barents Sea
Arctic Circle

NORWAY SWEDEN FINLAND
St Petersburg
ESTONIA
LATVIA
LITHUANIA
RUSS. FED.
Moscow

DENMARK GERMANY POLAND BELARUS
Berlin Kiev
CZECH REP. SLOVAKIA UKRAINE
Paris LIECH. SWITZ. AUSTRIA HUNGARY MOLDOVA
MACO SLOVENIA ROMANIA
ANDORRA CROATIA B-H BULGARIA
SAN MARINO ITALY Bucharest
VATICAN CITY Rome MACEDONIA GEORGIA ARMENIA AZERBAIJAN
ALBANIA GREECE Istanbul Ankara AZER.
TUNISIA MALTA Athens TURKEY
CYPRUS SYRIA
Mediterranean Sea LEBANON Baghdad
ISRAEL IRAQ
Alexandria Cairo JORDAN
ALGERIA El Giza
LIBYA EGYPT KUWAIT
BAHRAIN Riyadh QATAR
NIGER SAUDI ARABIA UAE
CHAD ARABIA OMAN
SUDAN ERITREA YEMEN
NIGERIA DJIBOUTI
CAMEROON CENTRAL AFRICAN REPUBLIC ETHIOPIA SOMALIA
EQUATORIAL GUINEA
TOME & PRINCIPE GABON CONGO UGANDA KENYA
CONGO (DEM. REP.) RWANDA BURUNDI TANZANIA
Kinshasa Lake Victoria
ANGOLA (Cabinda) Lake Tanganyika
ANGOLA ZAMBIA MALAWI
NAMIBIA ZIMBABWE MOZAMBIQUE
BOTSWANA
SWAZILAND
LESOTHO
SOUTH AFRICA

KAZAKHSTAN
Aral Sea Lake Balkhash
UZBEKISTAN KYRGYZSTAN
TURKMENISTAN TAJIKISTAN
Tehran
IRAN AFGHANISTAN
PAKISTAN
Karachi
Delhi Kanpur
Ahmadabad Calcutta
Bombay INDIA Chittagong
Pune Hyderabad
Madras Andaman Is (to India)
Bangalore
Laccadive Is (to India)
SRI LANKA
Nicobar Is (to India)
MALDIVES

MONGOLIA
Harbin
Changchun
Shenyang NORTH KOREA
Beijing Dalian Pyongyang
Tianjin Qingdao SOUTH KOREA Seoul
Jinan Pusan Taegu
CHINA Nanjing Shanghai
Xian
Chengdu Wuhan
Chongqing Ryukyu Is (to Japan)
Taipei
NEPAL BHUTAN TAIWAN
BANGLADESH Dhaka Macao (to Portugal) Guangzhou Hong Kong
MYANMAR LAOS Hanoi
Rangoon VIETNAM
THAILAND Parcel Is (disputed)
Bangkok CAMBODIA South China Sea Manila PHILIPPINES
Ho Chi Minh City Spratly Is (disputed)
BRUNEI
MALAYSIA
SINGAPORE PALAU
INDONESIA
Jakarta Java Sea
Surabaya

JAPAN
Nagoya Tokyo
Osaka Yokohama
Sea of Japan

PACIFIC OCEAN

Wake Island (to US)
Northern Mariana Is (to US)
MARSHALL ISLANDS
Guam (to US) MICRONESIA
NAURU KIRIBATI
PAPUA NEW GUINEA
SOLOMON ISLANDS TUVALU
Ashmore & Cartier Islands (to Australia)
Coral Sea Islands (to Australia) VANUATU
New Caledonia (to France) FIJI

Arabian Sea
Bay of Bengal
Socotra (to Yemen)
SEYCHELLES
British Indian Ocean Territory (to UK)
Agalega Islands (to Mauritius)
COMOROS
Mayotte (to France)
MADAGASCAR
Tromelin (to Réunion)
Rodrigues (to Mauritius)
Réunion (to France) MAURITIUS
INDIAN OCEAN
Christmas Island (to Australia)
Cocos (Keeling) Islands (to Australia)

AUSTRALIA
Sydney
Melbourne
Lord Howe Island (to Australia)
Norfolk Island (to Australia)
NEW ZEALAND

Tropic of Cancer
Equator
Tropic of Capricorn

Amsterdam Island
St Paul Island
Prince Edward Islands (to South Africa)
French Southern & Antarctic Territories (to France)
Crozet Islands
Kerguelen
Heard & McDonald Islands (to Australia)

Bouvet Island (to Norway)

Macquarie Island (to Australia)
Auckland Islands (to NZ) Antipodes Islands (to NZ)
Bounty Islands (to NZ)
Campbell Island (to NZ)

INDIAN OCEAN

ANTARCTICA
(All territorial claims are held in abeyance under the 1959 Antarctic Treaty)
Antarctic Circle

ARCTIC OCEAN

SCALE 1:66,000,000
(projection: Wagner VII)

Km
0 250 500 1,000 1,500 2,000
Miles
0 250 500 1,000 1,500 2,000

STATES AND BOUNDARIES

THERE ARE OVER 190 SOVEREIGN STATES in the world today; in 1950 there were only 82. Over the last half-century, national self-determination has been a driving force for many states with a history of colonialism and oppression. As more borders are added to the world map, the number of international border disputes increases. In many cases, where the impetus toward independence has been religious or ethnic, disputes with minority groups have also caused violent internal conflict. While many newly formed states have moved peacefully toward independence, successfully establishing government by multiparty democracy, dictatorship by military regime or individual despot is often the result of the internal power struggles that characterize the early stages in the lives of new nations.

THE NATURE OF POLITICS

Democracy is a broad term: it can range from the ideal of multiparty elections and fair representation to, in countries such as Singapore and Indonesia, a thin disguise for single-party rule. In despotic regimes, on the other hand, a single, often personal authority has total power; institutions such as parliament and the military are mere instruments of the dictator.

The Stars and Stripes is a potent symbol of the US's status as a federal democracy.

Types of government

- Multiparty democracy for more than 10 yrs
- Multiparty/transitional democracy within last 10 yrs
- Single-party government
- Military regime
- Monarchy or theocracy
- State of unrest/civil war

THE CHANGING WORLD MAP

DECOLONIZATION

In 1950, large areas of the world remained under the control of a handful of European countries (*page xxviii*). The process of decolonization had begun in Asia, where, following the Second World War, much of southern and southeastern Asia sought and achieved self-determination. In the 1960s, a host of African states achieved independence, so that by 1965, most of the larger tracts of the European overseas empires had been substantially eroded. The final major stage in decolonization came with the breakup of the Soviet Union and the Eastern bloc after 1990. The process continues today, as the last toeholds of European colonialism, often tiny island nations, press increasingly for independence.

Iran is one of the world's true theocracies; Islam has an impact on every aspect of political life.

Saddam Hussein overthrew his predecessor in 1979. Since then he has promoted an extreme personality cult, with autocratic control over 19.3 million Iraqis.

NEW NATIONS 1945–1965

NEW NATIONS 1965–1996

Icons of communism, including statues of former leaders such as Lenin and Stalin, were destroyed when the Soviet bloc was dismantled in 1989, creating several new nations.

North Korea is an independent communist republic. Power is concentrated in the hands of Kim Jong Il.

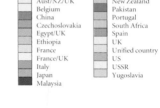

South Africa became a democracy in 1994, when elections ended 45 years of white rule.

Administration at the time of independence

Australia	Netherlands
Aust/NZ/UK	New Zealand
Belgium	Pakistan
China	Portugal
Czechoslovakia	South Africa
Egypt/UK	Spain
Ethiopia	UK
France	Unified country
France/UK	US
Italy	USSR
Japan	Yugoslavia
Malaysia	

In Brunei the Sultan has ruled by decree since 1962; power is closely tied to the royal family. The Sultan's brothers are responsible for finance and foreign affairs.

LINES ON THE MAP

THE DETERMINATION OF INTERNATIONAL BOUNDARIES can be based on a variety of criteria. Many of the borders between older states follow physical boundaries; some mirror religious and ethnic differences; others are the legacy of complex histories of conflict and colonialism, while others have been imposed by international agreements or arbitration.

POST COLONIAL BORDERS

WHEN THE EUROPEAN COLONIAL EMPIRES IN AFRICA were dismantled during the second half of the 20th century, the outlines of the new African states mirrored colonial boundaries. These boundaries had been drawn up by colonial administrators, often based on inadequate geographical knowledge. Such arbitrary boundaries were imposed on people of different languages, racial groups, religions, and customs. This confused legacy often led to civil and international war.

Dates from which current boundaries have existed

- 1990–1993
- 1966–1989
- 1946–1965
- 1915–1945
- 1850–1914
- 1800–1849
- Pre-1800

The conflict that has plagued many African countries since independence has caused millions of people to become refugees.

PHYSICAL BORDERS

MANY OF THE WORLD'S COUNTRIES are divided by physical borders: lakes, rivers, mountains. The demarcation of such boundaries can, however, lead to disputes. Control of waterways, water supplies and fisheries are frequent sources of international friction.

ENCLAVES

THE SHIFTING POLITICAL MAP over the course of history has frequently led to anomalous situations. Parts of national territories may become isolated by territorial agreement, forming an enclave. The West German part of the city of Berlin, which until 1989 lay several hundred miles within East German territory, was a famous example.

Since the independence of Lithuania and Belarus, the peoples of the Russian enclave of Kaliningrad have become physically isolated.

ANTARCTICA

WHEN ANTARCTIC EXPLORATION began a century ago, seven nations – Australia, Argentina, Britain, Chile, France, New Zealand, and Norway – laid claim to the new territory. In 1961 the Antarctic Treaty, signed by 39 nations, agreed to hold all territorial claims in abeyance.

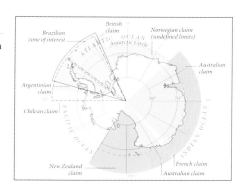

WORLD BOUNDARIES

GEOMETRIC BORDERS

STRAIGHT LINES and lines of longitude and latitude have occasionally been used to determine international boundaries. The world's longest international boundary, between Canada and the US, follows the 49th parallel for over one-third of its course. Many Canadian, American, and Australian internal administrative boundaries are similarly determined using a geometric solution.

The 49th parallel forms the boundary between much of the US and Canada.

LAKE BORDERS

Countries that lie next to lakes usually place their borders in the middle of the lake. The Lake Nyasa border between Malawi and Tanzania, however, runs along Tanzania's shore.

Complicated agreements between colonial powers led to the awkward division of Lake Nyasa

RIVER BORDERS

Rivers alone account for one-sixth of the world's borders. Many great rivers form boundaries between a number of countries. Changes in a river's course and interruptions of its natural flow can lead to disputes, particularly in areas where water is scarce. The center of the river's course is the nominal boundary line.

The Danube forms all or part of the border between nine European nations.

MOUNTAIN BORDERS

Mountain ranges form natural barriers and are the basis for many major borders, particularly in Europe and Asia. The watershed is the conventional boundary demarcation line, but its accurate determination is often problematic.

The Pyrenees form a natural mountain border between France and Spain.

SHIFTING BOUNDARIES – POLAND

BORDERS BETWEEN COUNTRIES can change dramatically over time. The nations of eastern Europe have been particularly affected by changing boundaries. Poland is an example of a country whose boundaries have changed so significantly that it has literally moved around Europe. At the start of the 16th century, Poland was the largest nation in Europe. Between 1772 and 1795, it was absorbed into Prussia, Austria, and Russia, and it effectively ceased to exist. After the First World War, Poland became an independent country once more, but its borders changed again after the Second World War following invasions by both Soviet Russia and Nazi Germany.

In 1634, Poland was the largest nation in Europe, its eastern boundary reaching toward Moscow.

From 1772–1795, Poland was gradually partitioned among Austria, Russia, and Prussia. Its eastern boundary receded by over 100 miles (160 km).

Following the First World War, Poland was reinstated as an independent state, but it was less than half the size it had been in 1634.

After the Second World War, the Baltic Sea border was extended westward, but much of the eastern territory was annexed by Russia.

INTERNATIONAL DISPUTES

THERE ARE MORE THAN 60 DISPUTED BORDERS or territories in the world today. Although many of these disputes can be settled by peaceful negotiation, some areas have become a focus for international conflict. Ethnic tensions have been a major source of territorial disagreement throughout history, as has the ownership of and access to valuable natural resources. The turmoil of the post-colonial era in many parts of Africa is partly a result of the 19th-century "carve-up" of the continent, which created the potential for conflict by drawing often arbitrary lines through linguistic and cultural areas.

JAMMU AND KASHMIR

DISPUTES OVER JAMMU AND KASHMIR have caused three serious wars between India and Pakistan since 1947. Pakistan wishes to annex the largely Muslim territory, while India refuses to cede any territory or to hold a referendum, and also lays claim to the entire territory. Most international maps show the line of control agreed in 1972 as the de facto border. In addition, both Pakistan and India have territorial disputes with neighbouring China. The situation is further complicated by a Kashmiri independence movement, active since the late 1980s.

Indian army troops maintain their positions in the mountainous terrain of northern Kashmir.

NORTH AND SOUTH KOREA

SINCE 1953, the de facto border between North and South Korea has been a ceasefire line that straddles the 38th Parallel and is designated as a demilitarized zone. Both countries have heavy fortifications and troop concentrations behind this zone.

The so-called green line divides Cyprus into Greek and Turkish sectors.

CYPRUS

CYPRUS WAS PARTITIONED in 1974, following an invasion by Turkish troops. The south is now the Greek Cypriot Republic of Cyprus, while the self-proclaimed Turkish Republic of Northern Cyprus is recognized only by Turkey.

TURKISH REPUBLIC OF NORTHERN CYPRUS

Heavy fortifications are in place on the border between North and South Korea.

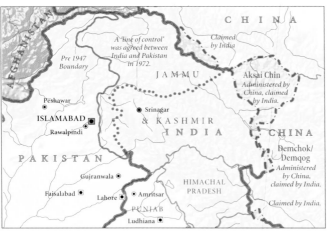

THE FALKLAND ISLANDS

THE BRITISH DEPENDENT TERRITORY of the Falkland Islands was invaded by Argentina in 1982, sparking a full-scale war with the UK. In 1995, the UK and Argentina reached an agreement on the exploitation of oil reserves around the islands.

British warships exchange fire during the war with Argentina in 1982.

Disputed territories and borders

- Countries involved in active territorial or border disputes
- Disputed borders
- Undefined borders
- Disputed territories

ISRAEL

ISRAEL WAS CREATED IN 1947 following the UN Resolution (147) on Palestine. Until 1979 Israel had no borders, only ceasefire lines from a series of wars in 1948, 1967, and 1973. Treaties with Egypt in 1979 and Jordan in 1994 led to these borders being defined and agreed. Negotiations over disputed territories with Lebanon and Syria, and the issue of self-government with the Palestinians, continue.

- ● Israeli settlement
- ○ Major settlement
- ▲ Palestinian settlement
- ▨ Area under Palestinian control

Barbed-wire fences surround a settlement in the Golan Heights.

YUGOSLAVIA

FOLLOWING THE DISINTEGRATION in 1990 of the communist state of Yugoslavia, the breakaway states of Croatia and Bosnia-Herzegovina came into conflict with the parent state (consisting of Serbia and Montenegro). Warfare focused on ethnic and territorial ambitions in Bosnia. The tenuous Dayton Accord of 1995 sought to recognize the post-1990 borders, whilst providing for ethnic partition. It required international peace-keeping troops to maintain the terms of the peace.

- ▨ Invaded by Serbia
- ▨ Muslim/Croat federation

THE SPRATLY ISLANDS

THE SITE OF POTENTIAL OIL and natural gas reserves, the Spratly Islands in the South China Sea have been claimed by China, Vietnam, Taiwan, Malaysia, and the Philippines since the Japanese gave up a wartime claim in 1951.

Most claimant states have small military garrisons on the Spratly Islands.

- ● Occupied by Taiwan
- ● Occupied by Philippines
- ● Occupied by Malaysia
- ● Occupied by China
- ● Occupied by Vietnam

ATLAS
OF THE
WORLD

THE MAPS IN THIS ATLAS ARE ARRANGED CONTINENT BY CONTINENT, STARTING FROM THE INTERNATIONAL DATE LINE AND MOVING EAST. THE MAPS PROVIDE A UNIQUE VIEW OF TODAY'S WORLD, COMBINING TRADITIONAL CARTOGRAPHIC TECHNIQUES WITH THE LATEST REMOTE-SENSED AND DIGITAL TECHNOLOGY.

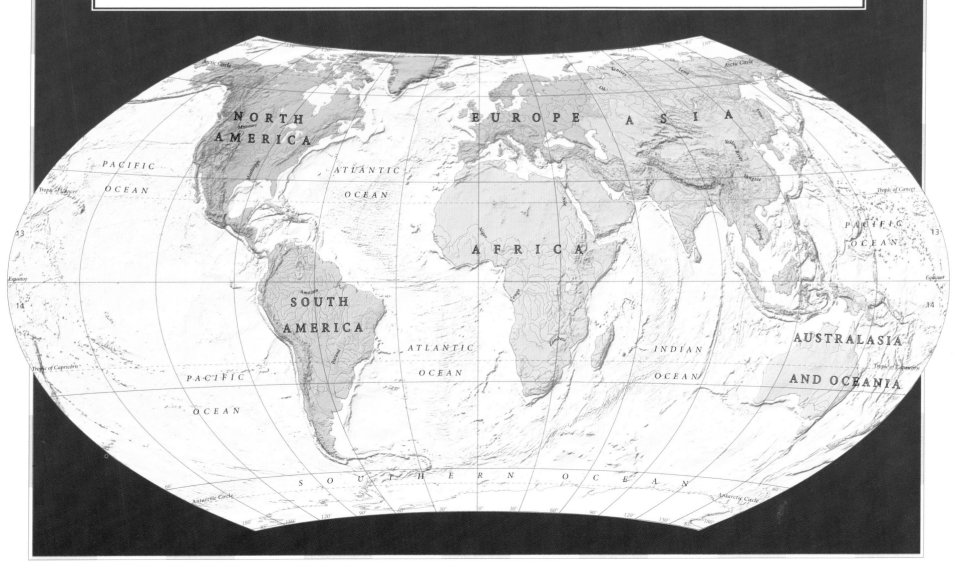

EURASIAN PLATE
NORTH AMERICAN PLATE

Khrebet Cherskogo

Franz Josef Land

East Siberian
Sea

A R C T I C   O C E A N

North Pole

Nordaustlandet

Greenland Sea

Norwegian Sea

Sea of
Okhotsk

Khrebet Kolymskiy

Kamchatka

Koryakskoye Nagor'ye

Chukchi
Sea

Kap
Morris Jesup

Queen
Elizabeth Islands

Ellesmere
Island

King Frederik
VIII Land

Iceland

Kuril Trench

Northwest Pacific
Basin

Komandorskaya
Basin

Anadyrskiy
Zaliv

Cape Prince
of Wales

Bering Strait

Point Barrow

Beaufort Sea

McClure Strait

Banks Island

Parry Islands

Jones Sound

Viscount Melville Sound

Lancaster Sound

Baffin Bay

King Christian X Land

Denmark Strait

Bering
Sea

Aleutian
Basin

Seward
Peninsula

Norton
Sound

Colville

Yukon

Mackenzie
Bay

Prince
of
Wales
Island

McClintock Channel

Boothia
Peninsula

Gulf
of
Boothia

Davis Strait

Baffin Island

King
VI Coast

Bowers Ridge

Atka

Nunivak
Island

St Lawrence
Island

Brooks Range

Koyukuk

Yukon

Porcupine

Arctic Red River

Peel

Victoria Island

Coronation Gulf

Queen Maud
Gulf

Boothia

Greenland

Aleutian Islands

Kuskokwim Bay

Bristol
Bay

Kuskokwim

Alaska

Mount
McKinley
(Denali)
6194m

Range

Stewart

Yukon

Great Bear Lake

Copper mine

Arctic Circle

Garry Lake

Baker Lake

Foxe Basin

Southampton
Island

Nettilling Lake

Cumberland
Sound

Frobisher Bay

Aleutian Trench

NORTH AMERICAN PLATE

PACIFIC PLATE

Alaska Peninsula

Aleutian Range

Kenai
Mountains

Kodiak
Island

Gulf of
Alaska

Mount Logan
5959m

Tanana

Liard

Mackenzie

Back

Thelon

Dubawnt Lake

Kasan

Foxe
Channel

Amadjuak
Lake

Péninsule
d' Ungava

Labrador
Sea

Alaska Range

Patton Seamount

Cowie Seamount

NORTH AMERICAN PLATE

PACIFIC PLATE

Alexander
Archipelago

Coast Mountains

Skeena

Peace

Hay

Great Slave Lake

Athabasca

Lake Athabasca

Wollaston Lake

Reindeer Lake

Great
Whale

Churchill

Nelson

Coats Island

Mansel
Island

Belcher
Islands

Hudson Strait

Arnaud

Rivière
aux Feuilles

Rivière
aux Mélèzes

Ungava
Bay

Gilbert Seamounts

Morton Seamount

Union Seamount

Queen Charlotte Islands

Fraser

Thompson

North Saskatchewan

South Saskatchewan

Lake Winnipeg

Severn

Winisk

Attawapiskat

Moose

James
Bay

La Grande Rivière

Lac Mistassini

N O R T H

Canadian

Shield

George

Labrador

Caniapiscau

Laurentian
Highland

Cobb Seamount

Vancouver
Island

Cascadia
Basin

JUAN DE FUCA PLATE

Astoria
Fan

Columbia

Coast Ranges

Cascade Range

Mount Rainier
4392m

Mount St Helens 2549m

Clark Fork

Yellowstone

Missouri

Souris

Lake of the Woods

Lake Manitoba

Winnipeg

Lake Nipigon

Lake Superior

Ottawa

Saguenay

St Lawrence

Lake Champlain

Mendocino Fracture Zone

Pioneer Fracture Zone

Gorda Ridge

Delgada
Fan

Columbia
Plateau

Harney Basin

Hells
Canyon

Snake

Salmon

Owyhee

Bighorn

Powder

Cheyenne

Black Hills

Lake Oahe

North Platte

Niobrara

Red River

Minnesota

Mississippi

Des Moines

Wisconsin

Illinois

Lake Michigan

Lake Huron

Georgian Bay

Lake Erie

Lake Ontario

Niagara Falls

Ontario

Toronto

Hudson

P A C I F I C   O C E A N

Murray Fracture Zone

Moonless
Mountains

San Francisco Bay

Monterey Bay

Sacramento

San Joaquin

Sierra Nevada

Coast Ranges

Great Basin

Great Salt Lake

Mount Whitney 4418m

Death Valley
-86m

Lake Mead

Mojave
Desert

Lake Powell

Mount Elbert 4399m

A M E R I C A

Arkansas

Kansas

South Platte

Platte

Missouri

Great Plains

St Louis

Cumberland Plateau

Tennessee

Alleghney Mountains

Appalachian Mountains

Blue Ridge

Roanoke

Delaware Bay

Chesapeake Bay

Cape Hatteras

Mount Mitchell 2037m

Long Island

Connecticut

Tropic of Cancer

Molokai Fracture Zone

Colorado

Grand
Canyon

Colorado
Plateau

Painted Desert

Humphreys
Peak 3851m

Baldy Peak 3476m

Sonoran
Desert

Gila

Rio Grande

Pecos

Canadian

Arkansas

Red River

Mississippi

Alabama

Chattahoochee

Apalachee

Savannah

Cape Lookout

Cape Fear

Clarion Fracture Zone

Alijos Rocks

Lower California

Gulf of California

Rio Yaqui

Rio Grande

Colorado

Mississippi
Delta

Galveston Bay

Sigsbee Escarpment

Mississippi Fan

Sigsbee Escarpment

Gulf of Mexico

Mexico
Basin

Tampa Bay

Lake Okeechobee

The
Everglades

Blake
Plateau

Blake-Bahama Basin

Cape Canaveral

Straits of Florida

Bahamas

Cuba

Cabo San
Lucas

Sierra Madre Occidental

Rio Grande de Santiago

Revillagigedo
Islands

Sierra Madre Oriental

Campeche Bank

Yucatan
Peninsula

Yucatan
Channel

Yucatan Basin

Great

Mathematicians
Seamounts

Lago de Chapala

Popocatépetl
5452m

Citlaltépetl
5700m

Bay of
Campeche

East Pacific Rise

Sierra Madre del Sur

NORTH AMERICAN PLATE

COCOS PLATE

NORTH AMERICAN PLATE

CARIBBEAN PLATE

Golfo de
Tehuantepec

Gulf of Honduras

Nicaraguan
Rise

Cayman Trench

Jamaica

Caribbean

Península
de la Guajira

Orozco Fracture Zone

PACIFIC PLATE

COCOS PLATE

Clipperton Fracture Zone

Clipperton Seamounts

Clipperton
Island

Tehuantepec Ridge

Middle America Trench

Golfo de
Fonseca

CARIBBEAN PLATE

COCOS PLATE

La Mosquitia

Lago de Nicaragua

Mosquito
Gulf

Gulf of Darién

Colombian
Basin

Equator

Siqueiros Fracture Zone

Albatross
Plateau

Guatemala

Basin

Berlanga Rise

Cocos Ridge

Mosquito Gulf

Gulf of
Panama

Isthmus of Panama

Península
de Azuero

NAZCA PLATE

Cordillera Occidental

Colón Ridge

Panama
Basin

Cordillera Central

NORTH AMERICA

North America is the world's third largest continent, with a total area of 9,358,340 sq miles (24,238,000 sq km) including Greenland and the Caribbean Islands. It lies wholly within the Northern Hemisphere.

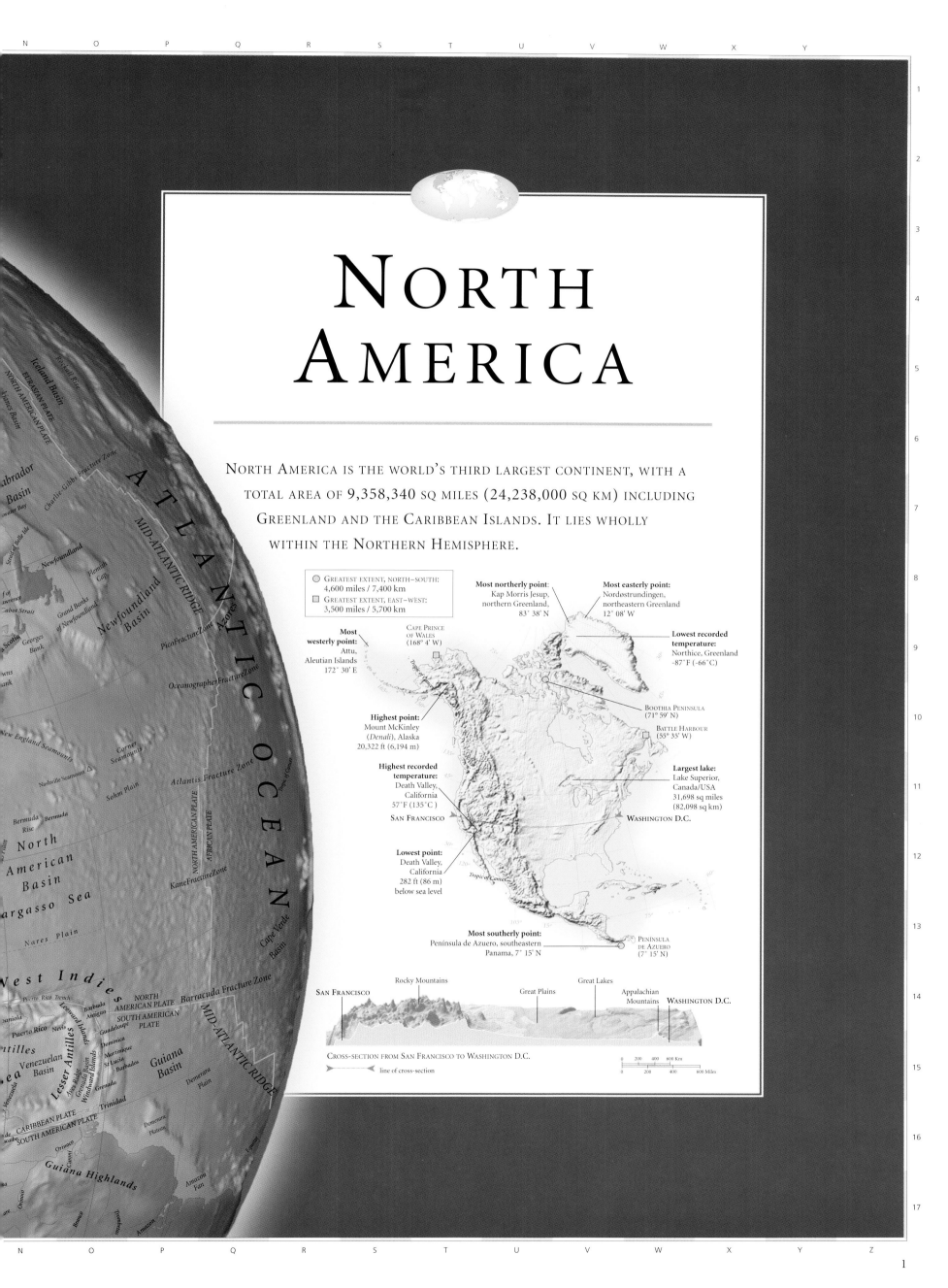

- ◉ Greatest extent, north–south: 4,600 miles / 7,400 km
- ▢ Greatest extent, east–west: 3,500 miles / 5,700 km

Most northerly point: Kap Morris Jesup, northern Greenland, 83° 38' N

Most easterly point: Nordøstrundingen, northeastern Greenland 12° 08' W

Most westerly point: Attu, Aleutian Islands 172° 30' E

CAPE PRINCE OF WALES (168° 4' W)

Lowest recorded temperature: Northice, Greenland -87°F (-66°C)

BOOTHIA PENINSULA (71° 59' N)

BATTLE HARBOUR (55° 35' W)

Highest point: Mount McKinley (*Denali*), Alaska 20,322 ft (6,194 m)

Largest lake: Lake Superior, Canada/USA 31,698 sq miles (82,098 sq km)

Highest recorded temperature: Death Valley, California 57°F (135°C)

SAN FRANCISCO

WASHINGTON D.C.

Lowest point: Death Valley, California 282 ft (86 m) below sea level

Most southerly point: Península de Azuero, southeastern Panama, 7° 15' N

PENÍNSULA DE AZUERO (7° 15' N)

SAN FRANCISCO — Rocky Mountains — Great Plains — Great Lakes — Appalachian Mountains — WASHINGTON D.C.

CROSS-SECTION FROM SAN FRANCISCO TO WASHINGTON D.C.

➤ line of cross-section

0 200 400 600 Km
0 200 400 600 Miles

Iceland Basin · EURASIAN PLATE · NORTH AMERICAN PLATE · Rockall Rise · Rosemary Bank · Aegir Basin · Labrador Basin · Charlie Gibbs Fracture Zone · MID-ATLANTIC RIDGE · ATLANTIC OCEAN · Newfoundland · Flemish Cap · Newfoundland Basin · Grand Banks of Newfoundland · Pico Fracture Zone · Azores · Oceanographer Fracture Zone · New England Seamounts · Corner Seamounts · Nashville Seamount · Sohm Plain · Atlantis Fracture Zone · NORTH AMERICAN PLATE · AFRICAN PLATE · Bermuda · Bermuda Rise · North American Basin · Kane Fracture Zone · Sargasso Sea · Nares Plain · Cape Verde Basin · West Indies · NORTH AMERICAN PLATE · Barracuda Fracture Zone · SOUTH AMERICAN PLATE · MID-ATLANTIC RIDGE · Puerto Rico Trench · Leeward Islands · Barbuda · Antigua · Guadeloupe · Dominica · Martinique · St Lucia · Barbados · Grenada · Lesser Antilles · Windward Islands · Grenada Basin · Venezuelan Basin · Guiana Basin · Demerara Plain · CARIBBEAN PLATE · SOUTH AMERICAN PLATE · Orinoco · Guiana Highlands · Amazon Fan · Tropic of Cancer

PHYSICAL NORTH AMERICA

The North American continent can be divided into a number of major structural areas: the Western Cordillera, the Canadian Shield, the Great Plains and Central Lowlands, and the Appalachians. Other smaller regions include the Gulf Atlantic Coastal Plain, which borders the southern coast of North America from the southern Appalachians to the Great Plains. This area includes the expanding Mississippi Delta. A chain of volcanic islands, running in an arc around the margin of the Caribbean Plate, lie to the east of the Gulf of Mexico.

THE CANADIAN SHIELD

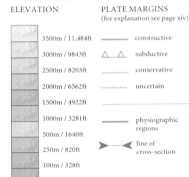

Spanning northern Canada and Greenland, this geologically stable plain forms the heart of the continent, containing rocks more than two billion years old. A long history of weathering and repeated glaciation has scoured the region, leaving flat plains, gentle hummocks, numerous small basins and lakes, and the bays and islands of the Arctic.

The hard bedrock of the Canadian Shield is slowly rising

Hudson Bay was depressed by the ice sheet to form North America's largest basin

Once overlain by sedimentary rocks, erosion has reexposed the ancient Laurentian Highlands

Section across the Canadian Shield showing where the ice sheet has depressed the underlying rock and formed bays and islands.

THE WESTERN CORDILLERA

About 80 million years ago the Pacific and North American plates collided, uplifting the Western Cordillera. This consists of the Aleutian, Coast, Cascade, and Sierra Nevada mountains, and the inland Rocky Mountains. These run parallel from the Arctic to Mexico.

The weight of the ice sheet, 1.8 miles (3 km) thick, has depressed the land to 0.6 miles (1 km) below sea level

This computer-generated view shows the ice-covered island of Greenland without its ice cap.

Strata have been thrust eastward along fault lines

The Rocky Mountain Trench is the longest linear fault on the continent

Volcanic rock

Cross-section through the Western Cordillera showing direction of mountain-building.

MAP KEY

ELEVATION

	3500m / 11,484ft
	3000m / 9843ft
	2500m / 8203ft
	2000m / 6562ft
	1500m / 4922ft
	1000m / 3281ft
	500m / 1640ft
	250m / 820ft
	100m / 328ft
	sea level

PLATE MARGINS
(for explanation see page xiv)

constructive
subductive
conservative
uncertain

physiographic regions

line of cross-section

SCALE 1:38,000,000
(projection: Lambert Azimuthal Equal Area)

THE GREAT PLAINS & CENTRAL LOWLANDS

DEPOSITS LEFT by retreating glaciers and rivers have made this vast flat area very fertile. In the north this is the result of glaciation, with deposits up to one mile (1.7 km) thick, covering the basement rock. To the south and west, the massive Missouri/Mississippi river system has for centuries deposited silt across the plains, creating broad, flat floodplains and deltas.

Sedimentary layers overlay domed basement rock

Upland rivers drain south toward the Mississippi Basin

Confluence of the Missouri and Mississippi Rivers

Section across the Great Plains and Central Lowlands showing river systems and structure.

THE APPALACHIANS

THE APPALACHIAN MOUNTAINS, uplifted some 400 million years ago, are some of the oldest in the world. They have been lowered and rounded by erosion and now slope gently toward the Atlantic across a broad coastal plain.

Horizontal strata

Sedimentary strata folded and faulted into ridges and valleys

Softer strata has been crumpled against the harder basement rock

Hard basement rock

Cross-section through the Appalachians showing the numerous folds, which have subsequently been weathered to create a rounded relief.

Map labels

ASIA
Bering Strait
Aleutian Islands
Bering Sea
Aleutian Range
Alaska Range
Gulf of Alaska
Brooks Range
Beaufort Sea
Mount McKinley 6194m
Mackenzie Delta
Mackenzie Mountains
Mackenzie
Great Bear Lake
Great Slave Lake
Lake Athabasca
Reindeer Lake
CANADIAN SHIELD
Hudson Bay
Hudson Strait
Foxe Basin
Baffin Island
Baffin Bay
Greenland
ATLANTIC OCEAN
Davis Strait
Labrador Sea
Labrador
Laurentian Highlands
Newfoundland
Nova Scotia
St Lawrence
Cape Cod
Lake Winnipeg
Lake Manitoba
Lake Superior
Lake Huron
Lake Michigan
Lake Ontario
Lake Erie
Great Lakes
GREAT PLAINS
CENTRAL LOWLANDS
ROCKY MOUNTAINS
WESTERN CORDILLERA
COAST MOUNTAINS
NORTH AMERICAN PLATE
PACIFIC PLATE
PACIFIC OCEAN
Mount Rainier 4392m
Mount St Helens 2549m
Cascade Range
Great Basin
Great Salt Lake
Coast Ranges
Sierra Nevada
San Joaquin
San Andreas Fault
Death Valley 86m
Mojave Desert
Grand Canyon
Colorado Plateau
Colorado
Missouri
Ohio
Arkansas
Mississippi
APPALACHIAN MOUNTAINS
APPALACHIANS
GULF ATLANTIC COASTAL PLAIN
Sonoran Desert
Gulf of California
Lower California
Sierra Madre Occidental
Rio Grande
Sierra Madre Oriental
Mississippi Delta
Gulf of Mexico
Citlaltépetl 5700m
Sierra Madre del Sur
Yucatan Peninsula
NORTH AMERICAN PLATE
CARIBBEAN PLATE
COCOS PLATE
Isthmus of Panama
Lago de Nicaragua
Caribbean Sea
Greater Antilles
Lesser Antilles
West Indies
SOUTH AMERICAN PLATE
SOUTH AMERICA

CLIMATE

"Tornado alley" in the Mississippi Valley suffers frequent tornadoes.

NORTH AMERICA'S climate includes extremes ranging from freezing Arctic conditions in Alaska and Greenland, to desert in the southwest, and tropical conditions in southeastern Florida, the Caribbean, and Central America. Central and southern regions can experience severe storms including tornadoes and hurricanes.

Much of the southwest is semi-desert, receiving less than 12 inches (300 mm) of rainfall a year.

Climate
- ice cap
- tundra
- subarctic
- cool continental
- warm humid
- semiarid
- arid
- humid equatorial
- tropical
- ☼ daily hours of sunshine, January
- ☼ daily hours of sunshine, July
- → direction of hurricanes
- ⊙ tornado zones

TEMPERATURE

Average January temperature

Average July temperature

Temperature
- below –22°F (–30°C)
- –22 to –4°F (–30 to –20°C)
- –4 to 14°F (–20 to –10°C)
- 14 to 32°F (–10 to 0°C)
- 32 to 50°F (0 to 10°C)
- 50°F (10 to 20°C)
- 68 to 86°F (20 to 30°C)
- above 86°F (30°C)

RAINFALL

Average January rainfall

Average July rainfall

Rainfall
- 0 – 1 in (0 – 25 mm)
- 1 – 2 in (25 – 50 mm)
- 2 – 4 in (50 – 100 mm)
- 4 – 8 in (100 – 200 mm)
- 8 – 12 in (200 – 300 mm)
- 12 – 16 in (300 – 400 mm)
- 16 – 20 in (400 – 500 mm)
- above 20 in (500 mm)

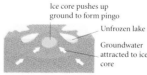

The lush, green mountains of the Lesser Antilles receive annual rainfall of up to 360 inches (9,000 mm).

Map labels: Nome, Fairbanks, Aklavik, Coppermine, Resolute, Eismitte, Haines Junction, Frobisher Bay, Juneau, Fort Vermillon, Churchill, Happy Valley - Goose Bay, Fort St John, Torbay, Vancouver, Winnipeg, Montréal, Medicine Hat, Toronto, Boise, Sioux City, New York, Salt Lake City, Denver, San Francisco, Cape Hatteras, Las Vegas, Phoenix, Atlanta, Los Angeles, Little Rock, Houston, Miami, Guaymas, New Orleans, Nassau, Chihuahua, Santo Domingo, Fort-de-France, Mérida, Kingston, Acapulco, San Salvador, San José

SHAPING THE CONTINENT

GLACIAL PROCESSES affect much of northern Canada, Greenland, and the Western Cordillera. Along the western coast of North America, Central America, and the Caribbean, underlying plates moving together lead to earthquakes and volcanic eruptions. The vast river systems, fed by mountain streams, constantly erode and deposit material along their paths.

VOLCANIC ACTIVITY

[1] Mount St. Helens volcano (right) in the Cascade Range erupted violently in May 1980, killing 57 people and leveling large areas of forest. The lateral blast filled a valley with debris for 15 miles (25 km).

- Molten rock at volcano's core
- Vertical eruption
- Lateral explosion increases extent of damage
- Landslide fills valley

VOLCANIC ACTIVITY: ERUPTION OF MOUNT ST. HELENS

SEISMIC ACTIVITY

[5] The San Andreas Fault (above) places much of the North America's West Coast under constant threat from earthquakes. It is caused by the Pacific Plate grinding at a faster rate past the North American Plate, though in the same direction.

- Pacific Plate
- San Andreas Fault
- Fault is caused by faster movement of Pacific Plate
- North American Plate

SEISMIC ACTIVITY: ACTION OF THE SAN ANDREAS FAULT

RIVER EROSION

[6] The Grand Canyon (above) in the Colorado Plateau was created by the downward erosion of the Colorado River, combined with the gradual uplift of the plateau, over the past 30 million years. The contours of the canyon formed as the softer rock layers eroded into gentle slopes, and the hard rock layers into cliffs. The depth varies from 3,855–6,560 ft (1,175–2,000 m).

- Soft rock is easily eroded into gentle slopes
- Hard rock resists erosion
- Colorado River cuts down through rock

RIVER EROSION: FORMATION OF THE GRAND CANYON

PERIGLACIATION

[2] The ground in the far north is nearly always frozen: the surface thaws only in summer. This freeze–thaw process produces features such as pingos (left); formed by the freezing of groundwater. With each successive winter ice accumulates, producing a mound with a core of ice.

- Ice core pushes up ground to form pingo
- Unfrozen lake
- Groundwater attracted to ice core

PERIGLACIATION: FORMATION OF A PINGO IN THE MACKENZIE DELTA

THE EVOLVING LANDSCAPE

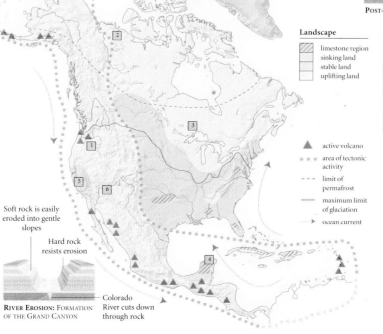

Landscape
- limestone region
- sinking land
- stable land
- uplifting land
- ▲ active volcano
- ⚬ area of tectonic activity
- --- limit of permafrost
- — maximum limit of glaciation
- ⚬ ocean current

POST-GLACIAL LAKES

[3] A chain of lakes from Great Bear Lake to the Great Lakes (above) was created as the ice retreated northward. Glaciers scoured hollows in the softer lowland rock. Glacial deposits at the lip of the hollows, and ridges of harder rock, trapped water to form lakes.

- Retreating glacier
- Ice-scoured hollow filled with glacial meltwater to form a lake
- Harder rock creates a barrier between lakes
- Softer lowland rock

POST-GLACIAL LAKES: FORMATION OF THE GREAT LAKES

WEATHERING

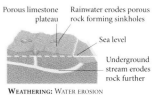

[4] The Yucatan Peninsula is a vast, flat limestone plateau in southern Mexico. Weathering action from both rainwater and underground streams has enlarged fractures in the rock to form caves and hollows, called sinkholes (above).

- Porous limestone plateau
- Rainwater erodes porous rock forming sinkholes
- Sea level
- Underground stream erodes rock further

WEATHERING: WATER EROSION ON THE YUCATAN PENINSULA

POLITICAL NORTH AMERICA

Democracy is well established in some parts of the continent but is a recent phenomenon in others. The economically dominant nations of Canada and the US have a long democratic tradition but elsewhere, notably in the countries of Central America, political turmoil has been more common. In Nicaragua and Haiti, harsh dictatorships have only recently been superseded by democratically elected governments. North America's largest countries, Canada, Mexico, and the US have federal–state systems, sharing political power between national and state governments. The US has intervened militarily on several occasions in Central America and the Caribbean to protect its strategic interests.

TRANSPORTATION

In the 19th century, railroads opened up the North American continent. Air transportation is now more common for long-distance passenger travel, although railroads are still extensively used for bulk freight transportation. Waterways like the Mississippi River are important for the transportation of bulk materials, and the Panama Canal is a vital link between the Pacific and Atlantic Oceans. In the 20th century, road transportation has increased dramatically, with the introduction of cheap, mass-produced cars and extensive highway construction.

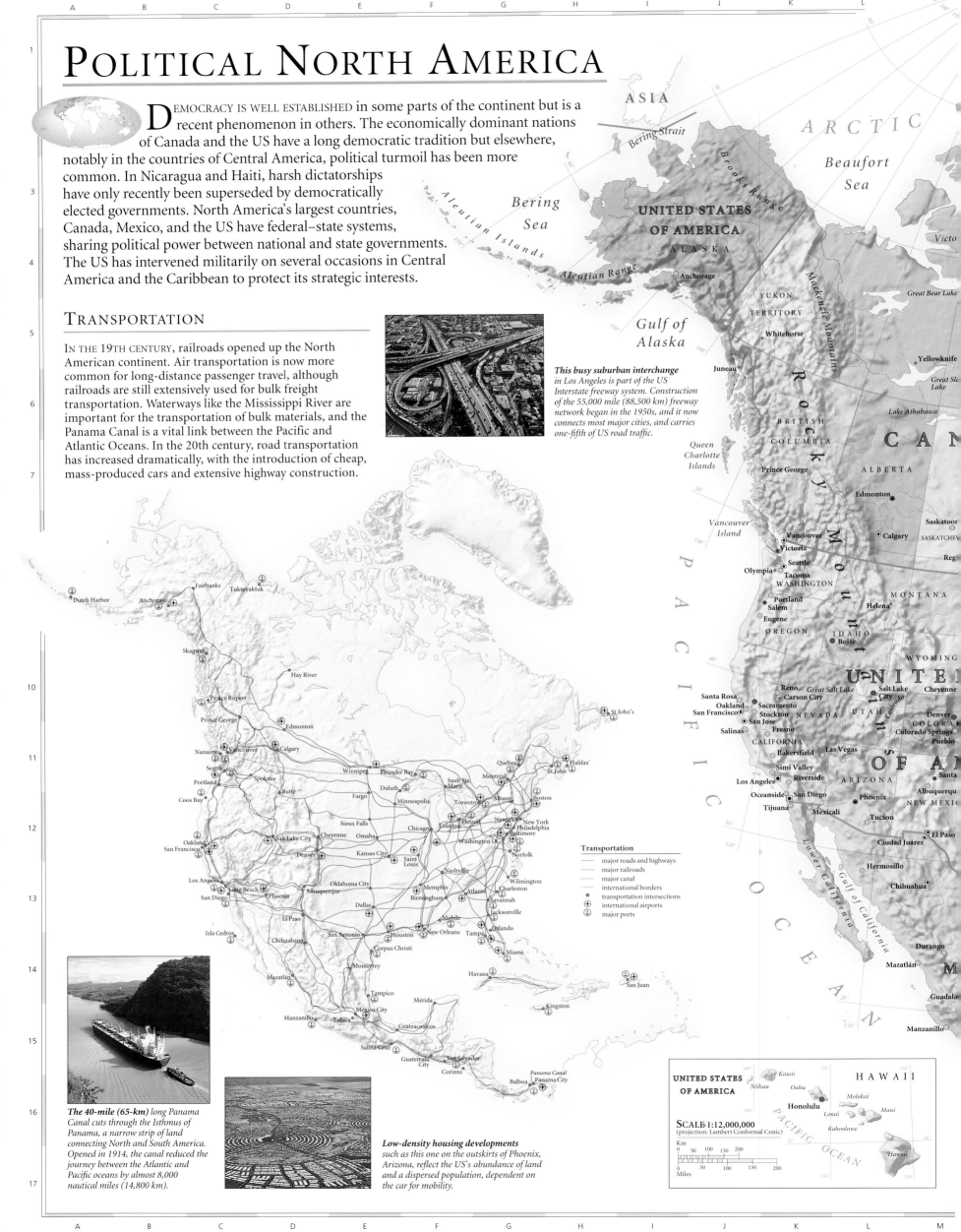

This busy suburban interchange in Los Angeles is part of the US Interstate freeway system. Construction of the 55,000 mile (88,500 km) freeway network began in the 1950s, and it now connects most major cities, and carries one-fifth of US road traffic.

Transportation
—— major roads and highways
—— major railroads
—— major canal
—— international borders
• transportation intersections
⊕ international airports
⊕ major ports

The 40-mile (65-km) long Panama Canal cuts through the Isthmus of Panama, a narrow strip of land connecting North and South America. Opened in 1914, the canal reduced the journey between the Atlantic and Pacific oceans by almost 8,000 nautical miles (14,800 km).

Low-density housing developments such as this one on the outskirts of Phoenix, Arizona, reflect the US's abundance of land and a dispersed population, dependent on the car for mobility.

UNITED STATES OF AMERICA

SCALE 1:12,000,000
(projection: Lambert Conformal Conic)

HAWAII

S T U V Y Z

Language groups
- Native American
- Germanic
- Romance
- Eskimo-Aleut
- Uninhabited

ESKIMO-ALEUT
ATHABASCAN
ALGONQUIN
FRENCH
ENGLISH
ENGLISH/SPANISH
UTO-AZTECAN
MAYAN
SPANISH
FRENCH/ENGLISH
ENGLISH SPANISH
ENGLISH
FRENCH
CREOLE
CREOLE

Ellesmere Island

Baffin Bay

Greenland (to Denmark)

Baffin Island

Davis Strait

NUUK

Foxe Basin

NORTHWEST TERRITORIES

Labrador Sea

MAP KEY

POPULATION
- ◼ above 5 million
- ◼ 1 million to 5 million
- ◻ 500,000 to 1 million
- ◻ 100,000 to 500,000
- ⊕ 50,000 to 100,000
- ○ 10,000 to 50,000
- below 10,000
- ● State / Province capital
- ○ Country capital

BORDERS
- full international border
- state border

Hudson Strait

Hudson Bay

Reindeer Lake

MANITOBA

Lake Winnipeg

QUÉBEC

Newfoundland

St. John's

NEWFOUNDLAND AND LABRADOR

ONTARIO

Winnipeg

Thunder Bay

Lake Superior

St Pierre & Miquelon *(to France)*

PRINCE EDWARD ISLAND

NEW BRUNSWICK

Charlottetown

Québec

Fredericton

NOVA SCOTIA

Halifax

MAINE

NORTH DAKOTA

MINNESOTA

Bismarck

Lake Huron

MICHIGAN

Oshawa

Toronto

Hamilton

Lake Ontario

Montréal

St. Lawrence

OTTAWA

Augusta

VERMONT

NEW HAMPSHIRE

Concord

Boston

Albany

Rochester

NEW YORK

Providence

MASSACHUSETTS

RHODE ISLAND

Hartford

CONNECTICUT

Saint Paul

Minneapolis

WISCONSIN

Madison

Milwaukee

Lansing

Lake Erie

Detroit

Buffalo

Newark

New York

Sioux Falls

SOUTH DAKOTA

IOWA

Chicago

Toledo

Cleveland

PENNSYLVANIA

Philadelphia

NEW JERSEY

Trenton

NEBRASKA

Des Moines

Davenport

ILLINOIS

INDIANA

OHIO

Columbus

Pittsburgh

Harrisburg

Baltimore

Dover

DELAWARE

Lincoln

Omaha

Springfield

Indianapolis

Cincinnati

WEST VIRGINIA

WASHINGTON DC

MARYLAND

Annapolis

Topeka

Kansas City

Saint Louis

Louisville

Frankfort

Charleston

Richmond

Jefferson City

Ohio

KANSAS

MISSOURI

Evansville

KENTUCKY

VIRGINIA

Norfolk

Wichita

Springfield

Nashville

Raleigh

Arkansas

TENNESSEE

NORTH CAROLINA

Charlotte

Tulsa

ARKANSAS

Memphis

Columbia

SOUTH CAROLINA

Oklahoma City

Little Rock

Birmingham

Atlanta

GEORGIA

OKLAHOMA

MISSISSIPPI

ALABAMA

Columbus

Savannah

Fort Worth

Dallas

Shreveport

Jackson

Montgomery

TEXAS

LOUISIANA

Jacksonville

Austin

Baton Rouge

Mobile

Talahassee

Houston

New Orleans

San Antonio

Orlando

Tampa

Mississippi Delta

Saint Petersburg

FLORIDA

Corpus Christi

Fort Lauderdale

Miami

Rio Grande

Monterrey

Gulf of Mexico

NASSAU

BAHAMAS

West Indies

British Virgin Islands

Virgin Islands *(to US)*

Anguilla *(to UK)*

Tampico

HAVANA

Santa Clara

CUBA

Santiago de Cuba

Turks & Caicos Islands *(to UK)*

Puerto Rico *(to US)*

SAN JUAN

DOMINICAN REPUBLIC

ANTIGUA & BARBUDA

Guadeloupe *(to France)*

Greater Antilles

HAITI

PORT-AU-PRINCE

SANTO DOMINGO

ST KITTS & NEVIS

Montserrat *(to UK)*

DOMINICA

Martinique *(to France)*

ST LUCIA

San Luis Potosí

Mérida

Yucatan Peninsula

Cayman Islands *(to UK)*

Guapuato

Querétaro

Morelia

Toluca

MEXICO CITY

Puebla

JAMAICA

KINGSTON

Navassa Island *(to US)*

BARBADOS

ST VINCENT & THE GRENADINES

GRENADA

Villahermosa

Acapulco

Caribbean Sea

Aruba *(to Neth.)*

Lesser Antilles

TRINIDAD & TOBAGO

PORT-OF-SPAIN

BELIZE

BELMOPAN

GUATEMALA

GUATEMALA CITY

HONDURAS

San Pedro Sula

TEGUCIGALPA

SAN SALVADOR

EL SALVADOR

NICARAGUA

Lake Nicaragua

MANAGUA

Netherlands Antilles *(to Neth.)*

SOUTH AMERICA

SAN JOSÉ

PANAMA CITY

COSTA RICA

PANAMA

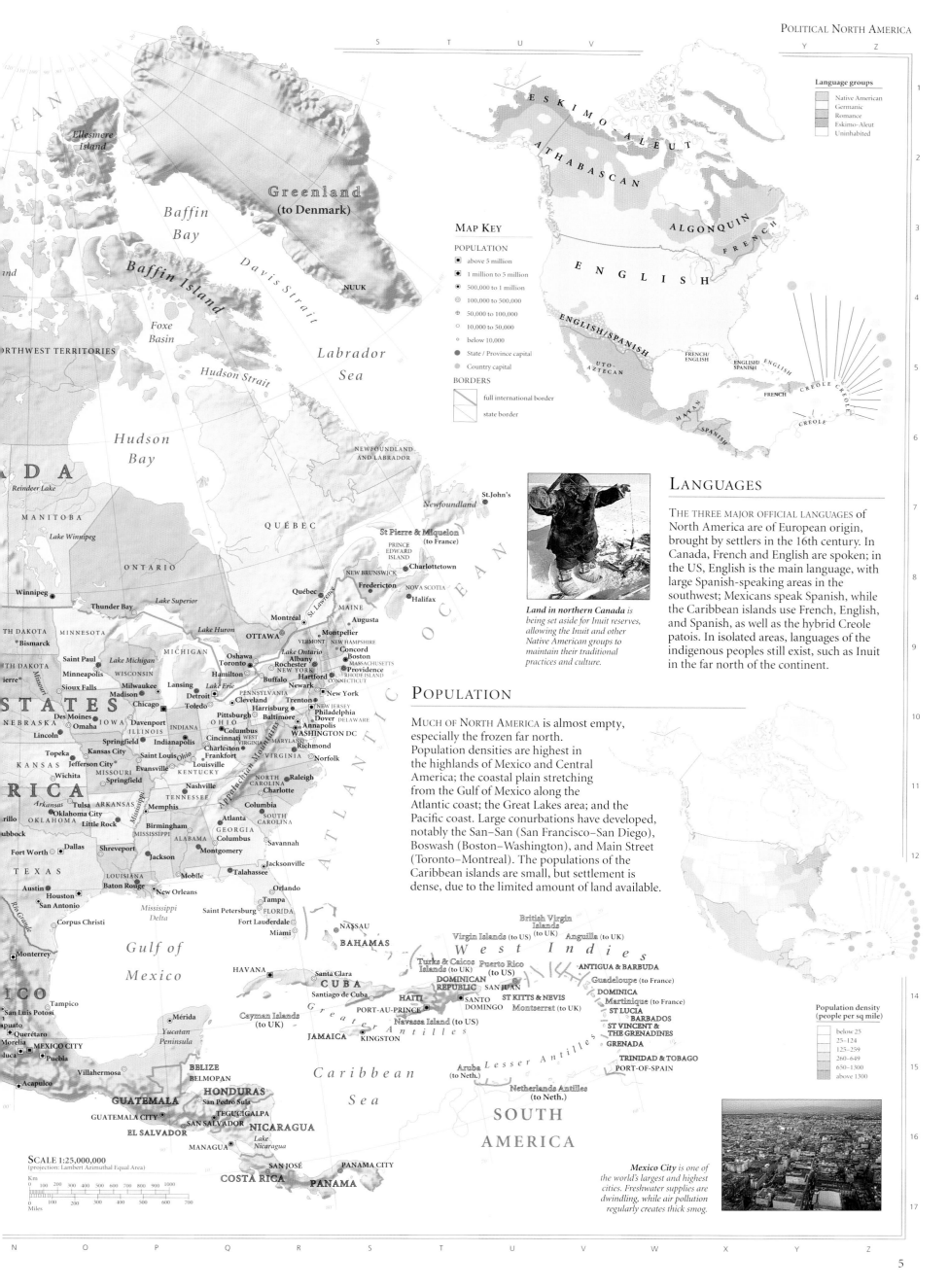

Land in northern Canada is being set aside for Inuit reserves, allowing the Inuit and other Native American groups to maintain their traditional practices and culture.

LANGUAGES

THE THREE MAJOR OFFICIAL LANGUAGES of North America are of European origin, brought by settlers in the 16th century. In Canada, French and English are spoken; in the US, English is the main language, with large Spanish-speaking areas in the southwest; Mexicans speak Spanish, while the Caribbean islands use French, English, and Spanish, as well as the hybrid Creole patois. In isolated areas, languages of the indigenous peoples still exist, such as Inuit in the far north of the continent.

POPULATION

MUCH OF NORTH AMERICA is almost empty, especially the frozen far north. Population densities are highest in the highlands of Mexico and Central America; the coastal plain stretching from the Gulf of Mexico along the Atlantic coast; the Great Lakes area; and the Pacific coast. Large conurbations have developed, notably the San–San (San Francisco–San Diego), Boswash (Boston–Washington), and Main Street (Toronto–Montreal). The populations of the Caribbean islands are small, but settlement is dense, due to the limited amount of land available.

Population density (people per sq mile)
- below 25
- 25–124
- 125–259
- 260–649
- 650–1300
- above 1300

Mexico City is one of the world's largest and highest cities. Freshwater supplies are dwindling, while air pollution regularly creates thick smog.

SCALE 1:25,000,000
(projection: Lambert Azimuthal Equal Area)

Km 0 100 200 300 400 500 600 700 800 900 1000

Miles 0 100 200 300 400 500 600 700

N O P Q R S T U V W X Y Z

NORTH AMERICAN RESOURCES

THE TWO NORTHERN COUNTRIES of Canada and the US are richly endowed with natural resources that have helped to fuel economic development. The US is the world's largest economy, although today it is facing stiff competition from the Far East. Mexico has relied on oil revenues but there are hopes that the North American Free Trade Agreement (NAFTA) will encourage trade growth with Canada and the US. The poorer countries of Central America and the Caribbean depend largely on cash crops and tourism.

STANDARD OF LIVING

THE US AND CANADA have one of the highest overall standards of living in the world. However, many people still live in poverty, especially in urban ghettos and some rural areas. Central America and the Caribbean are markedly poorer than their wealthier northern neighbors. Haiti is the poorest country in the western hemisphere.

Standard of Living
(UN Human Development Index)

high

low

INDUSTRY

THE MODERN, INDUSTRIALIZED economies of the US and Canada contrast sharply with those of Mexico, Central America, and the Caribbean. Manufacturing is especially important in the US; vehicle production is concentrated around the Great Lakes, while electronic and hi-tech industries are increasingly found in the western and southern states. Mexico depends on oil exports and assembly work, taking advantage of cheap labor. Many Central American and Caribbean countries rely heavily on agricultural exports.

After its purchase from Russia in 1867, Alaska's frozen lands were largely ignored by the US. Oil reserves similar in magnitude to those in eastern Texas were discovered in Prudhoe Bay, Alaska, in 1968, but freezing temperatures and a fragile environment hamper oil extraction.

South of San Francisco, "Silicon Valley" is both a national and international center for hi-tech industries, electronic industries, and research institutions.

Multinational companies rely on cheap labor and tax benefits to assemble vehicles in Mexican factories.

Fish such as cod, flounder, and plaice are caught in the Grand Banks off the Newfoundland coast, and processed in many North Atlantic coastal settlements.

The twin towers of the World Trade Center dominate the Manhattan skyline. New York is one of the world's leading trade and finance centers.

Industry

✈ aerospace	🖨 printing & publishing	
♦ brewing	⚗ research & development	
🚗 car/vehicle manufacture	⚓ shipbuilding	
🧪 chemicals	⚙ sugar processing	
🛡 defense	☩ textiles	
💻 electronics	🌲 timber processing	
⚙ engineering	🚬 tobacco processing	
🎬 film industry		
💲 finance	♦ coal	
🍴 food processing	⚒ oil	
🖥 hi-tech industry	◊ gas	
⚒ iron & steel	• industrial cities	
💊 pharmaceuticals	▨ major industrial areas	

GNP per capita (US$)

0–1999
2000–4999
5000–9999
10,000–19,999
20,000–24,999
25,000+

Map labels

ARCTIC OCEAN

RUSS. FED.

Bering Strait

Beaufort Sea

Greenland (to Denmark)

Baffin Bay

Bering Sea

Prudhoe Bay

U.S.A

Gulf of Alaska

Labrador Sea

Hudson Strait

Hudson Bay

CANADA

Vancouver
Calgary
Seattle
Winnipeg
Portland
Montréal
Boston
Albany
New York
Minneapolis
Toronto
Buffalo
Milwaukee
Detroit
Cleveland
Chicago
Pittsburgh
Philadelphia
Dayton
Cincinnati
Baltimore

UNITED STATES OF AMERICA

San Francisco
Saint Louis
Denver
Kansas City
Wichita
Nashville
Greensboro
Charlotte
Tulsa
Los Angeles
Phoenix
Birmingham
Atlanta
San Diego
Tijuana
Ciudad Juárez
El Paso
Dallas
Houston
Jacksonville
New Orleans
Orlando
Tampa
Miami

PACIFIC OCEAN

ATLANTIC OCEAN

Monterrey

Gulf of Mexico

BAHAMAS

MEXICO

Guadalajara

Mexico City

West Indies

Turks & Caicos Islands (to UK)
Virgin Islands (to US)
British Virgin Islands (to UK)
Anguilla (to UK)
Puerto Rico (to US)
ST KITTS & NEVIS
ANTIGUA & BARBUDA
Montserrat (to UK)
Guadeloupe (to France)
DOMINICA
ST LUCIA
BARBADOS
ST VINCENT & THE GRENADINES
GRENADA
TRINIDAD & TOBAGO
Port-of-Spain

CUBA
Havana
HAITI
Port-au-Prince
DOMINICAN REPUBLIC
San Juan
Santo Domingo
Cayman Islands (to UK)
JAMAICA
Navassa Island (to US)
Greater Antilles
Lesser Antilles
Aruba (to Neth.)
Netherlands Antilles (to Neth.)
Caribbean Sea

BELIZE
GUATEMALA
Guatemala City
HONDURAS
Tegucigalpa
EL SALVADOR
San Salvador
NICARAGUA
Managua
COSTA RICA
San José
PANAMA
Panama City
VENEZUELA
COLOMBIA

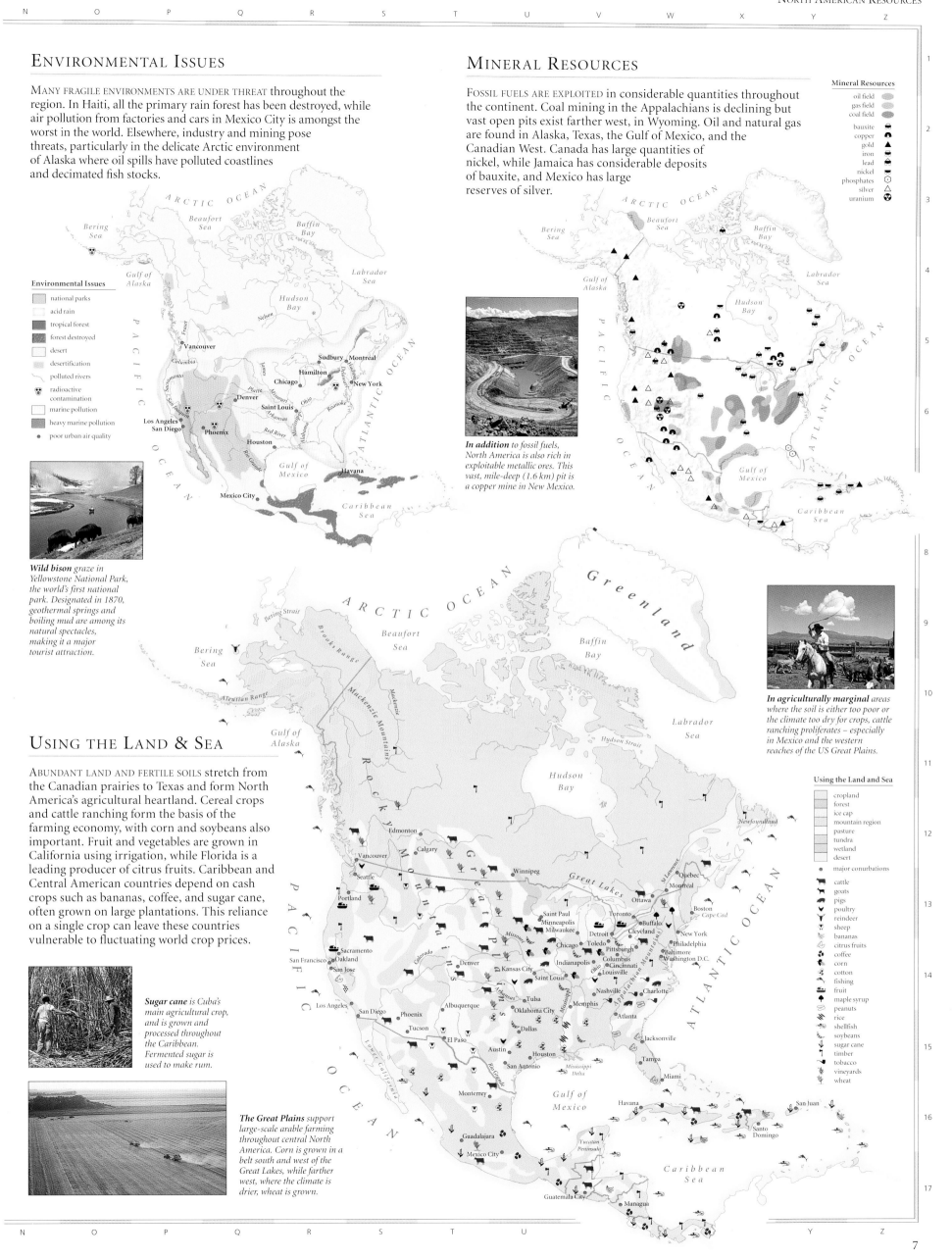

ENVIRONMENTAL ISSUES

MANY FRAGILE ENVIRONMENTS ARE UNDER THREAT throughout the region. In Haiti, all the primary rain forest has been destroyed, while air pollution from factories and cars in Mexico City is amongst the worst in the world. Elsewhere, industry and mining pose threats, particularly in the delicate Arctic environment of Alaska where oil spills have polluted coastlines and decimated fish stocks.

Environmental Issues
- national parks
- acid rain
- tropical forest
- forest destroyed
- desert
- desertification
- polluted rivers
- radioactive contamination
- marine pollution
- heavy marine pollution
- poor urban air quality

Wild bison graze in Yellowstone National Park, the world's first national park. Designated in 1870, geothermal springs and boiling mud are among its natural spectacles, making it a major tourist attraction.

MINERAL RESOURCES

FOSSIL FUELS ARE EXPLOITED in considerable quantities throughout the continent. Coal mining in the Appalachians is declining but vast open pits exist farther west, in Wyoming. Oil and natural gas are found in Alaska, Texas, the Gulf of Mexico, and the Canadian West. Canada has large quantities of nickel, while Jamaica has considerable deposits of bauxite, and Mexico has large reserves of silver.

Mineral Resources
- oil field
- gas field
- coal field
- bauxite
- copper
- gold
- iron
- lead
- nickel
- phosphates
- silver
- uranium

In addition to fossil fuels, North America is also rich in exploitable metallic ores. This vast, mile-deep (1.6 km) pit is a copper mine in New Mexico.

In agriculturally marginal areas where the soil is either too poor or the climate too dry for crops, cattle ranching proliferates – especially in Mexico and the western reaches of the US Great Plains.

USING THE LAND & SEA

ABUNDANT LAND AND FERTILE SOILS stretch from the Canadian prairies to Texas and form North America's agricultural heartland. Cereal crops and cattle ranching form the basis of the farming economy, with corn and soybeans also important. Fruit and vegetables are grown in California using irrigation, while Florida is a leading producer of citrus fruits. Caribbean and Central American countries depend on cash crops such as bananas, coffee, and sugar cane, often grown on large plantations. This reliance on a single crop can leave these countries vulnerable to fluctuating world crop prices.

Using the Land and Sea
- cropland
- forest
- ice cap
- mountain region
- pasture
- tundra
- wetland
- desert
- major conurbations
- cattle
- goats
- pigs
- poultry
- reindeer
- sheep
- bananas
- citrus fruits
- coffee
- corn
- cotton
- fishing
- fruit
- maple syrup
- peanuts
- rice
- shellfish
- soybeans
- sugar cane
- timber
- tobacco
- vineyards
- wheat

Sugar cane is Cuba's main agricultural crop, and is grown and processed throughout the Caribbean. Fermented sugar is used to make rum.

The Great Plains support large-scale arable farming throughout central North America. Corn is grown in a belt south and west of the Great Lakes, while farther west, where the climate is drier, wheat is grown.

CANADA: WESTERN PROVINCES

Alberta, British Columbia, Manitoba, Saskatchewan, Yukon Territory

THE MOUNTAINS OF THE WEST COAST, incorporating British Columbia and the Yukon Territory, descend into the vast, flat prairies of Alberta, Saskatchewan, and Manitoba. The empty lands and fertile soils of the prairie provinces attracted migrants, and the descendants of early European immigrants still make up a large proportion of the population. The mechanization of agriculture has reduced the need for labor, and rural population densities remain low. The majority of the people live within 100 miles (160 km) of the southern Canada–US border, and in British Columbia, one of the leading Canadian provinces in terms of economic wealth. The Yukon Territory, in the far north, remains a relatively unspoiled wilderness, containing large, untapped mineral reserves. This province has a significant population of Native American people, many of whom maintain a traditional lifestyle.

USING THE LAND & SEA

WHEAT FARMING IS THE MAINSTAY of the economy of Alberta, Manitoba and Saskatchewan, which contain 82% of Canada's farmland. Cattle are also raised on the prairies. Forestry and fishing are the most prominent resource-based industries in British Columbia. Despite the mountainous terrain, fruit and specialized grains can be grown in the Okanagan and Fraser valleys.

Land use and agricultural distribution

- cattle
- cereals
- fishing
- fruit
- timber
- major towns

- pasture
- cropland
- forest
- wetland
- barren
- tundra

THE URBAN/RURAL POPULATION DIVIDE

77% urban | 23% rural

0 10 20 30 40 50 60 70 80 90 100

POPULATION DENSITY
6 people per sq mile
(2 people per sq km)

TOTAL LAND AREA
1,224,449 sq miles
(3,172,150 sq km)

Large, highly mechanized and often very specialized farms, requiring huge investment but little labor, characterize modern farming in the prairies.

TRANSPORTATION & INDUSTRY

THE WESTERN PROVINCES contain a wealth of mineral resources. Alberta holds the bulk of Canada's fossil fuels; the other provinces contain reserves of metallic ores, such as zinc, lead, and silver. Isolation from markets has slowed the development of manufacturing, restricting it to the large cities like Vancouver, Winnipeg, and Calgary. Hydroelectric power is widely exploited, though there is increasing concern about potential ecological damage.

TRANSPORTATION NETWORK

82,438 miles (135,145 km)

6,459 miles (10,401 km)

10,811 miles (17,410 km)

None

The transportation network of the western provinces is dominated by east–west routes that weave through mountain passes and spread across the plains. Access to some northern areas is restricted to air travel.

Major industry and infrastructure

- aerospace
- chemicals
- coal
- engineering
- food processing
- hydroelectric power
- mining
- oil & gas
- timber processing
- major towns
- international airports
- major roads
- major industrial areas

The Fraser River valley is a major area of settlement in British Columbia. Railroads cross the Rocky Mountains via this valley.

Established in 1907, Jasper National Park lies in the heart of the Rocky Mountains. It is noted for its spectacular alpine scenery and contains part of the large Columbia Icefield.

Much of the Yukon Territory is uninhabited tundra. Industry is based on the extraction of mineral resources, and to a lesser extent, on the scattered forests of the south.

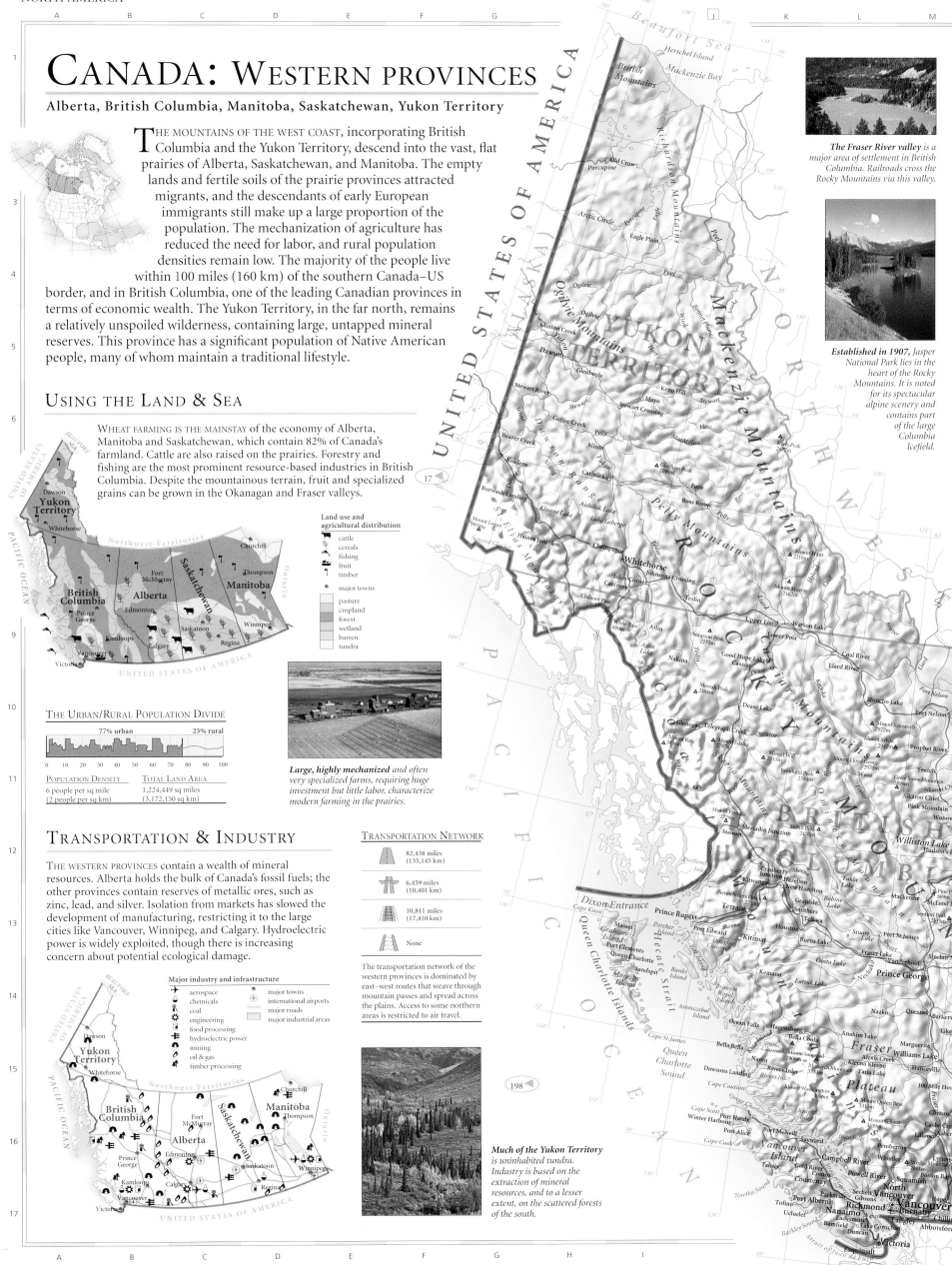

ENVIRONMENTAL ISSUES

MANY FRAGILE ENVIRONMENTS ARE UNDER THREAT throughout the region. In Haiti, all the primary rain forest has been destroyed, while air pollution from factories and cars in Mexico City is amongst the worst in the world. Elsewhere, industry and mining pose threats, particularly in the delicate Arctic environment of Alaska where oil spills have polluted coastlines and decimated fish stocks.

Environmental Issues
- national parks
- acid rain
- tropical forest
- forest destroyed
- desert
- desertification
- polluted rivers
- radioactive contamination
- marine pollution
- heavy marine pollution
- poor urban air quality

Wild bison graze in Yellowstone National Park, the world's first national park. Designated in 1870, geothermal springs and boiling mud are among its natural spectacles, making it a major tourist attraction.

MINERAL RESOURCES

FOSSIL FUELS ARE EXPLOITED in considerable quantities throughout the continent. Coal mining in the Appalachians is declining but vast open pits exist farther west, in Wyoming. Oil and natural gas are found in Alaska, Texas, the Gulf of Mexico, and the Canadian West. Canada has large quantities of nickel, while Jamaica has considerable deposits of bauxite, and Mexico has large reserves of silver.

Mineral Resources
- oil field
- gas field
- coal field
- bauxite
- copper
- gold
- iron
- lead
- nickel
- phosphates
- silver
- uranium

In addition to fossil fuels, North America is also rich in exploitable metallic ores. This vast, mile-deep (1.6 km) pit is a copper mine in New Mexico.

In agriculturally marginal areas where the soil is either too poor or the climate too dry for crops, cattle ranching proliferates – especially in Mexico and the western reaches of the US Great Plains.

USING THE LAND & SEA

ABUNDANT LAND AND FERTILE SOILS stretch from the Canadian prairies to Texas and form North America's agricultural heartland. Cereal crops and cattle ranching form the basis of the farming economy, with corn and soybeans also important. Fruit and vegetables are grown in California using irrigation, while Florida is a leading producer of citrus fruits. Caribbean and Central American countries depend on cash crops such as bananas, coffee, and sugar cane, often grown on large plantations. This reliance on a single crop can leave these countries vulnerable to fluctuating world crop prices.

Using the Land and Sea
- cropland
- forest
- ice cap
- mountain region
- pasture
- tundra
- wetland
- desert
- major conurbations
- cattle
- goats
- pigs
- poultry
- reindeer
- sheep
- bananas
- citrus fruits
- coffee
- corn
- cotton
- fishing
- fruit
- maple syrup
- peanuts
- rice
- shellfish
- soybeans
- sugar cane
- timber
- tobacco
- vineyards
- wheat

Sugar cane is Cuba's main agricultural crop, and is grown and processed throughout the Caribbean. Fermented sugar is used to make rum.

The Great Plains support large-scale arable farming throughout central North America. Corn is grown in a belt south and west of the Great Lakes, while farther west, where the climate is drier, wheat is grown.

THE LANDSCAPE

THE MASSIVE ROCKY MOUNTAINS form a continental divide between rivers flowing eastward and westward. The interior plains lie east of the mountains, stretching from the Arctic Circle south into the US. Covered with glacial deposits from the last Ice Age, these are interspersed with hilly regions and long, steep escarpments.

MAP KEY

POPULATION
- ◉ 500,000 to 1 million
- ◎ 100,000 to 500,000
- ⊕ 50,000 to 100,000
- ○ 10,000 to 50,000
- ○ below 10,000

ELEVATION
- 6000m / 19,686ft
- 4000m / 13,124ft
- 3000m / 9843ft
- 2000m / 6562ft
- 1000m / 3281ft
- 500m / 1640ft
- 250m / 820ft
- 100m / 328ft
- sea level

SCALE 1:7,500,000
(projection: Lambert Conformal Conic)

Km
0 25 50 100 150 200 250

Miles
0 25 50 100 150 200 250

Mount Logan rises 19,551 ft (5,959 m). It is the highest peak in Canada.

The Rocky Mountain Trench is the longest linear fault in the world. It has formed a straight, flat-bottomed valley between 2 and 9 miles (4–15 km) wide, and up to 3,280 ft (1,000 m) deep.

Hundreds of islands dot the fjord-indented coast of British Columbia; the largest is Vancouver Island.

Three major passes cut through the Rocky Mountains: Yellowhead, Kicking Horse, and Crowsnest. They are all used as transportation routes through the mountains.

The Cypress Hills rise to 4,806 ft (1,465 m) above the surrounding plain. Having escaped the last glaciation, they contain unique plant and animal life. The silvery lupine, bunchberry, and lodgepole pine all grow in the cool, moist climate of the hills.

The Columbia Icefield in the Rocky Mountains is the source of two major rivers, the Athabasca and the North Saskatchewan.

The badlands of Alberta were created when east-flowing rivers, swollen by meltwater at the end of the last Ice Age, cut deep, wide canyons producing eroded, barren landscapes.

South Saskatchewan River

Vegetated island
River flow is diverted by deposited sediments
Bar
Sand flat

Braided rivers are shallow and fast-flowing. The interlaced branches form when excess sediments, which can no longer be transported, are deposited. The sediments collect in the river channel forming bars and sand flats. Islands form when the bars are colonized by vegetation.

The Alberta and Saskatchewan plains bear strong testament to past glaciations. The Assiniboine, Saskatchewan, and Qu'Appelle Rivers occupy flat-bottomed, steep-sided valleys eroded during the last Ice Age by glacial meltwater.

Across the tundra of northern Manitoba, widespread permafrost inhibits water from permeating the soil. This causes rivers like the Churchill to flow in many channels, which can be frozen for up to six months during the winter.

The Nelson and Churchill rivers drain northward across the Canadian Shield to Hudson Bay. The shield covers three-fifths of Saskatchewan.

Setting Lake

Ancient granite outcrops, part of the Canadian Shield, are scattered across the surface of Setting Lake, which was initially formed by meltwater from the last Ice Age.

The lowlands of Manitoba are a basin that once held the vast post-glacial Lake Agassiz, remnants of which include Lake Winnipeg, Lake Winnipegosis, and Lake Manitoba.

CANADA: EASTERN PROVINCES

New Brunswick, Newfoundland and Labrador, Nova Scotia, Ontario,
Prince Edward Island, Québec, *St. Pierre & Miquelon* (to France)

COLONIZED BY BOTH THE ENGLISH AND THE FRENCH during the 16th century, Canada's eastern provinces are still marked by their dual influences. They contain the last fragment of once-sizeable French territories, the islands of St. Pierre and Miquelon. French remains Canada's second official language and Québec's first language. The population of the eastern provinces is highly concentrated in the south, especially along the border with the US. A recent decline in fishing in the Atlantic provinces has encouraged a steady flow of westerly migration to more properous regions. The north, around Hudson Bay, remains snow-covered for most of the year and the indigenous Inuit make up the bulk of its sparse population.

Rocher Percé is 290 ft (88 m) high. Lying off the southeastern coast of Québec, it is a sanctuary for seabirds.

SCALE 1:7,000,000
(projection: Lambert Conformal Conic)

Km
0   25   50   100   150   200   250

Miles
0   25   50   100   150   200   250

MAP KEY

POPULATION

- 500,000 to 1 million
- 100,000 to 500,000
- 50,000 to 100,000
- 10,000 to 50,000
- below 10,000

ELEVATION

500m / 1640ft
250m / 820ft
100m / 328ft
sea level

ONTARIO

QUÉBEC

NORTHWEST TERRITORIES

MANITOBA

UNITED STATES OF AMERICA

Hudson Bay

James Bay

Péninsule d' Ungava

Lake Superior

Lake Huron

Lake Michigan

Lake Erie

Lake Ontario

Georgian Bay

Lake Nipigon

OTTAWA

Toronto

Montréal

Québec

Thunder Bay

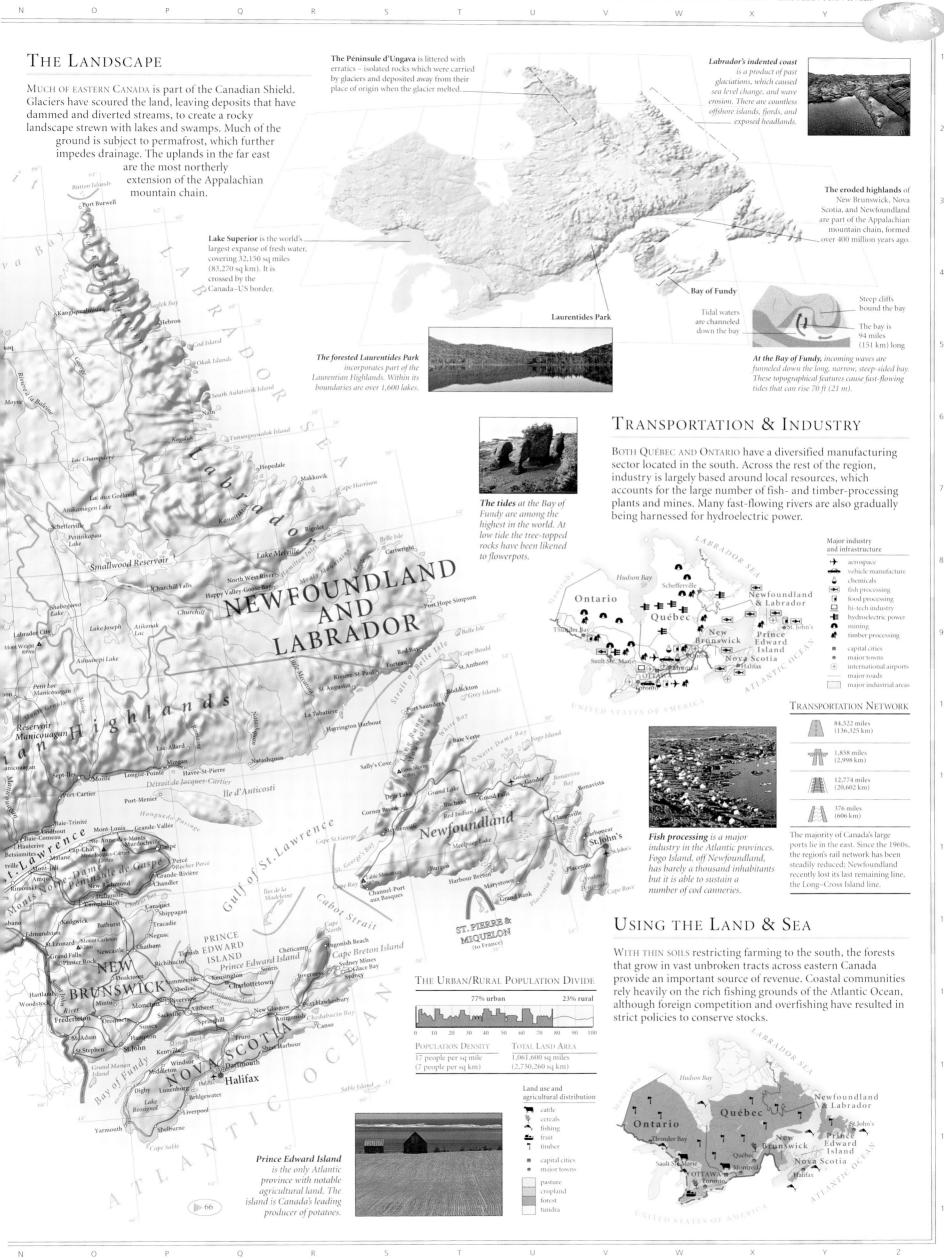

THE LANDSCAPE

MUCH OF EASTERN CANADA is part of the Canadian Shield. Glaciers have scoured the land, leaving deposits that have dammed and diverted streams, to create a rocky landscape strewn with lakes and swamps. Much of the ground is subject to permafrost, which further impedes drainage. The uplands in the far east are the most northerly extension of the Appalachian mountain chain.

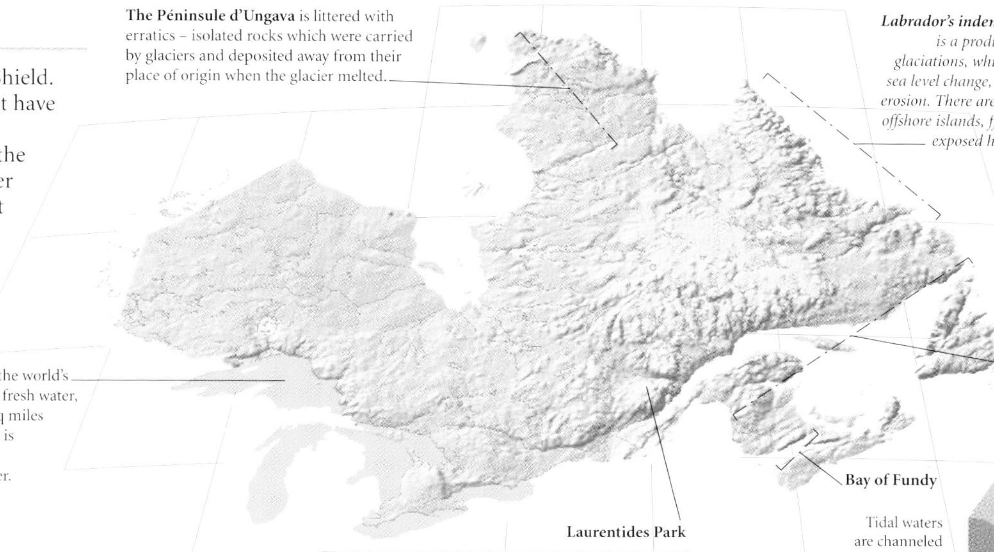

Laurentides Park
Bay of Fundy

The Péninsule d'Ungava is littered with erratics – isolated rocks which were carried by glaciers and deposited away from their place of origin when the glacier melted.

Lake Superior is the world's largest expanse of fresh water, covering 32,150 sq miles (83,270 sq km). It is crossed by the Canada–US border.

Labrador's indented coast *is a product of past glaciations, which caused sea level change, and wave erosion. There are countless offshore islands, fjords, and exposed headlands.*

The eroded highlands of New Brunswick, Nova Scotia, and Newfoundland are part of the Appalachian mountain chain, formed over 400 million years ago.

The forested Laurentides Park *incorporates part of the Laurentian Highlands. Within its boundaries are over 1,600 lakes.*

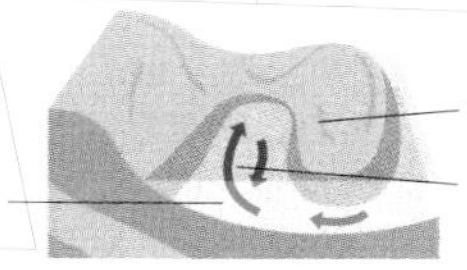

Tidal waters are channeled down the bay
Steep cliffs bound the bay
The bay is 94 miles (151 km) long

At the Bay of Fundy, *incoming waves are funneled down the long, narrow, steep-sided bay. These topographical features cause fast-flowing tides that can rise 70 ft (21 m).*

LABRADOR SEA
Labrador
NEWFOUNDLAND AND LABRADOR
Newfoundland
Gulf of St. Lawrence
Cabot Strait
PRINCE EDWARD ISLAND
NEW BRUNSWICK
NOVA SCOTIA
ATLANTIC OCEAN
ST. PIERRE & MIQUELON (to France)
Halifax
St. John's
Smallwood Reservoir
Lake Melville
Île d'Anticosti
Péninsule de Gaspé
Cape Breton Island
Bay of Fundy
Strait of Belle Isle

66

The tides *at the Bay of Fundy are among the highest in the world. At low tide the tree-topped rocks have been likened to flowerpots.*

TRANSPORTATION & INDUSTRY

BOTH QUÉBEC AND ONTARIO have a diversified manufacturing sector located in the south. Across the rest of the region, industry is largely based around local resources, which accounts for the large number of fish- and timber-processing plants and mines. Many fast-flowing rivers are also gradually being harnessed for hydroelectric power.

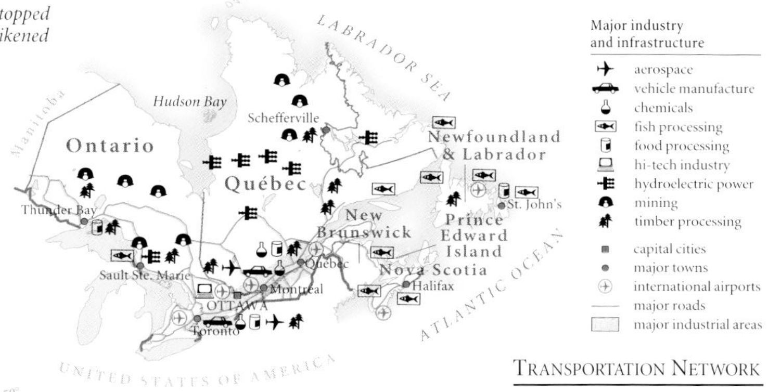

LABRADOR SEA
Hudson Bay
Ontario
Québec
Newfoundland & Labrador
New Brunswick
Prince Edward Island
Nova Scotia
ATLANTIC OCEAN
UNITED STATES OF AMERICA
Major industry and infrastructure
aerospace
vehicle manufacture
chemicals
fish processing
food processing
hi-tech industry
hydroelectric power
mining
timber processing
capital cities
major towns
international airports
major roads
major industrial areas

TRANSPORTATION NETWORK

Roads	84,522 miles (136,325 km)
Highways	1,858 miles (2,998 km)
Railways	12,774 miles (20,602 km)
Waterways	376 miles (606 km)

The majority of Canada's large ports lie in the east. Since the 1960s, the region's rail network has been steadily reduced; Newfoundland recently lost its last remaining line, the Long-Cross Island line.

Fish processing *is a major industry in the Atlantic provinces. Fogo Island, off Newfoundland, has barely a thousand inhabitants but it is able to sustain a number of cod canneries.*

USING THE LAND & SEA

WITH THIN SOILS restricting farming to the south, the forests that grow in vast unbroken tracts across eastern Canada provide an important source of revenue. Coastal communities rely heavily on the rich fishing grounds of the Atlantic Ocean, although foreign competition and overfishing have resulted in strict policies to conserve stocks.

THE URBAN/RURAL POPULATION DIVIDE

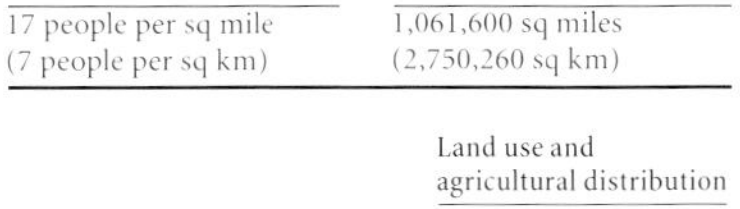

77% urban
23% rural
0 10 20 30 40 50 60 70 80 90 100

POPULATION DENSITY	TOTAL LAND AREA
17 people per sq mile (7 people per sq km)	1,061,600 sq miles (2,750,260 sq km)

LABRADOR SEA
Hudson Bay
Ontario
Québec
Newfoundland & Labrador
New Brunswick
Prince Edward Island
Nova Scotia
ATLANTIC OCEAN
UNITED STATES OF AMERICA
Land use and agricultural distribution
cattle
cereals
fishing
fruit
timber
capital cities
major towns
pasture
cropland
forest
tundra

Prince Edward Island *is the only Atlantic province with notable agricultural land. The island is Canada's leading producer of potatoes.*

SOUTHEASTERN CANADA

Southern Ontario, Southern Québec

THE SOUTHERN PARTS of Québec and Ontario form the economic heart of Canada. The two provinces are divided by their language and culture; in Québec, French is the main language, while English is spoken in Ontario. Separatist sentiment has led to a provincial referendum on the question of Québec having a sovereignty association with Canada. The region contains Canada's capital, Ottawa, and its two largest cities: Toronto, the center of commerce, and Montréal, the cultural and administrative heart of French Canada.

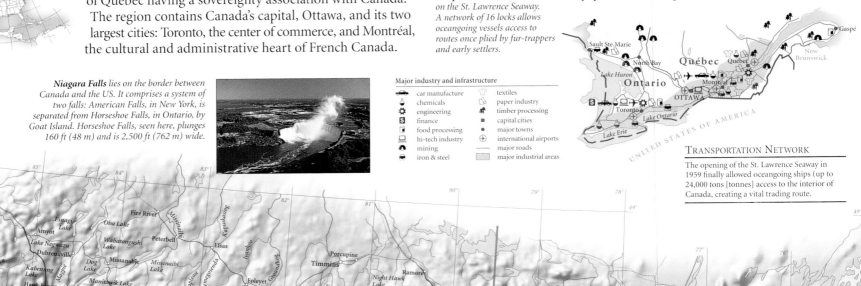

The port at Montréal is situated on the St. Lawrence Seaway. A network of 16 locks allows oceangoing vessels access to routes once plied by fur-trappers and early settlers.

TRANSPORTATION & INDUSTRY

THE CITIES OF SOUTHERN QUÉBEC AND ONTARIO, and their suburbs, form the heart of Canadian manufacturing industry. Toronto is Canada's leading financial center, and Ontario's motor and aerospace industries have developed around the city. A major center for nickel mining lies to the north of Toronto. Most of Québec's industry is located in Montréal, the oldest port in North America. Chemicals, paper manufacture, and the construction of transportation equipment are leading industrial activities.

TRANSPORTATION NETWORK

The opening of the St. Lawrence Seaway in 1959 finally allowed oceangoing ships (up to 24,000 tons [tonnes] access to the interior of Canada, creating a vital trading route.

Niagara Falls lies on the border between Canada and the US. It comprises a system of two falls: American Falls, in New York, is separated from Horseshoe Falls, in Ontario, by Goat Island. Horseshoe Falls, seen here, plunges 160 ft (48 m) and is 2,500 ft (762 m) wide.

Major industry and infrastructure

- car manufacture
- chemicals
- engineering
- finance
- food processing
- hi-tech industry
- mining
- iron & steel
- textiles
- paper industry
- timber processing
- capital cities
- major towns
- international airports
- major roads
- major industrial areas

MAP KEY

POPULATION

- 1 million to 5 million
- 500,000 to 1 million
- 100,000 to 500,000
- 50,000 to 100,000
- 10,000 to 50,000
- below 10,000

ELEVATION

- 500m/1640ft
- 250m/820ft
- 100m/328ft
- sea level

Montréal, on the banks of the St. Lawrence River, is Québec's leading metropolitan center and one of Canada's two largest cities – Toronto is the other. Montréal clearly reflects French culture and traditions.

USING THE LAND & SEA

THE PRODUCTIVE NIAGARA "FRUIT BELT" on the shores of Lake Erie and Lake Ontario is a major farming region, although available farmland is being challenged by urban expansion. Québec is Canada's leading producer of maple syrup and dairy products. In the north, farmland gives way to extensive forested areas, partly used for commercial logging. Fishing occurs in Atlantic waters and in the Great Lakes.

THE URBAN/RURAL POPULATION DIVIDE

urban 87%   rural 13%

0 10 20 30 40 50 60 70 80 90 100

POPULATION DENSITY	TOTAL LAND AREA
64 people per sq mile	214,230 sq miles
(25 people per sq km)	(555,000 sq km)

Land use and agricultural distribution

- cattle
- fish
- cereals
- fruit
- maple syrup
- timber
- tobacco
- capital cities
- major towns
- pasture
- cropland
- forest

Pumpkins are just one of the crops grown in the Niagara "fruit belt." The mild climate, moderated by the lakes, allows the cultivation of a wide range of fruit and vegetables, including cherries, apples, peaches, grapes, and asparagus. Fruit and vegetable growing is confined to southern Canada, due to the colder climate and short growing season of the northern regions.

In contrast to the boreal forest, which spans northern Canada, the Gaspé Peninsula (Peninsule de Gaspé) is covered with a band of mixed coniferous–deciduous woodland, including sugar and red maple, cedar, and eastern hemlock.

THE LANDSCAPE

THE HEART OF SOUTHEASTERN CANADA is the lowland area surrounding the St. Lawrence River, the principal outlet for the Great Lakes. The lowlands are bordered to the east by an extension of the Appalachian mountain chain and to the north by the Canadian Shield. The Champlain Sea, which flooded the area during the last glacial period, deposited clay over much of the area.

The wooded Gaspé Peninsula (Peninsule de Gaspé) includes the Notre Dame and Shickshock Mountains (Monts Chic-Choc). These are a northerly outcrop of the Appalachian mountain chain.

The Laurentide Scarp, along the north shore of the St. Lawrence River, is a 2,000-ft (610-m) escarpment, marking the rim of the Canadian Shield.

In 1971, large quantities of marine clay liquefied and flowed into the Saguenay River, killing 30 people. Large landslides often occur on waterlogged slopes.

The flat plains of the St. Lawrence Valley were formed when the area was inundated by the Champlain Sea during the last glacial period.

SCALE 1:3,000,000
(projection: Lambert Conformal Conic)

Km
0 10 20 30 40 50 60 70 80

Miles
0 10 20 30 40 50 60 70 80

Lake Superior

Lake Huron

Point Pelee is a world-famous site for bird migration. Over 250 species of bird have been sighted on the sandspit which forms the southern tip of the Canadian mainland.

Lake Erie

Lake Ontario

The Great Lakes moderate the climate of the area surrounding the St. Lawrence River. Their water, which cools more slowly than the land, acts as a reservoir for warmth, extending the growing season into the early autumn.

Mount Royal, around which the city of Montréal has developed, is the result of an igneous intrusion that occurred between 135 and 65 million years ago.

Riverbank or bluff

Earthflow

Sand

Clay

River

In the lowlands around the St. Lawrence, earthflows have developed along gentle riverbanks where sand overlies clay, making the surface layers very unstable. When the slope's natural equilibrium is disturbed, an earthflow can occur.

13

CANADA

CANADA IS THE SECOND LARGEST COUNTRY in the world, and with only about one-tenth of its land area inhabited, it is one of the most sparsely populated. Canada became a confederation in 1867, though Newfoundland did not join until 1949. As a founding member of the UN and of the Commonwealth, Canada has played an important role in international affairs. A constitutional crisis, focusing on the French-speaking Québécois, Inuit, and Native American land rights, has dominated politics in the 1990s. In 1999, part of the Northwest Territories, Nunavut, will become a self-governing Inuit homeland.

The Selwyn Mountains
in northwestern Canada form part of the Rocky Mountains. The highest point, Keele Peak, rises 9,750 ft (2,972 m).

TRANSPORTATION & INDUSTRY

ABUNDANT ENERGY in the form of coal, oil, natural gas, and hydroelectric power underpins Canadian industry. Over 75% of manufacturing is concentrated in the Great Lakes–St. Lawrence region, including prospering aerospace, transportation and hi-tech industries. Across Canada as a whole, manufacturing has developed around a diversified, high-quality resource base and a wide range of metallic and nonmetallic minerals.

Major industry and infrastructure

- aerospace
- car manufacture
- chemicals
- engineering
- food processing
- hi-tech industry
- hydroelectric power
- oil & gas
- mining
- timber processing
- capital cities
- major towns
- international airports
- major roads
- major industrial areas

Canada has one of the world's highest rates of energy consumption per person. It is endowed with vast hydroelectric potential from which more than 60% of its electricity requirements are generated.

TRANSPORTATION NETWORK

549,460 miles (884,272 km)	4,860 miles (7,819 km)
120,546 miles (194,000 km)	1,864 miles (3,000 km)

In recent years the road network has been expanded, especially links to remote areas. Meanwhile, for long-distance travel, air transportation now supersedes the declining rail network, which focuses mainly on east–west routes.

THE LANDSCAPE

GLACIERS ON ISLANDS IN THE ARCTIC OCEAN are the last remnants of the ice sheet that once covered and shaped Canada. Hudson Bay is the center of the Canadian Shield, a huge, eroded plateau marked at its southern extremity by a string of lakes running southeastward from Great Bear Lake to the Great Lakes. In contrast to the rolling relief of the Shield and the central lowland region, the Rocky Mountains rise to peaks of over 13,000 ft (4,000 m), stretching 500 miles (800 km) along the west coast.

Along the northeastern coast of Baffin Island the mountains rise to 8,000 ft (2,440 m). Glaciers move down through the valleys to the sea, eroding wide U-shaped valleys.

Top layer thaws in the summer

Permanently frozen ground

Permanently frozen ground known as permafrost is common in Canada's northern tundra. It thickens farther north, becoming hundreds of yards deep in parts of the Arctic.

Marginal areas of permafrost thaw in summer

Unfrozen ground where temperature is more moderate

The Mackenzie River, flowing north over the permafrost, forms a wide river channel with many tributaries. Together with the Peel River it has created a long, narrow delta at its mouth. The entire river freezes during the winter.

Great Bear Lake

Exposure to three phases of mountain-building and subsequent erosion over millions of years has molded the ancient Canadian Shield into a series of basins and ridges.

The Rocky Mountains were formed some 80 million years ago, when the Pacific Plate was driven under the North American Plate, forcing up the land.

Isolated pillars, known as hoodoos near Red Deer River in the badlands of Alberta are a product of wind and water erosion, especially flash floods. The badlands lie in the rain shadow of the Rocky Mountains, which creates a semiarid climate.

Fertile prairies stretch from the southern rim of the Canadian Shield south into the US.

The Great Lakes lie on the Canada–US border. The basins they now occupy were carved by repeated ice advance. Once, Lakes Superior, Huron, and Michigan formed one large lake, Lake Nipissing.

The St. Lawrence River is 2,350 miles (3,782 km) long. It flows from the western shore of Lake Superior through the Great Lakes and on to the Atlantic Ocean. From December to April, the St. Lawrence Seaway freezes between Lake Ontario and Montréal.

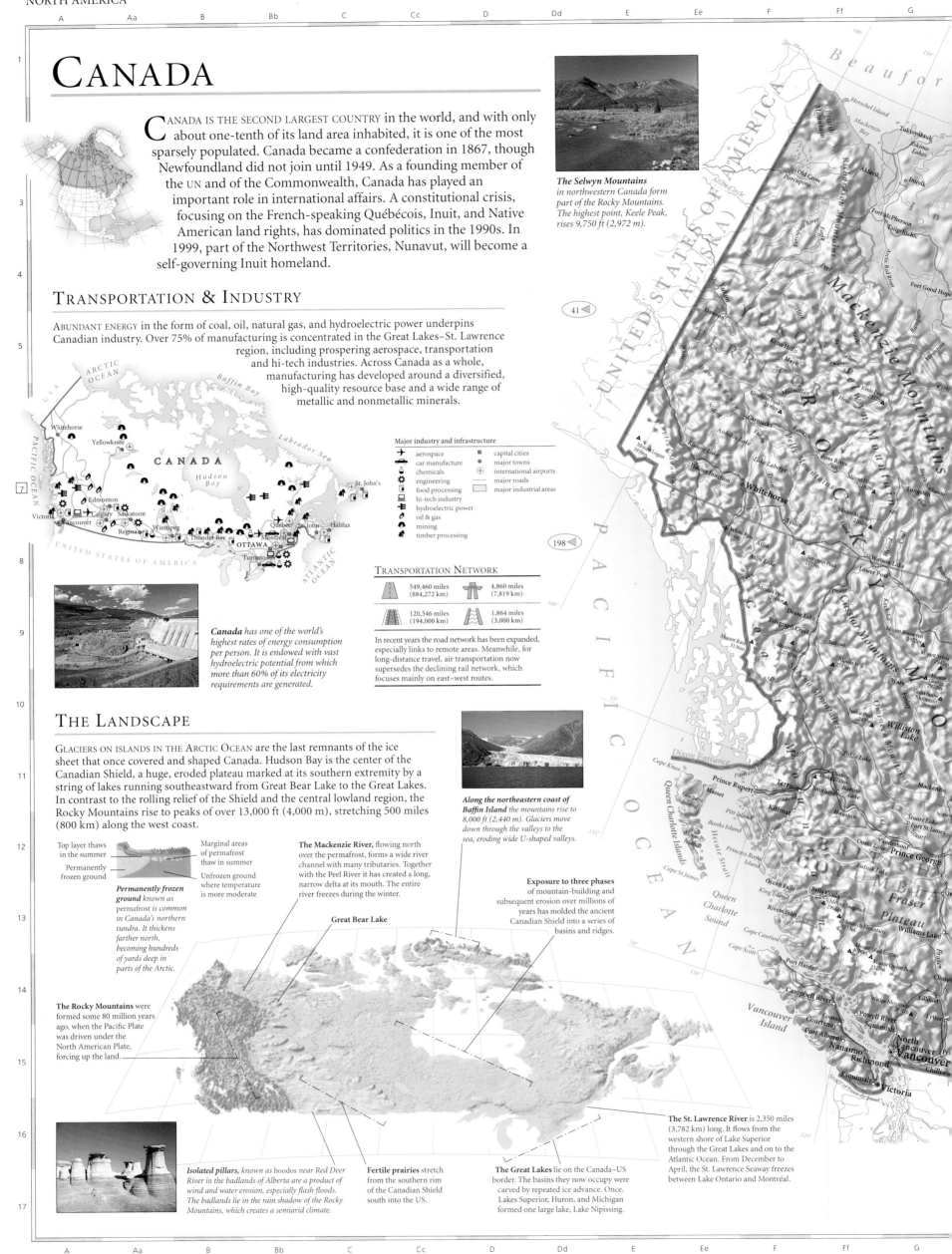

Viscount Melville Sound
Banks Island
Cape Kellett
Sachs Harbour
Prince of Wales Strait
Prince Albert Peninsula
Passage Point
Peel Point
Stefansson Island
206
Hadley Bay
McClintock Channel
Peel Sound
Somerset Island
Prince of Wales Island
Franklin Strait
Prince Regent Inlet
Boothia Peninsula
Gulf of Boothia
Brodeur Peninsula
Borden Peninsula
Admiralty Inlet
Baffin
Amundsen Gulf
Cape Bathurst
Cape Lambton
Cape Parry
Cape Wollaston
Holman
Zeta Lake
Victoria Island
Gateshead Island
Larsen Sound
Franklin Bay
Cape Lyon
Prince Albert Sound
Paulatuk
Wollaston Peninsula
Dolphin & Union Strait
Kitikmeot
Cambridge Bay
King William Island
Gjoa Haven
Jenny Lind Island
Queen Maud Gulf
Adelaide Peninsula
Bowes Point
Taloyoak
Pelly Bay
Simpson Peninsula
Committee Bay
Wales Island
Cape Englefield
Cape Chipman
Igloolik
Jens Munk Island
Hall Beach
Melville Peninsula
Rowley Island
Baird Peninsula
Prince Charles Island
Air Force Island
Nettilling Lake
Foxe Basin
Bluenose Lake
Rae
Cape Krusenstern
Coronation Gulf
Kent Peninsula
Coppermine
Repulse Bay
Vansittart Island
Cape Dorchester
Foxe Peninsula
Cape Dorset
Foxe Channel
Salisbury Island
NORTHWEST TERRITORIES
Hood
Burnside
Great Bear Lake
Echo Bay
Takijuq Lake
Wells
Déline
Fort Norman
Wager Bay
Southampton Island
Coral Harbour
Roes Welcome Sound
Nottingham Island
Evans Strait
Ivujivik
Garry Lake
Back
Hottah Lake
Aberdeen Lake
Baker Lake
Quoich
Chesterfield Inlet
Cape Kendall
Cape Low
Fisher Strait
Coats Island
Mansel Island
Aylmer Lake
Thelon
Clinton-Colden Lake
Hanbury
Keewatin
Rankin Inlet
Dubawnt Lake
Yathkyed Lake
Whale Cove
Wrigley
Lac La Martre
Yellowknife
Snare
Fort Smith
Willowlake
Rae-Edzo
Reliance
Fort Simpson
Lutselk'e
Snowdrift
Nonacho Lake
Kazan
Ottawa Islands
Eskimo Point
Arviat
Fort Providence
Great Slave Lake
Fort Resolution
Trout
Taltson
Hay River
Pine Point
Thoa
Dubawnt
Tha-Anne
Thlewiaza
Hudson Bay
Wholdaia Lake
Kasba Lake
Nueltin Lake
Petitot
Bistcho Lake
Steen River
Fort Smith
Slave
Nejanilini Lake
Selwyn Lake
Uranium City
Caribou Mountains
Peace
Phelps Lake
Seal
Cape Churchill
Churchill
Fort Chipewyan
Lake Athabasca
Black Lake
Lac Brochet
Tadoule Lake
High Level
Fort Vermilion
Lake Claire
Pasfield Lake
Wollaston Lake
Cape Tatnam
South Seal
Southern Indian Lake
Birch Mountains
Cree Lake
Reindeer Lake
Fort Severn
Winisk
Clear Hills
Chinchaga
Fort St.John
Manning
SASKATCHEWAN
Lynn Lake
Waskaiowaka Lake
Gillam
Nelson
Hayes
Severn
ALBERTA
Wabasca
Clearwater
Turnor Lake
Foster Lakes
Leaf Rapids
Granville Lake
Split Lake
Grimshaw
Fairview
Peace River
Athabasca
Fort McMurray
La Loche
Frobisher Lake
Macoun Lake
Thompson
Dawson Creek
Smoky
Desmarais
Utikuma Lake
Churchill Lake
Reindeer
Grande Prairie
High Prairie
Lesser Slave Lake
Peter Pond Lake
Buffalo Narrows
Pinehouse Lake
Missinipe
Burntwood
Sipiwesk Lake
Wapiti
Valleyview
Slave Lake
Wallace Mountain
Swan Hills
Kississing Lake
Wabowden
Oxford Lake
Gods Lake
Big Trout Lake
Winisk Lake
Athabasca
Primrose Lake
La Ronge
Lac La Ronge
Creighton
Flin Flon
Molson Lake
Sachigo Lake
Grande Cache
Whitecourt
Barrhead
Westlock
Cold Lake
Grand Centre
Beaver
Deschambault Lake
Amisk Lake
Island Lake
Attawapiskat
Morinville
St.Albert
Fort Saskatchewan
St.Paul
Meadow Lake
Montreal Lake
MANITOBA
Mount Robson
Edson
Hinton
Spruce Grove
Stony Plain
Edmonton
North Saskatchewan
St.Walburg
Tobin Lake
Saskatchewan
The Pas
Cedar Lake
Grand Rapids
Lake Winnipeg
Sandy Lake
North Caribou Lake
Attawapiskat Lake
Drayton Valley
Pembina
Devon
Leduc
Vegreville
Vermilion
Lloydminster
Prince Albert
Nipawin
Pasquia Hills
Hudson Bay
Poplar
Berens
Pipestone
ONTARIO
Rocky Mountain House
Wetaskiwin
Camrose
Wainwright
North Battleford
Melfort
Tisdale
Lake Winnipegosis
Ogoki
Ponoka
Battleford
Porcupine Hills
Swan River
Gypsumville
Kinbasket Lake
Lacombe
Stettler
Unity
Humboldt
Mount Columbia
Sylvan Lake
Innisfail
Red Deer
Martensville
Saskatoon
Quill Lakes
Duck Mountain
Trout Lake
Lake St.Joseph
Armstrong
Olds
Biggar
Lanigan
Watrous
Wynyard
Canora
Kamsack
Lake Nipigon
Didsbury
Kicking Horse Pass
Drumheller
Airdrie
Rosetown
Outlook
Yorkton
Dauphin
Red Lake
Ear Falls
Lac Seul
Golden
Banff
Canmore
Strathmore
Oyen
Kindersley
Last Mountain Lake
Melville
Esterhazy
Riding Mountain
Lake Manitoba
Eriksdale
Gimli
Sioux Lookout
Salmon Arm
Calgary
Okotoks
Lake Diefenbaker
Fort Qu'Appelle
Indian Head
Neepawa
Stonewall
Selkirk
Beausejour
Pinawa
Kenora
Dryden
Nipigon
Invermere
High River
South Saskatchewan
Lumsden
Regina
Qu'Appelle
Minnedosa
Portage la Prairie
Winnipeg
Eagle Lake
Lac des Milles Lacs
Kelowna
Claresholm
Travers Reservoir
Swift Current
Moose Jaw
Moosomin
Brandon
Assiniboine
Carman
Steinbach
Rainy Lake
Atikokan
Thunder Bay
Crowsnest Pass
Fort Macleod
Kimberley
Lethbridge
Redcliff
Medicine Hat
Old Wives Lake
Virden
Melita
Killarney
Morden
Winkler
Altona
Red River
Fort Frances
Cranbrook
Pincher Creek
Coaldale
Taber
Maple Creek
Weyburn
Carlyle
Estevan
Lake of the Woods
Rainy River
Lake Superior
Cardston
Raymond
Milk River
Cypress Hills
Assiniboia
Val Marie
Wood Mountain
Rockglen
UNITED STATES OF AMERICA
SCALE 1:9,250,000
Projection: Lambert Azimuthal Equal Area
17
H
Hh
I
Ii
J
Jj
K
Kk
L
Ll
M
Mm

SCALE 1: 8,750,000
(projection: Lambert Azimuthal Equal Area)

Km
0 25 50   100   150   200   250   300
Miles
0   25   50   100   150   200   250

C A N A D A

WASHINGTON

Seattle
Bellingham
Mount Vernon
Everett
Glacier Peak
Wenatchee
Ellensburg
Mount Rainier
Yakima
Richland
The Dalles
Pendleton
La Grande
Baker
Columbia Basin
Snake River
Walla Walla
Kennewick
Hermiston

OREGON

Spokane
Coeur d'Alene
Moscow
Lewiston
Clearwater Mountains
Bitterroot Range
Sandpoint
Kalispell
Libby
Flathead Lake
Lake Pend Oreille
Cut Bank
Shelby
Conrad
Great Falls

MONTANA

Havre
Malta
Glasgow
Wolf Point
Fort Peck Lake
Missouri River
Sidney
Glendive
Miles City

NORTH DAKOTA

Bottineau
Rugby
Minot
Williston
Lake Sakakawea
Dickinson
Mandan
Bismarck
Bowman

Devils Lake
Grand Forks
Crookston
Jamestown
Valley City
Fargo
Moorhead
Wahpeton

Lake of the Woods
Upper Red Lake
Lower Red Lake
Lake Winnibigoshish
Grand Rapids
Leech Lake

MINNESOTA

Bemidji
Fergus Falls
Brainerd
Mille Lacs Lake
Saint Cloud
Morris
Willmar
Minneapolis
Charles Lindbergh
Red Wing
New Ulm
Mankato
Rochester

IDAHO

Boise
Nampa
Caldwell
Ketchum
Mountain Home
Shoshone
Twin Falls
Burley
Pocatello
Idaho Falls
Rexburg

Salmon River Mountains
Snake River Plain

Missoula
Anaconda
Butte
Helena
Dillon
Bozeman
Livingston
Billings
Hardin
Yellowstone River
Billings

Yellowstone Lake
Grand Teton
Cody
Cloud Peak
Sheridan
Buffalo
Gillette
Devils Tower
Belle Fourche
Spearfish
Lead
Newcastle
Rapid City
Black Hills
Harney Peak 2207m
Hot Springs
Pine Ridge
Chadron

SOUTH DAKOTA

Mobridge
Lake Oahe
Aberdeen
Redfield
Watertown
Huron
Pierre
Lake Sharpe
Mitchell
Brookings
Sioux Falls
Winner

WYOMING

Thermopolis
Riverton
Casper
Douglas
Cody
Gannett Peak 4207m

Great Divide Basin

Rock Springs
Green River
Rawlins
Laramie
Cheyenne
Fort Collins
Loveland
Greeley

NEBRASKA

Chadron
Alliance
Scottsbluff
Kimball
Wild Horse Hill 1281m
Sand Hills
Valentine
O'Neill
Norfolk
North Platte
Ogallala
Lexington
Kearney
Grand Island
Columbus
Fremont
Omaha
Council Bluffs
Lincoln
Beatrice

IOWA

Des Moines
Creston
Clarinda
Maryville
Saint Joseph

NEVADA

Winnemucca
Elko
Battle Mountain
Austin
Ely
Great Salt Lake Desert
Great Salt Lake
Brigham City
Ogden
Salt Lake City
Tooele
Provo
Nephi
Delta
Price
Richfield

UTAH

Uinta Mountains
Kings Peak 4123m
Vernal
Flaming Gorge Reservoir

COLORADO

Craig
Steamboat Springs
White River
Roan Plateau
Grand Junction
Montrose
Vail
Aspen
Glenwood Springs
Boulder
Denver
Aurora
Limon
Colorado Springs
Canon City
Pueblo
La Junta
Lamar

KANSAS

Colby
Burlington
Goodland
Hays
Salina
Great Bend
Hutchinson
McPherson
Newton
Wichita
Dodge City
Garden City
Pratt
Liberal

Humboldt River
Walker Lake
Hawthorne
Tonopah
Wheeler Peak 3981m

CALIFORNIA

Las Vegas
Henderson
Lake Mead
Mojave Desert
San Bernardino
Riverside
Santa Ana
El Cajon
Escondido
Palm Springs

ARIZONA

Kingman
Needles
Lake Havasu City
Prescott
Wickenburg
Flagstaff
Humphreys Peak 3851m
Grand Canyon
Colorado Plateau
Painted Desert
Phoenix
Scottsdale
Mesa
Globe
Casa Grande
Sonoran Desert
Yuma
Gila River
Tucson
Green Valley
Nogales
Safford

NEW MEXICO

Gallup
Grants
Albuquerque
Santa Fe
Los Alamos
Taos
Sangre de Cristo Mountains
Socorro
Vaughn
Roswell
Clovis
Portales
Silver City
Deming
Las Cruces
Alamogordo
Artesia
Carlsbad
Hobbs

MEXICO

El Paso
Van Horn
Alpine
Pecos
Fort Stockton
Del Rio
Eagle Pass

TEXAS

Amarillo
Pampa
Dumas
Dalhart
Canyon
Hereford
Tucumcari
Plainview
Lubbock
Brownfield
Lamesa
Snyder
Big Spring
Midland
Odessa
San Angelo
Brownwood
Llano Estacado
Edwards Plateau
Abilene
Fort Worth
Arlington
Dallas
Waco
Temple
Killeen
Austin
San Antonio
New Braunfels
Seguin
Uvalde
Victoria
Houston
Pasadena
Beaumont
Galveston
Corpus Christi
Laredo
McAllen
Harlingen
Brownsville

OKLAHOMA

Guymon
Woodward
Enid
Clinton
El Reno
Oklahoma City
Norman
Chickasha
Lawton
Altus
Vernon
Wichita Falls
Ardmore
Durant
Denton
Sherman
Paris

KANSAS
Kansas City
Topeka
Lawrence
Emporia
Wichita
Coffeyville
Ponca City
Tulsa
Broken Arrow
Muskogee
McAlester

MISSOURI
Springfield
Joplin
Fort Scott
Fort Smith

MAP KEY

POPULATION

- ■ above 5 million
- ◉ 1 million to 5 million
- ◎ 500,000 to 1 million
- ◉ 100,000 to 500,000
- ⊕ 50,000 to 100,000
- ○ 10,000 to 50,000
- ∘ below 10,000

ELEVATION

- 4000m / 13,124ft
- 3000m / 9843ft
- 2000m / 6562ft
- 1000m / 3281ft
- 500m / 1640ft
- 250m / 820ft
- 100m / 328ft
- sea level

The Sonoran Desert in southwestern Arizona stretches into Mexico and merges to the northwest with California's Mojave Desert. Much of the southwest is very arid, especially the "rain-starved" areas between the Coast Ranges and the Rocky Mountains.

THE UNITED STATES OF AMERICA

CONTERMINOUS US (FOR ALASKA AND HAWAII SEE PAGES 40–41)

THE US'S PROGRESSION FROM FRONTIER TERRITORY to economic and political superpower has taken less than 200 years. The 48 contiguous states, along with the outlying states of Alaska and Hawaii, are part of a federal union, held together by the guiding principles of the US Constitution, which embodies the ideals of democracy and liberty for all. Abundant fertile land and a rich resource base fueled and sustained US economic development. With the spread of agriculture and the growth of trade and industry came the need for a larger workforce, which was supplied by millions of immigrants, many seeking an escape from poverty and political or religious persecution. Immigration continues today, particularly from Central America and Asia.

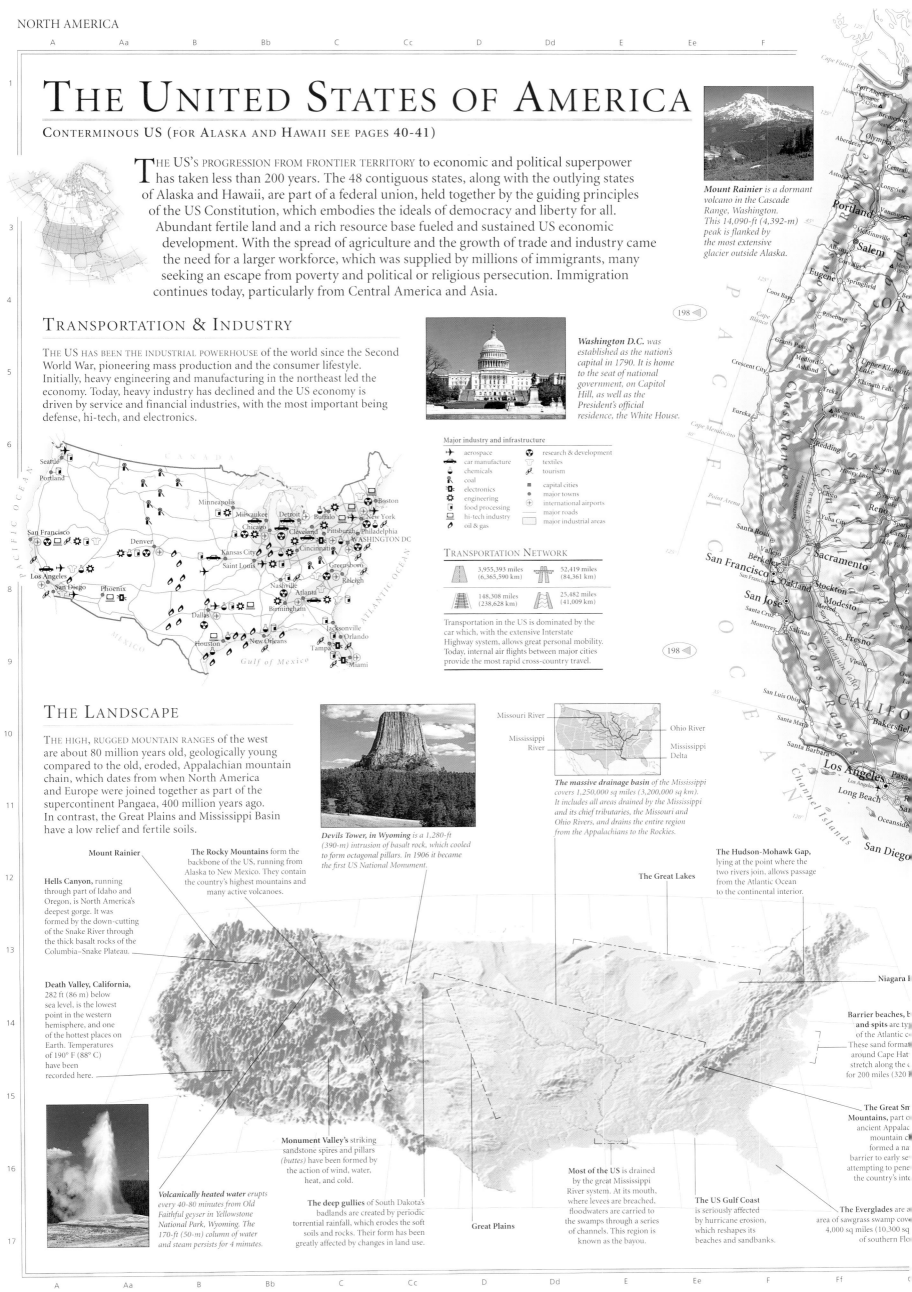

Mount Rainier is a dormant volcano in the Cascade Range, Washington. This 14,090-ft (4,392-m) peak is flanked by the most extensive glacier outside Alaska.

TRANSPORTATION & INDUSTRY

THE US HAS BEEN THE INDUSTRIAL POWERHOUSE of the world since the Second World War, pioneering mass production and the consumer lifestyle. Initially, heavy engineering and manufacturing in the northeast led the economy. Today, heavy industry has declined and the US economy is driven by service and financial industries, with the most important being defense, hi-tech, and electronics.

Washington D.C. was established as the nation's capital in 1790. It is home to the seat of national government, on Capitol Hill, as well as the President's official residence, the White House.

Major industry and infrastructure

- aerospace
- car manufacture
- chemicals
- coal
- electronics
- engineering
- food processing
- hi-tech industry
- oil & gas
- research & development
- textiles
- tourism
- capital cities
- major towns
- international airports
- major roads
- major industrial areas

TRANSPORTATION NETWORK

3,955,393 miles (6,365,590 km)	52,419 miles (84,361 km)
148,308 miles (238,628 km)	25,482 miles (41,009 km)

Transportation in the US is dominated by the car which, with the extensive Interstate Highway system, allows great personal mobility. Today, internal air flights between major cities provide the most rapid cross-country travel.

198

198

THE LANDSCAPE

THE HIGH, RUGGED MOUNTAIN RANGES of the west are about 80 million years old, geologically young compared to the old, eroded, Appalachian mountain chain, which dates from when North America and Europe were joined together as part of the supercontinent Pangaea, 400 million years ago. In contrast, the Great Plains and Mississippi Basin have a low relief and fertile soils.

Devils Tower, in Wyoming is a 1,280-ft (390-m) intrusion of basalt rock, which cooled to form octagonal pillars. In 1906 it became the first US National Monument.

Missouri River
Mississippi River
Ohio River
Mississippi Delta

The massive drainage basin of the Mississippi covers 1,250,000 sq miles (3,200,000 sq km). It includes all areas drained by the Mississippi and its chief tributaries, the Missouri and Ohio Rivers, and drains the entire region from the Appalachians to the Rockies.

Mount Rainier

Hells Canyon, running through part of Idaho and Oregon, is North America's deepest gorge. It was formed by the down-cutting of the Snake River through the thick basalt rocks of the Columbia–Snake Plateau.

The Rocky Mountains form the backbone of the US, running from Alaska to New Mexico. They contain the country's highest mountains and many active volcanoes.

The Hudson-Mohawk Gap, lying at the point where the two rivers join, allows passage from the Atlantic Ocean to the continental interior.

The Great Lakes

Death Valley, California, 282 ft (86 m) below sea level, is the lowest point in the western hemisphere, and one of the hottest places on Earth. Temperatures of 190° F (88° C) have been recorded here.

Niagara F

Barrier beaches, b and spits are typ of the Atlantic co These sand format around Cape Hat stretch along the c for 200 miles (320 k

The Great Sm Mountains, part o ancient Appalac mountain ch formed a na barrier to early se attempting to pene the country's inte

Volcanically heated water erupts every 40-80 minutes from Old Faithful geyser in Yellowstone National Park, Wyoming. The 170-ft (50-m) column of water and steam persists for 4 minutes.

Monument Valley's striking sandstone spires and pillars *(buttes)* have been formed by the action of wind, water, heat, and cold.

The deep gullies of South Dakota's badlands are created by periodic torrential rainfall, which erodes the soft soils and rocks. Their form has been greatly affected by changes in land use.

Great Plains

Most of the US is drained by the great Mississippi River system. At its mouth, where levees are breached, floodwaters are carried to the swamps through a series of channels. This region is known as the bayou.

The US Gulf Coast is seriously affected by hurricane erosion, which reshapes its beaches and sandbanks.

The Everglades is an area of sawgrass swamp cove 4,000 sq miles (10,300 sq of southern Fle

USING THE LAND & SEA

THE MAJORITY OF CANADA's agricultural land is found in the prairies, which cover 140 million acres (57 million ha) and support wheat and grain-fed cattle. More specialized crops, such as fruit and vegetables, are grown in pockets of agricultural land in the east and west. Of Canada's many islands, only Prince Edward Island has notable farmland. Further north, boreal forests, exploited for timber, run in an almost unbroken arc, giving way to uncultivable tundra and ice sheets in the far north.

Land use and agricultural distribution

- cattle
- cereals
- fishing
- fruit
- timber

- capital cities
- major towns

- pasture
- cropland
- forest
- wetland
- mountain region
- barren
- tundra

THE URBAN/RURAL POPULATION DIVIDE

urban 78%   rural 22%

0 10 20 30 40 50 60 70 80 90 100

POPULATION DENSITY
8 people per sq mile
(3 people per sq km)

TOTAL LAND AREA
3,559,294 sq miles
(9,220,970 sq km)

The climate and topography of the prairies makes them ideal for farming. Long summer days, moderate temperatures, limited rainfall, and flat plains provide excellent conditions for growing wheat.

Ottawa was selected by Queen Victoria as the Canadian capital in 1858. Prior to this date it was a notorious work camp centered around the lumber industry. Today, the city is known as "Silicon Valley North," due to its concentration of hi-tech industries.

MAP KEY

POPULATION

- 500,000 to 1 million
- 100,000 to 500,000
- 50,000 to 100,000
- 10,000 to 50,000
- below 10,000

ELEVATION

- 6000m / 19,686ft
- 4000m / 13,124ft
- 3000m / 9843ft
- 2000m / 6562ft
- 1000m / 3281ft
- 500m / 1640ft
- 250m / 820ft
- 100m / 328ft
- sea level

The Great Lakes are drained by the St. Lawrence River, which flows down through a wide tectonic depression. It forms a broad estuary for much of its course, the width varying from 1.2 miles (1.9 km) in the upper reaches to 90 miles (145 km) at its mouth.

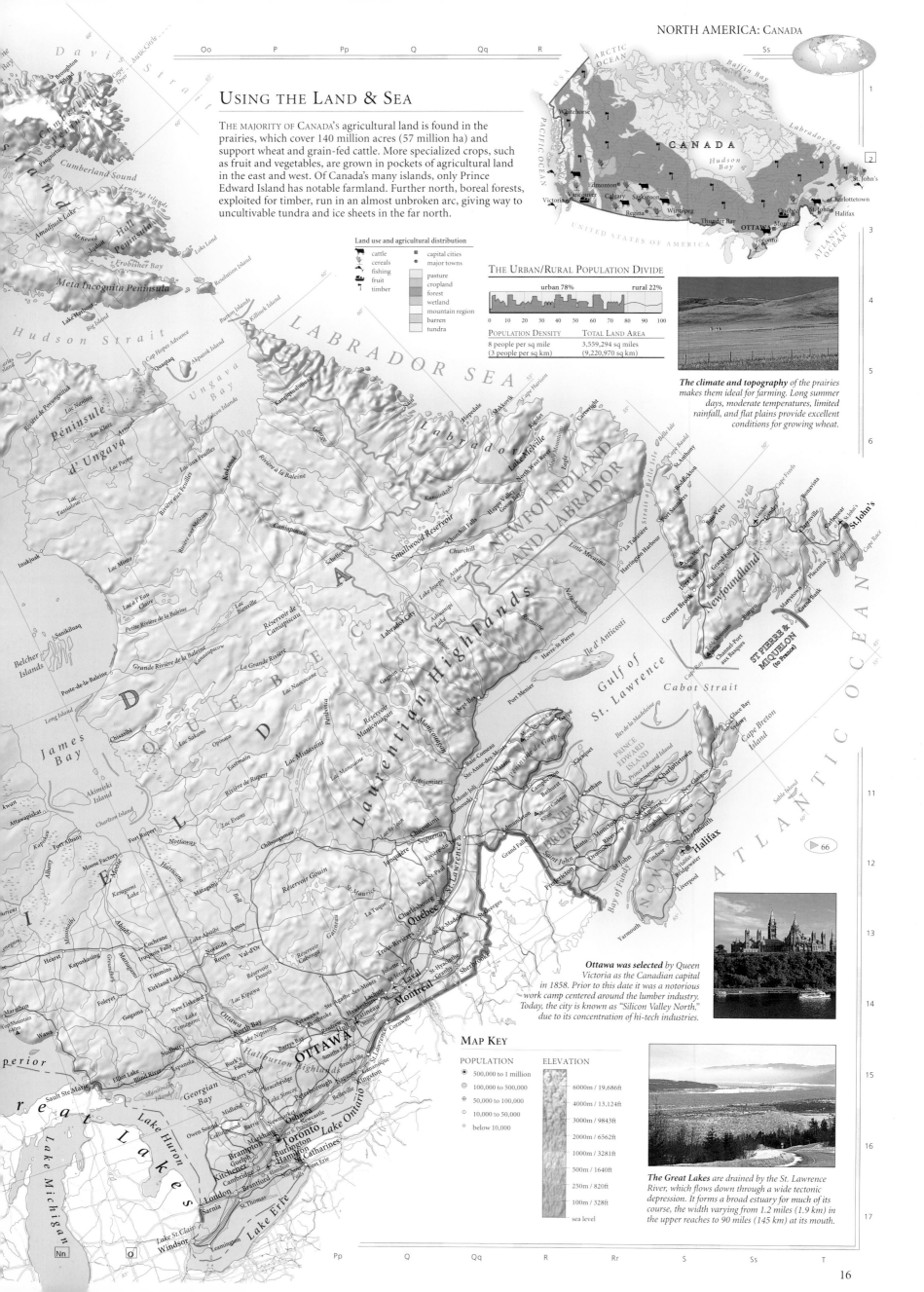

The clear waters of Niagara Falls cascade 190 ft (58 m) into the gorge below. It is one of North America's most famous spectacles and a leading tourist attraction. The falls are slowly receding and the gorge may one day stretch from Lake Ontario to Lake Erie.

USING THE LAND & SEA

OVER HALF OF THE US is used for agriculture, typified by the large cereal grain farms and cattle ranches of the Great Plains and Midwest prairie regions. Although wheat and corn are still primary crops, a diverse range of fruits and vegetables are grown in the fertile areas, particularly near the east and west coasts. Despite the abundance of cultivable land, inadequate soil management has resulted in a third of the topsoil being lost through wind and water erosion.

THE URBAN/RURAL POPULATION DIVIDE

urban 75%   rural 25%

0 10 20 30 40 50 60 70 80 90 100

POPULATION DENSITY	TOTAL LAND AREA
72 people per sq mile	3,538,307 sq miles
(28 people per sq km)	(9,166,600 sq km)

Land use and agricultural distribution

cattle	corn	capital cities
pigs	peanuts	major towns
poultry	shellfish	pasture
citrus fruits	soybeans	cropland
cotton	timber	forest
fishing	tobacco	wetland
fruit	wheat	desert
		mountain region

Fakahatchee Strand is part of the extensive subtropical swamps in the Florida Everglades. The swamps support a wide variety of animal life, including many rare birds, fish, alligators, and crocodiles.

Farming on the Great Plains and in the Midwest is characterized by large-scale, mechanized wheat farms.

USA: NORTHEASTERN STATES

Connecticut, Maine, Massachusetts, New Hampshire, New Jersey, New York, Pennsylvania, Rhode Island, Vermont

THE INDENTED COAST AND VAST WOODLANDS of the northeastern states were the original core area for European expansion. The rustic character of New England prevails after nearly four centuries, while the great Atlantic seaboard cities have formed an almost continuous urban region. Over 20 million immigrants entered New York between 1855 and 1924, and the northeast became the industrial center of the US. After the decline of mining and heavy manufacturing, economic dynamism has been restored with the growth of hi-tech and service industries.

Chelsea, in Vermont, is surrounded by trees in their fall foliage. Tourism and agriculture dominate the economy of this self-consciously rural state, where no town exceeds 30,000 people.

MAP KEY

POPULATION
- above 5 million
- 1 million to 5 million
- 500,000 to 1 million
- 100,000 to 500,000
- 50,000 to 100,000
- 10,000 to 50,000
- below 10,000

ELEVATION
- 1000m / 3281ft
- 500m / 1640ft
- 250m / 820ft
- 100m / 328ft
- sea level

TRANSPORTATION & INDUSTRY

THE PRINCIPAL SEABOARD CITIES grew up on trade and manufacturing. They are now global centers of commerce and corporate administration, dominating the regional economy. Research and development facilities support an expanding electronics and communications sector throughout the region. Pharmaceutical and chemical industries are important in New Jersey and Pennsylvania.

TRANSPORTATION NETWORK

340,090 miles (544,144 km)	4,813 miles 7,700 km
12,872 miles (20,592 km)	2,108 miles (3,389 km)

New York's commercial success is tied historically to its transportation connections. The Erie Canal, completed in 1825, opened up the Great Lakes and the interior to New York's markets and carried a stream of immigrants into the Midwest.

Major industry and infrastructure
- chemicals
- coal
- defense
- electronics
- engineering
- finance
- hi-tech industry
- iron & steel
- pharmaceuticals
- printing & publishing
- research & development
- textiles
- timber processing
- major towns
- international airports
- major roads
- major industrial area

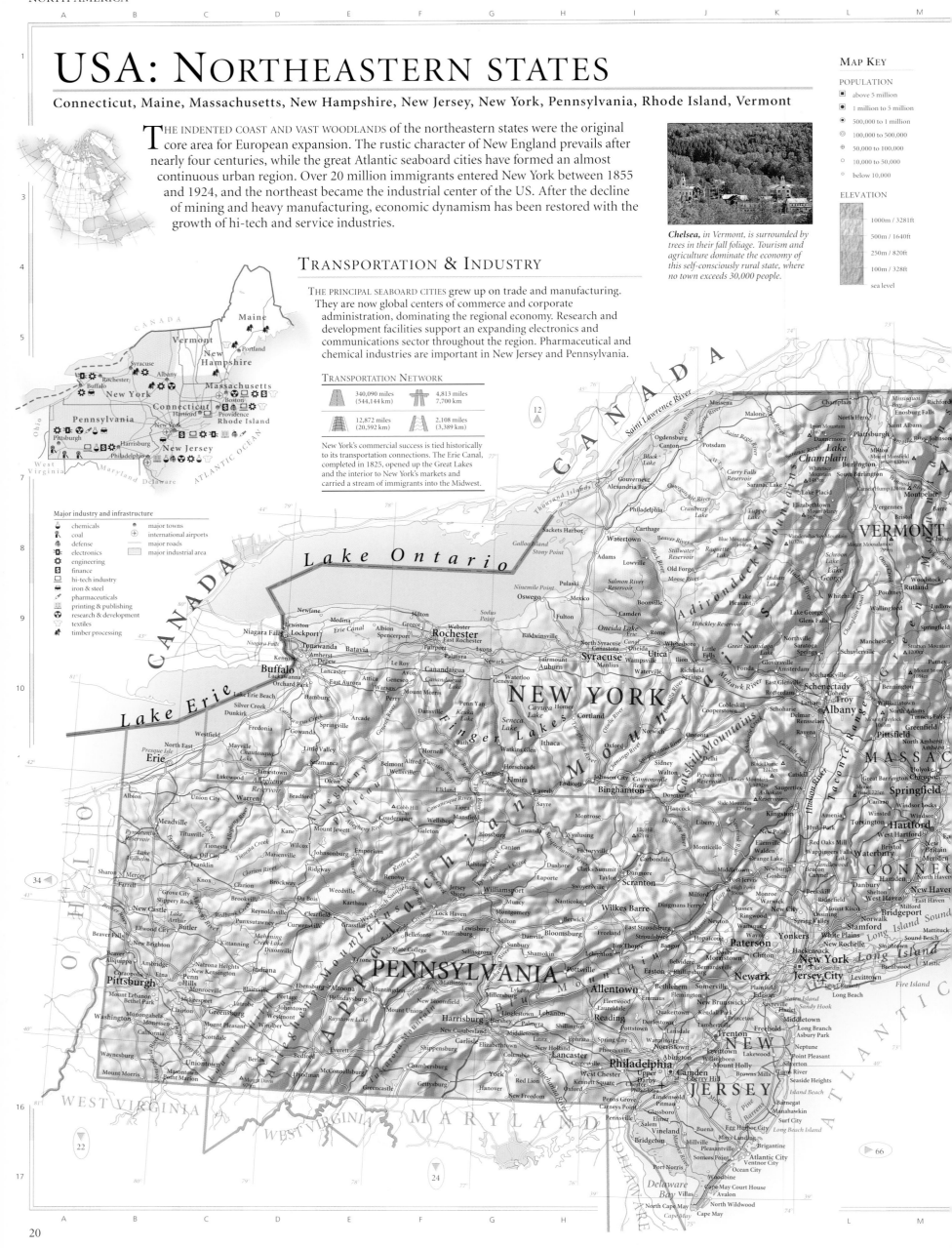

The Hancock Tower dominates the skyline of Boston's business district. New England's principal city has grown through land reclamation within Massachusetts Bay.

USING THE LAND & SEA

PENNSYLVANIA HAS a large rural population and a major agribusiness sector dominated by livestock-raising. Fruit, vegetables, and nursery plants are grown throughout the region, with fishing on the coast. Cranberries and maple syrup are traditional products in New England. Large areas of cropland in the north have been returned to forest this century.

Land use and agricultural distribution
- cattle
- poultry
- cranberries
- fishing
- fodder
- fruit
- maple syrup
- timber
- major towns
- pasture
- cropland
- forest

THE URBAN/RURAL POPULATION DIVIDE

urban 78%   rural 22%

0 10 20 30 40 50 60 70 80 90 100

POPULATION DENSITY	TOTAL LAND AREA
277 people per sq mile	161,096 sq miles
(107 people per sq km)	(417,222 sq km)

Foreign competition and a depletion of the stocks in the Atlantic fishing grounds caused a decline in fishing in the seaboard states. Recent years have seen a gradual recovery; Massachusetts now annually ranks third or fourth in the US in terms of the value of fish caught.

THE LANDSCAPE

THE MARSHY LOWLANDS of the Atlantic Coastal Plain dwindle toward the north, giving way to the rocky coast of Maine. Uplifted over 400 million years ago, the Appalachian Mountains have since been carved into several discrete ranges by the region's main rivers and heavily denuded by successive glacial advances. This broad upland belt, with the younger Adirondack Mountains, is bounded by the Great Lakes in the northwest.

The islands, inlets, and promontories of Maine's coast extend 3,500 miles (5,630 km). The tidal range is particularly high, varying between 12 and 24 ft (3.7–7.3 m).

The narrow Finger Lakes of northwestern New York State were formed by glaciers cutting into deep deposits of material from an earlier ice advance.

The Adirondack Mountains were formed when the deeply buried basement rocks were forced upward in a dome by as much as 2 miles (3 km).

The lower Connecticut River has cut down into the flat, clay valley floor, which previously formed the bed of an ice-dammed lake.

Deposits of glacial till from the last Ice Age are up to 1,000 ft (300 m) deep around Lake Ontario.

The Genesee River in New York State has eroded a canyon 800 ft (240 m) deep through the Appalachians. The river continued to cut downward as the land was uplifted.

Green Mountains

Niagara Falls
1000m / 3281ft
500m / 1640ft
250m / 820ft
100m / 328ft
sea level

Lake Erie, receiving water flowing from the rest of the Great Lakes, drains via Niagara Falls, into Lake Ontario, which lies 325 ft (99 m) below.

Cape Cod

Resistant rock
River fed by water from the Great Lakes
Force of water continues to undercut cliffs
Softer rock is eroded more quickly

Niagara Falls was created where the Niagara River reached an escarpment capped by hard limestone. This was gradually eroded exposing softer rock strata. Plunging water continues to erode the softer strata causing the falls to recede upstream.

The waterfalls at Dingmans Ferry are typical of those found in villages on the "Fall-line," where rivers drop from the Appalachians to the coastal lowlands. These locations provide waterpower and are often at the navigable head of the river.

Dingmans Ferry

The Atlantic Coastal Plain is part of the continental shelf, which extends several hundred miles out to sea, providing a rich environment for marine life.

Rising sea levels have flooded river valleys along the coast, creating rias such as Long Island Sound.

Cape Cod, Long Island, and the islands between them mark the top of a great terminal moraine, formed on the front of the ice sheet that once covered the land. This ridge of deposited material was subsequently flooded by rising seas.

At Provincetown, Cape Cod, complex and powerful ocean currents continue to modify the shoreline, washing away some 3 ft (1 m) of the lower cape each year, while extending the beaches in the north.

SCALE 1:2,750,000
(projection: Lambert Conformal Conic)

Km
0 5 10 20 30 40 50 60 70 80 90 100

Miles
0 5 10 20 30 40 50 60 70 80 90 100

USA: MID-EASTERN STATES

Delaware, District of Columbia, Kentucky, Maryland, North Carolina,
South Carolina, Tennessee, Virginia, West Virginia

KEY EVENTS IN AMERICAN HISTORY took place in this diverse region, which became the front line between the North and the South during the Civil War of the 1860s. Strong regional contrasts exist between the fertile coastal plains, the isolated upcountry of the Appalachian Mountains, and the cotton-growing areas of the Mississippi lowlands to the west. While coal mining, a traditional industry in the Appalachians, has declined in recent years leaving much rural poverty, service industries elsewhere have increased, especially in Washington D.C., the nation's capital.

MAP KEY

POPULATION

- ◉ 500,000 to 1 million
- ◎ 100,000 to 500,000
- ⊕ 50,000 to 100,000
- ○ 10,000 to 50,000
- ∘ below 10,000

ELEVATION

- 6000m / 19,686ft
- 4000m / 13,124ft
- 3000m / 9843ft
- 2000m / 6562ft
- 1000m / 3281ft
- 500m / 1640ft
- 250m / 820ft
- 100m / 328ft
- sea level

SCALE 1:3,000,000
(projection: Lambert Conformal Conic)

Km 0 5 10 20 30 40 50 60 70 80
Miles 0 5 10 20 30 40 50 60 70 80

The Bluegrass region of Kentucky centers on the town of Lexington. This exceptionally fertile rolling plain is well known for its thoroughbred horse-breeding ranches.

TRANSPORTATION & INDUSTRY

IN THE URBANIZED NORTHEAST, manufacturing remains important, alongside a burgeoning service sector. North Carolina is a major center for industrial research and development. Traditional industries include Tennessee whiskey and textiles in South Carolina. The decline of open-cast coal mining in the Appalachians has been hastened by environmental controls, although adventure tourism is a flourishing new industry.

Major industry and infrastructure

- adventure tourism
- car manufacture
- coal
- electronics
- engineering
- finance
- food processing
- hi-tech industry
- mining
- research & development
- textiles
- ■ capital cities
- ■ major towns
- ✈ international airports
- — major roads
- major industrial areas

TRANSPORTATION NETWORK

- 452,218 miles (723,548 km)
- 5,737 miles (8,267 km)
- 18,336 miles (29,503 km)
- 4,404 miles (7,081 km)

Tennessee's rivers are part of an important inland bulk transportation network. Memphis connects with New Orleans in the south, and with cities as distant as Minneapolis, Sioux City, Chicago, and Pittsburgh, via the Mississippi and its tributaries.

THE LANDSCAPE

THE EASTERN TRIBUTARIES OF THE MISSISSIPPI drain the interior lowlands. The Cumberland Plateau and the parallel ranges of the Appalachians have been successively uplifted and eroded over time, with the eastern side reduced to a series of foothills, known as the Piedmont. The broad coastal plain gradually falls away into salt marshes, lagoons, and offshore bars, broken by flooded estuaries along the shores of the Atlantic.

The Mammoth Cave is part of an extensive cave system in the limestone region of southwestern Kentucky. It stretches for over 300 miles (485 km) on five different levels and contains three rivers and three lakes.

The Mississippi River and its tributary the Ohio River form the western border of the region.

The Cumberland Plateau is the most southwesterly part of the Appalachians. Big Black Mountain, at 4,180 ft (1,274 m), is the highest point in the range.

The Great Smoky Mountains form the western escarpment of the Appalachians. The region is heavily forested, with over 130 species of trees.

The Blue Ridge Mountains are a steep ridge culminating in Mount Mitchell, the highest point in the Appalachians, at 6,684 ft (2,037 m).

Natural Bridge in eastern Kentucky is an arch 78 ft (26 m) long and 65 ft (20 m) high. It has been shaped out of resistant sandstone by gradual weathering processes that removed the softer rock lying underneath.

The Allegheny Mountains form the northwestern edge of the Appalachian mountain chain. Continuous folding has formed rich seams of bituminous coal.

Appalachian Mountains

Farmland on the eastern shores of Chesapeake Bay is sustained by artificial drainage. The area also provides refuge for a variety of waterfowl.

The many inlets of Chesapeake Bay are the flooded tributaries of the main river valley, which have been inundated by rising sea levels.

Salt marshes such as Great Dismal Swamp develop where the coast is sheltered. Vast areas of such marshland have been reclaimed for farmland and settlement.

Cape Hatteras is the easternmost point of an offshore barrier island, a wave-deposited sand-bar which has become permanent, establishing its own vegetation.

Barrier islands

Tidal inlet

Barrier island

These intertidal mud flats become submerged at high tide

Barrier islands are common along the coasts of North and South Carolina. As sea levels rise, wave action builds up ridges of sand and pebbles parallel to the coast, separated by lagoons or intertidal mud flats, which are flooded at high tide.

Map labels

INDIANA, ILLINOIS, MISSOURI, ARKANSAS, MISSISSIPPI, ALABAMA, KENTUCKY, TENNESSEE

Louisville, Nashville, Memphis, Chattanooga, Paducah, Bowling Green, Clarksville, Murfreesboro, Jackson

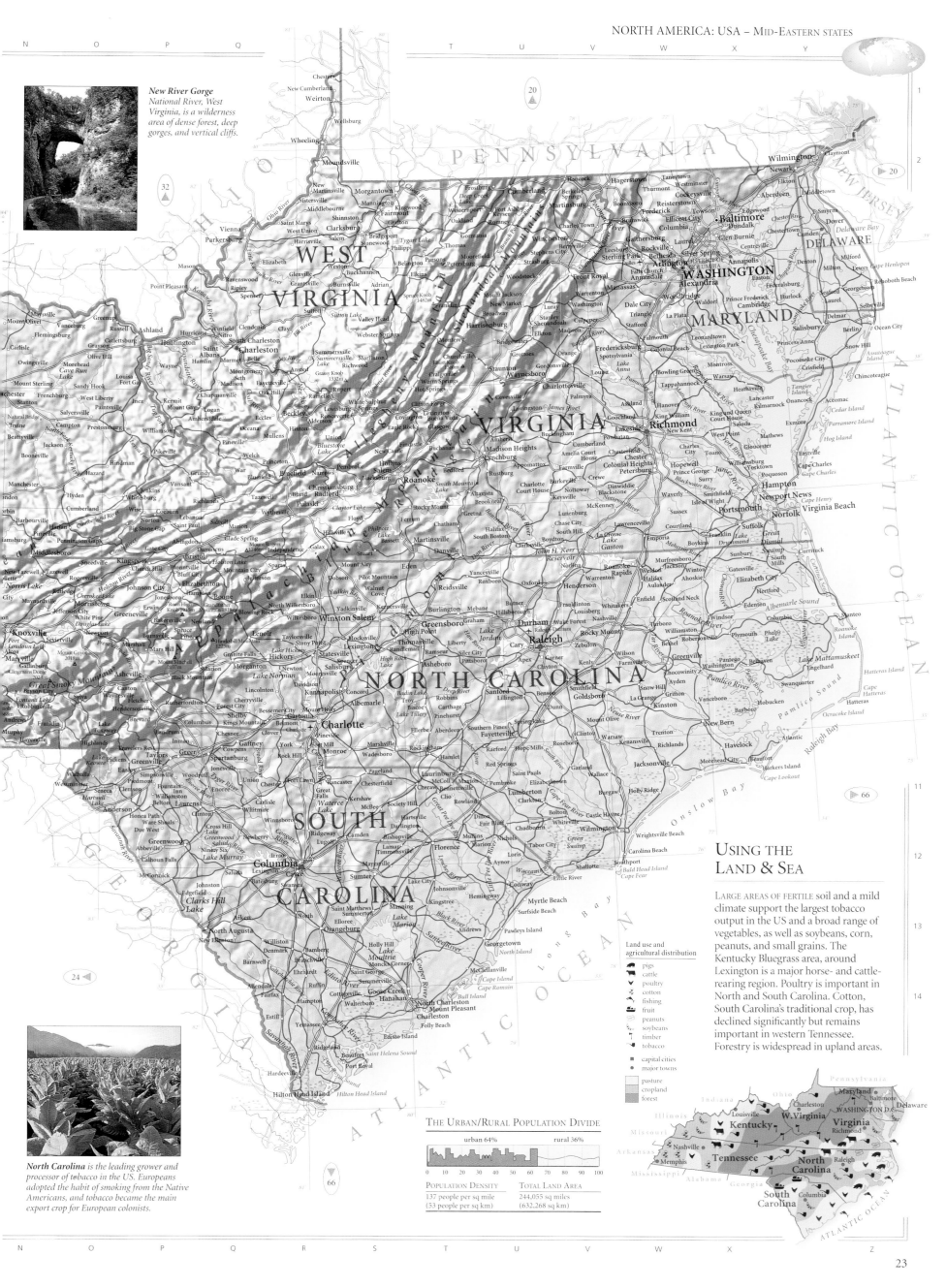

New River Gorge
National River, West Virginia, is a wilderness area of dense forest, deep gorges, and vertical cliffs.

North Carolina is the leading grower and processor of tobacco in the US. Europeans adopted the habit of smoking from the Native Americans, and tobacco became the main export crop for European colonists.

USING THE LAND & SEA

LARGE AREAS OF FERTILE soil and a mild climate support the largest tobacco output in the US and a broad range of vegetables, as well as soybeans, corn, peanuts, and small grains. The Kentucky Bluegrass area, around Lexington is a major horse- and cattle-rearing region. Poultry is important in North and South Carolina. Cotton, South Carolina's traditional crop, has declined significantly but remains important in western Tennessee. Forestry is widespread in upland areas.

Land use and agricultural distribution

- pigs
- cattle
- poultry
- cotton
- fishing
- fruit
- peanuts
- soybeans
- timber
- tobacco
- ■ capital cities
- ● major towns
- pasture
- cropland
- forest

THE URBAN/RURAL POPULATION DIVIDE

urban 64%   rural 36%

0 10 20 30 40 50 60 70 80 90 100

POPULATION DENSITY	TOTAL LAND AREA
137 people per sq mile	244,055 sq miles
(53 people per sq km)	(632,268 sq km)

USA: SOUTHERN STATES

Alabama, Florida, Georgia, Louisiana, Mississippi

THE SOUTH HAS MAINTAINED a separate identity and outlook throughout the history of the US. Defeat in the Civil War (1861–65) brought chronic poverty to the former confederate states, while the subsequent liberation of four million slaves began a struggle that continued until the 1960s, when the Civil Rights movement achieved an end to legal racial segregation. Many parts of the South have experienced rapid change. Tourism and retirement communities, together with agriculture, have fueled growth in Florida, while defense-related industries have boosted the growth of cities such as Miami and Atlanta. Many people retain a strong attachment to their history and culture, evidenced by Creole-speaking Cajuns in Louisiana and Hispanic communities in South Florida.

TRANSPORTATION & INDUSTRY

FLORIDA'S TOURIST TRADE is only part of a flourishing service sector, which has swelled the principal cities of the south. Petroleum and mineral extraction has made the Gulf Coast a major industrial region. Traditional textile production remains important in Georgia, while advanced new industries have grown from the NASA Space Program.

TRANSPORTATION NETWORK

441,625 miles (706,600 km)

5116 miles (8186 km)

16,597 miles (26,555 km)

6179 miles (9942 km)

Atlanta's Hartsfield International airport is one of the busiest in the world. A dramatic rise in the use of regional air transportation has helped to integrate the major cities of the Southern states.

The French Quarter is the traditional cultural center of New Orleans, one of the historic Southern cities. The city once thrived on the cotton trade but now relies mainly on tourism and on oil from the Gulf of Mexico.

Major industry and infrastructure

- ✈ aerospace
- 🚗 car manufacture
- ⚗ chemicals
- ⛏ coal
- 🛡 defense
- ▣ electronics
- ⚙ engineering
- 🏭 food processing
- ⛽ oil
- 🧵 textiles
- 🏖 tourism
- • major towns
- ✈ international airports
- — major roads
- ▨ major industrial areas

The cypress swamps of the Mississippi Delta form in the backswamps behind the levees of the river and in the multitude of subsiding delta basins.

THE LANDSCAPE

THE BLUE RIDGE MOUNTAINS in the north are skirted by the gentle hills of the Piedmont, whose rivers drain south onto the great flat expanse of the coastal plain. Sandy barrier beaches and islands dominate the seashore, tracing around the swampy limestone arm of Florida. The Mississippi meanders toward its delta in the west, crossing the thickly mantled alluvial plain of the interior lowlands.

Cathedral Caverns, near Huntsville, Alabama, is a system of vast limestone caves, with a main opening 1,000 ft (300 m) high and 150 ft (50 m) wide.

The Yazoo River flows parallel to the Mississippi through a common floodplain. The confluence of the rivers is deferred downstream because flood deposition has built the Mississippi channel up above the level of the Yazoo.

At De Soto Falls, Alabama, the Little River descends into the deepest canyon east of the Mississippi, with sheer cliff walls up to 700 ft (230 m) high.

Brasstown Bald, in the Blue Ridge Mountains of Georgia, is the region's highest point, at 4,784 ft (1,485 m).

The Mississippi is the world's third longest river and moves over a billion tons (tonnes) of sediment a year, creating deep alluvial plains. Flooding is a constant threat in lowland areas.

Piedmont

In Providence Canyon, Georgia, the Chattahoochee River has cut straight down through the sandy bedrock, to leave sheer rock faces and pinnacles that have been smoothed by subsequent weathering.

Sandbars, deposited by waves breaking offshore, form barrier beaches along much of the coastline, creating sheltered lagoons and salt marshes behind them.

Mississippi Delta

The delta of the Mississippi over 5,000 years ago

Present-day delta

Delta lobe

Atchafalaya Bay

Lake Okeechobee is actually a shallow, slow-moving river, 150 miles (240 km) long and 50 miles (80 km) wide.

Across Florida the coastal plain is mostly less than 75 ft (25 m) above sea level. The land is underlain by limestone pitted with hollows that have been filled by over 10,000 lakes.

Over the last 5,000 years, the lower course of the Mississippi has moved back and forth over great distances. These changes, caused by varying sediment loads and human modification, have resulted in a "bird's foot" delta with several lobes, each reflecting the river's different historic position.

The Everglades lie in a limestone hollow formed over two million years ago, which has gradually become filled with swamp deposits.

Florida Keys

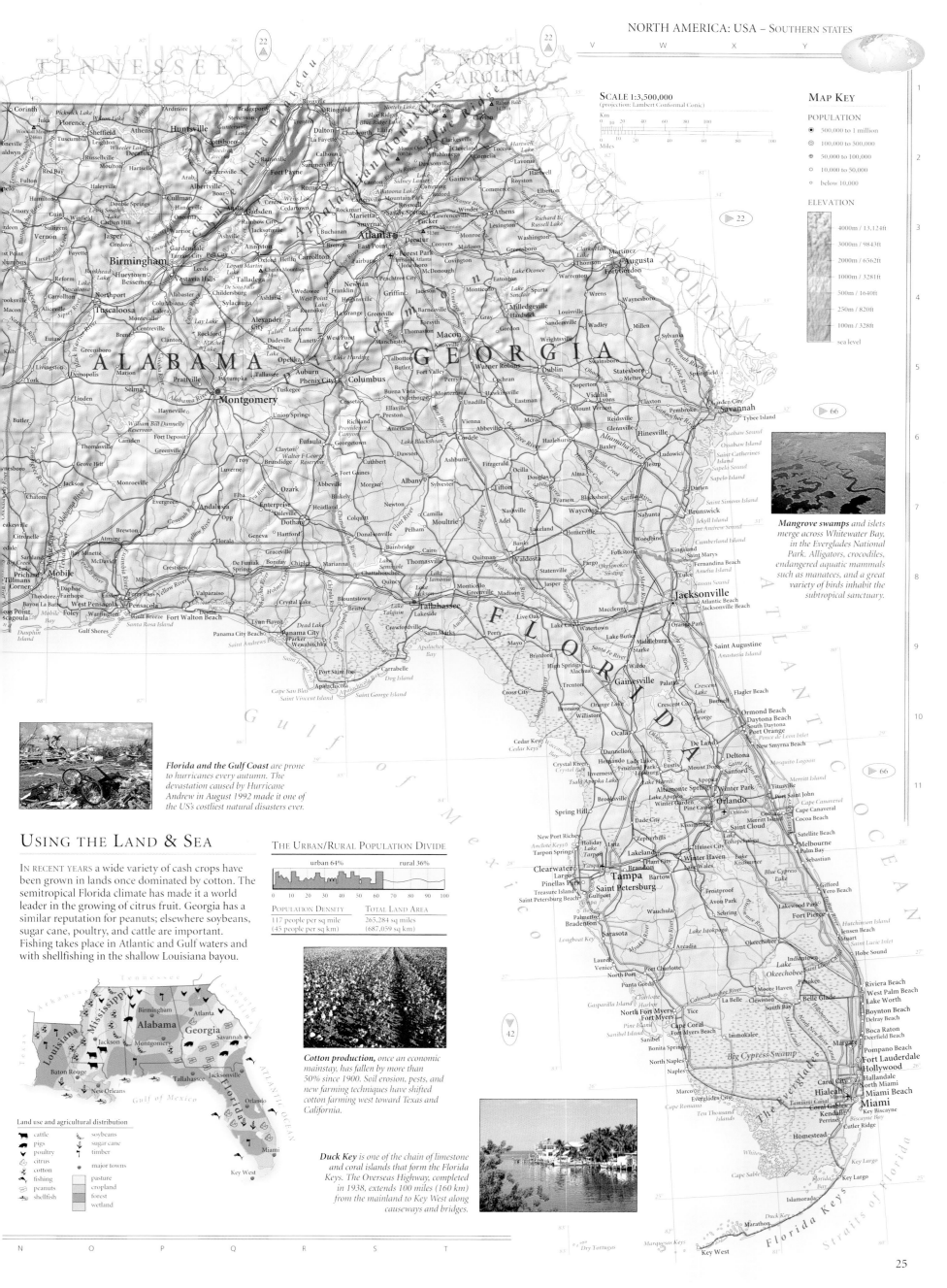

SCALE 1:3,500,000
(projection: Lambert Conformal Conic)

MAP KEY

POPULATION
◉ 500,000 to 1 million
◎ 100,000 to 500,000
⊕ 50,000 to 100,000
⊙ 10,000 to 50,000
○ below 10,000

ELEVATION
4000m / 13,124ft
3000m / 9843ft
2000m / 6562ft
1000m / 3281ft
500m / 1640ft
250m / 820ft
100m / 328ft

sea level

Mangrove swamps and islets merge across Whitewater Bay, in the Everglades National Park. Alligators, crocodiles, endangered aquatic mammals such as manatees, and a great variety of birds inhabit the subtropical sanctuary.

Florida and the Gulf Coast are prone to hurricanes every autumn. The devastation caused by Hurricane Andrew in August 1992 made it one of the US's costliest natural disasters ever.

USING THE LAND & SEA

IN RECENT YEARS a wide variety of cash crops have been grown in lands once dominated by cotton. The semitropical Florida climate has made it a world leader in the growing of citrus fruit. Georgia has a similar reputation for peanuts; elsewhere soybeans, sugar cane, poultry, and cattle are important. Fishing takes place in Atlantic and Gulf waters and with shellfishing in the shallow Louisiana bayou.

THE URBAN/RURAL POPULATION DIVIDE

urban 64%	rural 36%

0 10 20 30 40 50 60 70 80 90 100

POPULATION DENSITY	TOTAL LAND AREA
117 people per sq mile	265,284 sq miles
(45 people per sq km)	(687,059 sq km)

Cotton production, once an economic mainstay, has fallen by more than 50% since 1900. Soil erosion, pests, and new farming techniques have shifted cotton farming west toward Texas and California.

Land use and agricultural distribution
- cattle
- pigs
- poultry
- citrus
- cotton
- peanuts
- shellfish
- soybeans
- sugar cane
- timber
- major towns
- pasture
- cropland
- forest
- wetland

Duck Key is one of the chain of limestone and coral islands that form the Florida Keys. The Overseas Highway, completed in 1938, extends 100 miles (160 km) from the mainland to Key West along causeways and bridges.

USA: TEXAS

IRST EXPLORED BY SPANIARDS moving north from Mexico in search of gold, Texas was controlled by Spain and then by Mexico, before becoming an independent republic in 1836 and joining the Union of States in 1845. During the 19th century, many migrants who came to Texas raised cattle on the abundant land; in the 20th century, they were joined by prospectors attracted by the promise of oil riches. Today, although natural resources, especially oil, still form the basis of its wealth, the diversified Texan economy includes thriving hi-tech and financial industries. The major urban centers, home to 80% of the population, lie in the south and east, and include Houston, the oil city, and Dallas–Fort Worth. Hispanic influences remain strong, especially in southern and western Texas.

Dallas was founded in 1841 as a prairie trading post and its development was stimulated by the arrival of railroads. Cotton and then oil funded the town's early growth. Today, the modern, high-rise skyline of Dallas reflects the city's position as a leading center of banking, insurance, and the petroleum industry in the southwest.

USING THE LAND

COTTON PRODUCTION AND LIVESTOCK-RAISING, particularly cattle, dominate farming, although crop failures and the demands of local markets have led to some diversification. Following the introduction of modern farming techniques, cotton production spread out of the east into the plains of western Texas. Cattle ranches are widespread, while sheep and goats are raised on the dry Edwards Plateau.

Land use and agricultural distribution
- cattle
- goats
- sheep
- cereals
- cotton
- major towns

pasture
cropland
forest
barren

THE URBAN/RURAL POPULATION DIVIDE

urban 80%   rural 20%

0 10 20 30 40 50 60 70 80 90 100

POPULATION DENSITY
66 people per sq mile
(26 people per sq km)

TOTAL LAND AREA
267,338 sq miles
(692,402 sq km)

38

The huge cattle ranches of Texas developed during the 19th century when land was plentiful and could be acquired cheaply. Today, more cattle and sheep are raised in Texas than in any other state.

THE LANDSCAPE

TEXAS IS MADE UP OF A SERIES of massive steps descending from the mountains and high plains of the west and northwest to the coastal lowlands in the southeast. Many of the state's borders are delineated by water. The Rio Grande flows from the Rocky Mountains to the Gulf of Mexico, marking the border with Mexico.

Cap Rock Escarpment juts out of the plains, running 200 miles (320 km) from north to south. Its height varies from 300 ft (90 m) rising to sheer cliffs up to 1,000 ft (300 m).

42

The Llano Estacado or Staked Plain in northern Texas is known for its harsh environment. In the north, freezing winds carrying ice and snow sweep down from the Rocky Mountains. To the south, sandstorms frequently blow up, scouring anything in their paths. Flash floods, in the wide, flat riverbeds that remain dry for most of the year, are another hazard.

The Guadalupe Mountains lie in the southern Rocky Mountains. They incorporate Guadalupe Peak, the highest in Texas, rising 8,749 ft (2,667 m).

The Rio Grande flows from the Rocky Mountains through semi-arid land, supporting sparse vegetation. The river actually shrinks along its course, losing more water through evaporation and seepage than it gains from its tributaries and rainfall.

Big Bend National Park

Flowing through 1,500-ft (450-m) high gorges, the shallow, muddy Rio Grande makes a 90° bend. This marks the southern border of Big Bend National Park, and gives it its name. The area is a mixture of forested mountains, deserts, and canyons.

The Red River flows for 1,300 miles (2,090 km), marking most of the northern border of Texas. A dam and reservoir along its course provide vital irrigation and hydroelectric power to the surrounding area.

Sabine River

Extensive forests of pine and cypress grow in the eastern corner of the coastal lowlands where the average rainfall is 45 inches (1,145 mm) a year. This is higher than the rest of the state and over twice the average in the west.

In the coastal lowlands of southeastern Texas the Earth's crust is warping, causing the land to subside and allowing the sea to invade. Around Galveston, the rate of downward tilting is 6 inches (15 cm) per year.

Edwards Plateau is a limestone outcrop. It is part of the Great Plains, bounded to the southeast by the Balcones Escarpment, which marks the southerly limit of the plains.

Laguna Madre in southern Texas has been almost completely cut off from the sea by Padre Island. This sandbank was created by wave action, carrying and depositing material along the coast, in a process known as longshore drift.

Padre Island

Oil deposits

Oil trapped by fault

Oil deposits migrate through reservoir rocks such as shale

Oil accumulates beneath impermeable cap rock

Impermeable rock strata

Salt dome

Oil deposits are found beneath much of Texas. They collect as oil migrates upward through porous layers of rock until it is trapped, either by a cap of rock above a salt dome or by a fault line that exposes impermeable rock through which the oil cannot rise.

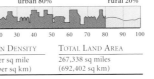

TRANSPORTATION & INDUSTRY

INDUSTRY IN THE 20TH CENTURY has largely concentrated on the processing of local raw materials, especially oil – deposits have been discovered underneath 65% of the state's area. The technological demands of the oil industry and defense-related institutions, particularly NASA, have stimulated the development of numerous electronics and hi-tech firms which, alongside many national corporate headquarters, are based in Dallas–Fort Worth and Houston.

Major industry and infrastructure

chemicals		mining	
defense		oil	
engineering		textiles	
finance		major towns	
food processing		international airports	
gas		major roads	
hi-tech industry		major industrial areas	

TRANSPORTATION NETWORK

293,509 miles (496,614 km)	3,229 miles (5,166 km)
10,681 miles (17,089 km)	845 miles (1,359 km)

The sheer size of Texas promoted the development of an extensive road and rail network. The highway system, although well developed, is concentrated in the east.

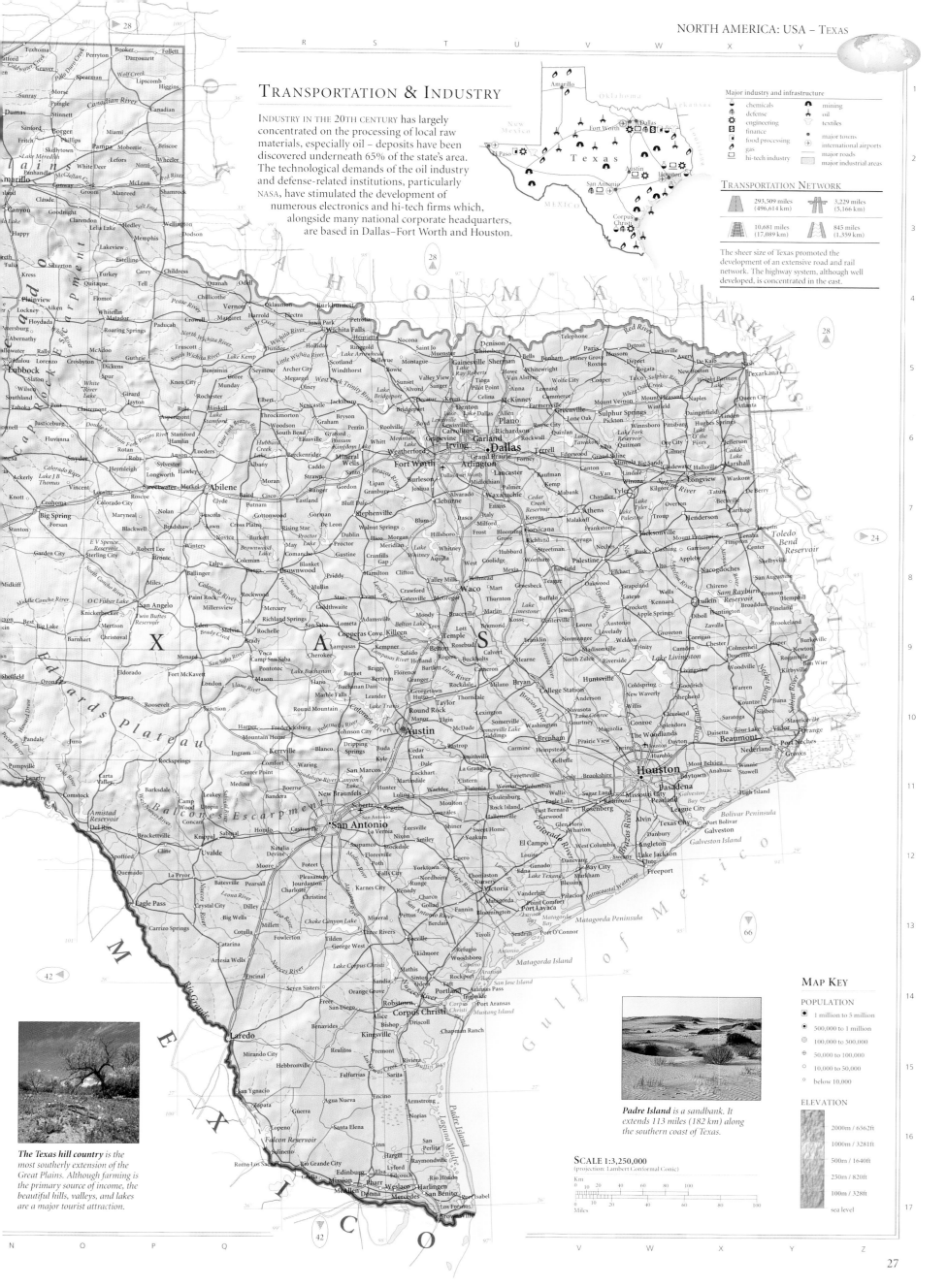

The Texas hill country is the most southerly extension of the Great Plains. Although farming is the primary source of income, the beautiful hills, valleys, and lakes are a major tourist attraction.

Padre Island is a sandbank. It extends 113 miles (182 km) along the southern coast of Texas.

MAP KEY

POPULATION

- 1 million to 5 million
- 500,000 to 1 million
- 100,000 to 500,000
- 50,000 to 100,000
- 10,000 to 50,000
- below 10,000

ELEVATION

- 2000m / 6562ft
- 1000m / 3281ft
- 500m / 1640ft
- 250m / 820ft
- 100m / 328ft
- sea level

SCALE 1:3,250,000
(projection: Lambert Conformal Conic)

USA: SOUTH MIDWESTERN STATES

Arkansas, Kansas, Missouri, Oklahoma

THE EXPANSION OF THE US focused on this region in the mid-19th century. Settlers spread from the confluence of the Missouri and Mississippi Rivers up onto the Great Plains. This treeless expanse, which early explorers had called the Great American Desert, was turned into one of the world's richest agricultural regions. But periodic droughts, coupled with overintensive farming, led to the "dustbowl" soil erosion crisis of the 1930s, the abandonment of many farms, and a mass exodus to the West Coast. The land has since recovered, although the mechanization of agriculture has led to a decline in the rural population. In recent years, suburban residential development has spread rapidly across the wooded Ozark Plateau in the east of the region.

TRANSPORTATION & INDUSTRY

THE PROCESSING OF AGRICULTURAL PRODUCTS, such as brewing and meatpacking, has traditionally been important in these states. In Kansas and Oklahoma, diversified manufacturing now supplements income from fossil fuels; Wichita has become a world center for aeronautical engineering, an industry that also employs many people in neighboring Missouri.

Major industry and infrastructure

- ✈ aerospace
- ✿ engineering
- S finance
- food processing
- ◊ gas
- mining
- ⚓ oil
- vehicle manufacture
- • major towns
- ✈ international airports
- — major roads
- major industrial areas

Agricultural produce from the plains is moved by barges along the Mississippi. The river now carries a far greater tonnage of freight than any other waterway system in the US.

TRANSPORTATION NETWORK

380,307 miles (608,491 km)	4,068 miles (6,508 km)
16,185 miles (25,896 km)	1,994 miles (3,208 km)

The Arkansas River and its tributaries allow access to over half of the US's navigable inland waterways. A system of locks and dams along the river provides Tulsa, in Oklahoma, with a navigable water route to the Gulf of Mexico.

MAP KEY

POPULATION

- ◎ 100,000 to 500,000
- ⊕ 50,000 to 100,000
- ○ 10,000 to 50,000
- ◦ below 10,000

ELEVATION

- 1000m / 3281ft
- 500m / 1640ft
- 250m / 820ft
- 100m / 328ft
- sea level

THE LANDSCAPE

MOST OF THE REGION consists of high, treeless plains, which gradually descend east from the Rocky Mountains. Drainage follows this slope, with rivers flowing toward the alluvial lowlands of the Mississippi in the southeast. Between the plains and the lowlands lie various ranges of wooded hills, including the deeply incised Ozark Plateau.

Collapsed limestone caverns led to the formation of Big Basin in Kansas, a depression 100 ft (33 m) deep and 1 mile (1.6 km) wide.

The Great Salt Plains of northern Oklahoma cover 45 sq miles (116 sq km). The arid, white flats were left by the gradual evaporation of an ancient salt lake.

Underground water reserves

The Ogallala Aquifer, beneath the Great Plains, is the largest known source of underground water in the world. There is concern about the rapid depletion of this finite water supply by irrigation.

Flint Hills is the region's easternmost major escarpment. Steep, grassy uplands are interspersed with rocky, wooded ravines and outcrops of limestone and chert.

Missouri River

Red River

Devil's Den is a dry badland area. The rugged landscape, strewn with large boulders, is the eroded remnant of a spur extending from the Arbuckle Mountains to the west.

Ouachita Mountains

The Mississippi, North America's longest river, is joined by the Missouri, its main tributary, on a floodplain which spreads south to the Gulf of Mexico.

The Ozark Plateau is a wooded, hilly region of rivers and narrow, winding lakes. The Lake of the Ozarks was created by the damming of the Osage River in 1930.

Lake Ouachita, in Arkansas, is one of a number of irregularly-shaped lakes found among the ridges of the Ouachita Mountains.

Mississippi River

Crowleys Ridge is a long, sandy ridge, rising from the Mississippi floodplain. It was formed over thousands of years, by the deposition of sand blown eastward from the Great Plains.

SCALE 1:3,000,000
(projection: Lambert Conformal Conic)

Km
0 5 10 20 30 40 50 60 70

Miles
0 5 10 20 30 40 50 60 70

The landscape of northeastern Kansas is interlaced by rivers that have cut broad wooded valleys through the gentle hills. All the rivers in Kansas form part of the massive Missouri/Mississippi drainage basin.

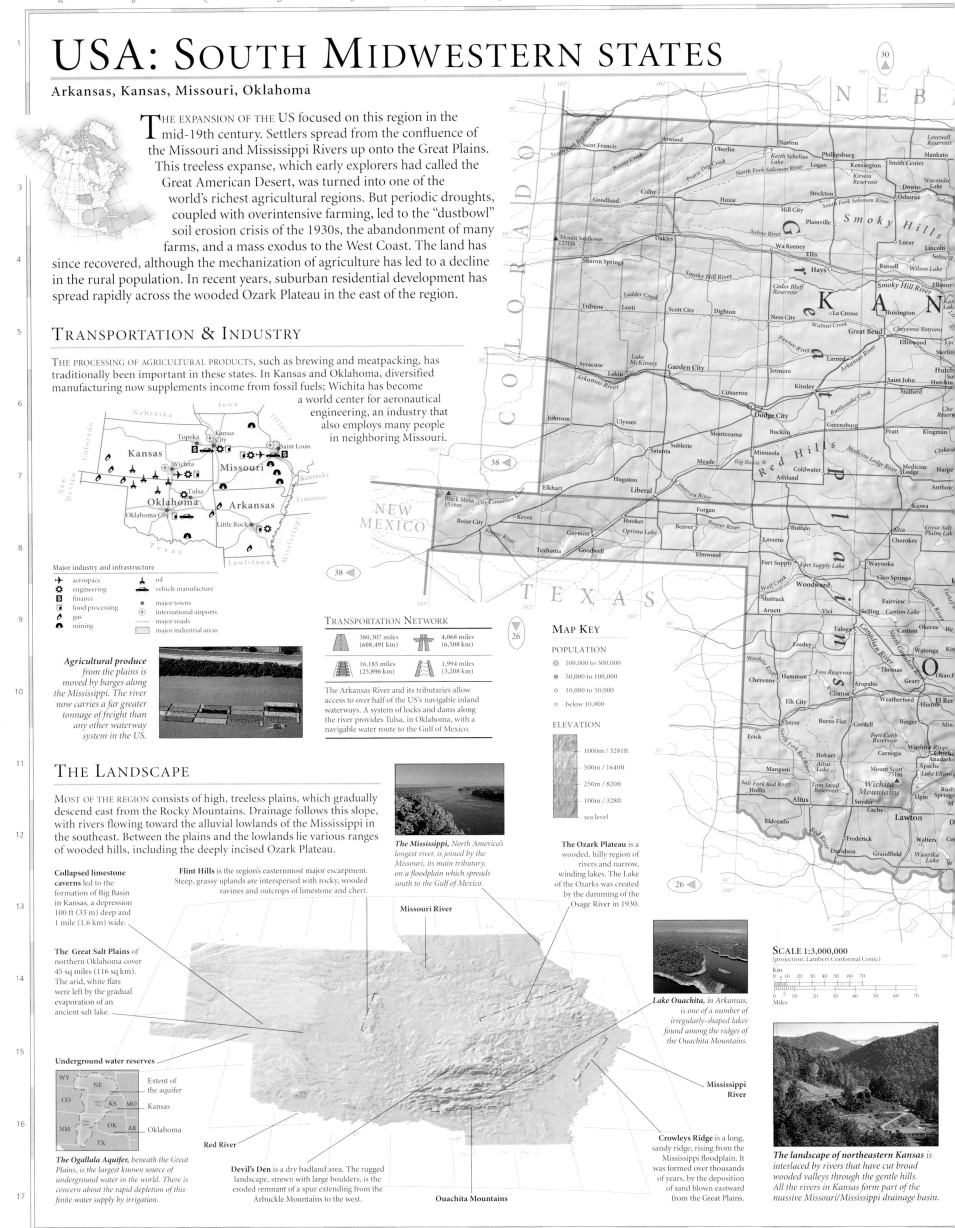

Gateway Arch, in Saint Louis, Missouri, is 634 ft (192 m) high. The huge steel arch symbolizes the city's historic role as the "Gateway to the West."

USING THE LAND

THE PROBLEMS of a harsh continental climate, with severe winters and hot, dry summers, are partially offset by the rich soils of the plains. Kansas is a major cereal crop producer, ranking first in US production of wheat and sorghum. Rainfall increases toward the east, favoring the cultivation of soybeans, cotton, and rice, with corn concentrated in Missouri. Huge herds of cattle are raised in Oklahoma, Kansas, and Missouri.

A combine harvester works the land on the Great Plains. A hundred years ago this region, also known as the prairies – the French word for pasture – was covered with tall, wild grasses.

THE URBAN/RURAL POPULATION DIVIDE

urban 65%   rural 35%

0 10 20 30 40 50 60 70 80 90 100

POPULATION DENSITY
48 people per sq mile
(19 people per sq km)

TOTAL LAND AREA
274,900 sq miles
(712,177 sq km)

Land use and agricultural distribution

- cattle
- poultry
- cereals
- corn
- cotton
- fodder
- rice
- soybeans
- major towns
- pasture
- cropland
- forest

USA: UPPER PLAINS STATES

Iowa, Minnesota, Nebraska, North Dakota, South Dakota

Lying at the very heart of the North American continent, much of this region was acquired from France as part of the Louisiana Purchase in 1803. The area was largely bypassed by the early waves of westward migrants. When Europeans did settle during the 19th century, they displaced the Native Americans who lived on the plains. The settlers planted arable crops and raised cattle on the immensely fertile prairie land, founding an agrarian tradition that flourishes today. Most of this region remains rural; of the five states, only in Minnesota has there been significant diversification away from agriculture and resource-based industries into the hi-tech and service sectors.

USING THE LAND

THE POPULAR IMAGE of these states as agricultural is entirely justified; prairies stretch uninterrupted across most of the area. Croplands fall into two regions: the wheat belt of the plains and the corn belt of the central US. Cash crops, such as soybeans, are grown to supplement incomes. Livestock, particularly pigs and cattle, are raised throughout this region.

Dark, fertile prairie soil in the southeast provides Minnesota's most productive farmland. Hot, humid summers create a long growing season for corn cultivation.

THE URBAN/RURAL POPULATION DIVIDE

urban 64%   rural 36%

0 10 20 30 40 50 60 70 80 90 100

POPULATION DENSITY
28 people per sq mile
(11 people per sq km)

TOTAL LAND AREA
365,287 sq miles
(946,056 sq km)

Land use and agricultural distribution
- cattle
- pigs
- corn
- soybeans
- wheat
- major towns
- pasture
- cropland
- forest
- wetland

TRANSPORTATION & INDUSTRY

FOOD PROCESSING and the production of farm machinery are supported by the large agricultural sector. Mineral exploitation is also an important activity: gold is mined in the ore-rich Black Hills of South Dakota, and both North Dakota and Nebraska are emerging as major petroleum producers.

Water erosion along the Little Missouri River has carried away sedimentary deposits, creating rugged landscapes known as badlands.

TRANSPORTATION NETWORK

504,522 miles (807,235 km)
3,422 miles (5,475 km)
16,940 miles (27,104 km)
683 miles (1,098 km)

Nebraska's central location makes it an important transportation artery for east–west traffic. Minnesota's road network radiates out of the hub of the twin cities Minneapolis–Saint Paul.

Major industry and infrastructure
- coal
- engineering
- electronics
- finance
- food processing
- oil & gas
- mining
- major towns
- international airports
- major roads
- major industrial areas

THE LANDSCAPE

THESE STATES STRADDLE the Great Plains and the lowlands of the central US, with Minnesota lying in a transition zone between the eastern forests and the prairies. The region was shaped by repeated ice advances and retreats, leaving a flat relief broken only by the numerous lakes and broad river networks that drain the prairies.

Escarpment   Ridge   Hollows are formed in permeable strata by small mudslides

Water flowing into gullies erodes back the escarpment

Badlands are formed by stormwater run-off. This flows down the impermeable strata of the escarpment and saturates the permeable strata, leading to mudslides and the formation of gullies.

North Dakota Badlands

The Minnesota landscape contains many post-glacial features, including its numerous lakes, boulder-strewn hills, and mineral-rich deposits.

Although it escaped the last glaciation, the limestone bedrock of southeastern Minnesota has been eroded by surface and subterranean streams, leaving a network of underground caverns and steep-sided valleys.

In the Badlands of North and South Dakota, horizontal layers of sandstone have been eroded by rivers, leaving a landscape of narrow gullies, sharp crests, and pinnacles.

South Dakota Badlands

Chimney Rock is a remnant of an ancient land surface, eroded by the North Platte River. The tip of its spire stands 500 ft (150 m) above the plain.

Missouri River

Mississippi River

In northeastern Iowa, the Mississippi and its tributaries have deeply incised the underlying bedrock creating a hilly terrain, with bluffs standing 300 ft (90 m) above the valley.

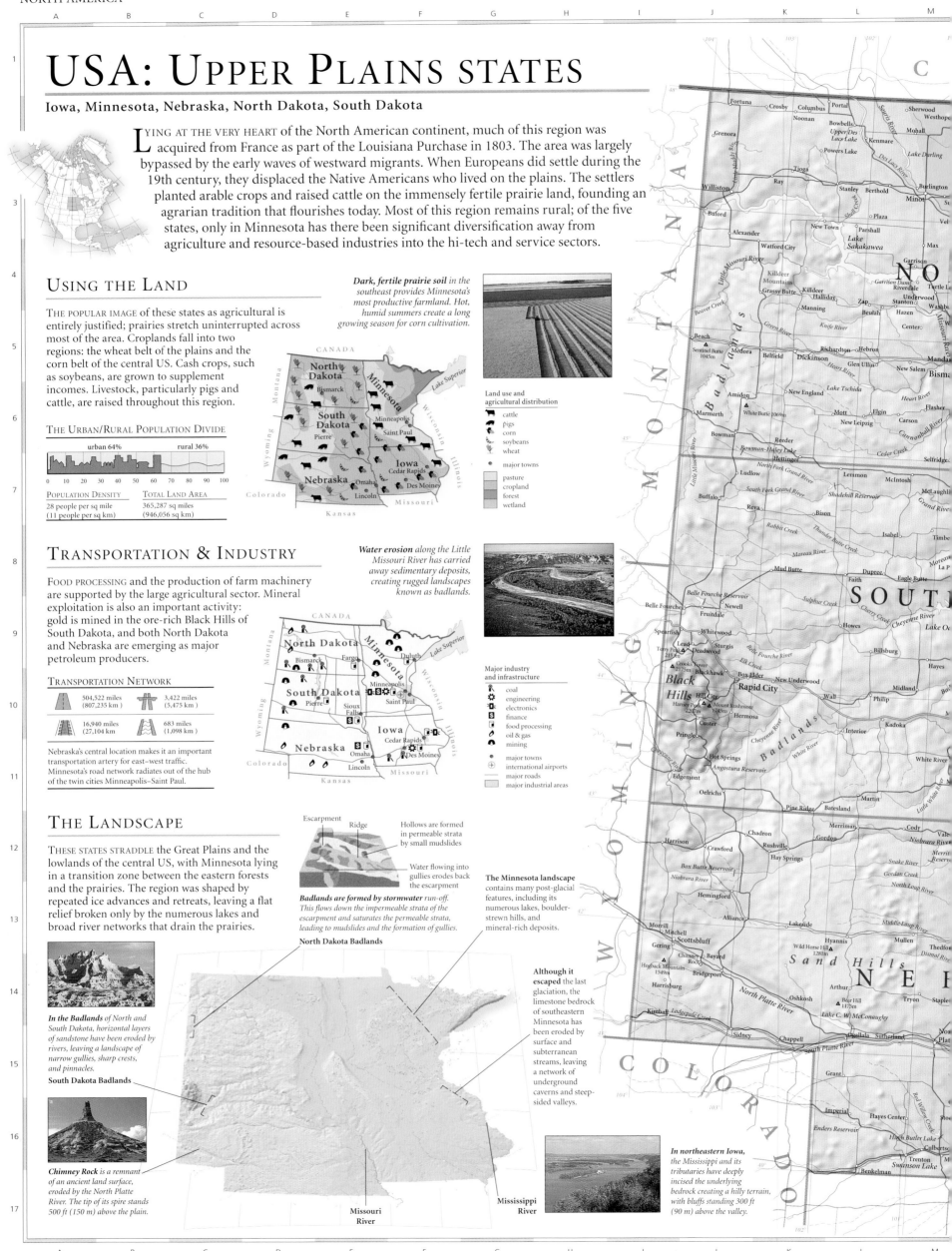

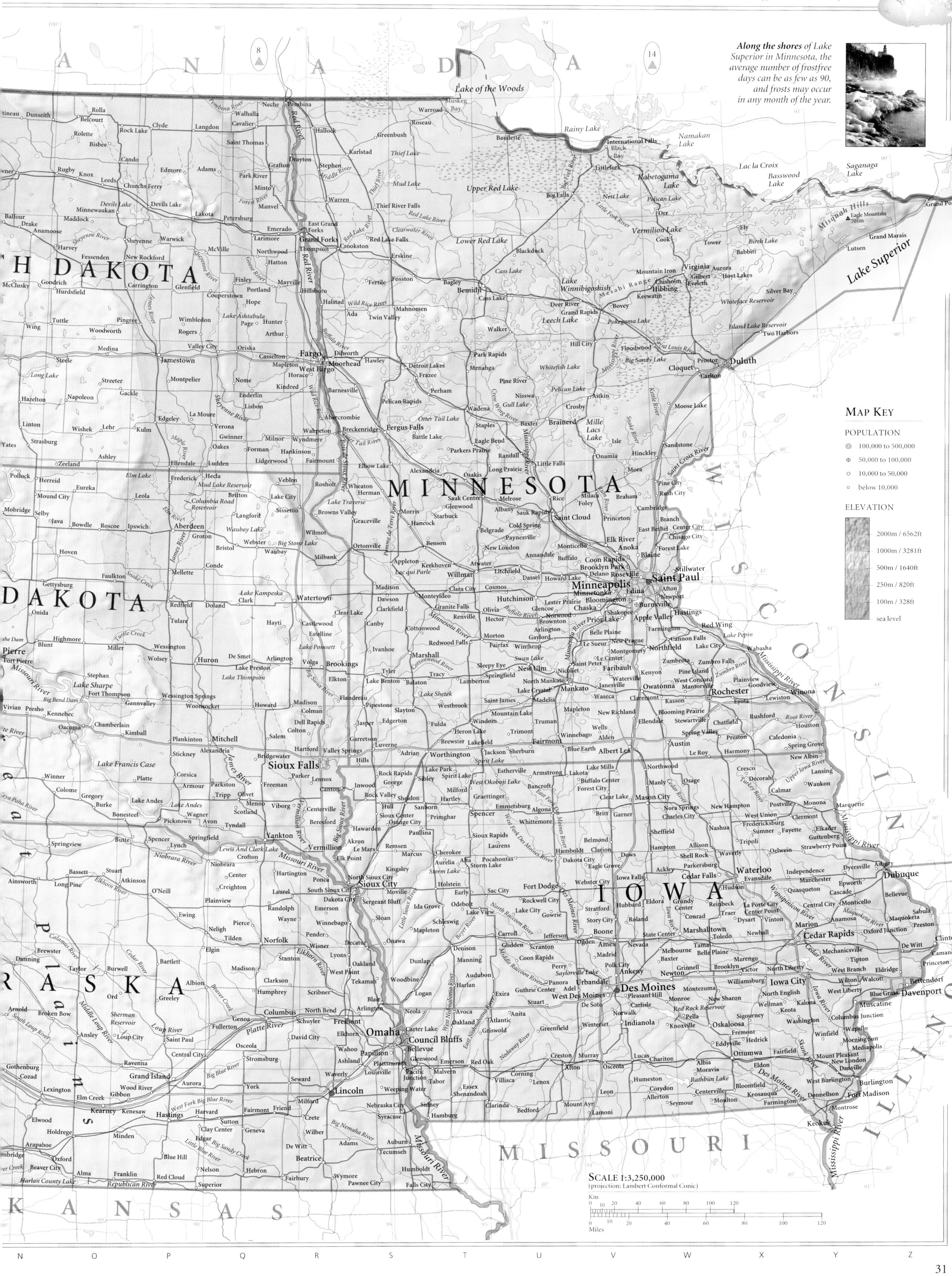

Along the shores of Lake Superior in Minnesota, the average number of frostfree days can be as few as 90, and frosts may occur in any month of the year.

CANADA

NORTH DAKOTA

SOUTH DAKOTA

MINNESOTA

WISCONSIN

IOWA

NEBRASKA

ILLINOIS

MISSOURI

KANSAS

Lake Superior

Lake of the Woods

Rainy Lake

Lower Red Lake *Upper Red Lake*

Minneapolis Saint Paul

Duluth

Fargo Moorhead

Sioux Falls

Sioux City

Des Moines

Omaha Council Bluffs

Lincoln

Cedar Rapids

Rochester

Waterloo

Davenport

Dubuque

MAP KEY

POPULATION

◎ 100,000 to 500,000
⊕ 50,000 to 100,000
⊙ 10,000 to 50,000
○ below 10,000

ELEVATION

2000m / 6562ft
1000m / 3281ft
500m / 1640ft
250m / 820ft
100m / 328ft
sea level

SCALE 1:3,250,000
(projection: Lambert Conformal Conic)

Km 0 10 20 40 60 80 100 120
Miles 0 10 20 40 60 80 100 120

USA: GREAT LAKES STATES

Illinois, Indiana, Michigan, Ohio, Wisconsin

THE STATES BORDERING THE GREAT LAKES developed rapidly in the second half of the 19th century as a result of improvements in communications: railroads to the west and waterways to the south and east. Fertile land and good links with growing eastern cities encouraged the development of agriculture and food processing. Migrants from Europe and other parts of the US flooded into the region and for much of this century the region's economy boomed. However, in recent years heavy industry has declined, earning the region the unwanted label, the "Rustbelt."

TRANSPORTATION & INDUSTRY

THE GREAT LAKES REGION IS THE CENTER of the US car industry. Since the early part of this century, its prosperity has been closely linked to the fortunes of automobile manufacturing. Iron and steel production has expanded to meet demand from this industry. In the 1970s, nationwide recession, cheaper foreign competition in the automobile sector, pollution in and around the Great Lakes, and the collapse of the meatpacking industry, centered in Chicago, forced these states to diversify their industrial base. New industries have emerged, notably electronics, service, and financial industries.

TRANSPORTATION NETWORK

540,682 miles (865,091 km)	6,550 miles (10,480 km)
24,928 miles (39,884 km)	2,330 miles (3,748 km)

Few areas of the US have a comparable system. Chicago is a principal transportation terminus with a dense network of roads, railroads, and Interstate freeways that radiates out from the city.

Ever since Ransom Olds and Henry Ford started mass-producing automobiles in Detroit early this century, the city's name has become synonymous with the American automotive industry.

Major industry and infrastructure

- car manufacture
- coal
- electronics
- engineering
- finance
- food processing
- iron & steel
- oil
- research & development
- textiles
- major towns
- international airports
- major roads
- major industrial areas

THE LANDSCAPE

MUCH OF THIS REGION shows the impact of glaciation, which lasted until about 10,000 years ago, and extended as far south as Illinois and Ohio. Although the relief of the region slopes toward the Great Lakes, because the ice sheets blocked northerly drainage, most of the rivers today flow southward, forming part of the massive Mississippi/Missouri drainage basin.

The dunes near Sleeping Bear Point rise 400 ft (120 m) from the banks of Lake Michigan. They are constantly resculpted by wind.

Lake Michigan

Lake Erie is the shallowest of the five Great Lakes. Its average depth is about 62 ft (19 m). Storms sweeping across from Canada erode its shores and cause the silting of its harbors.

The many lakes and marshes of Wisconsin and Michigan are the result of the glacial erosion and deposition, which occurred during the last Ice Age.

Southwestern Wisconsin is known as a "driftless" area. Unlike most of the region, low hills protected it from erosion by the advancing ice sheet.

Most of the water used in northern Illinois is pumped from underground reservoirs. Due to increased demand, many areas now face a water shortage. Around Joliet, the water table has been lowered by more than 700 ft (210 m) over the 20th century.

Illinois plains

The plains of Illinois are characteristic of drift landscapes, scoured and flattened by glacial erosion and covered with fertile glacial deposits.

Mississippi River

Relic landforms from the last glaciation, such as shallow basins and ridges, cover all but the south of this region. Ridges, known as moraines, up to 300 ft (100 m) high, lie to the south of Lake Michigan.

Ohio River

Unlike the level prairie to the north, southern Indiana is relatively rugged. Limestone in the hills has been dissolved by water, producing features such as sinkholes and underground caves.

The Appalachian Plateau stretches eastward from Ohio. It is dissected by streams flowing west into the Mississippi and Ohio Rivers.

Glacial till

- Present-day river or stream
- Channels caused by outwash from melting glacier
- Most recent till deposits
- Older till sheet
- Bedrock

As a result of successive glacial depositions, the total depth of till along the former southern margin of the Laurentide ice sheet can exceed 1,300 ft (400 m).

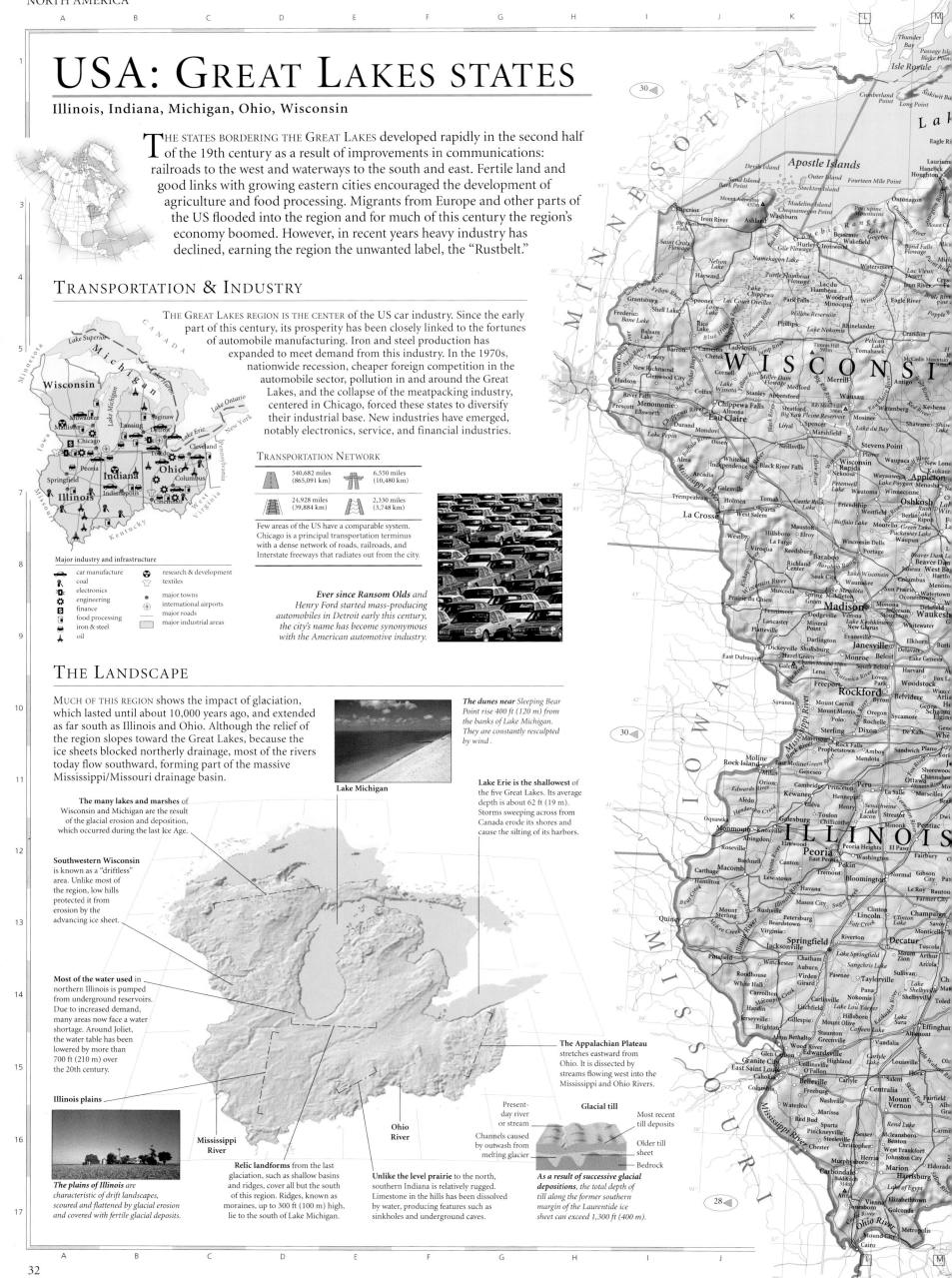

THE URBAN/RURAL POPULATION DIVIDE

urban 74%   rural 26%

0 10 20 30 40 50 60 70 80 90 100

POPULATION DENSITY	TOTAL LAND AREA
169 people per sq mile (65 people per sq km)	248,283 sq miles (643,028 sq km)

USING THE LAND

THE VARIED SOILS AND CLIMATE of this region have allowed for the development of different types of agriculture. Corn and soybeans are the main crops produced, although Michigan is best known for growing fruit, particularly cherries and apples. About 80% of Wisconsin's agricultural income is derived from livestock and dairy farming. Pig breeding is important in both Illinois and Indiana.

Land use and agricultural distribution

cattle   major towns
pigs   pasture
poultry   cropland
corn   forest
fruit
soybeans
timber

Farms like this one stretch across more than 80% of Illinois, covering 56,000 sq miles (145,000 sq km). The state is the leading US producer of soybeans, which are used for animal feed and oil.

Lake Superior is the largest of the Great Lakes and attracts millions of tourists each year. Valuable mineral deposits such as iron and copper are mined close to its shores.

SCALE 1:3,750,000
(projection: Lambert Conformal Conic)

Km
0 20 40 60 80 100

Miles
0 20 40 60 80 100

Although large-scale agribusiness has mostly replaced family farming in the Midwest, some communities, such as the Amish people in Ohio, retain traditional farming methods, cultivating their small holdings using limited machinery.

MAP KEY

POPULATION

◙ 1 million to 5 million
◉ 500,000 to 1 million
◎ 100,000 to 500,000
⊕ 50,000 to 100,000
⊙ 10,000 to 50,000
○ below 10,000

ELEVATION

1000m / 3281ft
500m / 1640ft
250m / 820ft
100m / 328ft
sea level

USA: NORTH MOUNTAIN STATES

Idaho, Montana, Oregon, Washington, Wyoming

THE REMOTENESS OF THE NORTH MOUNTAIN STATES, coupled with their rugged landscape, ensured that this was one of the last areas settled by Europeans in the 19th century. Fur-trappers and gold-prospectors followed the Snake River westward as it wound its way through the Rocky Mountains. The states of the northwest have pioneered many conservationist policies, with the first US National Park opened in Yellowstone in 1872. More recently, the Cascades and Rocky Mountains have become havens for adventure tourism. The mountains still serve to isolate the western seaboard from the rest of the continent. This isolation has encouraged West Coast cities to expand their trade links with countries of the Pacific Rim.

The Snake River has cut down into the basalt of the Columbia Basin to form Hells Canyon, the deepest in the US, with cliffs up to 7,900 ft (2,408 m) high.

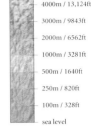

Fine-textured volcanic soils in the hilly Palouse region of eastern Washington are susceptible to erosion.

USING THE LAND

WHEAT FARMING IN THE EAST gives way to cattle ranching as rainfall decreases. Irrigated farming in the Snake River valley produces large yields of potatoes and other vegetables. Dairying and fruit-growing take place in the wet western lowlands between the mountain ranges.

THE URBAN/RURAL POPULATION DIVIDE

urban 70%   rural 30%

0 10 20 30 40 50 60 70 80 90 100

POPULATION DENSITY
20 people per sq mile
(8 people per sq km)

TOTAL LAND AREA
493,782 sq miles
(1,278,846 sq km)

SCALE 1:3,750,000
(projection: Lambert Conformal Conic)

Km 0 10 20   40   60   80   100
Miles 0 10 20   40   60   80   100

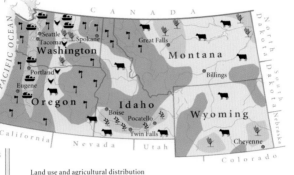

Land use and agricultural distribution

- 🐄 cattle
- 🦃 poultry
- 🌾 cereals
- 🍎 fruit
- 🥔 potatoes
- 🌲 timber
- ● major towns
- pasture
- cropland
- forest

198 ◀

TRANSPORTATION & INDUSTRY

MINERALS AND TIMBER are extremely important in this region. Uranium, precious metals, copper, and coal are all mined, the latter in vast open-cast pits in Wyoming; oil and natural gas are extracted farther north. Manufacturing, notably related to the aerospace and electronics industries, is important in western cities.

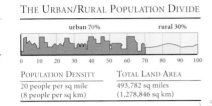

TRANSPORTATION NETWORK

- 347,857 miles (556,571 km)
- 4,200 miles (6,720 km)
- 12,354 miles (19,766 km)
- 1,108 miles (1,782 km)

Major industry and infrastructure

- △ adventure tourism
- ✈ aerospace
- coal
- chemicals
- electronics
- food processing
- mining
- oil & gas
- timber processing
- ● major towns
- ⊕ international airports
- major roads
- major industrial areas

The Union Pacific Railroad has been in service across Wyoming since 1867. The route through the Rocky Mountains is now shared with the Interstate 80, a major east–west highway.

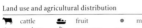

Seattle lies in one of Puget Sound's many inlets. The city receives oil and other resources from Alaska, and benefits from expanding trade across the Pacific.

Crater Lake, Oregon, is 6 miles (10 km) wide and 1,800 ft (600 m) deep. It marks the site of a volcanic cone, which collapsed after an eruption within the last 7,000 years.

THE LANDSCAPE

THE ROCKY MOUNTAINS are flanked by lower parallel ranges, which spread onto the Great Plains in the east and surmount the broad lava plateau that extends westward. The Cascade Range divides the Columbia Basin from the coastlands, where the low areas around Puget Sound are broken by the steep, volcanic Olympic Mountains and the wooded hills of the Coast Ranges.

Molten rock cools, forming parallel columns

Surrounding strata eroded away

Molten rock wells up from the Earth's core

Devil's Tower in Wyoming is an igneous intrusion, formed below the Earth's surface. Molten rock intruded through cracks in the overlying strata and cooled. Over time, the softer rock layers have been eroded away, leaving only the tower standing.

Glacial valleys on the seaward side of the Olympic Mountains receive about 142 inches (3,600 mm) of rain per year, supporting the only true rain forest of the northern hemisphere.

The Cascades are glacially scoured volcanic mountains, the highest of which is Mount Rainier, a dormant volcano 14,409 ft (4,392 m) high.

Coast Ranges

The plateaus of the Columbia and Snake Rivers represent one of the world's largest accumulations of lava. Over 5 million years ago, successive flows of molten basalt buried the existing land surface by up to 450 ft (150 m).

Mount St. Helens erupted in 1980, killing 57 people and devastating a huge area.

Puget Sound

Columbia Basin

Grand Coulee and the lesser *coulées* (ravines) were cut by cataclysmic floods, from the release of an ice-dammed lake, at the end of the last Ice Age.

The contorted rock shapes at "Craters of the Moon" National Monument in Idaho were left 2,000 years ago by the sporadic upwelling of viscous lava from fissures in the basalt plateau.

The Continental Divide, or watershed, crosses the Lewis Range. From here, rivers flow west to Hudson Bay, south to the Gulf of Mexico and east to the Pacific Ocean.

Rocky Mountains

Piney Buttes are the remnants of an older, higher land surface gradually weathered and eroded into isolated outcrops with flat tops and steep sides.

Great Plains

Devil's Tower

Water from the hot springs in Yellowstone National Park deposits minerals as it cools in rock pools. Long periods of deposition have created these rock terraces.

USA: CALIFORNIA & NEVADA

THE GOLD RUSH OF 1849 attracted the first major wave of European settlers to the West Coast. The pleasant climate, beautiful scenery, and dynamic economy continue to attract immigrants – despite the ever-present danger of earthquakes – and California has become the US's most populous state. The overwhelmingly urban population is concentrated in the vast conurbations of Los Angeles, San Francisco, and San Diego; new immigrants include people from South Korea, the Philippines, Vietnam, and Mexico. Nevada's arid lands were initially exploited for minerals; in recent years, revenue from mining has been superseded by income from the tourist and gambling centers of Las Vegas and Reno.

MAP KEY

POPULATION

- 1 million to 5 million
- 500,000 to 1 million
- 100,000 to 500,000
- 50,000 to 100,000
- 10,000 to 50,000
- below 10,000

ELEVATION

- 4000m / 13,124ft
- 3000m / 9843ft
- 2000m / 6562ft
- 1000m / 3281ft
- 500m / 1640ft
- 250m / 820ft
- 100m / 328ft
- sea level

SCALE 1:3,000,000
(projection: Lambert Conformal Conic)

Km 0 5 10 20 30 40 50 60 70 80
Miles 0 5 10 20 30 40 50 60 70 80

TRANSPORTATION & INDUSTRY

NEVADA'S RICH MINERAL RESERVES ushered in a period of mining wealth that has now been replaced by revenue generated from gambling. California supports a broad set of activities including defense-related industries and research and development facilities. "Silicon Valley," near San Francisco, is a world-leading center for microelectronics, while tourism and the Los Angeles film industry also generate large incomes.

Gambling was legalized in Nevada in 1931. Las Vegas has since become the center of this multimillion dollar industry.

Major industry and infrastructure

- aerospace
- car manufacture
- defense
- film industry
- finance
- food processing
- gambling
- hi-tech industry
- mining
- pharmaceuticals
- research & development
- textiles
- tourism
- major towns
- international airports
- major roads
- major industrial areas

TRANSPORTATION NETWORK

211,459 miles (338,334 km)	
2,944 miles (4,710 km)	
7,872 miles (12,595 km)	
190 miles (306 km)	

In California, the motor vehicle is a vital part of daily life, and an extensive freeway system runs throughout the state, which has a greater *per capita* car ownership than anywhere else in the world.

THE LANDSCAPE

THE BROAD CENTRAL VALLEY divides California's coastal mountains from the Sierra Nevada. The San Andreas Fault, running beneath much of the state, is the site of frequent earth tremors and sometimes more serious earthquakes. East of the Sierra Nevada, the landscape is characterized by the basin and range topography with stony deserts and many salt lakes.

Rising molten rock causes stretching of the Earth's crust

Extensive cracking (faulting) uplifted a series of ridges

As ridges are eroded they fill intervening valleys with sediments

Molten rock (magma) welling up to form a dome in the Earth's interior, causes the brittle surface rocks to stretch and crack. Some areas were uplifted to form mountains (ranges), while others sank to form flat valleys (basins).

The General Sherman sequoia tree in Sequoia National Park is 3,000 years old. At 275 ft (84 m), it is one of the largest living things on Earth.

Most of California's agriculture is confined to the fertile and extensively irrigated Central Valley, running between the Coast Ranges and the Sierra Nevada. It incorporates the San Joaquin and Sacramento valleys.

The dramatic granitic rock formations of Half Dome and El Capitan, and the verdant coniferous forests, attract millions of visitors annually to Yosemite National Park in the Sierra Nevada.

The Great Basin dominates most of Nevada's topography, containing large open basins, punctuated by eroded features such as *buttes* and *mesas*. River flow tends to be seasonal, depending on spring showers and winter snowmelt.

Sierra Nevada

Wheeler Peak is home to some of the world's oldest living trees, bristlecone pines, which live for up to 5,000 years.

When the Hoover Dam across the Colorado River was completed in 1936, it created Lake Mead, one of the largest artificial lakes in the world, extending for 115 miles (285 km) upstream.

The San Andreas Fault is a transverse fault which extends for 650 miles (1,050 km) through California. Major earthquakes occur when the land either side of the fault moves at different rates. San Francisco was devastated by an earthquake in 1906.

Death Valley

Named by migrating settlers in 1849, Death Valley is the driest, hottest place in North America, as well as being the lowest point on land in the western hemisphere, at 282 ft (86 m) below sea level.

The sparsely populated Mojave Desert receives less than 8 inches (200 mm) of rainfall a year. It is used extensively for testing weapons and other military purposes.

The Salton Sea was created accidentally between 1905 and 1907 when an irrigation channel from the Colorado River broke its banks and formed this salty 300-sq-mile (777-sq-km) landlocked lake.

Amargosa Desert

The Sierra Nevada create a "rainshadow," preventing rain from reaching much of Nevada. Pacific air masses, passing over the mountains, are stripped of their moisture.

USING THE LAND

CALIFORNIA is the leading agricultural producer in the US, although low rainfall makes irrigation essential. The long growing season and abundant sunshine allow many crops to be grown in the fertile Central Valley, including grapes, citrus fruits, vegetables, and cotton. Almost 17 million acres (6.8 million ha) of California's forests are used commercially. Nevada's arid climate and poor soil are largely unsuitable for agriculture; 85% of its land is state-owned and large areas are used for underground of testing nuclear weapons.

Land use and agricultural distribution

- cattle
- citrus fruits
- fruit
- irrigation
- timber
- vineyards
- major towns
- pasture
- cropland
- forest
- desert

Without considerable irrigation, this fertile valley at Palm Springs would still be part of the Sonoran Desert. California's farmers account for about 80% of the state's total water usage.

THE URBAN/RURAL POPULATION DIVIDE

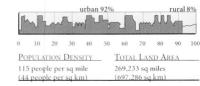

urban 92%   rural 8%

0 10 20 30 40 50 60 70 80 90 100

POPULATION DENSITY
115 people per sq mile
(44 people per sq km)

TOTAL LAND AREA
269,233 sq miles
(697,286 sq km)

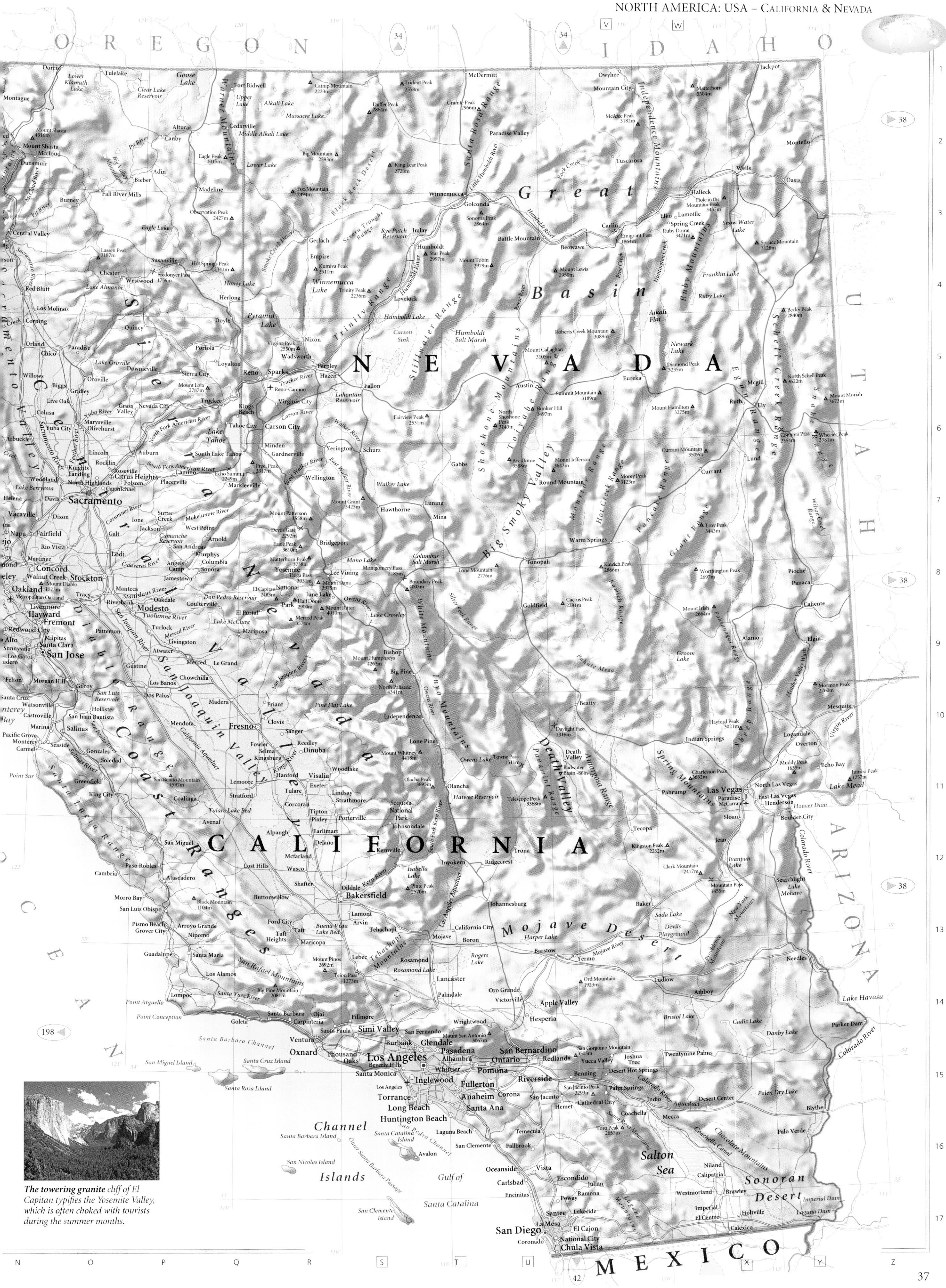

OREGON

IDAHO

UTAH

ARIZONA

MEXICO

NEVADA

CALIFORNIA

Great Basin

Sierra

Nevada

Central Valley

San Joaquin Valley

Mojave Desert

Sonoran Desert

Death Valley

Pacific Ocean

Sacramento

San Jose

Oakland

Fresno

Bakersfield

Los Angeles

San Diego

Las Vegas

Reno

Carson City

Stockton

Modesto

The towering granite cliff of El Capitan typifies the Yosemite Valley, which is often choked with tourists during the summer months.

USA: South Mountain states

Arizona, Colorado, New Mexico, Utah

THIS ARID REGION, CHARACTERIZED BY EXPANSIVE PLATEAUS and spectacular canyons, is home to several distinct peoples. The ruins of cliff dwellings built a thousand years ago by the Anasazi people still exist today, and Native Americans own one-third of the land in Arizona. Spanish and Mexican conquest and settlement left a Hispanic presence which is strongest in New Mexico. The Mormons, who came to the Great Salt Lake seeking religious freedom in 1847, were among the earliest Anglo-American settlers and now make up over 70% of Utah's population. The region's mineral wealth has driven rapid development this century, yet the constraints of a fragile environment, including widespread water shortages, may limit prospects for growth.

When water evaporates it leaves a salt pan

Mudflats

Lake is fed by seasonal snowmelt

Water level of lake varies according to quantity of run-off received from snowmelt

The Great Salt Lake is an ephemeral lake; it can remain dry for extended periods, leaving a pan of evaporated mineral salts in its center.

THE LANDSCAPE

THE ARID, ROCKY EXPANSE of the Colorado Plateau is dissected by the immense canyons of the Colorado River. Desert lies to the north and south and branches of the Rocky Mountains run east and west. The Great Salt Lake and Desert lie within the Great Basin, a barren region of parallel mountain ranges that extends into Arizona.

Over 13 million years of weathering has created thousands of spires and pinnacles from the alternating rock strata of Bryce Canyon.

Lake Powell

The Rio Grande has its source in several meltwater streams that have cut deep valleys into the platform of the San Juan Mountains.

The parallel basins and ridges, which run north–south along the Great Basin, reflect a major series of block-faults in the underlying bedrock.

Sand dunes, 600 ft (180 m) high, have been deposited in San Luis Valley, by winds funneled through the San Juan and Sangre de Cristo mountains in the Rockies.

Parts of the Grand Canyon, which cuts through the Colorado Plateau, are 16 miles (25 km) wide. The Colorado River has cut down 6,262 ft (2,000 m), exposing rock strata more than 2 billion years old.

Rainbow Bridge is the world's largest natural arch. The 309-ft (94-m) span probably began to grow when the sandstone spur of a meandering creek was breached during a flash flood.

The striking color effects seen in the Painted Desert come from minerals such as gypsum and hematite, combined with ambient heat and dust.

Petrified Forest

Shifting gypsum sands produce a constantly changing land surface, overwhelming plants and any other obstacles in Tularosa Valley.

Carlsbad Caverns

In the arid landscape of Petrified Forest National Park in Arizona, the grain of prehistoric trees has been preserved as a fossil imprint in the rocks. The bog-preserved trees were gradually turned to stone by seeping mineral-rich water.

The intricate stalactites of Carlsbad Caverns have grown with the seepage of calcium-rich water over the last 100,000 years. The huge caves are home to around 100,000 Mexican freetail bats.

TRANSPORTATION & INDUSTRY

NEW INDUSTRIES HAVE HELPED reduce the region's dependence on the extraction of minerals and fossil fuels. Precision manufacture has grown rapidly, particularly in Arizona and Colorado. Salt Lake City and Denver are well-established financial centers and New Mexico, the main US producer of uranium, is a prominent region for nuclear research. Colorado is the most important US center for winter sports.

TRANSPORTATION NETWORK

232,434 miles (373,986 km)	4,059 miles (6,515 km)
8,627 miles (13,881 km)	none

The Colorado Rockies are crossed by 32 mountain passes, some as high as 12,183 ft (3,713 m). The Eisenhower Tunnel west of Denver carries Interstate High way 70 straight through the Continental

Glen Canyon Dam on the Colorado River was completed in 1964. It provides hydroelectric power and irrigation water as part of a long-term federal project to harness the river.

Major industry and infrastructure

- chemicals
- coal
- defense
- finance
- food processing
- hi-tech industry
- oil & gas
- mining
- research & development
- winter sports
- major towns
- international airports
- major roads
- major industrial areas

The flat tablelands (mesas), and the isolated pinnacles (buttes) which rise from the floor of Monument Valley are the resistant remnants of an earlier land surface, gradually cut back by erosion under arid conditions.

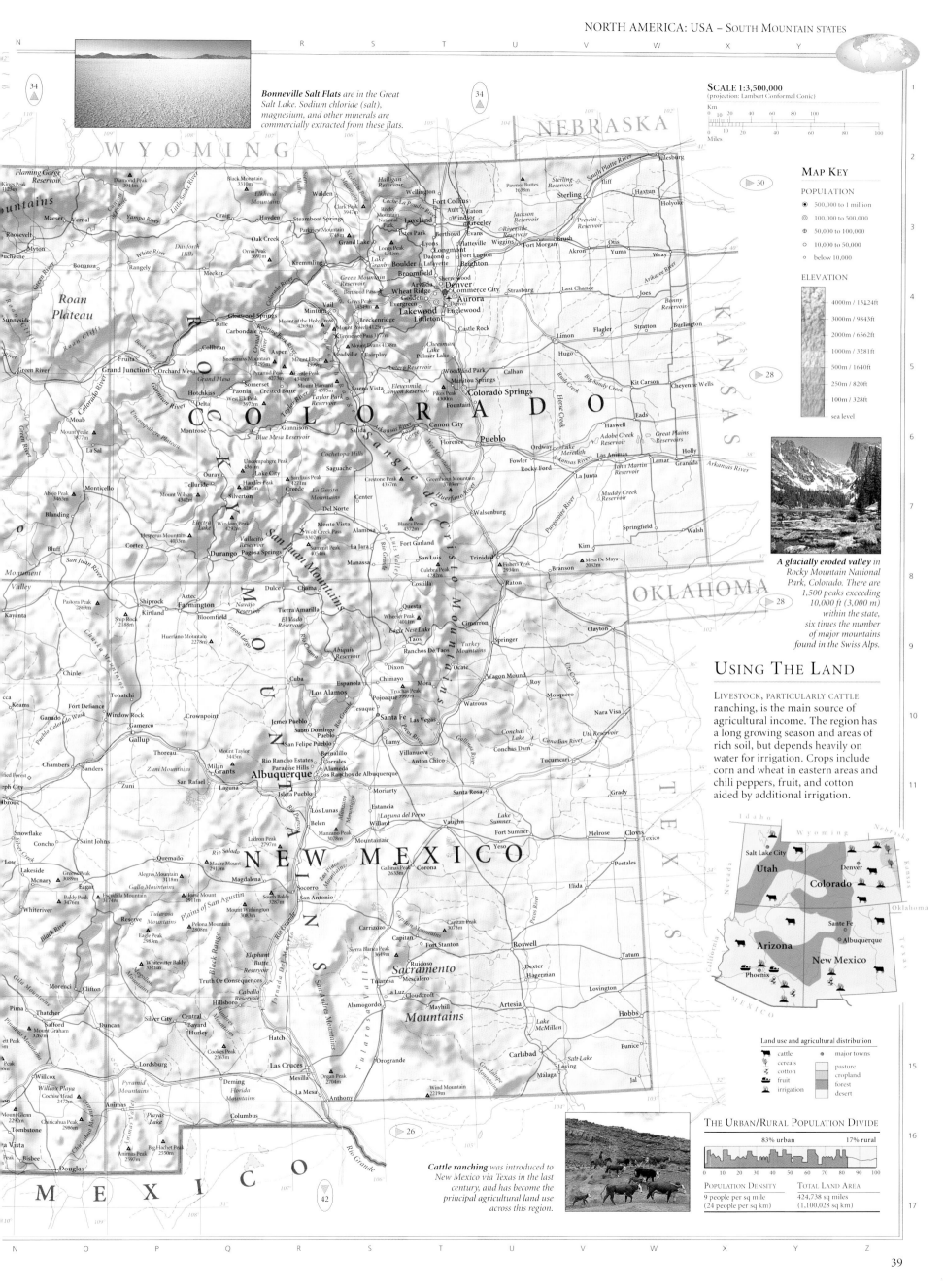

Bonneville Salt Flats are in the Great Salt Lake. Sodium chloride (salt), magnesium, and other minerals are commercially extracted from these flats.

SCALE 1:3,500,000
(projection: Lambert Conformal Conic)

Km
Miles

MAP KEY

POPULATION

⊙ 500,000 to 1 million
⊕ 100,000 to 500,000
⊕ 50,000 to 100,000
○ 10,000 to 50,000
○ below 10,000

ELEVATION

4000m / 13,124ft
3000m / 9843ft
2000m / 6562ft
1000m / 3281ft
500m / 1640ft
250m / 820ft
100m / 328ft
sea level

A glacially eroded valley in Rocky Mountain National Park, Colorado. There are 1,500 peaks exceeding 10,000 ft (3,000 m) within the state, six times the number of major mountains found in the Swiss Alps.

USING THE LAND

LIVESTOCK, PARTICULARLY CATTLE ranching, is the main source of agricultural income. The region has a long growing season and areas of rich soil, but depends heavily on water for irrigation. Crops include corn and wheat in eastern areas and chili peppers, fruit, and cotton aided by additional irrigation.

Land use and agricultural distribution

🐄 cattle
🌾 cereals
cotton
🍎 fruit
irrigation

• major towns
pasture
cropland
forest
desert

THE URBAN/RURAL POPULATION DIVIDE

83% urban   17% rural

POPULATION DENSITY	TOTAL LAND AREA
9 people per sq mile	424,738 sq miles
(24 people per sq km)	(1,100,028 sq km)

Cattle ranching was introduced to New Mexico via Texas in the last century, and has become the principal agricultural land use across this region.

USA: Hawaii

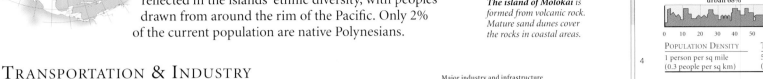

THE 122 ISLANDS of the Hawaiian archipelago, part of Polynesia, are the peaks of the world's largest volcanoes. They rise approximately 6 miles (9.7 km) from the floor of the Pacific Ocean. The largest, the island of Hawaii, remains highly active. Hawaii became the 50th state in 1959. A tradition of receiving immigrant workers is reflected in the islands' ethnic diversity, with peoples drawn from around the rim of the Pacific. Only 2% of the current population are native Polynesians.

The island of Molokai is formed from volcanic rock. Mature sand dunes cover the rocks in coastal areas.

USING THE LAND & SEA

THE ICE-FREE COASTLINE of Alaska provides access to salmon fisheries and more than 5.5 million acres (2.2 million ha) of forest. Most of Alaska is uncultivable, and around 90% of food is imported. Barley, hay, and hothouse products are grown around Anchorage, where dairy farming is also concentrated.

THE URBAN/RURAL POPULATION DIVIDE

urban 68% rural 32%

POPULATION DENSITY	TOTAL LAND AREA
1 person per sq mile (0.3 people per sq km)	586,412 sq miles (1,518,800 sq km)

A raft of timber from the Tongass Forest is hauled by a tug, bound for the pulp mills of the Alaskan coast between Juneau and Ketchikan.

TRANSPORTATION & INDUSTRY

TOURISM DOMINATES the economy, with over half of the population employed in the service industry. The naval base at Pearl Harbor is also a major of employer. Industry is concentrated on the island of Oahu and relies mostly on imported materials, while agricultural produce is processed locally.

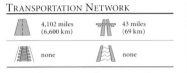

Major industry and infrastructure

- food processing
- military base
- textiles
- tourism
- major towns
- international airports
- major roads
- major industrial areas

TRANSPORTATION NETWORK

4,102 miles (6,600 km)	43 miles (69 km)
none	none

Hawaii relies on ocean-surface transportation. Honolulu is the main focus of this network, bringing foreign trade and the markets of mainland US to Hawaii's outer islands.

Haleakala's extinct volcanic crater is the world's largest. The giant caldera, containing many secondary cones, is 2,000 ft (600 m) deep and 20 miles (32 km) in circumference.

SCALE 1:3,500,000
(projection: Lambert Conformal Conic)

MAP KEY

POPULATION
- ◎ 100,000 to 500,000
- ⊕ 50,000 to 100,000
- ○ 10,000 to 50,000
- ○ below 10,000

ELEVATION
- 4000m / 13,124ft
- 3000m / 9843ft
- 2000m / 6562ft
- 1000m / 3281ft
- 500m / 1640ft
- 250m / 820ft
- 100m / 328ft
- sea level

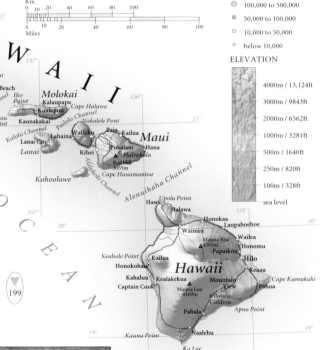

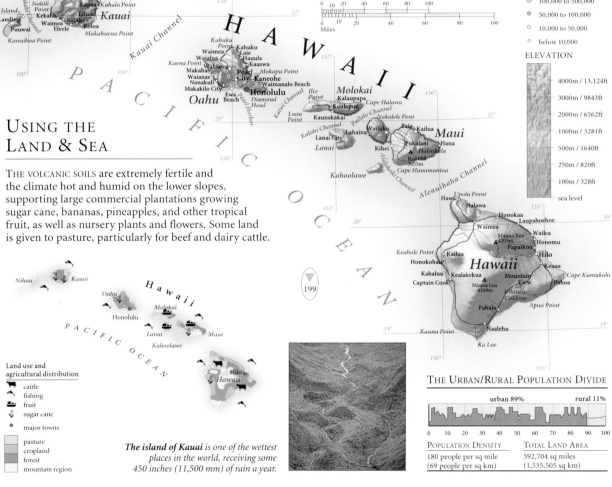

USING THE LAND & SEA

THE VOLCANIC SOILS are extremely fertile and the climate hot and humid on the lower slopes, supporting large commercial plantations growing sugar cane, bananas, pineapples, and other tropical fruit, as well as nursery plants and flowers. Some land is given to pasture, particularly for beef and dairy cattle.

Land use and agricultural distribution
- cattle
- fishing
- fruit
- sugar cane
- major towns
- pasture
- cropland
- forest
- mountain region

The island of Kauai is one of the wettest places in the world, receiving some 450 inches (11,500 mm) of rain a year.

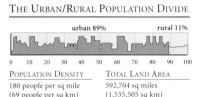

THE URBAN/RURAL POPULATION DIVIDE

urban 89% rural 11%

POPULATION DENSITY	TOTAL LAND AREA
180 people per sq mile (69 people per sq km)	592,704 sq miles (1,535,505 sq km)

CHUKCHI SEA

RUSSIAN FEDERATION

BERING SEA

Saint Lawrence Island

Nunivak Island

Kuskokwim Bay

Pribilof Islands

MAP KEY

POPULATION
- ◎ 100,000 to 500,000
- ⊕ 50,000 to 100,000
- ○ 10,000 to 50,000
- ○ below 10,000

ELEVATION
- 4000m / 13,124ft
- 3000m / 9843ft
- 2000m / 6562ft
- 1000m / 3281ft
- 500m / 1640ft
- 250m / 820ft
- 100m / 328ft
- sea level

SCALE 1:8,000,000
(projection: Lambert Conformal Conic)

Near Islands

Aleutian Islands

Rat Islands

Andreanof Islands

Fox Islands

PACIFIC OCEAN

USA: ALASKA

JUST OVER HALF A MILLION people live in Alaska, a wilderness of ice, forest, mountains, and plains, purchased from Russia in 1867 and covering twice the area of Texas. The discovery of large oil reserves has brought prosperity to the US's "last frontier," while advancing the need to preserve natural habitats and the traditional livelihoods of indigenous peoples, such as the Aleuts and Inupiaq.

Land use and agricultural distribution

- fishing
- reindeer
- fruit
- major towns
- forest
- barren
- tundra

THE LANDSCAPE

THE MOUNTAINS OF THE PACIFIC COAST culminate in the heavily glaciated Alaska Range and extend west to the Alaska Peninsula and the great volcanic arc of the Aleutian Islands. The interior plains are drained by the Yukon River and bounded by the bare, jagged peaks of the Brooks Range to the north.

The Yukon Delta is a fan of alluvial material eroded by the Yukon River and its tributaries. It is approximately twice the size of the Mississippi Delta.

Yukon River

Brooks Range

West Fork Glacier

The ten highest mountains in the US are all in the Alaska Range; Mount McKinley (Denali), at 20,321 ft (6,194 m), is the highest.

Alaska Range

The arc of the Aleutian Islands marks the boundary between the Eurasian and Pacific tectonic plates.

Fjords are found along the coast where valleys, deeply excavated by large glaciers, were inundated by rising seas.

By August, the Alaska Range is covered with autumnal tundra vegetation.

West Fork Glacier

The surging ice mass shears along the glacier margin

Deep crevasses divide the front of the surging glacier into large ice blocks

Surging glaciers make rapid and dramatic advances, normally after periods of snow accumulation. West Fork Glacier in the Susitna River Basin traveled 2.5 miles (4 km) in 1987.

TRANSPORTATION & INDUSTRY

LARGE AREAS OF ALASKA are undeveloped, and much of the existing infrastructure is a legacy of Cold War military investment. Mineral ores, including gold, have been mined for over a century, but the oil business now dominates the economy. Processing industries such as paper-pulp mills supply Japan and other markets on the Pacific Rim.

TRANSPORTATION NETWORK

13,524 miles (21,760 km)		49 miles (78 km)	
482 miles (772 km)		none	

Nearly 80 million gallons of oil are pumped through the Trans-Alaska Pipeline every day. The oil takes six days to travel the 789 miles (1,262 km) from Prudhoe Bay to Valdez.

Major industry and infrastructure

- fish processing
- gold mining
- oil
- timber processing
- major towns
- international airports
- major roads

The Trans-Alaska Pipeline has carried crude oil from Prudhoe Bay since 1977. The oilfield is the largest in the US and is estimated to be equal to the biggest oilfields of the Persian Gulf.

SCALE 1:6,250,000
(projection: Lambert Conformal Conic)

Km
0 25 50   100   150   200

0   25   50   100   150   200
Miles

The rugged, desert landscape of the Sierra Madre del Sur is a product of complex tectonic processes, where the fold mountains in western North America, running north–south, meet the Caribbean mountain arc, which runs east–west.

Wave action has cut steep cliffs into the igneous rocks of Isla Cedros, off the Pacific coast of Baja California. The island is home to sea lions, reptiles, and deer.

MEXICO

MEXICO POSSESSES rich mineral resources, limited agricultural land, and the world's largest and fastest growing Spanish-speaking population. Most Mexicans are *mestizo* – of Hispanic and Native American heritage – although Amerindian communities still exist in the south, 400 years after Spain destroyed the Aztec empire. Much of the arid north is sparsely inhabited, while Mexico City is becoming the world's most populous city. Conflict with the US has long overshadowed Mexico's development, but the North American Free Trade Agreement offers a more benign relationship, which may offset Mexico's hyperinflation, foreign debt, unequal wealth distribution, and political instability.

USING THE LAND & SEA

CORN OCCUPIES much of the cultivated area. Commercial plantations of coffee, sugar, vanilla, and cotton are found along the Gulf coastal plain and in irrigated parts of the arid north, which is otherwise used for extensive ranching. Fishing is important, particularly shellfish for export. A soaring population has created the need for grain imports since 1980.

THE URBAN/RURAL POPULATION DIVIDE

urban 74%   rural 26%

0 10 20 30 40 50 60 70 80 90 100

POPULATION DENSITY	TOTAL LAND AREA
119 people per sq mile (46 people per sq km)	755,865 sq miles (1,958,200 sq km)

Land use and agricultural distribution

- cattle
- coffee
- corn
- cotton
- fishing
- shellfish
- sugar cane
- timber
- vanilla

- capital cities
- major towns

- pasture
- cropland
- forest
- desert

Coffee beans spread out to dry in the sun. Coffee, grown mainly on the Gulf coastal plain, is Mexico's most valuable export crop.

MEXICO: ADMINISTRATIVE REGIONS

ⓓ DISTRITO FEDERAL

MAP KEY

POPULATION

- ■ above 5 million
- ■ 1 million to 5 million
- ◉ 500,000 to 1 million
- ◎ 100,000 to 500,000
- ⊕ 50,000 to 100,000
- ⊙ 10,000 to 50,000
- ○ below 10,000

ELEVATION

- 4000m / 13,124ft
- 3000m / 9843ft
- 2000m / 6562ft
- 1000m / 3281ft
- 500m / 1640ft
- 250m / 820ft
- 100m / 328ft
- sea level

THE LANDSCAPE

THE GREAT CENTRAL PLATEAU rises gently southward from the Río Grande, isolated from the coastal plains by the Sierra Madre Oriental and Occidental. The two ranges converge from the east and west respectively, culminating in high volcanic peaks around Mexico City. Further ranges of the Sierra Madre rise to the south of the Balsas Basin, skirted by the low-lying Isthmus of Tehuantepec (*Istmo de Tehuantepec*) and Yucatan Peninsula.

The long, narrow, extremely arid peninsula of Baja (lower) California is an elongated granite block, separated from the mainland by the flooded rift valley of the Gulf of California (*Golfo de California*).

Wave action has constructed sandbars that shelter lagoons along the shore of the Gulf coastal plain.

The dormant cone of Volcán Pico de Orizaba is, at 18,700 ft (5,700 m), the highest peak in Mexico. In North America, only Mount McKinley and Mount Logan are taller.

Sierra Madre Oriental

Río Grande

The heavily forested Isthmus of Tehuantepec (*Istmo de Tehuantepec*) is a *graben*, a low-lying trough created by downward movement of the bedrock between two fault lines.

Tropical rain forest abounds in the Yucatan Peninsula, a broad, low limestone shelf. Rivers are rare due to the porous nature of limestone, so the forest is fed mainly by streams and underground water.

Formation of the Gulf of California

Direction of plate movement

Baja California

Gulf of California

Transform fault

Spreading oceanic ridge

Edge of continental crust

The Gulf of California (*Golfo de California*) *began to open out about 4 million years ago as a result of rifting and plate displacement along transform faults.*

Sierra Madre Occidental

Río Balsas

Popocatépetl

Popocatépetl is a dormant volcano, part of the Pacific "Ring of Fire." The crater is over half a mile (1 km) wide.

The unstable, earthquake-prone, upland basin around Mexico City was once a region of shallow lakes. Flood control measures and domestic consumption over the last four centuries have caused the virtual disappearance of this surface water.

The highlands of Chiapas are a series of *horsts*, blocks of land thrust upward between two fault lines. Volcanic cones have developed where lava has flowed out from the faults.

TRANSPORTATION & INDUSTRY

OIL AND GAS ON THE GULF COAST are Mexico's main sources of export income. Metal mining has declined but the country remains a leading global producer of silver. Manufacturing is heavily concentrated around the metropolitan area of Mexico City, while the duty-free movement of goods in the US border region, under the *Maquiladora* (twin plant) scheme, has created new hi-tech and service growth centers.

Major industry and infrastructure

brewing		oil & gas
car manufacture		textiles
chemicals		
electronics		capital cities
fish processing		major towns
maquiladoras		international airports
mining		major roads
		major industrial areas

A stone figure reclines by the Temple of Warriors, within the Mayan city of Chichén-Itzá. The Maya civilization flourished across the Yucatan Peninsula between 200 and 900 AD.

TRANSPORTATION NETWORK

151,951 miles (373,986 km)

1,935 miles (3,116 km)

12,684 miles (20,425 km)

1,801 miles (2,900 km)

Fast, modern highways or *autopistas* now link Mexico City with Toluca, Puebla, and other satellite cities, yet distant centers like Chihuahua are still served by narrow roads and an outdated railroad network.

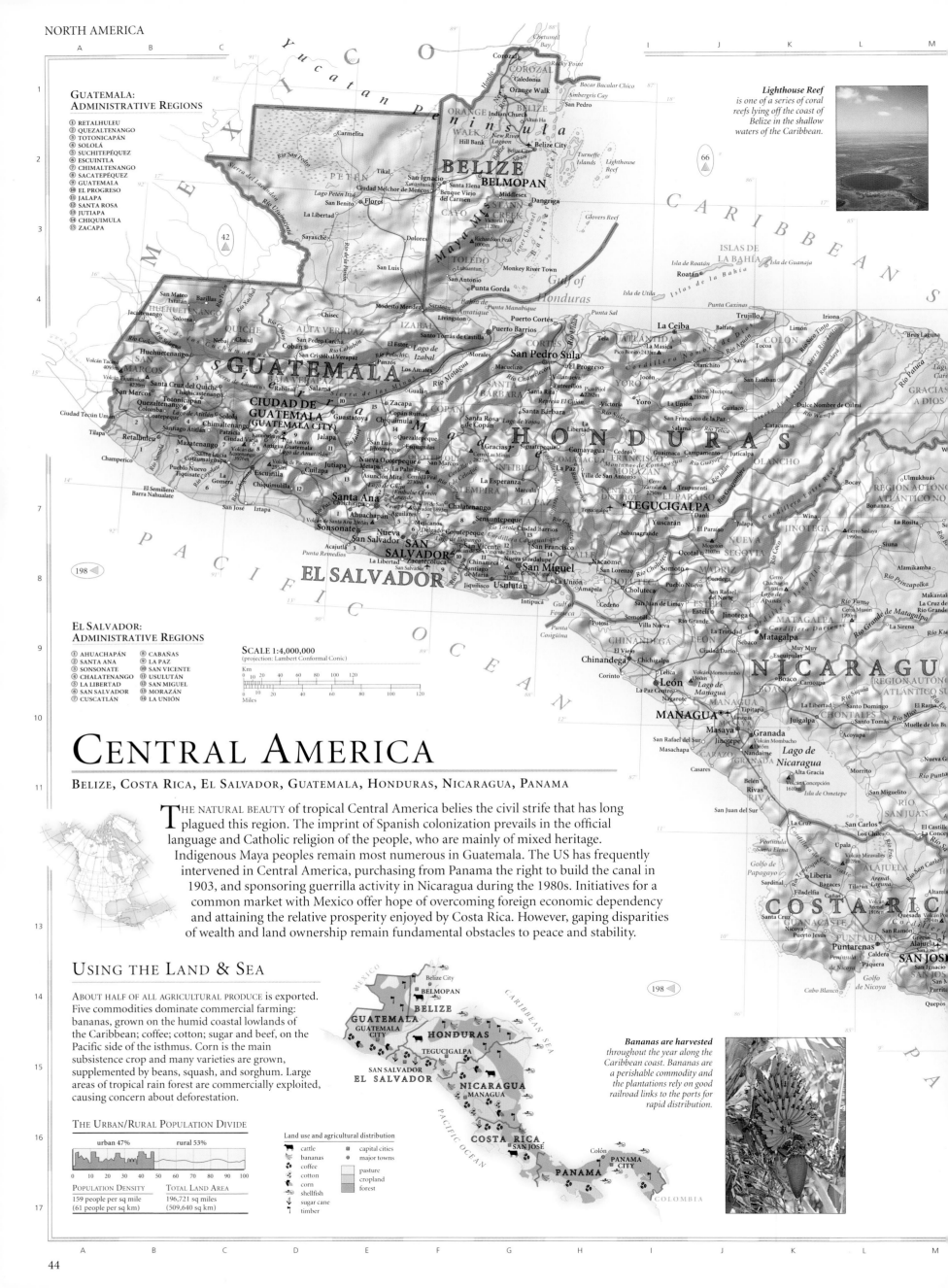

GUATEMALA: ADMINISTRATIVE REGIONS

① RETALHULEU
② QUEZALTENANGO
③ TOTONICAPÁN
④ SOLOLÁ
⑤ SUCHITEPÉQUEZ
⑥ ESCUINTLA
⑦ CHIMALTENANGO
⑧ SACATEPÉQUEZ
⑨ GUATEMALA
⑩ EL PROGRESO
⑪ JALAPA
⑫ SANTA ROSA
⑬ JUTIAPA
⑭ CHIQUIMULA
⑮ ZACAPA

Lighthouse Reef is one of a series of coral reefs lying off the coast of Belize in the shallow waters of the Caribbean.

EL SALVADOR: ADMINISTRATIVE REGIONS

① AHUACHAPÁN
② SANTA ANA
③ SONSONATE
④ CHALATENANGO
⑤ LA LIBERTAD
⑥ SAN SALVADOR
⑦ CUSCATLÁN
⑧ CABAÑAS
⑨ LA PAZ
⑩ SAN VICENTE
⑪ USULUTÁN
⑫ SAN MIGUEL
⑬ MORAZÁN
⑭ LA UNIÓN

SCALE 1:4,000,000
(projection: Lambert Conformal Conic)

Km
0 10 20   40   60   80   100   120

Miles
0   10   20   40   60   80   100   120

CENTRAL AMERICA

Belize, Costa Rica, El Salvador, Guatemala, Honduras, Nicaragua, Panama

The natural beauty of tropical Central America belies the civil strife that has long plagued this region. The imprint of Spanish colonization prevails in the official language and Catholic religion of the people, who are mainly of mixed heritage. Indigenous Maya peoples remain most numerous in Guatemala. The US has frequently intervened in Central America, purchasing from Panama the right to build the canal in 1903, and sponsoring guerrilla activity in Nicaragua during the 1980s. Initiatives for a common market with Mexico offer hope of overcoming foreign economic dependency and attaining the relative prosperity enjoyed by Costa Rica. However, gaping disparities of wealth and land ownership remain fundamental obstacles to peace and stability.

USING THE LAND & SEA

About half of all agricultural produce is exported. Five commodities dominate commercial farming: bananas, grown on the humid coastal lowlands of the Caribbean; coffee; cotton; sugar and beef, on the Pacific side of the isthmus. Corn is the main subsistence crop and many varieties are grown, supplemented by beans, squash, and sorghum. Large areas of tropical rain forest are commercially exploited, causing concern about deforestation.

THE URBAN/RURAL POPULATION DIVIDE

urban 47%   rural 53%

0 10 20 30 40 50 60 70 80 90 100

POPULATION DENSITY   TOTAL LAND AREA
159 people per sq mile   196,721 sq miles
(61 people per sq km)   (509,640 sq km)

Land use and agricultural distribution

- cattle
- bananas
- coffee
- cotton
- corn
- shellfish
- sugar cane
- timber

- ◼ capital cities
- ◼ major towns
- pasture
- cropland
- forest

Bananas are harvested throughout the year along the Caribbean coast. Bananas are a perishable commodity and the plantations rely on good railroad links to the ports for rapid distribution.

THE LANDSCAPE

THE SIERRA MADRE RANGE spreads west from Mexico, between the narrow Pacific coastal plain and the limestone lowland of Petén. Parallel hill ranges sweep across Honduras and extend south, past the Caribbean Mosquito Coast, to Lakes Managua and Nicaragua. The Cordillera Central rises to the south, gradually descending to Lake Gatún (*Lago Gatún*). A highly active volcanic belt runs along the Pacific seaboard from Mexico to Costa Rica.

Over 40 active volcanoes line the Pacific coast north of Panama, including Volcán Tajumulco. At 13,846 ft (4,220 m), it is the highest point in Central America.

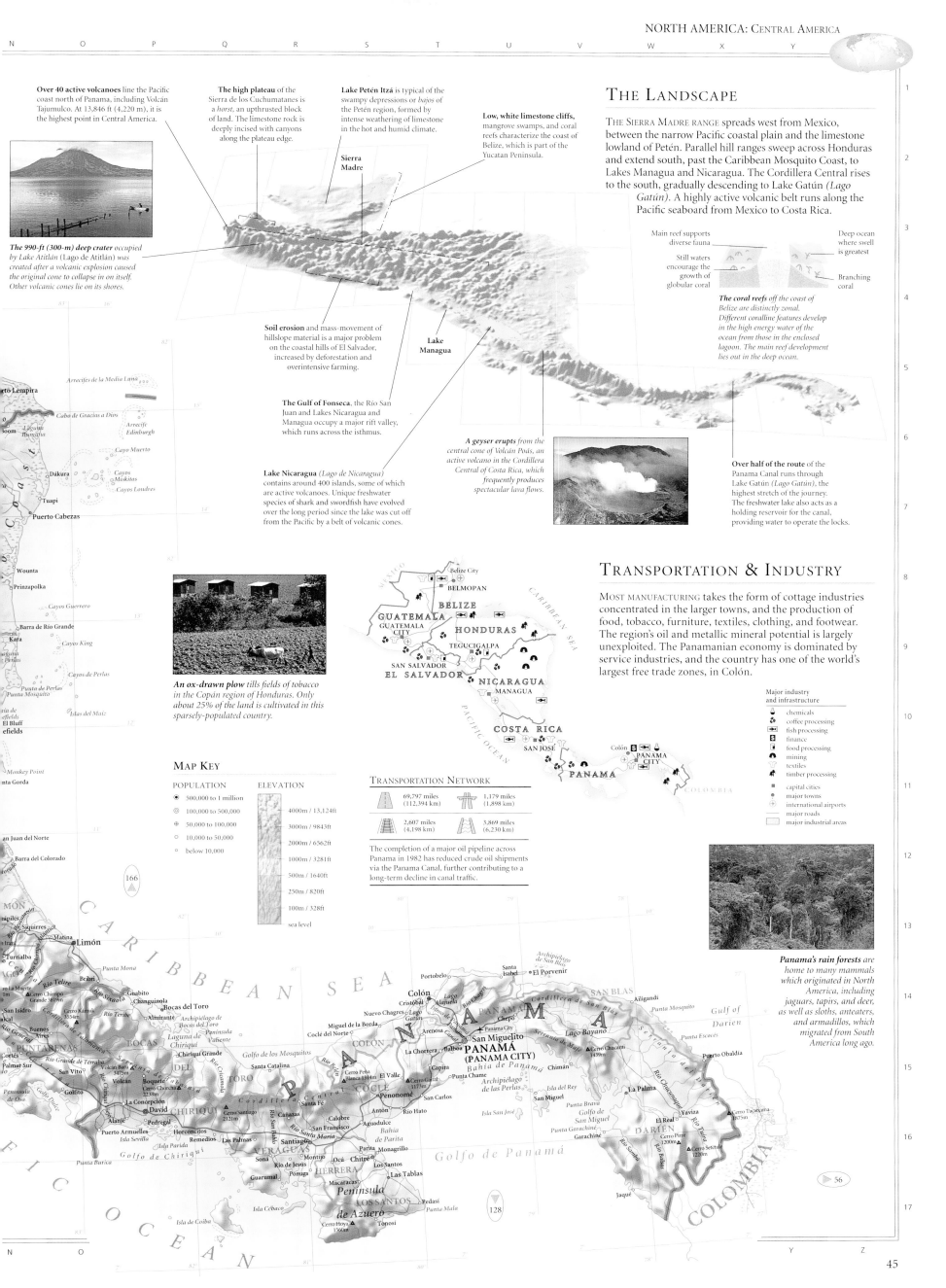

The 990-ft (300-m) deep crater occupied by Lake Atitlán (Lago de Atitlán) was created after a volcanic explosion caused the original cone to collapse in on itself. Other volcanic cones lie on its shores.

The high plateau of the Sierra de los Cuchumatanes is a *horst*, an upthrusted block of land. The limestone rock is deeply incised with canyons along the plateau edge.

Lake Petén Itzá is typical of the swampy depressions or *bajos* of the Petén region, formed by intense weathering of limestone in the hot and humid climate.

Low, white limestone cliffs, mangrove swamps, and coral reefs characterize the coast of Belize, which is part of the Yucatan Peninsula.

Sierra Madre

Lake Managua

Soil erosion and mass-movement of hillslope material is a major problem on the coastal hills of El Salvador, increased by deforestation and overintensive farming.

The Gulf of Fonseca, the Río San Juan and Lakes Nicaragua and Managua occupy a major rift valley, which runs across the isthmus.

Lake Nicaragua (*Lago de Nicaragua*) contains around 400 islands, some of which are active volcanoes. Unique freshwater species of shark and swordfish have evolved over the long period since the lake was cut off from the Pacific by a belt of volcanic cones.

A geyser erupts from the central cone of Volcán Poás, an active volcano in the Cordillera Central of Costa Rica, which frequently produces spectacular lava flows.

Main reef supports diverse fauna

Still waters encourage the growth of globular coral

Deep ocean where swell is greatest

Branching coral

The coral reefs off the coast of Belize are distinctly zonal. Different coralline features develop in the high energy water of the ocean from those in the enclosed lagoon. The main reef development lies out in the deep ocean.

Over half of the route of the Panama Canal runs through Lake Gatún (*Lago Gatún*), the highest stretch of the journey. The freshwater lake also acts as a holding reservoir for the canal, providing water to operate the locks.

TRANSPORTATION & INDUSTRY

MOST MANUFACTURING takes the form of cottage industries concentrated in the larger towns, and the production of food, tobacco, furniture, textiles, clothing, and footwear. The region's oil and metallic mineral potential is largely unexploited. The Panamanian economy is dominated by service industries, and the country has one of the world's largest free trade zones, in Colón.

An ox-drawn plow tills fields of tobacco in the Copán region of Honduras. Only about 25% of the land is cultivated in this sparsely-populated country.

MAP KEY

POPULATION
◉ 500,000 to 1 million
◎ 100,000 to 500,000
⊕ 50,000 to 100,000
○ 10,000 to 50,000
○ below 10,000

ELEVATION
4000m / 13,124ft
3000m / 9843ft
2000m / 6562ft
1000m / 3281ft
500m / 1640ft
250m / 820ft
100m / 328ft
sea level

TRANSPORTATION NETWORK
69,797 miles (112,394 km)	1,179 miles (1,898 km)
2,607 miles (4,198 km)	3,869 miles (6,230 km)

The completion of a major oil pipeline across Panama in 1982 has reduced crude oil shipments via the Panama Canal, further contributing to a long-term decline in canal traffic.

Major industry and infrastructure
- chemicals
- coffee processing
- fish processing
- finance
- food processing
- mining
- textiles
- timber processing
- ■ capital cities
- ● major towns
- ✈ international airports
- major roads
- major industrial areas

MEXICO

Belize City
BELMOPAN
BELIZE
GUATEMALA
GUATEMALA CITY
HONDURAS
TEGUCIGALPA
SAN SALVADOR
EL SALVADOR
NICARAGUA
MANAGUA
CARIBBEAN SEA
PACIFIC OCEAN
COSTA RICA
SAN JOSÉ
Colón
PANAMA CITY
PANAMA
COLOMBIA

Panama's rain forests are home to many mammals which originated in North America, including jaguars, tapirs, and deer, as well as sloths, anteaters, and armadillos, which migrated from South America long ago.

Arrecifes de la Media Luna
Cabo de Gracias a Dios
Arrecife Edinburgh
Laguna Bismuna
Dákura
Cayo Muerto
Cayos Miskitos
Cayos Londres
Tuapi
Puerto Cabezas
Wounta
Prinzapolka
Cayos Guerrero
Cayos King
Barra de Río Grande
Kara
Cayos Perlas
Punta de Perlas
Punta Mosquito
Islas del Maíz
El Bluff
Monkey Point
Punta Gorda
San Juan del Norte
Barra del Colorado

166

CARIBBEAN SEA
Limón
Turrialba
Bribri
Punta Mona
Matina
Squirres
Cerro Chirripó Grande 3810m
Guabito
Río Sixaola
Bocas del Toro
Changuinola
Almirante
Río Teribe
Portobelo
Santa Isabela
El Porvenir
Archipiélago de San Blas
Ailigandi
Punta Mosquito
Gulf of Darien
Nuevo Chagres
Colón
Cristóbal
Lago Alajuela
Lago Gatún
SAN BLAS
Cordillera de San Blas
Miguel de la Borda
Coclé del Norte
Chepo
Arenosa
Panamá Viejo
San Miguelito
PANAMÁ (PANAMA CITY)
Serranía del Darién
Cerro Chucanti 1439m
Puerto Obaldia
Cerro Kamúk 3554m
Cerro Chorcha 2238m
San Isidro
Buenos Aires
Río General
Río Grande de Térraba
PUNTARENAS
Palmar Sur
Cortés
Península de Osa
Golfito
Golfo Dulce
Volcán Barú 3475m
Boquete
Cerro Pando 2121m
Puerto Armuelles
Isla Parida
Punta Burica
La Concepción
David
Alanje
Pedregal
Horconcitos
Remedios
CHIRIQUÍ
Las Palmas
Golfo de Chiriquí
Chiriquí Grande
Santa Catalina
VERAGUAS
Cerro Santiago 2121m
Cañazas
Río San Pablo
Soná
Santa Fé
San Francisco
Calobre
Río de Jesús
Aguadulce
Guarumal
Montijo
Río Santa María
COCLÉ
El Valle
La Chorrera
Capira
Cerro Peña Blanca 1314m
Penonomé
Anton
Río Hato
San Carlos
Punta Chame
Balboa
Golfo de los Mosquitos
Chimán
Bahía de Panamá
Cerro Gaital 1173m
Archipiélago de las Perlas
Isla del Rey
San Miguel
Punta Brava
La Palma
HERRERA
Parita
Chitré
Los Santos
Macaracas
Monagrillo
Pesé
Pedasí
Peninsula de Azuero
Cerro Hoya 1560m
Tonosí
Punta Mala
Isla de Coiba
Isla Cébaco
LOS SANTOS
Las Tablas
Golfo de Panamá
El Real
Yaviza
DARIÉN
Cerro Tacarcuna 1875m
Cerro Pirre 1200m
Cerro Setetulo 1220m
Río Tuira
Río Balsas
Río Sambú
COLOMBIA
Garachiné
Golfo de San Miguel
Punta Garachiné

PACIFIC OCEAN

128
56

The Caribbean's virgin rain forest, seen here in Jamaica, is increasingly at risk from agricultural, industrial, and tourist development. On some islands, the rain forest has virtually disappeared.

The large bar which lies submerged in front of Marina Cay in the British Virgin Islands, has been built up by waves, depositing a bank of sand, which partially encloses the islet.

THE CARIBBEAN

BAHAMAS, GREATER ANTILLES, LESSER ANTILLES

THE ISLANDS KNOWN AS THE WEST INDIES form a great arc that trails eastward from the Gulf of Mexico almost to Venezuela, enclosing the Caribbean Sea. During the period of European colonization, which began in the 16th century, Britain, France, Spain, and the Netherlands struggled for control of the area. Some countries remained politically tied to their colonial rulers until late in the 20th century, and most islands' economies still bear the legacy of the plantation system. A diverse mix of peoples, with roots in Africa, East Asia, and Europe, replaced the indigenous population. Their unique and remarkably homogeneous culture is reflected in the various Creole languages and musical forms, such as reggae and calypso.

USING THE LAND & SEA

AGRICULTURE has long been the basis of most Caribbean economies. Much agricultural land is set aside for cash crops, such as sugar, spices, citrus fruits, bananas, and cocoa, which are grown for export. Diversification is being encouraged to reduce the islands' reliance on imported grain and vulnerability to price fluctuations.

THE URBAN/RURAL POPULATION DIVIDE

urban 55%   rural 45%

| 0 | 10 | 20 | 30 | 40 | 50 | 60 | 70 | 80 | 90 | 100 |

POPULATION DENSITY
396 people per sq mile
(153 people per sq km)

TOTAL LAND AREA
88,396 sq miles
(229,005 sq km)

SCALE 1:5,500,000
(projection: Lambert Conformal Conic)

Market traders in St. George's, the capital of Grenada, sell a wide variety of fresh fruit and vegetables. The island is known particularly for its spices and is the world's leading producer of nutmeg.

SCALE 1:2,500,000

Land use and agricultural distribution

- cattle
- bananas
- coffee
- fishing
- shellfish
- sugar cane
- tobacco
- major towns
- pasture
- cropland
- forest

MAP KEY

POPULATION
- 1 million to 5 million
- 500,000 to 1 million
- 100,000 to 500,000
- 50,000 to 100,000
- 10,000 to 50,000
- below 10,000

ELEVATION
- 3000m / 9843ft
- 2000m / 6562ft
- 1000m / 3281ft
- 500m / 1640ft
- 250m / 820ft
- 100m / 328ft
- sea level

TRANSPORTATION & INDUSTRY

CARIBBEAN INDUSTRY remains, with few exceptions, agricultural and export-led, or service-based, supporting the flourishing tourist industry. However, several countries including Jamaica, Barbados, Trinidad and Tobago, and Puerto Rico have developed important mineral industries. Cuba is attempting to diversify its economy by importing capital goods to start up new manufacturing businesses.

Cruise ships, *such as this one moored at Castries in St. Lucia, have become a popular mode for tourist travel around the Caribbean islands, stopping off at several islands for sightseeing and shopping.*

This rock stack *on the coast of St. Martin in the Leeward Islands has been created by wave action that undercuts the cliffs, forming an arch. Continued wave action weakened the arch, which eventually collapsed leaving a single tower of rock.*

TRANSPORTATION NETWORK

60,831 miles (97,956 km)	357 miles (575 km)
10,310 miles (16,602 km)	211 miles (340 km)

Air links are well developed between most of the Caribbean islands. The importance of the tourist trade has recently encouraged many countries to upgrade their paved roads.

Major industry and infrastructure

- fish processing
- finance
- mining
- oil refining
- sugar refining
- tourism
- major towns
- international airports
- major roads
- major industrial areas

Bahamas, Havana, Cuba, Camagüey, Cayman Islands, Santiago de Cuba, Jamaica, Kingston, Hispaniola, Port-au-Prince, Santo Domingo, San Juan, Puerto Rico, Greater Antilles, ATLANTIC OCEAN, CARIBBEAN SEA, Leeward Islands, Windward Islands, Lesser Antilles, Barbados, Tobago, Trinidad, SOUTH AMERICA

PUERTO RICO (to US) — SCALE 1:2,500,000

GUADELOUPE (to France) — SCALE 1:2,500,000

The Pitons, *in St. Lucia, are two volcanic domes; the tallest is 2,620 ft (798 m) high. Their steep slopes are covered in thick forest.*

DOMINICAN REPUBLIC, SANTO DOMINGO, PUERTO RICO (to US), SAN JUAN, BRITISH VIRGIN ISLANDS (to UK), ROAD TOWN, CHARLOTTE AMALIE, VIRGIN ISLANDS (to US), ANGUILLA (to UK), THE VALLEY, NETHERLANDS ANTILLES (to Netherlands), ANTIGUA & BARBUDA, ST JOHN'S, BASSETERRE, ST KITTS & NEVIS, PLYMOUTH, MONTSERRAT (to UK), GUADELOUPE (to France), BASSE-TERRE, DOMINICA, ROSEAU, MARTINIQUE (to France), FORT-DE-FRANCE, ST LUCIA, CASTRIES, BARBADOS, BRIDGETOWN, ST VINCENT & THE GRENADINES, KINGSTOWN, GRENADA, ST GEORGE'S, TRINIDAD & TOBAGO, PORT-OF SPAIN, ARUBA (to Netherlands), ORANJESTAD, NETHERLANDS ANTILLES (to Netherlands), WILLEMSTAD, Lesser Antilles, Leeward Islands, Windward Islands, VENEZUELA

DOMINICA — SCALE 1:2,000,000

MARTINIQUE (to France) — SCALE 1:2,500,000

ST LUCIA — SCALE 1:2,000,000

BARBADOS — SCALE 1:2,000,000

St Vincent — SCALE 1:2,000,000

GRENADA — SCALE 1:2,000,000

Trinidad — SCALE 1:2,500,000

66

56

SOUTH AMERICA

REACHING FROM THE HUMID TROPICS DOWN INTO THE COLD SOUTH
ATLANTIC, SOUTH AMERICA HAS AN AREA OF 6,886,000 SQ MILES
(17,835,000 SQ KM). THERE ARE 12 SEPARATE COUNTRIES, WITH THE
LARGEST, BRAZIL, COVERING ALMOST HALF OF THE CONTINENT.

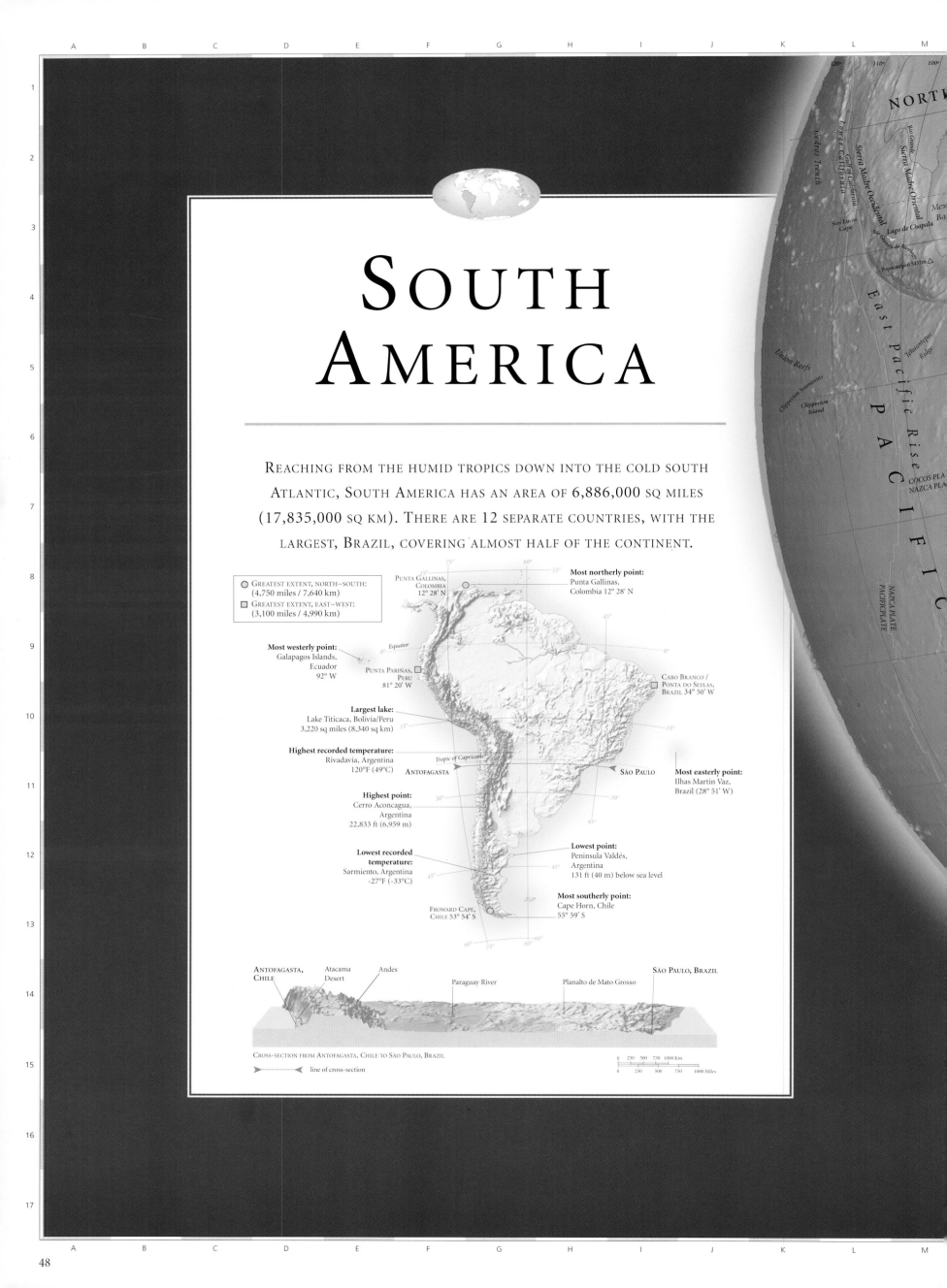

- ○ GREATEST EXTENT, NORTH–SOUTH:
  (4,750 miles / 7,640 km)
- □ GREATEST EXTENT, EAST–WEST:
  (3,100 miles / 4,990 km)

PUNTA GALLINAS,
COLOMBIA
12° 28' N

Most northerly point:
Punta Gallinas,
Colombia 12° 28' N

Most westerly point:
Galapagos Islands,
Ecuador
92° W

PUNTA PARIÑAS,
PERU
81° 20' W

CABO BRANCO /
PONTA DO SEIXAS,
BRAZIL 34° 50' W

Largest lake:
Lake Titicaca, Bolivia/Peru
3,220 sq miles (8,340 sq km)

Highest recorded temperature:
Rivadavia, Argentina
120°F (49°C)

ANTOFAGASTA

SÃO PAULO

Most easterly point:
Ilhas Martin Vaz,
Brazil (28° 51' W)

Highest point:
Cerro Aconcagua,
Argentina
22,833 ft (6,959 m)

**Lowest recorded
temperature:**
Sarmiento, Argentina
-27°F (-33°C)

Lowest point:
Peninsula Valdés,
Argentina
131 ft (40 m) below sea level

Most southerly point:
Cape Horn, Chile
55° 59' S

FROWARD CAPE,
CHILE 53° 54' S

ANTOFAGASTA,
CHILE

Atacama
Desert

Andes

Paraguay River

Planalto de Mato Grosso

SÃO PAULO, BRAZIL

CROSS-SECTION FROM ANTOFAGASTA, CHILE TO SÃO PAULO, BRAZIL

◄───── line of cross-section

| 0 | 250 | 500 | 750 | 1000 Km |
| 0 | 250 | 500 | 750 | 1000 Miles |

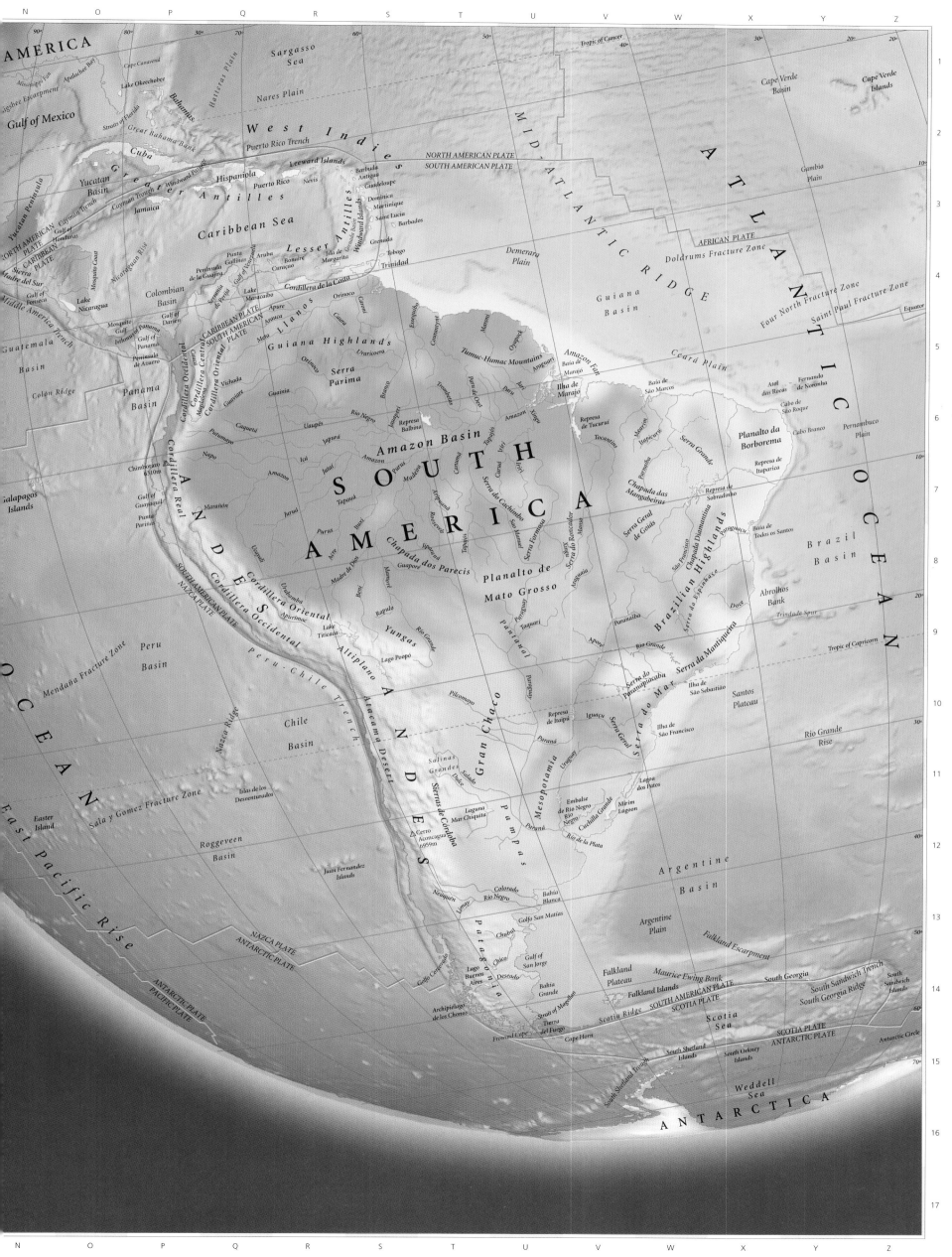

N O P Q R S T U V W X Y Z

AMERICA

Mississippi Fan
Apalachee Bay
Cape Canaveral
Sargasso
Sea
Sigsbee Escarpment
Hatteras Plain
Gulf of Mexico
Lake Okeechobee
Straits of Florida
Bahamas
Nares Plain
West Indies
Great Bahama Bank
Cuba
Yucatan Peninsula
Yucatan Basin
Greater Antilles
Cayman Trench
Puerto Rico Trench
Windward Passage
Hispaniola
Puerto Rico
Leeward Islands
Nevis
Barbuda
Antigua
Guadeloupe
NORTH AMERICAN PLATE
SOUTH AMERICAN PLATE
Dominica
Martinique
Saint Lucia
Barbados

MID-ATLANTIC RIDGE
ATLANTIC

Tropic of Cancer
Cape Verde Basin
Cape Verde Islands

AFRICAN PLATE

NORTH AMERICAN PLATE
CARIBBEAN PLATE
Sierra Madre del Sur
Cayman Trench
Jamaica
Caribbean Sea
Lesser Antilles
Grenada
Tobago
Trinidad
Doldrums Fracture Zone
Gambia Plain

Middle America Trench
Gulf of Fonseca
Mosquito Coast
Nicaraguan Rise
Colombian Basin
Punta Gallinas
Isla de Margarita
Bonaire
Aruba
Curaçao
Península de la Guajira
Cordillera de la Costa
Demerara Plain
Guiana Basin
Four North Fracture Zone
Saint Paul Fracture Zone
Equator

Guatemala Basin
Lake Nicaragua
Mosquito Gulf
Gulf of Darién
Serranía de Perijá
Lake Maracaibo
Apure
Arauca
Orinoco
Caroni
Caura
CARIBBEAN PLATE
SOUTH AMERICAN PLATE
Esequibo
Ceará Plain

Colón Ridge
Gulf of Panama
Isthmus of Panama
Cordillera Occidental
Cordillera Central
Cordillera Oriental
Magdalena
Llanos
Meta
Vichada
Guiana Highlands
Uraricoera
Tumuc-Humac Mountains
Oyapock
Amazon Fan
Baía de Marajó
Baía de São Marcos
Atol das Rocas
Fernando de Noronha

Panama Basin
Península de Azuero
Guaviare
Serra Parima
Branco
Pará de Oter
Jari
Amapá
Xingu
Ilha de Marajó
Represa de Tucuruí
Baía de São Marcos
Mearim
Itapicuru
Planalto da Borborema
Cabo Branco
Pernambuco Plain

Galapagos Islands
Chimborazo 6310m
Gulf of Guayaquil
Cordillera Real
Caquetá
Putumayo
Guainía
Rio Negro
Uaupés
Japurá
Juruapeá
Represa Balbina
Amazon Basin
Madeira
Tapajós
Caxiri
Iriri
Tocantins
SOUTH
São Francisco
Serra Grande
Represa de Itaparica

Napo
Punta Pariñas
Marañón
Cordillera Real
Içá
Jutaí
Amazon
Purus
Juruá
Tapauá
AMERICA
Teles Pires
São Manuel
Serra do Cachimbo
Araguaia
Chapada das Mangabeiras
Serra Geral de Goiás
Represa de Sobradinho

Peru Basin
Mendaña Fracture Zone
Cordillera Oriental
Cordillera Occidental
NAZCA PLATE
SOUTH AMERICAN PLATE
ANDES
Urubamba
Apurímac
Madre de Dios
Beni
Mamoré
Chapada dos Parecis
Guaporé
Planalto de Mato Grosso
Xingu
Serra do Roncador
Serra Formosa
Araguaia
Manso
Brazilian Highlands
Chapada Diamantina
São Francisco
Doce
Abrolhos Bank
Brazil Basin

Yungas
Lake Titicaca
Rapulo
Rio Grande
Paraguay
Taquari
Pantanal
Serra da Espinhaço
Trindade Spur

OCEAN
Nazca Ridge
Peru-Chile Trench
Altiplano
Lago Poopó
Pilcomayo
Apore
Rio Grande
Paranaíba
Serra da Mantiqueira
Tropic of Capricorn

Chile Basin
Atacama Desert
Gran Chaco
Represa de Itaipu
Iguaçu
Paraná
Serra Geral
Serra do Paranapiacaba
Serra da Mantiqueira
Ilha de São Sebastião
Santos Plateau

Sala y Gomez Fracture Zone
Islas de los Desventurados
Salinas Grandes
Salado
Dulce
Mesopotamia
Uruguay
Serra do Mar
Ilha de São Francisco
Rio Grande Rise

Easter Island
Roggeveen Basin
Juan Fernandez Islands
Sierras de Córdoba
Laguna Mar Chiquita
Pampas
Paraná
Embalse de Río Negro
Río Negro
Cuchilla Grande
Mirim Lagoon
Lagoa dos Patos

Cerro Aconcagua 6959m
Neuquén
Colorado
Rio Negro
Bahía Blanca
Río de la Plata
Argentine Basin

East Pacific Rise
ANDES
Limay
Golfo San Matías
Argentine Plain

NAZCA PLATE
ANTARCTIC PLATE
Chubut
Chico
Gulf of San Jorge
Falkland Escarpment

ANTARCTIC PLATE
PACIFIC PLATE
Patagonia
Lago Buenos Aires
Deseado
Bahía Grande
Falkland Plateau
Maurice Ewing Bank
South Georgia
South Sandwich Trench
South Sandwich Islands

Archipiélago de los Chonos
Golfo Corcovado
Strait of Magellan
Tierra del Fuego
Falkland Islands
South Georgia Ridge
SOUTH AMERICAN PLATE
SCOTIA PLATE

Prowland Cape
Cape Horn
Scotia Ridge
SOUTH AMERICAN PLATE
SCOTIA PLATE
Scotia Sea
SCOTIA PLATE
ANTARCTIC PLATE
Antarctic Circle

South Shetland Trough
South Shetland Islands
South Orkney Islands
Weddell Sea

ANTARCTICA

PHYSICAL SOUTH AMERICA

THREE MAJOR PHYSIOGRAPHICAL REGIONS characterize South America. The oldest, the ancient Brazilian Shield and the smaller Guyana and Patagonian shields, form the stable core of the continent. Stretching along the entire west coast are the younger Andean fold mountains with many summits rising to 20,000 ft (6,100 m). These two diverse regions are separated by a number of sedimentary basins carrying South America's large river systems to the sea. These include the massive Amazon Basin and the basin of the Gran Chaco.

THE AMAZON BASIN AND GUYANA SHIELD

THE AMAZON RIVER occupies a large depression in the Earth's crust, formed by the uplift of the Andes. It is covered by thick volcanic deposits and layers of alluvium – these have been laid down by the Amazon's many tributaries. To the north is the smaller Guyana Shield.

Headwaters of the Amazon rise in the Andes / Thick alluvium deposits / Mouths of the Amazon

Section across northern South America showing Amazon Basin and its drainage pattern.

SCALE 1:27,500,000
(projection: Lambert Azimuthal Equal Area)

THE ANDEAN UPLANDS

THE ANDEAN UPLANDS run along the west coast of South America. They are being uplifted as the Nazca Plate is subducted beneath the South American Plate. They contain some of the world's largest volcanoes, such as Cotopaxi, and Lake Titicaca, which occupies a dormant site. The far south has many large ice sheets and a fragmented coastline.

Nazca Plate / South American Plate / Volcanic intrusions

Cross-section through the Andes showing the subduction of the Nazca Plate beneath the South American Plate.

MAP KEY

ELEVATION

6000m / 19,686ft
4000m / 13,124ft
3000m / 9843ft
2000m / 6562ft
1500m / 4922ft
1000m / 3281ft
500m / 1640ft
250m / 820ft
100m / 328ft
sea level

PLATE MARGINS
(for explanation see page xiv)

—— constructive
△ △ destructive
—— conservative
········ uncertain

—— physiographic regions
◄ line of cross-section

THE BRAZILIAN SHIELD AND GRAN CHACO

THE IMMENSE BRAZILIAN SHIELD underlies more than one-third of South America. It is pitted with numerous volcanic intrusions, and a large basaltic plateau exists between the Paraná River and the Atlantic Ocean. The flat Gran Chaco lies to the west of the Shield, covered by sedimentary deposits eroded from the Andes, and transported by South America's mighty rivers.

Young, folded Andes Mountains / Volcanic intrusions / Major rivers drain to the south through the Gran Chaco / Ancient resistant shield

Section across central South America showing the flat basin of the Gran Chaco and the ancient Brazilian Shield.

Map labels

Punta Gallinas, Gulf of Venezuela, Gulf of Darien, Gulf of Panama, Lake Maracaibo, Cauca, Orinoco, Llanos, Pakaraima Mountains, GUYANA SHIELD, Guiana Highlands, Tumuc-Humac Mountains, Rio Negro, Cordillera Occidental, Cordillera Central, Cordillera Oriental, Magdalena, Japurá, Putumayo, Cotopaxi 5897m, Chimborazo 6310m, Gulf of Guayaquil, Marañón, Amazon, Madre de Dios, Purus, Madeira, Represa Balbina, Amazon, Tapajós, Xingu, Serra dos Carajás, Ilha de Marajó, Cabo de São Roque, Planalto de Borborema, Tocantins, BRAZILIAN SHIELD, Araguaia, Serra Formosa, Serra do Cachimbo, Chapada dos Parecis, Guaporé, Planalto de Mato Grosso, Serra do Roncador, Serra Dourada, Serra do Espinhaço, São Francisco, Represa de Sobradinho, Brazilian Highlands, Punta Negra, Nevado Huascarán 6768m, Ucayali, Lake Titicaca, Lago Poopó, Altiplano, Pantanal, Serra do Caiapó, Serra de Maracaju, Serra da Mantiqueira, Nevado Ojos del Salado 6880m, Atacama Desert, Pilcomayo, Gran Chaco, Paraguay, Paraná, Serra Geral, Serra do Mar, Uruguay, Mesopotamia, Lagoa dos Patos, Mirim Lagoon, Cerro Aconcagua 6959m, Salado, Pampas, Rio de la Plata, Colorado, Rio Negro, Península Valdés, Isla de Chiloé, Lago Colhué Huapí, Gulf of San Jorge, Golfo de Peñas, Río Deseado, Patagonia, PATAGONIAN SHIELD, Bahía Grande, Falkland Islands, Tierra del Fuego, Strait of Magellan, Cape Horn, COCOS PLATE, NAZCA PLATE, SOUTH AMERICAN PLATE, ANTARCTIC PLATE, SCOTIA PLATE, PACIFIC OCEAN, ATLANTIC OCEAN

CLIMATE

THE CLIMATE OF SOUTH AMERICA is influenced by three principal factors: the seasonal shift of high pressure air masses over the tropics, cold ocean currents along the western coast, which affect temperature and precipitation, and the mountain barrier produced by the Andes, which creates a rain shadow over much of the south.

Mild winters and cool summers typify the extensive Pampas grasslands of Argentina.

Chile's hyperarid Atacama Desert is renowned as one of the driest places on Earth.

Climate
- tundra
- cool continental
- warm humid
- semiarid
- arid
- humid equatorial
- tropical
- ☼ daily hours of sunshine, January
- ☼ daily hours of sunshine, July
- → cold wind

TEMPERATURE

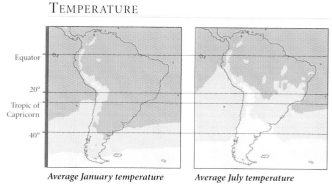

Average January temperature   *Average July temperature*

Temperature
- below -22°F (-30°C)
- -22 to -4°F (-30 to -20°C)
- -4 to 14°F (-20 to -10°C)
- 14 to 32°F (-10 to 0°C)
- 32 to 50°F (0 to 10°C)
- 50°F (10 to 20°C)
- 68 to 86°F (20 to 30°C)
- above 86°F (30°C)

RAINFALL

Average January rainfall   *Average July rainfall*

Rainfall
- 0–1 in (0–25 mm)
- 1–2 in (25–50 mm)
- 2–4 in (50–100 mm)
- 4–8 in (100–200 mm)
- 8–12 in (200–300 mm)
- 12–16 in (300–400 mm)
- 16–20 in (400–500 mm)
- more than 20 in (500 mm)

Maracaibo, Caracas, Georgetown, Cayenne, Bogotá, Quito, Belém, Manaus, Altos, Lima, Recife, La Paz, Brasília, Santa Cruz, Belo Horizonte, La Quiaca, Rio de Janeiro, Antofagasta, Asunción, Córdoba, Porto Alegre, Santiago, Buenos Aires, Montevideo, Concepción, Stanley

Equator   Tropic of Capricorn   Pamperos

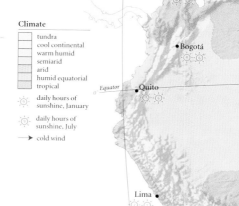
Tropical conditions are found across more than half of South America. When both rainfall and temperatures are high, hot, humid rain forests prevail.

SHAPING THE CONTINENT

SOUTH AMERICA'S ACTIVE TECTONIC BELT has been extensively folded over millions of years; landslides are still frequent in the mountains. The large river systems that erode the mountains flow across resistant shield areas, depositing sediment. Present-day glaciation affects the distinctive landscape of the far south.

MASS MOVEMENT
[6] Debris slides are common in the highlands of South America (*left*). They occur where soil on a slope is saturated with rainwater and therefore less stable. The actual slides are often triggered by earthquakes.

Scarp face left after soil has moved to the base of the slope
Failure plane
Toe of debris slide

MASS MOVEMENT: A SECTION OF A DEBRIS SLIDE

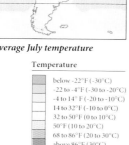

THE EVOLVING LANDSCAPE

CHEMICAL WEATHERING
[1] Table mountains (*left*) are the eroded remnants of an ancient upland. As water percolates along cracks in these high, flat-topped mountains it forms intricate cave systems. Chemical weathering also isolates large blocks which then collapse, accumulating as rockfalls at the foot of scarp slopes.

Smooth summit dissected by deep gorges
Rainfall
Runoff surges down caverns as waterfalls

CHEMICAL WEATHERING: EROSION OF THE GUYANA SHIELD

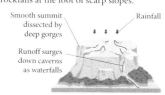

RIVER SYSTEMS
[2] Along the Amazon (*above*) there is a great variation in rates of erosion. As the headwaters of the Amazon flow down from the Andes, they erode and transport vast quantities of sediment, and are known as whitewaters. Across the shield areas erosion rates are very low. These rivers, carrying rotting vegetation, are called blackwaters.

Whitewater river   Blackwater river
Little erosion in shield areas
Confluence of whitewater with blackwater

RIVER SYSTEMS: SUSPENDED SEDIMENTS IN THE AMAZON

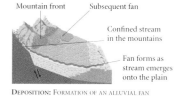

FOLDING
[5] Folding occurs beneath the surface under high temperatures and pressures. Rocks become sufficiently malleable to flow and not fracture as tectonic plates collide. In the Valley of the Moon in Chile (*above*), anticlines (or upfolds) and synclines (or troughs) have been exploited by erosion.

Fold axis
Anticline
Syncline
Fold axis

FOLDING: SYNCLINES AND ANTICLINES

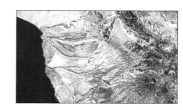

DEPOSITION
[4] Large alluvial fans are found extensively across South America (*above*). Confined mountain rivers, carrying large quantities of eroded material, emerge from a mountain gorge onto the plains, where they deposit their load in huge fans.

Mountain front   Subsequent fan
Confined stream in the mountains
Fan forms as stream emerges onto the plain

DEPOSITION: FORMATION OF AN ALLUVIAL FAN

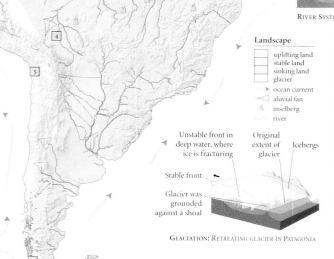

Landscape
- uplifting land
- stable land
- sinking land
- glacier
- ocean current
- aluvial fan
- inselberg
- river

Unstable front in deep water, where ice is fracturing
Original extent of glacier
Icebergs
Stable front
Glacier was grounded against a shoal

GLACIATION: RETREATING GLACIER IN PATAGONIA

GLACIATION
[3] As fjord glaciers in Patagonia (*above*) retreat, they become grounded on shoals. In deeper water the base of the glacier becomes unstable, and icebergs break off (calve) until the glacier snout grounds once more.

POLITICAL SOUTH AMERICA

MODERN SOUTH AMERICA'S POLITICAL BOUNDARIES have their origins in the territorial endeavors of explorers during the 16th century, who claimed almost the entire continent for Portugal and Spain. The Portuguese land in the east later evolved into the federal state of Brazil, while the Spanish vice-royalties eventually emerged as separate independent nation-states in the early 19th century. South America's growing population has become increasingly urbanized, with the growth of coastal cities into large conurbations like Rio de Janeiro and Buenos Aires. In Brazil, Argentina, Chile, and Uruguay, a succession of military dictatorships has given way to fragile, but strengthening, democracies.

Europe retains a small foothold in South America. Kourou in French Guiana is the site chosen by the European Space Agency to launch the Ariane rocket. As a result of its status as a French overseas department, French Guiana is actually part of the European Union.

SCALE 1:21,500,000
(projection: Lambert Azimuthal Equal Area)

TRANSPORTATION

MOST MAJOR ROAD AND RAIL ROUTES are confined to the coastal regions by the imposing natural barriers of the Andes Mountains and the Amazon Basin. Few major cross-continental routes exist, although Buenos Aires serves as a transportation center for the main rail links to La Paz and Valparaíso, while the construction of the Trans-Amazon and Pan-American Highways have made direct road travel possible from Recife to Lima and from Puerto Montt up the coast into Central America. A new waterway project is planned to transform the Paraguay River into a major shipping route, although it involves considerable wetlands destruction.

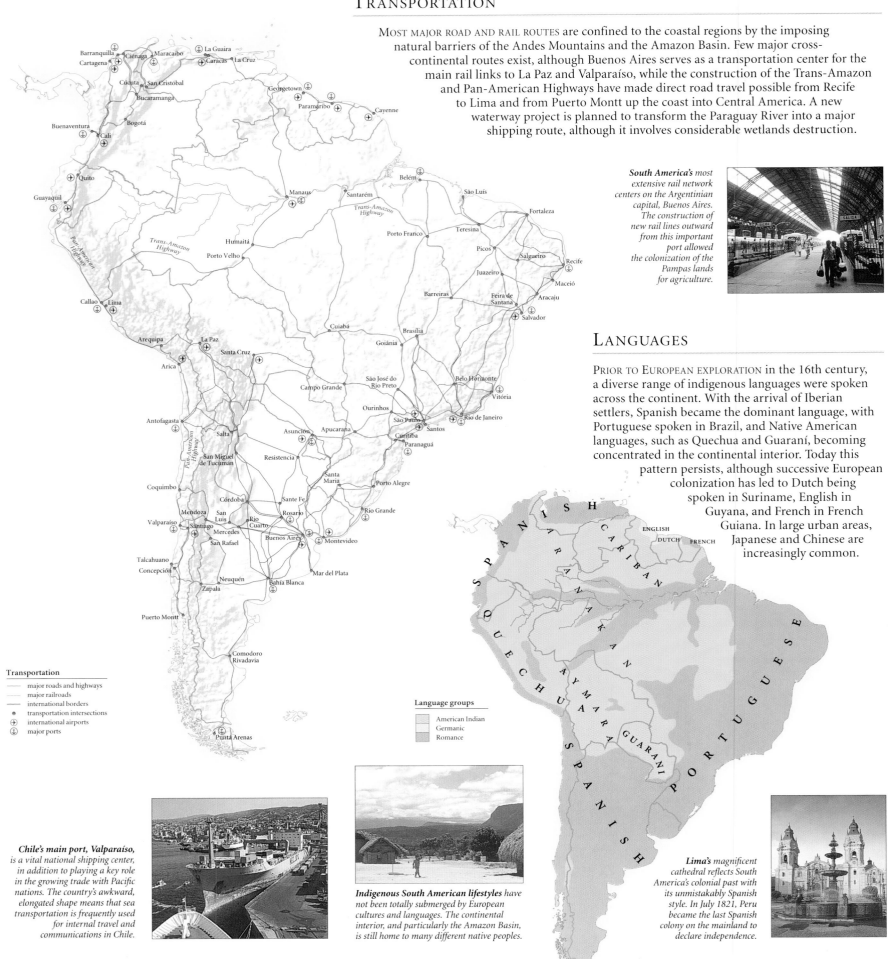

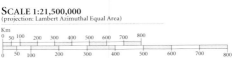

South America's most extensive rail network centers on the Argentinian capital, Buenos Aires. The construction of new rail lines outward from this important port allowed the colonization of the Pampas lands for agriculture.

LANGUAGES

PRIOR TO EUROPEAN EXPLORATION in the 16th century, a diverse range of indigenous languages were spoken across the continent. With the arrival of Iberian settlers, Spanish became the dominant language, with Portuguese spoken in Brazil, and Native American languages, such as Quechua and Guaraní, becoming concentrated in the continental interior. Today this pattern persists, although successive European colonization has led to Dutch being spoken in Suriname, English in Guyana, and French in French Guiana. In large urban areas, Japanese and Chinese are increasingly common.

Transportation
— major roads and highways
— major railroads
— international borders
• transportation intersections
⊕ international airports
⊥ major ports

Language groups
American Indian
Germanic
Romance

Chile's main port, Valparaíso, is a vital national shipping center, in addition to playing a key role in the growing trade with Pacific nations. The country's awkward, elongated shape means that sea transportation is frequently used for internal travel and communications in Chile.

Indigenous South American lifestyles have not been totally submerged by European cultures and languages. The continental interior, and particularly the Amazon Basin, is still home to many different native peoples.

Lima's magnificent cathedral reflects South America's colonial past with its unmistakably Spanish style. In July 1821, Peru became the last Spanish colony on the mainland to declare independence.

Caribbean Sea

NORTH AMERICA

Gulf of Darien

Gulf of Panama

PANAMA

Santa Marta
Barranquilla
Cartagena
Maracaibo
Valledupar
Cabimas
Valencia
Maracay
CARACAS
Cumaná
TRINIDAD & TOBAGO

Gulf of Venezuela
Lake Maracaibo
Monteria
Cúcuta
Barinas
San Cristóbal
Ciudad Guayana

Venezuelan territorial claim

Bucaramanga

Medellín
Manizales
Pereira
Armenia
Ibagué
BOGOTÁ

GEORGETOWN
Linden
PARAMARIBO
CAYENNE

VENEZUELA

GUYANA

SURINAME

French Guiana (to France)

Surinamese territorial claims

Cali

COLOMBIA

Llanos

Orinoco

Rio Negro

Guiana Highlands

Pasto

Boa Vista
RORAIMA

AMAPÁ

Esmeraldas

Macapá

QUITO

ECUADOR

Marañón

Japurá

Amazon

Represa Balbina

Belém

Equator

Portoviejo
Ambato
Riobamba
Babahoyo
Cuenca

Putumayo

Manaus

Santarém

São Luís

Guayaquil
Machala

AMAZONAS

PARÁ

MARANHÃO

Fortaleza

Ecuadorean territorial claims

Iquitos

Amazon Basin

Jurua

Purus

Madeira

Tapajós

Xingu

Tocantins

Araguaia

Teresina

CEARÁ

RIO GRANDE DO NORTE

Natal

Piura

Amazon

PIAUÍ

PARAÍBA

João Pessoa

Chiclayo

ACRE

Porto Velho

PERU

Rio Branco

RONDÔNIA

Palmas do Tocantins

TOCANTINS

PERNAMBUCO

Juazeiro

Jaboatão

Recife

ALAGOAS

Maceió

Trujillo

Madre de Dios

B R A Z I L

Represa de Sobradinho

SERGIPE

Aracaju

Callao
LIMA

Huancayo

Cusco

MATO GROSSO

Planalto de Mato Grosso

Cuiabá

BAHIA

São Francisco

Brazilian Highlands

Salvador

Arequipa

Lake Titicaca

LA PAZ

Cochabamba

BRASÍLIA

DISTRITO FEDERAL

Goiânia

Tacna
Oruro
Arica

BOLIVIA

SUCRE

Santa Cruz

GOIÁS

MINAS GERAIS

Belo Horizonte

Iquique

Lago Poopó

Campo Grande

Ribeirão Preto

Vitória

ESPÍRITO SANTO

Tocopilla

Pilcomayo

MATO GROSSO DO SUL

Paraná

SÃO PAULO

Juiz de Fora

Antofagasta

PARAGUAY

Londrina

Campinas
Osasco
Sorocaba

Nova Iguaçu
Duque de Caxias
RIO DE JANEIRO
Niterói

San Salvador de Jujuy

Gran Chaco

ASUNCIÓN

São Paulo
Santo André

Santos

Rio de Janeiro

Salta

Formosa

Ciudad del Este

PARANÁ

Curitiba

Tropic of Capricorn

San Miguel de Tucumán

Villarrica

SANTA CATARINA

Santiago del Estero

Resistencia

Corrientes

Posadas

Florianópolis

Atacama Desert

La Rioja

RIO GRANDE

Santa Maria

DO SUL

Porto Alegre

Córdoba

Santa Fe

San Juan

Mendoza

San Luis

Paraná
Rosario

Tacuarembó
Melo

URUGUAY

Viña del Mar
Valparaíso
SANTIAGO

CHILE

ARGENTINA

BUENOS AIRES
La Plata

Rio de la Plata

MONTEVIDEO

Linares

Paraná

Pampas

Salado

Santa Rosa

Concepción

Lota

Temuco
Valdivia

Neuquén

Colorado

Bahía Blanca

Mar del Plata

Rio Negro

PATAGONIA

Puerto Montt

Lago Colhué Huapí

Rawson

Golfo de Penas

Gulf of San Jorge

Deseado

Bahía Grande
Río Gallegos

Falkland Islands (to UK)

STANLEY

Punta Arenas

Strait of Magellan

Ushuaia

Beagle Channel

Cape Horn

PACIFIC OCEAN

ATLANTIC OCEAN

MAP KEY

POPULATION

- ■ above 5 million
- ▣ 1 million to 5 million
- ⊡ 500,000 to 1 million
- ⊞ 100,000 to 500,000
- ⊕ 50,000 to 100,000
- ○ 10,000 to 50,000
- ○ below 10,000
- ● Country capital
- ● State capital

BORDERS

- full international border
- disputed de facto border
- disputed territorial claim border
- state border

In April 1960, Brazil's government began the move from Rio de Janeiro to Brasília, a futuristic city built in the sparsely populated interior. Brasília is now the federal capital of Brazil.

Rapid urbanization has been a feature of most South American countries in the latter half of the 20th century. In many cases, this unchecked growth has led to the development of sprawling slums, lacking adequate water and sewage facilities.

Perched high in the Andes like many of the cities in western South America, La Paz, Bolivia is the world's highest capital city at over 11,500 ft (3,500 m).

POPULATION

ALMOST HALF OF SOUTH AMERICA'S population lives in Brazil but, due to the large uninhabited expanses of the Amazon Basin, its overall population density is much lower than in other countries. During the 20th century the most important population trend has been the movement from rural to urban areas, giving rise to great population concentrations in large cities like São Paulo, Rio de Janeiro, Caracas, Lima, Bogotá, and Buenos Aires.

Population density (people per sq mile)
- 0–10
- 11–23
- 24–36
- 37–49
- 50–75
- above 75

SOUTH AMERICAN RESOURCES

Agriculture still provides the largest single form of employment in South America, though rural unemployment and poverty continue to drive people toward the huge coastal cities in search of jobs and opportunities. Mineral and fuel resources, although substantial, are distributed unevenly; few countries have both fossil fuels and minerals. To break dependence on industries based on raw materials, boost manufacturing, and improve infrastructure, governments borrowed heavily from the World Bank in the 1960s and 1970s. This led to the accumulation of massive debts that are unlikely to be repaid. Today, Brazil dominates the continent's economic output, followed by Argentina. Recently, the less-developed western side of South America has benefited from its geographical position at the eastern edge of the Pacific Rim. Chile, for example, is increasingly exporting raw materials to Japan.

***Ciudad Guayana** is a planned industrial complex in eastern Venezuela, built as an iron and steel center to exploit the nearby iron ore reserves.*

Industry

Symbol	Industry	Symbol	Industry
✈	aerospace		narcotics
	brewing		pharmaceuticals
	car/vehicle manufacture		printing & publishing
	chemicals		shipbuilding
	electronics		sugar processing
	engineering		textiles
	finance		timber processing
	fish processing		tobacco processing
	food processing		oil
	hi-tech industry		gas
	iron & steel	●	industrial cities
	meat processing	△	
	metal refining		major industrial areas

***The cold Peru Current** flows north from the Antarctic along the Pacific coast of Peru, providing rich nutrients for one of the world's largest fishing grounds. Overexploitation has severely reduced Peru's anchovy catch.*

STANDARD OF LIVING

Financial disparities throughout the continent create a wide gulf between affluent landowners and the chronically poor in inner-city slums. The illicit production of cocaine, and the hugely influential drug barons who control its distribution, contribute to the violent disorder and corruption that affect northwestern South America, destabilizing local governments and economies.

Standard of Living
(UN Human Development Index)

low — high

***Both Argentina and Chile** are now exploring the southernmost tip of the continent in search of oil. Here in Punta Arenas, a drilling rig is being prepared for exploratory drilling in the Strait of Magellen.*

GNP per capita (US$)

	0–499
	500–999
	1,000–1,499
	1,500–2,999
	3,000–5,999
	6,000+

INDUSTRY

Argentina and Brazil are South America's most industrialized countries and São Paulo is the continent's leading industrial center. Long-term government investment in Brazilian industry has encouraged a diverse industrial base; engineering, steel production, food processing, textile manufacture, and chemicals predominate. The illegal production of cocaine is economically significant in the Andean countries of Colombia and Bolivia. In Venezuela, the oil-dominated economy has left the country vulnerable to global price fluctuations. Food processing and mineral exploitation are common throughout the less industrially developed parts of the continent, including Bolivia, Chile, Ecuador, and Peru.

Map labels: Caribbean Sea, PANAMA, Gulf of Panama, Barranquilla, Cartagena, Maracaibo, Barquisimeto, Caracas, Valencia, Ciudad Guayana, Georgetown, Paramaribo, VENEZUELA, GUYANA, SURINAME, French Guiana (to France), Medellín, Bogotá, Cali, COLOMBIA, ATLANTIC OCEAN, Quito, ECUADOR, Guayaquil, Iquitos, Amazon Basin, Manaus, Belém, Fortaleza, PERU, Chiclayo, Chimbote, Lima, Cusco, BRAZIL, Natal, Recife, Maceió, Arequipa, La Paz, BOLIVIA, Santa Cruz, Sucre, Brasília, Salvador, PACIFIC OCEAN, Arica, Iquique, Chuquicamata, Antofagasta, PARAGUAY, Belo Horizonte, Asunción, Ciudad del Este, São Paulo, Rio de Janeiro, Curitiba, San Miguel de Tucumán, Corrientes, Córdoba, Santa Fe, Rosario, URUGUAY, Rio Grande, Valparaíso, Mendoza, Santiago, Buenos Aires, Montevideo, Talca, Concepción, ARGENTINA, CHILE, Valdivia, Neuquén, Bahía Blanca, Comodoro Rivadavia, Gulf of San Jorge, Falkland Islands (to UK), Bahía Grande, Punta Arenas, Cape Horn

ENVIRONMENTAL ISSUES

THE AMAZON BASIN is one of the last great wilderness areas left on Earth. The tropical rain forests which grow there are a valuable genetic resource, containing innumerable unique plants and animals. The forests are increasingly under threat from new and expanding settlements and "slash and burn" farming techniques, which clear land for the raising of beef cattle, causing land degradation and soil erosion.

Clouds of smoke billow from the burning Amazon rain forest. Over 25,000 sq miles (60,000 sq km) of virgin rain forest are being cleared annually, destroying an ancient, irreplaceable, natural resource and biodiverse habitat.

Environmental Issues

- national parks
- tropical forest
- forest destroyed
- desert
- desertification
- polluted rivers
- marine pollution
- heavy marine pollution
- poor urban air quality

MINERAL RESOURCES

OVER A QUARTER OF THE WORLD'S known copper reserves are found at the Chuquicamata mine in northern Chile, and other metallic minerals such as tin are found along the length of the Andes. The discovery of oil and gas at Venezuela's Lake Maracaibo in 1917 turned the country into one of the world's leading oil producers. In contrast, South America is virtually devoid of coal, the only significant deposit being on the peninsula of Guajira in Colombia.

Copper is Chile's largest export, most of which is mined at Chuquicamata. Along the length of the Andes, metallic minerals like copper and tin are found in abundance, formed by the excessive pressures and heat involved in mountain-building.

Mineral Resources

- oil field
- gas field
- coal field
- bauxite
- copper
- diamonds
- gold
- iron
- lead
- silver
- tin

USING THE LAND & SEA

MANY FOODS NOW COMMON WORLDWIDE originated in South America. These include the potato, tomato, squash, and cassava. Today, large herds of beef cattle roam the temperate grasslands of the Pampas, supporting an extensive meatpacking trade in Argentina, Uruguay, and Paraguay. Corn is grown as a staple crop across the continent and coffee is grown as a cash crop in Brazil and Colombia. Coca plants grown in Bolivia, Peru, and Colombia provide most of the world's cocaine. Fish and shellfish are caught off the western coast, especially anchovies off Peru, shrimps off Ecuador, and pilchards off Chile.

South America, and Brazil in particular, now leads the world in coffee production, mainly growing Coffea arabica in large plantations. Coffee beans are harvested, roasted, and brewed to produce the world's second most popular drink, after tea.

The Pampas region of southeast South America is characterized by extensive, flat plains and populated by cattle and ranchers (gauchos). Argentina is a major world producer of beef, much of which is exported to the US for use in hamburgers.

High in the Andes, hardy alpacas graze on the barren land. Alpacas are thought to have been domesticated by the Incas, whose nobility wore robes made from their wool. Today, they are still reared and prized for their soft, warm fleeces.

Using the Land and Sea

- barren land
- cropland
- desert
- forest
- mountain region
- pasture
- major conurbations
- cattle
- pigs
- sheep
- bananas
- corn
- citrus fruits
- cocoa
- cotton
- coffee
- fishing
- oil palms
- peanuts
- rubber
- shellfish
- soybeans
- sugar cane
- vineyards
- wheat

NORTHERN SOUTH AMERICA

COLOMBIA, GUYANA, SURINAME, VENEZUELA, *French Guiana* (to France)

Fringed by the Pacific and Atlantic oceans and the Caribbean Sea, South America's northern region has a rich range of natural resources, some exploited for centuries by colonial powers, including the Spanish, French, Dutch, and British, others still to be fully explored. The prospects for further economic development in Colombia, Guyana, and Suriname are blighted by drug-related violence and political instability. Venezuela, despite huge incomes from its oil reserves, remains less developed in other industrial sectors.

French Guiana is an overseas *département* of France, now seeking greater autonomy. Most of the major population centers, such as Bogotá, have grown up in the temperate conditions of the high Andes or, like Caracas, at strategic points along the Caribbean coast.

Flowers grown in Colombia are exported all over the world, and include fine carnations and roses. Here, workers are cutting roses that have been grown in plastic greenhouses.

MAP KEY

POPULATION

- ■ 1 million to 5 million
- ● 500,000 to 1 million
- ◉ 100,000 to 500,000
- ⊕ 50,000 to 100,000
- ○ 10,000 to 50,000
- · below 10,000

ELEVATION

- 4000m / 13,124ft
- 3000m / 9843ft
- 2000m / 6562ft
- 1000m / 3281ft
- 500m / 1640ft
- 250m / 820ft
- 100m / 328ft
- sea level

Scattered farms and villages have grown up on the gentle slopes of this Colombian river valley, utilizing the fertile soils for farming.

Large open squares, like the Plaza Bolívar in Bogotá, are characteristic of many cities founded by the Spanish.

SCALE 1:6,500,000
(projection: Lambert Azimuthal Equal Area)

Km 0 25 50 100 150 200
Miles 0 25 50 100 150 200

The Orinoco River flows from its source in the southern Guiana Highlands to form a broad delta on Venezuela's Atlantic coast. One of its distributary channels opens into a wide bay called the Serpent's Mouth.

Transportation & Industry

Many mineral resources are mined in Colombia, including fuels, gold, and precious and semiprecious stones. Revenues from coffee and exports of illegal narcotics are crucial to the economy. Venezuela's major economic activity is the oil industry around Lake Maracaibo (*Lago de Maracaibo*). Sugar and bauxite are exported from Guyana and Suriname.

Transportation Network

🛣	153,755 miles (247,593km)
🛤	925 miles (1,490 km)
🚂	2,541 miles (4,092 km)
	18,233 miles (29,360 km)

Rivers are an important means of transportation in Colombia; many are extensively navigable. The Pan-American Highway runs through Colombia. In Venezuela, much infrastructure investment is linked to the oil industry.

Major industry and infrastructure
- chemicals
- S finance
- food processing
- iron & steel
- narcotics
- mining
- oil
- oil refining
- pharmaceuticals
- textiles
- timber processing
- ■ capital cities
- ■ major towns
- ✈ international airports
- — major roads
- ▨ major industrial areas

Vast oil reserves around Lake Maracaibo (*Lago de Maracaibo*) form the focus of Venezuelan industry. Incomes from oil are used to invest in other industries and in the development of infrastructure.

Using the Land

The Andean basins support cereal grains and potatoes. Livestock graze at higher altitudes and on the drier tropical grasslands known as the *llanos*; hardy goats are reared in scrubland areas. Grown at higher elevations, coffee is an important cash crop, as is cotton, sugar cane, bananas, citrus fruits, cocoa, and rice, farmed on the Caribbean lowlands. Coca is the most widely grown narcotic plant, with heroin poppies grown in Colombia and marijuana in lowland areas throughout the region.

Land use and agricultural distribution
- cattle
- goats
- bananas
- cereals
- coffee
- cotton
- sugar cane
- ■ capital cities
- • major towns
- pasture
- cropland
- forest
- wetlands
- mountain region

The Urban/Rural Population Divide

urban 78%   rural 22%

POPULATION DENSITY
50 people per sq mile
(19 people per sq km)

TOTAL LAND AREA
1,111,317 sq miles
(2,879,060 sq km)

The Landscape

At its northernmost reaches, in western Colombia and Venezuela, the great Andean mountain chain splits into three distinct ranges: the Cordillera Oriental, Cordillera Central, and Cordillera Occidental, intercut by a complex series of lesser ranges and basins. The relief becomes lower toward the coast and the interior plains of the northern Amazon Basin, rising again into the tropical hills of the Guiana Highlands.

The Sierra Nevada de Santa Marta is a granite massif that rises sharply from the Caribbean lowlands to snow-covered peaks, the tallest of which is 18,947 ft (5,775 m) high.

Lake Maracaibo (*Lago de Maracaibo*) is not a true lake but a shallow inlet of the Caribbean Sea. It is the main source of Venezuela's oil.

The drainage basin of the Magdalena River and the Cauca, its main tributary, covers over 20% of Colombia's total surface area.

In the Guiana Highlands, Venezuela's most remote region, the ancient crystalline rocks contain deposits of iron ore, gold, and diamonds.

Angel Falls (*Salto Ángel*), at 3,212 ft (979 m), is the world's highest waterfall.

Igneous intrusions into the crystalline plateau that forms most of central Guyana have led to the formation of the many rapids that characterize Guyana's rivers.

Guyana Shield
- Alluvial plains
- Inselbergs
- Table mountains

The Guyana Shield is one of the oldest land surfaces in the world – probably formed more than 4 billion years ago. Chemical weathering over millions of years has created flat-topped table mountains and large numbers of inselbergs.

Over 80% of Suriname is covered by tropical rain forest.

Cordillera Occidental

Cordillera Central

Cordillera Oriental

Colombia's eastern lowlands are known locally as *llanos*, meaning "grasslands."

The Potaru River descends 741 ft (226 m) over a sandstone ledge at the Kaieteur Falls in Guyana.

Potaru River

Most of the land in French Guiana is low-lying; here, the rocks of the Guiana Highlands have been eroded by rivers flowing toward the sea.

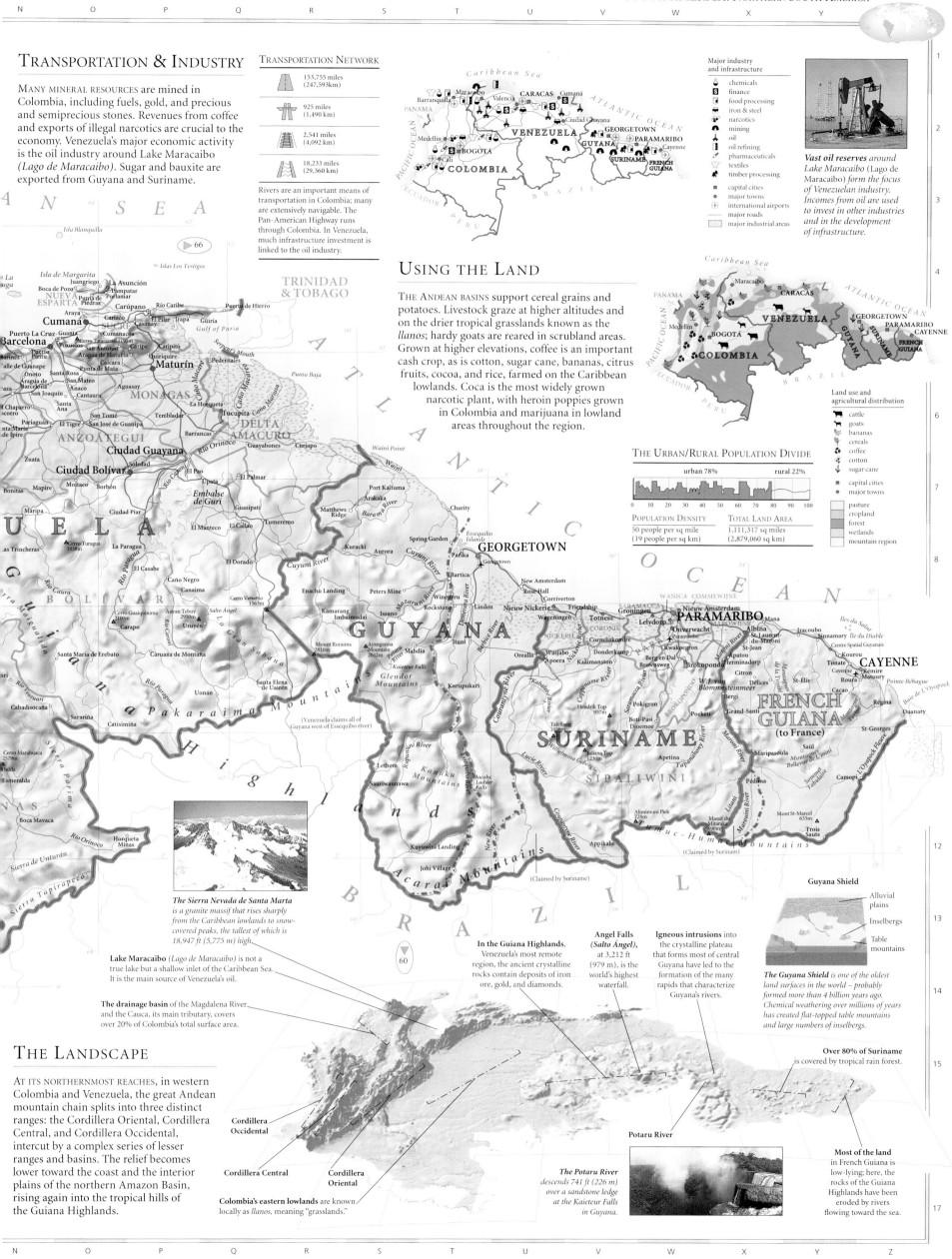

WESTERN SOUTH AMERICA

BOLIVIA, ECUADOR, PERU

THE THREE STATES OF WESTERN SOUTH AMERICA share a similar geography and recent history. Dominated by the Inca empire until Spanish conquest in the 16th century, they achieved independence from Spain in the early 19th century. The precipitous terrain of the Andes presents severe difficulties for overland transportation and continues to be a barrier to national unity and stability. Although Ecuador is now a relatively stable democracy, the military is highly influential in Peru and Bolivia, while the drug trade and associated corruption discourages external aid and economic progress. Wealth and power are still largely concentrated in the hands of a small elite of families who attained their position during the Spanish colonial period. Land rights and political recognition for indigenous peoples are becoming increasingly important issues, particularly in Ecuador.

Ecuador's capital city, Quito, lies high in the Andes, nestling between snowcapped peaks. At 9,350 ft (2,850 m), Quito is the second highest capital in the world – La Paz in Bolivia is the highest.

THE LANDSCAPE

BOLIVIA, PERU, AND ECUADOR each possess a high Andean mountain region and an eastern region consisting of tropical lowlands and the Andean slope leading down to them. Toward the south of the region, the mountains widen to form the high plateau of the Altiplano. Peru and Ecuador also have fertile lowland coastal plains. A wide variety of environments include *selva* (tropical rain forest), *montaña* (mountain forest), and grassland.

There are many large and active volcanoes in the Andes. Magma generated in the heart of the volcano erupts in a huge cloud of ash. Ashfall deposits are common throughout the Andes and the rock produced is known as andesite. This is rapidly soaked by heavy rain, causing massive flows of debris.

Falling ash
Lava flows
Magma chamber
Eruption column
Subduction zone
Zone of magma generation

Rapidly flowing tributaries of the Amazon, which rise in the Andes, run eastward through the front ranges to reach the tropical lowlands. They cut valleys which are so deep that tropical environments can be found extending well into mountainous areas.

Much of eastern Ecuador is covered by the tropical rain forest of the Amazon Basin.

Rolling hills and level plains typify the *montaña* and *selva* region, which makes up more than 65% of Peru.

The Bolivian oriente covers more than two-thirds of the country. It includes *llanos* (low alluvial plains), massive swamps, flooded bottomlands, savannah grassland, and tropical forests.

Cotopaxi is the world's highest active volcano, with a peak 19,347 ft (5,897 m) high. A massive eruption in 1877 caused a mudflow which destroyed everything in its path for 150 miles (240 km).

The coastal floodplains are the source of Ecuador's richest soils, enabling the cultivation of a wide range of crops.

The steepness of the Andean slopes means that avalanches and debris flows are an ever-present danger. A landslide starting from Nevado Huascarán in Peru in 1970 killed 20,000 people in 2.5 minutes when it engulfed an inhabited valley.

The Peruvian Andes are relatively young mountains which are continually being uplifted, making the area very unstable, with frequent earthquakes. The transportation difficulties that they present continue to form a barrier to national unity.

The Altiplano is a flat, high plateau lying between the Cordillera Occidental and the Cordillera Oriental at a height of up to 12,500 ft (3,800 m). At its margins lie many spurs and alluvial fans.

Bolivian Andes

Nevado de Illampu and Nevado de Ancohuma, at 21,275 ft (6,485 m) and 21,490 ft (6,550 m) respectively, form Illampu, the highest mountain in the Bolivian Andes.

Lake Titicaca

Lake Titicaca, which forms part of the border between Peru and Bolivia, is the largest lake in South America. It is the highest significant body of water in the world, situated at an altitude of 12,507 ft (3,812 m).

SCALE 1:7,750,000
(projection: Lambert Azimuthal Equal Area)

Km
Miles

MAP KEY

POPULATION

- above 5 million
- 1 million to 5 million
- 500,000 to 1 million
- 100,000 to 500,000
- 50,000 to 100,000
- 10,000 to 50,000
- below 10,000

ELEVATION

- 6000m / 19,686ft
- 4000m / 13,124ft
- 3000m / 9843ft
- 2000m / 656ft
- 1000m / 328ft
- 500m / 1640ft
- 250m / 820ft
- 100m / 328ft
- sea level

ECUADOREAN ADMINISTRATIVE REGIONS

1. CARCHI
2. TUNGURAHUA
3. BOLÍVAR
4. CHIMBORAZO
5. ZAMORA-CHINCHIPE

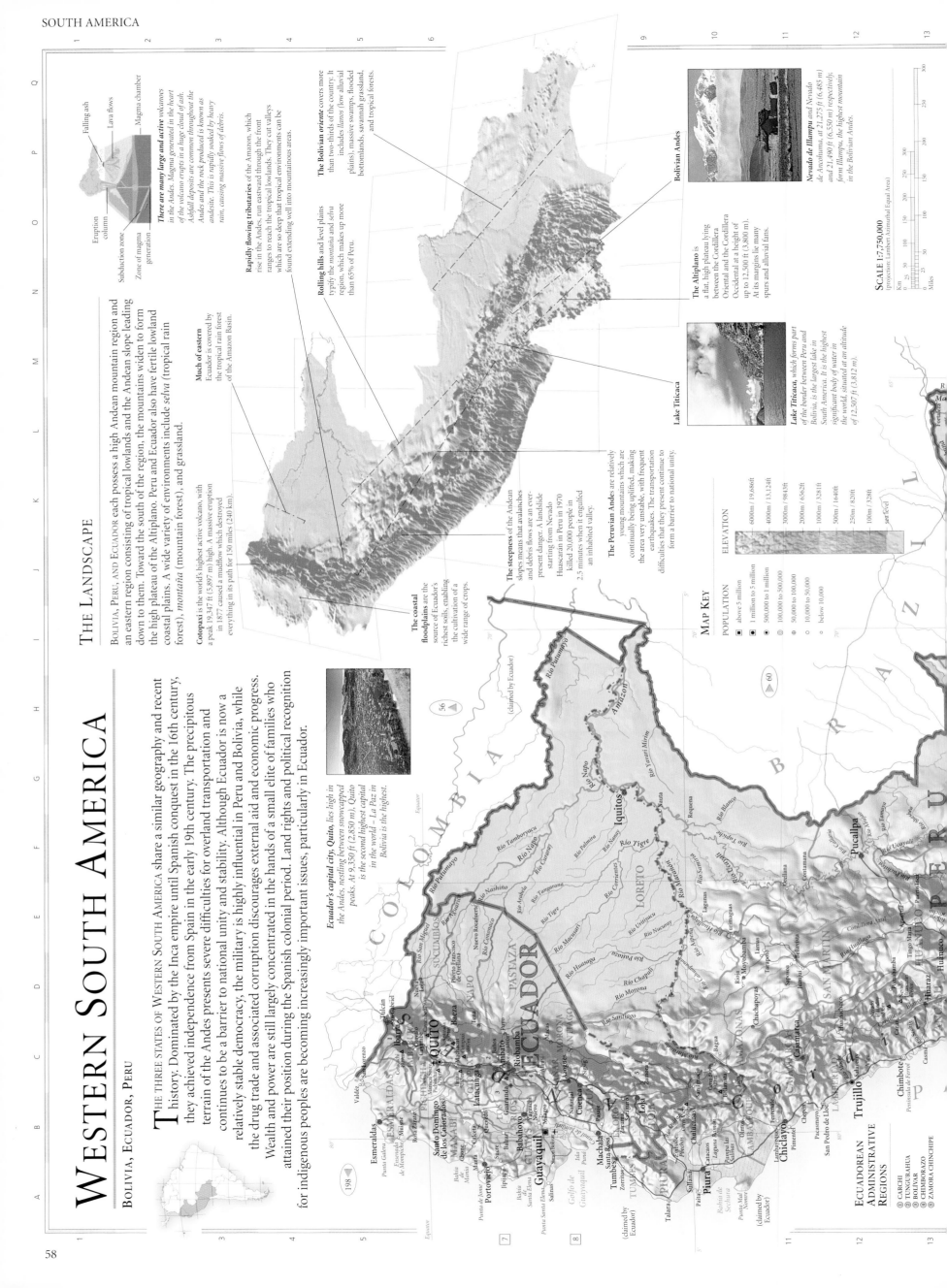

Llamas, along with alpacas and vicuñas, are indigenous to South America. They thrive in Andean conditions and their wool is both exported and used in the manufacture of local textiles.

BOLIVIA'S TWO CAPITALS

LA PAZ – legislative and administrative capital
SUCRE – legal capital

THE URBAN/RURAL POPULATION DIVIDE

urban 64%   rural 36%

POPULATION DENSITY	TOTAL LAND AREA
41 people per sq mile	1,019,515 sq miles
(16 people per sq km)	(2,641,230 sq km)

Clearance of the forest in coca-growing regions is encouraged by the Bolivian government. The inaccessible terrain makes policing the growers very difficult. Coca is a popular crop because it is simple to grow and to transport, and is very profitable when illegally processed as cocaine.

USING THE LAND & SEA

THE COASTAL REGIONS support a variety of cash crops including rice, sugar cane, bananas, coffee, and cocoa, watered by rainfall or by irrigation schemes. The grasslands of the high *sierra* are mainly used for grazing a wide range of livestock; cattle and sheep are reared, along with pigs, and the indigenous llama and alpaca. Subsistence crops, especially potatoes and cereal grains, are grown lower down the mountain flanks. Despite government incentives to grow alternative crops, coca, used for cocaine, is the Bolivian and Peruvian *oriente's* most profitable commercial crop.

Land use and agricultural distribution

- cattle
- sheep
- bananas
- cereals
- cocoa
- coffee
- fishing
- rubber
- sugar cane

- capital cities
- major towns

- pasture
- cropland
- forest
- mountain region
- desert
- wetlands

The Galápagos Islands are mainly composed of lava, with very little vegetation near the coasts, although the wetter inland slopes are mantled with forest.

The ancient city of Machupicchu, in the Peruvian Andes, was built prior to the Inca period. Its impressive ruins reflect a culture which had developed a high degree of sophistication.

A colony of marine iguanas basks on the rocks of Isla Fernandina in the Galápagos Islands. Charles Darwin's theory of evolution was inspired by the differences he found between the animal species on neighboring islands in the Galápagos.

Galápagos Islands
(Archipiélago de Colón)

GALÁPAGOS
(to Ecuador)

(same scale as main map)

TRANSPORTATION & INDUSTRY

THE MOUNTAIN REGIONS are rich in minerals including lead, copper, silver, gold, zinc, and tungsten, although high production and transportation costs have meant that they are expensive to extract and vulnerable to price collapses. Foreign debt remains a major burden, hampering industrial development. Manufacturing tends to be on a small scale and concentrates on products for local needs, including textiles, food processing, and pharmaceuticals. Narcotics are an important, though illegal, export.

Major industry and infrastructure

- car manufacture
- chemicals
- engineering
- fish processing
- food processing
- iron & steel
- mining
- narcotics
- oil
- pharmaceuticals
- shipbuilding
- capital cities
- major towns
- international airports
- major roads
- major industrial areas

In Potosí, Bolivia, silver has been mined for over 400 years.

TRANSPORTATION NETWORK

96,070 miles (154,702 km)	4,417 miles (7,112 km)	14,960 miles (24,090 km)
		none

By the year 2000, a transcontinental highway should link Ilo, on Peru's Pacific coast, to Porto Esperança in Brazil, via Puerto Suárez in Bolivia. Establishing port facilities on the Pacific coast is crucial to landlocked Bolivia's further development.

59

BRAZIL

B RAZIL IS THE LARGEST COUNTRY in South America, with a population of
nearly 160 million – greater than the combined total of the whole of the
rest of the continent. The 26 states which make up the federal republic of
Brazil are administered from the purpose-built capital, Brasília. Tropical
rain forest, covering more than one-third of the country, contains rich
natural resources, but great tracts are sacrificed on a daily basis to agriculture,
industry, and urban expansion. Most of Brazil's multiethnic population now live
in cities, some of which are vast areas of urban sprawl. São Paulo is one of the
world's biggest conurbations, with more than 17 million inhabitants. Although
prosperity is a reality for some, many people still live in great poverty, and mounting
foreign debts continue to damage Brazil's prospects of economic advancement.

USING THE LAND

BRAZIL HAS IMMENSE NATURAL RESOURCES, including minerals and
hardwoods, many of which are found in the fragile rain forest.
Brazil is the world's leading coffee grower and a major producer
of livestock, sugar, and orange juice concentrate. Soybeans for
animal feed, particularly for poultry, have become the country's
most significant crop.

Land use and
agricultural distribution
- cattle
- pigs
- sheep
- citrus fruits
- coffee
- cotton
- soybeans
- sugar cane
- timber

■ capital cities
● major towns

pasture cropland forest

THE URBAN/RURAL POPULATION DIVIDE

urban 77%   rural 23%

POPULATION DENSITY	TOTAL LAND AREA
44 people per sq mile	3,286,472 sq miles
(17 people per sq km)	(8,511,970 sq km)

0 10 20 30 40 50 60 70 80 90 100

THE LANDSCAPE

THE AMAZON BASIN, containing the largest area of
tropical rain forest on Earth, covers nearly half of Brazil.
It is bordered by two shield areas: in the south by the
Brazilian Highlands, and in the north by the Guiana
Highlands. The east coast is dominated by a great
escarpment which runs for 1,600 miles (2,565 km).

*The fecundity of parts of
Brazil's rain forest is the
result of exceptionally high
levels of rainfall and the
quantities of silt deposited by
the Amazon River system.*

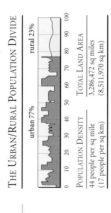

*The Pantanal region in the
south of Brazil is an extension
of the Gran Chaco plain. The
swamps and marshes of this area
are renowned for their beauty
and abundant and unique
wildlife, including wildfowl and
these caimans, a type of crocodile.*

Pantanal swamps

Brazil's highest mountain is the Pico da
Neblina. It was discovered as recently as
1962. It is 9,888 ft (3,014 m) high.

The floodplains which
border the Amazon River
are made up of a variety
of different features
including shallow lakes
and swamps, mangrove
forests in the tidal
delta area, and fertile
levees on riverbanks
and point bars.

Guiana Highlands

The Amazon Basin is the largest river basin
in the world. The Amazon River and over
a thousand tributaries drain an area of
2,375,000 sq miles (6,150,000 sq km)
and carry one-fifth of the world's
fresh water out to sea.

The ancient Brazilian Highlands have a
varied topography. Their plateaus, hills, and deep
valleys are bordered by highly-eroded mountains
containing important mineral deposits. They are
drained by three great river systems, the Amazon,
the Paraguay–Paraná, and the São Francisco.

The São Francisco Basin has a climate unique
in Brazil. Known as the "drought polygon," it
has almost no rain during the dry season,
leading to regular disastrous droughts.

The northeastern scrublands
are known as the *caatinga*, a
virtually impenetrable thorny
woodland, sometimes intermixed
with cacti where water is scarce.

**The famous Sugar Loaf
Mountain** (*Pão de Açúcar*)
which overlooks Rio de
Janeiro is a fine example of
a volcanic plug – a domed
core of solidified lava left
after the slopes of the original
volcano have eroded away.

Deep natural harbors such as
Baía de Guanabara were created
where the steep slopes of the
Serra da Mantiqueira plunge
directly into the ocean.

Hillslope gullying

Direction of growth
Overland water flow
Gully
Rainfall
Water seeps
through
hillslope

*Large-scale gullies
are common in Brazil,
particularly on hillslopes from
which vegetation has been
removed. Gullies grow
headward (up the slope),
aided by a combination
of erosion through water
seepage and rainwater runoff.*

*The Iguaçu River surges over the
spectacular Iguaçu Falls (Saltos do
Iguaçu) toward the Paraná River.
Falls like these are increasingly under
pressure from large-scale hydroelectric
projects such as that at Itaipú.*

MAP KEY

POPULATION
■ above 5 million
■ 1 million to 5 million
◎ 500,000 to 1 million
⊕ 100,000 to 500,000
○ 50,000 to 100,000
○ 10,000 to 50,000
○ below 10,000

ELEVATION
3000m/9843ft
2000m/6562ft
1000m/3281ft
500m/1640ft
250m/820ft
100m/328ft
sea level

Picinguaba Beach lies in Serra do Mar State Park in São Paulo state. São Paulo's beaches stretch for 240 miles (400 km) along the Atlantic coast.

A **gaucho** wearing traditional clothing herds beef cattle on the grasslands of the Rio Grande do Sul in southern Brazil.

TRANSPORTATION & INDUSTRY

BRAZILIAN INDUSTRY is diverse and well developed, partly as a result of past government incentives, including the prohibition of imports. Industries which have benefited include car manufacture, petrochemicals, and microelectronics. Textiles, clothing, and footwear are among Brazil's most successful exports. The country's service and tourist industries are also expanding rapidly.

SCALE 1:12,750,000
(projection: Lambert Azimuthal Equal Area)

Km
Miles

TRANSPORTATION NETWORK

1,032,008 miles
(1,661,850 km)

2,105 miles
(5,000 km)

13,738 miles
(22,123 km)

31,069 miles
(50,000 km)

An extensive new road network is being built to link Brazil's main centers. Investment is needed to update the antiquated railroad system. In São Paulo, the subway system is being extended to accommodate the expanding population.

Brazil's urban population has grown by over 6% per year since the mid-1970s. At current population levels, this represents a rate of nearly 6 million people annually. In Rio de Janeiro prosperous neighborhoods exist alongside over 450 shantytowns or favelas, some of which house as many as 250,000 people.

Major industry and infrastructure

car manufacture
chemicals
electronics
finance
food processing
iron & steel

mining
oil
printing & publishing
textiles
timber processing
tourism

capital cities
major towns
international airports
major roads
major industrial areas

Eastern South America

URUGUAY, NORTHEAST ARGENTINA, SOUTHEAST BRAZIL.

T HE VAST CONURBATIONS OF RIO DE JANEIRO, São Paulo, and Buenos Aires form the core of South America's highly-urbanized eastern region. São Paulo state, with almost 34 million inhabitants, is among the world's 20 most powerful economies, and São Paulo is the fastest growing city on the continent. Rio de Janeiro and Buenos Aires, transformed in the last hundred years from port cities into great metropolitan areas each with more than 10 million inhabitants, typify the unstructured growth and wealth disparities of South America's great cities. In Uruguay, over half of the population lives in the capital, Montevideo, which faces Buenos Aires across the Plate River (Rio de la Plata). Immigration from the countryside has created severe pressure on the urban infrastructure, particularly on available housing, leading to a profusion of crowded shanty settlements (favelas or barrios).

USING THE LAND

MOST OF URUGUAY and the Pampas of northern Argentina are devoted to raising livestock, especially cattle and sheep, which are central to both countries' economies. Soybeans, first produced in Brazil's Rio Grande do Sul, are now more widely grown for large-scale export, as are cereal grains, sugar cane, and grapes. Subsistence crops, including potatoes, corn, and sugar beets, are grown on the remaining arable land.

Land use and agricultural distribution

- cattle
- sheep
- cereals
- coffee
- fruit
- soybeans
- sugar cane
- pasture
- cropland
- forest
- wetlands
- barren land
- capital cities
- major towns

TRANSPORTATION & INDUSTRY

SOUTHEAST BRAZIL IS HOME TO MUCH of the important motor and capital goods industry, largely based around São Paulo; iron and steel production is also concentrated in this region. Uruguay's economy continues to be based mainly on the export of livestock products, including meat and leather goods. Buenos Aires is Argentina's chief port, and the region has a varied and sophisticated economic base including service-based industries such as finance and publishing, as well as primary processing.

Major industry and infrastructure

- car manufacture
- chemicals
- engineering
- finance
- food processing
- iron & steel
- meat processing
- printing & publishing
- shipbuilding
- textiles
- timber processing
- capital cities
- major towns
- international airports
- major roads
- major industrial areas

TRANSPORTATION NETWORK

Throughout the region, road networks need to be expanded to cope with urban development. Plans are underway to build a road tunnel under the Plate River (Rio de la Plata) to link Montevideo and Buenos Aires.

MAP KEY

POPULATION

- above 5 million
- 1 million to 5 million
- 500,000 to 1 million
- 100,000 to 500,000
- 50,000 to 100,000
- 10,000 to 50,000
- below 10,000

ELEVATION

- 2000m / 6562ft
- 1000m / 3281ft
- 500m / 1640ft
- 250m / 820ft
- 100m / 328ft
- sea level

SCALE 1: 6,250,000
(projection: Lambert Azimuthal Equal Area)

Soybeans are harvested, pressed, and processed into soycake, which is used as animal feed. The cake is fed mainly to chickens on large-scale factory farms, and the growth in soy production has been an important factor in the expansion of the Brazilian poultry trade.

The rolling grasslands of Uruguay are ideally suited to the rearing of cattle, which are concentrated in great herds throughout the region.

The Itaipú dam on the Paraná River is one of the largest hydroelectric projects in the world, financed by both Brazil and Paraguay.

Rio de Janeiro's annual carnival, Mardi Gras, which ushers in the start of Lent, is an extravagant five-day parade through the city, characterized by fantastically decorated floats, exuberant dancing, and samba music.

THE LANDSCAPE

THE SOUTHERN REACHES of the Brazilian Highlands follow the Atlantic coast to form low, rolling hills in the northeast of Uruguay. Much of South America's mid-eastern region and all of Uruguay has a gentle relief with land rarely rising above 300 ft (100 m). Argentina's northeast comprises two main regions: a long, narrow lowland known as Mesopotamia; and part of the Pampas grasslands.

In winter, polar air masses and the cyclonic storms associated with them, can bring heavy rain, frosts, and even snow, as far north as São Paulo.

Tracing the edge of São Paulo state, the Paraná River drains the Brazilian Highlands, finally reaching the sea at the Plate River (Río de la Plata). Along with the Paraguay River, it is at the center of a controversial plan to turn the largely unnavigable route into a vast shipping canal.

The Serra do Mar runs along the Atlantic coast toward Porto Alegre. South of this, the land slopes away to become lower and more level in Uruguay.

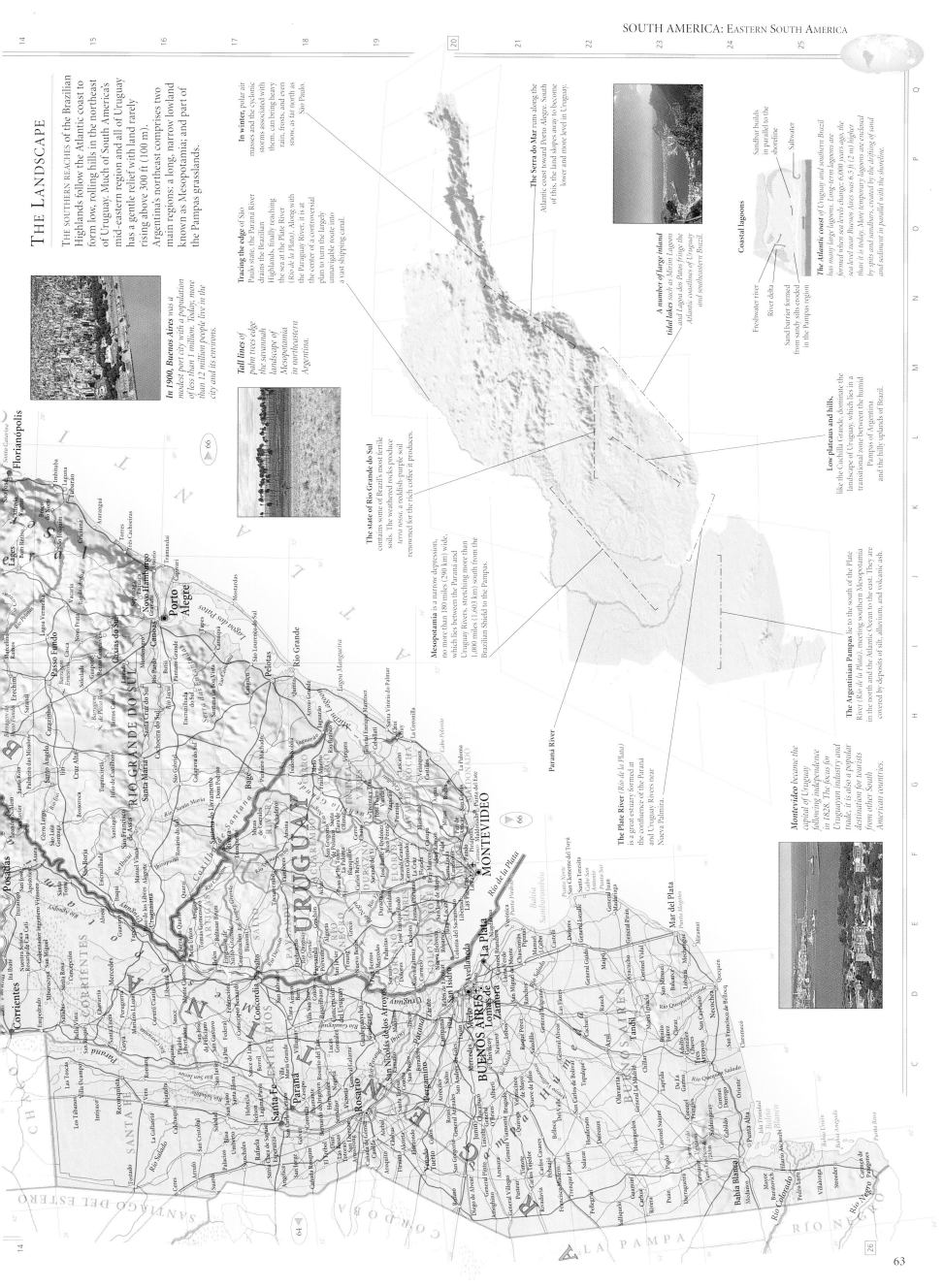

A number of large inland tidal lakes such as Mirim Lagoon and Lagoa dos Patos fringe the Atlantic coastlines of Uruguay and southeastern Brazil.

Tall lines of palm trees edge the savannah landscape of Mesopotamia in northeastern Argentina.

In 1900, Buenos Aires was a modest port city with a population of less than 1 million. Today, more than 12 million people live in the city and its environs.

The state of Rio Grande do Sul contains some of Brazil's most fertile soils. The weathered rocks produce terra rossa, a reddish-purple soil renowned for the rich coffee it produces.

Mesopotamia is a narrow depression, no more than 180 miles (290 km) wide, which lies between the Paraná and Uruguay Rivers, stretching more than 1,000 miles (1,603 km) south from the Brazilian Shield to the Pampas.

Low plateaus and hills, like the Cuchilla Grande, dominate the landscape of Uruguay, which lies in a transitional zone between the humid Pampas of Argentina and the hilly uplands of Brazil.

The Argentinian Pampas lie to the south of the Plate River (Río de la Plata), meeting southern Mesopotamia in the north and the Atlantic Ocean to the east. They are covered by deposits of silt, alluvium, and volcanic ash.

Montevideo became the capital of Uruguay following independence in 1828. The focus for Uruguayan industry and trade, it is also a popular destination for tourists from other South American countries.

The Plate River (Río de la Plata) is a great estuary formed at the confluence of the Paraná and Uruguay Rivers near Nueva Palmira.

Coastal lagoons

Sandbar builds in parallel to the shoreline

Saltwater

Freshwater river

River delta

Sand barrier formed from sandy silts eroded in the Pampas region

The Atlantic coast of Uruguay and southern Brazil has many large lagoons. Long-term lagoons are formed when sea levels change; 6,000 years ago, the sea level near Buenos Aires was 6.5 ft (2 m) higher than it is today. More temporary lagoons are enclosed by spits and sandbars, created by the drifting of sand and sediment in parallel with the shoreline.

Parana River

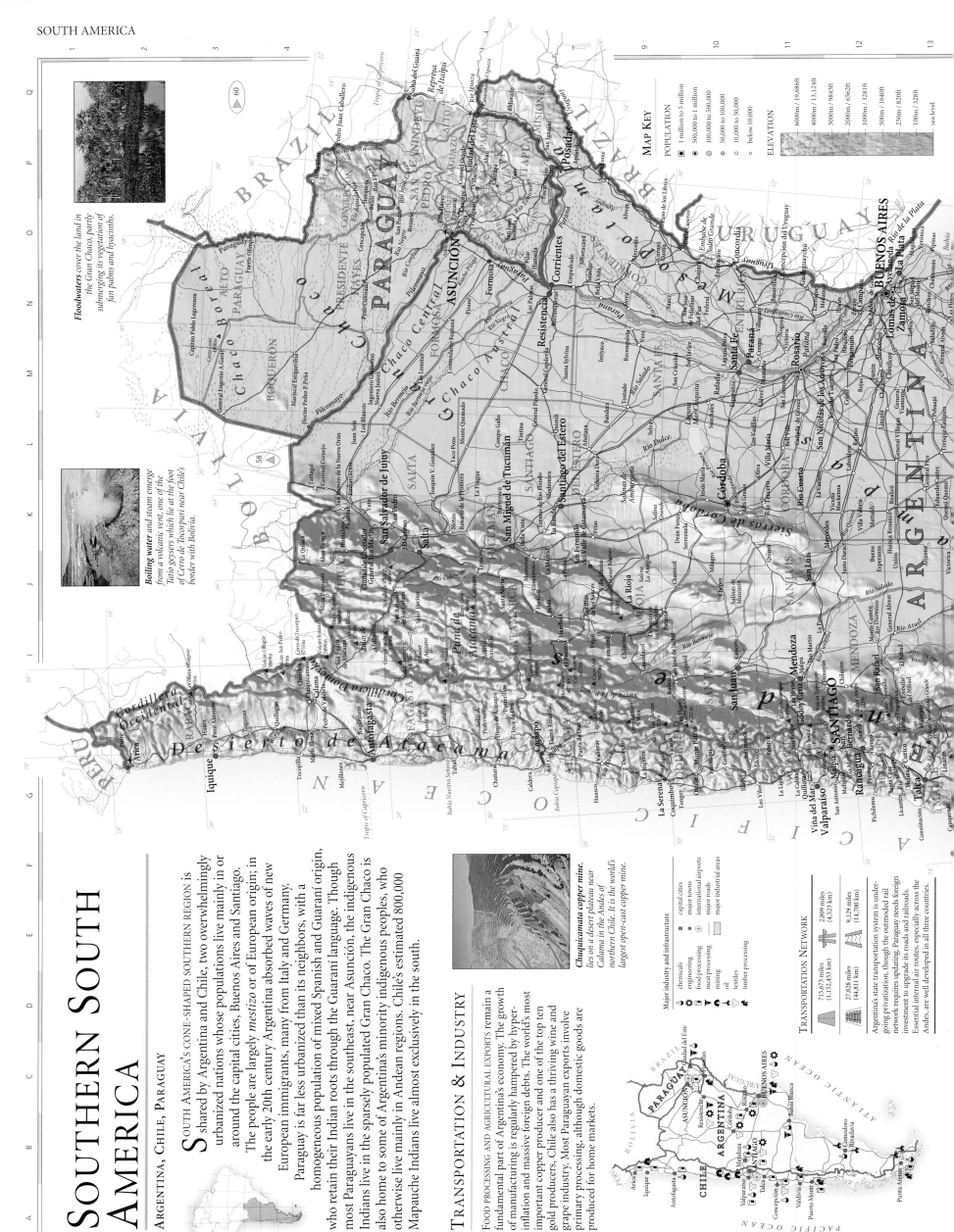

SOUTHERN SOUTH AMERICA

ARGENTINA, CHILE, PARAGUAY

SOUTH AMERICA'S CONE-SHAPED SOUTHERN REGION IS shared by Argentina and Chile, two overwhelmingly urbanized nations whose populations live mainly in or around the capital cities, Buenos Aires and Santiago. The people are largely *mestizo* or of European origin; in the early 20th century Argentina absorbed waves of new European immigrants, many from Italy and Germany. Paraguay is far less urbanized than its neighbors, with a homogeneous population of mixed Spanish and Guaraní origin, who retain their Indian roots through the Guaraní language. Though most Paraguayans live in the southeast, near Asunción, the indigenous Indians live in the sparsely populated Gran Chaco. The Gran Chaco is also home to some of Argentina's minority indigenous peoples, who otherwise live mainly in Andean regions. Chile's estimated 800,000 Mapauche Indians live almost exclusively in the south.

TRANSPORTATION & INDUSTRY

FOOD PROCESSING AND AGRICULTURAL EXPORTS remain a fundamental part of Argentina's economy. The growth of manufacturing is regularly hampered by hyperinflation and massive foreign debts. The world's most important copper producer and one of the top ten gold producers, Chile also has a thriving wine and grape industry. Most Paraguayan exports involve primary processing, although domestic goods are produced for home markets.

Floodwaters cover the land in the Gran Chaco, partly submerging its vegetation of fan palms and hyacinths.

Boiling water and steam emerge from a volcanic vent, one of the Tatio geysers which lie at the foot of Cerro de Tocorpuri near Chile's border with Bolivia.

Chuquicamata copper mine, lies on a desert plateau near Calama in the Andes of northern Chile. It is the world's largest open-cast copper mine.

TRANSPORTATION NETWORK

715,673 miles (1,152,453 km)	2,809 miles (4,523 km)
27,828 miles (44,811 km)	9,129 miles (14,700 km)

Argentina's state transportation system is undergoing privatization, though the outmoded rail network requires updating. Paraguay needs foreign investment to upgrade its roads and railroads. Essential internal air routes, especially across the Andes, are well developed in all three countries.

Major industry and infrastructure

chemicals
engineering
food processing
meat processing
mining
oil
textiles
timber processing

capital cities
major towns
international airports
major roads
major industrial areas

MAP KEY

POPULATION

- 1 million to 5 million
- 500,000 to 1 million
- 100,000 to 500,000
- 50,000 to 100,000
- 10,000 to 50,000
- below 10,000

ELEVATION

6000m / 19,686ft	
4000m / 13,124ft	
3000m / 9843ft	
2000m / 6562ft	
1000m / 3281ft	
500m / 1640ft	
250m / 820ft	
100m / 328ft	
sea level	

THE LANDSCAPE

THE ANDES RUN FROM NORTH TO SOUTH, forming a precipitous natural border between Chile and Argentina. East of the Andes are the scrublands of the Gran Chaco and the plains of the Pampas, which extend northward toward Paraguay. In the far southwest, Chile's indented Pacific coastline has many features typical of areas which have been affected by glaciation.

The Atacama Desert (Desierto de Atacama) in Chile is one of the driest places on Earth where some areas have never recorded any rain. It contains a number of salt lakes.

Most of the highest mountains in Chile's northern Andes are volcanoes, like Volcán Lascar and Volcán Rutana.

Cerro Aconcagua in the central Andes is the tallest mountain in the whole chain, rising to 22,834 ft (6,959 m).

Alluvial deposits from the many rivers in central Chile have created rich soils, ideal for a wide range of agriculture.

Cape Horn is the most southerly point of South America. The severity of the "Roaring Forties" winds makes the Horn one of the world's most treacherous shipping regions.

The Patagonian ice sheet is the world's third largest ice field, covering 6,560 sq miles (17,000 sq km). Patagonia also contains many typical features from past glaciations. These include glacial lakes, U-shaped valleys, fjords, and deep-cut channels.

Patagonia divides into two zones, with the Andes in the west, and the lower main plateau, extending east toward the Atlantic. It is a desolate area with climatic extremes; dark lava fields scattered with light bunchgrass give a "leopard skin" effect to the landscape.

Landlocked Paraguay relies on its river system for access to the sea and to produce hydroelectric power. The most important river system is the Paraguay–Paraná, which provides links into neighboring countries including Brazil, Uruguay, and Argentina.

The Gran Chaco combines poor drainage; extremely hot temperatures, and thorn-infested scrub to make it one of South America's most inhospitable regions.

The Pampas derive their name from an Indian word meaning flat surface. The dry, western region is largely desert, while the east is well-watered, supporting temperate grasses.

The Andean mountain system, which forms Argentina's western border, was created by folding and faulting, following the convergence of the Nazca and South American tectonic plates.

Argentinian Pampas

Rainfall

Windblown particles

Ice-capped Andes are source of loess

Jet stream

Thick layer of loess sediments

A thick, fertile layer of loess lies in the basin underlying the Argentinian Pampas. It has been laid down following successive periods of glaciation. The minute loess particles are transported as dust and deposited by a downward air motion, or following rainfall.

Andes

Great blocks of ice break away from the jagged blue peaks of these ice mountains to form icebergs off the coast of Patagonia, Argentina's most southerly region.

USING THE LAND & SEA

THE RICH PLAINS OF THE PAMPAS support massive herds of cattle, producing meat, milk, and hides essential to the domestic and export markets of both Argentina and Paraguay. Wheat and fruit are Argentina's other major agricultural products. A wide range of soft fruits, citrus fruits, and more specialized crops such as grapes for wine and the table, along with walnuts, are grown in Chile's fertile Central Valley, while the landscape to the south is dominated by forestry, mainly growing commercial radiata pine. Paraguay is self-sufficient in wheat and other staples. Cotton, coffee, tobacco, and oil sources such as soybeans, are the major export crops.

Charred tree stumps surround a cattle enclosure on the island of Tierra del Fuego in southern Argentina. Forest clearance to provide grazing land for cattle is of major environmental concern.

THE URBAN/RURAL POPULATION DIVIDE

urban 83%   rural 17%

POPULATION DENSITY
35 people per sq mile
(13 people per sq km)

TOTAL LAND AREA
1,498,757 sq miles
(3,882,790 sq km)

Land use and agricultural distribution

capital cities
major towns

pasture
cropland
forest
barren land
mountain region

cattle
sheep
cereals
fruit
grapes
timber

SCALE 1:8,750,000
(projection: Lambert Azimuthal Equal Area)

FALKLAND ISLANDS
(to UK)

STANLEY
East Falkland
West Falkland

65

THE ATLANTIC OCEAN

THE ATLANTIC IS THE YOUNGEST OF THE WORLD'S OCEANS, formed about 180 million years ago when the landmasses of the eastern and western hemispheres separated. Its underwater topography is dominated by the Mid-Atlantic Ridge, a huge mountain system running north to south along the center of the ocean. Although most of the ridge's peaks lie below the sea, some emerge as volcanic islands, like Iceland and the Azores. The Atlantic contains a wealth of resources, including substantial oil and gas reserves and rich fishing grounds. Until the 1950s, the north Atlantic was the world's busiest shipping route; cheaper air transportation and alternate routes have shifted patterns of world trade.

RESOURCES

DEVELOPMENT OF THE OIL AND GAS RESERVES in the Atlantic began in the 1940s around the Gulf of Mexico. Since then other areas have been exploited, including the North Sea, the west coast of Africa and the area east of Newfoundland and Nova Scotia. There is also extensive mining of sand, gravel, and shell deposits by the US and UK. For centuries, the north Atlantic's fishing grounds have been more heavily utilized than other oceans, leading to a serious decline in many fish stocks.

Resources (including wildlife)
- fish
- whales
- aggregates
- oil & gas
- major towns
- major ports

Surtsey near Iceland, lies on the Mid-Atlantic Ridge. The island was formed in 1963 following a volcanic eruption caused by sea-floor spreading.

On January 5, 1993, the oil tanker Braer ran aground in the Shetland Islands, spilling 83,660 tons (85,000 tonnes) of light crude oil into the ocean, devastating the local marine ecosystem.

Fishing in the seas around northwestern Europe dates back more than 1,500 years. The high nutrient content of the seas makes them ideal breeding grounds for many species of fish.

AZORES (to Portugal)

SCALE 1:6,500,000

MADEIRA (to Portugal)

SCALE 1:2,500,000

ISLAS CANARIAS (CANARY ISLANDS) (to Spain)

SCALE 1:6,500,000

BERMUDA (to UK)

SCALE 1:500,000

SCALE 1:43,000,000
(projection Mollweide)

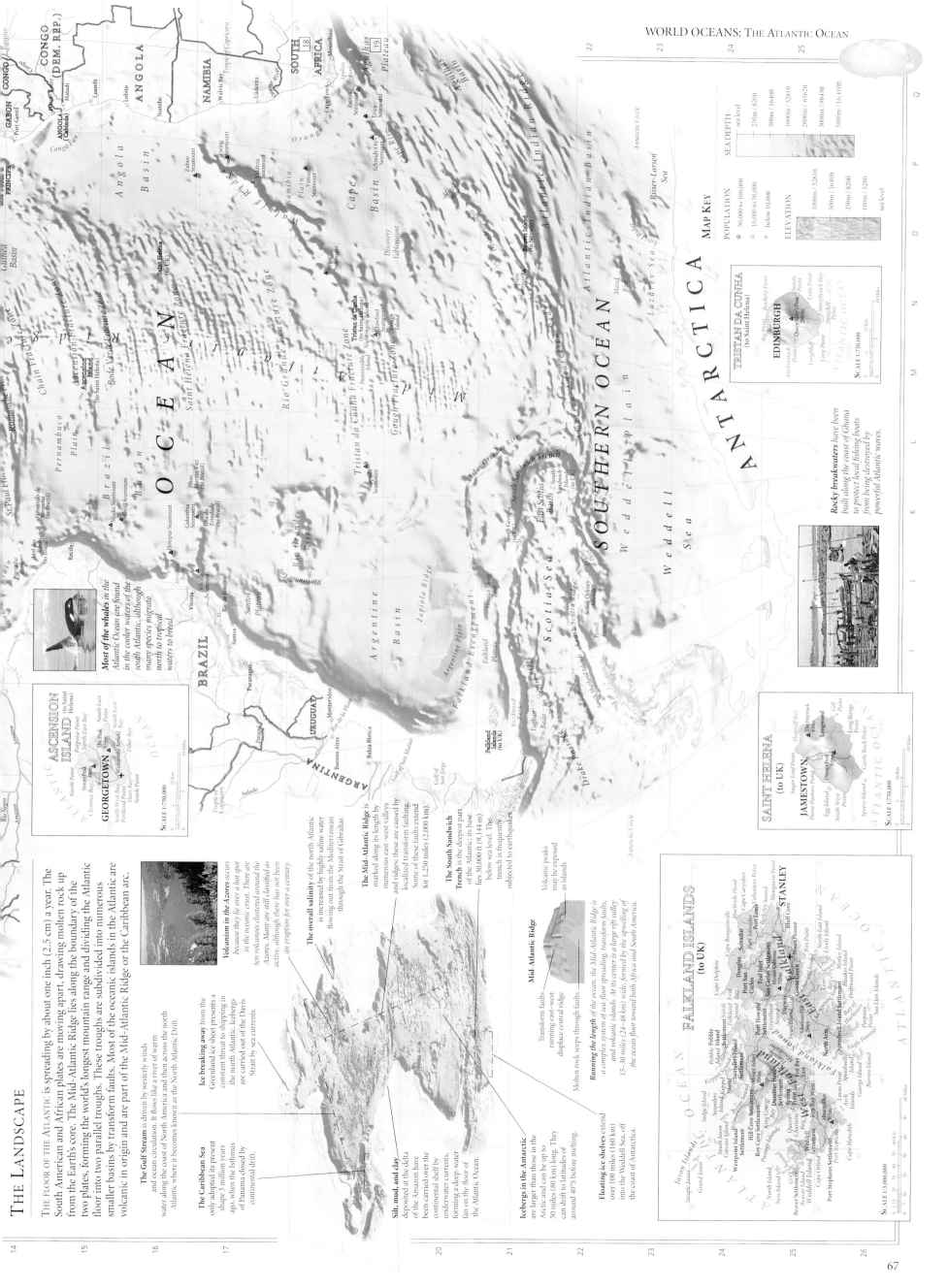

THE LANDSCAPE

THE FLOOR OF THE ATLANTIC is spreading by about one inch (2.5 cm) a year. The South American and African plates are moving apart, drawing molten rock up from the Earth's core. The Mid-Atlantic Ridge lies along the boundary of the two plates, forming the world's longest mountain range and dividing the Atlantic floor into two parallel troughs. These troughs are subdivided into numerous smaller basins by transform faults. Most of the oceanic islands in the Atlantic are volcanic in origin and are part of the Mid-Atlantic Ridge or the Caribbean arc.

The Gulf Stream is driven by westerly winds and ocean circulation. It flows like a river of warm water along the coast of North America and then across the north Atlantic where it becomes known as the North Atlantic Drift.

Ice breaking away from the Greenland ice sheet presents a constant threat to shipping in the north Atlantic. Icebergs are carried out of the Davis Strait by sea currents.

The Caribbean Sea only adopted its present shape 3 million years ago, when the Isthmus of Panama closed by continental drift.

Silt, mud, and clay deposited at the delta of the Amazon have been carried over the continental shelf by underwater currents, forming a deep-water fan on the floor of the Atlantic Ocean.

Icebergs in the Antarctic are larger than those in the Arctic and can be up to 50 miles (80 km) long. They can drift to latitudes of around 40°S before melting.

Floating ice shelves extend over 100 miles (160 km) into the Weddell Sea, off the coast of Antarctica.

Most of the whales in the Atlantic Ocean are found in the cooler waters of the south Atlantic, although many species migrate north to tropical waters to breed.

Volcanism in the Azores occurs because they lie over a hot spot in the oceanic crust. There are ten volcanoes clustered around the Azores. Many are still classified as active, although there has not been an eruption for over a century.

The overall salinity of the north Atlantic is increased by highly saline water flowing out from the Mediterranean through the Strait of Gibraltar.

The Mid-Atlantic Ridge is marked along its length by numerous east–west valleys and ridges; these are caused by localized transform faulting. Some of these faults extend for 1,250 miles (2,000 km).

The South Sandwich Trench is the deepest part of the Atlantic; its base lies 30,000 ft (9,144 m) below sea level. The trench is frequently subjected to earthquakes.

Volcanic peaks may be exposed as islands.

Running the length of the ocean, the Mid-Atlantic Ridge is a complex system of sea-floor spreading, transform faults, and volcanic islands. At its center is a large rift valley 15–30 miles (24–48 km) wide, formed by the upwelling of the ocean floor toward both Africa and South America.

Transform faults running east–west displace central ridge

Molten rock seeps through faults

Mid-Atlantic Ridge

Rocky breakwaters have been built along the coast of Ghana to protect local fishing boats from being destroyed by powerful Atlantic waves.

MAP KEY

POPULATION
- ■ 50,000 to 100,000
- ● 10,000 to 50,000
- ○ below 10,000

SEA DEPTH
sea level	
250m / 820ft	
500m / 1640ft	
1000m / 3281ft	
2000m / 6562ft	
3000m / 9843ft	

ELEVATION
1000m / 3281ft	
500m / 1640ft	
250m / 820ft	
100m / 328ft	
sea level	

TRISTAN DA CUNHA
(to Saint Helena)

EDINBURGH

Big Point · Rookery Point
The Ponds
Sandy Point
Anchorstock · Stonybeach Bay · Stony Hill
Crawfords Point
Queen Mary's Peak 2060m
Longbluff · Noble Point
Cave Point
ATLANTIC OCEAN
SCALE 1:750,000

SAINT HELENA
(to UK)

JAMESTOWN
Sugar Loaf Point · Flagstaff Bay
Flagstaff Bay
The Haystack
Longwood
Egg Island · Diana's Peak 823m · Long Range Point
South West Point
Speery Island · Castle Rock Point
ATLANTIC OCEAN
SCALE 1:750,000

ASCENSION ISLAND
(to Saint Helena)

GEORGETOWN
North Point · South East Bay · South East Bay
Sisters Peak · Porpoise Point
Clarence Bay · Wideawake Airfield
The Peak 859m
South West Bay · Portland Point
Mars Bay · Pillar Bay
South Point
ATLANTIC OCEAN
SCALE 1:750,000

FALKLAND ISLANDS
(to UK)

STANLEY

Jason Islands · Steeple Jason · Grand Jason · Flat Jason · South Jason · North Fur Island
Sedge Island
Saunders Island · Keppel Island · Pebble Island · Cape Dolphin
South Jason · Carcass Island · Westpoint Island · Hill Cove Settlement · Roy Cove Settlement · Passage Island · Port San Carlos · Douglas Settlement · Cape Carysfort · Macbride Head · Cape Bougainville · Volunteer Point
New Island · Port Howard Settlement · San Carlos Settlement · Teal Inlet · Berkeley Sound · Port Louis
Beaver Settlement · Queen Charlotte Bay · Mount Adam 700m · Darwin · Mount Usborne 705m · Bluff Cove · Mount Pleasant
Weddell Island · Spring Point · Port San Salvador · North Arm · Fox Bay West · Goose Green
George Island · Lively Island · Motley Island
Mount Maria · Fox Bay East · Speedwell Island · Bleaker Island
Arch Islands · Speedwell Island Settlement · Sea Lion Islands
Barren Island · Driftwood Point
Port Stephens Settlement · Cape Meredith · Eagle Passage · Porpoise Point
FALKLAND SOUND
West Falkland · East Falkland
ATLANTIC OCEAN
SCALE 1:3,000,000

AFRICA

THE WORLD'S SECOND LARGEST CONTINENT, AFRICA COVERS AN
AREA OF 11,712,434 SQ MILES (30,335,000 SQ KM). IT HAS
53 SEPARATE COUNTRIES, INCLUDING MADAGASCAR IN THE
INDIAN OCEAN – THE HIGHEST NUMBER OF ANY CONTINENT.

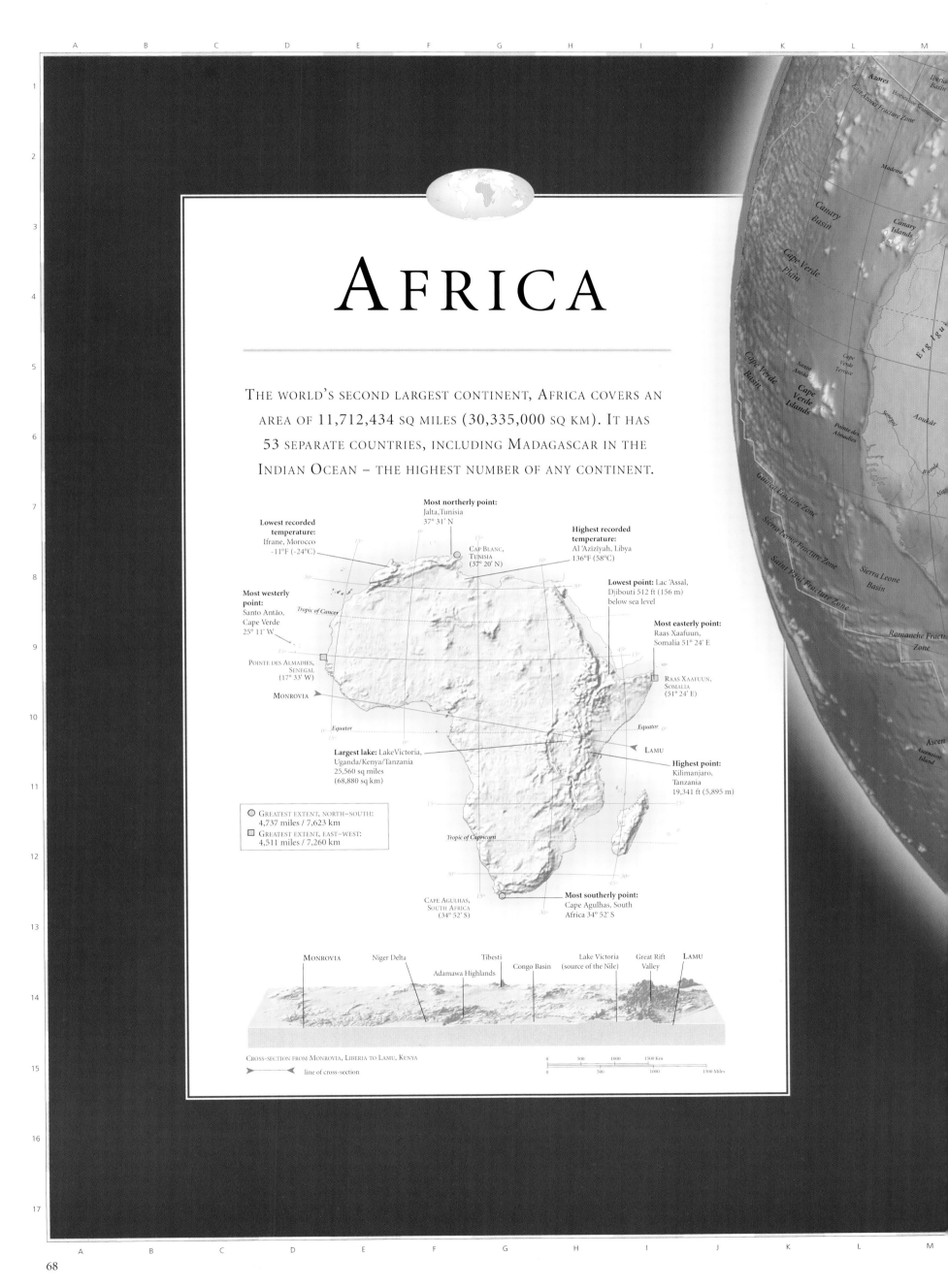

Most northerly point:
Jalta, Tunisia
37° 31' N

**Lowest recorded
temperature:**
Ifrane, Morocco
-11°F (-24°C)

CAP BLANC,
TUNISIA
(37° 20' N)

**Highest recorded
temperature:**
Al 'Azīzīyah, Libya
136°F (58°C)

**Most westerly
point:**
Santo Antão,
Cape Verde
25° 11' W

Tropic of Cancer

Lowest point: Lac 'Assal,
Djibouti 512 ft (156 m)
below sea level

Most easterly point:
Raas Xaafuun,
Somalia 51° 24' E

POINTE DES ALMADIES,
SENEGAL
(17° 33' W)

RAAS XAAFUUN,
SOMALIA
(51° 24' E)

MONROVIA

Equator   *Equator*

Largest lake: LakeVictoria,
Uganda/Kenya/Tanzania
25,560 sq miles
(68,880 sq km)

LAMU

Highest point:
Kilimanjaro,
Tanzania
19,341 ft (5,895 m)

○ GREATEST EXTENT, NORTH–SOUTH:
4,737 miles / 7,623 km
□ GREATEST EXTENT, EAST–WEST:
4,511 miles / 7,260 km

Tropic of Capricorn

Most southerly point:
Cape Agulhas, South
Africa 34° 52' S

CAPE AGULHAS,
SOUTH AFRICA
(34° 52' S)

MONROVIA   Niger Delta   Tibesti   Congo Basin   Lake Victoria   Great Rift   LAMU
                                                                   (source of the Nile) Valley
              Adamawa Highlands

CROSS-SECTION FROM MONROVIA, LIBERIA TO LAMU, KENYA

▶   line of cross-section

0   500   1000   1500 Km
0   500   1000   1500 Miles

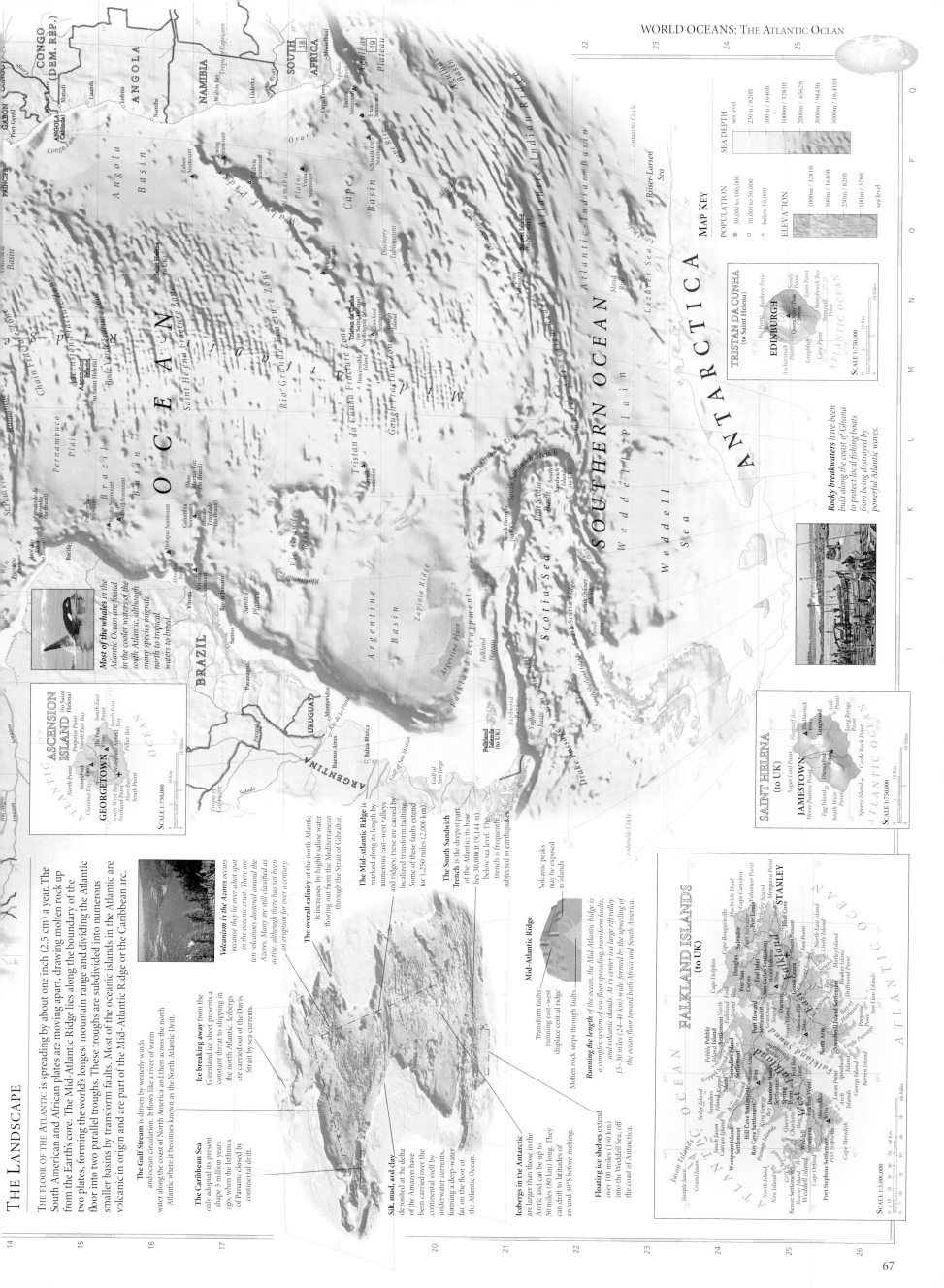

THE LANDSCAPE

THE FLOOR OF THE ATLANTIC is spreading by about one inch (2.5 cm) a year. The South American and African plates are moving apart, drawing molten rock up from the Earth's core. The Mid-Atlantic Ridge lies along the boundary of the two plates, forming the world's longest mountain range and dividing the Atlantic floor into two parallel troughs. These troughs are subdivided into numerous smaller basins by transform faults. Most of the oceanic islands in the Atlantic are volcanic in origin and are part of the Mid-Atlantic Ridge or the Caribbean arc.

Most of the whales in the Atlantic Ocean are found in the cooler waters of the south Atlantic, although many species migrate north to tropical waters to breed.

Volcanism in the Azores occurs because they lie over a hot spot in the oceanic crust. There are ten volcanoes clustered around the Azores. Many are still classified as active, although there has not been an eruption for over a century.

The overall salinity of the north Atlantic is increased by highly saline water flowing out from the Mediterranean through the Strait of Gibraltar.

The Mid-Atlantic Ridge is marked along its length by numerous east–west valleys and ridges; these are caused by localized transform faulting. Some of these faults extend for 1,250 miles (2,000 km).

The South Sandwich Trench is the deepest part of the Atlantic; its base lies 30,000 ft (9,144 m) below sea level. The trench is frequently subjected to earthquakes.

The Gulf Stream is driven by westerly winds and ocean circulation. It flows like a river of warm water along the coast of North America and then across the north Atlantic where it becomes known as the North Atlantic Drift.

Ice breaking away from the Greenland ice sheet presents a constant threat to shipping in the north Atlantic. Icebergs are carried out of the Davis Strait by sea currents.

The Caribbean Sea only adopted its present shape 3 million years ago, when the Isthmus of Panama closed by continental drift.

Silt, mud, and clay deposited at the delta of the Amazon have been carried over the continental shelf by underwater currents, forming a deep-water fan on the floor of the Atlantic Ocean.

Icebergs in the Antarctic are larger than those in the Arctic and can be up to 50 miles (80 km) long. They can drift to latitudes of around 40°S before melting.

Floating ice shelves extend over 100 miles (160 km) into the Weddell Sea, off the coast of Antarctica.

Mid-Atlantic Ridge

Transform faults running east–west displace central ridge

Molten rock seeps through faults

Volcanic peaks may be exposed as islands

Running the length of the ocean, the Mid-Atlantic Ridge is a complex system of sea-floor spreading, transform faults, and volcanic islands. At its center is a large rift valley 15–30 miles (24–48 km) wide, formed by the upwelling of the ocean floor toward both Africa and South America.

Rocky breakwaters have been built along the coast of Ghana to protect local fishing boats from being destroyed by powerful Atlantic waves.

MAP KEY

POPULATION
- ● 50,000 to 100,000
- ○ 10,000 to 50,000
- ○ below 10,000

SEA DEPTH
SEA LEVEL
- 250m / 820ft
- 500m / 1640ft
- 1000m / 3281ft
- 2000m / 6562ft
- 3000m / 9843ft
- 5000m / 16,410ft

ELEVATION
- 1000m / 3281ft
- 500m / 1640ft
- 250m / 820ft
- 100m / 328ft
- sea level

TRISTAN DA CUNHA
(to Saint Helena)

EDINBURGH

ATLANTIC OCEAN

SCALE 1:750,000

SAINT HELENA
(to UK)

JAMESTOWN

ATLANTIC OCEAN

SCALE 1:750,000

ASCENSION ISLAND (to Saint Helena)

GEORGETOWN

ATLANTIC OCEAN

SCALE 1:750,000

FALKLAND ISLANDS
(to UK)

STANLEY

ATLANTIC OCEAN

SCALE 1:3,000,000

N O P Q R S T U V W X Y Z

EUROPE

Iberian
Peninsula

Corsica

Adriatic
Sea

Sardinia

Balearic
Islands

Tyrrhenian
Sea

Sicily

Ionian
Sea

Lake Van

Caspian Sea

Lake Tuz

Anatolia

Aegean
Sea

Lake Urmia

Elburz Mountains

Qolleh-ye
Damāvand
5654m

Iranian
Plateau

ASIA

Mediterranean Sea

Sierra Nevada

Strait of
Gibraltar

EURASIAN PLATE
AFRICAN PLATE

Atlas Mountains

Grand Erg Occidental

Saharan Atlas

Malta

Gulf of
Sirte

Grand Erg
Oriental

Plateau du
Tademaït

Oued Saoura

S A H A R A

Erg Chech

Tassili
-n-Ajjer

Idhān
Murzuq

Ahaggar

Tamanrasset

Ténéré
du
Tafassâsset

Massif
de l'Aïr

Ténéré

Tibesti

Cyprus

Gulf of
Antalya

Sea of
Crete

Crete

Hellenic Trough

Taurus
Mountains

Jordan

Dead
Sea

Sinai

Suez
Canal

Nile Fan

Eastern Desert

Western
Desert

Qattara
Depression

Great Sand Sea

Libyan Desert

The Great
Oasis

Lake Nasser

Nubian
Desert

Nile

Wadi el Milk

Ouadi Haouach

Ouadi Howa

*Syrian
Desert*

Wādī al Bāṭin

Wādī al Ubayyid

Euphrates

Tigris

An
Nafūd

Red Sea

Zagros Mountains

IRANIAN PLATE
ARABIAN PLATE

Persian Gulf

Gulf of
Oman

Arabian

**Arabian
Peninsula**

Az
Zāhirah

Wahibah
Sands

Sea

Murray Ridge

Tropic of Cancer

ARABIAN PLATE
AFRICAN PLATE

Rub' al Khālī

East Sheba Ridge

Abāa-Fartak Trench

Socotra

Owen Fracture Zone

Azaouâd

Adrar des
Ifôghas

Vallée de
Tilemsi

Valée de
l'Azaouâk

Grand Erg de Bilma

Niger

Black Volta

Lake Chad

Komadugu Gana

Chari

Logone

S a h e l

Hadejia

Jos
Plateau

Shebshi
Mountains

Benoue

Bahr des Bongo

Massif des Bongo

Bangoran

Blue Nile

Lake Tana

Atbara

Gāsh

Tekezē

Lac
Assal

Buk

Abuna Mēda
4000m △

Wabē Shebelē

Gāsh

Gumi

Gulf of Aden

Horn
of
Africa

Raas
Xaafuun

Chain Ridge

Lake Volta

Oti

Katsina Ala

Niger

Niger
Delta

Benue

Niger Fan

Bioko

Cameroon
Mountain 4070m △

A F R I C A

Adamawa
Highlands

Koro

Uele

Ubangi

Itimbiri

Kibali

Aruwimi

Bomu

S u d d

White Nile

Ethiopian
Highlands

Baro

Gilo

Mendebo

Genalē

Dawa

Ogaden

Somali Basin

Somali
Plain

Equator

Guinea
Basin

Gulf of
Guinea

Principe

São Tomé

Ogooué

Zadié

Congo

**Congo
Basin**

Nepoko

Lomami

Maiko

Ulindi

Congo

Yei

White Nile

Didinga Hills

Lotagipi
Swamp

Lake
Rudolf

Cherangany
Hills

Lake
Albert

Lake
Edward

Lake
Kivu

Lake
Victoria

Grumeti

△ Mount Kenya
5200m

Huri
Hills

INDIAN

Seychelles

A T L A N T I C

Chain Fracture Zone

Congo Fan

Congo Canyon

Loge

Lualaba

Kasai

Kwilu

Lukuga

Lualaba

Gombe

Lake Tanganyika

Lake
Kisu

Lake
Mweru

Great Rift Valley

Mitumba Range

Lake Rukwa

Great Rift Valley

Ruvuma

Rufiji

Pemba
Zanzibar

Pemba Channel

Zanzibar Channel

OCEAN

Comoro Islands

Comoro
Basin

Tanjona
Bobaomby

**Angola
Basin**

Lucala

Cuango

Cuanza

Catumbela

Bié
Plateau

Cuanza

Kabompo

Luangwa

Muchinga Escarpment

Lake
Nyasa

Luangwa

Lūrio

Madagascar

Mascarene Plain

Mozambique Channel

Madagascar
Basin

Volcanae Ridge

Saint Helena

Cunene

Catumbela

Cuito

Caundo

Cubango

Zambezi

Lake Cabora
Bassa

Lake Kariba

Luenha

Zambezi

Sabi

Sambava

Tsiribihina

Tropic of Capricorn

M i d - A t l a n t i c   R i d g e

SOUTH AMERICAN PLATE
AFRICAN PLATE

South Atlantic Ridge

Omatako

Okavango
Delta

Eiseb

Ghanzi

Niewute
Pan

Chobe

Kafue Flats

Kafue

Limpopo

Olifants

Crocodile

Mangoky

Tanjona
Vohimena

Madagascar

**Madagascar
Plateau**

Walvis Ridge

Tristan da Cunha

Gough Island

Khomas
Hochland

**Kalahari
Desert**

Shashi

Molopo

Nossob

Auob

Namib Desert

Groot

Kuruman

Kuiseb

Karasberge

Orange River

Orange Fan

Dorine

Vaal

Orange River

Harts

Breë

Tugela

Limpopo

Natal
Valley

Natal
Basin

Mozambique Plateau

Southwest Indian Ridge

Discovery II Fracture Zone

Indomed Fracture Zone

Crozet
Islands

Cape of Good Hope

Cape Agulhas

Great Karoo

Breë

Drakensberg

Agulhas
Plateau

Prince Edward
Island

**Cape
Basin**

Cape Rise

Agulhas
Basin

AFRICAN PLATE
ANTARCTICA PLATE

Du Toit Fracture Zone

Prince Edward Fracture Zone

Crozet Plateau

Atlantic-Indian Ridge

N O P Q R S T U V W X Y Z

A B C D E F G H I J K L M

PHYSICAL AFRICA

THE STRUCTURE OF AFRICA was dramatically influenced by the breaking up of the supercontinent Gondwanaland about 160 million years ago and, more recently, rifting and hot spot activity. Today, much of Africa is remote from active plate boundaries and comprises a series of extensive plateaus and deep basins, which influence the drainage patterns of major rivers. The relief rises to the east, where volcanic uplands and vast lakes mark the Great Rift Valley. In the far north and south, sedimentary rocks have been folded to form the Atlas Mountains and the Great Karoo.

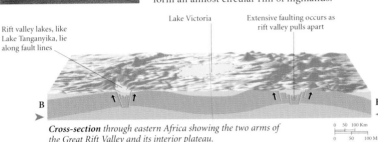

EAST AFRICA

THE GREAT RIFT VALLEY is the most striking feature of this region, running for 4,475 miles (7,200 km) from Lake Nyasa to the Red Sea. North of Lake Nyasa it splits into two arms and encloses an interior plateau, which contains Lake Victoria. A number of elongated lakes and volcanoes lie along the fault lines. To the west lies the Congo Basin, a vast, shallow depression, which rises to form an almost circular rim of highlands.

Rift valley lakes, like Lake Tanganyika, lie along fault lines

Lake Victoria

Extensive faulting occurs as rift valley pulls apart

B — B

Cross-section through eastern Africa showing the two arms of the Great Rift Valley and its interior plateau.

0   50   100 Km
0   50   100 Miles

NORTHERN AFRICA

NORTHERN AFRICA COMPRISES a system of basins and plateaus. The Tibesti and Ahaggar are volcanic uplands, whose uplift has been matched by subsidence within large surrounding basins. Many of the basins have been filled in with sand and gravel, creating the vast Saharan lands. The Atlas Mountains in the north were formed by convergence of the African and Eurasian plates.

The Earth's crust has been warped to form the Taoudenni Basin

Volcanic Ahaggar Mountains, formed by rising magma from a hot spot

Lake Chad lies in a sand-filled basin

A — A

Section across northern Africa showing filled in basins and uplifted plateaus.

0   250   500 Km
0   250   500 Miles

SCALE 1:36,000,000
(projection: Lambert Azimuthal Equal Area)

Km
0 100 200   400   600   800
0 100 200   400   600   800
Miles

MAP KEY

ELEVATION

5000m / 16,405ft
4000m / 13,124ft
3000m / 9843ft
2000m / 6562ft
1000m / 3281ft
500m / 1640ft
250m / 820ft
100m / 328ft
sea level
below sea level

PLATE MARGINS
(for explanation see page xiv)

constructive
destructive
conservative
uncertain

line of cross-section

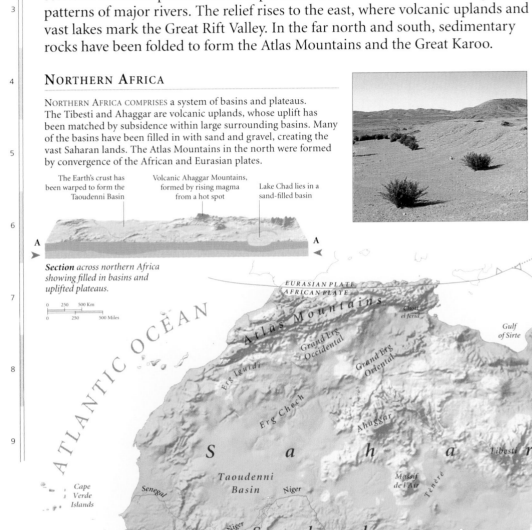

EURASIAN PLATE
AFRICAN PLATE

ANATOLIAN PLATE

AFRICAN PLATE

ARABIAN PLATE

ATLANTIC OCEAN

Atlas Mountains

Grand Erg Occidental

Grand Erg Oriental

Erg Iguidi

Erg Chech

Chott el Jerid

Gulf of Sirte

Nile Delta

Qattara Depression

Western Desert

Great Sand Sea

Libyan Desert

Nubian Desert

Lake Nasser

ASIA

Red Sea

ARABIAN PLATE

AFRICAN PLATE

S   a   h   a   r   a

Ahaggar

Taoudenni Basin

Massif de l'Aïr

Ténéré

Tibesti

Cape Verde Islands

Senegal

Niger

Niger

Sahel

A — A

White Volta

Lake Volta

Niger

Benue

Grain Coast

Ivory Coast   Gold Coast

Slave Coast

Bight of Benin

Niger Delta

Gulf of Guinea

São Tomé

Adamawa Highlands

Cameroon Mountain 4070m

Chari

Massif des Bongo

Congo (Zaire)

Congo Basin

Congo

Zaire

Kitumbanyi

White Nile

Blue Nile

Nile

Lake Tana

Ethiopian Highlands

Gulf of Aden

Horn of Africa

Sudd

Lake Rudolf

Shebeli

Juba

Great Rift Valley

Lake Albert
Lake Victoria

Kilimanjaro 5895m

Lake Tanganyika

B — B

Pemba Island
Zanzibar

Seychelles

ATLANTIC OCEAN

SOUTHERN AFRICA

THE GREAT ESCARPMENT marks the southern boundary of Africa's basement rock, and includes the Drakensberg range. It was uplifted when Gondwanaland fragmented about 160 million years ago and it has gradually been eroded back from the coast. To the north, the relief drops steadily, forming the Kalahari Basin. In the far south are the fold mountains of the Great Karoo.

Kalahari Basin, covered with the sandy plains of the Kalahari Desert

Boundary of the Great Escarpment

Uplift of the basement rock created a raised plateau

Drakensberg

C — C

Cross-section through southern Africa showing the boundary of the Great Escarpment.

0   100   200 Km
0   100   200 Miles

Bie Plateau

Zambezi

Lake Nyasa

Comoro Islands

Mozambique Channel

Madagascar

INDIAN OCEAN

Mauritius

Réunion

Okavango Delta

Namib Desert

Kalahari Basin

Kalahari Desert

Orange River

Limpopo

Zambezi

Drakensberg

Great Karoo

C — C

Cape of Good Hope

CLIMATE

THE CLIMATES OF AFRICA range from mediterranean to arid, savannah, and humid equatorial. In East Africa, where snow settles at the summit of volcanies such as Kilimanjaro, climate is also modified by altitude. The winds of the Sahara carry millions of tons of dust a year both northward and eastward.

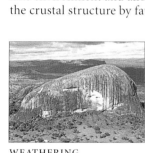

Savannah grasslands run in a belt across Africa; limited rainfall inhibits tree growth.

TEMPERATURE

Average January temperature

Average July temperature

Temperature

- 32 to 50° F (0 to 10°C)
- 0 to 68°F (10 to 20°C)
- 68 to 86°F (20 to 30°C)
- above 86°F (30°C)

The hot, equatorial basin of the Congo River receives over 48 inches (1,200 mm) of rainfall per year.

RAINFALL

Average January rainfall

Average July rainfall

Rainfall

- 0–1 in (0–25 mm)
- 1–2 in (25–50 mm)
- 2–4 in (50–100 mm)
- 4–8 in (100–200 mm)
- 8–12 in (200–300 mm)
- 12–16 in (300–400 mm)
- 16–20 in (400–500 mm)
- more than 20 in (500 mm)

Climate

- arid
- humid equatorial
- mediterranean
- semiarid
- tropical
- warm humid
- daily hours of sunshine, January
- daily hours of sunshine, July
- cold wind
- hot wind

Casablanca, Marrakech, Algiers, Cairo, Tamanrasset, Nouakchott, Dakar, Bamako, Conakry, Ouagadougou, Niamey, Bilma, Abéché, Khartoum, Port Sudan, Djibouti, Abidjan, Lagos, Wau, Mogadishu, Bata, Douala, Libreville, Bangui, Kisangani, Nairobi, Mombassa, Kinshasa, Dar es Salaam, Luanda, Pemba, Lusaka, Harare, Antananarivo, Windhoek, Pretoria, Maputo, Durban, Cape Town

Sirocco, Sirocco, Ghibli, Khamsin, Harmattan, Harmattan, July Winds, July Winds, Haboob, Haboob, July Winds

Tropic of Cancer, Equator, Tropic of Capricorn

SHAPING THE CONTINENT

AFRICAN LANDSCAPES are shaped by the intensity of climatic extremes and by tectonic action. High aridity, wind action, and infrequent but heavy rainstorms lead to the migration of sand dunes and dramatic flash flooding across much of the north and west. In the wetter areas, high precipitation increases the rate of weathering. To the east, the rift system has created a volcanic and lake environment and allowed rivers to erode weaknesses left in the crustal structure by faults.

THE EVOLVING LANDSCAPE

GROUNDWATER

[1] Oases are found in desert areas such as the Sahara *(left)*. Groundwater migrates through permeable rock strata, confined between two impermeable layers. Oases form either when the permeable rocks come near to the surface, or at a fault line, when water is able to seep up to the surface through the crushed rocks at the fault.

Rainwater feeds the aquifer
Water migrates up through fault
Aquifer exposed near the surface
Groundwater trapped between impermeable strata

GROUNDWATER: RECHARGE OF AN OASIS

RIVER SYSTEMS

[2] The Zambezi River *(above)* drops 360 ft (110 m) over the Victoria Falls into a zigzag gorge. The river has eroded the gorge along lines of weakness in the bedrock, created by fault lines running in two directions.

Old site of Victoria Falls
River plunges over falls
Fault and joint lines running in two directions
Zigzag gorge of the Zambezi

RIVER SYSTEMS: RETREATING OF THE VICTORIA FALLS

Exfoliated layers
External stresses act on the surface of the inselberg
Joints or cracks caused by expansion and contraction

WEATHERING: FORMATION OF AN INSELBERG

WEATHERING

[6] Inselbergs *(above)*, found extensively across West Africa, are exposed remnants of an extensive upland area. Erosion of the surrounding uplands leaves a resistant rock outcrop. Its spheroidal shape is the result of "onionskin" weathering, the exfoliating of layers, due to repeated expansion and contraction.

EPHEMERAL CHANNELS

[5] Wadis *(above)* drain much of northern Africa. These drybed courses are flooded only after infrequent, but intense, storms in the uplands cause water to surge along their channels.

Heavy rainfall runs off of mountains
Water collects and floods the dry channel

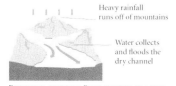

EPHEMERAL CHANNELS: FLASH FLOODING OF A WADI

Sand is gradually blown up the back slope
Deposition on the slip face
Build up of sand produces strata inside the dune

WIND EROSION: MIGRATION OF A DUNE

WIND EROSION

[4] Dunes like this in the Namib Desert *(left)* are wind-blown accumulations of sand, which slowly migrate. Wind action moves sand up the shallow back slope; when the sand reaches the crest of the dune it is deposited on the slip face.

Landscape

- sinking land
- stable land
- uplifting land
- escarpment
- ocean current
- rift
- active volcano
- inselberg
- oasis
- river
- wadi
- waterfall

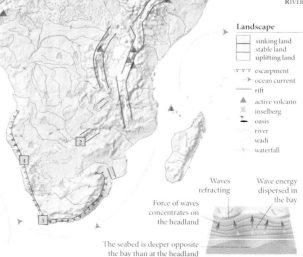

Waves refracting
Wave energy dispersed in the bay
Force of waves concentrates on the headland
The seabed is deeper opposite the bay than at the headland

COASTAL PROCESSES: EROSION OF A BAY

COASTAL PROCESSES

[3] Houtbaai *(above)*, in southern Africa, is constantly being modified by wave action. As waves approach the indented coastline, they reach the shallow water of the headland, slowing down and reducing in length. This causes them to bend or refract, concentrating their erosive force at the headlands.

POLITICAL AFRICA

THE CURRENT POLITICAL MAP OF MODERN AFRICA emerged after the Second World War. Over the next half-century, all of the countries formerly controlled by European powers gained independence from their colonial rulers – only Liberia and Ethiopia were never colonized. The postcolonial era has not been an easy period for many countries, but there have been moves toward multiparty democracy in much of West Africa, and in Zambia, Tanzania, and Kenya. In South Africa, democratic elections replaced the internationally-condemned apartheid system only in 1994. Other countries have still to find political stability; corruption in government and ethnic tensions are serious problems. National infrastructures, based on the colonial transportation systems built to exploit Africa's resources, are often inappropriate for independent economic development.

LANGUAGES

THREE MAJOR WORLD LANGUAGES act as *lingua francas* across the African continent: Arabic in North Africa; English in southern and eastern Africa and Nigeria; and French in Central and West Africa and in Madagascar. A huge number of African languages are spoken as well – over 2,000 have been recorded, with more than 400 in Nigeria alone – reflecting the continuing importance of traditional cultures and values. In the north of the continent, the extensive use of Arabic reflects Middle Eastern influences while Bantu is widely spoken across much of southern Africa.

OFFICIAL AFRICAN LANGUAGES

Official languages

- French
- English
- Arabic
- Portuguese
- Swahili
- Ahmaric
- Spanish
- French/English
- French/Arabic
- English/Swahili

Language groups

- Afro-Asiatic (Hamito-Semitic)
- Niger-Congo
- Sudanic
- Saharan
- Khoisan
- Indo-European
- Austronesian

Islamic influences are evident throughout North Africa. The Great Mosque at Kairouan, Tunisia, is Africa's holiest Islamic place.

In northeastern Nigeria, people speak Kanuri – a dialect of the Saharan language group.

TRANSPORTATION

AFRICAN RAILROADS WERE BUILT to aid the exploitation of natural resources, and most offer passage only from the interior to the coastal cities, leaving large parts of the continent untouched – five landlocked countries have no railroads at all. The Congo (Zaire), Nile, and Niger River networks offer limited access to the continental interior, as a number of waterfalls and cataracts prevent navigation from the sea. Many roads were developed in the 1960s and 1970s, but economic difficulties make the maintenance and expansion of these networks difficult.

South Africa has the largest concentration of railroads in Africa. Over 20,000 miles (32,000 km) of routes have been built since 1870.

Transportation
- major roads and highways
- major railroads
- major canal
- international borders
- transportation intersections
- international airports
- major ports

Traditional means of transportation, such as the camel, are still widely used across the less accessible parts of Africa.

The Congo (Zaire) River, though not suitable for river transportation along its entire length, forms a vital link for people and goods in its navigable inland reaches.

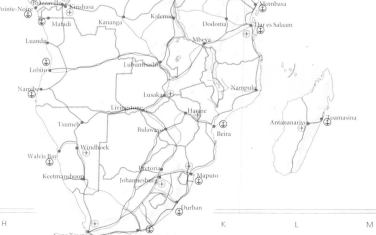

W   X   Y   Z

SCALE 1:27,500,000
(projection: Lambert Azimuthal Equal Area)

Km
0   100   200   400   600   800   1000

Miles
0   100   200   300   400   500   600   700   800   900   1000

MAP KEY

POPULATION

- above 5 million
- 1 million to 5 million
- 500,000 to 1 million
- 100,000 to 500,000
- 50,000 to 100,000
- 10,000 to 50,000
- Country capital

SPAIN / ITALY / Mediterranean Sea

Ceuta (to Spain), Melilla (to Spain), ALGIERS, Tizi Ouzou, Annaba, Bizerte, TUNIS, Chlef, Blida, Béjaïa, Oran, Sidi Bel Abbès, Sétif, Constantine, Kairouan, Fès, Oujda, Tlemcen, Batna, Sfax, Meknès, Khouribga, RABAT, Gabès, MALTA, GREECE, Crete

TUNISIA, TRIPOLI, Mişrātah, Gulf of Sirte, Benghazi

CYPRUS, SYRIA, LEBANON, ISRAEL, JORDAN

Alexandria, Port Said, Ismâ'iliya, Tanta, CAIRO, Beni Suef, El Giza, El Faiyûm, El Minya, Asyût, Sohâg, Qena, Luxor, Aswân

ATLAS Mountains, Grand Erg Oriental

A L G E R I A

Erg Chech, Ahaggar, S a h a r a, Tibesti, Libyan Desert

L I B Y A

E G Y P T

SAUDI ARABIA, Red Sea, Nubian Desert, Lake Nasser, Tropic of Cancer, Port Sudan

M A L I, N I G E R, C H A D

NIAMEY, Maradi, Zinder, Lake Chad, NDJAMENA, Omdurman, Khartoum North, Kassala, ASMARA, ERITREA, KHARTOUM, Wad Medani, DJIBOUTI, DJIBOUTI, Gulf of Aden

BURKINA, Sokoto, Katsina, Kano, Gusau, Zaria, Kaduna, Maiduguri, Maroua, El Obeid, Blue Nile, Lake Tana, Hargeysa

OUAGADOUGOU, Bobo-Dioulasso, BENIN, Natitingou, Tamale, Parakou, NIGERIA, ABUJA, Jos, Garoua, Sarh, Moundou, SUDAN, ADDIS ABABA, Diré Dawa, Ethiopian Highlands, Horn of Africa

GHANA, Lake Volta, Shaki, Oyo, Ogbomosho, Oshogbo, Ibadan, Benue, Adamawa Highlands, White Nile, Sudd

Kumasi, Abeokuta, Cotonou, PORTO-NOVO, Enugu, Onitsha, Aba, Calabar, Bafoussam, Douala, YAOUNDÉ, CENTRAL AFRICAN REPUBLIC, BANGUI, Ubangi

LOMÉ, Lagos, Port Harcourt, EQUATORIAL GUINEA, MALABO, CAMEROON, ACCRA, ACCRA

SAO TOMÉ & PRINCIPE, SÃO TOMÉ, LIBREVILLE, Mbandaka, Congo (Zaire), Congo, Kisangani, UGANDA, KAMPALA, KENYA, Lake Albert, Lake Rudolf, Marka, SOMALIA, ETHIOPIA, Shebeli

Port-Gentil, GABON, CONGO, CONGO (DEM. REP.), Basin, RWANDA, Bukavu, KIGALI, Lake Victoria, Mwanza, Kisumu, NAIROBI, Kismaayo, MOGADISHU, Equator

BRAZZAVILLE, KINSHASA, Ilebo, BUJUMBURA, BURUNDI, Mombasa, Tanga, VICTORIA

ANGOLA (Cabinda), Matadi, Kikwit, Kananga, Kalemie, Lake Tanganyika, DODOMA, Zanzibar, Dar Es Salaam, SEYCHELLES

LUANDA, Mbuji-Mayi, TANZANIA

Kolwezi, Likasi, Lubumbashi, MALAWI, COMOROS, MORONI, Mayotte (to France)

A N G O L A, Chingola, Mufulira, Kitwe, Ndola, Luanshya, Lake Nyasa, Nacala, Nampula, Mahajanga

Huambo, ZAMBIA, LUSAKA, Kabwe, LILONGWE, Blantyre, Zambezi

Namibe, Lubango, Zambezi, HARARE, MOZAMBIQUE, Beira

NAMIBIA, ZIMBABWE, Toamasina, ANTANANARIVO, MADAGASCAR, INDIAN OCEAN

Bulawayo, MAURITIUS, Fianarantsoa, Réunion (to France), PORT LOUIS

BOTSWANA, Kalahari Desert, Namib Desert, WINDHOEK, Mahalapye, Limpopo

GABORONE, Johannesburg, PRETORIA, MAPUTO, Soweto, MBABANE, SWAZILAND, Welkom, Orange River, Kimberley, MASERU, Bloemfontein, Pietermaritzburg

SOUTH AFRICA, LESOTHO, Drakensberg, Cape Town, Bellville, East London, Port Elizabeth, Cape of Good Hope

ATLANTIC OCEAN

POPULATION

AFRICA HAS A rapidly growing population of more than 500 million people, yet over 75% of the continent remains sparsely populated. Most Africans still live a traditional rural lifestyle, though urbanization is increasing as people move to the cities in search of employment. The greatest population densities occur where water is more readily available, such as in the Nile Valley, the coasts of North and West Africa, along the Niger, in the eastern African highlands, and in South Africa.

Population density
(people per sq mile)

- below 130
- 130–259
- 260–379
- 380–519
- 520–780
- above 780

A thin layer of smog blankets the dusty streets of Cairo, Africa's most populous city and home to almost seven million people. Cairo grew by about 1,500 people per day in the first half of the 1990s.

Thriving street markets in Gambia's capital, Banjul, trade a variety of locally grown produce. Africa's population is still predominantly rural.

AFRICAN RESOURCES

THE ECONOMIES OF MOST AFRICAN COUNTRIES are dominated by subsistence and cash crop agriculture, with limited industrialization. Manufacturing is largely confined to South Africa. Many countries depend on a single resource, such as copper or gold, or a cash crop, such as coffee, for export income, which can leave them vulnerable to fluctuations in world commodity prices. In order to diversify their economies and develop a wider industrial base, overseas investment is being actively sought by many African governments.

INDUSTRY

MANY AFRICAN INDUSTRIES concentrate on the extraction and processing of raw materials. These include the oil industry, food processing, mining, and textile production. South Africa accounts for more than half of the continent's industrial output, with much of the remainder coming from the countries along the northern coast. Over 60% of Africa's workforce is employed in agriculture.

The unspoiled natural splendor of wildlife reserves, like the Serengeti National Park in Tanzania, attract tourists from around the globe to Africa. The tourist industry in Kenya and Tanzania is particularly well developed, where it accounts for almost 10% of GNP.

STANDARD OF LIVING

SINCE THE 1960s most countries in Africa have seen significant improvements in life expectancy, health care, and education. However, 18 of the 20 most deprived countries in the world are African, and the continent as a whole lies well behind the rest of the world in terms of many basic human needs.

Standard of Living
(UN Human Development Index)

high

low

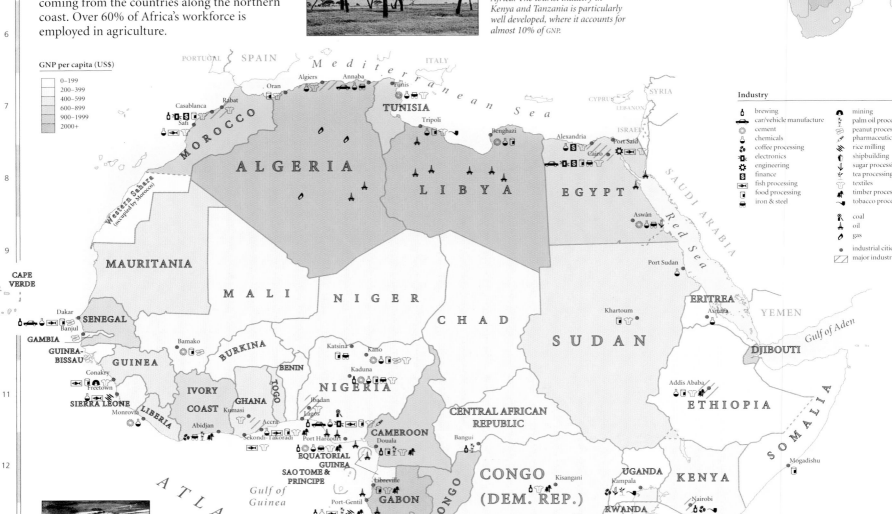

GNP per capita (US$)

0–199
200–399
400–599
600–899
900–1999
2000+

Industry

brewing
car/vehicle manufacture
cement
chemicals
coffee processing
electronics
engineering
finance
fish processing
food processing
iron & steel

mining
palm oil processing
peanut processing
pharmaceuticals
rice milling
shipbuilding
sugar processing
tea processing
textiles
timber processing
tobacco processing

coal
oil
gas

industrial cities
major industrial areas

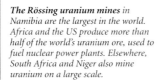

The discovery of oil in the swampy Niger Delta during the 1960s made Nigeria one of Africa's richer nations. As world oil prices fell in the 1980s, the Nigerian economy faltered.

Exotic rugs and brightly colored textiles are sold in a street market along the banks of the Nile River in Luxor, Egypt.

The Rössing uranium mines in Namibia are the largest in the world. Africa and the US produce more than half of the world's uranium ore, used to fuel nuclear power plants. Elsewhere, South Africa and Niger also mine uranium on a large scale.

ENVIRONMENTAL ISSUES

ONE OF AFRICA'S most serious environmental problems occurs in marginal areas such as the Sahel where scrub and forest clearance, often for cooking fuel, combined with overgrazing, is causing desertification. Game reserves in southern and eastern Africa have helped to preserve many endangered animals, although the needs of growing populations have led to conflict over land use, and poaching is a serious problem.

Environmental Issues
- national parks
- tropical forest
- forest destroyed
- desert
- desertification
- polluted rivers
- radioactive contamination
- marine pollution
- heavy marine pollution
- poor urban air quality

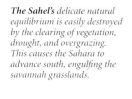

The Sahel's delicate natural equilibrium is easily destroyed by the clearing of vegetation, drought, and overgrazing. This causes the Sahara to advance south, engulfing the savannah grasslands.

MINERAL RESOURCES

AFRICA'S ANCIENT PLATEAUS contain some of the world's most substantial reserves of precious stones and metals. Over 40% of the world's gold is mined in South Africa; Zambia has great copper deposits; and diamonds are mined in Botswana, Congo (Dem. Rep.), and South Africa. Oil has brought great economic benefits to Algeria, Libya, and Nigeria.

Mineral Resources
- oil field
- gas field
- coal field
- bauxite
- copper
- diamonds
- gold
- iron
- phosphates
- tin
- uranium

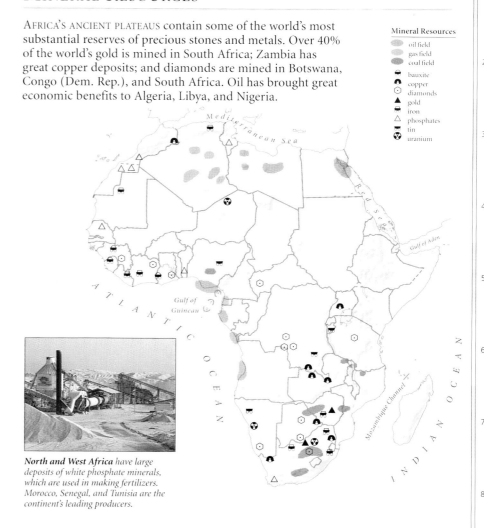

North and West Africa have large deposits of white phosphate minerals, which are used in making fertilizers. Morocco, Senegal, and Tunisia are the continent's leading producers.

Workers on a tea plantation gather one of Africa's most important cash crops, providing a valuable source of income. Coffee, rubber, bananas, cotton, and cocoa are also widely grown as cash crops.

USING THE LAND & SEA

SOME OF AFRICA'S MOST PRODUCTIVE agricultural land is found in the eastern volcanic uplands, where fertile soils support a wide range of valuable export crops including vegetables, tea, and coffee. The most widely-grown crop is corn, and peanuts are particularly important in West Africa. Without intensive irrigation, cultivation is not possible in desert regions and unreliable rainfall in other areas limits crop production. Pastoral herding is most commonly found in these marginal lands. Substantial local fishing industries are found along coasts and in vast lakes such as Lake Nyasa and Lake Victoria.

Surrounded by desert, the fertile floodplains of the Nile Valley and Delta have been extensively irrigated, farmed, and settled since 3000 BCE.

Using the Land and Sea
- cropland
- forest
- pasture
- desert
- wetland
- major conurbations
- cattle
- goats
- sheep
- bananas
- corn
- citrus fruits
- cocoa
- cotton
- coffee
- dates
- fishing
- fruit
- oil palms
- olives
- peanuts
- rice
- rubber
- shellfish
- sugar cane
- tea
- tobacco
- vineyards

NORTH AFRICA

ALGERIA, EGYPT, LIBYA, MOROCCO, TUNISIA, WESTERN SAHARA

FRINGED BY THE MEDITERRANEAN along the northern coast and by the arid Sahara in the south, North Africa reflects the influence of many invaders, both European and, most importantly, Arab, giving the region an almost universal Islamic flavor and a common Arabic language. The countries lying to the west of Egypt are often referred to as the Maghreb, an Arabic term for "west." Today, Morocco and Tunisia exploit their culture and landscape for tourism, while rich oil and gas deposits aid development in Libya and Algeria, despite political turmoil. Egypt, with its fertile, Nile-watered agricultural land and varied industrial base, is the most populous nation.

THE LANDSCAPE

THE ATLAS MOUNTAINS, which run through much of Morocco, northern Algeria, and Tunisia, are part of the fold mountain system, which also runs through much of southern Europe. They recede to the south and east, becoming a steppe landscape before meeting the Sahara desert, which covers more than 90% of the region. The sediments of the Sahara overlie an ancient plateau of crystalline rock, some of which is more than four billion years old.

These rock piles in Algeria's Ahaggar Mountains are the result of weathering caused by extremes of temperature. Great cracks or joints appear in the rocks, which are then worn smooth by the wind.

MAP KEY

POPULATION

- ■ above 5 million
- ■ 1 million to 5 million
- ◉ 500,000 to 1 million
- ◎ 100,000 to 500,000
- ⊕ 50,000 to 100,000
- ⊙ 10,000 to 50,000
- ○ below 10,000

ELEVATION

4000m / 13,124ft
3000m / 9843ft
2000m / 6562ft
1000m / 3281ft
500m / 1640ft
250m / 820ft
100m / 328ft
sea level

The town of Tiznit, Morocco, lies in an oasis in the desert. Crops and trees grow on the fertile land surrounding the town.

SCALE 1:11,000,000
(projection: Lambert Azimuthal Equal Area)

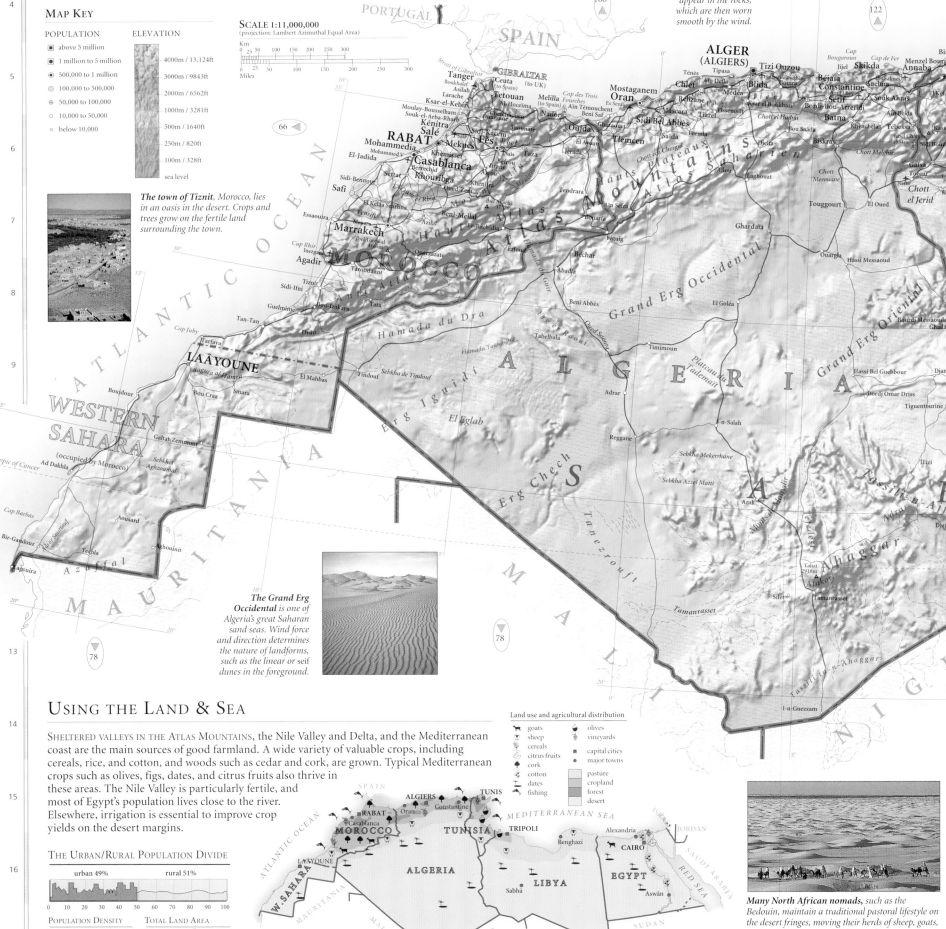

The Grand Erg Occidental is one of Algeria's great Saharan sand seas. Wind force and direction determines the nature of landforms, such as the linear or seif dunes in the foreground.

USING THE LAND & SEA

SHELTERED VALLEYS IN THE ATLAS MOUNTAINS, the Nile Valley and Delta, and the Mediterranean coast are the main sources of good farmland. A wide variety of valuable crops, including cereals, rice, and cotton, and woods such as cedar and cork, are grown. Typical Mediterranean crops such as olives, figs, dates, and citrus fruits also thrive in these areas. The Nile Valley is particularly fertile, and most of Egypt's population lives close to the river. Elsewhere, irrigation is essential to improve crop yields on the desert margins.

Land use and agricultural distribution
- goats
- sheep
- cereals
- citrus fruits
- cork
- cotton
- olives
- vineyards
- ■ capital cities
- • major towns
- pasture
- cropland
- forest
- desert

THE URBAN/RURAL POPULATION DIVIDE

urban 49%	rural 51%

0 10 20 30 40 50 60 70 80 90 100

POPULATION DENSITY
56 people per sq mile
(22 people per sq km)

TOTAL LAND AREA
2,215,020 sq miles
(5,738,394 sq km)

Many North African nomads, such as the Bedouin, maintain a traditional pastoral lifestyle on the desert fringes, moving their herds of sheep, goats, and camels from place to place and across country borders in order to find sufficient grazing land.

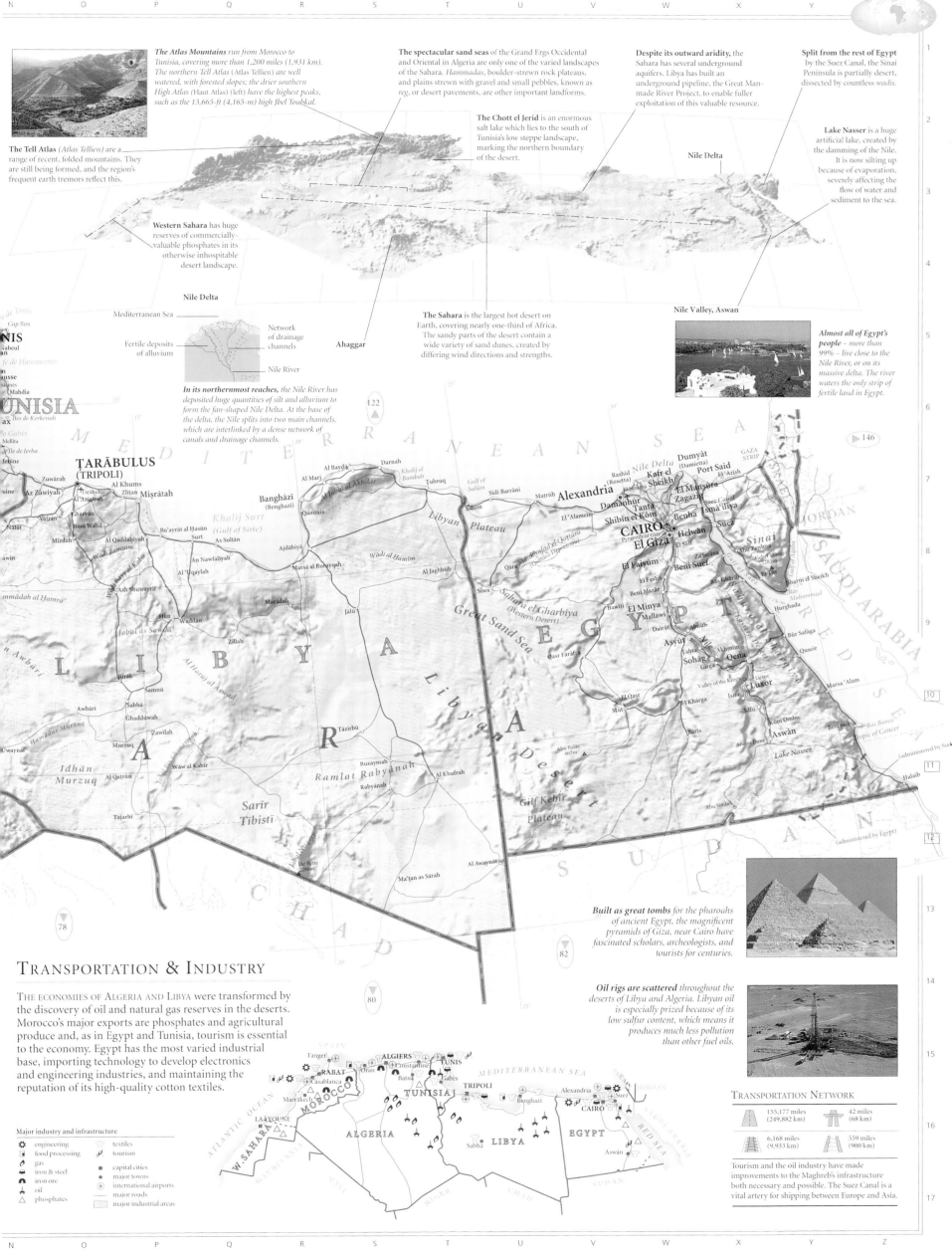

The Atlas Mountains *run from Morocco to Tunisia, covering more than 1,200 miles (1,931 km). The northern Tell Atlas (Atlas Tellien) are well watered, with forested slopes; the drier southern High Atlas (Haut Atlas) (left) have the highest peaks, such as the 13,665-ft (4,165-m) high Jbel Toubkal.*

The spectacular sand seas of the Grand Ergs Occidental and Oriental in Algeria are only one of the varied landscapes of the Sahara. *Hammadas*, boulder-strewn rock plateaus, and plains strewn with gravel and small pebbles, known as *reg*, or desert pavements, are other important landforms.

Despite its outward aridity, the Sahara has several underground aquifers. Libya has built an underground pipeline, the Great Man-made River Project, to enable fuller exploitation of this valuable resource.

Split from the rest of Egypt by the Suez Canal, the Sinai Peninsula is partially desert, dissected by countless *wadis*.

The Tell Atlas (*Atlas Tellien*) are a range of recent, folded mountains. They are still being formed, and the region's frequent earth tremors reflect this.

The Chott el Jerid is an enormous salt lake which lies to the south of Tunisia's low steppe landscape, marking the northern boundary of the desert.

Lake Nasser is a huge artificial lake, created by the damming of the Nile. It is now silting up because of evaporation, severely affecting the flow of water and sediment to the sea.

Western Sahara has huge reserves of commercially-valuable phosphates in its otherwise inhospitable desert landscape.

Mediterranean Sea

Network of drainage channels

Fertile deposits of alluvium

Nile River

Nile Delta

The Sahara is the largest hot desert on Earth, covering nearly one-third of Africa. The sandy parts of the desert contain a wide variety of sand dunes, created by differing wind directions and strengths.

Ahaggar

Nile Valley, Aswan

Almost all of Egypt's people – more than 99% – live close to the Nile River, or on its massive delta. The river waters the only strip of fertile land in Egypt.

In its northernmost reaches, the Nile River has deposited huge quantities of silt and alluvium to form the fan-shaped Nile Delta. At the base of the delta, the Nile splits into two main channels, which are interlinked by a dense network of canals and drainage channels.

Built as great tombs for the pharoahs of ancient Egypt, the magnificent pyramids of Giza, near Cairo have fascinated scholars, archeologists, and tourists for centuries.

Oil rigs are scattered throughout the deserts of Libya and Algeria. Libyan oil is especially prized because of its low sulfur content, which means it produces much less pollution than other fuel oils.

TRANSPORTATION & INDUSTRY

THE ECONOMIES OF ALGERIA AND LIBYA were transformed by the discovery of oil and natural gas reserves in the deserts. Morocco's major exports are phosphates and agricultural produce and, as in Egypt and Tunisia, tourism is essential to the economy. Egypt has the most varied industrial base, importing technology to develop electronics and engineering industries, and maintaining the reputation of its high-quality cotton textiles.

Major industry and infrastructure

⚙ engineering	🧵 textiles
🍴 food processing	⚑ tourism
⬡ gas	
▣ iron & steel	■ capital cities
◆ iron ore	• major towns
⬢ oil	✈ international airports
△ phosphates	— major roads
	▨ major industrial areas

TRANSPORTATION NETWORK

155,177 miles (249,882 km)		42 miles (68 km)	
6,168 miles (9,933 km)		559 miles (900 km)	

Tourism and the oil industry have made improvements to the Maghreb's infrastructure both necessary and possible. The Suez Canal is a vital artery for shipping between Europe and Asia.

WEST AFRICA

Benin, Burkina, Cape Verde, Gambia, Ghana, Guinea, Guinea-Bissau, Ivory Coast, Liberia, Mali, Mauritania, Niger, Nigeria, Senegal, Sierra Leone, Togo

WEST AFRICA IS AN IMMENSELY DIVERSE REGION, encompassing the desert landscapes and mainly Muslim populations of the southern Saharan countries, and the tropical rain forests of the more humid south, with a great variety of local languages and cultures. The rich natural resources and accessibility of the area were quickly exploited by Europeans; most of the Africans captured by slave traders came from this region, causing serious depopulation. The very different influences of West Africa's leading colonial powers, Britain and France, remain today, reflected in the languages and institutions of the countries they once governed.

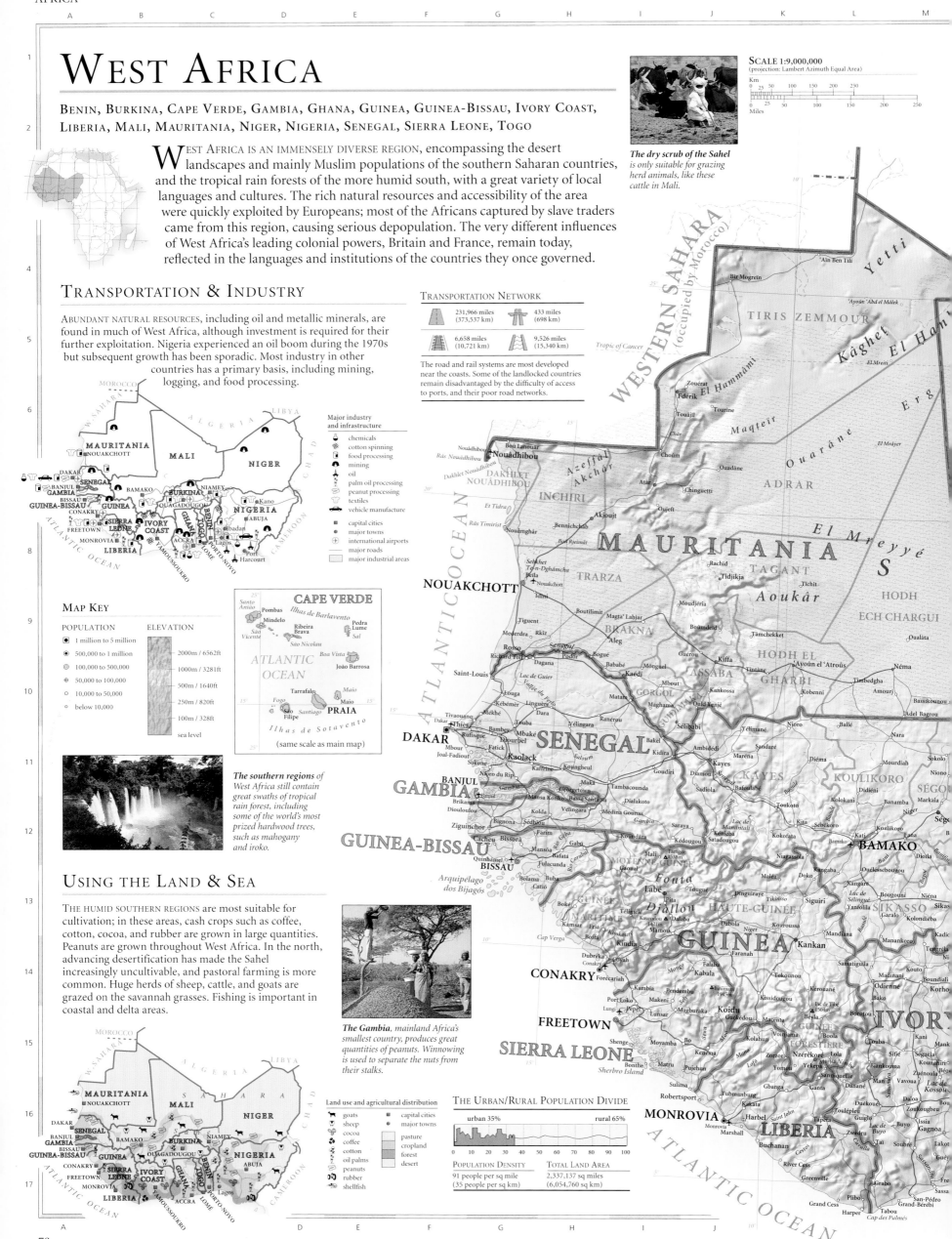

The dry scrub of the Sahel *is only suitable for grazing herd animals, like these cattle in Mali.*

SCALE 1:9,000,000
(projection: Lambert Azimuth Equal Area)

TRANSPORTATION & INDUSTRY

ABUNDANT NATURAL RESOURCES, including oil and metallic minerals, are found in much of West Africa, although investment is required for their further exploitation. Nigeria experienced an oil boom during the 1970s but subsequent growth has been sporadic. Most industry in other countries has a primary basis, including mining, logging, and food processing.

TRANSPORTATION NETWORK

231,966 miles (373,537 km)	433 miles (698 km)
6,658 miles (10,721 km)	9,526 miles (15,340 km)

The road and rail systems are most developed near the coasts. Some of the landlocked countries remain disadvantaged by the difficulty of access to ports, and their poor road networks.

Major industry and infrastructure

- chemicals
- cotton spinning
- food processing
- mining
- oil
- palm oil processing
- peanut processing
- textiles
- vehicle manufacture
- capital cities
- major towns
- international airports
- major roads
- major industrial areas

MAP KEY

POPULATION
- 1 million to 5 million
- 500,000 to 1 million
- 100,000 to 500,000
- 50,000 to 100,000
- 10,000 to 50,000
- below 10,000

ELEVATION
- 2000m / 6562ft
- 1000m / 3281ft
- 500m / 1640ft
- 250m / 820ft
- 100m / 328ft
- sea level

CAPE VERDE

Santo Antão, Ilhas de Barlavento, Pombas, Mindelo, São Vicente, Ribeira Brava, Pedra Lume, Sal, São Nicolau, Boa Vista, ATLANTIC OCEAN, João Barrosa, Tarrafal, Maio, Fogo, São Filipe, Santiago, Maio, PRAIA, Ilhas de Sotavento

(same scale as main map)

The southern regions of West Africa still contain great swaths of tropical rain forest, including some of the world's most prized hardwood trees, such as mahogany and iroko.

USING THE LAND & SEA

THE HUMID SOUTHERN REGIONS are most suitable for cultivation; in these areas, cash crops such as coffee, cotton, cocoa, and rubber are grown in large quantities. Peanuts are grown throughout West Africa. In the north, advancing desertification has made the Sahel increasingly uncultivable, and pastoral farming is more common. Huge herds of sheep, cattle, and goats are grazed on the savannah grasses. Fishing is important in coastal and delta areas.

The Gambia, mainland Africa's smallest country, produces great quantities of peanuts. Winnowing is used to separate the nuts from their stalks.

Land use and agricultural distribution
- goats
- sheep
- cocoa
- coffee
- cotton
- oil palms
- peanuts
- rubber
- shellfish
- capital cities
- major towns
- pasture
- cropland
- forest
- desert

THE URBAN/RURAL POPULATION DIVIDE

urban 35%　　　　　　rural 65%

POPULATION DENSITY	TOTAL LAND AREA
91 people per sq mile (35 people per sq km)	2,337,137 sq miles (6,054,760 sq km)

THE LANDSCAPE

THERE ARE TWO MAJOR TOPOGRAPHICAL AREAS in West Africa: the northern deserts are part of the Saharan region that stretches across the whole continent; the grasslands of the Sahel and the southern Guinea coast are part of Africa's central plateau. The landscape is generally low, rarely rising above 1,500 ft (457 m) and consists mainly of plains, broken by an occasional high plateau or mountain range.

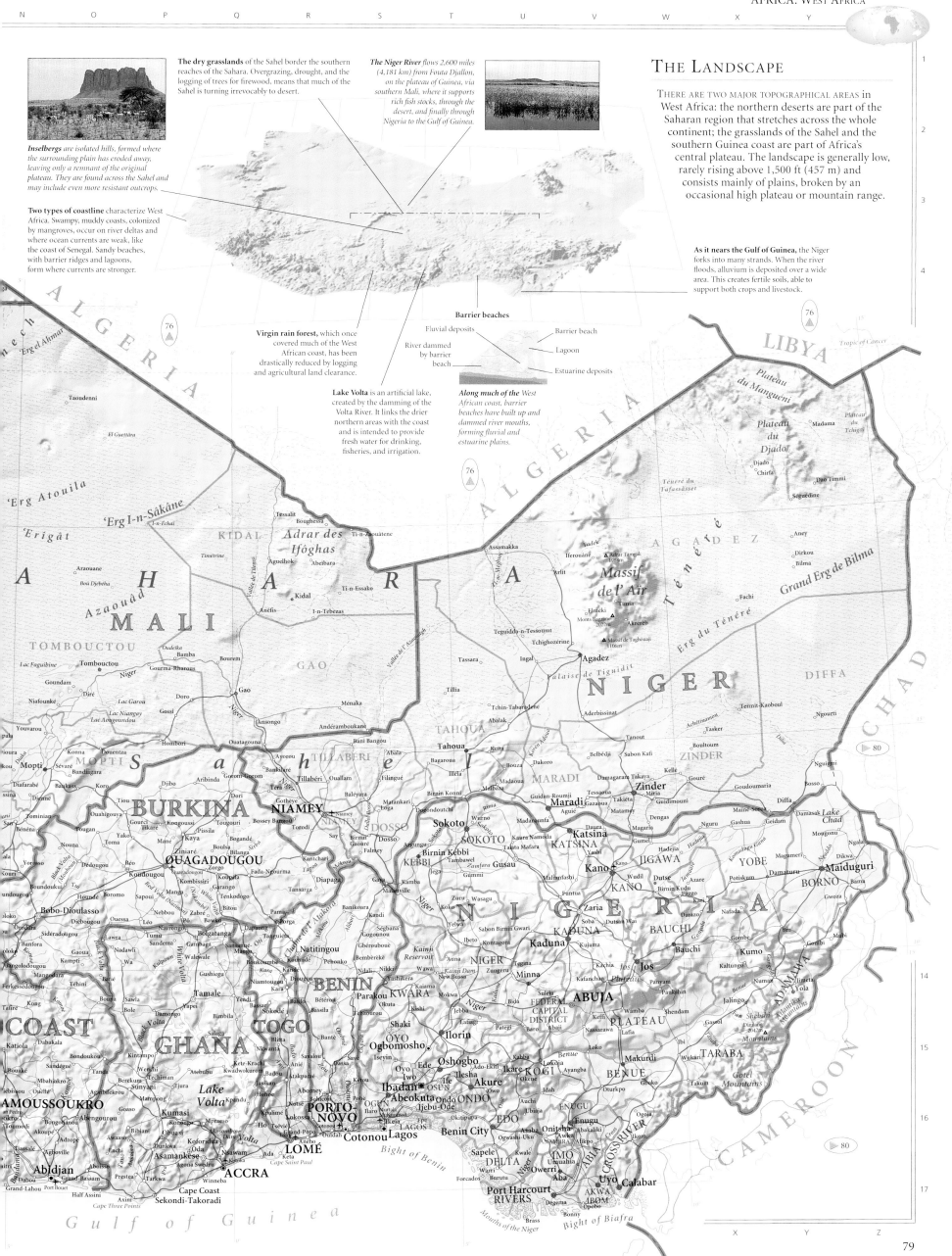

The dry grasslands of the Sahel border the southern reaches of the Sahara. Overgrazing, drought, and the logging of trees for firewood, means that much of the Sahel is turning irrevocably to desert.

Inselbergs are isolated hills, formed where the surrounding plain has eroded away, leaving only a remnant of the original plateau. They are found across the Sahel and may include even more resistant outcrops.

Two types of coastline characterize West Africa. Swampy, muddy coasts, colonized by mangroves, occur on river deltas and where ocean currents are weak, like the coast of Senegal. Sandy beaches, with barrier ridges and lagoons, form where currents are stronger.

The Niger River flows 2,600 miles (4,181 km) from Fouta Djallon, on the plateau of Guinea, via southern Mali, where it supports rich fish stocks, through the desert, and finally through Nigeria to the Gulf of Guinea.

As it nears the Gulf of Guinea, the Niger forks into many strands. When the river floods, alluvium is deposited over a wide area. This creates fertile soils, able to support both crops and livestock.

Virgin rain forest, which once covered much of the West African coast, has been drastically reduced by logging and agricultural land clearance.

Barrier beaches
Fluvial deposits
River dammed by barrier beach
Barrier beach
Lagoon
Estuarine deposits

Lake Volta is an artificial lake, created by the damming of the Volta River. It links the drier northern areas with the coast and is intended to provide fresh water for drinking, fisheries, and irrigation.

Along much of the West African coast, barrier beaches have built up and dammed river mouths, forming fluvial and estuarine plains.

CENTRAL AFRICA

CAMEROON, CENTRAL AFRICAN REPUBLIC, CHAD, CONGO, CONGO (DEMOCRATIC REPUBLIC OF), EQUATORIAL GUINEA, GABON, SAO TOME & PRINCIPE

THE GREAT RAIN FOREST BASIN of the Congo (Zaire) River embraces most of remote Central Africa. The interior was largely unknown to Europeans until late in the 19th century, when its tribal kingdoms were split principally between France and Belgium, with Sao Tome and Principe the lone Portuguese territory, and Equatorial Guinea controlled by Spain. Open democracy and regional economic integration are important goals for these nations, several of which have only recently emerged from restrictive regimes, and investment is needed to improve transportation infrastructures. Many of the small, fast-growing, and increasingly urban population speak French, the regional *lingua franca*, along with several hundred Pygmy, Bantu, and Sudanic dialects.

TRANSPORTATION & INDUSTRY

LARGE RESERVES OF VALUABLE MINERALS are found in Central Africa: copper, cobalt, manganese, zinc, and tin are mined in Congo (Dem. Rep.) and Cameroon; diamonds in the Central African Republic; and manganese in Gabon. Cameroon, Gabon, Congo (Dem. Rep.), and Congo have oil deposits and oil has also been recently discovered in Chad. Other export industries are based on the processing of goods such as palm oil and rubber.

The ancient rocks of Congo (Dem. Rep.) hold immense and varied mineral reserves. This open pit copper mine is at Kolwezi in the far south.

Major industry and infrastructure

- brewing
- chemicals
- cobalt
- copper
- diamonds
- food processing
- manganese
- oil
- palm oil processing
- textiles
- tin
- capital cities
- major towns
- international airports
- major roads
- major industrial areas

TRANSPORTATION NETWORK

181,633 miles (292,485 km)	
342 miles (550 km)	
4,774 miles (7,688 km)	
15,261 miles (24,475 km)	

The Trans-Gabon railroad, which began operating in 1987, has opened up new sources of timber and manganese. Elsewhere, much investment is needed to update and improve road, rail, and water transportation.

THE LANDSCAPE

LAKE CHAD LIES in a desert basin bounded by the volcanic Tibesti Mountains in the north, plateaus in the east and, in the south, the broad watershed of the Congo Basin. The vast circular depression of the Congo is isolated from the coastal plain by the granite Massif du Chaillu. To the northwest, the volcanoes and fold mountains of the Cameroon Ridge (*Dorsale Camerounaise*) extend as islands into the Gulf of Guinea. The high fold mountains fringing the east of the Congo Basin fall steeply to the lakes of the Great Rift Valley.

A plug of resistant lava, at the southwestern end of the Cameroon Ridge (Dorsale Camerounaise), is all that remains of an eroded volcano.

The volcanic massif of Cameroon Mountain occupies an area that remains volcanically active.

Gulf of Guinea

Massif du Chaillu

The Tibesti Mountains are the highest in the Sahara. They were pushed up by the movement of the African Plate over a hot spot, which first formed the northern Ahaggar Mountains and is now thought to lie under the Great Rift Valley.

The Congo (Zaire) River is second only to the Amazon in the volume of water it carries, and in the size of its drainage basin.

Lake Tanganyika, the world's second deepest lake, is the largest of a series of linear "ribbon" lakes occupying a trench within the Great Rift Valley.

Rich mineral deposits in "Copper Belt" of Congo (Dem. Rep.) were formed under intense heat and pressure, when the ancient African Shield was uplifted to form the region's mountains.

Virgin tropical rain forest is found in the Ruwenzori range Congo (Dem. Rep.) and Ugandan border.

The lakelike expansion of the Congo (Zaire) River, in Stanley Pool, is the lowest point of the interior basin, though the river still descends more than 1,000 ft (300 m) to reach the sea.

Lake Chad is the remnant of an inland sea, which once occupied much of the surrounding basin. A series of droughts since the 1970s has reduced the area of this shallow freshwater lake to about 1,000 sq miles (2,599 sq km).

Broad, shallow basin

Waterfalls and cataracts

Submarine canyon

The Congo (Zaire) River flows sluggishly through the rain forest of the interior basin. Toward the coast, the river drops steeply in a series of waterfalls and cataracts. At this point, the erosional power of the river becomes so great that it has formed a deep submarine canyon offshore.

The vast sandflats surrounding Lake Chad were once covered by water. Changing climatic patterns caused the lake to shrink, and desert now covers much of its previous area.

MAP KEY

POPULATION

- 1 million to 5 million
- 500,000 to 1 million
- 100,000 to 500,000
- 50,000 to 100,000
- 10,000 to 50,000
- below 10,000

ELEVATION

- 4000m / 13,124ft
- 3000m / 9843ft
- 2000m / 6562ft
- 1000m / 3281ft
- 500m / 1640ft
- 250m / 820ft
- 100m / 328ft
- sea level

SCALE 1:9,500,000
(projection: Lambert Azimuthal Equal Area)

The great Congo (Zaire) River forms part of the border between Congo and Congo (Dem. Rep.). The river flows quickly. A series of falls and rapids makes it only partly navigable.

USING THE LAND

CASH CROPS FOR EXPORT include cocoa, coffee, and rubber. Shifting cultivation is widely practiced, and plantains are the staple food of the equatorial region, grown with yam and taro. Cassava, guinea corn (sorghum), and millet are the main subsistence crops in savannah areas. Cattle farming is limited to areas free of tsetse fly, and fish from the interior rivers are an important protein source.

Land use and agricultural distribution

- cattle
- cocoa
- coffee
- cotton
- palms
- peanuts
- rubber
- timber
- capital cities
- major towns

pasture
cropland
forest
desert

THE URBAN/RURAL POPULATION DIVIDE

urban 34%   rural 76%

POPULATION DENSITY
33 people per sq mile
(13 people per sq km)

TOTAL LAND AREA
2,023,939 sq miles
(5,243,364 sq km)

High-quality timber is floated to Port-Gentil, Gabon, via the Ogooué River. Timber provides important export revenue for several countries, though there has been concern about the uncontrolled logging of rare tropical woods.

EAST AFRICA

BURUNDI, DJIBOUTI, ERITREA, ETHIOPIA, KENYA, RWANDA, SOMALIA, SUDAN, TANZANIA, UGANDA

THE COUNTRIES OF EAST AFRICA divide into two distinct cultural regions. Sudan and the "Horn" nations have been influenced by the Middle East. Ethiopia was the home of one of the earliest Christian civilizations, and Sudan reflects both Muslim and Christian influences. The southern countries share a closer cultural affinity with other sub-Saharan nations. Some of Africa's most densely populated countries lie in this region, and the needs of a growing number of people have put pressure on marginal lands and fragile environments. Although most East African economies remain strongly agricultural, Kenya has developed a varied industrial base.

THE LANDSCAPE

EAST AFRICA'S MOST SIGNIFICANT landscape feature is the Great Rift Valley. This formed during the most recent phase of continental movement, when the rigid basement rocks cracked and buckled. Great blocks of land were raised and lowered, creating huge flat-bottomed valleys and steep escarpments, sometimes covered by volcanic extrusions in highland areas.

Ephemeral lake forms at far edge of slope

Boundary fault

Central block slopes toward main fault

The eastern arm of the Great Rift Valley is gradually being pulled apart. The forces on one side are greater than the other, however, causing the land to slope. This affects regional drainage that migrates down the slope.

This dome at Gonder, in Ethiopia, is a volcanic intrusion, formed when molten rock pushed up the surface of the Earth and then solidified, leaving an outcrop of igneous rock.

Lava flows on uplifted areas either side of the eastern branch of the Great Rift Valley gave the Ethiopian Highlands – a series of high, wide plateaus – their distinctive rounded appearance and fertile soils.

Kilimanjaro

An extinct volcano, Kilimanjaro is Africa's highest mountain, rising 19,340 ft (5,895 m). It is one of the few places in Africa where snow settles, allowing glacier ice to form.

A vast plateau lies between the eastern and western rift valleys in Kenya, Uganda, and western Tanzania. It has been leveled by long periods of erosion to form a peneplain, but is dotted with inselbergs – outcrops of more resistant rocks.

The Kassala region in eastern Sudan is watered by the Atbara River, an important tributary of the Nile. Most of the population is engaged in agriculture, growing cotton and cereals.

Lake Victoria occupies the two vast basin between the two arms of the Great Rift Valley. It is the world's second largest lake in terms of surface area, extending 26,828 sq miles (69,484 sq km). The lake contains numerous islands and coral reefs.

Lake Tanganyika lies 8,202 ft (2,500 m) above sea level. It has a depth of nearly 16,400 ft (5,000 m). The lake traces the valley floor for some 400 miles (644 km) of the western arm of the Great Rift Valley.

The tiny countries of Rwanda and Burundi are mainly mountainous, with large areas of inaccessible tropical rain forest.

Much of northern Sudan is covered by desert. However, in the tropical wetlands of the southern Sudd region, annual rainfall can sometimes exceed 40 inches (1,000 mm).

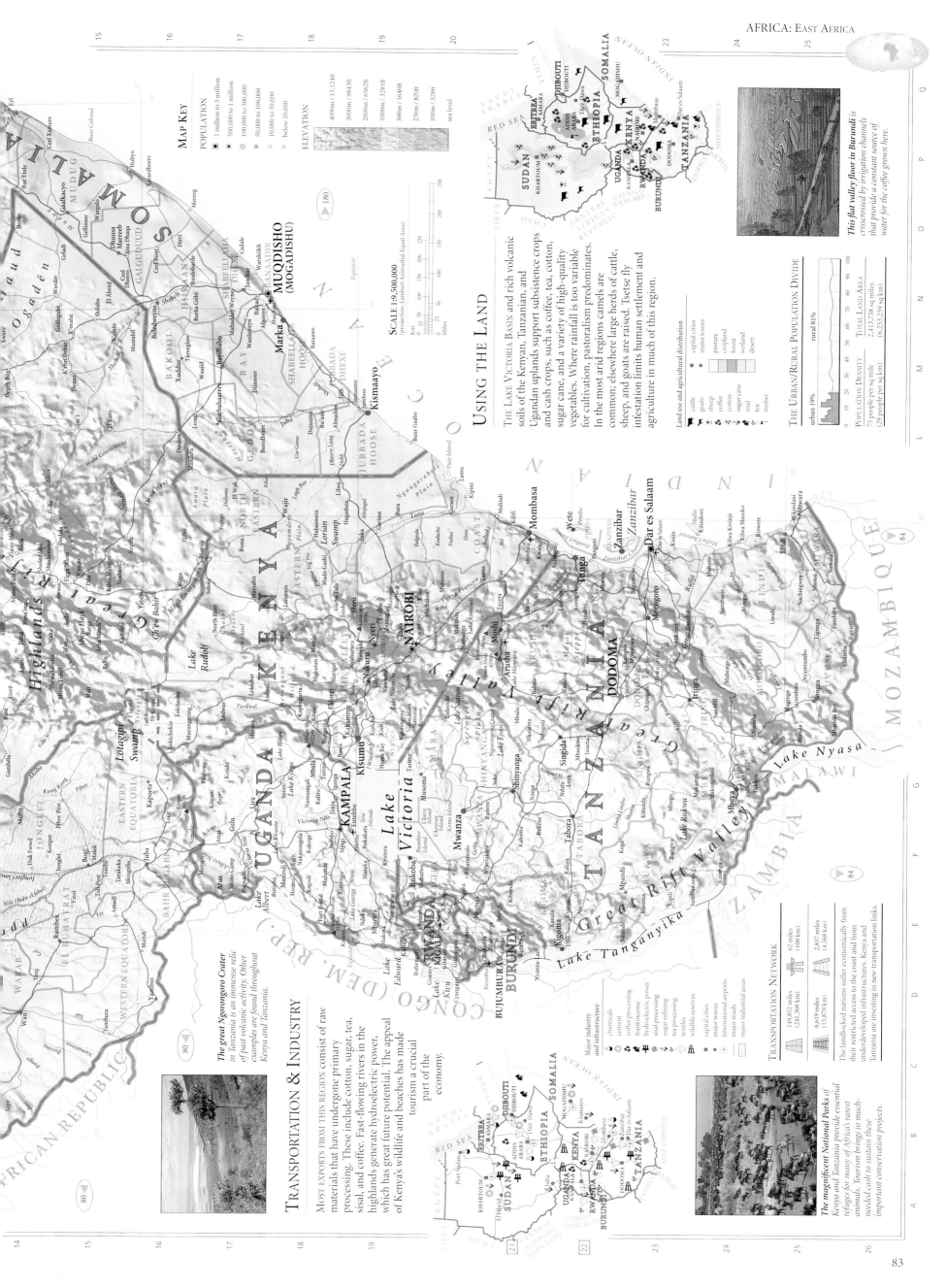

Map Key

POPULATION
- 1 million to 5 million
- 500,000 to 1 million
- 100,000 to 500,000
- 50,000 to 100,000
- 10,000 to 50,000
- below 10,000

ELEVATION
- 4000m / 13,124ft
- 3000m / 9843ft
- 2000m / 6562ft
- 1000m / 3281ft
- 500m / 1640ft
- 250m / 820ft
- 100m / 328ft
- sea level

SCALE 1:9,500,000
(projection: Lambert Azimuthal Equal Area)

USING THE LAND

THE LAKE VICTORIA BASIN and rich volcanic soils of the Kenyan, Tanzanian, and Ugandan uplands support subsistence crops and cash crops, such as coffee, tea, cotton, sugar cane, and a variety of high-quality vegetables. Where rainfall is too variable for cultivation, pastoralism predominates. In the more arid regions camels are common; elsewhere large herds of cattle, sheep, and goats are raised. Tsetse fly infestation limits human settlement and agriculture in much of this region.

Land use and agricultural distribution

- capital cities
- major towns
- cattle
- goats
- sheep
- coffee
- cotton
- pasture
- cropland
- forest
- wetland
- desert
- sugar cane
- sisal
- tea
- timber

THE URBAN/RURAL POPULATION DIVIDE

urban 19% — rural 81%

POPULATION DENSITY
75 people per sq mile
(29 people per sq km)

TOTAL LAND AREA
2,413,758 sq miles
(6,253,259 sq km)

This flat valley floor in Burundi is crisscrossed by irrigation channels that provide a constant source of water for the coffee grown here.

TRANSPORTATION & INDUSTRY

MOST EXPORTS FROM THIS REGION consist of raw materials that have undergone primary processing. These include cotton, sugar, tea, sisal, and coffee. Fast-flowing rivers in the highlands generate hydroelectric power, which has great future potential. The appeal of Kenya's wildlife and beaches has made tourism a crucial part of the economy.

The great Ngorongoro Crater in Tanzania is an immense relic of past volcanic activity. Other examples are found throughout Kenya and Tanzania.

Major industry and infrastructure
- chemicals
- cement
- coffee processing
- frankincense
- hydroelectric power
- sisal processing
- sugar refining
- tea processing
- textiles
- wildlife reserves
- capital cities
- major towns
- international airports
- major roads
- major industrial areas

TRANSPORTATION NETWORK

62 miles (100 km)

149,852 miles (241,308 km)

2,837 miles (4,568 km)

8,619 miles (13,879 km)

The landlocked nations suffer economically from their restricted access to the coast and from underdeveloped infrastructures. Kenya and Tanzania are investing in new transportation links.

The magnificent National Parks of Kenya and Tanzania provide essential refuges for many of Africa's rarest animals. Tourism brings in much-needed cash to sustain these important conservation projects.

SOUTHERN AFRICA

ANGOLA, BOTSWANA, LESOTHO, MALAWI, MOZAMBIQUE, NAMIBIA,
SOUTH AFRICA, SWAZILAND, ZAMBIA, ZIMBABWE

AFRICA'S VAST SOUTHERN PLATEAU has been a contested homeland for
disparate peoples for many centuries. The European incursion
began with the slave trade and quickened in the 19th century, when
the discovery of enormous mineral wealth secured South Africa's
regional economic dominance. The struggle against white minority
rule led to strife in Namibia, Zimbabwe, and the former Portuguese
territories of Angola and Mozambique. South Africa's notorious
apartheid laws, which denied basic human rights to more than 75%
of the people, led to the state being internationally ostracized until 1994,
when the first fully democratic elections inaugurated a new era of racial justice.

TRANSPORTATION & INDUSTRY

SOUTH AFRICA, the world's largest exporter of gold,
has a varied economy that generates about 75% of
the region's income and draws migrant labor from
neighboring states. Angola exports petroleum;
Botswana and Namibia rely on diamond mining;
and Zambia is seeking to diversify its economy
to compensate for declining copper reserves.

*Almost all new mining
ventures in Zimbabwe are
now subject to government
control. This mine at Bindura
in northeastern Zimbabwe
produces nickel, one of the
country's top three minerals
in terms of economic value.*

THE LANDSCAPE

MOST OF SOUTHERN AFRICA rests on a concave plateau
comprising the Kalahari basin and a mountainous fringe,
skirted by a coastal plain that widens out in Mozambique. The
plateau extends north, toward the Planalto de Bié in Angola, the
Congo Basin, and the lake-filled troughs of the Great Rift Valley.
The eastern region is drained by the Zambezi and Limpopo
Rivers, and the Orange is the major western river.

*Thousands of years of evaporating
water have produced the Etosha Pan, one
of the largest salt flats in the world. Lake
and river sediments in the area indicate
that the region was once less arid.*

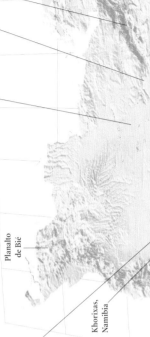

*Finger Rock, near Khorixas,
Namibia is a remnant of a former
land surface, which has been
denuded by erosion over the last
5 million years. These occasional
stacks of partially weathered rocks
interrupt the plains of the dry
southern interior.*

TRANSPORTATION NETWORK

196,477 miles (316,388 km)	1,267 miles (2,040 km)
24,137 miles (38,868 km)	5,090 miles (8,196 km)

Southern Africa's Cape-gauge rail network is by far
the largest on the continent. About two-thirds of
the 20,000-mile (32,000-km) system lies within
South Africa. Lines such as the Harare–Bulawayo
route have become corridors for industrial growth.

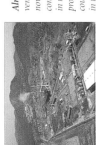

*Following a series of droughts,
this baobab tree in Zimbabwe now
stands alone in a field once filled by
sugar cane. The thick trunk and
small leaves of the baobab help it to
conserve water, enabling it to
survive even in drought conditions.*

At Victoria Falls, the Zambezi River has cut
a spectacular gorge by taking advantage of
large joints in the basalt, which were first
formed as the lava cooled and contracted.

*The fast-flowing Zambezi
River cuts a deep, wide
channel as it flows along the
Zimbabwe/Zambia border.*

Lake Nyasa occupies one of
the deep troughs of the
Great Rift Valley, where the
land has been displaced
downward by as much
as 3,000 ft (920 m).

Great Rift Valley

Bushveld intrusion

Limpopo River

Volcanic lava, over 250 million years
old, caps the peaks of the Drakensberg
range, which lie on the mountainous rim
of southern Africa's interior plateau.

The Okavango/Cubango River flows
from the Planalto de Bié to the
swamplands of the Okavango Delta, one
of the world's largest inland deltas, where
it divides into countless distributary
channels, feeding out into the desert.

Planalto de Bié

Khorixas, Namibia

Namib Desert

The Kalahari Desert
is the largest continuous
sand surface in the
world. Iron oxide gives a
distinctive red color to
the windblown sand,
which, in eastern areas
covers the bedrock to a
depth of 200 ft (60 m).

The mountains of the
Little Karoo are composed
of sedimentary rocks that
have been substantially
folded and faulted.

Broad, flat-topped mountains characterize the
Great Karoo, which have been cut from level rock
strata under extremely arid conditions.

The Orange River, one of the
longest in Africa, rises in Lesotho
and is the only major river in the
south which flows westward,
rather than to the east coast.

MAP KEY

POPULATION

- ● 1 million to 5 million
- ◉ 500,000 to 1 million
- ⊙ 100,000 to 500,000
- ⊕ 50,000 to 100,000
- ○ 10,000 to 50,000
- ∘ below 10,000

ELEVATION

	3000m/9843ft
	2000m/6562ft
	1000m/3281ft
	500m/1640ft
	250m/820ft
	100m/328ft
	sea level

Bushveld intrusion

Granite

Chromite

Gabbro and peridotite

Magnetite

Platinum

Platinum minerals

*The Bushveld intrusion lies on South
Africa's high "veld." Molten magma
intruded into the Earth's crust creating
a saucer-shaped feature, more than
180 miles (300 km) across, containing
regular layers of precious minerals,
overlain by a dome of granite.*

SOUTH AFRICA'S THREE CAPITALS

PRETORIA – administrative capital
CAPE TOWN – legislative capital
BLOEMFONTEIN – judicial capital

SCALE 1:9,500,000
(projection: Lambert Azimuthal Equal Area)

Major industry and infrastructure

car manufacture	gold
coal	oil
copper	textiles
diamonds	uranium
food processing	wildlife reserves

- capital cities
- major towns
- international airports
- major roads
- major industrial areas

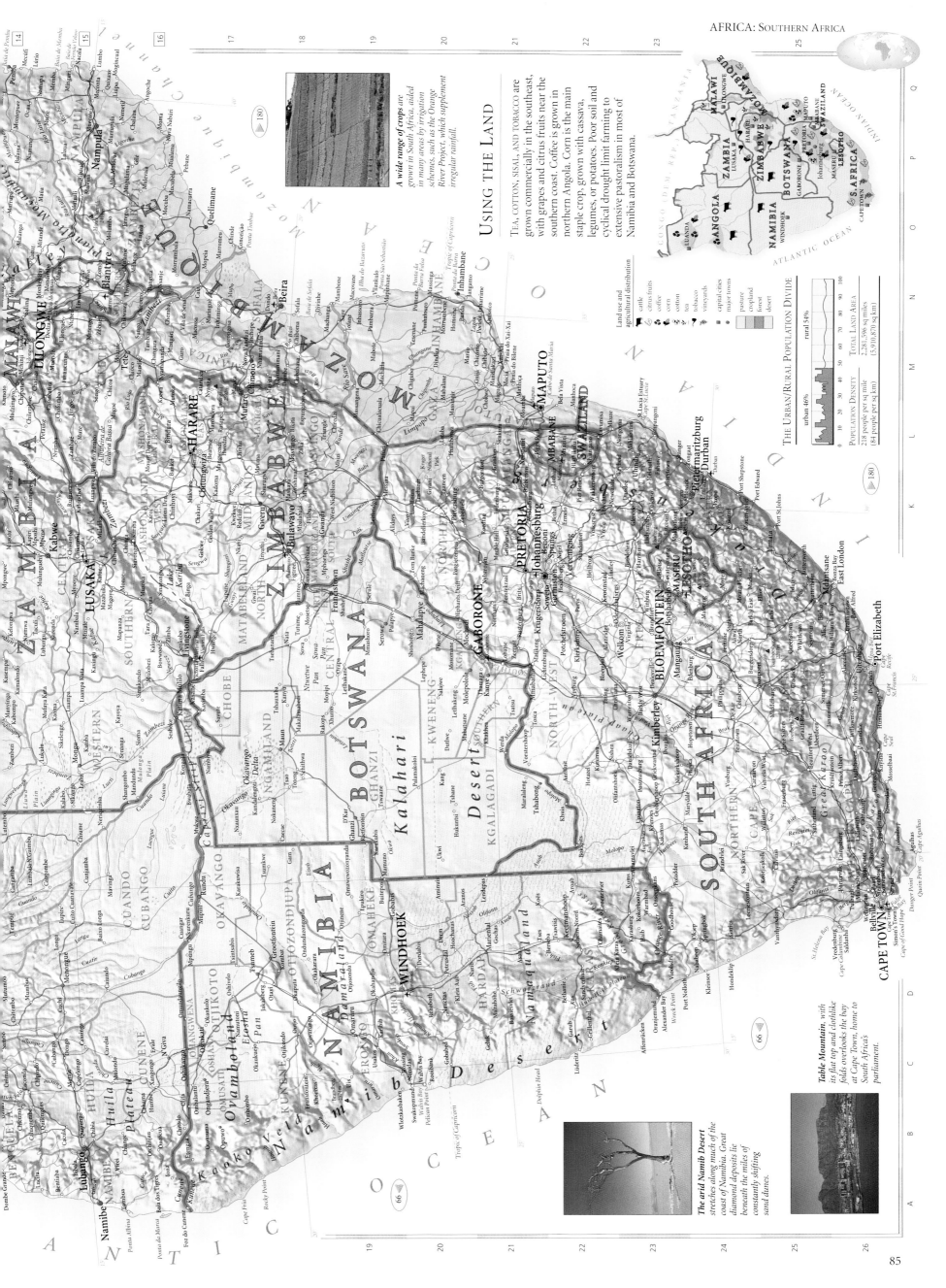

A wide range of crops are grown in South Africa, aided in many areas by irrigation schemes, such as the Orange River Project, which supplement irregular rainfall.

USING THE LAND

TEA, COTTON, SISAL, AND TOBACCO are grown commercially in the southeast, with grapes and citrus fruits near the southern coast. Coffee is grown in northern Angola. Corn is the main staple crop, grown with cassava, legumes, or potatoes. Poor soil and cyclical drought limit farming to extensive pastoralism in most of Namibia and Botswana.

land use and
agricultural distribution

- cattle
- citrus fruits
- coffee
- corn
- cotton
- tea
- tobacco
- vineyards
- capital cities
- major towns

pasture cropland forest desert

THE URBAN/RURAL POPULATION DIVIDE

urban 46% rural 54%

POPULATION DENSITY
218 people per sq mile
(84 people per sq km)

TOTAL LAND AREA
2,281,596 sq miles
(5,910,870 sq km)

The arid Namib Desert stretches along much of the coast of Namibia. Great diamond deposits lie beneath the miles of constantly shifting sand dunes.

Table Mountain, with its flat top and clothlike folds overlooks the bay at Cape Town, home to South Africa's parliament.

ARCTIC OCEAN

North Pole

Greenland

King Frederik
VIII Land

King Christian X Land

Ellesmere Island

Greenland
Sea

Spitsbergen

EURASIAN PLATE
NORTH AMERICAN PLATE

Bjørnøya

Jan Mayen Fracture Zone
Jan Mayen

Kolbeinsey Ridge

Iceland
Plateau

Jan Mayen Ridge

Voring Plateau

Norwegian
Basin

Severnaya
Zemlya

Ostrov
Rudol'fa

Franz Josef Land

Kara Sea

Poluostrov Taymyr

Novaya Zemlya

Barents
Sea

Baydaratskaya Guba

Poluostrov Yamal

Gulf of Ob

Yenisey

Ob'

West Siberian
Plain

A S I

U r a l M o u n t a i n s

Barents
Trough

Tromsøflaket
North Cape Nordkinn

Murmansk Rise

Kara Strait

Ostrov
Kolguyev

Poluostrov
Kanin

Pechora

Gora Narodnaya

Vorkuta

Denmark Strait

Arctic Circle

Bjargtangar

ReykjanesRidge

Iceland

Vatnajökull

Iceland
Plateau

Faeroe-Iceland Ridge

Norwegian Sea

Vesterålen
Lofoten

Kebnekaise
2117m

Kjølen

Scandinavia

Traena
Bank

Gäldhøpiggen
2469m

Fugløya Bank
Inarijärvi

Torneälven

Kemijoki
Oulujoki

White Sea

Onega Bay

Northern Dvina

Lake
Ladoga

Kola Peninsula
Ozero
Imandra

Mezen

Timanskiy Kryazh

Northern Dvina

Vaga

Ozero
Vygozero

Lake
Onega

Vyg

Sukhona

Yug

Vychegda

Tobol

Iset'

Chusovaya

Ufa

Belaya

Iceland
Basin

Hatton Ridge

Rockall
Rise

Feni Ridge

Rockall Trough

ATLANTIC OCEAN

Porcupine
Plain

Bill Bailey's
Bank

Faeroe Islands

Faeroe-Shetland Trough

Shetland
Islands

Orkney Islands

Outer Hebrides

Ben Nevis
1343m
Grampian
Mountains

Viking Bank

Norwegian Trench

Umeälven

Ljungan

Ljusnan

Gilma

Gulf of Bothnia

Åland

Vänern

Vättern

Gotland

Gulf of Finland

Lake
Peipus
Lake Pskov

Western Dvina

Gulf of
Riga

Baltic Sea

Lake Ilmen
Msta

Rybinsk
Reservoir

Beloye
Ozero

Sheksna

Unzha

Gor'kiy
Reservoir

Moskva

Oka

Sura
Kuybyshev
Reservoir

Volga Upland

Volga

Samara

Ural

ReykjanesRidge

North
Sea

Jutland
Bank

Great
Fisher
Bank

Skagerrak

Kattegat

Sjælland

North European Plain

Western Dvina

Valdai

Central Russian Upland

Kama

Vyatka

Votkinsk
Reservoir

Belaya

British
Isles

Ireland

Irish Sea

Shannon

Pennines

Snowdon
1085m

North Channel

Britain

Trent
Severn

The Fens

St George's
Channel

Thames

Strait of Dover

Harz

Dogger
Bank

German
Bight

Frisian Islands

Elbe

Oder

Vistula

Warta

Bug

Pripet
Marshes

Desna

Dnieper

Don

Sym

Central Russian Upland

Khoper

Medveditsa

Don

Kirghiz Ste

Celtic Sea
Celtic
Shelf

Land's End

English Channel

Channel Islands

Bristol Channel

E U R O P E

Neman

Dnieper
Lowlands

Podil's'ka Vysochina

Kremenchuk
Reservoir

Dnieper

Tsimlyansk
Reservoir

Donets

Cas

Charcot Seamounts

Azores-Biscay Rise

Theta Gap
Galicia
Bank

Iberian
Plain

Biscay
Plain

Bay of
Biscay

Seine

Marne

Loire

Meuse

Ardennes

Rhine

Vienne

Cher

Creuse

Massif
Central

Saône

Black
Forest

Vosges

Danube

Lake Constance

Alps

Dolomites

Bakony

Lake Balaton

Great
Hungarian
Plain

Drava

Sava

Tisza

Carpathian
Mountains

Siret

Prut

Dniester

Southern Bug

Black Sea Lowland

Sea of
Azov

Crimea

Kerch Strait

Sea of
Azov

Gulf of
Lion

Cordillera Cantábrica

Miño

Douro

Duero

Aragón

Pyrenees

Aneto 3404m

Garonne

Dordogne

Lot

Cévennes

Rhône

Isère

Mont
Blanc
4807m

Lake Geneva

Lake Garda

Po

Arno

Ligurian
Sea

Apennines

Adriatic Sea

Dinaric Alps

Drina

Danube

Balkan Mountains

Transylvanian Alps

Mureș

Olt

Black Sea

Iberian
Plain

Cordillera Cantábrica

Sistema Ibérico

Sistema Central

Ebro

Tagus

Júcar

Gulf of
Valencia

Corsica

Tyrrhenian
Sea

Corno Grande
2912m

Adriatic
Basin

Lake Scutari

Rhodope Mountains

Maritsa

Sea of
Marmara

Iberian
Peninsula

Cabo
da Roca

Tagus Plain

Guadiana

Sierra Morena

Guadalquivir

Segura

Balearic Islands

Balearic Plain

Sardinia

Strait of Bonifacio

Tyrrhenian
Basin

Gulf of
Taranto

Strait of Otranto

Pindus Mountains

Lake
Ohrid

Lake
Prespa

Adriatic
Sea

Aegean
Sea

Anatolia

Lake Tuz

Gorringe
Ridge

Cape
Saint Vincent

Punta de
Tarifa

Sistemas Béticos

Sierra Nevada

Alboran Sea

Strait of
Gibraltar

Rif

Oued Chélif

Sebou

Mediterranean Sea

EURASIAN PLATE
AFRICAN PLATE

Mount Etna
3340m

Strait of Sicily

Sicily

Malta

Ionian Sea

Ionian
Basin

Peloponnese

Mirtoan
Sea

Sea of Crete

Crete

Gávdos

Mediterranean Ridge

Karpathos Strait

Kaso Strait

Rhodes

Taurus Mountains

Gulf of
Antalya

Cyprus

Cyprus
Basin

ARABIAN PLA
AFRICAN PLA

Levantine
Basin

Nile Fan

Horseshoe Seamounts

Ampère Seamount

Seine Plain

Seine Seamount

Dacia Seamount

Madeira

Agadir Canyon

Middle Atlas

High Atlas

Atlas Mountains

Tell Atlas

Saharan Atlas

Oum er Rbia

Moulouya

Chott el Jerid

Gulf of
Sidra

Canary Islands

'Erg Iguidi

Grand Erg Occidental

Grand Erg Oriental

Western Desert

Libyan Desert

Nile

Erg Chech

S a h a r a

A F R I C A

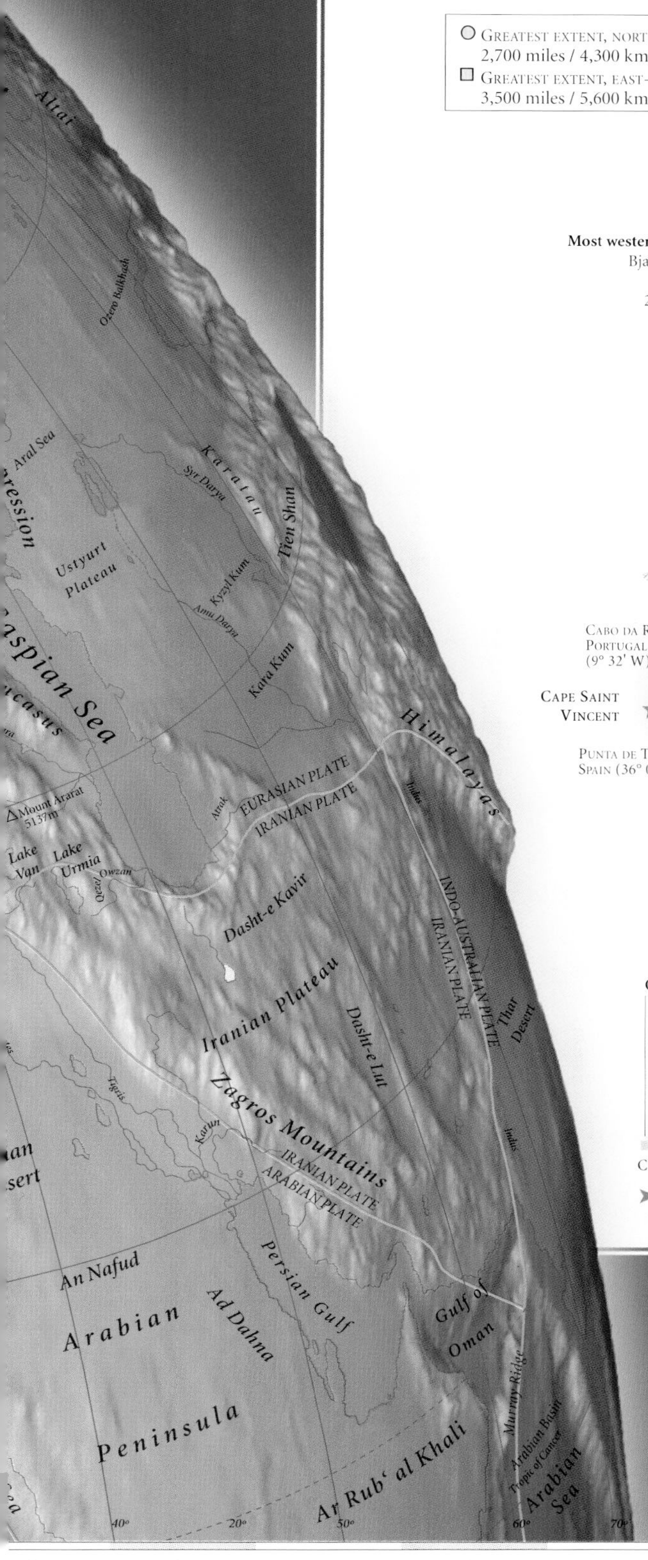
Altai
Aral Sea
Syr Darya
Karatau
Tien Shan
Ustyurt Plateau
Kyzyl Kum
Amu Darya
Kara Kum
Caspian Sea
Himalayas
EURASIAN PLATE
IRANIAN PLATE
Mount Ararat 5137m
Lake Van
Lake Urmia
Dasht-e Kavir
INDO-AUSTRALIAN PLATE
IRANIAN PLATE
Thar Desert
Iranian Plateau
Dasht-e Lut
Zagros Mountains
IRANIAN PLATE
ARABIAN PLATE
An Nafud
Arabian Peninsula
Ad Dahna
Persian Gulf
Gulf of Oman
Murray Ridge
Arabian Basin
Tropic of Cancer
Arabian Sea
Ar Rub' al Khali

EUROPE

EUROPE IS THE WORLD'S SECOND SMALLEST CONTINENT, COVERING 4,053,309 SQ MILES (10,498,000 SQ KM). IT COMPRISES 44 SEPARATE COUNTRIES, INCLUDING TURKEY AND THE RUSSIAN FEDERATION. THE GREATER PARTS OF THESE NATIONS, HOWEVER, LIE IN ASIA.

○ GREATEST EXTENT, NORTH–SOUTH: 2,700 miles / 4,300 km
□ GREATEST EXTENT, EAST–WEST 3,500 miles / 5,600 km

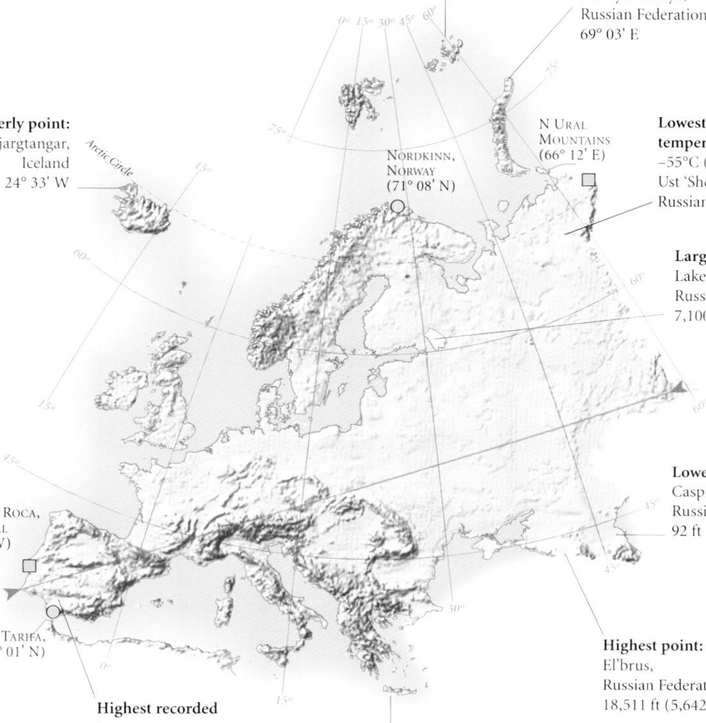
Most northerly point:
Ostrov Rudol'fa, Russian Federation 81° 47' N
Most easterly point:
Mys Flissingskiy, Novaya Zemlya, Russian Federation, 69° 03' E
Most westerly point:
Bjargtangar, Iceland 24° 33' W
Arctic Circle
NORDKINN, NORWAY (71° 08' N)
N URAL MOUNTAINS (66° 12' E)
Lowest recorded temperature:
–55°C (–67°F), Ust 'Shchugor, Russian Federation
Largest lake:
Lake Ladoga, Russian Federation 7,100 sq miles (18,300 sq km)
URAL MOUNTAINS
Lowest point:
Caspian Depression Russian Federation 92 ft (28 m) below sea level
CABO DA ROCA, PORTUGAL (9° 32' W)
CAPE SAINT VINCENT
PUNTA DE TARIFA, SPAIN (36° 01' N)
Highest point:
El'brus, Russian Federation 18,511 ft (5,642 m)
Highest recorded temperature:
122°F (50°C), Seville, Spain
Most southerly point:
Gávdos, Greece 34 °51' N

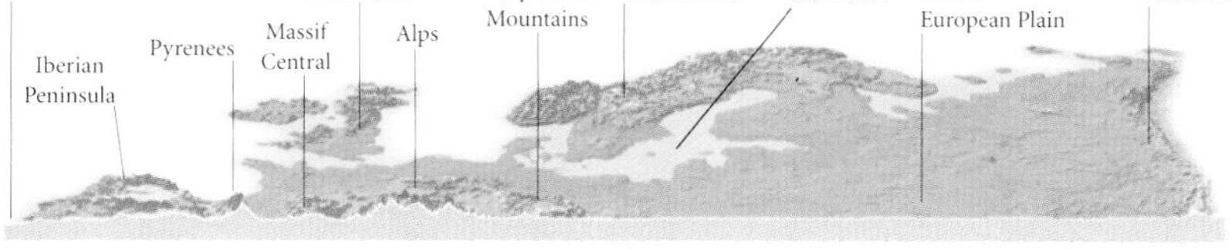
CAPE SAINT VINCENT
Iberian Peninsula
Pyrenees
Massif Central
British Isles
Alps
Carpathian Mountains
Scandinavia
Baltic Sea
North European Plain
URAL MOUNTAINS
0 200 400 Km
0 200 400 Miles

CROSS-SECTION FROM CAPE SAINT VINCENT, PORTUGAL TO THE URAL MOUNTAINS, RUSSIAN FEDERATION

line of cross-section

PHYSICAL EUROPE

THE PHYSICAL DIVERSITY of Europe belies its relatively small size. To the northwest and south it is enclosed by mountains. The older, rounded Atlantic Highlands of Scandinavia and the British Isles lie to the north; the younger, rugged peaks of the Alpine Uplands are in the south. The North European Plain lies in between, stretching 2,485 miles (4,000 km) from The Fens in England to the Ural Mountains in Russia. South of the plain lies a series of gently folded sedimentary rocks separated by ancient plateaus, known as massifs.

THE NORTH EUROPEAN PLAIN

RISING LESS THAN 1,000 ft (300 m) above sea level, the North European Plain strongly reflects past glaciation. Ridges of both coarse moraine and finer, windblown deposits have accumulated over much of the region. The ice sheet also diverted a number of river channels from their original courses.

Glacial lakes

Rivers were diverted from their original course by the ice sheet

A layer of glacial sediments covers the North European Plain

Section across the North European Plain showing its low relief and drainage.

0 100 200 Km
0 100 200 Miles

THE ATLANTIC HIGHLANDS

THE ATLANTIC HIGHLANDS were formed over 500 million years ago during the Caledonian mountain-building period, by compression against the Scandinavian Shield. The highlands were once part of a continuous mountain chain, now divided by the North Sea and a submerged rift valley.

The Atlantic Highlands continue in the British Isles

Rift valley buried by sediments

North Sea

Atlantic Highlands in Norway

Rocks affected by ancient mountain-building

Scandinavian Shield

Cross-section through northeastern Europe showing the continuous mountain chain and rift valley system.

0 100 200 Km
0 100 200 Miles

SCALE 1:23,000,000
(projection: Lambert Azimuthal Equal Area)

Km
0 100 200 400 600
0 50 100 200 300 400 500 600
Miles

MAP KEY

ELEVATION

4000m / 13,124ft
3000m / 9843ft
2000m / 6562ft
1000m / 3281ft
500m / 1640ft
250m / 820ft
100m / 328ft
sea level

PLATE MARGINS
(for explanation see page xiv)

———— constructive
△ △ destructive
———— conservative
.... uncertain

———— physiographic regions

▷◁ line of cross-section

Map labels

NORTH AMERICAN PLATE
EURASIAN PLATE
Iceland

ATLANTIC OCEAN

Norwegian Sea

Faeroe Islands

Shetland Islands

Outer Hebrides

British Isles
Ireland
Shannon
Britain
The Fens
Thames
English Channel

North Sea
Jylland

Vänern
Vättern

ATLANTIC HIGHLANDS
SCANDINAVIAN SHIELD
Kola Peninsula
White Sea
Barents Sea
Novaya Zemlya
Kara Sea
Ostrov Kolguyev

Northern Dvina

Lake Onega
Lake Ladoga
Gulf of Bothnia
Gulf of Riga
Baltic Sea
Western Dvina

NORTH EUROPEAN PLAIN

Central Russian Upland

Ural Mountains

Rhine
Elbe
Oder
Vistula
Dnieper
Dniester
Don
Volga
Volga Upland

PLATEAUX AND LOWLANDS
Seine
Loire
Ardennes
Garonne
Bay of Biscay
Massif Central
Pyrenees
Ebro
Duero
Iberian Peninsula
Guadalquivir
Tagus

Mt Blanc 4807m
ALPS
Po
Danube
Corsica
Sardinia
Balearic Islands

Carpathian Mountains
Great Hungarian Plain
Danube
Balkan Mountains
DINARIC ALPS
Adriatic Sea
Vesuvius 1171m
Etna 3263m
Sicily
Malta
Tyrrhenian Sea
Ionian Sea
Crete
Aegean Sea
Peloponnese

Crimea
Sea of Azov
Caspian Sea
Caucasus
El'brus 5642m
Black Sea

ASIA

EURASIAN PLATE
AFRICAN PLATE
Mediterranean Sea
EURASIAN PLATE
ANATOLIAN PLATE
AFRICAN PLATE

THE PLATEAUS AND LOWLANDS

THE UPLIFTED PLATEAUS or massifs of southern central Europe are the result of long-term erosion, later followed by uplift. They are the source areas of many of the rivers that drain Europe's lowlands. In some of the higher reaches, fractures have enabled igneous rocks from deep in the Earth to reach the surface.

Igneous rocks have intruded into the Massif Central

Older, eroded massifs lie behind the arc of the Alps

Tectonically formed basins

Po Valley

Great Hungarian Plain

Cross-section through the plateaus and lowlands showing the lower elevation of the ancient massifs.

0 100 200 Km
0 100 200 Miles

THE ALPINE UPLANDS

THE COLLISION OF the African and European continents, which began about 65 million years ago, folded and then uplifted a series of mountain ranges running across southern Europe and into Asia. Two major lines of folding can be traced: one includes the Pyrenees, the Alps, and the Carpathian Mountains; the other incorporates the Apennines and the Dinaric Alps.

European basement rock

Alps

Weak sedimentary strata have been folded

African Plate moved northward

The Apennines

Cross-section through the Alps showing folding and faulting caused by plate tectonics.

0 50 100 Km
0 50 100 Miles

CLIMATE

EUROPE EXPERIENCES few extremes in either rainfall or temperature, with the exception of the far north and south. Along the west coast, the warm currents of the North Atlantic Drift moderate temperatures. Although east–west air movement is relatively unimpeded by relief, the Alpine Uplands halt the progress of north–south air masses, protecting most of the Mediterranean from cold, north winds.

Frost grips *northern and eastern Europe during the long cold winters. Lakes and rivers frequently freeze.*

TEMPERATURE

Arctic Circle
60°N
40°N

GLACIATION: DEVELOPMENT OF A GLACIER

Average July temperature

Temperature

	below -30°C (-22°F)
	-30 to -20°C (-22 to -4°F)
	-20 to -10°C (-4 to 14°F)
	-10 to 0°C (14 to 32°F)
	0 to 10°C (32 to 50°F)
	10 to 20°C (50 to 60°F)
	20 to 30°C (68 to 86°F)
	above 30°C (86°F)

RAINFALL

Arctic Circle
60°N
40°N

Average January rainfall

Average July rainfall

Rainfall

	0–25 mm (0–1 in)
	25–50 mm (1–2 in)
	50–100 mm (2–4 in)
	100–200 mm (4–8 in)
	200–300 mm (8–12 in)
	300–400 mm (12–16 in)
	400–500 mm (16–20 in)
	more than 500 mm (20 in)

Mild temperatures *and frequent rainfall contribute to the fertile farmland found over much of northwestern Europe.*

Dusty Sirocco *winds from Africa help to create the semiarid scrubland common across the Mediterranean coastlands of southern Europe.*

Climate

	tundra
	subarctic
	cool continental
	warm humid
	mediterranean
	semi-arid
☼	daily hours of sunshine, January
☼	daily hours of sunshine, July
→	cold wind
→	hot wind

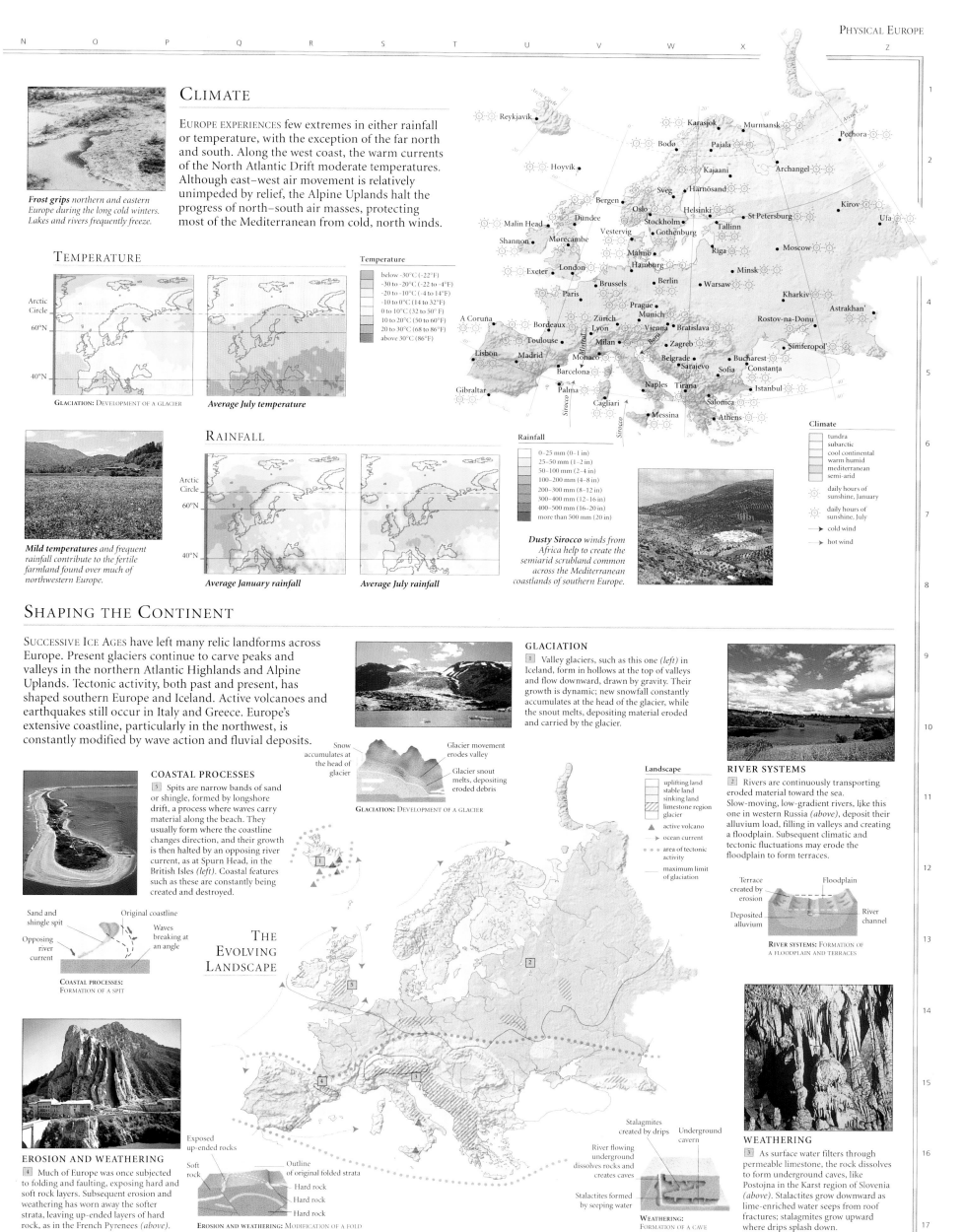

SHAPING THE CONTINENT

SUCCESSIVE ICE AGES have left many relic landforms across Europe. Present glaciers continue to carve peaks and valleys in the northern Atlantic Highlands and Alpine Uplands. Tectonic activity, both past and present, has shaped southern Europe and Iceland. Active volcanoes and earthquakes still occur in Italy and Greece. Europe's extensive coastline, particularly in the northwest, is constantly modified by wave action and fluvial deposits.

GLACIATION

1 Valley glaciers, such as this one *(left)* in Iceland, form in hollows at the top of valleys and flow downward, drawn by gravity. Their growth is dynamic; new snowfall constantly accumulates at the head of the glacier, while the snout melts, depositing material eroded and carried by the glacier.

Snow accumulates at the head of glacier

Glacier movement erodes valley

Glacier snout melts, depositing eroded debris

GLACIATION: DEVELOPMENT OF A GLACIER

COASTAL PROCESSES

5 Spits are narrow bands of sand or shingle, formed by longshore drift, a process where waves carry material along the beach. They usually form where the coastline changes direction, and their growth is then halted by an opposing river current, as at Spurn Head, in the British Isles *(left)*. Coastal features such as these are constantly being created and destroyed.

Sand and shingle spit

Original coastline

Opposing river current

Waves breaking at an angle

COASTAL PROCESSES: FORMATION OF A SPIT

Landscape

	uplifting land
	stable land
	sinking land
	limestone region
	glacier
▲	active volcano
●	ocean current
⋯	area of tectonic activity
—	maximum limit of glaciation

RIVER SYSTEMS

2 Rivers are continuously transporting eroded material toward the sea. Slow-moving, low-gradient rivers, like this one in western Russia *(above)*, deposit their alluvium load, filling in valleys and creating a floodplain. Subsequent climatic and tectonic fluctuations may erode the floodplain to form terraces.

Terrace created by erosion

Floodplain

Deposited alluvium

River channel

RIVER SYSTEMS: FORMATION OF A FLOODPLAIN AND TERRACES

THE EVOLVING LANDSCAPE

EROSION AND WEATHERING

4 Much of Europe was once subjected to folding and faulting, exposing hard and soft rock layers. Subsequent erosion and weathering has worn away the softer strata, leaving up-ended layers of hard rock, as in the French Pyrenees *(above)*.

Exposed up-ended rocks

Soft rock

Outline of original folded strata

Hard rock

Hard rock

Hard rock

EROSION AND WEATHERING: MODIFICATION OF A FOLD

WEATHERING

3 As surface water filters through permeable limestone, the rock dissolves to form underground caves, like Postojna in the Karst region of Slovenia *(above)*. Stalactites grow downward as lime-enriched water seeps from roof fractures; stalagmites grow upward where drips splash down.

Stalagmites created by drips

Underground cavern

River flowing underground dissolves rocks and creates caves

Stalactites formed by seeping water

WEATHERING: FORMATION OF A CAVE

POLITICAL EUROPE

THE POLITICAL BOUNDARIES OF EUROPE have changed many times, especially during the 20th century in the aftermath of two world wars, the breakup of the empires of Austria–Hungary, Nazi Germany, and more recently, the collapse of communism in eastern Europe. The fragmentation of the former Yugoslavia has again altered the political map of Europe, highlighting a trend toward nationalism and devolution. In contrast, economic federalism is growing. In 1958, the formation of the European Economic Community (now the European Union or EU) began a move toward economic and political union.

The Brandenburg Gate in Berlin is a potent symbol of German reunification. In 1961 a wall was built in the road beneath it to stop the flow of refugees to the West. The road was opened again in 1989 when the wall was destroyed and East and West Germany were reunited.

POPULATION

EUROPE IS A DENSELY POPULATED, urbanized continent; in Belgium and the United Kingdom, over 90% of people live in urban areas. The highest population densities are found in an area stretching east from southern Britain and northern France, into Germany. The northern fringes are only sparsely populated.

Demand for space in densely populated European cities like London has led to the development of high-rise offices and urban sprawl.

Population density
(people per sq mile)

- below 130
- 130–259
- 260–379
- 380–519
- 520–780
- above 780

Traditional lifestyles still persist in many remote and rural parts of Europe, especially in the south, east, and in the far north.

MAP KEY

POPULATION

- ■ above 5 million
- ■ 1 million to 5 million
- ◉ 500,000 to 1 million
- ◎ 100,000 to 500,000
- ⊕ 50,000 to 100,000
- ○ 10,000 to 50,000
- ● Country capital

SCALE 1:15,500,000
(projection: Lambert Azimuthal Equal Area)

Km
0 50 100 200 300 400 500 600 700 800 900 1000
0 50 100 200 300 400 500 600 700
Miles

(Map labels)

Denmark Strait · Arctic Circle · REYKJAVIK · ICELAND · Norwegian Sea · Faeroe Islands (to Denmark) · Shetland Islands · Outer Hebrides · Orkney Islands · Bergen · Stavanger · Kristiansand · NORWAY · SWEDEN · Trondheim · OSLO · Uppsala · Örebro · STOCKHOLM · Vänern · Vättern · Gothenburg · Jönköping · Gotland · Ventspils · FINLAND · Tampere · Åland · Turku · HELSINKI · TALLINN · ESTONIA · St Petersburg · Murmansk · Gulf of Bothnia

ATLANTIC OCEAN · North Sea · SCOTLAND · Aberdeen · Glasgow · Dundee · NORTHERN IRELAND · Edinburgh · Belfast · Newcastle upon Tyne · REPUBLIC OF IRELAND · Isle of Man (to UK) · DUBLIN · Liverpool · Leeds · UNITED · Manchester · Sheffield · WALES · Birmingham · KINGDOM · Cardiff · ENGLAND · LONDON · Thames · Southampton · Channel Islands (to UK) · English Channel

DENMARK · Ålborg · COPENHAGEN · Odense · Helsingborg · Malmö · Baltic Sea · RIGA · LATVIA · Liepāja · Western Dvina · LITHUANIA · Kaunas · Vitsyebsk · RUSS. FED. (Kaliningrad) · Kaliningrad · VILNIUS · MINSK · Gdańsk · Bydgoszcz · Vistula · BELARUS · Babruysk · Homy · Brest · POLAND · WARSAW · Poznań · Łódź · Wrocław · Kraków · L'viv · UK

NETH. · AMSTERDAM · THE HAGUE · Groningen · Hamburg · Bremen · Rotterdam · Nijmegen · Hannover · Elbe · BERLIN · Oder · Antwerp · BELGIUM · Liege · Düsseldorf · GERMANY · Leipzig · Dresden · Łódź · BRUSSELS · Bonn · Rhine · Frankfurt am Main · PRAGUE · le Havre · LUXEMBOURG · Nuremberg · CZECH REPUBLIC · Seine · PARIS · LUXEMBOURG · Strasbourg · Stuttgart · Rennes · Orléans · Munich · SLOVAKIA · St-Nazaire · Nantes · Loire · FRANCE · Salzburg · VIENNA · BRATISLAVA · Győr · Chernivtsi · MOLDOVA · Limoges · Zürich · BERN · AUSTRIA · BUDAPEST · Miskolc · Bay of Biscay · Bordeaux · SWITZERLAND · Innsbruck · Alps · HUNGARY · Geneva · Alps · LIECHTENSTEIN · Cluj-Napoca · CHIŞINĂU · Lyon · Milan · LJUBLJANA · Danube · Turin · Verona · SLOVENIA · ZAGREB · ROMANIA · A Coruña · Po · Venice · Trieste · Braşov · Rhône · Genoa · Bologna · CROATIA · Porto · Marseille · Nice · Florence · BOS. & HERZ. · BELGRADE · PORTUGAL · Douro · Valladolid · Pyrenees · MONACO · Pisa · SAN MARINO · SARAJEVO · SERBIA · BUCHAREST · Constanţa · LISBON · Tagus · MADRID · Zaragoza · ANDORRA LA VELLA · ANDORRA · Corsica · Adriatic Sea · Mostar · Danube · Ruse · Setúbal · SPAIN · Barcelona · ITALY · YUGOSLAVIA · BULGARIA · Var · Seville · Córdoba · Valencia · Eivissa · Mallorca · Menorca · Sardinia · MONTENEGRO · SOFIA · Stara Zagora · Burgas · Gibraltar (to UK) · Cádiz · Málaga · Murcia · Palma · Balearic Islands · VATICAN CITY · ROME · Bari · TIRANA · SKOPJE · MACEDONIA · Istanbul · Ceuta (to Spain) · Naples · ALBANIA · Lárisa · Aegean Sea · Melilla (to Spain) · Mediterranean Sea · Tyrrhenian Sea · Cagliari · GREECE · Salonica · Palermo · Sicily · Messina · Piraeus · ATHENS · Catania · Cosenza · Ionian Sea · MALTA · VALLETTA · Sea · Iráklejo · Crete

Overcoming natural barriers, the Brenner Autobahn, one of the main routes across the Alps, links Innsbruck, Austria, with Verona, Italy.

Transportation

— major roads and highways
— major railroads
— international borders
• transportation intersections
⊕ major international airports
⚓ major ports

Novaya Zemlya

Kara Sea

Barents Sea

White Sea

Lake Onega

Arkhangel'sk

Northern Dvina

R U S S I A N

F E D E R A T I O N

Vologda

Perm'

Kirov

Yaroslavl'

Nizhniy Novgorod

Ufa

Kazan'

MOSCOW

Ul'yanovsk

Tol'yatti

Samara

Orenburg

Tula

K A Z A K H S T A N

Saratov

Voronezh

Volgograd

Kharkiv

Volga

Astrakhan'

I N E

ipropetrovs'k

Donets'k

Rostov-na-Donu

Dniepr

Sea of Azov

Stavropol'

Simferopol'

Novorossiysk

Groznyy

Caspian Sea

C a u c a s u s

GEORGIA

AZERBAIJAN

Black Sea

E Y

Reykjavik

Vorkuta

Murmansk

Archangel

Perm'

Trondheim

Bergen

Oslo

Helsinki

St Petersburg

Vologda

Kirov

Stockholm

Tallinn

Nizhniy Novgorod

Samara

Aberdeen
Grangemouth

Newcastle upon Tyne

Middlesbrough

Gothenburg

Riga

Moscow

Dublin

Liverpool

Copenhagen

Helsingborg

Kaliningrad

Vilnius

Minsk

London

Amsterdam

Hamburg

Gdansk

Southampton

Rotterdam

Berlin

Poznan

Warsaw

Brest

le Havre

Antwerp

Brussels

Frankfurt am Main

Kiev

Kharkiv

Volgograd

St-Nazaire

Paris

Strasbourg

Nuremberg

Prague

Rostov-na-Donu

Astrakhan'

A Coruna

Bordeaux

Bilbao

Bern

Munich

Innsbruck

Vienna

Bratislava

Budapest

Odesa

Novorossiysk

Lyon

Milan

Verona

Trieste

Ljubljana

Zagreb

Lisbon

Genoa

Bologna

Belgrade

Bucharest

Constanta

Madrid

Marseille

Rome

Sofia

Varna

Istanbul

Barcelona

Valencia

Naples

Salonica

Cadiz

Gibraltar

Piraeus

Athens

Valletta

Transportation

DESPITE ITS FRAGMENTED GEOGRAPHY and many natural frontiers, communications in Europe are well developed. Extensive highway links allow rapid road transportation. High-speed rail connections like France's TGV (*Train à Grande Vitesse*), and the Channel Tunnel have improved rail travel. Outdated communication infrastructures in parts of eastern Europe, and insufficient transportation links across the Alps, however, remain weak parts of the network.

Languages

THERE ARE THREE MAIN EUROPEAN language groups: Germanic languages predominate in central and northern Europe; Romance languages in western and Mediterranean Europe and Romania; and Slavic languages are spoken in eastern Europe and the Russian Federation. Isolated pockets of local languages, such as Basque and Gaelic, persist and frequently provide a focus for national identity.

Language groups

Turkic
Albanian
Finnic/Ugric
Germanic
Slavic
Romance
Basque
Baltic
Celtic
Greek

ICELANDIC

FAEROESE

NORWEGIAN

LAPPISH (SAMI)

SWEDISH

FINNISH

R U S S I A N

GAELIC

ENGLISH

ESTONIAN

IRISH

ENGLISH

DANISH

LATVIAN

LITHUANIAN

WELSH

FRISIAN

RUSSIAN

BELARUS

BRETON

DUTCH

GERMAN

POLISH

UKRAINIAN

FRENCH

GERMAN

CZECH

SLOVAK

HUNGARIAN

ROMANIAN

PORTUGUESE

GALICIAN

BASQUE

FRENCH

ITALIAN

SLOVENE

SERBO-CROAT

BULGARIAN

MACEDONIAN

TURKISH

SPANISH

CATALAN

FRENCH

ITALIAN

ALBANIAN

GREEK

CATALAN

ITALIAN

MALTESE

The architecture of the Grand Place lies at the heart of Brussels – home city to one of the EU headquarters.

EUROPEAN RESOURCES

Europe's large tracts of fertile, accessible land, combined with its generally temperate climate, have allowed a greater percentage of land to be used for agricultural purposes than on any other continent. Extensive coal and iron ore deposits were used to create steel and manufacturing industries during the 19th and 20th centuries. Today, although natural resources have been largely exploited, and heavy industry is of declining importance, the growth of hi-tech and service industries has enabled Europe to maintain its wealth.

INDUSTRY

Europe's wealth was generated by the rise of industry and colonial exploitation during the 19th century. The mining of abundant natural resources made Europe the industrial center of the world. Adaptation has been essential in the changing world economy, and a move to service-based industries has been widespread except in eastern Europe, where heavy industry still dominates.

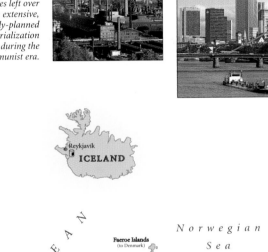

Countries like Hungary are still struggling to modernize inefficient factories left over from extensive, centrally-planned industrialization during the communist era.

Other power sources are becoming more attractive as fossil fuels run out; 16% of Europe's electricity is now provided by hydroelectric power.

Frankfurt am Main is an example of a modern service-based city. The skyline is dominated by headquarters from the worlds of banking and commerce.

STANDARD OF LIVING

Living standards in western Europe are among the highest in the world, although there is a growing sector of homeless, jobless people. Eastern Europeans have lower overall standards of living – a legacy of stagnated economies.

Standard of Living
(UN Human Development Index)

low

high

Skiing brings millions of tourists to the slopes every year. This means that even unproductive, marginal land generates income in the French, Swiss, Italian, and Austrian Alps.

GNP per capita (US$)

below 1,999
2,000–4,999
5,000–9,999
10,000–19,999
20,000–24,999
above 25,000

Industry

aerospace	food processing	wine
brewing	hi-tech industry	coal
car/vehicle manufacture	iron & steel	oil
chemicals	pharmaceuticals	gas
defense	printing & publishing	
electronics	shipbuilding	industrial cities
engineering	textiles	major industrial areas
finance	timber processing	

(Map labels:) ATLANTIC OCEAN · Norwegian Sea · Faeroe Islands (to Denmark) · ICELAND · Reykjavik · Barents Sea · Novaya Zemlya · Ostrov Kolguyev · Murmansk · Archangel · RUSSIAN FEDERATION · Perm' · Cherepovets · Yaroslavl' · Ivanovo · Nizhniy Novgorod · Kazan' · Ufa · Moscow · Tol'yatti · Ryazan' · Samara · Tula · Saratov · Voronezh · Volgograd · Kursk · Rostov-na-Donu · KAZAKHSTAN · Caspian Sea · GEORGIA · Black Sea · Trondheim · Bergen · Oslo · SWEDEN · NORWAY · FINLAND · Turku · Helsinki · St Petersburg · Tallinn · ESTONIA · Stockholm · Gothenburg · Gulf of Bothnia · LATVIA · Riga · LITHUANIA · Vilnius · Minsk · BELARUS · Kiev · UKRAINE · Kharkiv · Dnipropetrovs'k · Donets'k · Kryvyy Rih · MOLDOVA · Odesa · ROMANIA · Bucharest · Ploesti · Constanta · Varna · BULGARIA · Sofia · Salonica · GREECE · Athens · Piraeus · TURKEY · Istanbul · Aegean Sea · Ionian Sea · Crete · MALTA · Sicily · Palermo · Naples · Taranto · ITALY · Rome · VATICAN CITY · SAN MARINO · Sardinia · Corsica · Tyrrhenian Sea · Mediterranean Sea · Balearic Islands · SPAIN · Madrid · Barcelona · Seville · Gibraltar (to UK) · Ceuta (to Spain) · Melilla (to Spain) · MOROCCO · PORTUGAL · Lisbon · Porto · A Coruña · Bay of Biscay · ANDORRA · Marseille · MONACO · Toulouse · Bordeaux · Nantes · Lyon · FRANCE · Paris · Rouen · Lille · BELG. · Brussels · Liège · LUX. · Metz · Strasbourg · Stuttgart · Munich · SWITZ. · Zürich · LIECH. · AUSTRIA · Vienna · Linz · Innsbruck · SLVN. · Ljubljana · Zagreb · CROATIA · BOSNIA & HERZ. · YUGOSLAVIA · Belgrade · ALBANIA · MACED. · Milan · Turin · Genoa · Venice · Bologna · Florence · Channel Islands (to UK) · UNITED KINGDOM · London · Cardiff · Birmingham · Manchester · Liverpool · Newcastle upon Tyne · Glasgow · Belfast · REPUBLIC OF IRELAND · Dublin · Isle of Man (to UK) · North Sea · DENMARK · Copenhagen · Malmö · NETH. · Amsterdam · Rotterdam · Antwerp · Essen · Cologne · GERMANY · Frankfurt am Main · Hamburg · Berlin · Hanover · Leipzig · Dresden · POLAND · Poznań · Łódź · Warsaw · Wrocław · Kraków · Katowice · CZECH REP. · Prague · SLOVAKIA · Bratislava · Budapest · HUNGARY · Gdańsk · RUSS. FED. (Kaliningrad) · Baltic Sea*

Environmental Issues

Environmental Issues

national parks	marine pollution
acid rain	heavy marine pollution
polluted rivers	• poor urban air quality
☢ radioactive contamination	

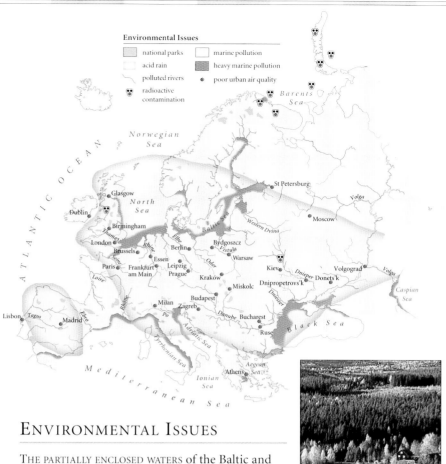

MINERAL RESOURCES

FOSSIL FUELS ARE EUROPE'S main mineral resource, although fuel demand far outstrips production. Sizeable coal reserves remain in the Donbass in Ukraine, Germany's Ruhr Valley, Poland, and in the British Isles. Oil and gas reserves are found mainly in the North Sea, and in the Volga Basin.

Mineral Resources

oil field
gas field
coal field

bauxite
iron
lead
mercury
potassium ▲
uranium △
zinc

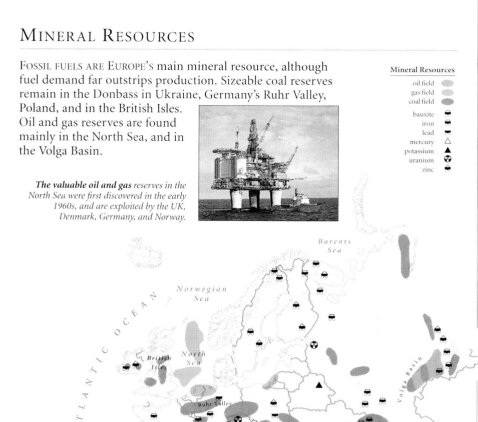

The valuable oil and gas reserves in the North Sea were first discovered in the early 1960s, and are exploited by the UK, Denmark, Germany, and Norway.

ENVIRONMENTAL ISSUES

THE PARTIALLY ENCLOSED WATERS of the Baltic and Mediterranean seas have become heavily polluted, while the Barents Sea is contaminated with spent nuclear fuel from Russia's navy. Acid rain, caused by emissions from factories and power stations, is actively destroying northern forests. As a result, pressure is growing to safeguard Europe's natural environment and prevent further deterioration.

Coniferous forest covers vast stretches of northern Scandinavia and the Russian Federation. Pollutants from other parts of Europe mixing with rainfall are causing defoliation and serious damage to many forests.

The Camargue in the Rhône Delta, southern France, is a protected wetland area, famous for its native population of white horses, and unique bird and plant life.

USING THE LAND & SEA

EUROPE'S SWELLING URBAN POPULATION and the outward expansion of many cities has created acute competition for land. Despite this, European resourcefulness has maximized land potential, and over half of Europe's land is still used for a wide variety of agricultural purposes. Land in northern Europe is used for cattle-rearing, pasture, and arable crops. Toward the Mediterranean, the mild climate allows for the growing of olives, sunflowers, tobacco, citrus fruits, and grapes for wine. EU subsidies, however, have resulted in massive overproduction and a land "set-aside" policy has been introduced.

Using the Land and Sea

cropland
forest
ice cap
mountain region
pasture
tundra
wetland
• major conurbations

cattle
goats
pigs
poultry
reindeer
sheep
cereals
citrus fruits
cotton
fishing
fodder
fruit
olive oil
potatoes
rice
root crops
roses
shellfish
sunflowers
timber
tobacco

Bulgarian roses are one of the many diverse crops grown in Europe. Rose oil, extracted from the petals, is used in perfume-making.

Lowland pastures are used for dairy farming. Good transportation links and refrigeration allow fresh milk to be distributed throughout Europe.

SCANDINAVIA, FINLAND & ICELAND

DENMARK, NORWAY, SWEDEN, FINLAND, ICELAND

JUTTING INTO THE ARCTIC CIRCLE, this northern swath of Jeurope has some of the continent's harshest environments, but benefits from great reserves of oil, gas, and natural evergreen forests. While most early settlers came from the south, migrants to Finland came from the east, bringing a distinct language and culture. Since the late 19th century, the Scandinavian states have developed strong egalitarian traditions. Today, their social welfare systems are among the most extensive in the world, and standards of living are high. The Lapps, or Saami, maintain their traditional lifestyle in the northern regions of Norway, Sweden, and Finland.

THE LANDSCAPE

GLACIERS UP TO 10,000 ft (3,000 m) deep covered most of Scandinavia and Finland during the last Ice Age. The effects of glaciation mark the entire landscape, from the mountains to the lowlands, across the tundra landscape of Lapland and the lake districts of Sweden and Finland.

Geysers are a by-product of Iceland's volcanic activity. Geysir, Iceland's largest spring, gives them their name.

The Lofoten Islands were one of the first areas exposed as the ice sheet melted.

Halti Mountain is Finland's highest point, at 4,356 ft (1,328 m).

Lapland, north of the Arctic Circle, is an area of undulating fells and plains, known as tundra. The subsoil is permanently frozen and therefore impermeable. There are many peat bogs. Pools reappear in the summer when the surface thaws.

Finland's landscape was fashioned by ice action. Glaciers gouged out its distinctive shallow lake basins, such as Oulujärvi, and left debris, called moraines, in their wake.

Oulujärvi

Scandinavia is still recovering from the last Ice Age, when ice depressed the land by 2,000 ft (600 m). This gradual uplift is known as isostatic rebound.

Area of maximum yearly uplift 0.3 in/yr (9 mm/yr)

Slower rates of uplift 0.1 in/yr (3 mm/yr)

The fjords on the western coast of Norway were once gentle river valleys. Their deep floors and steep sides were carved out by glaciers during the last Ice Age, and they were later flooded by the sea.

Fjords

Sjælland coast

On the coast of Sjælland, these cliffs have been eroded by the sea, exposing layers of chalk and limestone.

USING THE LAND & SEA

THE COLD CLIMATE, short growing season, poorly developed soil, steep slopes, and exposure to high winds across northern regions all mean that most agriculture is concentrated, along with the population, in the south. Most of Finland and much of Norway and Sweden are covered by dense forests of pine, spruce, and birch, which supply the timber industries.

Land use and agricultural distribution

- fishing
- pigs
- reindeer
- sheep
- timber
- capital cities
- major towns
- pasture
- cropland
- forest
- mountain region
- tundra

THE URBAN/RURAL POPULATION DIVIDE

urban 84%   rural 16%

POPULATION DENSITY	TOTAL LAND AREA
269 people per sq mile (104 people per sq km)	329,380 sq miles (853,090 sq km)

ARCTIC OCEAN
BARENTS SEA
GREENLAND SEA
SVALBARD
Spitsbergen
(to Norway)

ATLANTIC OCEAN
GREENLAND SEA
ICELAND
REYKJAVÍK

Strait of Denmark
ICELAND
NORÐURLAND
AUSTURLAND
SUÐURLAND
REYKJAVÍK

SCALE 1:5,000,000
(projection: Lambert Conformal Conic)

RUSSIAN FEDERATION
FINLAND
Tampere
Turku
HELSINKI
STOCKHOLM
Uppsala
SWEDEN
Norrköping
OSLO
Bergen
NORWAY
Trondheim
Copenhagen
DENMARK
Malmö
GERMANY
BALTIC SEA
NORTH SEA
NORWEGIAN SEA
ICELAND
REYKJAVÍK
ATLANTIC OCEAN

ARCTIC OCEAN
BARENTS SEA
RUSSIAN FEDERATION
LAPPI
LAPLAND
NORRBOTTEN
Arctic Circle

Sweden is one of the world's largest producers of wood and wood-based products. The traditional transportation of logs, by floating them down rivers, has now been largely replaced by the use of trucks.

MAP KEY

POPULATION

- ◉ 500,000 to 1 million
- ◎ 100,000 to 500,000
- ⊕ 50,000 to 100,000
- ⊕ 10,000 to 50,000
- ∘ below 10,000

ELEVATION

- 2000m / 6562ft
- 1000m / 3281ft
- 500m / 1640ft
- 250m / 820ft
- 100m / 328ft
- sea level

TRANSPORTATION & INDUSTRY

NORWAY DERIVES ITS PREMIER INDUSTRY, the production of oil and gas, from the North Sea, while Denmark exploits its own oil and gas reserves. Hydroelectric power is a major industry, particularly in Sweden and Iceland. Timber processing remains significant in Finland and Sweden, but metal and engineering industries are increasingly important. In Iceland, fish products are the main source of export earnings.

Major industry and infrastructure

- ✿ car manufacture
- ✿ engineering
- fish processing
- geothermal power
- hydroelectric power
- nuclear power
- oil & gas
- timber processing
- ■ capital cities
- ∘ major towns
- ⊕ international airports
- + major roads
- major industrial areas

TRANSPORTATION NETWORK

238,725 miles (384,192 km)	total road network
1,255 miles (2,020 km)	total motorway/expressway
14,903 miles (23,984 km)	total rail network
15,715 miles (25,292 km)	total waterways

Roads now reach most areas, but the railroads are less developed. Much of the north is not served by rail and must rely on air and sea transportation for long distance travel and for transporting freight.

The use of geothermal power in Iceland began half a century ago. Today geothermal power stations supply 86% of the country's domestic heating requirements.

Along with traditional reindeer herding, many Lapp herders now also earn their living by fishing and farming, or working in cities. Tourism provides some with an extra source of income.

RUSSIAN FEDERATION

ARCTIC OCEAN

FINLAND

HELSINKI

SWEDEN

STOCKHOLM

NORWAY

OSLO

DENMARK

COPENHAGEN

NORTH SEA

NORWEGIAN SEA

BALTIC SEA

GERMANY

GREENLAND SEA

ICELAND

REYKJAVIK

ATLANTIC OCEAN

NORTH SEA

SOUTHERN SCANDINAVIA

DENMARK, SOUTHERN NORWAY, SOUTHERN SWEDEN

Scandinavia's economic and political hub is the more habitable and accessible southern region. Many of the area's major cities are on the southern coasts, including Oslo and Stockholm, the capitals of Norway and Sweden. In Denmark, most of the population and the capital, Copenhagen, are located on its many islands. A cultural unity links the three Scandinavian countries. Their main languages, Danish, Swedish, and Norwegian, are mutually intelligible, and they all retain their monarchies, though the parliaments have legislative control.

USING THE LAND

Agriculture in southern Scandinavia is highly mechanized, even though farms are small. Denmark is the most intensively farmed country and its western pastureland is used mainly for pig farming. Cereal crops, including wheat, barley, and oats, predominate in eastern Denmark and in the far south of Sweden. Southern Norway and Sweden have large tracts of forest, which are exploited for logging.

THE URBAN/RURAL POPULATION DIVIDE

urban 87% | rural 13%

POPULATION DENSITY
152 people per sq mile
(61 people per sq km)

TOTAL LAND AREA
173,487 sq miles
(456,564 sq km)

Land use and agricultural distribution

- cattle
- pigs
- sheep
- cereals
- fodder
- root crops
- timber
- capital cities
- major towns
- pasture
- cropland
- forest
- mountain region

THE LANDSCAPE

Southern Scandinavia, with the exception of Norway, has a flatter terrain than the rest of the region. Denmark and southern Sweden are both extensions of the North European Plain. In this area, because of glacial deposition rather than erosion, the soils are deeper and more fertile.

Acid rain, caused by industrial pollution carried north from elsewhere in Europe, harms plant and animal life in Scandinavian forests and lakes. The region's surface rocks lack lime to neutralize the acid, making the problem more serious.

In the past, glaciers such as this one in Olden, Norway, were much larger. Today, many are retreating to yield the spectacular glacial scenery.

Limestone pillars eroded by the sea dot the coast of Gotland and surrounding islands.

Distinctive low ridges, called eskers, are found across southern Sweden. They are formed from sand and gravel deposits left by retreating glaciers.

The peak of Glittertind in the Jotunheimen mountains is 8,044 ft (2,452 m) high.

The lakes of southern Sweden are all that remains of a time when the land was completely flooded. The land rose as the ice that covered the area melted, leaving lakes in shallow, ice-scoured depressions. Sweden has over 90,000 lakes.

Vänern, in Sweden, is the largest lake in Scandinavia. It covers an area of 2,080 sq miles (5,390 sq km).

Denmark's flat and fertile soils are formed on glacial deposits between 100–160 ft (30–50 m) deep.

When the ice retreated, the valley was flooded by the sea
Old valley floor
Sea level
Erosion by glaciers deepened existing river valleys

Sognefjorden is the deepest of Norway's many fjords. It drops to 4,291 ft (1,308 m) below sea level.

Olden

Sognefjorden

MAP KEY

POPULATION
- 500,000 to 1 million
- 100,000 to 500,000
- 50,000 to 100,000
- 10,000 to 50,000
- below 10,000

ELEVATION
- 2000m / 6562ft
- 1000m / 3281ft
- 500m / 1640ft
- 250m / 820ft
- 100m / 328ft
- sea level

SCALE 1:2,900,000
(projection: Lambert Conformal Conic)

In Norway, winters are longer and colder inland than in coastal areas, where the warm North Atlantic Drift moderates the climate.

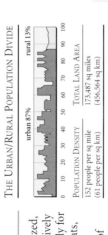

NORWAY
SWEDEN
DENMARK
OSLO
STOCKHOLM
COPENHAGEN

NORWEGIAN SEA
NORTH SEA
BALTIC SEA

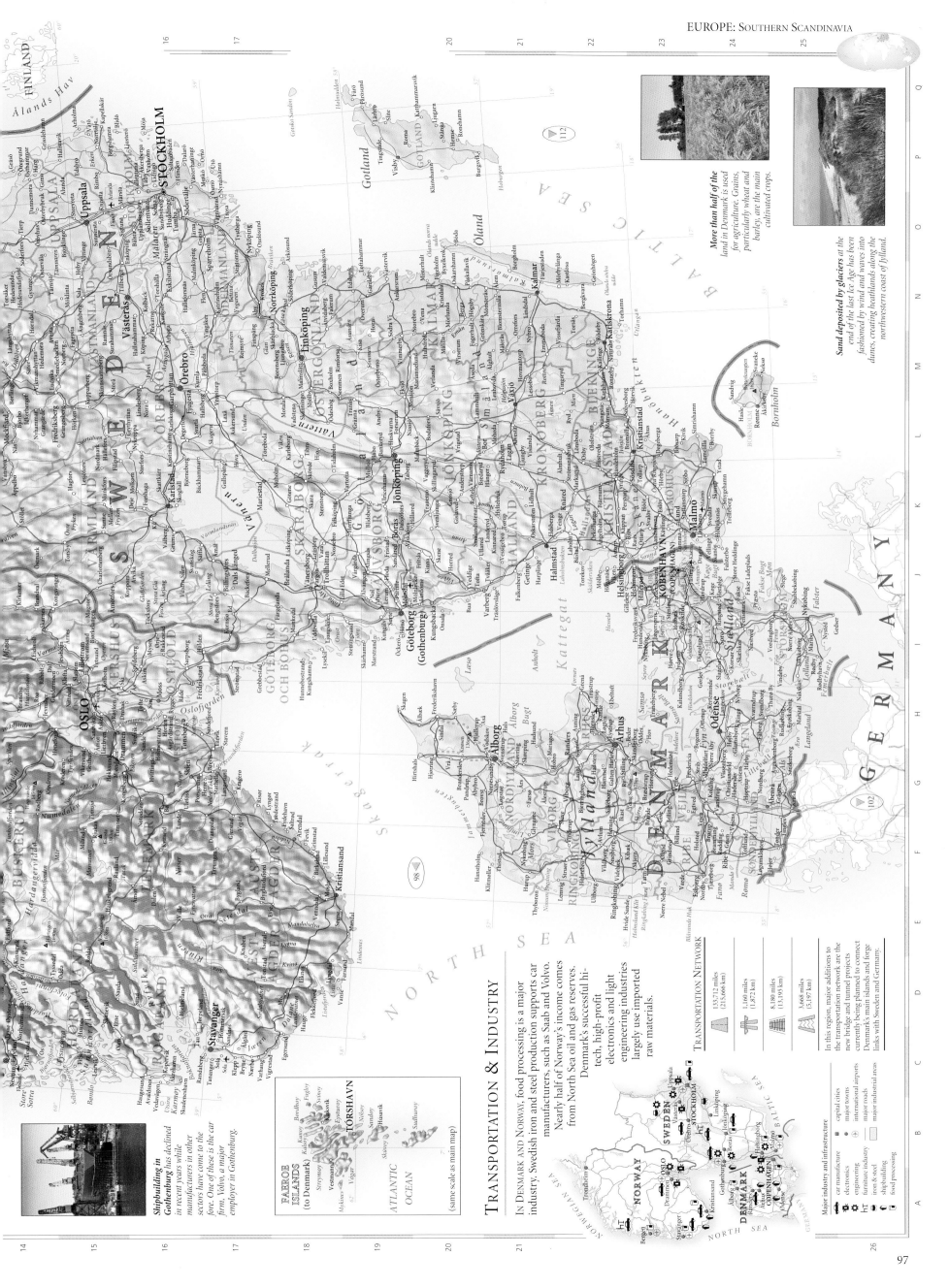

More than half of the land in Denmark is used for agriculture. Grains, particularly wheat and barley, are the main cultivated crops.

Sand deposited by glaciers at the end of the last Ice Age has been fashioned by wind and waves into dunes, creating heathlands along the northwestern coast of Jylland.

Shipbuilding in Gothenburg has declined in recent years while manufacturers in other sectors have come to the fore. One of these is the car firm, Volvo, a major employer in Gothenburg.

FAEROE ISLANDS (to Denmark)

ATLANTIC OCEAN

(same scale as main map)

TRANSPORTATION & INDUSTRY

IN DENMARK AND NORWAY, food processing is a major industry. Swedish iron and steel production supports car manufacturers, such as Saab and Volvo. Nearly half of Norway's income comes from North Sea oil and gas reserves. Denmark's successful hi-tech, high-profit electronics and light engineering industries largely use imported raw materials.

TRANSPORTATION NETWORK

133,712 miles (215,666 km)	
1,160 miles (1,872 km)	
8,180 miles (13,195 km)	
3,668 miles (5,197 km)	

In this region, major additions to the transportation network are the new bridge and tunnel projects currently being planned to connect Denmark's main islands and forge links with Sweden and Germany.

Major industry and infrastructure

- car manufacture
- electronics
- engineering
- furniture industry
- iron & steel
- shipbuilding
- food processing
- capital cities
- major towns
- international airports
- major roads
- major industrial areas

97

THE BRITISH ISLES

UNITED KINGDOM, REPUBLIC OF IRELAND

THE BRITISH ISLES have played a central role in European and world history for centuries. England, Wales, Scotland, and Northern Ireland together form the United Kingdom (UK), while the southern portion of Ireland is an independent country, self-governing since 1921. England has often been the politically and economically dominant partner in the UK. The other partners, however, maintain independent cultures and distinct national identities, and Celtic languages are still spoken by some people. Southeastern England is the most densely populated part of this region, with more than nine million people living in and around London.

TRANSPORTATION & INDUSTRY

THE BRITISH ISLES' INDUSTRIAL BASE was founded primarily on coal, iron, and textiles, situated largely in the north. Today, the most productive sectors include hi-tech industries clustered mainly in southeastern England, chemicals, finance, and the service sector, particularly tourism.

The UK's congested roads have become a major focus of environmental concern in recent years. No longer an island, the UK was finally linked to continental Europe by the Channel Tunnel in 1994.

Major industry and infrastructure

- car manufacture
- chemicals
- engineering
- hi-tech industry
- iron & steel
- tourism

- capital cities
- major towns
- international airports
- major roads
- major industrial areas

TRANSPORTATION NETWORK

278,898 miles (448,844 km)	1,927 miles (3,101 km)
11,514 miles (18,530 km)	2,255 miles (3,629 km)

Clew Bay, in western Ireland, is characteristic of the heavily indented west coast, where deep wide-mouthed bays separate the mountains of Mayo, Donegal, and Kerry as they thrust out into the Atlantic Ocean.

THE LANDSCAPE

RUGGED UPLANDS dominate the landscape of Scotland, Wales, and northern England. All of the peaks in the British Isles over 4,000 ft (1,219 m) lie in highland Scotland. Lowland England rises into several ranges of rolling hills, including the older Mendips, and the Cotswolds and the Chilterns, which were formed at the same time as the Alps in southern Europe.

The Pennines, sometimes called "the backbone of England," are formed of limestones and grits.

Ullswater in the Lake District fills a deep valley formed by glacial erosion.

The Fens are a low-lying area reclaimed from the sea.

Chiltern Hills

The Cotswold Hills are characterized by a series of limestone ridges overlooking clay vales.

Durdle Door

Coastal erosion around the British Isles forms striking features, such as this limestone arch, known as Durdle Door, in Dorset.

Lake District

Mendip Hills

Dartmoor, studded with tors, is an exposed part of a vast granite dome, formed when molten rock intruded into the Earth's crust.

Black Ven, Lyme Regis

Much of the south coast is subject to landslides. Following heavy rain, porous sandstones feed water into the underlying, less permeable clays, which then crumble and slide into the sea.

- Cracks
- Sandstone
- Clay
- Limestone
- Water
- Mudslide
- Sea

MAP KEY

POPULATION

- above 5 million
- 1 million to 5 million
- 500,000 to 1 million
- 100,000 to 500,000
- 50,000 to 100,000
- 10,000 to 50,000
- below 10,000

ELEVATION

- 1000m / 3281ft
- 500m / 1640ft
- 250m / 820ft
- 100m / 328ft
- sea level

The lowlands of Scotland, drained by the Tay, Forth, and Clyde Rivers, are centered on a rift valley. The region contains valuable coal reserves.

Ben Nevis, at 4,409 ft (1,343 m), is the highest peak in the UK.

Over 600 islands, mostly uninhabited, lie west and north of the Scottish mainland.

Thousands of hexagonal basalt columns form Giant's Causeway on the north coast of Antrim. These were created by volcanic activity.

The British Isles have no large-scale river systems. The Shannon is the longest, at 230 miles (370 km).

Snowdon is the highest mountain in England and Wales, reaching 3,556 ft (1,085 m).

Peat bogs dot the poorly-drained Irish lowlands.

The valley of Glen Coe in the Scottish Highlands is a U-shaped valley, typical of the north and west of the British Isles, where glaciers shaped much of the landscape.

Map labels

Shetland Islands

Orkney Islands

SCOTLAND

Aberdeen

Dundee

Edinburgh

Glasgow

North Sea

English Channel

LONDON

UNITED KINGDOM

REPUBLIC OF IRELAND

DUBLIN

ATLANTIC OCEAN

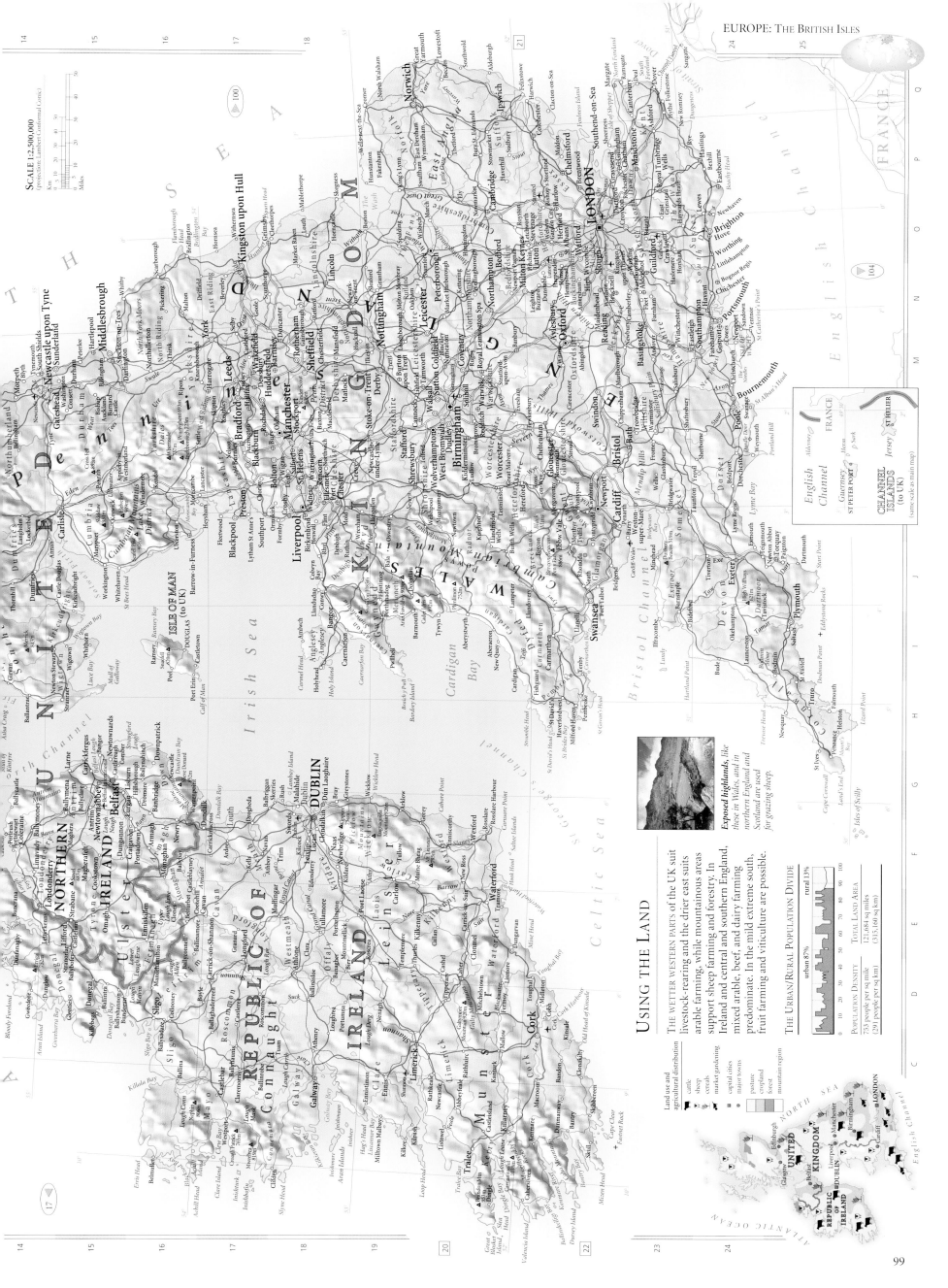

SCALE 1:2,500,000
(projection: Lambert Conformal Conic)

Exposed highlands, like these in Wales, and in northern England and Scotland are used for grazing sheep.

USING THE LAND

THE WETTER WESTERN PARTS of the UK suit livestock-rearing and the drier east suits arable farming, while mountainous areas support sheep farming and forestry. In Ireland and central and southern England, mixed arable, beef, and dairy farming predominate. In the mild extreme south, fruit farming and viticulture are possible.

THE URBAN/RURAL POPULATION DIVIDE

urban 87%   rural 13%

POPULATION DENSITY	TOTAL LAND AREA
753 people per sq mile (291 people per sq km)	121,684 sq miles (315,160 sq km)

Land use and agricultural distribution

- cattle
- sheep
- cereals
- market gardening
- capital cities
- major towns

pasture
cropland
forest
mountain region

THE LOW COUNTRIES

BELGIUM, LUXEMBOURG, NETHERLANDS

ONE OF NORTHWESTERN EUROPE'S strategic crossroads, the Low Countries are united by a common history. They have often been used as a battleground in European wars. For over a thousand years they were ruled by foreign powers. Even after they achieved independence, the three countries maintained close links, later forming the world's first totally free labor and goods market, the Benelux Economic Union, which became the core of the European Community (now the European Union or EU). These states have remained at the forefront of wider European cooperation; Brussels, The Hague, and Luxembourg host the major institutions of the EU.

THE LANDSCAPE

THE MAIN GEOGRAPHICAL REGIONS of the Netherlands are the northern glacial heathlands, the low-lying lands of the Rhine and Maas/Meuse, the reclaimed polders, and the dune coast and islands. Belgium includes part of the Ardennes, together with the coalfields on its northern flanks, and the fertile Flanders Plain.

Extensive sand dune systems along the coast have prevented flooding of the land. Behind the dunes, marshy land is drained to form polders, usable land suitable for agriculture.

Sand dunes

Since the Middle Ages the people of the Netherlands have used ditches and drainage dykes to reclaim land from the sea. These reclaimed areas are known as polders.

Sea
Dune system
Polder
Drainage ditch

The loess soils of the Flanders Plain in western Belgium provide excellent conditions for arable farming.

Uplifted and folded 220 million years ago, the Ardennes have since been reduced to relatively level plateaus, then sharply incised by rivers such as the Maas/Meuse.

Ardennes

Hautes Fagnes is the highest part of Belgium. The bogs and streams in this upland region are the result of high rainfall and low temperatures.

Heathlands are found along the coast of the Netherlands. Much of the coast was breached by the sea in the 5th century, creating its distinctive inlets and islands.

Schoorl

One-third of the Netherlands lies below sea level and flooding is a constant threat. Dams have been built across the mouths of many rivers to contain floodwaters.

The parallel valleys of the Maas/Meuse and Rhine Rivers were created when the Rhine was deflected from its previous course by the ice sheet which formed during the last Ice Age.

Silts and sands eroded by the Rhine throughout its course are deposited to form a delta on the west coast of the Netherlands.

TRANSPORTATION & INDUSTRY

IN THE WESTERN NETHERLANDS, a massive, sprawling industrialized zone encompasses many new hi-tech and service industries. Belgium's central region has emerged as the country's light manufacturing and services center. Luxembourg city is home to more than 160 banks and the European headquarters of many international companies.

The Low Countries hold a key position on the North Sea, containing Europe's two largest ports, Rotterdam and Antwerp, which are connected to a comprehensive system of inland waterways.

TRANSPORTATION NETWORK

155,154 miles (249,697 km)	1,065 miles (1,714 km)
4,280 miles (6,888 km)	4,369 miles (7,031 km)

Major industry and infrastructure
- aerospace
- finance
- engineering
- hi-tech industry
- pharmaceuticals
- textiles
- capital cities
- major towns
- international airports
- major roads
- major industrial areas

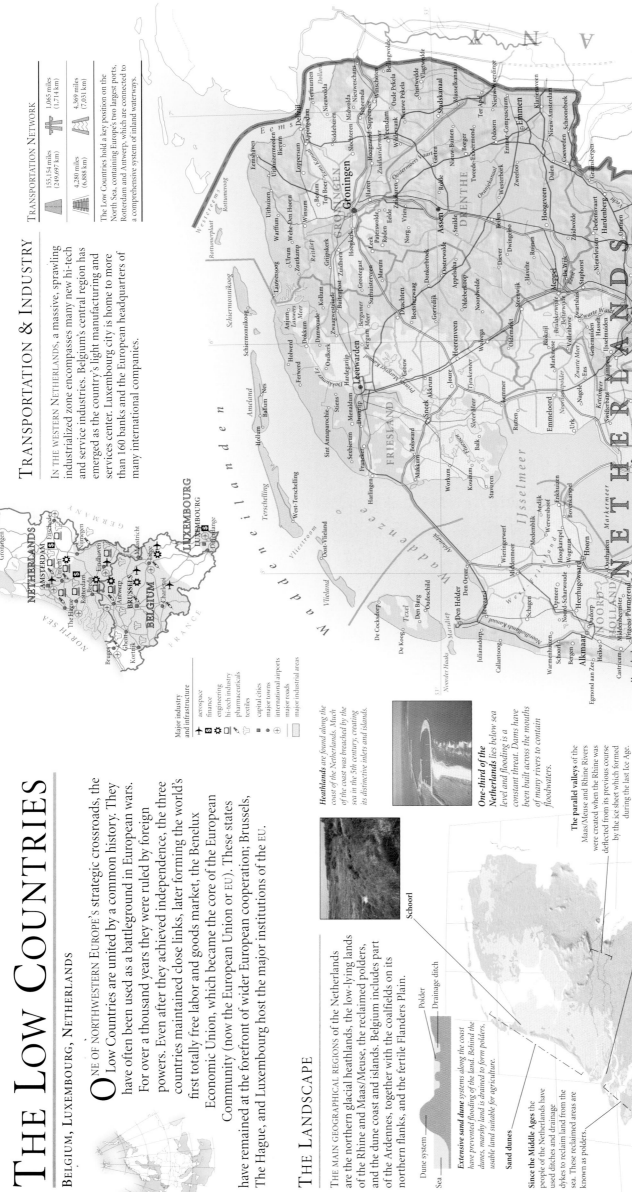

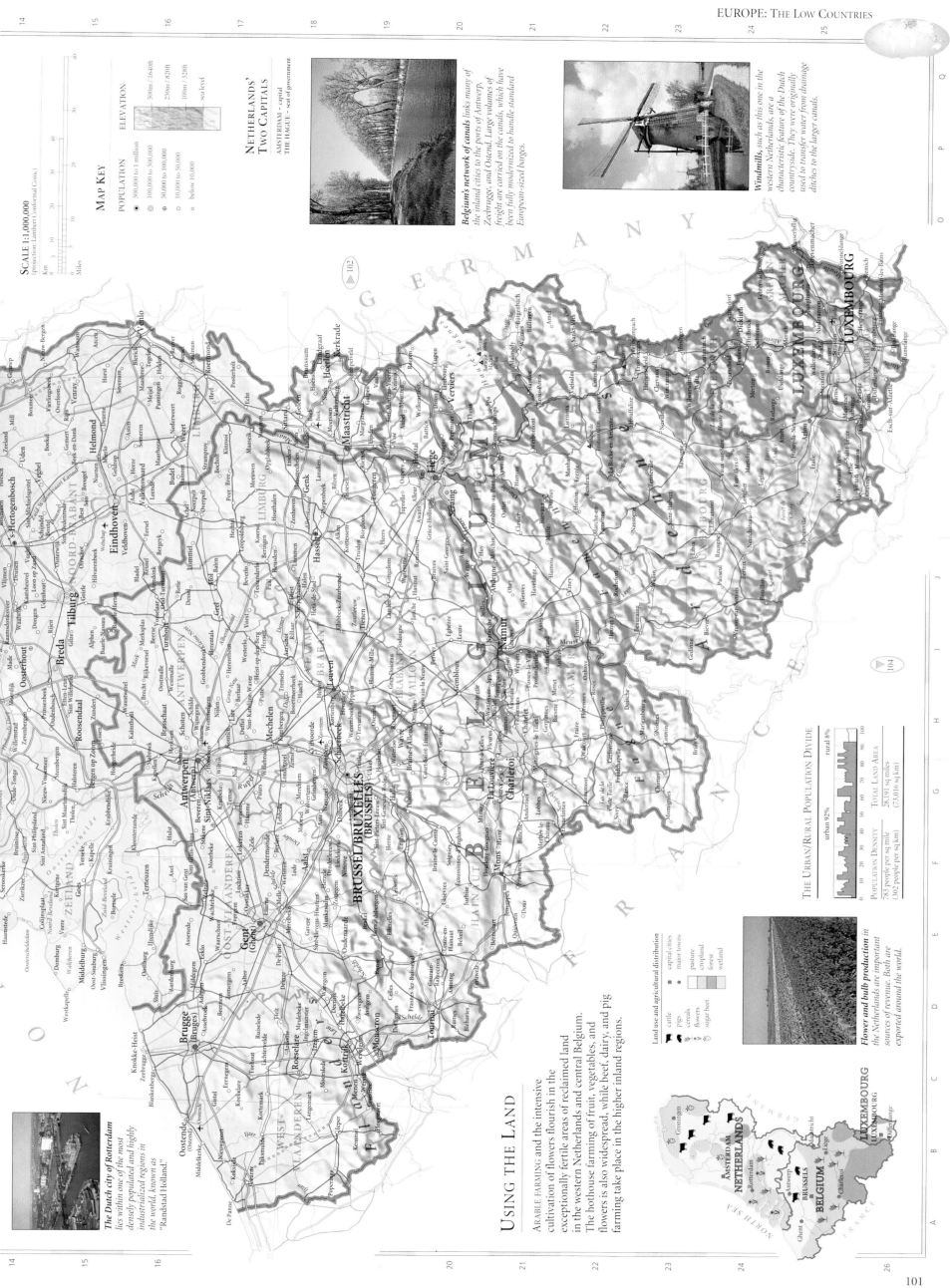

SCALE 1:1,000,000
(Projection: Lambert Conformal Conic)

MAP KEY

POPULATION

- 500,000 to 1 million
- 100,000 to 500,000
- 50,000 to 100,000
- 10,000 to 50,000
- below 10,000

ELEVATION

- 500m/1640ft
- 250m/820ft
- 100m/328ft
- sea level

NETHERLANDS' TWO CAPITALS

AMSTERDAM - capital
THE HAGUE - seat of government

Belgium's network of canals links many of the inland cities to the ports of Antwerp, Zeebrugge, and Ostend. Large volumes of freight are carried on the canals, which have been fully modernized to handle standard European-sized barges.

Windmills, such as this one in the western Netherlands, are a characteristic feature of the Dutch countryside. They were originally used to transfer water from drainage ditches to the larger canals.

The Dutch city of Rotterdam lies within one of the most densely populated and highly industrialized regions in the world, known as "Randstad Holland."

USING THE LAND

ARABLE FARMING and the intensive cultivation of flowers flourish in the exceptionally fertile areas of reclaimed land in the western Netherlands and central Belgium. The hothouse farming of fruit, vegetables, and flowers is also widespread, while beef, dairy, and pig farming take place in the higher inland regions.

Flower and bulb production in the Netherlands are important sources of revenue. Both are exported around the world.

Land use and agricultural distribution

- cattle
- pigs
- cereals
- flowers
- sugar beet
- capital cities
- major towns
- pasture
- cropland
- forest
- wetland

THE URBAN/RURAL POPULATION DIVIDE

urban 92%   rural 8%

POPULATION DENSITY	TOTAL LAND AREA
783 people per sq mile (302 people per sq km)	28,191 sq miles (73,016 sq km)

101

GERMANY

DESPITE THE DEVASTATION of its industry and infrastructure during the Second World War and its separation from East Germany during the Cold War, West Germany made a rapid recovery in the following generation to become Europe's most formidable economic power. When the Berlin Wall was dismantled in 1989, Germany was politically united for the first time in 40 years. Complete social and economic unity remain a longer-term goal, as East German industry and society adapt to a free market. Germany has been a key player in the creation of the European Union (EU) and in moves toward adopting a single European currency.

USING THE LAND

GERMANY HAS A LARGE, efficient agricultural sector, producing more than three-quarters of its own food. The major crops grown are cereals and sugar beet on the more fertile soils, and root crops, rye, oats, and fodder on the poorer soils of the northern plains and central uplands. Southern Germany is also a principal producer of high-quality wines. Vineyards cover the slopes surrounding the Rhine and its tributaries.

Land use and
agricultural distribution
- cattle
- pigs
- cereals
- sugar beet
- vineyards
- capital cities
- major towns
- pasture
- cropland
- forest

THE URBAN/RURAL POPULATION DIVIDE

urban 86%   rural 14%

POPULATION DENSITY	TOTAL LAND AREA
593 people per sq mile	13,804 sq miles
(229 people per sq km)	(356,910 sq km)

The Moselle River flows through the Rhine State Uplands (Rheinisches Schiefergebirge). During a period of uplift, preexisting river meanders were deeply incised, to form its present dramatic incised.

THE LANDSCAPE

THE PLAINS OF NORTHERN GERMANY, the volcanic plateaus and mountains of the central uplands, and the Bavarian Alps are the three principal geographic regions in Germany. North to south the land rises steadily from barely 300 ft (90 m) in the plains to 6,500 ft (2,000 m) in the Bavarian Alps, which are a small but distinct region in the far south.

The Harz Mountains were formed 300 million years ago. They are block-faulted mountains, formed when a section of the Earth's crust was thrust up between two faults.

The heathlands of northern Germany are covered by glacial deposits of sandy outwash soil, which makes them largely infertile. They only support sheep and solitary trees.

Lüneburg Heath
(*Lüneburger Heide*)

Much of the landscape of northern Germany has been shaped by glaciation. During the last Ice Age, the ice sheet advanced as far the northern slopes of the central uplands.

Müritz Lake covers 45 sq miles (117 sq km), but is only 108 ft (33 m) deep. It lies in a shallow valley formed by meltwater flowing out from a retreating ice sheet. These valleys are known as *Urstromtäler*.

The Elbe flows in wide meanders across the North German Plain to the North Sea. At its mouth it is 10 miles (16 km) wide.

Elbe River

Part of the floor of the Rhine Rift Valley was let down between two parallel faults in the Earth's crust.
Rhine Rift Valley

Fault lines
Rhine
Downfaulted block

The Rhine is Germany's principal waterway and one of Europe's longest rivers, flowing 820 miles (1,320 km).

The Danube rises in the Black Forest (*Schwarzwald*) and flows east, across a wide valley, on its course to the Black Sea.

Zugspitze, the highest peak in Germany at 9,719 ft (2,962 m), was formed during the Alpine mountain-building period, 30 million years ago.

SCALE 1:2,250,000
(projection Lambert Conformal Conic)

The Bavarian Alps straddle the country's southern border at an average height of 6,500 ft (2,000 m).

In the Black Forest (Schwarzwald), in southwestern Germany, woodland cloaks sandstone and granite hills, which contain rich mineral springs.

TRANSPORTATION & INDUSTRY

TODAY, THE MAIN INDUSTRIES which contribute to Germany's economic power are industrial machine building, electronics, chemicals, and car manufacturing, including the famous Mercedes and BMW firms. While the introduction of a free market in the east has forced the closure of many less efficient companies there, west German manufacturers have moved in to set up new plants and businesses.

Germany has a complex network of inland waterways. The Rhine and Danube are at the center of a vast canal system that links central and eastern Europe to the north.

Major industry and infrastructure

- car manufacture
- chemicals
- hi-tech industry
- iron & steel
- mining
- precision engineering
- research & development
- shipbuilding
- capital cities
- major cities
- major towns
- international airports
- major roads
- major industrial areas

TRANSPORTATION NETWORK

- 386,056 miles (621,297 km)
- 3,406 miles (5,482 km)
- 26,098 miles (42,000 km)
- 4,598 miles (7,100 km)

MAP KEY

POPULATION
- 1 million to 5 million
- 500,000 to 1 million
- 100,000 to 500,000
- 50,000 to 100,000
- 10,000 to 50,000
- below 10,000

ELEVATION
- 2000m / 6562ft
- 1000m / 3281ft
- 500m / 1640ft
- 250m / 820ft
- 100m / 328ft
- sea level

FRANCE

FRANCE, MONACO

E UROPE'S SECOND LARGEST NATION and the founder of modern Republican government, France is a major center of culture and fashion, and a leading producer of both agricultural and industrial goods. It has played a leading role in European events for centuries, and remains a key player in the push toward European unity. The Paris Basin is the most highly populated area; Île de France is home to over nine million people. Large parts of France remain thinly populated, particularly the mountainous Massif Central, Pyrenees, and southern Alps.

The chalk cliffs of Normandy (Normandie) and southeastern England form part of a single geological region, now divided in two by the English Channel.

THE LANDSCAPE

FRANCE'S LANDSCAPE was fashioned by two phases of mountain-building. The northwestern peninsula, the Massif Central, and the Vosges date from 220 million years ago. The complex folds of the Alps and Pyrenees, the gently-folded Jura, and the low-lying sedimentary areas of the Paris, Garonne, and Rhône basins started to form 65 million years ago.

The coast of Brittany (*Bretagne*) is highly indented where deep valleys in the northwestern peninsula were drowned by the sea.

The Normandy (*Normandie*) coastline is characterized by high chalk cliffs.

The coastline of France is 2,141 miles (3,427 km) long.

The Paris Basin consists of a layered sequence of sedimentary rocks. Fertile soils over much of the area make good agricultural land.

The gently rounded summits of the Vosges are over 200 million years old.

The folded Jura form low ridges and long narrow valleys.

The Biscay coast, like the Mediterranean, is characterized by flat sandy beaches, interspersed with lagoons.

Garonne Basin

The Alps were forced up during several phases of mountain-building beginning 65 million years ago.

The Dordogne Region contains spectacular examples of limestone scenery, including caves and gorges.

The Pyrenees form a natural border between France and Spain.

The ancient Massif Central, disturbed by the formation of the Alps, was subject to volcanism that only ceased during the last 10,000 years.

Rhône Delta

Rhône Basin

Rhône

Corsica's northeastern peninsula has dramatic cliffs of folded limestone.

Delta plain

The marshes of the Camargue

The volcanic landscape of the Auvergne, where the cones of its extinct volcanoes have worn away to leave "plugs" of lava.

Deposition in the Rhône Delta is wave-dominated. Sea currents carry river sediments extending the delta plain westward.

TRANSPORTATION & INDUSTRY

TODAY THE MAIN FRENCH GROWTH INDUSTRIES are hi-tech, including microelectronics, telecommunications, and aerospace. Other important sectors are the nuclear industry, rivaled in scale only by that of the US, car manufacturing, dominated by the giants Renault and Peugeot, and a highly diversified tourist industry.

Major industry and infrastructure

- aerospace industry
- car manufacture
- chemicals
- engineering
- hi-tech industry
- nuclear power
- tourism
- capital cities
- major towns
- international airports
- major roads
- major industrial areas

TRANSPORTATION NETWORK

516,359 miles (831,000 km)	4,142 miles (6,680 km)
21,170 miles (34,070 km)	5,270 miles (8,500 km)

The French TGV (*Train à Grande Vitesse*) leads the world in high-speed train technology, and provides a service which is faster, door-to-door, than air travel.

SCALE 1:2,750,000
(projection: Lambert Conformal Conic)

MAP KEY

POPULATION

- ■ above 5 million
- ■ 1 million to 5 million
- ◉ 500,000 to 1 million
- ◎ 100,000 to 500,000
- ⊕ 50,000 to 100,000
- ○ 10,000 to 50,000
- ○ below 10,000

ELEVATION

- 4000m / 13,124ft
- 3000m / 9843ft
- 2000m / 6562ft
- 1000m / 3281ft
- 500m / 1640ft
- 250m / 820ft
- 100m / 328ft
- sea level

USING THE LAND

FRANCE IS WESTERN EUROPE'S leading agricultural producer, yet it is the beneficiary of high levels of EU subsidy. The variation in climate and soils across the country provides great potential for agriculture and forestry, reflected in the range of products cultivated, including cereal crops, olives, herbs, and grapes for its famous wines.

Land use and agricultural distribution

- cattle
- cereals
- market gardening
- sugar beet
- vineyards
- ● capital cities
- ● major towns
- pasture
- cropland
- forest
- mountain region

The Romans first introduced winemaking to France when they occupied the region. Traditional vineyards can be found all over France, producing many of the world's classic wines.

THE URBAN/RURAL POPULATION DIVIDE

urban 74%   rural 26%

POPULATION DENSITY	TOTAL LAND AREA
269 people per sq mile (104 people per sq km)	212,930 sq mile (551,500 sq km)

The rugged hills and cliffs of Corsica were uplifted when the African Plate and Eurasian Plate collided. During the Ice Age frost action created their present form.

Corse (Corsica)

In the sunny climate of southern France, olives, grapes, peppers, garlic, and lavender now grow in place of the forests that once covered much of the area.

(same scale as main map)

THE IBERIAN PENINSULA

ANDORRA, GIBRALTAR, PORTUGAL, SPAIN *(Azores, Canary Islands, Madeira on p.66)*

THE IBERIAN PENINSULA is separated from the rest of Europe by the Pyrenees, and at its most southerly point is only 5 miles (8 km) from North Africa. The location of Iberia has been central to its diverse history. The Greeks, Carthaginians, Romans, Visigoths, and most recently the Moors, invaded Iberia at various times. For much of the 20th century, both Spain and Portugal were governed by right-wing dictators. Since the establishment of democratic governments in the mid-1970s, modernization has been rapid and both countries are now among the most popular of European holiday destinations.

USING THE LAND

THE PRINCIPAL CROPS grown in Iberia are cereals, especially wheat and barley. Both countries are major wine producers, most notably of Rioja, sherry, and port. Sheep are kept throughout the region and citrus fruits thrive on the Mediterranean coast. The successful forest industry in Iberia produces two-thirds of the world's cork.

The steep, terraced slopes of the Douro Valley in northern Portugal, are used to cultivate grapes. These are harvested to produce Portugal's famous port wine.

THE URBAN/RURAL POPULATION DIVIDE

urban 69%   rural 31%

0 10 20 30 40 50 60 70 80 90 100

POPULATION DENSITY
481 people per sq mile
(186 people per sq km)

TOTAL LAND AREA
230,569 sq miles
(597,170 sq km)

Land use and agricultural distribution
- sheep
- cereals
- citrus fruit
- olives
- vineyards
- cork
- capital cities
- major towns
- pasture
- cropland
- forest
- mountain region

TRANSPORTATION & INDUSTRY

SINCE THE 1970s, the economies of Spain and Portugal have expanded and diversified. In both countries, tourism has outstripped agriculture in economic importance. Spain's resource base is varied, including coal, iron, and the world's largest reserves of mercury. Portugal is a leading producer of tungsten ore.

TRANSPORTATION NETWORK

241,720 miles
(388,990 km)

1,552 miles
(2,529 km)

11,793 miles
(18,979 km)

1,159 miles
(1,865 km)

Radiating from Madrid, the road network in Spain dates from the 18th century, but now includes many highways. Portugal's road system has been completely modernized in recent years.

Major industry and infrastructure
- car manufacture
- chemicals
- engineering
- fish processing
- mining
- textiles
- tourism
- capital cities
- major towns
- international airports
- major roads
- major industrial areas

The eroded cliffs of the Algarve in southern Portugal were carved by Atlantic waves. The numerous rocky bays and beaches, and the region's pleasant climate, have made it a popular tourist destination.

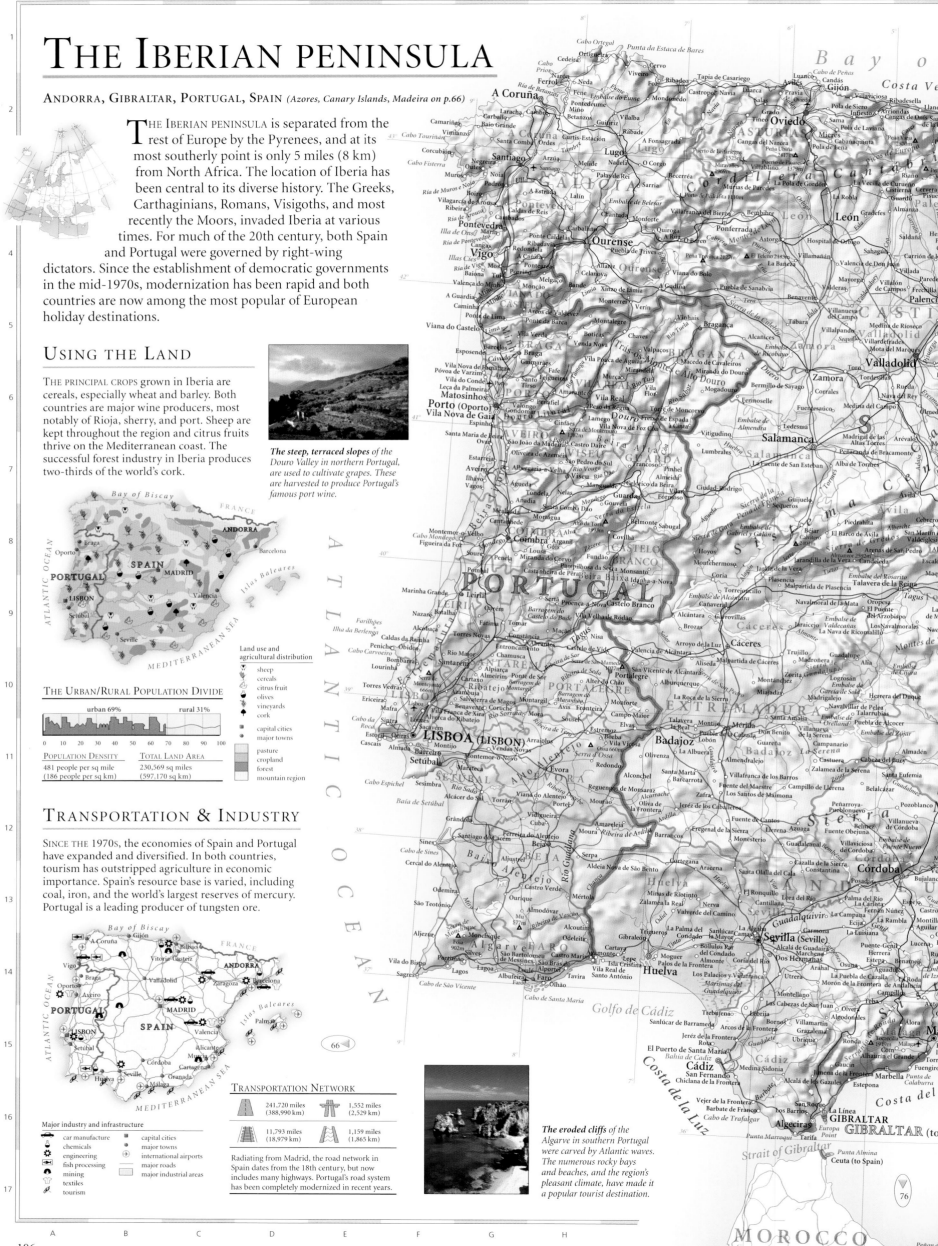

The climate in northwestern Spain is milder in both summer and winter than in the rest of the country, creating a verdant environment more commonly associated with northwestern Europe.

MAP KEY

POPULATION

- 1 million to 5 million
- 500,000 to 1 million
- 100,000 to 500,000
- 50,000 to 100,000
- 10,000 to 50,000
- below 10,000

ELEVATION

- 3000m / 9843ft
- 2000m / 6562ft
- 1000m / 3281ft
- 500m / 1640ft
- 250m / 820ft
- 100m / 328ft
- sea level

SCALE 1:2,750,000
(projection: Lambert Conformal Conic)

Km 0 10 20 30 40 50 60 70 80

Miles 0 10 20 30 40 50 60 70 80

Bay of Biscay

MEDITERRANEAN SEA

Golfo de Valencia

Islas Baleares (Balearic Islands)

Menorca (Minorca)

Mallorca (Majorca)

Eivissa (Ibiza)

Formentera

Cabrera

THE LANDSCAPE

A VAST PLATEAU, the Meseta dominates the center of the peninsula, enclosed by the Cordillera Cantábrica to the north and the Sierra Morena to the south. It is drained by three major rivers, the Douro/Duero, the Tagus, and the Guadalquivir. The peninsula experiences great variations in climate and rainfall, both regionally and locally.

The Pyrenees form Iberia's northeastern boundary, running for some 270 miles (440 km) and dividing it from the rest of Europe.

The Ebro River has formed the peninsula's largest delta. Recently, sediment flows have been seriously disturbed by nearby reservoirs.

On the northeastern coast, sea level changes are evident from wave-cut beaches which rise up to 200 ft (60 m) above the present sea level.

Cordillera Cantábrica

Douro/Duero River

The Meseta averages 1,970 ft (600 m) in height and is now largely dry and treeless.

Tagus River

Mountain front

Weathered material

Pediment

Pediments are characteristic of semiarid lands across Iberia. A pediment is a flat, low-lying, eroded platform, cut into the bedrock. Weathered material is transported by streams and deposited in broad fan shapes on the pediment.

The Guadalquivir River brings vital irrigation water to the plains, and like many of Iberia's rivers, it is prone to flooding.

Sierra Morena

The Sierra Nevada in southern Spain contain Iberia's highest peak, Mulhacén, which rises 11,418 ft (3,481 m).

The Balearic Islands (Islas Baleares) are characterized by jagged limestones and plains.

In the Sierra de los Filabres deforestation and overgrazing, which cause soil erosion, have created semidesert badlands.

THE ITALIAN PENINSULA

ITALY, SAN MARINO, VATICAN CITY

THE ITALIAN PENINSULA is a land of great contrasts. Until unification in 1860, Italy was a collection of independent city states, whose competitiveness during the Renaissance resulted in the architectural and artistic magnificence of cities such as Rome, Florence, and Venice. The majority of Italy's population and economic activity is concentrated in the north, centered on the sophisticated industrial city of Milan. Southern Italy, called the *Mezzogiorno*, has a harsh and difficult terrain, and remains far less developed than the north. Attempts to attract industry and investment in the south are frequently deterred by the entrenched network of organized crime and corruption.

THE LANDSCAPE

THE MAINLY MOUNTAINOUS and hilly Italian peninsula took its present form following a collision between the African and Eurasian tectonic plates. The Alps in the northwest rise to a high point of 15,772 ft (4,807 m) at Mont Blanc (*Monte Bianco*) on the French border, while the Apennines (*Appennino*) form a rugged backbone that runs the entire length of the country.

The island of Sardinia is an ancient land mass, an uplifted section of very old igneous rocks. Its rugged mountainous regions provide pasture for sheep and goats, while its valleys support some agriculture.

Mont Blanc (*Monte Bianco*)

Costa Smeralda

The Dolomites (*Alpi Dolomitiche*) *are formed of thick limestones, overlying weaker marine strata. They have distinctive serrated peaks and many massive landslides occur.*

The distinctive square shape of the Gulf of Taranto (*Golfo di Taranto*) was defined by numerous block faults. Earthquakes are common in this region.

Vesuvius (*Vesuvio*)

The Apennines (*Appennino*) are the source of most of Italy's rivers. They run 823 miles (1,324 km) down the length of the peninsula.

The Po Valley once formed part of the Adriatic Sea. Sediments of gravel, sand, and clay washed down from the Alps gradually filled it to form a broad, cultivable plain.

The Pontine Marshes (*Agro Pontino*) are bounded by low sandhills that prevent natural drainage.

Sardinia is the second largest island in the Mediterranean Sea. The highest point is Punta La Marmora at 6,017 ft (1,834 m).

Sicily is the largest island in the Mediterranean at 9,926 sq miles (25,708 sq km)

The southeastern tip of Sicily lies 95 miles (152 km) from the northern African mainland and is part of the same geological region.

The Strait of Messina (*Stretto di Messina*) is between 2 and 12 miles (3–19 km) wide. It is a rich fishing ground.

Present-day crater has developed within the old crater of Monte Somma

Old crater

Vesuvius (*Vesuvio*)

Monte Somma

Old crater

There have been four volcanoes on the site of Vesuvius since volcanic activity began here more than 10,000 years ago.

USING THE LAND

ITALY PRODUCES 95% of its own food. The best farming land is in the Po Valley in northern Italy, where soft wheat and rice are grown. Irrigation is essential to agriculture in much of the south. Italy is a major producer and exporter of citrus fruits, olives, tomatoes, and wine.

THE URBAN/RURAL POPULATION DIVIDE

urban 69%   rural 31%

TOTAL LAND AREA
116,320 sq miles
(301,270 sq km)

POPULATION DENSITY
497 people per sq mile
(196 people per sq km)

Land use and agricultural distribution

- cattle
- cereals
- citrus fruits
- olive oil
- rice
- vineyards

- capital cities
- major towns

- pasture
- cropland
- forest
- mountain region

SCALE 1:2,500,000
(projection: Lambert Conformal Conic)

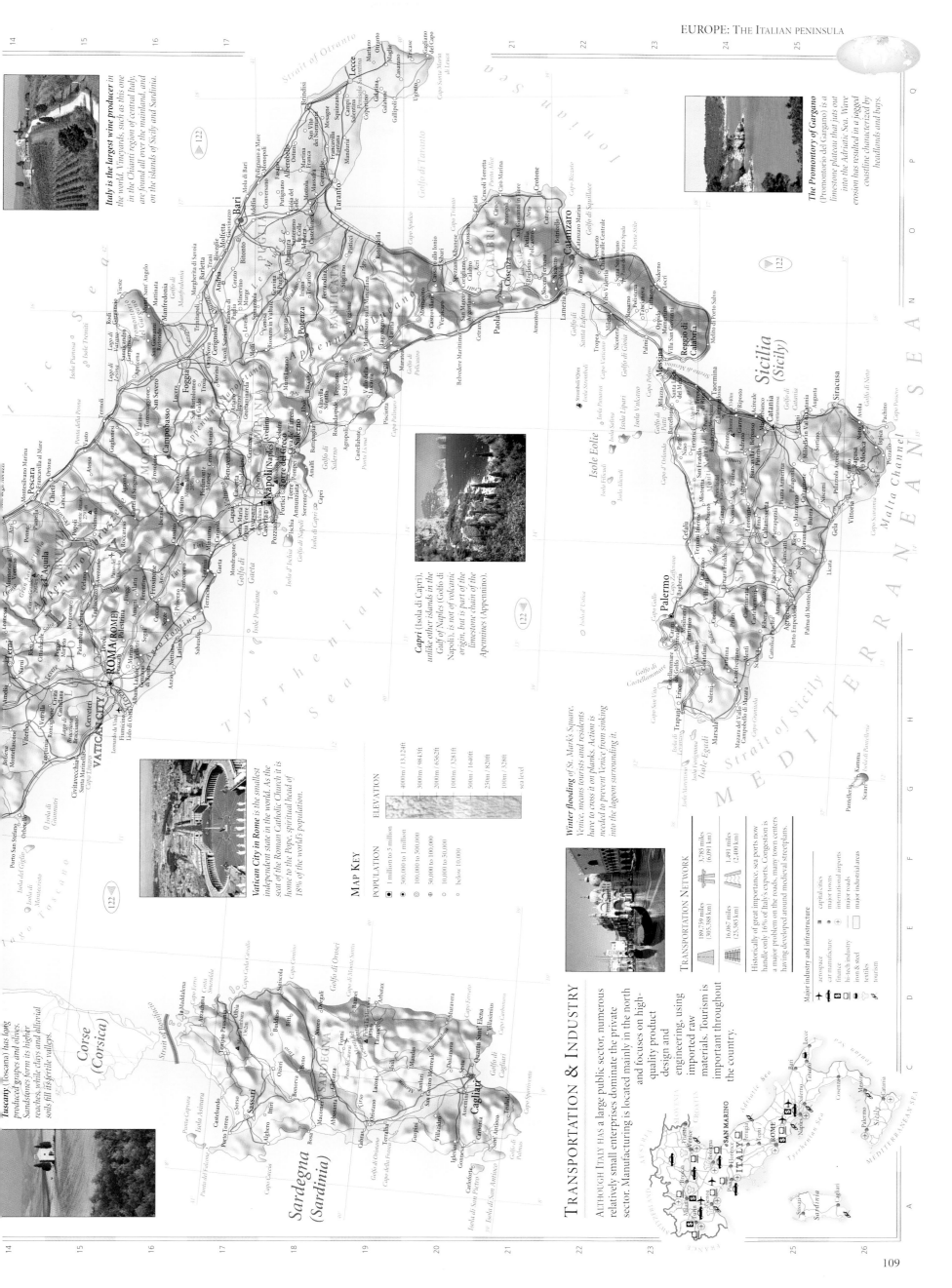

Italy is the largest wine producer in the world. Vineyards, such as this one in the Chianti region of central Italy, are found all over the mainland, and on the islands of Sicily and Sardinia.

The Promontory of Gargano (Promontorio del Gargano) is a limestone plateau that juts out into the Adriatic Sea. Wave erosion has resulted in a jagged coastline characterized by headlands and bays.

Capri (Isola di Capri), unlike other islands in the Gulf of Naples (Golfo di Napoli), is not of volcanic origin, but is part of the limestone chain of the Apennines (Appennino).

Vatican City in Rome is the smallest independent state in the world. As the seat of the Roman Catholic Church it is home to the Pope, spiritual head of 18% of the world's population.

Winter flooding of St. Mark's Square, Venice, means tourists and residents have to cross it on planks. Action is needed to prevent Venice from sinking into the lagoon surrounding it.

Tuscany (Toscana) has long produced grapes and olives. Sandstones form its higher reaches, while clays and alluvial soils fill its fertile valleys.

MAP KEY

POPULATION

● 1 million to 5 million
◉ 500,000 to 1 million
◎ 100,000 to 500,000
⊕ 50,000 to 100,000
○ 10,000 to 50,000
° below 10,000

ELEVATION

4000m / 13,124ft
3000m / 9843ft
2000m / 6562ft
1000m / 3281ft
500m / 1640ft
250m / 820ft
100m / 328ft
sea level

TRANSPORTATION & INDUSTRY

ALTHOUGH ITALY HAS a large public sector, numerous relatively small enterprises dominate the private sector. Manufacturing is located mainly in the north and focuses on high-quality product design and engineering, using imported raw materials. Tourism is important throughout the country.

TRANSPORTATION NETWORK

189,759 miles (305,388 km)	3,785 miles (6,091 km)
16,067 miles (25,585 km)	1,491 miles (2,400 km)

Historically of great importance, sea ports now handle only 16% of Italy's exports. Congestion is a major problem on the roads, many town centers having developed around medieval streetplans.

Major industry and infrastructure

aerospace
car manufacture
finance
hi-tech industry
iron & steel
textiles
tourism

capital cities
major towns
international airports
major roads
major industrial areas

Corse (Corsica)

Sardegna (Sardinia)

Sicilia (Sicily)

Stretto di Messina

MEDITERRANEAN SEA

THE ALPINE STATES

AUSTRIA, LIECHTENSTEIN, SLOVENIA, SWITZERLAND

THE ALPINE COUNTRIES of Austria, Switzerland, Liechtenstein, and Slovenia form a narrow strip across western Europe's geographical core, lying on the main north–south trading routes across the Alps. Switzerland, politically neutral since 1815, is an important international meeting place and houses one of the headquarters of the United Nations, although not a member itself. Once at the heart of the great Habsburg Empire, Austria has been a fully independent nation since 1955, and maintains a deserved reputation as an international center of culture. Slovenia declared independence from the former Yugoslavia in 1991 and despite initial economic hardship, is now starting to achieve the prosperity enjoyed by its Alpine neighbors.

USING THE LAND

THE ALPINE REGION'S mountainous terrain discourages cultivation over much of the land area. The primary agricultural activity is raising dairy and beef cattle on the pastureland of the lower mountain slopes. Austria is self-supporting in grains, and crops such as wheat, barley, and grapes are grown in the eastern Austrian lowlands. Woodlands are more prevalent in the eastern Alps; both Austria and Slovenia have large tracts of forest.

Land use and agricultural distribution

- cattle
- pigs
- cereals
- vineyards
- capital cities
- major towns
- pasture
- cropland
- forest
- mountain region

The Matterhorn, on the Swiss–Italian border, is one of the highest mountains in the Alps, at 14,692 ft (4,478 m). The term "horn" refers to its distinctive peak, formed by three glaciers eroding hollows, known as cirques, in each of its sides.

THE LANDSCAPE

THE ALPS OCCUPY THREE-FIFTHS OF SWITZERLAND, most of southern Austria, and the northwest of Slovenia. They were formed by the collision of the African and Eurasian tectonic plates, which began 65 million years ago. Their complex geology is reflected in the differing heights and rock types of the various ranges. The Rhine flows along Liechtenstein's border with Switzerland, creating a broad floodplain in the north and west of Liechtenstein. In the far northeast and east are a number of lowland regions, including the Vienna Basin, Burgenland, and the plain of the Danube. Slovenia's major rivers flow across the lower eastern regions; in the west, the rivers flow underground through the limestone Karst region.

Original height after uplift and folding

Folded strata are overturned, creating a *nappe*

Eurasian Plate

Present-day height of Alps

African Plate

The convergence of the African and Eurasian plates compressed and folded huge masses of rock strata. As the plates continued to move together, the folded strata were overturned, creating complex nappes. Much of the rock strata has since been eroded, resulting in the current topography of the Alps.

Constricted as it cuts through ridges in the Alps, the Danube meanders across the lowlands, where uplift combined with river erosion has deepened meanders.

The Vienna Basin lies mainly below 390 ft (120 m). It gradually subsided and filled with sediment as the Alps were uplifted.

Neusiedler See straddles the border of Austria and Hungary; the area around it provides some of the best wine-growing land in Austria.

The mountains of the Jura form a natural border between Switzerland and France. Their marine limestones date from more than 200 million years ago. When the Alps were folded, the Jura were folded into a series of parallel ridges and troughs.

Tectonic activity has resulted in dramatic changes in land height over very short distances. Lake Geneva, lying at 1,221 ft (372 m) is only 43 miles (70 km) away from the 15,772-ft (4,807-m) peak of Mont Blanc, on the France–Italy border.

The Bernese Alps (*Berner Alpen*) contain the Aletsch, which at 15 miles (24 km) is the longest Alpine glacier.

The Rhine, like other major Alpine rivers, follows a broad, flat trough between the mountains. Along part of its course, the Rhine forms the boundary between Switzerland and Liechtenstein.

The deep, blue lakes of the Karst region of Slovenia are part of a drainage network that runs largely underground through this limestone area.

Karst region, Slovenia

The first road through the Brenner Pass was built in 1772, although it has been used as a mountain route since Roman times. It is the lowest of the main Alpine passes at 4,298 ft (1,374 m).

The limestone cave system at Postojna extends for more than 10 miles (16 km) and includes caverns reaching 125 ft (40 m) in height and width.

The Tauern range in the central Austrian Alps contains the highest mountain in Austria, the towering Grossglockner, rising 12,461 ft (3,798 m).

The Austrian Alps comprise three distinct mountain ranges, separated by deep trenches. The northern and southern ranges are rugged limestone, while the Tauern range is made of crystalline rocks.

THE URBAN/RURAL POPULATION DIVIDE

58% urban　　　42% rural

0 10 20 30 40 50 60 70 80 90 100

POPULATION DENSITY
454 people per sq mile
(175 people per sq km)

TOTAL LAND AREA
36,390 sq miles
(94,275 sq km)

In this mountainous region, the flatter, more accessible areas are often used for both cattle grazing and recreation.

These converging glaciers are marked by dark lines of moraine. This eroded material is carried by glaciers and deposited as the ice melts.

SCALE 1:1,750,000
(projection: Lambert Conformal Conic)

Km
0 5 10 20 30 40 50 60

Miles
0 5 10 20 30 40 50 60

TRANSPORTATION & INDUSTRY

ALL FOUR NATIONS concentrate on high-quality manufacturing and services. Austrian iron and steel production is complemented by construction industries; and Slovenia, traditionally the industrial powerhouse of the western Balkans, has increasingly diversified industries. Liechtenstein and Switzerland, lacking raw materials, produce pharmaceuticals and precision instruments, like watches, and act as international banking centers. The spectacular scenery of the region encourages tourism all year round.

TRANSPORTATION NETWORK

120,180 miles (193,526 km)	1,890 miles (3,041 km)
7,481 miles (12,047 km)	1,027 miles (1,654 km)

Tunnels and passes through the Alps are an important feature of this region. The NEAT project, providing two new high-speed rail links between Basel and Milan, was given approval in 1992.

The Austrian Tirol contains some of the most spectacular Alpine scenery. Snow cover is a permanent feature in the highest reaches.

MAP KEY

POPULATION

- 1 million to 5 million
- 500,000 to 1 million
- 100,000 to 500,000
- 50,000 to 100,000
- 10,000 to 50,000
- below 10,000

ELEVATION

4000m / 13,124ft
3000m / 9843ft
2000m / 6562ft
1000m / 3281ft
500m / 1640ft
250m / 820ft
100m / 328ft
sea level

Major industry and infrastructure

- car manufacture
- chemicals
- engineering
- finance
- food processing
- iron & steel
- pharmaceuticals
- textiles
- tourism
- watchmaking
- winter sports
- capital cities
- major towns
- international airports
- major roads
- major industrial areas

The Schönbrunn Palace, in Vienna, was the summer residence of the Habsburg monarchy. Today, it is a major tourist attraction.

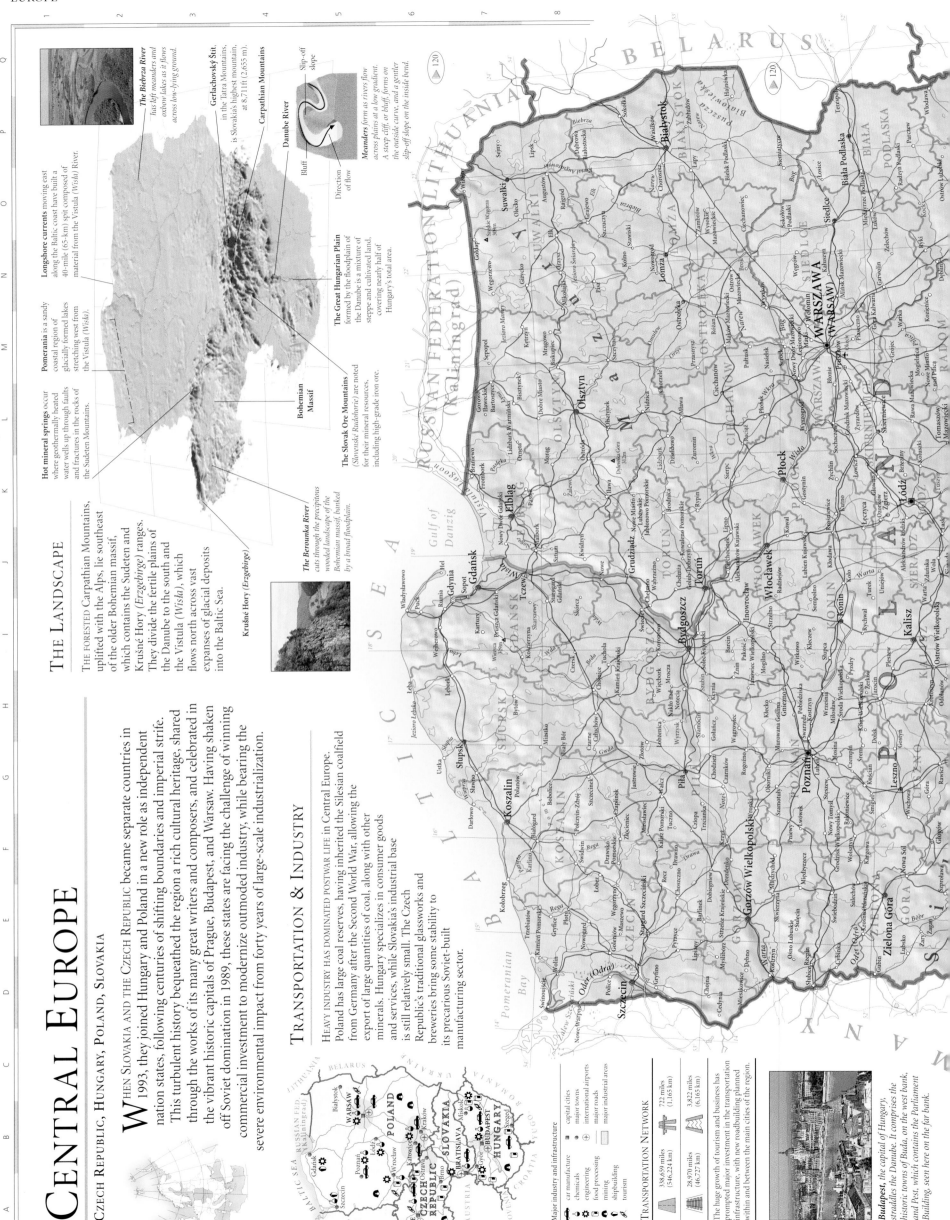

CENTRAL EUROPE

CZECH REPUBLIC, HUNGARY, POLAND, SLOVAKIA

WHEN SLOVAKIA AND THE CZECH REPUBLIC became separate countries in 1993, they joined Hungary and Poland in a new role as independent nation states, following centuries of shifting boundaries and imperial strife. This turbulent history bequeathed the region a rich cultural heritage, shared through the works of its many great writers and composers, and celebrated in the vibrant historic capitals of Prague, Budapest, and Warsaw. Having shaken off Soviet domination in 1989, these states are facing the challenge of winning commercial investment to modernize outmoded industry, while bearing the severe environmental impact from forty years of large-scale industrialization.

THE LANDSCAPE

THE FORESTED Carpathian Mountains, uplifted with the Alps, lie southeast of the older Bohemian massif, which contains the Sudeten and Krušné Hory (Erzgebirge) ranges. They divide the fertile plains of the Danube to the south and the Vistula (Wisła), which flows north across vast expanses of glacial deposits into the Baltic Sea.

Hot mineral springs occur where geothermally heated water wells up through faults and fractures in the rocks of the Sudeten Mountains.

Pomerania is a sandy coastal region of glacially formed lakes stretching west from the Vistula (Wisła).

Longshore currents moving east along the Baltic coast have built a 40-mile (65-km) spit composed of material from the Vistula (Wisła) River.

The Biebrza River has left meanders and oxbow lakes as it flows across low-lying ground.

Gerlachovský Štít, in the Tatra Mountains, is Slovakia's highest mountain, at 8,711ft (2,655 m).

Carpathian Mountains

Danube River

The Great Hungarian Plain formed by the floodplain of the Danube is a mixture of steppe and cultivated land, covering nearly half of Hungary's total area.

The Slovak Ore Mountains (Slovenské Rudohorie) are noted for their mineral resources, including high-grade iron ore.

Bohemian Massif

Krušné Hory (Erzgebirge)

The Berounka River cuts through the precipitous wooded landscape of the Bohemian massif, banked by a broad floodplain.

Slip-off slope

Bluff

Direction of flow

Meanders form as rivers flow across plains at a low gradient. A steep cliff, or bluff, forms on the outside curve, and a gentler slip-off slope on the inside bend.

TRANSPORTATION & INDUSTRY

HEAVY INDUSTRY HAS DOMINATED POSTWAR LIFE in Central Europe. Poland has large coal reserves, having inherited the Silesian coalfield from Germany after the Second World War, allowing the export of large quantities of coal, along with other minerals. Hungary specializes in consumer goods and services, while Slovakia's industrial base is still relatively small. The Czech Republic's traditional glassworks and breweries bring some stability to its precarious Soviet-built manufacturing sector.

Major industry and infrastructure

car manufacture
chemicals
engineering
food processing
mining
shipbuilding
tourism

capital cities
major towns
international airports
major roads
major industrial areas

TRANSPORTATION NETWORK

338,659 miles (546,224 km)	722 miles (1,165 km)	
28,970 miles (46,727 km)	3,822 miles (6,165 km)	

The huge growth of tourism and business has prompted major investment in the transportation infrastructure, with new roadbuilding planned within and between the main cities of the region.

Budapest, the capital of Hungary, straddles the Danube. It comprises the historic towns of Buda, on the west bank, and Pest, which contains the Parliament Building, seen here on the far bank.

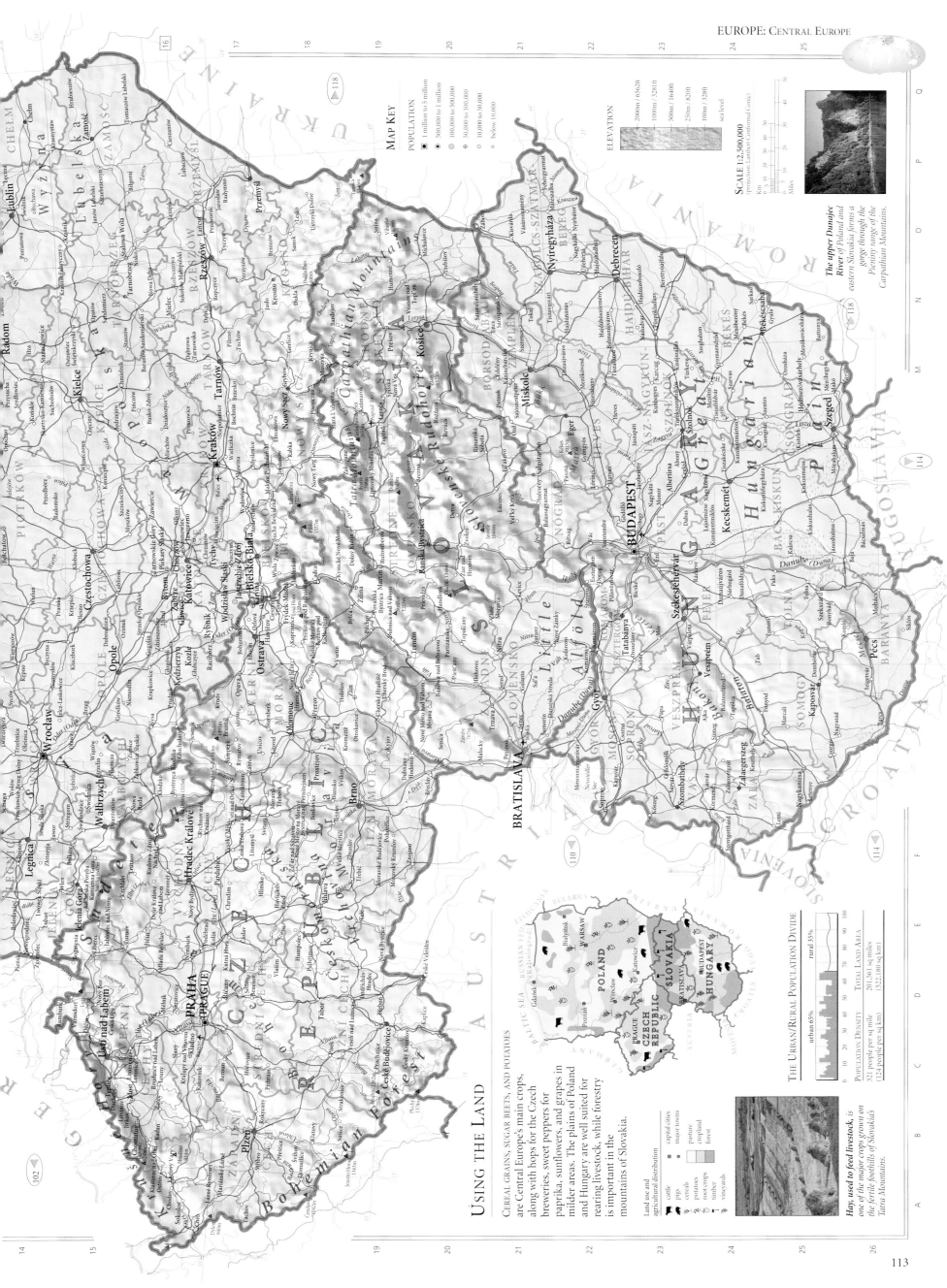

USING THE LAND

CEREAL GRAINS, SUGAR BEETS, AND POTATOES are Central Europe's main crops, along with hops for the Czech breweries, sunflowers, and grapes in milder areas. The plains of Poland and Hungary are well suited for rearing livestock, while forestry is important in the mountains of Slovakia.

The upper Dunajec River of Poland and eastern Slovakia forms a gorge through the Pieniny range of the Carpathian Mountains.

Hay, used to feed livestock, is one of the major crops grown on the fertile foothills of Slovakia's Tatra Mountains.

Land use and agricultural distribution
- cattle
- pigs
- cereals
- potatoes
- root crops
- timber
- vineyards

capital cities
major towns
pasture
cropland
forest

THE URBAN/RURAL POPULATION DIVIDE

urban 65%   rural 35%

POPULATION DENSITY
321 people per sq mile
(124 people per sq km)

TOTAL LAND AREA
201,561 sq miles
(522,180 sq km)

SCALE 1:2,500,000
(projection: Lambert Conformal Conic)

MAP KEY

POPULATION
- 1 million to 5 million
- 500,000 to 1 million
- 100,000 to 500,000
- 50,000 to 100,000
- 10,000 to 50,000
- below 10,000

ELEVATION
- 2000m / 6562ft
- 1000m / 3281ft
- 500m / 1640ft
- 250m / 820ft
- 100m / 328ft
- sea level

THE WESTERN BALKANS

ALBANIA, BOSNIA & HERZEGOVINA, CROATIA, MACEDONIA, YUGOSLAVIA

FOR 46 YEARS THE FEDERATION of Yugoslavia held together the most diverse ethnic region in Europe, along the picturesque mountain hinterland of the Dalmatian coast. Economic collapse resulted in internal tensions. The Serbian government regained central control over the previously autonomous regions of Kosovo and Vojvodina. In June 1991 Croatia and Slovenia (page 110) declared independence and Yugoslavia fragmented into five new nations. Bosnia and Herzegovina was devastated as Serbs and Croats struggled to establish ethnically exclusive territories, while the Bosnian government sought to preserve the country's multiethnic character. Albania is slowly emerging from the long isolation imposed by the communist Hoxha regime.

Hot, dry summers and mild winters offer excellent conditions for viticulture in Montenegro. The precipitous Dinaric Alps have kept this region relatively isolated for centuries.

THE LANDSCAPE

THE TISZA, SAVA, AND DRAVA RIVERS drain the broad northern lowland, meeting the Danube after it crosses the Hungarian border. In the west, the Dinaric Alps divide the Adriatic Sea from the interior. Mainland valleys and elongated islands run parallel to the steep Dalmatian (*Dalmacija*) coastline, following alternating bands of resistant limestone.

SCALE 1:2,500,000
(projection: Lambert Conformal Conic)

Km
0 5 10 20 30 40 50 60 70

Miles
0 10 20 30 40 50

The river floodplains of the Pannonian Basin are flanked by terraces of gravel and wind-blown glacial deposits, known as loess.

Tisza River

At least 70% of all fresh water in the Western Balkans drains into the Black Sea, mostly via the Danube (Dunav).

Drava River

Sava River

The elongated islands, promontories and straits of the Dalmatian (Dalmacija) coast were formed as the Adriatic Sea rose to flood valleys running parallel to the shore.

Dalmatian (Dalmacija) coast

Limestone cliffs along the Dalmatian (Dalmacija) shoreline are heavily eroded, as saltwater dissolves the rock along existing horizontal cracks, or joints. This tends to form a platform of rock at the foot of the cliff.

Polijes in the Kosovo region

Sheer limestone walls enclose all sides

Flat polje floor

Underground drainage along joints in the rock

Spring at foot of cliff

Rain and underground water dissolve limestone along massive vertical joints (cracks). This creates poljes: depressions several miles across with steep walls and broad, flat floors.

At Iron Gate (Derdap), on the border with Romania, the Danube narrows and cuts through foothills of the Balkan and Carpathian mountains, forming the deepest gorge in Europe.

A major earthquake at Skopje, Macedonia, in 1963 killed 1,000 people. The whole region lies on an active crustal plate margin.

Lake Ohrid

A series of river valleys breaking through the Dinaric Alps from the lowlands of western Albania give access to the interior.

Lake Ohrid borders Albania and Macedonia. Ohrid is the deepest lake in the Western Balkans, reaching depths of 938 ft (286 m).

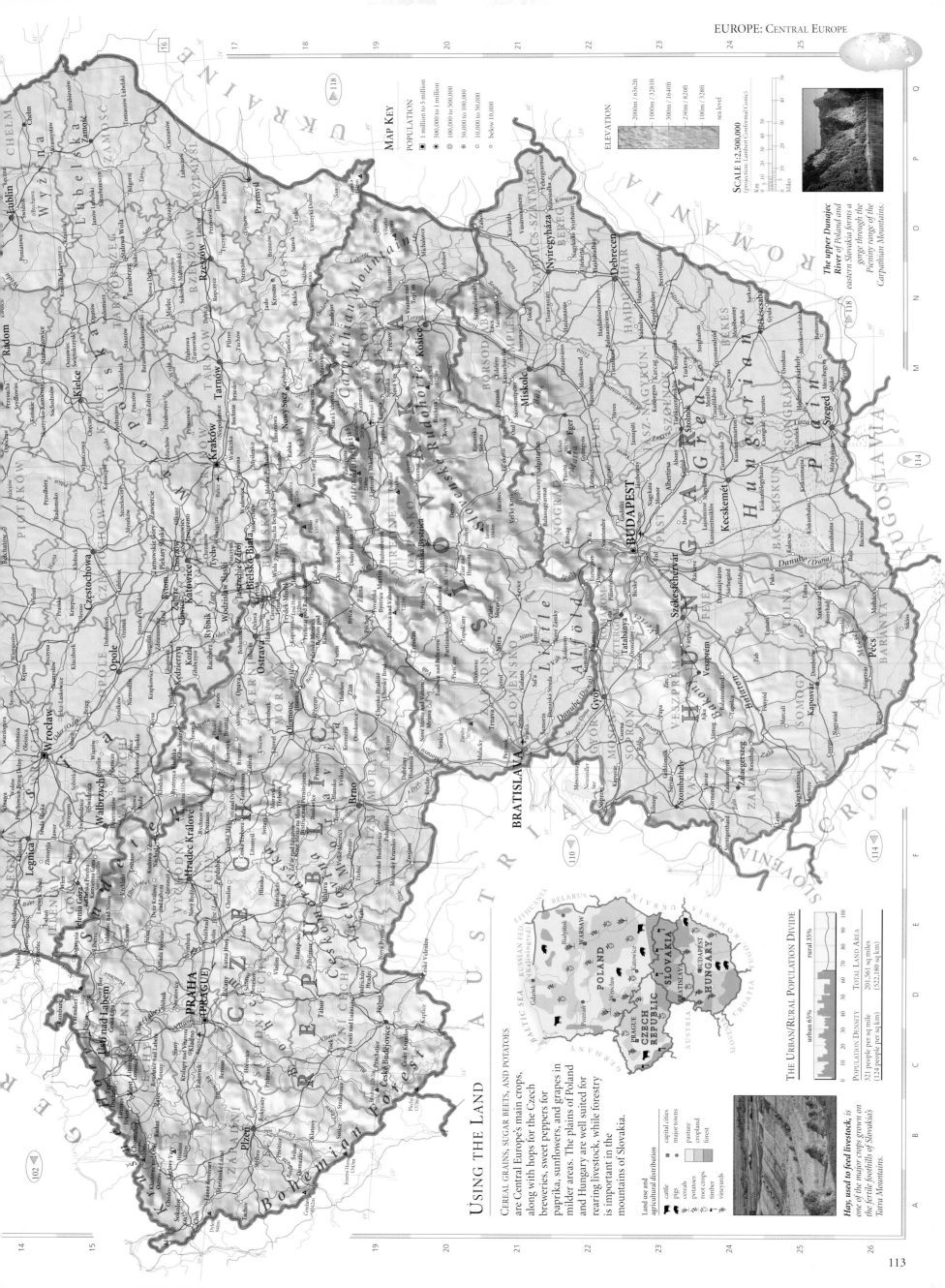

MAP KEY

POPULATION

- ● 1 million to 5 million
- ◉ 500,000 to 1 million
- ⊕ 100,000 to 500,000
- ○ 50,000 to 100,000
- ○ 10,000 to 50,000
- ○ below 10,000

ELEVATION

- 2000m / 6562ft
- 1000m / 3281ft
- 500m / 1640ft
- 250m / 820ft
- 100m / 328ft
- sea level

SCALE 1:2,500,000
(projection: Lambert Conformal Conic)

The upper Dunajec River of Poland and eastern Slovakia forms a gorge through the Pieniny range of the Carpathian Mountains.

USING THE LAND

CEREAL GRAINS, SUGAR BEETS, AND POTATOES are Central Europe's main crops, along with hops for the Czech breweries, sweet peppers for paprika, sunflowers, and grapes in milder areas. The plains of Poland and Hungary are well suited for rearing livestock, while forestry is important in the mountains of Slovakia.

Land use and agricultural distribution

- 🐄 cattle
- 🐖 pigs
- ✿ cereals
- ✿ potatoes
- ✿ root crops
- ▲ timber
- ♦ vineyards

- ■ capital cities
- ● major towns
- pasture
- cropland
- forest

Hay, used to feed livestock, is one of the major crops grown on the fertile foothills of Slovakia's Tatra Mountains.

THE URBAN/RURAL POPULATION DIVIDE

urban 65%   rural 35%

POPULATION DENSITY
321 people per sq mile
(124 people per sq km)

TOTAL LAND AREA
201,561 sq miles
(522,180 sq km)

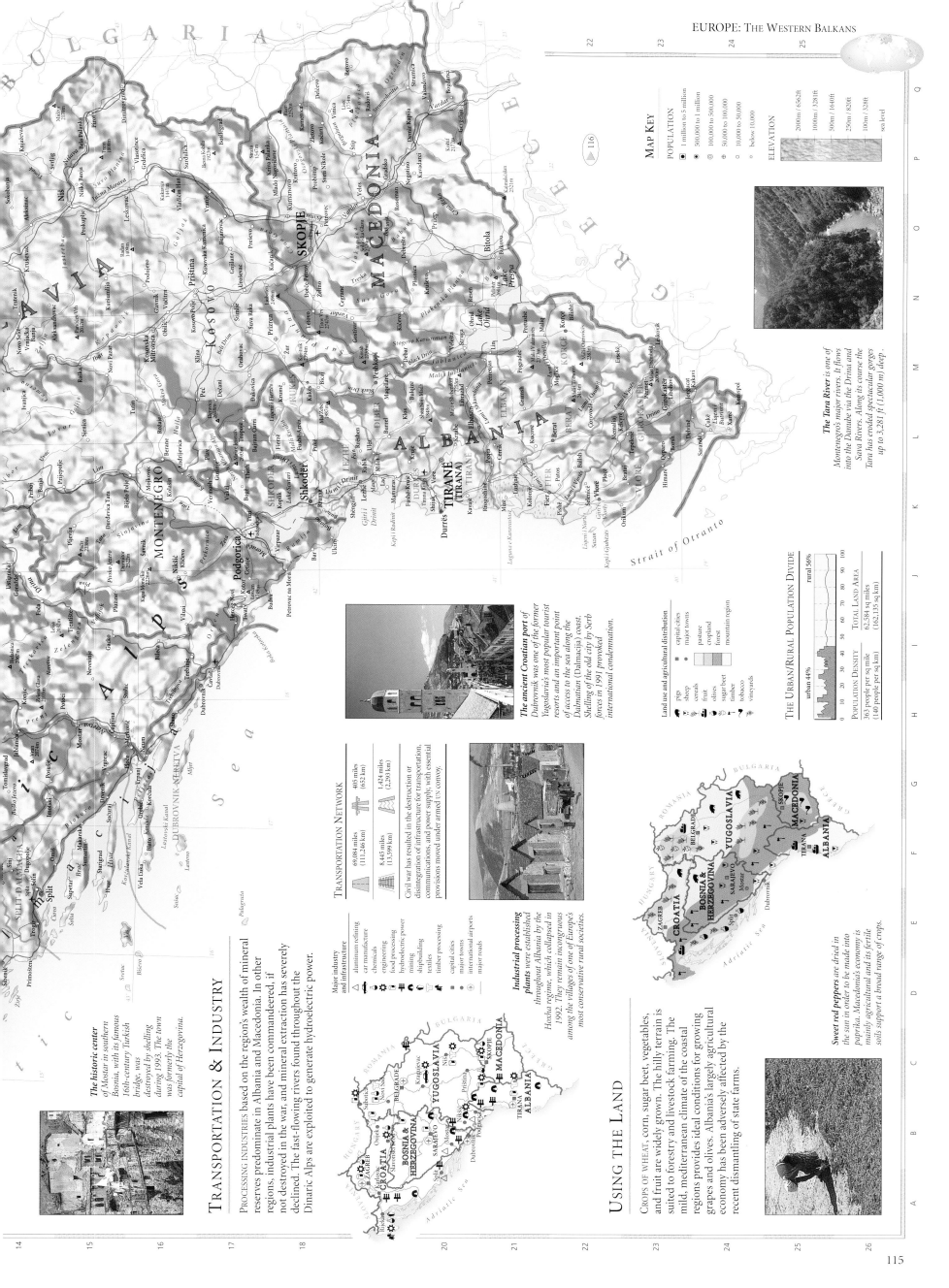

MAP KEY

POPULATION

- ● 1 million to 5 million
- ⊚ 500,000 to 1 million
- ⊙ 100,000 to 500,000
- ⊕ 50,000 to 100,000
- ⊙ 10,000 to 50,000
- ○ below 10,000

ELEVATION

- 2000m / 6562ft
- 1000m / 3281ft
- 500m / 1640ft
- 250m / 820ft
- 100m / 328ft
- sea level

▲ 116

The Tara River is one of Montenegro's major rivers. It flows into the Danube via the Drina and Sava Rivers. Along its course the Tara has eroded spectacular gorges up to 3,281 ft (1,000 m) deep.

The ancient Croatian port of Dubrovnik was one of the former Yugoslavia's most popular tourist resorts and an important point of access to the sea along the Dalmatian (Dalmacija) coast. Shelling of the old city by Serb forces in 1991 provoked international condemnation.

Land use and agricultural distribution

- capital cities
- major towns
- pigs
- sheep
- cereals — pasture
- fruit — cropland
- olives — forest
- sugar beet — mountain region
- timber
- tobacco
- vineyards

THE URBAN/RURAL POPULATION DIVIDE

urban 44%   rural 56%

POPULATION DENSITY	TOTAL LAND AREA
363 people per sq mile (140 people per sq km)	62,584 sq miles (162,135 sq km)

Civil war has resulted in the destruction or disintegration of infrastructure for transportation, communications, and power supply, with essential provisions moved under armed UN convoy.

TRANSPORTATION NETWORK

69,084 miles (111,246 km)	405 miles (652 km)
8,445 miles (13,599 km)	1,424 miles (2,293 km)

Industrial processing plants were established throughout Albania by the Hoxha regime, which collapsed in 1992. They remain incongruous among the villages of one of Europe's most conservative rural societies.

TRANSPORTATION & INDUSTRY

PROCESSING INDUSTRIES based on the region's wealth of mineral reserves predominate in Albania and Macedonia. In other regions, industrial plants have been commandeered, if not destroyed in the war, and mineral extraction has severely declined. The fast-flowing rivers found throughout the Dinaric Alps are exploited to generate hydroelectric power.

Major industry and infrastructure

- △ aluminum refining
- ⚙ car manufacture
- chemicals
- engineering
- food processing
- hydroelectric power
- mining
- shipbuilding
- textiles
- timber processing
- capital cities
- major towns
- international airports
- major roads

The historic center of Mostar in southern Bosnia, with its famous 16th-century Turkish bridge, was destroyed by shelling during 1993. The town was formerly the capital of Herzegovina.

USING THE LAND

CROPS OF WHEAT, corn, sugar beet, vegetables, and fruit are widely grown. The hilly terrain is suited to forestry and livestock farming. The mild, mediterranean climate of the coastal regions provides ideal conditions for growing grapes and olives. Albania's largely agricultural economy has been adversely affected by the recent dismantling of state farms.

Sweet red peppers are dried in the sun in order to be made into paprika. Macedonia's economy is mainly agricultural and its fertile soils support a broad range of crops.

BULGARIA & GREECE

Including EUROPEAN TURKEY

G REECE IS RENOWNED as the original hearth of Western civilization. Its rugged terrain and numerous islands have profoundly affected its development, creating a strong agricultural and maritime tradition. In the past 50 years, this formerly rural society has rapidly urbanized, with more than half of the population now living in the capital, Athens, and in the northern city of Salonica. Bulgaria, dominated for centuries by the Ottoman Turks, became part of the eastern bloc after the Second World War, only slowly emerging from Soviet influence in 1989. Moves toward democracy have led to some political instability and Bulgaria has been slow to align its economy with the rest of Europe.

TRANSPORTATION & INDUSTRY

S OVIET INVESTMENT introduced heavy industry into Bulgaria and the processing of agricultural produce, such as tobacco, is important throughout the country. Both countries have substantial shipyards and Greece has one of the world's largest merchant fleets. Many small craft workshops, producing textiles and processed foods, are clustered around Greek cities. The service and construction sectors have profited from the successful tourist industry.

Major industry and infrastructure
- chemicals
- engineering
- food processing
- shipbuilding
- textiles
- tourism
- capital cities
- major towns
- international airports
- major roads
- major industrial areas

TRANSPORTATION NETWORK

103,930 miles (167,650 km)	
345 miles (557 km)	
345 miles (557 km)	
294 miles (474 km)	

Bulgaria's railroads require investment to revive an outdated infrastructure. In Greece, despite a developing road network, ferry-boats remain the most effective form of transportation in many areas.

THE LANDSCAPE

B ULGARIA'S BALKAN MOUNTAINS divide the Danubian Plain (*Dunavska Ravnina*) and Maritsa Basin, meeting the Black Sea in the east along sandy beaches. The steep Rhodope Mountains form a natural barrier with Greece, while the younger Pindus form a rugged central spine. This descends into the Aegean Sea to give a vast archipelago of more than 2,000 islands, the largest of which is Crete.

Mount Olympus is the mythical home of the Greek Gods and, at 9,570 ft (2,917 m), the highest mountain in Greece.

Limestone rocks exposed by erosion of metamorphic rocks

Ancient metamorphic rock, formed miles below the surface

Younger limestones created in shallow seas

Mount Olympus is a composite of rocks formed by two major tectonic events. First the older metamorphic rocks were thrust over the limestones, then two million years ago regional warping and subsequent erosion reexposed the limestone.

The Peloponnese consists of several mountainous peninsulas, linked to the mainland by the Isthmus of Corinth. The Corinth Canal (*Dôrýga Korínthou*), built in 1893, cuts through the isthmus, linking the Aegean and Ionian Seas.

The Danube, Europe's second longest river, forms most of Bulgaria's northern border. The Danubian Plain (*Dunavska Ravnina*), extending from the southern bank, is extremely fertile.

The Arda River cuts through the Rhodope Mountains in rugged, rocky gorges.

Balkan Mountains

Maritsa Basin

Rhodope Mountains

The islands of Crete, Kýthira, Kárpathos, and Rhodes are part of an arc that bends southeastward from the Peloponnese, forming the southern boundary of the Aegean.

Layers of black volcanic ash still cover the island of Thíra. This volcano last erupted 3,500 years ago, but still shows signs of volcanic activity.

Rhodes

Kárpathos

Crete

Kýthira

Corinth Canal (*Dôrýga Korínthou*)

Rhodope Mountains

Pindus Mountains

Mount Olympus

SCALE 1:2,500,000
(projection: Lambert Conformal Conic)

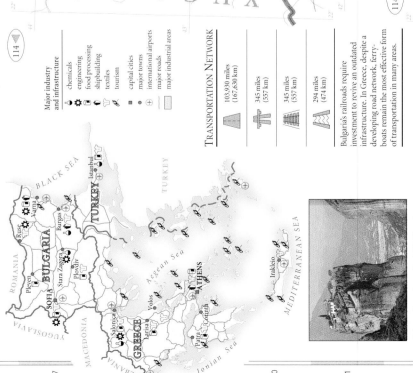

A towering pinnacle at Metéora in central Greece is home to the monastery of Roussánou. The 24 rock towers that dominate the plain of Thessaly (Thessalía) are remnants of an old plateau. Long-term weathering along fissures in the rock has worn away the rest of the plateau.

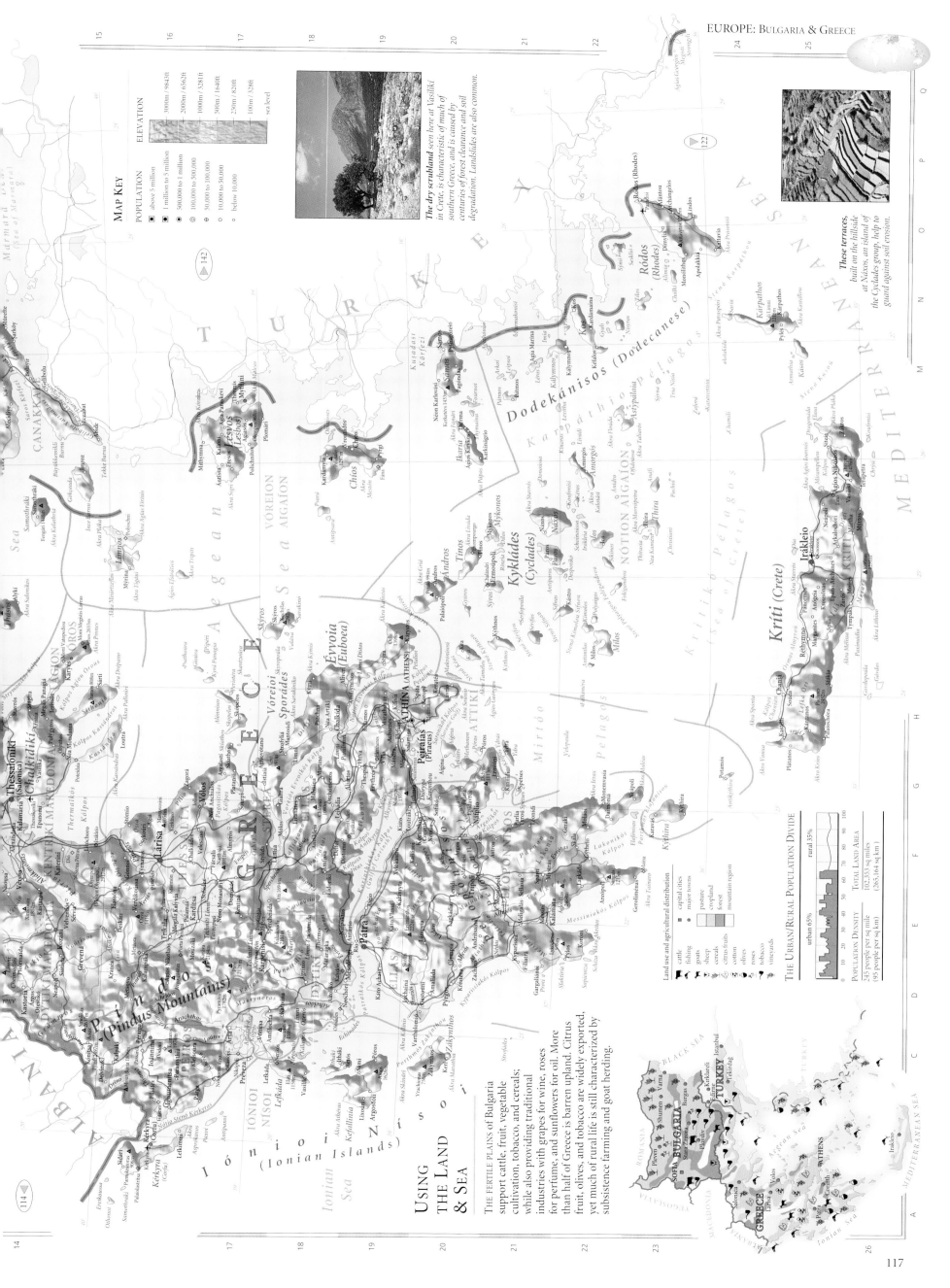

MAP KEY

POPULATION

- ■ above 5 million
- ■ 1 million to 5 million
- ◉ 500,000 to 1 million
- ⊕ 100,000 to 500,000
- ⊙ 50,000 to 100,000
- ○ 10,000 to 50,000
- ○ below 10,000

ELEVATION

- 3000m / 9843ft
- 2000m / 6562ft
- 1000m / 3281ft
- 500m / 1640ft
- 250m / 820ft
- 100m / 328ft
- sea level

The dry scrubland seen here at Vasilikí in Crete, is characteristic of much of southern Greece, and is caused by centuries of forest clearance and soil degradation. Landslides are also common.

These terraces, built on the hillside at Náxos, an island of the Cyclades group, help to guard against soil erosion.

USING THE LAND & SEA

THE FERTILE PLAINS of Bulgaria support cattle, fruit, vegetable cultivation, tobacco, and cereals; while also providing traditional industries with grapes for wine, roses for perfume, and sunflowers for oil. More than half of Greece is barren upland. Citrus fruit, olives, and tobacco are widely exported, yet much of rural life is still characterized by subsistence farming and goat herding.

Land use and agricultural distribution

- cattle
- goats
- sheep
- cereals
- citrus fruits
- cotton
- olives
- roses
- tobacco
- vineyards

- ● capital cities
- ● major towns
- pasture
- cropland
- forest
- mountain region

THE URBAN/RURAL POPULATION DIVIDE

urban 65%   rural 35%

POPULATION DENSITY
245 people per sq mile
(95 people per sq km)

TOTAL LAND AREA
102,353 sq miles
(265,164 sq km)

Selected map labels: ALBANIA, TURKEY, GREECE, Thessaloníki (Salonica), Chalkidiki, Lárisa, THESSALÍA, Vólos, Píndos (Pindus Mountains), PELOPÓNNISOS, Pátra, ATHÍNA (ATHENS), Peiraiás (Piraeus), ATTIKÍ, Évvoia (Euboea), Vóreioi Sporádes, Lésvos (Lesbos), Chíos, Límnos, Samothráki, Kykládes (Cyclades), Náxos, Ándros, Tínos, Mýkonos, Amorgós, NÓTION AIGAÍON, VÓREION AIGAÍON, Aegean Sea, Dodekánisos (Dodecanese), Ródos (Rhodes), Kárpathos, Kríti (Crete), Irákleio, Chaniá, Réthymno, Sitía, Kritikó Pélagos (Sea of Crete), MEDITERRANEAN SEA, Mirtóo Pélagos, Iónioi Nísoi (Ionian Islands), Kérkyra (Corfu), Kefallinía, Zákynthos, Ionian Sea

ROMANIA, MOLDOVA & UKRAINE

THE INDUSTRIAL, SOCIAL, AND CULTURAL makeup of Romania and the former Soviet states of Moldova and Ukraine still bears the imprint of their communist past. As part of the USSR, Ukraine was a leading agricultural, industrial, and energy producer. These industries, like those in Moldova and Romania, are now being reoriented more firmly toward Western markets. As a result of shifting borders, and Soviet policy actively encouraging Russian immigration into other Soviet states like Ukraine and Moldova, all three countries contain large numbers of foreign nationals. Moldovans and Romanians are still close in terms of language and culture, although Moldova is striving to remain an independent nation.

USING THE LAND

THE FERTILE BLACK SOILS of Ukraine, often called "the breadbasket of Europe," have enabled the cultivation of a variety of cereals and vegetables, which are widely exported. Romania and Moldova also grow cereals, sunflowers, and vegetables, and are noted particularly for the quality of their wines.

The fertile lands and tolerant climate of Moldova are ideally suited to growing grapes for wine.

Land use and agricultural distribution

- cattle
- pigs
- poultry
- sheep
- cereals
- cotton
- sugar beet
- sunflowers
- vineyards
- capital cities
- major towns
- pasture
- cropland
- forest
- wetland

THE URBAN/RURAL POPULATION DIVIDE

urban 62% | rural 38%

0 10 20 30 40 50 60 70 80 90 100

POPULATION DENSITY
238 people per sq mile
(92 people per sq km)

TOTAL LAND AREA
334,947 sq miles
(867,740 sq km)

Glacial lakes are found throughout the Transylvanian Alps (Carpaţii Meridionali), although the mountains no longer have any permanent snow cover.

TRANSPORTATION & INDUSTRY

HEAVY INDUSTRY using local raw materials characterizes much of this region. The industrial heartland of Ukraine, specializing in metal and machine-building industries, is based around its vast mineral reserves in the Donbass region. In Moldova, food processing draws on produce from its agricultural sector. Romanian industry relies both on local raw materials and imported iron, steel, and oil.

Major industry and infrastructure

- car manufacture
- chemicals
- coal
- engineering
- food processing
- mining
- oil & gas
- textiles
- tourism
- capital cities
- major towns
- international airports
- major roads
- major industrial areas

TRANSPORTATION NETWORK

223,834 miles (361,024 km)	70 miles (113 km)
21,989 miles (35,466 km)	3,796 miles (6,124 km)

Increased industrialization has necessitated the upgrading of road and rail networks in all three countries. Modernization has tended to focus only on major cities and industrial areas.

During the 1960s and 1970s, many industries, like this carbon factory, developed using the mineral resources on the flanks of the Transylvanian Alps (Carpaţii Meridionali).

SCALE 1:3,250,000
(projection: Lambert Conformal Conic)

Km
0 10 20 30 40 50 60 70 80 90 100

Miles
0 10 20 30 40 50 60 70 80 90 100

MAP KEY

POPULATION

- 1 million to 5 million
- 500,000 to 1 million
- 100,000 to 500,000
- 50,000 to 100,000
- 10,000 to 50,000
- below 10,000

ELEVATION

2000m / 6562ft
1000m / 3281ft
500m / 1640ft
250m / 820ft
100m / 328ft
sea level

The Swallow's Nest castle, in Yalta, is one of many tourist resorts on the Crimean (Krym) coast, dubbed the "Russian Riviera."

THE LANDSCAPE

VAST FLAT LOWLANDS and gently rolling hills cover most of southeastern Europe. In the southwest, the Carpathian Mountains form a gentle arc. To the south of the Carpathian Mountains lies the Danube Plain, across which the Danube River flows to the Black Sea. To the north and east, the hills of Moldova level out into low plains, running east to the steppes of Ukraine.

Divided into crystalline massifs, the southern arm of the Carpathian Mountains, the Transylvanian Alps (Carpații Meridionali), extend 170 miles (274 km) across southwestern Romania.

The Apuseni Mountains (*Munții Apuseni*) are rich in mineral deposits, including gold and iron ore.

Transylvanian Alps (*Carpații Meridionali*)

Uplifted and folded at the same time as the Alps, some 250 miles (400 km) of the eastern Carpathian Mountains contain ancient volcanic cones and craters.

The Codrii Hills dominate the landscape of central Moldova; they are intersected by deep, flat valleys and ravines.

Steppe landscape covers two-thirds of Ukraine. These flat, treeless grasslands extend from central Europe to central Asia.

Most of the major rivers in southeastern Europe, like the Danube, the Dniester, and Dnieper, flow south and east to the Black Sea.

The Danube forms a natural border between Romania and Bulgaria.

The three branches of the Danube Delta (*Delta Dunării*) form a triangle of wetlands covering some 1,950 sq miles (5,050 sq km).

At Kryms'ki Hory, three flat-topped, parallel limestone ridges run 80 miles (128 km) along the southern coast of the Crimean (Krym) Peninsula.

Balkas are common throughout Ukraine. They are large U-shaped valleys, formed during the last Ice Age, which contain narrower, deep valleys. These were incised by a sudden flow of water, following an icemelt.

Water has eroded a new post-glacial valley

Old glaciated valley

Counterclockwise currents have created the sandspits that fringe the Sea of Azov.

RUSSIAN FEDERATION

U K R A I N E

Black Sea

Sea of Azov

Gulf of Taganrog

KYYIV (KIEV)

CHIȘINĂU

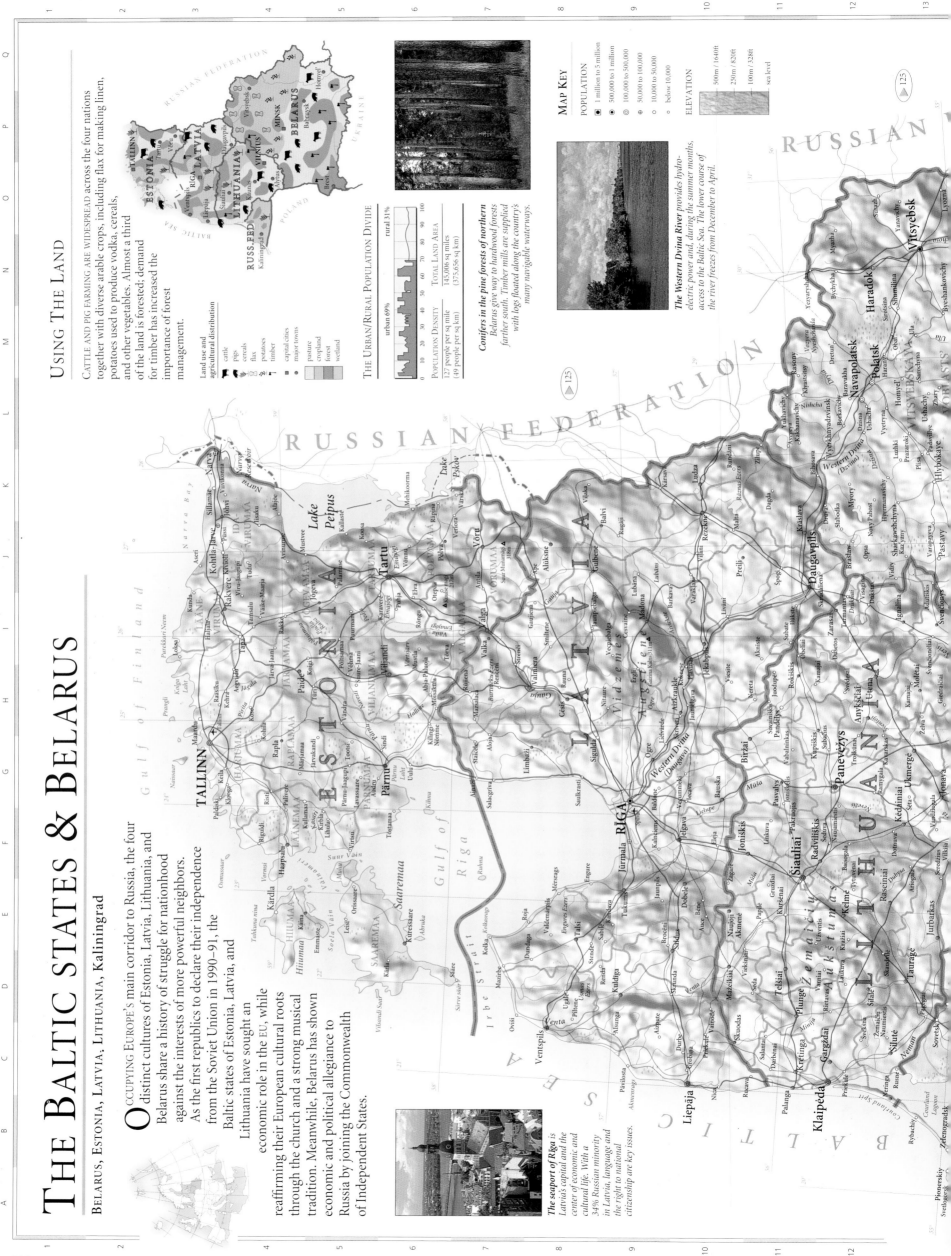

THE BALTIC STATES & BELARUS

BELARUS, ESTONIA, LATVIA, LITHUANIA, KALININGRAD

OCCUPYING EUROPE's main corridor to Russia, the four distinct cultures of Estonia, Latvia, Lithuania, and Belarus share a history of struggle for nationhood against the interests of more powerful neighbors. As the first republics to declare their independence from the Soviet Union in 1990–91, the Baltic states of Estonia, Latvia, and Lithuania have sought an economic role in the EU, while reaffirming their European cultural roots through the church and a strong musical tradition. Meanwhile, Belarus has shown economic and political allegiance to Russia by joining the Commonwealth of Independent States.

The seaport of Riga is Latvia's capital and the center of economic and cultural life. With a 34% Russian minority in Latvia, language and the right to national citizenship are key issues.

USING THE LAND

CATTLE AND PIG FARMING ARE WIDESPREAD across the four nations together with diverse arable crops, including flax for making linen, potatoes used to produce vodka, cereals, and other vegetables. Almost a third of the land is forested; demand for timber has increased the importance of forest management.

Land use and agricultural distribution

- cattle
- pigs
- flax
- potatoes
- timber
- capital cities
- major towns

- pasture
- cropland
- forest
- wetland

Conifers in the pine forests of northern Belarus give way to hardwood forests farther south. Timber mills are supplied with logs floated along the country's many navigable waterways.

The Western Dvina River provides hydro-electric power and, during the summer months, access to the Baltic Sea. The lower course of the river freezes from December to April.

THE URBAN/RURAL POPULATION DIVIDE

urban 69%   rural 31%

TOTAL LAND AREA
145,006 sq miles
(375,656 sq km)

POPULATION DENSITY
127 people per sq mile
(49 people per sq km)

MAP KEY

POPULATION
- ◉ 1 million to 5 million
- ◉ 500,000 to 1 million
- ⊕ 100,000 to 500,000
- ⊕ 50,000 to 100,000
- ⊕ 10,000 to 50,000
- ○ below 10,000

ELEVATION
- 500m / 1640ft
- 250m / 820ft
- 100m / 328ft
- sea level

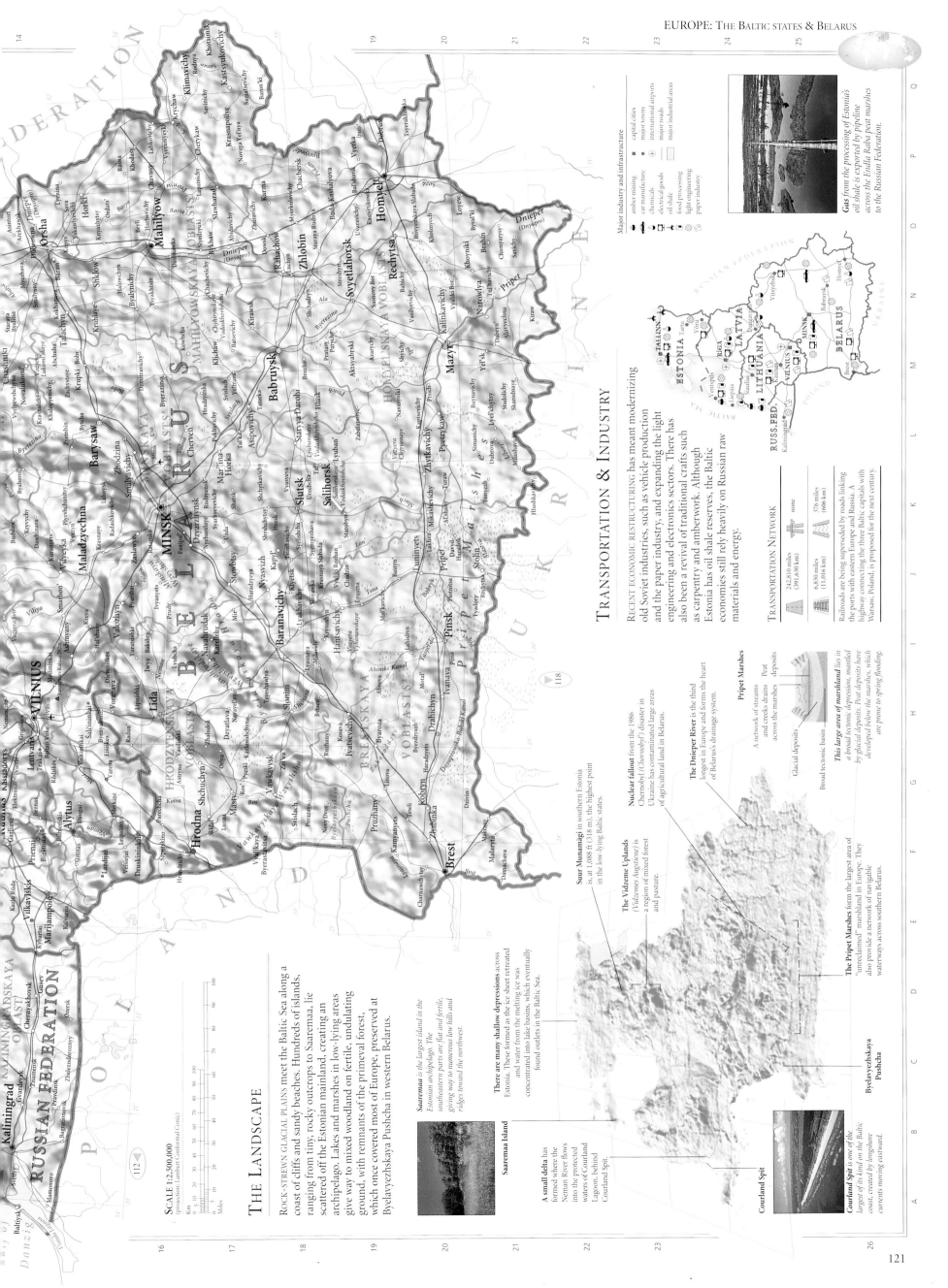

The Landscape

ROCK-STREWN GLACIAL PLAINS meet the Baltic Sea along a coast of cliffs and sandy beaches. Hundreds of islands, ranging from tiny, rocky outcrops to Saaremaa, lie scattered off the Estonian mainland, creating an archipelago. Lakes and marshes in low-lying areas give way to mixed woodland on fertile, undulating ground, with remnants of the primeval forest, which once covered most of Europe, preserved at Byelavyezhskaya Pushcha in western Belarus.

Saaremaa is the largest island in the Estonian archipelago. The southeastern parts are flat and fertile, giving way to numerous low hills and ridges toward the northwest.

Saaremaa Island

A small delta has formed where the Neman River flows into the protected waters of Courland Lagoon, behind Courland Spit.

There are many shallow depressions across Estonia. These formed as the ice sheet retreated and water from the melting ice was concentrated into lake basins, which eventually found outlets in the Baltic Sea.

Courland Spit

Courland Spit is one of the largest of its kind on the Baltic coast, created by longshore currents moving eastward.

SCALE 1:2,500,000

Projection: Lambert Conformal Conic

Transportation & Industry

RECENT ECONOMIC RESTRUCTURING has meant modernizing old Soviet industries, such as vehicle production and the paper industry, and expanding the light engineering and electronics sectors. There has also been a revival of traditional crafts such as carpentry and amberwork. Although Estonia has oil shale reserves, the Baltic economies still rely heavily on Russian raw materials and energy.

Major industry and infrastructure

- amber mining
- car manufacture
- chemicals
- electrical goods
- oil/shale
- food processing
- light engineering
- paper industry

- capital cities
- major towns
- international airports
- major roads
- major industrial areas

Gas from the processing of Estonia's oil shale is exported by pipeline across the Endla Raba peat marshes to the Russian Federation.

TRANSPORTATION NETWORK

242,810 miles (391,630 km)		none
6,830 miles (11,016 km)		376 miles (606 km)

Railroads are being superseded by roads linking the ports with eastern Europe and Russia. A highway connecting the three Baltic capitals with Warsaw, Poland, is proposed for the next century.

The Videzme Uplands (*Vidzemes Augstiene*) is a region of mixed forest and pasture.

Suur Munamägi in southern Estonia is, at 1,088 ft (318 m), the highest point in the low-lying Baltic states.

Nuclear fallout from the 1986 Chernobyl (*Chornobyl*) disaster in Ukraine has contaminated large areas of agricultural land in Belarus.

The Dnieper River is the third longest in Europe and forms the heart of Belarus's drainage system.

The Pripet Marshes form the largest area of "unreclaimed" marshland in Europe. They also provide a network of navigable waterways across southern Belarus.

Pripet Marshes

A network of streams and creeks drains across the marshes.

Peat deposits

This large area of marshland lies in a broad tectonic depression, mantled by glacial deposits. Peat deposits have developed below the marshes, which are prone to spring flooding.

Glacial deposits

Broad tectonic basin

Byelavyezhskaya Pushcha

RUSSIAN FEDERATION

KALININGRADSKAYA OBLAST'

POLAND

UKRAINE

ESTONIA

LATVIA

LITHUANIA

BELARUS

RUSS. FED.

TALLINN

RIGA

VILNIUS

MINSK

Kaliningrad

THE MEDITERRANEAN

THE MEDITERRANEAN SEA stretches over 2,500 miles (4,000 km) east to west, separating Europe from Africa. At its westernmost point it is connected to the Atlantic Ocean through the Strait of Gibraltar. In the east, the Suez Canal, opened in 1869, gives passage to the Indian Ocean. In the northeast, linked by the Sea of Marmara, lies the Black Sea. The Mediterranean is bordered by 28 states and territories, and more than 100 million people live on its shores and islands. Throughout history, the Mediterranean has been a focal area for many great empires and civilizations, reflected in the variety of cultures found on its shores. Since the 1960s, development along the southern coast of Europe has expanded rapidly to accommodate increasing numbers of tourists and to enable the exploitation of oil and gas reserves. This has resulted in rising levels of pollution, threatening the future of the sea.

TRANSPORTATION & INDUSTRY

THE OPENING OF THE SUEZ CANAL in 1869 made the Mediterranean a key shipping route to Asia. Oil and gas reserves, although comparatively small on a world scale, are being explored and exploited off the coasts of Libya, Greece, Italy, Spain, and Tunisia. The Mediterranean's greatest natural resources are its miles of beaches and warm sea. Over half the world's income from tourism is generated in the Mediterranean.

Benidorm is one of the most popular resorts on Spain's Costa Blanca. Many of the Mediterranean's coastal resorts have grown up since the 1950s, expanding from small fishing villages to large resorts catering almost exclusively to tourists.

USING THE LAND & SEA

A QUARTER OF THE FISH SPECIES found in the Mediterranean are economically important. Sardines are the main catch in northern and western regions and aquaculture, including oyster farming, is becoming increasingly important in the eastern Mediterranean. Olives, citrus fruit, cork trees, and grapes thrive in the Mediterranean climate, enjoying hot, dry summers and mild, wet winters. Italy and Spain are world leaders in commercial olive production.

The growing of citrus fruits, such as lemons, limes, oranges, and grapefruit, is common along the coasts surrounding the Mediterranean.

Land use and agricultural distribution

- goats
- sheep
- cereals
- citrus fruits
- cork
- fishing
- olive oil
- sunflowers
- tobacco
- vineyards
- major towns

- pasture
- cropland
- forest
- mountain region
- wetland
- desert

THE LANDSCAPE

THE MEDITERRANEAN SEA IS ALMOST TOTALLY LANDLOCKED, joined to the Atlantic Ocean through the Strait of Gibraltar, which is only 8 miles (13 km) wide. Lying on an active plate margin, sea floor movements have formed a variety of basins, troughs, and ridges. A submarine ridge running from Tunisia to the island of Sicily divides the Mediterranean into two distinct basins. The western basin is characterized by broad, smooth abyssal (ocean) plains. In contrast, the eastern basin is dominated by a large ridge system, running east to west.

The narrow Strait of Gibraltar inhibits water exchange between the Mediterranean Sea and the Atlantic Ocean, producing a high degree of salinity and a low tidal range within the Mediterranean. The lack of tides has encouraged the build-up of pollutants in many semienclosed bays.

The Dalmatian (Dalmacija) *coast* has many long, elongated islands parallel to the mainland. These were created when rising sea levels drowned valleys running parallel with the coast.

Main surface current

Denser, more saline currents flow back to Atlantic

Dense currents sink below surface

Because the Mediterranean is almost enclosed by land, its circulation is quite different from the oceans. There is one major current which flows in from the Atlantic and moves east. Currents flowing back to the Atlantic are denser and flow below the main current.

The Ionian Basin is the deepest in the Mediterranean, reaching depths of 16,800 ft (5,121 m).

Industrial pollution flowing from the Dniep[er] and Danube Rivers has destroyed a lar[ge] proportion of the fish population that used [to] inhabit the upper layers of the Black Se[a]

The eastern basin of the Mediterranean contains many features which indicate the force of a colliding plate margin, including volcanoes, earthquake zones, ridges, and seamounts.

The Atlas Mountains are a range of fold mountains that lie in Morocco and Algeria. They run parallel to the Mediterranean, forming a topographical and climatic divide between the Mediterranean coast and the western Sahara.

The edge of the Eurasian Plate is edged by a continental shelf. In the Mediterranean Sea this is widest at the Ebro Fan, where it extends 60 miles (96 km).

Beneath the Strait of Sicily lies a submarine ridge which rises to 1,200 ft (360 m) below sea level. It divides the eastern and western basins of the Mediterranean.

An arc of active submarine, island, and mainland volcanoes, including Etna and Vesuvius, lie in and around southern Italy. The area is also susceptible to earthquakes and landslides.

The shallow basin of the Aegean contains numerous small islands, many of volcanic origin.

Nutrient-flows into the easter[n] Mediterranean and sediment-flo[ws] to the Nile Delta have been severe[ly] decreased by the building of t[he] Aswan Dam across the Nile in Egy[pt] causing the delta to shrin[k]

66 ◀

66 ◀

▼
76

ATLANTIC OCEAN

A Coruña
Cabo Ortegal
Cabo Fisterra
Gijón
Vigo
Ourense
Cordillera Cant[abrica]
Porto
Vila Nova de Gaia
Douro
Valladolid
Embalse de Almendra
Salamanca
Sistema Cen[tral]
Cabo Carvoeiro
LISBOA (LISBON)
Tagus
Setúbal
Cabo da Roca
Badajoz
Guadiana
S P[AIN]
PORTUGAL
Cabo de São Vicente
Sierra Morena
Golfo de Cádiz
Huelva
Guadalquivir
Sevilla (Seville)
Córdoba
Jaén
Jerez de la Frontera
Granada
Cádiz
Málaga
Algeciras
GIBRALTAR (to UK)
Strait of Gibraltar
Costa d[el]
Cap Spartel
Ceuta (to Spain)
Alborán Sea
Tanger
Tétouan
Melilla (to Spain)
Kénitra
RABAT
Salé
Casablanca
Mohammedia
Fès
Safi
Meknès
MOROCCO
Cap Beddouza
Oued er Rbia
Moyen Atlas
Tensift
Marrakech
Beni-Mellal
Haut Atlas
A t l a s

EUROPE
Marseille
Venice
Nice
Madrid
Rome
Barcelona
Sevastopol'
BLACK SEA
Naples
Dubrovnik
Valencia
İstanbul
İzmir
Ankara
Oran
Algiers
Athens
Tunis
MEDITERRANEAN SEA
Beirut
Tel Aviv-Yafo
Tripoli
Benghazi
Alexandria
Cairo
AFRICA
ASIA
ATLANTIC OCEAN

THE RUSSIAN FEDERATION

Summer beds of moss and lichen scatter a 90% surface cover of ice across the islands of Franz Josef Land (Zemlya Frantsa-Iosifa), the northernmost land in the eastern hemisphere.

THE COLD WAR ERA OF GLOBAL RELATIONS was concluded in 1991 with the formal dissolution of the Soviet Union. The Russian Federation declared its separate sovereignty from the foundering communist empire following independence declarations from a number of former Soviet republics. As the leading member of the Commonwealth of Independent States, the Russian Federation has a central role in the development of post-Soviet Eurasia. Crossing 11 time zones, the Russian Federation is almost twice the size of the US, and with more than 150 ethnic minorities and 21 autonomous republics, regionalist dissent within its own territory remains a danger.

MAP KEY

POPULATION

- ▣ above 5 million
- ◉ 1 million to 5 million
- ◎ 500,000 to 1 million
- ◉ 100,000 to 500,000
- ⊕ 50,000 to 100,000
- ○ 10,000 to 50,000
- ∘ below 10,000

ELEVATION

- 4000m / 13,124ft
- 3000m / 9843ft
- 2000m / 6562ft
- 1000m / 3281ft
- 500m / 1640ft
- 250m / 820ft
- 100m / 328ft
- sea level

USING THE LAND

THE MAIN AGRICULTURAL REGIONS follow the belt of rich, black *chernozem* soils between Ukraine and Novosibirsk, producing cereals, fodder, and a broad range of crops for industrial use. Small pockets of pastureland are also found in this region. Large areas of terrain are uncultivable, and the constraints of a severe climate force the Federation to be partly dependent on imported grain. The wilds of Siberia are given over to hunting and reindeer herding, and contain the world's largest timber reserves.

Land use and agricultural distribution

- cattle
- cereals
- root crops
- timber
- capital cities
- major towns
- pasture
- cropland
- forest
- desert
- mountain region
- barren

THE RUSSIAN FEDERATION: ADMINISTRATIVE REGIONS

1. PSKOVSKAYA OBLAST'
2. YAROSLAVSKAYA OBLAST'
3. IVANOVSKAYA OBLAST'
4. SMOLENSKAYA OBLAST'
5. MOSKOVSKAYA OBLAST
6. VLADIMIRSKAYA OBLAST'
7. RESPUBLIKA MARIY EL
8. CHUVASHSKAYA RESPUBLIKA
9. KALUZHSKAYA OBLAST'
10. TUL'SKAYA OBLAST'
11. RYAZANSKAYA OBLAST'
12. RESPUBLIKA MORDOVIYA
13. UL'YANOVSKAYA OBLAST'
14. SAMARSKAYA OBLAST'
15. BRYANSKAYA OBLAST'
16. ORLOVSKAYA OBLAST'

17. LIPETSKAYA OBLAST'
18. TAMBOVSKAYA OBLAST'
19. KURSKAYA OBLAST'
20. BELGORODSKAYA OBLAST'
21. VORONEZHSKAYA OBLAST'
22. KRASNODARSKIY KRAY
23. RESPUBLIKA ADYGEYA
24. KARACHAYEVO-CHERKESSKAYA RESPUBLIKA
25. KABARDINO-BALKARSKAYA RESPUBLIKA
26. RESPUBLIKA SEVERNAYA OSETIYA
27. INGUSHSKAYA RESPUBLIKA
28. CHECHENSKAYA RESPUBLIKA
29. YEVREYSKAYA AVTONOMNAYA OBLAST'

THE URBAN/RURAL POPULATION DIVIDE

urban 74%   rural 26%

0 10 20 30 40 50 60 70 80 90 100

POPULATION DENSITY	TOTAL LAND AREA
23 people per sq mile	65,592,800 sq miles
(9 people per sq km)	(17,075,400 sq km)

N Nn O Oo P Pp Q Qq R Rr S Ss

SCALE 1:7,500,000
(projection: Lambert Conformal Conic)

Km
0 25 50 100 150 200 250 300
0 25 50 100 150 200 250 300
Miles

St. Peter's Castle, in Bodrum, southwestern Turkey, is a crusader's castle. It is one of many ancient ruins found along the shores of the Mediterranean, reflecting different civilizations and the strategic importance of many coastal towns.

Zafer Burnu
(Akrotiri Andréa)

Yenierenköy
(Agialoúsa)

Dipkarpaz
(Rizokárpason)

Lapta
(Lapíthos)
Girne (Akanthoú)
Tatlısu

Trikomon
Değirmenlik
(Kythréa)
Yeniboğaziçi

NICOSIA
Vadili
(Vatilí)
Athienou
Paralimni

Kato Lakatámeia

Gazimağusa
(Ammóchostos, Famagusta)

Agía Nápa

Aradíppou
Lárnaka (Lárnaca)

Akrotíri Gkréko

Dekéleia
Sovereign
Base Area
(to UK)

Lemesós (Limassol)
Kólpos Akrotiríou
Akrotíri Gátas

SCALE 1:2,000,000
(projection: Lambert Conformal Conic)

Km
0 5 10 20 30 40 50
0 5 10 20 30 40 50
Miles

TURKEY OCCUPIED the northern part of Cyprus ... Greek Cypriots remained in control of the south. ... as effectively partitioned and a UN buffer ... rently divides the two areas. In 1983 the ... the island proclaimed itself the Turkish ... of North Cyprus. It is only ... d by Turkey.

UKRAINE
Mykolayiv
Kherson
Nova Kakhovka
Odesa
MOLDOVA

Sea of Azov

RUSSIAN FEDERATION

Taganrog
Mariupol'
Berdyans'k
Melitopol'
Yeysk
Kerch
Krasnodar
Novorossiysk
Stavropol'
Nevinnomyssk
Maykop
Cherkessk
Kislovodsk
Pyatigorsk
Nal'chik
Vladikavkaz

ROMANIA
Ploiești
BUCUREȘTI (BUCHAREST)
Constanța

Sevastopol'
Simferopol'
Yevpatoriya

Sochi
Sokhumi
Sukhumi

GEORGIA
K'ut'aisi
P'ot'i
Bat'umi

BULGARIA
Pleven
Shumen
Varna
Burgas
Stara Zagora
Sliven
Plovdiv
Edirne
SOFIYA (SOFIA)

Niš
Leskovac
Priština
SKOPJE
MACEDONIA
Bitola

BLACK SEA

Sinop
Samsun
Ordu
Trabzon
Zonguldak
Erzurum

İstanbul
İzmit
Adapazarı
Bursa
Bandırma
Çanakkale
Balıkesir
Edremit
Kütahya
Eskişehir
ANKARA
Kırıkkale
Çorum
Sivas

GREECE
Thessaloniki (Salonica)
Lárisa
Pátra

TURKEY

Manisa
Uşak
İzmir
Aydın
Denizli
Isparta
Konya
Kayseri
Malatya
Gaziantep

ATHINA (ATHENS)
Peiraías (Piraeus)
Korinthos (Corinth)
Spárti
Pýlos

Bodrum
Antalya
Mersin
Adana
Osmaniye
İskenderun
Halab

Irákleio
Kríti (Crete)

CYPRUS
NICOSIA
Lemesós (Limassol)
Lárnaka

SYRIA
Al Lādhiqīyah (Latakia)
Hamāh
Himş

LEBANON
Tripoli
BEYROUTH (BEIRUT)
DIMASHQ (DAMASCUS)
Hefa

ISRAEL
Tel Aviv-Yafo
JERUSALEM
Gaza

WEST BANK
AMMAN
JORDAN
Az Zarqa'
Irbid

MEDITERRANEAN SEA

EGYPT
Alexandria
Port Said
Dumyât (Damietta)
Rashid (Rosetta)
Kafr el-Sheikh
El Mansûra
El Mahalla el Kubra
İsmâ'ilîya
Tanta
Zagazig
Benha
CAIRO
El Gîza
Shubrâ el Kheima
Helwân
Suez
El Faiyûm
Beni Suef
El Minya

SAUDI ARABIA

Sinai
Gulf of Suez
Gulf of Aqaba
Red Sea

MAP KEY

POPULATION
■ above 5 million
■ 1 million to 5 million
⊙ 500,000 to 1 million
⊙ 100,000 to 500,000
⊕ 50,000 to 100,000
○ 10,000 to 50,000
○ below 10,000

ELEVATION
4000m / 13,124ft
3000m / 9843ft
2000m / 6562ft
1000m / 3281ft
500m / 1640ft
250m / 820ft
100m / 328ft
sea level

SEA DEPTH
sea level
250m / 820ft
500m / 1640ft
1000m / 3281ft
2000m / 6562ft
3000m / 9843ft

The Suez Canal links the Mediterranean with the Red Sea, providing an important shipping route between Europe and Asia.

Beirut is Lebanon's largest city. In the 1960s and 70s it was the chief financial, commercial, and transportation center for the Arab states. In 1975 civil war broke out. Rebuilding is under way, however, many buildings bear the scars of the war, which only ended in 1990.

Major industry and infrastructure

- fishing port
- oil & gas
- tourism
- major towns
- international airports
- major roads
- major industrial areas

Monte Carlo is just one of the luxurious resorts scattered along the Riviera, which stretches along the coast from Cannes in France to La Spezia in Italy. The region's mild winters and hot summers have attracted wealthy tourists since the early 19th century.

CYPRUS

In 1974 while Gr... Cyprus v... zone cur... north of ... Republic ... recogniz...

Oxygen in the Black Sea is dissolved only in its upper layers; at depths below 230–300 ft (70–100 m) the sea is "dead" and can support no life other than specially adapted bacteria.

The city of Venice is built on an archipelago of islands and mudflats in the middle of a lagoon at the head of the Adriatic Sea. The city's numerous canals follow water routes between the original 118 islands.

Cyprus is the third largest Mediterranean island after Sardinia and Sicily. The island is mountainous and contains two main ranges, the Troodos and the Kyrenia Mountains.

Both the Dead Sea in Jordan and the Gulf of Aqaba are extensions of the Great Rift Valley, which runs through eastern Africa.

The Suez Canal, opened in 1869, extends 100 miles (160 km) from Port Said to the Gulf of Suez.

MALTA

SCALE 1:900,000
(projection: Lambert Conformal Conic)

0   10   20 Km
0   10   20 Miles

Commercial fisheries are found throughout the Mediterranean. Operations have traditionally been small-scale. As elsewhere, high demand has caused a decline in fish stocks.

A **fishing trawler** lies at anchor in the icy waters of Karaginskiy Zaliv, at the northern end of the Kamchatka Peninsula (Poluostrov Kamchatka) in eastern Siberia. The Russian Federation's fishing fleet is the largest in the world and operates worldwide.

The shores of Lake Baikal (Ozero Baykal) are a mixture of forest and the grassy steppe seen here. The lake freezes to a depth of 33 ft (10 m) in winter.

SCALE 1:13,800,000
(projection: Lambert Conformal Conic)

The Kamchatka Peninsula
(Poluostrov Kamchatka) *is a volcanic area on the margins of the Eurasian Plate, forming part of the Pacific "Ring of Fire." The volcano Vulkan Klyuchevskaya Sopka, at 15,585 ft (4,750 m), is the highest mountain in Siberia.*

TRANSPORTATION & INDUSTRY

RAW MATERIALS, particularly fossil fuels, ores, and precious metals are abundant, yet often found at sites far from habitation. This inherent "friction of distance" problem was met starting in the 1930s by Soviet commitment to heavy industry and the strategic location of plants east of the Urals. It has left a pattern of isolated and often vast industrial complexes, in remote areas from Vladivostok to Murmansk, in the far north and across European Russia, with lighter manufacturing concentrated in urban areas.

Major industry and infrastructure

- ✈ aerospace
- 🚗 car manufacture
- ⚗ chemicals
- ⚙ engineering
- 🔥 gas
- 🛢 iron & steel
- ⛏ mining
- oil
- textiles
- 🌲 timber processing
- ■ capital cities
- ● major towns
- ✈ international airports
- — major roads
- major industrial areas

TRANSPORTATION NETWORK

🛣	545,042 miles (879,100 km)
🛤	None
🚉	53,988 miles (87,079 km)
🚉	76,694 miles (123,700 km)

The recent growth of trade with China and East Asia has put pressure on Siberia's inadequate road and rail network, prompting increased use of the Amur River for freight transportation.

Novosibirsk was established at the point where the Trans–Siberian railroad crosses the Ob' River. It grew as an industrial center under the Soviet Union and is now Siberia's largest city.

THE LANDSCAPE

THE URAL MOUNTAINS (*Ural'skiye Gory*) divide the fertile North European Plain from the West Siberian Plain (*Zapadno-Sibirskaya Ravnina*), the world's largest area of flat ground, crossed by giant rivers flowing north to the Kara Sea (*Karskoye More*). The land rises to the Central Siberian Plateau (*Srednesibirskoye Ploskogor'ye*) and becomes more mountainous to the southeast. These immense topographic regions intersect with latitudinal vegetation bands. The tundra of the extreme north gives way to a vast area of coniferous woodland, known as *taiga*, which is larger than the Amazon rain forest. This belt turns to mixed forest and then steppe grasslands toward the south.

Polygon shapes create patterned ground

Permafrost

Permanent ice wedges up to 16 ft (5 m) deep

Patterned ground *is a permafrost feature found extensively across northern Russia. Seasonal contraction of the permafrost creates polygonal cracks, which are filled by ice wedges.*

The Khatanga River meanders slowly across the Poluostrov Taymyr, a low-lying tundra landscape which floods in the spring thaw, until the water can escape to the sea.

Poluostrov Taymyr

The mountains of Verkhoyanskiy Khrebet were formed by movement between the Eurasian and North American plates, during the same period of folding that created the Urals.

Central Siberian Plateau (*Srednesibirskoye Ploskogor'ye*)

Kara Sea (*Karskoye More*)

The North European Plain is marked by huge moraine ridges left by the Scandinavian Ice Sheet and by long intermoraine drainage channels, known as *Urstromtäler*.

The Ural Mountains (*Ural'skiye Gory*) extend 2,500 miles (4,020 km). They were formed over 280 million years ago, folded as the East European and Siberian plates moved closer together.

West Siberian Plain (*Zapadno-Sibirskaya Ravnina*)

The Yenisey is one of the world's longest rivers, and also among the most languid, dropping only 500 ft (152 m) over 1,200 miles (2,000 km).

Lake Baikal (*Ozero Baykal*), occupies a rift valley and is the world's deepest lake, over 1 mile (1.6 km) in depth. It is fed by over 300 rivers and drained by just one, the Angara.

Yukagirskoye Ploskogor'ye is a rolling plain with isolated drumlins, domelike features resulting from glacial deposition.

NORTHERN EUROPEAN RUSSIA

REACHING INTO THE ARCTIC CIRCLE, this region of lakeland, forest, and tundra is historically bound to Europe by St. Petersburg, the old imperial capital of Czarist Russia and home to one-third of the region's population. Communist rule from Moscow left the north politically marginalized, contributing to the present problems of outmoded industry, poor infrastructure, and serious environmental neglect. However, with borders embracing Finland, Norway, the Baltic, and the northern sea route to the Atlantic, the region's success in foreign trade is now of prime importance to the Russian economy.

St. Peter and Paul Fortress is the oldest building in St. Petersburg, founded by Peter the Great in 1703 as a modern, European capital for Russia.

THE LANDSCAPE

THE ANCIENT BEDROCK of the Scandinavian Shield lies exposed across the glacially scoured Khibiny Mountains of the Kola Peninsula *(Kol'skiy Poluostrov)*, becoming mantled with till toward the North European Plain. The Valdai Hills *(Valdayskaya Vozvyshennost')* form an important watershed for the plain's rivers, while thick forest veils a complicated topography of moraines, lakes, and ground disturbed by frost action. The Ural Mountains *(Ural'skiye Gory)* form a border with Asia in the east.

The Khibiny Mountains were formed by volcanic intrusions into the Scandinavian Shield, over 570 million years ago.

Kola Peninsula (Kol'skiy Poluostrov)

The Kola Peninsula (Kol'skiy Poluostrov) *is part of the Scandinavian Shield, an area of ancient bedrock underlying Scandinavia. Rocks more than 2.5 billion years old are exposed across the peninsula.*

Karst features, including sinkholes, lakes, and caverns, are found in limestone outcrops across the plain of the Severnaya Dvina and Mezen' Rivers.

The low-lying plains of the Pechora, Mezen', and Severnaya Dvina Rivers were flooded by the sea, while the land was still isostatically depressed following the last Ice Age, a process which has hidden the landforms created by glacial deposition.

Retreating glacier
Meltwater channels
Terminal moraine

Terminal moraines are crescent-shaped ridges of glacial deposits, widely found in central Russia. Detritus is carried by the glacier and deposited at its terminus (snout) as it melts, marking the limit of the ice advance.

Two of Europe's biggest rivers, the Volga and Western Dvina, rise in the swampy uplands of the Valdai Hills *(Valdayskaya Vozvyshennost')*.

Lake Onega (Onezhskoye Ozero) *is the remnant of a body of water which, 12,000 years ago, connected the White Sea (Beloye More) with Gulf of Finland and the Baltic Sea.*

Ural Mountains *(Ural'skiye Gory)*

USING THE LAND & SEA

THE COLD CLIMATE confines agriculture mainly to southern and western provinces, where dairy farming predominates and arable land is given over to fodder crops as well as flax, potatoes, oats, and rye. Areas beyond the northern margins of cultivation are used for forestry, hunting, herding, and fishing, with some vegetables grown in hothouses around urban areas.

RUSSIAN FEDERATION

Land use and agricultural distribution
- cattle
- fishing
- reindeer
- timber
- fodder
- major towns
- pasture
- cropland
- forest
- mountain region
- wetland
- tundra
- barren
- ice

THE URBAN/RURAL POPULATION DIVIDE

urban 74%   rural 26%

0 10 20 30 40 50 60 70 80 90 100

POPULATION DENSITY
27 people per sq mile
10 people per sq km

TOTAL LAND AREA
829,398 sq miles
(2,148,700 sq km)

Many rapids are found along the 175-mile (280-km) course of the Suna River.

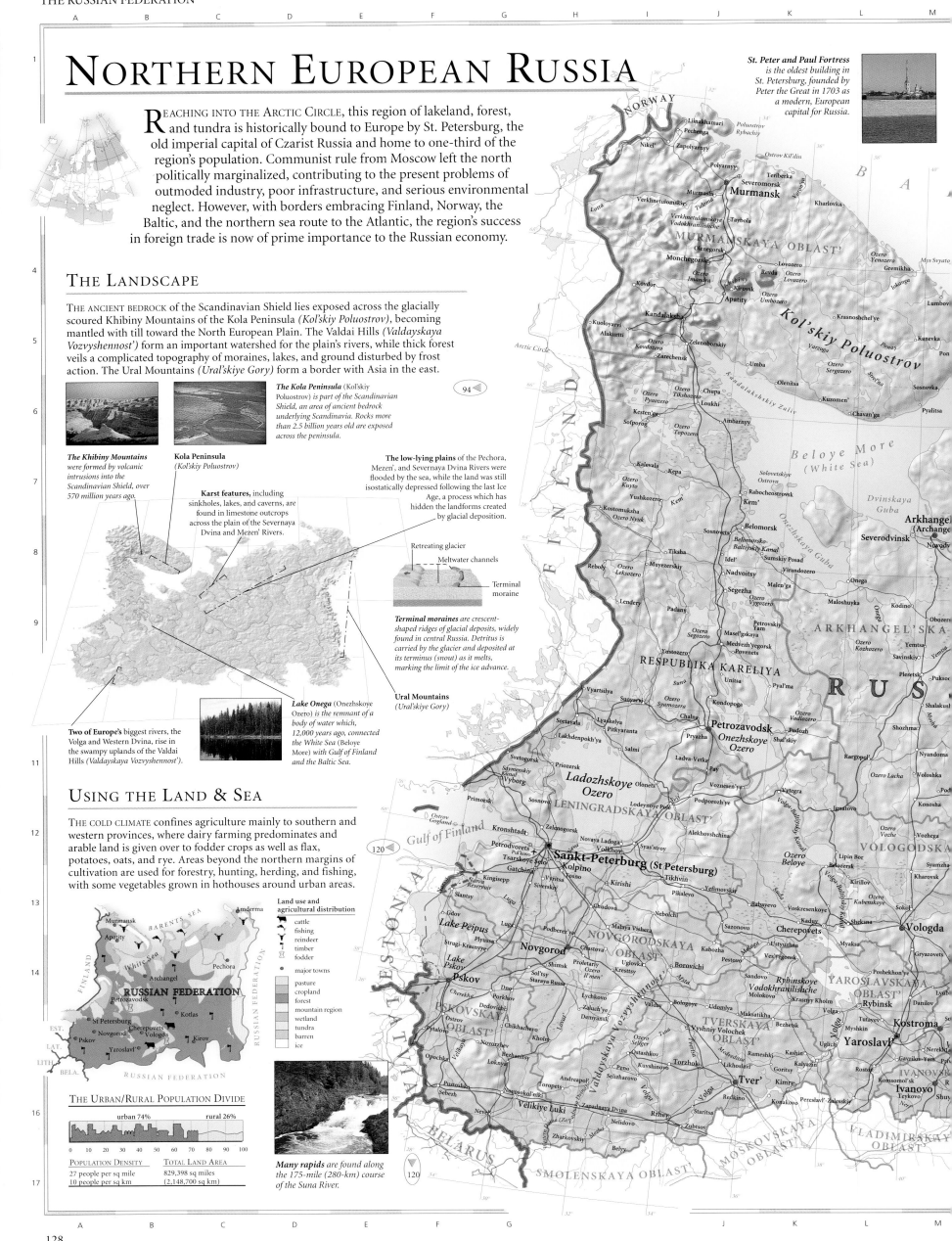

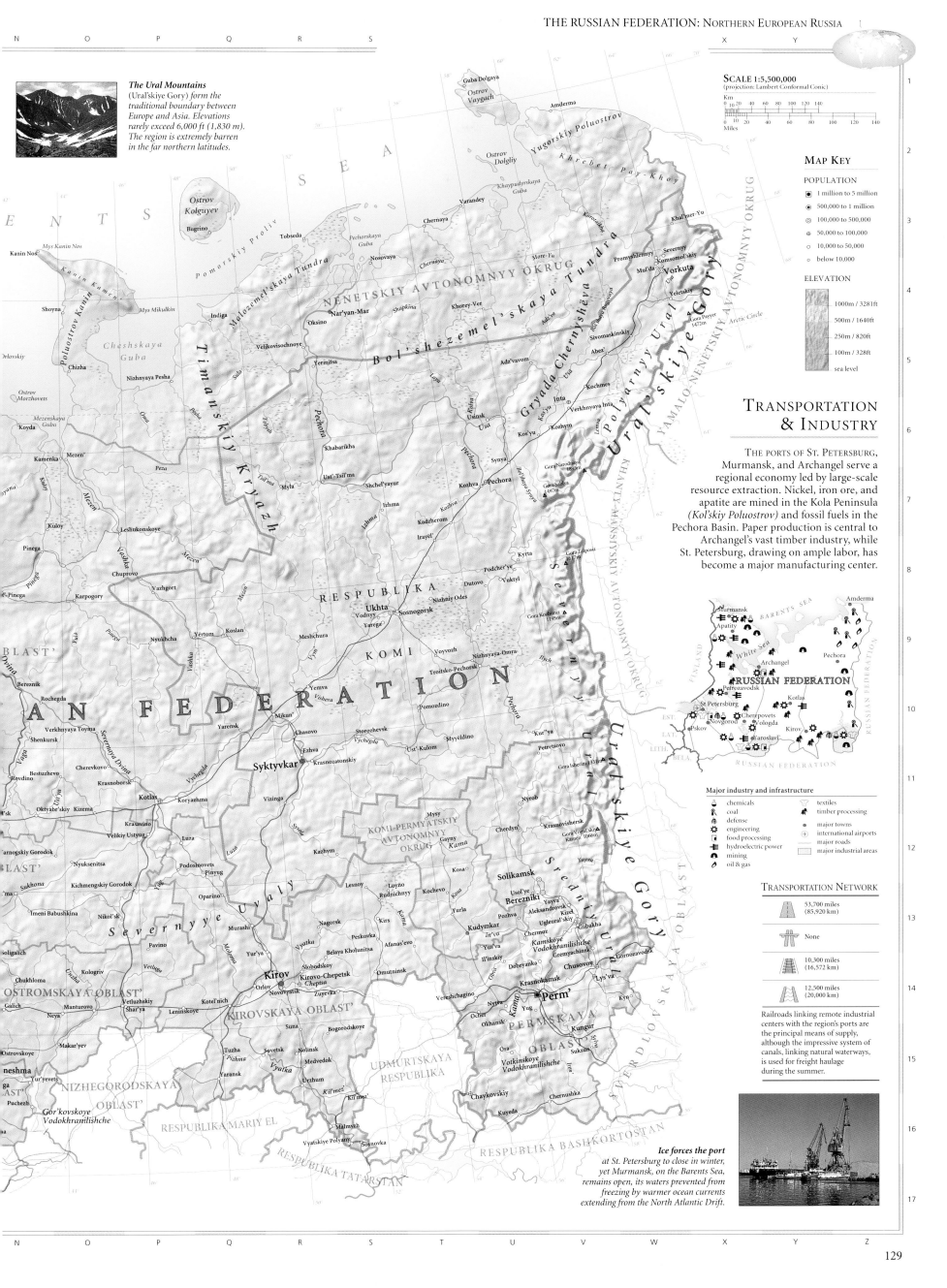

The Ural Mountains
(Ural'skiye Gory) form the traditional boundary between Europe and Asia. Elevations rarely exceed 6,000 ft (1,830 m). The region is extremely barren in the far northern latitudes.

SCALE 1:5,500,000
(projection: Lambert Conformal Conic)

MAP KEY

POPULATION

- 1 million to 5 million
- 500,000 to 1 million
- 100,000 to 500,000
- 50,000 to 100,000
- 10,000 to 50,000
- below 10,000

ELEVATION

1000m / 3281ft
500m / 1640ft
250m / 820ft
100m / 328ft
sea level

TRANSPORTATION & INDUSTRY

THE PORTS OF ST. PETERSBURG, Murmansk, and Archangel serve a regional economy led by large-scale resource extraction. Nickel, iron ore, and apatite are mined in the Kola Peninsula (Kol'skiy Poluostrov) and fossil fuels in the Pechora Basin. Paper production is central to Archangel's vast timber industry, while St. Petersburg, drawing on ample labor, has become a major manufacturing center.

Major industry and infrastructure

- chemicals
- coal
- defense
- engineering
- food processing
- hydroelectric power
- mining
- oil & gas
- textiles
- timber processing
- major towns
- international airports
- major roads
- major industrial areas

TRANSPORTATION NETWORK

53,700 miles (85,920 km)

None

10,300 miles (16,572 km)

12,500 miles (20,000 km)

Railroads linking remote industrial centers with the region's ports are the principal means of supply, although the impressive system of canals, linking natural waterways, is used for freight haulage during the summer.

Ice forces the port
at St. Petersburg to close in winter, yet Murmansk, on the Barents Sea, remains open, its waters prevented from freezing by warmer ocean currents extending from the North Atlantic Drift.

129

Kaliningrad has been a Russian enclave since 1945. The port is an important center for the Russian Federation's Baltic fishing fleet.

St. Basil's Cathedral, completed in 1561, stands in Moscow's Red Square next to the Kremlin, which was the original fortified stronghold of the city.

SOUTHERN EUROPEAN RUSSIA

THIS REGION, DIVIDED FROM ASIA by desert, seas, and mountains, has exerted a powerful influence both east and west since the 13th century. More than 70 years of communist rule produced a highly urbanized, industrial society dominated by Moscow, which was the capital of the Soviet Union until 1991. Almost two-thirds of the Russian Federation's population live in this core area, with a relatively high *per capita* share of its wealth.

However, the rapid growth of a market economy has caused great social upheaval, with rising crime and political instability.

THE LANDSCAPE

ANCIENT FOLDS in the deep sedimentary strata of the North European Plain have created a sequence of high and low regions. The Central Russian Upland (*Srednerusskaya Vozvyshennost'*) in the west is deeply incised by rivers draining into the lowland of the Oka and Don rivers. In the east, the Volga, Europe's longest river, divides the Volga Uplands (*Privolzhskaya Vozvyshennost'*) from the foothills of the Ural Mountains (*Ural'skiye Gory*), flowing south to the Caspian Sea. The Caucasus Mountains and the Black Sea form a natural border to the southwest.

A plantation of Scots pine helps consolidate the loose sandy soils of the Meshchera Lowland (*Meshcherskaya Nizina*), which lies on the bed of an old glacial lake.

The Smolensk-Moscow Upland (*Smolensko-Moskovskaya Vozvyshennost'*) is a series of terminal moraine ridges marking the southern extent of the last glaciation.

Glacial till covers the bedrock to the north of the North European Plain, giving a gentle surface relief.

The lowland of the Oka and Don Rivers lies over a broad trough, between the upfolds of the Volga Uplands (*Privolzhskaya Vozvyshennost'*) to the east, and the Central Russian Upland (*Srednerusskaya Vozvyshennost'*) to the west.

The southern Ural Mountains (*Ural'skiye Gory*) consist of several parallel ranges of ancient fold mountains running from north to south.

Ice and water have formed escarpments and columns in the resistant chalk strata south of the Central Russian Upland (*Srednerusskaya Vozvyshennost'*).

The floodplain of the Volga forms a long oasis of verdant vegetation, contrasting with the aridity of the surrounding Caspian hinterland.

The marshlands of the Volga Delta are visited by over 260 species of bird each year, migrating between South Africa and Arctic Siberia.

The Caspian Depression is a large downfold (or syncline) which became flooded, forming the Caspian Sea. The shoreline is 98 ft (30 m) below sea level.

The Caucasus Mountains run from the Black Sea to the Caspian Sea and include El' brus which, at 18,511 ft (5,642 m), is the highest point in all of Europe.

Drifting sand occupies large areas of the south, creating dunes up to 50 ft (15 m) high.

Salt dome

Sedimentary strata

Salt dome is forced up and through the rock strata

Salts are forced upward by denser overlying strata

Salt domes, rounded hills up to 500 ft (150 m) high, are produced as less dense rock salts are displaced under the extreme pressure of denser, overlying strata and forced up toward the surface creating domes. They are widespread in the Caspian Depression.

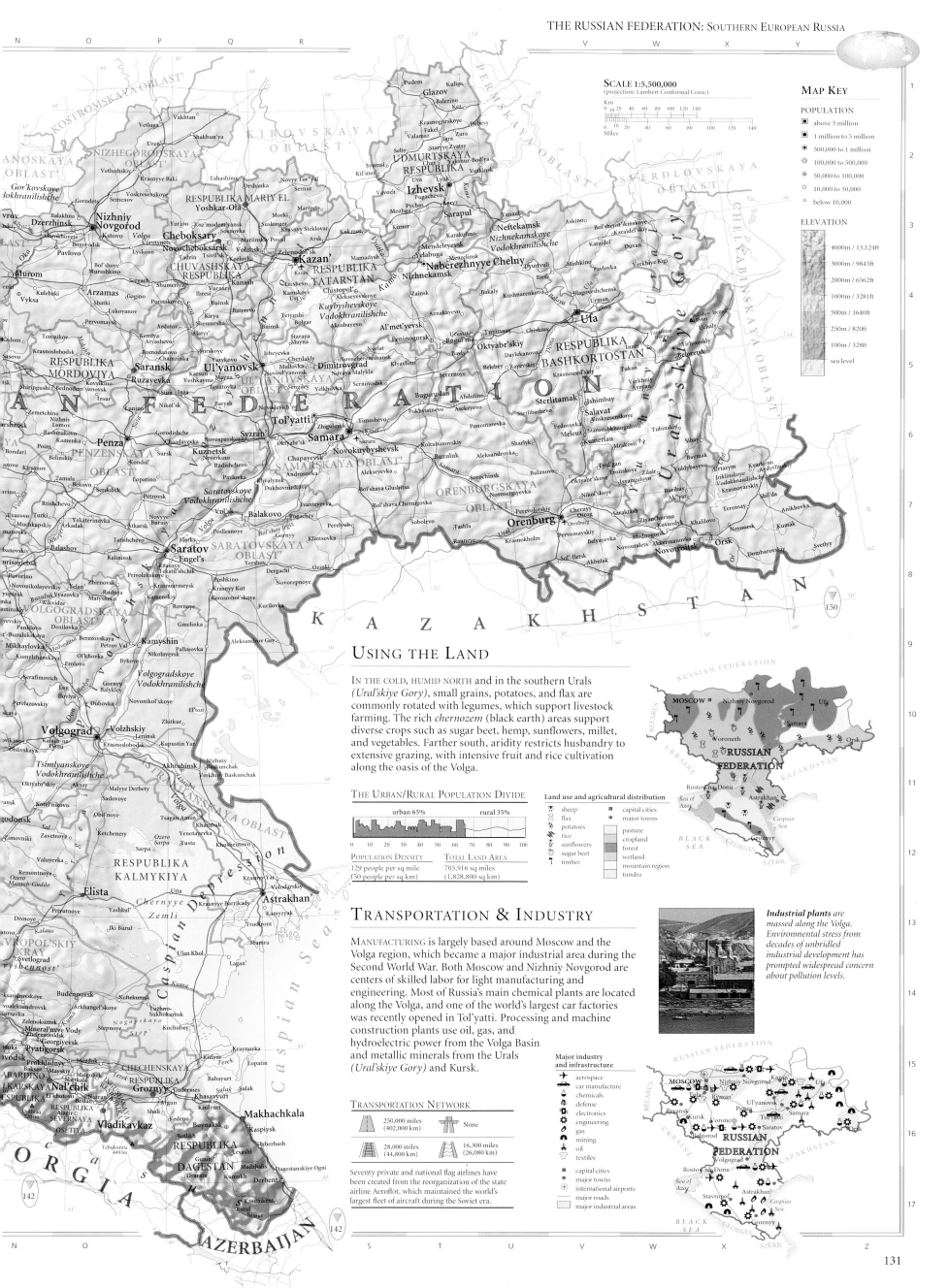

SCALE 1:5,500,000
(projection: Lambert Conformal Conic)

MAP KEY

POPULATION

- above 5 million
- 1 million to 5 million
- 500,000 to 1 million
- 100,000 to 500,000
- 50,000 to 100,000
- 10,000 to 50,000
- below 10,000

ELEVATION

- 4000m / 13,124ft
- 3000m / 9843ft
- 2000m / 6562ft
- 1000m / 3281ft
- 500m / 1640ft
- 250m / 820ft
- 100m / 328ft
- sea level

USING THE LAND

IN THE COLD, HUMID NORTH and in the southern Urals (*Ural'skiye Gory*), small grains, potatoes, and flax are commonly rotated with legumes, which support livestock farming. The rich *chernozem* (black earth) areas support diverse crops such as sugar beet, hemp, sunflowers, millet, and vegetables. Farther south, aridity restricts husbandry to extensive grazing, with intensive fruit and rice cultivation along the oasis of the Volga.

THE URBAN/RURAL POPULATION DIVIDE

urban 65%   rural 35%

0 10 20 30 40 50 60 70 80 90 100

POPULATION DENSITY	TOTAL LAND AREA
129 people per sq mile (50 people per sq km)	705,916 sq miles (1,828,800 sq km)

Land use and agricultural distribution

- sheep
- flax
- potatoes
- rice
- sunflowers
- sugar beet
- timber
- capital cities
- major towns
- pasture
- cropland
- forest
- wetland
- mountain region
- tundra

TRANSPORTATION & INDUSTRY

MANUFACTURING is largely based around Moscow and the Volga region, which became a major industrial area during the Second World War. Both Moscow and Nizhniy Novgorod are centers of skilled labor for light manufacturing and engineering. Most of Russia's main chemical plants are located along the Volga, and one of the world's largest car factories was recently opened in Tol'yatti. Processing and machine construction plants use oil, gas, and hydroelectric power from the Volga Basin and metallic minerals from the Urals (*Ural'skiye Gory*) and Kursk.

Industrial plants are massed along the Volga. Environmental stress from decades of unbridled industrial development has prompted widespread concern about pollution levels.

TRANSPORTATION NETWORK

250,000 miles (402,000 km)		None	
28,000 miles (44,800 km)		16,300 miles (26,080 km)	

Seventy private and national flag airlines have been created from the reorganization of the state airline Aeroflot, which maintained the world's largest fleet of aircraft during the Soviet era.

Major industry and infrastructure

- aerospace
- car manufacture
- chemicals
- defense
- electronics
- engineering
- gas
- mining
- oil
- textiles
- capital cities
- major towns
- international airports
- major roads
- major industrial areas

ASIA

ASIA, THE WORLD'S LARGEST CONTINENT, COVERS 16,838,365 SQ MILES
(43,608,000 SQ KM). IT COMPRISES 48 SEPARATE COUNTRIES,
INCLUDING 97% OF TURKEY AND 72% OF THE RUSSIAN FEDERATION.
ALMOST 60% OF THE WORLD'S POPULATION LIVES IN ASIA.

○ GREATEST EXTENT NORTH–SOUTH:
(4,000 miles / 6,440 km)
□ GREATEST EXTENT EAST–WEST:
(6,000 miles / 9,650 km)

Most northerly point:
Mys Articesku,
Russian Federation
81° 12' N

Most easterly point:
Mys Dezhneva,
Russian Federation
169° 40' W

MYS DEZHNEVA,
RUSSIAN FEDERATION
169° 40' W

Largest lake:
Caspian Sea
143,205 sq miles
(371,000 sq km)

Lowest recorded temperature:
Verkhoyansk,
Russian Federation
-90°F (-68°C)

MYS CHELYUSKIN,
RUSSIAN FEDERATION
77° 44' N

Most westerly point:
Bozca Adası,
Turkey 26° 2' E

BABA BUR-NU,
TURKEY
26° 4' E

KAGOSHIMA

Highest point:
Mount Everest,
China/Nepal
29,029 ft (8,848 m)

HODEIDA

Highest recorded temperature:
Tirat Tsvi, Israel
129°F (54°C)

TANJONG PIAI,
MALAYSIA
1° 16' N

Lowest point:
Dead Sea,
Israel/Jordan
1,286 ft (392 m)
below sea level

Most southerly point:
Pulau Pamana, Indonesia 11' S

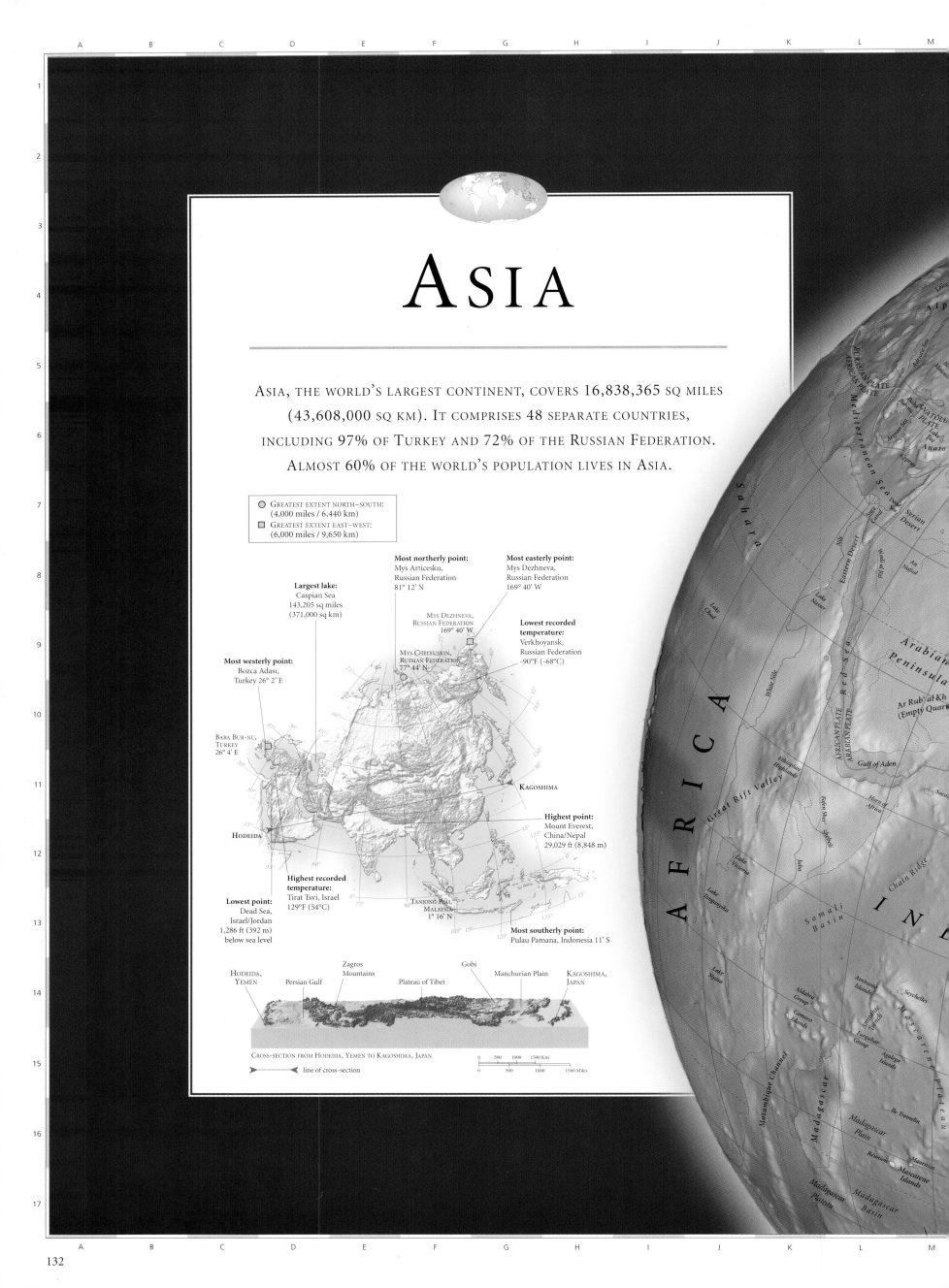

HODEIDA, YEMEN — Persian Gulf — Zagros Mountains — Plateau of Tibet — Gobi — Manchurian Plain — KAGOSHIMA, JAPAN

CROSS-SECTION FROM HODEIDA, YEMEN TO KAGOSHIMA, JAPAN

► ——— line of cross-section

0 500 1000 1500 Km

0 500 1000 1500 Miles

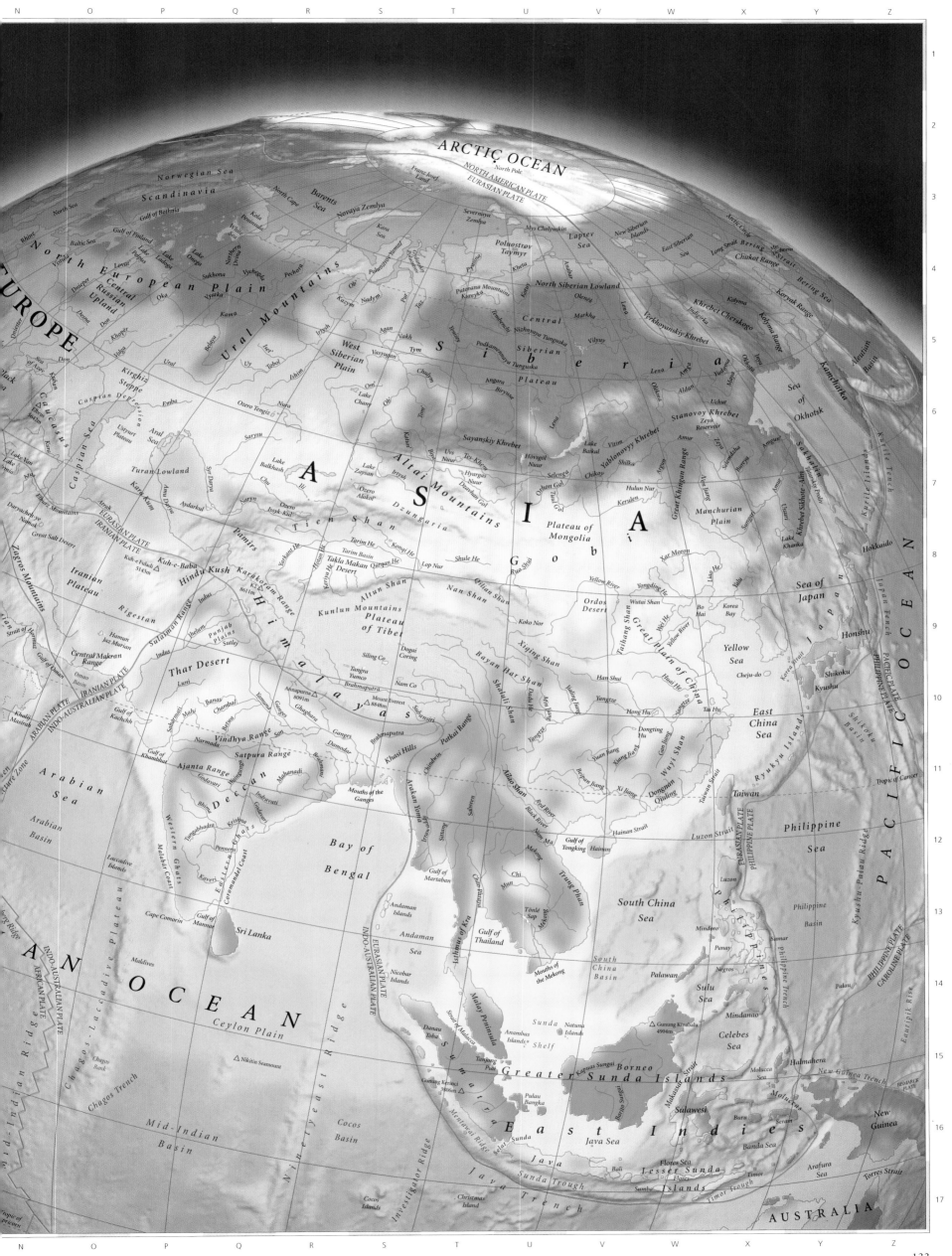

ARCTIC OCEAN
North Pole
NORTH AMERICAN PLATE
EURASIAN PLATE

EUROPE

ASIA

INDIAN OCEAN

AUSTRALIA

133

ASIAN RESOURCES

ALTHOUGH AGRICULTURE REMAINS THE ECONOMIC MAINSTAY of most Asian countries, the number of people employed in agriculture has steadily declined, as new industries have been developed during the past 30 years. China, Indonesia, Malaysia, Thailand, and Turkey have all experienced far-reaching structural changes in their economies, while the breakup of the former Soviet Union has created a new economic challenge in the Central Asian republics. The countries of the Persian Gulf illustrate the rapid transformation from rural nomadism to modern, urban society, which oil wealth has brought to parts of the continent. Asia's most economically dynamic countries, Japan, Singapore, South Korea, and Taiwan, fringe the Pacific Ocean and are known as the Pacific Rim. In contrast, other Southeast Asian countries like Laos and Cambodia remain both economically and industrially underdeveloped.

INDUSTRY

JAPANESE INDUSTRY LEADS THE CONTINENT in both productivity and efficiency; electronics, hi-tech industries, car manufacture, and shipbuilding are important. In recent years, the so-called economic "tigers" of the Pacific Rim such as Taiwan and South Korea are now challenging Japan's economic dominance. Heavy industries such as engineering, chemicals, and steel typify the industrial complexes along the corridor created by the Trans–Siberian Railway, the Fergana Valley in Central Asia, and also much of the huge industrial plain of east China. The discovery of oil in the Persian Gulf has brought immense wealth to countries that previously relied on subsistence agriculture on marginal desertland.

STANDARD OF LIVING

DESPITE JAPAN'S HIGH STANDARDS OF LIVING, and southwestern Asia's oil-derived wealth, immense disparities exist throughout the continent. Afghanistan remains one of the world's most underdeveloped nations, as do the mountain states of Nepal and Bhutan. Rapid population growth is exacerbating poverty and overcrowding in many parts of India and Bangladesh.

Standard of Living
(UN Human Development Index)

low

high

Industry

- ✈ aerospace
- 🍺 brewing
- 🚗 car/vehicle manufacture
- cement
- 🧪 chemicals
- electronics
- ⚙ engineering
- finance
- 🐟 fish processing
- food processing
- 🖥 hi-tech industry
- iron & steel
- 💊 pharmaceuticals
- 🖨 printing & publishing
- 🚢 shipbuilding
- sugar processing
- tea processing
- ⊤ textiles
- timber processing
- tobacco processing
- coal
- oil
- gas
- ● industrial cities
- ⧄ major industrial areas

On a small island on the southern tip of the Malay Peninsula lies Singapore, one of the Pacific Rim's most vibrant economic centers. Multinational banking and finance form the core of the city's wealth.

GNP per capita (US$)

- 0–499
- 500–999
- 1,000–4,999
- 5,000–9,999
- 10,000–19,999
- 2,0000+

ARCTIC OCEAN

PACIFIC OCEAN

Sea of Okhotsk

RUSSIAN FEDERATION

Yekaterinburg
Chelyabinsk
Magnitogorsk
Omsk
Novosibirsk
Kemerovo
Novokuznietsk
Krasnoyarsk
Bratsk
Irkutsk
Yakutsk
Khabarovsk
Vladivostok
Trans–Siberian Railway
Trans–Siberian Railway

Istanbul
Izmir
Ankara
GEORGIA
Tbilisi
TURKEY
ARMENIA
Yerevan
AZERB.
Baku
CYPRUS
LEBANON
Beirut
SYRIA
Damascus
Tel Aviv–Yafo
ISRAEL
JORDAN
Amman
Kirkuk
Baghdad
IRAQ
Basra
Kuwait
KUWAIT
SAUDI ARABIA
Ad Damman
BAHRAIN
QATAR
Riyadh
Jedda
Abu Dhabi
U.A.E.
Dubai
Gulf of Oman
OMAN
YEMEN
Gulf of Aden

Caspian Sea
KAZAKHSTAN
Karaganda
Aral Sea
UZBEKISTAN
Tashkent
Ashgabat
TURKMENISTAN
Dushanbe
Farghona
KYRGYZSTAN
TAJIKISTAN
Tehran
Isfahan
IRAN
AFGHANISTAN
Rawalpindi
Lahore
PAKISTAN
Karachi
Ahmadabad
Delhi
Kanpur
Indore
Jamshedpur
Nagpur
INDIA
Bombay
Bangalore
Madras
SRI LANKA

Urumqi
Alma-Ata
MONGOLIA
Ulan Bator
Harbin
Shenyang
Beijing
Tianjin
Taiyuan
Jinan
Lanzhou
Xi'an
Zhengzhou
Nanjing
Shanghai
Wuhan
Chengdu
Chongqing
Kunming
Guangzhou
Hong Kong
CHINA
NORTH KOREA
Pyongyang
Seoul
SOUTH KOREA
Pusan
Dalian
Qingdao
JAPAN
Tokyo
Nagoya
Kobe
Taipei
TAIWAN

NEPAL
BHUTAN
BANGLADESH
Dhaka
Chittagong
Calcutta
Mandalay
MYANMAR
Hanoi
LAOS
Da Nang
THAILAND
Bangkok
CAMBODIA
VIETNAM
Ho Chi Minh City
Rangoon
South China Sea
Manila
PHILIPPINES

Arabian Sea

Red Sea

MALAYSIA
BRUNEI
Kuala Lumpur
Singapore
SINGAPORE
INDONESIA
Jakarta
Surabaya

INDIAN OCEAN

Iron and steel, engineering, and shipbuilding typify the industries of eastern China's industrial cities, especially the nation's leading manufacturing center, Shanghai.

Traditional industries are still crucial to many rural economies across Asia. Here, on the Vietnamese coast, salt has been extracted from seawater by evaporation and is being loaded into a truck to take to market.

ENVIRONMENTAL ISSUES

THE TRANSFORMATION OF UZBEKISTAN by the former Soviet Union into the world's second largest producer of cotton led to the diversion of several major rivers for irrigation. Starved of this water, the Aral Sea diminished in volume by over 50% in 30 years, irreversibly altering the ecology of the area. Heavy industries in eastern China have polluted coastal waters, rivers, and urban air, while in Myanmar, Malaysia, and Indonesia, ancient hardwood rain forests are being cut down faster than they can regenerate.

Environmental Issues
- tropical forest
- forest destroyed
- desert
- desertification
- acid rain
- polluted rivers
- marine pollution
- heavy marine pollution
- radioactive contamination
- poor urban air quality

The long-term environmental impact of the Gulf War (1991) is still uncertain. As Iraqi troops left Kuwait, equipment was abandoned to rust and thousands of oil wells were set on fire, pouring crude oil into the Persian Gulf.

Although Siberia remains a quintessentially frozen, inhospitable wasteland, vast untapped mineral reserves – especially the oil and gas of the West Siberian Plain – have lured industrial development to the area since the 1950s and 1960s.

MINERAL RESOURCES

AT LEAST 60% OF THE WORLD'S known oil and gas deposits are found in Asia; notably the vast oil fields of the Persian Gulf, and the less-exploited oil and gas fields of the Ob' Basin in western Siberia. Immense coal reserves in Siberia and China have been utilized to support large steel industries. Southeast Asia has some of the world's largest deposits of tin, found in a belt running down the Malay Peninsula to Indonesia.

Mineral Resources
- oil field
- gas field
- coal field
- chromite
- copper
- gold
- iron
- lead
- nickel
- platinum
- tin
- wolfram

USING THE LAND & SEA

VAST AREAS OF ASIA REMAIN UNCULTIVATED as a result of unsuitable climatic and soil conditions. In favorable areas such as river deltas, farming is intensive. Rice is the staple crop of most Asian countries, grown in paddy fields on waterlogged alluvial plains and terraced hillsides, and often irrigated for higher yields. Across the black-earth region of the Eurasian steppe in southern Siberia and Kazakhstan, wheat farming is the dominant activity. Cash crops, like tea in Sri Lanka and dates in the Arabian Peninsula, are grown for export, and provide valuable income. The sovereignty of the rich fishing grounds in the South China Sea is disputed by China, Malaysia, Taiwan, the Philippines, and Vietnam, because of potential oil reserves.

Using the Land and Sea
- cropland
- desert
- forest
- mountain region
- pasture
- tundra
- wetland
- major conurbations
- cattle
- pigs
- goats
- sheep
- coconuts
- corn
- cotton
- dates
- fishing
- fruit
- jute
- oil palms
- peanuts
- rice
- rubber
- shellfish
- soy beans
- sugar beet
- sugar cane
- tea
- timber
- wheat

Date palms have been cultivated in oases throughout the Arabian Peninsula since antiquity. In addition to the fruit, palms are used for timber, fuel, rope, and for making vinegar, syrup, and a liquor known as arrack.

Rice terraces blanket the landscape across the small Indonesian island of Bali. The large amounts of water needed to grow rice have resulted in Balinese farmers organizing water-control cooperatives.

POLITICAL ASIA

ASIA IS THE WORLD'S LARGEST CONTINENT, encompassing many different and discrete realms, from the desert Arab lands of the southwest to the subtropical archipelago of Indonesia; from the vast barren wastes of Siberia to the fertile river valleys of China and South Asia, seats of some of the world's most ancient civilizations. The collapse of the Soviet Union has fragmented the north of the continent into the Siberian portion of the Russian Federation and the new republics of Central Asia. Strong religious traditions heavily influence the politics of South and Southwest Asia. Hindu and Muslim rivalries threaten to upset the political equilibrium in South Asia, where India – in terms of population – remains the world's largest democracy. Communist China is the last great world empire. A population giant, it is still relatively closed to the western world, while on its doorstep, the economically progressive and dynamic Pacific Rim countries, led by Japan, continue to assert their worldwide economic force.

Population density
(people per sq mile)

	below 25
	26–124
	125–259
	260–649
	650–10,400
	above 10,400

POPULATION

SOME OF THE WORLD'S MOST POPULOUS and least populous regions are in Asia. The plains of eastern China, the Ganges River in India, Japan, and the Indonesian island of Java, all have very high population densities. In contrast, parts of Siberia and the Plateau of Tibet are virtually uninhabited. China has the world's greatest population – 20% of the globe's total – while India, with the second largest, is likely to overtake China within 20 years.

Calcutta's 12 million inhabitants bustle through a maze of crowded, narrow streets. The population density in India's largest city reaches almost 85,000 per sq mile (33,000 per sq km).

Map labels

ARCTIC OCEAN
East Siberian Sea
Laptev Sea
Kara Sea
Indigirka
Kolyma
Yana
Lena
Olenek
Anabar
Kheta
Kureyka
Central Siberian Plateau
Noril'sk
Arctic Circle
Ob'
West Siberian Plain
Yekaterinburg
Chelyabinsk
Ural Mountains
Ural'sk
Tobol
Ishim
Irtysh
Ob'
Rudnyy
Omsk
Tomsk
Novosibirsk
Novokuznetsk
Krasnoyarsk
Yenisey
Angara
Stony Tunguska
Lower Tunguska
Chulym
Yakutsk
Vilyuy
Aldan
Lena
Vitim
Lake Baikal
Irkutsk
Amur
Argun
Sühbaatar
Choybalsan
Erdenet
Ulan Bator
MONGOLIA
Gobi
Inner Mongolia

RUSSIAN FEDERATION
EUROPE
Siberia

Istanbul
Black Sea
Ankara
TURKEY
Anatolia
Adana
CYPRUS
Nicosia
LEBANON
Beirut
Tripoli
Haifa
Tel Aviv-Yafo
Gaza
ISRAEL
Jerusalem
Amman
JORDAN
SYRIA
Damascus
Aleppo
Gaziantep
ARMENIA
Yerevan
GEORGIA
Sokhumi
Bat'umi
K'ut'aisi
T'bilisi
Gäncä
AZERB.
AZERB.
Baku
Tabriz
Mosul
Kirkuk
Euphrates
Tigris
Baghdad
An Najaf
IRAQ
Basra
KUWAIT
Kuwait
SAUDI ARABIA
Riyadh
At Ta'if
Jedda
Red Sea
Tropic of Cancer
AFRICA
Arabian Peninsula
Ar Rub' al Khali (Empty Quarter)
Sana
Ta'izz
YEMEN
Aden
Gulf of Aden
Socotra (to Yemen)

AFRICA
Caspian Sea
Aktau
Aral Sea
Syr Darya
Amu Darya
Dashkhovuz
UZBEKISTAN
TURKMENISTAN
Ashgabat
Tashkent
Zhambyl
Bishkek
Alma-Ata
Karakol
KYRGYZSTAN
Osh
Dushanbe
TAJIKISTAN
Balkh
Qal'eh-ye Now
Herat
Kabul
Jalalabad
AFGHANISTAN
Kandahar
Quetta
Zahedan
Kerman
Shiraz
Esfahan
Ahvaz
IRAN
Iranian Plateau
Tehran
Qom
Gorgan
Mashhad
Bandar-e 'Abbas
Manama
BAHRAIN
QATAR
Doha
Abu Dhabi
U.A.E.
Ar Rustaq
Muscat
Sur
OMAN
Persian Gulf
Gulf of Oman
Arabian Sea

KAZAKHSTAN
Akmola
Karaganda
Zhezkazgan
Semipalatinsk
Balkhash
Kzyl-Orda
Lake Balkhash
Urumqi
Altai Mountains
Tien Shan
Tarim He
Takla Makan Desert
Kunlun Mountains
Plateau of Tibet
CHINA
Lanzhou
Xi'an
Luoyang
Zhengzhou
Handan
Taiyuan
Shijiazhuang
Baoding
Beijing
Baotou
Datong
Yellow River
Mianyang
Chengdu
Leshan
Chongqing
Guiyang
Liuzhou
Nanning
Kunming
Yangtze
Mekong
Salween
Brahmaputra

Srinagar
Islamabad
Jammu
Peshawar
Gujranwala
Faisalabad
Lahore
Multan
Ludhiana
PAKISTAN
Karachi
Larkana
Shikarpur
Hyderabad
Thar Desert
Indus
Delhi
New Delhi
Jaipur
Bareilly
Agra
Kanpur
Lucknow
NEPAL
Kathmandu
Thimphu
BHUTAN
Rangpur
Guwahati
Patna
Varanasi
Ganges
INDIA
Ahmadabad
Vadodara
Bhopal
Indore
Surat
Nagpur
Narmada
Jamshedpur
Khulna
Calcutta
BANGLADESH
Dhaka
Brahmanbaria
Chittagong
MYANMAR
Mandalay
Pakokku
Taunggyi
Bhubaneshwar
Bombay
Pune
Solapur
Hyderabad
Godavari
Krishna
Vijayawada
Hubli
Bangalore
Mysore
Madras
Coimbatore
Cochin
Jaffna
Trivandrum
SRI LANKA
Colombo
Bay of Bengal
Andaman Islands (to India)
Andaman Sea
Nicobar Islands (to India)
INDIAN OCEAN

Irrawaddy
Salween
Mekong
Prome
Pegu
Rangoon
Bassein
Bogale
Chiang Mai
THAILAND
Bangkok
Batdambang
Phnom Penh
CAMBODIA
Louangphabang
Vientiane
Pakxe
LAOS
VIETNAM
Ha Noi
Hai Phong
Vinh
Da Nang
Da Lat
Ho Chi Minh City
Gulf of Thailand
Kota Bharu
Taiping
Medan
Kuala Lumpur
SINGAPORE
Singapore
MALAYSIA
Sumatra
Jambi
Padang
Palembang
Jakarta
Bandung
Equator

PHYSICAL ASIA

THE STRUCTURE OF ASIA can be divided into two distinct regions. The landscape of northern Asia consists of old mountain chains, shields, plateaus, and basins, like the Ural Mountains in the west and the Central Siberian Plateau in the east. To the south of this region are a series of plateaus and basins, including the vast Plateau of Tibet and the Tarim Basin. In contrast, the landscapes of southern Asia are much younger, formed by tectonic activity beginning about 65 million years ago, leading to an almost continuous mountain chain running from Europe, across much of Asia, and culminating in the mighty Himalayan mountain belt, formed when the Indo-Australian Plate collided with the Eurasian Plate. These mountains are still being uplifted. North of the mountains lies a belt of deserts, including the Gobi and the Takla Makan. In the far south, tectonic activity has formed narrow island arcs, extending over 4,000 miles (7,000 km). To the west lies the Arabian Shield, once part of the African Plate. As it was rifted apart from Africa, the Arabian Plate collided with the Eurasian Plate, uplifting the Zagros Mountains.

SHAPING THE LANDSCAPE

IN THE NORTH, melting of extensive permafrost leads to typical periglacial features such as thermokarst. In the arid areas, wind action transports sand, creating extensive dune systems. An active tectonic margin in the south causes continued uplift and volcanic and seismic activity, but also high rates of weathering and erosion. Across the continent, huge rivers erode and transport vast quantities of sediment, depositing it on the plains or forming large deltas.

PERIGLACIATION

1 Permafrost is widespread across northern Siberia. When ground ice, which makes up a large proportion of the soil layer, melts, it contracts and extensive ground subsidence occurs. Over time, this process leads to depressions in the landscape and the gradual movement of soil down slopes. Eventually the accumulation of water in the depressions leads to thermokarstic lakes (left).

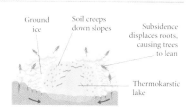

PERIGLACIATION: FORMATION OF THERMOKARST

THE EVOLVING LANDSCAPE

Landscape

- limestone region
- sinking land
- stable land
- uplifting land
- ▲ active volcano
- ● ● ● area of tectonic activity
- – – – limit of permafrost
- → ocean current

RIVER SYSTEMS

2 Vast river systems flow across Asia, many originating in the Himalayas and the Plateau of Tibet. Seasonal melting of snow and monsoon rains swell the river flow, leading to flooding and erosion. The Yellow River (above) gets its color from the high level of eroded material from the loess plateau.

Snowmelt — Monsoon rains
Yellow River dissects loess plateau — Carries large sediment load

RIVER SYSTEMS: EROSION OF THE LOESS PLATEAU BY THE YELLOW RIVER

TECTONIC ACTIVITY

7 The Dead Sea (above) lies in a pull-apart basin. The sliding of the African Plate against the Arabian Plate, at unequal rates, led to the sinking of blocks of crust. This depression has been filled by the waters of the Dead Sea and Lake Tiberias (Sea of Galilee). The plates continue to move, causing intermittent earthquakes.

Arabian Plate — Blocks of the Earth's crust sink, creating a basin
Dead Sea
African Plate

TECTONIC ACTIVITY: THE FORMATION OF A PULL-APART BASIN

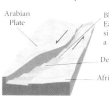

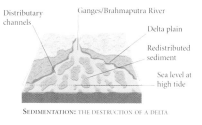

CHEMICAL WEATHERING

3 Tower karsts are widespread across southern China (above) and Vietnam. It is thought that the karstic towers were formed under a soil cover, where small depressions in the limestone bedrock began to be weathered by soil water acids, eventually creating larger hollows. This process continued over millions of years, deepening the hollows and leaving steep-sided limestone hills.

Old soil cover — Hollow being eroded by soil water acidity
Limestone hills — Eroded hollow

CHEMICAL WEATHERING: FORMATION OF TOWER KARST

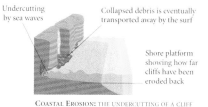

SEDIMENTATION

6 The Ganges/Brahmaputra is a tide-dominated delta (above). The two rivers transport huge quantities of mountain sediment, which is deposited on the delta plain. This debris is then redistributed by tidal currents, to form extensions to the bars, beach ridges, and deltaic deposits.

Distributary channels — Ganges/Brahmaputra River
Delta plain
Redistributed sediment
Sea level at high tide

SEDIMENTATION: THE DESTRUCTION OF A DELTA

COASTAL EROSION

5 The erosion of cliffs along the coast of Indonesia (above) and Thailand occurs when waves and currents undermine the base leading to the collapse of material. The surf then gradually erodes this material away, exposing the cliff to further undercutting. This process eventually creates shore platforms.

Undercutting by sea waves — Collapsed debris is eventually transported away by the surf
Shore platform showing how far cliffs have been eroded back

COASTAL EROSION: THE UNDERCUTTING OF A CLIFF

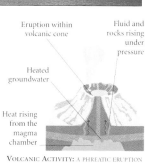

VOLCANIC ACTIVITY

4 Volcanic eruptions occur frequently across Southeast Asia's island arcs (above). Low-level eruptions occur when groundwater, superheated by underlying magma, becomes pressurized, forcing hot fluid and rocks up through cracks in the volcanic cone. This is known as a phreatic eruption.

Eruption within volcanic cone — Fluid and rocks rising under pressure
Heated groundwater
Heat rising from the magma chamber

VOLCANIC ACTIVITY: A PHREATIC ERUPTION

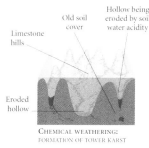

SIBERIAN PLATEAU AND PLAIN

THE WEST SIBERIAN PLAIN is one of the largest in the world, and contains a vast system of marshes. The whole area is covered by glacial deposits, underlain by the Angara Shield, a remnant of the ancient continent of Laurasia. The flat relief of the region and thick surface deposits result in poor drainage; this, combined with the freezing and thawing of the extensive permafrost layer, leads to the formation of the vast swamps that cover the area. Many of the north-flowing rivers are also frozen for up to half of the year.

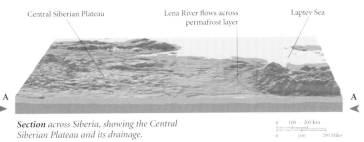

Central Siberian Plateau   Lena River flows across permafrost layer   Laptev Sea

Section across Siberia, showing the Central Siberian Plateau and its drainage.

0   100   200 Km
0   100   200 Miles

THE ARABIAN SHIELD AND IRANIAN PLATEAU

APPROXIMATELY FIVE MILLION YEARS AGO, rifting of the continental crust split the Arabian Plate from the African Plate and flooded the Red Sea. As this rift spread, the Arabian Plate collided with the Eurasian Plate, transforming part of the Tethys seabed into the Zagros Mountains, which run northwest–southeast across western Iran.

The confluence of the Tigris and Euphrates on the Mesopotamian Depression   Zagros Mountains   Folded sedimentary rock strata   Iranian Plateau

Cross-section through southwestern Asia, showing the Mesopotamian Depression, the folded Zagros Mountains, and the Iranian Plateau.

0   50   100 Km
0   50   100 Miles

THE TURAN BASIN AND KAZAKH UPLANDS

THE TURAN BASIN AND KAZAKH UPLANDS are a complex mixture of mountain foothills, an arid limestone plateau, and deserts including the Kyzl Kum and Kara Kum. In the center of the Turan Lowland – an area of inland drainage – is the desiccated Aral Sea, reduced to a fraction of its former size because of the diversion of its flow into irrigation channels. The only rivers with sufficient water to cross this arid region are the Syr Dayra and Amu Dayra.

THE INDIAN SHIELD AND HIMALAYAN SYSTEM

THE LARGE SHIELD AREA beneath the Indian subcontinent is between 2.5 and 3.5 billion years old. As the floor of the southern Indian Ocean spread, it pushed the Indian Shield north. It was eventually driven beneath the Plateau of Tibet. This process closed up the ancient Tethys Sea and uplifted the world's highest mountain chain, the Himalayas. Much of the uplifted rock strata was from the seabed of the Tethys Sea, partly accounting for the weakness of the rocks and the high levels of erosion found in the Himalayas.

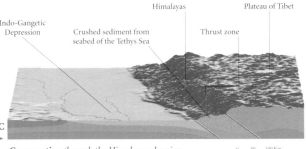

Indo-Gangetic Depression   Himalayas   Plateau of Tibet   Crushed sediment from seabed of the Tethys Sea   Thrust zone

Cross-section through the Himalayas showing thrust faulting of the rock strata.

0   50   100 Km
0   50   100 Miles

CENTRAL ASIAN PLATEAUS AND BASINS

THE PLATEAU OF TIBET lies north of the Himalayas and covers 965,250 sq miles (2,500,000 sq km); its average elevation is 16,500 ft (5,000 m). The region is noted for its extreme aridity. In the south, the Himalayan mountain belt blocks moisture-bearing winds. The pressure from the Indo-Australian Plate against the plateau is causing both uplift and, when combined with the downward force caused by the weight of the plateau, extension east and west of the more malleable underlying crust. The brittle upper rock layers are extensively faulted.

Mantle   Weight of plateau contributes to east–west extension of the crust   Extension of brittle upper crust leads to extensive faulting across the Plateau of Tibet   Malleable lower crust stretching east and west

Cross-section across the Plateau of Tibet, showing uplift and crustal extension caused by the collision of the Indo-Australian and Eurasian plates.

0   200   400 Km
0   200   400 Miles

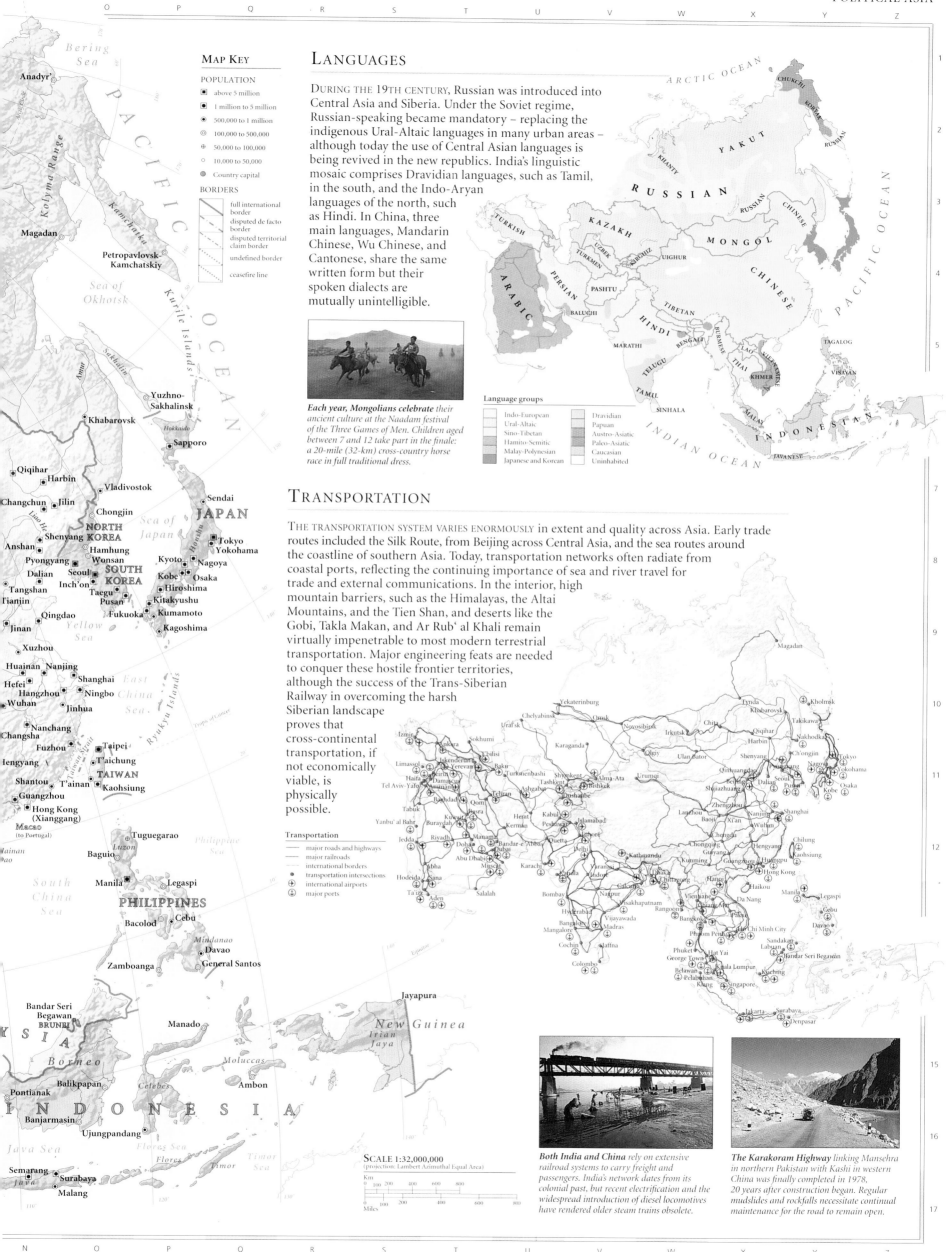

MAP KEY

POPULATION
- above 5 million
- 1 million to 5 million
- 500,000 to 1 million
- 100,000 to 500,000
- 50,000 to 100,000
- 10,000 to 50,000
- Country capital

BORDERS
- full international border
- disputed de facto border
- disputed territorial claim border
- undefined border
- ceasefire line

LANGUAGES

DURING THE 19TH CENTURY, Russian was introduced into Central Asia and Siberia. Under the Soviet regime, Russian-speaking became mandatory – replacing the indigenous Ural-Altaic languages in many urban areas – although today the use of Central Asian languages is being revived in the new republics. India's linguistic mosaic comprises Dravidian languages, such as Tamil, in the south, and the Indo-Aryan languages of the north, such as Hindi. In China, three main languages, Mandarin Chinese, Wu Chinese, and Cantonese, share the same written form but their spoken dialects are mutually unintelligible.

Each year, Mongolians celebrate their ancient culture at the Naadam festival of the Three Games of Men. Children aged between 7 and 12 take part in the finale: a 20-mile (32-km) cross-country horse race in full traditional dress.

Language groups
- Indo-European
- Ural-Altaic
- Sino-Tibetan
- Hamito-Semitic
- Malay-Polynesian
- Japanese and Korean
- Dravidian
- Papuan
- Austro-Asiatic
- Paleo-Asiatic
- Caucasian
- Uninhabited

TRANSPORTATION

THE TRANSPORTATION SYSTEM VARIES ENORMOUSLY in extent and quality across Asia. Early trade routes included the Silk Route, from Beijing across Central Asia, and the sea routes around the coastline of southern Asia. Today, transportation networks often radiate from coastal ports, reflecting the continuing importance of sea and river travel for trade and external communications. In the interior, high mountain barriers, such as the Himalayas, the Altai Mountains, and the Tien Shan, and deserts like the Gobi, Takla Makan, and Ar Rub' al Khali remain virtually impenetrable to most modern terrestrial transportation. Major engineering feats are needed to conquer these hostile frontier territories, although the success of the Trans-Siberian Railway in overcoming the harsh Siberian landscape proves that cross-continental transportation, if not economically viable, is physically possible.

Transportation
- major roads and highways
- major railroads
- international borders
- transportation intersections
- international airports
- major ports

SCALE 1:32,000,000
(projection: Lambert Azimuthal Equal Area)

Km
0 100 200 400 600 800

Miles
0 100 200 400 600 800

Both India and China rely on extensive railroad systems to carry freight and passengers. India's network dates from its colonial past, but recent electrification and the widespread introduction of diesel locomotives have rendered older steam trains obsolete.

The Karakoram Highway linking Mansehra in northern Pakistan with Kashi in western China was finally completed in 1978, 20 years after construction began. Regular mudslides and rockfalls necessitate continual maintenance for the road to remain open.

CLIMATE

THE CLIMATE OF ASIA exhibits marked differences from region to region, with freezing polar conditions in the north, hot and cold deserts in central regions, and subtropical conditions throughout the south. Much of this variation can be attributed to enormous mountain barriers and internal depressions found across the continent. Monsoon winds, which reverse semiannually, cause alternate wet and dry seasons across southern Asia. These air masses moving north from the ocean are stripped of their moisture over the Himalayas, causing arid conditions across the Plateau of Tibet. Both the south and east are susceptible to tropical cyclones or typhoons.

Treeless, frozen plains, with permanently frozen soil layers characterize much of Siberia. Even during the summer, only the top 2–3 ft (1 m) of soil thaws.

Tundralike marshes are found alongside vast sand dunes in the Takla Makan Desert in China. In the spring, windstorms of hurricane force can send dust as high as 13,000 ft (4,000 m) into the air.

The Gobi Desert experiences major extremes in climate, with winter temperatures sometimes falling below -40°F (-40°C) and summer temperatures exceeding 113°F (45°C).

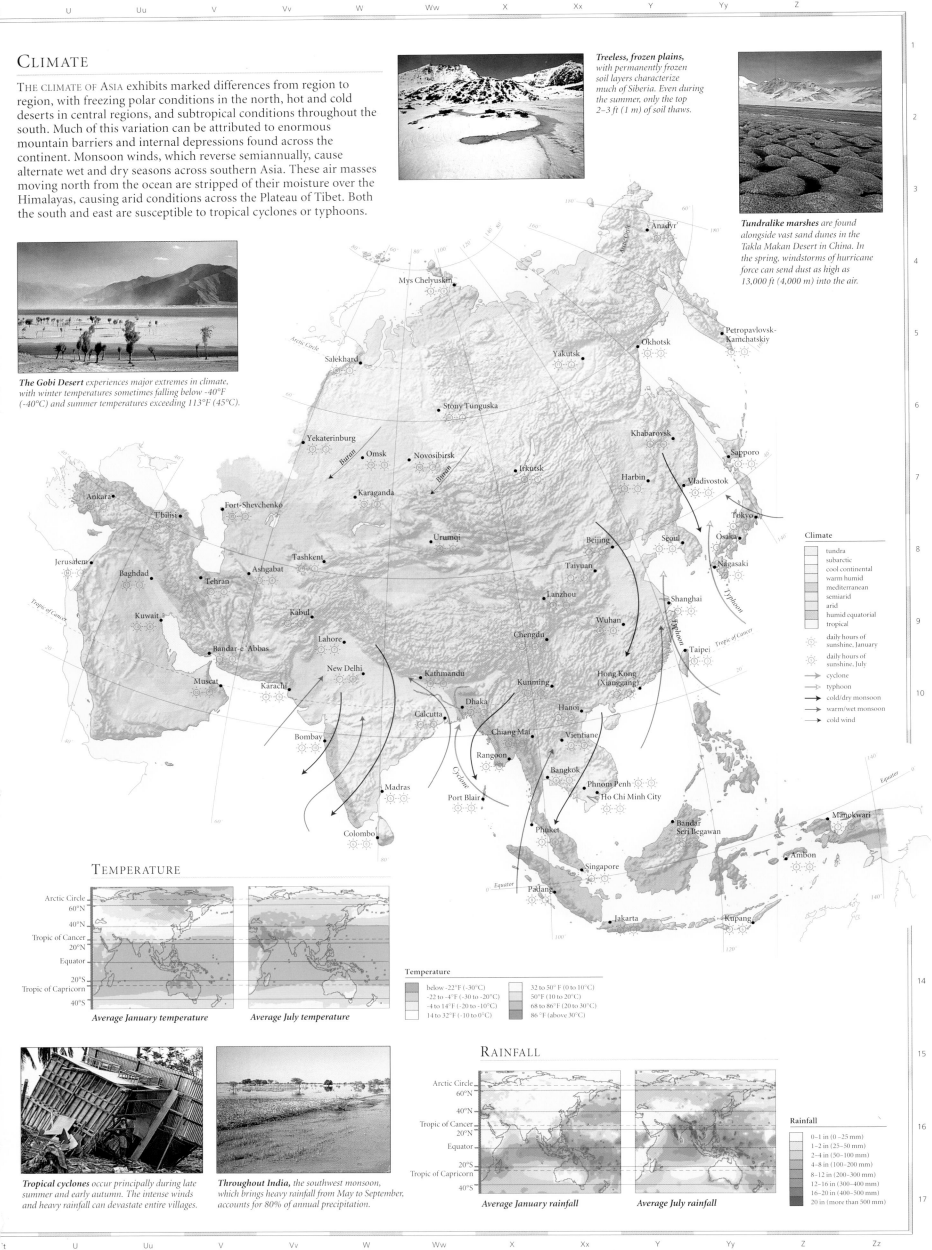

Climate
- tundra
- subarctic
- cool continental
- warm humid
- mediterranean
- semiarid
- arid
- humid equatorial
- tropical
- ☼ daily hours of sunshine, January
- ☼ daily hours of sunshine, July
- → cyclone
- → typhoon
- → cold/dry monsoon
- → warm/wet monsoon
- → cold wind

TEMPERATURE

Average January temperature

Average July temperature

Temperature
below -22°F (-30°C)	32 to 50° F (0 to 10°C)
-22 to -4°F (-30 to -20°C)	50°F (10 to 20°C)
-4 to 14°F (-20 to -10°C)	68 to 86°F (20 to 30°C)
14 to 32°F (-10 to 0°C)	86 °F (above 30°C)

RAINFALL

Average January rainfall

Average July rainfall

Rainfall
- 0–1 in (0 –25 mm)
- 1–2 in (25–50 mm)
- 2–4 in (50–100 mm)
- 4–8 in (100–200 mm)
- 8–12 in (200–300 mm)
- 12–16 in (300–400 mm)
- 16–20 in (400–500 mm)
- 20 in (more than 500 mm)

Tropical cyclones occur principally during late summer and early autumn. The intense winds and heavy rainfall can devastate entire villages.

Throughout India, the southwest monsoon, which brings heavy rainfall from May to September, accounts for 80% of annual precipitation.

EAST SIBERIAN MOUNTAINS

THE FOLD MOUNTAINS along the coast of northeast Asia are formed from folded sedimentary strata from an ancient sea shelf. The peninsula of Kamchatka, in the far northeast, extends 600 miles (1,000 km) into the Pacific Ocean. The mountain range continues as the Kurile Island arc. Kamchatka lies at the boundary of the Eurasian and Pacific plates, and contains 74 volcanoes, of which only 13 are still active.

SCALE 1:30,000,000
(projection: Lambert Azimuthal Equal Area)

Km 0 100 200 400 600 800

Miles 0 100 200 400 600 800

MAP KEY

ELEVATION

	6000m / 19,686ft
	4000m / 13,124ft
	3000m / 9843ft
	2000m / 6562ft
	1000m / 3281ft
	500m / 1640ft
	250m / 820ft
	100m / 328ft
	sea level

PLATE MARGINS
(for explanation see page xiv)

———— constructive

△△△ destructive

———— conservative

·········· uncertain

———— physiographic regions

➤—➤ line of cross-section

EAST ASIAN PLAINS AND UPLANDS

SEVERAL, SMALL, ISOLATED shield areas, such as the Shandong Peninsula, are found in East Asia. Between these stable shield areas, large river systems like the Yangtze and the Yellow River have deposited thick layers of sediment, forming extensive alluvial plains. The largest of these is the Great Plain of China, the relief of which does not rise above 300 ft (100 m).

COASTAL LOWLANDS AND ISLAND ARCS

THE COASTAL PLAINS that fringe Southeast Asia contain many large delta systems, caused by high levels of rainfall and the erosion of the Himalayas, the Plateau of Tibet, and relict loess deposits. To the south is an extensive island archipelago, lying on the drowned Sunda Shelf. Most of these islands are volcanic in origin, caused by the subduction of the Indo-Australian Plate beneath the Eurasian Plate.

Cross-section through Southeast Asia, showing the subduction zone between the Indo-Australian and Eurasian plates and the island arc.

TURKEY & THE CAUCASUS

ARMENIA, AZERBAIJAN, GEORGIA, TURKEY

THIS REGION OCCUPIES THE FRAGMENTED JUNCTION between Europe, Asia, and the Russian Federation. Sunni Islam provides a common identity for the secular state of Turkey, which the revered leader Kemal Atatürk established out of the remnants of the Ottoman Empire after the First World War. Turkey has a broad resource base and expanding trade links with Europe, but the east is relatively undeveloped and strife between the state and a large Kurdish minority has yet to be resolved. Georgia is similarly challenged by ethnic separatism, while the Christian state of Armenia and the mainly Muslim and oil-rich Azerbaijan are locked in conflict over the territory of Nagornyy Karabakh.

TRANSPORTATION & INDUSTRY

TURKEY LEADS THE REGION'S well diversified economy. Petrochemicals, textiles, engineering, and food processing are the main industries. Azerbaijan is able to export oil, while the other states rely heavily on hydro-electric power and imported fuel. Georgia produces precision machinery. War and earthquake damage have devastated Armenia's infrastructure.

Azerbaijan has substantial oil reserves, located in and around the Caspian Sea. They were some of the earliest oil fields in the world to be exploited.

Major industry and infrastructure

- carpetweaving
- cement
- chemicals
- coal
- engineering
- food processing
- oil
- textiles
- tourism
- vehicle manufacture
- ■ capital cities
- ● major towns
- ✈ international airports
- — major roads
- ▨ major industrial areas

TRANSPORTATION NETWORK

279,352 miles
(449,642 km)

513 miles
(826 km)

8,020 miles
(12,914 km)

745 miles
(1,200 km)

Physical and political barriers limit communications between Armenia, Georgia, and Azerbaijan severely. Turkey has a relatively well-developed transportation network.

USING THE LAND & SEA

TURKEY IS LARGELY SELF-SUFFICIENT in food. The irrigated Black Sea coastlands have the world's highest yields of hazelnuts. Tobacco, cotton, golden raisins, tea, and figs are the region's main cash crops and a great range of fruit and vegetables are grown. Wine grapes are among the labor-intensive crops that allow full use of limited agricultural land in the Caucasus. Sturgeon fishing is particularly important in Azerbaijan.

Land use and agricultural distribution

- cattle
- goats
- cotton
- fishing
- fruit
- hazelnuts
- olives
- sugar beet
- tobacco
- vineyards
- ■ capital cities
- ● major towns
- pasture
- cropland
- forest

THE URBAN/RURAL POPULATION DIVIDE

urban 62%   rural 38%

0 10 20 30 40 50 60 70 80 90 100

POPULATION DENSITY
206 people per sq mile
(80 people per sq km)

TOTAL LAND AREA
368,912 sq miles
(955,730 sq km)

For many centuries, Istanbul has held tremendous strategic importance as a crucial gateway between Europe and Asia. Founded by the Greeks as Byzantium, the city became the center of the East Roman Empire and was known as Constantinople to the Romans. Beginning in the 15th century, the city became the center of the great Ottoman Empire.

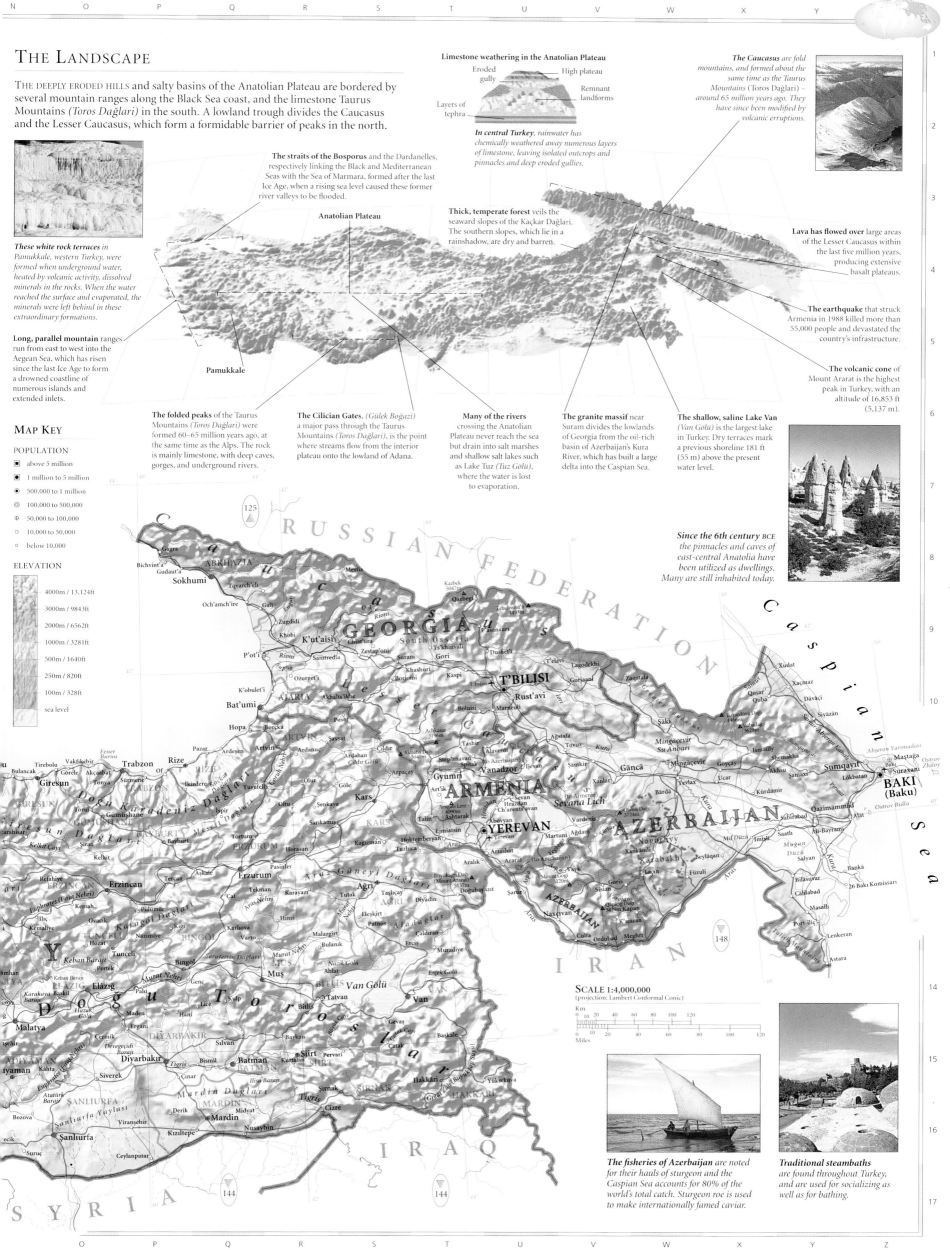

THE LANDSCAPE

THE DEEPLY ERODED HILLS and salty basins of the Anatolian Plateau are bordered by several mountain ranges along the Black Sea coast, and the limestone Taurus Mountains (*Toros Dağlari*) in the south. A lowland trough divides the Caucasus and the Lesser Caucasus, which form a formidable barrier of peaks in the north.

These white rock terraces in Pamukkale, western Turkey, were formed when underground water, heated by volcanic activity, dissolved minerals in the rocks. When the water reached the surface and evaporated, the minerals were left behind in these extraordinary formations.

Long, parallel mountain ranges run from east to west into the Aegean Sea, which has risen since the last Ice Age to form a drowned coastline of numerous islands and extended inlets.

The straits of the Bosporus and the Dardanelles, respectively linking the Black and Mediterranean Seas with the Sea of Marmara, formed after the last Ice Age, when a rising sea level caused these former river valleys to be flooded.

Anatolian Plateau

Thick, temperate forest veils the seaward slopes of the Kaçkar Dağlari. The southern slopes, which lie in a rainshadow, are dry and barren.

Limestone weathering in the Anatolian Plateau
Eroded gully — High plateau
— Remnant landforms
Layers of tephra

In central Turkey, rainwater has chemically weathered away numerous layers of limestone, leaving isolated outcrops and pinnacles and deep eroded gullies.

The Caucasus are fold mountains, and formed about the same time as the Taurus Mountains (Toros Dağlari) – around 65 million years ago. They have since been modified by volcanic eruptions.

Lava has flowed over large areas of the Lesser Caucasus within the last five million years, producing extensive basalt plateaus.

The earthquake that struck Armenia in 1988 killed more than 55,000 people and devastated the country's infrastructure.

The volcanic cone of Mount Ararat is the highest peak in Turkey, with an altitude of 16,853 ft (5,137 m).

Pamukkale

The folded peaks of the Taurus Mountains (*Toros Dağlari*) were formed 60–65 million years ago, at the same time as the Alps. The rock is mainly limestone, with deep caves, gorges, and underground rivers.

The Cilician Gates, (*Gülek Boğazi*) a major pass through the Taurus Mountains (*Toros Dağlari*), is the point where streams flow from the interior plateau onto the lowland of Adana.

Many of the rivers crossing the Anatolian Plateau never reach the sea but drain into salt marshes and shallow salt lakes such as Lake Tuz (*Tuz Gölü*), where the water is lost to evaporation.

The granite massif near Suram divides the lowlands of Georgia from the oil-rich basin of Azerbaijan's Kura River, which has built a large delta into the Caspian Sea.

The shallow, saline Lake Van (*Van Gölü*) is the largest lake in Turkey. Dry terraces mark a previous shoreline 181 ft (55 m) above the present water level.

Since the 6th century BCE the pinnacles and caves of east-central Anatolia have been utilized as dwellings. Many are still inhabited today.

MAP KEY

POPULATION
- ■ above 5 million
- ▣ 1 million to 5 million
- ▣ 500,000 to 1 million
- ◉ 100,000 to 500,000
- ⊕ 50,000 to 100,000
- ○ 10,000 to 50,000
- ○ below 10,000

ELEVATION
- 4000m / 13,124ft
- 3000m / 9843ft
- 2000m / 6562ft
- 1000m / 3281ft
- 500m / 1640ft
- 250m / 820ft
- 100m / 328ft
- sea level

SCALE 1:4,000,000
(projection: Lambert Conformal Conic)

Km
0 10 20 40 60 80 100 120
Miles

The fisheries of Azerbaijan are noted for their hauls of sturgeon and the Caspian Sea accounts for 80% of the world's total catch. Sturgeon roe is used to make internationally famed caviar.

Traditional steambaths are found throughout Turkey, and are used for socializing as well as for bathing.

THE NEAR EAST

IRAQ, ISRAEL, JORDAN, LEBANON, SYRIA

SOME OF THE WORLD'S OLDEST CIVILIZATIONS developed in this region – the Fertile Crescent – which is venerated by Jews, Muslims, and Christians, but torn by competing religious, ethnic, and national claims to the land. Turkish Ottoman rule ended with the First World War and the region was divided into areas administered by Britain and France. The UN endorsed calls for a Jewish homeland in what was then Palestine and in 1948 the state of Israel was declared. Hostility toward the Jewish state led to a series of wars but since 1977, and especially since 1993, a peace process between Israel and her neighbors has been evolving. Since independence, Syria has played a leading role in Middle Eastern politics. The once-prosperous state of Lebanon is emerging from a ruinous factional war, while Iraq's great oil wealth has funded military campaigns against Iran and Kuwait and the stifling of internal dissent, leading to international ostracization.

USING THE LAND & SEA

WATER SCARCITY limits cropland to the north and to areas watered principally by the Tigris, Euphrates, and Jordan Rivers. In Israel, new irrigation techniques are allowing cultivation in the arid Negev. Wheat is the chief grain and large areas of scrub support herds of livestock. Commercial produce includes dates, tobacco, citrus fruits, olives, grapes, and cotton, which is Syria's main export crop. Fishing is still important in the Mediterranean.

THE URBAN/RURAL POPULATION DIVIDE

urban 63%   rural 37%

POPULATION DENSITY
145 people per sq mile
(56 people per sq km)

TOTAL LAND AREA
325,460 sq miles
(843,160 sq km)

Land use and agricultural distribution

- sheep
- cereals
- citrus fruits
- cotton
- dates
- fishing
- rice
- tobacco
- capital cities
- major towns
- pasture
- cropland
- wetland
- desert

TRANSPORTATION & INDUSTRY

THE PETROCHEMICAL INDUSTRY is well established, and central to the economies of Syria and Iraq, which was the world's second largest oil exporter before the war with Iran which began in 1980. Lebanon has traditionally been a center for commerce, while Israel has a well-diversified economy with an expanding tourist industry, despite few natural resources.

TRANSPORTATION NETWORK

62,624 miles (100,844 km)

1,000 miles (1,600 km)

3,897 miles (6,275 km)

498 miles (802 km)

Major industry and infrastructure
- car manufacture
- cement
- chemicals
- electronics
- finance
- food processing
- iron & steel
- oil
- oil refining
- textiles
- capital cities
- major towns
- international airports
- major roads
- major industrial areas

Jordan's seaport of Al 'Aqabah is connected to Damascus in Syria by road and rail. This route to the Red Sea provides for large exports of phosphate and trade with states in the Persian Gulf.

The Dome of the Rock in Jerusalem is a magnificent mosque, revered by Muslims. Close by is the Western Wall, the city's most sacred Jewish landmark and the Church of the Holy Sepulchre, a famous Christian place of worship.

The city of Petra, carved from spectacular rose-colored limestone, lies deep within a canyon in southern Jordan. Revenues from the spice trade funded the construction of the city which was built by the Nabatean people in about 400 BCE.

Water and wind erosion over thousands of years have created the Canyon of the Oasis at En 'Avedat in the Negev Desert (HaNegev). Extreme diurnal temperature fluctuations, coupled with wind erosion, have caused layers of rock to crack and peel away.

THE LANDSCAPE

THE AL JAZIRAH PLATEAU divides the Euphrates and Tigris Rivers, which cross the Mesopotamian plain to reach their confluence in the southeast. The rocky Syrian Desert extends west to the northern extremity of the Great Rift Valley, which runs from the mountains of Lebanon to the Gulf of Aqaba. The Jordan River flows south along this trough into the Dead Sea, divided from the Mediterranean coastal plain by a steep-sided plateau.

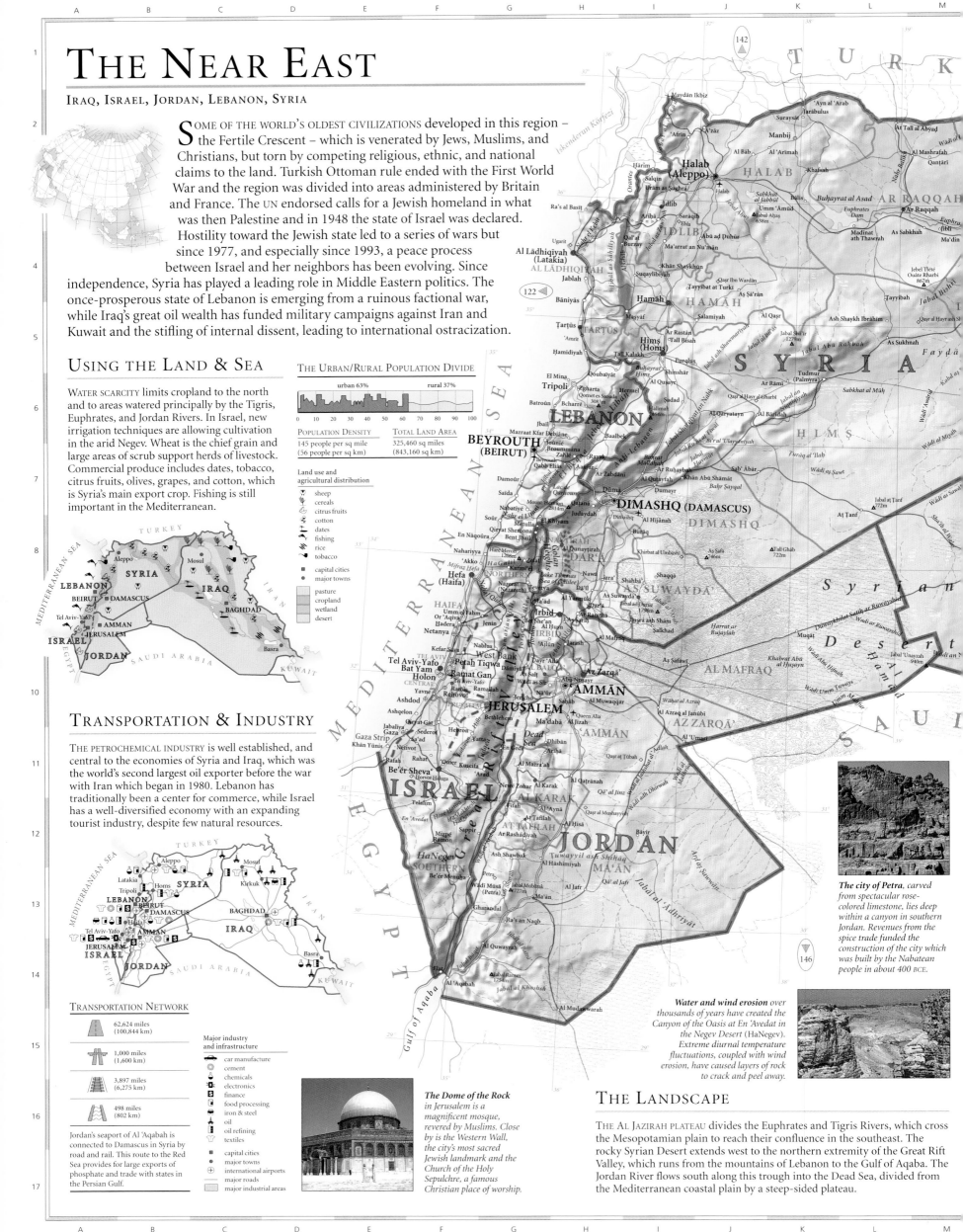

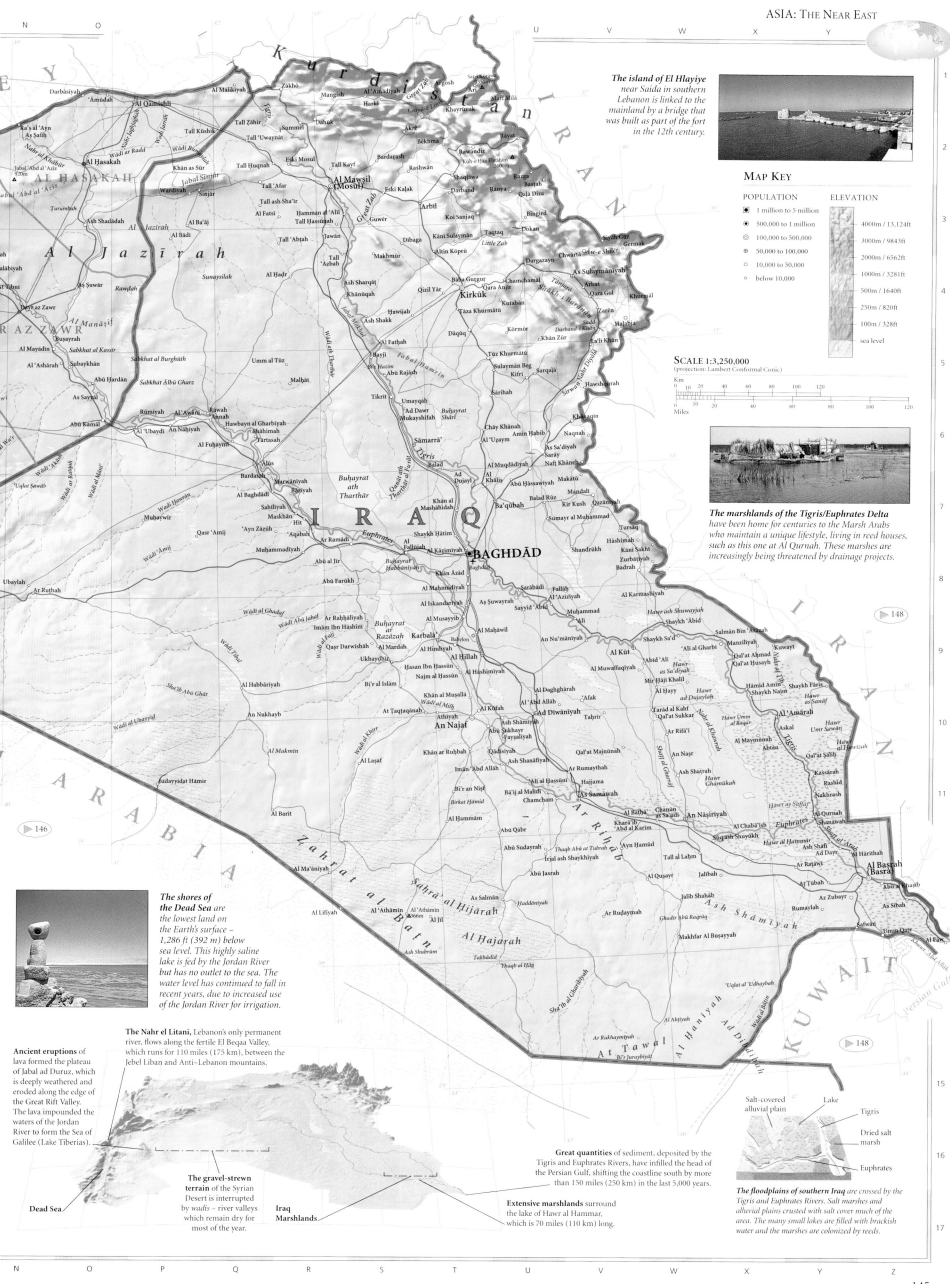

The island of El Hlayiye near Saida in southern Lebanon is linked to the mainland by a bridge that was built as part of the fort in the 12th century.

MAP KEY

POPULATION

- ◼ 1 million to 5 million
- ◉ 500,000 to 1 million
- ⊕ 100,000 to 500,000
- ⊕ 50,000 to 100,000
- ⊙ 10,000 to 50,000
- ○ below 10,000

ELEVATION

- 4000m / 13,124ft
- 3000m / 9843ft
- 2000m / 6562ft
- 1000m / 3281ft
- 500m / 1640ft
- 250m / 820ft
- 100m / 328ft
- sea level

SCALE 1:3,250,000
(projection: Lambert Conformal Conic)

Km 0 10 20 40 60 80 100 120

Miles 0 10 20 40 60 80 100 120

The marshlands of the Tigris/Euphrates Delta have been home for centuries to the Marsh Arabs who maintain a unique lifestyle, living in reed houses, such as this one at Al Qurnah. These marshes are increasingly being threatened by drainage projects.

The shores of the Dead Sea are the lowest land on the Earth's surface – 1,286 ft (392 m) below sea level. This highly saline lake is fed by the Jordan River but has no outlet to the sea. The water level has continued to fall in recent years, due to increased use of the Jordan River for irrigation.

Ancient eruptions of lava formed the plateau of Jabal ad Duruz, which is deeply weathered and eroded along the edge of the Great Rift Valley. The lava impounded the waters of the Jordan River to form the Sea of Galilee (Lake Tiberias).

The Nahr el Litani, Lebanon's only permanent river, flows along the fertile El Beqaa Valley, which runs for 110 miles (175 km), between the Jebel Liban and Anti–Lebanon mountains.

The gravel-strewn terrain of the Syrian Desert is interrupted by *wadis* – river valleys which remain dry for most of the year.

Iraq Marshlands

Great quantities of sediment, deposited by the Tigris and Euphrates Rivers, have infilled the head of the Persian Gulf, shifting the coastline south by more than 150 miles (250 km) in the last 5,000 years.

Extensive marshlands surround the lake of Hawr al Hammar, which is 70 miles (110 km) long.

The floodplains of southern Iraq are crossed by the Tigris and Euphrates Rivers. Salt marshes and alluvial plains crusted with salt cover much of the area. The many small lakes are filled with brackish water and the marshes are colonized by reeds.

Salt-covered alluvial plain — Lake — Tigris — Dried salt marsh — Euphrates

THE ARABIAN PENINSULA

BAHRAIN, KUWAIT, OMAN, QATAR, SAUDI ARABIA, UNITED ARAB EMIRATES (UAE), YEMEN

HUGE EXPANSES OF DESERT cover much of the Arabian Peninsula, limiting settlement to oases, the mountains along the Red Sea, and coastal belts. The most populous area is the fertile highlands of Yemen. The Islamic faith and Arabic language give the region a cultural and religious unity, and the Saudi city of Mecca is Islam's most holy place, visited by over two million pilgrims each year. More than half of the world's oil reserves are contained in this region, and the exploitation of oil and gas has brought great wealth, particularly to Saudi Arabia. Yemen and Oman are the least developed of the Arabian states, with large rural populations. Within Saudi Arabia over two-thirds of the people live in urban areas.

USING THE LAND

MOST OF THE ARABIAN PENINSULA is unsuited to settled agriculture, making irrigation and land reclamation projects essential. The narrow coastal plain and isolated oases, commonly amounting to less than 1% of the land area, are used to cultivate grains, coffee, and exotic fruits. Goats, sheep, and camels are widespread throughout the region.

THE URBAN/RURAL POPULATION DIVIDE

urban 42%	rural 58%

0 10 20 30 40 50 60 70 80 90 100

POPULATION DENSITY	TOTAL LAND AREA
29 people per sq mile (11 people per sq km)	1,147,856 sq miles (2,973,720 sq km)

Land use and agricultural distribution

goats · sheep · cereals · coffee · dates · fruit

capital cities · major towns · pasture · cropland · desert

The fertile soils of Yemen have encouraged the settlement of almost all of the land from sea level up to the mountains at 10,000 ft (3,050 m). In the higher reaches, elaborate terraces have been constructed to facilitate crop cultivation.

THE LANDSCAPE

A PLATEAU MORE THAN 2,500 ft (760 m) high extends across much of the Arabian Peninsula. The plateau slopes eastward from the massive, rifted escarpment along the coast of the Red Sea, to the shallow waters of the Persian Gulf. The interior is characterized by *cuestas* and valleys, drained by a system of *wadis*. A crescent of sand and gravel deserts lies to the east.

The An Nafud Desert is covered with *barchan* dunes varying between 30–100 ft (10–30 m) high. The "horns" of the crescent-shaped dunes reflect the direction in which they are being moved by the wind.

Inselbergs are dotted over a wide area of the Najd Plateau. These resistant remnants of the ancient basement rock are left standing when the softer surrounding rock has been worn away.

Evaporation
Extra high tidal level
Normal level of tidal range
Crusted layer left behind

A sabkha is a flat, salt-encrusted plain that occurs near the coast just above the high water mark. Flooding by seawater leads to saturation of the land with saline-rich groundwater. As this evaporates, a cracked layer of sand cemented together with salt, gypsum, and calcium carbonate, is left behind.

Across the Najd Plateau the flat relief is broken by *mesas*; steep-sided rock plateaus and *cuestas*; ridges with one steep and one gentle slope.

Few areas in the Arabian Peninsula have rivers flowing through them. Most are drained by seasonal watercourses, called *wadis*.

The Hejaz (*Al Ḥijāz*) and Asir Mountains form part of the same geological region as the highlands of Sudan and Eritrea, to which they were once joined. They were separated when faulting opened the Red Sea, more than 50 million years ago.

Ar Rub' al Khali, also known as the Empty Quarter, is the most arid part of the Arabian Peninsula. It is the largest uninterrupted sand desert in the world. Ridges of sand up to 25 miles (40 km) long, run northeast-southwest, giving characteristic linear dunes.

The Jabal an Nabi Shu'ayb in Yemen is the highest point in the peninsula, rising to 12,336 ft (3,760 m).

The Arabian Shield underpins the west of the peninsula. It is a fragment of the ancient continent, Gondwanaland, which was separated by rifting millions of years ago.

Every Muslim must make at least one pilgrimage or hajj to Mecca (Makkah), in Saudi Arabia, during their lifetime. The cloth-covered shrine is called the Ka'bah, and is regarded by Muslims as the most sacred place on Earth.

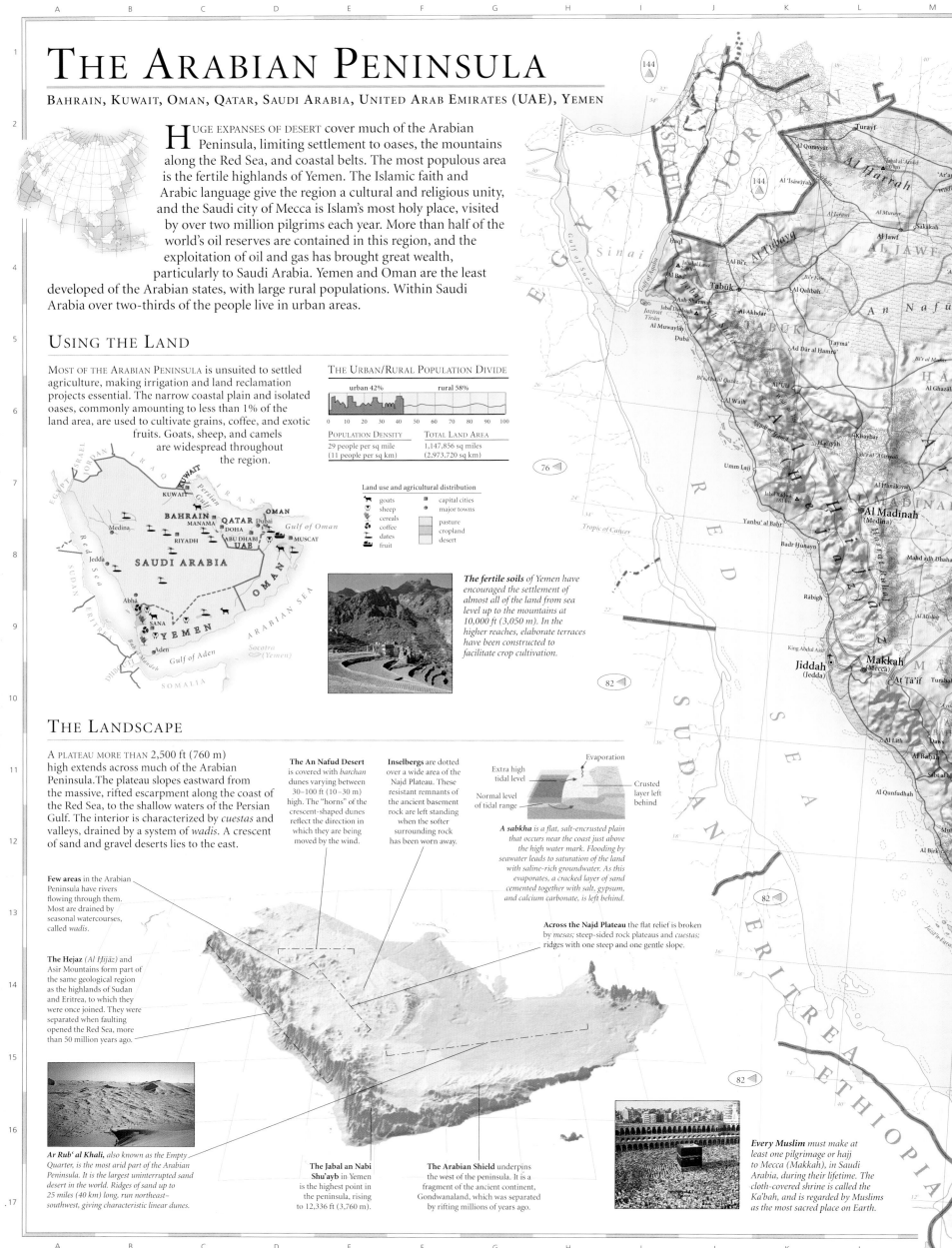

TRANSPORTATION & INDUSTRY

THE EXTRACTION AND REFINING OF OIL AND GAS are the major industrial activities in the Arabian Peninsula. The region also has an active construction sector, with many Arab cities reflecting the wealth generated by the oil industry. The service sector is dominated by financial and technical institutions, which, like the construction sector, mainly serve the oil industry. Traditional crafts such as carpet weaving are found in rural areas.

Saudi Arabia contains the world's largest oil reserves, lying mainly along the Persian Gulf coast. Each day the region produces 8.3 million barrels of oil. Here, in the desert, excess oil is being burned off.

TRANSPORTATION NETWORK

139,180 miles (224,122 km)		373 miles (600 km)	
848 miles (1,365 km)		none	

Internal surface transportation is poorly developed across the peninsula. Along the coast, commerical routes have developed, but connections between bordering states rely on major airports.

Major industry and infrastructure

- cement
- chemicals
- iron & steel
- oil
- oil refining
- food processing
- capital cities
- major towns
- international airports
- major roads
- major industrial areas

Seasonal watercourses or wadis drain much of the interior of the Arabian Peninsula. Although they remain dry for most of the year, they are prone to flash floods after heavy rains.

MAP KEY

POPULATION

- 1 million to 5 million
- 500,000 to 1 million
- 100,000 to 500,000
- 50,000 to 100,000
- 10,000 to 50,000
- below 10,000

ELEVATION

3000m / 9843ft
2000m / 6562ft
1000m / 3281ft
500m / 1640ft
250m / 820ft
100m / 328ft
sea level

SCALE 1:7,500,000
(projection: Lambert Conformal Conic)

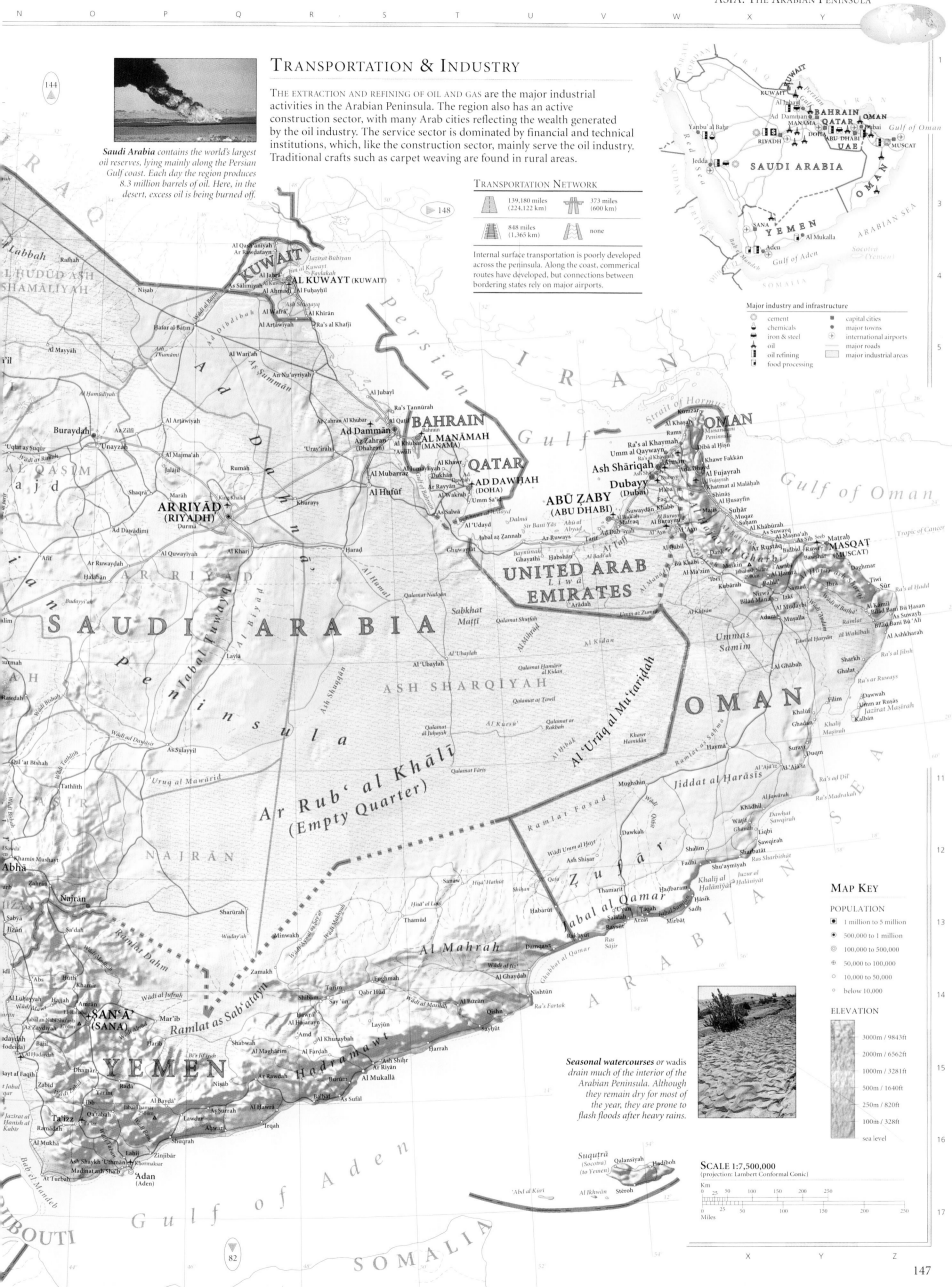

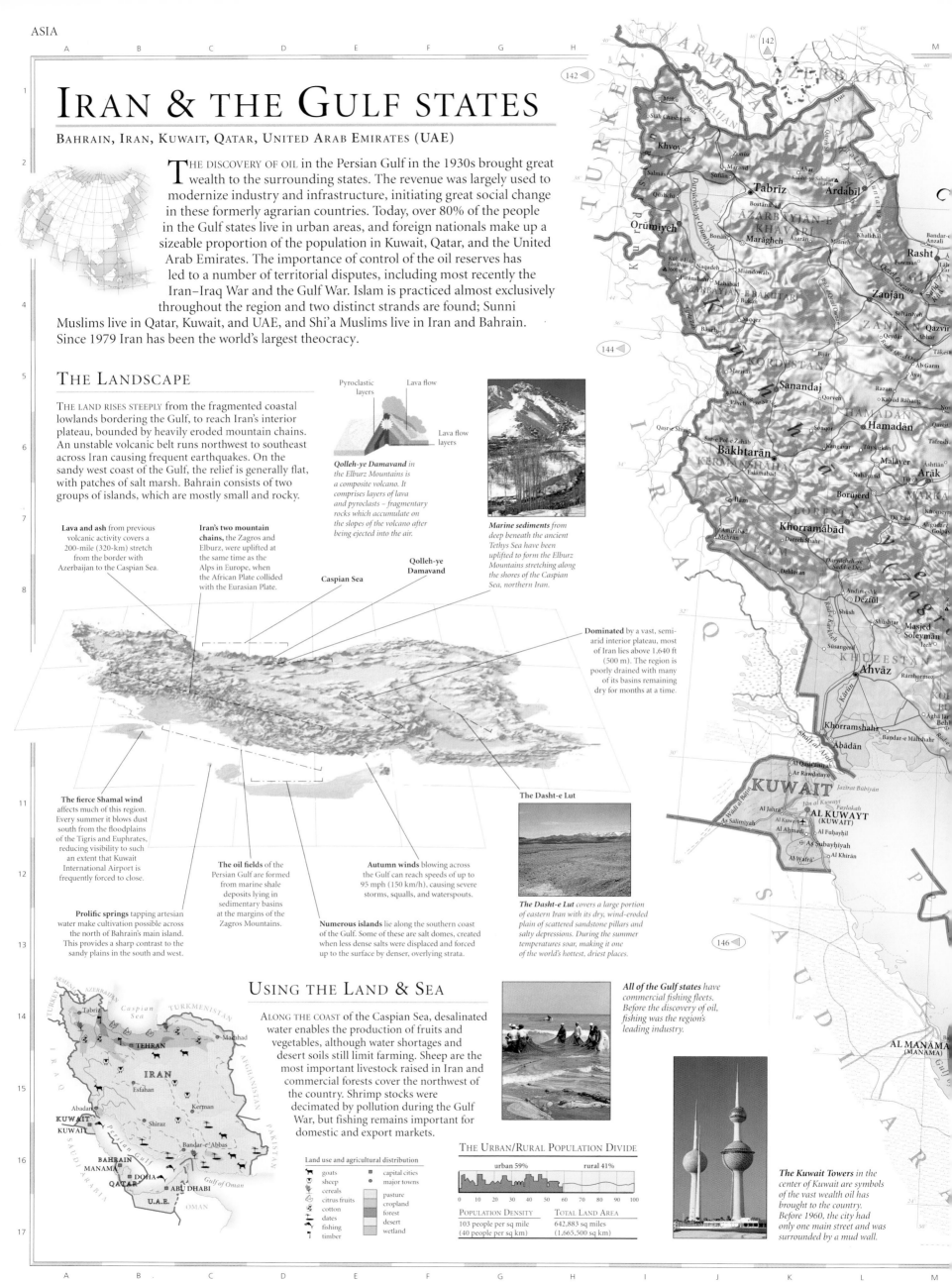

IRAN & THE GULF STATES

BAHRAIN, IRAN, KUWAIT, QATAR, UNITED ARAB EMIRATES (UAE)

THE DISCOVERY OF OIL in the Persian Gulf in the 1930s brought great wealth to the surrounding states. The revenue was largely used to modernize industry and infrastructure, initiating great social change in these formerly agrarian countries. Today, over 80% of the people in the Gulf states live in urban areas, and foreign nationals make up a sizeable proportion of the population in Kuwait, Qatar, and the United Arab Emirates. The importance of control of the oil reserves has led to a number of territorial disputes, including most recently the Iran–Iraq War and the Gulf War. Islam is practiced almost exclusively throughout the region and two distinct strands are found; Sunni Muslims live in Qatar, Kuwait, and UAE, and Shi'a Muslims live in Iran and Bahrain. Since 1979 Iran has been the world's largest theocracy.

THE LANDSCAPE

THE LAND RISES STEEPLY from the fragmented coastal lowlands bordering the Gulf, to reach Iran's interior plateau, bounded by heavily eroded mountain chains. An unstable volcanic belt runs northwest to southeast across Iran causing frequent earthquakes. On the sandy west coast of the Gulf, the relief is generally flat, with patches of salt marsh. Bahrain consists of two groups of islands, which are mostly small and rocky.

Qolleh-ye Damavand in the Elburz Mountains is a composite volcano. It comprises layers of lava and pyroclasts – fragmentary rocks which accumulate on the slopes of the volcano after being ejected into the air.

Marine sediments from deep beneath the ancient Tethys Sea have been uplifted to form the Elburz Mountains stretching along the shores of the Caspian Sea, northern Iran.

Lava and ash from previous volcanic activity covers a 200-mile (320-km) stretch from the border with Azerbaijan to the Caspian Sea.

Iran's two mountain chains, the Zagros and Elburz, were uplifted at the same time as the Alps in Europe, when the African Plate collided with the Eurasian Plate.

Caspian Sea

Qolleh-ye Damavand

Dominated by a vast, semi-arid interior plateau, most of Iran lies above 1,640 ft (500 m). The region is poorly drained with many of its basins remaining dry for months at a time.

The fierce Shamal wind affects much of this region. Every summer it blows dust south from the floodplains of the Tigris and Euphrates, reducing visibility to such an extent that Kuwait International Airport is frequently forced to close.

Prolific springs tapping artesian water make cultivation possible across the north of Bahrain's main island. This provides a sharp contrast to the sandy plains in the south and west.

The oil fields of the Persian Gulf are formed from marine shale deposits lying in sedimentary basins at the margins of the Zagros Mountains.

Autumn winds blowing across the Gulf can reach speeds of up to 95 mph (150 km/h), causing severe storms, squalls, and waterspouts.

Numerous islands lie along the southern coast of the Gulf. Some of these are salt domes, created when less dense salts were displaced and forced up to the surface by denser, overlying strata.

The Dasht-e Lut

The Dasht-e Lut covers a large portion of eastern Iran with its dry, wind-eroded plain of scattered sandstone pillars and salty depressions. During the summer temperatures soar, making it one of the world's hottest, driest places.

USING THE LAND & SEA

ALONG THE COAST of the Caspian Sea, desalinated water enables the production of fruits and vegetables, although water shortages and desert soils still limit farming. Sheep are the most important livestock raised in Iran and commercial forests cover the northwest of the country. Shrimp stocks were decimated by pollution during the Gulf War, but fishing remains important for domestic and export markets.

All of the Gulf states have commercial fishing fleets. Before the discovery of oil, fishing was the region's leading industry.

The Kuwait Towers in the center of Kuwait are symbols of the vast wealth oil has brought to the country. Before 1960, the city had only one main street and was surrounded by a mud wall.

Land use and agricultural distribution

- goats
- sheep
- cereals
- citrus fruits
- cotton
- dates
- fishing
- timber

- capital cities
- major towns

- pasture
- cropland
- forest
- desert
- wetland

THE URBAN/RURAL POPULATION DIVIDE

urban 59%   rural 41%

0 10 20 30 40 50 60 70 80 90 100

POPULATION DENSITY	TOTAL LAND AREA
103 people per sq mile (40 people per sq km)	642,883 sq miles (1,665,500 sq km)

Map labels:

TURKEY, ARMENIA, AZERBAIJAN, Mākū, Khvoy, Salmās, Orūmiyeh, Tabrīz, Ardabīl, Marāgheh, Rasht, Zanjān, Sanandaj, Hamadān, Bākhtarān, Khorramābād, Arāk, Borūjerd, Ahvāz, Khorramshahr, Ābādān, KUWAIT, AL KUWAYT (KUWAIT), Al Jahrā', Al Ahmadī, SAUDI ARABIA, IRAQ, AL MANĀMAH (MANAMA)

Lower left map:

TURKEY, ARMENIA, AZERBAIJAN, Caspian Sea, TURKMENISTAN, Tabriz, TEHRAN, Mashhad, AFGHANISTAN, IRAN, Esfahan, Kerman, Abadan, KUWAIT, Shiraz, PAKISTAN, BAHRAIN, MANAMA, Bandar-e Abbas, QATAR, DOHA, ABU DHABI, U.A.E., OMAN, Gulf of Oman, Persian Gulf, SAUDI ARABIA

Many volcanoes lie in Iran's 1,200-mile (1,930-km) volcanic belt, including the country's highest peak, the now-extinct Qolleh-ye Damavand at 18,600 ft (5,671 m).

Extensive oil and gas exploitation in the Gulf region has allowed the economic transformation of the Gulf states. Kuwait and the United Arab Emirates today have the highest per capita incomes in the world.

TRANSPORTATION & INDUSTRY

BOTH ONSHORE AND OFFSHORE oil reserves are exploited throughout the region. Kuwait not only extracts but also refines 80% of its oil. Bahrain has diversified its economy to become the main commercial and financial center in the Gulf. Iran produces a wide range of products: textile mills are widespread and carpet weaving is an important export industry.

Major industry and infrastructure

- carpet manufacture
- chemicals
- finance
- food processing
- oil
- oil refining
- textiles
- capital city
- major towns
- international airports
- major roads
- major industrial areas

TRANSPORTATION NETWORK

92,308 miles (148,644 km)	478 miles (770 km)
3,010 miles (4,847 km)	81 miles (130 km)

Major towns and neighboring countries are linked by adequate road networks, although rural areas are less well served. Bahrain is linked to the mainland by a 15-mile (25-km) causeway.

MAP KEY

POPULATION

- above 5 million
- 1 million to 5 million
- 500,000 to 1 million
- 100,000 to 500,000
- 50,000 to 100,000
- 10,000 to 50,000
- below 10,000

ELEVATION

- 4000m / 13,124ft
- 3000m / 9843ft
- 2000m / 6562ft
- 1000m / 3281ft
- 500m / 1640ft
- 250m / 820ft
- 100m / 328ft
- sea level

SCALE 1:5,500,000
(projection: Lambert Conformal Conic)

Km
0 10 20 40 60 80 100 120 140 160 180 200
Miles
0 10 20 40 60 80 100 120 140 160 180 200

KAZAKHSTAN

ABUNDANT NATURAL RESOURCES lie in the immense steppe grasslands, deserts, and central plateau of the former Soviet republic of Kazakhstan. An intensive program of industrial and agricultural development to exploit these resources during the Soviet era resulted in catastrophic industrial pollution, including fallout from nuclear testing and the shrinkage of the Aral Sea. Since independence, the government has encouraged foreign investment and liberalized the economy to promote growth. The adoption of Kazakh as the national language is intended to encourage a new sense of national identity in a state where living conditions for the majority remain harsh, both in cramped urban centers and impoverished rural areas.

TRANSPORTATION & INDUSTRY

THE SINGLE MOST IMPORTANT INDUSTRY in Kazakhstan is mining, based around extensive oil deposits near the Caspian Sea, the world's largest chromium mine, and vast reserves of iron ore. Recent foreign investment has helped to develop industries including food processing and steel manufacture, and to expand the exploitation of mineral resources. The Russian space program is still based in Baykonur, near Zhezkazgan, in central Kazakhstan.

Major industry and infrastructure

- ⚗ chemicals
- ⚙ engineering
- 🐟 fish processing
- 🍴 food processing
- △ iron & steel
- △ metallurgy
- ⚒ mining
- ♦ oil
- ■ capital cities
- ● major towns
- + international airports
- major roads
- major industrial areas

TRANSPORTATION NETWORK

🛣	103,623 miles (166,864 km)
🛤	none
🚂	8,786 miles (14,148 km)
	none

Industrial areas in the north and east are well-connected to Russia. Air and rail links with Germany and China have been established through foreign investment. Better access to Baltic ports is being sought.

Foreign investment is being actively sought by the Kazakh government in order to fully exploit the potential of the country's rich mineral reserves, found in such places as this open-cast coal mine, in Kazakhstan.

MAP KEY

POPULATION
- ⊙ 1 million to 5 million
- ⊙ 500,000 to 1 million
- ⊙ 100,000 to 500,000
- ⊕ 50,000 to 100,000
- ○ 10,000 to 50,000
- ○ below 10,000

ELEVATION
- 4000m / 13,124ft
- 3000m / 9843ft
- 2000m / 6562ft
- 1000m / 3281ft
- 500m / 1640ft
- 250m / 820ft
- 100m / 328ft
- sea level

USING THE LAND & SEA

THE REARING OF LARGE HERDS of sheep and goats on the steppe grasslands forms the core of Kazakh agriculture. Arable cultivation and cotton-growing in pasture and desert areas was encouraged during the Soviet era, but relative yields are low. The heavy use of fertilizers and the diversion of natural water sources for irrigation has degraded much of the land.

THE URBAN/RURAL POPULATION DIVIDE

urban 58%   rural 42%

0 10 20 30 40 50 60 70 80 90 100

POPULATION DENSITY	TOTAL LAND AREA
16 people per sq mile (6 people per sq km)	1,048,878 sq miles (2,717,300 sq km)

Land use and agricultural distribution

- cattle
- goats
- sheep
- cotton
- fishing
- wheat
- ■ capital cities
- ● major towns
- pasture
- cropland
- forest
- mountain region
- desert

The nomadic peoples who moved their herds around the steppe grasslands are now largely settled, although echoes of their traditional lifestyle, in particular their superb riding skills, remain.

SCALE 1:6,250,000
(projection: Lambert Conformal Conic)

Km
0 25 50 100 150 200 250

Miles
0 25 50 100 150 200 250

THE LANDSCAPE

STRETCHING MORE THAN 1,250 MILES (2,000 km) from the Caspian Sea in the west to China in the east, more than 40% of Kazakhstan is covered by steppe grasslands, which give way to barren desert in the south. The land rises eastward toward the mineral-rich central plateau, to form the Altai Mountains.

1960 **1996** **2010**

Since 1960, the Aral Sea has shrunk by 40%, become extremely saline, and lost all but five of its once-abundant fish species. Factors in this ecological disaster include the excessive use of fertilizers, defoliants, and the diversion of its main source rivers for the irrigation of desert lands.

The Caspian Sea is the largest body of inland water in the world.

The desert of Peski Bol'shiye Barsuki is mainly sandy, displaying a number of classic dune formations. Groundwater supports a small amount of vegetation.

A large number of salt lakes fill depressions in the rolling uplands of central Kazakhstan.

The Altai Mountains lie on Kazakhstan's eastern borders with China and the Russian Federation. Cold and largely barren, they are the source of many of the rivers which flow across the steppe.

Altai Mountains

Tien Shan

Aral Sea

Khrebet Kanchingiz

Its waters taken for industry and irrigation, the Syr Darya, one of Kazakhstan's major rivers, now barely reaches the Aral Sea, which it used to fill. Like many Kazakh rivers it has been heavily polluted with chemicals and its flow has been restricted by up to 60%.

The waters of Lake Balkhash (*Ozero Balkhash*), unlike those of the Aral Sea, are still able to support a fishing industry.

The central Kazakh Uplands (*Kazakhskiy Melkosopochnik*) contain much of the country's mineral riches. The landscape is largely flat with occasional rocky outcrops and hillocks.

Immense stretches of steppe grasslands characterize much of the Kazakh landscape. These lowland areas have been used for arable cultivation in recent years, although problems with irrigation have meant that much of the land is being allowed to revert to its natural vegetation and pastoral usage.

Rows of pine trees edge this valley near Alma-Ata, the capital of Kazakhstan. The snow-covered slopes in the background are used for skiing.

151

CENTRAL ASIA

KYRGYZSTAN, TAJIKISTAN, TURKMENISTAN, UZBEKISTAN

THE FOUR REPUBLICS that declared independence in 1991 were created in the early years of the former Soviet Union, promoting ethnic divisions in a region whose common focus, since the 8th century, has been Islam. Traditional rural, nomadic ways of life have survived the Soviet era, while the benefits of modern industry and grand irrigation schemes have resulted in severe pollution in the delicate, arid steppe environment, particularly in Uzbekistan.

Many ethnic minority groups are scattered among the four republics, with isolated communities in the mountains of Kyrgyzstan. The current Islamic revival has brought hope of greater regional unity, in spite of religious factionalism which, in 1992, plunged Tajikistan into civil war.

The desert of the Kara Kum (Garagumy) occupies over 70% of Turkmenistan; its wind-scoured surface of dune ridges and depressions severely limits human settlement.

The southern shoreline of the Aral Sea has retreated over 30 miles (48 km) since 1960. A major cause is the diversion of water from the Amu Darya River for irrigation via the Garagumskiy Kanal.

MAP KEY

POPULATION

- 1 million to 5 million
- 500,000 to 1 million
- 100,000 to 500,000
- 50,000 to 100,000
- 10,000 to 50,000
- below 10,000

ELEVATION

6000m / 19,686ft	
4000m / 13,124ft	
3000m / 9843ft	
2000m / 6562ft	
1000m / 3281ft	
500m / 1640ft	
250m / 820ft	
100m / 328ft	
sea level	

TRANSPORTATION & INDUSTRY

FOSSIL FUELS ARE extracted and processed in all four republics, with scope for further exploitation. Agriculture provides raw materials for many industries, including food and textiles processing, and the manufacture of leather goods, clothing, and carpets. Farm machinery is also produced.

TRANSPORTATION NETWORK

98,925 miles (159,300 km)		None	
3,974 miles (6,400 km)		1,242 miles (2,000 km)	

The Kara Kum Canal (Garagumskiy Kanal) runs for 870 miles (1,400 km) from the Amu Darya River to the Caspian Sea. The canal is principally used for irrigation but is navigable for 280 miles (450 km).

Major industry and infrastructure

- carpet weaving
- chemicals
- engineering
- food processing
- oil & gas
- textiles
- capital cities
- major towns
- international airports
- major roads
- major industrial areas

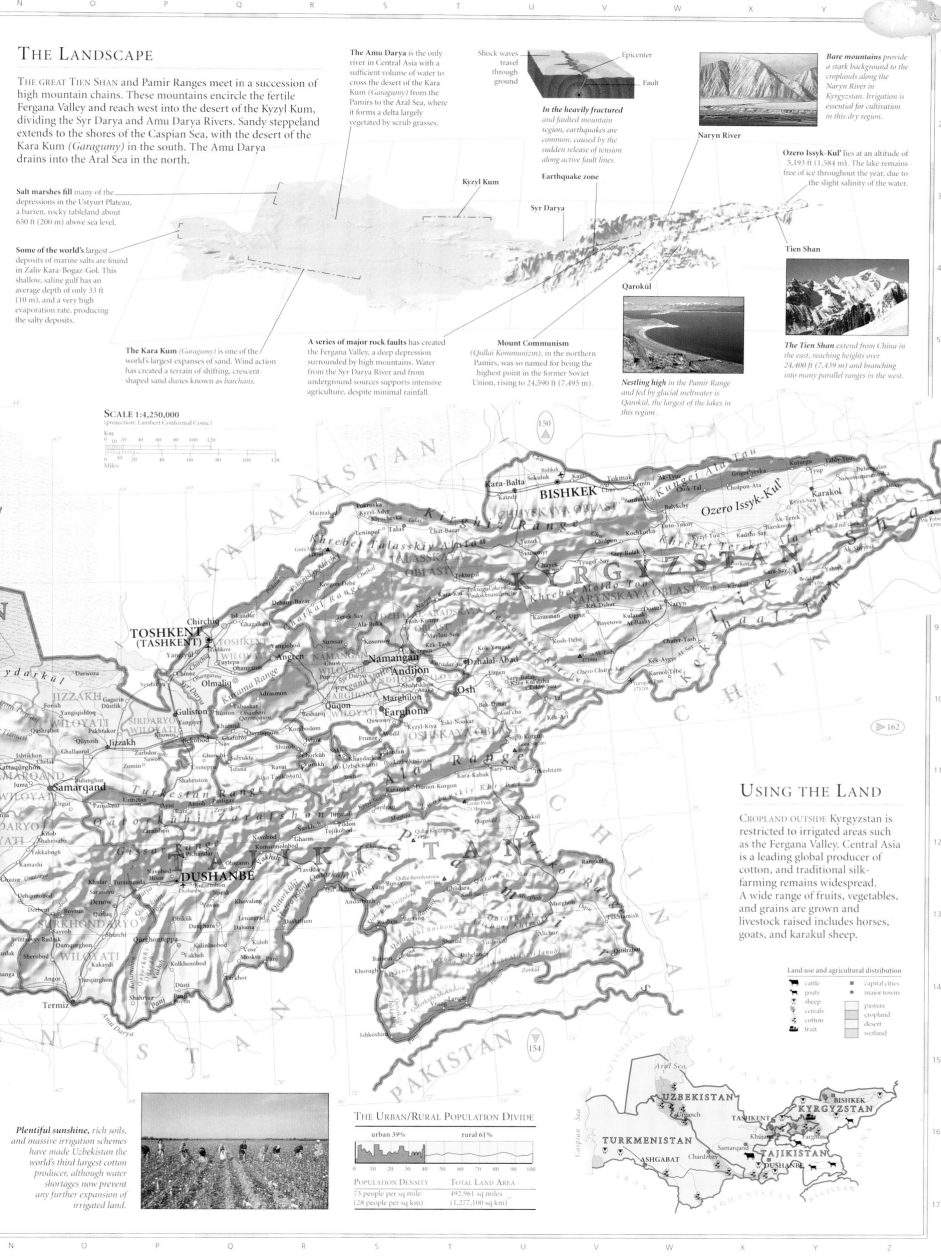

THE LANDSCAPE

THE GREAT TIEN SHAN and Pamir Ranges meet in a succession of high mountain chains. These mountains encircle the fertile Fergana Valley and reach west into the desert of the Kyzyl Kum, dividing the Syr Darya and Amu Darya Rivers. Sandy steppeland extends to the shores of the Caspian Sea, with the desert of the Kara Kum (Garagumy) in the south. The Amu Darya drains into the Aral Sea in the north.

Salt marshes fill many of the depressions in the Ustyurt Plateau, a barren, rocky tableland about 650 ft (200 m) above sea level.

Some of the world's largest deposits of marine salts are found in Zaliv Kara-Bogaz-Gol. This shallow, saline gulf has an average depth of only 33 ft (10 m), and a very high evaporation rate, producing the salty deposits.

The Kara Kum (Garagumy) is one of the world's largest expanses of sand. Wind action has created a terrain of shifting, crescent-shaped sand dunes known as barchans.

The Amu Darya is the only river in Central Asia with a sufficient volume of water to cross the desert of the Kara Kum (Garagumy) from the Pamirs to the Aral Sea, where it forms a delta largely vegetated by scrub grasses.

A series of major rock faults has created the Fergana Valley, a deep depression surrounded by high mountains. Water from the Syr Darya River and from underground sources supports intensive agriculture, despite minimal rainfall.

In the heavily fractured and faulted mountain region, earthquakes are common, caused by the sudden release of tension along active fault lines.

Earthquake zone

Kyzyl Kum

Syr Darya

Naryn River

Mount Communism (Qullai Kommunizm), in the northern Pamirs, was so named for being the highest point in the former Soviet Union, rising to 24,590 ft (7,495 m).

Nestling high in the Pamir Range and fed by glacial meltwater is Qarokül, the largest of the lakes in this region.

Qarokül

Bare mountains provide a stark background to the croplands along the Naryn River in Kyrgyzstan. Irrigation is essential for cultivation in this dry region.

Ozero Issyk-Kul' lies at an altitude of 5,193 ft (1,584 m). The lake remains free of ice throughout the year, due to the slight salinity of the water.

Tien Shan

The Tien Shan extend from China in the east, reaching heights over 24,400 ft (7,439 m) and branching into many parallel ranges in the west.

SCALE 1:4,250,000
(projection: Lambert Conformal Conic)

USING THE LAND

CROPLAND OUTSIDE Kyrgyzstan is restricted to irrigated areas such as the Fergana Valley. Central Asia is a leading global producer of cotton, and traditional silk-farming remains widespread. A wide range of fruits, vegetables, and grains are grown and livestock raised includes horses, goats, and karakul sheep.

Land use and agricultural distribution

cattle	capital cities
goats	major towns
sheep	pasture
cereals	cropland
cotton	desert
fruit	wetland

Plentiful sunshine, rich soils, and massive irrigation schemes have made Uzbekistan the world's third largest cotton producer, although water shortages now prevent any further expansion of irrigated land.

THE URBAN/RURAL POPULATION DIVIDE

urban 39%   rural 61%

POPULATION DENSITY	TOTAL LAND AREA
73 people per sq mile	492,961 sq miles
(28 people per sq km)	(1,277,100 sq km)

AFGHANISTAN & PAKISTAN

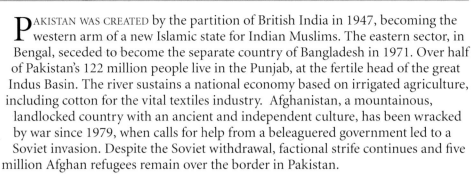

The town of Bamian lies high in the Hindu Kush, 250 miles (420 km) west of the Afghan capital, Kabul. It contains two huge statues of Buddha and a number of sanctuaries and cells carved in the rock. In 1222, the ancient city was destroyed by Chinghiz Khan.

PAKISTAN WAS CREATED by the partition of British India in 1947, becoming the western arm of a new Islamic state for Indian Muslims. The eastern sector, in Bengal, seceded to become the separate country of Bangladesh in 1971. Over half of Pakistan's 122 million people live in the Punjab, at the fertile head of the great Indus Basin. The river sustains a national economy based on irrigated agriculture, including cotton for the vital textiles industry. Afghanistan, a mountainous, landlocked country with an ancient and independent culture, has been wracked by war since 1979, when calls for help from a beleaguered government led to a Soviet invasion. Despite the Soviet withdrawal, factional strife continues and five million Afghan refugees remain over the border in Pakistan.

TRANSPORTATION & INDUSTRY

PAKISTAN IS HIGHLY dependent on the cotton textiles industry, although diversified manufacture is expanding around cities such as Karachi and Lahore. Afghanistan's limited industry is based mainly on the processing of agricultural raw materials and includes traditional crafts such as carpet weaving.

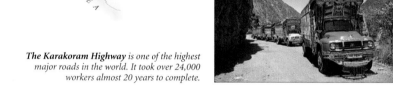

Major industry and infrastructure

- carpet weaving
- chemicals
- engineering
- finance
- food processing
- iron & steel
- oil & gas
- textiles
- ● capital cities
- ○ major towns
- ✈ international airports
- — major roads
- major industrial areas

TRANSPORTATION NETWORK

🛣	82,740 miles (133,237 km)
	None
🚂	7,855 miles (12,649 km)
	745 miles (1,200 km)

The Karakoram Highway was completed after 20 years of construction in 1978. It breaches the Himalayan mountain barrier and provides a commercial motor route linking lowland Pakistan and China.

The Karakoram Highway is one of the highest major roads in the world. It took over 24,000 workers almost 20 years to complete.

THE LANDSCAPE

AFGHANISTAN'S TOPOGRAPHY is dominated by the mountains of the Hindu Kush, which spread south and west into numerous mountain spurs. The dry plateau of southwestern Afghanistan extends into Pakistan and the hills which overlook the great Indus Basin. In northern Pakistan the Hindu Kush, Himalayan and Karakoram ranges meet to form one of the world's highest mountain regions.

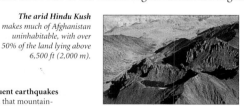

The arid Hindu Kush makes much of Afghanistan uninhabitable, with over 50% of the land lying above 6,500 ft (2,000 m).

Frequent earthquakes mean that mountain-building processes are continuing in this region, as the Indo-Australian Plate drifts northward, colliding with the Eurasian Plate.

Mountain chains running southwest from the Hindu Kush into Pakistan form a barrier to the humid winds that blow from the Indian Ocean, creating arid conditions across southern Afghanistan.

The Indus Basin is part of the Indus–Ganges lowland, a vast depression which has been filled with layers of sediment over the last 50 million years. These deposits are estimated to be over 16,400 ft (5,000 m) deep.

The Indus Delta is prone to heavy flooding and high levels of salinity. It remains a largely uncultivated wilderness area.

The Hunza River rises in the northern Karakoram Range, running for 120 miles (193 km) before joining the Gilgit River.

Hunza River

The plains and foothills which extend from the northern slopes of the Hindu Kush are part of the great grassy steppe of Central Asia.

K2 (Mount Godwin Austen), in the Karakoram Range, is the second highest mountain in the world, at an altitude of 28,251 ft (8,611 m).

Hindu Kush

Some of the largest glaciers outside the polar regions are found in the Karakoram Range, including Siachen Glacier (Siachen Muztagh), which is 30 miles (72 km) long.

Himalayas

The soils of the Punjab Plain are nourished by enormous quantities of sediment, carried from the Himalayas by the five tributaries of the Indus River.

Glacis covered by coarse-grained sediment

Sediments washed down from mountains accumulate on glacis slopes

Bedrock

Fine sediments deposited on salt flats are removed by wind erosion.

Glacis are gentle, debris-covered slopes which lead into saltflats or deserts. They typically occur at the base of mountains in arid regions such as Afghanistan.

SCALE 1:4,500,000
(projection: Lambert Conformal Conic)

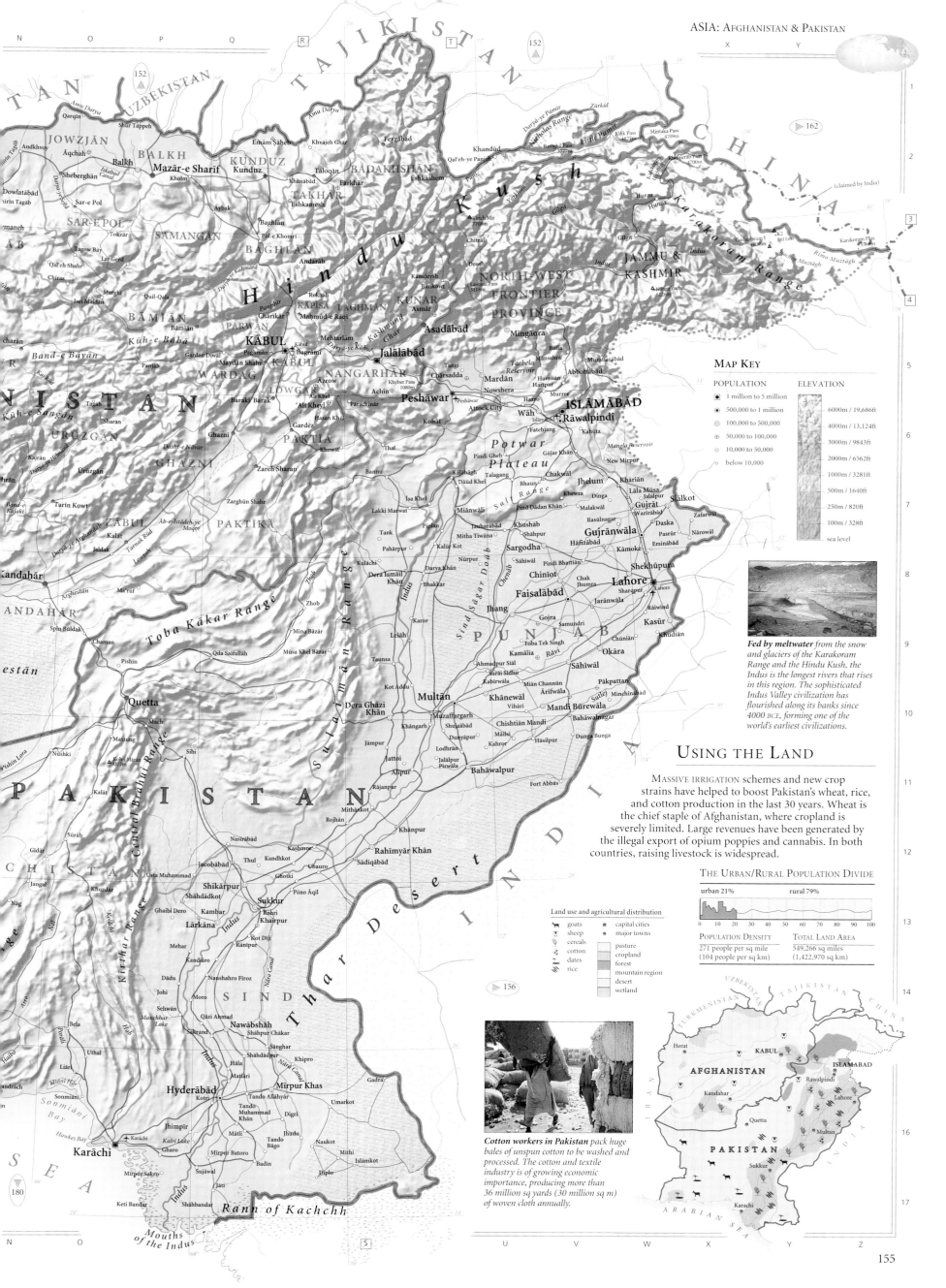

MAP KEY

POPULATION

- 1 million to 5 million
- 500,000 to 1 million
- 100,000 to 500,000
- 50,000 to 100,000
- 10,000 to 50,000
- below 10,000

ELEVATION

6000m / 19,686ft	
4000m / 13,124ft	
3000m / 9843ft	
2000m / 6562ft	
1000m / 3281ft	
500m / 1640ft	
250m / 820ft	
100m / 328ft	
sea level	

Fed by meltwater from the snow and glaciers of the Karakoram Range and the Hindu Kush, the Indus is the longest rivers that rises in this region. The sophisticated Indus Valley civilization has flourished along its banks since 4000 BCE, forming one of the world's earliest civilizations.

USING THE LAND

MASSIVE IRRIGATION schemes and new crop strains have helped to boost Pakistan's wheat, rice, and cotton production in the last 30 years. Wheat is the chief staple of Afghanistan, where cropland is severely limited. Large revenues have been generated by the illegal export of opium poppies and cannabis. In both countries, raising livestock is widespread.

THE URBAN/RURAL POPULATION DIVIDE

urban 21%   rural 79%

POPULATION DENSITY	TOTAL LAND AREA
271 people per sq mile	549,266 sq miles
(104 people per sq km)	(1,422,970 sq km)

Land use and agricultural distribution

- goats
- sheep
- cereals
- cotton
- dates
- rice
- capital cities
- major towns
- pasture
- cropland
- forest
- mountain region
- desert
- wetland

Cotton workers in Pakistan pack huge bales of unspun cotton to be washed and processed. The cotton and textile industry is of growing economic importance, producing more than 36 million sq yards (30 million sq m) of woven cloth annually.

SOUTH ASIA

BANGLADESH, BHUTAN, INDIA, MALDIVES, NEPAL, PAKISTAN, SRI LANKA

MORE THAN ONE-FIFTH of the world's population lives in the South Asian subcontinent. Great cultural diversity has come from a long succession of foreign invaders, including Hindu Aryans, Islamic Moguls, and the British, whose empire incorporated the princely states of the Maharajas and extended to the borders of Nepal and Bhutan in the Himalayas. Half a century after independence, India is the world's largest democracy, and, at the current rate of growth, may overtake China as the world's most populous country within the next century. There are points of tension in the region over claims for independence by the Sikhs in the Indian Punjab and the Tamil separatists in Sri Lanka, and the long-standing dispute with Pakistan over Jammu and Kashmir in the north.

The towering Karakoram and Hindu Kush ranges, formed at the same time as the Himalayas, dominate Pakistan's northern borders. K2, on the border of northern Pakistan, is the second highest mountain on Earth, at 28,252 ft (8,611 m).

THE LANDSCAPE

SOUTHERN ASIA is effectively isolated from the rest of Asia by desert along the western flank of Pakistan, and a continuous wall of mountains, dominated by the Himalayas, to the north and east. The great basins of the Indus and Ganges separate this mountain fringe from the rolling plateau of the Indian peninsula, which is bordered by a line of coastal hills, the Eastern and Western Ghats.

The Indus River flows more than 1,100 miles (1,800 km) from southwestern Tibet to its mouth on the Arabian Sea. It has an estimated catchment area of 371,853 sq miles (963,100 sq km).

The coast of western Pakistan is a staircase of folded rock strata caused by successive periods of rapid uplift.

The Himalayas are the highest and most extensive mountain system in the world. They were formed when the Indo-Australian Plate collided with the Eurasian Plate about 40 million years ago, thrusting up huge masses of land and creating a "ripple" effect, which formed lesser mountain ranges in Tibet and Southeast Asia. Mount Everest is the world's tallest mountain at 28,372 ft (8,848 m).

The Indus Valley near Skardu in northern Pakistan has been partially filled by great quantities of eroded sediment. Most of this is carried from the region's bare slopes by swollen rivers during the spring thaw and mass movement activity.

Almost all of Bangladesh lies in the immense delta formed by the Ganges and the Brahmaputra, which merge and flow out into the Bay of Bengal.

Ganges Delta

Deccan Plateau

The Deccan Plateau covers an area of more than 123,553 sq miles (320,000 sq km). It is formed of deep layers of volcanic basalt, reaching thicknesses of more than 9,800 ft (3,000 m) toward the coast. Distinctive stepped valleys cut in the basalt plateau by rivers are known as "traps."

Layers of volcanic basalt

Stepped valleys or "traps"

Eastern Ghats

Coastal deposition has formed many typical features along the western coast of Sri Lanka. These include spits and bars, sometimes enclosing lagoons.

Trivandrum in southern India normally receives the first of the monsoon rains, which are essential to southern Asian agriculture and moderate the extreme summer heat. The monsoon then moves northward over a period of about two months.

The Western Ghats are formed by a fault scarp that runs unbroken for more than 930 miles (1,500 km). They reach their highest point at the southern Cardamon Hills.

Bharatpur

Rivers flowing from the Himalayas into a broad depression in northern India have formed marshes around Bharatpur. They are now a sanctuary for numerous bird species.

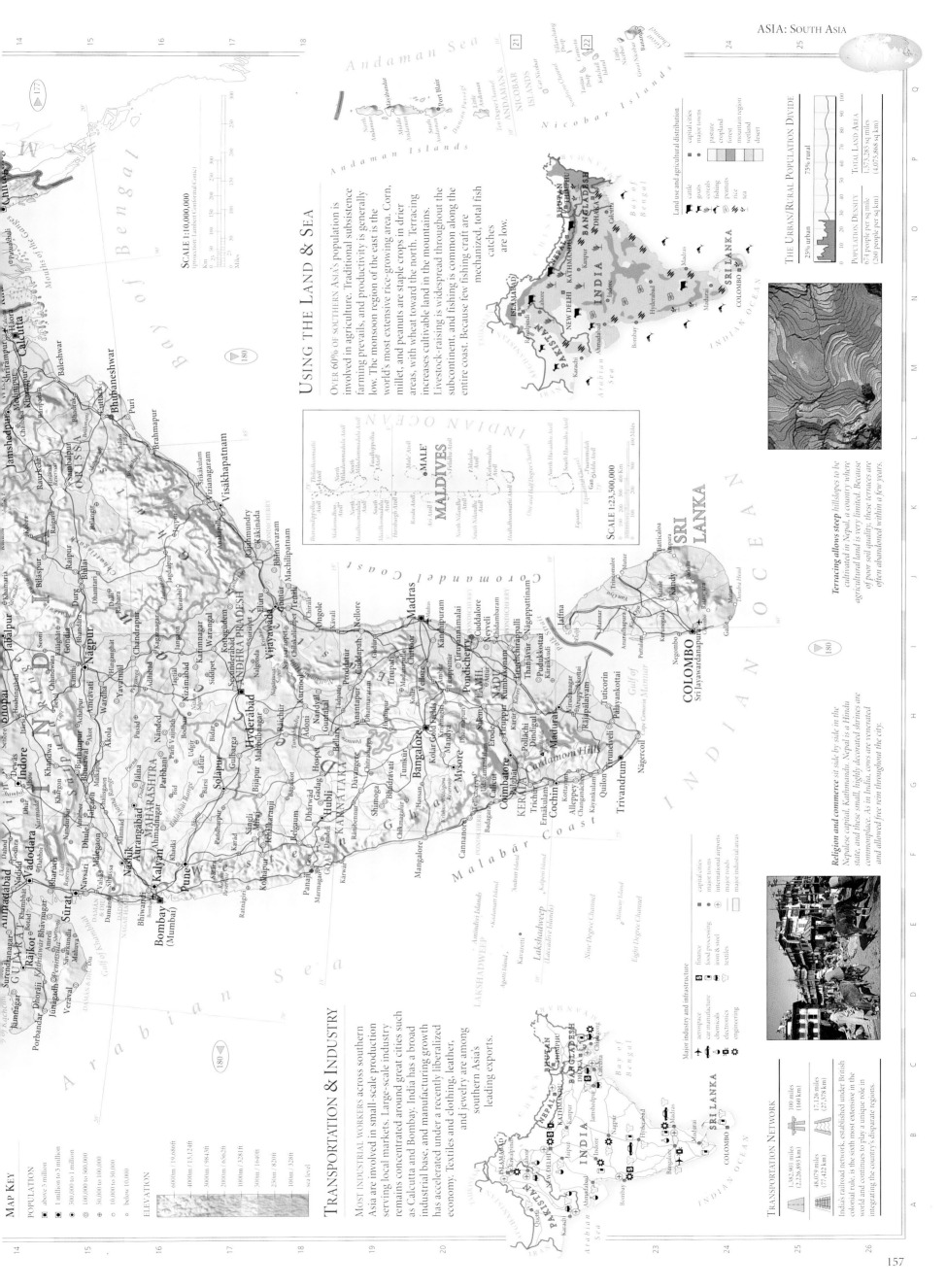

USING THE LAND & SEA

OVER 60% OF SOUTHERN ASIA'S population is involved in agriculture. Traditional subsistence farming prevails, and productivity is generally low. The monsoon region of the east is the world's most extensive rice-growing area. Corn, millet, and peanuts are staple crops in drier areas, with wheat toward the north. Terracing increases cultivable land in the mountains. Livestock-raising is widespread throughout the subcontinent, and fishing is common along the entire coast. Because few fishing craft are mechanized, total fish catches are low.

Land use and agricultural distribution

- capital cities
- major towns

pasture · cereals
cropland · peanuts
forest · rice
mountain region · tea
wetland
desert

- cattle
- goats · fishing

THE URBAN/RURAL POPULATION DIVIDE

25% urban   75% rural

POPULATION DENSITY
674 people per sq mile
(260 people per sq km)

TOTAL LAND AREA
1,573,285 sq miles
(4,075,868 sq km)

Terracing allows steep hillslopes to be cultivated in Nepal, a country where agricultural land is very limited. Because of poor soil quality, these terraces are often abandoned within a few years.

Religion and commerce sit side by side in the Nepalese capital, Kathmandu. Nepal is a Hindu state, and these small, highly decorated shrines are commonplace. As in India, cows are venerated and allowed free rein throughout the city.

TRANSPORTATION & INDUSTRY

MOST INDUSTRIAL WORKERS across southern Asia are involved in small-scale production serving local markets. Large-scale industry remains concentrated around great cities such as Calcutta and Bombay. India has a broad industrial base, and manufacturing growth has accelerated under a recently liberalized economy. Textiles and clothing, leather, and jewelry are among southern Asia's leading exports.

Major industry and infrastructure

- aerospace · finance
- car manufacture · food processing
- chemicals · iron & steel
- electronics · textiles
- engineering

- capital cities
- major towns
- international airports
- major roads
- major industrial areas

TRANSPORTATION NETWORK

1,382,901 miles (2,226,893 km) — 100 miles (160 km)

48,079 miles (77,422 km) — 17,126 miles (27,578 km)

India's railroad network, established under British colonial rule, is the sixth most extensive in the world and continues to play a unique role in integrating the country's disparate regions.

Map Key

POPULATION

- above 5 million
- 1 million to 5 million
- 500,000 to 1 million
- 100,000 to 500,000
- 50,000 to 100,000
- 10,000 to 50,000
- below 10,000

ELEVATION

6000m / 19,686ft
4000m / 13,124ft
3000m / 9843ft
2000m / 6562ft
1000m / 3281ft
500m / 1640ft
250m / 820ft
100m / 328ft
sea level

SCALE 1:10,000,000
(projection: Lambert Conformal Conic)

SCALE 1:23,500,000

MALDIVES

MALE

INDIAN OCEAN

SRI LANKA

COLOMBO
Sri Jayawardanapura

NORTHERN INDIA & THE HIMALAYAN STATES

BANGLADESH, BHUTAN, NEPAL, Arunachal Pradesh, Assam, Bihar, Chandigarh, Delhi, Haryana, Himachal Pradesh, Jammu & Kashmir, Manipur, Meghalaya, Mizoram, Nagaland, Punjab, Rajasthan, Sikkim, Tripura, Uttar Pradesh, West Bengal

THE GANGES AND BRAHMAPUTRA river basins and the massive mountain barrier of the Himalayas define this region's landscape and have served to reinforce potent cultural and religious differences among its people. Hinduism pervades most aspects of national life and is a growing political force within India, a secular country that also encompasses the center of Sikhism in Amritsar and the world's largest Muslim minority. Nepal is a crowded mountain state that faces severe ecological problems due to deforestation, while the tiny Himalayan Buddhist kingdom of Bhutan is emerging from long-term isolation to welcome selected visitors. The Muslim state of Bangladesh, formerly East Pakistan, is one of the world's most densely populated countries and one of the poorest, with more than 120 million people living largely on the massive Ganges/Brahmaputra Delta. Many Bangladeshis live under threat of repeated, catastrophic floods.

SCALE 1:5,750,000
(projection: Lambert Conformal Conic)

The Golden Temple in Amritsar, the most sacred shrine of the Sikh religion, was the scene of violent clashes between Sikh separatists and government forces in 1984.

MAP KEY

POPULATION

- ▣ 1 million to 5 million
- ◉ 500,000 to 1 million
- ◎ 100,000 to 500,000
- ⊕ 50,000 to 100,000
- ⊙ 10,000 to 50,000
- ○ below 10,000

ELEVATION

- 6000m / 19,686ft
- 4000m / 13,124ft
- 3000m / 9843ft
- 2000m / 6562ft
- 1000m / 3281ft
- 500m / 1640ft
- 250m / 820ft
- 100m / 328ft
- sea level

TRANSPORTATION & INDUSTRY

TEXTILES, ENGINEERING, chemicals, and electronics are leading industries in northern India. The plateau of Chota Nagpur provides ore for iron and steel production in the major industrial region northeast of Calcutta. Bangladesh processes jute, and Nepal has a small manufacturing sector based on agricultural produce, while Bhutan's limited industry is concentrated in the southern lowland area.

Major industry and infrastructure

- adventure tourism
- car manufacture
- chemicals
- coal
- electronics
- engineering
- finance
- food processing
- iron & steel
- jute processing
- oil
- tea processing
- textiles
- ■ capital cities
- ▪ major towns
- ✈ international airports
- ✈ major roads
- major industrial areas

TRANSPORTATION NETWORK

Over 60% of Bangladesh's internal trade is carried by boat. The country has a very disjointed land transportation network, with no bridges over the Brahmaputra and few road crossings on the Ganges River.

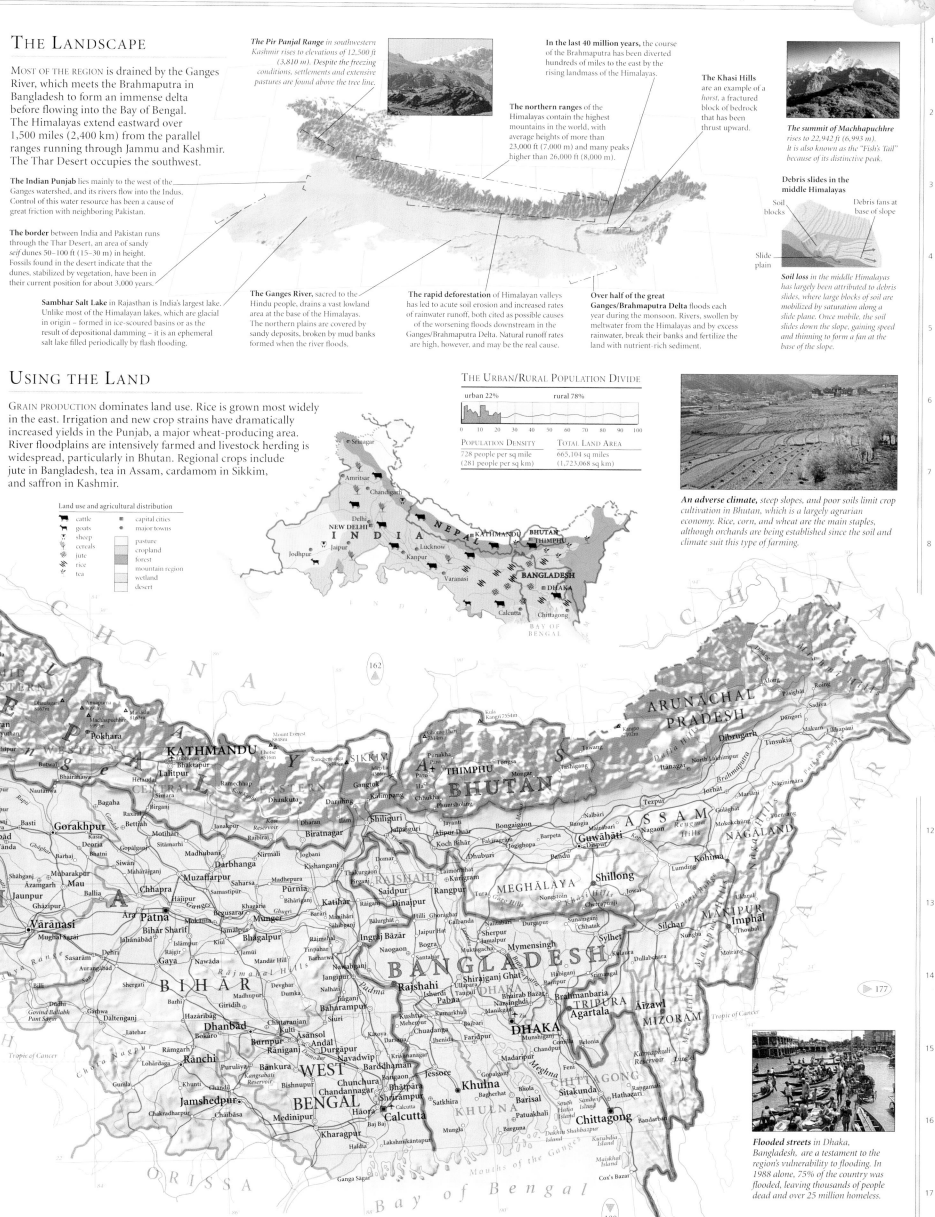

THE LANDSCAPE

MOST OF THE REGION is drained by the Ganges River, which meets the Brahmaputra in Bangladesh to form an immense delta before flowing into the Bay of Bengal. The Himalayas extend eastward over 1,500 miles (2,400 km) from the parallel ranges running through Jammu and Kashmir. The Thar Desert occupies the southwest.

The Indian Punjab lies mainly to the west of the Ganges watershed, and its rivers flow into the Indus. Control of this water resource has been a cause of great friction with neighboring Pakistan.

The border between India and Pakistan runs through the Thar Desert, an area of sandy *seif* dunes 50–100 ft (15–30 m) in height. Fossils found in the desert indicate that the dunes, stabilized by vegetation, have been in their current position for about 3,000 years.

Sambhar Salt Lake in Rajasthan is India's largest lake. Unlike most of the Himalayan lakes, which are glacial in origin – formed in ice-scoured basins or as the result of depositional damming – it is an ephemeral salt lake filled periodically by flash flooding.

The Pir Panjal Range *in southwestern Kashmir rises to elevations of 12,500 ft (3,810 m). Despite the freezing conditions, settlements and extensive pastures are found above the tree line.*

In the last 40 million years, the course of the Brahmaputra has been diverted hundreds of miles to the east by the rising landmass of the Himalayas.

The northern ranges of the Himalayas contain the highest mountains in the world, with average heights of more than 23,000 ft (7,000 m) and many peaks higher than 26,000 ft (8,000 m).

The Khasi Hills are an example of a *horst*, a fractured block of bedrock that has been thrust upward.

The summit of Machhapuchhre *rises to 22,942 ft (6,993 m). It is also known as the "Fish's Tail" because of its distinctive peak.*

Debris slides in the middle Himalayas

Soil blocks · Debris fans at base of slope · Slide plain

Soil loss *in the middle Himalayas has largely been attributed to debris slides, where large blocks of soil are mobilized by saturation along a slide plane. Once mobile, the soil slides down the slope, gaining speed and thinning to form a fan at the base of the slope.*

The Ganges River, sacred to the Hindu people, drains a vast lowland area at the base of the Himalayas. The northern plains are covered by sandy deposits, broken by mud banks formed when the river floods.

The rapid deforestation of Himalayan valleys has led to acute soil erosion and increased rates of rainwater runoff, both cited as possible causes of the worsening floods downstream in the Ganges/Brahmaputra Delta. Natural runoff rates are high, however, and may be the real cause.

Over half of the great Ganges/Brahmaputra Delta floods each year during the monsoon. Rivers, swollen by meltwater from the Himalayas and by excess rainwater, break their banks and fertilize the land with nutrient-rich sediment.

USING THE LAND

GRAIN PRODUCTION dominates land use. Rice is grown most widely in the east. Irrigation and new crop strains have dramatically increased yields in the Punjab, a major wheat-producing area. River floodplains are intensively farmed and livestock herding is widespread, particularly in Bhutan. Regional crops include jute in Bangladesh, tea in Assam, cardamom in Sikkim, and saffron in Kashmir.

THE URBAN/RURAL POPULATION DIVIDE

urban 22%   rural 78%

POPULATION DENSITY	TOTAL LAND AREA
728 people per sq mile	665,104 sq miles
(281 people per sq km)	(1,723,068 sq km)

Land use and agricultural distribution

cattle · goats · sheep · cereals · jute · rice · tea

capital cities · major towns · pasture · cropland · forest · mountain region · wetland · desert

An adverse climate, *steep slopes, and poor soils limit crop cultivation in Bhutan, which is a largely agrarian economy. Rice, corn, and wheat are the main staples, although orchards are being established since the soil and climate suit this type of farming.*

Flooded streets *in Dhaka, Bangladesh, are a testament to the region's vulnerability to flooding. In 1988 alone, 75% of the country was flooded, leaving thousands of people dead and over 25 million homeless.*

SOUTHERN INDIA & SRI LANKA

Sri Lanka, Andhra Pradesh, Dadra & Nagar Haveli, Daman & Diu, Goa, Gujarat, Karnataka, Kerala, Lakshadweep, Madhya Pradesh, Maharashtra, Orissa, Pondicherry, Tamil Nadu

THE UNIQUE AND HIGHLY INDEPENDENT southern states of India reflect the diverse and decentralized nature of that country, which has fourteen official languages. The southern half of the peninsula was beyond the reach of early invaders from the north and retained the distinct and ancient culture of Dravidian peoples such as the Tamils, whose language is spoken in preference to Hindi throughout southern India. The interior plateau of southern India is less densely populated than the coastal lowlands, where the European colonial imprint is strongest. Urban and industrial growth is accelerating, but southern India's vast population remains predominantly rural. The island of Sri Lanka has two distinct cultural groups; the mainly Buddhist Sinhalese majority, and the Tamil minority whose struggle for a homeland in the northeast has led to prolonged civil war.

USING THE LAND & SEA

RICE IS THE MAIN staple in the east, in Sri Lanka, and along the humid Malabar Coast. Peanuts are grown on the Deccan Plateau, with wheat, corn, and chickpeas, toward the north. Sri Lanka is a leading exporter of tea, coconuts, and rubber. Cotton plantations supply local mills around Nagpur and Bombay. Fishing supports many communities in Kerala and the Laccadive Islands.

Commercial plantations, growing tea (seen here), cardamom, coffee, coconuts, and rubber, occupy about half the agricultural land in Kerala, necessitating food imports for local consumption.

Land use and agricultural distribution

- cattle
- goats
- cereals
- cotton
- fishing
- peanuts
- rice
- rubber
- tea

- capital cities
- major towns
- pasture
- cropland
- forest
- wetland

THE URBAN/RURAL POPULATION DIVIDE

urban 29%	rural 71%

POPULATION DENSITY	TOTAL LAND AREA
650 people per sq mile (251 people per sq km)	698,295 sq miles (1,809,054 sq km)

THE LANDSCAPE

THE UNDULATING DECCAN PLATEAU underlies most of southern India. It slopes gently down toward the east and is largely enclosed by the Ghats coastal hill ranges. The Western Ghats run continuously along the Arabian Sea coast, while the Eastern Ghats are interrupted by rivers which follow the slope of the plateau and flow across broad lowlands into the Bay of Bengal. The plateaus and basins of Sri Lanka's central highlands are surrounded by a broad plain.

The Rann of Kachchh tidal marshes encircle the low-lying Kachchh Peninsula. For several months during the rainy season the water level of the marshes rises and Kachchh becomes an island.

The Konkan coast, which runs between Daman and Goa, is characterized by rocky headlands and bays with crescent shaped beaches. Flooded river valleys known as rias extend inland.

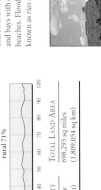

The Western Ghats run north–south marking the western boundary of the Deccan Plateau. Their height rises to the south where their summits reach altitudes of 8,000 ft (2,500 m).

Along the northern boundary of the Deccan Plateau, old basement rocks are interspersed with younger sedimentary strata. This creates spectacular scarplands that are cut by numerous waterfalls, along the softer sedimentary strata.

The interior uplands of southern India are broadly known as the Deccan Plateau. River erosion of the plateau's volcanic rock has created distinctive stepped valleys called traps.

The island of Sri Lanka is essentially an extension of the Deccan Plateau. It lies on the Indian continental shelf and is composed of the same hard, crystalline rocks.

Deep layers of river sediment have created a broad lowland plain along the eastern coast, with rivers such as the Krishna forming extensive deltas.

Adam's Bridge

- Ocean currents cause sediment build up
- Sri Lanka
- Relict of ancient tombolo
- Adam's Bridge

Adam's Bridge (Rama's Bridge) is a chain of sandy shoals lying about 4 ft (1.2 m) under the sea between India and Sri Lanka. They once formed the world's longest tombolo, or land bridge, before the sea level began to rise several thousand years ago.

TRANSPORTATION & INDUSTRY

SOUTH INDIA HAS a broad industrial base, with three leading regions around Bombay, Bangalore, and Ahmadabad. Cotton mills and chemical plants make use of cheap hydroelectric power generated in the Western Ghats. Light engineering and textiles are well established to the south and west of Madras. Sri Lanka's industry is based mainly on the processing of agricultural products.

Major industry and infrastructure

- ✈ aerospace
- 🚗 car manufacture
- ⚗ chemicals
- ⚙ electronics
- engineering
- food processing
- iron & steel
- pharmaceuticals
- printing & publishing
- shipbuilding
- tea processing
- textiles
- tobacco processing
- capital cities
- major towns
- ✈ international airports
- major roads
- major industrial areas

TRANSPORTATION NETWORK

India's hard-surfaced road network has grown almost tenfold since independence, yet many villages are still only accessible on foot, even in densely-populated rural areas.

The great triumphal arch of Charminar, built in 1591, epitomizes the fine Islamic architecture, which the Moghuls brought from the north to Hyderabad, the capital of Andhra Pradesh.

Bombay is one of the largest and most densely populated cities in the world. It is the center of India's textile trade and has important finance and commerce sectors.

Sea pencils thrive on the coral reefs around the coast of the Laccadive Islands and Sri Lanka. The reefs support an amazing diversity of marine life, but are increasingly under threat from growing coastal populations.

Local fisheries around Sri Lanka afford great potential for exploitation. Development, however, has been hampered by technological constraints. Most fishermen live on the coastal fringes and operate on a small scale.

MAP KEY

POPULATION
- ■ above 5 million
- ● 1 million to 5 million
- ● 500,000 to 1 million
- ⊕ 100,000 to 500,000
- ○ 50,000 to 100,000
- ○ 10,000 to 50,000
- ○ below 10,000

ELEVATION
- 2000m / 6562ft
- 1000m / 3281ft
- 500m / 1640ft
- 250m / 820ft
- 100m / 328ft
- sea level

SCALE 1:6,250,000
(projection: Lambert Conformal Conic)

MAINLAND EAST ASIA

CHINA, MONGOLIA, NORTH KOREA, SOUTH KOREA, TAIWAN, *Macao* (to Portugal)

CHINA, THE WORLD'S MOST POPULOUS NATION, has an unbroken cultural history, longer than that of any other country, and is rapidly emerging as a leading world power. When Mao Zedong established communist rule in 1949, China had become a backward feudal empire, stricken by civil war and more than a century of European and Japanese incursions. The closed regime withstood the traumas of rapid industrialization, communal farming, and the brutal purges of the Cultural Revolution. Since the 1980s it has introduced economic reforms, led by expanded foreign trade. China's population is concentrated heavily in the east and, despite accelerating urban growth, remains predominantly rural. One cultural group, the Han, make up over 90% of the people, while five "Autonomous Regions" have been established in the south and west for the main ethnic minorities.

TRANSPORTATION & INDUSTRY

LARGE-SCALE INDUSTRIAL growth has always been a priority of the communist government. Metals and machine production, chemicals, and engineering are among the leading industries, concentrated in the major cities of the east coast. Textiles and clothing manufacture, the main consumer-goods sector, is relatively well dispersed, with a few significant centers such as Shanghai, Beijing, and Hong Kong.

Major industry and infrastructure

- car manufacture
- chemicals
- electronics
- engineering
- finance
- food processing
- iron & steel
- shipbuilding
- textiles
- capital cities
- major towns
- international airports
- major roads
- major industrial areas

TRANSPORTATION NETWORK

734,473 miles (1,182,727 km)
1,182 miles (1,904 km)
41,798 miles (67,308 km)
70,495 miles (113,519 km)

Steam trains use China's abundant coal and are still the main form of passenger and goods transportation. The railroad network is now struggling to meet a constantly increasing demand.

Coal is China's most abundant mineral resource. This mine at Fuxin in Liaoning province is used to provide coal for a nearby power station.

THE LANDSCAPE

THE EAST ASIAN landmass is arranged in three distinct levels, the highest of which is the Plateau of Tibet in the southwest. The arid uplands of northwestern China form a barren middle step. The main rivers flow eastward from these two platforms to the East China and South China Sea coasts, across a broad region of alluvial lowlands and low hills.

Paektu-san, at 9,023 ft (2,750 m), is North Korea's highest peak. It is an extinct volcanic cone now filled by a crater lake.

The loess plateau of northern China is the world's greatest expanse of loess, a loose soil made up of wind-blown material. The plateau has been heavily eroded by tributaries of the Yellow River.

Shifting sand dunes are found in the arid west of the northeast China Plain, while the eastern part of this great expanse is wet and swampy.

The Gobi Desert extends across the Nei Mongol Gaoyuan, a vast saucer-shaped upland surrounded by a rim of higher mountains.

Fine soils eroded by river

Thick blanket of loess

Loess soil particles are small and granular and easily transported and deposited by the winds that scour the plains. In northern China, deposits of loess can be up to 3,000 ft (1,000 m) thick. Loess-based soils are very fertile, but clearing land for agriculture quickly destabilizes the soil and allows it to be eroded.

Plateau of Tibet

Tarim Basin (Tarim Pendi)

Paektu-san

North China Plain

The Yangtze is China's longest river and the principal navigable waterway.

The Plateau of Tibet occupies about a quarter of China's total area. The Yangtze, Mekong, Indus, and Brahmaputra Rivers all originate in the south and east of the plateau.

The Himalayas extend along the southwestern edge of the Plateau of Tibet, forming a continuous mountain barrier over 1,500 miles (2,500 km) long.

Warm, humid conditions have caused intensive erosion of southern China's karst areas, producing spectacular jagged peaks and vast caves in the limestone.

Sichuan Pendi

Gansu province, through which the ancient Silk Route passes on its way to the west, is characterized by extensive loess deposits that are terraced and used for crop cultivation.

Although it is over 20 years since his death, the legacy of Chairman Mao Zedong, architect of the Great Proletariat Cultural Revolution, is still very much in evidence across China's landscape. In 1959 Mao launched a 20-year period of industrialization and socioeconomic realignment, rejecting western ideals and social codes.

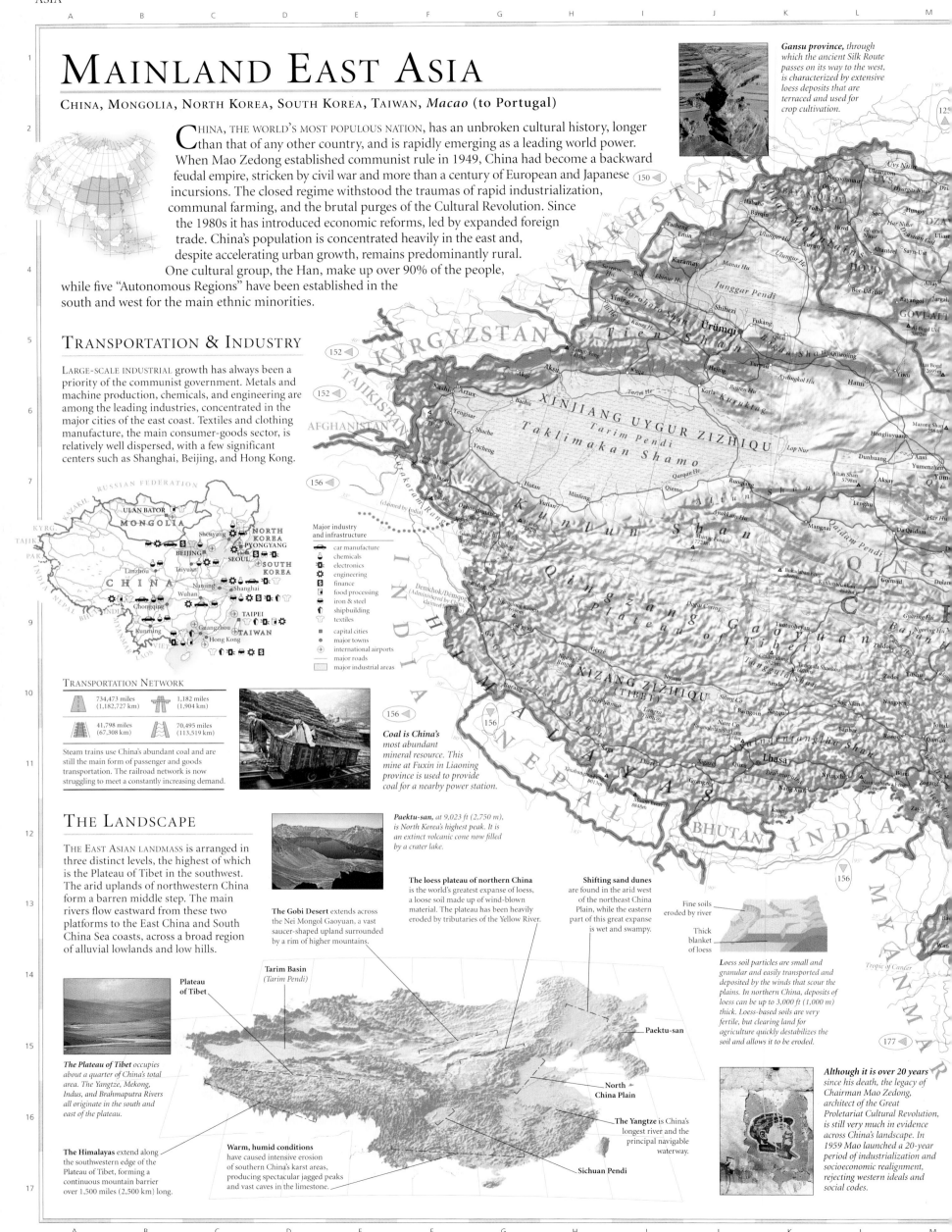

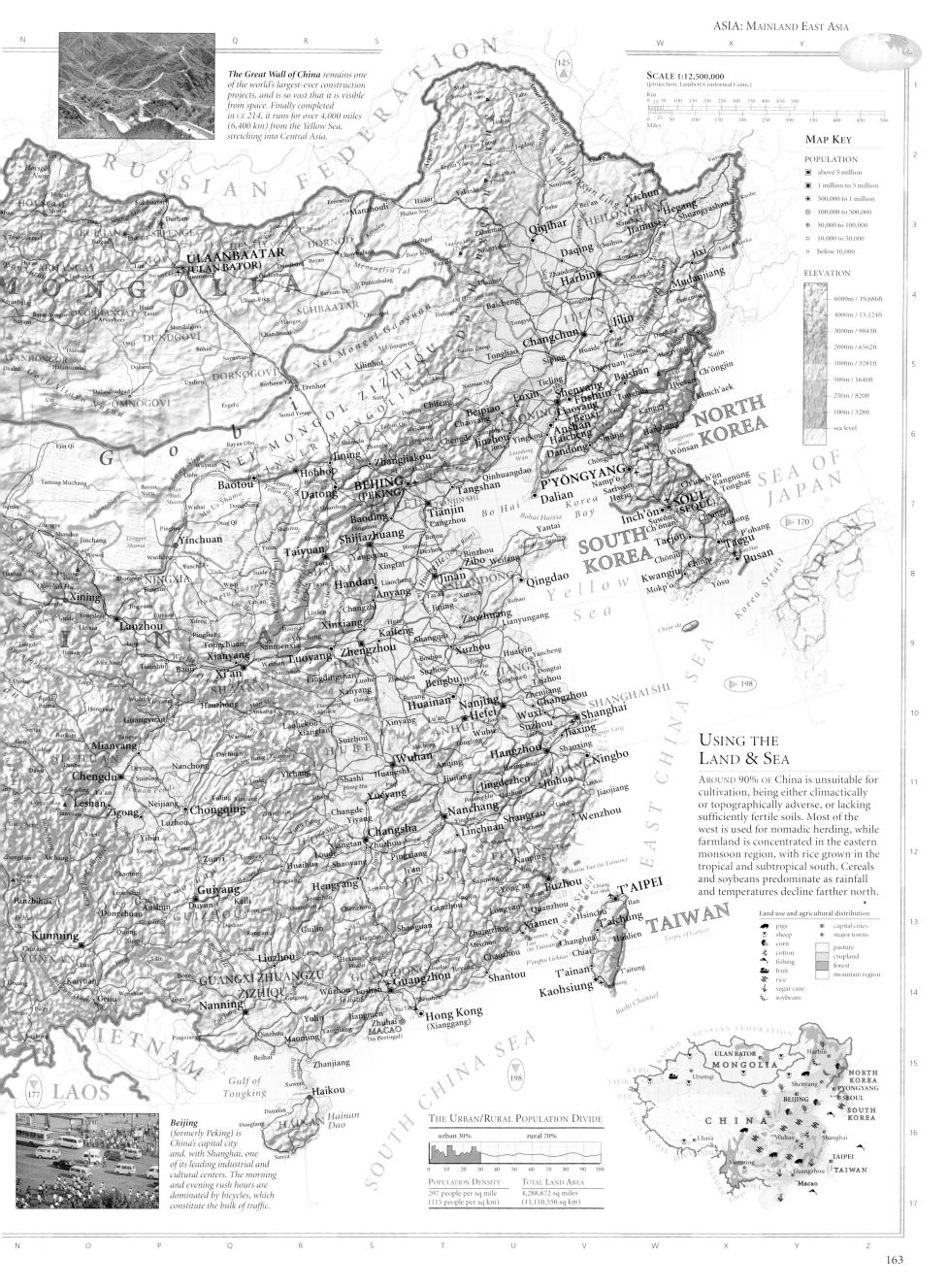

The Great Wall of China remains one of the world's largest-ever construction projects, and is so vast that it is visible from space. Finally completed in CE 214, it runs for over 4,000 miles (6,400 km) from the Yellow Sea, stretching into Central Asia.

SCALE 1:12,500,000
(projection: Lambert Conformal Conic)

Km
0 25 50 | 100 | 150 | 200 | 250 | 300 | 350 | 400 | 450 | 500

Miles
0 25 50 | 100 | 150 | 200 | 250 | 300 | 350 | 400 | 450 | 500

MAP KEY

POPULATION

- ■ above 5 million
- ■ 1 million to 5 million
- ◉ 500,000 to 1 million
- ◉ 50,000 to 100,000
- ◉ 10,000 to 50,000
- ○ below 10,000

ELEVATION

- 6000m / 19,686ft
- 4000m / 13,124ft
- 3000m / 9843ft
- 2000m / 6562ft
- 1000m / 3281ft
- 500m / 1640ft
- 250m / 820ft
- 100m / 328ft
- sea level

USING THE LAND & SEA

AROUND 90% OF China is unsuitable for cultivation, being either climactically or topographically adverse, or lacking sufficiently fertile soils. Most of the west is used for nomadic herding, while farmland is concentrated in the eastern monsoon region, with rice grown in the tropical and subtropical south. Cereals and soybeans predominate as rainfall and temperatures decline farther north.

Land use and agricultural distribution

- pigs
- sheep
- corn
- cotton
- fishing
- fruit
- rice
- sugar cane
- soybeans
- ● capital cities
- ● major towns
- pasture
- cropland
- forest
- mountain region

Beijing (formerly Peking) is China's capital city and, with Shanghai, one of its leading industrial and cultural centers. The morning and evening rush hours are dominated by bicycles, which constitute the bulk of traffic.

THE URBAN/RURAL POPULATION DIVIDE

urban 30%   rural 70%

0 10 20 30 40 50 60 70 80 90 100

POPULATION DENSITY
297 people per sq mile
(115 people per sq km)

TOTAL LAND AREA
4,288,672 sq miles
(11,110,550 sq km)

WESTERN CHINA

Gansu, Ningxia, Qinghai, Tibet, Xinjiang

THE PLATEAUS AND BASINS of China's dry, desolate western domain are sparsely populated and largely undeveloped, although they have rich mineral reserves; they also form a critical buffer zone for China, in a geographically important and culturally sensitive part of the Asian continent. Across most of the west, the Han Chinese are outnumbered by a range of cultural groups, including the Uygur, the largest group of the various seminomadic Muslim peoples from Central Asia. The remote, inhospitable Plateau of Tibet is the world's coldest and highest plateau. It has been occupied by the Chinese since 1958. Tibet is one of western China's five "Autonomous Regions," but its reclusive Buddhist culture has been systematically undermined by the Chinese government.

MAP KEY

POPULATION

- ▣ 1 million to 5 million
- ◉ 500,000 to 1 million
- ◎ 100,000 to 500,000
- ⊕ 50,000 to 100,000
- ○ 10,000 to 50,000
- ○ below 10,000

ELEVATION

- 6000m / 19,686ft
- 4000m / 13,124ft
- 3000m / 9843ft
- 2000m / 6562ft
- 1000m / 3281ft
- 500m / 1640ft
- 250m / 820ft
- 100m / 328ft
- sea level

SCALE 1:7,000,000
(projection: Lambert Conformal Conic)

The Lhasa He is one of the many rivers that drains the vast Plateau of Tibet. From its source in the Nyainqêntanglha Shan range and fed by the spring meltwater, it eventually joins the upper Brahmaputra 40 miles (65 km) southeast of Lhasa.

USING THE LAND

AGRICULTURE IS CONSTRAINED by the cold, dry climate and lack of fertile soils in the region, although irrigation and greenhouse farming are increasing agricultural potential. Large quantities of fruits, like melons and grapes, are grown at the oases of Hami and Turpan in Xinjiang, and new irrigation schemes have greatly increased cotton and wheat production in the Tarim Basin *(Tarim Pendi)*. Most of the great area of Tibet and Qinghai is devoted to pastoralism. Sheep are the principal livestock.

Land use and agricultural distribution

- 🐐 goats
- 🐑 sheep
- cereals
- cotton
- grapes
- melons
- oases
- ● major towns
- pasture
- cropland
- forest
- mountain region
- desert

The Potola Palace, in Tibet's capital, Lhasa, was the former residence of the Dalai Lama, Tibetan Buddhism's spiritual leader. Tibet remains only sparsely populated; forming more than 20% of China's landmass, it supports less than 1% of its population.

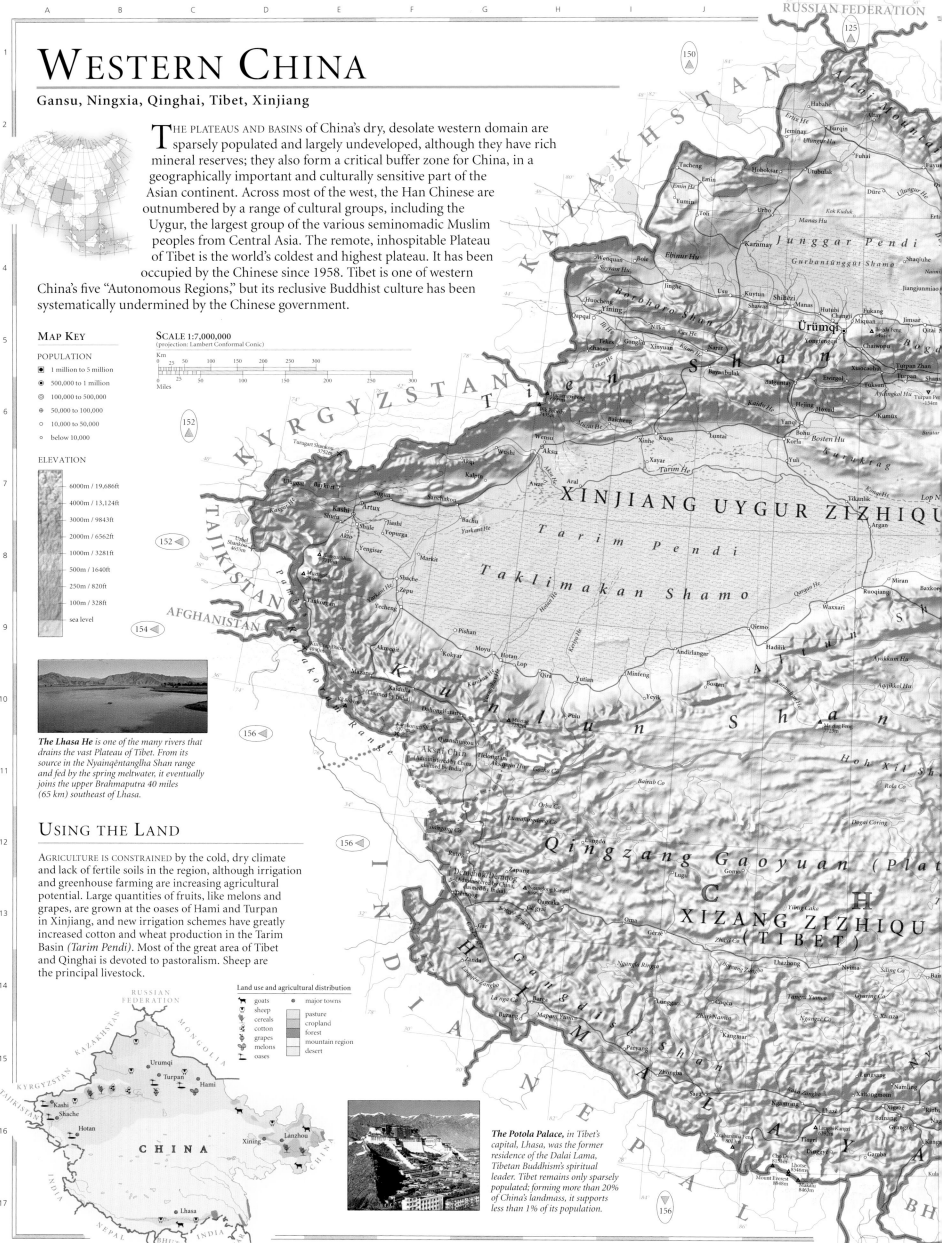

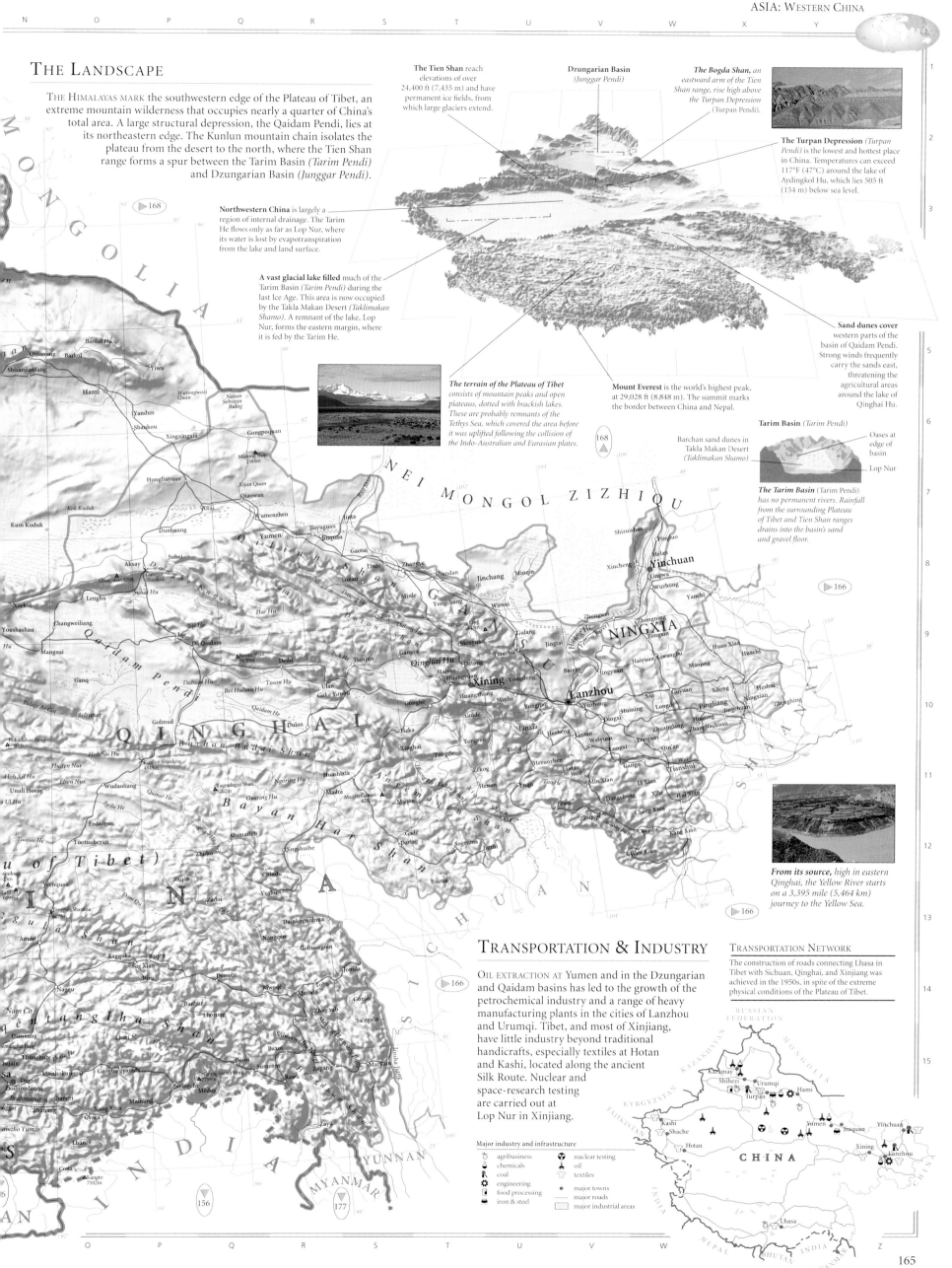

THE LANDSCAPE

THE HIMALAYAS MARK the southwestern edge of the Plateau of Tibet, an extreme mountain wilderness that occupies nearly a quarter of China's total area. A large structural depression, the Qaidam Pendi, lies at its northeastern edge. The Kunlun mountain chain isolates the plateau from the desert to the north, where the Tien Shan range forms a spur between the Tarim Basin (*Tarim Pendi*) and Dzungarian Basin (*Junggar Pendi*).

The Tien Shan reach elevations of over 24,400 ft (7,435 m) and have permanent ice fields, from which large glaciers extend.

Dzungarian Basin (*Junggar Pendi*)

The Bogda Shan, an eastward arm of the Tien Shan range, rise high above the Turpan Depression (*Turpan Pendi*).

The Turpan Depression (*Turpan Pendi*) is the lowest and hottest place in China. Temperatures can exceed 117°F (47°C) around the lake of Aydingkol Hu, which lies 505 ft (154 m) below sea level.

Northwestern China is largely a region of internal drainage. The Tarim He flows only as far as Lop Nur, where its water is lost by evapotranspiration from the lake and land surface.

A vast glacial lake filled much of the Tarim Basin (*Tarim Pendi*) during the last Ice Age. This area is now occupied by the Takla Makan Desert (*Taklimakan Shamo*). A remnant of the lake, Lop Nur, forms the eastern margin, where it is fed by the Tarim He.

The terrain of the Plateau of Tibet consists of mountain peaks and open plateaus, dotted with brackish lakes. These are probably remnants of the Tethys Sea, which covered the area before it was uplifted following the collision of the Indo-Australian and Eurasian plates.

Mount Everest is the world's highest peak, at 29,028 ft (8,848 m). The summit marks the border between China and Nepal.

Sand dunes cover western parts of the basin of Qaidam Pendi. Strong winds frequently carry the sands east, threatening the agricultural areas around the lake of Qinghai Hu.

Tarim Basin (*Tarim Pendi*)

Barchan sand dunes in Takla Makan Desert (*Taklimakan Shamo*)

Oases at edge of basin

Lop Nur

The Tarim Basin (Tarim Pendi) has no permanent rivers. Rainfall from the surrounding Plateau of Tibet and Tien Shan ranges drains into the basin's sand and gravel floor.

From its source, high in eastern Qinghai, the Yellow River starts on a 3,395 mile (5,464 km) journey to the Yellow Sea.

TRANSPORTATION & INDUSTRY

OIL EXTRACTION AT Yumen and in the Dzungarian and Qaidam basins has led to the growth of the petrochemical industry and a range of heavy manufacturing plants in the cities of Lanzhou and Urumqi. Tibet, and most of Xinjiang, have little industry beyond traditional handicrafts, especially textiles at Hotan and Kashi, located along the ancient Silk Route. Nuclear and space-research testing are carried out at Lop Nur in Xinjiang.

TRANSPORTATION NETWORK

The construction of roads connecting Lhasa in Tibet with Sichuan, Qinghai, and Xinjiang was achieved in the 1950s, in spite of the extreme physical conditions of the Plateau of Tibet.

Major industry and infrastructure

- agribusiness
- chemicals
- coal
- engineering
- food processing
- iron & steel
- nuclear testing
- oil
- textiles
- major towns
- major roads
- major industrial areas

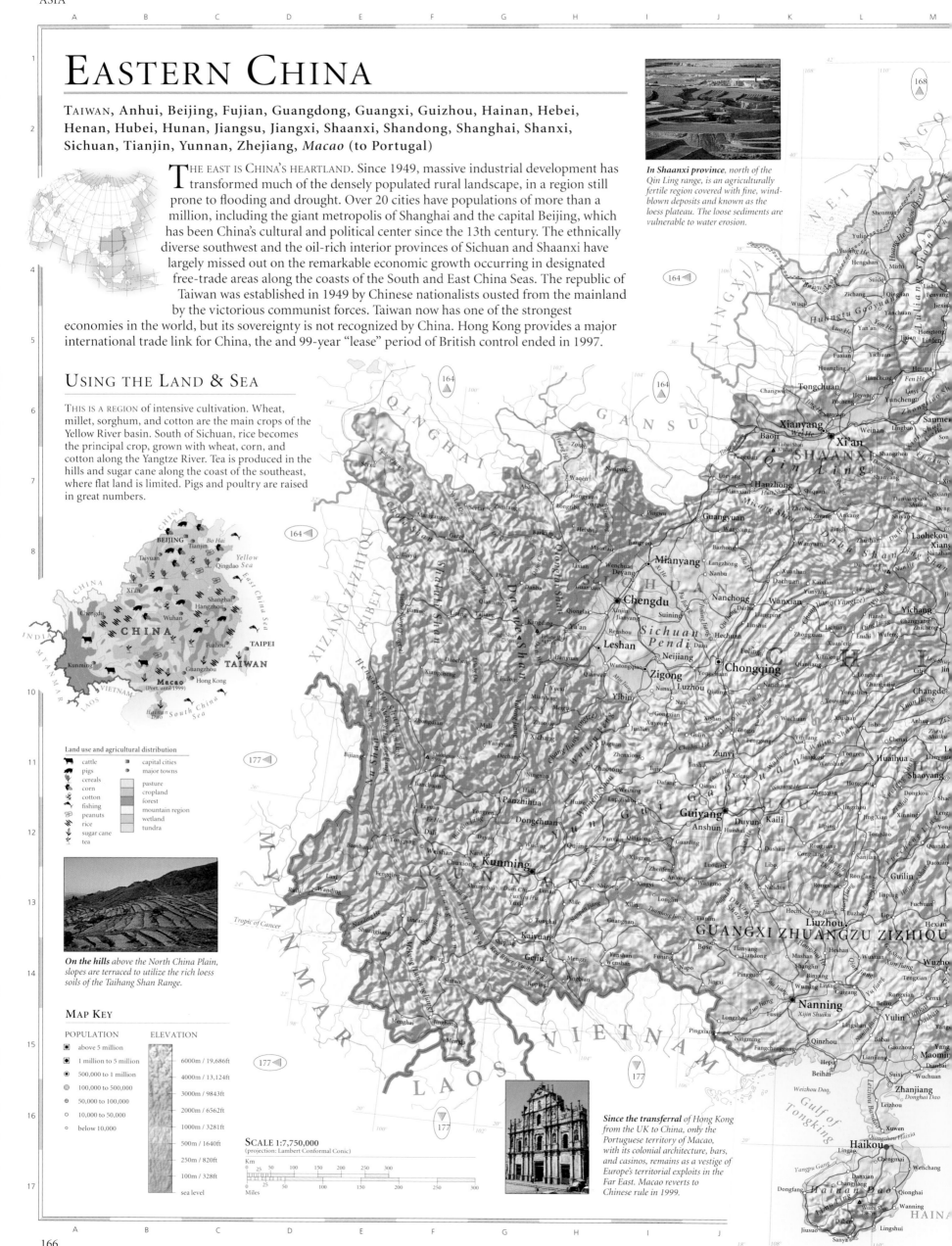

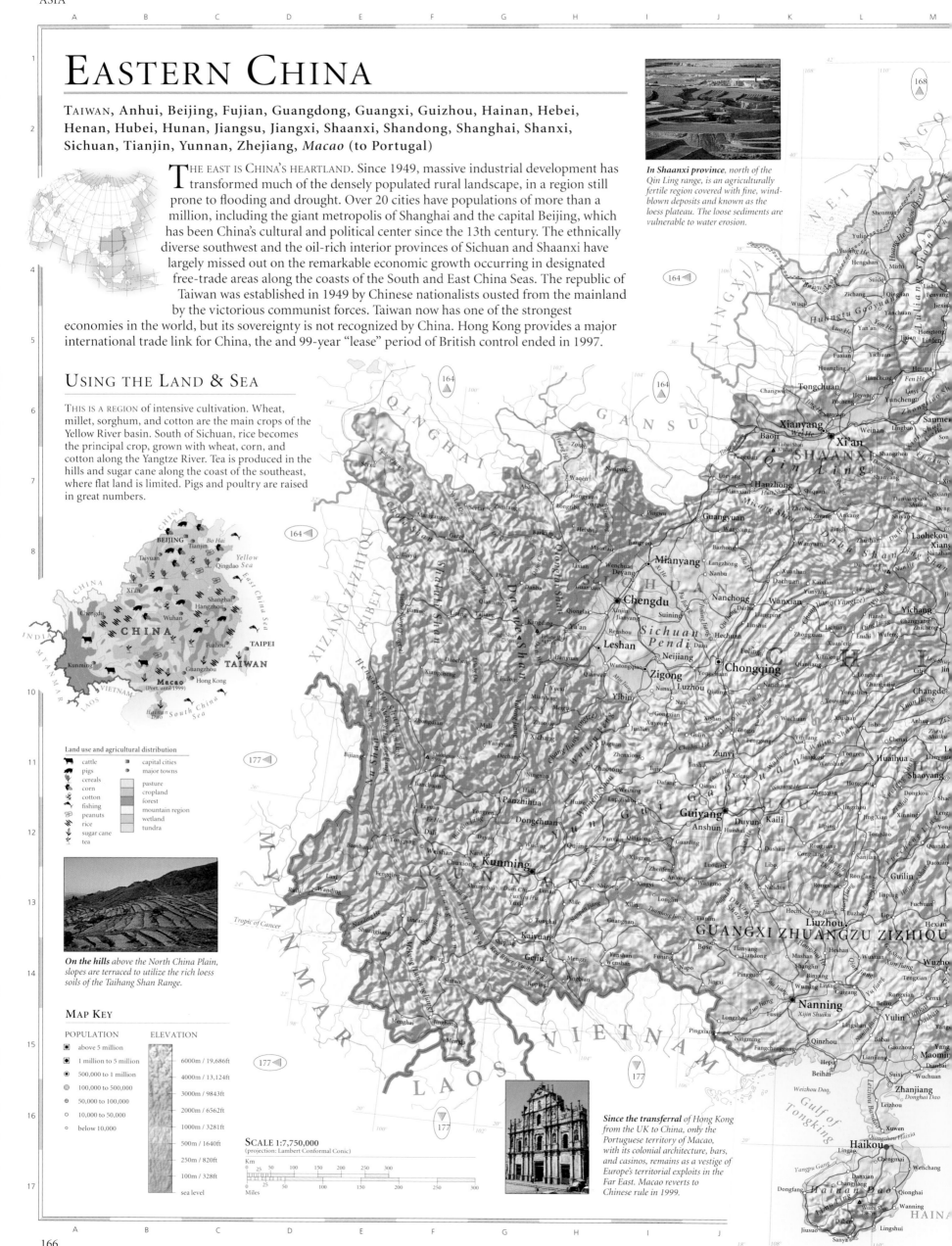

EASTERN CHINA

TAIWAN, Anhui, Beijing, Fujian, Guangdong, Guangxi, Guizhou, Hainan, Hebei, Henan, Hubei, Hunan, Jiangsu, Jiangxi, Shaanxi, Shandong, Shanghai, Shanxi, Sichuan, Tianjin, Yunnan, Zhejiang, *Macao* (to Portugal)

THE EAST IS CHINA'S HEARTLAND. Since 1949, massive industrial development has transformed much of the densely populated rural landscape, in a region still prone to flooding and drought. Over 20 cities have populations of more than a million, including the giant metropolis of Shanghai and the capital Beijing, which has been China's cultural and political center since the 13th century. The ethnically diverse southwest and the oil-rich interior provinces of Sichuan and Shaanxi have largely missed out on the remarkable economic growth occurring in designated free-trade areas along the coasts of the South and East China Seas. The republic of Taiwan was established in 1949 by Chinese nationalists ousted from the mainland by the victorious communist forces. Taiwan now has one of the strongest economies in the world, but its sovereignty is not recognized by China. Hong Kong provides a major international trade link for China, the and 99-year "lease" period of British control ended in 1997.

In Shaanxi province, north of the Qin Ling range, is an agriculturally fertile region covered with fine, wind-blown deposits and known as the loess plateau. The loose sediments are vulnerable to water erosion.

USING THE LAND & SEA

THIS IS A REGION of intensive cultivation. Wheat, millet, sorghum, and cotton are the main crops of the Yellow River basin. South of Sichuan, rice becomes the principal crop, grown with wheat, corn, and cotton along the Yangtze River. Tea is produced in the hills and sugar cane along the coast of the southeast, where flat land is limited. Pigs and poultry are raised in great numbers.

Land use and agricultural distribution

cattle	capital cities
pigs	major towns
cereals	pasture
corn	cropland
cotton	forest
fishing	mountain region
peanuts	wetland
rice	tundra
sugar cane	
tea	

On the hills above the North China Plain, slopes are terraced to utilize the rich loess soils of the Taihang Shan Range.

MAP KEY

POPULATION

- ■ above 5 million
- ■ 1 million to 5 million
- ◉ 500,000 to 1 million
- ◎ 100,000 to 500,000
- ⊕ 50,000 to 100,000
- ○ 10,000 to 50,000
- ○ below 10,000

ELEVATION

- 6000m / 19,686ft
- 4000m / 13,124ft
- 3000m / 9843ft
- 2000m / 6562ft
- 1000m / 3281ft
- 500m / 1640ft
- 250m / 820ft
- 100m / 328ft
- sea level

SCALE 1:7,750,000
(projection: Lambert Conformal Conic)

Km 0 25 50 100 150 200 250 300
Miles 0 25 50 100 150 200 250 300

Since the transferral of Hong Kong from the UK to China, only the Portuguese territory of Macao, with its colonial architecture, bars, and casinos, remains as a vestige of Europe's territorial exploits in the Far East. Macao reverts to Chinese rule in 1999.

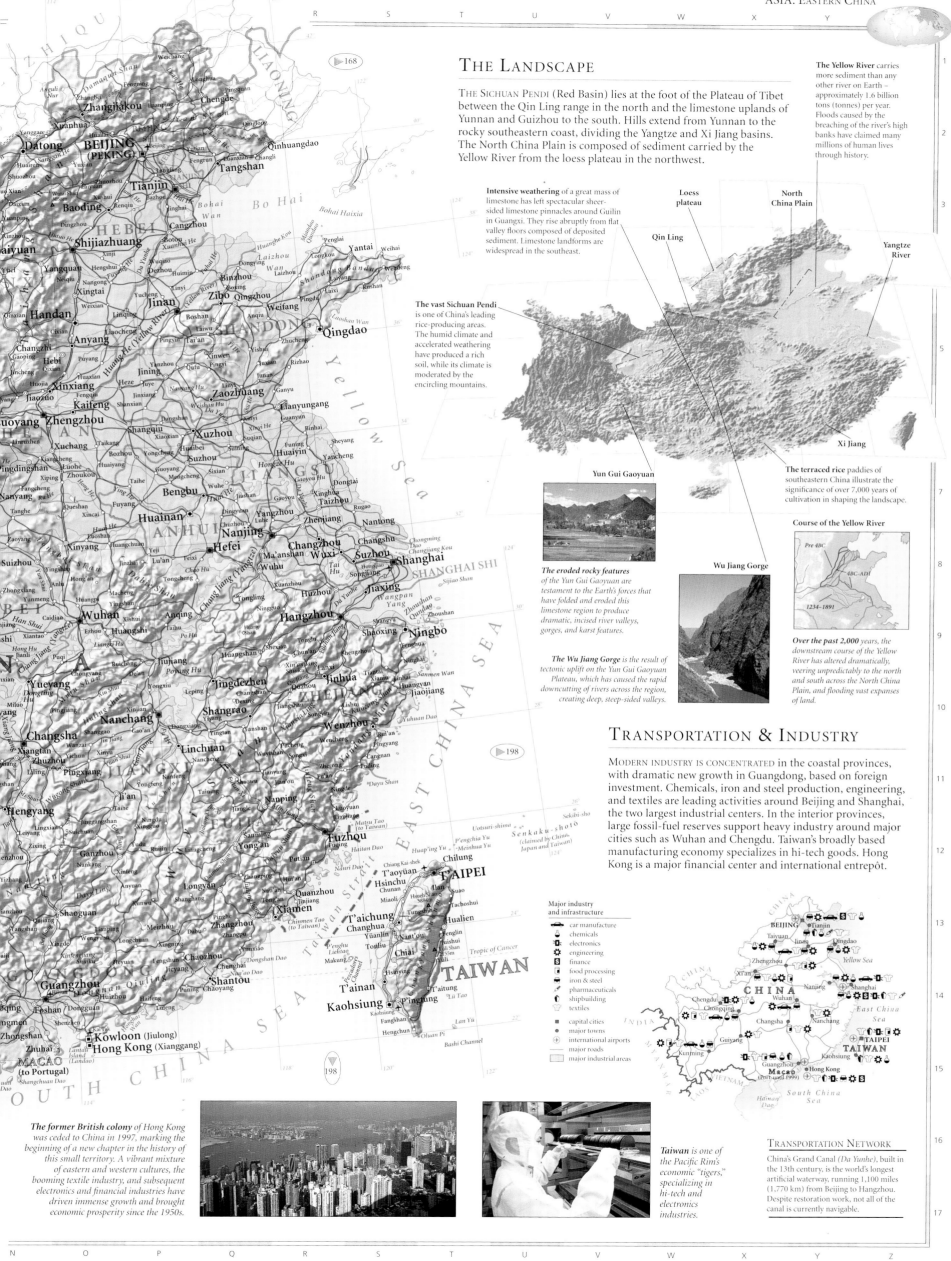

THE LANDSCAPE

THE SICHUAN PENDI (Red Basin) lies at the foot of the Plateau of Tibet between the Qin Ling range in the north and the limestone uplands of Yunnan and Guizhou to the south. Hills extend from Yunnan to the rocky southeastern coast, dividing the Yangtze and Xi Jiang basins. The North China Plain is composed of sediment carried by the Yellow River from the loess plateau in the northwest.

The Yellow River carries more sediment than any other river on Earth – approximately 1.6 billion tons (tonnes) per year. Floods caused by the breaching of the river's high banks have claimed many millions of human lives through history.

Intensive weathering of a great mass of limestone has left spectacular sheer-sided limestone pinnacles around Guilin in Guangxi. They rise abruptly from flat valley floors composed of deposited sediment. Limestone landforms are widespread in the southeast.

Loess plateau

North China Plain

Qin Ling

Yangtze River

The vast Sichuan Pendi is one of China's leading rice-producing areas. The humid climate and accelerated weathering have produced a rich soil, while its climate is moderated by the encircling mountains.

Xi Jiang

The terraced rice paddies of southeastern China illustrate the significance of over 7,000 years of cultivation in shaping the landscape.

Yun Gui Gaoyuan

The eroded rocky features of the Yun Gui Gaoyuan are testament to the Earth's forces that have folded and eroded this limestone region to produce dramatic, incised river valleys, gorges, and karst features.

Wu Jiang Gorge

The Wu Jiang Gorge is the result of tectonic uplift on the Yun Gui Gaoyuan Plateau, which has caused the rapid downcutting of rivers across the region, creating deep, steep-sided valleys.

Course of the Yellow River

Pre 4BC

4BC–AD1

1234–1891

Over the past 2,000 years, the downstream course of the Yellow River has altered dramatically, veering unpredictably to the north and south across the North China Plain, and flooding vast expanses of land.

TRANSPORTATION & INDUSTRY

MODERN INDUSTRY IS CONCENTRATED in the coastal provinces, with dramatic new growth in Guangdong, based on foreign investment. Chemicals, iron and steel production, engineering, and textiles are leading activities around Beijing and Shanghai, the two largest industrial centers. In the interior provinces, large fossil-fuel reserves support heavy industry around major cities such as Wuhan and Chengdu. Taiwan's broadly based manufacturing economy specializes in hi-tech goods. Hong Kong is a major financial center and international entrepôt.

Major industry and infrastructure

- car manufacture
- chemicals
- electronics
- engineering
- finance
- food processing
- iron & steel
- pharmaceuticals
- shipbuilding
- textiles
- capital cities
- major towns
- international airports
- major roads
- major industrial areas

The former British colony of Hong Kong was ceded to China in 1997, marking the beginning of a new chapter in the history of this small territory. A vibrant mixture of eastern and western cultures, the booming textile industry, and subsequent electronics and financial industries have driven immense growth and brought economic prosperity since the 1950s.

Taiwan is one of the Pacific Rim's economic "tigers," specializing in hi-tech and electronics industries.

TRANSPORTATION NETWORK

China's Grand Canal (Da Yunhe), built in the 13th century, is the world's longest artificial waterway, running 1,100 miles (1,770 km) from Beijing to Hangzhou. Despite restoration work, not all of the canal is currently navigable.

NORTHEASTERN CHINA, MONGOLIA & KOREA

MONGOLIA, NORTH KOREA, SOUTH KOREA, Heilongjiang, Inner Mongolia, Jilin, Liaoning

THIS NORTHERLY REGION has been a domain of shifting borders and competing colonial powers for centuries. Mongolia was the heartland of Chinghiz Khan's vast Mongol empire in the 13th century, while northeastern China was home to the Manchus, China's last ruling dynasty (1644–1911). The mineral and forest wealth of the northeast helped to make it China's principal region of heavy industry, although the outdated state factories now face decline. South Korea's state-led market economy has grown dramatically, and Seoul is now one of the world's largest cities. The austere communist regime of North Korea has isolated itself from the expanding markets of the Pacific Rim and faces continuing economic stagnation.

The Eurasian steppe stretches from the mouth of the Danube in Europe, to Mongolia. In Mongolia, nomadic people have lived in felt huts, called yurts or gers, for thousands of years.

MAP KEY

POPULATION

- ◼ above 5 million
- ◼ 1 million to 5 million
- ◉ 500,000 to 1 million
- ◎ 100,000 to 500,000
- ⊕ 50,000 to 100,000
- ⊕ 10,000 to 50,000
- ○ below 10,000

ELEVATION

- 4000m / 13,124ft
- 3000m / 9843ft
- 2000m / 6562ft
- 1000m / 3281ft
- 500m / 1640ft
- 250m / 820ft
- 100m / 328ft
- sea level

SCALE 1:7,000,000
(projection: Lambert Conformal Conic)

Km
0 25 50 100 150 200

Miles
0 25 50 100 150 200

THE LANDSCAPE

THE GREAT NORTH CHINA PLAIN is largely enclosed by mountain ranges, including the Great and Lesser Khingan ranges *(Da Hinggan Ling* and *Xiao Hinggan Ling)* in the north, and the Changbai Shan, which extend south into the rugged peninsula of Korea. The broad steppeland plateau of Nei Mongol Gaoyuan borders the southeastern edge of the great cold desert of the Gobi, which extends west across the southern reaches of Mongolia. In northwest Mongolia, the Altai Mountains and various lesser ranges are interspersed with lakeland basins.

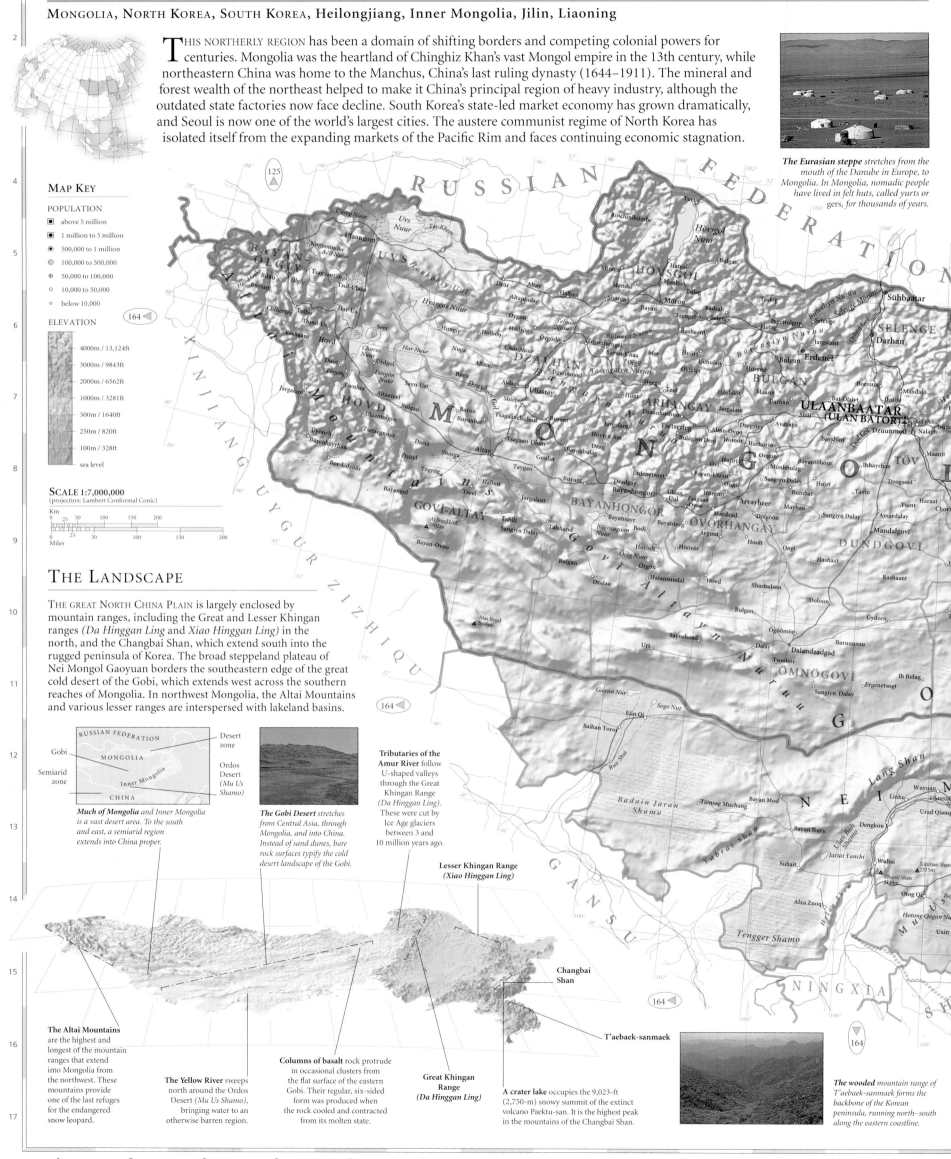

Much of Mongolia and Inner Mongolia is a vast desert area. To the south and east, a semiarid region extends into China proper.

The Gobi Desert stretches from Central Asia, through Mongolia, and into China. Instead of sand dunes, bare rock surfaces typify the cold desert landscape of the Gobi.

Tributaries of the Amur River follow U-shaped valleys through the Great Khingan Range *(Da Hinggan Ling).* These were cut by Ice Age glaciers between 3 and 10 million years ago.

Lesser Khingan Range *(Xiao Hinggan Ling)*

Changbai Shan

T'aebaek-sanmaek

The Altai Mountains are the highest and longest of the mountain ranges that extend into Mongolia from the northwest. These mountains provide one of the last refuges for the endangered snow leopard.

The Yellow River sweeps north around the Ordos Desert *(Mu Us Shamo),* bringing water to an otherwise barren region.

Columns of basalt rock protrude in occasional clusters from the flat surface of the eastern Gobi. Their regular, six-sided form was produced when the rock cooled and contracted from its molten state.

Great Khingan Range *(Da Hinggan Ling)*

A crater lake occupies the 9,023-ft (2,750-m) snowy summit of the extinct volcano Paektu-san. It is the highest peak in the mountains of the Changbai Shan.

The wooded mountain range of T'aebaek-sanmaek forms the backbone of the Korean peninsula, running north–south along the eastern coastline.

TRANSPORTATION & INDUSTRY

NORTH KOREA'S CENTRALLY PLANNED ECONOMY is strongly oriented toward heavy industry, while South Korea has a broad manufacturing base that includes textiles, steel, electronics, and one of the world's largest shipbuilding industries. Mongolia and Inner Mongolia's great mineral resource potential is largely undeveloped. The heavy industrial region around Shenyang produces iron, steel, chemicals, and cement on a massive scale.

Major industry and infrastructure

car manufacture		pharmaceuticals	
chemicals		shipbuilding	
coal		textiles	
electronics		capital cities	
engineering		major towns	
finance		international airports	
food processing		major roads	
iron & steel		major industrial areas	

TRANSPORTATION NETWORK

Liaoning has China's most comprehensive railroad network, the legacy of the Japanese occupation of Manchuria, earlier this century. The railroads are used primarily for freight transportation.

Ulan Bator, the Mongolian capital, bears many of the hallmarks of Soviet-style central planning. This is the result of economic and industrial assistance from the Soviet Union following Mongolian independence in 1921.

While North Korea has remained politically and economically isolated from the rest of the world, South Korea has enjoyed immense economic growth. It has benefited considerably from US economic aid in the aftermath of the Korean War of 1950–1953.

USING THE LAND & SEA

MONGOLIA AND INNER MONGOLIA rely heavily on livestock farming, with only about 1% of the land area cultivated. Northeastern China produces wheat, corn, soybeans, and sugar beet. The cool climate limits the range of crops, and large upland areas of the northeast remain forested. Rice is the staple food of North and South Korea. The latter has become a leading ocean-fishing nation.

Land use and agricultural distribution

goats	capital cities
pigs	major towns
sheep	pasture
corn	cropland
fishing	forest
rice	mountain region
soybeans	desert
sugar beet	
wheat	

JAPAN

IN THE YEARS SINCE THE END of the Second World War, Japan has become the most dynamic industrial nation in the world. The country is composed of a string of over 4,000 islands. They lie in the northwest Pacific in a great northeast–southwest arc. Four major islands – Hokkaido, Honshu, Shikoku, and Kyushu – are home to the great majority of Japan's population of 124 million people, although the mountainous terrain of the central region means that most cities are situated on the coast. A densely populated industrial belt stretches along much of Honshu's southern coast, and includes Japan's crowded capital, Tokyo. Alongside its spectacular economic growth and the increasing westernization of its cities, Japan still maintains a highly individual culture, reflected in its traditional food, formal behavioral codes, unique Shinto religion, and reverence for the emperor, who is officially regarded as a god.

TRANSPORTATION & INDUSTRY

JAPAN IS THE WORLD'S second largest market economy, outranked only by the US. Technological development, particularly of computers, electronic goods, cars, and motorcycles, is second to none. Japanese industry invests in its workforce and in long-term research and development to maintain the high standard of its products and a reputation for innovation. Japanese businesses are now global, both in their manufacturing bases and in the distribution of goods.

Major industry and infrastructure

- brewing
- car manufacture
- chemicals
- hi-tech industry
- engineering
- finance
- iron & steel
- research & development
- shipbuilding
- textiles
- winter sports

- ■ capital cities
- • major towns
- ⊕ international airports
- major roads
- major industrial areas

TRANSPORTATION NETWORK

691,076 miles (1,112,844 km)		2,423 miles (3,900 km)	
12,577 miles (20,254 km)		1,099 miles (1,770 km)	

Japanese road construction traditionally lagged behind that of its extensive and technologically advanced railroad network. The road network's relative lack of development has led to severe urban congestion, although expressways have now been built in some cities.

Known in the west as the "bullet train," the Shinkansen is the second-fastest train in the world. It speeds past the snow-capped peak of Mount Fuji between the cities of Tokyo and Osaka.

USING THE LAND & SEA

ALTHOUGH ONLY ABOUT 11% OF JAPAN is suitable for cultivation, substantial government support, a favorable climate, and intensive farming methods enable the country to be virtually self-sufficient in rice production. Northern Hokkaido, the largest and most productive farming region, has an open terrain and climate similar to that of the American Midwest, and produces more than half of Japan's cereal grain requirements. Farmers are being encouraged to diversify by growing fruits, vegetables, and wheat, as well as raising livestock.

Land use and agricultural distribution

- cattle
- pigs
- fishing
- cereals
- citrus fruits
- fruit
- herbs
- rice
- root crops
- tobacco
- ■ capital cities
- • major towns
- pasture
- cropland
- forest

THE URBAN/RURAL POPULATION DIVIDE

urban 77%   rural 23%

0 10 20 30 40 50 60 70 80 90 100

POPULATION DENSITY	TOTAL LAND AREA
847 people per sq mile (327 people per sq km)	145,869 sq miles (377,800 sq km)

Cutting terraces maximizes the limited agricultural land, enabling Japan to produce large quantities of rice.

The Kobe earthquake in January 1995 highlighted Japan's vulnerability to earthquakes, despite technological advances. It shattered much of the infrastructure of this important port. More than 5,000 people died as buildings and overhead highways collapsed and fires broke out.

A number of new volcanoes have emerged in Japan this century, existing alongside older cones. This volcano, on the island of Kyushu in Aso-Kuju National Park, is now dormant and covered with grass.

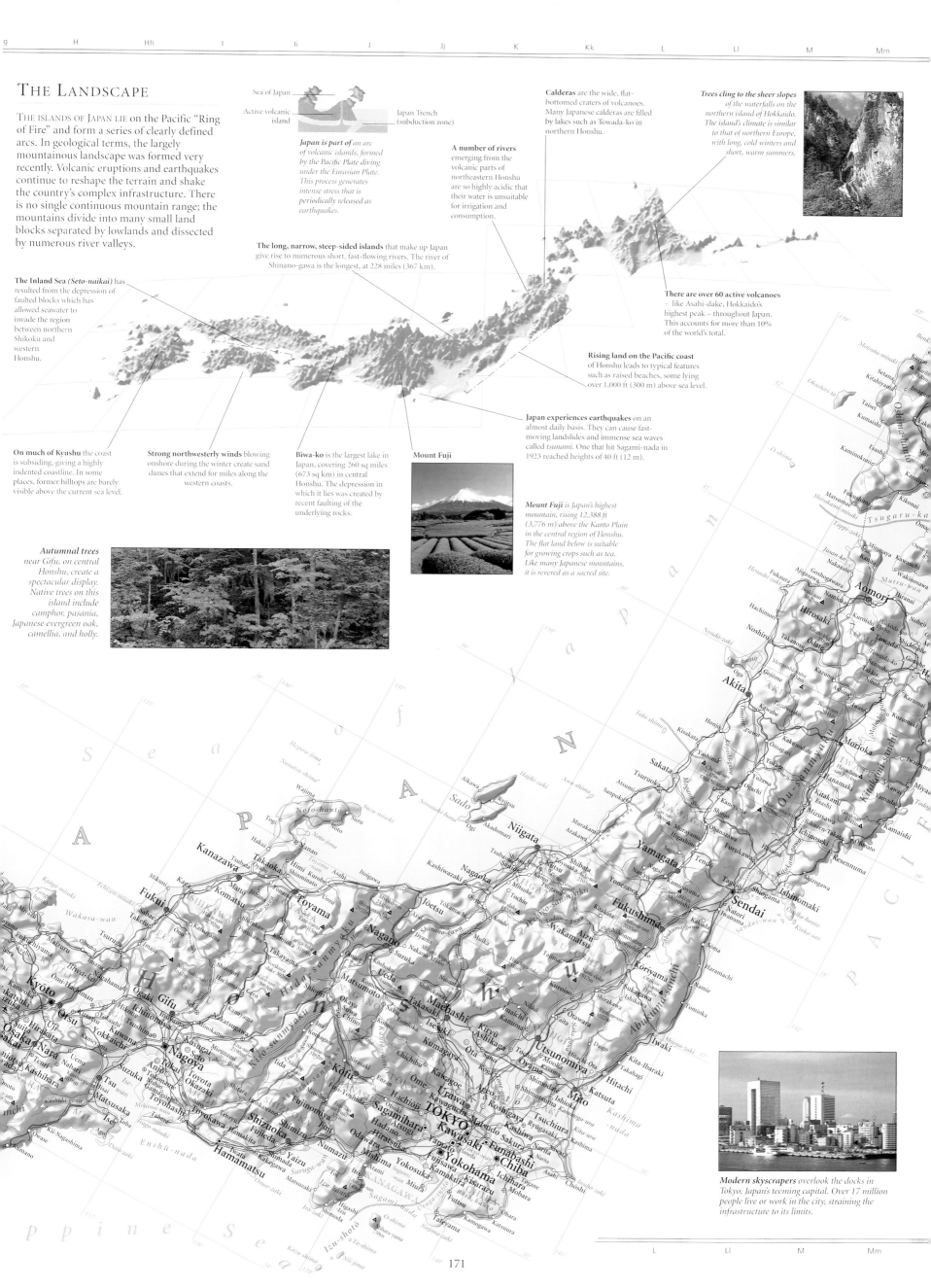

THE LANDSCAPE

THE ISLANDS OF JAPAN LIE on the Pacific "Ring of Fire" and form a series of clearly defined arcs. In geological terms, the largely mountainous landscape was formed very recently. Volcanic eruptions and earthquakes continue to reshape the terrain and shake the country's complex infrastructure. There is no single continuous mountain range; the mountains divide into many small land blocks separated by lowlands and dissected by numerous river valleys.

Japan is part of an arc of volcanic islands, formed by the Pacific Plate diving under the Eurasian Plate. This process generates intense stress that is periodically released as earthquakes.

Sea of Japan
Active volcanic island
Japan Trench (subduction zone)

Calderas are the wide, flat-bottomed craters of volcanoes. Many Japanese calderas are filled by lakes such as Towada-ko in northern Honshu.

A number of rivers emerging from the volcanic parts of northeastern Honshu are so highly acidic that their water is unsuitable for irrigation and consumption.

Trees cling to the sheer slopes of the waterfalls on the northern island of Hokkaido. The island's climate is similar to that of northern Europe, with long, cold winters and short, warm summers.

The long, narrow, steep-sided islands that make up Japan give rise to numerous short, fast-flowing rivers. The river of Shinano-gawa is the longest, at 228 miles (367 km).

There are over 60 active volcanoes – like Asahi-dake, Hokkaido's highest peak – throughout Japan. This accounts for more than 10% of the world's total.

The Inland Sea *(Seto-naikai)* has resulted from the depression of faulted blocks which has allowed seawater to invade the region between northern Shikoku and western Honshu.

Rising land on the Pacific coast of Honshu leads to typical features such as raised beaches, some lying over 1,000 ft (300 m) above sea level.

Japan experiences earthquakes on an almost daily basis. They can cause fast-moving landslides and immense sea waves called *tsunami*. One that hit Sagami-nada in 1923 reached heights of 40 ft (12 m).

On much of Kyushu the coast is subsiding, giving a highly indented coastline. In some places, former hilltops are barely visible above the current sea level.

Strong northwesterly winds blowing onshore during the winter create sand dunes that extend for miles along the western coasts.

Biwa-ko is the largest lake in Japan, covering 260 sq miles (673 sq km) in central Honshu. The depression in which it lies was created by recent faulting of the underlying rocks.

Mount Fuji

Mount Fuji is Japan's highest mountain, rising 12,388 ft (3,776 m) above the Kanto Plain in the central region of Honshu. The flat land below is suitable for growing crops such as tea. Like many Japanese mountains, it is revered as a sacred site.

Autumnal trees near Gifu, on central Honshu, create a spectacular display. Native trees on this island include camphor, pasania, Japanese evergreen oak, camellia, and holly.

Modern skyscrapers overlook the docks in Tokyo, Japan's teeming capital. Over 17 million people live or work in the city, straining the infrastructure to its limits.

171

Malaysia exports a greater tonnage of tropical timber than any other country in the world. Much of it comes from Sarawak in Borneo. Although in principle logging is allowed only on a sustainable basis, environmentalists fear that the rain forest in Sarawak will have disappeared by the early 21st century.

This tiny island near Kota Kinabalu, in Sabah, eastern Malaysia, is a part of a designated national park. Thickly forested, it is surrounded by broad, sandy beaches and shallow inland seas.

MALAYSIA

SOUTH CHINA SEA

MAP KEY

POPULATION
- ■ above 5 million
- ■ 1 million to 5 million
- ▣ 500,000 to 1 million
- ⊕ 100,000 to 500,000
- ⊕ 50,000 to 100,000
- ⊙ 10,000 to 50,000
- ○ below 10,000

ELEVATION
- 4000m / 13,124ft
- 3000m / 9843ft
- 2000m / 6562ft
- 1000m / 3281ft
- 500m / 1640ft
- 250m / 820ft
- 100m / 328ft
- sea level

SCALE 1:6,250,000
(projection: Mercator)

Km
0 25 50 100 150

Miles
0 25 50 100 150

Throughout Southeast Asia, where agricultural land is at a premium, terraces are cut into the slopes to maximize the area available for cultivation. These terraces on the Indonesian island of Bali are used to support rice paddies.

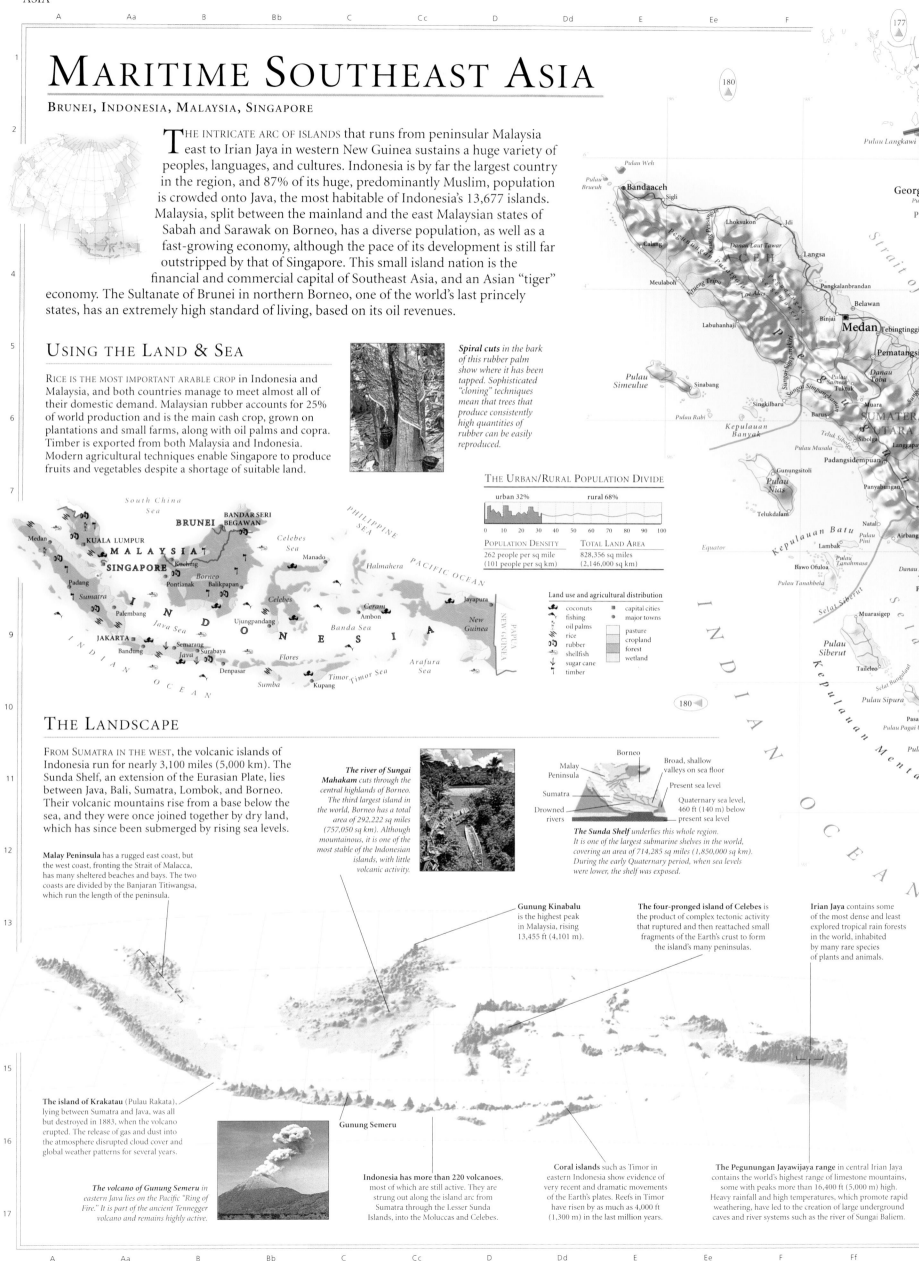

Maritime Southeast Asia

Brunei, Indonesia, Malaysia, Singapore

The intricate arc of islands that runs from peninsular Malaysia east to Irian Jaya in western New Guinea sustains a huge variety of peoples, languages, and cultures. Indonesia is by far the largest country in the region, and 87% of its huge, predominantly Muslim, population is crowded onto Java, the most habitable of Indonesia's 13,677 islands. Malaysia, split between the mainland and the east Malaysian states of Sabah and Sarawak on Borneo, has a diverse population, as well as a fast-growing economy, although the pace of its development is still far outstripped by that of Singapore. This small island nation is the financial and commercial capital of Southeast Asia, and an Asian "tiger" economy. The Sultanate of Brunei in northern Borneo, one of the world's last princely states, has an extremely high standard of living, based on its oil revenues.

Using the Land & Sea

Rice is the most important arable crop in Indonesia and Malaysia, and both countries manage to meet almost all of their domestic demand. Malaysian rubber accounts for 25% of world production and is the main cash crop, grown on plantations and small farms, along with oil palms and copra. Timber is exported from both Malaysia and Indonesia. Modern agricultural techniques enable Singapore to produce fruits and vegetables despite a shortage of suitable land.

Spiral cuts in the bark of this rubber palm show where it has been tapped. Sophisticated "cloning" techniques mean that trees that produce consistently high quantities of rubber can be easily reproduced.

The Urban/Rural Population Divide

urban 32%   rural 68%

0 10 20 30 40 50 60 70 80 90 100

Population Density
262 people per sq mile
(101 people per sq km)

Total Land Area
828,356 sq miles
(2,146,000 sq km)

Land use and agricultural distribution

- coconuts
- fishing
- oil palms
- rice
- rubber
- shellfish
- sugar cane
- timber
- capital cities
- major towns
- pasture
- cropland
- forest
- wetland

The Landscape

From Sumatra in the west, the volcanic islands of Indonesia run for nearly 3,100 miles (5,000 km). The Sunda Shelf, an extension of the Eurasian Plate, lies between Java, Bali, Sumatra, Lombok, and Borneo. Their volcanic mountains rise from a base below the sea, and they were once joined together by dry land, which has since been submerged by rising sea levels.

The river of Sungai Mahakam cuts through the central highlands of Borneo. The third largest island in the world, Borneo has a total area of 292,222 sq miles (757,050 sq km). Although mountainous, it is one of the most stable of the Indonesian islands, with little volcanic activity.

Borneo
Malay Peninsula
Sumatra
Drowned rivers
Broad, shallow valleys on sea floor
Present sea level
Quaternary sea level, 460 ft (140 m) below present sea level

The Sunda Shelf underlies this whole region. It is one of the largest submarine shelves in the world, covering an area of 714,285 sq miles (1,850,000 sq km). During the early Quaternary period, when sea levels were lower, the shelf was exposed.

Malay Peninsula has a rugged east coast, but the west coast, fronting the Strait of Malacca, has many sheltered beaches and bays. The two coasts are divided by the Banjaran Titiwangsa, which run the length of the peninsula.

Gunung Kinabalu is the highest peak in Malaysia, rising 13,455 ft (4,101 m).

The four-pronged island of Celebes is the product of complex tectonic activity that ruptured and then reattached small fragments of the Earth's crust to form the island's many peninsulas.

Irian Jaya contains some of the most dense and least explored tropical rain forests in the world, inhabited by many rare species of plants and animals.

The island of Krakatau (Pulau Rakata), lying between Sumatra and Java, was all but destroyed in 1883, when the volcano erupted. The release of gas and dust into the atmosphere disrupted cloud cover and global weather patterns for several years.

Gunung Semeru

The volcano of Gunung Semeru in eastern Java lies on the Pacific "Ring of Fire." It is part of the ancient Tennegger volcano and remains highly active.

Indonesia has more than 220 volcanoes, most of which are still active. They are strung out along the island arc from Sumatra through the Lesser Sunda Islands, into the Moluccas and Celebes.

Coral islands such as Timor in eastern Indonesia show evidence of very recent and dramatic movements of the Earth's plates. Reefs in Timor have risen by as much as 4,000 ft (1,300 m) in the last million years.

The Pegunungan Jayawijaya range in central Irian Jaya contains the world's highest range of limestone mountains, some with peaks more than 16,400 ft (5,000 m) high. Heavy rainfall and high temperatures, which promote rapid weathering, have led to the creation of large underground caves and river systems such as the river of Sungai Baliem.

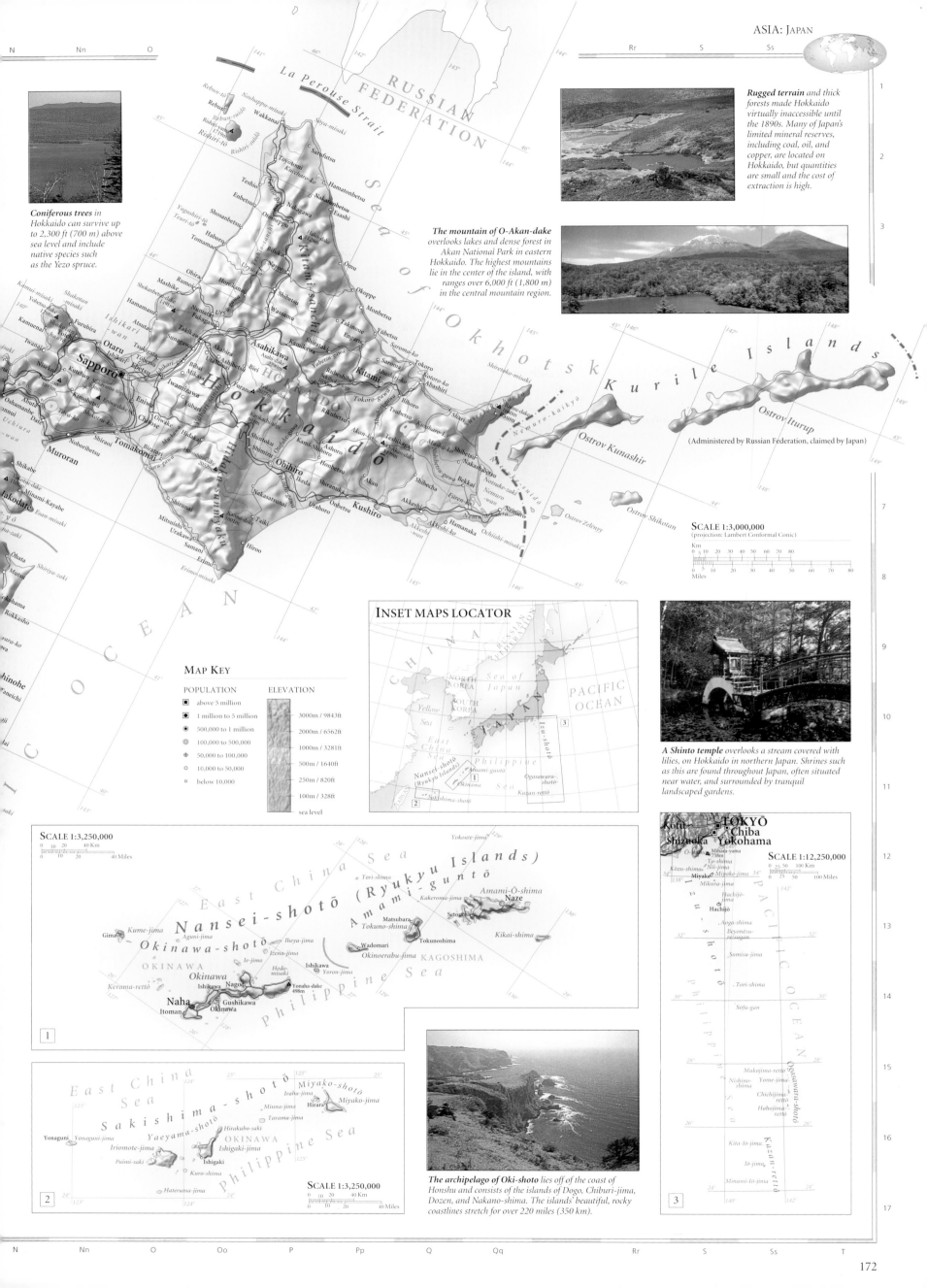

Coniferous trees in Hokkaido can survive up to 2,300 ft (700 m) above sea level and include native species such as the Yezo spruce.

Rugged terrain and thick forests made Hokkaido virtually inaccessible until the 1890s. Many of Japan's limited mineral reserves, including coal, oil, and copper, are located on Hokkaido, but quantities are small and the cost of extraction is high.

The mountain of O-Akan-dake overlooks lakes and dense forest in Akan National Park in eastern Hokkaido. The highest mountains lie in the center of the island, with ranges over 6,000 ft (1,800 m) in the central mountain region.

A Shinto temple overlooks a stream covered with lilies, on Hokkaido in northern Japan. Shrines such as this are found throughout Japan, often situated near water, and surrounded by tranquil landscaped gardens.

The archipelago of Oki-shoto lies off the coast of Honshu and consists of the islands of Dogo, Chiburi-jima, Dozen, and Nakano-shima. The islands' beautiful, rocky coastlines stretch for over 220 miles (350 km).

SCALE 1:3,000,000
(projection: Lambert Conformal Conic)

INSET MAPS LOCATOR

MAP KEY

POPULATION

- ■ above 5 million
- ▣ 1 million to 5 million
- ◉ 500,000 to 1 million
- ◎ 100,000 to 500,000
- ⊕ 50,000 to 100,000
- ○ 10,000 to 50,000
- ○ below 10,000

ELEVATION

- 3000m / 9843ft
- 2000m / 6562ft
- 1000m / 3281ft
- 500m / 1640ft
- 250m / 820ft
- 100m / 328ft
- sea level

SCALE 1:3,250,000

Nansei-shotō (Ryukyu Islands)
Amami-guntō
Okinawa-shotō

SCALE 1:3,250,000

Sakishima-shotō
Miyako-shotō
Yaeyama-shotō

SCALE 1:12,250,000

TOKYO
Chiba
Yokohama

MAINLAND SOUTHEAST ASIA & THE PHILIPPINES

CAMBODIA, LAOS, MYANMAR, PHILIPPINES, THAILAND, VIETNAM

THICKLY FORESTED MOUNTAINS intercut by the broad valleys of five great rivers characterize the landscape of Southeast Asia's mainland countries. Agriculture remains the main activity for much of the population, which is concentrated in the river floodplains and deltas. Linked ethnic and cultural roots give the region a distinct identity. Most people on the mainland are Theravada Buddhists, and the Philippines is the only predominantly Christian country in Southeast Asia. Foreign intervention began in the 16th century with the opening of the spice trade; Cambodia, Laos, and Vietnam were French colonies until the end of the Second World War; Myanmar was under British control; and the Philippines was controlled by Spain and the US in the 20th century. Only Thailand was never colonized. Today, Thailand and the Philippines are poised to play a leading role in the economic development of the Pacific Rim, and Laos and Vietnam have begun to mend the devastation of the Vietnam War, and to develop their economies. With continuing political instability and a shattered infrastructure, Cambodia faces an uncertain future, while Myanmar is seeking investment and the ending of its 30-year isolation from the world community.

The Irrawaddy River is Myanmar's vital central artery, watering the rice paddies and providing a rich source of fish, as well as an important transportation link, particularly for local traffic.

Commercial logging, still widespread in Myanmar, has now been stopped in Thailand because of overexploitation of the tropical rain forest.

THE LANDSCAPE

A SERIES OF MOUNTAIN RANGES runs north–south through the mainland, formed as the result of the collision between the Eurasian Plate and the Indian subcontinent, which created the Himalayas. They are interspersed by the valleys of a number of great rivers. On their passage to the sea, these rivers have deposited sediment, forming huge, fertile floodplains and deltas. The Philippines' 7,000 islands are mountainous and volcanic, with narrow coastal plains.

Lake Taal on the Philippine island of Luzon lies within the crater of an immense volcano that has erupted twice in the 20th century, first in 1911 and again in 1965, causing the deaths of more than 3,200 people.

The Irrawaddy River runs virtually north–south, draining the plains of northern Myanmar. The Irrawaddy Delta is the country's main rice-growing area.

Hkakabo Razi is the highest point in mainland Southeast Asia. It rises 19,300 ft (5,885 m) at the border between China and Myanmar.

Mountains dominate the Laotian landscape, with more than 90% of the land lying more than 600 ft (180 m) above sea level. The mountains of the Chaine Annamitique form the country's eastern border.

The Red River Delta in northern Vietnam is fringed to the north by steep-sided, round-topped limestone hills, typical of karst scenery.

Mindanao has five mountain ranges, many of which have large numbers of active volcanoes. Lying just west of the Philippine Trench, which forms the boundary between the colliding Philippine and Eurasian plates, the entire island chain is subject to earthquakes and volcanic activity.

The fast-flowing waters of the Mekong River cascade over this waterfall in Champasak province in Laos. The force of the water erodes rocks at the base of the fall.

Salween River

The Mekong River flows through southern China and Myanmar, then for much of its length forms the border between Laos and Thailand, flowing through Cambodia before terminating in a vast delta on the southern Vietnamese coast.

The coastline of the Isthmus of Kra

Longshore drift

Spit

Eroded coastline

Wave attack

Lagoon

Bohol

Malay Peninsula

Tonle Sap, a freshwater lake, drains into the Mekong Delta via the Mekong River. It is the largest lake in Southeast Asia.

Thailand

The coast of the Isthmus of Kra, in southeast Thailand, has many small, precipitous islands like these, formed by chemical erosion on limestone, which is weathered along vertical cracks. The humidity of the climate in Southeast Asia increases the rate of weathering.

The east and west coasts of the Isthmus of Kra differ greatly. The tectonically uplifting west coast is exposed to the harsh southwesterly monsoon and is heavily eroded. On the east coast, longshore currents produce depositional features such as spits and lagoons.

Bohol in the southern Philippines is famous for its so-called "chocolate hills." There are more than 1,000 of these regular mounds on the island. The hills are limestone in origin, the smoothed remains of an earlier cycle of erosion. Their brown appearance in the dry season gives the hills their name.

U   Uu   V   Vv   W   Ww   X   Xx   Y   Yy   Z

Transportation & Industry

Singapore has a thriving economy based on international trade and finance. Annual trade through the port is among the highest of any port in the world. Indonesia still depends on natural resources, particularly wood, petroleum, and gas, although the economy is rapidly diversifying, with manufactured exports including garments, consumer electronics, and footwear. A high-profile aircraft industry has developed in Bandung. Malaysia has a fast-growing and varied manufacturing sector, although oil, gas, and timber remain important resource-based industries.

Major industry and infrastructure

- aerospace
- copra processing
- chemicals
- electronics
- engineering
- finance
- food processing
- iron & steel
- oil
- shipbuilding
- timber processing
- textiles
- capital cities
- major towns
- international airports
- major roads
- major industrial areas

Ranks of gleaming skyscrapers, new highways, and infrastructure construction reflect the investment that is pouring into Southeast Asian cities like the Malaysian capital, Kuala Lumpur. Traditional housing and markets still exist between the new developments. Many of the city's inhabitants subsist at a level far removed from the prosperity implied by its outward modernity.

Transportation Network

160,350 miles (258,213 km)	
188 miles (302 km)	
5,482 miles (8,828 km)	
15,523 miles (32,903km)	

Singapore's subway system, completed in 1991, is among the most efficient in the world. Malaysia has several fast, modern highways and most roads are paved. Indonesia's many islands make improvement of the shipping infrastructure a priority.

Although Indonesia is now a mainly Muslim country, relicts of other civilizations are found throughout its many islands. These scattered columns are the ruins of a Hindu settlement that flourished on Java more than a thousand years ago.

PHILIPPINES

PHILIPPINES

PHILIPPINE

▶ 198

177

Sulu
Sea

Pulau Balambangan

Balabac Strait

Pulau Banggi

Tiga Tarok

Kudat

Teluk Marudu

Teluk Paitan

Kanibongan

Tuaran

Gunung Kinabalu 4101m

Sungai Sugut

Ranau

Kota Kinabalu

Teluk Kimanis

Kuala Penyu

Tambunan

LABUAN

Pulau Labuan

Labuan

Keningau

SABAH

Sandakan

Sungai Labuk

Teluk Labuk

Sungai Kinabatangan

Sungai Segama

Lahad Datu

Banjar Seri
Begawan

Brunei Bay

Tenom

BANDAR
SERI
BEGAWAN
BRUNEI

Teluk
Lahad Datu

Pulau Timbun Mata
Pulau Bum Bun

Tawau

Pulau Sebatik

Celebes

Sea

Kepulauan
Kawio

Kepulauan
Nanusa

Pulau
Karakelong

Pulau
Sangihe

Melanguane

Kepulauan Talaud

Pulau Salibabu

Damau

Pulau
Kaburuang

Pulau Mandul

Sebuku Teluk

Sungai Sembakung

Sungai Sesayap

Pulau Bunyu

Bunyu

Tahuna

Tarakan

Pulau Tarakan

Pulau Mapat

Kepulauan Sangir

Ulu

Pulau Siau

Pulau
Tahulandang

Kepulauan
Loloda Utara

Tanjung Bisoa

Sopi

Pulau
Morotai

Sabatai

Tanjungbatu

Teluk
Pantai

Pulau Marattua

Gunung Antu 750m

Serai

Pulau Bangka

Galela

Tobelo

Pediwang

Iga

Salumpaga

Tolitoli

Oan

Teluk Bilang

Lanu

Teluk Paleleh

SULAWESI
UTARA

Manado

Tomohon

Bitung

Airmadidi

Tondano

Danau Tondano

Amurang

Pulau Mayu

Bobopayo

Kusu

Dodaga

Ternate

Pulau Ternate

Pulau Tidore

Pulau
Halmahera

Buli

Teluk Buli

Bico

Tompo

Teluk
Dondo

Leok

Teluk Dampal

Gunung Malino 2499m

Pegunungan Paleleh

Lemito

Kuandang

Danau
Limboto

Gunung Balowa 1970m

Kotamobagu

Molibagu

Soasiu

Pulau Makian

Mafa

Teluk
Weda

Pulau
Kasiruta

Pulau
Bacan

Molucca

Sea

Kepulauan
Bacan

Pulau Mandioli

Selat Obi

Gani

Kep

Ha

Molosipat

Bubaa

Gorontalo

Teluk Gorontalo

KALIMANTAN TIMUR

Gunung Menyapa 2000m

Muarawahau

Sangkulirang

Kepulauan
Togian

Pulau
Batudaka

Pulau Boano

Pegunungan
Ogoamas

Towera

Donggala

Tetc

Teluk Tambu

Gulf of
Tomini

Dondo

Toima

Teluk Poh

Selat Walea

Teluk
Uebonti

Maliku

Bolaang

Teku

Selat Peleng

Balo

Pulau Bisu

Kawassi

Pulau Obi

Sepasu

Tenggarong

Tanjung Ayu

Samarinda

Sangasanga

Lohjanan

Tanjung Bayur

Danau
Semayang

Danau Melintang

Danau Jempang

Palu

Pakuli

Danau
Lindu

Lambogo

Tambarana

Gimpu

Poso

Pandiri

Pegunungan Balingara

SULAWESI

TENGAH

Luwuk

Pulau Peleng

Pelei

Kembani

Pulau Banggai

Kepulauan
Banggai

Penu

Pulau Mangole

Capalulu

Sepese

Pulau Gomumu

Longiram

n
t
a
n

Muaratewe

Waru

Muarakaman

Balikpapan

Teluk Balikpapan

Sungai Telen

Sungai Wahau

Karosa

Babana

Tentena

Taripa

Baturebe

Pegunungan
Tokalekaju

Tobamawu

Danau Poso

Mamuju

Pulau Reneng

Pegunungan
Pompangeo

Saroako

Pulau Luka

Teluk Tolo

Kepulauan Banggai

Pulau Taliabu

Tano

Sanana

Pulau
Sanana

Kepulauan Sula

Ceram

Maluku

Dayu

Sungai Barito

Tanjung

Pegunungan Meratus

Amuntai

Kandangan

Negara

Rantau

KALIMANTAN
SELATAN

Banjarmasin

Martapura

Kotabaru

Pulau
Laut

Karambu

Pelaihari

Pulau Sebuku

Makassar Strait

Teluk Adang

Teluk Mamuju

Malunda

Rantepao

Pegunungan Quarles

Sulawesi
(Celebes)

Masamba

Danau Matana

Wotu

Usu

Mahalona

Danau Towuti

Kepulauan
Salabangka

Kendari

Kepulauan
Trcko

Pulau Manui

Gunung Kaubalamada 2729m

Waflia

Pulau
Mandioli

Lasahata

Tanjung N

Piru

Namlea

Danau
Rana

Pulau Buru

Pulau Boano

Pulau
Kelang

Luhu

Pulau
Manipa

Watawa

Pulau Seram

Halong

Ambon

Pulau Ambon

Pulau
Haruku

Sea

MALU

Elara

Tifu

Majene

Teluk
Mandar

Polewali

Enrekang

SULAWESI

SELATAN

Teluk
Lebani

Sungai
Sedeng

Parepare

Anabanua

Singkang

Danau Tempe

Watampone

Teluk Bone

Malamala

Wiau

Asera

Pegunungan
Mekongga

Pegunungan
Mekongga

Kolaka

SULAWESI

TENGGARA

Pulau Padamarang

Pulau Wowoni

Pulau Staring

Pulau Wowoni

Kakea

Banda Sea

Kepulauan
Penyu

Kepulauan
Lucipara

Ambelau

Kepulauan

Sulamu

I   N   D   O   N   E   S   I   A

Kepulauan
Laut Kecil

Kepulauan
Balabalangan

Maros

Ujungpandang

Takalar

Kepulauan
Pabbiring

Sungai Walanae

Bugingkalo

Pising

Selat Tioro

Tampo

Raha

Pulau Muna

Bonelipu

Teluk
Kolowanawatobo

Kamaru

Kepulauan
Langkesi

Jeneponto

Bulukumba

Pulau
Kabaena

Baubau

Pulau
Kaledupa

Kepulauan
Tukangbesi

Pulau Karamain

mbo-besar

Benteng

Selat Selayar

Pulau Kabia

Kepulauan
Macan

Pulau
Batuata

Pulau
Binongko

Kepulauan
Bonerate

Pulau
Kangean

Kepulauan
Kangean

Kepulauan
Sabalana

Pulau
Tanahjampea

Pulau Kalao

Pulau Bonerate

Pulau Kalaotoa

Flores

Sea

Bondokodi

Walakubak

Pulau Sumba

Waingapu

Baing

Savu Sea

Kepulauan
Sawu

Pulau Sawu

Selat Roti

Pulau Roti

Kupang

Toineke

Timor Sea

Bali Sea

Bali

ingaraja

vangi

Tejakula

Danau Batur

BALI

Denpasar

Ngurah Rai

Nusa
Penida

Mataram

Kuta

Pulau
Lombok

Bayan

NUSA TENGGARA BARAT

Kubu

Pulau Moyo

Alas

Sumbawabesar

Taliwang

Sumbawa

Lunyuk

Gunung Tambora 1400m

Teluk Saleh

Dompu

Teluk Sanggar

Gunung Api 1949m

Sangeang

Raba

Teluk Bima

Komodo

Gerampi

Komodo

Labuhanbajo

Ruteng

Pota

Teluk Palu

Bajawa

Endeh

Pulau Lomblen

Larantuka

Maumere

Flores

Kepulauan Alor

Pulau Alor

Pulau
Lomblen

Kabir

Labala

Pulau Pantar

Kepulauan
Solor

Pulau Solor

Kepulauan Alor

Pulau
Kambing

Mahana

TIMOR TIMUR

Kefamenanu

Gunung Kekrsnu 2670m

Soe

Nikiniki

Sulamu

Nikiniki

NUSA TENGGARA TIMUR

Pulau Wetar

Selat Romang

Pulau Romang

Kepulauan
Leti

Pulau
Moa

Dili

Manatuto

Lospalos

Tutuala

Selat Wetar

Selat Ombai

Selat Ombai

Pante Makasar

Suai

Kefamenanu

Kepulauan

Pu

N   U   S   A   T   E   N   G   G   A   R   A   (L   e   s   s   e   r   S   u   n   d   a   I   s   l   a   n   d   s   )

Timor Sea

USING THE LAND & SEA

THE FERTILE FLOODPLAINS of rivers such as the Mekong and Salween, and the humid climate, enable the production of rice throughout the region. Cambodia, Myanmar, and Laos still have substantial forests, producing hardwoods such as teak and rosewood. Cash crops include tropical fruits such as coconuts, bananas, and pineapples, rubber, oil palm, sugar cane, and the jute substitute, kenaf. Pigs and cattle are the main livestock raised. Large quantities of marine and freshwater fish are caught throughout the region.

▶ 162

Land use and agricultural distribution

- cattle
- pigs
- bananas
- coconuts
- fishing
- oil palms
- rice
- rubber
- sugar cane
- timber
- ■ capital cities
- ■ major towns

pasture
cropland
forest
mountain region

THE URBAN/RURAL POPULATION DIVIDE

urban 22%   rural 78%

0 10 20 30 40 50 60 70 80 90 100

POPULATION DENSITY	TOTAL LAND AREA
253 people per sq mile (98 people per sq km)	733,828 sq miles (1,901,110 sq km)

The Paracel Islands and the Spratly Islands are two strategically sensitive island groups, disputed by several surrounding countries. The Paracels are claimed by China, Taiwan, and Vietnam, though only China has actually occupied them. The Spratlys are claimed by China, Taiwan, Vietnam, Malaysia, and the Philippines and are particularly important because they lie on oil and gas deposits.

▶ 198

The walled city of Hue, in central Vietnam, was built in the 19th century in the style of a Chinese city. It is the site of a number of religious monuments, including the Thien-Mu Pagoda.

180 ◀

◀ 173

Transportation & Industry

Industrial manufacturing has become increasingly important in Thailand, Vietnam, and the Philippines in recent years. The assembling of component-based electrical and electronic goods is becoming more common throughout this region, with foreign companies benefiting from low labor costs and the upgrading of technology. The economies of Myanmar and Cambodia are still based on agricultural produce and the processing of raw materials. Tin is the region's most important metal, and nickel, copper, and chromite are also mined, although the quantities produced are not significant on a global scale. Thailand's successful tourist industry is the country's highest earner of foreign exchange.

Transportation Network

	130,235 miles (209,718 km)		None
	7,087 miles (11,413 km)		20,433 miles (32,903 km)

Transportation development has concentrated on the building of road networks. Water and sea transportation remain important, although air links have improved, particularly in Thailand and the Philippines.

Major industry and infrastructure

- chemicals
- electronics
- engineering
- finance
- food processing
- iron & steel
- oil & gas
- mining
- shipbuilding
- textiles
- timber processing
- capital cities
- major towns
- international airports
- major roads
- major industrial areas

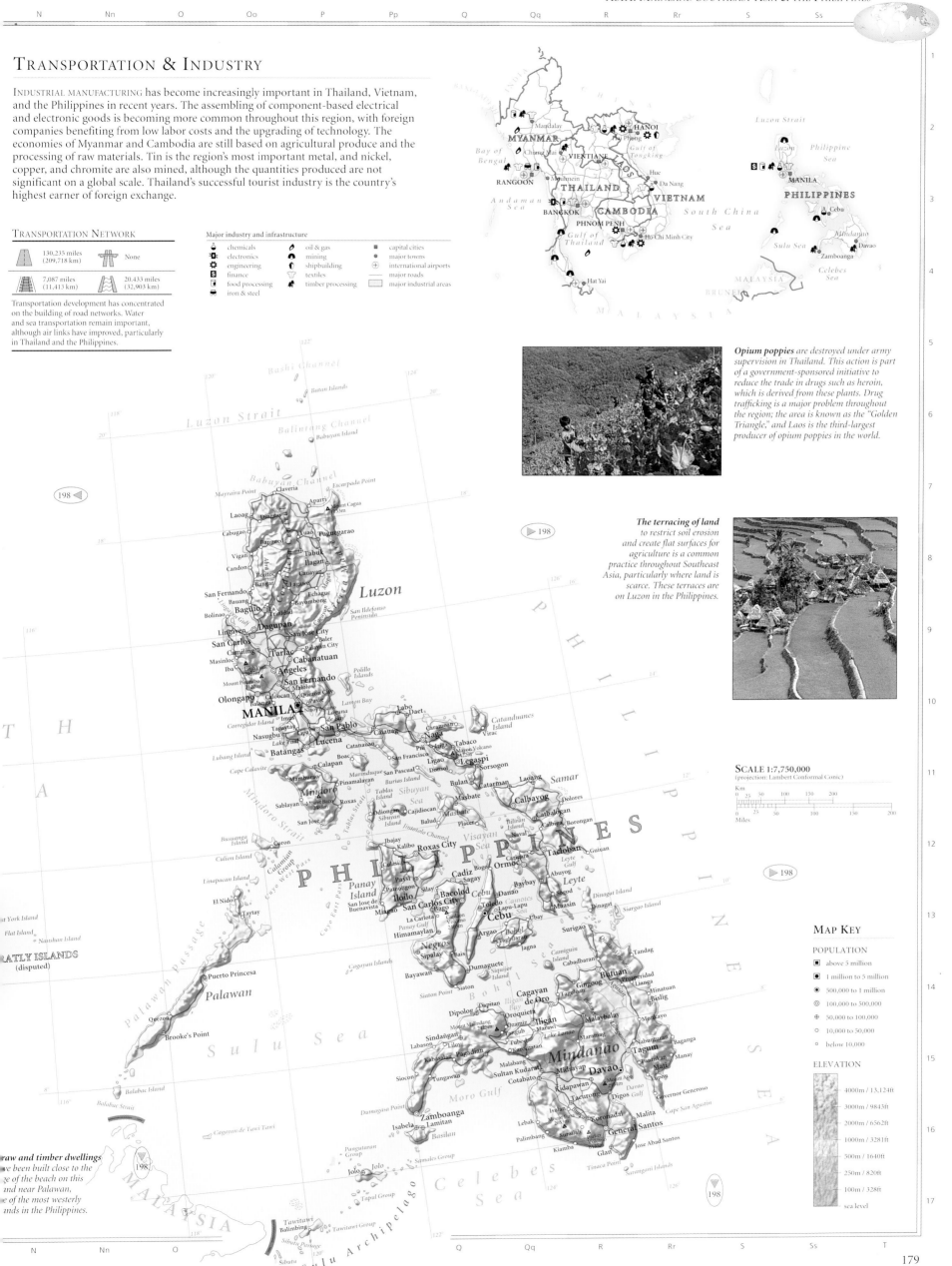

Opium poppies are destroyed under army supervision in Thailand. This action is part of a government-sponsored initiative to reduce the trade in drugs such as heroin, which is derived from these plants. Drug trafficking is a major problem throughout the region; the area is known as the "Golden Triangle," and Laos is the third-largest producer of opium poppies in the world.

The terracing of land to restrict soil erosion and create flat surfaces for agriculture is a common practice throughout Southeast Asia, particularly where land is scarce. These terraces are on Luzon in the Philippines.

SCALE 1:7,750,000
(projection: Lambert Conformal Conic)

Map Key

Population

- above 5 million
- 1 million to 5 million
- 500,000 to 1 million
- 100,000 to 500,000
- 50,000 to 100,000
- 10,000 to 50,000
- below 10,000

Elevation

	4000m / 13,124ft
	3000m / 9843ft
	2000m / 6562ft
	1000m / 3281ft
	500m / 1640ft
	250m / 820ft
	100m / 328ft
	sea level

raw and timber dwellings ... have been built close to the ... ge of the beach on this ... nd near Palawan, ... e of the most westerly ... nds in the Philippines.

THE INDIAN OCEAN

DESPITE BEING THE SMALLEST of the three major oceans, the evolution of the Indian Ocean was the most complex. The ocean basin was formed during the breakup of the supercontinent Gondwanaland, when the Indian subcontinent moved northeast, Africa moved west, and Australia separated from Antarctica. Like the Pacific Ocean, the warm waters of the Indian Ocean are punctuated by coral atolls and islands. About one-fifth of the world's population – over a billion people – live on its shores. Those people living along the northern coasts are constantly threatened by flooding and typhoons caused by the monsoon winds.

THE LANDSCAPE

THE INDIAN OCEAN BEGAN FORMING about 150 million years ago, but in its present form it is relatively young, only about 36 million years old. Along the three subterranean mountain chains of its mid-ocean ridge the sea floor is still spreading. The Indian Ocean has fewer trenches than other oceans and only a narrow continental shelf around most of its surrounding land.

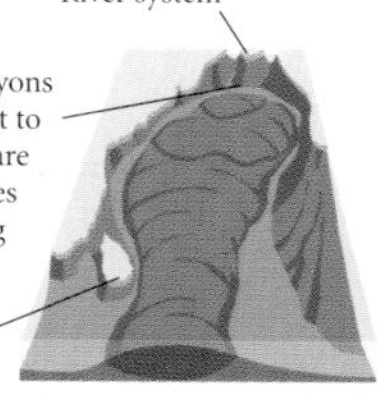

Sediments come from Ganges/Brahmaputra River system

Submarine canyons transport sediment to fan – some of these are more than 1,500 miles (2,500 km) long

Sri Lanka

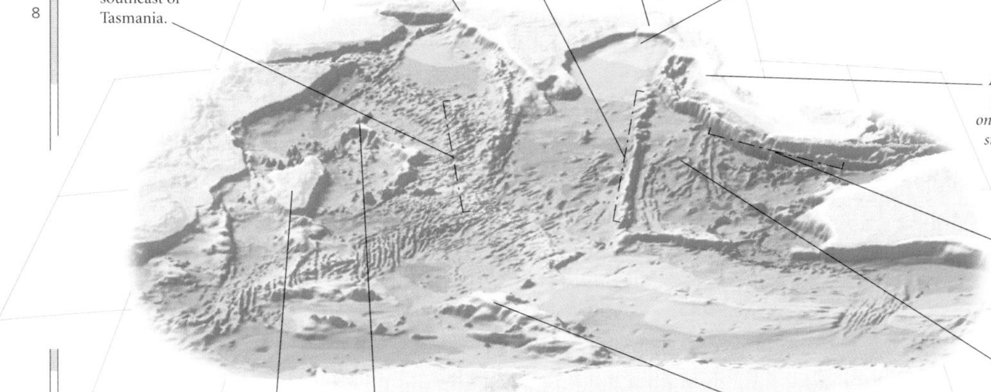

The mid-oceanic ridge runs from the Arabian Sea. It diverges east of Madagascar. One arm runs southwest to join the Mid-Atlantic Ridge, the other branches southeast, joining the Pacific-Antarctic Ridge, southeast of Tasmania.

The Ninetyeast Ridge takes its name from the line of longitude it follows. It is the world's longest and straightest undersea ridge.

Two of the world's largest rivers flow into the Indian Ocean; the Indus and the Ganges/Brahmaputra. Both have deposited enormous fans of sediment.

The Ganges Fan is one of the world's largest submarine accumulations of sediment, extending far beyond Sri Lanka. It is fed by the Ganges/Brahmaputra River system, whose sediment is carried through a network of underwater canyons at the edge of the continental shelf.

Indus River

The relief of Madagascar rises from a low-lying coastal strip in the east, to the central plateau. The plateau is also a major watershed separating Madagascar's three main river basins.

The central group of the Seychelles are mountainous, granite islands. They have a narrow coastal belt and lush, tropical vegetation cloaks the highlands.

The Kerguelen Islands in the Southern Ocean were created by a hot spot in the Earth's crust. The islands were formed in succession as the Antarctic Plate moved slowly over the hot spot.

A large proportion of the coast of Thailand, on the Isthmus of Kra, is stabilized by mangrove thickets. They act as an important breeding ground for wildlife.

The Java Trench is the world's longest. Running 1,600 miles (2,570 km) from the southwest of Java, it is only 50 miles (80 km) wide.

The circulation in the northern Indian Ocean is controlled by the monsoon winds. Biannually these winds reverse their pattern, causing a reversal in the surface currents and alternating high and low pressure conditions over Asia and Australia.

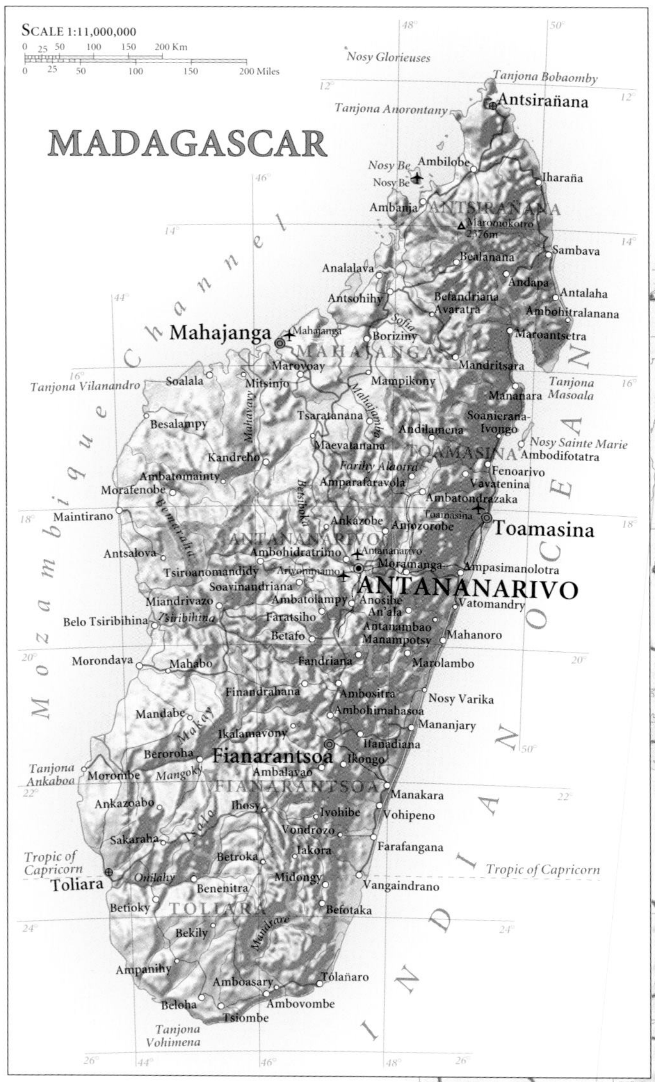

RESOURCES

MANY OF THE SMALL ISLANDS in the Indian Ocean rely exclusively on tuna-fishing and tourism to maintain their economies. Most fisheries are artisanal, although large-scale tuna-fishing does take place in the Seychelles, Mauritius, and the western Indian Ocean. Nonliving resources include oil in the Persian Gulf, pearls in the Red Sea, and tin from deposits off the shores of Burma, Thailand, and Indonesia.

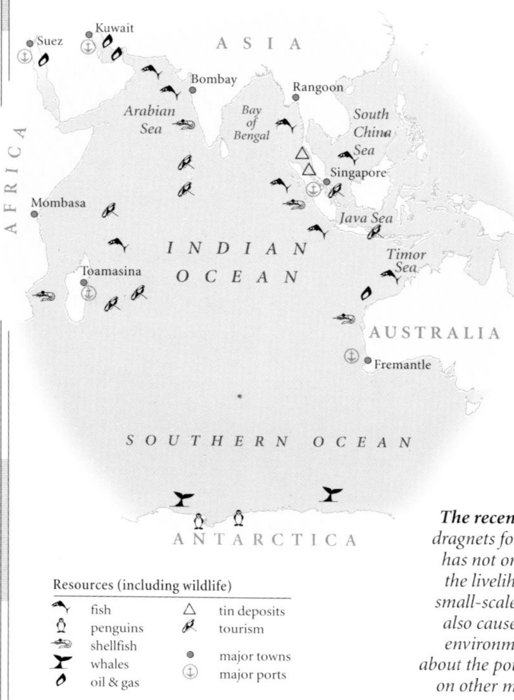

The recent use of large dragnets for tuna-fishing has not only threatened the livelihoods of many small-scale fisheries, but also caused widespread environmental concern about the potential impact on other marine species.

Resources (including wildlife)

- fish
- penguins
- shellfish
- whales
- oil & gas
- tin deposits
- tourism
- major towns
- major ports

SCALE 1:11,000,000

MADAGASCAR

Nosy Glorieuses
Tanjona Bobaomby
Antsirañana
Tanjona Anorontany

Iharaña
Ambilobe
Nosy Be
Ambanja

Sambava

Analalava
Antsohihy
Andapa
Antalaha
Mahajanga
Ambodifotatra
Maroantsetra

Soalala
Mitsinjo
Mandritsara
Tanjona Masoala

Besalampy
Kandreho
Maevatanana
Tsaratanana
Soanierana Ivongo
Nosy Sainte Marie

Morafenobe
Fenoarivo
Toamasina

Maintirano
Ankazobe
ANTANANARIVO
Watomandry

Antsalova
Tsiroanomandidy
Arivonimamo
Moramanga

Miandrivazo
Antanifotsy
Mahanoro

Belo Tsiribihina
Betafo
Marolambo

Morondava
Mahabo
Nosy Varika

Mandabe
Fianarantsoa
Mananjary

Berorodha
Manakara

Tanjona Ankaboa
Morombe
Vohipeno

Ankazoabo
Ihosy
Farafangana

Sakaraha
Betroka
Vangaindrano

Toliara
Betioky
Befotaka

Bekily
Amboasary

Ampanihy
Ambovombe

Beloha
Tôlañaro

Tanjona Vohimena

Madagascar inset scale text continues

SCALE 1:4,500,000

Grande Comore
Mitsamiouli
Mbéni
Koimbani
MORONI
Hahaya
La Kartala
Mitsoudjé
Foumbouni
Dembéni

COMOROS

Mohéli
Anjouan
Moutsamudu
Ouani
Miringoni
Fomboni
Sima
Domoni
Nioumachoua
Ouanani
Moya
Mramani

MAYOTTE
(to France)

Dzaoudzi
Pamandzi
MAMOUDZOU
Bandrélé

Comoro Islands

Mozambique Channel

SCALE 1:2,000,000

Inner Islands
Île Aride
Praslin
Curieuse
Les Sœurs
Cousin
Grand Sœur
Île du Nord
Félicité
Mount Dauban
La Digue
Marianne

SEYCHELLES

Mamelles
Silhouette
Mahé
North Point
Île aux Récifs

VICTORIA
Sainte Anne
Île au Cerf
Frégate
Morne Seychellois
Île Thérèse
Mahé
Cascade
Anse Boileau
Pointe Lazare
Baie Lazare
Quatre Bornes
Pointe Police

Coral reefs support an enormous diversity of animal and plant life. Many species of tiny tropical fish, like these squirrel fish, live and feed around the profusion of reefs and atolls in the Indian Ocean.

The steeper eastern side of Madagascar is drained by numerous short, fast-flowing rivers. In contrast, larger, more languid rivers flow across the west. Both erode huge quantities of Madagascar's red soil.

There are over 1,300 small coral islands in the Maldives, but only about 200 are inhabited. Based around an ancient submerged volcanic mountain range, all the islands are low-lying and none rise more than 6 ft (1.8 m) above sea level.

SCALE 1:42,000,000
(projection: Mollweide)

Km
0 200 400 600 800 1000

Miles
0 200 400 600 800 1000

ASIA

KUWAIT
IRAN
BAHRAIN
QATAR
UAE
Doha
Dubai
Abu Dhabi
UAE
Ad
Bandar-e 'Abbās
PAKISTAN
Gwadar
Karachi
Indus
ARABIA
OMAN
Mina' Qābūs
Salalah
YEMEN
Socotra
Bombay
Narmada
INDIA
Bhávnagar
Mangalore
Goaduari
Krishna
Madras
Visakhapatnam
Bay of Bengal
Ganges Fan
Ganges
Brahmaputra
BANGLADESH
Dhaka
Calcutta
Chittagong
Irrawaddy
MYANMAR
Rangoon
Salween
Mekong
Gulf of Tongking
CHINA
LAOS
VIETNAM
THAILAND
CAMBODIA
Gulf of Thailand
TAIWAN
Ryukyu Islands
Tropic of Cancer
East China Sea
Philippine Sea
PHILIPPINES
South China Sea

Laccadive Islands (to India)
Cochin
Tuticorin
Trincomalee
Colombo
Sri Lanka
SRI LANKA
MALDIVES
Ceylon Plain
Andaman Islands (to India)
Andaman Basin
Nicobar Islands (to India)
Bedawan
Klang
Singapore
MALAYSIA
Sumatra
Borneo
Celebes Sea
Sulu Sea
Sunda Molucca

Arabian Basin
Arabian Sea
Carlsberg Ridge
Chain Ridge
Owen Fracture Zone
Somali Basin
Amirante Islands
Seychelles Bank
Mahe
Chagos-Laccadive Plateau
Mid-Indian Ridge
Chagos Trench
Ninetyeast Ridge
Mid-Indian Basin
Investigator Ridge
Java Trench
Mentawai
Kepulauan
Cocos Basin
Java Ridge
Java Sea
INDONESIA
Celebes
New Guinea
Arafura Sea
Banda
Geram

HELLES
Mascarene Plateau
Saya de Malha Bank
Nazareth Bank
Cargados Carajos Bank
Chagos Archipelago
Diego Garcia
British Indian Ocean Territory (to UK)
Cocos Islands (to Australia)
Christmas Island (to Australia)
Ashmore & Cartier Islands (to Australia)
Timor
Timor Sea
Bali
Lombok
Sumbawa
Sumba
Roo Rise
North Australian Basin
Sahul Shelf
Bonaparte Gulf
Darwin
Joseph Bonaparte Gulf
Gulf of Carpentaria
Wyndham

INDIAN

Mascarene Basin
Agalega Islands (to Mauritius)
Toamasina
MAURITIUS
Rodrigues (to Mauritius)
Réunion (to France)
Mascarene Islands
Egeria Fracture Zone
Amsterdam Fracture Zone
Osborn Plateau
Wharton Basin
Wallaby Plateau
Cuvier Basin
Cuvier Plateau
Gascoyne Plain
Exmouth Plateau
Rowley Shoals
Port Hedland
Broome
Tropic of Capricorn

Madagascar Basin
Mauritius Trench
Batavia Seamount
Gulden Draak Seamount
Perth Basin
Naturaliste Plateau
Geraldton
Fremantle
Bunbury
Albany
Shark Bay
AUSTRALIA
Port Augusta
Murray
Adelaide
Darling
Melbourne

OCEAN

Broken Ridge
East Indiaman Ridge
Diamantina Fracture Zone
Great Australian Bight
South Australian Basin
Naturaliste Plateau
King Island
Bass Strait
Tasmania
Kangaroo Island
South Australian Plain
Tasman Plateau

Crozet Basin
Amsterdam Island
St. Paul Island
Southeast Indian Ridge
South Indian Basin
Crozet Plateau
Crozet Islands
French Southern & Antarctic Territories (to France)
Kerguelen
Kerguelen Plateau
Heard & McDonald Islands (to Australia)
Lena Tablemount

SOUTHERN OCEAN

The island of Mauritius is volcanic in origin. Its central plateau is bounded by mountains which may once have formed the rim of a volcanic crater.

Derby Plain
Banzare Seamounts
Pryd z Bay
Antarctic Circle

ANTARCTICA

INSET MAP KEY

POPULATION
⊙ 500,000 to 1 million
◎ 100,000 to 500,000
⊕ 50,000 to 100,000
○ 10,000 to 50,000
· below 10,000

ELEVATION
3000m / 9843ft
2000m / 6562ft
1000m / 3281ft
500m / 1640ft
250m / 820ft
100m / 328ft
sea level

OCEAN MAP KEY

SEA DEPTH
sea level
250m / 820ft
500m / 1640ft
1000m / 3281ft
2000m / 6562ft
3000m / 9843ft

(to France)
SCALE 1:2,000,000
0 5 10 20 30 Km
0 10 20 30 Miles

RÉUNION
ST-DENIS
Ste-Marie
Le Port
Ste-Suzanne
St-Paul
Gillot
Ste-Suzanne
Salazie
St-Benoit
Pointe des Aigrettes
Piton des Neiges 3070m
Trois-Bassins
Cilaos
La Plaine-des-Palmistes
St-Leu
Ste-Rose
Pointe au Sel
Piton de la Fournaise 2632m
Le Tampon
St-Louis
St-Pierre
St-Joseph
St-Philippe
Pointe de la Table
Point de la Rivière
St-Étienne
St-André
INDIAN OCEAN

MAURITIUS

Canonniers Point
Flat Island
Round Island
Gunner's Quoin
Île D'Ambre
Triolet
Goodlands
Pamplemousses
Rivière du Rempart
PORT LOUIS
Beau Bassin
Rose Hill
Centre de Flacq
Quatre Bornes
Mont du Rempart
Bel Air
Tamarin
Vacoas
Curepipe
Mahebourg
Piton de la Petite
Rivière Noire 826m
Rose Belle
Chemin Grenier
Souillac
Ramgoolam
Seewoosagur
Pointe Sud Ouest
INDIAN OCEAN
SCALE 1:2,000,000
0 5 10 20 30 Km
0 10 20 30 Miles

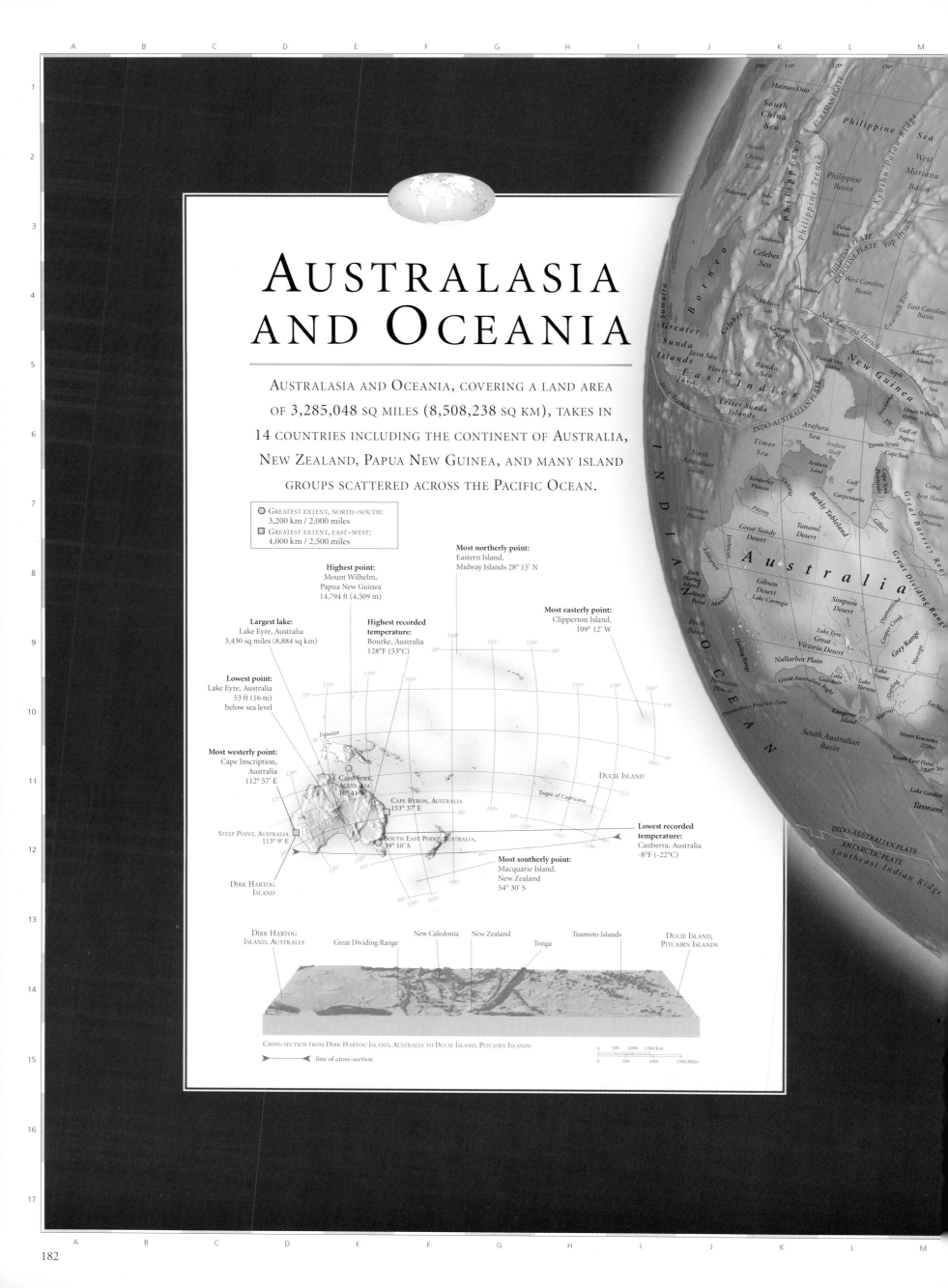

AUSTRALASIA AND OCEANIA

AUSTRALASIA AND OCEANIA, COVERING A LAND AREA
OF 3,285,048 SQ MILES (8,508,238 SQ KM), TAKES IN
14 COUNTRIES INCLUDING THE CONTINENT OF AUSTRALIA,
NEW ZEALAND, PAPUA NEW GUINEA, AND MANY ISLAND
GROUPS SCATTERED ACROSS THE PACIFIC OCEAN.

○ GREATEST EXTENT, NORTH–SOUTH:
3,200 km / 2,000 miles
□ GREATEST EXTENT, EAST–WEST:
4,000 km / 2,500 miles

Highest point:
Mount Wilhelm,
Papua New Guinea
14,794 ft (4,509 m)

Most northerly point:
Eastern Island,
Midway Islands 28° 15' N

Most easterly point:
Clipperton Island,
109° 12' W

Largest lake:
Lake Eyre, Australia
3,430 sq miles (8,884 sq km)

**Highest recorded
temperature:**
Bourke, Australia
128°F (53°C)

Lowest point:
Lake Eyre, Australia
53 ft (16 m)
below sea level

Most westerly point:
Cape Inscription,
Australia
112° 57' E

CAPE YORK,
AUSTRALIA
10° 41' S

CAPE BYRON, AUSTRALIA
153° 37' E

DUCIE ISLAND

STEEP POINT, AUSTRALIA
113° 9' E

SOUTH EAST POINT, AUSTRALIA,
39° 10' S

**Lowest recorded
temperature:**
Canberra, Australia
-8°F (-22°C)

DIRK HARTOG
ISLAND

Most southerly point:
Macquarie Island,
New Zealand
54° 30' S

DIRK HARTOG
ISLAND, AUSTRALIA

Great Dividing Range

New Caledonia

New Zealand

Tonga

Tuamoto Islands

DUCIE ISLAND,
PITCAIRN ISLANDS

CROSS-SECTION FROM DIRK HARTOG ISLAND, AUSTRALIA TO DUCIE ISLAND, PITCAIRN ISLANDS

◄ line of cross-section

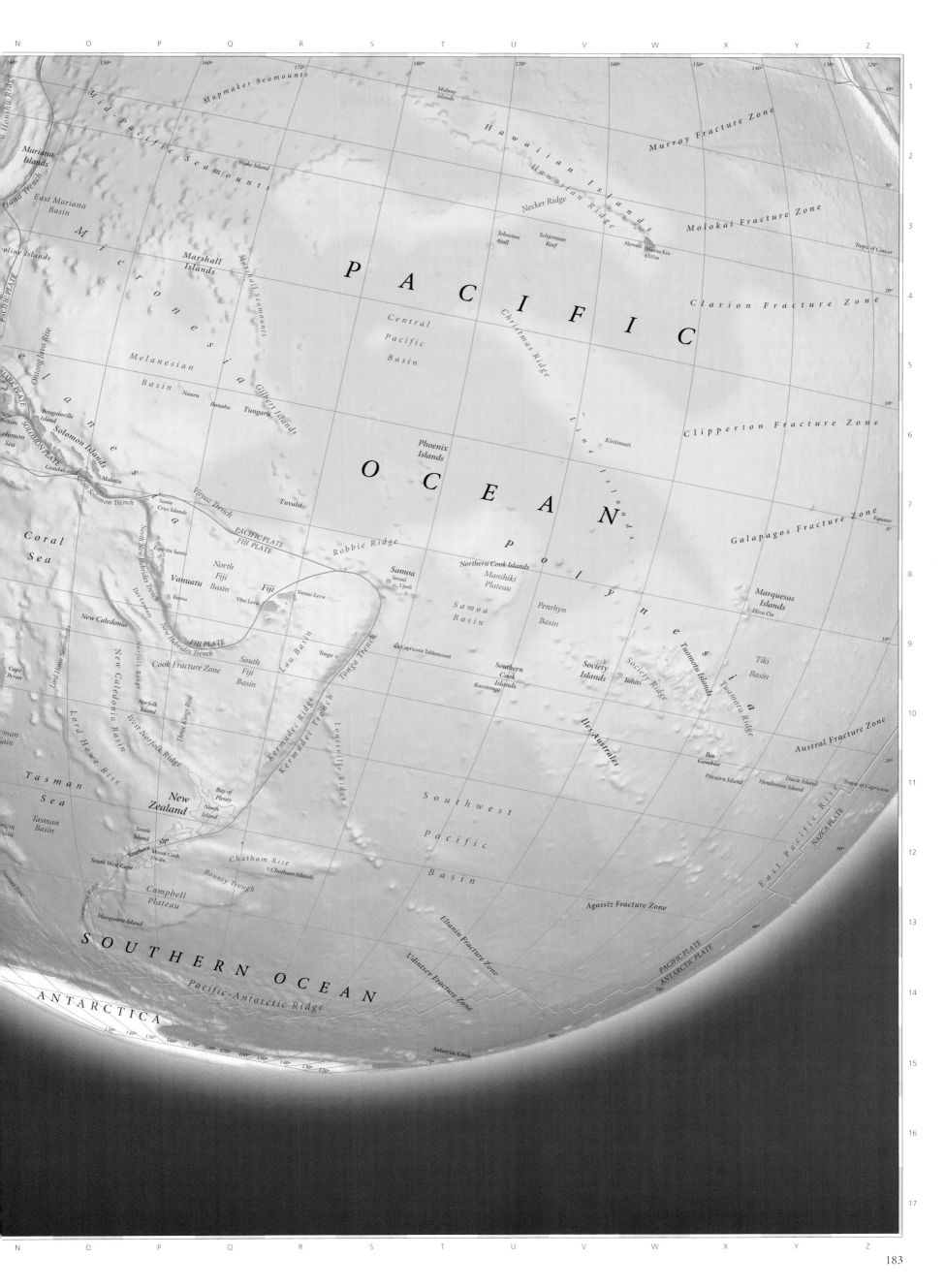

N O P Q R S T U V W X Y Z
1 2 3 4 5 6 7 8 9 10 11 12 13 14 15 16 17
PACIFIC OCEAN
SOUTHERN OCEAN
ANTARCTICA
Mapmaker Seamounts
Mid-Pacific Seamounts
Midway Islands
Hawaiian Islands
Hawaiian Ridge
Murray Fracture Zone
Mariana Islands
Wake Island
East Mariana Basin
Necker Ridge
Molokai Fracture Zone
Micronesia
Johnston Atoll
Schjetman Reef
Hawaii
Mauna Kea 4205m
Tropic of Cancer
Marshall Islands
Marshall Seamounts
Clarion Fracture Zone
Central Pacific Basin
Christmas Ridge
Ontong Java Rise
Melanesian Basin
Melanesia
Nauru
Banaba
Tungaru
Gilbert Islands
Line Islands
Bougainville Island
Solomon Islands
Solomon Sea
SOLOMON PLATE
Clipperton Fracture Zone
Kiritimati
Phoenix Islands
Guadalcanal
Malaita
South Solomon Trench
Santa Cruz Islands
Vityaz Trench
Tuvalu
PACIFIC PLATE
FIJI PLATE
Galapagos Fracture Zone
Equator
Coral Sea
North New Hebrides Trench
Espiritu Santo
Robbie Ridge
Polynesia
North Fiji Basin
Vanuatu
Samoa
Savaii
Upoli
Northern Cook Islands
Manihiki Plateau
Fiji
Vanua Levu
Viti Levu
Tanna
Iles Loyaute
Marquesas Islands
Hiva Oa
New Caledonia
Samoa Basin
Penrhyn Basin
New Hebrides Trench
Lau Basin
Tonga
Tonga Trench
Capricorn Tablemount
Lord Howe Seamounts
Norfolk Ridge
New Caledonia Basin
Cook Fracture Zone
South Fiji Basin
Southern Cook Islands
Rarotonga
Society Islands
Tahiti
Society Ridge
Tuamotu Islands
Tuamotu Ridge
Tiki Basin
Cape Byron
Norfolk Island
Three Kings Rise
West Norfolk Ridge
Kermadec Ridge
Kermadec Trench
Louisville Ridge
Iles Australes
Lord Howe Rise
Austral Fracture Zone
Iles Gambier
Pitcairn Island
Henderson Island
Ducie Island
Tropic of Capricorn
Tasman Sea
New Zealand
Bay of Plenty
North Island
Southwest Pacific Basin
Tasman Basin
South Island
Southern Alps
Mount Cook 3764m
South West Cape
East Pacific Rise
NAZCA PLATE
Chatham Rise
Chatham Islands
Bounty Trough
Campbell Plateau
Macquarie Ridge
Macquarie Island
Agassiz Fracture Zone
Eltanin Fracture Zone
Udintsev Fracture Zone
PACIFIC PLATE
ANTARCTIC PLATE
Pacific-Antarctic Ridge
Antarctic Circle

POLITICAL AUSTRALASIA AND OCEANIA

Western Australia's mineral wealth has transformed its state capital, Perth, into one of Australia's major cities. Perth is one of the world's most isolated cities. It is more than 2,500 miles (4,000 km) from the population centers of the eastern seaboard.

Vast expanses of ocean separate this geographically fragmented realm, characterized more by each country's isolation than by any political unity. Australia's and New Zealand's traditional ties with the UK, as members of the British Commonwealth, are now in question as Australasian and Oceanian nations increasingly look to forge new relationships with neighboring Asian countries like Japan. External influences have featured strongly in the politics of the islands of the Pacific; the various territories of Micronesia were largely under American control until the late 1980s. France, New Zealand, the US, and the UK still have territories under colonial rule in Polynesia. The testing of nuclear weapons by Western superpowers was widespread during the Cold War period, but has now been discontinued.

POPULATION

DENSITY OF SETTLEMENT in the region is generally low. Australia is one of the least densely populated countries on Earth with over 80% of its population living within 25 miles (40 km) of the coast – mostly in the southeast of the country. New Zealand, and the island groups of Melanesia, Micronesia, and Polynesia, are much more densely populated, although many of the smaller islands remain uninhabited.

Population density
(people per sq mile)

- below 10
- 10–62
- 63–130
- 131–259
- 260–519
- 520–780
- above 780

The myriad of small coral islands that are scattered across the Pacific Ocean are often uninhabited. They offer little shelter from the weather, often no fresh water, and only limited food supplies.

The planes of the Australian Royal Flying Doctor Service are able to cover large expanses of barren land quickly, bringing medical treatment to the most inaccessible and faraway places.

LANGUAGES

ENGLISH IS SPOKEN THROUGHOUT New Zealand and Australia, superimposed upon a mosaic of indigenous languages. Many, such as the Papuan dialects and languages – of which there are more than 700 – are only spoken by relatively small numbers of people, although Maori is spoken extensively in parts of New Zealand. In Papua New Guinea, Melanesian Pidgin, derived from English, has become the *lingua franca*. Across Australasia and Oceania, languages can be divided into the many dialects of Austronesian, spoken in Micronesia and Polynesia, and the numerous Papuan languages of Melanesia.

Language groups
- Australian
- Papuan
- Germanic
- Malay-Polynesian
- Uninhabited

SCALE 1:32,000,000
(projection: Lambert Azimuthal Equal Area)

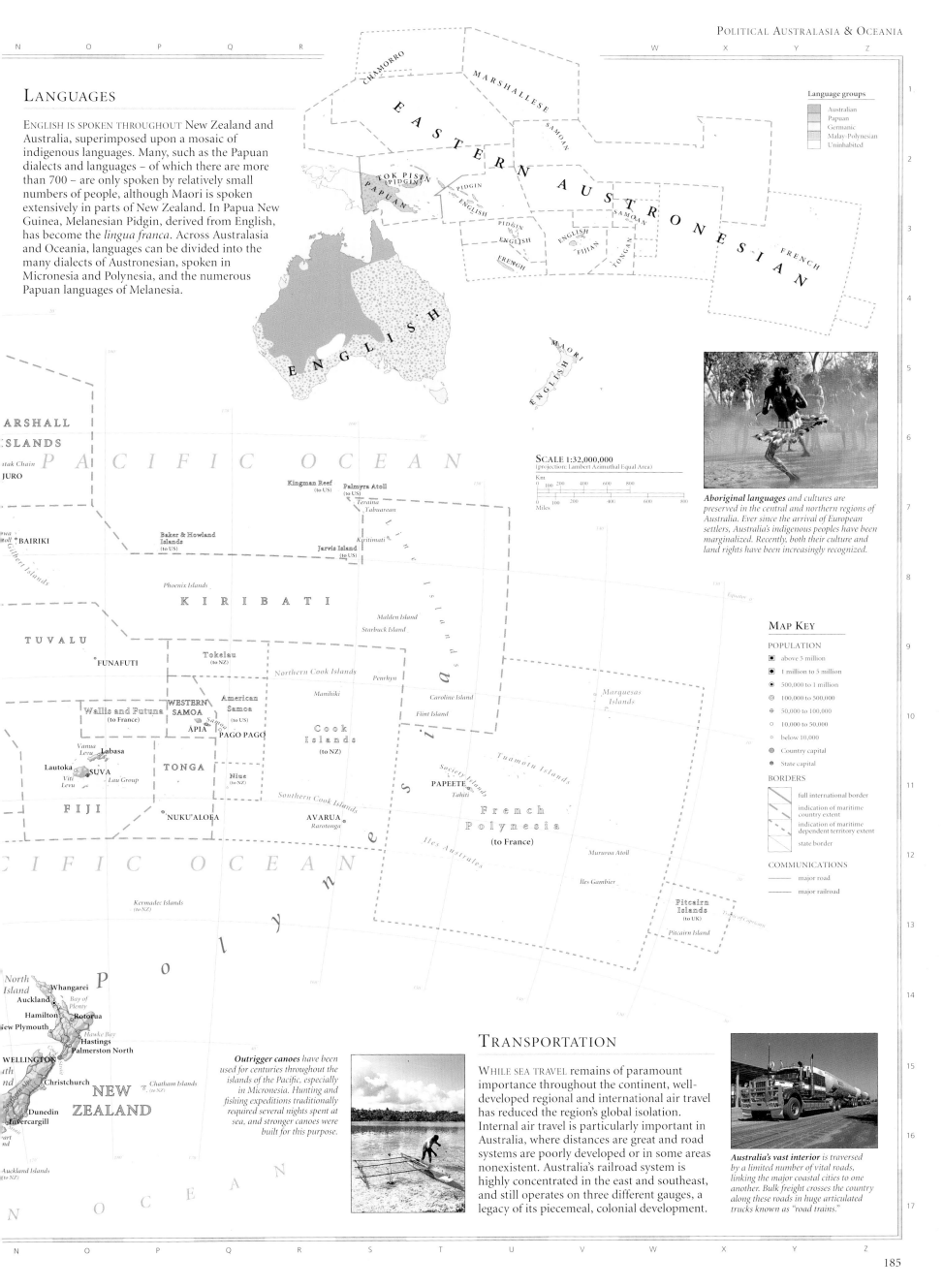

Aboriginal languages *and cultures are preserved in the central and northern regions of Australia. Ever since the arrival of European settlers, Australia's indigenous peoples have been marginalized. Recently, both their culture and land rights have been increasingly recognized.*

MAP KEY

POPULATION
- ■ above 5 million
- ■ 1 million to 5 million
- ◉ 500,000 to 1 million
- ◎ 100,000 to 500,000
- ⊕ 50,000 to 100,000
- ○ 10,000 to 50,000
- ∘ below 10,000
- ● Country capital
- ∙ State capital

BORDERS
- full international border
- indication of maritime country extent
- indication of maritime dependent territory extent
- state border

COMMUNICATIONS
- major road
- major railroad

TRANSPORTATION

WHILE SEA TRAVEL remains of paramount importance throughout the continent, well-developed regional and international air travel has reduced the region's global isolation. Internal air travel is particularly important in Australia, where distances are great and road systems are poorly developed or in some areas nonexistent. Australia's railroad system is highly concentrated in the east and southeast, and still operates on three different gauges, a legacy of its piecemeal, colonial development.

Outrigger canoes *have been used for centuries throughout the islands of the Pacific, especially in Micronesia. Hunting and fishing expeditions traditionally required several nights spent at sea, and stronger canoes were built for this purpose.*

Australia's vast interior *is traversed by a limited number of vital roads, linking the major coastal cities to one another. Bulk freight crosses the country along these roads in huge articulated trucks known as "road trains."*

AUSTRALASIAN AND OCEANIAN RESOURCES

NATURAL RESOURCES ARE OF MAJOR ECONOMIC IMPORTANCE throughout Australasia and Oceania. Australia in particular is a top world exporter of raw materials such as coal, iron ore, and bauxite, while New Zealand's agricultural economy is dominated by sheep-raising. Trade with western Europe has declined significantly in the last 20 years, and the Pacific Rim countries of Southeastern Asia are now the main trading partners, as well as a source of new settlers to the region. Australasia and Oceania's greatest resources are its climate and environment; tourism increasingly provides a vital source of income for the whole continent.

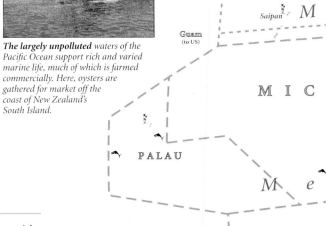

The largely unpolluted waters of the Pacific Ocean support rich and varied marine life, much of which is farmed commercially. Here, oysters are gathered for market off the coast of New Zealand's South Island.

Huge flocks of sheep are a common sight in New Zealand, where they outnumber people by 20 to 1. New Zealand is one of the world's largest exporters of wool and frozen lamb.

STANDARD OF LIVING

IN MARKED CONTRAST TO ITS NEIGHBOR, Australia, with one of the world's highest life expectancies and standards of living, Papua New Guinea is one of the world's least developed countries. In addition, high population growth and urbanization rates throughout the islands of the Pacific contribute to overcrowding. In Australia and New Zealand, the Aboriginal and Maori people have been isolated, although recently their land ownership rights have begun to be recognized in an effort to ease their social and economic isolation, and to improve living standards.

Standard of Living
(UN Human Development Index)

low
high
figures unavailable

ENVIRONMENTAL ISSUES

THE PROSPECT OF RISING SEA LEVELS poses a threat to many low-lying islands in the Pacific. The testing of nuclear weapons, once common throughout the region, was finally discontinued in 1996. Australia's ecological balance has been irreversibly altered by the introduction of alien species. Although it has the world's largest underground water reserve, the Great Artesian Basin, the availability of fresh water in Australia remains critical. Periodic droughts combined with overgrazing lead to desertification and increase the risk of devastating bush fires.

Environmental Issues

- national parks
- tropical forest
- forest destroyed
- desert
- desertification
- polluted rivers
- radioactive contamination
- marine pollution
- heavy marine pollution
- poor urban air quality

In 1946 Bikini Atoll, in the Marshall Islands, was chosen as the site for Operation Crossroads – investigating the effects of atomic bombs upon naval vessels. Further nuclear tests continued until 1958. The long-term environmental effects are unknown.

Northern Mariana Islands (to US)

Saipan

Mi

Guam (to US)

MICRO

PALAU

Me

PAPUA NEW GUINEA

New Guinea

Port Moresby

Arafura Sea

Torres Strait

Timor Sea

Darwin

Gulf of Carpentaria

Great Barrier Re

Townsville

AUSTRALIA

INDIAN OCEAN

Adelaide

Geel

Perth

Bikini Atoll

Eniwetak Atoll

SOUTHER

Malden Island

INDIAN OCEAN

Murchison

Darling

Murray

Sydney

Coral Sea

PACIFIC OCEAN

Fangataufa

Tasman Sea

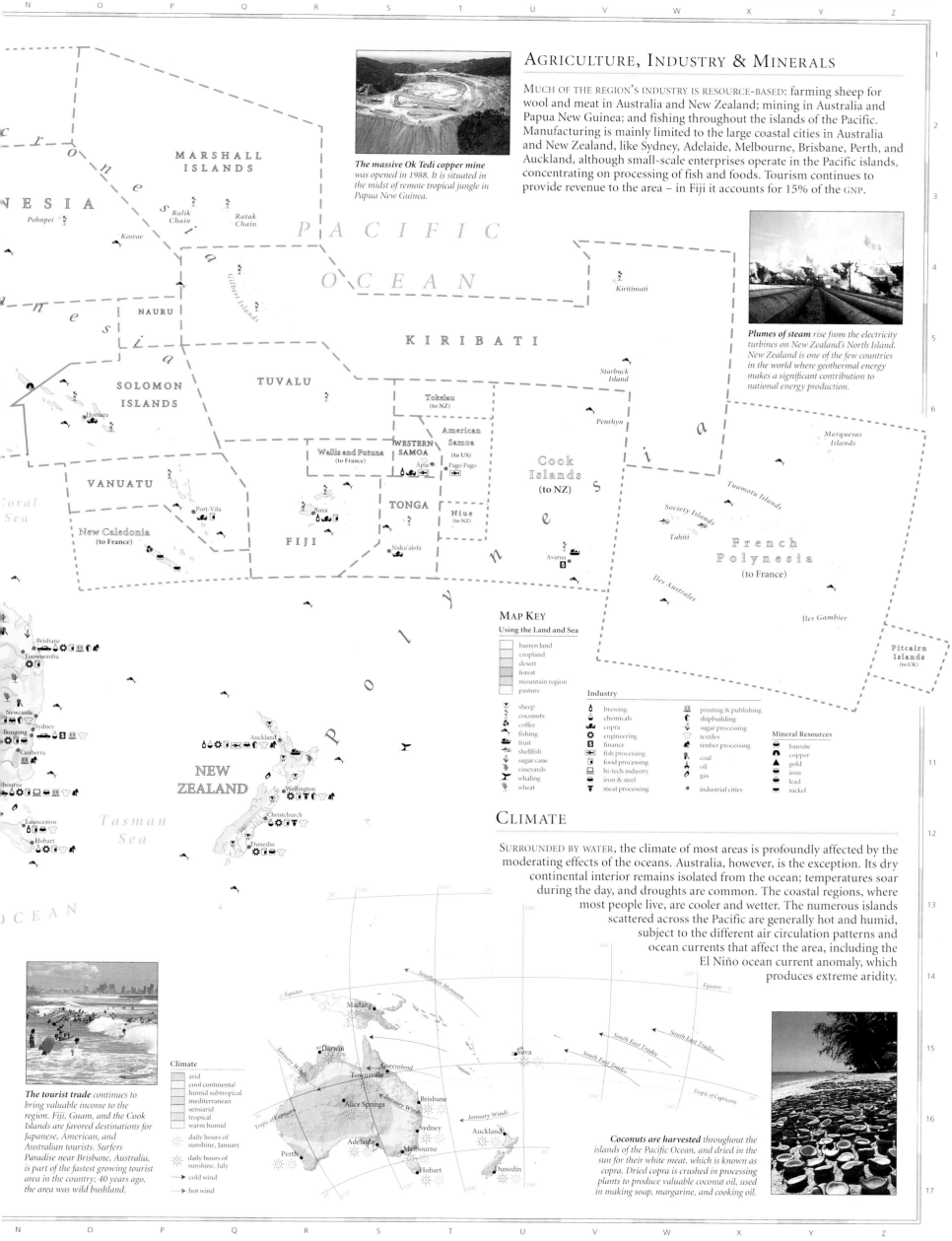

AGRICULTURE, INDUSTRY & MINERALS

MUCH OF THE REGION'S INDUSTRY IS RESOURCE-BASED: farming sheep for wool and meat in Australia and New Zealand; mining in Australia and Papua New Guinea; and fishing throughout the islands of the Pacific. Manufacturing is mainly limited to the large coastal cities in Australia and New Zealand, like Sydney, Adelaide, Melbourne, Brisbane, Perth, and Auckland, although small-scale enterprises operate in the Pacific islands, concentrating on processing of fish and foods. Tourism continues to provide revenue to the area – in Fiji it accounts for 15% of the GNP.

The massive Ok Tedi copper mine was opened in 1988. It is situated in the midst of remote tropical jungle in Papua New Guinea.

Plumes of steam rise from the electricity turbines on New Zealand's North Island. New Zealand is one of the few countries in the world where geothermal energy makes a significant contribution to national energy production.

MAP KEY

Using the Land and Sea

- barren land
- cropland
- desert
- forest
- mountain region
- pasture

sheep	**Industry**	
coconuts	brewing	printing & publishing
coffee	chemicals	shipbuilding
fishing	copra	sugar processing
fruit	engineering	textiles
shellfish	finance	timber processing
sugar cane	fish processing	**Mineral Resources**
vineyards	food processing	bauxite
whaling	hi-tech industry	coal	copper
wheat	iron & steel	oil	gold
	meat processing	gas	iron
		industrial cities	lead
			nickel

CLIMATE

SURROUNDED BY WATER, the climate of most areas is profoundly affected by the moderating effects of the oceans. Australia, however, is the exception. Its dry continental interior remains isolated from the ocean; temperatures soar during the day, and droughts are common. The coastal regions, where most people live, are cooler and wetter. The numerous islands scattered across the Pacific are generally hot and humid, subject to the different air circulation patterns and ocean currents that affect the area, including the El Niño ocean current anomaly, which produces extreme aridity.

Climate

- arid
- cool continental
- humid subtropical
- mediterranean
- semiarid
- tropical
- warm humid
- daily hours of sunshine, January
- daily hours of sunshine, July
- cold wind
- hot wind

The tourist trade continues to bring valuable income to the region. Fiji, Guam, and the Cook Islands are favored destinations for Japanese, American, and Australian tourists. Surfers Paradise near Brisbane, Australia, is part of the fastest growing tourist area in the country; 40 years ago, the area was wild bushland.

Coconuts are harvested throughout the islands of the Pacific Ocean, and dried in the sun for their white meat, which is known as copra. Dried copra is crushed in processing plants to produce valuable coconut oil, used in making soap, margarine, and cooking oil.

AUSTRALIA

Australia is the world's smallest continent, a stable landmass lying between the Indian and Pacific oceans. Previously home to its aboriginal peoples only, since the end of the 18th century immigration has transformed the face of the country. Initially settlers came mainly from western Europe, particularly the UK, and for years Australia remained wedded to its British colonial past. More recent immigrants have come from eastern Europe, and from Asian countries such as Japan, South Korea, and Indonesia. Australia is now forging strong trading links with these "Pacific Rim" countries and its economic future seems to lie with Asia and the Americas, rather than Europe, its traditional partner.

Uluru (Ayers Rock), the world's largest freestanding rock, is a massive outcrop of red sandstone in Australia's desert center. Wind and sandstorms have ground the rock into the smooth curves seen here. Uluru is revered as a sacred site by many aboriginal peoples.

USING THE LAND

Over 165 million sheep are dispersed in vast herds around the country, contributing to a major export industry. Cattle-ranching is important, particularly in the west. Wheat, and grapes for Australia's wine industry, are grown mainly in the south. Much of the country is desert, unsuitable for agriculture unless irrigation is used.

THE URBAN/RURAL POPULATION DIVIDE

urban 87%   rural 13%

0 10 20 30 40 50 60 70 80 90 100

POPULATION DENSITY
5 people per sq mile
(2 people per sq km)

TOTAL LAND AREA
2,967,893 sq miles
(7,686,850 sq km)

Land use and agricultural distribution

- cattle
- sheep
- cereals
- sugar cane
- timber
- vineyards
- capital cities
- major towns
- pasture
- cropland
- forest
- desert
- mountain region

Lines of ripening vines stretch for miles in Barossa Valley, a major wine-growing region near Adelaide.

THE LANDSCAPE

Australia consists of many eroded plateaus, lying firmly in the middle of the Indo-Australian Plate. It is the world's flattest continent, and the driest, after Antarctica. The coasts tend to be more hilly and fertile, especially in the east. The mountains of the Great Dividing Range form a natural barrier between the eastern coastal areas and the flat, dry plains and desert regions of the Australian "outback."

The Great Barrier Reef is the world's largest area of coral islands and reefs. It runs for about 1,240 miles (2,000 km) along the Queensland coast.

The ancient Kimberley Plateau is the source of some of Australia's richest mineral deposits, including diamonds.

Arnhem Land

Uluru (Ayers Rock)

The tropical rain forest of the Cape York Peninsula contains more than 600 different varieties of tree.

Great Artesian Basin

The Pinnacles are a series of rugged sandstone pillars. Their strange shapes have been formed by water and wind erosion.

More than half of Australia rests on a uniform shield over 600 million years old. It is one of the Earth's original geological plates.

The Nullarbor Plain is a low-lying limestone plateau which is so flat that the Trans-Australian Railway runs through it in a straight line for more than 300 miles (483 km).

The Simpson Desert has a number of large salt pans, created by the evaporation of past rivers and now sourced by seasonal rains. Some are crusted with gypsum, but most are covered by common salt crystals.

The Lake Eyre Basin, lying 51 ft (16 m) below sea level, is one of the largest inland drainage systems in the world, covering an area of more than 500,000 sq miles (1,300,000 sq km).

Tasmania has the same geological structure as the Australian Alps. During the last period of glaciation, 18,000 years ago, sea levels were some 300 ft (100 m) lower and it was joined to the mainland.

The Great Dividing Range forms a watershed between east- and west-flowing rivers. Erosion has created deep valleys, gorges, and waterfalls where rivers tumble over escarpments on their way to the sea.

Murray/Darling River

Australian Alps

Great Artesian Basin

Rainwater replenishes aquifer

Lake Eyre

Aquifers from which artesian water is obtained

Underground water movements

The Great Artesian Basin underlies nearly 20% of the total area of Australia, providing a valuable store of underground water, essential to Australian agriculture. The ephemeral rivers which drain into the northern part of the basin have highly braided courses and, in consequence, the area is known as "channel country."

SCALE 1:10,500,000
(projection: Lambert Conformal Conic)

Km
0 25 50 100 150 200 250 300 350
Miles
0 25 50 100 150 200 250 350

MAP KEY

POPULATION
- 1 million to 5 million
- 500,000 to 1 million
- 100,000 to 500,000
- 50,000 to 100,000
- 10,000 to 50,000
- below 10,000

ELEVATION
- 2000m / 6562ft
- 1000m / 3281ft
- 500m / 1640ft
- 250m / 820ft
- 100m / 328ft
- sea level

Map labels:

INDIAN OCEAN

Great Sandy Desert

Little Sandy Desert

Gibson Desert

WESTERN AUSTRALIA

Cape Londonderry
Cape Bougainville
Kalumburu
Bigge Island
Bonaparte Archipelago
Heywood Islands
Adele Island
Collier Bay
Kimberley Plateau
Lombadina
Derby
Broome
Fitzroy River
Dampier Archipelago
Dampier
Karratha
Port Hedland
Wickham
Whim Creek
Roebourne
De Grey River
Marble Bar
Lake Dora
Lake Auld
Percival Lakes
Tobin Lake
Barrow Island
Onslow
Fortescue River
Hamersley Range
Wittenoom
Lake Disappointment
North West Cape
Exmouth
Exmouth Gulf
Learmonth
Ashburton River
Tom Price
Paraburdoo
Mount Mehany 1251m
Newman
Coral Bay
Barlee Range
Kenneth Range
Mount Augustus 1106m
Kulmarina Roadhouse
Minilya
Lake Macleod
Waldburg Range
Carnarvon Range
Gascoyne River
Gascoyne Junction
Robinson Range
Lake Gregory
Lake Carnegie
Bernier Island
Shark Bay
Wiluna
Lake Way
Lake Wells
Dorre Island
Denham
Murchison River
Meekatharra
Lake Throssell
Dirk Hartog Island
Lake Annean
Lake Austin
Lake Yeo
AUSTRALIA
Kalbarri
Lake Mason
Mount Magnet
Leonora
Lake Carey
Yalgoo
Lake Ballard
Geraldton
Mongers Lake
Menzies
Lake Rebecca
Lake Moore
Kalgoorlie
Coolgardie
Kitchener
Wubin
Pithara
Southern Cross
Kambalda
Lake Lefroy
Moora
The Pinnacles
Merredin
Lake Cowan
Balladonia
Gingin
Wanneroo
Northam
York
Lake Johnston
Norseman
Lake Dundas
Perth
Fremantle
Brookton
Kondinin
Lake King
Rockingham
Narrogin
Wagin
Esperance
Mandurah
Ravensthorpe
Bunbury
Collie
Katanning
Busselton
Bridgetown
Mount Barker
Margaret River
Manjimup
Cape Leeuwin
Augusta
Pemberton
Albany
Tower Peak
Tropic of Capricorn
PACIFIC OCEAN
Timor Sea
Darwin
Townsville
Alice Springs
AUSTRALIA
Brisbane
Perth
Sydney
Adelaide
CANBERRA
Melbourne
Hobart

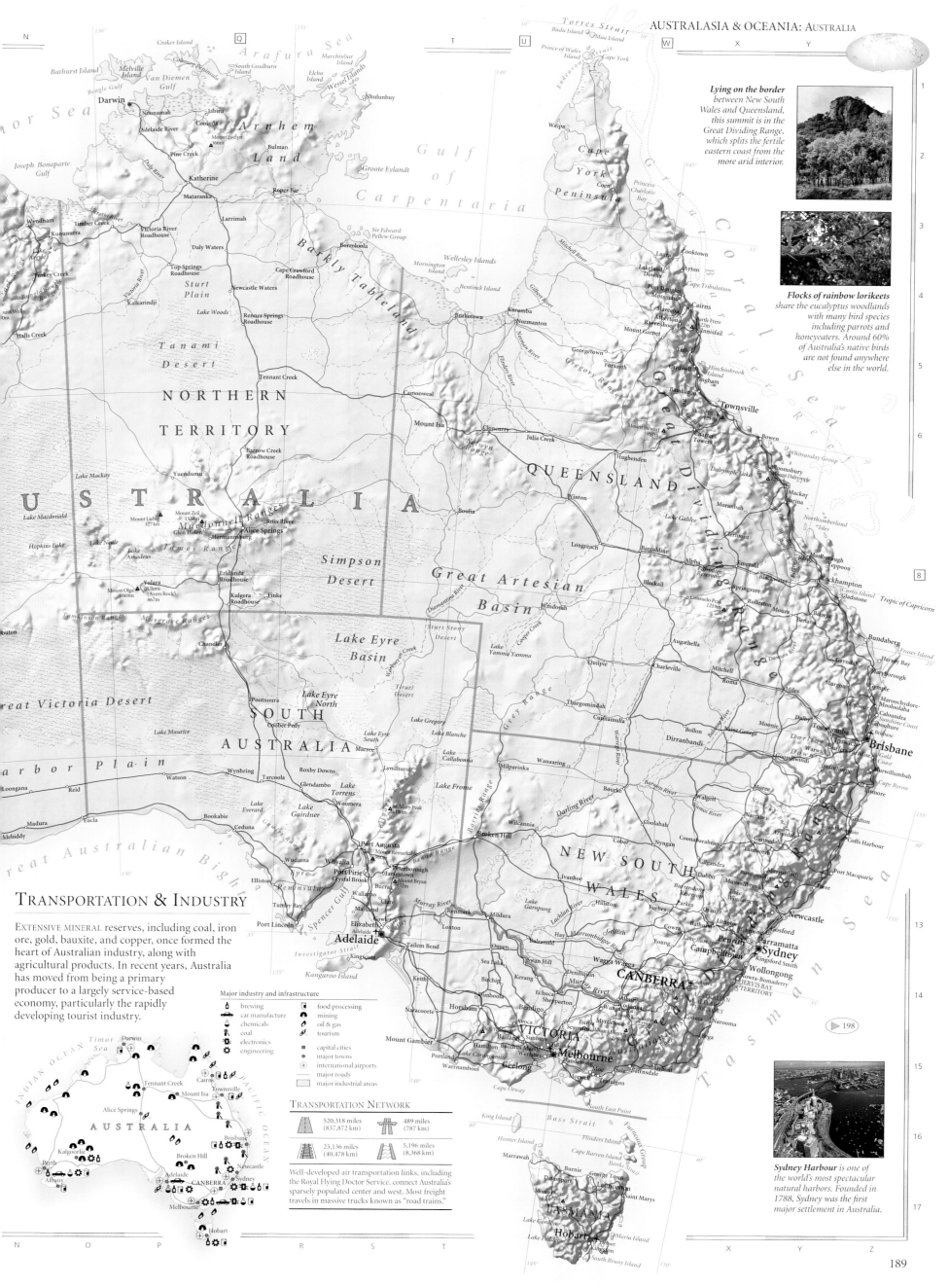

Lying on the border between New South Wales and Queensland, this summit is in the Great Dividing Range, which splits the fertile eastern coast from the more arid interior.

Flocks of rainbow lorikeets share the eucalyptus woodlands with many bird species including parrots and honeyeaters. Around 60% of Australia's native birds are not found anywhere else in the world.

TRANSPORTATION & INDUSTRY

EXTENSIVE MINERAL reserves, including coal, iron ore, gold, bauxite, and copper, once formed the heart of Australian industry, along with agricultural products. In recent years, Australia has moved from being a primary producer to a largely service-based economy, particularly the rapidly developing tourist industry.

Major industry and infrastructure

- brewing
- car manufacture
- chemicals
- coal
- electronics
- engineering
- food processing
- mining
- oil & gas
- tourism
- capital cities
- major towns
- international airports
- major roads
- major industrial areas

TRANSPORTATION NETWORK

520,318 miles (837,872 km)		489 miles (787 km)	
25,136 miles (40,478 km)		5,196 miles (8,368 km)	

Well-developed air transportation links, including the Royal Flying Doctor Service, connect Australia's sparsely populated center and west. Most freight travels in massive trucks known as "road trains."

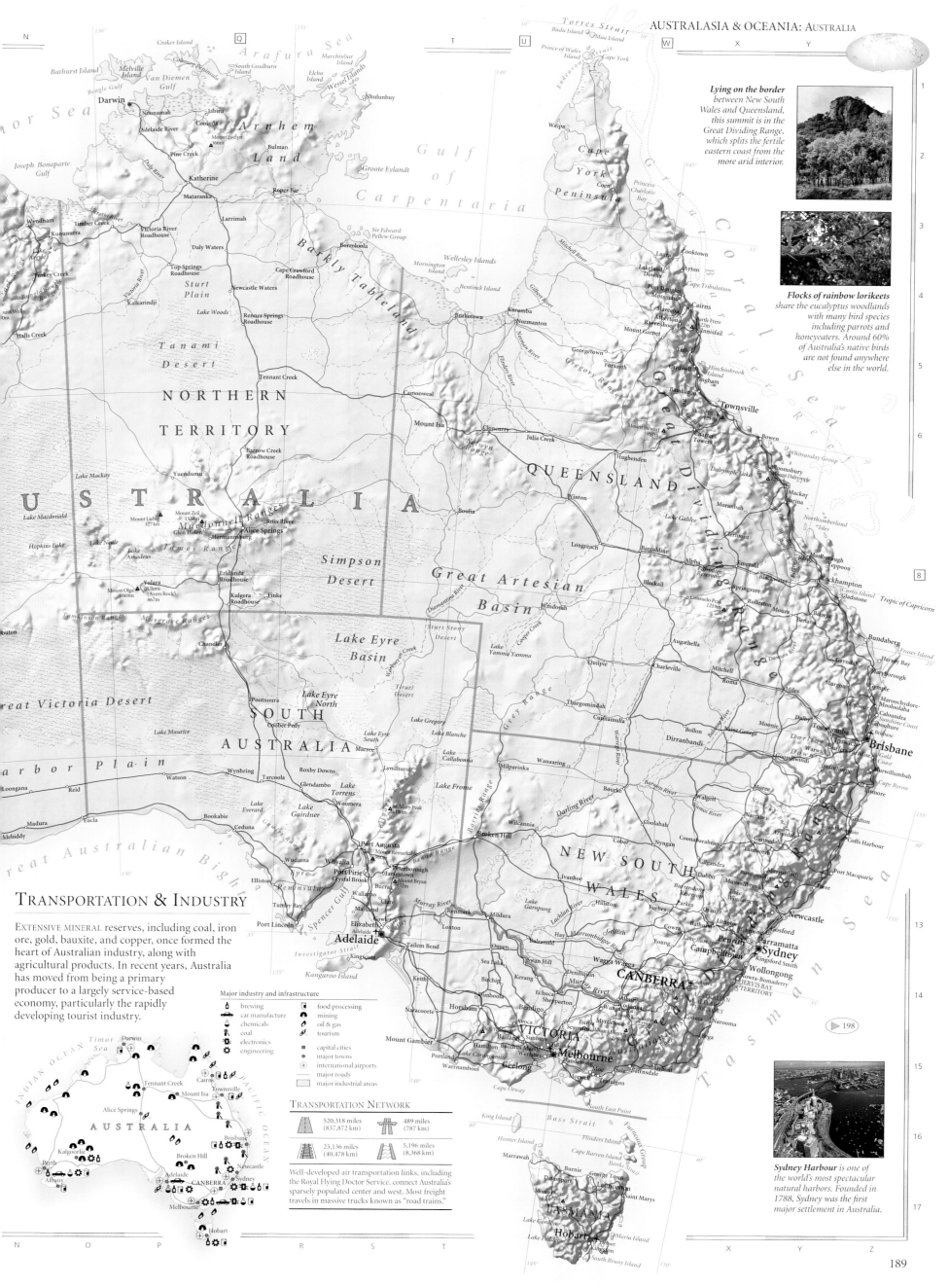

Sydney Harbour is one of the world's most spectacular natural harbors. Founded in 1788, Sydney was the first major settlement in Australia.

▶ 198

189

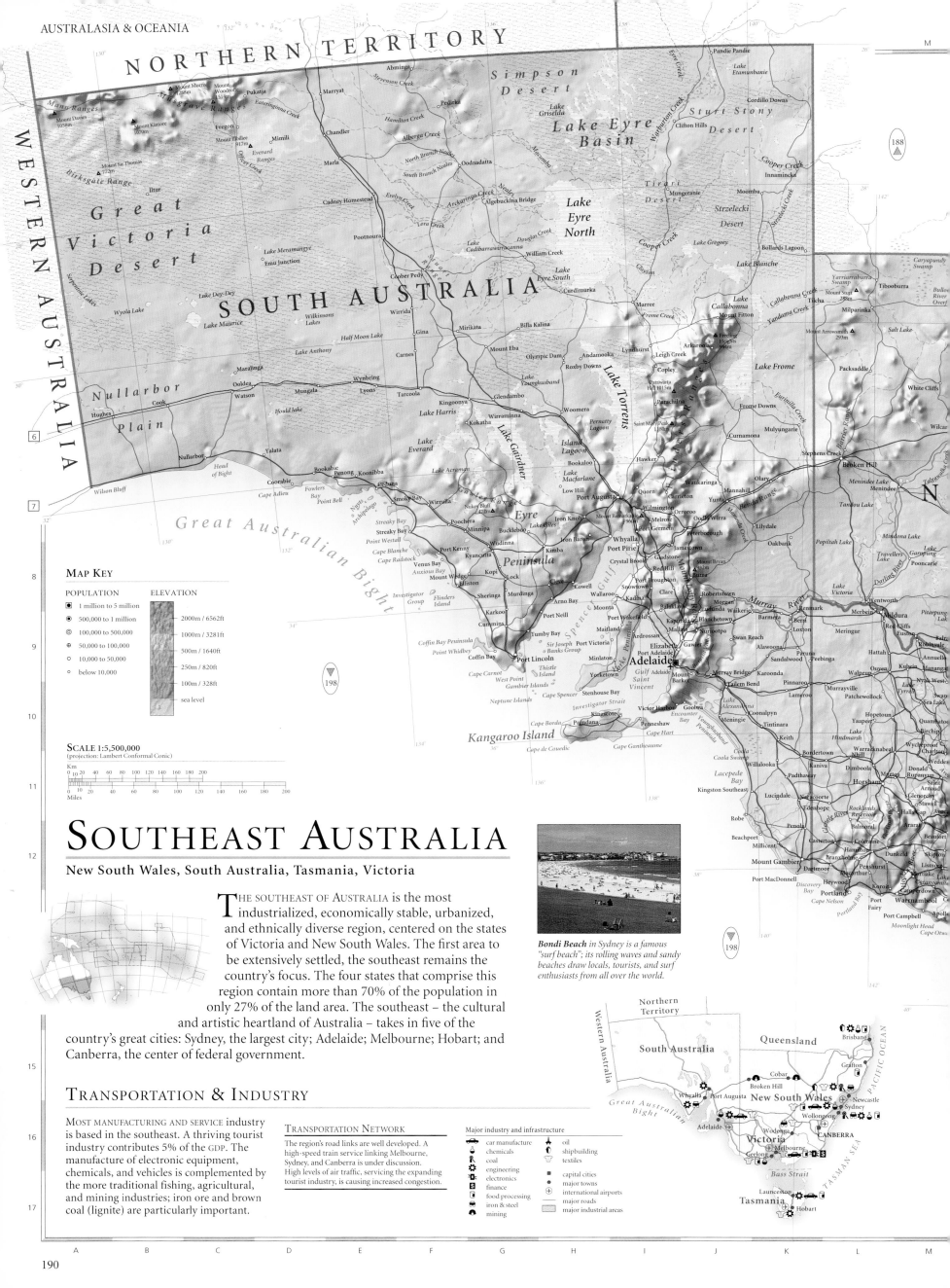

NORTHERN TERRITORY

WESTERN AUSTRALIA

SOUTH AUSTRALIA

Great Victoria Desert

Simpson Desert

Lake Eyre Basin

Lake Eyre North

Sturt Stony Desert

Nullarbor Plain

Great Australian Bight

Eyre Peninsula

Spencer Gulf

Adelaide

Kangaroo Island

MAP KEY

POPULATION

- ■ 1 million to 5 million
- ◉ 500,000 to 1 million
- ◎ 100,000 to 500,000
- ⊕ 50,000 to 100,000
- ⊙ 10,000 to 50,000
- ○ below 10,000

ELEVATION

- 2000m / 6562ft
- 1000m / 3281ft
- 500m / 1640ft
- 250m / 820ft
- 100m / 328ft
- sea level

SCALE 1:5,500,000
(projection: Lambert Conformal Conic)

Km
0 10 20 40 60 80 100 120 140 160 200

Miles
0 10 20 40 60 80 100 120 140 160 200

SOUTHEAST AUSTRALIA

New South Wales, South Australia, Tasmania, Victoria

THE SOUTHEAST OF AUSTRALIA is the most industrialized, economically stable, urbanized, and ethnically diverse region, centered on the states of Victoria and New South Wales. The first area to be extensively settled, the southeast remains the country's focus. The four states that comprise this region contain more than 70% of the population in only 27% of the land area. The southeast – the cultural and artistic heartland of Australia – takes in five of the country's great cities: Sydney, the largest city; Adelaide; Melbourne; Hobart; and Canberra, the center of federal government.

Bondi Beach in Sydney is a famous "surf beach"; its rolling waves and sandy beaches draw locals, tourists, and surf enthusiasts from all over the world.

TRANSPORTATION & INDUSTRY

MOST MANUFACTURING AND SERVICE industry is based in the southeast. A thriving tourist industry contributes 5% of the GDP. The manufacture of electronic equipment, chemicals, and vehicles is complemented by the more traditional fishing, agricultural, and mining industries; iron ore and brown coal (lignite) are particularly important.

TRANSPORTATION NETWORK

The region's road links are well developed. A high-speed train service linking Melbourne, Sydney, and Canberra is under discussion. High levels of air traffic, servicing the expanding tourist industry, is causing increased congestion.

Major industry and infrastructure

- car manufacture
- chemicals
- coal
- engineering
- electronics
- finance
- food processing
- iron & steel
- mining
- oil
- shipbuilding
- textiles
- ■ capital cities
- ● major towns
- ⊕ international airports
- major roads
- major industrial areas

Northern Territory

Western Australia

South Australia

Queensland

New South Wales

Victoria

Tasmania

PACIFIC OCEAN

TASMAN SEA

Bass Strait

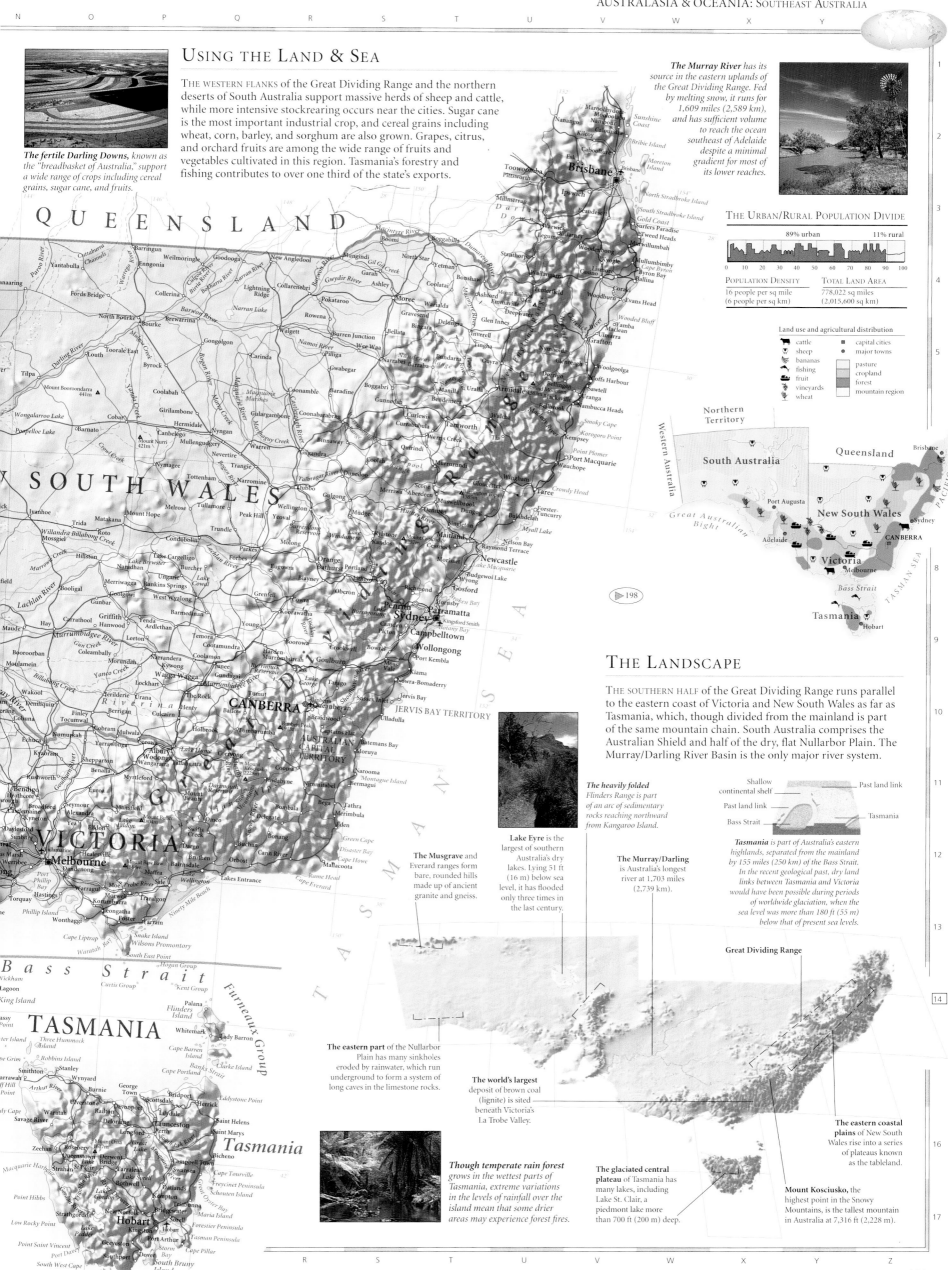

USING THE LAND & SEA

THE WESTERN FLANKS of the Great Dividing Range and the northern deserts of South Australia support massive herds of sheep and cattle, while more intensive stockrearing occurs near the cities. Sugar cane is the most important industrial crop, and cereal grains including wheat, corn, barley, and sorghum are also grown. Grapes, citrus, and orchard fruits are among the wide range of fruits and vegetables cultivated in this region. Tasmania's forestry and fishing contributes to over one third of the state's exports.

The fertile Darling Downs, known as the "breadbasket of Australia," support a wide range of crops including cereal grains, sugar cane, and fruits.

The Murray River has its source in the eastern uplands of the Great Dividing Range. Fed by melting snow, it runs for 1,609 miles (2,589 km), and has sufficient volume to reach the ocean southeast of Adelaide despite a minimal gradient for most of its lower reaches.

THE URBAN/RURAL POPULATION DIVIDE

89% urban   11% rural

0 10 20 30 40 50 60 70 80 90 100

POPULATION DENSITY
16 people per sq mile
(6 people per sq km)

TOTAL LAND AREA
778,022 sq miles
(2,015,600 sq km)

Land use and agricultural distribution

- cattle
- sheep
- bananas
- fishing
- fruit
- vineyards
- wheat
- capital cities
- major towns
- pasture
- cropland
- forest
- mountain region

THE LANDSCAPE

THE SOUTHERN HALF of the Great Dividing Range runs parallel to the eastern coast of Victoria and New South Wales as far as Tasmania, which, though divided from the mainland is part of the same mountain chain. South Australia comprises the Australian Shield and half of the dry, flat Nullarbor Plain. The Murray/Darling River Basin is the only major river system.

The heavily folded Flinders Range is part of an arc of sedimentary rocks reaching northward from Kangaroo Island.

The Musgrave and Everard ranges form bare, rounded hills made up of ancient granite and gneiss.

Lake Eyre is the largest of southern Australia's dry lakes. Lying 51 ft (16 m) below sea level, it has flooded only three times in the last century.

The Murray/Darling is Australia's longest river at 1,703 miles (2,739 km).

Shallow continental shelf
Past land link
Past land link
Bass Strait
Past land link
Tasmania

Tasmania is part of Australia's eastern highlands, separated from the mainland by 155 miles (250 km) of the Bass Strait. In the recent geological past, dry land links between Tasmania and Victoria would have been possible during periods of worldwide glaciation, when the sea level was more than 180 ft (55 m) below that of present sea levels.

Great Dividing Range

The eastern part of the Nullarbor Plain has many sinkholes eroded by rainwater, which run underground to form a system of long caves in the limestone rocks.

The world's largest deposit of brown coal (lignite) is sited beneath Victoria's La Trobe Valley.

Though temperate rain forest grows in the wettest parts of Tasmania, extreme variations in the levels of rainfall over the island mean that some drier areas may experience forest fires.

The glaciated central plateau of Tasmania has many lakes, including Lake St. Clair, a piedmont lake more than 700 ft (200 m) deep.

The eastern coastal plains of New South Wales rise into a series of plateaus known as the tableland.

Mount Kosciusko, the highest point in the Snowy Mountains, is the tallest mountain in Australia at 7,316 ft (2,228 m).

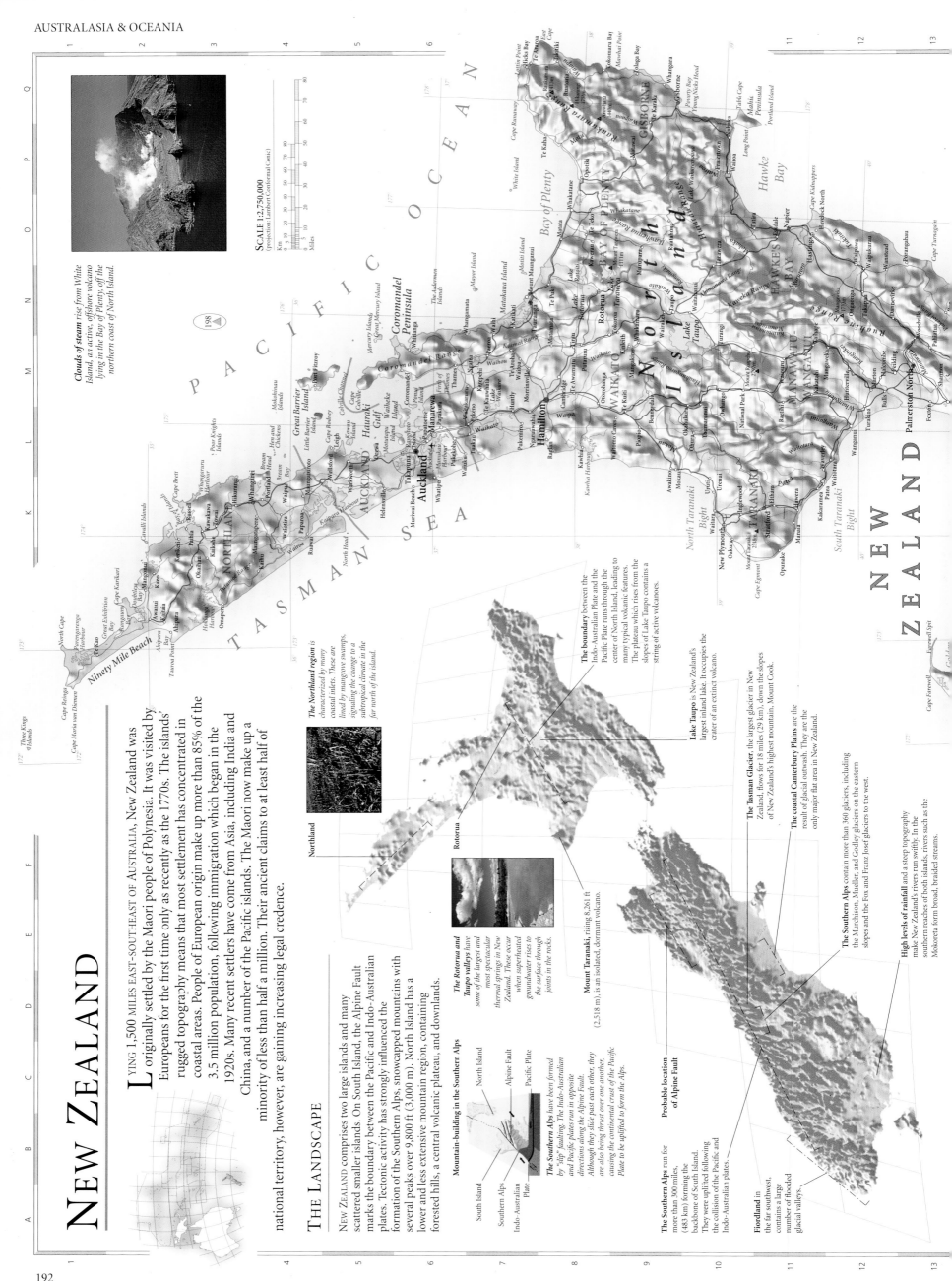

NEW ZEALAND

L YING 1,500 MILES EAST-SOUTHEAST OF AUSTRALIA, New Zealand was originally settled by the Maori people of Polynesia. It was visited by Europeans for the first time only as recently as the 1770s. The islands' rugged topography means that most settlement has concentrated in coastal areas. People of European origin make up more than 85% of the 3.5 million population, following immigration which began in the 1920s. Many recent settlers have come from Asia, including India and China, and a number of the Pacific islands. The Maori now make up a minority of less than half a million. Their ancient claims to at least half of national territory, however, are gaining increasing legal credence.

THE LANDSCAPE

NEW ZEALAND comprises two large islands and many scattered smaller islands. On South Island, the Alpine Fault marks the boundary between the Pacific and Indo-Australian plates. Tectonic activity has strongly influenced the formation of the Southern Alps, snowcapped mountains with several peaks over 9,800 ft (3,000 m). North Island has a lower and less extensive mountain region, containing forested hills, a central volcanic plateau, and downlands.

Mountain-building in the Southern Alps

North Island

Alpine Fault

Pacific Plate

South Island

Southern Alps

Indo-Australian Plate

The Southern Alps have been formed by "slip" faulting. The Indo-Australian and Pacific plates run in opposite directions along the Alpine Fault. Although they slide past each other, they are also being thrust over one another, causing the continental crust of the Pacific Plate to be uplifted to form the Alps.

Probable location of Alpine Fault

The Southern Alps run for more than 300 miles, (483 km) forming the backbone of South Island. They were uplifted following the collision of the Pacific and Indo-Australian plates.

Fiordland in the far southwest, contains a large number of flooded glacial valleys.

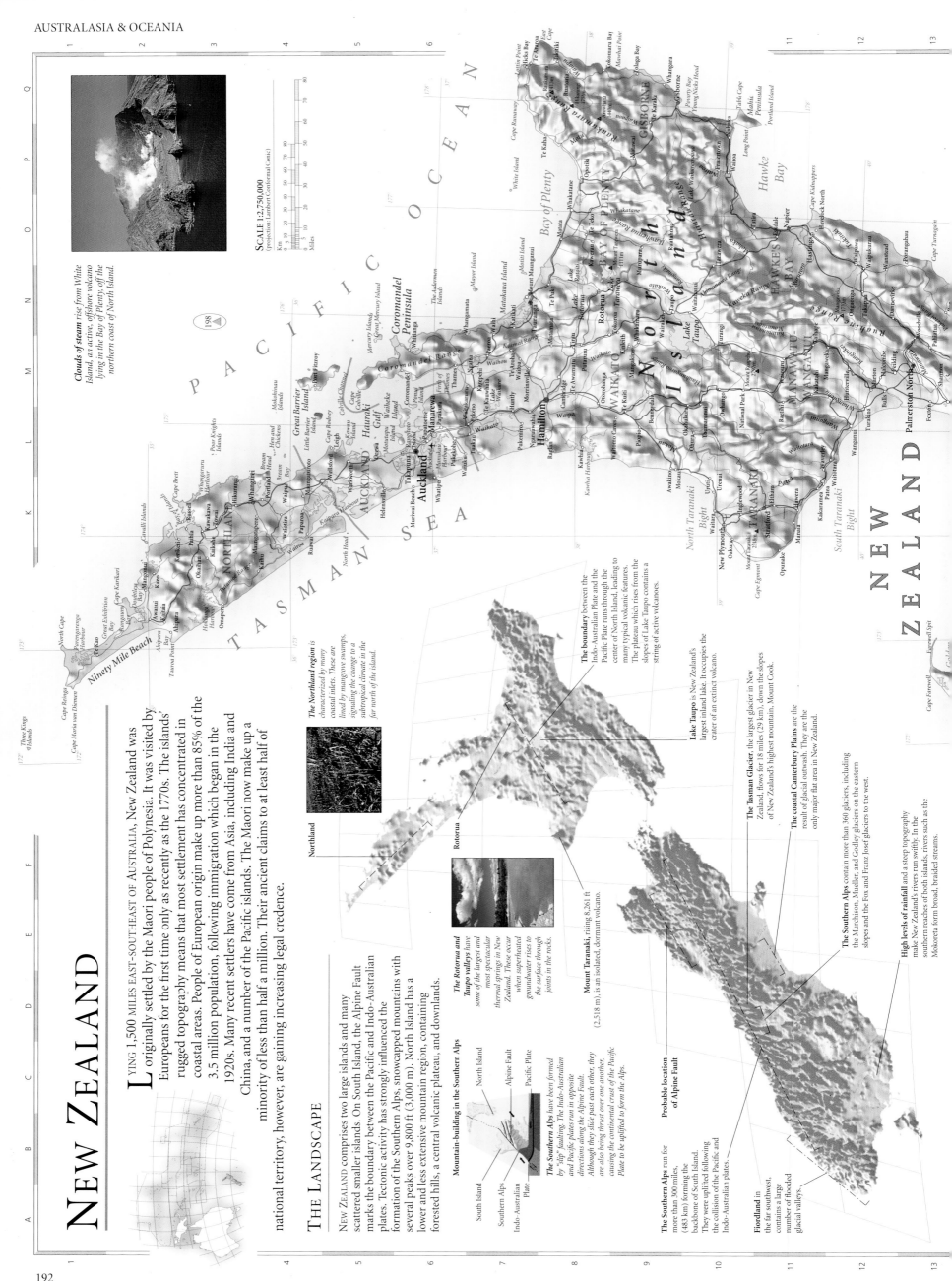
Northland

The Northland region is characterized by many coastal inlets. These are lined by mangrove swamps, signaling the change to a subtropical climate in the far north of the island.

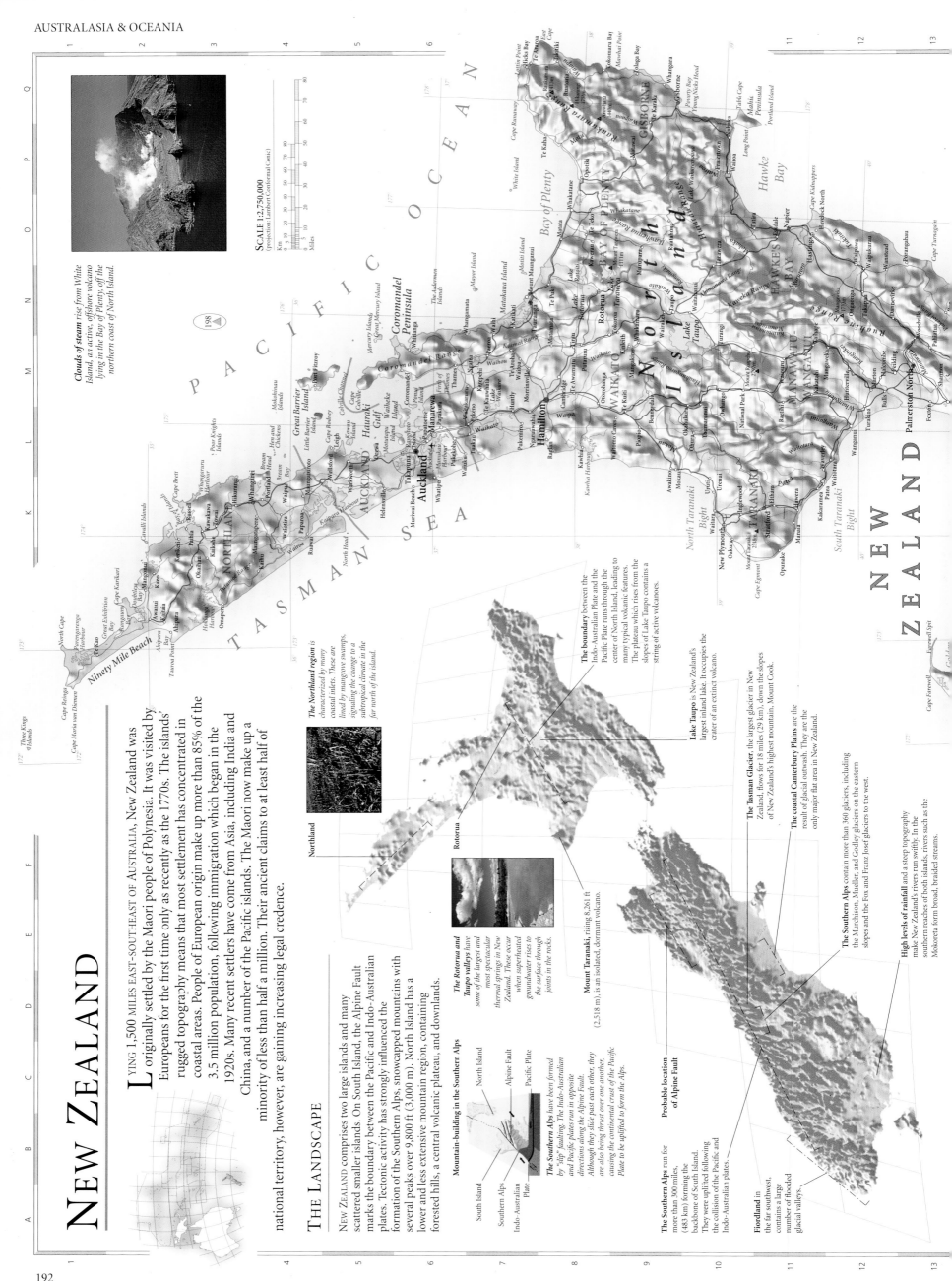
Rotorua

The Rotorua and Taupo valleys have some of the largest and most spectacular thermal springs in New Zealand. These occur when superheated groundwater rises to the surface through joints in the rocks.

Mount Taranaki, rising 8,261 ft (2,518 m), is an isolated, dormant volcano.

The boundary between the Indo-Australian Plate and the Pacific Plate runs through the center of North Island, leading to many typical volcanic features. The plateau which rises from the slopes of Lake Taupo contains a string of active volcanoes.

Lake Taupo is New Zealand's largest inland lake. It occupies the crater of an extinct volcano.

The Tasman Glacier, the largest glacier in New Zealand, flows for 18 miles (29 km), down the slopes of New Zealand's highest mountain, Mount Cook.

The coastal Canterbury Plains are the result of glacial outwash. They are the only major flat area in New Zealand.

The Southern Alps contain more than 360 glaciers, including the Murchison, Mueller, and Godley glaciers on the eastern slopes and the Fox and Franz Josef glaciers to the west.

High levels of rainfall and a steep topography make New Zealand's rivers run swiftly. In the southern reaches of both islands, rivers such as the Mokoreta form broad, braided streams.

Clouds of steam rise from White Island, an active, offshore volcano lying in the Bay of Plenty, off the northern coast of North Island.

SCALE 1:2,750,000
(projection: Lambert Conformal Conic)

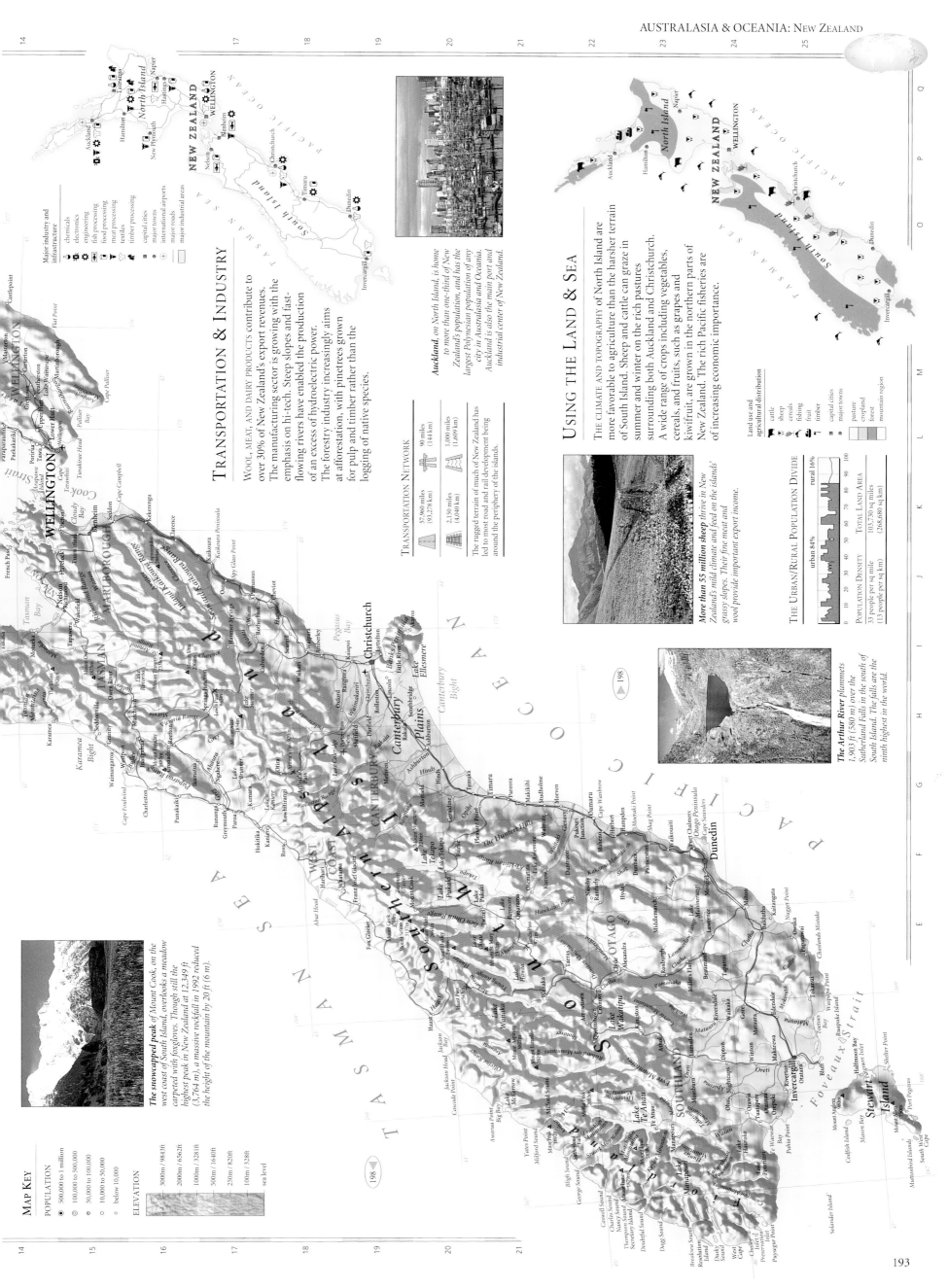

Major industry and infrastructure

- chemicals
- electronics
- engineering
- fish processing
- food processing
- meat processing
- textiles
- timber processing
- capital cities
- major towns
- international airports
- major roads
- major industrial areas

NEW ZEALAND

North Island

Napier
Tauranga
Hastings
WELLINGTON
Hamilton
New Plymouth
Auckland
Nelson
Blenheim
Christchurch
Timaru
Dunedin
Invercargill

South Island

PACIFIC OCEAN
TASMAN SEA

TRANSPORTATION & INDUSTRY

WOOL, MEAT, AND DAIRY PRODUCTS contribute to over 30% of New Zealand's export revenues. The manufacturing sector is growing with the emphasis on hi-tech. Steep slopes and fast-flowing rivers have enabled the production of an excess of hydroelectric power. The forestry industry increasingly aims at afforestation, with pinetrees grown for pulp and timber rather than the logging of native species.

Auckland, on North Island, is home to more than one-third of New Zealand's population, and has the largest Polynesian population of any city in Australasia and Oceania. Auckland is also the main port and industrial center of New Zealand.

TRANSPORTATION NETWORK

57,960 miles (93,278 km)	90 miles (144 km)
2,150 miles (4,040 km)	1,000 miles (1,609 km)

The rugged terrain of much of New Zealand has led to most road and rail development being around the periphery of the islands.

USING THE LAND & SEA

THE CLIMATE AND TOPOGRAPHY of North Island are more favorable to agriculture than the harsher terrain of South Island. Sheep and cattle can graze in summer and winter on the rich pastures surrounding both Auckland and Christchurch. A wide range of crops including vegetables, cereals, and fruits, such as grapes and kiwifruit, are grown in the northern parts of New Zealand. The rich Pacific fisheries are of increasing economic importance.

NEW ZEALAND

North Island
Napier
Auckland
Hamilton
WELLINGTON
Christchurch
Dunedin
Invercargill

South Island
PACIFIC OCEAN
TASMAN SEA

Land use and agricultural distribution

- cattle
- sheep
- cereals
- fruit
- timber
- capital cities
- major towns
- pasture
- cropland
- forest
- mountain region

More than 55 million sheep thrive in New Zealand's mild climate and feed on the islands' grassy slopes. Their fine meat and wool provide important export income.

THE URBAN/RURAL POPULATION DIVIDE

urban 84% / rural 16%

POPULATION DENSITY	TOTAL LAND AREA
33 people per sq mile (13 people per sq km)	103,730 sq miles (268,680 sq km)

The Arthur River plummets 1,903 ft (580 m) over the Sutherland Falls in the south of South Island. The falls are the ninth highest in the world.

MAP KEY

POPULATION

- 500,000 to 1 million
- 100,000 to 500,000
- 50,000 to 100,000
- 10,000 to 50,000
- below 10,000

ELEVATION

- 3000m / 9843ft
- 2000m / 6562ft
- 1000m / 3281ft
- 500m / 1640ft
- 250m / 820ft
- 100m / 328ft
- sea level

The snowcapped peak of Mount Cook, on the west coast of South Island, overlooks a meadow carpeted with foxgloves. Though still the highest peak in New Zealand at 12,349 ft (3,764 m), a massive rockfall in 1992 reduced the height of the mountain by 20 ft (6 m).

Map labels — South Island

WELLINGTON
Cook Strait
MARLBOROUGH
Nelson
Blenheim
TASMAN
Kaikoura
WEST COAST
Greymouth
Hokitika
Christchurch
Canterbury Plains
SOUTHERN ALPS
Mount Cook
Lake Tekapo
Lake Pukaki
Timaru
OTAGO
Oamaru
Queenstown
Lake Wakatipu
Dunedin
FIORDLAND
SOUTHLAND
Invercargill
Stewart Island
Foveaux Strait

TASMAN SEA
PACIFIC OCEAN

A B C D E F G H I J K L M

PAPUA NEW GUINEA & THE SOLOMON ISLANDS

Cut off by inaccessible, largely mountainous terrain, the peoples of Papua New Guinea have maintained a remarkable diversity of language and culture. There are over 750 separate languages, and yet more distinct tribes. Much of the country remains isolated, with many of the indigenous inhabitants of the interior living as hunter-gatherers. To the east of Papua New Guinea, the Solomons form an archipelago of several hundred islands, scattered over an area of 252,897 sq miles (655,000 sq km). The Solomon Islanders, a mainly Melanesian people, live on the six largest islands.

USING THE LAND & SEA

Most agriculture in Papua New Guinea is at a subsistence level, with more than two-thirds of the land used for rough grazing, particularly for pigs. The tropical rain forest is a rich timber resource. The Solomon Islanders rely heavily on coconuts for export revenue and fishing, mainly for tuna, is a staple industry.

TRANSPORTATION & INDUSTRY

Papua New Guinea has substantial mineral resources including the world's largest copper reserves at Panguna on Bougainville Island; gold, and potential oil and natural gas. Political instability on Bougainville and an undeveloped infrastructure deters the investment necessary for exploition of these reserves. The Solomon Islanders rely mainly on copra and timber with some production of palm oil and cocoa. Traditional crafts are made for the tourist market and for export.

TRANSPORTATION NETWORK

🛣	416 miles (670 km)
	None
🚆	None
	6,794 miles (10,940 km)

Much of Papua New Guinea and the Solomons is inaccessible by road. A network of airstrips serves even remote villages on the islands. The Solomons' airport has been extended to take jumbo jets to improve connections for tourism.

The slopes of this extinct volcano near Talasea on the island of New Britain have been almost entirely colonized by rain forest vegetation.

Major industry and infrastructure

- 🍺 beverages
- ☕ coffee processing
- copra processing
- 🍴 food processing
- ⛏ mining
- 👕 textiles
- 🌲 timber processing

- ■ capital cities
- ● major towns
- ✈ international airports
- — major roads

Land use and agricultural distribution

- 🍌 bananas
- cocoa
- coconuts
- fishing
- oil palms
- rubber
- timber

- ■ capital cities
- ● major towns
- cropland
- forest
- wetland

Over 70% of Papua New Guinea is covered by dense, tropical rain forest, sustained by high levels of rainfall. Uncontrolled logging in the formerly inaccessible rain forest has led to species loss and soil erosion on steep slopes.

THE URBAN/RURAL POPULATION DIVIDE

urban 15%   rural 85%

0 10 20 30 40 50 60 70 80 90 100

POPULATION DENSITY	TOTAL LAND AREA
15 people per sq mile (6 people per sq km)	290,210 sq miles (751,840 sq km)

MAP KEY

POPULATION

- ◉ 100,000 to 500,000
- ⊕ 50,000 to 100,000
- ⊙ 10,000 to 50,000
- ○ below 10,000

ELEVATION

- 4000m / 13,124ft
- 3000m / 9843ft
- 2000m / 6562ft
- 1000m / 3281ft
- 500m / 1640ft
- 250m / 820ft
- 100m / 328ft
- sea level

Huli tribesmen from Southern Highlands Province in Papua New Guinea parade in ceremonial dress, their powdered wigs decorated with exotic plumage and their faces and bodies painted with colored pigments.

SCALE 1:5,500,000
(projection: Mercator)

Km
0 10 20 40 60 80 100 120 140 160 180 200

0 10 20 40 60 80 100 120 140 160 180 200
Miles

N O P Q R S T U V W X Y

THE LANDSCAPE

THE PLATE MARGIN between the Pacific and Indo-Australian plates runs through the mainland of Papua New Guinea, which is dominated by steep and forested mountain ranges. The 600 or so outer islands are mainly high, volcanic islands, fringed by coral reefs. The Solomons comprise six large volcanic islands which form two parallel chains, and several hundred small islands and atolls.

The Sepik River drains the lowlands north of the Central Range, flowing eastward into the Bismarck Sea.

The Bismarck Range is precipitous, rugged, and covered in dense vegetation, rising to 14,793 ft (4,509 m) at Mount Wilhelm in central Papua New Guinea.

Most of Papua New Guinea's outlying islands, including New Britain, Bougainville Island, and New Ireland, are precipitous and of volcanic origin.

The Star Mountains include some of the most remote terrain on Earth. The area is rich in gold and copper.

Huon Peninsula

A series of coral reefs can be seen in the clear waters off Cape Esperance on the island of Guadalcanal in the Solomons.

Cape Esperance

Southern Papua New Guinea is part of the Indo-Australian Plate. New Guinea only became separated physically from Australia about 8,000 years ago, following the flooding of the Torres Strait.

The lowland plains in the south and north of the main island are swampy, and contain fertile alluvial soil. This contrasts with the mountainous islands in the rest of Papua New Guinea where soils are generally thin and nutrients are retained in the existing vegetation.

Kikori River

Papua New Guinea's rivers, though fairly short, carry extremely high sediment loads, largely due to soil erosion. This is caused by a combination of very steep slopes and heavy rainfall, and is made worse by forest clearance, particularly "slash and burn" techniques and mine operations.

The Owen Stanley Range contains several of Papua New Guinea's highest peaks, the greatest of which is Mount Victoria at 13,200 ft (4,035 m).

Kavachi is an active submarine volcano near New Georgia, which erupts every few years.

The Louisiade Archipelago contains 10 volcanic islands and numerous coral islets. Tagula Island is the largest of the islands, containing the archipelago's highest peak at 2,645 ft (806 m).

Huon Peninsula

Caves and undercut cliffs mark former shoreline

Stream cuts down through recently exposed land

Former level of beach

Current beach

Uplift of the land in tectonically active regions can lead to former coastlines being lifted beyond the reach of the sea. New cliffs and caves are formed at a lower level, and rivers cut down through the lower land to reach sea level once more.

SOLOMON ISLANDS

PACIFIC OCEAN

TEMOTU

Duff Islands

Reef Islands

Tinakula

Nendö Noka

Lata Santa Cruz Islands

Utupua

Vanikolo

(same scale as main map)

Lying close to the banks of the Sepik River in northern Papua New Guinea, this building is known as the Spirit House. It is constructed from leaves and twigs, ornately woven and trimmed into geometric patterns. The house is decorated with a mask and topped by a carved statue.

Matthias Group
Emirau Island

el Channel

New Hanover
Tsukul
North Cape Kavieng
an
Dyaul Island

Tatau Island
Simberi Island
Tabar Islands
Tabar Island
Konos
Konogogo
Namatanai
Lihir Group
Lihir Island
Tanga Islands
Boang Island
Malendok Island
Feni Islands

PACIFIC OCEAN

Nuguria Islands

NEW IRELAND

New Ireland

St. George's Channel

Cape Lambert
Rabaul
Kokopo
Gazelle Peninsula
Toriu
Mount Konogaiang
Ambitle Island
Babase Island
Taron
Cape St. George

Green Islands
Pinipel Island
Nissan Island

Tulun Islands

Takuu Islands

Nukumanu Islands

Willaumez Peninsula
Lolobau Island
Open Bay
Mount Bamus
Wide Bay

Lemankoa
Buka Island
Hutjena

Ontong Java Atoll

Kimbe Bay
Hoskins
Kimbe
Ubai
Talasea
Nakanai Mountains
Pomio
Lau
EAST NEW BRITAIN

NORTH SOLOMONS

Roncador Reef

Gasmata

New Britain

Mount Balbi
Wakunai

SOLOMON SEA

SOLOMON SEA

Torokina
Empress Augusta Bay
Arawa Kieta
Panguna

Bougainville Island

Buin

Nukiki

Fauro
Shortland Islands Strait
Shortland Island

Panggoe
Liru
Choiseul
Rob Roy
Vaghena

Kia
Baolo
ISABEL
Santa Isabel
Buala
Mount Sasari

Dai Island

MALAITA

Treasury Islands

WESTERN

New Georgia Sound

Malu'u
Kwailibesi
Auki
Malaita
Olomburi
Bannani

Vella Lavella
Ranongga
Gizo
Ringgi
Munda
Rendova

New Georgia Islands

Mongga
Kolombangara
New Georgia
Vangunu
Nggatokae

Blanche Channel
Tetepare

Kolokofa
Kaolo
San Jorge

Sikaiana

D'Entrecasteaux Islands
Losuia
Kiriwina Island
Kitava Island
Vakuta Island
Madau Island
Woodlark Island
Guasopa

Goodenough Island
Fergusson Island
Esa'ala
Normanby Island
Schulea

Russell Islands
Yandina
Cape Esperance
Savo
Tulaghi
Florida Islands

CENTRAL

Tambea
HONIARA
Henderson Field
Tangarare
Mount Popomanaseu
Guadalcanal
Nduindui
Avuavu

Tarapaina
Maramasike
Apio

Olawa Island

NEA

Milne Bay
Alotau
Ahioma
Sideia Island
Samarai
Suau

Louisiade Archipelago

Conflict Group

Misima Island
Bwagaoia

Pocklington Reef

SOLOMON ISLANDS

GUADALCANAL

CENTRAL

Three Sisters Islands
Heuru
Kirakira San Cristobal
Star Harbour
Hauraha

The Calvados Chain
Tagula

MAKIRA

Tagula Island

Rossel Island

Bellona

Lavanggu
Rennell

THE PACIFIC OCEAN

THE PACIFIC IS THE WORLD'S LARGEST AND DEEPEST OCEAN. It is nearly twice the area of the Atlantic and contains almost three times as much water. The ocean is dotted with islands and surrounded by some of the world's most populous states; over half the world's population lives on its shores. The Pacific is bordered by active plate margins known as the "Ring of Fire," causing earthquakes and tsunamis, and creating volcanic islands and subterranean mountain chains. The largest underwater mountains break the surface as island arcs. The fisheries of the Pacific are some of the most productive in the world and provide a vital resource for many of the Pacific islands. Since the Second World War there has been a shift in trading patterns, with a considerable growth in trade between the US and the countries of the Pacific Rim.

INSET MAP KEY

POPULATION

○ below 10,000

ELEVATION

1000m / 3281ft
500m / 1640ft
250m / 820ft
100m / 328ft
sea level

OCEAN MAP KEY

SEA DEPTH

sea level
250m / 820ft
500m / 1640ft
1000m / 3281ft
2000m / 6562ft
3000m / 9843ft
5000m / 16,410ft

SCALE 1:50,000,000
(projection: Mollweide)

Km 0 200 400 600 800 1000
Miles 0 200 400 600 800 1000

AMERICAN SAMOA AND WESTERN SAMOA

AMERICAN SAMOA AND WESTERN SAMOA are part of the island archipelago of Polynesia. The two most populous islands are Tutuila in American Samoa and Upolu in Western Samoa. Although the economies of both of these states remain predominantly resource-based, both are expanding their light manufacturing sectors, and the US administration is the primary employer in American Samoa. Fishing is particularly important: 25% of all tuna consumed in the US is processed and canned in Pago Pago.

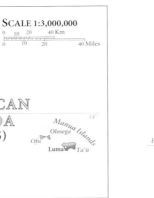

Japan is one of the major trading nations within the Pacific, importing iron and steel from Australia, and grain from the US. The major exports from the Pacific Rim are electronics, precision equipment, and motor cars.

SCALE 1:3,000,000
0 10 20 40 Km
0 10 20 40 Miles

WESTERN SAMOA
ÁPIA Upolu
Savai'i
AMERICAN SAMOA (to US)
PAGO PAGO
Tutuila
Manua Islands
PACIFIC OCEAN

Many of the buildings in Western Samoa reflect the country's colonial past. Once a colony of New Zealand, Western Samoa is now an independent state; American Samoa remains an unincorporated territory of the US.

THE RING OF FIRE

THE ACTIVE PLATE MARGINS surrounding the Pacific have created numerous land and island volcanoes along its border. The actual basin of the Pacific is made up of a number of separate tectonic plates which move away from each other, colliding with other plates. When they collide, the thinner oceanic plates are forced beneath the thicker continental plates, forming deep ocean trenches and high ridges. These collision zones, known as subduction zones, are characterized by intense seismic and volcanic activity.

RESOURCES

MANY OF THE SMALL ISLANDS in the Pacific rely heavily on marine resources to provide valuable export incomes. These fisheries tend to be small-scale and are forced to compete with the large commercial fleets from Japan and the Russian Federation. Although many metallic mineral deposits have been discovered in the Pacific, few are exploited. The major areas of oil and gas extraction are off the coast of Vietnam, along the Kamchatka Peninsula, and off the coast of Alaska. The numerous reefs which fringe the islands of the Pacific are harvested for corals.

Farms such as this black pearl oyster farm in Tahiti are widespread throughout the Pacific. The culturing or farming of marine organisms, such as mollusks and crustaceans, has been practiced for hundreds of years.

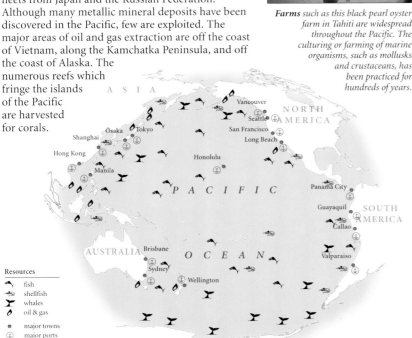

Resources
⌐ fish
⌐ shellfish
Y whales
○ oil & gas
● major towns
● major ports

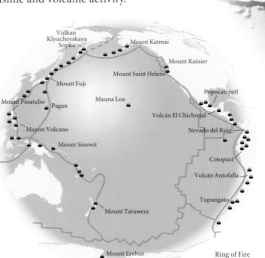

Vulkan Klyuchevskaya Sopka
Mount Katmai
Mount Rainier
Mount Saint Helens
Mount Fuji
Popocatepetl
Mount Pinatubo
Pagan
Mauna Loa
Volcán El Chichonal
Mayon Volcano
Nevado del Ruiz
Mount Sinewit
Cotopaxi
Volcán Antofalla
Tupungato
Mount Tarawera
Mount Erebus

Ring of Fire
— plate boundaries
● major volcanoes

Mayon Volcano in the Philippines is one of many active volcanoes on the Pacific "Ring of Fire." It is noted for its perfect conical shape; the base of the cone is 80 miles (130 km) in circumference.

The Hawaiian volcanoes lie in the center of a plate, not on a plate margin, and are known as intraplate volcanoes. They are associated with hot spots, where a plume of hot molten rock rises to the surface as the plate moves over it.

MELANESIA

Fiji, Vanuatu, *New Caledonia* (to France)

THREE MAIN ISLAND groups make up the area of southern Melanesia in the southwestern Pacific: the independent countries of Fiji and Vanuatu and the French overseas territory of New Caledonia. The major Melanesian island group, the Solomon Islands, lies to the east of Papua New Guinea (pages 194–95). Most of the larger islands are volcanic in origin; the smaller ones are mainly coral atolls and are largely uninhabited. The economy in all three island groups is increasingly driven by tourism, not necessarily to the benefit of other economic activities.

VANUATU

A STRING OF MOUNTAINOUS VOLCANIC ISLANDS covering more than 800 sq miles (1,300 sq km) of the south Pacific, Vanuatu achieved independence from France and the UK in 1980. The majority of the population relies on subsistence fishing and agriculture. Once-important copra and cocoa exports are declining as a result of cost-effective substitutes from elsewhere, and alternatives are being explored. There is further resource potential in the forests and fishing grounds, and beef and arable farming are of growing importance. Tourism, accounting for 40% of the GDP, is the fastest-growing sector of the economy, and further expansion is planned.

SCALE 1:6,000,000
(projection: Lambert Conformal Conic)

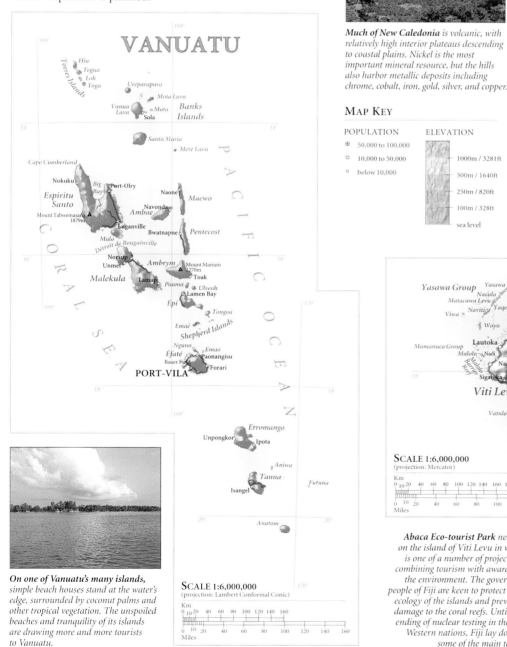

On one of Vanuatu's many islands, simple beach houses stand at the water's edge, surrounded by coconut palms and other tropical vegetation. The unspoiled beaches and tranquility of its islands are drawing more and more tourists to Vanuatu.

SCALE 1:6,000,000
(projection: Lambert Conformal Conic)

NEW CALEDONIA (France)

NEW CALEDONIA, a French overseas territory known as Kanaky by its indigenous peoples, comprises a large main island 260 miles (418 km) long and many smaller islands and atolls. Socioeconomic inequality, unemployment, and the issue of independence have caused tension between the Kanaks and the French-speaking expatriate population. This has resulted in a long history of political violence, although a referendum on independence is promised for 1998. New Caledonia produces 25% of the world's nickel, and improved incomes from tourism and agriculture have benefited the economy.

SCALE 1:6,000,000
(projection: Lambert Conformal Conic)

Much of New Caledonia is volcanic, with relatively high interior plateaus descending to coastal plains. Nickel is the most important mineral resource, but the hills also harbor metallic deposits including chrome, cobalt, iron, gold, silver, and copper.

MAP KEY

POPULATION
- ⊕ 50,000 to 100,000
- ○ 10,000 to 50,000
- ○ below 10,000

ELEVATION
- 1000m / 3281ft
- 500m / 1640ft
- 250m / 820ft
- 100m / 328ft
- sea level

FIJI

FIJI IS A VOLCANIC ARCHIPELAGO in the southwestern Pacific consisting of two large islands and 880 smaller islets, and covering a total area of 7,054 sq miles (18,270 sq km). The majority of the population lives on the two largest islands. The people are split fairly evenly between Indo-Fijians, who arrived when Fiji was still a British colony, and the indigenous Fijians who have, since 1987, controlled the government. Sugar and copra are the most important crops in a diversified agricultural base and forestry is becoming increasingly important. A relatively varied economy has potential for mineral and hydroelectric exploitation, while Fiji's climate and location on the main Pacific air routes are an impetus to tourism.

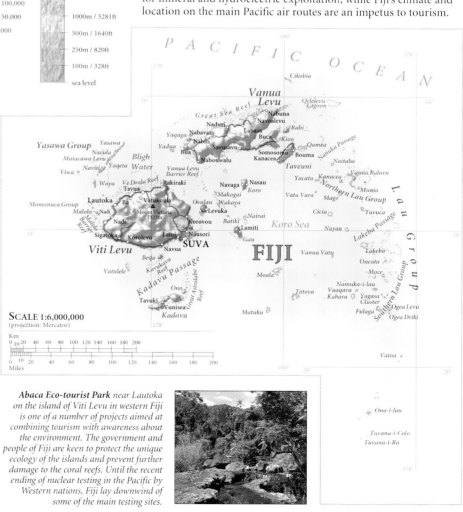

Abaca Eco-tourist Park near Lautoka on the island of Viti Levu in western Fiji is one of a number of projects aimed at combining tourism with awareness about the environment. The government and people of Fiji are keen to protect the unique ecology of the islands and prevent further damage to the coral reefs. Until the recent ending of nuclear testing in the Pacific by Western nations, Fiji lay downwind of some of the main testing sites.

SCALE 1:6,000,000
(projection: Mercator)

MICRONESIA

MARSHALL ISLANDS, MICRONESIA, NAURU, PALAU, Guam, Northern Mariana Islands, Wake Island

THE MICRONESIAN ISLANDS lie in the western reaches of the Pacific Ocean and are all part of the same volcanic zone. The Federated States of Micronesia is the largest group, with more than 600 atolls and forested volcanic islands in an area of more than 1,120 sq miles (2,900 sq km). Micronesia is a mixture of former colonies, overseas territories, and dependencies. Most of the region still relies on aid and subsidies to sustain economies limited by resources, isolation, and an emigrating population drawn to New Zealand and Australia by the attractions of a western lifestyle.

PALAU

PALAU IS AN ARCHIPELAGO OF OVER 200 ISLANDS, only eight of which are inhabited. It was the last remaining UN Trust Territory in the Pacific, controlled by the US until 1994, when it became independent. The economy operates on a subsistence level, with coconuts and cassava as the principal crops. Fishing licenses and tourism provide foreign currency.

SCALE 1:750,000

SCALE 1:6,000,000

GUAM (to US)

LYING AT THE SOUTHERN END of the Mariana Islands, Guam is an important US military base and tourist destination. Social and political life is dominated by the indigenous Chamorro, who make up just under half of the population, although the increasing prevalence of western culture threatens Guam's traditional social stability.

The tranquility of these coastal lagoons, at Inarajan in southern Guam, belies the fact that the island lies in a region where typhoons are common.

GUAM
(to US)

AGANA

SCALE 1:825,000

NORTHERN MARIANA ISLANDS (to US)

A US COMMONWEALTH TERRITORY, the Northern Marianas comprise the whole of the Mariana archipelago except for Guam. The islands retain their close links with the US and continue to receive American aid. Tourism, though bringing in much-needed revenue, has speeded the decline of the traditional subsistence economy. Most of the population lives on Saipan.

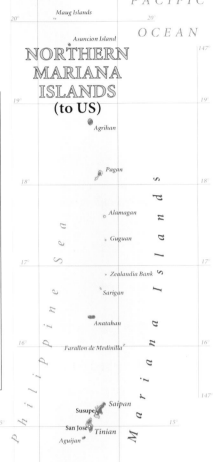

NORTHERN MARIANA ISLANDS (to US)

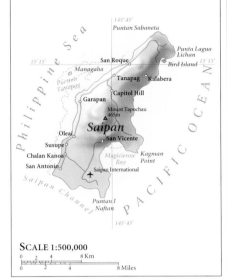

Saipan

SCALE 1:500,000

The Palau Islands have numerous hidden lakes and lagoons. These sustain their own ecosystems, which have developed in isolation. This has produced adaptations in the animals and plants that are often unique to each lake.

SCALE 1:5,000,000

MICRONESIA

A MIXTURE OF HIGH VOLCANIC ISLANDS and low-lying coral atolls, the Federated States of Micronesia include all of the Caroline Islands except Palau. Pohnpei, Kosrae, Chuuk, and Yap are the four main island cluster states, each of which has its own language, with English remaining the official language. Nearly half of the population is concentrated on Pohnpei, the largest island. Independent since 1979, the islands continue to receive considerable aid from the US that supplements an economy based primarily on fishing and copra processing.

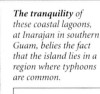

Yap

SCALE 1:825,000

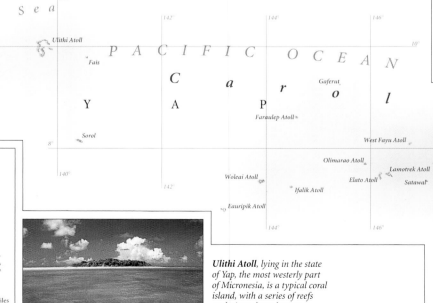

Ulithi Atoll, lying in the state of Yap, the most westerly part of Micronesia, is a typical coral island, with a series of reefs enclosing a large lagoon.

MARSHALL ISLANDS

A GROUP OF 34 WIDELY SCATTERED ATOLLS in the central Pacific Ocean, the Marshall Islands include some of the largest atolls in the world, formed from low coral islands with sandy beaches and enclosing vast lagoons. Formerly under US protection as part of the UN Trust Territory of the Pacific Islands, and including the former US nuclear testing sites of Bikini Atoll and Enewetak Atoll, the Marshall Islands became self-governing in 1979. The economy is reliant on American aid and on the rent paid by the US for its missile base on Kwajalein Atoll.

SCALE 1:1,000,000

Majuro Atoll is the Marshall Islands' capital and commercial center. Almost half of the population live on the narrow islands, often in overcrowded conditions.

SCALE 1:6,500,000

NAURU

A FORMER BRITISH COLONY, the tiny island of Nauru, with an area of only 8.2 sq miles (21.2 sq km), has been exploited for its substantial phosphate deposits by the UK, Australia, and New Zealand. Since independence in 1968, Nauru's phosphate industry has made its citizens some of the wealthiest in the world, and scars from the vast mining operation pit the island's landscape. Phosphate reserves are now virtually exhausted, and investment overseas will form the bulk of Nauru's income in the future.

SCALE 1:200,000

A series of coral pinnacles stand exposed in the shallow water off the coast of Nauru. Much of the island has an extraordinary "lunar" landscape, created by years of phosphate extraction.

WAKE ISLAND (to US)

AN UNINCORPORATED TERRITORY of the US with a tiny population, Wake Island remains strategically important to US forces, and has been used as a base in several conflicts. Formed by the rim of an extinct underwater volcano, it is now used as an emergency airstrip for trans-Pacific flights and as a stopover for cargo planes.

SCALE 1:650,000

Canoes, built following tradition, are still important in Micronesia, and are used for transportation and fishing. This large canoe, on Satawal, in the state of Yap, needs nearly 20 people to return it to the boathouse.

SCALE 1:1,500,000

SCALE 1:250,000

SCALE 1:500,000

SCALE 1:8,000,000

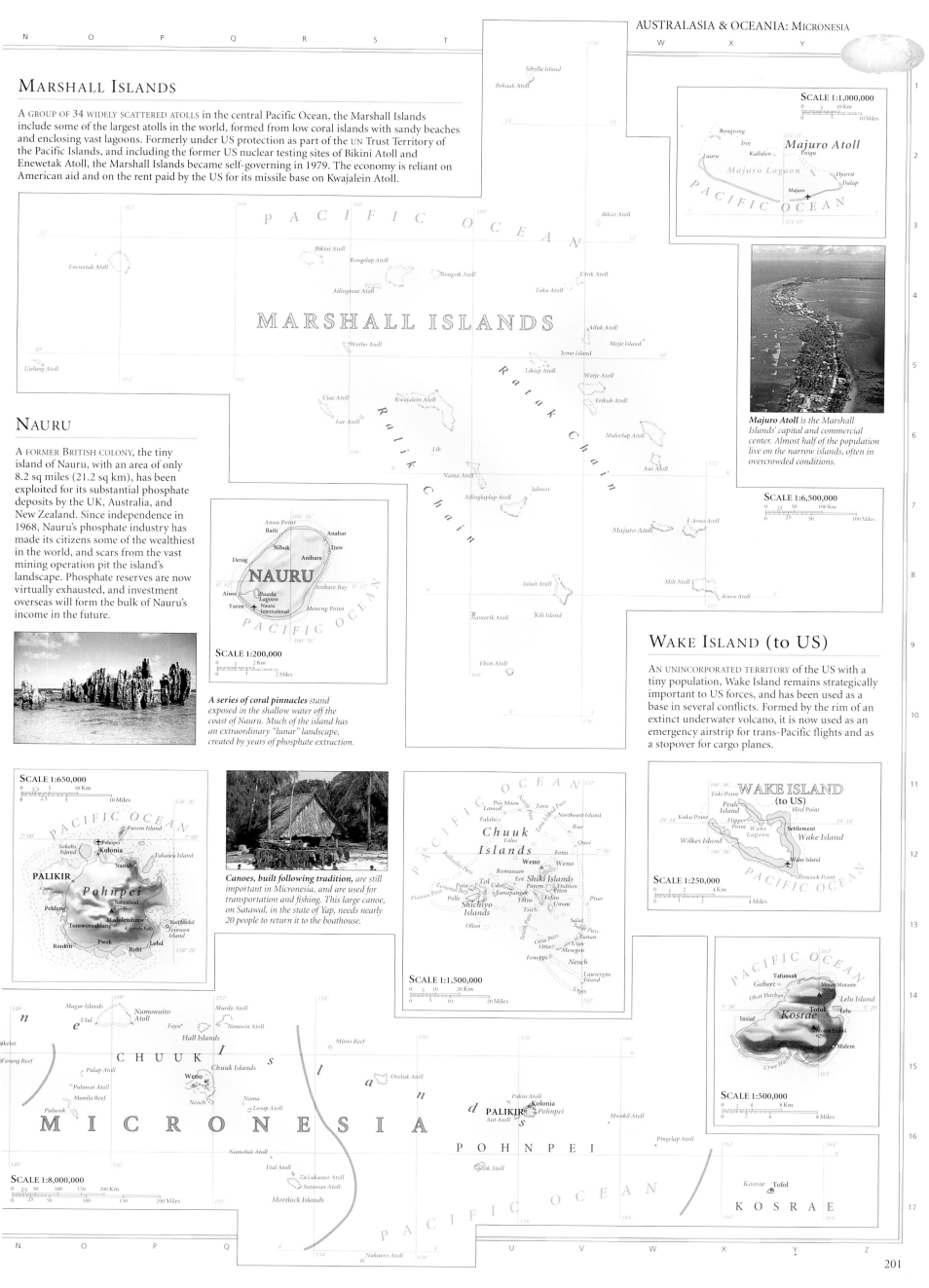

THE LANDSCAPE

ALTHOUGH IT IS STILL THE LARGEST OCEAN, the basin of the Pacific has been gradually decreasing in size due to the movement of the Indo-Australian Plate. Its oldest parts are about 135 million years old. The eastern border of the Pacific is characterized by a continuous mountain chain running the length of the North and South American continents. The eastern basin has a low, uninterrupted relief, at depths averaging 15,000 ft (4,570 m). In contrast, the western Pacific is scattered with island arcs and bounded by a series of deep ocean trenches. An almost continuous chain of volcanoes surrounds the ocean and an active mid-ocean ridge runs northeast–southwest.

Micronesia consists of numerous small, oceanic islands in the western Pacific. The Micronesian islands are all oceanic in origin, rising directly up from the ocean floor.

The Emperor Seamounts were formed over 40 million years ago. Like other islands and seamounts of the same era, they trend in a north–south direction. Younger chains run northwest–southeast.

Turbidity currents are sinking masses of sediment-laden water. Their erosive force creates deep, narrow submarine canyons along the continental shelf to the ocean floor, where the sediments are deposited.

Continental shelf
Sediment-laden current
Submarine canyon
Ocean floor

The Mariana Trench marks a subduction zone between the Pacific Plate and the Philippine Plate. It is the world's deepest trench, reaching depths of 36,201 ft (11,034 m).

The Tonga Trench lies north of New Zealand's North Island. The trench reaches average depths of 34,448 ft (10,500 m), which is more than twice the average depth of the ocean.

The Pacific mid-ocean ridge is spreading at a rate of 6.5 inches (15 cm) a year. The northeastern part is no longer apparent, having merged with the strike-slip fault systems of North America.

The Peru–Chile Trench is the longest trench in the Pacific, extending 3,660 miles (5,900 km), and following the line of the Andes mountain range down the west coast of South America.

Bora-Bora

Bora-Bora's twin mountain peaks are the remnants of an ancient volcano, now surrounded by a large lagoon, fringed with coral.

Northern Chile

The powerful erosive capacity of Pacific waves can be seen along this stretch of coastline in northern Chile. Wave erosion has cut back the bedrock, exposing numerous rock layers.

TONGA

THE KINGDOM OF TONGA lies in the southwest Pacific, about 2,000 miles (3,000 km) off the east coast of Australia. It comprises 169 islands of which only 36 are permanently inhabited. The majority of the population live on the largest island, Tongatapu. There are only three sizeable towns and the main commercial center is the capital Nuku'alofa. Tonga's economy is based mainly on agriculture; coconuts, bananas, and vanilla are grown as cash crops for export. Although there is some light manufacturing, growing land shortages have forced increased migration to New Zealand and Australia.

The islands of Tonga fall into two belts; those in the east are low coral islands, while those in the west are high and volcanic. Four of the islands still contain active volcanoes. The mountainous western islands are covered with verdant tropical vegetation.

Coral reefs and atolls are found throughout the warm waters of the south Pacific. Reefs build up from the skeletons of millions of coral polyps – tiny sea creatures that cling to the reef and secrete calcium carbonate around their bodies, forming a hard protective skeleton.

SCALE 1:1,000,000

SCALE 1:6,000,000

TONGA

Arctic Circle

RUSSIAN
FEDERATION

UNITED STATES OF
AMERICA
(ALASKA)

NORTH

CANADA

Anadyr

Magadan

Sea of
Okhotsk

Kamchatka

Bering
Sea

Gulf of
Anadyr

Saint Lawrence
Island

Saint Matthew
Island

Nunivak
Island

Bristol
Bay

Anchorage

Gulf of
Alaska

Kodiak Island

Patton
Seamount

Pratt
Seamount

Welker
Seamount

Queen
Charlotte
Islands

Vancouver
Island

Vancouver

Sakhalin

Petropavlovsk-
Kamchatskiy

Komandorskiye
Ostrova

Attu Island

Aleutian Basin

Pribilof Islands

Unimak Island

Unalaska Island

Aleutian Islands

Gilbert Seamounts

Seattle

Cascadia
Basin

Columbia

Kurile Basin

Amchitka Island

Aleutian Trench

Comstock Seamount

Endeavour
Seamount

Vladivostok

Kurile Islands

Harris Seamount

Tufts Plain

Japan
Basin

Hokkaido

Emperor Seamounts

Chinook Trough

Mendocino Fracture Zone

Gorda
Ridge

NORTH
KOREA

Wonsan

Sea of
Japan

Honshu

Northwest Pacific

Basin

Chinook Trough

San Francisco

UNITED

SOUTH
KOREA

Pusan

Tokyo

Kammu
Seamount

Murray Fracture Zone

Moonless Mountain

Osaka

Nagoya

JAPAN

Midway
Islands
(to US)

Kure Atoll

Hawaiian Islands
(to US)

Guadalupe
(to Mexico)

Long Beach

Kyushu

Shikoku

Salmon Bank

Lisianski
Island

Channel Islands

Makarov Seamount

Mapmaker Seamounts

Necker
Island

Cedros

Marcus Island
(to Japan)

Hess
Tablemount

Kauai

Oahu

Molokai

Honolulu

Revillagigedo Island
(to Mexico)

West
Mariana
Basin

Mariana
Islands

East
Mariana
Basin

Wake Island
(to US)

Johnston Atoll
(to US)

Hawaii

Clarion Fracture Zone

Guam
(to US)

Mariana Trench

Northern Mariana
Islands (to US)

Eniwetok

Bikini

Mountains

Vityaz Seamount

PACIFIC

Challenger Deep

Caroline Ridge

MARSHALL
ISLANDS

Central
Pacific

Magellan
Rise

Kingman Reef
(to US)

Palmyra Atoll
(to US)

Tabuaeran

Clipperton Fracture Zone

Yap

Caroline Islands

MICRONESIA

Basin

Kiritimati

PALAU

Ontong Java Rise

Melanesian
Basin

Baker & Howland
Islands (To US)

Jarvis Island
(to US)

Galapagos Fracture Zone

Galle
Rise

NAURU

Banaba

Kanton

Nova

KIRIBATI

Endebury
Island

Admiralty
Islands

New Guinea Trench

Bismarck Archipelago

New Ireland

Phoenix
Islands

Malden
Island

Starbuck
Island

Marquesas
Islands

Hiva Oa

Nukuhiva

Marquesas Fracture Zone

New Guinea

New Britain

SOLOMON ISLANDS

TUVALU

Robbie Ridge

Tokelau
(to NZ)

Northern Cook Islands

Manihiki
Plateau

Penrhyn

Vostok
Island

Flint
Island

Caroline
Island

Tuamotu

Tiki
Basin

Tuamotu Fracture Zone

PAPUA NEW GUINEA

Lae

Solomon Sea

Santa Cruz
Islands

Hazel Holme Bank

Rotuma

WESTERN
SAMOA

American
Samoa
(to US)

Cook Islands
(to NZ)

Rangiroa

Tahiti

Port
Moresby

Louisiade
Archipelago

Wells & Futuna
(to France)

Samoa

Penrhyn
Basin

Bora-Bora

Mehetia

Australia

Fracture Zone

Coral Sea

Queensland
Plateau

VANUATU

North
Fiji
Basin

FIJI

TONGA

Niue
(to NZ)

Samoa
Basin

French Polynesia
(to France)

Iles Gambier

Henderson
Island

Ducie Island

Osprey Reef

Coral Sea
Islands
(to Australia)

Iles Chesterfield

Iles Loyauté

New Caledonia
(to France)

Southern
Cook Islands

Rarotonga

Mauke

President Thiers
Seamount

Rapa

Pitcairn
Island

Pitcairn Islands
(to UK)

Ducie Island

AUSTRALIA

Great Barrier Reef

Brisbane

New Caledonia Basin

Horizon Deep

South Fiji
Basin

Ozbourn
Seamount

Iles Australes

Southwest

Pacific

East Pacific Rise

Darling

Lord Howe
Island
(to Australia)

Norfolk Island
(to Australia)

Kermadec
Islands
(to NZ)

Basin

Sydney

Balls Pyramid

Lord Howe Rise

Kermadec Trench

Northland
Plateau

Gascoyne
Tablemount

Auckland

Rankumara
Plain

Valerie
Guyot

Agassiz Fracture Zone

Melbourne

King Island

Tasman Plain

North
Island

Chatham Rise

Kangaroo
Island

Furneaux
Group

Tasman
Sea

Challenger
Plateau

Wellington

Chatham Islands (to NZ)

Hobart

Tasmania

East
Tasman
Plateau

NEW
ZEALAND

South Island

Menard Fracture Zone

Tasman Basin

Dunedin

Bounty Trough

Bounty Islands (to NZ)

Antipodes Islands (to NZ)

South
Australian
Basin

Campbell
Plateau

Antipodes Islands (to NZ)

Bollons
Tablemount

Indian Ridge

Tasman Fracture Zone

Macquarie Ridge

Auckland
Islands
(to NZ)

Campbell Island (to NZ)

Eltanin Fracture Zone

Macquarie Island
(to Australia)

Udintsev Fracture Zone

South
Indian
Basin

Pacific Antarctic Ridge

SOUTHERN OCEAN

Southeast Pacific

Basin

Bellingshausen

De Gerlache

Antarctic Circle

Balleny Islands
(to NZ)

Amundsen Plain

Marie Byrd
Seamount

Peter I Island
(to Norway)

Wave action has eroded this shoreline
near Port Campbell in southeastern
Australia, leaving isolated pinnacles of
rock cut off from the main coastline.
They are known as the "Twelve Apostles."

Scott Island
(to NZ)

Iselin Seamount

Scott Shoal

Amundsen Sea

Bellingshausen
Sea

ANTARCTICA

POLYNESIA

KIRIBATI, TUVALU, Cook Islands, Easter Island, French Polynesia, Niue, Pitcairn Islands, Tokelau, Wallis & Futuna

THE NUMEROUS ISLAND GROUPS OF POLYNESIA lie to the east of Australia, scattered over a vast area in the south Pacific. The islands are a mixture of low-lying coral atolls, some of which enclose lagoons, and the tips of great underwater volcanoes. The populations on the islands are small, and most people are of Polynesian origin, as are the Maori of New Zealand. Local economies remain simple, relying mainly on subsistence crops, mineral deposits, many of which are now exhausted, fishing, and tourism.

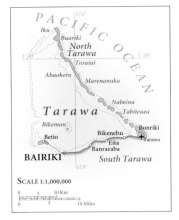

SCALE 1:1,000,000

With the exception of Banaba, *all the islands in Kiribati's three groups are low-lying coral atolls. This aerial view shows the sparsely vegetated islands, intercut by many small lagoons.*

KIRIBATI

A FORMER BRITISH COLONY, Kiribati became independent in 1979. Banaba's phosphate deposits ran out in 1980, following decades of exploitation by the British. Economic development remains slow and most agriculture is at a subsistence level, although coconuts provide export income, and underwater agriculture is being developed.

TUVALU

TUVALU IS A CHAIN of nine coral atolls, 360 miles (579 km) long with a land area of just over 9 sq miles (23 sq km). It is one of the world's smallest and most isolated states. As the Ellice Islands, Tuvalu was linked to the Gilbert Islands (now part of Kiribati) as a British colony until independence in 1978. Politically and socially conservative, Tuvaluans live by fishing and subsistence farming.

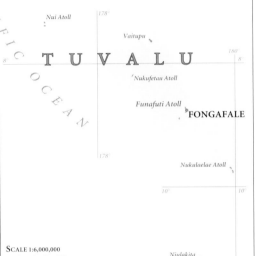

Funafuti Atoll *contains more than 40% of Tuvalu's people, giving it an extremely high population density.*

SCALE 1:500,000

SCALE 1:6,000,000

TOKELAU (to New Zealand)

A LOW-LYING CORAL ATOLL, Tokelau is a dependent territory of New Zealand with few natural resources. Although a 1990 cyclone destroyed crops and infrastructure, a tuna cannery and the sale of fishing licenses have raised revenue. A catamaran link between the islands has increased their potential for tourism. Tokelau's small size and economic weakness make independence from New Zealand unlikely.

Fishermen cast their nets *to catch small fish in the shallow waters off Atafu Atoll, the most westerly island in Tokelau.*

SCALE 1:2,000,000

WALLIS & FUTUNA (to France)

IN CONTRAST TO OTHER FRENCH overseas territories in the south Pacific, the inhabitants of Wallis and Futuna have shown little desire for greater autonomy. A subsistence economy produces a variety of tropical crops, while foreign currency remittances come from expatriates and from the sale of licenses to Japanese and Korean fishing fleets.

SCALE 1:1,000,000

SCALE 1:1,000,000

COOK ISLANDS (to New Zealand)

A MIXTURE OF CORAL ATOLLS and volcanic peaks, the Cook Islands achieved self-government in 1965 but exist in free association with New Zealand. A diverse economy includes pearl and giant-clam farming and an ostrich farm, as well as tourism and banking. A 1991 friendship treaty with France provides for French surveillance of territorial waters.

NIUE (to New Zealand)

NIUE, the world's largest coral island, is self-governing but exists in free association with New Zealand. Tropical fruits are grown for local consumption; tourism and the sale of postage stamps provide foreign currency. The lack of local job prospects has led more than 10,000 Niueans to emigrate to New Zealand, which has now invested heavily in Niue's economy in the hope of reversing this trend.

Palm trees *fringe the white sands of a beach on Aitutaki in the Southern Cook Islands, where tourism is of increasing economic importance.*

SCALE 1:1,000,000

Waves have cut back *the original coastline, exposing a sandy beach, near Mutalau in the northeast corner of Niue.*

SCALE 1:325,000

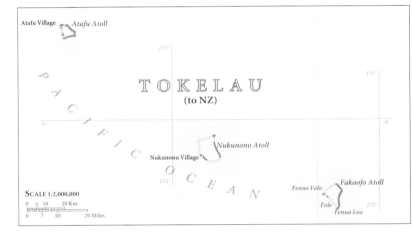

SCALE 1:20,000,000

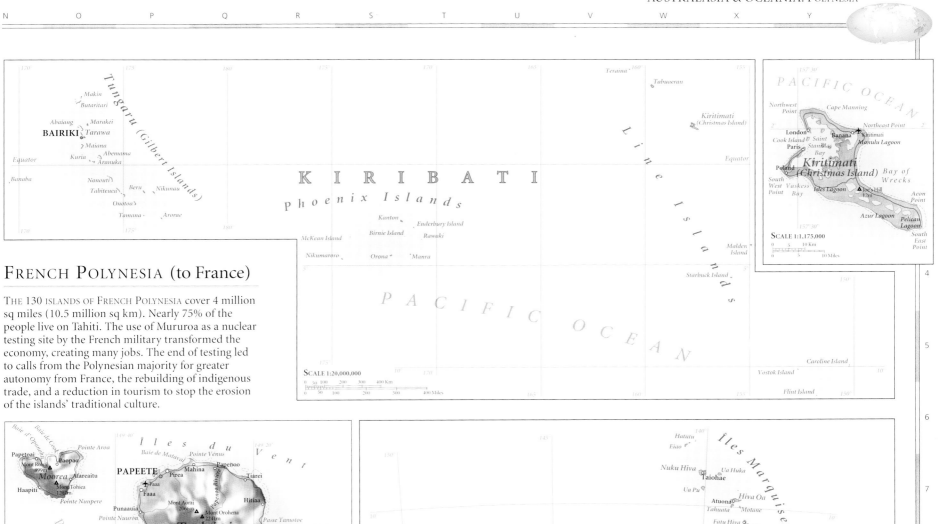

PACIFIC OCEAN

Kiritimati (Christmas Island)

Northwest Point · Cape Manning · Northeast Point
London · Banana · Kiritimati · Manulu Lagoon
Cook Island · Saint Stanislas · Bay
Paris · Poland · *Kiritimati (Christmas Island)* · Bay of Wrecks
South West Point · South West Bay · Isles Lagoon · Aeon Point
Azur Lagoon · Pelican Lagoon · South East Point

SCALE 1:1,175,000

KIRIBATI

Tungaru (Gilbert Islands)

Makin · Butaritari · Abaiang · Marakei · **BAIRIKI** · Tarawa · Maiana · Kuria · Abemama · Aranuka · Banaba · Nonouti · Tabiteuea · Beru · Nikunau · Onotoa · Tamana · Arorae

Phoenix Islands

Kanton · Enderbury Island · Rawaki · McKean Island · Birnie Island · Nikumaroro · Orona · Manra

Line Islands

Teraina · Tabuaeran · Kiritimati (Christmas Island) · Malden Island · Starbuck Island · Caroline Island · Vostok Island · Flint Island

SCALE 1:20,000,000

PACIFIC OCEAN

FRENCH POLYNESIA (to France)

THE 130 ISLANDS of FRENCH POLYNESIA cover 4 million sq miles (10.5 million sq km). Nearly 75% of the people live on Tahiti. The use of Mururoa as a nuclear testing site by the French military transformed the economy, creating many jobs. The end of testing led to calls from the Polynesian majority for greater autonomy from France, the rebuilding of indigenous trade, and a reduction in tourism to stop the erosion of the islands' traditional culture.

Îles du Vent

Baie d'Opunohu · Baie de Cook · Pointe Aroa · Papetoai · Paopao · *Moorea* · Mont Rotui 899m · Atareaitu · Mont Tohiea 1200m · Haapiti · Pointe Nuupere · Pointe Venus · Baie de Matavai · Pointe Venus · Papenoo · **PAPEETE** · Faaa · Pirae · Mahina · Tiarei · Faaa · Hitiaa · Punaauia · Mont Aorai 2066m · Mont Orohena 2241m · Paea · Mont Tetufera 1799m · Faaone · *Tahiti* · Passe Tamotoe · Baie de Taravao · Maraa · Mataiea · Papara · Teahupoo · Vairao · Afaahiti · Taravao · Tautira · Isthme de Taravao · *Presqu'île de Taiarapu* · Mont Ronui 1332m · Récif Tepace

POINTE MARAA · POINTE MAHONO · PACIFIC OCEAN

SCALE 1:1,000,000

The traditional Tahitian welcome for visitors, who are greeted by parties of canoes, has become a major tourist attraction.

PITCAIRN ISLANDS (to UK)

BRITAIN'S MOST ISOLATED DEPENDENCY, Pitcairn Island was first populated by mutineers from the HMS *Bounty* in 1790. Emigration is further depleting the already limited gene pool of the island's inhabitants, with associated social and health problems. Barter, fishing, and subsistence farming form the basis of the economy, although postage stamp sales provide foreign currency earnings, and offshore mineral exploitation may boost the economy in future.

PITCAIRN ISLANDS (to UK)

Oeno Island · Henderson Island · Ducie Island · Pitcairn Island

PACIFIC OCEAN

SCALE 1:10,000,000

The Pitcairn Islanders rely on regular airdrops from New Zealand and periodic visits by supply vessels to provide them with basic commodities.

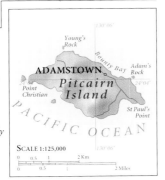

Pitcairn Island

Young's Rock · Bounty Bay · Adam's Rock · **ADAMSTOWN** · Point Christian · *Pitcairn Island* · St Paul's Point · PACIFIC OCEAN

SCALE 1:125,000

FRENCH POLYNESIA (to France)

Îles Marquises

Hatutu · Eiao · Nuku Hiva · Ua Huka · Taiohae · Ua Pu · Hiva Oa · Atuona · Tahuata · Motane · Fatu Hiva · Omoa

Îles Tuamotu

Îles du Roi George · Îles du Désappointement · Mataiva · Tikehau · Ahe · Manihi · Takaroa · Takapoto · Tepoto · Napuka · Rangiroa · Îles Palliser · Tikei · Pukapuka · Makatea · Aratika · Toau · Kauehi · Takume · Fangatau · Fakahina · Niau · Fakarava · Raraka · Katiu · Makemo · Raroia · Faaite · Tahanea · Nihiru · Tehuata · Tatakoto · Anaa · Haraiki · Marutea · Hikueru · Tauere · Amanu · Reitoru · Marokau · Hao · Akiaki · Vahitahi · Pukarua · Reao · Ravahere · Nengonengo · Paraoa · Vairaatea · Pinaki · Manuhangi · Ahunui · Mehetia · Hereheretue · Îles du Duc de Gloucester · Vanavana · Tureia · Groupe Acteon · Tenararo · Marutea · Tematangi · Mururoa · Maria · Fangataufa · Îles Gambier · Mangareva · Temoe

Moorea · PAPEETE · *Tahiti*

Îles Sous le Vent / Îles du Vent / Archipel de la Société

Motu One · Manuae · Maupihaa · Tupai · Bora-Bora · Fare · Maupiti · Tahaa · Huahine · Tetiaroa · Raiatea · Moorea · Maiao · PAPEETE · Tahiti

Îles Australes

Maria · Rimatara · Rurutu · Tubuai · Raevavae · Rapa Iti · Marotiri

SCALE 1:14,500,000

EASTER ISLAND (to Chile)

ONE OF THE MOST EASTERLY ISLANDS in Polynesia, Easter Island *(Isla de Pascua)* – also known as Rapa Nui – is part of Chile. The mainly Polynesian inhabitants support themselves by farming, which is mainly of a subsistence nature, and includes cattle rearing and growing crops such as sugar cane, bananas, corn, gourds, and potatoes. In recent years, tourism has become the most important source of income, and the island sustains a small commercial airport.

Easter Island (Isla de Pascua) (to Chile)

Punta San Juan · Playa de Anakena · Punta Rosalia · Naunau · Cabo Norte · Maunga Terevaka 506m · Anse de La Pérouse · Cabo O'Higgins · Ahu Tepeu · Maunga Pukatiki 370m · Ahu Akivi · Motu Tautara · Ahu Akivi · Rano Raraku · Cabo Roggewein · Hanga Roa · Maunga Tangaroa 77m · Vaihu · Punta Baja · Mataveri · Punta Akahanga · Punta Cuidado · Rano-Kau · Ahu Vinapu · Cabo Sur · Orongo · Motu Nui

PACIFIC OCEAN

SCALE 1:500,000

The Naunau, a series of huge stone statues, overlook Playa de Anakena, on Easter Island. Carved out of a soft volcanic rock, they were erected between 400 and 900 years ago.

ANTARCTICA

T HE ICE-COVERED CONTINENT of Antarctica, which is the Earth's most southerly region, has drawn explorers and entrepreneurs seeking challenge and riches in its wintry lands for over 200 years. The extreme climate has deterred any large-scale settlement of the continent, and though commercial hunters built outposts in the past, habitation is now limited to scientific bases. The Antarctic Treaty, which came into force in 1961, provides for international governance and scientific cooperation instead of potential territorial conflict.

RESOURCES

MANY ORE MINERALS, including iron and gold, are found in the Antarctic, and there are also coal reserves in the Transantarctic Mountains. The severe conditions and environmental importance of the region mean that exploitation of potential mineral resources is both uneconomic and undesirable. The unique wildlife and landscape draw a small number of tourists annually.

Most settlements in Antarctica are research bases such as this one at Rothera on Adelaide Island, although there is a small Chilean settlement on King George Island.

Resources (including wildlife)
- coal
- fish
- minerals
- oil & gas
- penguins
- seals
- whales
- polar research base

THE LANDSCAPE

THERE ARE TWO DISTINCT PARTS to Antarctica: Lesser Antarctica, a series of ice-covered, mountainous islands joined together by the ice, and the high plateau of Greater Antarctica. The Ross Sea and the Weddell Sea are outliers of the Atlantic and Pacific oceans – deep bays partially covered by thick ice shelves.

On Elephant Island, the coast is edged by glaciers, although the land is not permanently covered by ice.

Grease ice   Pancake ice   Sea-ice sheet   Ice floe

Pack ice forms out at sea in freezing temperatures. At the outer limits, grease ice congeals on the surface of the ocean. This is then spun around by wind and waves into irregular "pancakes," freezing and breaking up several times before bonding together again to form sea-ice sheets, which finally cement into enormous ice floes.

During the winter the seas surrounding Antarctica freeze, increasing the size of the continent by 100%.

Upper Wright Valley

Limit of summer pack ice

Limit of winter pack ice

Elephant Island

Many volcanoes, some of them still active, can be found in the mountains of the Antarctic Peninsula.

High winds carrying snow form huge snowdrifts. The erosive power of the wind-borne snow can also sculpt the ice sheet to produce landforms known as *sastrugi*, which align with the direction of the wind.

The Lambert Glacier is the largest glacier system in the world, up to 50 miles (80 km) wide at its seaward limit, and reaching 180 miles (300 km) into the interior by way of the Prince Charles Mountains.

Antarctica is the highest continent on Earth, because of the great thickness of ice which overlays the land. In places the ice alone can reach up to 15,700 ft (4,800 m) thick. Much of the basement rock of west Antarctica lies below sea level, pushed down by the weight of the ice.

The mountainous Antarctic Peninsula is formed of rocks 65–225 million years old, overlain by more recent rocks and glacial deposits. It is connected to the Andes in South America by a submarine ridge.

Nearly half – 44% – of the Antarctic coastline is bounded by ice shelves, like the Ronne Ice Shelf, which float on the Ocean. These are joined to the inland ice sheet by dome-shaped ice "rises."

More than 30% of Antarctic ice is contained in the Ross Ice Shelf.

The barren, flat-bottomed Upper Wright Valley was once filled by a glacier, but is now dry, strewn with boulders and pebbles. In some dry valleys, there has been no rain for over 2 million years.

Large colonies of seabirds live in the extremely harsh Antarctic climate. The Emperor penguins seen here, the smaller Adélie penguin, the Antarctic petrel, and the South Polar skua are the only birds that breed exclusively on the continent.

TERRITORIAL CLAIMS
- Argentinian claim
- Brazilian zone of interest
- British claim
- Norwegian undefined limit
- Australian claim
- Chilean claim
- French claim
- Australian claim
- New Zealand claim

Research Stations on King George Island
- Arctowski (to Poland)
- Artigas (to Uruguay)
- Bellingshausen (to Russian Federation)
- Comandante Ferraz (to Brazil)
- Great Wall (to China)
- Jubany (to Argentina)
- King Sejong (to South Korea)
- Teniente Rodolfo Marsh (to Chile)

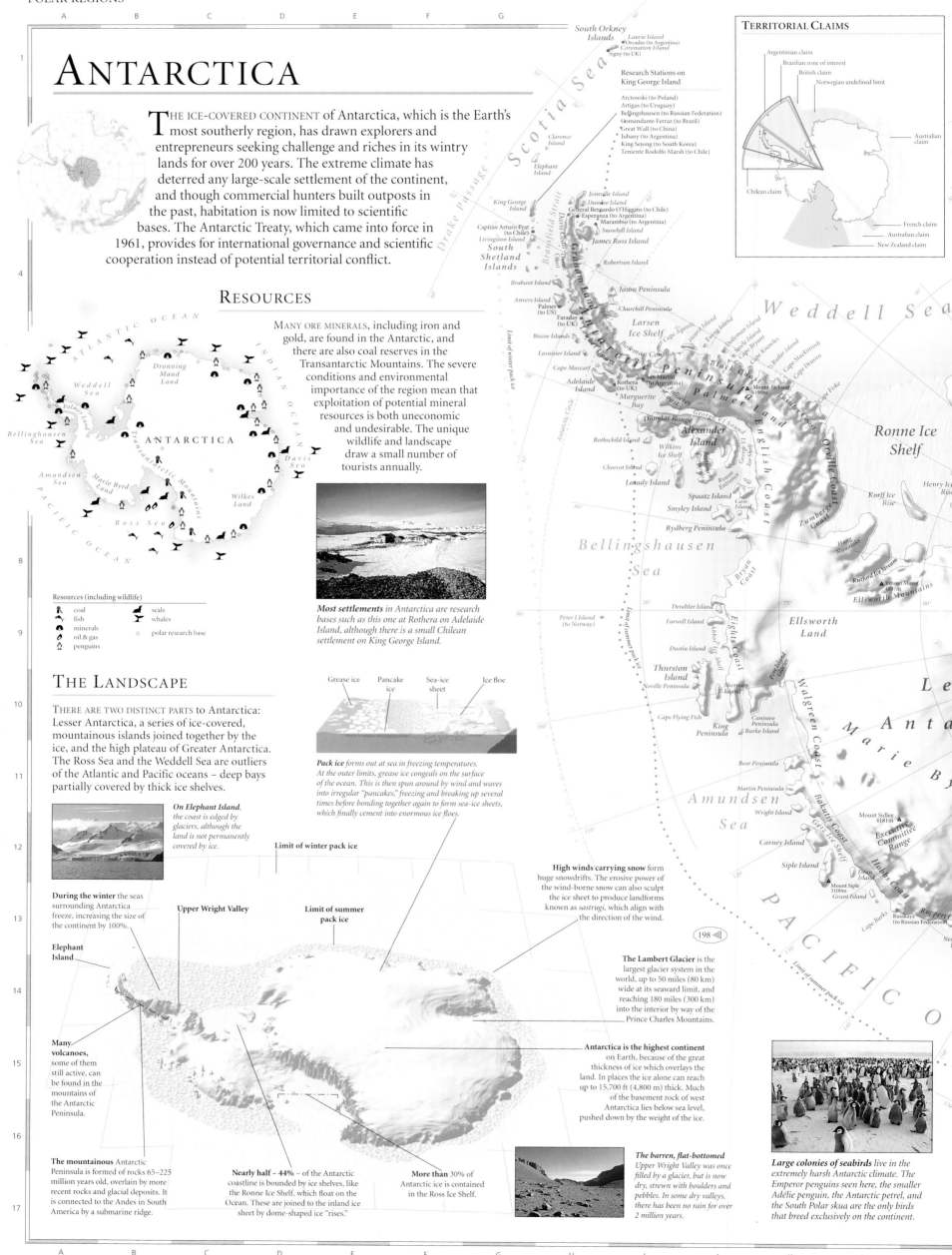

The sun sets over the Antarctic Peninsula for more than six months during the winter. However, there are more hours of sunshine during the brief Antarctic summer than most equatorial countries receive in a whole year.

▶ 180

66

ATLANTIC OCEAN

Antarctic Circle

INDIAN OCEAN

Limit of summer pack ice

Cape Norvegia
Georg von Neumayer (to Germany)
Sanae (to South Africa)
Fimbul Ice Shelf
Maitri (to India)
Novolazarevskaya (to Russian Federation)
Princess Astrid Kyst
Riiser-Larsen Ice Shelf
Kronprinsesse Mårtha Kyst
Børg Massif
Mühlig-Hofmann Mountains
Wohlthat Mountains
Prinsesse Ragnhild Kyst
Prins Harald Kyst
Lützow Holmbukta
Riiser-Larsen Peninsula
Lyddan Island
Maudheimvidda
Fimbutheimen
Dronning Maud Land
Asuka (to Japan)
Sør Rondane Mountains
Syowa (to Japan)
Molodezhnaya (to Russian Federation)
Casey Bay
Amundsen Bay
Cape Batterbee
Brunt Ice Shelf
Belgica Mountains
Thyer Glacier
Kronprins Olav Kyst
Nye Mountains
Napier Mountains
Halley (to UK)
Caird Coast
Thorshavnheiane
Mount Victor 2588m
Enderby Land
Mount Elkins 2300m
Coats Land
Luitpold Coast
Belgrano II (to Argentina)
Theron Mountains
Slessor Glacier
Dismal Mountains
Edward VIII Bay
Law Promontory
Kemp Land
Hansen Mountains
Mawson (to Australia)
Filchner Ice Shelf
Recovery Glacier
Gustav Bull Mountains
Mac. Robertson Land
Mount Menzies 3355m
Lars Christensen Coast
Cape Darnley
kner land
Pensacola Mountains
Support Force Glacier
Prince Charles Mountains
Lambert Glacier
Amery Ice Shelf
Gillock Island
Mackenzie Bay
Foundation Ice Stream
Princess Elizabeth Land
Ingrid Christensen Coast
Zhongshan (to China)
Prydz Bay
Davis (to Australia)
West Ice Shelf
King Leopold and Queen Astrid Land
Mikhaylov Island
ANTARCTICA
Amundsen-Scott (to US)
South Pole
Greater Antarctica
Philippi Glacier
Davis Sea
Whitmore Mountains
Mount Seelig
Wilhelm II Land
Mirny (to Russian Federation)
er tica
Horlick Mountains
Transantarctic Mountains
Vostok (to Russian Federation)
+ South Geomagnetic Pole
Northcliffe Glacier
Masson Island
Gould Coast
Queen Maud Mountains
Beardmore Glacier
Mount Kirkpatrick 4528m
Denman Glacier
Mill Island
Land
Siple Coast
Ross Ice Shelf
Mount Markham 4351m
Nimrod Glacier
Byrd Glacier
Mount McClintock 3492m
Scott Glacier
Bowman Island
Knox Coast
Wilkes Land
Rockefeller Plateau
Shirase Coast
Roosevelt Island
Shackleton Coast
Hillary Coast
Victoria Land
Vincennes Bay
unders Coast
Edward VII Peninsula
Salzburger Bay
Mount Lister 4026m
Scott Base (to NZ)
McMurdo Base (to US)
Ross Island
Mount Erebus 3794m
Scott Coast
Casey (to Australia)
Budd Coast
Cape Poinsett
Ross Sea
Drygalski Ice Tongue
Sabrina Coast
Cape Waldron
Coulman Island
Terre Adélie
Banzare Coast
Dalton Iceberg Tongue
Borchgrevink Coast
George V Land
Wilkes Coast
Cape Goodenough
Oates Land
Cape Adare
Mount Minto 4163m
Rennick Glacier
George V Coast
Adélie Coast
Cape Keltie
Dumont d'Urville (to France)
Porpoise Bay
Leningradskaya
Ninnis Glacier
Mertz Glacier
Cape Carr
Cape Cheetham
Cape Freshfield
Cape Hudson
Dumont d'Urville Sea
Dibble Iceberg Tongue
Antarctic Circle
Limit of summer pack ice
Ballen“y Islands
Scott Island

MAP KEY

ELEVATION

ice cap
ice shelf
exposed land

SCALE 1:14,750,000
(projection: Lambert Azimuthal Equal Area)

Km
0 25 50 100 150 200 250 300 350 400 450 500
0 25 50 100 150 200 250 300 400 500
Miles

Immense, flat-topped icebergs are formed when blocks of ice break away from the main ice sheet. Though the exposed area is enormous, the volume of ice concealed beneath the water may be many times greater.

THE ARCTIC

THREE CONTINENTS, ASIA, NORTH AMERICA, AND EUROPE, reach into the Arctic Circle at their northernmost limits, almost entirely encircling the Arctic Ocean. Despite the region's extraordinarily harsh climate, it has been inhabited for thousands of years by peoples such as the European Lapps, the Russian Nenet, and the North American Inuit, who draw a living from fishing, herding, and hunting. More recently, particularly in the Russian Arctic, opportunities to exploit oil and other mineral reserves have encouraged immigration. Pollution of the Arctic's unique ecology and damage to the traditional lifestyles of many native peoples have been the unfortunate results of this activity, and international cooperation is needed to safeguard the future of the region.

MAP KEY

POPULATION

- ▪ above 5 million
- ▪ 1 million to 5 million
- ◉ 500,000 to 1 million
- ◎ 100,000 to 500,000
- ⊕ 50,000 to 100,000
- ⊙ 10,000 to 50,000
- ○ below 10,000

SEA DEPTH

- sea level
- 250m / 820ft
- 500m / 1640ft
- 1000m / 3281ft
- 2000m / 6562ft
- 3000m / 9843ft

SCALE 1:21,000,000
(projection: Lambert Azimuthal Equal Area)

Km 100 200 300 400 500 600
Miles 100 200 300 400 500 600

Windblown snow etches deep patterns in the ice sheet. Known as sastrugi, the patterns align with the direction of the wind.

RESOURCES

LARGE QUANTITIES of coal, oil, and natural gas are to be found in the basins of the Arctic Ocean and in northern Canada, Alaska, and the Russian Federation. The cost and difficulty of extraction and, more recently, awareness of damage to the environment have limited exploitation to coastal regions. The unfrozen waters have stocks of fish, including cod, flounder, and haddock. Quotas have now been put in place to restrict the number of fish caught annually. Reindeer are herded in large numbers by many of the native Arctic peoples. Most grain and vegetables are imported from elsewhere.

Bering Sea

ARCTIC OCEAN

Inuvik
Tiksi
Noril'sk
Qaanaaq
Reykjavík
Murmansk

NORTH AMERICA
ASIA
EUROPE
ATLANTIC OCEAN

Icebreakers are ships with specially strengthened hulls designed to break a path through the ice. They are used to keep important routes open during the winter, when falling temperatures cause much of the Arctic Ocean to freeze over.

Resources

- ♠ coal
- ⌐ fish
- ♣ mining
- ♠ oil & gas
- ☢ radioactive contamination
- ● major towns
- ⊕ major ports

THE LANDSCAPE

THE ARCTIC OCEAN comprises two large ocean basins divided by three submarine ridges, the greatest of which, the Lomonosov Ridge, is a huge underwater mountain range that has an average height of more than 10,000 ft (3,000 m). The lands that encircle the Arctic Ocean are underlain by great shield areas of ancient rocks, which were heavily glaciated during the last Ice Age.

Icebergs are constantly broken up and reshaped by wind and the oceans. This flat-topped iceberg has been undercut, leaving a craggy ice cliff.

A complex and ancient mountain system, extending from the Queen Elizabeth Islands to eastern Greenland, was formed more than 245 million years ago.

The Canadian Shield underlies almost all of the Canadian Arctic. A very stable plateau of ancient rock, it is now covered by glacial lakes and sediment, that supports tundra vegetation.

The Arctic Ocean is the world's smallest ocean, with a total area of 5,440,000 sq miles (15,100,000 sq km).

At a latitude of more than 75° N, the Arctic Ocean is almost permanently covered with pack ice, though high winds and the movement of the seas can cause the ice to crack and break up.

In the more southerly reaches of the Arctic, like Siberia, much of the land is covered by permafrost. In the summer, higher temperatures warm the frozen ground, causing a number of typical phenomena. These include solifluction, the fast downhill movement of topsoil layers; freeze/thaw activity, which patterns the ground into regular polygonal shapes; and the formation of large domes with a frozen ice core, known as pingos.

Lomonosov Ridge

Lomonosov Ridge

Arctic ice shelf

Much of Greenland is covered by a massive ice sheet more than 650,000 sq miles (1,683,400 sq km) in extent. The weight of the ice has depressed the central land area to form a basin lying more than 1,000 ft (300 m) below sea level. Only at the edges of the island is bare rock visible.

Iceland has five major glaciers, sustained by heavy snowfall. Parts of the ice cap cover active volcanoes, such as Bárdharbunga, which periodically erupt causing the melted ice to form a great lake at the glacier margins.

Crevasses occur at the edge of the ice sheet

Ice sheet

Iceberg

Seawater melts the edge of the ice sheet

At the boundary of the Arctic ice shelves, seawater flows under the ice, causing melting and forming crevasses on the surface. This eventually weakens blocks of ice, which break away as icebergs. This process is known as calving.

CANADA
NORTH AMERICA
Great Bear Lake
Great Slave Lake
Coppermine
Bathurst Inlet
Cambridge Bay
King William Island
Booth Peninsula
Churchill
Southampton Island
Hudson Bay
Coats Island
Repulse Bay
Melville Peninsula
Mansel Island
Foxe Basin
Prince Charles Island
Ivujivik
Inukjuak
Hudson Strait
Lake Harbour
Baffin Island
Ungava Bay
Cape Chidley
Davis Strait
Maniitsoq
Labrador Sea
NUUK
Nain
Paamiut
Ivittuut
Labrador Basin
Qaqortoq
Narsaq
Nanortalik
Uummannarsuaq Eirik Ridge
ATLANTIC

V   W   X   Y

ATLANTIC OCEAN

INDIAN OCEAN

The sun sets over the Antarctic Peninsula for more than six months during the winter. However, there are more hours of sunshine during the brief Antarctic summer than most equatorial countries receive in a whole year.

180

Antarctic Circle

Limit of summer pack ice

Cape Norvegia

Georg von Neumayer (to Germany)

Sanae (to South Africa)
Fimbul Ice Shelf
Maitri (to India)
Novolazarevskaya (to Russian Federation)

Mühlig-Hofmann Mountains

Prinsesse Astrid Kyst

Wohlthat Mountains

Prinsesse Ragnhild Kyst

Prins Harald Kyst

Riiser-Larsen Peninsula

Lützow-Holmbukta

Syowa (to Japan)

Molodezhnaya (to Russian Federation)

Casey Bay

Amundsen Bay

Cape Batterbee

Kronprinsesse Martha Kyst

Borg Massif

Dronning Maud Land

Fimbutheimen

Sør Rondane Mountains

Yukia (to Japan)

Belgica Mountains

Thyer Glacier

Kronprins Olav Kyst

Nye Mountains

Napier Mountains

Mount Elkins 2300m

Lyddan Island

Maudheimvidda

Thorshavnheiane

Mount Victor 2588m

Enderby Land

Dismal Mountains

Law Promontory

Edward VIII Gulf

Riiser-Larsen Ice Shelf

Brunt Ice Shelf

Stancomb-Wills Glacier

Kemp Land

Hansen Mountains

Mawson Coast

Mawson (to Australia)

Halley (to UK)
Caird Coast

Coats Land

Luitpold Coast

Belgrano II (to Argentina)

Theron Mountains

Slessor Glacier

Filchner Ice Shelf

Recovery Glacier

Mac. Robertson Land

Mount Menzies 3355m

Prince Charles Mountains

Gustav Bull Mountains

Lars Christensen Coast

Cape Darnley

Berkner Land

Pensacola Mountains

Support Force Glacier

Foundation Ice Stream

Lambert Glacier

Amery Ice Shelf

Gillock Island

Ingrid Christensen Coast

Mackenzie Bay

Princess Elizabeth Land

Zhongshan (to China)

Prydz Bay

Davis (to Australia)

A N T A R C T I C A

Transantarctic Mountains

South Pole

Amundsen-Scott (to US)

Greater

Antarctica

Wilhelm II Land

West Ice Shelf

King Leopold and Queen Astrid Land

Mikhaylov Island

Philippi Glacier

Davis Sea

Whitmore Mountains
Mount Seelig

Horlick Mountains

Wisconsin Range

Queen Maud Mountains

Beardmore Glacier

Gould Coast

Dufek Coast

Mount Kirkpatrick 4528m

Mount Markham 4351m

Nimrod Glacier

Vostok (to Russian Federation)

South Geomagnetic Pole

Mirny (to Russian Federation)

Queen Mary Coast

Northcliffe Glacier

Denman Glacier

Masson Island

Shackleton Ice Shelf

Mill Island

Bowman Island

Land

Siple Coast

Shackleton Coast

Byrd Glacier

Mount McClintock 3492m

Hillary Coast

Wilkes Land

Vincennes Bay

Rockefeller Plateau

Shirase Coast

Ross Ice Shelf

Roosevelt Island

Saunders Coast

Edward VII Peninsula

Sulzberger Bay

Mount Lister 4025m

Scott Base (to NZ)

Ross Island

McMurdo Base (to US)

Mount Erebus 3794m

Scott Coast

Victoria Land

Budd Coast

Casey (to Australia)

Cape Poinsett

Cape Waldron

Drygalski Ice Tongue

Sabrina Coast

Dalton Iceberg Tongue

Ross Sea

Coulman Island

Borchgrevink Coast

Terre Adélie

Banzare Coast

Cape Goodenough

Porpoise Bay

Limit of summer pack ice

Cape Adare

Mount Minto 4163m

Oates Land

Rennick Glacier

George V Land

George V Coast

Ninnis Glacier

Mertz Glacier

Wilkes Coast

Cape Keltie

Dumont d'Urville (to France)

Adélie Coast

Dibble Iceberg Tongue

Cape Cheetham

Leningradskaya

Cape Freshfield

Cape Hudson

Cape Carey

Dumont d'Urville Sea

Ballenek Islands

Scott Island

Antarctic Circle

Limit of summer pack ice

MAP KEY

ELEVATION

ice cap

ice shelf

exposed land

SCALE 1:14,750,000
(projection: Lambert Azimuthal Equal Area)

Km
0 25 50 100 150 200 250 300 350 400 450 500

Miles
0 25 50   100   150   200   250   300   350   400   450   500

Immense, flat-topped icebergs are formed when blocks of ice break away from the main ice sheet. Though the exposed area is enormous, the volume of ice concealed beneath the water may be many times greater.

The aurora borealis, or northern lights are colored bands of light that appear in northern latitudes. Light is emitted when dust particles from the Sun react with gases in the Earth's atmosphere.

N O P Q R S T U V W X Y

Map labels

Bering Sea
Aleutian Basin
Komandorskaya Basin
Karaginskiy Zaliv
Poluostrov Kamchatka
Sea of Okhotsk
Shirshov Ridge
Mys Olyutorskiy
Mys Navarin
Pakhachi
Zaliv Shelikhova
Mys Tolstoy
Magadan
Okhotsk

Bristol Bay
Alaska Peninsula
Kodiak Island
Gulf of Alaska
Nunivak Island
Saint Matthew Island
Anadyrskiy Zaliv
Mys Olyutorskiy
Anadyr

Cook Inlet
Anchorage
Norton Sound
Saint Lawrence Island
Provideniya Zaliv
Anadyr
Manily

UNITED STATES OF AMERICA
ALASKA
Nome
Cape Prince of Wales
Seward Peninsula
Bering Strait
Chukotskiy Poluostrov
Uelen
Arctic Circle

Limit of winter pack ice
198

Kotzebue Sound
Vankarem

Inuvik
Tuktoyaktuk
Cape Bathurst
Prudhoe Bay
Barrow
Point Hope
Pevek
Chukchi Sea
Proliv Longa
Ostrov Vrangelya
Ambarchik
Kolyma
East Siberian Sea

Limit of summer pack ice
Limit of permanent ice cap

Beaufort Sea
Amundsen Gulf
Banks Island
Northwind Plain
Chukchi Plain
Chukchi Plateau
Canada Plain
Canada Basin

RUSSIAN FEDERATION
Proliv Dmitriya Lapteva
Ostrov Novaya Sibir'
Buorkhaya Guba
Tiksi
Olenek
Laptev Sea
Ust'-Olenek

Victoria Island
McClure Strait
Prince Patrick Island
Melville Island
Mackenzie King Island
Prince Gustaf Adolf Sea
Ellef Ringnes Island
Axel Heiberg Island

ARCTIC OCEAN
Wrangel Plain
Mendeleyev Ridge
Makarov Basin
Alpha Cordillera
Novosibirskiye Ostrova

Khatangskiy Zaliv
Ozero Taymyr
Khatanga
Poluostrov Taymyr

Queen Elizabeth Islands
North Geomagnetic Pole
North Pole
Lomonosov Ridge
Fram Basin
Nansen Cordillera
Nansen Basin
Ostrov Bol'shevik
Ostrov Komsomolets
Severnaya Zemlya
Ostrov Oktyabr'skoy Revolyutsii
Noril'sk

Devon Island
Lancaster Sound
Somerset Island
Resolute
Ellesmere Island
Nares Strait
Cape Columbia
Alert
Knud Rasmussen Land
Kap Morris Jesup
Lincoln Sea
Barents Plain
Franz Josef Land
Novaya Zemlya
Dikson
Yeniseyskiy Zaliv
Yenisey
Kara Sea
Ostrov Belyy
Gydanskiy Poluostrov

Baffin Basin
Innaanganeq
Qaanaaq
Savissivik
Qimusseriarsuaq

Wandel Sea
Independence Fjord
Nord
Svyataya Anna Trough
East Novaya Zemlya Trough
Poluostrov Yamal
Baydaratskaya Guba
Vorkuta

Baffin Bay
Kullorsuaq
Upernavik
SVALBARD (to Norway)
Spitsbergen
Longyearbyen
Barents Sea
Bjørnøya
Ostrov Kotel'nyy
Nar'yan-Mar
Pechora

GREENLAND (to Denmark)
Uummannaq
Qeqertarsuaq
Qasigiannguit
Kong Christian X Land
Kong Frederik VIII Land
Peterman Bjerg
Daneborg
Barents Trough
North Cape
Poluostrov Kanin

Greenland Plain
Greenland Sea
Kong Oscar Fjord
Murmansk Rise
Murmansk
Kola Peninsula
Archangel
White Sea
Northern Dvina

Kong Christian IX Land
Mont Forel 3360m
Aputiteeq
Gunnbjørn Fjeld 3700m
Ittoqqortoormiit
Kangikajik
JAN MAYEN (to Norway)
Mohns Ridge
Hammerfest
Fugløy
Tromsø
Lapland
Onezhskoye Ozero

Ammassalik
Kong Christian IX Kyst
Kangerlussuaq
Norwegian Sea
Iceland Plateau
NORWAY
FINLAND
Gulf of Bothnia
Ladozhskoye Ozero

Denmark Strait
Akureyri
Voring Plateau
SWEDEN
Voring Plateau
MOSCOW

Reykjanes Basin
REYKJAVÍK
Arctic Circle
Norwegian Basin
HELSINKI
Gulf of Finland

ICELAND
Faeroe-Iceland Ridge
TALLINN
ESTONIA

Reykjanes Ridge
FAEROE ISLANDS (to Denmark)
Bill Baileys Bank
OSLO
STOCKHOLM
RIGA
LATVIA

Iceland Basin
Faeroe Bank
Shetland Islands
Orkney Islands
Baltic Sea
Norwegian Trench

94
198
125

EUROPE

Polar bears range for great distances over the Arctic pack ice in search of food. They are formidable hunters that live mainly on seals. In December and January, mother bears give birth to their cubs in dens dug deep beneath the snow.

THE TIME ZONES

The numbers at the top of the map indicate the number of hours each time zone is ahead or behind Greenwich Mean Time (GMT). The clocks and 24-hour times given at the bottom of the map show the time in each time zone when it is 12:00 hours noon GMT.

COUNTRIES OF THE WORLD

THERE ARE CURRENTLY 192 independent countries in the world – more than at any previous time – and 59 dependencies. Antarctica is the only land area on Earth that is not officially part of, and does not belong to, any single country.

In 1950, the world comprised 82 countries. In the decades following, many more states came into being as they achieved independence from their former colonial rulers. Most recently, the breakup of the former Soviet Union in 1991, and the former Yugoslavia in 1992, swelled the ranks of independent states.

COUNTRY FACTFILE KEY

Formation Date of independence / date current borders were established
Population Total population / population density – based on total land area / percentage of urban-based population
Languages An asterisk (*) denotes the official language(s)
Calorie consumption Average number of calories consumed daily per person

---

AFGHANISTAN
Central Asia

Official name Islamic State of Afghanistan
Formation 1919 / 1919
Capital Kabul
Population 20.1 million / 80 people per sq mile (31 people per sq km) / 20%
Total area 251,770 sq miles (652,090 sq km)
Languages Persian*, Pashtu*, Dari, Uzbek, Turkmen
Religions Sunni Muslim 84%, Shi'a Muslim 15%, other 1%
Ethnic mix Pashtun 38%, Tajik 25%, Hazara 19%, Uzbek 6%, other 12%
Government Mujahideen coalition
Currency Afghani = 100 puls
Literacy rate 29%
Calorie consumption 1,523 kilocalories

ALGERIA
Northern Africa

Official name Democratic and Popular Republic of Algeria
Formation 1962 / 1962
Capital Algiers
Population 27.9 million / 31 people per sq mile (12 people per sq km) / 53%
Total area 919,590 sq miles (2,381,740 sq km)
Languages Arabic*, Berber, French
Religions Muslim 99%, Christian & Jewish 1%
Ethnic mix Arab and Berber 99%, European 1%
Government Military regime
Currency Dinar = 100 centimes
Literacy rate 57%
Calorie consumption 2,897 kilocalories

ANGOLA
Southern Africa

Official name Republic of Angola
Formation 1975 / 1975
Capital Luanda
Population 11.1 million / 23 people per sq mile (9 people per sq km) / 30%
Total area 481,551 sq miles (1,246,700 sq km)
Languages Portuguese*, Umbundu, Kimbundu, Kongo
Religions Roman Catholic / Protestant 64%, traditional beliefs 34%, other 2%
Ethnic mix Ovimbundu 37%, Kimbundu 25%, Bakongo 13%, other 25%
Government Multiparty republic
Currency Kwanza = 100 lwei
Literacy rate 42%
Calorie consumption 1,839 kilocalories

ARGENTINA
South America

Official name Republic of Argentina
Formation 1816 / 1925
Capital Buenos Aires
Population 34.6 million / 34 people per sq mile (13 people per sq km) / 87%
Total area 1,068,296 sq miles (2,766,890 sq km)
Languages Spanish*, Italian, English, German, French, Amerindian languages
Religions Roman Catholic 90%, Jewish 2%, other 8%
Ethnic mix White 85%, other (including *mestizo* and Amerindian) 15%
Government Multiparty republic
Currency Peso = 100 centavos
Literacy rate 95%
Calorie consumption 2,880 kilocalories

ARMENIA
Southwestern Asia

Official name Republic of Armenia
Formation 1991 / 1991
Capital Yerevan
Population 3.6 million / 314 people per sq mile (121 people per sq km) / 68%
Total area 11,505 sq miles (29,000 sq km)
Languages Armenian*, Azerbaijani, Russian, Kurdish
Religions Armenian Apostolic 90%, other Christian and Muslim 10%
Ethnic mix Armenian 93%, Azerbaijani 3%, Russian, Kurdish 4%
Government Multiparty republic
Currency Dram = 100 louma
Literacy rate 99%
Calorie consumption NOT AVAILABLE

AUSTRIA
Central Europe

Official name Republic of Austria
Formation 1918 / 1945
Capital Vienna
Population 8 million / 251 people per sq mile (97 people per sq km) / 55%
Total area 32,375 sq miles (83,850 sq km)
Languages German*, Croatian, Slovene, Hungarian (Magyar)
Religions Roman Catholic 85%, Protestant 6%, other 9%
Ethnic mix German 99%, other (including Hungarian, Slovene, Croat) 1%
Government Multiparty republic
Currency Schilling = 100 groschen
Literacy rate 99%
Calorie consumption 3,497 kilocalories

AZERBAIJAN
Southwestern Asia

Official name Azerbaijani Republic
Formation 1991 / 1991
Capital Baku
Population 7.6 million / 228 people per sq mile (88 people per sq km) / 55%
Total area 33,436 sq miles (86,600 sq km)
Languages Azerbaijani*, Russian, Armenian
Religions Muslim 83%, Armenian Apostolic, Russian Orthodox 17%
Ethnic mix Azerbaijani 83%, Russian 6%, Armenian 6%, other 5%
Government Multiparty republic
Currency Manat = 100 gopik
Literacy rate 97%
Calorie consumption NOT AVAILABLE

ALBANIA
Southeastern Europe

Official name Republic of Albania
Formation 1912 / 1913
Capital Tirana
Population 3.4 million / 321 people per sq mile (124 people per sq km) / 36%
Total area 11,100 sq miles (28,750 sq km)
Languages Albanian*, Greek, Macedonian
Religions Muslim 70%, Greek Orthodox 20%, Roman Catholic 10%
Ethnic mix Albanian 96%, Greek 2%, other (including Macedonian) 2%
Government Multiparty republic
Currency Lek = 100 qindars
Literacy rate 72%
Calorie consumption 2,605 kilocalories

ANDORRA
Southwestern Europe

Official name Principality of Andorra
Formation 1278 / 1278
Capital Andorra la Vella
Population 64,000 / 357 people per sq mile (138 people per sq km) / 94%
Total area 181 sq miles (468 sq km)
Languages Catalan*, Spanish, French, Portuguese
Religions Roman Catholic 86%, other 14%
Ethnic mix Catalan 61%, Spanish Castilian 30%, other 9%
Government Parliamentary democracy
Currency French franc, Spanish peseta
Literacy rate 100%
Calorie consumption 3,708 kilocalories

ANTIGUA & BARBUDA
West Indies

Official name Antigua and Barbuda
Formation 1981 / 1981
Capital St. John's
Population 65,000 / 384 people per sq mile (148 people per sq km) / 36%
Total area 170 sq miles (440 sq km)
Languages English*, English Creole
Religions Protestant 87%, Roman Catholic 10%, other 3%
Ethnic mix Black 98%, other 2%
Government Parliamentary democracy
Currency E. Caribbean $ = 100 cents
Literacy rate 96%
Calorie consumption 2,458 kilocalories

AUSTRALIA
Australasia & Oceania

Official name Commonwealth of Australia
Formation 1901 / 1901
Capital Canberra
Population 17.8 million / 5 people per sq mile (2 people per sq km) / 85%
Total area 2,967,893 sq miles (7,686,850 sq km)
Languages English*, Greek, Italian, Malay, Vietnamese, Aboriginal
Religions Protestant 60%, Roman Catholic 26%, other 14%
Ethnic mix Caucasian 95%, Asian 4%, Aboriginal and other 1%
Government Parliamentary democracy
Currency Australian $ = 100 cents
Literacy rate 99%
Calorie consumption 3,179 kilocalories

BAHAMAS
West Indies

Official name Commonwealth of the Bahamas
Formation 1973 / 1973
Capital Nassau
Population 300,000 / 78 people per sq mile (30 people per sq km) / 85%
Total area 5,359 sq miles (13,880 sq km)
Languages English*, English Creole
Religions Protestant 76%, Roman Catholic 19%, other 5%
Ethnic mix Black 85%, White 15%
Government Parliamentary democracy
Currency Bahamian $ = 100 cents
Literacy rate 98%
Calorie consumption 2,624 kilocalories

Bahrain
Southwestern Asia

Official name State of Bahrain
Formation 1971 / 1971
Capital Manama
Population 600,000 / 2,286 people per sq mile (882 people per sq km) / 89%
Total area 263 sq miles (680 sq km)
Languages Arabic*, English, Urdu
Religions Muslim (Shi'a majority) 85%, Christian 7%, other 8%
Ethnic mix Arab 73%, South Asian 14%, Persian 8%, other 5%
Government Absolute monarchy (emirate)
Currency Dinar = 1,000 fils
Literacy rate 84%
Calorie consumption NOT AVAILABLE

Bangladesh
Southern Asia

Official name People's Republic of Bangladesh
Formation 1971 / 1971
Capital Dhaka
Population 120.4 million / 2,330 people per sq mile (899 people per sq km) / 17%
Total area 55,598 sq miles (143,998 sq km)
Languages Bengali*, Urdu, Chakma, Marma, Garo, Khasi
Religions Muslim 83%, Hindu 16%, other 1%
Ethnic mix Bengali 98%, other 2%
Government Multiparty republic
Currency Taka = 100 paisa
Literacy rate 35%
Calorie consumption 2,019 kilocalories

Barbados
West Indies

Official name Barbados
Formation 1966 / 1966
Capital Bridgetown
Population 300,000 / 1,809 people per sq mile (698 people per sq km) / 46%
Total area 166 sq miles (430 sq km)
Languages English*, English Creole
Religions Protestant 94%, Roman Catholic 5%, other 1%
Ethnic mix Black 80%, mixed 15%, White 4%, other 1%
Government Parliamentary democracy
Currency Barbados $ = 100 cents
Literacy rate 99%
Calorie consumption 3,207 kilocalories

Belarus
Eastern Europe

Official name Republic of Belarus
Formation 1991 / 1991
Capital Minsk
Population 10.1 million / 127 people per sq mile (49 people per sq km) / 68%
Total area 80,154 sq miles (207,600 sq km)
Languages Belarus*, Russian
Religions Russian Orthodox 60%, Roman Catholic 8%, other 32%
Ethnic mix Belarus 78%, Russian 13%, Polish 4%, other 5%
Government Multiparty republic
Currency Rouble = 100 kopeks
Literacy rate 98%
Calorie consumption NOT AVAILABLE

Belgium
Northwestern Europe

Official name Kingdom of Belgium
Formation 1830 / 1830
Capital Brussels
Population 10.1 million / 798 people per sq mile (308 people per sq km) / 97%
Total area 12,780 sq miles (33,100 sq km)
Languages French*, Dutch*, German, Flemish
Religions Roman Catholic 75%, other 25%
Ethnic mix Flemish 58%, Walloon 32%, other European 6%, other 4%
Government Constitutional monarchy
Currency Franc = 100 centimes
Literacy rate 99%
Calorie consumption: 3,681 kilocalories

Belize
Central America

Official name Belize
Formation 1981 / 1981
Capital Belmopan
Population 200,000 /23 people per sq mile (9 people per sq km) / 47%
Total area 8,865 sq miles (22,960 sq km)
Languages English*, English Creole, Spanish
Religions Christian 87%, other 13%
Ethnic mix *mestizo* 44%, Creole 30%, Indian 11%, Garifuna 8%, other 7%
Government Parliamentary democracy
Currency Belizean $ =100 cents
Literacy rate 95%
Calorie consumption 2,662 kilocalories

Benin
Western Africa

Official name Republic of Benin
Formation 1960 / 1960
Capital Porto-Novo
Population 5.4 million / 127 people per sq mile (49 people per sq km) / 30%
Total area 43,480 sq miles (112,620 sq km)
Languages French*, Fon, Adja, Yoruba
Religions Traditional beliefs 70%, Muslim 15%, Christian 15%
Ethnic mix Fon 39%, Yoruba 12%, Adja 10%, other 39%
Government Multiparty republic
Currency CFA franc = 100 centimes
Literacy rate 23%
Calorie consumption 2,532 kilocalories

Bhutan
Southeastern Asia

Official name Kingdom of Bhutan
Formation 1949 / 1865
Capital Thimphu
Population 1.6 million / 88 people per sq mile (34 people per sq km) / 6%
Total area 18,147 sq miles (47,000 sq km)
Languages Dzongkha*, Nepali, Assamese
Religions Mahayana Buddhist 70%, Hindu 24%, Muslim 5%, other 1%
Ethnic mix Bhutia 61%, Gurung 15%, Assamese 13%, other 11%
Government Constitutional monarchy
Currency Ngultrum = 100 chetrum
Literacy rate 38%
Calorie consumption 2,553 kilocalories

Bolivia
South America

Official name Republic of Bolivia
Formation 1825 / 1938
Capitals La Paz / Sucre
Population 7.4 million / 18 people per sq mile (7 people per sq km) / 58%
Total area 424,162 sq miles (1,098,580 sq km)
Languages Spanish*, Quechua*, Aymará*
Religions Roman Catholic 95%, other 5%
Ethnic mix Indian 55%, *mestizo* 27%, White 10%, other 8%
Government Multiparty republic
Currency Boliviano = 100 centavos
Literacy rate 83%
Calorie consumption 2,094 kilocalories

Bosnia & Herzegovina
Southeastern Europe

Official name Republic of Bosnia and Herzegovina
Formation 1992 / 1992
Capital Sarajevo
Population 3.5 million / 176 people per sq mile (68 people per sq km) / 36%
Total area 19,741 sq miles (51,130 sq km)
Languages Serbian*, Croatian*
Religions Muslim 40%, Orthodox Catholic 31%, other 29%
Ethnic mix Bosnian 44%, Serb 31%, Croat 17%, other 8%
Government Multiparty republic
Currency Dinar = 100 para
Literacy rate 93%
Calorie consumption NOT AVAILABLE

Botswana
Southern Africa

Official name Republic of Botswana
Formation 1966 / 1966
Capital Gaborone
Population 1.5 million / 8 people per sq mile (3 people per sq km) / 25%
Total area 224,600 sq miles (581,730 sq km)
Languages English*, Tswana, Shona, San
Religions Traditional beliefs 50%, Christian 50%
Ethnic mix Tswana 75%, Shona 12%, San 3%, other 10%
Government Multiparty republic
Currency Pula = 100 thebe
Literacy rate 67%
Calorie consumption 2,266 kilocalories

Brazil
South America

Official name Federative Republic of Brazil
Formation 1822 / 1929
Capital Brasília
Population 161.8 million / 49 people per sq mile (19 people per sq km) / 76%
Total area 3,286,472 sq miles (8,511,970 sq km)
Languages Portuguese*, German, Italian
Religions Roman Catholic 90%, other 10%
Ethnic mix White (Portuguese, Italian, German, Japanese) 55%, mixed 38%, Black 6%, other 1%
Government Multiparty republic
Currency Real = 100 centavos
Literacy rate 80%
Calorie consumption 2,824 kilocalories

Brunei
Southeastern Asia

Official name Sultanate of Brunei
Formation 1984 / 1984
Capital Bandar Seri Begawan
Population 300,000 / 148 people per sq mile (57 people per sq km) / 58%
Total area 2,228 sq miles (5,770 sq km)
Languages Malay*, English, Chinese
Religions Muslim 63%, Buddhist 14%, Christian 10%, other 13%
Ethnic mix Malay 69%, Chinese 18%, other 13%
Government Absolute monarchy
Currency Brunei $ = 100 cents
Literacy rate 89%
Calorie consumption 2,745 kilocalories

Bulgaria
Southeastern Europe

Official name Republic of Bulgaria
Formation 1908 / 1923
Capital Sofia
Population 8.8 million / 207 people per sq mile (80 people per sq km) / 69%
Total area 42,822 sq miles (110,910 sq km)
Languages Bulgarian*, Turkish, Macedonian, Romany, Armenian
Religions Christian 85%, Muslim 13%, Jewish 1%, other 1%
Ethnic mix Bulgarian 85%, Turkish 9%, Macedonian 3%, Gypsy 3%
Government Multiparty republic
Currency Lev = 100 stoninki
Literacy rate 98%
Calorie consumption 2,831 kilocalories

Burkina
Western Africa

Official name Burkina Faso
Formation 1960 / 1960
Capital Ouagadougou
Population 10.3 million / 98 people per sq mile (38 people per sq km) / 22%
Total area 105,870 sq miles (274,200 sq km)
Languages French*, Mossi, Fulani
Religions Traditional beliefs 65%, Muslim 25%, Christian 10%
Ethnic mix Mossi 45%, Mande 10%, Fulani 10%, other 35%
Government Multiparty republic
Currency CFA franc = 100 centimes
Literacy rate 18%
Calorie consumption 2,387 kilocalories

Burundi
Central Africa

Official name Republic of Burundi
Formation 1962 / 1962
Capital Bujumbura
Population 6.4 million / 648 people per sq mile (250 people per sq km) / 7%
Total area 10,750 sq miles (27,830 sq km)
Languages Kirundi*, French*, Swahili
Religions Christian 68%, traditional beliefs 32%
Ethnic mix Hutu 85%, Tutsi 13%, Twa pygmy 1%, other 1%
Government Multiparty republic
Currency Franc = 100 centimes
Literacy rate 50%
Calorie consumption 1,941 kilocalories

Cambodia
Southeastern Asia

Official name Kingdom of Cambodia
Formation 1953 / 1953
Capital Phnom Penh
Population 10.3 million / 150 people per sq mile (58 people per sq km) / 19%
Total area 69,000 sq miles (181,040 sq km)
Languages Khmer*, French, Chinese, Vietnamese
Religions Buddhist 88%, Muslim 2%, other 10%
Ethnic mix Khmer 94%, Chinese 4%, other 2%
Government Constitutional monarchy
Currency Riel = 100 sen
Literacy rate 35%
Calorie consumption 2,021 kilocalories

Cameroon
Central Africa

Official name Republic of Cameroon
Formation 1960 / 1960
Capital Yaoundé
Population 12.5 million / 73 people per sq mile (28 people per sq km) / 42%
Total area 183,570 miles (475,440 sq km)
Languages English*, French*, Fang, Bulu, Yaundé, Duala
Religions Traditional beliefs 51%, Christian 33%, Muslim 16%
Ethnic mix Bamileke and Manum 20%, Fang 19%, other 61%
Government Multiparty republic
Currency CFA franc = 100 centimes
Literacy rate 54%
Calorie consumption 1,981 kilocalories

Canada
North America

Official name Canada
Formation 1867 / 1949
Capital Ottawa
Population 29.5 million / 8 people per sq mile (3 people per sq km) / 77%
Total area 3,851,788 sq miles (9,976,140 sq km)
Languages English*, French*, Chinese, Italian, German, Portuguese, Inuit
Religions Roman Catholic 46%, Protestant 30%, other 24%
Ethnic mix British origin 40%, French origin 27%, other 33%
Government Parliamentary democracy
Currency Canadian $ = 100 cents
Literacy rate 96%
Calorie consumption 3,094 kilocalories

Cape Verde
Atlantic Ocean

Official Name Republic of Cape Verde
Formation 1975 / 1975
Capital Praia
Population 400,000 / 257 people per sq mile (99 people per sq km) / 49%
Total area 1,556 sq miles (4,030 sq km)
Languages Portuguese*, Creole
Religions Roman Catholic 98%, Protestant 2%
Ethnic mix Creole (*mestizo*) 71%, Black 28%, White 1%
Government Multiparty republic
Currency Escudo = 100 centavos
Literacy rate 63%
Calorie consumption 2,805 kilocalories

Central African Republic
Central Africa

Official name Central African Republic
Formation 1960 / 1960
Capital Bangui
Population 3.3 million / 13 people per sq mile (5 people per sq km) / 38%
Total area 240,530 sq miles (622,980 sq km)
Languages French*, Sango, Banda, Gbaya
Religions Christian 50%, traditional beliefs 27%, Muslim 15%, other 8%
Ethnic mix Baya 34%, Banda 27%, Mandjia 21%, other 18%
Government Multiparty republic
Currency CFA franc = 100 centimes
Literacy rate 38%
Calorie consumption 1,690 kilocalories

Chad
Central Africa

Official name Republic of Chad
Formation 1960 / 1960
Capital N'Djamena
Population 6.4 million / 19 people per sq mile (5 people per sq km) / 21%
Total area 495,752 sq miles (1,284,000 sq km)
Languages French*, Sara, Maba
Religions Muslim 44%, Christian 33%, traditional beliefs 23%
Ethnic mix Bagirmi, Sara, and Kreish 31%, Sudanic Arab 26%, Teda 7%, other 36%
Government Transitional
Currency CFA franc = 100 centimes
Literacy rate 45%
Calorie consumption 1,989 kilocalories

Chile
South America

Official name Republic of Chile
Formation 1818 / 1929
Capital Santiago
Population 14.3 million / 49 people per sq mile (19 people per sq km) / 84%
Total area 292,258 sq miles (756,950 sq km)
Languages Spanish*, Indian languages
Religions Roman Catholic 89%, Protestant 11%
Ethnic mix White and *mestizo* 92%, Indian 6%, other 2%
Government Multiparty republic
Currency Peso = 100 centavos
Literacy rate 94%
Calorie consumption 2,582 kilocalories

China
Eastern Asia

Official name People's Republic of China
Formation 1949 / 1950
Capital Beijing
Population 1.2 billion / 340 people per sq mile (131 people per sq km) / 28%
Total area 3,628,166 sq miles (9,396,960 sq km)
Languages Mandarin*, Wu, Cantonese, Hsiang, Min, Hakka, Kan
Religions Confucianist 20%, Buddhist 6%, Taoist 2%, other 72%
Ethnic mix Han 93%, Zhaung 1%, other 6%
Government Single-party republic
Currency Yuan = 10 jiao = 100 fen
Literacy rate 78%
Calorie consumption 2,727 kilocalories

Colombia
South America

Official name Republic of Colombia
Formation 1819 / 1922
Capital Bogotá
Population 35.1 million / 88 people per sq mile (34 people per sq km) / 71%
Total area 439,733 sq miles (1,138,910 sq km)
Languages Spanish*, Amerindian languages, English Creole
Religions Roman Catholic 95%, other 5%
Ethnic mix *mestizo* 58%, White 20%, mixed 14%, other 8%
Government Multiparty republic
Currency Peso = 100 centavos
Literacy rate 87%
Calorie consumption 2,677 kilocalories

Comoros
Indian Ocean

Official name Federal Islamic Republic of the Comoros
Formation 1975 / 1975
Capital Moroni
Population 600,000 / 814 people per sq mile (314 people per sq km) / 29%
Total area 861 sq miles (2,230 sq km)
Languages Arabic*, French*, Comoran
Religions Muslim 86%, Roman Catholic 14%
Ethnic mix Comorian 96%, other 4%
Government Islamic republic
Currency Franc = 100 centimes
Literacy rate 48%
Calorie consumption 1,897 kilocalories

Congo
Central Africa

Official name Republic of the Congo
Formation 1960 / 1960
Capital Brazzaville
Population 2.6 million / 21 people per sq km (8 people per sq km) / 56%
Total area 132,040 sq miles (342,000 sq km)
Languages French*, Kongo, Teke, Lingala
Religions Roman Catholic 50%, traditional beliefs 48%, other 2%
Ethnic mix Bakongo 48%, Teke 17%, Mboshi 17%, other 18%
Government Multiparty republic
Currency CFA franc = 100 centimes
Literacy rate 57%
Calorie consumption 2,296 kilocalories

Congo (Democratic Republic of) *see* **Zaire**

Costa Rica
Central America

Official name Republic of Costa Rica
Formation 1821 / 1838
Capital San José
Population 3.4 million / 174 people per sq mile (67 people per sq km) / 48%
Total area 19,730 miles (51,100 sq km)
Languages Spanish*, English Creole, Bribri, Cabecar
Religions Roman Catholic 95%, other 5%
Ethnic mix White / *mestizo* 96%, Black 2%, Amerindian 2%
Government Multiparty republic
Currency Colón = 100 centimos
Literacy rate 93%
Calorie consumption 2,883 kilocalories

Croatia
Southeastern Europe

Official name Republic of Croatia
Formation 1991 / 1991
Capital Zagreb
Population 4.5 million / 207 people per sq mile (80 people per sq km) / 51%
Total area 21,830 sq miles (56,540 sq km)
Languages Croatian*, Serbian, Hungarian (Magyar), Slovenian
Religions Roman Catholic 77%, Eastern Orthodox 11%, Protestant 1%, Muslim 1%, other 10%
Ethnic mix Croat 80%, Serb 12%, Hungarian, Slovenian, other 8%
Government Multiparty republic
Currency Kuna = 100 lipa
Literacy rate 97%
Calorie consumption NOT AVAILABLE

Cuba
West Indies

Official name Republic of Cuba
Formation 1902 / 1898
Capital Havana
Population 10.8 million / 251 people per sq mile (97 people per sq km) / 75%
Total area 42,803 sq miles (110,860 sq km)
Languages Spanish*, English, French
Religions Roman Catholic 85%, other 15%
Ethnic mix White 66%, Afro-European 22%, other 12%
Government Socialist republic
Currency Peso = 100 centavos
Literacy rate 94%
Calorie consumption 2,833 kilocalories

CYPRUS
Southeastern Europe

Official name Republic of Cyprus
Formation 1960 / 1983
Capital Nicosia
Population 700,000 / 197 people per
sq mile (76 people per sq km) / 53%
Total area 3,572 sq miles (9,251 sq km)
Languages Greek*, Turkish, English
Religions Greek Orthodox 77%,
Muslim 18%, other 5%
Ethnic mix Greek 77%, Turkish 18%,
other (mainly British) 5%
Government Multiparty republic
Currency Cypriot £ / Turkish lira
Literacy rate 94%
Calorie consumption 3,779 kilocalories

CZECH REPUBLIC
Central Europe

Official name Czech Republic
Formation 1993 / 1993
Capital Prague
Population 10.3 million / 339 people per
sq mile (131 people per sq km) / 65%
Total area 30,260 sq miles (78,370 sq km)
Languages Czech*, Slovak, Romany,
Hungarian (Magyar)
Religions Roman Catholic 44%, Protestant 6%,
other Christian 12%, other 38%
Ethnic mix Czech 85%, Moravian 13%, other 2%
Government Multiparty republic
Currency Koruna = 100 halura
Literacy rate 99%
Calorie consumption 3,156 kilocalories

DENMARK
Northern Europe

Official name Kingdom of Denmark
Formation AD 960 / 1953
Capital Copenhagen
Population 5.2 million / 319 people per
sq mile (123 people per sq km) / 85%
Total area 16,629 sq miles (43,069 sq km)
Languages Danish*, Faeroese, Inuit
Religions Evangelical Lutheran 91%
other Christian 9%
Ethnic mix Danish 96%, Faeroese &
Inuit 1%, other 3%
Government Constitutional monarchy
Currency Krone = 100 øre
Literacy rate 100%
Calorie consumption 3,664 kilocalories

DJIBOUTI
East Africa

Official name Republic of Djibouti
Formation 1977 / 1977
Capital Djibouti
Population 600,000 / 67 people per
sq mile (26 people per sq km) / 81%
Total area 8,958 sq miles
(23,200 sq km)
Languages Arabic*, French*, Somali, Afar
Religions Christian 87%, other 13%
Ethnic mix Issa 35%, Afar 20%, Gadaboursis
and Isaaks 28%, other 17%
Government Single-party republic
Currency Franc = 100 centimes
Literacy rate 43%
Calorie consumption 2,338 kilocalories

DOMINICA
West Indies

Official name Commonwealth
of Dominica
Formation 1978 / 1978
Capital Roseau
Population 71,000 / 246 people per
sq mile (95 people per sq km) / 57%
Total area 290 sq miles (750 sq km)
Languages English*, French Creole, Carib, Cocoy
Religions Roman Catholic 77%,
Protestant 15%, other 8%
Ethnic mix Black 98%, Amerindian 2%
Government Multiparty republic
Currency E. Caribbean $ = 100 cents
Literacy rate 97%
Calorie consumption 2,778 kilocalories

DOMINICAN REPUBLIC
West Indies

Official name Dominican Republic
Formation 1865 / 1865
Capital Santo Domingo
Population 7.8 million / 417 people per
sq mile (161 people per sq km) / 62%
Total area 18,815 sq miles
(48,730 sq km)
Languages Spanish*, French Creole
Religions Roman Catholic 95%, other 5%
Ethnic mix Afro-European 73%,
White 16%, Black 11%
Government Multiparty republic
Currency Peso = 100 centavos
Literacy rate 83%
Calorie consumption 2,286 kilocalories

ECUADOR
South America

Official name Republic of Ecuador
Formation 1830 / 1942
Capital Quito
Population 11.5 million / 109 people per
sq mile (42 people per sq km) / 56%
Total area 109,483 sq miles (283,560 sq km)
Languages Spanish*, Quechua, other
Amerindian languages
Religions Roman Catholic 95%, other 5%
Ethnic mix *mestizo* 55%, Amerindian 25%,
Black 10%, White 10%
Government Multiparty republic
Currency Sucre = 100 centavos
Literacy rate 87%
Calorie consumption 2,583 kilocalories

EGYPT
Northern Africa

Official name Arab Republic of Egypt
Formation 1936 / 1982
Capital Cairo
Population 62.9 million / 163 people per
sq mile (63 people per sq km) / 44%
Total area 386,660 sq miles (1,001,450 sq km)
Languages Arabic*, French, English, Berber,
Greek, Armenian
Religions Muslim 94%, other 6%
Ethnic mix Eastern Hamitic 90%,
other (including Greek, Armenian) 10%
Government Multiparty republic
Currency Pound = 100 piastres
Literacy rate 48%
Calorie consumption 3,335 kilocalories

EL SALVADOR
Central America

Official name Republic of El Salvador
Formation 1856 / 1838
Capital San Salvador
Population 5.8 million / 726 people per
sq mile (280 people per sq km) / 44%
Total area 8,124 sq miles
(21,040 sq km)
Languages Spanish*, Nahua
Religions Roman Catholic 75%, other 25%
Ethnic mix *mestizo* 89%, Amerindian 10%,
White 1%
Government Multiparty republic
Currency Colón = 100 centavos
Literacy rate 73%
Calorie consumption 2,663 kilocalories

EQUATORIAL GUINEA
Central Africa

Official name Republic of
Equatorial Guinea
Formation 1968 / 1968
Capital Malabo
Population 400,000 / 36 people per
sq mile (14 people per sq km) / 39%
Total area 10,830 sq miles (28,050 sq km)
Languages Spanish*, Fang, Bubi
Religions Christian 89%, other 11%
Ethnic mix Fang 72%, Bubi 14%,
Duala 3%, other 11%
Government Multiparty republic
Currency CFA franc = 100 centimes
Literacy rate 50%
Calorie consumption NOT AVAILABLE

ERITREA
Eastern Africa

Official name State of Eritrea
Formation 1993 / 1993
Capital Asmara
Population 3.5 million / 96 people per
sq mile (37 people per sq km) / 22%
Total area 36,170 sq miles (93,680 sq km)
Languages Tigrinya*, Arabic*, Tigre
Religions Coptic Christian 45%,
Muslim 45%, other 10%
Ethnic mix Nine main ethnic groups
Government Provisional military
government
Currency Ethiopian birr = 100 cents
Literacy rate 20%
Calorie consumption 1,610 kilocalories

ESTONIA
Northeastern Europe

Official name Republic of Estonia
Formation 1991 / 1991
Capital Tallinn
Population 1.6 million / 86 people per
sq mile (37 people per sq km) / 72%
Total area 17,423 sq miles (45,125 sq km)
Languages Estonian*, Russian
Religions Evangelical Lutheran 98%, Eastern
Orthodox, Baptist 2%
Ethnic mix Estonian 62%, Russian 30%,
Ukrainian 3%, other 5%
Government Multiparty republic
Currency Kroon = 100 cents
Literacy rate 99%
Calorie consumption NOT AVAILABLE

ETHIOPIA
Eastern Africa

Official name Federal Democratic Republic
of Ethiopia
Formation 1903 / 1993
Capital Addis Ababa
Population 55.1 million / 130 people per
sq mile (50 people per sq km) / 13%
Total area 435,605 sq miles (1,128,221 sq km)
Languages Amharic*, English, Arabic
Religions Muslim 43%, Christian 37%,
traditional beliefs, other 20%,
Ethnic mix Oromo 40%, Amhara
and Tigrean 32%, other 28%
Government Multiparty republic
Currency Birr = 100 cents
Literacy rate 24%
Calorie consumption 1,610 kilocalories

FIJI
Australasia & Oceania

Official name Sovereign Democratic
Republic of Fiji
Formation 1970 / 1970
Capital Suva
Population 800,000 / 114 people per
sq mile (44 people per sq km) / 40%
Total area 7,054 sq miles (18,270 sq km)
Languages English*, Fijian, Hindu, Urdu
Religions Christian 52%, Hindu 8%,
Muslim 38%, other 2%
Ethnic mix Native Fijian 49%,
Indo-Fijian 46%, other 5%
Government Multiparty republic
Currency Fiji $ = 100 cents
Literacy rate 87%
Calorie consumption 3,089 kilocalories

FINLAND
Northern Europe

Official name Republic of Finland
Formation 1917 / 1917-1920
Capital Helsinki
Population 5.1 million / 44 people per
sq mile (17 people per sq km) / 62%
Total area 130,552 sq miles (338,130 sq km)
Languages Finnish*, Swedish*, Lappish
Religions Evangelical Lutheran 89%,
Greek Orthodox 1%, other 10%
Ethnic mix Finnish 93%, Swedish 6%,
other (including Sami) 1%
Government Multiparty republic
Currency Markka = 100 pennia
Literacy rate 99%
Calorie consumption 3,018 kilocalories

FRANCE
Western Europe

Official name French Republic
Formation 1685 / 1919-1920
Capital Paris
Population 58 million / 272 people per
sq mile (105 people per sq km) / 73%
Total area 212,930 sq miles (551,500 sq km)
Languages French*, Provençal, Breton,
Catalan, Basque
Religions Roman Catholic 90%,
Protestant 2%, Jewish 1%, other 7%
Ethnic mix French 92%, North African 3%,
other 5%
Government Multiparty republic
Currency Franc = 100 centimes
Literacy rate 99%
Calorie consumption 3,633 kilocalories

GABON
Central Africa

Official name Gabonese Republic
Formation 1960 / 1960
Capital Libreville
Population 1.3 million / 13 people per
sq mile (5 people per sq km) / 48%
Total area 103,347 sq miles (267,670 sq km)
Languages French*, Fang, Punu, Sira,
Nzebi, Mpongwe
Religions Roman Catholic, other Christian 96%,
Muslim 2%, other 2%
Ethnic mix Fang 36%, Mpongwe 15%,
Mbete 14%, other 35%
Government Multiparty republic
Currency CFA franc = 100 centimes
Literacy rate 61%
Calorie consumption 2,500 kilocalories

GAMBIA
Western Africa

Official name Republic of the Gambia
Formation 1965 / 1965
Capital Banjul
Population 1.1 million / 286 people per
sq mile (110 people per sq km) / 24%
Total area 4,363 sq miles (11,300 sq km)
Languages English*, Mandinka, Fulani,
Wolof, Diola, Soninke
Religions Muslim 85%, Christian 9%,
traditional beliefs 6%
Ethnic mix Mandinka 41%, Fulani 14%,
Wolof 13%, other 32%
Government Military regime
Currency Dalasi = 100 butut
Literacy rate 64%
Calorie consumption 2,360 kilocalories

GEORGIA
Southwestern Asia

Official name Republic of Georgia
Formation 1991 / 1991
Capital Tbilisi
Population 5.5 million / 206 people per
sq mile (79 people per sq km) / 57%
Total area 26,911 sq miles (69,700 sq km)
Languages Georgian*, Russian
Religions Georgian Orthodox 70%,
Russian Orthodox 10%, other 20%
Ethnic mix Georgian 69%, Armenian 9%,
Russian 6%, other 16%
Government Republic
Currency Coupons
Literacy rate 99%
Calorie consumption NOT AVAILABLE

GERMANY
Northern Europe

Official name Federal Republic of Germany
Formation 1871 / 1990
Capital Berlin
Population 81.6 million / 604 people per
sq mile (33 people per sq km) / 86%
Total area 137,800 sq miles
(356,910 sq km)
Languages German*, Sorbian, Turkish
Religions Protestant 45%, Roman
Catholic 37%, other 18%
Ethnic mix German 92%, other 8%
Government Multiparty republic
Currency Deutsche Mark = 100 pfennigs
Literacy rate 99%
Calorie consumption 3,344 kilocalories

GHANA
Western Africa

Official name Republic of Ghana
Formation 1957 / 1957
Capital Accra
Population 17.5 million / 197 people per
sq mile (76 people per sq km) / 35%
Total area 92,100 sq miles (238,540 sq km)
Languages English*, Akan, Mossi, Ewe
Religions Traditional beliefs 38%,
Muslim 30%, Christian 24%, other 8%
Ethnic mix Akan 52%, Mossi 15%,
Ewe 12%, Ga 8%, other 13%
Government Multiparty republic
Currency Cedi = 100 pesewas
Literacy rate 61%
Calorie consumption 2,199 kilocalories

GREECE
Southeastern Europe

Official name Hellenic Republic
Formation 1830 / 1945-1947
Capital Athens
Population 10.5 million / 207 people per
sq mile (80 people per sq km) / 64%
Total area 50,961 sq miles (131,990 sq km)
Languages Greek*, Turkish, Albanian,
Macedonian
Religions Greek Orthodox 98%,
Muslim 1%, other 1%
Ethnic mix Greek 98%, other 2%
Government Multiparty republic
Currency Drachma = 100 lepta
Literacy rate 95%
Calorie consumption 3,815 kilocalories

GRENADA
West Indies

Official name Grenada
Formation 1974 / 1974
Capital St. George's
Population 92,000 / 705 people per
sq mile (271 people per sq km) / 17%
Total area 131 sq miles (340 sq km)
Languages English*, English Creole
Religions Roman Catholic 68%,
Protestant 32%
Ethnic mix Black 84%, Afro-European 13%,
South Asian 3%
Government Parliamentary democracy
Currency E. Caribbean $ = 100 cents
Literacy rate 98%
Calorie consumption 2,402 kilocalories

GUATEMALA
Central America

Official name Republic of Guatemala
Formation 1838 / 1838
Capital Guatemala City
Population 10.6 million / 255 people per
sq mile (98 people per sq km) / 40%
Total area 42,043 sq miles (108,890 sq km)
Languages Spanish*, Quiché,
Mam, Kekchí
Religions Christian 99%, other 1%
Ethnic mix Amerindian 55%, *ladino*
(European-Amerindian, White) 45%
Government Multiparty republic
Currency Quetzal = 100 centavos
Literacy rate 54%
Calorie consumption 2,255 kilocalories

GUINEA
Western Africa

Official name Republic of Guinea
Formation 1958 / 1958
Capital Conakry
Population 6.7 million / 70 people per
sq mile (27 people per sq km) / 28%
Total area 94,926 sq miles (245,860 sq km)
Languages French*, Fulani, Malinke,
Soussou, Kissi
Religions Muslim 85%, Christian 8%,
traditional beliefs 7%
Ethnic mix Fulani 40%, Malinke 25%,
Susu 12%, other 23%
Government Multiparty republic
Currency Franc = 100 centimes
Literacy rate 33%
Calorie consumption 2,389 kilocalories

GUINEA-BISSAU
Western Africa

Official name Republic of Guinea-Bissau
Formation 1974 / 1974
Capital Bissau
Population 1.1 million / 102 people per
sq mile (39 people per sq km) / 21%
Total area 13,940 sq miles (36,120 sq km)
Languages Portuguese*, Balante, Fulani, Malinke
Religions Traditional beliefs 54%,
Muslim 38%, Christian 8%
Ethnic mix Balante 27%, Fulani 22%,
Malinke 12%, other 39%
Government Multiparty republic
Currency Peso = 100 centavos
Literacy rate 36%
Calorie consumption 2,556 kilocalories

GUYANA
South America

Official name Cooperative Republic of Guyana
Formation 1966 / 1966
Capital Georgetown
Population 800,000 / 10 people per sq
mile (4 people per sq km) / 35%
Total area 83,000 sq miles (214,970 sq km)
Languages English*, English Creole, Hindi,
Tamil, English
Religions Christian 57%, Hindu 33%,
Muslim 9%, other 1%
Ethnic mix South Asian 51%, Black and
mixed 43%, other 6%
Government Multiparty republic
Currency Guyana $ = 100 cents
Literacy rate 98%
Calorie consumption 2,384 kilocalories

HAITI
West Indies

Official name Republic of Haiti
Formation 1804 / 1804
Capital Port-au-Prince
Population 7.2 million / 679 people per
sq mile (261 people per sq km) / 30%
Total area 10,714 sq miles (27,750 sq km)
Languages French*, French Creole*,
Religions Roman Catholic 80%,
Protestant 16%, Voodoo 4%
Ethnic mix Black 95%,
Afro-European 5%
Government Multiparty republic
Currency Gourde = 100 centimes
Literacy rate 35%
Calorie consumption 1,706 kilocalories

HONDURAS
Central America

Official name Republic of Honduras
Formation 1838 / 1838
Capital Tegucigalpa
Population 5.7 million / 133 people per
sq mile (51 people per sq km) / 42%
Total area 43,278 sq miles (112,090 sq km)
Languages Spanish*, English Creole,
Garifuna, Amerindian languages
Religions Roman Catholic 97%, other 3%
Ethnic mix *mestizo* 90%, Amerindian 7%,
Garifuna (Black Carib) 2%, White 1%
Government Multiparty republic
Currency Lempira = 100 centavos
Literacy rate 71%
Calorie consumption 2,305 kilocalories

HUNGARY
Central Europe

Official name Republic of Hungary
Formation 1918 / 1945
Capital Budapest
Population 10.1 million / 282 people per
sq mile (109 people per sq km) / 63%
Total area 35,919 sq miles (93,030 sq km)
Languages Hungarian (Magyar)*, German, Slovak
Religions Roman Catholic 68%,
Protestant 25%, other 7%
Ethnic mix Hungarian (Magyar) 90%,
German 2%, other 8%
Government Multiparty republic
Currency Forint = 100 filler
Literacy rate 99%
Calorie consumption 3,503 kilocalories

ICELAND
Northwestern Europe

Official name Republic of Iceland
Formation 1944 / 1944
Capital Reykjavík
Population 300,000 / 8 people per sq mile (3 people per sq km) / 91%
Total area 39,770 sq miles (103,000 sq km)
Languages Icelandic*, English
Religions Evangelical Lutheran 96%, other Christian 3%, other 1%
Ethnic mix Icelandic (Norwegian-Celtic descent) 98%, other 2%
Government Constitutional republic
Currency Krona = 100 aurar
Literacy rate 100%
Calorie consumption 3,058 kilocalories

INDIA
Southern Asia

Official name Republic of India
Formation 1947 / 1961
Capital New Delhi
Population 935.7 million / 816 people per sq mile (315 people per sq km) / 26%
Total area 1,269,338 sq miles (3,287,590 sq km)
Languages Hindi*, English*, Urdu, Bengali, Marathi, Telugu, Tamil, Bihari
Religions Hindu 83%, Muslim 11%, Christian 2%, Sikh 2%, other 2%
Ethnic mix Indo-Aryan 72%, Dravidian 25%, Mongoloid and other 3%
Government Multiparty republic
Currency Rupee = 100 paisa
Literacy rate 52%
Calorie consumption 2,395 kilocalories

INDONESIA
Southeastern Asia

Official name Republic of Indonesia
Formation 1949 / 1963
Capital Jakarta
Population 197.6 million / 282 people per sq mile (109 people per sq km) / 33%
Total area 735,555 sq miles (1,904,570 sq km)
Languages Bahasa Indonesia*, 250 (est.) languages or dialects
Religions Muslim 87%, Christian 10%, Hindu 2%, Buddhist 1%
Ethnic mix Javanese 45%, Sundanese 14%, Madurese 8%, other 33%
Government Multiparty republic
Currency Rupiah = 100 sen
Literacy rate 82%
Calorie consumption 2,752 kilocalories

IRAN
Southwestern Asia

Official name Islamic Republic of Iran
Formation 1906 / 1906
Capital Tehran
Population 67.3 million / 106 people per sq mile (41 people per sq km) / 57%
Total area 636,293 sq miles (1,648,000 sq km)
Languages Farsi (Persian)*, Azerbaijani, Giaki, Mazanderani, Kurdish, Baluchi, Arabic, Turkmen
Religions Shi'a Muslim 95%, Sunni Muslim 4%, other 1%
Ethnic mix Persian 52%, Azerbaijani 24%, Kurdish 9%, other 15%
Government Islamic Republic
Currency Rial = 100 dinars
Literacy rate 72%
Calorie consumption 2,860 kilocalories

IRAQ
Southwestern Asia

Official name Republic of Iraq
Formation 1932 / 1981
Capital Baghdad
Population 20.4 million / 122 people per sq mile (47 people per sq km) / 73%
Total area 169,235 sq miles (438,320 sq km)
Languages Arabic*, Kurdish, Turkish, Farsi (Persian)
Religions Shi'a Muslim 63%, Sunni Muslim 34%, other 3%
Ethnic mix Arab 79%, Kurdish 16%, Persian 3%, Turkish 2%
Government Single-party republic
Currency Dinar = 1,000 fils
Literacy rate 60%
Calorie consumption 2,121 kilocalories

IRELAND
Northwestern Europe

Official name Republic of Ireland
Formation 1921 / 1922
Capital Dublin
Population 3.6 million / 135 people per sq mile (52 people per sq km) / 57%
Total area 27,155 sq miles (70,280 sq km)
Languages English*, Irish Gaelic*
Religions Roman Catholic 93%, Protestant 5%, other 2%
Ethnic mix Irish 95%, other 5%
Government Multiparty republic
Currency Irish pound = 100 pence
Literacy rate 99%
Calorie consumption 3,847 kilocalories

ISRAEL
Southwestern Asia

Official name State of Israel
Formation 1948 / 1982
Capital Jerusalem
Population 5.6 million / 713 people per sq mile (275 people per sq km) / 91%
Total area 7,992 sq miles (20,700 sq km)
Languages Hebrew*, Arabic, Yiddish
Religions Jewish 83%, Muslim 13%, Christian 2%, other 2%
Ethnic mix Jewish 83%, Arab 17%
Government Multiparty republic
Currency New shekel = 100 agorat
Literacy rate 95%
Calorie consumption 3,050 kilocalories

ITALY
Southern Europe

Official name Italian Republic
Formation 1871 / 1954
Capital Rome
Population 57.2 million / 505 people per sq mile (195 people per sq km) / 67%
Total area 116,320 sq miles (301,270 sq km)
Languages Italian*, German, French, Rhaeto-Romanic, Sardinian
Religions Roman Catholic 99%, other 1%
Ethnic mix Italian 98%, other 2%
Government Multiparty republic
Currency Lira = 100 centesimi
Literacy rate 97%
Calorie consumption 3,561 kilocalories

IVORY COAST
Western Africa

Official name Republic of the Ivory Coast
Formation 1960 / 1960
Capital Yamoussoukro
Population 14.5 million / 117 people per sq mile (45 people per sq km) / 42%
Total area 124,503 sq miles (322,463 sq km)
Languages French*, Akran, Kru, Voltaic
Religions Traditional beliefs 63%, Muslim 25%, Christian 12%
Ethnic mix Baoule 23%, Bété 18%, Kru 17%, Malinke 15%, other 27%
Government Multiparty republic
Currency CFA franc = 100 centimes
Literacy rate 54%
Calorie consumption 2,491 kilocalories

JAMAICA
West Indies

Official name Jamaica
Formation 1962 / 1962
Capital Kingston
Population 2.4 million / 577 people per sq mile (222 people per sq km) / 52%
Total area 4,243 sq miles (10,990 sq km)
Languages English*, English Creole
Religions Christian 60%, other 40%
Ethnic mix Black 75%, mixed 15%, South Asian 5%, other 5%
Government Parliamentary democracy
Currency Jamaican $ = 100 cents
Literacy rate 98%
Calorie consumption 2,607 kilocalories

JAPAN
Eastern Asia

Official name Japan
Formation 1868 / 1945
Capital Tokyo
Population 125.1 million / 834 people per sq mile (322 people per sq km) / 77%
Total area 145,869 sq miles (377,800 sq km)
Languages Japanese*, Korean, Chinese
Religions Shinto and Buddhist 76%, Buddhist 16%, other 8%
Ethnic mix Japanese 99.4%, other 0.6%
Government Constitutional monarchy
Currency Yen = 100 sen
Literacy rate 99%
Calorie consumption 2,903 kilocalories

JORDAN
Southwestern Asia

Official name Hashemite Kingdom of Jordan
Formation 1946 / 1976
Capital Amman
Population 5.4 million / 159 people per sq mile (61 people per sq km) / 70%
Total area 34,440 sq miles (89,210 sq km)
Languages Arabic*
Religions Muslim 95%, Christian 5%
Ethnic mix Arab 98%, (Palestinian 49%), Armenian 1%, Circassian 1%
Government Constitutional monarchy
Currency Dinar = 1,000 fils
Literacy rate 83% Urban
Calorie consumption 3,022 kilocalories

KAZAKHSTAN
Central Asia

Official Name Republic of Kazakhstan
Formation 1991 / 1991
Capital Alma-Ata
Population 17.1 million / 16 people per sq mile (6 people per sq km) / 58%
Total area 1,049,150 sq miles (2,717,300 sq km)
Languages Kazakh*, Russian, German
Religions Muslim 47%, other 53% (mostly Russian Orthodox and Lutheran)
Ethnic mix Kazakh 40%, Russian 38%, Ukrainian 6%, other 16%
Government Multiparty republic
Currency Tenge = 100 tein
Literacy rate 97%
Calorie consumption NOT AVAILABLE

KENYA
Eastern Africa

Official name Republic of Kenya
Formation 1963 / 1963
Capital Nairobi
Population 28.3 million / 130 people per sq mile (50 people per sq km) / 25%
Total area 224,081 sq miles (580,370 sq km)
Languages Swahili*, English, Kikuyu, Luo, Kamba
Religions Christian 66%, traditional beliefs 26%, other 8%
Ethnic mix Kikuyu 21%, Luhya 14%, Kamba 11%, other 54%
Government Multiparty republic
Currency Shilling = 100 cents
Literacy rate 69%
Calorie consumption 2,075 kilocalories

KIRIBATI
Australasia & Oceania

Official Name Republic of Kiribati
Formation 1979 / 1979
Capital Bairiki
Population 77,000 / 281 people per sq mile (108 people per sq km) / 36%
Total area 274 sq miles (710 sq km)
Languages English*, Kiribati
Religions Roman Catholic 53%, Protestant 40%, other Christian 4%, other 3%
Ethnic mix I-Kiribati 98%, other 2%
Government Multiparty republic
Currency Australian $ = 100 cents
Literacy rate 98%
Calorie consumption 2,651 kilocalories

KUWAIT
Southwestern Asia

Official name State of Kuwait
Formation 1961 / 1981
Capital Kuwait
Population 1.5 million / 218 people per sq mile (84 people per sq km) / 95%
Total area 6,880 sq miles (17,820 sq km)
Languages Arabic*, English
Religions Muslim 92%, Christian 6%, other 2%
Ethnic mix Arab 85%, South Asian 9%, Persian 4%, other 2%
Government Constitutional monarchy
Currency Dinar = 1,000 fils
Literacy rate 73%
Calorie consumption 2,523 kilocalories

KYRGYZSTAN
Central Asia

Official name Kyrgyz Republic
Formation 1991 / 1991
Capital Bishkek
Population 4.7 million / 62 people per sq mile (24 people per sq km) / 39%
Total area 76,640 sq miles (198,500 sq km)
Languages Kyrgyz*, Russian*, Uzbek
Religions Muslim 65%, other (mostly Russian Orthodox) 35%
Ethnic mix Kyrgyz 52%, Russian 21%, Uzbek 13%, other (mostly Kazakh and Tajik) 14%
Government Multiparty republic
Currency Som =100 teen
Literacy rate 97%
Calorie consumption NOT AVAILABLE

LAOS
Southeastern Asia

Official name Lao People's Democratic Republic
Formation 1953 / 1953
Capital Vientiane
Population 4.9 million / 54 people per sq mile (21 people per sq km) / 20%
Total area 91, 428 sq miles (236,800 sq km)
Languages Lao*, Miao, Yao
Religions Buddhist 85%, Christian 2%, other 13%
Ethnic mix Lao Loum 56%, Lao Theung 34%, Lao Soung 10%
Government Single-party republic
Currency Kip = 100 cents
Literacy rate 57%
Calorie consumption 2,259 kilocalories

LATVIA
Northeastern Europe

Official name Republic of Latvia
Formation 1991 / 1991
Capital Riga
Population 2.6 million / 104 people per sq mile (40 people per sq km) / 72%
Total area 24,938 sq miles (64,589 sq km)
Languages Latvian*, Russian
Religions Evangelical Lutheran 85%, other Christian 15%
Ethnic mix Latvian 52%, Russian 34%, Belarus 5%, other 9%
Government Multiparty republic
Currency Lats = 100 santimi
Literacy rate 99%
Calorie consumption NOT AVAILABLE

LEBANON
Southwestern Asia

Official name Republic of Lebanon
Formation 1944 / 1944
Capital Beirut
Population 3 million / 762 people per sq mile (293 people per sq km) / 86%
Total area 4,015 sq miles (10,400 sq km)
Languages Arabic*, French, Armenian, Assyrian
Religions Muslim (mainly Shi'a) 57%, Christian (mainly Maronite) 43%
Ethnic mix Arab 93% (Lebanese 83%, Palestinian 10%), other 7%
Government Multiparty republic
Currency Pound = 100 piastres
Literacy rate 91%
Calorie consumption 3,317 kilocalories

LESOTHO
Southern Africa

Official name Kingdom of Lesotho
Formation 1966 / 1966
Capital Maseru
Population 2.1 million / 10 people per sq mile (27 people per sq km) / 21%
Total area 11,718 sq miles (30,350 sq km)
Languages English*, Sesotho*, Zulu
Religions Christian 93%, other 7%
Ethnic mix Basotho 99%, other 1%
Government Constitutional monarchy
Currency Loti = 100 lisente
Literacy rate 69%
Calorie consumption 2,201 kilocalories

LIBERIA
Western Africa

Official name Republic of Liberia
Formation 1847 / 1889–1907
Capital Monrovia
Population 3 million / 80 people per sq mile (27 people per sq km) / 44%
Total area 43,000 sq miles (111,370 sq km)
Languages English*, Kpelle, Bassa, Vai, Kru, Grebo, Kissi, Gola
Religions Traditional beliefs 70%, Muslim 20%, Christian 10%
Ethnic mix Kpelle 20%, Bassa 14%, Americo-Liberians 5%, other 61%
Government Transitional
Currency Liberian $ = 100 cents
Literacy rate 39%
Calorie consumption 1,640 kilocalories

LIBYA
Northern Africa

Official name Socialist People's Libyan Arab Jamahiriya
Formation 1951 / 1951
Capital Tripoli
Population 5.4 million / 8 people per sq mile (3 people per sq km) / 84%
Total area 679,358 sq miles (1,759,540 sq km)
Languages Arabic*, Tuareg
Religions Muslim 97%, other 3%
Ethnic mix Arab and Berber 97%, other 3%
Government Socialist *jamahiriya* (state of the masses)
Currency Dinar = 1,000 dirhams
Literacy rate 64%
Calorie consumption 3,308 kilocalories

LIECHTENSTEIN
Southeastern Europe

Official name Principality of Liechtenstein
Formation 1719 / 1719
Capital Vaduz
Population 30,630 / 495 people per sq mile (191 people per sq km) / 87%
Total area 62 sq miles (160 sq km)
Languages German*, Alemannish, Italian
Religions Roman Catholic 87%, Protestant 8%, other 5%
Ethnic mix Liechtensteiner 63%, Swiss 15%, German 9%, other 13%
Government Constitutional monarchy
Currency Swiss franc = 100 centimes
Literacy rate 100%
Calorie consumption NOT AVAILABLE

LITHUANIA
Northeastern Europe

Official name Republic of Lithuania
Formation 1991 / 1991
Capital Vilnius
Population 3.7 million / 148 people per sq mile (57 people per sq km) / 70%
Total area 25,174 sq miles (65,200 sq km)
Languages Lithuanian*, Russian
Religions Roman Catholic 87%, Russian Orthodox 10%, other 3%
Ethnic mix Lithuanian 80%, Russian 9%, Polish 8%, other 3%
Government Multiparty republic
Currency Litas = 100 centas
Literacy rate 98%
Calorie consumption NOT AVAILABLE

LUXEMBOURG
Northwestern Europe

Official name Grand Duchy of Luxembourg
Formation 1890 / 1890
Capital Luxembourg
Population 400,000 / 403 people per sq mile (155 people per sq km) / 88%
Total area 998 sq miles (2,586 sq km)
Languages Letzeburgish*, French, Portuguese, Italian
Religions Roman Catholic 97%, other 3%
Ethnic mix Luxemburger 72%, Portuguese 9%, Italian 5%, other 14%
Government Constitutional monarchy
Currency Franc = 100 centimes
Literacy rate 99% Urban
Calorie consumption 3,681 kilocalories

MACEDONIA
Southeastern Europe

Official name Former Yugoslav Republic of Macedonia
Formation 1991 / 1991
Capital Skopje
Population 2.2 million / 223 people per sq mile (86 people per sq km) / 59%
Total area 9,929 sq miles (25,715 sq km)
Languages Macedonian, Serbian, Croatian (no official language)
Religions Christian 80%, Muslim 20%
Ethnic mix Macedonian 67%, Albanian 20%, Turkish 4%, other 9%
Government Multiparty republic
Currency Denar = 100 deni
Literacy rate 89%
Calorie consumption NOT AVAILABLE

MADAGASCAR
Indian Ocean

Official name Democratic Republic of Madagascar
Formation 1960 / 1960
Capital Antananarivo
Population 14.8 million / 65 people per sq mile (25 people per sq km) / 25%
Total area 226,660 sq miles (587,040 sq km)
Languages Malagasy*, French*
Religions Traditional beliefs 52%, Christian 41%, Muslim 7%
Ethnic mix Merina 26%, Betsimisaraka 15%, Betsileo 12%, other 47%
Government Multiparty republic
Currency Franc = 100 centimes
Literacy rate 81%
Calorie consumption 2,135 kilocalories

MALAWI
Southern Africa

Official name Republic of Malawi
Formation 1964 / 1964
Capital Lilongwe
Population 11.1 million / 307 people per sq mile (118 people per sq km) / 12%
Total area 45,745 sq miles (118,480 sq km)
Languages English*, Chewa, Lomwe, Yao
Religions Christian 66%, traditional beliefs 18%, other 16%
Ethnic mix Maravi 55%, Lomwe 17%, Yao 13%, other 15%
Government Multiparty republic
Currency Kwacha = 100 tambala
Literacy rate 49%
Calorie consumption 1,825 kilocalories

MALAYSIA
Southeastern Asia

Official name Malaysia
Formation 1957 / 1965
Capital Kuala Lumpur
Population 20.1 million / 158 people per sq mile (61 people per sq km) / 51%
Total area 127,317 sq miles (329,750 sq km)
Languages Malay*, Chinese, Tamil
Religions Muslim 53%, Buddhist and Confucianist 30%, other 17%
Ethnic mix Malay and Aboriginal 60%, Chinese 30%, Indian 8%, other 2%
Government Federal constitutional monarchy
Currency Ringgit = 100 cents
Literacy rate 78%
Calorie consumption 2,888 kilocalories

MALDIVES
Indian Ocean

Official name Republic of Maldives
Formation 1965 / 1965
Capital Male
Population 300,000 / 2,591 people per
  sq mile (1,000 people per sq km) / 26%
Total area 116 sq miles (300 sq km)
Languages Divehi (Maldivian)*,
  Sinhala, Tamil
Religions Sunni Muslim 100%
Ethnic mix Maldivian 99%,
  other 1%
Government Republic
Currency Rufiyaa = 100 laari
Literacy rate 91%
Calorie consumption 2,580 kilocalories

MALI
Western Africa

Official name Republic of Mali
Formation 1960 / 1960
Capital Bamako
Population 10.8 million / 24 people per
  sq mile (9 people per sq km) / 25%
Total area 478,837 sq miles (1,240,190 sq km)
Languages French*, Bambara, Fulani,
  Senufo, Soninké
Religions Muslim 80%, traditional
  beliefs 18%, Christian 2%
Ethnic mix Bambara 31%, Fulani 13%,
  Senufo 12%, other 44%
Government Multiparty republic
Currency CFA franc = 100 centimes
Literacy rate 32%
Calorie consumption 2,278 kilocalories

MALTA
Southern Europe

Official name Republic of Malta
Formation 1964 / 1964
Capital Valletta
Population 400,000 / 3,239 people per
  sq mile (1,250 people per sq km) / 88%
Total area 124 sq miles (320 sq km)
Languages Maltese*, English*
Religions Roman Catholic 98%, other
  (mostly Anglican) 2%
Ethnic mix Maltese (mixed Arab, Sicilian, Norman,
  Spanish, Italian, English) 98%, other 2%
Government Multiparty republic
Currency Lira = 100 cents
Literacy rate 86%
Calorie consumption 3,486 kilocalories

MARSHALL ISLANDS
Australasia & Oceania

Official name Republic of the
  Marshall Islands
Formation 1986 / 1986
Capital Majuro
Population 52,000 / 744 people per
  sq mile (287 people per sq km) / 28%
Total area 70 sq miles (181 sq km)
Languages English*, Marshallese*
Religions Protestant 80%, Roman
  Catholic 15%, other 5%
Ethnic mix Marshallese 90%,
  other Pacific Islanders 10%
Government Republic
Currency US $ = 100 cents
Literacy rate 91%
Calorie consumption NOT AVAILABLE

MAURITANIA
Western Africa

Official name Islamic Republic
  of Mauritania
Formation 1960 / 1960
Capital Nouakchott
Population 2.3 million / 5 people per
  sq mile (2 people per sq km) / 50%
Total area 395,953 sq miles (1,025,520 sq km)
Languages French*, Hassaniyah Arabic, Wolof
Religions Muslim 100%
Ethnic mix Maure 80%, Wolof 7%,
  Tukulor 5%, other 8%
Government Multiparty republic
Currency Ouguiya = 5 khoums
Literacy rate 34%
Calorie consumption 2,685 kilocalories

MAURITIUS
Indian Ocean

Official name Republic of Mauritius
Formation 1968 / 1968
Capital Port Louis
Population 1.1 million / 1,542 people
  per sq mile (595 people per sq km) / 41%
Total area 718 sq miles (1,860 sq km)
Languages English*, French Creole, Hindi,
  Urdu, Tamil, Chinese
Religions Hindu 52%, Roman
  Catholic, 26%, Muslim 17%, other 5%
Ethnic mix Creole 55%, South
  Asian 40%, Chinese 3%, other 2%
Government Multiparty republic
Currency Rupee = 100 cents
Literacy rate 79%
Calorie consumption 2,690 kilocalories

MEXICO
North America

Official name United Mexican States
Formation 1836 / 1867
Capital Mexico City
Population 93.7 million / 127 people
  per sq mile (49 people per sq km) / 74%
Total area 756,061 sq miles (1,958,200 sq km)
Languages Spanish*, Mayan dialects
Religions Roman Catholic 89%,
  Protestant 6%, other 5%
Ethnic mix *mestizo* 55%, Amerindian 30%,
  White 6%, other 9%
Government Multiparty republic
Currency Peso = 100 centavos
Literacy rate 89%
Calorie consumption 3,146 kilocalories

MICRONESIA
Australasia & Oceania

Official name Federated States of Micronesia
Formation 1986 / 1986
Capital Palikir
Population 107,000 / 394 people per
  sq mile (152 people per sq km) / 36%
Total area 1,120 sq miles (2,900 sq km)
Languages English*, Trukese,
  Pohnpeian, Mortlockese, Kosrean
Religions Roman Catholic 50%,
  Protestant 48%, other 2%
Ethnic mix Micronesian 99%, other 1%
Government Republic
Currency US $ = 100 cents
Literacy rate 90%
Calorie consumption NOT AVAILABLE

MOLDOVA
Southeastern Europe

Official name Republic of Moldova
Formation 1991 / 1991
Capital Chişinău
Population 4.4 million / 339 people per
  sq mile (131 people per sq km) / 49%
Total area 13,000 sq miles (33, 700 sq km)
Languages Moldovan*, Russian, Romanian
Religions Romanian Orthodox 98%,
  Jewish 1%, other 1%
Ethnic mix Moldovan (Romanian) 65%,
  Ukrainian 14%, Russian 13%, other 8%
Government Multiparty republic
Currency Leu = 100 bani
Literacy rate 96%
Calorie consumption NOT AVAILABLE

MONACO
Southern Europe

Official name Principality of Monaco
Formation 1861 / 1861
Capital Monaco
Population 31,000 / 41,332 people per
  sq mile (15,897 people per sq km) / 100%
Total area 0.75 sq miles (1.95 sq km)
Languages French*, Italian, Monégasque,
  English
Religions Roman Catholic 95%, other 5%
Ethnic mix French 47%, Monégasque 17%,
  Italian 16%, other 20%
Government Constitutional monarchy
Currency French franc = 100 centimes
Literacy rate 99%
Calorie consumption NOT AVAILABLE

MONGOLIA
Eastern Asia

Official name Mongolia
Formation 1924 / 1911
Capital Ulan Bator
Population 2.4 million / 5 people per
  sq mile (2 people per sq km) / 59%
Total area 604,247 sq miles (1,565,000 sq km)
Languages Khalkha Mongol*, Turkic,
  Russian, Chinese
Religions Predominantly Tibetan Buddhist,
  with a Muslim minority
Ethnic mix Khalkha Mongol 90%,
  Kazakh 4%, Chinese 2%, other 4%
Government Multiparty republic
Currency Tughrik = 100 möngös
Literacy rate 81%
Calorie consumption 1,899 kilocalories

MOROCCO
Northern Africa

Official name Kingdom of Morocco
Formation 1956 / 1956
Capital Rabat
Population 27 million / 155 people per
  sq mile (60 people per sq km) / 47%
Total area 269,757 sq miles
  (698,670 sq km)
Religions Muslim 99%,
  other 1%
Ethnic mix Arab and Berber 99%,
  European 1%
Government Constitutional monarchy
Currency Dirham = 100 centimes
Literacy rate 44%
Calorie consumption 2,984 kilocalories

MOZAMBIQUE
Southern Africa

Official name Republic of Mozambique
Formation 1975 / 1975
Capital Maputo
Population 16 million / 135 people per
  sq mile (20 people per sq km) / 30%
Total area 309,493 sq miles (801,590 sq km)
Languages Portuguese*, Makua,
  Tsonga, Sena, Lomwe
Religions Traditional beliefs 60%,
  Christian 30%, Muslim 10%
Ethnic mix Makua-Lomwe 47%, Tsonga 23%,
  Malawi 12%, other 18%
Government Multiparty republic
Currency Metical = 100 centavos
Literacy rate 40%
Calorie consumption 1,680 kilocalories

MYANMAR
Southeastern Asia

Official name Union of Myanmar
Formation 1948 / 1948
Capital Rangoon
Population 46.5 million / 184 people per
  sq mile (71 people per sq km) / 25%
Total area 261,200 sq miles (676,550 sq km)
Languages Burmese*, Karen, Mon
Religions Buddhist 89%, Muslim 4%,
  other 7%
Ethnic mix Burman 68%, Shan 9%,
  Karen 6%, Rakhine 4%, other 13%
Government Military regime
Currency Kyat = 100 pyas
Literacy rate 81%
Calorie consumption 2,598 kilocalories

NAMIBIA
Southern Africa

Official name Republic of Namibia
Formation 1990 / 1994
Capital Windhoek
Population 1.5 million / 5 people per
  sq mile (2 people per sq km) / 34%
Total area 318,260 sq miles (824,290 sq km)
Languages English*, Afrikaans,
  Ovambo, Kavango, Bergdama
Religions Christian 90%, other 10%
Ethnic mix Ovambo 50%, Kavango 9%,
  Herero 7%, Damara 7%, other 27%
Government Multiparty republic
Currency Rand = 100 cents
Literacy rate 40%
Calorie consumption 2,134 kilocalories

NAURU
Australasia & Oceania

Official name Republic of Nauru
Formation 1968 / 1968
Capital No official capital
Population 10,000 / 1,233 people per
  sq mile (476 people per sq km) / 100%
Total area 8.2 sq miles (21.2 sq km)
Languages Nauruan*, English, Kiribati,
  Chinese, Tuvaluan
Religions Christian 95%, other 5%
Ethnic mix Nauruan 58%, other Pacific
  Islanders 26%, Chinese 8%, European 8%
Government Parliamentary democracy
Currency Australian $ = 100 cents
Literacy rate 99%
Calorie consumption NOT AVAILABLE

NEPAL
Southern Asia

Official name Kingdom of Nepal
Formation 1769 / 1769
Capital Kathmandu
Population 21.4 million / 404 people per
  sq mile (156 people per sq km) / 12%
Total area 54,363 sq miles (140,800 sq km)
Languages Nepali*, Maithilli, Bhojpuri
Religions Hindu 90%, Buddhist 5%,
  Muslim 3%, other 2%
Ethnic mix Nepalese 58%, Bihari 19%,
  Tamang 6%, other 17%
Government Constitutional monarchy
Currency Rupee = 100 paisa
Literacy rate 26%
Calorie consumption 1,957 kilocalories

NETHERLANDS
Northwestern Europe

Official name Kingdom of the Netherlands
Formation 1815 / 1890
Capitals Amsterdam, The Hague
Population 15.5 million / 1,188 people per
  sq mile (457 people per sq km) / 89%
Total area 14,410 sq miles
  (37,330 sq km)
Languages Dutch*, Frisian
Religions Roman Catholic 36%,
  Protestant 27%, other 37%
Ethnic mix Dutch 96%, other 4%
Government Constitutional monarchy
Currency Guilder = 100 cents
Literacy rate 99%
Calorie consumption 3,222 kilocalories

NEW ZEALAND
Australasia & Oceania

Official name New Zealand
Formation 1947 / 1947
Capital Wellington
Population 3.6 million / 34 people per
  sq mile (13 people per sq km) / 86%
Total area 103,730 sq miles (268,680 sq km)
Languages English, Maori
Religions Protestant 62%,
  Roman Catholic 18%, other 20%
Ethnic mix European 88%, Maori 9%,
  other 3%
Government Constitutional monarchy
Currency NZ $ = 100 cents
Literacy rate 99%
Calorie consumption 3,669 kilocalories

NICARAGUA
Central America

Official name Republic of Nicaragua
Formation 1838 / 1838
Capital Managua
Population 4.4 million / 96 people per
  sq mile (37 people per sq km) / 62%
Total area 50,193 sq miles
  (130,000 sq km)
Languages Spanish*, English Creole, Miskito
Religions Roman Catholic 95%, other 5%
Ethnic mix *mestizo* 69%, White 17%,
  Black 9%, Amerindian 5%
Government Multiparty republic
Currency Córdoba = 100 pence
Literacy rate 65%
Calorie consumption 2,293 kilocalories

NIGER
Western Africa

Official name Republic of Niger
Formation 1960 / 1960
Capital Niamey
Population 9.2 million / 18 people per
  sq mile (7 people per sq km) / 16%
Total area 489,188 sq miles (1,267,000 sq km)
Languages French*, Hausa, Djerma, Fulani,
  Tuareg, Teda
Religions Muslim 85%, traditional
  beliefs 14%, Christian 1%
Ethnic mix Hausa 56%, Djerma 22%,
  Fulani 9%, other 13%
Government Multiparty republic
Currency CFA franc = 100 centimes
Literacy rate 28%
Calorie consumption 2,257 kilocalories

NIGERIA
Western Africa

Official name Federal Republic of Nigeria
Formation 1960 / 1960
Capital Abuja
Population 111.7 million / 319 people per
  sq mile (123 people per sq km) / 37%
Total area 356,668 sq miles (923,770 sq km)
Languages English*, Hausa, Yoruba, Ibo
Religions Muslim 50%, Christian 40%,
  traditional beliefs 10%
Ethnic mix Hausa 21%, Yoruba 20%,
  Ibo 17%, Fulani 9%, other 33%
Government Military regime
Currency Naira = 100 kobo
Literacy rate 53%
Calorie consumption 2,124 kilocalories

NORTH KOREA
Eastern Asia

Official name Democratic People's Republic
  of Korea
Formation 1948 / 1948
Capital Pyongyang
Population 23.9 million / 515 people per
  sq mile (198 people per sq km) / 60%
Total area 46,540 sq miles (120,540 sq km)
Languages Korean*, Chinese
Religions Traditional beliefs 16%, Ch'ondogyo
  14%, Buddhist 2%, nonreligious 68%
Ethnic mix Korean 99%, other 1%
Government Single-party republic
Currency Won = 100 chon
Literacy rate 99%
Calorie consumption 2,833 kilocalories

NORWAY
Northern Europe

Official name Kingdom of Norway
Formation 1905 / 1930
Capital Oslo
Population 4.3 million / 36 people per
  sq mile (14 people per sq km) / 73%
Total area 125,060 sq miles (323,900 sq km)
Languages Norwegian* (Bokmal and
  Nynorsk), Lappish, Finnish
Religions Evangelical Lutheran 88%,
  other Christian 12%
Ethnic mix Norwegian 95%, Lapp 1%, other 4%
Government Constitutional monarchy
Currency Krone = 100 øre
Literacy rate 99%
Calorie consumption 3,244 kilocalories

OMAN
Southwestern Asia

Official name Sultanate of Oman
Formation 1650 / 1951
Capital Muscat
Population 2.2 million / 26 people per
  sq mile (10 people per sq km) / 12%
Total area 82,030 sq miles (212,460 sq km)
Languages Arab*, Baluchi
Religions Ibadi Muslim 75%, other
  Muslim 11%, Hindu 14%
Ethnic mix Arab 75%, Baluchi 15%, Other 15%
Government Monarchy with
  Consultative Council
Currency Rial = 1,000 baizas
Literacy rate 44%
Calorie consumption 3,013 kilocalories

PAKISTAN
Southern Asia

Official name Islamic Republic of Pakistan
Formation 1947 / 1972
Capital Islamabad
Population 140.5 million / 472 people per
  sq mile (182 people per sq km) / 33%
Total area 307,374 sq miles (796,100 sq km)
Main languages Urdu*, Punjabi, Sindhi,
  Pashtu, Baluchi
Religions Sunni Muslim 77%, Shi'a Muslim
  20%, Hindu 2%, Christian 1%
Ethnic mix Punjabi 56%, Sindhi 13%,
  Pashtun 8%, other 23%
Government Multiparty republic
Currency Rupee = 100 paisa
Literacy rate 38% Urban
Calorie consumption 2,315 kilocalories

PALAU
Australasia & Oceania

Official name Palau
Formation 1994 / 1994
Capital Oreor
Population 16,200 /83 people per
  sq mile (32 people per sq km) / 52%
Total area 192 sq miles (497 sq km)
Languages Palauan, English,
  Sonsorolese-Tobian (no official language)
Religions Christian 70%, traditional
  beliefs 30%
Ethnic mix Palauan 99%, 1% Other
Government Multiparty republic
Currency US $ = 100 cents
Literacy rate 92%
Calorie consumption NOT AVAILABLE

PANAMA
Central America

Official name Republic of Panama
Formation 1903 / 1914
Capital Panama City
Population 2.6 million / 88 people per
  sq mile (34 people per sq km) / 52%
Total area 29,761 sq miles (77,080 sq km)
Languages Spanish*, English Creole,
  Amerindian languages
Religions Roman Catholic 93%, other 7%
Ethnic mix *mestizo* 70%, Black 14%,
  White 10%, Amerindian 6%
Government Multiparty republic
Currency Balboa = 100 centesimos
Literacy rate 91%
Calorie consumption 2,242 kilocalories

PAPUA NEW GUINEA
Australasia & Oceania

Official name Independent State of Papua
  New Guinea
Formation 1975 / 1975
Capital Port Moresby
Population 4.3 million / 23 people per
  sq mile (9 people per sq km) / 15%
Total area 178,700 sq miles (462, 840 sq km)
Languages Pidgin English*, Motu*,
  750 (est.) native languages
Religions Christian 66%, other 34%
Ethnic mix Papuan 85%, other 15%
Government Parliamentary democracy
Currency Kina = 100 toea
Literacy rate 72%
Calorie consumption 2,613 kilocalories

PARAGUAY
South America

Official name Paraguay
Formation 1811 / 1938
Capital Asunción
Population 5 million / 34 people per
  sq mile (13 people per sq km) / 51%
Total area 157,046 sq miles
  (406,750 sq km)
Languages Spanish*, Guaraní
Religions Roman Catholic 90%,
  other 10%
Ethnic mix *mestizo* 95%, White 3%,
  Amerindian 2%
Government Multiparty republic
Literacy rate 92%
Calorie consumption 2,670 kilocalories

PERU
South America

Official name Republic of Peru
Formation 1824 / 1942
Capital Lima
Population 23.8 million / 49 people per sq mile (19 people per sq km) / 71%
Total area 496,223 sq miles (1,285,220 sq km)
Languages Spanish*, Quechua, Aymará
Religions Roman Catholic 95%, other 5%
Ethnic mix Amerindian 45%, *mestizo* 37%, White 15%, other 3%
Government Multiparty republic
Currency New sol = 100 centimos
Literacy rate 89%
Calorie consumption 1,882 kilocalories

PHILIPPINES
Southwestern Asia

Official name Republic of the Philippines
Formation 1946 / 1946
Capital Manila
Population 67.6 million / 588 people per sq mile (227 people per sq km) / 51%
Total area 115,831 sq miles (300,000 sq km)
Languages Pilipino*, English, Cebuano, Hiligaynon, Samaran, Bikol
Religions Roman Catholic 83%, Protestant 9%, Muslim 5%, other 3%
Ethnic mix Filipino 96%, Chinese 2%, other 2%
Government Multiparty republic
Currency Peso = 100 centavos
Literacy rate 95%
Calorie consumption 2,257 kilocalories

POLAND
Northern Europe

Official name Republic of Poland
Formation 1918 / 1945
Capital Warsaw
Population 38.4 million / 327 people per sq mile (126 people per sq km) / 63%
Total area 120,720 sq miles (312,680 sq km)
Languages Polish*, German
Religions Roman Catholic 95%, other Christian 5%
Ethnic mix Polish 98%, other 2%
Government Multiparty republic
Currency Zloty = 100 groszy
Literacy rate 99%
Calorie consumption 3,301 kilocalories

PORTUGAL
Southwestern Europe

Official name Republic of Portugal
Formation 1140 / 1640
Capital Lisbon
Population 9.8 million / 277 people per sq mile (107 people per sq km) / 34%
Total area 35,670 sq miles (92,390 sq km)
Languages Portuguese*
Religions Roman Catholic 97%, Protestant 1%, other 2%
Ethnic mix Portuguese 98%, African 1%, other 1%
Government Multiparty republic
Currency Escudo = 100 centavos
Literacy rate 86%
Calorie consumption 3,634 kilocalories

QATAR
Southwestern Asia

Official name State of Qatar
Formation 1971 / 1971
Capital Doha
Population 600,000 / 143 people per sq mile (55 people per sq km) / 90%
Total area 4,247 sq miles (11,000 sq km)
Languages Arabic*, Farsi (Persian), Urdu, Hindi, English
Religions Sunni Muslim 86%, Hindu 10%, Christian 4%
Ethnic mix Arab 40%, South Asian 35%, Persian 12%, other 13%
Government Absolute monarchy
Currency Riyal = 100 dirhams
Literacy rate 79%
Calorie consumption NOT AVAILABLE

ROMANIA
Southeastern Europe

Official name Romania
Formation 1947 / 1947
Capital Bucharest
Population 22.8 million /257 people per sq mile (99 people per sq km) / 54%
Total area 91,700 sq miles (237,500 sq km)
Languages Romanian*, Hungarian,
Religions Romanian Orthodox 70%, Roman Catholic 6%, Protestant 6%, other 18%
Ethnic mix Romanian 89%, Hungarian 8%, other (including Gypsy) 3%
Government Multiparty republic
Currency Leu = 100 bani
Literacy rate 97%
Calorie consumption 3,051 kilocalories

RUSSIAN FEDERATION
Europe / Asia

Official name Russian Federation
Formation 1991 / 1991
Capital Moscow
Population 147 million /23 people per sq mile (9 people per sq km) / 75%
Total area 6,592,800 sq miles (17,075,400 sq km)
Languages Russian*, Tatar, Ukrainian
Religions Russian Orthodox 80%, other (including Jewish, Muslim) 20%
Ethnic mix Russian 80%, Tatar 4%, Ukrainian 3%, other 13%
Currency Rouble = 100 kopeks
Literacy rate 98%
Calorie consumption NOT AVAILABLE

RWANDA
Central Africa

Official name Rwandese Republic
Formation 1962 / 1962
Capital Kigali
Population 8 million / 788 people per sq mile (304 people per sq km) / 6%
Total area 10,170 sq miles (26,340 sq km)
Languages Kinyarwanda*, French*, Kiswahili, English
Religions Christian 74%, traditional beliefs 25%, other 1%
Ethnic mix Hutu 90%, Tutsi 9%, Twa pygmy 1%
Government Multiparty republic
Currency Franc = 100 centimes
Literacy rate 61%
Calorie consumption 1,821 kilocalories

SAINT KITTS & NEVIS
West Indies

Official name Federation of Saint Christopher and Nevis
Formation 1983 / 1983
Capital Basseterre
Population 44,000 / 295 people per sq mile (114 people per sq km) / 41%
Total area 139 sq miles (360 sq km)
Languages English*, English Creole
Religions Protestant 85%, Roman Catholic 10%, other Christian 5%
Ethnic mix Black 95%, mixed 5%
Government Parliamentary democracy
Currency E. Caribbean $ = 100 cents
Literacy rate 97%
Calorie consumption 2,419 kilocalories

SAINT LUCIA
West Indies

Official name Saint Lucia
Formation 1979 / 1979
Capital Castries
Population 145,000 / 617 people per sq mile (238 people per sq km) / 47%
Total area 239 sq miles (620 sq km)
Languages English*, French Creole, Hindi, Urdu
Religions Roman Catholic 90%, other 10%
Ethnic mix Black 90%, Afro-European 6%, South Asian 4%
Government Parliamentary democracy
Currency E. Caribbean $ = 100 cents
Literacy rate 93%
Calorie consumption 2,588 kilocalories

SAINT VINCENT & THE GRENADINES *West Indies*

Official name Saint Vincent and the Grenadines
Formation 1979 / 1979
Capital Kingstown
Population 111,000 / 845 people per sq mile (326 people per sq km) / 43%
Total area 131 sq miles (340 sq km)
Languages English*, English Creole
Religions Protestant 62% Roman Catholic 19%, other 19%
Ethnic mix Black 82%, mixed 14%, White 3%, South Asian 1%
Government Parliamentary democracy
Currency E. Caribbean $ = 100 cents
Literacy rate 84%
Calorie consumption 2,347 kilocalories

SAN MARINO
Southern Europe

Official name Republic of San Marino
Formation CE 301 / 1862
Capital San Marino
Population 24,000 / 1,018 people per sq mile (393 people per sq km) / 90%
Total area 24 sq miles (61 sq km)
Languages Italian*
Religions Roman Catholic 96%, other 4%
Ethnic mix Sammarinese 95%, other 5%
Government Multiparty republic
Currency Italian lira = 100 centesimi
Literacy rate 96%
Calorie consumption 3,561 kilocalories

SAO TOME & PRINCIPE
Western Africa

Official name Democratic Republic of Sao Tome and Principe
Formation 1975 / 1975
Capital São Tomé
Population 125,000 / 337 people per sq mile (130 people per sq km) / 44%
Total area 372 sq miles (964 sq km)
Languages Portuguese, Portuguese Creole
Religions Roman Catholic 90%, other Christian 10%
Ethnic mix Black 90%, Portuguese and Creole 10%
Government Multiparty republic
Currency Dobra = 100 centimos
Literacy rate 57%
Calorie consumption 2,129 kilocalories

SAUDI ARABIA
Southwestern Asia

Official name Kingdom of Saudi Arabia
Formation 1932 / 1981
Capital Riyadh
Population 17.9 million / 21 people per sq mile (8 people per sq km) / 78%
Total area 829,995 sq miles (2,149,690 sq km)
Languages Arabic*
Religions Sunni Muslim 85%, Shi'a Muslim 14%, Christian 1%
Ethnic mix Arab 90%, Yemeni 8%, other Arab 1%, other 1%
Government Absolute monarchy
Currency Riyal = 100 malalah
Literacy rate 63%
Calorie consumption 2,735 kilocalories

SENEGAL
Western Africa

Official name Republic of Senegal
Formation 1960 / 1960
Capital Dakar
Population 8.3 million /111 people per sq mile (43 people per sq km) / 41%
Total area 75,950 sq miles (196,720 sq km)
Languages French*, Wolof, Fulani, Serer
Religions Muslim 92%, traditional beliefs 6%, Christian 2%
Ethnic mix Wolof 46%, Fulani 25%, Serer 16%, other 13%
Government Multiparty republic
Currency CFA franc = 100 centimes
Literacy rate 33%
Calorie consumption 2,262 kilocalories

SEYCHELLES
Indian Ocean

Official name Republic of Seychelles
Formation 1976 / 1976
Capital Victoria
Population 73,000 / 700 people per sq mile (270 people per sq km) / 52%
Total area 108 sq miles (280 sq km)
Languages Creole*, French, English
Religions Roman Catholic 90%, other 10%
Ethnic mix Seychellois (mixed African, South Asian and European) 95%, Chinese and South Asian 5%
Government Multiparty republic
Currency Rupee = 100 cents
Literacy rate 58%
Calorie consumption 2,287 kilocalories

SIERRA LEONE
Western Africa

Official name Republic of Sierra Leone
Formation 1961 / 1961
Capital Freetown
Population 4.5 million / 163 people per sq mile (63 people per sq km) / 34%
Total area 27,699 sq miles (71,740 sq km)
Languages English*, Krio (Creole), Mende, Temne
Religions Traditional beliefs 52%, Muslim 40%, Christian 8%
Ethnic mix Mende 34%, Temne 31%, Limba 9%, Kono 5%, other 21%
Government Military regime
Currency Leone = 100 cents
Literacy rate 31%
Calorie consumption 1,694 kilocalorie

SINGAPORE
Southeastern Asia

Official name Republic of Singapore
Formation 1965 / 1965
Capital Singapore
Population 2.8 million / 11,894 people per sq mile (4,590 people per sq km) / 100%
Total area 239 sq miles (620 sq km)
Languages Malay*, Chinese, Tamil, English
Religions Buddhist 30%, Christian 20%, Muslim 17%, other 33%
Ethnic mix Chinese 76%, Malay 15%, South Asian 7%, other 2%
Government Multiparty democracy
Currency Singapore $ = 100 cents
Literacy rate 91%
Calorie consumption 3,128 kilocalories

SLOVAKIA
Central Europe

Official name Slovak Republic
Formation 1993 / 1993
Capital Bratislava
Population 5.4 million / 285 people per sq mile (110 people per sq km) / 57%
Total area 19,100 sq miles (49,500 sq km)
Languages Slovak*, Hungarian (Magyar), Romany, Czech
Religions Roman Catholic 80%, Protestant 12%, other 8%
Ethnic mix Slovak 85%, Hungarian 9%, Czech 1%, other 5%
Government Multiparty republic
Currency Koruna = 100 halierov
Literacy rate 99%
Calorie consumption 3,156 kilocalories

SLOVENIA
Central Europe

Official name Republic of Slovenia
Formation 1991 / 1991
Capital Ljubljana
Population 1.9 million / 244 people per sq mile (94 people per sq km) / 62%
Total area 7,820 sq miles (20,250 sq km)
Languages Slovene*, Serbian, Croatian
Religions Roman Catholic 96%, Muslim 1%, other 3%
Ethnic mix Slovene 92%, Croat 3%, Serb 1%, other 4%
Government Multiparty republic
Currency Tolar = 100 stotins
Literacy rate 99%
Calorie consumption NOT AVAILABLE

SOLOMON ISLANDS
Australasia & Oceania

Official name Solomon Islands
Formation 1978 / 1978
Capital Honiara
Population 400,000 / 36 people per sq mile (14 people per sq km) / 16%
Total area 111,583 sq miles (289,000 sq km)
Languages English*, 87 (established) native languages
Religions Christian 91%, other 9%
Ethnic mix Melanesian 94%, other 6%
Government Parliamentary democracy
Currency Solomon Is $ = 100 cents
Literacy rate 24%
Calorie consumption 2,173 kilocalories

SOMALIA
Eastern Africa

Official name Somali Democratic Republic
Formation 1960 / 1960
Capital Mogadishu
Population 9.3 million / 39 people per sq mile (15 people per sq km) / 25%
Total area 246,200 sq miles (637,660 sq km)
Languages Somali*, Arabic, English
Religions Sunni Muslim 99%, other (including Christian) 1%
Ethnic mix Somali 98%, Bantu, Arab and other 2%
Government Transitional
Currency Shilling = 100 cents
Literacy rate 24%
Calorie consumption 1,499 kilocalories

SOUTH AFRICA
Southern Africa

Official name Republic of South Africa
Formation 1910 / 1934
Capitals Pretoria, Cape Town, Bloemfontein
Population 41.5 million / 88 people per sq mile (34 people per sq km) / 50%
Total area 471,443 sq miles (1,221,040 sq km)
Languages Afrikaans*, English, 11 African languages
Religions Protestant 55%, Roman Catholic 9%, Hindu 1%, Muslim 1%, other 34%
Ethnic mix Black 75%, White 14%, mixed 9%, South Asian 2%
Government Multiparty republic
Currency Rand = 100 cents
Literacy rate 82%
Calorie consumption 2,695 kilocalories

SOUTH KOREA
Eastern Asia

Official name Republic of Korea
Formation 1948 / 1948
Capital Seoul
Population 45 million / 1,182 people per sq mile (456 people per sq km) / 77%
Total area 38,232 sq miles (99,020 sq km)
Languages Korean*, Chinese
Religions Mahayana Buddhist 47%, Protestant 38%, Roman Catholic 11%, Confucianist 3%, other 1%
Ethnic mix Korean 99.9% other 0.1%
Government Multiparty republic
Currency Won = 100 chon
Literacy rate 97%
Calorie consumption 3,285 kilocalories

SPAIN
Southeastern Europe

Official name Kingdom of Spain
Formation 1492 / 1713
Capital Madrid
Population 39.6 million / 205 people per sq mile (79 people per sq km) / 76%
Total area 194,900 sq miles (504,780 sq km)
Languages Castilian Spanish*, Catalan*, Galician*, Basque*
Religions Roman Catholic 99%, other 1%
Ethnic mix Castilian Spanish 72%, Catalan 16%, Galician 7%, other 5%
Government Constitutional monarchy
Currency Peseta = 100 céntimos
Literacy rate 95%
Calorie consumption 3,708 kilocalories

SRI LANKA
Southern Asia

Official name Democratic Socialist Republic of Sri Lanka
Formation 1948 / 1948
Capital Colombo
Population 18.4 million / 736 people per sq mile (284 people per sq km) / 22%
Total area 25,332 sq miles (65,610 sq km)
Languages Sinhala*, Tamil, English
Religions Buddhist 70%, Hindu 15%, Christian 8%, Muslim 7%
Ethnic mix Sinhalese 74%, Tamil 18%, other 8%
Government Multiparty republic
Currency Rupee = 100 cents
Literacy rate 90%
Calorie consumption 2,273 kilocalories

SUDAN
Eastern Africa

Official name Republic of Sudan
Formation 1956 / 1956
Capital Khartoum
Population 28.1 million / 31 people per sq mile (12 people per sq km) / 23%
Total area 967,493 sq miles (2,505,815 sq km)
Languages Arabic*, Dinka, Nuer, Nubian, Beja, Zande, Bari, Fur
Religions Muslim 70%, traditional beliefs 20%, Christian 5%, other 5%
Ethnic mix Arab 51%, Dinka 13%, Nuba 9%, Beja 7%, other 20%
Government Military regime
Currency Pound = 100 piastres
Literacy rate 46%
Calorie consumption 2,202 kilocalories

SURINAME
South America

Official name Republic of Suriname
Formation 1975 / 1975
Capital Paramaribo
Population 400,000 / 5 people per sq mile (2 people per sq km) / 49%
Total area 63,039 sq miles (163,270 sq km)
Languages Dutch*, Pidgin English (Taki-Taki), Hindi, Javanese, Carib
Religions Christian 48%, Hindu 27%, Muslim 20%, other 5%
Ethnic mix South Asian 37%, Creole 31%, Javanese 15%, other 17%
Government Multiparty republic
Currency Guilder = 100 cents
Literacy rate 93%
Calorie consumption 2,547 kilocalories

SWAZILAND
Southern Africa

Official name Kingdom of Swaziland
Formation 1968 / 1968
Capital Mbabane
Population 900,000 / 135 people per sq mile (52 people per sq km) / 29%
Total area 6,703 sq miles (17,360 sq km)
Languages Siswati*, English*, Zulu
Religions Christian 60%, traditional beliefs 40%
Ethnic mix Swazi 95%, other 5%
Government Executive monarchy
Currency Lilangeni = 100 cents
Literacy rate 77%
Calorie consumption 2,706 kilocalories

SWEDEN
Northern Europe

Official name Kingdom of Sweden
Formation 1809 / 1905
Capital Stockholm
Population 8.8 million / 50 people per sq mile (20 people per sq km) / 83%
Total area 173,730 sq miles (449,960 sq km)
Languages Swedish*, Finnish, Lappish
Religions Evangelical Lutheran 94%, Roman Catholic 2%, other 4%
Ethnic mix Swedish 87%, Finnish and Lapp 1%, other European 12%
Government Constitutional monarchy
Currency Krona = 100 öre
Literacy rate 99%
Calorie consumption 2,972 kilocalories

Switzerland
Central Europe

Official name Swiss Confederation
Formation 1815 / 1815
Capital Bern
Population 7.2 million / 469 people per sq mile (181 people per sq km) / 60%
Total area 15,940 sq miles (41,290 sq km)
Languages German*, French*, Italian*, Romansch*
Religions Roman Catholic 48%, Protestant 44%, other 8%
Ethnic mix German 65%, French 18%, Italian 10%, other 7%
Government Federal republic
Currency Franc = 100 centimes
Literacy rate 99%
Calorie consumption 3,379 kilocalories

Syria
Southwestern Asia

Official name Syrian Arab Republic
Formation 1946 / 1946
Capital Damascus
Population 14.7 million / 207 people per sq mile (80 people per sq km) / 51%
Total area 71,500 sq miles (185,180 sq km)
Languages Arabic*, French, Kurdish, Armenian, Circassian, Turkmen
Religions Sunni Muslim 74%, other Muslim 16%, Christian 10%
Ethnic mix Arab 90%, other 10%
Government Single-party republic
Currency Pound = 100 piastres
Literacy rate 71%
Calorie consumption 3,175 kilocalories

Taiwan
Eastern Asia

Official name Republic of China
Formation 1949 / 1949
Capital Taipei
Population 20.9 million / 1,682 people per sq mile (649 people per sq km) / 69%
Total area 13,969 sq miles (36,179 sq km)
Languages Mandarin*, Amoy Chinese, Hakka Chinese
Religions Buddhist, Confucianist, Taoist 93%, other 7%
Ethnic mix Taiwanese 84%, mainland Chinese 14%, other 2%
Government Multiparty republic
Currency New Taiwan $ = 100 cents
Literacy rate 94%
Calorie consumption NOT AVAILABLE

Tajikistan
Central Asia

Official name Republic of Tajikistan
Formation 1991 / 1991
Capital Dushanbe
Population 6.1 million / 111 people per sq mile (43 people per sq km) / 32%
Total area 55,251 sq miles (143,100 sq km)
Main languages Tajik*, Uzbek, Russian
Religions Sunni Muslim 85%, Shi'a Muslim 5%, other 10%
Ethnic mix Tajik 62%, Uzbek 24%, Russian 4%, Tatar 2%, other 8%
Government Single-party republic
Currency Tajik rouble = 100 kopeks
Literacy rate 98%
Calorie consumption NOT AVAILABLE

Tanzania
Eastern Africa

Official name United Republic of Tanzania
Formation 1964 / 1964
Capital Dodoma
Population 29.7 million / 88 people per sq mile (34 people per sq km) / 22%
Total area 364,900 sq miles (945,090 sq km)
Languages English*, Swahili, Sukuma, Chagga, Nyamwezi, Hehe, Makonde
Religions Traditional beliefs 42%, Muslim 31%, Christian 27%
Ethnic mix 120 ethnic Bantu groups 99%, other 1%
Government Single-party republic
Currency Shilling = 100 cents
Literacy rate 68%
Calorie consumption 2,018 kilocalories

Thailand
Southeastern Asia

Official name Kingdom of Thailand
Formation 1882 / 1887
Capital Bangkok
Population 58.8 million / 298 people per sq mile (115 people per sq km) / 19%
Total area 198,116 sq miles (513,120 sq km)
Languages Thai*, Chinese, Malay, Khmer, Mon, Karen
Religions Buddhist 95%, other 5%
Ethnic mix Thai 75%, Chinese 14%, Malay 4%, other 7%
Government Constitutional monarchy
Currency Baht = 100 stangs
Literacy rate 94%
Calorie consumption 2,432 kilocalories

Togo
Western Africa

Official name Togolese Republic
Formation 1960 / 1960
Capital Lomé
Population 4.1 million / 195 people per sq mile (75 people per sq km) / 30%
Total area 21,927 sq miles (56,790 sq km)
Languages French*, Ewe, Kabye, Gurma
Religions Traditional beliefs 70%, Christian 20%, Muslim 10%
Ethnic mix Ewe 43%, Kabye 26%, Gurma 16%, other 15%
Government Multiparty republic
Currency CFA franc = 100 centimes
Literacy rate 52%
Calorie consumption 2,242 kilocalories

Tonga
Australasia & Oceania

Official name Kingdom of Tonga
Formation 1970 / 1970
Capital Nuku'alofa
Population 98,000 / 352 people per sq mile (136 people per sq km) / 21%
Total area 290 sq miles (750 sq km)
Languages Tongan*, English
Religions Protestant 82%, Roman Catholic 18%
Ethnic mix Tongan 98%, other 2%
Government Constitutional monarchy
Currency Pa'anga = 100 seniti
Literacy rate 99%
Calorie consumption 2,946 kilocalories

Trinidad & Tobago
West Indies

Official name Republic of Trinidad and Tobago
Formation 1962 / 1962
Capital Port-of-Spain
Population 1.3 million / 656 people per sq mile (253 people per sq km) / 70%
Total area 1,981 sq miles (5,130 sq km)
Languages English*, English Creole, Hindi, French, Spanish
Religions Christian 58%, Hindu 30%, Muslim 8%, other 4%
Ethnic mix Black 43%, South Asian 40%, mixed 14%, other 3%
Government Multiparty republic
Currency Trinidad & Tobago $ = 100 cents
Literacy rate 98%
Calorie consumption 2,585 kilocalories

Tunisia
Northern Africa

Official name Republic of Tunisia
Formation 1956 / 1956
Capital Tunis
Population 8.9 million / 148 people per sq mile (57 people per sq km) / 56%
Total area 63,170 sq miles (163,610 sq km)
Languages Arabic*, French
Religions Muslim 98%, Christian 1%, other 1%
Ethnic mix Arab and Berber 98%, European 1%, other 1%
Government Multiparty republic
Currency Dinar = 1,000 millimes
Literacy rate 67%
Calorie consumption 3,330 kilocalories

Turkey
Asia / Europe

Official name Republic of Turkey
Formation 1923 / 1939
Capital Ankara
Population 61.9 million / 207 people per sq mile (80 people per sq km) / 64%
Total area 300,950 sq miles (779,450 sq km)
Languages Turkish*, Kurdish, Arabic, Circassian, Armenian
Religions Muslim 99%, other 1%
Ethnic mix Turkish 80%, Kurdish 17%, other 3%
Government Multiparty republic
Currency Turkish lira = 100 krural
Literacy rate 82%
Calorie consumption 3,429 kilocalories

Turkmenistan
Central Asia

Official name Turkmenistan
Formation 1991 / 1991
Capital Ashgabat
Population 4.1 million / 21 people per sq mile (8 people per sq km) / 45%
Total area 188,455 sq miles (488,100 sq km)
Languages Turkmen*, Uzbek, Russian
Religions Muslim 85%, Eastern Orthodox 10%, other 5%
Ethnic mix Turkmen 72%, Russian 9%, Uzbek 9%, other 10%
Government Single-party republic
Currency Manat = 100 tenge
Literacy rate 98%
Calorie consumption NOT AVAILABLE

Tuvalu
Australasia & Oceania

Official name Tuvalu
Formation 1978 / 1978
Capital Fongafale
Population 9,000 / 997 people per sq mile (346 people per sq km) / 31%
Total area 10 sq miles (26 sq km)
Languages Tuvaluan*, Kiribati, English
Religions Protestant 97%, other 3%
Ethnic mix Tuvaluan 95% other 5%
Government Constitutional monarchy
Currency Australian $ = 100 cents
Literacy rate 95%
Calorie consumption NOT AVAILABLE

Uganda
Eastern Africa

Official name Republic of Uganda
Formation 1962 / 1962
Capital Kampala
Population 21.3 million / 277 people per sq mile (107 people per sq km) / 12%
Total area 91,073 sq miles (235,880 sq km)
Languages English*, Luganda, Nkole, Chiga, Lango, Acholi, Teso
Religions Christian 66%, traditional beliefs 18%, Muslim 16%
Ethnic mix Buganda 18%, Banyoro 14%, Teso 9%, other 59%
Government Multiparty republic
Currency Shilling = 100 cents
Literacy rate 62%
Calorie consumption 2,159 kilocalories

Ukraine
Eastern Europe

Official name Ukraine
Formation 1991 / 1991
Capital Kiev
Population 51.4 million / 220 people per sq mile (85 people per sq km) / 69%
Total area 223,090 sq miles (603,700 sq km)
Languages Ukrainian*, Russian, Tatar
Religions Mostly Ukrainian Orthodox, with Roman Catholic, Protestant and Jewish minorities
Ethnic mix Ukrainian 73%, Russian 22%, other (including Tatar) 5%
Government Multiparty republic
Currency Karbovanets (coupons)
Literacy rate 98%
Calorie consumption NOT AVAILABLE

United Arab Emirates
Southwestern Asia

Official name United Arab Emirates
Formation 1971 / 1971
Capital Abu Dhabi
Population 1.9 million / 9 people per sq mile (23 people per sq km) / 82%
Total area 32,278 sq miles (83,600 sq km)
Languages Arabic*, Farsi (Persian), Urdu, Hindi, English
Religions Sunni Muslim 77%, Shi'a Muslim 19%, other 4%
Ethnic mix South Asian 50%, Emirian 19%, other Arab 23%, other 8%
Government Federation of monarchs
Currency Dirham = 100 fils
Literacy rate 79%
Calorie consumption 3,384 kilocalories

United Kingdom
Northwestern Europe

Official name United Kingdom of Great Britain and Northern Ireland
Formation 1801 / 1922
Capital London
Population 58.3 million / 625 people per sq mile (241 people per sq km) / 89%
Total area 94,550 sq miles (244,880 sq km)
Languages English*, Welsh, Scottish, Gaelic
Religions Protestant 52%, Roman Catholic 9%, Muslim 3%, other 36%
Ethnic mix English 81%, Scottish 10%, Welsh 2%, other 7%
Government Constitutional monarchy
Currency Pound sterling = 100 pence
Literacy rate 99%
Calorie consumption 3,317 kilocalories

United States
North America

Official name United States of America
Formation 1787 / 1959
Capital Washington D.C.
Population 263.3 million / 75 people per sq mile (29 people per sq km) / 76%
Total area 3,681,760 sq miles (9,372,610 sq km)
Languages English*, Spanish, Italian, German, French, Polish, Chinese, Greek
Religions Protestant 56%, Roman Catholic 28%, Jewish 2%, other 14%
Ethnic mix White (including Hispanic) 83%, Black 13%, other 4%
Government Multiparty republic
Currency US $ = 100 cents
Literacy rate 99%
Calorie consumption 3,732 kilocalories

Uruguay
South America

Official name Oriental Republic of Uruguay
Formation 1828 / 1909
Capital Montevideo
Population 3.2 million / 122 people per sq mile (18 people per sq km) / 90%
Total area 67,494 sq miles (174,810 sq km)
Languages Spanish*
Religions Roman Catholic 66%, Protestant 2%, Jewish 2%, other 30%
Ethnic mix European 88%, *mestizo* 8% Black 4%
Government Multiparty republic
Currency Peso = 100 centimes
Literacy rate 97%
Calorie consumption 2,750 kilocalories

Uzbekistan
Central Asia

Official name Republic of Uzbekistan
Formation 1991 / 1991
Capital Tashkent
Population 22.8 million / 132 people per sq mile (51 people per sq km) / 41%
Total area 439,733 sq miles (1,138,910 sq km)
Languages Uzbek*, Russian
Religions Muslim 88%, other (mostly Eastern Orthodox) 12%
Ethnic mix Uzbek 71%, Russian 8%, Tajik 5%, Kazakh 4%, other 12%
Government Single-party republic
Currency Sum = 100 teen
Literacy rate 97%
Calorie consumption NOT AVAILABLE

Vanuatu
Australasia & Oceania

Official name Republic of Vanuatu
Formation 1980 / 1980
Capital Port-Vila
Population 200,000 / 41 people per sq mile (16 people per sq km) / 19%
Total area 4,706 sq miles (12,190 sq km)
Languages Bislama*, English, French
Religions Protestant 77%, Roman Catholic 15%, traditional beliefs 8%
Ethnic mix Ni-Vanuatu 98%, other 2%
Government Multiparty republic
Currency Vatu = 100 centimes
Literacy rate 70%
Calorie consumption 2,739 kilocalories

Vatican City
Southern Europe

Official name Vatican City State
Formation 1929 / 1929
Capital Not applicable
Population 1,000 / 5,890 people per sq mile (2,273 people per sq km) /100%
Total area 0.17 sq miles (0.44 sq km)
Languages Italian*, Latin*
Religions Roman Catholic 100%
Ethnic mix Italian 90%, Swiss 10% (including the Swiss Guard, responsible for papal security)
Government Papal Commission
Currency Italian lira = 100 centesimi
Literacy rate 100%
Calorie consumption 3,561 kilocalories

Venezuela
South America

Official name Republic of Venezuela
Formation 1830 / 1929
Capital Caracas
Population 21.8 million / 65 people per sq mile (25 people per sq km) / 91%
Total area 352,143 sq miles (912,050 sq km)
Languages Spanish*, Amerindian languages
Religions Roman Catholic 96%, Protestant 2%, other 2%
Ethnic mix *mestizo* 67%, White 21%, Black 10%, Amerindian 2%
Government Multiparty republic
Currency Bolívar = 100 centimos
Literacy rate 91%
Calorie consumption 2,618 kilocalories

Vietnam
Southeastern Asia

Official name Socialist Republic of Vietnam
Formation 1976 / 1976
Capital Hanoi
Population 74.5 million / 593 people per sq mile (229 people per sq km) / 20%
Total area 127,243 sq miles (329,560 sq km)
Languages Vietnamese*, Chinese, Thai, Khmer, Muong
Religions Buddhist 55%, Roman Catholic 7%, Muslim 1%, other 37%
Ethnic mix Vietnamese 88%, Chinese 4%, Thai 2%, other 6%
Government Single-party republic
Currency Dong = 10 hao = 100 xu
Literacy rate 94%
Calorie consumption 2,250 kilocalories

Western Samoa
Australasia & Oceania

Official name Independent State of Western Samoa
Formation 1962 / 1962
Capital Apia
Population 169,000 / 155 people per sq mile (60 people per sq km) / 21%
Total area 1,027 sq miles (2,840 sq km)
Languages Samoan*, English*
Religions Protestant 74%, Roman Catholic 26%
Ethnic mix Samoan 93%, other 7%
Government Parliamentary state
Currency Tala = 100 sene
Literacy rate 92%
Calorie consumption 2,828 kilocalories

Yemen
Southwestern Asia

Official name Republic of Yemen
Formation 1990 / 1990
Capital Sana
Population 14.5 million / 70 people per sq mile (27 people per sq km) / 31%
Total area 203,849 sq miles (527,970 sq km)
Languages Arabic*, Hindi, Tamil, Urdu
Religions Sunni Muslim 55%, Shi'a Muslim 42%, other 3%
Ethnic mix Arab 95%, Afro-Arab 3%, South Asian, African, European 2%
Government Multiparty republic
Currency Rial (North), Dinar (South) – both are legal currency
Literacy rate 41%
Calorie consumption 2,203 kilocalories

Yugoslavia (Serbia & Montenegro) *Europe*

Official name Federal Republic of Yugoslavia
Formation 1992 / 1992
Capital Belgrade
Population 10.8 million / 1,088 people per sq mile (420 people per sq km) / 50%
Total area 9,929 sq miles (25,715 sq km)
Languages Serbian*, Croatian, Albanian
Religions Roman Catholic, Eastern Orthodox 65%, Muslim 19%, other 16%
Ethnic mix Serb 63%, Albanian 14%, Montenegrin 6%, other 17%
Government Multiparty republic
Currency Dinar = 100 para
Literacy rate 93%
Calorie consumption NOT AVAILABLE

Zaire *now called* Congo (Democratic Republic of)
Central Africa

Official name Republic of Zaire
Formation 1960 / 1960
Capital Kinshasa
Population 43.9 million / 49 people per sq mile (19 people per sq km) / 29%
Total area 905,563 sq miles (2,345,410 sq km)
Languages French*, Kiswahili, Tshiluba, Lingala
Religions Christian 70%, traditional beliefs 20%, Muslim 10%
Ethnic mix Bantu 23%, Hamitic 23%, other 54%
Government Transitional
Currency New zaire = 100 makuta
Literacy rate 77%
Calorie consumption 2,060 kilocalories

Zambia
Southern Africa

Official name Republic of Zambia
Formation 1964 / 1964
Capital Lusaka
Population 9.5 million / 34 people per sq mile (13 people per sq km) / 42%
Total area 285,992 sq miles (740,720 sq km)
Languages English*, Bemba*, Nyanja*, Tonga, Kaonde, Lunda
Religions Christian 63%, Traditional beliefs 35%, other 2%
Ethnic mix Bemba 36%, Maravi 18%, Tonga 15%, other 31%
Government Multiparty republic
Currency Kwacha = 100 ngwee
Literacy rate 78%
Calorie consumption 1,931 kilocalories

Zimbabwe
Southern Africa

Official name Republic of Zimbabwe
Formation 1980 / 1980
Capital Harare
Population 11.3 million / 75 people per sq mile (29 people per sq km) / 30%
Total area 150,800 sq miles (390,580 sq km)
Languages English*, Shona, Ndebele
Religions Syncretic (Christian and traditional beliefs) 50%, Christian 26%, traditional beliefs 24%
Ethnic mix Shona 71%, Ndebele 16%, other 11%, White, Asian 2%
Government Multiparty republic
Currency Zimbabwe $ = 100 cents
Literacy rate 85%
Calorie consumption 1,985 kilocalories

GLOSSARY

THIS GLOSSARY lists most geographical, technical, and foreign language terms that appear in the text, followed by a brief definition of the term. Any acronyms used in the text are also listed. Terms in italics are for cross-reference and indicate that the word is defined separately in the glossary.

A

Aboriginal The original (*indigenous*) inhabitants of a country or continent. Particularly used in reference to Australia.

Abyssal plain A broad *plain* found in the depths of the ocean, more than 10,000 ft (3,000 m) below sea level.

Acid rain Rain, sleet, snow, or mist that has absorbed waste gases from fossil-fueled power stations and vehicle exhaust fumes, becoming more acid. It causes severe environmental damage.

Adaptation The gradual evolution of plants and animals to enhance their abilites to survive and reproduce in their *environment*.

Afforestation The planting of new forest in areas that were once forested but have been cleared.

Agribusiness A term applied to activities such as growing crops, rearing animals, or manufacturing of farm machinery, that eventually leads to the supply of agricultural produce at market.

Air mass A huge, homogeneous mass of air, within which horizontal patterns of temperature and *humidity* are consistent. Air masses are separated by *fronts*.

Alliance An agreement between two or more nations, to work together to achieve common purposes.

Alluvial fan A large fan-shaped deposit of fine sediments deposited by a river as it emerges from a narrow, mountain valley onto a broad, open *plain*.

Alluvium Material deposited by rivers. Today usually applied only to finer particles of silt and clay.

Alpine Mountain *environment* between the *tree line* and the level of permanent snow cover.

Alpine mountains Ranges of mountains formed from 30 million to 65 million years ago by *folding*, in west and central Europe.

Amerindian A term applied to people *indigenous* to Mexico, Central and South America.

Animal husbandry The business of rearing animals.

Antarctic circle The parallel that lies at a *latitude* of 66° 32' S.

Anticline A geological *fold* that forms an arch shape, curving upward in the rock *strata*.

Anticyclone An area of relatively high atmospheric pressure.

Aquaculture Collective term for the farming of produce derived from the sea, including fish-farming and the cultivation of shellfish and plants such as seaweed.

Aquifer A body of rock that can absorb water. Also applied to any rock strata that have sufficient porosity to yield *groundwater* through wells or springs.

Arable Land that has been plowed and is in use for cultivation, or is suitable for growing crops.

Archipelago A group or chain of islands.

Arctic Circle The parallel that lies at a *latitude* of 66° 32' N.

Arête A thin, jagged mountain ridge that divides two adjacent *cirques*, found in regions where *glaciation* has occurred.

Arid Dry. An area of low rainfall, where the rate of *evaporation* may be greater than that of *precipitation*. Often defined as those areas that receive less than one inch (25 mm) of rain a year. Only drought-resistant plants can survive in these areas.

Artesian well A naturally occurring source of underground water, stored in an *aquifer*.

Artisanal Small-scale, manual operation, such as fishing, using little or no machinery.

ASEAN Association of Southeast Asian Nations. Established in 1967 to promote economic, social, and cultural cooperation. Its members include Brunei, Indonesia, Malaysia, Philippines, Singapore, and Thailand.

Aseismic A region where *earthquake* activity has ceased.

Asteroid A minor planet circling the Sun, mainly between the orbits of Mars and Jupiter.

Asthenosphere A zone of hot, partially melted rock, which underlies the *lithosphere*, within the Earth's *crust*.

Atmosphere The envelope of odorless, colorless, and tasteless gases surrounding the Earth, consisting of *oxygen* (23%), *nitrogen* (75%), argon (1%), and *carbon dioxide* (0.03%), as well as tiny proportions of other gases.

Atmospheric pressure The pressure created by the action of gravity on the gases surrounding the Earth.

Atoll A ring-shaped island or *coral reef* often enclosing a *lagoon* of seawater.

Avalanche The rapid movement of a mass of snow and ice down a steep slope. Similar movements of other materials are described as rock avalanches or *landslides* and sand avalanches.

B

Badlands A landscape that has been heavily eroded and dissected by rainwater, and supports little or no vegetation.

Back slope The gentler windward slope of a sand *dune* or gentler slope of a *cuesta*.

Bajos An *alluvial fan* deposited by a river at the base of mountains and hills that encircle *desert* areas.

Bar, coastal An offshore strip of sand or shingle, either above or below the water. Usually parallel to the shore but sometimes crescent-shaped or at an oblique angle.

Barchan A crescent-shaped sand *dune*, formed where wind direction is very consistent. The horns of the crescent point downwind, and where there is enough sand, the barchan is mobile.

Barrio A Spanish term for the shantytowns – settlements of shacks – that are clustered around many South and Central American cities (*see also Favela*).

Basalt Dark, fine-grained *igneous rock* that is formed near the Earth's surface from rapidly cooling *lava*.

Base level The level below which flowing water cannot erode the land.

Basement rock A mass of ancient rock, often of *Precambrian age*, covered by a layer of more recent *sedimentary rocks*. Commonly associated with *shield* areas.

Beach Shore of a sea or lake where waves break and there is an accumulation of loose sand, mud, gravel, or pebbles.

Bedrock Solid, consolidated, and relatively unweathered rock, found on the surface of the land or just below a layer of soil or *weathered* rock.

Biodiversity The quantity of animal or plant species in a given area.

Biomass The total mass of organic matter – plants and animals – in a given area. It is usually measured in kilograms per square meter. Plant biomass is proportionally greater than that of animals, except in cities.

Biosphere The zone just above and below the Earth's surface where all plants and animals live.

Blizzard A severe windstorm with snow and sleet. Visibility is often severely restricted.

Bluff The steep bank of a *meander*, formed by the erosive action of a river.

Boreal forest Tracts of mainly coniferous forest found in northern *latitudes*.

Breccia A type of rock composed of sharp fragments, cemented by a fine-grained material such as clay.

Butte An isolated, flat-topped hill with steep or vertical sides, buttes are the eroded remnants of a former land surface.

C

Caatinga Portuguese (Brazilian) term for thorny woodland growing in areas of pale granitic soils.

CACM Central American Common Market. Established in 1960 to further economic ties between its members, which are Costa Rica, El Salvador, Guatemala, Honduras, and Nicaragua.

Calcite Hexagonal crystals of calcium carbonate.

Caldera A huge volcanic vent, often containing a number of smaller vents, and sometimes a crater lake.

Carbon cycle The transfer of carbon to and from the *atmosphere*. This occurs on land through *photosynthesis*. In the sea, *carbon dioxide* is absorbed, some returning to the air and some taken up into the bodies of sea creatures.

Carbon dioxide A colorless, odorless gas (CO_2) that makes up 0.03% of the *atmosphere*.

Carbonation The process in which rocks are broken down by carbonic acid. Carbon dioxide in the air dissolves in rainwater, forming carbonic acid. *Limestone* terrain can be eaten away rapidly.

Cash crop A single crop grown specifically for export sale, instead of local use. Typical examples include coffee, tea, and citrus fruits.

Cassava A type of grain meal, used to produce tapioca. A staple crop in many parts of Africa.

Castle kopje Hill or rock outcrop, especially in southern Africa, where steep sides, and a summit composed of blocks, give a castlelike appearance.

Cataracts A series of stepped waterfalls created as a river flows over a band of hard, resistant rock.

Causeway A raised route through marshland or a body of water.

CEEAC Economic Community of Central African States. Established in 1983 to promote regional cooperation and if possible, establish a common market between 11 Central African nations.

Chemical weathering The chemical reactions leading to the decomposition of rocks. Types of chemical weathering include *carbonation, hydrolysis,* and *oxidation*.

Chernozem A fertile soil, also known as "black earth" consisting of a layer of dark topsoil rich in decaying vegetation, overlying a lighter chalky layer.

Cirque Found in mountain regions, an armchair-shaped basin with a steep back, or rear, wall and a raised rock lip, often containing a lake (or *tarn*). The cirque floor has been eroded by a *glacier*, while the back wall is eroded both by a *glacier* and by *weathering*.

Climate The average weather conditions in a given area over a period of years, sometimes defined as 30 years or more.

Cold War A period of hostile relations between the US and the former Soviet Union and their allies after World War II.

Composite volcano Also known as a strato-volcano, the volcanic cone is composed of alternating deposits of *lava* and *pyroclastic* material.

Compound A substance made up of *elements* chemically combined in a consistent way.

Condensation The process in which a gas changes into a liquid. For example, water vapor in the *atmosphere* condenses around tiny airborne particles to form droplets of water.

Confluence The point at which two rivers meet.

Conglomerate Rock composed of large, water worn, or rounded pebbles, held together by a natural cement.

Coniferous forest A forest type containing trees that are generally, but not necessarily, *evergreen* and have slender, needlelike leaves. Coniferous trees reproduce by means of seeds contained in a cone.

Continental drift The theory that the continents of today are fragments of one or more prehistoric *supercontinents* that have moved across the Earth's surface, creating ocean basins. The theory has been superseded by a more sophisticated theory, known as *plate tectonics*.

Continental shelf An area of the continental *crust*, below sea level, that slopes gently. It is separated from the deep ocean by a much more steeply inclined *continental slope*.

Continental slope A steep slope running from the edge of the *continental shelf* to the ocean floor.

Conurbation A vast metropolitan area created by the expansion of towns and cities into a virtually continuous urban area.

Cool continental A rainy *climate* with warm summers [warmest month below 76°F (22°C)] and often severe winters [coldest month below 32°F (0°C)].

Copra The dried white kernel of a coconut, from which coconut oil is extracted.

Coral reef An underwater barrier created by colonies of the coral polyp. Polyps secrete a protective skeleton of calcium carbonate, and reefs develop as live polyps build on the skeletons of dead generations.

Core The center of the Earth, consisting of a dense mass of iron and nickel. It is thought that the outer core is molten or liquid, and that the hot inner core is solid due to extremely high pressures.

Coriolis effect A deflecting force caused by the rotation of the Earth. In the northern hemisphere a body, such as an *air mass* or ocean current, is deflected to the right, and in the southern hemisphere to the left. This prevents winds from blowing straight from areas of high to low pressure.

Coulée A term for a ravine or gully created by river *erosion*.

Craton A large block of the Earth's *crust* that has remained stable for a long period of *geological time*. It is made up of ancient *shield* rocks.

Cretaceous A period of *geological time* beginning about 145 million years ago and lasting until about 65 million years ago.

Crevasse A deep crack in a *glacier*.

Crust The hard, thin, outer shell of the Earth. The crust floats on the *mantle*, which is softer and more dense. Under the oceans (oceanic crust) the crust is 3.7–6.8 miles (6–11 km) thick. Continental crust averages 18–24 miles (30–40 km).

Crystalline rock Rocks formed when molten *magma* crystallizes (*igneous rocks*) or when heat or pressure cause recrystallization (*metamorphic rocks*). Crystalline rocks are distinct from *sedimentary rocks*.

Cuesta A hill that rises into a steep slope on one side but has a gentler gradient on its other slope.

Cyclone An area of low *atmospheric pressure*, occurring where the air is warm and relatively low in density, causing low level winds to spiral. *Hurricanes* and *typhoons* are tropical cyclones.

D

De facto
1 Government or other activity that takes place, or exists in reality if not by right.
2 A border that exists in practice, but is not officially recognized by all of the countries it adjoins.

Deciduous forest A forest of trees that shed their leaves annually at a particular time or season. In *temperate* climates the fall of leaves occurs in the autumn. Some *coniferous* trees, such as the larch, are deciduous. Deciduous vegetation contrasts with *evergreen*, which keeps its leaves for more than a year.

Defoliant Chemical spray used to remove foliage (leaves) from trees.

Deforestation The act of cutting down and clearing large areas of forest for human activities, such as agriculture or urban development.

Delta Low-lying, fan-shaped area at the mouth of a river, formed by the *deposition* of successive layers of *sediment*. Slowing as it enters the sea, a river deposits sediment and may, as a result, split into numerous smaller channels, known as *distributaries*.

Denudation The combined effect of *weathering, erosion,* and *mass movement*, which, over long periods of time, exposes underlying rocks.

Deposition The laying down of material that has accumulated:
(*1*) after being *eroded* and then transported by physical forces such as wind, ice, or water;
(*2*) as organic remains, such as coal and coral;
(*3*) as the result of *evaporation* and chemical *precipitation*.

Depression
1 In climatic terms, a large low pressure system.
2 A complex *fold*, producing a large valley that incorporates both a *syncline* and an *anticline*.

Desert An *arid* region of low rainfall with little vegetation or animal life, except that which has adapted to the dry conditions. The term is now applied not only to hot tropical and subtropical regions, but to arid areas of the continental interiors and to the ice deserts of the *Arctic* and *Antarctic*.

Desertification The gradual extension of *desert* conditions in *arid* or *semiarid* regions, as a result of climatic change or human activity, such as overgrazing and *deforestation*.

Despot A ruler with absolute power. Despots are often associated with oppressive regimes.

Detritus Piles of rock deposited by an erosive agent such as a river or *glacier*.

Distributary Common at *deltas*, a minor branch of a river that does not rejoin the main stream.

Diurnal Something that occurs on a daily basis. Diurnal temperature refers to the variation in temperature over the course of a full day and night.

Divide A term describing the area of high ground separating two *drainage basins*.

Donga A steep-sided *gully*, resulting from *erosion* by a river or by floods.

Dormant A term used to describe a *volcano* that is not currently erupting. Dormant *volcanoes* are different from extinct *volcanoes* since they are still considered likely to erupt in the future.

Drainage basin The area drained by a single river system. Its boundary is marked by a *watershed* or *divide*.

Drought A long period of continuously low rainfall.

Drumlin A long, streamlined hillock composed of material deposited by a *glacier*. They often occur in groups known as swarms.

Dune A mound or ridge of sand, shaped, and often moved, by the wind. They are found in hot *deserts* and on low-lying coasts where onshore winds blow across sandy beaches.

Dyke A wall constructed in low-lying areas to contain floodwaters or protect the land from high tides.

E

Earthflow The rapid movement of soil and other loose surface material down a slope, when saturated with water. It is similar to a *mudflow* but does not flow as fast due to a lower percentage of water.

Earthquake Sudden movements of the Earth's *crust*, causing the ground to shake. Frequently occurring at *tectonic plate* margins, the shock, or series of shocks, spreads out from an *epicenter*.

EC The European Community (*see* EU).

Ecosystem A system of living organisms – plants and animals – interacting with their *environment*.

ECOWAS Economic Community of West African States. Established in 1975, it incorporates 16 West African states and aims to promote closer regional and economic cooperation.

Element
1 A constituent of the *climate* – *precipitation, humidity*, temperature, *atmospheric pressure*, or wind.
2 A substance that cannot be separated into simpler substances by chemical means.

El Niño A climatic phenomenon, the El Niño effect occurs about 14 times every century and leads to major shifts in global air circulation. It is associated with unusually warm currents off the coasts of Peru, Ecuador, and Chile. The anomaly can last for up to two years.

Environment The conditions created by the surroundings (both natural and artificial) within which an organism lives. In human geography the word includes the surrounding economic, cultural, and social conditions.

Eon (aeon) Traditionally a long, but not indefinite, period of *geological time*.

Ephemeral A nonpermanent feature, the term is often used in connection with seasonal rivers or lakes in dry areas.

Epicenter The point on the Earth's surface directly above the underground origin – or focus – of an *earthquake*.

Equator The line of *latitude* that lies equidistant between the North and South Poles.

Erg An extensive area of sand *dunes*, particularly in the Sahara Desert.

Erosion The processes that wear away the surface of the land. *Glaciers*, wind, rivers, waves, and currents all carry debris that causes erosion. Some definitions also include *mass movement* due to gravity as an agent of erosion.

Escarpment A steep slope at the margin of a level, upland surface. In a landscape created by *folding*, escarpments (or scarps) frequently lie behind a more gentle backward slope.

Esker A narrow, winding ridge of sand and gravel deposited by streams of water flowing beneath or at the edge of a *glacier*.

Erratic A rock transported by a *glacier* and deposited some distance from its place of origin.

Eustacy A worldwide fall or rise in ocean levels.

EU The European Union. Established in 1965, it was formerly known as the EEC (European Economic Community) and then the EC (European Community). Its members are Austria, Belgium, Denmark, Finland, France, Germany, Greece, Ireland, Italy, Luxembourg, Netherlands, Portugal, Spain, Sweden, and the UK. It seeks to establish an integrated European common market and eventual federation.

Evaporation The process in which a liquid or solid is turned into a gas or vapor. It also refers to the diffusion of water vapor into the *atmosphere* from exposed water surfaces such as lakes and seas.

Evapotranspiration The loss of moisture from the Earth's surface through a combination of *evaporation*, and *transpiration* from the leaves of plants.

Evergreen Plants with long-lasting leaves that are not shed annually or seasonally.

Exfoliation A type of *weathering* in which scalelike flakes of rock are peeled or broken off by the development of salt crystals in water within the rocks. *Groundwater*, which contains dissolved salts, seeps to the surface and evaporates, precipitating a film of salt crystals. These crystals expand and cause fine cracks. As the cracks grow, flakes of rock break off.

Extrusive rock *Igneous* rock formed when molten material, *magma*, pours forth at the Earth's surface and cools rapidly. It usually has a glassy texture.

F

Factionalism The actions of one or more minority political group acting against the interests of the majority government.

Fault A fracture or crack in rock, where strains (*tectonic* movement) have caused blocks to move, vertically or laterally, relative to each other.

Fauna Collective name for the animals of a particular period of time, or region.

Favela Brazilian term for the shantytowns of temporary huts that lie around the edge of many South and Central American cities.

Ferrel cell A component in the global pattern of air circulation, which rises in the colder *latitudes* (60° N and S) and descends in warmer *latitudes* (30° N and S). The Ferrel cell forms part of the world's three-cell air circulation pattern, with the *Hadley* and Polar cells.

Fissure A deep crack in a rock or a *glacier*.

Fjord A deep, narrow inlet, created when the sea inundates the *U-shaped valley* created by a *glacier*.

Flash flood A sudden, short-lived rise in the water level of a river or stream, or surge of water down a dry river channel, or *wadi*, caused by heavy rainfall.

Flax A plant used to make linen.

Floodplain The broad, flat part of a river valley, adjacent to the river itself, formed by *sediment* deposited during flooding.

Flora The collective name for the plants of a particular period of time or region.

Flow The movement of a river within its banks, particularly in terms of the speed and volume of water.

Fold A bend in the rock *strata* of the Earth's *crust*, resulting from compression.

Fossil The remains, or traces, of a dead organism preserved in the Earth's *crust*.

Fossil dune A *dune* formed in a once-*arid* region that is now wetter. *Dunes* normally move with the wind, but in these cases vegetation makes them stable.

Fossil fuel Fuel – coal, natural gas, or oil – composed of the fossilized remains of plants and animals.

Front The boundary between two *air masses* that contrast sharply in temperature and *humidity*.

Frontal depression An area of low pressure caused by rising warm air. They are generally 600–1,200 miles (1,000–2,000 km) in diameter. Within *depressions* there are both warm and cold fronts.

Frost shattering A form of *weathering* where water freezes in cracks, causing expansion. As temperatures fluctuate and the ice melts and refreezes, it eventually causes the rocks to shatter and fragments of rock to break off.

G

Gaucho South American term for a stock herder or cowboy who works on the grassy *plains* of Paraguay, Uruguay, and Argentina.

Geological timescale The chronology of the Earth's history as revealed in its rocks. Geological time is divided into a number of periods: *eon*, era, period, epoch, age, and chron (the shortest). These units are not of uniform length.

Geosyncline A concave fold (*syncline*) or large depression in the Earth's *crust*, extending hundreds of miles. This basin contains a deep layer of sediment, especially at its center, from the land masses around it.

Geothermal energy Heat derived from hot rocks within the Earth's *crust* and resulting in hot springs, steam, or hot rocks at the surface. The energy is generated by rock movements, and from the breakdown of radioactive elements occurring under intense pressure.

GDP Gross Domestic Product. The total value of goods and services produced by a country excluding income from foreign countries.

Geyser A jet of steam and hot water that intermittently erupts from vents in the ground in areas that are, or were, *volcanic*. Some geysers occasionally reach heights of 196 ft (60 m).

Ghetto An area of a city or region occupied by an overwhelming majority of people from one racial or religious group, who may be subject to persecution or containment.

Glaciation The growth of *glaciers* and *ice sheets*, and their impact on the landscape.

Glacier A body of ice moving downslope under the influence of gravity and consisting of compacted and frozen snow. A glacier is distinct from an *ice sheet*, which is wider and less confined by features of the landscape.

Glacio-eustacy A worldwide change in the level of the oceans, caused when the formation of *ice sheets* takes up water or when their melting returns water to the ocean. The formation of *ice sheets* in the *Pleistocene* epoch, for example, caused sea level to drop by about 320 ft (100 m).

Glaciofluvial To do with glacial *meltwater*, the landforms it creates, and its processes; *erosion*, transportation, and *deposition*. Glaciofluvial effects are more powerful and rapid when they occur within or beneath the *glacier*, rather than beyond its edge.

Glacis A gentle slope or *pediment*.

Global warming An increase in the average temperature of the Earth. At present the *greenhouse effect* is thought to contribute to this.

GNP Gross National Product. The total value of goods and services produced by a country.

Gondwanaland The *supercontinent* thought to have existed over 200 million years ago in the southern hemisphere. Gondwanaland is believed to have comprised today's Africa, Madagascar, Australia, parts of South America, *Antarctica*, and the Indian subcontinent.

Graben A block of rock let down between two parallel *faults*. Where the graben occurs within a valley, the structure is known as a *rift valley*.

Grease ice Slicks of ice that form in *Antarctic* seas, when ice crystals are bonded together by wind and wave action.

Greenhouse effect A change in the temperature of the *atmosphere*. Short-wave solar radiation travels through the *atmosphere* unimpeded to the Earth's surface, while outgoing, long-wave terrestrial radiation is absorbed by materials that reradiate it back to the Earth. Radiation trapped in this way, by water vapor, carbon dioxide, and other "greenhouse gases," keeps the Earth warm. As more *carbon dioxide* is released into the atmosphere by the burning of *fossil fuels*, the greenhouse effect may cause a global increase in temperature.

Groundwater Water that has seeped into the pores, cavities, and cracks of rocks or into soil and water held in an *aquifer*.

Gully A deep, narrow channel eroded in the landscape by *ephemeral* streams.

Guyot A small, flat-topped submarine mountain, formed as a result of subsidence that occurs during *sea-floor spreading*.

Gypsum A soft mineral *compound* (hydrated calcium sulfate), used as the basis of many forms of plaster, including plaster of Paris.

H

Hadley cell A large-scale component in the global pattern of air circulation. Warm air rises over the *Equator* and blows at high altitude toward the poles, sinking in subtropical regions (30° N and 30° S) and creating high pressure. The air then flows at the surface toward the *Equator* in the form of trade winds. There is one cell in each hemisphere. The Hadley cell is named after G. Hadley, who published his theory in 1735.

Hamada An Arabic word for a plateau of bare rock in a *desert*.

Hanging valley A tributary valley that ends suddenly, high above the bed of the main valley. The effect is found where the main valley has been more deeply eroded by a *glacier*, than has the tributary valley. A stream in a hanging valley will descend to the floor of the main valley as a waterfall or *cataract*.

Headward The action of a river eroding back upstream, as opposed to the normal process of downstream *erosion*. Headward *erosion* is often associated with *gullying*.

Hoodos Pinnacles of rock that have been worn away by *weathering* in *semiarid* regions.

Horst A block of the Earth's *crust* that has been left protruding from the Earth's surface by the sinking of adjoining blocks along fault lines.

Hot spot A region of the Earth's *crust* where high thermal activity occurs, often leading to volcanic eruptions. Hot spots often occur far from plate boundaries, but their movement is associated with *plate tectonics*.

Humid equatorial Rainy *climate* with no winter, where the coolest month is generally above 64°F (18°C).

Humidity The relative amount of moisture held in the Earth's *atmosphere*.

Hurricane
1 A tropical *cyclone* occurring in the Caribbean and western North Atlantic.
2 A wind of more than 65 knots (47 mph).

Hydroelectric power Energy produced by harnessing the rapid movement of water down steep mountain slopes to drive turbines that generate electricity.

Hydrolysis The chemical breakdown of rocks in reaction with water, forming new compounds.

I

Ice Age A period in the Earth's history when surface temperatures in the temperate *latitudes* were much lower and *ice sheets* expanded considerably. There have been *ice ages* from *Precambrian* times onward. The most recent began two million years ago and ended 10,000 years ago.

Ice cap A permanent dome of ice in highland areas. The term ice cap is often seen as distinct from *ice sheet*, which denotes a much wider covering of ice. The term is also used to describe the very extensive *polar* and Greenland ice caps.

Ice floe A large, flat mass of ice floating free on the ocean surface. It is usually formed after the breakup of winter ice by heavy storms.

Ice sheet A continuous, very thick layer of ice and snow. The term is usually used to denote ice masses that are continental in extent.

Ice shelf A floating mass of ice attached to the edge of a coast. The seaward edge is usually a sheer cliff up to 100 ft (30 m) high.

Ice wedge Massive blocks of ice up to 6.5 ft (2 m) wide at the top and extending 32 ft (10 m) deep. They are found in cracks in *polygonally-patterned* ground in *periglacial* regions.

Iceberg A large mass of ice in a lake or a sea that has broken off from a floating *ice sheet* (an *ice shelf*) or from a *glacier*.

Igneous rock Rock formed when molten material, *magma*, from the hot, lower layers of the Earth's *crust* cools, solidifies, and crystallizes, either within the Earth's *crust* (*intrusive*) or on the surface (*extrusive*).

IMF International Monetary Fund. Established in 1944 as a UN agency, it contains 175 members from around the world and is concerned with world monetary stability and economic development.

Incised meander A *meander* where the river, following its original course, cuts deeply into *bedrock*. This may occur when a mature, meandering river begins to erode its bed much more vigorously after the surrounding land has been uplifted.

Indigenous People, plants, or animals that are native to a particular region.

Infrastructure The communications and services – roads, railroads, and telecommunications – necessary for the functioning of a country or region.

Inselberg An isolated, steep-sided hill, rising from a low *plain* in *semiarid* and *savannah* landscapes. Inselbergs are usually composed of a rock, such as granite, which resists *erosion*.

Interglacial A period of global *climate*, between two *ice ages*, when temperatures rise and *ice sheets* and *glaciers* retreat.

Intraplate volcano A *volcano* that lies in the center of one of the Earth's *tectonic plates*, instead of, as is more common, at its edge. They are thought to have been formed by a *hot spot*.

Intrusion (intrusive igneous rock) Rock formed when molten material, *magma*, penetrates existing rocks below the Earth's surface before cooling and solidifying. These rocks cool more slowly than extrusive rock and therefore tend to have coarser grains.

Irrigation The artificial supply of agricultural water to dry areas, often involving the creation of canals and the diversion of natural watercourses.

Island arc A curved chain of islands. Typically, such an arc fringes an ocean trench, formed at the margin between two *tectonic plates*. As one plate overrides another, *earthquakes* and volcanic activity are common. The islands themselves are often volcanic cones.

Isostasy The state of equilibrium that the Earth's *crust* maintains as its lighter and heavier parts float on the denser underlying mantle.

Isthmus A narrow strip of land connecting two larger landmasses or islands.

J

Jet stream A narrow belt of westerly winds in the *troposphere*, at altitudes above 39,000 ft (12,000 m). Jet streams tend to blow more strongly in winter and include: the subtropical jet stream; the *polar* front jet stream in mid-*latitudes*; the *Arctic* jet stream; and the *polar*-night jet stream.

Joint A crack in a rock, formed where blocks of rock have not shifted relative to each other, as is the case with a *fault*. Joints are created by *folding*; by shrinkage in *igneous rock* as it cools or *sedimentary rock* as it dries out; and by the release of pressure in a rock mass when overlying materials are removed by *erosion*.

Jute A plant fiber used to make coarse ropes, sacks, and matting.

K

Kame A mound of stratified sand and gravel with steep sides, deposited in a *crevasse* by *meltwater* running over a *glacier*. When the ice retreats, this forms an undulating terrain of hummocks.

Karst A barren *limestone* landscape created by carbonic acid in streams and rainwater, in areas where *limestone* is close to the surface. Typical features include caverns, towerlike hills, *sinkholes*, and flat limestone pavements.

Kettle hole A round hollow formed in a glacial deposit by a detached block of glacial ice, which later melted. They can fill with water to form kettle-lakes.

L

Lagoon A shallow stretch of coastal saltwater behind a partial barrier such as a sandbank or *coral reef*. Lagoon is also used to describe the water encircled by an *atoll*.

LAIA Latin American Integration Association. Established in 1980, its members are Argentina, Bolivia, Brazil, Chile, Colombia, Ecuador, Mexico, Paraguay, Peru, Uruguay, and Venezuela. It aims to promote economic cooperation between member states.

Landslide The sudden downslope movement of a mass of rock or earth on a slope, caused either by heavy rain, the impact of waves, an *earthquake*, or human activity.

Laterite A hard red deposit left by *chemical weathering* in tropical conditions, and consisting mainly of oxides of iron and aluminum.

Latitude The angular distance from the *Equator* to a given point on the Earth's surface. Imaginary lines of *latitude* running parallel to the Equator encircle the Earth, and are measured in degrees north or south of the Equator. The Equator is 0°, the poles 90° South and North respectively. Also called parallels.

Laurasia In the theory of *continental drift*, the northern part of the great *supercontinent* of *Pangaea*. Laurasia is said to consist of North America, Greenland, and all of Eurasia north of the Indian subcontinent.

Lava The molten rock, *magma*, that erupts onto the Earth's surface through a *volcano*, or through a *fault* or crack in the Earth's *crust*. Lava refers to the rock both in its molten, and in its later solidified, form.

Leaching The process in which water dissolves minerals and moves them down through layers of soil or rock.

Levée A raised bank alongside the channel of a river. Levées are either manufactured or formed naturally in times of flood when the river overflows its channel, slows, and deposits much of its *sediment* load.

Lichen An organism that is the symbiotic product of an algae and a fungus. Lichens form in tight crusts on stones and trees, and are resistant to extreme cold. They are often found in tundra regions.

Lignite Low-grade coal, also known as brown coal. Found in large deposits in eastern Europe.

Limestone A porous *sedimentary* rock formed from carbonate materials.

Lingua franca The language adopted as the common language between speakers whose native languages are different. This is common in former colonial nations.

Lithosphere The rigid upper layer of the Earth, consisting of the *crust* and the upper part of the *mantle*.

Llanos Vast grassland *plains* of northern South America.

Loess Fine-grained, yellow deposits of unstratified silts and sands. Loess is believed to be wind-carried *sediment* created in the last *Ice Age*. Some deposits may have been redistributed by rivers later. Loess-derived soils are of a high quality, fertile, and easy to work.

Longitude A division of the Earth that pinpoints how far east or west a given place is from the Prime Meridian (0°), which runs through the Royal Observatory at Greenwich, England (UK). Imaginary lines of longitude are drawn around the world from pole to pole. The world is divided into 360 degrees.

Longshore drift The movement of sand and silt along the coast, carried by waves hitting the beach at an angle.

M

Magma Underground, molten rock that is very hot and highly charged with gas. It is generated at great pressure, at depths 10 miles (16 km) or more below the Earth's surface. It can issue as *lava* at the Earth's surface or, more often, solidify below the surface as *intrusive igneous rock*.

Mantle The layer of the Earth between the *crust* and the *core*. It is about 1,800 miles (2,900 km) thick. The uppermost layer of the mantle is the soft, 125-mile (200-km) thick *asthenosphere* on which the more rigid *lithosphere* floats.

Maquiladoras Factories on the Mexican side of the Mexico/US border, that are allowed to import raw materials and components duty-free and use low-cost labor to assemble the goods, finally exporting them for sale in the US.

Market gardening The intensive growing of fruits and vegetables close to large local markets.

Mass movement Downslope movement of weathered materials such as rock, often helped by rainfall or glacial *meltwater*. Mass movement may be a gradual process or rapid, as in a *landslide* or rockfall.

Massif A single very large mountain or an area of mountains with uniform characteristics and clearly defined boundaries.

Meander A looplike bend in a river. It is usually found in the lower, mature reaches of a river but can form wherever the valley is wide and the slope is gentle.

Mediterranean climate A temperate *climate* of hot, dry summers and warm, damp winters. This is typical of the western fringes of the world's continents in the warm temperate regions between *latitudes* of 30° and 40° (north and south).

Meltwater Water resulting from the melting of a *glacier* or *ice sheet*.

Mesa A broad, flat-topped hill, characteristic of *arid* regions.

Mesosphere A layer of the Earth's *atmosphere*, between the *stratosphere* and the *thermosphere*. Extending from about 25–50 miles (40–80 km) above the surface of the Earth.

Mestizo A person of mixed *Amerindian* and European origin.

Metallurgy The refining and working of metals.

Metamorphic rocks Rocks that have been altered from their original form, in terms of texture, composition, and structure by intense heat, pressure, or by the introduction of new chemical substances, or a combination of more than one of these.

Meteor A body of rock, metal, or other material that travels through space at great speeds. Meteors are visible as they enter the Earth's *atmosphere* as shooting stars and fireballs.

Meteorite The remains of a *meteor* that has fallen to Earth.

Meteoroid A *meteor* that is still traveling in space, outside the Earth's *atmosphere*.

Mezzogiorno A term applied to the southern portion of Italy.

Milankovitch hypothesis A theory suggesting that there are a series of cycles that slightly alter the Earth's position when rotating around the Sun. The cycles identified all affect the amount of *radiation* that the Earth receives at different *latitudes*. The theory is seen as a key factor in the cause of *ice ages*.

Millet A grain crop, forming part of the staple diet in much of Africa.

Mistral A strong, dry, cold, northerly or northwesterly wind that blows from the Massif Central of France to the Mediterranean Sea. It is common in winter and its cold blasts can cause crop damage in the Rhône Delta, in France.

Mohorovičić discontinuity (Moho) The structural divide at the margin between the Earth's *crust* and the *mantle*. On average it is 20 miles (35 km) below the continents and 6 miles (10 km) below the oceans. The different densities of the *crust* and the mantle cause *earthquake* waves to accelerate at this point.

Monarchy A form of government in which the head of state is a single hereditary monarch. The monarch may be a mere figurehead, or may retain significant authority.

Monsoon A wind that changes direction biannually. The change is caused by the reversal of pressure over landmasses and the adjacent oceans. Because the inflowing moist winds bring rain, the term monsoon is also used to refer to the rain itself. The term is derived from and most commonly refers to the seasonal winds of southern and eastern Asia.

Montaña Mountain areas along the west coast of South America.

Moraine Debris, transported and deposited by a *glacier* or *ice sheet* in unstratified, mixed piles of rock, boulders, pebbles, and clay.

Mountain-building The formation of *fold* mountains by tectonic activity. Also known as orogeny, mountain-building often occurs on the margin where two *tectonic plates* collide. The periods when most mountain-building occurred are known as orogenic phases and lasted many millions of years.

Mudflow An *avalanche* of mud that occurs when a mass of soil is drenched by rain or melting snow. It is a type of *mass movement* and is faster than an *earthflow* because it is lubricated by water.

N

Nappe A mass of rocks that has been overfolded by repeated thrust *faulting*.

NAFTA The North American Free Trade Association. Established in 1994 between Canada, Mexico, and the US to set up a free-trade zone.

NASA The North American Space Agency. It is a government body and was established in 1958 to develop manned and unmanned space programs.

NATO The North Atlantic Trade Organization. Established in 1949 to promote mutual defense and cooperation between its members, which are Belgium, Canada, Denmark, France, Germany, Greece, Iceland, Italy, Luxembourg, the Netherlands, Norway, Portugal, Spain, Turkey, UK, and US.

Nitrogen The odorless, colorless gas that makes up 78% of the atmosphere. Within the soil, it is a vital nutrient for plants.

Nomads (nomadic) Wandering communities that move around in search of suitable pasture for their herds of animals.

Nuclear fusion A technique used to create a new nucleus by the merging of two lighter ones, resulting in the release of large quantities of energy.

O

Oasis A fertile area in the middle of a *desert*, usually watered by an underground *aquifer*.

Oceanic ridge A mid-ocean ridge formed, according to the theory of *plate tectonics*, when plates drift apart and hot *magma* pours through to form new oceanic *crust*.

Oligarchy The government of a state by a small, exclusive group of people, such as an elite class or a family group.

Onionskin weathering The *weathering* away or *exfoliation* of a rock or outcrop by the peeling off of surface layers.

Oriente A flatter region lying to the east of the Andes in South America.

Outwash plain *Glaciofluvial* material (typically clay, sand, and gravel) carried beyond an *ice sheet* by *meltwater* streams, forming a broad, flat deposit.

Oxbow lake A crescent-shaped lake formed on a river *floodplain* when a river erodes the outside bend of a *meander*, making the neck of the *meander* narrower until the river cuts across the neck. The meander is cut off and is dammed off with sediment, creating an oxbow lake. Also known as a cut-off lake or mortlake.

Oxidation A form of *chemical weathering* where *oxygen* dissolved in water reacts with minerals in rocks – particularly iron – to form oxides. Oxidation causes brown or yellow staining on rocks and eventually leads to the breakdown of the rock.

Oxygen A colorless, odorless gas that is one of the main constituents of the Earth's *atmosphere* and is essential to life on Earth.

Ozone layer A layer of enriched *oxygen* (O_3) within the stratosphere, mostly between 18–50 miles (30–80 km) above the Earth's surface. It is vital to the existence of life on Earth because it absorbs harmful shortwave ultraviolet radiation, while allowing beneficial longer wave ultraviolet radiation to penetrate to the Earth's surface.

P

Pacific Rim The name given to the economically dynamic countries bordering the Pacific Ocean.

Pack ice Ice masses more than 10 ft (3 m) thick that form on the sea surface and are not attached to a landmass.

Pancake ice Thin disks of ice, up to 8 ft (2.4 m) wide, that form when slicks of *grease ice* are tossed together by winds and stormy seas.

Pangaea In the theory of *continental drift*, Pangaea is the original great land mass that began to split about 190 million years ago. The southern portion is called *Gondwanaland* and the northern is called *Laurasia*. They were separated by the Tethys Sea.

Pastoralism Grazing of livestock– usually sheep, goats, or cattle. Pastoralists in many drier areas have traditionally been *nomadic*.

Parallel *see Latitude.*

Peat Ancient, partially decomposed vegetation found in wet, boggy conditions where there is little *oxygen*. It is the first stage in the development of coal and is often dried for use as fuel. It is also used to improve soil quality.

Pediment A gently sloping ramp of *bedrock* below a steeper slope, often found at mountain edges in *desert* areas, but also in other climatic zones. Pediments may include depositional elements such as *alluvial fans*.

Peninsula A thin strip of land surrounded on three of its sides by water. Large examples include Florida and Korea.

Per capita Latin term meaning "for each person."

Periglacial Regions on the edges of *ice sheets* or *glaciers* or, more commonly, cold regions experiencing intense frost action, *permafrost*, or both. Periglacial climates bring long, freezing winters and short, mild summers.

Permafrost Permanently frozen ground, typical of *Arctic* regions. Although a layer of soil above the permafrost melts in summer, the melted water does not drain through the permafrost.

Permeable rocks Rocks through which water can seep, because they are either porous or cracked.

Pharmaceuticals The manufacture of medicinal drugs.

Phreatic eruption A volcanic eruption that occurs when *lava* combines with *groundwater*, superheating the water and causing a sudden emission of steam at the surface.

Physical weathering (mechanical weathering) The breakdown of rocks by physical, as opposed to chemical, processes. Examples include: changes in pressure or temperature; the effect of windblown sand; the pressure of expanding salt crystals in cracks within rock; and the expansion and contraction of water within rock as it freezes and thaws.

Pingo A dome of earth with a core of ice, found in *tundra* regions. Pingos are formed either when *groundwater* freezes and expands, pushing up the land surface, or when trapped, freezing water in a lake expands and pushes up lake *sediments* to form the pingo dome.

Placer A belt of mineral-bearing rock *strata* lying at or close to the Earth's surface, from which minerals can be extracted easily.

Plain A flat, level region of land, often relatively low-lying.

Plateau A highland tract of flat land.

Plate *see Tectonic plates.*

Plate tectonics The study of *tectonic plates* that helps to explain *continental drift*, mountain formation, and volcanic activity. The movement of tectonic plates may be explained by the currents of rock rising and falling from within the Earth's *mantle* as it heats up and then cools. The boundaries of the plates are known as plate margins and most mountains, *earthquakes*, and *volcanoes* occur at these margins. Constructive margins are moving apart; destructive margins are crunching together; and conservative margins are sliding past one another.

Pleistocene A period of *geological time* spanning from about 5.2 million years ago to 1.6 million years ago.

Plutonic rock *Igneous* rocks found deep below the surface. They are coarse-grained because they cooled and solidified slowly.

Polar The zones within the *Arctic* and *Antarctic* circles.

Polje A long, broad *depression* found in *karst* (*limestone*) regions.

Polygonal patterning The ground patterning that is typically found in areas where the soil is subject to severe frost action, often in *periglacial* regions.

Porosity A measure of how much water can be held within a rock or a soil. Porosity is measured as the percentage of holes or pores in a material, compared to its total volume. For example, the porosity of slate is less than 1%, while that of gravel is 25–35%.

Prairies Originally a French word for grassy *plains* with few or no trees.

Precambrian The earliest period of *geological time* dating from over 570 million years ago.

Precipitation The fall of moisture from the *atmosphere* onto the surface of the Earth, whether as dew, hail, rain, sleet, or snow.

Pyramidal peak A steep, isolated mountain summit, formed when the back walls of three or more *cirques* are cut back and move toward each other. The cliffs around such a horned peak, or horn, are divided by sharp *arêtes*. The Matterhorn in the Swiss Alps is an example.

Pyroclasts Fragments of rock ejected during volcanic eruptions.

Q

Quaternary The current period of *geological time*, which started about 1.6 million years ago.

R

Radiation The emission of energy in the form of particles or waves. Radiation from the sun includes heat, light, ultraviolet rays, gamma rays, and X-rays. Only some of the solar energy radiated into space reaches the Earth.

Rain forest Dense forests in tropical zones with high rainfall, temperature, and *humidity*. Strictly, the term applies to the equatorial rain forest in tropical lowlands with constant rainfall and no seasonal change. The Congo and Amazon basins are examples. The term is applied more loosely to lush forest in other climates. Within rain forests organic life is dense and varied: at least 40% of all plant and animal species are found here and there may be as many as 100 tree species per 2.5 acres (1 ha).

Rainshadow An area that experiences low rainfall because of its position on the leeward side of a mountain range.

Reg A large area of stony *desert*, where tightly packed gravel lies on top of clayey sand. A reg is formed where the wind blows away the finer sand.

Remote-sensing Method of obtaining information about the *environment* using unmanned equipment, such as a satellite, that relays the information to a point where it is collected and used.

Resistance The capacity of a rock to resist *denudation*, by processes such as *weathering* and *erosion*.

Ria A flooded *V-shaped river valley* or estuary, flooded by a rise in sea level (*eustacy*) or sinking land. It is shorter than a *fjord* and gets deeper as it meets the sea.

Rift valley A long, narrow depression in the Earth's *crust*, formed by the sinking of rocks between two *faults*.

River channel The trough that contains a river and is molded by the flow of the water within it.

Roche moutonée A rock found in a glaciated valley. The side facing the flow of the *glacier* has been smoothed and rounded, while the other side has been left more rugged because the *glacier*, as it flowed over the rock, has plucked out frozen fragments and carried them away.

Runoff Water draining from a land surface by flowing across it.

S

Sabkha The floor of an isolated *depression* that occurs in an *arid environment*. It is usually covered by salt deposits and devoid of vegetation.

SADC Southern African Development Community. Established in 1992 to promote economic integration between its member states, which are Angola, Botswana, Lesotho, Malawi, Mauritius, Mozambique, Namibia, South Africa, Swaziland, Tanzania, Zambia, and Zimbabwe.

Salt plug A rounded hill produced by the upward doming of rock *strata* caused by the movement of salt or other evaporite deposits under intense pressure.

Sastrugi Ice ridges formed by wind action. They lie parallel to the direction of the wind.

Savannah Open grassland found between the zone of *deserts*, and that of tropical *rain forests* in the tropics and subtropics. Scattered trees and shrubs are found in some kinds of savannah. A savannah *climate* usually has wet and dry seasons.

Scarp *see Escarpment.*

Scree Piles of rock fragments beneath a cliff or rock face, caused by mechanical *weathering*, especially *frost shattering*, where the expansion and contraction of freezing and thawing water within the rock gradually breaks it up.

Sea-floor spreading The process where *tectonic plates* move apart, allowing hot *magma* to erupt and solidify. This forms a new sea floor and, ultimately, widens the ocean.

Seamount An isolated, submarine mountain or hill, probably of volcanic origin.

Season A period of time linked to regular changes in the weather, especially the intensity of solar *radiation*.

Sediment Grains of rock transported and deposited by rivers, sea, ice, or wind.

Sedimentary rocks Rocks formed from the debris of preexisting rocks or of organic material. They are found in many *environments* – on the ocean floor, on beaches, in rivers, and in *deserts*. Organically-formed sedimentary rocks include coal and chalk. Other sedimentary rocks, such as flint, are formed by chemical processes. Most of these rocks contain *fossils*, which can be used to date them.

Seif A sand *dune* that lies parallel to the direction of the prevailing wind. Seifs form steep-sided ridges, sometimes extending for miles.

Seismic activity Movement within the Earth, such as an *earthquake* or *tremor*.

Selva A region of wet forest found in the Amazon Basin.

Semiarid, semidesert The *climate* and landscape that lies between *savannah* and *desert* or between *savannah* and a *mediterranean* climate. In semiarid conditions there is a little more moisture than in a true *desert*. More patches of drought-resistant vegetation can survive here.

Shale (marine shale) A compacted *sedimentary rock*, with fine-grained particles. Marine shale is formed on the seabed. Fuel such as oil may be extracted from it.

Sheetwash Water that runs downhill in thin sheets without forming channels. It can cause *sheet erosion*.

Sheet erosion The washing away of soil by a thin film or sheet of water, known as *sheetwash*.

Shield A vast stable block of the Earth's *crust* that has experienced little or no *mountain-building*.

Sierra The Spanish word for mountains.

Sinkhole A circular *depression* in a *limestone* region. They are formed by the collapse of an underground cave system or the *chemical weathering* of the *limestone*.

Sisal A plant fiber used to make matting.

Slash and burn A farming technique involving the cutting down and burning of scrub forest, to create agricultural land. After a number of seasons this land is abandoned and the process is repeated. This practice is common in Africa and South America.

Slip face The steep leeward side of a sand *dune* or slope. Opposite side to a *back slope*.

Soil A thin layer of rock particles mixed with the remains of dead plants and animals. This occurs naturally on the surface of the Earth and provides a medium for plants to grow in.

Soil creep The very gradual downslope movement of rock debris and soil, under the influence of gravity. This is a type of *mass movement*.

Soil erosion The wearing away of soil more quickly than it is replaced by natural processes. Soil can be carried away by wind as well as by water. Human activities, such as overgrazing and the clearing of land for farming, accelerate the process in many areas.

Solar energy Energy derived from the Sun. Solar energy is converted into other forms of energy. For example, the wind and waves, as well as the creation of plant material in photosynthesis, depend on solar energy.

Solifluction A kind of *soil creep*, where water in the surface layer has saturated the soil and rock debris, which slips slowly downhill. It often happens when frozen top-layer deposits thaw, leaving behind the frozen layers below.

Sorghum A type of grass found in South America, similar to sugar cane. When refined it is used to make molasses.

Spit A thin linear deposit of sand or shingle extending from the seashore. Spits are formed as angled waves shift sand along the beach, eventually extending a ridge of sand beyond a change in the angle of the coast. Spits are common where the coastline bends, especially at estuaries.

Squash A type of edible gourd.

Stack A tall, isolated pillar of rock near a coastline, created as wave action erodes away the adjacent rock.

Stalactite A tapering cylinder of mineral deposit, hanging from the roof of a cave in a *karst* area. It is formed by calcium carbonate dissolved in water that drips through the roof of a *limestone* cavern.

Stalagmite A cone of calcium carbonate, similar to a *stalactite*, rising from the floor of a *limestone* cavern and formed when drops of water fall from the roof of a *limestone* cave. If the water has dripped from a *stalactite* above the stalagmite, the two may join to form a continuous pillar.

Staple crop The main crop upon which a country is economically and or physically reliant. For example, the major crop grown for large-scale local consumption in southern Asia is rice.

Steppe Large areas of dry grassland in the northern hemisphere – particularly found in southeastern Europe and central Asia.

Strata The plural of stratum, a distinct, virtually horizontal layer of deposited material, lying parallel to other layers.

Stratosphere A layer of the *atmosphere*, above the *troposphere*, extending from about 7–30 miles (11–50 km) above the Earth's surface. In the lower part of the stratosphere, the temperature is relatively stable and there is little moisture.

Strike-slip fault Occurs where plates move sideways past each other and blocks of rocks move horizontally in relation to each other, not up or down as is the case with normal *faults*.

Subduction zone A region where two *tectonic plates* collide, forcing one beneath the other. Typically, a dense oceanic plate dips below a lighter continental plate, melting in the heat of the *asthenosphere*. This is why the zone is also called a destructive margins (*see Plate tectonics*). These zones are characterized by *earthquakes*, *volcanoes*, *mountain-building*, and the development of *oceanic trenches* and *island arcs*.

Submarine canyon A steep-sided valley that extends along the *continental shelf* to the ocean floor. Often formed by *turbidity currents*.

Submarine fan Deposits of silt and *alluvium*, carried by large rivers forming great fan-shaped deposits on the ocean floor.

Subsistence agriculture An agricultural practice in which enough food is produced to support the farmer and his or her dependents, but not providing any surplus to generate an income.

Subtropical A term loosely applied to *climates* that are nearly tropical or tropical for a part of the year – areas north or south of the *tropics* but outside the *temperate zone*.

Supercontinent A large continent that breaks up to form smaller continents or that forms when smaller continents merge. In the theory of *continental drift*, the supercontinents are *Pangaea*, *Gondwanaland*, and *Laurasia*.

Sustainable development An approach to development, particularly applied to economies around the world that exploit natural resources without destroying them or damaging the *environment*.

Syncline A basin-shaped downfold in rock *strata*, created when the *strata* are compressed, for example, where *tectonic plates* collide.

T

Tableland A highland area with a flat or gently undulating surface.

Taiga The belt of *coniferous* forest found in the north of Asia and North America. The conifers are adapted to survive low temperatures and long periods of snowfall.

Tarn A Scottish term for a small mountain lake, usually found at the head of a *glacier*.

Tectonic plates Plates, or tectonic plates, are the rigid slabs that form the Earth's outer shell, the *lithosphere*. Eight big plates and several smaller ones have been identified.

Temperate A moderate *climate* without extremes of temperature, typical of the mid-*latitudes* between the *tropics* and the *polar* circles.

Theocracy A state governed by religious laws. Today, the world's largest theocracy is Iran.

Thermokarst Subsidence created by the thawing of ground ice in *periglacial* areas, creating depressions.

Thermosphere A layer of the Earth's *atmosphere* that lies above the *mesophere*, about 60–300 miles (100–500 km) above the Earth

Terraces Steps cut into steep slopes to create flat surfaces for cultivating crops. They also help to reduce soil *erosion* on unconsolidated slopes. They are most common in heavily populated parts of Southeast Asia.

Till Unstratified glacial deposits or drift left by a *glacier* or *ice sheet*. Till includes mixtures of clay, sand, gravel, and boulders.

Topography The typical shape and features of a given area such as land height and terrain.

Tombolo A large sand *spit* that attaches part of the mainland to an island.

Tornado A violent, spiraling windstorm with a center of very low pressure. Wind speeds reach 200 mph (320 km/h) and there is often thunder and heavy rain.

Transform fault In *plate tectonics*, a *fault* of continental scale, such as the San Andreas Fault, where two plates slide past each other, staying close together. The jerky, uneven movement creates *earthquakes* but does not destroy or add to the Earth's *crust*

Transpiration The loss of water vapor through the pores (or stomata) of plants. The process helps return moisture to the *atmosphere*.

Trap An area of fine-grained *igneous rock* that has been extruded and cooled on the Earth's surface in stages, forming a series of steps or terraces.

Tree line The line beyond which trees cannot grow, dependent on *latitude* and altitude, as well as local factors such as soil.

Tremor A slight *earthquake*.

Trench (oceanic trench) A long, deep trough in the ocean floor, formed, according to the theory of *plate tectonics*, when two plates collide and one dives under the other, creating a *subduction zone*.

Tropics The zone between the *Tropic of Cancer* and the *Tropic of Capricorn* where the *climate* is hot. The term can also be applied to denote areas even further north or south of the *Equator*, where the climate is similar to that of the true tropics.

Tropic of Cancer A line of *latitude* or an imaginary circle around the Earth, lying at 23° 28' N.

Tropic of Capricorn A line of *latitude* or an imaginary circle around the Earth, lying at 23° 28' S.

Troposphere The lowest layer of the Earth's *atmosphere*. From the surface, it reaches a height of between 4–10 miles (7–16 km). It is the most turbulent zone of the atmosphere and accounts for the generation of most of the world's weather. The layer above it is called the *stratosphere*.

Tsunami A huge wave created by shock waves from an *earthquake* under the sea. Reaching speeds of up to 600 mph (960 km/h), the wave may increase to heights of 50 ft (15 m) on entering coastal waters. It can cause great damage.

Tundra The treeless *plains* of the *Arctic Circle*, found south of the *polar* region of permanent ice and snow, and north of the belt of *coniferous* forests known as *taiga*. In this region of long, very cold winters, vegetation is usually limited to mosses, *lichens*, sedges, and rushes, although flowers and dwarf shrubs blossom in the brief summer.

Turbidity current An oceanic feature. A turbidity current is a mass of *sediment*-laden water that has substantial erosive power. Turbidity currents are thought to contribute to the formation of *submarine canyons*.

Typhoon A kind of *hurricane* (or tropical cyclone) bringing violent winds and heavy rain, a typhoon can do great damage. They occur in the South China Sea, especially around the Philippines.

U

U-shaped valley A river valley that has been deepened and widened by a *glacier*. They are characteristically flat-bottomed and steep-sided and generally much deeper than river valleys.

UN United Nations. Established in 1945, it contains 184 nations and aims to maintain international peace and security, and to promote cooperation over economic, social, cultural, and humanitarian problems.

UNICEF United Nations Children's Fund. A UN organization set up to promote family- and child-related programs.

Urstromtäler A German word used to describe *meltwater* channels that flowed along the front edge of the advancing *ice sheet* during the last *Ice Age*, 18,000–20,000 years ago.

V

V-shaped valley A typical valley eroded by a river in its upper course.

Virgin rain forest Tropical *rain forest* in its original state, untouched by human activity, such as logging, clearance for agriculture, settlement, or roadbuilding.

Viticulture The cultivation of grapes for wine.

Volcano An opening or vent in the Earth's *crust* where molten rock, *magma*, erupts. Volcanoes tend to be conical but may also occur as a crack in the Earth's surface or a hole blasted through a mountain. The *magma* is accompanied by other materials such as gas, steam, and fragments of rock, known as *pyroclasts*. Volcanoes tend to occur on destructive or constructive *tectonic plate* margins.

W–Z

Wadi The dry bed left by a torrent of water. Wadis are also classified as an *ephemeral* stream, found in *arid* and *semiarid* regions that are subject to sudden and often severe flash flooding.

Warm humid climate A rainy climate with warm summers and mild winters.

Water cycle The continuous circulation of water between the Earth's surface and the *atmosphere*. The processes include *evaporation* and *transpiration* of moisture into the atmosphere, and its return as *precipitation*, some of which flows into lakes and oceans.

Water table The upper level of *groundwater* saturation in permeable rock *strata*.

Watershed The dividing line between one *drainage basin* – an area where all streams flow into a single river system – and another. Watershed also means the whole drainage basin of a single river system, referred to as its catchment area.

Waterspout A rotating column of water in the form of cloud, mist, and spray that form on open water. Often has the appearance of a small *tornado*.

Weathering The decay and breakup of rocks at or near the Earth's surface, caused by water, wind, heat, ice, organic material, or the *atmosphere*. *Physical weathering* includes the effects of frost and temperature changes. Biological weathering includes the effects of plant roots, burrowing animals, and the acids produced by animals, especially as they decay after death. *Carbonation* and *hydrolysis* are among many kinds of *chemical weathering*.

Geographical Names

The following glossary lists all geographical terms occurring on the maps and in main-entry names in the Index-Gazetteer. These terms may precede, follow, or be run together with the proper element of the name; where they precede it the term is reversed for indexing purposes, for example, Poluostrov Yamal is indexed as Yamal, Puluostrov.

Key
Geographical term *Language*, Term

A

Å *Danish, Norwegian*, River
Āb *Persian*, River
Adrar *Berber*, Mountains
Agía, Ágios *Greek*, Saint
Air *Indonesian*, River
Ákra *Greek*, Cape, point
Alpen *German*, Alps
Alt- *German*, Old
Altiplanicie *Spanish*, Plateau
Älve(en) *Swedish*, River
-ån *Swedish*, River
Anse *French*, Bay
'Aqabat *Arabic*, Pass
Archipiélago *Spanish*, Archipelago
Arcipelago *Italian*, Archipelago
Arquipélago *Portuguese*, Archipelago
Arrecife(s) *Spanish*, Reef(s)
Aru *Tamil*, River
Augstiene *Latvian*, Upland
Aukštuma *Lithuanian*, Upland
Aust- *Norwegian*, Eastern
Avtonomnyy Okrug *Russian*, Autonomous district
Āw *Kurdish*, River
'Ayn *Arabic*, Spring, well
'Ayoûn *Arabic*, Wells

B

Baelt *Danish*, Strait
Bahía *Spanish*, Bay
Baḩr *Arabic*, River
Baía *Portuguese*, Bay
Baie *French*, Bay
Bañado *Spanish*, Marshland
Bandao *Chinese*, Peninsula
Banjaran *Malay*, Mountain range
Barajı *Turkish*, Dam
Barragem *Portuguese*, Reservoir
Bassin *French*, Basin
Batang *Malay*, Stream
Beinn, Ben *Gaelic*, Mountain
-berg *Afrikaans, Norwegian*, Mountain
Besar *Indonesian, Malay*, Big
Birkat, Birket *Arabic*, Lake, well, cistern
Boğazi *Turkish*, Lake
Boka *Serbo-Croatian*, Bay
Bol'sh-aya, -iye, -oy, -oye *Russian*, Big
Botigh(i) *Uzbek*, Depression basin
-bre(en) *Norwegian*, Glacier
Bredning *Danish*, Bay
Bucht *German*, Bay
Bugt(en) *Danish*, Bay
Buḩayrat *Arabic*, Lake, reservoir
Buḩeirat *Arabic*, Lake
Bukit *Malay*, Mountain
-bukta *Norwegian*, Bay
bukten *Swedish*, Bay
Bulag *Mongolian*, Spring
Bulak *Uighur*, Spring
Burnu *Turkish*, Cape, point
Buuraha *Somali*, Mountains

C

Cabo *Portuguese*, Cape
Caka *Tibetan*, Salt lake
Canal *Spanish*, Channel
Cap *French*, Cape
Capo *Italian*, Cape, headland
Cascada *Portuguese*, Waterfall
Cayo(s) *Spanish*, Islet(s), rock(s)
Cerro *Spanish*, Mountain
Chaîne *French*, Mountain range
Chapada *Portuguese*, Hills, upland
Chau *Cantonese*, Island
Chāy *Turkish*, River
Chhâk *Cambodian*, Bay
Chhu *Tibetan*, River
-chŏsuji *Korean*, Reservoir
Chott *Arabic*, Depression, salt lake
Chūli *Uzbek*, Grassland, steppe
Ch'ün-tao *Chinese*, Island group
Chuŏr Phnum *Cambodian*, Mountains
Ciudad *Spanish*, City, town
Co *Tibetan*, Lake
Colline(s) *French*, Hill(s)
Cordillera *Spanish*, Mountain range
Costa *Spanish*, Coast
Côte *French*, Coast
Coxilha *Portuguese*, Mountains
Cuchilla *Spanish*, Mountains

D

Daban *Mongolian, Uighur*, Pass
Daği *Azerbaijani, Turkish*, Mountain
Dağlari *Azerbaijani, Turkish*, Mountains
-dake *Japanese*, Peak
-dal(en) *Norwegian*, Valley
Danau *Indonesian*, Lake
Dao *Chinese*, Island
Đao *Vietnamese*, Island
Daryā *Persian*, River
Daryācheh *Persian*, Lake
Dasht *Persian*, Desert, plain
Dawḩat *Arabic*, Bay
Denizi *Turkish*, Sea
Dere *Turkish*, Stream
Desierto *Spanish*, Desert
Dili *Azerbaijani*, Spit
-do *Korean*, Island
Dooxo *Somali*, Valley
Düzü *Azerbaijani*, Steppe
-dwīp *Bengali*, Island

E

-eilanden *Dutch*, Islands
Embalse *Spanish*, Reservoir
Ensenada *Spanish*, Bay
Erg *Arabic*, Dunes
Estany *Catalan*, Lake
Estero *Spanish*, Inlet
Estrecho *Spanish*, Strait
Étang *French*, Lagoon, lake
-ey *Icelandic*, Island
Ezero *Bulgarian, Macedonian*, Lake
Ezers *Latvian*, Lake

F

Feng *Chinese*, Peak
Fjord *Danish*, Fjord
-fjord(en) *Danish, Norwegian, Swedish*, fjord
-fjørdhur *Faeroese*, Fjord
Fleuve *French*, River
Fliegu *Maltese*, Channel
-fljór *Icelandic*, River
-flói *Icelandic*, Bay
Forêt *French*, Forest

G

-gan *Japanese*, Rock
-gang *Korean*, River
Ganga *Hindi, Nepali, Sinhala*, River
Gaoyuan *Chinese*, Plateau
Garagumy *Turkmen*, Sands
-gawa *Japanese*, River
Gebel *Arabic*, Mountain
-gebirge *German*, Mountain range
Ghadīr *Arabic*, Well
Ghubbat *Arabic*, Bay
Gjiri *Albanian*, Bay
Gol *Mongolian*, River
Golfe *French*, Gulf
Golfo *Italian, Spanish*, Gulf
Göl(ü) *Turkish*, Lake
Golyam, -a *Bulgarian*, Big
Gora *Russian, Serbo-Croatian*, Mountain
Góra *Polish*, Mountain
Gory *Russian*, Mountain
Gryada *Russian*, Ridge
Guba *Russian*, Bay
-gundo *Korean*, Island group
Gunung *Malay*, Mountain

H

Ḩadd *Arabic*, Spit
-haehyŏp *Korean*, Strait
Haff *German*, Lagoon
Hai *Chinese*, Bay, lake, sea
Haixia *Chinese*, Strait
Hamada *Arabic*, Plateau
Ḩammādat *Arabic*, Plateau
Hāmūn *Persian*, Lake
-hantō *Japanese*, Peninsula
Har, Haré *Hebrew*, Mountain
Ḩarrat *Arabic*, Lava-field
Hav(et) *Danish, Swedish*, Sea
Hawr *Arabic*, Lake
Hāyk' *Amharic*, Lake
He *Chinese*, River
-hegység *Hungarian*, Mountain range
Heide *German*, Heath, moorland
Helodrano *Malagasy*, Bay
Higashi- *Japanese*, East(ern)
Ḩişā' *Arabic*, Well
Hka *Burmese*, River
-ho *Korean*, Lake
Hô *Korean*, Reservoir
Ḩolot *Hebrew*, Dunes
Hora *Belarus, Czech*, Mountain
Hrada *Belarus*, Mountain, ridge
Hsi *Chinese*, River
Hu *Chinese*, Lake
Huk *Danish*, Point

I

Île(s) *French*, Island(s)
Ilha(s) *Portuguese*, Island(s)
Ilhéu(s) *Portuguese*, Islet(s)
Imeni *Russian*, In the name of
Inish- *Gaelic*, Island
Insel(n) *German*, Island(s)
Irmağı, Irmak *Turkish*, River
Isla(s) *Spanish*, Island(s)
Isola (Isole) *Italian*, Island(s)

J

Jabal *Arabic*, Mountain
Jāl *Arabic*, Ridge
-järv *Estonian*, Lake
-järvi *Finnish*, Lake
Jazā'ir *Arabic*, Islands
Jazīrat *Arabic*, Island
Jazīreh *Persian*, Island
Jebel *Arabic*, Mountain
Jezero *Serbo-Croatian*, Lake
Jezioro *Polish*, Lake
Jiang *Chinese*, River
-jima *Japanese*, Island
Jižní *Czech*, Southern
-jõgi *Estonian*, River
-joki *Finnish*, River
-jökull *Icelandic*, Glacier
Jūn *Arabic*, Bay
Juzur *Arabic*, Islands

K

Kaikyō *Japanese*, Strait
-kaise *Lappish*, Mountain
Kali *Nepali*, River
Kalnas *Lithuanian*, Mountain
Kalns *Latvian*, Mountain
Kang *Chinese*, Harbor
Kangri *Tibetan*, Mountain(s)
Kaôh *Cambodian*, Island
Kapp *Norwegian*, Cape
Káto *Greek*, Lower
Kavīr *Persian*, Desert
K'edi *Georgian*, Mountain range
Kediet *Arabic*, Mountain
Kepi *Albanian*, Cape, point
Kepulauan *Indonesian, Malay*, Island group
Khalīg, Khalīj *Arabic*, Gulf
Khawr *Arabic*, Inlet
Khola *Nepali*, River
Khrebet *Russian*, Mountain range
Ko *Thai*, Island
-ko *Japanese*, Inlet, lake
Kólpos *Greek*, Bay
-kopf *German*, Peak
Körfäzi *Azerbaijani*, Bay
Körfezi *Turkish*, Bay
Kõrgustik *Estonian*, Upland
Kosa *Russian, Ukrainian*, Spit
Koshi *Nepali*, River
Kou *Chinese*, Rivermouth
Kowtal *Persian*, Pass
Kray *Russian*, Region, territory
Kryazh *Russian*, Ridge
Kuduk *Uighur*, Well
Kūh(hā) *Persian*, Mountain(s)
-kul' *Russian*, Lake
Kŭl(i) *Tajik, Uzbek*, Lake
-kundo *Korean*, Island group
-kysten *Norwegian*, Coast
Kyun *Burmese*, Island

L

Laaq *Somali*, Watercourse
Lac *French*, Lake
Lacul *Romanian*, Lake
Lagh *Somali*, Stream
Lago *Italian, Portuguese, Spanish*, Lake
Lagoa *Portuguese*, Lagoon
Laguna *Italian, Spanish*, Lagoon, lake
Laht *Estonian*, Bay
Laut *Indonesian*, Bay
Lembalemba *Malagasy*, Plateau
Lerr *Armenian*, Mountain
Lerrnashght'a *Armenian*, Mountain range
Les *Czech*, Forest
Lich *Armenian*, Lake
Liehtao *Chinese*, Island group
Liqeni *Albanian*, Lake
Límni *Greek*, Lake
Ling *Chinese*, Mountain range
Llano *Spanish*, Plain, prairie
Lumi *Albanian*, River
Lyman *Ukrainian*, Estuary

M

Madīnat *Arabic*, City, town
Mae Nam *Thai*, River
-mägi *Estonian*, Hill
Maja *Albanian*, Mountain
Mal *Albanian*, Mountains
Mal-aya, -oye, -yy, *Russian*, Small
-man *Korean*, Bay
Mar *Spanish*, Lake
Marios *Lithuanian*, Lake
Massif *French*, Mountains
Meer *German*, Lake
-meer *Dutch*, Lake
Melkosopochnik *Russian*, Plain
-meri *Estonian*, Sea
Mifraz *Hebrew*, Bay
Minami- *Japanese*, South(ern)
-misaki *Japanese*, Cape, point
Monkhafad *Arabic*, Depression
Montagne(s) *French*, Mountain(s)
Montañas *Spanish*, Mountains
Mont(s) *French*, Mountain(s)
Monte *Italian, Portuguese*, Mountain
More *Russian*, Sea
Mörön *Mongolian*, River
Mys *Russian*, Cape, point

N

-nada *Japanese*, Open stretch of water
Nagor'ye *Russian*, Upland
Naḩal *Hebrew*, River
Nahr *Arabic*, River
Nam *Laotian*, River
Namakzār *Persian*, Salt desert
Né-a, -on, -os *Greek*, New
Nedre- *Norwegian*, Lower
-neem *Estonian*, Cape, point
Nehri *Turkish*, River
-nes *Norwegian*, Cape, point
Nevado *Spanish*, Mountain (snow-capped)
Nieder- *German*, Lower
Nishi- *Japanese*, West(ern)
-nísi *Greek*, Island
Nisoi *Greek*, Islands
Nizhn-eye, -iy, -iye, -yaya *Russian*, Lower
Nizmennost' *Russian*, Lowland, plain
Nord *Danish, French, German*, North
Norte *Portuguese, Spanish*, North
Nos *Bulgarian*, Point, spit
Nosy *Malagasy*, Island
Nov-a, -i, *Bulgarian, Serbo-Croatian*, New
Nov-aya, -o, -oye, -yy, -yye *Russian*, New
Now-a, -e, -y *Polish*, New
Nur *Mongolian*, Lake
Nuruu *Mongolian*, Mountains
Nuur *Mongolian*, Lake
Nyzovyna *Ukrainian*, Lowland, plain

O

-ø *Danish*, Island
Ober- *German*, Upper
Oblast' *Russian*, Province
Órmos *Greek*, Bay
Orol(i) *Uzbek*, Island
Øster- *Norwegian*, Eastern
Ostrov(a) *Russian*, Island(s)
Otok *Serbo-Croatian*, Island
Oued *Arabic*, Watercourse
-oy *Faeroese*, Island
-øy(a) *Norwegian*, Island
Oya *Sinhala*, River
Ozero *Russian, Ukrainian*, Lake

P

Passo *Italian*, Pass
Pegunungan *Indonesian, Malay*, Mountain range
Pélagos *Greek*, Sea
Pendi *Chinese*, Basin
Penisola *Italian*, Peninsula
Pertuis *French*, Strait
Peski *Russian*, Sands
Phanom *Thai*, Mountain
Phou *Laotian*, Mountain
Pi *Chinese*, Point
Pic *Catalan, French*, Peak
Pico *Portuguese, Spanish*, Peak
-piggen *Danish*, Peak
Pik *Russian*, Peak
Pivostriv *Ukrainian*, Peninsula
Planalto *Portuguese*, Plateau
Planina, Planini *Bulgarian, Macedonian, Serbo-Croatian*, Mountain range
Plato *Russian*, Plateau
Ploskogor'ye *Russian*, Upland
Poluostrov *Russian*, Peninsula
Ponta *Portuguese*, Point
Porthmós *Greek*, Strait
Pótamos *Greek*, River
Presa *Spanish*, Dam
Prokhod *Bulgarian*, Pass
Proliv *Russian*, Strait
Pulau *Indonesian, Malay*, Island
Pulu *Malay*, Island
Punta *Spanish*, Point
Pushcha *Belarus*, Forest
Puszcza *Polish*, Forest

Q

Qā' *Arabic*, Depression
Qalamat *Arabic*, Well
Qatorkŭh(i) *Tajik*, Mountain
Qiuling *Chinese*, Hills
Qolleh *Persian*, Mountain
Qu *Tibetan*, Stream
Quan *Chinese*, Well
Qulla(i) *Tajik*, Peak
Qundao *Chinese*, Island group

R

Raas *Somali*, Cape
-rags *Latvian*, Cape
Ramlat *Arabic*, Sands
Ra's *Arabic*, Cape, headland, point
Ravnina *Bulgarian, Russian*, Plain
Récif *French*, Reef
Recife *Portuguese*, Reef
Reka *Bulgarian*, River
Represa (Rep.) *Portuguese, Spanish*, Reservoir
Reshteh *Persian*, Mountain range
Respublika *Russian*, Republic, first-order administrative division
Respublika(si) *Uzbek*, Republic, first-order administrative division
-retsugan *Japanese*, Chain of rocks
-rettō *Japanese*, Island chain
Riacho *Spanish*, Stream
Riban' *Malagasy*, Mountains
Rio *Portuguese*, River
Río *Spanish*, River
Riu *Catalan*, River
Rivier *Dutch*, River
Rivière *French*, River
Rowd *Pashtu*, River
Rt *Serbo-Croatian*, Point
Rūd *Persian*, River
Rūdkhāneh *Persian*, River
Rudohorie *Slovak*, Mountains
Ruisseau *French*, Stream

S

-saar *Estonian*, Island
-saari *Finnish*, Island
Sabkhat *Arabic*, Salt marsh
Sāgar(a) *Hindi*, Lake, reservoir
Şaḩrā' *Arabic*, Desert
Saint, Sainte *French*, Saint
Salar *Spanish*, Salt pan
Salto *Portuguese, Spanish*, Waterfall
Samudra *Sinhala*, Reservoir
-san *Japanese, Korean*, Mountain
-sanchi *Japanese*, Mountains
-sandur *Icelandic*, Beach
Sankt *German, Swedish*, Saint
-sanmaek *Korean*, Mountain range
-sanmyaku *Japanese*, Mountain range
San, Santa, Santo *Italian, Portuguese, Spanish*, Saint
São *Portuguese*, Saint
Sarir *Arabic*, Desert
Sebkha, Sebkhet *Arabic*, Depression, salt marsh
Sedlo *Czech*, Pass
See *German*, Lake
Selat *Indonesian*, Strait
Selatan *Indonesian*, Southern
-selkä *Finnish*, Lake, ridge
Selseleh *Persian*, Mountain range
Serra *Portuguese*, Mountain
Serranía *Spanish*, Mountain
-seto *Japanese*, Channel, strait
Sever-naya, -noye, -nyy, -o *Russian*, Northern
Sha'īb *Arabic*, Watercourse
Shākh *Kurdish*, Mountain
Shamo *Chinese*, Desert
Shan *Chinese*, Mountain(s)
Shankou *Chinese*, Pass
Shanmo *Chinese*, Mountain range
Shaţţ *Arabic*, Distributary
Shet' *Amharic*, River
Shi *Chinese*, Municipality
-shima *Japanese*, Island
Shiqqat *Arabic*, Depression
-shotō *Japanese*, Group of islands
Shuiku *Chinese*, Reservoir
Shŭrkhog(i) *Uzbek*, Salt marsh
Sierra *Spanish*, Mountains
Sint *Dutch*, Saint
-sjø(en) *Norwegian*, Lake
-sjön *Swedish*, Lake
Solonchak *Russian*, Salt lake
Solonchakovyye Vpadiny *Russian*, Salt basin, wetlands
Sơn *Vietnamese*, Mountain
Sông *Vietnamese*, River
Sør- *Norwegian*, Southern
-spitze *German*, Peak
Star-á, -é *Czech*, Old
Star-aya, -oye, -yy, -yye *Russian*, Old
Stenó *Greek*, Strait
Step' *Russian*, Steppe
Štít *Slovak*, Peak
Stœng *Cambodian*, River
Stolovaya Strana *Russian*, Plateau
Stredné *Slovak*, Middle
Střední *Czech*, Middle
Stretto *Italian*, Strait
Su Anbari *Azerbaijani*, Reservoir
-suidō *Japanese*, Channel, strait
Sund *Swedish*, Sound, strait
Sungai *Indonesian, Malay*, River
Suu *Turkish*, River

T

Tal *Mongolian*, Plain
Tandavan' *Malagasy*, Mountain range
Tangorombohitr' *Malagasy*, Mountain massif
Tanjung *Indonesian, Malay*, Cape, point
Tao *Chinese*, Island
Ţaraq *Arabic*, Hills
Tassili *Berber*, Mountain, plateau
Tau *Russian*, Mountain(s)
Taungdan *Burmese*, Mountain range
Techníti Límni *Greek*, Reservoir
Tekojärvi *Finnish*, Reservoir
Teluk *Indonesian, Malay*, Bay
Tengah *Indonesian*, Middle
Terara *Amharic*, Mountain
Timur *Indonesian*, Eastern
-tind(an) *Norwegian*, Peak
Tizma(si) *Uzbek*, Mountain range, ridge
-tō *Japanese*, Island
Tog *Somali*, Valley
-tōge *Japanese*, Pass
Togh(i) *Uzbek*, Mountain
Tônlé *Cambodian*, Lake
Top *Dutch*, Peak
-tunturi *Finnish*, Mountain
Ţurāq *Arabic*, Hills
Tur'at *Arabic*, Channel

U

Udde(n) *Swedish*, Cape, point
'Uqlat *Arabic*, Well
Utara *Indonesian*, Northern
Uul *Mongolian*, Mountains

V

Väin *Estonian*, Strait
Vallée *French*, Valley
-vatn *Icelandic*, Lake
-vatnet *Norwegian*, Lake
Velayat *Turkmen*, Province
-vesi *Finnish*, Lake
Vestre- *Norwegian*, Western
-vidda *Norwegian*, Plateau
-vík *Icelandic*, Bay
-viken *Swedish*, Bay, inlet
Vinh *Vietnamese*, Bay
Víztárloló *Hungarian*, Reservoir
Vodaskhovishcha *Belarus*, Reservoir
Vodokhranilishche (Vdkhr.) *Russian*, Reservoir
Vodoskhovyshche (Vdskh.) *Ukrainian*, Reservoir
Volcán *Spanish*, Volcano
Vostochn-o, yy *Russian*, Eastern
Vozvyshennost' *Russian*, Upland, plateau
Vozyera *Belarus*, Lake
Vpadina *Russian*, Depression
Vrchovina *Czech*, Mountains
Vrha *Macedonian*, Peak
Vychodné *Slovak*, Eastern
Vysochyna *Ukrainian*, Upland
Vysočina *Czech*, Upland

W

Waadi *Somali*, Watercourse
Wādī *Arabic* Watercourse
Wāḩat, Wâhat *Arabic*, Oasis
Wald *German*, Forest
Wan *Chinese*, Bay
Way *Indonesian*, River
Webi *Somali*, River
Wenz *Amharic*, River
Wiloyat(i) *Uzbek*, Province
Wyżyna *Polish*, Upland
Wzgórza *Polish*, Upland
Wzvyshsha *Belarus*, Upland

X

Xé *Laotian*, River
Xi *Chinese*, Stream

Y

-yama *Japanese*, Mountain
Yanchi *Chinese*, Salt lake
Yang *Chinese*, Bay
Yanhu *Chinese*, Salt lake
Yarımadası *Azerbaijani, Turkish*, Peninsula
Yaylası *Turkish*, Plateau
Yazovir *Bulgarian*, Reservoir
Yoma *Burmese*, Mountains
Ytre- *Norwegian*, Outer
Yü *Chinese*, Island
Yunhe *Chinese*, Canal
Yuzhn-o, -yy *Russian*, Southern

Z

-zaki *Japanese*, Cape, point
Zaliv *Bulgarian, Russian*, Bay
-zan *Japanese*, Mountain
Zangbo *Tibetan*, River
Zapadn-aya, -o, -yy *Russian*, Western
Západné *Slovak*, Western
Západní *Czech*, Western
Zatoka *Polish, Ukrainian*, Bay
-zee *Dutch*, Sea
Zemlya *Russian*, Earth, land
Zizhiqu *Chinese*, Autonomous region

25 de Mayo – Acalayong

Index

Glossary of Abbreviations

This glossary provides a comprehensive guide to the abbreviations used in this Atlas and in the Index-Gazetteer.

A

abbrev. abbreviated
Afr. Afrikaans
Alb. Albanian
Amh. Amharic
anc. ancient
approx. approximately
Ar. Arabic
Arm. Armenian
ASEAN Association of South East Asian Nations
ASSR Autonomous Soviet Socialist Republic
Aust. Australian
Az. Azerbaijani
Azerb. Azerbaijan

B

Basq. Basque
BCE Before the Common Era
Bel. Belarus
Ben. Bengali
Ber. Berber
B-H Bosnia-Herzegovina
bn billion (one thousand million)
BP British Petroleum
Bret. Breton
Brit. British
Bul. Bulgarian
Bur. Burmese

C

C central
C. Cape
°C degrees (Centigrade)
CACM Central America Common Market
Cam. Cambodian
Cant. Cantonese
CAR Central African Republic
Cast. Castilian
Cat. Catalan
CE Common Era
CEEAC Central America Common Market
Chin. Chinese
CIS Commonwealth of Independent States
cm centimeter(s)
Cro. Croat
Cz. Czech
Czech Rep. Czech Republic

D

Dan. Danish
Dom. Rep. Dominican Republic
Dut. Dutch

E

E east
EC see EU
EEC see EU
ECOWAS Economic Community of West African States
ECU European Currency Unit
EMS European Monetary System
Eng. English
est estimated
Est. Estonian
EU European Union (previously European Community [EC], European Economic Community [EEC])

F

°F degrees Fahrenheit
Faer. Faeroese
Fij. Fijian
Fin. Finnish
Fr. French
Fris. Frisian
ft foot/feet
FYROM Former Yugoslav Republic of Macedonia

G

g gram(s)
Gael. Gaelic
Gal. Galician
GDP Gross Domestic Product (the total value of goods and services produced by a country excluding income from foreign countries)
Geor. Georgian
Ger. German
Gk Greek
GNP Gross National Product (the total value of goods and services produced by a country)

H

Heb. Hebrew
HEP hydroelectric power
Hind. Hindi
hist. historical
Hung. Hungarian

I

I. Island
Icel. Icelandic
in inch(es)
In. Inuit (Eskimo)
Ind. Indonesian
Intl International
Ir. Irish
Is Islands
It. Italian

J

Jap. Japanese

K

Kaz. Kazakh
kg kilogram(s)
Kir. Kirghiz
km kilometer(s)
km² square kilometer (singular)
Kor. Korean
Kurd. Kurdish

L

L. Lake
LAIA Latin American Integration Association
Lao. Laotian
Lapp. Lappish
Lat. Latin
Latv. Latvian
Liech. Liechtenstein
Lith. Lithuanian
Lux. Luxembourg

M

m million/meter(s)
Mac. Macedonian
Maced. Macedonia
Mal. Malay
Malg. Malagasy
Malt. Maltese
mi. mile(s)
Mong. Mongolian
Mt. Mountain
Mts Mountains

N

N north
NAFTA North American Free Trade Agreement
Nep. Nepali
Neth. Netherlands
Nic. Nicaraguan
Nor. Norwegian
NZ New Zealand

P

Pash. Pashtu
PNG Papua New Guinea
Pol. Polish
Poly. Polynesian
Port. Portuguese
prev. previously

R

Rep. Republic
Res. Reservoir
Rmsch. Romansch
Rom. Romanian
Rus. Russian
Russ. Fed. Russian Federation

S

S south
SADC Southern Africa Development Community
SCr. Serbo-Croatian
Sinh. Sinhala
Slvk. Slovak
Slvn. Slovene
Som. Somali
Sp. Spanish
St., St Saint
Strs. Straits
Swa. Swahili
Swe. Swedish
Switz. Switzerland

T

Taj. Tajik
Th. Thai
Thai. Thailand
Tib. Tibetan
Turk. Turkish
Turkm. Turkmenistan

U

UAE United Arab Emirates
Uigh. Uighur
UK United Kingdom
Ukr. Ukrainian
UN United Nations
Urd. Urdu
US/USA United States of America
USSR Union of Soviet Socialist Republic
Uzb. Uzbek

V

var. variant
Vdkhr. Vodokhranilishche (Russian for reservoir)
Vdskh. Vodoskhovyshche (Ukrainian for reservoir)
Vtn. Vietnamese

W

W west
Wel. Welsh

Y

Yugo. Yugoslavia

This index lists all the placenames and features shown on the regional and continental maps in this Atlas. Placenames are referenced to the largest scale map on which they appear. The policy followed throughout the Atlas is to use the local spelling or local name at regional level; commonly-used English language names may occasionally be added (in parentheses) where this is an aid to identification e.g. Firenze (Florence). English names, where they exist, have been used for all international features e.g. oceans and country names; they are also used on the continental maps and in the introductory World Today section; these are then fully cross-referenced to the local names found on the regional maps. The index also contains commonly-found alternative names and variant spellings, which are also fully cross-referenced.

All main entry names are those of settlements unless otherwise indicated by the use of italicized definitions or representative symbols, which are keyed at the foot of each page.

1

25 de Mayo *see* Veinticinco de Mayo
143 *Y13* **26 Bakı Komissarı** *Rus.* Imeni 26 Bakinskikh Komissarov. SE Azerbaijan
26 Baku Komissarlary Adyndaky *see* Imeni 26 Bakinskikh Komissarov
8 *M16* **100 Mile House** *var.* Hundred Mile House. British Columbia, SW Canada

A

Aa *see* Gauja
Aabenraa *see* Åbenrå
Aabybro *see* Åbybro
103 *C16* **Aachen** *Dut.* Aken, *Fr.* Aix-la-Chapelle; *anc.* Aquae Grani, Aquisgranum. Nordrhein-Westfalen, W Germany
Aaiún *see* Laâyoune
Aakirkeby *see* Åkirkeby
Aalborg *see* Ålborg
Aalborg Bugt *see* Ålborg Bugt
103 *J21* **Aalen** Baden-Württemberg, S Germany
Aalestrup *see* Ålestrup
100 *I11* **Aalsmeer** Noord-Holland, C Netherlands
101 *F18* **Aalst** *Fr.* Alost. Oost-Vlaanderen, C Belgium
101 *K18* **Aalst** Noord-Brabant, S Netherlands
100 *O12* **Aalten** Gelderland, E Netherlands
101 *D17* **Aalter** Oost-Vlaanderen, NW Belgium
Aanaar *see* Inari
Aanaarjävri *see* Inarijärvi
95 *M17* **Äänekoski** Keski-Suomi, C Finland
144 *H7* **Aanjar** *var.* 'Anjar. C Lebanon
85 *G21* **Aansluit** Northern Cape, N South Africa
Aar *see* Aare
110 *F7* **Aarau** Aargau, N Switzerland
110 *D8* **Aarberg** Bern, W Switzerland
101 *D16* **Aardenburg** Zeeland, SW Netherlands
110 *D8* **Aare** *var.* Aar. ≈ W Switzerland
110 *F7* **Aargau** *Fr.* Argovie. ◐ *canton* N Switzerland
Aarhus *see* Århus
Aarlen *see* Arlon
Aars *see* Års
101 *I17* **Aarschot** Vlaams Brabant, C Belgium
Aassi, Nahr el *see* Orontes
Aat *see* Ath
166 *G7* **Aba** *prev.* Ngawa. Sichuan, C China
79 *V17* **Aba** Abia, S Nigeria
81 *P16* **Aba** Haut-Zaïre, NE Zaire
146 *J6* **Abā al Qazāz, Bi'r** *well* NW Saudi Arabia
Abā as Su'ūd *see* Najrān
61 *G14* **Abacaxis, Rio** ≈ NW Brazil
Abaco Island *see* Great Abaco/Little Abaco
Abaco Island *see* Great Abaco, N Bahamas
148 *K10* **Ābādān** Khūzestān, SW Iran
149 *O10* **Ābādeh** Fārs, C Iran
76 *H8* **Abadla** W Algeria
61 *M20* **Abaeté** Minas Gerais, SE Brazil
169 *Q10* **Abag Qi** *var.* Xin Hot. Nei Mongol Zizhiqu, N China
64 *P7* **Abaí** Caazapá, S Paraguay
203 *O2* **Abaiang** *var.* Apia; *prev.* Charlotte Island. *atoll* Tungaru, W Kiribati
Abaj *see* Abay
79 *U15* **Abaji** Federal Capital District, C Nigeria
39 *O7* **Abajo Peak** ▲ Utah, W USA
79 *V16* **Abakaliki** Enugu, S Nigeria
126 *Hh15* **Abakan** Respublika Khakasiya, S Russian Federation
126 *Hh15* **Abakan** ≈ S Russian Federation
79 *S11* **Abala** Tillabéri, SW Niger
79 *U11* **Abalak** Tahoua, C Niger
121 *N14* **Abalyanka** *Rus.* Obolyanka. ≈ N Belarus
126 *Ii14* **Aban** Krasnoyarskiy Kray, S Russian Federation
149 *P9* **Āb Anbār-e Kān Sorkh** Yazd, C Iran
59 *G16* **Abancay** Apurímac, SE Peru
202 *H2* **Abaokoro** *atoll* Tungaru, W Kiribati
Abariringa *see* Kanton
149 *P10* **Abarkū** Yazd, C Iran
172 *Qq5* **Abashiri** *var.* Abasiri. Hokkaidō, NE Japan
172 *Q6* **Abashiri-gawa** ≈ Hokkaidō, NE Japan
172 *Q5* **Abashiri-ko** ◎ Hokkaidō, NE Japan
Abasiri *see* Abashiri
43 *P10* **Abasolo** Tamaulipas, C Mexico
194 *L16* **Abau** Central, S PNG
151 *R10* **Abay** *var.* Abaj. Karaganda, C Kazakhstan
83 *I15* **Ābaya Hāyk'** *Eng.* Lake Margherita, *It.* Abbaia. ◎ SW Ethiopia
Ābay Wenz *see* Blue Nile
126 *Hh15* **Abaza** Respublika Khakasiya, S Russian Federation
Abbaia *see* Ābaya Hāyk'
149 *Q13* **Āb Bārīk** Fārs, S Iran
109 *C18* **Abbasanta** Sardegna, Italy, C Mediterranean Sea
Abbatis Villa *see* Abbeville
32 *M3* **Abbaye, Point** *headland* Michigan, N USA
Abbazia *see* Opatija
Abbé, Lake *see* Abhe, Lake
105 *N2* **Abbeville** *anc.* Abbatis Villa. Somme, N France
25 *R7* **Abbeville** Alabama, S USA
25 *U6* **Abbeville** Georgia, SE USA
24 *I9* **Abbeville** Louisiana, S USA
23 *P12* **Abbeville** South Carolina, SE USA
99 *B20* **Abbeyfeale** *Ir.* Mainistir na Féile. SW Ireland
108 *D8* **Abbiategrasso** Lombardia, NW Italy
95 *I14* **Abborrträsk** Norrbotten, N Sweden
204 *J9* **Abbot Ice Shelf** *ice shelf* Antarctica
8 *M17* **Abbotsford** British Columbia, SW Canada
32 *K6* **Abbotsford** Wisconsin, N USA
155 *U5* **Abbottābād** North-West Frontier Province, NW Pakistan
121 *M14* **Abchuha** *Rus.* Obchuga. Minskaya Voblasts', NW Belarus
100 *I10* **Abcoude** Utrecht, C Netherlands
145 *N2* **'Abd al 'Azīz, Jabal** ⛰ NE Syria
147* *U17* **'Abd al Kūrī** *island* SE Yemen
145 *Z13* **'Abd Allāh, Khawr** *bay* Iraq/Kuwait
131 *U6* **Abdulino** Orenburgskaya Oblast', W Russian Federation
80 *J10* **Abéché** *var.* Abécher, Abeshr. Ouaddaï, SE Chad
Abécher *see* Abéché
149 *S8* **Āb-e Garm va Sard** Khorāsān, E Iran
79 *R8* **Abeïbara** Kidal, NE Mali
107 *P5* **Abejar** Castilla-León, N Spain
56 *E9* **Abejorral** Antioquia, W Colombia
Abela *see* Ávila
Abellinum *see* Avellino
94 *Q2* **Abeløya** *island* Kong Karls Land, E Svalbard
82 *I13* **Ābeltī** C Ethiopia
203 *O2* **Abemama** *var.* Apamama; *prev.* Roger Simpson Island. *atoll* Tungaru, W Kiribati
176 *Yy14* **Abemaree** *var.* Abemarre. Irian Jaya, E Indonesia
79 *O16* **Abengourou** E Ivory Coast
97 *G24* **Åbenrå** *var.* Aabenraa, *Ger.* Apenrade. Sønderjylland, SW Denmark
103 *L22* **Abens** ≈ SE Germany
79 *S16* **Abeokuta** Ogun, SW Nigeria
99 *I20* **Aberaeron** SW Wales, UK
Aberbrothock *see* Arbroath
Abercorn *see* Mbala
31 *R6* **Abercrombie** North Dakota, N USA
191 *T7* **Aberdeen** New South Wales, SE Australia
9 *T15* **Aberdeen** Saskatchewan, S Canada
85 *H25* **Aberdeen** Eastern Cape, S South Africa
98 *L9* **Aberdeen** *anc.* Devana. NE Scotland, UK
23 *X2* **Aberdeen** Maryland, NE USA
25 *N3* **Aberdeen** Mississippi, S USA
23 *T10* **Aberdeen** North Carolina, SE USA
31 *P8* **Aberdeen** South Dakota, N USA
34 *F8* **Aberdeen** Washington, NW USA
98 *K9* **Aberdeen** *cultural region* NE Scotland, UK
15 *K6* **Aberdeen Lake** ◎ Northwest Territories, NE Canada
98 *J10* **Aberfeldy** C Scotland, UK
99 *K21* **Abergavenny** *anc.* Gobannium. SE Wales, UK
Abergwaun *see* Fishguard
Abermarre *see* Abemaree
27 *N5* **Abernathy** Texas, SW USA
Abersee *see* Wolfgangsee
Abertawe *see* Swansea
Aberteifi *see* Cardigan
34 *I15* **Abert, Lake** ◎ Oregon, NW USA
99 *I20* **Aberystwyth** W Wales, UK
Abeshr *see* Abéché
108 *F10* **Abetone** Toscana, C Italy
129 *V5* **Abez'** Respublika Komi, NW Russian Federation
148 *M5* **Āb Garm** Zanjān, NW Iran
147 *N12* **Abhā** 'Asīr, SW Saudi Arabia
148 *M5* **Abhar** Zanjān, NW Iran
Abhé Bad/Ābhē Bid Hāyk' *see* Abhe, Lake
82 *K12* **Abhe, Lake** *var.* Lake Abbé, *Amh.* Ābhē Bid Hāyk', *Som.* Abhé Bad. ◎ Djibouti/Ethiopia
79 *V17* **Abia** ◐ *state* SE Nigeria
145 *V9* **'Abīd 'Alī** E Iraq
121 *O17* **Abidavichy** *Rus.* Obidovichi. Mahilyowskaya Voblasts', E Belarus
117 *L15* **Abide** Çanakkale, NW Turkey
79 *N17* **Abidjan** S Ivory Coast
Āb-i-Istāda *see* Īstādeh-ye Moqor, Āb-e-
29 *N4* **Abilene** Kansas, C USA
27 *Q7* **Abilene** Texas, SW USA
Abindonia *see* Abingdon
99 *M21* **Abingdon** *anc.* Abindonia. S England, UK
32 *K12* **Abingdon** Illinois, N USA
23 *P8* **Abingdon** Virginia, NE USA
Abingdon *see* Pinta, Isla
20 *J15* **Abington** Pennsylvania, NE USA
130 *K14* **Abinsk** Krasnodarskiy Kray, SW Russian Federation
39 *R9* **Abiquiu Reservoir** ⊡ New Mexico, SW USA
94 *I10* **Abisko** Norrbotten, N Sweden
10 *G12* **Abitibi** ≈ Ontario, S Canada
10 *H12* **Abitibi, Lake** ◎ Ontario, S Canada
82 *J10* **Ābīy Ādī** N Ethiopia
120 *H6* **Abja-Paluoja** Viljandimaa, S Estonia
143 *Q8* **Abkhazia** ◐ *autonomous republic* NW Georgia
190 *F1* **Abminga** South Australia
77 *W9* **Abnûb** C Egypt
Åbo *see* Turku
Åbo-Björneborg *see* Turku-Pori
158 *G9* **Abohar** Punjab, N India
79 *O17* **Aboisso** SE Ivory Coast
80 *H5* **Abo, Massif d'** ⛰ NW Chad
79 *R16* **Abomey** S Benin
81 *F16* **Abong Mbang** Est, SE Cameroon
113 *L23* **Abony** Pest, C Hungary
80 *J11* **Abou-Déïa** Salamat, SE Chad
Aboudouhour *see* Abū aḍ Ḍuhūr
Abou Kémal *see* Abū Kamāl
Abou Simbel *see* Abu Simbel
143 *T12* **Abovyan** C Armenia
179 *P8* **Abra** ≈ Luzon, N Philippines
147 *P15* **Abrād, Wādī** *seasonal river* W Yemen
Abraham Bay *see* The Carlton
106 *G10* **Abrantes** *var.* Abrántes. Santarém, C Portugal
64 *J4* **Abra Pampa** Jujuy, N Argentina
Abrashlare *see* Brezovo
56 *G7* **Abrego** Norte de Santander, N Colombia
Abrene *see* Pytalovo
42 *C7* **Abreojos, Punta** *headland* W Mexico
67 *J16* **Abrolhos Bank** *undersea feature* W Atlantic Ocean
121 *H19* **Abrova** *Rus.* Obrovo. Brestskaya Voblasts', SW Belarus
118 *G11* **Abrud** *Ger.* Gross-Schlatten, *Hung.* Abrudbánya. Alba, SW Romania
Abrudbánya *see* Abrud
120 *E6* **Abruka** *island* SW Estonia
109 *J15* **Abruzzese, Appennino** ⛰ C Italy
109 *J14* **Abruzzi** ◐ *region* C Italy
147 *N14* **'Abs** *var.* Sūq 'Abs. W Yemen
35 *T12* **Absaroka Range** ⛰ Montana/Wyoming, NW USA
143 *Z11* **Abşeron Yarımadası** *Rus.* Apsheronskiy Poluostrov. *peninsula* E Azerbaijan
149 *N6* **Āb Shīrīn** Eşfahān, C Iran
145 *X10* **Abtān** SE Iraq
111 *R6* **Abtenau** Salzburg, NW Austria
170 *Dd12* **Abu** Yamaguchi, Honshū, SW Japan
158 *E14* **Ābu** Rājasthān, N India
144 *I4* **Abū aḍ Ḍuhūr** *Fr.* Aboudouhour. Idlib, NW Syria
149 *P17* **Abū al Abyaḍ** *island* C UAE
144 *K10* **Abū al Ḩuşayn, Khabrat** ◎ N Jordan
145 *R8* **Abū al Jīr** C Iraq
145 *Y12* **Abū al Khaşīb** *var.* Abul Khasib. SE Iraq
145 *U12* **Abū at Tubrah, Thaqb** *well* S Iraq
77 *V11* **Abu Balâs** ▲ SW Egypt
Abu Dhabi *see* Abū Z̧aby
145 *R8* **Abū Farūkh** C Iraq
82 *C12* **Abu Gabra** Southern Darfur, W Sudan
145 *P10* **Abū Ghār, Sha'īb** *dry watercourse* S Iraq
82 *G7* **Abu Hamed** River Nile, N Sudan
145 *O5* **Abū Ḩardān** *var.* Hajîne. Dayr az Zawr, E Syria
145 *T7* **Abū Ḩāssawīyah** E Iraq
144 *K10* **Abū Ḩifnah, Wādī** *dry watercourse* N Jordan
79 *V15* **Abuja** ● (Nigeria) Federal Capital District, C Nigeria
145 *R9* **Abū Jahaf, Wādī** *dry watercourse* C Iraq
58 *F12* **Abujao, Río** ≈ E Peru
145 *U12* **Abū Jasrah** S Iraq
145 *O6* **Abū Kamāl** *Fr.* Abou Kémal. Dayr az Zawr, E Syria
175 *Q11* **Abuki, Pegunungan** ⛰ Sulawesi, C Indonesia
171 *Ll14* **Abukuma-gawa** ≈ Honshū, C Japan
171 *Ll15* **Abukuma-sanchi** ⛰ Honshū, C Japan
Abula *see* Ávila
Abul Khasib *see* Abū al Khaşīb
81 *K16* **Abumombazi** *var.* Abumonbazi. Equateur, N Zaire
Abumonbazi *see* Abumombazi
61 *D15* **Abunã** Rondônia, W Brazil
58 *K13* **Abunã, Rio** *var.* Río Abuná. ≈ Bolivia/Brazil
144 *G10* **Abū Nuşayr** *var.* Abu Nuseir. 'Ammān, W Jordan
Abu Nuseir *see* Abū Nuşayr
145 *T12* **Abū Qabr** S Iraq
144 *K5* **Abū Raḩbah, Jabal** ⛰ C Syria
145 *S5* **Abū Rajāsh** N Iraq
145 *W13* **Abū Raqrāq, Ghadīr** *well* S Iraq
158 *E14* **Ābu Road** Rājasthān, N India
82 *I6* **Abu Shagara, Ras** *headland* NE Sudan
77 *W12* **Abu Simbel** *var.* Abou Simbel, Abū Sunbul. *ancient monument* S Egypt
145 *U12* **Abū Sudayrah** S Iraq
145 *T10* **Abū Şukhayr** S Iraq
Abū Sunbul *see* Abu Simbel
172 *Nn6* **Abuta** Hokkaidō, NE Japan
193 *E18* **Abut Head** *headland* South Island, NZ
82 *E9* **Abu 'Urug** Northern Kordofan, C Sudan
82 *K12* **Ābuyē Mēda** ▲ C Ethiopia
179 *R13* **Abuyog** Leyte, C Philippines
82 *D11* **Abu Zabad** Western Kordofan, C Sudan
Abū Z̧abī *see* Abū Z̧aby
149 *P16* **Abū Z̧aby** *var.* Abū Z̧abī, *Eng.* Abu Dhabi. ● (UAE) Abū Z̧aby, C UAE
77 *X8* **Abu Zenîma** E Egypt
97 *N17* **Åby** Östergötland, S Sweden
Abyaḍ, Al Baḩr al *see* White Nile
97 *G20* **Åbybro** *var.* Aabybro. Nordjylland, N Denmark
82 *D13* **Abyei** Western Kordofan, S Sudan
Abyla *see* Ávila
Abymes *see* les Abymes
Abyssinia *see* Ethiopia
Açâba *see* Assaba
56 *F11* **Acacias** Meta, C Colombia
60 *L13* **Açailandia** Maranhão, E Brazil
Acaill *see* Achill Island
44 *E8* **Acajutla** Sonsonate, W El Salvador
81 *D17* **Acalayong** SW Equatorial Guinea

◆ Country
● Country Capital
◇ Dependent Territory
○ Dependent Territory Capital
◐ Administrative Region
✕ International Airport
▲ Mountain
⛰ Mountain Range
Volcano
≈ River
◎ Lake
⊡ Reservoir

Acámbaro – Ajax, Mount

43 *N13* **Acámbaro** Guanajuato, C Mexico

56 *C6* **Acandí** Chocó, NW Colombia

106 *H4* **A Cañiza** *var.* La Cañiza. Galicia, NW Spain

42 *J11* **Acaponeta** Nayarit, C Mexico

42 *J11* **Acaponeta, Río de** ≈ C Mexico

43 *O16* **Acapulco** *var.* Acapulco de Juárez. Guerrero, S Mexico

Acapulco de Juárez *see* Acapulco

57 *T13* **Acarai Mountains** *Sp.* Serra Acaraí. ⛰ Brazil/Guyana

Acaraí, Serra *see* Acarai Mountains

60 *O13* **Acaraú** Ceará, NE Brazil

56 *J6* **Acarigua** Portuguesa, N Venezuela

44 *C6* **Acatenango, Volcán de** 🌋 S Guatemala

43 *Q15* **Acatlán** *var.* Acatlán de Osorio. Puebla, S Mexico

Acatlán de Osorio *see* Acatlán

43 *S15* **Acayucan** *var.* Acayucán. Veracruz-Llave, E Mexico

Accho *see* 'Akko

23 *Y5* **Accomac** Virginia, NE USA

79 *Q17* **Accra** ● (Ghana) SE Ghana

99 *L17* **Accrington** NW England, UK

63 *B19* **Acebal** Santa Fe, C Argentina

173 *Ee4* **Aceh** *off.* Daerah Istimewa Aceh, *var.* Acheen, Achin, Atchin, Atjeh. ⬖ *autonomous district* NW Indonesia

109 *M18* **Acerenza** Basilicata, S Italy

109 *K17* **Acerra** *anc.* Acerrae. Campania, S Italy

Acerrae *see* Acerra

Ach'asar Lerr *see* Achkasar

59 *J17* **Achacachi** La Paz, W Bolivia

56 *K7* **Achaguas** Apure, C Venezuela

160 *H12* **Achalpur** *prev.* Elichpur, Ellichpur. Mahārāshtra, C India

63 *F18* **Achar** Tacuarembó, C Uruguay

117 *H19* **Acharnés** *var.* Aharnes; *prev.* Akharnaí. Attikí, C Greece

Acheen *see* Aceh

101 *K16* **Achel** Limburg, NE Belgium

117 *D16* **Achelóos** *var.* Akhelóös, Aspropótamos; *anc.* Achelous. ≈ W Greece

Achelous *see* Achelóos

169 *W8* **Acheng** Heilongjiang, NE China

111 *N6* **Achenkirch** Tirol, W Austria

103 *L24* **Achenpass** *pass* Austria/Germany

111 *N7* **Achensee** ◎ W Austria

103 *F22* **Achern** Baden-Württemberg, SW Germany

117 *C16* **Acherón** ≈ W Greece

79 *W11* **Achétinamou** ≈ S Niger

158 *J12* **Achhnera** Uttar Pradesh, N India

44 *C7* **Achiguate, Río** ≈ S Guatemala

99 *A16* **Achill Head** *Ir.* Ceann Acla. *headland* W Ireland

99 *A16* **Achill Island** *Ir.* Acaill. *island* W Ireland

102 *H11* **Achim** Niedersachsen, NW Germany

155 *S5* **Achīn** Nangarhār, E Afghanistan

Achin *see* Aceh

126 *Hh14* **Achinsk** Krasnoyarskiy Kray, S Russian Federation

168 *E5* **Achit Nuur** ◎ NW Mongolia

143 *T11* **Achkasar** *Arm.* Ach'asar Lerr. ▲ Armenia/Georgia

130 *K13* **Achuyevo** Krasnodarskiy Kray, SW Russian Federation

83 *F16* **Achwa** *var.* Aswa. ≈ N Uganda

142 *E15* **Acıgöl** *salt lake* SW Turkey

109 *L24* **Acireale** Sicilia, Italy, C Mediterranean Sea

Aciris *see* Agri

27 *N7* **Ackerly** Texas, SW USA

24 *M4* **Ackerman** Mississippi, S USA

31 *W13* **Ackley** Iowa, C USA

46 *J5* **Acklins Island** *island* SE Bahamas

Acla, Ceann *see* Achill Head

64 *H11* **Aconcagua, Cerro** ▲ W Argentina

Açores/Açores, Arquipélago dos/Açores, Ilhas dos *see* Azores

106 *H2* **A Coruña** *Cast.* La Coruña, *Eng.* Corunna; *anc.* Caronium. Galicia, NW Spain

44 *L10* **Acoyapa** Chontales, S Nicaragua

108 *H13* **Acquapendente** Lazio, C Italy

108 *J13* **Acquasanta Terme** Marche, C Italy

108 *I13* **Acquasparta** Lazio, C Italy

108 *C9* **Acqui Terme e Bagni** Piemonte, NW Italy

Acrae *see* Palazzola Acreide

190 *F7* **Acraman, Lake** *salt lake* South Australia

61 *A15* **Acre** *off.* Estado do Acre. ⬖ *state* W Brazil

Acre *see* 'Akko

61 *C16* **Acre, Rio** ≈ W Brazil

109 *N20* **Acri** Calabria, SW Italy

Acte *see* Ágion Óros

203 *Y12* **Actéon, Groupe** *island group* Îles Tuamotu, SE French Polynesia

13 *P12* **Acton-Vale** Québec, SE Canada

43 *P13* **Actopan** *var.* Actopán. Hidalgo, C Mexico

61 *P14* **Açu** *var.* Assu. Rio Grande do Norte, E Brazil

Acunum Acusio *see* Montélimar

79 *Q17* **Ada** SE Ghana

31 *R5* **Ada** Minnesota, N USA

33 *R12* **Ada** Ohio, N USA

29 *O12* **Ada** Oklahoma, C USA

114 *L8* **Ada** Serbia, N Yugoslavia

Ada Bazar *see* Adapazarı

42 *D3* **Adair, Bahía de** *bay* NW Mexico

106 *M7* **Adaja** ≈ N Spain

40 *H17* **Adak Island** *island* Aleutian Islands, Alaska, USA

Adalia *see* Antalya

Adalia, Gulf of *see* Antalya Körfezi

147 *X9* **Adam** N Oman

Adama *see* Nazrēt

62 *I8* **Adamantina** São Paulo, S Brazil

81 *E14* **Adamaoua** *Eng.* Adamawa. ⬖ *province* N Cameroon

70 *F11* **Adamaoua, Massif d'** *Eng.* Adamawa Highlands. *plateau* NW Cameroon

79 *Y14* **Adamawa** ⬖ *state* E Nigeria

Adamawa *see* Adamaoua

Adamawa Highlands *see* Adamaoua, Massif d'

108 *F6* **Adamello** ▲ N Italy

83 *J14* **Ādamī Tulu** C Ethiopia

65 *M23* **Adam, Mount** ▲ West Falkland, Falkland Islands

31 *R16* **Adams** Nebraska, C USA

20 *H8* **Adams** New York, NE USA

31 *Q3* **Adams** North Dakota, N USA

161 *I23* **Adam's Bridge** *chain of shoals* NW Sri Lanka

34 *H10* **Adams, Mount** ▲ Washington, NW USA

Adam's Peak *see* Sri Pada

203 *R16* **Adam's Rock** *island* Pitcairn Island, Pitcairn Islands

203 *P16* **Adamstown** ○ (Pitcairn Islands) Pitcairn Island, Pitcairn Islands

22 *G10* **Adamsville** Tennessee, S USA

27 *S9* **Adamsville** Texas, SW USA

147 *O17* **'Adan** *Eng.* Aden. SW Yemen

142 *K16* **Adana** *var.* Seyhan. Adana, S Turkey

142 *K16* **Adana** *var.* Seyhan. ⬖ *province* S Turkey

Adâncata *see* Horlivka

175 *Nn10* **Adang, Teluk** *bay* Borneo, C Indonesia

142 *F11* **Adapazarı** *prev.* Ada Bazar. Sakarya, NW Turkey

82 *H8* **Adarama** River Nile, NE Sudan

205 *Q16* **Adare, Cape** *headland* Antarctica

108 *E6* **Adda** *anc.* Addua. ≈ N Italy

82 *A13* **Adda** ≈ W Sudan

149 *Q17* **Aḍ Ḍab'īyah** Abū Ẓaby, C UAE

149 *O18* **Aḍ Ḍafrah** *desert* S UAE

147 *Q6* **Ad Dahnā'** *desert* E Saudi Arabia

76 *A11* **Ad Dakhla** *var.* Dakhla. SW Western Sahara

Ad Dalanj *see* Dilling

Ad Damar *see* Ed Damer

Ad Damazīn *see* Ed Damazin

Ad Dāmir *see* Ed Damer

181 *N2* **Ad Dammām** *desert* NE Saudi Arabia

147 *R6* **Ad Dammān** *var.* Dammām. Ash Sharqīyah, NE Saudi Arabia

Ad Dāmūr *see* Damoûr

146 *K5* **Ad Dār al Ḥamrā'** Tabūk, NW Saudi Arabia

146 *M13* **Ad Darb** Jīzān, SW Saudi Arabia

147 *O8* **Ad Dawādimī** Ar Riyāḍ, C Saudi Arabia

149 *N16* **Ad Dawḥah** *Eng.* Doha. ● (Qatar) C Qatar

149 *N16* **Ad Dawḥah** *Eng.* Doha. ✕ C Qatar

145 *S6* **Ad Dawr** N Iraq

145 *Y12* **Ad Dayr** *var.* Dayr, Shahbān. E Iraq

Addi Arkay *see* Ādī Ārk'ay

145 *X15* **Ad Dibdibah** *physical region* Iraq/Kuwait

Aḍ Ḍiffah *see* Libyan Plateau

Addis Ababa *see* Ādīs Ābeba

Addison *see* Webster Springs

145 *U10* **Ad Dīwānīyah** *var.* Diwaniyah. C Iraq

Addua *see* Adda

157 *K22* **Addu Atoll** *atoll* S Maldives

Ad Dujail *see* Ad Dujayl

145 *T7* **Ad Dujayl** *var.* Ad Dujail. N Iraq

Ad Duwaym/Ad Duwēm *see* Ed Dueim

101 *D16* **Adegem** Oost-Vlaanderen, NW Belgium

25 *U7* **Adel** Georgia, SE USA

31 *U14* **Adel** Iowa, C USA

190 *I9* **Adelaide** South Australia

46 *H2* **Adelaide** New Providence, N Bahamas

190 *I9* **Adelaide** ✕ South Australia

204 *H6* **Adelaide Island** *island* Antarctica

15 *K4* **Adelaide Peninsula** *peninsula* Northwest Territories, N Canada

189 *P2* **Adelaide River** Northern Territory, N Australia

78 *M10* **'Adel Bagrou** Hodh ech Chargui, SE Mauritania

194 *I11* **Adelbert Range** ⛰ N PNG

188 *K3* **Adele Island** *island* Western Australia

109 *O17* **Adelfia** Puglia, SE Italy

205 *V16* **Adélie Coast** *physical region* Antarctica

205 *V14* **Adélie, Terre** *physical region* Antarctica

Adelnau *see* Odolanów

Adelsberg *see* Postojna

Aden *see* 'Adan

147 *Q17* **Aden, Gulf of** *gulf* SW Arabian Sea

79 *V10* **Aderbissinat** Agadez, C Niger

Adhaim *see* Al 'Uẓaym

149 *R16* **Adh Dhayd** *var.* Al Dhaid. Ash Shāriqah, NE UAE

146 *M4* **'Adhfā'** *spring/well* NW Saudi Arabia

144 *I13* **'Ādhriyāt, Jabāl al** ⛰ S Jordan

194 *L12* **Adi** ≈ New Britain, C PNG

82 *I10* **Ādī Ārk'ay** *var.* Addi Arkay. N Ethiopia

190 *C7* **Adieu, Cape** *headland* South Australia

108 *H8* **Adige** *Ger.* Etsch. ≈ N Italy

82 *J10* **Ādīgrat** N Ethiopia

160 *I13* **Ādilabād** *var.* Ādilābād. Andhra Pradesh, C India

37 *P2* **Adin** California, W USA

176 *Vv12* **Adi, Pulau** *island* E Indonesia

20 *K8* **Adirondack Mountains** ⛰ New York, NE USA

82 *J13* **Ādīs Ābeba** *Eng.* Addis Ababa. ● (Ethiopia) C Ethiopia

82 *J13* **Ādīs Ābeba** ✕ C Ethiopia

82 *I11* **Ādīs Zemen** NW Ethiopia

Adi Ugri *see* Mendefera

143 *N15* **Adıyaman** Adıyaman, SE Turkey

143 *N15* **Adıyaman** ⬖ *province* S Turkey

118 *L11* **Adjud** Vrancea, E Romania

47 *T6* **Adjuntas** C Puerto Rico

Adjuntas, Presa de las *see* Vicente Guerrero, Presa

Ādkup *see* Erikub Atoll

130 *L15* **Adler** Krasnodarskiy Kray, SW Russian Federation

Adler *see* Orlice

110 *G7* **Adliswil** Zürich, NW Switzerland

15 *L1* **Admiralty Inlet** *fjord* Baffin Island, Northwest Territories, NE Canada

34 *G7* **Admiralty Inlet** *inlet* Washington, NW USA

41 *X13* **Admiralty Island** *island* Alexander Archipelago, Alaska, USA

194 *K8* **Admiralty Islands** *island group* N PNG

142 *B14* **Adnan Menderes** ✕ (İzmir) İzmir, W Turkey

39 *V6* **Adobe Creek Reservoir** ⊟ Colorado, C USA

79 *T16* **Ado-Ekiti** Ondo, SW Nigeria

Adola *see* Kibre Mengist

63 *C23* **Adolfo González Chaues** Buenos Aires, E Argentina

161 *H17* **Ādoni** Andhra Pradesh, C India

104 *K15* **Adour** *anc.* Aturus. ≈ SW France

Adowa *see* Ādwa

107 *O15* **Adra** Andalucía, S Spain

109 *L24* **Adrano** Sicilia, Italy, C Mediterranean Sea

76 *I9* **Adrar** C Algeria

78 *K7* **Adrar** ⬖ *region* C Mauritania

76 *L11* **Adrar** ⛰ SE Algeria

76 *A12* **Adrar Souttouf** ⛰ SW Western Sahara

Adrasman *see* Adrasmon

153 *Q10* **Adrasmon** *Rus.* Adrasman. NW Tajikistan

80 *K10* **Adré** Ouaddaï, E Chad

108 *H9* **Adria** *anc.* Atria, Hadria, Hatria. Veneto, NE Italy

33 *R10* **Adrian** Michigan, N USA

31 *S11* **Adrian** Minnesota, N USA

29 *R5* **Adrian** Missouri, C USA

26 *M2* **Adrian** Texas, SW USA

23 *S4* **Adrian** West Virginia, NE USA

Adrianople/Adrianopolis *see* Edirne

123 *Mm8* **Adriatic Basin** *undersea feature* Adriatic Sea, N Mediterranean Sea

Adriatico, Mare *see* Adriatic Sea

108 *L13* **Adriatic Sea** *Alb.* Deti Adriatik, *It.* Mare Adriatico, *SCr.* Jadransko More, *Slvn.* Jadransko Morje. *sea* N Mediterranean Sea

Adriatik, Deti *see* Adriatic Sea

Adua *see* Ādwa

Aduana del Sásabe *see* Sásabe

81 *O17* **Adusa** Haut-Zaïre, NE Zaire

120 *J13* **Adutiškis** Švenčionys, E Lithuania

29 *Y7* **Advance** Missouri, C USA

67 *D25* **Adventure Sound** *bay* East Falkland, Falkland Islands

82 *J10* **Ādwa** *var.* Adowa, *It.* Adua. N Ethiopia

126 *M8* **Adycha** ≈ NE Russian Federation

130 *L14* **Adygeya, Respublika** ⬖ *autonomous republic* SW Russian Federation

152 *C11* **Adzhikui** *Turkm.* Ajyguyy. Balkanskiy Velayat, W Turkmenistan

79 *N17* **Adzopé** SE Ivory Coast

129 *U4* **Adz'va** ≈ NW Russian Federation

129 *U5* **Adz'vavom** Respublika Komi, NW Russian Federation

Ædua *see* Autun

117 *K19* **Aegean Islands** *island group* Greece/Turkey

Aegean North *see* Vóreion Aigaíon

117 *I17* **Aegean Sea** *Gk.* Aigaíon Pélagos, Aigaío Pélagos, *Turk.* Ege Denizi. *sea* NE Mediterranean Sea

Aegean South *see* Nótion Aigaíon

120 *H3* **Aegviidu** *Ger.* Charlottenhof. Harjumaa, NW Estonia

Aegyptus *see* Egypt

Aelana *see* Al 'Aqabah

Aelok *see* Ailuk Atoll

Aelōninae *see* Ailinginae Atoll

Aelōnļapļap *see* Ailinglaplap Atoll

Æmilia *see* Emilia-Romagna

Æmilianum *see* Millau

Aemona *see* Ljubljana

Aenaria *see* Ischia

Aeolian Islands *see* Eolie, Isole

203 *Z3* **Aeon Point** *headland* Kiritimati, NE Kiribati

97 *G24* **Ærø** *Ger.* Arrö. *island* C Denmark

97 *H24* **Ærøskøbing** Fyn, C Denmark

Æsernia *see* Isernia

106 *G3* **A Estrada** Galicia, NW Spain

117 *C18* **Aetós** Itháki, Iónioi Nísoi, Greece, C Mediterranean Sea

203 *Q8* **Afaahiti** Tahiti, W French Polynesia

145 *U10* **'Afak** C Iraq

Afanasjevo *see* Afanas'yevo

129 *T14* **Afanas'yevo** *var.* Afanasjevo. Kirovskaya Oblast', NW Russian Federation

Afándou *see* Afántou

117 *O23* **Afántou** *var.* Afándou. Ródos, Dodekánisos, Greece, Aegean Sea

Afar Depression *see* Danakil Desert

203 *O7* **Afareaitu** Moorea, W French Polynesia

146 *L7* **'Afariyah, Bi'r al** *well* NW Saudi Arabia

Afars et des Issas, Territoire Français des *see* Djibouti

85 *D22* **Affenrücken** Karas, SW Namibia

Afghānestān, Dowlat-e Eslāmī-ye *see* Afghanistan

154 *M6* **Afghanistan** *off.* Islamic State of Afghanistan, *Per.* Dowlat-e Eslāmī-ye Afghānestān; *prev.* Republic of Afghanistan. ◆ *islamic state* C Asia

Afgoi *see* Afgooye

83 *N17* **Afgooye** *It.* Afgoi. Shabeellaha Hoose, S Somalia

147 *N8* **'Afīf** Ar Riyāḍ, C Saudi Arabia

79 *V17* **Afikpo** Abia, S Nigeria

Afiun Karahissar *see* Afyon

96 *H7* **Åfjord** Sør-Trøndelag, C Norway

111 *V6* **Aflenz Kurort** Steiermark, E Austria

76 *J6* **Aflou** N Algeria

83 *L18* **Afmadow** Jubbada Hoose, S Somalia

41 *Q14* **Afognak Island** *island* Alaska, USA

106 *J2* **A Fonsagrada** Galicia, NW Spain

194 *L15* **Afore** Northern, S PNG

61 *O15* **Afrânio** Pernambuco, E Brazil

68-69 **Africa** *continent*

70 *L11* **Africa, Horn of** *physical region* Ethiopia/Somalia

180 *K11* **Africana Seamount** *undersea feature* SW Indian Ocean

88 *A14* **African Plate** *tectonic feature*

144 *I2* **'Afrīn** Ḥalab, N Syria

142 *M15* **Afşin** Kahramanmaraş, C Turkey

100 *J7* **Afsluitdijk** *dam* N Netherlands

31 *U15* **Afton** Iowa, C USA

31 *W9* **Afton** Minnesota, N USA

29 *R8* **Afton** Oklahoma, C USA

142 *F14* **Afyon** *prev.* Afyonkarahisar. Afyon, W Turkey

142 *F14* **Afyon** *var.* Afiun Karahissar, Afyonkarahisar. ⬖ *province* W Turkey

Afyonkarahisar *see* Afyon

Agadès *see* Agadez

79 *V10* **Agadez** *prev.* Agadès. Agadez, C Niger

79 *W8* **Agadez** ⬖ *department* N Niger

76 *E8* **Agadir** SW Morocco

66 *M9* **Agadir Canyon** *undersea feature* SE Atlantic Ocean

151 *R12* **Agadyr'** Zhezkazgan, C Kazakhstan

181 *O7* **Agalega Islands** *island group* N Mauritius

44 *K6* **Agalta, Sierra de** ⛰ E Honduras

126 *Gg10* **Agan** ≈ C Russian Federation

196 *B16* **Agana** *var.* Agaña. ○ (Guam) NW Guam

196 *B15* **Agana Bay** *bay* NW Guam

196 *C16* **Agana Field** ✕ (Agana) C Guam

171 *Kk13* **Agano-gawa** ≈ Honshū, C Japan

196 *B17* **Aga Point** *headland* S Guam

160 *G9* **Agar** Madhya Pradesh, C India

83 *I14* **Āgaro** W Ethiopia

159 *V15* **Agartala** Tripura, NE India

204 *I5* **Agassiz, Cape** *headland* Antarctica

183 *V13* **Agassiz Fracture Zone** *tectonic feature* S Pacific Ocean

196 *B16* **Agat** W Guam

196 *B16* **Agat Bay** *bay* W Guam

151 *P13* **Agat, Gory** *hill* C Kazakhstan

Agatha *see* Agde

117 *M20* **Agathónisi** *island* Dodekánisos, Greece, Aegean Sea

176 *Y13* **Agats** Irian Jaya, E Indonesia

161 *C21* **Agatti Island** *island* Lakshadweep, India, N Indian Ocean

40 *D16* **Agattu Island** *island* Aleutian Islands, Alaska, USA

40 *D16* **Agattu Strait** *strait* Aleutian Islands, Alaska, USA

12 *B8* **Agawa** ≈ Ontario, S Canada

12 *B8* **Agawa Bay** *lake bay* Ontario, S Canada

79 *N17* **Agboville** SE Ivory Coast

143 *V12* **Ağdam** *Rus.* Agdam. SW Azerbaijan

105 *P16* **Agde** *anc.* Agatha. Hérault, S France

105 *P16* **Agde, Cap d'** *headland* S France

Agedabia *see* Ajdābiyā

104 *L14* **Agen** *anc.* Aginnum. Lot-et-Garonne, SW France

Agendicum *see* Sens

171 *K16* **Ageo** Saitama, Honshū, S Japan

111 *R5* **Ager** ≈ N Austria

Agere Hiywet *see* Hāgere Hiywet

110 *G8* **Ägerisee** ◎ W Switzerland

148 *M10* **Āghā Jārī** Khūzestān, SW Iran

41 *P15* **Aghiyuk Island** *island* Alaska, USA

76 *B12* **Aghouinit** SE Western Sahara

Aghri Dagh *see* Büyükağrı Dağı

76 *B10* **Aghzoumal, Sebkhet** *var.* Sebjet Agsumal. *salt lake* E Western Sahara

117 *F15* **Agiá** *var.* Ayiá. Thessalía, C Greece

42 *G7* **Agiabampo, Estero de** *estuary* NW Mexico

124 *Nn4* **Agía Fýlaxis** *var.* Ayia Phyla. S Cyprus

Agialoúsa *see* Yenierenköy

117 *M21* **Agía Marína** Léros, Dodekánisos, Greece, Aegean Sea

124 *Oo3* **Agía Nápa** *var.* Ayia Napa. E Cyprus

117 *L16* **Agía Paraskeví** Lésvos, E Greece

117 *J15* **Agías Eirínis, Ákra** *headland* Límnos, E Greece

117 *L17* **Agiasós** *var.* Ayiásos, Ayiássos. Lésvos, E Greece

Aginnum *see* Agen

126 *K16* **Aginskiy Buryatskiy Avtonomnyy Okrug** ⬖ *autonomous district* S Russian Federation

126 *Kk16* **Aginskoye** Aginskiy Buryatskiy Avtonomnyy Okrug, S Russian Federation

117 *I14* **Ágion Óros** *Eng.* Mount Athos. ⬖ *monastic republic* NE Greece

117 *H14* **Ágion Óros** *var.* Akte, Aktí; *anc.* Acte. *peninsula* NE Greece

116 *D13* **Ágios Achílleios** *religious building* Dytikí Makedonía, N Greece

117 *J16* **Ágios Efstrátios** *var.* Áyios Evstrátios, Hagios Evstrátios. *island* E Greece

117 *H20* **Ágios Geórgios** *island* Kykládes, Greece, Aegean Sea

117 *Q23* **Ágios Geórgios** *island* SE Greece

117 *E21* **Ágios Ilías** ▲ S Greece

117 *K25* **Ágios Ioannis, Ákra** *headland* Kríti, Greece, E Mediterranean Sea

117 *L20* **Ágios Kírykos** *var.* Áyios Kírikos. Ikaría, Dodekánisos, Greece, Aegean Sea

117 *D16* **Ágios Nikolaos** Thessalía, C Greece

117 *K25* **Ágios Nikólaos** *var.* Áyios Nikólaos. Kríti, Greece, E Mediterranean Sea

Ágios Sérgios *see* Yeniboğaziçi

117 *H14* **Agíou Órous, Kólpos** *gulf* N Greece

109 *K24* **Agira** *anc.* Agyrium. Sicilia, Italy, C Mediterranean Sea

117 *G20* **Agkístri** *island* S Greece

116 *G12* **Ágkistro** *var.* Angistro. ▲ NE Greece

105 *O17* **Agly** ≈ S France

Agnetheln *see* Agnita

12 *E10* **Agnew Lake** ◎ Ontario, S Canada

79 *O16* **Agnibilékrou** E Ivory Coast

118 *I11* **Agnita** *Ger.* Agnetheln, *Hung.* Szentágota. Sibiu, SW Romania

109 *K15* **Agnone** Molise, C Italy

171 *Hh17* **Ago** Mie, Honshū, SW Japan

108 *C8* **Agogna** ≈ N Italy

79 *P17* **Agona Swedru** *var.* Swedru. SE Ghana

Agordat *see* Akurdet

Agosta *see* Augusta

105 *N15* **Agout** ≈ S France

158 *J12* **Āgra** Uttar Pradesh, N India

Agra and Oudh, United Provinces of *see* Uttar Pradesh

Agram *see* Zagreb

107 *U5* **Agramunt** Cataluña, NE Spain

107 *Q5* **Agreda** Castilla-León, N Spain

143 *S13* **Ağrı** *var.* Karaköse; *prev.* Karakılısse. Ağrı, NE Turkey

143 *S13* **Ağrı** ⬖ *province* NE Turkey

109 *N19* **Agri** *anc.* Aciris. ≈ S Italy

Agri Dagi *see* Büyükağrı Dağı

109 *J24* **Agrigento** *Gk.* Akragas; *prev.* Girgenti. Sicilia, Italy, C Mediterranean Sea

196 *K4* **Agrihan** *island* N Northern Mariana Islands

117 *D18* **Agrínio** *prev.* Agrinion. Dytikí Ellás, W Greece

Agrinion *see* Agrínio

117 *G17* **Agriovótano** Évvoia, C Greece

109 *L18* **Agropoli** Campania, S Italy

131 *T3* **Agryz** Udmurtskaya Respublika, NW Russian Federation

143 *U11* **Ağstafa** *Rus.* Akstafa. NW Azerbaijan

Agsumal, Sebjet *see* Aghzoumal, Sebkhet

42 *J11* **Agua Brava, Laguna** *lagoon* W Mexico

56 *F7* **Aguachica** Cesar, N Colombia

61 *J20* **Água Clara** Mato Grosso do Sul, SW Brazil

46 *D5* **Aguada de Pasajeros** Cienfuegos, C Cuba

56 *J5* **Aguada Grande** Lara, N Venezuela

47 *S5* **Aguadilla** W Puerto Rico

45 *S16* **Aguadulce** Coclé, S Panama

106 *L14* **Aguadulce** Andalucía, S Spain

43 *O8* **Agualeguas** Nuevo León, NE Mexico

42 *L9* **Aguanaval, Río** ≈ C Mexico

44 *J5* **Aguán, Río** ≈ N Honduras

27 *R16* **Agua Nueva** Texas, SW USA

62 *J8* **Aguapeí, Rio** ≈ S Brazil

63 *E14* **Aguapey, Río** ≈ NE Argentina

42 *G3* **Agua Prieta** Sonora, NW Mexico

106 *G5* **A Guardia** *var.* Laguardia, La Guardia. Galicia, NW Spain

58 *E6* **Aguarico, Río** ≈ Ecuador/Peru

57 *O6* **Aguasay** Monagas, NE Venezuela

42 *M12* **Aguascalientes** Aguascalientes, C Mexico

42 *L12* **Aguascalientes** ⬖ *state* C Mexico

59 *I18* **Aguas Calientes, Río** ≈ S Peru

107 *R7* **Aguasvivas** ≈ NE Spain

62 *J7* **Água Vermelha, Represa de** ⊟ S Brazil

58 *E12* **Aguaytía** Ucayali, C Peru

106 *I5* **A Gudiña** *var.* La Gudiña. Galicia, NW Spain

106 *G7* **Águeda** Aveiro, N Portugal

106 *J8* **Águeda** ≈ Portugal/Spain

79 *Q8* **Aguelhok** Kidal, NE Mali

79 *V12* **Aguié** Maradi, S Niger

196 *K8* **Aguijan** *island* S Northern Mariana Islands

106 *M14* **Aguilar** *var.* Aguilar de la Frontera. Andalucía, S Spain

106 *M3* **Aguilar de Campóo** Castilla-León, N Spain

Aguilar de la Frontera *see* Aguilar

44 *F7* **Aguilares** San Salvador, C El Salvador

107 *Q14* **Aguilas** Murcia, SE Spain

42 *L15* **Aguililla** Michoacán de Ocampo, SW Mexico

85 *F26* **Agulhas** *var.* L'Agulhas. Western Cape, SW South Africa

180 *J11* **Agulhas Bank** *undersea feature* SW Indian Ocean

180 *K11* **Agulhas Basin** *undersea feature* SW Indian Ocean

85 *F26* **Agulhas, Cape** *Afr.* Kaap Agulhas. *headland* SW South Africa

Agulhas, Kaap *see* Agulhas, Cape

62 *O9* **Agulhas Negras, Pico das** ▲ SE Brazil

180 *K11* **Agulhas Plateau** *undersea feature* SW Indian Ocean

172 *Oo14* **Aguni-jima** *island* Nansei-shotō, SW Japan

Agurain *see* Salvatierra

179 *Rr15* **Agusan** ≈ Mindanao, S Philippines

56 *G5* **Agustín Codazzi** *var.* Codazzi. Cesar, N Colombia

Agyrium *see* Agira

76 *L12* **Ahaggar** *high plateau region* SE Algeria

Ahal Welayaty *see* Akhalskiy Velayat

148 *K2* **Ahar** Āžarbāyjān-e Khāvarī, NW Iran

Aharnes *see* Acharnés

144 *J3* **Aḥaş, Jabal** ▲ NW Syria

144 *J3* **Aḥaş, Jebal** ⛰ W Syria

193 *G16* **Ahaura** ≈ South Island, NZ

102 *E13* **Ahaus** Nordrhein-Westfalen, NW Germany

203 *U9* **Ahe** *atoll* Îles Tuamotu, C French Polynesia

192 *N10* **Ahimanawa Range** ⛰ North Island, NZ

121 *I19* **Ahinski Kanal** *Rus.* Oginskiy Kanal. *canal* SW Belarus

195 *N16* **Ahioma** SE PNG

192 *I2* **Ahipara** Northland, North Island, NZ

192 *I2* **Ahipara Bay** *bay* SE Tasman Sea

41 *N13* **Ahklun Mountains** ⛰ Alaska, USA

143 *R14* **Ahlat** Bitlis, E Turkey

103 *F14* **Ahlen** Nordrhein-Westfalen, W Germany

160 *D10* **Ahmadābād** *var.* Ahmedabad. Gujarāt, W India

149 *R10* **Ahmadābād** Kermān, C Iran

Ahmadi *see* Al Aḥmadī

Ahmad Khel *see* Ḥasan Khēl

161 *F14* **Ahmadnagar** *var.* Ahmednagar. Mahārāshtra, W India

155 *T9* **Ahmadpur Siāl** Punjab, E Pakistan

79 *N5* **Aḥmar, 'Erg el** *desert* N Mali

82 *K13* **Ahmar Mountains** ⛰ C Ethiopia

Ahmedabad *see* Ahmadābād

Ahmednagar *see* Ahmadnagar

116 *N12* **Ahmetbey** Kırklareli, NW Turkey

12 *H12* **Ahmic Lake** ◎ Ontario, S Canada

202 *G12* **Ahoa** Île Uvea, E Wallis and Futuna

42 *G8* **Ahomé** Sinaloa, C Mexico

23 *X8* **Ahoskie** North Carolina, SE USA

103 *D17* **Ahr** ≈ W Germany

149 *N12* **Ahram** *var.* Ahrom. Būshehr, S Iran

102 *J9* **Ahrensburg** Schleswig-Holstein, N Germany

Ahrom *see* Ahram

95 *L17* **Ähtäri** Vaasa, W Finland

42 *K12* **Ahuacatlán** Nayarit, C Mexico

44 *E7* **Ahuachapán** Ahuachapán, W El Salvador

44 *A9* **Ahuachapán** ⬖ *department* W El Salvador

203 *V16* **Ahu Akivi** *var.* Siete Moai. *ancient monument* Easter Island, Chile, E Pacific Ocean

203 *W11* **Ahunui** *atoll* Îles Tuamotu, C French Polynesia

193 *E20* **Ahuriri** ≈ South Island, NZ

97 *L22* **Åhus** Kristianstad, S Sweden

Ahu Tahira *see* Ahu Vinapu

203 *V16* **Ahu Tepeu** *ancient monument* Easter Island, Chile, E Pacific Ocean

203 *V17* **Ahu Vinapu** *var.* Ahu Tahira. *ancient monument* Easter Island, Chile, E Pacific Ocean

148 *L9* **Ahvāz** *var.* Ahwāz; *prev.* Nāsiri. Khūzestān, SW Iran

Ahvenanmaa *see* Åland

147 *Q16* **Aḥwar** SW Yemen

Ahwāz *see* Ahvāz

Aibak *see* Āybak

103 *K22* **Aichach** Bayern, SE Germany

171 *I16* **Aichi** *off.* Aichi-ken, *var.* Aiti. ⬖ *prefecture* Honshū, SW Japan

Aïdin *see* Aydın

176 *Ww12* **Aiduna** Irian Jaya, E Indonesia

Aidussina *see* Ajdovščina

194 *F13* **Aiema** ≈ W PNG

Aifir, Clochán an *see* Giant's Causeway

Aigaíon Pélagos/Aigaío Pélagos *see* Aegean Sea

111 *S3* **Aigen im Mülkreis** Oberösterreich, N Austria

117 *G20* **Aígina** *var.* Aíyina, Egina. Aígina, C Greece

117 *G20* **Aígina** *island* S Greece

117 *E18* **Aígio** *var.* Egio; *prev.* Aíyion. Dytikí Ellás, S Greece

110 *C10* **Aigle** Vaud, SW Switzerland

105 *P14* **Aigoual, Mont** ▲ S France

181 *O16* **Aigrettes, Pointe des** *headland* W Réunion

63 *G19* **Aiguá** *var.* Aigua. Maldonado, S Uruguay

105 *S13* **Aigues** ≈ SE France

105 *N10* **Aigurande** Indre, C France

Ai-hun *see* Heihe

171 *K11* **Aikawa** Niigata, Sado, C Japan

23 *Q13* **Aiken** South Carolina, SE USA

27 *N4* **Aiken** Texas, SW USA

166 *F13* **Ailao Shan** ⛰ SW China

45 *W14* **Ailigandí** San Blas, NE Panama

201 *R4* **Ailinginae Atoll** *var.* Aelōninae. *atoll* Ralik Chain, SW Marshall Islands

201 *T7* **Ailinglaplap Atoll** *var.* Aelōnlaplap. *atoll* Ralik Chain, S Marshall Islands

Aillionn, Loch *see* Allen, Lough

98 *H13* **Ailsa Craig** *island* SW Scotland, UK

201 *V5* **Ailuk Atoll** *var.* Aelok. *atoll* Ratak Chain, NE Marshall Islands

126 *Mm12* **Aim** Khabarovskiy Kray, E Russian Federation

105 *R11* **Ain** ⬖ *department* E France

105 *S10* **Ain** ≈ E France

Aïn Aïssa *see* Ayn 'Īsá

120 *G7* **Ainaži** *Est.* Heinaste, *Ger.* Hainasch. Limbaži, N Latvia

76 *L6* **Aïn Beida** NE Algeria

78 *K4* **'Aïn Ben Tili** Tiris Zemmour, N Mauritania

76 *J5* **Aïn Defla** *var.* Aïn Eddefla. N Algeria

Aïn Eddefla *see* Aïn Defla

76 *L5* **Ain El Bey** ✕ (Constantine) NE Algeria

Ain Īsa *see* Ayn 'Īsá

117 *C19* **Aínos** ▲ Kefallinía, Iónioi Nísoi, Greece, C Mediterranean Sea

107 *T4* **Ainsa** Aragón, NE Spain

76 *I7* **Aïn Sefra** NW Algeria

31 *N13* **Ainsworth** Nebraska, C USA

Aintab *see* Gaziantep

76 *H5* **Aïn Témouchent** N Algeria

194 *H11* **Aiome** Madang, N PNG

Aïoun el Atrous/Aïoun el Atroûss *see* 'Ayoûn el 'Atroûs

56 *E11* **Aipe** Huila, C Colombia

58 *D9* **Aipena, Río** ≈ N Peru

59 *L19* **Aiquile** Cochabamba, C Bolivia

Aïr *see* Aïr, Massif de l'

196 *E10* **Airai** Babeldaob, C Palau

196 *E10* **Airai** ✕ (Oreor) Babeldaob, N Palau

173 *Ff8* **Airbangis** Sumatera, NW Indonesia

9 *Q16* **Airdrie** Alberta, SW Canada

98 *I12* **Airdrie** S Scotland, UK

Air du Azbine *see* Aïr, Massif de l'

99 *M17* **Aire** ≈ N England, UK

104 *K15* **Aire-sur-l'Adour** Landes, SW France

105 *O1* **Aire-sur-la-Lys** Pas-de-Calais, N France

16 *N2* **Air Force Island** *island* Baffin Island, Northwest Territories, NE Canada

174 *L11* **Airhitam, Teluk** *bay* Borneo, C Indonesia

175 *Rr7* **Airmadidi** Sulawesi, N Indonesia

79 *V8* **Aïr, Massif de l'** *var.* Aïr, Air du Azbine, Asben. ⛰ NC Niger

110 *G10* **Airolo** Ticino, S Switzerland

104 *K9* **Airvault** Deux-Sèvres, W France

103 *K19* **Aisch** ≈ S Germany

65 *G20* **Aisén** *off.* Región Aisén del General Carlos Ibañez del Campo, *var.* Aysen. ⬖ *region* S Chile

8 *H7* **Aishihik Lake** ◎ Yukon Territory, W Canada

105 *P3* **Aisne** ⬖ *department* N France

105 *R4* **Aisne** ≈ NE France

111 *T4* **Aist** ≈ N Austria

116 *K13* **Aisými** Anatolikí Makedonía kai Thráki, NE Greece

107 *S11* **Aitana** ▲ E Spain

194 *F9* **Aitape** *var.* Eitape. Sandaun, NW PNG

Aiti *see* Aichi

31 *V6* **Aitkin** Minnesota, N USA

117 *D18* **Aitolikó** *var.* Etoliko; *prev.* Aitolikón. Dytikí Ellás, C Greece

Aitolikón *see* Aitolikó

202 *L15* **Aitutaki** *island* S Cook Islands

118 *H11* **Aiud** *Ger.* Strassburg, *Hung.* Nagyenyed; *prev.* Engeten. Alba, SW Romania

120 *I9* **Aiviekste** ≈ C Latvia

201 *Q8* **Aiwo** SW Nauru

196 *E8* **Aiwokako Passage** *passage* Babeldaob, N Palau

Aix *see* Aix-en-Provence

105 *S15* **Aix-en-Provence** *var.* Aix; *anc.* Aquae Sextiae. Bouches-du-Rhône, SE France

Aix-la-Chapelle *see* Aachen

105 *T11* **Aix-les-Bains** Savoie, E France

194 *E11* **Aiyang, Mount** ▲ NW PNG

Aíyina *see* Aígina

Aíyion *see* Aígio

159 *W15* **Āīzawl** Mizoram, NE India

120 *H9* **Aizkraukle** Aizkraukle, S Latvia

120 *C9* **Aizpute** Liepāja, W Latvia

171 *L14* **Aizu-Wakamatsu** *var.* Aizuwakamatu. Fukushima, Honshū, C Japan

Aizuwakamatu *see* Aizu-Wakamatsu

104 *E2* **Ajaccio** Corse, France, C Mediterranean Sea

104 *E2* **Ajaccio, Golfe d'** *gulf* Corse, France, C Mediterranean Sea

43 *Q15* **Ajalpán** Puebla, S Mexico

160 *F13* **Ajanta Range** ⛰ C India

143 *R10* **Ajaria** ⬖ *autonomous republic* SW Georgia

Ajastan *see* Armenia

95 *G14* **Ajaureforsen** Västerbotten, N Sweden

193 *H17* **Ajax, Mount** ▲ South Island, NZ

◆ Country
● Country Capital
◇ Dependent Territory
○ Dependent Territory Capital
⬖ Administrative Region
✕ International Airport
▲ Mountain
⛰ Mountain Range
🌋 Volcano
≈ River
◎ Lake
⊟ Reservoir

AJ BOGD UUL – ALFIÓS

168 F9 **Aj Bogd Uul** ▲ SW Mongolia
77 R8 **Ajdābiyā** *var.* Agedabia, Ajdābiyah. NE Libya
Ajdābiyah *see* Ajdābiyā
111 S12 **Ajdovščina** *Ger.* Haidenschaft, *It.* Aidussina. W Slovenia
171 Mm8 **Ajigasawa** Aomori, Honshū, C Japan
Ajjinena *see* El Geneina
113 H23 **Ajka** Veszprém, W Hungary
144 G9 **'Ajlūn** Irbid, N Jordan
144 H9 **'Ajlūn, Jabal** ▲ W Jordan
149 R15 **'Ajmān** *var.* Ajman, 'Ujmān. 'Ajmān, NE UAE
158 G12 **Ajmer** *var.* Ajmere. Rājasthān, N India
38 J15 **Ajo** Arizona, SW USA
107 N2 **Ajo, Cabo de** *headland* N Spain
38 J16 **Ajo Range** ▲ Arizona, SW USA
Ajyguyy *see* Adzhikui
Akaba *see* Al 'Aqabah
172 P5 **Akabira** Hokkaidō, NE Japan
171 K12 **Akadomari** Niigata, Sado, C Japan
83 E20 **Akagera** *var.* Kagera. ~ Rwanda/Tanzania *see also* Kagera
203 W16 **Akahanga, Punta** *headland* Easter Island, Chile, E Pacific Ocean
171 Ii16 **Akaishi-dake** ▲ Honshū, S Japan
171 J16 **Akaishi-sanmyaku** ▲ Honshū, S Japan
82 J13 **Āk'ak'i** C Ethiopia
161 G15 **Akalkot** Mahārāshtra, W India
Akamagaseki *see* Shimonoseki
172 Q7 **Akan** Hokkaidō, NE Japan
172 Q6 **Akan-ko** ◎ Hokkaidō, NE Japan
Akanthoú *see* Tatlısu
193 I19 **Akaroa** Canterbury, South Island, NZ
82 E6 **Akasha** Northern, N Sudan
170 G14 **Akashi** *var.* Akasi. Hyōgo, Honshū, SW Japan
145 N7 **'Akāsh, Wādī** *var.* Wādī 'Ukash. *dry watercourse* W Iraq
Akasi *see* Akashi
94 K11 **Äkäsjokisuu** Lappi, N Finland
143 S11 **Akbaba Dağı** ▲ Armenia/Turkey
142 B15 **Akbük Limanı** *bay* W Turkey
131 V8 **Akbulak** Orenburgskaya Oblast', W Russian Federation
143 O11 **Akçaabat** Trabzon, NE Turkey
143 N15 **Akçadağ** Malatya, C Turkey
142 G11 **Akçakoca** Bolu, NW Turkey
Akchakaya, Vpadina *see* Akdzhakaya, Vpadina
78 H7 **Akchâr** *desert* W Mauritania
151 S12 **Akchatau** *Kaz.* Aqshataū. Zhezkazgan, C Kazakhstan
142 L13 **Akdağlar** ▲ C Turkey
142 E17 **Ak Dağları** ▲ SW Turkey
142 K13 **Akdağmadeni** Yozgat, C Turkey
Akdar, Jebel *see* Akhḑar al Jabal
152 G8 **Akdepe** *prev.* Ak-Tepe, Leninsk, *Turkm.* Lenin. Dashkhovuzskiy Velayat, N Turkmenistan
Ak-Dere *see* Byala
124 O3 **Akdoğan** *Gk.* Lýsi. C Cyprus
126 Hh16 **Ak-Dovurak** Respublika Tyva, S Russian Federation
152 F9 **Akdzhakaya, Vpadina** *var.* Vpadina Akchakaya. *depression* N Turkmenistan
175 Tt7 **Akelamo** Pulau Halmahera, E Indonesia
Aken *see* Aachen
Akermanceaster *see* Bath
97 P15 **Åkersberga** Stockholm, C Sweden
97 H15 **Akershus** ⬖ *county* S Norway
81 L16 **Aketi** Haut-Zaïre, N Zaire
Akgyr Erezi *see* Gryada Akkyr
152 E12 **Akhalskiy Velayat** *Turkm.* Ahal Welayaty. ⬖ *province* C Turkmenistan
143 S10 **Akhalts'ikhe** SW Georgia
Akhangaran *see* Ohangaron
Akharnaí *see* Acharnés
77 R7 **Akhḑar, Al Jabal al** *hill range* NE Libya
Akhelóös *see* Achelóos
41 Q15 **Akhiok** Kodiak Island, Alaska, USA
142 C13 **Akhisar** Manisa, W Turkey
77 X10 **Akhmīm** *anc.* Panopolis. C Egypt
158 H6 **Akhnūr** Jammu and Kashmir, NW India
131 P11 **Akhtuba** ~ SW Russian Federation
131 P11 **Akhtubinsk** Astrakhanskaya Oblast', SW Russian Federation
Akhtyrka *see* Okhtyrka
170 F15 **Aki** Kōchi, Shikoku, SW Japan
41 N12 **Akiachak** Alaska, USA
41 N12 **Akiak** Alaska, USA
203 X11 **Akiaki** *atoll* Îles Tuamotu, E French Polynesia
10 H9 **Akimiski Island** *island* Northwest Territories, C Canada
142 K17 **Akıncı Burnu** *headland* S Turkey
Akıncılar *see* Selçuk
119 U10 **Akinovka** Zaporiz'ka Oblast', S Ukraine
97 M24 **Åkirkeby** *var.* Aakirkeby. Bornholm, E Denmark
171 M10 **Akita** Akita, Honshū, C Japan
171 M10 **Akita** *off.* Akita-ken. ⬖ *prefecture* Honshū, C Japan
78 H8 **Akjoujt** *prev.* Fort-Repoux. Inchiri, W Mauritania
94 H11 **Akkajaure** ◎ N Sweden
Akkala *see* Oqqal'a
161 L25 **Akkaraipattu** Eastern Province, E Sri Lanka
94 H11 **Akkavare** ▲ N Sweden
151 P13 **Akkense** Zhezkazgan, C Kazakhstan
Akkerman *see* Bilhorod-Dnistrovs'kyy
131 W8 **Akkermanovka** Orenburgskaya Oblast', W Russian Federation
172 Qq7 **Akkeshi** Hokkaidō, NE Japan
172 Qq7 **Akkeshi-ko** ◎ Hokkaidō, NE Japan
172 Qq8 **Akkeshi-wan** *bay* NW Pacific Ocean
144 F8 **'Akko** *Eng.* Acre, *Fr.* Saint-Jean-d'Acre; *Bibl.* Accho, Ptolemaïs. Northern, N Israel
151 T14 **Akkol'** *Kaz.* Aqkōl. Almaty, SE Kazakhstan
151 Q16 **Akkol'** *Kaz.* Aqkōl. Zhambyl, S Kazakhstan
150 M11 **Akkol', Ozero** *prev.* Ozero Zhaman-Akkol'. ◎ C Kazakhstan
100 L6 **Akkrum** Friesland, N Netherlands
150 F12 **Akkystau** *Kaz.* Aqqystaū. Atyrau, SW Kazakhstan
14 Ff3 **Aklavik** Northwest Territories, NW Canada
120 B9 **Akmenrags** *headland* W Latvia
164 E9 **Akmeqit** Xinjiang Uygur Zizhiqu, NW China
152 J14 **Akmeydan** Maryyskiy Velayat, C Turkmenistan
151 Q9 **Akmola** *Kaz.* Aqmola; *prev.* Akmolinsk, Tselinograd. Akmola, N Kazakhstan
151 P9 **Akmola** *off.* Akmolinskaya Oblast', *Kaz.* Aqmola Oblysy; *prev.* Tselinogradskaya Oblast. ⬖ *province* C Kazakhstan
Akmolinsk/Akmolinskaya Oblast' *see* Akmola
Aknavásár *see* Târgu Ocna
120 I11 **Akniste** Jēkabpils, S Latvia
170 G14 **Akō** Hyōgo, Honshū, SW Japan
83 G14 **Akobo** Jonglei, SE Sudan
83 G14 **Akobo** *var.* Åkobowenz. ~ Ethiopia/Sudan
Åkobowenz *see* Akobo
160 H12 **Akola** Mahārāshtra, C India
Akordat *see* Akurdet
79 Q16 **Akosombo Dam** *dam* SE Ghana
160 H12 **Akot** Mahārāshtra, C India
79 N16 **Akoupé** SE Ivory Coast
10 M3 **Akpatok Island** *island* Northwest Territories, E Canada
164 G7 **Akqi** Xinjiang Uygur Zizhiqu, NW China
144 I2 **Akrād, Jabal al** ▲ N Syria
Akragas *see* Agrigento
94 H3 **Akranes** Vesturland, W Iceland
145 S2 **Ākrē** *Ar.* 'Aqrah. N Iraq
97 C16 **Åkrehamn** Rogaland, S Norway
79 V9 **Akrérèb** Agadez, C Niger
117 D22 **Akrítas, Ákra** *headland* S Greece
39 V3 **Akron** Colorado, C USA
31 R12 **Akron** Iowa, C USA
33 U12 **Akron** Ohio, N USA
Akrotiri *see* Akrotírion
Akrotiri Bay *see* Akrotírion Kólpos
124 N4 **Akrotírion** *var.* Akrotiri. *UK air base* S Cyprus
124 Nn4 **Akrotírion, Kólpos** *var.* Akrotiri Bay. *bay* S Cyprus
123 Mm4 **Akrotiri Sovereign Base Area** *UK military installation* S Cyprus
164 F11 **Aksai Chin** *Chin.* Aksayqin. *disputed region* China/India
Aksaj *see* Aksay
142 I15 **Aksaray** Aksaray, C Turkey
142 I15 **Aksaray** ⬖ *province* C Turkey
165 P8 **Aksay** *var.* Aksay Kazakzu Zizhixian. Gansu, N China
150 G8 **Aksay** *var.* Aksaj, *Kaz.* Aqsay. Zapadnyy Kazakhstan, NW Kazakhstan
131 O11 **Aksay** Volgogradskaya Oblast', SW Russian Federation
153 W10 **Aksay** *var.* Toxkan He. ~ China/Kyrgyzstan
Aksay Kazakzu Zizhixian *see* Aksay
Aksayqin *see* Aksai Chin
164 G11 **Aksayqin Hu** ◎ NW China
142 G14 **Akşehir** Konya, W Turkey
142 G14 **Akşehir Gölü** ◎ C Turkey
142 G16 **Akseki** Antalya, SW Turkey
126 L15 **Aksenovo-Zilovskoye** Chitinskaya Oblast', S Russian Federation
126 Kk16 **Aksha** Chitinskaya Oblast', S Russian Federation
151 V11 **Akshatau, Khrebet** ▲ E Kazakhstan
153 Y8 **Ak-Shyyrak** Issyk-Kul'skaya Oblast', E Kyrgyzstan
Akstafa *see* Ağstafa
164 H7 **Aksu** Xinjiang Uygur Zizhiqu, NW China
151 R8 **Aksu** *Kaz.* Aqsū. Akmola, N Kazakhstan
151 T8 **Aksu** *var.* Jermak, *Kaz.* Ermak; *prev.* Yermak. Pavlodar, NE Kazakhstan
151 W13 **Aksu** *Kaz.* Aqsū. Taldykorgan, SE Kazakhstan
151 V13 **Aksu** *Kaz.* Aqsū. ~ SE Kazakhstan
151 X11 **Aksuat** *Kaz.* Aqsūat. Semipalatinsk, E Kazakhstan
151 Y11 **Aksuat** *Kaz.* Aqsūat. Vostochnyy Kazakhstan, SE Kazakhstan
131 S4 **Aksubayevo** Respublika Tatarstan, W Russian Federation
164 H7 **Aksu He** *Rus.* Sary-Dzhaz. ~ China/Kyrgyzstan *see also* Sary-Dzhaz
82 J10 **Āksum** N Ethiopia
151 O12 **Aktas** *Kaz.* Aqtas. Zhezkazgan, C Kazakhstan
Aktash *see* Oqtosh
153 V9 **Ak-Tash, Gora** ▲ C Kyrgyzstan
151 R10 **Aktau** *Kaz.* Aqtaū. Karaganda, C Kazakhstan
150 E11 **Aktau** *Kaz.* Aqtaū; *prev.* Shevchenko. Mangistau, W Kazakhstan
Aktau, Khrebet *see* Oqtogh, SW Tajikistan
Aktau, Khrebet *see* Oqtow Tizmasi, C Uzbekistan
Akte *see* Ágion Óros
Ak-Tepe *see* Akdepe
153 X7 **Ak-Terek** Issyk-Kul'skaya Oblast', E Kyrgyzstan
Aktí *see* Ágion Óros
164 E8 **Akto** Xinjiang Uygur Zizhiqu, NW China
151 V12 **Aktogay** *Kaz.* Aqtoghay. Semipalatinsk, E Kazakhstan
151 T12 **Aktogay** *Kaz.* Aqtoghay. Zhezkazgan, C Kazakhstan
121 M18 **Aktsyabrski** *Rus.* Oktyabr'skiy; *prev.* Karpilovka. Homyel'skaya Voblasts', SE Belarus
150 I10 **Aktyubinsk** *Kaz.* Aqtöbe. Aktyubinsk, NW Kazakhstan
150 H11 **Aktyubinsk** *off.* Aktyubinskaya Oblast', *Kaz.* Aqtöbe Oblysy. ⬖ *province* W Kazakhstan
153 W7 **Ak-Tyuz** *var.* Aktyuz. Chuyskaya Oblast', N Kyrgyzstan
81 J17 **Akula** Equateur, NW Zaire
170 Bb15 **Akune** Kagoshima, Kyūshū, SW Japan
40 L16 **Akun Island** *island* Aleutian Islands, Alaska, USA
82 J9 **Akurdet** *var.* Agordat, Akordat. C Eritrea
79 T16 **Akure** Ondo, SW Nigeria
94 J2 **Akureyri** Nordhurland Eystra, N Iceland
40 L17 **Akutan** Akutan Island, Alaska, USA
40 K17 **Akutan Island** *island* Aleutian Islands, Alaska, USA
79 V17 **Akwa Ibom** ⬖ *state* SE Nigeria
Akyab *see* Sittwe
131 W7 **Ak"yar** Respublika Bashkortostan, W Russian Federation
151 Y11 **Akzhar** *Kaz.* Aqzhar. Vostochnyy Kazakhstan, E Kazakhstan
96 F13 **Ål** Buskerud, S Norway
121 N18 **Ala** *Rus.* Ola. ~ SE Belarus
22 H11 **Alabama** *off.* State of Alabama; *also known as* Camellia State, Heart of Dixie, The Cotton State, Yellowhammer State. ⬖ *state* S USA
25 P6 **Alabama River** ~ Alabama, S USA
25 P4 **Alabaster** Alabama, S USA
145 U10 **Al 'Abd Allāh** *var.* Al Abdullah. S Iraq
Al Abdullah *see* Al 'Abd Allāh
145 W14 **Al Abṭīyah** *well* S Iraq
153 S9 **Ala-Buka** Dzhalal-Abadskaya Oblast', W Kyrgyzstan
194 K15 **Alabule** ~ C PNG
142 J12 **Alaca** Çorum, N Turkey
142 K10 **Alaçam** Samsun, N Turkey
Alacant *see* Alicante
25 V9 **Alachua** Florida, SE USA
143 S13 **Aladağlar** ▲ W Turkey
142 K15 **Ala Dağları** ▲ C Turkey
131 O16 **Alagir** Respublika Severnaya Osetiya, SW Russian Federation
108 B6 **Alagna Valsesia** Valle d'Aosta, NW Italy
105 P12 **Alagnon** ~ C France
61 P16 **Alagoas** *off.* Estado de Alagoas. ⬖ *state* E Brazil
61 P17 **Alagoinhas** Bahia, E Brazil
107 R5 **Alagón** Aragón, NE Spain
106 J9 **Alagón** ~ W Spain
95 K16 **Alahärmä** Vaasa, W Finland
al Ahdar *see* Al Akhḑar
148 K12 **Al Aḩmadī** *var.* Ahmadi. E Kuwait
Al Ain *see* Al 'Ayn
107 Z8 **Alaior** *prev.* Alayor. Menorca, Spain, W Mediterranean Sea
153 T11 **Alai Range** *Rus.* Alayskiy Khrebet. ▲ Kyrgyzstan/Tajikistan
Alais *see* Alès
147 X11 **Al 'Ajā'iz** E Oman
147 X11 **Al 'Ajā'iz** *oasis* SE Oman
95 L16 **Alajärvi** Vaasa, W Finland
120 K4 **Alajõe** Ida-Virumaa, NE Estonia
44 M13 **Alajuela** Alajuela, C Costa Rica
44 L12 **Alajuela** *off.* Provincia de Alajuela. ⬖ *province* N Costa Rica
45 T14 **Alajuela, Lago** ◎ C Panama
40 M11 **Alakanuk** Alaska, USA
146 K5 **Al Akhḑar** *var.* al Ahdar. Tabūk, NW Saudi Arabia
Alaköl *see* Alakol', Ozero
151 X13 **Alakol', Ozero** *Kaz.* Alaköl. ◎ SE Kazakhstan
128 I5 **Alakurtti** Murmanskaya Oblast', NW Russian Federation
40 F10 **Alalakeiki Channel** *channel* Hawaii, USA, C Pacific Ocean
Al 'Alamayn *see* El 'Alamein
145 R1 **Al 'Amādīyah** N Iraq
196 K5 **Alamagan** *island* C Northern Mariana Islands
145 X10 **Al 'Amārah** *var.* Amara. E Iraq
82 J11 **Ālamat'ā** NE Ethiopia
39 R11 **Alameda** New Mexico, SW USA
124 Pp15 **'Alam el Rûm, Râs** *headland* N Egypt
Alamícamba *see* Alamikamba
44 M8 **Alamikamba** *var.* Alamícamba. Región Autónoma Atlántico Norte, NE Nicaragua
26 K11 **Alamito Creek** ~ Texas, SW USA
42 M8 **Alamitos, Sierra de los** ▲ NE Mexico
37 X9 **Alamo** Nevada, W USA
22 F9 **Alamo** Tennessee, S USA
43 Q12 **Álamo** Veracruz-Llave, C Mexico
39 S14 **Alamogordo** New Mexico, SW USA
38 J12 **Alamo Lake** ⊡ Arizona, SW USA
42 H7 **Álamos** Sonora, NW Mexico
39 S7 **Alamosa** Colorado, C USA
95 J20 **Åland** *var.* Aland Islands, *Fin.* Ahvenanmaa. ⬖ *province* SW Finland
95 J19 **Åland** *Fin.* Ahvenanmaa. *island* SW Finland
90 K9 **Åland** *var.* Aland Islands, *Fin.* Ahvenanmaa. *island group* SW Finland
Aland Islands *see* Åland
Aland Sea *see* Ålands Hav
97 Q14 **Ålands Hav** *var.* Aland Sea. *strait* Baltic Sea/Gulf of Bothnia
45 P16 **Alanje** Chiriquí, SW Panama
27 O2 **Alanreed** Texas, SW USA
142 G17 **Alanya** Antalya, S Turkey
25 U7 **Alapaha River** ~ Florida/Georgia, SE USA
125 Ee11 **Alapayevsk** Sverdlovskaya Oblast', C Russian Federation
Alappuzha *see* Alleppey
144 F14 **Al 'Aqabah** *var.* Akaba, Aqaba, 'Aqaba; *anc.* Aelana, Elath. Ma'ān, SW Jordan
Al 'Arabīyah as Su'ūdīyah *see* Saudi Arabia
al Araïch *see* Larache
107 Q10 **Alarcón** Castilla-La Mancha, C Spain
107 Q9 **Alarcón, Embalse de** ⊡ C Spain
144 J2 **Al 'Arīmah** *Fr.* Arime. Ḩalab, N Syria
Al 'Arīsh *see* El 'Arîsh
147 R5 **Al Arṭāwīyah** SE Kuwait
147 P6 **Al Arṭāwīyah** Ar Riyāḑ, N Saudi Arabia
175 O16 **Alas** Sumbawa, S Indonesia
Alasca, Golfo de *see* Alaska, Gulf of
142 D14 **Alaşehir** Manisa, W Turkey
145 N5 **Al 'Ashārah** *var.* Ashara. Dayr az Zawr, E Syria
Al Ashkhara *see* Al Ashkharah
147 Z9 **Al Ashkharah** *var.* Al Ashkhara. NE Oman
41 P8 **Alaska** *off.* State of Alaska; *also known as* Land of the Midnight Sun, The Last Frontier, Seward's Folly; *prev.* Russian America. ⬖ *state* NW USA
41 T13 **Alaska, Gulf of** *var.* Golfo de Alasca. *gulf* Canada/USA
41 O15 **Alaska Peninsula** *peninsula* Alaska, USA
41 Q11 **Alaska Range** ▲ Alaska, USA
173 Ee4 **Alas, Lae** ~ Sumatera, NW Indonesia
Al-Asnam *see* Chlef
175 O16 **Alas, Selat** *strait* Nusa Tenggara, C Indonesia
108 B10 **Alassio** Liguria, NW Italy
Alat *see* Olot
143 Y12 **Älät** *Rus.* Alyat; *prev.* Alyaty-Pristan'. SE Azerbaijan
145 S13 **Al 'Athāmīn** S Iraq
41 P7 **Alatna River** ~ Alaska, USA
109 J15 **Alatri** Lazio, C Italy
Alattio *see* Alta
131 P5 **Alatyr'** Chuvashskaya Respublika, W Russian Federation
58 C7 **Alausí** Chimborazo, C Ecuador
107 O3 **Álava** *Basq.* Araba. ⬖ *province* País Vasco, N Spain
143 T11 **Alaverdi** N Armenia
Alavo *see* Alavus
95 N14 **Ala-Vuokki** Oulu, E Finland
95 K17 **Alavus** *Swe.* Alavo. Vaasa, W Finland
Al 'Awābī *see* Awābī
145 P6 **Al 'Awānī** W Iraq
77 U12 **Al Awaynāt** SE Libya
Al Awaynāt *see* Al 'Uwaynāt
190 K9 **Alawoona** South Australia
Alaykel'/Alay-Kuu *see* Këk-Art
149 R17 **Al 'Ayn** *var.* Al Ain. Abū Ẓaby, E UAE
149 R17 **Al 'Ayn** *var.* Al Ain. ✕ Abū Ẓaby, E UAE
144 G12 **Al 'Aynā** Al Karak, W Jordan
Alayor *see* Alaior
Alayskiy Khrebet *see* Alai Range
127 N7 **Alazeya** ~ NE Russian Federation
145 U8 **Al 'Azīzīyah** *var.* Aziziya. E Iraq
123 L14 **Al 'Azīzīyah** NW Libya
144 I10 **Al Azraq al Janūbī** Az Zarqā', N Jordan
108 B9 **Alba** *anc.* Alba Pompeia. Piemonte, NW Italy
27 V6 **Alba** Texas, SW USA
118 G11 **Alba** ⬖ *county* W Romania
145 P3 **Al Ba'āj** N Iraq
144 J2 **Al Bāb** Ḩalab, N Syria
118 G10 **Albac** *Hung.* Fehérvölgy; *prev.* Álbák. Alba, SW Romania
107 Q11 **Albacete** Castilla-La Mancha, C Spain
107 P11 **Albacete** ⬖ *province* Castilla-La Mancha, C Spain
146 I4 **Al Bad'** Tabūk, NW Saudi Arabia
106 L7 **Alba de Tormes** Castilla-León, N Spain
145 P3 **Al Bādī** N Iraq
147 V8 **Al Badī'ah** ✕ (Abū Ẓaby) Abū Ẓaby, C UAE
149 P17 **Al Badī'ah** *var.* Al Bedei'ah. *spring/well* C UAE
145 Q7 **Al Baghdādī** *var.* Khān al Baghdādī. SW Iraq
Al Bāha *see* Al Bāḩah
146 M11 **Al Bāḩah** *var.* Al Bāha. Al Bāḩah, SW Saudi Arabia
146 M11 **Al Bāḩah** *off.* Minţaqat al Bāḩah. ⬖ *province* W Saudi Arabia
Al Baḩrayn *see* Bahrain
107 S11 **Albaida** País Valenciano, E Spain
118 H11 **Alba Iulia** *Ger.* Weissenburg, *Hung.* Gyulafehérvár; *prev.* Bălgrad, Karlsburg, Károly-Fehérvár. Alba, W Romania
Álbák *see* Albac
144 G10 **Al Balqā'** *off.* Muḩāfaẓat al Balqā', *var.* Balqā'. ⬖ *governorate* NW Jordan
12 F11 **Alban** Ontario, S Canada
105 O15 **Alban** Tarn, S France
10 K11 **Albanel, Lac** ◎ Québec, SE Canada
115 L20 **Albania** *off.* Republic of Albania, *Alb.* Republika e Shqipërisë, Shqipëria; *prev.* People's Socialist Republic of Albania. ◆ *republic* SE Europe
Albania *see* Aubagne
109 H15 **Albano Laziale** Lazio, C Italy
188 J14 **Albany** Western Australia
25 S7 **Albany** Georgia, SE USA
33 P13 **Albany** Indiana, N USA
22 L8 **Albany** Kentucky, S USA
31 U7 **Albany** Minnesota, N USA
29 R2 **Albany** Missouri, C USA
20 L10 **Albany** *state capital* New York, NE USA
34 G12 **Albany** Oregon, NW USA
27 Q6 **Albany** Texas, SW USA
10 F10 **Albany** ~ Ontario, S Canada
Alba Pompeia *see* Alba
Alba Regia *see* Székesfehérvár
144 J6 **Al Bāridah** *var.* Bāridah. Ḩimş, C Syria
145 Q11 **Al Barīt** S Iraq
107 R8 **Albarracín** Aragón, NE Spain
145 Y12 **Al Baṣrah** *Eng.* Basra; *hist.* Busra, Bussora. SE Iraq
145 V11 **Al Baṭḩā'** SE Iraq
147 X8 **Al Bāṭinah** *var.* Batinah. *coastal region* N Oman
1 H16 **Albatross Plateau** *undersea feature* E Pacific Ocean
Al Batrūn *see* Batroûn
124 Nn14 **Al Bayḑā'** *var.* Beida. NE Libya
147 P16 **Al Bayḑā'** *var.* Al Beida. SW Yemen
Al Bedei'ah *see* Al Badī'ah
Al Beida *see* Al Bayḑā'
23 S10 **Albemarle** *var.* Albermarle. North Carolina, SE USA
Albemarle Island *see* Isabela, Isla
23 N8 **Albemarle Sound** *inlet* W Atlantic Ocean
108 B10 **Albenga** Liguria, NW Italy
106 L8 **Alberche** ~ C Spain
105 O17 **Albères, Chaîne des** *var.* les Albères, Montes Albères. ▲ France/Spain
Albères, Montes *see* Albères, Chaîne des
190 F2 **Alberga Creek** *seasonal river* South Australia
106 G7 **Albergaria-a-Velha** Aveiro, N Portugal
107 S10 **Alberic** País Valenciano, E Spain
Albermarle *see* Albemarle
109 P18 **Alberobello** Puglia, SE Italy
110 J7 **Alberschwende** Vorarlberg, W Austria
105 O3 **Albert** Somme, N France
9 O12 **Alberta** ⬖ *province* SW Canada
194 K14 **Albert Edward, Mount** ▲ S PNG
Albert Edward Nyanza *see* Edward, Lake
63 C20 **Alberti** Buenos Aires, E Argentina
113 K23 **Albertirsa** Pest, C Hungary
101 I16 **Albertkanaal** *canal* N Belgium
81 P17 **Albert, Lake** *var.* Albert Nyanza, Lac Mobutu Sese Seko. ◎ Uganda/Zaire
31 V11 **Albert Lea** Minnesota, N USA
83 F16 **Albert Nile** ~ NW Uganda
Albert Nyanza *see* Albert, Lake
105 T11 **Albertville** Savoie, E France
25 Q2 **Albertville** Alabama, S USA
Albertville *see* Kalemie
105 N15 **Albi** *anc.* Albiga. Tarn, S France
31 W15 **Albia** Iowa, C USA
Albiga *see* Albi
57 X9 **Albina** Marowijne, NE Suriname
85 A15 **Albina, Ponta** *headland* SW Angola
32 M16 **Albion** Illinois, N USA
33 P11 **Albion** Indiana, N USA
31 P14 **Albion** Nebraska, C USA
20 E9 **Albion** New York, NE USA
20 B12 **Albion** Pennsylvania, NE USA
Al Biqā' *see* El Beqaa
146 J4 **Al Bi'r** *var.* Bi'r Ibn Hirmās. Tabūk, NW Saudi Arabia
146 M12 **Al Birk** Makkah, SW Saudi Arabia
147 Q9 **Al Biyāḑ** *desert* C Saudi Arabia
100 H13 **Alblasserdam** Zuid-Holland, SW Netherlands
107 T8 **Albocácer** *var.* Albocasser. País Valenciano, E Spain
Albocasser *see* Albocácer
97 H19 **Albæk** Nordjylland, N Denmark
Albona *see* Labin
107 O17 **Alborán, Isla de** *island* S Spain
Alborán, Mar de *see* Alboran Sea
107 N17 **Alboran Sea** *Sp.* Mar de Alborán. *sea* SW Mediterranean Sea
97 G20 **Ålborg** *var.* Aalborg, Ålborg-Nørresundby; *anc.* Alburgum. Nordjylland, N Denmark
97 H21 **Ålborg Bugt** *var.* Aalborg Bugt. *bay* N Denmark
Ålborg-Nørresundby *see* Ålborg
149 O5 **Alborz, Reshteh-ye Kūhhā-ye** *Eng.* Elburz Mountains. ▲ N Iran
107 Q14 **Albox** Andalucía, S Spain
103 H23 **Albstadt** Baden-Württemberg, SW Germany
106 G14 **Albufeira** Beja, S Portugal
145 P5 **Ālbū Gharz, Sabkhat** ◎ W Iraq
107 O15 **Albuñol** Andalucía, S Spain
39 Q11 **Albuquerque** New Mexico, SW USA
147 W8 **Al Buraymī** *var.* Buraimi. N Oman
149 R17 **Al Buraymī** *var.* Buraimi. *spring/well* Oman/UAE
Al Burayqah *see* Marsá al Burayqah
Alburgum *see* Ålborg
106 I10 **Alburquerque** Extremadura, W Spain
189 V14 **Albury** New South Wales, SE Australia
191 P11 **Albury-Wodonga** New South Wales/Victoria, SE Australia
147 T14 **Al Buzūn** SE Yemen
95 G17 **Alby** Västernorrland, C Sweden
Albyn, Glen *see* Mor, Glen
106 G12 **Alcácer do Sal** Setúbal, W Portugal
Alcalá de Chisvert *see* Alcalá de Chivert
107 T8 **Alcalá de Chivert** *var.* Alcalá de Chisvert. País Valenciano, E Spain
106 K14 **Alcalá de Guadaira** Andalucía, S Spain
107 O8 **Alcalá de Henares** *Ar.* Alkal'a; *anc.* Complutum. Madrid, C Spain
106 K16 **Alcalá de los Gazules** Andalucía, S Spain
107 N14 **Alcalá La Real** Andalucía, S Spain
109 I23 **Alcamo** Sicilia, Italy, C Mediterranean Sea
107 T4 **Alcanadre** ~ NE Spain
107 T8 **Alcanar** Cataluña, NE Spain
106 J5 **Alcañices** Castilla-León, N Spain
107 T7 **Alcañiz** Aragón, NE Spain
106 I9 **Alcántara** Extremadura, W Spain
106 J9 **Alcántara, Embalse de** ⊡ W Spain
107 R13 **Alcantarilla** Murcia, SE Spain
107 P11 **Alcaraz** Castilla-La Mancha, C Spain
107 P12 **Alcaraz, Sierra de** ▲ C Spain
106 I12 **Alcarrache** ~ SW Spain
107 T6 **Alcarràs** Cataluña, NE Spain
107 N14 **Alcaudete** Andalucía, S Spain
Alcázar *see* Ksar-el-Kebir
107 O10 **Alcázar de San Juan** *anc.* Alce. Castilla-La Mancha, C Spain
Alcazarquivir *see* Ksar-el-Kebir
Alce *see* Alcázar de San Juan
59 B17 **Alcebo, Volcán** ▲ Galapagos Islands, Ecuador, E Pacific Ocean
145 X12 **Al Chabā'ish** *var.* Al Kaba'ish. SE Iraq
119 Y7 **Alchevs'k** *prev.* Kommunarsk, Voroshilovsk. Luhans'ka Oblast', E Ukraine
Alcira *see* Alzira
23 N9 **Alcoa** Tennessee, S USA
106 F9 **Alcobaça** Leiria, C Portugal
107 N8 **Alcobendas** Madrid, C Spain
Alcoi *see* Alcoy
107 P7 **Alcolea del Pinar** Castilla-La Mancha, C Spain
106 I11 **Alconchel** Extremadura, W Spain
107 S9 **Alcora** País Valenciano, E Spain
107 N8 **Alcorcón** Madrid, C Spain
107 S7 **Alcorisa** Aragón, NE Spain
63 B19 **Alcorta** Santa Fe, C Argentina
106 H14 **Alcoutim** Faro, S Portugal
35 W15 **Alcova** Wyoming, C USA
107 S11 **Alcoy** *var.* Alcoi. País Valenciano, E Spain
107 Y9 **Alcúdia, Badia d'** *bay* Mallorca, Spain, W Mediterranean Sea
180 M7 **Aldabra Group** *island group* SW Seychelles
145 U10 **Al Daghghārah** C Iraq
42 J5 **Aldama** Chihuahua, N Mexico
43 P11 **Aldama** Tamaulipas, C Mexico
126 Ll12 **Aldan** Respublika Sakha (Yakutiya), NE Russian Federation
126 Mm12 **Aldan** ~ NE Russian Federation
168 G7 **Aldar** Dzavhan, W Mongolia
al Dar al Baida *see* Rabat
99 Q20 **Aldeburgh** E England, UK
107 P5 **Aldehuela de Calatañazor** Castilla-León, N Spain
Aldeia Nova *see* Aldeia Nova de São Bento
106 H13 **Aldeia Nova de São Bento** *var.* Aldeia Nova. Beja, S Portugal
31 V11 **Alden** Minnesota, N USA
192 N6 **Aldermen Islands, The** *island group* N NZ
99 L25 **Alderney** *island* Channel Islands
99 N22 **Aldershot** S England, UK
23 R6 **Alderson** West Virginia, NE USA
Al Dhaid *see* Adh Dhayd
32 J11 **Aledo** Illinois, N USA
78 H9 **Aleg** Brakna, SW Mauritania
66 Q10 **Alegranza** *island* Islas Canarias, Spain, NE Atlantic Ocean
39 P12 **Alegres Mountain** ▲ New Mexico, SW USA
63 F15 **Alegrete** Rio Grande do Sul, S Brazil
63 C16 **Alejandra** Santa Fe, C Argentina
200 Oo12 **Alejandro Selkirk, Isla** *island* Islas Juan Fernández, Chile, E Pacific Ocean
128 I12 **Alekhovshchina** Leningradskaya Oblast', NW Russian Federation
41 O13 **Aleknagik** Alaska, USA
Aleksandriya *see* Oleksandriya
Aleksandropol' *see* Gyumri
130 L3 **Aleksandrov** Vladimirskaya Oblast', W Russian Federation
115 N14 **Aleksandrovac** Serbia, C Yugoslavia
131 R9 **Aleksandrov Gay** Saratovskaya Oblast', W Russian Federation
131 U6 **Aleksandrovka** Orenburgskaya Oblast', W Russian Federation
Aleksandrovka *see* Oleksandrivka
116 J8 **Aleksandrovo** Loveshka Oblast, N Bulgaria
129 V13 **Aleksandrovsk** Permskaya Oblast', NW Russian Federation
Aleksandrovsk *see* Zaporizhzhya
131 N14 **Aleksandrovskoye** Stavropol'skiy Kray, SW Russian Federation
127 O14 **Aleksandrovsk-Sakhalinskiy** Ostrov Sakhalin, Sakhalinskaya Oblast', SE Russian Federation
112 J10 **Aleksandrów Kujawski** Włocławek, C Poland
112 K12 **Aleksandrów Łódzki** Łódź, C Poland
Alekseevka *see* Alekseyevka
151 Q8 **Alekseyevka** *Kaz.* Alekseevka. Akmola, C Kazakhstan
151 P7 **Alekseyevka** *Kaz.* Alekseevka. Kokshetau, N Kazakhstan
151 Z10 **Alekseyevka** *Kaz.* Alekseevka. Vostochnyy Kazakhstan, E Kazakhstan
131 S7 **Alekseyevka** Samarskaya Oblast', W Russian Federation
126 Jj13 **Alekseyevsk** Irkutskaya Oblast', C Russian Federation
131 R4 **Alekseyevskoye** Respublika Tatarstan, W Russian Federation
130 K5 **Aleksin** Tul'skaya Oblast', W Russian Federation
115 O14 **Aleksinac** Serbia, SE Yugoslavia
202 G11 **Alele** Île Uvea, E Wallis and Futuna
97 N20 **Ålem** Kalmar, S Sweden
104 L6 **Alençon** Orne, N France
60 I12 **Alenquer** Pará, NE Brazil
40 G10 **Alenuihaha Channel** *channel* Hawaii, USA, C Pacific Ocean
Alep/Aleppo *see* Ḩalab
104 F2 **Aléria** Corse, France, C Mediterranean Sea
207 Q11 **Alert** Ellesmere Island, Northwest Territories, N Canada
105 Q14 **Alès** *prev.* Alais. Gard, S France
118 G9 **Aleşd** *Hung.* Élesd. Bihor, SW Romania
108 C9 **Alessandria** *Fr.* Alexandrie. Piemonte, N Italy
97 G21 **Ålestrup** *var.* Aalestrup. Viborg, NW Denmark
96 D9 **Ålesund** Møre og Romsdal, S Norway
110 E10 **Aletschhorn** ▲ SW Switzerland
207 S1 **Aleutian Basin** *undersea feature* Bering Sea
40 H17 **Aleutian Islands** *island group* Alaska, USA
41 P14 **Aleutian Range** ▲ Alaska, USA
1 B5 **Aleutian Trench** *undersea feature* S Bering Sea
127 O10 **Alevina, Mys** *headland* E Russian Federation
13 Q6 **Alex** ~ Québec, SE Canada
30 J3 **Alexander** North Dakota, N USA
41 W14 **Alexander Archipelago** *island group* Alaska, USA
Alexanderbaai *see* Alexander Bay
85 D23 **Alexander Bay** *Afr.* Alexanderbaai. Northern Cape, W South Africa
25 Q5 **Alexander City** Alabama, S USA
204 J6 **Alexander Island** *island* Antarctica
Alexander Range *see* Kirghiz Range
191 O12 **Alexandra** Victoria, SE Australia
193 D22 **Alexandra** Otago, South Island, NZ
117 F14 **Alexándreia** *var.* Alexándria. Kentrikí Makedonía, N Greece
Alexandretta *see* İskenderun
Alexandretta, Gulf of *see* İskenderun Körfezi
13 N13 **Alexandria** Ontario, SE Canada
124 Q15 **Alexandria** *Ar.* Al Iskandarīyah. N Egypt
46 J12 **Alexandria** C Jamaica
118 J15 **Alexandria** Teleorman, S Romania
33 P13 **Alexandria** Indiana, N USA
22 M4 **Alexandria** Kentucky, S USA
24 H7 **Alexandria** Louisiana, S USA
31 T7 **Alexandria** Minnesota, N USA
31 Q11 **Alexandria** South Dakota, N USA
23 W4 **Alexandria** Virginia, NE USA
Alexándria *see* Alexándreia
20 I7 **Alexandria Bay** New York, NE USA
Alexandrie *see* Alessandria
190 J10 **Alexandrina, Lake** ◎ South Australia
116 K13 **Alexandroúpoli** *var.* Alexandroúpolis, *Turk.* Dedeagaç, Dedeagach. Anatolikí Makedonía kai Thráki, NE Greece
Alexandroúpolis *see* Alexandroúpoli
8 L15 **Alexis Creek** British Columbia, SW Canada
126 Gg15 **Aleysk** Altayskiy Kray, S Russian Federation
145 S8 **Al Fallūjah** *var.* Falluja. C Iraq
107 R8 **Alfambra** ~ E Spain
Al Faqa *see* Faq'
147 R15 **Al Farḑah** C Yemen
107 Q4 **Alfaro** La Rioja, N Spain
107 U5 **Alfarràs** Cataluña, NE Spain
Al Fāshir *see* El Fasher
Al Fashn *see* El Fashn
116 M7 **Alfatar** Razgradska Oblast, NE Bulgaria
145 S5 **Al Fatḩah** C Iraq
145 Q3 **Al Fatsī** N Iraq
145 Z13 **Al Fāw** *var.* Fao. SE Iraq
Al Fayyūm *see* El Faiyûm
117 D20 **Alfeiós** *prev.* Alfiós, *anc.* Alpheius, Alpheus. ~ S Greece
102 I13 **Alfeld** Niedersachsen, C Germany
Alfiós *see* Alfeiós

◆ Country ● Country Capital ◇ Dependent Territory ○ Dependent Territory Capital ⬖ Administrative Region ✕ International Airport ▲ Mountain ▲ Mountain Range Volcano ~ River ◎ Lake ⊡ Reservoir

221

ALFÖLD – ALVARO OBREGÓN, PRESA

Alföld *see* Great Hungarian Plain
96 C11 **Ålfotbreen** *glacier* S Norway
21 P9 **Alfred** Maine, NE USA
20 F11 **Alfred** New York, NE USA
63 K14 **Alfredo Vagner** Santa Catarina, S Brazil
96 M12 **Alfta** Gävleborg, C Sweden
146 K12 **Al Fuḥayḥīl** *var.* Fahaheel. SE Kuwait
145 Q6 **Al Fuḥaymī** C Iraq
149 S16 **Al Fujayrah** *Eng.* Fujairah. Al Fujayrah, NE UAE
149 S16 **Al Fujayrah** *Eng.* Fujairah. ✕ Al Fujayrah, NE UAE
Al Furāt *see* Euphrates
150 I10 **Alga** *Kaz.* Algha. Aktyubinsk, NW Kazakhstan
150 G9 **Algabas** Zapadnyy Kazakhstan, NW Kazakhstan
97 C17 **Ålgård** Rogaland, S Norway
106 G14 **Algarve** *cultural region* S Portugal
190 G3 **Algebuckina Bridge** South Australia
106 K16 **Algeciras** Andalucía, SW Spain
107 S10 **Algemesí** País Valenciano, E Spain
Al-Genain *see* El Geneina
123 I11 **Alger** *var.* Algiers, El Djazaïr, Al Jazair. ● (Algeria) N Algeria
76 H9 **Algeria** *off.* Democratic and Popular Republic of Algeria. ◆ *republic* N Africa
123 J9 **Algerian Basin** *var.* Balearic Plain *undersea feature* W Mediterranean Sea
Algha *see* Alga
144 I4 **Al Ghāb** ◎ NW Syria
147 X10 **Al Ghābah** *var.* Ghaba. C Oman
147 U14 **Al Ghayḍah** E Yemen
146 M6 **Al Ghazālah** Ḥā'il, NW Saudi Arabia
109 B17 **Alghero** Sardegna, Italy, C Mediterranean Sea
97 M20 **Älghult** Kronoberg, S Sweden
Al Ghurdaqah *see* Hurghada
Algiers *see* Alger
107 S10 **Alginet** País Valenciano, E Spain
85 I26 **Algoa Bay** *bay* S South Africa
106 L15 **Algodonales** Andalucía, S Spain
107 N9 **Algodor** ≈ C Spain
Al Golea *see* El Goléa
33 N6 **Algoma** Wisconsin, N USA
31 U12 **Algona** Iowa, C USA
22 L8 **Algood** Tennessee, S USA
107 O2 **Algorta** País Vasco, N Spain
63 E18 **Algorta** Río Negro, W Uruguay
Al Haba *see* Haba
145 Q10 **Al Habbārīyah** S Iraq
Al Hadhar *see* Al Ḥaḍr
145 Q4 **Al Ḥaḍr** *var.* Al Hadhar; *anc.* Hatra. NW Iraq
145 T13 **Al Ḥajarah** *desert* S Iraq
147 W8 **Al Ḥajār al Gharbī** ▲▲ N Oman
147 Y8 **Al Ḥajar ash Sharqī** ▲▲ NE Oman
147 R15 **Al Hajarayn** C Yemen
144 L10 **Al Ḥamād** *desert* Jordan/Saudi Arabia
Al Hamad *see* Syrian Desert
77 N9 **Al Ḥamādah al Ḥamrā'** *var.* Al Ḥamrā'. *desert* NW Libya
107 N15 **Alhama de Granada** Andalucía, S Spain
107 R13 **Alhama de Murcia** Murcia, SE Spain
37 T15 **Alhambra** California, W USA
145 T12 **Al Ḥammām** S Iraq
147 X8 **Al Ḥamrā'** NE Oman
Al Ḥamrā' *see* Al Ḥamādah al Ḥamrā'
147 O6 **Al Ḥamūdīyah** *spring/well* N Saudi Arabia
146 M7 **Al Ḥanākīyah** Al Madīnah, W Saudi Arabia
145 W14 **Al Ḥanīyah** *escarpment* Iraq/Saudi Arabia
145 Y12 **Al Hārithah** SE Iraq
146 L3 **Al Ḥarrah** *desert* NW Saudi Arabia
77 Q10 **Al Harūj al Aswad** *desert* C Libya
Al Hasaifin *see* Al Ḥusayfin
145 N2 **Al Ḥasakah** *var.* Al Hasijah, El Haseke, *Fr.* Hassetché. Al Ḥasakah, NE Syria
145 O2 **Al Ḥasakah** *off.* Muḥāfaẓat al Ḥasakah, *var.* Al Hasakah, Āl Hasakah, Hasakah, Hassakeh. ◈ *governorate* NE Syria
145 T9 **Al Hāshimīyah** C Iraq
144 G13 **Al Hāshimīyah** Ma'ān, S Jordan
Al Hasijah *see* Al Ḥasakah
106 M15 **Alhaurín el Grande** Andalucía, S Spain
147 Q16 **Al Ḥawrā** S Yemen
145 V10 **Al Ḥayy** *var.* Kut al Hai, Kūt al Ḥayy. E Iraq
147 U11 **Al Ḥibāk** *desert* E Saudi Arabia
144 H8 **Al Hījānah** *var.* Hejanah, Hijanah. Dimashq, W Syria
146 K7 **Al Ḥijāz** *Eng.* Hejaz. *physical region* NW Saudi Arabia
Al Hilbeh *see* 'Ulayyānīyah, Bi'r al
145 T9 **Al Ḥillah** *var.* Hilla. C Iraq
145 T9 **Al Hindīyah** *var.* Hindiya. C Iraq
144 G12 **Al Ḥisā** Aṭ Ṭafīlah, W Jordan
76 G5 **Al-Hoceïma** *var.* al Hoceima, Al-Hoceima, Alhucemas; *prev.* Villa Sanjurjo. N Morocco
Alhucemas *see* Al-Hoceïma
107 N17 **Alhucemas, Peñon de** *island group* S Spain
147 N15 **Al Ḥudaydah** *Eng.* Hodeida. W Yemen
147 N15 **Al Ḥudaydah** *Eng.* Hodeida. ✕ W Yemen
146 M4 **Al Ḥudūd ash Shamālīyah** *var.* Minṭaqat al Ḥudūd ash Shamālīyah, *Eng.* Northern Border Region. ◈ *province* N Saudi Arabia
147 S7 **Al Hufūf** *var.* Hofuf. Ash Sharqīyah, NE Saudi Arabia
al-Hurma *see* Al Khurmah
147 X7 **Al Ḥusayfīn** *var.* Al Hasaifin. N Oman
144 G9 **Al Ḥuṣn** *var.* Husn. Irbid, N Jordan
145 U9 **'Alī** E Iraq
106 L10 **Alia** Extremadura, W Spain
149 P9 **'Alīābād** Yazd, C Iran
'Alīābad *see* Qā'emshahr
107 S7 **Aliaga** Aragón, NE Spain
142 B13 **Aliağa** İzmir, W Turkey
Aliákmon *see* Aliákmonas
117 F14 **Aliákmonas** *prev.* Aliákmon, *anc.* Haliacmon. ≈ N Greece
145 W9 **'Alī al Gharbī** E Iraq
145 U11 **'Alī al Ḥassūnī** S Iraq
117 G18 **Alíartos** Stereá Ellás, C Greece
143 Y12 **Äli-Bayramlı** *Rus.* Ali-Bayramly. SE Azerbaijan
Ali-Bayramly *see* Äli-Bayramlı
116 P12 **Alibey Barajı** ⊠ NW Turkey
79 S13 **Alibori** ≈ N Benin
114 M10 **Alibunar** Serbia, NE Yugoslavia
107 S12 **Alicante** *Cat.* Alacant; *Lat.* Lucentum. País Valenciano, SE Spain
107 S12 **Alicante** ◈ *province* País Valenciano, SE Spain
107 S12 **Alicante** ✕ Murcia, E Spain
85 I25 **Alice** Eastern Cape, S South Africa
27 S14 **Alice** Texas, SW USA
85 I25 **Alicedale** Eastern Cape, S South Africa
67 B25 **Alice, Mount** *hill* West Falkland, Falkland Islands
109 P20 **Alice, Punta** *headland* S Italy
189 Q7 **Alice Springs** Northern Territory, C Australia
25 N4 **Aliceville** Alabama, S USA
153 U13 **Alichur** SE Tajikistan
153 U14 **Alichuri Janubí, Qatorkŭhi** *Rus.* Yuzhno-Alichurskiy Khrebet. ▲▲ SE Tajikistan
153 U13 **Alichuri Shimolí, Qatorkŭhi** *Rus.* Severo-Alichurskiy Khrebet. ▲▲ SE Tajikistan
109 K22 **Alicudi, Isola** *island* Isole Eolie, S Italy
158 J11 **Alīgarh** Uttar Pradesh, N India
148 M7 **Alīgūdarz** Lorestān, W Iran
1 F12 **Alijos, Islas** *island group* California, SW USA
155 R6 **'Alī Kbel** *Pash.* 'Alī Khēl. Paktīkā, E Afghanistan
Ali Khel *see* 'Alī Kheyl, Paktīā, Afghanistan
'Alī Khēl *see* 'Alī Kbel, Paktīkā, Afghanistan
155 R6 **'Alī Kheyl** *var.* Ali Khel, Jajı. Paktīā, SE Afghanistan
147 V17 **Al Ikhwān** *island group* SE Yemen
Aliki *see* Alykí
81 H19 **Alima** ≈ C Congo
Al Imārāt al 'Arabīyah al Muttaḥidah *see* United Arab Emirates
194 M12 **Alimbit** ≈ New Britain, C PNG
117 N23 **Alimía** *island* Dodekánisos, Greece, Aegean Sea
57 V12 **Alimimuni Piek** ▲ S Suriname
81 K15 **Alindao** Basse-Kotto, S Central African Republic
97 J18 **Alingsås** Älvsborg, S Sweden
83 K18 **Alinjugul** *spring/well* E Kenya
155 S11 **Alīpur** Punjab, E Pakistan
159 T12 **Alīpur Duār** West Bengal, NE India
20 B14 **Aliquippa** Pennsylvania, NE USA
82 L12 **'Ali Sabieh** *var.* 'Alī Sabīḥ. S Djibouti
'Alī Sabīḥ *see* 'Ali Sabieh
146 K3 **Al 'Īsāwīyah** Al Jawf, NW Saudi Arabia
106 J10 **Aliseda** Extremadura, W Spain
145 T8 **Al Iskandarīyah** C Iraq
Al Iskandarīyah *see* Alexandria
127 Oo5 **Aliskerovo** Chukotskiy Avtonomnyy Okrug, NE Russian Federation
116 H13 **Alistráti** Kentrikí Makedonía, NE Greece
41 P15 **Alitak Bay** *bay* Kodiak Island, Alaska, USA
Al Ittiḥād *see* Madīnat ash Sha'b
117 H18 **Alivéri** *var.* Alivérion. Évvoia, C Greece
Alivérion *see* Alivéri
Aliwal-Noord *see* Aliwal North
85 I24 **Aliwal North** *Afr.* Aliwal-Noord. Eastern Cape, SE South Africa
124 Nn15 **Al Jabal al Akhḍar** ▲▲ NE Libya
144 H13 **Al Jafr** Ma'ān, S Jordan
77 T8 **Al Jaghbūb** NE Libya
148 K11 **Al Jahrā'** *var.* Al Jahrah, Jahra. C Kuwait
Al Jahrah *see* Al Jahrā'
Al Jamāhīrīyah al 'Arabīyah al Lībīyah ash Sha'bīyah al Ishtirāk *see* Libya
146 K3 **Al Jarāwī** *spring/well* NW Saudi Arabia
147 X11 **Al Jawārah** *oasis* SE Oman
146 L3 **Al Jawf** *var.* Jauf. Al Jawf, NW Saudi Arabia
146 L4 **Al Jawf** *off.* Minṭaqat al Jawf. ◈ *province* N Saudi Arabia
Al Jawlān *see* Golan Heights
Al Jazair *see* Alger
145 N4 **Al Jazīrah** *physical region* Iraq/Syria
106 F14 **Aljezur** Faro, S Portugal
145 S13 **Al Jīl** S Iraq
144 G11 **Al Jīzah** *var.* Jiza. 'Ammān, N Jordan
Al Jīzah *see* El Gîza
Al Jubail *see* Al Jubayl
147 S6 **Al Jubayl** *var.* Al Jubail. Ash Sharqīyah, NE Saudi Arabia
147 T10 **Āl Juḥaysh, Qalamat** *well* SE Saudi Arabia
149 N15 **Al Jumaylīyah** N Qatar
Al Junaynah *see* El Geneina
106 G13 **Aljustrel** Beja, S Portugal
Al Kaba'ish *see* Al Chabā'ish
Al-Kadhimain *see* Al Kāẓimīyah
Al Kāf *see* El Kef
Alkal'a *see* Alcalá de Henares
37 W4 **Alkali Flat** *salt flat* Nevada, W USA
37 Q1 **Alkali Lake** ◎ Nevada, W USA
147 Z9 **Al Kāmil** NE Oman
144 G11 **Al Karak** *var.* El Kerak, Karak, Kerak; *anc.* Kir Moab, Kir of Moab. Al Karak, W Jordan
144 G12 **Al Karak** *off.* Muḥāfaẓat al Karak. ◈ *governorate* W Jordan
145 W8 **Al Karmashīyah** E Iraq
Al-Kashaniya *see* Al Qash'ānīyah
Al-Kasr al-Kebir *see* Ksar-el-Kebir
145 T8 **Al Kāẓimīyah** *var.* Al-Kadhimain, Kadhimain. C Iraq
101 J18 **Alken** Limburg, NE Belgium
147 X8 **Al Khābūrah** *var.* Khabura. N Oman
Al Khalīl *see* Hebron
145 T7 **Al Khāliṣ** C Iraq
Al Khaluf *see* Khalūf
Al Khārijah *see* El Khârga
147 Q8 **Al Kharj** Ar Riyāḍ, C Saudi Arabia
147 W6 **Al Khaṣab** *var.* Khasab. N Oman
Al Khaur *see* Al Khawr
149 N15 **Al Khawr** *var.* Al Khaur, Al Khor. N Qatar
148 K12 **Al Khīrān** *var.* Al Khiran. SE Kuwait
147 W9 **Al Khīrān** *spring/well* NW Oman
Al Khiyām *see* El Khiyam
Al-Khobar *see* Al Khubar
Al Khor *see* Al Khawr
147 S6 **Al Khubar** *var.* Al-Khobar. Ash Sharqīyah, NE Saudi Arabia
77 T11 **Al Khufrah** SE Libya
123 L14 **Al Khums** *var.* Homs, Khoms, Khums. NW Libya
147 R15 **Al Khuraybah** C Yemen
146 M9 **Al Khurmah** *var.* al-Hurma. Makkah, W Saudi Arabia
147 V9 **Al Kidan** *desert* NE Saudi Arabia
100 H9 **Alkmaar** Noord-Holland, NW Netherlands
145 T10 **Al Kūfah** *var.* Kufa. S Iraq
147 T10 **Al Kursū'** *desert* E Saudi Arabia
145 V9 **Al Kūt** *var.* Kūt al 'Amārah, Kut al Imara. E Iraq
Al-Kuwait *see* Al Kuwayt
Al Kuwayr *see* Guwēr
148 K11 **Al Kuwayt** *var.* Al-Kuwait, *Eng.* Kuwait, Kuwait City; *prev.* Qurein. ● (Kuwait) E Kuwait
148 K11 **Al Kuwayt** ✕ C Kuwait
117 G19 **Alkyonidón, Kólpos** *gulf* C Greece
147 N4 **Al Labbah** *physical region* N Saudi Arabia
144 G4 **Al Lādhiqīyah** *Eng.* Latakia, *Fr.* Lattaquié; *anc.* Laodicea, Laodicea ad Mare. Al Lādhiqīyah, W Syria
144 H4 **Al Lādhiqīyah** *off.* Muḥāfaẓat al Ļādhiqīyah, *var.* Al Lathqiyah, Latakia, Lattakia. ◈ *governorate* W Syria
21 R2 **Allagash River** ≈ Maine, NE USA
158 M13 **Allahābād** Uttar Pradesh, N India
149 S3 **Allāh Dāgh, Reshteh-ye** ▲▲ NE Iran
41 Q8 **Allakaket** Alaska, USA
126 Mm11 **Allakh-Yun'** ≈ NE Russian Federation
9 T15 **Allan** Saskatchewan, S Canada
177 Ff6 **Allanmyo** Magwe, C Myanmar
85 I22 **Allanridge** Free State, C South Africa
106 H4 **Allariz** Galicia, NW Spain
145 R11 **Al Laṣaf** *var.* Al Lussuf. S Iraq
Al Lathqiyah *see* Al Lādhiqīyah
25 S2 **Allatoona Lake** ⊠ Georgia, SE USA
85 J19 **Alldays** Northern, NE South Africa
Alle *see* Łyna
33 P10 **Allegan** Michigan, N USA
19 Qq8 **Allegheny Mountains** ▲▲ NE USA
20 E12 **Allegheny Plateau** ▲▲ New York/Pennsylvania, NE USA
20 D11 **Allegheny Reservoir** ⊠ New York/Pennsylvania, NE USA
20 E12 **Allegheny River** ≈ New York/Pennsylvania, NE USA
24 K9 **Allemands, Lac des** ◎ Louisiana, S USA
27 U6 **Allen** Texas, SW USA
23 R14 **Allendale** South Carolina, SE USA
43 N6 **Allende** Coahuila de Zaragoza, NE Mexico
43 O9 **Allende** Nuevo León, NE Mexico
99 D16 **Allen, Lough** *Ir.* Loch Aillionn. ◎ NW Ireland
193 B26 **Allen, Mount** ▲ Stewart Island, Southland, SW NZ
111 V2 **Allensteig** Niederösterreich, N Austria
Allenstein *see* Olsztyn
20 I14 **Allentown** Pennsylvania, NE USA
161 G23 **Alleppey** *var.* Alappuzha; *prev.* Alleppi. Kerala, SW India
Alleppi *see* Alleppey
102 J12 **Aller** ≈ NW Germany
31 V16 **Allerton** Iowa, C USA
101 K19 **Alleur** Liège, E Belgium
103 J25 **Allgäuer Alpen** ▲▲ Austria/Germany
30 J13 **Alliance** Nebraska, C USA
33 U12 **Alliance** Ohio, N USA
105 O10 **Allier** ◈ *department* N France
145 R13 **Al Līfīyah** S Iraq
46 J13 **Alligator Pond** C Jamaica
23 Y9 **Alligator River** ≈ North Carolina, SE USA
31 W12 **Allison** Iowa, C USA
12 G14 **Alliston** Ontario, S Canada
146 L11 **Al Līth** Makkah, SW Saudi Arabia
Al Liwā' *see* Līwā
98 J12 **Alloa** C Scotland, UK
105 U14 **Allos** Alpes-de-Haute-Provence, SE France
110 D6 **Allschwil** Basel-Land, NW Switzerland
Al Lubnān *see* Lebanon
147 N14 **Al Luḥayyah** W Yemen
12 K12 **Allumettes, Île des** *island* Québec, SE Canada
Al Lussuf *see* Al Laṣaf
111 S5 **Alm** ≈ N Austria
13 Q7 **Alma** Québec, SE Canada
29 S10 **Alma** Arkansas, C USA
25 V7 **Alma** Georgia, SE USA
29 P4 **Alma** Kansas, C USA
33 Q8 **Alma** Michigan, N USA
31 O17 **Alma** Nebraska, C USA
32 I7 **Alma** Wisconsin, N USA
145 R12 **Al Ma'ānīyah** S Iraq
Alma-Ata/Alma-Atinskaya Oblast' *see* Almaty
Almacellas *see* Almacelles
107 T5 **Almacelles** *var.* Almacellas. Cataluña, NE Spain
106 F11 **Almada** Setúbal, W Portugal
106 L11 **Almadén** Castilla-La Mancha, C Spain
68 L6 **Almadies, Pointe des** *headland* W Senegal
146 L7 **Al Madīnah** *Eng.* Medina. Al Madīnah, W Saudi Arabia
146 L7 **Al Madīnah** *off.* Minṭaqat al Madīnah. ◈ *province* W Saudi Arabia
144 H9 **Al Mafraq** *var.* Mafraq. Al Mafraq, N Jordan
144 J10 **Al Mafraq** *off.* Muḥāfaẓat al Mafraq. ◈ *governorate* NW Jordan
147 R15 **Al Maghārīm** C Yemen
107 N11 **Almagro** Castilla-La Mancha, C Spain
Al Maḥallah al Kubrá *see* El Maḥalla el Kubra
145 T9 **Al Maḥāwīl** *var.* Khān al Maḥāwīl. C Iraq
Al Mahdīyah *see* Mahdia
145 T8 **Al Maḥmūdīyah** *var.* Mahmudiya. C Iraq
147 T14 **Al Mahrah** ▲▲ E Yemen
147 P7 **Al Majma'ah** Ar Riyāḍ, C Saudi Arabia
145 Q11 **Al Makmīn** *well* S Iraq
145 Q1 **Al Mālikīyah** *var.* Malkiye. Al Ḥasakah, N Syria
Almalyk *see* Olmaliq
Al Mamlakah al Urdunīyah al Hāshimīyah *see* Jordan
Al Mamlakah *see* Morocco
149 Q18 **Al Manādir** *var.* Al Manadir. *desert* Oman/UAE
148 L15 **Al Manāmah** *Eng.* Manama. ● (Bahrain) N Bahrain
145 O5 **Al Manāṣif** ▲▲ E Syria
37 O4 **Almanor, Lake** ⊠ California, W USA
107 R11 **Almansa** Castilla-La Mancha, C Spain
Al Manṣūrah *see* El Manṣûra
106 L3 **Almanza** Castilla-León, N Spain
106 L8 **Almanzor** ▲ W Spain
107 P14 **Almanzora** ≈ SE Spain
145 S9 **Al Mardah** C Iraq
Al-Mariyya *see* Almería
77 R7 **Al Marj** *var.* Barka, *It.* Barce. NE Libya
144 L2 **Al Mashrafah** Ar Raqqah, N Syria
147 X8 **Al Maṣna'ah** *var.* Al Muṣana'a. NE Oman
107 T9 **Almassora** País Valenciano, E Spain
Almatinskaya Oblast' *see* Almaty
151 U15 **Almaty** *var.* Alma-Ata. ● (Kazakhstan) Almaty, SE Kazakhstan
151 S14 **Almaty** *off.* Almatinskaya Oblast', *Kaz.* Almaty Oblysy; *prev.* Alma-Atinskaya Oblast'. ◈ *province* SE Kazakhstan
151 U15 **Almaty** ✕ Almaty, SE Kazakhstan
Almaty Oblysy *see* Almaty
al-Mawailih *see* Al Muwayliḥ
145 R3 **Al Mawṣil** *Eng.* Mosul. N Iraq
145 N5 **Al Mayādīn** *var.* Mayadin, *Fr.* Meyadine. Dayr az Zawr, E Syria
145 X10 **Al Maymūnah** *var.* Maimuna. SE Iraq
147 N5 **Al Mayyāh** Ḥā'il, N Saudi Arabia
Al Ma'zam *see* Al Ma'zim
107 P6 **Almazán** Castilla-León, N Spain
147 W8 **Al Ma'zim** *var.* Al Ma'zam. NW Oman
126 Kk11 **Almaznyy** Respublika Sakha (Yakutiya), NE Russian Federation
Al Mazra' *see* Al Mazra'ah
144 G11 **Al Mazra'ah** *var.* Al Mazra', Mazra'a. Al Karak, W Jordan
103 G15 **Alme** ≈ W Germany
106 I7 **Almeida** Guarda, N Portugal
106 G10 **Almeirim** Santarém, C Portugal
100 O10 **Almelo** Overijssel, E Netherlands
107 S9 **Almenara** País Valenciano, E Spain
107 P12 **Almenaras** ▲ S Spain
107 P5 **Almenar de Soria** Castilla-León, N Spain
106 J6 **Almendra, Embalse de** ⊠ Castilla-León, NW Spain
106 J11 **Almendralejo** Extremadura, W Spain
100 J10 **Almere** *var.* Almere-stad. Flevoland, C Netherlands
100 J10 **Almere-Buiten** Flevoland, C Netherlands
100 J10 **Almere-Haven** Flevoland, C Netherlands
Almere-stad *see* Almere
107 P15 **Almería** *Ar.* Al-Mariyya; *anc.* Unci, *Lat.* Portus Magnus. Andalucía, S Spain
107 P14 **Almería** ◈ *province* Andalucía, S Spain
107 P15 **Almería, Golfo de** *gulf* S Spain
131 S5 **Al'met'yevsk** Respublika Tatarstan, W Russian Federation
97 L21 **Älmhult** Kronoberg, S Sweden
147 U9 **Al Miḥrāḍ** *desert* NE Saudi Arabia
Al Mīnā' *see* El Mina
106 L17 **Almina, Punta** *headland* Ceuta, Spain, N Africa
Al Minyā *see* El Minya
Al Miqdādīyah *see* Al Muqdādīyah
45 P14 **Almirante** Bocas del Toro, NW Panama
Almirós *see* Almyrós
146 M9 **Al Mislaḥ** *spring/well* W Saudi Arabia
Almissa *see* Omiš
106 G13 **Almodôvar** *var.* Almodóvar. Beja, S Portugal
106 M11 **Almodóvar del Campo** Castilla-La Mancha, C Spain
107 Q9 **Almodóvar del Pinar** Castilla-La Mancha, C Spain
33 S9 **Almont** Michigan, N USA
12 L13 **Almonte** Ontario, SE Canada
106 J14 **Almonte** Andalucía, S Spain
106 K9 **Almonte** ≈ W Spain
158 K9 **Almora** Uttar Pradesh, N India
106 M8 **Almorox** Castilla-La Mancha, C Spain
147 S7 **Al Mubarraz** Ash Sharqīyah, E Saudi Arabia
Al Muḍaibī *see* Al Muḍaybī
144 G15 **Al Mudawwarah** Ma'ān, SW Jordan
147 Y9 **Al Muḍaybī** *var.* Al Muḍaibī. NE Oman
Almudébar *see* Almudévar
107 S5 **Almudévar** *var.* Almudébar. Aragón, NE Spain
147 S15 **Al Mukallā** *var.* Mukalla. SE Yemen
147 N16 **Al Mukhā** *Eng.* Mocha. SW Yemen
107 N15 **Almuñécar** Andalucía, S Spain
145 U7 **Al Muqdādīyah** *var.* Al Miqdādīyah. C Iraq
146 L3 **Al Murayr** *spring/well* NW Saudi Arabia
142 M12 **Almus** Tokat, N Turkey
Al Muṣana'a *see* Al Maṣna'ah
145 T9 **Al Musayyib** *var.* Musaiyib. C Iraq
145 V9 **Al Muwaffaqīyah** S Iraq
144 H10 **Al Muwaqqar** *var.* El Muwaqqar. 'Ammān, W Jordan
146 J5 **Al Muwayliḥ** *var.* al-Mawailih. Tabūk, NW Saudi Arabia
117 F17 **Almyrós** *var.* Almirós. Thessalía, C Greece
117 I24 **Almyroú, Órmos** *bay* Krití, Greece, E Mediterranean Sea
Al Nūwfalīyah *see* An Nawfalīyah
98 L13 **Alnwick** N England, UK
Al Obayyid *see* El Obeid
Al Odaid *see* Al 'Udayd
202 B16 **Alofi** ○ (Niue) W Niue
202 A16 **Alofi Bay** *bay* W Niue, C Pacific Ocean
202 E13 **Alofi, Île** *island* S Wallis and Futuna
202 E13 **Alofitai** Île Alofi, W Wallis and Futuna
Aloha State *see* Hawaii
120 G7 **Aloja** Limbaži, N Latvia
159 X10 **Along** Arunāchel Pradesh, NE India
117 H16 **Alónnisos** *island* Vóreioi Sporádes, Greece, Aegean Sea
106 M15 **Álora** Andalucía, S Spain
175 Rr15 **Alor, Kepulauan** *island group* E Indonesia
175 Rr16 **Alor, Pulau** *prev.* Ombai. *island* Kepulauan Alor, E Indonesia
175 R16 **Alor, Selat** *strait* Flores Sea/Savu Sea
173 G2 **Alor Setar** *var.* Alor Star, Alur Setar. Kedah, Peninsular Malaysia
Alost *see* Aalst
160 F9 **Ālot** Madhya Pradesh, C India
195 N16 **Alotau** Milne Bay, SE PNG
176 Yy15 **Alotip** Irian Jaya, E Indonesia
Al Oued *see* El Oued
37 R12 **Alpaugh** California, W USA
Alpen *see* Alps
33 R6 **Alpena** Michigan, N USA
Alpes *see* Alps
105 S14 **Alpes-de-Haute-Provence** ◈ *department* SE France
105 U14 **Alpes-Maritimes** ◈ *department* SE France
189 W8 **Alpha** Queensland, E Australia
207 R9 **Alpha Cordillera** *var.* Alpha Ridge. *undersea feature* Arctic Ocean
Alpha Ridge *see* Alpha Cordillera
Alpheius *see* Alfeiós
101 I15 **Alphen** Noord-Brabant, S Netherlands
100 H11 **Alphen aan den Rijn** *var.* Alphen. Zuid-Holland, C Netherlands
Alpheus *see* Alfeiós
Alpi *see* Alps
106 G10 **Alpiarça** Santarém, C Portugal
26 K10 **Alpine** Texas, SW USA
110 F8 **Alpnach** Unterwalden, W Switzerland
110 D11 **Alps** *Fr.* Alpes, *Ger.* Alpen, *It.* Alpi. ▲▲ C Europe
147 W8 **Al Qābil** *var.* Qabil. N Oman
Al Qaḍārif *see* Gedaref
77 P8 **Al Qaddāḥīyah** N Libya
Al Qadmouss *see* Al Qadmūs
Al Qāhirah *see* Cairo
146 K4 **Al Qalībah** Tabūk, NW Saudi Arabia
145 O1 **Al Qāmishlī** *var.* Kamishli, Qamishly. Al Ḥasakah, NE Syria
144 I6 **Al Qaryatayn** *var.* Qaryatayn, *Fr.* Qariateïne. Ḥimṣ, C Syria
148 K11 **Al Qash'ānīyah** *var.* Al-Kashaniya. NE Kuwait
147 N7 **Al Qaṣīm** *off.* Minṭaqat Qaṣīm, Qassim. ◈ *province* C Saudi Arabia
144 J5 **Al Qaṣr** Ḥimṣ, C Syria
Al Qaṣr *see* El Qaṣr
Al Qaṣrayn *see* Kasserine
147 S6 **Al Qaṭīf** Ash Sharqīyah, NE Saudi Arabia
144 G11 **Al Qaṭrānah** *var.* El Qatrani, Qatrana. Al Karak, W Jordan
77 P11 **Al Qaṭrūn** SW Libya
Al Qayrawān *see* Kairouan
Al-Qsar al-Kbir *see* Ksar-el-Kebir
Al Qubayyāt *see* Qoubaïyât
Al Qudayr *see* Al Qadr
Al Quds/Al Quds ash Sharīf *see* Jerusalem
144 G8 **Al Qunayṭirah** *var.* El Kuneitra, El Quneitra, Kuneitra, Qunaytra. Al Qunayṭirah, SW Syria
144 G8 **Al Qunayṭirah** *off.* Muḥāfaẓat al Qunayṭirah, *var.* El Q'unayṭirah, Qunaytirah, *Fr.* Kuneitra. ◈ *governorate* SW Syria
146 M11 **Al Qunfudhah** Makkah, SW Saudi Arabia
146 K2 **Al Qurayyāt** Al Jawf, NW Saudi Arabia
145 Y11 **Al Qurnah** *var.* Kurna. SE Iraq
145 V12 **Al Quṣayr** S Iraq
144 I6 **Al Quṣayr** *var.* El Quseir, Quṣayr, *Fr.* Kousseir. Ḥimṣ, W Syria
Al Quṣayr *see* Quseir
144 H7 **Al Quṭayfah** *var.* Quṭayfah, Qutayfe, Quteife, *Fr.* Kouteifé. Dimashq, W Syria
147 P8 **Al Quwayīyah** Ar Riyāḍ, C Saudi Arabia
Al Quwayr *see* Guwēr
144 F14 **Al Quwayrah** *var.* El Quweira. Ma'ān, SW Jordan
Al Rayyan *see* Ar Rayyān
Al Rbeil *see* Ar Rubayl
Al Ruweis *see* Ar Ruways
97 G24 **Als** *Ger.* Alsen. *island* SW Denmark
105 U5 **Alsace** *Ger.* Elsass; *anc.* Alsatia. ◈ *region* NE France
9 R16 **Alsask** Saskatchewan, S Canada
107 P3 **Alsasua** Navarra, N Spain
Alsatia *see* Alsace
103 C16 **Alsdorf** Nordrhein-Westfalen, W Germany
8 G8 **Alsek** ≈ Canada/USA
Alsen *see* Als
103 F19 **Alsenz** ≈ W Germany
103 H17 **Alsfeld** Hessen, C Germany
121 K20 **Al'shany** *Rus.* Ol'shany. Brestskaya Voblasts', SW Belarus
Alsókubin *see* Dolný Kubín
120 C9 **Alsunga** Kuldīga, W Latvia
Alt *see* Olt
94 K9 **Alta** *Fin.* Alattio. Finnmark, N Norway
31 T12 **Alta** Iowa, C USA
110 I7 **Altach** Vorarlberg, W Austria
94 K9 **Altaelva** ≈ N Norway
94 J8 **Altafjorden** *fjord* NE Norwegian Sea
64 K10 **Alta Gracia** Córdoba, C Argentina
44 K11 **Alta Gracia** Rivas, SW Nicaragua
56 H4 **Altagracia** Zulia, NW Venezuela
56 M5 **Altagracia de Orituco** Guárico, N Venezuela
Altai *see* Altai Mountains
133 T7 **Altai Mountains** *var.* Altai, *Chin.* Altay Shan, *Rus.* Altay. ▲▲ Asia/Europe
25 V6 **Altamaha River** ≈ Georgia, SE USA
60 J13 **Altamira** Pará, NE Brazil
56 D12 **Altamira** Huila, S Colombia
44 M13 **Altamira** Alajuela, N Costa Rica
43 Q11 **Altamira** Tamaulipas, C Mexico
32 L15 **Altamont** Illinois, N USA
29 Q7 **Altamont** Kansas, C USA
34 H16 **Altamont** Oregon, NW USA
22 K10 **Altamont** Tennessee, S USA
25 X11 **Altamonte Springs** Florida, SE USA
109 O17 **Altamura** *anc.* Lupatia. Puglia, SE Italy
42 H9 **Altamura, Isla** *island* C Mexico
168 G7 **Altan** Dzavhan, W Mongolia
168 G6 **Altanbulag** Dzavhan, N Mongolia
Altan Emel *see* Xin Barag Youqi
168 J8 **Altan-Ovoo** Arhangay, C Mongolia
168 E7 **Altanteel** Hovd, W Mongolia
42 F3 **Altar** Sonora, NW Mexico
42 D2 **Altar, Desierto de** *var.* Sonoran Desert. *desert* Mexico/USA *see also* Sonoran Desert
107 Q8 **Alta, Sierra** ▲ N Spain
42 H9 **Altata** Sinaloa, C Mexico
44 D4 **Alta Verapaz** *off.* Departamento de Alta Verapaz. ◈ *department* C Guatemala
109 L18 **Altavilla Silentia** Campania, S Italy
23 T7 **Altavista** Virginia, NE USA
164 L2 **Altay** Xinjiang Uygur Zizhiqu, NW China
168 G5 **Altay** Dzavhan, N Mongolia
168 G8 **Altay** Govĭ-Altay, W Mongolia
Altay *see* Altai Mountains
126 H16 **Altay, Respublika** *var.* Gornyy Altay; *prev.* Gorno-Altayskaya Respublika. ◈ *autonomous republic* S Russian Federation
Altay Shan *see* Altai Mountains
125 G15 **Altayskiy Kray** ◈ *territory* S Russian Federation
Altbetsche *see* Bečej
103 L20 **Altdorf** Bayern, SE Germany
110 G8 **Altdorf** *var.* Altorf. Uri, C Switzerland
107 T11 **Altea** País Valenciano, E Spain
102 L10 **Alte Elde** ≈ N Germany
103 M16 **Altenburg** Thüringen, E Germany
Altenburg *see* București, Romania
Altenburg *see* Baia de Criș, Romania
102 P12 **Alte Oder** ≈ NE Germany
106 H10 **Alter do Chão** Portalegre, C Portugal
94 I10 **Altevatnet** ◎ N Norway
29 V12 **Altheimer** Arkansas, C USA
111 T9 **Althofen** Kärnten, S Austria
116 H7 **Altimir** Oblast Montana, NW Bulgaria
142 K11 **Altınkaya Barajı** ⊠ N Turkey
145 S3 **Altin Köprü** *var.* Altun Kupri. N Iraq
142 E13 **Altıntaş** Kütahya, W Turkey
59 K18 **Altiplano** *physical region* W South America
Altkanischa *see* Kanjiža
105 U7 **Altkirch** Haut-Rhin, NE France
Altlublau *see* Stará L'ubovňa
102 L12 **Altmark** *cultural region* N Germany
Altmoldowa *see* Moldova Veche
27 W8 **Alto** Texas, SW USA
106 H11 **Alto Alentejo** *physical region* S Portugal
61 I19 **Alto Araguaia** Mato Grosso, C Brazil
60 L12 **Alto Bonito** Pará, NE Brazil
85 O15 **Alto Molócuè** Zambézia, NE Mozambique
32 K15 **Alton** Illinois, N USA
29 W8 **Alton** Missouri, C USA
9 X17 **Altona** Manitoba, S Canada
20 E14 **Altoona** Pennsylvania, NE USA
32 J6 **Altoona** Wisconsin, N USA
64 N3 **Alto Paraguay** *off.* Departamento del Alto Paraguay. ◈ *department* N Paraguay
61 L17 **Alto Paraíso de Goiás** Goiás, S Brazil
64 P6 **Alto Paraná** *off.* Departamento del Alto Paraná. ◈ *department* E Paraguay
Alto Paraná *see* Paraná
61 L15 **Alto Parnaíba** Maranhão, E Brazil
58 H13 **Alto Purús, Río** ≈ E Peru
Altorf *see* Altdorf
65 H19 **Alto Río Senguer** *var.* Alto Río Senguerr. Chubut, S Argentina
43 Q13 **Altotonga** Veracruz-Llave, E Mexico
103 N23 **Altötting** Bayern, SE Germany
Altpasua *see* Stara Pazova
168 I5 **Altraga** Hövsgöl, N Mongolia
Alt-Schwanenburg *see* Gulbene
Altsohl *see* Zvolen
110 I7 **Altstätten** Sankt Gallen, NE Switzerland
44 G1 **Altun Ha** *ruins* Belize, N Belize
Altun Kupri *see* Altin Köprü
164 D8 **Altun Shan** ▲ C China
164 L9 **Altun Shan** *var.* Altyn Tagh. ▲▲ NW China
37 P2 **Alturas** California, W USA
28 K12 **Altus** Oklahoma, C USA
28 K11 **Altus Lake** ⊠ Oklahoma, C USA
Altvater *see* Praděd
Altyn Tagh *see* Altun Shan
Alu *see* Shortland Island
al-'Ubaila *see* Al 'Ubaylah
145 O6 **Al 'Ubaydī** W Iraq
147 T9 **Al 'Ubaylah** *var.* al-'Ubaila. Ash Sharqīyah, E Saudi Arabia
147 T9 **Al 'Ubaylah** *spring/well* E Saudi Arabia
Al Ubayyiḍ *see* El Obeid
147 T7 **Al 'Udayd** *var.* Al Odaid. Abū Ẓaby, W UAE
120 J8 **Alūksne** *Ger.* Marienburg. Alūksne, NE Latvia
146 K6 **Al 'Ulā** Al Madīnah, NW Saudi Arabia
181 N4 **Alula-Fartak Trench** *var.* Illaue Fartak Trench. *undersea feature* W Indian Ocean
144 I11 **Al 'Umarī** 'Ammān, E Jordan
33 S13 **Alum Creek Lake** ⊠ Ohio, N USA
65 H15 **Aluminé** Neuquén, C Argentina
97 O14 **Alunda** Uppsala, C Sweden
119 T14 **Alupka** Respublika Krym, S Ukraine
77 P8 **Al 'Uqaylah** N Libya
Al Uqṣur *see* Luxor
Al Urdunn *see* Jordan
173 G6 **Alur Panal** *bay* Sumatera, W Indonesia
147 V10 **Al 'Urūq al Mu'tariḍah** *salt lake* SE Saudi Arabia
145 Q7 **Ālūs** C Iraq
119 T13 **Alushta** Respublika Krym, S Ukraine
77 N11 **Al 'Uwaynāt** *var.* Al Awaynāt. SW Libya
145 T6 **Al 'Uẓaym** *var.* Adhaim. E Iraq
28 L8 **Alva** Oklahoma, C USA
106 H8 **Alva** ≈ N Portugal
97 J18 **Älvängen** Älvsborg, S Sweden
12 F14 **Alvanley** Ontario, S Canada
43 S14 **Alvarado** Veracruz-Llave, E Mexico
27 T7 **Alvarado** Texas, SW USA
60 D13 **Alvarães** Amazonas, NW Brazil
42 G6 **Alvaro Obregón, Presa** ⊠ W Mexico

222
◆ Country ● Country Capital ◇ Dependent Territory ○ Dependent Territory Capital ◈ Administrative Region ✕ International Airport ▲ Mountain ▲▲ Mountain Range Volcano ≈ River ◎ Lake ⊠ Reservoir

ALVDAL – ANGRA DO HEROÍSMO

96 H10 **Alvdal** Hedmark, S Norway
96 K12 **Älvdalen** Kopparberg, C Sweden
63 E15 **Alvear** Corrientes, NE Argentina
106 F10 **Alverca do Ribatejo** Lisboa, C Portugal
97 L20 **Alvesta** Kronoberg, S Sweden
96 D13 **Ålvik** Hordaland, S Norway
27 W12 **Alvin** Texas, SW USA
96 O13 **Älvkarleby** Uppsala, C Sweden
27 S5 **Alvord** Texas, SW USA
95 G18 **Älvros** Jämtland, C Sweden
97 J19 **Älvsborg** ◐ *county* S Sweden
94 J13 **Älvsbyn** Norrbotten, N Sweden
148 K12 **Al Wafrā'** SE Kuwait
146 J6 **Al Wajh** Tabūk, NW Saudi Arabia
149 N16 **Al Wakrah** *var.* Wakra. C Qatar
144 M8 **al Walaj, Sha'īb** *dry watercourse* W Iraq
158 I11 **Alwar** Rājasthān, N India
147 Q5 **Al Wari'ah** Ash Sharqīyah, N Saudi Arabia
161 G22 **Alwaye** Kerala, SW India
168 K14 **Alxa Zuoqi** *var.* Ehen Hudag. Nei Mongol Zizhiqu, N China
Al Yaman *see* Yemen
144 G9 **Al Yarmūk** Irbid, N Jordan
Alyat/Alyaty-Pristan' *see* Älät
117 I14 **Alykí** *var.* Aliki. Thásos, N Greece
121 F14 **Alytus** *Pol.* Olita. Alytus, S Lithuania
103 N23 **Alz** ≈ SE Germany
35 Y11 **Alzada** Montana, NW USA
126 I14 **Alzamay** Irkutskaya Oblast', S Russian Federation
101 M25 **Alzette** ≈ S Luxembourg
107 S10 **Alzira** *var.* Alcira ; *anc.* Saetabicula, Suero. País Valenciano, E Spain
Al Zubair *see* Az Zubayr
189 O8 **Amadeus, Lake** *seasonal lake* Northern Territory, C Australia
83 E15 **Amadi** Western Equatoria, SW Sudan
16 Nn3 **Amadjuak Lake** ◎ Baffin Island, Northwest Territories, N Canada
97 J23 **Amager** *island* E Denmark
170 Cc13 **Amagi** Fukuoka, Kyūshū, SW Japan
171 J17 **Amagi-san** ▲ Honshū, S Japan
175 Tt11 **Amahai** *var.* Masohi. Pulau Seram, E Indonesia
40 M16 **Amak Island** *island* Alaska, USA
170 Bb14 **Amakusa-nada** *gulf* Kyūshū, SW Japan
97 J16 **Åmål** Älvsborg, S Sweden
56 E8 **Amalfi** Antioquia, N Colombia
109 L18 **Amalfi** Campania, S Italy
117 D19 **Amaliáda** *var.* Amaliás. Dytikí Ellás, S Greece
Amaliás *see* Amaliáda
160 F12 **Amalner** Mahārāshtra, C India
176 X12 **Amamapare** Irian Jaya, E Indonesia
61 H21 **Amambaí, Serra de** *var.* Cordillera de Amambay, Serra de Amambay. ▲▲ Brazil/Paraguay *see also* Amambay, Cordillera de
64 P4 **Amambay** *off.* Departamento del Amambay. ◐ *department* E Paraguay
64 P5 **Amambay, Cordillera de** *var.* Serra de Amambaí, Serra de Amambay. ▲▲ Brazil/Paraguay *see also* Amambaí, Serra de
Amambay, Serra de *see* Amambaí, Serra de/Amambay, Cordillera de
172 Q13 **Amami-guntō** *island group* SW Japan
172 Qq13 **Amami-Ō-shima** *island* S Japan
194 E10 **Amanab** Sandaun, NW PNG
108 J13 **Amandola** Marche, C Italy
109 N21 **Amantea** Calabria, SW Italy
203 W10 **Amanu** *island* Îles Tuamotu, C French Polynesia
60 J10 **Amapá** Amapá, NE Brazil
60 J11 **Amapá** *off.* Estado de Amapá; *prev.* Território de Amapá. ◐ *state* NE Brazil
44 H8 **Amapala** Valle, S Honduras
Amara *see* Al 'Amārah
106 H6 **Amarante** Porto, N Portugal
177 G5 **Amarapura** Mandalay, C Myanmar
168 L9 **Amardalay** Dundgovĭ, C Mongolia
106 I12 **Amareleja** Beja, S Portugal
37 V11 **Amargosa Range** ▲▲ California, W USA
27 N2 **Amarillo** Texas, SW USA
Amarinthos *see* Amárynthos
109 K15 **Amaro, Monte** ▲ C Italy
117 H18 **Amárynthos** *var.* Amarinthos. Évvoia, C Greece
Amasia *see* Amasya
142 K12 **Amasya** *anc.* Amasia. Amasya, N Turkey
142 K11 **Amasya** ◐ *province* N Turkey
44 F4 **Amatique, Bahía de** *bay* Gulf of Honduras, W Caribbean Sea
44 D6 **Amatitlán, Lago de** ◎ S Guatemala
109 J14 **Amatrice** Lazio, C Italy
202 C8 **Amatuku** *atoll* C Tuvalu
101 J20 **Amay** Liège, E Belgium
50 F7 **Amazon** *Sp.* Amazonas. ≈ Brazil/Peru
61 C14 **Amazonas** *off.* Estado do Amazonas. ◐ *state* N Brazil
56 G15 **Amazonas** *off.* Comisaría del Amazonas. ◐ *province* SE Colombia
58 C10 **Amazonas** *off.* Departamento de Amazonas. ◐ *department* N Peru
56 M12 **Amazonas** *off.* Territorio Amazonas. ◐ *federal territory* S Venezuela
Amazonas *see* Amazon
50 F7 **Amazon Basin** *basin* N South America
49 V5 **Amazon Fan** *undersea feature* W Atlantic Ocean
60 K11 **Amazon, Mouths of the** *delta* NE Brazil
197 C12 **Ambae** *var.* Aoba, Omba. *island* C Vanuatu
158 I9 **Ambāla** Haryāna, NW India
161 J26 **Ambalangoda** Southern Province, SW Sri Lanka
161 K26 **Ambalantota** Southern Province, S Sri Lanka
180 I6 **Ambalavao** Fianarantsoa, C Madagascar
56 E10 **Ambalema** Tolima, C Colombia
81 E17 **Ambam** Sud, S Cameroon
180 J2 **Ambanja** Antsiranana, N Madagascar
127 O5 **Ambarchik** Respublika Sakha (Yakutiya), NE Russian Federation
64 K9 **Ambargasta, Salinas de** *salt lake* C Argentina
128 J6 **Ambarnyy** Respublika Kareliya, NW Russian Federation
58 C7 **Ambato** Tungurahua, C Ecuador
180 I5 **Ambatolampy** Antananarivo, C Madagascar
180 H4 **Ambatomainty** Mahajanga, W Madagascar
180 J4 **Ambatondrazaka** Toamasina, C Madagascar
175 Ss12 **Ambelau, Pulau** *see* Ambelau, Pulau
103 L20 **Amberg** *var.* Amberg in der Oberpfalz. Bayern, SE Germany
Amberg in der Oberpfalz *see* Amberg
44 H1 **Ambergris Cay** *island* NE Belize
105 S11 **Ambérieu-en-Bugey** Ain, E France
193 I18 **Amberley** Canterbury, South Island, NZ
105 P11 **Ambert** Puy-de-Dôme, C France
Ambianum *see* Amiens
78 J11 **Ambidédi** Kayes, SW Mali
160 M10 **Ambikāpur** Madhya Pradesh, C India
180 J2 **Ambilobe** Antsiranana, N Madagascar
195 Q10 **Ambitle Island** *island* Feni Islands, NE PNG
41 O7 **Ambler** Alaska, USA
Amblève *see* Amel
Ambo *see* Hägere Hiywet
180 I8 **Amboasary** Toliara, S Madagascar
180 J4 **Ambodifotatra** *var.* Ambodifototra. Toamasina, E Madagascar
Amboenten *see* Ambunten
180 I5 **Ambohidratrimo** Antananarivo, C Madagascar
180 I6 **Ambohimahasoa** Fianarantsoa, SE Madagascar
180 K3 **Ambohitralanana** Antsiranana, NE Madagascar
176 X10 **Amboi, Kepulauan** *island group* E Indonesia
Amboina *see* Ambon
104 M8 **Amboise** Indre-et-Loire, C France
175 T11 **Ambon** *prev.* Amboina, Amboyna. Pulau Ambon, E Indonesia
175 T12 **Ambon, Pulau** *island* E Indonesia
83 J20 **Amboseli, Lake** ◎ Kenya/Tanzania
180 I6 **Ambositra** Fianarantsoa, SE Madagascar
180 I8 **Ambovombe** Toliara, S Madagascar
37 W14 **Amboy** California, W USA
32 L11 **Amboy** Illinois, N USA
Amboyna *see* Ambon
Ambracia *see* Árta
20 B14 **Ambridge** Pennsylvania, NE USA
Ambrim *see* Ambrym
84 A11 **Ambriz** Bengo, NW Angola
Ambrizete *see* N'Zeto
197 C13 **Ambrym** *var.* Ambrim. *island* C Vanuatu
174 Mm14 **Ambunten** *prev.* Amboenten. Pulau Madura, E Indonesia
194 G10 **Ambunti** East Sepik, NW PNG
161 I20 **Āmbūr** Tamil Nādu, SE India
40 E17 **Amchitka Island** *island* Aleutian Islands, Alaska, USA
40 F17 **Amchitka Pass** *strait* Aleutian Islands, Alaska, USA
147 R15 **'Amd** C Yemen
80 J10 **Am Dam** Ouaddaï, E Chad
176 Uu15 **Amdassa** Pulau Yamdena, E Indonesia
129 U1 **Amderma** Nenetskiy Avtonomnyy Okrug, NW Russian Federation
165 N14 **Amdo** Xizang Zizhiqu, W China
42 K13 **Ameca** Jalisco, SW Mexico
43 P14 **Amecameca** *var.* Amecameca de Juárez. México, C Mexico
Amecameca de Juárez *see* Amecameca
63 A20 **Ameghino** Buenos Aires, E Argentina
101 M21 **Amel** *Fr.* Amblève. Liège, E Belgium
100 K4 **Ameland** *Fris.* It Amelân. *island* Waddeneilanden, N Netherlands
Amelân, It *see* Ameland
109 H14 **Amelia** Umbria, C Italy
23 V6 **Amelia Court House** Virginia, NE USA
25 W8 **Amelia Island** *island* Florida, SE USA
20 L12 **Amenia** New York, NE USA
America *see* United States of America
67 M21 **America-Antarctica Ridge** *undersea feature* S Atlantic Ocean
America in Miniature *see* Maryland
62 L9 **Americana** São Paulo, S Brazil
35 Q15 **American Falls** Idaho, NW USA
35 Q15 **American Falls Reservoir** ⊡ Idaho, NW USA
38 L3 **American Fork** Utah, W USA
198 D8 **American Samoa** ◇ *US unincorporated territory* W Polynesia
25 S6 **Americus** Georgia, SE USA
100 K12 **Amerongen** Utrecht, C Netherlands
100 K11 **Amersfoort** Utrecht, C Netherlands
99 N21 **Amersham** SE England, UK
32 I5 **Amery** Wisconsin, N USA
205 W6 **Amery Ice Shelf** *ice shelf* Antarctica
31 V13 **Ames** Iowa, C USA
21 P10 **Amesbury** Massachusetts, NE USA
Amestratus *see* Mistretta
117 F18 **Amfíkleia** *var.* Amfiklia. Stereá Ellás, C Greece
Amfiklia *see* Amfíkleia
117 D17 **Amfilochía** *var.* Amfilokhía. Dytikí Ellás, C Greece
Amfilokhía *see* Amfilochía
116 H13 **Amfípoli** *anc.* Amphipolis. *site of ancient city* Kentrikí Makedonía, NE Greece
117 F18 **Ámfissa** Stereá Ellás, C Greece
126 M11 **Amga** Respublika Sakha (Yakutiya), NE Russian Federation
126 M11 **Amga** ≈ NE Russian Federation
Amgalang *see* Xin Barag Zuoqi
195 N12 **Amgen** ≈ New Britain, C PNG
127 P4 **Amguema** ≈ NE Russian Federation
127 Nn14 **Amgun'** ≈ SE Russian Federation
11 P15 **Amherst** Nova Scotia, SE Canada
20 M11 **Amherst** Massachusetts, NE USA
20 D10 **Amherst** New York, NE USA
26 M4 **Amherst** Texas, SW USA
23 U6 **Amherst** Virginia, NE USA
Amherst *see* Kyaikkami
12 C18 **Amherstburg** Ontario, S Canada
23 Q6 **Amherstdale** West Virginia, NE USA
12 K15 **Amherst Island** *island* Ontario, SE Canada
Amida *see* Diyarbakır
30 J6 **Amidon** North Dakota, N USA
105 O3 **Amiens** *anc.* Ambianum, Samarobriva. Somme, N France
145 P8 **'Āmij, Wādī** *var.* Wadi 'Amiq. *dry watercourse* W Iraq
142 L17 **Amik Ovası** ◎ S Turkey
Amilhayt, Wādī *see* Umm al Ḥayt, Wādī
Amíndaion/Amindeo *see* Amýntaio
161 C21 **Amīndivi Islands** *island group* Lakshadweep, India, N Indian Ocean
145 U6 **Āmīn Ḥabīb** E Iraq
85 E20 **Aminuis** Omaheke, E Namibia
'Amīq, Wadi *see* 'Āmij, Wādī
148 J7 **Amīrābād** Īlām, NW Iran
Amirante Bank *see* Amirante Ridge
181 N6 **Amirante Basin** *undersea feature* W Indian Ocean
181 N6 **Amirante Islands** *var.* Amirantes Group. *island group* C Seychelles
181 N7 **Amirante Ridge** *var.* Amirante Bank. *undersea feature* W Indian Ocean
Amirantes Group *see* Amirante Islands
181 N7 **Amirante Trench** *undersea feature* W Indian Ocean
176 Z12 **Amisibil** Irian Jaya, E Indonesia
9 U13 **Amisk Lake** ◎ Saskatchewan, C Canada
Amistad, Presa de la *see* Amistad Reservoir
27 O12 **Amistad Reservoir** *var.* Presa de la Amistad. ⊡ Mexico/USA
Amisus *see* Samsun
24 K8 **Amite** *var.* Amite City. Louisiana, S USA
Amite City *see* Amite
29 T12 **Amity** Arkansas, C USA
160 H11 **Amla** *prev.* Amulla. Madhya Pradesh, C India
40 I17 **Amlia Island** *island* Aleutian Islands, Alaska, USA
99 I18 **Amlwch** NW Wales, UK
Ammaia *see* Portalegre
144 H10 **'Ammān** *var.* Amman; *anc.* Philadelphia, *Bibl.* Rabbah Ammon, Rabbath Ammon. ● (Jordan) 'Ammān, NW Jordan
144 H10 **'Ammān** *off.* Muḥāfaẓat 'Ammān. ◐ *governorate* NW Jordan
95 N14 **Ammänsaari** Oulu, E Finland
94 H13 **Ammarnäs** Västerbotten, N Sweden
207 O15 **Ammassalik** *var.* Angmagssalik. S Greenland
103 K24 **Ammer** ≈ SE Germany
103 K24 **Ammersee** ◎ SE Germany
100 J13 **Ammerzoden** Gelderland, C Netherlands
Ammóchostos *see* Gazimağusa
Ammóchostos, Kólpos *see* Gazimağusa Körfezi
Amnok-kang *see* Yalu
Amoea *see* Portalegre
Amoentai *see* Amuntai
Amoerang *see* Amurang
149 O4 **Āmol** *var.* Amul. Māzandarān, N Iran
117 K21 **Amorgós** Amorgós, Kykládes, Greece, Aegean Sea
117 K22 **Amorgós** *island* Kykládes, Greece, Aegean Sea
25 N3 **Amory** Mississippi, S USA
10 I13 **Amos** Québec, SE Canada
97 G15 **Åmot** Buskerud, S Norway
97 E15 **Åmot** Telemark, S Norway
97 J15 **Åmotfors** Värmland, C Sweden
78 L10 **Amourj** Hodh ech Chargui, SE Mauritania
Amoy *see* Xiamen
180 H7 **Ampanihy** Toliara, SW Madagascar
161 L25 **Ampara** *var.* Amparai. Eastern Province, E Sri Lanka
180 J4 **Amparafaravola** Toamasina, E Madagascar
Amparai *see* Ampara
62 M9 **Amparo** São Paulo, S Brazil
180 J5 **Ampasimanolotra** Toamasina, E Madagascar
59 H17 **Ampato, Nevado** ▲ S Peru
103 L23 **Amper** ≈ SE Germany
66 M9 **Ampère Seamount** *undersea feature* E Atlantic Ocean
Amphipolis *see* Amfípoli
178 M10 **Amphitrite Group** *island group* N Paracel Islands
176 U15 **Amplawas** *var.* Emplawas. Pulau Babar, E Indonesia
107 U7 **Amposta** Cataluña, NE Spain
13 V7 **Amqui** Québec, SE Canada
147 O14 **'Amrān** W Yemen
Amraoti *see* Amrāvati
160 H12 **Amrāvati** *prev.* Amraoti. Mahārāshtra, C India
160 C11 **Amreli** Gujarāt, W India
110 H6 **Amriswil** Thurgau, NE Switzerland
144 H5 **'Amrīt** *ruins* Ṭarṭūs, W Syria
158 H7 **Amritsar** Punjab, N India
158 I10 **Amroha** Uttar Pradesh, N India
102 G7 **Amrum** *island* NW Germany
95 I15 **Åmsele** Västerbotten, N Sweden
100 I10 **Amstelveen** Noord-Holland, C Netherlands
100 I10 **Amsterdam** ● (Netherlands) Noord-Holland, C Netherlands
20 K10 **Amsterdam** New York, NE USA
181 Q11 **Amsterdam Fracture Zone** *tectonic feature* S Indian Ocean
181 R11 **Amsterdam Island** *island* NE French Southern and Antarctic Territories
111 U4 **Amstetten** Niederösterreich, N Austria
80 J11 **Am Timan** Salamat, SE Chad
152 L12 **Amu-Bukhoro Kanali** *var.* Aral-Bukhorskiy Kanal. *canal* C Uzbekistan
145 O1 **'Āmūdah** *var.* Amude. Al Ḥasakah, N Syria
152 M14 **Amu-Dar'ya** Lebapskiy Velayat, NE Turkmenistan
153 O15 **Amu Darya** *Rus.* Amudar'ya, *Taj.* Dar"yoi Amu, *Turkm.* Amyderya, *Uzb.* Amudaryo; *anc.* Oxus. ≈ C Asia
Amudar'ya/Amudaryo/Amu, Dar"yoi *see* Amu Darya
Amude *see* 'Āmūdah
146 L3 **'Amūd, Jabal al** ▲ NW Saudi Arabia
40 J17 **Amukta Island** *island* Aleutian Islands, Alaska, USA
40 I17 **Amukta Pass** *strait* Aleutian Islands, Alaska, USA
Amul *see* Āmol
Amulla *see* Amla
Amundsen Basin *see* Fram Basin
205 X3 **Amundsen Bay** *bay* Antarctica
205 P10 **Amundsen Coast** *physical region* Antarctica
15 H2 **Amundsen Gulf** *gulf* Northwest Territories, N Canada
199 L16 **Amundsen Plain** *undersea feature* S Pacific Ocean
205 Q9 **Amundsen-Scott** *US research station* Antarctica
204 J11 **Amundsen Sea** *sea* S Pacific Ocean
96 M12 **Amungen** ◎ C Sweden
175 N10 **Amuntai** *prev.* Amoentai. Borneo, C Indonesia
133 W6 **Amur** *Chin.* Heilong Jiang. ≈ China/Russian Federation
175 Rr7 **Amurang** *prev.* Amoerang. Sulawesi, C Indonesia
175 Rr7 **Amurang, Teluk** *bay* Sulawesi, C Indonesia
107 O3 **Amurrio** País Vasco, N Spain
127 Nn15 **Amursk** Khabarovskiy Kray, SE Russian Federation
126 M14 **Amurskaya Oblast'** ◐ *province* SE Russian Federation
82 G7 **'Amur, Wadi** ≈ NE Sudan
117 C17 **Amvrakikós Kólpos** *gulf* W Greece
Amvrosiyevka *see* Amvrosiyivka
119 X8 **Amvrosiyivka** *Rus.* Amvrosiyevka. Donets'ka Oblast', SE Ukraine
Amyderya *see* Amu Darya
116 E13 **Amýntaio** *var.* Amindeo; *prev.* Amíndaion. Dytikí Makedonía, N Greece
12 B6 **Amyot** Ontario, S Canada
203 U10 **Anaa** *atoll* Îles Tuamotu, C French Polynesia
Anabanoea *see* Anabanua
175 Pp12 **Anabanua** *prev.* Anabanoea. Sulawesi, C Indonesia
201 R8 **Anabar** NE Nauru
126 K7 **Anabar** ≈ NE Russian Federation
An Abhainn Mhór *see* Blackwater
57 O6 **Anaco** Anzoátegui, NE Venezuela
35 Q10 **Anaconda** Montana, NW USA
34 H7 **Anacortes** Washington, NW USA
28 M11 **Anadarko** Oklahoma, C USA
116 N12 **Ana Dere** ≈ NW Turkey
106 G8 **Anadia** Aveiro, N Portugal
Anadolu Dağları *see* Doğu Karadeniz Dağları
127 Pp5 **Anadyr'** Chukotskiy Avtonomnyy Okrug, NE Russian Federation
127 P5 **Anadyr'** ≈ NE Russian Federation
Anadyr, Gulf of *see* Anadyrskiy Zaliv
133 X4 **Anadyrskiy Khrebet** *var.* Chukot Range. ▲▲ NE Russian Federation
127 Q4 **Anadyrskiy Zaliv** *Eng.* Gulf of Anadyr. *gulf* NE Russian Federation
117 K22 **Anáfi** *anc.* Anaphe. *island* Kykládes, Greece, Aegean Sea
109 J15 **Anagni** Lazio, C Italy
'Ānah *see* 'Annah
37 T15 **Anaheim** California, W USA
8 L15 **Anahim Lake** British Columbia, SW Canada
40 B8 **Anahola** Kauai, Hawaii, USA, C Pacific Ocean
27 X11 **Anahuac** Texas, SW USA
43 O7 **Anáhuac** Nuevo León, NE Mexico
161 G22 **Anai Mudi** ▲ S India
Anaiza *see* 'Unayzah
161 M15 **Anakāpalle** Andhra Pradesh, E India
203 W15 **Anakena, Playa de** *beach* Easter Island, Chile, E Pacific Ocean
41 Q7 **Anaktuvuk Pass** Alaska, USA
41 Q6 **Anaktuvuk River** ≈ Alaska, USA
180 J3 **Analalava** Mahajanga, NW Madagascar
46 F6 **Ana Maria, Golfo de** *gulf* C Cuba
Anambas Islands *see* Anambas, Kepulauan
174 I5 **Anambas, Kepulauan** *var.* Anambas Islands. *island group* W Indonesia
79 U17 **Anambra** ◐ *state* SE Nigeria
31 N4 **Anamoose** North Dakota, N USA
31 Y13 **Anamosa** Iowa, C USA
142 H17 **Anamur** İçel, S Turkey
142 H17 **Anamur Burnu** *headland* S Turkey
170 Ff16 **Anan** Tokushima, Shikoku, SW Japan
160 O12 **Ānandadur** Orissa, E India
161 H18 **Anantapur** Andhra Pradesh, S India
158 H5 **Anantnāg** *var.* Islamabad. Jammu and Kashmir, NW India
Ananyev *see* Anan'yiv
119 O9 **Anan'yiv** *Rus.* Ananyev. Odes'ka Oblast', SW Ukraine
130 J14 **Anapa** Krasnodarskiy Kray, SW Russian Federation
Anaphe *see* Anáfi
61 K18 **Anápolis** Goiás, C Brazil
149 R10 **Anār** Kermān, C Iran
Anár *see* Inari
149 P7 **Anārak** Eṣfahān, C Iran
Anar Dara *see* Anār Darreh
154 J7 **Anār Darreh** *var.* Anar Dara. Farāh, W Afghanistan
Anárjohka *see* Inarijoki
25 X9 **Anastasia Island** *island* Florida, SE USA
196 K7 **Anatahan** *island* C Northern Mariana Islands
132 M6 **Anatolia** *plateau* C Turkey
88 F14 **Anatolian Plate** *tectonic feature* Asia/Europe
116 H13 **Anatolikí Makedonía kai Thráki** *Eng.* Macedonia East and Thrace. ◐ *region* NE Greece
197 D17 **Anatom** *var.* Aneityum; *prev.* Kéamu. *island* S Vanuatu
64 L8 **Añatuya** Santiago del Estero, N Argentina
An Baile Meánach *see* Ballymena
An Bhearú *see* Barrow
An Bhóinn *see* Boyne
An Blascaod Mór *see* Great Blasket Island
An Cabhán *see* Cavan
An Caisleán Nua *see* Newcastle
An Caisleán Riabhach *see* Castlereagh, Northern Ireland, UK
An Caisleán Riabhach *see* Castlerea, Ireland
58 C13 **Ancash** *off.* Departamento de Ancash. ◐ *department* W Peru
An Cathair *see* Caher
104 J8 **Ancenis** Loire-Atlantique, NW France
An Chanáil Ríoga *see* Royal Canal
An Cheacha *see* Caha Mountains
41 R11 **Anchorage** Alaska, USA
41 R12 **Anchorage** ✕ Alaska, USA
41 Q13 **Anchor Point** Alaska, USA
An Chorr Chríochach *see* Cookstown
67 M24 **Anchorstack Point** *headland* W Tristan da Cunha
An Clár *see* Clare
An Clochán *see* Clifden
An Clochán Liath *see* Dunglow
25 U12 **Anclote Keys** *island group* Florida, SE USA
An Cóbh *see* Cobh
59 J17 **Ancohuma, Nevado de** ▲ W Bolivia
An Comar *see* Comber
59 D14 **Ancón** Lima, W Peru
108 J12 **Ancona** Marche, C Italy
Ancuabe *see* Ancuabi
84 Q13 **Ancuabi** *var.* Ancuabe. Cabo Delgado, NE Mozambique
65 F17 **Ancud** *prev.* San Carlos de Ancud. Los Lagos, S Chile
65 G17 **Ancud, Golfo de** *gulf* S Chile
Ancyra *see* Ankara
169 V8 **Anda** Heilongjiang, NE China
59 G16 **Andahuaylas** Apurímac, S Peru
An Daingean *see* Dingle
159 R15 **Andāl** West Bengal, NE India
96 E9 **Åndalsnes** Møre og Romsdal, S Norway
106 K13 **Andalucía** *Eng.* Andalusia. ◐ *autonomous community* S Spain
25 P7 **Andalusia** Alabama, S USA
Andalusia *see* Andalucía
157 Q21 **Andaman and Nicobar Islands** *var.* Andamans and Nicobars. ◐ *union territory* India, NE Indian Ocean
181 T4 **Andaman Basin** *undersea feature* NE Indian Ocean
157 P19 **Andaman Islands** *island group* India, NE Indian Ocean
181 T4 **Andaman Sea** *sea* NE Indian Ocean
59 K19 **Andamarca** Oruro, C Bolivia
176 V10 **Andamata** Irian Jaya, E Indonesia
190 H5 **Andamooka** South Australia
147 Y9 **'Andām, Wādī** *seasonal river* NE Oman
180 J3 **Andapa** Antsiranana, NE Madagascar
155 R4 **Andarāb** *var.* Banow. Baghlān, NE Afghanistan
Andarbag *see* Andarbogh
153 S13 **Andarbogh** *Rus.* Andarbag, Anderbak. S Tajikistan
111 Z5 **Andau** Burgenland, E Austria
Andaung Pech *see* Bâ Kêv
110 I10 **Andeer** Graubünden, S Switzerland
94 H9 **Andenes** Nordland, C Norway
101 J20 **Andenne** Namur, SE Belgium
79 S11 **Andéramboukane** Gao, E Mali
Anderbak *see* Andarbogh
101 G18 **Anderlecht** Brussels, C Belgium
101 G21 **Anderlues** Hainaut, S Belgium
110 G9 **Andermatt** Uri, C Switzerland
103 E17 **Andernach** *anc.* Antunnacum. Rheinland-Pfalz, SW Germany
196 D15 **Andersen Air Force Base** *air base* NE Guam
41 R9 **Anderson** Alaska, USA
37 N4 **Anderson** California, W USA
33 P13 **Anderson** Indiana, N USA
29 R8 **Anderson** Missouri, C USA
23 P11 **Anderson** South Carolina, SE USA
27 V10 **Anderson** Texas, SW USA
15 Gg3 **Anderson** ≈ Northwest Territories, NW Canada
97 K20 **Anderstorp** Jönköping, S Sweden
56 D9 **Andes** Antioquia, W Colombia
49 P7 **Andes** ▲▲ W South America
31 P12 **Andes, Lake** ◎ South Dakota, N USA
94 H9 **Andfjorden** *fjord* E Norwegian Sea
161 H16 **Andhra Pradesh** ◐ *state* E India
100 J8 **Andijk** Noord-Holland, NW Netherlands
153 S10 **Andijon** *Rus.* Andizhan. Andijon Wiloyati, E Uzbekistan
153 S10 **Andijon Wiloyati** *Rus.* Andizhanskaya Oblast'. ◐ *province* E Uzbekistan
Andikíthira *see* Antikýthira
180 J4 **Andilamena** Toamasina, C Madagascar
148 L8 **Andīmeshk** *var.* Andimishk; *prev.* Salehābād. Khūzestān, SW Iran
Andimishk *see* Andīmeshk
Andipáros *see* Antíparos
Andipaxi *see* Antípaxoi
Andípsara *see* Antípsara
142 L16 **Andırın** Kahramanmaraş, S Turkey
164 J8 **Andirlangar** Xinjiang Uygur Zizhiqu, NW China
Andírrion *see* Antírrio
Ándissa *see* Ántissa
Andizhan *see* Andijon
Andizhanskaya Oblast' *see* Andijon Wiloyati
155 N2 **Andkhvoy** Fāryāb, N Afghanistan
107 Q2 **Andoain** País Vasco, N Spain
176 W9 **Andoi** Irian Jaya, E Indonesia
169 Y15 **Andong** *Jap.* Antō. E South Korea
111 R4 **Andorf** Oberösterreich, N Austria
107 S7 **Andorra** Aragón, NE Spain
107 V4 **Andorra** *off.* Principality of Andorra, *Cat.* Valls d'Andorra, *Fr.* Vallée d'Andorre. ◆ *monarchy* SW Europe
Andorra *see* Andorra la Vella
107 V4 **Andorra la Vella** *var.* Andorra, *Fr.* Andorre la Vielle, *Sp.* Andorra la Vieja. ● (Andorra) C Andorra
Andorra la Vieja *see* Andorra la Vella
Andorra, Valls d'/Andorre, Vallée d' *see* Andorra
Andorre la Vielle *see* Andorra la Vella
99 M22 **Andover** S England, UK
29 N6 **Andover** Kansas, C USA
94 G10 **Andøya** *island* C Norway
62 I8 **Andradina** São Paulo, S Brazil
Andraitx *see* Andratx
41 N10 **Andreafsky River** ≈ Alaska, USA
40 H17 **Andreanof Islands** *island group* Aleutian Islands, Alaska, USA
128 H16 **Andreapol'** Tverskaya Oblast', W Russian Federation
Andreas, Cape *see* Zafer Burnu
Andreevka *see* Andreyevka
23 N10 **Andrews** North Carolina, SE USA
23 T13 **Andrews** South Carolina, SE USA
26 M7 **Andrews** Texas, SW USA
181 N5 **Andrew Tablemount** *var.* Gora Andryu. *undersea feature* W Indian Ocean
151 W13 **Andreyevka** *Kaz.* Andreevka. Taldykorgan, SW Kazakhstan
109 N17 **Andria** Puglia, SE Italy
115 K16 **Andrijevica** Montenegro, SW Yugoslavia
117 E20 **Andrítsaina** Pelopónnisos, S Greece
An Droichead Nua *see* Newbridge
Androna *see* Khirbat al Andarīn
Andropov *see* Rybinsk
117 J19 **Ándros** Ándros, Kykládes, Greece, Aegean Sea
117 J20 **Ándros** *island* Kykládes, Greece, Aegean Sea
21 O7 **Androscoggin River** ≈ Maine/New Hampshire, NE USA
46 F3 **Andros Island** *island* NW Bahamas
131 R7 **Androsovka** Samarskaya Oblast', W Russian Federation
46 G3 **Andros Town** Andros Island, NW Bahamas
161 D21 **Āndrott Island** *island* Lakshadweep, India, N Indian Ocean
119 N5 **Andrushivka** Zhytomyrs'ka Oblast', N Ukraine
113 K17 **Andrychów** Bielsko-Biała, S Poland
Andryu, Gora *see* Andrew Tablemount
94 I10 **Andselv** Troms, N Norway
81 O17 **Andudu** Haut-Zaïre, NE Zaire
107 N13 **Andújar** *anc.* Illiturgis. Andalucía, SW Spain
84 C12 **Andulo** Bié, W Angola
105 Q14 **Anduze** Gard, S France
An Earagail *see* Errigal
97 L19 **Aneby** Jönköping, S Sweden
Anécho *see* Aného
79 Q9 **Anéfis** Kidal, NE Mali
47 U8 **Anegada** *island* NE British Virgin Islands
63 B25 **Anegada, Bahía** *bay* E Argentina
47 U9 **Anegada Passage** *passage* Anguilla/British Virgin Islands
79 R17 **Aného** *var.* Anécho; *prev.* Petit-Popo. S Togo
Aneityum *see* Anatom
119 N10 **Anenii Noi** *Rus.* Novyye Aneny. C Moldova
194 L12 **Anepmete** New Britain, E PNG
107 U4 **Aneto** ▲ NE Spain
Ānew *see* Annau
Ānewetak *see* Enewetak Atoll
79 Y8 **Aney** Agadez, NE Niger
An Fheoir *see* Nore
126 Ii13 **Angara** ≈ C Russian Federation
126 J15 **Angarsk** Irkutskaya Oblast', S Russian Federation
95 G17 **Ånge** Västernorrland, C Sweden
Ángel *see* Úhlava
42 D4 **Ángel de la Guarda, Isla** *island* NW Mexico
179 P10 **Angeles** *off.* Angeles City. Luzon, N Philippines
Angeles City *see* Angeles
Angel Falls *see* Ángel, Salto
97 J22 **Ängelholm** Kristianstad, S Sweden
63 A17 **Angélica** Santa Fe, C Argentina
27 W8 **Angelina River** ≈ Texas, SW USA
57 Q9 **Ángel, Salto** *Eng.* Angel Falls. *waterfall* E Venezuela
97 M15 **Ängelsberg** Västmanland, C Sweden
37 P8 **Angels Camp** California, W USA
111 W7 **Anger** Steiermark, SE Austria
Angerapp *see* Ozersk
Angerburg *see* Węgorzewo
95 H15 **Ångermanälven** ≈ N Sweden
102 P11 **Angermünde** Brandenburg, NE Germany
104 K7 **Angers** *anc.* Juliomagus. Maine-et-Loire, NW France
13 W7 **Angers** ≈ Québec, SE Canada
95 J16 **Ängesön** *island* N Sweden
Angistro *see* Ágkistro
116 H13 **Angítis** ≈ NE Greece
178 J14 **Ângk Tasaôm** *prev.* Angtassom. Takêv, S Cambodia
193 C25 **Anglem, Mount** ▲ Stewart Island, Southland, SW NZ
99 I18 **Anglesey** *cultural region* NW Wales, UK
99 I18 **Anglesey** *island* NW Wales, UK
104 I15 **Anglet** Pyrénées-Atlantiques, SW France
27 W12 **Angleton** Texas, SW USA
Anglia *see* England
12 H9 **Angliers** Québec, SE Canada
Anglo-Egyptian Sudan *see* Sudan
Angmagssalik *see* Ammassalik
178 I8 **Ang Nam Ngum** ◎ C Laos
81 N16 **Ango** Haut-Zaïre, N Zaire
85 Q15 **Angoche** Nampula, E Mozambique
65 G14 **Angol** Araucanía, C Chile
33 Q11 **Angola** Indiana, N USA
84 A9 **Angola** *off.* Republic of Angola; *prev.* People's Republic of Angola, Portuguese West Africa. ◆ *republic* SW Africa
67 P15 **Angola Basin** *undersea feature* E Atlantic Ocean
41 X13 **Angoon** Admiralty Island, Alaska, USA
153 O14 **Angor** Surkhondaryo Wiloyati, S Uzbekistan
Angora *see* Ankara
194 H10 **Angoram** East Sepik, NW PNG
42 H8 **Angostura** Sinaloa, C Mexico
Angostura *see* Ciudad Bolívar
43 U17 **Angostura, Presa de la** ⊡ SE Mexico
30 J11 **Angostura Reservoir** ⊡ South Dakota, N USA
104 L11 **Angoulême** *anc.* Iculisma. Charente, W France
104 K11 **Angoumois** *cultural region* W France
66 O2 **Angra do Heroísmo** Terceira, Azores, Portugal, NE Atlantic Ocean

◆ Country ● Country Capital ◇ Dependent Territory ○ Dependent Territory Capital ◐ Administrative Region ✕ International Airport ▲ Mountain ▲▲ Mountain Range Ⓡ Volcano ≈ River ◎ Lake ⊡ Reservoir

◆ COUNTRY   ◇ DEPENDENT TERRITORY   ★ ADMINISTRATIVE REGION   ▲ MOUNTAIN   ✦ VOLCANO   ⊗ LAKE
● COUNTRY CAPITAL   ○ DEPENDENT TERRITORY CAPITAL   ✈ INTERNATIONAL AIRPORT   ▲ MOUNTAIN RANGE   ⚓ RIVER   ⊞ RESERVOIR

Arcos de la Frontera – ‘Asīr

106 K15 **Arcos de la Frontera** Andalucía, S Spain
106 G5 **Arcos de Valdevez** Viana do Castelo, N Portugal
61 P15 **Arcoverde** Pernambuco, E Brazil
104 H5 **Arcovest, Pointe de l'** *headland* NW France
Arctic-Mid Oceanic Ridge *see* Nansen Cordillera
207 R8 **Arctic Ocean** *ocean*
14 G4 **Arctic Red River** ⁓ Northwest Territories/Yukon Territory, NW Canada
Arctic Red River *see* Tsiigehtchic
41 S6 **Arctic Village** Alaska, USA
204 H1 **Arctowski** *Polish research station* South Shetland Islands, Antarctica
116 L12 **Arda** *var.* Ardhas, *Gk.* Ardas. ⁓ Bulgaria/Greece *see also* Ardas
148 L2 **Ardabīl** *var.* Ardebil. Ardabīl, NW Iran
148 L2 **Ardabīl** *off.* Ostān-e Ardabīl. ◆ *province* NW Iran
143 R11 **Ardahan** Kars, NE Turkey
149 P8 **Ardakān** Yazd, C Iran
96 E12 **Årdalstangen** Sogn og Fjordane, S Norway
143 R11 **Ardanuç** Artvin, NE Turkey
116 L12 **Ardas** *var.* Ardhas, *Bul.* Arda. ⁓ Bulgaria/Greece *see also* Arda
144 I13 **Arḍ aṣ Ṣawwān** *var.* Ardh es Suwwān. *plain* S Jordan
131 P5 **Ardatov** Respublika Mordoviya, W Russian Federation
12 G12 **Ardbeg** Ontario, S Canada
Ardeal *see* Transylvania
Ardebil *see* Ardabīl
105 Q13 **Ardèche** ⁓ C France
105 Q13 **Ardèche** ◆ *department* E France
99 F17 **Ardee** *Ir.* Baile Átha Fhirdhia. NE Ireland
105 Q3 **Ardennes** ◆ *department* NE France
101 J23 **Ardennes** *physical region* Belgium/France
143 Q11 **Ardeşen** Rize, NE Turkey
149 O7 **Ardestān** *var.* Ardistan. Eşfahān, C Iran
110 I9 **Ardez** Graubünden, SE Switzerland
Ardhas *see* Arda/Ardas
Ardh es Suwwān *see* Arḍ aṣ Ṣawwān
106 I12 **Ardila, Ribeira de** *Sp.* Ardilla. ⁓ Portugal/Spain *see also* Ardilla
9 T17 **Ardill** Saskatchewan, S Canada
106 I12 **Ardilla** *Port.* Ribeira de Ardila. ⁓ Portugal/Spain *see also* Ardila, Ribeira de
42 M11 **Ardilla, Cerro la** ▲ C Mexico
116 J12 **Ardino** Khaskovska Oblast, S Bulgaria
Ardistan *see* Ardestān
191 P9 **Ardlethan** New South Wales, SE Australia
Ard Mhacha *see* Armagh
25 P1 **Ardmore** Alabama, S USA
29 N13 **Ardmore** Oklahoma, C USA
22 J10 **Ardmore** Tennessee, S USA
98 G10 **Ardnamurchan, Point of** *headland* N Scotland, UK
101 C17 **Ardooie** West-Vlaanderen, W Belgium
190 I9 **Ardrossan** South Australia
118 H9 **Ardusat** *Hung.* Erdőszáda. Maramureş, N Romania
95 F16 **Åre** Jämtland, C Sweden
81 P16 **Arebi** Haut-Zaïre, NE Zaire
47 T5 **Arecibo** C Puerto Rico
176 W10 **Aredo** Irian Jaya, E Indonesia
61 P14 **Areia Branca** Rio Grande do Norte, E Brazil
121 O14 **Arekhawsk** *Rus.* Orekhovsk. Vitsyebskaya Voblasts', N Belarus
Arel *see* Arlon
Arelas/Arelate *see* Arles
Arenal, Embalse de *see* Arenal Laguna
44 L12 **Arenal Laguna** *var.* Embalse de Arenal. ◎ NW Costa Rica
44 L13 **Arenal, Volcán** ⚠ NW Costa Rica
36 K6 **Arena, Point** *headland* California, W USA
61 H17 **Arenápolis** Mato Grosso, W Brazil
42 G10 **Arena, Punta** *headland* W Mexico
106 L8 **Arenas de San Pedro** Castilla-León, N Spain
65 I24 **Arenas, Punta de** *headland* S Argentina
63 B20 **Arenaza** Buenos Aires, E Argentina
97 F17 **Arendal** Aust-Agder, S Norway
101 J16 **Arendonk** Antwerpen, N Belgium
45 T15 **Arenosa** Panamá, N Panama
Arensburg *see* Kuressaare
107 W5 **Arenys de Mar** Cataluña, NE Spain
108 C9 **Arenzano** Liguria, NW Italy
117 F22 **Areópoli** *prev.* Areópolis. Pelopónnisos, S Greece
Areópolis *see* Areópoli
59 H18 **Arequipa** Arequipa, SE Peru
59 G17 **Arequipa** *off.* Departamento de Arequipa. ◆ *department* SW Peru
63 B19 **Arequito** Santa Fe, C Argentina
106 M7 **Arévalo** Castilla-León, N Spain
108 H12 **Arezzo** *anc.* Arretium. Toscana, C Italy
107 Q4 **Arga** ⁓ N Spain
Argaeus *see* Erciyes Dağı
117 G17 **Argalastí** Thessalía, C Greece
107 O10 **Argamasilla de Alba** Castilla-La Mancha, C Spain
164 L8 **Argan** Xinjiang Uygur Zizhiqu, NW China
107 O8 **Arganda** Madrid, C Spain
106 H8 **Arganil** Coimbra, N Portugal
179 Qq14 **Argao** Cebu, C Philippines
159 V15 **Argartala** Tripura, NE India
126 K9 **Arga-Sala** ⁓ NE Russian Federation
105 P17 **Argelès-sur-Mer** Pyrénées-Orientales, S France
105 T15 **Argens** ⁓ SE France
108 H9 **Argenta** Emilia-Romagna, N Italy
104 K5 **Argentan** Orne, N France
105 N12 **Argentat** Corrèze, C France
108 A9 **Argentera** Piemonte, NE Italy
105 N5 **Argenteuil** Val-d'Oise, N France
64 K13 **Argentina** *off.* Republic of Argentina. ◆ *republic* S South America
Argentina Basin *see* Argentine Basin
Argentine Abyssal Plain *see* Argentine Plain
67 I19 **Argentine Basin** *var.* Argentina Basin. *undersea feature* SW Atlantic Ocean
67 I20 **Argentine Plain** *var.* Argentine Abyssal Plain. *undersea feature* SW Atlantic Ocean
Argentine Rise *see* Falkland Plateau
65 H22 **Argentino, Lago** ◎ S Argentina
104 K8 **Argenton-Château** Deux-Sèvres, W France
104 M9 **Argenton-sur-Creuse** Indre, C France
Argentoratum *see* Strasbourg
118 I12 **Argeş** ◆ *county* S Romania
118 K14 **Argeş** ⁓ S Romania
155 O8 **Arghandāb, Daryā-ye** ⁓ SE Afghanistan
Arghastān *see* Arghestān
155 O8 **Arghestān** *Pash.* Arghastān. ⁓ SE Afghanistan
Argirocastro *see* Gjirokastër
82 E7 **Argo** Northern, N Sudan
181 P7 **Argo Fracture Zone** *tectonic feature* C Indian Ocean
117 F20 **Argolikós Kólpos** *gulf* S Greece
105 R4 **Argonne** *physical region* NE France
174 Mm15 **Argopuro, Gunung** ▲ Jawa, S Indonesia
117 F20 **Árgos** Pelopónnisos, S Greece
145 S1 **Argōsh** N Iraq
117 D14 **Árgos Orestikó** Dytikí Makedonía, N Greece
117 B19 **Argostóli** *var.* Argostólion. Kefallinía, Iónioi Nísoi, Greece, C Mediterranean Sea
Argostólion *see* Argostóli
Argovie *see* Aargau
37 O14 **Arguello, Point** *headland* California, W USA
131 P16 **Argun** Chechenskaya Respublika, SW Russian Federation
163 T2 **Argun** *Chin.* Ergun He, *Rus.* Argun'. ⁓ China/Russian Federation
79 T12 **Argungu** Kebbi, NW Nigeria
168 J9 **Arguut** Övörhangay, C Mongolia
189 N3 **Argyle, Lake** *salt lake* Western Australia
98 G12 **Argyll** *cultural region* W Scotland, UK
Argyrokastron *see* Gjirokastër
168 I7 **Arhangay** ◆ *province* C Mongolia
Arhangelos *see* Archángelos
97 P14 **Arholma** Stockholm, C Sweden
97 G22 **Århus** *var.* Aarhus. Århus, C Denmark
97 G22 **Århus** ◆ *county* C Denmark
145 T1 **Ārī** E Iraq
194 M12 **Aria** ⁓ New Britain, E PNG
Aria *see* Herāt
170 C13 **Ariake-kai** *bay* NE East China Sea
85 F22 **Ariamsvlei** Karas, SE Namibia
109 L17 **Ariano Irpino** Campania, S Italy
56 F11 **Ariari, Río** ⁓ C Colombia
157 K19 **Ari Atoll** *atoll* C Maldives
79 P11 **Aribinda** N Burkina
64 G2 **Arica** *hist.* San Marcos de Arica. Tarapacá, N Chile
56 H16 **Arica** Amazonas, S Colombia
64 G2 **Arica** ✕ Tarapacá, N Chile
170 G16 **Arida** Wakayama, Honshū, SW Japan
116 E13 **Aridaía** *var.* Aridea, Aridhaía. Dytikí Makedonía, N Greece
Aridea *see* Aridaía
180 I15 **Aride, Île** *island* Inner Islands, NE Seychelles
Aridhaía *see* Aridaía
105 N17 **Ariège** ◆ *department* S France
104 M16 **Ariège** *var.* la Riege. ⁓ Andorra/France
118 H11 **Arieş** ⁓ W Romania
155 U10 **Ārifwāla** Punjab, E Pakistan
Ariguaní *see* El Difícil
144 G11 **Arīḥā** Al Karak, W Jordan
144 I3 **Arīḥā** *var.* Arīhā. Idlib, W Syria
Arīḥā *see* Jericho
39 W4 **Arikaree River** ⁓ Colorado/Nebraska, C USA
170 Bb12 **Arikawa** Nagasaki, Nakadōri-jima, SW Japan
114 L13 **Arilje** Serbia, W Yugoslavia
47 U14 **Arima** Trinidad, Trinidad and Tobago
Arime *see* Al 'Arīmah
Ariminum *see* Rimini
61 H16 **Arinos, Rio** ⁓ W Brazil
42 M14 **Ario de Rosales** *var.* Ario de Rosáles. Michoacán de Ocampo, SW Mexico
120 F12 **Ariogala** Raseiniai, C Lithuania
49 T7 **Aripuanã** ⁓ W Brazil
61 E15 **Ariquemes** Rondônia, W Brazil
124 R5 **'Arīsh, Wādi el** ⁓ NE Egypt
56 K6 **Arismendi** Barinas, C Venezuela
8 J14 **Aristazabal Island** *island* SW Canada
62 F13 **Aristóbulo del Valle** Misiones, NE Argentina
180 I5 **Arivonimamo** ✕ (Antananarivo) Antananarivo, C Madagascar
Arixang *see* Wenquan
107 Q6 **Ariza** Aragón, NE Spain
64 I6 **Arizaro, Salar de** *salt lake* NW Argentina
64 K13 **Arizona** San Luis, C Argentina
38 J12 **Arizona** *off.* State of Arizona; also known as Copper State, Grand Canyon State. ◆ *state* SW USA
42 G4 **Arizpe** Sonora, NW Mexico
97 J16 **Årjäng** Värmland, C Sweden
149 P8 **Arjenān** Yazd, C Iran
94 I13 **Arjeplog** Norrbotten, N Sweden
56 E5 **Arjona** Bolívar, N Colombia
107 N13 **Arjona** Andalucía, S Spain
127 N11 **Arka** Khabarovskiy Kray, E Russian Federation
24 L2 **Arkabutla Lake** ▣ Mississippi, S USA
131 O7 **Arkadak** Saratovskaya Oblast', W Russian Federation
29 T13 **Arkadelphia** Arkansas, C USA
117 J25 **Arkalochóri** *prev.* Arkalohori, Arkalokhórion. Kríti, Greece, E Mediterranean Sea
Arkalohori/Arkalokhórion *see* Arkalochóri
151 O10 **Arkalyk** *Kaz.* Arqalyq. Turgay, C Kazakhstan
29 U10 **Arkansas** *off.* State of Arkansas; also known as The Land of Opportunity. ◆ *state* S USA
29 W14 **Arkansas City** Arkansas, C USA
29 O7 **Arkansas City** Kansas, C USA
18 Kk10 **Arkansas River** ⁓ C USA
190 J5 **Arkaroola** South Australia
Arkhángelos *see* Archángelos
128 L8 **Arkhangel'sk** *Eng.* Archangel. Arkhangel'skaya Oblast', NW Russian Federation
128 L9 **Arkhangel'skaya Oblast'** ◆ *province* NW Russian Federation
131 O14 **Arkhangel'skoye** Stavropol'skiy Kray, SW Russian Federation
127 N16 **Arkhara** Amurskaya Oblast', S Russian Federation
99 G19 **Arklow** *Ir.* An tInbhear Mór. SE Ireland
117 M20 **Arkoí** *island* Dodekánisos, Greece, Aegean Sea
29 R11 **Arkoma** Oklahoma, C USA
102 O7 **Arkona, Kap** *headland* NE Germany
97 N17 **Arkösund** Östergötland, S Sweden
126 H4 **Arkticheskogo Instituta, Ostrova** *island* N Russian Federation
97 O15 **Arlanda** ✕ (Stockholm) Stockholm, C Sweden
152 C11 **Arlan, Gora** ▲ W Turkmenistan
107 O5 **Arlanza** ⁓ N Spain
107 N5 **Arlanzón** ⁓ N Spain
105 R15 **Arles** *var.* Arles-sur-Rhône; *anc.* Arelas, Arelate. Bouches-du-Rhône, SE France
Arles-sur-Rhône *see* Arles
105 O17 **Arles-sur-Tech** Pyrénées-Orientales, S France
31 U9 **Arlington** Minnesota, N USA
31 R15 **Arlington** Nebraska, C USA
34 J11 **Arlington** Oregon, NW USA
31 R10 **Arlington** South Dakota, N USA
22 E10 **Arlington** Tennessee, S USA
27 T6 **Arlington** Texas, SW USA
23 W4 **Arlington** Virginia, NE USA
34 H7 **Arlington** Washington, NW USA
32 M10 **Arlington Heights** Illinois, N USA
79 U8 **Arlit** Agadez, C Niger
101 L24 **Arlon** *Dut.* Aarlen, *Ger.* Arel; *Lat.* Orolaunum. Luxembourg, SE Belgium
29 R7 **Arma** Kansas, C USA
99 F16 **Armagh** *Ir.* Ard Mhacha. S Northern Ireland, UK
99 F16 **Armagh** *cultural region* S Northern Ireland, UK
104 K15 **Armagnac** *cultural region* S France
105 Q7 **Armançon** ⁓ C France
62 K10 **Armando Laydner, Represa** ▣ S Brazil
117 M24 **Armathía** *island* SE Greece
130 M14 **Armavir** Krasnodarskiy Kray, SW Russian Federation
56 E10 **Armenia** Quindío, W Colombia
143 T12 **Armenia** *off.* Republic of Armenia, *var.* Ajastan, *Arm.* Hayastani Hanrapetut'yun; *prev.* Armenian Soviet Socialist Republic. ◆ *republic* SW Asia
Armenierstadt *see* Gherla
105 O1 **Armentières** Nord, N France
42 K14 **Armería** Colima, SW Mexico
191 T5 **Armidale** New South Wales, SE Australia
31 P11 **Armour** South Dakota, N USA
63 B18 **Armstrong** Santa Fe, C Argentina
9 N16 **Armstrong** British Columbia, SW Canada
10 D11 **Armstrong** Ontario, S Canada
31 U11 **Armstrong** Iowa, C USA
27 S16 **Armstrong** Texas, SW USA
119 S11 **Armyans'k** *Rus.* Armyansk. Respublika Krym, S Ukraine
117 H14 **Arnaía** *var.* Arnea. Kentrikí Makedonía, N Greece
123 Mm3 **Arnaoúti, Akrotíri** *var.* Arnaoútis, Cape Arnaouti. *headland* W Cyprus
Arnaouti, Cape/Arnaoútis *see* Arnaoúti, Akrotíri
10 L4 **Arnaud** ⁓ Québec, E Canada
105 Q8 **Arnay-le-Duc** Côte d'Or, C France
Arnea *see* Arnaía
107 Q4 **Arnedo** La Rioja, N Spain
97 I14 **Årnes** Akershus, S Norway
95 E15 **Årnes** Sør-Trøndelag, S Norway
28 K9 **Arnett** Oklahoma, C USA
100 L12 **Arnhem** Gelderland, SE Netherlands
189 Q2 **Arnhem Land** *physical region* Northern Territory, N Australia
108 F11 **Arno** ⁓ C Italy
Arṇo *see* Arno Atoll
201 W7 **Arno Atoll** *var.* Arṇo. *atoll* Ratak Chain, NE Marshall Islands
190 H8 **Arno Bay** South Australia
37 Q8 **Arnold** California, W USA
29 X5 **Arnold** Missouri, C USA
31 N15 **Arnold** Nebraska, C USA
111 R10 **Arnoldstein** *Slvn.* Pod Klošter. Kärnten, S Austria
105 N9 **Arnon** ⁓ C France
47 P14 **Arnos Vale** ✕ (Kingstown) Saint Vincent, SE Saint Vincent and the Grenadines
94 I8 **Arnøy** *island* N Norway
12 L12 **Arnprior** Ontario, SE Canada
103 G15 **Arnsberg** Nordrhein-Westfalen, W Germany
103 K16 **Arnstadt** Thüringen, C Germany
Arnswalde *see* Choszczno
56 K5 **Aroa** Yaracuy, N Venezuela
85 E21 **Aroab** Karas, SE Namibia
117 E19 **Aroania** ▲ S Greece
203 O6 **Aroa, Pointe** *headland* Moorea, W French Polynesia
Aroe Islands *see* Aru, Kepulauan
103 H15 **Arolsen** Niedersachsen, C Germany
108 C7 **Arona** Piemonte, NE Italy
21 R3 **Aroostook River** ⁓ Canada/USA
Arop Island *see* Long Island
40 M12 **Aropuk Lake** ◎ Alaska, USA
203 P4 **Arorae** *atoll* Tungaru, W Kiribati
202 G16 **Arorangi** Rarotonga, S Cook Islands
110 I9 **Arosa** Graubünden, S Switzerland
106 F4 **Arousa, Ría de** *estuary* E Atlantic Ocean
176 Uu16 **Aro Usu, Tanjung** *headland* Pulau Selaru, SE Indonesia
192 P8 **Arowhana** ▲ North Island, NZ
143 V12 **Arp'a** *Az.* Arpaçay. ⁓ Armenia/Azerbaijan
143 S11 **Arpaçay** Kars, NE Turkey
Arpaçay *see* Arp'a
Arqalyq *see* Arkalyk
155 N14 **Arra** ⁓ SW Pakistan
Arrabona *see* Győr
Arrah *see* Āra
Ar Rahad *see* Er Rahad
145 R9 **Ar Raḥḥālīyah** C Iraq
62 Q10 **Arraial do Cabo** Rio de Janeiro, SE Brazil
106 H11 **Arraiolos** Évora, S Portugal
145 R8 **Ar Ramādī** *var.* Ramadi, Rumadiya. SW Iraq
144 J6 **Ar Rāmī** Ḩimş, C Syria
Ar Rams *see* Rams
144 H9 **Ar Ramthā** *var.* Ramtha. Irbid, N Jordan
98 H13 **Arran, Isle of** *island* SW Scotland, UK
144 L3 **Ar Raqqah** *var.* Rakka; *anc.* Nicephorium. Ar Raqqah, N Syria
144 L3 **Ar Raqqah** *off.* Muḩāfaẓat al Raqqah, *var.* Raqqah, *Fr.* Rakka. ◆ *governorate* N Syria
105 O2 **Arras** *anc.* Nemetocenna. Pas-de-Calais, N France
Ar Raşāfah *see* Ar Ruşāfah
Arrasate *see* Mondragón
144 G12 **Ar Rashādīyah** Aţ Ţafīlah, W Jordan
144 I5 **Ar Rastan** *var.* Rastāne. Ḩimş, W Syria
145 X12 **Ar Raṭāwī** E Iraq
104 L15 **Arrats** ⁓ S France
147 N10 **Ar Rawḍah** Makkah, S Saudi Arabia
147 Q15 **Ar Rawḍah** S Yemen
148 K11 **Ar Rawḍatayn** *var.* Raudhatain. N Kuwait
149 N16 **Ar Rayyān** *var.* Al Rayyan. C Qatar
104 L17 **Arreau** Hautes-Pyrénées, S France
66 Q11 **Arrecife** *var.* Arrecife de Lanzarote, Puerto Arrecife. Lanzarote, Islas Canarias, NE Atlantic Ocean
Arrecife de Lanzarote *see* Arrecife
45 P6 **Arrecife Edinburgh** *reef* NE Nicaragua
63 C19 **Arrecifes** Buenos Aires, E Argentina
45 O5 **Arrecifes de la Media Luna** *reef* E Honduras
104 F6 **Arrée, Monts d'** ▲ NW France
Ar Refā'ī *see* Ar Rifā'ī
Arretium *see* Arezzo
Arriaca *see* Guadalajara
111 S9 **Arriach** Kärnten, S Austria
43 T16 **Arriaga** Chiapas, SE Mexico
43 N12 **Arriaga** San Luis Potosí, C Mexico
145 W10 **Ar Rifā'ī** *var.* Ar Refā'ī. SE Iraq
145 V12 **Ar Riḩāb** *salt flat* S Iraq
106 L2 **Arriondas** Asturias, N Spain
147 R7 **Ar Riyāḑ** *Eng.* Riyadh. ● (Saudi Arabia) Ar Riyāḑ, C Saudi Arabia
147 O8 **Ar Riyāḑ** *off.* Minţaqat ar Riyāḑ. ◆ *province* C Saudi Arabia
147 S15 **Ar Riyān** S Yemen
Arrö *see* Ærø
63 H18 **Arroio Grande** Rio Grande do Sul, S Brazil
104 K15 **Arros** ⁓ S France
105 Q9 **Arroux** ⁓ C France
27 R5 **Arrowhead, Lake** ▣ Texas, SW USA
190 L5 **Arrowsmith, Mount** *hill* New South Wales, SE Australia
193 D21 **Arrowtown** Otago, South Island, NZ
63 D17 **Arroyo Barú** Entre Ríos, E Argentina
106 J10 **Arroyo de la Luz** Extremadura, W Spain
65 J16 **Arroyo de la Ventana** Río Negro, SE Argentina
37 P13 **Arroyo Grande** California, W USA
Ar Ru'ays *see* Ar Ruways
147 R11 **Ar Rub' al Khālī** *Eng.* Empty Quarter, Great Sandy Desert. *desert* SW Asia
145 V13 **Ar Rudaymah** S Iraq
63 A16 **Arrufó** Santa Fe, C Argentina
144 I7 **Ar Ruḩaybah** *var.* Ruhaybeh, *Fr.* Rouhaïbé. Dimashq, W Syria
145 V15 **Ar Rukhaymīyah** *well* S Iraq
145 U11 **Ar Rumaythah** *var.* Rumaitha. S Iraq
147 X8 **Ar Rustāq** *var.* Rostak, Rustaq. N Oman
145 N8 **Ar Ruṭbah** *var.* Rutba. SW Iraq
146 M3 **Ar Rūthīyah** *spring/well* NW Saudi Arabia
ar-Ruwaida *see* Ar Ruwaydah
147 O8 **Ar Ruwaydah** *var.* ar-Ruwaida. Jīzān, C Saudi Arabia
149 N15 **Ar Ruways** *var.* Al Ruweis, Ar Ru'ays, Ruwais. N Qatar
149 O17 **Ar Ruways** *var.* Ar Ru'ays. Abū Ẓaby, W UAE
97 G21 **Års** *var.* Aars. Nordjylland, N Denmark
Arsanias *see* Murat Nehri
127 Nn18 **Arsen'yev** Primorskiy Kray, SE Russian Federation
161 G19 **Arsikere** Karnātaka, W India
131 R3 **Arsk** Respublika Tatarstan, W Russian Federation
96 N10 **Årskogen** Gävleborg, C Sweden
124 N3 **Ársos** C Cyprus
96 N13 **Årsunda** Gävleborg, C Sweden
Arta *see* Árachthos
117 C17 **Árta** *anc.* Ambracia. Ípeiros, W Greece
143 T12 **Artashat** S Armenia
42 M15 **Arteaga** Michoacán de Ocampo, SW Mexico
127 Nn18 **Artem** Primorskiy Kray, SE Russian Federation
46 C4 **Artemisa** La Habana, W Cuba
119 W7 **Artemivs'k** Donets'ka Oblast', E Ukraine
126 I14 **Artemovsk** Krasnoyarskiy Kray, S Russian Federation
126 Kk13 **Artemovskiy** Irkutskaya Oblast', C Russian Federation
125 Ee13 **Artemovskiy** Sverdlovskaya Oblast', C Russian Federation
107 U5 **Artesa de Segre** Cataluña, NE Spain
39 U14 **Artesia** New Mexico, SW USA
27 Q14 **Artesia Wells** Texas, SW USA
110 G8 **Arth** Schwyz, C Switzerland
12 F15 **Arthur** Ontario, S Canada
32 M14 **Arthur** Illinois, N USA
30 L14 **Arthur** Nebraska, C USA
31 Q5 **Arthur** North Dakota, N USA
193 B21 **Arthur** ⁓ South Island, NZ
20 B13 **Arthur, Lake** ▣ Pennsylvania, NE USA
191 N15 **Arthur River** ⁓ Tasmania, SE Australia
193 G18 **Arthur's Pass** Canterbury, South Island, NZ
193 G17 **Arthur's Pass** *pass* South Island, NZ
46 I3 **Arthur's Town** Cat Island, C Bahamas
46 M9 **Artibonite, Rivière de l'** ⁓ C Haiti
63 E16 **Artigas** *prev.* San Eugenio, San Eugenio del Cuareim. Artigas, N Uruguay
63 E16 **Artigas** ◆ *department* N Uruguay
204 H1 **Artigas** *Uruguayan research station* Antarctica
143 T11 **Art'ik** W Armenia
197 G4 **Art, Île** *island* Îles Belep, W New Caledonia
105 O2 **Artois** *cultural region* N France
142 L12 **Artova** Tokat, N Turkey
107 Y9 **Artrutx, Cap d'** *var.* Cabo Dartuch. *headland* Menorca, Spain, W Mediterranean Sea
Artsiz *see* Artsyz
119 N11 **Artsyz** *Rus.* Artsiz. Odes'ka Oblast', SW Ukraine
164 E7 **Artux** Xinjiang Uygur Zizhiqu, NW China
143 R11 **Artvin** Artvin, NE Turkey
143 R11 **Artvin** ◆ *province* NE Turkey
152 G14 **Artyk** Akhalskiy Velayat, C Turkmenistan
81 Q16 **Aru** Haut-Zaïre, NE Zaire
106 I4 **A Rúa** *var.* La Rúa. Galicia, NW Spain
83 E17 **Arua** NW Uganda
Aruángua *see* Luangwa
47 O15 **Aruba** *var.* Oruba. ◇ *Dutch autonomous region* S West Indies
49 Q4 **Aruba** *island* Aruba, Lesser Antilles
Aru Islands *see* Aru, Kepulauan
176 Ww14 **Aru, Kepulauan** *Eng.* Aru Islands; *prev.* Aroe Islands. *island group* E Indonesia
159 W10 **Arunāchal Pradesh** *prev.* North East Frontier Agency, North East Frontier Agency of Assam. ◆ *state* NE India
169 U7 **Arun Qi** Nei Mongol Zizhiqu, N China
161 H23 **Aruppukkottai** Tamil Nādu, SE India
176 Ww9 **Aruri, Selat** *strait* Irian Jaya, E Indonesia
83 I20 **Arusha** Arusha, N Tanzania
83 I21 **Arusha** ◆ *region* E Tanzania
83 I20 **Arusha** ✕ Arusha, N Tanzania
56 C9 **Arusí, Punta** *headland* NW Colombia
174 Ll10 **Arut, Sungai** ⁓ Borneo, C Indonesia
161 J23 **Aruvi Aru** ⁓ NW Sri Lanka
81 M17 **Aruwimi** *var.* Ituri (upper course). ⁓ NE Zaire
Árva *see* Orava
39 T4 **Arvada** Colorado, C USA
Arvand Rūd *see* 'Arab, Shaṭṭ al
168 J8 **Arvayheer** Övörhangay, C Mongolia
15 L8 **Arviat** *prev.* Eskimo Point. Northwest Territories, C Canada
95 I14 **Arvidsjaur** Norrbotten, N Sweden
97 J15 **Arvika** Värmland, C Sweden
94 J8 **Årviksand** Troms, N Norway
37 S13 **Arvin** California, W USA
151 P7 **Arykbalyk** *Kaz.* Aryqbalyq. Kokshetau, N Kazakhstan
Aryqbalyq *see* Arykbalyk
151 P17 **Arys'** *Kaz.* Arys. Yuzhnyy Kazakhstan, S Kazakhstan
Arys *see* Orzysz
Arys Köli *see* Arys, Ozero
151 O14 **Arys, Ozero** *Kaz.* Arys Köli. ◎ C Kazakhstan
109 D16 **Arzachena** Sardegna, Italy, C Mediterranean Sea
131 O4 **Arzamas** Nizhegorodskaya Oblast', W Russian Federation
147 V13 **Arzāt** S Oman
106 H3 **Arzúa** Galicia, NW Spain
113 A16 **Aš** *Ger.* Asch. Západní Čechy, W Czech Republic
97 H15 **Ås** Akershus, S Norway
97 H20 **Aså** Nordjylland, N Denmark
85 E21 **Asab** Karas, S Namibia
79 U16 **Asaba** Delta, S Nigeria
155 S4 **Asadābād** *var.* Asadābād; *prev.* Chaghasarāy. Kunar, E Afghanistan
144 K3 **Asad, Buḩayrat al** ◎ N Syria
65 H20 **Asador, Pampa del** *plain* S Argentina
171 Kk17 **Asahi** Chiba, Honshū, S Japan
171 J13 **Asahi** Toyama, Honshū, SW Japan
172 Pp5 **Asahi-dake** ▲ Hokkaidō, N Japan
170 Ff13 **Asahi-gawa** ⁓ Honshū, SW Japan
172 P5 **Asahikawa** Hokkaidō, N Japan
153 S10 **Asaka** *Rus.* Assake; *prev.* Leninsk. Andijon Wiloyati, E Uzbekistan
79 P17 **Asamankese** SE Ghana
171 Jj15 **Asama-yama** ▲ Honshū, S Japan
196 B15 **Asan** W Guam
196 B15 **Asan Point** *headland* W Guam
159 R15 **Āsānsol** West Bengal, NE India
176 V9 **Asbakin** Irian Jaya, E Indonesia
Asben *see* Aïr, Massif de l'
125 Ee11 **Asbest** Sverdlovskaya Oblast', C Russian Federation
13 Q12 **Asbestos** Québec, SE Canada
31 Y13 **Asbury** Iowa, C USA
20 K15 **Asbury Park** New Jersey, NE USA
43 Z12 **Ascención, Bahiá de la** *bay* NW Caribbean Sea
42 J3 **Ascensión** Chihuahua, N Mexico
67 M14 **Ascension Fracture Zone** *tectonic feature* C Atlantic Ocean
67 G14 **Ascension Island** ◇ *dependency of St.Helena* C Atlantic Ocean
67 N16 **Ascension Island** *island* C Atlantic Ocean
Asch *see* Aš
111 S3 **Aschach an der Donau** Oberösterreich, N Austria
103 H18 **Aschaffenburg** Bayern, SW Germany
103 F14 **Ascheberg** Nordrhein-Westfalen, W Germany
103 L14 **Aschersleben** Sachsen-Anhalt, C Germany
108 G12 **Asciano** Toscana, C Italy
108 J13 **Ascoli Piceno** *anc.* Asculum Picenum. Marche, C Italy
109 M17 **Ascoli Satriano** *anc.* Asculub, Ausculum Apulum. Puglia, SE Italy
110 G11 **Ascona** Ticino, S Switzerland
Asculub *see* Ascoli Satriano
Asculum Picenum *see* Ascoli Piceno
82 L11 **Āseb** *var.* Assab, *Amh.* Āseb. SE Eritrea
97 M20 **Åseda** Kronoberg, S Sweden
131 T6 **Asekeyevo** Orenburgskaya Oblast', W Russian Federation
194 J13 **Aseki** Morobe, C PNG
83 J14 **Āsela** *var.* Asella, Aselle, Asselle. C Ethiopia
95 H15 **Åsele** Västerbotten, N Sweden
Asella/Aselle *see* Āsela
96 K12 **Åsen** Kopparberg, C Sweden
116 J11 **Asenovgrad** *prev.* Stanimaka. Plovdivska Oblast, S Bulgaria
175 Q11 **Asera** Sulawesi, C Indonesia
97 E17 **Åseral** Vest-Agder, S Norway
120 J3 **Aseri** *var.* Asserien, *Ger.* Asserin. Ida-Virumaa, NE Estonia
42 J10 **Aserradero** Durango, W Mexico
97 H16 **Åsgårdstrand** Vestfold, S Norway
125 E11 **Asha** Chelyabinskaya Oblast', C Russian Federation
Ashara *see* Al 'Ashārah
25 T6 **Ashburn** Georgia, SE USA
193 G19 **Ashburton** Canterbury, South Island, NZ
193 G19 **Ashburton** ⁓ South Island, NZ
188 H8 **Ashburton River** ⁓ Western Australia
151 V10 **Ashchysu** ⁓ E Kazakhstan
8 M16 **Ashcroft** British Columbia, SW Canada
144 E10 **Ashdod** *anc.* Azotos, *Lat.* Azotus. Central, W Israel
29 S14 **Ashdown** Arkansas, C USA
23 T9 **Asheboro** North Carolina, SE USA
9 X15 **Ashern** Manitoba, S Canada
23 P10 **Asheville** North Carolina, SE USA
10 E8 **Asheweig** ⁓ Ontario, C Canada
29 V9 **Ash Flat** Arkansas, C USA
191 T4 **Ashford** New South Wales, SE Australia
99 P22 **Ashford** SE England, UK
38 K11 **Ash Fork** Arizona, SW USA
152 F13 **Ashgabat** *prev.* Ashkhabad, Poltoratsk. ● (Turkmenistan) Akhalskiy Velayat, C Turkmenistan
152 F13 **Ashgabat** ✕ Akhalskiy Velayat, C Turkmenistan
29 T7 **Ash Grove** Missouri, C USA
171 K15 **Ashikaga** *var.* Asikaga. Tochigi, Honshū, S Japan
171 Mm10 **Ashiro** Iwate, Honshū, C Japan
170 E16 **Ashizuri-misaki** *headland* Shikoku, SW Japan
Ashkelon *see* Ashqelon
Ashkhabad *see* Ashgabat
25 Q4 **Ashland** Alabama, S USA
28 K7 **Ashland** Kansas, C USA
23 P5 **Ashland** Kentucky, S USA
21 S2 **Ashland** Maine, NE USA
24 M1 **Ashland** Mississippi, S USA
29 U4 **Ashland** Missouri, C USA
31 S15 **Ashland** Nebraska, C USA
33 T12 **Ashland** Ohio, N USA
34 G15 **Ashland** Oregon, NW USA
23 W6 **Ashland** Virginia, NE USA
32 K3 **Ashland** Wisconsin, N USA
22 I8 **Ashland City** Tennessee, S USA
191 S4 **Ashley** New South Wales, SE Australia
31 O7 **Ashley** North Dakota, N USA
181 W7 **Ashmore and Cartier Islands** ◇ *Australian external territory* E Indian Ocean
121 I14 **Ashmyany** *Rus.* Oshmyany. Hrodzyenskaya Voblasts', W Belarus
20 K12 **Ashokan Reservoir** ▣ New York, NE USA
172 Pp6 **Ashoro** Hokkaidō, NE Japan
144 E10 **Ashqelon** *var.* Ashkelon. Southern, C Israel
Ashraf *see* Behshahr
145 O3 **Ash Shadādah** *var.* Ash Shaddādah, Jisr ash Shadadi, Shaddādī, Shedadi, Tell Shedadi. Al Ḩasakah, NE Syria
Ash Shaddādah *see* Ash Shadādah
145 Y12 **Ash Shāfī** E Iraq
145 R4 **Ash Shakk** *var.* Shaykh. C Iraq
Ash Sham/Ash Shām *see* Dimashq
145 T10 **Ash Shāmīyah** *var.* Shamiya. C Iraq
145 Y13 **Ash Shāmīyah** *var.* Al Bādiyah al Janūbīyah. *desert* S Iraq
145 T11 **Ash Shanāfīyah** *var.* Ash Shināfīyah. S Iraq
144 G13 **Ash Sharāh** *var.* Esh Sharā. ▲ W Jordan
149 R16 **Ash Shāriqah** *Eng.* Sharjah. Ash Shāriqah, NE UAE
149 R16 **Ash Shāriqah** *var.* Sharjah. ✕ Ash Shāriqah, NE UAE
146 I4 **Ash Sharmah** *var.* Šarma. Tabūk, NW Saudi Arabia
145 R4 **Ash Sharqāṭ** NW Iraq
147 S10 **Ash Sharqīyah** *off.* Al Minṭaqah ash Sharqīyah, *Eng.* Eastern Region. ◆ *province* E Saudi Arabia
145 W11 **Ash Shaṭrah** *var.* Shatra. SE Iraq
144 G13 **Ash Shawbak** Ma'ān, W Jordan
144 L5 **Ash Shaykh Ibrāhīm** Ḩimş, C Syria
147 O17 **Ash Shaykh 'Uthmān** SW Yemen
147 S15 **Ash Shiḩr** SE Yemen
Ash Shināfīyah *see* Ash Shanāfīyah
147 V12 **Ash Shişar** *var.* Shisur. SW Oman
145 S13 **Ash Shubrūm** *well* S Iraq
147 R4 **Ash Shuqayq** *var.* As Shageeg. *desert* S Kuwait
147 R10 **Ash Shuqqān** *desert* E Saudi Arabia
77 O9 **Ash Shuwayrif** *var.* Ash Shwayrif. N Libya
Ash Shwayrif *see* Ash Shuwayrif
33 U10 **Ashtabula** Ohio, N USA
31 Q5 **Ashtabula, Lake** ▣ North Dakota, N USA
143 T12 **Ashtarak** W Armenia
148 M6 **Āshtiān** *var.* Āshtiyān. Markazī, W Iran
Āshtiyān *see* Āshtiān
35 R13 **Ashton** Idaho, NW USA
11 O10 **Ashuanipi Lake** ◎ Newfoundland and Labrador, E Canada
13 P6 **Ashuapmushuan** ⁓ Québec, SE Canada
25 Q3 **Ashville** Alabama, S USA
33 S14 **Ashville** Ohio, N USA
32 K3 **Ashwabay, Mount** *hill* Wisconsin, N USA
176 Uu7 **Asia, Kepulauan** *island group* E Indonesia
160 N13 **Āsika** Orissa, E India
Asikaga *see* Ashikaga
95 M18 **Asikkala** *var.* Vääksy. Häme, S Finland
76 G5 **Asilah** N Morocco
'Aṣī, Nahr al *see* Orontes
109 B16 **Asinara, Isola** *island* W Italy
126 H13 **Asino** Tomskaya Oblast', C Russian Federation
121 O14 **Asintorf** *Rus.* Osintorf. Vitsyebskaya Voblasts', N Belarus
121 L17 **Asipovichy** *Rus.* Osipovichi. Mahilyowskaya Voblasts', C Belarus
147 N12 **'Asīr** *off.* Minṭaqat 'Asīr. ◆ *province* SW Saudi Arabia

◆ Country ● Country Capital ◇ Dependent Territory ○ Dependent Territory Capital ◆ Administrative Region ✕ International Airport ▲ Mountain ▲ Mountain Range ⚠ Volcano ⁓ River ◎ Lake ▣ Reservoir

'Asīr – Ayakagytma

146 M11 'Asīr Eng. Asir. ⛰ SW Saudi Arabia
145 X10 Askal E Iraq
143 P13 Aşkale Erzurum, NE Turkey
119 T11 Askaniya-Nova Khersons'ka Oblast', S Ukraine
97 H15 Asker Akershus, S Norway
97 L17 Askersund Örebro, C Sweden
Askī Kalak see Eski Kaļak
97 I15 Askim Østfold, S Norway
131 V3 Askino Respublika Bashkortostan, W Russian Federation
117 D14 Áskio ⛰ N Greece
158 L9 Askot Uttar Pradesh, N India
96 C12 Askvoll Sogn og Fjordane, S Norway
142 A13 Aslan Burnu headland W Turkey
142 L16 Aslantaş Barajı ▣ S Turkey
155 S4 Asmār var. Bar Kunar. Kunar, E Afghanistan
82 I9 Asmara Amh. Āsmera. ● (Eritrea) C Eritrea
Āsmera see Asmara
97 L21 Åsnen ◎ S Sweden
117 F19 Asopós ≈ S Greece
176 X10 Asori Irian Jaya, E Indonesia
82 G12 Āsosa W Ethiopia
34 M10 Asotin Washington, NW USA
Aspadana see Eşfahān
Aspang see Aspang Markt
111 X6 Aspang Markt var. Aspang. Niederösterreich, E Austria
107 S12 Aspe País Valenciano, E Spain
39 R5 Aspen Colorado, C USA
27 P6 Aspermont Texas, SW USA
Asphaltites, Lacus see Dead Sea
Aspinwall see Colón
193 C20 Aspiring, Mount ▲ South Island, NZ
117 B16 Asprókavos, Ákra headland Kérkyra, Iónioi Nísoi, Greece, C Mediterranean Sea
Aspropótamos see Achelóos
Assab see Aseb
78 J10 Assaba var. Açâba. ◈ region S Mauritania
144 L4 As Sabkhah var. Sabkha. Ar Raqqah, NE Syria
145 U6 As Sa'dīyah E Iraq
Assad, Lake see Asad, Buḩayrat al
144 I8 Aş Şafā ▲ S Syria
144 I10 Aş Şafāwī Al Mafraq, N Jordan
Aş Şaff see El Şaff
145 N2 Aş Şafīḩ Al Ḩasakah, N Syria
Aş Şaḩrā' al Gharbīyah see Sahara el Gharbîya
Aş Şaḩrā' ash Sharqīyah see Sahara el Sharqîya
Assake see Asaka
As Salamīyah see Salamīyah
147 Q4 As Salimi var. Salemy. SW Kuwait
148 J11 As Sālimīyah W Kuwait
69 W7 'Assal, Lac ◎ C Djibouti
As Sallūm see Salûm
145 T13 As Salmān S Iraq
144 G10 As Salṭ var. Salt. Al Balqā', NW Jordan
148 M16 As Salwā var. Salwa, Salwah. S Qatar
159 V12 Assam ◈ state NE India
Assamaka see Assamakka
79 T8 Assamakka var. Assamaka. Agadez, NW Niger
145 U11 As Samāwah var. Samawa. S Iraq
As Saqia al Hamra see Saguia al Hamra
144 J4 Aş Şā'rān Ḩamāh, C Syria
144 G9 Aş Şarīḩ Irbid, N Jordan
23 Z5 Assateague Island island Maryland, NE USA
145 O6 As Sayyāl var. Sayyāl. Dayr az Zawr, E Syria
101 G18 Asse Vlaams Brabant, C Belgium
101 D16 Assebroek West-Vlaanderen, NW Belgium
Asselle see Āsela
109 C20 Assemini Sardegna, Italy, C Mediterranean Sea
100 N7 Assen Drenthe, NE Netherlands
101 E16 Assenede Oost-Vlaanderen, NW Belgium
97 G24 Assens Fyn, C Denmark
Asserien/Asserin see Aseri
101 I21 Assesse Namur, SE Belgium
As Shageeg see Ash Shuqayq
147 Y8 As Sīb var. Seeb. NE Oman
145 Z13 As Sībah var. Sibah. SE Iraq
9 T17 Assiniboia Saskatchewan, S Canada
9 V15 Assiniboine ≈ Manitoba, S Canada
9 P16 Assiniboine, Mount ▲ Alberta/British Columbia, SW Canada
Assiout see Asyût
62 J9 Assis São Paulo, S Brazil
108 I13 Assisi Umbria, C Italy
Assiut see Asyût
Assling see Jesenice
Assouan see Aswân
Assu see Açu
Assuan see Aswân
148 K12 Aş Şubayḩīyah var. Subiyah. S Kuwait
147 R16 As Sufāl S Yemen
144 L5 As Sukhnah var. Sukhne, Fr. Soukhné. Ḩimş, C Syria
145 U4 As Sulaymānīyah var. Sulaimaniya, Kurd. Slēmānī. NE Iraq
147 P11 As Sulayyil Ar Riyāḍ, S Saudi Arabia
123 M16 As Sulṭān N Libya
147 Q5 Aş Şummān desert N Saudi Arabia
147 Q16 Aş Şurrah SW Yemen
145 N4 Aş Şuwār var. Şuwār. Dayr az Zawr, E Syria
144 H9 As Suwaydā' var. El Suweida, Es Suweida, Suweida, Fr. Soueida. As Suwaydā', SW Syria
144 H9 As Suwaydā' off. Muḩāfaẓat as Suwaydā', var. As Suwaydā, Suwayda, Suweida, Fr. Soueida. ◈ governorate S Syria
147 Z9 As Suwayḩ NE Oman
147 X8 As Suwayq var. Suwaik. N Oman
145 T8 Aş Şuwayrah var. Suwaira. E Iraq
As Suways see Suez
Asta Colonia see Asti
Astacus see İzmit
117 M23 Astakída island SE Greece
148 M3 Āstāneh Gīlān, NW Iran
Asta Pompeia see Asti
143 Y14 Astara S Azerbaijan
Astarabad see Gorgān
101 L15 Asten Noord-Brabant, SE Netherlands
Asterābād see Gorgān
108 C8 Asti anc. Asta Colonia, Asta Pompeia, Hasta Colonia, Hasta Pompeia. Piemonte, NW Italy
Astigi see Ecija
Astipálaia see Astypálaia
154 L16 Astola Island island SW Pakistan
158 H4 Astor Jammu and Kashmir, NW India
106 K4 Astorga anc. Asturica Augusta. Castilla-León, N Spain
34 F10 Astoria Oregon, NW USA
1 F8 Astoria Fan undersea feature E Pacific Ocean
97 J22 Åstorp Kristianstad, S Sweden
Astrabad see Gorgān
131 Q13 Astrakhan' Astrakhanskaya Oblast', SW Russian Federation
Astrakhan-Bazar see Cälilabad
131 Q11 Astrakhanskaya Oblast' ◈ province SW Russian Federation
95 J15 Åsträsk Västerbotten, N Sweden
Astrida see Butare
67 O22 Astrid Ridge undersea feature S Atlantic Ocean
194 J11 Astrolabe Bay inlet N PNG
197 I4 Astrolabe, Récifs de l' reef C New Caledonia
124 Nn3 Astromerítis N Cyprus
117 F20 Ástros Pelopónnisos, S Greece
121 G16 Astryna Rus. Ostryna. Hrodzyenskaya Voblasts', W Belarus
106 J2 Asturias ◈ autonomous community NW Spain
Asturias see Oviedo
Asturica Augusta see Astorga
117 L22 Astypálaia var. Astipálaia, It. Stampalia. island Kykládes, Greece, Aegean Sea
198 Aa8 Āsuisui, Cape headland Savai'i, W Western Samoa
205 S2 Asuka Japanese research station Antarctica
64 O6 Asunción ● (Paraguay) Central, S Paraguay
64 O6 Asunción ✕ Central, S Paraguay
196 K3 Asuncion Island island N Northern Mariana Islands
44 E6 Asunción Mita Jutiapa, SE Guatemala
Asunción Nochixtlán see Nochixtlán
42 E3 Asunción, Río ≈ NW Mexico
97 M18 Åsunden ◎ S Sweden
120 K11 Asvyeya Rus. Osveya. Vitsyebskaya Voblasts', N Belarus
Aswa see Achwa
77 X11 Aswân var. Assouan, Assuan; anc. Syene. SE Egypt
77 X11 Aswân High Dam dam SE Egypt
77 W9 Asyût var. Assiout, Assiut, Siut; anc. Lycopolis. C Egypt
200 R15 Ata island Tongatapu Group, SW Tonga
64 G8 Atacama off. Región de Atacama. ◈ region C Chile
Atacama Desert see Atacama, Desierto de
64 H4 Atacama, Desierto de Eng. Atacama Desert. desert N Chile
64 I6 Atacama, Puna de ⛰ NW Argentina
64 I5 Atacama, Salar de salt lake N Chile
56 E11 Ataco Tolima, C Colombia
202 H8 Atafu Atoll island NW Tokelau
202 H8 Atafu Village Atafu Atoll, NW Tokelau
76 K12 Atakor ⛰ SE Algeria
79 R14 Atakora, Chaîne de l' var. Atakora Mountains. ⛰ N Benin
Atakora Mountains see Atakora, Chaîne de l'
79 R16 Atakpamé C Togo
152 F11 Atakui Akhalskiy Velayat, C Turkmenistan
60 B13 Atalaia do Norte Amazonas, N Brazil
171 J17 Atami Shizuoka, Honshū, S Japan
78 I7 Aţâr Adrar, W Mauritania
168 G10 Atas Bogd ▲ SW Mongolia
37 P12 Atascadero California, W USA
27 S13 Atascosa River ≈ Texas, SW USA
151 R11 Atasu Zhezkazgan, C Kazakhstan
151 R12 Atasu ≈ C Kazakhstan
200 Qq15 Atata island Tongatapu Group, S Tonga
142 H10 Atatürk ✕ (İstanbul) İstanbul, NW Turkey
143 N16 Atatürk Barajı ▣ S Turkey
Atax see Aude
82 G8 Atbara var. 'Aţbārah. River Nile, NE Sudan
82 H8 Atbara var. Nahr 'Aţbarah. ≈ Eritrea/Sudan
'Aţbārah/'Aţbarah, Nahr see Atbara
151 P9 Atbasar Akmola, N Kazakhstan
At-Bashi see At-Bashy
153 W9 At-Bashy var. At-Bashi. Narynskaya Oblast', C Kyrgyzstan
24 I10 Atchafalaya Bay bay Louisiana, S USA
24 I8 Atchafalaya River ≈ Louisiana, S USA
Atchin see Aceh
29 Q3 Atchison Kansas, C USA
79 P16 Atebubu C Ghana
107 Q6 Ateca Aragón, NE Spain
42 K11 Atengo, Río ≈ C Mexico
Aternum see Pescara
109 K15 Atessa Abruzzi, C Italy
Ateste see Este
101 E19 Ath var. Aat. Hainaut, SW Belgium
9 Q13 Athabasca Alberta, SW Canada
9 Q12 Athabasca var. Athabaska. ≈ Alberta, SW Canada
9 R10 Athabasca, Lake ◎ Alberta/Saskatchewan, SW Canada
Athabaska see Athabasca
117 C16 Athamánon ⛰ C Greece
99 F17 Athboy Ir. Baile Átha Buí. E Ireland
Athenae see Athína
99 C18 Athenry Ir. Baile Átha an Rí. W Ireland
25 P2 Athens Alabama, S USA
25 T3 Athens Georgia, SE USA
33 T14 Athens Ohio, N USA
22 M10 Athens Tennessee, S USA
27 V7 Athens Texas, SW USA
Athens see Athína
117 B18 Athéras, Ákra headland Kefallinía, Iónioi Nísoi, Greece, C Mediterranean Sea
189 W4 Atherton Queensland, NE Australia
83 I19 Athi ≈ S Kenya
124 O3 Athiénou SE Cyprus
117 H19 Athína Eng. Athens; prev. Athínai, anc. Athenae. ● (Greece) Attikí, C Greece
Athínai see Athína
145 S10 Athīyah C Iraq
99 D18 Athlone Ir. Baile Átha Luain. C Ireland
161 F16 Athni Karnātaka, W India
193 C23 Athol Southland, South Island, NZ
21 N11 Athol Massachusetts, NE USA
117 I15 Áthos ⛰ NE Greece
Athos, Mount see Ágion Óros
Ath Thawrah see Madīnat ath Thawrah
147 P5 Ath Thumāmī spring/well N Saudi Arabia
101 L25 Athus Luxembourg, SE Belgium
99 E19 Athy Ir. Baile Átha Í. C Ireland
80 I10 Ati Batha, C Chad
83 F16 Atiak NW Uganda
59 G17 Atico Arequipa, SW Peru
107 O6 Atienza Castilla-La Mancha, C Spain
41 Q6 Atigun Pass pass Alaska, USA
10 B12 Atikokan Ontario, S Canada
11 O9 Atikonak Lac ◎ Newfoundland and Labrador, E Canada
44 C6 Atitlán, Lago de ◎ W Guatemala
202 L16 Atiu island S Cook Islands
Atjeh see Aceh
127 O9 Atka Magadanskaya Oblast', E Russian Federation
40 H17 Atka Atka Island, Alaska, USA
40 H17 Atka Island island Aleutian Islands, Alaska, USA
131 O7 Atkarsk Saratovskaya Oblast', W Russian Federation
29 U11 Atkins Arkansas, C USA
31 O13 Atkinson Nebraska, C USA
176 U10 Atkri Irian Jaya, E Indonesia
43 O13 Atlacomulco var. Atlacomulco de Fabela. México, C Mexico
Atlacomulco de Fabela see Atlacomulco
25 S3 Atlanta state capital Georgia, SE USA
33 R6 Atlanta Michigan, N USA
27 X6 Atlanta Texas, SW USA
31 T15 Atlantic Iowa, C USA
23 Y10 Atlantic North Carolina, SE USA
25 W8 Atlantic Beach Florida, SE USA
20 J17 Atlantic City New Jersey, NE USA
180 L14 Atlantic-Indian Basin undersea feature SW Indian Ocean
180 K13 Atlantic-Indian Ridge undersea feature SW Indian Ocean
56 E4 Atlántico off. Departamento del Atlántico. ◈ province NW Colombia
66-67 Atlantic Ocean ocean
44 K7 Atlántico Norte, Región Autónoma prev. Zelaya Norte. ◈ autonomous region NE Nicaragua
44 L10 Atlántico Sur, Región Autónoma prev. Zelaya Sur. ◈ autonomous region SE Nicaragua
44 I5 Atlántida ◈ department N Honduras
79 Y15 Atlantika Mountains ⛰ E Nigeria
66 J10 Atlantis Fracture Zone tectonic feature NW Atlantic Ocean
76 H7 Atlas Mountains ⛰ NW Africa
127 Pp13 Atlasova, Ostrov island SE Russian Federation
127 Pp10 Atlasovo Kamchatskaya Oblast', E Russian Federation
123 H13 Atlas Saharien var. Saharan Atlas. ⛰ Algeria/Morocco
Atlas, Tell see Atlas Tellien
123 Gg10 Atlas Tellien Eng. Tell Atlas. ⛰ N Algeria
8 I9 Atlin British Columbia, W Canada
8 I9 Atlin Lake ◎ British Columbia, W Canada
43 P14 Atlixco Puebla, S Mexico
96 B11 Atløyna island S Norway
161 I17 Ātmakūr Andhra Pradesh, C India
25 O8 Atmore Alabama, S USA
103 J20 Atmühl ≈ S Germany
96 H11 Atna ≈ S Norway
170 E12 Atō Yamaguchi, Honshū, SW Japan
59 L21 Atocha Potosí, S Bolivia
29 P12 Atoka Oklahoma, C USA
29 O12 Atoka Lake var. Atoka Reservoir. ▣ Oklahoma, C USA
Atoka Reservoir see Atoka Lake
35 Q14 Atomic City Idaho, NW USA
42 L10 Atotonilco Zacatecas, C Mexico
42 M13 Atotonilco el Alto var. Atotonilco. Jalisco, SW Mexico
79 N7 Atouila, 'Erg desert N Mali
43 N16 Atoyac var. Atoyac de Alvarez. Guerrero, S Mexico
Atoyac de Alvarez see Atoyac
43 P15 Atoyac, Río ≈ S Mexico
41 O5 Atqasuk Alaska, USA
152 C13 Atrak Per. Rūd-e Atrak, Rus. Atrek, Turkm. Etrek. ≈ Iran/Turkmenistan
Atrak, Rūd-e see Atrak
97 J20 Ätran ≈ S Sweden
56 C7 Atrato, Río ≈ NW Colombia
Atrek see Atrak
109 K14 Atri Abruzzi, C Italy
Atria see Adria
171 Jj16 Atsugi var. Atugi. Kanagawa, Honshū, S Japan
171 L12 Atsumi Yamagata, Honshū, C Japan
172 Oo4 Atsuta Hokkaidō, NE Japan
176 Y13 Atsy Irian Jaya, E Indonesia
149 Q17 Aţ Ţaff desert C UAE
144 G12 Aţ Ţafilah var. Et Tafila, Tafila. Aţ Ţafilah, W Jordan
144 G12 Aţ Ţafilah off. Muḩāfaẓat aţ Ţafilah. ◈ governorate W Jordan
146 L10 Aţ Ţā'if Makkah, W Saudi Arabia
Attaleia/Attalia see Antalya
25 Q3 Attalla Alabama, S USA
144 L2 At Tall al Abyaḍ var. Tall al Abyaḍ, Tell Abyad, Fr. Tell Abiad. Ar Raqqah, N Syria
144 L7 Aţ Ţanf Ḩimş, S Syria
Attapu see Samakhixai
145 S10 Aţ Ţaqţaqānah C Iraq
117 O23 Attávytos ▲ Ródos, Dodekánisos, Greece, Aegean Sea
145 V15 At Tawal desert Iraq/Saudi Arabia
10 G9 Attawapiskat Ontario, C Canada
10 F9 Attawapiskat ≈ Ontario, S Canada
10 D9 Attawapiskat Lake ◎ Ontario, C Canada
At Taybé see Ţayyibah
103 F16 Attendorn Nordrhein-Westfalen, W Germany
111 R5 Attersee Salzburg, NW Austria
111 R5 Attersee ◎ N Austria
101 L24 Attert Luxembourg, SE Belgium
144 M4 At Tibnī var. Tibnī. Dayr az Zawr, NE Syria
33 N13 Attica Indiana, N USA
20 E10 Attica New York, NE USA
Attica see Attikí
11 N7 Attikamagen Lake ◎ Newfoundland and Labrador, E Canada
117 H20 Attikí Eng. Attica. ◈ region C Greece
21 O12 Attleboro Massachusetts, NE USA
111 R5 Attnang Oberösterreich, N Austria
155 U6 Attock City Punjab, E Pakistan
Attopeu see Samakhixai
27 X8 Attoyac River ≈ Texas, SW USA
40 D16 Attu Attu Island, Alaska, USA
145 Y12 Aţ Ţūbah E Iraq
146 K4 Aţ Ţubayq plain Jordan/Saudi Arabia
40 C16 Attu Island island Aleutian Islands, Alaska, USA
Aţ Ţūr see El Ţûr
161 J21 Āttūr Tamil Nādu, SE India
147 N17 At Turbah SW Yemen
64 I12 Atuel, Río ≈ C Argentina
Atugi see Atsugi
203 X7 Atuona Hiva Oa, NE French Polynesia
Aturus see Adour
97 M18 Åtvidaberg Östergötland, S Sweden
37 P9 Atwater California, W USA
31 T8 Atwater Minnesota, N USA
28 I2 Atwood Kansas, C USA
33 U12 Atwood Lake ▣ Ohio, N USA
131 P5 Atyashevo Respublika Mordoviya, W Russian Federation
150 F12 Atyrau prev. Gur'yev. Atyrau, W Kazakhstan
150 E11 Atyrau off. Atyrauskaya Oblast', var. Kaz. Atyraū Oblysy; prev. Gur'yevskaya Oblast'. ◈ province W Kazakhstan
Atyraū Oblysy/Atyrauskaya Oblast' see Atyrau
110 J7 Au Vorarlberg, NW Austria
194 G8 Aua Island island NW PNG
105 S16 Aubagne anc. Albania. Bouches-du-Rhône, SE France
101 L25 Aubange Luxembourg, SE Belgium
105 Q6 Aube ◈ department N France
105 R6 Aube ≈ N France
101 L19 Aubel Liège, E Belgium
105 Q13 Aubenas Ardèche, E France
105 O8 Aubigny-sur-Nère Cher, C France
105 O13 Aubin Aveyron, S France
105 O13 Aubrac, Monts d' ⛰ S France
38 J10 Aubrey Cliffs cliff Arizona, SW USA
25 R5 Auburn Alabama, S USA
37 P6 Auburn California, W USA
32 K14 Auburn Illinois, N USA
33 Q11 Auburn Indiana, N USA
22 J7 Auburn Kentucky, S USA
21 P8 Auburn Maine, NE USA
21 N11 Auburn Massachusetts, NE USA
31 S16 Auburn Nebraska, C USA
20 H10 Auburn New York, NE USA
34 H8 Auburn Washington, NW USA
105 N11 Aubusson Creuse, C France
120 E10 Auce Ger. Autz. Dobele, SW Latvia
104 L15 Auch Lat. Augusta Auscorum, Elimberrum. Gers, S France
79 U16 Auchi Edo, S Nigeria
25 T9 Aucilla River ≈ Florida/Georgia, SE USA
192 L6 Auckland Auckland, North Island, NZ
192 K5 Auckland off. Auckland Region. ◈ region North Island, NZ
192 L6 Auckland ✕ Auckland, North Island, NZ
199 Ii15 Auckland Islands island group S NZ
105 O16 Aude ◈ department S France
105 N16 Aude anc. Atax. ≈ S France
Audenarde see Oudenaarde
Audern see Audru
104 E6 Audierne Finistère, NW France
104 E6 Audierne, Baie d' bay NW France
105 U7 Audincourt Doubs, E France
120 G5 Audru Ger. Audern. Pärnumaa, SW Estonia
31 T14 Audubon Iowa, C USA
103 N17 Aue Sachsen, E Germany
102 H12 Aue ≈ NW Germany
102 L9 Auerbach Bayern, SE Germany
103 M17 Auerbach Sachsen, E Germany
110 I10 Auererrhein ≈ SW Switzerland
103 N17 Auersberg ▲ E Germany
189 W9 Augathella Queensland, E Australia
33 Q12 Auglaize River ≈ Ohio, N USA
85 F22 Augrabies Falls waterfall W South Africa
33 R7 Au Gres River ≈ Michigan, N USA
Augsbourg see Augsburg
103 K22 Augsburg Fr. Augsbourg; anc. Augusta Vindelicorum. Bayern, S Germany
188 I14 Augusta Western Australia
109 L25 Augusta It. Agosta. Sicilia, Italy, C Mediterranean Sea
29 O6 Augusta Arkansas, C USA
25 V3 Augusta Georgia, SE USA
29 W11 Augusta Kansas, C USA
21 Q7 Augusta state capital Maine, NE USA
35 Q8 Augusta Montana, NW USA
Augusta see London
Augusta Auscorum see Auch
Augusta Emerita see Mérida
Augusta Praetoria see Aosta
Augusta Suessionum see Soissons
Augusta Trajana see Stara Zagora
Augusta Treverorum see Trier
Augusta Vangionum see Worms
Augusta Vindelicorum see Augsburg
97 G24 Augustenborg Ger. Augustenburg. Sønderjylland, SW Denmark
Augustenburg see Augustenborg
41 Q13 Augustine Island island Alaska, USA
12 L9 Augustines, Lac des ◎ Québec, SE Canada
Augustobona Tricassium see Troyes
Augustodunum see Autun
Augustodurum see Bayeux
Augustoritum Lemovicensium see Limoges
112 O8 Augustów Rus. Avgustov. Suwałki, NE Poland
Augustow Canal see Augustowski, Kanał
112 O8 Augustowski, Kanał Eng. Augustow Canal, Rus. Avgustovskiy Kanal. canal NE Poland
188 I9 Augustus, Mount ▲ Western Australia
195 X15 Auki Malaita, N Solomon Islands
23 W8 Aulander North Carolina, SE USA
188 L7 Auld, Lake salt lake Western Australia
Aulie Ata/Auliye-Ata see Zhambyl
108 E10 Aulla Toscana, C Italy
104 F6 Aulne ≈ NW France
Aulong see Ulong
39 T3 Ault Colorado, C USA
105 N3 Aumale Seine-Maritime, N France
Auminzatau, Gory see Owminzatovo-Toshi
79 T14 Auna Niger, W Nigeria
97 H21 Auning Århus, C Denmark
198 Cc9 Aunu'u Island island W American Samoa
85 E20 Auob var. Oup. ≈ Namibia/South Africa
95 K19 Aura Turku-Pori, SW Finland
111 R5 Aurach ≈ N Austria
Aural, Phnom see Aôral, Phnum
159 O14 Aurangābād Bihār, N India
160 F13 Aurangābād Mahārāshtra, C India
201 V7 Aur Atoll atoll E Marshall Islands
104 G7 Auray Morbihan, NW France
96 G13 Aurdal Oppland, S Norway
96 F8 Aure Møre og Romsdal, S Norway
31 T12 Aurelia Iowa, C USA
Aurelia Aquensis see Baden-Baden
Aurelianum see Orléans
123 J12 Aurès, Massif de l' ⛰ NE Algeria
102 F10 Aurich Niedersachsen, NW Germany
105 O13 Aurillac Cantal, C France
Aurine, Alpi see Zillertaler Alpen
Aurium see Ourense
12 H15 Aurora Ontario, S Canada
57 S8 Aurora NW Guyana
39 T4 Aurora Colorado, C USA
32 M11 Aurora Illinois, N USA
33 Q15 Aurora Indiana, N USA
31 W4 Aurora Minnesota, N USA
29 S8 Aurora Missouri, C USA
31 P16 Aurora Nebraska, C USA
38 J5 Aurora Utah, W USA
Aurora see San Francisco, Philippines
Aurora see Maewo, Vanuatu
96 F10 Aursjøen ◎ S Norway
96 I9 Aursunden ◎ S Norway
85 D21 Aus Karas, SW Namibia
Ausa see Vic
12 E16 Ausable ≈ Ontario, S Canada
33 O3 Au Sable Point headland Michigan, N USA
33 S7 Au Sable Point headland Michigan, N USA
33 R6 Au Sable River ≈ Michigan, N USA
59 H16 Ausangate, Nevado ▲ C Peru
Auschwitz see Oświęcim
Ausculum Apulum see Ascoli Satriano
107 Q4 Ausejo La Rioja, N Spain
Aussig see Ústí nad Labem
97 F17 Aust-Agder ◈ county S Norway
94 P2 Austfonna glacier NE Svalbard
33 P15 Austin Indiana, N USA
31 W11 Austin Minnesota, N USA
37 U5 Austin Nevada, W USA
27 S10 Austin state capital Texas, S USA
188 J10 Austin, Lake salt lake Western Australia
33 V11 Austintown Ohio, N USA
27 V9 Austonio Texas, SW USA
Australes, Archipel des see Australes, Îles
Australes et Antarctiques Françaises, Terres see French Southern and Antarctic Territories
203 T14 Australes, Îles var. Archipel des Australes, Îles Tubuai, Tubuai Islands, Eng. Austral Islands. island group SW French Polynesia
183 Y11 Austral Fracture Zone tectonic feature S Pacific Ocean
189 O7 Australia off. Commonwealth of Australia. ◆ commonwealth republic
182 M8 Australia continent
191 Q12 Australian Alps ⛰ SE Australia
191 R11 Australian Capital Territory prev. Federal Capital Territory. ◈ territory SE Australia
Australie, Bassin Nord de l' see North Australian Basin
Austral Islands see Australes, Îles
Austrava see Ostrov
111 T6 Austria off. Republic of Austria, Ger. Österreich. ◆ republic C Europe
94 K3 Austurland ◈ region SE Iceland
94 G10 Austvågøy island C Norway
60 G13 Autazes Amazonas, N Brazil
104 M16 Auterive Haute-Garonne, S France
Autesiodorum see Auxerre
105 N2 Authie ≈ N France
Autissiodorum see Auxerre
42 K14 Autlán var. Autlán de Navarro. Jalisco, SW Mexico
Autlán de Navarro see Autlán
Autricum see Chartres
105 Q9 Autun anc. Ædua, Augustodunum. Saône-et-Loire, C France
Autz see Auce
101 H20 Auvelais Namur, S Belgium
105 P11 Auvergne ◈ region C France
104 M12 Auvézère ≈ W France
105 P7 Auxerre anc. Autesiodorum, Autissiodorum. Yonne, C France
105 N2 Auxi-le-Château Pas-de-Calais, N France
105 S8 Auxonne Côte d'Or, C France
57 P9 Auyan Tebuy ▲ SE Venezuela
105 O10 Auzances Creuse, C France
29 U8 Ava Missouri, C USA
148 M5 Āvaj Zanjān, W Iran
97 C15 Avaldsnes Rogaland, S Norway
105 Q8 Avallon Yonne, C France
104 K6 Avaloirs, Mont des ▲ NW France
37 S16 Avalon Santa Catalina Island, California, W USA
20 J17 Avalon New Jersey, NE USA
11 V13 Avalon Peninsula peninsula Newfoundland, Newfoundland and Labrador, E Canada
62 K10 Avaré São Paulo, S Brazil
Avaricum see Bourges
202 H16 Avarua ○ (Cook Islands) Rarotonga, S Cook Islands
202 H16 Avarua Harbour harbor Rarotonga, S Cook Islands
Avasfelsőfalu see Negreşti-Oaş
40 L17 Avatanak Island island Aleutian Islands, Alaska, USA
202 B16 Avatele S Niue
202 H16 Avatiu Rarotonga, S Cook Islands
202 H15 Avatiu Harbour harbor Rarotonga, S Cook Islands
Avdeyevka see Avdiyivka
116 J13 Ávdira Anatolikí Makedonía kai Thráki, NE Greece
119 X8 Avdiyivka Rus. Avdeyevka. Donets'ka Oblast', SE Ukraine
168 K7 Avdzaga C Mongolia
106 G6 Ave ≈ N Portugal
106 G7 Aveiro anc. Talabriga. Aveiro, W Portugal
106 G7 Aveiro ◈ district N Portugal
Avela see Ávila
101 D18 Avelgem West-Vlaanderen, W Belgium
63 D20 Avellaneda Buenos Aires, E Argentina
109 L17 Avellino anc. Abellinum. Campania, S Italy
37 Q12 Avenal California, W USA
Avenio see Avignon
96 E8 Averoya island S Norway
109 K17 Aversa Campania, S Italy
35 N9 Avery Idaho, NW USA
27 W5 Avery Texas, SW USA
Aves, Islas de see Las Aves, Islas
Avesnes see Avesnes-sur-Helpe
105 Q2 Avesnes-sur-Helpe var. Avesnes. Nord, N France
66 G12 Aves Ridge undersea feature SE Caribbean Sea
97 M14 Avesta Kopparberg, C Sweden
105 O14 Aveyron ◈ department S France
105 N14 Aveyron ≈ S France
109 J15 Avezzano Abruzzi, C Italy
117 D16 Avgó ▲ C Greece
Avgustov see Augustów
Avgustovskiy Kanal see Augustowski, Kanał
98 J9 Aviemore N Scotland, UK
193 F21 Aviemore, Lake ◎ South Island, NZ
105 R15 Avignon anc. Avenio. Vaucluse, SE France
106 M7 Ávila var. Avila; anc. Abela, Abula, Abyla, Avela. Castilla-León, C Spain
106 L8 Ávila ◈ province Castilla-León, C Spain
106 K2 Avilés Asturias, NW Spain
120 J4 Avinurme Ger. Awinorm. Ida-Virumaa, NE Estonia
106 H10 Avis Portalegre, C Portugal
97 F22 Avlum Ringkøbing, C Denmark
190 M11 Avoca Victoria, SE Australia
31 T14 Avoca Iowa, C USA
190 M11 Avoca River ≈ Victoria, SE Australia
109 L25 Avola Sicilia, Italy, C Mediterranean Sea
20 F10 Avon New York, NE USA
31 P12 Avon South Dakota, N USA
99 M23 Avon ≈ S England, UK
99 L20 Avon ≈ C England, UK
38 K13 Avondale Arizona, SW USA
25 X13 Avon Park Florida, SE USA
104 J5 Avranches Manche, N France
105 O3 Avre ≈ N France
195 X16 Avuavu var. Kolotambu. Guadalcanal, C Solomon Islands
Avveel see Ivalo, Finland
Avveel see Ivalojoki, Finland
Avvil see Ivalo
79 O17 Awaaso var. Awaso. SW Ghana
147 X8 'Awābī var. Al 'Awābī. NE Oman
170 G15 Awaji-shima island SW Japan
192 L9 Awakino Waikato, North Island, NZ
148 M15 'Awālī C Bahrain
101 K19 Awans Liège, E Belgium
192 I2 Awanui Northland, North Island, NZ
154 M14 Awārān Baluchistān, SW Pakistan
83 K16 Awara Plain plain NE Kenya
82 M13 Āwarē E Ethiopia
144 M6 'Awāriḑ, Wādī dry watercourse E Syria
193 B20 Awarua Point headland South Island, NZ
83 J14 Āwasa S Ethiopia
82 K13 Āwash C Ethiopia
82 K12 Āwash var. Hawash. ≈ C Ethiopia
171 Kk11 Awa-shima island C Japan
Awaso see Awaaso
164 H7 Awat Xinjiang Uygur Zizhiqu, NW China
193 J15 Awatere ≈ South Island, NZ
77 O10 Awbārī SW Libya
77 N9 Awbārī, Idhān var. Edeyen d'Oubari. desert Algeria/Libya
82 C13 Aweil Northern Bahr el Ghazal, SW Sudan
98 H11 Awe, Loch ◎ W Scotland, UK
79 U16 Awka Anambra, SW Nigeria
41 O6 Awuna River ≈ Alaska, USA
Awwinorm see Avinurme
Ax see Dax
Axarfjördhur see Öxarfjördhur
105 N17 Axat Aude, S France
101 F16 Axel Zeeland, SW Netherlands
207 P9 Axel Heiberg Island var. Axel Heiburg. island Northwest Territories, N Canada
Axel Heiburg see Axel Heiberg Island
79 O17 Axim S Ghana
116 F13 Axiós var. Vardar. ≈ Greece/FYR Macedonia see also Vardar
105 N17 Ax-les-Thermes Ariège, S France
171 Gg14 Ayabe Kyōto, Honshū, SW Japan
122 F13 Ayachi, Jbel ▲ C Morocco
63 D22 Ayacucho Buenos Aires, E Argentina
59 F15 Ayacucho Ayacucho, S Peru
59 E16 Ayacucho off. Departamento de Ayacucho. ◈ department SW Peru
151 W11 Ayaguz Kaz. Ayaköz; prev. Sergiopol. Semipalatinsk, E Kazakhstan
151 V12 Ayaguz Kaz. Ayaköz. ≈ E Kazakhstan
Ayakagytma see Oyoqighitma

◆ Country
● Country Capital
◇ Dependent Territory
○ Dependent Territory Capital
◈ Administrative Region
✕ International Airport
▲ Mountain
⛰ Mountain Range
▲ Volcano
≈ River
◎ Lake
▣ Reservoir

AYAKKUDUK – BAKER LAKE

Ayakkuduk *see* Oyoqquduq
164 *L10* **Ayakkum Hu** ◎ NW China
Ayaköz *see* Ayaguz
106 *H14* **Ayamonte** Andalucía, S Spain
127 *N12* **Ayan** Khabarovskiy Kray, E Russian Federation
142 *J10* **Ayancık** Sinop, N Turkey
57 *S9* **Ayanganna Mountain** ▲ C Guyana
79 *U16* **Ayangba** Kogi, C Nigeria
127 *P6* **Ayanka** Koryakskiy Avtonomnyy Okrug, E Russian Federation
56 *E7* **Ayapel** Córdoba, NW Colombia
142 *H12* **Ayaş** Ankara, N Turkey
59 *I16* **Ayaviri** Puno, S Peru
155 *P3* **Āybak** *var.* Aibak, Haibak; ***prev.*** Samangān. Samangān, NE Afghanistan
153 *N10* **Aydarkŭl** ***Rus.*** Ozero Aydarkul'. ◎ C Uzbekistan
Aydarkul', Ozero *see* Aydarkŭl
23 *W10* **Ayden** North Carolina, SE USA
142 *C15* **Aydın** ***var.*** Aïdin; ***anc.*** Tralles. Aydın, SW Turkey
142 *C15* **Aydın** ***var.*** Aïdin. ⬖ *province* SW Turkey
142 *I17* **Aydıncık** İçel, S Turkey
142 *C15* **Aydın Dağları** ▲▲ W Turkey
164 *L6* **Aydingkol Hu** ◎ NW China
131 *X7* **Aydyrlinskiy** Orenburgskaya Oblast', W Russian Federation
107 *S4* **Ayerbe** Aragón, NE Spain
Ayers Rock *see* Uluru
Ayeyarwady *see* Irrawaddy
Ayiá *see* Agiá
Ayia Napa *see* Agía Nápa
Ayia Phyla *see* Agía Fýlaxis
Ayiásos/Ayiássos *see* Agiasós
Áyios Evstrátios *see* Ágios Efstrátios
Áyios Kírikos *see* Ágios Kírykos
Áyios Nikólaos *see* 3Ágios Nikólaos
Ayios Seryios *see* Yeniboğaziçi
82 *I11* **Āykel** NW Ethiopia
126 *K10* **Aykhal** Respublika Sakha (Yakutiya), NE Russian Federation
12 *J12* **Aylen Lake** ◎ Ontario, SE Canada
99 *N21* **Aylesbury** SE England, UK
107 *O6* **Ayllón** Castilla-León, N Spain
12 *F17* **Aylmer** Ontario, S Canada
12 *L12* **Aylmer** Québec, SE Canada
13 *R12* **Aylmer, Lac** ◎ Québec, SE Canada
15 *J6* **Aylmer Lake** ◎ Northwest Territories, NW Canada
151 *V14* **Aynabulak** Taldykorgan, SE Kazakhstan
144 *K2* **'Ayn al 'Arab** Ḩalab, N Syria
Aynayn *see* 'Aynīn
145 *V12* **'Ayn Ḩamūd** S Iraq
153 *P12* **Ayní** ***prev.*** Rus. Varzimanor Ayni. W Tajikistan
146 *M10* **'Aynīn** ***var.*** Aynayn. *spring/well* SW Saudi Arabia
23 *U12* **Aynor** South Carolina, SE USA
145 *Q7* **'Ayn Zāzūh** C Iraq
159 *N12* **Ayodhya** Uttar Pradesh, N India
127 *O5* **Ayon, Ostrov** *island* NE Russian Federation
107 *R11* **Ayora** País Valenciano, E Spain
79 *Q11* **Ayorou** Tillabéri, W Niger
81 *E16* **Ayos** Centre, S Cameroon
78 *L5* **'Ayoûn 'Abd el Mâlek** *well* N Mauritania
78 *K10* **'Ayoûn el 'Atroûs** ***var.*** Aïoun el Atrous, Aïoun el Atroûss. Hodh el Gharbi, SE Mauritania
98 *I13* **Ayr** W Scotland, UK
98 *I13* **Ayr** ≈ W Scotland, UK
98 *I13* **Ayrshire** *cultural region* SW Scotland, UK
Aysen *see* Aisén
82 *L12* **Āysha** E Ethiopia
152 *K8* **Aytim** Nawoiy Wiloyati, N Uzbekistan
189 *W4* **Ayton** Queensland, NE Australia
116 *M9* **Aytos** Burgaska Oblast, E Bulgaria
176 *Uu7* **Ayu, Kepulauan** *island group* E Indonesia
A Yun Pa *see* Cheo Reo
175 *O8* **Ayu, Tanjung** *headland* Borneo, N Indonesia
42 *K13* **Ayutla** Jalisco, C Mexico
43 *P16* **Ayutlá** ***var.*** Ayutla de los Libres. Guerrero, S Mexico
Ayutla de los Libres *see* Ayutlá
178 *H11*. **Ayutthaya** ***var.*** Phra Nakhon Si Ayutthaya. Phra Nakhon Si Ayutthaya, C Thailand
142 *B13* **Ayvalık** Balıkesir, W Turkey
101 *L20* **Aywaille** Liège, E Belgium
147 *R13* **'Aywat aş Şay'ar, Wādī** *seasonal river* N Yemen
Azaffal *see* Azeffâl
107 *T9* **Azahar, Costa del** *coastal region* E Spain
107 *S6* **Azaila** Aragón, NE Spain
106 *F10* **Azambuja** Lisboa, C Portugal
159 *N13* **Āzamgarh** Uttar Pradesh, N India
79 *O9* **Azaouâd** *desert* C Mali
79 *S10* **Azaouagh, Vallée de l'** ***var.*** Azaouak. ≈ W Niger
Azaouak *see* Azaouagh, Vallée de l'
63 *F14* **Azara** Misiones, NE Argentina
148 *K3* **Āzarān** Āžarbāyjān-e Khāvarī, N Iran
Azärbaycan/Azärbaycan Respublikası *see* Azerbaijan
148 *I4* **Āžarbāyjān-e Bākhtarī** ***off.*** Ostān-e Āžarbāyjān-e Bākhtarī, ***var.*** Āžarbāyjān-e Gharbī, ***Eng.*** West Azerbaijan. ⬖ *province* NW Iran
Āžarbāyjān-e Gharbī *see* Āžarbāyjān-e Bākhtarī
148 *J3* **Āžarbāyjān-e Khāvarī** ***off.*** Ostān-e Āžarbāyjān-e Khāvarī, ***var.*** Āžarbāyjān-e Sharqī, ***Eng.*** East Azerbaijan. ⬖ *province* NW Iran
Āžarbāyjān-e Sharqī *see* Āžarbāyjān-e Khāvarī
79 *W13* **Azare** Bauchi, N Nigeria
121 *M19* **Azarychy** ***Rus.*** Ozarichi. Homyel'skaya Voblasts', SE Belarus
104 *L8* **Azay-le-Rideau** Indre-et-Loire, C France
144 *I2* **A'zāz** Ḩalab, NW Syria
78 *H7* **Azeffâl** ***var.*** Azaffal. *desert* Mauritania/Western Sahara
143 *V12* **Azerbaijan** ***off.*** Azerbaijani Republic, ***Az.*** Azärbaycan, Azärbaycan Respublikası; ***prev.*** Azerbaijan SSR. ◆ *republic* SE Asia
151 *T7* **Azhbulat, Ozero** ◎ NE Kazakhstan
76 *F7* **Azilal** C Morocco
Azimabad *see* Patna
21 *O6* **Aziscohos Lake** ⊠ Maine, NE USA
Azizbekov *see* Vayk'
Azizie *see* Telish
Aziziya *see* Al 'Azīzīyah
131 *T4* **Aznakayevo** Respublika Tatarstan, W Russian Federation
58 *C8* **Azogues** Cañar, S Ecuador
66 *N2* **Azores** ***var.*** Açores, Ilhas dos Açores, ***Port.*** Arquipélago dos Açores. *island group* Portugal, NE Atlantic Ocean
66 *L8* **Azores-Biscay Rise** *undersea feature* E Atlantic Ocean
Azotos/Azotus *see* Ashdod
80 *K11* **Azoum, Bahr** *seasonal river* SE Chad
130 *L12* **Azov** Rostovskaya Oblast', SW Russian Federation
130 *J13* **Azov, Sea of** ***Rus.*** Azovskoye More, ***Ukr.*** Azovs'ke More. *sea* NE Black Sea
Azovs'ke More/Azovskoye More *see* Azov, Sea of
Azraq, Bahr el *see* Blue Nile
144 *I10* **Azraq, Wāḩat al** *oasis* N Jordan
Āzro *see* Āzrow
76 *G6* **Azrou** C Morocco
155 *R5* **Āzrow** ***var.*** Āzro. Lowgar, E Afghanistan
39 *P8* **Aztec** New Mexico, SW USA
38 *M13* **Aztec Peak** ▲ Arizona, SW USA
47 *N9* **Azua** ***var.*** Azua de Compostela. S Dominican Republic
Azua de Compostela *see* Azua
106 *K12* **Azuaga** Extremadura, W Spain
58 *B8* **Azuay** ⬖ *province* W Ecuador
170 *Bb11* **Azuchi-Ō-shima** *island* SW Japan
107 *O11* **Azuer** ≈ C Spain
45 *S17* **Azuero, Península de** *peninsula* S Panama
64 *I6* **Azufre, Volcán** ***var.*** Volcán Lastarria. ▲ N Chile
118 *J12* **Azuga** Prahova, SE Romania
63 *C22* **Azul** Buenos Aires, E Argentina
64 *I8* **Azul, Cerro** ▲ NW Argentina
58 *E12* **Azul, Cordillera** ▲▲ C Peru
171 *Ll14* **Azuma-san** ▲ Honshū, C Japan
105 *V15* **Azur, Côte d'** *coastal region* SE France
203 *Z3* **Azur Lagoon** ◎ Kiritimati, E Kiribati
'Azza *see* Gaza
Az Zāb al Kabīr *see* Great Zab
144 *H7* **Az Zabdānī** ***var.*** Zabadani. Dimashq, W Syria
147 *W8* **Aẓ Ẓāhirah** *desert* NW Oman
147 *S6* **Aẓ Ẓahrān** ***Eng.*** Dhahran. Ash Sharqīyah, NE Saudi Arabia
147 *R6* **Aẓ Ẓahrān al Khubar** ***var.*** Dhahran Al Khobar. ✕ Ash Sharqīyah, NE Saudi Arabia
Az Zaqāzīq *see* Zagazig
144 *H10* **Az Zarqā'** ***var.*** Zarqa. Az Zarqā', NW Jordan
144 *I11* **Az Zarqā'** ***off.*** Muḩāfaẓat az Zarqā', ***var.*** Zarqa. ⬖ *governorate* N Jordan
77 *O7* **Az Zāwiyah** ***var.*** Zawia. NW Libya
147 *N15* **Az Zaydīyah** W Yemen
76 *I11* **Azzel Matti, Sebkha** ***var.*** Sebkra Azz el Matti. *salt flat* C Algeria
147 *P6* **Az Zilfī** Ar Riyāḑ, N Saudi Arabia
145 *Y13* **Az Zubayr** ***var.*** Al Zubair. SE Iraq
Az Zuqur *see* Jabal Zuuqar, Jazīrat

B

197 *H14* **Ba** ***prev.*** Mba. Viti Levu, W Fiji
Ba *see* Đa Răng
175 *R18* **Baa** Pulau Rote, C Indonesia
197 *G5* **Baaba, Île** *island* Îles Belep, W New Caledonia
144 *H7* **Baalbek** ***var.*** Ba'labakk; ***anc.*** Heliopolis. E Lebanon
110 *G8* **Baar** Zug, N Switzerland
83 *L17* **Baardheere** ***var.*** Bardere, ***It.*** Bardera. Gedo, SW Somalia
82 *Q12* **Baargaal** Bari, NE Somalia
101 *I15* **Baarle-Hertog** Antwerpen, N Belgium
101 *I15* **Baarle-Nassau** Antwerpen, N Belgium
100 *J11* **Baarn** Utrecht, C Netherlands
116 *D13* **Baba** ***var.*** Buševa, ***Gk.*** Varnoús. ▲▲ FYR Macedonia/Greece
78 *H10* **Bababé** Brakna, W Mauritania
142 *G10* **Baba Burnu** *headland* NW Turkey
119 *N13* **Babadag** Tulcea, SE Romania
143 *X10* **Babadağ Dağı** ▲ NE Azerbaijan
Babadayhan *see* Babadaykhan
152 *H14* **Babadaykhan** ***Turkm.*** Babadayhan; ***prev.*** Kirovsk. Akhalskiy Velayat, C Turkmenistan
152 *G14* **Babadurmaz** Akhalskiy Velayat, C Turkmenistan
116 *M12* **Babaeski** Kırklareli, NW Turkey
145 *T4* **Bāba Gurgur** N Iraq
58 *B7* **Babahoyo** ***prev.*** Bodegas. Los Ríos, C Ecuador
155 *P5* **Bābā, Kūh-e** ▲▲ C Afghanistan
175 *P10* **Babana** Sulawesi, C Indonesia
176 *U16* **Babar, Kepulauan** *island group* E Indonesia
176 *U15* **Babar, Pulau** *island* Kepulauan Babar, E Indonesia
158 *G4* **Bābāsar Pass** *pass* India/Pakistan
195 *Q10* **Babase Island** *island* Feni Islands, NE PNG
152 *C9* **Babashy** ▲▲ W Turkmenistan
174 *Ll15* **Babat** Jawa, S Indonesia
174 *I10* **Babat** Sumatera, W Indonesia
Babatag, Khrebet *see* Bobotogh, Qatorkŭhi
83 *H21* **Babati** Arusha, NE Tanzania
128 *J13* **Babayevo** Vologodskaya Oblast', NW Russian Federation
131 *Q15* **Babayurt** Respublika Dagestan, SW Russian Federation
35 *P6* **Babb** Montana, NW USA
31 *X4* **Babbitt** Minnesota, N USA
196 *E9* **Babeldaob** ***var.*** Babeldaop, Babelthuap. *island* N Palau
Babeldaop *see* Babeldaob
147 *N17* **Bab el Mandeb** *strait* Gulf of Aden/Red Sea
Babelthuap *see* Babeldaob
113 *K17* **Babia Góra** ***var.*** Babia Hora. ▲ Czech Republic/Poland
Babia Hora *see* Babia Góra
Babian Jiang *see* Black River
Babichi *see* Babichy
121 *N19* **Babichy** ***Rus.*** Babichi. Homyel'skaya Voblasts', SE Belarus
114 *I10* **Babina Greda** Vukovar-Srijem, E Croatia
8 *K13* **Babine Lake** ◎ British Columbia, SW Canada
176 *Vv10* **Babo** Irian Jaya, E Indonesia
149 *O4* **Bābol** ***var.*** Babul, Balfrush, Barfrush; ***prev.*** Barfurush. Māzandarān, N Iran
149 *O4* **Bābolsar** ***var.*** Babulsar; ***prev.*** Meshed-i-Sar. Māzandarān, N Iran
38 *L16* **Baboquivari Peak** ▲ Arizona, SW USA
81 *G15* **Baboua** Nana-Mambéré, W Central African Republic
121 *M17* **Babruysk** ***Rus.*** Bobruysk. Mahilyowskaya Voblasts', E Belarus
Babu *see* Hexian
Babul *see* Bābol
Babulsar *see* Bābolsar
115 *O19* **Babuna** ≈ C FYR Macedonia
115 *O19* **Babuna** ▲▲ C FYR Macedonia
154 *K7* **Bābūs, Dasht-e** ***Pash.*** Bebas, Dasht-i. ▲▲ W Afghanistan
126 *Jj16* **Babushkin** Respublika Buryatiya, S Russian Federation
179 *P7* **Babuyan Channel** *channel* N Philippines
179 *Pp7* **Babuyan Island** *island* N Philippines
145 *T9* **Babylon** *site of ancient city* C Iraq
114 *J9* **Bač** ***Ger.*** Batsch. Serbia, NW Yugoslavia
60 *M13* **Bacabal** Maranhão, E Brazil
43 *Y14* **Bacalar** Quintana Roo, SE Mexico
43 *Y14* **Bacalar Chico, Boca** *strait* SE Mexico
175 *Ss8* **Bacan, Kepulauan** *island group* E Indonesia
175 *T8* **Bacan, Pulau** ***prev.*** Batjan. *island* Maluku, E Indonesia
118 *L10* **Bacău** ***Hung.*** Bákó. Bacău, NE Romania
118 *K11* **Bacău** ⬖ *county* E Romania
Băc Bô, Vinh *see* Tongking, Gulf of
178 *Jj5* **Băc Can** Băc Thai, N Vietnam
105 *T5* **Baccarat** Meurthe-et-Moselle, NE France
191 *N12* **Bacchus Marsh** Victoria, SE Australia
42 *H4* **Bacerac** Sonora, NW Mexico
118 *L10* **Băceşti** Vaslui, E Romania
178 *Jj6* **Băc Giang** Ha Băc, N Vietnam
56 *I5* **Bachaquero** Zulia, NW Venezuela
Bacher *see* Pohorje
120 *M13* **Bacheykava** ***Rus.*** Bocheykovo. Vitsyebskaya Voblasts', N Belarus
42 *I5* **Bachíniva** Chihuahua, N Mexico
164 *G8* **Bachu** Xinjiang Uygur Zizhiqu, NW China
15 *J6* **Back** ≈ Northwest Territories, N Canada
114 *K10* **Bačka Palanka** ***prev.*** Palanka. Serbia, NW Yugoslavia
114 *K8* **Bačka Topola** ***Hung.*** Topolya; ***prev. Hung.*** Bácstopolya. Serbia, N Yugoslavia
97 *J17* **Bäckefors** Älvsborg, S Sweden
Bäckermühle Schulzenmühle *see* Żywiec
97 *L16* **Bäckhammar** Värmland, C Sweden
114 *K9* **Bački Petrovac** ***Hung.*** Petrőcz; ***prev.*** Petrovac, Petrovácz. Serbia, NW Yugoslavia
103 *I21* **Backnang** Baden-Württemberg, SW Germany
178 *J15* **Bac Liêu** ***var.*** Vinh Loi. Minh Hai, S Vietnam
178 *Jj6* **Băc Ninh** Ha Băc, N Vietnam
42 *G4* **Bacoachi** Sonora, NW Mexico
179 *Q13* **Bacolod** ***off.*** Bacolod City. Negros, C Philippines
179 *P12* **Baco, Mount** ▲ Mindoro, N Philippines
113 *K25* **Bácsalmás** Bács-Kiskun, S Hungary
Bácsjózseffalva *see* Žednik
113 *J24* **Bács-Kiskun** ***off.*** Bács-Kiskun Megye. ⬖ *county* S Hungary
Bácsszenttamás *see* Srbobran
Bácstopolya *see* Bačka Topola
Bactra *see* Balkh
161 *F21* **Badagara** Kerala, SW India
103 *M24* **Bad Aibling** Bayern, SE Germany
168 *I13* **Badain Jaran Shamo** *desert* N China
106 *I11* **Badajoz** ***anc.*** Pax Augusta. Extremadura, W Spain
106 *J11* **Badajoz** ⬖ *province* Extremadura, W Spain
155 *S2* **Badakhshān** ⬖ *province* NE Afghanistan
107 *W6* **Badalona** ***anc.*** Baetulo. Cataluña, E Spain
160 *O11* **Bādāmapāhārh** Orissa, E India
158 *K8* **Badarīnāth** ▲ N India
174 *Jj8* **Badas, Kepulauan** *island group* W Indonesia
111 *S6* **Bad Aussee** Salzburg, E Austria
33 *S8* **Bad Axe** Michigan, N USA
103 *G16* **Bad Berleburg** Nordrhein-Westfalen, W Germany
103 *L17* **Bad Blankenburg** Thüringen, C Germany
Bad Borseck *see* Borsec
103 *G18* **Bad Camberg** Hessen, W Germany
102 *L8* **Bad Doberan** Mecklenburg-Vorpommern, N Germany
103 *N14* **Bad Düben** Sachsen, E Germany
111 *X4* **Baden** ***var.*** Baden bei Wien; ***anc.*** Aquae Panoniae, Thermae Pannonicae. Niederösterreich, NE Austria
110 *F9* **Baden** Aargau, N Switzerland
103 *G21* **Baden-Baden** ***anc.*** Aurelia Aquensis. Baden-Württemberg, SW Germany
Baden bei Wien *see* Baden
103 *G22* **Baden-Württemberg** ***Fr.*** Bade-Wurtemberg. ⬖ *state* SW Germany
114 *A10* **Baderna** Istra, NW Croatia
Bade-Wurtemberg *see* Baden-Württemberg
103 *H20* **Bad Fredrichshall** Baden-Württemberg, S Germany
102 *P11* **Bad Freienwalde** Brandenburg, NE Germany
111 *Q8* **Badgastein** ***var.*** Gastein. Salzburg, NW Austria
Badger State *see* Wisconsin
154 *L4* **Bādghīs** ⬖ *province* NW Afghanistan
111 *T5* **Bad Hall** Oberösterreich, N Austria
103 *J14* **Bad Harzburg** Niedersachsen, C Germany
103 *I16* **Bad Hersfeld** Hessen, C Germany
100 *I10* **Badhoevedorp** Noord-Holland, C Netherlands
111 *Q8* **Bad Hofgastein** Salzburg, NW Austria
Bad Homburg *see* Bad Homburg vor der Höhe
103 *G18* **Bad Homburg vor der Höhe** ***var.*** Bad Homburg. Hessen, W Germany
103 *E17* **Bad Honnef** Nordrhein-Westfalen, W Germany
155 *Q17* **Badīn** Sind, SE Pakistan
23 *S10* **Badin Lake** ⊠ North Carolina, SE USA
42 *I8* **Badiraguato** Sinaloa, C Mexico
111 *R6* **Bad Ischl** Oberösterreich, N Austria
Badjawa *see* Bajawa
103 *J18* **Bad Kissingen** Bayern, SE Germany
Bad Königswart *see* Lázně Kynžvart
103 *F19* **Bad Kreuznach** Rheinland-Pfalz, SW Germany
103 *F24* **Bad Krozingen** Baden-Württemberg, SW Germany
103 *G16* **Bad Laasphe** Nordrhein-Westfalen, W Germany
30 *J6* **Badlands** *physical region* North Dakota, N USA
103 *K16* **Bad Langensalza** Thüringen, C Germany
111 *T3* **Bad Leonfelden** Oberösterreich, N Austria
103 *I20* **Bad Mergentheim** Baden-Württemberg, SW Germany
103 *H17* **Bad Nauheim** Hessen, W Germany
103 *E17* **Bad Neuenahr-Arhweiler** Rheinland-Pfalz, W Germany
Bad Neustadt *see* Bad Neustadt an der Saale
103 *J18* **Bad Neustadt an der Saale** ***var.*** Bad Neustadt. Berlin, C Germany
Badnur *see* Betūl
176 *Yy15* **Bado** Irian Jaya, E Indonesia
102 *H13* **Bad Oeynhausen** Nordrhein-Westfalen, NW Germany
102 *J9* **Bad Oldesloe** Schleswig-Holstein, N Germany
79 *Q16* **Badou** C Togo
Bad Polzin *see* Połczyn-Zdrój
102 *H13* **Bad Pyrmont** Niedersachsen, C Germany
111 *X9* **Bad Radkersburg** Steiermark, SE Austria
145 *V8* **Badrah** E Iraq
168 *J6* **Badrah** Hövsgöl, N Mongolia
103 *N24* **Bad Reichenhall** Bayern, SE Germany
146 *K8* **Badr Ḩunayn** Al Madīnah, W Saudi Arabia
30 *M10* **Bad River** ≈ South Dakota, N USA
32 *K4* **Bad River** ≈ Wisconsin, N USA
102 *H13* **Bad Salzuflen** Nordrhein-Westfalen, NW Germany
103 *J16* **Bad Salzungen** Thüringen, C Germany
111 *V8* **Bad Sankt Leonhard im Lavanttal** Kärnten, S Austria
102 *K9* **Bad Schwartau** Schleswig-Holstein, N Germany
103 *L24* **Bad Tölz** Bayern, SE Germany
189 *U1* **Badu Island** *island* Queensland, NE Australia
161 *K25* **Badulla** Uva Province, C Sri Lanka
111 *X5* **Bad Vöslau** Niederösterreich, NE Austria
103 *I24* **Bad Waldsee** Baden-Württemberg, S Germany
37 *U11* **Badwater Basin** *depression* California, W USA
103 *J20* **Bad Windsheim** Bayern, C Germany
103 *J23* **Bad Wörishofen** Bayern, S Germany
102 *G10* **Bad Zwischenahn** Niedersachsen, NW Germany
106 *M13* **Baena** Andalucía, S Spain
Baeterrae/Baeterrae Septimanorum *see* Béziers
Baetic Cordillera/Baetic Mountains *see* Béticos, Sistemas
Baetulo *see* Badalona
59 *K18* **Baeza** Napo, NE Ecuador
107 *N13* **Baeza** Andalucía, S Spain
81 *D15* **Bafang** Ouest, W Cameroon
78 *H12* **Bafatá** C Guinea-Bissau
155 *U5* **Baffa** North-West Frontier Province, NW Pakistan
15 *Ll1* **Baffin** ⬖ *district* Northwest Territories, NE Canada
207 *O11* **Baffin Basin** *undersea feature* N Labrador Sea
207 *N12* **Baffin Bay** *bay* Canada/Greenland
27 *T15* **Baffin Bay** *inlet* Texas, SW USA
206 *M12* **Baffin Island** *island* Northwest Territories, NE Canada
81 *E15* **Bafia** Centre, C Cameroon
79 *R14* **Bafilo** NE Togo
78 *J12* **Bafing** *headstream* W Africa
78 *J12* **Bafoulabé** Kayes, W Mali
81 *D15* **Bafoussam** Ouest, W Cameroon
149 *R9* **Bāfq** Yazd, C Iran
142 *L10* **Bafra** Samsun, N Turkey
142 *L10* **Bafra Burnu** *headland* N Turkey
149 *S12* **Bāft** Kermān, S Iran
81 *N18* **Bafwabalinga** Haut-Zaïre, NE Zaire
81 *N18* **Bafwaboli** Haut-Zaïre, NE Zaire
81 *N17* **Bafwasende** Haut-Zaïre, NE Zaire
194 *J11* **Bagabag Island** *island* N PNG
44 *K13* **Bagaces** Guanacaste, NW Costa Rica
159 *O12* **Bagaha** Bihār, N India
161 *F16* **Bāgalkot** Karnātaka, W India
83 *J22* **Bagamoyo** Pwani, E Tanzania
174 *Gg4* **Bagan Datuk** ***var.*** Bagan Datok. Perak, Peninsular Malaysia
179 *Rr15* **Baganga** Mindanao, S Philippines
174 *Gg6* **Bagansiapiapi** ***var.*** Pasirpangarayan. Sumatera, W Indonesia
Bagaria *see* Bagheria
79 *T11* **Bagaroua** Tahoua, W Niger
81 *I20* **Bagata** Bandundu, W Zaire
Bagdad *see* Baghdād
126 *Kk15* **Bagdarin** Respublika Buryatiya, S Russian Federation
63 *G17* **Bagé** Rio Grande do Sul, S Brazil
Bagenalstown *see* Muine Bheag
105 *P16* **Bages et de Sigean, Étang de** ◎ S France
35 *W17* **Baggs** Wyoming, C USA
160 *F11* **Bāgh** Madhya Pradesh, C India
145 *T8* **Baghdād** ***var.*** Bagdad, ***Eng.*** Baghdad. ● (Iraq) C Iraq
145 *T8* **Baghdād** ✕ C Iraq
159 *T16* **Bagherhat** Khulna, S Bangladesh
109 *J23* **Bagheria** ***var.*** Bagaria. Sicilia, Italy, C Mediterranean Sea
149 *S10* **Bāghīn** Kermān, C Iran
155 *Q3* **Baghlān** Baghlān, NE Afghanistan
155 *Q3* **Baghlān** ***var.*** Bāghlān. ⬖ *province* NE Afghanistan
154 *M7* **Bāghrān** Helmand, S Afghanistan
31 *T4* **Bagley** Minnesota, N USA
108 *H10* **Bagnacavallo** Emilia-Romagna, C Italy
104 *K16* **Bagnères-de-Bigorre** Hautes-Pyrénées, S France
104 *L17* **Bagnères-de-Luchon** Hautes-Pyrénées, S France
108 *F11* **Bagni di Lucca** Toscana, C Italy
108 *H11* **Bagno di Romagna** Emilia-Romagna, C Italy
105 *R14* **Bagnols-sur-Cèze** Gard, S France
168 *M14* **Bag Nur** ◎ N China
179 *Q13* **Bago** ***off.*** Bago City. Negros, C Philippines
Bago *see* Pegu
78 *M13* **Bagoé** ≈ Ivory Coast/Mali
Bagrāmē *see* Bagrāmī
155 *R5* **Bagrāmī** ***var.*** Bagrāmē. Kābul, E Afghanistan
121 *B14* **Bagrationovsk** ***Ger.*** Preussisch Eylau. Kaliningradskaya Oblast', W Russian Federation
Bagrax *see* Bohu
Bagrax Hu *see* Bosten Hu
58 *C10* **Bagua** Amazonas, NE Peru
179 *P9* **Baguio** ***off.*** Baguio City. Luzon, N Philippines
79 *V9* **Bagzane, Monts** ▲ N Niger
Bāḩah, Minţaqat al *see* Al Bāḩah
Bahama Islands *see* Bahamas
46 *H3* **Bahamas** ***off.*** Commonwealth of the Bahamas. ◆ *commonwealth republic* N West Indies
1 *L13* **Bahamas** ***var.*** Bahama Islands. *island group* N West Indies
159 *S15* **Baharampur** ***prev.*** Berhampore. West Bengal, NE India
175 *Nn6* **Bahau, Sungai** ≈ Borneo, N Indonesia
155 *U10* **Bahāwalnagar** Punjab, E Pakistan
155 *T11* **Bahāwalpur** Punjab, E Pakistan
142 *L16* **Bahçe** Adana, S Turkey
166 *J8* **Ba He** ≈ C China
Bäherden *see* Bakharden
61 *N16* **Bahia** ***off.*** Estado da Bahia. ⬖ *state* E Brazil
63 *B24* **Bahía Blanca** Buenos Aires, E Argentina
42 *L15* **Bahía Bufadero** Michoacán de Ocampo, SW Mexico
65 *J19* **Bahía Bustamante** Chubut, SE Argentina
42 *D5* **Bahía de los Ángeles** Baja California, NW Mexico
42 *C6* **Bahía de Tortugas** Baja California Sur, W Mexico
44 *J4* **Bahía, Islas de la** ***Eng.*** Bay Islands. *island group* N Honduras
42 *E5* **Bahía Kino** Sonora, NW Mexico
42 *E9* **Bahía Magdalena** ***var.*** Puerto Magdalena. Baja California Sur, W Mexico
56 *C8* **Bahía Solano** ***var.*** Ciudad Mutis, Solano. Chocó, W Colombia
82 *I11* **Bahir Dar** ***var.*** Bahr Dar, Bahrdar Giyorgis. NW Ethiopia
147 *X8* **Bahlā'** ***var.*** Bahlah, Bahlat. NW Oman
Bāhla *see* Bālān
Bahlah/Bahlat *see* Bahlā'
158 *M11* **Bahraich** Uttar Pradesh, N India
149 *M14* **Bahrain** ***off.*** State of Bahrain, Dawlat al Bahrayn, ***Ar.*** Al Baḩrayn; ***prev.*** Bahrein, ***anc.*** Tylos or Tyros. ◆ *monarchy* SW Asia
148 *M14* **Bahrain** ✕ C Bahrain
148 *M15* **Bahrain, Gulf of** *gulf* Persian Gulf, NW Arabian Sea
144 *I7* **Baḩrat Mallāḩah** ◎ W Syria
Bahrayn, Dawlat al *see* Bahrain
Bahr Dar/Bahrdar Giyorgis *see* Bahir Dar
Bahrein *see* Bahrain
83 *E16* **Bahr el Gabel** ⬖ *state* S Sudan
82 *E13* **Bahr ez Zaref** ≈ C Sudan
69 *R8* **Bahr Kameur** ≈ N Central African Republic
Bahr Tabariya, Sea of *see* Tiberias, Lake
149 *W15* **Bāhū Kalāt** Sīstān va Balūchestān, SE Iran
120 *N13* **Bahushewsk** ***Rus.*** Bogushëvsk. Vitsyebskaya Voblasts', NE Belarus
Bai *see* Tagow Bāy
118 *G13* **Baia de Aramă** Mehedinţi, SW Romania
118 *G11* **Baia de Criş** ***Ger.*** Altenburg, ***Hung.*** Körösbánya. Hunedoara, SW Romania
85 *A16* **Baia dos Tigres** Namibe, SW Angola
84 *A13* **Baia Farta** Benguela, W Angola
118 *H9* **Baia Mare** ***Ger.*** Frauenbach, ***Hung.*** Nagybánya; ***prev.*** Neustadt. Maramureş, NW Romania
118 *H8* **Baia Sprie** ***Ger.*** Mittelstadt, ***Hung.*** Felsőbánya. Maramureş, NW Romania
80 *G13* **Baïbokoum** Logone-Oriental, SW Chad
166 *F12* **Baicao Ling** ▲▲ SW China
169 *U9* **Baicheng** ***var.*** Pai-ch'eng; ***prev.*** T'aon-an. Jilin, NE China
164 *I6* **Baicheng** ***var.*** Bay. Xinjiang Uygur Zizhiqu, NW China
118 *J13* **Băicoi** Prahova, SE Romania
Baidoa *see* Baydhabo
13 *U6* **Baie-Comeau** Québec, SE Canada
13 *T7* **Baie-des-Bacon** Québec, SE Canada
13 *S8* **Baie-des-Rochers** Québec, SE Canada
13 *U6* **Baie-des-Sables** Québec, SE Canada
10 *K11* **Baie-du-Poste** Québec, SE Canada
180 *H17* **Baie Lazare** Mahé, NE Seychelles
47 *Y5* **Baie-Mahault** Basse Terre, C Guadeloupe
13 *R9* **Baie-St-Paul** Québec, SE Canada
13 *V5* **Baie-Trinité** Québec, SE Canada
11 *T11* **Baie Verte** Newfoundland, Newfoundland and Labrador, SE Canada
Baiguan *see* Shangyu
145 *U11* **Bā'ij al Mahdī** S Iraq
Baiji *see* Bayjī
Baikal, Lake *see* Baykal, Ozero
Bailādila *see* Kirandul
Baile an Chaistil *see* Ballycastle
Baile an Róba *see* Ballinrobe
Baile an tSratha *see* Ballintra
Baile Átha an Rí *see* Athenry
Baile Átha Buí *see* Athboy
Baile Átha Cliath *see* Dublin
Baile Átha Fhirdhia *see* Ardee
Baile Átha Í *see* Athy
Baile Átha Luain *see* Athlone
Baile Átha Troim *see* Trim
Baile Brigín *see* Balbriggan
Baile Easa Dara *see* Ballysadare
118 *I13* **Băile Govora** Vâlcea, SW Romania
118 *F13* **Băile Herculane** ***Ger.*** Herkulesbad, ***Hung.*** Herkulesfürdő. Caraş-Severin, SW Romania
Baile Locha Riach *see* Loughrea
Baile Mhistéala *see* Mitchelstown
Baile Monaidh *see* Ballymoney
107 *N12* **Bailén** Andalucía, S Spain
Baile na hInse *see* Ballynahinch
Baile na Lorgan *see* Castleblayney
Baile na Mainistreach *see* Newtownabbey
Baile Nua na hArda *see* Newtownards
118 *I12* **Băile Olăneşti** Vâlcea, SW Romania
118 *H14* **Băileşti** Dolj, SW Romania
Bailingmiao *see* Darhan Muminggan Lianheqi
60 *K11* **Bailique, Ilha** *island* NE Brazil
105 *O1* **Bailleul** Nord, N France
80 *H12* **Ba Illi** Chari-Baguirmi, SW Chad
165 *V12* **Bailong Jiang** ≈ C China
84 *C13* **Bailundo** ***Port.*** Vila Teixeira da Silva. Huambo, C Angola
165 *T13* **Baima** ***var.*** Sêraitang. Qinghai, C China
176 *W14* **Baimun** Pulau Workai, E Indonesia
194 *H14* **Baimuru** Gulf, S PNG
164 *M16* **Bainang** Xizang Zizhiqu, W China
25 *S8* **Bainbridge** Georgia, SE USA
175 *Pp17* **Baing** Pulau Sumba, SE Indonesia
164 *M14* **Baingoin** Xizang Zizhiqu, W China
106 *G2* **Baio Grande** Galicia, NW Spain
106 *G4* **Baiona** Galicia, NW Spain
169 *V7* **Baiquan** Heilongjiang, NE China
Bā'ir *see* Bāyir
164 *I11* **Bairab Co** ◎ W China
27 *Q7* **Baird** Texas, SW USA
41 *N7* **Baird Mountains** ▲▲ Alaska, USA
15 *Mm2* **Baird Peninsula** *peninsula* Baffin Island, Northwest Territories, NE Canada
Baireuth *see* Bayreuth
202 *H3* **Bairiki** ● (Kiribati) Tarawa, NW Kiribati
169 *S11* **Bairin Youqi** ***var.*** Daban. Nei Mongol Zizhiqu, N China
169 *S10* **Bairin Zuoqi** ***var.*** Lindong. Nei Mongol Zizhiqu, N China
151 *P17* **Bairkum** ***Kaz.*** Bayyrqum. Yuzhnyy Kazakhstan, S Kazakhstan
191 *P12* **Bairnsdale** Victoria, SE Australia
179 *Q14* **Bais** Negros, S Philippines
104 *L15* **Baïse** ***var.*** Baise. ≈ S France
169 *W11* **Baishan** ***prev.*** Hunjiang. Jilin, NE China
120 *F12* **Baisogala** Radviliškis, C Lithuania
201 *Q7* **Baiti** N Nauru
106 *G13* **Baixo Alentejo** *physical region* S Portugal
66 *P5* **Baixo, Ilhéu de** *island* Madeira, Portugal, NE Atlantic Ocean
85 *E15* **Baixo Longa** Cuando Cubango, SE Angola
165 *V10* **Baiyin** Gansu, C China
166 *E8* **Baiyü** Sichuan, C China
167 *N14* **Baiyun** ✕ (Guangzhou) Guangdong, S China
166 *K4* **Baiyu Shan** ▲▲ C China
113 *J25* **Baja** Bács-Kiskun, S Hungary
42 *C4* **Baja California** ⬖ *state* NW Mexico
42 *C4* **Baja California** ***Eng.*** Lower California. *peninsula* NW Mexico
42 *E9* **Baja California Sur** ⬖ *state* W Mexico
Bājah *see* Béja
Bajan *see* Bayan
203 *V16* **Baja, Punta** *headland* Easter Island, Chile, E Pacific Ocean
42 *B4* **Baja, Punta** *headland* NW Mexico
57 *R5* **Baja, Punta** *headland* NE Venezuela
44 *D5* **Baja Verapaz** ***off.*** Departamento de Baja Verapaz. ⬖ *department* C Guatemala
175 *Q16* **Bajawa** ***prev.*** Badjawa. Flores, S Indonesia
159 *S16* **Baj Baj** ***prev.*** Budge-Budge. West Bengal, E India
147 *N15* **Bājil** W Yemen
191 *U4* **Bajimba, Mount** ▲ New South Wales, SE Australia
114 *K13* **Bajina Bašta** Serbia, W Yugoslavia
159 *U14* **Bajitpur** Dhaka, E Bangladesh
114 *K8* **Bajmok** Serbia, NW Yugoslavia
Bajo Boquete *see* Boquete
115 *L17* **Bajram Curri** Kukës, N Albania
81 *J14* **Bakala** Ouaka, C Central African Republic
131 *T4* **Bakaly** Respublika Bashkortostan, W Russian Federation
Bakan *see* Shimonoseki
151 *U14* **Bakanas** ***Kaz.*** Baqanas. Almaty, SE Kazakhstan
151 *V12* **Bakanas** ***Kaz.*** Baqanas. ≈ E Kazakhstan
151 *U14* **Bakbakty** ***Kaz.*** Baqbaqty. Almaty, SE Kazakhstan
126 *Gg13* **Bakchar** Tomskaya Oblast', C Russian Federation
78 *I11* **Bakel** E Senegal
37 *W13* **Baker** California, W USA
24 *J8* **Baker** Louisiana, S USA
35 *Y9* **Baker** Montana, NW USA
34 *L12* **Baker** Oregon, NW USA
199 *Jj8* **Baker and Howland Islands** ◇ *US unincorporated territory* W Polynesia
38 *L12* **Baker Butte** ▲ Arizona, SW USA
41 *X15* **Baker Island** *island* Alexander Archipelago, Alaska, USA
15 *Kk6* **Baker Lake** Northwest Territories, N Canada
15 *Kk6* **Baker Lake** ◎ Northwest Territories, N Canada

◆ Country
● Country Capital
◇ Dependent Territory
○ Dependent Territory Capital
⬖ Administrative Region
✕ International Airport
▲ Mountain
▲▲ Mountain Range
Ѫ Volcano
≈ River
◎ Lake
⊠ Reservoir

BAKERSFIELD – BARAKĪ BARAK

37 R13 **Bakersfield** California, W USA
26 M9 **Bakersfield** Texas, SW USA
23 P9 **Bakersville** North Carolina, SE USA
Bakhābi *see* Bū Khābi
152 E12 **Bakharden** *Turkm.* Bäherden; *prev.* Bakherden. Akhalskiy Velayat, C Turkmenistan
152 F12 **Bakhardok** *Turkm.* Bokurdak. Akhalskiy Velayat, C Turkmenistan
149 U5 **Bākharz, Kuhhā-ye** ▲ NE Iran
158 D13 **Bākhāsar** Rājasthān, NW India
Bakhchisaray *see* Bakhchysaray
119 T13 **Bakhchysaray** *Rus.* Bakhchisaray. Respublika Krym, S Ukraine
Bakherden *see* Bakharden
119 R3 **Bakhmach** Chernihivs'ka Oblast', N Ukraine
126 Hh11 **Bakhta** Krasnoyarskiy Kray, C Russian Federation
148 K6 **Bākhtarān** *prev.* Kermānshāh, Qahremānshahr. Kermānshāhān, W Iran
Bākhtarān *see* Kermānshāhān
149 Q11 **Bakhtegān, Daryācheh-ye** ◎ C Iran
151 X12 **Bakhty** Semipalatinsk, E Kazakhstan
143 Z11 **Bakı** *Eng.* Baku. ● (Azerbaijan) E Azerbaijan
143 Z11 **Bakı** ✕ E Azerbaijan
142 C13 **Bakır Çayı** ⩫ W Turkey
94 L1 **Bakkafjördhur** Austurland, NE Iceland
94 L1 **Bakkaflói** *sea area* W Norwegian Sea
83 I15 **Bako** SW Ethiopia
78 L15 **Bako** NW Ivory Coast
Bákó *see* Bacău
113 H23 **Bakony** *Eng.* Bakony Mountains, *Ger.* Bakonywald. ▲ W Hungary
Bakony Mountains/ Bakonywald *see* Bakony
83 M16 **Bakool** *off.* Gobolka Bakool. ◆ *region* W Somalia
81 L15 **Bakouma** Mbomou, SE Central African Republic
131 N15 **Baksan** Kabardino-Balkarskaya Respublika, SW Russian Federation
121 I16 **Bakshty** Hrodzyenskaya Voblasts', W Belarus
Baku *see* Bakı
204 K12 **Bakutis Coast** *physical region* Antarctica
Bakwanga *see* Mbuji-Mayi
151 O15 **Bakyrly** Yuzhnyy Kazakhstan, S Kazakhstan
12 H13 **Bala** Ontario, S Canada
99 J19 **Bala** NW Wales, UK
142 I13 **Balâ** Ankara, C Turkey
179 O16 **Balabac Island** *island* W Philippines
Balabac, Selat *see* Balabac Strait
175 O1 **Balabac Strait** *var.* Selat Balabac. *strait* Malaysia/Philippines
Ba'labakk *see* Baalbek
175 O10 **Balabalangan, Kepulauan** *island group* N Indonesia
197 H4 **Balabio, Île** *island* Province Nord, W New Caledonia
118 I14 **Balaci** Teleorman, S Romania
145 S7 **Balad** N Iraq
145 U7 **Balad Rūz** E Iraq
126 J15 **Balagansk** Irkutskaya Oblast', S Russian Federation
160 J11 **Bālāghāt** Madhya Pradesh, C India
161 F14 **Bālāghāt Range** ▲ W India
104 E1 **Balagne** *physical region* Corse, France, C Mediterranean Sea
107 U5 **Balaguer** Cataluña, NE Spain
107 S3 **Balaïtous** *var.* Pic de Balaitous, Pic de Balaïtous. ▲ France/Spain
Balaitous, Pic de *see* Balaïtous
131 O3 **Balakhna** Nizhegorodskaya Oblast', W Russian Federation
126 I14 **Balakhta** Krasnoyarskiy Kray, S Russian Federation
190 I9 **Balaklava** South Australia
Balakleya *see* Balakliya
119 V6 **Balakliya** *Rus.* Balakleya. Kharkivs'ka Oblast', E Ukraine
131 Q7 **Balakovo** Saratovskaya Oblast', W Russian Federation
85 P14 **Balama** Cabo Delgado, N Mozambique
175 Nn1 **Balambangan, Pulau** *island* East Malaysia
154 L3 **Bālā Morghāb** Laghmān, NW Afghanistan
158 E11 **Bālān** *prev.* Bāhla. Rājasthān, NW India
118 J10 **Bălan** *Hung.* Balánbánya. Harghita, C Romania
Balánbánya *see* Bălan
179 P10 **Balanga** Luzon, N Philippines
160 M12 **Balāngīr** *prev.* Bolangir. Orissa, E India
131 N8 **Balashov** Saratovskaya Oblast', W Russian Federation
Balasore *see* Bāleshwar
113 K21 **Balassagyarmat** Nógrád, N Hungary
31 S10 **Balaton** Minnesota, N USA
113 H24 **Balaton** *var.* Lake Balaton, *Ger.* Plattensee. ◎ W Hungary
113 I23 **Balatonfüred** *var.* Füred. Veszprém, W Hungary
Balaton, Lake *see* Balaton
118 I11 **Bălăușeri** *Ger.* Bladenmarkt, *Hung.* Balavásár. Mureș, C Romania
Balavásár *see* Bălăușeri
107 Q11 **Balazote** Castilla-La Mancha, C Spain
Balázsfalva *see* Blaj
121 F14 **Balbieriškis** Prienai, S Lithuania
195 S12 **Balbi, Mount** ▲ Bougainville Island, NE PNG
60 F11 **Balbina, Represa** ⊡ NW Brazil
45 T15 **Balboa** Panamá, C Panama
99 G17 **Balbriggan** *Ir.* Baile Brigín. E Ireland
Balbunar *see* Kubrat
83 N17 **Balcad** Shabeellaha Dhexe, C Somalia
63 D23 **Balcarce** Buenos Aires, E Argentina
9 U16 **Balcarres** Saskatchewan, S Canada
116 O8 **Balchik** Varnenska Oblast, NE Bulgaria
193 E24 **Balclutha** Otago, South Island, NZ
27 Q12 **Balcones Escarpment** *escarpment* Texas, SW USA
20 F14 **Bald Eagle Creek** ⩫ Pennsylvania, NE USA
Baldenburg *see* Biały Bór
23 V12 **Bald Head Island** *island* North Carolina, SE USA
29 W10 **Bald Knob** Arkansas, C USA
32 K17 **Bald Knob** *hill* Illinois, N USA
Baldohn *see* Baldone
120 G9 **Baldone** *Ger.* Baldohn. Riga, W Latvia
24 I9 **Baldwin** Louisiana, S USA
33 P7 **Baldwin** Michigan, N USA
29 Q4 **Baldwin City** Kansas, C USA
41 N8 **Baldwin Peninsula** *headland* Alaska, USA
20 H9 **Baldwinsville** New York, NE USA
25 N2 **Baldwyn** Mississippi, S USA
9 W15 **Baldy Mountain** ▲ Manitoba, S Canada
35 T7 **Baldy Mountain** ▲ Montana, NW USA
39 O13 **Baldy Peak** ▲ Arizona, SW USA
Bâle *see* Basel
107 X9 **Baleares** ◆ *autonomous community* E Spain
107 X11 **Baleares, Islas** *Eng.* Balearic Islands. *island group* Spain, W Mediterranean Sea
Baleares Major *see* Mallorca
Balearic Islands *see* Baleares, Islas
Balearic Plain *see* Algerian Basin
Balearis Minor *see* Menorca
174 M6 **Baleh, Batang** ⩫ East Malaysia
10 J8 **Baleine, Grande Rivière de la** ⩫ Québec, E Canada
10 K7 **Baleine, Petite Rivière de la** ⩫ Québec, SE Canada
11 N6 **Baleine, Rivière à la** ⩫ Québec, E Canada
101 J16 **Balen** Antwerpen, N Belgium
179 P9 **Baler** Luzon, N Philippines
160 P11 **Bāleshwar** *prev.* Balasore. Orissa, E India
126 L16 **Baley** Chitinskaya Oblast', S Russian Federation
79 S12 **Baléyara** Tillabéri, W Niger
131 T1 **Balezino** Udmurtskaya Respublika, NW Russian Federation
44 J4 **Balfate** Colón, N Honduras
9 O17 **Balfour** British Columbia, SW Canada
31 N3 **Balfour** North Dakota, N USA
Balfrush *see* Bābol
126 I16 **Balgazyn** Respublika Tyva, S Russian Federation
9 U16 **Balgonie** Saskatchewan, S Canada
Bālgrad *see* Alba Iulia
83 J19 **Balguda** *spring/well* S Kenya
164 K6 **Balguntay** Xinjiang Uygur Zizhiqu, NW China
147 R16 **Balḥāf** S Yemen
158 F13 **Bāli** Rājasthān, N India
175 O16 **Bali** ◆ *province* S Indonesia
175 N16 **Bali** *island* C Indonesia
113 K16 **Balice** ✕ (Kraków) Kraków, S Poland
176 Yy13 **Baliem, Sungai** ⩫ Irian Jaya, E Indonesia
142 C12 **Balıkesir** Balıkesir, W Turkey
142 C12 **Balıkesir** ◆ *province* NW Turkey
144 L3 **Balīkh, Nahr** ⩫ N Syria
175 O9 **Balikpapan** Borneo, C Indonesia
175 O9 **Balikpapan, Teluk** *bay* Borneo, C Indonesia
Bali, Laut *see* Bali Sea
195 O11 **Balima** ⩫ New Britain, C PNG
179 P17 **Balimbing** Tawitawi, SW Philippines
194 G14 **Balimo** Western, SW PNG
Balinc *see* Balinț
175 Qq9 **Balingara, Pegunungan** ▲ Sulawesi, N Indonesia
103 H23 **Balingen** Baden-Württemberg, SW Germany
118 F11 **Balinț** *Hung.* Bálinc. Timiș, W Romania
179 Pp6 **Balintang Channel** *channel* N Philippines
144 K3 **Bālis** Ḥalab, N Syria
175 N15 **Bali Sea** *Ind.* Laut Bali. *sea* C Indonesia
175 N16 **Bali, Selat** *strait* C Indonesia
100 K7 **Balk** Friesland, N Netherlands
124 O7 **Balkan Mountains** *Bul./SCr.* Stara Planina. ▲ Bulgaria/Yugoslavia
152 B9 **Balkanskiy Velayat** *Turkm.* Balkan Welayaty. ◆ *province* W Turkmenistan
Balkan Welayaty *see* Balkanskiy Velayat
151 P8 **Balkashino** Akmola, N Kazakhstan
155 O2 **Balkh** *anc.* Bactra. Balkh, N Afghanistan
155 P2 **Balkh** ◆ *province* N Afghanistan
151 T13 **Balkhash** *Kaz.* Balqash. Zhezkazgan, SE Kazakhstan
Balkhash, Lake *see* Balkhash, Ozero
151 T13 **Balkhash, Ozero** *Eng.* Lake Balkhash, *Kaz.* Balqash. ◎ SE Kazakhstan
Balla Balla *see* Mbalabala
98 H10 **Ballachulish** N Scotland, UK
188 M12 **Balladonia** Western Australia
99 C16 **Ballaghaderreen** *Ir.* Bealach an Doirín. C Ireland
94 H10 **Ballangen** Nordland, NW Norway
99 H14 **Ballantrae** W Scotland, UK
191 N12 **Ballarat** Victoria, SE Australia
188 K11 **Ballard, Lake** *salt lake* Western Australia
Ballari *see* Bellary
78 L11 **Ballé** Koulikoro, W Mali
42 D7 **Ballenas, Bahía de** *bay* W Mexico
42 D5 **Ballenas, Canal de** *channel* NW Mexico
205 R17 **Balleny Islands** *island group* Antarctica
42 J7 **Balleza** *var.* San Pablo Balleza. Chihuahua, N Mexico
116 M13 **Ballı** Tekirdağ, NW Turkey
159 O13 **Ballia** Uttar Pradesh, N India
191 V4 **Ballina** New South Wales, SE Australia
99 C16 **Ballina** *Ir.* Béal an Átha. W Ireland
99 D16 **Ballinamore** *Ir.* Béal an Átha Móir. NW Ireland
99 D18 **Ballinasloe** *Ir.* Béal Átha na Sluaighe. W Ireland
27 P8 **Ballinger** Texas, SW USA
99 C17 **Ballinrobe** *Ir.* Baile an Róba. W Ireland
99 A21 **Ballinskelligs Bay** *Ir.* Bá na Scealg. *inlet* SW Ireland
99 D15 **Ballintra** *Ir.* Baile an tSratha. NW Ireland
105 T7 **Ballon d'Alsace** ▲ NE France
Ballon de Guebwiller *see* Grand Ballon
115 K21 **Ballsh** *var.* Ballshi. Fier, SW Albania
Ballshi *see* Ballsh
100 K4 **Ballum** Friesland, N Netherlands
99 F16 **Ballybay** *Ir.* Béal Átha Beithe. N Ireland
99 E14 **Ballybofey** *Ir.* Bealach Féich. NW Ireland
99 G14 **Ballycastle** *Ir.* Baile an Chaistil. N Northern Ireland, UK
99 G15 **Ballyclare** *Ir.* Bealach Cláir. E Northern Ireland, UK
99 E16 **Ballyconnell** *Ir.* Béal Átha Conaill. N Ireland
99 C17 **Ballyhaunis** *Ir.* Beál Átha hAmhnais. W Ireland
99 G14 **Ballymena** *Ir.* An Baile Meánach. NE Northern Ireland, UK
99 F14 **Ballymoney** *Ir.* Baile Monaidh. NE Northern Ireland, UK
99 G15 **Ballynahinch** *Ir.* Baile na hInse. SE Northern Ireland, UK
99 D16 **Ballysadare** *Ir.* Baile Easa Dara. NW Ireland
99 D15 **Ballyshannon** *Ir.* Béal Átha Seanaidh. NW Ireland
65 H19 **Balmaceda** Aisén, S Chile
65 G23 **Balmaceda, Cerro** ▲ S Chile
113 N22 **Balmazújváros** Hajdú-Bihar, E Hungary
110 E10 **Balmhorn** ▲ SW Switzerland
190 L12 **Balmoral** Victoria, SE Australia
26 K9 **Balmorhea** Texas, SW USA
Balneario Claromecó *see* Claromecó
175 R9 **Balo** Sulawesi, N Indonesia
Balochistān *see* Baluchistān
84 B13 **Balombo** *Port.* Norton de Matos, Vila Norton de Matos. Benguela, W Angola
84 B13 **Balombo** ⩫ W Angola
189 X10 **Balonne River** ⩫ Queensland, E Australia
158 E13 **Bālotra** Rājasthān, N India
Balqā'/Balqā', Muḥāfaẓat al *see* Al Balqā'
Balqash *see* Balkhash/ Balkhash, Ozero
158 M12 **Balrāmpur** Uttar Pradesh, N India
190 M9 **Balranald** New South Wales, SE Australia
118 H14 **Balș** Olt, S Romania
12 H11 **Balsam Creek** Ontario, S Canada
32 I5 **Balsam Lake** Wisconsin, N USA
12 I14 **Balsam Lake** ◎ Ontario, SE Canada
61 M14 **Balsas** Maranhão, E Brazil
42 M15 **Balsas, Río** *var.* Río Mexcala. ⩫ S Mexico
45 W16 **Balsas, Río** ⩫ SE Panama
121 O18 **Bal'shavik** *Rus.* Bol'shevik. Homyel'skaya Voblasts', SE Belarus
97 O15 **Bålsta** Uppsala, C Sweden
110 E7 **Balsthal** Solothurn, NW Switzerland
119 O8 **Balta** Odes'ka Oblast', SW Ukraine
121 H14 **Baltaji Voke** Vilnius, SE Lithuania
107 N5 **Baltanás** Castilla-León, N Spain
63 E16 **Baltasar Brum** Artigas, N Uruguay
118 M9 **Bălți** *Rus.* Bel'tsy. N Moldova
Baltic Port *see* Paldiski
120 B10 **Baltic Sea** *Ger.* Ostee, *Rus.* Baltiskoye More. *sea* N Europe
23 X3 **Baltimore** Maryland, NE USA
33 T13 **Baltimore** Ohio, N USA
Baltischport/Baltiski *see* Paldiski
Baltiskoye More *see* Baltic Sea
121 A14 **Baltiysk** *Ger.* Pillau. Kaliningradskaya Oblast', W Russian Federation
Baltkrievija *see* Belarus
194 K9 **Baluan Island** *island* N PNG
Balūchestān va Sīstān *see* Sīstān va Balūchestān
154 M12 **Baluchistān** *var.* Balochistān, Beluchistan. ◆ *province* SW Pakistan
179 Q12 **Balud** Masbate, N Philippines
174 Mm6 **Balui, Batang** ⩫ East Malaysia
159 S13 **Bālurghat** West Bengal, NE India
120 J8 **Balvi** Balvi, NE Latvia
194 H12 **Balyer River** Western Highlands, C PNG
153 W7 **Balykchy** *Kir.* Ysyk-Köl; *prev.* Issyk-Kul', Rybach'ye. Issyk-Kul'skaya Oblast', NE Kyrgyzstan
58 B7 **Balzar** Guayas, W Ecuador
110 I8 **Balzers** S Liechtenstein
149 T12 **Bam** Kermān, SE Iran
79 Y13 **Bama** Borno, NE Nigeria
78 L12 **Bamako** ● (Mali) Capital District, SW Mali
79 P10 **Bamba** Gao, C Mali
44 M8 **Bambana, Río** ⩫ NE Nicaragua
81 J15 **Bambari** Ouaka, C Central African Republic
189 W5 **Bambaroo** Queensland, NE Australia
103 K19 **Bamberg** Bayern, SE Germany
23 R14 **Bamberg** South Carolina, SE USA
81 M16 **Bambesa** Haut-Zaïre, N Zaire
78 G11 **Bambey** W Senegal
81 H16 **Bambio** Sangha-Mbaéré, SW Central African Republic
85 I24 **Bamboesberge** ▲ S South Africa
81 D14 **Bamenda** Nord-Ouest, W Cameroon
8 K17 **Bamfield** Vancouver Island, British Columbia, SW Canada
152 E12 **Bami** *Turkm.* Bamy. Akhalskiy Velayat, C Turkmenistan
155 P4 **Bāmīān** *var.* Bāmiān. Bāmīān, NE Afghanistan
155 O4 **Bāmīān** ◆ *province* C Afghanistan
81 J14 **Bamingui** Bamingui-Bangoran, C Central African Republic
80 J13 **Bamingui** ⩫ N Central African Republic
80 J13 **Bamingui-Bangoran** ◆ *prefecture* N Central African Republic
149 V13 **Bampūr** Sīstān va Balūchestān, SE Iran
194 G14 **Bamu** ⩫ SW PNG
Bamy *see* Bami
Bán *see* Bánovce nad Bebravou
83 N17 **Banaadir** *off.* Gobolka Banaadir. ◆ *region* S Somalia
203 N3 **Banaba** *var.* Ocean Island. *island* Tungaru, W Kiribati
61 O14 **Banabuiú, Açude** ⊡ NE Brazil
59 O19 **Bañados del Izozog** *salt lake* SE Bolivia
99 D18 **Banagher** *Ir.* Beannchar. C Ireland
81 M17 **Banalia** Haut-Zaïre, N Zaire
78 L12 **Banamba** Koulikoro, W Mali
42 G4 **Banámichi** Sonora, NW Mexico
189 Y9 **Banana** Queensland, E Australia
203 Z2 **Banana** *prev.* Main Camp. Kiritimati, E Kiribati
61 K16 **Bananal, Ilha do** *island* C Brazil
25 Y12 **Banana River** *lagoon* Florida, SE USA
157 Q22 **Bananga** Andaman and Nicobar Islands, India, NE Indian Ocean
Banaras *see* Vārānasi
116 N13 **Banarlı** Tekirdağ, NW Turkey
158 H12 **Banās** ⩫ N India
77 Z11 **Banâs, Râs** *headland* E Egypt
114 N10 **Banatski Karlovac** Serbia, NE Yugoslavia
147 P16 **Banā, Wādī** *dry watercourse* SW Yemen
142 E14 **Banaz** Uşak, W Turkey
142 E14 **Banaz Çayı** ⩫ W Turkey
165 P14 **Banbar** Xizang Zizhiqu, W China
99 G15 **Banbridge** *Ir.* Droichead na Banna. SE Northern Ireland, UK
Ban Bua Yai *see* Bua Yai
99 M21 **Banbury** S England, UK
178 H7 **Ban Chiang Dao** Chiang Mai, NW Thailand
98 K9 **Banchory** NE Scotland, UK
12 J13 **Bancroft** Ontario, SE Canada
35 R15 **Bancroft** Idaho, NW USA
31 U11 **Bancroft** Iowa, C USA
160 I9 **Bānda** Madhya Pradesh, C India
158 L13 **Bānda** Uttar Pradesh, N India
173 E3 **Bandaaceh** *var.* Banda Atjeh; *prev.* Koetaradja, Kutaradja, Kutaraja. Sumatera, W Indonesia
Banda Atjeh *see* Bandaaceh
176 U12 **Banda, Kepulauan** *island group* E Indonesia
Banda, Laut *see* Banda Sea
79 N17 **Bandama** *var.* Bandama Fleuve. ⩫ S Ivory Coast
79 N15 **Bandama Blanc** ⩫ C Ivory Coast
Bandama Fleuve *see* Bandama
Bandar 'Abbās *see* Bandar-e 'Abbās
159 W16 **Bandarban** Chittagong, SE Bangladesh
82 Q13 **Bandarbeyla** *var.* Bender Beila, Bender Beyla. Bari, NE Somalia
149 R14 **Bandar-e 'Abbās** *var.* Bandar 'Abbās; *prev.* Gombroon. Hormozgān, S Iran
148 M3 **Bandar-e Anzalī** Gīlān, NW Iran
149 N12 **Bandar-e Būshehr** *var.* Būshehr, *Eng.* Bushire. Būshehr, S Iran
148 M11 **Bandar-e Gonāveh** *var.* Ganāveh; *prev.* Gonāveh. Būshehr, SW Iran
149 R14 **Bandar-e Khamīr** Hormozgān, S Iran
149 Q14 **Bandar-e Langeh** *var.* Bandar-e Lengeh, Lingeh. Hormozgān, S Iran
Bandar-e Lengeh *see* Bandar-e Langeh
148 L10 **Bandar-e Māhshahr** *var.* Māh-Shahr; *prev.* Bandar-e Ma'shūr. Khūzestān, SW Iran
Bandar-e Ma'shūr *see* Bandar-e Māhshahr
149 O14 **Bandar-e Nakhīlū** Hormozgān, S Iran
Bandar-e Shāh *see* Bandar-e Torkaman
149 P4 **Bandar-e Torkaman** *var.* Bandar-e Torkeman, Bandar-e Torkman; *prev.* Bandar-e Shāh. Māzandarān, N Iran
Bandar-e Torkeman/Bandar-e Torkman *see* Bandar-e Torkaman
Bandar Kassim *see* Boosaaso
174 Ii13 **Bandarlampung** *prev.* Tanjungkarang, Teloekbetoeng, Telukbetung. Sumatera, W Indonesia
Bandar Maharani *see* Muar
Bandar Masulipatnam *see* Machilipatnam
Bandar Penggaram *see* Batu Pahat
175 N3 **Bandar Seri Begawan** *prev.* Brunei Town. ● (Brunei) N Brunei
174 Mm3 **Bandar Seri Begawan** ✕ N Brunei
175 Ss13 **Banda Sea** *var.* Laut Banda. *sea* E Indonesia
106 H5 **Bande** Galicia, NW Spain
61 G15 **Bandeirantes** Mato Grosso, W Brazil
61 N20 **Bandeira, Pico da** ▲ SE Brazil
85 K19 **Bandelierkop** Northern, NE South Africa
64 L8 **Bandera** Santiago del Estero, N Argentina
27 Q11 **Bandera** Texas, SW USA
42 J13 **Banderas, Bahía de** *bay* W Mexico
79 O11 **Bandiagara** Mopti, C Mali
158 I12 **Bāndīkūī** Rājasthān, N India
142 C11 **Bandırma** *var.* Penderma. Balıkesir, NW Turkey
Bandjarmasin *see* Banjarmasin
Bandoeng *see* Bandung
99 C21 **Bandon** *Ir.* Droicheadna Bandan. SW Ireland
34 E14 **Bandon** Oregon, NW USA
178 J8 **Ban Dong Bang** Nong Khai, E Thailand
178 I6 **Ban Donkon** Oudômxai, N Laos
180 J14 **Bandrélé** SE Mayotte
81 H20 **Bandundu** *prev.* Banningville. Bandundu, W Zaire
81 I21 **Bandundu** *off.* Région de Bandundu. ◆ *region* W Zaire
174 Jj14 **Bandung** *prev.* Bandoeng. Jawa, C Indonesia
118 L15 **Băneasa** Constanța, SW Romania
148 J4 **Bāneh** Kordestān, N Iran
46 I7 **Banes** Holguín, E Cuba
9 P16 **Banff** Alberta, SW Canada
98 K8 **Banff** NE Scotland, UK
98 K8 **Banff** *cultural region* NE Scotland, UK
Bánffyhunyad *see* Huedin
79 N14 **Banfora** SW Burkina
161 H19 **Bangalore** Karnātaka, S India
159 S16 **Bangaon** West Bengal, NE India
179 P9 **Bangar** Luzon, N Philippines
81 L15 **Bangassou** Mbomou, SE Central African Republic
194 K12 **Bangeta, Mount** ▲ C PNG
175 Qq10 **Banggai, Kepulauan** *island group* C Indonesia
175 R9 **Banggai, Pulau** *island* Kepulauan Banggai, N Indonesia
176 X11 **Banggelapa** Irian Jaya, E Indonesia
Banggi *see* Banggi, Pulau
175 O1 **Banggi, Pulau** *var.* Banggi. *island* East Malaysia
124 N15 **Banghāzī** *Eng.* Bengazi, Benghazi, *It.* Bengasi. NE Libya
Bang Hieng *see* Xé Banghiang
174 K8 **Bangkai, Tanjung** *var.* Bankai. *headland* Borneo, N Indonesia
174 M14 **Bangkalan** Pulau Madura, C Indonesia
175 S6 **Bangka, Pulau** *island* N Indonesia
174 J10 **Bangka, Pulau** *island* W Indonesia
174 Ii10 **Bangka, Selat** *strait* Sumatera, W Indonesia
175 Rr6 **Bangka, Selat** *var.* Selat Likupang. *strait* Sulawesi, N Indonesia
174 Gg8 **Bangkinang** Sumatera, W Indonesia
174 H10 **Bangko** Sumatera, W Indonesia
Bangkok *see* Krung Thep
Bangkok, Bight of *see* Krung Thep, Ao
159 T14 **Bangladesh** *off.* People's Republic of Bangladesh; *prev.* East Pakistan. ◆ *republic* S Asia
178 Kk13 **Ba Ngoi** Khanh Hoa, S Vietnam
158 K5 **Bangong Co** *var.* Pangong Tso. ◎ China/India *see also* Pangong Tso
99 G15 **Bangor** *Ir.* Beannchar. E Northern Ireland, UK
99 I18 **Bangor** NW Wales, UK
21 R6 **Bangor** Maine, NE USA
20 I14 **Bangor** Pennsylvania, NE USA
69 R8 **Bangoran** ⩫ S Central African Republic
Bang Phra *see* Trat
Bang Pla Soi *see* Chon Buri
27 Q8 **Bangs** Texas, SW USA
178 H13 **Bang Saphan** *var.* Bang Saphan Yai. Prachuap Khiri Khan, SW Thailand
Bang Saphan Yai *see* Bang Saphan
38 I8 **Bangs, Mount** ▲ Arizona, SW USA
95 E15 **Bangsund** Nord-Trøndelag, C Norway
179 P8 **Bangued** Luzon, N Philippines
81 I15 **Bangui** ● (Central African Republic) Ombella-Mpoko, SW Central African Republic
81 I15 **Bangui** ✕ Ombella-Mpoko, SW Central African Republic
85 N16 **Bangula** Southern, S Malawi
Bangwaketse *see* Southern
84 K12 **Bangweulu, Lake** *var.* Lake Bengweulu. ◎ N Zambia
Banhā *see* Benha
Ban Hat Yai *see* Hat Yai
178 I8 **Ban Hin Heup** Viangchan, C Laos
Ban Houayxay/Ban Houei Sai *see* Houayxay
178 H12 **Ban Hua Hin** *var.* Hua Hin. Prachuap Khiri Khan, SW Thailand
81 L14 **Bani** Haute-Kotto, E Central African Republic
79 N12 **Bani** ⩫ S Mali
47 O9 **Baní** S Dominican Republic
Banias *see* Bāniyās
79 S11 **Bani Bangou** Tillabéri, SW Niger
78 M12 **Banifing** *var.* Ngorolaka. ⩫ Burkina/Mali
79 R13 **Banikoara** N Benin
Banī Mazār *see* Beni Mazâr
116 K8 **Baniski Lom** ⩫ N Bulgaria
23 U7 **Banister River** ⩫ Virginia, NE USA
Banī Suwayf *see* Beni Suef
77 O8 **Banī Walīd** NW Libya
144 H5 **Bāniyās** *var.* Banias, Baniyas, Paneas. Ṭarṭūs, W Syria
115 K14 **Banja** Serbia, W Yugoslavia
Banjak, Kepulauan *see* Banyak, Kepulauan
114 J12 **Banja Koviljača** Serbia, W Yugoslavia
114 G11 **Banja Luka** NW Bosnia and Herzegovina
175 N11 **Banjarmasin** *prev.* Bandjarmasin. Borneo, C Indonesia
Banjoewangi *see* Banyuwangi
78 F11 **Banjul** *prev.* Bathurst. ● (Gambia) W Gambia
78 F11 **Banjul** ✕ W Gambia
Banjuwangi *see* Banyuwangi
Bank *see* Bankä
143 Y13 **Bankä** *Rus.* Bank. SE Azerbaijan
178 Jj11 **Ban Kadian** *var.* Ban Kadiene. Champasak, S Laos
Ban Kadiene *see* Ban Kadian
Bankai *see* Bangkai, Tanjung
178 Gg15 **Ban Kam Phuam** Phangnga, SW Thailand
Ban Kantang *see* Kantang
79 O11 **Bankass** Mopti, S Mali
97 L19 **Bankeryd** Jönköping, S Sweden
85 K16 **Banket** Mashonaland West, N Zimbabwe
178 Jj11 **Ban Khamphô** Attapu, S Laos
25 O4 **Bankhead Lake** ⊡ Alabama, S USA
79 Q11 **Bankilaré** Tillabéri, SW Niger
Banks, Îles *see* Banks Islands
8 I14 **Banks Island** *island* British Columbia, SW Canada
15 Hh1 **Banks Island** *island* Banks Island, Northwest Territories, NW Canada
197 C10 **Banks Islands** *Fr.* Îles Banks. *island group* N Vanuatu
25 U8 **Banks Lake** ◎ Georgia, SE USA
34 K8 **Banks Lake** ⊡ Washington, NW USA
193 I19 **Banks Peninsula** *peninsula* South Island, NZ
191 Q15 **Banks Strait** *strait* SW Tasman Sea
Ban Kui Nua *see* Kui Buri
159 R16 **Bānkura** West Bengal, NE India
178 I8 **Ban Lakxao** *var.* Lak Sao. Bolikhamxai, C Laos
178 H17 **Ban Lam Phai** Songkhla, SW Thailand
Ban Mae Sot *see* Mae Sot
Ban Mae Suai *see* Mae Suai
Ban Mak Khaeng *see* Udon Thani
177 G3 **Banmauk** Sagaing, N Myanmar
Banmo *see* Bhamo
178 Jj10 **Ban Mun-Houamuang** S Laos
99 F14 **Bann** *var.* Lower Bann, Upper Bann. ⩫ N Northern Ireland, UK
178 Jj10 **Ban Nadou** Salavan, S Laos
178 J10 **Ban Nakala** Savannakhét, S Laos
178 I8 **Ban Nakha** Viangchan, C Laos
178 Jj9 **Ban Nakham** Khammouan, S Laos
178 I8 **Ban Namoun** Xaignabouli, N Laos
178 Hh17 **Ban Nang Sata** Yala, SW Thailand
178 Gg15 **Ban Na San** Surat Thani, SW Thailand
178 Ii7 **Ban Nasi** Xiangkhoang, N Laos
46 I3 **Bannerman Town** Eleuthera Island, C Bahamas
37 V15 **Banning** California, W USA
Banningville *see* Bandundu
178 Jj11 **Ban Nongsim** Champasak, S Laos
155 S7 **Bannu** *prev.* Edwardesabad. North-West Frontier Province, NW Pakistan
Bañolas *see* Banyoles
58 C7 **Baños** Tungurahua, C Ecuador
Bánovce *see* Bánovce nad Bebravou
113 I19 **Bánovce nad Bebravou** *var.* Bánovce, *Hung.* Bán. Západné Slovensko, W Slovakia
114 I12 **Banovići** E Bosnia and Herzegovina
Banow *see* Andarāb
Ban Pak Phanang *see* Pak Phanang
178 Hh7 **Ban Pan Nua** Lampang, NW Thailand
178 I10 **Ban Phai** Khon Kaen, E Thailand
178 Jj9 **Ban Phou A Douk** Khammouan, C Laos
178 I8 **Ban Phu** Uthai Thani, W Thailand
178 H11 **Ban Pong** Ratchaburi, W Thailand
202 I3 **Banraeaba** Tarawa, W Kiribati
178 Gg11 **Ban Sai Yok** Kanchanaburi, W Thailand
Ban Sattahip/Ban Sattahipp *see* Sattahip
Ban Sichon *see* Sichon
Ban Si Racha *see* Siracha
113 J19 **Banská Bystrica** *Ger.* Neusohl, *Hung.* Besztercebánya. Stredné Slovensko, C Slovakia
178 J8 **Ban Söppheung** Bolikhamxai, C Laos
Ban Sop Prap *see* Sop Prap
158 G15 **Bānswāra** Rājasthān, N India
178 Gg15 **Ban Ta Khun** Surat Thani, SW Thailand
Ban Takua Pa *see* Takua Pa
178 Jj9 **Ban Talak** Khammouan, C Laos
79 R15 **Bantè** W Benin
178 Ii8 **Ban Thabôk** Bolikhamxai, C Laos
178 Jj10 **Ban Tôp** Savannakhét, S Laos
99 B21 **Bantry** *Ir.* Beanntraí. SW Ireland
99 A21 **Bantry Bay** *Ir.* Bá Bheanntraí. *bay* SW Ireland
174 L15 **Bantul** *prev.* Bantoel. Jawa, C Indonesia
161 F19 **Bantvāl** *var.* Bantwāl. Karnātaka, E India
Bantwāl *see* Bantvāl
116 N9 **Banya** Burgaska Oblast, E Bulgaria
173 Ee6 **Banyak, Kepulauan** *prev.* Kepulauan Banjak. *island group* NW Indonesia
107 U8 **Banya, La** *headland* E Spain
81 E14 **Banyo** Adamaoua, NW Cameroon
107 X4 **Banyoles** *var.* Bañolas. Cataluña, NE Spain
178 H16 **Ban Yong Sata** Trang, SW Thailand
174 Mm16 **Banyuwangi** *var.* Banjuwangi; *prev.* Banjoewangi. Jawa, S Indonesia
205 X14 **Banzare Coast** *physical region* Antarctica
181 Q14 **Banzare Seamounts** *undersea feature* S Indian Ocean
Banzart *see* Bizerte
Baochang *see* Taibus Qi
167 O3 **Baoding** *var.* Pao-ting; *prev.* Tsingyuan. Hebei, E China
Baoebaoe *see* Baubau
Baoi, Oileán *see* Dursey Island
166 J6 **Baoji** *var.* Pao-chi, Paoki. Shaanxi, C China
195 V14 **Baolo** Santa Isabel, N Solomon Islands
178 K13 **Bao Lôc** Lâm Đông, S Vietnam
169 Z7 **Baoqing** Heilongjiang, NE China
Baoqing *see* Shaoyang
81 H15 **Baoro** Nana-Mambéré, W Central African Republic
166 E12 **Baoshan** *var.* Pao-shan. Yunnan, SW China
169 N13 **Baotou** *var.* Pao-t'ou, Paotow. Nei Mongol Zizhiqu, N China
78 L14 **Baoulé** ⩫ S Mali
78 K12 **Baoulé** ⩫ W Mali
105 O2 **Bapaume** Pas-de-Calais, N France
12 J13 **Baptiste Lake** ◎ Ontario, SE Canada
Baqanas *see* Bakanas
Baqbaqty *see* Bakbakty
165 P14 **Baqên** *var.* Dartang. Xizang Zizhiqu, W China
144 F14 **Bāqir, Jabal** ▲ S Jordan
145 T7 **Ba'qūbah** *var.* Qubba. C Iraq
64 H5 **Baquedano** Antofagasta, N Chile
118 M6 **Bar** Vinnyts'ka Oblast', C Ukraine
115 J18 **Bar** *It.* Antivari. Montenegro, SW Yugoslavia
82 E10 **Bara** Northern Kordofan, C Sudan
83 M18 **Baraawe** *It.* Brava. Shabeellaha Hoose, S Somalia
158 M12 **Bāra Banki** Uttar Pradesh, N India
125 G13 **Barabinsk** Novosibirskaya Oblast', C Russian Federation
32 L8 **Baraboo** Wisconsin, N USA
32 K8 **Baraboo Range** *hill range* Wisconsin, N USA
Baracaldo *see* San Vicente de Barakaldo
13 Y6 **Barachois** Québec, SE Canada
46 J7 **Baracoa** Guantánamo, E Cuba
63 C19 **Baradero** Buenos Aires, E Argentina
191 R6 **Baradine** New South Wales, SE Australia
Baraf Daja Islands *see* Damar, Kepulauan
160 M12 **Baragarh** Orissa, E India
83 I17 **Baragoi** Rift Valley, W Kenya
47 N9 **Barahona** SW Dominican Republic
159 W13 **Barail Range** ▲ NE India
82 I9 **Baraka** *var.* Barka, *Ar.* Khawr Barakah. *seasonal river* Eritrea/Sudan
82 G10 **Barakat** Gezira, C Sudan
Barakī *see* Barakī Barak
155 Q6 **Barakī Barak** *var.* Barakī, Baraki Rajan. Lowgar, E Afghanistan

◆ Country ● Country Capital ◇ Dependent Territory ○ Dependent Territory Capital ◆ Administrative Region ✕ International Airport ▲ Mountain ▲ Mountain Range ⚠ Volcano ⩫ River ◎ Lake ⊡ Reservoir

Baraki Rajan see Baraki Barak
160 N11 **Bārākot** Orissa, E India
Baram see Baram, Batang
57 S7 **Barama River** ≈ N Guyana
161 E14 **Bārāmati** Mahārāshtra, W India
174 Mm4 **Baram, Batang** var. Baram, Barram. ≈ East Malaysia
158 H5 **Bārāmūla** Jammu and Kashmir, NW India
121 N14 **Baran'** Vitsyebskaya Voblasts', NE Belarus
158 I14 **Bārān** Rājasthān, N India
145 U4 **Barānān, Shākh-i** ▲ E Iraq
121 I17 **Baranavichy** Pol. Baranowicze, Rus. Baranovichi. Brestskaya Voblasts', SW Belarus
127 Oo5 **Baranikha** Chukotskiy Avtonomnyy Okrug, NE Russian Federation
118 M4 **Baranivka** Zhytomyrs'ka Oblast', N Ukraine
41 W14 **Baranof Island** island Alexander Archipelago, Alaska, USA
Baranovichi/Baranowicze see Baranavichy
113 N15 **Baranów Sandomierski** Tarnobrzeg, SE Poland
113 I26 **Baranya** off. Baranya Megye. ◐ county S Hungary
159 R13 **Barāri** Bihār, NE India
24 L10 **Barataria Bay** bay Louisiana, S USA
Barat Daya, Kepulauan see Damar, Kepulauan
120 L12 **Baravukha** Rus. Borovukha. Vitsyebskaya Voblasts', N Belarus
56 E11 **Baraya** Huila, C Colombia
61 M21 **Barbacena** Minas Gerais, SE Brazil
56 B13 **Barbacoas** Nariño, SW Colombia
56 L6 **Barbacoas** Aragua, N Venezuela
47 Z13 **Barbados** ◆ commonwealth republic SE West Indies
49 S3 **Barbados** island Barbados
107 U11 **Barbaria, Cap de** var. Cabo de Berberia. headland Formentera, E Spain
116 N13 **Barbaros** Tekirdağ, NW Turkey
76 A11 **Barbas, Cap** headland S Western Sahara
107 T5 **Barbastro** Aragón, NE Spain
106 K16 **Barbate** ≈ SW Spain
106 K16 **Barbate de Franco** Andalucía, S Spain
85 K21 **Barberton** Mpumalanga, NE South Africa
33 U12 **Barberton** Ohio, N USA
104 K12 **Barbezieux-St-Hilaire** Charente, W France
56 G9 **Barbosa** Santander, C Colombia
23 N7 **Barbourville** Kentucky, S USA
47 W9 **Barbuda** island N Antigua and Barbuda
189 W8 **Barcaldine** Queensland, E Australia
Barcarozsnyó see Râşnov
106 I11 **Barcarrota** Extremadura, W Spain
Barcău see Berettyó
Barce see Al Marj
109 L23 **Barcellona** var. Barcellona Pozzo di Gotto. Sicilia, Italy, C Mediterranean Sea
Barcellona Pozzo di Gotto see Barcellona
107 W6 **Barcelona** anc. Barcino, Barcinona. Cataluña, E Spain
57 N5 **Barcelona** Anzoátegui, NE Venezuela
107 S5 **Barcelona** ◐ province Cataluña, NE Spain
107 W6 **Barcelona** ✕ Cataluña, E Spain
105 U14 **Barcelonnette** Alpes-de-Haute-Provence, SE France
60 E12 **Barcelos** Amazonas, N Brazil
106 G5 **Barcelos** Braga, N Portugal
112 I10 **Barcin** Ger. Bartschin. Bydgoszcz, C Poland
Barcino/Barcinona see Barcelona
Barcoo see Cooper Creek
113 H26 **Barcs** Somogy, SW Hungary
143 W11 **Bärdä** Rus. Barda. C Azerbaijan
80 H5 **Bardaï** Borkou-Ennedi-Tibesti, N Chad
145 R2 **Bardaṛash** N Iraq
145 Q7 **Bardasah** SW Iraq
159 S16 **Barddhamān** West Bengal, NE India
113 N18 **Bardejov** Ger. Bartfeld, Hung. Bártfa. Východné Slovensko, NE Slovakia
107 R4 **Bárdenas Reales** physical region N Spain
Bardera/Bardere see Baardheere
Bardesīr see Bardsīr
94 K3 **Bardharbunga** ▲ C Iceland
Bardhë, Drini i see Beli Drim
108 E9 **Bardi** Emilia-Romagna, C Italy
108 A8 **Bardonecchia** Piemonte, W Italy
99 H19 **Bardsey Island** island NW Wales, UK
149 S11 **Bardsīr** var. Bardesīr, Mashīz. Kermān, C Iran
22 L6 **Bardstown** Kentucky, S USA
Barduli see Barletta
22 G7 **Bardwell** Kentucky, S USA
158 K11 **Bareilly** var. Bareli. Uttar Pradesh, N India
Bareli see Bareilly
100 H13 **Barendrecht** Zuid-Holland, SW Netherlands
104 M3 **Barentin** Seine-Maritime, N France
94 N3 **Barentsburg** Spitsbergen, W Svalbard
Barentsevo More/Barents Havet see Barents Sea
94 O3 **Barentsøya** island E Svalbard
207 T11 **Barents Plain** undersea feature N Barents Sea
129 P3 **Barents Sea** Nor. Barents Havet, Rus. Barentsevo More. sea Arctic Ocean
207 U14 **Barents Trough** undersea feature SW Barents Sea
82 I9 **Barentu** W Eritrea
104 J3 **Barfleur** Manche, N France
104 J3 **Barfleur, Pointe de** headland N France
Barfrush/Barfurush see Bābol
164 H14 **Barga** Xizang Zizhiqu, W China
107 N9 **Bargas** Castilla-La Mancha, C Spain
83 I15 **Bargē** SW Ethiopia
108 A9 **Barge** Piemonte, NE Italy
159 U16 **Barguna** Khulna, S Bangladesh
Bārguşad see Vorotan
126 K15 **Barguzin** Respublika Buryatiya, S Russian Federation
159 O13 **Barhaj** Uttar Pradesh, N India
191 N10 **Barham** New South Wales, SE Australia
158 J12 **Barhan** Uttar Pradesh, N India
21 S7 **Bar Harbor** Mount Desert Island, Maine, NE USA
159 R14 **Barharwa** Bihār, NE India
159 P15 **Barhi** Bihār, N India
109 O17 **Bari** var. Bari delle Puglie; anc. Barium. Puglia, SE Italy
82 P12 **Bari** off. Gobolka Bari. ◐ region NE Somalia
178 K14 **Ba Ria** Ba Ria-Vung Tau, S Vietnam
Bāridah see Al Bāridah
Bari delle Puglie see Bari
Barikot see Barikowṭ
155 T4 **Barikowṭ** var. Barikot. Kunar, NE Afghanistan
44 C4 **Barillas** var. Santa Cruz Barillas. Huehuetenango, NW Guatemala
56 J6 **Barinas** Barinas, W Venezuela
56 I7 **Barinas** off. Estado Barinas; prev. Zamora. ◐ state C Venezuela
56 I6 **Barinitas** Barinas, NW Venezuela
160 P11 **Bāripada** Orissa, E India
62 K9 **Bariri** São Paulo, S Brazil
77 W11 **Bâris** S Egypt
158 G14 **Bari Sādri** Rājasthān, N India
159 U16 **Barisal** Khulna, S Bangladesh
173 G7 **Barisan, Pegunungan** ▲▲ Sumatera, W Indonesia
175 N10 **Barito, Sungai** ≈ Borneo, C Indonesia
Barium see Bari
Barka see Baraka
Barka see Al Marj
166 H8 **Barkam** Sichuan, C China
120 J9 **Barkava** Madona, C Latvia
8 M15 **Barkerville** British Columbia, SW Canada
12 J12 **Bark Lake** ◎ Ontario, SE Canada
22 H7 **Barkley, Lake** ⊠ Kentucky/Tennessee, S USA
8 K17 **Barkley Sound** inlet British Columbia, W Canada
85 J24 **Barkly East** Afr. Barkly-Oos. Eastern Cape, SE South Africa
Barkly-Oos see Barkly East
189 S4 **Barkly Tableland** plateau Northern Territory/Queensland, N Australia
Barkly-Wes see Barkly West
85 H22 **Barkly West** Afr. Barkly-Wes. Northern Cape, N South Africa
165 O5 **Barkol** var. Barkol Kazak Zizhixian. Xinjiang Uygur Zizhiqu, NW China
165 O5 **Barkol Hu** ◎ NW China
Barkol Kazak Zizhixian see Barkol
32 J3 **Bark Point** headland Wisconsin, N USA
27 P11 **Barksdale** Texas, SW USA
Bar Kunar see Asmār
118 L11 **Bârlad** prev. Birlad. Vaslui, E Romania
118 M11 **Bârlad** prev. Birlad. ≈ E Romania
78 D9 **Barlavento, Ilhas de** var. Windward Islands. island group N Cape Verde
105 R5 **Bar-le-Duc** var. Bar-sur-Ornain. Meuse, NE France
188 K11 **Barlee, Lake** ◎ Western Australia
188 H8 **Barlee Range** ▲▲ Western Australia
109 N16 **Barletta** anc. Barduli. Puglia, SE Italy
112 E10 **Barlinek** Ger. Berlinchen. Gorzów, W Poland
29 S11 **Barling** Arkansas, C USA
176 Vv10 **Barma** Irian Jaya, E Indonesia
191 Q9 **Barmedman** New South Wales, SE Australia
Barmen-Elberfeld see Wuppertal
158 D12 **Bārmer** Rājasthān, NW India
190 K9 **Barmera** South Australia
99 I19 **Barmouth** NW Wales, UK
160 F10 **Barnagar** Madhya Pradesh, C India
158 H9 **Barnāla** Punjab, NW India
99 L15 **Barnard Castle** N England, UK
191 O6 **Barnato** New South Wales, SE Australia
126 H14 **Barnaul** Altayskiy Kray, C Russian Federation
111 V8 **Bärnbach** Steiermark, SE Austria
20 K16 **Barnegat** New Jersey, NE USA
25 S4 **Barnesville** Georgia, SE USA
31 R6 **Barnesville** Minnesota, N USA
33 U13 **Barnesville** Ohio, N USA
100 K11 **Barneveld** var. Barnveld. Gelderland, C Netherlands
27 O9 **Barnhart** Texas, SW USA
29 P8 **Barnsdall** Oklahoma, C USA
99 M17 **Barnsley** N England, UK
21 Q12 **Barnstable** Massachusetts, NE USA
99 I23 **Barnstaple** SW England, UK
Barnveld see Barneveld
23 Q14 **Barnwell** South Carolina, SE USA
69 U8 **Baro** var. Baro Wenz. ≈ Ethiopia/Sudan
79 U15 **Baro** Niger, C Nigeria
Baro see Baro Wenz
Baroda see Vadodara
155 U2 **Baroghil Pass** var. Kowtal-e Barowghil. pass Afghanistan/Pakistan
121 Q17 **Baron'ki** Rus. Boron'ki. Mahilyowskaya Voblasts', E Belarus
190 J9 **Barossa Valley** valley South Australia
Barouï see Salisbury
83 H14 **Baro Wenz** var. Baro, Nahr Barū. ≈ Ethiopia/Sudan
159 U12 **Barpeta** Assam, NE India
33 S7 **Barques, Pointe Aux** headland Michigan, N USA
56 I5 **Barquisimeto** Lara, NW Venezuela
61 N16 **Barra** Bahia, E Brazil
98 E9 **Barra** island NW Scotland, UK
191 T5 **Barraba** New South Wales, SE Australia
62 L9 **Barra Bonita** São Paulo, S Brazil
66 J12 **Barracuda Fracture Zone** var. Fifteen Twenty Fracture Zone. tectonic feature SW Atlantic Ocean
66 G11 **Barracuda Ridge** undersea feature N Atlantic Ocean
45 N12 **Barra del Colorado** Limón, NE Costa Rica
45 N9 **Barra de Río Grande** Región Autónoma Atlántico Sur, E Nicaragua
84 A11 **Barra do Cuanza** Luanda, NW Angola
62 O9 **Barra do Piraí** Rio de Janeiro, SE Brazil
63 D16 **Barra do Quaraí** Rio Grande do Sul, SE Brazil
61 G14 **Barra do São Manuel** Pará, N Brazil
85 N19 **Barra Falsa, Ponta da** headland S Mozambique
98 E10 **Barra Head** headland NW Scotland, UK
Barram see Baram, Batang
62 O9 **Barra Mansa** Rio de Janeiro, SE Brazil
59 D14 **Barranca** Lima, W Peru
56 F8 **Barrancabermeja** Santander, N Colombia
56 H4 **Barrancas** La Guajira, N Colombia
56 J6 **Barrancas** Barinas, NW Venezuela
57 Q6 **Barrancas** Monagas, NE Venezuela
56 F6 **Barranco de Loba** Bolívar, N Colombia
106 I12 **Barrancos** Beja, S Portugal
64 N7 **Barranqueras** Chaco, N Argentina
56 E4 **Barranquilla** Atlántico, N Colombia
85 N20 **Barra, Ponta da** headland S Mozambique
107 P11 **Barrax** Castilla-La Mancha, C Spain
21 N11 **Barre** Massachusetts, NE USA
20 M7 **Barre** Vermont, NE USA
61 M17 **Barreiras** Bahia, E Brazil
106 F11 **Barreiro** Setúbal, W Portugal
67 C26 **Barren Island** island S Falkland Islands
22 K7 **Barren River Lake** ⊠ Kentucky, S USA
62 L7 **Barretos** São Paulo, S Brazil
9 P14 **Barrhead** Alberta, SW Canada
12 G14 **Barrie** Ontario, S Canada
9 N16 **Barrière** British Columbia, SW Canada
12 H8 **Barrière, Lac** ◎ Québec, SE Canada
190 L6 **Barrier Range** hill range New South Wales, SE Australia
44 G3 **Barrier Reef** reef E Belize
196 C16 **Barrigada** C Guam
Barrington Island see Santa Fe, Isla
191 T7 **Barrington Tops** ▲ New South Wales, SE Australia
191 O4 **Barringun** New South Wales, SE Australia
61 K18 **Barro Alto** Goiás, S Brazil
61 N14 **Barro Duro** Piauí, NE Brazil
32 I5 **Barron** Wisconsin, N USA
12 J12 **Barron** ≈ Ontario, SE Canada
63 H15 **Barros Cassal** Rio Grande do Sul, S Brazil
47 P14 **Barrouallie** Saint Vincent, W Saint Vincent and the Grenadines
41 O4 **Barrow** Alaska, USA
99 E20 **Barrow** Ir. An Bhearú. ≈ SE Ireland
189 Q6 **Barrow Creek Roadhouse** Northern Territory, N Australia
99 J16 **Barrow-in-Furness** NW England, UK
188 G7 **Barrow Island** island Western Australia
41 O4 **Barrow, Point** headland Alaska, USA
9 V14 **Barrows** Manitoba, S Canada
99 J22 **Barry** S Wales, UK
12 J12 **Barry's Bay** Ontario, SE Canada
150 K14 **Barsakel'mes, Ostrov** island SW Kazakhstan
153 S14 **Barsem** S Tajikistan
151 V11 **Barshatas** Semipalatinsk, E Kazakhstan
161 F14 **Bārsi** Mahārāshtra, W India
102 I13 **Barsinghausen** Niedersachsen, C Germany
153 X8 **Barskoon** Issyk-Kul'skaya Oblast', E Kyrgyzstan
102 F10 **Barssel** Niedersachsen, NW Germany
37 U14 **Barstow** California, W USA
26 L8 **Barstow** Texas, SW USA
105 R6 **Bar-sur-Aube** Aube, NE France
Bar-sur-Ornain see Bar-le-Duc
105 Q6 **Bar-sur-Seine** Aube, N France
153 S13 **Bartang** S Tajikistan
153 T13 **Bartang** ≈ SE Tajikistan
Bartenstein see Bartoszyce
Bártfa/Bartfeld see Bardejov
102 N7 **Barth** Mecklenburg-Vorpommern, NE Germany
29 W13 **Bartholomew, Bayou** ≈ Arkansas/Louisiana, S USA
57 T8 **Bartica** N Guyana
142 H10 **Bartın** Zonguldak, N Turkey
189 W4 **Bartle Frere** ▲ Queensland, E Australia
29 P8 **Bartlesville** Oklahoma, C USA
31 P14 **Bartlett** Nebraska, C USA
22 E10 **Bartlett** Tennessee, S USA
27 T9 **Bartlett** Texas, SW USA
38 L13 **Bartlett Reservoir** ⊠ Arizona, SW USA
21 N6 **Barton** Vermont, NE USA
112 L7 **Bartoszyce** Ger. Bartenstein. Olsztyn, N Poland
25 W12 **Bartow** Florida, SE USA
Bartschin see Barcin
176 V10 **Baru** Irian Jaya, E Indonesia
173 G6 **Barumun, Sungai** ≈ Sumatera, W Indonesia
Barū, Nahr see Baro Wenz
174 M16 **Barung, Nusa** island S Indonesia
173 Ff6 **Barus** Sumatera, NW Indonesia
168 L10 **Baruunsuu** Ömnögovĭ, S Mongolia
169 P8 **Baruun-Urt** Sühbaatar, E Mongolia
45 P15 **Barú, Volcán** var. Volcán de Chiriquí. ※ W Panama
101 K21 **Barvaux** Luxembourg, SE Belgium
44 M13 **Barva, Volcán** ※ NW Costa Rica
119 W6 **Barvinkove** Kharkivs'ka Oblast', E Ukraine
160 G11 **Barwāh** Madhya Pradesh, C India
Bärwalde Neumark see Mieszkowice
160 F11 **Barwāni** Madhya Pradesh, C India
191 P5 **Barwon River** ≈ New South Wales, SE Australia
121 L15 **Barysaw** Rus. Borisov. Minskaya Voblasts', NE Belarus
131 Q6 **Barysh** Ul'yanovskaya Oblast', W Russian Federation
119 Q4 **Baryshivka** Kyyivs'ka Oblast', N Ukraine
81 J17 **Basankusu** Equateur, NW Zaire
119 N11 **Basarabeasca** Rus. Bessarabka. SE Moldova
118 M14 **Basarabi** Constanța, SW Romania
42 H6 **Basaseachic** Chihuahua, NW Mexico
107 O2 **Basauri** País Vasco, N Spain
63 D18 **Basavilbaso** Entre Ríos, E Argentina
110 E6 **Basel** Eng. Basle, Fr. Bâle. Basel-Stadt, NW Switzerland
110 E7 **Basel** Eng. Basle, Fr. Bâle. ◐ canton NW Switzerland
149 T14 **Bashākerd, Kūhhā-ye** ▲▲ SE Iran
9 Q15 **Bashaw** Alberta, SW Canada
152 K16 **Bashbedeng** Maryyskiy Velayat, S Turkmenistan
85 J24 **Bashee** ≈ S South Africa
167 T15 **Bashi Channel** Chin. Pa-shih Hai-hsia. channel Philippines/Taiwan
Bashkiria see Bashkortostan, Respublika
125 Dd12 **Bashkortostan, Respublika** prev. Bashkiria. ◐ autonomous republic W Russian Federation
131 N6 **Bashmakovo** Penzenskaya Oblast', W Russian Federation
152 J10 **Bashsakarba** Lebapskiy Velayat, NE Turkmenistan
119 R9 **Bashtanka** Mykolayivs'ka Oblast', S Ukraine
195 O17 **Basilaki Island** island SE PNG
24 H8 **Basile** Louisiana, S USA
109 M18 **Basilicata** ◐ region S Italy
35 V13 **Basin** Wyoming, C USA
99 N22 **Basingstoke** S England, UK
149 U8 **Bāsīrān** Khorāsān, E Iran
114 B10 **Baška** It. Bescanuova. Primorje-Gorski Kotar, NW Croatia
143 T15 **Başkale** Van, SE Turkey
12 L10 **Baskatong, Réservoir** ⊠ Québec, SE Canada
143 O14 **Baskil** Elâzığ, E Turkey
Basle see Basel
160 H9 **Bāsoda** Madhya Pradesh, C India
81 L17 **Basoko** Haut-Zaïre, N Zaire
Basque Country, The see País Vasco
Basra see Al Başrah
105 U5 **Bas-Rhin** ◐ department NE France
Bassam see Grand-Bassam
9 Q16 **Bassano** Alberta, SW Canada
108 H7 **Bassano del Grappa** Veneto, NE Italy
79 Q15 **Bassar** var. Bassari. NW Togo
Bassari see Bassar
180 L9 **Bassas da India** island group W Madagascar
110 D7 **Bassecourt** Jura, W Switzerland
177 Ff8 **Bassein** var. Pathein. Irrawaddy, SW Myanmar
81 J15 **Basse-Kotto** ◐ prefecture S Central African Republic
107 V5 **Bassella** Cataluña, NE Spain
104 J5 **Basse-Normandie** Eng. Lower Normandy. ◐ region N France
47 Q11 **Basse-Pointe** N Martinique
78 H12 **Basse Santa Su** E Gambia
Basse-Saxe see Niedersachsen
47 X6 **Basse-Terre** ○ (Guadeloupe) Basse Terre, SW Guadeloupe
47 X6 **Basse Terre** island W Guadeloupe
47 V10 **Basseterre** ● (Saint Kitts and Nevis) Saint Kitts, Saint Kitts and Nevis
31 O13 **Bassett** Nebraska, C USA
23 S7 **Bassett** Virginia, NE USA
39 N15 **Bassett Peak** ▲ Arizona, SW USA
78 M10 **Bassikounou** Hodh ech Chargui, SE Mauritania
79 R15 **Bassila** W Benin
Bass, Îlots de see Marotiri
33 O11 **Bass Lake** Indiana, N USA
191 O14 **Bass Strait** strait SE Australia
102 H11 **Bassum** Niedersachsen, NW Germany
31 X3 **Basswood Lake** ◎ Canada/USA
97 J21 **Båstad** Kristianstad, S Sweden
145 U2 **Baştah** E Iraq
159 N12 **Basti** Uttar Pradesh, N India
104 F1 **Bastia** Corse, France, C Mediterranean Sea
101 L23 **Bastogne** Luxembourg, SE Belgium
24 I5 **Bastrop** Louisiana, S USA
27 T11 **Bastrop** Texas, SW USA
95 J15 **Bastuträsk** Västerbotten, N Sweden
121 J19 **Bastyn'** Rus. Bostyn'. Brestskaya Voblasts', SW Belarus
Basuo see Dongfang
Basutoland see Lesotho
121 O15 **Basya** ≈ E Belarus
119 V8 **Basyl'kivka** Dnipropetrovs'ka Oblast', E Ukraine
81 F21 **Bas-Zaïre** off. Région du Bas-Zaïre. ◐ region SW Zaire
81 D17 **Bata** NW Equatorial Guinea
81 D17 **Bata** ✕ S Equatorial Guinea
Batae Coritanorum see Leicester
126 M8 **Batagay** Respublika Sakha (Yakutiya), NE Russian Federation
126 L18 **Batagay-Alyta** Respublika Sakha (Yakutiya), NE Russian Federation
114 L10 **Batajnica** Serbia, N Yugoslavia
142 H15 **Bataklık Gölü** ◎ S Turkey
116 H11 **Batak, Yazovir** ⊠ SW Bulgaria
158 H7 **Batāla** Punjab, N India
106 F9 **Batalha** Leiria, C Portugal
81 N17 **Batama** Haut-Zaïre, NE Zaire
126 L10 **Batamay** Respublika Sakha (Yakutiya), NE Russian Federation
174 I7 **Batam, Pulau** island Kepulauan Riau, W Indonesia
166 F9 **Batang** Sichuan, C China
174 Kk14 **Batang** Jawa, C Indonesia
81 I14 **Batangafo** Ouham, NW Central African Republic
179 P11 **Batangas** off. Batangas City. Luzon, N Philippines
Bătania see Battonya
179 Pp6 **Batan Islands** island group N Philippines
62 L8 **Batatais** São Paulo, S Brazil
20 E10 **Batavia** New York, NE USA
Batavia see Jakarta
181 T9 **Batavia Seamount** undersea feature E Indian Ocean
130 L12 **Bataysk** Rostovskaya Oblast', SW Russian Federation
12 B9 **Batchawana** ≈ Ontario, S Canada
12 B9 **Batchawana Bay** Ontario, S Canada
178 Ii12 **Bătdâmbâng** prev. Battambang. Bătdâmbâng, NW Cambodia
81 G20 **Batéké, Plateaux** plateau S Congo
191 S11 **Batemans Bay** New South Wales, SE Australia
23 Q13 **Batesburg** South Carolina, SE USA
30 K12 **Batesland** South Dakota, N USA
29 V10 **Batesville** Arkansas, C USA
33 Q14 **Batesville** Indiana, N USA
24 L2 **Batesville** Mississippi, S USA
27 Q13 **Batesville** Texas, SW USA
46 J13 **Bath** E Jamaica
99 L22 **Bath** hist. Akermanceaster, anc. Aquae Calidae, Aquae Solis. SW England, UK
21 Q8 **Bath** Maine, NE USA
20 F11 **Bath** New York, NE USA
Bath see Berkeley Springs
80 I10 **Batha** off. Préfecture du Batha. ◐ prefecture C Chad
80 I10 **Batha** seasonal river C Chad
147 Y8 **Baṭḥā', Wādī al** dry watercourse NE Oman
158 H9 **Bathinda** Punjab, NW India
100 M11 **Bathmen** Overijssel, E Netherlands
47 Z14 **Bathsheba** E Barbados
191 R8 **Bathurst** New South Wales, SE Australia
11 O13 **Bathurst** New Brunswick, SE Canada
Bathurst see Banjul
15 Gg2 **Bathurst, Cape** headland Northwest Territories, NW Canada
206 L8 **Bathurst Inlet** Northwest Territories, N Canada
15 J4 **Bathurst Inlet** inlet Northwest Territories, N Canada
189 N1 **Bathurst Island** island Northern Territory, N Australia
207 O9 **Bathurst Island** island Parry Islands, Northwest Territories, N Canada
79 O14 **Batié** SW Burkina
197 J14 **Batiki** prev. Mbatiki. island C Fiji
Batinah see Al Bāṭinah
147 Y9 **Bāṭin, Wādī al** dry watercourse SW Asia
13 P9 **Batiscan** ≈ Québec, SE Canada
142 F16 **Batı Toroslar** ▲▲ SW Turkey
Batjan see Bacan, Pulau
Batlle y Ordóñez see José Batlle y Ordóñez
191 Q10 **Batlow** New South Wales, SE Australia
143 Q15 **Batman** var. Iluh. Batman, SE Turkey
143 Q15 **Batman** ◐ province SE Turkey
76 L6 **Batna** NE Algeria
Batoe see Batu, Kepulauan
168 K7 **Bat-Öldziyt** Töv, C Mongolia
24 J8 **Baton Rouge** state capital Louisiana, S USA
81 G15 **Batouri** Est, E Cameroon
144 G14 **Batrā', Jibāl al** ▲ S Jordan
144 G6 **Batroûn** var. Al Batrūn. N Lebanon
Batsch see Bač
Batsevichi see Batsevichy
121 M17 **Batsevichy** Rus. Batsevichi. Mahilyowskaya Voblasts', E Belarus
94 M7 **Båtsfjord** Finnmark, N Norway
Battambang see Bătdâmbâng
205 X3 **Batterbee, Cape** headland Antarctica
161 L24 **Batticaloa** Eastern Province, E Sri Lanka
101 L19 **Battice** Liège, E Belgium
109 L18 **Battipaglia** Campania, S Italy
9 R15 **Battle** ≈ Alberta/Saskatchewan, SW Canada
Battle Born State see Nevada
33 Q10 **Battle Creek** Michigan, N USA
29 T7 **Battlefield** Missouri, C USA
9 S15 **Battleford** Saskatchewan, S Canada
31 S6 **Battle Lake** Minnesota, N USA
37 U3 **Battle Mountain** Nevada, W USA
113 M25 **Battonya** Rom. Bătania. Békés, SE Hungary
175 Qq14 **Batuata, Pulau** island C Indonesia
175 Q8 **Batudaka, Pulau** island N Indonesia
173 F8 **Batu, Kepulauan** prev. Batoe. island group W Indonesia
143 Q10 **Bat'umi** W Georgia
174 H6 **Batu Pahat** prev. Bandar Penggaram. Johor, Peninsular Malaysia
175 Q10 **Baturebe** Sulawesi, N Indonesia
126 H13 **Baturino** Tomskaya Oblast', C Russian Federation
119 R3 **Baturyn** Chernihivs'ka Oblast', N Ukraine
144 F10 **Bat Yam** Tel Aviv, C Israel
131 Q4 **Batyrevo** Chuvashskaya Respublika, W Russian Federation
Batys Qazaqstan Oblysy see Zapadnyy Kazakhstan
104 F5 **Batz, Île de** island NW France
174 L7 **Bau** Sarawak, East Malaysia
179 P9 **Bauang** Luzon, N Philippines
175 Qq13 **Baubau** var. Baoebaoe. Pulau Buton, C Indonesia
79 W14 **Bauchi** Bauchi, NE Nigeria
79 W14 **Bauchi** ◐ state C Nigeria
104 H7 **Baud** Morbihan, NW France
31 T2 **Baudette** Minnesota, N USA
200 Nn10 **Bauer Basin** undersea feature E Pacific Ocean
197 C14 **Bauer Field** var. Port Vila. ✕ (Port-Vila) Éfaté, C Vanuatu
11 T9 **Bauld, Cape** headland Newfoundland, Newfoundland and Labrador, E Canada
105 T8 **Baume-les-Dames** Doubs, E France
195 X15 **Baunani** Malaita, N Solomon Islands
103 I15 **Baunatal** Hessen, C Germany
109 D18 **Baunei** Sardegna, Italy, C Mediterranean Sea
59 M15 **Baures, Río** ≈ N Bolivia
62 K9 **Bauru** São Paulo, S Brazil
Baushar see Bawshar
120 G10 **Bauska** Ger. Bauske. Bauska, S Latvia
Bauske see Bauska
103 Q15 **Bautzen** Lus. Budyšin. Sachsen, E Germany
Bauzanum see Bolzano
Bavaria see Bayern
111 N7 **Bavarian Alps** Ger. Bayrische Alpen. ▲▲ Austria/Germany
Bavière see Bayern
42 H4 **Bavispe, Río** ≈ NW Mexico
131 T5 **Bavly** Respublika Tatarstan, W Russian Federation
174 Kk10 **Bawal, Pulau** island N Indonesia
174 Mm10 **Bawan** Borneo, C Indonesia
191 O12 **Baw Baw, Mount** ▲ Victoria, SE Australia
176 W11 **Bawe** Irian Jaya, E Indonesia
174 M13 **Bawean, Pulau** island S Indonesia
174 L15 **Bawen** Jawa, S Indonesia
77 V9 **Bawīṭī** N Egypt
79 Q13 **Bawku** N Ghana
178 Gg7 **Bawlakè** Kayah State, C Myanmar
173 Ff8 **Bawo Ofuloa** Pulau Tanahmasa, W Indonesia
147 Y8 **Bawshar** var. Baushar. NE Oman
Ba Xian see Bazhou
164 M8 **Baxkorgan** Xinjiang Uygur Zizhiqu, W China
25 V6 **Baxley** Georgia, SE USA
165 R15 **Baxoi** Xizang Zizhiqu, W China
31 W14 **Baxter** Iowa, C USA
31 U6 **Baxter** Minnesota, N USA
29 R8 **Baxter Springs** Kansas, C USA
83 M17 **Bay** off. Gobolka Bay. ◐ region SW Somalia
Bay see Baicheng
46 H7 **Bayamo** Granma, E Cuba
47 U5 **Bayamón** E Puerto Rico
169 W8 **Bayan** Heilongjiang, NE China
175 Nn16 **Bayan** prev. Bajan. Pulau Lombok, C Indonesia
168 I6 **Bayan** Arhangay, C Mongolia
169 P7 **Bayan** Dornod, E Mongolia
169 N9 **Bayan** Dornogovĭ, SE Mongolia
168 F7 **Bayan** Govĭ-Altay, W Mongolia
169 O8 **Bayan** Hentiy, C Mongolia
158 I12 **Bayāna** Rājasthān, N India
155 N5 **Bāyān, Band-e** ▲▲ C Afghanistan
168 H8 **Bayanbulag** Bayanhongor, C Mongolia
169 N7 **Bayanbulag** Hentiy, C Mongolia
164 J5 **Bayanbulak** Xinjiang Uygur Zizhiqu, W China
126 Jj15 **Bayanday** Ust'-Ordynskiy Buryatskiy Avtonomnyy Okrug, S Russian Federation
Bayan Gol see Dengkou
168 F8 **Bayangol** Govĭ-Altay, SW Mongolia
165 R12 **Bayan Har Shan** var. Bayan Khar. ▲▲ C China
168 I8 **Bayanhongor** Bayanhongor, C Mongolia
168 H9 **Bayanhongor** ◐ province C Mongolia
Bayan Khar see Bayan Har Shan
173 G3 **Bayan Lepas** ✕ (George Town) Pinang, Peninsular Malaysia
168 K13 **Bayan Mod** Nei Mongol Zizhiqu, N China
168 K13 **Bayan Nuru** Nei Mongol Zizhiqu, N China
169 N12 **Bayan Obo** Nei Mongol Zizhiqu, N China
45 V15 **Bayano, Lago** ◎ E Panama
168 C5 **Bayan-Ölgiy** ◐ province NW Mongolia
168 F9 **Bayan-Ovoo** Govĭ-Altay, SW Mongolia
168 H9 **Bayansayr** Bayanhongor, C Mongolia
165 Q9 **Bayan Shan** ▲ C China
168 J9 **Bayanteeg** Övörhangay, C Mongolia
168 L8 **Bayantöhöm** Töv, C Mongolia
168 H6 **Bayan-Uhaa** Dzavhan, C Mongolia
168 J8 **Bayan-Ulaan** Övörhangay, C Mongolia
Bayan Ul Hot see Xi Ujimqin Qi
30 J14 **Bayard** Nebraska, C USA
39 P15 **Bayard** New Mexico, SW USA
105 T13 **Bayard, Col** pass SE France
169 O8 **Bayasgalant** Sühbaatar, E Mongolia
142 J12 **Bayat** Çorum, N Turkey
179 Q14 **Bayawan** Negros, C Philippines
149 R10 **Bayāẓ** Kermān, C Iran
179 R13 **Baybay** Leyte, C Philippines
23 X10 **Bayboro** North Carolina, SE USA
143 P12 **Bayburt** Bayburt, NE Turkey
143 P12 **Bayburt** ◐ province NE Turkey
33 R8 **Bay City** Michigan, N USA
27 V12 **Bay City** Texas, SW USA
125 G7 **Baydaratskaya Guba** var. Baydarata Bay. bay N Russian Federation
83 M16 **Baydhabo** var. Baydhowa, Isha Baydhabo, It. Baidoa. Bay, SW Somalia
Baydhowa see Baydhabo
103 N21 **Bayerischer Wald** ▲▲ SE Germany
103 K21 **Bayern** Eng. Bavaria, Fr. Bavière. ◐ state SE Germany
153 V9 **Bayetovo** Narynskaya Oblast', C Kyrgyzstan
104 K4 **Bayeux** anc. Augustodurum. Calvados, N France
12 E15 **Bayfield** ≈ Ontario, S Canada
151 O15 **Baygakum** Kaz. Bäygequm. Kzyl-Orda, S Kazakhstan
Bäygequm see Baygakum
142 C14 **Bayındır** İzmir, SW Turkey
144 H13 **Bāyir** var. Bā'ir. Ma'ān, S Jordan
Bay Islands see Bahía, Islas de la
145 R5 **Bayjī** var. Baiji. N Iraq
151 Q16 **Baykadam** Kaz. Bayqadam. Zhambyl, S Kazakhstan
126 K15 **Baykal, Ozero** Eng. Lake Baikal. ◎ S Russian Federation
126 J16 **Baykal'sk** Irkutskaya Oblast', S Russian Federation
143 R15 **Baykan** Siirt, SE Turkey
126 Ii12 **Baykit** Evenkiyskiy Avtonomnyy Okrug, C Russian Federation
151 N12 **Baykonur** Zhezkazgan, C Kazakhstan
164 E7 **Baykurt** Xinjiang Uygur Zizhiqu, W China
12 I9 **Bay, Lac** ◎ Québec, SE Canada
179 Pp11 **Bay, Laguna de** ◎ Luzon, N Philippines
131 W6 **Baymak** Respublika Bashkortostan, W Russian Federation
25 O8 **Bay Minette** Alabama, S USA
149 O17 **Baynūnah** desert W UAE
192 O8 **Bay of Plenty** off. Bay of Plenty Region. ◐ region North Island, NZ
203 Z3 **Bay of Wrecks** bay Kiritimati, E Kiribati
179 P9 **Bayombong** Luzon, N Philippines
104 I15 **Bayonne** anc. Lapurdum. Pyrénées-Atlantiques, SW France
24 H4 **Bayou D'Arbonne Lake** ⊠ Louisiana, S USA
25 N9 **Bayou La Batre** Alabama, S USA
Bayou State see Mississippi
Bayqadam see Baykadam
Bayram-Ali see Bayramaly
152 J14 **Bayramaly** prev. Bayram-Ali. Maryyskiy Velayat, S Turkmenistan
103 L19 **Bayreuth** var. Baireuth. Bayern, SE Germany
Bayrische Alpen see Bavarian Alps
Bayrūt see Beyrouth
24 L9 **Bay Saint Louis** Mississippi, S USA
Baysān see Bet She'an
168 L8 **Bayshint** Töv, C Mongolia

◆ Country ● Country Capital ◇ Dependent Territory ○ Dependent Territory Capital ◐ Administrative Region ✕ International Airport ▲ Mountain ▲▲ Mountain Range ※ Volcano ≈ River ◎ Lake ⊠ Reservoir

Bays, Lake of – Bentinck Island

12 H13 **Bays, Lake of** ◎ Ontario, S Canada
24 M6 **Bay Springs** Mississippi, S USA
Bay State *see* Massachusetts
Baysun *see* Boysun
12 H13 **Baysville** Ontario, S Canada
147 N15 **Bayt al Faqīh** W Yemen
164 M4 **Baytik Shan** ▲▲ China/Mongolia
Bayt Laḥm *see* Bethlehem
27 W11 **Baytown** Texas, SW USA
175 O9 **Bayur, Tanjung** *headland* Borneo, N Indonesia
123 U16 **Bayy al Kabīr, Wādī** *dry watercourse* NW Libya
Bayyrqum *see* Bairkum
107 P14 **Baza** Andalucía, S Spain
143 X10 **Bazardüzü Dağı** *Rus.* Gora Bazardyuzyu. ▲ N Azerbaijan
Bazardyuzyu, Gora *see* Bazardüzü Dağı
Bazargic *see* Dobrich
85 N18 **Bazaruto, Ilha do** *island* SE Mozambique
104 K14 **Bazas** Gironde, SW France
107 O14 **Baza, Sierra de** ▲▲ S Spain
166 J8 **Bazhong** Sichuan, C China
167 P3 **Bazhou** *prev.* Baxian, Ba Xian. Hebei, E China
12 M9 **Bazin** ≈ Québec, SE Canada
Bazin *see* Pezinok
145 Q7 **Bāzīyah** C Iraq
144 H6 **Bcharré** *var.* Bcharreh, Bsharrī, Bsherri. NE Lebanon
Bcharreh *see* Bcharré
30 J5 **Beach** North Dakota, N USA
190 K12 **Beachport** South Australia
99 O23 **Beachy Head** *headland* SE England, UK
20 K13 **Beacon** New York, NE USA
65 J25 **Beagle Channel** *channel* Argentina/Chile
189 O1 **Beagle Gulf** *gulf* Northern Territory, N Australia
Bealach an Doirín *see* Ballaghaderreen
Bealach Cláir *see* Ballyclare
Bealach Féich *see* Ballybofey
180 J3 **Bealanana** Mahajanga, NE Madagascar
Béal an Átha *see* Ballina
Béal an Átha Móir *see* Ballinamore
Béal an Mhuirhead *see* Belmullet
Béal Átha Beithe *see* Ballybay
Béal Átha Conaill *see* Ballyconnell
Béal Átha hAmhnais *see* Ballyhaunis
Béal Átha na Sluaighe *see* Ballinasloe
Béal Átha Seanaidh *see* Ballyshannon
Bealdovuopmi *see* Peltovuoma
Béal Feirste *see* Belfast
Béal Tairbirt *see* Belturbet
Beanna Boirche *see* Mourne Mountains
Beannchar *see* Banagher, Ireland
Beannchar *see* Bangor, Northern Ireland, UK
Beanntraí *see* Bantry
25 N2 **Bear Creek** ≈ Alabama/Mississippi, S USA
32 J13 **Bear Creek** ≈ Illinois, N USA
29 U13 **Bearden** Arkansas, C USA
205 Q10 **Beardmore Glacier** *glacier* Antarctica
32 K13 **Beardstown** Illinois, N USA
30 L14 **Bear Hill** ▲ Nebraska, C USA
Bear Island *see* Bjørnøya
12 H12 **Bear Lake** Ontario, S Canada
38 M1 **Bear Lake** ◎ Idaho/Utah, NW USA
41 U11 **Bear, Mount** ▲ Alaska, USA
104 J16 **Béarn** *cultural region* SW France
204 J11 **Bear Peninsula** *peninsula* Antarctica
158 I7 **Beās** ≈ India/Pakistan
107 P3 **Beasain** País Vasco, N Spain
107 O12 **Beas de Segura** Andalucía, S Spain
47 N10 **Beata, Cabo** *headland* SW Dominican Republic
47 N10 **Beata, Isla** *island* SW Dominican Republic
66 F11 **Beata Ridge** *undersea feature* N Caribbean Sea
31 R17 **Beatrice** Nebraska, C USA
85 L16 **Beatrice** Mashonaland East, NE Zimbabwe
9 N11 **Beatton** ≈ British Columbia, W Canada
9 N11 **Beatton River** British Columbia, W Canada
37 V10 **Beatty** Nevada, W USA
23 N6 **Beattyville** Kentucky, S USA
181 X16 **Beau Bassin** W Mauritius
105 R15 **Beaucaire** Gard, S France
12 J8 **Beauchastel, Lac** ◎ Québec, SE Canada
12 I10 **Beauchêne, Lac** ◎ Québec, SE Canada
191 V3 **Beaudesert** Queensland, E Australia
190 M12 **Beaufort** Victoria, SE Australia
23 X11 **Beaufort** North Carolina, SE USA
23 R15 **Beaufort** South Carolina, SE USA
40 M11 **Beaufort Sea** *sea* Arctic Ocean
Beaufort-Wes *see* Beaufort West
85 G25 **Beaufort West** *Afr.* Beaufort-Wes. Western Cape, SW South Africa
105 N7 **Beaugency** Loiret, C France
21 R1 **Beau Lake** ◎ Maine, NE USA
98 I8 **Beauly** N Scotland, UK
101 G21 **Beaumont** Hainaut, S Belgium
193 E23 **Beaumont** Otago, South Island, NZ
24 M7 **Beaumont** Mississippi, S USA
27 X10 **Beaumont** Texas, SW USA
104 M15 **Beaumont-de-Lomagne** Tarn-et-Garonne, S France
104 L6 **Beaumont-sur-Sarthe** Sarthe, NW France
105 R8 **Beaune** Côte d'Or, C France
13 R9 **Beaupré** Québec, SE Canada
104 J8 **Beaupréau** Maine-et-Loire, NW France
101 I22 **Beauraing** Namur, SE Belgium
105 R12 **Beaurepaire** Isère, E France
9 Y16 **Beausejour** Manitoba, S Canada
105 N4 **Beauvais** *anc.* Bellovacum, Caesaromagus. Oise, N France
9 S13 **Beauval** Saskatchewan, C Canada
104 I9 **Beauvoir-sur-Mer** Vendée, NW France
41 R8 **Beaver** Alaska, USA
28 J8 **Beaver** Oklahoma, C USA
20 B14 **Beaver** Pennsylvania, NE USA
38 K6 **Beaver** Utah, W USA
8 L9 **Beaver** ≈ British Columbia/Yukon Territory, W Canada
9 S13 **Beaver** ≈ Saskatchewan, C Canada
31 N17 **Beaver City** Nebraska, C USA
8 G6 **Beaver Creek** Yukon Territory, W Canada
33 R14 **Beavercreek** Ohio, N USA
41 S8 **Beaver Creek** ≈ Alaska, USA
28 H3 **Beaver Creek** ≈ Kansas/Nebraska, C USA
30 J5 **Beaver Creek** ≈ Montana/North Dakota, N USA
31 Q14 **Beaver Creek** ≈ Nebraska, C USA
27 Q4 **Beaver Creek** ≈ Texas, SW USA
32 M8 **Beaver Dam** Wisconsin, N USA
32 M8 **Beaver Dam Lake** ◎ Wisconsin, N USA
20 B14 **Beaver Falls** Pennsylvania, NE USA
35 P12 **Beaverhead Mountains** ▲▲ Idaho/Montana, NW USA
35 Q12 **Beaverhead River** ≈ Montana, NW USA
67 A25 **Beaver Island** *island* W Falkland Islands
33 P5 **Beaver Island** *island* Michigan, N USA
29 S9 **Beaver Lake** ⊡ Arkansas, C USA
9 N13 **Beaverlodge** Alberta, W Canada
20 I8 **Beaver River** ≈ New York, NE USA
28 J8 **Beaver River** ≈ Oklahoma, C USA
20 B13 **Beaver River** ≈ Pennsylvania, NE USA
67 A25 **Beaver Settlement** Beaver Island, W Falkland Islands
Beaver State *see* Oregon
12 H14 **Beaverton** Ontario, S Canada
34 G11 **Beaverton** Oregon, NW USA
158 G12 **Beāwar** Rājasthān, N India
Bebas, Dasht-i *see* Bābūs, Dasht-e
62 L8 **Bebedouro** São Paulo, S Brazil
103 I16 **Bebra** Hessen, C Germany
43 W12 **Becal** Campeche, SE Mexico
13 Q11 **Bécancour** ≈ Québec, SE Canada
99 Q19 **Beccles** E England, UK
114 L9 **Bečej** *Ger.* Altbetsche, *Hung.* Óbecse, Rácz-Becse; *prev.* Magyar-Becse, Stari Bečej. Serbia, N Yugoslavia
106 I3 **Becerréa** Galicia, NW Spain
76 H7 **Béchar** *prev.* Colomb-Béchar. W Algeria
41 O14 **Becharof Lake** ◎ Alaska, USA
118 F15 **Bechet** *var.* Bechetu. Dolj, SW Romania
Bechetu *see* Bechet
23 R6 **Beckley** West Virginia, NE USA
103 G14 **Beckum** Nordrhein-Westfalen, W Germany
27 X7 **Beckville** Texas, SW USA
37 X4 **Becky Peak** ▲ Nevada, W USA
118 I9 **Beclean** *Hung.* Bethlen; *prev.* Betlen. Bistriţa-Năsăud, N Romania
Bécs *see* Wien
113 H18 **Bečva** *Ger.* Betschau, *Pol.* Beczwa. ≈ E Czech Republic
Beczwa *see* Bečva
105 P15 **Bédarieux** Hérault, S France
122 Dd12 **Beddouza, Cap** *headland* W Morocco
82 I13 **Bedelē** W Ethiopia
153 Y8 **Bedel Pass** *Rus.* Pereval Bedel. *pass* China/Kyrgyzstan
Bedel, Pereval *see* Bedel Pass
97 H22 **Beder** Århus, C Denmark
99 N20 **Bedford** E England, UK
33 O15 **Bedford** Indiana, N USA
31 U16 **Bedford** Iowa, C USA
22 L4 **Bedford** Kentucky, S USA
20 D15 **Bedford** Pennsylvania, NE USA
23 T6 **Bedford** Virginia, NE USA
99 N20 **Bedfordshire** *cultural region* E England, UK
131 N5 **Bednodem'yanovsk** Penzenskaya Oblast', W Russian Federation
100 N5 **Bedum** Groningen, NE Netherlands
29 V11 **Beebe** Arkansas, C USA
47 T9 **Beef Island** ✕ (Road Town) Tortola, E British Virgin Islands
Beehive State *see* Utah
101 L18 **Beek** Limburg, SE Netherlands
101 L18 **Beek** ✕ (Maastricht) Limburg, SE Netherlands
101 K14 **Beek-en-Donk** Noord-Brabant, S Netherlands
144 F13 **Be'ér Menuḥa** Southern, S Israel
101 D16 **Beernem** West-Vlaanderen, NW Belgium
101 I16 **Beerse** Antwerpen, N Belgium
Beersheba *see* Be'ér Sheva'
144 E11 **Be'ér Sheva'** *var.* Beersheba, *Ar.* Bir es Saba. Southern, S Israel
100 J13 **Beesd** Gelderland, C Netherlands
101 M16 **Beesel** Limburg, SE Netherlands
85 J21 **Beestekraal** North-West, N South Africa
204 J7 **Beethoven Peninsula** *peninsula* Alexander Island, Antarctica
Beetstersweach *see* Beetsterzwaag
100 M6 **Beetsterzwaag** *Fris.* Beetstersweach. Friesland, N Netherlands
27 S13 **Beeville** Texas, SW USA
81 J18 **Befale** Equateur, NW Zaire
Befandriana *see* Befandriana Avaratra
180 J3 **Befandriana Avaratra** *var.* Befandriana, Befandriana Nord. Mahajanga, NW Madagascar
Befandriana Nord *see* Befandriana Avaratra
81 K18 **Befori** Equateur, N Zaire
180 I7 **Befotaka** Fianarantsoa, S Madagascar
191 R11 **Bega** New South Wales, SE Australia
104 G5 **Bégard** Côtes d'Armor, NW France
114 M9 **Begejski Kanal** *canal* NE Yugoslavia
151 V9 **Begen'** Semipalatinsk, E Kazakhstan
96 G13 **Begna** ≈ S Norway
Begoml' *see* Byahoml'
Begovat *see* Bekobod
159 Q13 **Begusarai** Bihār, NE India
149 R9 **Behābād** Yazd, C Iran
Behagle *see* Laï
57 Z10 **Béhague, Pointe** *headland* E French Guiana
Behar *see* Bihār
148 M10 **Behbahān** *var.* Behbehān. Khūzestān, SW Iran
Behbehān *see* Behbahān
46 G3 **Behring Point** Andros Island, W Bahamas
149 P4 **Behshahr** *prev.* Ashraf. Māzandarān, N Iran
169 V6 **Bei'an** Heilongjiang, NE China
Beibunar *see* Sredishte
Beibu Wan *see* Tongking, Gulf of
Beida *see* Al Bayḍā'
82 H13 **Beigi** W Ethiopia
166 L16 **Beihai** Guangxi Zhuangzu Zizhiqu, S China
165 Q10 **Bei Hulsan Hu** ◎ C China
167 N13 **Bei Jiang** ≈ S China
167 O2 **Beijing** *var.* Pei-ching, *Eng.* Peking; *prev.* Pei-p'ing. *country/municipality capital* (China) Beijing Shi, E China
167 P2 **Beijing** ✕ Beijing Shi, E China
Beijing *see* Beijing Shi
167 O2 **Beijing Shi** *var.* Beijing, Jing, Pei-ching, *Eng.* Peking; *prev.* Pei-p'ing. ◐ *municipality* E China
78 G8 **Beïla** Trarza, W Mauritania
100 N7 **Beilen** Drenthe, NE Netherlands
166 L15 **Beiliu** Guangxi Zhuangzu Zizhiqu, S China
165 O12 **Beilu He** ≈ W China
Beilul *see* Beylul
98 H8 **Beinn Dearg** ▲ N Scotland, UK
Beinn MacDuibh *see* Ben Macdui
166 I12 **Beipan Jiang** ≈ S China
169 T12 **Beipiao** Liaoning, NE China
85 N17 **Beira** Sofala, C Mozambique
85 N17 **Beira** ✕ Sofala, C Mozambique
106 I7 **Beira Alta** *former province* N Portugal
106 H9 **Beira Baixa** *former province* C Portugal
106 G8 **Beira Litoral** *former province* N Portugal
Beirut *see* Beyrouth
Beisān *see* Bet She'an
9 Q16 **Beiseker** Alberta, SW Canada
85 K19 **Beitbridge** Matabeleland South, S Zimbabwe
118 G10 **Beiuş** *Hung.* Belényes. Bihor, NW Romania
169 U12 **Beizhen** Liaoning, NE China
106 H12 **Beja** *anc.* Pax Julia. Beja, SE Portugal
106 G13 **Beja** ◐ *district* S Portugal
76 M5 **Béja** *var.* Bājah. N Tunisia
123 Ii11 **Bejaïa** *var.* Bejaia, *Fr.* Bougie; *anc.* Saldae. NE Algeria
106 K8 **Béjar** Castilla-León, N Spain
Bejraburi *see* Phetchaburi
Bekaa Valley *see* El Beqaa
Bekabad *see* Bekobod
Békás *see* Bicaz
174 J14 **Bekasi** Jawa, C Indonesia
Bek-Budi *see* Qarshi
152 A8 **Bekdash** Balkanskiy Velayat, NW Turkmenistan
153 T10 **Bek-Dzhar** Oshskaya Oblast', SW Kyrgyzstan
113 N24 **Békés** *Rom.* Bichiş. Békés, SE Hungary
113 M24 **Békés** *off.* Békés Megye. ◐ *county* SE Hungary
113 M24 **Békéscsaba** *Rom.* Bichiş-Ciaba. Békés, SE Hungary
145 S2 **Bēkhma** E Iraq
180 H7 **Bekily** Toliara, S Madagascar
172 Qq7 **Bekkai** Hokkaidō, NE Japan
153 Q11 **Bekobod** *Rus.* Bekabad; *prev.* Begovat. Toshkent Wiloyati, E Uzbekistan
131 O7 **Bekovo** Penzenskaya Oblast', W Russian Federation
Bél *see* Beliu
158 M13 **Bela** Uttar Pradesh, N India
155 N15 **Bela** Baluchistān, SW Pakistan
81 F15 **Bélabo** Est, C Cameroon
114 N10 **Bela Crkva** *Ger.* Weisskirchen, *Hung.* Fehértemplom. Serbia, W Yugoslavia
181 Y16 **Bel Air** *var.* Rivière Sèche. E Mauritius
106 L12 **Belalcázar** Andalucía, S Spain
115 P15 **Bela Palanka** Serbia, SE Yugoslavia
121 H16 **Belarus** *off.* Republic of Belarus, *var.* Belorussia, *Latv.* Baltkrievija; *prev.* Belorussian SSR, *Rus.* Belorusskaya SSR. ◆ *republic* E Europe
Belau *see* Palau
61 H21 **Bela Vista** Mato Grosso do Sul, SW Brazil
85 L21 **Bela Vista** Maputo, S Mozambique
173 Ff4 **Belawan** Sumatera, W Indonesia
Běla Woda *see* Weisswasser
131 U4 **Belaya** ≈ W Russian Federation
127 N7 **Belaya Gora** Respublika Sakha (Yakutiya), NE Russian Federation
130 M11 **Belaya Kalitiva** Rostovskaya Oblast', SW Russian Federation
129 R14 **Belaya Kholunitsa** Kirovskaya Oblast', NW Russian Federation
Belaya Tserkov' *see* Bila Tserkva
79 V11 **Belbédji** Zinder, S Niger
112 K13 **Bełchatów** *var.* Belchatow. Piotrków, C Poland
Belcher, Îles *see* Belcher Islands
10 H7 **Belcher Islands** *Fr.* Îles Belcher. *island group* Northwest Territories, SE Canada
107 S6 **Belchite** Aragón, NE Spain
31 O2 **Belcourt** North Dakota, N USA
33 P9 **Belding** Michigan, N USA
131 U5 **Belebey** Respublika Bashkortostan, W Russian Federation
83 N16 **Beledweyne** *var.* Belet Huen, *It.* Belet Uen. Hiiraan, C Somalia
152 B10 **Belek** Balkanskiy Velayat, W Turkmenistan
60 L12 **Belém** *var.* Pará. *state capital* Pará, N Brazil
67 I14 **Belém Ridge** *undersea feature* C Atlantic Ocean
39 R12 **Belen** New Mexico, SW USA
64 I7 **Belén** Catamarca, NW Argentina
56 G9 **Belén** Boyacá, C Colombia
44 J11 **Belén** Rivas, SW Nicaragua
64 O5 **Belén** Concepción, C Paraguay
63 D16 **Belén** Salto, N Uruguay
63 D20 **Belén de Escobar** Buenos Aires, E Argentina
116 J7 **Belene** Loveshka Oblast, N Bulgaria
116 J7 **Belene, Ostrov** *island* N Bulgaria
45 R15 **Belén, Río** ≈ C Panama
Belényes *see* Beiuş
197 G4 **Belep, Îles** *island group* W New Caledonia
106 H3 **Belesar, Embalse de** ⊡ NW Spain
Belet Huen/Belet Uen *see* Beledweyne
130 J5 **Belëv** Tul'skaya Oblast', W Russian Federation
99 G15 **Belfast** *Ir.* Béal Feirste. ◐ E Northern Ireland, UK
21 R7 **Belfast** Maine, NE USA
99 G15 **Belfast International** ✕ E Northern Ireland, UK
99 G15 **Belfast Lough** *Ir.* Loch Lao *inlet* E Northern Ireland, UK
30 K5 **Belfield** North Dakota, N USA
105 U7 **Belfort** Territoire-de-Belfort, E France
Belgard *see* Białogard
161 E17 **Belgaum** Karnātaka, W India
Belgian Congo *see* Zaire
205 T3 **Belgica Mountains** ▲▲ Antarctica
België/Belgique *see* Belgium
101 F20 **Belgium** *off.* Kingdom of Belgium, *Dut.* België, *Fr.* Belgique. ◆ *monarchy* NW Europe
130 J8 **Belgorod** Belgorodskaya Oblast', W Russian Federation
Belgorod-Dnestrovskiy *see* Bilhorod-Dnistrovs'kyy
130 J8 **Belgorodskaya Oblast'** ◐ *province* W Russian Federation
Belgrad *see* Beograd
31 T8 **Belgrade** Minnesota, N USA
35 S11 **Belgrade** Montana, NW USA
Belgrade *see* Beograd
205 N5 **Belgrano II** *Argentinian research station* Antarctica
23 X9 **Belhaven** North Carolina, SE USA
109 I23 **Belice** *anc.* Hypsas. ≈ Sicilia, Italy, C Mediterranean Sea
Belice *see* Belize/Belize City
115 M16 **Beli Drim** *Alb.* Drini i Bardhë. ≈ Albania/Yugoslavia
Beligrad *see* Berat
196 C8 **Beliliou** *prev.* Peleliu. *island* S Palau
116 L8 **Beli Lom, Yazovir** ⊡ NE Bulgaria
114 I8 **Beli Manastir** *Hung.* Pélmonostor; *prev.* Monostor. Osijek-Baranja, NE Croatia
104 J13 **Bélin-Béliet** Gironde, SW France
81 F17 **Bélinga** Ogooué-Ivindo, NE Gabon
23 S4 **Belington** West Virginia, NE USA
131 O6 **Belinskiy** Penzenskaya Oblast', W Russian Federation
174 I9 **Belinyu** Pulau Bangka, W Indonesia
174 Jj11 **Belitung, Pulau** *island* W Indonesia
118 F10 **Beliu** *Hung.* Bél. Arad, W Romania
116 I9 **Beli Vit** ≈ NW Bulgaria
44 G2 **Belize** *Sp.* Belice; *prev.* British Honduras, Colony of Belize. ◆ *commonwealth republic* Central America
44 F2 **Belize** *Sp.* Belice. ◐ *district* NE Belize
44 G2 **Belize** ≈ Belize/Guatemala
Belize *see* Belize City
44 G2 **Belize City** *var.* Belize, *Sp.* Belice. Belize, NE Belize
44 G2 **Belize City** ✕ Belize, NE Belize
Beljak *see* Villach
41 N16 **Belkofski** Alaska, USA
126 L4 **Bel'kovskiy, Ostrov** *island* Novosibirskiye Ostrova, NE Russian Federation
12 J8 **Bell** ≈ Québec, SE Canada
8 J15 **Bella Bella** British Columbia, SW Canada
104 M10 **Bellac** Haute-Vienne, C France
8 K15 **Bella Coola** British Columbia, SW Canada
108 D6 **Bellagio** Lombardia, N Italy
33 P6 **Bellaire** Michigan, N USA
108 D6 **Bellano** Lombardia, N Italy
161 G17 **Bellary** *var.* Ballari. Karnātaka, S India
191 S5 **Bellata** New South Wales, SE Australia
63 D16 **Bella Unión** Artigas, N Uruguay
63 C14 **Bella Vista** Corrientes, NE Argentina
64 J7 **Bella Vista** Tucumán, N Argentina
64 P4 **Bella Vista** Amambay, C Paraguay
58 B10 **Bellavista** Cajamarca, N Peru
58 D11 **Bellavista** San Martín, N Peru
191 U6 **Bellbrook** New South Wales, SE Australia
29 V5 **Belle** Missouri, C USA
23 Q5 **Belle** West Virginia, NE USA
33 R13 **Bellefontaine** Ohio, N USA
20 F14 **Bellefonte** Pennsylvania, NE USA
30 J9 **Belle Fourche** South Dakota, N USA
30 J9 **Belle Fourche Reservoir** ⊡ South Dakota, N USA
30 K9 **Belle Fourche River** ≈ South Dakota/Wyoming, N USA
105 S10 **Bellegarde-sur-Valserine** Ain, E France
25 Y14 **Belle Glade** Florida, SE USA
104 G8 **Belle Île** *island* NW France
11 T9 **Belle Isle** *island* Belle Isle, Newfoundland and Labrador, E Canada
11 S10 **Belle Isle, Strait of** *strait* Newfoundland and Labrador, E Canada
Bellenz *see* Bellinzona
31 W14 **Belle Plaine** Iowa, C USA
31 V9 **Belle Plaine** Minnesota, N USA
12 I9 **Belleterre** Québec, SE Canada
12 J15 **Belleville** Ontario, SE Canada
105 R10 **Belleville** Rhône, E France
32 K15 **Belleville** Illinois, N USA
29 N3 **Belleville** Kansas, C USA
31 Z13 **Bellevue** Iowa, C USA
31 S15 **Bellevue** Nebraska, C USA
33 S11 **Bellevue** Ohio, N USA
27 S5 **Bellevue** Texas, SW USA
34 H8 **Bellevue** Washington, NW USA
57 Y11 **Bellevue de l'Inini, Montagnes** ▲▲ S French Guiana
105 S11 **Belley** Ain, E France
Bellin *see* Kangirsuk
191 V6 **Bellingen** New South Wales, SE Australia
99 L14 **Bellingham** N England, UK
34 H6 **Bellingham** Washington, NW USA
Belling Hausen Mulde *see* Southeast Pacific Basin
204 H2 **Bellingshausen** *Russian research station* South Shetland Islands, Antarctica
Bellingshausen *see* Motu One
Bellingshausen Abyssal Plain *see* Bellingshausen Plain
200 N16 **Bellingshausen Plain** *var.* Bellingshausen Abyssal Plain. *undersea feature* SE Pacific Ocean
204 I8 **Bellingshausen Sea** *sea* Antarctica
100 P6 **Bellingwolde** Groningen, NE Netherlands
110 H11 **Bellinzona** *Ger.* Bellenz. Ticino, S Switzerland
27 T8 **Bellmead** Texas, SW USA
56 E8 **Bello** Antioquia, W Colombia
63 B21 **Bellocq** Buenos Aires, E Argentina
Bello Horizonte *see* Belo Horizonte
195 W17 **Bellona** *var.* Mungiki. *island* S Solomon Islands
Bellovacum *see* Beauvais
190 D7 **Bell, Point** *headland* South Australia
22 F9 **Bells** Tennessee, S USA
27 U5 **Bells** Texas, SW USA
94 N3 **Bellsund** *inlet* SW Svalbard
108 H6 **Belluno** Veneto, NE Italy
64 L11 **Bell Ville** Córdoba, C Argentina
85 E26 **Bellville** Western Cape, SW South Africa
27 U11 **Bellville** Texas, SW USA
106 L12 **Belmez** Andalucía, S Spain
31 V12 **Belmond** Iowa, C USA
20 E11 **Belmont** New York, NE USA
23 R10 **Belmont** North Carolina, SE USA
61 O18 **Belmonte** Bahia, E Brazil
106 I8 **Belmonte** Castelo Branco, C Portugal
107 P10 **Belmonte** Castilla-La Mancha, C Spain
44 G2 **Belmopan** ● (Belize) Cayo, C Belize
99 B16 **Belmullet** *Ir.* Béal an Mhuirhead. W Ireland
126 Mm15 **Belogorsk** Amurskaya Oblast', SE Russian Federation
Belogorsk *see* Bilohirs'k
116 F7 **Belogradchik** Oblast Montana, NW Bulgaria
180 H8 **Beloha** Toliara, S Madagascar
61 M20 **Belo Horizonte** *prev.* Bello Horizonte. *state capital* Minas Gerais, SE Brazil
28 M3 **Beloit** Kansas, C USA
32 L9 **Beloit** Wisconsin, N USA
Belokorovichi *see* Bilokorovychi
126 H15 **Belokurikha** Altayskiy Kray, S Russian Federation
128 J8 **Belomorsk** Respublika Kareliya, NW Russian Federation
128 J8 **Belomorsko-Baltiyskiy Kanal** *Eng.* White Sea-Baltic Canal, White Sea Canal. *canal* NW Russian Federation
159 V15 **Belonia** Tripura, NE India
Belopol'ye *see* Bilopillya
107 O4 **Belorado** Castilla-León, N Spain
130 L14 **Belorechensk** Krasnodarskiy Kray, SW Russian Federation
131 W5 **Beloretsk** Respublika Bashkortostan, W Russian Federation
Belorussia *see* Belarus
Belorussian SSR *see* Belarus
Belorusskaya Gryada *see* Byelaruskaya Hrada
Belorusskaya SSR *see* Belarus
Beloshchel'ye *see* Nar'yan-Mar
116 N8 **Beloslav** Varnenska Oblast, NE Bulgaria
Belostok *see* Białystok
180 H5 **Belo Tsiribihina** *var.* Belo-sur-Tsiribihina. Toliara, W Madagascar
Belovár *see* Bjelovar
Belovezhskaya Pushcha *see* Białowieska, Puszcza/Byelavyezhskaya Pushcha
116 H10 **Belovo** Plovdivska Oblast, W Bulgaria
126 H14 **Belovo** Kemerovskaya Oblast', S Russian Federation
Belovodsk *see* Bilovods'k
125 Ff9 **Beloyarskiy** Khanty-Mansiyskiy Avtonomnyy Okrug, N Russian Federation
128 K7 **Beloye More** *Eng.* White Sea. *sea* NW Russian Federation
128 K13 **Beloye, Ozero** ◎ NW Russian Federation
116 J10 **Belozem** Plovdivska Oblast, C Bulgaria
128 K13 **Belozërsk** Vologodskaya Oblast', NW Russian Federation
101 E20 **Belœil** Hainaut, SW Belgium
110 D8 **Belp** Bern, W Switzerland
110 D8 **Belp** ✕ (Bern) Bern, C Switzerland
109 L24 **Belpasso** Sicilia, Italy, C Mediterranean Sea
33 U14 **Belpre** Ohio, N USA
100 M8 **Belterwijde** ◎ N Netherlands
29 R4 **Belton** Missouri, C USA
23 P11 **Belton** South Carolina, SE USA
27 T9 **Belton** Texas, SW USA
27 S9 **Belton Lake** ⊡ Texas, SW USA
Bel'tsy *see* Bălţi
99 E16 **Belturbet** *Ir.* Béal Tairbirt. N Ireland
Beluchistan *see* Baluchistān
151 Z9 **Belukha, Gora** ▲ Kazakhstan/Russian Federation
109 M20 **Belvedere Marittimo** Calabria, SW Italy
32 L10 **Belvidere** Illinois, N USA
20 J14 **Belvidere** New Jersey, NE USA
Bely *see* Belyy
131 V8 **Belyayevka** Orenburgskaya Oblast', W Russian Federation
Belynichi *see* Byalynichy
128 H17 **Belyy** *var.* Bely, Beyj. Tverskaya Oblast', W Russian Federation
130 J6 **Belyye Berega** Bryanskaya Oblast', W Russian Federation
126 H5 **Belyy, Ostrov** *island* N Russian Federation
126 H12 **Belyy Yar** Tomskaya Oblast', C Russian Federation
102 N13 **Belzig** Brandenburg, NE Germany
24 K4 **Belzoni** Mississippi, S USA
180 H4 **Bemaraha** *var.* Plateau du Bemaraha. ▲▲ W Madagascar
84 B10 **Bembe** Uíge, NW Angola
79 S14 **Bembèrèkè** *var.* Bimbéréké. N Benin
106 K12 **Bembézar** ≈ SW Spain
106 J3 **Bembibre** Castilla-León, N Spain
31 T4 **Bemidji** Minnesota, N USA
100 L12 **Bemmel** Gelderland, SE Netherlands
176 U11 **Bemu** Pulau Seram, E Indonesia
Benāb *see* Bonāb
107 T5 **Benabarre** *var.* Benavarn. Aragón, NE Spain
Benaco *see* Garda, Lago di
81 L20 **Bena-Dibele** Kasai Oriental, C Zaire
107 R9 **Benageber, Embalse de** ⊡ E Spain
191 O11 **Benalla** Victoria, SE Australia
106 M14 **Benamejí** Andalucía, S Spain
Benares *see* Vārānasi
Benavarn *see* Benabarre
106 F10 **Benavente** Santarém, C Portugal
106 K5 **Benavente** Castilla-León, N Spain
27 S15 **Benavides** Texas, SW USA
98 F8 **Benbecula** *island* NW Scotland, UK
Bencovazzo *see* Benkovac
34 H13 **Bend** Oregon, NW USA
190 K7 **Benda Range** ▲▲ South Australia
191 T6 **Bendemeer** New South Wales, SE Australia
Bender *see* Tighina
Bender Beila/Bender Beyla *see* Bandarbeyla
Bender Cassim/Bender Qaasim *see* Boosaaso
Bendery *see* Tighina
191 N11 **Bendigo** Victoria, SE Australia
120 E10 **Bēne** Dobele, SW Latvia
100 K13 **Beneden-Leeuwen** Gelderland, C Netherlands
103 L24 **Benediktenwand** ▲ S Germany
Benemérita de San Cristóbal *see* San Cristóbal
79 N12 **Bénéna** Ségou, S Mali
180 I7 **Benenitra** Toliara, S Madagascar
Beneschau *see* Benešov
Beneški Zaliv *see* Venice, Gulf of
113 D17 **Benešov** *Ger.* Beneschau. Střední Čechy, W Czech Republic
126 Ll3 **Benetta, Ostrov** *island* Novosibirskiye Ostrova, NE Russian Federation
109 L17 **Benevento** *anc.* Beneventum, Malventum. Campania, S Italy
Beneventum *see* Benevento
181 S3 **Bengal, Bay of** *bay* N Indian Ocean
81 M17 **Bengamisa** Haut-Zaïre, N Zaire
Bengasi *see* Banghāzī
174 Ll15 **Bengawan, Sungai** ≈ Jawa, S Indonesia
Bengazi *see* Banghāzī
167 P7 **Bengbu** *var.* Peng-pu. Anhui, E China
34 L9 **Benge** Washington, NW USA
Benghazi *see* Banghāzī
174 H7 **Bengkalis** Pulau Bengkalis, W Indonesia
174 H6 **Bengkalis, Pulau** *island* W Indonesia
174 Kk7 **Bengkayang** Borneo, C Indonesia
Bengkoelen/Bengkoeloe *see* Bengkulu
174 H12 **Bengkulu** *prev.* Bengkoeloe, Benkoelen, Benkulen. Sumatera, W Indonesia
174 H11 **Bengkulu** *off.* Propinsi Bengkulu; *prev.* Bengkoelen, Benkoelen, Benkulen. ◐ *province* W Indonesia
84 A11 **Bengo** ◐ *province* W Angola
97 J16 **Bengtsfors** Älvsborg, S Sweden
84 B13 **Benguela** *var.* Benguella. Benguela, W Angola
85 A14 **Benguela** ◐ *province* W Angola
Benguella *see* Benguela
Bengweulu, Lake *see* Bangweulu, Lake
124 Qq15 **Benha** *var.* Banhā. N Egypt
198 G6 **Benham Seamount** *undersea feature* W Philippine Sea
98 H6 **Ben Hope** ▲ N Scotland, UK
81 P18 **Beni** Nord Kivu, NE Zaire
59 L15 **Beni** *var.* El Beni. ◐ *department* N Bolivia
76 H8 **Beni Abbès** W Algeria
107 T8 **Benicarló** País Valenciano, E Spain
107 T9 **Benicasim** País Valenciano, E Spain
107 T12 **Benidorm** País Valenciano, SE Spain
77 W9 **Beni Mazâr** *var.* Banī Mazār. C Egypt
122 F12 **Beni-Mellal** C Morocco
79 R14 **Benin** *off.* Republic of Benin; *prev.* Dahomey. ◆ *republic* W Africa
79 S17 **Benin, Bight of** *gulf* W Africa
79 U16 **Benin City** Edo, SW Nigeria
59 K16 **Beni, Río** ≈ N Bolivia
123 Gg11 **Beni Saf** *var.* Beni-Saf. NW Algeria
107 T11 **Benissa** País Valenciano, E Spain
124 Qq17 **Beni Suef** *var.* Banī Suwayf. N Egypt
9 V15 **Benito** Manitoba, S Canada
Benito *see* Uolo, Río
63 C23 **Benito Juárez** Buenos Aires, E Argentina
43 P14 **Benito Juaréz Internacional** ✕ (México) México, S Mexico
27 P5 **Benjamin** Texas, SW USA
60 B13 **Benjamin Constant** Amazonas, N Brazil
42 F4 **Benjamín Hill** Sonora, NW Mexico
65 F19 **Benjamín, Isla** *island* Archipiélago de los Chonos, S Chile
172 N5 **Benkei-misaki** *headland* Hokkaidō, NE Japan
30 L17 **Benkelman** Nebraska, C USA
98 I7 **Ben Klibreck** ▲ N Scotland, UK
Benkoelen *see* Bengkulu
114 D13 **Benkovac** *It.* Bencovazzo. Zadar-Knin, S Croatia
Benkulen *see* Bengkulu
98 I11 **Ben Lawers** ▲ C Scotland, UK
98 J9 **Ben Macdui** *var.* Beinn MacDuibh. ▲ C Scotland, UK
98 G11 **Ben More** ▲ W Scotland, UK
98 I11 **Ben More** ▲ C Scotland, UK
98 H7 **Ben More Assynt** ▲ N Scotland, UK
193 E20 **Benmore, Lake** ◎ South Island, NZ
100 L12 **Bennekom** Gelderland, SE Netherlands
23 T11 **Bennettsville** South Carolina, SE USA
98 H10 **Ben Nevis** ▲ N Scotland, UK
192 M9 **Benneydale** Waikato, North Island, NZ
Bennichab *see* Bennichchāb
78 H8 **Bennichchāb** *var.* Bennichab. Inchiri, W Mauritania
20 L10 **Bennington** Vermont, NE USA
193 E20 **Ben Ohau Range** ▲▲ South Island, NZ
85 J21 **Benoni** Gauteng, NE South Africa
180 J2 **Be, Nosy** *var.* Nossi-Bé. *island* NW Madagascar
Bénoué *see* Benue
44 F2 **Benque Viejo del Carmen** Cayo, W Belize
103 G19 **Bensheim** Hessen, W Germany
39 N16 **Benson** Arizona, SW USA
31 S8 **Benson** Minnesota, N USA
23 U10 **Benson** North Carolina, SE USA
175 Pp14 **Benteng** Pulau Selayar, C Indonesia
85 A14 **Bentiaba** Namibe, SW Angola
189 T4 **Bentinck Island** *island* Wellesley Islands, Queensland, N Australia

◆ Country ● Country Capital ◇ Dependent Territory ○ Dependent Territory Capital ◐ Administrative Region ✕ International Airport ▲ Mountain ▲▲ Mountain Range Volcano ≈ River ◎ Lake ⊡ Reservoir

BENTIU – BILANGA

82 E13 **Bentiu** Wahda, S Sudan
144 G8 **Bent Jbaïl** *var.* Bint Jubayl. S Lebanon
9 Q15 **Bentley** Alberta, SW Canada
63 I15 **Bento Gonçalves** Rio Grande do Sul, S Brazil
29 Y7 **Benton** Arkansas, C USA
32 L16 **Benton** Illinois, N USA
22 H7 **Benton** Kentucky, S USA
24 G5 **Benton** Louisiana, S USA
29 U12 **Benton** Missouri, C USA
22 M10 **Benton** Tennessee, S USA
33 O10 **Benton Harbor** Michigan, N USA
29 S9 **Bentonville** Arkansas, C USA
79 U16 **Benue** ◐ *state* SE Nigeria
80 F13 **Benue** *Fr.* Bénoué. ~ Cameroon/Nigeria
174 Hh6 **Benut** Johor, Peninsular Malaysia
169 V12 **Benxi** *prev.* Pen-ch'i, Penhsihu, Penki. Liaoning, NE China
Benyakoni *see* Byenyakoni
114 K10 **Beočin** Serbia, N Yugoslavia
Beodericsworth *see* Bury St Edmunds
114 M11 **Beograd** *Eng.* Belgrade, *Ger.* Belgrad; *anc.* Singidunum. ● (Yugoslavia) Serbia, N Yugoslavia
114 L11 **Beograd** *Eng.* Belgrade. ✕ Serbia, N Yugoslavia
78 M16 **Béoumi** C Ivory Coast
37 V3 **Beowawe** Nevada, W USA
176 Ww8 **Bepondi, Pulau** *see* Bepondi, Pulau
170 D13 **Beppu** Ōita, Kyūshū, SW Japan
170 Dd14 **Beppu-wan** *bay* SW Japan
197 H15 **Beqa** *prev.* Mbengga. *island* W Fiji
Beqa Barrier Reef *see* Kavukavu Reef
47 Y14 **Bequia** *island* C Saint Vincent and the Grenadines
115 L16 **Berane** *prev.* Ivangrad. Montenegro, SW Yugoslavia
115 L21 **Berat** *var.* Berati, *SCr.* Beligrad. Berat, C Albania
115 L21 **Berat** ◐ *district* C Albania
Berătău *see* Berettyó
Berati *see* Berat
Beraun *see* Berounka, Czech Republic
Beraun *see* Beroun, Czech Republic
175 O6 **Berau, Sungai** ~ Borneo, N Indonesia
176 V10 **Berau, Teluk** *var.* MacCluer Gulf. *bay* Irian Jaya, E Indonesia
82 G8 **Berber** River Nile, NE Sudan
82 N12 **Berbera** Woqooyi Galbeed, NW Somalia
81 H16 **Berbérati** Mambéré-Kadéï, SW Central African Republic
Berberia, Cabo de *see* Barbaria, Cap de
57 T9 **Berbice River** ~ NE Guyana
Berchid *see* Berrechid
105 N2 **Berck-Plage** Pas-de-Calais, N France
27 T13 **Berclair** Texas, SW USA
119 W10 **Berda** ~ SE Ukraine
Berdichev *see* Berdychiv
126 Ll11 **Berdigestyakh** Respublika Sakha (Yakutiya), NE Russian Federation
126 H14 **Berdsk** Novosibirskaya Oblast', C Russian Federation
119 W10 **Berdyans'k** *Rus.* Berdyansk; *prev.* Osipenko. Zaporiz'ka Oblast', SE Ukraine
119 W10 **Berdyans'ka Kosa** *spit* SE Ukraine
119 V10 **Berdyans'ka Zatoka** *gulf* S Ukraine
119 N5 **Berdychiv** *Rus.* Berdichev. Zhytomyrs'ka Oblast', N Ukraine
22 M6 **Berea** Kentucky, S USA
Beregovo/Beregszász *see* Berehove
118 G8 **Berehove** *Cz.* Berehovo, *Hung.* Beregszász, *Rus.* Beregovo. Zakarpats'ka Oblast', W Ukraine
Berehovo *see* Berehove
194 J15 **Bereina** Central, S PNG
47 O12 **Berekua** S Dominica
79 O16 **Berekum** W Ghana
77 Y11 **Berenice** *var.* Minā Baranīs. SE Egypt
15 L14 **Berens** ~ Manitoba/Ontario, C Canada
9 X14 **Berens River** Manitoba, C Canada
31 R12 **Beresford** South Dakota, N USA
118 J4 **Berestechko** Volyns'ka Oblast', NW Ukraine
118 M11 **Bereşti** Galaţi, E Romania
119 U6 **Berestova** ~ E Ukraine
Beretău *see* Berettyó
113 N23 **Berettyó** *Rom.* Barcău; *prev.* Berătău, Beretău. ~ Hungary/Romania
113 N23 **Berettyóújfalu** Hajdú-Bihar, E Hungary
Berëza/Bereza Kartuska *see* Byaroza
119 Q4 **Berezan'** Kyyivs'ka Oblast', N Ukraine
119 Q10 **Berezanka** Mykolayivs'ka Oblast', S Ukraine
118 J6 **Berezhany** *Pol.* Brzeżany. Ternopil's'ka Oblast', W Ukraine
Berezina *see* Byerezino
Berezino *see* Byerazino
119 P10 **Berezivka** *Rus.* Berezovka. Odes'ka Oblast', SW Ukraine
119 Q2 **Berezna** Chernihivs'ka Oblast', NE Ukraine
118 L3 **Berezne** Rivnens'ka Oblast', NW Ukraine
119 R9 **Bereznehuvate** Mykolayivs'ka Oblast', S Ukraine
129 N10 **Bereznik** Arkhangel'skaya Oblast', NW Russian Federation
129 U13 **Berezniki** Permskaya Oblast', NW Russian Federation
Berezovka *see* Berezivka
125 Ff9 **Berezovo** Khanty-Mansiyskiy Avtonomnyy Okrug, N Russian Federation
131 O9 **Berezovskaya** Volgogradskaya Oblast', SW Russian Federation
126 H14 **Berezovskiy** Kemerovskaya Oblast', S Russian Federation
127 N14 **Berezovyy** Khabarovskiy Kray, E Russian Federation
85 E25 **Berg** ~ W South Africa
Berg *see* Berg bei Rohrbach
107 V4 **Berga** Cataluña, NE Spain
97 N20 **Berga** Kalmar, S Sweden
142 B13 **Bergama** İzmir, W Turkey
108 E7 **Bergamo** *anc.* Bergomum. Lombardia, N Italy
107 P3 **Bergara** País Vasco, N Spain
111 S3 **Berg bei Rohrbach** *var.* Berg. Oberösterreich, N Austria
195 O11 **Bergberg** ~ New Britain, C Papau New Guinea
102 I11 **Bergen** Mecklenburg-Vorpommern, NE Germany
103 O16 **Bergen** Niedersachsen, NW Germany
100 H8 **Bergen** Noord-Holland, NW Netherlands
96 C13 **Bergen** Hordaland, S Norway
Bergen *see* Mons
57 W9 **Berg en Dal** Brokopondo, C Suriname
101 G15 **Bergen op Zoom** Noord-Brabant, S Netherlands
104 L13 **Bergerac** Dordogne, SW France
101 J16 **Bergeyk** Noord-Brabant, S Netherlands
103 D16 **Bergheim** Nordrhein-Westfalen, W Germany
57 X10 **Bergi** Sipaliwini, E Suriname
103 E16 **Bergisch Gladbach** Nordrhein-Westfalen, W Germany
103 F14 **Bergkamen** Nordrhein-Westfalen, W Germany
97 N21 **Bergkvara** Kalmar, S Sweden
Bergomum *see* Bergamo
100 K13 **Bergse Maas** ~ S Netherlands
97 P15 **Bergshamra** Stockholm, C Sweden
96 N10 **Bergsjö** Gävleborg, C Sweden
95 J14 **Bergsviken** Norrbotten, N Sweden
100 L6 **Bergum** *Fris.* Burgum. Friesland, N Netherlands
100 M6 **Bergumer Meer** ◎ N Netherlands
96 N12 **Bergviken** ◎ C Sweden
174 I9 **Berhala, Selat** *strait* Sumatera, W Indonesia
Berhampore *see* Baharampur
127 Q9 **Beringa, Ostrov** *island* E Russian Federation
101 J17 **Beringen** Limburg, NE Belgium
41 T12 **Bering Glacier** *glacier* Alaska, USA
Beringov Proliv *see* Bering Strait
127 Q5 **Beringovskiy** Chukotskiy Avtonomnyy Okrug, NE Russian Federation
199 K2 **Bering Sea** *sea* N Pacific Ocean
40 L9 **Bering Strait** *Rus.* Beringov Proliv. *strait* Bering Sea/Chukchi Sea
Berislav *see* Beryslav
107 O15 **Berja** Andalucía, S Spain
96 H9 **Berkåk** Sør-Trøndelag, S Norway
100 N11 **Berkel** ~ Germany/Netherlands
37 N8 **Berkeley** California, W USA
67 E24 **Berkeley Sound** *sound* NE Falkland Islands
23 V2 **Berkeley Springs** *var.* Bath. West Virginia, NE USA
205 N6 **Berkner Island** *island* Antarctica
116 G8 **Berkovitsa** Oblast Montana, NW Bulgaria
99 M22 **Berkshire** *cultural region* S England, UK
101 H17 **Berlaar** Antwerpen, N Belgium
Berlanga *see* Berlanga de Duero
107 P6 **Berlanga de Duero** *var.* Berlanga. Castilla-León, N Spain
1 I16 **Berlanga Rise** *undersea feature* E Pacific Ocean
101 F17 **Berlare** Oost-Vlaanderen, NW Belgium
106 E9 **Berlenga, Ilha da** *island* C Portugal
94 M7 **Berlevåg** Finnmark, N Norway
102 O12 **Berlin** ● (Germany) Berlin, NE Germany
23 Z4 **Berlin** Maryland, NE USA
21 O7 **Berlin** New Hampshire, NE USA
20 D16 **Berlin** Pennsylvania, NE USA
32 L7 **Berlin** Wisconsin, N USA
102 O12 **Berlin** ◐ *state* NE Germany
Berlinchen *see* Barlinek
33 U12 **Berlin Lake** ⊡ Ohio, N USA
191 R11 **Bermagui** New South Wales, SE Australia
42 L8 **Bermejillo** Durango, C Mexico
64 M6 **Bermejo (viejo), Río** ~ N Argentina
64 L5 **Bermejo, Río** ~ N Argentina
64 I10 **Bermejo, Río** ~ W Argentina
107 P2 **Bermeo** País Vasco, N Spain
106 K6 **Bermillo de Sayago** Castilla-León, N Spain
108 E6 **Bermina, Pizzo** *Rmsch.* Piz Bernina. ▲ Italy/Switzerland *see also* Bernina, Piz
66 A12 **Bermuda** *var.* Bermuda Islands, Bermudas; *prev.* Somers Islands. ◇ *UK crown colony* NW Atlantic Ocean
1 N11 **Bermuda** *var.* Great Bermuda, Long Island, Main Island. *island* Bermuda
Bermuda Islands *see* Bermuda
Bermuda-New England Seamount Arc *see* New England Seamounts
1 N11 **Bermuda Rise** *undersea feature* C Sargasso Sea
Bermudas *see* Bermuda
110 D8 **Bern** *Fr.* Berne. ● (Switzerland) Bern, W Switzerland
110 D9 **Bern** *Fr.* Berne. ◐ *canton* W Switzerland
39 R11 **Bernalillo** New Mexico, SW USA
12 H12 **Bernard Lake** ◎ Ontario, S Canada
63 B18 **Bernardo de Irigoyen** Santa Fe, NE Argentina
20 J14 **Bernardsville** New Jersey, NE USA
65 K14 **Bernasconi** La Pampa, C Argentina
102 O12 **Bernau** Brandenburg, NE Germany
104 L4 **Bernay** Eure, N France
103 L14 **Bernburg** Sachsen-Anhalt, C Germany
111 X5 **Berndorf** Niederösterreich, NE Austria
33 Q12 **Berne** Indiana, N USA
Berne *see* Bern
110 D10 **Berner Alpen** *var.* Berner Oberland, *Eng.* Bernese Oberland. ▲▲ SW Switzerland
Berner Oberland/Bernese Oberland *see* Berner Alpen
111 Y2 **Bernhardsthal** Niederösterreich, N Austria
24 H4 **Bernice** Louisiana, S USA
29 Y8 **Bernie** Missouri, C USA
188 G9 **Bernier Island** *island* Western Australia
Bernina Pass *see* Bernina, Passo del
110 J10 **Bernina, Passo del** *Eng.* Bernina Pass. *pass* SE Switzerland
110 J10 **Bernina, Piz** *It.* Pizzo Bermina. ▲ Italy/Switzerland *see also* Bermina, Pizzo
101 E20 **Bernissart** Hainaut, SW Belgium
103 E18 **Bernkastel-Kues** Rheinland-Pfalz, W Germany
Beroea *see* Ḥalab
180 H6 **Beroroha** Toliara, SW Madagascar
Béroubouay *see* Gbéroubouè
113 C17 **Beroun** *Ger.* Beraun. Střední Čechy, W Czech Republic
113 C16 **Berounka** *Ger.* Beraun. ~ W Czech Republic
115 Q18 **Berovo** E FYR Macedonia
76 F6 **Berrechid** *var.* Berchid. W Morocco
105 R15 **Berre, Étang de** ◎ SE France
105 S15 **Berre-l'Étang** Bouches-du-Rhône, SE France
190 K9 **Berri** South Australia
33 O10 **Berrien Springs** Michigan, N USA
191 O10 **Berrigan** New South Wales, SE Australia
105 N9 **Berry** *cultural region* C France
37 N7 **Berryessa, Lake** ◎ California, W USA
46 G2 **Berry Islands** *island group* N Bahamas
29 T9 **Berryville** Arkansas, C USA
23 V3 **Berryville** Virginia, NE USA
85 D21 **Berseba** Karas, S Namibia
119 O8 **Bershad'** Vinnyts'ka Oblast', C Ukraine
30 L3 **Berthold** North Dakota, N USA
39 T3 **Berthoud** Colorado, C USA
39 S4 **Berthoud Pass** *pass* Colorado, C USA
81 F15 **Bertoua** Est, E Cameroon
30 I10 **Bertram** Texas, SW USA
65 G22 **Bertrand, Cerro** ▲ S Argentina
101 J23 **Bertrix** Luxembourg, SE Belgium
203 P3 **Beru** *var.* Peru. *atoll* Tungaru, W Kiribati
Beruni *see* Beruniy
152 I9 **Beruniy** *var.* Biruni, *Rus.* Beruni. Qoraqalpoghiston Respublikasi, W Uzbekistan
60 F13 **Beruri** Amazonas, NW Brazil
20 H14 **Berwick** Pennsylvania, NE USA
98 K12 **Berwick** *cultural region* SE Scotland, UK
98 L12 **Berwick-upon-Tweed** N England, UK
119 S10 **Beryslav** *Rus.* Berislav. Khersons'ka Oblast', S Ukraine
Berytus *see* Beyrouth
180 H4 **Besalampy** Mahajanga, W Madagascar
105 T8 **Besançon** *anc.* Besontium, Vesontio. Doubs, E France
105 P10 **Besbre** ~ C France
Bescanuova *see* Baška
Besdan *see* Bezdan
Besed' *see* Byesyedz'
153 R10 **Beshariq** *Rus.* Besharyk; *prev.* Kirovo. Farghona Wiloyati, E Uzbekistan
Besharyk *see* Beshariq
152 L9 **Beshbuloq** *Rus.* Beshbulak. Nawoiy Wiloyati, N Uzbekistan
Beshenkovichi *see* Byeshankovichy
152 M13 **Beshkent** Qashqadaryo Wiloyati, S Uzbekistan
Beshulak *see* Beshbuloq
176 Uu8 **Besir** Irian Jaya, E Indonesia
114 L10 **Beška** Serbia, N Yugoslavia
Beskra *see* Biskra
131 O16 **Beslan** Respublika Severnaya Osetiya, SW Russian Federation
115 P16 **Besna Kobila** ▲ SE Yugoslavia
143 N16 **Besni** Adıyaman, S Turkey
Besontium *see* Besançon
124 Nn2 **Beşparmak Dağları** *Eng.* Kyrenia Mountains. ▲▲ N Cyprus
Bessarabka *see* Basarabeasca
94 O2 **Bessels, Kapp** *headland* C Svalbard
25 P4 **Bessemer** Alabama, S USA
32 K3 **Bessemer** Michigan, N USA
23 Q10 **Bessemer City** North Carolina, SE USA
104 M10 **Bessines-sur-Gartempe** Haute-Vienne, C France
101 K15 **Best** Noord-Brabant, S Netherlands
27 N9 **Best** Texas, SW USA
129 O11 **Bestuzhevo** Arkhangel'skaya Oblast', NW Russian Federation
126 M11 **Bestyakh** Respublika Sakha (Yakutiya), NE Russian Federation
Beszterce *see* Bistriţa
Besztercebánya *see* Banská Bystrica
180 I5 **Betafo** Antananarivo, C Madagascar
106 H2 **Betanzos** Galicia, NW Spain
106 G2 **Betanzos, Ría de** *estuary* NW Spain
81 G15 **Bétaré Oya** Est, E Cameroon
107 S9 **Bétera** País Valenciano, E Spain
79 R15 **Bétérou** C Benin
85 K21 **Bethal** Mpumalanga, NE South Africa
32 K15 **Bethalto** Illinois, N USA
85 D21 **Bethanie** *var.* Bethanien, Bethany. Karas, S Namibia
Bethanien *see* Bethanie
29 N10 **Bethany** Missouri, C USA
29 S2 **Bethany** Oklahoma, C USA
Bethany *see* Bethanie
41 N12 **Bethel** Alaska, USA
21 P7 **Bethel** Maine, NE USA
23 W9 **Bethel** North Carolina, SE USA
20 B15 **Bethel Park** Pennsylvania, NE USA
23 W3 **Bethesda** Maryland, NE USA
85 J22 **Bethlehem** Free State, C South Africa
20 I14 **Bethlehem** Pennsylvania, NE USA
144 F10 **Bethlehem** *Ar.* Bayt Laḥm, *Heb.* Bet Leḥem. C West Bank
Bethlen *see* Beclean
85 I24 **Bethulie** Free State, C South Africa
105 O1 **Béthune** Pas-de-Calais, N France
104 M3 **Béthune** ~ N France
106 M14 **Béticos, Sistemas** *var.* Sistema Penibético, *Eng.* Baetic Cordillera, Baetic Mountains. ▲▲ S Spain
56 I6 **Betijoque** Trujillo, NW Venezuela
61 M20 **Betim** Minas Gerais, SE Brazil
202 H3 **Betio** Tarawa, W Kiribati
180 H7 **Betioky** Toliara, S Madagascar
Bet Leḥem *see* Bethlehem
Betlen *see* Beclean
178 H17 **Betong** Yala, SW Thailand
81 I16 **Bétou** La Likouala, N Congo
151 P14 **Betpak-Dala** *Kaz.* Betpaqdala. *plateau* S Kazakhstan
Betpaqdala *see* Betpak-Dala
180 H7 **Betroka** Toliara, S Madagascar
Betschau *see* Bečva
144 G9 **Bet She'an** *Ar.* Baysān, Beisān; *anc.* Scythopolis. Northern, N Israel
13 T6 **Betsiamites** Québec, SE Canada
13 T6 **Betsiamites** ~ Québec, SE Canada
180 I4 **Betsiboka** ~ N Madagascar
101 M25 **Bettembourg** Luxembourg, S Luxembourg
101 M23 **Bettendorf** Diekirch, NE Luxembourg
31 Z14 **Bettendorf** Iowa, C USA
77 R13 **Bette, Pic** *var.* Bikkū Bitti, *It.* Picco Bette. ▲ S Libya
Bette, Picco *see* Bette, Pic
159 P12 **Bettiah** Bihār, N India
41 Q7 **Bettles** Alaska, USA
97 N17 **Bettna** Södermanland, C Sweden
160 H11 **Betūl** *prev.* Badnur. Madhya Pradesh, C India
160 H9 **Betwa** ~ C India
103 F16 **Betzdorf** Rheinland-Pfalz, W Germany
84 C9 **Béu** Uíge, NW Angola
33 P6 **Beulah** Michigan, N USA
30 L5 **Beulah** North Dakota, N USA
100 M8 **Beulakerwijde** ◎ N Netherlands
100 L13 **Beuningen** Gelderland, SE Netherlands
Beuthen *see* Bytom
105 N7 **Beuvron** ~ C France
101 F16 **Beveren** Oost-Vlaanderen, N Belgium
23 T9 **B.Everett Jordan Reservoir** *var.* Jordan Lake. ⊡ North Carolina, SE USA
99 N17 **Beverley** E England, UK
Beverley *see* Beverly
101 J17 **Beverlo** Limburg, NE Belgium
21 P11 **Beverly** Massachusetts, NE USA
34 J9 **Beverly** *var.* Beverley. Washington, NW USA
37 S15 **Beverly Hills** California, W USA
103 I14 **Beverungen** Nordrhein-Westfalen, C Germany
100 H9 **Beverwijk** Noord-Holland, W Netherlands
110 C10 **Bex** Vaud, W Switzerland
99 P23 **Bexhill** *var.* Bexhill-on-Sea. SE England, UK
Bexhill-on-Sea *see* Bexhill
142 E17 **Bey Dağları** ▲▲ SW Turkey
Beyj *see* Belyy
142 E10 **Beykoz** İstanbul, NW Turkey
78 K15 **Beyla** Guinée-Forestière, SE Guinea
143 X12 **Beylǎqan** *prev.* Zhdanov. SW Azerbaijan
82 L10 **Beylul** *var.* Beilul. SE Eritrea
150 H14 **Beyneu** *Kaz.* Beyneū. Mangistau, SW Kazakhstan
Beyneū *see* Beyneu
172 Ss14 **Beyonēsu-retsugan** *Eng.* Bayonnaise Rocks. *island group* SE Japan
142 G12 **Beypazarı** Ankara, NW Turkey
161 F21 **Beypore** Kerala, SW India
144 G7 **Beyrouth** *var.* Bayrūt, *Eng.* Beirut; *anc.* Berytus. ● (Lebanon) W Lebanon
144 G7 **Beyrouth** ✕ W Lebanon
142 G15 **Beyşehir** Konya, SW Turkey
142 G15 **Beyşehir Gölü** ◎ C Turkey
110 J7 **Bezau** Vorarlberg, NW Austria
114 J8 **Bezdan** *Ger.* Besdan, *Hung.* Bezdán. Serbia, NW Yugoslavia
Bezdezh *see* Byezdzyezh
128 G15 **Bezhanitsy** Pskovskaya Oblast', W Russian Federation
128 K15 **Bezhetsk** Tverskaya Oblast', W Russian Federation
105 P16 **Béziers** *anc.* Baeterrae, Baeterrae Septimanorum, Julia Beterrae. Hérault, S France
Bezmein *see* Byuzmeyin
Bezwada *see* Vijayawāda
160 P12 **Bhadrak** *var.* Bhadrakh. Orissa, E India
Bhadrakh *see* Bhadrak
161 F19 **Bhadra Reservoir** ⊡ SW India
161 F18 **Bhadrāvati** Karnātaka, SW India
159 R14 **Bhāgalpur** Bihār, NE India
Bhairab *see* Bhairab Bazar
159 U14 **Bhairab Bazar** *var.* Bhairab. Dhaka, C Bangladesh
159 O11 **Bhairahawa** Western, S Nepal
155 S8 **Bhakkar** Punjab, E Pakistan
159 P11 **Bhaktapur** Central, C Nepal
178 Gg3 **Bhamo** *var.* Banmo. Kachin State, N Myanmar
Bhāmragad *see* Bhāmragarh
160 K13 **Bhāmragarh** *var.* Bhāmragad. Mahārāshtra, C India
160 J12 **Bhandāra** Mahārāshtra, C India
Bhārat *see* India
158 J12 **Bharatpur** *prev.* Bhurtpore. Rājasthān, N India
160 D11 **Bharūch** Gujarāt, W India
161 E18 **Bhatkal** Karnātaka, W India
159 O13 **Bhatni** *var.* Bhatni Junction. Uttar Pradesh, N India
Bhatni Junction *see* Bhatni
159 S16 **Bhātpāra** West Bengal, NE India
155 U7 **Bhaun** Punjab, E Pakistan
Bhaunagar *see* Bhāvnagar
160 M13 **Bhavānīpātna** Orissa, E India
161 H21 **Bhavānīsāgar Reservoir** ⊡ S India
160 D11 **Bhāvnagar** *prev.* Bhaunagar. Gujarāt, W India
Bheanntraí, Bá *see* Bantry Bay
Bheara, Béal an *see* Gweebarra Bay
160 K12 **Bhilai** Madhya Pradesh, C India
158 G13 **Bhīlwāra** Rājasthān, N India
161 E14 **Bhīma** ~ S India
161 K16 **Bhīmavaram** Andhra Pradesh, E India
160 I7 **Bhind** Madhya Pradesh, C India
158 E13 **Bhīnmāl** Rājasthān, N India
Bhir *see* Bīd
160 D13 **Bhiwandi** Mahārāshtra, W India
158 H10 **Bhiwāni** Haryāna, N India
158 L13 **Bhognīpur** Uttar Pradesh, N India
159 U16 **Bhola** Khulna, S Bangladesh
160 H10 **Bhopāl** Madhya Pradesh, C India
161 J14 **Bhopālpatnam** Madhya Pradesh, C India
161 E14 **Bhor** Mahārāshtra, W India
160 O12 **Bhubaneshwar** *prev.* Bhubaneswar, Bhuvaneshwar. Orissa, E India
Bhubaneswar *see* Bhubaneshwar
160 B9 **Bhuj** Gujarāt, W India
Bhuket *see* Phuket
Bhurtpore *see* Bharatpur
Bhusaval *see* Bhusāwal
160 G12 **Bhusāwal** *prev.* Bhusaval. Mahārāshtra, C India
159 T12 **Bhutan** *off.* Kingdom of Bhutan, *var.* Druk-yul. ◆ *monarchy* S Asia
Bhuvaneshwar *see* Bhubaneshwar
149 T15 **Bīābān, Kūh-e** ▲▲ S Iran
79 V18 **Biafra, Bight of** *var.* Bight of Bonny. *bay* W Africa
176 X9 **Biak** Irian Jaya, E Indonesia
176 Ww9 **Biak, Pulau** *island* E Indonesia
112 P12 **Biała Podlaska** Biała Podlaska, E Poland
112 O12 **Biała Podlaska** *off.* Województwo Bialskopodlaskie. ◐ *province* E Poland
112 F7 **Białogard** *Ger.* Belgard. Koszalin, NW Poland
Białostockie, Województwo *see* Białystok
112 P10 **Białowieska, Puszcza** *Bel.* Byelavyezhskaya Pushcha, *Rus.* Belovezhskaya Pushcha. *physical region* Belarus/Poland *see also* Byelavyezhskaya Pushcha
Bialskopodlaskie, Województwo *see* Biała Podlaska
112 G8 **Biały Bór** *Ger.* Baldenburg. Koszalin, NW Poland
112 P9 **Białystok** *Rus.* Belostok, Bielostok. Białystok, E Poland
112 O10 **Białystok** *off.* Województwo Białostockie, *Rus.* Belostok, Bielostok. ◐ *province* E Poland
109 L24 **Biancavilla** *prev.* Inessa. Sicilia, Italy, C Mediterranean Sea
Bianco, Monte *see* Blanc, Mont
78 L15 **Biankouma** W Ivory Coast
178 I7 **Bia, Phou** *var.* Pou Bia. ▲ C Laos
Bia, Pou *see* Bia, Phou
149 R5 **Biārjmand** Semnān, N Iran
104 I15 **Biarritz** Pyrénées-Atlantiques, SW France
110 H10 **Biasca** Ticino, S Switzerland
63 E17 **Biassini** Salto, N Uruguay
172 Oo5 **Bibai** Hokkaidō, NE Japan
85 B15 **Bibala** *Port.* Vila Arriaga. Namibe, SW Angola
106 I4 **Bibei** ~ NW Spain
Biberach *see* Biberach an der Riss
103 I23 **Biberach an der Riss** *var.* Biberach, *Ger.* Biberach an der Riß. Baden-Württemberg, S Germany
110 E7 **Biberist** Solothurn, NW Switzerland
79 O16 **Bibiani** SW Ghana
114 C13 **Bibinje** Zadar-Knin, W Croatia
Biblical Gebal *see* Jbaïl
118 I5 **Bibrka** *Pol.* Bóbrka, *Rus.* Bobrka. L'vivs'ka Oblast', NW Ukraine
119 N10 **Bic** ~ S Moldova
115 M18 **Bicaj** Kukës, NE Albania
118 K10 **Bicaz** *Hung.* Békás. Neamţ, NE Romania
191 Q16 **Bicheno** Tasmania, SE Australia
Bichiş *see* Békés
Bichiş-Ciaba *see* Békéscsaba
Bichitra *see* Phichit
143 P8 **Bichvint'a** *Rus.* Pitsunda. NW Georgia
13 T7 **Bic, Île du** *island* Québec, SE Canada
34 J10 **Bickleton** Washington, NW USA
38 L6 **Bicknell** Utah, W USA
175 Tt7 **Bicoli** Pulau Halmahera, E Indonesia
113 J22 **Bicske** Fejér, C Hungary
161 F14 **Bīd** *prev.* Bhir. Mahārāshtra, W India
79 U15 **Bida** Niger, C Nigeria
161 H15 **Bīdar** Karnātaka, C India
147 Y8 **Bidbid** NE Oman
21 P9 **Biddeford** Maine, NE USA
100 L9 **Biddinghuizen** Flevoland, C Netherlands
35 X11 **Biddle** Montana, NW USA
99 J23 **Bideford** SW England, UK
84 D13 **Bié** ◐ *province* C Angola
37 O2 **Bieber** California, W USA
112 O9 **Biebrza** ~ NE Poland
172 P5 **Biei** Hokkaidō, NE Japan
110 D8 **Biel** *Fr.* Bienne. Bern, W Switzerland
102 G13 **Bielefeld** Nordrhein-Westfalen, NW Germany
110 D8 **Bieler See** *Fr.* Lac de Bienne. ◎ W Switzerland
Bielitz/Bielitz-Biala *see* Bielsko-Biała
108 C7 **Biella** Piemonte, N Italy
Bielostok *see* Białystok
Bielskie, Województwo/Bielsko *see* Bielsko-Biała
113 J17 **Bielsko-Biała** *Ger.* Bielitz, Bielitz-Biala. Bielsko-Biała, S Poland
113 J17 **Bielsko-Biała** *off.* Województwo Bielskie, *var.* Bielsko. ◐ *province* S Poland
112 P10 **Bielsk Podlaski** Białystok, E Poland
Bien Bien *see* Điện Biên
Biên Đông *see* South China Sea
9 V17 **Bienfait** Saskatchewan, S Canada
178 Jj14 **Biên Hoa** Đông Nai, S Vietnam
Bienne *see* Biel
Bienne, Lac de *see* Bieler See
10 K8 **Bienville, Lac** ◎ Québec, C Canada
84 D13 **Bié, Planalto do** *var.* Bié Plateau. *plateau* C Angola
Bié Plateau *see* Bié, Planalto do
110 B9 **Bière** Vaud, W Switzerland
100 O4 **Bierum** Groningen, NE Netherlands
100 I13 **Biesbos** *var.* Biesbosch. *wetland* S Netherlands
Biesbosch *see* Biesbos
101 H21 **Biesme** Namur, S Belgium
103 H21 **Bietigheim-Bissingen** Baden-Württemberg, SW Germany
101 I23 **Bièvre** Namur, SE Belgium
81 D18 **Bifoun** Moyen-Ogooué, NW Gabon
172 Pp3 **Bifuka** Hokkaidō, NE Japan
142 C11 **Biga** Çanakkale, NW Turkey
142 C13 **Bigadiç** Balıkesir, W Turkey
28 J7 **Big Basin** *basin* Kansas, C USA
193 B20 **Big Bay** *bay* South Island, NZ
197 B12 **Big Bay** *bay* C Vanuatu
33 O5 **Big Bay de Noc** ◎ Michigan, N USA
33 N3 **Big Bay Point** *headland* Michigan, N USA
35 R10 **Big Belt Mountains** ▲▲ Montana, NW USA
31 N10 **Big Bend Dam** *dam* South Dakota, N USA
26 K12 **Big Bend National Park** *national park* Texas, S USA
24 K5 **Big Black River** ~ Mississippi, S USA
29 O3 **Big Blue River** ~ Kansas/Nebraska, C USA
26 M10 **Big Canyon** ~ Texas, SW USA
35 N12 **Big Creek** Idaho, NW USA
25 N8 **Big Creek Lake** ⊡ Alabama, S USA
25 X15 **Big Cypress Swamp** *wetland* Florida, SE USA
41 S9 **Big Delta** Alaska, USA
32 K6 **Big Eau Pleine Reservoir** ⊡ Wisconsin, N USA
21 P5 **Bigelow Mountain** ▲ Maine, NE USA
31 U3 **Big Falls** Minnesota, N USA
35 P8 **Bigfork** Montana, NW USA
31 U3 **Big Fork River** ~ Minnesota, N USA
9 S15 **Biggar** Saskatchewan, S Canada
188 L3 **Bigge Island** *island* Western Australia
37 O5 **Biggs** California, W USA
34 I11 **Biggs** Oregon, NW USA
12 K13 **Big Gull Lake** ◎ Ontario, SE Canada
39 P16 **Big Hachet Peak** ▲ New Mexico, SW USA
35 P11 **Big Hole River** ~ Montana, NW USA
35 V13 **Bighorn Basin** *basin* Wyoming, C USA
35 U11 **Bighorn Lake** ◎ Montana/Wyoming, N USA
35 W13 **Bighorn Mountains** ▲▲ Wyoming, C USA
38 J13 **Big Horn Peak** ▲ Arizona, SW USA
35 V11 **Bighorn River** ~ Montana/Wyoming, NW USA
16 O5 **Big Island** *island* Northwest Territories, NE Canada
41 O16 **Big Koniuji Island** *island* Shumagin Islands, Alaska, USA
27 N9 **Big Lake** Texas, SW USA
21 T5 **Big Lake** ◎ Maine, NE USA
32 I3 **Big Manitou Falls** *waterfall* Wisconsin, N USA
37 R2 **Big Mountain** ▲ Nevada, W USA
110 G10 **Bignasco** Ticino, S Switzerland
31 R16 **Big Nemaha River** ~ Nebraska, C USA
78 G12 **Bignona** SW Senegal
Bigorra *see* Tarbes
Bigosovo *see* Bihosava
37 S10 **Big Pine** California, W USA
37 Q14 **Big Pine Mountain** ▲ California, W USA
29 V6 **Big Piney Creek** ~ Missouri, C USA
67 M24 **Big Point** *headland* N Tristan da Cunha
33 P8 **Big Rapids** Michigan, N USA
32 K6 **Big Rib River** ~ Wisconsin, N USA
12 L14 **Big Rideau Lake** ◎ Ontario, SE Canada
9 T14 **Big River** Saskatchewan, C Canada
29 X5 **Big River** ~ Missouri, C USA
33 N7 **Big Sable Point** *headland* Michigan, N USA
35 S7 **Big Sandy** Montana, NW USA
27 W6 **Big Sandy** Texas, SW USA
39 V5 **Big Sandy Creek** ~ Colorado, C USA
31 Q16 **Big Sandy Creek** ~ Nebraska, C USA
31 V5 **Big Sandy Lake** ◎ Minnesota, N USA
38 J11 **Big Sandy River** ~ Arizona, SW USA
23 P5 **Big Sandy River** ~ S USA
25 V6 **Big Satilla Creek** ~ Georgia, SE USA
31 R12 **Big Sioux River** ~ Iowa/South Dakota, N USA
37 U7 **Big Smoky Valley** *valley* Nevada, W USA
27 N7 **Big Spring** Texas, SW USA
21 Q5 **Big Squaw Mountain** ▲ Maine, NE USA
23 O7 **Big Stone Gap** Virginia, NE USA
31 Q8 **Big Stone Lake** ◎ Minnesota/South Dakota, N USA
24 K4 **Big Sunflower River** ~ Mississippi, S USA
35 T11 **Big Timber** Montana, NW USA
10 D8 **Big Trout Lake** Ontario, C Canada
12 I12 **Big Trout Lake** ◎ Ontario, SE Canada
37 O2 **Big Valley Mountains** ▲▲ California, W USA
27 Q13 **Big Wells** Texas, SW USA
12 F11 **Bigwood** Ontario, S Canada
114 D11 **Bihać** NW Bosnia and Herzegovina
159 P14 **Bihār** *prev.* Behar. ◐ *state* N India
Bihār *see* Bihār Sharīf
83 F20 **Biharamulo** Kagera, NW Tanzania
159 R13 **Bihārīganj** Bihār, NE India
159 P14 **Bihār Sharīf** *var.* Bihār. Bihār, N India
118 F10 **Bihor** ◐ *county* NW Romania
172 Q6 **Bihoro** Hokkaidō, NE Japan
120 K11 **Bihosava** *Rus.* Bigosovo. Vitsyebskaya Voblasts', NW Belarus
Bijagos Archipelago *see* Bijagós, Arquipélago dos
78 G13 **Bijagós, Arquipélago dos** *var.* Bijagos Archipelago. *island group* W Guinea-Bissau
161 F16 **Bijāpur** Karnātaka, C India
148 K5 **Bījār** Kordestān, W Iran
114 J11 **Bijeljina** NE Bosnia and Herzegovina
115 K15 **Bijelo Polje** Montenegro, SW Yugoslavia
166 E11 **Bijiang** *prev.* Zhiziluo. Yunnan, SW China
166 I11 **Bijie** Guizhou, S China
158 J10 **Bijnor** Uttar Pradesh, N India
158 F11 **Bīkāner** Rājasthān, NW India
201 V3 **Bikar Atoll** *var.* Pikaar. *atoll* Ratak Chain, N Marshall Islands
202 H3 **Bikeman** *atoll* Tungaru, W Kiribati
202 I3 **Bikenebu** Tarawa, W Kiribati
127 Nn16 **Bikin** Khabarovskiy Kray, SE Russian Federation
127 Nn16 **Bikin** ~ SE Russian Federation
201 R3 **Bikini Atoll** *var.* Pikinni. *atoll* Ralik Chain, NW Marshall Islands
85 L17 **Bikita** Masvingo, E Zimbabwe
Bikkū Bitti *see* Bette, Pic
81 I19 **Bikoro** Equateur, W Zaire
147 Z9 **Bilād Banī Bū 'Alī** NE Oman
147 Z9 **Bilād Banī Bū Ḥasan** NE Oman
147 X9 **Bilād Manaḥ** *var.* Manaḥ. NE Oman
79 Q12 **Bilanga** C Burkina

◆ Country ● Country Capital ◇ Dependent Territory ○ Dependent Territory Capital ◐ Administrative Region ✕ International Airport ▲ Mountain ▲▲ Mountain Range ※ Volcano ~ River ◎ Lake ⊡ Reservoir

231

BILANG, TELUK – BOCHOLT

175 *Q7* **Bilang, Teluk** *bay* Sulawesi, N Indonesia
158 *F12* **Bilāra** Rājasthān, N India
158 *K10* **Bilāri** Uttar Pradesh, N India
144 *J5* **Bil'ās, Jabal al** ⛰ C Syria
158 *I8* **Bilāspur** Himāchal Pradesh, N India
160 *L11* **Bilāspur** Madhya Pradesh, C India
173 *G6* **Bila, Sungai** ≈ Sumatera, W Indonesia
143 *Y13* **Biläsuvar** ***Rus.*** Bilyasuvar; ***prev.*** Pushkino. SE Azerbaijan
119 *O5* **Bila Tserkva** ***Rus.*** Belaya Tserkov'. Kyyivs'ka Oblast', N Ukraine
178 *H11* **Bilauktaung Range** ***var.*** Thanintari Taungdan. ⛰ Myanmar/Thailand
107 *O2* **Bilbao** ***Basq.*** Bilbo. País Vasco, N Spain
Bilbo *see* Bilbao
94 *H2* **Bíldudalur** Vestfirdhir, NW Iceland
115 *I16* **Bileća** S Bosnia and Herzegovina
142 *E12* **Bilecik** Bilecik, NW Turkey
142 *F12* **Bilecik** ◈ *province* NW Turkey
118 *E11* **Biled** ***Ger.*** Billed, ***Hung.*** Billéd. Timiş, W Romania
113 *O15* **Biłgoraj** Zamość, SE Poland
119 *P11* **Bilhorod-Dnistrovs'kyy** ***Rus.*** Belgorod-Dnestrovskiy, ***Rom.*** Cetatea Albă; ***prev.*** Akkerman, ***anc.*** Tyras. Odes'ka Oblast', SW Ukraine
81 *M16* **Bili** Haut-Zaïre, N Zaire
127 *Oo5* **Bilibino** Chukotskiy Avtonomnyy Okrug, NE Russian Federation
178 *Gg8* **Bilin** Mon State, S Myanmar
179 *Qq12* **Biliran Island** *island* C Philippines
115 *N21* **Bilisht** ***var.*** Bilishti. Korçë, SE Albania
Bilishti *see* Bilisht
191 *N10* **Billabong Creek** ***var.*** Moulamein Creek. *seasonal river* New South Wales, SE Australia
190 *G4* **Billa Kalina** South Australia
207 *Q17* **Bill Baileys Bank** *undersea feature* N Atlantic Ocean
Billed/Billéd *see* Biled
159 *N14* **Billi** Uttar Pradesh, N India
99 *M15* **Billingham** N England, UK
35 *U11* **Billings** Montana, NW USA
97 *J16* **Billingsfors** Älvsborg, S Sweden
Bill of Cape Clear, The *see* Clear, Cape
30 *L9* **Billsburg** South Dakota, N USA
97 *F23* **Billund** Ribe, W Denmark
38 *L11* **Bill Williams Mountain** ▲ Arizona, SW USA
38 *I12* **Bill Williams River** ≈ Arizona, SW USA
79 *Y8* **Bilma** Agadez, NE Niger
79 *Y8* **Bilma, Grand Erg de** *desert* NE Niger
189 *Y9* **Biloela** Queensland, E Australia
114 *G8* **Bilo Gora** ⛰ N Croatia
119 *U13* **Bilohirs'k** ***Rus.*** Belogorsk; ***prev.*** Karasubazar. Respublika Krym, S Ukraine
118 *M3* **Bilokorovychi** ***Rus.*** Belokorovichi. Zhytomyrs'ka Oblast', N Ukraine
119 *X5* **Bilokurakine** Luhans'ka Oblast', E Ukraine
119 *T3* **Bilopillya** ***Rus.*** Belopol'ye. Sums'ka Oblast', NE Ukraine
119 *Y6* **Bilovods'k** ***Rus.*** Belovodsk. Luhans'ka Oblast', E Ukraine
24 *M9* **Biloxi** Mississippi, S USA
119 *R10* **Bilozerka** Khersons'ka Oblast', S Ukraine
119 *W7* **Bilozers'ke** Donets'ka Oblast', E Ukraine
100 *J11* **Bilthoven** Utrecht, C Netherlands
80 *K9* **Biltine** Biltine, E Chad
80 *J9* **Biltine** ***off.*** Préfecture de Biltine. ◈ *prefecture* E Chad
168 *D5* **Bilüü** Bayan-Ölgiy, W Mongolia
Bilwi *see* Puerto Cabezas
Bilyasuvar *see* Biläsuvar
119 *O11* **Bilyayivka** Odes'ka Oblast', SW Ukraine
101 *K18* **Bilzen** Limburg, NE Belgium
Bimbéréké *see* Bembèrèkè
191 *R10* **Bimberi Peak** ▲ New South Wales, SE Australia
79 *Q15* **Bimbila** E Ghana
81 *I15* **Bimbo** Ombella-Mpoko, SW Central African Republic
46 *F2* **Bimini Islands** *island group* W Bahamas
160 *I9* **Bīna** Madhya Pradesh, C India
149 *T4* **Bīnālūd, Kūh-e** ⛰ NE Iran
101 *F20* **Binche** Hainaut, S Belgium
Bindloe Island *see* Marchena, Isla
85 *L16* **Bindura** Mashonaland Central, NE Zimbabwe
107 *T5* **Binefar** Aragón, NE Spain
85 *J16* **Binga** Matabeleland North, W Zimbabwe
191 *T5* **Bingara** New South Wales, SE Australia
103 *F18* **Bingen am Rhein** Rheinland-Pfalz, SW Germany
28 *M11* **Binger** Oklahoma, C USA
Bingerau *see* Węgrów
Bin Ghalfān, Jazā'ir *see* Ḥalāniyāt, Juzur al
21 *Q6* **Bingham** Maine, NE USA
20 *H11* **Binghamton** New York, NE USA
Bin Ghanīmah, Jabal *see* Bin Ghunaymah, Jabal
77 *P11* **Bin Ghunaymah, Jabal** ***var.*** Jabal Bin Ghanīmah. ⛰ C Libya
145 *U3* **Bingird** NE Iraq
143 *P14* **Bingöl** Bingöl, E Turkey
143 *P14* **Bingöl** ◈ *province* E Turkey
167 *R6* **Binhai** ***var.*** Binhai Xian, Dongkan. Jiangsu, E China
Binhai Xian *see* Binhai
178 *Kk12* **Binh Đinh** ***var.*** An Nhon. Binh Đinh, C Vietnam
178 *Kk10* **Binh Sơn** ***var.*** Châu Ô. Quang Ngai, C Vietnam
Binimani *see* Bintimani
173 *Ff5* **Binjai** Sumatera, W Indonesia
191 *R6* **Binnaway** New South Wales, SE Australia
110 *E6* **Binningen** Basel-Land, NW Switzerland
175 *R13* **Binongko, Pulau** *island* Kepulauan Tukangbesi, C Indonesia
174 *Gg3* **Bintang, Banjaran** ⛰ Peninsular Malaysia
174 *I7* **Bintan, Pulau** *island* Kepulauan Riau, W Indonesia
78 *J14* **Bintimani** ***var.*** Binimani. ▲ NE Sierra Leone
Bint Jubayl *see* Bent Jbaïl
174 *M5* **Bintulu** Sarawak, East Malaysia
176 *Vv10* **Bintuni** ***prev.*** Steenkool. Irian Jaya, E Indonesia
176 *Vv10* **Bintuni, Teluk** *bay* Irian Jaya, E Indonesia
169 *W8* **Bin Xian** Heilongjiang, NE China
166 *K14* **Binyang** Guangxi Zhuangzu Zizhiqu, S China
167 *Q4* **Binzhou** Shandong, E China
65 *G14* **Bío Bío** ***off.*** Región del Bío Bío. ◈ *region* C Chile
65 *G14* **Bío Bío, Río** ≈ C Chile
81 *C16* **Bioco, Isla de** ***var.*** Bioko, ***Eng.*** Fernando Po, ***Sp.*** Fernando Póo; ***prev.*** Macías Nguema Biyogo. *island* NW Equatorial Guinea
114 *D13* **Biograd na Moru** ***It.*** Zaravecchia. Zadar-Knin, S Croatia
Bioko *see* Bioco, Isla de
115 *F14* **Biokovo** ⛰ S Croatia
Biorra *see* Birr
Bipontium *see* Zweibrücken
149 *W13* **Bīrag, Kūh-e** ⛰ SE Iran
77 *O10* **Birāk** ***var.*** Brak. C Libya
145 *S10* **Bi'r al Islām** C Iraq
160 *N11* **Biramitrapur** Orissa, E India
145 *T11* **Bi'r an Niṣf** S Iraq
80 *L12* **Birao** Vakaga, NE Central African Republic
164 *M6* **Biratar Bulak** *well* NW China
159 *R12* **Biratnagar** Eastern, SE Nepal
172 *Oo6* **Biratori** Hokkaidō, NE Japan
41 *S8* **Birch Creek** Alaska, USA
40 *M11* **Birch Creek** ≈ Alaska, USA
9 *T14* **Birch Hills** Saskatchewan, S Canada
190 *M10* **Birchip** Victoria, SE Australia
31 *X4* **Birch Lake** ◎ Minnesota, N USA
9 *Q11* **Birch Mountains** ⛰ Alberta, W Canada
9 *V15* **Birch River** Manitoba, S Canada
46 *H12* **Birchs Hill** *hill* W Jamaica
41 *R11* **Birchwood** Alaska, USA
196 *I5* **Bird Island** *island* S Northern Mariana Islands
143 *N16* **Birecik** Şanlıurfa, S Turkey
158 *M10* **Birendranagar** ***var.*** Surkhet. Mid Western, W Nepal
Bir es Saba *see* Be'ér Sheva'
76 *A12* **Bir-Gandouz** SW Western Sahara
159 *P12* **Birganj** Central, C Nepal
83 *B14* **Biri** ≈ W Sudan
Bi'r Ibn Hirmās *see* Al Bi'r
176 *Yy10* **Biri, Sungai** ≈ Irian Jaya, E Indonesia
149 *U8* **Bīrjand** Khorāsān, E Iran
145 *T11* **Birkat Ḥāmid** *well* S Iraq
97 *F18* **Birkeland** Aust-Agder, S Norway
103 *E19* **Birkenfeld** Rheinland-Pfalz, SW Germany
99 *K18* **Birkenhead** NW England, UK
111 *W7* **Birkfeld** Steiermark, SE Austria
190 *A2* **Birksgate Range** ⛰ South Australia
Bîrlad *see* Bârlad
99 *K20* **Birmingham** C England, UK
25 *P4* **Birmingham** Alabama, S USA
99 *M20* **Birmingham** ✈ C England, UK
Bir Moghrein *see* Bîr Mogreïn
78 *J4* **Bîr Mogreïn** ***var.*** Bir Moghrein; ***prev.*** Fort-Trinquet. Tiris Zemmour, N Mauritania
203 *S4* **Birnie Island** *atoll* Phoenix Islands, C Kiribati
Birni-Ngaouré *see* Birnin Gaouré
79 *S12* **Birnin Gaouré** ***var.*** Birni-Ngaouré. Dosso, SW Niger
79 *S12* **Birnin Kebbi** Kebbi, NW Nigeria
Birni-Nkonni *see* Birnin Konni
79 *T12* **Birnin Konni** ***var.*** Birni-Nkonni. Tahoua, SW Niger
79 *W13* **Birnin Kudu** Jigawa, N Nigeria
127 *N16* **Birobidzhan** Yevreyskaya Avtonomnaya Oblast', SE Russian Federation
99 *D18* **Birr** ***var.*** Parsonstown, ***Ir.*** Biorra. C Ireland
191 *P4* **Birrie River** ≈ New South Wales/Queensland, SE Australia
110 *D7* **Birse** ≈ NW Switzerland
Birsen *see* Biržai
110 *E6* **Birsfelden** Basel-Land, NW Switzerland
131 *U4* **Birsk** Respublika Bashkortostan, W Russian Federation
121 *F14* **Birštonas** Prienai, C Lithuania
165 *P14* **Biru** Xinjiang Uygur Zizhiqu, W China
Biruni *see* Beruniy
126 *Ii14* **Biryusa** ≈ C Russian Federation
126 *Ii14* **Biryusinsk** Irkutskaya Oblast', C Russian Federation
120 *G10* **Biržai** ***Ger.*** Birsen. Biržai, NE Lithuania
123 *Jj17* **Birżebbuġa** SE Malta
Bisanthe *see* Tekirdağ
175 *T9* **Bisa, Pulau** *island* Maluku, E Indonesia
39 *N17* **Bisbee** Arizona, SW USA
31 *O2* **Bisbee** North Dakota, N USA
Biscaia, Baía de *see* Biscay, Bay of
104 *I13* **Biscarrosse et de Parentis, Étang de** ◎ SW France
106 *M1* **Biscay, Bay of** ***Sp.*** Golfo de Vizcaya, ***Port.*** Baía de Biscaia. *bay* France/Spain
25 *Z16* **Biscayne Bay** *bay* Florida, SE USA
66 *M7* **Biscay Plain** *undersea feature* SE Bay of Biscay
109 *N17* **Bisceglie** Puglia, SE Italy
Bischoflack *see* Škofja Loka
Bischofsburg *see* Biskupiec
111 *Q7* **Bischofshofen** Salzburg, NW Austria
103 *P15* **Bischofswerda** Sachsen, E Germany
105 *V5* **Bischwiller** Bas-Rhin, NE France
23 *T10* **Biscoe** North Carolina, SE USA
204 *G5* **Biscoe Islands** *island group* Antarctica
12 *E9* **Biscotasi Lake** ◎ Ontario, S Canada
12 *E9* **Biscotasing** Ontario, S Canada
56 *J6* **Biscucuy** Portuguesa, NW Venezuela
116 *K11* **Biser** Khaskovska Oblast, SE Bulgaria
115 *D15* **Biševo** ***It.*** Busi. *island* SW Croatia
147 *N12* **Bīshah, Wādī** *dry watercourse* C Saudi Arabia
153 *U7* **Bishkek** ***var.*** Pishpek; ***prev.*** Frunze. ● (Kyrgyzstan) Chuyskaya Oblast', N Kyrgyzstan
153 *U7* **Bishkek** ✈ Chuyskaya Oblast', N Kyrgyzstan
159 *R16* **Bishnupur** West Bengal, NE India
85 *J25* **Bisho** Eastern Cape, S South Africa
37 *S9* **Bishop** California, W USA
27 *S15* **Bishop** Texas, SW USA
99 *L15* **Bishop Auckland** N England, UK
Bishop's Lynn *see* King's Lynn
99 *O21* **Bishop's Stortford** E England, UK
23 *S12* **Bishopville** South Carolina, SE USA
144 *M5* **Bishrī, Jabal** ⛰ E Syria
169 *U4* **Bishui** Heilongjiang, NE China
83 *G17* **Bisina, Lake** ***prev.*** Lake Salisbury. ◎ E Uganda
Biskara *see* Biskra
76 *L6* **Biskra** ***var.*** Beskra, Biskara. NE Algeria
112 *M8* **Biskupiec** ***Ger.*** Bischofsburg. Olsztyn, N Poland
179 *Rr15* **Bislig** Mindanao, S Philippines
29 *X6* **Bismarck** Missouri, C USA
30 *M5* **Bismarck** *state capital* North Dakota, N USA
194 *K9* **Bismarck Archipelago** *island group* NE PNG
133 *Z16* **Bismarck Plate** *tectonic feature* W Pacific Ocean
194 *I12* **Bismarck Range** ⛰ N PNG
194 *J10* **Bismarck Sea** *sea* W Pacific Ocean
143 *P15* **Bismil** Dıyarbakır, SE Turkey
45 *N6* **Bismuna, Laguna** *lagoon* NE Nicaragua
Bisnulok *see* Phitsanulok
175 *T6* **Bisoa, Tanjung** *headland* Pulau Halmahera, N Indonesia
30 *K7* **Bison** South Dakota, N USA
95 *H17* **Bispfors** Jämtland, C Sweden
78 *G13* **Bissau** ● (Guinea-Bissau) W Guinea-Bissau
78 *G13* **Bissau** ✈ W Guinea-Bissau
101 *M24* **Bissen** Luxembourg, C Luxembourg
78 *G12* **Bissorā** W Guinea-Bissau
9 *O10* **Bistcho Lake** ◎ Alberta, W Canada
24 *G5* **Bistineau, Lake** ⊠ Louisiana, S USA
Bistrica *see* Ilirska Bistrica
118 *I9* **Bistriţa** ***Ger.*** Bistritz, ***Hung.*** Beszterce; ***prev.*** Nösen. Bistriţa-Năsăud, N Romania
118 *K10* **Bistriţa** ***Ger.*** Bistritz. ≈ NE Romania
118 *I9* **Bistriţa-Năsăud** ◈ *county* N Romania
Bistritz *see* Bistriţa
Bistritz ober Pernstein *see* Bystřice nad Pernštejnem
158 *L11* **Biswān** Uttar Pradesh, N India
112 *M7* **Bisztynek** Olsztyn, N Poland
81 *E17* **Bitam** Woleu-Ntem, N Gabon
103 *D18* **Bitburg** Rheinland-Pfalz, SW Germany
105 *U4* **Bitche** Moselle, NE France
80 *I11* **Bitkine** Guéra, C Chad
143 *R15* **Bitlis** Bitlis, SE Turkey
143 *R14* **Bitlis** ◈ *province* E Turkey
Bitoeng *see* Bitung
115 *N20* **Bitola** ***Turk.*** Monastir; ***prev.*** Bitolj. S FYR Macedonia
Bitolj *see* Bitola
109 *O17* **Bitonto** ***anc.*** Butuntum. Puglia, SE Italy
79 *Q13* **Bitou** ***var.*** Bittou. SE Burkina
161 *C20* **Bitra Island** *island* Lakshadweep, India, N Indian Ocean
103 *M14* **Bitterfeld** Sachsen-Anhalt, E Germany
34 *O9* **Bitterroot Range** ⛰ Idaho/Montana, NW USA
35 *P10* **Bitterroot River** ≈ Montana, NW USA
109 *D18* **Bitti** Sardegna, Italy, C Mediterranean Sea
Bittou *see* Bitou
175 *S7* **Bitung** ***prev.*** Bitoeng. Sulawesi, C Indonesia
62 *I12* **Bituruna** Paraná, S Brazil
79 *Y13* **Biu** Borno, E Nigeria
Biumba *see* Byumba
171 *H14* **Biwa-ko** ◎ Honshū, SW Japan
176 *Y13* **Biwarlaut** Irian Jaya, E Indonesia
29 *P10* **Bixby** Oklahoma, C USA
126 *H15* **Biya** ≈ S Russian Federation
Biy-Khem *see* Bol'shoy Yenisey
126 *H15* **Biysk** Altayskiy Kray, S Russian Federation
170 *Ff14* **Bizen** Okayama, Honshū, SW Japan
Bizerta *see* Bizerte
123 *K11* **Bizerte** ***Ar.*** Banzart, ***Eng.*** Bizerta. N Tunisia
Bizkaia *see* Vizcaya
94 *G2* **Bjargtangar** *headland* W Iceland
Bjärnå *see* Perniö
97 *K22* **Bjärnum** Kristianstad, S Sweden
95 *I16* **Bjästa** Västernorrland, C Sweden
115 *I14* **Bjelašnica** ▲ SE Bosnia and Herzegovina
114 *C10* **Bjelolasica** ▲ NW Croatia
114 *F8* **Bjelovar** ***Hung.*** Belovár. Bjelovar-Bilogora, N Croatia
114 *F8* **Bjelovar-Bilogora** ***off.*** Bjelovarsko-Bilogorska Županija. ◈ *province* NE Croatia
Bjelovarsko-Bilogorska Županija *see* Bjelovar-Bilogora
94 *H10* **Bjerkvik** Nordland, C Norway
97 *G21* **Bjerringbro** Viborg, NW Denmark
Bjeshkët e Namuna *see* North Albanian Alps
97 *L14* **Björbo** Kopparberg, C Sweden
97 *I15* **Bjørkelangen** Akershus, S Norway
97 *O14* **Björklinge** Uppsala, C Sweden
95 *I14* **Björksele** Västerbotten, N Sweden
95 *I16* **Björna** Västernorrland, C Sweden
97 *C14* **Bjørnafjorden** *fjord* S Norway
97 *L16* **Björneborg** Värmland, C Sweden
Björneborg *see* Pori
97 *E14* **Bjornesfjorden** ◎ S Norway
94 *M9* **Bjørnevatn** Finnmark, N Norway
207 *T13* **Bjørnøya** ***Eng.*** Bear Island. *island* N Norway
95 *I15* **Bjurholm** Västerbotten, N Sweden
97 *J22* **Bjuv** Malmöhus, S Sweden
78 *M12* **Bla** Ségou, W Mali
189 *W8* **Blackall** Queensland, E Australia
31 *V2* **Black Bay** *lake bay* Minnesota, N USA
29 *N9* **Black Bear Creek** ≈ Oklahoma, C USA
99 *K17* **Blackburn** NW England, UK
47 *W10* **Blackburne** ✈ (Plymouth) E Montserrat
41 *T11* **Blackburn, Mount** ▲ Alaska, USA
37 *N5* **Black Butte Lake** ⊠ California, W USA
204 *J5* **Black Coast** *physical region* Antarctica
9 *Q16* **Black Diamond** Alberta, SW Canada
20 *K11* **Black Dome** ▲ New York, NE USA
115 *L18* **Black Drin** ***Alb.*** Lumi i Drinit të Zi, ***SCr.*** Crni Drim. ≈ Albania/FYR Macedonia
10 *D6* **Black Duck** ≈ Ontario, C Canada
31 *U4* **Blackduck** Minnesota, N USA
35 *R14* **Blackfoot** Idaho, NW USA
35 *P9* **Blackfoot River** ≈ Montana, NW USA
Black Forest *see* Schwarzwald
30 *J10* **Blackhawk** South Dakota, N USA
30 *I10* **Black Hills** ⛰ South Dakota/Wyoming, N USA
9 *T10* **Black Lake** ◎ Saskatchewan, C Canada
33 *Q5* **Black Lake** ◎ Michigan, N USA
20 *I7* **Black Lake** ◎ New York, NE USA
24 *G6* **Black Lake** ⊠ Louisiana, S USA
28 *F7* **Black Mesa** ▲ Oklahoma, C USA
23 *P10* **Black Mountain** North Carolina, SE USA
37 *P13* **Black Mountain** ▲ California, W USA
39 *Q2* **Black Mountain** ▲ Colorado, C USA
98 *K1* **Black Mountains** ⛰ SE Wales, UK
38 *H10* **Black Mountains** ⛰ Arizona, SW USA
35 *Q16* **Black Pine Peak** ▲ Idaho, NW USA
99 *K17* **Blackpool** NW England, UK
39 *Q14* **Black Range** ⛰ New Mexico, SW USA
46 *I12* **Black River** W Jamaica
12 *J14* **Black River** ≈ Ontario, SE Canada
133 *U12* **Black River** ***Chin.*** Babian Jiang, Lixian Jiang, ***Fr.*** Rivière Noire, ***Vtn.*** Sông Đa. ≈ China/Vietnam
46 *I12* **Black River** ≈ W Jamaica
41 *T7* **Black River** ≈ Alaska, USA
39 *N13* **Black River** ≈ Arizona, SW USA
29 *X7* **Black River** ≈ Arkansas/Missouri, C USA
24 *I7* **Black River** ≈ Louisiana, S USA
33 *S8* **Black River** ≈ Michigan, N USA
33 *Q5* **Black River** ≈ Michigan, N USA
20 *I8* **Black River** ≈ New York, NE USA
23 *T13* **Black River** ≈ South Carolina, SE USA
32 *J7* **Black River** ≈ Wisconsin, N USA
32 *J7* **Black River Falls** Wisconsin, N USA
37 *R3* **Black Rock Desert** *desert* Nevada, W USA
Black Sand Desert *see* Garagumy
23 *S7* **Blacksburg** Virginia, NE USA
142 *H10* **Black Sea** ***var.*** Euxine Sea, ***Bul.*** Cherno More, ***Rom.*** Marea Neagră, ***Rus.*** Chernoye More, ***Turk.*** Karadeniz, ***Ukr.*** Chorne More. *sea* Asia/Europe
119 *Q10* **Black Sea Lowland** ***Ukr.*** Prychornomors'ka Nyzovyna. *depression* SE Europe
35 *S17* **Blacks Fork** ≈ Wyoming, C USA
25 *V7* **Blackshear** Georgia, SE USA
25 *S6* **Blackshear, Lake** ⊠ Georgia, SE USA
99 *A16* **Blacksod Bay** ***Ir.*** Cuan an Fhóid Duibh. *inlet* W Ireland
23 *V7* **Blackstone** Virginia, NE USA
79 *O14* **Black Volta** ***var.*** Borongo, Mouhoun, Moun Hou, ***Fr.*** Volta Noire. ≈ W Africa
25 *O5* **Black Warrior River** ≈ Alabama, S USA
189 *X8* **Blackwater** Queensland, E Australia
99 *D20* **Blackwater** ***Ir.*** An Abhainn Mhór. ≈ S Ireland
29 *T4* **Blackwater River** ≈ Missouri, C USA
23 *W7* **Blackwater River** ≈ Virginia, NE USA
Blackwater State *see* Nebraska
29 *N8* **Blackwell** Oklahoma, C USA
27 *P7* **Blackwell** Texas, SW USA
101 *J15* **Bladel** Noord-Brabant, S Netherlands
Bladenmarkt *see* Bălăuşeri
116 *G11* **Blagoevgrad** ***prev.*** Gorna Dzhumaya. Sofiyska Oblast, W Bulgaria
126 *Gg14* **Blagoveshchenka** Altayskiy Kray, S Russian Federation
126 *M16* **Blagoveshchensk** Amurskaya Oblast', SE Russian Federation
131 *V4* **Blagoveshchensk** Respublika Bashkortostan, W Russian Federation
104 *I7* **Blain** Loire-Atlantique, NW France
31 *V8* **Blaine** Minnesota, N USA
34 *H6* **Blaine** Washington, NW USA
9 *T15* **Blaine Lake** Saskatchewan, S Canada
31 *S14* **Blair** Nebraska, C USA
98 *J10* **Blairgowrie** C Scotland, UK
20 *C15* **Blairsville** Pennsylvania, NE USA
118 *H11* **Blaj** ***Ger.*** Blasendorf, ***Hung.*** Balázsfalva. Alba, SW Romania
66 *F9* **Blake-Bahama Ridge** *undersea feature* W Atlantic Ocean
25 *S7* **Blakely** Georgia, SE USA
66 *E10* **Blake Plateau** ***var.*** Blake Terrace. *undersea feature* W Atlantic Ocean
32 *M1* **Blake Point** *headland* Michigan, N USA
Blake Terrace *see* Blake Plateau
63 *B24* **Blanca, Bahía** *bay* E Argentina
58 *C12* **Blanca, Cordillera** ⛰ W Peru
107 *T12* **Blanca, Costa** *physical region* SE Spain
39 *S7* **Blanca Peak** ▲ Colorado, C USA
26 *I9* **Blanca, Sierra** ▲ Texas, SW USA
123 *K11* **Blanc, Cap** *headland* N Tunisia
Blanc, Cap *see* Nouâdhibou, Râs
33 *R12* **Blanchard River** ≈ Ohio, N USA
190 *E8* **Blanche, Cape** *headland* South Australia
195 *U15* **Blanche Channel** *channel* NW Solomon Islands
190 *J4* **Blanche, Lake** ◎ South Australia
33 *R14* **Blanchester** Ohio, N USA
190 *J9* **Blanchetown** South Australia
47 *U13* **Blanchisseuse** Trinidad, Trinidad and Tobago
105 *T11* **Blanc, Mont** ***It.*** Monte Bianco. ▲ France/Italy
27 *R11* **Blanco** Texas, SW USA
44 *K14* **Blanco, Cabo** *headland* NW Costa Rica
34 *D14* **Blanco, Cape** *headland* Oregon, NW USA
64 *H10* **Blanco, Río** ≈ W Argentina
58 *F10* **Blanco, Río** ≈ NE Peru
13 *O9* **Blanc, Réservoir** ⊠ Québec, SE Canada
23 *R7* **Bland** Virginia, NE USA
94 *I2* **Blanda** ≈ N Iceland
39 *O7* **Blanding** Utah, W USA
107 *X5* **Blanes** Cataluña, NE Spain
105 *N3* **Blangy-sur-Bresle** Seine-Maritime, N France
113 *C18* **Blanice** ***Ger.*** Blanitz. ≈ SE Czech Republic
Blanitz *see* Blanice
101 *C16* **Blankenberge** West-Vlaanderen, NW Belgium
103 *D17* **Blankenheim** Nordrhein-Westfalen, W Germany
27 *R8* **Blanket** Texas, SW USA
57 *O3* **Blanquilla, Isla** ***var.*** La Blanquilla. *island* N Venezuela
Blanquilla, La *see* Blanquilla, Isla
63 *F18* **Blanquillo** Durazno, C Uruguay
113 *G18* **Blansko** ***Ger.*** Blanz. Jižní Morava, SE Czech Republic
85 *N15* **Blantyre** ***var.*** Blantyre-Limbe. Southern, S Malawi
85 *N15* **Blantyre** ✈ Southern, S Malawi
Blantyre-Limbe *see* Blantyre
Blanz *see* Blansko
100 *J10* **Blaricum** Noord-Holland, C Netherlands
Blasendorf *see* Blaj
Blatnitsa *see* Durankulak
115 *F15* **Blato** ***It.*** Blatta. Dubrovnik-Neretva, S Croatia
Blatta *see* Blato
110 *E10* **Blatten** Valais, SW Switzerland
103 *J20* **Blaufelden** Baden-Württemberg, SW Germany
97 *E23* **Blävands Huk** *headland* W Denmark
104 *G6* **Blavet** ≈ NW France
104 *J12* **Blaye** Gironde, SW France
191 *R8* **Blayney** New South Wales, SE Australia
67 *D25* **Bleaker Island** *island* SE Falkland Islands
111 *T10* **Bled** ***Ger.*** Veldes. NW Slovenia
101 *D20* **Bléharies** Hainaut, SW Belgium
111 *U9* **Bleiburg** ***Slvn.*** Pliberk. Kärnten, S Austria
103 *L17* **Bleiloch-Stausee** ⊠ C Germany
100 *H12* **Bleiswijk** Zuid-Holland, W Netherlands
97 *L22* **Blekinge** ◈ *county* S Sweden
12 *D17* **Blenheim** Ontario, S Canada
193 *K15* **Blenheim** Marlborough, South Island, NZ
101 *M15* **Blerick** Limburg, SE Netherlands
Blesae *see* Blois
27 *V13* **Blessing** Texas, SW USA
12 *I10* **Bleu, Lac** ◎ Québec, SE Canada
Blibba *see* Blitta
123 *I11* **Blida** ***var.*** El Boulaida, El Boulaïda. N Algeria
97 *P15* **Blidö** Stockholm, C Sweden
97 *K18* **Blidsberg** Älvsborg, S Sweden
193 *A21* **Bligh Sound** *sound* South Island, NZ
197 *H13* **Bligh Water** *strait* NW Fiji
12 *D11* **Blind River** Ontario, S Canada
33 *R11* **Blissfield** Michigan, N USA
174 *Ll16* **Blitar** Jawa, C Indonesia
79 *R15* **Blitta** ***prev.*** Blibba. C Togo
21 *O13* **Block Island** *island* Rhode Island, NE USA
21 *O13* **Block Island Sound** *sound* Rhode Island, NE USA
100 *H10* **Bloemendaal** Noord-Holland, W Netherlands
85 *H23* **Bloemfontein** ***var.*** Mangaung. ● (South Africa-judicial capital) Free State, C South Africa
85 *I22* **Bloemhof** North-West, NW South Africa
104 *M7* **Blois** ***anc.*** Blesae. Loir-et-Cher, C France
100 *L8* **Blokzijl** Overijssel, N Netherlands
97 *N20* **Blomstermåla** Kalmar, S Sweden
94 *I2* **Blönduós** Nordhurland Vestra, N Iceland
112 *L11* **Błonie** Warszawa, C Poland
99 *C14* **Bloody Foreland** ***Ir.*** Cnoc Fola. *headland* NW Ireland
33 *N15* **Bloomfield** Indiana, N USA
31 *X16* **Bloomfield** Iowa, C USA
29 *Y8* **Bloomfield** Missouri, C USA
39 *P9* **Bloomfield** New Mexico, SW USA
27 *U7* **Blooming Grove** Texas, SW USA
31 *W10* **Blooming Prairie** Minnesota, N USA
32 *L13* **Bloomington** Illinois, N USA
33 *O15* **Bloomington** Indiana, N USA
31 *V9* **Bloomington** Minnesota, N USA
27 *U13* **Bloomington** Texas, SW USA
20 *H14* **Bloomsburg** Pennsylvania, NE USA
189 *X7* **Bloomsbury** Queensland, NE Australia
174 *Ll14* **Blora** Jawa, C Indonesia
20 *G12* **Blossburg** Pennsylvania, NE USA
27 *V5* **Blossom** Texas, SW USA
127 *Oo3* **Blossom, Mys** *headland* Wrangel Island, NE Russian Federation
25 *R8* **Blountstown** Florida, SE USA
23 *P8* **Blountville** Tennessee, S USA
23 *Q9* **Blowing Rock** North Carolina, SE USA
110 *J8* **Bludenz** Vorarlberg, W Austria
38 *L6* **Blue Bell Knoll** ▲ Utah, W USA
25 *Y12* **Blue Cypress Lake** ◎ Florida, SE USA
31 *U11* **Blue Earth** Minnesota, N USA
23 *Q7* **Bluefield** Virginia, NE USA
23 *R7* **Bluefield** West Virginia, NE USA
45 *N10* **Bluefields** Región Autónoma Atlántico Sur, SE Nicaragua
45 *N10* **Bluefields, Bahía de** *bay* W Caribbean Sea
31 *Z14* **Blue Grass** Iowa, C USA
Bluegrass State *see* Kentucky
Blue Hen State *see* Delaware
21 *S7* **Blue Hill** Maine, NE USA
31 *P16* **Blue Hill** Nebraska, C USA
32 *J5* **Blue Hills** *hill range* Wisconsin, N USA
36 *L3* **Blue Lake** California, W USA
Blue Law State *see* Connecticut
39 *Q6* **Blue Mesa Reservoir** ⊠ Colorado, C USA
29 *S12* **Blue Mountain** ▲ Arkansas, C USA
21 *O6* **Blue Mountain** ▲ New Hampshire, NE USA
20 *K8* **Blue Mountain** ▲ New York, NE USA
20 *H15* **Blue Mountain** *ridge* Pennsylvania, NE USA
46 *H10* **Blue Mountain Peak** ▲ E Jamaica
191 *S8* **Blue Mountains** ⛰ New South Wales, SE Australia
34 *L11* **Blue Mountains** ⛰ Oregon/Washington, NW USA
82 *G12* **Blue Nile** ◈ *state* E Sudan
82 *H12* **Blue Nile** ***var.*** Abai, Bahr el Azraq, ***Amh.*** Ābay Wenz, ***Ar.*** An Nīl al Azraq. ≈ Ethiopia/Sudan
15 *Hh4* **Bluenose Lake** ◎ Northwest Territories, NW Canada
29 *O3* **Blue Rapids** Kansas, C USA
25 *S1* **Blue Ridge** Georgia, SE USA
19 *Q10* **Blue Ridge** ***var.*** Blue Ridge Mountains. ⛰ North Carolina/Virginia, E USA
25 *S1* **Blue Ridge Lake** ⊠ Georgia, SE USA
Blue Ridge Mountains *see* Blue Ridge
9 *N15* **Blue River** British Columbia, SW Canada
29 *O12* **Blue River** ≈ Oklahoma, C USA
29 *R4* **Blue Springs** Missouri, C USA
23 *R6* **Bluestone Lake** ⊠ West Virginia, NE USA
193 *C25* **Bluff** Southland, South Island, NZ
39 *O8* **Bluff** Utah, W USA
23 *P8* **Bluff City** Tennessee, S USA
67 *E24* **Bluff Cove** East Falkland, Falkland Islands
27 *S7* **Bluff Dale** Texas, SW USA
191 *N15* **Bluff Hill Point** *headland* Tasmania, SE Australia
33 *Q12* **Bluffton** Indiana, N USA
33 *R12* **Bluffton** Ohio, N USA
27 *T7* **Blum** Texas, SW USA
103 *G24* **Blumberg** Baden-Württemberg, SW Germany
62 *K13* **Blumenau** Santa Catarina, S Brazil
31 *N9* **Blunt** South Dakota, N USA
34 *H15* **Bly** Oregon, NW USA
41 *R13* **Blying Sound** *sound* Alaska, USA
99 *M14* **Blyth** N England, UK
37 *Y16* **Blythe** California, W USA
29 *Y9* **Blytheville** Arkansas, C USA
119 *V7* **Blyznyuky** Kharkivs'ka Oblast', E Ukraine
78 *I15* **Bo** S Sierra Leone
97 *G16* **Bø** Telemark, S Norway
179 *Pp11* **Boac** Marinduque, N Philippines
44 *K10* **Boaco** Boaco, S Nicaragua
44 *J10* **Boaco** ◈ *department* C Nicaragua
81 *I15* **Boali** Ombella-Mpoko, SW Central African Republic
Boalsert *see* Bolsward
194 *K13* **Boana** Morobe, C PNG
195 *Q10* **Boang Island** *island* Tanga Islands, NE PNG
33 *V12* **Boardman** Ohio, N USA
34 *J11* **Boardman** Oregon, NW USA
12 *F13* **Boat Lake** ◎ Ontario, S Canada
60 *F10* **Boa Vista** *state capital* Roraima, NW Brazil
78 *D9* **Boa Vista** *island* Ilhas de Barlavento, E Cape Verde
25 *Q2* **Boaz** Alabama, S USA
166 *L15* **Bobai** Guangxi Zhuangzu Zizhiqu, S China
180 *J1* **Bobaomby, Tanjona** ***Fr.*** Cap d'Ambre. *headland* N Madagascar
161 *M14* **Bobbili** Andhra Pradesh, E India
108 *D9* **Bobbio** Emilia-Romagna, C Italy
12 *I14* **Bobcaygeon** Ontario, SE Canada
Bober *see* Bóbr
105 *O5* **Bobigny** Seine-St-Denis, N France
79 *N13* **Bobo-Dioulasso** SW Burkina
112 *G8* **Bobolice** ***Ger.*** Bublitz. Koszalin, NW Poland
175 *T7* **Bobopayo** Pulau Halmahera, E Indonesia
153 *P13* **Bobotogh, Qatorkŭhi** ***Rus.*** Khrebet Babatag. ⛰ Tajikistan/Uzbekistan
116 *G10* **Bobovdol** Sofiyska Oblast, W Bulgaria
121 *M15* **Bobr** Minskaya Voblasts', NW Belarus
121 *M15* **Bobr** ≈ C Belarus
113 *E14* **Bóbr** ***Eng.*** Bobrawa, ***Ger.*** Bober. ≈ SW Poland
Bobrawa *see* Bóbr
Bobrik *see* Bobryk
Bobrinets *see* Bobrynets'
Bobrka/Bóbrka *see* Bibrka
130 *L8* **Bobrov** Voronezhskaya Oblast', W Russian Federation
119 *Q4* **Bobrovytsya** Chernihivs'ka Oblast', N Ukraine
Bobruysk *see* Babruysk
121 *J19* **Bobryk** ***Rus.*** Bobrik. ≈ SW Belarus
119 *Q8* **Bobrynets'** ***Rus.*** Bobrinets. Kirovohrads'ka Oblast', C Ukraine
12 *K14* **Bobs Lake** ◎ Ontario, SE Canada
56 *I6* **Bobures** Zulia, NW Venezuela
44 *H1* **Boca Bacalar Chico** *headland* N Belize
114 *G11* **Bočac** NW Bosnia and Herzegovina
43 *R14* **Boca del Río** Veracruz-Llave, S Mexico
57 *O4* **Boca de Pozo** Nueva Esparta, NE Venezuela
61 *C15* **Boca do Acre** Amazonas, N Brazil
57 *N12* **Boca Mavaca** Amazonas, S Venezuela
81 *G14* **Bocaranga** Ouham-Pendé, W Central African Republic
25 *Z15* **Boca Raton** Florida, SE USA
45 *P14* **Bocas del Toro** Bocas del Toro, NW Panama
45 *P15* **Bocas del Toro** ***off.*** Provincia de Bocas del Toro. ◈ *province* NW Panama
45 *P15* **Bocas del Toro, Archipiélago de** *island group* NW Panama
44 *L7* **Bocay** Jinotega, N Nicaragua
107 *N6* **Boceguillas** Castilla-León, N Spain
Bocheykovo *see* Bacheykava
113 *L17* **Bochnia** Tarnów, SE Poland
101 *K16* **Bocholt** Limburg, NE Belgium
103 *D14* **Bocholt** Nordrhein-Westfalen, W Germany

232
◆ Country ● Country Capital ◇ Dependent Territory ○ Dependent Territory Capital ◈ Administrative Region ✈ International Airport ▲ Mountain ⛰ Mountain Range Volcano ≈ River ◎ Lake ⊠ Reservoir

Bochum – Boston Mountains

103 E15 **Bochum** Nordrhein-Westfalen, W Germany
104 F2 **Bocognano** Corse, France, C Mediterranean Sea
56 I6 **Boconó** Trujillo, NW Venezuela
118 F12 **Bocşa** Ger. Bokschen, Hung. Boksánbánya. Caraş-Severin, SW Romania
81 H15 **Boda** Lobaye, SW Central African Republic
96 L12 **Boda** Kopparberg, C Sweden
97 O20 **Böda** Kalmar, S Sweden
97 L19 **Bodafors** Jönköping, S Sweden
126 Kk13 **Bodaybo** Irkutskaya Oblast', E Russian Federation
24 G5 **Bodcau, Bayou** var. Bodcau Creek. ≈ Louisiana, S USA
Bodcau Creek see Bodcau, Bayou
46 D8 **Bodden Town** var. Boddentown. Grand Cayman, SW Cayman Islands
103 K14 **Bode** ≈ C Germany
36 L7 **Bodega Head** headland California, W USA
Bodegas see Babahoyo
100 H11 **Bodegraven** Zuid-Holland, C Netherlands
80 H8 **Bodélé** depression W Chad
94 J13 **Boden** Norrbotten, N Sweden
Bodensee see Constance, Lake, C Europe
67 M15 **Bode Verde Fracture Zone** tectonic feature E Atlantic Ocean
161 H14 **Bodhan** Andhra Pradesh, C India
168 I9 **Bodĭ** Bayanhongor, C Mongolia
161 H22 **Bodināyakkanūr** Tamil Nādu, SE India
110 H10 **Bodio** Ticino, S Switzerland
99 I24 **Bodmin** SW England, UK
99 I24 **Bodmin Moor** moorland SW England, UK
94 G12 **Bodø** Nordland, C Norway
61 H20 **Bodoquena, Serra da** ▲ SW Brazil
142 B16 **Bodrum** Muğla, SW Turkey
Bodzafordulő see Întorsura Buzăului
101 L14 **Boekel** Noord-Brabant, SE Netherlands
Boeloekoemba see Bulukumba
105 Q11 **Boën** Loire, E France
81 K18 **Boende** Equateur, C Zaire
27 R11 **Boerne** Texas, SW USA
Boeroe see Buru, Pulau
Boetoeng see Buton, Pulau
24 I5 **Boeuf River** ≈ Arkansas/Louisiana, S USA
78 H14 **Boffa** Guinée-Maritime, W Guinea
Bó Finne, Inis see Inishbofin
Boga see Bogë
177 Ff9 **Bogale** Irrawaddy, SW Myanmar
24 L8 **Bogalusa** Louisiana, S USA
79 Q12 **Bogandé** C Burkina
81 I15 **Bogangolo** Ombella-Mpoko, C Central African Republic
191 Q7 **Bogan River** ≈ New South Wales, SE Australia
27 W5 **Bogata** Texas, SW USA
113 D14 **Bogatynia** Ger. Reichenau. Jelenia Góra, SW Poland
142 K13 **Boğazlıyan** Yozgat, C Turkey
81 J17 **Bogbonga** Equateur, NW Zaire
164 J14 **Bogcang Zangbo** ≈ W China
164 L5 **Bogda Feng** ▲ NW China
116 I9 **Bogdan** ▲ C Bulgaria
115 Q20 **Bogdanci** SE FYR Macedonia
164 M5 **Bogda Shan** var. Po-ko-to Shan. ▲ NW China
115 K17 **Bogë** var. Boga. Shkodër, N Albania
Bogendorf see Łuków
97 G23 **Bogense** Fyn, C Denmark
191 T3 **Boggabilla** New South Wales, SE Australia
191 S6 **Boggabri** New South Wales, SE Australia
194 I10 **Bogia** Madang, N PNG
99 N23 **Bognor Regis** SE England, UK
179 Qq13 **Bogo** Cebu, C Philippines
Bogodukhov see Bohodukhiv
189 V15 **Bogong, Mount** ▲ Victoria, SE Australia
174 J14 **Bogor** Dut. Buitenzorg. Jawa, C Indonesia
130 L5 **Bogoroditsk** Tul'skaya Oblast', W Russian Federation
131 O3 **Bogorodsk** Nizhegorodskaya Oblast', W Russian Federation
Bogorodskoje see Bogorodskoye
127 Nn14 **Bogorodskoye** Khabarovskiy Kray, SE Russian Federation
129 R15 **Bogorodskoye** var. Bogorodskoje. Kirovskaya Oblast', NW Russian Federation
56 F10 **Bogotá** prev. Santa Fe, Santa Fe de Bogotá. ● (Colombia) Cundinamarca, C Colombia
159 T14 **Bogra** Rajshahi, N Bangladesh
Bogschan see Boldu
126 Ii13 **Boguchany** Krasnoyarskiy Kray, C Russian Federation
130 M9 **Boguchar** Voronezhskaya Oblast', W Russian Federation
78 H10 **Bogué** Brakna, SW Mauritania
24 K8 **Bogue Chitto** ≈ Louisiana/Mississippi, S USA
Bogushëvsk see Bahushewsk
Boguslav see Bohuslav
46 K12 **Bog Walk** C Jamaica
167 Q3 **Bo Hai** var. Gulf of Chihli. gulf NE China
167 R3 **Bohai Haixia** strait NE China
167 Q3 **Bohai Wan** bay NE China
113 C17 **Bohemia** Cz. Čechy, Ger. Böhmen. cultural and historical region W Czech Republic
113 B18 **Bohemian Forest** Cz. Ceský Les, Šumava, Ger. Böhmerwald. ▲ C Europe
Bohemian-Moravian Highlands see Českomoravská Vrchovina
79 R16 **Bohicon** S Benin
111 S11 **Bohinjska Bistrica** Ger. Wocheiner Feistritz. NW Slovenia
Bohkká see Pokka
Böhmen see Bohemia
Böhmerwald see Bohemian Forest
Böhmisch-Krumau see Český Krumlov
Böhmisch-Leipa see Česká Lípa
Böhmisch-Mährische Höhe see Českomoravská Vrchovina
Böhmisch-Trübau see Česká Třebová
119 U5 **Bohodukhiv** Rus. Bogodukhov. Kharkivs'ka Oblast', E Ukraine
179 Qq14 **Bohol** island C Philippines
179 Qq15 **Bohol Sea** var. Mindanao Sea. sea S Philippines
118 I7 **Bohorodchany** Ivano-Frankivs'ka Oblast', W Ukraine
168 M9 **Böhöt** Dundgovĭ, C Mongolia
164 K6 **Bohu** var. Bagrax. Xinjiang Uygur Zizhiqu, NW China
113 I17 **Bohumín** Ger. Oderberg; prev. Neuoderberg, Nový Bohumín. Severní Morava, E Czech Republic
119 P6 **Bohuslav** Rus. Boguslav. Kyyivs'ka Oblast', N Ukraine
60 F11 **Boiaçu** Roraima, N Brazil
109 K16 **Boiano** Molise, C Italy
13 R8 **Boilleau** Québec, SE Canada
61 O17 **Boipeba, Ilha de** island SE Brazil
106 G3 **Boiro** Galicia, NW Spain
33 Q5 **Bois Blanc Island** island Michigan, N USA
31 R7 **Bois de Sioux River** ≈ Minnesota, N USA
35 N14 **Boise** var. Boise City. state capital Idaho, NW USA
28 G8 **Boise City** Oklahoma, C USA
35 N14 **Boise River, Middle Fork** ≈ Idaho, NW USA
Bois, Lac des see Woods, Lake of the
Bois-le-Duc see 's-Hertogenbosch
9 W17 **Boissevain** Manitoba, S Canada
13 T7 **Boisvert, Pointe au** headland Québec, SE Canada
102 K10 **Boizenburg** Mecklenburg-Vorpommern, N Germany
Bojador see Boujdour
115 K18 **Bojana** Alb. Bunë. ≈ Albania/Yugoslavia see also Bunë
149 S3 **Bojnūrd** var. Bujnurd. Khorāsān, N Iran
174 Ll15 **Bojonegoro** prev. Bodjonegoro. Jawa, C Indonesia
201 T1 **Bokaak Atoll** var. Bokak, Taongi. atoll Ratak Chain, NE Marshall Islands
Bokak see Bokaak Atoll
159 Q15 **Bokāro** Bihār, N India
81 I18 **Bokatola** Equateur, NW Zaire
78 H13 **Boké** Guinée-Maritime, W Guinea
Bokhara see Bukhoro
191 Q4 **Bokharra River** ≈ New South Wales/Queensland, SE Australia
Bo Kheo see Bâ Kêv
97 C16 **Boknafjorden** fjord S Norway
80 H11 **Bokoro** Chari-Baguirmi, W Chad
81 K19 **Bokota** Equateur, NW Zaire
178 Gg13 **Bokpyin** Tenasserim, S Myanmar
Boksánbánya/Bokschen see Bocşa
85 F21 **Bokspits** Kgalagadi, SW Botswana
81 K18 **Bokungu** Equateur, C Zaire
Bokurdak see Bakhardok
80 G10 **Bol** Lac, W Chad
175 Qq9 **Bolaang** Sulawesi, N Indonesia
78 G13 **Bolama** SW Guinea-Bissau
Bolangir see Balāngir
Bolanos see Bolanos, Mount, Guam
Bolaños see Bolaños de Calatrava, Spain
107 N11 **Bolaños de Calatrava** var. Bolaños. Castilla-La Mancha, C Spain
196 B17 **Bolanos, Mount** var. Bolanos. ▲ S Guam
42 L12 **Bolaños, Río** ≈ C Mexico
117 M14 **Bolayır** Çanakkale, NW Turkey
104 L3 **Bolbec** Seine-Maritime, N France
118 L13 **Boldu** var. Bogschan. Buzău, SE Romania
152 H8 **Boldumsaz** prev. Kalinin, Kalininsk, Porsy. Dashkhovuzskiy Velayat, N Turkmenistan
164 I4 **Bole** var. Bortala. Xinjiang Uygur Zizhiqu, NW China
79 O15 **Bole** NW Ghana
81 J19 **Boleko** Equateur, W Zaire
113 E14 **Bolesławiec** Ger. Bunzlau. Jelenia Góra, SW Poland
131 R4 **Bolgar** prev. Kuybyshev. Respublika Tatarstan, W Russian Federation
79 P14 **Bolgatanga** N Ghana
Bolgrad see Bolhrad
119 N12 **Bolhrad** Rus. Bolgrad. Odes'ka Oblast', SW Ukraine
169 Y8 **Boli** Heilongjiang, NE China
81 I19 **Bolia** Bandundu, W Zaire
95 J14 **Boliden** Västerbotten, N Sweden
176 Uu11 **Bolifar** Pulau Seram, E Indonesia
179 Oo9 **Bolinao** Luzon, N Philippines
29 T6 **Bolivar** Missouri, C USA
22 F10 **Bolivar** Tennessee, S USA
56 C12 **Bolívar** Cauca, SW Colombia
56 F7 **Bolívar** off. Departmento de Bolívar. ◐ province N Colombia
58 A13 **Bolívar** ◐ province C Ecuador
57 N9 **Bolívar** off. Estado Bolívar. ◐ state SE Venezuela
27 X12 **Bolivar Peninsula** headland Texas, SW USA
56 I6 **Bolívar, Pico** ▲ W Venezuela
59 K17 **Bolivia** off. Republic of Bolivia. ◆ republic W South America
114 O13 **Boljevac** Serbia, E Yugoslavia
Bolkenhain see Bolków
130 J5 **Bolkhov** Orlovskaya Oblast', W Russian Federation
113 F14 **Bolków** Ger. Bolkenhain. Jelenia Góra, SW Poland
190 K3 **Bollards Lagoon** South Australia
105 R14 **Bollene** Vaucluse, SE France
96 N12 **Bollnäs** Gävleborg, C Sweden
189 W10 **Bollon** Queensland, C Australia
199 Jj14 **Bollons Tablemount** undersea feature S Pacific Ocean
95 H17 **Bollstabruk** Västernorrland, C Sweden
Bolluilos de Par del Condado see Bollulos Par del Condado
106 J14 **Bollulos Par del Condado** var. Bolluilos de Par del Condado. Andalucía, S Spain
97 K21 **Bolmen** ◎ S Sweden
143 T10 **Bolnisi** S Georgia
81 H19 **Bolobo** Bandundu, W Zaire
127 N14 **Bolodek** Khabarovskiy Kray, SE Russian Federation
108 G10 **Bologna** Emilia-Romagna, N Italy
128 I15 **Bologoye** Tverskaya Oblast', W Russian Federation
81 J18 **Bolomba** Equateur, NW Zaire
43 X13 **Bolónchén de Rejón** var. Bolonchén de Rejón. Campeche, SE Mexico
126 H14 **Bolotnoye** Novosibirskaya Oblast', C Russian Federation
116 J13 **Boloústra, Ákra** headland NE Greece
178 Jj10 **Bolovens, Plateau des** plateau S Laos
108 H13 **Bolsena** Lazio, C Italy
109 G14 **Bolsena, Lago di** ◎ C Italy
130 B3 **Bol'shakovo** Ger. Kreuzingen; prev. Gross-Skaisgirren. Kaliningradskaya Oblast', W Russian Federation
126 J6 **Bol'shaya Balakhnya** ≈ N Russian Federation
Bol'shaya Berëstovitsa see Vyalikaya Byerastavitsa
131 S7 **Bol'shaya Chernigovka** Samarskaya Oblast', W Russian Federation
131 S7 **Bol'shaya Glushitsa** Samarskaya Oblast', W Russian Federation
150 H9 **Bol'shaya Khobda** Kaz. Ülkenqobda. ≈ Kazakhstan/Russian Federation
126 Jj8 **Bol'shaya Kuonamka** ≈ NE Russian Federation
130 M12 **Bol'shaya Martynovka** Rostovskaya Oblast', SW Russian Federation
126 I13 **Bol'shaya Murta** Krasnoyarskiy Kray, C Russian Federation
129 V4 **Bol'shaya Rogovaya** ≈ NW Russian Federation
129 U7 **Bol'shaya Synya** ≈ NW Russian Federation
151 V9 **Bol'shaya Vladimirovka** Semipalatinsk, E Kazakhstan
125 G13 **Bol'sherech'ye** Omskaya Oblast', C Russian Federation
127 Pp12 **Bol'sheretsk** Kamchatskaya Oblast', E Russian Federation
131 W3 **Bol'sheust'ikinskoye** Respublika Bashkortostan, W Russian Federation
Bol'shevik see Bal'shavik
126 Ii3 **Bol'shevik, Ostrov** island Severnaya Zemlya, N Russian Federation
129 U4 **Bol'shezemel'skaya Tundra** physical region NW Russian Federation
150 J13 **Bol'shiye Barsuki, Peski** desert SW Kazakhstan
125 Ff12 **Bol'shiye Uki** Omskaya Oblast', C Russian Federation
127 O6 **Bol'shoy Anyuy** ≈ NE Russian Federation
126 K6 **Bol'shoy Begichev, Ostrov** island NE Russian Federation
131 O4 **Bol'shoye Murashkino** Nizhegorodskaya Oblast', W Russian Federation
131 W4 **Bol'shoy Iremel'** ▲ W Russian Federation
131 R7 **Bol'shoy Irgiz** ≈ W Russian Federation
126 M5 **Bol'shoy Lyakhovskiy, Ostrov** island NE Russian Federation
126 Ll13 **Bol'shoy Nimnyr** Respublika Sakha (Yakutiya), NE Russian Federation
Bol'shoy Rozhan see Vyaliki Rozhan
150 E10 **Bol'shoy Uzen'** Kaz. Ülkenözen. ≈ Kazakhstan/Russian Federation
126 Ii15 **Bol'shoy Yenisey** var. Biy-Khem. ≈ S Russian Federation
42 K6 **Bolson de Mapimi** ▲ NW Mexico
100 K6 **Bolsward** Fris. Boalsert. Friesland, N Netherlands
107 T4 **Boltaña** Aragón, NE Spain
12 G15 **Bolton** Ontario, S Canada
99 K17 **Bolton** prev. Bolton-le-Moors. NW England, UK
23 V12 **Bolton** North Carolina, SE USA
Bolton-le-Moors see Bolton
142 G11 **Bolu** Bolu, NW Turkey
142 G11 **Bolu** ◐ province NW Turkey
195 N15 **Bolubolu** Goodenough Island, S PNG
94 H1 **Bolungarvík** Vestfirdhir, NW Iceland
165 O10 **Boluntay** Qinghai, W China
142 F14 **Bolvadin** Afyon, W Turkey
116 M10 **Bolyarovo** prev. Pashkeni. Burgaska Oblast, SE Bulgaria
108 G6 **Bolzano** Ger. Bozen; anc. Bauzanum. Trentino-Alto Adige, N Italy
81 F22 **Boma** Bas-Zaïre, W Zaire
191 R12 **Bombala** New South Wales, SE Australia
106 F10 **Bombarral** Leiria, C Portugal
160 D13 **Bombay** Guj. Mumbai. Mahārāshtra, W India
160 D13 **Bombay** ✕ Mahārāshtra, W India
176 Vv11 **Bomberai** ≈ Irian Jaya, E Indonesia
176 Vv11 **Bomberai, Jazirah** peninsula Irian Jaya, E Indonesia
176 Vv11 **Bomberai, Semenanjung** headland Irian Jaya, E Indonesia
83 F18 **Bombo** S Uganda
81 I17 **Bomboma** Equateur, NW Zaire
61 I14 **Bom Futuro** Pará, N Brazil
165 Q15 **Bomi** var. Bowo, Zhamo. Xizang Zizhiqu, W China
81 N17 **Bomili** Haut-Zaïre, NE Zaire
61 N17 **Bom Jesus da Lapa** Bahia, E Brazil
62 Q8 **Bom Jesus do Itabapoana** Rio de Janeiro, SE Brazil
97 C15 **Bømlafjorden** fjord S Norway
97 B15 **Bømlo** island S Norway
126 M14 **Bomnak** Amurskaya Oblast', SE Russian Federation
81 I17 **Bomongo** Equateur, NW Zaire
63 K14 **Bom Retiro** Santa Catarina, S Brazil
81 L15 **Bomu** var. Mbomou, Mbomu, M'Bomu. ≈ Central African Republic/Zaire
148 J3 **Bonāb** var. Benāb, Bunab. Āžarbāyjān-e Khāvarī, N Iran
47 Q16 **Bonaire** island E Netherlands Antilles
41 U11 **Bona, Mount** ▲ Alaska, USA
194 M16 **Bonando** ≈ SE Papau New Guinea
191 Q12 **Bonang** Victoria, SE Australia
44 L7 **Bonanza** Región Autónoma Atlántico Norte, NE Nicaragua
39 O4 **Bonanza** Utah, W USA
47 O9 **Bonao** C Dominican Republic
188 L3 **Bonaparte Archipelago** island group Western Australia
34 K6 **Bonaparte, Mount** ▲ Washington, NW USA
41 N11 **Bonasila Dome** ▲ Alaska, USA
47 T15 **Bonasse** Trinidad, Trinidad and Tobago
13 X7 **Bonaventure** Québec, SE Canada
13 X7 **Bonaventure** ≈ Québec, SE Canada
11 V11 **Bonavista** Newfoundland, Newfoundland and Labrador, SE Canada
11 U11 **Bonavista Bay** inlet NW Atlantic Ocean
123 Kk11 **Bon, Cap** headland N Tunisia
81 E19 **Bonda** Ogooué-Lolo, C Gabon
131 N6 **Bondari** Tambovskaya Oblast', W Russian Federation
108 G9 **Bondeno** Emilia-Romagna, C Italy
32 L4 **Bond Falls Flowage** ◎ Michigan, N USA
81 L16 **Bondo** Haut-Zaïre, N Zaire
175 P17 **Bondokodi** Pulau Sumba, S Indonesia
79 O15 **Bondoukou** E Ivory Coast
Boudoukui/Bondoukuy see Boundoukui
174 Mm15 **Bondowoso** Jawa, C Indonesia
35 S14 **Bondurant** Wyoming, C USA
Bone see Watampone, Indonesia
Bône see Annaba, Algeria
32 I5 **Bone Lake** ◎ Wisconsin, N USA
175 R12 **Bonelipu** Pulau Buton, C Indonesia
175 Q14 **Bonerate, Kepulauan** var. Macan. island group C Indonesia
175 Pp15 **Bonerate, Pulau** island Kepulauan Bonerate, C Indonesia
31 O12 **Bonesteel** South Dakota, N USA
64 I8 **Bonete, Cerro** ▲ N Argentina
175 Pp11 **Bone, Teluk** bay Sulawesi, C Indonesia
110 D6 **Bonfol** Jura, NW Switzerland
159 U12 **Bongaigaon** Assam, NE India
81 K17 **Bongandanga** Equateur, NW Zaire
80 L13 **Bongo, Massif des** var. Chaine des Mongos. ▲ NE Central African Republic
80 G12 **Bongor** Mayo-Kébbi, SW Chad
79 N16 **Bongouanou** E Ivory Coast
178 Kk11 **Bồng Sơn** var. Hoai Nhơn. Bình Định, C Vietnam
27 U5 **Bonham** Texas, SW USA
Bonhard see Bonyhád
105 U6 **Bonhomme, Col du** pass NE France
104 F3 **Bonifacio** Corse, France, C Mediterranean Sea
Bonifacio, Bocche de/Bonifacio, Bouches de see Bonifacio, Strait of
104 F3 **Bonifacio, Strait of** Fr. Bouches de Bonifacio, It. Bocche de Bonifacio. strait C Mediterranean Sea
25 Q8 **Bonifay** Florida, SE USA
Bonin Islands see Ogasawara-shotō
199 H6 **Bonin Trench** undersea feature NW Pacific Ocean
25 W15 **Bonita Springs** Florida, SE USA
44 I5 **Bonito, Pico** ▲ N Honduras
103 E17 **Bonn** Nordrhein-Westfalen, W Germany
94 H11 **Bonnåsjøen** Nordland, C Norway
12 J12 **Bonnechere** Ontario, SE Canada
12 J12 **Bonnechere** ≈ Ontario, SE Canada
35 N7 **Bonners Ferry** Idaho, NW USA
29 R4 **Bonner Springs** Kansas, C USA
104 L6 **Bonnétable** Sarthe, NW France
29 X6 **Bonne Terre** Missouri, C USA
8 J5 **Bonnet Plume** ≈ Yukon Territory, NW Canada
104 M6 **Bonneval** Eure-et-Loir, C France
105 T10 **Bonneville** Haute-Savoie, E France
38 J3 **Bonneville Salt Flats** salt flat Utah, W USA
79 U18 **Bonny** Rivers, S Nigeria
Bonny, Bight of see Biafra, Bight of
39 W4 **Bonny Reservoir** ⊡ Colorado, C USA
9 R14 **Bonnyville** Alberta, SW Canada
109 C18 **Bono** Sardegna, Italy, C Mediterranean Sea
176 Xx10 **Bonoi** Irian Jaya, E Indonesia
Bononia see Vidin, Bulgaria
Bononia see Boulogne-sur-Mer, France
109 B18 **Bonorva** Sardegna, Italy, C Mediterranean Sea
32 M15 **Bonpas Creek** ≈ Illinois, N USA
202 I3 **Bonriki** Tarawa, W Kiribati
191 T4 **Bonshaw** New South Wales, SE Australia
78 I16 **Bonthe** SW Sierra Leone
179 P8 **Bontoc** Luzon, N Philippines
194 M16 **Bonua** ≈ S PNG
27 Y9 **Bon Wier** Texas, SW USA
113 J25 **Bonyhád** Ger. Bonhard. Tolna, S Hungary
Bonzabaai see Bonza Bay
85 J25 **Bonza Bay** Afr. Bonzabaai. Eastern Cape, S South Africa
190 D7 **Bookabie** South Australia
190 H6 **Bookaloo** South Australia
39 P5 **Book Cliffs** cliff Colorado/Utah, W USA
175 Tt9 **Boo, Kepulauan** island group E Indonesia
27 P1 **Booker** Texas, SW USA
78 K15 **Boola** Guinée-Forestière, SE Guinea
191 O8 **Booligal** New South Wales, SE Australia
101 G17 **Boom** Antwerpen, N Belgium
45 N6 **Boom** var. Boon. Región Autónoma Atlántico Norte, NE Nicaragua
191 S3 **Boomi** New South Wales, SE Australia
Boon see Boom
31 V13 **Boone** Iowa, C USA
23 Q8 **Boone** North Carolina, SE USA
29 S11 **Booneville** Arkansas, C USA
23 N6 **Booneville** Kentucky, S USA
25 N2 **Booneville** Mississippi, S USA
23 V3 **Boonsboro** Maryland, NE USA
168 H9 **Böön Tsagaan Nuur** ◎ S Mongolia
36 L6 **Boonville** California, W USA
33 N16 **Boonville** Indiana, N USA
29 U4 **Boonville** Missouri, C USA
20 I9 **Boonville** New York, NE USA
82 M12 **Boorama** Woqooyi Galbeed, NW Somalia
191 O6 **Booroondarra, Mount** hill New South Wales, SE Australia
191 N9 **Booroorban** New South Wales, SE Australia
191 R9 **Boorowa** New South Wales, SE Australia
101 H17 **Boortmeerbeek** Vlaams Brabant, C Belgium
82 P11 **Boosaaso** var. Bandar Kassim, Bender Qaasim, Bosaso, It. Bender Cassim. Bari, N Somalia
21 Q8 **Boothbay Harbor** Maine, NE USA
Boothia Felix see Boothia Peninsula
15 Kk2 **Boothia, Gulf of** gulf Northwest Territories, NE Canada
15 K2 **Boothia Peninsula** prev. Boothia Felix. peninsula Northwest Territories, NE Canada
81 E18 **Booué** Ogooué-Ivindo, NE Gabon
103 J21 **Bopfingen** Baden-Württemberg, S Germany
103 F18 **Boppard** Rheinland-Pfalz, W Germany
64 M4 **Boquerón** off. Departamento de Boquerón. ◐ department W Paraguay
45 P15 **Boquete** var. Bajo Boquete. Chiriquí, W Panama
42 J6 **Boquilla, Presa de la** ⊡ N Mexico
42 L5 **Boquillas** var. Boquillas del Carmen. Coahuila de Zaragoza, NE Mexico
Boquillas del Carmen see Boquillas
126 I11 **Bor** Krasnoyarskiy Kray, C Russian Federation
83 F15 **Bor** Jonglei, S Sudan
97 L20 **Bor** Jönköping, S Sweden
142 J15 **Bor** Niğde, S Turkey
114 P12 **Bor** Serbia, E Yugoslavia
203 S10 **Bora-Bora** island Îles Sous le Vent, W French Polynesia
178 Ii10 **Borabu** Maha Sarakham, E Thailand
35 P13 **Borah Peak** ▲ Idaho, NW USA
Boralday see Burunday
97 J19 **Borås** Älvsborg, S Sweden
149 N11 **Borāzjān** var. Borazjān. Būshehr, S Iran
Borazjan see Borāzjān
60 G13 **Borba** Amazonas, N Brazil
106 H11 **Borba** Évora, S Portugal
Borbetomagus see Worms
57 O7 **Borbón** Bolívar, E Venezuela
61 Q15 **Borborema, Planalto da** plateau NE Brazil
118 M14 **Borcea, Braţul** ≈ S Romania
Borchalo see Marneuli
205 R15 **Borchgrevink Coast** physical region Antarctica
143 Q11 **Borçka** Artvin, NE Turkey
100 N11 **Borculo** Gelderland, E Netherlands
190 G10 **Borda, Cape** headland South Australia
104 K13 **Bordeaux** anc. Burdigala. Gironde, SW France
9 T15 **Borden** Saskatchewan, S Canada
12 D8 **Borden Lake** ◎ Ontario, S Canada
15 L1 **Borden Peninsula** peninsula Baffin Island, Northwest Territories, NE Canada
190 K11 **Bordertown** South Australia
94 H2 **Bordheyri** Vestfirdhir, NW Iceland
108 B11 **Bordighera** Liguria, NW Italy
76 K5 **Bordj-Bou-Arreridj** var. Bordj Bou Arreridj, Bordj Bou Arréridj. N Algeria
123 I10 **Bordj El Bahri, Cap de** headland N Algeria
76 L10 **Bordj Omar Driss** E Algeria
149 N13 **Bord Khūn** Hormozgān, S Iran
153 V7 **Bordunskiy** Chuyskaya Oblast', N Kyrgyzstan
97 M17 **Borensberg** Östergötland, S Sweden
Borgå see Porvoo
94 L2 **Borgarfjördhur** Austurland, NE Iceland
94 H3 **Borgarnes** Vesturland, W Iceland
95 G14 **Børgefjellet** ▲ C Norway
100 O7 **Borger** Drenthe, NE Netherlands
27 N2 **Borger** Texas, SW USA
97 N20 **Borgholm** Kalmar, S Sweden
109 N22 **Borgia** Calabria, SW Italy
101 J18 **Borgloon** Limburg, NE Belgium
205 P2 **Borg Massif** ▲ Antarctica
24 L9 **Borgne, Lake** ◎ Louisiana, S USA
108 C7 **Borgomanero** Piemonte, NE Italy
108 G10 **Borgo Panigale** ✕ (Bologna) Emilia-Romagna, N Italy
109 J15 **Borgorose** Lazio, C Italy
108 A9 **Borgo San Dalmazzo** Piemonte, N Italy
108 G11 **Borgo San Lorenzo** Toscana, C Italy
108 C7 **Borgosesia** Piemonte, NE Italy
108 E9 **Borgo Val di Taro** Emilia-Romagna, C Italy
108 G6 **Borgo Valsugana** Trentino-Alto Adige, N Italy
169 O11 **Borhoyn Tal** Dornogovĭ, SE Mongolia
178 Ii8 **Borikhan** var. Borikhane. Bolikhamxai, C Laos
Borikhane see Borikhan
Borislav see Boryslav
131 N8 **Borisoglebsk** Voronezhskaya Oblast', W Russian Federation
Borisov see Barysaw
Borisovgrad see Pŭrvomay
Borispol' see Boryspil'
180 I3 **Boriziny** Mahajanga, NW Madagascar
107 Q5 **Borja** Aragón, NE Spain
Borjas Blancas see Les Borges Blanques
143 S10 **Borjomi** Rus. Borzhomi. C Georgia
120 L12 **Borkavichy** Rus. Borkovichi. Vitsyebskaya Voblasts', N Belarus
103 H16 **Borken** Hessen, C Germany
103 E14 **Borken** Nordrhein-Westfalen, W Germany
94 H10 **Borkenes** Troms, N Norway
80 H7 **Borkou-Ennedi-Tibesti** off. Préfecture du Borkou-Ennedi-Tibesti. ◐ prefecture N Chad
Borkovichi see Borkavichy
102 E9 **Borkum** island NW Germany
83 K17 **Bor, Lagh** var. Lak Bor. dry watercourse NE Kenya
Bor, Lak see Bor, Lagh
97 M14 **Borlänge** Kopparberg, C Sweden
108 C9 **Bormida** ≈ NW Italy
108 F6 **Bormio** Lombardia, N Italy
103 M16 **Borna** Sachsen, E Germany
100 O10 **Borne** Overijssel, E Netherlands
101 F17 **Bornem** Antwerpen, N Belgium
174 M6 **Borneo** island Brunei/Indonesia/Malaysia
103 E16 **Bornheim** Nordrhein-Westfalen, W Germany
97 L24 **Bornholm** ◐ county E Denmark
97 L24 **Bornholm** island E Denmark
79 Y13 **Borno** ◐ state NE Nigeria
106 K15 **Bornos** Andalucía, S Spain
168 L7 **Bornuur** Töv, C Mongolia
126 I14 **Borodino** Krasnoyarskiy Kray, S Russian Federation
119 O4 **Borodyanka** Kyyivs'ka Oblast', N Ukraine
126 M10 **Borogontsy** Respublika Sakha (Yakutiya), NE Russian Federation
164 I5 **Borohoro Shan** ▲ NW China
79 O13 **Boromo** SW Burkina
37 T13 **Boron** California, W USA
179 R12 **Borongan** Samar, C Philippines
Borongo see Black Volta
Boron'ki see Baron'ki
Borosjenő see Ineu
Borossebes see Sebiş
78 L15 **Borotou** NW Ivory Coast
119 W6 **Borova** Kharkivs'ka Oblast', E Ukraine
116 H8 **Borovan** Oblast Montana, NW Bulgaria
128 I14 **Borovichi** Novgorodskaya Oblast', W Russian Federation
Borovlje see Ferlach
114 J9 **Borovo** Vukovar-Srijem, NE Croatia
151 Q7 **Borovoye** Kaz. Būrabay. Kokshetau, N Kazakhstan
130 K4 **Borovsk** Kaluzhskaya Oblast', W Russian Federation
125 F12 **Borovskiy** Tyumenskaya Oblast', C Russian Federation
151 N7 **Borovskoy** Kustanay, N Kazakhstan
Borovukha see Baravukha
97 L23 **Borrby** Kristianstad, S Sweden
189 R3 **Borroloola** Northern Territory, N Australia
118 F9 **Bors** Bihor, NW Romania
118 I9 **Borşa** Hung. Borsa. Maramureş, N Romania
118 J10 **Borsec** Ger. Bad Borseck, Hung. Borszék. Harghita, C Romania
94 K8 **Børselv** Finnmark, N Norway
115 L23 **Borsh** var. Borshi. Vlorë, S Albania
Borshchev see Borshchiv
118 K7 **Borshchiv** Pol. Borszczów, Rus. Borshchev. Ternopil's'ka Oblast', W Ukraine
Borshi see Borsh
113 L20 **Borsod-Abaúj-Zemplén** off. Borsod-Abaúj-Zemplén Megye. ◐ county NE Hungary
101 E15 **Borssele** Zeeland, SW Netherlands
Borszczów see Borshchiv
Borszék see Borsec
Bortala see Bole
105 O12 **Bort-les-Orgues** Corrèze, C France
Bor u České Lípy see Nový Bor
168 E8 **Bor-Udzüür** Hovd, W Mongolia
149 N9 **Borūjen** Chahār Maḩall va Bakhtiārī, C Iran
148 L7 **Borūjerd** var. Burujird. Lorestān, W Iran
118 H6 **Boryslav** Pol. Borysław, Rus. Borislav. L'vivs'ka Oblast', NW Ukraine
Borysław see Boryslav
119 P4 **Boryspil'** Rus. Borispol'. Kyyivs'ka Oblast', N Ukraine
119 P4 **Boryspil'** Rus. Borispol'. ✕ (Kyyiv) Kyyivs'ka Oblast', N Ukraine
Borzhomi see Borjomi
119 R3 **Borzna** Chernihivs'ka Oblast', NE Ukraine
126 L16 **Borzya** Chitinskaya Oblast', S Russian Federation
109 B18 **Bosa** Sardegna, Italy, C Mediterranean Sea
114 F10 **Bosanska Dubica** NW Bosnia and Herzegovina
114 G10 **Bosanska Gradiška** N Bosnia and Herzegovina
114 F10 **Bosanska Kostajnica** NW Bosnia and Herzegovina
114 E11 **Bosanska Krupa** NW Bosnia and Herzegovina
114 H10 **Bosanski Brod** N Bosnia and Herzegovina
114 E10 **Bosanski Novi** NW Bosnia and Herzegovina
114 E11 **Bosanski Petrovac** NW Bosnia and Herzegovina
114 I10 **Bosanski Šamac** N Bosnia and Herzegovina
114 E12 **Bosansko Grahovo** W Bosnia and Herzegovina
Bosaso see Boosaaso
194 G13 **Bosavi, Mount** ▲ W PNG
166 J14 **Bose** Guangxi Zhuangzu Zizhiqu, S China
167 Q5 **Boshan** Shandong, E China
115 P16 **Bosilegrad** prev. Bosiljgrad. Serbia, SE Yugoslavia
Bosiljgrad see Bosilegrad
Bösing see Pezinok
100 H12 **Boskoop** Zuid-Holland, C Netherlands
113 G18 **Boskovice** Ger. Boskowitz. Jižní Morava, SE Czech Republic
Boskowitz see Boskovice
114 I10 **Bosna** ≈ N Bosnia and Herzegovina
176 X9 **Bosnabraidi** Irian Jaya, E Indonesia
114 H12 **Bosnia and Herzegovina** off. Republic of Bosnia and Herzegovina. ◆ republic SE Europe
81 J16 **Bosobolo** Equateur, NW Zaire
171 K17 **Bōsō-hantō** peninsula Honshū, S Japan
Bosora see Buşrá ash Shām
Bosphorus/Bosporus see İstanbul Boğazı
Bosporus Cimmerius see Kerch Strait
Bosporus Thracius see İstanbul Boğazı
Bosra see Buşrá ash Shām
81 H14 **Bossangoa** Ouham, C Central African Republic
Bossé Bangou see Bossey Bangou
81 I15 **Bossembélé** Ombella-Mpoko, C Central African Republic
81 H15 **Bossentélé** Ouham-Pendé, W Central African Republic
79 R12 **Bossey Bangou** var. Bossé Bangou. Tillabéri, SW Niger
24 G5 **Bossier City** Louisiana, S USA
85 D20 **Bossiesvlei** Hardap, S Namibia
79 Y11 **Bosso** Diffa, SE Niger
63 F15 **Bossoroca** Rio Grande do Sul, S Brazil
164 J10 **Bostan** Xinjiang Uygur Zizhiqu, W China
148 K3 **Bostānābād** Āžarbāyjān-e Khāvarī, N Iran
164 K6 **Bosten Hu** var. Bagrax Hu. ◎ NW China
99 O18 **Boston** prev. St.Botolph's Town. E England, UK
21 O11 **Boston** state capital Massachusetts, NE USA
8 M17 **Boston Bar** British Columbia, SW Canada
29 T10 **Boston Mountains** ▲ Arkansas, C USA

◆ Country ● Country Capital ◇ Dependent Territory ○ Dependent Territory Capital ◐ Administrative Region ✕ International Airport ▲ Mountain ▲ Mountain Range ▲ Volcano ≈ River ◎ Lake ⊡ Reservoir

BOSTONNAIS – BROOKVILLE

13 P8 **Bostonnais** Québec, SE Canada
Bostyn' *see* Bastyn'
114 J10 **Bosut** E Croatia
160 C11 **Botād** Gujarāt, W India
191 T9 **Botany Bay** *inlet* New South Wales, SE Australia
85 G18 **Boteti** *var.* Botletle. N Botswana
116 J9 **Botev** ▲ C Bulgaria
116 H9 **Botevgrad** *prev.* Orkhaniye. Sofiyska Oblast, W Bulgaria
95 J16 **Bothnia, Gulf of** ***Fin.*** Pohjanlahti, ***Swe.*** Bottniska Viken. *gulf* N Baltic Sea
191 P17 **Bothwell** Tasmania, SE Australia
106 H5 **Boticas** Vila Real, N Portugal
57 W10 **Boti-Pasi** Sipaliwini, C Suriname
Botletle *see* Boteti
131 P16 **Botlikh** Chechenskaya Respublika, SW Russian Federation
119 N10 **Botna** E Moldova
118 I9 **Botoşani** ***Hung.*** Botosány. Botoşani, NE Romania
118 K8 **Botoşani** ◈ *county* NE Romania
Botosány *see* Botoşani
167 P4 **Botou** ***prev.*** Bozhen. Hebei, E China
101 M20 **Botrange** ▲ E Belgium
109 O21 **Botricello** Calabria, SW Italy
85 I23 **Botshabelo** Free State, C South Africa
95 J15 **Botsmark** Västerbotten, N Sweden
85 G19 **Botswana** ***off.*** Republic of Botswana. ◆ *republic* S Africa
31 N2 **Bottineau** North Dakota, N USA
Bottniska Viken *see* Bothnia, Gulf of
62 L9 **Botucatu** São Paulo, S Brazil
78 M16 **Bouaflé** C Ivory Coast
79 N16 **Bouaké** ***var.*** Bwake. C Ivory Coast
81 G14 **Bouar** Nana-Mambéré, W Central African Republic
76 H7 **Bouarfa** NE Morocco
113 B19 **Boubín** ▲ SW Czech Republic
81 I14 **Bouca** Ouham, W Central African Republic
13 T5 **Boucher** Québec, SE Canada
105 R15 **Bouches-du-Rhône** ◈ *department* SE France
76 C9 **Bou Craa** ***var.*** Bu Craa. NW Western Sahara
79 O9 **Boû Djébéha** *oasis* C Mali
110 C8 **Boudry** Neuchâtel, W Switzerland
188 L2 **Bougainville, Cape** *headland* Western Australia
67 E24 **Bougainville, Cape** *headland* East Falkland, Falkland Islands
197 B12 **Bougainville, Détroit de** ***Eng.*** Bougainville Strait. *strait* C Vanuatu
195 S13 **Bougainville Island** *island* NE PNG
195 T13 **Bougainville Strait** *strait* N Solomon Islands
Bougainville Strait *see* Bougainville, Détroit de
176 U8 **Bouganville, Selat** *strait* Irian Jaya, E Indonesia
123 J11 **Bougaroun, Cap** *headland* NE Algeria
79 R8 **Boughessa** Kidal, NE Mali
Bougie *see* Béjaïa
78 L13 **Bougouni** Sikasso, SW Mali
101 J24 **Bouillon** Luxembourg, SE Belgium
76 K5 **Bouira** ***var.*** Bouïra. N Algeria
76 D8 **Bou-Izakarn** SW Morocco
76 B9 **Boujdour** ***var.*** Bojador. W Western Sahara
76 G5 **Boukhalef** ✕ (Tanger) N Morocco
Boukombé *see* Boukoumbé
79 R14 **Boukoumbé** ***var.*** Boukombé. C Benin
78 G6 **Boû Lanouâr** Dakhlet Nouâdhibou, W Mauritania
39 T4 **Boulder** Colorado, C USA
35 R10 **Boulder** Montana, NW USA
37 X12 **Boulder City** Nevada, W USA
189 T7 **Boulia** Queensland, C Australia
13 N10 **Boullé** Québec, SE Canada
104 J9 **Boulogne** NW France
Boulogne *see* Boulogne-sur-Mer
104 L16 **Boulogne-sur-Gesse** Haute-Garonne, S France
105 N1 **Boulogne-sur-Mer** ***var.*** Boulogne; ***anc.*** Bononia, Gesoriacum, Gessoriacum. Pas-de-Calais, N France
197 I7 **Bouloupari** Province Sud, S New Caledonia
79 Q12 **Boulsa** C Burkina
79 W11 **Boultoum** Zinder, C Niger
197 K13 **Bouma** Taveuni, N Fiji
81 G16 **Boumba** SE Cameroon
78 J9 **Boûmdeïd** ***var.*** Boumdeït. Assaba, S Mauritania
Boumdeït *see* Boûmdeïd
117 C17 **Boumistós** ▲ W Greece
79 O15 **Bouna** NE Ivory Coast
21 P4 **Boundary Bald Mountain** ▲ Maine, NE USA
37 S8 **Boundary Peak** ▲ Nevada, W USA
78 M14 **Boundiali** N Ivory Coast
81 G19 **Boundji** Cuvette, C Congo
79 O13 **Boundoukui** ***var.*** Bondoukui, Bondoukuy. W Burkina
38 L2 **Bountiful** Utah, W USA
Bounty Basin *see* Bounty Trough
203 Q16 **Bounty Bay** *bay* Pitcairn Island, C Pacific Ocean
199 Jj14 **Bounty Islands** *island group* S NZ
183 Q13 **Bounty Trough** ***var.*** Bounty Basin. *undersea feature* S Pacific Ocean
197 I6 **Bourail** Province Sud, C New Caledonia
29 V5 **Bourbeuse River** Missouri, C USA
105 Q9 **Bourbon-Lancy** Saône-et-Loire, C France
33 N11 **Bourbonnais** Illinois, N USA
105 O10 **Bourbonnais** *cultural region* C France
105 S7 **Bourbonne-les-Bains** Haute-Marne, N France
Bourbon Vendée *see* la Roche-sur-Yon
76 M8 **Bourdj Messaouda** E Algeria
79 Q10 **Bourem** Gao, C Mali
Bourg *see* Bourg-en-Bresse
105 N11 **Bourganeuf** Creuse, C France
Bourgas *see* Burgas
Bourge-en-Bresse *see* Bourg-en-Bresse
105 S10 **Bourg-en-Bresse** ***var.*** Bourg, Bourge-en-Bresse. Ain, E France
105 O8 **Bourges** ***anc.*** Avaricum. Cher, C France
105 T11 **Bourget, Lac du** ◎ E France
105 P8 **Bourgogne** ***Eng.*** Burgundy. ◈ *region* E France
105 S11 **Bourgoin-Jallieu** Isère, E France
105 R14 **Bourg-St-Andéol** Ardèche, E France
105 U11 **Bourg-St-Maurice** Savoie, E France
110 C11 **Bourg St.Pierre** Valais, SW Switzerland
78 H8 **Boû Rjeimât** *well* W Mauritania
191 P5 **Bourke** New South Wales, SE Australia
99 M24 **Bournemouth** S England, UK
101 M23 **Bourscheid** Diekirch, NE Luxembourg
76 K6 **Bou Saâda** ***var.*** Bou Saada. N Algeria
38 I13 **Bouse Wash** Arizona, SW USA
105 N10 **Boussac** Creuse, C France
104 M16 **Boussens** Haute-Garonne, S France
80 H12 **Bousso** ***prev.*** Fort-Bretonnet. Chari-Baguirmi, S Chad
78 H9 **Boutilimit** Trarza, SW Mauritania
67 D21 **Bouvet Island** ◇ *Norwegian dependency* S Atlantic Ocean
79 U11 **Bouza** Tahoua, SW Niger
111 R10 **Bovec** ***Ger.*** Flitsch, ***It.*** Plezzo. NW Slovenia
100 J8 **Bovenkarspel** Noord-Holland, NW Netherlands
31 V5 **Bovey** Minnesota, N USA
34 M9 **Bovill** Idaho, NW USA
26 L4 **Bovina** Texas, SW USA
109 M17 **Bovino** Puglia, SE Italy
63 C17 **Bovril** Entre Ríos, E Argentina
30 L2 **Bowbells** North Dakota, N USA
9 Q16 **Bow City** Alberta, SW Canada
31 O8 **Bowdle** South Dakota, N USA
189 X6 **Bowen** Queensland, NE Australia
198 B4 **Bowers Ridge** *undersea feature* S Bering Sea
15 Jj4 **Bowes Point** *headland* Northwest Territories, N Canada
27 S5 **Bowie** Texas, SW USA
9 R17 **Bow Island** Alberta, SW Canada
Bowkān *see* Būkān
22 J7 **Bowling Green** Kentucky, S USA
29 V3 **Bowling Green** Missouri, C USA
33 R11 **Bowling Green** Ohio, N USA
23 W5 **Bowling Green** Virginia, NE USA
30 J6 **Bowman** North Dakota, N USA
16 N3 **Bowman Bay** *bay* NW Atlantic Ocean
204 I5 **Bowman Coast** *physical region* Antarctica
30 J7 **Bowman-Haley Lake** ▣ North Dakota, N USA
205 Z11 **Bowman Island** *island* Antarctica
Bowo *see* Bomi
191 S9 **Bowral** New South Wales, SE Australia
194 K14 **Bowutu Mountains** ▲▲ C PNG
85 I16 **Bowwood** Southern, S Zambia
30 I12 **Box Butte Reservoir** ▣ Nebraska, C USA
30 J10 **Box Elder** South Dakota, N USA
97 M18 **Boxholm** Östergötland, S Sweden
Bo Xian/Boxian *see* Bozhou
167 Q4 **Boxing** Shandong, E China
101 L14 **Boxmeer** Noord-Brabant, SE Netherlands
101 J14 **Boxtel** Noord-Brabant, S Netherlands
142 J10 **Boyabat** Sinop, N Turkey
56 F9 **Boyacá** ***off.*** Departamento de Boyacá. ◈ *province* C Colombia
119 O4 **Boyarka** Kyyivs'ka Oblast', N Ukraine
24 H7 **Boyce** Louisiana, S USA
35 U11 **Boyd** Montana, NW USA
27 S6 **Boyd** Texas, SW USA
23 V8 **Boydton** Virginia, NE USA
Boyer Ahmadī va Kohkīlūyeh *see* Kohkīlūyeh va Būyer Aḩmadī
31 T13 **Boyer River** Iowa, C USA
23 W8 **Boykins** Virginia, NE USA
9 Q13 **Boyle** Alberta, SW Canada
99 D16 **Boyle** ***Ir.*** Mainistirna Búille. C Ireland
99 F17 **Boyne** ***Ir.*** An Bhóinn. E Ireland
33 Q5 **Boyne City** Michigan, N USA
25 Z14 **Boynton Beach** Florida, SE USA
153 O13 **Boysun** ***Rus.*** Baysun. Surkhondaryo Wiloyati, S Uzbekistan
Bozau *see* Întorsura Buzăului
142 C14 **Boz Dağları** ▲▲ W Turkey
35 S11 **Bozeman** Montana, NW USA
Bozen *see* Bolzano
81 J16 **Bozene** Equateur, NW Zaire
167 P7 **Bozhou** ***var.*** Boxian, Bo Xian. Anhui, E China
142 H16 **Bozkır** Konya, S Turkey
142 K13 **Bozok Yaylası** *plateau* C Turkey
81 H14 **Bozoum** Ouham-Pendé, W Central African Republic
143 N16 **Bozova** Sanlıurfa, S Turkey
Bozrah *see* Buşrá ash Shām
142 E12 **Bozüyük** Bilecik, NW Turkey
108 B9 **Bra** Piemonte, NW Italy
204 G4 **Brabant Island** *island* Antarctica
115 F15 **Brač** ***var.*** Brach, ***It.*** Brazza; ***anc.*** Brattia. *island* S Croatia
Bracara Augusta *see* Braga
109 H15 **Bracciano** Lazio, C Italy
109 H14 **Bracciano, Lago di** ◎ C Italy
12 H13 **Bracebridge** Ontario, S Canada
Brach *see* Brač
95 G17 **Bräcke** Jämtland, C Sweden
27 P12 **Brackettville** Texas, SW USA
99 N22 **Bracknell** S England, UK
63 K14 **Braço do Norte** Santa Catarina, S Brazil
118 G11 **Brad** ***Hung.*** Brád. Hunedoara, SW Romania
109 N18 **Bradano** S Italy
25 V13 **Bradenton** Florida, SE USA
12 H14 **Bradford** Ontario, S Canada
99 L17 **Bradford** N England, UK
29 W10 **Bradford** Arkansas, C USA
20 D12 **Bradford** Pennsylvania, NE USA
29 T15 **Bradley** Arkansas, C USA
27 P7 **Bradshaw** Texas, SW USA
27 Q9 **Brady** Texas, SW USA
27 Q9 **Brady Creek** Texas, SW USA
98 J10 **Braemar** NE Scotland, UK
118 K8 **Brăeşti** Botoşani, NW Romania
106 G5 **Braga** ***anc.*** Bracara Augusta. Braga, NW Portugal
106 G5 **Braga** ◈ *district* N Portugal
118 J15 **Bragadiru** Teleorman, S Romania
63 C20 **Bragado** Buenos Aires, E Argentina
106 J5 **Bragança** ***Eng.*** Braganza; ***anc.*** Julio Briga. Bragança, NE Portugal
106 I5 **Bragança** ◈ *district* N Portugal
62 N9 **Bragança Paulista** São Paulo, S Brazil
Braganza *see* Bragança
Bragin *see* Brahin
31 V7 **Braham** Minnesota, N USA
Brahe *see* Brda
Brahestad *see* Raahe
121 O20 **Brahin** ***Rus.*** Bragin. Homyel'skaya Voblasts', SE Belarus
159 U15 **Brahmanbaria** Chittagong, E Bangladesh
160 O12 **Brāhmani** E India
160 N13 **Brahmapur** Orissa, E India
133 S10 **Brahmaputra** ***var.*** Padma, Tsangpo, ***Ben.*** Jamuna, ***Chin.*** Yarlung Zangbo Jiang, ***Ind.*** Bramaputra, Dihang, Siang. S Asia
99 H19 **Braich y Pwll** *headland* NW Wales, UK
191 R10 **Braidwood** New South Wales, SE Australia
32 M11 **Braidwood** Illinois, N USA
118 M13 **Brăila** Brăila, E Romania
118 L13 **Brăila** ◈ *county* SE Romania
101 G19 **Braine-l'Alleud** Walloon Brabant, C Belgium
101 F19 **Braine-le-Comte** Hainaut, SW Belgium
31 U6 **Brainerd** Minnesota, N USA
101 J19 **Braives** Liège, E Belgium
85 H23 **Brak** C South Africa
Brak *see* Birāk
101 E18 **Brakel** Oost-Vlaanderen, SW Belgium
100 J13 **Brakel** Gelderland, C Netherlands
78 H9 **Brakna** ◈ *region* S Mauritania
97 J17 **Brålanda** Älvsborg, S Sweden
Bramaputra *see* Brahmaputra
97 F23 **Bramming** Ribe, W Denmark
12 G15 **Brampton** Ontario, S Canada
102 F12 **Bramsche** Niedersachsen, NW Germany
118 J12 **Bran** ***Ger.*** Törzburg, ***Hung.*** Törcsvár. Braşov, S Romania
31 W8 **Branch** Minnesota, N USA
23 R14 **Branchville** South Carolina, SE USA
49 Y6 **Branco, Cabo** *headland* E Brazil
60 F11 **Branco, Rio** N Brazil
110 J8 **Brand** Vorarlberg, W Austria
85 B18 **Brandberg** ▲ NW Namibia
97 H14 **Brandbu** Oppland, S Norway
97 F22 **Brande** Ringkøbing, W Denmark
Brandebourg *see* Brandenburg
102 M12 **Brandenburg** ***var.*** Brandenburg an der Havel. Brandenburg, NE Germany
22 K5 **Brandenburg** Kentucky, S USA
102 N12 **Brandenburg** ***off.*** Freie und Hansestadt Hamburg, ***Fr.*** Brandebourg. ◈ *state* NE Germany
Brandenburg an der Havel *see* Brandenburg
85 I23 **Brandfort** Free State, C South Africa
9 W16 **Brandon** Manitoba, S Canada
25 V12 **Brandon** Florida, SE USA
24 L6 **Brandon** Mississippi, S USA
99 A20 **Brandon Mountain** ***Ir.*** Cnoc Bréanainn. ▲ SW Ireland
Brandsen *see* Coronel Brandsen
97 I14 **Brandval** Hedmark, S Norway
85 F24 **Brandvlei** Northern Cape, W South Africa
25 U9 **Branford** Florida, SE USA
112 K7 **Braniewo** ***Ger.*** Braunsberg. Elbląg, N Poland
204 H3 **Bransfield Strait** *strait* Antarctica
39 U8 **Branson** Colorado, C USA
29 T8 **Branson** Missouri, C USA
12 G16 **Brantford** Ontario, S Canada
104 L12 **Brantôme** Dordogne, SW France
190 L12 **Branxholme** Victoria, SE Australia
Brasil *see* Brazil
61 C16 **Brasiléia** Acre, W Brazil
61 K18 **Brasília** ● (Brazil) Distrito Federal, C Brazil
Braslav *see* Braslaw
120 J12 **Braslaw** ***Pol.*** Brasław, ***Rus.*** Braslav. Vitsyebskaya Voblasts', N Belarus
118 J12 **Braşov** ***Ger.*** Kronstadt, ***Hung.*** Brassó; ***prev.*** Oraşul Stalin. Braşov, C Romania
118 I12 **Braşov** ◈ *county* C Romania
176 W7 **Bras, Pulau** *island* Kepulauan Mapia, E Indonesia
79 U18 **Brass** Rivers, S Nigeria
101 H16 **Brasschaat** ***var.*** Brasschaet. Antwerpen, N Belgium
Brasschaet *see* Brasschaat
175 O4 **Brassey, Banjaran** ***var.*** Brassey Range. ▲▲ East Malaysia
Brassey Range *see* Brassey, Banjaran
Brassó *see* Braşov
25 T1 **Brasstown Bald** ▲ Georgia, SE USA
115 K22 **Brataj** Vlorë, SW Albania
116 J10 **Bratan** ***var.*** Morozov. ▲ C Bulgaria
113 F21 **Bratislava** ***Ger.*** Pressburg, ***Hung.*** Pozsony. ● (Slovakia) Západné Slovensko, SW Slovakia
116 H10 **Bratiya** ▲ C Bulgaria
126 J14 **Bratsk** Irkutskaya Oblast', C Russian Federation
119 Q8 **Brats'ke** Mykolayivs'ka Oblast', S Ukraine
126 J14 **Bratskoye Vodokhranilishche** ***Eng.*** Bratsk Reservoir. ▣ S Russian Federation
Bratsk Reservoir *see* Bratskoye Vodokhranilishche
Brattia *see* Brač
96 D9 **Brattvåg** Møre og Romsdal, S Norway
114 K12 **Bratunac** E Bosnia and Herzegovina
116 J10 **Bratya Daskalovi** ***prev.*** Grozdovo. Khaskovska Oblast, C Bulgaria
111 U2 **Braunau** N Austria
Braunau *see* Braunau am Inn
111 Q4 **Braunau am Inn** ***var.*** Braunau. Oberösterreich, N Austria
Braunsberg *see* Braniewo
102 J13 **Braunschweig** ***Eng./Fr.*** Brunswick. Niedersachsen, N Germany
Brava *see* Baraawe
107 Y6 **Brava, Costa** *coastal region* NE Spain
45 V16 **Brava, Punta** *headland* E Panama
97 N17 **Bråviken** *inlet* S Sweden
58 B10 **Bravo, Cerro** ▲ N Peru
Bravo del Norte, Río/Bravo, Río *see* Grande, Rio
37 X17 **Brawley** California, W USA
99 G18 **Bray** ***Ir.*** Bré. E Ireland
61 G16 **Brazil** ***off.*** Federative Republic of Brazil, ***Port.*** Repùblica Federativa do Brasil, ***Sp.*** Brasil; ***prev.*** United States of Brazil. ◆ *federal republic* South America
67 K15 **Brazil Basin** ***var.*** Brazilian Basin, Brazil'skaya Kotlovina. *undersea feature* W Atlantic Ocean
Brazilian Basin *see* Brazil Basin
Brazilian Highlands *see* Central, Planalto
Brazil'skaya Kotlovina *see* Brazil Basin
27 U10 **Brazos River** Texas, SW USA
176 Yy13 **Brazza** Irian Jaya, E Indonesia
Brazza *see* Brač
81 G21 **Brazzaville** ● (Congo) Capital District, S Congo
81 G21 **Brazzaville** ✕ Le Pool, S Congo
114 J11 **Brčko** NE Bosnia and Herzegovina
112 H8 **Brda** ***Ger.*** Brahe. N Poland
Bré *see* Bray
193 A23 **Breaksea Sound** *sound* South Island, NZ
192 L4 **Bream Bay** *bay* North Island, NZ
192 L4 **Bream Head** *headland* North Island, NZ
Bréanainn, Cnoc *see* Brandon Mountain
47 S6 **Brea, Punta** *headland* W Puerto Rico
24 I9 **Breaux Bridge** Louisiana, S USA
118 J13 **Breaza** Prahova, SE Romania
174 K14 **Brebes** Jawa, C Indonesia
98 K10 **Brechin** E Scotland, UK
101 H15 **Brecht** Antwerpen, N Belgium
39 S4 **Breckenridge** Colorado, C USA
31 R6 **Breckenridge** Minnesota, N USA
27 R6 **Breckenridge** Texas, SW USA
99 J21 **Brecknock** *cultural region* SE Wales, UK
65 G25 **Brecknock, Península** *headland* S Chile
113 G19 **Břeclav** ***Ger.*** Lundenburg. Jižní Morava, SE Czech Republic
99 J21 **Brecon** E Wales, UK
99 J21 **Brecon Beacons** ▲▲ S Wales, UK
101 I14 **Breda** Noord-Brabant, S Netherlands
97 K20 **Bredaryd** Jönköping, S Sweden
85 F26 **Bredasdorp** Western Cape, SW South Africa
95 H16 **Bredbyn** Västernorrland, N Sweden
125 E13 **Bredy** Chelyabinskaya Oblast', C Russian Federation
101 K17 **Bree** Limburg, NE Belgium
69 T15 **Breede** S South Africa
100 I7 **Breezand** Noord-Holland, NW Netherlands
115 P18 **Bregalnica** E FYR Macedonia
110 I6 **Bregenz** ***anc.*** Brigantium. Vorarlberg, W Austria
110 J7 **Bregenzer Wald** ▲▲ W Austria
116 F6 **Bregovo** Oblast Montana, NW Bulgaria
104 H5 **Bréhat, Île de** *island* NW France
94 H2 **Breidhafjördhur** *bay* W Iceland
94 L3 **Breidhdalsvík** Austurland, E Iceland
110 H9 **Breil** ***Ger.*** Brigels. Graubünden, S Switzerland
94 J8 **Breivikbotn** Finnmark, N Norway
96 I9 **Brekken** Sør-Trøndelag, S Norway
96 G7 **Brekstad** Sør-Trøndelag, S Norway
96 B10 **Bremangerlandet** *island* S Norway
Brême *see* Bremen
102 H11 **Bremen** ***Fr.*** Brême. Bremen, NW Germany
25 R3 **Bremen** Georgia, SE USA
33 O11 **Bremen** Indiana, N USA
102 H10 **Bremen** ***off.*** Freie Hansestadt Bremen, ***Fr.*** Brême. ◈ *state* N Germany
102 G9 **Bremerhaven** Bremen, NW Germany
Bremersdorp *see* Manzini
34 G8 **Bremerton** Washington, NW USA
102 H10 **Bremervörde** Niedersachsen, NW Germany
27 U9 **Bremond** Texas, SW USA
27 U10 **Brenham** Texas, SW USA
110 M8 **Brenner** Tirol, W Austria
Brenner, Col du/Brennero, Passo del *see* Brenner Pass
110 M8 **Brenner Pass** ***var.*** Brenner Sattel, ***Fr.*** Col du Brenner, ***Ger.*** Brennerpass, ***It.*** Passo del Brennero. *pass* Austria/Italy
Brenner Sattel *see* Brenner Pass
110 G10 **Brenno** SW Switzerland
108 F7 **Breno** Lombardia, N Italy
25 O5 **Brent** Alabama, S USA
108 H7 **Brenta** NE Italy
99 P21 **Brentwood** E England, UK
20 L14 **Brentwood** Long Island, New York, NE USA
108 F7 **Brescia** ***anc.*** Brixia. Lombardia, N Italy
101 D15 **Breskens** Zeeland, SW Netherlands
Breslau *see* Wrocław
108 H5 **Bressanone** ***Ger.*** Brixen. Trentino-Alto Adige, N Italy
98 M2 **Bressay** *island* NE Scotland, UK
104 K9 **Bressuire** Deux-Sèvres, W France
121 F20 **Brest** ***Pol.*** Brześć nad Bugiem, ***Rus.*** Brest-Litovsk; ***prev.*** Brześć Litewski. Brestskaya Voblasts', SW Belarus
104 F5 **Brest** Finistère, NW France
Brest-Litovsk *see* Brest
114 A10 **Brestova** Istra, NW Croatia
Brestskaya Oblast' *see* Brestskaya Voblasts'
121 G19 **Brestskaya Voblasts'** ***prev.*** Rus. Brestskaya Oblast'. ◈ *province* SW Belarus
104 G6 **Bretagne** ***Eng.*** Brittany; ***Lat.*** Britannia Minor. ◈ *region* NW France
118 G12 **Bretea-Română** ***Hung.*** Oláhbrettye; ***prev.*** Bretea-Romînă. Hunedoara, W Romania
Bretea-Romînă *see* Bretea-Română
105 O3 **Breteuil** Oise, N France
104 I10 **Breton, Pertuis** *inlet* W France
24 L10 **Breton Sound** *sound* Louisiana, S USA
192 K2 **Brett, Cape** *headland* North Island, NZ
103 G21 **Bretten** Baden-Württemberg, SW Germany
101 K15 **Breugel** Noord-Brabant, S Netherlands
108 B6 **Breuil** ***It.*** Cervinia. Valle d'Aosta, NW Italy
100 I11 **Breukelen** Utrecht, C Netherlands
23 P10 **Brevard** North Carolina, SE USA
40 L9 **Brevig Mission** Alaska, USA
97 G16 **Brevik** Telemark, S Norway
191 P5 **Brewarrina** New South Wales, SE Australia
21 R6 **Brewer** Maine, NE USA
31 T11 **Brewster** Minnesota, N USA
31 N14 **Brewster** Nebraska, C USA
33 U12 **Brewster** Ohio, N USA
191 O8 **Brewster, Lake** ◎ New South Wales, SE Australia
25 P7 **Brewton** Alabama, S USA
Brezhnev *see* Naberezhnyye Chelny
111 W12 **Brežice** ***Ger.*** Rann. E Slovenia
116 G9 **Breznik** Sofiyska Oblast, W Bulgaria
113 K19 **Brezno** ***Ger.*** Bries, Briesen, ***Hung.*** Breznóbánya; ***prev.*** Brezno nad Hronom. Stredné Slovensko, C Slovakia
Breznóbánya/Brezno nad Hronom *see* Brezno
118 I12 **Brezoi** Vâlcea, SW Romania
116 J10 **Brezovo** ***prev.*** Abrashlare. Plovdivska Oblast, C Bulgaria
81 K14 **Bria** Haute-Kotto, C Central African Republic
105 U13 **Briançon** ***anc.*** Brigantio. Hautes-Alpes, SE France
38 K7 **Brian Head** ▲ Utah, W USA
105 O7 **Briare** Loiret, C France
191 V2 **Bribie Island** *island* Queensland, E Australia
45 O14 **Bribrí** Limón, E Costa Rica
118 L8 **Briceni** ***var.*** Brinceni, ***Rus.*** Brichany. N Moldova
Bricgstow *see* Bristol
Brichany *see* Briceni
101 M24 **Bridel** Luxembourg, C Luxembourg
99 J22 **Bridgend** S Wales, UK
12 I14 **Bridgenorth** Ontario, SE Canada
25 Q1 **Bridgeport** Alabama, S USA
37 R8 **Bridgeport** California, W USA
20 L13 **Bridgeport** Connecticut, NE USA
33 N15 **Bridgeport** Illinois, N USA
30 J14 **Bridgeport** Nebraska, C USA
27 S6 **Bridgeport** Texas, SW USA
23 S3 **Bridgeport** West Virginia, NE USA
27 S5 **Bridgeport, Lake** ▣ Texas, SW USA
35 U11 **Bridger** Montana, NW USA
20 I17 **Bridgeton** New Jersey, NE USA
188 J14 **Bridgetown** Western Australia
47 Y14 **Bridgetown** ● (Barbados) SW Barbados
191 P17 **Bridgewater** Tasmania, SE Australia
11 P16 **Bridgewater** Nova Scotia, SE Canada
21 P12 **Bridgewater** Massachusetts, NE USA
31 Q11 **Bridgewater** South Dakota, N USA
23 U5 **Bridgewater** Virginia, NE USA
21 P8 **Bridgton** Maine, NE USA
99 K23 **Bridgwater** SW England, UK
99 K22 **Bridgwater Bay** *bay* SW England, UK
99 O16 **Bridlington** E England, UK
99 O16 **Bridlington Bay** *bay* E England, UK
191 P15 **Bridport** Tasmania, SE Australia
99 K24 **Bridport** S England, UK
105 O5 **Brie** *cultural region* N France
Brieg *see* Brzeg
Briel *see* Brielle
100 G12 **Brielle** ***var.*** Briel, Bril, ***Eng.*** The Brill. Zuid-Holland, SW Netherlands
110 E9 **Brienz** Bern, C Switzerland
110 E9 **Brienzer See** ◎ SW Switzerland
Bries/Briesen *see* Brezno
Brietzig *see* Brzesko
105 S4 **Briey** Meurthe-et-Moselle, NE France
110 E10 **Brig** ***Fr.*** Brigue, ***It.*** Briga. Valais, SW Switzerland
Briga *see* Brig
103 G24 **Brigach** S Germany
20 K17 **Brigantine** New Jersey, NE USA
Brigantio *see* Briançon
Brigantium *see* Bregenz
Brigels *see* Breil
27 S9 **Briggs** Texas, SW USA
38 L1 **Brigham City** Utah, W USA
12 J15 **Brighton** Ontario, SE Canada
99 O23 **Brighton** SE England, UK
39 T4 **Brighton** Colorado, C USA
32 K15 **Brighton** Illinois, N USA
105 T16 **Brignoles** Var, W France
Brigue *see* Brig
107 O7 **Brihuega** Castilla-La Mancha, C Spain
114 A10 **Brijuni** ***It.*** Brioni. *island group* NW Croatia
78 G12 **Brikama** W Gambia
Bril *see* Brielle
Brill, The *see* Brielle
103 G15 **Brilon** Nordrhein-Westfalen, W Germany
Brinceni *see* Briceni
109 Q18 **Brindisi** ***anc.*** Brundisium, Brundusium. Puglia, SE Italy
29 W11 **Brinkley** Arkansas, C USA
Brioni *see* Brijuni
105 P12 **Brioude** ***anc.*** Brivas. Haute-Loire, C France
Briovera *see* St-Lô
191 U2 **Brisbane** Queensland, E Australia
191 V2 **Brisbane** ✕ Queensland, E Australia
27 P2 **Briscoe** Texas, SW USA
108 H10 **Brisighella** Emilia-Romagna, C Italy
110 G11 **Brissago** Ticino, S Switzerland
99 K22 **Bristol** ***anc.*** Bricgstow. SW England, UK
20 M12 **Bristol** Connecticut, NE USA
25 R9 **Bristol** Florida, SE USA
21 N9 **Bristol** New Hampshire, NE USA
31 Q8 **Bristol** South Dakota, N USA
23 P8 **Bristol** Tennessee, S USA
20 M8 **Bristol** Vermont, NE USA
41 N14 **Bristol Bay** *bay* Alaska, USA
99 I22 **Bristol Channel** *inlet* England/Wales, UK
37 W14 **Bristol Lake** ◎ California, W USA
29 P10 **Bristow** Oklahoma, C USA
88 C10 **Britain** ***var.*** Great Britain. *island* UK
Britannia Minor *see* Bretagne
8 L12 **British Columbia** ***Fr.*** Colombie-Britannique. ◈ *province* SW Canada
British Guiana *see* Guyana
British Honduras *see* Belize
181 Q7 **British Indian Ocean Territory** ◇ *UK dependent territory* C Indian Ocean
88 B9 **British Isles** *island group* NW Europe
8 I1 **British Mountains** ▲▲ Yukon Territory, NW Canada
British North Borneo *see* Sabah
British Solomon Islands Protectorate *see* Solomon Islands
47 S8 **British Virgin Islands** ***var.*** Virgin Islands. ◇ *UK dependent territory* E West Indies
85 J21 **Brits** North-West, N South Africa
85 H24 **Britstown** Northern Cape, W South Africa
12 F12 **Britt** Ontario, S Canada
31 V12 **Britt** Iowa, C USA
Brittany *see* Bretagne
31 Q7 **Britton** South Dakota, N USA
Briva Curretia *see* Brive-la-Gaillarde
Briva Isarae *see* Pontoise
Brivas *see* Brioude
Brive *see* Brive-la-Gaillarde
104 M12 **Brive-la-Gaillarde** ***prev.*** Brive, ***anc.*** Briva Curretia. Corrèze, C France
107 O4 **Briviesca** Castilla-León, N Spain
Brixen *see* Bressanone
Brixia *see* Brescia
151 S15 **Brlik** ***prev.*** Novotroickoje, Novotroitskoye. Zhambyl, SE Kazakhstan
113 G18 **Brno** ***Ger.*** Brünn. Jižní Morava, SE Czech Republic
98 G7 **Broad Bay** *bay* NW Scotland, UK
27 X8 **Broaddus** Texas, SW USA
191 O12 **Broadford** Victoria, SE Australia
98 G9 **Broadford** N Scotland, UK
98 J13 **Broad Law** ▲ S Scotland, UK
25 U3 **Broad River** Georgia, SE USA
23 N8 **Broad River** North Carolina/South Carolina, SE USA
189 Y8 **Broadsound Range** ▲▲ Queensland, E Australia
35 X11 **Broadus** Montana, NW USA
23 U4 **Broadway** Virginia, NE USA
120 E9 **Brocēni** Saldus, SW Latvia
9 U11 **Brochet** Manitoba, C Canada
9 U10 **Brochet, Lac** ◎ Manitoba, C Canada
13 S5 **Brochet, Lac au** ◎ Québec, SE Canada
103 K14 **Brocken** ▲ C Germany
21 O12 **Brockton** Massachusetts, NE USA
12 L14 **Brockville** Ontario, SE Canada
20 D13 **Brockway** Pennsylvania, NE USA
Brod/Bród *see* Slavonski Brod
15 Kk1 **Brodeur Peninsula** *peninsula* Baffin Island, Northwest Territories, NE Canada
98 H13 **Brodick** W Scotland, UK
Brod na Savi *see* Slavonski Brod
112 K9 **Brodnica** ***Ger.*** Buddenbrock. Toruń, N Poland
114 G10 **Brod-Posavina** ***off.*** Brodsko-Posavska Županija. ◈ *province* NE Croatia
118 J5 **Brody** L'vivs'ka Oblast', NW Ukraine
97 G22 **Brædstrup** Vejle, C Denmark
100 I10 **Broek-in-Waterland** Noord-Holland, C Netherlands
34 L13 **Brogan** Oregon, NW USA
112 N10 **Brok** Ostrołęka, E Poland
29 P9 **Broken Arrow** Oklahoma, C USA
191 T9 **Broken Bay** *bay* New South Wales, SE Australia
31 N15 **Broken Bow** Nebraska, C USA
29 R13 **Broken Bow** Oklahoma, C USA
29 R12 **Broken Bow Lake** ▣ Oklahoma, C USA
190 L6 **Broken Hill** New South Wales, SE Australia
181 S10 **Broken Ridge** *undersea feature* S Indian Ocean
194 H10 **Broken Water Bay** *bay* W Bismarck Sea
57 W10 **Brokopondo** Brokopondo, NE Suriname
57 W10 **Brokopondo** ◈ *district* C Suriname
Bromberg *see* Bydgoszcz
97 L22 **Bromölla** Kristianstad, S Sweden
99 L20 **Bromsgrove** W England, UK
97 G20 **Brønderslev** Nordjylland, N Denmark
108 D8 **Broni** Lombardia, N Italy
8 K11 **Bronlund Peak** ▲ British Columbia, W Canada
95 F14 **Brønnøysund** Nordland, C Norway
25 V10 **Bronson** Florida, SE USA
33 Q11 **Bronson** Michigan, N USA
27 X8 **Bronson** Texas, SW USA
109 L24 **Bronte** Sicilia, Italy, C Mediterranean Sea
27 P8 **Bronte** Texas, SW USA
27 Y9 **Brookeland** Texas, SW USA
179 O15 **Brooke's Point** Palawan, W Philippines
29 T3 **Brookfield** Missouri, C USA
24 K7 **Brookhaven** Mississippi, S USA
34 E16 **Brookings** Oregon, NW USA
31 R10 **Brookings** South Dakota, N USA
31 W14 **Brooklyn** Iowa, C USA
31 U8 **Brooklyn Park** Minnesota, N USA
23 U7 **Brookneal** Virginia, NE USA
9 R16 **Brooks** Alberta, SW Canada
27 V11 **Brookshire** Texas, SW USA
40 L8 **Brooks Mountain** ▲ Alaska, USA
40 M11 **Brooks Range** ▲▲ Alaska, USA
33 O12 **Brookston** Indiana, N USA
25 V11 **Brooksville** Florida, SE USA
25 N4 **Brooksville** Mississippi, S USA
188 J13 **Brookton** Western Australia
33 Q14 **Brookville** Indiana, N USA
20 D13 **Brookville** Pennsylvania, NE USA

◆ Country
● Country Capital
◇ Dependent Territory
○ Dependent Territory Capital
◈ Administrative Region
✕ International Airport
▲ Mountain
▲▲ Mountain Range
Volcano
River
◎ Lake
▣ Reservoir

Brookville Lake – Butawal

33 Q14 **Brookville Lake** ⊡ Indiana, N USA
188 K5 **Broome** Western Australia
39 S4 **Broomfield** Colorado, C USA
Broos *see* Orăştie
98 J7 **Brora** N Scotland, UK
98 I7 **Brora** ∽ N Scotland, UK
97 F23 **Brørup** Ribe, W Denmark
97 L23 **Brösarp** Kristianstad, S Sweden
118 J9 **Broşteni** Suceava, NE Romania
104 M6 **Brou** Eure-et-Loir, C France
Broucsella *see* Brussel/Bruxelles
Broughton Bay *see* Tongjosŏn-man
16 I1 **Broughton Island** Northwest Territories, NE Canada
144 G7 **Broummâna** C Lebanon
24 I9 **Broussard** Louisiana, S USA
100 E13 **Brouwersdam** *dam* SW Netherlands
100 E13 **Brouwershaven** Zeeland, SW Netherlands
119 P4 **Brovary** Kyyivs'ka Oblast', N Ukraine
97 G20 **Brovst** Nordjylland, N Denmark
33 S8 **Brown City** Michigan, N USA
26 M6 **Brownfield** Texas, SW USA
35 Q7 **Browning** Montana, NW USA
35 R6 **Brown, Mount** ▲ Montana, NW USA
194 K15 **Brown River** ∽ S PNG
1 M9 **Browns Bank** *undersea feature* NW Atlantic Ocean
33 O14 **Brownsburg** Indiana, N USA
20 J16 **Browns Mills** New Jersey, NE USA
46 J12 **Browns Town** C Jamaica
33 P15 **Brownstown** Indiana, N USA
31 R8 **Browns Valley** Minnesota, N USA
22 K7 **Brownsville** Kentucky, S USA
22 F9 **Brownsville** Tennessee, S USA
27 T17 **Brownsville** Texas, SW USA
57 W10 **Brownsweg** Brokopondo, C Suriname
31 U9 **Brownton** Minnesota, N USA
21 R5 **Brownville Junction** Maine, NE USA
27 R8 **Brownwood** Texas, SW USA
27 R8 **Brownwood Lake** ⊡ Texas, SW USA
106 I9 **Brozas** Extremadura, W Spain
121 M18 **Brozha** Mahilyowskaya Voblasts', E Belarus
105 O2 **Bruay-en-Artois** Pas-de-Calais, N France
105 P2 **Bruay-sur-l'Escaut** Nord, N France
12 F13 **Bruce Peninsula** *peninsula* Ontario, S Canada
22 H9 **Bruceton** Tennessee, S USA
27 T9 **Bruceville** Texas, SW USA
103 G21 **Bruchsal** Baden-Württemberg, SW Germany
111 Q7 **Bruck** Salzburg, NW Austria
Bruck *see* Bruck an der Mur
111 Y4 **Bruck an der Leitha** Niederösterreich, NE Austria
111 V7 **Bruck an der Mur** *var.* Bruck. Steiermark, C Austria
103 M24 **Bruckmühl** Bayern, SE Germany
173 Dd3 **Brueuh, Pulau** *island* NW Indonesia
Bruges *see* Brugge
110 F6 **Brugg** Aargau, NW Switzerland
101 C16 **Brugge** *Fr.* Bruges. West-Vlaanderen, NW Belgium
111 R9 **Bruggen** Kärnten, S Austria
103 E16 **Brühl** Nordrhein-Westfalen, W Germany
101 F14 **Bruinisse** Zeeland, SW Netherlands
174 L5 **Bruit, Pulau** *island* East Malaysia
12 K10 **Brûlé, Lac** ◎ Québec, SE Canada
32 M4 **Brule River** ∽ Michigan/Wisconsin, N USA
101 H23 **Brûly** Namur, S Belgium
61 N17 **Brumado** Bahia, E Brazil
100 M11 **Brummen** Gelderland, E Netherlands
96 H13 **Brumunddal** Hedmark, S Norway
25 Q6 **Brundidge** Alabama, S USA
Brundisium/Brundusium *see* Brindisi
35 N15 **Bruneau River** ∽ Idaho, NW USA
Bruneck *see* Brunico
174 Mm4 **Brunei** *off.* Sultanate of Brunei, *Mal.* Negara Brunei Darussalam. ◆ *monarchy* SE Asia
175 N3 **Brunei Bay** *var.* Teluk Brunei. *bay* N Brunei
Brunei, Teluk *see* Brunei Bay
Brunei Town *see* Bandar Seri Begawan
108 H5 **Brunico** *Ger.* Bruneck. Trentino-Alto Adige, N Italy
Brünn *see* Brno
193 G17 **Brunner, Lake** ◎ South Island, NZ
101 M18 **Brunssum** Limburg, SE Netherlands
25 W7 **Brunswick** Georgia, SE USA
21 Q8 **Brunswick** Maine, NE USA
23 V3 **Brunswick** Maryland, NE USA
29 T3 **Brunswick** Missouri, C USA
33 T11 **Brunswick** Ohio, N USA
Brunswick *see* Braunschweig
65 H24 **Brunswick, Peninsula** *headland* S Chile
113 H17 **Bruntál** *Ger.* Freudenthal. Severní Morava, E Czech Republic
205 N3 **Brunt Ice Shelf** *ice shelf* Antarctica
Brusa *see* Bursa
39 U3 **Brush** Colorado, C USA
44 M5 **Brus Laguna** Gracias a Dios, E Honduras
62 K13 **Brusque** Santa Catarina, S Brazil
Brussa *see* Bursa
101 E18 **Brussel** *var.* Brussels, *Fr.* Bruxelles, *Ger.* Brüssel; *anc.* Broucsella. ● (Belgium) Brussels, C Belgium *see also* Bruxelles
Brüssel/Brussels *see* Brussel/Bruxelles
119 O5 **Brusyliv** Zhytomyrs'ka Oblast', N Ukraine
191 Q12 **Bruthen** Victoria, SE Australia
Bruttium *see* Calabria
Brüx *see* Most
101 E18 **Bruxelles** *var.* Brussels, *Dut.* Brussel, *Ger.* Brüssel; *anc.* Broucsella. ● (Belgium) Brussels, C Belgium *see also* Brussel
56 J7 **Bruzual** Apure, W Venezuela
33 Q11 **Bryan** Ohio, N USA
27 U10 **Bryan** Texas, SW USA
204 J4 **Bryan Coast** *physical region* Antarctica
126 I13 **Bryanka** Krasnoyarskiy Kray, C Russian Federation
119 Y7 **Bryanka** Luhans'ka Oblast', E Ukraine
190 J8 **Bryan, Mount** ▲ South Australia
130 I6 **Bryansk** Bryanskaya Oblast', W Russian Federation
130 H6 **Bryanskaya Oblast'** ◐ *province* W Russian Federation
204 J5 **Bryant, Cape** *headland* Antarctica
29 U8 **Bryant Creek** ∽ Missouri, C USA
38 K8 **Bryce Canyon** *canyon* Utah, W USA
121 O15 **Bryli** *Rus.* Bryli. Mahilyowskaya Voblasts', E Belarus
97 C17 **Bryne** Rogaland, S Norway
27 R6 **Bryson** Texas, SW USA
23 N10 **Bryson City** North Carolina, SE USA
12 K11 **Bryson, Lac** ◎ Québec, SE Canada
130 K13 **Bryukhovetskaya** Krasnodarskiy Kray, SW Russian Federation
113 H15 **Brzeg** *Ger.* Brieg; *anc.* Civitas Altae Ripae. Opole, SW Poland
113 G14 **Brzeg Dolny** *Ger.* Dyhernfurth. Wrocław, SW Poland
Brześć Litewski/Brześć nad Bugiem *see* Brest
113 L17 **Brzesko** *Ger.* Brietzig. Tarnów, SE Poland
Brzeżany *see* Berezhany
112 K12 **Brzeziny** Skierniewice, C Poland
Brzostowica Wielka *see* Vyalikaya Byerastavitsa
113 O17 **Brzozów** Krosno, SE Poland
Bsharrī/Bsherri *see* Bcharré
197 I13 **Bua** Vanua Levu, N Fiji
97 J20 **Bua** Halland, S Sweden
84 M13 **Bua** ∽ C Malawi
Bua *see* Čiovo
83 L18 **Bu'aale** *It.* Buale. Jubbada Dhexe, SW Somalia
201 Q8 **Buada Lagoon** *lagoon* Nauru, C Pacific Ocean
195 W14 **Buala** Santa Isabel, E Solomon Islands
Buale *see* Bu'aale
202 H1 **Buariki** *atoll* Tungaru, W Kiribati
178 I10 **Bua Yai** *var.* Ban Bua Yai. Nakhon Ratchasima, E Thailand
77 P8 **Bu'ayrāt al Ḩasūn** *var.* Buwayrāt al Hasūn. C Libya
78 H13 **Buba** S Guinea-Bissau
175 Qq7 **Bubaa** Sulawesi, N Indonesia
83 D20 **Bubanza** NW Burundi
85 K18 **Bubi** *prev.* Bubye. ∽ S Zimbabwe
148 L11 **Būbiyan, Jazirat** *island* E Kuwait
Bublitz *see* Bobolice
Bubye *see* Bubi
197 J13 **Buca** *prev.* Mbutha. Vanua Levu, N Fiji
142 F16 **Bucak** Burdur, SW Turkey
56 G8 **Bucaramanga** Santander, N Colombia
109 M18 **Buccino** Campania, S Italy
118 K9 **Bucecea** Botoşani, NE Romania
118 J6 **Buchach** *Pol.* Buczacz. Ternopil's'ka Oblast', W Ukraine
191 Q12 **Buchan** Victoria, SE Australia
78 J17 **Buchanan** *prev.* Grand Bassa. SW Liberia
25 R3 **Buchanan** Georgia, SE USA
33 O11 **Buchanan** Michigan, N USA
23 T6 **Buchanan** Virginia, NE USA
27 R10 **Buchanan Dam** Texas, SW USA
27 R10 **Buchanan, Lake** ⊡ Texas, SW USA
98 L8 **Buchan Ness** *headland* NE Scotland, UK
11 T12 **Buchans** Newfoundland, Newfoundland and Labrador, SE Canada
Bucharest *see* Bucureşti
103 H20 **Buchen** Baden-Württemberg, SW Germany
102 I10 **Buchholz in der Nordheide** Niedersachsen, NW Germany
110 I8 **Buchs** Aargau, N Switzerland
110 F7 **Buchs** Sankt Gallen, NE Switzerland
102 H13 **Bückeburg** Niedersachsen, NW Germany
38 K14 **Buckeye** Arizona, SW USA
Buckeye State *see* Ohio
23 S4 **Buckhannon** West Virginia, NE USA
27 T9 **Buckholts** Texas, SW USA
98 K8 **Buckie** NE Scotland, UK
12 M12 **Buckingham** Québec, SE Canada
23 U6 **Buckingham** Virginia, NE USA
99 N21 **Buckinghamshire** *cultural region* SE England, UK
41 N8 **Buckland** Alaska, USA
190 G7 **Buckleboo** South Australia
28 K7 **Bucklin** Kansas, C USA
29 T3 **Bucklin** Missouri, C USA
38 I12 **Buckskin Mountains** ▲▲ Arizona, SW USA
21 R7 **Bucksport** Maine, NE USA
84 A9 **Buco Zau** Cabinda, NW Angola
Bu Craa *see* Bou Craa
118 K14 **Bucureşti** *Eng.* Bucharest, *Ger.* Bukarest; *prev.* Altenburg, *anc.* Cetatea Damboviţei. ● (Romania) Bucureşti, S Romania
33 S12 **Bucyrus** Ohio, N USA
Buczacz *see* Buchach
96 E9 **Bud** Møre og Romsdal, S Norway
27 S11 **Buda** Texas, SW USA
121 O18 **Buda-Kashalyova** *Rus.* Buda-Koshelëvo. Homyel'skaya Voblasts', SE Belarus
Buda-Koshelëvo *see* Buda-Kashalyova
177 G4 **Budalin** Sagaing, C Myanmar
113 J22 **Budapest** *off.* Budapest Főváros, *SCr.* Budimpešta. ● (Hungary) Pest, N Hungary
158 K11 **Budaun** Uttar Pradesh, N India
147 O9 **Budayyi'ah** *oasis* C Saudi Arabia
205 Y12 **Budd Coast** *physical region* Antarctica
Buddenbrock *see* Brodnica
109 C17 **Budduso** Sardegna, Italy, C Mediterranean Sea
99 I23 **Bude** SW England, UK
24 J7 **Bude** Mississippi, S USA
101 K16 **Budel** Noord-Brabant, SE Netherlands
102 I8 **Büdelsdorf** Schleswig-Holstein, N Germany
131 O14 **Budënnovsk** Stavropol'skiy Kray, SW Russian Federation
118 K14 **Budeşti** Călăraşi, SE Romania
Budgewoi *see* Budgewoi Lake
191 T8 **Budgewoi Lake** *var.* Budgewoi. New South Wales, SE Australia
94 I2 **Búdhardalur** Vesturland, W Iceland
Budimpešta *see* Budapest
81 J16 **Budjala** Equateur, NW Zaire
108 G10 **Budrio** Emilia-Romagna, C Italy
Budslav *see* Budslaw
121 K14 **Budslaw** *Rus.* Budslav. Minskaya Voblasts', N Belarus
Budua *see* Budva
174 Ll5 **Budu, Tanjung** *headland* East Malaysia
115 J17 **Budva** *It.* Budua. Montenegro, SW Yugoslavia
Budweis *see* České Budějovice
Budyšin *see* Bautzen
81 D16 **Buea** Sud-Ouest, SW Cameroon
105 S13 **Buëch** ∽ SE France
20 J17 **Buena** New Jersey, NE USA
64 K12 **Buena Esperanza** San Luis, C Argentina
56 C11 **Buenaventura** Valle del Cauca, W Colombia
42 I4 **Buenaventura** Chihuahua, N Mexico
59 M18 **Buena Vista** Santa Cruz, C Bolivia
42 G10 **Buenavista** Baja California Sur, W Mexico
39 S5 **Buena Vista** Colorado, C USA
25 S5 **Buena Vista** Georgia, SE USA
23 T6 **Buena Vista** Virginia, NE USA
46 F5 **Buena Vista, Bahia de** *bay* N Cuba
37 R13 **Buena Vista Lake Bed** ◎ California, W USA
107 P8 **Buendía, Embalse de** ⊡ C Spain
65 F16 **Bueno, Río** ∽ S Chile
64 N12 **Buenos Aires** *hist.* Santa Maria del Buen Aire. ● (Argentina) Buenos Aires, E Argentina
45 O15 **Buenos Aires** Puntarenas, SE Costa Rica
63 C20 **Buenos Aires** *off.* Provincia de Buenos Aires. ◐ *province* E Argentina
65 H19 **Buenos Aires, Lago** *var.* Lago General Carrera. ◎ Argentina/Chile
56 C13 **Buesaco** Nariño, SW Colombia
31 U8 **Buffalo** Minnesota, N USA
28 K8 **Buffalo** Missouri, C USA
20 D10 **Buffalo** New York, NE USA
29 T6 **Buffalo** Oklahoma, C USA
30 J7 **Buffalo** South Dakota, N USA
27 V8 **Buffalo** Texas, SW USA
35 W12 **Buffalo** Wyoming, C USA
31 U11 **Buffalo Center** Iowa, C USA
26 M3 **Buffalo Lake** ⊡ Texas, SW USA
32 K7 **Buffalo Lake** ⊡ Wisconsin, N USA
9 S12 **Buffalo Narrows** Saskatchewan, C Canada
29 U9 **Buffalo River** ∽ Arkansas, C USA
31 R5 **Buffalo River** ∽ Minnesota, N USA
22 I10 **Buffalo River** ∽ Tennessee, S USA
32 J6 **Buffalo River** ∽ Wisconsin, N USA
46 L12 **Buff Bay** E Jamaica
25 T3 **Buford** Georgia, SE USA
30 J3 **Buford** North Dakota, N USA
35 Y17 **Buford** Wyoming, C USA
118 J14 **Buftea** Bucureşti, S Romania
86 I9 **Bug** *Bel.* Zakhodni Buh, *Eng.* Western Bug, *Rus.* Zapadnyy Bug, *Ukr.* Zakhidnyy Buh. ∽ E Europe
56 D11 **Buga** Valle del Cauca, W Colombia
168 F7 **Buga** Dzavhan, W Mongolia
105 O17 **Bugarach, Pic du** ▲ S France
152 B12 **Bugdayly** Balkanskiy Velayat, W Turkmenistan
Buggs Island Lake *see* John H.Kerr Reservoir
Bughotu *see* Santa Isabel
175 Q12 **Bugingkalo** Sulawesi, C Indonesia
Bugingkaro *see* Bungingkolu, Tanjung
66 P6 **Bugio** *island* Madeira, Portugal, NE Atlantic Ocean
94 M8 **Bugøynes** Finnmark, N Norway
129 Q3 **Bugrino** Nenetskiy Avtonomnyy Okrug, NW Russian Federation
131 T5 **Bugul'ma** Respublika Tatarstan, W Russian Federation
Būgūr *see* Luntai
131 T6 **Buguruslan** Orenburgskaya Oblast', W Russian Federation
165 R9 **Buh He** ∽ C China
35 O15 **Buhl** Idaho, NW USA
103 F22 **Bühl** Baden-Württemberg, SW Germany
118 K10 **Buhuşi** Bacău, E Romania
Buie d'Istria *see* Buje
99 J20 **Builth Wells** E Wales, UK
195 S13 **Buin** Bougainville Island, NE PNG
110 J9 **Buin, Piz** ▲ Austria/Switzerland
131 Q4 **Buinsk** Chuvashskaya Respublika, W Russian Federation
131 Q4 **Buinsk** Respublika Tatarstan, W Russian Federation
169 R8 **Buir Nur** *Mong.* Buyr Nuur. ◎ China/Mongolia *see also* Buyr Nuur
100 M5 **Buitenpost** *Fris.* Bûtenpost. Friesland, N Netherlands
Buitenzorg *see* Bogor
85 F19 **Buitepos** Omaheke, E Namibia
107 N7 **Buitrago del Lozoya** Madrid, C Spain
Buj *see* Buy
106 M13 **Bujalance** Andalucía, S Spain
115 O17 **Bujanovac** Serbia, SE Yugoslavia
107 S6 **Bujaraloz** Aragón, NE Spain
114 A9 **Buje** *It.* Buie d'Istria. Istra, NW Croatia
Bujnurd *see* Bojnūrd
83 D21 **Bujumbura** *prev.* Usumbura. ● (Burundi) W Burundi
83 D20 **Bujumbura** ✕ W Burundi
126 L15 **Bukachacha** Chitinskaya Oblast', S Russian Federation
165 N11 **Bukadaban Feng** ▲ C China
195 R11 **Buka Island** *island* NE PNG
83 F18 **Bukakata** S Uganda
81 N24 **Bukama** Shaba, SE Zaire
148 J4 **Būkān** *var.* Bowkān. Āzarbāyjān-e Bākhtarī, NW Iran
Bukantau, Gory *see* Bŭkantow-Toghi
152 K8 **Bŭkantow-Toghi** *Rus.* Gory Bukantau. ▲▲ N Uzbekistan
Bukarest *see* Bucureşti
81 O19 **Bukavu** *prev.* Costermansville. Sud Kivu, E Zaire
83 F21 **Bukene** Tabora, NW Tanzania
147 W8 **Bū Khābī** *var.* Bakhābī. NW Oman
Bukhara *see* Bukhoro
Bukharskaya Oblast' *see* Bukhoro Wiloyati
152 L11 **Bukhoro** *var.* Bokhara, *Rus.* Bukhara. Bukhoro Wiloyati, C Uzbekistan
152 J11 **Bukhoro Wiloyati** *Rus.* Bukharskaya Oblast'. ◐ *province* C Uzbekistan
174 I12 **Bukitkemuning** Sumatera, W Indonesia
173 G8 **Bukittinggi** *prev.* Fort de Kock. Sumatera, W Indonesia
113 L21 **Bükk** ▲▲ NE Hungary
83 F19 **Bukoba** Kagera, NW Tanzania
115 N20 **Bukovo** S FYR Macedonia
110 G6 **Bülach** Zürich, NW Switzerland
Bülaevo *see* Bulayevo
168 I6 **Bulag** Hövsgöl, N Mongolia
168 M7 **Bulag** Töv, C Mongolia
168 I8 **Bulagiyn Denj** Arhangay, C Mongolia
191 U7 **Bulahdelah** New South Wales, SE Australia
176 Yy15 **Bulaka, Sungai** ∽ Irian Jaya, E Indonesia
179 Qq12 **Bulan** Luzon, N Philippines
143 N11 **Bulancak** Giresun, N Turkey
158 J10 **Bulandshahr** Uttar Pradesh, N India
143 R14 **Bulanık** Muş, E Turkey
131 U7 **Bulanovo** Orenburgskaya Oblast', W Russian Federation
85 J17 **Bulawayo** *var.* Buluwayo. Matabeleland North, SW Zimbabwe
85 J17 **Bulawayo** ✕ Matabeleland North, SW Zimbabwe
151 Q6 **Bulayevo** *Kaz.* Bülaevo. Severnyy Kazakhstan, N Kazakhstan
142 D15 **Buldan** Denizli, SW Turkey
160 G12 **Buldāna** Mahārāshtra, C India
40 E16 **Buldir Island** *island* Aleutian Islands, Alaska, USA
Buldur *see* Burdur
168 H9 **Bulgan** Bayanhongor, C Mongolia
168 K6 **Bulgan** Bulgan, N Mongolia
168 F7 **Bulgan** Hovd, W Mongolia
168 J5 **Bulgan** Hövsgöl, N Mongolia
168 J10 **Bulgan** Ömnögovĭ, S Mongolia
168 J7 **Bulgan** ◐ *province* N Mongolia
116 H10 **Bulgaria** *off.* Republic of Bulgaria, *Bul.* Bălgariya; *prev.* People's Republic of Bulgaria. ◆ *republic* SE Europe
Bŭlgariya *see* Bulgaria
116 L9 **Bŭlgarka** ▲ E Bulgaria
175 T7 **Buli** Pulau Halmahera, E Indonesia
175 Tt7 **Buli, Teluk** *bay* Pulau Halmahera, E Indonesia
166 J13 **Buliu He** ∽ S China
Bullange *see* Büllingen
106 M11 **Bullaque** ∽ C Spain
107 Q13 **Bullas** Murcia, SE Spain
82 M12 **Bullaxaar** Woqooyi Galbeed, NW Somalia
110 C9 **Bulle** Fribourg, SW Switzerland
193 G15 **Buller** ∽ South Island, NZ
191 P12 **Buller, Mount** ▲ Victoria, SE Australia
38 H11 **Bullhead City** Arizona, SW USA
101 N21 **Büllingen** *Fr.* Bullange. Liège, E Belgium
Bullion State *see* Missouri
23 T14 **Bull Island** *island* South Carolina, SE USA
190 M4 **Bulloo River Overflow** *wetland* New South Wales, SE Australia
192 M12 **Bulls** Manawatu-Wanganui, North Island, NZ
23 T14 **Bulls Bay** *bay* South Carolina, SE USA
29 U9 **Bull Shoals Lake** ⊡ Arkansas/Missouri, C USA
189 Q2 **Bulman** Northern Territory, N Australia
168 I6 **Bulnayn Nuruu** ▲▲ N Mongolia
194 I13 **Bulolo** Morobe, C PNG
175 Qq7 **Bulowa, Gunung** ▲ Sulawesi, N Indonesia
Bulqiza *see* Bulqizë
115 L19 **Bulqizë** *var.* Bulqiza. Dibër, C Albania
Bulsar *see* Valsād
175 R7 **Buludawa Keten, Pegunungan** ▲▲ Sulawesi, N Indonesia
175 Pp13 **Bulukumba** *prev.* Boeloekoemba. Sulawesi, C Indonesia
153 O11 **Bulunghur** *Rus.* Bulungur; *prev.* Krasnogvardeysk. Samarqand Wiloyati, C Uzbekistan
81 I21 **Bulungu** Bandundu, SW Zaire
Bulungur *see* Bulunghur
Buluwayo *see* Bulawayo
81 K17 **Bumba** Equateur, N Zaire
124 O15 **Bumbah, Khalīj al** *gulf* N Libya
168 K8 **Bumbat** Övörhangay, C Mongolia
83 F19 **Bumbire Island** *island* N Tanzania
175 Oo4 **Bum Bun, Pulau** *island* East Malaysia
83 J17 **Buna** North Eastern, NE Kenya
27 Y10 **Buna** Texas, SW USA
Bunab *see* Bonāb
Bunai *see* M'bunai
153 S13 **Bunay** S Tajikistan
188 I13 **Bunbury** Western Australia
99 E14 **Buncrana** *Ir.* Bun Cranncha. NW Ireland
Bun Cranncha *see* Buncrana
189 Z9 **Bundaberg** Queensland, E Australia
191 T5 **Bundarra** New South Wales, SE Australia
102 G13 **Bünde** Nordrhein-Westfalen, NW Germany
158 H13 **Bündi** Rājasthān, N India
194 I12 **Bundi** Madang, N PNG
Bun Dobhráin *see* Bundoran
99 D15 **Bundoran** *Ir.* Bun Dobhráin. NW Ireland
115 K18 **Bunë** *SCr.* Bojana. ∽ Albania/Yugoslavia *see also* Bojana
179 R16 **Bunga** ∽ Mindanao, S Philippines
173 Ff10 **Bungalaut, Selat** *strait* W Indonesia
178 I8 **Bung Kan** Nong Khai, E Thailand
189 N4 **Bungle Bungle Range** ▲▲ Western Australia
84 C10 **Bungo** Uíge, NW Angola
83 G18 **Bungoma** Western, W Kenya
170 Dd15 **Bungo-suidō** *strait* SW Japan
170 Dd13 **Bungo-Takada** Ōita, Kyūshū, SW Japan
102 K8 **Bungsberg** *hill* N Germany
Bungur *see* Bunyu
81 P17 **Bunia** Haut-Zaïre, NE Zaire
37 U6 **Bunker Hill** ▲ Nevada, W USA
24 I7 **Bunkie** Louisiana, S USA
25 X10 **Bunnell** Florida, SE USA
107 S10 **Buñol** País Valenciano, E Spain
100 K11 **Bunschoten** Utrecht, C Netherlands
142 K14 **Bünyan** Kayseri, C Turkey
175 Oo5 **Bunyu** *var.* Bungur. Borneo, N Indonesia
175 Oo5 **Bunyu, Pulau** *island* N Indonesia
Bunzlau *see* Bolesławiec
Buoddobohki *see* Patoniva
126 L6 **Buorkhaya Guba** *bay* N Russian Federation
176 Z15 **Bupul** Irian Jaya, E Indonesia
83 K19 **Bura** Coast, SE Kenya
82 P12 **Buraan** Sanaag, N Somalia
Būrabay *see* Borovoye
Buraida *see* Buraydah
Buraimi *see* Al Buraymi
151 Y11 **Buran** Vostochnyy Kazakhstan, E Kazakhstan
164 G15 **Burang** Xizang Zizhiqu, W China
Burao *see* Burco
144 I8 **Burāq** Dar'ā, S Syria
147 O6 **Buraydah** *var.* Buraida. Al Qaşīm, N Saudi Arabia
37 S15 **Burbank** California, W USA
33 N11 **Burbank** Illinois, N USA
191 Q8 **Burcher** New South Wales, SE Australia
82 N13 **Burco** *var.* Burao, Bur'o. Togdheer, NW Somalia
152 L13 **Burdalyk** Lebapskiy Velayat, E Turkmenistan
189 W6 **Burdekin River** ∽ Queensland, NE Australia
29 O7 **Burden** Kansas, C USA
Burdigala *see* Bordeaux
142 E15 **Burdur** *var.* Buldur. Burdur, SW Turkey
142 E15 **Burdur** *var.* Buldur. ◐ *province* SW Turkey
142 E15 **Burdur Gölü** *salt lake* SW Turkey
67 H21 **Burdwood Bank** *undersea feature* SW Atlantic Ocean
82 I12 **Burē** NW Ethiopia
82 H13 **Burē** W Ethiopia
95 J15 **Bureå** Västerbotten, N Sweden
103 G14 **Büren** Nordrhein-Westfalen, W Germany
168 K6 **Bürengiyn Nuruu** ▲▲ N Mongolia
168 E8 **Bürenhayrhan** Hovd, W Mongolia
Bürewāla *see* Mandi Būrewāla
127 N17 **Bureya** ∽ SE Russian Federation
94 J9 **Burfjord** Troms, N Norway
102 L13 **Burg** *var.* Burg an der Ihle, Burg bei Magdeburg. Sachsen-Anhalt, C Germany
Burg an der Ihle *see* Burg
116 N10 **Burgas** *var.* Bourgas. Burgaska Oblast, E Bulgaria
116 N9 **Burgas** ✕ Burgaska Oblast, E Bulgaria
Burgas *see* Burgaska Oblast
116 L9 **Burgaska Oblast** *var.* Burgas. ◐ *province* E Bulgaria
116 N10 **Burgaski Zaliv** *gulf* E Bulgaria
116 M10 **Burgasko Ezero** *lagoon* E Bulgaria
23 V11 **Burgaw** North Carolina, SE USA
Burg bei Magdeburg *see* Burg
110 E8 **Burgdorf** Bern, NW Switzerland
111 Y7 **Burgenland** *off.* Land Burgenland. ◐ *state* SE Austria
11 S13 **Burgeo** Newfoundland, Newfoundland and Labrador, SE Canada
85 I24 **Burgersdorp** Eastern Cape, SE South Africa
85 K20 **Burgersfort** Mpumalanga, NE South Africa
103 N23 **Burghausen** Bayern, SE Germany
145 O5 **Burghūth, Sabkhat al** ◎ E Syria
103 M20 **Burglengenfeld** Bayern, SE Germany
43 P9 **Burgos** Tamaulipas, C Mexico
107 N4 **Burgos** Castilla-León, N Spain
107 N4 **Burgos** ◐ *province* Castilla-León, N Spain
Burgstadlberg *see* Hradiště
97 P20 **Burgsvik** Gotland, SE Sweden
Burgum *see* Bergum
Burgundy *see* Bourgogne
165 Q11 **Burhan Budai Shan** ▲▲ C China
142 B12 **Burhaniye** Balıkesir, W Turkey
160 G12 **Burhānpur** Madhya Pradesh, C India
179 Q11 **Burias Island** *island* C Philippines
131 W7 **Buribay** Respublika Bashkortostan, W Russian Federation
45 O17 **Burica, Punta** *headland* Costa Rica/Panama
178 I10 **Buriram** *var.* Buri Ram, Puriramya. Buri Ram, E Thailand
107 S10 **Burjassot** País Valenciano, E Spain
83 N16 **Burka Giibi** Hiiraan, C Somalia
153 X8 **Burkan** ∽ E Kyrgyzstan
27 R4 **Burkburnett** Texas, SW USA
31 O12 **Burke** South Dakota, N USA
8 K15 **Burke Channel** *channel* British Columbia, W Canada
204 J10 **Burke Island** *island* Antarctica
22 L7 **Burkesville** Kentucky, S USA
189 T4 **Burketown** Queensland, NE Australia
27 Q8 **Burkett** Texas, SW USA
27 Y9 **Burkeville** Texas, SW USA
23 V7 **Burkeville** Virginia, NE USA
79 O12 **Burkina** *off.* Burkina Faso; *prev.* Upper Volta. ◆ *republic* W Africa
Burkina Faso *see* Burkina
204 L13 **Burks, Cape** *headland* Antarctica
12 H12 **Burk's Falls** Ontario, S Canada
103 H23 **Burladingen** Baden-Württemberg, S Germany
27 T7 **Burleson** Texas, SW USA
35 P15 **Burley** Idaho, NW USA
150 G8 **Burlin** Zapadnyy Kazakhstan, NW Kazakhstan
12 G16 **Burlington** Ontario, S Canada
39 W4 **Burlington** Colorado, C USA
31 Y15 **Burlington** Iowa, C USA
29 P5 **Burlington** Kansas, C USA
23 T9 **Burlington** North Carolina, SE USA
30 M3 **Burlington** North Dakota, N USA
20 L7 **Burlington** Vermont, NE USA
32 M9 **Burlington** Wisconsin, N USA
29 Q1 **Burlington Junction** Missouri, C USA
Burma *see* Myanmar
8 L17 **Burnaby** British Columbia, SW Canada
119 O12 **Burnas, Ozero** ◎ SW Ukraine
27 S10 **Burnet** Texas, SW USA
37 O3 **Burney** California, W USA
191 O16 **Burnie** Tasmania, SE Australia
99 L17 **Burnley** NW England, UK
151 Q16 **Burnoye** Zhambyl, S Kazakhstan
159 R15 **Burnpur** West Bengal, NE India
34 K14 **Burns** Oregon, NW USA
28 K11 **Burns Flat** Oklahoma, C USA
22 M7 **Burnside** Kentucky, S USA
15 I15 **Burnside** ∽ Northwest Territories, NW Canada
34 L15 **Burns Junction** Oregon, NW USA
8 L13 **Burns Lake** British Columbia, SW Canada
31 V9 **Burnsville** Minnesota, N USA
23 P9 **Burnsville** North Carolina, SE USA
23 R4 **Burnsville** West Virginia, NE USA
12 I13 **Burnt River** ∽ Ontario, SE Canada
12 I11 **Burntroot Lake** ◎ Ontario, SE Canada
9 W12 **Burntwood** ∽ Manitoba, C Canada
Bur'o *see* Burco
164 L2 **Burqin** Xinjiang Uygur Zizhiqu, NW China
190 J8 **Burra** South Australia
191 S9 **Burragorang, Lake** ⊡ New South Wales, SE Australia
98 K5 **Burray** *island* NE Scotland, UK
115 L19 **Burrel** *var.* Burreli. Dibër, C Albania
Burreli *see* Burrel
191 R8 **Burrendong Reservoir** ⊡ New South Wales, SE Australia
191 R5 **Burren Junction** New South Wales, SE Australia
107 T9 **Burriana** País Valenciano, E Spain
191 R10 **Burrinjuck Reservoir** ⊡ New South Wales, SE Australia
38 I12 **Burro Creek** ∽ Arizona, SW USA
42 M5 **Burro, Serranías del** ▲▲ NW Mexico
64 K7 **Burruyacú** Tucumán, N Argentina
142 E12 **Bursa** *var.* Brussa; *prev.* Brusa, *anc.* Prusa. Bursa, NW Turkey
142 D12 **Bursa** *var.* Brusa, Brussa. ◐ *province* NW Turkey
77 Y9 **Būr Safāga** *var.* Būr Safājah. E Egypt
Būr Safājah *see* Būr Safāga
Būr Sa'īd *see* Port Said
83 O14 **Bur Tinle** Mudug, C Somalia
33 Q5 **Burt Lake** ◎ Michigan, N USA
Burtnieks *see* Burtnieku Ezers
120 H7 **Burtnieku Ezers** *var.* Burtnieks. ◎ N Latvia
33 Q9 **Burton** Michigan, N USA
Burton on Trent *see* Burton upon Trent
99 M19 **Burton upon Trent** *var.* Burton on Trent, Burton-upon-Trent. C England, UK
95 J15 **Burträsk** Västerbotten, N Sweden
151 S14 **Burubaytal** *prev.* Burylbaytal. Zhambyl, SE Kazakhstan
Burujird *see* Borūjerd
Burultokay *see* Fuhai
147 R15 **Burūm** SE Yemen
151 U16 **Burunday** *Kaz.* Boralday. Almaty, SE Kazakhstan
83 D21 **Burundi** *off.* Republic of Burundi; *prev.* Kingdom of Burundi, Urundi. ◆ *republic* C Africa
175 S11 **Buru, Pulau** *prev.* Boeroe. *island* E Indonesia
79 T17 **Burutu** Delta, S Nigeria
8 G7 **Burwash Landing** Yukon Territory, W Canada
31 O14 **Burwell** Nebraska, C USA
99 L17 **Bury** NW England, UK
126 K15 **Buryatiya, Respublika** *prev.* Buryatskaya ASSR. ◐ *autonomous republic* S Russian Federation
Buryatskaya ASSR *see* Buryatiya, Respublika
Burylbaytal *see* Burubaytal
119 S3 **Buryn'** Sums'ka Oblast', NE Ukraine
99 P20 **Bury St Edmunds** *hist.* Beodericsworth. E England, UK
116 G8 **Bŭrziya** ∽ NW Bulgaria
108 D9 **Busalla** Liguria, NW Italy
179 R17 **Busa, Mount** ▲ Mindanao, S Philippines
Busan *see* Pusan
145 N5 **Buşayrah** Dayr az Zawr, E Syria
Buševa *see* Baba
149 N12 **Būshehr** *off.* Ostān-e Būshehr. ◐ *province* SW Iran
Būshehr/Bushire *see* Bandar-e Būshehr
27 N2 **Bushland** Texas, SW USA
32 J12 **Bushnell** Illinois, N USA
Busi *see* Biševo
83 G18 **Busia** SE Uganda
Busiasch *see* Buziaş
81 K16 **Businga** Equateur, NW Zaire
81 J18 **Busira** ∽ NW Zaire
118 I5 **Bus'k** *Rus.* Busk. L'vivs'ka Oblast', W Ukraine
97 E14 **Buskerud** ◐ *county* S Norway
115 F14 **Buško Jezero** ⊡ SW Bosnia and Herzegovina
113 M15 **Busko-Zdrój** Kielce, SE Poland
Busra *see* Al Başrah, Iraq
Buşrá *see* Buşrá ash Shām, Syria
144 H9 **Buşrá ash Shām** *var.* Bosora, Bosra, Bozrah, Buşrá. Dar'ā, S Syria
188 I13 **Busselton** Western Australia
83 C14 **Busseri** ∽ W Sudan
108 F9 **Busseto** Emilia-Romagna, C Italy
108 A8 **Bussoleno** Piemonte, NE Italy
Bussora *see* Al Başrah
100 J10 **Bussum** Noord-Holland, C Netherlands
43 N7 **Bustamante** Nuevo León, NE Mexico
65 I23 **Bustamante, Punta** *headland* S Argentina
Bustan *see* Bŭston
118 J12 **Buşteni** Prahova, SE Romania
108 D7 **Busto Arsizio** Lombardia, N Italy
153 Q10 **Bŭston** *Rus.* Buston. NW Tajikistan
152 I9 **Bŭston** *Rus.* Bustan. Qoraqalpoghiston Respublikasi, W Uzbekistan
179 P12 **Busuanga Island** *island* Calamian Group, W Philippines
102 H8 **Büsum** Schleswig-Holstein, N Germany
81 M16 **Buta** Haut-Zaïre, N Zaire
83 E20 **Butare** *prev.* Astrida. S Rwanda
203 O2 **Butaritari** *atoll* Tungaru, W Kiribati
Butawal *see* Butwal

◆ Country ● Country Capital ◇ Dependent Territory ○ Dependent Territory Capital ◐ Administrative Region ✕ International Airport ▲ Mountain ▲▲ Mountain Range Volcano ∽ River ◎ Lake ⊡ Reservoir

BUTE – CAMPBELLSVILLE

98 H13 **Bute** cultural region SW Scotland, UK
168 K6 **Büteeliyn Nuruu** ▲ N Mongolia
8 L16 **Bute Inlet** fjord British Columbia, W Canada
98 H12 **Bute, Island of** island SW Scotland, UK
81 P18 **Butembo** Nord Kivu, NE Zaire
Bûtenpost see Buitenpost
109 K25 **Butera** Sicilia, Italy, C Mediterranean Sea
101 M20 **Bütgenbach** Liège, E Belgium
Butha Qi see Zalantun
177 F5 **Buthidaung** Arakan State, W Myanmar
63 I16 **Butiá** Rio Grande do Sul, S Brazil
83 F17 **Butiaba** NW Uganda
25 N6 **Butler** Alabama, S USA
25 S5 **Butler** Georgia, SE USA
33 Q11 **Butler** Indiana, N USA
29 R5 **Butler** Missouri, C USA
20 B14 **Butler** Pennsylvania, NE USA
204 K5 **Butler Island** island Antarctica
23 U8 **Butner** North Carolina, SE USA
175 Qq13 **Buton, Pulau** var. Pulau Butung; prev. Boetoeng. island C Indonesia
175 Qq13 **Buton, Selat** strait C Indonesia
Bütow see Bytów
115 L23 **Butrintit, Liqeni i** ◎ S Albania
25 N3 **Buttahatchee River** ≈ Alabama/Mississippi, S USA
35 Q10 **Butte** Montana, NW USA
31 O12 **Butte** Nebraska, C USA
173 G3 **Butterworth** Pinang, Peninsular Malaysia
85 J25 **Butterworth** var. Gcuwa. Eastern Cape, SE South Africa
11 O3 **Button Islands** island group Northwest Territories, NE Canada
37 R13 **Buttonwillow** California, W USA
179 R14 **Butuan** off. Butuan City. Mindanao, S Philippines
Butung, Pulau see Buton, Pulau
Butuntum see Bitonto
130 M8 **Buturlinovka** Voronezhskaya Oblast', W Russian Federation
159 O11 **Butwal** var. Butawal. Western, C Nepal
103 G17 **Butzbach** Hessen, W Germany
102 L9 **Bützow** Mecklenburg-Vorpommern, N Germany
82 N13 **Buuhoodle** Togdheer, N Somalia
83 N16 **Buulobarde** var. Buulo Berde. Hiiraan, C Somalia Africa
Buulo Berde see Buulobarde
82 P12 **Buuraha Cal Miskaat** ▲▲ NE Somalia
83 L19 **Buur Gaabo** Jubbada Hoose, S Somalia
101 M22 **Buurgplaatz** ▲ N Luxembourg
Buwayrat al Hasūn see Bu'ayrāt al Ḩasūn
102 I10 **Buxtehude** Niedersachsen, NW Germany
99 L18 **Buxton** C England, UK
128 M14 **Buy** var. Buj. Kostromskaya Oblast', NW Russian Federation
168 G7 **Buyanbat** Govĭ-Altay, W Mongolia
168 H8 **Buyant** Bayanhongor, C Mongolia
168 D6 **Buyant** Bayan-Ölgiy, W Mongolia
168 H7 **Buyant** Dzavhan, C Mongolia
169 N9 **Buyant** Hentiy, C Mongolia
169 N10 **Buyant-Uhaa** Dornogovĭ, SE Mongolia
168 M7 **Buyant Ukha** × (Ulaanbaatar) Töv, N Mongolia
131 Q16 **Buynaksk** Respublika Dagestan, SW Russian Federation
121 L20 **Buynavichy** Rus. Buynovichi. Homyel'skaya Voblasts', SE Belarus
Buynovichi see Buynavichy
78 L16 **Buyo** SW Ivory Coast
78 L16 **Buyo, Lac de** ⊟ W Ivory Coast
169 R7 **Buyr Nuur** var. Buir Nur. ◎ China/Mongolia see also Buir Nur
143 T13 **Büyükağrı Dağı** var. Aghri Dagh, Agri Dagi, Koh I Noh, Masis, Eng. Great Ararat, Mount Ararat. ▲ E Turkey
143 R15 **Büyük Çayı** ≈ NE Turkey
116 O13 **Büyük Çekmece** İstanbul, NW Turkey
116 N12 **Büyükkarıştıran** Kırklareli, NW Turkey
117 L14 **Büyükkemikli Burnu** headland NW Turkey
142 E15 **Büyükmenderes Nehri** ≈ SW Turkey
Büyükzap Suyu see Great Zab
104 M9 **Buzançais** Indre, C France
118 K13 **Buzău** Buzău, SE Romania
118 K13 **Buzău** ◈ county SE Romania
118 L12 **Buzău** ≈ E Romania
77 S11 **Buzaymah** var. Bzīmah. SE Libya
170 D13 **Buzen** Fukuoka, Kyūshū, SW Japan
118 F12 **Buziaș** Ger. Busiasch, Hung. Buziásfürdő; prev. Buziás. Timiș, W Romania
Buziásfürdő see Buziaș
85 M18 **Búzi, Rio** ≈ C Mozambique
119 Q10 **Buz'kyy Lyman** bay S Ukraine
Büzmeyin see Byuzmeyin
151 O8 **Buzuluk** Turgay, C Kazakhstan
131 T6 **Buzuluk** Orenburgskaya Oblast', W Russian Federation
131 N8 **Buzuluk** ≈ SW Russian Federation
21 P12 **Buzzards Bay** Massachusetts, NE USA
21 P13 **Buzzards Bay** bay Massachusetts, NE USA
85 G16 **Bwabata** Caprivi, NE Namibia
195 P17 **Bwagaoia** Misima Island, SE PNG
Bwake see Bouaké
197 C12 **Bwatnapne** Pentecost, C Vanuatu
121 K14 **Byahoml'** Rus. Begoml'. Vitsyebskaya Voblasts', N Belarus
116 J8 **Byala** Razgradska Oblast, N Bulgaria
116 N9 **Byala** prev. Ak-Dere. Varnenska Oblast, NE Bulgaria
Byala Reka see Erydropótamos
116 H8 **Byala Slatina** Oblast Montana, NW Bulgaria
121 N15 **Byalynichy** Rus. Belynichi. Mahilyowskaya Voblasts', E Belarus
Bybles see Jbail
121 G19 **Byaroza** Pol. Bereza Kartuska, Rus. Berëza. Brestskaya Voblasts', SW Belarus
113 O14 **Bychawa** Lublin, SE Poland
Bychikha see Bychykha
120 N11 **Bychykha** Rus. Bychikha. Vitsyebskaya Voblasts', NE Belarus
113 I14 **Byczyna** Ger. Pitschen. Opole, SW Poland
Bydgoskie, Województwo see Bydgoszcz
112 I10 **Bydgoszcz** Ger. Bromberg. Bydgoszcz, W Poland
112 H9 **Bydgoszcz** off. Województwo Bydgoskie, Ger. Bromberg. ◈ province W Poland
121 I17 **Byelaruskaya Hrada** Rus. Belorusskaya Gryada. ridge N Belarus
121 G18 **Byelavyezhskaya Pushcha** Pol. Puszcza Białowieska, Rus. Belovezhskaya Pushcha. forest Belarus/Poland see also Białowieska, Puszcza
121 H15 **Byenyakoni** Rus. Benyakoni. Hrodzyenskaya Voblasts', W Belarus
121 M16 **Byerazino** Rus. Berezino. Minskaya Voblasts', C Belarus
120 L13 **Byerazino** Rus. Berezino. Vitsyebskaya Voblasts', N Belarus
121 L14 **Byerezino** Rus. Berezina. ≈ C Belarus
120 M13 **Byeshankovichy** Rus. Beshenkovichi. Vitsyebskaya Voblasts', N Belarus
33 U13 **Byesville** Ohio, N USA
121 P18 **Byesyedz'** Rus. Besed'. ≈ SE Belarus
121 H19 **Byezdzyezh** Rus. Bezdezh. Brestskaya Voblasts', SW Belarus
95 J15 **Bygdeå** Västerbotten, N Sweden
96 E12 **Bygdin** ◎ S Norway
95 J15 **Bygdsiljum** Västerbotten, N Sweden
97 E17 **Bygland** Aust-Agder, S Norway
97 E17 **Byglandsfjord** Aust-Agder, S Norway
121 N16 **Bykhaw** Rus. Bykhov. Mahilyowskaya Voblasts', E Belarus
Bykhov see Bykhaw
131 P9 **Bykovo** Volgogradskaya Oblast', SW Russian Federation
126 L6 **Bykovskiy** Respublika Sakha (Yakutiya), NE Russian Federation
205 R12 **Byrd Glacier** glacier Antarctica
12 K10 **Byrd, Lac** ◎ Québec, SE Canada
191 P5 **Byrock** New South Wales, SE Australia
32 L10 **Byron** Illinois, N USA
191 V4 **Byron Bay** New South Wales, SE Australia
191 V4 **Byron, Cape** headland New South Wales, E Australia
65 F21 **Byron, Isla** island S Chile
Byron Island see Nikunau
67 B24 **Byron Sound** sound NW Falkland Islands
126 J5 **Byrranga, Gora** ▲▲ N Russian Federation
95 J14 **Byske** Västerbotten, N Sweden
113 K18 **Bystrá** ▲ N Slovakia
113 F18 **Bystřice nad Pernštejnem** Ger. Bistritz ober Pernstein. Jižní Morava, SE Czech Republic
Bystrovka see Kemin
113 G16 **Bystrzyca Kłodzka** Ger. Habelschwerdt. Wałbrzych, SW Poland
113 I18 **Bytča** Stredné Slovensko, NW Slovakia
121 L15 **Bytcha** Rus. Bytcha. Minskaya Voblasts', NE Belarus
Byteń/Byten' see Bytsyen'
113 J16 **Bytom** Ger. Beuthen. Katowice, S Poland
112 H7 **Bytów** Ger. Bütow. Słupsk, NW Poland
121 H18 **Bytsyen'** Pol. Byteń, Rus. Byten'. Brestskaya Voblasts', SW Belarus
83 E19 **Byumba** var. Biumba. N Rwanda
152 F13 **Byuzmeyin** Turkm. Büzmeyin; prev. Bezmein. Akhalskiy Velayat, C Turkmenistan
121 O20 **Byval'ki** Homyel'skaya Voblasts', SE Belarus
97 O20 **Byxelkrok** Kalmar, S Sweden
Byzantium see İstanbul
Bzīmah see Buzaymah

C

64 O6 **Caacupé** Cordillera, S Paraguay
64 P6 **Caaguazú** off. Departamento de Caaguazú. ◈ department C Paraguay
84 C13 **Caála** var. Kaala, Robert Williams, Port. Vila Robert Williams. Huambo, C Angola
64 P7 **Caazapá** Caazapá, S Paraguay
64 P7 **Caazapá** off. Departamento de Caazapá. ◈ department SE Paraguay
83 P15 **Cabaad, Raas** headland C Somalia
179 R14 **Cabadbaran** Mindanao, S Philippines
57 N10 **Cabadisocaña** Amazonas, S Venezuela
46 F5 **Cabaiguán** Sancti Spíritus, C Cuba
Caballeria, Cabo see Cavalleria, Cap de
39 Q14 **Caballo Reservoir** ⊟ New Mexico, SW USA
42 L6 **Caballos Mesteños, Llano de los** plain N Mexico
106 L2 **Cabañaquinta** Asturias, N Spain
44 B9 **Cabañas** ◈ department E El Salvador
179 P10 **Cabanatuan** off. Cabanatuan City. Luzon, N Philippines
13 T8 **Cabano** Québec, SE Canada
106 L11 **Cabeza del Buey** Extremadura, W Spain
47 V5 **Cabezas de San Juan** headland E Puerto Rico
107 N2 **Cabezón de la Sal** Cantabria, N Spain
Cabhán see Cavan
63 B23 **Cabildo** Buenos Aires, E Argentina
Cabillonum see Chalon-sur-Saône
56 H5 **Cabimas** Zulia, NW Venezuela
84 A9 **Cabinda** var. Kabinda. Cabinda, NW Angola
84 A9 **Cabinda** var. Kabinda. ◈ province NW Angola
35 N7 **Cabinet Mountains** ▲▲ Idaho/Montana, NW USA
84 B11 **Cabiri** Bengo, NW Angola
65 J20 **Cabo Blanco** Santa Cruz, SE Argentina
84 P13 **Cabo Delgado** off. Província de Cabo Delgado. ◈ province NE Mozambique
12 L9 **Cabonga, Réservoir** ⊟ Québec, SE Canada
29 V7 **Cabool** Missouri, C USA
191 V2 **Caboolture** Queensland, E Australia
Cabora Bassa, Lake see Cahora Bassa, Albufeira de
42 F3 **Caborca** Sonora, NW Mexico
Cabo San Lucas see San Lucas
29 V11 **Cabot** Arkansas, C USA
12 F12 **Cabot Head** headland Ontario, S Canada
16 Ss10 **Cabot Strait** strait E Canada
Cabo Verde, Ilhas do see Cape Verde
106 M14 **Cabra** Andalucía, S Spain
109 B19 **Cabras** Sardegna, Italy, C Mediterranean Sea
196 A15 **Cabras Island** island W Guam
47 O8 **Cabrera** N Dominican Republic
107 X10 **Cabrera** anc. Capraria. island Islas Baleares, Spain, W Mediterranean Sea
106 J4 **Cabrera** ≈ NW Spain
107 Q15 **Cabrera, Sierra** ▲▲ S Spain
9 S16 **Cabri** Saskatchewan, S Canada
107 R10 **Cabriel** ≈ E Spain
57 M7 **Cabruta** Guárico, C Venezuela
179 Oo8 **Cabugao** Luzon, N Philippines
56 G10 **Cabuyaro** Meta, C Colombia
62 I13 **Caçador** Santa Catarina, S Brazil
44 G8 **Cacaguatique, Cordillera** var. Cordillera. ▲▲ NE El Salvador
114 L13 **Čačak** Serbia, C Yugoslavia
57 Y10 **Cacao** NE French Guiana
63 H16 **Caçapava do Sul** Rio Grande do Sul, S Brazil
23 U3 **Cacapon River** ≈ West Virginia, NE USA
109 J23 **Caccamo** Sicilia, Italy, C Mediterranean Sea
109 A17 **Caccia, Capo** headland Sardegna, Italy, C Mediterranean Sea
61 G18 **Cáceres** Mato Grosso, W Brazil
106 J10 **Cáceres** Ar. Qazris. Extremadura, W Spain
106 J9 **Cáceres** ◈ province Extremadura, W Spain
Cachacrou see Scotts Head Village
63 C21 **Cacharí** Buenos Aires, E Argentina
28 L12 **Cache** Oklahoma, C USA
8 M16 **Cache Creek** British Columbia, SW Canada
37 N6 **Cache Creek** ≈ California, W USA
39 S3 **Cache La Poudre River** ≈ Colorado, C USA
Cacheo see Cacheu
29 W11 **Cache River** ≈ Arkansas, C USA
32 L17 **Cache River** ≈ Illinois, N USA
78 G12 **Cacheu** var. Cacheo. W Guinea-Bissau
61 I15 **Cachimbo** Pará, NE Brazil
61 H15 **Cachimbo, Serra do** ▲▲ C Brazil
84 D13 **Cachingues** Bié, C Angola
56 G7 **Cáchira** Norte de Santander, N Colombia
63 H16 **Cachoeira do Sul** Rio Grande do Sul, S Brazil
61 O20 **Cachoeiro de Itapemirim** Espírito Santo, SE Brazil
84 E12 **Cacolo** Lunda Sul, NE Angola
85 C14 **Caconda** Huíla, C Angola
84 A9 **Cacongo** Cabinda, NW Angola
37 U9 **Cactus Peak** ▲ Nevada, W USA
84 A11 **Cacuaco** Luanda, NW Angola
85 B14 **Cacula** Huíla, SW Angola
69 R12 **Caculuvar** ≈ SW Angola
61 O19 **Caçumba, Ilha** island SE Brazil
57 N10 **Cacuri** Amazonas, S Venezuela
83 N17 **Cadale** Shabeellaha Dhexe, E Somalia
107 X4 **Cadaqués** Cataluña, NE Spain
113 J18 **Čadca** Hung. Csaca. Stredné Slovensko, N Slovakia
29 P13 **Caddo** Oklahoma, C USA
27 R6 **Caddo** Texas, SW USA
27 X6 **Caddo Lake** ⊟ Louisiana/Texas, SW USA
29 S12 **Caddo Mountains** ▲▲ Arkansas, C USA
43 O8 **Cadereyta** Nuevo León, NE Mexico
99 J19 **Cader Idris** ▲ NW Wales, United Kingdom
190 F3 **Cadibarrawirracanna, Lake** salt lake South Australia
12 J7 **Cadillac** Québec, SE Canada
9 T17 **Cadillac** Saskatchewan, S Canada
104 K13 **Cadillac** Gironde, SW France
33 P7 **Cadillac** Michigan, N USA
107 V4 **Cadí, Torre de** ▲ NE Spain
179 Q13 **Cadiz** off. Cadiz City. Negros, C Philippines
22 H7 **Cadiz** Kentucky, S USA
33 U13 **Cadiz** Ohio, N USA
106 J15 **Cádiz** anc. Gades, Gadier, Gadir, Gadire. Andalucía, SW Spain
106 K15 **Cádiz** ◈ province Andalucía, SW Spain
106 I15 **Cadiz, Bahía de** bay SW Spain
Cadiz City see Cadiz
106 H15 **Cádiz, Golfo de** Eng. Gulf of Cadiz. gulf Portugal/Spain
Cadiz, Gulf of see Cádiz, Golfo de
37 X14 **Cadiz Lake** ◎ California, W USA
190 E2 **Cadney Homestead** South Australia
Cadurcum see Cahors
85 F17 **Caecae** Ngamiland, NW Botswana
104 K4 **Caen** Calvados, N France
Caene/Caenepolis see Qena
Caerdydd see Cardiff
Caer Glou see Gloucester
Caer Gybi see Holyhead
Caerleon see Chester
Caer Luel see Carlisle
99 I18 **Caernarfon** var. Caernarvon, Carnarvon. NW Wales, UK
99 H18 **Caernarfon Bay** bay NW Wales, UK
99 I19 **Caernarvon** cultural region NW Wales, UK
Caernarvon see Caernarfon
Caesaraugusta see Zaragoza
Caesarea Mazaca see Kayseri
Caesarobriga see Talavera de la Reina
Caesarodunum see Tours
Caesaromagus see Beauvais
Caesena see Cesena
61 N17 **Caetité** Bahia, E Brazil
64 J6 **Cafayate** Salta, N Argentina
179 Pp9 **Cagayan** ≈ Luzon, N Philippines
179 R15 **Cagayan de Oro** off. Cagayan de Oro City. Mindanao, S Philippines
179 Oo17 **Cagayan de Tawi Tawi** island S Philippines
179 Pp14 **Cagayan Islands** island group C Philippines
33 O14 **Cagles Mill Lake** ⊟ Indiana, N USA
108 I12 **Cagli** Marche, C Italy
109 C20 **Cagliari** anc. Caralis. Sardegna, Italy, C Mediterranean Sea
109 C20 **Cagliari, Golfo di** gulf Sardegna, Italy, C Mediterranean Sea
105 U15 **Cagnes-sur-Mer** Alpes-Maritimes, SE France
56 L5 **Cagua** Aragua, N Venezuela
179 Pp8 **Cagua, Mount** ▲ Luzon, N Philippines
56 F13 **Caguán, Río** ≈ SW Colombia
47 U6 **Caguas** E Puerto Rico
25 P5 **Cahaba River** ≈ Alabama, S USA
44 E5 **Cahabón, Río** ≈ C Guatemala
85 B15 **Cahama** Cunene, SW Angola
99 B21 **Caha Mountains** Ir. An Cheacha. ▲▲ SW Ireland
99 D20 **Caher** Ir. An Cathair. S Ireland
99 A21 **Cahersiveen** Ir. Cathair Saidhbhín. SW Ireland
32 K15 **Cahokia** Illinois, N USA
85 L15 **Cahora Bassa, Albufeira de** var. Lake Cabora Bassa. ⊟ NW Mozambique
99 G20 **Cahore Point** Ir. Rinn Chathóir. headland SE Ireland
104 M14 **Cahors** anc. Cadurcum. Lot, S France
58 D9 **Cahuapanas, Río** ≈ N Peru
118 M12 **Cahul** Rus. Kagul. S Moldova
Cahul, Lacul see Kahul, Ozero
85 N16 **Caia** Sofala, C Mozambique
61 J19 **Caiapó, Serra do** ▲▲ C Brazil
46 F5 **Caibarién** Villa Clara, C Cuba
57 O5 **Caicara** Monagas, NE Venezuela
61 P14 **Caicó** Rio Grande do Norte, E Brazil
46 M6 **Caicos Islands** island group W Turks and Caicos Islands
46 L5 **Caicos Passage** strait Bahamas/Turks and Caicos Islands
167 O9 **Caidian** prev. Hanyang. Hubei, C China
Caiffa see Ḩefa
188 M12 **Caiguna** Western Australia
Caillí, Ceann see Hag's Head
42 J11 **Caimanero, Laguna del** var. Laguna del Camaronero. lagoon E Pacific Ocean
119 N10 **Căinari** Rus. Kaynary. C Moldova
59 L19 **Caine, Río** ≈ C Bolivia
Caiphas see Ḩefa
205 N4 **Caird Coast** physical region Antarctica
98 J9 **Cairn Gorm** ▲ C Scotland, UK
98 J9 **Cairngorm Mountains** ▲▲ C Scotland, UK
41 P12 **Cairn Mountain** ▲ Alaska, USA
189 W4 **Cairns** Queensland, NE Australia
124 Qq16 **Cairo** Ar. Al Qāhirah, var. El Qâhira. ● (Egypt) N Egypt
25 T8 **Cairo** Georgia, SE USA
32 L17 **Cairo** Illinois, N USA
77 V8 **Cairo** × C Egypt
Caiseal see Cashel
Caisleán an Bharraigh see Castlebar
Caisleán na Finne see Castlefinn
98 J6 **Caithness** cultural region N Scotland, UK
85 D15 **Caiundo** Cuando Cubango, S Angola
58 C11 **Cajamarca** prev. Caxamarca. Cajamarca, NW Peru
58 B11 **Cajamarca** off. Departamento de Cajamarca. ◈ department N Peru
105 N14 **Cajarc** Lot, S France
179 Q12 **Cajidiocan** Sibuyan Island, C Philippines
44 G6 **Cajón, Represa El** ⊟ NW Honduras
60 N12 **Caju, Ilha do** island NE Brazil
Cakaubalavu Reef see Kavukavu Reef
165 R10 **Caka Yanhu** ◎ C China
114 E7 **Čakovec** Ger. Csakathurn, Hung. Csáktornya; prev. Ger. Tschakathurn. Medimurje, N Croatia
79 V17 **Calabar** Cross River, S Nigeria
12 K13 **Calabogie** Ontario, SE Canada
56 L6 **Calabozo** Guárico, C Venezuela
109 N20 **Calabria** anc. Bruttium. ◈ region SW Italy
106 M16 **Calaburra, Punta de** headland S Spain
118 G14 **Calafat** Dolj, SW Romania
Calafate see El Calafate
107 Q4 **Calahorra** La Rioja, N Spain
105 N1 **Calais** Pas-de-Calais, N France
21 T5 **Calais** Maine, NE USA
Calais, Pas de see Dover, Strait of
Calalen see Kallalen
64 H4 **Calama** Antofagasta, N Chile
Calamianes see Calamian Group
179 P13 **Calamian Group** var. Calamianes. island group W Philippines
107 R7 **Calamocha** Aragón, NE Spain
31 N14 **Calamus River** ≈ Nebraska, C USA
118 G12 **Călan** Ger. Kalan, Hung. Pusztakalán. Hunedoara, SW Romania
107 S7 **Calanda** Aragón, NE Spain
173 E4 **Calang** Sumatera, W Indonesia
179 P11 **Calapan** Mindoro, N Philippines
Călăras see Călărași
118 M9 **Călărași** var. Călăras, Rus. Kalarash. C Moldova
118 L14 **Călărași** Călărași, SE Romania
118 K14 **Călărași** ◈ county SE Romania
56 E10 **Calarca** Quindío, W Colombia
107 Q12 **Calasparra** Murcia, SE Spain
109 I23 **Calatafimi** Sicilia, Italy, C Mediterranean Sea
107 Q6 **Calatayud** Aragón, NE Spain
179 Pp11 **Calauag** Luzon, N Philippines
37 P8 **Calaveras River** ≈ California, W USA
179 Oo11 **Calavite, Cape** headland Mindoro, N Philippines
179 Qq12 **Calbayog** off. Calbayog City. Samar, C Philippines
179 R12 **Calbiga** Samar, C Philippines
24 G9 **Calcasieu Lake** ◎ Louisiana, S USA
24 H8 **Calcasieu River** ≈ Louisiana, S USA
58 B6 **Calceta** Manabí, W Ecuador
63 B16 **Calchaquí** Santa Fe, C Argentina
64 J6 **Calchaquí, Río** ≈ NW Argentina
60 J10 **Calçoene** Amapá, NE Brazil
159 S16 **Calcutta** West Bengal, NE India
159 S16 **Calcutta** × West Bengal, N India
56 E9 **Caldas** off. Departamento de Caldas. ◈ province W Colombia
106 F10 **Caldas da Rainha** Leiria, W Portugal
106 G3 **Caldas de Reis** var. Caldas de Reyes. Galicia, NW Spain
Caldas de Reyes see Caldas de Reis
60 F13 **Caldeirão** Amazonas, NW Brazil
64 G7 **Caldera** Atacama, N Chile
44 L14 **Caldera** Puntarenas, W Costa Rica
107 N10 **Calderina** ▲ C Spain
143 T13 **Çaldıran** Van, E Turkey
34 M14 **Caldwell** Idaho, NW USA
29 N8 **Caldwell** Kansas, C USA
12 G15 **Caledon** Ontario, S Canada
85 I23 **Caledon** var. Mohokare. ≈ Lesotho/South Africa
44 G1 **Caledonia** Corozal, N Belize
12 G16 **Caledonia** Ontario, S Canada
31 X11 **Caledonia** Minnesota, N USA
107 X5 **Calella** var. Calella de la Costa. Cataluña, NE Spain
Calella de la Costa see Calella
25 P4 **Calera** Alabama, S USA
65 I19 **Caleta Olivia** Santa Cruz, SE Argentina
37 X17 **Calexico** California, W USA
99 H16 **Calf of Man** island SW Isle of Man
9 Q16 **Calgary** Alberta, SW Canada
9 Q16 **Calgary** × Alberta, SW Canada
39 U5 **Calhan** Colorado, C USA
66 O5 **Calheta** Madeira, Portugal, NE Atlantic Ocean
25 R2 **Calhoun** Georgia, SE USA
22 I6 **Calhoun** Kentucky, S USA
24 M3 **Calhoun City** Mississippi, S USA
23 P12 **Calhoun Falls** South Carolina, SE USA
56 D11 **Cali** Valle del Cauca, W Colombia
29 V9 **Calico Rock** Arkansas, C USA
161 F21 **Calicut** var. Kozhikode. Kerala, SW India
37 Y9 **Caliente** Nevada, W USA
29 U5 **California** Missouri, C USA
20 B15 **California** Pennsylvania, NE USA
37 Q12 **California** off. State of California; also known as El Dorado, The Golden State. ◈ state W USA
37 P11 **California Aqueduct** aqueduct California, W USA
37 T13 **California City** California, W USA
42 F6 **California, Golfo de** Eng. Gulf of California; prev. Sea of Cortez. gulf W Mexico
California, Gulf of see California, Golfo de
143 Y13 **Călilabad** Rus. Dzhalilabad; prev. Astrakhan-Bazar. S Azerbaijan
118 I12 **Călimănești** Vâlcea, SW Romania
118 J9 **Călimani, Munții** ▲▲ N Romania
Calinisc see Cupcina
37 X17 **Calipatria** California, W USA
Calisia see Kalisz
36 M7 **Calistoga** California, W USA
85 G25 **Calitzdorp** Western Cape, SW South Africa
43 W12 **Calkiní** Campeche, E Mexico
190 K4 **Callabonna Creek** var. Tilcha Creek. seasonal river New South Wales/South Australia
190 J4 **Callabonna, Lake** ◎ South Australia
104 G5 **Callac** Côtes d'Armor, NW France
37 U5 **Callaghan, Mount** ▲ Nevada, W USA
Callain see Callan
99 E19 **Callan** Ir. Callain. S Ireland
12 H11 **Callander** Ontario, S Canada
98 I11 **Callander** C Scotland, UK
100 H7 **Callantsoog** Noord-Holland, NW Netherlands
59 D14 **Callao** Callao, W Peru
59 D15 **Callao** off. Departamento del Callao. ◈ constitutional province W Peru
58 F11 **Callaria, Río** ≈ E Peru
Callatis see Mangalia
9 Q13 **Calling Lake** Alberta, W Canada
Callosa de Ensarriá see Callosa d'En Sarrià
107 T11 **Callosa d'En Sarrià** var. Callosa de Ensarriá. País Valenciano, E Spain
107 S12 **Callosa de Segura** País Valenciano, E Spain
31 X11 **Calmar** Iowa, C USA
Calmar see Kalmar
45 R16 **Calobre** Veraguas, C Panama
179 P10 **Caloocan** municipality Luzon, N Philippines
25 X14 **Caloosahatchee River** ≈ Florida, SE USA
191 V2 **Caloundra** Queensland, E Australia
107 T11 **Calpe** País Valenciano, E Spain
43 P14 **Calpulalpan** Tlaxcala, S Mexico
109 K25 **Caltagirone** Sicilia, Italy, C Mediterranean Sea
109 J24 **Caltanissetta** Sicilia, Italy, C Mediterranean Sea
84 E11 **Caluango** Lunda Norte, NE Angola
84 C12 **Calucinga** Bié, W Angola
84 B12 **Calulo** Cuanza Sul, NW Angola
85 B14 **Caluquembe** Huíla, W Angola
82 Q11 **Caluula** Bari, NE Somalia
104 K4 **Calvados** ◈ department N France
195 P17 **Calvados Chain, The** island group SE PNG
27 U9 **Calvert** Texas, SW USA
22 H7 **Calvert City** Kentucky, S USA
104 E1 **Calvi** Corse, France, C Mediterranean Sea
42 L12 **Calvillo** Aguascalientes, C Mexico
85 F24 **Calvinia** Northern Cape, W South Africa
106 K8 **Calvitero** ▲ W Spain
103 G22 **Calw** Baden-Württemberg, SW Germany
Calydon see Kalydón
107 N11 **Calzada de Calatrava** Castilla-La Mancha, C Spain
Cama see Kama
84 C11 **Camabatela** Cuanza Norte, NW Angola
66 Q5 **Camacha** Porto Santo, Madeira, Portugal, NE Atlantic Ocean
12 L8 **Camachigama, Lac** ◎ Québec, SE Canada
42 M9 **Camacho** Zacatecas, C Mexico
84 D13 **Camacupa** var. General Machado, Port. Vila General Machado. Bié, C Angola
56 L7 **Camaguán** Guárico, C Venezuela
46 G6 **Camagüey** prev. Puerto Príncipe. Camagüey, C Cuba
46 G5 **Camagüey, Archipiélago de** island group C Cuba
42 D5 **Camalli, Sierra de** ▲ NW Mexico
59 G18 **Camana** var. Camaná. Arequipa, SW Peru
31 Z14 **Camanche** Iowa, C USA
37 P8 **Camanche Reservoir** ⊟ California, W USA
63 I16 **Camaquã** Rio Grande do Sul, S Brazil
63 H16 **Camaquã, Rio** ≈ S Brazil
66 P6 **Câmara de Lobos** Madeira, Portugal, NE Atlantic Ocean
105 U16 **Camarat, Cap** headland SE France
43 O8 **Camargo** Tamaulipas, C Mexico
105 R15 **Camargue** physical region SE France
106 F2 **Camariñas** Galicia, NW Spain
Camaronero, Laguna del see Caimanero, Laguna del
65 J18 **Camarones** Chaco, S Argentina
65 J18 **Camarones, Bahía** bay S Argentina
106 J14 **Camas** Andalucía, S Spain
178 J15 **Ca Mau** prev. Quan Long. Minh Hai, S Vietnam
84 E11 **Camaxilo** Lunda Norte, NE Angola
106 G3 **Cambados** Galicia, NW Spain
Cambay, Gulf of see Khambhāt, Gulf of
Camberia see Chambéry
99 N22 **Camberley** SE England, UK
178 Ii12 **Cambodia** off. Kingdom of Cambodia, var. Democratic Kampuchea, Roat Kampuchea, Cam. Kampuchea; prev. People's Democratic Republic of Kampuchea. ◆ republic SE Asia
104 I16 **Cambo-les-Bains** Pyrénées-Atlantiques, SW France
105 P2 **Cambrai** Flem. Kambryk; prev. Cambray, anc. Cameracum. Nord, N France
Cambray see Cambrai
106 H2 **Cambre** Galicia, NW Spain
37 O12 **Cambria** California, W USA
99 J20 **Cambrian Mountains** ▲▲ C Wales, UK
12 G16 **Cambridge** Ontario, S Canada
46 I12 **Cambridge** W Jamaica
192 M8 **Cambridge** Waikato, North Island, NZ
99 O20 **Cambridge** Lat. Cantabrigia. E England, UK
34 M12 **Cambridge** Idaho, NW USA
32 K11 **Cambridge** Illinois, N USA
23 Y4 **Cambridge** Maryland, NE USA
21 O11 **Cambridge** Massachusetts, NE USA
31 V7 **Cambridge** Minnesota, N USA
31 N16 **Cambridge** Nebraska, C USA
33 U13 **Cambridge** Ohio, NE USA
15 J3 **Cambridge Bay** district capital Victoria Island, Northwest Territories, NW Canada
99 O20 **Cambridgeshire** cultural region E England, UK
107 U6 **Cambrils de Mar** Cataluña, NE Spain
Cambundi-Catembo see Nova Gaia
143 N11 **Çam Burnu** headland N Turkey
191 S9 **Camden** New South Wales, SE Australia
25 O6 **Camden** Alabama, S USA
29 U14 **Camden** Arkansas, C USA
23 Y3 **Camden** Delaware, NE USA
21 R7 **Camden** Maine, NE USA
20 I16 **Camden** New Jersey, NE USA
20 I9 **Camden** New York, NE USA
23 R12 **Camden** South Carolina, SE USA
22 H8 **Camden** Tennessee, S USA
27 X9 **Camden** Texas, SW USA
41 S5 **Camden Bay** bay S Beaufort Sea
29 U6 **Camdenton** Missouri, C USA
Camellia State see Alabama
20 M7 **Camels Hump** ▲ Vermont, NE USA
119 N8 **Camenca** Rus. Kamenka. N Moldova
Cameracum see Cambrai
24 G9 **Cameron** Louisiana, S USA
27 T9 **Cameron** Texas, SW USA
32 J5 **Cameron** Wisconsin, N USA
8 M12 **Cameron** ≈ British Columbia, W Canada
193 A24 **Cameron Mountains** ▲▲ South Island, NZ
81 D15 **Cameroon** off. Republic of Cameroon, Fr. Cameroun. ◆ republic W Africa
81 D15 **Cameroon Mountain** ▲ SW Cameroon
Cameroon Ridge see Camerounaise, Dorsale
Cameroun see Cameroon
81 E14 **Camerounaise, Dorsale** Eng. Cameroon Ridge. ridge NW Cameroon
179 R14 **Camiguin Island** island S Philippines
179 P10 **Camiling** Luzon, N Philippines
25 T7 **Camilla** Georgia, SE USA
106 G5 **Caminha** Viana do Castelo, N Portugal
37 P7 **Camino** California, W USA
142 B15 **Çamiçi Gölü** ◎ SW Turkey
109 J24 **Cammarata** Sicilia, Italy, C Mediterranean Sea
44 K10 **Camoapa** Boaco, S Nicaragua
60 O13 **Camocim** Ceará, E Brazil
108 D10 **Camogli** Liguria, NW Italy
189 S5 **Camooweal** Queensland, C Australia
57 Y11 **Camopi** E French Guiana
157 Q22 **Camorta** island Nicobar Islands, India, NE Indian Ocean
179 R13 **Camotes Sea** sea C Philippines
44 I6 **Campamento** Olancho, C Honduras
63 D19 **Campana** Buenos Aires, E Argentina
65 F21 **Campana, Isla** island S Chile
106 K11 **Campanario** Extremadura, W Spain
109 L17 **Campania** Eng. Champagne. ◈ region S Italy
29 Y8 **Campbell** Missouri, C USA
193 K15 **Campbell, Cape** headland South Island, NZ
12 J14 **Campbellford** Ontario, SE Canada
33 R13 **Campbell Hill** hill Ohio, N USA
199 J14 **Campbell Island** island S NZ
183 P13 **Campbell Plateau** undersea feature SW Pacific Ocean
8 K17 **Campbell River** Vancouver Island, British Columbia, SW Canada
22 L6 **Campbellsville** Kentucky, S USA

◆ Country ● Country Capital ◇ Dependent Territory ○ Dependent Territory Capital ◈ Administrative Region × International Airport ▲ Mountain ▲▲ Mountain Range Volcano ≈ River ◎ Lake ⊟ Reservoir

Legend (bottom):
◆ COUNTRY ● COUNTRY CAPITAL ◇ DEPENDENT TERRITORY ○ DEPENDENT TERRITORY CAPITAL ◆ ADMINISTRATIVE REGION ▲ MOUNTAIN ◆ VOLCANO ◎ LAKE ☙ RIVER ✈ INTERNATIONAL AIRPORT ▲ MOUNTAIN RANGE ◎ RESERVOIR

CARTWRIGHT – CHADAN

11 S8 **Cartwright** Newfoundland and Labrador, E Canada
57 P9 **Caruana de Montaña** Bolívar, SE Venezuela
61 Q15 **Caruaru** Pernambuco, E Brazil
57 P5 **Carúpano** Sucre, NE Venezuela
Carusbur *see* Cherbourg
60 M12 **Carutapera** Maranhão, E Brazil
29 Y9 **Caruthersville** Missouri, C USA
105 O1 **Carvin** Pas-de-Calais, N France
60 E12 **Carvoeiro** Amazonas, NW Brazil
106 E10 **Carvoeiro, Cabo** *headland* C Portugal
23 U9 **Cary** North Carolina, SE USA
190 M3 **Caryapundy Swamp** *wetland* New South Wales/Queensland, SE Australia
67 E24 **Carysfort, Cape** *headland* East Falkland, Falkland Islands
76 F6 **Casablanca** *Ar.* Dar-el-Beida. NW Morocco
62 M8 **Casa Branca** São Paulo, S Brazil
38 L14 **Casa Grande** Arizona, SW USA
108 C8 **Casale Monferrato** Piemonte, NW Italy
108 E8 **Casalpusterlengo** Lombardia, N Italy
56 H10 **Casanare** *off.* Intendencia de Casanare. ◈ *province* C Colombia
57 P5 **Casanay** Sucre, NE Venezuela
26 K11 **Casa Piedra** Texas, SW USA
109 Q19 **Casarano** Puglia, SE Italy
44 J11 **Casares** Carazo, W Nicaragua
107 R10 **Casas Ibáñez** Castilla-La Mancha, C Spain
63 I14 **Casca** Rio Grande do Sul, S Brazil
180 I17 **Cascade** Mahé, NE Seychelles
35 N13 **Cascade** Idaho, NW USA
31 Y13 **Cascade** Iowa, C USA
35 R9 **Cascade** Montana, NW USA
193 B20 **Cascade Point** *headland* South Island, NZ
34 G13 **Cascade Range** ⛰ Oregon/Washington, NW USA
35 N12 **Cascade Reservoir** ▣ Idaho, NW USA
1 E8 **Cascadia Basin** *undersea feature* NE Pacific Ocean
106 E11 **Cascais** Lisboa, C Portugal
13 W7 **Cascapédia** ≈ Québec, SE Canada
61 I22 **Cascavel** Ceará, E Brazil
62 G11 **Cascavel** Paraná, S Brazil
108 I13 **Cascia** Umbria, C Italy
108 F11 **Cascina** Toscana, C Italy
21 Q8 **Casco Bay** *bay* Maine, NE USA
204 J7 **Case Island** *island* Antarctica
108 B8 **Caselle** ✕ (Torino) Piemonte, NW Italy
109 K17 **Caserta** Campania, S Italy
13 N8 **Casey** Québec, SE Canada
32 M14 **Casey** Illinois, N USA
205 Y12 **Casey** *Australian research station* Antarctica
205 W3 **Casey Bay** *bay* Antarctica
82 Q11 **Caseyr, Raas** *headland* NE Somalia
99 D20 **Cashel** *Ir.* Caiseal. S Ireland
56 G6 **Casigua** Zulia, W Venezuela
63 B19 **Casilda** Santa Fe, C Argentina
Casim *see* General Toshevo
191 V4 **Casino** New South Wales, SE Australia
Casinum *see* Cassino
113 E17 **Čáslav** *Ger.* Tschaslau. Střední Čechy, C Czech Republic
58 C13 **Casma** Ancash, C Peru
178 J7 **Ca, Sông** ≈ N Vietnam
109 K17 **Casoria** Campania, S Italy
107 T6 **Caspe** Aragón, NE Spain
35 X15 **Casper** Wyoming, C USA
86 M10 **Caspian Depression** *Kaz.* Kaspīy Mangy Oypaty, *Rus.* Prikaspiyskaya Nizmennost'. *depression* Kazakhstan/Russian Federation
139 Kk8 **Caspian Sea** *Az.* Xäzär Dänizi, *Kaz.* Kaspiy Tengizi, *Per.* Baḩr-e Khazar, Daryā-ye Khazar, *Rus.* Kaspiyskoye More. *inland sea* Asia/Europe
85 L14 **Cassacatiza** Tete, NW Mozambique
Cassai *see* Kasai
84 F13 **Cassamba** Moxico, E Angola
109 N20 **Cassano allo Ionio** Calabria, SE Italy
33 S8 **Cass City** Michigan, N USA
Cassel *see* Kassel
12 M13 **Casselman** Ontario, SE Canada
31 R5 **Casselton** North Dakota, N USA
61 M16 **Cássia** *var.* Santa Rita de Cassia. Bahia, E Brazil
8 J9 **Cassiar** British Columbia, W Canada
8 K10 **Cassiar Mountains** ⛰ British Columbia, W Canada
85 C15 **Cassinga** Huíla, SW Angola
109 J16 **Cassino** *prev.* San Germano; *anc.* Casinum. Lazio, C Italy
31 T4 **Cass Lake** Minnesota, N USA
31 T4 **Cass Lake** ◎ Minnesota, N USA
33 P10 **Cassopolis** Michigan, N USA
33 S8 **Cass River** ≈ Michigan, N USA
29 S8 **Cassville** Missouri, C USA
Castamoni *see* Kastamonu
60 L12 **Castanhal** Pará, NE Brazil
106 G8 **Castanheira de Pêra** Leiria, C Portugal
43 N7 **Castaños** Coahuila de Zaragoza, NE Mexico
110 I10 **Castasegna** Graubünden, SE Switzerland
108 D8 **Casteggio** Lombardia, N Italy
109 K23 **Castelbuono** Sicilia, Italy, C Mediterranean Sea
109 K15 **Castel di Sangro** Abruzzi, C Italy
108 H7 **Castelfranco Veneto** Veneto, NE Italy
104 K14 **Casteljaloux** Lot-et-Garonne, SW France
109 L18 **Castellabate** *var.* Santa Maria di Castellabate. Campania, S Italy
109 I23 **Castellammare del Golfo** Sicilia, Italy, C Mediterranean Sea
109 H22 **Castellammare, Golfo di** *gulf* Sicilia, Italy, C Mediterranean Sea
105 U15 **Castellane** Alpes-de-Haute-Provence, SE France
109 O18 **Castellaneta** Puglia, SE Italy
108 E9 **Castel l'Arquato** Emilia-Romagna, C Italy
63 E21 **Castelli** Buenos Aires, E Argentina
107 T9 **Castelló de la Plana** *var.* Castellón. País Valenciano, E Spain
107 S8 **Castellón** ◈ *province* País Valenciano, E Spain
Castellón *see* Castelló de la Plana
107 S7 **Castellote** Aragón, NE Spain
105 N16 **Castelnaudary** Aude, S France
104 L16 **Castelnau-Magnoac** Hautes-Pyrénées, S France
108 F10 **Castelnovo ne' Monti** Emilia-Romagna, C Italy
Castelnuovo *see* Herceg-Novi
106 H9 **Castelo Branco** Castelo Branco, C Portugal
106 H8 **Castelo Branco** ◈ *district* C Portugal
106 I10 **Castelo de Vide** Portalegre, C Portugal
106 G9 **Castelo do Bode, Barragem do** ▣ C Portugal
108 G10 **Castel San Pietro** Emilia-Romagna, C Italy
109 B17 **Castelsardo** Sardegna, Italy, C Mediterranean Sea
104 M14 **Castelsarrasin** Tarn-et-Garonne, S France
109 I24 **Casteltermini** Sicilia, Italy, C Mediterranean Sea
109 H24 **Castelvetrano** Sicilia, Italy, C Mediterranean Sea
190 L12 **Casterton** Victoria, SE Australia
104 J15 **Castets** Landes, SW France
108 H12 **Castiglione del Lago** Umbria, C Italy
108 F13 **Castiglione della Pescaia** Toscana, C Italy
108 F8 **Castiglione delle Stiviere** Lombardia, N Italy
106 M9 **Castilla-La Mancha** ◈ *autonomous community* NE Spain
106 L5 **Castilla-León** *var.* Castillia y Leon. ◈ *autonomous community* NW Spain
107 N10 **Castilla Nueva** *cultural region* C Spain
107 N6 **Castilla Vieja** *cultural region* N Spain
Castillia y Leon *see* Castilla-León
Castillo de Locubim *see* Castillo de Locubín
107 N14 **Castillo de Locubín** *var.* Castillo de Locubim. Andalucía, S Spain
104 K13 **Castillon-la-Bataille** Gironde, SW France
65 I19 **Castillo, Pampa del** *plain* S Argentina
63 G19 **Castillos** Rocha, SE Uruguay
99 B16 **Castlebar** *Ir.* Caisleán an Bharraigh. W Ireland
99 F16 **Castleblayney** *Ir.* Baile na Lorgan. N Ireland
47 O11 **Castle Bruce** E Dominica
38 M5 **Castle Dale** Utah, W USA
38 I14 **Castle Dome Peak** ▲ Arizona, SW USA
99 J14 **Castle Douglas** S Scotland, UK
99 E14 **Castlefinn** *Ir.* Caisleán na Finne. NW Ireland
99 M17 **Castleford** N England, UK
9 O17 **Castlegar** British Columbia, SW Canada
66 B12 **Castle Harbour** *inlet* Bermuda, NW Atlantic Ocean
23 V12 **Castle Hayne** North Carolina, SE USA
99 B20 **Castleisland** *Ir.* Oileán Ciarral. SW Ireland
191 N12 **Castlemaine** Victoria, SE Australia
39 R5 **Castle Peak** ▲ Colorado, C USA
35 O13 **Castle Peak** ▲ Idaho, NW USA
192 N13 **Castlepoint** Wellington, North Island, NZ
99 D17 **Castlerea** *Ir.* An Caisleán Riabhach. W Ireland
99 G15 **Castlereagh** *Ir.* An Caisleán Riabhach. N Northern Ireland, UK
191 R6 **Castlereagh River** ≈ New South Wales, SE Australia
39 T5 **Castle Rock** Colorado, C USA
32 K7 **Castle Rock Lake** ▣ Wisconsin, N USA
67 G25 **Castle Rock Point** *headland* S Saint Helena
99 I16 **Castletown** SE Isle of Man
31 R9 **Castlewood** South Dakota, N USA
9 R15 **Castor** Alberta, SW Canada
12 M13 **Castor** ≈ Ontario, SE Canada
29 X7 **Castor River** ≈ Missouri, C USA
Castra Albiensium *see* Castres
Castra Regina *see* Regensburg
105 N15 **Castres** *anc.* Castra Albiensium. Tarn, S France
100 H9 **Castricum** Noord-Holland, W Netherlands
47 S11 **Castries** ● (Saint Lucia) N Saint Lucia
62 J11 **Castro** Paraná, S Brazil
65 F17 **Castro** Los Lagos, W Chile
106 H7 **Castro Daire** Viseu, N Portugal
106 M13 **Castro del Río** Andalucía, S Spain
Castrogiovanni *see* Enna
106 H14 **Castro Marim** Faro, S Portugal
106 J2 **Castropol** Asturias, N Spain
107 O2 **Castro-Urdiales** *var.* Castro Urdiales. Cantabria, N Spain
106 G13 **Castro Verde** Beja, S Portugal
109 N19 **Castrovillari** Calabria, SW Italy
37 N10 **Castroville** California, W USA
27 R12 **Castroville** Texas, SW USA
106 K11 **Castuera** Extremadura, W Spain
63 F19 **Casupá** Florida, S Uruguay
193 A22 **Caswell Sound** *sound* South Island, NZ
143 Q13 **Çat** Erzurum, NE Turkey
44 K6 **Catacamas** Olancho, C Honduras
58 A10 **Catacaos** Piura, NW Peru
24 I7 **Catahoula Lake** ◎ Louisiana, S USA
143 S15 **Çatak** Van, SE Turkey
143 S15 **Çatak Çayi** ≈ SE Turkey
116 O12 **Çatalca** İstanbul, NW Turkey
116 O12 **Çatalca Yarımadası** *physical region* NW Turkey
64 H6 **Catalina** Antofagasta, N Chile
Catalonia *see* Cataluña
107 U5 **Cataluña** *Cat.* Catalunya; *Eng.* Catalonia. ◈ *autonomous community* N Spain
Catalunya *see* Cataluña
64 I7 **Catamarca** *off.* Provincia de Catamarca. ◈ *province* NW Argentina
Catamarca *see* San Fernando del Valle de Catamarca
179 Pp11 **Catanauan** Luzon, N Philippines
85 M16 **Catandica** Manica, C Mozambique
179 Qq11 **Catanduanes Island** *island* N Philippines
62 K8 **Catanduva** São Paulo, S Brazil
109 L24 **Catania** Sicilia, Italy, C Mediterranean Sea
109 M24 **Catania, Golfo di** *gulf* Sicilia, Italy, C Mediterranean Sea
47 U5 **Cataño** *var.* Cantaño. E Puerto Rico
109 O21 **Catanzaro** Calabria, SW Italy
109 O22 **Catanzaro Marina** *var.* Marina di Catanzaro. Calabria, S Italy
27 Q14 **Catarina** Texas, SW USA
179 Qq12 **Catarman** Samar, C Philippines
107 S10 **Catarroja** País Valenciano, E Spain
23 R11 **Catawba River** ≈ North Carolina/South Carolina, SE USA
179 R12 **Catbalogan** Samar, C Philippines
12 I14 **Catchacoma** Ontario, SE Canada
43 S15 **Catemaco** Veracruz-Llave, SE Mexico
Cathair na Mart *see* Westport
Cathair Saidhbhín *see* Cahersiveen
33 P5 **Cat Head Point** *headland* Michigan, N USA
25 Q2 **Cathedral Caverns** *cave* Alabama, S USA
37 V16 **Cathedral City** California, W USA
26 K10 **Cathedral Mountain** ▲ Texas, SW USA
34 G10 **Cathlamet** Washington, NW USA
78 G13 **Catió** S Guinea-Bissau
57 O10 **Catisimiña** Bolívar, SE Venezuela
46 J3 **Cat Island** *island* C Bahamas
10 B9 **Cat Lake** Ontario, S Canada
23 P5 **Catlettsburg** Kentucky, S USA
193 D24 **Catlins** ≈ South Island, NZ
37 R1 **Catnip Mountain** ▲ Nevada, W USA
43 Z11 **Catoche, Cabo** *headland* SE Mexico
29 P9 **Catoosa** Oklahoma, C USA
43 N10 **Catorce** San Luis Potosí, C Mexico
65 I14 **Catriel** Río Negro, C Argentina
64 K13 **Catriló** La Pampa, C Argentina
60 F11 **Catrimani** Roraima, N Brazil
60 E10 **Catrimani, Rio** ≈ N Brazil
20 K11 **Catskill** New York, NE USA
20 K11 **Catskill Creek** ≈ New York, NE USA
20 J11 **Catskill Mountains** ⛰ New York, NE USA
20 D11 **Cattaraugus Creek** ≈ New York, NE USA
Cattaro *see* Kotor
Cattaro, Bocche di *see* Kotorska, Boka
109 I24 **Cattolica Eraclea** Sicilia, Italy, C Mediterranean Sea
85 B14 **Catumbela** ≈ W Angola
85 N14 **Catur** Niassa, N Mozambique
84 C10 **Cauale** ≈ NE Angola
179 Pp9 **Cauayan** Luzon, N Philippines
56 C12 **Cauca** *off.* Departamento del Cauca. ◈ *province* SW Colombia
49 P5 **Cauca** ≈ SE Venezuela
60 P13 **Caucaia** Ceará, E Brazil
56 E7 **Cauca, Río** ≈ N Colombia
56 E7 **Caucasia** Antioquia, NW Colombia
143 Q8 **Caucasus** *Rus.* Kavkaz. ⛰ Georgia/Russian Federation
64 I10 **Caucete** San Juan, W Argentina
107 R11 **Caudete** Castilla-La Mancha, C Spain
105 P2 **Caudry** Nord, N France
84 D11 **Caungula** Lunda Norte, NE Angola
64 G13 **Cauquenes** Maule, C Chile
57 N8 **Caura, Río** ≈ C Venezuela
13 V7 **Causapscal** Québec, SE Canada
119 N10 **Căuşeni** *Rus.* Kaushany. E Moldova
104 M14 **Caussade** Tarn-et-Garonne, S France
104 K17 **Cauterets** Hautes-Pyrénées, S France
8 J15 **Caution, Cape** *headland* British Columbia, SW Canada
46 H7 **Cauto** ≈ E Cuba
Cauvery *see* Kāveri
104 L3 **Caux, Pays de** *physical region* N France
109 L18 **Cava de' Tirreni** Campania, S Italy
106 G6 **Cávado** ≈ N Portugal
Cavaia *see* Kavajë
105 R15 **Cavaillon** Vaucluse, SE France
105 U16 **Cavalaire-sur-Mer** Var, SE France
108 G6 **Cavalese** *Ger.* Gablös. Trentino-Alto Adige, N Italy
31 Q2 **Cavalier** North Dakota, N USA
78 L17 **Cavalla** *var.* Cavally, Cavally Fleuve. ≈ Ivory Coast/Liberia
107 Y8 **Cavalleria, Cap de** *var.* Cabo Caballeria. *headland* Menorca, Spain, W Mediterranean Sea
192 K2 **Cavalli Islands** *island group* N NZ
Cavally/Cavally Fleuve *see* Cavalla
99 E16 **Cavan** *Ir.* Cabhán. N Ireland
99 E16 **Cavan** *Ir.* An Cabhán. *cultural region* N Ireland
108 H8 **Cavarzare** Veneto, NE Italy
29 W9 **Cave City** Arkansas, C USA
22 K7 **Cave City** Kentucky, S USA
67 M25 **Cave Point** *headland* S Tristan da Cunha
23 N5 **Cave Run Lake** ▣ Kentucky, S USA
60 K11 **Caviana de Fora, Ilha** *var.* Ilha Caviana. *island* N Brazil
Caviana, Ilha *see* Caviana de Fora, Ilha
115 I16 **Cavtat** *It.* Ragusavecchia. Dubrovnik-Neretva, SE Croatia
Cawnpore *see* Kānpur
Caxamarca *see* Cajamarca
60 N13 **Caxias** Amazonas, W Brazil
60 A13 **Caxias** Maranhão, E Brazil
63 I15 **Caxias do Sul** Rio Grande do Sul, S Brazil
44 J4 **Caxinas, Punta** *headland* N Honduras
84 B11 **Caxito** Bengo, NW Angola
142 F14 **Çay** Afyon, W Turkey
42 L15 **Cayacal, Punta** *var.* Punta Mongrove. *headland* S Mexico
58 C6 **Cayambe** Pichincha, N Ecuador
58 C6 **Cayambe** ▲ N Ecuador
23 R12 **Cayce** South Carolina, SE USA
57 Y10 **Cayenne** ○ (French Guiana) NE French Guiana
57 Y10 **Cayenne** ✕ NE French Guiana
46 K10 **Cayes** *var.* Les Cayes. SW Haiti
47 U6 **Cayey** C Puerto Rico
47 U6 **Cayey, Sierra de** ⛰ E Puerto Rico
105 N14 **Caylus** Tarn-et-Garonne, S France
46 E8 **Cayman Brac** *island* E Cayman Islands
46 D8 **Cayman Islands** ◇ *UK dependent territory* W West Indies
66 D11 **Cayman Trench** *undersea feature* NW Caribbean Sea
49 O3 **Cayman Trough** *undersea feature* NW Caribbean Sea
82 O13 **Caynabo** Togdheer, N Somalia
44 F3 **Cayo** ◈ *district* SW Belize
Cayo *see* San Ignacio
45 N9 **Cayos Guerrero** *reef* E Nicaragua
45 O9 **Cayos King** *reef* E Nicaragua
46 E4 **Cay Sal** *islet* SW Bahamas
12 G16 **Cayuga** Ontario, S Canada
27 V8 **Cayuga** Texas, SW USA
20 G10 **Cayuga Lake** ◎ New York, NE USA
106 K13 **Cazalla de la Sierra** Andalucía, S Spain
118 L14 **Căzăneşti** Ialomiţa, SE Romania
104 M16 **Cazères** Haute-Garonne, S France
114 E10 **Cazin** NW Bosnia and Herzegovina
84 G13 **Cazombo** Moxico, E Angola
107 O13 **Cazorla** Andalucía, S Spain
Cazza *see* Sušac
106 L4 **Cea** ≈ NW Spain
Ceadâr-Lunga *see* Ciadîr-Lunga
Ceanannas *see* Kells
Ceann Toirc *see* Kanturk
60 O13 **Ceará** *off.* Estado do Ceará. ◈ *state* C Brazil
Ceará *see* Fortaleza
Ceara Abyssal Plain *see* Ceará Plain
61 Q14 **Ceará Mirim** Rio Grande do Norte, E Brazil
66 J13 **Ceará Plain** *var.* Ceara Abyssal Plain. *undersea feature* W Atlantic Ocean
66 I13 **Ceará Ridge** *undersea feature* C Atlantic Ocean
Ceatharlach *see* Carlow
45 Q17 **Cébaco, Isla** *island* SW Panama
42 K7 **Ceballos** Durango, C Mexico
63 G19 **Cebollatí** Rocha, E Uruguay
63 G19 **Cebollatí, Río** ≈ E Uruguay
107 P5 **Cebollera** ▲ N Spain
106 M8 **Cebreros** Castilla-León, N Spain
179 Qq14 **Cebu** *off.* Cebu City. Cebu, C Philippines
179 Qq13 **Cebu** *island* C Philippines
109 J16 **Ceccano** Lazio, C Italy
Čechy *see* Bohemia
108 F12 **Cecina** Toscana, C Italy
28 K4 **Cedar Bluff Reservoir** ▣ Kansas, C USA
32 M8 **Cedarburg** Wisconsin, N USA
38 J7 **Cedar City** Utah, W USA
27 T11 **Cedar Creek** Texas, SW USA
30 L7 **Cedar Creek** ≈ North Dakota, N USA
27 U7 **Cedar Creek Reservoir** ▣ Texas, SW USA
31 W13 **Cedar Falls** Iowa, C USA
33 N8 **Cedar Grove** Wisconsin, N USA
23 Y6 **Cedar Island** *island* Virginia, NE USA
25 U11 **Cedar Key** Cedar Keys, Florida, SE USA
25 U11 **Cedar Keys** *island group* Florida, SE USA
9 V14 **Cedar Lake** ◎ Manitoba, C Canada
12 I11 **Cedar Lake** ◎ Ontario, SE Canada
26 M6 **Cedar Lake** ◎ Texas, SW USA
31 X13 **Cedar Rapids** Iowa, C USA
31 X14 **Cedar River** ≈ Iowa/Minnesota, C USA
31 O14 **Cedar River** ≈ Nebraska, C USA
33 P8 **Cedar Springs** Michigan, N USA
25 R3 **Cedartown** Georgia, SE USA
29 O7 **Cedar Vale** Kansas, C USA
37 Q2 **Cedarville** California, W USA
106 H1 **Cedeira** Galicia, NW Spain
44 H8 **Cedeño** Choluteca, S Honduras
43 N10 **Cedral** San Luis Potosí, C Mexico
44 I6 **Cedros** Francisco Morazán, C Honduras
42 M9 **Cedros** Zacatecas, C Mexico
42 B5 **Cedros, Isla** *island* W Mexico
199 Mm6 **Cedros Trench** *undersea feature* E Pacific Ocean
190 E7 **Ceduna** South Australia
112 D10 **Cedynia** *Ger.* Zehden. Szczecin, W Poland
82 P12 **Ceelaayo** Sanaag, N Somalia
83 O16 **Ceel Buur** *It.* El Bur; Galguduud, C Somalia
83 N15 **Ceel Dheere** *var.* Ceel Dher, *It.* El Dere. Galguduud, C Somalia
Ceel Dher *see* Ceel Dheere
83 P14 **Ceel Xamure** Mudug, E Somalia
82 O12 **Ceerigaabo** *var.* Erigabo, Erigavo. Sanaag, N Somalia
109 J23 **Cefalù** *anc.* Cephaloedium. Sicilia, Italy, C Mediterranean Sea
107 N6 **Cega** ≈ N Spain
113 K23 **Cegléd** *prev.* Czegléd. Pest, C Hungary
115 N18 **Čegrane** W FYR Macedonia
107 Q13 **Cehegín** Murcia, SE Spain
142 K12 **Çekerek** Yozgat, N Turkey
109 J15 **Celano** Abruzzi, C Italy
106 H4 **Celanova** Galicia, NW Spain
44 F6 **Celaque, Cordillera de** ⛰ W Honduras
43 N13 **Celaya** Guanajuato, C Mexico
Celebes *see* Sulawesi
198 Ff8 **Celebes Basin** *undersea feature* SE South China Sea
175 Qq4 **Celebes Sea** *Ind.* Laut Sulawesi. *sea* Indonesia/Philippines
43 W12 **Celestún** Yucatán, E Mexico
33 Q12 **Celina** Ohio, N USA
22 L8 **Celina** Tennessee, S USA
27 U5 **Celina** Texas, SW USA
114 G11 **Čelinac Donji** N Bosnia and Herzegovina
111 V10 **Celje** *Ger.* Cilli. C Slovenia
113 G23 **Celldömölk** Vas, W Hungary
102 J12 **Celle** *var.* Zelle. Niedersachsen, N Germany
101 D19 **Celles** Hainaut, SW Belgium
106 I7 **Celorico da Beira** Guarda, N Portugal
Celovec *see* Klagenfurt
66 M7 **Celtic Sea** *Ir.* An Mhuir Cheilteach. *sea* SW British Isles
66 N7 **Celtic Shelf** *undersea feature* E Atlantic Ocean
116 L13 **Çeltik Gölu** ◎ NW Turkey
115 M14 **Čemerno** ⛰ C Yugoslavia
175 Oo16 **Cempi, Teluk** *bay* Nusa Tenggara, S Indonesia
107 Q12 **Cenajo, Embalse del** ▣ S Spain
107 P4 **Cenicero** La Rioja, N Spain
108 E9 **Ceno** ≈ NW Italy
104 K13 **Cenon** Gironde, SW France
12 K13 **Centennial Lake** ◎ Ontario, SE Canada
Centennial State *see* Colorado
39 S7 **Center** Colorado, C USA
31 Q13 **Center** Nebraska, C USA
30 M5 **Center** North Dakota, N USA
27 X8 **Center** Texas, SW USA
31 W8 **Center City** Minnesota, N USA
38 L5 **Centerfield** Utah, W USA
22 K9 **Center Hill Lake** ▣ Tennessee, S USA
31 X13 **Center Point** Iowa, C USA
27 R11 **Center Point** Texas, SW USA
31 W16 **Centerville** Iowa, C USA
29 W7 **Centerville** Missouri, C USA
31 R12 **Centerville** South Dakota, N USA
22 I9 **Centerville** Tennessee, S USA
27 V9 **Centerville** Texas, SW USA
42 M5 **Centinela, Picacho del** ▲ NE Mexico
108 G9 **Cento** Emilia-Romagna, N Italy
Centrafricaine, République *see* Central African Republic
41 S8 **Central** Alaska, USA
39 P15 **Central** New Mexico, SW USA
85 H18 **Central** ◈ *district* E Botswana
144 E10 **Central** ◈ *district* C Israel
83 I19 **Central** ◈ *province* C Kenya
84 M13 **Central** ◈ *region* C Malawi
159 P12 **Central** ◈ *zone* C Nepal
194 J15 **Central** ◈ *province* S PNG
65 I21 **Central** ◈ *department* C Paraguay
195 W15 **Central** *off.* Central Province. ◈ *province* S Solomon Islands
85 J14 **Central** ◈ *province* C Zambia
119 P11 **Central** ✕ (Odesa) Odes'ka Oblast', SW Ukraine
Central *see* Centre
81 H14 **Central African Republic** *var.* République Centrafricaine, *abbrev.* CAR; *prev.* Ubangi-Shari, Oubangui-Chari, Territoire de l'Oubangui-Chari. ◆ *republic* C Africa
198 G6 **Central Basin Trough** *undersea feature* W Pacific Ocean
Central Borneo *see* Kalimantan Tengah
155 P12 **Central Brāhui Range** ⛰ W Pakistan
Central Celebes *see* Sulawesi Tengah
31 Y13 **Central City** Iowa, C USA
22 I6 **Central City** Kentucky, S USA
31 P15 **Central City** Nebraska, C USA
50 D6 **Central, Cordillera** ⛰ W Bolivia
56 D11 **Central, Cordillera** ⛰ W Colombia
44 M13 **Central, Cordillera** ⛰ C Costa Rica
47 N9 **Central, Cordillera** ⛰ C Dominican Republic
45 R16 **Central, Cordillera** ⛰ C Panama
179 P8 **Central, Cordillera** ⛰ Luzon, N Philippines
47 S6 **Central, Cordillera** ⛰ Puerto Rico
44 H7 **Central District** *var.* Tegucigalpa. ◈ *district* C Honduras
32 L15 **Centralia** Illinois, N USA
29 U4 **Centralia** Missouri, C USA
34 G9 **Centralia** Washington, NW USA
Central Indian Ridge *see* Mid-Indian Ridge
Central Java *see* Jawa Tengah
Central Kalimantan *see* Kalimantan Tengah
154 L14 **Central Makrān Range** ⛰ W Pakistan
199 J8 **Central Pacific Basin** *undersea feature* C Pacific Ocean
61 M19 **Central, Planalto** *var.* Brazilian Highlands. ⛰ E Brazil
34 F15 **Central Point** Oregon, NW USA
161 K25 **Central Province** ◈ *province* C Sri Lanka
Central Provinces and Berar *see* Madhya Pradesh
194 G11 **Central Range** ⛰ NW PNG
Central Russian Upland *see* Srednerusskaya Vozvyshennost'
Central Siberian Plateau/Central Siberian Uplands *see* Srednesibirskoye Ploskogor'ye
106 K8 **Central, Sistema** ⛰ C Spain
Central Sulawesi *see* Sulawesi Tengah
37 N3 **Central Valley** California, W USA
37 P8 **Central Valley** *valley* California, W USA
25 Q3 **Centre** Alabama, S USA
81 E15 **Centre** *Eng.* Central. ◈ *province* C Cameroon
104 M8 **Centre** ◈ *region* N France
181 Y16 **Centre de Flacq** E Mauritius
57 Y9 **Centre Spatial Guyanais** *space station* N French Guiana
25 O5 **Centreville** Alabama, S USA
23 X3 **Centreville** Maryland, NE USA
24 J7 **Centreville** Mississippi, S USA
Centum Cellae *see* Civitavecchia
166 M14 **Cenxi** Guangxi Zhuangzu Zizhiqu, S China
Ceos *see* Kéa
Cephaloedium *see* Cefalù
114 I9 **Čepin** *Hung.* Csepén. Osijek-Baranja, E Croatia
174 Ll15 **Cepu** *prev.* Tjepoe, Tjepu. Jawa, C Indonesia
Ceram *see* Seram, Pulau
175 T10 **Ceram Sea** *Ind.* Laut Seram. *sea* E Indonesia
198 G9 **Ceram Trough** *undersea feature* W Pacific Ocean
Cerasus *see* Giresun
38 I10 **Cerbat Mountains** ⛰ Arizona, SW USA
105 P17 **Cerbère, Cap** *headland* S France
106 F13 **Cercal do Alentejo** Setúbal, S Portugal
113 A18 **Čerchov** *Ger.* Czerkow. ▲ W Czech Republic
105 O13 **Cère** ≈ C France
63 A16 **Ceres** Santa Fe, C Argentina
61 K18 **Ceres** Goiás, C Brazil
Ceresio *see* Lugano, Lago di
105 O17 **Céret** Pyrénées-Orientales, S France
56 E6 **Cereté** Córdoba, NW Colombia
180 I17 **Cerf, Île au** *island* Inner Islands, NE Seychelles
101 G22 **Cerfontaine** Namur, S Belgium
Cergy-Pontoise *see* Pontoise
109 N16 **Cerignola** Puglia, SE Italy
Cerigo *see* Kýthira
105 O9 **Cérilly** Allier, C France
142 I11 **Çerkeş** Çankırı, N Turkey
142 D10 **Çerkezköy** Tekirdağ, NW Turkey
111 T12 **Cerknica** *Ger.* Zirknitz. SW Slovenia
111 S11 **Cerkno** W Slovenia
118 F10 **Cermei** *Hung.* Csermő. Arad, W Romania
143 O15 **Çermik** Dıyarbakır, SE Turkey
114 I10 **Cerna** Vukovar-Srijem, E Croatia
Cernăuţi *see* Chernivtsi
118 M14 **Cernavodă** Constanţa, SW Romania
105 U7 **Cernay** Haut-Rhin, NE France
Černice *see* Schwarzach
43 O8 **Cerralvo** Nuevo León, NE Mexico
42 G9 **Cerralvo, Isla** *island* W Mexico
109 L16 **Cerreto Sannita** Campania, S Italy
115 L20 **Cërrik** *var.* Cerriku. Elbasan, C Albania
Cerriku *see* Cërrik
43 O11 **Cerritos** San Luis Potosí, C Mexico
62 K11 **Cerro Azul** Paraná, S Brazil
63 F18 **Cerro Chato** Treinta y Tres, E Uruguay
63 F19 **Cerro Colorado** Florida, S Uruguay
58 E13 **Cerro de Pasco** Pasco, C Peru
63 G18 **Cerro Largo** ◈ *department* NE Uruguay
63 G14 **Cêrro Largo** Rio Grande do Sul, S Brazil
44 E7 **Cerrón Grande, Embalse** ▣ N El Salvador
65 I14 **Cerros Colorados, Embalse** ◎ W Argentina
107 V5 **Cervera** Cataluña, NE Spain
106 M3 **Cervera del Pisuerga** Castilla-León, N Spain
107 Q5 **Cervera del Río Alhama** La Rioja, N Spain
109 H15 **Cerveteri** Lazio, C Italy
108 H10 **Cervia** Emilia-Romagna, N Italy
108 J7 **Cervignano del Friuli** Friuli-Venezia Giulia, NE Italy
109 L17 **Cervinara** Campania, S Italy
Cervinia *see* Breuil
108 B6 **Cervino, Monte** *var.* Matterhorn. ▲ Italy/Switzerland *see also* Matterhorn
104 F2 **Cervione** Corse, France, C Mediterranean Sea
106 I1 **Cervo** Galicia, NW Spain
56 F5 **Cesar** *off.* Departamento del Cesar. ◈ *province* N Colombia
108 H10 **Cesena** *anc.* Caesena. Emilia-Romagna, N Italy
108 I10 **Cesenatico** Emilia-Romagna, N Italy
120 H8 **Cēsis** *Ger.* Wenden. Cēsis, C Latvia
113 D15 **Česká Lípa** *Ger.* Böhmisch-Leipa. Severní Čechy, N Czech Republic
Česká Republika *see* Czech Republic
113 F17 **Česká Třebová** *Ger.* Böhmisch-Trübau. Východní Čechy, E Czech Republic
113 D19 **České Budějovice** *Ger.* Budweis. Jižní Čechy, SW Czech Republic
113 D19 **České Velenice** Jižní Čechy, S Czech Republic
113 E18 **Českomoravská Vrchovina** *var.* Českomoravská Vysočina, *Eng.* Bohemian-Moravian Highlands, *Ger.* Böhmisch-Mährische Höhe. ⛰ S Czech Republic
Českomoravská Vysočina *see* Českomoravská Vrchovina
113 C19 **Český Krumlov** *var.* Böhmisch-Krumau, *Ger.* Krummau. Jižní Čechy, SW Czech Republic
Ceský Les *see* Bohemian Forest
114 F8 **Česma** ≈ N Croatia
142 A14 **Çeşme** İzmir, W Turkey
Cess *see* Cestos
191 T8 **Cessnock** New South Wales, SE Australia
78 K17 **Cestos** *var.* Cess. ≈ S Liberia
120 I9 **Cesvaine** Madona, E Latvia
118 G14 **Cetate** Dolj, SW Romania
Cetatea Albă *see* Bilhorod-Dnistrovs'kyy
115 J17 **Cetinje** *It.* Cettigne. Montenegro, SW Yugoslavia
109 N20 **Cetraro** Calabria, S Italy
Cette *see* Sète
196 A17 **Cetti Bay** *bay* SW Guam
Cettigne *see* Cetinje
106 L17 **Ceuta** *var.* Sebta. Ceuta, Spain, N Africa
90 C16 **Ceuta** *enclave* Spain, N Africa
108 B9 **Ceva** Piemonte, NE Italy
105 P14 **Cévennes** ⛰ S France
110 G10 **Cevio** Ticino, S Switzerland
142 K16 **Ceyhan** Adana, S Turkey
142 K17 **Ceyhan Nehri** ≈ S Turkey
143 P17 **Ceylanpınar** Şanlıurfa, SE Turkey
Ceylon *see* Sri Lanka
181 R6 **Ceylon Plain** *undersea feature* N Indian Ocean
Ceyre to the Caribs *see* Marie-Galante
105 Q14 **Cèze** ≈ S France
152 H15 **Chaacha** *Turkm.* Chäche. Akhalskiy Velayat, S Turkmenistan
131 P6 **Chaadayevka** Penzenskaya Oblast', W Russian Federation
178 H12 **Cha-Am** Phetchaburi, SW Thailand
149 W15 **Chābahār** *var.* Chāh Bahār, Chahbar. Sīstān va Balūchestān, SE Iran
63 B19 **Chabas** Santa Fe, C Argentina
105 T10 **Chablais** *physical region* E France
63 B20 **Chacabuco** Buenos Aires, E Argentina
44 K8 **Chachagón, Cerro** ▲ N Nicaragua
58 C10 **Chachapoyas** Amazonas, NW Peru
Chäche *see* Chaacha
121 O18 **Chachersk** *Rus.* Chechersk. Homyel'skaya Voblasts', SE Belarus
121 N16 **Chachevichy** *Rus.* Chechevichi. Mahilyowskaya Voblasts', E Belarus
63 B14 **Chaco** *off.* Provincia de Chaco. ◈ *province* NE Argentina
Chaco *see* Gran Chaco
64 M6 **Chaco Austral** *physical region* N Argentina
64 M3 **Chaco Boreal** *physical region* N Paraguay
64 M6 **Chaco Central** *physical region* N Argentina
41 Y15 **Chacon, Cape** *headland* Prince of Wales Island, Alaska, USA
80 H9 **Chad** *off.* Republic of Chad, *Fr.* Tchad. ◆ *republic* C Africa
126 Hh16 **Chadan** Respublika Tyva, S Russian Federation

◆ Country
● Country Capital
◇ Dependent Territory
○ Dependent Territory Capital
◈ Administrative Region
✕ International Airport
▲ Mountain
⛰ Mountain Range
Volcano
≈ River
◎ Lake
▣ Reservoir

23 U12 **Chadbourn** North Carolina, SE USA
85 L14 **Chadiza** Eastern, E Zambia
69 Q7 **Chad, Lake** Fr. Lac Tchad. ◊ C Africa
126 J13 **Chadobets** ✍ C Russian Federation
30 J12 **Chadron** Nebraska, C USA
Chadyr-Lunga see Ciadîr-Lunga
169 W14 **Chaeryŏng** SW North Korea
107 P17 **Chafarinas, Islas** island group S Spain
29 Y7 **Chaffee** Missouri, C USA
154 L12 **Chāgai Hills** var. Chāh Gay. ▲ Afghanistan/Pakistan
126 M12 **Chagda** Respublika Sakha (Yakutiya), NE Russian Federation
Chaghasarāy see Asadābād
155 N5 **Chaghcharān** var. Chakhcharan, Cheghcheran, Qala Āhangarān. Ghowr, C Afghanistan
105 R9 **Chagny** Saône-et-Loire, C France
181 Q7 **Chagos Archipelago** var. Oil Islands. island group British Indian Ocean Territory
133 O15 **Chagos Bank** undersea feature C Indian Ocean
133 O14 **Chagos-Laccadive Plateau** undersea feature N Indian Ocean
181 Q7 **Chagos Trench** undersea feature N Indian Ocean
45 T14 **Chagres, Río** ✍ C Panama
47 U14 **Chaguanas** Trinidad, Trinidad and Tobago
56 M6 **Chaguaramas** Guárico, N Venezuela
152 C9 **Chagyl** Balkanskiy Velayat, NW Turkmenistan
Chahārmahāl and Bakhtīāri see Chahār Mahall va Bakhtīāri
148 M9 **Chahār Mahall va Bakhtīāri** off. Ostān-e Chahār Mahall va Bakhtīāri, var. Chahārmahall and Bakhtīyāri. ◊ province SW Iran
149 V13 **Chāh Derāz** Sīstān va Balūchestān, SE Iran
Chāh Gay see Chāgai Hills
178 Hh10 **Chai Badan** Lop Buri, C Thailand
159 Q16 **Chāibāsa** Bihār, N India
81 E19 **Chaillu, Massif du** ▲ C Gabon
178 Hh10 **Chai Nat** var. Chainat, Jayanath. Chai Nat, C Thailand
67 M14 **Chain Fracture Zone** tectonic feature E Atlantic Ocean
181 N5 **Chain Ridge** undersea feature W Indian Ocean
Chairn, Ceann an see Carnsore Point
164 L5 **Chaiwopu** Xinjiang Uygur Zizhiqu, W China
178 I10 **Chaiyaphum** var. Jayabum. Chaiyaphum, C Thailand
64 N10 **Chajarí** Entre Ríos, E Argentina
44 C5 **Chajul** Quiché, W Guatemala
85 K16 **Chakari** Mashonaland West, N Zimbabwe
154 J9 **Chakhānsūr** Nīmrūz, SW Afghanistan
Chakhānsūr see Nīmrūz
Chakhcharan see Chaghcharān
155 V8 **Chak Jhumra** var. Jhumra. Punjab, E Pakistan
152 I16 **Chaknakdysonga** Akhalskiy Velayat, S Turkmenistan
159 P16 **Chakradharpur** Bihār, N India
158 J8 **Chakrāta** Uttar Pradesh, N India
155 U7 **Chakwāl** Punjab, NE Pakistan
59 F17 **Chala** Arequipa, SW Peru
104 K12 **Chalais** Charente, W France
110 D10 **Chalais** Valais, SW Switzerland
117 J20 **Chalándri** var. Halandri; prev. Khalándrion. prehistoric site Sýros, Kykládes, Greece, Aegean Sea
196 H6 **Chalan Kanoa** Saipan, S Northern Mariana Islands
196 L16 **Chalan Pago** C Guam
Chalap Dalam/Chalap Dalan see Chehel Abdālān, Kūh-e
44 F7 **Chalatenango** Chalatenango, N El Salvador
44 A9 **Chalatenango** ◊ department NW El Salvador
85 P15 **Chalaua** Nampula, NE Mozambique
83 I16 **Chalbi Desert** desert N Kenya
44 D7 **Chalchuapa** Santa Ana, W El Salvador
Chalcidice see Chalkidikí
Chalcis see Chalkída
105 N6 **Châlette-sur-Loing** Loiret, C France
13 U4 **Chaleur Bay** Fr. Baie des Chaleurs. bay New Brunswick/Québec, E Canada
Chaleurs, Baie des see Chaleur Bay
59 G16 **Chalhuanca** Apurímac, S Peru
160 F12 **Chālisgaon** Mahārāshtra, C India
117 N23 **Chálki** island Dodekánisos, Greece, Aegean Sea
117 F16 **Chalkída** var. Halkida; prev. Khalkís, anc. Chalcis. Évvoia, E Greece
117 G14 **Chalkidikí** var. Khalkidhikí; anc. Chalcidice. peninsula NE Greece
193 A24 **Chalky Inlet** inlet South Island, NZ
41 S7 **Chalkyitsik** Alaska, USA
104 I9 **Challans** Vendée, NW France
59 K19 **Challapata** Oruro, SW Bolivia
199 H7 **Challenger Deep** undersea feature W Pacific Ocean
200 Nn12 **Challenger Fracture Zone** tectonic feature SE Pacific Ocean
199 Ii13 **Challenger Plateau** undersea feature E Tasman Sea
35 P13 **Challis** Idaho, NW USA

24 L9 **Chalmette** Louisiana, S USA
128 J11 **Chalna** Respublika Kareliya, NW Russian Federation
105 Q5 **Châlons-en-Champagne** prev. Châlons-sur-Marne, hist. Arcae Remorum, anc. Carolopois. Marne, NE France
Châlons-sur-Marne see Châlons-en-Champagne
105 R9 **Chalon-sur-Saône** anc. Cabillonum. Saône-et-Loire, C France
Chaltel, Cerro see Fitzroy, Monte
149 N4 **Chālūs** Māzandarān, N Iran
104 M11 **Châlus** Haute-Vienne, C France
101 N20 **Cham** Bayern, SE Germany
110 F7 **Cham** Zug, N Switzerland
39 R8 **Chama** New Mexico, SW USA
Cha Mai see Thung Song
85 E22 **Chamaites** Karas, S Namibia
155 O9 **Chaman** Baluchistān, SW Pakistan
39 R9 **Chama, Río** ✍ New Mexico, SW USA
158 I6 **Chamba** Himāchal Pradesh, N India
83 I25 **Chamba** Ruvuma, S Tanzania
156 H12 **Chambal** ✍ C India
9 U16 **Chamberlain** Saskatchewan, S Canada
31 O11 **Chamberlain** South Dakota, N USA
21 R3 **Chamberlain Lake** ◎ Maine, NE USA
41 S5 **Chamberlin, Mount** ▲ Alaska, USA
39 O11 **Chambers** Arizona, SW USA
20 F16 **Chambersburg** Pennsylvania, NE USA
33 N5 **Chambers Island** island Wisconsin, N USA
105 T11 **Chambéry** anc. Cambería. Savoie, E France
84 L12 **Chambeshi** Northern, NE Zambia
84 L12 **Chambeshi** ✍ NE Zambia
76 M6 **Chambi, Jebel** var. Jabal ash Sha'nabi. ▲ W Tunisia
13 Q7 **Chambord** Québec, SE Canada
194 G10 **Chambri Lake** ◎ W PNG
145 U11 **Chamcham** S Iraq
145 T4 **Chamchamāl** N Iraq
42 J14 **Chamela** Jalisco, SW Mexico
64 J9 **Chamical** La Rioja, C Argentina
117 L23 **Chamíli** island Kykládes, Greece, Aegean Sea
178 Ii13 **Chámnar** Kaôh Kông, SW Cambodia
158 K9 **Chamoli** Uttar Pradesh, N India
105 U11 **Chamonix-Mont-Blanc** Haute-Savoie, E France
160 L11 **Chāmpa** Madhya Pradesh, C India
8 H8 **Champagne** Yukon Territory, W Canada
105 Q5 **Champagne** cultural region N France
Champagne see Campania
105 Q5 **Champagne-Ardenne** ◆ region N France
105 S9 **Champagnole** Jura, E France
32 M13 **Champaign** Illinois, N USA
178 J11 **Champasak** Champasak, S Laos
105 U6 **Champ de Feu** ▲ NE France
11 O7 **Champdoré, Lac** ◎ Québec, NE Canada
44 B4 **Champerico** Retalhuleu, SW Guatemala
110 C11 **Champéry** Valais, SW Switzerland
20 L9 **Champlain** New York, NE USA
20 L9 **Champlain Canal** canal New York, NE USA
13 P13 **Champlain, Lac** ◎ Québec, SE Canada
20 L7 **Champlain, Lake** ◎ Canada/USA
105 S7 **Champlitte** Haute-Saône, E France
43 W13 **Champotón** Campeche, SE Mexico
106 G12 **Chamusca** Santarém, C Portugal
121 O20 **Chamrysy** Rus. Chemerisy. Homyel'skaya Voblasts', SE Belorussia
131 P5 **Chamzinka** Respublika Mordoviya, W Russian Federation
Chanáil Mhór, An see Grand Canal
Chanak see Çanakkale
64 G7 **Chañaral** Atacama, N Chile
106 H13 **Chança** var. Chanza. ✍ Portugal/Spain
59 D14 **Chancay** Lima, W Peru
Chan-chiang/Chanchiang see Zhanjiang
41 R7 **Chandalar** Alaska, USA
41 R6 **Chandalar River** ✍ Alaska, USA
158 L10 **Chandan Chauki** Uttar Pradesh, N India
159 S16 **Chandannagar** prev. Chandernagor. West Bengal, NE India
158 K10 **Chandausi** Uttar Pradesh, N India
24 M10 **Chandeleur Islands** island group Louisiana, S USA
24 M10 **Chandeleur Sound** sound N Gulf of Mexico
158 F8 **Chandigarh** Punjab, N India
159 Q16 **Chāndil** Bihār, NE India
190 I3 **Chandler** South Australia
13 Q7 **Chandler** Québec, SE Canada
38 L14 **Chandler** Arizona, SW USA
27 V7 **Chandler** Oklahoma, C USA
27 V7 **Chandler** Texas, SW USA
41 Q6 **Chandler River** ✍ Alaska, USA
58 H13 **Chandles, Río** ✍ C Brazil

169 N9 **Chandmanï** Dornogovĭ, SE Mongolia
22 J13 **Chandos Lake** ◎ Ontario, SE Canada
159 U15 **Chandpur** Chittagong, C Bangladesh
160 I13 **Chandrapur** Mahārāshtra, C India
85 J15 **Changa** Southern, S Zambia
Chang'an see Rong'an, Guangxi Zhuangzu Zizhiqu, China
161 G23 **Changanācheri** Kerala, SW India
85 M19 **Changane** ✍ S Mozambique
85 M16 **Changara** Tete, NW Mozambique
169 X11 **Changbai** var. Changbai Chaoxianzu Zizhixian. Jilin, NE China
169 X11 **Changbai Chaoxianzu Zizhixian** see Changbai
169 V10 **Changbai Shan** ▲ NE China
166 M10 **Changchun** var. Ch'angch'un, Ch'ang-ch'un; prev. Hsinking. Jilin, NE China
166 I13 **Changde** Hunan, S China
167 S13 **Changhua** Jap. Shoka. C Taiwan
174 I7 **Changi** ✕ (Singapore) E Singapore
164 L5 **Changji** Xinjiang Uygur Zizhiqu, W China
163 O13 **Chang Jiang** var. Yangtze Kiang, Eng. Yangtze. ✍ C China
166 L17 **Changjiang** prev. Shiliu. Hainan, S China
167 S8 **Changjiang Kou** delta E China
178 I13 **Chang, Ko** island S Thailand
167 Q2 **Changli** Hebei, E China
169 V10 **Changling** Jilin, NE China
167 N11 **Changsha** var. Ch'angsha, Ch'ang-sha. Hunan, S China
167 Q10 **Changshan** Zhejiang, SE China
169 X11 **Changshan Qundao** island group NE China
167 S8 **Changshu** var. Ch'ang-shu. Jiangsu, E China
169 V11 **Changtu** Liaoning, NE China
45 P14 **Changuinola** Bocas del Toro, NW Panama
165 N9 **Changweiliang** Qinghai, W China
166 K6 **Changwu** Shaanxi, C China
169 U13 **Changxing Dao** island N China
166 M9 **Changyang** Hubei, C China
169 W14 **Changyŏn** SW North Korea
167 N5 **Changzhi** Shanxi, C China
167 R8 **Changzhou** Jiangsu, E China
117 H24 **Chaniá** var. Hania, Khaniá, Eng. Canea; anc. Cydonia. Kriti, Greece, E Mediterranean Sea
117 H24 **Chanión, Kólpos** gulf Kríti, Greece, E Mediterranean Sea
80 I12 **Chankári** var. Shari. ✍ Central African Republic/Chad
80 G11 **Chari-Baguirmi** off. Préfecture du Chari-Baguirmi. ◊ prefecture SW Chad
31 V15 **Chariton** Iowa, C USA
29 U3 **Chariton River** ✍ Missouri, C USA
57 T7 **Charity** NW Guyana
33 R7 **Charity Island** island Michigan, N USA
Chärjew see Chardzhev
Chärjew Oblasty see Lebapskiy Velayat
Charkhlik/Charkhliq see Ruoqiang
104 J11 **Charleroi** Hainaut, S Belgium
9 V12 **Charles** Manitoba, C Canada
13 R10 **Charlesbourg** Québec, SE Canada
23 Y7 **Charles, Cape** headland Virginia, NE USA
31 W12 **Charles City** Iowa, C USA
23 W6 **Charles City** Virginia, NE USA
105 O5 **Charles de Gaulle** ✕ (Paris) Seine-et-Marne, N France
10 K7 **Charles Island** island Northwest Territories, NE Canada
Charles Island see Santa María, Isla
18 Mm5 **Charles-Lindbergh** ✕ (Minneapolis/Saint Paul) Minnesota, N USA
32 K9 **Charles Mound** hill Illinois, N USA
193 A22 **Charles Sound** sound South Island, NZ
193 G15 **Charleston** West Coast, South Island, NZ
29 Z7 **Charleston** Arkansas, C USA
32 M14 **Charleston** Illinois, N USA
22 L6 **Charleston** Mississippi, S USA
29 S11 **Charleston** Missouri, C USA
23 T15 **Charleston** South Carolina, SE USA
23 Q5 **Charleston** state capital West Virginia, NE USA
12 L14 **Charleston Lake** ◎ Ontario, SE Canada
37 W11 **Charleston Peak** ▲ Nevada, W USA
47 W10 **Charlestown** Nevis, Saint Kitts and Nevis
33 P16 **Charlestown** Indiana, N USA
20 M9 **Charlestown** New Hampshire, NE USA
23 V3 **Charles Town** West Virginia, NE USA
189 W9 **Charleville** Queensland, E Australia
105 R3 **Charleville-Mézières** Ardennes, N France
33 R5 **Charlevoix** Michigan, N USA
33 Q6 **Charlevoix, Lake** ◎ Michigan, N USA
41 T9 **Charley River** ✍ Alaska, USA
66 J6 **Charlie-Gibbs Fracture Zone** tectonic feature N Atlantic Ocean
105 Q10 **Charlieu** Loire, E France
33 Q10 **Charlotte** Michigan, N USA
23 R10 **Charlotte** North Carolina, SE USA
22 I8 **Charlotte** Tennessee, S USA
22 L7 **Charlotte** Vermont, NE USA
23 R10 **Charlotte** ✕ North Carolina, SE USA
47 R9 **Charlotte Amalie** prev. Saint Thomas. ◆ (Virgin Islands (US)) Saint Thomas, N Virgin Islands (US)
23 T12 **Charlotte Court House** Virginia, NE USA
25 W14 **Charlotte Harbor** inlet Florida, SE USA

12 D7 **Chapleau** ✍ Ontario, S Canada
9 T16 **Chaplin** Saskatchewan, S Canada
130 M6 **Chaplygin** Lipetskaya Oblast', W Russian Federation
119 S11 **Chaplynka** Khersons'ka Oblast', S Ukraine
15 L3 **Chapman, Cape** headland Northwest Territories, NE Canada
27 T15 **Chapman Ranch** Texas, SW USA
Chapman's see Okwa
23 P5 **Chapmanville** West Virginia, NE USA
30 K15 **Chappell** Nebraska, C USA
Chapra see Chhapra
58 D9 **Chapuli, Río** ✍ N Peru
78 I6 **Châr** well N Mauritania
126 Kk13 **Chara** Chitinskaya Oblast', S Russian Federation
126 Kk13 **Chara** ✍ C Russian Federation
56 G8 **Charala** Santander, C Colombia
43 N10 **Charcas** San Luis Potosí, C Mexico
27 T13 **Charco** Texas, SW USA
204 H7 **Charcot Island** island Antarctica
66 M8 **Charcot Seamounts** undersea feature E Atlantic Ocean
151 P17 **Chardara** Yuzhnyy Kazakhstan, S Kazakhstan
151 P17 **Chardarinskoye Vodokhranilishche** ◎ S Kazakhstan
33 U11 **Chardon** Ohio, N USA
46 K9 **Chardonnières** SW Haiti
152 K12 **Chardzhev** prev. Chardzhou, Chardzhui, Leninsk-Turkmenski, Turkm. Chärjew. Lebapskiy Velayat, E Turkmenistan
Chardzhevskaya Oblast' see Lebapskiy Velayat
Chardzhou/Chardzhui see Chardzhev
104 L11 **Charente** ◆ department W France
104 J11 **Charente** ✍ W France
104 J10 **Charente-Maritime** ◆ department W France
143 U12 **Ch'arents'avan** C Armenia
117 D15 **Chásia** ▲ C Greece
31 V9 **Chaska** Minnesota, N USA
193 D25 **Chaslands Mistake** headland South Island, NZ
129 R11 **Chasovo** Respublika Komi, NW Russian Federation
128 H14 **Chastova** Novgorodskaya Oblast', NW Russian Federation
149 R9 **Chāt** Māzandarān, N Iran
Chatak see Chhatak
41 R9 **Chatanika** Alaska, USA
41 R9 **Chatanika River** ✍ Alaska, USA
153 T8 **Chat-Bazar** Talasskaya Oblast', NW Kyrgyzstan
23 S2 **Cheat River** ✍ NE USA
113 A16 **Cheb** Ger. Eger. Západní Čechy, W Czech Republic
131 Q3 **Cheboksary** Chuvashskaya Respublika, W Russian Federation
33 Q5 **Cheboygan** Michigan, N USA
Chechaouèn see Chefchaouen
Chechenia see Chechenskaya Respublika
131 O15 **Chechenskaya Respublika** Eng. Chechenia, Chechnia, Rus. Chechnya. ◆ autonomous republic SW Russian Federation
69 N4 **Chech, Erg** desert Algeria/Mali
Chechersk see Chachersk
Chechevichi see Chachevichy
Che-chiang see Zhejiang
Chechnia/Chechnya see Chechenskaya Respublika
169 Y15 **Chech'ŏn Jap.** Teisen. N South Korea
113 L15 **Chęciny** Kielce, S Poland
29 O4 **Checotah** Oklahoma, C USA
11 R15 **Chedabucto Bay** inlet Nova Scotia, E Canada
177 F7 **Cheduba Island** island W Myanmar
39 T5 **Cheesman Lake** ◎ Colorado, C USA
205 S16 **Cheetham, Cape** headland Antarctica
58 B11 **Chepén** La Libertad, C Peru
45 U14 **Chepes** La Rioja, C Argentina
45 U14 **Chepo** Panamá, C Panama
Chepping Wycombe see High Wycombe
129 R14 **Cheptsa** ✍ NW Russian Federation
32 K3 **Chequamegon Point** headland Wisconsin, N USA
105 O8 **Cher** ◆ department C France
104 M8 **Cher** ✍ C France
Cherangani Hills see Cherangany Hills
83 H17 **Cherangany Hills** var. Cherangani Hills. ▲ W Kenya
34 G9 **Chehalis** Washington, NW USA
34 G9 **Chehalis River** ✍ Washington, NW USA
154 M6 **Chehel Abdālān, Kūh-e** var. Chalap Dalam, Pash. Chalap Dalan. ▲ C Afghanistan
117 D14 **Cheimadítis, Límni** ◎ N Greece
105 U15 **Cheiron, Mont** ▲ SE France
169 X17 **Cheju Jap.** Saishū. S South Korea
183 Q12 **Cheju Island** island Chatham Island, NZ
169 X17 **Cheju-do Jap.** Saishū; prev. Quelpart. island S South Korea
169 X17 **Cheju-haehyŏp** strait S South Korea
Chekiang see Zhejiang
Chekichler see Chekishlyar
152 B13 **Chekishlyar Turkm.** Chekichler. Balkanskiy Velayat, W Turkmenistan
196 F8 **Chelab** Babeldaob, N Palau
153 N11 **Chelak Rus.** Chelek. Samarqand Wiloyati, C Uzbekistan
34 J7 **Chelan, Lake** ◎ Washington, NW USA
Chelek see Chelak
152 A11 **Cheleken** Balkanskiy Velayat, W Turkmenistan
Chélif/Chéliff see Chelif, Oued

76 J5 **Chelif, Oued** var. Chélif, Chéliff, Chellif, Shellif. ✍ N Algeria
150 K12 **Chelkar** Aktyubinsk, W Kazakhstan
Chelkar, Ozero see Shalkar, Ozero
Chellif see Chelif, Oued
113 P14 **Chełm Rus.** Kholm. Chełm, E Poland
113 P14 **Chełm** off. Województwo Chełmskie, Rus. Kholm. ◆ province E Poland
112 I9 **Chełmno Ger.** Culm, Kulm. Toruń, N Poland
12 F10 **Chelmsford** Ontario, S Canada
99 P21 **Chelmsford** E England, UK
Chełm
112 J9 **Chełmża Ger.** Culmsee, Kulmsee. Toruń, N Poland
29 Q8 **Chelsea** Oklahoma, C USA
20 M8 **Chelsea** Vermont, NE USA
99 L21 **Cheltenham** C England, UK
107 R9 **Chelva** País Valenciano, E Spain
125 Ee12 **Chelyabinsk** Chelyabinskaya Oblast', C Russian Federation
125 E12 **Chelyabinskaya Oblast'** ◊ province C Russian Federation
126 Jj4 **Chelyuskin, Mys** headland N Russian Federation
126 H15 **Chemal** Altayskiy Kray, S Russian Federation
43 Y12 **Chemax** Yucatán, SE Mexico
85 N16 **Chemba** Sofala, C Mozambique
84 J13 **Chembe** Luapula, NE Zambia
152 J17 **Chemenibit** Maryyskiy Velayat, S Turkmenistan
Chemerisy see Chamyarysy
118 K7 **Chemerivtsi** Khmel'nyts'ka Oblast', W Ukraine
104 J8 **Chemillé** Maine-et-Loire, NW France
181 X17 **Chemin Grenier** S Mauritius
103 N16 **Chemnitz** prev. Karl-Marx-Stadt. Sachsen, E Germany
Chemulpo see Inch'ŏn
34 H14 **Chemult** Oregon, NW USA
20 G12 **Chemung River** ✍ New York/Pennsylvania, NE USA
155 U8 **Chenāb** ✍ India/Pakistan
41 S9 **Chena Hot Springs** Alaska, USA
20 J11 **Chenango River** ✍ New York, NE USA
174 Gg3 **Chenderoh, Tasik** ◎ Peninsular Malaysia
13 Q11 **Chêne, Rivière du** ✍ Québec, SE Canada
34 L8 **Cheney** Washington, NW USA
28 M6 **Cheney Reservoir** ◎ Kansas, C USA
Chengchiatun see Liaoyuan
Ch'eng-chou/Chengchow see Zhengzhou
167 P1 **Chengde** var. Jehol. Hebei, E China
166 I9 **Chengdu** var. Chengtu, Ch'eng-tu. Sichuan, C China
167 Q14 **Chenghai** Guangdong, S China
Chenghsien see Zhengzhou
166 L17 **Chengmai** Hainan, S China
Chengtu/Ch'eng-tu see Chengdu
166 L12 **Cheng Xian** Gansu, C China
Chenkiang see Zhenjiang
Chennai see Madras
166 L11 **Chenôve** Côte d'Or, C France
166 L11 **Chenxi** Hunan, S China
Chen Xian/Chenxian/Chen Xiang see Chenzhou
167 N12 **Chenzhou** var. Chenxian, Chen Xian, Chen Xiang. Hunan, S China
178 Kk12 **Cheo Reo** var. A Yun Pa. Gia Lai, S Vietnam
116 I11 **Chepelare** Plovdivska Oblast, S Bulgaria
116 I11 **Chepelarska Reka** ✍ S Bulgaria
58 B11 **Chepén** La Libertad, C Peru
131 R5 **Cherdakly** Ul'yanovskaya Oblast', W Russian Federation
129 T2 **Cherdyn'** Permskaya Oblast', NW Russian Federation
126 J15 **Cherekha** ✍ W Russian Federation
126 J15 **Cheremkhovo** Irkutskaya Oblast', S Russian Federation
126 Hh15 **Cheremushki** Respublika Khakastya, S Russian Federation
Cheren see Keren
128 X13 **Cherepovets** Vologodskaya Oblast', NW Russian Federation
129 O11 **Cherevkovo** Arkhangel'skaya Oblast', NW Russian Federation
76 I6 **Chergui, Chott ech** salt lake NW Algeria
Cherikov see Cherykaw
119 Q6 **Cherkas'ka Oblast'** var. Cherkasy, Rus. Cherkasskaya Oblast'. ◊ province C Ukraine
Cherkasskaya Oblast' see Cherkas'ka Oblast'
Cherkasy see Cherkas'ka Oblast'
119 Q6 **Cherkasy Rus.** Cherkassy. Cherkas'ka Oblast', C Ukraine

● COUNTRY ◇ DEPENDENT TERRITORY ✕ ADMINISTRATIVE REGION ▲ MOUNTAIN ▼ VOLCANO ◎ LAKE
● COUNTRY CAPITAL ○ DEPENDENT TERRITORY CAPITAL ✕ INTERNATIONAL AIRPORT ▲ MOUNTAIN RANGE ✍ RIVER ▫ RESERVOIR

239

Cherkasy see Cherkas'ka Oblast'
130 M15 **Cherkessk** Karachayevo-Cherkesskaya Respublika, SW Russian Federation
125 G13 **Cherlak** Omskaya Oblast', C Russian Federation
125 Fj14 **Cherlakskiy** Omskaya Oblast', C Russian Federation
129 U13 **Chermoz** Permskaya Oblast', NW Russian Federation
Chernavchitsy see Charnawchytsy
129 T3 **Chernaya** Nenetskiy Avtonomnyy Okrug, NW Russian Federation
129 T4 **Chernaya** NW Russian Federation
Chernigov see Chernihiv
Chernigovskaya Oblast' see Chernihivs'ka Oblast'
119 Q2 **Chernihiv** Rus. Chernigov, NE Ukraine
Chernihiv see Chernihivs'ka Oblast'
119 V9 **Chernihivka** Zaporiz'ka Oblast', SE Ukraine
119 P2 **Chernihivs'ka Oblast'** var. Chernihiv, Rus. Chernigovskaya Oblast'. ◆ province NE Ukraine
116 I9 **Cherni Osŭm** N Bulgaria
118 J8 **Chernivets'ka Oblast'** var. Chernivtsi, Rus. Chernovitskaya Oblast'. ◆ province W Ukraine
116 I9 **Cherni Vit** NW Bulgaria
116 G10 **Cherni Vrŭkh** W Bulgaria
118 K8 **Chernivtsi** Ger. Czernowitz, Rom. Cernăuţi, Rus. Chernovtsy. Chernivets'ka Oblast', W Ukraine
118 M7 **Chernivtsi** Vinnyts'ka Oblast', C Ukraine
Chernivtsi see Chernivets'ka Oblast'
Chernobyl' see Chornobyl'
126 Hh15 **Chernogorsk** Respublika Khakasiya, S Russian Federation
Cherno More see Black Sea
Chernomorskoye see Chornomors'ke
151 T7 **Chernoretskoye** Pavlodar, NE Kazakhstan
Chernovitskaya Oblast' see Chernivets'ka Oblast'
Chernovtsy see Chernivtsi
151 U8 **Chernoye** Pavlodar, NE Kazakhstan
Chernoye More see Black Sea
129 U16 **Chernushka** Permskaya Oblast', NW Russian Federation
119 N4 **Chernyakhiv** Rus. Chernyakhov. Zhytomyrs'ka Oblast', N Ukraine
Chernyakhov see Chernyakhiv
121 C14 **Chernyakhovsk** Ger. Insterburg. Kaliningradskaya Oblast', W Russian Federation
130 K8 **Chernyanka** Belgorodskaya Oblast', W Russian Federation
129 V5 **Chernysheva, Gryada** NW Russian Federation
150 J14 **Chernysheva, Zaliv** gulf SW Kazakhstan
126 L15 **Chernyshevsk** Chitinskaya Oblast', S Russian Federation
126 K11 **Chernyshevskiy** Respublika Sakha (Yakutiya), NE Russian Federation
131 P13 **Chernyye Zemli** plain SW Russian Federation
Chërnyy Irtysh see Ertix He
131 V7 **Chërnyy Otrog** Orenburgskaya Oblast', W Russian Federation
31 T12 **Cherokee** Iowa, C USA
28 M8 **Cherokee** Oklahoma, C USA
27 R9 **Cherokee** Texas, SW USA
23 O8 **Cherokee Lake** Tennessee, S USA
Cherokees, Lake O' The see Grand Lake O' The Cherokees
46 N1 **Cherokee Sound** Great Abaco, N Bahamas
159 V13 **Cherrapunji** Meghālaya, NE India
30 L9 **Cherry Creek** South Dakota, N USA
20 J16 **Cherry Hill** New Jersey, NE USA
29 Q7 **Cherryvale** Kansas, C USA
23 Q10 **Cherryville** North Carolina, SE USA
Cherski Range see Cherskogo, Khrebet
127 O5 **Cherskiy** Respublika Sakha (Yakutiya), NE Russian Federation
126 Mm6 **Cherskogo, Khrebet** var. Cherski Range. NE Russian Federation
Cherso see Cres
130 L10 **Chertkovo** Rostovskaya Oblast', SW Russian Federation
Cherven' see Chervyen'
116 H8 **Cherven Bryag** Loveshka Oblast', NW Bulgaria
118 M4 **Chervonoarmiys'k** Zhytomyrs'ka Oblast', N Ukraine
Chervonograd see Chervonohrad
118 I4 **Chervonohrad** Rus. Chervonograd. L'vivs'ka Oblast', NW Ukraine
119 W6 **Chervonooskil's'ke Vodoskhovyshche** Rus. Krasnoosol'skoye Vodokhranilishche. NE Ukraine
Chervonoye, Ozero see Chyrvonaye, Vozyera
119 S4 **Chervonozavods'ke** Poltavs'ka Oblast', C Ukraine
121 L16 **Chervyen'** Rus. Cherven'. Minskaya Voblasts', C Belorussia
121 P16 **Cherykaw** Rus. Cherikov. Mahilyowskaya Voblasts', E Belorussia
33 R9 **Chesaning** Michigan, N USA
23 X5 **Chesapeake Bay** inlet NE USA
Cheshevlya see Tsyeshawlya

99 K18 **Cheshire** cultural region C England, UK
129 P5 **Chëshskaya Guba** var. Archangel Bay, Chesha Bay, Dvina Bay. bay NW Russian Federation
12 F14 **Chesley** Ontario, S Canada
23 Q10 **Chesnee** South Carolina, SE USA
99 K18 **Chester** Wel. Caerleon; hist. Legaceaster, Lat. Deva, Devana Castra. C England, UK
37 O4 **Chester** California, W USA
32 K16 **Chester** Illinois, N USA
33 N11 **Chester** Montana, NW USA
20 S7 **Chester** Pennsylvania, NE USA
23 R1 **Chester** South Carolina, SE USA
27 X9 **Chester** Texas, SW USA
23 W6 **Chester** Virginia, NE USA
23 M18 **Chesterfield** C England, UK
23 S11 **Chesterfield** South Carolina, SE USA
23 W6 **Chesterfield** Virginia, NE USA
199 I10 **Chesterfield, Îles** island group NW New Caledonia
15 Ll6 **Chesterfield Inlet** Northwest Territories, NW Canada
15 L6 **Chesterfield** inlet Northwest Territories, N Canada
23 Y3 **Chester River** Delaware/Maryland, NE USA
23 X3 **Chestertown** Maryland, NE USA
21 R4 **Chesuncook Lake** Maine, NE USA
32 J5 **Chetek** Wisconsin, N USA
11 R14 **Chéticamp** Nova Scotia, SE Canada
29 Q8 **Chetopa** Kansas, C USA
43 Y14 **Chetumal** var. Payo Obispo. Quintana Roo, SE Mexico
Chetumal, Bahía/Chetumal, Bahía de see Chetumal Bay
44 G1 **Chetumal Bay** var. Bahía Chetumal, Bahía de Chetumal. bay Belize/Mexico
8 H7 **Chetwynd** British Columbia, W Canada
40 M11 **Chevak** Alaska, USA
38 M12 **Chevelon Creek** Arizona, SW USA
193 J17 **Cheviot** Canterbury, South Island, NZ
98 L13 **Cheviot Hills** hill range England/Scotland, UK
98 L13 **Cheviot, The** England/Scotland, UK
13 R7 **Chicoutimi** Québec, SE Canada
13 Q8 **Chicoutimi** Québec, SE Canada
12 M11 **Chevreuil, Lac du** Québec, SE Canada
83 I16 **Ch'ew Bahir** var. Lake Stefanie. Ethiopia/Kenya
34 L7 **Chewelah** Washington, NW USA
28 K10 **Cheyenne** Oklahoma, C USA
35 Z17 **Cheyenne** state capital Wyoming, C USA
28 L5 **Cheyenne Bottoms** Kansas, C USA
18 Kk6 **Cheyenne River** South Dakota/Wyoming, N USA
39 W5 **Cheyenne Wells** Colorado, C USA
110 C9 **Cheyres** Vaud, W Switzerland
Chezdi-Oşorheiu see Târgu Secuiesc
159 P13 **Chhapra** prev. Chapra. Bihār, N India
159 V13 **Chhatak** var. Chatak. Chittagong, NE Bangladesh
160 J9 **Chhatarpur** Madhya Pradesh, C India
160 N13 **Chhatrapur** prev. Chatrapur. Orissa, E India
160 L12 **Chhattisgarh** plain C India
160 I11 **Chhindwāra** Madhya Pradesh, C India
Chhlong see Phumĭ Chhlong
Chhuk see Phumĭ Chhuk
159 T12 **Chhukha** SW Bhutan
167 S14 **Chiai** var. Chia-i, Chiayi, Kiayi, Jap. Kagi. C Taiwan
Chia-mu-ssu see Jiamusi
85 B15 **Chiange** Port. Vila de Almoster. Huíla, SW Angola
Chiang-hsi see Jiangxi
167 S12 **Chiang Kai-shek** ✈ (T'aipei) N Taiwan
178 I8 **Chiang Khan** Loei, E Thailand
178 H7 **Chiang Mai** var. Chiangmai, Chiengmai, Kiangmai. Chiang Mai, NW Thailand
178 H7 **Chiang Mai** ✈ Chiang Mai, NW Thailand
178 Hh6 **Chiang Rai** var. Chianpai, Chienrai, Muang Chiang Rai. Chiang Rai, NW Thailand
Chiang-su see Jiangsu
Chianning/Chiang-ning see Nanjing
Chianpai see Chiang Rai
108 G12 **Chianti** cultural region C Italy
43 V16 **Chiapa** see Chiapa de Cerzo
43 V16 **Chiapa de Cerzo** var. Chiapa. Chiapas, SE Mexico
43 U16 **Chiapas** ◆ state SE Mexico
108 J12 **Chiaravalle** Marche, C Italy
109 N22 **Chiaravalle Centrale** Calabria, SW Italy
108 E7 **Chiari** Lombardia, N Italy
110 H12 **Chiasso** Ticino, S Switzerland
143 S9 **Chiat'ura** C Georgia
43 P15 **Chiautla** var. Chiautla de Tapia. Puebla, S Mexico
Chiautla de Tapia see Chiautla
108 D10 **Chiavari** Liguria, NW Italy
108 E6 **Chiavenna** Lombardia, N Italy
Chiayi see Chiai
Chiazza see Piazza Armerina
172 S12 **Chiba** var. Tiba. Chiba, Honshū, S Japan
171 K17 **Chiba** off. Chiba-ken, var. Tiba. ◆ prefecture Honshū, S Japan
85 M18 **Chibabava** Sofala, C Mozambique

85 B15 **Chibia** Port. João de Almeida, Vila João de Almeida. Huíla, SW Angola
119 N13 **Chilia, Brațul** SE Romania
Chilia-Nouă see Kiliya
85 M18 **Chiboma** Sofala, C Mozambique
84 J12 **Chibondo** Luapula, N Zambia
84 K11 **Chibote** Luapula, NE Zambia
10 K12 **Chibougamau** Québec, SE Canada
170 Ffj1 **Chiburi-jima** island Oki-shotō, SW Japan
85 M20 **Chibuto** Gaza, S Mozambique
33 N11 **Chicago** Illinois, N USA
33 N11 **Chicago Heights** Illinois, N USA
13 W6 **Chic-Chocs, Monts** Eng. Shickshock Mountains. ▲ Québec, SE Canada
41 W13 **Chichagof Island** island Alexander Archipelago, Alaska, USA
59 K20 **Chichas, Cordillera de** ▲ SW Bolivia
43 X12 **Chichén-Itzá, Ruinas** ruins Yucatán, SE Mexico
99 Q23 **Chichester** SE England, UK
171 Ij16 **Chichibu** var. Titibu. Saitama, Honshū, S Japan
44 C5 **Chichicastenango** Quiché, W Guatemala
44 I9 **Chichigalpa** Chinandega, W Nicaragua
Ch'i-ch'i-ha-erh see Qiqihar
172 T16 **Chichijima-rettō** Eng. Beechy Group. island group SE Japan
56 K4 **Chichiriviche** Falcón, N Venezuela
41 R11 **Chickaloon** Alaska, USA
22 L10 **Chickamauga Lake** ☒ Tennessee, S USA
25 N7 **Chickasawhay River** ☒ Mississippi, S USA
28 M11 **Chickasha** Oklahoma, C USA
41 T9 **Chicken** Alaska, USA
106 J16 **Chiclana de la Frontera** Andalucía, S Spain
58 B11 **Chiclayo** Lambayeque, NW Peru
37 N5 **Chico** California, W USA
43 L15 **Chicoa** Tete, NW Mozambique
85 M19 **Chicomo** Gaza, S Mozambique
20 M11 **Chicopee** Massachusetts, NE USA
65 I19 **Chico, Río** ☒ SE Argentina
65 I21 **Chico, Río** ☒ S Argentina
29 W14 **Chicot, Lake** ☒ Arkansas, C USA
13 R7 **Chicoutimi** Québec, SE Canada
13 Q8 **Chicoutimi** ☒ Québec, SE Canada
85 L19 **Chicualacuala** Gaza, SW Mozambique
85 B14 **Chicuma** Benguela, C Angola
161 J21 **Chidambaram** Tamil Nādu, SE India
206 K13 **Chidley, Cape** headland Newfoundland and Labrador, E Canada
103 N24 **Chiemsee** ☒ SE Germany
Chiengmai see Chiang Mai
Chienrai see Chiang Rai
108 B8 **Chieri** Piemonte, NW Italy
108 F8 **Chiese** ☒ N Italy
109 K14 **Chieti** var. Teate. Abruzzi, C Italy
101 E19 **Chièvres** Hainaut, SW Belgium
169 S12 **Chifeng** var. Ulanhad. Nei Mongol Zizhiqu, N China
84 I13 **Chifumage** ☒ E Angola
84 M13 **Chifunda** Eastern, NE Zambia
151 S14 **Chiganak** var. Čiganak. Zhambyl, SE Kazakhstan
41 P15 **Chiginagak, Mount** ▲ Alaska, USA
43 P13 **Chignahuapan** Puebla, S Mexico
41 O15 **Chignik** Alaska, USA
85 M19 **Chigombe** ☒ S Mozambique
56 D7 **Chigorodó** Antioquia, NW Colombia
85 M19 **Chigubo** Gaza, S Mozambique
168 D6 **Chihertey** Bayan-Ölgiy, W Mongolia
Chih-fu see Yantai
Chihli see Hebei
Chihli, Gulf of see Bo Hai
42 J6 **Chihuahua** Chihuahua, N Mexico
42 J6 **Chihuahua** ◆ state N Mexico
151 O15 **Chiili** Kzyl-Orda, S Kazakhstan
28 M7 **Chikaskia River** ☒ Kansas/Oklahoma, C USA
161 H19 **Chik Ballāpur** Karnātaka, W India
128 G15 **Chikhachevo** Pskovskaya Oblast', W Russian Federation
161 F19 **Chikmagalūr** Karnātaka, W India
133 V7 **Chikoy** ☒ C Russian Federation
85 J15 **Chikumbi** Lusaka, C Zambia
84 M13 **Chikwa** Eastern, NE Zambia
85 N15 **Chikwawa** var. Chikwana. Southern, S Malawi
161 J16 **Chilakalūrupet** Andhra Pradesh, E India
152 L14 **Chilan** Lebapskiy Velayat, E Turkmenistan
43 P16 **Chilapa** var. Chilapa de Alvarez. Guerrero, S Mexico
Chilapa de Alvarez see Chilapa
161 J25 **Chilaw** North Western Province, W Sri Lanka
59 D15 **Chilca** Lima, W Peru
27 P4 **Childress** Texas, SW USA
23 Z5 **Childersburg** Alabama, S USA
65 G14 **Chile** off. Republic of Chile. ◆ republic SW South America
49 R10 **Chile Basin** undersea feature E Pacific Ocean
65 H20 **Chile Chico** Aisén, W Chile
64 H12 **Chilecito** La Rioja, NW Argentina
85 L14 **Chilembwe** Eastern, NE Zambia

200 O13 **Chile Rise** undersea feature SE Pacific Ocean
119 N13 **Chilia, Brațul** ☒ SE Romania
Chilia-Nouă see Kiliya
151 V15 **Chilik** Almaty, SE Kazakhstan
151 V15 **Chilik** ☒ SE Kazakhstan
160 O13 **Chilika Lake** var. Chilka Lake. ☒ E India
84 J13 **Chililabombwe** Copperbelt, C Zambia
Chi-lin see Jilin
Chilka Lake see Chilika Lake
8 H9 **Chilkoot Pass** pass British Columbia, W Canada
Chill Ala, Cuan see Killala Bay
64 G13 **Chillán** Bío Bío, C Chile
63 C22 **Chillar** Buenos Aires, E Argentina
Chill Chiaráin, Cuan see Kilkieran Bay
32 K12 **Chillicothe** Illinois, N USA
29 S3 **Chillicothe** Missouri, C USA
33 S14 **Chillicothe** Ohio, N USA
27 Q4 **Chillicothe** Texas, SW USA
8 M17 **Chilliwack** British Columbia, SW Canada
Chill Mhantáin, Ceann see Wicklow Head
Chill Mhantáin, Sléibhte see Wicklow Mountains
110 C10 **Chillon** Vaud, W Switzerland
152 C11 **Chil'mamedkum, Peski** Turkm. Chälmämetgum. desert W Turkmenistan
Chilmämetgum see Chil'mamedkum, Peski
65 F17 **Chiloé, Isla de** var. Isla Grande de Chiloé. island W Chile
34 H15 **Chiloquin** Oregon, NW USA
43 O16 **Chilpancingo** var. Chilpancingo de los Bravos. Guerrero, S Mexico
Chilpancingo de los Bravos see Chilpancingo
99 N21 **Chiltern Hills** hill range S England, UK
32 M7 **Chilton** Wisconsin, N USA
84 F11 **Chiluage** Lunda Sul, NE Angola
84 M12 **Chilumba** prev. Deep Bay. Northern, N Malawi
167 T12 **Chilung** var. Keelung, Jap. Kirun, Kirun'; prev. Sp. Santissima Trinidad. N Taiwan
85 N15 **Chilwa, Lake** var. Lago Chirua, NE Mozambique; prev. Lago Shirwa. ☒ SE Malawi
178 J10 **Chi, Mae Nam** ☒ E Thailand
44 C6 **Chimaltenango** Chimaltenango, C Guatemala
44 A2 **Chimaltenango** off. Departamento de Chimaltenango. ◆ department C Guatemala
45 V15 **Chimán** Panamá, E Panama
85 M17 **Chimanimani** prev. Mandidzudzure, Melsetter. Manicaland, E Zimbabwe
101 G21 **Chimay** Hainaut, S Belgium
39 S10 **Chimayo** New Mexico, SW USA
58 A13 **Chimbay** see Chimboy
58 C7 **Chimborazo** ◆ province C Ecuador
58 C12 **Chimborazo** ▲ C Ecuador
58 B11 **Chimbote** Ancash, W Peru
152 H7 **Chimboy** Rus. Chimbay. Qoraqalpoghiston Respublikasi, NW Uzbekistan
194 H12 **Chimbu** ◆ province C PNG
56 F6 **Chimichagua** Cesar, N Colombia
Chimishliya see Cimişlia
Chimkent see Shymkent
Chimkentskaya Oblast' see Yuzhnyy Kazakhstan
30 I14 **Chimney Rock** rock Nebraska, C USA
85 M17 **Chimoio** Manica, C Mozambique
84 K11 **Chimpembe** Northern, NE Zambia
43 O8 **China** Nuevo León, NE Mexico
162 M9 **China** off. People's Republic of China, Chin. Chung-hua Jen-min Kung-ho-kuo, Zhonghua Renmin Gongheguo; prev. Chinese Empire. ◆ republic E Asia
China Lake see China
21 Q7 **China Lake** ☒ California, W USA
44 H9 **Chinameca** San Miguel, E El Salvador
Chi-nan/Chinan see Jinan
44 H9 **Chinandega** Chinandega, NW Nicaragua
44 H9 **Chinandega** ◆ department NW Nicaragua
China, People's Republic of see China
China, Republic of see Taiwan
26 J11 **Chinati Mountains** ▲ Texas, SW USA
Chinaz see Chinoz
59 E15 **Chincha Alta** Ica, SW Peru
9 N11 **Chinchaga** ☒ Alberta, W Canada
23 Y6 **Chincoteague** Assateague Island, Virginia, NE USA
Chin-chiang see Quanzhou
Chinchilla see Chinchilla de Monte Aragón
107 Q11 **Chinchilla de Monte Aragón** var. Chinchilla. Castilla-La Mancha, C Spain
85 D10 **Chinchiná** Caldas, W Colombia
107 O8 **Chinchón** Madrid, C Spain
43 Z14 **Chinchorro, Banco** island SE Mexico
Chin-chou/Chinchow see Jinzhou
85 O17 **Chinde** Zambézia, NE Mozambique
165 V14 **Chŏ-do** island SW North Korea
169 V14 **Chin-do** Jap. Chin-tō. island SW South Korea
165 R13 **Chindu** Qinghai, C China
177 G2 **Chindwin** ☒ W Myanmar
Chinese Empire see China
152 L10 **Chingeldi** Rus. Chingildi. Nawoiy Wiloyati, N Uzbekistan
Ch'ing Hai see Qinghai Hu

Chingildi see Chingeldi
150 H9 **Chingirlau** Kaz. Shynghyrlaü. Zapadnyy Kazakhstan, W Kazakhstan
84 J13 **Chingola** Copperbelt, C Zambia
Ching-Tao/Ch'ing-tao see Qingdao
84 C13 **Chinguar** Huambo, C Angola
78 I7 **Chinguetti** var. Chinguetti. Adrar, C Mauritania
169 Z16 **Chinhae** Jap. Chinkai. S South Korea
177 Ff4 **Chin Hills** ▲ W Myanmar
85 K16 **Chinhoyi** prev. Sinoia. Mashonaland West, N Zimbabwe
41 Q12 **Chiniak, Cape** headland Kodiak Island, Alaska, USA
12 B9 **Chiniguchi Lake** ☒ Ontario, S Canada
155 U8 **Chiniot** Punjab, E Pakistan
155 U10 **Chintian Mandi** Punjab, E Pakistan
166 F11 **Chishui He** ☒ C China
Chisimaio/Chisimayu see Kismaayo
119 N10 **Chişinău** Rus. Kishinev. ● (Moldova) C Moldova
119 N10 **Chişinău** C Moldova
Chişinău-Criş see Chişineu-Criş
118 F10 **Chişineu-Criş** Hung. Kşjenő; prev. Chişinău-Criş. Arad, W Romania
84 C15 **Chinko** ☒ C Central African Republic
39 O9 **Chinle** Arizona, SW USA
167 R13 **Chinmen Tao** var. Jinmen Dao, Quemoy. island W Taiwan
Chinnereth see Tiberias, Lake
110 C10 **Chillon** Vaud, W Switzerland
84 J13 **Chisamba** Central, C Zambia
108 A8 **Chisone** ☒ NW Italy
26 K2 **Chisos Mountains** ▲ Texas, SW USA
41 T10 **Chistochina** Alaska, USA
131 P4 **Chistopol'** Respublika Tatarstan, W Russian Federation
151 O8 **Chistopol'ye** Kokshetau, N Kazakhstan
85 B16 **Chitado** Cunene, SW Angola
Chitaldroog/Chitaldrug see Chitradurga
85 C15 **Chitanda** S Angola
85 F10 **Chitato** Lunda Norte, NE Angola
41 T11 **Chitina** Alaska, USA
41 T11 **Chitina River** ☒ Alaska, USA
126 Kk14 **Chitinskaya Oblast'** ◆ province S Russian Federation
84 M11 **Chitipa** prev. Fort Hill. Northern, NW Malawi
172 Oo6 **Chitose** var. Titose. Hokkaidō, NE Japan
161 G18 **Chitradurga** prev. Chitaldroog, Chitaldrug. Karnātaka, W India
155 T3 **Chitral** North-West Frontier Province, NW Pakistan
45 S19 **Chitré** Herrera, S Panama
159 O16 **Chittagong** Ben. Cháttagám. Chittagong, SE Bangladesh
159 U16 **Chittagong** ◆ division E Bangladesh
159 Q15 **Chittaranjan** West Bengal, NE India
158 G14 **Chittaurgarh** Rājasthān, N India
161 I21 **Chittoor** Andhra Pradesh, E India
85 K16 **Chitungwiza** prev. Chitungwiza. Mashonaland East, NE Zimbabwe
84 F12 **Chiúmbe** var. Tshiumbe. ☒ Angola/Zaire
85 F15 **Chiume** Moxico, E Angola
84 K13 **Chiundaponde** Northern, NE Zambia
108 H13 **Chiusi** Toscana, C Italy
56 J5 **Chivacoa** Yaracuy, N Venezuela
108 B8 **Chivasso** Piemonte, NW Italy
85 L17 **Chivhu** prev. Enkeldoorn. Midlands, C Zimbabwe
63 C20 **Chivilcoy** Buenos Aires, E Argentina
84 D4 **Chiweta** Northern, N Malawi
64 D4 **Chixoy, Río** var. Río Negro, Río Salinas. ☒ Guatemala/Mexico
84 H13 **Chizela** North Western, NW Zambia
129 O5 **Chizha** Nenetskiy Avtonomnyy Okrug, NW Russian Federation
161 I21 **Chizha** Andhra Pradesh, E India
155 N4 **Chiras** Ghowr, N Afghanistan
158 H11 **Chiráwa** Rājasthān, N India
Chirchik see Chirchiq
153 Q9 **Chirchiq** Rus. Chirchik. Toshkent Wiloyati, E Uzbekistan
153 P10 **Chirchiq** ☒ E Uzbekistan
Chire see Shire
85 L18 **Chiredzi** Masvingo, SE Zimbabwe
79 X7 **Chirfa** Agadez, N Niger
56 F6 **Chiriguaná** Cesar, N Colombia
41 P15 **Chirikof Island** island Alaska, USA
45 O16 **Chiriquí** off. Provincia de Chiriquí. ◆ province SW Panama
45 P17 **Chiriquí, Golfo de** Eng. Chiriquí Gulf. gulf SW Panama
45 P15 **Chiriquí Grande** Bocas del Toro, W Panama
Chiriquí Gulf see Chiriquí, Golfo de
45 P15 **Chiriquí, Laguna de** lagoon NW Panama
45 O16 **Chiriquí Viejo, Río** ☒ NW Panama
Chiriquí, Volcán de see Barú, Volcán
85 N15 **Chiromo** Southern, S Malawi
116 J10 **Chirpan** Khaskovska Oblast', C Bulgaria
45 N14 **Chirripó Atlántico, Río** ☒ E Costa Rica
Chirripó, Cerro see Chirripó Grande, Cerro
45 N14 **Chirripó Grande, Cerro** var. Cerro Chirripó. ▲ SE Costa Rica
45 N13 **Chirripó, Río** var. Río Chirripó del Pacífico. ☒ NE Costa Rica
Chohtan see Chauhtan

9 U14 **Choiceland** Saskatchewan, S Canada
195 U13 **Choiseul** var. Lauru. island NW Solomon Islands
65 M23 **Choiseul Sound** sound East Falkland, Falkland Islands
42 H7 **Choix** Sinaloa, C Mexico
112 D10 **Chojna** Szczecin, W Poland
112 H8 **Chojnice** Ger. Konitz. Bydgoszcz, NW Poland
113 F14 **Chojnów** Ger. Hainau, Haynau. Legnica, W Poland
171 Ll11 **Chōkai-san** ▲ Honshū, N Japan
178 I11 **Chok Chai** Nakhon Ratchasima, C Thailand
82 I12 **Ch'ok'ē** var. Choke Mountains. ▲ NW Ethiopia
27 R13 **Choke Canyon Lake** ☒ Texas, SW USA
Choke Mountains see Ch'ok'ē
151 T15 **Chokpar** Kaz. Shoqpar. Zhambyl, S Kazakhstan
153 T16 **Chok-Tal** var. Choktal. Issyk-Kul'skaya Oblast', E Kyrgyzstan
126 Mm6 **Chokurdakh** Respublika Sakha (Yakutiya), NE Russian Federation
85 L20 **Chókuè** Gaza, S Mozambique
196 F8 **Chol** Babeldaob, N Palau
166 I68 **Chola Shan** ▲ C China
104 J8 **Cholet** Maine-et-Loire, NW France
65 H14 **Cholila** Chubut, W Argentina
Cholo see Thyolo
153 V8 **Cholpon** Narynskaya Oblast', C Kyrgyzstan
153 V7 **Cholpon-Ata** Issyk-Kul'skaya Oblast', E Kyrgyzstan
44 I9 **Choluteca** Choluteca, S Honduras
44 I8 **Choluteca** ◆ department S Honduras
44 G6 **Choluteca, Río** ☒ SW Honduras
85 I15 **Choma** Southern, S Zambia
159 T11 **Chomo Lhari** ▲ NW Bhutan
178 H7 **Chom Thong** Chiang Mai, NW Thailand
113 B15 **Chomutov** Ger. Komotau. Severní Čechy, NW Czech Republic
126 K12 **Chona** ☒ C Russian Federation
169 X15 **Ch'ŏnan** Jap. Tenan. W South Korea
178 Hh12 **Chon Buri** prev. Bang Pla Soi. Chon Buri, S Thailand
58 B6 **Chone** Manabí, W Ecuador
169 W13 **Ch'ŏngch'ŏn-gang** ☒ W North Korea
169 Y11 **Ch'ŏngjin** NE North Korea
169 W13 **Ch'ŏngju** NE North Korea
167 S8 **Chongming Dao** island E China
166 J10 **Chongqing** var. Ch'ung-ching, Ch'ung-ch'ing, Chungking, Pahsien, Tchongking, Yuzhou. Sichuan, C China
Chóngup see Chŏngŭp
167 O10 **Chongyang** Hubei, C China
169 Y16 **Chŏnju** prev. Chŏngŭp, Jap. Seiyu. SW South Korea
169 Y15 **Chŏnju** Jap. Zenshū. SW South Korea
Chonnacht see Connaught
168 E9 **Chonogol** Sühbaatar, E Mongolia
65 F19 **Chonos, Archipiélago de los** island group S Chile
44 K10 **Chontales** ◆ department S Nicaragua
178 J12 **Chơn Thanh** Sông Be, S Vietnam
164 K17 **Cho Oyu** var. Qowowuyag. ▲ China/Nepal see also Qowowuyag
118 G7 **Chop** Cz. Čop, Hung. Csap. Zakarpats'ka Oblast', W Ukraine
23 Y3 **Choptank River** ☒ Maryland, NE USA
Chorcaí, Cuan see Cork Harbour
45 P15 **Chorcha, Cerro** ▲ W Panama
Chorku see Chorkŭh
153 R11 **Chorkŭh** Rus. Chorku. N Tajikistan
99 K17 **Chorley** NW England, UK
Chorne More see Black Sea
119 R5 **Chornobay** Cherkas'ka Oblast', C Ukraine
119 O3 **Chornobyl'** Rus. Chernobyl'. Kyyivs'ka Oblast', N Ukraine
119 R12 **Chornomors'ke** Rus. Chernomorskoye. Respublika Krym, S Ukraine
119 R4 **Chornukhy** Poltavs'ka Oblast', C Ukraine
Chorokh/Chorokhi see Çoruh Nehri
112 O9 **Choroszcz** Białystok, NE Poland
118 K6 **Chortkiv** Rus. Chortkov. Ternopil's'ka Oblast', W Ukraine
Chortkov see Chortkiv
Chorum see Çorum
112 M9 **Chorzele** Ostrołęka, NE Poland
113 I16 **Chorzów** Ger. Königshütte; prev. Królewska Huta. Katowice, S Poland
169 W12 **Ch'osan** N Korea
Chŏsen-kaikyō see Korea Strait
171 Kk17 **Chōshi** var. Tyōsi. Chiba, Honshū, S Japan
65 H14 **Chos Malal** Neuquén, W Argentina
Chosŏn-minjujuŭi-inmin-kanghwaguk see North Korea
112 E9 **Choszczno** Ger. Arnswalde. Gorzów, W Poland
159 O15 **Chota Nāgpur** plateau N India
33 R8 **Choteau** Montana, NW USA
10 H6 **Chouart** ☒ Québec, SE Canada
78 I7 **Choûm** Adrar, C Mauritania
28 Q9 **Chouteau** Oklahoma, C USA
23 X8 **Chowan River** ☒ North Carolina, SE USA

● COUNTRY   ◆ ADMINISTRATIVE REGION   ▲ MOUNTAIN   ▲ VOLCANO   ☒ LAKE
● COUNTRY CAPITAL   ✈ INTERNATIONAL AIRPORT   ▲ MOUNTAIN RANGE   ☒ RIVER   ☒ RESERVOIR
◇ DEPENDENT TERRITORY
○ DEPENDENT TERRITORY CAPITAL

◆ COUNTRY
● COUNTRY CAPITAL
◇ DEPENDENT TERRITORY
○ DEPENDENT TERRITORY CAPITAL
◆ ADMINISTRATIVE REGION
✕ INTERNATIONAL AIRPORT
▲ MOUNTAIN
▲ MOUNTAIN RANGE
▲ VOLCANO
⊠ RIVER
⊗ LAKE
⊗ RESERVOIR

Cordeiro – Culbertson

62 Q9 **Cordeiro** Rio de Janeiro, SE Brazil
25 T6 **Cordele** Georgia, SE USA
28 L11 **Cordell** Oklahoma, C USA
105 N14 **Cordes** Tarn, S France
64 O6 **Cordillera** *off.* Departamento de la Cordillera. ◐ *department* C Paraguay
190 K1 **Cordillo Downs** South Australia
64 K10 **Córdoba** Córdoba, C Argentina
43 R14 **Córdoba** Veracruz-Llave, E Mexico
106 M13 **Córdoba** *var.* Cordoba, *Eng.* Cordova; *anc.* Corduba. Andalucía, SW Spain
64 K11 **Córdoba** *off.* Provincia de Córdoba. ◐ *province* C Argentina
56 D7 **Córdoba** *off.* Departamento de Córdoba. ◐ *province* NW Colombia
106 L13 **Córdoba** ◐ *province* Andalucía, S Spain
64 K10 **Córdoba, Sierras de** ▲ C Argentina
25 O3 **Cordova** Alabama, S USA
41 S12 **Cordova** Alaska, USA
Cordova/Corduba *see* Córdoba
Corentyne River *see* Courantyne River
Corfu *see* Kérkyra
106 J9 **Coria** Extremadura, W Spain
106 J14 **Coria del Río** Andalucía, S Spain
191 S8 **Coricudgy, Mount** ▲ New South Wales, SE Australia
109 N20 **Corigliano Calabro** Calabria, SW Italy
Corinium/Corinium Dobunorum *see* Cirencester
25 N1 **Corinth** Mississippi, S USA
Corinth *see* Kórinthos
Corinth Canal *see* Dióryga Korinthou
Corinth, Gulf of/Corinthiacus Sinus *see* Korinthiakós Kólpos
Corinthus *see* Kórinthos
44 I9 **Corinto** Chinandega, NW Nicaragua
99 C21 **Cork** *Ir.* Corcaigh. S Ireland
99 C21 **Cork** *Ir.* Corcaigh. *cultural region* SW Ireland
99 C21 **Cork** ✕ SW Ireland
99 D21 **Cork Harbour** *Ir.* Cuan Chorcaí. *inlet* SW Ireland
109 I23 **Corleone** Sicilia, Italy, C Mediterranean Sea
116 N13 **Çorlu** Tekirdağ, NW Turkey
116 N12 **Çorlu Çayı** ∿ NW Turkey
Cormaiore *see* Courmayeur
9 V13 **Cormorant** Manitoba, C Canada
25 T2 **Cornelia** Georgia, SE USA
62 J10 **Cornélio Procópio** Paraná, S Brazil
57 V9 **Corneliskondre** Sipaliwini, N Suriname
32 J5 **Cornell** Wisconsin, N USA
11 S12 **Corner Brook** Newfoundland, Newfoundland and Labrador, E Canada
Corner Rise Seamounts *see* Corner Seamounts
66 I9 **Corner Seamounts** *var.* Corner Rise Seamounts. *undersea feature* NW Atlantic Ocean
118 M9 **Corneşti** *Rus.* Korneshty. C Moldova
Corneto *see* Tarquinia
Cornhusker State *see* Nebraska
29 X8 **Corning** Arkansas, C USA
37 N5 **Corning** California, W USA
31 U15 **Corning** Iowa, C USA
20 G11 **Corning** New York, NE USA
Corn Islands *see* Maíz, Islas del
109 J14 **Corno Grande** ▲ C Italy
13 N13 **Cornwall** Ontario, SE Canada
99 H25 **Cornwall** *cultural region* SW England, UK
99 G25 **Cornwall, Cape** *headland* SW England, UK
56 J4 **Coro** *prev.* Santa Ana de Coro. Falcón, NW Venezuela
59 J18 **Corocoro** La Paz, W Bolivia
59 K17 **Coroico** La Paz, W Bolivia
192 M5 **Coromandel** Waikato, North Island, NZ
161 K20 **Coromandel Coast** *coast* E India
192 M5 **Coromandel Peninsula** *peninsula* North Island, NZ
192 M6 **Coromandel Range** ▲ North Island, NZ
179 P12 **Coron** Busuanga Island, W Philippines
37 T15 **Corona** California, W USA
39 T12 **Corona** New Mexico, SW USA
9 U17 **Coronach** Saskatchewan, S Canada
37 U17 **Coronado** California, W USA
45 N15 **Coronado, Bahía de** *bay* S Costa Rica
9 R15 **Coronation** Alberta, SW Canada
15 I4 **Coronation Gulf** *gulf* Northwest Territories, N Canada
204 I1 **Coronation Island** *island* Antarctica
41 X14 **Coronation Island** *island* Alexander Archipelago, Alaska, USA
63 B18 **Coronda** Santa Fe, C Argentina
65 F14 **Coronel** Bío Bío, C Chile
63 D20 **Coronel Brandsen** *var.* Brandsen. Buenos Aires, E Argentina
64 K4 **Coronel Cornejo** Salta, N Argentina
63 B24 **Coronel Dorrego** Buenos Aires, E Argentina
64 P6 **Coronel Oviedo** Caaguazú, SE Paraguay
63 B23 **Coronel Pringles** Buenos Aires, E Argentina
63 B23 **Coronel Suárez** Buenos Aires, E Argentina
63 E22 **Coronel Vidal** Buenos Aires, E Argentina
57 V9 **Coronie** ◐ *district* NW Suriname
59 G17 **Coropuna, Nevado** ▲ S Peru
Çorovoda *see* Çorovodë
115 L22 **Çorovodë** *var.* Çorovoda. Berat, S Albania
191 P11 **Corowa** New South Wales, SE Australia
44 G1 **Corozal** Corozal, N Belize
56 E6 **Corozal** Sucre, NW Colombia
44 G1 **Corozal** ◐ *district* N Belize
27 T14 **Corpus Christi** Texas, SW USA
27 T14 **Corpus Christi Bay** *inlet* Texas, SW USA
27 R14 **Corpus Christi, Lake** ⊡ Texas, SW USA
65 F16 **Corral** Los Lagos, C Chile
107 O9 **Corral de Almaguer** Castilla-La Mancha, C Spain
106 K6 **Corrales** Castilla-León, N Spain
39 R11 **Corrales** New Mexico, SW USA
Corrán Tuathail *see* Carrauntoohil
108 F9 **Correggio** Emilia-Romagna, C Italy
179 P11 **Corregidor Island** *island* NW Philippines
61 M16 **Corrente** Piauí, E Brazil
61 I19 **Correntes, Rio** ∿ SW Brazil
105 N12 **Corrèze** ◐ *department* C France
99 C17 **Corrib, Lough** *Ir.* Loch Coirib. ◎ W Ireland
63 C14 **Corrientes** Corrientes, NE Argentina
63 D15 **Corrientes** *off.* Provincia de Corrientes. ◐ *province* NE Argentina
46 A5 **Corrientes, Cabo** *headland* W Cuba
42 I13 **Corrientes, Cabo** *headland* SW Mexico
Corrientes, Provincia de *see* Corrientes
63 C16 **Corrientes, Río** ∿ NE Argentina
58 E8 **Corrientes, Río** ∿ Ecuador/Peru
27 W9 **Corrigan** Texas, SW USA
57 U9 **Corriverton** E Guyana
Corriza *see* Korçë
191 Q11 **Corryong** Victoria, SE Australia
104 F2 **Corse** *Eng.* Corsica. ◐ *region* France, C Mediterranean Sea
104 E1 **Corse** *Eng.* Corsica. *island* France, C Mediterranean Sea
104 F1 **Corse, Cap** *headland* Corse, France, C Mediterranean Sea
104 E2 **Corse-du-Sud** ◐ *department* Corse, France, C Mediterranean Sea
31 P11 **Corsica** South Dakota, N USA
Corsica *see* Corse
27 U7 **Corsicana** Texas, SW USA
104 F2 **Corte** Corse, France, C Mediterranean Sea
65 G16 **Corte Alto** Los Lagos, S Chile
106 I13 **Cortegana** Andalucía, S Spain
45 N15 **Cortés** *var.* Ciudad Cortés. Puntarenas, SE Costa Rica
44 G5 **Cortés** ◐ *department* NW Honduras
39 P8 **Cortez** Colorado, C USA
Cortez, Sea of *see* California, Golfo de
108 H6 **Cortina d'Ampezzo** Veneto, NE Italy
20 H11 **Cortland** New York, NE USA
33 V11 **Cortland** Ohio, N USA
108 H12 **Cortona** Toscana, C Italy
78 H13 **Corubal, Rio** ∿ E Guinea-Bissau
106 G10 **Coruche** Santarém, C Portugal
Çoruh *see* Rize
143 R11 **Çoruh Nehri** *Geor.* Chorokhi, *Rus.* Chorokh. ∿ Georgia/Turkey
142 K12 **Çorum** *var.* Chorum. Çorum, N Turkey
142 J12 **Çorum** *var.* Chorum. ◐ *province* N Turkey
61 H19 **Corumbá** Mato Grosso do Sul, S Brazil
12 D16 **Corunna** Ontario, S Canada
Corunna *see* A Coruña
34 F12 **Corvallis** Oregon, NW USA
66 M1 **Corvo** *var.* Ilha do Corvo. *island* Azores, Portugal, NE Atlantic Ocean
Corvo, Ilha do *see* Corvo
33 O16 **Corydon** Indiana, N USA
31 V16 **Corydon** Iowa, C USA
Cos *see* Kos
42 I9 **Cosalá** Sinaloa, C Mexico
43 R15 **Cosamaloapan** *var.* Cosamaloapan de Carpio. Veracruz-Llave, E Mexico
Cosamaloapan de Carpio *see* Cosamaloapan
109 N21 **Cosenza** *anc.* Consentia. Calabria, SW Italy
33 T13 **Coshocton** Ohio, N USA
44 H9 **Cosigüina, Punta** *headland* NW Nicaragua
31 T9 **Cosmos** Minnesota, N USA
105 O8 **Cosne-sur-Loire** Nièvre, C France
110 B9 **Cossonay** Vaud, W Switzerland
Cossyra *see* Pantelleria
49 R4 **Costa, Cordillera de la** *var.* Cordillera de Venezuela. ▲ N Venezuela
44 K13 **Costa Rica** *off.* Republic of Costa Rica. ◆ *republic* Central America
45 N15 **Costeña, Fila** ▲ S Costa Rica
Costermansville *see* Bukavu
118 I14 **Costeşti** Argeş, SW Romania
39 S8 **Costilla** New Mexico, SW USA
37 O7 **Cosumnes River** ∿ California, W USA
103 O16 **Coswig** Sachsen, E Germany
103 M14 **Coswig** Sachsen-Anhalt, E Germany
Cosyra *see* Pantelleria
179 R16 **Cotabato** Mindanao, S Philippines
58 C5 **Cotacachi** ▲ N Ecuador
59 L21 **Cotagaita** Potosí, S Bolivia
105 V15 **Côte d'Azur** *prev.* Nice. ✕ (Nice) Alpes-Maritimes, SE France
Côte d'Ivoire *see* Ivory Coast
105 R8 **Côte d'Or** *cultural region* C France
105 R7 **Côte d'Or** ◐ *department* E France
Côte Française des Somalis *see* Djibouti
104 J4 **Cotentin** *peninsula* N France
104 G6 **Côtes d'Armor** *prev.* Côtes-du-Nord. ◐ *department* NW France
Côtes-du Nord *see* Côtes d'Armor
Cöthen *see* Köthen
Côtière, Chaine *see* Coast Mountains
42 M13 **Cotija** *var.* Cotija de la Paz. Michoacán de Ocampo, SW Mexico
Cotija de la Paz *see* Cotija
79 R16 **Cotonou** *var.* Kotonu. S Benin
79 R16 **Cotonou** ✕ S Benin
58 B6 **Cotopaxi** *prev.* León. ◐ *province* C Ecuador
58 C6 **Cotopaxi** ⩕ N Ecuador
Cotrone *see* Crotone
99 L21 **Cotswold Hills** *var.* Cotswolds. *hill range* S England, UK
Cotswolds *see* Cotswold Hills
34 F13 **Cottage Grove** Oregon, NW USA
23 S14 **Cottageville** South Carolina, SE USA
103 P14 **Cottbus** *prev.* Kottbus. Brandenburg, E Germany
29 U9 **Cotter** Arkansas, C USA
108 A9 **Cottian Alps** *Fr.* Alpes Cottiennes, *It.* Alpi Cozie. ▲ France/Italy
Cottiennes, Alpes *see* Cottian Alps
Cotton State, The *see* Alabama
24 G4 **Cotton Valley** Louisiana, S USA
38 L12 **Cottonwood** Arizona, SW USA
34 M10 **Cottonwood** Idaho, NW USA
31 S9 **Cottonwood** Minnesota, N USA
27 Q7 **Cottonwood** Texas, SW USA
29 O5 **Cottonwood Falls** Kansas, C USA
38 L3 **Cottonwood Heights** Utah, W USA
31 S10 **Cottonwood River** ∿ Minnesota, N USA
47 O9 **Cotuí** C Dominican Republic
27 Q13 **Cotulla** Texas, SW USA
Cotyora *see* Ordu
104 I11 **Coubre, Pointe de la** *headland* W France
20 E12 **Coudersport** Pennsylvania, NE USA
13 S9 **Coudres, Île aux** *island* Québec, SE Canada
190 G11 **Couedic, Cape de** *headland* South Australia
Couentrey *see* Coventry
104 I6 **Couesnon** ∿ NW France
34 H10 **Cougar** Washington, NW USA
104 L10 **Couhé** Vienne, W France
34 K8 **Coulee City** Washington, NW USA
205 Q15 **Coulman Island** *island* Antarctica
105 P5 **Coulommiers** Seine-et-Marne, N France
12 K11 **Coulonge** ∿ Québec, SE Canada
12 K11 **Coulonge Est** ∿ Québec, SE Canada
37 Q9 **Coulterville** California, W USA
40 M9 **Council** Alaska, USA
34 M12 **Council** Idaho, NW USA
31 S15 **Council Bluffs** Iowa, C USA
29 O5 **Council Grove** Kansas, C USA
29 O5 **Council Grove Lake** ⊡ Kansas, C USA
34 G7 **Coupeville** Washington, NW USA
57 U12 **Courantyne River** *var.* Corantijn Rivier, Corentyne River. ∿ Guyana/Suriname
101 G21 **Courcelles** Hainaut, S Belgium
110 C7 **Courgenay** Jura, NW Switzerland
130 B2 **Courland Lagoon** *Ger.* Kurisches Haff, *Rus.* Kurskiy Zaliv. *lagoon* Lithuania/Russian Federation
120 B12 **Courland Spit** *Lith.* Kuršių Nerija, *Rus.* Kurshskaya Kosa. *spit* Lithuania/Russian Federation
108 A6 **Courmayeur** *prev.* Cormaiore. Valle d'Aosta, NW Italy
110 D7 **Courroux** Jura, NW Switzerland
8 K17 **Courtenay** Vancouver Island, British Columbia, SW Canada
23 W7 **Courtland** Virginia, NE USA
27 V10 **Courtney** Texas, SW USA
32 J4 **Court Oreilles, Lac** ◎ Wisconsin, N USA
Courtrai *see* Kortrijk
101 H19 **Court-Saint-Étienne** Walloon Brabant, C Belgium
24 G6 **Coushatta** Louisiana, S USA
180 I16 **Cousin** *island* Inner Islands, NE Seychelles
180 I16 **Cousine** *island* Inner Islands, NE Seychelles
104 J4 **Coutances** *anc.* Constantia. Manche, N France
104 K12 **Coutras** Gironde, SW France
47 U14 **Couva** Trinidad, Trinidad and Tobago
110 B8 **Couvet** Neuchâtel, W Switzerland
101 H22 **Couvin** Namur, S Belgium
118 K12 **Covasna** *Ger.* Kowasna, *Hung.* Kovászna. Covasna, E Romania
118 J11 **Covasna** ◐ *county* E Romania
12 E12 **Cove Island** *island* Ontario, S Canada
36 M5 **Covelo** California, W USA
99 M20 **Coventry** *anc.* Couentrey. C England, UK
Cove of Cork *see* Cobh
23 U5 **Covesville** Virginia, NE USA
106 I8 **Covilhã** Castelo Branco, E Portugal
25 T3 **Covington** Georgia, SE USA
33 N13 **Covington** Indiana, N USA
22 M3 **Covington** Kentucky, S USA
24 K8 **Covington** Louisiana, S USA
33 Q13 **Covington** Ohio, N USA
22 F9 **Covington** Tennessee, S USA
23 S6 **Covington** Virginia, NE USA
191 Q8 **Cowal, Lake** *seasonal lake* New South Wales, SE Australia
9 W15 **Cowan** Manitoba, S Canada
20 F12 **Cowanesque River** ∿ New York/Pennsylvania, NE USA
188 L12 **Cowan, Lake** ◎ Western Australia
13 P13 **Cowansville** Québec, SE Canada
190 H8 **Cowell** South Australia
99 M23 **Cowes** S England, UK
29 Q10 **Coweta** Oklahoma, C USA
1 D6 **Cowie Seamount** *undersea feature* NE Pacific Ocean
34 G10 **Cowlitz River** ∿ Washington, NW USA
23 Q11 **Cowpens** South Carolina, SE USA
191 R8 **Cowra** New South Wales, SE Australia
Coxen Hole *see* Roatán
61 I19 **Coxim** Mato Grosso do Sul, S Brazil
61 I19 **Coxim, Rio** ∿ SW Brazil
Coxin Hole *see* Roatán
159 V17 **Cox's Bazar** Chittagong, S Bangladesh
78 H14 **Coyah** Conakry, W Guinea
42 K5 **Coyame** Chihuahua, N Mexico
26 L9 **Coyanosa Draw** ∿ Texas, SW USA
Coyhaique *see* Coihaique
44 C7 **Coyolate, Río** ∿ S Guatemala
Coyote State *see* South Dakota
42 I10 **Coyotitán** Sinaloa, C Mexico
43 N15 **Coyuca** *var.* Coyuca de Catalán. Guerrero, S Mexico
43 O16 **Coyuca** *var.* Coyuca de Benítez. Guerrero, S Mexico
Coyuca de Benítez/Coyuca de Catalán *see* Coyuca
31 N15 **Cozad** Nebraska, C USA
Cozie, Alpi *see* Cottian Alps
Cozmeni *see* Kitsman'
42 E3 **Cozón, Cerro** ▲ NW Mexico
43 Z12 **Cozumel** Quintana Roo, E Mexico
43 Z12 **Cozumel, Isla** *island* SE Mexico
34 K8 **Crab Creek** ∿ Washington, NW USA
46 H12 **Crab Pond Point** *headland* W Jamaica
Cracovia/Cracow *see* Kraków
85 I25 **Cradock** Eastern Cape, S South Africa
41 Y14 **Craig** Prince of Wales Island, Alaska, USA
39 Q3 **Craig** Colorado, C USA
99 F15 **Craigavon** C Northern Ireland, UK
23 T5 **Craigsville** Virginia, NE USA
103 J21 **Crailsheim** Baden-Württemberg, S Germany
118 H14 **Craiova** Dolj, SW Romania
8 K12 **Cranberry Junction** British Columbia, SW Canada
20 J8 **Cranberry Lake** ◎ New York, NE USA
9 V13 **Cranberry Portage** Manitoba, C Canada
9 P17 **Cranbrook** British Columbia, SW Canada
32 M5 **Crandon** Wisconsin, N USA
34 K14 **Crane** Oregon, NW USA
26 M9 **Crane** Texas, SW USA
Crane *see* The Crane
27 S8 **Cranfills Gap** Texas, SW USA
21 O12 **Cranston** Rhode Island, NE USA
Cranz *see* Zelenogradsk
61 L15 **Craolândia** Tocantins, E Brazil
104 J7 **Craon** Mayenne, NW France
205 V16 **Crary, Cape** *headland* Antarctica
Crasna *see* Kraszna
34 G14 **Crater Lake** ◎ Oregon, NW USA
194 I13 **Crater Mount** ▲ C PNG
35 P14 **Craters of the Moon National Monument** *national park* Idaho, NW USA
61 O14 **Crateús** Ceará, E Brazil
Crathis *see* Crati
109 N20 **Crati** *anc.* Crathis. ∿ S Italy
9 U16 **Craven** Saskatchewan, S Canada
56 I8 **Cravo Norte** Arauca, E Colombia
30 J12 **Crawford** Nebraska, C USA
27 T8 **Crawford** Texas, SW USA
9 O17 **Crawford Bay** British Columbia, SW Canada
67 M19 **Crawford Seamount** *undersea feature* S Atlantic Ocean
33 O13 **Crawfordsville** Indiana, N USA
25 T9 **Crawfordville** Florida, SE USA
99 O23 **Crawley** SE England, UK
35 S10 **Crazy Mountains** ▲ Montana, NW USA
9 T11 **Cree** ∿ Saskatchewan, C Canada
39 R7 **Creede** Colorado, C USA
42 I6 **Creel** Chihuahua, N Mexico
9 S11 **Cree Lake** ◎ Saskatchewan, C Canada
9 V13 **Creighton** Saskatchewan, C Canada
31 Q13 **Creighton** Nebraska, C USA
105 O4 **Creil** Oise, N France
108 E8 **Crema** Lombardia, N Italy
108 E8 **Cremona** Lombardia, N Italy
Creole State *see* Louisiana
114 M10 **Crepaja** *Hung.* Cserépalja. Serbia, N Yugoslavia
105 O4 **Crépy-en-Valois** Oise, N France
114 B10 **Cres** *It.* Cherso. Primorje-Gorski Kotar, NW Croatia
114 A11 **Cres** *It.* Cherso; *anc.* Crexa. *island* W Croatia
34 H14 **Crescent** Oregon, NW USA
36 K1 **Crescent City** California, W USA
25 W10 **Crescent City** Florida, SE USA
178 M10 **Crescent Group** *island group* C Paracel Islands
25 W10 **Crescent Lake** ◎ Florida, SE USA
31 X11 **Cresco** Iowa, C USA
63 B18 **Crespo** Entre Ríos, E Argentina
56 E5 **Crespo** ✕ (Cartagena) Bolívar, NW Colombia
105 R13 **Crest** Drôme, E France
39 R5 **Crested Butte** Colorado, C USA
33 S12 **Crestline** Ohio, N USA
9 O17 **Creston** British Columbia, SW Canada
31 U15 **Creston** Iowa, C USA
35 V16 **Creston** Wyoming, C USA
39 S7 **Crestone Peak** ▲ Colorado, C USA
25 P8 **Crestview** Florida, SE USA
123 Gg10 **Cretan Trough** *undersea feature* Aegean Sea, C Mediterranean Sea
31 R16 **Crete** Nebraska, C USA
Crete *see* Kríti
105 O5 **Créteil** Val-de-Marne, N France
Crete, Sea of/Creticum, Mare *see* Kritikó Pélagos
107 X4 **Creus, Cap de** *headland* NE Spain
105 N10 **Creuse** ◐ *department* C France
104 L9 **Creuse** ∿ C France
105 T4 **Creutzwald** Moselle, NE France
107 S12 **Crevillente** País Valenciano, E Spain
99 L18 **Crewe** C England, UK
23 V7 **Crewe** Virginia, NE USA
Crexa *see* Cres
45 Q15 **Cricamola, Río** ∿ NW Panama
63 K14 **Criciúma** Santa Catarina, S Brazil
98 J11 **Crieff** C Scotland, UK
114 B10 **Crikvenica** *It.* Cirquenizza; *prev.* Cirkvenica, Crjkvenica. Primorje-Gorski Kotar, NW Croatia
Crimea/Crimean Oblast *see* Krym, Respublika
103 M16 **Crimmitschau** *var.* Krimmitschau. Sachsen, E Germany
118 G11 **Crişcior** *Hung.* Kristyor. Hunedoara, W Romania
23 Y5 **Crisfield** Maryland, NE USA
33 P3 **Crisp Point** *headland* Michigan, N USA
61 L19 **Cristalina** Goiás, C Brazil
46 J7 **Cristal, Sierra del** ▲ E Cuba
45 T14 **Cristóbal** Colón, C Panama
56 F4 **Cristóbal Colón, Pico** ▲ N Colombia
Cristur/Cristuru Săcuiesc *see* Cristuru Secuiesc
118 I11 **Cristuru Secuiesc** *prev.* Cristur, Cristuru Săcuiesc, Sitaş Cristuru, *Ger.* Kreutz, *Hung.* Székelykeresztúr, Szitás-Keresztúr. Harghita, C Romania
118 F10 **Crişul Alb** *var.* Weisse Kreisch, *Ger.* Weisse Körös, *Hung.* Fehér-Körös. ∿ Hungary/Romania
118 F10 **Crişul Negru** *Ger.* Schwarze Körös, *Hung.* Fekete-Körös. ∿ Hungary/Romania
118 G10 **Crişul Repede** *var.* Schnelle Kreisch, *Ger.* Schnelle Körös, *Hung.* Sebes-Körös. ∿ Hungary/Romania
119 N10 **Criuleni** *Rus.* Kriulyany. C Moldova
Crivadia Vulcanului *see* Vulcan
Crjkvenica *see* Crikvenica
115 O17 **Crna Gora** ▲ FYR Macedonia/Yugoslavia
Crna Gora *see* Montenegro
115 O20 **Crna Reka** ∿ S FYR Macedonia
Crni Drim *see* Black Drin
111 V10 **Črni Vrh** ▲ NE Slovenia
111 V13 **Črnomelj** *Ger.* Tschernembl. SE Slovenia
99 A17 **Croagh Patrick** *Ir.* Cruach Phádraig. ▲ W Ireland
114 D9 **Croatia** *off.* Republic of Croatia, *Ger.* Kroatien, *SCr.* Hrvatska. ◆ *republic* SE Europe
Croce, Picco di *see* Wilde Kreuzspitze
13 P8 **Croche** ∿ Québec, SE Canada
175 Nn3 **Crocker, Banjaran** *var.* Crocker Range. ▲ East Malaysia
Crocker Range *see* Crocker, Banjaran
27 V9 **Crockett** Texas, SW USA
69 V14 **Crocodile** *var.* Krokodil. ∿ N South Africa
Crocodile *see* Limpopo
22 I7 **Crofton** Kentucky, S USA
31 Q12 **Crofton** Nebraska, C USA
Croia *see* Krujë
105 R16 **Croisette, Cap** *headland* SE France
104 G8 **Croisic, Pointe du** *headland* NW France
105 S13 **Croix Haute, Col de la** *pass* E France
13 U5 **Croix, Pointe à la** *headland* Québec, SE Canada
12 F13 **Croker, Cape** *headland* Ontario, S Canada
189 P1 **Croker Island** *island* Northern Territory, N Australia
98 I8 **Cromarty** N Scotland, UK
101 M21 **Crombach** Liège, E Belgium
99 Q18 **Cromer** E England, UK
193 D22 **Cromwell** Otago, South Island, NZ
193 H16 **Cronadun** West Coast, South Island, NZ
41 O11 **Crooked Creek** Alaska, USA
46 K5 **Crooked Island** *island* SE Bahamas
46 J5 **Crooked Island Passage** *channel* SE Bahamas
34 I13 **Crooked River** ∿ Oregon, NW USA
31 R4 **Crookston** Minnesota, N USA
30 I10 **Crooks Tower** ▲ South Dakota, N USA
33 T14 **Crooksville** Ohio, N USA
191 R9 **Crookwell** New South Wales, SE Australia
12 L14 **Crosby** Ontario, SE Canada
99 K17 **Crosby** *var.* Great Crosby. NW England, UK
31 U6 **Crosby** Minnesota, N USA
30 K2 **Crosby** North Dakota, N USA
27 O5 **Crosbyton** Texas, SW USA
79 V16 **Cross** ∿ Cameroon/Nigeria
25 U10 **Cross City** Florida, SE USA
Crossen *see* Krosno Odrzańskie
29 V14 **Crossett** Arkansas, C USA
99 K15 **Cross Fell** ▲ N England, UK
9 P16 **Crossfield** Alberta, SW Canada
23 Q12 **Cross Hill** South Carolina, SE USA
21 U6 **Cross Island** *island* Maine, NE USA
9 X13 **Cross Lake** Manitoba, C Canada
24 F5 **Cross Lake** ⊡ Louisiana, S USA
38 I12 **Crossman Peak** ▲ Arizona, SW USA
27 Q7 **Cross Plains** Texas, SW USA
79 V17 **Cross River** ◐ *state* SE Nigeria
22 L9 **Crossville** Tennessee, S USA
33 S8 **Croswell** Michigan, N USA
12 K13 **Crotch Lake** ◎ Ontario, SE Canada
Croton/Crotona *see* Crotone
109 O21 **Crotone** *var.* Cotrone; *anc.* Croton, Crotona. Calabria, SW Italy
35 V11 **Crow Agency** Montana, NW USA
191 U7 **Crowdy Head** *headland* New South Wales, SE Australia
27 Q4 **Crowell** Texas, SW USA
191 O6 **Crowl Creek** *seasonal river* New South Wales, SE Australia
24 H9 **Crowley** Louisiana, S USA
37 S9 **Crowley, Lake** ⊡ California, W USA
29 X10 **Crowleys Ridge** *hill range* Arkansas, C USA
194 J11 **Crown Island** *island* N Papau New Guinea
33 N11 **Crown Point** Indiana, N USA
39 P10 **Crownpoint** New Mexico, SW USA
35 R10 **Crow Peak** ▲ Montana, NW USA
9 P17 **Crowsnest Pass** *pass* Alberta/British Columbia, SW Canada
31 T6 **Crow Wing River** ∿ Minnesota, N USA
99 O22 **Croydon** SE England, UK
181 P11 **Crozet Basin** *undersea feature* S Indian Ocean
181 O12 **Crozet Islands** *island group* French Southern and Antarctic Territories
181 N12 **Crozet Plateau** *var.* Crozet Plateaus. *undersea feature* SW Indian Ocean
Crozet Plateaus *see* Crozet Plateau
104 E6 **Crozon** Finistère, NW France
Cruacha Dubha, Na *see* Macgillycuddy's Reeks
Cruach Phádraig *see* Croagh Patrick
118 M14 **Crucea** Constanţa, SE Romania
46 E5 **Cruces** Cienfuegos, C Cuba
109 O20 **Crucoli Torretta** Calabria, SW Italy
43 P9 **Cruillas** Tamaulipas, C Mexico
66 K9 **Cruiser Tablemount** *undersea feature* E Atlantic Ocean
63 G14 **Cruz Alta** Rio Grande do Sul, S Brazil
46 G8 **Cruz, Cabo** *headland* S Cuba
62 N9 **Cruzeiro** São Paulo, S Brazil
62 H10 **Cruzeiro do Oeste** Paraná, S Brazil
61 A15 **Cruzeiro do Sul** Acre, W Brazil
25 U11 **Crystal Bay** *bay* Florida, SE USA
190 I8 **Crystal Brook** South Australia
9 X17 **Crystal City** Manitoba, S Canada
29 X5 **Crystal City** Missouri, C USA
27 P13 **Crystal City** Texas, SW USA
32 M4 **Crystal Falls** Michigan, N USA
25 Q8 **Crystal Lake** Florida, SE USA
33 O6 **Crystal Lake** ◎ Michigan, N USA
25 V11 **Crystal River** Florida, SE USA
39 Q5 **Crystal River** ∿ Colorado, C USA
24 K6 **Crystal Springs** Mississippi, S USA
Csaca *see* Čadca
Csakathurn/Csáktornya *see* Čakovec
Csap *see* Chop
Csepén *see* Čepin
Cserépalja *see* Crepaja
Csermő *see* Cermei
Csíkszereda *see* Miercurea-Ciuc
113 L24 **Csongrád** Csongrád, SE Hungary
113 L24 **Csongrád** *off.* Csongrád Megye. ◐ *county* SE Hungary
113 H22 **Csorna** Győr-Moson-Sopron, NW Hungary
Csucsa *see* Ciucea
113 G25 **Csurgó** Somogy, SW Hungary
Csurog *see* Čurug
56 L5 **Cúa** Miranda, N Venezuela
84 C11 **Cuale** Malanje, NW Angola
69 T12 **Cuando** *var.* Kwando. ∿ S Africa
85 E15 **Cuando Cubango** *var.* Kuando-Kubango. ◐ *province* SE Angola
85 E16 **Cuangar** Cuando Cubango, S Angola
84 D11 **Cuango** Lunda Norte, NE Angola
84 C10 **Cuango** Uíge, NW Angola
84 C10 **Cuango** *var.* Kwango. ∿ Angola/Zaire *see also* Kwango
Cuan, Loch *see* Strangford Lough
84 C12 **Cuanza** *var.* Kwanza. ∿ C Angola
84 B11 **Cuanza Norte** *var.* Kuanza Norte. ◐ *province* NE Angola
84 B12 **Cuanza Sul** *var.* Kuanza Sul. ◐ *province* NE Angola
63 E16 **Cuareim, Río** *var.* Rio Quaraí. ∿ Brazil/Uruguay *see also* Quaraí, Rio
85 D15 **Cuatir** ∿ S Angola
42 M7 **Cuatro Ciénegas** *var.* Cuatro Ciénegas de Carranza. Coahuila de Zaragoza, NE Mexico
Cuatro Ciénegas de Carranza *see* Cuatro Ciénegas
42 I6 **Cuauhtémoc** Chihuahua, N Mexico
43 P14 **Cuautla** Morelos, S Mexico
106 H12 **Cuba** Beja, S Portugal
29 W6 **Cuba** Missouri, C USA
39 R10 **Cuba** New Mexico, SW USA
46 E6 **Cuba** *off.* Republic of Cuba. ◆ *republic* W West Indies
49 O2 **Cuba** *island* W West Indies
84 B13 **Cubal** Benguela, W Angola
85 C15 **Cubango** *var.* Kuvango, *Port.* Vila Artur de Paiva, Vila da Ponte. Huíla, SW Angola
85 D16 **Cubango** *var.* Kavango, Kavengo, Kubango, Okavango, Okavanggo. ∿ S Africa *see also* Okavango
56 H8 **Cubará** Boyacá, N Colombia
142 I12 **Çubuk** Ankara, N Turkey
85 D14 **Cuchi** Cuando Cubango, C Angola
44 C5 **Cuchumatanes, Sierra de los** ▲ W Guatemala
Cuculaya, Rio *see* Kukalaya, Rio
84 E12 **Cucumbi** *prev.* Trás-os-Montes. Lunda Sul, NE Angola
56 G7 **Cúcuta** *var.* San José de Cúcuta. Norte de Santander, N Colombia
33 N9 **Cudahy** Wisconsin, N USA
161 J21 **Cuddalore** Tamil Nādu, SE India
161 I18 **Cuddapah** Andhra Pradesh, S India
106 M6 **Cuéllar** Castilla-León, N Spain
84 D13 **Cuemba** *var.* Coemba. Bié, C Angola
58 B8 **Cuenca** Azuay, S Ecuador
107 Q9 **Cuenca** *anc.* Conca. Castilla-La Mancha, C Spain
107 P9 **Cuenca** ◐ *province* Castilla-La Mancha, C Spain
42 L9 **Cuencamé** *var.* Cuencamé de Ceniceros. Durango, C Mexico
Cuencamé de Ceniceros *see* Cuencamé
107 Q8 **Cuenca, Serranía de** ▲ C Spain
Cuera *see* Chur
107 P5 **Cuerda del Pozo, Embalse de la** ⊡ N Spain
43 O14 **Cuernavaca** Morelos, S Mexico
27 T12 **Cuero** Texas, SW USA
46 I7 **Cueto** Holguín, E Cuba
43 Q13 **Cuetzalán** *var.* Cuetzalán del Progreso. Puebla, S Mexico
Cuetzalán del Progreso *see* Cuetzalán
107 Q14 **Cuevas de Almanzora** Andalucía, S Spain
107 T8 **Cuevas de Vinromá** País Valenciano, E Spain
118 H12 **Cugir** *Hung.* Kudzsir. Alba, SW Romania
61 H18 **Cuiabá** *prev.* Cuyabá. *state capital* Mato Grosso, SW Brazil
61 H19 **Cuiabá, Rio** ∿ SW Brazil
43 R15 **Cuicatlán** *var.* San Juan Bautista Cuicatlán. Oaxaca, SE Mexico
203 W16 **Cuidado, Punta** *headland* Easter Island, Chile, E Pacific Ocean
Cuidad Presidente Stroessner *see* Ciudad del Este
Cúige *see* Connaught
Cúige Laighean *see* Leinster
Cúige Mumhan *see* Munster
100 L13 **Cuijck** Noord-Brabant, SE Netherlands
Cúil an tSúdaire *see* Portarlington
44 D7 **Cuilapa** Santa Rosa, S Guatemala
44 B5 **Cuilco, Río** ∿ W Guatemala
Cúil Mhuine *see* Collooney
Cúil Raithin *see* Coleraine
85 C14 **Cuima** Huambo, C Angola
85 E16 **Cuito** *var.* Kwito. ∿ SE Angola
85 E15 **Cuito Cuanavale** Cuando Cubango, E Angola
43 N14 **Cuitzeo, Lago de** ◎ C Mexico
29 W4 **Cuivre River** ∿ Missouri, C USA
Çuka *see* Çukë
174 Hh4 **Cukai** *var.* Chukai, Kemaman. Terengganu, Peninsular Malaysia
115 L23 **Çukë** *var.* Çuka. Vlorë, S Albania
Cularo *see* Grenoble
179 Pp13 **Culasi** Panay Island, C Philippines
35 Y7 **Culbertson** Montana, NW USA

◆ Country
● Country Capital
◇ Dependent Territory
○ Dependent Territory Capital
◐ Administrative Region
✕ International Airport
▲ Mountain
▲ Mountain Range
⩕ Volcano
∿ River
◎ Lake
⊡ Reservoir

CULBERTSON – DATONG SHAN

30 *M16* **Culbertson** Nebraska, C USA
191 *P10* **Culcairn** New South Wales, SE Australia
47 *W5* **Culebra** *var.* Dewey. E Puerto Rico
47 *W6* **Culebra, Isla de** *island* E Puerto Rico
39 *T8* **Culebra Peak** ▲ Colorado, C USA
106 *J5* **Culebra, Sierra de la** ▲▲ NW Spain
100 *J12* **Culemborg** Gelderland, C Netherlands
143 *V14* **Culfa** ***Rus.*** Dzhul'fa. SW Azerbaijan
191 *P4* **Culgoa River** ≈ New South Wales/Queensland, SE Australia
42 *I9* **Culiacán** *var.* Culiacán Rosales, Culiacán-Rosales. Sinaloa, C Mexico
Culiacán-Rosales/Culiacán Rosales *see* Culiacán
179 *P13* **Culion Island** *island* Calamian Group, W Philippines
107 *P14* **Cúllar-Baza** Andalucía, S Spain
107 *S10* **Cullera** País Valenciano, E Spain
25 *P3* **Cullman** Alabama, S USA
110 *B10* **Cully** Vaud, W Switzerland
Culm *see* Chełmno
Culmsee *see* Chełmża
23 *V4* **Culpeper** Virginia, NE USA
Culpepper Island *see* Darwin, Isla
193 *I17* **Culverden** Canterbury, South Island, NZ
57 *N5* **Cumaná** Sucre, NE Venezuela
57 *O5* **Cumanacoa** Sucre, NE Venezuela
56 *C13* **Cumbal, Nevado de** *elevation* S Colombia
23 *O7* **Cumberland** Kentucky, S USA
23 *U2* **Cumberland** Maryland, NE USA
23 *V6* **Cumberland** Virginia, NE USA
197 *A11* **Cumberland, Cape** *var.* Cape Nahoi. *headland* Espiritu Santo, N Vanuatu
9 *V14* **Cumberland House** Saskatchewan, C Canada
25 *W8* **Cumberland Island** *island* Georgia, SE USA
22 *L7* **Cumberland, Lake** ▣ Kentucky, S USA
16 *O1* **Cumberland Peninsula** *peninsula* Baffin Island, Northwest Territories, NE Canada
1 *K11* **Cumberland Plateau** *plateau* E USA
32 *L1* **Cumberland Point** *headland* Michigan, N USA
23 *O7* **Cumberland River** ≈ Kentucky/Tennessee, S USA
16 *O2* **Cumberland Sound** *inlet* Baffin Island, Northwest Territories, NE Canada
98 *I12* **Cumbernauld** S Scotland, UK
99 *K15* **Cumbria** *cultural region* NW England, UK
99 *K15* **Cumbrian Mountains** ▲▲ NW England, UK
25 *S2* **Cumming** Georgia, SE USA
Cummin in Pommern *see* Kamień Pomorski
190 *G9* **Cummins** South Australia
98 *I13* **Cumnock** W Scotland, UK
42 *G4* **Cumpas** Sonora, NW Mexico
142 *H16* **Çumra** Konya, C Turkey
65 *G15* **Cunco** Araucanía, C Chile
56 *E9* **Cundinamarca** *off.* Departamento de Cundinamarca. ◈ *province* C Colombia
43 *U15* **Cunduacán** Tabasco, SE Mexico
85 *C16* **Cunene** ◈ *province* S Angola
85 *A16* **Cunene** *var.* Kunene. ≈ Angola/Namibia *see also* Kunene
108 *A9* **Cuneo** ***Fr.*** Coni. Piemonte, NW Italy
85 *E15* **Cunjamba** Cuando Cubango, E Angola
189 *V10* **Cunnamulla** Queensland, E Australia
94 *K8* **Cuokkarašša** ▲ N Norway
108 *B7* **Cuorgne** Piemonte, NE Italy
98 *K11* **Cupar** E Scotland, UK
118 *L8* **Cupcina** ***Rus.*** Kupchino; ***prev.*** Calinisc, Kalinisk. N Moldova
56 *C8* **Cupica** Chocó, W Colombia
56 *C8* **Cupica, Golfo de** *gulf* W Colombia
114 *N13* **Ćuprija** Serbia, E Yugoslavia
Cura *see* Villa de Cura
47 *P16* **Curaçao** *island* Netherlands Antilles
58 *H13* **Curanja, Río** ≈ E Peru
58 *F7* **Curaray, Rio** ≈ Ecuador/Peru
118 *K14* **Curcani** Călărași, SE Romania
190 *H4* **Curdimurka** South Australia
105 *P7* **Cure** ≈ C France
181 *Y16* **Curepipe** C Mauritius
57 *R6* **Curiapo** Delta Amacuro, NE Venezuela
Curia Rhaetorum *see* Chur
64 *G12* **Curicó** Maule, C Chile
Curieta *see* Krk
180 *I15* **Curieuse** *island* Inner Islands, NE Seychelles
61 *C16* **Curitiba** Acre, W Brazil
62 *K12* **Curitiba** *prev.* Curytiba. *state capital* Paraná, S Brazil
62 *J13* **Curitibanos** Santa Catarina, S Brazil
191 *S6* **Curlewis** New South Wales, SE Australia
190 *J6* **Curnamona** South Australia
85 *A15* **Curoca** ≈ SW Angola
191 *T6* **Currabubula** New South Wales, SE Australia
61 *Q14* **Currais Novos** Rio Grande do Norte, E Brazil
37 *W7* **Currant** Nevada, W USA
37 *W6* **Currant Mountain** ▲ Nevada, W USA
46 *H2* **Current** Eleuthera Island, C Bahamas
29 *W8* **Current River** ≈ Arkansas/Missouri, C USA
190 *M14* **Currie** Tasmania, SE Australia
23 *Y8* **Currituck** North Carolina, SE USA
23 *Y8* **Currituck Sound** *sound* North Carolina, SE USA
41 *R11* **Curry** Alaska, USA
Curtbunar *see* Tervel
118 *I13* **Curtea de Argeș** *var.* Curtea-de-Arges. Argeș, S Romania
118 *E10* **Curtici** ***Ger.*** Kurtitsch, ***Hung.*** Kürtös. Arad, W Romania
30 *M16* **Curtis** Nebraska, C USA
106 *H2* **Curtis-Estación** Galicia, NW Spain
191 *O14* **Curtis Group** *island group* Tasmania, SE Australia
189 *Y8* **Curtis Island** *island* Queensland, SE Australia
60 *K11* **Curuá, Ilha do** *island* NE Brazil
49 *U7* **Curuá, Rio** ≈ N Brazil
61 *A14* **Curuçá, Rio** ≈ NW Brazil
114 *L9* **Čurug** ***Hung.*** Csurog. Serbia, N Yugoslavia
63 *D16* **Curuzú Cuatiá** Corrientes, NE Argentina
61 *M19* **Curvelo** Minas Gerais, SE Brazil
20 *E14* **Curwensville** Pennsylvania, NE USA
32 *M3* **Curwood, Mount** ▲ Michigan, N USA
Curytiba *see* Curitiba
Curzola *see* Korčula
44 *A10* **Cuscatlán** ◈ *department* C El Salvador
59 *H15* **Cusco** *var.* Cuzco. Cusco, C Peru
59 *H15* **Cusco** *off.* Departamento de Cusco; *var.* Cuzco. ◈ *department* C Peru
29 *O9* **Cushing** Oklahoma, C USA
27 *W8* **Cushing** Texas, SW USA
42 *I6* **Cusihuiriachic** Chihuahua, N Mexico
105 *P10* **Cusset** Allier, C France
25 *S6* **Cusseta** Georgia, SE USA
30 *J10* **Custer** South Dakota, N USA
Cüstrin *see* Kostrzyn
35 *Q7* **Cut Bank** Montana, NW USA
Cutch, Gulf of *see* Kachchh, Gulf of
25 *S6* **Cuthbert** Georgia, SE USA
9 *S15* **Cut Knife** Saskatchewan, S Canada
25 *Y16* **Cutler Ridge** Florida, SE USA
24 *K10* **Cut Off** Louisiana, S USA
65 *I15* **Cutral-Có** Neuquén, C Argentina
109 *O21* **Cutro** Calabria, SW Italy
191 *O4* **Cuttaburra Channels** *seasonal river* New South Wales, SE Australia
160 *O12* **Cuttack** Orissa, E India
85 *C15* **Cuvelai** Cunene, SW Angola
81 *G18* **Cuvette** *var.* Région de la Cuvette. ◈ *province* C Congo
181 *V9* **Cuvier Basin** *undersea feature* E Indian Ocean
181 *U9* **Cuvier Plateau** *undersea feature* E Indian Ocean
84 *B12* **Cuvo** ≈ W Angola
102 *H9* **Cuxhaven** Niedersachsen, NW Germany
Cuyabá *see* Cuiabá
179 *Pp13* **Cuyo East Pass** *passage* C Philippines
179 *P13* **Cuyo West Pass** *passage* C Philippines
Cuyuni, Río *see* Cuyuni River
57 *S8* **Cuyuni River** *var.* Río Cuyuni. ≈ Guyana/Venezuela
Cuzco *see* Cusco
99 *K22* **Cwmbran** ***Wel.*** Cwmbrân. SW Wales, UK
30 *K15* **C.W.McConaughy, Lake** ▣ Nebraska, C USA
83 *D20* **Cyangugu** SW Rwanda
112 *D11* **Cybinka** ***Ger.*** Ziebingen. Zielona Góra, W Poland
Cyclades *see* Kykládes
Cydonia *see* Chaniá
Cymru *see* Wales
22 *M5* **Cynthiana** Kentucky, S USA
9 *S17* **Cypress Hills** ▲▲ Alberta/Saskatchewan, SW Canada
Cypro-Syrian Basin *see* Cyprus Basin
123 *Mm1* **Cyprus** *off.* Republic of Cyprus, ***Gk.*** Kypros, ***Turk.*** Kıbrıs, Kıbrıs Cumhuriyeti. ◆ *republic* E Mediterranean Sea
86 *L14* **Cyprus** ***Gk.*** Kypros, ***Turk.*** Kıbrıs. *island* E Mediterranean Sea
123 *Gg10* **Cyprus Basin** *var.* Cypro-Syrian Basin. *undersea feature* E Mediterranean Sea
Cythera *see* Kýthira
Cythnos *see* Kýthnos
112 *F9* **Czaplinek** ***Ger.*** Tempelburg. Koszalin, NW Poland
Czarna Woda *see* Wda
112 *G8* **Czarne** Słupsk, NW Poland
112 *G10* **Czarnków** Piła, NW Poland
113 *E17* **Czech Republic** ***Cz.*** Česká Republika. ◆ *republic* C Europe
Czegléd *see* Cegléd
112 *G12* **Czempiń** Poznań, W Poland
Czenstochau *see* Częstochowa
Czerkow *see* Čerchov
Czernowitz *see* Chernivtsi
112 *I8* **Czersk** Bydgoszcz, NW Poland
113 *J15* **Częstochowa** ***Ger.*** Czenstochau, Tschenstochau, ***Rus.*** Chenstokhov. Częstochowa, S Poland
113 *J15* **Częstochowa** *off.* Województwo częstochowskie, ***Ger.*** Czenstochau, Tschenstochau, ***Rus.*** Chenstokhov. ◈ *province* S Poland
Częstochowskie, Województwo *see* Częstochowa
112 *F10* **Człopa** ***Ger.*** Schloppe. Piła, W Poland
112 *H8* **Człuchów** ***Ger.*** Schlochau. Słupsk, NW Poland

D

169 *V9* **Da'an** *var.* Dalai. Jilin, NE China
13 *S10* **Daaquam** Québec, SE Canada
Daawo, Webi *see* Dawa Wenz
56 *I4* **Dabajuro** Falcón, NW Venezuela
79 *N15* **Dabakala** NE Ivory Coast
Daban *see* Bairin Youqi
113 *K23* **Dabas** Pest, C Hungary
166 *L8* **Daba Shan** ▲▲ C China
146 *J5* **Dabbāgh, Jabal** ▲ NW Saudi Arabia
56 *D8* **Dabeiba** Antioquia, NW Colombia
166 *L17* **Daben** Hainan, S China
160 *E11* **Dabhoi** Gujarāt, W India
167 *P8* **Dabie Shan** ▲▲ C China
78 *J13* **Dabola** Haute-Guinée, C Guinea
79 *N17* **Dabou** S Ivory Coast
112 *P8* **Dąbrowa Białostocka** Białystok, NE Poland
113 *M16* **Dąbrowa Tarnowska** Tarnów, SE Poland
121 *M20* **Dabryn'** ***Rus.*** Dobryn'. Homyel'skaya Voblasts', SE Belorussia
165 *P10* **Dabsan Hu** ◎ C China
167 *Q13* **Dabu** *prev.* Huliao. Guangdong, S China
118 *H15* **Dăbuleni** Dolj, SW Romania
Dacca *see* Dhaka
103 *L23* **Dachau** Bayern, SE Germany
166 *K8* **Dachuan** *prev.* Daxian, Da Xian. Sichuan, C China
Dacia Bank *see* Dacia Seamount
66 *M10* **Dacia Seamount** *var.* Dacia Bank. *undersea feature* E Atlantic Ocean
39 *T3* **Dacono** Colorado, C USA
Đăc Tô *see* Đak Tô
Dacura *see* Dákura
25 *W12* **Dade City** Florida, SE USA
158 *L10* **Dadeldhura** *var.* Dandeldhura. Far Western, W Nepal
25 *Q5* **Dadeville** Alabama, S USA
105 *N15* **Dadou** ≈ S France
160 *D12* **Dādra and Nagar Haveli** ◈ *union territory* W India
155 *P14* **Dādu** Sind, SE Pakistan
178 *K11* **Da Du Bǫloc** Kon Tum, C Vietnam
166 *G9* **Dadu He** ≈ C China
Daegu *see* Taegu
Daerah Istimewa Aceh *see* Aceh
179 *Q11* **Daet** Luzon, N Philippines
166 *I11* **Dafang** Guizhou, S China
159 *W11* **Dafla Hills** ▲▲ NE India
9 *U15* **Dafoe** Saskatchewan, S Canada
78 *G10* **Dagana** N Senegal
Dagana *see* Dahana, Tajikistan
Dagana *see* Massakory, Chad
120 *K11* **Dagda** Krāslava, SE Latvia
Dagden *see* Hiiumaa
Dagden-Sund *see* Soela Väin
131 *P16* **Dagestan, Respublika** *prev.* Dagestanskaya ASSR, ***Eng.*** Daghestan. ◈ *autonomous republic* SW Russian Federation
Dagestanskaya ASSR *see* Dagestan, Respublika
131 *R17* **Dagestanskiye Ogni** Respublika Dagestan, SW Russian Federation
193 *A23* **Dagg Sound** *sound* South Island, NZ
Daghestan *see* Dagestan, Respublika
147 *Y8* **Daghmar** NE Oman
Dağlıq Qarabağ *see* Nagornyy Karabakh
Dagö *see* Hiiumaa
56 *D11* **Dagua** Valle del Cauca, W Colombia
166 *H11* **Daguan** Yunnan, SW China
179 *P9* **Dagupan** *off.* Dagupan City. Luzon, N Philippines
165 *N16* **Dagzê** Xizang Zizhiqu, W China
153 *Q13* **Dahana** ***Rus.*** Dagana, Dakhana. SW Tajikistan
169 *V10* **Dahei Shan** ▲▲ N China
169 *T7* **Da Hinggan Ling** ***Eng.*** Great Khingan Range. ▲▲ NE China
Dahlac Archipelago *see* Dahlak Archipelago
82 *K9* **Dahlak Archipelago** *var.* Dahlac Archipelago. *island group* E Eritrea
25 *T2* **Dahlonega** Georgia, SE USA
103 *O14* **Dahme** Brandenburg, E Germany
102 *O13* **Dahme** ≈ E Germany
147 *O14* **Dahm, Ramlat** *desert* NW Yemen
160 *E10* **Dāhod** *prev.* Dohad. Gujarāt, W India
Dahomey *see* Benin
164 *G10* **Dahongliutan** Xinjiang Uygur Zizhiqu, NW China
Dahra *see* Dara
145 *R2* **Dahūk** *var.* Dohuk, ***Kurd.*** Dihōk. N Iraq
118 *J15* **Daia** Giurgiu, S Romania
171 *L15* **Daigo** Ibaraki, Honshū, S Japan
169 *O13* **Dai Hai** ◎ N China
Daihoku *see* T'aipei
195 *X14* **Dai Island** *island* N Solomon Islands
177 *G8* **Daik-u** Pegu, SW Myanmar
144 *H9* **Dā'īl** Dar'ā, S Syria
178 *Kk12* **Đai Lanh** Khanh Hoa, S Vietnam
167 *Q13* **Daimao Shan** ▲▲ SE China
107 *N11* **Daimiel** Castilla-La Mancha, C Spain
117 *F22* **Daimoniá** Pelopónnisos, S Greece
Dainan *see* T'ainan
27 *W6* **Daingerfield** Texas, SW USA
Daingin, Bá an *see* Dingle Bay
165 *R13* **Dainkognubma** Xizang Zizhiqu, W China
171 *Hh17* **Daiō-zaki** *headland* Honshū, SW Japan
Dairbhre *see* Valencia Island
63 *B22* **Daireaux** Buenos Aires, E Argentina
Dairen *see* Dalian
77 *W9* **Dairûț** *var.* Dayrūț. C Egypt
170 *Ff12* **Dai-sen** ▲ Kyūshū, SW Japan
27 *X10* **Daisetta** Texas, SW USA
199 *Gg5* **Daitō-jima** *island group* SW Japan
199 *Gg5* **Daitō Ridge** *undersea feature* N Philippine Sea
167 *N3* **Daixian** *var.* Dai Xian. Shanxi, C China
167 *Q12* **Daiyun Shan** ▲▲ SE China
46 *M8* **Dajabón** NW Dominican Republic
166 *G8* **Dajin Chuan** ≈ C China
154 *J6* **Dak** ◎ W Afghanistan
78 *F11* **Dakar** ● (Senegal) W Senegal
78 *F11* **Dakar** ✕ W Senegal
178 *K11* **Đak Glây** Kon Tum, C Vietnam
Dakhana *see* Dahana
159 *U16* **Dakhin Shahbazpur Island** *island* S Bangladesh
Dakhla *see* Ad Dakhla
78 *F7* **Dakhlet Nouâdhibou** ◈ *region* NW Mauritania
Đak Lap *see* Kiên Đưc
178 *K13* **Đak Nông** Đăc Lăc, S Vietnam
79 *U11* **Dakoro** Maradi, S Niger
31 *U12* **Dakota City** Iowa, C USA
31 *R13* **Dakota City** Nebraska, C USA
115 *M17* **Đakovica** *var.* Djakovica, ***Alb.*** Gjakovë. Serbia, S Yugoslavia
114 *I10* **Đakovo** *var.* Djakovo, ***Hung.*** Diakovár. Osijek-Baranja, E Croatia
Dakshin *see* Deccan
178 *K11* **Đak Tô** *var.* Đăc Tô. Kon Tum, C Vietnam
45 *N7* **Dákura** *var.* Dacura. Región Autónoma Atlántico Norte, NE Nicaragua
97 *I14* **Dal** Akershus, S Norway
84 *E12* **Dala** Lunda Sul, E Angola
110 *J8* **Dalaas** Vorarlberg, W Austria
78 *I13* **Dalaba** Moyenne-Guinée, W Guinea
Dalai *see* Da'an
Dalain Hob *see* Ejin Qi
Dalai Nor *see* Hulun Nur
169 *Q11* **Dalai Nur** *salt lake* N China
Dala-Jarna *see* Järna
97 *M14* **Dalälven** ≈ C Sweden
142 *D16* **Dalaman** Muğla, SW Turkey
142 *C16* **Dalaman** ✕ Muğla, SW Turkey
142 *D16* **Dalaman Çayı** ≈ SW Turkey
168 *K11* **Dalandzadgad** Ömnögovĭ, S Mongolia
97 *D17* **Dalane** *physical region* S Norway
201 *Z2* **Dalap-Uliga-Djarrit** *var.* Delap-Uliga-Darrit, D-U-D. *island group* Ratak Chain, SE Marshall Islands
96 *L13* **Dalarna** *prev.* ***Eng.*** Dalecarlia. *cultural region* C Sweden
97 *P16* **Dalarö** Stockholm, C Sweden
178 *Kk13* **Đa Lat** Lâm Đông, S Vietnam
168 *J11* **Dalay** Ömnögovĭ, S Mongolia
154 *L12* **Dālbandin** *var.* Dāl Bandin. Baluchistān, SW Pakistan
97 *J17* **Dalbosjön** *lake bay* S Sweden
189 *Y10* **Dalby** Queensland, E Australia
96 *D13* **Dale** Hordaland, S Norway
96 *C12* **Dale** Sogn og Fjordane, S Norway
34 *K12* **Dale** Oregon, NW USA
27 *T11* **Dale** Texas, SW USA
Dalecarlia *see* Dalarna
23 *W4* **Dale City** Virginia, NE USA
22 *L8* **Dale Hollow Lake** ▣ Kentucky/Tennessee, S USA
100 *O8* **Dalen** Drenthe, NE Netherlands
97 *E15* **Dalen** Telemark, S Norway
177 *F4* **Daletme** Chin State, W Myanmar
25 *Q7* **Daleville** Alabama, S USA
100 *M9* **Dalfsen** Overijssel, E Netherlands
26 *M1* **Dalhart** Texas, SW USA
11 *O13* **Dalhousie** New Brunswick, SE Canada
158 *I6* **Dalhousie** Himāchal Pradesh, N India
166 *F12* **Dali** *var.* Xiaguan. Yunnan, SW China
Dali *see* Idálion
169 *U14* **Dalian** *var.* Dairen, Dalien, Lüda, Ta-lien, ***Rus.*** Dalny. Liaoning, NE China
107 *O15* **Dalías** Andalucía, S Spain
Dalien *see* Dalian
Dalijan *see* Delījān
114 *J9* **Dalj** ***Hung.*** Dalja. Osijek-Baranja, E Croatia
Dalja *see* Dalj
34 *F12* **Dallas** Oregon, NW USA
27 *U6* **Dallas** Texas, SW USA
27 *T7* **Dallas-Fort Worth** ✕ Texas, SW USA
160 *K12* **Dalli Rājhara** Madhya Pradesh, C India
41 *X15* **Dall Island** *island* Alexander Archipelago, Alaska, USA
40 *M12* **Dall Lake** ◎ Alaska, USA
79 *S12* **Dallol Bosso** *seasonal river* W Niger
147 *U7* **Dalmā** *island* W UAE
115 *E14* **Dalmacija** ***Eng.*** Dalmatia, ***Ger.*** Dalmatien, ***It.*** Dalmazia. *cultural region* S Croatia
Dalmatia/Dalmatien/Dalmazia *see* Dalmacija
127 *Nn17* **Dal'negorsk** Primorskiy Kray, SE Russian Federation
127 *Nn17* **Dal'nerechensk** Primorskiy Kray, SE Russian Federation
Dalny *see* Dalian
78 *M16* **Daloa** C Ivory Coast
166 *J11* **Dalou Shan** ▲▲ S China
189 *X7* **Dalrymple Lake** ◎ Queensland, E Australia
12 *H14* **Dalrymple Lake** ◎ Ontario, S Canada
189 *X7* **Dalrymple, Mount** ▲ Queensland, E Australia
95 *K20* **Dalsbruk** ***Fin.*** Taalintehdas. Turku-Pori, SW Finland
97 *K19* **Dalsjöfors** Älvsborg, S Sweden
97 *J17* **Dals Långed** *var.* Långed. Älvsborg, S Sweden
159 *O15* **Dāltenganj** *prev.* Daltonganj. Bihār, N India
25 *R2* **Dalton** Georgia, SE USA
Daltonganj *see* Dāltenganj
205 *X14* **Dalton Iceberg Tongue** *ice feature* Antarctica
94 *J1* **Dalvík** Nordhurland Eystra, N Iceland
37 *N8* **Daly City** California, W USA
189 *P2* **Daly River** ≈ Northern Territory, N Australia
189 *Q3* **Daly Waters** Northern Territory, N Australia
121 *F20* **Damachava** *var.* Damachova, ***Pol.*** Domaczewo, ***Rus.*** Domachëvo. Brestskaya Voblasts', SW Belorussia
Damachova *see* Damachava
79 *W11* **Damagaram Takaya** Zinder, S Niger
160 *D12* **Damān** Damān and Diu, W India
160 *B12* **Damān and Diu** ◈ *union territory* W India
77 *V7* **Damanhûr** *anc.* Hermopolis Parva. N Egypt
Damão *see* Damān
167 *O1* **Damaqun Shan** ▲▲ E China
81 *I15* **Damara** Ombella-Mpoko, S Central African Republic
85 *D18* **Damaraland** *physical region* C Namibia
175 *T15* **Damar, Kepulauan** *var.* Baraf Daja Islands, Kepulauan Barat Daya. *island group* C Indonesia
174 *Gg4* **Damar Laut** Perak, Peninsular Malaysia
175 *Tt15* **Damar, Pulau** *island* Maluku, E Indonesia
Damas *see* Dimashq
79 *Y12* **Damasak** Borno, NE Nigeria
Damasco *see* Dimashq
23 *Q8* **Damascus** Virginia, NE USA
Damascus *see* Dimashq
79 *X13* **Damaturu** Yobe, NE Nigeria
175 *Ss4* **Damau** Pulau Kaburuang, N Indonesia
149 *O5* **Damāvand, Qolleh-ye** ▲ N Iran
84 *B10* **Damba** Uíge, NW Angola
116 *M12* **Dambaslar** Tekirdağ, NW Turkey
118 *J13* **Dâmbovița** *prev.* Dîmbovița. ◈ *county* SE Romania
118 *J13* **Dâmbovița** *prev.* Dîmbovița. ≈ S Romania
181 *Y15* **D'Ambre, Île** *island* NE Mauritius
161 *K24* **Dambulla** Central Province, C Sri Lanka
46 *K9* **Dame-Marie** SW Haiti
46 *J9* **Dame Marie, Cap** *headland* SW Haiti
149 *Q4* **Dāmghān** Semnān, N Iran
Damietta *see* Dumyât
144 *G10* **Dāmiyā** Al Balqā', NW Jordan
152 *G11* **Damla** Dashkhovuzskiy Velayat, N Turkmenistan
Dammām *see* Ad Dammān
102 *G12* **Damme** Niedersachsen, NW Germany
159 *R15* **Dāmodar** ≈ NE India
160 *J9* **Damoh** Madhya Pradesh, C India
79 *P15* **Damongo** NW Ghana
144 *G7* **Damoûr** *var.* Ad Dāmūr. W Lebanon
175 *Pp7* **Dampal, Teluk** *bay* Sulawesi, C Indonesia
188 *H7* **Dampier** Western Australia
188 *H6* **Dampier Archipelago** *island group* Western Australia
176 *Uu9* **Dampier, Selat** *strait* Irian Jaya, E Indonesia
194 *L12* **Dampier Strait** *strait* NE PNG
147 *U14* **Damqawt** *var.* Damqut. E Yemen
165 *O13* **Dam Qu** ≈ C China
Damqut *see* Damqawt
178 *Ii13* **Dâmrei, Chuŏr Phmun** ***Fr.*** Chaîne de l'Éléphant. ▲▲ SW Cambodia
110 *C7* **Damvant** Jura, NW Switzerland
Damwâld *see* Damwoude
100 *L5* **Damwoude** ***Fris.*** Damwâld. Friesland, N Netherlands
165 *N15* **Damxung** Xizang Zizhiqu, W China
82 *K11* **Danakil Desert** *var.* Afar Depression, Danakil Plain. *desert* E Africa
Danakil Plain *see* Danakil Desert
37 *R8* **Dana, Mount** ▲ California, W USA
78 *L16* **Danané** W Ivory Coast
178 *Kk10* **Đă Nâng** *prev.* Tourane. Quang Nam-Đa Năng, C Vietnam
179 *Qq13* **Danao** *var.* Danao City. Cebu, C Philippines
166 *G9* **Danba** Sichuan, C China
Danborg *see* Daneborg
20 *L13* **Danbury** Connecticut, NE USA
27 *W12* **Danbury** Texas, SW USA
37 *X15* **Danby Lake** ◎ California, W USA
204 *H4* **Danco Coast** *physical region* Antarctica
84 *B11* **Dande** ≈ NW Angola
Dandeldhura *see* Dadeldhura
161 *E17* **Dandeli** Karnātaka, W India
191 *O12* **Dandenong** Victoria, SE Australia
169 *V13* **Dandong** *var.* Tan-tung; *prev.* An-tung. Liaoning, NE China
207 *Q14* **Daneborg** *var.* Danborg. N Greenland
27 *V12* **Danevang** Texas, SW USA
Dänew *see* Deynau
12 *L12* **Danford Lake** Québec, SE Canada
21 *T4* **Danforth** Maine, NE USA
39 *P3* **Danforth Hills** ▲▲ Colorado, C USA
Dangara *see* Danghara
165 *V12* **Dangchang** Gansu, C China
Dangchengwan *see* Subei
84 *B10* **Dange** Uíge, NW Angola
Dangerous Archipelago *see* Tuamotu, Îles
85 *E26* **Danger Point** *headland* SW South Africa
153 *Q13* **Danghara** ***Rus.*** Dangara. SW Tajikistan
165 *P8* **Danghe Nanshan** ▲▲ W China
82 *I12* **Dangila** *var.* Dānglā. NW Ethiopia
165 *P8* **Dangjin Shankou** *pass* N China
Dangla *see* Tanggula Shan
Dānglā *see* Dangila, NW Ethiopia
Dangme Chu *see* Manās
159 *Y11* **Dāngori** Assam, NE India
Dang Raek, Phanom/Dangrek, Chaîne des *see* Dângrêk, Chuŏr Phnum
178 *Ii11* **Dângrêk, Chuŏr Phnum** *var.* Phanom Dang Raek, Phanom Dong Rak, ***Fr.*** Chaîne des Dangrek. ▲▲ Cambodia/Thailand
44 *G3* **Dangriga** *prev.* Stann Creek. Stann Creek, E Belize
167 *P6* **Dangshan** Anhui, E China
35 *T15* **Daniel** Wyoming, C USA
85 *H22* **Daniëlskuil** Northern Cape, N South Africa
21 *N12* **Danielson** Connecticut, NE USA
128 *M15* **Danilov** Yaroslavskaya Oblast', W Russian Federation
131 *O9* **Danilovka** Volgogradskaya Oblast', SW Russian Federation
Danish West Indies *see* Virgin Islands (US)
166 *L7* **Dan Jiang** ≈ C China
166 *M7* **Danjiangkou Shuiku** ▣ C China
147 *W8* **Ḑank** *var.* Dhank. NW Oman
158 *J7* **Dankhar** Himāchal Pradesh, N India
130 *L6* **Dankov** Lipetskaya Oblast', W Russian Federation
44 *J7* **Danlí** El Paraíso, S Honduras
Danmark *see* Denmark
Danmarksstraedet *see* Denmark Strait
97 *O14* **Dannemora** Uppsala, C Sweden
20 *L6* **Dannemora** New York, NE USA
102 *K11* **Dannenberg** Niedersachsen, N Germany
192 *N12* **Dannevirke** Manawatu-Wanganui, North Island, NZ
23 *U8* **Dan River** ≈ Virginia, NE USA
178 *Hh9* **Dan Sai** Loei, C Thailand
20 *F10* **Dansville** New York, NE USA
Dantzig *see* Gdańsk
88 *E12* **Danube** ***Bul.*** Dunav, ***Cz.*** Dunaj, ***Ger.*** Donau, ***Hung.*** Duna, ***Rom.*** Dunărea. ≈ C Europe
Danubian Plain *see* Dunavska Ravnina
177 *Ff8* **Danubyu** Irrawaddy, SW Burma
Danum *see* Doncaster
21 *P11* **Danvers** Massachusetts, NE USA
29 *T11* **Danville** Arkansas, C USA
33 *N13* **Danville** Illinois, N USA
33 *O14* **Danville** Indiana, N USA
31 *Y15* **Danville** Iowa, C USA
22 *M6* **Danville** Kentucky, S USA
20 *G14* **Danville** Pennsylvania, NE USA
23 *T6* **Danville** Virginia, NE USA
166 *L17* **Danxian** *var.* Dan Xian, Nada. Hainan, S China
Danzig *see* Gdańsk
Danziger Bucht *see* Danzig, Gulf of
112 *J6* **Danzig, Gulf of** *var.* Gulf of Gdańsk, ***Ger.*** Danziger Bucht, ***Pol.*** Zakota Gdańska, ***Rus.*** Gdan'skaya Bukhta. *gulf* N Poland
166 *F10* **Daocheng** Sichuan, C China
Daokou *see* Huaxian
106 *H7* **Dão, Rio** ≈ N Portugal
Daosa *see* Dausa
79 *Y7* **Dao Timmi** Agadez, NE Niger
166 *M13* **Daoxian** *var.* Dao Xian. Hunan, S China
79 *Q14* **Dapaong** N Togo
25 *N8* **Daphne** Alabama, S USA
179 *Qq15* **Dapitan** Mindanao, S Philippines
165 *P9* **Da Qaidam** Qinghai, C China
169 *V8* **Daqing** Heilongjiang, NE China
169 *O13* **Daqing Shan** ▲▲ N China
Daqm *see* Duqm
145 *T5* **Dāqūq** *var.* Tāwūq. N Iraq
78 *G10* **Dara** *var.* Dahra. NW Senegal
144 *H9* **Dar'ā** *var.* Der'a, ***Fr.*** Déraa. Dar'ā, SW Syria
144 *H8* **Dar'ā** *off.* Muḩāfaẓat Dar'ā, *var.* Dará, Derá, Derrá. ◈ *governorate* S Syria
149 *Q12* **Dārāb** Fārs, S Iran
118 *K8* **Darabani** Botoșani, NW Romania
Daraj *see* Dirj
148 *M8* **Dārān** Eșfahān, W Iran
178 *Kk12* **Đa Răng, Sông** *var.* Ba. ≈ S Vietnam
126 *Kk16* **Darasun** Chitinskaya Oblast', S Russian Federation
Daraut-Kurgan *see* Daroot-Korgon
79 *W13* **Darazo** Bauchi, E Nigeria
145 *S3* **Darband** N Iraq
145 *V4* **Darband-i Khān, Sadd** *dam* NE Iraq
145 *N1* **Darbāsīyah** *var.* Derbisīye. Al Ḩasakah, N Syria
120 *C11* **Darbėnai** Kretinga, NW Lithuania
159 *Q13* **Darbhanga** Bihār, N India
40 *M9* **Darby, Cape** *headland* Alaska, USA
114 *I9* **Darda** ***Hung.*** Dárda. Osijek-Baranja, E Croatia
29 *T11* **Dardanelle** Arkansas, C USA
29 *S11* **Dardanelle, Lake** ▣ Arkansas, C USA
Dardanelles *see* Çanakkale Boğazı
Dardanelli *see* Çanakkale
Dar-el-Beida *see* Casablanca
142 *M14* **Darende** Malatya, C Turkey
83 *J22* **Dar es Salaam** Dar es Salaam, E Tanzania
83 *J22* **Dar es Salaam** ✕ Pwani, E Tanzania
193 *H18* **Darfield** Canterbury, South Island, NZ
108 *F7* **Darfo** Lombardia, N Italy
82 *B10* **Darfur** *var.* Darfur Massif. *cultural region* W Sudan
Darfur Massif *see* Darfur
152 *J10* **Dargan-Ata** *var.* Darganata. Lebapskiy Velayat, NE Turkmenistan
Darganata *see* Dargan-Ata
149 *T3* **Dargaz** *var.* Darreh Gaz; *prev.* Moḩammadābād. Khorāsān, NE Iran
145 *U4* **Dargazayn** NE Iraq
191 *P12* **Dargo** Victoria, SE Australia
168 *K7* **Darhan** Bulgan, C Mongolia
169 *N8* **Darhan** Hentiy, C Mongolia
168 *L6* **Darhan** Selenge, N Mongolia
169 *N12* **Darhan Muminggan Lianheqi** *var.* Bailingmiao. Nei Mongol Zizhiqu, N China
25 *W7* **Darien** Georgia, SE USA
45 *W16* **Darién** *off.* Provincia del Darién. ◈ *province* SE Panama
Darién, Golfo del *see* Darien, Gulf of
45 *X14* **Darien, Gulf of** ***Sp.*** Golfo del Darién. *gulf* S Caribbean Sea
Darien, Isthmus of *see* Panamá, Istmo de
44 *K9* **Dariense, Cordillera** ▲▲ C Nicaragua
45 *W15* **Darién, Serranía del** ▲▲ Colombia/Panama
Dario *see* Ciudad Darío
Dariorigum *see* Vannes
Dariv *see* Darvi
Darj *see* Dirj
Darjeeling *see* Darjiling
159 *S12* **Darjiling** *prev.* Darjeeling. West Bengal, NE India
Darkehnen *see* Ozersk
165 *S12* **Darlag** Qinghai, C China
191 *T3* **Darling Downs** *hill range* Queensland, E Australia
30 *M2* **Darling, Lake** ▣ North Dakota, N USA
188 *I12* **Darling Range** ▲▲ Western Australia
190 *L8* **Darling River** ≈ New South Wales, SE Australia
99 *M15* **Darlington** N England, UK
23 *T12* **Darlington** South Carolina, SE USA
32 *K9* **Darlington** Wisconsin, N USA
112 *G7* **Darłowo** Koszalin, NW Poland
103 *G19* **Darmstadt** Hessen, SW Germany
77 *S7* **Darnah** *var.* Dérna. NE Libya
105 *S6* **Darney** Vosges, NE France
190 *M7* **Darnick** New South Wales, SE Australia
205 *Y6* **Darnley, Cape** *headland* Antarctica
107 *R7* **Daroca** Aragón, NE Spain
153 *S11* **Daroot-Korgon** *var.* Daraut-Kurgan. Oshskaya Oblast', SW Kyrgyzstan
63 *A23* **Darragueira** *var.* Darregueira. Buenos Aires, E Argentina
Darregueira *see* Darragueira
Darreh Gaz *see* Dargaz
148 *K7* **Darreh Shahr** *var.* Darreh-ye Shahr. Īlām, W Iran
Darreh-ye Shahr *see* Darreh Shahr
34 *I7* **Darrington** Washington, NW USA
27 *P1* **Darrouzett** Texas, SW USA
159 *S15* **Darsana** *var.* Darshana. Khulna, N Bangladesh
Darshana *see* Darsana
102 *M7* **Darss** *peninsula* NE Germany
102 *M7* **Darsser Ort** *headland* NE Germany
99 *J24* **Dart** ≈ SW England, UK
Dartang *see* Baqên
99 *P22* **Dartford** SE England, UK
190 *L12* **Dartmoor** Victoria, SE Australia
99 *I24* **Dartmoor** *moorland* SW England, UK
11 *Q15* **Dartmouth** Nova Scotia, SE Canada
99 *J24* **Dartmouth** SW England, UK
13 *Y6* **Dartmouth** ≈ Québec, SE Canada
191 *Q11* **Dartmouth Reservoir** ◎ Victoria, SE Australia
Dartuch, Cabo *see* Artrutx, Cap d'
194 *G15* **Daru** Western, SW PNG
114 *G9* **Daruvar** ***Hung.*** Daruvár. Bjelovar-Bilogora, NE Croatia
152 *F10* **Darvaza** ***Turkm.*** Derweze. Akhalskiy Velayat, C Turkmenistan
Darvaza *see* Darwoza
Darvazskiy Khrebet *see* Darvoz, Qatorkŭhi
168 *F8* **Darvi** *var.* Dariv. Govĭ-Altay, W Mongolia
154 *L9* **Darvīshān** *var.* Darweshan, Garmser. Helmand, S Afghanistan
153 *R13* **Darvoz, Qatorkŭhi** ***Rus.*** Darvazskiy Khrebet. ▲▲ C Tajikistan
Darweshan *see* Darvīshān
65 *J15* **Darwin** Río Negro, S Argentina
189 *O1* **Darwin** *prev.* Palmerston, Port Darwin. *territory capital* Northern Territory, N Australia
67 *D24* **Darwin** *var.* Darwin Settlement. East Falkland, Falkland Islands
64 *H8* **Darwin, Cordillera** ▲▲ N Chile
59 *B17* **Darwin, Volcán** ⩚ Galapagos Islands, Ecuador, E Pacific Ocean
153 *O10* **Darwoza** ***Rus.*** Darvaza. Jizzakh Wiloyati, C Uzbekistan
155 *S8* **Darya Khān** Punjab, E Pakistan
151 *O15* **Dar'yalyktakyr, Ravnina** *plain* S Kazakhstan
149 *T11* **Dārzīn** Kermān, S Iran
166 *L8* **Dashennongjia** ▲ C China
Dashhowuz *see* Dashkhovuz
Dashhowuz Welayaty *see* Dashkhovuzskiy Velayat
121 *O16* **Dashkawka** ***Rus.*** Dashkovka. Mahilyowskaya Voblasts', E Belorussia
152 *H8* **Dashkhovuz** ***Turkm.*** Dashhowuz; ***prev.*** Tashauz. Dashkhovuzskiy Velayat, N Turkmenistan
Dashkhovuz *see* Dashkhovuzskiy Velayat
152 *E9* **Dashkhovuzskiy Velayat** *var.* Dashkhovuz, ***Turkm.*** Dashhowuz Welayaty. ◈ *province* N Turkmenistan
Dashköpri *see* Tashkepri
Dashkovka *see* Dashkawka
154 *J15* **Dasht** ≈ SW Pakistan
Dashtidzhum *see* Dashtijum
153 *R13* **Dashtijum** ***Rus.*** Dashtidzhum. SW Tajikistan
155 *W7* **Daska** Punjab, NE Pakistan
Đa, Sông *see* Black River
79 *R15* **Dassa** *var.* Dassa-Zoumé. S Benin
Dassa-Zoumé *see* Dassa
31 *U8* **Dassel** Minnesota, N USA
158 *H3* **Dastegil Sar** *var.* Disteghil Sār. ▲ N India
142 *C16* **Datça** Muğla, SW Turkey
172 *Nn6* **Date** Hokkaidō, NE Japan
160 *I8* **Datia** *prev.* Duttia. Madhya Pradesh, C India
165 *T10* **Datong** Qinghai, C China
167 *N2* **Datong** *var.* Tatung, Ta-t'ung. Shanxi, C China
165 *S9* **Datong He** ≈ C China
165 *S9* **Datong Shan** ▲▲ C China

◆ Country
● Country Capital
◇ Dependent Territory
○ Dependent Territory Capital
◈ Administrative Region
✕ International Airport
▲ Mountain
▲▲ Mountain Range
⩚ Volcano
≈ River
◎ Lake
▣ Reservoir

174 Kk6 **Datu, Tanjung** *headland* Indonesia/Malaysia
Daua *see* Dawa Wenz
180 H16 **Dauban, Mount** ▲ Silhouette, NE Seychelles
155 T7 **Dáüd Khel** Punjab, E Pakistan
121 G15 **Daugai** Alytus, S Lithuania
Daugava *see* Western Dvina
120 J11 **Daugavpils** *Ger.* Dünaburg; *prev.* Rus. Dvinsk. *municipality* Daugavpils, SE Latvia
Dauka *see* Dawkah
Daulatabad *see* Maláyer
103 D18 **Daun** Rheinland-Pfalz, W Germany
161 E14 **Daund** *prev.* Dhond. Mahárăshtra, W India
178 Gg2 **Daung Kyun** *island* S Myanmar
9 W15 **Dauphin** Manitoba, S Canada
105 S13 **Dauphiné** *cultural region* E France
25 N9 **Dauphin Island** *island* Alabama, S USA
9 X15 **Dauphin River** Manitoba, S Canada
79 V12 **Daura** Katsina, N Nigeria
158 H12 **Dausa** *prev.* Daosa. Rájasthán, N India
Dauwa *see* Dawwah
143 Y10 **Däväçi** *Rus.* Divichi. NE Azerbaijan
161 F18 **Dávangere** Karnátaka, W India
179 Rr16 **Davao** *off.* Davao City. Mindanao, S Philippines
179 Rr16 **Davao Gulf** *gulf* Mindanao, S Philippines
13 Q11 **Daveluyville** Québec, SE Canada
31 Z14 **Davenport** Iowa, C USA
34 L8 **Davenport** Washington, NW USA
45 P16 **David** Chiriquí, W Panama
13 O11 **David** ✈ Québec, SE Canada
31 R15 **David City** Nebraska, C USA
Davíd-Gorodok *see* Davyd-Haradok
9 T16 **Davidson** Saskatchewan, S Canada
23 R10 **Davidson** North Carolina, SE USA
28 K12 **Davidson** Oklahoma, C USA
41 S6 **Davidson Mountains** ▲ Alaska, USA
180 M8 **Davie Ridge** *undersea feature* W Indian Ocean
190 A1 **Davies, Mount** ▲ South Australia
37 O7 **Davis** California, W USA
29 N12 **Davis** Oklahoma, C USA
205 Y7 **Davis** *Australian research station* Antarctica
204 H3 **Davis Coast** *physical region* Antarctica
20 C16 **Davis, Mount** ▲ Pennsylvania, NE USA
26 K9 **Davis Mountains** ▲ Texas, SW USA
205 Z9 **Davis Sea** *sea* Antarctica
67 O20 **Davis Seamounts** *undersea feature* N Atlantic Ocean
206 M13 **Davis Strait** *strait* Baffin Bay/Labrador Sea
131 U5 **Davlekanovo** Respublika Bashkortostan, W Russian Federation
110 J9 **Davos** *Rmsch.* Tavau. Graubünden, E Switzerland
121 J20 **Davyd-Haradok** *Pol.* Dawidgródek, *Rus.* David-Gorodok. Brestskaya Voblasts', SW Belorussia
169 U12 **Dawa** Liaoning, NE China
147 O11 **Dawásir, Wádi ad** *dry watercourse* S Saudi Arabia
83 K15 **Dawa Wenz** *var.* Daua, Webi Daawo. ✍ E Africa
Dawaymah, Birkat ad *see* Umm al Baqar, Hawr
Dawei *see* Tavoy
121 K14 **Dawhinava** *Rus.* Dolginovo. Minskaya Voblasts', N Belorussia
Dawidgródek *see* Davyd-Haradok
147 V12 **Dawkah** *var.* Dauka. SW Oman
Dawlat Qatar *see* Qatar
26 M3 **Dawn** Texas, SW USA
146 M11 **Daws** Al Báhah, SW Saudi Arabia
8 H5 **Dawson** *var.* Dawson City. Yukon Territory, NW Canada
25 S6 **Dawson** Georgia, SE USA
31 S9 **Dawson** Minnesota, N USA
Dawson City *see* Dawson
9 T16 **Dawson Creek** British Columbia, W Canada
8 H7 **Dawson Range** ▲ Yukon Territory, W Canada
189 T9 **Dawson River** ✍ Queensland, E Australia
8 J15 **Dawsons Landing** British Columbia, SW Canada
22 I7 **Dawson Springs** Kentucky, S USA
25 V2 **Dawsonville** Georgia, SE USA
166 G8 **Dawu** Sichuan, C China
Dawu *see* Maqén
Dawukou *see* Shizuishan
147 Y10 **Dawwah** *var.* W Oman
104 J15 **Dax** *Ax*; *anc.* Aquae Augustae, Aquae Tarbelicae. Landes, SW France
Da Xian/Daxian *see* Dachuan
166 G9 **Daxue Shan** ▲ C China
166 G12 **Dayao** Yunnan, SW China
Dayishan *see* Gaoyou
191 N12 **Daylesford** Victoria, SE Australia
37 U12 **Daylight Pass** *pass* California, W USA
63 D17 **Daymán, Río** ✍ N Uruguay
Dayr *see* Ad Dayr
144 G10 **Dayr 'Alá** *var.* Deir 'Alla. Al Balqá', N Jordan
145 N4 **Dayr az Zawr** *var.* Deir ez Zor. Dayr az Zawr, E Syria
144 M5 **Dayr az Zawr** *off.* Muḥáfaẓat Dayr az Zawr, *var.* Dayr Az-Zor. ◆ *governorate* E Syria
Dayr Az-Zor *see* Dayr az Zawr
Dayrút *see* Dairút
183 R14 **Daysland** Alberta, SW Canada
33 R14 **Dayton** Ohio, N USA
22 L11 **Dayton** Tennessee, S USA
27 W11 **Dayton** Texas, SW USA
34 L10 **Dayton** Washington, NW USA

25 X10 **Daytona Beach** Florida, SE USA
175 N10 **Dayu** Poso, C Indonesia
167 O13 **Dayu Ling** ▲ S China
167 R7 **Da Yunhe** *Eng.* Grand Canal. *canal* E China
167 S11 **Dayu Shan** *island* SE China
166 J9 **Dazhu** Sichuan, C China
166 J9 **Dazu** Sichuan, C China
85 H24 **De Aar** Northern Cape, C South Africa
204 K5 **Deacon, Cape** *headland* Antarctica
8 L19 **Deadhorse** Alaska, USA
35 T12 **Dead Indian Peak** ▲ Wyoming, C USA
25 R9 **Dead Lake** ⊜ Florida, SE USA
46 J4 **Deadman's Cay** Long Island, C Bahamas
144 G11 **Dead Sea** *var.* Lacus Asphaltites, *Ar.* Al Baḥr al Mayyit, Baḥrat Lūṭ, *Heb.* Yam HaMelaḥ. *salt lake* Israel/Jordan
30 J9 **Deadwood** South Dakota, N USA
99 Q22 **Deal** SE England, UK
85 I22 **Dealesville** Free State, C South Africa
Dealnu *see* Tana/Teno
167 P10 **De'an** Jiangxi, S China
64 K9 **Deán Funes** Córdoba, C Argentina
204 L12 **Dean Island** *island* Antarctica
9 N3 **Dearborn** Michigan, N USA
29 R3 **Dearborn** Missouri, C USA
34 K9 **Deary** Idaho, NW USA
188 J6 **De Grey River** ✍ Western Australia
8 J10 **Dease** ✍ British Columbia, W Canada
8 J10 **Dease Lake** British Columbia, W Canada
104 L4 **Deauville** Calvados, N France
119 X7 **Debal'tseve** *Rus.* Debal'tsevo. Donets'ka Oblast', SE Ukraine
Debal'tsevo *see* Debal'tseve
115 M19 **Debar** *Ger.* Dibra, *Turk.* Debre. W FYR Macedonia
41 O9 **Debauch Mountain** ▲ Alaska, USA
De Behagle *see* Laï
27 X7 **De Berry** Texas, SW USA
131 T2 **Debesy** Udmurtskaya Respublika, NW Russian Federation
113 N16 **Debica** Tarnów, SE Poland
De Bildt *see* De Bilt
100 J11 **De Bilt** *var.* De Bildt. Utrecht, C Netherlands
127 O9 **Debin** Magadanskaya Oblast', E Russian Federation
112 N13 **Dęblin** *Rus.* Ivangorod. Lublin, E Poland
112 D10 **Dębno** Gorzów, W Poland
41 S10 **Deborah, Mount** ▲ Alaska, USA
35 N8 **De Borgia** Montana, NW USA
82 J13 **Debra Birhan** *see* Debre Birhan
Debra Marcos *see* Debre Mark'os
Debra Tabor *see* Debre Tabor
Debre *see* Debar
82 J13 **Debre Birhan** *var.* Debra Birhan. C Ethiopia
113 N22 **Debrecen** *Ger.* Debreczin, *Rom.* Debreţin; *prev.* Debreczen. Hajdú-Bihar, E Hungary
Debrecen/Debreczin *see* Debrecen
82 I12 **Debre Mark'os** *var.* Debra Marcos. NW Ethiopia
115 N19 **Debreše** SW FYR Macedonia
82 J11 **Debre Tabor** *var.* Debra Tabor. NW Ethiopia
Debreţin *see* Debrecen
82 J13 **Debre Zeyt** C Ethiopia
115 L16 **Dečani** Serbia, S Yugoslavia
25 P2 **Decatur** Alabama, S USA
25 S3 **Decatur** Georgia, SE USA
33 L13 **Decatur** Illinois, N USA
33 P11 **Decatur** Indiana, N USA
31 S14 **Decatur** Nebraska, C USA
27 T5 **Decatur** Texas, SW USA
22 L9 **Decaturville** Tennessee, S USA
105 O13 **Decazeville** Aveyron, S France
161 H17 **Deccan** *Hind.* Dakshin. *plateau* C India
12 J8 **Decelles, Réservoir** ⊜ Québec, SE Canada
10 K2 **Déception** Québec, NE Canada
166 G11 **Dechang** Sichuan, C China
113 C15 **Děčín** *Ger.* Tetschen. Severní Čechy, NW Czech Republic
105 P9 **Decize** Nièvre, C France
100 I6 **De Cocksdorp** Noord-Holland, NW Netherlands
31 X11 **Decorah** Iowa, C USA
Dedeagaç/Dedeagach *see* Alexandroúpoli
196 C15 **Dededo** N Guam
100 N9 **Dedemsvaart** Overijssel, E Netherlands
21 O11 **Dedham** Massachusetts, NE USA
85 H19 **Dedo, Cerro** ▲ SW Argentina
79 Q13 **Dédougou** W Burkina
128 G15 **Dedovichi** Pskovskaya Oblast', W Russian Federation
169 V6 **Dedu** *var.* Qingshan. Heilongjiang, NE China
161 J24 **Deduru Oya** ✍ W Sri Lanka
82 J13 **Dedza** Central, S Malawi
85 N14 **Dedza Mountain** ▲ C Malawi
99 J19 **Dee** *Wel.* Afon Dyfrdwy. ✍ England/Wales, UK
98 K9 **Dee** ✍ NE Scotland, UK
23 T4 **Deep Bay** *see* Chilumba
23 T4 **Deep Creek Lake** ⊜ Maryland, NE USA
38 J4 **Deep Creek Range** ▲ Utah, W USA
29 P10 **Deep Fork** ✍ Oklahoma, C USA
12 J11 **Deep River** Ontario, SE Canada
23 T10 **Deep River** North Carolina, SE USA
191 U4 **Deepwater** New South Wales, SE Australia
33 U4 **Deer Creek Lake** ⊜ Ohio, N USA

25 Z15 **Deerfield Beach** Florida, SE USA
41 N8 **Deering** Alaska, USA
40 M16 **Deer Island** Alaska, USA
21 S7 **Deer Isle** *island* Maine, NE USA
11 S11 **Deer Lake** Newfoundland, Newfoundland and Labrador, SE Canada
101 D18 **Deerlijk** West-Vlaanderen, W Belgium
35 Q10 **Deer Lodge** Montana, NW USA
34 L8 **Deer Park** Washington, NW USA
31 U5 **Deer River** Minnesota, N USA
Deés *see* Dej
33 R11 **Defiance** Ohio, N USA
25 Q8 **De Funiak Springs** Florida, SE USA
97 L23 **Degeberga** Kristianstad, S Sweden
106 H12 **Degebe, Ribeira** ✍ S Portugal
82 M13 **Degeh Bur** SE Ethiopia
18 U9 **Dégelis** Québec, SE Canada
79 U17 **Degema** Rivers, S Nigeria
97 L16 **Degerfors** Örebro, C Sweden
200 N16 **De Gerlache Seamounts** *undersea feature* SE Pacific Ocean
103 N21 **Deggendorf** Bayern, SE Germany
124 Nn2 **Değirmenlik** *Gk.* Kythréa. N Cyprus
82 I11 **Degoma** NW Ethiopia
29 T12 **De Gordyk** *see* Gorredijk
29 T12 **De Gray Lake** ⊜ Arkansas, C USA
130 M10 **Degtevo** Rostovskaya Oblast', SW Russian Federation
149 X13 **Dehak** Sistán va Balúchestán, SE Iran
149 R9 **Deh 'Ali** Kermán, C Iran
149 S13 **Dehbárez** *var.* Rúdán. Hormozgán, S Iran
149 P10 **Deh Bíd** Fárs, C Iran
148 M10 **Deh Dasht** Kohkilúyeh va Búyer Aḥmadí, SW Iran
77 N8 **Dehibat** SE Tunisia
148 L8 **Dehlí** *see* Delhi
148 K8 **Dehlorán** Ílám, W Iran
153 N13 **Dehqonobod** *Rus.* Dekhkanabad. Qashqadaryo Wiloyati, S Uzbekistan
159 O14 **Dehra Dún** Uttar Pradesh, N India
159 O14 **Deh Shú** *var.* Deshu. Helmand, S Afghanistan
101 D17 **Deinze** Oost-Vlaanderen, NW Belgium
Deir 'Alla *see* Dayr 'Allá
Deir ez Zor *see* Dayr az Zawr
118 H9 **Dej** *Hung.* Dés; *prev.* Deés. Cluj, NW Romania
97 K15 **Deje** Värmland, C Sweden
176 Y14 **De Jongs, Tanjung** *headland* Irian Jaya, SE Indonesia
De Jouwer *see* Joure
32 M10 **De Kalb** Illinois, N USA
24 M5 **De Kalb** Mississippi, S USA
27 W5 **De Kalb** Texas, SW USA
81 K20 **Dekese** Kasai Occidental, C Zaire
180 H13 **Dembéni** Grande Comore, NW Comoros
81 I14 **Dékoa** Kémo, C Central African Republic
100 H6 **De Koog** Noord-Holland, NW Netherlands
32 M9 **Delafield** Wisconsin, N USA
63 C23 **De La Garma** Buenos Aires, E Argentina
12 K10 **Delahey, Lac** ⊜ Québec, SE Canada
82 E11 **Delami** Southern Kordofan, C Sudan
25 X11 **De Land** Florida, SE USA
37 R12 **Delano** California, W USA
31 V8 **Delano** Minnesota, N USA
38 K6 **Delano Peak** ▲ Utah, W USA
Delap-Uliga-Darrit *see* Dalap-Uliga-Djarrit
154 F17 **Delárám** Faráh, SW Afghanistan
40 F17 **Delarof Islands** *island group* Aleutian Islands, Alaska, USA
32 M9 **Delavan** Wisconsin, N USA
33 S3 **Delaware** Ohio, N USA
20 J14 **Delaware** ◆ *state* NE USA
33 R11 **Delaware** *off.* State of Delaware; *also known as* Blue Hen State, Diamond State, First State. ◆ *state* NE USA
20 I17 **Delaware Bay** *bay* NE USA
26 J8 **Delaware Mountains** ▲ Texas, SW USA
20 I12 **Delaware River** ✍ NE USA
29 Q3 **Delaware River** ✍ Kansas, C USA
20 J14 **Delaware Water Gap** *valley* New Jersey/Pennsylvania, NE USA
103 G14 **Delbrück** Nordrhein-Westfalen, W Germany
9 Q15 **Delburne** Alberta, SW Canada
180 M12 **Del Cano Rise** *undersea feature* SW Indian Ocean
115 Q18 **Delčevo** NE FYR Macedonia
115 O18 **Delcommune, Lac** *see* Nzilo, Lac
100 O10 **Delden** Overijssel, E Netherlands
191 R12 **Delegate** New South Wales, SE Australia
110 D7 **Delémont** *Ger.* Delsberg. Jura, NW Switzerland
83 N17 **De Leon** Texas, SW USA
117 R7 **Delfoí** Stereá Ellás, C Greece
100 G12 **Delft** Zuid-Holland, W Netherlands
161 J23 **Delft** *island* NW Sri Lanka
100 O5 **Delfzijl** Groningen, NE Netherlands
67 P18 **Delgada Fan** *undersea feature* NE Pacific Ocean
44 F17 **Delgado** San Salvador, SW El Salvador
84 E6 **Delgado, Cabo** *headland* N Mozambique
82 E6 **Delgo** Northern, N Sudan
165 R10 **Delhi** *var.* Delingha. Qinghai, C China
158 I10 **Delhi** *var.* Dehlí, *Hind.* Dilli; *hist.* Shahjahanabad. Delhi, N India

24 J5 **Delhi** Louisiana, S USA
20 J11 **Delhi** New York, NE USA
158 I10 **Delhi** ◆ *union territory* NW India
142 J17 **Deli Burnu** *headland* N Turkey
57 X10 **Délices** C French Guiana
142 J12 **Delice Çayı** ✍ C Turkey
42 J6 **Delicias** *var.* Ciudad Delicias. Chihuahua, N Mexico
149 N7 **Delíján** *var.* Dalíján, Dilíján. Markazí, W Iran
114 P12 **Deli Jovan** ▲ E Yugoslavia
Déli-Kárpátok *see* Carpaţii Meridionali
15 H6 **Déline** *prev.* Fort Franklin. Northwest Territories, NW Canada
Delingha *see* Delhi
13 Q7 **Delisle** Québec, SE Canada
9 T15 **Delisle** Saskatchewan, S Canada
103 M15 **Delitzsch** Sachsen, E Germany
35 Q2 **Dell** Montana, NW USA
26 I7 **Dell City** Texas, SW USA
105 U7 **Delle** Territoire-de-Belfort, E France
38 J9 **Dellenbaugh, Mount** ▲ Arizona, SW USA
31 R11 **Dell Rapids** South Dakota, N USA
23 Y4 **Delmar** Maryland, NE USA
20 I10 **Delmar** New York, NE USA
102 G11 **Delmenhorst** Niedersachsen, NW Germany
23 R14 **Delmar** South Carolina, SE USA
97 G23 **Denmark** *off.* Kingdom of Denmark, *Dan.* Danmark; *anc.* Hafnia. ◆ *monarchy* N Europe
94 H1 **Denmark Strait** *var.* Danmarksstraedet. *strait* Greenland/Iceland
47 T11 **Dennery** E Saint Lucia
100 I7 **Den Oever** Noord-Holland, NW Netherlands
153 O13 **Denow** *Rus.* Denau. Surkhondaryo Wiloyati, S Uzbekistan
175 N16 **Denpasar** *prev.* Paloe. Bali, C Indonesia
118 E12 **Denta** Timiş, W Romania
23 Y3 **Denton** Maryland, NE USA
27 T6 **Denton** Texas, SW USA
195 O15 **D'Entrecasteaux Islands** *island group* SE PNG
39 T4 **Denver** *state capital* Colorado, C USA
18 K8 **Denver** ✈ Colorado, C USA
26 L6 **Denver City** Texas, SW USA
158 J9 **Deoband** Uttar Pradesh, N India
160 E13 **Deolali** Mahárăshtra, W India
160 I10 **Deori** Madhya Pradesh, C India
159 O12 **Deoria** Uttar Pradesh, N India
101 A17 **De Panne** West-Vlaanderen, W Belgium
56 M5 **Dependencia Federal** *off.* Territorio Dependencia Federal. ◆ *federal dependency* N Venezuela
Dependencia Federal, Territorio *see* Dependencia Federal
Désse *see* Desè
103 M14 **Dessau** Sachsen-Anhalt, E Germany
101 J16 **Dessel** Antwerpen, N Belgium
Dessie *see* Desè
Destêrro *see* Florianópolis
25 P9 **Destin** Florida, SE USA
Destná *see* Velká Deštná
200 Oo11 **Desventurados, Islas de los** *island group* W Chile
105 N1 **Desvres** Pas-de-Calais, N France
118 E12 **Deta** *Ger.* Detta. Timiş, W Romania
103 H14 **Detmold** Nordrhein-Westfalen, W Germany
33 S9 **Detroit** Michigan, N USA
27 W5 **Detroit** Texas, SW USA
33 S8 **Detroit** ✈ Canada/USA
31 S6 **Detroit Lakes** Minnesota, N USA
33 S10 **Detroit Metropolitan** ✈ Michigan, N USA
Detta *see* Deta
178 T11 **Det Udom** Ubon Ratchathani, E Thailand
113 K20 **Detva** *Hung.* Gyeva. Stredné Slovensko, C Slovakia
81 M15 **Deua** Kasai Occidental, SE Central African Republic
188 L4 **Derby** Western Australia
99 M19 **Derby** C England, UK
29 N7 **Derby** Kansas, C USA
99 L18 **Derbyshire** *cultural region* C England, UK
113 C16 **Derdap** *physical region* E Yugoslavia
118 G11 **Dej** *see* Gönnoi
176 X11 **Derew** ✍ Irian Jaya, E Indonesia
131 R8 **Dergachi** Saratovskaya Oblast', W Russian Federation
Dergachi *see* Derhachi
99 C17 **Derg, Lough** *Ir.* Loch Deirgeirt. ⊜ W Ireland
119 V3 **Derhachi** *Rus.* Dergachi. Kharkiv'ska Oblast', E Ukraine
24 G8 **De Ridder** Louisiana, S USA
143 P16 **Derik** Mardin, SE Turkey
85 E20 **Derm** Hardap, C Namibia
150 M14 **Dermentobe** *prev.* Dyurmen'tyube. Kzyl-Orda, S Kazakhstan
29 W14 **Dermott** Arkansas, C USA
118 G11 **Derna** *see* Darnah
125 Ff11 **Dern'yanska** *Rus.* Tyumenskaya Oblast', C Russian Federation
41 S10 **Denali** *see* McKinley, Mount
82 N13 **Denan** SE Ethiopia
104 I4 **Deroute, Passage de la** *strait* Channel Islands/France
142 L12 **Develi** Kayseri, C Turkey
100 M11 **Deventer** Overijssel, E Netherlands
13 O10 **Devenyns, Lac** ⊜ Québec, SE Canada
98 K8 **Deveron** ✍ NE Scotland, UK
159 R14 **Devghar** *prev.* Deoghar. Bihár, N India
191 O16 **Derwent Bridge** Tasmania, SE Australia
191 O17 **Derwent, River** ✍ Tasmania, SE Australia
29 R10 **Devil's Den** *plateau* Arkansas, C USA
37 R7 **Devils Gate** *pass* California, W USA
31 P3 **Devils Lake** North Dakota, N USA

33 R10 **Devils Lake** ⊜ Michigan, N USA
31 O3 **Devils Lake** ⊜ North Dakota, N USA
37 W13 **Devils Playground** *desert* California, W USA
27 O11 **Devils River** ✍ Texas, SW USA
35 Y12 **Devils Tower** ▲ Wyoming, C USA
116 I11 **Devin** *prev.* Dovlen. Plovdivska Oblast', SW Bulgaria
27 R12 **Devine** Texas, SW USA
158 H13 **Devlí** Rájasthán, N India
116 N8 **Devnya** *prev.* Devne. Varnenska Oblast', NE Bulgaria
33 U14 **Devola** Ohio, S USA
115 M21 **Devoll, Lumi i** *var.* Devoll. SE Albania
9 Q14 **Devon** Alberta, SW Canada
9 S14 **Devon** *cultural region* SW England, UK
207 N10 **Devon Island** *prev.* North Devon Island. *island* Parry Islands, Northwest Territories, NE Canada
191 O16 **Devonport** Tasmania, SE Australia
142 H11 **Devrek** Zonguldak, N Turkey
160 G10 **Dewás** Madhya Pradesh, C India
De Westereen *see* Zwaagwesteinde
29 P8 **Dewey** Oklahoma, C USA
Dewey *see* Culebra
100 M8 **De Wijk** Drenthe, NE Netherlands
31 W12 **De Witt** Arkansas, C USA
31 Z14 **De Witt** Iowa, C USA
31 R16 **De Witt** Nebraska, C USA
99 M17 **Dewsbury** N England, UK
167 Q10 **Dexing** Jiangxi, S China
29 Y8 **Dexter** Missouri, C USA
39 U14 **Dexter** New Mexico, SW USA
166 I8 **Deyang** Sichuan, C China
190 C4 **Dey–Dey, Lake** *salt lake* South Australia
149 S7 **Deyhúk** Khorásán, E Iran
152 K12 **Deynau** *var.* Dyanev, *Turkm.* Dänew. Lebapskiy Velayat, NE Turkmenistan
148 L8 **Dezful** *var.* Dizful. Khúzestán, SW Iran
133 X4 **Dezhneva, Mys** *headland* NE Russian Federation
167 P4 **Dezhou** Shandong, E China
Dezh Sháhpúr *see* Maríván
159 U14 **Dhaka** *prev.* Dacca. ● (Bangladesh) Dhaka, C Bangladesh
159 T15 **Dhaka** ◆ *division* C Bangladesh
Dhali *see* Idálion
147 O15 **Dhamár** W Yemen
160 K12 **Dhamtari** Madhya Pradesh, C India
159 Q15 **Dhanbád** Bihár, N India
158 L10 **Dhangadhi** *var.* Dhangarhi. Far Western, W Nepal
Dhangarhi *see* Dhangadhi
Dhank *see* Dank
159 R12 **Dhankuta** Eastern, E Nepal
158 I6 **Dhaola Dhár** ▲ NE India
160 F10 **Dhár** Madhya Pradesh, C India
159 R12 **Dharan** *var.* Dharan Bazar. Eastern, E Nepal
161 H21 **Dháräpuram** Tamil Nádu, SE India
161 H20 **Dharmapuri** Tamil Nádu, SE India
161 H18 **Dharmavaram** Andhra Pradesh, E India
160 M11 **Dharmjaygarh** Madhya Pradesh, C India
158 I7 **Dharmsála** *prev.* Dharmshála. Himáchal Pradesh, NW India
161 F17 **Dhárwád** *prev.* Dharwar. Karnátaka, SW India
Dharwar *see* Dhárwád
159 O10 **Dhaulágiri** ▲ C Nepal
83 L18 **Dheere Laaq** *var.* Lak Dera; *It.* Lach Dera. *seasonal river* Kenya/Somalia
124 O3 **Dhekélia Sovereign Base Area** *UK military installation* E Cyprus
124 O3 **Dhekélia** *Eng.* Dhekelia. SE Cyprus. *UK air base* SE Cyprus
115 M22 **Dhëmbelit, Majaë** ▲ S Albania
160 O12 **Dhënkánál** Orissa, E India
Dheskáti *see* Deskáti
144 G11 **Dhíbán** 'Ammán, NW Jordan
Dhidhimótikhon *see* Didymóteicho
Dhíkti Ori *see* Díkti
144 I12 **Dhirwah, Wádi adh** *dry watercourse* C Jordan
Dhístomon *see* Dístomo
Dhodhekánisos *see* Dodekánisos
Dhodhóni *see* Dodóni
Dhofar *see* Zufár
Dhomokós *see* Domokós
Dhond *see* Daund
161 H17 **Dhone** Andhra Pradesh, C India
160 B11 **Dhoráji** Gujarát, W India
Dhráma *see* Dráma
85 C10 **Dhrángadhra** Gujarát, W India
Dhrepanon, Akra *see* Drépano, Akra
160 F12 **Dhule** *prev.* Dhulia. Mahárăshtra, C India
Dhulia *see* Dhule
160 B11 **Dhún Dealgan, Cuan** *see* Dundalk Bay
Dhún Droma, Cuan *see* Dundrum Bay
Dhún na nGall, Bá *see* Donegal Bay
Dhú Shaykh *see* Qazániyah
82 Q13 **Dhuudo** Bari, NE Somalia
83 N15 **Dhuusa Marreeb** *var.* Dusa Marreb, *It.* Dusa Mareb. C Somalia
117 J24 **Día** *island* SE Greece
57 Y9 **Diable, Île du** *var.* Devil's Island. *island* N French Guiana
13 N12 **Diable, Rivière du** ✍ Québec, SE Canada

◆ COUNTRY
◆ COUNTRY CAPITAL
◇ DEPENDENT TERRITORY
○ DEPENDENT TERRITORY CAPITAL
◆ ADMINISTRATIVE REGION
✕ INTERNATIONAL AIRPORT
▲ MOUNTAIN
▲ MOUNTAIN RANGE
✕ VOLCANO
✍ RIVER
⊜ LAKE
□ RESERVOIR

37 N8 **Diablo, Mount** ▲ California, W USA
37 O9 **Diablo Range** ▲ California, W USA
26 I8 **Diablo, Sierra** ▲ Texas, SW USA
47 O11 **Diablotins, Morne** ▲ N Dominica
79 N11 **Diafarabé** Mopti, C Mali
79 N11 **Diaka** ♒ SW Mali
Diakovár see Đakovo
78 I12 **Dialakoto** S Senegal
8 B18 **Diamante** Entre Ríos, E Argentina
64 I12 **Diamante, Río** ♒ C Argentina
61 M19 **Diamantina** Minas Gerais, SE Brazil
61 N17 **Diamantina, Chapada** ▲ E Brazil
181 U11 **Diamantina Fracture Zone** tectonic feature E Indian Ocean
189 T8 **Diamantina River** ♒ Queensland/South Australia
40 I10 **Diamond Head** headland Oahu, Hawaii, USA, C Pacific Ocean
39 P2 **Diamond Peak** ▲ Colorado, C USA
37 W5 **Diamond Peak** ▲ Nevada, W USA
Diamond State see Delaware
78 J11 **Diamou** Kayes, SW Mali
97 I23 **Dianalund** Vestsjælland, C Denmark
67 G25 **Diana's Peak** ▲ C Saint Helena
166 M16 **Dianbai** Guangdong, S China
166 G13 **Dian Chi** ⊚ SW China
108 B10 **Diano Marina** Liguria, NW Italy
79 R13 **Diapaga** E Burkina
Diarbekr see Diyarbakır
109 J15 **Diavolo, Passo del** pass C Italy
83 I18 **Díaz** Santa Fe, C Argentina
147 W6 **Dibā al Ḥiṣn** var. Dibah, Dibba. Ash Shāriqah, NE UAE
145 S3 **Dībaga** N Iraq
Dībā al Ḥiṣn see Dibā al Ḥiṣn
81 L22 **Dibaya** Kasai Occidental, S Zaire
Dibba see Dibā al Ḥiṣn
205 W15 **Dibble Iceberg Tongue** ice feature Antarctica
115 L19 **Dibër** ♦ district E Albania
85 I20 **Dibete** Central, SE Botswana
27 W9 **Diboll** Texas, SW USA
Dibra see Debar
159 X11 **Dibrugarh** Assam, NE India
56 G4 **Dibulla** La Guajira, N Colombia
27 O5 **Dickens** Texas, SW USA
21 R2 **Dickey** Maine, NE USA
32 K9 **Dickeyville** Wisconsin, N USA
30 K5 **Dickinson** North Dakota, N USA
1 E6 **Dickins Seamount** undersea feature NE Pacific Ocean
29 O13 **Dickson** Oklahoma, C USA
22 J9 **Dickson** Tennessee, S USA
Dicle see Tigris
Dicsőszentmárton see Târnăveni
100 M12 **Didam** Gelderland, E Netherlands
169 Y8 **Didao** Heilongjiang, NE China
78 L12 **Didiéni** Koulikoro, W Mali
Didimo see Dídymo
Didimóteiho see Didymóteicho
83 K17 **Didimtu** spring/well NE Kenya
69 U9 **Didinga Hills** ▲ S Sudan
9 Q16 **Didsbury** Alberta, SW Canada
158 G11 **Didwāna** Rājasthān, N India
117 G20 **Dídymo** var. Didimo. ▲ S Greece
116 L12 **Didymóteicho** var. Dhidhimótikhon, Didimotiho. Anatolikí Makedonía kai Thráki, NE Greece
105 O13 **Die** Drôme, E France
79 O13 **Diébougou** SW Burkina
Diedenhofen see Thionville
9 S16 **Diefenbaker, Lake** ⊚ Saskatchewan, S Canada
64 H7 **Diego de Almagro** Atacama, N Chile
65 F23 **Diego de Almagro, Isla** island S Chile
63 A20 **Diego de Alvear** Santa Fe, C Argentina
181 Q7 **Diego Garcia** island S British Indian Ocean Territory
Diégo-Suarez see Antsirañana
101 M23 **Diekirch** Diekirch, C Luxembourg
101 L23 **Diekirch** ♦ district N Luxembourg
78 K11 **Diéma** Kayes, W Mali
104 J7 **Diemel** ♒ W Germany
100 I10 **Diemen** Noord-Holland, C Netherlands
Diemrich see Deva
178 I16 **Điện Biên** Biên, Dien Bien Phu. Lai Châu, N Vietnam
178 J8 **Dien Bien Phu** see Điện Biên
178 J8 **Điện Châu** Nghệ An, N Vietnam
101 K18 **Diepenbeek** Limburg, NE Belgium
100 N11 **Diepenheim** Overijssel, E Netherlands
100 M10 **Diepenveen** Overijssel, E Netherlands
102 G12 **Diepholz** Niedersachsen, NW Germany
104 M3 **Dieppe** Seine-Maritime, N France
100 M12 **Dieren** Gelderland, E Netherlands
29 S13 **Dierks** Arkansas, C USA
101 J17 **Diest** Vlaams Brabant, C Belgium
110 F7 **Dietikon** Zürich, NW Switzerland
105 R13 **Dieulefit** Drôme, E France
75 T8 **Dieuze** Moselle, NE France
121 H15 **Dieveniškės** Šalčininkai, SE Lithuania
100 N7 **Diever** Drenthe, NE Netherlands
103 F17 **Diez** Rheinland-Pfalz, W Germany
79 Y10 **Diffa** Diffa, SE Niger
101 L25 **Differdange** Luxembourg, SW Luxembourg
11 O16 **Digby** Nova Scotia, SE Canada
29 J5 **Dighton** Kansas, C USA

105 T14 **Digne** var. Digne-les-Bains. Alpes-de-Haute-Provence, SE France
Digne-les-Bains see Digne
Digoel see Digul, Sungai
105 Q10 **Digoin** Saône-et-Loire, C France
179 Rr16 **Digos** Mindanao, S Philippines
176 Z13 **Digri** Sind, SE Pakistan
176 Z13 **Digul Barat, Sungai** ♒ Irian Jaya, E Indonesia
176 Z13 **Digul, Sungai** prev. Digoel. ♒ Irian Jaya, E Indonesia
176 Z13 **Digul Timur, Sungai** ♒ Irian Jaya, E Indonesia
Dihang see Brahmaputra
159 X10 **Dihāng** ♒ NE India
Dihōk see Dahūk
83 L17 **Diinsoor** Bay, S Somalia
101 H17 **Dijle** ♒ C Belgium
105 R8 **Dijon** anc. Divio. Côte d'Or, C France
95 H14 **Dikanäs** Västerbotten, N Sweden
83 L17 **Dikhil** SW Djibouti
142 B13 **Dikili** İzmir, W Turkey
101 B17 **Diksmuide** var. Dixmuide, Fr. Dixmude. West-Vlaanderen, W Belgium
126 Hh6 **Dikson** Taymyrskiy (Dolgano-Nenetskiy) Avtonomnyy Okrug, N Russian Federation
117 K25 **Dikti** var. Dhíkti Óri. ▲ Kríti, Greece, E Mediterranean Sea
79 X14 **Dikwa** Borno, NE Nigeria
83 J15 **Dila** S Ethiopia
101 G18 **Dilbeek** Vlaams Brabant, C Belgium
175 S16 **Dili** var. Dilli, Dilly. Timor, C Indonesia
79 Y11 **Dilia** var. Dillia. ♒ SE Niger
178 K13 **Di Linh** Lâm Đồng, S Vietnam
103 G16 **Dillenburg** Hessen, W Germany
27 Q13 **Dilley** Texas, SW USA
Dilli see Delhi, India
Dili see Dili, Indonesia
Dilia see Dilia
82 E11 **Dilling** var. Ad Dalanj. Southern Kordofan, C Sudan
103 D20 **Dillingen** Saarland, SW Germany
Dillingen see Dillingen an der Donau
103 J22 **Dillingen an der Donau** var. Dillingen. Bayern, S Germany
41 O13 **Dillingham** Alaska, USA
35 Q12 **Dillon** Montana, NW USA
23 T13 **Dillon** South Carolina, SE USA
33 T13 **Dillon Lake** ⊚ Ohio, N USA
Dilly see Dili
81 K24 **Dilolo** Shaba, S Zaire
117 J20 **Dílos** island Kykládes, Greece, Aegean Sea
31 R5 **Dilworth** Minnesota, N USA
144 H7 **Dimashq** var. Ash Shām, Esh Sham, Eng. Damascus, Fr. Damas, It. Damasco. ● (Syria) Dimashq, SW Syria
144 I8 **Dimashq** off. Muḥāfaẓat Dimashq, var. Damascus, Ar. Ash Sham, Ash Shām, Damasco, Esh Sham, Fr. Damas. ♦ governorate S Syria
144 I7 **Dimashq** x Dimashq, S Syria
81 L21 **Dimbelenge** Kasai Occidental, C Zaire
79 N16 **Dimbokro** E Ivory Coast
190 L11 **Dimboola** Victoria, SE Australia
Dimbovita see Dâmbovița
116 K11 **Dimitrovgrad** Khaskovska Oblast, S Bulgaria
131 R5 **Dimitrovgrad** Ul'yanovskaya Oblast', W Russian Federation
115 Q15 **Dimitrovgrad** prev. Caribrod. Serbia, SE Yugoslavia
Dimitrovo see Pernik
Dimlang see Vogel Peak
26 M3 **Dimmitt** Texas, SW USA
116 F7 **Dimovo** Oblast Montana, NW Bulgaria
8 A16 **Dimpolis** Acre, W Brazil
117 O23 **Dimylía** Ródos, Dodekánisos, Greece, Aegean Sea
179 R13 **Dinagat** Dinagat Island, S Philippines
179 Rr13 **Dinagat Island** island S Philippines
159 S13 **Dinajpur** Rajshahi, NW Bangladesh
104 I6 **Dinan** Côtes d'Armor, NW France
101 I21 **Dinant** Namur, S Belgium
142 H15 **Dinar** Afyon, SW Turkey
114 F13 **Dinara** ▲ W Croatia
Dinara see Dinaric Alps
104 I5 **Dinard** Ille-et-Vilaine, NW France
114 F13 **Dinaric Alps** var. Dinara. ▲ Bosnia and Herzegovina/Croatia
149 N10 **Dinār, Kūh-e** ▲ C Iran
Dinbych see Denbigh
161 H22 **Dindigul** Tamil Nādu, SE India
85 M19 **Dindiza** Gaza, S Mozambique
155 V7 **Dinga** Punjab, E Pakistan
81 M21 **Dinga** Bandundu, SW Zaire
164 L16 **Dinggyé** Xizang Zizhiqu, W China
99 A20 **Dingle** Ir. An Daingean. SW Ireland
99 A20 **Dingle Bay** Ir. Bá an Daingin. bay SW Ireland
20 I13 **Dingmans Ferry** Pennsylvania, NE USA
103 M23 **Dingolfing** Bayern, SE Germany
179 P8 **Dingras** Luzon, N Philippines
78 J13 **Dinguiraye** Haute-Guinée, N Guinea
98 I8 **Dingwall** N Scotland, UK
165 V10 **Dingxi** Gansu, C China
167 Q7 **Dingyuan** Anhui, E China
167 O3 **Dingzhou** Hebei, E China
178 K8 **Đinh Lâp** Lang Sơn, N Vietnam
178 K14 **Đinh Quan** Đồng Nai, S Vietnam
102 E13 **Dinkel** ♒ Germany/Netherlands
103 K21 **Dinkelsbühl** Bayern, S Germany
103 D14 **Dinslaken** Nordrhein-Westfalen, W Germany
37 R11 **Dinuba** California, W USA

23 W7 **Dinwiddie** Virginia, NE USA
100 N13 **Dinxperlo** Gelderland, E Netherlands
117 F14 **Dío** anc. Dium. site of ancient city Kentrikí Makedonía, N Greece
Diófás see Nucet
78 M12 **Dioīla** Koulikoro, W Mali
117 G19 **Dióryga Korínthou** Eng. Corinth Canal. canal S Greece
79 N12 **Diouloulou** SW Senegal
78 G12 **Dioura** Mopti, W Mali
78 I11 **Diourbel** W Senegal
158 L10 **Dipāyal** Far Western, W Nepal
124 Oo2 **Dipkarpaz** Gk. Rízokárpaso, Rízokárpason. NE Cyprus
155 R17 **Diplo** Sind, SE Pakistan
179 Qq15 **Dipolog** var. Dipolog City. Mindanao, S Philippines
193 C23 **Dipton** Southland, South Island, NZ
78 L13 **Diré** Tombouctou, C Mali
82 O13 **Diré Dawa** E Ethiopia
117 H18 **Dírfys** var. Dirfis. ♒ Évvoia, C Greece
117 H18 **Dírfys** var. Dirfis. ▲ Évvoia, C Greece
77 N9 **Dirj** var. Daraj, Darj. S W Libya
188 G10 **Dirk Hartog Island** island Western Australia
189 X11 **Dirranbandi** Queensland, E Australia
83 O16 **Dirri** Galguduud, C Somalia
79 N6 **Dirschau** see Tczew
34 E10 **Dirty Devil River** ♒ Utah, W USA
34 E10 **Disappointment, Cape** headland Washington, NW USA
188 L8 **Disappointment, Lake** salt lake Western Australia
191 R12 **Disaster Bay** bay New South Wales, SE Australia
46 J11 **Discovery Bay** C Jamaica
190 K13 **Discovery Bay** inlet SE Australia
69 Y15 **Discovery II Fracture Zone** tectonic feature SW Indian Ocean
Discovery Seamount/Discovery Seamounts see Discovery Tablemount
67 O19 **Discovery Tablemount** var. Discovery Seamount, Discovery Seamounts. undersea feature SW Indian Ocean
110 G9 **Disentis** Rmsch. Mustér. Graubünden, S Switzerland
41 Z9 **Dishna** River ♒ Alaska, USA
205 X4 **Dismal Mountains** ▲ Antarctica
30 M14 **Dismal River** ♒ Nebraska, C USA
Disna see Dzisna
101 I19 **Dison** Liège, E Belgium
159 V12 **Dispur** Assam, NE India
13 R13 **Disraeli** Québec, SE Canada
117 F18 **Dístomo** prev. Dhístomon. Stereá Ellás, C Greece
117 H20 **Dístos, Límni** ⊚ Évvoia, C Greece
61 L18 **Distrito Federal** Eng. Federal District. ♦ federal district C Brazil
43 P14 **Distrito Federal** ♦ federal district S Mexico
56 L4 **Distrito Federal** off. Territorio Distrito Federal. ♦ federal district N Venezuela
Distrito Federal, Territorio see Distrito Federal
118 J10 **Ditrău** Hung. Ditró. Harghita, C Romania
Ditró see Ditrău
160 B12 **Diu** Damān and Diu, W India
179 Rr14 **Diuata Mountains** ▲ Mindanao, S Philippines
Dium see Dío
111 S13 **Divača** SW Slovenia
104 K5 **Dives** ♒ N France
104 L5 **Divichi** see Dāväçi
35 Q11 **Divide** Montana, NW USA
85 N18 **Divinhe** Sofala, E Mozambique
61 L20 **Divinópolis** Minas Gerais, SE Brazil
126 I14 **Divnogorsk** Krasnoyarskiy Kray, S Russian Federation
131 N13 **Divnoye** Stavropol'skiy Kray, SW Russian Federation
78 M17 **Divo** S Ivory Coast
Divodurum Mediomatricum see Metz
143 N13 **Divriği** Sivas, C Turkey
Diwaniyah see Ad Dīwānīyah
145 V5 **Dīyālá, Nahr** var. Rudkhaneh-ye Sīrvān, Sirwan. ♒ Iran/Iraq see also Sīrvān, Rudkhaneh-ye
143 P15 **Diyarbakır** var. Diarbekr; anc. Amida. Diyarbakır, SE Turkey
143 P15 **Diyarbakır** var. Diarbekr. ♦ province SE Turkey
Dizful see Dezfūl
81 F16 **Dja** ♒ SE Cameroon
Djadié see Zadié
79 X7 **Djado** Agadez, NE Niger
79 X6 **Djado, Plateau du** ▲ NE Niger
Djailolo see Halmahera, Pulau
Djajapura see Jayapura
Djakarta see Jakarta
Djakovica see Đakovica
Djakovo see Đakovo
81 G20 **Djambala** Plateaux, C Congo
Djambi see Jambi, Sumatera, W Indonesia
Djambi see Hari, Batang, Sumatera, W Indonesia
76 M11 **Djanet** prev. Fort Charlet. SE Algeria
76 J8 **Djelfa** var. El Djelfa. N Algeria
81 M14 **Djéma** Haut-Mbomou, E Central African Republic
Djenepolnto see Jenepolnto
79 N12 **Djenné** var. Jenné. Mopti, C Mali
Djérablous see Jarāblus
Djerba see Jerba, Île de
81 F15 **Djérem** ♒ C Cameroon
81 L22 **Djevdjelija** see Gevgelija
79 P11 **Djibo** N Burkina
82 L12 **Djibouti** var. Jibuti. ● (Djibouti) E Djibouti
82 L12 **Djibouti** off. Republic of Djibouti, var. Jibuti; prev. French Somaliland, French Territory of the Afars and Issas, Fr. Côte Française des Somalis, Territoire Française des Afars et des Issas. ♦ republic E Africa
82 L12 **Djidjel/Djidjelli** see Jijel
57 W10 **Djoemoe** Sipaliwini, C Suriname
81 K18 **Djokjakarta** see Yogyakarta
81 K18 **Djoku-Punda** Kasai Occidental, C Zaire
81 F17 **Djolu** Equateur, N Zaire
79 R4 **Djorce Petrov** see Đorče Petrov
81 F17 **Djoua** ♒ Congo/Gabon
79 R4 **Djougou** W Benin
80 I8 **Djoum** Sud, S Cameroon
81 P17 **Djourab, Erg du** dunes N Chad
81 P17 **Djugu** Haut-Zaïre, NE Zaire
94 L3 **Djúpivogur** Austurland, SE Iceland
96 L13 **Djura** Kopparberg, C Sweden
85 G18 **Djurdjevac** var. Đurđevac. ▲
207 U6 **D'Kar** Ghanzi, NW Botswana
83 J14 **Dodola** S Ethiopia
130 J7 **Dmitriya Lapteva, Proliv** strait N Russian Federation
130 K3 **Dmitriyev-L'govskiy** Kurskaya Oblast', W Russian Federation
Dmitriyevsk see Makiyivka
130 K3 **Dmitrovichi** var. Dzmitravichy
130 M12 **Dmitrov** Moskovskaya Oblast', W Russian Federation
130 J6 **Dmitrov-Orlovskiy** Orlovskaya Oblast', W Russian Federation
119 R3 **Dmytrivka** Chernihivs'ka Oblast', N Ukraine
Dnepr see Dnieper
143 N15 **Dneprodzerzhinsk** see Dniprodzerzhyns'k
Dneprodzerzhinskoye Vodokhranilishche see Dniprodzerzhyns'ke Vodoskhovyshche
Dnepropetrovsk see Dnipropetrovs'k
Dnepropetrovskaya Oblast' see Dnipropetrovs'ka Oblast'
Dneprorudnoye see Dniprorudne
Dnestr see Dniester
119 R3 **Dnestrovskiy Liman** see Dnistrovs'kyy Lyman
88 H11 **Dnieper** Bel. Dnyapro, Rus. Dnepr, Ukr. Dnipro. ♒ E Europe
119 P3 **Dnieper Lowland** Bel. Prydnyaprowskaya Nizina, Ukr. Prydniprovs'ka Nyzovyna. lowlands Belorussia/Ukraine
118 M8 **Dniester** Rom. Nistru, Rus. Dnestr, Ukr. Dnister; anc. Tyras. ♒ Moldova/Ukraine
119 T7 **Dnipro** see Dnieper
Dniprodzerzhyns'k Rus. Dneprodzerzhinsk; prev. Kamenskoye. Dnipropetrovs'ka Oblast', E Ukraine
119 T7 **Dniprodzerzhyns'ke Vodoskhovyshche** Rus. Dneprodzerzhinskoye Vodokhranilishche. ⊚ C Ukraine
119 U7 **Dnipropetrovs'k** Rus. Dnepropetrovsk; prev. Yekaterinoslav. Dnipropetrovs'ka Oblast', E Ukraine
119 U8 **Dnipropetrovs'k** x Dnipropetrovs'ka Oblast', S Ukraine
119 X8 **Dnipropetrovs'ka Oblast'** var. Dnipropetrovs'k, Rus. Dnepropetrovskaya Oblast'. ♦ province E Ukraine
119 U9 **Dniprorudne** Rus. Dneprorudnoye. Zaporiz'ka Oblast', SE Ukraine
119 Q11 **Dniprovs'kyy Lyman** Rus. Dneprovskiy Liman. bay S Ukraine
119 R3 **Dnistrovs'kyy Lyman** Rus. Dnestrovskiy Liman. inlet S Ukraine
Dnister see Dniester
128 G14 **Dno** Pskovskaya Oblast', W Russian Federation
129 U2 **Dnyapro** see Dnieper
121 H20 **Dnyaprowska-Buhski, Kanal** Rus. Dneprovsko-Bugskiy Kanal. canal SW Belorussia
168 J9 **Döbögön** Övörhangay, C Mongolia
109 C20 **Doba** Logone-Oriental, S Chad
121 F15 **Dobele** Ger. Doblen. W Latvia
103 Q15 **Döbeln** Sachsen, E Germany
176 Vv9 **Doberai, Jazirah** Dut. Vogelkop. peninsula Irian Jaya, E Indonesia
114 F10 **Dobiegniew** Ger. Woldenberg Neumark. Gorzów, W Poland
83 K18 **Dobli** spring/well SW Somalia
176 W13 **Dobo** Pulau Wamar, E Indonesia
114 H12 **Doboj** N Bosnia and Herzegovina
114 I9 **Dobrá Lom** Montana, NW Bulgaria
119 X8 **Dobra** ♒ Lipetskaya Oblast', W Russian Federation
130 J6 **Dobranka** Volgogradskaya Oblast', SW Russian Federation
108 H8 **Dolo** Veneto, NE Italy
Dolomites/Dolomiti see Dolomitiche, Alpi

80 I10 **Djédaa** Batha, C Chad
76 J6 **Djelfa** var. El Djelfa. N Algeria
81 M14 **Djéma** Haut-Mbomou, E Central African Republic
79 N12 **Djenné** var. Jenné. Mopti, C Mali
81 F15 **Djérem** ♒ C Cameroon
81 L22 **Djevdjelija** see Gevgelija
79 P11 **Djibo** N Burkina
82 L12 **Djibouti** var. Jibuti. ● (Djibouti) E Djibouti
82 L12 **Djibouti** off. Republic of Djibouti, var. Jibuti; prev. French Somaliland, French Territory of the Afars and Issas, Fr. Côte Française des Somalis, Territoire Française des Afars et des Issas. ♦ republic E Africa
82 L12 **Djidjel/Djidjelli** see Jijel
57 W10 **Djoemoe** Sipaliwini, C Suriname
81 K18 **Djokjakarta** see Yogyakarta
81 K18 **Djoku-Punda** Kasai Occidental, C Zaire
81 F17 **Djolu** Equateur, N Zaire
79 R4 **Djorce Petrov** see Đorče Petrov
81 F17 **Djoua** ♒ Congo/Gabon
79 R4 **Djougou** W Benin
80 I8 **Djoum** Sud, S Cameroon
81 P17 **Djourab, Erg du** dunes N Chad
81 P17 **Djugu** Haut-Zaïre, NE Zaire
94 L3 **Djúpivogur** Austurland, SE Iceland
96 L13 **Djura** Kopparberg, C Sweden
85 G18 **Djurdjevac** var. Đurđevac. ▲
207 U6 **D'Kar** Ghanzi, NW Botswana
83 J14 **Dodola** S Ethiopia
130 J7 **Dmitriya Lapteva, Proliv** strait N Russian Federation
130 K3 **Dmitriyev-L'govskiy** Kurskaya Oblast', W Russian Federation
Dmitriyevsk see Makiyivka
130 K3 **Dmitrovichi** var. Dzmitravichy
130 M12 **Dmitrov** Moskovskaya Oblast', W Russian Federation
130 J6 **Dmitrov-Orlovskiy** Orlovskaya Oblast', W Russian Federation
119 R3 **Dmytrivka** Chernihivs'ka Oblast', N Ukraine
164 I12 **Dogai Coring** var. Lake Montcalm. ⊚ W China
143 N15 **Doğanşehir** Malatya, C Turkey
86 E9 **Dogger Bank** undersea feature C North Sea
25 S10 **Dog Island** island Florida, SE USA
12 C7 **Dog Lake** ⊚ Ontario, S Canada
158 B9 **Dogliani** Piemonte, NE Italy
170 G11 **Dōgo** island Oki-shotō, SW Japan
79 S12 **Dogondoutchi** Dosso, SW Niger
170 F13 **Dōgo-yama** var. Dōgo-san. ▲ Kyūshū, SW Japan
Dogrular see Pravda
143 T13 **Doğubayazit** Ağrı, E Turkey
143 P12 **Doğu Karadeniz Dağları** var. Anadolu Dağları. ▲ NE Turkey
47 X11 **Dohad** see Dāhod
47 X11 **Doha** see Ad Dawḥah
Dohuk see Dahūk
165 N16 **Doilungdêqên** Xizang Zizhiqu, W China
116 F12 **Doïranis, Límnis** Bul. Ezero Doyransko. ⊚ N Greece
118 M8 **Doire** see Londonderry
101 H22 **Doische** Namur, S Belgium
61 P17 **Dois de Julho** x (Salvador) Bahia, NE Brazil
62 H12 **Dois Vizinhos** Paraná, S Brazil
82 H10 **Doka** Gedaref, E Sudan
145 T3 **Dokan** var. Dūkān. E Iraq
96 H13 **Dokka** Oppland, S Norway
100 L5 **Dokkum** Friesland, N Netherlands
100 L5 **Dokkumer Ee** ♒ N Netherlands
78 K13 **Doko** Haute-Guinée, NE Guinea
130 K13 **Dokshitsy** see Dokshytsy
121 K13 **Dokshytsy** Rus. Dokshitsy. Vitsyebskaya Voblasts', N Belorussia
119 X8 **Dokuchayevs'k** var. Dokuchayevsk. Donets'ka Oblast', SE Ukraine
155 Y4 **Dokuri, Pulau** see Yos Sudarso, Pulau
31 P9 **Doland** South Dakota, N USA
65 B18 **Dolavón** Chaco, S Argentina
13 P6 **Dolbeau** Québec, SE Canada
104 J5 **Dol-de-Bretagne** Ille-et-Vilaine, NW France
66 D13 **Doldrums Fracture Zone** tectonic feature W Atlantic Ocean
105 S8 **Dôle** Jura, E France
99 J19 **Dolgellau** NW Wales, UK
130 K11 **Dolgino** see Dawhinava
99 M17 **Dolgi, Ostrov** see Dolgiy, Ostrov
99 M17 **Dolgiy, Ostrov** var. Ostrov Dolgi. island NW Russian Federation
46 K12 **Don Christophers Point** headland C Jamaica
57 V9 **Donderkamp** Sipaliwini, NW Suriname
109 C20 **Dolianova** Sardegna, Italy, C Mediterranean Sea
108 C6 **Dolina** see Dolyna
103 G23 **Dolinskaya** see Dolyns'ka
161 K26 **Dondra Head** headland S Sri Lanka
109 C20 **Dolo** Veneto, NE Italy
Dolomites/Dolomiti see Dolomitiche, Alpi

113 I15 **Dobrodzień** Ger. Guttentag. Częstochowa, S Poland
Dobrogea see Dobruja
119 W7 **Dobropillya** Rus. Dobropol'ye. Donets'ka Oblast', SE Ukraine
Dobropol'ye see Dobropillya
119 P8 **Dobrovelychkivka** Kirovohrads'ka Oblast', C Ukraine
116 O7 **Dobruja** var. Dobrudja, Bul. Dobrudzha, Rom. Dobrogea. physical region Bulgaria/Romania
121 P19 **Dobrush** Homyel'skaya Voblasts', SE Belorussia
129 U14 **Dobryanka** Permskaya Oblast', NW Russian Federation
119 P2 **Dobryanka** Chernihivs'ka Oblast', N Ukraine
Dobryn' see Dabryn'
82 L12 **Dobson** North Carolina, SE USA
61 N20 **Doce, Rio** ♒ SE Brazil
95 I16 **Docksta** Västernorrland, C Sweden
43 N10 **Doctor Arroyo** Nuevo León, NE Mexico
64 L4 **Doctor Pedro P. Peña** Boquerón, W Paraguay
175 T7 **Dodaga** Pulau Halmahera, E Indonesia
161 G21 **Dodda Betta** ▲ S India
117 M22 **Dodekánisos** var. Nóties Sporádes, Eng. Dodecanese; prev. Dhodhekánisos. island group SE Greece
29 L3 **Dodge City** Kansas, C USA
32 J6 **Dodgeville** Wisconsin, N USA
99 H25 **Dodman Point** headland SW England, UK
83 J14 **Dodola** S Ethiopia
83 H22 **Dodoma** ● (Tanzania) Dodoma, C Tanzania
83 H22 **Dodoma** ♦ region C Tanzania
117 C16 **Dodóni** var. Dhodhóni. site of ancient city Ípeiros, W Greece
35 U7 **Dodson** Montana, NW USA
27 P3 **Dodson** Texas, SW USA
100 M12 **Doesburg** Gelderland, E Netherlands
100 N12 **Doetinchem** Gelderland, E Netherlands
164 H13 **Dogai Coring** var. Lake Montcalm. ⊚ W China
164 H13 **Dogaru**
60 L13 **Dom Eliseu** Pará, NE Brazil
105 O13 **Dôme, Puy de** ▲ C France
38 H13 **Dome Rock Mountains** ▲ Arizona, SW USA
121 K21 **Domesnes, Cape** see Kolkasrags
64 G8 **Domeyko** Atacama, N Chile
64 H5 **Domeyko, Cordillera** ▲ N Chile
104 K5 **Domfront** Orne, N France
176 Xx10 **Dom, Gunung** ▲ Irian Jaya, E Indonesia
47 X11 **Dominica** off. Commonwealth of Dominica. ♦ republic E West Indies
49 S3 **Dominica** island Dominica
Dominica Channel see Martinique Passage
45 N15 **Dominical** Puntarenas, SE Costa Rica
47 Q8 **Dominican Republic** ♦ republic C West Indies
47 X11 **Dominica Passage** passage E Caribbean Sea
101 K21 **Donoússa** island Kykládes, Greece, Aegean Sea
37 P8 **Don Pedro Reservoir** ⊞ California, W USA
130 L4 **Domodedovo** x (Moskva) Moskovskaya Oblast', W Russian Federation
108 C6 **Domodossola** Piemonte, NE Italy
117 F17 **Domokós** var. Dhomokós. Stereá Ellás, C Greece
180 I14 **Domoni** Anjouan, SE Comoros
63 G16 **Dom Pedrito** Rio Grande do Sul, S Brazil
Dompoe see Dompu
175 Oo16 **Dompu** prev. Dompoe. Sumbawa, C Indonesia
100 L5 **Domschale** see Domžale
111 U11 **Domuyo, Volcán** ▲ W Argentina
111 U11 **Domžale** Ger. Domschale. C Slovenia
131 O10 **Don** var. Duna, Tanais. ♒ SW Russian Federation
98 K9 **Don** ♒ NE Scotland, UK
193 M11 **Donald** Victoria, SE Australia
24 J7 **Donaldsonville** Louisiana, S USA
25 S8 **Donalsonville** Georgia, SE USA
Donau see Danube
103 G23 **Donaueschingen** Baden-Württemberg, SW Germany
103 K22 **Donaumoos** wetland S Germany
103 K22 **Donauwörth** Bayern, S Germany
111 U7 **Donawitz** Steiermark, SE Austria
115 N18 **Don Benito** Extremadura, W Spain
99 M17 **Doncaster** anc. Danum. N England, UK
129 U2 **Dondo** Sofala, C Mozambique
57 V9 **Dondo** Cuanza Norte, NW Angola
175 Q9 **Dondo** Sulawesi, N Indonesia
175 Pp7 **Dondo, Teluk** bay Sulawesi, N Indonesia
161 K26 **Dondra Head** headland S Sri Lanka
168 F7 **Dörgön Nuur** ⊚ NW Mongolia
79 Q12 **Dori** N Burkina
85 G23 **Doring** ♒ S South Africa
103 E16 **Dormagen** Nordrhein-Westfalen, W Germany
110 E6 **Dornach** Solothurn, NW Switzerland
Dorna Watra see Vatra Dornei
110 J7 **Dornbirn** Vorarlberg, W Austria
98 J7 **Dornoch** N Scotland, UK
98 J7 **Dornoch Firth** inlet N Scotland, UK
131 O9 **Dornod** ♦ province SE Mongolia
Dornogovi see Dornogovi
57 P10 **Doro** Tombouctou, S Mali
118 L14 **Dorohoi** Botoșani, NE Romania
113 J22 **Dorog** Komárom-Esztergom, N Hungary

119 W8 **Donets'ka Oblast'** var. Donets'k, Rus. Donetskaya Oblast'; prev. Rus. Stalinskaya Oblast'. ♦ province SE Ukraine
Donetska Oblast' see Donets'ka Oblast'
69 P8 **Donga** ♒ Cameroon/Nigeria
25 O13 **Donchuan** Yunnan, SW China
101 I14 **Dongen** Noord-Brabant, S Netherlands
166 K17 **Dongfang** var. Basuo. Hainan, S China
169 Z7 **Dongfanghong** Heilongjiang, NE China
169 W11 **Dongfeng** Jilin, NE China
175 P9 **Donggala** Sulawesi, C Indonesia
175 V13 **Donggou** Liaoning, NE China
167 O14 **Dongguan** Guangdong, S China
178 K9 **Đông Ha** Quang Tri, C Vietnam
178 I9 **Dong Hai** see East China Sea
178 M16 **Dong Hai Dao** island S China
178 Ij9 **Đông Hơi** Quang Binh, C Vietnam
110 H10 **Dongio** Ticino, S Switzerland
85 C14 **Dongka** see Binhai
166 L11 **Dongkou** Hunan, S China
82 E7 **Dongliao** see Liaoyuan
85 K13 **Đông-nai** see Đông Nai, Sông
178 K13 **Đông Nai, Sông** var. Dong-nai, Dong Noi, Donnai. ♒ S Vietnam
167 O14 **Dongnan Qiuling** plateau SE China
169 Y9 **Dongning** Heilongjiang, NE China
85 K13 **Đông Noi** see Đông Nai, Sông
85 C14 **Dongo** Huíla, C Angola
82 E7 **Dongola** var. Donqola, Dunqulah. Northern, N Sudan
81 I11 **Dongou** La Likouala, NE Congo
5 K8 **Đông Phu Sông Bé**, S Vietnam
87 T14 **Dông Rak, Phanom** see Dângrêk, Chuor Phnum
167 Q14 **Dongshan Dao** island SE China
169 N14 **Dongsheng** Nei Mongol Zizhiqu, N China
71 R7 **Dongtai** Jiangsu, E China
167 N10 **Dongting Hu** var. Tung-t'ing Hu. ⊚ S China
101 D14 **Dongxiang** Jiangxi, S China
167 Q4 **Dongying** Shandong, E China
29 X8 **Doniphan** Missouri, C USA
167 S13 **Donji Lapac** Zadar-Knin, C Croatia
114 E11 **Donji Miholjac** Osijek-Baranja, NE Croatia
114 H8 **Donji Milanovac** Serbia, E Yugoslavia
114 G12 **Donji Vakuf** C Bosnia and Herzegovina
100 M6 **Donkerbroek** Friesland, N Netherlands
178 Hh11 **Don Muang** x (Krung Thep) Nonthaburi, C Thailand
79 R13 **Donna** Texas, SW USA
13 Q10 **Donnacona** Québec, SE Canada
31 Y16 **Donnellson** Iowa, C USA
190 K13 **Donnelly** Alberta, W Canada
103 F19 **Donnersberg** ▲ W Germany
79 Donoso see Miguel de la Borda
107 P2 **Donostia-San Sebastián** País Vasco, N Spain
101 K21 **Donoússa** island Kykládes, Greece, Aegean Sea
37 P8 **Don Pedro Reservoir** ⊞ California, W USA
130 L5 **Donskoy** Tul'skaya Oblast', W Russian Federation
179 Q12 **Donsol** Luzon, N Philippines
83 L16 **Doolow** SE Ethiopia
41 Q7 **Doonerak, Mount** ▲ Alaska, USA
100 J12 **Doorn** Utrecht, C Netherlands
33 N6 **Doornik** see Tournai
82 P13 **Door Peninsula** peninsula Wisconsin, N USA
82 P13 **Dooxo Nugaaleed** var. Nogal Valley. valley E Somalia
166 G8 **Do Qu** ♒ C China
108 B7 **Dora Baltea** anc. Duria Major. ♒ NW Italy
188 K7 **Dora, Lake** salt lake Western Australia
108 A8 **Dora Riparia** anc. Duria Minor. ♒ NW Italy
110 E6 **Dorbiljin** see Emin
119 V8 **Dorbod** var. Dorbod Mongolzu Zizhixian, Talkang. Heilongjiang, NE China
Dorbod Mongolzu Zizhixian see Dorbod
115 N18 **Đorče Petrov** var. Đjorče Petrov, Gorče Petrov. N FYR Macedonia
12 E13 **Dorchester** Ontario, S Canada
99 L24 **Dorchester** anc. Durnovaria. S England, UK
15 Mm4 **Dorchester, Cape** headland Baffin Island, Northwest Territories, N Canada
124 I13 **Dordabis** Khomas, C Namibia
104 L12 **Dordogne** ♦ department SW France
105 N12 **Dordogne** ♒ W France
100 H13 **Dordrecht** var. Dordt, Dort. Zuid-Holland, SW Netherlands
Dordt see Dordrecht
105 P11 **Dore** ♒ C France
9 S13 **Doré Lake** ⊚ Saskatchewan, C Canada
105 O13 **Dore, Monts** ▲ C France
103 D18 **Dorfen** Bayern, SE Germany
109 D18 **Dorgali** Sardegna, Italy, C Mediterranean Sea
168 F7 **Dörgön Nuur** ⊚ NW Mongolia

Dorogobuzh – Dynów

130 I4 **Dorogobuzh** Smolenskaya Oblast', W Russian Federation
118 K8 **Dorohoi** Botoşani, NE Romania
95 H15 **Dorotea** Västerbotten, N Sweden
Dorpat see Tartu
188 G10 **Dorre Island** island Western Australia
191 U5 **Dorrigo** New South Wales, SE Australia
37 N1 **Dorris** California, W USA
12 H13 **Dorset** Ontario, SE Canada
99 K23 **Dorset** cultural region S England, UK
103 E14 **Dorsten** Nordrhein-Westfalen, W Germany
Dort see Dordrecht
103 F15 **Dortmund** Nordrhein-Westfalen, W Germany
102 F12 **Dortmund-Ems-Kanal** canal W Germany
142 L17 **Dörtyol** Hatay, S Turkey
148 L7 **Do Rūd** var. Dow Rūd, Durud. Lorestān, W Iran
81 O15 **Doruma** Haut-Zaïre, N Zaire
13 O12 **Dorval** × (Montréal) Québec, SE Canada
47 T5 **Dos Bocas, Lago** ◎ C Puerto Rico
106 K14 **Dos Hermanas** Andalucía, S Spain
Dospad Dagh see Rhodope Mountains
37 P10 **Dos Palos** California, W USA
116 I11 **Dospat** Plovdivska Oblast, SW Bulgaria
116 H11 **Dospat, Yazovir** ⊠ SW Bulgaria
102 M11 **Dosse** ~ NE Germany
79 S12 **Dosso** Dosso, SW Niger
79 S12 **Dosso** ◐ department SW Niger
150 G12 **Dossor** Atyrau, SW Kazakhstan
153 V9 **Dostuk** Narynskaya Oblast', C Kyrgyzstan
151 X13 **Dostyk** prev. Druzhba. Taldykorgan, SE Kazakhstan
25 R7 **Dothan** Alabama, S USA
41 T9 **Dot Lake** Alaska, USA
120 F12 **Dotnuva** Kėdainiai, C Lithuania
101 D19 **Dottignies** Hainaut, W Belgium
105 P2 **Douai** prev. Douay, anc. Duacum. Nord, N France
12 L9 **Douaire, Lac** ◎ Québec, SE Canada
81 D16 **Douala** var. Duala. Littoral, W Cameroon
81 D16 **Douala** × Littoral, W Cameroon
104 F6 **Douarnenez** Finistère, NW France
104 E6 **Douarnenez, Baie de** bay NW France
Douay see Douai
27 O6 **Double Mountain Fork Brazos River** ~ Texas, SW USA
25 O3 **Double Springs** Alabama, S USA
105 T8 **Doubs** ◐ department E France
110 C8 **Doubs** ~ France/Switzerland
193 A22 **Doubtful Sound** sound South Island, NZ
192 J2 **Doubtless Bay** bay North Island, NZ
27 X9 **Doucette** Texas, SW USA
104 K8 **Doué-la-Fontaine** Maine-et-Loire, NW France
79 O11 **Douentza** Mopti, S Mali
67 D24 **Douglas** East Falkland, Falkland Islands
99 I16 **Douglas** ○ (Isle of Man) E Isle of Man
85 H23 **Douglas** Northern Cape, C South Africa
41 X13 **Douglas** Alexander Archipelago, Alaska, USA
39 O17 **Douglas** Arizona, SW USA
25 U7 **Douglas** Georgia, SE USA
35 Y15 **Douglas** Wyoming, C USA
8 J14 **Douglas Channel** channel British Columbia, W Canada
190 G3 **Douglas Creek** seasonal river South Australia
33 P5 **Douglas Lake** ◎ Michigan, N USA
23 O9 **Douglas Lake** ⊠ Tennessee, S USA
41 Q13 **Douglas, Mount** ▲ Alaska, USA
204 I6 **Douglas Range** ▲▲ Alexander Island, Antarctica
124 N10 **Doukáto, Ákra** headland Lefkáda, W Greece
105 O2 **Doullens** Somme, N France
Douma see Dūmā
81 F15 **Doumé** Est, E Cameroon
101 E21 **Dour** Hainaut, S Belgium
61 K18 **Dourada, Serra** ▲▲ S Brazil
61 I21 **Dourados** Mato Grosso do Sul, S Brazil
105 N5 **Dourdan** Essonne, N France
106 I6 **Douro** Sp. Duero. ~ Portugal/Spain see also Duero
106 G6 **Douro Litoral** former province N Portugal
Douvres see Dover
104 K15 **Douze** ~ SW France
191 P17 **Dover** Tasmania, SE Australia
99 Q22 **Dover** Fr. Douvres; Lat. Dubris Portus. SE England, UK
19 R8 **Dover** state capital Delaware, NE USA
21 P9 **Dover** New Hampshire, NE USA
20 J14 **Dover** New Jersey, NE USA
33 U12 **Dover** Ohio, N USA
22 H8 **Dover** Tennessee, S USA
99 Q23 **Dover, Strait of** var. Straits of Dover, Fr. Pas de Calais. strait England, UK/France
Dover, Straits of see Dover, Strait of
Dovlen see Devin
96 G11 **Dovre** Oppland, S Norway
96 G10 **Dovrefjell** plateau S Norway
Dovsk see Dowsk
85 M14 **Dowa** Central, C Malawi
33 O10 **Dowagiac** Michigan, N USA
149 N10 **Dow Gonbadān** var. Do Gonbadān, Gonbadān. Kohkīlūyeh va Būyer Aḩmadī, SW Iran
154 M2 **Dowlatābād** Fāryāb, N Afghanistan
99 G16 **Down** cultural region SE Northern Ireland, UK
35 R16 **Downey** Idaho, NW USA
37 P5 **Downieville** California, W USA
99 G16 **Downpatrick** Ir. Dún Pádraig. SE Northern Ireland, UK
28 M3 **Downs** Kansas, C USA
20 J12 **Downsville** New York, NE USA
Dow Rūd see Do Rūd
31 V12 **Dows** Iowa, C USA
121 O17 **Dowsk** Rus. Dovsk. Homyel'skaya Voblasts', SE Belorussia
37 Q4 **Doyle** California, W USA
20 I15 **Doylestown** Pennsylvania, NE USA
Doyransko, Ezero see Doïranis, Límnis
116 I8 **Doyrentsi** Loveshka Oblast, N Bulgaria
170 Ff11 **Dōzen** island Oki-shotō, SW Japan
12 K9 **Dozois, Réservoir** ⊠ Québec, SE Canada
76 D9 **Drâa** seasonal river S Morocco
Drâa, Hammada du see Dra, Hamada du
Drabble see José Enrique Rodó
119 Q5 **Drabiv** Cherkas'ka Oblast', C Ukraine
Drable see José Enrique Rodó
105 U13 **Drac** ~ E France
Drač/Drac see Durrës
62 I8 **Dracena** São Paulo, S Brazil
100 M6 **Drachten** Friesland, N Netherlands
94 H11 **Drag** Nordland, C Norway
118 L14 **Dragalina** Călăraşi, SE Romania
118 J14 **Drăgăneşti-Vlaşca** Teleorman, S Romania
118 I13 **Drăgăşani** Vâlcea, SW Romania
116 G9 **Dragoman** Sofiyska Oblast, W Bulgaria
117 L25 **Dragonáda** island SE Greece
Dragonera, Isla see Sa Dragonera
47 T14 **Dragon's Mouths, The** strait Trinidad and Tobago/Venezuela
97 J23 **Dragør** København, E Denmark
116 F10 **Dragovishtsa** Sofiyska Oblast, W Bulgaria
105 U15 **Draguignan** Var, SE France
76 E9 **Dra, Hamada du** var. Hammada du Drâa, Haut Plateau du Dra. plateau W Algeria
Dra, Haut Plateau du see Dra, Hamada du
121 H19 **Drahichyn** Pol. Drohiczyn Poleski, Rus. Drogichin. Brestskaya Voblasts', SW Belorussia
31 N4 **Drake** North Dakota, N USA
85 K23 **Drakensberg** ▲▲ Lesotho/South Africa
204 F3 **Drake Passage** passage Atlantic Ocean/Pacific Ocean
116 L8 **Dralfa** Razgradska Oblast, N Bulgaria
116 I12 **Dráma** var. Dhráma. Anatolikí Makedonía kai Thráki, NE Greece
Dramburg see Drawsko Pomorskie
97 H15 **Drammen** Buskerud, S Norway
97 H15 **Drammensfjorden** fjord S Norway
94 H1 **Drangajökull** ▲ NW Iceland
97 F16 **Drangedal** Telemark, S Norway
94 I2 **Drangsnes** Vestfirdhir, NW Iceland
Drann see Dravinja
111 T10 **Drau** var. Drava, Eng. Drave, Hung. Dráva. ~ C Europe see also Drava
86 I11 **Drava** var. Drau, Eng. Drave, Hung. Dráva. ~ C Europe see also Drau
Dráva see Drau/Drava
Drave see Drau/Drava
111 W10 **Dravinja** Ger. Drann. ~ NE Slovenia
111 V9 **Dravograd** Ger. Unterdrauburg; prev. Spodnji Dravograd. N Slovenia
112 F10 **Drawa** ~ NW Poland
112 F9 **Drawno** Gorzów, NW Poland
112 F9 **Drawsko Pomorskie** Ger. Dramburg. Koszalin, NW Poland
31 R3 **Drayton** North Dakota, N USA
9 P14 **Drayton Valley** Alberta, SW Canada
194 F10 **Dreikikir** East Sepik, NW PNG
Dreikirchen see Teiuş
100 N7 **Drenthe** ◐ province NE Netherlands
117 H15 **Drépano, Ákra** var. Akra Dhrepanon. headland N Greece
Drepanum see Trapani
12 D17 **Dresden** Ontario, S Canada
103 O16 **Dresden** Sachsen, E Germany
22 G8 **Dresden** Tennessee, S USA
120 M11 **Dretun'** Rus. Dretun'. Vitsyebskaya Voblasts', N Belorussia
104 M5 **Dreux** anc. Drocae, Durocasses. Eure-et-Loir, C France
96 I11 **Drevsjø** Hedmark, S Norway
24 K3 **Drew** Mississippi, S USA
112 F10 **Drezdenko** Ger. Driesen. Gorzów, W Poland
100 J12 **Driebergen** var. Driebergen-Rijsenburg. Utrecht, C Netherlands
Driebergen-Rijsenburg see Driebergen
Driesen see Drezdenko
99 N16 **Driffield** E England, UK
67 D25 **Driftwood Point** headland East Falkland, Falkland Islands
35 S14 **Driggs** Idaho, NW USA
Drin see Drinit, Lumi i
114 K12 **Drina** ~ Bosnia and Herzegovina/Yugoslavia
Drin, Gulf of see Drinit, Gjiri i
115 K18 **Drinit, Gjiri i** var. Pellg i Drinit, Eng. Gulf of Drin. gulf NW Albania
115 L17 **Drinit, Lumi i** var. Drin. ~ NW Albania
Drinit, Pellg i see Drinit, Gjiri i
Drinit të Zi, Lumi i see Black Drin
115 L22 **Drino** var. Drino, Drinos Pótamos, Alb. Lumi i Drinos. ~ Albania/Greece
Drinos, Lumi i/Drínos Pótamos see Drino
27 S11 **Dripping Springs** Texas, SW USA
27 S15 **Driscoll** Texas, SW USA
24 H5 **Driskill Mountain** ▲ Louisiana, S USA
Drissa see Drysa
96 G10 **Driva** ~ S Norway
114 E13 **Drniš** It. Dernis. Šibenik, S Croatia
97 H15 **Drøbak** Akershus, S Norway
118 G13 **Drobeta-Turnu Severin** prev. Turnu Severin. Mehedinţi, SW Romania
Drocae see Dreux
118 M8 **Drochia** Rus. Drokiya. N Moldova
99 F17 **Drogheda** Ir. Droichead Átha. NE Ireland
Drogichin see Drahichyn
Drogobych see Drohobych
Drohiczyn Poleski see Drahichyn
118 H6 **Drohobych** Pol. Drohobycz, Rus. Drogobych. L'vivs'ka Oblast', NW Ukraine
Drohobycz see Drohobych
Droichead Átha see Drogheda
Droicheadna Bandan see Bandon
Droichead na Banna see Banbridge
Droim Mór see Dromore
Drokiya see Drochia
105 R13 **Drôme** ◐ department E France
105 S13 **Drôme** ~ E France
99 G15 **Dromore** Ir. Droim Mór. SE Northern Ireland, UK
108 A9 **Dronero** Piemonte, NE Italy
104 L12 **Dronne** ~ SW France
205 Q3 **Dronning Maud Land** physical region Antarctica
100 K6 **Dronrijp** Fris. Dronryp. Friesland, N Netherlands
Dronryp see Dronrijp
100 L9 **Dronten** Flevoland, C Netherlands
Drontheim see Trondheim
104 L13 **Dropt** ~ SW France
155 T4 **Drosh** North-West Frontier Province, NW Pakistan
Drossen see Ośno Lubuskie
Drug see Durg
152 I9 **Drujba** Rus. Druzhba. Khorazm Wiloyati, W Uzbekistan
120 I12 **Drūkšiai** ◎ NE Lithuania
Druk-yul see Bhutan
9 Q16 **Drumheller** Alberta, SW Canada
35 Q10 **Drummond** Montana, NW USA
33 R4 **Drummond Island** island Michigan, N USA
Drummond Island see Tabiteuea
23 X7 **Drummond, Lake** ◎ Virginia, NE USA
13 P12 **Drummondville** Québec, SE Canada
41 T11 **Drum, Mount** ▲ Alaska, USA
29 O9 **Drumright** Oklahoma, C USA
101 J14 **Drunen** Noord-Brabant, S Netherlands
Druskienniki see Druskininkai
121 F15 **Druskininkai** Pol. Druskienniki. Druskininkai, S Lithuania
100 K13 **Druten** Gelderland, SE Netherlands
120 K11 **Druya** Vitsyebskaya Voblasts', NW Belorussia
119 S2 **Druzhba** Sums'ka Oblast', NE Ukraine
Druzhba see Dostyk, Kazakhstan
Druzhba see Drujba, Uzbekistan
126 Mm7 **Druzhina** Respublika Sakha (Yakutiya), NE Russian Federation
119 X7 **Druzhkivka** Donets'ka Oblast', E Ukraine
114 E12 **Drvar** W Bosnia and Herzegovina
115 G15 **Drvenik** Split-Dalmacija, SE Croatia
116 K9 **Dryanovo** Loveshka Oblast, C Bulgaria
28 G7 **Dry Cimarron River** ~ Kansas/Oklahoma, C USA
10 B11 **Dryden** Ontario, C Canada
26 M11 **Dryden** Texas, SW USA
205 Q14 **Drygalski Ice Tongue** ice feature Antarctica
120 L11 **Drysa** Rus. Drissa. ~ N Belorussia
25 V17 **Dry Tortugas** island Florida, SE USA
81 D15 **Dschang** Ouest, W Cameroon
56 J5 **Duaca** Lara, N Venezuela
Duacum see Douai
Duala see Douala
47 N9 **Duarte, Pico** ▲ C Dominican Republic
146 J5 **Dubā** Tabūk, NW Saudi Arabia
Dubai see Dubayy
119 N9 **Dubăsari** Rus. Dubossary. NE Moldova
119 N9 **Dubăsari Reservoir** ⊠ NE Moldova
15 J8 **Dubawnt** ~ Northwest Territories, NW Canada
15 K7 **Dubawnt Lake** ◎ Northwest Territories, N Canada
32 L6 **Du Bay, Lake** ⊠ Wisconsin, N USA
147 U7 **Dubayy** Eng. Dubai. Dubayy, NE UAE
147 W7 **Dubayy** Eng. Dubai. × Dubayy, NE UAE
191 R7 **Dubbo** New South Wales, SE Australia
110 G7 **Dübendorf** Zürich, NW Switzerland
99 F18 **Dublin** Ir. Baile Átha Cliath; anc. Eblana. ● (Ireland), E Ireland
25 U5 **Dublin** Georgia, SE USA
27 R7 **Dublin** Texas, SW USA
99 G18 **Dublin** Ir. Baile Átha Cliath; anc. Eblana. cultural region E Ireland
99 G18 **Dublin Airport** × E Ireland
201 V12 **Dublon** var. Tonoas. island Chuuk Islands, C Micronesia
130 K2 **Dubna** Moskovskaya Oblast', W Russian Federation
113 G19 **Dubňany** Ger. Dubnian. Jižní Morava, SE Czech Republic
Dubnian see Dubňany
113 I19 **Dubnica nad Váhom** Hung. Máriatölgyes; prev. Dubnicz. Stredné Slovensko, NW Slovakia
Dubnicz see Dubnica nad Váhom
118 K4 **Dubno** Rivnens'ka Oblast', NW Ukraine
20 D13 **Du Bois** Pennsylvania, NE USA
35 R13 **Dubois** Idaho, NW USA
35 T14 **Dubois** Wyoming, C USA
Dubossary see Dubăsari
131 O10 **Dubovka** Volgogradskaya Oblast', SW Russian Federation
78 H14 **Dubréka** Guinée-Maritime, SW Guinea
12 B7 **Dubreuilville** Ontario, S Canada
Dubris Portus see Dover
121 L20 **Dubrova** Rus. Dubrova. Homyel'skaya Voblasts', SE Belorussia
130 I5 **Dubrovka** Bryanskaya Oblast', W Russian Federation
115 H16 **Dubrovnik** It. Ragusa. Dubrovnik-Neretva, SE Croatia
115 I16 **Dubrovnik** × Dubrovnik-Neretva, SE Croatia
115 F16 **Dubrovnik-Neretva** off. Dubrovačko-Neretvanska Županija. ◐ province SE Croatia
Dubrovno see Dubrowna
118 L2 **Dubrovytsya** Rivnens'ka Oblast', NW Ukraine
121 O14 **Dubrowna** Rus. Dubrovno. Vitsyebskaya Voblasts', N Belorussia
31 Z13 **Dubuque** Iowa, C USA
120 E12 **Dubysa** ~ C Lithuania
178 K12 **Đưc Cơ** Gia Lai, C Vietnam
203 V12 **Duc de Gloucester, Îles du** Eng. Duke of Gloucester Islands. island group C French Polynesia
113 C15 **Duchcov** Ger. Dux. Severní Čechy, NW Czech Republic
39 N3 **Duchesne** Utah, W USA
203 P17 **Ducie Island** atoll E Pitcairn Islands
9 W15 **Duck Bay** Manitoba, S Canada
25 X17 **Duck Key** island Florida Keys, Florida, SE USA
9 T14 **Duck Lake** Saskatchewan, S Canada
9 V15 **Duck Mountain** ▲▲ Manitoba, S Canada
22 I9 **Duck River** ~ Tennessee, S USA
22 M10 **Ducktown** Tennessee, S USA
178 Kk11 **Đưc Phô** Quang Ngai, C Vietnam
178 J8 **Đưc Tho** Ha Tinh, N Vietnam
178 Kk13 **Đưc Trong** var. Liên Nghia. Lâm Đông, S Vietnam
D-U-D see Dalap-Uliga-Djarrit
101 M25 **Dudelange** var. Forge du Sud, Ger. Dudelingen. Luxembourg, S Luxembourg
Dudelingen see Dudelange
103 J15 **Duderstadt** Niedersachsen, C Germany
159 N15 **Dūdhi** Uttar Pradesh, N India
126 I8 **Dudinka** Taymyrskiy (Dolgano-Nenetskiy) Avtonomnyy Okrug, N Russian Federation
99 L20 **Dudley** C England, UK
160 G13 **Dudna** ~ C India
78 L16 **Duékoué** W Ivory Coast
106 M5 **Dueñas** Castilla-León, N Spain
106 K4 **Duerna** ~ NW Spain
107 O6 **Duero** Port. Douro. ~ Portugal/Spain see also Douro
Duesseldorf see Düsseldorf
23 P12 **Due West** South Carolina, SE USA
205 P11 **Dufek Coast** physical region Antarctica
101 H17 **Duffel** Antwerpen, C Belgium
37 S2 **Duffer Peak** ▲ Nevada, W USA
195 X7 **Duff Islands** island group E Solomon Islands
Dufour, Pizzo/Dufour, Punta see Dufour Spitze
110 E12 **Dufour Spitze** It. Pizzo Dufour, Punta Dufour. ▲ Italy/Switzerland
114 D9 **Duga Resa** Karlovac, C Croatia
24 H5 **Dugdemona River** ~ Louisiana, S USA
160 J12 **Duggipar** Mahārāshtra, C India
114 B13 **Dugi Otok** var. Isola Grossa, It. Isola Lunga. island W Croatia
115 F14 **Dugopolje** Split-Dalmacija, S Croatia
166 L8 **Du He** ~ C China
56 M11 **Duida, Cerro** ▲ S Venezuela
Duinekerke see Dunkerque
103 E15 **Duisburg** prev. Duisburg-Hamborn. Nordrhein-Westfalen, W Germany
Duisburg-Hamborn see Duisburg
101 F14 **Duiveland** island SW Netherlands
100 M12 **Duiven** Gelderland, E Netherlands
145 W10 **Dujaylah, Hawr ad** ◎ S Iraq
83 L18 **Dujuuma** Shabeellaha Hoose, S Somalia
Dūkān see Dokan
41 Z14 **Duke Island** island Alexander Archipelago, Alaska, USA
Dukelský Priesmy/Dukelský Průsmyk see Dukla Pass
Duke of Gloucester Islands see Duc de Gloucester, Îles du
83 F14 **Duk Faiwil** Jonglei, SE Sudan
147 T7 **Dukhān** C Qatar
Dukhan Heights see Dukhān, Jabal
149 N16 **Dukhān, Jabal** var. Dukhan Heights. hill range S Qatar
131 Q7 **Dukhovnitskoye** Saratovskaya Oblast', W Russian Federation
130 H4 **Dukhovshchina** Smolenskaya Oblast', W Russian Federation
Dukielska, Przełęcz see Dukla Pass
113 N17 **Dukla** Krosno, SE Poland
Duklai Hág see Dukla Pass
113 N18 **Dukla Pass** Cz. Dukelský Průsmyk, Ger. Dukla-Pass, Hung. Duklai Hág, Pol. Przełęcz Dukielska, Slvk. Dukelský Priesmy. pass Poland/Slovakia
Dukou see Panzhihua
120 I12 **Dūkštas** Ignalina, E Lithuania
168 M8 **Dulaan** Hentiy, C Mongolia
165 R10 **Dulan** var. Qagan Us. Qinghai, C China
39 R8 **Dulce** New Mexico, SW USA
45 N16 **Dulce, Golfo** gulf S Costa Rica
Dulce, Golfo see Izabal, Lago de
44 K6 **Dulce Nombre de Culmí** Olancho, C Honduras
64 L9 **Dulce, Río** ~ C Argentina
126 M9 **Dulgalakh** ~ NE Russian Federation
116 M8 **Dŭlgopol** Varnenska Oblast, NE Bulgaria
159 V14 **Dullabchara** Assam, NE India
22 D3 **Dulles** × (Washington DC) Virginia, NE USA
103 E14 **Dülmen** Nordrhein-Westfalen, W Germany
116 M7 **Dulovo** Razgradska Oblast, NE Bulgaria
31 W5 **Duluth** Minnesota, N USA
144 H7 **Dūmā** Fr. Douma. Dimashq, SW Syria
179 Pp16 **Dumagasa Point** headland Mindanao, S Philippines
179 Qq14 **Dumaguete** var. Dumaguete City. Negros, C Philippines
174 Gg6 **Dumai** Sumatera, W Indonesia
191 T4 **Dumaresq River** ~ New South Wales/Queensland, SE Australia
29 W13 **Dumas** Arkansas, C USA
27 N1 **Dumas** Texas, SW USA
144 I7 **Ḑumayr** Dimashq, W Syria
98 I12 **Dumbarton** W Scotland, UK
98 I12 **Dumbarton** cultural region C Scotland, UK
197 J7 **Dumbéa** Province Sud, S New Caledonia
113 K19 **Ďumbier** Ger. Djumbir, Hung. Gyömbér. ▲ C Slovakia
118 I11 **Dumbrăveni** Ger. Elisabethstedt, Hung. Erzsébetváros; prev. Ebesfalva, Eppeschdorf, Ibaşfalău. Sibiu, C Romania
118 L12 **Dumbrăveni** Vrancea, E Romania
99 J14 **Dumfries** S Scotland, UK
99 J14 **Dumfries** cultural region SW Scotland, UK
159 R15 **Dumka** Bihār, NE India
Dümmer see Dümmersee
102 G12 **Dümmersee** var. Dümmer. ◎ NW Germany
12 J11 **Dumoine** ~ Québec, SE Canada
12 J10 **Dumoine, Lac** ◎ Québec, SE Canada
205 V16 **Dumont d'Urville** French research station Antarctica
205 W15 **Dumont d'Urville Sea** S Pacific Ocean
12 K11 **Dumont, Lac** ◎ Québec, SE Canada
77 W7 **Dumyāṭ** Eng. Damietta. N Egypt
Duna see Don, Russian Federation
Duna see Danube, C Europe
Düna see Western Dvina
Dünaburg see Daugavpils
113 J24 **Dunaföldvár** Tolna, C Hungary
Dunaj see Wien, Austria
Dunaj see Danube, C Europe
113 L18 **Dunajec** ~ S Poland
113 H21 **Dunajská Streda** Hung. Dunaszerdahely. Západné Slovensko, SW Slovakia
Dunapentele see Dunaújváros
Dunărea see Danube
118 M13 **Dunărea Veche, Braţul** ~ SE Romania
119 N13 **Dunării, Delta** delta SE Romania
Dunaszerdahely see Dunajská Streda
113 J23 **Dunaújváros** prev. Dunapentele, Sztálinváros. Fejér, C Hungary
Dunav see Danube
116 J8 **Dunavska Ravnina** Eng. Danubian Plain. plain N Bulgaria
116 G7 **Dunavtsi** Oblast Montana, NW Bulgaria
Dunayevtsy see Dunayivtsi
118 L7 **Dunayivtsi** Rus. Dunayevtsy. Khmel'nyts'ka Oblast', NW Ukraine
193 F22 **Dunback** Otago, South Island, NZ
8 L17 **Duncan** Vancouver Island, British Columbia, SW Canada
39 O15 **Duncan** Arizona, SW USA
28 M12 **Duncan** Oklahoma, C USA
Duncan Island see Pinzón, Isla
157 Q20 **Duncan Passage** strait Andaman Sea/Bay of Bengal
98 K6 **Duncansby Head** headland N Scotland, UK
12 G12 **Dunchurch** Ontario, S Canada
120 D7 **Dundaga** Talsi, NW Latvia
12 G14 **Dundalk** Ontario, S Canada
99 F16 **Dundalk** Ir. Dún Dealgan. NE Ireland
23 X3 **Dundalk** Maryland, NE USA
99 F16 **Dundalk Bay** Ir. Cuan Dhún Dealgan. bay NE Ireland
12 G16 **Dundas** Ontario, S Canada
188 L12 **Dundas, Lake** salt lake Western Australia
169 O7 **Dundbürd** Hentiy, E Mongolia
Dún Dealgan see Dundalk
13 N13 **Dundee** Québec, SE Canada
85 K22 **Dundee** KwaZulu/Natal, E South Africa
98 K11 **Dundee** E Scotland, UK
33 R10 **Dundee** Michigan, N USA
27 R5 **Dundee** Texas, SW USA
204 H3 **Dundee Island** island Antarctica
168 L9 **Dundgovĭ** ◐ province C Mongolia
99 G16 **Dundrum Bay** Ir. Cuan Dhún Droma. inlet NW Irish Sea
176 Y11 **Dundu** ~ Irian Jaya, E Indonesia
9 T15 **Dundurn** Saskatchewan, S Canada
168 E6 **Dund-Us** Hovd, W Mongolia
193 F23 **Dunedin** Otago, South Island, NZ
191 R7 **Dunedoo** New South Wales, SE Australia
99 D14 **Dunfanaghy** Ir. Dún Fionnachaidh. NW Ireland
98 J12 **Dunfermline** C Scotland, UK
Dún Fionnachaidh see Dunfanaghy
155 V10 **Dunga Bunga** Punjab, E Pakistan
99 F15 **Dungannon** Ir. Dún Geanainn. C Northern Ireland, UK
Dun Garbháin see Dungarvan
158 F15 **Dūngarpur** Rājasthān, N India
99 E21 **Dungarvan** Ir. Dun Garbháin. S Ireland
103 N21 **Dungau** cultural region SE Germany
Dún Geanainn see Dungannon
99 P23 **Dungeness** headland SE England, UK
65 I23 **Dungeness, Punta** headland S Argentina
Dungloe see Dunglow
99 D14 **Dunglow** var. Dungloe, Ir. An Clochán Liath. NW Ireland
191 T7 **Dungog** New South Wales, SE Australia
81 O16 **Dungu** Haut-Zaïre, NE Zaire
174 Hh3 **Dungun** var. Kuala Dungun. Terengganu, Peninsular Malaysia
82 I6 **Dungûnab** Red Sea, NE Sudan
13 P13 **Dunham** Québec, SE Canada
Dunheved see Launceston
Dunholme see Durham
169 X10 **Dunhua** Jilin, NE China
165 P8 **Dunhuang** Gansu, N China
190 L12 **Dunkeld** Victoria, SE Australia
105 O1 **Dunkerque** Eng. Dunkirk, Flem. Duinekerke; prev. Dunquerque. Nord, N France
99 K23 **Dunkery Beacon** ▲ SW England, UK
20 C11 **Dunkirk** New York, NE USA
Dunkirk see Dunkerque
79 P17 **Dunkwa** SW Ghana
99 G18 **Dún Laoghaire** Eng. Dunleary; prev. Kingstown. E Ireland
31 S14 **Dunlap** Iowa, C USA
22 L10 **Dunlap** Tennessee, S USA
Dunleary see Dún Laoghaire
Dún Mánmhaí see Dunmanway
99 B21 **Dunmanway** Ir. Dún Mánmhaí. SW Ireland
20 I13 **Dunmore** Pennsylvania, NE USA
23 U10 **Dunn** North Carolina, SE USA
Dún na nGall see Donegal
25 V11 **Dunnellon** Florida, SE USA
98 J6 **Dunnet Head** headland N Scotland, UK
31 N14 **Dunning** Nebraska, C USA
67 B24 **Dunnose Head Settlement** West Falkland, Falkland Islands
12 G17 **Dunnville** Ontario, S Canada
Dún Pádraig see Downpatrick
Dunquerque see Dunkerque
Dunqulah see Dongola
98 L12 **Duns** SE Scotland, UK
31 N2 **Dunseith** North Dakota, N USA
37 N2 **Dunsmuir** California, W USA
99 N21 **Dunstable** Lat. Durocobrivae. E England, UK
193 D21 **Dunstan Mountains** ▲▲ South Island, NZ
105 O9 **Dun-sur-Auron** Cher, C France
193 F21 **Duntroon** Canterbury, South Island, NZ
155 T10 **Dunyāpur** Punjab, E Pakistan
169 U5 **Duobukur He** ~ NE China
169 R12 **Duolun** var. Dolonnur. Nei Mongol Zizhiqu, N China
178 Ii14 **Dương Đông** Kiên Giang, S Vietnam
116 G10 **Dupnitsa** prev. Marek, Stanke Dimitrov. Sofiyska Oblast, W Bulgaria
30 L8 **Dupree** South Dakota, N USA
35 Q7 **Dupuyer** Montana, NW USA
147 Y11 **Duqm** var. Daqm. E Oman
53 X9 **Duque de Caxias** Rio de Janeiro, SE Brazil
65 F23 **Duque de York, Isla** island S Chile
189 N4 **Durack Range** ▲▲ Western Australia
Dura Europus see Aş Şālihīyah
142 K10 **Durağan** Sinop, N Turkey
105 S15 **Durance** ~ SE France
33 R9 **Durand** Michigan, N USA
32 I6 **Durand** Wisconsin, N USA
197 L7 **Durand, Récif** reef SE New Caledonia
42 K10 **Durango** var. Victoria de Durango. Durango, W Mexico
107 P3 **Durango** País Vasco, N Spain
39 Q8 **Durango** Colorado, C USA
42 J9 **Durango** ◐ state C Mexico
116 O7 **Durankulak** Rom. Răcari; prev. Blatnitsa, Duranulac. Varnenska Oblast, NE Bulgaria
24 L4 **Durant** Mississippi, S USA
29 P13 **Durant** Oklahoma, C USA
Duranulac see Durankulak
107 N6 **Duratón** ~ N Spain
63 E19 **Durazno** var. San Pedro de Durazno. Durazno, C Uruguay
63 E19 **Durazno** ◐ department C Uruguay
Durazzo see Durrës
85 K23 **Durban** var. Port Natal. KwaZulu/Natal, E South Africa
85 K23 **Durban** × KwaZulu/Natal, E South Africa
120 C9 **Durbe** Ger. Durben. Liepāja, W Latvia
Durben see Durbe
101 K21 **Durbuy** Luxembourg, SE Belgium
107 N15 **Dúrcal** Andalucía, S Spain
114 F8 **Đurđevac** Ger. Sankt Georgen, Hung. Szentgyörgy; prev. Djurdjevac, Gjurgjevac. Koprivnica-Križevci, N Croatia
115 K15 **Đurđevica Tara** Montenegro, SW Yugoslavia
99 L24 **Durdle Door** natural arch S England, UK
164 L3 **Düre** Xinjiang Uygur Zizhiqu, W China
103 D16 **Düren** anc. Marcodurum. Nordrhein-Westfalen, W Germany
160 K12 **Durg** prev. Drug. Madhya Pradesh, C India
159 U13 **Durgapur** Dhaka, N Bangladesh
159 R15 **Durgāpur** West Bengal, NE India
12 F14 **Durham** Ontario, S Canada
99 M14 **Durham** hist. Dunholme. N England, UK
23 U9 **Durham** North Carolina, SE USA
99 L15 **Durham** cultural region N England, UK
174 Gg7 **Duri** Sumatera, W Indonesia
Duria Major see Dora Baltea
Duria Minor see Dora Riparia
Durlas see Thurles
147 P8 **Ḑurmā** Ar Riyāḑ, C Saudi Arabia
115 J15 **Durmitor** ▲ N Yugoslavia
98 H6 **Durness** N Scotland, UK
111 Y3 **Dürnkrut** Niederösterreich, E Austria
Durnovaria see Dorchester
Durobrivae see Rochester
Durocasses see Dreux
Durocobrivae see Dunstable
Durocortorum see Reims
Durostorum see Silistra
Durovernum see Canterbury
115 K20 **Durrës** var. Durrësi, Dursi, It. Durazzo, SCr. Drač, Turk. Draç. Durrës, W Albania
115 K19 **Durrës** ◐ district W Albania
Durrësi see Durrës
99 A21 **Dursey Island** Ir. Oileán Baoi. island SW Ireland
Dursi see Durrës
Durud see Do Rūd
116 P12 **Durusu** İstanbul, NW Turkey
116 O12 **Durusu Gölü** ◎ NW Turkey
144 I9 **Durūz, Jabal ad** ▲ SW Syria
192 K13 **D'Urville Island** island C NZ
176 Xx9 **D'Urville, Tanjung** headland Irian Jaya, E Indonesia
Dusa Mareb/Dusa Marreb see Dhuusa Marreeb
120 I11 **Dusetos** Zarasai, NE Lithuania
152 H14 **Dushak** Akhalskiy Velayat, S Turkmenistan
166 K12 **Dushan** Guizhou, S China
153 P13 **Dushanbe** var. Dyushambe; prev. Stalinabad, Taj. Stalinobod. ● (Tajikistan) W Tajikistan
153 P13 **Dushanbe** × W Tajikistan
143 T9 **Dushet'i** E Georgia
20 H13 **Dushore** Pennsylvania, NE USA
193 A23 **Dusky Sound** sound South Island, NZ
103 E15 **Düsseldorf** var. Duesseldorf. Nordrhein-Westfalen, W Germany
153 P14 **Dŭsti** Rus. Dusti. SW Tajikistan
204 I9 **Dustin Island** island Antarctica
153 O10 **Dŭstlik** Jizzakh Wiloyati, C Uzbekistan
Dutch East Indies see Indonesia
Dutch Guiana see Suriname
40 L17 **Dutch Harbor** Unalaska Island, Alaska, USA
38 J3 **Dutch Mount** ▲ Utah, W USA
Dutch New Guinea see Irian Jaya
Dutch West Indies see Netherlands Antilles
85 H20 **Dutlwe** Kweneng, S Botswana
69 V16 **Du Toit Fracture Zone** tectonic feature SW Indian Ocean
129 U8 **Dutovo** Respublika Komi, NW Russian Federation
79 V13 **Dutsan Wai** var. Dutsen Wai. Kaduna, C Nigeria
79 W13 **Dutse** Jigawa, N Nigeria
Dutsen Wai see Dutsan Wai
Duttia see Datia
12 E17 **Dutton** Ontario, S Canada
38 L7 **Dutton, Mount** ▲ Utah, W USA
168 E7 **Duut** Hovd, W Mongolia
12 K11 **Duval, Lac** ◎ Québec, SE Canada
131 W3 **Duvan** Respublika Bashkortostan, W Russian Federation
144 L9 **Duwaykhilat Satīḩ ar Ruwayshid** seasonal river SE Jordan
Dux see Duchcov
166 J13 **Duyang Shan** ▲▲ S China
178 Jj15 **Duyên Hai** Tra Vinh, S Vietnam
166 K12 **Duyun** Guizhou, S China
142 G11 **Düzce** Bolu, NW Turkey
Duzdab see Zāhedān
Duzenkyr, Khrebet see Duzkyr, Khrebet
152 I16 **Duzkyr, Khrebet** prev. Khrebet Duzenkyr. ▲▲ S Turkmenistan
Dvina Bay see Chëshskaya Guba
Dvinsk see Daugavpils
128 L7 **Dvinskaya Guba** bay NW Russian Federation
114 E10 **Dvor** Sisak-Moslavina, C Croatia
119 W5 **Dvorichna** Kharkivs'ka Oblast', E Ukraine
113 F16 **Dvůr Králové nad Labem** Ger. Königinhof an der Elbe. Východní Čechy, NE Czech Republic
160 A10 **Dwārka** Gujarāt, W India
32 M12 **Dwight** Illinois, N USA
100 N8 **Dwingeloo** Drenthe, NE Netherlands
35 N10 **Dworshak Reservoir** ⊠ Idaho, NW USA
Dyal see Dyaul Island
Dyanev see Deynau
Dyatlovo see Dzyatlava
195 N9 **Dyaul Island** var. Djaul, Dyal. island NE PNG
22 G8 **Dyer** Tennessee, S USA
16 O1 **Dyer, Cape** headland Baffin Island, Northwest Territories, NE Canada
22 F8 **Dyersburg** Tennessee, S USA
31 Y13 **Dyersville** Iowa, C USA
99 I21 **Dyfed** cultural region SW Wales, UK
Dyfrdwy, Afon see Dee
Dyhernfurth see Brzeg Dolny
113 E19 **Dyje** var. Thaya. ~ Austria/Czech Republic see also Thaya
119 T5 **Dykanska** Poltavs'ka Oblast', C Ukraine
194 L15 **Dyke Ackland Bay** inlet E PNG
131 N16 **Dykhtau** ▲ SW Russian Federation
113 A16 **Dyleń** Ger. Tillenberg. ▲ NW Czech Republic
112 K9 **Dylewska Góra** ▲ N Poland
119 O4 **Dymer** Kyyivs'ka Oblast', N Ukraine
119 W7 **Dymytrov** Rus. Dimitrov. Donets'ka Oblast', SE Ukraine
113 O17 **Dynów** Przemyśl, SE Poland

◆ Country ● Country Capital ◇ Dependent Territory ○ Dependent Territory Capital ◐ Administrative Region × International Airport ▲ Mountain ▲▲ Mountain Range Volcano ~ River ◎ Lake ⊠ Reservoir

◆ COUNTRY · ● COUNTRY CAPITAL · ◇ DEPENDENT TERRITORY · ○ DEPENDENT TERRITORY CAPITAL · ◆ ADMINISTRATIVE REGION · × INTERNATIONAL AIRPORT · ▲ MOUNTAIN · ▲ MOUNTAIN RANGE · ≈ VOLCANO · ≈ RIVER · ◎ LAKE · ◙ RESERVOIR

El Boulaida – Era

El Boulaida/El Boulaïda see Blida
9 T16 Elbow Saskatchewan, S Canada
31 S7 Elbow Lake Minnesota, N USA
131 N16 El'brus var. Gora El'brus. ▲ SW Russian Federation
El'brus, Gora see El'brus
130 M15 El'brusskiy Karachayevo-Cherkesskaya Respublika, SW Russian Federation
83 D14 El Buhayrat var. Lakes State. ⬖ state S Sudan
El Bur see Ceel Buur
100 L10 Elburg Gelderland, E Netherlands
107 O6 El Burgo de Osma Castilla-León, C Spain
Elburz Mountains see Alborz, Reshteh-ye Kūhhā-ye
37 V17 El Cajon California, W USA
65 H22 El Calafate var. Calafate. Santa Cruz, S Argentina
57 Q8 El Callao Bolívar, E Venezuela
27 U12 El Campo Texas, SW USA
56 I7 El Cantón Barinas, W Venezuela
37 Q8 El Capitan ▲ California, W USA
56 H5 El Carmelo Zulia, NW Venezuela
64 J5 El Carmen Jujuy, NW Argentina
56 E5 El Carmen de Bolívar Bolívar, NW Colombia
57 O8 El Casabe Bolívar, SE Venezuela
44 M12 El Castillo de La Concepción Río San Juan, SE Nicaragua
El Cayo see San Ignacio
37 X17 El Centro California, W USA
57 N6 El Chaparro Anzoátegui, NE Venezuela
107 S12 Elche var. Elx-Elche; anc. Ilici, Lat. Illicis. País Valenciano, E Spain
107 Q12 Elche de la Sierra Castilla-La Mancha, C Spain
43 U15 El Chichonal, Volcán ⛰ SE Mexico
42 C2 El Chinero Baja California, NW Mexico
189 R1 Elcho Island island Wessel Islands, Northern Territory, N Australia
65 H18 El Corcovado Chubut, SW Argentina
107 R12 Elda País Valenciano, E Spain
102 M10 Elde ≈ NE Germany
100 L12 Elden Gelderland, E Netherlands
83 J16 El Der spring/well S Ethiopia
El Dere see Ceel Dheere
42 E3 El Desemboque Sonora, NW Mexico
56 F5 El Difícil var. Ariguaní. Magdalena, N Colombia
126 Mm11 El'dikan Respublika Sakha (Yakutiya), NE Russian Federation
El Djazaïr see Alger
El Djelfa see Djelfa
31 X15 Eldon Iowa, C USA
29 U5 Eldon Missouri, C USA
56 E13 El Doncello Caquetá, S Colombia
31 W13 Eldora Iowa, C USA
62 G12 Eldorado Misiones, NE Argentina
42 I9 El Dorado Sinaloa, C Mexico
29 U14 El Dorado Arkansas, C USA
32 M17 Eldorado Illinois, N USA
29 O6 El Dorado Kansas, C USA
28 K12 Eldorado Oklahoma, C USA
27 O9 Eldorado Texas, SW USA
57 Q8 El Dorado Bolívar, E Venezuela
56 F10 El Dorado ✕ (Bogotá) Cundinamarca, C Colombia
El Dorado see California
29 O6 El Dorado Lake ⊡ Kansas, C USA
29 S6 El Dorado Springs Missouri, C USA
83 H18 Eldoret Rift Valley, W Kenya
31 Z14 Eldridge Iowa, C USA
97 J21 Eldsberga Halland, S Sweden
27 R4 Electra Texas, SW USA
39 Q7 Electra Lake ⊡ Colorado, C USA
40 B8 Eleele Haw. 'Ele'ele. Kauai, Hawaii, USA, C Pacific Ocean
Elefantes see Olifants
117 H19 Elefsína prev. Elevsís. Attikí, C Greece
117 G19 Eléftheres anc. Eleutherae. site of ancient city Attikí/Stereá Ellás, C Greece
116 I13 Eleftheroúpoli prev. Elevtheroúpolis. Anatolikí Makedonía kai Thráki, NE Greece
76 F10 El Eglab ▲▲ SW Algeria
120 F10 Eleja Jelgava, C Latvia
Elek see Ilek
121 G14 Elektrėnai Kaišiadorys, SE Lithuania
130 L3 Elektrostal' Moskovskaya Oblast', W Russian Federation
83 H15 Elemi Triangle disputed region Kenya/Sudan
56 G16 El Encanto Amazonas, S Colombia
39 R14 Elephant Butte Reservoir ⊡ New Mexico, SW USA
Éléphant, Chaîne de l' see Dâmrei, Chuŏr Phnum
204 G2 Elephant Island island South Shetland Islands, Antarctica
Elephant River see Olifants
El Escorial see San Lorenzo de El Escorial
Élesd see Aleşd
116 F11 Eleshnitsa ≈ W Bulgaria
143 S13 Eleşkirt Ağrı, E Turkey
44 F5 El Estor Izabal, E Guatemala
Eleutherae see Eléftheres
46 I2 Eleuthera Island island N Bahamas
39 S5 Elevenmile Canyon Reservoir ⊡ Colorado, C USA
29 W8 Eleven Point River ≈ Arkansas/Missouri, C USA
Elevsís see Elefsína
Elevtheroúpolis see Eleftheroúpoli
77 W8 El Faiyûm var. Al Fayyūm. N Egypt
82 B10 El Fasher var. Al Fāshir. Northern Darfur, W Sudan
77 W8 El Fashn var. Al Fashn. C Egypt
El Ferrol/El Ferrol del Caudillo see Ferrol
41 W13 Elfin Cove Chichagof Island, Alaska, USA
107 W4 El Fluvià ≈ NE Spain
42 H7 El Fuerte Sinaloa, W Mexico
82 D11 El Fula Western Kordofan, C Sudan
El Gedaref see Gedaref
82 A10 El Geneina var. Ajjinena, Al-Genain, Al Junaynah. Western Darfur, W Sudan
98 J8 Elgin NE Scotland, UK
32 M10 Elgin Illinois, N USA
31 P14 Elgin Nebraska, C USA
37 Y9 Elgin Nevada, W USA
30 L6 Elgin North Dakota, N USA
28 M12 Elgin Oklahoma, C USA
27 T10 Elgin Texas, SW USA
127 N9 El'ginskiy Respublika Sakha (Yakutiya), NE Russian Federation
77 W8 El Giza var. Al Jīzah, Gîza, Gizeh. N Egypt
76 J8 El Goléa var. Al Golea. C Algeria
42 D2 El Golfo de Santa Clara Sonora, NW Mexico
83 G18 Elgon, Mount ▲ E Uganda
96 I10 Elgpiggen ▲ S Norway
107 T4 El Grado Aragón, NE Spain
42 L6 El Guaje, Laguna ⊡ NE Mexico
56 H6 El Guayabo Zulia, W Venezuela
79 O6 El Guettâra oasis N Mali
78 J6 El Ḥammâmi desert N Mauritania
78 M5 El Ḥank cliff N Mauritania
El Haseke see Al Ḥasakah
82 H10 El Hawata Gedaref, E Sudan
El Higo see Higos
176 Uu16 Eliase Pulau Selaru, E Indonesia
Elías Piña see Comendador
27 R6 Eliasville Texas, SW USA
Elichpur see Achalpur
39 V13 Elida New Mexico, SW USA
117 F18 Elikónas ▲▲ C Greece
69 T10 Elila ≈ W Zaire
41 N9 Elim Alaska, USA
Elimberrum see Auch
Eliocroca see Lorca
63 B16 Elisa Santa Fe, C Argentina
Elisabethstedt see Dumbrăveni
Élisabethville see Lubumbashi
131 O13 Elista Respublika Kalmykiya, SW Russian Federation
190 I9 Elizabeth South Australia
23 Q3 Elizabeth West Virginia, NE USA
21 Q9 Elizabeth, Cape headland Maine, NE USA
23 Y8 Elizabeth City North Carolina, SE USA
23 P8 Elizabethton Tennessee, S USA
32 M17 Elizabethtown Illinois, N USA
22 K6 Elizabethtown Kentucky, S USA
20 L7 Elizabethtown New York, NE USA
23 U11 Elizabethtown North Carolina, SE USA
20 G15 Elizabethtown Pennsylvania, NE USA
76 E6 El-Jadida prev. Mazagan. W Morocco
El Jafr see Jafr, Qā' al
82 F11 El Jebelein White Nile, E Sudan
112 N8 Ełk Ger. Lyck. Suwałki, NE Poland
112 O8 Ełk ≈ NE Poland
31 Y12 Elkader Iowa, C USA
82 G9 El Kamlin Gezira, C Sudan
35 N11 Elk City Idaho, NW USA
28 K10 Elk City Oklahoma, C USA
29 P7 Elk City Lake ⊡ Kansas, C USA
36 M5 Elk Creek California, W USA
30 J10 Elk Creek ≈ South Dakota, N USA
76 M5 El Kef var. Al Kāf, Le Kef. NW Tunisia
76 F7 El Kelâa Srarhna var. Kal al Sraghna. C Morocco
El Kerak see Al Karak
9 P17 Elkford British Columbia, SW Canada
El Khalil see Hebron
82 E7 El Khandaq Northern, N Sudan
77 W10 El Khârga var. Al Khārijah. C Egypt
33 P11 Elkhart Indiana, N USA
28 H7 Elkhart Kansas, C USA
27 V8 Elkhart Texas, SW USA
32 M7 Elkhart Lake ◎ Wisconsin, N USA
El Khartûm see Khartoum
39 Q3 Elkhead Mountains ▲▲ Colorado, C USA
20 I12 Elk Hill ▲ Pennsylvania, NE USA
144 G8 El Khiyam var. Al Khiyām, Khiam. S Lebanon
31 S15 Elkhorn Nebraska, C USA
32 M9 Elkhorn Wisconsin, N USA
31 R14 Elkhorn River ≈ Nebraska, C USA
131 O16 El'khotovo Respublika Severnaya Osetiya, SW Russian Federation
116 L10 Elkhovo prev. Kizilagach. Burgaska Oblast, SE Bulgaria
23 R8 Elkin North Carolina, SE USA
23 S4 Elkins West Virginia, NE USA
205 X3 Elkins, Mount ▲ Antarctica
12 G8 Elk Lake Ontario, S Canada
110 L7 Elk Lake ◎ Michigan, N USA
20 F12 Elkland Pennsylvania, NE USA
37 W3 Elko Nevada, W USA
El Kôm see Al Kawm
9 R14 Elk Point Alberta, SW Canada
31 R12 Elk Point South Dakota, N USA
31 V8 Elk River Minnesota, N USA
22 J10 Elk River ≈ Alabama/Tennessee, S USA
23 R4 Elk River ≈ West Virginia, NE USA
22 I7 Elkton Kentucky, S USA
23 Y2 Elkton Maryland, NE USA
31 R10 Elkton South Dakota, N USA
22 I10 Elkton Tennessee, S USA
23 U5 Elkton Virginia, NE USA
El Kuneitra see Al Qunayṭirah
83 L15 El Kure SE Ethiopia
82 D12 El Lagowa Western Kordofan, C Sudan
41 S12 Ellamar Alaska, USA
Ellás see Greece
25 S6 Ellaville Georgia, SE USA
207 P9 Ellef Ringnes Island island Northwest Territories, N Canada
31 V10 Ellendale Minnesota, N USA
31 P7 Ellendale North Dakota, N USA
38 M6 Ellen, Mount ▲ Utah, W USA
34 I9 Ellensburg Washington, NW USA
20 K12 Ellenville New York, NE USA
Ellep see Lib
23 T10 Ellerbe North Carolina, SE USA
207 P10 Ellesmere Island island Queen Elizabeth Islands, Northwest Territories, N Canada
193 H19 Ellesmere, Lake ◎ South Island, NZ
99 K18 Ellesmere Port C England, UK
33 O14 Ellettsville Indiana, N USA
101 E19 Ellezelles Hainaut, SW Belgium
15 Jj4 Ellice ≈ Northwest Territories, NE Canada
Ellice Islands see Tuvalu
Ellichpur see Achalpur
23 W3 Ellicott City Maryland, NE USA
25 S2 Ellijay Georgia, SE USA
29 W7 Ellington Missouri, C USA
28 L5 Ellinwood Kansas, C USA
85 J24 Elliot Eastern Cape, SE South Africa
12 D10 Elliot Lake Ontario, S Canada
189 X6 Elliot, Mount ▲ Queensland, E Australia
23 T5 Elliott Knob ▲ Virginia, NE USA
28 K4 Ellis Kansas, C USA
190 F8 Elliston South Australia
24 M7 Ellisville Mississippi, S USA
107 V5 El Llobregat ≈ NE Spain
98 L9 Ellon NE Scotland, UK
Ellore see Elūru
23 S13 Elloree South Carolina, SE USA
28 M4 Ellsworth Kansas, C USA
21 S7 Ellsworth Maine, NE USA
32 I6 Ellsworth Wisconsin, N USA
28 M11 Ellsworth, Lake ⊡ Oklahoma, C USA
204 K9 Ellsworth Land physical region Antarctica
204 L9 Ellsworth Mountains ▲▲ Antarctica
103 J21 Ellwangen Baden-Württemberg, S Germany
20 B14 Ellwood City Pennsylvania, NE USA
110 H8 Elm Glarus, NE Switzerland
34 G9 Elma Washington, NW USA
124 Qq15 El Maḥalla el Kubra var. Al Maḥallah al Kubrá, Mahalla el Kubra. N Egypt
76 E9 El Mahbas var. Mahbés. SW Western Sahara
65 H17 El Maitén Chubut, W Argentina
142 E16 Elmalı Antalya, SW Turkey
82 G10 El Manaqil Gezira, C Sudan
56 M12 El Mango Amazonas, S Venezuela
77 W7 El Manṣûra var. Al Manṣūrah, Manṣûra. N Egypt
57 P8 El Manteco Bolívar, E Venezuela
31 O16 Elm Creek Nebraska, C USA
El Mediyya see Médéa
79 Y9 Elméki Agadez, C Niger
110 K7 Elmen Tirol, W Austria
20 J16 Elmer New Jersey, NE USA
144 G6 El Mina var. Al Mīnā'. N Lebanon
77 W9 El Minya var. Al Minyā, Minya. C Egypt
12 F15 Elmira Ontario, S Canada
20 G11 Elmira New York, NE USA
38 K13 El Mirage Arizona, SW USA
31 O7 Elm Lake ⊡ South Dakota, N USA
El Mojân see San Rafael
107 N7 El Molar Madrid, C Spain
78 L7 El Mrâyer well C Mauritania
78 L5 El Mreïti well N Mauritania
78 L8 El Mreyyé desert E Mauritania
31 P8 Elm River ≈ North Dakota/South Dakota, N USA
102 I9 Elmshorn Schleswig-Holstein, N Germany
82 D12 El Muglad Western Kordofan, C Sudan
El Muwaqqar see Al Muwaqqar
12 G14 Elmvale Ontario, S Canada
32 K12 Elmwood Illinois, N USA
28 J8 Elmwood Oklahoma, C USA
105 P17 Elne anc. Illiberis. Pyrénées-Orientales, S France
56 F11 El Nevado, Cerro elevation C Colombia
179 Oo13 El Nido Palawan, W Philippines
64 I12 El Nihuil Mendoza, W Argentina
77 W7 El Nouzha ✕ (Alexandria) N Egypt
82 E10 El Obeid var. Al Obayyid, Al Ubayyiḍ. Northern Kordofan, C Sudan
43 O13 El Oro México, S Mexico
58 B8 El Oro ⬖ province SW Ecuador
63 B19 Elortondo Santa Fe, C Argentina
56 J8 Elorza Apure, C Venezuela
El Ouâdi see El Oued
76 L7 El Oued var. Al Oued, El Ouâdi, El Wad. NE Algeria
38 L15 Eloy Arizona, SW USA
57 Q7 El Palmar Bolívar, E Venezuela
42 K8 El Palmito Durango, W Mexico
57 P7 El Pao Bolívar, E Venezuela
56 K5 El Pao Cojedes, N Venezuela
44 J7 El Paraíso El Paraíso, S Honduras
44 I7 El Paraíso ⬖ department SE Honduras
32 L12 El Paso Illinois, N USA
26 G8 El Paso Texas, SW USA
26 G8 El Paso ✕ Texas, SW USA
107 U7 El Perello Cataluña, NE Spain
57 P5 El Pilar Sucre, NE Venezuela
44 F7 El Pital, Cerro ▲ El Salvador/Honduras
37 Q9 El Portal California, W USA
42 J3 El Porvenir Chihuahua, N Mexico
45 U14 El Porvenir San Blas, N Panama
107 W6 El Prat de Llobregat Cataluña, NE Spain
44 H5 El Progreso Yoro, NW Honduras
44 A2 El Progreso off. Departamento de El Progreso. ⬖ department C Guatemala
El Progreso see Guastatoya
106 L9 El Puente del Arzobispo Castilla-La Mancha, C Spain
106 J15 El Puerto de Santa María Andalucía, S Spain
64 I8 El Puesto Catamarca, NW Argentina
El Qâhira see Cairo
77 V10 El Qaşr var. Al Qaşr. C Egypt
El Qatrani see Al Qaṭrānah
42 I10 El Quelite Sinaloa, C Mexico
64 G9 Elqui, Río ≈ N Chile
El Quneitra see Al Qunayṭirah
El Quseir see Al Quşayr
El Quweira see Al Quwayrah
147 O15 El-Rahaba ✕ (Şan'ā') W Yemen
44 M10 El Rama Región Autónoma Atlántico Sur, SE Nicaragua
45 W16 El Real var. El Real de Santa María. Darién, SE Panama
El Real de Santa María see El Real
28 M10 El Reno Oklahoma, C USA
42 K9 El Rodeo Durango, C Mexico
106 J13 El Ronquillo Andalucía, S Spain
9 S16 Elrose Saskatchewan, S Canada
32 K8 Elroy Wisconsin, N USA
27 S17 Elsa Texas, SW USA
77 W8 El Ṣaff var. Aş Şaff. N Egypt
42 J10 El Salto Durango, C Mexico
44 D8 El Salvador off. Republica de El Salvador. ◆ republic Central America
56 K7 El Samán de Apure Apure, C Venezuela
12 D7 Elsas Ontario, S Canada
Elsass see Alsace
42 J5 El Sáuz Chihuahua, N Mexico
29 W4 Elsberry Missouri, C USA
47 P9 El Seibo var. Santa Cruz de El Seibo, Santa Cruz del Seibo. E Dominican Republic
44 B7 El Semillero Barra Nahualate Escuintla, SW Guatemala
Elsene see Ixelles
165 N11 Elsen Nur ◎ C China
38 L6 Elsinore Utah, W USA
Elsinore see Helsingør
101 L18 Elsloo Limburg, SE Netherlands
62 G13 El Soberbio Misiones, NE Argentina
57 N6 El Socorro Guárico, C Venezuela
56 L6 El Sombrero Guárico, N Venezuela
100 L10 Elspeet Gelderland, E Netherlands
100 L12 Elst Gelderland, E Netherlands
103 O15 Elsterwerda Brandenburg, E Germany
42 J4 El Sueco Chihuahua, N Mexico
El Suweida see As Suwaydā'
El Suweis see Suez
56 D12 El Tambo Cauca, SW Colombia
183 T13 Eltanin Fracture Zone tectonic feature SE Pacific Ocean
107 X5 El Ter ≈ NE Spain
192 K11 Eltham Taranaki, North Island, NZ
57 O6 El Tigre Anzoátegui, NE Venezuela
El Tigrito see San José de Guanipa
56 J5 El Tocuyo Lara, N Venezuela
131 Q10 El'ton Volgogradskaya Oblast', SW Russian Federation
34 K10 Eltopia Washington, NW USA
63 A18 El Trébol Santa Fe, C Argentina
42 J13 El Tuito Jalisco, SW Mexico
77 X8 El Ṭûr var. Aṭ Ṭūr. NE Egypt
161 K16 Elūru prev. Ellore. Andhra Pradesh, E India
120 H13 Elva Ger. Elwa. Tartumaa, SE Estonia
39 R9 El Vado Reservoir ⊡ New Mexico, SW USA
45 S15 El Valle Coclé, C Panama
106 I11 Elvas Portalegre, C Portugal
56 K7 El Venado Apure, C Venezuela
107 V6 El Vendrell Cataluña, NE Spain
96 I13 Elverum Hedmark, S Norway
44 I9 El Viejo Chinandega, NW Nicaragua
56 G7 El Viejo, Cerro ▲ C Colombia
56 H6 El Vigía Mérida, NW Venezuela
107 Q4 El Villar de Arnedo La Rioja, N Spain
61 A14 Elvira Amazonas, W Brazil
Elwa see Elva
El Wad see El Oued
83 K17 El Wak North Eastern, NE Kenya
35 R7 Elwell, Lake ⊡ Montana, NW USA
33 P13 Elwood Indiana, N USA
29 R3 Elwood Kansas, C USA
31 N16 Elwood Nebraska, C USA
Elx-Elche see Elche
99 O20 Ely E England, UK
31 X4 Ely Minnesota, N USA
37 X6 Ely Nevada, W USA
El Yopal see Yopal
33 T11 Elyria Ohio, N USA
47 S9 El Yunque ▲ E Puerto Rico
103 F23 Elz ≈ SW Germany
197 C14 Emae island Shepherd Islands, C Vanuatu
120 I5 Emajõgi Ger. Embach. ≈ SE Estonia
Emāmrūd see Shāhrūd
155 Q2 Emām Ṣāḩeb var. Emam Saheb, Hazarat Imam. Kunduz, NE Afghanistan
Emāmshahr see Shāhrūd
97 M20 Emån ≈ S Sweden
197 D14 Emao island C Vanuatu
150 J11 Emba Kaz. Embi. Aktyubinsk, W Kazakhstan
150 H12 Emba Kaz. Zhem. ≈ W Kazakhstan
Embach see Emajõgi
64 K5 Embarcación Salta, N Argentina
32 M15 Embarras River ≈ Illinois, N USA
Embi see Emba
83 I19 Embu Eastern, C Kenya
102 E10 Emden Niedersachsen, NW Germany
31 Q4 Emerado North Dakota, N USA
189 X8 Emerald Queensland, E Australia
Emerald Isle see Montserrat
59 J15 Emero, Río ≈ W Bolivia
9 Y17 Emerson Manitoba, S Canada
31 T15 Emerson Iowa, C USA
31 R13 Emerson Nebraska, C USA
38 M5 Emery Utah, W USA
Emesa see Ḥimş
142 E13 Emet Kütahya, W Turkey
194 G14 Emeti Western, SW PNG
37 V3 Emigrant Pass pass Nevada, W USA
80 I6 Emi Koussi ▲ N Chad
Emilia see Emilia-Romagna
43 V15 Emiliano Zapata Chiapas, SE Mexico
108 E9 Emilia-Romagna prev. Emilia, anc. Æmilia. ⬖ region N Italy
164 J3 Emin var. Dorbiljin. Xinjiang Uygur Zizhiqu, NW China
155 W8 Eminābād Punjab, E Pakistan
22 L5 Eminence Kentucky, S USA
29 W7 Eminence Missouri, C USA
116 N9 Emine, Nos headland E Bulgaria
164 I3 Emin He ≈ NW China
195 N8 Emirau Island island N PNG
142 F13 Emirdağ Afyon, W Turkey
97 M21 Emmaboda Kalmar, S Sweden
120 E5 Emmaste Hiiumaa, W Estonia
20 I15 Emmaus Pennsylvania, NE USA
191 U4 Emmaville New South Wales, SE Australia
110 E9 Emme ≈ W Switzerland
100 L8 Emmeloord Flevoland, N Netherlands
100 O8 Emmen Drenthe, NE Netherlands
110 F8 Emmen Luzern, C Switzerland
103 F23 Emmendingen Baden-Württemberg, SW Germany
100 P8 Emmer-Compascuum Drenthe, NE Netherlands
103 D14 Emmerich Nordrhein-Westfalen, W Germany
31 U12 Emmetsburg Iowa, C USA
34 M14 Emmett Idaho, NW USA
40 M10 Emmonak Alaska, USA
Emona see Ljubljana
Emonti see East London
26 L12 Emory Peak ▲ Texas, SW USA
42 F6 Empalme Sonora, NW Mexico
85 L23 Empangeni KwaZulu/Natal, E South Africa
63 C14 Empedrado Corrientes, NE Argentina
199 I13 Emperor Seamounts undersea feature NW Pacific Ocean
199 J3 Emperor Trough undersea feature N Pacific Ocean
37 R4 Empire Nevada, W USA
Empire State of the South see Georgia
Emplawas see Amplawas
108 F11 Empoli Toscana, C Italy
29 P5 Emporia Kansas, C USA
23 W7 Emporia Virginia, NE USA
20 E13 Emporium Pennsylvania, NE USA
195 S12 Empress Augusta Bay inlet Bougainville Island, PNG
Empty Quarter see Ar Rub' al Khālī
102 E10 Ems Dut. Eems. ≈ NW Germany
102 F13 Emsdetten Nordrhein-Westfalen, NW Germany
Ems-Hunte Canal see Küstenkanal
102 F10 Ems-Jade-Kanal canal NW Germany
102 F11 Emsland cultural region NW Germany
190 D3 Emu Junction South Australia
169 T3 Emur He ≈ NE China
57 R8 Enachu Landing NW Guyana
95 F16 Enafors Jämtland, C Sweden
96 N11 Enånger Gävleborg, C Sweden
98 G7 Enard Bay bay NW Scotland, UK
Enareträsk see Inarijärvi
176 X12 Enarotali Irian Jaya, E Indonesia
171 I15 Ena-san ▲ Honshū, S Japan
144 E12 En 'Avedat well S Israel
172 P2 Enbetsu Hokkaidō, NE Japan
63 H16 Encantadas, Serra das ▲▲ S Brazil
42 E7 Encantado, Cerro ▲ NW Mexico
64 P7 Encarnación Itapúa, S Paraguay
42 M12 Encarnación de Díaz Jalisco, SW Mexico
79 O17 Enchi SW Ghana
27 Q14 Encinal Texas, SW USA
37 U17 Encinitas California, W USA
27 S16 Encino Texas, SW USA
56 H6 Encontrados Zulia, NW Venezuela
190 I10 Encounter Bay inlet South Australia
63 F15 Encruzilhada Rio Grande do Sul, S Brazil
63 H16 Encruzilhada do Sul Rio Grande do Sul, S Brazil
113 M20 Encs Borsod-Abaúj-Zemplén, NE Hungary
199 M3 Endeavour Seamount undersea feature N Pacific Ocean
189 V1 Endeavour Strait strait Queensland, NE Australia
175 Q16 Endeh Flores, S Indonesia
97 G23 Endelave island C Denmark
203 T4 Enderbury Island atoll Phoenix Islands, C Kiribati
9 N16 Enderby British Columbia, SW Canada
205 W4 Enderby Land physical region Antarctica
181 N14 Enderby Plain undersea feature S Indian Ocean
31 Q6 Enderlin North Dakota, N USA
Endersdorf see Jędrzejów
30 K16 Enders Reservoir ⊡ Nebraska, C USA
20 H11 Endicott New York, NE USA
41 P7 Endicott Mountains ▲▲ Alaska, USA
120 I5 Endla Raba wetland C Estonia
119 T9 Enerhodar Zaporiz'ka Oblast', SE Ukraine
59 F14 Ene, Río ≈ C Peru
201 N4 Enewetak Atoll var. Ānewetak, Eniwetok. atoll Ralik Chain, W Marshall Islands
116 L13 Enez Edirne, NW Turkey
23 W8 Enfield North Carolina, SE USA
194 G12 Enga ⬖ province W PNG
47 Q9 Engaño, Cabo headland E Dominican Republic
172 Q5 Engaru Hokkaidō, NE Japan
144 F11 'En Gedi Southern, E Israel
110 F9 Engelberg Unterwalden, C Switzerland
23 Y9 Engelhard North Carolina, SE USA
131 P8 Engel's Saratovskaya Oblast', W Russian Federation
103 G24 Engen Baden-Württemberg, SW Germany
Engeten see Aiud
174 H13 Enggano, Pulau island W Indonesia
82 J8 Enghershatu ▲ N Eritrea
101 F19 Enghien Dut. Edingen. Hainaut, SW Belgium
29 V12 England Arkansas, C USA
99 M20 England Lat. Anglia. national region UK
15 L2 Englefield, Cape headland Northwest Territories, NE Canada
12 H8 Englehart Ontario, S Canada
39 T4 Englewood Colorado, C USA
33 O16 English Indiana, N USA
41 Q13 English Bay Alaska, USA
English Bazar see Ingrāj Bāzār
99 N25 English Channel var. The Channel, Fr. la Manche. channel NW Europe
204 J7 English Coast physical region Antarctica
107 S11 Enguera País Valenciano, E Spain
120 E8 Engure Tukums, W Latvia
120 E8 Engures Ezers ◎ NW Latvia
143 R9 Enguri Rus. Inguri. ≈ NW Georgia
Engyum see Gangi
28 M9 Enid Oklahoma, C USA
24 L3 Enid Lake ⊡ Mississippi, S USA
201 Y2 Enigu island Ratak Chain, SE Marshall Islands
Enikale Strait see Kerch Strait
153 Z8 Enil'chek Issyk-Kul'skaya Oblast', E Kyrgyzstan
117 F17 Enipéfs ≈ C Greece
172 O4 Eniwa Hokkaidō, NE Japan
172 O6 Eniwa-dake ⛰ Hokkaidō, NE Japan
Eniwetok see Enewetak Atoll
Enkeldoorn see Chivhu
127 Nn11 Enken, Mys headland NE Russian Federation
100 J8 Enkhuizen Noord-Holland, NW Netherlands
111 Q4 Enknach ≈ N Austria
97 N15 Enköping Uppsala, C Sweden
109 K24 Enna var. Castrogiovanni, Henna. Sicilia, Italy, C Mediterranean Sea
82 D11 En Nahud Western Kordofan, C Sudan
144 F8 En Nâqoûra var. An Nāqūrah. SW Lebanon
En Nazira see Nagerat
80 K8 Ennedi plateau E Chad
103 E15 Ennepetal Nordrhein-Westfalen, W Germany
191 P4 Enngonia New South Wales, SE Australia
99 C19 Ennis Ir. Inis. W Ireland
35 R11 Ennis Montana, NW USA
27 U7 Ennis Texas, SW USA
99 F20 Enniscorthy Ir. Inis Córthaidh. SE Ireland
99 E15 Enniskillen var. Inniskilling, Ir. Inis Ceithleann. SW Northern Ireland, UK
99 B19 Ennistimon Ir. Inis Díomáin. W Ireland
111 T4 Enns Oberösterreich, N Austria
111 T4 Enns ≈ C Austria
95 O16 Eno Pohjois-Karjala, SE Finland
26 M5 Enochs Texas, SW USA
95 N17 Enonkoski Mikkeli, SE Finland
94 K10 Enontekiö Lapp. Eanodat. Lappi, N Finland
23 Q11 Enoree South Carolina, SE USA
23 P11 Enoree River ≈ South Carolina, SE USA
20 M6 Enosburg Falls Vermont, NE USA
175 P11 Enrekang Sulawesi, C Indonesia
47 N10 Enriquillo SW Dominican Republic
47 N9 Enriquillo, Lago ◎ SW Dominican Republic
100 L9 Ens Flevoland, N Netherlands
100 P11 Enschede Overijssel, E Netherlands
42 B2 Ensenada Baja California, NW Mexico
103 E20 Ensheim ✕ (Saarbrücken) Saarland, W Germany
166 L9 Enshi Hubei, C China
171 Hh17 Enshū-nada gulf SW Japan
25 O8 Ensley Florida, SE USA
Enso see Svetogorsk
83 F18 Entebbe S Uganda
83 F18 Entebbe ✕ C Uganda
103 M18 Entenbühl ▲ Czech Republic/Germany
100 N10 Enter Overijssel, E Netherlands
25 Q7 Enterprise Alabama, S USA
34 L11 Enterprise Oregon, NW USA
38 J7 Enterprise Utah, W USA
34 J8 Entiat Washington, NW USA
107 P15 Entinas, Punta de las headland S Spain
110 F8 Entlebuch Luzern, W Switzerland
110 F8 Entlebuch valley C Switzerland
65 I22 Entrada, Punta headland S Argentina
105 O13 Entraygues-sur-Truyère Aveyron, S France
197 G3 Entrecasteaux, Récifs d' reef N New Caledonia
63 C17 Entre Ríos off. Provincia de Entre Ríos. ⬖ province NE Argentina
44 K7 Entre Ríos, Cordillera ▲▲ Honduras/Nicaragua
106 G9 Entroncamento Santarém, C Portugal
176 Z10 Entrop Irian Jaya, E Indonesia
79 V16 Enugu Enugu, S Nigeria
79 U16 Enugu ⬖ state SE Nigeria
127 Pp3 Enurmino Chukotskiy Avtonomnyy Okrug, NE Russian Federation
56 E9 Envigado Antioquia, W Colombia
61 B15 Envira Amazonas, W Brazil
Enyélé see Enyellé
81 I16 Enyellé var. Enyélé. La Likouala, NE Congo
103 H21 Enz ≈ SW Germany
171 J16 Enzan Yamanashi, Honshū, S Japan
106 I2 Eo ≈ NW Spain
Eochaill see Youghal
Eochaille, Cuan see Youghal Bay
109 K22 Eolie, Isole var. Isole Lipari, Eng. Aeolian Islands, Lipari Islands. island group S Italy
201 U12 Eot island Chuuk, C Micronesia
117 J25 Epáno Archánes var. Áno Arkhánai; prev. Epáno Arkhánai. Kríti, Greece, E Mediterranean Sea
Epáno Arkhánai see Epáno Archánes
117 G14 Epanomí Kentrikí Makedonía, N Greece
100 M10 Epe Gelderland, E Netherlands
79 S16 Epe Lagos, S Nigeria
81 I17 Epéna La Likouala, NE Congo
Eperies/Eperjes see Prešov
105 Q4 Épernay anc. Sparnacum. Marne, N France
38 L5 Ephraim Utah, W USA
20 H15 Ephrata Pennsylvania, NE USA
34 J8 Ephrata Washington, NW USA
197 C13 Épi island C Vanuatu
107 R6 Épila Aragón, NE Spain
105 T6 Épinal Vosges, NE France
Epiphania see Ḥamāh
Epirus see Ípeiros
124 N4 Episkopí SW Cyprus
Episkopi Bay see Episkopí, Kólpos
124 N4 Episkopí, Kólpos var. Episkopi Bay. bay SE Cyprus
Epitoli see Pretoria
Epoon see Ebon Atoll
Eporedia see Ivrea
Eppeschdorf see Dumbrăveni
103 H21 Eppingen Baden-Württemberg, SW Germany
85 E18 Epukiro Omaheke, E Namibia
31 Y13 Epworth Iowa, C USA
149 O10 Eqlīd var. Iqlid. Fārs, C Iran
Equality State see Wyoming
81 J18 Equateur off. Région de l' Equateur. ⬖ region N Zaire
157 K22 Equatorial Channel channel S Maldives
81 B17 Equatorial Guinea off. Republic of Equatorial Guinea. ◆ republic C Africa
194 H14 Era ≈ S PNG

◆ Country ◉ Country Capital ◇ Dependent Territory ○ Dependent Territory Capital ⬖ Administrative Region ✕ International Airport ▲ Mountain ▲▲ Mountain Range ⛰ Volcano ≈ River ◎ Lake ⊡ Reservoir

◆ COUNTRY   ◇ DEPENDENT TERRITORY   ◇ ADMINISTRATIVE REGION   ▲ MOUNTAIN   ▲ VOLCANO   ☒ LAKE
● COUNTRY CAPITAL   ○ DEPENDENT TERRITORY CAPITAL   ✈ INTERNATIONAL AIRPORT   ▲ MOUNTAIN RANGE   ↔ RIVER   ☒ RESERVOIR

102 I6 **Flensburg** Schleswig-Holstein, N Germany
102 J6 **Flensburger Förde** inlet Denmark/Germany
104 K5 **Flers** Orne, N France
97 C14 **Flesland** ✕ (Bergen) Hordaland, S Norway
Flessingue see Vlissingen
23 P10 **Fletcher** North Carolina, SE USA
33 R6 **Fletcher Pond** ◎ Michigan, N USA
104 L15 **Fleurance** Gers, S France
110 B8 **Fleurier** Neuchâtel, W Switzerland
101 H20 **Fleurus** Hainaut, S Belgium
105 N7 **Fleury-les-Aubrais** Loiret, C France
100 K10 **Flevoland** ◆ province C Netherlands
Flickertail State see North Dakota
110 H9 **Flims** Glarus, NE Switzerland
190 F8 **Flinders Island** island Investigator Group, South Australia
191 P14 **Flinders Island** island Furneaux Group, Tasmania, SE Australia
190 I6 **Flinders Ranges** ▲ South Australia
189 U5 **Flinders River** ↗ Queensland, NE Australia
9 V13 **Flin Flon** Manitoba, C Canada
99 K18 **Flint** NE Wales, UK
33 R9 **Flint** Michigan, N USA
99 J18 **Flint** cultural region NE Wales, UK
29 O7 **Flint Hills** hill range Kansas, C USA
203 Y6 **Flint Island** island Line Islands, E Kiribati
25 S4 **Flint River** ↗ Georgia, SE USA
33 R9 **Flint River** ↗ Michigan, N USA
201 X12 **Flipper Point** headland C Wake Island
96 I13 **Flisa** Hedmark, S Norway
96 I13 **Flisa** ↗ S Norway
126 Hh4 **Flissingskiy, Mys** headland Novaya Zemlya, NW Russian Federation
see also Bovec
107 U6 **Flix** Cataluña, NE Spain
97 J19 **Floda** Älvsborg, S Sweden
103 O16 **Flöha** E Germany
27 O4 **Flomot** Texas, SW USA
31 V5 **Floodwood** Minnesota, N USA
32 M15 **Flora** Illinois, N USA
105 P14 **Florac** Lozère, S France
25 Q8 **Florala** Alabama, S USA
105 S4 **Florange** Moselle, NE France
Floreana, Isla see Santa María, Isla
25 O2 **Florence** Alabama, S USA
35 L14 **Florence** Arizona, SW USA
39 T6 **Florence** Colorado, C USA
29 O5 **Florence** Kansas, C USA
22 M4 **Florence** Kentucky, S USA
34 E13 **Florence** Oregon, NW USA
23 T12 **Florence** South Carolina, SE USA
27 S9 **Florence** Texas, SW USA
Florence see Firenze
63 E19 **Florencia** Caquetá, S Colombia
101 H21 **Florennes** Namur, S Belgium
Florentia see Firenze
65 J18 **Florentino Ameghino, Embalse** ◎ S Argentina
101 J24 **Florenville** Luxembourg, SE Belgium
44 E3 **Flores** Petén, N Guatemala
63 E19 **Flores** ◆ department S Uruguay
175 Pp16 **Flores** island Nusa Tenggara, C Indonesia
66 M1 **Flores** island Azores, Portugal, NE Atlantic Ocean
Floreshty see Florești
Flores, Lago de see Petén Itzá, Lago
175 P15 **Flores, Laut** see Flores Sea
175 P15 **Flores Sea** Ind. Laut Flores. sea C Indonesia
118 M8 **Florești** Rus. Floreshty. N Moldova
27 S12 **Floresville** Texas, SW USA
61 N14 **Floriano** Piauí, E Brazil
63 K14 **Florianópolis** prev. Destêrro. state capital Santa Catarina, S Brazil
46 G6 **Florida** Camagüey, C Cuba
63 F19 **Florida** Florida, S Uruguay
63 F19 **Florida** ◆ department S Uruguay
25 U9 **Florida** off. State of Florida; also known as Peninsular State, Sunshine State. ◆ state SE USA
23 Y17 **Florida Bay** bay Florida, SE USA
56 G8 **Floridablanca** Santander, N Colombia
195 X15 **Florida Islands** island group C Solomon Islands
23 Y17 **Florida Keys** island group Florida, SE USA
39 Q16 **Florida Mountains** ▲ New Mexico, SW USA
66 D10 **Florida, Straits of** strait Atlantic Ocean/Gulf of Mexico
116 E12 **Flórina** var. Phlórina. Dytikí Makedonía, N Greece
29 X4 **Florissant** Missouri, C USA
96 C11 **Florø** Sogn og Fjordane, S Norway
117 L22 **Floúda, Ákra** headland Astypálaia, Kykládes, Greece, Aegean Sea
23 S7 **Floyd** Virginia, NE USA
27 N4 **Floydada** Texas, SW USA
100 K7 **Fluessen** ◎ N Netherlands
107 U5 **Flúmen** ↗ NE Spain
109 C20 **Flumendosa** ↗ Sardegna, Italy, C Mediterranean Sea
33 R9 **Flushing** Michigan, N USA
Flushing see Vlissingen
27 O6 **Fluvanna** Texas, SW USA
194 F14 **Fly** ↗ Indonesia/PNG

204 I10 **Flying Fish, Cape** headland Thurston Island, Antarctica
Flylån see Vlieland
200 Ss13 **Foa** island Ha'apai Group, C Tonga
9 U15 **Foam Lake** Saskatchewan, S Canada
115 J14 **Foča** SE Bosnia and Herzegovina
118 L12 **Focșani** Vrancea, E Romania
Fogaras/Fogarasch see Făgăraș
109 M16 **Foggia** Puglia, SE Italy
Foggo see Faggo
78 D10 **Fogo, Ilhas de Sotavento**, SW Cape Verde
11 U11 **Fogo Island** island Newfoundland and Labrador, E Canada
111 U7 **Fohnsdorf** Steiermark, SE Austria
102 H7 **Föhr** island NW Germany
106 F14 **Fóia** ▲ S Portugal
12 I10 **Foins, Lac aux** ◎ Québec, SE Canada
105 N17 **Foix** Ariège, S France
130 I5 **Fokino** Bryanskaya Oblast', W Russian Federation
96 G11 **Folda** fjord C Norway
94 G11 **Folda** fjord C Norway
95 F14 **Foldereid** Nord-Trøndelag, C Norway
95 E14 **Foldfjorden** fjord C Norway
Földvár see Feldioara
117 J22 **Folégandros** island Kykládes, Greece, Aegean Sea
25 O9 **Foley** Alabama, S USA
12 E7 **Foley** Minnesota, N USA
12 E7 **Foleyet** Ontario, S Canada
41 Y15 **Folgefonni** glacier S Norway
108 I13 **Foligno** Umbria, C Italy
99 Q23 **Folkestone** SE England, UK
25 W8 **Folkston** Georgia, SE USA
96 H10 **Folldal** Hedmark, S Norway
27 P1 **Follett** Texas, SW USA
108 F13 **Follonica** Toscana, C Italy
23 T15 **Folly Beach** South Carolina, SE USA
37 O7 **Folsom** California, W USA
118 M12 **Fomba** ↗ C Madagascar
180 H14 **Fomboni** Mohéli, S Comoros
25 X4 **Fonda** New York, NE USA
9 K10 **Fond du Lac** Saskatchewan, S Canada
32 M8 **Fond du Lac** Wisconsin, N USA
9 T10 **Fond-du-Lac** ↗ Saskatchewan, C Canada
202 C9 **Fongafale** var. Funafuti. ● (Tuvalu) Funafuti Atoll, SE Tuvalu
202 G8 **Fongafale** atoll C Tuvalu
109 C18 **Fonni** Sardegna, Italy, C Mediterranean Sea
201 V12 **Fono** island Chuuk, C Micronesia
56 G4 **Fonseca** La Guajira, N Colombia
Fonseca, Golfo de see Fonseca, Gulf of
44 H8 **Fonseca, Gulf of** Sp. Golfo de Fonseca. gulf Central America
105 O6 **Fontainebleau** Seine-et-Marne, N France
65 G19 **Fontana, Lago** ◎ W Argentina
23 N10 **Fontana Lake** ◎ North Carolina, SE USA
109 L24 **Fontanarossa** ✕ (Catania) Sicilia, Italy, C Mediterranean Sea
9 N11 **Fontas** ↗ British Columbia, W Canada
60 D12 **Fonte Boa** Amazonas, N Brazil
104 J10 **Fontenay-le-Comte** Vendée, NW France
35 T16 **Fontenelle Reservoir** ◎ Wyoming, C USA
200 Ss12 **Fonualei** island Vava'u Group, N Tonga
113 H24 **Foochow** see Fuzhou
41 Q1 **Foraker, Mount** ▲ Alaska, USA
197 D14 **Forari** Éfaté, C Vanuatu
105 U4 **Forbach** Moselle, NE France
191 Q8 **Forbes** New South Wales, SE Australia
79 T17 **Forcados** Delta, S Nigeria
105 S14 **Forcalquier** Alpes-de-Haute-Provence, SE France
103 K19 **Forchheim** Bayern, SE Germany
176 V14 **Fordate, Pulau** island Kepulauan Tanimbar, E Indonesia
37 R13 **Ford City** California, W USA
96 D11 **Førde** Sogn og Fjordane, S Norway
33 N4 **Ford River** ↗ Michigan, N USA
191 O4 **Fords Bridge** New South Wales, SE Australia
22 H6 **Fordsville** Kentucky, S USA
29 U13 **Fordyce** Arkansas, C USA
78 I14 **Forécariah** Guinée-Maritime, SW Guinea
207 O14 **Forel, Mont** ▲ SE Greenland
9 R17 **Foremost** Alberta, SW Canada
12 E8 **Forest** Ontario, S Canada
24 L5 **Forest** Mississippi, S USA
31 V11 **Forest** Ohio, N USA
31 V11 **Forest City** Iowa, C USA
23 P9 **Forest City** North Carolina, SE USA
34 G11 **Forest Grove** Oregon, NW USA
191 P17 **Forestier Peninsula** peninsula Tasmania, SE Australia
25 S3 **Forest Lake** Minnesota, N USA
25 S3 **Forest Park** Georgia, SE USA
31 Q3 **Forest River** ↗ North Dakota, N USA
13 T6 **Forestville** Québec, SE Canada
98 K10 **Forfar** E Scotland, UK
28 J8 **Forgan** Oklahoma, C USA
Forge du Sud see Dudelange
103 J24 **Forggensee** ◎ S Germany
153 N10 **Forish** Rus. Farish. Jizzakh Wiloyati, C Uzbekistan
29 S14 **Forked Deer River** ↗ Tennessee, S USA

34 F7 **Forks** Washington, NW USA
94 N2 **Forlandsundet** sound W Svalbard
108 H10 **Forlì** anc. Forum Livii. Emilia-Romagna, N Italy
31 Q7 **Forman** North Dakota, N USA
99 K17 **Formby** NW England, UK
107 V11 **Formentera** island Islas Baleares, Spain, W Mediterranean Sea
Formentor, Cabo de see Formentor, Cap de
107 Y9 **Formentor, Cap de** var. Cabo de Formentor, Cape Formentor. headland Mallorca, Spain, W Mediterranean Sea
Formentor, Cape see Formentor, Cap de
109 L12 **Formia** Lazio, C Italy
64 O7 **Formosa** Formosa, NE Argentina
64 M6 **Formosa** off. Provincia de Formosa. ◆ province NE Argentina
Formosa/Formo'sa see Taiwan
61 N17 **Formosa, Serra** ▲ C Brazil
Formosa Strait see Taiwan Strait
97 H15 **Fornebu** ✕ (Oslo) Akershus, S Norway
27 U6 **Forney** Texas, SW USA
97 H21 **Fornæs** headland C Denmark
108 E9 **Fornovo di Taro** Emilia-Romagna, C Italy
119 T14 **Foros** Respublika Krym, S Ukraine
Føroyar see Faeroe Islands
98 I8 **Forres** NE Scotland, UK
29 X11 **Forrest City** Arkansas, C USA
41 Y15 **Forrester Island** island Alexander Archipelago, Alaska, USA
27 N7 **Forsan** Texas, SW USA
189 V5 **Forsayth** Queensland, NE Australia
97 L19 **Forserum** Jönköping, S Sweden
97 K15 **Forshaga** Värmland, C Sweden
93 N15 **Forssa** Häme, SW Finland
103 Q14 **Forst** Lus. Barść Łużyca. Brandenburg, E Germany
191 U7 **Forster-Tuncurry** New South Wales, SE Australia
25 U5 **Forsyth** Georgia, SE USA
29 T8 **Forsyth** Missouri, C USA
25 W10 **Forsyth** Montana, NW USA
155 U11 **Fort Abbās** Punjab, E Pakistan
21 X7 **Fort Albany** Ontario, C Canada
58 L13 **Fortaleza** Pando, N Bolivia
60 P13 **Fortaleza** prev. Ceará. state capital Ceará, NE Brazil
61 D16 **Fortaleza** Rondônia, W Brazil
58 C13 **Fortaleza, Río** ↗ W Peru
Fort-Archambault see Sarh
23 U3 **Fort Ashby** West Virginia, NE USA
9 N12 **Fort Augustus** N Scotland, UK
Fort-Bayard see Zhanjiang
35 S8 **Fort Benton** Montana, NW USA
37 Q1 **Fort Bidwell** California, W USA
36 L5 **Fort Bragg** California, W USA
33 N16 **Fort Branch** Indiana, N USA
Fort-Bretonnet see Bousso
35 T17 **Fort Bridger** Wyoming, C USA
Fort-Cappolani see Tidjikja
Fort Charlet see Djanet
Fort-Chimo see Kuujjuaq
9 R10 **Fort Chipewyan** Alberta, C Canada
Fort Cobb Lake see Fort Cobb Reservoir
28 L11 **Fort Cobb Reservoir** var. Fort Cobb. Lake. ◎ Oklahoma, C USA
39 T3 **Fort Collins** Colorado, C USA
12 K12 **Fort-Coulonge** Québec, SE Canada
Fort-Crampel see Kaga Bandoro
Fort-Dauphin see Tôlañaro
26 K10 **Fort Davis** Texas, SW USA
39 O10 **Fort Defiance** Arizona, SW USA
47 Q12 **Fort-de-France** prev. Fort-Royal. ● (Martinique) W Martinique
47 P12 **Fort-de-France, Baie de** bay W Martinique
Fort de Kock see Bukittinggi
25 P6 **Fort Deposit** Alabama, S USA
11 S10 **Fort Dodge** Iowa, C USA
108 E11 **Forte dei Marmi** Toscana, C Italy
25 P9 **Fort Erie** Ontario, S Canada
188 H7 **Fortescue River** ↗ Western Australia
21 S2 **Fort Fairfield** Maine, NE USA
Fort-Foureau see Kousséri
10 A11 **Fort Frances** Ontario, S Canada
Fort Franklin see Déline
23 P5 **Fort Gay** West Virginia, NE USA
23 T8 **Fort Garland** Colorado, C USA
Fort George see La Grande Rivière
15 Q9 **Fort Gibson** Oklahoma, C USA
15 **Fort Gibson Lake** ◎ Oklahoma, C USA
15 **Fort Good Hope** var. Good Hope. Northwest Territories, NW Canada
25 V4 **Fort Gordon** Georgia, SE USA
34 J12 **Fort Gouraud** see Fdérik
98 I11 **Forth** ↗ C Scotland, UK
98 K12 **Forth, Firth of** estuary E Scotland, UK
123 R3 **Forthton** Ontario, SE Canada
13 U8 **Fortie** Québec, SE Canada
31 T6 **Fortin General Eugenio Garay** see General Eugenio A. Garay
Fort Jameson see Chipata
Fort Johnston see Mangochi

21 R1 **Fort Kent** Maine, NE USA
Fort-Lamy see Ndjamena
25 Z15 **Fort Lauderdale** Florida, SE USA
23 R11 **Fort Lawn** South Carolina, SE USA
15 Gg9 **Fort Liard** var. Liard. Northwest Territories, W Canada
46 M8 **Fort-Liberté** NE Haiti
23 N9 **Fort Loudoun Lake** ◎ Tennessee, S USA
39 T3 **Fort Lupton** Colorado, C USA
9 R12 **Fort MacKay** Alberta, C Canada
9 Q17 **Fort Macleod** var. MacLeod. Alberta, SW Canada
31 Y16 **Fort Madison** Iowa, C USA
Fort Manning see Mchinji
27 P9 **Fort McKavett** Texas, SW USA
9 R12 **Fort McMurray** Alberta, C Canada
14 F3 **Fort McPherson** var. McPherson. Northwest Territories, NW Canada
23 R11 **Fort Mill** South Carolina, SE USA
Fort-Millot see Ngouri
39 U3 **Fort Morgan** Colorado, C USA
25 W14 **Fort Myers** Florida, SE USA
25 W15 **Fort Myers Beach** Florida, SE USA
8 M10 **Fort Nelson** British Columbia, W Canada
8 M10 **Fort Nelson** ↗ British Columbia, W Canada
15 Gg6 **Fort Norman** var. Norman. Northwest Territories, NW Canada
27 P9 **Fort Payne** Alabama, S USA
35 W7 **Fort Peck** Montana, NW USA
35 V8 **Fort Peck Lake** ◎ Montana, NW USA
25 Y13 **Fort Pierce** Florida, SE USA
31 N10 **Fort Pierre** South Dakota, N USA
83 E18 **Fort Portal** SW Uganda
15 Hh8 **Fort Providence** var. Providence. Northwest Territories, W Canada
9 U16 **Fort Qu'Appelle** Saskatchewan, S Canada
Fort-Repoux see Akjoujt
15 I8 **Fort Resolution** var. Resolution. Northwest Territories, W Canada
35 T13 **Fortress Mountain** ▲ Wyoming, C USA
Fort Rosebery see Mansa
Fort-Rousset see Owando
Fort-Royal see Fort-de-France
10 I10 **Fort Rupert** prev. Rupert House. Québec, C Canada
9 N12 **Fort St.James** British Columbia, SW Canada
9 N12 **Fort St.John** British Columbia, W Canada
Fort Sandeman see Zhob
9 Q14 **Fort Saskatchewan** Alberta, SW Canada
29 R6 **Fort Scott** Kansas, C USA
10 E6 **Fort Severn** Ontario, C Canada
33 R12 **Fort Shawnee** Ohio, N USA
150 E14 **Fort-Shevchenko** Mangistau, W Kazakhstan
Fort-Sibut see Sibut
15 I9 **Fort Simpson** var. Simpson. Northwest Territories, W Canada
15 I9 **Fort Smith** district capital Northwest Territories, W Canada
29 R10 **Fort Smith** Arkansas, C USA
15 I7 **Fort Smith** ◆ district Northwest Territories, W Canada
39 T13 **Fort Stanton** New Mexico, SW USA
26 L9 **Fort Stockton** Texas, SW USA
39 U12 **Fort Sumner** New Mexico, SW USA
28 K8 **Fort Supply** Oklahoma, C USA
28 K8 **Fort Supply Lake** ◎ Oklahoma, C USA
31 O10 **Fort Thompson** South Dakota, N USA
Fort-Trinquet see Bîr Mogreïn
107 R12 **Fortuna** Murcia, SE Spain
36 K3 **Fortuna** California, W USA
31 N2 **Fortuna** North Dakota, N USA
25 T5 **Fort Valley** Georgia, SE USA
9 P11 **Fort Vermilion** Alberta, W Canada
Fort Victoria see Masvingo
33 P12 **Fortville** Indiana, N USA
25 P9 **Fort Walton Beach** Florida, SE USA
33 P12 **Fort Wayne** Indiana, N USA
98 H10 **Fort William** N Scotland, UK
27 T6 **Fort Worth** Texas, SW USA
30 M7 **Fort Yates** North Dakota, N USA
41 S7 **Fort Yukon** Alaska, USA
Forum Alieni see Ferrara
Forum Julii see Fréjus
Forum Livii see Forlì
109 P18 **Fosen** physical region S Norway
96 H7 **Fosen** physical region S Norway
167 N14 **Foshan** var. Fatshan, Fo-shan, Namhoi. Guangdong, S China
Fossa Claudia see Chioggia
108 B9 **Fossano** Piemonte, NW Italy
101 H21 **Fosses-la-Ville** Namur, S Belgium
34 J12 **Fossil** Oregon, NW USA
31 E9 **Fossil Lake** ◎ Oregon, NW USA
108 I11 **Fossombrone** Marche, C Italy
28 M10 **Foss Reservoir** var. Foss Lake. ◎ Oklahoma, C USA
31 S4 **Fosston** Minnesota, N USA
190 I13 **Foster** Victoria, SE Australia
9 T12 **Foster Lakes** ◎ Saskatchewan, C Canada
31 T12 **Fostoria** Ohio, N USA
79 D19 **Fougamou** Ngounié, C Gabon
104 J6 **Fougères** Ille-et-Vilaine, NW France
29 S14 **Fouke** Arkansas, C USA

98 K2 **Foula** island NE Scotland, UK
67 D24 **Foul Bay** bay East Falkland, Falkland Islands
99 P21 **Foulness Island** island SE England, UK
193 F15 **Foulwind, Cape** headland South Island, NZ
81 E15 **Foumban** Ouest, NW Cameroon
180 H13 **Foumbouni** Grande Comore, NW Comoros
205 N8 **Foundation Ice Stream** glacier Antarctica
39 T5 **Fountain** Colorado, C USA
38 L4 **Fountain Green** Utah, W USA
23 P11 **Fountain Inn** South Carolina, SE USA
29 S11 **Fourche LaFave River** ↗ Arkansas, C USA
39 S13 **Four Corners** Wyoming, C USA
102 G7 **Fourmies** Nord, N France
105 Q2 **Four Mountains, Islands of** island group Aleutian Islands, Alaska, USA
181 P17 **Fournaise, Piton de la** ▲ E Réunion
12 J8 **Fournière, Lac** ◎ Québec, SE Canada
117 L20 **Foúrnoi** island Dodekánisos, Greece, Aegean Sea
66 G5 **Four North Fracture Zone** tectonic feature W Atlantic Ocean
Fouron-Saint-Martin see Sint-Martens-Voeren
32 L5 **Fourteen Mile Point** headland Michigan, N USA
78 M3 **Fouta Djallon** var. Futa Jallon. ▲ W Guinea
193 C25 **Foveaux Strait** strait S NZ
37 Q11 **Fowler** California, W USA
39 U6 **Fowler** Colorado, C USA
33 N12 **Fowler** Indiana, N USA
190 D7 **Fowlers Bay** bay South Australia
37 R13 **Fowlerton** Texas, SW USA
148 M3 **Fowman** var. Fuman, Fumen. Gīlān, NW Iran
67 C25 **Fox Bay East** West Falkland, Falkland Islands
67 C25 **Fox Bay West** West Falkland, Falkland Islands
12 J14 **Foxboro** Ontario, SE Canada
9 O14 **Fox Creek** Alberta, W Canada
66 G5 **Fox Basin** see Northwest Territories, N Canada
66 G5 **Foxe Channel** channel Northwest Territories, N Canada
97 I16 **Foxen** ◎ C Sweden
16 N4 **Foxe Peninsula** peninsula Baffin Island, Northwest Territories, N Canada
193 E19 **Fox Glacier** West Coast, South Island, NZ
40 L17 **Fox Islands** island Aleutian Islands, Alaska, USA
32 M10 **Fox Lake** Illinois, N USA
9 V12 **Fox Mine** Manitoba, C Canada
37 R3 **Fox Mountain** ▲ Nevada, W USA
67 E25 **Fox Point** headland East Falkland, Falkland Islands
32 M11 **Fox River** ↗ Illinois/Wisconsin, N USA
32 I7 **Fox River** ↗ Wisconsin, N USA
192 L13 **Foxton** Manawatu-Wanganui, North Island, NZ
9 S16 **Fox Valley** Saskatchewan, S Canada
9 W16 **Foxwarren** Manitoba, S Canada
99 E14 **Foyle, Lough** Ir. Loch Feabhail. inlet N Ireland
204 H5 **Foyn Coast** physical region Antarctica
106 I2 **Foz** Galicia, NW Spain
62 H12 **Foz do Areia, Represa de** ◎ S Brazil
61 A16 **Foz do Breu** Acre, W Brazil
85 A16 **Foz do Cunene** Namibe, SW Angola
62 G12 **Foz do Iguaçu** Paraná, S Brazil
60 C12 **Foz do Mamoriá** Amazonas, NW Brazil
101 H21 **Fraire** Namur, S Belgium
101 L21 **Fraiture, Baraque de** hill SE Belgium
95 H17 **Fränsta** Västernorrland, C Sweden
126 H1 **Frantsa-Iosifa, Zemlya** Eng. Franz Josef Land. island group N Russian Federation
193 E18 **Franz Josef Glacier** West Coast, South Island, NZ
Franz Josef Land see Frantsa-Iosifa, Zemlya
Franz-Josef Spitze see Gerlachovský Štít
109 A19 **Frasca, Capo della** headland Sardegna, Italy, C Mediterranean Sea
109 I15 **Frascati** Lazio, C Italy
85 G24 **Fraserburg** Western Cape, SW South Africa
98 L8 **Fraserburgh** NE Scotland, UK
189 Z9 **Fraser Island** var. Great Sandy Island. island Queensland, E Australia
8 L14 **Fraser Lake** British Columbia, SW Canada
8 L15 **Fraser Plateau** plateau British Columbia, SW Canada
192 P10 **Frasertown** Hawke's Bay, North Island, NZ
101 J22 **Frasnes-lez-Buissenal** Hainaut, SW Belgium
102 B8 **Frauenbach** see Baia Mare
Frauenburg see Saldus, Latvia
Frauenburg see Frombork, Poland
110 H6 **Frauenfeld** Thurgau, NE Switzerland
111 Z5 **Frauenkirchen** Burgenland, E Austria

44 H6 **Francisco Morazán** prev. Tegucigalpa. ◆ department C Honduras
85 I8 **Francistown** North East, NE Botswana
Franconia Forest see Frankenwald
Franconian Jura see Fränkische Alb
100 K6 **Franeker** Fris. Frjentsjer. Friesland, N Netherlands
103 H16 **Frankenberg** Hessen, C Germany
103 J20 **Frankenhöhe** hill range C Germany
33 R8 **Frankenmuth** Michigan, N USA
103 I18 **Frankenstein** hill W Germany
Frankenstein/Frankenstein in Schlesien see Ząbkowice Śląskie
103 L18 **Frankenthal** Rheinland-Pfalz, W Germany
Frankenwald Eng. Franconian Forest. ▲ C Germany
46 J12 **Frankfield** C Jamaica
12 J14 **Frankford** Ontario, SE Canada
29 O3 **Frankfort** Kansas, C USA
22 L5 **Frankfort** state capital Kentucky, S USA
Frankfort on the Main see Frankfurt am Main
Frankfurt see Słubice, Poland
Frankfurt see Frankfurt am Main, Germany
103 G18 **Frankfurt am Main** var. Frankfurt, Fr. Francfort; prev. Eng. Frankfort on the Main. Hessen, SW Germany
102 Q12 **Frankfurt an der Oder** Brandenburg, E Germany
103 L21 **Fränkische Alb** var. Frankenalb, Eng. Franconian Jura. ▲ S Germany
103 I18 **Fränkische Saale** ↗ C Germany
103 L19 **Fränkische Schweiz** hill range C Germany
33 P14 **Franklin** Indiana, N USA
22 J7 **Franklin** Kentucky, S USA
24 J9 **Franklin** Louisiana, S USA
31 O17 **Franklin** Nebraska, C USA
23 N10 **Franklin** North Carolina, SE USA
20 C13 **Franklin** Pennsylvania, NE USA
27 U9 **Franklin** Tennessee, S USA
27 X6 **Franklin** Texas, SW USA
23 X4 **Franklin** West Virginia, NE USA
32 M9 **Franklin** Wisconsin, N USA
37 W4 **Franklin Lake** ◎ Nevada, W USA
193 B22 **Franklin Mountains** ▲ South Island, NZ
41 R5 **Franklin Mountains** ▲ Alaska, USA
41 N4 **Franklin, Point** headland Alaska, USA
191 O17 **Franklin River** ↗ Tasmania, SE Australia
15 I5 **Franklin Strait** strait Northwest Territories, N Canada
24 K8 **Franklinton** Louisiana, S USA
23 U9 **Franklinton** North Carolina, SE USA
27 V7 **Frankston** Texas, SW USA
35 U12 **Frannie** Wyoming, C USA
13 U5 **Franquelin** Québec, SE Canada
85 C18 **Fransfontein** Kunene, NW Namibia

63 D19 **Fray Bentos** Río Negro, W Uruguay
63 F19 **Fray Marcos** Florida, S Uruguay
31 S6 **Frazee** Minnesota, N USA
106 M5 **Frechilla** Castilla-León, N Spain
32 I4 **Frederic** Wisconsin, N USA
97 G23 **Fredericia** Vejle, C Denmark
21 X4 **Frederick** Maryland, NE USA
31 P7 **Frederick** Oklahoma, C USA
31 O10 **Frederick** South Dakota, N USA
31 X12 **Fredericksburg** Texas, SW USA
27 R10 **Fredericksburg** Texas, SW USA
23 W5 **Fredericksburg** Virginia, NE USA
41 X13 **Frederick Sound** sound Alaska , USA
29 X6 **Fredericktown** Missouri, C USA
62 H13 **Frederico Westphalen** Rio Grande do Sul, S Brazil
11 O15 **Fredericton** New Brunswick, SE Canada
Frederikshåb see Paamiut
97 H19 **Frederikshavn** prev. Fladstrand. Nordjylland, N Denmark
97 I22 **Frederikssund** Frederiksborg, E Denmark
47 W3 **Frederiksted** Saint Croix, S Virgin Islands (US)
97 I22 **Frederiksværk** Frederiksborg, E Denmark
56 E9 **Fredonia** Antioquia, W Colombia
38 K8 **Fredonia** Arizona, SW USA
29 C11 **Fredonia** Kansas, C USA
20 C11 **Fredonia** New York, NE USA
Fredonyer Pass pass California, W USA
95 I15 **Fredrika** Västerbotten, N Sweden
97 L14 **Fredriksberg** Kopparberg, C Sweden
Fredrikshald see Halden
Fredrikshamn see Hamina
97 H16 **Fredrikstad** Østfold, S Norway
32 K16 **Freeburg** Illinois, N USA
20 K15 **Freehold** New Jersey, NE USA
20 H14 **Freeland** Pennsylvania, NE USA
190 J5 **Freeling Heights** ▲ South Australia
37 Q7 **Freel Peak** ▲ California, W USA
16 T7 **Freels, Cape** headland Newfoundland, Newfoundland and Labrador, E Canada
31 Q11 **Freeman** South Dakota, N USA
46 G1 **Freeport** Grand Bahama Island, N Bahamas
32 L10 **Freeport** Illinois, N USA
20 W12 **Freeport** Texas, SW USA
46 G1 **Freeport** ✕ Grand Bahama Island, N Bahamas
27 R14 **Freer** Texas, SW USA
85 I22 **Free State** ◆ Free State Province; prev. Orange Free State, Afr. Oranje Vrystaat. ◆ province C South Africa
Free State see Maryland
78 G15 **Freetown** ● (Sierra Leone) W Sierra Leone
180 J16 **Frégate** island Inner Islands, NE Seychelles
106 J12 **Fregenal de la Sierra** Extremadura, W Spain
190 G2 **Fregon** South Australia
104 H5 **Fréhel, Cap** headland NW France
103 N7 **Frei** Møre og Romsdal, S Norway
103 O16 **Freiberg** Sachsen, E Germany
103 O16 **Freiberger Mulde** ↗ E Germany
Freiburg see Freiburg im Breisgau, Germany
Freiburg see Fribourg, Switzerland
103 F23 **Freiburg im Breisgau** var. Freiburg, Fr. Fribourg-en-Brisgau. Baden-Württemberg, SW Germany
Freiburg in Schlesien see Świebodzice
Freie Hansestadt Bremen see Bremen
Freie und Hansestadt Hamburg see Brandenburg
103 L22 **Freising** Bayern, SE Germany
111 T3 **Freistadt** Oberösterreich, N Austria
Freistadtl see Hlohovec
103 O16 **Freital** Sachsen, E Germany
Freiwaldau see Jeseník
104 J6 **Freixo de Espada à Cinta** Bragança, N Portugal
188 I13 **Fremantle** Western Australia
37 N9 **Fremont** California, W USA
33 Q11 **Fremont** Indiana, N USA
31 W15 **Fremont** Iowa, C USA
33 P8 **Fremont** Michigan, N USA
31 R15 **Fremont** Nebraska, C USA
31 T14 **Fremont** Ohio, N USA
35 O6 **Fremont** ↗ Utah, W USA
35 T14 **Fremont Peak** ▲ Wyoming, C USA
38 M6 **Fremont River** ↗ Utah, W USA
23 O9 **French Broad River** ↗ Tennessee, S USA
23 N5 **Frenchburg** Kentucky, S USA
20 C12 **French Creek** ↗ Pennsylvania, NE USA
34 K15 **Frenchglen** Oregon, NW USA
57 Y10 **French Guiana** var. Guiana, Guyane. ◆ French overseas department N South America
French Guinea see Guinea
33 O15 **French Lick** Indiana, N USA
193 J14 **French Pass** Marlborough, South Island, NZ

● Country
◆ Country Capital
◇ Dependent Territory
○ Dependent Territory Capital
◆ Administrative Region
✕ International Airport
▲ Mountain
▲ Mountain Range
✕ Volcano
↗ River
◎ Lake
◎ Reservoir

FRENCH POLYNESIA – GARGNÄS

203 T11 French Polynesia ◇ French overseas territory C Polynesia
French Republic see France
12 F11 French River ≈ Ontario, S Canada
French Somaliland see Djibouti
181 P12 French Southern and Antarctic Territories Fr. Terres Australes et Antarctiques Françaises. ◇ French overseas territory S Indian Ocean
French Sudan see Mali
French Territory of the Afars and Issas see Djibouti
French Togoland see Togo
76 J6 Frenda NW Algeria
113 I18 Frenštát pod Radhoštěm Ger. Frankstadt. Severní Morava, E Czech Republic
78 M17 Fresco S Ivory Coast
205 U16 Freshfield, Cape headland Antarctica
42 L10 Fresnillo var. Fresnillo de González Echeverría. Zacatecas, C Mexico
Fresnillo de González Echeverría see Fresnillo
37 Q10 Fresno California, W USA
Freu, Cabo del see Freu, Cap des
107 Y9 Freu, Cap des var. Cabo del Freu. headland Mallorca, Spain, W Mediterranean Sea
103 G22 Freudenstadt Baden-Württemberg, SW Germany
Freudenthal see Bruntál
191 Q17 Freycinet Peninsula peninsula Tasmania, SE Australia
78 H14 Fria Guinée-Maritime, W Guinea
85 A17 Fria, Cape headland NW Namibia
37 Q10 Friant California, W USA
64 K8 Frías Santiago del Estero, N Argentina
110 D9 Fribourg Ger. Freiburg. Fribourg, W Switzerland
110 C9 Fribourg Ger. Freiburg. ◐ canton W Switzerland
Fribourg-en-Brisgau see Freiburg im Breisgau
34 G7 Friday Harbor San Juan Islands, Washington, NW USA
194 F11 Frieda ≈ NW PNG
Friedau see Ormož
103 K23 Friedberg Bayern, S Germany
103 H18 Friedberg Hessen, W Germany
Friedeberg Neumark see Strzelce Krajeńskie
Friedek-Mistek see Frýdek-Místek
Friedland see Pravdinsk
103 I24 Friedrichshafen Baden-Württemberg, S Germany
Friedrichstadt see Jaunjelgava
31 Q16 Friend Nebraska, C USA
Friendly Islands see Tonga
57 V9 Friendship Coronie, N Suriname
32 L7 Friendship Wisconsin, N USA
111 T8 Friesach Kärnten, S Austria
Friesche Eilanden see Frisian Islands
103 F22 Friesenheim Baden-Württemberg, SW Germany
Friesische Inseln see Frisian Islands
100 K6 Friesland ◐ province N Netherlands
62 Q10 Frio, Cabo headland SE Brazil
26 M3 Friona Texas, SW USA
44 L12 Frío, Río ≈ N Costa Rica
27 R13 Frio River ≈ Texas, SW USA
101 M25 Frisange Luxembourg, S Luxembourg
Frisches Haff see Vistula Lagoon
38 J6 Frisco Peak ▲ Utah, W USA
86 F9 Frisian Islands Dut. Friesche Eilanden, Ger. Friesische Inseln. island group N Europe
20 L12 Frissell, Mount ▲ Connecticut, NE USA
97 J19 Fristad Älvsborg, S Sweden
27 N2 Fritch Texas, SW USA
97 J19 Fritsla Älvsborg, S Sweden
103 H16 Fritzlar Hessen, C Germany
108 H6 Friuli-Venezia Giulia ◐ region NE Italy
Frjentsjer see Franeker
206 L13 Frobisher Bay inlet Baffin Island, Northwest Territories, NE Canada
Frobisher Bay see Iqaluit
9 S12 Frobisher Lake ◎ Saskatchewan, C Canada
96 G7 Frohavet sound C Norway
Frohenbruck see Veselí nad Lužnicí
111 V7 Frohnleiten Steiermark, SE Austria
101 G22 Froidchapelle Hainaut, S Belgium
131 O9 Frolovo Volgogradskaya Oblast', SW Russian Federation
112 K7 Frombork Ger. Frauenburg. Elbląg, N Poland
99 L22 Frome SW England, UK
190 I4 Frome Creek seasonal river South Australia
190 J6 Frome Downs South Australia
190 J5 Frome, Lake salt lake South Australia
Fronicken see Wronki
106 H10 Fronteira Portalegre, C Portugal
42 M7 Frontera Coahuila de Zaragoza, NE Mexico
43 U14 Frontera Tabasco, SE Mexico
42 G3 Fronteras Sonora, NW Mexico
105 Q16 Frontignan Hérault, S France
56 D8 Frontino Antioquia, NW Colombia
23 V4 Front Royal Virginia, NE USA
109 J16 Frosinone anc. Frusino. Lazio, C Italy
109 K16 Frosolone Molise, C Italy
27 U7 Frost Texas, SW USA
23 U2 Frostburg Maryland, NE USA
25 X13 Frostproof Florida, SE USA
Frostviken see Kvarnbergsvattnet
97 M15 Frövi Örebro, C Sweden
96 F7 Frøya island W Norway
39 P5 Fruita Colorado, C USA
30 J9 Fruitdale South Dakota, N USA
25 W11 Fruitland Park Florida, SE USA
Frumentum see Formentera
153 S11 Frunze Oshskaya Oblast', SW Kyrgyzstan
Frunze see Bishkek
119 O9 Frunzivka Odes'ka Oblast', SW Ukraine
Frusino see Frosinone
110 E9 Frutigen Bern, W Switzerland
113 I17 Frýdek-Místek Ger. Friedek-Mistek. Severní Morava, SE Czech Republic
200 Qq16 Fua'amotu Tongatapu, S Tonga
202 A9 Fuafatu island Funafuti Atoll, C Tuvalu
202 A9 Fuagea island Funafuti Atoll, C Tuvalu
202 B8 Fualifeke atoll C Tuvalu
202 A8 Fualopa island Funafuti Atoll, C Tuvalu
157 K22 Fuammulah var. Gnaviyani Atoll. atoll S Maldives
167 R11 Fu'an Fujian, SE China
Fu-chien see Fujian
Fu-chou see Fuzhou
170 F13 Fuchū var. Hutyû. Hiroshima, Honshū, SW Japan
166 M13 Fuchuan Guangxi Zhuangzu Zizhiqu, S China
172 N11 Fudai Iwate, Honshū, C Japan
167 S11 Fuding Fujian, SE China
83 J20 Fudua spring/well S Kenya
106 M16 Fuengirola Andalucía, S Spain
106 J12 Fuente de Cantos Extremadura, W Spain
106 J11 Fuente del Maestre Extremadura, W Spain
106 L12 Fuente Obejuna Andalucía, S Spain
106 L6 Fuentesaúco Castilla-León, N Spain
64 O3 Fuerte Olimpo var. Olimpo. Alto Paraguay, NE Paraguay
42 H8 Fuerte, Río ≈ C Mexico
66 Q11 Fuerteventura island Islas Canarias, Spain, NE Atlantic Ocean
147 S14 Fughmah var. Faghman, Fugma. C Yemen
94 M2 Fuglehuken headland W Svalbard
207 T15 Fugloya Bank undersea feature E Norwegian Sea
Fugma see Fughmah
83 K16 Fugugo spring/well NE Kenya
164 L2 Fuhai var. Burultokay. Xinjiang Uygur Zizhiqu, NW China
167 P10 Fu He ≈ S China
Fuhkien see Fujian
102 J9 Fuhlsbüttel ✕ (Hamburg) Hamburg, N Germany
103 L14 Fuhne ≈ C Germany
Fu-hsin see Fuxin
Fujairah see Al Fujayrah
171 J17 Fuji var. Huzi. Shizuoka, Honshū, S Japan
167 Q12 Fujian var. Fu-chien, Fuhkien, Fujian Sheng, Fukien, Min. ◐ province SE China
166 I9 Fu Jiang ≈ C China
Fujian Sheng see Fujian
171 I17 Fujieda var. Huzieda. Shizuoka, Honshū, S Japan
Fuji, Mount/Fujiyama see Fuji-san
169 Y7 Fujin Heilongjiang, NE China
171 J16 Fujinomiya var. Huzinomiya. Shizuoka, Honshū, S Japan
171 J16 Fuji-san var. Fujiyama, Eng. Mount Fuji. ▲ Honshū, SE Japan
171 Jj17 Fujisawa var. Huzisawa. Kanagawa, Honshū, S Japan
171 J16 Fuji-Yoshida var. Huziyosida. Yamanashi, Honshū, S Japan
172 Oo4 Fukagawa var. Hukagawa. Hokkaidō, NE Japan
164 L5 Fukang Xinjiang Uygur Zizhiqu, W China
171 M8 Fukaura Aomori, Honshū, C Japan
200 R15 Fukave island Tongatapu Group, S Tonga
Fukien see Fujian
171 Gg14 Fukuchiyama var. Hukutiyama. Kyōto, Honshū, SW Japan
170 B12 Fukue var. Hukue. Nagasaki, Fukue-jima, SW Japan
170 B12 Fukue-jima island Gotō-rettō, SW Japan
171 Hh13 Fukui var. Hukui. Fukui, Honshū, SW Japan
171 Hh14 Fukui off. Fukui-ken, var. Hukui. ◐ prefecture Honshū, SW Japan
170 C12 Fukuoka var. Hukuoka; hist. Najima. Fukuoka, Kyūshū, SW Japan
170 Cc13 Fukuoka off. Fukuoka-ken, var. Hukuoka. ◐ prefecture Kyūshū, SW Japan
171 L13 Fukushima var. Hukusima. Fukushima, Honshū, C Japan
171 Mm7 Fukushima Hokkaidō, NE Japan
171 Kk14 Fukushima off. Fukushima-ken, var. Hukusima. ◐ prefecture Honshū, C Japan
170 F14 Fukuyama var. Hukuyama. Hiroshima, Honshū, SW Japan
78 G13 Fulacunda C Guinea-Bissau
133 P8 Fūlādī, Kūh-e ▲ E Afghanistan
197 K16 Fulaga island Lau Group, E Fiji
103 I17 Fulda Hessen, C Germany
31 S10 Fulda Minnesota, N USA
103 I16 Fulda ≈ C Germany
Fülek see Fil'akovo
Fulin see Hanyuan
166 K10 Fuling Sichuan, C China
37 T15 Fullerton California, SE USA
31 P15 Fullerton Nebraska, C USA
110 M8 Fulpmes Tirol, W Austria
22 G8 Fulton Kentucky, S USA
25 N2 Fulton Mississippi, S USA
29 V4 Fulton Missouri, C USA
20 H9 Fulton New York, NE USA
Fuman/Fumen see Fowman
105 R3 Fumay Ardennes, N France
104 M13 Fumel Lot-et-Garonne, SW France
171 K17 Funabashi var. Hunabasi. Chiba, Honshū, S Japan
202 B10 Funafara atoll C Tuvalu
202 C9 Funafuti ✕ Funafuti Atoll, C Tuvalu
Funafuti see Fongafale
202 F8 Funafuti Atoll atoll C Tuvalu
202 B9 Funangongo atoll C Tuvalu
95 F17 Funäsdalen Jämtland, C Sweden
66 O6 Funchal Madeira, Portugal, NE Atlantic Ocean
66 P5 Funchal ✕ Madeira, Portugal, NE Atlantic Ocean
56 F5 Fundación Magdalena, N Colombia
106 I8 Fundão var. Fundão. Castelo Branco, C Portugal
11 O16 Fundy, Bay of bay Canada/USA
Fünen see Fyn
56 C13 Fúnes Nariño, SW Colombia
Fünfkirchen see Pécs
85 M19 Funhalouro Inhambane, S Mozambique
167 R6 Funing Jiangsu, E China
166 I14 Funing Yunnan, SW China
166 M7 Funiu Shan ▲▲ C China
79 U13 Funtua Katsina, N Nigeria
167 R12 Fuqing Fujian, SE China
85 M14 Furancungo Tete, NW Mozambique
172 P5 Furano var. Hurano. Hokkaidō, NE Japan
118 I15 Furculeşti Teleorman, S Romania
Füred see Balatonfüred
172 Qq7 Füren-ko ◎ Hokkaidō, NE Japan
149 R12 Fürg Fārs, S Iran
Furluk see Fârliug
Fürmanov see Furmanovka
151 S15 Furmanovka Kaz. Fūrmanov. Zhambyl, S Kazakhstan
150 E9 Furmanovo Zapadnyy Kazakhstan, W Kazakhstan
61 L20 Furnas, Represa de ⊠ SE Brazil
191 Q14 Furneaux Group island group Tasmania, SE Australia
Furnes see Veurne
166 J10 Furong Jiang ≈ S China
144 I5 Furqlus Ḥimṣ, W Syria
102 F12 Fürstenau Niedersachsen, NW Germany
111 X8 Fürstenfeld Steiermark, SE Austria
103 L23 Fürstenfeldbruck Bayern, S Germany
102 P12 Fürstenwalde Brandenburg, NE Germany
103 K20 Fürth Bayern, S Germany
111 W3 Furth bei Göttweig Niederösterreich, NW Austria
172 O4 Furubira Hokkaidō, NE Japan
96 L12 Furudal Kopparberg, C Sweden
171 Ii14 Furukawa Gifu, Honshū, SW Japan
171 M12 Furukawa var. Hurukawa. Miyagi, Honshū, C Japan
56 F10 Fusagasugá Cundinamarca, C Colombia
Fusan see Pusan
Fushë-Arëzi/Fushë-Arrësi see Fushë-Arrëz
115 L18 Fushë-Arrëz var. Fushë-Arëzi, Fushë-Arrësi. Shkodër, N Albania
Fushë-Kruja see Fushë-Krujë
115 K19 Fushë-Krujë var. Fushë-Kruja. Durrës, C Albania
169 V12 Fushun var. Fou-shan, Fu-shun. Liaoning, NE China
Fusin see Fuxin
110 G10 Fusio Ticino, S Switzerland
169 X11 Fusong Jilin, NE China
103 K24 Füssen Bayern, S Germany
166 K15 Fusui prev. Funan. Guangxi Zhuangzu Zizhiqu, S China
Futa Jallon see Fouta Djallon
65 G18 Futaleufú Los Lagos, S Chile
114 K10 Futog Serbia, NW Yugoslavia
171 K17 Futtsu var. Huttu. Chiba, Honshū, S Japan
197 E16 Futuna island S Vanuatu
202 D12 Futuna, Île island S Wallis and Futuna
167 Q11 Futun Xi ≈ SE China
166 L5 Fuxian var. Fu Xian. Shaanxi, C China
Fuxian see Wafangdian
166 G13 Fuxian Hu ◎ SW China
169 U12 Fuxin var. Fou-hsin, Fu-hsin, Fusin. Liaoning, NE China
Fuxing see Wangmo
167 P7 Fuyang Anhui, E China
167 O4 Fuyang He ≈ E China
169 U7 Fuyu Heilongjiang, NE China
Fuyu/Fu-yü see Songyuan
169 Z6 Fuyuan Heilongjiang, NE China
164 M3 Fuyun var. Koktokay. Xinjiang Uygur Zizhiqu, NW China
113 L22 Füzesabony Heves, E Hungary
167 R12 Fuzhou var. Foochow, Fu-chou. Fujian, SE China
Fuzhou see Linchuan
143 W13 Füzuli Rus. Fizuli. SW Azerbaijan
121 I20 Fyadory Rus. Fëdory. Brestskaya Voblasts', SW Belarus
97 G24 Fyn off. Fyns Amt, var. Fünen. ◐ county C Denmark
97 G23 Fyn Ger. Fünen. island C Denmark
98 H12 Fyne, Loch inlet W Scotland, UK
97 E16 Fyresvatnet ◎ S Norway
FYR Macedonia/FYROM see Macedonia, FYR
Fyzabad see Feyzābād

G

83 O14 Gaalkacyo var. Galka'yo, It. Galcaio. Mudug, C Somalia
Gabakly see Kabakly
116 H8 Gabare Oblast Montana, NW Bulgaria
104 K15 Gabas ≈ SW France
37 T7 Gabbs Nevada, W USA
84 B12 Gabela Cuanza Sul, W Angola
Gaberones see Gaborone
201 X14 Gabert island Caroline Islands, E Micronesia
76 M7 Gabès var. Qābis. E Tunisia
76 M6 Gabès, Golfe de Ar. Khalīj Qābis. gulf E Tunisia
Gablonz an der Neisse see Jablonec nad Nisou
Gablös see Cavalese
81 E18 Gabon off. Gabonese Republic. ◆ republic C Africa
85 I20 Gaborone prev. Gaberones. ● (Botswana) South East, SE Botswana
85 I20 Gaborone ✕ South East, SE Botswana
106 K8 Gabriel y Galán, Embalse de ⊠ W Spain
149 U15 Gābrik, Rūd-e ≈ SE Iran
116 J9 Gabrovo Loveshka Oblast, C Bulgaria
78 H12 Gabú prev. Nova Lamego. E Guinea-Bissau
31 O6 Gackle North Dakota, N USA
115 I15 Gacko S Bosnia and Herzegovina
161 F17 Gadag Karnātaka, W India
95 G15 Gäddede Jämtland, C Sweden
165 S12 Gadê Qinghai, C China
Gades/Gadier/Gadir/Gadire see Cádiz
107 P15 Gádor, Sierra de ▲▲ S Spain
155 S15 Gadra Sind, SE Pakistan
25 Q3 Gadsden Alabama, S USA
38 H15 Gadsden Arizona, SW USA
Gadyach see Hadyach
81 H15 Gadzi Mambéré-Kadéï, SW Central African Republic
118 J13 Găeşti Dâmboviţa, S Romania
109 J17 Gaeta Lazio, C Italy
109 J17 Gaeta, Golfo di var. Gulf of Gaeta. gulf C Italy
196 L14 Gaferut atoll Caroline Islands, W Micronesia
23 Q10 Gaffney South Carolina, SE USA
Gäfle see Gävle
Gäfleborg see Gävleborg
76 M6 Gafsa var. Qafṣah. W Tunisia
Gafurov see Ghafurov
130 J3 Gagarin Smolenskaya Oblast', W Russian Federation
153 O10 Gagarin Jizzakh Wiloyati, C Uzbekistan
103 G21 Gaggenau Baden-Württemberg, SW Germany
196 F16 Gagil Tamil var. Gagil-Tomil. island Caroline Islands, W Micronesia
Gagil-Tomil see Gagil Tamil
131 O4 Gagino Nizhegorodskaya Oblast', W Russian Federation
109 Q19 Gagliano del Capo Puglia, SE Italy
96 L13 Gagnef Kopparberg, C Sweden
78 M17 Gagnoa C Ivory Coast
11 N10 Gagnon Québec, E Canada
Gago Coutinho see Lumbala N'Guimbo
175 T8 Gag, Pulau island E Indonesia
143 P8 Gagra NW Georgia
33 S13 Gahanna Ohio, N USA
149 R13 Gahkom Hormozgān, S Iran
Gahnpa see Ganta
59 Q19 Gaiba, Laguna ◎ E Bolivia
159 T13 Gaibanda var. Gaibandah. Rajshahi, NW Bangladesh
Gaibandah see Gaibanda
Gaibhlte, Cnoc Mór na n see Galtymore Mountain
111 R9 Gail ≈ S Austria
103 I21 Gaildorf Baden-Württemberg, S Germany
105 N15 Gaillac var. Gaillac-sur-Tarn. Tarn, S France
Gaillac-sur-Tarn see Gaillac
Gaillimh see Galway
Gaillimhe, Cuan na see Galway Bay
111 Q9 Gailtaler Alpen ▲▲ S Austria
65 J17 Gaimán Chaco, S Argentina
22 K8 Gainesboro Tennessee, S USA
25 V10 Gainesville Florida, SE USA
25 T2 Gainesville Georgia, SE USA
29 U8 Gainesville Missouri, C USA
27 T5 Gainesville Texas, SW USA
111 X5 Gainfarn Niederösterreich, NE Austria
99 N18 Gainsborough E England, UK
190 G6 Gairdner, Lake salt lake South Australia
94 I8 Gaissane ▲▲ N Norway
45 T15 Gaital, Cerro ▲ C Panama
23 W3 Gaithersburg Maryland, NE USA
169 U13 Gaizhou Liaoning, NE China
Gaiziņ see Gaiziņa Kalns
120 I9 Gaiziņa Kalns var. Gaiziņ. ▲ E Latvia
Gajac see Villeneuve-sur-Lot
174 L15 Gajahmungkur, Danau ◎ Jawa, S Indonesia
41 S10 Gakona Alaska, USA
Galaassiya see Galaosiyo
Galāgil see Jalājil
Galam, Pulau see Gelam, Pulau
64 J6 Galán, Cerro ▲ NW Argentina
113 H21 Galanta Hung. Galánta. Západné Slovensko, SW Slovakia
152 L11 Galaosiye Rus. Galaassiya. Bukhoro Wiloyati, C Uzbekistan
59 B17 Galápagos off. Provincia de Galápagos. ◐ province Ecuador, E Pacific Ocean
199 M9 Galapagos Fracture Zone tectonic feature E Pacific Ocean
200 O10 Galapagos Rise undersea feature E Pacific Ocean
98 K13 Galashiels SE Scotland, UK
118 M12 Galaţi Ger. Galatz. Galaţi, E Romania
118 L12 Galaţi ◐ county E Romania
109 Q19 Galatina Puglia, SE Italy
109 Q19 Galatone Puglia, SE Italy
Galatz see Galaţi
23 R8 Galax Virginia, NE USA
Galaymor see Kala-i-Mor
Galcaio see Gaalkacyo
66 P11 Gáldar Gran Canaria, Islas Canarias, Spain NE Atlantic Ocean
96 F11 Galdhøpiggen ▲ S Norway
42 I4 Galeana Chihuahua, N Mexico
43 O9 Galeana Nuevo León, NE Mexico
62 P9 Galeão ✕ (Rio de Janeiro) Rio de Janeiro, SE Brazil
175 T6 Galela Pulau Halmahera, E Indonesia
41 O9 Galena Alaska, USA
32 K10 Galena Illinois, N USA
27 R7 Galena Kansas, C USA
29 T8 Galena Missouri, C USA
47 V15 Galeota Point headland Trinidad, Trinidad and Tobago
107 P13 Galera Andalucía, S Spain
47 Y16 Galera Point headland Trinidad, Trinidad and Tobago
58 A5 Galera, Punta headland NW Ecuador
32 K12 Galesburg Illinois, N USA
32 J7 Galesville Wisconsin, N USA
20 F12 Galeton Pennsylvania, NE USA
118 H9 Gâlgău Hung. Galgó; prev. Gilgău. Sălaj, NW Romania
Galgó see Gâlgău
Galgóc see Hlohovec
83 N15 Galguduud off. Gobolka Galguduud. ◐ region E Somalia
143 Q9 Gali W Georgia
129 N14 Galich Kostromskaya Oblast', NW Russian Federation
116 H7 Galiche Oblast Montana, NW Bulgaria
106 H3 Galicia anc. Gallaecia. ◐ autonomous community NW Spain
66 M8 Galicia Bank undersea feature E Atlantic Ocean
Galilee see HaGalil
189 W7 Galilee, Lake ◎ Queensland, NE Australia
Galilee, Sea of see Tiberias, Lake
108 E11 Galileo Galilei ✕ (Pisa) Toscana, C Italy
33 S12 Galion Ohio, N USA
Galka'yo see Gaalkacyo
82 H11 Gallabat Gedaref, E Sudan
Gallaecia see Galicia
108 C7 Gallarate Lombardia, NW Italy
29 S2 Gallatin Missouri, C USA
22 J8 Gallatin Tennessee, S USA
35 R11 Gallatin Peak ▲ Montana, NW USA
35 R12 Gallatin River ≈ Montana/Wyoming, NW USA
161 J26 Galle prev. Point de Galle. Southern Province, SW Sri Lanka
107 S5 Gállego ≈ NE Spain
200 N9 Gallego Rise undersea feature E Pacific Ocean
Gallegos see Río Gallegos
65 H23 Gallegos, Río ≈ Argentina/Chile
Gallia see France
24 K10 Galliano Louisiana, S USA
117 G14 Gallikós ≈ N Greece
39 S12 Gallinas Peak ▲ New Mexico, SW USA
56 H3 Gallinas, Punta headland NE Colombia
39 T11 Gallinas River ≈ New Mexico, SW USA
109 Q19 Gallipoli Puglia, SE Italy
Gallipoli see Gelibolu
Gallipoli Peninsula see Gelibolu Yarımadası
33 T15 Gallipolis Ohio, N USA
94 J12 Gällivare Norrbotten, N Sweden
111 T4 Gallneukirchen Oberösterreich, N Austria
107 Q7 Gallo ≈ C Spain
95 G17 Gällö Jämtland, C Sweden
109 I23 Gallo, Capo headland Sicilia, Italy, C Mediterranean Sea
39 P13 Gallo Mountains ▲ New Mexico, SW USA
20 G8 Galloo Island island New York, NE USA
99 H15 Galloway, Mull of headland S Scotland, UK
39 P10 Gallup New Mexico, SW USA
107 R5 Gallur Aragón, NE Spain
Gâlma see Guelma
37 O8 Galt California, W USA
76 C10 Galtat-Zemmour C Western Sahara
97 G22 Galten Århus, C Denmark
99 D20 Galtymore Mountain Ir. Cnoc Mór na nGaibhlte. ▲ S Ireland
99 D20 Galty Mountains Ir. Na Gaibhlte. ▲▲ S Ireland
32 K11 Galva Illinois, N USA
27 X12 Galveston Texas, SW USA
27 W11 Galveston Bay inlet Texas, SW USA
27 W12 Galveston Island island Texas, SW USA
63 B18 Gálvez Santa Fe, C Argentina
99 C18 Galway Ir. Gaillimh. W Ireland
99 B18 Galway Ir. Gaillimh. cultural region W Ireland
99 B18 Galway Bay Ir. Cuan na Gaillimhe. bay W Ireland
85 F18 Gam Otjozondjupa, NE Namibia
194 G14 Gama ≈ SW PNG
171 Hh16 Gamagōri Aichi, Honshū, SW Japan
56 F7 Gamarra Cesar, N Colombia
Gâmas see Kaamanen
164 L17 Gamba Xizang Zizhiqu, W China
79 P14 Gambaga NE Ghana
83 G14 Gambēla W Ethiopia
40 K10 Gambell Saint Lawrence Island, Alaska, USA
78 E12 Gambia off. Republic of The Gambia, The Gambia. ◆ republic W Africa
78 I12 Gambia Fr. Gambie. ≈ W Africa
66 K12 Gambia Plain undersea feature E Atlantic Ocean
Gambie see Gambia
33 T13 Gambier Ohio, N USA
203 Y13 Gambier, Îles island group E French Polynesia
190 G10 Gambier Islands island group South Australia
81 H19 Gamboma Plateaux, E Congo
81 G16 Gamboula Mambéré-Kadéï, SW Central African Republic
39 P10 Gamerco New Mexico, SW USA
143 V12 Gamiş Dağı ▲ W Azerbaijan
Gamlakarleby see Kokkola
97 N18 Gamleby Kalmar, S Sweden
Gammelstad see Gammelstaden
95 J14 Gammelstaden var. Gammelstad. Norrbotten, N Sweden
Gammouda see Sidi Bouzid
161 J25 Gampaha Western Province, W Sri Lanka
161 K25 Gampola Central Province, C Sri Lanka
176 Uu8 Gam, Pulau island E Indonesia
178 Jj5 Gâm, Sông ≈ N Vietnam
94 L7 Gamvik Finnmark, N Norway
156 H13 Gan Addu Atoll, C Maldives
Gan see Gansu, China
Gan see Jiangxi, China
Ganaane see Juba
39 O10 Ganado Arizona, SW USA
27 U12 Ganado Texas, SW USA
12 L14 Gananoque Ontario, SE Canada
Ganāveh see Bandar-e Gonāveh
143 V11 Gäncä Rus. Gyandzha; prev. Kirovabad, Yelisavetpol. W Azerbaijan
Ganchi see Ghonchí
Gand see Gent
84 B13 Ganda var. Mariano Machado, Port. Vila Mariano Machado. Benguela, W Angola
81 L22 Gandajika Kasai Oriental, S Zaire
159 O12 Gandak Nep. Nārāyāni. ≈ India/Nepal
11 U11 Gander Newfoundland, Newfoundland and Labrador, SE Canada
11 U11 Gander ✕ Newfoundland, Newfoundland and Labrador, E Canada
102 G11 Ganderkesee Niedersachsen, NW Germany
107 T7 Gandesa Cataluña, NE Spain
160 B10 Gāndhīdhām Gujarāt, W India
160 D10 Gāndhīnagar Gujarāt, W India
160 F9 Gāndhi Sāgar ◎ C India
107 T11 Gandía País Valenciano, E Spain
165 O10 Gang Qinghai, W China
158 G9 Gangānagar Rājasthān, NW India
158 I12 Gangāpur Rājasthān, N India
159 S17 Ganga Sāgar West Bengal, NE India
Gangavathi see Gangāwati
161 G17 Gangāwati var. Gangavathi. Karnātaka, C India
165 S9 Gangca var. Shaliuhe. Qinghai, C China
164 H14 Gangdisê Shan Eng. Kailas Range. ▲▲ W China
105 Q15 Ganges Hérault, S France
159 P13 Ganges Ben. Padma. ≈ Bangladesh/India see also Padma
Ganges Cone see Ganges Fan
181 S3 Ganges Fan var. Ganges Cone. undersea feature N Bay of Bengal
159 U17 Ganges, Mouths of the delta Bangladesh/India
109 K23 Gangi anc. Engyum. Sicilia, Italy, C Mediterranean Sea
158 K8 Gangotri Uttar Pradesh, N India
Gangra see Çankırı
159 S11 Gangtok Sikkim, N India
165 W11 Gangu Gansu, C China
169 U5 Gan He ≈ NE China
175 T9 Gani Pulau Halmahera, E Indonesia
167 O12 Gan Jiang ≈ S China
152 H15 Gannaly Akhalskiy Velayat, S Turkmenistan
169 U7 Gannan Heilongjiang, NE China
105 P10 Gannat Allier, C France
35 T14 Gannett Peak ▲ Wyoming, C USA
31 O10 Gannvalley South Dakota, N USA
111 Y3 Gänserndorf Niederösterreich, NE Austria
Gansos, Lago dos see Goose Lake
165 T9 Gansu var. Gan, Gansu Sheng, Kansu. ◐ province N China
Gansu Sheng see Gansu
78 K16 Ganta var. Gahnpa. NE Liberia
190 H11 Gantheaume, Cape headland South Australia
Gantsevichi see Hantsavichy
167 Q6 Ganyu var. Qingkou. Jiangsu, E China
150 D12 Ganyushkino Atyrau, SW Kazakhstan
167 O12 Ganzhou Jiangxi, S China
79 Q10 Gao Gao, E Mali
79 R10 Gao ◐ region SE Mali
167 O10 Gao'an Jiangxi, S China
167 N5 Gaoping Shanxi, C China
165 S8 Gaotai Gansu, N China
Gaoth Dobhair see Gweedore
79 O14 Gaoua SW Burkina
78 I13 Gaoual Moyenne-Guinée, N Guinea
Gaoxiong see Kaohsiung
167 R7 Gaoyou var. Dayishan. Jiangsu, E China
167 R7 Gaoyou Hu ◎ E China
166 M15 Gaozhou Guangdong, S China
105 T13 Gap anc. Vapincum. Hautes-Alpes, SE France
164 G13 Gar var. Gar Xincun. Xizang Zizhiqu, W China
Garabekevyul/Garabekewül see Karabekaul
Garabogazköl see Kara-Bogaz-Gol
45 V16 Garachiné Darién, SE Panama
45 V16 Garachiné, Punta headland SE Panama
Garagan see Karagan
56 G10 Garagoa Boyacá, C Colombia
Garagöl see Karagel'
Garagum see Garagumy
Garagum Kanaly see Garagumskiy Kanal
152 E12 Garagumskiy Kanal var. Kara Kum Canal, Karakumskiy Kanal, Turkm. Garagum Kanaly. canal C Turkmenistan
152 F12 Garagumy var. Qara Qum, Eng. Black Sand Desert, Kara Kum, Turkm. Garagum; prev. Peski Karakumy. desert C Turkmenistan
191 S4 Garah New South Wales, SE Australia
66 O11 Garajonay ▲ Gomera, Islas Canarias, Spain NE Atlantic Ocean
116 M8 Gara Khitrino Varnenska Oblast, NE Bulgaria
78 L13 Garalo Sikasso, SW Mali
Garam see Hron
Garamäbnyyaz see Karamet-Niyaz
Garamszentkereszt see Žiar nad Hronom
79 Q13 Garango S Burkina
61 Q15 Garanhuns Pernambuco, E Brazil
196 H5 Garapan Saipan, S Northern Mariana Islands
Gárassavon see Kaaresuvanto
80 J13 Garba Bamingui-Bangoran, N Central African Republic
83 L16 Garbahaarrey It. Garba Harre. Gedo, SW Somalia
Garba Harre see Garbahaarrey
83 J18 Garba Tula Eastern, C Kenya
29 N9 Garber Oklahoma, C USA
36 L4 Garberville California, W USA
102 I12 Garbsen Niedersachsen, N Germany
62 K9 Garça São Paulo, S Brazil
106 L10 García de Solá, Embalse de ⊠ C Spain
105 Q14 Gard ◐ department S France
105 Q14 Gard ≈ S France
108 F7 Garda, Lago di var. Benaco, Eng. Lake Garda, Ger. Gardasee. ◎ NE Italy
Garda, Lake see Garda, Lago di
Gardan Divāl see Gardan Dīwāl
155 Q5 Gardan Dīwāl var. Gardan Divāl. Wardag, C Afghanistan
105 S15 Gardanne Bouches-du-Rhône, SE France
Gardasee see Garda, Lago di
102 L12 Gardelegen Sachsen-Anhalt, C Germany
12 B10 Garden ≈ Ontario, S Canada
25 X6 Garden City Georgia, SE USA
28 I6 Garden City Kansas, C USA
29 S5 Garden City Missouri, C USA
27 N8 Garden City Texas, SW USA
25 P3 Gardendale Alabama, S USA
33 P5 Garden Island island Michigan, N USA
24 M11 Garden Island Bay bay Louisiana, S USA
33 O5 Garden Peninsula peninsula Michigan, N USA
Garden State see New Jersey
97 I14 Gardermoen Akershus, S Norway
Gardeyz see Gardēz
155 Q6 Gardēz var. Gardeyz, Gordiaz. Paktīā, E Afghanistan
95 G14 Gardiken ◎ N Sweden
21 Q7 Gardiner Maine, NE USA
35 S12 Gardiner Montana, NW USA
21 N13 Gardiners Island island New York, NE USA
Gardner Island see Nikumaroro
21 T6 Gardner Lake ◎ Maine, NE USA
37 Q6 Gardnerville Nevada, W USA
Gardo see Qardho
108 F7 Gardone Val Trompia Lombardia, N Italy
Garegegasnjárga see Karigasniemi
40 F17 Gareloi Island island Aleutian Islands, Alaska, USA
108 B10 Garessio Piemonte, NE Italy
34 M9 Garfield Washington, NW USA
33 U11 Garfield Heights Ohio, N USA
Gargaliani see Gargaliánoi
117 D21 Gargaliánoi var. Gargaliani. Pelopónnisos, S Greece
109 N15 Gargano, Promontorio del headland SE Italy
110 J8 Gargellen Graubünden, W Switzerland
95 I14 Gargnäs Västerbotten, N Sweden

◆ Country ● Country Capital ◇ Dependent Territory ○ Dependent Territory Capital ◐ Administrative Region ✕ International Airport ▲ Mountain ▲▲ Mountain Range ✱ Volcano ≈ River ◎ Lake ⊠ Reservoir

GARGŽDAI – GILLOT

120 C11 **Gargždai** Gargždai, W Lithuania
160 J13 **Garhchiroli** Mahārāshtra, C India
159 O15 **Garhwa** Bihār, N India
176 Ww11 **Gariau** Irian Jaya, E Indonesia
85 E24 **Garies** Northern Cape, W South Africa
83 K19 **Garissa** Coast, E Kenya
23 V11 **Garland** North Carolina, SE USA
27 T6 **Garland** Texas, SW USA
36 L1 **Garland** Utah, W USA
108 D8 **Garlasco** Lombardia, N Italy
121 F14 **Garliava** Kaunas, S Lithuania
Garm see Gharm
148 M9 **Garm, Āb-e** var. Rūd-e Khersān. ∽ SW Iran
103 K25 **Garmisch-Partenkirchen** Bayern, S Germany
149 O5 **Garmsār** prev. Qishlaq. Semnān, N Iran
Garmser see Darvishān
31 V12 **Garner** Iowa, C USA
23 U9 **Garner** North Carolina, SE USA
29 Q5 **Garnett** Kansas, C USA
101 M25 **Garnich** Luxembourg, SW Luxembourg
190 M8 **Garnpung, Lake** salt lake New South Wales, SE Australia
Garoe see Garoowe
Garoet see Garut
159 U13 **Gāro Hills** hill range NE India
104 K13 **Garonne** anc. Garumna. ∽ S France
82 P13 **Garoowe** var. Garoe. Nugaal, N Somalia
80 F12 **Garoua** var. Garua. Nord, N Cameroon
81 G14 **Garoua Boulaï** Est, E Cameroon
79 O10 **Garou, Lac** ◎ C Mali
194 M11 **Garove Island** island Witu Islands, C PNG
97 L16 **Garphyttan** Örebro, C Sweden
31 R11 **Garretson** South Dakota, N USA
33 Q11 **Garrett** Indiana, N USA
35 Q10 **Garrison** Montana, NW USA
30 M4 **Garrison** North Dakota, N USA
27 X8 **Garrison** Texas, SW USA
30 L4 **Garrison Dam** dam North Dakota, N USA
106 J9 **Garrovillas** Extremadura, W Spain
Garrygala see Kara-Kala
15 J6 **Garry Lake** ◎ Northwest Territories, N Canada
Gars see Gars am Kamp
111 W3 **Gars am Kamp** var. Gars. Niederösterreich, NE Austria
83 K20 **Garsen** Coast, S Kenya
Garshy see Karshi
12 F10 **Garson** Ontario, S Canada
111 T5 **Garsten** Oberösterreich, N Austria
Gartar see Qianning
104 M10 **Gartempe** ∽ C France
Gartog see Markam
Garua see Garoua
85 D21 **Garub** Karas, SW Namibia
Garumna see Garonne
174 Jj15 **Garut** prev. Garoet. Jawa, C Indonesia
193 C20 **Garvie Mountains** ▲ South Island, NZ
112 N12 **Garwolin** Siedlce, E Poland
27 U12 **Garwood** Texas, SW USA
Gar Xincun see Gar
33 N11 **Gary** Indiana, N USA
27 X7 **Gary** Texas, SW USA
170 E12 **Garyū-san** ▲ Kyūshū, SW Japan
164 G13 **Gar Zangbo** ∽ W China
166 F8 **Garzê** Sichuan, C China
56 E12 **Garzón** Huila, S Colombia
152 B13 **Gasan-Kuli** var. Esenguly. Balkanskiy Velayat, W Turkmenistan
33 P13 **Gas City** Indiana, N USA
104 K15 **Gascogne** Eng. Gascony. cultural region S France
Gascogne, Golfe de see Gascony, Gulf of
28 V5 **Gasconade River** ∽ Missouri, C USA
Gascony see Gascogne
104 H15 **Gascony, Gulf of** var. Golfe de Gascogne. gulf France/Spain
188 H9 **Gascoyne Junction** Western Australia
181 V8 **Gascoyne Plain** undersea feature E Indian Ocean
188 H9 **Gascoyne River** ∽ Western Australia
199 I12 **Gascoyne Tablemount** undersea feature N Tasman Sea
69 U6 **Gash** var. Nahr al Qāsh. ∽ W Sudan
155 X3 **Gasherbrum** ▲ NE Pakistan
165 N9 **Gas Hu** ◎ C China
79 X12 **Gashua** Yobe, NE Nigeria
176 Uu9 **Gasim** Irian Jaya, E Indonesia
195 N12 **Gasmata** New Britain, E PNG
25 V14 **Gasparilla Island** island Florida, SE USA
174 Jj11 **Gaspar, Selat** strait W Indonesia
13 Y6 **Gaspé** Québec, SE Canada
13 Z6 **Gaspé, Cap de** headland Québec, SE Canada
13 X6 **Gaspé, Péninsule de** var. Péninsule de la Gaspésie. peninsula Québec, SE Canada
Gaspésie, Péninsule de la see Gaspé, Péninsule de
171 Ll12 **Gas-san** ▲ Honshū, C Japan
79 W15 **Gassol** Taraba, E Nigeria
Gastein see Badgastein
23 R10 **Gastonia** North Carolina, SE USA
23 V8 **Gaston, Lake** ⊞ North Carolina/Virginia, SE USA
117 D19 **Gastoúni** Dytikí Ellás, S Greece
65 I17 **Gastre** Chubut, S Argentina
Gat see Ghāt
107 P15 **Gata, Cabo de** headland S Spain
Gata, Cape see Gátas, Akrotíri
107 T11 **Gata de Gorgos** País Valenciano, E Spain
118 E12 **Gătaia** Ger. Gataja, Hung. Gátalja; prev. Gáttája. Timiș, W Romania
Gataja/Gátalja see Gătaia
124 Nn4 **Gátas, Akrotíri** var. Cape Gata. headland S Cyprus
106 J8 **Gata, Sierra de** ▲ W Spain
128 G13 **Gatchina** Leningradskaya Oblast', NW Russian Federation
23 P8 **Gate City** Virginia, NE USA
99 M14 **Gateshead** NE England, UK
15 Jj2 **Gateshead Island** island Northwest Territories, N Canada
23 X8 **Gatesville** North Carolina, SE USA
27 S8 **Gatesville** Texas, SW USA
12 L12 **Gatineau** Québec, SE Canada
12 L11 **Gatineau** ∽ Ontario/Québec, SE Canada
23 N9 **Gatlinburg** Tennessee, S USA
Gatooma see Kadoma
Gáttája see Gătaia
45 T14 **Gatún, Lago** ⊞ C Panama
61 N14 **Gaturiano** Piauí, NE Brazil
99 O22 **Gatwick** ✕ (London) SE England, UK
197 J15 **Gau** prev. Ngau. island C Fiji
Gaua see Santa Maria
106 L16 **Gaucín** Andalucía, S Spain
Gauhāti see Guwāhāti
120 I8 **Gauja** Ger. Aa. ∽ Estonia/Latvia
120 I7 **Gaujiena** Alūksne, NE Latvia
Gaul/Gaule see France
96 H9 **Gauldalen** valley S Norway
23 R5 **Gauley River** ∽ West Virginia, NE USA
101 D19 **Gaurain-Ramecroix** Hainaut, SW Belgium
97 F15 **Gausta** ▲ S Norway
85 J21 **Gauteng** off. Gauteng Province; prev. Pretoria-Witwatersrand-Vereeniging. ⬖ province NE South Africa
Gauteng see Germiston, South Africa
Gauteng see Johannesburg, South Africa
176 Y10 **Gauttier, Pegunungan** ▲ Irian Jaya, E Indonesia
149 P14 **Gāvbandī** Hormozgān, S Iran
117 H25 **Gavdopoúla** island SE Greece
117 H26 **Gávdos** island SE Greece
104 K16 **Gave de Pau** var. Gave-de-Pay. ∽ SW France
Gave-de-Pay see Gave de Pau
104 J16 **Gave d'Oloron** ∽ SW France
101 E18 **Gavere** Oost-Vlaanderen, NW Belgium
96 N13 **Gävle** var. Gäfle; prev. Gefle. Gävleborg, C Sweden
96 M11 **Gävleborg** var. Gäfleborg, Gefleborg. ⬖ county C Sweden
96 O13 **Gävlebukten** bay C Sweden
128 L16 **Gavrilov-Yam** Yaroslavskaya Oblast', W Russian Federation
195 P15 **Gawa Island** island SE Papau New Guinea
190 I9 **Gawler** South Australia
190 G7 **Gawler Ranges** hill range South Australia
Gawso see Goaso
168 H11 **Gaxun Nur** ◎ N China
159 P14 **Gaya** Bihār, N India
79 S13 **Gaya** Dosso, SW Niger
Gaya see Kyjov
33 Q6 **Gaylord** Michigan, N USA
31 U9 **Gaylord** Minnesota, N USA
189 Y9 **Gayndah** Queensland, E Australia
129 T12 **Gayny** Komi-Permyatskiy Avtonomnyy Okrug, NW Russian Federation
Gaysin see Haysyn
Gayvorno see Hayvoron
144 E11 **Gaza** Ar. Ghazzah, Heb. 'Azza. NE Gaza Strip
85 L20 **Gaza** off. Província de Gaza. ⬖ province SW Mozambique
152 I9 **Gaz-Achak** Turkm. Gazojak. Lebapskiy Velayat, NE Turkmenistan
Gazalkent see Ghazalkent
152 C11 **Gazandzhyk** Turkm. Gazanjyk; prev. Kazandzhik. Balkanskiy Velayat, W Turkmenistan
Gazanjyk see Gazandzhyk
79 V12 **Gazaoua** Maradi, S Niger
144 E11 **Gaza Strip** Ar. Qiṭā' Ghazzah. disputed region SW Asia
195 P11 **Gazelle Peninsula** headland New Britain, E PNG
197 J5 **Gazelle, Récif de la** reef C New Caledonia
Gazgan see Ghozghon
Gazi Antep see Gaziantep
142 M16 **Gaziantep** var. Gazi Antep; prev. Aintab, Antep. Gaziantep, S Turkey
142 M17 **Gaziantep** var. Gazi Antep. ⬖ province S Turkey
116 M13 **Gaziköy** Tekirdağ, NW Turkey
124 O3 **Gazimağusa** var. Famagusta, Gk. Ammóchostos. E Cyprus
124 Nn2 **Gazimağusa Körfezi** var. Famagusta Bay, Gk. Kólpos Ammóchostos. bay E Cyprus
152 K11 **Gazli** Bukhoro Wiloyati, C Uzbekistan
Gazojak see Gaz-Achak
81 K15 **Gbadolite** Equateur, NW Zaire
78 K16 **Gbanga** var. Gbarnga. N Liberia
Gbarnga see Gbanga
79 S14 **Gbéroubouè** var. Béroubouay. N Benin
79 W16 **Gboko** Benue, S Nigeria
Gcuwa see Butterworth
112 J7 **Gdańsk** Fr. Dantzig, Ger. Danzig. Gdańsk, N Poland
112 J7 **Gdańsk** off. Województwo Gdańskie, Fr. Dantzig, Ger. Danzig. ⬖ province N Poland
Gdan'skaya Bukhta/Gdańsk, Gulf of see Danzig, Gulf of
Gdańska, Zakota see Danzig, Gulf of
Gdańskie, Województwo see Gdańsk
Gdingen see Gdynia
128 F13 **Gdov** Pskovskaya Oblast', W Russian Federation
112 I6 **Gdynia** Ger. Gdingen. Gdańsk, N Poland
28 M10 **Geary** Oklahoma, C USA
Geavvú see Kevo
78 H12 **Gêba, Rio** ∽ C Guinea-Bissau
175 Tt8 **Gebe, Pulau** island E Indonesia
142 E11 **Gebze** Kocaeli, NW Turkey
124 O2 **Geçitkale** Gk. Lefkonico, Lefkónikon. NE Cyprus
82 H10 **Gedaref** var. Al Qaḍārif, El Gedaref. Gedaref, E Sudan
82 H10 **Gedaref** ⬖ state E Sudan
82 B11 **Gedid Ras el Fil** Southern Darfur, W Sudan
101 I23 **Gedinne** Namur, SE Belgium
142 E13 **Gediz** Kütahya, W Turkey
142 C14 **Gediz Nehri** ∽ W Turkey
83 N14 **Gedlegubē** SE Ethiopia
83 L17 **Gedo** off. Gobolka Gedo. ⬖ region SW Somalia
97 I25 **Gedser** Storstrøm, SE Denmark
101 I16 **Geel** var. Gheel. Antwerpen, N Belgium
191 N13 **Geelong** Victoria, SE Australia
Ge'e'mu see Golmud
101 I14 **Geertruidenberg** Noord-Brabant, S Netherlands
102 H10 **Geeste** ∽ NW Germany
102 J10 **Geesthacht** Schleswig-Holstein, N Germany
191 P17 **Geeveston** Tasmania, SE Australia
Gefle see Gävle
Gefleborg see Gävleborg
164 G13 **Gê'gyai** Xizang Zizhiqu, W China
79 X12 **Geidam** Yobe, NE Nigeria
9 T11 **Geikie** ∽ Saskatchewan, C Canada
96 F13 **Geilo** Buskerud, S Norway
96 E10 **Geiranger** Møre og Romsdal, S Norway
103 I22 **Geislingen** var. Geislingen an der Steige. Baden-Württemberg, SW Germany
Geislingen an der Steige see Geislingen
83 F20 **Geita** Mwanza, NW Tanzania
97 G15 **Geithus** Buskerud, S Norway
166 H14 **Gejiu** var. Kochiu. Yunnan, S China
Gëkdepe see Geok-Tepe
152 E9 **Geklengkui, Solonchak** var. Solonchak Goklenkuy. salt marsh NW Turkmenistan
83 D14 **Gel** ∽ W Sudan
109 K25 **Gela** prev. Terranova di Sicilia. Sicilia, Italy, C Mediterranean Sea
Gëladaindong see Glandaindong
83 N14 **Geladī** SE Ethiopia
174 Kk11 **Gelam, Pulau** var. Pulau Galam. island N Indonesia
100 L11 **Gelderland** prev. Eng. Guelders. ⬖ province E Netherlands
100 J13 **Geldermalsen** Gelderland, C Netherlands
103 D14 **Geldern** Nordrhein-Westfalen, W Germany
101 K15 **Geldrop** Noord-Brabant, SE Netherlands
101 L17 **Geleen** Limburg, SE Netherlands
130 K14 **Gelendzhik** Krasnodarskiy Kray, SW Russian Federation
Gelib see Jilib
142 B11 **Gelibolu** Eng. Gallipoli. Çanakkale, NW Turkey
117 L14 **Gelibolu Yarımadası** Eng. Gallipoli Peninsula. peninsula NW Turkey
Gelinting, Teluk see Geliting, Teluk
175 Qq16 **Geliting, Teluk** var. Teluk Gelinting. bay Nusa Tenggara, S Indonesia
83 O14 **Gellinsor** Mudug, C Somalia
103 H18 **Gelnhausen** Hessen, C Germany
103 E14 **Gelsenkirchen** Nordrhein-Westfalen, W Germany
85 C20 **Geluk** Hardap, SW Namibia
101 H20 **Gembloux** Namur, Belgium
194 I12 **Gembogl** Chimbu, C PNG
81 J16 **Gemena** Equateur, NW Zaire
101 L14 **Gemert** Noord-Brabant, SE Netherlands
142 E11 **Gemlik** Bursa, NW Turkey
Gem of the Mountains see Idaho
108 J6 **Gemona del Friuli** Friuli-Venezia Giulia, NE Italy
Gem State see Idaho
Genalē Wenz see Juba
174 Ll7 **Genali, Danau** ◎ Borneo, N Indonesia
101 G19 **Genappe** Walloon Brabant, C Belgium
143 P14 **Genç** Bingöl, E Turkey
Genck see Genk
100 M9 **Genemuiden** Overijssel, E Netherlands
65 K14 **General Acha** La Pampa, C Argentina
63 C21 **General Alvear** Buenos Aires, E Argentina
64 I12 **General Alvear** Mendoza, W Argentina
63 B20 **General Arenales** Buenos Aires, E Argentina
63 D21 **General Belgrano** Buenos Aires, E Argentina
204 H3 **General Bernardo O'Higgins** Chilean research station Antarctica
43 O8 **General Bravo** Nuevo León, NE Mexico
64 M7 **General Capdevila** Chaco, N Argentina
General Carrera, Lago see Buenos Aires, Lago
43 N9 **General Cepeda** Coahuila de Zaragoza, NE Mexico
65 K15 **General Conesa** Río Negro, E Argentina
63 G18 **General Enrique Martínez** Treinta y Tres, E Uruguay
64 L3 **General Eugenio A. Garay** var. Fortín General Eugenio Garay; prev. Yrendagüé. Nueva Asunción, NW Paraguay
63 C18 **General Galarza** Entre Ríos, E Argentina
63 E22 **General Guido** Buenos Aires, E Argentina
General José F.Uriburu see Zárate
63 E22 **General Juan Madariaga** Buenos Aires, E Argentina
43 O16 **General Juan N Alvarez** ✕ (Acapulco) Guerrero, S Mexico
63 B22 **General La Madrid** Buenos Aires, E Argentina
63 E21 **General Lavalle** Buenos Aires, E Argentina
General Machado see Camacupa
64 I8 **General Manuel Belgrano, Cerro** ▲ W Argentina
43 O8 **General Mariano Escobero** ✕ (Monterrey) Nuevo León, NE Mexico
63 B20 **General O'Brien** Buenos Aires, E Argentina
64 K13 **General Pico** La Pampa, C Argentina
64 M7 **General Pinedo** Chaco, N Argentina
63 B20 **General Pinto** Buenos Aires, E Argentina
63 E22 **General Pirán** Buenos Aires, E Argentina
45 N15 **General, Río** ∽ S Costa Rica
65 I15 **General Roca** Río Negro, C Argentina
179 Rr17 **General Santos** off. General Santos City. Mindanao, S Philippines
43 O9 **General Terán** Nuevo León, NE Mexico
116 N7 **General Toshevo** Rom. I.G.Duca, prev. Casim, Kasimköj. Varnenska Oblast, NE Bulgaria
63 B20 **General Viamonte** Buenos Aires, E Argentina
63 A20 **General Villegas** Buenos Aires, E Argentina
Gênes see Genova
20 E11 **Genesee River** ∽ New York/Pennsylvania, NE USA
32 K11 **Geneseo** Illinois, N USA
20 F10 **Geneseo** New York, NE USA
59 L14 **Geneshuaya, Río** ∽ N Bolivia
25 Q8 **Geneva** Alabama, S USA
32 M10 **Geneva** Illinois, N USA
31 Q16 **Geneva** Nebraska, C USA
20 G10 **Geneva** New York, NE USA
33 U10 **Geneva** Ohio, NE USA
Geneva see Genève
110 B10 **Geneva, Lake** Fr. Lac de Genève, Lac Léman, le Léman, Ger. Genfer See. ◎ France/Switzerland
110 A10 **Genève** Eng. Geneva, Ger. Genf, It. Ginevra. Genève, SW Switzerland
110 A11 **Genève** Eng. Geneva, Ger. Genf, It. Ginevra. ⬖ canton SW Switzerland
110 A10 **Genève** var. Geneva. ✕ Vaud, SW Switzerland
Genève, Lac de see Geneva, Lake
Genf see Genève
Genfer See see Geneva, Lake
169 S5 **Gen He** ∽ NE China
Genichesk see Heniches'k
106 L14 **Genil** ∽ S Spain
101 K18 **Genk** var. Genck. Limburg, NE Belgium
170 Cc12 **Genkai-nada** gulf Kyūshū, SW Japan
109 C19 **Gennargentu, Monti del** ▲ Sardegna, Italy, C Mediterranean Sea
101 M14 **Gennep** Limburg, SE Netherlands
32 M10 **Genoa** Illinois, N USA
31 Q15 **Genoa** Nebraska, C USA
Genoa see Genova
Genoa, Gulf of see Genova, Golfo di
108 D10 **Genova** Eng. Genoa, Fr. Gênes; anc. Genua. Liguria, NW Italy
108 D10 **Genova, Golfo di** Eng. Gulf of Genoa. gulf NW Italy
59 C17 **Genovesa, Isla** var. Tower Island. island Galapagos Islands, Ecuador, E Pacific Ocean
Genshū see Wŏnju
101 E17 **Gent** Eng. Ghent, Fr. Gand. Oost-Vlaanderen, NW Belgium
174 J15 **Genteng** Jawa, C Indonesia
102 M12 **Genthin** Sachsen-Anhalt, E Germany
29 R9 **Gentry** Arkansas, C USA
Genua see Genova
109 I15 **Genzano di Roma** Lazio, C Italy
Geokchay see Göyçay
152 F13 **Geok-Tepe** var. Gëkdepe, Turkm. Gökdepe. Akhalskiy Velayat, C Turkmenistan
126 Gg1 **George, Zemlya** Eng. George Land. island Zemlya Frantsa-Iosifa, N Russian Federation
85 G26 **George** Western Cape, S South Africa
31 S11 **George** Iowa, C USA
11 O5 **George** ∽ Newfoundland and Labrador/Québec, E Canada
67 C25 **George Island** island S Falkland Islands
191 R10 **George, Lake** ◎ New South Wales, SE Australia
83 E18 **George, Lake** ◎ SW Uganda
25 W10 **George, Lake** ◎ Florida, SE USA
20 L8 **George, Lake** ⊞ New York, NE USA
George Land see George, Zemlya
Georgenburg see Jurbarkas
George River see Kangiqsualujjuaq
66 G8 **Georges Bank** undersea feature W Atlantic Ocean
193 A21 **George Sound** sound South Island, NZ
67 F15 **Georgetown** ○ (Ascension Island) NW Ascension Island
189 V5 **Georgetown** Queensland, NE Australia
191 P15 **George Town** Tasmania, SE Australia
46 I4 **George Town** Great Exuma Island, C Bahamas
46 D8 **George Town** var. Georgetown. ○ (Cayman Islands) Grand Cayman, SW Cayman Islands
78 H12 **Georgetown** E Gambia
57 T8 **Georgetown** ● (Guyana) N Guyana
173 Ff3 **George Town** var. Penang, Pinang. Pinang, Peninsular Malaysia
47 Y14 **Georgetown** Saint Vincent, Saint Vincent and the Grenadines
23 Y4 **Georgetown** Delaware, NE USA
25 R6 **Georgetown** Georgia, SE USA
22 M5 **Georgetown** Kentucky, S USA
23 T13 **Georgetown** South Carolina, SE USA
27 S10 **Georgetown** Texas, SW USA
57 T8 **Georgetown** ✕ N Guyana
205 U16 **George V Coast** physical region Antarctica
205 T15 **George V Land** physical region Antarctica
204 J7 **George VI Ice Shelf** ice shelf Antarctica
204 J6 **George VI Sound** sound Antarctica
27 S14 **George West** Texas, SW USA
143 R9 **Georgia** off. Republic of Georgia, Geor. Sak'art'velo, Rus. Gruzinskaya SSR, Gruziya; prev. Georgian SSR. ◆ republic SW Asia
25 S5 **Georgia** off. State of Georgia; also known as Empire State of the South, Peach State. ⬖ state SE USA
12 F12 **Georgian Bay** lake bay Ontario, S Canada
8 L17 **Georgia, Strait of** strait British Columbia, W Canada
Georgi Dimitrov see Kostenets
Georgi Dimitrov, Yazovir see Koprinka, Yazovir
116 M9 **Georgi Traykov, Yazovir** ⊞ NE Bulgaria
Georgiu-Dezh see Liski
151 W10 **Georgiyevka** Semipalatinsk, E Kazakhstan
151 T6 **Georgiyevka** Zhambyl, SE Kazakhstan
131 N15 **Georgiyevsk** Stavropol'skiy Kray, SW Russian Federation
102 G13 **Georgsmarienhütte** Niedersachsen, NW Germany
205 O1 **Georg von Neumayer** German research station Antarctica
103 M16 **Gera** Thüringen, E Germany
103 K16 **Gera** ∽ C Germany
101 E19 **Geraardsbergen** Oost-Vlaanderen, SW Belgium
117 F21 **Geráki** Pelopónnisos, S Greece
29 W5 **Gerald** Missouri, C USA
49 V8 **Geral de Goiás, Serra** ▲ E Brazil
193 G20 **Geraldine** Canterbury, South Island, NZ
188 H11 **Geraldton** Western Australia
10 E11 **Geraldton** Ontario, S Canada
62 J12 **Geral, Serra** ▲ S Brazil
175 P16 **Gerampi** Sumbawa, S Indonesia
105 U6 **Gérardmer** Vosges, NE France
Gerasa see Jarash
Gerdauen see Zheleznodorozhnyy
41 Q11 **Gerdine, Mount** ▲ Alaska, USA
142 H11 **Gerede** Bolu, N Turkey
142 H11 **Gerede Çayı** ∽ N Turkey
154 M8 **Gereshk** Helmand, SW Afghanistan
103 L24 **Geretsried** Bayern, S Germany
107 Q14 **Gérgal** Andalucía, S Spain
194 K13 **Gerhards, Cape** headland C PNG
30 I14 **Gering** Nebraska, C USA
37 R3 **Gerlach** Nevada, W USA
Gerlachfalvi Csúcs/Gerlachovka see Gerlachovský Štít
113 L18 **Gerlachovský Štít** var. Gerlachovka, Ger. Gerlsdorfer Spitze, Hung. Gerlachfalvi Csúcs; prev. Stalinov Štít, Ger. Franz-Josef Spitze, Hung. Ferencz-József Csúcs. ▲ N Slovakia
110 E8 **Gerlafingen** Solothurn, NW Switzerland
Gerlsdorfer Spitze see Gerlachovský Štít
145 V3 **Germak** E Iraq
German East Africa see Tanzania
Germanicopolis see Çankırı
Germanicum, Mare/German Ocean see North Sea
Germanovichi see Hyermanavichy
German Southwest Africa see Namibia
22 E10 **Germantown** Tennessee, S USA
103 I15 **Germany** off. Federal Republic of Germany, Ger. Bundesrepublik Deutschland, Deutschland. ◆ federal republic N Europe
103 L23 **Germering** Bayern, SE Germany
85 J21 **Germiston** var. Gauteng. Gauteng, NE South Africa
Gernika see Gernika-Lumo
107 P2 **Gernika-Lumo** var. Gernika, Guernica, Guernica y Lumo. País Vasco, N Spain
171 Ii15 **Gero** Gifu, Honshū, SW Japan
117 F22 **Gerolimenas** Pelopónnisos, S Greece
107 W5 **Gerona** ⬖ province Cataluña, NE Spain
Gerona see Girona
101 H21 **Gerpinnes** Hainaut, S Belgium
104 L15 **Gers** ⬖ department S France
104 L14 **Gers** ∽ S France
Gerunda see Girona
142 K10 **Gerze** Sinop, N Turkey
164 I13 **Gêrzê** Xizang Zizhiqu, W China
Gesoriacum/Gessoriacum see Boulogne-sur-Mer
101 J21 **Gesves** Namur, SE Belgium
95 J20 **Geta** Åland, SW Finland
107 N8 **Getafe** Madrid, C Spain
97 J21 **Getinge** Halland, S Sweden
20 F16 **Gettysburg** Pennsylvania, NE USA
31 N8 **Gettysburg** South Dakota, N USA
204 K12 **Getz Ice Shelf** ice shelf Antarctica
143 S15 **Gevaş** Van, SE Turkey
Gevgeli see Gevgelija
115 Q20 **Gevgelija** var. Devđelija, Djevdjelija, Turk. Gevgeli. SE FYR Macedonia
105 T10 **Gex** Ain, E France
94 I3 **Geysir** physical region SW Iceland
142 F11 **Geyve** Sakarya, NW Turkey
82 G10 **Gezira** ⬖ state E Sudan
111 V3 **Gföhl** Niederösterreich, N Austria
85 H22 **Ghaap Plateau** Afr. Ghaapplato. plateau C South Africa
Ghaapplato see Ghaap Plateau
Ghaba see Al Ghābah
144 J8 **Ghāb, Tall** ▲ SE Syria
145 Q9 **Ghadaf, Wādī al** dry watercourse C Iraq
Ghadamès see Ghadāmis
76 M9 **Ghadāmis** var. Ghadamès, Rhadames. W Libya
147 Y10 **Ghadan** E Oman
77 O10 **Ghaddūwah** C Libya
153 Q11 **Ghafurov** Rus. Gafurov; prev. Sovetabad. NW Tajikistan
157 N12 **Ghāghara** ∽ S Asia
155 P13 **Ghaibi Dero** Sind, SE Pakistan
147 Y10 **Ghalat** E Oman
153 O11 **Ghallaorol** Jizzakh Wiloyati, C Uzbekistan
145 W11 **Ghamūkah, Hawr** ◎ S Iraq
79 P15 **Ghana** off. Republic of Ghana. ◆ republic W Africa
147 X12 **Ghānah** spring/well S Oman
Ghanongga see Ranongga
Ghansi/Ghansiland see Ghanzi
85 F18 **Ghanzi** var. Khanzi. Ghanzi, W Botswana
85 G19 **Ghanzi** var. Ghansi, Ghansiland, Khanzi. ⬖ district C Botswana
69 T14 **Ghanzi** var. Knanzi. ∽ Botswana/South Africa
Ghap'an see Kapan
144 F13 **Gharandal** Ma'ān, SW Jordan
Gharbt, Jabal al see Liban, Jebel
76 K7 **Ghardaïa** N Algeria
145 U14 **Gharibīyah, Sha'īb al** ∽ S Iraq
153 R12 **Gharm** Rus. Garm. C Tajikistan
155 P17 **Gharo** Sind, SE Pakistan
145 W10 **Gharrāf, Shaṭṭ al** ∽ S Iraq
Gharvān see Gharyān
77 O7 **Gharyān** var. Gharvān. NW Libya
76 M11 **Ghāt** var. Gat. SW Libya
Ghawdex see Gozo
147 U8 **Ghayathi** Abū Ẓaby, W UAE
Ghazāl, Baḥr al see Ghazal, Bahr el
80 H9 **Ghazal, Bahr el** var. Soro. seasonal river C Chad
82 E13 **Ghazal, Bahr el** var. Baḥr al Ghazāl. ∽ S Sudan
153 Q9 **Ghazalkent** Rus. Gazalkent. Toshkent Wiloyati, E Uzbekistan
76 H6 **Ghazaouet** NW Algeria
158 I10 **Ghāziābād** Uttar Pradesh, N India
159 O13 **Ghāzīpur** Uttar Pradesh, N India
155 Q6 **Ghaznī** var. Ghazni. Ghaznī, E Afghanistan
155 P7 **Ghaznī** ⬖ province SE Afghanistan
Ghazzah see Gaza
Gheel see Geel
Ghelizâne see Relizane
Ghent see Gent
Gheorghe Brațul see Sfântu Gheorghe, Brațul
Gheorghe Gheorghiu-Dej see Onești
118 J10 **Gheorgheni** prev. Gheorghieni, Sînt-Miclăuș, Ger. Niklasmarkt, Hung. Gyergyószentmiklós. Harghita, C Romania
Gheorghieni see Gheorgheni
118 H10 **Gherla** Ger. Neuschliss, Hung. Szamosújvár; prev. Armenierstadt. Cluj, NW Romania
Gheweifat see Ghuwayfāt
152 L11 **Ghijduwon** Rus. Gizhduvan. Bukhoro Wiloyati, C Uzbekistan
Ghilan see Gīlān
109 C18 **Ghilarza** Sardegna, Italy, C Mediterranean Sea
Ghilizane see Relizane
Ghimbi see Gimbi
Ghiriș see Câmpia Turzii
104 F2 **Ghisonaccia** Corse, France, C Mediterranean Sea
Ghizo see Gizo
153 Q11 **Ghonchí** Rus. Ganchi. NW Tajikistan
Ghor see Ghowr
159 T13 **Ghoraghat** Rajshahi, NW Bangladesh
155 R13 **Ghotki** Sind, SE Pakistan
154 M5 **Ghowr** var. Ghor. ⬖ province C Afghanistan
152 M10 **Ghozghon** Rus. Gazgan. Nawoiy Wiloyati, C Uzbekistan
153 T13 **Ghūdara** var. Gudara, Rus. Kudara. SE Tajikistan
159 R13 **Ghugri** ∽ N India
153 S14 **Ghund** Rus. Gunt. ∽ SE Tajikistan
Ghurdaqah see Hurghada
154 J5 **Ghūrīān** Herāt, W Afghanistan
147 T8 **Ghuwayfāt** var. Gheweifat. Abū Ẓaby, W UAE
123 Mm17 **Ghuzayyil, Sabkhat** salt lake N Libya
153 N13 **Ghuzor** Rus. Guzar. Qashqadaryo Wiloyati, S Uzbekistan
117 G17 **Giáltra** Évvoia, C Greece
Giamame see Jamaame
116 F13 **Giannitsá** var. Yiannitsá. Kentrikí Makedonía, N Greece
109 F14 **Giannutri, Isola di** island Archipelago Toscano, C Italy
98 F13 **Giant's Causeway** Ir. Clochán an Aifir. lava flow N Northern Ireland, UK
178 J15 **Gia Rai** Minh Hai, S Vietnam
109 L24 **Giarre** Sicilia, Italy, C Mediterranean Sea
46 I7 **Gibara** Holguín, E Cuba
31 O16 **Gibbon** Nebraska, C USA
34 K11 **Gibbon** Oregon, NW USA
35 P11 **Gibbonsville** Idaho, NW USA
66 A13 **Gibb's Hill** hill S Bermuda
94 I9 **Gibostad** Troms, N Norway
106 I14 **Gibraleón** Andalucía, S Spain
106 L16 **Gibraltar** ○ (Gibraltar) S Gibraltar
106 L16 **Gibraltar** ◇ UK dependent territory SW Europe
Gibraltar, Détroit de/Gibraltar, Estrecho de see Gibraltar, Strait of
106 J17 **Gibraltar, Strait of** Fr. Détroit de Gibraltar, Sp. Estrecho de Gibraltar. strait Atlantic Ocean/Mediterranean Sea
33 S11 **Gibsonburg** Ohio, N USA
32 M13 **Gibson City** Illinois, N USA
188 L8 **Gibson Desert** desert Western Australia
8 L17 **Gibsons** British Columbia, SW Canada
155 N12 **Gīdār** Baluchistān, SW Pakistan
161 I17 **Giddalūr** Andhra Pradesh, E India
27 U10 **Giddings** Texas, SW USA
29 Y8 **Gideon** Missouri, C USA
83 I15 **Gīdolē** SW Ethiopia
120 H13 **Giedraičiai** Molėtai, E Lithuania
105 O7 **Gien** Loiret, C France
103 G17 **Giessen** Hessen, W Germany
100 O6 **Gieten** Drenthe, NE Netherlands
25 Y13 **Gifford** Florida, SE USA
15 Ll1 **Gifford** ∽ Baffin Island, Northwest Territories, NE Canada
102 J12 **Gifhorn** Niedersachsen, N Germany
9 P13 **Gift Lake** Alberta, W Canada
171 Hh15 **Gifu** var. Gihu. Gifu, Honshū, SW Japan
171 Hh14 **Gifu** off. Gifu-ken, var. Gihu. ⬖ prefecture Honshū, SW Japan
130 M13 **Gigant** Rostovskaya Oblast', SW Russian Federation
42 E8 **Giganta, Sierra de la** ▲ W Mexico
56 E12 **Gigante** Huila, S Colombia
116 I7 **Gigen** Loveshka Oblast, NW Bulgaria
Giggiga see Jijiga
98 G12 **Gigha Island** island SW Scotland, UK
109 E14 **Giglio, Isola del** island Archipelago Toscano, C Italy
Gihu see Gifu
106 L2 **Gijón** Asturias, NW Spain
83 D20 **Gikongoro** SW Rwanda
38 K14 **Gila Bend** Arizona, SW USA
38 J14 **Gila Bend Mountains** ▲ Arizona, SW USA
39 N14 **Gila Mountains** ▲ Arizona, SW USA
38 I15 **Gila Mountains** ▲ Arizona, SW USA
148 M4 **Gīlān** off. Ostān-e Gīlān; var. Ghilan, Guilan. ⬖ province NW Iran
Gilani see Gnjilane
38 L14 **Gila River** ∽ Arizona, SW USA
31 W4 **Gilbert** Minnesota, N USA
Gilbert Islands see Tungaru
8 L16 **Gilbert, Mount** ▲ British Columbia, SW Canada
189 U4 **Gilbert River** ∽ Queensland, NE Australia
1 C6 **Gilbert Seamounts** undersea feature NE Pacific Ocean
35 S7 **Gildford** Montana, NW USA
85 P15 **Gilé** Zambézia, NE Mozambique
32 K4 **Gile Flowage** ◎ Wisconsin, N USA
190 G7 **Giles, Lake** salt lake South Australia
77 U12 **Gilf Kebir Plateau** Ar. Haḍabat al Jilf al Kabīr. plateau SW Egypt
191 R6 **Gilgandra** New South Wales, SE Australia
Gilgau see Gălgău
83 I19 **Gilgil** Rift Valley, SW Kenya
191 S4 **Gil Gil Creek** ∽ New South Wales, SE Australia
155 V3 **Gilgit** Jammu and Kashmir, NE Pakistan
155 V3 **Gilgit** ∽ N Pakistan
9 X11 **Gillam** Manitoba, C Canada
97 J22 **Gilleleje** Frederiksborg, E Denmark
32 K14 **Gillespie** Illinois, N USA
29 W13 **Gillett** Arkansas, C USA
35 X12 **Gillette** Wyoming, C USA
99 P22 **Gillingham** SE England, UK
205 X6 **Gillock Island** island Antarctica
181 O16 **Gillot** ✕ (St-Denis) N Réunion

◆ Country ● Country Capital ◇ Dependent Territory ○ Dependent Territory Capital ⬖ Administrative Region ✕ International Airport ▲ Mountain ▲ Mountain Range Volcano ∽ River ◎ Lake ⊞ Reservoir

GILL POINT – GOTTWALDOV

67 H25 **Gill Point** *headland* E Saint Helena
32 M12 **Gilman** Illinois, N USA
27 W6 **Gilmer** Texas, SW USA
Gilolo *see* Halmahera, Pulau
83 G14 **Gīlo Wenz** ≈ SW Ethiopia
37 O10 **Gilroy** California, W USA
194 H12 **Giluwe, Mount** ▲ W PNG
126 M14 **Gilyuy** ≈ SE Russian Federation
101 I14 **Gilze** Noord-Brabant, S Netherlands
172 O14 **Gima** Okinawa, Kume-jima, SW Japan
82 H13 **Gīmbī** *It.* Ghimbi. W Ethiopia
47 T12 **Gimie, Mount** ▲ C Saint Lucia
9 X16 **Gimli** Manitoba, S Canada
Gimma *see* Jīma
97 O14 **Gimo** Uppsala, C Sweden
104 L15 **Gimone** ≈ S France
Gimpoe *see* Gimpu
175 Pp9 **Gimpu** *prev.* Gimpoe. Sulawesi, C Indonesia
190 F5 **Gina** South Australia
Ginevra *see* Genève
101 J19 **Gingelom** Limburg, NE Belgium
188 I12 **Gingin** Western Australia
179 R14 **Gingoog** Mindanao, S Philippines
83 K14 **Gīnīr** S Ethiopia
Giohar *see* Jawhar
109 O17 **Gióia del Colle** Puglia, SE Italy
109 M22 **Gioia, Golfo di** *gulf* S Italy
Giona *see* Gkióna
117 I16 **Gioúra** *island* Vóreioi Sporádes, Greece, Aegean Sea
109 O17 **Giovinazzo** Puglia, SE Italy
Gipeswic *see* Ipswich
Gipuzkoa *see* Guipúzcoa
Giran *see* Ilan
32 K14 **Girard** Illinois, N USA
29 R7 **Girard** Kansas, C USA
27 O6 **Girard** Texas, SW USA
56 E10 **Girardot** Cundinamarca, C Colombia
180 M7 **Giraud Seamount** *undersea feature* SW Indian Ocean
85 A15 **Giraul** ≈ SW Angola
98 L9 **Girdle Ness** *headland* NE Scotland, UK
143 N11 **Giresun** *var.* Kerasunt; *anc.* Cerasus, Pharnacia. Giresun, NE Turkey
143 N12 **Giresun** *var.* Kerasunt. ◐ *province* NE Turkey
143 N12 **Giresun Dağları** ▲▲ N Turkey
77 X10 **Girga** *var.* Girgeh, Jirjā. C Egypt
Girgeh *see* Girga
Girgenti *see* Agrigento
194 H10 **Girgir, Cape** *headland* NW PNG
159 Q15 **Girīdīh** Bihār, NE India
191 P6 **Girilambone** New South Wales, SE Australia
Girin *see* Jilin
124 R12 **Girne** *Gk.* Kerýneia, Kyrenia. N Cyprus
107 X5 **Girona** *var.* Gerona; *anc.* Gerunda. Cataluña, NE Spain
104 J12 **Gironde** ◐ *department* SW France
104 J11 **Gironde** *estuary* SW France
107 V5 **Gironella** Cataluña, NE Spain
105 N15 **Girou** ≈ S France
99 H14 **Girvan** W Scotland, UK
26 M9 **Girvin** Texas, SW USA
192 Q9 **Gisborne** Gisborne, North Island, NZ
192 P9 **Gisborne** *off.* Gisborne District. ◐ *unitary authority* North Island, NZ
Giseifu *see* Ŭijŏngbu
Gisenye *see* Gisenyi
83 D19 **Gisenyi** *var.* Gisenye. NW Rwanda
97 K20 **Gislaved** Jönköping, S Sweden
105 N4 **Gisors** Eure, N France
Gissar *see* Hisor
153 P12 **Gissar Range** *Rus.* Gissarskiy Khrebet. ▲▲ Tajikistan/Uzbekistan
Gissarskiy Khrebet *see* Gissar Range
101 B16 **Gistel** West-Vlaanderen, W Belgium
110 F9 **Giswil** Unterwalden, C Switzerland
117 B16 **Gitánes** *ancient monument* Ípeiros, W Greece
83 E20 **Gitarama** C Rwanda
83 E20 **Gitega** C Burundi
Githio *see* Gýtheio
110 H11 **Giubiasco** Ticino, S Switzerland
108 K13 **Giulianova** Abruzzi, C Italy
Giulie, Alpi *see* Julian Alps
Giumri *see* Gyumri
118 M13 **Giurgeni** Ialomiţa, SE Romania
118 J15 **Giurgiu** Giurgiu, S Romania
118 J14 **Giurgiu** ◐ *county* SE Romania
97 F22 **Give** Vejle, C Denmark
105 R2 **Givet** Ardennes, N France
105 R11 **Givors** Rhône, E France
85 K19 **Giyani** Northern, NE South Africa
82 I13 **Giyon** C Ethiopia
Gîza/Gizeh *see* El Gîza
77 V8 **Giza, Pyramids of** *ancient monument* N Egypt
Gizhduvan *see* Ghijduwon
127 Oo8 **Gizhiga** Magadanskaya Oblast', E Russian Federation
127 Oo8 **Gizhiginskaya Guba** *bay* E Russian Federation
195 T14 **Gizo** Gizo, NW Solomon Islands
195 T14 **Gizo** *var.* Ghizo. *island* NW Solomon Islands
112 N7 **Giżycko** *Ger.* Lötzen. Suwałki, NE Poland
Gízymałów *see* Hrymayliv
Gjakovë *see* Đakovica
96 F12 **Gjende** ◎ S Norway
97 F17 **Gjerstad** Aust-Agder, S Norway
Gjilan *see* Gnjilane
Gjinokastër *see* Gjirokastër
115 L23 **Gjirokastër** *var.* Gjirokastra; *prev.* Gjinokastër, *Gk.* Argyrokastron, *It.* Argirocastro. Gjirokastër, S Albania
115 L22 **Gjirokastër** ◐ *district* S Albania
Gjirokastra *see* Gjirokastër
15 K3 **Gjoa Haven** King William Island, Northwest Territories, NW Canada
96 H13 **Gjøvik** Oppland, S Norway
115 J22 **Gjuhëzës, Kepi i** *headland* SW Albania
Gjurgjevac *see* Đurđevac
117 E18 **Gkióna** *var.* Giona. ▲▲ C Greece
124 Oo3 **Gkréko, Akrotíri** *var.* Cape Greco, Pidálion. *headland* E Cyprus
101 I18 **Glabbeek-Zuurbemde** Vlaams Brabant, C Belgium
11 R14 **Glace Bay** Cape Breton Island, Nova Scotia, SE Canada
9 O16 **Glacier** British Columbia, SW Canada
41 W12 **Glacier Bay** *inlet* Alaska, USA
34 I7 **Glacier Peak** ▲ Washington, NW USA
23 Q7 **Glade Spring** Virginia, NE USA
27 W7 **Gladewater** Texas, SW USA
189 Y8 **Gladstone** Queensland, E Australia
190 I8 **Gladstone** South Australia
9 X16 **Gladstone** Manitoba, S Canada
33 O5 **Gladstone** Michigan, N USA
29 R4 **Gladstone** Missouri, C USA
33 Q7 **Gladwin** Michigan, N USA
97 J15 **Glafsfjorden** ◎ C Sweden
94 H2 **Gláma** *physical region* NW Iceland
86 F7 **Glåma** ≈ SE Norway
114 F13 **Glamoč** W Bosnia and Herzegovina
99 J22 **Glamorgan** *cultural region* S Wales, UK
97 G24 **Glamsbjerg** Fyn, C Denmark
179 Rr17 **Glan** Mindanao, S Philippines
97 M17 **Glan** ◎ S Sweden
111 T9 **Glan** ≈ SE Austria
103 F19 **Glan** ≈ W Germany
165 N13 **Glandaindong** *var.* Gêladaindong. ▲ C China
Glaris *see* Glarus
110 H9 **Glarner Alpen** *Eng.* Glarus Alps. ▲▲ E Switzerland
110 H8 **Glarus** Glarus, E Switzerland
110 H9 **Glarus** *Fr.* Glaris. ◐ *canton* C Switzerland
Glarus Alps *see* Glarner Alpen
29 N3 **Glasco** Kansas, C USA
98 I12 **Glasgow** S Scotland, UK
22 K7 **Glasgow** Kentucky, S USA
29 T4 **Glasgow** Missouri, C USA
35 W7 **Glasgow** Montana, NW USA
23 T6 **Glasgow** Virginia, NE USA
98 I12 **Glasgow** ✕ W Scotland, UK
9 S14 **Glaslyn** Saskatchewan, S Canada
20 I16 **Glassboro** New Jersey, NE USA
26 L10 **Glass Mountains** ▲▲ Texas, SW USA
99 K23 **Glastonbury** SW England, UK
Glatz *see* Kłodzko
103 N16 **Glauchau** Sachsen, E Germany
Glavn'a Morava *see* Velika Morava
115 N16 **Glavnik** Serbia, S Yugoslavia
131 T1 **Glazov** Udmurtskaya Respublika, NW Russian Federation
Głda *see* Gwda
111 U8 **Gleinalpe** ▲▲ SE Austria
111 W8 **Gleisdorf** Steiermark, SE Austria
Gleiwitz *see* Gliwice
41 S11 **Glenallen** Alaska, USA
104 F7 **Glénan, Îles** *island group* NW France
193 G21 **Glenavy** Canterbury, South Island, NZ
8 H5 **Glenboyle** Yukon Territory, NW Canada
23 X3 **Glen Burnie** Maryland, NE USA
38 L8 **Glen Canyon** *canyon* Utah, W USA
38 L8 **Glen Canyon Dam** *dam* Arizona, SW USA
32 K15 **Glen Carbon** Illinois, N USA
12 E17 **Glencoe** Ontario, S Canada
85 K22 **Glencoe** KwaZulu/Natal, E South Africa
31 U9 **Glencoe** Minnesota, N USA
98 H10 **Glen Coe** *valley* N Scotland, UK
38 K13 **Glendale** Arizona, SW USA
37 S15 **Glendale** California, W USA
190 G5 **Glendambo** South Australia
35 Y8 **Glendive** Montana, NW USA
35 Y15 **Glendo** Wyoming, C USA
57 S10 **Glendor Mountians** ▲▲ C Guyana
190 K12 **Glenelg River** ≈ South Australia/Victoria, SE Australia
31 P4 **Glenfield** North Dakota, N USA
27 V12 **Glen Flora** Texas, SW USA
189 P7 **Glen Helen** Northern Territory, N Australia
191 U5 **Glen Innes** New South Wales, SE Australia
33 P6 **Glen Lake** ◎ Michigan, N USA
8 I7 **Glenlyon Peak** ▲ Yukon Territory, W Canada
39 N16 **Glenn, Mount** ▲ Arizona, SW USA
35 N15 **Glenns Ferry** Idaho, NW USA
25 W6 **Glennville** Georgia, SE USA
8 J10 **Glenora** British Columbia, W Canada
190 M11 **Glenorchy** Victoria, SE Australia
191 V5 **Glenreagh** New South Wales, SE Australia
35 X15 **Glenrock** Wyoming, C USA
98 K11 **Glenrothes** E Scotland, UK
20 L9 **Glens Falls** New York, NE USA
99 D14 **Glenties** *Ir.* Na Gleannta. NW Ireland
30 L5 **Glen Ullin** North Dakota, N USA
23 R4 **Glenville** West Virginia, NE USA
29 T12 **Glenwood** Arkansas, C USA
31 S15 **Glenwood** Iowa, C USA
31 T7 **Glenwood** Minnesota, N USA
38 L5 **Glenwood** Utah, W USA
32 I5 **Glenwood City** Wisconsin, N USA
39 Q4 **Glenwood Springs** Colorado, C USA
110 F10 **Gletsch** Valais, S Switzerland
Glevum *see* Gloucester
31 U14 **Glidden** Iowa, C USA
114 E9 **Glina** Sisak-Moslavina, NE Croatia
96 F11 **Glittertind** ▲ S Norway
113 J16 **Gliwice** *Ger.* Gleiwitz. Katowice, S Poland
38 M14 **Globe** Arizona, SW USA
Globino *see* Hlobyne
110 L9 **Glockturm** ▲ SW Austria
118 L9 **Glodeni** *Rus.* Glodyany. N Moldova
111 S9 **Glödnitz** Kärnten, S Austria
Glodyany *see* Glodeni
Glogau *see* Głogów
111 W6 **Gloggnitz** Niederösterreich, E Austria
112 F13 **Głogów** *Ger.* Glogau, Glogow. Legnica, W Poland
113 I16 **Głogówek** *Ger.* Oberglogau. Opole, SW Poland
94 G12 **Glomfjord** Nordland, C Norway
96 I12 **Glomma** *var.* Glommen. ≈ S Norway
Glommen *see* Glomma
95 I14 **Glommersträsk** Norrbotten, N Sweden
180 I1 **Glorieuses, Nosy** *island group* N Madagascar
67 C25 **Glorious Hill** *hill* East Falkland, Falkland Islands
40 J12 **Glory of Russia Cape** *headland* Saint Matthew Island, Alaska, USA
24 J7 **Gloster** Mississippi, S USA
191 U7 **Gloucester** New South Wales, SE Australia
194 L12 **Gloucester** New Britain, E PNG
99 L21 **Gloucester** *hist.* Caer Glou, *Lat.* Glevum. C England, UK
21 P10 **Gloucester** Massachusetts, NE USA
23 X6 **Gloucester** Virginia, NE USA
99 K21 **Gloucestershire** *cultural region* C England, UK
33 T14 **Glouster** Ohio, N USA
44 H3 **Glovers Reef** *reef* E Belize
20 K10 **Gloversville** New York, NE USA
112 K12 **Głowno** Łódź, C Poland
113 H16 **Głubczyce** *Ger.* Leobschütz. Opole, SW Poland
130 L11 **Glubokiy** Rostovskaya Oblast', SW Russian Federation
151 W9 **Glubokoye** Vostochnyy Kazakhstan, E Kazakhstan
Glubokoye *see* Hlybokaye
113 H16 **Głuchołazy** *Ger.* Ziegenhais. Opole, SW Poland
102 I9 **Glückstadt** Schleswig-Holstein, N Germany
Glukhov *see* Hlukhiv
Glushkevichi *see* Hlushkavichy
Glusk/Glussk *see* Hlusk
Glybokaya *see* Hlyboka
97 F21 **Glyngøre** Viborg, NW Denmark
131 Q9 **Gmelinka** Volgogradskaya Oblast', SW Russian Federation
111 U2 **Gmünd** Kärnten, S Austria
111 R8 **Gmünd** Niederösterreich, N Austria
Gmünd *see* Schwäbisch Gmünd
111 S5 **Gmunden** Oberösterreich, N Austria
Gmundner See *see* Traunsee
96 N10 **Gnarp** Gävleborg, C Sweden
111 W8 **Gnas** Steiermark, SE Austria
Gnesen *see* Gniezno
97 O16 **Gnesta** Södermanland, C Sweden
112 H11 **Gniezno** *Ger.* Gnesen. Poznań, C Poland
115 O17 **Gnjilane** *var.* Gilani, *Alb.* Gjilan. Serbia, S Yugoslavia
97 K20 **Gnosjö** Jönköping, S Sweden
161 E17 **Goa** *prev.* Old Goa, Vela Goa, Velha Goa. Goa, W India
161 E17 **Goa** *var.* Old Goa. ◐ *state* W India
44 H7 **Goascorán, Río** ≈ El Salvador/ Honduras
79 O16 **Goaso** *var.* Gawso. W Ghana
83 K14 **Goba** *It.* Gobbà. S Ethiopia
85 C20 **Gobabed** Erongo, W Namibia
85 E19 **Gobabis** Omaheke, E Namibia
Gobannium *see* Abergavenny
66 M7 **Goban Spur** *undersea feature* NW Atlantic Ocean
Gobbà *see* Goba
65 H21 **Gobernador Gregores** Santa Cruz, S Argentina
63 F14 **Gobernador Ingeniero Virasoro** Corrientes, NE Argentina
168 L12 **Gobi** *desert* China/Mongolia
170 G16 **Gobō** Wakayama, Honshū, SW Japan
103 D14 **Goch** Nordrhein-Westfalen, W Germany
85 E20 **Gochas** Hardap, S Namibia
161 I14 **Godāvari** *var.* Godavari. ≈ C India
161 L16 **Godāvari, Mouths of the** *delta* E India
13 V5 **Godbout** Québec, SE Canada
13 U5 **Godbout** ≈ Québec, SE Canada
13 U5 **Godbout Est** ≈ Québec, SE Canada
29 N6 **Goddard** Kansas, C USA
12 E15 **Goderich** Ontario, S Canada
Godhavn *see* Qeqertarsuaq
160 E10 **Godhra** Gujarāt, W India
Göding *see* Hodonín
113 K22 **Gödöllő** Pest, N Hungary
64 H11 **Godoy Cruz** Mendoza, W Argentina
9 Y11 **Gods** ≈ Manitoba, C Canada
9 Y13 **Gods Lake** Manitoba, C Canada
9 X13 **Gods Lake** ◎ Manitoba, C Canada
Godthaab/Godthåb *see* Nuuk
Godwin Austen, Mount *see* K2
Goede Hoop, Kaap de *see* Good Hope, Cape of
Goedgegun *see* Nhlangano
Goeie Hoop, Kaap die *see* Good Hope, Cape of
11 O7 **Goélands, Lac aux** ◎ Québec, SE Canada
100 E13 **Goeree** *island* SW Netherlands
101 F15 **Goes** Zeeland, SW Netherlands
Goettingen *see* Göttingen
21 O10 **Goffstown** New Hampshire, NE USA
12 E8 **Gogama** Ontario, S Canada
170 Ee12 **Gō-gawa** ≈ Honshū, SW Japan
32 L3 **Gogebic, Lake** ◎ Michigan, N USA
32 K3 **Gogebic Range** *hill range* Michigan/Wisconsin, N USA
143 V13 **Gogi, Mount** *Arm.* Gogi Lerr, *Az.* Küküdağ. ▲ Armenia/Azerbaijan
128 F12 **Gogland, Ostrov** *island* NW Russian Federation
113 I15 **Gogolin** Opole, SW Poland
Gogonou *see* Gogounou
79 S14 **Gogounou** *var.* Gogonou. N Benin
158 I10 **Gohāna** Haryāna, N India
61 K18 **Goianésia** Goiás, C Brazil
61 K18 **Goiânia** *prev.* Goyania. *state capital* Goiás, C Brazil
61 K18 **Goiás** Goiás, C Brazil
61 J18 **Goiás** *off.* Estado de Goiás; *prev.* Goiaz, Goyaz. ◐ *state* C Brazil
Goiaz *see* Goiás
165 R14 **Goinsargoin** Xizang Zizhiqu, W China
62 H10 **Goio-Erê** Paraná, SW Brazil
101 I15 **Goirle** Noord-Brabant, S Netherlands
106 H8 **Góis** Coimbra, N Portugal
171 Gg16 **Gojō** *var.* Gozyô. Nara, Honshū, SW Japan
171 M10 **Gojōme** Akita, Honshū, NW Japan
155 U9 **Gojra** Punjab, E Pakistan
170 D15 **Gokase-gawa** ≈ Kyūshū, SW Japan
142 A11 **Gökçeada** *var.* Imroz Adası, *Gk.* Imbros. *island* NW Turkey
Gökçeada *see* İmroz
Gökdepe *see* Geok-Tepe
142 I10 **Gökırmak** ≈ N Turkey
Goklenkuy, Solonchak *see* Geklengkui, Solonchak
142 C16 **Gökova Körfezi** *gulf* SW Turkey
142 K15 **Göksu** ≈ S Turkey
142 L15 **Göksun** Kahramanmaraş, C Turkey
142 I17 **Göksu Nehri** ≈ S Turkey
85 J16 **Gokwe** Midlands, NW Zimbabwe
96 F13 **Gol** Buskerud, S Norway
159 X12 **Golāghāt** Assam, NE India
112 H10 **Gołańcz** Piła, W Poland
144 G8 **Golan Heights** *Ar.* Al Jawlān, *Heb.* HaGolan. ▲▲ SW Syria
Golārā *see* Ārān
Golaya Pristan *see* Hola Prystan'
149 T11 **Golbāf** Kermān, C Iran
142 M15 **Gölbaşı** Adıyaman, S Turkey
111 P9 **Gölbner** ▲ SW Austria
32 M17 **Golconda** Illinois, N USA
37 T3 **Golconda** Nevada, W USA
142 E11 **Gölcük** Kocaeli, NW Turkey
110 I7 **Goldach** Sankt Gallen, NE Switzerland
112 N7 **Gołdap** *Ger.* Goldap. Suwałki, NE Poland
34 E15 **Gold Beach** Oregon, NW USA
Goldberg *see* Złotoryja
70 D12 **Gold Coast** *coastal region* S Ghana
191 V3 **Gold Coast** *cultural region* Queensland, E Australia
41 R10 **Gold Creek** Alaska, USA
9 O16 **Golden** British Columbia, SW Canada
39 T4 **Golden** Colorado, C USA
192 I13 **Golden Bay** *bay* South Island, NZ
29 R7 **Golden City** Missouri, C USA
34 I11 **Goldendale** Washington, NW USA
Goldener Tisch *see* Zlatý Stôl
46 L13 **Golden Grove** E Jamaica
12 J12 **Golden Lake** ◎ Ontario, SE Canada
24 K10 **Golden Meadow** Louisiana, S USA
47 V10 **Golden Rock** ✕ (Basseterre) Saint Kitts, Saint Kitts and Nevis
Golden State, The *see* California
85 K16 **Golden Valley** Mashonaland West, N Zimbabwe
37 U9 **Goldfield** Nevada, W USA
Goldingen *see* Kuldīga
Goldmarkt *see* Zlatna
8 K17 **Gold River** Vancouver Island, British Columbia, SW Canada
23 V10 **Goldsboro** North Carolina, SE USA
26 M8 **Goldsmith** Texas, SW USA
27 R8 **Goldthwaite** Texas, SW USA
143 R11 **Göle** Kars, NE Turkey
Golema Ada *see* Ostrovo
116 H9 **Golema Planina** ▲▲ W Bulgaria
116 F9 **Golemi Vrŭkh** ▲ W Bulgaria
112 D8 **Goleniów** *Ger.* Gollnow. Szczecin, NW Poland
37 Q14 **Goleta** California, W USA
45 O16 **Golfito** Puntarenas, SE Costa Rica
27 T13 **Goliad** Texas, SW USA
115 L14 **Golija** ▲▲ SW Yugoslavia
115 O16 **Goljak** ▲▲ SE Yugoslavia
142 M12 **Gölköy** Ordu, N Turkey
Gollel *see* Lavumisa
111 X3 **Göllersbach** ≈ NE Austria
Gollnow *see* Goleniów
Golmo *see* Golmud
165 P10 **Golmud** *var.* Ge'e'mu, Golmo, *Chin.* Ko-erh-mu. Qinghai, C China
104 F1 **Golo** ≈ Corse, France, C Mediterranean Sea
Golovanevsk *see* Holovanivs'k
Golovchin *see* Halowchyn
41 N9 **Golovin** Alaska, USA
148 M7 **Golpāyegān** *var.* Gulpaigan. Eşfahān, W Iran
Golshan *see* Ţabas
Gol'shany *see* Hal'shany
98 J7 **Golspie** N Scotland, UK
114 O11 **Golubac** Serbia, NE Yugoslavia
112 J9 **Golub-Dobrzyń** Toruń, N Poland
151 S7 **Golubovka** Pavlodar, N Kazakhstan
84 B11 **Golungo Alto** Cuanza Norte, NW Angola
116 M8 **Golyama Kamchiya** ≈ E Bulgaria
116 L8 **Golyama Reka** ≈ N Bulgaria
116 H11 **Golyama Syutkya** ▲ SW Bulgaria
116 I12 **Golyam Perelik** ▲ S Bulgaria
116 I11 **Golyam Persenk** ▲ S Bulgaria
125 F12 **Golyshmanovo** Tyumenskaya Oblast', C Russian Federation
81 P19 **Goma** Nord Kivu, NE Zaire
171 Gg16 **Gomadan-zan** ▲ Honshū, SW Japan
Gomati *see* Gumti
79 X14 **Gombe** Bauchi, E Nigeria
69 U10 **Gombe** *var.* Igombe. ≈ E Tanzania
79 Y14 **Gombi** Adamawa, E Nigeria
Gombroon *see* Bandar-e 'Abbās
Gomel' *see* Homyel'
Gomel'skaya Oblast' *see* Homyel'skaya Voblasts'
66 N11 **Gomera** *island* Islas Canarias, Spain, NE Atlantic Ocean
42 I5 **Gómez Farias** Chihuahua, N Mexico
42 L8 **Gómez Palacio** Durango, C Mexico
164 J13 **Gomo** Xizang Zizhiqu, W China
175 T11 **Gomumu, Pulau** *see* Gomumu, Pulau
149 T6 **Gonābād** *var.* Gunabad. Khorāsān, NE Iran
46 L8 **Gonaïves** *var.* Les Gonaïves. N Haiti
126 M13 **Gonam** ≈ NE Russian Federation
46 L9 **Gonâve, Canal de la** *var.* Canal de Sud. *channel* N Caribbean Sea
46 K9 **Gonâve, Golfe de la** *gulf* N Caribbean Sea
Gonāveh *see* Bandar-e Gonāveh
46 K9 **Gonâve, Île de la** *island* C Haiti
Gonbadān *see* Dow Gonbadān
149 Q3 **Gonbad-e Kāvūs** *var.* Gunbad-i-Qawus. Māzandarān, N Iran
158 M12 **Gonda** Uttar Pradesh, N India
Gondar *see* Gonder
82 I11 **Gonder** *var.* Gondar. NW Ethiopia
80 J13 **Gondey** Moyen-Chari, S Chad
160 J12 **Gondia** Mahārāshtra, C India
106 G6 **Gondomar** Porto, NW Portugal
142 C12 **Gönen** Balıkesir, W Turkey
142 C12 **Gönen Çayı** ≈ NW Turkey
165 O15 **Gongbo'gyamda** Xizang Zizhiqu, W China
165 N16 **Gonggar** Xizang Zizhiqu, W China
166 G9 **Gongga Shan** ▲ C China
165 T10 **Gonghe** Qinghai, C China
164 I5 **Gongliu** *var.* Tokkuztara. Xinjiang Uygur Zizhiqu, NW China
79 W14 **Gongola** ≈ E Nigeria
Gongoleh State *see* Jonglei
191 P5 **Gongolgon** New South Wales, SE Australia
165 Q6 **Gongpoquan** Gansu, N China
166 I10 **Gongxian** *var.* Gong Xian. Sichuan, C China
Gongzhuling *see* Huaide
165 S14 **Gonjo** Xizang Zizhiqu, W China
109 B20 **Gonnesa** Sardegna, Italy, C Mediterranean Sea
Gonni/Gónnos *see* Gónnoi
117 F15 **Gónnoi** *var.* Gonni, Gónnos; *prev.* Derelí. Thessalía, C Greece
172 N9 **Gonohe** Aomori, Honshū, C Japan
170 Cc11 **Gōnoura** Nagasaki, Iki, SW Japan
37 O11 **Gonzales** California, W USA
24 J9 **Gonzales** Louisiana, S USA
27 T12 **Gonzales** Texas, SW USA
43 P11 **González** Tamaulipas, C Mexico
23 V6 **Goochland** Virginia, NE USA
195 N16 **Goodenough Bay** *inlet* SE PNG
205 X14 **Goodenough, Cape** *headland* Antarctica
195 N15 **Goodenough Island** *var.* Morata. *island* SE PNG
Good Hope *see* Fort Good Hope
41 N8 **Goodhope Bay** *bay* Alaska, USA
85 D26 **Good Hope, Cape of** *Afr.* Kaap de Goede Hoop, Kaap die Goeie Hoop. *headland* SW South Africa
Good Hope, Cape of *see* Yamsursba, Tanjung
8 K10 **Good Hope Lake** British Columbia, W Canada
85 E23 **Goodhouse** Northern Cape, W South Africa
35 O15 **Gooding** Idaho, NW USA
28 H3 **Goodland** Kansas, C USA
181 Y15 **Goodlands** NW Mauritius
22 J8 **Goodlettsville** Tennessee, S USA
41 N13 **Goodnews** Alaska, USA
27 O3 **Goodnight** Texas, SW USA
191 Q4 **Goodooga** New South Wales, SE Australia
31 N4 **Goodrich** North Dakota, N USA
27 W10 **Goodrich** Texas, SW USA
31 X10 **Goodview** Minnesota, N USA
28 H8 **Goodwell** Oklahoma, C USA
99 N17 **Goole** E England, UK
191 O8 **Goolgowi** New South Wales, SE Australia
190 I10 **Goolwa** South Australia
189 Y11 **Goondiwindi** Queensland, E Australia
100 O11 **Goor** Overijssel, E Netherlands
Goose Bay *see* Happy Valley-Goose Bay
35 V13 **Gooseberry Creek** ≈ Wyoming, C USA
23 S14 **Goose Creek** South Carolina, SE USA
65 M23 **Goose Green** East Falkland, Falkland Islands
17 G6 **Goose Lake** *var.* Lago dos Gansos. ◎ California/Oregon, W USA
31 Q4 **Goose River** ≈ North Dakota, N USA
159 T16 **Gopalganj** Dhaka, S Bangladesh
159 O12 **Gopālganj** Bihār, N India
Gopher State *see* Minnesota
103 I22 **Göppingen** Baden-Württemberg, SW Germany
112 G13 **Góra** *Ger.* Guhrau. Leszno, W Poland
112 M12 **Góra Kalwaria** Warszawa, C Poland
159 O12 **Gorakhpur** Uttar Pradesh, N India
Gorany *see* Harany
115 J14 **Goražde** SE Bosnia and Herzegovina
Gorbovichi *see* Harbavichy
Gorče Petrov *see* Đorče Petrov
1 E9 **Gorda Ridges** *undersea feature* NE Pacific Ocean
Gordiaz *see* Gardēz
80 K12 **Gordil** Vakaga, N Central African Republic
25 U5 **Gordon** Georgia, SE USA
30 K12 **Gordon** Nebraska, C USA
27 R7 **Gordon** Texas, SW USA
30 L13 **Gordon Creek** ≈ Nebraska, C USA
65 I25 **Gordon, Isla** *island* S Chile
191 O17 **Gordon, Lake** ◎ Tasmania, SE Australia
191 O17 **Gordon River** ≈ Tasmania, SE Australia
23 V5 **Gordonsville** Virginia, NE USA
82 H13 **Gorē** W Ethiopia
193 D24 **Gore** Southland, South Island, NZ
80 H13 **Goré** Logone-Oriental, S Chad
12 D11 **Gore Bay** Manitoulin Island, Ontario, S Canada
27 Q5 **Goree** Texas, SW USA
143 O11 **Görele** Giresun, NE Turkey
21 N6 **Gore Mountain** ▲ Vermont, NE USA
41 R13 **Gore Point** *headland* Alaska, USA
39 R4 **Gore Range** ▲▲ Colorado, C USA
99 F19 **Gorey** *Ir.* Guaire. SE Ireland
149 R12 **Gorgāb** Kermān, S Iran
149 Q4 **Gorgān** *var.* Astarabad, Astrabad, Gurgan; *prev.* Asterābād, *anc.* Hyrcania. Māzandarān, N Iran
149 Q4 **Gorgān, Rūd-e** ≈ N Iran
78 I10 **Gorgol** ◐ *region* S Mauritania
108 D12 **Gorgona, Isola di** *island* Archipelago Toscano, C Italy
21 P8 **Gorham** Maine, NE USA
143 T10 **Gori** C Georgia
100 I13 **Gorinchem** *var.* Gorkum. Zuid-Holland, C Netherlands
143 V13 **Goris** SE Armenia
128 K16 **Goritsy** Tverskaya Oblast', W Russian Federation
108 J7 **Gorizia** *Ger.* Görz. Friuli-Venezia Giulia, NE Italy
118 G13 **Gorj** ◐ *county* SW Romania
Gorjanci *see* Žumberačka Gora
Görkau *see* Jirkov
Gorki *see* Horki
Gor'kiy *see* Nizhniy Novgorod
Gor'kiy Reservoir *see* Gor'kovskoye Vodokhranilishche
125 D9 **Gor'kovskoye Vodokhranilishche** *Eng.* Gor'kiy Reservoir. ⊠ W Russian Federation
Gorkum *see* Gorinchem
97 I23 **Gørlev** Vestsjælland, E Denmark
113 M17 **Gorlice** Nowy Sącz, S Poland
103 Q15 **Görlitz** Sachsen, E Germany
Görlitz *see* Zgorzelec
Gorlovka *see* Horlivka
27 R7 **Gorman** Texas, SW USA
23 T3 **Gormania** West Virginia, NE USA
Gorna Dzhumaya *see* Blagoevgrad
116 K8 **Gorna Oryakhovitsa** Loveshka Oblast, N Bulgaria
116 J8 **Gorna Studena** Loveshka Oblast, N Bulgaria
Gornja Mužlja *see* Mužlja
111 X9 **Gornja Radgona** *Ger.* Oberradkersburg. NE Slovenia
114 M13 **Gornji Milanovac** Serbia, C Yugoslavia
114 G13 **Gornji Vakuf** SW Bosnia and Herzegovina
126 H15 **Gorno-Altaysk** Respublika Altay, S Russian Federation
Gorno-Altayskaya Respublika *see* Altay, Respublika
126 K13 **Gorno-Chuyskiy** Irkutskaya Oblast', C Russian Federation
129 V14 **Gornozavodsk** Permskaya Oblast', NW Russian Federation
127 O16 **Gornozavodsk** Ostrov Sakhalin, Sakhalinskaya Oblast', SE Russian Federation
126 Gg15 **Gornyak** Altayskiy Kray, S Russian Federation
131 R8 **Gornyy** Saratovskaya Oblast', W Russian Federation
Gornyy Altay *see* Altay, Respublika
131 O10 **Gornyy Balykley** Volgogradskaya Oblast', SW Russian Federation
82 I13 **Goroch'an** ▲ W Ethiopia
Gorodenka *see* Horodenka
131 O3 **Gorodets** Nizhegorodskaya Oblast', W Russian Federation
Gorodets *see* Haradzyets
Gorodeya *see* Haradzyeya
131 P6 **Gorodishche** Penzenskaya Oblast', W Russian Federation
Gorodishche *see* Horodyshche
Gorodnya *see* Horodnya
Gorodok *see* Haradok
Gorodok/Gorodok Yagellonski *see* Horodok
130 M13 **Gorodovikovsk** Respublika Kalmykiya, SW Russian Federation
194 I12 **Goroka** Eastern Highlands, C PNG
Gorokhov *see* Horokhiv
131 N3 **Gorokhovets** Vladimirskaya Oblast', W Russian Federation
79 Q11 **Gorom-Gorom** NE Burkina
176 V12 **Gorong, Kepulauan** *island group* E Indonesia
85 M17 **Gorongosa** Sofala, C Mozambique
176 Uu12 **Gorong, Pulau** *island* Kepulauan Gorong, E Indonesia
175 R8 **Gorontalo** Sulawesi, C Indonesia
175 Qq8 **Gorontalo, Teluk** *bay* Sulawesi, C Indonesia
Gorontalo, Teluk *see* Tomini, Gulf of
112 L7 **Górowo Iławeckie** *Ger.* Landsberg. Olsztyn, N Poland
100 M7 **Gorredijk** *Fris.* De Gordyk. Friesland, N Netherlands
86 C14 **Gorringe Ridge** *undersea feature* E Atlantic Ocean
100 M11 **Gorssel** Gelderland, E Netherlands
111 T8 **Görtschitz** ≈ S Austria
Goryn *see* Horyn'
Görz *see* Gorizia
112 E10 **Gorzów** *off.* Województwo Gorzowskie. ◐ *province* W Poland
Gorzowskie, Województwo *see* Gorzów
112 E10 **Gorzów Wielkopolski** *Ger.* Landsberg, Landsberg an der Warthe. Gorzów, W Poland
110 G9 **Göschenen** Uri, C Switzerland
195 N16 **Goschen Strait** *strait* SE PNG
171 Kk13 **Gosen** Niigata, Honshū, C Japan
191 T8 **Gosford** New South Wales, SE Australia
33 P11 **Goshen** Indiana, N USA
20 K13 **Goshen** New York, NE USA
Goshoba *see* Koshoba
171 Mm8 **Goshogawara** *var.* Gosyogawara. Aomori, Honshū, C Japan
152 I8 **Goshquduq Qum** *var.* Tosquduq Qumlari, *Rus.* Peski Taskuduk. *desert* W Uzbekistan
103 J14 **Goslar** Niedersachsen, C Germany
29 Y9 **Gosnell** Arkansas, C USA
114 C11 **Gospić** Lika-Senj, C Croatia
99 N23 **Gosport** S England, UK
96 D9 **Gossa** *island* S Norway
110 H7 **Gossau** Sankt Gallen, NE Switzerland
101 G20 **Gosselies** *var.* Goss'lies. Hainaut, S Belgium
79 P10 **Gossi** Tombouctou, C Mali
Goss'lies *see* Gosselies
115 N18 **Gostivar** W FYR Macedonia
Gostomel' *see* Hostomel'
112 G12 **Gostyń** *var.* Gostyn. Leszno, W Poland
112 K11 **Gostynin** Płock, C Poland
Gosyogawara *see* Goshogawara
97 J18 **Göta Älv** ≈ S Sweden
97 N17 **Göta kanal** *canal* S Sweden
97 K18 **Götaland** *cultural region* S Sweden
97 H17 **Göteborg** *Eng.* Gothenburg. Göteborg och Bohus, S Sweden
97 H17 **Göteborg och Bohus** *var.* Göteborg and Bohus. ◐ *county* S Sweden
79 X16 **Gotel Mountains** ▲▲ E Nigeria
97 K17 **Götene** Skaraborg, S Sweden
Gotera *see* San Francisco
103 K16 **Gotha** Thüringen, C Germany
31 N15 **Gothenburg** Nebraska, C USA
Gothenburg *see* Göteborg
79 R12 **Gothèye** Tillabéri, SW Niger
Gothland *see* Gotland
97 P19 **Gotland** *var.* Gothland, Gottland. ◐ *county* SE Sweden
97 O18 **Gotland** *island* SE Sweden
170 B12 **Gotō-rettō** *island group* SW Japan
116 H12 **Gotse Delchev** *prev.* Nevrokop. Sofiyska Oblast, SW Bulgaria
97 P17 **Gotska Sandön** *island* SE Sweden
170 Ee12 **Gōtsu** *var.* Gôtu. Shimane, Honshū, SW Japan
103 I15 **Göttingen** *var.* Goettingen. Niedersachsen, C Germany
Gottland *see* Gotland
95 I16 **Gottne** Västernorrland, C Sweden
Gottschee *see* Kočevje
Gottwaldov *see* Zlín

◆ Country
● Country Capital
◇ Dependent Territory
○ Dependent Territory Capital
◐ Administrative Region
✕ International Airport
▲ Mountain
▲▲ Mountain Range
Volcano
≈ River
◎ Lake
⊠ Reservoir

GÔTU – GREVENMACHER

Gôtu see Gôtsu
Goturdepe see Koturdepe
110 I7 **Götzis** Vorarlberg, NW Austria
100 H12 **Gouda** Zuid-Holland, C Netherlands
78 I11 **Goudiri** var. Goudiry. E Senegal
Goudiry see Goudiri
79 X12 **Goudoumaria** Diffa, S Niger
13 R9 **Gouffre, Rivière du** ~ Québec, SE Canada
67 M19 **Gough Fracture Zone** tectonic feature S Atlantic Ocean
67 M19 **Gough Island** island Tristan da Cunha, S Atlantic Ocean
13 N8 **Gouin, Réservoir** ⊠ Québec, SE Canada
12 B10 **Goulais River** Ontario, S Canada
191 R9 **Goulburn** New South Wales, SE Australia
191 O11 **Goulburn River** ~ Victoria, SE Australia
205 O10 **Gould Coast** physical region Antarctica
Goulimime see Guelmime
116 F13 **Gouménissa** Kentrikí Makedonía, N Greece
79 O10 **Goundam** Tombouctou, NW Mali
80 H12 **Goundi** Moyen-Chari, S Chad
80 G12 **Gounou-Gaya** Mayo-Kébbi, SW Chad
79 O12 **Gourci** var. Gourcy. NW Burkina
Gourcy see Gourci
104 M13 **Gourdon** Lot, S France
79 W11 **Gouré** Zinder, SE Niger
104 G6 **Gourin** Morbihan, NW France
79 P10 **Gourma-Rharous** Tombouctou, C Mali
105 N4 **Gournay-en-Bray** Seine-Maritime, N France
80 J6 **Gouro** Borkou-Ennedi-Tibesti, N Chad
106 H8 **Gouveia** Guarda, N Portugal
20 I7 **Gouverneur** New York, NE USA
101 L21 **Gouvy** Luxembourg, E Belgium
47 R14 **Gouyave** var. Charlotte Town. NW Grenada
Goverla, Gora see Hoverla, Hora
61 N20 **Governador Valadares** Minas Gerais, SE Brazil
179 Rr16 **Governor Generoso** Mindanao, S Philippines
46 I2 **Governor's Harbour** Eleuthera Island, C Bahamas
168 F9 **Govĭ-Altay** ◆ province SW Mongolia
168 I10 **Govĭ Altayn Nuruu** ▲ S Mongolia
160 L9 **Govind Ballabh Pant Sāgar** ⊠ C India
158 I7 **Govind Sagar** ⊠ NE India
153 N14 **Govurdak** Turkm. Gowurdak; prev. Guardak. Lebapskiy Velayat, E Turkmenistan
20 D11 **Gowanda** New York, NE USA
154 J10 **Gowd-e Zereh, Dasht-e** var. Guad-i-Zirreh. marsh SW Afghanistan
12 F8 **Gowganda** Ontario, S Canada
12 G8 **Gowganda Lake** ◎ Ontario, S Canada
31 U13 **Gowrie** Iowa, C USA
Gowurdak see Govurdak
63 C15 **Goya** Corrientes, NE Argentina
Goyania see Goiânia
143 X11 **Göyçay** Rus. Geokchay. C Azerbaijan
Goymat see Koymat
Goymatdag see Koymatdag, Gory
142 F12 **Göynük** Bolu, NW Turkey
172 N12 **Goyō-san** ▲ Honshū, C Japan
80 K11 **Goz Beïda** Ouaddaï, SE Chad
164 H11 **Gozha Co** ◎ W China
123 J15 **Gozo** Malt. Ghawdex. island N Malta
82 H9 **Göz Regeb** Kassala, NE Sudan
Gozyô see Gojō
85 H25 **Graaff-Reinet** Eastern Cape, S South Africa
Graasten see Gråsten
78 L17 **Grabo** SW Ivory Coast
114 P11 **Grabovica** Serbia, E Yugoslavia
112 I13 **Grabów nad Prosną** Kalisz, SW Poland
110 I8 **Grabs** Sankt Gallen, NE Switzerland
114 D12 **Gračac** Zadar-Knin, C Croatia
114 I11 **Gračanica** NE Bosnia and Herzegovina
12 L11 **Gracefield** Québec, SE Canada
101 K19 **Grâce-Hollogne** Liège, E Belgium
25 R8 **Graceville** Florida, SE USA
31 R8 **Graceville** Minnesota, N USA
44 G6 **Gracias** Lempira, W Honduras
Gracias see Lempira
44 L5 **Gracias a Dios** ◆ department E Honduras
45 O6 **Gracias a Dios, Cabo de** headland Honduras/Nicaragua
66 O2 **Graciosa** var. Ilha Graciosa. island Azores, Portugal, NE Atlantic Ocean
66 Q11 **Graciosa** island Islas Canarias, Spain, NE Atlantic Ocean
Graciosa, Ilha see Graciosa
114 I11 **Gradačac** N Bosnia and Herzegovina
61 J15 **Gradaús, Serra dos** ▲ C Brazil
106 L3 **Gradefes** Castilla-León, N Spain
Gradizhsk see Hradyz'k
108 J7 **Grado** Friuli-Venezia Giulia, NE Italy
106 K2 **Grado** Asturias, N Spain
115 P19 **Gradsko** C FYR Macedonia
39 V11 **Grady** New Mexico, SW USA
114 E8 **Grad Zagreb** ◆ province NC Croatia
31 T12 **Graettinger** Iowa, C USA
103 M23 **Grafing** Bayern, SE Germany
27 S6 **Graford** Texas, SW USA
191 V5 **Grafton** New South Wales, SE Australia
31 Q3 **Grafton** North Dakota, N USA
23 S3 **Grafton** West Virginia, NE USA
23 T9 **Graham** North Carolina, SE USA
27 R6 **Graham** Texas, SW USA
Graham Bell Island see Greem-Bell, Ostrov
8 I13 **Graham Island** island Queen Charlotte Islands, British Columbia, SW Canada
21 S6 **Graham Lake** ◎ Maine, NE USA
204 H4 **Graham Land** physical region Antarctica
39 N15 **Graham, Mount** ▲ Arizona, SW USA
Grahamstad see Grahamstown
85 I25 **Grahamstown** Afr. Grahamstad. Eastern Cape, S South Africa
70 C12 **Grain Coast** coastal region S Liberia
174 Mm16 **Grajagan** Jawa, S Indonesia
174 Mm16 **Grajagan, Teluk** bay Jawa, S Indonesia
61 L14 **Grajaú** Maranhão, E Brazil
60 M13 **Grajaú, Rio** ~ NE Brazil
112 O8 **Grajewo** Łomża, NE Poland
97 F24 **Gram** Sønderjylland, SW Denmark
105 N13 **Gramat** Lot, S France
24 H5 **Grambling** Louisiana, S USA
117 C14 **Grámmos** ▲ Albania/Greece
98 I9 **Grampian Mountains** ▲ C Scotland, UK
190 L12 **Grampians, The** ▲ Victoria, SE Australia
100 O9 **Gramsbergen** Overijssel, E Netherlands
115 L21 **Gramsh** var. Gramshi. Elbasan, C Albania
Gramshi see Gramsh
Gran see Hron, Slovakia
Gran see Esztergom, Hungary
56 F11 **Granada** Meta, C Colombia
44 J10 **Granada** Granada, SW Nicaragua
107 N14 **Granada** Andalucía, S Spain
39 W6 **Granada** Colorado, C USA
44 J11 **Granada** ◆ department SW Nicaragua
107 N14 **Granada** ◆ province Andalucía, S Spain
65 I21 **Gran Antiplanicie Central** plain S Argentina
99 E17 **Granard** Ir. Gránard. C Ireland
63 J20 **Gran Bajo** basin S Argentina
65 J15 **Gran Bajo del Gualicho** basin E Argentina
65 I21 **Gran Bajo de San Julián** basin SE Argentina
27 S7 **Granbury** Texas, SW USA
13 P12 **Granby** Québec, SE Canada
29 S8 **Granby** Missouri, C USA
39 S3 **Granby, Lake** ⊠ Colorado, C USA
66 O12 **Gran Canaria** var. Grand Canary. island Islas Canarias, Spain, NE Atlantic Ocean
49 T11 **Gran Chaco** var. Chaco. lowland plain South America
47 R14 **Grand Anse** SW Grenada
Grand-Anse see Portsmouth
46 G1 **Grand Bahama Island** island N Bahamas
Grand Balé see Tui
105 U7 **Grand Ballon** Ger. Ballon de Guebwiller. ▲ NE France
11 T13 **Grand Bank** Newfoundland, Newfoundland and Labrador, SE Canada
66 I7 **Grand Banks of Newfoundland** undersea feature NW Atlantic Ocean
Grand Bassa see Buchanan
79 N17 **Grand-Bassam** var. Bassam. SE Ivory Coast
12 E16 **Grand Bend** Ontario, S Canada
78 L17 **Grand-Bérébi** var. Grand-Béréby. SW Ivory Coast
Grand-Béréby see Grand-Bérébi
47 X11 **Grand-Bourg** Marie-Galante, SE Guadeloupe
46 M6 **Grand Caicos** var. Middle Caicos. island C Turks and Caicos Islands
12 K12 **Grand Calumet, Île du** island Québec, SE Canada
99 E18 **Grand Canal** Ir. An Chanáil Mhór. canal C Ireland
Grand Canary see Gran Canaria
38 K10 **Grand Canyon** Arizona, SW USA
38 J9 **Grand Canyon** canyon Arizona, SW USA
Grand Canyon State see Arizona
46 D8 **Grand Cayman** island SW Cayman Islands
9 R14 **Grand Centre** Alberta, SW Canada
78 L17 **Grand Cess** SE Liberia
110 D12 **Grand Combin** ▲ S Switzerland
34 K8 **Grand Coulee** Washington, NW USA
34 J8 **Grand Coulee** valley Washington, NW USA
47 X5 **Grand Cul-de-Sac Marin** bay N Guadeloupe
Grand Duchy of Luxembourg see Luxembourg
65 I22 **Grande, Bahía** bay S Argentina
9 N14 **Grande Cache** Alberta, W Canada
105 U12 **Grande Casse** ▲ E France
180 G12 **Grande Comore** var. Njazidja, Great Comoro. island NW Comoros
63 G18 **Grande, Cuchilla** hill range E Uruguay
47 S5 **Grande de Añasco, Río** ~ W Puerto Rico
Grande de Chiloé, Isla see Chiloé, Isla de
60 J12 **Grande de Gurupá, Ilha** river island NE Brazil
59 K21 **Grande de Lipez, Río** ~ SW Bolivia
47 U6 **Grande de Loíza, Río** ~ E Puerto Rico
47 T5 **Grande de Manatí, Río** ~ C Puerto Rico
44 L9 **Grande de Matagalpa, Río** ~ C Nicaragua
42 K12 **Grande de Santiago, Río** var. Santiago. ~ C Mexico
45 O15 **Grande de Térraba, Río** var. Río Térraba. ~ SE Costa Rica
10 J9 **Grande Deux, Réservoir la** ⊠ Québec, E Canada
62 O10 **Grande, Ilha** island SE Brazil
9 O13 **Grande Prairie** Alberta, W Canada
76 I8 **Grand Erg Occidental** desert W Algeria
76 L9 **Grand Erg Oriental** desert Algeria/Tunisia
61 J20 **Grande, Rio** ~ S Brazil
2 F15 **Grande, Rio** var. Río Bravo, Sp. Río Bravo del Norte, Bravo del Norte. ~ Mexico/USA
59 M18 **Grande, Río** ~ C Bolivia
13 Y7 **Grande-Rivière** Québec, SE Canada
13 Y6 **Grande Rivière** ~ Québec, SE Canada
46 M8 **Grande-Rivière-du-Nord** N Haiti
64 K9 **Grande, Salina** var. Gran Salitral. salt lake C Argentina
13 S7 **Grandes-Bergeronnes** Québec, SE Canada
49 W6 **Grande, Serra** ▲ W Brazil
42 K4 **Grande, Sierra** ▲ N Mexico
105 S12 **Grandes Rousses** ▲ E France
65 K17 **Grandes, Salinas** salt lake E Argentina
47 Y5 **Grande Terre** island E West Indies
13 X5 **Grande-Vallée** Québec, SE Canada
47 Y5 **Grande Vigie, Pointe de la** headland Grande Terre, N Guadeloupe
11 N14 **Grand Falls** New Brunswick, SE Canada
11 T11 **Grand Falls** Newfoundland, Newfoundland and Labrador, SE Canada
26 L9 **Grandfalls** Texas, SW USA
23 P9 **Grandfather Mountain** ▲ North Carolina, SE USA
28 L13 **Grandfield** Oklahoma, C USA
9 N17 **Grand Forks** British Columbia, SW Canada
31 R4 **Grand Forks** North Dakota, N USA
33 O9 **Grand Haven** Michigan, N USA
Grandichi see Hrandzichy
31 P15 **Grand Island** Nebraska, C USA
33 O3 **Grand Island** island Michigan, N USA
24 K10 **Grand Isle** Louisiana, S USA
67 A23 **Grand Jason** island Jason Islands, NW Falkland Islands
39 P5 **Grand Junction** Colorado, C USA
22 F10 **Grand Junction** Tennessee, S USA
12 J9 **Grand-Lac-Victoria** Québec, SE Canada
12 J9 **Grand lac Victoria** ◎ Québec, SE Canada
79 N17 **Grand-Lahou** var. Grand Lahu. S Ivory Coast
Grand Lahu see Grand-Lahou
39 S3 **Grand Lake** Colorado, C USA
11 S11 **Grand Lake** ◎ Newfoundland, Newfoundland and Labrador, E Canada
24 G9 **Grand Lake** ◎ Louisiana, S USA
33 R5 **Grand Lake** ◎ Michigan, N USA
33 Q13 **Grand Lake** ⊠ Ohio, N USA
29 R9 **Grand Lake O' The Cherokees** var. Lake O' The Cherokees. ⊠ Oklahoma, C USA
33 Q9 **Grand Ledge** Michigan, N USA
104 I8 **Grand-Lieu, Lac de** ◎ NW France
21 U6 **Grand Manan Channel** channel Canada/USA
11 O15 **Grand Manan Island** island New Brunswick, SE Canada
31 Y4 **Grand Marais** Minnesota, N USA
13 P10 **Grand-Mère** Québec, SE Canada
39 P5 **Grand Mesa** ▲ Colorado, C USA
110 C10 **Grand Muveran** ▲ W Switzerland
106 G12 **Grândola** Setúbal, S Portugal
Grand Paradis see Gran Paradiso
197 G4 **Grand Passage** passage N New Caledonia
79 R16 **Grand-Popo** S Benin
31 Z3 **Grand Portage** Minnesota, N USA
27 T6 **Grand Prairie** Texas, SW USA
9 W14 **Grand Rapids** Manitoba, C Canada
33 P9 **Grand Rapids** Michigan, N USA
31 V5 **Grand Rapids** Minnesota, N USA
197 G5 **Grand Récif de Koumac** reef W New Caledonia
197 J8 **Grand Récif Sud** reef S New Caledonia
12 L10 **Grand-Remous** Québec, SE Canada
12 F15 **Grand River** ~ Ontario, S Canada
33 P9 **Grand River** ~ Michigan, N USA
29 T3 **Grand River** ~ Missouri, C USA
30 M7 **Grand River** ~ South Dakota, N USA
47 Q11 **Grand' Rivière** N Martinique
34 F11 **Grand Ronde** Oregon, NW USA
34 L11 **Grand Ronde River** ~ Oregon/Washington, NW USA
Grand-Saint-Bernard, Col du see Great Saint Bernard Pass
27 V6 **Grand Saline** Texas, SW USA
57 X10 **Grand-Santi** W French Guiana
Grandsee see Grandson
110 B9 **Grandson** prev. Grandsee. Vaud, W Switzerland
180 J16 **Grand Sœur** island Les Sœurs, NE Seychelles
35 S14 **Grand Teton** ▲ Wyoming, C USA
33 P5 **Grand Traverse Bay** lake bay Michigan, N USA
47 N6 **Grand Turk** ○ (Turks and Caicos Islands) Grand Turk Island, S Turks and Caicos Islands
47 N6 **Grand Turk Island** island SE Turks and Caicos Islands
105 S13 **Grand Veymont** ▲ E France
9 W15 **Grandview** Manitoba, S Canada
29 R4 **Grandview** Missouri, C USA
38 I10 **Grand Wash Cliffs** cliff Arizona, SW USA
12 J8 **Granet, Lac** ◎ Québec, SE Canada
97 L14 **Grangärde** Kopparberg, C Sweden
46 H12 **Grange Hill** W Jamaica
98 J12 **Grangemouth** C Scotland, UK
27 T10 **Granger** Texas, SW USA
34 J10 **Granger** Washington, NW USA
35 T17 **Granger** Wyoming, C USA
Granges see Grenchen
97 L14 **Grängesberg** Kopparberg, C Sweden
35 N11 **Grangeville** Idaho, NW USA
8 K13 **Granisle** British Columbia, SW Canada
32 K15 **Granite City** Illinois, N USA
31 S9 **Granite Falls** Minnesota, N USA
23 Q9 **Granite Falls** North Carolina, SE USA
38 K12 **Granite Mountain** ▲ Arizona, SW USA
35 T12 **Granite Peak** ▲ Montana, NW USA
37 T2 **Granite Peak** ▲ Nevada, W USA
38 J3 **Granite Peak** ▲ Utah, W USA
Granite State see New Hampshire
109 H24 **Granitola, Capo** headland Sicilia, Italy, C Mediterranean Sea
193 H15 **Granity** West Coast, South Island, NZ
Gran Lago see Nicaragua, Lago de
65 J18 **Gran Laguna Salada** ◎ S Argentina
Gran Malvina see West Falkland
97 L18 **Gränna** Jönköping, S Sweden
107 W5 **Granollers** var. Granollérs. Cataluña, NE Spain
108 A7 **Gran Paradiso** Fr. Grand Paradis. ▲ NW Italy
Gran Pilastro see Hochfeiler
Gran Salitral see Grande, Salina
Gran San Bernardo, Passo di see Great Saint Bernard Pass
Gran Santiago see Santiago
109 J14 **Gran Sasso d'Italia** ▲ C Italy
102 N11 **Gransee** Brandenburg, NE Germany
30 L15 **Grant** Nebraska, C USA
29 R1 **Grant City** Missouri, C USA
99 N19 **Grantham** E England, UK
67 D24 **Grantham Sound** sound East Falkland, Falkland Islands
204 K13 **Grant Island** island Antarctica
47 Z14 **Grantley Adams** ✕ (Bridgetown) SE Barbados
37 S7 **Grant, Mount** ▲ Nevada, W USA
98 J9 **Grantown-on-Spey** N Scotland, UK
37 W8 **Grant Range** ▲ Nevada, W USA
39 Q11 **Grants** New Mexico, SW USA
32 I4 **Grantsburg** Wisconsin, N USA
34 F15 **Grants Pass** Oregon, NW USA
38 K3 **Grantsville** Utah, W USA
23 R4 **Grantsville** West Virginia, NE USA
104 I5 **Granville** Manche, N France
9 V12 **Granville Lake** ◎ Manitoba, C Canada
27 V8 **Grapeland** Texas, SW USA
27 T6 **Grapevine** Texas, SW USA
85 K20 **Graskop** Mpumalanga, NE South Africa
97 P14 **Gräsö** Uppsala, C Sweden
95 I19 **Gräsö** island C Sweden
105 U15 **Grasse** Alpes-Maritimes, SE France
20 E14 **Grassflat** Pennsylvania, NE USA
35 U9 **Grassrange** Montana, NW USA
20 J6 **Grass River** ~ New York, NE USA
37 P6 **Grass Valley** California, W USA
191 N14 **Grassy** Tasmania, SE Australia
30 K4 **Grassy Butte** North Dakota, N USA
23 R5 **Grassy Knob** ▲ West Virginia, NE USA
97 G24 **Gråsten** var. Graasten. Sønderjylland, SW Denmark
97 J18 **Grästorp** Skaraborg, S Sweden
Gratianopolis see Grenoble
111 V8 **Gratwein** Steiermark, SE Austria
Gratz see Graz
110 I9 **Graubünden** Fr. Grisons, It. Grigioni. ◆ canton SE Switzerland
Graudenz see Grudziądz
105 N15 **Graulhet** Tarn, S France
107 T4 **Graus** Aragón, NE Spain
63 I16 **Gravataí** Rio Grande do Sul, S Brazil
100 L13 **Grave** Noord-Brabant, SE Netherlands
9 T17 **Gravelbourg** Saskatchewan, S Canada
105 N1 **Gravelines** Nord, N France
Graven see Grez-Doiceau
12 H13 **Gravenhurst** Ontario, S Canada
35 O10 **Grave Peak** ▲ Idaho, NW USA
104 I11 **Grave, Pointe de** headland W France
191 S4 **Gravesend** New South Wales, SE Australia
99 P22 **Gravesend** SE England, UK
109 N17 **Gravina di Puglia** Eng. Gravina in Puglia. Puglia, SE Italy
Gravina in Puglia see Gravina di Puglia
105 S8 **Gray** Haute-Saône, E France
25 T4 **Gray** Georgia, SE USA
34 F9 **Grayland** Washington, NW USA
41 N10 **Grayling** Alaska, USA
33 Q6 **Grayling** Michigan, N USA
34 F9 **Grays Harbor** inlet Washington, NW USA
23 O5 **Grayson** Kentucky, S USA
39 S4 **Grays Peak** ▲ Colorado, C USA
32 M16 **Grayville** Illinois, N USA
111 V8 **Graz** prev. Gratz. Steiermark, SE Austria
106 L15 **Grazalema** Andalucía, S Spain
115 P15 **Grdelica** Serbia, SE Yugoslavia
46 H1 **Great Abaco** var. Abaco Island. island N Bahamas
Great Admiralty Island see Manus Island
Great Alfold see Great Hungarian Plain
Great Ararat see Büyükağrı Dağı
189 U8 **Great Artesian Basin** lowlands Queensland, C Australia
197 I15 **Great Astrolabe Reef** reef Kadavu, SW Fiji
189 O12 **Great Australian Bight** bight S Australia
66 E11 **Great Bahama Bank** undersea feature E Gulf of Mexico
192 M4 **Great Barrier Island** island N NZ
189 X4 **Great Barrier Reef** reef Queensland, NE Australia
20 L11 **Great Barrington** Massachusetts, NE USA
1 F10 **Great Basin** basin W USA
15 H5 **Great Bear Lake** Fr. Grand Lac de l'Ours. ◎ Northwest Territories, NW Canada
Great Belt see Storebælt
28 L5 **Great Bend** Kansas, C USA
Great Bermuda see Bermuda
99 A20 **Great Blasket Island** Ir. An Blascaod Mór. island SW Ireland
Great Britain see Britain
157 Q23 **Great Channel** channel Andaman Sea/Indian Ocean
177 F10 **Great Coco Island** island SW Myanmar
Great Crosby see Crosby
23 X7 **Great Dismal Swamp** wetland North Carolina/Virginia, SE USA
35 V16 **Great Divide Basin** basin Wyoming, C USA
189 W7 **Great Dividing Range** ▲ NE Australia
12 D12 **Great Duck Island** island Ontario, S Canada
Great Elder Reservoir see Waconda Lake
205 V8 **Greater Antarctica** var. East Antarctica. physical region Antarctica
46 G8 **Greater Antilles** island group West Indies
133 V16 **Greater Sunda Islands** var. Sunda Islands. island group Indonesia
Greater Warsaw see Warszawa
192 I1 **Great Exhibition Bay** inlet North Island, NZ
46 H4 **Great Exuma Island** island C Bahamas
35 R8 **Great Falls** Montana, NW USA
23 R11 **Great Falls** South Carolina, SE USA
86 F9 **Great Fisher Bank** undersea feature C North Sea
Great Glen see Mor, Glen
Great Grimsby see Grimsby
46 I4 **Great Guana Cay** island C Bahamas
66 I5 **Great Hellefiske Bank** undersea feature N Atlantic Ocean
113 L24 **Great Hungarian Plain** var. Great Alfold, Plain of Hungary, Hung. Alföld. plain SE Europe
46 L7 **Great Inagua** var. Inagua Islands. island S Bahamas
Great Indian Desert see Thar Desert
85 G25 **Great Karoo** var. Great Karroo, High Veld, Afr. Groot Karoo, Hoë Karoo. plateau region S South Africa
Great Karroo see Great Karoo
Great Kei see Groot-Kei
Great Khingan Range see Da Hinggan Ling
12 E11 **Great La Cloche Island** island Ontario, S Canada
191 P16 **Great Lake** ◎ Tasmania, SE Australia
Great Lake see Tônlé Sap
16 O16 **Great Lakes** lakes Ontario, Canada/USA
Great Lakes State see Michigan
99 L20 **Great Malvern** W England, UK
192 M5 **Great Mercury Island** island N NZ
Great Meteor Seamount see Great Meteor Tablemount
66 K10 **Great Meteor Tablemount** var. Great Meteor Seamount. undersea feature E Atlantic Ocean
33 Q14 **Great Miami River** ~ Ohio, N USA
157 Q24 **Great Nicobar** island Nicobar Islands, India, NE Indian Ocean
69 T4 **Great Oasis, The** var. Khârga Oasis. oasis S Egypt
99 O19 **Great Ouse** var. Ouse. ~ E England, UK
191 Q17 **Great Oyster Bay** bay Tasmania, SE Australia
46 I13 **Great Pedro Bluff** headland W Jamaica
23 T12 **Great Pee Dee River** ~ North Carolina/South Carolina, SE USA
133 W9 **Great Plain of China** plain E China
2 F12 **Great Plains** var. High Plains. plains Canada/USA
39 W6 **Great Plains Reservoirs** ⊠ Colorado, C USA
21 Q13 **Great Point** headland Nantucket Island, Massachusetts, NE USA
70 I13 **Great Rift Valley** var. Rift Valley. depression Asia/Africa
83 I23 **Great Ruaha** ~ S Tanzania
20 K10 **Great Sacandaga Lake** ⊠ New York, NE USA
110 C12 **Great Saint Bernard Pass** Fr. Col du Grand-Saint-Bernard, It. Passo di Gran San Bernardo. pass Italy/Switzerland
46 F1 **Great Sale Cay** island N Bahamas
Great Salt Desert see Kavīr, Dasht-e
38 K1 **Great Salt Lake** salt lake Utah, W USA
38 J3 **Great Salt Lake Desert** plain Utah, W USA
28 M8 **Great Salt Plains Lake** ⊠ Oklahoma, C USA
77 T9 **Great Sand Sea** desert Egypt/Libya
188 L6 **Great Sandy Desert** desert Western Australia
Great Sandy Desert see Ar Rub' al Khālī
Great Sandy Island see Fraser Island
197 I13 **Great Sea Reef** reef Vanua Levu, N Fiji
40 H17 **Great Sitkin Island** island Aleutian Islands, Alaska, USA
15 I8 **Great Slave Lake** Fr. Grand Lac des Esclaves. ◎ Northwest Territories, NW Canada
23 O10 **Great Smoky Mountains** ▲ North Carolina/Tennessee, SE USA
8 L11 **Great Snow Mountain** ▲ British Columbia, W Canada
66 A12 **Great Sound** bay Bermuda, NW Atlantic Ocean
188 M10 **Great Victoria Desert** desert South Australia/Western Australia
204 H2 **Great Wall** Chinese research station South Shetland Islands, Antarctica
21 T7 **Great Wass Island** island Maine, NE USA
99 Q19 **Great Yarmouth** var. Yarmouth. E England, UK
145 S1 **Great Zab** Ar. Az Zāb al Kabīr, Kurd. Zē-i Bādinān, Turk. Büyükzap Suyu. ~ Iraq/Turkey
97 I17 **Grebbestad** Göteborg och Bohus, S Sweden
Grebenka see Hrebinka
44 M13 **Grecia** Alajuela, C Costa Rica
63 E18 **Greco** Río Negro, W Uruguay
Greco, Cape see Gkréko, Akrotíri
106 L8 **Gredos, Sierra de** ▲ W Spain
20 F9 **Greece** New York, NE USA
117 E17 **Greece** off. Hellenic Republic, Gk. Ellás; anc. Hellas. ◆ republic SE Europe
Greece Central see Stereá Ellás
Greece West see Dytikí Ellás
39 T3 **Greeley** Colorado, C USA
31 P14 **Greeley** Nebraska, C USA
126 Hh1 **Greem-Bell, Ostrov** Eng. Graham Bell Island. island Zemlya Frantsa-Iosifa, N Russian Federation
32 M6 **Green Bay** Wisconsin, N USA
33 N6 **Green Bay** lake bay Michigan/Wisconsin, N USA
23 S5 **Greenbrier River** ~ West Virginia, NE USA
31 S2 **Greenbush** Minnesota, N USA
191 R12 **Green Cape** headland New South Wales, SE Australia
33 O14 **Greencastle** Indiana, N USA
20 F16 **Greencastle** Pennsylvania, NE USA
29 T2 **Green City** Missouri, C USA
23 O9 **Greeneville** Tennessee, S USA
37 O11 **Greenfield** California, W USA
33 P14 **Greenfield** Indiana, N USA
31 U15 **Greenfield** Iowa, C USA
20 M11 **Greenfield** Massachusetts, NE USA
29 S7 **Greenfield** Missouri, C USA
33 S14 **Greenfield** Ohio, N USA
22 G8 **Greenfield** Tennessee, S USA
32 M9 **Greenfield** Wisconsin, N USA
29 T9 **Green Forest** Arkansas, C USA
39 T7 **Greenhorn Mountain** ▲ Colorado, C USA
Green Island see Lü Tao
195 R10 **Green Islands** var. Nissan Islands. island group NE PNG
9 S14 **Green Lake** Saskatchewan, C Canada
32 L8 **Green Lake** ◎ Wisconsin, N USA
207 O14 **Greenland** Dan. Grønland, Inuit Kalaallit Nunaat. ◇ Danish external territory NE North America
86 D4 **Greenland** island NE North America
207 R13 **Greenland Plain** undersea feature N Greenland Sea
94 J1 **Greenland Sea** sea Arctic Ocean
39 R4 **Green Mountain Reservoir** ⊠ Colorado, C USA
20 M8 **Green Mountains** ▲ Vermont, NE USA
Green Mountain State see Vermont
98 H12 **Greenock** W Scotland, UK
41 T5 **Greenough, Mount** ▲ Alaska, USA
194 E10 **Green River** Sandaun, NW PNG
39 N5 **Green River** Utah, W USA
35 U17 **Green River** Wyoming, C USA
18 Ii7 **Green River** ~ W USA
32 K11 **Green River** ~ Illinois, N USA
22 J7 **Green River** ~ Kentucky, S USA
30 K5 **Green River** ~ North Dakota, N USA
39 N6 **Green River** ~ Utah, W USA
35 T16 **Green River** ~ Wyoming, C USA
22 L7 **Green River Lake** ⊠ Kentucky, S USA
25 O5 **Greensboro** Alabama, S USA
25 U3 **Greensboro** Georgia, SE USA
23 T9 **Greensboro** North Carolina, SE USA
33 P14 **Greensburg** Indiana, N USA
28 K6 **Greensburg** Kansas, C USA
22 L7 **Greensburg** Kentucky, S USA
20 C15 **Greensburg** Pennsylvania, NE USA
39 O13 **Greens Peak** ▲ Arizona, SW USA
23 V12 **Green Swamp** wetland North Carolina, SE USA
23 O4 **Greenup** Kentucky, S USA
38 M16 **Green Valley** Arizona, SW USA
78 K17 **Greenville** var. Sino, Sinoe. SE Liberia
25 P6 **Greenville** Alabama, S USA
25 T8 **Greenville** Florida, SE USA
25 S4 **Greenville** Georgia, SE USA
32 L15 **Greenville** Illinois, N USA
22 I7 **Greenville** Kentucky, S USA
21 Q5 **Greenville** Maine, NE USA
33 P9 **Greenville** Michigan, N USA
24 J4 **Greenville** Mississippi, S USA
23 W9 **Greenville** North Carolina, SE USA
33 Q13 **Greenville** Ohio, N USA
21 O12 **Greenville** Rhode Island, NE USA
23 P11 **Greenville** South Carolina, SE USA
27 U6 **Greenville** Texas, SW USA
33 T12 **Greenwich** Ohio, N USA
29 S11 **Greenwood** Arkansas, C USA
33 O14 **Greenwood** Indiana, N USA
24 K4 **Greenwood** Mississippi, S USA
23 P12 **Greenwood** South Carolina, SE USA
23 Q12 **Greenwood, Lake** ⊠ South Carolina, SE USA
23 P11 **Greer** South Carolina, SE USA
29 V10 **Greers Ferry Lake** ⊠ Arkansas, C USA
29 S13 **Greeson, Lake** ⊠ Arkansas, C USA
31 O12 **Gregory** South Dakota, N USA
190 J3 **Gregory, Lake** salt lake South Australia
188 J9 **Gregory Lake** ◎ W Australia
189 V5 **Gregory Range** ▲ Queensland, E Australia
Greifenberg/Greifenberg in Pommern see Gryfice
Greifenhagen see Gryfino
102 O8 **Greifswald** Mecklenburg-Vorpommern, NE Germany
102 O8 **Greifswalder Bodden** bay NE Germany
111 U4 **Grein** Oberösterreich, N Austria
103 M17 **Greiz** Thüringen, C Germany
Gremicha/Gremiha see Gremikha
128 M4 **Gremikha** var. Gremicha, Gremiha. Murmanskaya Oblast', NW Russian Federation
129 V14 **Gremyachinsk** Permskaya Oblast', NW Russian Federation
97 H21 **Grenå** var. Grenaa. Århus, C Denmark
Grenaa see Grenå
24 L3 **Grenada** Mississippi, S USA
47 W15 **Grenada** ◆ commonwealth republic SE West Indies
49 S4 **Grenada** island Grenada
49 R4 **Grenada Basin** undersea feature W Atlantic Ocean
24 L3 **Grenada Lake** ⊠ Mississippi, S USA
47 Y14 **Grenadines, The** island group Grenada/St Vincent and the Grenadines
110 D7 **Grenchen** Fr. Granges. Solothurn, NW Switzerland
191 Q9 **Grenfell** New South Wales, SE Australia
9 V16 **Grenfell** Saskatchewan, S Canada
94 J1 **Grenivík** Nordhurland Eystra, N Iceland
105 S12 **Grenoble** anc. Cularo, Gratianopolis. Isère, E France
30 J2 **Grenora** North Dakota, N USA
94 N8 **Grense-Jakobselv** Finnmark, N Norway
47 S14 **Grenville** E Grenada
34 G11 **Gresham** Oregon, NW USA
Gresk see Hresk
108 B7 **Gressoney-St-Jean** Valle d'Aosta, NW Italy
24 K9 **Gretna** Louisiana, S USA
23 T7 **Gretna** Virginia, NE USA
100 F13 **Grevelingen** inlet S North Sea
102 F13 **Greven** Nordrhein-Westfalen, NW Germany
117 D15 **Grevená** Dytikí Makedonía, N Greece
103 D16 **Grevenbroich** Nordrhein-Westfalen, W Germany
101 N24 **Grevenmacher** Grevenmacher, E Luxembourg
101 M24 **Grevenmacher** ◆ district E Luxembourg

◆ Country ● Country Capital ◇ Dependent Territory ○ Dependent Territory Capital ◈ Administrative Region ✕ International Airport ▲ Mountain ▲ Mountain Range Volcano ~ River ◎ Lake ⊠ Reservoir

102 K9 **Grevesmülhen** Mecklenburg-
Vorpommern, N Germany
193 H16 **Grey** ≈ South Island, NZ
35 V12 **Greybull** Wyoming, C USA
35 U13 **Greybull River** ≈ Wyoming,
C USA
67 A24 **Grey Channel** sound
Falkland Islands
Greyerzer See see Gruyère,
Lac de la
11 T10 **Grey Islands** island group
Newfoundland and Labrador,
E Canada
20 L10 **Greylock, Mount**
▲ Massachusetts, NE USA
193 G17 **Greymouth** West Coast, South
Island, NZ
189 U10 **Grey Range** ▲ New South
Wales/Queensland, E Australia
99 G18 **Greystones Ir.** Na Clocha
Liatha. E Ireland
193 M14 **Greytown** Wellington, North
Island, NZ
85 K23 **Greytown** KwaZulu/Natal,
E South Africa
Greytown see San Juan del Norte
101 H19 **Grez-Doiceau Dut.** Graven.
Walloon Brabant, C Belgium
117 J19 **Griá, Ákra** headland Ándros,
Kykládes, Greece, Aegean Sea
131 N8 **Gribanovskiy** Voronezhskaya
Oblast', W Russian Federation
80 I13 **Gribingui** ≈ N Central
African Republic
37 U6 **Gridley** California, W USA
85 G23 **Griekwastad** Northern Cape,
C South Africa
25 S4 **Griffin** Georgia, SE USA
191 O9 **Griffith** New South Wales,
SE Australia
12 F13 **Griffith Island** island Ontario,
S Canada
23 W10 **Grifton** North Carolina, SE USA
Grigioni see Graubünden
121 H14 **Grigiškes** Trakai, SE Lithuania
119 N10 **Grigoriopol** C Moldova
153 X7 **Grigor'yevka** Issyk-Kul'skaya
Oblast', E Kyrgyzstan
200 Oo9 **Grijalva Ridge** undersea feature
E Pacific Ocean
43 U15 **Grijalva, Río** var. Tabasco.
≈ Guatemala/Mexico
100 N5 **Grijpskerk** Groningen,
NE Netherlands
85 C22 **Grillenthal** Karas, SW Namibia
81 J15 **Grimari** Ouaka, C Central
African Republic
Grimaylov see Hrymayliv
101 G18 **Grimbergen** Vlaams Brabant,
C Belgium
191 N15 **Grim, Cape** headland Tasmania,
SE Australia
102 N8 **Grimmen** Mecklenburg-
Vorpommern, NE Germany
12 G16 **Grimsby** Ontario, S Canada
99 O17 **Grimsby** prev. Great Grimsby.
E England, UK
94 J1 **Grimsey** var. Grimsey. island
N Iceland
9 O12 **Grimshaw** Alberta, W Canada
97 F18 **Grimstad** Aust-Agder, S Norway
94 H4 **Grindavík** Reykjanes,
W Iceland
110 F9 **Grindelwald** Bern,
S Switzerland
97 F23 **Grindsted** Ribe, W Denmark
31 W14 **Grinnell** Iowa, C USA
111 U10 **Grintavec** ▲ N Slovenia
190 H1 **Griselda, Lake** salt lake South
Australia
Grisons see Graubünden
97 P14 **Grisslehamn** Stockholm,
C Sweden
31 T15 **Griswold** Iowa, C USA
104 M1 **Griz Nez, Cap** headland
N France
114 P13 **Grljan** Serbia, E Yugoslavia
114 E11 **Grmeč** ▲ NW Bosnia and
Herzegovina
101 H16 **Grobbendonk** Antwerpen,
N Belgium
Grobin see Grobiņa
120 C10 **Grobiņa Ger.** Grobin. Liepāja,
W Latvia
85 K20 **Groblersdal** Mpumalanga,
NE South Africa
85 G23 **Groblershoop** Northern Cape,
W South Africa
Gródek Jagielloński see
Horodok
111 Q6 **Grödig** Salzburg, W Austria
113 H15 **Grodków** Opole, SW Poland
Grodnenskaya Oblast' see
Hrodzyenskaya Voblasts'
Grodno see Hrodna
112 L12 **Grodzisk Mazowiecki**
Warszawa, C Poland
112 F12 **Grodzisk Wielkopolski**
Poznań, W Poland
Grodzyanka see Hradzyanka
100 O12 **Groenlo** Gelderland,
E Netherlands
85 E22 **Groenrivier** Karas, SE Namibia
27 U8 **Groesbeck** Texas, SW USA
100 L13 **Groesbeek** Gelderland,
SE Netherlands
104 G7 **Groix, Îles de** island group
NW France
112 M13 **Grójec** Radom, C Poland
67 K15 **Gröll Seamount** undersea feature
C Atlantic Ocean
102 E13 **Gronau** var. Gronau in
Westfalen. Nordrhein-Westfalen,
NW Germany
Gronau in Westfalen
see Gronau
95 F15 **Grong** Nord-Trøndelag,
C Norway
97 N22 **Grönhögen** Kalmar, S Sweden
100 N5 **Groningen** Groningen,
NE Netherlands
57 W9 **Groningen** Saramacca,
N Suriname
100 N5 **Groningen** ♦ province
NE Netherlands
Grønland see Greenland

110 H11 **Grono** Graubünden,
S Switzerland
97 M20 **Grönskåra** Kalmar, S Sweden
27 O2 **Groom** Texas, SW USA
37 W9 **Groom Lake** ⊙ Nevada, W USA
85 H25 **Groot** ≈ S South Africa
189 S2 **Groote Eylandt** island Northern
Territory, N Australia
100 M6 **Grootegast** Groningen,
NE Netherlands
85 D17 **Grootfontein** Otjozondjupa,
N Namibia
85 E22 **Groot Karasberge**
▲ S Namibia
85 J25 **Groot-Kei Eng.** Great Kei.
≈ S South Africa
Groot Karoo see Great Karoo
85 J25 **Groot-Kei Eng.** Great Kei.
≈ S South Africa
47 T10 **Gros Islet** N Saint Lucia
46 L8 **Gros-Morne** NW Haiti
11 S11 **Gros Morne** ▲ Newfoundland,
Newfoundland and Labrador,
E Canada
105 R9 **Grosne** ≈ C France
47 S12 **Gros Piton** ▲ SW Saint Lucia
94 J4 **Grossa, Isola** see Dugi Otok
Grossbetschkerek see
Zrenjanin
Grosse Isper see Grosse Ysper
Grosse Kokel see Târnava Mare
103 M21 **Grosse Laaber** var. Grosse
Laber. ≈ SE Germany
Grosse Laber see Grosse Laaber
Grosse Morava see
Velika Morava
103 O15 **Grossenhain** Sachsen,
E Germany
111 Y4 **Grossenzersdorf**
Niederösterreich, NE Austria
103 R17 **Grosser Arber** ▲ SE Germany
103 I17 **Grosser Beerberg** ▲
C Germany
103 G18 **Grosser Feldberg** ▲
W Germany
111 O8 **Grosser Löffler It.** Monte
Lovello. ▲ Austria/Italy
111 N8 **Grosser Möseler** var. Mesule.
▲ Austria/Italy
102 J8 **Grosser Plöner See** ⊙
N Germany
103 O21 **Grosser Rachel** ▲ SE Germany
Grosser Sund see Suur Väin
13 V6 **Grosses-Roches** Québec,
SE Canada
111 P8 **Grosses Weiesbachhorn** var.
Wiesbachhorn. ▲ W Austria
108 F13 **Grosseto** Toscana, C Italy
103 M22 **Grosse Vils** ≈ SE Germany
111 U4 **Grosse Ysper** var. Grosse Isper.
≈ N Austria
103 G19 **Gross-Gerau** Hessen,
W Germany
111 U3 **Gross Gerungs**
Niederösterreich, N Austria
111 P8 **Grossglockner** ▲ W Austria
Grosskanizsa see Nagykanizsa
Gross-Karol see Carei
Grosskikinda see Kikinda
111 W9 **Grossklein** Steiermark,
SE Austria
Grosskoppe see Velká Deštná
Grossmeseritsch see
Velké Meziříčí
103 H19 **Grossostheim** Bayern,
C Germany
111 X7 **Grosspetersdorf** Burgenland,
SE Austria
111 T5 **Grossraming** Oberösterreich,
C Austria
103 P14 **Grossräschen** Brandenburg,
E Germany
Grossrauschenbach see Revúca
Gross-Sankt-Johannis see
Suure-Jaani
Gross-Schlatten see Abrud
111 V2 **Gross-Siegharts**
Niederösterreich, N Austria
Gross-Skaisgirren see
Bol'shakovo
Gross-Steffelsdorf see
Rimavská Sobota
Gross Strehlitz see Strzelce
Opolskie
111 O8 **Grossvenediger** ▲ W Austria
Grosswardein see Oradea
Gross Wartenberg see Syców
111 U11 **Grossuplje** C Slovenia
101 H17 **Grote Nete** ≈ N Belgium
96 E10 **Grotli** Oppland, S Norway
21 N13 **Groton** Connecticut, NE USA
31 P8 **Groton** South Dakota, N USA
109 P18 **Grottaglie** Puglia, SE Italy
109 L17 **Grottaminarda** Campania,
S Italy
108 K13 **Grottammare** Marche, C Italy
23 U5 **Grottoes** Virginia, NE USA
Grou see Greou
11 N10 **Groulx, Monts** ▲ Québec,
E Canada
12 E7 **Groundhog** ≈ Ontario,
S Canada
38 J1 **Grouse Creek** Utah, W USA
38 J1 **Grouse Creek Mountains**
▲ Utah, W USA
100 L6 **Grouw Fris.** Grou. Friesland,
N Netherlands
29 R8 **Grove** Oklahoma, C USA
21 S13 **Grove City** Ohio, N USA
20 B13 **Grove City** Pennsylvania,
NE USA
23 N3 **Grove Hill** Alabama, S USA
33 S15 **Grover** Wyoming, C USA
37 P12 **Grover City** California, W USA
27 Y11 **Groves** Texas, SW USA
21 O7 **Groveton** New Hampshire,
NE USA
27 W9 **Groveton** Texas, SW USA
38 J15 **Growler Mountains** ▲
Arizona, SW USA
Grozdovo see Bratya Daskalovi
127 P16 **Groznyy** Chechenskaya
Respublika, SW Russian
Federation
Grubeshov see Hrubieszów

114 G9 **Grubišno Polje** Bjelovar-
Bilogora, NE Croatia
Gruaire see Gorey
65 F18 **Guaiteca, Isla** island S Chile
46 G6 **Guajaba, Cayo** headland C Cuba
61 D16 **Guajará-Mirim** Rondônia,
W Brazil
Guajira see La Guajira
56 H3 **Guajira, Península de la**
peninsula N Colombia
44 J6 **Gualaco** Olancho, C Honduras
36 L7 **Gualala** California, W USA
44 E5 **Gualán** Zacapa, C Guatemala
63 C19 **Gualeguay** Entre Ríos,
E Argentina
63 D18 **Gualeguaychú** Entre Ríos,
E Argentina
63 C18 **Gualeguay, Río** ≈ E Argentina
63 K16 **Gualicho, Salina del** salt lake
S Argentina
196 B15 **Guam** ◇ US unincorporated
territory W Pacific Ocean
63 A22 **Guamblin, Isla** island
Archipiélago de los Chonos,
S Chile
42 H8 **Guamúchil** Sinaloa, C Mexico
56 H4 **Guana** var. Misión de Guana.
Zulia, NW Venezuela
46 C4 **Guanabacoa** La Habana,
N Cuba
44 K13 **Guanacaste off.** Provincia
de Guanacaste. ♦ province
NW Costa Rica
44 K12 **Guanacaste, Cordillera de**
▲ NW Costa Rica
42 J8 **Guanacaví** Durango, C Mexico
46 A5 **Guanahacabibes, Golfo de**
gulf W Cuba
44 K4 **Guanaja, Isla de** island Islas
de la Bahía, N Honduras
46 C4 **Guanajay** La Habana, W Cuba
43 N12 **Guanajuato** Guanajuato,
C Mexico
42 M12 **Guanajuato** ♦ state C Mexico
56 J6 **Guanare** Portuguesa,
N Venezuela
56 K7 **Guanare, Río** ≈ W Venezuela
56 J6 **Guanarito** Portuguesa,
NW Venezuela
166 M3 **Guancen Shan** ▲ C China
64 J9 **Guandacol** La Rioja,
W Argentina
46 A5 **Guane** Pinar del Río, W Cuba
167 N14 **Guangdong** var. Guangdong
Sheng, Kuang-tung, Kwangtung,
Yue. ♦ province S China
Guangdong Sheng see
Guangdong
Guanghua see Laohekou
Guangji see Kwangju
166 I13 **Guangnan** Yunnan, SW China
166 K14 **Guangxi** see Guangxi
Zhuangzu Zizhiqu
166 K14 **Guangxi Zhuangzu Zizhiqu**
var. Guangxi, Gui, Kuang-hsi,
Kwangsi, Eng. Kwangsi Chuang
Autonomous Region. ♦
autonomous region S China
166 J8 **Guangyuan** var. Kuang-yuan,
Kwangyuan. Sichuan, C China
167 N14 **Guangzhou** var. Kuang-chou,
Kwangchow, Eng. Canton.
Guangdong, S China
61 N19 **Guanhães** Minas Gerais,
SE Brazil
166 I12 **Guanling** var. Guanling
Bouyeizu Miaozu Zizhixian.
Guizhou, S China
**Guanling Bouyeizu Miaozu
Zizhixian** see Guanling
57 N5 **Guanta** Anzoátegui,
NE Venezuela
46 J8 **Guantánamo** Guantánamo,
SE Cuba
166 H9 **Guanxian** var. Guan Xian.
Sichuan, C China
167 Q6 **Guanyun** Jiangsu, E China
56 C12 **Guapi** Cauca, SW Colombia
45 N13 **Guápiles** Limón, NE Costa Rica
63 I15 **Guaporé** Rio Grande do Sul,
S Brazil
59 S8 **Guaporé, Río** var.
Río Iténez. ≈ Bolivia/Brazil see
also Iténez, Río
58 B7 **Guaranda** Bolívar, C Ecuador
62 H11 **Guaraniaçu** Paraná, S Brazil
61 O20 **Guarapari** Espírito Santo,
SE Brazil
62 H11 **Guarapuava** Paraná, S Brazil
62 J8 **Guararapes** São Paulo, S Brazil
107 S4 **Guara, Sierra de** ▲ NE Spain
62 N10 **Guaratinguetá** São Paulo,
S Brazil
106 I7 **Guarda** Guarda, N Portugal
106 I7 **Guarda** ♦ district N Portugal
Guardak see Govurdak
106 M3 **Guardo** Castilla-León, N Spain
106 K11 **Guareña** Extremadura, W Spain
62 I1 **Guaricana, Pico** ▲ S Brazil
62 L6 **Guárico** ♦ state Guárico,
N Venezuela
56 J7 **Guárico, Río** ≈ C Venezuela
46 J7 **Guarico, Punta** headland
E Cuba
50 G6 **Guiana Highlands** var.
Macizo de las Guayanas.
▲ N South America
Guiba see Juba
63 H16 **Guarujá** São Paulo, SE Brazil
62 I2 **Guarulhos** ✗ São Paulo,
SE Brazil
104 I7 **Guarumal** Veraguas, S Panama
63 E18 **Guasapo** see Guasopa
42 H8 **Guasave** Sinaloa, C Mexico
56 K7 **Guasdualito** Apure,
C Venezuela
57 Q7 **Guasipati** Bolívar, E Venezuela
195 Q15 **Guasopa** var. Guasapo.
Woodlark Island, SE PNG
44 J6 **Guaimaca** Francisco Morazán,
C Honduras
56 D7 **Guainía** off. Comisaría del
Guainía. ♦ province E Colombia
56 K12 **Guainía, Río** ≈
Colombia/Venezuela
57 Q9 **Guaiquinima, Cerro** elevation
SE Venezuela
64 O7 **Guairá off.** ♦ department
S Paraguay
62 G10 **Guaíra** Paraná, S Brazil
62 L7 **Guaíra** São Paulo, S Brazil
Guaire see Gorey
65 F18 **Guaiteca, Isla** island S Chile
46 G6 **Guajaba, Cayo** headland C Cuba
61 D16 **Guajará-Mirim** Rondônia,
W Brazil

85 M20 **Guijá** Gaza, S Mozambique
44 F7 **Güija, Lago de** ⊙
El Salvador/Guatemala
106 K8 **Guijuelo** Castilla-León, N Spain
Guilan see Gīlān
99 N22 **Guildford** SE England, UK
21 R5 **Guildford** Maine, NE USA
21 O7 **Guildhall** Vermont, NE USA
105 R13 **Guilherand** Ardèche, E France
166 L13 **Guilin** var. Kuei-lin, Kweilin.
Guangxi Zhuangzu Zizhiqu,
S China
13 J6 **Guillaume-Delisle, Lac**
⊙ Québec, NE Canada
105 U13 **Guillestre** Hautes-Alpes,
SE France
106 H6 **Guimarães** var. Guimarães.
Braga, N Portugal
60 D11 **Guimarães Rosas, Pico**
▲ NW Brazil
25 N3 **Guin** Alabama, S USA
Güina see Wina
78 I14 **Guinea off.** Republic of Guinea,
var. Guinée; prev. French Guinea,
People's Revolutionary Republic
of Guinea. ♦ republic W Africa
66 N13 **Guinea Basin** undersea feature
E Atlantic Ocean
78 E12 **Guinea-Bissau off.** Republic of
Guinea-Bissau, Fr. Guinée-Bissau,
Port. Guiné-Bissau; prev.
Portuguese Guinea. ♦ republic
W Africa
68 K7 **Guinea Fracture Zone** tectonic
feature E Atlantic Ocean
66 O13 **Guinea, Gulf of Fr.** Golfe de
Guinée. gulf E Atlantic Ocean
Guiné-Bissau see Guinea-Bissau
Guinée see Guinea
Guinée-Bissau see
Guinea-Bissau
78 K15 **Guinée-Forestière** ♦ state
SE Guinea
Guinée, Golfe de see Guinea,
Gulf of
78 H13 **Guinée-Maritime** ♦ state
W Guinea
46 C4 **Güines** La Habana, W Cuba
104 G5 **Guingamp** Côtes d'Armor,
NW France
107 P3 **Guipúzcoa Basq.** Gipuzkoa.
♦ province País Vasco, N Spain
97 G21 **Gudenå** var. Gudenaa.
≈ C Denmark
Gudenaa see Gudenå
131 P16 **Gudermes** Chechenskaya
Respublika, SW Russian
Federation
161 J18 **Gudūr** Andhra Pradesh, E India
152 B13 **Gudurolum** Balkanskiy Velayat,
W Turkmenistan
96 D13 **Gudvangen** Sogn og Fjordane,
S Norway
105 U7 **Guebwiller** Haut-Rhin,
NE France
Guécédou see Guékédou
12 K8 **Guéguen, Lac** ⊙ Québec,
SE Canada
78 J15 **Guékédou** var. Guécédou.
Guinée-Forestière, S Guinea
167 N14 **Guelb er Richât** physical region
C Mauritania
43 R16 **Guelatao** Oaxaca, SE Mexico
80 I7 **Guelb er Richât** physical region
C Mauritania
12 G15 **Guelph** Ontario, S Canada
104 I7 **Guémené-Penfao** Loire-
Atlantique, NW France
104 I7 **Guer** Morbihan, NW France
80 I1 **Guéra** ♦ Prefecture du Guéra.
♦ prefecture S Chad
104 H8 **Guérande** Loire-Atlantique,
NW France
80 K9 **Guéréda** Biltine, E Chad
105 N10 **Guéret** Creuse, C France
12 J16 **Gülek Boğazı** var. Cilician
Gates. pass S Turkey
194 I14 **Gulf** ♦ province S PNG
25 Q9 **Gulf Breeze** Florida, SE USA
25 V13 **Gulfport** Florida, SE USA
24 M9 **Gulfport** Mississippi, S USA
25 N9 **Gulf Shores** Alabama, S USA
Gulf, The see Persian Gulf
191 R7 **Gulgong** New South Wales,
SE Australia
166 I11 **Gulin** Sichuan, C China
176 V12 **Gulir** Pulau Kasiui, E Indonesia
143 V10 **Gulistan** see Guliston
153 P10 **Guliston Rus.** Gulistan. Sirdaryo
Wiloyati, E Uzbekistan
166 L14 **Gulja** see Yining
161 S11 **Gulkana** Alaska, USA
81 S17 **Gull Lake** Saskatchewan,
S Canada
33 P10 **Gull Lake** ⊙ Michigan, N USA
31 T6 **Gull Lake** ⊙ Minnesota, N USA
97 L16 **Gullspång** Skaraborg, S Sweden
158 H5 **Gulmarg** Jammu and Kashmir,
NW India
Gulpaigan see Golpāyegān
101 L18 **Gulpen** Limburg,
SE Netherlands
81 F17 **Gulu** NW Uganda
151 S13 **Gul'shad Kaz.** Gulshat.
Zhezkazgan, E Kazakhstan
79 U12 **Gulu** N Uganda
83 K10 **Gŭlŭbovo** Khaskovska Oblast,
C Bulgaria
166 I7 **Gulyantsi** Loveshka Oblast,
NW Bulgaria
Gulyaypole see Hulyaypole
79 W12 **Gumel** Jigawa, N Nigeria

107 N5 **Gumiel de Hizán** Castilla-
León, N Spain
194 I12 **Gumine** var. Gumire. Chimbu,
C PNG
Gumire see Gumine
159 P16 **Gumla** Bihār, N India
Gumma see Gunma
103 F16 **Gummersbach** Nordrhein-
Westfalen, W Germany
77 T13 **Gummi** Sokoto, NW Nigeria
Gumpolds see Humpolec
159 N13 **Gumti** var. Gomati. ≈ N India
Gümülcine/Gümüljina see
Komotini
3 O12 **Gümüşhane** var. Gümüşane,
Gumushkhane. Gümüşhane,
NE Turkey
3 O12 **Gümüşhane** var. Gümüşane,
Gumushkhane. ♦ province
NE Turkey
Gumushkhane see Gümüşhane
176 M13 **Gumzai** Pulau Kola, E Indonesia
160 H9 **Guna** Madhya Pradesh, C India
Gunabad see Gonābād
Gunbad-i-Qawus see Gonbad-e
Kāvūs
191 O9 **Gunbar** New South Wales,
SE Australia
191 O9 **Gun Creek** seasonal river New
South Wales, SE Australia
191 Q10 **Gundagai** New South Wales,
SE Australia
81 K17 **Gundji** Equateur, C Zaire
161 G20 **Gundlupet** Karnātaka, W India
142 G16 **Gündoğmuş** Antalya, S Turkey
143 O14 **Güney Doğu Toroslar** ▲
SE Turkey
81 J21 **Gungu** Bandundu, SW Zaire
131 P17 **Gunib** Respublika Dagestan,
SW Russian Federation
114 J11 **Gunja** Vukovar-Srijem,
E Croatia
33 P9 **Gun Lake** ⊙ Michigan, N USA
171 Ij15 **Gunma** off. Gunma-ken, var.
Gumma. ♦ prefecture Honshū,
S Japan
207 P15 **Gunnbjørn Fjeld** var.
Gunnbjörns Bjerge. ▲
C Greenland
191 S6 **Gunnedah** New South Wales,
SE Australia
181 Y15 **Gunner's Quoin** var. Coin de
Mire. island N Mauritius
39 R6 **Gunnison** Colorado, C USA
38 L5 **Gunnison** Utah, W USA
39 P5 **Gunnison River** ≈ Colorado,
C USA
23 X2 **Gunpowder River**
≈ Maryland, NE USA
Güns see Kőszeg
Gunsan see Kunsan
111 S4 **Gunskirchen** Oberösterreich,
N Austria
Gunt see Ghund
161 H17 **Guntakal** Andhra Pradesh,
C India
25 Q2 **Guntersville** Alabama, S USA
25 Q2 **Guntersville Lake** ⊟ Alabama,
S USA
111 X4 **Guntramsdorf**
Niederösterreich, E Austria
161 J16 **Guntúr** var. Guntur. Andhra
Pradesh, SE India
173 F7 **Gunungsitoli** Pulau Nias,
W Indonesia
161 M14 **Gunupur** Orissa, E India
103 J23 **Günz** ≈ S Germany
103 I22 **Günzburg** Bayern, S Germany
103 K21 **Gunzenhausen** Bayern,
S Germany
167 P7 **Guoyang** Anhui, E China
118 G11 **Gurahonţ Hung.** Honctő. Arad,
W Romania
Gurahumora see Gura
Humorului
118 K9 **Gura Humorului Ger.**
Gurahumora. Suceava,
NE Romania
164 K4 **Gurbantünggüt Shamo** desert
W China
158 H7 **Gurdāspur** Punjab, N India
27 T13 **Gurdon** Arkansas, C USA
Gurdzhaani see Gurjaani
Gurgan see Gorgān
158 I10 **Gurgaon** Haryāna, N India
61 M15 **Gurguéia, Rio** ≈ NE Brazil
57 Q7 **Guri, Embalse de**
⊟ E Venezuela
143 V10 **Gurjaani Rus.** Gurdzhaani.
E Georgia
111 T9 **Gurk Kärnten, S Austria**
111 T9 **Gurk Slvn.** Krka. ≈ S Austria
Gurkfeld see Krško
116 K9 **Gurkovo** prev. Kolupchii.
Khaskovska Oblast, C Bulgaria
111 S9 **Gurktaler Alpen** ▲ S Austria
152 H8 **Gurlan Rus.** Gurlen. Khorazm
Wiloyati, W Uzbekistan
Gurlen see Gurlan
85 K16 **Guro** Manica, C Mozambique
142 M14 **Gürün** Sivas, C Turkey
61 K16 **Gurupi** Tocantins, C Brazil
61 K16 **Gurupi, Rio** ≈ NE Brazil
79 Q14 **Gusau** Sokoto, N Nigeria
130 K12 **Gusev Ger.** Gumbinnen.
Kaliningradskaya Oblast',
W Russian Federation
152 I17 **Gushgy** prev. Kushka.
Maryyskiy Velayat,
S Turkmenistan
77 N13 **Gushiego** see Gushiegu
77 N13 **Gushiegu** var. Gushiego.
NE Ghana
172 P15 **Gushikawa** Okinawa, Okinawa,
SW Japan
115 L16 **Gusinje** Montenegro,
SW Yugoslavia
126 Jj16 **Gusinoozersk** Respublika
Buryatiya, S Russian Federation

♦ COUNTRY ◇ DEPENDENT TERRITORY ✦ ADMINISTRATIVE REGION ▲ MOUNTAIN ✦ VOLCANO ⊙ LAKE
● COUNTRY CAPITAL ○ DEPENDENT TERRITORY CAPITAL ✗ INTERNATIONAL AIRPORT ▲ MOUNTAIN RANGE ≈ RIVER ⊟ RESERVOIR

257

Gus'-Khrustal'nyy – Ḩaraḑ

130 M4 **Gus'-Khrustal'nyy** Vladimirskaya Oblast', W Russian Federation
109 B19 **Guspini** Sardegna, Italy, C Mediterranean Sea
111 X8 **Güssing** Burgenland, SE Austria
111 V6 **Gusswerk** Steiermark, E Austria
94 O2 **Gustav Adolf Land** *physical region* NE Svalbard
205 X5 **Gustav Bull Mountains** ▲ Antarctica
41 W13 **Gustavus** Alaska, USA
94 O1 **Gustav V Land** *physical region* NE Svalbard
37 P9 **Gustine** California, W USA
27 R8 **Gustine** Texas, SW USA
102 M9 **Güstrow** Mecklenburg-Vorpommern, NE Germany
97 N18 **Gusum** Östergötland, S Sweden
Guta/Gúta *see* Kolárovo
Gutenstein *see* Ravne na Koroškem
103 G14 **Gütersloh** Nordrhein-Westfalen, W Germany
29 N10 **Guthrie** Oklahoma, C USA
27 P5 **Guthrie** Texas, SW USA
31 U14 **Guthrie Center** Iowa, C USA
43 Q13 **Gutiérrez Zamora** Veracruz-Llave, E Mexico
Gutta *see* Kolárovo
31 Y12 **Guttenberg** Iowa, C USA
Guttentag *see* Dobrodzień
Guttstadt *see* Dobre Miasto
168 G8 **Guulin** Govĭ-Altay, C Mongolia
159 V12 **Guwāhāti** *prev.* Gauhāti. Assam, NE India
145 R3 **Guwēr** *var.* Al Kuwayr, Al Quwayr, Quwair. N Iraq
Guwlumayak *see* Kuuli-Mayak
57 R9 **Guyana** *off.* Cooperative Republic of Guyana; *prev.* British Guiana. ◆ *republic* N South America
23 P5 **Guyandotte River** ↝ West Virginia, NE USA
Guyane *see* French Guiana
Guyi *see* Sanjiang
28 H8 **Guymon** Oklahoma, C USA
152 L12 **Guynuk** Lebapskiy Velayat, NE Turkmenistan
23 O9 **Guyot, Mount** ▲ North Carolina/Tennessee, SE USA
191 U5 **Guyra** New South Wales, SE Australia
165 W10 **Guyuan** Ningxia, N China
Guzar *see* Ghuzor
124 N3 **Güzelyurt** *Gk.* Mórfou, Morphou. W Cyprus
124 N2 **Güzelyurt Körfezi** *var.* Morfou Bay, Morphou Bay, *Gk.* Kólpos Mórfou. *bay* W Cyprus
42 I3 **Guzmán** Chihuahua, N Mexico
121 B14 **Gvardeysk** *Ger.* Tapaiu. Kaliningradskaya Oblast', W Russian Federation
Gvardeyskoye *see* Hvardiys'ke
191 R5 **Gwabegar** New South Wales, SE Australia
154 J16 **Gwādar** *var.* Gwadur. Baluchistān, SW Pakistan
154 J16 **Gwādar East Bay** *bay* SW Pakistan
154 J16 **Gwādar West Bay** *bay* SW Pakistan
Gwadur *see* Gwādar
85 J17 **Gwai** Matabeleland North, W Zimbabwe
160 I7 **Gwalior** Madhya Pradesh, C India
85 J18 **Gwanda** Matabeleland South, SW Zimbabwe
81 N15 **Gwane** Haut-Zaïre, N Zaire
85 I17 **Gwayi** ↝ W Zimbabwe
112 G8 **Gwda** *var.* Głda, *Ger.* Küddow. ↝ NW Poland
99 C14 **Gweebarra Bay** *Ir.* Béal an Bheara. *inlet* W Ireland
99 D14 **Gweedore** *Ir.* Gaoth Dobhair. NW Ireland
Gwelo *see* Gweru
99 K21 **Gwent** *cultural region* S Wales, UK
85 K17 **Gweru** *prev.* Gwelo. Midlands, C Zimbabwe
31 Q7 **Gwinner** North Dakota, N USA
79 Y13 **Gwoza** Borno, NE Nigeria
Gwy *see* Wye
191 R4 **Gwydir River** ↝ New South Wales, SE Australia
99 I19 **Gwynedd** *var.* Gwyneth. *cultural region* NW Wales, UK
Gwyneth *see* Gwynedd
165 O16 **Gyaca** Xizang Zizhiqu, W China
Gya'gya *see* Saga
117 M22 **Gyalí** *var.* Yialí. *island* Dodekánisos, Greece, Aegean Sea
Gyandzha *see* Gäncä
164 M16 **Gyangzê** Xizang Zizhiqu, W China
164 L14 **Gyaring Co** ⊚ W China
165 Q12 **Gyaring Hu** ⊚ C China
117 I20 **Gyáros** *var.* Yioúra. *island* Kykládes, Greece, Aegean Sea
126 Hh7 **Gyda** Yamalo-Nenetskiy Avtonomnyy Okrug, N Russian Federation
126 H7 **Gydanskiy Poluostrov** *Eng.* Gyda Peninsula. *peninsula* N Russian Federation
Gyda Peninsula *see* Gydanskiy Poluostrov
Gyéres *see* Câmpia Turzii
Gyergyószentmiklós *see* Gheorgheni
Gyergyótölgyes *see* Tulgheş
Gyertyámos *see* Cărpiniş
Gyeva *see* Detva
Gyigang *see* Zayü
97 I23 **Gyldenløves Høy** *hill range* C Denmark
189 Z10 **Gympie** Queensland, E Australia
177 Ff7 **Gyobingauk** Pegu, SW Myanmar
113 M23 **Gyomaendrőd** Békés, SE Hungary
Gyömbér *see* Ďumbier
113 L22 **Gyöngyös** Heves, NE Hungary
113 H22 **Győr** *Ger.* Raab; *Lat.* Arrabona. Győr-Moson-Sopron, NW Hungary
113 G22 **Győr-Moson-Sopron** *off.* Győr-Moson-Sopron Megye. ◆ *county* NW Hungary
9 X15 **Gypsumville** Manitoba, S Canada
10 M4 **Gyrfalcon Islands** *island group* Northwest Territories, NE Canada
97 N14 **Gysinge** Gävleborg, C Sweden
117 F22 **Gýtheio** *var.* Githio; *prev.* Ýthion. Pelopónnisos, S Greece
152 L13 **Gyuichbirleshik** Lebapskiy Velayat, E Turkmenistan
113 N24 **Gyula** *Rom.* Jula. Békés, SE Hungary
Gyulafehérvár *see* Alba Iulia
Gyulovo *see* Roza
143 T11 **Gyumri** *var.* Giumri, *Rus.* Kumayri; *prev.* Aleksandropol', Leninakan. W Armenia
152 D13 **Gyunuzyndag, Gora** ▲ W Turkmenistan
152 D12 **Gyzylarbat** *prev.* Kizyl-Arvat. Balkanskiy Velayat, W Turkmenistan
Gyzylbaydak *see* Krasnoye Znamya
Gyzyletrek *see* Kizyl-Atrek
Gyzylgaya *see* Kizyl-Kaya
Gyzylsu *see* Kizyl-Su

H

159 T12 **Ha** W Bhutan
Haabai *see* Ha'apai Group
101 H17 **Haacht** Vlaams Brabant, C Belgium
111 T4 **Haag** Niederösterreich, NE Austria
204 L8 **Haag Nunataks** ▲ Antarctica
94 N2 **Haakon VII Land** *physical region* NW Svalbard
100 O11 **Haaksbergen** Overijssel, E Netherlands
101 E14 **Haamstede** Zeeland, SW Netherlands
200 Ss13 **Ha'ano** *island* Ha'apai Group, C Tonga
200 Ss13 **Ha'apai Group** *var.* Haabai. *island group* C Tonga
95 L15 **Haapajärvi** Oulu, C Finland
95 L17 **Haapamäki** Keski-Suomi, C Finland
95 L15 **Haapavesi** Oulu, C Finland
203 N7 **Haapiti** Moorea, W French Polynesia
120 F4 **Haapsalu** *Ger.* Hapsal. Läänemaa, W Estonia
Ha'Arava *see* 'Arabah, Wādī al
Haarby *see* Hårby
100 H10 **Haarlem** *prev.* Harlem. Noord-Holland, W Netherlands
193 D19 **Haast** West Coast, South Island, NZ
193 C20 **Haast** ↝ South Island, NZ
193 D20 **Haast Pass** *pass* South Island, NZ
200 R16 **Ha'atua** 'Eau, E Tonga
155 P15 **Hab** ↝ SW Pakistan
147 W7 **Haba** *var.* Al Haba. Dubayy, NE UAE
164 K2 **Habahe** *var.* Kaba. Xinjiang Uygur Zizhiqu, NW China
147 U13 **Ḩabarūt** *var.* Habrut. SW Oman
83 J18 **Habaswein** North Eastern, NE Kenya
101 L24 **Habay-la-Neuve** Luxembourg, SE Belgium
145 S8 **Ḩabbānīyah, Buḩayrat** ⊚ C Iraq
Habelschwerdt *see* Bystrzyca Kłodzka
159 V14 **Habiganj** Chittagong, NE Bangladesh
169 Q12 **Habirag** Nei Mongol Zizhiqu, N China
97 L19 **Habo** Skaraborg, S Sweden
127 P16 **Habomai Islands** *island group* Kuril'skiye Ostrova, SE Russian Federation
172 P3 **Haboro** Hokkaidō, NE Japan
159 S16 **Habra** West Bengal, NE India
Habrut *see* Ḩabarūt
149 P17 **Ḩabshān** Abū Ẓaby, C UAE
56 E14 **Hacha** Putumayo, S Colombia
172 Ss13 **Hachijō** Tōkyō, Hachijō-jima, SE Japan
172 Ss13 **Hachijō-jima** *var.* Hatizyô Zima. *island* Izu-shotō, SE Japan
171 I14 **Hachiman** Gifu, Honshū, SW Japan
171 M9 **Hachimori** Akita, Honshū, C Japan
172 N10 **Hachinohe** Aomori, Honshū, C Japan
171 Jj16 **Hachiōji** *var.* Hatiôzi. Tōkyō, Honshū, S Japan
95 G17 **Hackås** Jämtland, C Sweden
20 K14 **Hackensack** New Jersey, NE USA
Hadama *see* Nazrēt
171 J16 **Hadano** Kanagawa, Honshū, S Japan
147 W13 **Ḩadbaram** S Oman
145 U13 **Ḩaddānīyah** *well* S Iraq
98 K12 **Haddington** SE Scotland, UK
147 Z8 **Ḩadd, Ra's al** *headland* NE Oman
Haded *see* Xadeed
79 W12 **Hadejia** Jigawa, N Nigeria
79 W12 **Hadejia** ↝ N Nigeria
144 F9 **Ḩadera** Haifa, C Israel
Hadersleben *see* Haderslev
97 G24 **Haderslev** *Ger.* Hadersleben. Sønderjylland, SW Denmark
157 J21 **Hadhdhunmathi Atoll** *var.* Haddummati Atoll, Laamu Atoll. *atoll* S Maldives
Hadhramaut *see* Ḩaḑramawt
147 W17 **Ḩadīboh** Suquṭrā, SE Yemen
164 K9 **Hadilik** Xinjiang Uygur Zizhiqu, W China
142 H16 **Hadım** Konya, S Turkey
146 K7 **Hadīyah** Al Madīnah, W Saudi Arabia
15 J1 **Hadley Bay** *bay* Victoria Island, Northwest Territories, N Canada
178 Jj6 **Ha Đông** *var.* Hadong. Ha Tây, N Vietnam
147 R15 **Ḩaḑramawt** *Eng.* Hadhramaut. ▲ S Yemen
Hadria *see* Adria
Hadrianopolis *see* Edirne
Hadria Picena *see* Apricena
97 G22 **Hadsten** Århus, C Denmark
97 G21 **Hadsund** Nordjylland, N Denmark
119 S4 **Hadyach** *Rus.* Gadyach. Poltavs'ka Oblast', NE Ukraine
114 I13 **Hadžići** SE Bosnia and Herzegovina
169 W14 **Haeju** S North Korea
Haerbin/Haerhpin/Ha-erh-pin *see* Harbin
147 P5 **Ḩafar al Bāṭin** Ash Sharqīyah, N Saudi Arabia
9 T15 **Hafford** Saskatchewan, S Canada
142 M13 **Hafik** Sivas, N Turkey
155 V8 **Hāfizābād** Punjab, E Pakistan
94 H4 **Hafnarfjördhur** Reykjanes, W Iceland
Hafnia *see* København, Denmark
Hafnia *see* Denmark
Hafren *see* Severn
Hafun *see* Xaafuun
Hafun, Ras *see* Xaafuun, Raas
82 G10 **Hag 'Abdullah** Sinnar, E Sudan
83 K18 **Hagadera** North Eastern, E Kenya
144 G8 **HaGalil** *Eng.* Galilee. ▲ N Israel
12 G10 **Hagar** Ontario, S Canada
161 G18 **Hagari** *var.* Vedāvati. ↝ W India
102 M13 **Hagelberg** *hill* NE Germany
41 N14 **Hagemeister Island** *island* Alaska, USA
103 F15 **Hagen** Nordrhein-Westfalen, W Germany
102 K10 **Hagenow** Mecklenburg-Vorpommern, N Germany
8 K15 **Hagensborg** British Columbia, SW Canada
82 I13 **Hāgere Hiywet** *var.* Agere Hiywet, Ambo. C Ethiopia
35 O15 **Hagerman** Idaho, NW USA
39 U14 **Hagerman** New Mexico, SW USA
23 V2 **Hagerstown** Maryland, NE USA
12 G16 **Hagersville** Ontario, S Canada
104 J15 **Hagetmau** Landes, SW France
97 K14 **Hagfors** Värmland, C Sweden
95 G16 **Häggenås** Jämtland, C Sweden
170 Dd12 **Hagi** Yamaguchi, Honshū, SW Japan
178 J5 **Ha Giang** Ha Giang, N Vietnam
Hagios Evstrátios *see* Ágios Efstrátios
HaGolan *see* Golan Heights
105 T4 **Hagondange** Moselle, NE France
99 B18 **Hag's Head** *Ir.* Ceann Caillí. *headland* W Ireland
104 I3 **Hague, Cap de la** *headland* N France
105 V5 **Haguenau** Bas-Rhin, NE France
172 T16 **Hahajima-rettō** *island group* SE Japan
13 R8 **Há Há , Lac** ⊚ Québec, SE Canada
180 H13 **Hahaya** ✕ (Moroni) Grande Comore, NW Comoros
24 K9 **Hahnville** Louisiana, S USA
85 E22 **Haib** Karas, S Namibia
Haibak *see* Āybak
155 N15 **Haibo** ↝ SW Pakistan
169 U12 **Haicheng** Liaoning, NE China
Haida *see* Nový Bor
Haidarabad *see* Hyderābād
Haidenschaft *see* Ajdovščina
178 Jj6 **Hai Dương** Hai Hưng, N Vietnam
144 F9 **Haifa** ◆ *district* NW Israel
Haifa *see* Ḩefa
Haifa, Bay of *see* Ḩefa, Mifraẓ
167 P14 **Haifeng** Guangdong, S China
Haifong *see* Hai Phong
167 P3 **Hai He** ↝ E China
Haikang *see* Leizhou
166 L17 **Haikou** *var.* Hai-k'ou, Hoihow, *Fr.* Hoï-Hao. Hainan, S China
146 M6 **Ḩā'il** Ḩā'il, NW Saudi Arabia
147 N5 **Ḩā'il** *off.* Minṭaqah Ḩā'il. ◆ *province* N Saudi Arabia
Hai-la-erh *see* Hailar
169 S6 **Hailar** *var.* Hai-la-erh; *prev.* Hulun. Nei Mongol Zizhiqu, N China
169 S6 **Hailar He** ↝ NE China
35 P14 **Hailey** Idaho, NW USA
12 H9 **Haileybury** Ontario, S Canada
169 X9 **Hailin** Heilongjiang, NE China
Ḩā'il, Minṭaqah *see* Ḩā'il
Hailong *see* Meihekou
95 K14 **Hailuoto** *Swe.* Karlö. *island* W Finland
Haima *see* Haymā'
Haimen *see* Jiaojiang
166 M17 **Hainan** *var.* Hainan Sheng, Qiong. ◆ *province* S China
166 K17 **Hainan Dao** *island* S China
Hainan Sheng *see* Hainan
Hainan Strait *see* Qiongzhou Haixia
Hainasch *see* Ainaži
Hainau *see* Chojnów
101 E20 **Hainaut** ◆ *province* SW Belgium
Hainburg *see* Hainburg an der Donau
111 Z4 **Hainburg an der Donau** *var.* Hainburg. Niederösterreich, NE Austria
41 W12 **Haines** Alaska, USA
34 L12 **Haines** Oregon, NW USA
25 W11 **Haines City** Florida, SE USA
8 H8 **Haines Junction** Yukon Territory, W Canada
111 W4 **Hainfeld** Niederösterreich, NE Austria
103 N16 **Hainichen** Sachsen, E Germany
178 K6 **Hai Phong** *var.* Haifong, Haiphong. N Vietnam
167 S12 **Haitan Dao** *island* SE China
46 K8 **Haiti** *off.* Republic of Haiti. ◆ *republic* C West Indies
37 T11 **Haiwee Reservoir** ⊡ California, W USA
82 I7 **Haiya** Red Sea, NE Sudan
165 T10 **Haiyan** Qinghai, W China
166 M13 **Haiyang Shan** ▲ S China
165 V10 **Haiyuan** Ningxia, N China
Hajda *see* Nový Bor
113 M22 **Hajdú-Bihar** *off.* Hajdú-Bihar Megye. ◆ *county* E Hungary
113 N22 **Hajdúböszörmény** Hajdú-Bihar, E Hungary
113 N22 **Hajdúhadház** Hajdú-Bihar, E Hungary
113 N21 **Hajdúnánás** Hajdú-Bihar, E Hungary
113 N22 **Hajdúszoboszló** Hajdú-Bihar, E Hungary
148 I3 **Ḩājī Ebrāhīm, Kūh-e** ▲ Iran/Iraq
171 Kk11 **Hajiki-zaki** *headland* Sado, C Japan
Hajine *see* Abū Ḩardān
159 P13 **Hājīpur** Bihār, N India
147 N14 **Ḩajjah** W Yemen
145 U11 **Ḩajjama** S Iraq
149 R12 **Ḩājjīābād** Hormozgān, C Iran
145 U14 **Ḩājj, Thaqb al** *well* S Iraq
115 L16 **Hajla** ▲ SW Yugoslavia
112 P10 **Hajnówka** *Ger.* Hermhausen. Białystok, E Poland
177 Ff4 **Haka** Chin State, W Myanmar
Hakapehi *see* Punaauia
Hakâri *see* Hakkâri
143 T16 **Hakkâri** *var.* Çölemerik, Hakâri. Hakkâri, SE Turkey
143 T16 **Hakkâri** *var.* Hakkari. ◆ *province* SE Turkey
94 J12 **Hakkas** Norrbotten, N Sweden
171 Gg16 **Hakken-zan** ▲ Honshū, SW Japan
172 N9 **Hakkōda-san** ▲ Honshū, C Japan
172 Pp3 **Hako-dake** ▲ Hokkaidō, NE Japan
172 N7 **Hakodate** Hokkaidō, NE Japan
171 Ii12 **Hakui** Ishikawa, Honshū, SW Japan
202 B16 **Hakupu** SE Niue
171 I14 **Haku-san** ▲ Honshū, SW Japan
Hal *see* Halle
155 Q15 **Hāla** Sind, SE Pakistan
144 J3 **Ḩalab** *Eng.* Aleppo, *Fr.* Alep; *anc.* Beroea. Ḩalab, NW Syria
144 J3 **Ḩalab** *off.* Muḩāfaẓat Ḩalab, *var.* Aleppo, Halab. ◆ *governorate* NW Syria
144 J3 **Ḩalab** ✕ Ḩalab, NW Syria
147 O8 **Ḩalabān** *var.* Halibān. Ar Riyāḑ, C Saudi Arabia
145 V4 **Ḩalabja** NE Iraq
202 A16 **Halagigie Point** *headland* W Niue
77 Z11 **Halaib** SE Egypt
202 G12 **Halalo** Île Uvea, N Wallis and Futuna
Halandri *see* Chalándri
147 X13 **Ḩalānīyāt, Juzur al** *var.* Jazā'ir Bin Ghalfān, *Eng.* Kuria Muria Islands. *island group* S Oman
147 W13 **Ḩalānīyāt, Khalīj al** *Eng.* Kuria Muria Bay. *bay* S Oman
Halas *see* Kiskunhalas
40 G11 **Hālawa** *Haw.* Hālawa. Hawaii, USA, C Pacific Ocean
40 F9 **Halawa, Cape** *headland* Molokai, Hawaii, USA, C Pacific Ocean
168 H6 **Halban** Hövsgöl, N Mongolia
103 K14 **Halberstadt** Sachsen-Anhalt, C Germany
192 M12 **Halcombe** Manawatu-Wanganui, North Island, NZ
97 I16 **Halden** *prev.* Fredrikshald. Østfold, S Norway
102 L13 **Haldensleben** Sachsen-Anhalt, C Germany
Háldi *see* Halti
159 S17 **Haldia** West Bengal, NE India
158 K10 **Haldwāni** Uttar Pradesh, N India
40 F10 **Haleakala** *crater* Maui, Hawaii, USA, C Pacific Ocean
27 N4 **Hale Center** Texas, SW USA
101 J18 **Halen** Limburg, NE Belgium
25 O2 **Haleyville** Alabama, S USA
79 O17 **Half Assini** SW Ghana
37 R8 **Half Dome** ▲ California, W USA
193 C25 **Halfmoon Bay** *var.* Oban. Stewart Island, Southland, NZ
190 E5 **Half Moon Lake** *salt lake* South Australia
169 R7 **Halhgol** Dornod, E Mongolia
Haliacmon *see* Aliákmonas
Halibān *see* Ḩalabān
12 I13 **Haliburton** Ontario, SE Canada
12 I12 **Haliburton Highlands** *var.* Madawaska Highlands. *hill range* Ontario, SE Canada
11 Q15 **Halifax** Nova Scotia, SE Canada
99 L17 **Halifax** N England, UK
23 W8 **Halifax** North Carolina, SE USA
23 U7 **Halifax** Virginia, NE USA
11 Q15 **Halifax** ✕ Nova Scotia, SE Canada
149 T13 **Halīl Rūd** *seasonal river* SE Iran
144 I6 **Ḩalīmah** ▲ Lebanon/Syria
168 G8 **Haliun** Govĭ-Altay, W Mongolia
120 I3 **Haljala** *Ger.* Halljal. Lääne-Virumaa, N Estonia
41 Q4 **Halkett, Cape** *headland* Alaska, USA
Halkida *see* Chalkída
98 J6 **Halkirk** N Scotland, UK
13 X7 **Hall** ↝ Québec, SE Canada
Hall *see* Schwäbisch Hall
95 H15 **Hälla** Västerbotten, N Sweden
98 J6 **Halladale** ↝ N Scotland, UK
97 J21 **Halland** ◆ *county* S Sweden
25 Z15 **Hallandale** Florida, SE USA
97 K22 **Hallandsås** *physical region* S Sweden
15 M2 **Hall Beach** Northwest Territories, N Canada
101 G19 **Halle** *Fr.* Hal. Vlaams Brabant, C Belgium
103 M15 **Halle** *var.* Halle an der Saale. Sachsen-Anhalt, C Germany
Halle an der Saale *see* Halle
37 W3 **Halleck** Nevada, W USA
97 L15 **Hällefors** Örebro, C Sweden
97 N16 **Hälleforsnäs** Södermanland, C Sweden
111 Q6 **Hallein** Salzburg, N Austria
103 L15 **Halle-Neustadt** Sachsen-Anhalt, C Germany
27 U12 **Hallettsville** Texas, SW USA
205 N4 **Halley** *UK research station* Antarctica
30 L4 **Halliday** North Dakota, N USA
39 S2 **Halligan Reservoir** ⊡ Colorado, C USA
102 G7 **Halligen** *island group* N Germany
96 G13 **Hallingdal** *valley* S Norway
40 J12 **Hall Island** *island* Alaska, USA
Hall Island *see* Maiana
201 P15 **Hall Islands** *island group* C Micronesia
120 H6 **Halliste** ↝ S Estonia
Halljal *see* Haljala
95 I15 **Hallnäs** Västerbotten, N Sweden
31 R2 **Hallock** Minnesota, N USA
16 Oo3 **Hall Peninsula** *peninsula* Baffin Island, Northwest Territories, NE Canada
22 F9 **Halls** Tennessee, S USA
97 M16 **Hallsberg** Örebro, C Sweden
189 N5 **Halls Creek** Western Australia
190 L12 **Halls Gap** Victoria, SE Australia
97 N15 **Hallstahammar** Västmanland, C Sweden
111 R6 **Hallstatt** Salzburg, W Austria
111 R6 **Hallstätter See** ⊚ C Austria
97 P14 **Hallstavik** Stockholm, C Sweden
27 X7 **Hallsville** Texas, SW USA
105 P1 **Halluin** Nord, N France
Halmahera, Laut *see* Halmahera Sea
175 T7 **Halmahera, Pulau** *prev.* Djailolo, Gilolo, Jailolo. *island* E Indonesia
175 Tt8 **Halmahera Sea** *Ind.* Laut Halmahera. *sea* E Indonesia
97 J21 **Halmstad** Halland, S Sweden
175 T11 **Halong** Pulau Ambon, E Indonesia
121 N15 **Halowchyn** *Rus.* Golovchin. Mahilyowskaya Voblasts', E Belarus
97 H20 **Hals** Nordjylland, N Denmark
96 F8 **Halsa** Møre og Romsdal, S Norway
121 I15 **Hal'shany** *Rus.* Gol'shany. Hrodzyenskaya Voblasts', W Belarus
Hälsingborg *see* Helsingborg
31 R5 **Halstad** Minnesota, N USA
29 N6 **Halstead** Kansas, C USA
101 G15 **Halsteren** Noord-Brabant, S Netherlands
95 L16 **Halsua** Vaasa, W Finland
103 E14 **Haltern** Nordrhein-Westfalen, W Germany
94 J9 **Halti** *var.* Haltiatunturi, *Lapp.* Háldi. ▲ Finland/Norway
Haltiatunturi *see* Halti
118 J6 **Halych** Ivano-Frankivs'ka Oblast', W Ukraine
Halycus *see* Platani
105 P3 **Ham** Somme, N France
Hama *see* Ḩamāh
170 Ee12 **Hamada** Shimane, Honshū, SW Japan
148 L6 **Hamadān** *anc.* Ecbatana. Hamadān, W Iran
148 L6 **Hamadān** *off.* Ostān-e Hamadān. ◆ *province* W Iran
144 I5 **Ḩamāh** *var.* Hama; *anc.* Epiphania, *Bibl.* Hamath. Ḩamāh, W Syria
144 I5 **Ḩamāh** *off.* Muḩāfaẓat Ḩamāh, *var.* Hama. ◆ *governorate* C Syria
171 I17 **Hamakita** Shizuoka, Honshū, S Japan
172 O4 **Hamamasu** Hokkaidō, NE Japan
171 I17 **Hamamatsu** *var.* Hamamatu. Shizuoka, Honshū, S Japan
Hamamatu *see* Hamamatsu
172 Qq7 **Hamanaka** Hokkaidō, NE Japan
171 I17 **Hamana-ko** ⊚ Honshū, S Japan
96 I13 **Hamar** *prev.* Storhammer. Hedmark, S Norway
147 U10 **Ḩamār il Kidan, Qalamat** *well* E Saudi Arabia
170 G12 **Hamasaka** Hyōgo, Honshū, SW Japan
Hamath *see* Ḩamāh
172 Pp2 **Hamatonbetsu** Hokkaidō, NE Japan
161 K26 **Hambantota** Southern Province, SE Sri Lanka
194 G10 **Hambili** ↝ NW PNG
Hambourg *see* Hamburg
102 J9 **Hamburg** Hamburg, N Germany
29 V14 **Hamburg** Arkansas, C USA
31 S16 **Hamburg** Iowa, C USA
20 D10 **Hamburg** New York, NE USA
102 I10 **Hamburg** *Fr.* Hambourg. ◆ *state* N Germany
154 K5 **Hamdam Āb, Dasht-e** *Pash.* Dasht-i Hamdamab. ▲ W Afghanistan
Hamdamab, Dasht-i *see* Hamdam Āb, Dasht-e
20 M13 **Hamden** Connecticut, NE USA
146 K6 **Ḩamḑ, Wādī al** *dry watercourse* W Saudi Arabia
95 L18 **Häme** *Swe.* Tavastehus. ◆ *province* C Finland
95 K18 **Hämeenkyrö** Häme, SW Finland
95 L19 **Hämeenlinna** *Swe.* Tavastehus. Häme, SW Finland
HaMelah, Yam *see* Dead Sea
Hamelin *see* Hameln
102 I13 **Hameln** *Eng.* Hamelin. Niedersachsen, N Germany
188 I8 **Hamersley Range** ▲ Western Australia
169 Y12 **Hamgyŏng-sanmaek** ▲ N North Korea
169 X13 **Hamhŭng** C North Korea
165 O6 **Hami** *var.* Ha-mi, *Uigh.* Kumul, Qomul. Xinjiang Uygur Zizhiqu, NW China
145 X10 **Ḩāmid Amīn** E Iraq
147 W11 **Ḩamīdān, Khawr** *oasis* SE Saudi Arabia
144 H5 **Ḩamīdīyah** *var.* Hamīdīyé. Ṭarṭūs, W Syria
116 L12 **Hamidiye** Edirne, NW Turkey
Hamīdīyé *see* Ḩamīdīyah
190 L12 **Hamilton** Victoria, SE Australia
66 B12 **Hamilton** O (Bermuda) C Bermuda
12 G16 **Hamilton** Ontario, S Canada
192 M7 **Hamilton** Waikato, North Island, NZ
98 I12 **Hamilton** S Scotland, UK
25 N3 **Hamilton** Alabama, S USA
40 M10 **Hamilton** Alaska, USA
32 J13 **Hamilton** Illinois, N USA
29 S3 **Hamilton** Missouri, C USA
35 P10 **Hamilton** Montana, NW USA
27 S8 **Hamilton** Texas, SW USA
12 G16 **Hamilton** ✕ Ontario, SE Canada
66 I6 **Hamilton Bank** *undersea feature* SE Labrador Sea
190 E1 **Hamilton Creek** *seasonal river* South Australia
11 R8 **Hamilton Inlet** *inlet* Newfoundland and Labrador, E Canada
29 T12 **Hamilton, Lake** ⊡ Arkansas, C USA
37 W6 **Hamilton, Mount** ▲ Nevada, W USA
77 S8 **Ḩamīm, Wādī al** ↝ NE Libya
95 N19 **Hamina** *Swe.* Fredrikshamn. Kymi, S Finland
9 W16 **Hamiota** Manitoba, S Canada
158 L13 **Hamīrpur** Uttar Pradesh, N India
Hamīs Musait *see* Khamīs Mushayṭ
23 T11 **Hamlet** North Carolina, SE USA
27 P6 **Hamlin** Texas, SW USA
23 P5 **Hamlin** West Virginia, NE USA
33 O7 **Hamlin Lake** ⊚ Michigan, N USA
103 F14 **Hamm** *var.* Hamm in Westfalen. Nordrhein-Westfalen, W Germany
Ḩammāmāt, Khalīj al *see* Hammamet, Golfe de
77 N5 **Hammamet, Golfe de** *Ar.* Khalīj al Ḩammāmāt. *gulf* NE Tunisia
145 R3 **Ḩammān al 'Alīl** N Iraq
145 X12 **Ḩammār, Hawr al** ⊚ SE Iraq
95 J20 **Hammarland** Åland, SW Finland
95 H16 **Hammarstrand** Jämtland, C Sweden
95 O17 **Hammaslahti** Pohjois-Karjala, SE Finland
101 F17 **Hamme** Oost-Vlaanderen, NW Belgium
102 H10 **Hamme** ↝ NW Germany
97 G22 **Hammel** Århus, C Denmark
103 I18 **Hammelburg** Bayern, C Germany
101 H18 **Hamme-Mille** Walloon Brabant, C Belgium
102 H10 **Hamme-Oste-Kanal** *canal* NW Germany
95 G16 **Hammerdal** Jämtland, C Sweden
94 K8 **Hammerfest** Finnmark, N Norway
103 D14 **Hamminkeln** Nordrhein-Westfalen, W Germany
Hamm in Westfalen *see* Hamm
28 K10 **Hammon** Oklahoma, C USA
33 N11 **Hammond** Indiana, N USA
24 K8 **Hammond** Louisiana, S USA
101 K20 **Hamoir** Liège, E Belgium
101 J21 **Hamois** Namur, SE Belgium
101 K16 **Hamont** Limburg, NE Belgium
193 F22 **Hampden** Otago, South Island, NZ
21 R6 **Hampden** Maine, NE USA
99 M23 **Hampshire** *cultural region* S England, UK
11 O15 **Hampton** New Brunswick, SE Canada
29 U14 **Hampton** Arkansas, C USA
31 V12 **Hampton** Iowa, C USA
21 P10 **Hampton** New Hampshire, NE USA
23 R14 **Hampton** South Carolina, SE USA
23 P8 **Hampton** Tennessee, S USA
23 X7 **Hampton** Virginia, NE USA
96 L11 **Hamra** Gävleborg, C Sweden
82 D10 **Hamrat esh Sheikh** Northern Kordofan, C Sudan
145 S5 **Ḩamrīn, Jabal** ▲ N Iraq
123 Jj16 **Hamrun** C Malta
178 K14 **Ham Thuân Nam** Binh Thuân, S Vietnam
176 Ww11 **Hamuku** Irian Jaya, E Indonesia
Hāmūn, Daryācheh-ye *see* Şāberī, Hāmūn-e/Sīstān, Daryācheh-ye
Hamwih *see* Southampton
40 G10 **Hana** *Haw.* Hāna. Maui, Hawaii, USA, C Pacific Ocean
23 S14 **Hanahan** South Carolina, SE USA
40 B8 **Hanalei** Kauai, Hawaii, USA, C Pacific Ocean
178 Kk10 **Ha Nam** Quang Nam-Đa Nâng, C Vietnam
171 Mm11 **Hanamaki** Iwate, Honshū, C Japan
40 F10 **Hanamanioa, Cape** *headland* Maui, Hawaii, USA, C Pacific Ocean
202 B16 **Hanan** ✕ (Alofi) SW Niue
103 H18 **Hanau** Hessen, W Germany
15 J7 **Hanbury** ↝ Northwest Territories, NW Canada
Hâncești *see* Hincești
8 M15 **Hanceville** British Columbia, SW Canada
25 P3 **Hanceville** Alabama, S USA
Hancewicze *see* Hantsavichy
166 L6 **Hancheng** Shaanxi, C China
23 V2 **Hancock** Maryland, NE USA
32 M3 **Hancock** Michigan, N USA
31 S8 **Hancock** Minnesota, N USA
20 I12 **Hancock** New York, NE USA
82 Q12 **Handa** Bari, NE Somalia
167 O5 **Handan** *var.* Han-tan. Hebei, E China
97 P16 **Handen** Stockholm, C Sweden
83 J22 **Handeni** Tanga, E Tanzania
39 Q7 **Handies Peak** ▲ Colorado, C USA
113 J19 **Handlová** *Ger.* Krickerhäu, *Hung.* Nyitrabánya; *prev. Ger.* Kriegerhaj. Stredné Slovensko, C Slovakia
171 K17 **Haneda** ✕ (Tōkyō) Tōkyō, Honshū, S Japan
144 F13 **HaNegev** *Eng.* Negev. *desert* S Israel
37 Q11 **Hanford** California, W USA
203 V16 **Hanga Roa** Easter Island, Chile, E Pacific Ocean
168 H7 **Hangayn Nuruu** ▲ C Mongolia
Hang-chou/Hangchow *see* Hangzhou
97 K20 **Hånger** Jönköping, S Sweden
Hangö *see* Hanko
167 R9 **Hangzhou** *var.* Hang-chou, Hangchow. Zhejiang, SE China
168 F5 **Hanhöhiy Uul** ▲ NW Mongolia
Hanhowuz *see* Khauz-Khan
143 P15 **Hani** Diyarbakır, SE Turkey
Hania *see* Chaniá
147 R11 **Ḩanish al Kabīr, Jazīrat al** *island* SW Yemen
Hanka, Lake *see* Khanka, Lake
95 M17 **Hankasalmi** Keski-Suomi, C Finland
31 R7 **Hankinson** North Dakota, N USA
95 K20 **Hanko** *Swe.* Hangö. Uusimaa, SW Finland
Han-kou/Han-k'ou/Hankow *see* Wuhan
38 M6 **Hanksville** Utah, W USA
158 K6 **Hanle** Jammu and Kashmir, NW India
193 I17 **Hanmer Springs** Canterbury, South Island, NZ
9 R16 **Hanna** Alberta, SW Canada
29 V3 **Hannibal** Missouri, C USA
188 M3 **Hann, Mount** ▲ Western Australia
102 I12 **Hannover** *Eng.* Hanover. Niedersachsen, NW Germany
101 J19 **Hannut** Liège, C Belgium
97 L22 **Hanöbukten** *bay* S Sweden
178 Jj6 **Ha Nôi** *Eng.* Hanoi, *Fr.* Hanoï. ● (Vietnam) N Vietnam
12 F14 **Hanover** Ontario, S Canada
33 P15 **Hanover** Indiana, N USA
20 G16 **Hanover** Pennsylvania, NE USA
23 W6 **Hanover** Virginia, NE USA
Hanover *see* Hannover
65 G23 **Hanover, Isla** *island* S Chile
Hanselbeck *see* Érd
205 X5 **Hansen Mountains** ▲ Antarctica
166 M8 **Han Shui** ↝ C China
158 H10 **Hānsi** Haryāna, NW India
97 F20 **Hanstholm** Viborg, NW Denmark
Han-tan *see* Handan
164 H6 **Hantengri Feng** *var.* Pik Khan-Tengri. ▲ China/Kazakhstan *see also* Khan-Tengri, Pik
121 I18 **Hantsavichy** *Pol.* Hancewicze, *Rus.* Gantsevichi. Brestskaya Voblasts', SW Belarus
16 N2 **Hantzsch** ↝ Baffin Island, Northwest Territories, NE Canada
158 G9 **Hanumāngarh** Rājasthān, NW India
191 O9 **Hanwood** New South Wales, SE Australia
Hanyang *see* Caidian
Hanyang *see* Wuhan
166 H10 **Hanyuan** *var.* Fulin. Sichuan, C China
166 J7 **Hanzhong** Shaanxi, C China
203 W11 **Hao** *atoll* Îles Tuamotu, C French Polynesia
159 S16 **Hāora** *prev.* Howrah. West Bengal, NE India
80 K8 **Haouach, Ouadi** *dry watercourse* E Chad
Haoûârine *see* Ḩawārīn
94 K13 **Haparanda** Norrbotten, N Sweden
27 N3 **Happy** Texas, SW USA
36 M1 **Happy Camp** California, W USA
11 Q9 **Happy Valley-Goose Bay** *prev.* Goose Bay. Newfoundland and Labrador, E Canada
Hapsal *see* Haapsalu
158 J10 **Hāpur** Uttar Pradesh, N India
144 F12 **HaQatan, HaMakhtesh** ▲ S Israel
146 I4 **Ḩaql** Tabūk, NW Saudi Arabia
176 Vv13 **Har** Pulau Kai Besar, E Indonesia
168 M8 **Haraat** Dundgovĭ, C Mongolia
147 R8 **Ḩaraḑ** *var.* Haradh. Ash Sharqīyah, E Saudi Arabia

◆ Country ● Country Capital ◇ Dependent Territory ○ Dependent Territory Capital ◆ Administrative Region ✕ International Airport ▲ Mountain ▲ Mountain Range ✕ Volcano ↝ River ⊚ Lake ⊡ Reservoir

◆ COUNTRY ◇ DEPENDENT TERRITORY ◆ ADMINISTRATIVE REGION ▲ MOUNTAIN ▼ VOLCANO ◙ LAKE
● COUNTRY CAPITAL ○ DEPENDENT TERRITORY CAPITAL × INTERNATIONAL AIRPORT ▲ MOUNTAIN RANGE ◢ RIVER ◙ RESERVOIR

HEMNESBERGET – HOLLAND

94 G13 **Hemnesberget** Nordland, C Norway
27 Y8 **Hemphill** Texas, SW USA
27 V11 **Hempstead** Texas, SW USA
97 P20 **Hemse** Gotland, SE Sweden
95 F13 **Hemsedal** *valley* S Norway
165 T11 **Henan** *var.* Henan Mongolzu Zizhixian, Yêgainnyin. Qinghai, C China
167 N6 **Henan** *var.* Henan Sheng, Honan, Yu. ◆ *province* C China
192 L4 **Hen and Chickens** *island group* N NZ
Henan Mongolzu Zizhixian/ Henan Sheng *see* Henan
107 O7 **Henares** ~ C Spain
171 M8 **Henashi-zaki** *headland* Honshū, C Japan
104 I16 **Hendaye** Pyrénées-Atlantiques, SW France
142 F11 **Hendek** Sakarya, NW Turkey
63 B21 **Henderson** Buenos Aires, E Argentina
22 I5 **Henderson** Kentucky, S USA
37 X11 **Henderson** Nevada, W USA
23 V8 **Henderson** North Carolina, SE USA
22 G10 **Henderson** Tennessee, S USA
27 W7 **Henderson** Texas, SW USA
32 J12 **Henderson Creek** ~ Illinois, N USA
195 X16 **Henderson Field** ✕ (Honiara) Guadalcanal, C Solomon Islands
203 O17 **Henderson Island** *atoll* N Pitcairn Islands
23 O10 **Hendersonville** North Carolina, SE USA
22 J8 **Hendersonville** Tennessee, S USA
149 O14 **Hendorābī, Jazīreh-ye** *island* S Iran
57 V10 **Hendrik Top** *var.* Hendriktop. *elevation* C Suriname
Hendū Kosh *see* Hindu Kush
12 L12 **Heney, Lac** ◎ Québec, SE Canada
194 I12 **Henganofi** Eastern Highlands, C PNG
Hengchow *see* Hengyang
167 S15 **Hengchun** S Taiwan
165 R16 **Hengduan Shan** ▲▲ SW China
100 N12 **Hengelo** Gelderland, E Netherlands
100 O10 **Hengelo** Overijssel, E Netherlands
Hengnan *see* Hengyang
167 N11 **Hengshan** Hunan, S China
166 L4 **Hengshan** Shaanxi, C China
167 O4 **Hengshui** Hebei, E China
167 N12 **Hengyang** *var.* Hengnan, Heng-yang; *prev.* Hengchow. Hunan, S China
119 U11 **Heniches'k** *Rus.* Genichesk. Khersons'ka Oblast', S Ukraine
23 Z4 **Henlopen, Cape** *headland* Delaware, NE USA
Henna *see* Enna
96 M10 **Hennan** Gävleborg, C Sweden
104 G7 **Hennebont** Morbihan, NW France
32 L11 **Hennepin** Illinois, N USA
28 M9 **Hennessey** Oklahoma, C USA
102 N12 **Hennigsdorf** *var.* Hennigsdorf bei Berlin. Brandenburg, NE Germany
Hennigsdorf bei Berlin *see* Hennigsdorf
21 N9 **Henniker** New Hampshire, NE USA
27 S5 **Henrietta** Texas, SW USA
Henrique de Carvalho *see* Saurimo
32 L12 **Henry** Illinois, N USA
23 Y7 **Henry, Cape** *headland* Virginia, NE USA
29 P10 **Henryetta** Oklahoma, C USA
204 M7 **Henry Ice Rise** *ice cap* Antarctica
16 N1 **Henry Kater, Cape** *headland* Baffin Island, Northwest Territories, NE Canada
35 R13 **Henrys Fork** ~ Idaho, NW USA
12 E15 **Hensall** Ontario, S Canada
102 J9 **Henstedt-Ulzburg** Schleswig-Holstein, N Germany
169 N7 **Hentiy** ◆ *province* N Mongolia
168 M7 **Hentiyn Nuruu** ▲▲ N Mongolia
191 P10 **Henty** New South Wales, SE Australia
177 F8 **Henzada** Irrawaddy, SW Myanmar
103 G19 **Heppenheim** Hessen, W Germany
34 J11 **Heppner** Oregon, NW USA
166 L15 **Hepu** *prev.* Lianzhou. Guangxi Zhuangzu Zizhiqu, S China
94 J2 **Heradhsvötn** ~ C Iceland
Herakleion *see* Irákleio
154 K5 **Herāt** *var.* Herat; *anc.* Aria. Herāt, W Afghanistan
154 J5 **Herāt** ◆ *province* W Afghanistan
105 P14 **Hérault** ◆ *department* S France
105 P15 **Hérault** ~ S France
9 T16 **Herbert** Saskatchewan, S Canada
193 F22 **Herbert** Otago, South Island, NZ
40 J17 **Herbert Island** *island* Aleutian Islands, Alaska, USA
194 I12 **Herbert, Mount** ▲ C PNG
Herbertshöhe *see* Kokopo
13 Q7 **Hérbertville** Québec, SE Canada
103 G17 **Herborn** Hessen, W Germany
115 I17 **Herceg-Novi** *It.* Castelnuovo; *prev.* Ercegnovi. Montenegro, SW Yugoslavia
9 X10 **Herchmer** Manitoba, C Canada
194 K14 **Hercules Bay** *bay* E PNG
94 K2 **Herdhubreidh** ▲ C Iceland
44 M13 **Heredia** Heredia, C Costa Rica
44 M12 **Heredia** *off.* Provincia de Heredia. ◆ *province* N Costa Rica
99 K21 **Hereford** W England, UK
26 M3 **Hereford** Texas, SW USA
13 Q13 **Hereford, Mont** ▲ Québec, SE Canada
99 K21 **Herefordshire** *cultural region* W England, UK
203 U11 **Hereheretue** *atoll* Îles Tuamotu, C French Polynesia
107 N10 **Herencia** Castilla-La Mancha, C Spain
101 H18 **Herent** Vlaams Brabant, C Belgium
101 I16 **Herentals** *var.* Herenthals. Antwerpen, N Belgium
Herenthals *see* Herentals
101 H17 **Herenthout** Antwerpen, N Belgium
97 J23 **Herfølge** Roskilde, E Denmark
102 G13 **Herford** Nordrhein-Westfalen, NW Germany
29 O5 **Herington** Kansas, C USA
110 H7 **Herisau** *Fr.* Hérisau. Appenzell Ausser Rhoden, NE Switzerland
Héristal *see* Herstal
101 J18 **Herk-de-Stad** Limburg, NE Belgium
Herkulesbad/Herkulesfürdő *see* Băile Herculane
Herlen Gol/Herlen He *see* Kerulen
37 Q4 **Herlong** California, W USA
99 L26 **Herm** *island* Channel Islands
111 R9 **Hermagor** *Slvn.* Šmohor. Kärnten, S Austria
31 S7 **Herman** Minnesota, N USA
98 L1 **Herma Ness** *headland* NE Scotland, UK
29 V4 **Hermann** Missouri, C USA
189 Q8 **Hermannsburg** Northern Territory, N Australia
Hermannstadt *see* Sibiu
96 E12 **Hermansverk** Sogn og Fjordane, S Norway
144 H6 **Hermel** *var.* Hirmil. NE Lebanon
Hermhausen *see* Hajnówka
191 P6 **Hermidale** New South Wales, SE Australia
57 X9 **Herminadorp** Sipaliwini, NE Suriname
34 K11 **Hermiston** Oregon, NW USA
29 T6 **Hermitage** Missouri, C USA
194 J8 **Hermit Islands** *island group* N PNG
27 O7 **Hermleigh** Texas, SW USA
144 G7 **Hermon, Mount** *Ar.* Jabal ash Shaykh. ▲ S Syria
Hermopolis Parva *see* Damanhûr
30 J10 **Hermosa** South Dakota, N USA
42 F5 **Hermosillo** Sonora, NW Mexico
Hermoupolis *see* Ermoúpoli
113 N20 **Hernád** *var.* Hornád, *Ger.* Kundert. ~ Hungary/Slovakia
63 C18 **Hernández** Entre Ríos, E Argentina
25 V11 **Hernando** Florida, SE USA
24 L1 **Hernando** Mississippi, S USA
107 Q2 **Hernani** País Vasco, N Spain
101 F19 **Herne** Vlaams Brabant, C Belgium
103 E14 **Herne** Nordrhein-Westfalen, W Germany
97 F22 **Herning** Ringkøbing, W Denmark
Hernösand *see* Härnösand
124 Q13 **Herodotus Basin** *undersea feature* E Mediterranean Sea
124 Nn14 **Herodotus Trough** *undersea feature* C Mediterranean Sea
31 T11 **Heron Lake** Minnesota, N USA
Herowābād *see* Khalkhāl
97 G16 **Herre** Telemark, S Norway
31 N7 **Herreid** South Dakota, N USA
103 H22 **Herrenberg** Baden-Württemberg, S Germany
106 L14 **Herrera** Andalucía, S Spain
45 R17 **Herrera** *off.* Provincia de Herrera. ◆ *province* S Panama
106 L10 **Herrera del Duque** Extremadura, W Spain
106 M4 **Herrera de Pisuerga** Castilla-León, N Spain
43 Z13 **Herrero, Punta** *headland* SE Mexico
191 P16 **Herrick** Tasmania, SE Australia
32 L17 **Herrin** Illinois, N USA
22 M6 **Herrington Lake** ⊡ Kentucky, S USA
97 K18 **Herrljunga** Älvsborg, S Sweden
105 N16 **Hers** ~ S France
8 I1 **Herschel Island** *island* Yukon Territory, NW Canada
101 I17 **Herselt** Antwerpen, C Belgium
20 G15 **Hershey** Pennsylvania, NE USA
101 K19 **Herstal** *Fr.* Héristal. Liège, E Belgium
99 O21 **Hertford** E England, UK
23 X8 **Hertford** North Carolina, SE USA
99 O21 **Hertfordshire** *cultural region* E England, UK
189 Z9 **Hervey Bay** Queensland, E Australia
103 O14 **Herzberg** Brandenburg, E Germany
101 E18 **Herzele** Oost-Vlaanderen, NW Belgium
103 K20 **Herzogenaurach** Bayern, SE Germany
111 W4 **Herzogenburg** Niederösterreich, NE Austria
Herzogenbusch *see* 's-Hertogenbosch
105 N2 **Hesdin** Pas-de-Calais, N France
166 K14 **Heshan** Guangxi Zhuangzu Zizhiqu, S China
165 X10 **Heshui** *var.* Xihuachi. Gansu, C China
101 M25 **Hespérange** Luxembourg, SE Luxembourg
37 U14 **Hesperia** California, W USA
39 P7 **Hesperus Mountain** ▲ Colorado, C USA
8 J6 **Hess** ~ Yukon Territory, NW Canada
Hesse *see* Hessen
103 J21 **Hesselberg** ▲ S Germany
97 I22 **Hesselo** *island* E Denmark
103 H17 **Hessen** *Eng./Fr.* Hesse. ◆ *state* C Germany
199 J6 **Hess Tablemount** *undersea feature* C Pacific Ocean
29 N6 **Hesston** Kansas, C USA
99 K18 **Heswall** NW England, UK
159 P12 **Hetauda** Central, C Nepal
Hétfalu *see* Săcele
30 K7 **Hettinger** North Dakota, N USA
103 L14 **Hettstedt** Sachsen-Anhalt, C Germany
94 P3 **Heuglin, Kapp** *headland* SE Svalbard
195 Y16 **Heuru** San Cristobal, SE Solomon Islands
101 J17 **Heusden** Limburg, NE Belgium
100 J13 **Heusden** Noord-Brabant, S Netherlands
104 K3 **Hève, Cap de la** *headland* N France
101 H18 **Heverlee** Vlaams Brabant, C Belgium
113 L22 **Heves** Heves, NE Hungary
113 L22 **Heves** *off.* Heves Megye. ◆ *county* NE Hungary
Hevron *see* Hebron
47 Y13 **Hewanorra** ✕ (Saint Lucia) S Saint Lucia
166 M13 **Hexian** *var.* Babu, He Xian. Guangxi Zhuangzu Zizhiqu, S China
166 L6 **Heyang** Shaanxi, C China
Heydebrech *see* Kędzierzyn-Kozle
Heydekrug *see* Šilutė
99 K16 **Heysham** NW England, UK
167 O14 **Heyuan** Guangdong, S China
190 L12 **Heywood** Victoria, SE Australia
188 K3 **Heywood Islands** *island group* Western Australia
167 O6 **Heze** *var.* Caozhou. Shandong, E China
165 U11 **Hezheng** Gansu, C China
165 U11 **Hezuozhen** Gansu, C China
25 Z16 **Hialeah** Florida, SE USA
29 Q3 **Hiawatha** Kansas, C USA
38 M4 **Hiawatha** Utah, W USA
31 V4 **Hibbing** Minnesota, N USA
191 N17 **Hibbs, Point** *headland* Tasmania, SE Australia
Hibernia *see* Ireland
170 D12 **Hibiki-nada** *inlet* SW Japan
22 F8 **Hickman** Kentucky, S USA
23 Q9 **Hickory** North Carolina, SE USA
23 Q9 **Hickory, Lake** ◎ North Carolina, SE USA
192 Q7 **Hicks Bay** Gisborne, North Island, NZ
27 S8 **Hico** Texas, SW USA
172 Oo6 **Hidaka** Hokkaidō, NE Japan
171 Gg13 **Hidaka** Hyōgo, Honshū, SW Japan
172 P7 **Hidaka-sanmyaku** ▲▲ Hokkaidō, NE Japan
43 O6 **Hidalgo** *var.* Villa Hidalgo. Coahuila de Zaragoza, NE Mexico
43 N8 **Hidalgo** Nuevo León, NE Mexico
43 O10 **Hidalgo** Tamaulipas, C Mexico
43 O13 **Hidalgo** ◆ *state* C Mexico
42 J7 **Hidalgo del Parral** *var.* Parral. Chihuahua, N Mexico
171 J14 **Hida-sanmyaku** ▲▲ Honshū, S Japan
102 N7 **Hiddensee** *island* NE Germany
82 G6 **Hidiglib, Wadi** ~ NE Sudan
111 U6 **Hieflau** Salzburg, E Austria
197 H5 **Hienghène** Province Nord, C New Caledonia
Hierosolyma *see* Jerusalem
66 N12 **Hierro** *var.* Ferro. *island* Islas Canarias, Spain, NE Atlantic Ocean
170 Ee13 **Higashi-Hiroshima** *var.* Higasihirosima. Hiroshima, Honshū, SW Japan
171 J18 **Higashi-Izu** Shizuoka, Honshū, S Japan
171 Ll12 **Higashine** *var.* Higasine. Yamagata, Honshū, C Japan
170 C11 **Higashi-suidō** *strait* SW Japan
Higasihirosima *see* Higashi-Hiroshima
Higasine *see* Higashine
Higasiôsaka *see* Higashi-ôsaka
27 P1 **Higgins** Texas, SW USA
33 P7 **Higgins Lake** ◎ Michigan, N USA
29 S4 **Higginsville** Missouri, C USA
High Atlas *see* Haut Atlas
32 M5 **High Falls Reservoir** ⊡ Wisconsin, N USA
46 K12 **Highgate** C Jamaica
27 X11 **High Island** Texas, SW USA
33 O5 **High Island** *island* Michigan, N USA
32 K15 **Highland** Illinois, N USA
33 N10 **Highland Park** Illinois, N USA
23 O10 **Highlands** North Carolina, SE USA
9 O11 **High Level** Alberta, W Canada
31 O9 **Highmore** South Dakota, N USA
179 Oo10 **High Peak** ▲ Luzon, N Philippines
High Plains *see* Great Plains
23 S9 **High Point** North Carolina, SE USA
20 J13 **High Point** *hill* New Jersey, NE USA
9 P13 **High Prairie** Alberta, W Canada
9 Q16 **High River** Alberta, SW Canada
23 S9 **High Rock Lake** ⊡ North Carolina, SE USA
25 V9 **High Springs** Florida, SE USA
High Veld *see* Great Karoo
99 J24 **High Willhays** ▲ SW England, UK
99 N22 **High Wycombe** *prev.* Chepping Wycombe, Chipping Wycombe. SE England, UK
43 P12 **Higos** *var.* El Higo. Veracruz-Llave, E Mexico
104 I16 **Higuer, Cap** *headland* NE Spain
47 R5 **Higüero, Punta** *headland* W Puerto Rico
47 P9 **Higüey** *var.* Salvaleón de Higüey. E Dominican Republic
202 G11 **Hihifo** ✕ (Matā'utu) Île Uvea, N Wallis and Futuna
83 N16 **Hiiraan** *off.* Gobolka Hiiraan. ◆ *region* C Somalia
120 E4 **Hiiumaa** *off.* Hiiumaa Maakond. ◆ *province* W Estonia
120 D4 **Hiiumaa** *Ger.* Dagden, *Swe.* Dagö. *island* W Estonia
Hijanah *see* Al Hījānah
107 S6 **Híjar** Aragón, NE Spain
170 E13 **Hikari** Yamaguchi, Honshū, SW Japan
170 Ff15 **Hiketa** Kagawa, Shikoku, SW Japan
171 Hh15 **Hikone** Shiga, Honshū, SW Japan
170 D13 **Hiko-san** ▲ Kyūshū, SW Japan
203 V10 **Hikueru** *atoll* Îles Tuamotu, C French Polynesia
192 K3 **Hikurangi** Northland, North Island, NZ
192 Q8 **Hikurangi** ▲ North Island, NZ
199 J13 **Hikurangi Trench** *var.* Hikurangi Trough. *undersea feature* SW Pacific Ocean
Hikurangi Trough *see* Hikurangi Trench
202 B15 **Hikutavake** NW Niue
124 Nn14 **Hilāl, Ra's al** *headland* N Libya
63 A24 **Hilario Ascasubi** Buenos Aires, E Argentina
103 K17 **Hildburghausen** Thüringen, C Germany
103 E15 **Hilden** Nordrhein-Westfalen, W Germany
102 I13 **Hildesheim** Niedersachsen, N Germany
35 T9 **Hilger** Montana, NW USA
Hili *see* Hilli
Hilla *see* Al Ḥillah
47 O14 **Hillaby, Mount** ▲ N Barbados
97 K19 **Hillared** Älvsborg, S Sweden
205 R12 **Hillary Coast** *physical region* Antarctica
44 G2 **Hill Bank** Orange Walk, N Belize
35 O14 **Hill City** Idaho, NW USA
28 K3 **Hill City** Kansas, C USA
31 V5 **Hill City** Minnesota, N USA
30 J10 **Hill City** South Dakota, N USA
67 C24 **Hill Cove Settlement** West Falkland, Falkland Islands
100 H10 **Hillegom** Zuid-Holland, W Netherlands
97 J22 **Hillerød** Frederiksborg, E Denmark
38 M7 **Hillers, Mount** ▲ Utah, W USA
159 S13 **Hilli** *var.* Hili. Rajshahi, NW Bangladesh
31 R11 **Hills** Minnesota, N USA
32 L14 **Hillsboro** Illinois, N USA
29 N5 **Hillsboro** Kansas, C USA
29 X5 **Hillsboro** Missouri, C USA
21 N10 **Hillsboro** New Hampshire, NE USA
39 Q14 **Hillsboro** New Mexico, SW USA
31 R4 **Hillsboro** North Dakota, N USA
33 R14 **Hillsboro** Ohio, N USA
34 G11 **Hillsboro** Oregon, NW USA
27 T8 **Hillsboro** Texas, SW USA
32 K8 **Hillsboro** Wisconsin, N USA
25 Y14 **Hillsboro Canal** *canal* Florida, SE USA
47 Y15 **Hillsborough** Carriacou, N Grenada
99 G15 **Hillsborough** E Northern Ireland, UK
23 U9 **Hillsborough** North Carolina, SE USA
33 Q10 **Hillsdale** Michigan, N USA
191 O8 **Hillston** New South Wales, SE Australia
23 R7 **Hillsville** Virginia, NE USA
98 L2 **Hillswick** NE Scotland, UK
Hill Tippera *see* Tripura
40 H11 **Hilo** Hawaii, USA, C Pacific Ocean
20 F9 **Hilton** New York, NE USA
12 C10 **Hilton Beach** Ontario, S Canada
23 R16 **Hilton Head Island** South Carolina, SE USA
23 R16 **Hilton Head Island** *island* South Carolina, SE USA
101 J15 **Hilvarenbeek** Noord-Brabant, S Netherlands
100 J11 **Hilversum** Noord-Holland, C Netherlands
Hilwān *see* Helwân
158 J7 **Himāchal Pradesh** ◆ *state* NW India
Himalaya/Himalaya Shan *see* Himalayas
158 M9 **Himalayas** *var.* Himalaya, *Chin.* Himalaya Shan. ▲▲ S Asia
179 Q14 **Himamaylan** Negros, C Philippines
95 K15 **Himanka** Vaasa, W Finland
Himara *see* Himarë
115 L23 **Himarë** *var.* Himara. Vlorë, S Albania
144 M2 **Ḥimār, Wādī al** *dry watercourse* N Syria
160 D9 **Himatnagar** Gujarāt, W India
111 Y4 **Himberg** Niederösterreich, E Austria
171 J14 **Hime-gawa** ~ Honshū, S Japan
170 G14 **Himeji** *var.* Himezi. Hyōgo, Honshū, SW Japan
170 Dd13 **Hime-jima** *island* SW Japan
Himezi *see* Himeji
171 Ii13 **Himi** Toyama, Honshū, SW Japan
111 S9 **Himmelberg** Kärnten, S Austria
144 I5 **Ḥimṣ** *var.* Homs; *anc.* Emesa. Ḥimṣ, C Syria
144 K6 **Ḥimṣ** *off.* Muḥāfaẓat Ḥimṣ, *var.* Homs. ◆ *governorate* C Syria
144 I5 **Ḥimṣ, Buḥayrat** *var.* Buḥayrat Qaṭṭinah. ◎ W Syria
179 Rr15 **Hinatuan** Mindanao, S Philippines
119 N10 **Hînceşti** *var.* Hânceşti; *prev.* Kotovsk. C Moldova
46 M9 **Hinche** C Haiti
189 X5 **Hinchinbrook Island** *island* Queensland, NE Australia
41 S12 **Hinchinbrook Island** *island* Alaska, USA
99 M19 **Hinckley** C England, UK
31 V7 **Hinckley** Minnesota, N USA
38 K5 **Hinckley** Utah, W USA
20 J9 **Hinckley Reservoir** ⊡ New York, NE USA
158 I12 **Hindaun** Rājasthān, N India
Hindenburg/Hindenburg in Oberschlesien *see* Zabrze
Hindiya *see* Al Hindīyah
23 O6 **Hindman** Kentucky, S USA
190 L10 **Hindmarsh, Lake** ◎ Victoria, SE Australia
193 G19 **Hinds** Canterbury, South Island, NZ
193 G19 **Hinds** ~ South Island, NZ
97 H23 **Hindsholm** *island* C Denmark
155 S4 **Hindu Kush** *Per.* Hendū Kosh. ▲▲ Afghanistan/Pakistan
161 H19 **Hindupur** Andhra Pradesh, E India
9 O12 **Hines Creek** Alberta, W Canada
25 W6 **Hinesville** Georgia, SE USA
160 I12 **Hinganghāt** Mahārāshtra, C India
155 N15 **Hingol** ~ SW Pakistan
160 H13 **Hingoli** Mahārāshtra, C India
143 R13 **Hınıs** Erzurum, E Turkey
94 O2 **Hinlopenstretet** *strait* N Svalbard
94 G10 **Hinnøya** *island* C Norway
170 D15 **Hinokage** Miyazaki, Kyūshū, SW Japan
170 F11 **Hino-misaki** *headland* Honshū, SW Japan
110 H10 **Hinterrhein** ~ SW Switzerland
9 O14 **Hinton** Alberta, SW Canada
28 M10 **Hinton** Oklahoma, C USA
23 R6 **Hinton** West Virginia, NE USA
Hios *see* Chíos
43 N8 **Hipolito** Coahuila de Zaragoza, NE Mexico
Hipponium *see* Vibo Valentia
170 C12 **Hirado** Nagasaki, Hirado-shima, SW Japan
170 C12 **Hirado-shima** *island* SW Japan
171 Gg15 **Hirakata** Ōsaka, Honshū, SW Japan
172 P17 **Hirakubo-saki** *headland* Ishigaki-jima, SW Japan
160 M11 **Hīrākud Reservoir** ⊡ E India
Hir al Gharbi, Qasr al *see* Ḥayr al Gharbī, Qaṣr al
172 N9 **Hiranai** Aomori, Honshū, N Japan
172 Pp16 **Hirara** Okinawa, Miyako-jima, SW Japan
Qasr al Hir Ash Sharqī *see* Ḥayr ash Sharqī, Qaṣr al
170 F12 **Hirata** Shimane, Honshū, SW Japan
171 Jj17 **Hiratsuka** *var.* Hiratuka. Kanagawa, Honshū, S Japan
Hiratuka *see* Hiratsuka
142 I13 **Hirfanlı Barajı** ⊡ C Turkey
161 G18 **Hiriyūr** Karnātaka, W India
Hîrlău *see* Hârlău
154 K10 **Hirmand, Rūd-e** *var.* Daryā-ye Helmand. ~ Afghanistan/Iran *see also* Helmand, Daryā-ye
Hirmil *see* Hermel
172 P8 **Hiroo** Hokkaidō, NE Japan
171 Mm9 **Hirosaki** Aomori, Honshū, C Japan
170 E13 **Hiroshima** *var.* Hirosima. Hiroshima, Honshū, SW Japan
170 Ee13 **Hiroshima** *off.* Hiroshima-ken, *var.* Hirosima. ◆ *prefecture* Honshū, SW Japan
Hirosima *see* Hiroshima
Hirschberg/Hirschberg im Riesengebirge/Hirschberg in Schlesien *see* Jelenia Góra
105 Q3 **Hirson** Aisne, N France
Hîrşova *see* Hârşova
97 G19 **Hirtshals** Nordjylland, N Denmark
171 H16 **Hisai** Mie, Honshū, SW Japan
158 H10 **Hisār** Haryāna, NW India
194 J15 **Hisiu** Central, SW PNG
153 P13 **Hisor** *Rus.* Gissar. W Tajikistan
Hispalis *see* Sevilla
Hispana/Hispania *see* Spain
46 M7 **Hispaniola** *island* Dominion Republic/Haiti
66 F11 **Hispaniola Basin** *var.* Hispaniola Trough. *undersea feature* SW Atlantic Ocean
Hispaniola Trough *see* Hispaniola Basin
Histonium *see* Vasto
145 R7 **Hīt** SW Iraq
170 D14 **Hita** Ōita, Kyūshū, SW Japan
171 L16 **Hitachi** *var.* Hitati. Ibaraki, Honshū, S Japan
171 L15 **Hitachi-Ōta** *var.* Hitatiôta. Ibaraki, Honshū, S Japan
Hitati *see* Hitachi
Hitatiôta *see* Hitachi-Ōta
99 O21 **Hitchin** E England, UK
203 Q7 **Hitiaa** Tahiti, W French Polynesia
170 Cc15 **Hitoyoshi** *var.* Hitoyosi. Kumamoto, Kyūshū, SW Japan
Hitoyosi *see* Hitoyoshi
96 F7 **Hitra** *prev.* Hitteren. *island* S Norway
Hitteren *see* Hitra
197 B10 **Hiu** *island* Torres Islands, N Vanuatu
171 K14 **Hiuchiga-take** ▲ Honshū, C Japan
170 Ee14 **Hiuchi-nada** *gulf* S Japan
203 X7 **Hiva Oa** *island* Îles Marquises, N French Polynesia
22 M10 **Hiwassee Lake** ⊡ North Carolina, SE USA
22 M10 **Hiwassee River** ~ SE USA
97 H20 **Hjallerup** Nordjylland, N Denmark
97 M16 **Hjälmaren** *Eng.* Lake Hjalmar. ◎ C Sweden
Hjalmar, Lake *see* Hjälmaren
97 C14 **Hjellestad** Hordaland, S Norway
97 D16 **Hjelmeland** Rogaland, S Norway
96 G10 **Hjerkinn** Oppland, S Norway
97 L18 **Hjo** Skaraborg, S Sweden
97 G19 **Hjørring** Nordjylland, N Denmark
178 H1 **Hkakabo Razi** ▲ Myanmar/China
178 H1 **Hkring Bum** ▲ N Myanmar
85 L21 **Hlathikulu** *var.* Hlatikulu. S Swaziland
Hlatikulu *see* Hlathikulu
Hliboka *see* Hlyboka
113 F17 **Hlinsko** *var.* Hlinsko v Čechách. Východní Čechy, C Czech Republic
Hlinsko v Čechách *see* Hlinsko
119 S6 **Hlobyne** *Rus.* Globino. Poltavs'ka Oblast', NE Ukraine
113 H20 **Hlohovec** *Ger.* Freistadtl, *Hung.* Galgóc; *prev.* Frakštát. Západné Slovensko, W Slovakia
85 J23 **Hlotse** *var.* Leribe. NW Lesotho
113 I17 **Hlučín** *Ger.* Hultschin, *Pol.* Hulczyn. Severní Morava, E Czech Republic
119 S2 **Hlukhiv** *Rus.* Glukhov. Sums'ka Oblast', NE Ukraine
121 K21 **Hlushkavichy** *Rus.* Glushkevichi. Homyel'skaya Voblasts', SE Belarus
121 L18 **Hlusk** *Rus.* Glusk, Glussk. Mahilyowskaya Voblasts', E Belarus
118 K8 **Hlyboka** *Ger.* Hliboka, *Rus.* Glybokaya. Chernivets'ka Oblast', W Ukraine
120 K13 **Hlybokaye** *Rus.* Glubokoye. Vitsyebskaya Voblasts', N Belarus
79 Q16 **Ho** SE Ghana
178 Jj6 **Hoa Binh** Hoa Binh, N Vietnam
85 E20 **Hoachanas** Hardap, C Namibia
Hoai Nhơn *see* Bồng Sơn
178 Jj8 **Hoa Lac** Quang Binh, C Vietnam
178 J5 **Hoang Liên Sơn** ▲▲ N Vietnam
85 B17 **Hoanib** ~ NW Namibia
35 S15 **Hoback Peak** ▲ Wyoming, C USA
191 P17 **Hobart** *prev.* Hobarton, Hobart Town. *state capital* Tasmania, SE Australia
28 L11 **Hobart** Oklahoma, C USA
191 P17 **Hobart** ✕ Tasmania, SE Australia
Hobarton/Hobart Town *see* Hobart
39 W14 **Hobbs** New Mexico, SW USA
204 L12 **Hobbs Coast** *physical region* Antarctica
25 Z14 **Hobe Sound** Florida, SE USA
Hobicaurikány *see* Uricani
56 E12 **Hobo** Huila, S Colombia
101 G16 **Hoboken** Antwerpen, N Belgium
164 K3 **Hoboksar** *var.* Hoboksar Mongol Zizhixian. Xinjiang Uygur Zizhiqu, NW China
Hoboksar Mongol Zizhixian *see* Hoboksar
97 G21 **Hobro** Nordjylland, N Denmark
23 X10 **Hobucken** North Carolina, SE USA
97 O20 **Hoburgen** *headland* SE Sweden
83 P15 **Hobyo** *It.* Obbia. Mudug, E Somalia
111 R8 **Hochalmspitze** ▲ SW Austria
111 Q4 **Hochburg** Oberösterreich, N Austria
110 F8 **Hochdorf** Luzern, N Switzerland
111 N8 **Hochfeiler** *It.* Gran Pilastro. ▲ Austria/Italy
178 Jj14 **Hô Chi Minh** *var.* Ho Chi Minh City; *prev.* Saigon. S Vietnam
Ho Chi Minh City *see* Hô Chi Minh
110 I7 **Höchst** Vorarlberg, NW Austria
Höchstadt *see* Höchstadt an der Aisch
103 K19 **Höchstadt an der Aisch** *var.* Höchstadt. Bayern, C Germany
110 L9 **Hochwilde** *It.* L'Altissima. ▲ Austria/Italy
111 S7 **Hochwildstelle** ▲ C Austria
33 T14 **Hocking River** ~ Ohio, N USA
Hoctúm *see* Hoctún
43 X12 **Hoctún** *var.* Hoctúm. Yucatán, E Mexico
Hodeida *see* Al Ḥudaydah
22 K6 **Hodgenville** Kentucky, S USA
9 T17 **Hodgeville** Saskatchewan, S Canada
78 L9 **Hodh ech Chargui** ◆ *region* E Mauritania
Hodh el Garbi *see* Hodh el Gharbi
78 J10 **Hodh el Gharbi** *var.* Hodh el Garbi. ◆ *region* S Mauritania
113 L25 **Hódmezővásárhely** Csongrád, SE Hungary
76 J6 **Hodna, Chott El** *var.* Chott el-Hodna, *Ar.* Shatt al-Hodna. *salt lake* N Algeria
Hodna, Shatt al- *see* Hodna, Chott El
113 G19 **Hodonín** *Ger.* Göding. Jižní Morava, SE Czech Republic
168 G6 **Hödrögö** Dzavhan, N Mongolia
Hodság/Hodschag *see* Odžaci
41 R7 **Hodzana River** ~ Alaska, USA
Hoei *see* Huy
101 H19 **Hoeilaart** Vlaams Brabant, C Belgium
Hoë Karoo *see* Great Karoo
100 F12 **Hoek van Holland** *Eng.* Hook of Holland. Zuid-Holland, W Netherlands
100 L11 **Hoenderloo** Gelderland, E Netherlands
101 L18 **Hoensbroek** Limburg, SE Netherlands
169 Y11 **Hoeryŏng** NE North Korea
101 K18 **Hoeselt** Limburg, NE Belgium
100 K11 **Hoevelaken** Gelderland, C Netherlands
Hoey *see* Huy
103 M18 **Hof** Bayern, SE Germany
Höfdhakaupstadhur *see* Skagaströnd
Hofei *see* Hefei
103 G18 **Hofheim am Taunus** Hessen, W Germany
Hofmarkt *see* Odorheiu Secuiesc
94 L3 **Höfn** Austurland, SE Iceland
96 N13 **Hofors** Gävleborg, C Sweden
94 J6 **Hofsjökull** *glacier* C Iceland
94 J1 **Hofsós** Nordhurland Vestra, N Iceland
170 Dd13 **Hōfu** Yamaguchi, Honshū, SW Japan
Hofuf *see* Al Hufūf
97 J22 **Höganäs** Malmöhus, S Sweden
191 P14 **Hogan Group** *island group* Tasmania, SE Australia
25 R4 **Hogansville** Georgia, SE USA
41 P8 **Hogatza River** ~ Alaska, USA
30 I14 **Hogback Mountain** ▲ Nebraska, C USA
97 G14 **Høgevarde** ▲ S Norway
Högfors *see* Karkkila
33 P5 **Hog Island** *island* Michigan, N USA
23 Y6 **Hog Island** *island* Virginia, NE USA
Hogoley Islands *see* Chuuk Islands
97 N20 **Högsby** Kalmar, S Sweden
38 K1 **Hogup Mountains** ▲▲ Utah, W USA
103 E17 **Hohe Acht** ▲ W Germany
Hohenelbe *see* Vrchlabí
110 I7 **Hohenems** Vorarlberg, W Austria
Hohenmauth *see* Vysoké Mýto
Hohensalza *see* Inowrocław
Hohenstadt *see* Zábřeh
Hohenstein in Ostpreussen *see* Olsztynek
22 I9 **Hohenwald** Tennessee, S USA
103 L17 **Hohenwarte-Stausee** ⊡ C Germany
Hohes Venn *see* Hautes Fagnes
111 Q8 **Hohe Tauern** ▲▲ W Austria
169 O13 **Hohhot** *var.* Huhehot, Huhuohaote, *Mong.* Kukukhoto; *prev.* Kweisui, Kwesui. Nei Mongol Zizhiqu, N China
105 U6 **Hohneck** ▲ NE France
79 Q16 **Hohoe** E Ghana
170 D12 **Hōhoku** Yamaguchi, Honshū, SW Japan
165 O11 **Hoh Sai Hu** ◎ C China
165 N11 **Hoh Xil Hu** ◎ C China
164 L11 **Hoh Xil Shan** ▲▲ W China
178 Kk10 **Hôi An** *prev.* Faifo. Quang Nam-Đa Nang, C Vietnam
Hoï-Hao/Hoihow *see* Haikou
83 F17 **Hoima** W Uganda
28 L5 **Hoisington** Kansas, C USA
Hojagala *see* Khodzhakala
Hojambaz *see* Khodzhambas
97 H23 **Højby** Fyn, C Denmark
97 F24 **Højer** Sønderjylland, SW Denmark
170 Ee14 **Hōjō** *var.* Hôzyô. Ehime, Shikoku, SW Japan
192 J3 **Hokianga Harbour** *inlet* SE Tasman Sea
193 F17 **Hokitika** West Coast, South Island, NZ
172 P5 **Hokkai-dō** ◆ *territory* Hokkaidō, NE Japan
172 Oo5 **Hokkaidō** *prev.* Ezo, Yeso, Yezo. *island* NE Japan
97 G15 **Hokksund** Buskerud, S Norway
149 S4 **Hokmābād** Khorāsān, N Iran
Hokō *see* P'ohang
Hoko-guntō/Hoko-shotō *see* P'enghu Liehtao
143 T12 **Hoktemberyan** *Rus.* Oktemberyan. SW Armenia
96 F13 **Hol** Buskerud, S Norway
119 R11 **Hola Prystan'** *Rus.* Golaya Pristan. Khersons'ka Oblast', S Ukraine
97 I23 **Holbæk** Vestsjælland, E Denmark
168 G6 **Holboo** Dzavhan, W Mongolia
191 P10 **Holbrook** New South Wales, SE Australia
39 N11 **Holbrook** Arizona, SW USA
29 S5 **Holden** Missouri, C USA
38 K5 **Holden** Utah, W USA
29 O11 **Holdenville** Oklahoma, C USA
31 O16 **Holdrege** Nebraska, C USA
37 X3 **Hole in the Mountain Peak** ▲ Nevada, W USA
161 G20 **Hole Narsipur** Karnātaka, W India
113 H18 **Holešov** *Ger.* Holleschau. Jižní Morava, E Czech Republic
47 N14 **Holetown** *prev.* Jamestown. W Barbados
33 Q12 **Holgate** Ohio, N USA
46 I7 **Holguín** Holguín, SE Cuba
25 V12 **Holiday** Florida, SE USA
41 O12 **Holitna River** ~ Alaska, USA
96 J13 **Höljes** Värmland, C Sweden
111 X3 **Hollabrunn** Niederösterreich, NE Austria
38 L3 **Holladay** Utah, W USA
9 X16 **Holland** Manitoba, S Canada

◆ Country ● Country Capital ◇ Dependent Territory ○ Dependent Territory Capital ◆ Administrative Region ✕ International Airport ▲ Mountain ▲▲ Mountain Range Volcano ~ River ◎ Lake ⊡ Reservoir

◆ COUNTRY   ◇ DEPENDENT TERRITORY   ◈ ADMINISTRATIVE REGION   ▲ MOUNTAIN   ℟ VOLCANO   ☉ LAKE
● COUNTRY CAPITAL   ○ DEPENDENT TERRITORY CAPITAL   × INTERNATIONAL AIRPORT   ▲ MOUNTAIN RANGE   ≈ RIVER   ▨ RESERVOIR

261

HUITTINEN – IMPERIAL

95 K19 **Huittinen** Turku-Pori, SW Finland
43 O15 **Huitzuco** var. Huitzuco de los Figueroa. Guerrero, S Mexico
Huitzuco de los Figueroa see Huitzuco
165 W11 **Hui Xian** Gansu, C China
43 V17 **Huixtla** Chiapas, SE Mexico
166 H12 **Huize** Yunnan, SW China
100 J10 **Huizen** Noord-Holland, C Netherlands
167 O14 **Huizhou** Guangdong, S China
168 J6 **Hujirt** Arhangay, C Mongolia
168 J8 **Hujirt** Övörhangay, C Mongolia
168 K8 **Hujrt** Töv, C Mongolia
Hukagawa see Fukagawa
Hŭksan-chedo see Hŭksan-gundo
169 W17 **Hŭksan-gundo** var. Hŭksan-chedo. island group SW South Korea
Hukue see Fukue
Hukui see Fukui
85 G20 **Hukuntsi** Kgalagadi, SW Botswana
Hukuoka see Fukuoka
Hukusima see Fukushima
Hukutiyama see Fukuchiyama
Hukuyama see Fukuyama
169 W8 **Hulan** Heilongjiang, NE China
169 W8 **Hulan He** ≈ NE China
33 Q4 **Hulbert Lake** ◎ Michigan, N USA
Hulczyn see Hlučín
169 Z8 **Hulin** Heilongjiang, NE China
169 S9 **Hulingol** prev. Huolin Gol. Nei Mongol Zizhiqu, N China
12 L12 **Hull** Québec, SE Canada
31 S12 **Hull** Iowa, C USA
Hull see Kingston upon Hull
Hull Island see Orona
101 F16 **Hulst** Zeeland, SW Netherlands
169 Q7 **Hulstay** Dornod, NE Mongolia
Hultschin see Hlučín
97 M19 **Hultsfred** Kalmar, S Sweden
Hulun see Hailar
Hu-lun Ch'ih see Hulun Nur
169 Q6 **Hulun Nur** var. Hu-lun Ch'ih; prev. Dalai Nor. ◎ NE China
Hulwan/Hulwân see Helwân
119 V8 **Hulyaypole** Rus. Gulyaypole. Zaporiz'ka Oblast', SE Ukraine
169 V4 **Huma** Heilongjiang, NE China
47 V6 **Humacao** E Puerto Rico
169 U4 **Huma He** ≈ NE China
64 J5 **Humahuaca** Jujuy, N Argentina
61 E14 **Humaitá** Amazonas, N Brazil
64 N7 **Humaitá** Ñeembucú, S Paraguay
85 H26 **Humansdorp** Eastern Cape, S South Africa
29 S6 **Humansville** Missouri, C USA
42 J8 **Humaya, Río** ≈ C Mexico
85 C16 **Humbe** Cunene, SW Angola
99 N17 **Humber** estuary E England, UK
99 N17 **Humberside** cultural region E England, UK
Humberto see Umberto
27 W11 **Humble** Texas, SW USA
9 U15 **Humboldt** Saskatchewan, S Canada
31 U12 **Humboldt** Iowa, C USA
29 Q6 **Humboldt** Kansas, C USA
31 S17 **Humboldt** Nebraska, C USA
37 S3 **Humboldt** Nevada, W USA
22 G9 **Humboldt** Tennessee, S USA
36 K3 **Humboldt Bay** bay California, W USA
37 S4 **Humboldt Lake** ◎ Nevada, W USA
197 J7 **Humboldt, Mont** ▲ S New Caledonia
37 S4 **Humboldt River** ≈ Nevada, W USA
37 T5 **Humboldt Salt Marsh** wetland Nevada, W USA
191 P11 **Hume, Lake** ◎ New South Wales/Victoria, SE Australia
113 N19 **Humenné** Ger. Homenau, Hung. Homonna. Východné Slovensko, E Slovakia
31 V15 **Humeston** Iowa, C USA
56 J5 **Humocaro Bajo** Lara, N Venezuela
31 Q14 **Humphrey** Nebraska, C USA
37 S9 **Humphreys, Mount** ▲ California, W USA
38 L11 **Humphreys Peak** ▲ Arizona, SW USA
113 E17 **Humpolec** Ger. Gumpolds, Humpoletz. Jižní Čechy, C Czech Republic
Humpoletz see Humpolec
95 K19 **Humppila** Häme, SW Finland
34 F8 **Humptulips** Washington, NW USA
44 H7 **Humuya, Río** ≈ W Honduras
77 P9 **Hūn** N Libya
Hunabasi see Funabashi
94 I1 **Húnaflói** bay NW Iceland
166 M11 **Hunan** var. Hunan Sheng, Xiang. ◆ province S China
Hunan Sheng see Hunan
169 Y10 **Hunchun** Jilin, NE China
97 I22 **Hundested** Frederiksborg, E Denmark
Hundred Mile House see 100 Mile House
118 G12 **Hunedoara** Ger. Eisenmarkt, Hung. Vajdahunyad. Hunedoara, SW Romania
118 G12 **Hunedoara** ◆ county W Romania
103 I17 **Hünfeld** Hessen, C Germany
113 H23 **Hungary** off. Republic of Hungary, Ger. Ungarn, Hung. Magyarország, Rom. Ungaria, SCr. Mađarska, Ukr. Uhorshchyna; prev. Hungarian People's Republic. ◆ republic C Europe
Hungary, Plain of see Great Hungarian Plain
168 F6 **Hungiy** Dzavhan, W Mongolia
169 X13 **Hŭngnam** E North Korea
35 P8 **Hungry Horse Reservoir** ⊟ Montana, NW USA
Hungt'ou see Lan Yü
Hung-tse Hu see Hongze Hu
178 J6 **Hưng Yên** Hai Hưng, N Vietnam
Hunjiang see Baishan
97 I18 **Hunnebostrand** Göteborg och Bohus, S Sweden
103 E19 **Hunsrück** ▲▲ W Germany
99 P18 **Hunstanton** E England, UK
161 G20 **Hunsūr** Karnātaka, E India
168 I7 **Hunt** Arhangay, C Mongolia
102 G12 **Hunte** ≈ NW Germany
31 Q5 **Hunter** North Dakota, N USA
27 S11 **Hunter** Texas, SW USA
193 D20 **Hunter** ≈ South Island, NZ
191 N15 **Hunter Island** island Tasmania, SE Australia
20 K11 **Hunter Mountain** ▲ New York, NE USA
193 B23 **Hunter Mountains** ▲▲ South Island, NZ
191 S7 **Hunter River** ≈ New South Wales, SE Australia
34 L7 **Hunters** Washington, NW USA
193 F20 **Hunters Hills, The** hill range South Island, NZ
192 M12 **Hunterville** Manawatu-Wanganui, North Island, NZ
33 N16 **Huntingburg** Indiana, N USA
99 O20 **Huntingdon** E England, UK
20 E15 **Huntingdon** Pennsylvania, NE USA
22 G9 **Huntingdon** Tennessee, S USA
99 O20 **Huntingdonshire** cultural region C England, UK
33 P12 **Huntington** Indiana, N USA
34 L13 **Huntington** Oregon, NW USA
27 X9 **Huntington** Texas, SW USA
38 M5 **Huntington** Utah, W USA
23 P5 **Huntington** West Virginia, NE USA
37 T16 **Huntington Beach** California, W USA
37 W4 **Huntington Creek** ≈ Nevada, W USA
192 L7 **Huntly** Waikato, North Island, NZ
98 K8 **Huntly** NE Scotland, UK
8 K8 **Hunt, Mount** ▲ Yukon Territory, NW Canada
12 H12 **Huntsville** Ontario, S Canada
25 P2 **Huntsville** Alabama, S USA
29 S9 **Huntsville** Arkansas, C USA
29 U3 **Huntsville** Missouri, C USA
22 M8 **Huntsville** Tennessee, S USA
27 V10 **Huntsville** Texas, SW USA
38 L2 **Huntsville** Utah, W USA
43 W12 **Hunucmá** Yucatán, SE Mexico
155 W3 **Hunza** var. Karīmābād. Jammu and Kashmir, NE Pakistan
155 W3 **Hunza** ≈ NE Pakistan
Hunze see Oostermoers Vaart
164 H4 **Huocheng** var. Shuiding. Xinjiang Uygur Zizhiqu, NW China
167 N6 **Huojia** Henan, C China
Huolin Gol see Hulingol
197 F3 **Huon** reef N New Caledonia
194 K13 **Huon Gulf** gulf E PNG
194 K13 **Huon Peninsula** headland C PNG
Huoshao Dao see Lü Tao
Huoshao Tao see Lan Yü
Hupeh/Hupei see Hubei
Hurano see Furano
97 H14 **Hurdalssjøen** ◎ S Norway
12 E13 **Hurd, Cape** headland Ontario, S Canada
Hurdegaryp see Hardegarijp
31 N4 **Hurdsfield** North Dakota, N USA
168 J7 **Hüremt** Bulgan, C Mongolia
168 J8 **Hüremt** Övörhangay, C Mongolia
77 X9 **Hurghada** var. Al Ghurdaqah, Ghurdaqah. E Egypt
69 Y9 **Huri Hills** ▲▲ NW Kenya
39 P15 **Hurley** New Mexico, SW USA
32 K4 **Hurley** Wisconsin, N USA
23 Y4 **Hurlock** Maryland, NE USA
31 P10 **Huron** South Dakota, N USA
33 S6 **Huron, Lake** ◎ Canada/USA
33 N3 **Huron Mountains** hill range Michigan, N USA
38 J8 **Hurricane** Utah, W USA
23 P5 **Hurricane** West Virginia, NE USA
38 J8 **Hurricane Cliffs** cliff Arizona, SW USA
25 V6 **Hurricane Creek** ≈ Georgia, SE USA
96 E12 **Hurrungane** ▲ S Norway
103 E16 **Hürth** Nordrhein-Westfalen, W Germany
Hurukawa see Furukawa
193 I17 **Hurunui** ≈ South Island, NZ
97 F21 **Hurup** Viborg, NW Denmark
119 T14 **Hurzuf** Respublika Krym, S Ukraine
Huș see Huși
94 K1 **Húsavík** Nordhurland Eystra, NE Iceland
118 M10 **Huși** var. Huș. Vaslui, E Romania
97 L19 **Huskvarna** Jönköping, S Sweden
41 P8 **Huslia** Alaska, USA
Husn see Al Ḥuṣn
97 C15 **Husnes** Hordaland, S Norway
96 D8 **Hustadvika** sea area S Norway
Husté see Khust
102 H7 **Husum** Schleswig-Holstein, N Germany
95 I16 **Husum** Västernorrland, C Sweden
118 K6 **Husyatyn** Ternopil's'ka Oblast', W Ukraine
Huszt see Khust
168 K6 **Hutag** Bulgan, N Mongolia
28 M6 **Hutchinson** Kansas, C USA
31 U9 **Hutchinson** Minnesota, N USA
25 Y13 **Hutchinson Island** island Florida, SE USA
38 L11 **Hutch Mountain** ▲ Arizona, SW USA
147 O14 **Ḥūth** NW Yemen
195 R11 **Hutjena** Buka Island, NE PNG
111 T8 **Hüttenberg** Kärnten, S Austria
27 T10 **Hutto** Texas, SW USA
Huttu see Futtsu
110 E8 **Huttwil** Bern, W Switzerland
164 K5 **Hutubi** Xinjiang Uygur Zizhiqu, NW China
167 N4 **Hutuo He** ≈ C China
Hutyû see Fuchū
193 E20 **Huxley, Mount** ▲ South Island, NZ
101 J20 **Huy** Dut. Hoei, Hoey. Liège, E Belgium
167 R8 **Huzhou** var. Wuxing. Zhejiang, SE China
Huzi see Fuji
Huzieda see Fujieda
Huzinomiya see Fujinomiya
Huzisawa see Fujisawa
Huziyosida see Fuji-Yoshida
94 I2 **Hvammstangi** Nordhurland Vestra, N Iceland
94 K4 **Hvannadalshnúkur** ▲ S Iceland
115 E15 **Hvar** It. Lesina. Split-Dalmacija, S Croatia
115 F15 **Hvar** It. Lesina; anc. Pharus. island S Croatia
119 T13 **Hvardiys'ke** Rus. Gvardeyskoye. Respublika Krym, S Ukraine
94 I4 **Hveragerdhi** Sudhurland, SW Iceland
97 E22 **Hvide Sande** Ringkøbing, W Denmark
94 I3 **Hvítá** ≈ C Iceland
97 G15 **Hvittingfoss** Buskerud, S Norway
94 I4 **Hvolsvöllur** Sudhurland, SW Iceland
Hwach'ŏn-chŏsuji see P'aro-ho
Hwainan see Huainan
Hwalien see Hualien
85 I16 **Hwange** prev. Wankie. Matabeleland North, W Zimbabwe
Hwang-Hae see Yellow Sea
Hwangshih see Huangshi
85 L17 **Hwedza** Mashonaland East, E Zimbabwe
65 G20 **Hyades, Cerro** ▲ S Chile
21 Q12 **Hyannis** Massachusetts, NE USA
30 L13 **Hyannis** Nebraska, C USA
168 F6 **Hyargas Nuur** ◎ NW Mongolia
Hybla/Hybla Major see Paternò
41 Y14 **Hydaburg** Prince of Wales Island, Alaska, USA
193 F22 **Hyde** Otago, South Island, NZ
23 O7 **Hyden** Kentucky, S USA
20 K12 **Hyde Park** New York, NE USA
41 Z14 **Hyder** Alaska, USA
161 I15 **Hyderābād** var. Haidarabad. Andhra Pradesh, C India
155 Q16 **Hyderābād** var. Haidarabad. Sind, SE Pakistan
105 T16 **Hyères** Var, SE France
105 T16 **Hyères, Îles d'** island group S France
120 K12 **Hyermanavichy** Rus. Germanovichi. Vitsyebskaya Voblasts', N Belarus
169 X12 **Hyesan** NE North Korea
8 K8 **Hyland** ≈ Yukon Territory, NW Canada
97 K20 **Hyltebruk** Halland, S Sweden
20 D16 **Hyndman** Pennsylvania, NE USA
35 P14 **Hyndman Peak** ▲ Idaho, NW USA
170 G13 **Hyōgo** off. Hyōgo-ken. ◆ prefecture Honshū, SW Japan
170 G13 **Hyōno-sen** ▲ Kyūshū, SW Japan
Hypanis see Kuban'
Hypsas see Belice
Hyrcania see Gorgān
38 L1 **Hyrum** Utah, W USA
95 N14 **Hyrynsalmi** Oulu, C Finland
35 V10 **Hysham** Montana, NW USA
9 N13 **Hythe** Alberta, W Canada
99 Q23 **Hythe** SE England, UK
170 D15 **Hyūga** Miyazaki, Kyūshū, SW Japan
Hyvinge see Hyvinkää
95 L19 **Hyvinkää** Swe. Hyvinge. Uusimaa, S Finland

I

118 J9 **Iacobeni** Ger. Jakobeny. Suceava, NE Romania
Iader see Zadar
180 I7 **Iakora** Fianarantsoa, SE Madagascar
194 H12 **Ialibu** Southern Highlands, W PNG
118 K14 **Ialomiţa** var. Jalomitsa. ◆ county SE Romania
118 K14 **Ialomiţa** ≈ SE Romania
119 N10 **Ialoveni** Rus. Yaloveny. C Moldova
119 N11 **Ialpug** var. Ialpugul Mare, Rus. Yalpug. ≈ Moldova/Ukraine
Ialpugul Mare see Ialpug
25 T8 **Iamonia, Lake** ◎ Florida, SE USA
118 L13 **Ianca** Brăila, SE Romania
118 M10 **Iaşi** Ger. Jassy. Iaşi, NE Romania
118 L9 **Iaşi** Ger. Jassy, Yassy. ◆ county NE Romania
116 J13 **Íasmos** Anatolikí Makedonía kai Thráki, NE Greece
24 H6 **Iatt, Lake** ⊟ Louisiana, S USA
60 B11 **Iauretê** Amazonas, NW Brazil
179 Oo10 **Iba** Luzon, N Philippines
79 S16 **Ibadan** Oyo, SW Nigeria
56 E10 **Ibagué** Tolima, C Colombia
62 I10 **Ibaiti** Paraná, S Brazil
179 Pp12 **Ibajay** Panay Island, C Philippines
38 J4 **Ibapah Peak** ▲ Utah, W USA
115 M15 **Ibar** Alb. Ibër. ≈ C Yugoslavia
170 F14 **Ibara** Okayama, Honshū, SW Japan
171 Kk16 **Ibaraki** off. Ibaraki-ken. ◆ prefecture Honshū, S Japan
58 C5 **Ibarra** var. San Miguel de Ibarra. Imbabura, N Ecuador
Ibaşfalău see Dumbrăveni
147 O16 **Ibb** W Yemen
102 F13 **Ibbenbüren** Nordrhein-Westfalen, NW Germany
81 H16 **Ibenga** ≈ N Congo
Ibër see Ibar
59 I14 **Iberia** Madre de Dios, E Peru
Iberia see Spain
68 M1 **Iberian Basin** undersea feature E Atlantic Ocean
Iberian Mountains see Ibérico, Sistema
86 D12 **Iberian Peninsula** physical region Portugal/Spain
66 M8 **Iberian Plain** undersea feature E Atlantic Ocean
Ibérica, Cordillera see Ibérico, Sistema
107 P6 **Ibérico, Sistema** var. Cordillera Ibérica, Eng. Iberian Mountains. ▲▲ NE Spain
10 K7 **Iberville Lac d'** ◎ Québec, NE Canada
79 T14 **Ibeto** Niger, W Nigeria
79 W15 **Ibi** Taraba, C Nigeria
107 S11 **Ibi** País Valenciano, E Spain
61 L20 **Ibiá** Minas Gerais, SE Brazil
63 F15 **Ibicuí, Rio** ≈ S Brazil
63 C19 **Ibicuy** Entre Ríos, E Argentina
63 F16 **Ibirapuitã** ≈ S Brazil
Ibiza see Eivissa
144 J4 **Ibn Wardān, Qaşr** ruins Ḥamāh, C Syria
Ibo see Sassandra
196 E9 **Ibobang** Babeldaob, N Palau
176 Vv11 **Ibonma** Irian Jaya, E Indonesia
61 N17 **Ibotirama** Bahia, E Brazil
147 Y8 **Ibrā** NE Oman
131 Q4 **Ibresi** Chuvashskaya Respublika, W Russian Federation
147 X8 **'Ibrī** NW Oman
170 Bb16 **Ibusuki** Kagoshima, Kyūshū, SW Japan
59 E16 **Ica** Ica, SW Peru
59 E16 **Ica** off. Departamento de Ica. ◆ department SW Peru
60 C11 **Içana** Amazonas, NW Brazil
Icaria see Ikaría
60 B13 **Içá, Rio** var. Río Putumayo. ≈ NW South America see also Putumayo, Río
142 I17 **İçel** var. Ichili. ◆ province S Turkey
94 I3 **Iceland** off. Republic of Iceland, Dan. Island, Icel. Ísland. ◆ republic N Atlantic Ocean
88 B6 **Iceland** island N Atlantic Ocean
66 L5 **Iceland Basin** undersea feature N Atlantic Ocean
Icelandic Plateau see Iceland Plateau
207 Q15 **Iceland Plateau** var. Icelandic Plateau. undersea feature S Greenland Sea
161 E16 **Ichalkaranji** Mahārāshtra, W India
170 Cc15 **Ichifusa-yama** ▲ Kyūshū, SW Japan
171 K17 **Ichihara** var. Itihara. Chiba, Honshū, S Japan
Ichili see İçel
171 I15 **Ichinomiya** var. Itinomiya. Aichi, Honshū, SW Japan
171 Mm12 **Ichinoseki** var. Itinoseki. Iwate, Honshū, C Japan
119 R3 **Ichnya** Chernihivs'ka Oblast', NE Ukraine
59 L17 **Ichoa, Río** ≈ C Bolivia
I-ch'un see Yichun
Iconium see Konya
Iculisma see Angoulême
41 U12 **Icy Bay** inlet Alaska, USA
41 N5 **Icy Cape** headland Alaska, USA
41 W13 **Icy Strait** strait Alaska, USA
29 R13 **Idabel** Oklahoma, C USA
31 T13 **Ida Grove** Iowa, C USA
79 U16 **Idah** Kogi, S Nigeria
35 N13 **Idaho** off. State of Idaho; also known as Gem of the Mountains, Gem State. ◆ state NW USA
35 N14 **Idaho City** Idaho, NW USA
35 R14 **Idaho Falls** Idaho, NW USA
124 Nn3 **Idálion** var. Dali, Dhali. C Cyprus
27 N5 **Idalou** Texas, SW USA
106 I9 **Idanha-a-Nova** Castelo Branco, C Portugal
103 E19 **Idar-Oberstein** Rheinland-Pfalz, SW Germany
120 J3 **Ida-Virumaa** off. Ida-Viru Maakond. ◆ province NE Estonia
128 J8 **Idel'** Respublika Kareliya, NW Russian Federation
81 C15 **Idenao** Sud-Ouest, SW Cameroon
Idenburg-rivier see Taritatu, Sungai
Idensalmi see Iisalmi
168 I6 **Ider** Hövsgöl, C Mongolia
77 X10 **Idfu** var. Edfu. SE Egypt
Ídhi Óros see Ídi
Ídhra see Ýdra
173 F3 **Idi** Sumatera, W Indonesia
117 I25 **Ídi** var. Ídhi Óros. ▲ Kríti, Greece, E Mediterranean Sea
Idi Amin, Lac see Edward, Lake
108 G10 **Idice** ≈ N Italy
78 G9 **Idini** Trarza, W Mauritania
81 J21 **Idiofa** Bandundu, SW Zaire
41 O10 **Iditarod River** ≈ Alaska, USA
97 M14 **Idkerberget** Kopparberg, C Sweden
144 I3 **Idlib** Idlib, NW Syria
144 I4 **Idlib** off. Muḥāfaẓat Idlib. ◆ governorate NW Syria
Idra see Ýdra
96 J11 **Idre** Kopparberg, C Sweden
Idria see Idrija
111 S11 **Idrija** It. Idria. W Slovenia
103 G18 **Idstein** Hessen, W Germany
85 J25 **Idutywa** Eastern Cape, SE South Africa
Idzhevan see Ijevan
120 G9 **Iecava** Bauska, S Latvia
172 P14 **Ie-jima** var. Ii-shima. island Nansei-shotō, SW Japan
101 B18 **Ieper** Fr. Ypres. West-Vlaanderen, W Belgium
117 K25 **Ierápetra** Kríti, Greece, E Mediterranean Sea
117 G22 **Iérax, Ákra** headland S Greece
Ierisós see Ierissós
117 H14 **Ierissós** var. Ierisós. Kentrikí Makedonía, N Greece
118 I11 **Iernut** Hung. Radnót. Mureş, C Romania
108 J12 **Iesi** var. Jesi. Marche, C Italy
Iesolo see Jesolo
196 K16 **Ifalik Atoll** atoll Caroline Islands, C Micronesia
180 I6 **Ifanadiana** Fianarantsoa, SE Madagascar
79 T16 **Ife** Osun, SW Nigeria
79 V8 **Iferouâne** Agadez, N Niger
Iferten see Yverdon
94 L8 **Ifjord** Finnmark, N Norway
79 R8 **Ifôghas, Adrar des** var. Adrar des Iforas. ▲▲ NE Mali
Iforas, Adrar des see Ifôghas, Adrar des
190 D6 **Ifould lake** salt lake South Australia
76 G6 **Ifrane** C Morocco
175 T7 **Iga** Pulau Halmahera, E Indonesia
83 G18 **Iganga** SE Uganda
62 L7 **Igarapava** São Paulo, S Brazil
126 Hh9 **Igarka** Krasnoyarskiy Kray, N Russian Federation
Igaunija see Estonia
I.G.Duca see General Toshevo
Igel see Jihlava
96 N11 **Iggesund** Gävleborg, C Sweden
41 P7 **Igikpak, Mount** ▲ Alaska, USA
41 P13 **Igiugig** Alaska, USA
Iglau/Iglawa/Igława see Jihlava
109 B20 **Iglesias** Sardegna, Italy, C Mediterranean Sea
131 V4 **Iglino** Respublika Bashkortostan, W Russian Federation
Igló see Spišská Nová Ves
15 Ll2 **Igloolik** Northwest Territories, N Canada
10 B11 **Ignace** Ontario, S Canada
120 I12 **Ignalina** Ignalina, E Lithuania
131 Q5 **Ignatovka** Ul'yanovskaya Oblast', W Russian Federation
128 K12 **Ignatovo** Vologodskaya Oblast', NW Russian Federation
116 N11 **İğneada** Kırklareli, NW Turkey
124 P7 **İğneada Burnu** headland NW Turkey
Igombe see Gombe
117 B16 **Igoumenítsa** Ípeiros, W Greece
131 T2 **Igra** Udmurtskaya Respublika, NW Russian Federation
125 Ff9 **Igrim** Khanty-Mansiyskiy Avtonomnyy Okrug, N Russian Federation
62 G12 **Iguaçu, Rio** Sp. Río Iguazú. ≈ Argentina/Brazil see also Iguazú, Río
61 I22 **Iguaçu, Salto do** Sp. Cataratas del Iguazú; prev. Victoria Falls. waterfall Argentina/Brazil see also Iguazú, Cataratas del
43 O15 **Iguala** var. Iguala de la Independencia. Guerrero, S Mexico
107 V5 **Igualada** Cataluña, NE Spain
Iguala de la Independencia see Iguala
62 G12 **Iguazú, Cataratas del** Port. Salto do Iguaçu, prev. Victoria Falls. waterfall Argentina/Brazil see also Iguaçu, Salto do
64 Q6 **Iguazú, Río** Port. Rio Iguaçu. ≈ Argentina/Brazil see also Iguaçu, Rio
81 D19 **Iguéla** Ogooué-Maritime, SW Gabon
Iguid, Erg see Iguidi, 'Erg
69 M5 **Iguidi, 'Erg** var. Erg Iguid. desert Algeria/Mauritania
180 K2 **Iharaña** prev. Vohémar. Antsirañana, NE Madagascar
157 K18 **Ihavandippolhu Atoll** var. Ihavandiffulu Atoll. atoll N Maldives
168 M11 **Ih Bulag** Ömnogövĭ, S Mongolia
172 Pp14 **Iheya-jima** island Nansei-shotō, SW Japan
168 L8 **Ihhayrhan** Töv, C Mongolia
180 I6 **Ihosy** Fianarantsoa, S Madagascar
168 L7 **Ihsüüj** Töv, C Mongolia
95 L14 **Ii** Oulu, C Finland
171 Ii16 **Iida** Nagano, Honshū, S Japan
171 L13 **Iide-san** ▲ Honshū, C Japan
95 M14 **Iijoki** ≈ C Finland
120 J4 **Iisaku** Ger. Isaak. Ida-Virumaa, NE Estonia
95 M16 **Iisalmi** var. Idensalmi. Kuopio, C Finland
171 Jj14 **Iiyama** Nagano, Honshū, S Japan
170 D13 **Iizuka** Fukuoka, Kyūshū, SW Japan
79 S16 **Ijebu-Ode** Ogun, SW Nigeria
143 U11 **Ijevan** Rus. Idzhevan. N Armenia
100 H9 **IJmuiden** Noord-Holland, W Netherlands
100 M12 **IJssel** var. Yssel. ≈ Netherlands/Germany
100 J8 **IJsselmeer** prev. Zuider Zee. ◎ N Netherlands
100 L9 **IJsselmuiden** Overijssel, E Netherlands
100 I12 **IJsselstein** Utrecht, C Netherlands
63 G14 **Ijuí** Rio Grande do Sul, S Brazil
63 G14 **Ijuí, Rio** ≈ S Brazil
201 R8 **Ijuw** NE Nauru
101 E16 **IJzendijke** Zeeland, SW Netherlands
101 A18 **Ijzer** ≈ W Belgium
95 K18 **Ikaalinen** Häme, SW Finland
180 I6 **Ikalamavony** Fianarantsoa, SE Madagascar
193 G16 **Ikamatua** West Coast, South Island, NZ
79 U16 **Ikare** Ondo, SW Nigeria
117 L20 **Ikaría** var. Kariot, Nicaria, Nikaria; anc. Icaria. island Dodekánisos, Greece, Aegean Sea
97 F22 **Ikast** Ringkøbing, W Denmark
192 O9 **Ikawhenua Range** ▲▲ North Island, NZ
172 Pp7 **Ikeda** Hokkaidō, NE Japan
170 F15 **Ikeda** Tokushima, Shikoku, SW Japan
79 S16 **Ikeja** Lagos, SW Nigeria
81 L19 **Ikela** Equateur, C Zaire
116 H10 **Ikhtiman** Sofiyska Oblast, W Bulgaria
170 Cc12 **Iki** island SW Japan
131 O13 **Iki Burul** Respublika Kalmykiya, SW Russian Federation
170 C12 **Iki-suidō** strait SW Japan
170 Bb12 **Ikitsuki-shima** island SW Japan
143 P11 **İkizdere** Rize, NE Turkey
41 P14 **Ikolik, Cape** headland Kodiak Island, Alaska, USA
79 V17 **Ikom** Cross River, SE Nigeria
180 I6 **Ikongo** prev. Fort-Carnot. Fianarantsoa, SE Madagascar
41 P5 **Ikpikpuk River** ≈ Alaska, USA
202 H1 **Iku** prev. Lone Tree Islet. atoll Tungaru, W Kiribati
171 Gg14 **Ikuno** Hyōgo, Honshū, SW Japan
202 H16 **Ikurangi** ▲ Rarotonga, S Cook Islands
176 Xx12 **Ilaga** Irian Jaya, E Indonesia
179 Pp8 **Ilagan** Luzon, N Philippines
159 R12 **Ilam** Eastern, E Nepal
148 J7 **Īlām** var. Elam. Īlām, W Iran
148 J8 **Īlām** off. Ostān-e Īlām. ◆ province W Iran
167 T13 **Ilan** Jap. Giran. N Taiwan
152 G9 **Ilanly Obvodnitel'nyy Kanal** canal N Turkmenistan
126 Ii14 **Ilanskiy** Krasnoyarskiy Kray, S Russian Federation
110 H9 **Ilanz** Graubünden, S Switzerland
79 S16 **Ilaro** Ogun, SW Nigeria
59 I17 **Ilave** Puno, S Peru
112 K8 **Iława** Ger. Deutsch-Eylau. Olsztyn, N Poland
126 Ll11 **Il'benge** Respublika Sakha (Yakutiya), NE Russian Federation
Ile see Ili
9 S13 **Île-à-la-Crosse** Saskatchewan, C Canada
81 J21 **Ilebo** prev. Port-Francqui. Kasai Occidental, W Zaire
105 N5 **Île-de-France** ◆ region N France
150 I9 **Ilek** Kaz. Elek. ≈ Kazakhstan/Russian Federation
Ilerda see Lleida
79 T16 **Ilesha** Osun, SW Nigeria
197 J5 **Îles Loyauté, Province des** ◆ province E New Caledonia
9 X12 **Ilford** Manitoba, C Canada
99 I23 **Ilfracombe** SW England, UK
142 I11 **Ilgaz Dağları** ▲▲ N Turkey
142 G15 **Ilgın** Konya, W Turkey
62 I7 **Ilha Solteira** São Paulo, S Brazil
106 G7 **Ílhavo** Aveiro, N Portugal
61 O18 **Ilhéus** Bahia, E Brazil
133 R7 **Ili** Kaz. Ile, Rus. Reka Ili. ≈ China/Kazakhstan
Ili see Ili He
118 G11 **Ilia** Hung. Marosillye. Hunedoara, SW Romania
41 P13 **Iliamna** Alaska, USA
41 P13 **Iliamna Lake** ◎ Alaska, USA
143 N13 **Iliç** Erzincan, C Turkey
Il'ichevsk see Şărur, Azerbaijan
Il'ichevsk see Illichivs'k, Ukraine
Ilici see Elche
39 V2 **Iliff** Colorado, C USA
179 R15 **Iligan** off. Iligan City. Mindanao, S Philippines
179 R15 **Iligan Bay** bay S Philippines
164 I5 **Ili He** Rus. Ili. ≈ China/Kazakhstan
58 C6 **Iliniza** ▲ N Ecuador
Ilinski see Il'inskiy
129 U14 **Il'inskiy** var. Ilinski. Permskaya Oblast', NW Russian Federation
127 Oo15 **Il'inskiy** Ostrov Sakhalin, Sakhalinskaya Oblast', SE Russian Federation
20 I10 **Ilion** New York, NE USA
40 E9 **Ilio Point** headland Molokai, Hawaii, USA, C Pacific Ocean
111 T13 **Ilirska Bistrica** prev. Bistrica, Ger. Feistritz, Illyrisch-Feistritz, It. Villa del Nevoso. SW Slovenia
143 Q16 **Ilisu Barajı** ⊟ SE Turkey
161 G17 **Ilkal** Karnātaka, C India
99 M19 **Ilkeston** C England, UK
123 Jj17 **Il-Kullana** headland SW Malta
110 J8 **Ill** ≈ W Austria
105 U6 **Ill** ≈ NE France
64 G10 **Illapel** Coquimbo, C Chile
Illaue Fartak Trench see Alula-Fartak Trench
190 C2 **Illbillee, Mount** ▲ South Australia
104 I6 **Ille-et-Vilaine** ◆ department NW France
79 T11 **Illéla** Tahoua, SW Niger
103 J24 **Iller** ≈ S Germany
103 J23 **Illertissen** Bayern, S Germany
107 N8 **Illescas** Castilla-La Mancha, C Spain
Ille-sur-la-Têt see Ille-sur-Têt
105 O17 **Ille-sur-Têt** var. Ille-sur-la-Têt. Pyrénées-Orientales, S France
Illiberis see Elne
119 P11 **Illichivs'k** Rus. Il'ichevsk. Odes'ka Oblast', SW Ukraine
Illicis see Elche
104 M6 **Illiers-Combray** Eure-et-Loir, C France
32 K12 **Illinois** off. State of Illinois; also known as Prairie State, Sucker State. ◆ state C USA
32 J13 **Illinois River** ≈ Illinois, N USA
119 N6 **Illintsi** Vinnyts'ka Oblast', C Ukraine
Illiturgis see Andújar
76 M10 **Illizi** SE Algeria
29 Y7 **Illmo** Missouri, C USA
Illur co see Lorca
Illuro see Mataró
Illyrisch-Feistritz see Ilirska Bistrica
103 K16 **Ilm** ≈ C Germany
103 K17 **Ilmenau** Thüringen, C Germany
128 H14 **Il'men', Ozero** ◎ NW Russian Federation
59 H18 **Ilo** Moquegua, SW Peru
179 Q13 **Iloilo** off. Iloilo City. Panay Island, C Philippines
114 K10 **Ilok** Hung. Újlak. Serbia, NW Yugoslavia
95 O16 **Ilomantsi** Pohjois-Karjala, SE Finland
44 F8 **Ilopango, Lago de** volcanic lake C El Salvador
79 T15 **Ilorin** Kwara, W Nigeria
119 X8 **Ilovays'k** Rus. Ilovaysk. Donets'ka Oblast', SE Ukraine
131 O10 **Ilovlya** Volgogradskaya Oblast', SW Russian Federation
131 O10 **Ilovlya** ≈ SW Russian Federation
127 P8 **Il'pyrskiy** Koryakskiy Avtonomnyy Okrug, E Russian Federation
130 K14 **Il'skiy** Krasnodarskiy Kray, SW Russian Federation
190 B2 **Iltur** South Australia
176 Y11 **Ilugwa** Irian Jaya, E Indonesia
Iluh see Batman
120 I11 **Ilūkste** Daugvapils, SE Latvia
176 Uu12 **Ilur** Pulau Gorong, E Indonesia
34 F10 **Ilwaco** Washington, NW USA
152 H8 **Il'yaly** var. Yylanly. Dashkhovuzskiy Velayat, N Turkmenistan
Ilyasbaba Burnu see Tekke Burnu
129 U9 **Ilych** ≈ NW Russian Federation
103 O21 **Ilz** ≈ SE Germany
113 M14 **Iłża** Radom, SE Poland
170 Ee14 **Imabari** var. Imaharu. Ehime, Shikoku, SW Japan
172 N5 **Imagane** Hokkaidō, NE Japan
Imaharu see Imabari
171 K15 **Imaichi** var. Imaiti. Tochigi, Honshū, S Japan
Imaiti see Imaichi
171 Hh14 **Imajō** Fukui, Honshū, SW Japan
145 R9 **Imām Ibn Hāshim** C Iraq
145 T11 **Imān 'Abd Allāh** S Iraq
128 J4 **Imandra, Ozero** ◎ NW Russian Federation
170 E16 **Imano-yama** ▲ Shikoku, SW Japan
170 C13 **Imari** Saga, Kyūshū, SW Japan
Imarssuak Mid-Ocean Seachannel see Imarssuak Seachannel
66 J6 **Imarssuak Seachannel** var. Imarssuak Mid-Ocean Seachannel. channel N Atlantic Ocean
95 N18 **Imatra** Kymi, SE Finland
171 H14 **Imazu** Shiga, Honshū, SW Japan
58 C6 **Imbabura** ◆ province N Ecuador
57 R9 **Imbaimadai** W Guyana
63 K14 **Imbituba** Santa Catarina, S Brazil
29 W9 **Imboden** Arkansas, C USA
Imbros see Gökçeada
152 B11 **Imeni 26 Bakinskikh Komissarov** Turkm. 26 Baku Komissarlary Adyndaky. Balkanskiy Velayat, W Turkmenistan
Imeni 26 Bakinskikh Komissarov see 26 Bakı Komissarı
129 N13 **Imeni Babushkina** Vologodskaya Oblast', NW Russian Federation
130 J7 **Imeni Karla Libknekhta** Kurskaya Oblast', W Russian Federation
152 I14 **Imeni Mollanepesa** Maryyskiy Velayat, S Turkmenistan
127 N14 **Imeni Poliny Osipenko** Khabarovskiy Kray, SE Russian Federation
152 J15 **Imeni S.A.Niyazova** Maryyskiy Velayat, S Turkmenistan
Imeni Sverdlova Rudnik see Sverdlovs'k
196 E9 **Imeong** Babeldaob, N Palau
83 L14 **Īmī** SE Ethiopia
117 M21 **Imia** Turk. Kardak. island Dodekánisos, Greece, Aegean Sea
Imishli see İmişli
143 X12 **İmişli** Rus. Imishli. C Azerbaijan
169 X14 **Imjin-gang** ≈ North Korea/South Korea
37 S3 **Imlay** Nevada, W USA
33 S9 **Imlay City** Michigan, N USA
25 X15 **Immokalee** Florida, SE USA
79 U17 **Imo** ◆ state SE Nigeria
108 G10 **Imola** Emilia-Romagna, N Italy
194 E9 **Imonda** Sandaun, NW PNG
Imoschi see Imotski
115 G14 **Imotski** It. Imoschi. Split-Dalmacija, SE Croatia
61 L14 **Imperatriz** Maranhão, NE Brazil
108 B10 **Imperia** Liguria, NW Italy
59 E15 **Imperial** Lima, W Peru
37 X17 **Imperial** California, W USA
30 L16 **Imperial** Nebraska, C USA
26 M9 **Imperial** Texas, SW USA

262

◆ Country ● Country Capital ◇ Dependent Territory ○ Dependent Territory Capital ◆ Administrative Region ✕ International Airport ▲ Mountain ▲▲ Mountain Range Volcano ≈ River ◎ Lake ⊟ Reservoir

◆ COUNTRY   ◇ DEPENDENT TERRITORY   ◈ ADMINISTRATIVE REGION   ▲ MOUNTAIN   ✖ VOLCANO   ◎ LAKE
★ COUNTRY CAPITAL   ○ DEPENDENT TERRITORY CAPITAL   ✈ INTERNATIONAL AIRPORT   ▲ MOUNTAIN RANGE   ≈ RIVER   ☒ RESERVOIR

— J —

JEFFERSON – KAATSHEUVEL

31 U14 **Jefferson** Iowa, C USA
23 Q8 **Jefferson** North Carolina, SE USA
27 X6 **Jefferson** Texas, SW USA
32 M9 **Jefferson** Wisconsin, N USA
29 U5 **Jefferson City** *state capital* Missouri, C USA
35 R10 **Jefferson City** Montana, NW USA
23 N9 **Jefferson City** Tennessee, S USA
37 U7 **Jefferson, Mount** ▲ Nevada, W USA
34 H12 **Jefferson, Mount** ▲ Oregon, NW USA
22 L5 **Jeffersontown** Kentucky, S USA
33 P16 **Jeffersonville** Indiana, N USA
35 V15 **Jeffrey City** Wyoming, C USA
79 T13 **Jega** Kebbi, NW Nigeria
Jehol *see* Chengde
64 P5 **Jejui-Guazú, Río** ∽ E Paraguay
120 I10 **Jēkabpils** *Ger.* Jakobstadt. Jēkabpils, S Latvia
25 W7 **Jekyll Island** *island* Georgia, SE USA
174 L11 **Jelai, Sungai** ∽ Borneo, N Indonesia
Jelalabad *see* Jalālābād
113 H14 **Jelcz-Laskowice** Wrocław, SW Poland
113 E14 **Jelenia Góra** *Ger.* Hirschberg, Hirschberg im Riesengebirge, Hirschberg im Riesengebirge, Hirschberg in Schlesien. Jelenia Góra, SW Poland
113 E14 **Jelenia Góra** *off.* Województwo Jeleniogórskie, *Ger.* Hirschberg, Hirschberg im Riesengebirge, Hirschberg im Riesengebirge, Hirschberg in Schlesien. ◆ *province* SW Poland
Jeleniogórskie, Województwo *see* Jelenia Góra
159 S11 **Jelep La** *pass* N India
120 F9 **Jelgava** *Ger.* Mitau. Jelgava, C Latvia
114 L13 **Jelica** ▲ C Yugoslavia
22 M8 **Jellico** Tennessee, S USA
97 G23 **Jelling** Vejle, C Denmark
174 I5 **Jemaja, Pulau** *island* W Indonesia
Jemaluang *see* Jamaluang
101 E20 **Jemappes** Hainaut, S Belgium
174 M16 **Jember** *prev.* Djember. Jawa, C Indonesia
101 I20 **Jemeppe-sur-Sambre** Namur, S Belgium
39 R10 **Jemez Pueblo** New Mexico, SW USA
164 K2 **Jeminay** Xinjiang Uygur Zizhiqu, NW China
201 U5 **Jemo Island** *atoll* Ratak Chain, C Marshall Islands
175 Nn8 **Jempang, Danau** ◎ Borneo, N Indonesia
103 L16 **Jena** Thüringen, C Germany
24 I6 **Jena** Louisiana, S USA
110 I8 **Jenaz** Graubünden, SE Switzerland
111 N7 **Jenbach** Tirol, W Austria
175 P13 **Jeneponto** *prev.* Djeneponto. Sulawesi, C Indonesia
144 F9 **Jenin** N West Bank
23 P7 **Jenkins** Kentucky, S USA
29 P9 **Jenks** Oklahoma, C USA
Jenné *see* Djenné
111 X8 **Jennersdorf** Burgenland, SE Austria
24 H9 **Jennings** Louisiana, S USA
15 Jj4 **Jenny Lind Island** *island* Northwest Territories, N Canada
25 Y13 **Jensen Beach** Florida, SE USA
15 M2 **Jens Munk Island** *island* Northwest Territories, NE Canada
61 O17 **Jequié** Bahia, E Brazil
61 O18 **Jequitinhonha, Rio** ∽ E Brazil
Jerablus *see* Jarābulus
76 H6 **Jerada** NE Morocco
Jerash *see* Jarash
77 N7 **Jerba, Île de** *var.* Djerba, Jazīrat Jarbah. *island* E Tunisia
46 K9 **Jérémie** SW Haiti
Jerez *see* Jeréz de la Frontera, Spain
Jeréz *see* Jerez de García Salinas, Mexico
42 L11 **Jerez de García Salinas** *var.* Jeréz. Zacatecas, C Mexico
106 J15 **Jeréz de la Frontera** *var.* Jerez; *prev.* Xeres. Andalucía, SW Spain
106 I12 **Jeréz de los Caballeros** Extremadura, W Spain
Jergucati *see* Jorgucat
144 G10 **Jericho** *Ar.* Arīḥā, *Heb.* Yeriḥo. E West Bank
76 M7 **Jerid, Chott el** *var.* Shaṭṭ al Jarīd. *salt lake* SW Tunisia
191 O10 **Jerilderie** New South Wales, SE Australia
Jerischmarkt *see* Câmpia Turzii
94 K11 **Jerisjärvi** ◎ NW Finland
Jermer *see* Jaroměř
38 K11 **Jerome** Arizona, SW USA
35 O15 **Jerome** Idaho, NW USA
99 L26 **Jersey** *island* Channel Islands, NW Europe
20 K14 **Jersey City** New Jersey, NE USA
20 F13 **Jersey Shore** Pennsylvania, NE USA
32 K14 **Jerseyville** Illinois, N USA
106 K8 **Jerte** ∽ W Spain
144 F10 **Jerusalem** *Ar.* Al Quds, Al Quds ash Sharīf, *Heb.* Yerushalayim; *anc.* Hierosolyma. ● (Israel) Jerusalem, NE Israel
144 G10 **Jerusalem** ◆ *district* E Israel
191 S10 **Jervis Bay** New South Wales, SE Australia
191 S10 **Jervis Bay Territory** ◆ *territory* SE Australia
Jerwakant *see* Järvakandi
111 S10 **Jesenice** *Ger.* Assling. NW Slovenia
113 H16 **Jeseník** *Ger.* Freiwaldau. Severní Morava, E Czech Republic
Jesi *see* Iesi
108 I8 **Jesolo** *var.* Iesolo. Veneto, NE Italy
Jesselton *see* Kota Kinabalu
97 I14 **Jessheim** Akershus, S Norway
159 T15 **Jessore** Khulna, W Bangladesh
25 W6 **Jesup** Georgia, SE USA
43 S15 **Jesús Carranza** Veracruz-Llave, SE Mexico
64 K10 **Jesús María** Córdoba, C Argentina
28 K6 **Jetmore** Kansas, C USA
105 Q2 **Jeumont** Nord, N France
97 H14 **Jevnaker** Oppland, S Norway
Jewe *see* Jõhvi
27 V9 **Jewett** Texas, SW USA
21 N12 **Jewett City** Connecticut, NE USA
Jewish Autonomous Oblast *see* Yevreyskaya Avtonomnaya Oblast'
Jeypore/Jeypur *see* Jaypur, Orissa, India
Jeypore *see* Jaipur, Rājasthān, India
115 L17 **Jezercës, Maja e** ▲ N Albania
113 B18 **Jezerní Hora** ▲ SW Czech Republic
160 F10 **Jhābua** Madhya Pradesh, C India
158 H14 **Jhālāwār** Rājasthān, N India
155 U9 **Jhang** *var.* Jhang Sadar, Jhang Sadr. Punjab, NE Pakistan
Jhang Sadar/Jhang Sadr *see* Jhang
158 J13 **Jhānsi** Uttar Pradesh, N India
160 M11 **Jhārsuguda** Orissa, E India
155 V7 **Jhelum** Punjab, NE Pakistan
133 P9 **Jhelum** ∽ E Pakistan
159 T15 **Jhenida** Dhaka, W Bangladesh
155 P16 **Jhimpir** Sind, SE Pakistan
Jhind *see* Jind
155 R16 **Jhudo** Sind, SE Pakistan
Jhumra *see* Chak Jhumra
158 H11 **Jhunjhunūn** Rājasthān, N India
Ji *see* Hebei, China
Ji *see* Jilin, China
159 S14 **Jiāganj** West Bengal, NE India
166 J7 **Jialing Jiang** ∽ C China
169 Y7 **Jiamusi** *var.* Chia-mu-ssu, Kiamusze. Heilongjiang, NE China
167 O11 **Ji'an** Jiangxi, S China
169 W12 **Ji'an** Jilin, NE China
169 T13 **Jianchang** Liaoning, NE China
166 F11 **Jianchuan** Yunnan, SW China
164 M4 **Jiangjunmiao** Xinjiang Uygur Zizhiqu, W China
166 K11 **Jiangkou** Guizhou, S China
167 Q12 **Jiangle** Fujian, SE China
167 N15 **Jiangmen** Guangdong, S China
167 Q10 **Jiangshan** Zhejiang, SE China
167 Q7 **Jiangsu** *var.* Chiang-su, Jiangsu Sheng, Kiangsu, Su. ◆ *province* E China
Jiangsu Sheng *see* Jiangsu
167 O11 **Jiangxi** *var.* Chiang-hsi, Gan, Jiangxi Sheng, Kiangsi. ◆ *province* S China
Jiangxi Sheng *see* Jiangxi
166 I8 **Jiangyou** *prev.* Zhongba. Sichuan, C China
167 N9 **Jianli** Hubei, C China
167 Q11 **Jian'ou** Fujian, SE China
169 S12 **Jianping** Liaoning, NE China
166 L9 **Jianshi** Hubei, C China
133 V11 **Jian Xi** ∽ SE China
167 Q11 **Jianyang** Fujian, SE China
166 I9 **Jianyang** Sichuan, C China
169 X10 **Jiaohe** Jilin, NE China
167 S10 **Jiaojiang** *var.* Haimen. Zhejiang, SE China
167 N6 **Jiaozuo** Henan, C China
167 Q7 **Jiashan** *var.* Mingguan. Anhui, SE China
164 F8 **Jiashi** *var.* Payzawat. Xinjiang Uygur Zizhiqu, NW China
160 L9 **Jiāwān** Madhya Pradesh, C India
167 S9 **Jiaxing** Zhejiang, SE China
Jiayi *see* Chiai
169 X6 **Jiayin** *var.* Chaoyang. Heilongjiang, NE China
165 R8 **Jiayuguan** Gansu, N China
144 M4 **Jibli** Ar Raqqah, C Syria
118 H9 **Jibou** *Hung.* Zsibó. Sălaj, NW Romania
147 Z9 **Jibsh, Ra's al** *headland* E Oman
Jibuti *see* Djibouti
113 E15 **Jičín** *Ger.* Jitschin. Východní Čechy, N Czech Republic
146 K10 **Jiddah** *Eng.* Jedda. Makkah, W Saudi Arabia
147 W11 **Jiddat al Ḥarāsīs** *desert* C Oman
94 K9 **Jiesjavrre** ◎ N Norway
166 M4 **Jiexiu** Shanxi, C China
167 P14 **Jieyang** Guangdong, S China
121 F14 **Jieznas** Prienai, S Lithuania
Jifa', Bi'r *see* Jif'īyah, Bi'r
147 P15 **Jif'īyah, Bi'r** *var.* Bi'r Jifā'. *well* C Yemen
79 W13 **Jigawa** ◆ *state* N Nigeria
Jigerbent *see* Dzhigirbent
46 I7 **Jiguaní** Granma, E Cuba
165 T12 **Jigzhi** Qinghai, C China
Jih-k'a-tse *see* Xigazê
113 E18 **Jihlava** *Ger.* Iglau, *Pol.* Igława. Jižní Morava, S Czech Republic
113 E18 **Jihlava** *var.* Igel, *Ger.* Iglawa. ∽ S Czech Republic
Jihočeský Kraj *see* Jižní Čechy
Jihomoravský Kraj *see* Jižní Morava
76 L5 **Jijel** *var.* Djidjel; *prev.* Djidjelli. NE Algeria
118 L9 **Jijia** ∽ N Romania
82 L13 **Jijiga** *It.* Giggiga. E Ethiopia
107 S12 **Jijona** *var.* Xixona. País Valenciano, E Spain
Jilf al Kabīr, Haḍabat al *see* Gilf Kebir Plateau
83 L18 **Jilib** *It.* Gelib. Jubbada Dhexe, S Somalia
169 W10 **Jilin** *var.* Chi-lin, Girin, Kirin; *prev.* Yungki, Yunki. Jilin, NE China
169 W10 **Jilin** *var.* Chi-lin, Girin, Ji, Jilin Sheng, Kirin. ◆ *province* NE China
169 W11 **Jilin Hada Ling** ▲ NE China
Jilin Sheng *see* Jilin
169 S4 **Jiliu He** ∽ NE China
107 Q6 **Jiloca** ∽ N Spain
83 J14 **Jīma** *var.* Jimma, *It.* Gimma. SW Ethiopia
46 M9 **Jimaní** W Dominican Republic
118 E11 **Jimbolia** *Ger.* Hatzfeld, *Hung.* Zsombolya. Timiş, W Romania
106 K16 **Jimena de la Frontera** Andalucía, S Spain
42 K7 **Jiménez** Chihuahua, N Mexico
43 N5 **Jiménez** Coahuila de Zaragoza, NE Mexico
43 P9 **Jiménez** *var.* Santander Jiménez. Tamaulipas, C Mexico
42 L10 **Jiménez del Teul** Zacatecas, C Mexico
79 Y14 **Jimeta** Adamawa, E Nigeria
Jimma *see* Jīma
164 M5 **Jimsar** Xinjiang Uygur Zizhiqu, NW China
20 I14 **Jim Thorpe** Pennsylvania, NE USA
Jin *see* Shanxi, China
Jin *see* Tianjin Shi, China
167 P5 **Jinan** *var.* Chinan, Chi-nan, Tsinan. Shandong, E China
165 T8 **Jinchang** Gansu, N China
167 N5 **Jincheng** Shanxi, C China
Jinchengjiang *see* Hechi
158 I9 **Jind** *prev.* Jhind. Haryāna, NW India
191 Q11 **Jindabyne** New South Wales, SE Australia
113 O18 **Jindřichův Hradec** *Ger.* Neuhaus. Jižní Čechy, S Czech Republic
Jing *see* Beijing Shi, China
Jing *see* Jinghe, China
165 X10 **Jingchuan** Gansu, C China
167 Q10 **Jingdezhen** Jiangxi, S China
167 O12 **Jinggangshan** Jiangxi, S China
167 P3 **Jinghai** Tianjin Shi, E China
166 K6 **Jing He** ∽ C China
164 I4 **Jinghe** *var.* Jing. Xinjiang Uygur Zizhiqu, NW China
166 F15 **Jinghong** *var.* Yunjinghong. Yunnan, SW China
166 M9 **Jingmen** Hubei, C China
169 X10 **Jingpo Hu** ◎ NE China
166 M8 **Jing Shan** ▲ C China
165 V9 **Jingtai** *var.* Yitiaoshan. Gansu, C China
166 J14 **Jingxi** Guangxi Zhuangzu Zizhiqu, S China
166 L12 **Jing Xian** Hunan, E China
Jing Xian *see* Jingzhou
169 W11 **Jingyu** Jilin, NE China
165 V10 **Jingyuan** Gansu, C China
166 L12 **Jingzhou** *var.* Jing Xian. Hunan, S China
167 R10 **Jinhua** Zhejiang, SE China
169 P13 **Jining** Nei Mongol Zizhiqu, N China
167 P5 **Jining** Shandong, E China
83 G18 **Jinja** S Uganda
167 O11 **Jin Jiang** ∽ S China
167 R13 **Jinjiang** *var.* Qingyang. Fujian, SE China
176 W14 **Jin, Kepulauan** *island group* E Indonesia
Jinmen Dao *see* Chinmen Tao
44 J9 **Jinotega** Jinotega, NW Nicaragua
44 K7 **Jinotega** ◆ *department* N Nicaragua
44 J11 **Jinotepe** Carazo, SW Nicaragua
166 L13 **Jinping** *prev.* Sanjiang. Guizhou, S China
166 H14 **Jinping** Yunnan, SW China
Jinsen *see* Inch'ŏn
166 J11 **Jinsha** Guizhou, S China
163 N12 **Jinsha Jiang** ∽ SW China
166 M10 **Jinshi** Hunan, S China
165 R7 **Jinta** Gansu, N China
179 Q12 **Jintotolo Channel** *channel* C Philippines
167 Q12 **Jin Xi** ∽ SE China
169 T13 **Jinxi** Liaoning, NE China
169 U14 **Jinxian** Liaoning, NE China
167 P6 **Jinxiang** Shandong, E China
167 P8 **Jinzhai** *prev.* Meishan. Anhui, E China
169 T12 **Jinzhou** *var.* Chin-chou, Chinchow; *prev.* Chinhsien. Liaoning, NE China
144 H12 **Jinz, Qā' al** ◎ C Jordan
49 S8 **Jiparaná, Rio** ∽ W Brazil
58 A7 **Jipijapa** Manabí, W Ecuador
44 F8 **Jiquilisco** Usulután, S El Salvador
153 S12 **Jirgatol** *Rus.* Dzhirgatal'. C Tajikistan
Jirjā *see* Girga
113 B15 **Jirkov** *Ger.* Görkau. Severní Čechy, NW Czech Republic
Jiroft *see* Sabzvārān
166 L11 **Jishou** Hunan, S China
Jisr ash Shadadi *see* Ash Shadādah
118 I14 **Jitaru** Olt, S Romania
Jitschin *see* Jičín
118 H14 **Jiu** *Ger.* Schil, Schyl, *Hung.* Zsil, Zsily. ∽ S Romania
167 R11 **Jiufeng Shan** ▲ SE China
167 P9 **Jiujiang** Jiangxi, S China
167 O10 **Jiuling Shan** ▲ S China
166 G10 **Jiulong** Sichuan, C China
167 Q13 **Jiulong Jiang** ∽ SE China
167 Q13 **Jiulong Xi** ∽ SE China
165 R8 **Jiuquan** Gansu, N China
166 K17 **Jiusuo** Hainan, S China
169 W10 **Jiutai** Jilin, NE China
166 K13 **Jiuwan Dashan** ▲ S China
154 J16 **Jiwani** Baluchistān, SW Pakistan
169 Y8 **Jixi** Heilongjiang, NE China
169 Y7 **Jixian** Heilongjiang, NE China
166 M5 **Jixian** *var.* Ji Xian. Shanxi, C China
Jiza *see* Al Jīzah
147 N13 **Jīzān** *var.* Qīzān. Jīzān, SW Saudi Arabia
147 N13 **Jīzān** *var.* Minṭaqat Jīzān. ◆ *province* SW Saudi Arabia
146 K6 **Jīzl, Wādī al** *dry watercourse* W Saudi Arabia
113 C18 **Jižní Čechy** *off.* Jihočeský Kraj. ◆ *region* S Czech Republic
113 F19 **Jižní Morava** *off.* Jihomoravský Kraj. ◆ *region* SE Czech Republic
170 Ff12 **Jizō-zaki** *headland* Honshū, SW Japan
147 U14 **Jiz', Wādī al** *dry watercourse* E Yemen
153 O11 **Jizzakh** *Rus.* Dzhizak. Jizzakh Wiloyati, C Uzbekistan
153 N10 **Jizzakh Wiloyati** *Rus.* Dzhizakskaya Oblast'. ◆ *province* C Uzbekistan
62 I13 **Joaçaba** Santa Catarina, S Brazil
Joal *see* Joal-Fadiout
78 F11 **Joal-Fadiout** *prev.* Joal. W Senegal
78 E10 **João Barrosa** Boa Vista, E Cape Verde
João Belo *see* Xai-Xai
João de Almeida *see* Chibia
61 Q15 **João Pessoa** *prev.* Paraíba. *state capital* Paraíba, E Brazil
27 X7 **Joaquin** Texas, SW USA
64 K6 **Joaquín V.González** Salta, N Argentina
Joazeiro *see* Juazeiro
Jo'burg *see* Johannesburg
111 O7 **Jochberger Ache** ∽ W Austria
Jo-ch'iang *see* Ruoqiang
94 K12 **Jock** Norrbotten, N Sweden
44 I5 **Jocón** Yoro, N Honduras
107 O13 **Jódar** Andalucía, S Spain
158 F12 **Jodhpur** Rājasthān, NW India
101 I19 **Jodoigne** Walloon Brabant, C Belgium
97 I22 **Jægerspris** Frederiksborg, E Denmark
95 O16 **Joensuu** Pohjois-Karjala, SE Finland
97 C17 **Jæren** *physical region* S Norway
39 W4 **Joes** Colorado, C USA
203 Z3 **Joe's Hill** *hill* Kiritimati, NE Kiribati
171 Jj13 **Jōetsu** *var.* Zyôetu. Niigata, Honshū, C Japan
85 M18 **Jofane** Inhambane, S Mozambique
161 E18 **Jog** *waterfall* W India
159 R12 **Jogbani** Bihār, NE India
120 I5 **Jõgeva** *Ger.* Laisholm. Jõgevamaa, E Estonia
120 I4 **Jõgevamaa** *off.* Jõgeva Maakond. ◆ *province* E Estonia
149 S4 **Joghatāy** Khorāsān, NE Iran
159 U12 **Jogighopa** Assam, NE India
158 I7 **Jogindarnagar** Himāchal Pradesh, N India
Jogjakarta *see* Yogyakarta
171 Ii13 **Jōhana** Toyama, Honshū, SW Japan
85 J21 **Johannesburg** *var.* Egoli, Erautini, Gauteng, *abbrev.* Jo'burg. Gauteng, NE South Africa
37 T13 **Johannesburg** California, W USA
85 I21 **Johannesburg** ✕ Gauteng, NE South Africa
Johannisburg *see* Pisz
155 P14 **Johi** Sind, SE Pakistan
57 T13 **Johi Village** S Guyana
34 K13 **John Day** Oregon, NW USA
34 I11 **John Day River** ∽ Oregon, NW USA
20 L14 **John F Kennedy** ✕ (New York) Long Island, New York, NE USA
23 V8 **John H.Kerr Reservoir** *var.* Buggs Island Lake, Kerr Lake. ▣ North Carolina/Virginia, SE USA
39 V6 **John Martin Reservoir** ▣ Colorado, C USA
98 K6 **John o'Groats** N Scotland, UK
29 P5 **John Redmond Reservoir** ▣ Kansas, C USA
41 Q7 **John River** ∽ Alaska, USA
28 H6 **Johnson** Kansas, C USA
20 M7 **Johnson** Vermont, NE USA
20 D13 **Johnsonburg** Pennsylvania, NE USA
20 H11 **Johnson City** New York, NE USA
23 P8 **Johnson City** Tennessee, S USA
27 R10 **Johnson City** Texas, SW USA
37 S12 **Johnsondale** California, W USA
8 I8 **Johnsons Crossing** Yukon Territory, W Canada
23 T13 **Johnsonville** South Carolina, SE USA
23 Q13 **Johnston** South Carolina, SE USA
199 K6 **Johnston Atoll** ◇ *US unincorporated territory* C Pacific Ocean
183 Q3 **Johnston Atoll** *atoll* C Pacific Ocean
32 L17 **Johnston City** Illinois, N USA
188 K12 **Johnston, Lake** *salt lake* Western Australia
33 S13 **Johnstown** Ohio, N USA
20 D15 **Johnstown** Pennsylvania, NE USA
174 Hh6 **Johor** *var.* Johore. ◆ *state* Peninsular Malaysia
Johor Baharu *see* Johor Bahru
174 I6 **Johor Bahru** *var.* Johor Baharu, Johore Bahru. Johor, Peninsular Malaysia
Johore *see* Johor
Johore Bahru *see* Johor Bahru
120 K3 **Jõhvi** *Ger.* Jewe. Ida-Virumaa, NE Estonia
105 P7 **Joigny** Yonne, C France
Joinvile *see* Joinville
62 K12 **Joinville** *var.* Joinvile. Santa Catarina, S Brazil
105 R6 **Joinville** Haute-Marne, N France
204 H3 **Joinville Island** *island* Antarctica
43 O15 **Jojutla** *var.* Jojutla de Juárez. Morelos, S Mexico
Jojutla de Juárez *see* Jojutla
94 I12 **Jokkmokk** Norrbotten, N Sweden
94 L2 **Jökulsá á Dal** ∽ E Iceland
94 K2 **Jökulsá á Fjöllum** ∽ NE Iceland
Jokyakarta *see* Yogyakarta
32 M11 **Joliet** Illinois, N USA
13 O11 **Joliette** Québec, SE Canada
179 Pp17 **Jolo** Jolo Island, SW Philippines
96 D11 **Jølstervatnet** ◎ S Norway
174 Ll15 **Jombang** *prev.* Djombang. Jawa, S Indonesia
165 R14 **Jomda** Xizang Zizhiqu, W China
58 A6 **Jome, Punta de** *headland* W Ecuador
120 G13 **Jonava** *Ger.* Janow, *Pol.* Janów. Jonava, C Lithuania
152 L11 **Jondor** *Rus.* Zhondor. Bukhoro Wiloyati, C Uzbekistan
165 V11 **Jonê** Gansu, C China
29 X9 **Jonesboro** Arkansas, C USA
25 S4 **Jonesboro** Georgia, SE USA
32 L17 **Jonesboro** Illinois, N USA
24 H5 **Jonesboro** Louisiana, S USA
23 P8 **Jonesboro** Tennessee, S USA
21 T6 **Jonesport** Maine, NE USA
1 J4 **Jones Sound** *channel* Northwest Territories, N Canada
24 I6 **Jonesville** Louisiana, S USA
33 Q10 **Jonesville** Michigan, N USA
23 Q11 **Jonesville** South Carolina, SE USA
83 F14 **Jonglei** Jonglei, SE Sudan
83 F14 **Jonglei** *var.* Gongoleh State. ◆ *state* SE Sudan
83 F14 **Jonglei Canal** *canal* S Sudan
120 F11 **Joniškėlis** Pasvalys, N Lithuania
120 F10 **Joniškis** *Ger.* Janischken. Joniškis, N Lithuania
97 L19 **Jönköping** Jönköping, S Sweden
97 K20 **Jönköping** ◆ *county* S Sweden
13 Q7 **Jonquière** Québec, SE Canada
43 V15 **Jonuta** Tabasco, SE Mexico
104 K12 **Jonzac** Charente-Maritime, W France
29 R7 **Joplin** Missouri, C USA
35 W8 **Jordan** Montana, NW USA
153 S11 **Jordan** *var.* Iordan, *Rus.* Jardan. Farghona Wiloyati, E Uzbekistan
144 H12 **Jordan** *off.* Hashemite Kingdom of Jordan, *Ar.* Al Mamlakah al Urdunīyah al Hāshimīyah, Al Urdunn; *prev.* Transjordan. ◆ *monarchy* SW Asia
144 G9 **Jordan** *Ar.* Urdunn, *Heb.* HaYarden. ∽ SW Asia
Jordan Lake *see* B.Everett Jordan Reservoir
113 K17 **Jordanów** Nowy Sącz, S Poland
34 M15 **Jordan Valley** Oregon, NW USA
144 G9 **Jordan Valley** *valley* N Israel
59 D15 **Jorge Chávez International** *var.* Lima. ✕ (Lima) Lima, W Peru
115 L23 **Jorgucat** *var.* Jergucati, Jorgucati. Gjirokastër, S Albania
Jorgucati *see* Jorgucat
159 X12 **Jorhāt** Assam, NE India
95 J14 **Jörn** Västerbotten, N Sweden
39 R14 **Jornada Del Muerto** *valley* New Mexico, SW USA
95 N17 **Joroinen** Mikkeli, SE Finland
97 C16 **Jørpeland** Rogaland, S Norway
79 W14 **Jos** Plateau, C Nigeria
179 Rr17 **Jose Abad Santos** *var.* Trinidad. Mindanao, S Philippines
63 F19 **José Batlle y Ordóñez** *var.* Batlle y Ordóñez. Florida, C Uruguay
65 H18 **José de San Martín** Chubut, S Argentina
63 E19 **José Enrique Rodó** *var.* Rodó, José E.Rodo; *prev.* Drabble, Drable. Soriano, SW Uruguay
José E.Rodo *see* José Enrique Rodó
Josefsdorf *see* Žabalj
46 C4 **José Martí** ✕ (La Habana) Cuidad de La Habana, N Cuba
63 F19 **José Pedro Varela** *var.* José P.Varela. Lavalleja, S Uruguay
189 N2 **Joseph Bonaparte Gulf** *gulf* N Australia
39 N11 **Joseph City** Arizona, SW USA
11 O9 **Joseph, Lake** ◎ Newfoundland and Labrador, E Canada
12 G13 **Joseph, Lake** ◎ Ontario, S Canada
194 I11 **Josephstaal** Madang, N PNG
José P.Varela *see* José Pedro Varela
61 J14 **José Rodrigues** Pará, N Brazil
158 K9 **Joshimath** Uttar Pradesh, N India
27 T7 **Joshua** Texas, SW USA
37 V15 **Joshua Tree** California, W USA
79 V14 **Jos Plateau** *plateau* C Nigeria
104 H6 **Josselin** Morbihan, NW France
Jos Sudarso *see* Yos Sudarso, Pulau
96 E11 **Jostedalsbreen** *glacier* S Norway
96 F12 **Jotunheimen** ▲ S Norway
144 G7 **Joûnié** *var.* Juniyah. W Lebanon
27 R13 **Jourdanton** Texas, SW USA
100 L7 **Joure** *Fris.* De Jouwer. Friesland, N Netherlands
95 M18 **Joutsa** Keski-Suomi, C Finland
95 N18 **Joutseno** Kymi, SE Finland
94 M12 **Joutsijärvi** Lappi, NE Finland
110 A9 **Joux, Lac de** ◎ W Switzerland
46 D5 **Jovellanos** Matanzas, W Cuba
159 V13 **Jowai** Meghālaya, NE India
Jöwat *see* Jabwot
Jowhar *see* Jawhar
149 O12 **Jowkān** Fārs, S Iran
149 Q10 **Jowzam** Kermān, C Iran
155 N2 **Jowzjān** ◆ *province* N Afghanistan
Józseffalva *see* Žabalj
J.Storm Thurmond Reservoir *see* Clarks Hill Lake
47 T6 **Juana Díaz** C Puerto Rico
42 L9 **Juan Aldama** Zacatecas, C Mexico
1 E9 **Juan de Fuca Plate** *tectonic feature*
34 F7 **Juan de Fuca, Strait of** *strait* Canada/USA
Juan Fernandez Islands *see* Juan Fernández, Islas
200 Oo12 **Juan Fernández, Islas** *Eng.* Juan Fernandez Islands. *island group* W Chile
57 O4 **Juangriego** Nueva Esparta, NE Venezuela
58 D11 **Juanjuí** *var.* Juanjuy. San Martín, N Peru
Juanjuy *see* Juanjuí
95 N16 **Juankoski** Kuopio, C Finland
Juan Lacaze *see* Juan L.Lacaze
63 E20 **Juan L.Lacaze** *var.* Juan Lacaze, Puerto Sauce; *prev.* Sauce. Colonia, SW Uruguay
64 L5 **Juan Solá** Salta, N Argentina
65 F21 **Juan Stuven, Isla** *island* S Chile
61 H16 **Juará** Mato Grosso, W Brazil
43 N7 **Juárez** *var.* Villa Juárez. Coahuila de Zaragoza, NE Mexico
42 C2 **Juárez, Sierra de** ▲ NW Mexico
61 O15 **Juazeiro** *prev.* Joazeiro. Bahia, E Brazil
61 P14 **Juazeiro do Norte** Ceará, E Brazil
83 F15 **Juba** *var.* Jūbā. Bahr el Gabel, S Sudan
83 L17 **Juba** *Amh.* Genalē Wenz, *It.* Guiba, *Som.* Ganaane, Webi Jubba. ∽ Ethiopia/Somalia
204 H2 **Jubany** *Argentinian research station* Antarctica
Jubayl *see* Jbail
83 L18 **Jubbada Dhexe** *off.* Gobolka Jubbada Dhexe. ◆ *region* SW Somalia
83 K18 **Jubbada Hoose** ◆ *region* SW Somalia
Jubba, Webi *see* Juba
Jubbulpore *see* Jabalpur
Jubeil *see* Jbail
76 B9 **Juby, Cap** *headland* SW Morocco
107 R10 **Júcar** *var.* Jucar. ∽ C Spain
42 L12 **Juchipila** Zacatecas, C Mexico
43 S16 **Juchitán** *var.* Juchitán de Zaragosa. Oaxaca, SE Mexico
Juchitán de Zaragosa *see* Juchitán
144 G11 **Judaea** *cultural region* Israel/West Bank
144 F11 **Judaean Hills** *Heb.* Haré Yehuda. *hill range* E Israel
144 H8 **Judaydah** *Fr.* Jdaïdé. Dimashq, W Syria
145 P11 **Judayyidat Hāmir** S Iraq
111 U8 **Judenburg** Steiermark, C Austria
35 T8 **Judith River** ∽ Montana, NW USA
29 V11 **Judsonia** Arkansas, C USA
147 P14 **Jufrah, Wādī al** *dry watercourse* NW Yemen
Jugoslavija/Jugoslavija, Savezna Republika *see* Yugoslavia
44 K10 **Juigalpa** Chontales, S Nicaragua
167 T13 **Juishui** C Taiwan
102 E9 **Juist** *island* NW Germany
61 M21 **Juiz de Fora** Minas Gerais, SE Brazil
64 J5 **Jujuy** *off.* Provincia de Jujuy. ◆ *province* N Argentina
Jujuy *see* San Salvador de Jujuy
94 J11 **Jukkasjärvi** Norrbotten, N Sweden
Jula *see* Gyula, Hungary
Jūlā *see* Jālū, Libya
39 W2 **Julesburg** Colorado, C USA
Julia Beterrae *see* Béziers
59 I17 **Juliaca** Puno, SE Peru
189 U6 **Julia Creek** Queensland, C Australia
37 V17 **Julian** California, W USA
100 H7 **Julianadorp** Noord-Holland, NW Netherlands
111 S11 **Julian Alps** *Ger.* Julische Alpen, *It.* Alpi Giulie, *Slvn.* Julijske Alpe. ▲ Italy/Slovenia
57 V11 **Juliana Top** ▲ C Suriname
Julianehåb *see* Qaqortoq
Julijske Alpe *see* Julian Alps
42 J6 **Julimes** Chihuahua, N Mexico
Julio Briga *see* Bragança, Portugal
Juliobriga *see* Logroño, Spain
63 G15 **Júlio de Castilhos** Rio Grande do Sul, S Brazil
Juliomagus *see* Angers
Julische Alpen *see* Julian Alps
Jullundur *see* Jalandhar
153 N11 **Juma** *Rus.* Dzhuma. Samarqand Wiloyati, C Uzbekistan
167 O3 **Juma He** ∽ E China
83 L18 **Jumboo** Jubbada Hoose, S Somalia
37 Y11 **Jumbo Peak** ▲ Nevada, W USA
107 R12 **Jumilla** Murcia, SE Spain
159 N10 **Jumla** Mid Western, NW Nepal
Jummoo *see* Jammu
Jumna *see* Yamuna
Jumporn *see* Chumphon
32 K5 **Jump River** ∽ Wisconsin, N USA
160 B11 **Jūnāgadh** *var.* Junagarh. Gujarāt, W India
Junagarh *see* Jūnāgadh
167 Q6 **Junan** *prev.* Shizilu. Shandong, E China
64 G11 **Juncal, Cerro** ▲ C Chile
27 Q10 **Junction** Texas, SW USA
38 K6 **Junction** Utah, W USA
29 O4 **Junction City** Kansas, C USA
34 F13 **Junction City** Oregon, NW USA
62 M10 **Jundiaí** São Paulo, S Brazil
194 E13 **June** ∽ W PNG
41 X12 **Juneau** *state capital* Alaska, USA
32 M8 **Juneau** Wisconsin, N USA
107 U6 **Juneda** Cataluña, NE Spain
191 Q9 **Junee** New South Wales, SE Australia
37 R8 **June Lake** California, W USA
Jungbunzlau *see* Mladá Boleslav
164 L4 **Junggar Pendi** *Eng.* Dzungarian Basin. *basin* NW China
101 N24 **Junglinster** Grevenmacher, C Luxembourg
20 F14 **Juniata River** ∽ Pennsylvania, NE USA
63 B20 **Junín** Buenos Aires, E Argentina
59 E14 **Junín** Junín, C Peru
59 F14 **Junín** *off.* Departamento de Junín. ◆ *department* C Peru
65 H15 **Junín de los Andes** Neuquén, W Argentina
59 D14 **Junín, Lago de** ◎ C Peru
Juniyah *see* Joûnié
Junkseylon *see* Phuket
166 I11 **Junlian** Sichuan, C China
27 O11 **Juno** Texas, SW USA
94 J11 **Junosuando** Norrbotten, N Sweden
95 H16 **Junsele** Västernorrland, C Sweden
Junten *see* Sunch'ŏn
34 L14 **Juntura** Oregon, NW USA
95 N14 **Juntusranta** Oulu, E Finland
120 H11 **Juodupė** Rokiškis, NE Lithuania
121 H14 **Juozapinės Kalnas** ▲ SE Lithuania
101 K19 **Juprelle** Liège, E Belgium
82 D13 **Jur** ∽ C Sudan
105 S9 **Jura** ◆ *department* E France
110 C7 **Jura** ◆ *canton* NW Switzerland
110 B8 **Jura** *var.* Jura Mountains. ▲ France/Switzerland
98 G12 **Jura** *island* SW Scotland, UK
Juraciszki *see* Yuratsishki
56 C8 **Juradó** Chocó, NW Colombia
Jura Mountains *see* Jura
98 G12 **Jura, Sound of** *strait* W Scotland, UK
145 V15 **Juraybīyāt, Bi'r** *well* S Iraq
120 E13 **Jurbarkas** *Ger.* Georgenburg, Jurburg. Jurbarkas, W Lithuania
101 F20 **Jurbise** Hainaut, SW Belgium
Jurburg *see* Jurbarkas
120 F9 **Jūrmala** Riga, C Latvia
176 Ww13 **Jursian, Pulau** *island* E Indonesia
60 D13 **Juruá** Amazonas, NW Brazil
50 F7 **Juruá, Rio** *var.* Río Yuruá. ∽ Brazil/Peru
61 G16 **Juruena** Mato Grosso, W Brazil
61 G16 **Juruena** ∽ W Brazil
171 Mm8 **Jūsan-ko** ◎ Honshū, C Japan
27 O6 **Justiceburg** Texas, SW USA
Justinianopolis *see* Kirşehir
64 K11 **Justo Daract** San Luis, C Argentina
61 C14 **Jutaí** Amazonas, W Brazil
60 C13 **Jutaí, Rio** ∽ NW Brazil
102 N13 **Jüterbog** Brandenburg, E Germany
44 E6 **Jutiapa** Jutiapa, S Guatemala
44 A3 **Jutiapa** *off.* Departamento de Jutiapa. ◆ *department* SE Guatemala
44 J6 **Juticalpa** Olancho, C Honduras
84 I13 **Jutila** North Western, NW Zambia
Jutland *see* Jylland
86 F8 **Jutland Bank** *undersea feature* SE North Sea
95 N16 **Juuka** Pohjois-Karjala, E Finland
95 N17 **Juva** Mikkeli, SE Finland
Juvavum *see* Salzburg
46 A6 **Juventud, Isla de la** *var.* Isla de Pinos, *Eng.* Isle of Youth; *prev.* The Isle of the Pines. *island* W Cuba
Ju Xian *see* Juxian
167 Q5 **Juxian** *var.* Ju Xian. Shandong, E China
167 P6 **Juye** Shandong, E China
115 O15 **Južna Morava** *Ger.* Südliche Morava. ∽ SE Yugoslavia
97 I23 **Jyderup** Vestsjælland, E Denmark
97 F22 **Jylland** *Eng.* Jutland. *peninsula* W Denmark
Jyrgalan *see* Dzhergalan
95 M17 **Jyväskylä** Keski-Suomi, C Finland

K

155 X3 **K2** *Chin.* Qogir Feng, *Eng.* Mount Godwin Austen. ▲ China/Pakistan
40 D9 **Kaaawa** *Haw.* Ka'a'wa. Oahu, Hawaii, USA, C Pacific Ocean
83 G16 **Kaabong** NE Uganda
Kaaden *see* Kadaň
57 V9 **Kaaimanston** Sipaliwini, N Suriname
152 G14 **Kaakhka** *var.* Kaka. Akhalskiy Velayat, S Turkmenistan
Kaala *see* Caála
197 H5 **Kaala-Gomen** Province Nord, W New Caledonia
94 L9 **Kaamanen** *Lapp.* Gámas. Lappi, N Finland
Kaapstad *see* Cape Town
Kaarasjoki *see* Karasjok
Kaaresuanto *see* Karesuando
94 J10 **Kaaresuvanto** *Lapp.* Gárassavon. Lappi, N Finland
95 K19 **Kaarina** Turku-Pori, SW Finland
101 I14 **Kaatsheuvel** Noord-Brabant, S Netherlands

◆ Country ● Country Capital ◇ Dependent Territory ○ Dependent Territory Capital ◆ Administrative Region ✕ International Airport ▲ Mountain ▲ Mountain Range Volcano ∽ River ◎ Lake ▣ Reservoir

KAAVI – KAMUNDAN, SUNGAI

95 N16 **Kaavi** Kuopio, C Finland
Ka'a'wa see Kaaawa
176 Y15 **Kaba** Irian Jaya, E Indonesia
Kaba see Habahe
175 Q13 **Kabaena, Pulau** *island* C Indonesia
175 Q13 **Kabaena, Selat** *strait* Sulawesi, C Indonesia
152 J11 **Kabakly** *Turkm.* Gabakly. Lebapskiy Velayat, NE Turkmenistan
78 J14 **Kabala** N Sierra Leone
83 E19 **Kabale** SW Uganda
57 U10 **Kabalebo Rivier** ≈ W Suriname
81 N22 **Kabalo** Shaba, SE Zaire
81 O21 **Kabambare** Maniema, E Zaire
197 K15 **Kabara** *prev.* Kambara. *island* Lau Group, E Fiji
Kabardino-Balkaria see Kabardino-Balkarskaya Respublika
130 M15 **Kabardino-Balkarskaya Respublika** *Eng.* Kabardino-Balkaria. ⬖ *autonomous republic* SW Russian Federation
81 O19 **Kabare** Sud Kivu, E Zaire
176 Uu8 **Kabarei** Irian Jaya, E Indonesia
179 Q16 **Kabasalan** Mindanao, S Philippines
79 U15 **Kabba** Kogi, S Nigeria
94 I13 **Kåbdalis** Norrbotten, N Sweden
144 M6 **Kabd aş Şārim** *hill range* E Syria
12 B7 **Kabenung Lake** ◎ Ontario, S Canada
31 W3 **Kabetogama Lake** ◎ Minnesota, N USA
Kabia, Pulau see Kabin, Pulau
81 M22 **Kabinda** Kasai Oriental, SE Zaire
Kabinda see Cabinda
175 P13 **Kabin, Pulau** *var.* Pulau Kabia. *island* W Indonesia
175 Rr16 **Kabir** Pulau Pantar, S Indonesia
155 T10 **Kabīrwāla** Punjab, E Pakistan
176 U8 **Kable Bet** Irian Jaya, E Indonesia
80 I13 **Kabo** Ouham, NW Central African Republic
Kābol see Kābul
85 H14 **Kabompo** North Western, W Zambia
85 H14 **Kabompo** ≈ W Zambia
81 M22 **Kabongo** Shaba, SE Zaire
123 Kk12 **Kaboudia, Rass** *headland* E Tunisia
128 J14 **Kabozha** Novgorodskaya Oblast', W Russian Federation
149 U4 **Kabūd Gonbad** Khorāsān, NE Iran
148 L5 **Kabūd Rāhang** Hamadān, W Iran
84 L12 **Kabuko** Northern, NE Zambia
155 Q5 **Kābul** *var.* Kabul, *Per.* Kābol. ● (Afghanistan) Kābul, E Afghanistan
155 Q5 **Kābul** *Eng.* Kabul, *Per.* Kābol. ⬖ *province* E Afghanistan
155 Q5 **Kābul** ✖ Kābul, E Afghanistan
155 R5 **Kabul** *var.* Daryā-ye Kābul. ≈ Afghanistan/Pakistan *see also* Kābul, Daryā-ye
155 S5 **Kābul, Daryā-ye** *var.* Kabul. ≈ Afghanistan/Pakistan *see also* Kabul
81 O25 **Kabunda** Shaba, SE Zaire
175 Ss4 **Kaburuang, Pulau** *island* Kepulauan Talaud, N Indonesia
82 G8 **Kabushiya** River Nile, NE Sudan
85 J14 **Kabwe** Central, C Zambia
194 K12 **Kabwum** Morobe, C PNG
115 N17 **Kačanik** Serbia, S Yugoslavia
176 U8 **Kacepi** Pulau Gebe, E Indonesia
120 F13 **Kačerginė** Kaunas, C Lithuania
119 S13 **Kacha** Respublika Krym, S Ukraine
160 A10 **Kachchh, Gulf of** *var.* Gulf of Cutch, Gulf of Kutch. *gulf* W India
160 I11 **Kachchhidhāna** Madhya Pradesh, C India
155 Q11 **Kachchh, Rann of** *var.* Rann of Kachh, Rann of Kutch. *salt marsh* India/Pakistan
41 Q13 **Kachemak Bay** *bay* Alaska, USA
Kachh, Rann of see Kachchh, Rann of
79 V14 **Kachia** Kaduna, C Nigeria
178 Gg2 **Kachin State** ⬖ *state* N Myanmar
151 T7 **Kachiry** Pavlodar, NE Kazakhstan
126 Jj15 **Kachug** Irkutskaya Oblast', S Russian Federation
143 Q11 **Kaçkar Dağları** ▲▲ NE Turkey
161 C21 **Kadamatt Island** *island* Lakshadweep, India, N Indian Ocean
113 B15 **Kadaň** *Ger.* Kaaden. Severní Čechy, NW Czech Republic
178 Gg12 **Kadan Kyun** *prev.* King Island. *island* Mergui Archipelago, S Myanmar
197 I16 **Kadavu** *prev.* Kandavu. *island* S Fiji
197 I15 **Kadavu Passage** *channel* S Fiji
81 G16 **Kadéï** ≈ Cameroon/Central African Republic
Kadhimain see Al Kāẓimīyah
Kadijica see Kadiytsa
116 M13 **Kadıköy Barajı** ⊠ NW Turkey
190 I8 **Kadina** South Australia
142 H15 **Kadınhanı** Konya, C Turkey
78 M14 **Kadiolo** Sikasso, S Mali
142 L16 **Kadirli** Adana, S Turkey
116 G11 **Kadiytsa** *Mac.* Kadijica. ▲ Bulgaria/FYR Macedonia
30 L10 **Kadoka** South Dakota, N USA
131 N5 **Kadom** Ryazanskaya Oblast', W Russian Federation
85 K16 **Kadoma** *prev.* Gatooma. Mashonaland West, C Zimbabwe
82 E12 **Kadugli** Southern Kordofan, S Sudan
79 V14 **Kaduna** Kaduna, C Nigeria
79 V14 **Kaduna** ⬖ *state* C Nigeria
79 V15 **Kaduna** ≈ N Nigeria
128 K14 **Kaduy** Vologodskaya Oblast', NW Russian Federation
160 E13 **Kadwa** ≈ W India
127 Nn9 **Kadykchan** Magadanskaya Oblast', E Russian Federation
Kadzharan see K'ajaran
129 T7 **Kadzherom** Respublika Komi, NW Russian Federation
153 X8 **Kadzhi-Say** *Kir.* Kajisay. Issyk-Kul'skaya Oblast', NE Kyrgyzstan
78 I10 **Kaédi** Gorgol, S Mauritania
80 G12 **Kaélé** Extrême-Nord, N Cameroon
40 C9 **Kaena Point** *headland* Oahu, Hawaii, USA, C Pacific Ocean
192 J2 **Kaeo** Northland, North Island, NZ
169 X14 **Kaesŏng** *var.* Kaesŏng-si. S North Korea
Kaesŏng-si see Kaesŏng
Kaewieng see Kavieng
81 L24 **Kafakumba** Shaba, S Zaire
Kafan see Kapan
79 V14 **Kafanchan** Kaduna, C Nigeria
Kaffa see Feodosiya
78 G11 **Kaffrine** C Senegal
Kafiau see Kofiau, Pulau
117 I19 **Kafiréas, Ákra** *headland* Évvoia, C Greece
117 I19 **Kafiréos, Stenó** *strait* Évvoia/Kykládes, Greece, Aegean Sea
Kafirnigan see Kofarnihon
Kafo see Kafu
Kafr ash Shaykh/Kafrel Sheik see Kafr el Sheikh
77 W7 **Kafr el Sheikh** *var.* Kafr ash Shaykh, Kafrel Sheik. N Egypt
83 F17 **Kafu** *var.* Kafo. ≈ W Uganda
85 J15 **Kafue** Lusaka, SE Zambia
85 I14 **Kafue** ≈ C Zambia
69 T13 **Kafue Flats** *plain* C Zambia
171 I13 **Kaga** Ishikawa, Honshū, SW Japan
81 J14 **Kaga Bandoro** *prev.* Fort-Crampel. Nana-Grébizi, C Central African Republic
83 E18 **Kagadi** W Uganda
40 H17 **Kagalaska Island** *island* Aleutian Islands, Alaska, USA
Kagan see Kogon
Kaganovichabad see Kolkhozobod
Kagarlyk see Kaharlyk
170 F15 **Kagawa** *off.* Kagawa-ken. ⬖ *prefecture* Shikoku, SW Japan
160 J13 **Kagaznagar** Andhra Pradesh, C India
95 J14 **Kåge** Västerbotten, N Sweden
83 E19 **Kagera** *var.* Ziwa Magharibi, *Eng.* West Lake. ⬖ *region* NW Tanzania
83 E19 **Kagera** *var.* Akagera. ≈ Rwanda/Tanzania *see also* Akagera
78 L5 **Kâghet** *var.* Karet. *physical region* N Mauritania
Kagi see Chiai
143 S12 **Kağızman** Kars, NE Turkey
196 I6 **Kagman Point** *headland* Saipan, S Northern Mariana Islands
170 Bb15 **Kagoshima** *var.* Kagosima. Kagoshima, Kyūshū, SW Japan
172 Qq14 **Kagoshima** *off.* Kagoshima-ken, *var.* Kagosima. ⬖ *prefecture* Kyūshū, SW Japan
170 Bb16 **Kagoshima-wan** *bay* SW Japan
Kagosima see Kagoshima
194 H12 **Kagua** Southern Highlands, W PNG
Kagul see Cahul
Kagul, Ozero see Kahul, Ozero
40 B8 **Kahala Point** *headland* Kauai, Hawaii, USA, C Pacific Ocean
40 G12 **Kahaluu** *Haw.* Kahalu'u. Hawaii, USA, C Pacific Ocean
83 F21 **Kahama** Shinyanga, NW Tanzania
119 P5 **Kaharlyk** *Rus.* Kagarlyk. Kyyivs'ka Oblast', N Ukraine
174 Mm10 **Kahayan, Sungai** ≈ Borneo, C Indonesia
81 I22 **Kahemba** Bandundu, SW Zaire
193 A23 **Kaherekoau Mountains** ▲▲ South Island, NZ
149 W14 **Kahīrī** *var.* Kūhīrī. Sīstān va Balūchestān, SE Iran
103 L16 **Kahla** Thüringen, C Germany
103 G15 **Kahler Asten** ▲ W Germany
155 Q4 **Kahmard, Daryā-ye** *prev.* Darya-i-Surkhab. ≈ NE Afghanistan
149 T13 **Kahnūj** Kermān, SE Iran
29 V1 **Kahoka** Missouri, C USA
40 E10 **Kahoolawe** *island* Hawaii, USA, C Pacific Ocean
142 M16 **Kahramanmaraş** *var.* Kahraman Maraş, Maraş, Marash. Kahramanmaraş, S Turkey
142 L15 **Kahramanmaraş** *var.* Kahraman Maraş, Maraş, Marash. ⬖ *province* C Turkey
155 T11 **Kahror** *var.* Kahror Pakka. Punjab, E Pakistan
Kahror Pakka see Kahror
143 N15 **Kâhta** Adıyaman, S Turkey
40 D8 **Kahuku** Oahu, Hawaii, USA, C Pacific Ocean
40 D8 **Kahuku Point** *headland* Oahu, Hawaii, USA, C Pacific Ocean
118 M12 **Kahul, Ozero** *var.* Lacul Cahul, *Rus.* Ozero Kagul. ◎ Moldova/Ukraine
149 V11 **Kahūrak** Sīstān va Balūchestān, SE Iran
192 G13 **Kahurangi Point** *headland* South Island, NZ
155 V6 **Kahūta** Punjab, E Pakistan
79 S14 **Kaiama** Kwara, W Nigeria
194 J12 **Kaiapit** Morobe, C PNG
193 I18 **Kaiapoi** Canterbury, South Island, NZ
38 K9 **Kaibab Plateau** *plain* Arizona, SW USA
171 Gg14 **Kaibara** Hyōgo, Honshū, SW Japan
176 Vv13 **Kai Besar, Pulau** *island* Kepulauan Kai, E Indonesia
38 L9 **Kaibito Plateau** *plain* Arizona, SW USA
164 K6 **Kaidu He** *var.* Karaxahar. ≈ NW China
57 S10 **Kaieteur Falls** *waterfall* C Guyana
167 O6 **Kaifeng** Henan, C China
192 J3 **Kaihu** Northland, North Island, NZ
176 V13 **Kai Kecil, Pulau** *island* Kepulauan Kai, E Indonesia
176 V14 **Kai, Kepulauan** *prev.* Kei Islands. *island group* Maluku, SE Indonesia
192 J3 **Kaikohe** Northland, North Island, NZ
193 J16 **Kaikoura** Canterbury, South Island, NZ
193 J16 **Kaikoura Peninsula** *peninsula* South Island, NZ
Kailas Range see Gangdisê Shan
166 K12 **Kaili** Guizhou, S China
40 F10 **Kailua** Maui, Hawaii, USA, C Pacific Ocean
40 G11 **Kailua** *var.* Kailua-Kona, Kona. Hawaii, USA, C Pacific Ocean
Kailua-Kona see Kailua
194 E13 **Kaim** ≈ W PNG
176 Y13 **Kaima** Irian Jaya, E Indonesia
192 M7 **Kaimai Range** ▲▲ North Island, NZ
116 E13 **Kaïmaktsalán** ▲ Greece/FYR Macedonia
193 C20 **Kaimanawa Mountains** ▲▲ North Island, NZ
120 E4 **Käina** *Ger.* Keinis; *prev.* Keina. Hiiumaa, W Estonia
111 V7 **Kainach** ≈ SE Austria
170 G16 **Kainan** Tokushima, Shikoku, SW Japan
170 Ff16 **Kainan** Wakayama, Honshū, SW Japan
194 J12 **Kainantu** Eastern Highlands, C PNG
153 U7 **Kaindy** *Kir.* Kayyngdy. Chuyskaya Oblast', N Kyrgyzstan
79 T14 **Kainji Dam** *dam* W Nigeria
Kainji Lake see Kainji Reservoir
79 T14 **Kainji Reservoir** *var.* Kainji Lake. ⊠ W Nigeria
194 J14 **Kaintiba** *var.* Kamina. Gulf, S PNG
94 K12 **Kainulaisjärvi** Norrbotten, N Sweden
192 K5 **Kaipara Harbour** *harbor* North Island, NZ
158 I10 **Kairāna** Uttar Pradesh, N India
194 G9 **Kairiru Island** *island* NW PNG
76 M6 **Kairouan** *var.* Al Qayrawān. E Tunisia
Kaisaria see Kayseri
103 F20 **Kaiserslautern** Rheinland-Pfalz, SW Germany
120 G13 **Kaišiadorys** Kaišiadorys, S Lithuania
192 I2 **Kaitaia** Northland, North Island, NZ
167 O15 **Kai Tak** ✖ (Hong Kong) S China
193 E24 **Kaitangata** Otago, South Island, NZ
158 I9 **Kaithal** Haryāna, NW India
174 J11 **Kait, Tanjung** *headland* Sumatera, W Indonesia
40 E9 **Kaiwi Channel** *channel* Hawaii, USA, C Pacific Ocean
166 K9 **Kaixian** *var.* Kai Xian. Sichuan, C China
169 V11 **Kaiyuan** *var.* K'ai-yüan. Liaoning, NE China
166 H14 **Kaiyuan** Yunnan, SW China
41 O9 **Kaiyuh Mountains** ▲▲ Alaska, USA
95 M15 **Kajaani** *Swe.* Kajana. Oulu, C Finland
155 N7 **Kajaki, Band-e** ◎ C Afghanistan
Kajan see Kayan, Sungai
Kajana see Kajaani
143 V13 **K'ajaran** *Rus.* Kadzharan. SE Armenia
Kajisay see Kadzhi-Say
115 O20 **Kajmakčalan** ▲ S FYR Macedonia
Kajnar see Kaynar
155 N6 **Kajrān** Urūzgān, C Afghanistan
155 N5 **Kaj Rūd** ≈ C Afghanistan
Kaka see Kaakhka
10 C12 **Kakabeka Falls** Ontario, S Canada
85 F23 **Kakamas** Northern Cape, W South Africa
83 H18 **Kakamega** Western, W Kenya
114 H13 **Kakanj** C Bosnia and Herzegovina
193 F22 **Kakanui Mountains** ▲▲ South Island, NZ
192 K11 **Kakaramea** Taranaki, North Island, NZ
78 J16 **Kakata** C Liberia
192 M11 **Kakatahi** Manawatu-Wanganui, North Island, NZ
115 M23 **Kakavi** Gjirokastër, S Albania
153 O14 **Kakaydi** Surkhondaryo Wiloyati, S Uzbekistan
170 Ee13 **Kake** Hiroshima, Honshū, SW Japan
41 X13 **Kake** Kupreanof Island, Alaska, USA
175 R12 **Kakea** Pulau Wowoni, C Indonesia
171 Ii17 **Kakegawa** Shizuoka, Honshū, S Japan
172 Qq13 **Kakeromajima** Kagoshima, SW Japan
149 T6 **Kākhak** *var.* Kākhk. Khorāsān, E Iran
120 L11 **Kakhanavichy** *Rus.* Kokhanovichi. Vitsyebskaya Voblasts', N Belarus
41 P13 **Kakhonak** Alaska, USA
119 S10 **Kakhovka** Khersons'ka Oblast', S Ukraine
119 U9 **Kakhovs'ka Vodoskhovyshche** *Rus.* Kakhovskoye Vodokhranilishche. ⊠ SE Ukraine
Kakhovskoye Vodokhranilishche see Kakhovs'ka Vodoskhovyshche
119 T11 **Kakhovs'kyy Kanal** *canal* S Ukraine
Kakia see Khakhea
161 L16 **Kākināda** *prev.* Cocanada. Andhra Pradesh, E India
Käkisalmi see Priozersk
170 G14 **Kakogawa** Hyōgo, Honshū, SW Japan
83 F18 **Kakoge** C Uganda
151 O7 **Kak, Ozero** ◎ N Kazakhstan
Ka-Krem see Malyy Yenisey
Kakshaal-Too, Khrebet see Kokshaal-Tau
41 S5 **Kaktovik** Alaska, USA
171 Ll13 **Kakuda** Miyagi, Honshū, C Japan
171 M11 **Kakunodate** Akita, Honshū, C Japan
Kalaallit Nunaat see Greenland
155 T7 **Kālābāgh** Punjab, E Pakistan
175 Rr16 **Kalabahi** Pulau Alor, S Indonesia
196 I5 **Kalabera** Saipan, S Northern Mariana Islands
85 G14 **Kalabo** Western, W Zambia
130 M9 **Kalach** Voronezhskaya Oblast', W Russian Federation
125 G13 **Kalachinsk** Omskaya Oblast', C Russian Federation
131 N10 **Kalach-na-Donu** Volgogradskaya Oblast', SW Russian Federation
177 F5 **Kaladan** ≈ W Myanmar
12 K14 **Kaladar** Ontario, SE Canada
40 G13 **Ka Lae** *var.* South Cape, South Point. *headland* Hawaii, USA, C Pacific Ocean
85 G19 **Kalahari Desert** *desert* Southern Africa
40 B8 **Kalaheo** *Haw.* Kalāheo. Kauai, Hawaii, USA, C Pacific Ocean
Kalaikhum see Qal'aikhum
152 J16 **Kala-i-Mor** *Turkm.* Galaymor. Maryyskiy Velayat, S Turkmenistan
95 K15 **Kalajoki** Oulu, W Finland
Kalak see Eski Kaļak
Kal al Sraghna see El Kelâa Srarhna
34 G10 **Kalama** Washington, NW USA
Kalámai see Kalámata
117 G14 **Kalamariá** Kentrikí Makedonía, N Greece
117 E21 **Kalámata** *prev.* Kalámai. Pelopónnisos, S Greece
33 P10 **Kalamazoo** Michigan, N USA
33 P9 **Kalamazoo River** ≈ Michigan, N USA
Kalambaka see Kalampáka
119 S13 **Kalamits'ka Zatoka** *Rus.* Kalamitskiy Zaliv. *gulf* S Ukraine
Kalamitskiy Zaliv see Kalamits'ka Zatoka
117 H18 **Kálamos** Attikí, C Greece
117 C18 **Kálamos** *island* Iónioi Nísoi, Greece, C Mediterranean Sea
117 D15 **Kalampáka** *var.* Kalambaka. Thessalía, C Greece
Kalan see Călan, Romania
Kalan see Tunceli, Turkey
119 S11 **Kalanchak** Khersons'ka Oblast', S Ukraine
175 Pp15 **Kalao, Pulau** *island* Kepulauan Bonerate, W Indonesia
175 Q15 **Kalaotoa, Pulau** *island* W Indonesia
161 J24 **Kala Oya** ≈ NW Sri Lanka
Kalarash see Călăraşi
95 H17 **Kälarne** Jämtland, C Sweden
149 V15 **Kalar Rūd** ≈ SE Iran
178 I9 **Kalasin** *var.* Muang Kalasin. Kalasin, E Thailand
155 O8 **Kalāt** *Per.* Qalāt. Zābul, S Afghanistan
155 O11 **Kalāt** *var.* Kelat, Khelat. Baluchistān, SW Pakistan
117 J14 **Kalathriá, Ákra** *headland* Samothráki, NE Greece
200 R17 **Kalau** *island* Tongatapu Group, SE Tonga
40 E9 **Kalaupapa** Molokai, Hawaii, USA, C Pacific Ocean
131 N13 **Kalaus** ≈ SW Russian Federation
Kalávrita see Kalávryta
117 E19 **Kalávryta** *var.* Kalávrita. Dytikí Ellás, S Greece
147 Y10 **Kalbān** W Oman
188 H11 **Kalbarri** Western Australia
151 X10 **Kalbinskiy Khrebet** *Kaz.* Qalba Zhotasy. ▲▲ E Kazakhstan
150 G10 **Kaldygayty** ≈ W Kazakhstan
142 I12 **Kalecik** Ankara, N Turkey
175 R13 **Kaledupa, Pulau** *island* Kepulauan Tukangbesi, C Indonesia
81 O19 **Kalehe** Sud Kivu, E Zaire
81 P22 **Kalemie** *prev.* Albertville. Shaba, SE Zaire
177 Ff3 **Kalemyo** Sagaing, W Myanmar
84 H12 **Kalene Hill** North Western, NW Zambia
Kale Sultanie see Çanakkale
128 I7 **Kalevala** Respublika Kareliya, NW Russian Federation
177 Ff3 **Kalewa** Sagaing, C Myanmar
Kalgan see Zhangjiakou
41 Q12 **Kalgin Island** *island* Alaska, USA
188 L12 **Kalgoorlie** Western Australia
Kali see Sārda
117 E17 **Kaliakoúda** ▲ C Greece
116 O8 **Kaliakra, Nos** *headland* NE Bulgaria
117 F19 **Kaliánoi** Pelopónnisos, S Greece
179 Q13 **Kalibo** Panay Island, C Philippines
117 N24 **Kalí Límni** ▲ Kárpathos, SE Greece
81 N20 **Kalima** Maniema, E Zaire
174 M8 **Kalimantan** *Eng.* Indonesian Borneo. *geopolitical region* Borneo, C Indonesia
174 L8 **Kalimantan Barat** *off.* Propinsi Kalimantan Barat, *Eng.* West Borneo, West Kalimantan. ⬖ *province* N Indonesia
174 Mm11 **Kalimantan Selatan** *off.* Propinsi Kalimantan Selatan, *Eng.* South Borneo, South Kalimantan. ⬖ *province* N Indonesia
174 M9 **Kalimantan Tengah** *off.* Propinsi Kalimantan Tengah, *Eng.* Central Borneo, Central Kalimantan. ⬖ *province* N Indonesia
175 N7 **Kalimantan Timur** *off.* Propinsi Kalimantan Timur, *Eng.* East Borneo, East Kalimantan. ⬖ *province* N Indonesia
Kálimnos see Kálymnos
159 S12 **Kälimpang** West Bengal, NE India
Kalinin see Tver', Russian Federation
Kalinin see Boldumsaz, Turkmenistan
Kalininabad see Kalininobod
130 B3 **Kaliningrad** Kaliningradskaya Oblast', W Russian Federation
Kaliningrad see Kaliningradskaya Oblast'
130 A3 **Kaliningradskaya Oblast'** *var.* Kaliningrad. ⬖ *province and enclave* W Russian Federation
Kalinino see Tashir
153 P14 **Kalininobod** *Rus.* Kalininabad. SW Tajikistan
131 O8 **Kalininsk** Saratovskaya Oblast', W Russian Federation
Kalininsk see Boldumsaz
Kalinisk see Cupcina
121 M19 **Kalinkavichy** *Rus.* Kalinkovichi. Homyel'skaya Voblasts', SE Belarus
Kalinkovichi see Kalinkavichy
83 G18 **Kaliro** SE Uganda
Kalisch/Kalisch/Kalish/Kaliskie, Województwo see Kalisz
35 O7 **Kalispell** Montana, NW USA
112 I13 **Kalisz** *Ger.* Kalisch, *Rus.* Kalish; *anc.* Calisia. Kalisz, C Poland
112 H13 **Kalisz** *off.* Województwo Kaliskie, *Ger.* Kalisch. ⬖ *province* C Poland
112 F9 **Kalisz Pomorski** *Ger.* Kallies. Koszalin, NW Poland
130 M10 **Kalitva** ≈ SW Russian Federation
83 F21 **Kaliua** Tabora, C Tanzania
94 K13 **Kalix** Norrbotten, N Sweden
94 K12 **Kalixälven** ≈ N Sweden
94 J11 **Kalixfors** Norrbotten, N Sweden
151 T8 **Kalkaman** Pavlodar, NE Kazakhstan
Kalkandelen see Tetovo
189 O4 **Kalkarindji** Northern Territory, N Australia
33 P6 **Kalkaska** Michigan, N USA
95 F16 **Kall** Jämtland, C Sweden
201 X2 **Kallalen** *var.* Calalen. *island* Ratak Chain, SE Marshall Islands
120 J5 **Kallaste** *Ger.* Krasnogor. Tartumaa, SE Estonia
95 N16 **Kallavesi** ◎ SE Finland
117 F17 **Kallídromo** ▲▲ C Greece
Kallies see Kalisz Pomorski
97 M22 **Kallinge** Blekinge, S Sweden
117 L16 **Kalloní** Lésvos, E Greece
95 F16 **Kallsjön** ◎ C Sweden
97 N21 **Kalmar** *var.* Calmar. Kalmar, S Sweden
97 M19 **Kalmar** *var.* Calmar. ⬖ *county* S Sweden
97 N20 **Kalmarsund** *strait* S Sweden
154 L16 **Kalmat, Khor** *Eng.* Kalmat Lagoon. *lagoon* SW Pakistan
Kalmat Lagoon see Kalmat, Khor
119 X9 **Kal'mius** ≈ E Ukraine
101 H15 **Kalmthout** Antwerpen, N Belgium
Kalmykia/Kalmykiya-Khal'mg Tangch, Respublika see Kalmykiya, Respublika
131 O12 **Kalmykiya, Respublika** *var.* Respublika Kalmykiya-Khal'mg Tangch, *Eng.* Kalmykia; *prev.* Kalmytskaya ASSR. ⬖ *autonomous republic* SW Russian Federation
Kalmytskaya ASSR see Kalmykiya, Respublika
120 F9 **Kalnciems** Jelgava, C Latvia
116 L10 **Kalnitsa** ≈ SE Bulgaria
113 J24 **Kalocsa** Bács-Kiskun, S Hungary
116 J9 **Kalofer** Plovdivska Oblast, C Bulgaria
40 E10 **Kalohi Channel** *channel* C Pacific Ocean
85 I16 **Kalomo** Southern, S Zambia
31 X14 **Kalona** Iowa, C USA
117 K22 **Kalotási, Ákra** *headland* Amorgós, Kykládes, Greece, Aegean Sea
158 J8 **Kalpa** Himāchal Pradesh, N India
117 C15 **Kalpáki** Ípeiros, W Greece
161 C22 **Kalpeni Island** *island* Lakshadweep, India, N Indian Ocean
158 K13 **Kālpi** Uttar Pradesh, N India
164 G7 **Kalpin** Xinjiang Uygur Zizhiqu, NW China
152 K8 **Kalquduq** *Rus.* Kulkuduk. Nawoiy Wiloyati, N Uzbekistan
155 P16 **Kalri Lake** ◎ SE Pakistan
149 R5 **Kāl Shūr** N Iran
41 N11 **Kalskag** Alaska, USA
41 O9 **Kaltag** Alaska, USA
110 H7 **Kaltbrunn** Sankt Gallen, NE Switzerland
Kaltdorf see Pruszków
79 X14 **Kaltungo** Bauchi, E Nigeria
130 K4 **Kaluga** Kaluzhskaya Oblast', W Russian Federation
161 J26 **Kalu Ganga** ≈ S Sri Lanka
84 J13 **Kalulushi** Copperbelt, C Zambia
188 M2 **Kalumburu** Western Australia
97 H23 **Kalundborg** Vestsjælland, E Denmark
84 K11 **Kalungwishi** ≈ N Zambia
155 T8 **Kalūr Kot** Punjab, E Pakistan
118 I6 **Kalush** *Pol.* Kałusz. Ivano-Frankivs'ka Oblast', W Ukraine
Kałusz see Kalush
112 N11 **Kałuszyn** Siedlce, E Poland
161 J26 **Kalutara** Western Province, SW Sri Lanka
Kaluwawa see Fergusson Island
130 I5 **Kaluzhskaya Oblast'** ⬖ *province* W Russian Federation
121 E14 **Kalvarija** *Pol.* Kalwaria. Marijampolė, S Lithuania
95 K15 **Kälviä** Vaasa, W Finland
111 U6 **Kalwang** Steiermark, E Austria
Kalwaria see Kalvarija
160 D13 **Kalyān** Mahārāshtra, W India
128 K16 **Kalyazin** Tverskaya Oblast', W Russian Federation
117 D18 **Kalydón** *anc.* Calydon. *site of ancient city* Dytikí Ellás, C Greece
117 M21 **Kálymnos** *var.* Kálimnos. Kálymnos, Dodekánisos, Greece, Aegean Sea
117 M21 **Kálymnos** *var.* Kálimnos. *island* Dodekánisos, Greece, Aegean Sea
119 O5 **Kalynivka** Kyyivs'ka Oblast', N Ukraine
119 N6 **Kalynivka** Vinnyts'ka Oblast', C Ukraine
44 M10 **Kama** *var.* Cama. Región Autónoma Atlántico Sur, SE Nicaragua
125 E9 **Kama** ≈ NW Russian Federation
172 N12 **Kamaishi** *var.* Kamaisi. Iwate, Honshū, C Japan
Kamaisi see Kamaishi
120 H13 **Kamajai** Molėtai, E Lithuania
120 H11 **Kamajai** Rokiškis, NE Lithuania
171 Jj17 **Kamakura** Kanagawa, Honshū, S Japan
155 U9 **Kamālia** Punjab, NE Pakistan
85 I14 **Kamalondo** North Western, NW Zambia
142 I13 **Kaman** Kırşehir, C Turkey
81 O20 **Kamanyola** Sud Kivu, E Zaire
147 N14 **Kamarān** *island* W Yemen
57 R9 **Kamarang** W Guyana
161 I14 **Kāmāreddi** *var.* Kamareddy. Andhra Pradesh, C India
Kamareddy see Kāmāreddi
Kama Reservoir see Kamskoye Vodokhranilishche
154 K13 **Kamarod** Baluchistān, SW Pakistan
175 R13 **Kamaru** Pulau Buton, C Indonesia
153 N12 **Kamashi** Qashqadaryo Wiloyati, S Uzbekistan
79 S13 **Kamba** Kebbi, NW Nigeria
Kambaeng Petch see Kamphaeng Phet
188 L12 **Kambalda** Western Australia
155 P13 **Kambar** *var.* Qambar. Sind, SE Pakistan
Kambara see Kabara
78 I14 **Kambia** W Sierra Leone
175 S16 **Kambing, Pulau** *island* S Indonesia
Kambos see Kámpos
81 N25 **Kambove** Shaba, SE Zaire
Kambryk see Cambrai
127 Pp10 **Kamchatka** ≈ E Russian Federation
Kamchatka see Kamchatka, Poluostrov
Kamchatka Basin see Komandorskaya Basin
127 P11 **Kamchatka, Poluostrov** *Eng.* Kamchatka. *peninsula* E Russian Federation
127 Pp11 **Kamchatskaya Oblast'** ⬖ *province* E Russian Federation
127 Pp10 **Kamchatskiy Zaliv** *gulf* E Russian Federation
116 N9 **Kamchiya** ≈ E Bulgaria
116 L9 **Kamchiya, Yazovir** ◎ E Bulgaria
Kamdesh see Kāmdeysh
155 T4 **Kāmdeysh** *var.* Kamdesh. Kunar, E Afghanistan
170 Ee14 **Kamega-mori** ▲ Shikoku, SW Japan
120 M13 **Kamen'** *Rus.* Kamen'. Vitsyebskaya Voblasts', N Belarus
Kamenets see Kamyanyets
Kamenets-Podol'skaya Oblast' see Khmel'nyts'ka Oblast'
Kamenets-Podol'skiy see Kam"yanets'-Podil's'kyy
115 Q18 **Kamenica** NE FYR Macedonia
114 A11 **Kamenjak, Rt** *headland* NW Croatia
150 F8 **Kamenka** Zapadnyy Kazakhstan, NW Kazakhstan
129 O6 **Kamenka** Arkhangel'skaya Oblast', NW Russian Federation
130 L8 **Kamenka** Penzenskaya Oblast', W Russian Federation
131 O6 **Kamenka** Voronezhskaya Oblast', W Russian Federation
Kamenka see Camenca, Moldova
Kamenka see Kam"yanka, Ukraine
Kamenka-Bugskaya see Kam"yanka-Buz'ka
Kamenka Dneprovskaya see Kam"yanka-Dniprovs'ka
Kamen Kashirskiy see Kamin'-Kashyrs'kyy
126 Gg14 **Kamen'-na-Obi** Altayskiy Kray, S Russian Federation
130 L15 **Kamennomostskiy** Respublika Adygeya, SW Russian Federation
130 L11 **Kamenolomni** Rostovskaya Oblast', SW Russian Federation
131 P8 **Kamenskiy** Saratovskaya Oblast', W Russian Federation
127 P7 **Kamenskoye** Koryakskiy Avtonomnyy Okrug, E Russian Federation
Kamenskoye see Dniprodzerzhyns'k
130 L11 **Kamensk-Shakhtinskiy** Rostovskaya Oblast', SW Russian Federation
125 Ee11 **Kamensk-Ural'skiy** Sverdlovskaya Oblast', C Russian Federation
103 P15 **Kamenz** Sachsen, E Germany
171 Gg14 **Kameoka** Kyōto, Honshū, SW Japan
130 M3 **Kameshkovo** Vladimirskaya Oblast', W Russian Federation
171 H15 **Kameyama** Mie, Honshū, SW Japan
170 Cc10 **Kami-Agata** Nagasaki, Tsushima, SW Japan
35 N10 **Kamiah** Idaho, NW USA
Kamień Koszyrski see Kamin'-Kashyrs'kyy
112 H9 **Kamień Krajeński** *Ger.* Kamin in Westpreussen. Bydgoszcz, NW Poland
113 F15 **Kamienna Góra** *Ger.* Landeshut, Landeshut in Schlesien. Jelenia Góra, SW Poland
112 D8 **Kamień Pomorski** *Ger.* Cummin in Pommern. Szczecin, NW Poland
172 N7 **Kamiiso** Hokkaidō, NE Japan
81 L22 **Kamiji** Kasai Oriental, S Zaire
172 Pp5 **Kamikawa** Hokkaidō, NE Japan
170 Bb15 **Kami-Koshiki-jima** *island* SW Japan
81 M23 **Kamina** Shaba, S Zaire
Kamina see Kaintiba
44 C6 **Kaminaljuyú** *ruins* Guatemala, C Guatemala
Kamin in Westpreussen see Kamień Krajeński
118 J2 **Kamin'-Kashyrs'kyy** *Pol.* Kamień Koszyrski, *Rus.* Kamen Kashirskiy. Volyns'ka Oblast', NW Ukraine
172 N6 **Kaminokuni** Hokkaidō, NE Japan
171 Ll13 **Kaminoyama** Yamagata, Honshū, C Japan
171 Ii14 **Kamioka** Gifu, Honshū, SW Japan
41 Q13 **Kamishak Bay** *bay* Alaska, USA
172 Pp6 **Kami-Shihoro** Hokkaidō, NE Japan
Kamishli see Al Qāmishlī
Kamissar see Kamsar
170 Cc10 **Kami-Tsushima** Nagasaki, Tsushima, SW Japan
81 O20 **Kamituga** Sud Kivu, E Zaire
170 B17 **Kamiyaku** Kagoshima, Yaku-shima, SW Japan
9 N16 **Kamloops** British Columbia, SW Canada
109 G25 **Kamma** Sicilia, Italy, C Mediterranean Sea
199 I4 **Kammu Seamount** *undersea feature* N Pacific Ocean
111 U11 **Kamnik** *Ger.* Stein. C Slovenia
Kamniške Alpe see Savinjske Alpe
171 Kk13 **Kamo** Niigata, Honshū, C Japan
171 K17 **Kamogawa** Chiba, Honshū, S Japan
155 W8 **Kāmoke** Punjab, E Pakistan
84 L13 **Kamoto** Eastern, E Zambia
111 V3 **Kamp** ≈ N Austria
83 F18 **Kampala** ● (Uganda) S Uganda
174 H8 **Kampar, Sungai** ≈ Sumatera, W Indonesia
174 Ii10 **Kampa, Teluk** *bay* Pulau Bangka, W Indonesia
100 L9 **Kampen** Overijssel, E Netherlands
81 N20 **Kampene** Maniema, E Zaire
31 Q9 **Kampeska, Lake** ◎ South Dakota, N USA
178 Gg9 **Kamphaeng Phet** *var.* Kambaeng Petch. Kamphaeng Phet, W Thailand
Kampo see Campo, Cameroon
Kampo see Ntem, Cameroon/Equatorial Guinea
178 J13 **Kâmpóng Cham** *prev.* Kompong Cham. Kâmpóng Cham, C Cambodia
178 J13 **Kâmpóng Chhnăng** *prev.* Kompong. Kâmpóng Chhnăng, C Cambodia
178 Ii12 **Kâmpóng Khleăng** *prev.* Kompong Kleang. Siĕmréab, NW Cambodia
178 I14 **Kâmpóng Saôm** *prev.* Kompong Som, Sihanoukville. Kâmpóng Saôm, SW Cambodia
178 J13 **Kâmpóng Spoe** *prev.* Kompong Speu. Kâmpóng Spœ, S Cambodia
124 N3 **Kámpos** *var.* Kambos. NW Cyprus
178 Ii14 **Kâmpôt** Kâmpôt, SW Cambodia
Kamptee see Kāmthi
79 O14 **Kampti** SW Burkina
Kampuchea see Cambodia
174 I15 **Kampung Sirik** Sarawak, East Malaysia
176 Y13 **Kampung, Sungai** ≈ Irian Jaya, E Indonesia
176 Vv12 **Kamrau, Teluk** *bay* Irian Jaya, E Indonesia
9 V15 **Kamsack** Saskatchewan, S Canada
78 H13 **Kamsar** *var.* Kamissar. Guinée-Maritime, W Guinea
131 R4 **Kamskoye Ust'ye** Respublika Tatarstan, W Russian Federation
129 U14 **Kamskoye Vodokhranilishche** *var.* Kama Reservoir. ⊠ NW Russian Federation
160 I12 **Kāmthi** *prev.* Kamptee. Mahārāshtra, C India
Kamuela see Waimea
172 Nn5 **Kamuenai** Hokkaidō, NE Japan
172 P7 **Kamui-dake** ▲ Hokkaidō, NE Japan
172 Nn4 **Kamui-misaki** *headland* Hokkaidō, NE Japan
45 O15 **Kámuk, Cerro** ▲ SE Costa Rica
176 Vv9 **Kamundan, Sungai** ≈ Irian Jaya, E Indonesia

◆ Country
● Country Capital
◇ Dependent Territory
○ Dependent Territory Capital
⬖ Administrative Region
✖ International Airport
▲ Mountain
▲▲ Mountain Range
Volcano
≈ River
◎ Lake
⊠ Reservoir

176 X12 **Kamura, Sungai** ↗ Irian Jaya, E Indonesia
118 K7 **Kam"yanets'-Podil's'kyy** *Rus.* Kamenets-Podol'skiy. Khmel'nyts'ka Oblast', W Ukraine
119 Q6 **Kam"yanka** *Rus.* Kamenka. Cherkas'ka Oblast', C Ukraine
118 I5 **Kam"yanka-Buz'ka** *Rus.* Kamenka-Bugskaya. L'vivs'ka Oblast', NW Ukraine
119 T9 **Kam"yanka-Dniprovs'ka** *Rus.* Kamenka Dneprovskaya. Zaporiz'ka Oblast', SE Ukraine
121 F19 **Kamyanets** *Rus.* Kamenets. Brestskaya Voblasts', SW Belarus
131 P9 **Kamyshin** Volgogradskaya Oblast', SW Russian Federation
125 Ee11 **Kamyshlov** Sverdlovskaya Oblast', C Russian Federation
131 Q13 **Kamyzyak** Astrakhanskaya Oblast', SW Russian Federation
10 K8 **Kanaaupscow** ↗ Québec, C Canada
38 K8 **Kanab** Utah, W USA
38 K9 **Kanab Creek** ↗ Arizona/Utah, SW USA
197 J13 **Kanacea** *prev.* Kanathea. Taveuni, N Fiji
197 K14 **Kanacea** island Lau Group, E Fiji
40 G17 **Kanaga Island** island Aleutian Islands, Alaska, USA
40 G17 **Kanaga Volcano** ▲ Kanaga Island, Alaska, USA
171 J17 **Kanagawa** off. Kanagawa-ken. ◆ prefecture Honshū, S Japan
11 Q8 **Kanairiktok** ↗ Newfoundland and Labrador, E Canada
Kanaky see New Caledonia
81 K22 **Kananga** *prev.* Luluabourg. Kasai Occidental, S Zaire
Kananur see Cannanore
Kanara see Karnātaka
38 J7 **Kanarraville** Utah, W USA
131 Q4 **Kanash** Chuvashskaya Respublika, W Russian Federation
Kanathea see Kanacea
23 Q4 **Kanawha River** ↗ West Virginia, NE USA
171 I15 **Kanayama** Gifu, Honshū, SW Japan
171 I12 **Kanazawa** Ishikawa, Honshū, SW Japan
177 G4 **Kanbalu** Sagaing, C Myanmar
177 Ff8 **Kanbe** Yangon, SW Myanmar
178 H11 **Kanchanaburi** Kanchanaburi, W Thailand
Känchenjunga see Kangchenjunga
151 V11 **Kanchingiz, Khrebet** ▲ E Kazakhstan
161 J19 **Känchipuram** *prev.* Conjeeveram. Tamil Nādu, SE India
155 N8 **Kandahār** *Per.* Qandahār. Kandahār, S Afghanistan
155 N9 **Kandahār** *Per.* Qandahār. ◆ province SE Afghanistan
Kandalaksa see Kandalaksha
128 I5 **Kandalaksha** *var.* Kandalaksa, *Fin.* Kantalahti. Murmanskaya Oblast', NW Russian Federation
Kandalaksha Gulf/Kandalakshskaya Guba see Kandalakshskiy Zaliv
128 K6 **Kandalakshskiy Zaliv** *var.* Kandalaksha Guba, *Eng.* Kandalaksha Gulf. *bay* NW Russian Federation
Kandalengodi see Kandalengoti
85 G17 **Kandalengoti** *var.* Kandalengodi. Ngamiland, NW Botswana
175 N10 **Kandangan** Borneo, C Indonesia
Kandau see Kandava
120 E8 **Kandava** *Ger.* Kandau. Tukums, W Latvia
Kandavu see Kadavu
79 R14 **Kandé** *var.* Kanté. NE Togo
103 F23 **Kandel** ▲ SW Germany
194 G12 **Kandep** Enga, W PNG
155 R12 **Kandhkot** Sind, SE Pakistan
79 S13 **Kandi** N Benin
155 P14 **Kandiāro** Sind, SE Pakistan
142 F11 **Kandıra** Kocaeli, NW Turkey
191 S8 **Kandos** New South Wales, SE Australia
154 M16 **Kandrach** *var.* Kanrach. Baluchistān, SW Pakistan
180 I4 **Kandreho** Mahajanga, C Madagascar
194 M12 **Kandrian** New Britain, E PNG
Kandukur see Kondukūr
161 K25 **Kandy** Central Province, C Sri Lanka
20 D12 **Kane** Pennsylvania, NE USA
66 I11 **Kane Fracture Zone** tectonic feature N Atlantic Ocean
Kanêka see Kanêvka
80 G9 **Kanem** off. Préfecture du Kanem. ◆ prefecture W Chad
44 D9 **Kaneohe** *Haw.* Käne'ohe. Oahu, Hawaii, USA, C Pacific Ocean
Kanestron, Akra see Paliouri, Ákra
Kanëv see Kaniv
128 M5 **Kanëvka** *var.* Kanêka. Murmanskaya Oblast', NW Russian Federation
130 K13 **Kanevskaya** Krasnodarskiy Kray, SW Russian Federation
Kanevskoye Vodokhranilishche see Kaniv's'ke Vodoskhovyshche
171 Ll12 **Kaneyama** Yamagata, Honshū, C Japan
85 G20 **Kang** Kgalagadi, C Botswana
79 P15 **Kangaba** Koulikoro, SW Mali
142 M13 **Kangal** Sivas, C Turkey
149 U13 **Kangān** Büshehr, S Iran
149 S15 **Kangān** Hormozgān, SE Iran
173 G2 **Kangar** Perlis, Peninsular Malaysia
78 L13 **Kangaré** Sikasso, S Mali

190 F10 **Kangaroo Island** island South Australia
95 M17 **Kangasniemi** Mikkeli, SE Finland
148 K6 **Kangāvar** *var.* Kangāwar. Kermānshāhān, W Iran
Kangāwar see Kangāvar
159 S11 **Kangchenjunga** *var.* Känchenjunga. ▲ NE India
166 G9 **Kangding** Sichuan, C China
175 Nn14 **Kangean, Kepulauan** island group S Indonesia
175 N14 **Kangean, Pulau** island Kepulauan Kangean, S Indonesia
69 U8 **Kangen** *var.* Kangken. ↗ SE Sudan
207 Q15 **Kangerttittivaq** *Dan.* Scoresby Sund. *fjord* E Greenland
178 H2 **Kangfang** Kachin State, N Myanmar
176 Z13 **Kanggup** Irian Jaya, E Indonesia
169 X12 **Kanggye** var. Kanggyä. N North Korea
207 P15 **Kangikajik** *var.* Kap Brewster. headland E Greenland
11 N5 **Kangiqsualujjuaq** prev. George River, Port-Nouveau-Québec. Québec, E Canada
10 L2 **Kangiqsujuaq** prev. Maricourt, Wakeham Bay. Québec, E Canada
10 M4 **Kangirsuk** prev. Bellin, Payne. Québec, E Canada
164 J15 **Kangmar** Xizang Zizhiqu, W China
164 M16 **Kangmar** Xizang Zizhiqu, W China
169 Y14 **Kangnŭng** Jap. Kōryō. NE South Korea
81 D18 **Kango** Estuaire, NW Gabon
158 I7 **Kāngra** Himāchal Pradesh, NW India
159 O19 **Kangsabati Reservoir** ☒ NE India
165 O17 **Kangto** ▲ China/India
165 W12 **Kang Xian** var. Zuitaizi. Gansu, C China
177 Ff4 **Kani** Sagaing, C Myanmar
78 M15 **Kani** NW Ivory Coast
81 M23 **Kaniama** Shaba, S Zaire
Kanibadam see Konibodom
175 O2 **Kanibongan** Sabah, East Malaysia
193 F17 **Kaniere** West Coast, South Island, NZ
193 G17 **Kaniere, Lake** ☒ South Island, NZ
196 E17 **Kanifaay** Yap, W Micronesia
129 O4 **Kanin Kamen'** ▲ NW Russian Federation
129 N3 **Kanin Nos** Nenetskiy Avtonomnyy Okrug, NW Russian Federation
129 N3 **Kanin Nos, Mys** headland NW Russian Federation
129 O3 **Kanin, Poluostrov** peninsula NW Russian Federation
145 V8 **Kānī Sakht** E Iraq
143 T5 **Kānī Sulaymān** N Iraq
172 N8 **Kanita** Aomori, Honshū, C Japan
119 Q5 **Kaniv** Rus. Kanëv. Cherkas'ka Oblast', C Ukraine
190 K11 **Kaniva** Victoria, SE Australia
119 Q5 **Kaniv's'ke Vodoskhovyshche** Rus. Kanevskoye Vodokhranilishche. ☒ C Ukraine
114 L4 **Kanjiža** Ger. Altkanischa, Hung. Magyarkanizsa, Okanizsa; prev. Stara Kanjiža. Serbia, N Yugoslavia
95 K18 **Kankaanpää** Turku-Pori, SW Finland
32 M12 **Kankakee** Illinois, N USA
33 O11 **Kankakee River** ↗ Illinois/Indiana, N USA
78 N14 **Kankan** Haute-Guinée, E Guinea
160 K13 **Kānker** Madhya Pradesh, C India
78 J10 **Kankossa** Assaba, S Mauritania
178 Gg13 **Kanmaw Kyun** var. Kisseraing, Kitharang; island Mergui Archipelago, S Myanmar
170 E13 **Kanmuri-yama** ▲ Kyūshū, SW Japan
23 R10 **Kannapolis** North Carolina, SE USA
95 L16 **Kannonkoski** Keski-Suomi, C Finland
Kannur see Cannanore
95 K15 **Kannus** Vaasa, W Finland
79 V13 **Kano** Kano, N Nigeria
79 V13 **Kano** ◆ state N Nigeria
79 V13 **Kano** ↗ Kano, N Nigeria
170 F14 **Kan'onji** var. Kanonzi. Kagawa, Shikoku, SW Japan
Kanonzi see Kan'onji
28 M5 **Kanopolis Lake** ☒ Kansas, C USA
38 K5 **Kanosh** Utah, W USA
175 N10 **Kanowit** Sarawak, East Malaysia
170 Bb17 **Kanoya** Kagoshima, Kyūshū, SW Japan
158 H8 **Kānpur** Eng. Cawnpore. Uttar Pradesh, N India
Kanrach see Kandrách
171 Gg15 **Kansai** ✕ (Ōsaka) Ōsaka, Honshū, SW Japan
29 R9 **Kansas** Oklahoma, C USA
28 L5 **Kansas** off. State of Kansas; also known as Jayhawker State, Sunflower State. ◆ state C USA
29 R4 **Kansas City** Kansas, C USA
29 R3 **Kansas City** Missouri, C USA
29 R3 **Kansas City** ✕ Missouri, C USA
29 P4 **Kansas River** ↗ Kansas, C USA
126 I14 **Kansk** Krasnoyarskiy Kray, S Russian Federation
Kansu see Gansu
153 V7 **Kant** Chuyskaya Oblast', N Kyrgyzstan
Kantalahti see Kandalaksha
178 Gg16 **Kantang** var. Ban Kantang. Trang, SW Thailand
115 H25 **Kántanos** Kríti, Greece, E Mediterranean Sea

79 R12 **Kantchari** E Burkina
Kanté see Kandé
Kantemir see Cantemir
130 L9 **Kantemirovka** Voronezhskaya Oblast', W Russian Federation
178 J11 **Kantharalak** Si Sa Ket, E Thailand
Kantipur see Kathmandu
41 Q9 **Kantishna River** ↗ Alaska, USA
171 K16 **Kantō** physical region Honshū, SW Japan
203 S3 **Kanton** var. Abariringa, Canton Island; prev. Mary Island. atoll Phoenix Islands, C Kiribati
171 Jj15 **Kantō-sanchi** ▲ Honshū, S Japan
99 C20 **Kanturk** Ir. Ceann Toirc. SW Ireland
57 T11 **Kanuku Mountains** ▲ S Guyana
171 Kk15 **Kanuma** Tochigi, Honshū, S Japan
85 H20 **Kanye** Southern, SE Botswana
85 I14 **Kanyu** Ngamiland, C Botswana
177 G7 **Kanyutkwin** Pegu, C Myanmar
81 M24 **Kanzenze** Shaba, SE Zaire
200 Ss13 **Kao** island Kotu Group, W Tonga
167 S14 **Kaohsiung** var. Gaoxiong, Jap. Takao, Takow. S Taiwan
167 S14 **Kaohsiung** ✕ S Taiwan
Kaokoana see Kirakira
85 B17 **Kaoko Veld** ▲ N Namibia
78 G11 **Kaolack** var. Kaolak. W Senegal
Kaolak see Kaolack
Kaolan see Lanzhou
195 W15 **Kaolo** San Jorge, N Solomon Islands
40 B8 **Kapaa** Haw. Kapa'a. Kauai, Hawaii, USA, C Pacific Ocean
115 J16 **Kapa Moračka** ▲ SW Yugoslavia
143 V13 **Kapan** Rus. Kafan; prev. Ghap'an. SE Armenia
84 L13 **Kapandashila** Northern, NE Zambia
81 L23 **Kapanga** Shaba, S Zaire
151 U15 **Kapchagay** Kaz. Kapshaghay. Almaty, SE Kazakhstan
151 V13 **Kapchagayskoye Vodokhranilishche** Kaz. Qapshagay Böyeni. ☒ SE Kazakhstan
101 F15 **Kapelle** Zeeland, SW Netherlands
101 G16 **Kapellen** Antwerpen, N Belgium
97 P15 **Kapellskär** Stockholm, C Sweden
83 H18 **Kapenguria** Rift Valley, W Kenya
111 V6 **Kapfenberg** Steiermark, C Austria
85 J14 **Kapiri Mposhi** Central, C Zambia
155 R4 **Kāpīsā** ◆ province E Afghanistan
192 K13 **Kapiti Island** island C NZ
80 K9 **Kapka, Massif du** ▲ E Chad
Kaplamada see Kaubalatmada, Gunung
24 I9 **Kaplan** Louisiana, C USA
152 E9 **Kaplangky, Plato** ridge Turkmenistan/Uzbekistan
113 D19 **Kaplice** Ger. Kaplitz. Jižní Čechy, S Czech Republic
Kaplitz see Kaplice
Kapoche see Capoche
176 U10 **Kapocol** Irian Jaya, E Indonesia
178 Gg14 **Kapoe** Ranong, SW Thailand
83 S13 **Kapoeta** Eastern Equatoria, SE Sudan
113 I25 **Kapos** ↗ S Hungary
113 H22 **Kaposvár** Somogy, SW Hungary
96 H13 **Kapp** Oppland, S Norway
102 I7 **Kappeln** Schleswig-Holstein, N Germany
111 P7 **Kaprun** Salzburg, C Austria
Kapshaghay see Kapchagay
Kapstad see Cape Town
Kapsukas see Marijampolė
176 Yy10 **Kaptiau** Irian Jaya, E Indonesia
121 L19 **Kaptsevichy** Rus. Koptsevichi. Homyel'skaya Voblasts', SE Belarus
Kapuas Hulu, Banjaran/Kapuas Hulu, Pegunungan see Kapuas Mountains
174 M7 **Kapuas Mountains** Ind. Banjaran Kapuas Hulu, Pegunungan Kapuas Hulu. ▲ Indonesia/Malaysia
174 Kk8 **Kapuas, Sungai** ↗ Borneo, N Indonesia
175 N10 **Kapuas, Sungai** prev. Kapoeas. ↗ Borneo, C Indonesia
190 J9 **Kapunda** South Australia
158 H8 **Kapūrthala** Punjab, N India
175 L14 **Kapur Utara, Pegunungan** ▲ Jawa, S Indonesia
12 G12 **Kapuskasing** Ontario, S Canada
2 D6 **Kapuskasing** ↗ Ontario, S Canada
131 P11 **Kapustin Yar** Astrakhanskaya Oblast', SW Russian Federation
84 M11 **Kaputa** Northern, NE Zambia
113 G22 **Kapuvár** Győr-Moson-Sopron, NW Hungary
121 J17 **Kapyl'** Rus. Kopyl'. Minskaya Voblasts', C Belarus
45 N9 **Kara** var. Cara. Región Autónoma Atlántico Sur, SE Nicaragua
79 Q14 **Kara** ↗ N Togo
79 R14 **Kara** var. Lama-Kara. NE Togo
153 U7 **Kara-Balta** Chuyskaya Oblast', N Kyrgyzstan
151 P14 **Karabau** Atyrau, W Kazakhstan

152 E7 **Karabaur', Uval** Kaz. Korabawur Pastligi, Uzb. Qorabowur Kirlari. physical region Kazakhstan/Uzbekistan
152 L13 **Karabekaul** var. Garabekevyul, Turkm. Garabekewül. Lebapskiy Velayat, E Turkmenistan
152 K15 **Karabil', Vozvyshennost'** ▲ S Turkmenistan
152 A9 **Kara-Bogaz-Gol** var. Garabogaz. Balkanskiy Velayat, NW Turkmenistan
152 B9 **Kara-Bogaz-Gol, Zaliv** bay NW Turkmenistan
151 R15 **Karabogaz** Kaz. Qaraböget. Zhambyl, S Kazakhstan
142 H11 **Karabük** Zonguldak, N Turkey
152 Ii13 **Karabula** Krasnoyarskiy Kray, C Russian Federation
151 V14 **Karabulak** Kaz. Qarabulaq. Taldykorgan, SE Kazakhstan
151 Y11 **Karabulak** Kaz. Qarabulaq. Vostochnyy Kazakhstan, E Kazakhstan
151 Q17 **Karabulak** Kaz. Qarabulaq. Yuzhnyy Kazakhstan, S Kazakhstan
142 C17 **Kara Burnu** headland SW Turkey
150 K10 **Karabutak** Kaz. Qarabutaq. Aktyubinsk, W Kazakhstan
142 D12 **Karacabey** Bursa, NW Turkey
116 O12 **Karacaköy** İstanbul, NW Turkey
116 M12 **Karacaoğlan** Kırklareli, NW Turkey
Karachay-Cherkessia see Karachayevo-Cherkesskaya Respublika
130 L15 **Karachayevo-Cherkesskaya Respublika** Eng. Karachay-Cherkessia. ◆ autonomous republic SW Russian Federation
130 M15 **Karachayevsk** Karachayevo-Cherkesskaya Respublika, SW Russian Federation
130 J6 **Karachev** Bryanskaya Oblast', W Russian Federation
155 O16 **Karāchi** Sind, SE Pakistan
155 O16 **Karāchi** ✕ Sind, SE Pakistan
Karácsonkő see Piatra-Neamţ
161 E15 **Karād** Mahārāshtra, W India
142 H16 **Karadağ** ▲ S Turkey
153 T10 **Karadar'ya** Uzb. Qoradaryo. ↗ Kyrgyzstan/Uzbekistan
Karadeniz see Black Sea
Karadeniz Boğazı see İstanbul Boğazı
152 B13 **Karadepe** Balkanskiy Velayat, W Turkmenistan
Karadzhar see Qorajar
Karaferiye see Véroia
152 E13 **Karagan** Turkm. Garagan. Akhalskiy Velayat, C Turkmenistan
151 R10 **Karaganda** Kaz. Qaraghandy. Karaganda, C Kazakhstan
151 R10 **Karaganda** off. Karagandinskaya Oblast', Kaz. Qaraghandy Oblysy. ◆ province C Kazakhstan
Karagandinskaya Oblast' see Karaganda
151 T10 **Karagayly** Kaz. Qaraghayly. Karaganda, C Kazakhstan
152 A11 **Karagel'** Turkm. Garagöl. Balkanskiy Velayat, W Turkmenistan
127 Pp8 **Karaginskiy, Ostrov** island E Russian Federation
207 T1 **Karaginskiy Zaliv** bay E Russian Federation
143 P13 **Karagöl Dağları** ▲ NE Turkey
116 I13 **Karahisar** Edirne, NW Turkey
131 V3 **Karaidel'** Respublika Bashkortostan, W Russian Federation
131 V3 **Karaidel'skiy** Respublika Bashkortostan, W Russian Federation
116 L13 **Karaademir Barajı** ☒ NW Turkey
161 J21 **Kāraikāl** Pondicherry, SE India
161 I22 **Kāraikkudi** Tamil Nādu, SE India
151 Y11 **Kara Irtysh** Rus. Chërnyy Irtysh. ↗ NE Kazakhstan
149 N5 **Karaj** Tehrān, N Iran
174 H5 **Karak** Pahang, Peninsular Malaysia
Karak see Al Karak
153 T11 **Kara-Kabak** Oshskaya Oblast', SW Kyrgyzstan
152 D12 **Kara-Kala** var. Garrygala. Balkanskiy Velayat, W Turkmenistan
Karakala see Oqqal'a
Karakalpakstan, Respublika see Qoraqalpoghiston Respublikasi
Karakalpakya see Qoraqalpoghiston
Karak, Muḩāfaz̧at see Al Karak
Kara-Köl see Kara-Kul'
153 T12 **Karakol** prev. Przheval'sk. Issyk-Kul'skaya Oblast', NE Kyrgyzstan
153 X8 **Karakol** var. Karakolka. Issyk-Kul'skaya Oblast', NE Kyrgyzstan
Karakolka see Karakol
155 W2 **Karakoram Highway** road China/Pakistan
155 Z3 **Karakoram Pass** Chin. Karakoram Shankou. pass C Asia
158 I3 **Karakoram Shankou** see Karakoram Pass
Karaköse see Ağrı
151 P14 **Karakoyyn, Ozero** Kaz. Qaraqoyyn. ☒ C Kazakhstan
85 J9 **Karakubis** Ghanzi, C Botswana

153 T9 **Kara-Kul'** Kir. Kara-Köl. Dzhalal-Abadskaya Oblast', W Kyrgyzstan
Karakul' see Qarokŭl, Tajikistan
Karakul' see Qorakŭl, Uzbekistan
83 E22 **Karema** Rukwa, W Tanzania
Karen see Hualien
178 Gg8 **Karen State** var. Kawthule State, Kayin State. ◆ S Myanmar
94 J10 **Karesuando** Lapp. Kaaresuanto. Norrbotten, N Sweden
Karet see Kâghet
Kareyz-e-Elyäs/Kärez Iliäs see Käriz-e Elyäs
126 Gg12 **Kargasok** Tomskaya Oblast', C Russian Federation
126 Gg14 **Kargat** Novosibirskaya Oblast', C Russian Federation
142 J11 **Kargı** Çorum, N Turkey
158 I5 **Kargil** Jammu and Kashmir, NW India
128 L11 **Kargopol'** Arkhangel'skaya Oblast', NW Russian Federation
112 F12 **Kargowa** Ger. Unruhstadt. Zielona Góra, W Poland
79 X13 **Kari** Bauchi, E Nigeria
85 J15 **Kariba** Mashonaland West, N Zimbabwe
85 J16 **Kariba, Lake** ☒ Zambia/Zimbabwe
172 Nn5 **Kariba-yama** ▲ Hokkaidō, NE Japan
85 C19 **Karibib** Erongo, C Namibia
Karies see Karyés
94 L9 **Karigasniemi** Lapp. Garegeasnjárga. Lappi, N Finland
172 P6 **Karikachi-tōge** pass Hokkaidō, NE Japan
192 J2 **Karikari, Cape** headland North Island, NZ
Karimäbäd see Hunza
174 K10 **Karimata, Kepulauan** island group N Indonesia
174 K9 **Karimata, Pulau** island Kepulauan Karimata, N Indonesia
174 K10 **Karimata, Selat** strait W Indonesia
174 L13 **Karimunjawa, Pulau** island S Indonesia
161 I14 **Karīmnagar** Andhra Pradesh, C India
82 N12 **Karin** Woqooyi Galbeed, N Somalia
Kariot see Ikaría
95 L20 **Karis** Fin. Karjaa. Uusimaa, SW Finland
Káristos see Kárystos
154 J4 **Käriz-e Elyäs** var. Kareyz-e-Elyäs, Kärez Iliäs. Herät, NW Afghanistan
Karjaa see Karis
95 M19 **Kärkölä** Häme, S Finland
190 G9 **Karkoo** South Australia
120 D5 **Kärla** Saaremaa, W Estonia
Karleby see Kokkola
112 F7 **Karlino** Ger. Körlin an der Persante. Koszalin, NW Poland
Karlö see Hailuoto
Karl-Marx-Stadt see Chemnitz
114 C10 **Karlobag** Ger. Carlopago. Lika-Senj, W Croatia
114 D9 **Karlovac** Ger. Karlstadt, Hung. Károlyváros. Karlovac, C Croatia
114 C9 **Karlovac** ◆ province C Croatia
Karlovačka Županija see Karlovac
116 I9 **Karlovo** prev. Levskigrad. Plovdivska Oblast', C Bulgaria
113 A16 **Karlovy Vary** Ger. Karlsbad; prev. Carlsbad. Západní Čechy, W Czech Republic
97 L17 **Karlsborg** Skaraborg, S Sweden
97 L22 **Karlshamn** Blekinge, S Sweden
97 M22 **Karlskrona** Blekinge, S Sweden
103 G21 **Karlsruhe** var. Carlsruhe. Baden-Württemberg, SW Germany
97 K15 **Karlstad** Värmland, C Sweden
31 R3 **Karlstad** Minnesota, N USA
103 L18 **Karlstadt** Bayern, C Germany
Karlstadt see Karlovac
41 Q8 **Karluk** Kodiak Island, Alaska, USA
Karluk see Qarluq
121 O17 **Karma** Rus. Korma. Homyel'skaya Voblasts', SE Belarus
144 G6 **Karmi'el** var. Carmiel. Northern, N Israel
97 B16 **Karmøy** island S Norway
158 E14 **Karnāl** Haryāna, N India
159 W15 **Karnaphuli Reservoir** ☒ NE India
161 F17 **Karnātaka** var. Kanara; prev. Maisur, Mysore. ◆ state W India
27 S13 **Karnes City** Texas, SW USA

128 I10 **Kareliya, Respublika** prev. Karel'skaya ASSR, Eng. Karelia. ◆ autonomous republic NW Russian Federation
Karel'skaya ASSR see Kareliya, Respublika
153 U10 **Kara-Kul'dzha** Oshskaya Oblast', SW Kyrgyzstan
Karakul', Ozero see Qarokŭl
Kara Kum see Garagumy
Kara Kum Canal/Karakumskiy Kanal see Garagumskiy Kanal
Karakumy, Peski see Garagumy
85 E17 **Karakuwisa** Okavango, NE Namibia
126 Jj14 **Karakwia** Irkutskaya Oblast', S Russian Federation
175 N13 **Karamain, Pulau** island N Indonesia
142 I16 **Karaman** Karaman, S Turkey
142 H16 **Karaman** ◆ province S Turkey
116 M8 **Karamandere** ↗ N Bulgaria
164 J4 **Karamay** var. Karamai, Kelamayi, prev. Chin. K'o-la-ma-i. Xinjiang Uygur Zizhiqu, NW China
175 Nn11 **Karambu** Borneo, N Indonesia
193 H14 **Karamea** West Coast, South Island, NZ
193 H14 **Karamea** ↗ South Island, NZ
193 G15 **Karamea Bight** gulf South Island, NZ
152 L14 **Karamet-Niyaz** Turkm. Garamätbyyaz. Lebapskiy Velayat, E Turkmenistan
164 K10 **Karamiran He** ↗ NW China
176 Yy11 **Karamor, Pengunungan** ▲ Irian Jaya, E Indonesia
153 S11 **Karamyk** Oshskaya Oblast', SW Kyrgyzstan
175 Nn11 **Karangasem** Bali, S Indonesia
160 H12 **Karanja** Mahārāshtra, C India
158 F9 **Karanpur** var. Karanpura. Rājasthān, NW India
Karanpura see Karanpur
Karánsebes/Karansebesch see Caransebeș
151 T14 **Karaoy** Kaz. Qaraoy. Almaty, SE Kazakhstan
116 N7 **Karapelit** Rom. Stejarul. Varnenska Oblast, NE Bulgaria
142 I15 **Karapınar** Konya, C Turkey
85 D22 **Karas** ◆ district S Namibia
153 Y8 **Kara-Say** Issyk-Kul'skaya Oblast', SW Kyrgyzstan
85 C22 **Karasburg** Karas, S Namibia
Kara Sea see Karskoye More
Kara Su see Mesta/Néstos
151 N8 **Karasu** Kaz. Qarasū. Kustanay, N Kazakhstan
142 F11 **Karasu** Sakarya, NW Turkey
Karasubazar see Bilohirs'k
125 Q12 **Karasuk** Novosibirskaya Oblast', C Russian Federation
94 K9 **Karasjok** Fin. Kaarasjoki. Finnmark, N Norway
94 K9 **Karasjokka** ↗ N Norway
Kara Strait see Karskiye Vorota, Proliv
151 U13 **Karatal** Kaz. Qaratal. ↗ SE Kazakhstan
142 K17 **Karataş** Adana, S Turkey
151 Q16 **Karatau** Kaz. Qarataū. Zhambyl, S Kazakhstan
151 P16 **Karatau, Khrebet** var. Karatau, Kaz. Qarataū. ▲ S Kazakhstan
150 G13 **Karaton** Atyrau, W Kazakhstan
170 C12 **Karatsu** var. Karatu. Saga, Kyūshū, SW Japan
Karatu see Karatsu
126 Hh7 **Karaul** Taymyrskiy (Dolgano-Nenetskiy) Avtonomnyy Okrug, N Russian Federation
Karaulbazar see Qorowulbozor
Karauzyak see Qorauzak
117 D16 **Kárava** ▲ C Greece
117 F22 **Karavás** Kýthira, S Greece
115 J20 **Karavastasë, Laguna e** var. Kënet' e Karavastasë, Karavasta Lagoon. lagoon W Albania
Karavasta Lagoon see Karavastasë, Laguna e
174 Ii14 **Karawang** prev. Krawang. Jawa, C Indonesia
111 T11 **Karawanken** Slvn. Karavanke. ▲ Austria/Yugoslavia
143 N12 **Karayazı** Erzurum, NE Turkey
151 Q12 **Karazhal** Zhezkazgan, C Kazakhstan
145 S9 **Karbalā'** var. Kerbala, Kerbela. S Iraq
97 M14 **Kärböle** Gävleborg, C Sweden
113 M22 **Karcag** Jász-Nagykun-Szolnok, E Hungary
116 N7 **Kardam** Varnenska Oblast, NE Bulgaria
Kardak see Imia
117 M22 **Kardámaina** Kos, Dodekánisos, Greece, Aegean Sea
Kardamila see Kardámyla
117 L18 **Kardámyla** var. Kardamila, Kardhámila. Chíos, SE Greece
Kardeljevo see Ploče
Kardh see Qardho
Kardhámila see Kardámyla
Kardhítsa see Kardítsa
117 E16 **Kardítsa** var. Kardhítsa. Thessalía, C Greece
120 E4 **Kärdla** Ger. Kertel. Hiiumaa, W Estonia
121 I16 **Kärelichy** Pol. Korelicze, Rus. Korelichi. Hrodzyenskaya Voblasts', W Belarus

111 P9 **Karnische Alpen** It. Alpi Carniche. ▲ Austria/Italy
116 M9 **Karnobat** Burgaska Oblast, E Bulgaria
111 Q9 **Kärnten** off. Land Kärnten, Eng. Carinthia, Slvn. Koroška. ◆ state S Austria
Karnul see Kurnool
85 K16 **Karoi** Mashonaland West, N Zimbabwe
Karol see Carei
Károly-Fehérvár see Alba Iulia
Károlyváros see Karlovac
84 M12 **Karonga** Northern, N Malawi
153 W10 **Karool-Tëbë** Narynskaya Oblast', C Kyrgyzstan
190 I9 **Karoonda** South Australia
155 S9 **Karor** Punjab, E Pakistan
175 P10 **Karossa** Sulawesi, C Indonesia
Karpasía/Karpas Peninsula see Kárpasía
Karpaten see Carpathian Mountains
117 L22 **Karpáthio Pélagos** sea Dodekánisos, Greece, Aegean Sea
117 N24 **Kárpathos** Kárpathos, SE Greece
117 N24 **Kárpathos** It. Scarpanto; anc. Carpathos, Carpathus. island SE Greece
Kárpathos Strait see Karpathou, Stenó
117 N24 **Karpathou, Stenó** var. Karpathos Strait, Scarpanto Strait. strait Dodekánisos, Greece, Aegean Sea
Karpaty see Carpathian Mountains
117 E17 **Karpenísi** prev. Karpenísion. Stereá Ellás, C Greece
Karpenísion see Karpenísi
129 O8 **Karpogory** Arkhangel'skaya Oblast', NW Russian Federation
188 I7 **Karratha** Western Australia
143 S12 **Kars** var. Qars. Kars, NE Turkey
143 S12 **Kars** ◆ province NE Turkey
151 O12 **Karsakpay** Kaz. Qarsaqbay. Zhezkazgan, C Kazakhstan
95 L19 **Kärsämäki** Oulu, C Finland
120 K9 **Kärsava** var. Karsau; prev. Rus. Korsovka. Ludza, E Latvia
Karsau see Kärsava
152 A9 **Karshi** Turkm. Garshy. Balkanskiy Velayat, NW Turkmenistan
Karshi see Qarshi
Karshinskaya Step see Qarshi Chŭli
Karshinskiy Kanal see Qarshi Kanali
86 I5 **Karskiye Vorota, Proliv** Eng. Kara Strait. strait N Russian Federation
126 Gg5 **Karskoye More** Eng. Kara Sea. sea Arctic Ocean
95 L17 **Karstula** Länsi-Suomi, C Finland
125 Q5 **Karsun** Ul'yanovskaya Oblast', W Russian Federation
125 E12 **Kartaly** Chelyabinskaya Oblast', C Russian Federation
20 E13 **Karthaus** Pennsylvania, NE USA
112 H7 **Kartuzy** Gdańsk, NW Poland
172 N10 **Karumai** Iwate, Honshū, C Japan
189 U4 **Karumba** Queensland, NE Australia
148 L10 **Kārūn, Rūd-e** var. Rūd-e Kārūn. ↗ SW Iran
Kārūn, Rūd-e see Kārūn
94 K13 **Karungi** Norrbotten, N Sweden
94 K13 **Karunki** Lappi, N Finland
161 H21 **Kārūr** Tamil Nādu, SE India
95 K17 **Karvia** Turku-Pori, SW Finland
113 J17 **Karviná** Ger. Karwin, Pol. Karwina; prev. Nová Karvinná. Severní Morava, E Czech Republic
161 E17 **Kärwär** Karnātaka, W India
110 M7 **Karwendelgebirge** ▲ Austria/Germany
Karwin/Karwina see Karviná
117 I22 **Karyés** var. Karies. Ágion Óros, N Greece
126 Kk16 **Karymskoye** Chitinskaya Oblast', S Russian Federation
117 I19 **Kárystos** var. Káristos. Évvoia, C Greece

142 E17 **Kaş** Antalya, SW Turkey
41 Y14 **Kasaan** Prince of Wales Island, Alaska, USA
170 I20 **Kasai** Hyōgo, Honshū, SW Japan
81 K21 **Kasai** var. Cassai, Kassai. ↗ Angola/Zaire
81 K22 **Kasai Occidental** off. Région Kasai Occidental. ◆ region S Zaire
81 L21 **Kasai Oriental** off. Région Kasai Oriental. ◆ region S Zaire
81 J24 **Kasaji** Shaba, S Zaire
171 Kk16 **Kasama** Ibaraki, Honshū, S Japan
85 L14 **Kasama** Northern, N Zambia
85 H16 **Kasane** Chobe, NE Botswana
83 G22 **Kasanga** Rukwa, W Tanzania
81 G21 **Kasangulu** Bas-Zaire, W Zaire
161 E20 **Kāsaragod** Kerala, SW India
150 P13 **Kasari** var. Kasari Jõgi, Ger. Kasargen. ↗ W Estonia
Kasargen/Kasari Jõgi see Kasari
15 K9 **Kasba Lake** ☒ Northwest Territories, NE Canada
Kaschau see Košice
170 Bb16 **Kaseda** Kagoshima, Kyūshū, SW Japan
85 K9 **Kasempa** North Western, NW Zambia
81 O24 **Kasenga** Shaba, SE Zaire

◆ COUNTRY   ◇ DEPENDENT TERRITORY   ◆ ADMINISTRATIVE REGION   ▲ MOUNTAIN   ▲ VOLCANO   ☒ LAKE
● COUNTRY CAPITAL   ○ DEPENDENT TERRITORY CAPITAL   ✕ INTERNATIONAL AIRPORT   ▲ MOUNTAIN RANGE   ↗ RIVER   ☒ RESERVOIR

81 P17 **Kasenye** *var.* Kasenyi. Haut-Zaïre, NE Zaire
   Kasenyi *see* Kasenye
83 E18 **Kasese** SW Uganda
81 O19 **Kasese** Maniema, E Zaire
158 J11 **Käsganj** Uttar Pradesh, N India
149 U4 **Kashaf Rūd** ≈ NE Iran
149 N7 **Kāshān** Eşfahān, C Iran
130 M10 **Kashary** Rostovskaya Oblast', SW Russian Federation
41 O12 **Kashegelok** Alaska, USA
   Kashgar *see* Kashi
164 E7 **Kashi** *Chin.* Kaxgar, K'o-shih, *Uigh.* Kaxgar. Xinjiang Uygur Zizhiqu, NW China
171 Gg16 **Kashihara** *var.* Kashihara. Nara, Honshū, SW Japan
171 Kk17 **Kashima** Ibaraki, Honshū, S Japan
170 C13 **Kashima** *var.* Kasima. Saga, Kyūshū, SW Japan
171 L16 **Kashima-nada** *gulf* S Japan
128 K15 **Kashin** Tverskaya Oblast', W Russian Federation
158 K10 **Kāshīpur** Uttar Pradesh, N India
130 L4 **Kashira** Moskovskaya Oblast', W Russian Federation
171 K17 **Kashiwa** *var.* Kasiwa. Chiba, Honshū, S Japan
171 Jj13 **Kashiwazaki** *var.* Kasiwazaki. Niigata, Honshū, C Japan
   Kashkadar'inskaya Oblast' *see* Qashqadaryo Wiloyati
149 T5 **Kāshmar** *var.* Turshiz; *prev.* Solţānābād, Torshiz. Khorāsān, NE Iran
   Kashmir *see* Jammu and Kashmir
155 R12 **Kashmor** Sind, SE Pakistan
155 S5 **Kashmūnd Ghar** *Eng.* Kashmund Range. ▲ E Afghanistan
   Kashmund Range *see* Kashmūnd Ghar
   Kasi *see* Vārānasi
159 O12 **Kasia** Uttar Pradesh, N India
41 N2 **Kasigluk** Alaska, USA
   Kasihara *see* Kashihara
41 R12 **Kasilof** Alaska, USA
   Kasima *see* Kashima
   Kasimköj *see* General Toshevo
130 M4 **Kasimov** Ryazanskaya Oblast', W Russian Federation
81 P18 **Kasindi** Nord Kivu, E Zaire
175 S8 **Kasiruta, Pulau** *island* Kepulauan Bacan, E Indonesia
84 M12 **Kasitu** ≈ N Malawi
176 V12 **Kasiui, Pulau** *island* Kepulauan Watubela, E Indonesia
   Kasiwa *see* Kashiwa
   Kasiwazaki *see* Kashiwazaki
32 L14 **Kaskaskia River** ≈ Illinois, N USA
95 J17 **Kaskinen** *Swe.* Kaskö. Vaasa, W Finland
   Kaskö *see* Kaskinen
   Kas Kong *see* Kŏng, Kaôh
9 O17 **Kaslo** British Columbia, SW Canada
   Käsmark *see* Kežmarok
174 M10 **Kasongan** Borneo, C Indonesia
81 N21 **Kasongo** Maniema, E Zaire
81 H22 **Kasongo-Lunda** Bandundu, SW Zaire
117 M24 **Kásos** *island* S Greece
   Kasos Strait *see* Kasou, Stenó
117 M25 **Kasou, Stenó** *var.* Kasos Strait. *strait* Dodekánisos/Kríti, Greece, Aegean Sea
143 T10 **Kaspi** C Georgia
116 M8 **Kaspichan** Varnenska Oblast, NE Bulgaria
   Kaspiy Mangy Oypaty *see* Caspian Depression
131 Q16 **Kaspiysk** Respublika Dagestan, SW Russian Federation
   Kaspiyskiy *see* Lagan'
   Kaspiyskoye More/Kaspiy Tengizi *see* Caspian Sea
   Kassa *see* Košice
   Kassai *see* Kasai
82 I9 **Kassala** Kassala, E Sudan
82 I9 **Kassala** ◆ *state* NE Sudan
117 G15 **Kassándra** *prev.* Pallíni; *anc.* Pallene. *peninsula* NE Greece
117 G15 **Kassándras, Ákra** *headland* N Greece
117 H15 **Kassándras, Kólpos** *var.* Kólpos Toronaíos. *gulf* N Greece
145 Y11 **Kassárah** E Iraq
103 J15 **Kassel** *prev.* Cassel. Hessen, C Germany
76 M6 **Kasserine** *var.* Al Qaşrayn. W Tunisia
12 J14 **Kasshabog Lake** ◎ Ontario, SE Canada
145 O5 **Kassir, Sabkhat al** ◎ E Syria
31 W10 **Kasson** Minnesota, N USA
117 C18 **Kastaniés** Kentriki Makedonía, N Greece
117 C18 **Kastélli** Kríti, Greece, E Mediterranean Sea
   Kastellórizon *see* Megísti
97 N21 **Kastlösa** Kalmar, S Sweden
117 D14 **Kastoría** Dytiki Makedonía, N Greece
130 K7 **Kastornoye** Kurskaya Oblast', W Russian Federation
117 I21 **Kástro** Sífnos, Kykládes, Greece, Aegean Sea
97 J17 **Kastrup** ✈ (København) København, E Denmark
121 O18 **Kastsyukovichy** *Rus.* Kostyukovichi. Mahilyowskaya Voblasts', E Belarus

121 O18 **Kastsyukowka** *Rus.* Kostyukovka. Homyel'skaya Voblasts', SE Belarus
170 Cc12 **Kasuga** Fukuoka, Kyūshū, SW Japan
171 I15 **Kasugai** Aichi, Honshū, SW Japan
83 E21 **Kasulu** Kigoma, W Tanzania
171 Gg13 **Kasumi** Hyōgo, Honshū, SW Japan
171 Kk16 **Kasumiga-ura** ◎ Honshū, S Japan
131 R17 **Kasumkent** Respublika Dagestan, SW Russian Federation
84 M13 **Kasungu** Central, C Malawi
155 W9 **Kasūr** Punjab, E Pakistan
85 G15 **Kataba** Western, W Zambia
21 R4 **Katahdin, Mount** ▲ Maine, NE USA
81 M20 **Katako-Kombe** Kasai Oriental, C Zaire
41 T12 **Katalla** Alaska, USA
   Katana *see* Qatanā
126 J12 **Katanga** ≈ C Russian Federation
160 J11 **Katāngi** Madhya Pradesh, C India
188 J13 **Katanning** Western Australia
   Katawaz *see* Zarghūn Shahr
157 Q22 **Katchall** *island* Nicobar Islands, India, NE Indian Ocean
117 F14 **Kateríni** Kentriki Makedonía, N Greece
119 P7 **Katerynopil'** Cherkas'ka Oblast', C Ukraine
178 Gg3 **Katha** Sagaing, N Myanmar
189 P2 **Katherine** Northern Territory, N Australia
160 B11 **Kāthiāwār Peninsula** *peninsula* W India
159 P11 **Kathmandu** *prev.* Kantipur. ● (Nepal) Central, C Nepal
158 H7 **Kathua** Jammu and Kashmir, NW India
78 L12 **Kati** Koulikoro, SW Mali
159 R13 **Katihār** Bihār, NE India
192 N7 **Katikati** Bay of Plenty, North Island, NZ
85 H16 **Katima Mulilo** Caprivi, NE Namibia
79 N15 **Katiola** Ivory Coast
203 V10 **Katiu** *atoll* Îles Tuamotu, C French Polynesia
119 N22 **Katlabukh, Ozero** ◎ SW Ukraine
41 P14 **Katmai, Mount** ▲ Alaska, USA
160 J9 **Katni** Madhya Pradesh, C India
117 D19 **Káto Achaïa** *var.* Kato Ahaia. Dytiki Ellás, S Greece
   Kató Akhaía/Káto Akhaía *see* Káto Achaïa
124 Nn3 **Kato Lakatámeia** *var.* Kato Lakatamia. C Cyprus
   Kato Lakatamia *see* Kato Lakatámeia
81 N22 **Katompi** Shaba, SE Zaire
85 A14 **Katondwe** Lusaka, C Zambia
116 H12 **Káto Nevrokópi** *prev.* Káto Nevrokópion. Anatolikí Makedonía kai Thráki, NE Greece
   Káto Nevrokópion *see* Káto Nevrokópi
83 E18 **Katonga** ≈ S Uganda
117 F15 **Káto Ólympos** ▲ C Greece
117 D17 **Katoúna** Dytiki Ellás, C Greece
117 E19 **Káto Vlasií** Dytiki Makedonía, S Greece
113 J16 **Katowice** *Ger.* Kattowitz. Katowice, S Poland
113 I16 **Katowice** *off.* Województwo Katowickie, *Ger.* Kattowitz. ◆ *province* S Poland
   Katowickie, Województwo *see* Katowice
159 S15 **Kātoya** West Bengal, NE India
142 E16 **Katrançik Daği** ▲ SW Turkey
97 N16 **Katrineholm** Södermanland, C Sweden
98 I11 **Katrine, Loch** ◎ C Scotland, UK
79 V12 **Katsina** Katsina, N Nigeria
79 U12 **Katsina** ◆ *state* N Nigeria
79 P8 **Katsina Ala** ≈ S Nigeria
170 C11 **Katsumoto** Nagasaki, Iki, SW Japan
171 I16 **Katsuta** *var.* Katuta. Ibaraki, Honshū, S Japan
171 K17 **Katsuura** *var.* Katuura. Chiba, Honshū, S Japan
171 I14 **Katsuyama** *var.* Katuyama. Fukui, Honshū, SW Japan
170 Ff13 **Katsuyama** Okayama, Honshū, SW Japan
   Kattakurgan *see* Kattaqūrghon
153 N11 **Kattaqūrghon** *Rus.* Kattakurgan. Samarqand Wiloyati, C Uzbekistan
117 O23 **Kattavía** Ródos, Dodekánisos, Greece, Aegean Sea
97 I21 **Kattegat** *Dan.* Kattegatt. *strait* N Europe
   Kattegatt *see* Kattegat
97 P19 **Katthammarsvik** Gotland, SE Sweden
   Kattowitz *see* Katowice
127 N17 **Katun'** ≈ S Russian Federation
   Katuta *see* Katsuta
   Katuura *see* Katsuura
   Katuyama *see* Katsuyama
164 D7 **Katwa** ≈ NW China
164 J5 **Kax He** ≈ NW China
79 P12 **Kaya** C Burkina
121 O16 **Kayah State** ◆ *state* C Myanmar
126 J7 **Kayak Taymyrskiy (Dolgano-Nenetskiy) Avtonomnyy Okrug, N Russian Federation
41 T12 **Kayak Island** *island* Alaska, USA
116 M11 **Kayankulam** ≈ NW Turkey
179 G10 **Kayan, Sungai** ≈ Borneo, C Indonesia
175 N6 **Kayan, Sungai** *prev.* Kajan. ≈ Borneo, C Indonesia
150 J14 **Kaydak, Sor** *salt flat* SW Kazakhstan
8 K13 **Kaydanovo** *see* Dzyarzhynsk

103 I15 **Kaufungen** Hessen, C Germany
95 K17 **Kauhajoki** Vaasa, W Finland
95 K16 **Kauhava** Vaasa, W Finland
32 M7 **Kaukauna** Wisconsin, N USA
94 L11 **Kaukonen** Lappi, N Finland
40 A8 **Kaulakahi Channel** *channel* Hawaii, USA, C Pacific Ocean
40 E9 **Kaumakakai** Molokai, Hawaii, USA, C Pacific Ocean
40 F12 **Kauna Point** *headland* Hawaii, USA, C Pacific Ocean
120 F13 **Kaunas** *Ger.* Kauen, *Pol.* Kowno; *prev.* Rus. Kovno. Kaunas, C Lithuania
194 H10 **Kaup** East Sepik, NW PNG
79 U12 **Kaura Namoda** Sokoto, NW Nigeria
95 K16 **Kaustinen** Vaasa, W Finland
175 T7 **Kau, Teluk** *bay* Pulau Halmahera, E Indonesia
94 M10 **Kautokeino** Finnmark, N Norway
115 P19 **Kavadarci** *Turk.* Kavadar. S FYR Macedonia
   Kavaja *see* Kavajë
115 K20 **Kavajë** *It.* Cavaia, Kavaja. Tiranë, W Albania
117 F14 **Kavak Çayı** ≈ NW Turkey
116 I13 **Kavála** *prev.* Kaválla. Anatolikí Makedonía kai Thráki, NE Greece
116 I13 **Kaválas, Kólpos** *gulf* Aegean Sea, NE Greece
72 Nn17 **Kavalerovo** Primorskiy Kray, SE Russian Federation
161 J17 **Kāvali** Andhra Pradesh, E India
   Kaválla *see* Kavála
161 C21 **Kavango** *see* Cubango/Okavango
161 C21 **Kavaratti** Lakshadweep, SW India
116 O8 **Kavarna** Varnenska Oblast, NE Bulgaria
120 G12 **Kavarskas** Anykščiai, E Lithuania
   Kavengo *see* Cubango/Okavango
161 F20 **Kāveri** *var.* Cauvery. ≈ S India
195 N9 **Kavieng** *var.* Kaewieng. NE PNG
85 H16 **Kavimba** Chobe, NE Botswana
175 U15 **Kavkaz** *see* Caucasus
97 K23 **Kävlinge** Malmöhus, S Sweden
197 I15 **Kavukavu Reef** *var.* Kavanlik. Beqa Barrier Reef, Cakaubalavu Reef. *reef* Viti Levu, SW Fiji
84 G12 **Kavungo** Moxico, E Angola
171 M10 **Kawabe** Akita, Honshū, C Japan
171 K15 **Kawagoe** Saitama, Honshū, S Japan
171 J16 **Kawaguchi** *var.* Kawaguti. Saitama, Honshū, S Japan
   Kawaguti *see* Kawaguchi
172 N11 **Kawai** Iwate, Honshū, C Japan
40 A8 **Kawaihoa Point** *headland* Niihau, Hawaii, USA, C Pacific Ocean
192 K3 **Kawakawa** Northland, North Island, NZ
84 J13 **Kawama** North Western, NW Zambia
84 L11 **Kawambwa** Luapula, N Zambia
170 F14 **Kawanoe** Ehime, Shikoku, SW Japan
160 K11 **Kawardha** Madhya Pradesh, C India
12 J14 **Kawartha Lakes** ◎ Ontario, SE Canada
171 K17 **Kawasaki** Kanagawa, Honshū, S Japan
175 T9 **Kawassi** Pulau Obi, E Indonesia
172 N8 **Kawauchi** Aomori, Honshū, C Japan
192 L5 **Kawau Island** *island* N NZ
192 N10 **Kaweka Range** ▲ North Island, NZ
40 A10 **Kawelecht** *see* Puhja
81 K22 **Kawenda** Kasai Occidental, S Zaire
192 O8 **Kawerau** Bay of Plenty, North Island, NZ
120 J2 **Kawhia** Waikato, North Island, NZ
192 K8 **Kawhia Harbour** *inlet* North Island, NZ
37 V5 **Kawich Peak** ▲ Nevada, W USA
37 V9 **Kawich Range** ▲ Nevada, W USA
12 G12 **Kawigamog Lake** ◎ Ontario, S Canada
175 Rr3 **Kawio, Kepulauan** *island group* N Indonesia
178 Gg9 **Kawkareik** Karen State, S Myanmar
40 F11 **Kaw Lake** ◎ Oklahoma, C USA
177 N3 **Kawlin** Sagaing, N Myanmar
   Kawm Umbū *see* Kôm Ombo
   Kawthule State *see* Karen State
39 N10 **Kaxgar** *see* Kashi
31 O16 **Kéamu** *see* Anatom
38 L3 **Kearney** Nebraska, C USA
37 H20 **Kearns** Utah, W USA
143 O14 **Kéas, Stenó** *strait* SE Greece
143 O14 **Keban** C Turkey
41 T12 **Kebbi** ◆ *state* NW Nigeria
79 S13 **Kebbi** ◆ *state* NW Nigeria
78 G10 **Kébémèr** NW Senegal
76 M7 **Kebili** *var.* Qibli. C Tunisia
144 H4 **Kebir, Nahr el** ≈ NW Syria
82 A10 **Kebkabiya** Northern Darfur, W Sudan
33 R8 **Kebnekaise** ▲ N Sweden
149 N11 **Kāzerūn** Färs, S Iran
129 R12 **Kazhym** Respublika Komi, NW Russian Federation
   Kazi Ahmad *see* Qāzi Ahmad
   Kazi Magomed *see* Qazimämmäd
142 H16 **Kazımkarabekir** Karaman, S Turkey
113 M20 **Kazincbarcika** Borsod-Abaúj-Zemplén, NE Hungary
121 J17 **Kazlowshchyna** *Pol.* Kozlowszczyzna, *Rus.* Kozlovshchina. Hrodzyenskaya Voblasts', W Belarus
121 E14 **Kazlų Rūda** Marijampolė, S Lithuania
150 E9 **Kaztalovka** Zapadnyy Kazakhstan, W Kazakhstan

39 N9 **Kayenta** Arizona, SW USA
78 J11 **Kayes** Kayes, W Mali
78 J11 **Kayes** ◆ *region* SW Mali
151 U10 **Kaynar** *var.* Kajnar. Semipalatinsk, E Kazakhstan
   Kaynary *see* Căinari
85 H15 **Kayoya** Western, W Zambia
79 S13 **Kayrakkum** *see* Qayroqqum
   Kayrakkumskoye Vodokhranilishche *see* Qayroqqum, Obanbori
142 K14 **Kayseri** *var.* Kaisaria; *anc.* Caesarea Mazaca, Mazaca. Kayseri, C Turkey
142 K14 **Kayseri** ◆ *province* C Turkey
38 L2 **Kaysville** Utah, W USA
126 Hh8 **Kayyerkan** Taymyrskiy (Dolgano-Nenetskiy) Avtonomnyy Okrug, N Russian Federation
   Kayyngdy *see* Kaindy
12 L11 **Kazabazua** Québec, SE Canada
12 L12 **Kazabazua** ≈ Québec, SE Canada
126 M7 **Kazach'ye** Respublika Sakha (Yakutiya), NE Russian Federation
   Kazakdar'ya *see* Qozoqdar'ya
152 E9 **Kazakhlyshor, Solonchak** *var.* Solonchak Shorkazakhly. *salt marsh* NW Kazakhstan
   Kazakhskaya SSR/Kazakh Soviet Socialist Republic *see* Kazakhstan
151 R9 **Kazakhskiy Melkosopochnik** *Eng.* Kazakh Uplands, Kirghiz Steppe, *Kaz.* Saryarqa. *uplands* C Kazakhstan
150 L12 **Kazakhstan** *off.* Republic of Kazakhstan, *var.* Kazakstan, *Kaz.* Qazaqstan, Qazaqstan Respublikasy; *prev.* Kazakh Soviet Socialist Republic, *Rus.* Kazakhskaya SSR. ◆ *republic* C Asia
   Kazakh Uplands *see* Kazakhskiy Melkosopochnik
131 I25 **Kazakhstan** *var.* Kazalinsk. Kzyl-Orda, S Kazakhstan
131 N4 **Kazan'** Respublika Tatarstan, W Russian Federation
131 R4 **Kazan'** ✕ Respublika Tatarstan, W Russian Federation
15 K8 **Kazan** ≈ Northwest Territories, NW Canada
   Kazandzhik *see* Gazandzhyk
119 R8 **Kazanka** Mykolayivs'ka Oblast', S Ukraine
   Kazanketken *see* Qizqetkan
116 J9 **Kazanlŭk** *prev.* Kazanlik. Khaskovska Oblast, C Bulgaria
172 N11 **Kazan-rettō** *Eng.* Volcano Islands. *island group* SE Japan
125 F22 **Kazanskoye** Tyumenskaya Oblast', C Russian Federation
119 V12 **Kazantip, Mys** *headland* S Ukraine
153 U9 **Kazarman** Narynskaya Oblast', C Kyrgyzstan
   Kazatin *see* Kozyatyn
143 R8 **Kazbegi** *see* Kazbek
   Kazbegi *see* Qazbegi
143 T9 **Kazbek** *var.* Kazbegi, *Geor.* Mqinvartsveri. ▲ N Georgia
84 M13 **Kazembe** Eastern, NE Zambia
149 N11 **Kāzerūn** Färs, S Iran

39 U5 **Kelvington** Saskatchewan, S Canada
188 I8 **Kenneth Range** ▲ Western Australia
29 V9 **Kennett** Missouri, C USA
20 I16 **Kennett Square** Pennsylvania, NE USA
34 M7 **Kennewick** Washington, NW USA
10 E11 **Kenogami** ≈ Ontario, S Canada
13 Q7 **Kénogami, Lac** ◎ Québec, SE Canada
12 F7 **Kenogami Lake** Ontario, S Canada
8 I6 **Kenogamissi Lake** ◎ Ontario, S Canada
10 A11 **Kenora** Ontario, S Canada
33 N9 **Kenosha** Wisconsin, N USA
1 P14 **Kensington** Prince Edward Island, SE Canada
28 L3 **Kensington** Kansas, C USA
26 J9 **Kent** Oregon, NW USA
34 H11 **Kent** Washington, NW USA
99 P22 **Kent** *cultural region* SE England, UK
151 P16 **Kentau** Yuzhnyy Kazakhstan, S Kazakhstan
191 H14 **Kent Group** *island group* Tasmania, SE Australia
33 N12 **Kentland** Indiana, N USA
33 N13 **Kenton** Ohio, N USA
15 J4 **Kent Peninsula** *peninsula* Northwest Territories, N Canada
117 F14 **Kentriki Makedonía** ◆ *region* N Greece
22 J6 **Kentucky** *off.* Commonwealth of Kentucky; also known as The Bluegrass State. ◆ *state* C USA
22 M9 **Kentucky Lake** ◎ Kentucky/Tennessee, S USA
   Kentung *see* Keng Tung
1 P15 **Kentville** Nova Scotia, SE Canada
24 K8 **Kentwood** Louisiana, S USA
33 P9 **Kentwood** Michigan, N USA
83 H17 **Kenya** *off.* Republic of Kenya. ◆ *republic* E Africa
   Kenya, Mount *see* Kirinyaga
174 Hh3 **Kenyir, Tasik** *var.* Tasek Kenyir. ◆ Peninsular Malaysia
31 W10 **Kenyon** Minnesota, N USA
31 Y6 **Keokuk** Iowa, C USA
   Keonjiharjarh *see* Kendujhargarh
   Kéos *see* Kéa
31 X16 **Keosauqua** Iowa, C USA
31 X15 **Keota** Iowa, C USA
23 O11 **Keowee, Lake** ◎ South Carolina, SE USA
128 I7 **Kepa** *var.* Kepe. Respublika Kareliya, NW Russian Federation
   Kepe *see* Kepa
201 O13 **Kepirohi Falls** *waterfall* Pohnpei, E Micronesia
193 B22 **Kepler Mountains** ▲ South Island, NZ
113 I14 **Kepno** Kalisz, C Poland
67 C24 **Keppel Island** *island* N Falkland Islands
67 C24 **Keppel Sound** *sound* N Falkland Islands
142 D12 **Kepsut** Balikesir, NW Turkey
176 W12 **Kerai** Irian Jaya, E Indonesia
161 F22 **Kerak** *see* Al Karak
161 I21 **Kerala** ◆ *state* S India
194 H10 **Keram** ≈ N PNG
172 O14 **Kerama-rettō** *island group* SW Japan
191 N10 **Kerang** Victoria, SE Australia
117 H19 **Keratéa** *var.* Keratea. Attikí, C Greece
95 M19 **Kerava** *Swe.* Kervo. Uusimaa, S Finland
   Kerbala/Kerbela *see* Karbalā'
119 W12 **Kerch** *Rus.* Kerch'. Respublika Krym, SE Ukraine
   Kerchens'ka Protska/Kerchenskiy Proliv *see* Kerch Strait
119 V13 **Kerchens'ka Pyvostriv** *peninsula* S Ukraine
124 R4 **Kerch Strait** *var.* Bosporus Cimmerius, Enikale Strait, *Rus.* Kerchenskiy Proliv, *Ukr.* Kerchens'ka Protska. *strait* Black Sea/Sea of Azov
158 K8 **Kerdārnāth** Uttar Pradesh, N India
   Kerdilio *see* Kerdýlio
116 H13 **Kerdýlio** *var.* Kerdilio. ▲ N Greece
194 H14 **Kerema** Gulf, S PNG
   Keremitlik *see* Lyulyakovo
142 H9 **Kerempe Burnu** *headland* N Turkey
84 K9 **Keren** *var.* Cheren. E Eritrea
192 M6 **Kerepehi** Waikato, North Island, NZ
151 T19 **Kerey, Ozero** ◎ C Kazakhstan
69 I8 **Kergel** *see* Kézdi
181 S11 **Kerguelen** *island* C French Southern and Antarctic Territories
181 Q13 **Kerguelen Plateau** *undersea feature* S Indian Ocean
117 C20 **Keri** Zákynthos, Iónioi Nísoi, Greece, C Mediterranean Sea
83 H19 **Kericho** Rift Valley, W Kenya
192 K2 **Kerikeri** Northland, North Island, NZ
95 N18 **Kerimäki** Mikkeli, SE Finland
174 Gg10 **Kerinci, Danau** ◎ Sumatera, W Indonesia
174 Gg9 **Kerinci, Gunung** ▲ Sumatera, W Indonesia
   Keriya *see* Yutian
164 H9 **Keriya He** ≈ NW China

100 J9 **Kerkbuurt** Noord-Holland, C Netherlands

100 J13 **Kerkdriel** Gelderland, C Netherlands

77 N6 **Kerkenah, Îles de** *var.* Kerkenna Islands, *Ar.* Juzur Qarqannah. *island group* E Tunisia

Kerkenna Islands *see* Kerkenah, Îles de

117 M20 **Kerketévs** ▲ Sámos, Dodekánisos, Greece, Aegean Sea

31 T8 **Kerkhoven** Minnesota, N USA

152 M14 **Kerki** Lebapskiy Velayat, E Turkmenistan

152 M14 **Kerkichi** Lebapskiy Velayat, E Turkmenistan

117 F16 **Kerkíneo** *prehistoric site* Thessalía, C Greece

116 G12 **Kerkinitis, Límni** ⊜ N Greece

101 M18 **Kerkira** *see* Kérkyra

Kerkrade Limburg, SE Netherlands

Kerkuk *see* Kirkūk

117 B16 **Kérkyra** × Kérkyra, Iónioi Nísoi, Greece, C Mediterranean Sea

117 B16 **Kérkyra** *var.* Kérkira, *Eng.* Corfu. Kérkyra, Iónioi Nísoi, Greece, C Mediterranean Sea

117 A16 **Kérkyra** *var.* Kérkira, *Eng.* Corfu. *island* Iónioi Nísoi, Greece, C Mediterranean Sea

199 Jj12 **Kermadec Islands** *island group* NZ, SW Pacific Ocean

183 R10 **Kermadec Ridge** *undersea feature* SW Pacific Ocean

183 R11 **Kermadec Trench** *undersea feature* SW Pacific Ocean

149 S10 **Kermān** *var.* Kirman; *anc.* Carmana. Kermān, C Iran

149 R11 **Kermān** *off.* Ostān-e Kermān, *var.* Kirman; *anc.* Carmania. ◆ *province* SE Iran

149 U12 **Kermān, Biābān-e** *var.* Kerman Desert. *desert* SE Iran

149 Q9 **Kermānshāh** Yazd, C Iran

148 J6 **Kermānshāh** *off.* Ostān-e Kermānshāhān; *prev.* Bākhtarān. ◆ *province* W Iran

116 L10 **Kermen** Burgaska Oblast, E Bulgaria

26 L8 **Kermit** Texas, SW USA

23 P6 **Kermit** West Virginia, NE USA

23 S9 **Kernersville** North Carolina, SE USA

37 S12 **Kern River** ↔ California, W USA

37 S12 **Kernville** California, W USA

117 K21 **Kéros** *island* Kykládes, Greece, Aegean Sea

78 M14 **Kérouané** Haute-Guinée, SE Guinea

103 D16 **Kerpen** Nordrhein-Westfalen, W Germany

152 I11 **Kerpichli** Lebapskiy Velayat, NE Turkmenistan

26 M1 **Kerrick** Texas, SW USA

Kerr Lake *see* John H.Kerr Reservoir

9 S15 **Kerrobert** Saskatchewan, S Canada

27 Q11 **Kerrville** Texas, SW USA

99 B20 **Kerry** *Ir.* Ciarraí. *cultural region* SW Ireland

23 S11 **Kershaw** South Carolina, SE USA

Kertel *see* Kärdla

97 H23 **Kerteminde** Fyn, C Denmark

169 Q7 **Kerulen** *Chin.* Herlen He, *Mong.* Herlen Gol. ↔ China/Mongolia

Kervo *see* Kerava

Kerýneia *see* Girne

10 H11 **Kesagami Lake** ⊜ Ontario, SE Canada

95 O17 **Kesälahti** Pohjois-Karjala, SE Finland

142 B11 **Keşan** Edirne, NW Turkey

171 Mm12 **Kesennuma** Miyagi, Honshū, C Japan

169 V7 **Keshan** Heilongjiang, NE China

32 M6 **Keshena** Wisconsin, N USA

142 I13 **Keskin** Kırıkkale, C Turkey

95 L17 **Keski-Suomi** *Swe.* Mellersta Finland. ◆ *province* C Finland

Késmárk *see* Kežmarok

128 I6 **Kesten'ga** *var.* Kest Enga. Respublika Kareliya, NW Russian Federation

100 K12 **Kesteren** Gelderland, C Netherlands

12 H4 **Keswick** Ontario, S Canada

99 K15 **Keswick** NW England, UK

113 H24 **Keszthely** Zala, SW Hungary

126 Ih13 **Ket'** ↔ C Russian Federation

79 R17 **Keta** SE Ghana

174 Kk10 **Ketapang** Borneo, C Indonesia

131 O10 **Ketchenery** *prev.* Sovetskoye. Respublika Kalmykiya, SW Russian Federation

41 Y14 **Ketchikan** Revillagigedo Island, Alaska, USA

35 O14 **Ketchum** Idaho, NW USA

Kete/Kete Krakye *see* Kete-Krachi

79 Q15 **Kete-Krachi** *var.* Kete, Kete Krakye. E Ghana

100 L9 **Ketelmeer** *channel* E Netherlands

155 P17 **Keti Bandar** Sind, SE Pakistan

151 W16 **Ketmen', Khrebet** ▲ SE Kazakhstan

79 S16 **Kétou** SE Benin

112 M7 **Ketrzyn** *Ger.* Rastenburg. Olsztyn, NE Poland

99 O20 **Kettering** C England, UK

31 R13 **Kettering** Ohio, N USA

20 F13 **Kettle Creek** ↔ Pennsylvania, NE USA

34 L7 **Kettle Falls** Washington, NW USA

12 D16 **Kettle Point** *headland* Ontario, S Canada

31 N10 **Kettle River** ↔ Minnesota, N USA

194 E12 **Ketu** ↔ W PNG

---

20 G10 **Keuka Lake** ⊜ New York, NE USA

Keupriya *see* Primorsko

95 L17 **Keuruu** Keski-Suomi, C Finland

Kevevára *see* Kovin

94 L9 **Kevo** *Lapp.* Geavvú. Lappi, N Finland

46 M6 **Kew** North Caicos, N Turks and Caicos Islands

32 K11 **Kewanee** Illinois, N USA

33 N7 **Kewaunee** Wisconsin, N USA

32 M3 **Keweenaw Bay** ⊘ Michigan, N USA

33 N2 **Keweenaw Peninsula** *peninsula* Michigan, N USA

33 N2 **Keweenaw Point** *headland* Michigan, N USA

31 N12 **Keya Paha River** ↔ Nebraska/South Dakota, N USA

155 T10 **Khānewal** Punjab, NE Pakistan

155 S10 **Khāngarh** Punjab, E Pakistan

Khaniá *see* Chaniá

Khanka *see* Khonqa

169 Z8 **Khanka, Lake** *var.* Hsing-k'ai Hu, Lake Hanka, *Chin.* Xingkai Hu, *Rus.* Ozero Khanka. ⊜ China/Russian Federation

Khanka, Ozero *see* Khanka, Lake

Khankendi *see* Xankändi

Khanlar *see* Xanlar

126 Kk10 **Khannya** ↔ NE Russian Federation

155 S12 **Khānpur** Punjab, SE Pakistan

155 S12 **Khānpur** Punjab, E Pakistan

144 I4 **Khān Shaykhūn** *var.* Khan Sheikhun. Idlib, NW Syria

Khan Sheikhun *see* Khān Shaykhūn

151 S15 **Khantau** Zhambyl, S Kazakhstan

151 W16 **Khan Tengri, Pik** ▲ SE Kazakhstan

178 J9 **Khanthabouli** *prev.* Savannakhét, Savannakhét, S Laos

125 Ff10 **Khanty-Mansiysk** *prev.* Ostyako-Vogul'sk. Khanty-Mansiyskiy Avtonomnyy Okrug, C Russian Federation

129 V8 **Khanty-Mansiyskiy Avtonomnyy Okrug** ◆ *autonomous district* C Russian Federation

145 R4 **Khānūqah** C Iraq

144 E11 **Khān Yūnis** *var.* Khān Yūnus. S Gaza Strip

Khān Yūnus *see* Khān Yūnis

Khanzi *see* Ghanzi

145 V5 **Khān Zūr** E Iraq

178 H10 **Khao Laem Reservoir** ⊟ W Thailand

126 Kk17 **Khapcheranga** Chitinskaya Oblast', S Russian Federation

131 Q12 **Kharabali** Astrakhanskaya Oblast', SW Russian Federation

159 R16 **Kharagpur** West Bengal, NE India

145 V11 **Khārān** *var.* Khārān, Khāran, Khaur. C Iran

149 Q8 **Khārānaq** Yazd, C Iran

Kharbin *see* Harbin

152 H13 **Khardzhagaz** Akhalskiy Velayat, C Turkmenistan

158 M13 **Khārga Oasis** *see* Great Oasis, The

160 F11 **Khargon** Madhya Pradesh, C India

126 K16 **Kharilok** Chitinskaya Oblast', S Russian Federation

126 K16 **Khilok** ↔ S Russian Federation

130 K3 **Khimki** Moskovskaya Oblast', W Russian Federation

153 S12 **Khingou** Rus. Obi-Khingou. ↔ C Tajikistan

Khíos *see* Chíos

155 R15 **Khipro** Sind, SE Pakistan

145 S10 **Khirr, Wādī al** *dry watercourse* S Iraq

116 I11 **Khisarya** Plovdivska Oblast, C Bulgaria

Khiva *see* Khiwa

152 M9 **Khiwa** *Rus.* Khiva. Khorazm Wiloyati, W Uzbekistan

76 F7 **Khouribga** C Morocco

153 Q13 **Khovaling** *Rus.* Khavaling. SW Tajikistan

168 L6 **Khovd** *see* Hovd

178 G16 **Khlong Thom** Krabi, SW Thailand

178 I12 **Khlung** Chantaburi, S Thailand

Khmel'nik *see* Khmil'nyk

121 N20 **Khmel'nitskaya Oblast'** *see* Khmel'nyts'ka Oblast'

Khmel'nitskiy *see* Khmel 'nyts'kyy

118 K5 **Khmel'nyts'ka Oblast'** *var.* Khmel'nyts'kyy, *Rus.* Khmel'nitskaya Oblast'; *prev.* Kamenets-Podol'skaya Oblast'. ◆ *province* W Ukraine

Khmel 'nyts'kyy *see* Khmel'nyts'kyy

118 K5 **Khmel 'nyts'kyy** *Rus.* Khmel'nik; *prev.* Proskurov. Khmel'nyts'ka Oblast', W Ukraine

Khmel'nyts'kyy *see* Khmel'nyts'kyy

178 J10 **Khmuang** Nan Ubon Ratchathani, E Thailand

Khudal *see* Khādhil

155 V12 **Khudian** Punjab, E Pakistan

131 N8 **Khudzhand** *see* Khujand

---

126 J7 **Khatanga** Taymyrskiy (Dolgano-Nenetskiy) Avtonomnyy Okrug, N Russian Federation

126 J7 **Khatanga** ↔ N Russian Federation

128 H15 **Khatanga, Gulf of** *see* Khatangskiy Zaliv

Khandaparha *prev.* Khandpara. Orissa, E India

Khandpara *see* Khandaparha

155 T2 **Khandūd** *var.* Khandud, Wakhan. Badakhshān, NE Afghanistan

160 G11 **Khandwa** Madhya Pradesh, C India

126 Mm10 **Khandyga** Respublika Sakha (Yakutiya), NE Russian Federation

147 W7 **Khatmat al Malāḥah** N Oman

149 S16 **Khatmat al Malāḥah** Ash Shāriqah, E UAE

Khatoûniyé *see* Khātūnīyah

127 Q6 **Khatyrka** Chukotskiy Avtonomnyy Okrug, NE Russian Federation

152 I14 **Khauz-Khan** *Turkm.* Hanhowuz. Akhalskiy Velayat, S Turkmenistan

152 I14 **Khauzkhanskoye Vodokhranilishche** ⊟ S Turkmenistan

Khavaling *see* Khovaling

Khavast *see* Khowos

145 W10 **Khawrah, Nahr al** ↔ S Iraq

147 W7 **Khawr Barakah** *see* Baraka

147 W7 **Khawr Fakkān** *var.* Khor Fakkan. Ash Shāriqah, NE UAE

146 L6 **Khaybar** Al Madīnah, NW Saudi Arabia

Khaybar, Kowtal-e *see* Khyber Pass

153 S11 **Khaydarkan** *var.* Khaydarken. Oshskaya Oblast', SW Kyrgyzstan

Khaydarken *see* Khaydarkan

127 N8 **Khaypudyrskaya Guba** *bay* NW Russian Federation

145 S1 **Khayrūzuk** E Iraq

127 Nn16 **Khazar, Bahr-e/Khazar, Daryā-ye** *see* Caspian Sea

Khazarosp *see* Hazorasp

Khazretishi, Khrebet *see* Hazratishoh, Qatorkūhi

Khelat *see* Kalāt

76 F6 **Khemisset** NW Morocco

178 J10 **Khemmarat** *var.* Kemarat. Ubon Ratchathani, E Thailand

76 L6 **Khenchela** *var.* Khenchla. NE Algeria

Khenchla *see* Khenchela

76 G7 **Khénifra** C Morocco

119 R10 **Khersān, Rūd-e** *see* Garm, Āb-e

119 R10 **Kherson** Khersons'ka Oblast', S Ukraine

Kherson *see* Khersons'ka Oblast'

119 S14 **Kherson, Mys** *Mys* Khersonesskiy. *headland* S Ukraine

151 W15 **Khorgos** Taldykorgan, S Kazakhstan

126 K16 **Khorinsk** Respublika Buryatiya, S Russian Federation

85 C18 **Khorixas** Kunene, NW Namibia

147 O17 **Khormaksar** *var.* Aden. × ('Adan) SW Yemen

Khormal *see* Khurmal

Khormuj *see* Khvormūj

Khorog *see* Khorugh

119 S5 **Khorol** Poltavs'ka Oblast', NE Ukraine

148 L7 **Khorramābād** *var.* Khurramabad. Lorestān, W Iran

148 K10 **Khorramshahr** *var.* Khurramshahr, Muhammerah; *prev.* Mohammerah. Khūzestān, SW Iran

153 S14 **Khorugh** *Rus.* Khorog. S Tajikistan

131 Q12 **Khosheutovo** Astrakhanskaya Oblast', SW Russian Federation

Khotan *see* Hotan

126 K16 **Khotimsk** *see* Khotsimsk

127 R16 **Khotsimsk** *Rus.* Khotimsk. Mahilyowskaya Voblasts', E Belarus

118 K7 **Khotyn** *Rom.* Hotin, *Rus.* Khotin. Chernivets'ka Oblast', W Ukraine

76 F7 **Khouribga** C Morocco

---

178 Hh10 **Khok Samrong** Lop Buri, C Thailand

155 P2 **Kholm** *var.* Tashqurghan, *Pash.* Khulm. Balkh, N Afghanistan

Kholm *see* Chełm

Kholmech *see* Kholmyech

127 Oo16 **Kholmsk** Ostrov Sakhalin, Sakhalinskaya Oblast', SE Russian Federation

121 O19 **Kholmyech** *Rus.* Kholmech. Homyel'skaya Voblasts', SE Belarus

Kholopenichi *see* Khalopyenichy

85 D19 **Khomas** ◆ *district* C Namibia

85 D19 **Khomas Hochland** *var.* Khomasplato. *plateau* C Namibia

Khomasplato *see* Khomas Hochland

148 M7 **Khomein** *see* Khomeyn

Khomeini, Khumain. Markazi, W Iran

149 N8 **Khomeynīshahr** *prev.* Homāyūnshahr. Eşfahān, C Iran

Khoms *see* Al Khums

178 I9 **Khong Sedone** *see* Muang Khôngxédôn

178 I9 **Khon Kaen** *var.* Muang Khon Kaen. Khon Kaen, E Thailand

152 I9 **Khonqa** *Rus.* Khanka. Khorazm Wiloyati, W Uzbekistan

178 I9 **Khon San** Khon San, E Thailand

127 N8 **Khonuu** Respublika Sakha (Yakutiya), NE Russian Federation

131 N8 **Khopër** *var.* Khoper. ↔ SW Russian Federation

127 Nn16 **Khor** Khabarovskiy Kray, SE Russian Federation

127 Nn16 **Khor** ↔ SE Russian Federation

149 S16 **Khorāsān** *off.* Ostān-e Khorāsān, *var.* Khorassan, Khurasan. ◆ *province* NE Iran

Khorassan *see* Khorāsān

152 H9 **Khorat** *see* Nakhon Ratchasima

152 H9 **Khorazm Wiloyati** *Rus.* Khorezmskaya Oblast'. ◆ *province* W Uzbekistan

160 O13 **Khordha** *prev.* Khurda. Orissa, E India

129 U4 **Khorey-Ver** Nenetskiy Avtonomnyy Okrug, NW Russian Federation

Khorezmskaya Oblast' *see* Khorazm Wiloyati

Khor Fakkan *see* Khawr Fakkān

---

155 W2 **Khunjeráb Pass** *Chin.* Kunjirap Daban. *pass* China/Pakistan *see also* Kunjirap Daban

159 P16 **Khunti** Bihār, N India

178 Gg7 **Khun Yuam** Mae Hong Son, NW Thailand

Khurais *see* Khurayş

Khurasan *see* Khorāsān

147 R7 **Khurayş** *var.* Khurais. Ash Sharqīyah, C Saudi Arabia

Khurda *see* Khordha

158 I11 **Khurja** Uttar Pradesh, N India

145 V4 **Khurmal** *var.* Khormal. NE Iraq

Khurramabad *see* Khorramābād

Khurramshahr *see* Khorramshahr

82 D11 **Khuwei** Western Kordofan, C Sudan

Khust *Cz.* Chust, *Hustê, Hung.* Huszt. Zakarpats'ka Oblast', W Ukraine

155 U7 **Khushāb** Punjab, NE Pakistan

118 H8 **Khust** *Cz.* Chust, *Hustê, Hung.* Huszt. Zakarpats'ka Oblast', W Ukraine

155 O13 **Khuzdār** Baluchistān, SW Pakistan

148 L9 **Khūzestān** *off.* Ostān-e Khūzestān, *var.* Khuzistan; *prev.* Arabistan, *anc.* Susiana. ◆ *province* SW Iran

126 Jj15 **Khuzhir** Respublika Buryatiya, S Russian Federation

Khuzistan *see* Khūzestān

155 R2 **Khvājeh Ghār** *var.* Khwajaghar, Khwaja-i-Ghar. Takhār, NE Afghanistan

131 Q7 **Khvalynsk** Saratovskaya Oblast', W Russian Federation

149 N12 **Khvormūj** *var.* Khormuj. Būshehr, S Iran

148 I2 **Khvoy** *var.* Khoi, Khoy. Āzarbāyjān-e Bākhtarī, NW Iran

Khwajaghar/Khwaja-i-Ghar *see* Khvājeh Ghār

155 S5 **Khyber Pass** *var.* Kowtal-e Khaybar. *pass* Afghanistan/Pakistan

195 V14 **Kia** Santa Isabel, N Solomon Islands

179 R17 **Kiama** Mindanao, S Philippines

191 S10 **Kiama** New South Wales, SE Australia

29 Q12 **Kiamichi Mountains** ▲ Oklahoma, C USA

29 Q12 **Kiamichi River** ↔ Oklahoma, C USA

Kiamusze *see* Jiamusi

41 N7 **Kiana** Alaska, USA

126 K16 **Kiangmai** *see* Chiang Mai

Kiang-ning *see* Nanjing

Kiangsi *see* Jiangxi

Kiangsu *see* Jiangsu

83 I21 **Kibali** ↔ NE Dem. Rep. Congo

95 M14 **Kiantajärvi** ⊜ E Finland

117 F19 **Kiáto** *prev.* Kiáton. Pelopónnisos, S Greece

69 T9 **Kibali** *var.* Uele (upper course). ↔ NE Zaire

81 M17 **Kibangou** Le Niari, SW Congo

97 F22 **Kibæk** Ringkøbing, W Denmark

81 N20 **Kibondo** Maniema, E Zaire

83 N21 **Kibondo** Kigoma, NW Tanzania

83 J15 **Kibre Mengist** *var.* Adola. S Ethiopia

81 E20 **Kibungo** *var.* Kibungu. SE Rwanda

Kibungu *see* Kibungo

115 N19 **Kičevo** SW FYR Macedonia

129 P13 **Kichmengskiy Gorodok** Vologodskaya Oblast', NW Russian Federation

31 N9 **Kickapoo River** ↔ Wisconsin, N USA

9 P16 **Kicking Horse Pass** *pass* Alberta/British Columbia, SW Canada

79 Q8 **Kidal** Kidal, C Mali

79 Q8 **Kidal** ◆ *region* NE Mali

99 L20 **Kidderminster** C England, UK

78 I11 **Kidira** E Senegal

192 O11 **Kidnappers, Cape** *headland* North Island, NZ

102 J8 **Kiel** Schleswig-Holstein, N Germany

113 L15 **Kielce** *Rus.* Keltsy. Kielce, SE Poland

113 L15 **Kielce** *off.* Województwo Kieleckie, *Rus.* Keltsy. ◆ *province* SE Poland

Kieleckie, Województwo *see* Kielce

102 J7 **Kieler Förde** *inlet* N Germany

81 N24 **Kienge** Shaba, SE Zaire

195 O12 **Kieta** Bougainville Island, NE PNG

Kiev *see* Kyyiv

Kiev Reservoir *see* Kyyivs'ke Vodoskhovyshche

78 H9 **Kiffa** Assaba, S Mauritania

117 H19 **Kifisós** ↔ C Greece

117 H19 **Kifisós** ↔ C Greece

145 U5 **Kifrī** N Iraq

83 I21 **Kigali** ● (Rwanda) C Rwanda

81 E20 **Kigali** × C Rwanda

143 P13 **Kiğı** Bingöl, E Turkey

83 I22 **Kigoma** Kigoma, W Tanzania

83 I22 **Kigoma** ◆ *region* W Tanzania

40 F10 **Kihei** *Haw.* Kihei. Maui, Hawaii, USA, C Pacific Ocean

95 K17 **Kihniö** Häme, SW Finland

---

120 F6 **Kihnu** *var.* Kihnu Saar, *Ger.* Kühnö. *island* SW Estonia

Kihnu Saar *see* Kihnu

40 A8 **Kii Landing** Niihau, Hawaii, USA, C Pacific Ocean

95 L14 **Kiiminki** Oulu, C Finland

171 H16 **Kii-Nagashima** *var.* Nagashima. Mie, Honshū, SW Japan

171 Gg16 **Kii-sanchi** ▲ Honshū, SW Japan

94 L11 **Kiistala** Lappi, N Finland

170 Fj16 **Kii-suidō** *strait* S Japan

172 R14 **Kikai-shima** *var.* Kikaiga-shima. *island* Nansei-shotō, SW Japan

114 M8 **Kikinda** *Ger.* Grosskikinda, *Hung.* Nagykikinda; *prev.* Velika Kikinda. Serbia, N Yugoslavia

Kikládhes *see* Kykládes

172 N7 **Kikori** Gulf, S PNG

194 H14 **Kikori** ↔ W PNG

170 C14 **Kikuchi** *var.* Kikuti. Kumamoto, Kyūshū, SW Japan

Kikuti *see* Kikuchi

131 N8 **Kikvidze** Volgogradskaya Oblast', SW Russian Federation

12 I10 **Kikwissi, Lac** ⊜ Québec, SE Canada

81 I21 **Kikwit** Bandundu, W Zaire

97 K15 **Kil** Värmland, C Sweden

97 G15 **Kila** Skaraborg, C Sweden

40 B8 **Kilauea** *Haw.* Kilauea. Kauai, Hawaii, USA, C Pacific Ocean

40 H12 **Kilauea Caldera** *crater* Hawaii, USA, C Pacific Ocean

111 V4 **Kilb** Niederösterreich, C Austria

41 O12 **Kilbuck Mountains** ▲ Alaska, USA

169 Y12 **Kilchu** NE North Korea

99 F18 **Kilcock** *Ir.* Cill Choca. E Ireland

191 V2 **Kilcoy** Queensland, E Australia

99 F18 **Kildare** *Ir.* Cill Dara. E Ireland

99 F18 **Kildare** *Ir.* Cill Dara. *cultural region* E Ireland

128 K2 **Kil'din, Ostrov** *island* NW Russian Federation

27 W7 **Kilgore** Texas, SW USA

Kilien Mountains *see* Qilian Shan

116 K19 **Kilifarevo** Loveshka Oblast, C Bulgaria

83 I25 **Kilifi** Coast, SE Kenya

201 U9 **Kili Island** *var.* Köle. *island* Ralik Chain, S Marshall Islands

83 J23 **Kilimanjaro** ◆ *region* E Tanzania

83 J23 **Kilimanjaro** *var.* Uhuru Peak. ▲ NE Tanzania

Kilimbangara *see* Kolombangara

Kilinailau Islands *see* Tulun Islands

83 K23 **Kilindoni** Pwani, E Tanzania

120 H6 **Kilingi-Nõmme** *Ger.* Kurkund. Pärnumaa, SW Estonia

142 M17 **Kilis** Gaziantep, S Turkey

119 N12 **Kiliya** *Rom.* Chilia-Nouă. Odes'ka Oblast', SW Ukraine

99 B19 **Kilkee** *Ir.* Cill Chaoi. W Ireland

99 E19 **Kilkenny** *Ir.* Cill Chainnigh. S Ireland

99 E19 **Kilkenny** *Ir.* Cill Chainnigh. *cultural region* S Ireland

99 C17 **Kilkieran Bay** *Ir.* Cuan Chill Chiaráin. *bay* W Ireland

116 G13 **Kilkís** Kentrikí Makedonía, N Greece

99 C15 **Killala Bay** *Ir.* Cuan Chill Ala. *inlet* NW Ireland

8 L13 **Killam** Alberta, SW Canada

191 U3 **Killarney** Queensland, E Australia

9 W16 **Killarney** Manitoba, S Canada

12 E11 **Killarney** Ontario, S Canada

99 B20 **Killarney** *Ir.* Cill Airne. SW Ireland

30 K4 **Killdeer** North Dakota, N USA

30 K4 **Killdeer Mountains** ▲ North Dakota, N USA

47 Q14 **Killdeer River** ↔ Trinidad, Trinidad and Tobago

27 S9 **Killeen** Texas, SW USA

20 F6 **Killik River** ↔ Alaska, USA

41 P4 **Killinek Island** ◆ Northwest Territories, NE Canada

117 C19 **Killínis, Ákra** *headland* S Greece

99 D15 **Killybegs** *Ir.* Na Cealla Beaga. NW Ireland

Kilmain *see* Quelimane

97 X4 **Kilmarnock** W Scotland, UK

23 X6 **Kilmarnock** Virginia, NE USA

129 S16 **Kil'mez'** Kirovskaya Oblast', NW Russian Federation

131 S2 **Kil'mez'** Udmurtskaya Respublika, NW Russian Federation

129 S16 **Kil'mez'** ↔ NW Russian Federation

69 V11 **Kilombero** ↔ S Tanzania

95 N15 **Kilpisjärvi** Lappi, N Finland

99 F18 **Kilrush** *Ir.* Cill Rois. W Ireland

81 I24 **Kilwa** Shaba, SE Zaire

Kilwa *see* Kilwa Kivinje

83 J24 **Kilwa Kivinje** *var.* Kilwa. Lindi, SE Tanzania

83 J24 **Kilwa Masoko** Lindi, SE Tanzania

176 Uu11 **Kimaan** *var.* Kimaam; *prev.* Kimaam. Irian Jaya, E Indonesia

176 Uu11 **Kimaam** *see* Kimaan

116 F12 **Kilyos** Istanbul, NW Turkey

37 V3 **Kim** Colorado, C USA

176 V15 **Kimanis, Teluk** *bay* Sabah, East Malaysia

190 H8 **Kimba** South Australia

31 O14 **Kimball** Nebraska, C USA

31 Q11 **Kimball** South Dakota, N USA

81 I21 **Kimbao** Bandundu, SW Zaire

195 N12 **Kimbe** New Britain, E PNG

◆ COUNTRY ◇ DEPENDENT TERRITORY ◆ ADMINISTRATIVE REGION ▲ MOUNTAIN × VOLCANO ⊜ LAKE
● COUNTRY CAPITAL ○ DEPENDENT TERRITORY CAPITAL × INTERNATIONAL AIRPORT ▲ MOUNTAIN RANGE ↔ RIVER ⊟ RESERVOIR

KIMBE BAY – KOETAI

195 *N11* **Kimbe Bay** *inlet* New Britain, E PNG
9 *P17* **Kimberley** British Columbia, SW Canada
85 *H23* **Kimberley** Northern Cape, C South Africa
188 *M4* **Kimberley Plateau** *plateau* Western Australia
35 *P15* **Kimberly** Idaho, NW USA
169 *Y12* **Kimch'aek** *prev.* Sŏngjin. E North Korea
169 *Y15* **Kimch'ŏn** C South Korea
169 *Z16* **Kim Hae** *var.* Pusan. ✈ (Pusan) SE South Korea
Kími *see* Kými
95 *K20* **Kimito** *Swe.* Kemiö. Turku-Pori, SW Finland
172 *O6* **Kimobetsu** Hokkaidō, NE Japan
117 *I21* **Kímolos** *island* Kykládes, Greece, Aegean Sea
117 *I21* **Kímolou Sífnou, Stenó** *strait* Kykládes, Greece, Aegean Sea
130 *L5* **Kimovsk** Tul'skaya Oblast', W Russian Federation
169 *X15* **Kimpo** ✈ (Sŏul) NW South Korea
Kimpolung *see* Câmpulung Moldovenesc
128 *K16* **Kimry** Tverskaya Oblast', W Russian Federation
81 *H21* **Kimvula** Bas-Zaïre, SW Zaire
175 *Nn2* **Kinabalu, Gunung** ▲ East Malaysia
Kinabatangan *see* Kinabatangan, Sungai
175 *Oo3* **Kinabatangan, Sungai** *var.* Kinabatangan. ≈ East Malaysia
117 *L21* **Kínaros** *island* Kykládes, Greece, Aegean Sea
9 *O15* **Kinbasket Lake** ⊠ British Columbia, SW Canada
98 *I7* **Kinbrace** N Scotland, UK
12 *E14* **Kincardine** Ontario, S Canada
98 *K10* **Kincardine** *cultural region* E Scotland, UK
81 *K21* **Kinda** Kasai Occidental, SE Zaire
81 *M24* **Kinda** Shaba, SE Zaire
177 *Ff3* **Kindat** Sagaing, N Myanmar
111 *V6* **Kindberg** Steiermark, C Austria
24 *H8* **Kinder** Louisiana, S USA
100 *H13* **Kinderdijk** Zuid-Holland, SW Netherlands
99 *M17* **Kinder Scout** ▲ C England, UK
9 *S16* **Kindersley** Saskatchewan, S Canada
78 *I14* **Kindia** Guinée-Maritime, SW Guinea
66 *B11* **Kindley Field** *air base* E Bermuda
31 *R6* **Kindred** North Dakota, N USA
81 *N20* **Kindu** *prev.* Kindu-Port-Empain. Maniema, C Zaire
Kindu-Port-Empain *see* Kindu
131 *S6* **Kinel'** Samarskaya Oblast', W Russian Federation
129 *N15* **Kineshma** Ivanovskaya Oblast', W Russian Federation
King *see* King William's Town
146 *K10* **King Abdul Aziz** ✈ (Makkah) Makkah, W Saudi Arabia
23 *X6* **King and Queen Court House** Virginia, NE USA
King Charles Islands *see* Kong Karls Land
King Christian IX Land *see* Kong Christian IX Land
King Christian X Land *see* Kong Christian X Land
37 *O11* **King City** California, W USA
29 *R2* **King City** Missouri, C USA
40 *M16* **King Cove** Alaska, USA
28 *M10* **Kingfisher** Oklahoma, C USA
King Frederik VI Coast *see* Kong Frederik VI Kyst
King Frederik VIII Land *see* Kong Frederik VIII Land
67 *B24* **King George Bay** *bay* West Falkland, Falkland Islands
204 *G3* **King George Island** *var.* King George Land. *island* South Shetland Islands, Antarctica
10 *I6* **King George Islands** *island group* Northwest Territories, C Canada
King George Land *see* King George Island
128 *G13* **Kingisepp** Leningradskaya Oblast', NW Russian Federation
191 *N14* **King Island** *island* Tasmania, SE Australia
8 *J15* **King Island** *island* British Columbia, SW Canada
King Island *see* Kadan Kyun
Kingissepp *see* Kuressaare
147 *Q7* **King Khalid** ✈ (Ar Riyāḍ) Ar Riyāḍ, C Saudi Arabia
37 *S2* **King Lear Peak** ▲ Nevada, W USA
205 *Y8* **King Leopold and Queen Astrid Land** *physical region* Antarctica
188 *M4* **King Leopold Ranges** ▲▲ Western Australia
38 *I11* **Kingman** Arizona, SW USA
28 *M6* **Kingman** Kansas, C USA
199 *K7* **Kingman Reef** ◇ *US territory* C Pacific Ocean
81 *N20* **Kingombe** Maniema, E Zaire
190 *F5* **Kingoonya** South Australia
204 *J10* **King Peninsula** *peninsula* Antarctica
41 *P13* **King Salmon** Alaska, USA
37 *Q6* **Kings Beach** California, W USA
37 *R11* **Kingsburg** California, W USA
190 *I10* **Kingscote** South Australia
King's County *see* Offaly
204 *H2* **King Sejong** *South Korean research station* Antarctica
191 *T9* **Kingsford Smith** ✈ (Sydney) New South Wales, SE Australia
9 *P17* **Kingsgate** British Columbia, SW Canada
25 *W8* **Kingsland** Georgia, SE USA
31 *S13* **Kingsley** Iowa, C USA
99 *O19* **King's Lynn** *var.* Bishop's Lynn, Kings Lynn, Lynn, Lynn Regis. E England, UK
23 *Q10* **Kings Mountain** North Carolina, SE USA
188 *K4* **King Sound** *sound* Western Australia
39 *N2* **Kings Peak** ▲ Utah, W USA
23 *O8* **Kingsport** Tennessee, S USA
37 *R11* **Kings River** ≈ California, W USA
191 *P17* **Kingston** Tasmania, SE Australia
12 *K14* **Kingston** Ontario, SE Canada
46 *K13* **Kingston** ● (Jamaica) E Jamaica
193 *C22* **Kingston** Otago, South Island, NZ
21 *P12* **Kingston** Massachusetts, NE USA
29 *S3* **Kingston** Missouri, C USA
20 *K12* **Kingston** New York, NE USA
33 *S14* **Kingston** Ohio, N USA
21 *O13* **Kingston** Rhode Island, NE USA
22 *M9* **Kingston** Tennessee, S USA
37 *W12* **Kingston Peak** ▲ California, W USA
190 *J11* **Kingston Southeast** South Australia
99 *N17* **Kingston upon Hull** *var.* Hull. E England, UK
99 *N22* **Kingston upon Thames** SE England, UK
47 *P14* **Kingstown** ● (Saint Vincent and the Grenadines) Saint Vincent, Saint Vincent and the Grenadines
Kingstown *see* Dún Laoghaire
23 *T13* **Kingstree** South Carolina, SE USA
66 *L8* **Kings Trough** *undersea feature* E Atlantic Ocean
12 *C18* **Kingsville** Ontario, S Canada
27 *S15* **Kingsville** Texas, SW USA
23 *W6* **King William** Virginia, NE USA
15 *K3* **King William Island** *island* Northwest Territories, N Canada Arctic Ocean
85 *I25* **King William's Town** *var.* King, Kingwilliamstown. Eastern Cape, S South Africa
23 *T3* **Kingwood** West Virginia, NE USA
142 *C13* **Kınık** İzmir, W Turkey
81 *G21* **Kinkala** Le Pool, S Congo
171 *Mm14* **Kinka-san** *headland* Honshū, C Japan
192 *M8* **Kinleith** Waikato, North Island, NZ
97 *J19* **Kinna** Älvsborg, S Sweden
98 *L8* **Kinnaird Head** *var.* Kinnairds Head. *headland* NE Scotland, UK
97 *K20* **Kinnared** Halland, S Sweden
Kinneret, Yam *see* Tiberias, Lake
161 *K24* **Kinniyai** Eastern Province, NE Sri Lanka
95 *L16* **Kinnula** Keski-Suomi, C Finland
12 *I8* **Kinojévis** ≈ Québec, SE Canada
170 *G16* **Kino-kawa** ≈ Honshū, SW Japan
9 *U11* **Kinoosao** Saskatchewan, C Canada
101 *L17* **Kinrooi** Limburg, NE Belgium
98 *J11* **Kinross** C Scotland, UK
98 *J11* **Kinross** *cultural region* C Scotland, UK
99 *C21* **Kinsale** *Ir.* Cionn tSáile. SW Ireland
97 *D14* **Kinsarvik** Hordaland, S Norway
81 *G21* **Kinshasa** *prev.* Léopoldville. ● (Zaire) Kinshasa, W Zaire
81 *G21* **Kinshasa** *off.* Ville de Kinshasa, *var.* Kinshasa City. ⬖ *region* SW Zaire
81 *G21* **Kinshasa** ✈ Kinshasa, SW Zaire
Kinshasa City *see* Kinshasa
119 *U9* **Kins'ka** ≈ SE Ukraine
28 *K6* **Kinsley** Kansas, C USA
23 *W10* **Kinston** North Carolina, SE USA
79 *P15* **Kintampo** W Ghana
190 *B1* **Kintore, Mount** ▲ South Australia
98 *G13* **Kintyre** *peninsula* W Scotland, UK
98 *G13* **Kintyre, Mull of** *headland* W Scotland, UK
177 *G4* **Kin-u** Sagaing, C Myanmar
10 *G8* **Kinushseo** ≈ Ontario, C Canada
9 *P13* **Kinuso** Alberta, W Canada
160 *I13* **Kinwat** Mahārāshtra, C India
83 *F16* **Kinyeti** ▲ S Sudan
103 *I17* **Kinzig** ≈ SW Germany
197 *J13* **Kioa** *island* N Fiji
Kioga, Lake *see* Kyoga, Lake
28 *M8* **Kiowa** Kansas, C USA
29 *P12* **Kiowa** Oklahoma, C USA
Kiparissía *see* Kyparissía
12 *H10* **Kipawa, Lac** ◎ Québec, SE Canada
83 *G24* **Kipengere Range** ▲▲ SW Tanzania
83 *E23* **Kipili** Rukwa, W Tanzania
83 *K20* **Kipini** Coast, SE Kenya
9 *V16* **Kipling** Saskatchewan, S Canada
40 *M13* **Kipnuk** Alaska, USA
99 *F18* **Kippure** *Ir.* Cipiúr. ▲ E Ireland
81 *N25* **Kipushi** Shaba, SE Zaire
195 *Y17* **Kirakira** *var.* Kaokaona. San Cristobal, SE Solomon Islands
161 *K14* **Kirandul** *var.* Bailādila. Madhya Pradesh, C India
161 *I21* **Kīranūr** Tamil Nādu, SE India
121 *N21* **Kiraw** *Rus.* Kirovo. Homyel'skaya Voblasts', SE Belarus
121 *M17* **Kirawsk** *Rus.* Kirovsk; *prev.* Startsy. Mahilyowskaya Voblasts', E Belarus
120 *F5* **Kirbla** Läänemaa, W Estonia
27 *Y9* **Kirbyville** Texas, SW USA
116 *M12* **Kırcasalih** Edirne, NW Turkey
111 *W8* **Kirchbach** *var.* Kirchbach in Steiermark. Steiermark, SE Austria
Kirchbach in Steiermark *see* Kirchbach
110 *H7* **Kirchberg** Sankt Gallen, NE Switzerland
111 *S5* **Kirchdorf an der Krems** Oberösterreich, N Austria
Kirchheim *see* Kirchheim unter Teck
103 *I22* **Kirchheim unter Teck** *var.* Kirchheim. Baden-Württemberg, SW Germany
Kirdzhali *see* Kŭrdzhali
126 *Jj14* **Kirenga** ≈ S Russian Federation
126 *Jj13* **Kirensk** Irkutskaya Oblast', C Russian Federation
Kirghizia *see* Kyrgyzstan
151 *S16* **Kirghiz Range** *Rus.* Kirgizskiy Khrebet; *prev.* Alexander Range. ▲▲ Kazakhstan/Kyrgyzstan
Kirghiz SSR *see* Kyrgyzstan
Kirghiz Steppe *see* Kazakhskiy Melkosopochnik
Kirgizskaya SSR *see* Kyrgyzstan
Kirgizskiy Khrebet *see* Kirghiz Range
81 *I19* **Kiri** Bandundu, W Zaire
Kiriath-Arba *see* Hebron
203 *R3* **Kiribati** *off.* Republic of Kiribati. ◆ *republic* C Pacific Ocean
142 *L17* **Kırıkhan** Hatay, S Turkey
142 *I13* **Kırıkkale** Kırıkkale, C Turkey
142 *C10* **Kırıkkale** ⬖ *province* C Turkey
128 *L13* **Kirillov** Vologodskaya Oblast', NW Russian Federation
Kirin *see* Jilin
83 *I18* **Kirinyaga** *prev.* Mount Kenya. ⛰ C Kenya
128 *H13* **Kirishi** *var.* Kirisi. Leningradskaya Oblast', NW Russian Federation
170 *C16* **Kirishima-yama** ▲ Kyūshū, SW Japan
Kirisi *see* Kirishi
203 *Y2* **Kiritimati** ✈ Kiritimati, E Kiribati
203 *Y2* **Kiritimati** *prev.* Christmas Island. *atoll* Line Islands, E Kiribati
195 *O15* **Kiriwina Island** *Eng.* Trobriand Island. *island* SE PNG
195 *O15* **Kiriwina Islands** *var.* Trobriand Islands. *island group* S PNG
98 *K12* **Kirkcaldy** E Scotland, UK
99 *I14* **Kirkcudbright** S Scotland, UK
99 *I14* **Kirkcudbright** *cultural region* S Scotland, UK
Kirkee *see* Khadki
94 *M8* **Kirkenes** *var.* Kirkkoniemi. Finnmark, N Norway
97 *I14* **Kirkenær** Hedmark, S Norway
94 *J4* **Kirkjubæjarklaustur** Sudhurland, S Iceland
Kirk-Kilissa *see* Kırklareli
Kirkkoniemi *see* Kirkenes
95 *L20* **Kirkkonummi** *Swe.* Kyrkslätt. Uusimaa, S Finland
12 *G7* **Kirkland Lake** Ontario, S Canada
142 *C9* **Kırklareli** *prev.* Kirk-Kilissa. Kırklareli, NW Turkey
142 *I13* **Kırklareli** ⬖ *province* NW Turkey
193 *F20* **Kirkliston Range** ▲▲ South Island, NZ
12 *D10* **Kirkpatrick Lake** ◎ Ontario, S Canada
205 *Q11* **Kirkpatrick, Mount** ▲ Antarctica
29 *U2* **Kirksville** Missouri, C USA
145 *T4* **Kirkūk** *var.* Karkūk, Kerkuk. N Iraq
145 *U7* **Kir Kush** E Iraq
98 *K5* **Kirkwall** NE Scotland, UK
85 *H25* **Kirkwood** Eastern Cape, S South Africa
29 *X5* **Kirkwood** Missouri, C USA
Kirman *see* Kermān
Kir Moab/Kir of Moab *see* Al Karak
130 *I5* **Kirov** Kaluzhskaya Oblast', W Russian Federation
129 *R14* **Kirov** *prev.* Vyatka. Kirovskaya Oblast', NW Russian Federation
Kīrov *see* Kirovskiy, Kazakhstan
Kīrov *see* Kirova, Taldykorgan, Kazakhstan
151 *U13* **Kirova** *Kaz.* Kīrov. Taldykorgan, SE Kazakhstan
Kirovabad *see* Gäncä, Azerbaijan
Kirovabad *see* Panj, Tajikistan
Kirovakan *see* Vanadzor
Kirovo *see* Kiraw, Belarus
Kirovo/Kirovograd *see* Kirovohrad, Ukraine
Kirovo *see* Beshariq, Uzbekistan
129 *R14* **Kirovo-Chepetsk** Kirovskaya Oblast', NW Russian Federation
Kirovogradskaya Oblast'/Kirovohrad *see* Kirovohrads'ka Oblast'
119 *R7* **Kirovohrad** *Rus.* Kirovograd; *prev.* Kirovo, Yelizavetgrad, Zinov'yevsk. Kirovohrads'ka Oblast', C Ukraine
119 *P7* **Kirovohrads'ka Oblast'** *var.* Kirovohrad, *Rus.* Kirovogradskaya Oblast'. ⬖ *province* C Ukraine
128 *J4* **Kirovsk** Murmanskaya Oblast', NW Russian Federation
Kirovsk *see* Kirawsk, Belarus
Kirovsk *see* Babadaykhan, Turkmenistan
119 *X7* **Kirovs'k** Luhans'ka Oblast', E Ukraine
125 *Dd9* **Kirovskaya Oblast'** ⬖ *province* NW Russian Federation
119 *X8* **Kirov'ske** Donets'ka Oblast', E Ukraine
119 *U13* **Kirovs'ke** *Rus.* Kirovskoye. Respublika Krym, S Ukraine
151 *V14* **Kirovskiy** *Kaz.* Kīrov. Taldykorgan, SE Kazakhstan
127 *P12* **Kirovskiy** Kamchatskaya Oblast', E Russian Federation
Kirovskoye *see* Kyzyl-Adyr
Kirovskoye *see* Kirovs'ke
124 *Oo2* **Kırpaşa** *var.* Karpas Peninsula, *Gk.* Karpasía. *peninsula* NE Cyprus
152 *E11* **Kirpili** Akhalskiy Velayat, C Turkmenistan
98 *K10* **Kirriemuir** E Scotland, UK
129 *S13* **Kirs** Kirovskaya Oblast', NW Russian Federation
131 *N7* **Kirsanov** Tambovskaya Oblast', W Russian Federation
142 *J14* **Kirşehir** *anc.* Justinianopolis. Kirşehir, C Turkey
142 *I13* **Kirşehir** ⬖ *province* C Turkey
155 *P4* **Kīrthar Range** ▲▲ S Pakistan
39 *P9* **Kirtland** New Mexico, SW USA
Kirun/Kirun' *see* Chilung
94 *J11* **Kiruna** Norrbotten, N Sweden
81 *M18* **Kirundu** Haut-Zaïre, NE Zaire
28 *L3* **Kirwin Reservoir** ⊠ Kansas, C USA
131 *Q4* **Kirya** Chuvashskaya Respublika, W Russian Federation
171 *K15* **Kiryū** Gunma, Honshū, S Japan
97 *M18* **Kisa** Östergötland, S Sweden
171 *Ll11* **Kisakata** Akita, Honshū, C Japan
Kisalföld *see* Little Alföld
81 *L18* **Kisangani** *prev.* Stanleyville. Haut-Zaïre, NE Zaire
41 *N12* **Kisaralik River** ≈ Alaska, USA
171 *K17* **Kisarazu** Chiba, Honshū, S Japan
113 *I22* **Kisbér** Komárom-Esztergom, NW Hungary
9 *V17* **Kisbey** Saskatchewan, S Canada
126 *H14* **Kiselevsk** Kemerovskaya Oblast', S Russian Federation
159 *R13* **Kishanganj** Bihār, NE India
158 *G12* **Kishangarh** Rājasthān, N India
Kishegyes *see* Mali Iđoš
79 *S15* **Kishi** Oyo, W Nigeria
Kishinev *see* Chişinău
Kishiözen *see* Malyy Uzen'
171 *Gg15* **Kishiwada** *var.* Kisiwada. Ōsaka, Honshū, SW Japan
149 *P14* **Kīsh, Jazīreh-ye** *var.* Qeys. *island* S Iran
158 *I6* **Kishtwār** Jammu and Kashmir, NW India
83 *H19* **Kisii** Nyanza, SW Kenya
83 *J23* **Kisiju** Pwani, E Tanzania
Kisiwada *see* Kishiwada
Kisjenő *see* Chişineu-Criş
40 *E17* **Kiska Island** *island* Aleutian Islands, Alaska, USA
Kiskapus *see* Copşa Mică
113 *M22* **Kiskörei-víztároló** ⊠ E Hungary
Kis-Küküllo *see* Târnava Mică
113 *L24* **Kiskunfélegyháza** *var.* Félegyháza. Bács-Kiskun, C Hungary
113 *K25* **Kiskunhalas** *var.* Halas. Bács-Kiskun, S Hungary
113 *K24* **Kiskunmajsa** Bács-Kiskun, S Hungary
131 *N15* **Kislovodsk** Stavropol'skiy Kray, SW Russian Federation
83 *L18* **Kismaayo** *var.* Chisimayu, Kismayu, *It.* Chisimaio. Jubbada Hoose, S Somalia
Kismayu *see* Kismaayo
171 *Ii15* **Kiso-sanmyaku** ▲▲ Honshū, S Japan
Kisseraing *see* Kanmaw Kyun
78 *K14* **Kissidougou** Guinée-Forestière, S Guinea
25 *X12* **Kissimmee** Florida, SE USA
25 *X12* **Kissimmee, Lake** ◎ Florida, SE USA
25 *X13* **Kissimmee River** ≈ Florida, SE USA
9 *V13* **Kississing Lake** ◎ Manitoba, C Canada
113 *L24* **Kistelek** Csongrád, SE Hungary
Kistna *see* Krishna
113 *M23* **Kisújszállás** Jász-Nagykun-Szolnok, E Hungary
170 *F12* **Kisuki** Shimane, Honshū, SW Japan
83 *H18* **Kisumu** *prev.* Port Florence. Nyanza, W Kenya
Kisutzaneustadtl *see* Kysucké Nové Mesto
113 *O20* **Kisvárda** *Ger.* Kleinwardein. Szabolcs-Szatmár-Bereg, E Hungary
83 *J24* **Kiswere** Lindi, SE Tanzania
Kiszucaújhely *see* Kysucké Nové Mesto
78 *K12* **Kita** Kayes, W Mali
Kitab *see* Kitob
172 *N5* **Kitahiyama** Hokkaidō, NE Japan
171 *L15* **Kita-Ibaraki** Ibaraki, Honshū, S Japan
172 *Ss17* **Kita-Iō-jima** *Eng.* San Alessandro. *island* SE Japan
171 *Mm11* **Kitakami** Iwate, Honshū, C Japan
171 *M13* **Kitakami-gawa** ≈ Honshū, C Japan
172 *N11* **Kitakami-sanchi** ▲▲ Honshū, C Japan
171 *L13* **Kitakata** Fukushima, Honshū, C Japan
170 *D12* **Kitakyūshū** *var.* Kitakyûsyû. Fukuoka, Kyūshū, SW Japan
Kitakyûsyû *see* Kitakyūshū
83 *H18* **Kitale** Rift Valley, W Kenya
172 *Q5* **Kitami** Hokkaidō, NE Japan
172 *Pp4* **Kitami-sanchi** ▲▲ Hokkaidō, NE Japan
171 *Kk17* **Kita-ura** ◎ Honshū, S Japan
195 *O15* **Kitava Island** *island* Kiriwina Islands, SE PNG
39 *W5* **Kit Carson** Colorado, C USA
188 *M12* **Kitchener** Western Australia
12 *F16* **Kitchener** Ontario, S Canada
95 *O17* **Kitee** Pohjois-Karjala, SE Finland
83 *G16* **Kitgum** N Uganda
Kithareng *see* Kanmaw Kyun
Kíthira *see* Kýthira
Kíthnos *see* Kýthnos
15 *J3* **Kitikmeot** ⬖ *district* Northwest Territories, N Canada
8 *J13* **Kitimat** British Columbia, SW Canada
94 *L11* **Kitinen** ≈ N Finland
153 *N12* **Kitob** *Rus.* Kitab. Qashqadaryo Wiloyati, S Uzbekistan
118 *K7* **Kitsman'** *Ger.* Kotzman, *Rom.* Cozmeni, *Rus.* Kitsman. Chernivets'ka Oblast', W Ukraine
170 *Dd14* **Kitsuki** *var.* Kituki. Ōita, Kyūshū, SW Japan
20 *C14* **Kittanning** Pennsylvania, NE USA
21 *P10* **Kittery** Maine, NE USA
94 *L11* **Kittilä** Lappi, N Finland
111 *Z4* **Kittsee** Burgenland, E Austria
83 *J19* **Kitui** Eastern, S Kenya
Kituki *see* Kitsuki
83 *G22* **Kitunda** Tabora, C Tanzania
8 *K13* **Kitwanga** British Columbia, SW Canada
84 *J13* **Kitwe** *var.* Kitwe-Nkana. Copperbelt, C Zambia
Kitwe-Nkana *see* Kitwe
111 *O7* **Kitzbühel** Tirol, W Austria
111 *O7* **Kitzbüheler Alpen** ▲▲ W Austria
103 *J19* **Kitzingen** Bayern, SE Germany
159 *Q14* **Kiul** Bihār, NE India
194 *E12* **Kiunga** Western, SW PNG
95 *M16* **Kiuruvesi** Kuopio, C Finland
40 *M7* **Kivalina** Alaska, USA
94 *L13* **Kivalo** *ridge* C Finland
118 *J3* **Kivertsi** *Pol.* Kiwerce, *Rus.* Kivertsy. Volyns'ka Oblast', NW Ukraine
Kivertsy *see* Kivertsi
95 *L16* **Kivijärvi** Keski-Suomi, C Finland
97 *L23* **Kivik** Kristianstad, S Sweden
120 *J3* **Kiviõli** Ida-Virumaa, NE Estonia
Kivu, Lac *see* Kivu, Lake
69 *U10* **Kivu, Lake** *Fr.* Lac Kivu. ◎ Rwanda/Zaire
194 *G15* **Kiwai Island** *island* SW PNG
41 *N8* **Kiwalik** Alaska, USA
Kiwerce *see* Kivertsi
Kiyev *see* Kyyiv
151 *R10* **Kiyevka** Karaganda, C Kazakhstan
Kiyevskaya Oblast' *see* Kyyivs'ka Oblast'
Kiyevskoye Vodokhranilishche *see* Kyyivs'ke Vodoskhovyshche
142 *D10* **Kıyıköy** Kırklareli, NW Turkey
151 *O9* **Kiyma** Turgay, C Kazakhstan
129 *V13* **Kizel** Permskaya Oblast', NW Russian Federation
129 *O12* **Kizema** *var.* Kizëma. Arkhangel'skaya Oblast', NW Russian Federation
Kizilagach *see* Elkhovo
142 *H12* **Kızılcahamam** Ankara, N Turkey
142 *J10* **Kızıl Irmak** ≈ C Turkey
Kızılkoca *see* Şefaatli
Kizil Kum *see* Kyzyl Kum
143 *P16* **Kızıltepe** Mardin, SE Turkey
Ki Zil Uzen *see* Qezel Owzan
131 *Q16* **Kizilyurt** Respublika Dagestan, SW Russian Federation
131 *Q15* **Kizlyar** Respublika Dagestan, SW Russian Federation
131 *S3* **Kizner** Udmurtskaya Respublika, NW Russian Federation
Kizyl-Arvat *see* Gyzylarbat
152 *B13* **Kizyl-Atrek** *Turkm.* Gyzyletrek. Balkanskiy Velayat, W Turkmenistan
152 *D10* **Kizyl-Kaya** *Turkm.* Gyzylgaya. Balkanskiy Velayat, NW Turkmenistan
152 *A10* **Kizyl-Su** *Turkm.* Gyzylsu. Balkanskiy Velayat, W Turkmenistan
97 *H16* **Kjerkøy** *island* S Norway
Kjølen *see* Kölen
94 *L7* **Kjøllefjord** Finnmark, N Norway
94 *H11* **Kjøpsvik** Nordland, C Norway
174 *Ii9* **Klabat, Teluk** *bay* Pulau Bangka, W Indonesia
114 *I12* **Kladanj** E Bosnia and Herzegovina
176 *Xx16* **Kladar** Irian Jaya, E Indonesia
113 *C16* **Kladno** Střední Čechy, NW Czech Republic
114 *P11* **Kladovo** Serbia, E Yugoslavia
178 *Hh12* **Klaeng** Rayong, S Thailand
111 *T9* **Klagenfurt** *Slvn.* Celovec. Kärnten, S Austria
120 *B11* **Klaipėda** *Ger.* Memel. Klaipėda, NW Lithuania
174 *M15* **Klakah** Jawa, C Indonesia
36 *L2* **Klamath** California, W USA
34 *H16* **Klamath Falls** Oregon, NW USA
36 *M1* **Klamath Mountains** ▲▲ California/Oregon, W USA
36 *L2* **Klamath River** ≈ California/Oregon, W USA
174 *Gg5* **Klang** *var.* Kelang; *prev.* Port Swettenham. Selangor, Peninsular Malaysia
96 *J13* **Klarälven** ≈ Norway/Sweden
113 *B15* **Klášterec nad Ohří** *Ger.* Klösterle an der Eger. Severní Čechy, NW Czech Republic
174 *L15* **Klaten** Jawa, C Indonesia
113 *B18* **Klatovy** *Ger.* Klattau. Západní Čechy, SW Czech Republic
Klattau *see* Klatovy
Klausenburg *see* Cluj-Napoca
41 *Y14* **Klawock** Prince of Wales Island, Alaska, USA
100 *P8* **Klazienaveen** Drenthe, NE Netherlands
Kleck *see* Klyetsk
112 *H11* **Kłecko** Poznań, W Poland
112 *I11* **Kleczew** Konin, C Poland
8 *L15* **Kleena Kleene** British Columbia, SW Canada
85 *D20* **Klein Aub** Hardap, C Namibia
Kleine Donau *see* Mosoni-Duna
103 *O14* **Kleine Elster** ≈ E Germany
Kleine Kokel *see* Târnava Mică
101 *I16* **Kleine Nete** ≈ N Belgium
Kleines Ungarisches Tiefland *see* Little Alföld
85 *E22* **Klein Karas** Karas, S Namibia
Kleinkopisch *see* Copşa Mică
Klein-Marien *see* Väike-Maarja
Kleinschlatten *see* Zlatna
85 *D23* **Kleinsee** Northern Cape, W South Africa
Kleinwardein *see* Kisvárda
117 *C16* **Kleisoúra** Ípeiros, W Greece
97 *C17* **Klepp** Rogaland, S Norway
85 *I22* **Klerksdorp** North-West, N South Africa
130 *I5* **Kletnya** Bryanskaya Oblast', W Russian Federation
Kletsk *see* Klyetsk
103 *D14* **Kleve** *Eng.* Cleves, *Fr.* Clèves; *prev.* Cleve. Nordrhein-Westfalen, W Germany
115 *J16* **Kličevo** Montenegro, SW Yugoslavia
121 *M16* **Klichaw** *Rus.* Klichev. Mahilyowskaya Voblasts', E Belarus
Klichev *see* Klichaw
121 *Q16* **Klimavichy** *Rus.* Klimovichi. Mahilyowskaya Voblasts', E Belarus
116 *M7* **Kliment** Varnenska Oblast, NE Bulgaria
Klimovichi *see* Klimavichy
95 *G14* **Klimpfjäll** Västerbotten, N Sweden
130 *K3* **Klin** Moskovskaya Oblast', W Russian Federation
115 *M16* **Klina** Serbia, S Yugoslavia
113 *B15* **Klínovec** *Ger.* Keilberg. ▲ NW Czech Republic
97 *P19* **Klintehamn** Gotland, SE Sweden
131 *R8* **Klintsovka** Saratovskaya Oblast', W Russian Federation
130 *H6* **Klintsy** Bryanskaya Oblast', W Russian Federation
97 *K22* **Klippan** Kristianstad, S Sweden
94 *G13* **Klippen** Västerbotten, N Sweden
124 *Nn3* **Klírou** W Cyprus
116 *I9* **Klisura** Plovdivska Oblast, C Bulgaria
97 *F20* **Klitmøller** Viborg, NW Denmark
114 *F11* **Ključ** NW Bosnia and Herzegovina
113 *J14* **Kłobuck** Częstochowa, S Poland
112 *J11* **Kłodawa** Konin, C Poland
113 *G16* **Kłodzko** *Ger.* Glatz. Wałbrzych, SW Poland
97 *I14* **Kløfta** Akershus, S Norway
114 *P12* **Klokočevac** Serbia, E Yugoslavia
120 *G3* **Klooga** *Ger.* Lodensee. Harjumaa, NW Estonia
101 *F15* **Kloosterzande** Zeeland, SW Netherlands
115 *L19* **Klos** *var.* Klosi. Dibër, C Albania
Klosi *see* Klos
Klösterle an der Eger *see* Klášterec nad Ohří
111 *X3* **Klosterneuburg** Niederösterreich, NE Austria
110 *J9* **Klosters** Graubünden, SE Switzerland
110 *G7* **Kloten** Zürich, N Switzerland
110 *G7* **Kloten** ✈ (Zürich) Zürich, N Switzerland
102 *K12* **Klötze** Sachsen-Anhalt, C Germany
10 *K3* **Klotz, Lac** ◎ Québec, NE Canada
103 *O15* **Klotzsche** ✈ (Dresden) Sachsen, E Germany
8 *H7* **Kluane Lake** ◎ Yukon Territory, W Canada
Kluang *see* Keluang
113 *I14* **Kluczbork** *Ger.* Kreuzburg, Kreuzburg in Oberschlesien. Opole, SW Poland
41 *W12* **Klukwan** Alaska, USA
Klyastitsy *see* Klyastsitsy
120 *L11* **Klyastsitsy** *Rus.* Klyastitsy. Vitsyebskaya Voblasts', N Belarus
131 *T5* **Klyavlino** Samarskaya Oblast', W Russian Federation
86 *K9* **Klyaz'in** ≈ W Russian Federation
131 *N3* **Klyaz'ma** ≈ W Russian Federation
121 *J17* **Klyetsk** *Pol.* Kleck, *Rus.* Kletsk. Minskaya Voblasts', SW Belarus
153 *S8* **Klyuchevka** Talasskaya Oblast', NW Kyrgyzstan
127 *Pp10* **Klyuchevskaya Sopka, Vulkan** ⛰ E Russian Federation
127 *Pp10* **Klyuchi** Kamchatskaya Oblast', E Russian Federation
97 *D17* **Knaben** Vest-Agder, S Norway
Knanzi *see* Ghanzi
97 *K21* **Knäred** Halland, S Sweden
99 *M16* **Knaresborough** N England, UK
116 *H8* **Knezha** Oblast Montana, NW Bulgaria
27 *O9* **Knickerbocker** Texas, SW USA
30 *K5* **Knife River** ≈ North Dakota, N USA
8 *K16* **Knight Inlet** *inlet* British Columbia, W Canada
41 *S12* **Knight Island** *island* Alaska, USA
99 *K20* **Knighton** E Wales, UK
37 *O7* **Knights Landing** California, W USA
114 *E13* **Knin** Zadar-Knin, S Croatia
27 *Q12* **Knippal** Texas, SW USA
111 *U7* **Knittelfeld** Steiermark, C Austria
97 *O15* **Knivsta** Uppsala, C Sweden
115 *P14* **Knjaževac** Serbia, E Yugoslavia
29 *S4* **Knob Noster** Missouri, C USA
101 *D15* **Knokke-Heist** West-Vlaanderen, NW Belgium
97 *H20* **Knøsen** *hill* N Denmark
Knosós *see* Knossos
117 *J25* **Knossos** *Gk.* Knosós. *prehistoric site* Kríti, Greece, E Mediterranean Sea
27 *N7* **Knott** Texas, SW USA
204 *K5* **Knowles, Cape** *headland* Antarctica
33 *O11* **Knox** Indiana, N USA
31 *O3* **Knox** North Dakota, N USA
20 *C13* **Knox** Pennsylvania, NE USA
201 *X8* **Knox Atoll** *var.* Ņadikdik, Narikrik. *atoll* Ratak Chain, SE Marshall Islands
8 *H13* **Knox, Cape** *headland* Graham Island, British Columbia, SW Canada
27 *P5* **Knox City** Texas, SW USA
205 *Y11* **Knox Coast** *physical region* Antarctica
33 *T12* **Knox Lake** ⊠ Ohio, N USA
25 *T5* **Knoxville** Georgia, SE USA
32 *K12* **Knoxville** Illinois, N USA
31 *W15* **Knoxville** Iowa, C USA
23 *N9* **Knoxville** Tennessee, S USA
207 *P11* **Knud Rasmussen Land** *physical region* N Greenland
Knüll *see* Knüllgebirge
103 *I16* **Knüllgebirge** *var.* Knüll. ▲▲ C Germany
Knyazhevo *see* Sredishte
Knyazhitsy *see* Knyazhytsy
121 *O15* **Knyazhytsy** *Rus.* Knyazhitsy. Mahilyowskaya Voblasts', E Belarus
85 *G26* **Knysna** Western Cape, SW South Africa
176 *V10* **Koagas** Irian Jaya, E Indonesia
Koartac *see* Quaqtaq
174 *J10* **Koba** Pulau Bangka, W Indonesia
170 *C16* **Kobayashi** *var.* Kobayasi. Miyazaki, Kyūshū, SW Japan
Kobayasi *see* Kobayashi
171 *Gg14* **Kōbe** Hyōgo, Honshū, SW Japan
Kobelyaki *see* Kobelyaky
119 *T6* **Kobelyaky** *Rus.* Kobelyaki. Poltavs'ka Oblast', NE Ukraine
97 *J22* **København** *Eng.* Copenhagen; *anc.* Hafnia. ● (Denmark) Sjælland, København, E Denmark
97 *J23* **København** *off.* Københavns Amt. ⬖ *county* E Denmark
78 *K10* **Kobenni** Hodh el Gharbi, S Mauritania
176 *U11* **Kobi** Pulau Seram, E Indonesia
103 *F17* **Koblenz** *prev.* Coblenz, *Fr.* Coblence, *anc.* Confluentes. Rheinland-Pfalz, W Germany
110 *F6* **Koblenz** Aargau, N Switzerland
176 *Ww11* **Kobowre, Pegunungan** ▲▲ Irian Jaya, E Indonesia
160 *L11* **Kobra** Madhya Pradesh, C India
Kobrin *see* Kobryn
176 *W14* **Kobroor, Pulau** *island* Kepulauan Aru, E Indonesia
121 *G19* **Kobryn** *Pol.* Kobryn, *Rus.* Kobrin. Brestskaya Voblasts', SW Belarus
41 *O7* **Kobuk** Alaska, USA
41 *O7* **Kobuk River** ≈ Alaska, USA
143 *Q10* **K'obulet'i** W Georgia
126 *Ll10* **Kobyay** Respublika Sakha (Yakutiya), NE Russian Federation
142 *E11* **Kocaeli** ⬖ *province* NW Turkey
115 *P18* **Kočani** NE FYR Macedonia
114 *K12* **Koceljevo** Serbia, W Yugoslavia
111 *U12* **Kočevje** *Ger.* Gottschee. S Slovenia
159 *T12* **Koch Bihār** West Bengal, NE India
126 *J10* **Kochechum** ≈ N Russian Federation
103 *I20* **Kocher** ≈ SW Germany
129 *T13* **Kochevo** Komi-Permyatskiy Avtonomnyy Okrug, NW Russian Federation
170 *Ee15* **Kōchi** *var.* Kôti. Kōchi, Shikoku, SW Japan
170 *Ee15* **Kōchi** *off.* Kōchi-ken, *var.* Kôti. ⬖ *prefecture* Shikoku, SW Japan
Kochi *see* Cochin
Kochiu *see* Gejiu
Kochkor *see* Kochkorka
153 *V8* **Kochkorka** *Kir.* Kochkor. Narynskaya Oblast', C Kyrgyzstan
129 *V5* **Kochmes** Respublika Komi, NW Russian Federation
131 *P15* **Kochubey** Respublika Dagestan, SW Russian Federation
117 *I17* **Kochýlas** ▲ Skýros, Vóreioi Sporádes, Greece, Aegean Sea
112 *O13* **Kock** Lublin, E Poland
83 *J19* **Kodacho** *spring/well* S Kenya
161 *K24* **Koddiyar Bay** *bay* NE Sri Lanka
41 *Q14* **Kodiak** Kodiak Island, Alaska, USA
41 *Q14* **Kodiak Island** *island* Alaska, USA
160 *B12* **Kodīnār** Gujarāt, W India
128 *M9* **Kodino** Arkhangel'skaya Oblast', NW Russian Federation
126 *Ii13* **Kodinsk** Krasnoyarskiy Kray, C Russian Federation
82 *F12* **Kodok** Upper Nile, SE Sudan
119 *N8* **Kodyma** Odes'ka Oblast', SW Ukraine
101 *B17* **Koekelare** West-Vlaanderen, W Belgium
Koeln *see* Köln
Koepang *see* Kupang
Ko-erh-mu *see* Golmud
101 *J17* **Koersel** Limburg, NE Belgium
85 *E21* **Koës** Karas, SE Namibia
Koetai *see* Mahakam, Sunga

◆ COUNTRY
● COUNTRY CAPITAL
◇ DEPENDENT TERRITORY
○ DEPENDENT TERRITORY CAPITAL
⬖ ADMINISTRATIVE REGION
✈ INTERNATIONAL AIRPORT
▲ MOUNTAIN
▲▲ MOUNTAIN RANGE
⛰ VOLCANO
≈ RIVER
◎ LAKE
⊠ RESERVOIR

Koetaradja see Bandaaceh
38 I14 **Kofa Mountains** ▲ Arizona, SW USA
176 Z15 **Kofarau** Irian Jaya, E Indonesia
153 P13 **Kofarnihon** *Rus.* Kofarnikhon; *prev.* Ordzhonikidzeabad, *Taj.* Orjonikidzeobod, Yangi-Bazar. W Tajikistan
153 P14 **Kofarnihon** *Rus.* Kafirnigan. ↗ SW Tajikistan
Kofarnikhon see Kofarnihon
116 M11 **Kofçaz** Kırklareli, NW Turkey
176 U9 **Kofiau, Pulau** *var.* Kafiau. *island* Kepulauan Raja Ampat, E Indonesia
117 J25 **Kófinas** ▲ Kríti, Greece, E Mediterranean Sea
124 Nn4 **Kofinou** *var.* Kophinou. S Cyprus
111 V8 **Köflach** Steiermark, SE Austria
79 Q17 **Koforidua** SE Ghana
170 Ff12 **Kōfu** Tottori, Honshū, SW Japan
171 J15 **Kōfu** *var.* Kōhu. Yamanashi, Honshū, S Japan
171 K16 **Koga** Ibaraki, Honshū, S Japan
83 F22 **Koga** Tabora, C Tanzania
Kogălniceanu see Mihail Kogălniceanu
11 P6 **Kogaluk** ↗ Newfoundland and Labrador, E Canada
10 J4 **Kogaluk** ↗ Québec, NE Canada
126 Gg10 **Kogalym** Khanty-Mansiyskiy Avtonomnyy Okrug, C Russian Federation
97 J23 **Køge** Roskilde, E Denmark
97 J23 **Køge Bugt** *bay* E Denmark
79 U16 **Kogi** ◆ *state* C Nigeria
152 L11 **Kogon** *Rus.* Kagan. Bukhoro Wiloyati, C Uzbekistan
169 Y17 **Kōgŭm-do** *island* S South Korea
Kohalom see Rupea
155 T6 **Kohāt** North-West Frontier Province, NW Pakistan
120 G4 **Kohila** *Ger.* Koil. Raplamaa, NW Estonia
159 X13 **Kohima** Nāgāland, E India
Koh I Noh see Büyükağrı Dağı
148 L10 **Kohkīlūyeh va Būyer Aḥmadī** *off.* Ostān-e Kohkīlūyeh va Būyer Aḥmadī, *var.* Boyer Ahmadi va Kohkīlūyeh. ◆ *province* SW Iran
Kohsān see Kūhestān
120 J3 **Kohtla-Järve** Ida-Virumaa, NE Estonia
Kōhu see Kōfu
119 N10 **Kohyl'nyk** *Rom.* Cogîlnic. ↗ Moldova/Ukraine
171 K13 **Koide** Niigata, Honshū, C Japan
8 G7 **Koidern** Yukon Territory, W Canada
78 J15 **Koidu** E Sierra Leone
120 I4 **Koigi** Järvamaa, C Estonia
Koil see Kohila
180 H13 **Koimbani** Grande Comore, NW Comoros
145 T3 **Koi Sanjaq** *var.* Koysanjaq, Kūysanaq. N Iraq
95 O16 **Koitere** ◎ E Finland
Koivisto see Primorsk
169 Z16 **Kōje-do** *Jap.* Kyōsai-tō. *island* S South Korea
82 J13 **K'ok'a Hāyk'** ◎ C Ethiopia
Kokand see Qŭqon
190 F6 **Kokatha** South Australia
Kokcha see Kükcha
Kokchetav/Kokchetavskaya Oblast' see Kokshetau
95 K18 **Kokemäenjoki** ↗ SW Finland
176 X12 **Kokenau** *var.* Kokonau. Irian Jaya, E Indonesia
85 E22 **Kokerboom** Karas, SE Namibia
121 N14 **Kokhanava** *Rus.* Kokhanovo. Vitsyebskaya Voblasts', NE Belarus
Kokhanovichi see Kakhanavichy
Kokhanovo see Kokhanava
Kōk-Janggak see Kok-Yangak
95 K16 **Kokkola** *Swe.* Karleby; *prev.* Swe. Gamlakarleby. Vaasa, W Finland
164 L3 **Kok Kuduk** *well* N China
120 H9 **Koknese** Aizkraukle, C Latvia
79 T13 **Koko** Kebbi, W Nigeria
194 K15 **Kokoda** Northern, S PNG
78 K12 **Kokofata** Kayes, W Mali
41 N6 **Kokolik River** ↗ Alaska, USA
33 O13 **Kokomo** Indiana, N USA
Kokonau see Kokenau
Koko Nor see Qinghai Hu, China
Koko Nor see Qinghai, China
195 P10 **Kokopo** *var.* Kopopo; *prev.* Herbertshöhe. New Britain, E PNG
151 X10 **Kokpekti** *Kaz.* Kökpekti. Semipalatinsk, E Kazakhstan
151 X11 **Kokpekti** ↗ E Kazakhstan
41 P9 **Kokrines** Alaska, USA
41 P9 **Kokrines Hills** ▲ Alaska, USA
151 P17 **Koksaray** Yuzhnyy Kazakhstan, S Kazakhstan
153 X9 **Kokshaal-Tau** *Rus.* Khrebet Kakshaal-Too. ▲ China/Kyrgyzstan
151 P17 **Kokshetau** *Kaz.* Kökshetaū; *prev.* Kokchetav. Kokshetau, N Kazakhstan
151 P17 **Kokshetau** *off.* Kokshetauskaya Oblast', *Kaz.* Kökshetaū Oblysy; *prev.* Kokchetavskaya Oblast'. ◆ *province* N Kazakhstan
Kökshetaū Oblysy/Kokshetaūskaya Oblast' see Kokshetau
A17 **Koksijde** West-Vlaanderen, W Belgium
10 M4 **Koksoak** ↗ Québec, E Canada
85 K24 **Kokstad** KwaZulu/Natal, E South Africa
151 W13 **Koktal** *Kaz.* Köktal. Taldykorgan, SE Kazakhstan
151 Q12 **Koktas** ↗ C Kazakhstan
Kök-Tash see Kёk-Tash
151 T6 **Koktokay** see Fuyun

170 C16 **Kokubu** Kagoshima, Kyūshū, SW Japan
126 L15 **Kokuy** Chitinskaya Oblast', S Russian Federation
153 T9 **Kok-Yangak** *Kir.* Kōk-Janggak. Dzhalal-Abadskaya Oblast', W Kyrgyzstan
164 F9 **Kokyar** Xinjiang Uygur Zizhiqu, W China
155 O13 **Kolāchi** *var.* Kulachi. ↗ SW Pakistan
78 J15 **Kolahun** N Liberia
175 Q12 **Kolaka** Sulawesi, C Indonesia
Kolam see Quilon
K'o-la-ma-i see Karamay
Kola Peninsula see Kol'skiy Poluostrov
161 H19 **Kolār** Karnātaka, E India
161 H19 **Kolār Gold Fields** Karnātaka, E India
94 K11 **Kolari** Lappi, NW Finland
113 I21 **Kolárovo** *Ger.* Gutta; *prev.* Guta, *Hung.* Gúta. Západné Slovensko, SW Slovakia
115 K16 **Kolašin** Montenegro, SW Yugoslavia
158 F11 **Kolāyat** Rājasthān, NW India
97 N15 **Kolbäck** Västmanland, C Sweden
Kolbcha see Kowbcha
207 Q15 **Kolbeinsey Ridge** *undersea feature* Denmark Strait/ Norwegian Sea
Kolberg see Kołobrzeg
97 H15 **Kolbotn** Akershus, S Norway
113 N16 **Kolbuszowa** Rzeszów, SE Poland
130 L3 **Kol'chugino** Vladimirskaya Oblast', W Russian Federation
78 H12 **Kolda** S Senegal
97 G23 **Kolding** Vejle, C Denmark
81 M17 **Kole** Haut-Zaïre, N Zaire
81 K20 **Kole** Kasai Oriental, SW Zaire
Kōle see Kili Island
86 F6 **Kōlen** *Nor.* Kjølen. ▲ Norway/Sweden
Kolepom, Pulau see Yos Sudarso, Pulau
120 H3 **Kolga Laht** *Ger.* Kolko-Wiek. *bay* N Estonia
129 Q3 **Kolguyev, Ostrov** *island* NW Russian Federation
161 E16 **Kolhāpur** Mahārāshtra, SW India
157 K21 **Kolhumadulu Atoll** *var.* Kolumadulu Atoll, Thaa Atoll. *atoll* S Maldives
95 O16 **Koli** *var.* Kolinkylä. Pohjois-Karjala, E Finland
41 O13 **Koliganek** Alaska, USA
113 E16 **Kolín** *Ger.* Kolin. Středni Čechy, C Czech Republic
Kolinkylä see Koli
202 E12 **Koliu** Île Futuna, W Wallis and Futuna
120 E7 **Kolka** Talsi, NW Latvia
120 E7 **Kolkasrags** *prev. Eng.* Cape Domesnes. *headland* NW Latvia
153 P14 **Kolkhozobod** *Rus.* Kolkhozabad; *prev.* Kaganovichabad, Tugalan. SW Tajikistan
Kolki/Kolki see Kolky
118 K3 **Kolky** *Pol.* Kołki, *Rus.* Kolki. Volyns'ka Oblast', NW Ukraine
161 G20 **Kollegāl** Karnātaka, W India
100 M5 **Kollum** Friesland, N Netherlands
Kolmar see Colmar
103 E16 **Köln** *var.* Koeln, *Eng./Fr.* Cologne; *prev.* Cöln, *anc.* Colonia Agrippina, Oppidum Ubiorum. Nordrhein-Westfalen, W Germany
112 J9 **Kolno** Łomża, NE Poland
112 J12 **Koło** Konin, C Poland
40 B8 **Koloa** *Haw.* Kōloa. Kauai, Hawaii, USA, C Pacific Ocean
112 E7 **Kołobrzeg** *Ger.* Kolberg. Koszalin, NW Poland
130 H4 **Kologriv** Smolenskaya Oblast', W Russian Federation
202 E13 **Kolofau, Mont** ▲ Île Alofi, S Wallis and Futuna
129 O14 **Kologriv** Kostromskaya Oblast', W Russian Federation
78 L12 **Kolokani** Koulikoro, W Mali
79 N13 **Koloko** W Burkina
195 U14 **Kolombangara** *var.* Kilimbangara, Nduke. *island* New Georgia Islands, NW Solomon Islands
Kolomea see Kolomyya
130 L4 **Kolomna** Moskovskaya Oblast', W Russian Federation
118 J7 **Kolomyya** *Ger.* Kolomea. Ivano-Frankivs'ka Oblast', W Ukraine
78 K13 **Kolondiéba** Sikasso, SW Mali
200 R15 **Kolonga** Tongatapu, S Tonga
201 U16 **Kolonia** *var.* Colonia. Pohnpei, E Micronesia
Kolonja see Kolonjë
115 K21 **Kolonjë** *var.* Kolonja. Fier, C Albania
Kolonjë see Erseke
115 L21 **Kolonjë** see Avuavu
200 Q15 **Kolovai** Tongatapu, S Tonga
175 R13 **Kolowanawatobo, Teluk** *bay* Pulau Buton, C Indonesia
114 C9 **Kolpa** *Ger.* Kulpa, *SCr.* Kupa. ↗ Croatia/Slovenia
126 I12 **Kolpashevo** Tomskaya Oblast', C Russian Federation
128 I13 **Kolpino** Leningradskaya Oblast', NW Russian Federation
102 M10 **Kolpny** ↗ W Russian Federation
128 K5 **Kol'skiy Poluostrov** *Eng.* Kola Peninsula. *peninsula* NW Russian Federation
131 T6 **Koltubanovskiy** Orenburgskaya Oblast', W Russian Federation

114 L11 **Kolubara** ↗ C Yugoslavia
Kolupchii see Krupnik
112 K13 **Koluszki** Piotrków, C Poland
129 T6 **Kolva** ↗ NW Russian Federation
95 E14 **Kolvereid** Nord-Trøndelag, W Norway
154 L15 **Kolwa** Baluchistān, SW Pakistan
81 M24 **Kolwezi** Shaba, S Zaire
127 Nn7 **Kolyma** ↗ NE Russian Federation
Kolyma Lowland see Kolymskaya Nizmennost'
Kolyma Range/Kolymskiy, Khrebet see Kolymskoye Nagor'ye
127 Nn6 **Kolymskaya Nizmennost'** *Eng.* Kolyma Lowland. *lowlands* NE Russian Federation
127 Nn6 **Kolymskoye** Respublika Sakha (Yakutiya), NE Russian Federation
127 N17 **Kolymskoye Nagor'ye** *var.* Khrebet Kolymskiy, *Eng.* Kolyma Range. ▲ E Russian Federation
127 N17 **Kolyuchinskaya Guba** *bay* NE Russian Federation
151 W15 **Kol'zhat** Almaty, SE Kazakhstan
116 G8 **Kom** ▲ NW Bulgaria
82 I13 **Koma** C Ethiopia
79 X12 **Komadugu Gana** ↗ NE Nigeria
171 Ii15 **Komagane** Nagano, Honshū, S Japan
81 P17 **Komanda** Haut-Zaïre, NE Zaire
207 U1 **Komandorskaya Basin** *var.* Kamchatka Basin. *undersea feature* SW Bering Sea
129 Pp9 **Komandorskiye Ostrova** *Eng.* Commander Islands. *island group* E Russian Federation
Kománfalva see Comănești
113 I22 **Komárno** *Ger.* Komorn, *Hung.* Komárom. Západné Slovensko, SW Slovakia
113 I22 **Komárom** Komárom-Esztergom, NW Hungary
113 I22 **Komárom** see Komárno
113 I22 **Komárom-Esztergom** *off.* Komárom-Esztergom Megye. ◆ *county* N Hungary
171 I13 **Komatsu** *var.* Komatu. Ishikawa, Honshū, SW Japan
170 Ff15 **Komatsushima** Tokushima, Shikoku, SW Japan
Komatu see Komatsu
85 D17 **Kombat** Otjozondjupa, N Namibia
79 P13 **Kombissiri** see Kombissiri
79 P13 **Kombissiri** *var.* Kombissiguiri. C Burkina
196 E10 **Komebail Lagoon** *lagoon* N Palau
83 F20 **Kome Island** *island* N Tanzania
176 W13 **Komfane** Pulau Wokam, E Indonesia
119 P10 **Kominternivs'ke** Odes'ka Oblast', SW Ukraine
129 R12 **Komi-Permyatskiy Avtonomnyy Okrug** ◆ *autonomous district* W Russian Federation
129 R8 **Komi, Respublika** ◆ *autonomous republic* NW Russian Federation
113 I25 **Komló** Baranya, SW Hungary
Kommunarsk see Alchevs'k
153 S12 **Kommunizm, Qullai** ▲ E Tajikistan
194 G12 **Komo** Southern Highlands, W PNG
175 O16 **Komodo** Pulau Komodo, S Indonesia
175 O16 **Komodo, Pulau** *island* Nusa Tenggara, S Indonesia
207 Q14 **Kong Oscar Fjord** *fjord* E Greenland
79 N16 **Komoé** *var.* Komoé Fleuve. ↗ E Ivory Coast
Komoé Fleuve see Komoé
77 X11 **Kôm Ombo** *var.* Kawm Umbū. SE Egypt
81 F20 **Komono** La Lékoumou, SW Congo
176 V10 **Komoran** Irian Jaya, E Indonesia
176 V10 **Komoran, Pulau** *island* E Indonesia
Komorn see Komárno
171 J14 **Komoro** Nagano, Honshū, S Japan
Komornok see Comorâște
116 J13 **Komotiní** *var.* Gümülcine, *Turk.* Gümülcine. Anatolikí Makedonía kai Thráki, NE Greece
115 L19 **Komovi** ▲ SW Yugoslavia
Kompaniyivka Kirovohrads'ka Oblast', C Ukraine
194 H12 **Kompiam** Enga, W PNG
Kompong see Kâmpóng
Kompong Chhnang see Kâmpóng Chhnang
Kompong Cham see Kâmpóng Cham
Kompong Kleang see Kâmpóng Khleăng
Kompong Som see Kâmpóng Saôm
Kompong Speu see Kâmpóng Spoe
Kompong Thom see Kâmpóng Thum
Komrat see Comrat
Komsomol Komsomol'skiy, Atyrau, Kazakhstan
Komsomol see Komsomolets, Kustanay, Kazakhstan
151 R8 **Komsomolabad** see Komsolabad
Komsomolets *Kaz.* Komsomol. Kustanay, N Kazakhstan
126 I2 **Komsomolets, Ostrov** *island* Severnaya Zemlya, N Russian Federation
150 P13 **Komsomolets, Zaliv** *lake gulf* SW Kazakhstan
153 **Komsomolobod** *Rus.* Komsolabad. C Tajikistan

128 M16 **Komsomol'sk** Ivanovskaya Oblast', W Russian Federation
119 S6 **Komsomol's'k** Poltavs'ka Oblast', C Ukraine
152 M11 **Komsomol'skiy** *Kaz.*
150 G12 **Komsomol'skiy** *Kaz.* Komsomol. Atyrau, W Kazakhstan
129 W4 **Komsomol'skiy** Respublika Komi, NW Russian Federation
127 Nn15 **Komsomol'sk-na-Amure** Khabarovskiy Kray, SE Russian Federation
119 R3 **Komsomol'sk-na-Ustyurte** see Komsomol'sk-Ustyurt
150 K10 **Komsomol'skoye** Aktyubinsk, NW Kazakhstan
131 Q8 **Komsomol'skoye** Saratovskaya Oblast', W Russian Federation
152 G6 **Komsomol'sk-Ustyurt** *Rus.* Komsomol'sk-na-Ustyurte. Qoraqalpoghiston Respublikasi, NW Uzbekistan
151 P10 **Kon** ◎ C Kazakhstan
Kona see Kailua
128 K16 **Konakovo** Tverskaya Oblast', W Russian Federation
149 V15 **Konārak** Sīstān va Balūchestān, SE Iran
Konarhā see Kunar
29 O11 **Konawa** Oklahoma, C USA
176 V9 **Konda** Irian Jaya, E Indonesia
125 Ff11 **Konda** ↗ C Russian Federation
160 L13 **Kondagaon** Madhya Pradesh, C India
12 K10 **Kondiaronk, Lac** ◎ Québec, SE Canada
188 J13 **Kondinin** Western Australia
83 H21 **Kondoa** Dodoma, C Tanzania
131 P6 **Kondol'** Penzenskaya Oblast', W Russian Federation
116 N10 **Kondolovo** Burgaska Oblast', SE Bulgaria
128 J10 **Kondopoga** Respublika Kareliya, NW Russian Federation
Kondoz see Kunduz
161 J17 **Kondukūr** *var.* Kandukur. Andhra Pradesh, E India
Kondūz see Kunduz
197 H6 **Koné** Province Nord, W New Caledonia
Könekesir see Kёnekesir
Köneürgench see Kёneurgench
79 N15 **Kong** N Ivory Coast
41 S5 **Kongakut River** ↗ Alaska, USA
207 O14 **Kong Christian IX Land** *Eng.* King Christian IX Land. *physical region* SE Greenland
207 P13 **Kong Christian X Land** *Eng.* King Christian X Land. *physical region* E Greenland
207 N13 **Kong Frederik IX Land** *Eng.* King Frederik IX Land. *physical region* SW Greenland
207 Q12 **Kong Frederik VIII Land** *Eng.* King Frederik VIII Land. *physical region* NE Greenland
207 N15 **Kong Frederik VI Kyst** *Eng.* King Frederik VI Coast. *physical region* SE Greenland
178 I13 **Kông, Kaôh** *prev.* Kas Kong. *island* SW Cambodia
94 P2 **Kong Karls Land** *Eng.* King Charles Islands. *island group* SE Svalbard
83 G4 **Kong Kong** ↗ SE Sudan
Kongo see Congo
85 G16 **Kongola** Caprivi, NE Namibia
81 N21 **Kongolo** Shaba, E Zaire
82 Q2 **Kongor** Jonglei, SE Sudan
79 P9 **Kongoussi** N Burkina
97 G15 **Kongsberg** Buskerud, S Norway
94 Q2 **Kongsøya** *island* Kong Karls Land, E Svalbard
97 I14 **Kongsvinger** Hedmark, S Norway
178 Jj11 **Kông, Tônle** *Lao.* Xê Kong. ↗ Cambodia/Laos
164 E9 **Kongur Shan** ▲ NW China
83 I22 **Kongwa** Dodoma, C Tanzania
Kong, Xê see Kông, Tônle
Konia see Konya
153 N11 **Konibodom** *Rus.* Kanibadam. N Tajikistan
113 K15 **Koniecpol** Częstochowa, S Poland
Konieh see Konya
103 K23 **Königsbrunn** Bayern, S Germany
103 O24 **Königssee** ◎ SE Germany
103 H15 **Königstein** ▲ S Austria
111 U3 **Königswiesen** Oberösterreich, N Austria
103 E17 **Königswinter** Nordrhein-Westfalen, W Germany
231 M11 **Königwinkel** N Kenimekh. Nawoiy Wiloyati, N Uzbekistan
21 I12 **Konin** *Ger.* Kuhnau. Konin, C Poland
112 I12 **Konin** *off.* Województwo Konińskie, Województwo Konin. ◆ *province* C Poland
Koninkrijk der Nederlanden see Netherlands
Konińskie, Województwo see Konin
115 I20 **Konispol** *var.* Konispoli. Vlorë, S Albania
Konispoli see Konispol
117 C15 **Kónitsa** Ípeiros, W Greece
110 D8 **Köniz** Bern, W Switzerland
114 H14 **Konjic** ◆ S Bosnia and Herzegovina
84 H10 **Konkiep** ↗ S Namibia

85 D22 **Konkiep** ↗ S Namibia
78 I14 **Konkouré** ↗ W Guinea
79 O11 **Konna** Mopti, S Mali
195 P10 **Konogaiang, Mount** ▲ New Ireland, NE PNG
195 P10 **Konogogo** New Ireland, NE PNG
110 E9 **Konolfingen** Bern, W Switzerland
79 P16 **Konongo** C Ghana
195 O9 **Konos** New Ireland, NE PNG
128 M12 **Konosha** Arkhangel'skaya Oblast', NW Russian Federation
119 R3 **Konotop** Sums'ka Oblast', NE Ukraine
164 L7 **Konqi He** ↗ NW China
113 L14 **Końskie** Kielce, S Poland
Konstantinovka see Kostyantynivka
130 M11 **Konstantinovsk** Rostovskaya Oblast', SW Russian Federation
103 H24 **Konstanz** *var.* Constanz, *Eng.* Constance; *hist.* Kostnitz, *anc.* Constantia. Baden-Württemberg, S Germany
Konstanza see Constanța
79 T14 **Kontagora** Niger, W Nigeria
80 E13 **Kontcha** Nord, N Cameroon
101 G17 **Kontich** Antwerpen, N Belgium
95 O16 **Kontiolahti** Pohjois-Karjala, SE Finland
95 M15 **Kontiomäki** Oulu, C Finland
178 K11 **Kon Tum** *var.* Kontum. Kon Tum, C Vietnam
Konur see Sulakyurt
142 H15 **Konya** *var.* Konia, Konieh; *anc.* Iconium. Konya, C Turkey
142 H15 **Konya** *var.* Konia, Konieh. ◆ *province* C Turkey
151 W15 **Konyrolen** Taldykorgan, SE Kazakhstan
83 I19 **Konza** Eastern, S Kenya
100 I9 **Koog aan den Zaan** Noord-Holland, C Netherlands
190 E7 **Koonibba** South Australia
33 O11 **Koontz Lake** Indiana, N USA
176 V8 **Koor** Irian Jaya, E Indonesia
191 R9 **Koorawatha** New South Wales, SE Australia
120 I4 **Koosa** Tartumaa, E Estonia
9 **Kootenai** *var.* Kootenay. ↗ Canada/USA *see also* Kootenay
9 **Kootenay** *var.* Kootenai. ↗ Canada/USA *see also* Kootenai
85 F24 **Kootjieskolk** Northern Cape, W South Africa
115 M15 **Kopaonik** ▲ S Yugoslavia
Kopar see Koper
94 K1 **Kópasker** Nordhurland Eystra, N Iceland
94 H4 **Kópavogur** Reykjanes, W Iceland
111 S13 **Koper** *It.* Capodistria; *prev.* Kopar; *anc.* Capris. SW Slovenia
97 C16 **Kopervik** Rogaland, S Norway
Kopetdag, Khrebet see Koppeh Dāgh
125 Ee12 **Kopeysk** Kurganskaya Oblast', C Russian Federation
191 V6 **Kopi** South Australia
159 W12 **Kopili** ↗ NE India
97 M15 **Köping** Västmanland, C Sweden
115 K17 **Koplik** *var.* Kopliku. Shkodër, NW Albania
Kopliku see Koplik
96 I11 **Koppang** Hedmark, S Norway
97 L15 **Kopparberg** Örebro, C Sweden
96 J12 **Kopparberg** ◆ *county* C Sweden
149 S3 **Koppeh Dāgh** *var.* Khrebet Kopetdag. ▲ Iran/Turkmenistan
117 H19 **Kopríni** Attikí, C Greece
Koror see Oreor
Körös see Križevci
113 L23 **Körös** ↗ E Hungary
197 I14 **Koro Sea** *sea* C Fiji
119 X3 **Korosten'** Zhytomyrs'ka Oblast', NW Ukraine
119 N4 **Korostyshiv** *Rus.* Korostyshev. Zhytomyrs'ka Oblast', N Ukraine
129 V3 **Korotaikha** ↗ NW Russian Federation
126 H11 **Korotchayevo** Yamalo-Nenetskiy Avtonomnyy Okrug, N Russian Federation
80 I7 **Koro Toro** Borkou-Ennedi-Tibesti, N Chad
41 N16 **Korovin Island** *island* Shumagin Islands, Alaska, USA
197 I14 **Korovou** Viti Levu, W Fiji
115 M18 **Korab** ▲ Albania/FYR Macedonia
115 M18 **Korpilahti** Keski-Suomi, C Finland
95 M17 **Korpilombolo** Norrbotten, N Sweden
127 Oo16 **Korsakov** Ostrov Sakhalin, Sakhalinskaya Oblast', SE Russian Federation
97 J16 **Korsholm** *Fin.* Mustasaari. Vaasa, W Finland
97 J24 **Korsør** Vestsjælland, E Denmark
119 P6 **Korsun'-Shevchenkivs'kyy** *Rus.* Korsun'-Shevchenkovskiy. Cherkas'ka Oblast', C Ukraine
Korsun'-Shevchenkovskiy see Korsun'-Shevchenkivs'kyy
103 H15 **Korbach** Hessen, C Germany
115 M22 **Korçë** *var.* Korça, *Gk.* Korytsa, *It.* Corriza; *prev.* Koritsa. Korçë, SE Albania
115 L22 **Korçë** ◆ *district* SE Albania
103 C17 **Kortemark** West-Vlaanderen, NW Belgium
101 H18 **Kortenberg** Vlaams Brabant, C Belgium
101 K18 **Kortessem** Limburg, NE Belgium
101 C18 **Kortrijk** *Fr.* Courtrai. West-Vlaanderen, W Belgium

169 V13 **Korea Bay** *bay* China/ North Korea
Korea, Democratic People's Republic of see North Korea
169 Uu15 **Koreare** Pulau Yamdena, E Indonesia
Korea, Republic of see South Korea
169 Z17 **Korea Strait** *Jap.* Chōsen-kaikyō, *Kor.* Taehan-haehyŏp. *channel* Japan/South Korea
Korelichi/Korelicze see Karelichy
82 J11 **Korem** N Ethiopia
79 U11 **Korén Adoua** ↗ C Niger
130 I7 **Korenevo** Kurskaya Oblast', W Russian Federation
130 L13 **Korenovsk** Krasnodarskiy Kray, SW Russian Federation
118 L4 **Korets'** *Pol.* Korzec, *Rus.* Rivnens'ka Oblast', NW Ukraine
127 Pp8 **Korf** Koryakskiy Avtonomnyy Okrug, E Russian Federation
204 L7 **Korff Ice Rise** *ice cap* Antarctica
94 G13 **Korgen** Troms, N Norway
153 R9 **Korgon-Debe** Dzhalal-Abadskaya Oblast', W Kyrgyzstan
78 M14 **Korhogo** N Ivory Coast
117 F19 **Korinthiakós Kólpos** *Eng.* Gulf of Corinth; *anc.* Corinthiacus Sinus. *gulf* C Greece
117 F19 **Kórinthos** *Eng.* Corinth; *anc.* Corinthus. Pelopónnisos, S Greece
115 M18 **Koritnik** ▲ S Yugoslavia
Koritsa see Korçë
171 L14 **Kōriyama** Fukushima, Honshū, C Japan
142 E16 **Korkuteli** Antalya, SW Turkey
164 K6 **Korla** *Chin.* K'u-erh-lo. Xinjiang Uygur Zizhiqu, NW China
126 H11 **Korliki** Khanty-Mansiyskiy Avtonomnyy Okrug, C Russian Federation
Körlin an der Persante see Karlino
Korma see Karma
153 U9 **Kosh-Debe** *var.* Koshtebe. Narynskaya Oblast', C Kyrgyzstan
171 K16 **Koshigaya** *var.* Kosigaya. Saitama, Honshū, S Japan
170 B15 **Koshikijima-rettō** *var.* Koshikizima Rettō. *island group* SW Japan
151 W13 **Koshkarkol', Ozero** ◎ SE Kazakhstan
32 L9 **Koshkonong, Lake** ◎ Wisconsin, N USA
152 B10 **Koshoba** *Turkm.* Goshoba. Balkanskiy Velayat, NW Turkmenistan
171 J14 **Kōshoku** *var.* Kōsyoku. Nagano, Honshū, S Japan
Koshtebe see Kosh-Debe
Kōshū see Kwangju
113 N19 **Košice** *Ger.* Kaschau, *Hung.* Kassa. Východné Slovensko, E Slovakia
Kosigaya see Koshigaya
Kosikizima Rettō see Koshikijima-rettō
159 F13 **Kosi Reservoir** ◎ E Nepal
118 J8 **Kosiv** Ivano-Frankivs'ka Oblast', W Ukraine
151 O11 **Koskol'** Zhezkazgan, C Kazakhstan
129 Q9 **Koslan** Respublika Komi, NW Russian Federation
Köslin see Koszalin
152 M12 **Koson** *Rus.* Kasan. Qashqadaryo Wiloyati, S Uzbekistan
169 Y13 **Kosong** SE North Korea
153 S9 **Kosonsoy** *Rus.* Kasansay. Namangan Wiloyati, E Uzbekistan
115 M16 **Kosovo** *prev.* Autonomous Province of Kosovo and Metohija. *cultural region* S Yugoslavia
Kosovo see Kosova
Kosovo and Metohija, Autonomous Province of see Kosovo
115 N16 **Kosovo Polje** Serbia, S Yugoslavia
115 N16 **Kosovska Kamenica** Serbia, SE Yugoslavia
115 M16 **Kosovska Mitrovica** *Alb.* Mitrovicë; *prev.* Mitrovica, Titova Mitrovica. Serbia, S Yugoslavia
201 X17 **Kosrae** ◆ *state* E Micronesia
201 Y14 **Kosrae** *prev.* Kusaie. *island* Caroline Islands, E Micronesia
27 U7 **Kosse** Texas, SW USA
111 P6 **Kössen** Tirol, W Austria
78 M16 **Kossou, Lac de** ◎ C Ivory Coast
Kossukavak see Krumovgrad
114 F10 **Kostajnica** *var.* Hrvatska Kostajnica. Sisak-Moslavina, C Croatia
Kostamus see Kostomuksha
Kosten see Kościan
116 Hi0 **Kostenets** *prev.* Georgi Dimitrov. Sofiyska Oblast', W Bulgaria
82 H7 **Kosti** White Nile, C Sudan
Kostnitz see Constanz
115 N14 **Kostomuksha** *Fin.* Kostamus. Respublika Kareliya, NW Russian Federation
118 J3 **Kostopil'** *Rus.* Kostopol'. Rivnens'ka Oblast', NW Ukraine
Kostopol' see Kostopil'
128 M15 **Kostroma** Kostromskaya Oblast', NW Russian Federation
129 N14 **Kostroma** ↗ NW Russian Federation
129 N14 **Kostromskaya Oblast'** ◆ *province* NW Russian Federation
112 D12 **Kostrzyn** *Ger.* Cüstrin, Küstrin. Gorzów, W Poland
112 H11 **Kostrzyn** Poznań, C Poland
119 X7 **Kostyantynivka** *Rus.* Konstantinovka. Donets'ka Oblast', SE Ukraine
Kostyukovichi see Kastsyukovichy

191 O13 **Korumburra** Victoria, SE Australia
127 P8 **Koryak Range** see Koryakskoye Nagor'ye
127 P8 **Koryakskiy Avtonomnyy Okrug** ◆ *autonomous district* E Russian Federation
Koryakskiy Khrebet see Koryakskoye Nagor'ye
127 Pp7 **Koryakskoye Nagor'ye** *var.* Koryakskiy Khrebet, *Eng.* Koryak Range. ▲ NE Russian Federation
129 P11 **Koryazhma** Arkhangel'skaya Oblast', NW Russian Federation
Kёryô see Kangnŭng
119 Q2 **Koryukivka** Chernihivs'ka Oblast', N Ukraine
Korzec see Korets'
117 N21 **Kos** Kos, Dodekánisos, Greece, Aegean Sea
117 M21 **Kos** *It.* Coo; *anc.* Cos. *island* Dodekánisos, Greece, Aegean Sea
129 T12 **Kosa** *var.* Komi-Permyatskiy Avtonomnyy Okrug, NW Russian Federation
129 T13 **Kosa** ↗ NW Russian Federation
170 C11 **Ko-saki** *headland* Nagasaki, Tsushima, SW Japan
169 X13 **Kosan** SE North Korea
121 H18 **Kosava** *Rus.* Kosovo. Brestskaya Voblasts', SW Belarus
Kosch see Kosa
150 G12 **Koschagyl** *Kaz.* Qosshaghyl. Atyrau, W Kazakhstan
112 G12 **Kościan** *Ger.* Kosten. Leszno, W Poland
112 I7 **Kościerzyna** Gdańsk, NW Poland
24 J4 **Kosciusko** Mississippi, S USA
191 R11 **Kosciusko, Mount** ▲ New South Wales, SE Australia
120 H4 **Kose** Harjumaa, NW Estonia
116 G6 **Kosava** Oblast Montana, NW Bulgaria

● COUNTRY   ◇ DEPENDENT TERRITORY   ◆ ADMINISTRATIVE REGION   ▲ MOUNTAIN   ▼ VOLCANO   ◎ LAKE
● COUNTRY CAPITAL   ○ DEPENDENT TERRITORY CAPITAL   ✕ INTERNATIONAL AIRPORT   ▲ MOUNTAIN RANGE   ↗ RIVER   ◉ RESERVOIR

271

Kostyukovka see Kastsyukowka
Kôsyoku see Kōshoku
129 U6 Kos'yu Respublika Komi, NW Russian Federation
129 U6 Kos'yu ◊ NW Russian Federation
112 F7 Koszalin Ger. Köslin. Koszalin, NW Poland
112 F8 Koszalin off. Województwo Koszalińskie. Ger. Köslin. ◇ province NW Poland
Koszalińskie, Województwo see Koszalin
113 F22 Kőszeg Ger. Güns. Vas, W Hungary
158 H13 Kota prev. Kotah. Rājasthān, N India
174 H9 Kota Baru Sumatera, W Indonesia
175 Nn11 Kotabaru Pulau Laut, C Indonesia
Kotabaru see Jayapura
174 H2 Kota Bharu var. Kota Baharu, Kota Bahru. Kelantan, Peninsular Malaysia
Kotaboemi see Kotabumi
174 Ii12 Kotabumi prev. Kotaboemi. Sumatera, W Indonesia
155 S10 Kot Addu Punjab, E Pakistan
Kot Addu see Kota
175 Nn2 Kota Kinabalu prev. Jesselton. Sabah, East Malaysia
175 Nn2 Kota Kinabalu ✈ Sabah, East Malaysia
94 M12 Kotala Lappi, N Finland
Kotamobagoe see Kotamobagu
175 Rr7 Kotamobagu prev. Kotamobagoe. Sulawesi, C Indonesia
161 L14 Kotapad var. Kotapārh. Orissa, E India
Kotapārh see Kotapad
178 Gg17 Ko Ta Ru Tao island SW Thailand
174 L11 Kotawaringin, Teluk bay Borneo, C Indonesia
155 Q13 Kot Diji Sind, SE Pakistan
158 K9 Kotdwāra Uttar Pradesh, N India
129 Q14 Kotel'nich Kirovskaya Oblast', NW Russian Federation
131 N12 Kotel'nikovo Volgogradskaya Oblast', SW Russian Federation
126 Ll4 Kotel'nyy, Ostrov island Novosibirskiye Ostrova, N Russian Federation
119 T5 Kotel'va Poltavs'ka Oblast', C Ukraine
103 M14 Köthen var. Cöthen. Sachsen-Anhalt, C Germany
Kôti see Kōchi
83 G17 Kotido NE Uganda
95 M19 Kotka Kymi, S Finland
129 P11 Kotlas Arkhangel'skaya Oblast', NW Russian Federation
40 M10 Kotlik Alaska, USA
79 Q17 Kotoka ✈ (Accra) S Ghana
Kotonu see Cotonou
115 J17 Kotor It. Cattaro. Montenegro, SW Yugoslavia
Kotor see Kotoriba
114 F7 Kotoriba Hung. Kotor. Medimurje, N Croatia
115 I17 Kotorska, Boka It. Bocche di Cattaro. bay Montenegro, SW Yugoslavia
114 H11 Kotorsko N Bosnia and Herzegovina
114 G11 Kotor Varoš N Bosnia and Herzegovina
Koto Sho/Kotosho see Lan Yü
130 M7 Kotovsk Tambovskaya Oblast', W Russian Federation
119 O9 Kotovs'k Rus. Kotovsk. Odes'ka Oblast', SW Ukraine
Kotovsk see Hînceşti
121 G16 Kotra Rus. Kotra. ◄ W Belarus
155 P16 Kotri Sind, SE Pakistan
111 Q9 Kötschach Kärnten, S Austria
161 K15 Kottagūdem Andhra Pradesh, E India
161 F21 Kottappadi Kerala, SW India
161 G23 Kottayam Kerala, SW India
Kottbus see Cottbus
Kotte see Sri Jayawardanapura
81 K15 Kotto ◄ Central African Republic/Zaire
200 S13 Kotu Group island group W Tonga
152 B11 Koturdepe Turkm. Goturdepe. Balkanskiy Velayat, W Turkmenistan
126 J9 Kotuy ◄ N Russian Federation
85 M16 Kotwa Mashonaland East, NE Zimbabwe
41 N7 Kotzebue Alaska, USA
40 M7 Kotzebue Sound inlet Alaska, USA
Kotzenau see Chocianów
Kotzman see Kitsman'
79 N4 Kouandé N Benin
81 J15 Kouango Ouaka, S Central African Republic
79 O13 Koudougou C Burkina
100 K7 Koudum Friesland, N Netherlands
117 L25 Koufonísi island SE Greece
117 K21 Koufonísi island Kykládes, Greece, Aegean Sea
40 M8 Kougarok Mountain ▲ Alaska, USA
81 E20 Kouilou ◄ S Congo
78 L17 Koukdjuak ◄ Baffin Island, Northwest Territories, NE Canada
81 N3 Koúklia SW Cyprus
81 E19 Koulamoutou Ogooué-Lolo, C Gabon
78 L12 Koulikoro Koulikoro, SW Mali
78 L11 Kouli ◄ W French Guiana
197 H5 Koumac Province Nord, W New Caledonia
171 I13 Koumi Nagano, Honshū, N Japan
80 I13 Koumra Moyen-Chari, S Chad
Kounadougou see Koundougou
78 M15 Kounahiri C Ivory Coast
78 I12 Koundâra Moyenne-Guinée, NW Guinea
79 N13 Koundougou var. Kounadougou. C Burkina
78 H11 Koungheul C Senegal
151 T13 Kounradskiy Zhezkazgan, SE Kazakhstan
27 X10 Kountze Texas, SW USA
79 Q13 Koupéla C Burkina
79 Q13 Kouri Sikasso, SW Mali
57 Y9 Kourou N French Guiana
78 J12 Kouroú ◄ NE Greece
78 K14 Kouroussa Haute-Guinée, C Guinea
Kousseir see Al Quşayr
80 G11 Kousséri prev. Fort-Foureau. Extrême-Nord, NE Cameroon
Kouteifé see Al Qutayfah
78 M13 Koutiala Sikasso, S Mali
78 M14 Kouto NW Ivory Coast
95 N19 Kouvola Kymi, S Finland
81 G18 Kouyou ◄ C Congo
114 M10 Kovačica Hung. Antalfalva; prev. Kovacsica. Serbia, N Yugoslavia
Kovacsica see Kovačica
Kővárhosszúfalu see Satulung
Kovászna see Covasna
128 I4 Kovdor Murmanskaya Oblast', NW Russian Federation
128 I5 Kovdozero, Ozero ◎ NW Russian Federation
118 J3 Kovel' Pol. Kowel. Volyns'ka Oblast', NW Ukraine
114 M12 Kovin Hung. Kevevára; prev. Temes-Kubin. Serbia, NE Yugoslavia
Kovno see Kaunas
131 N3 Kovrov Vladimirskaya Oblast', W Russian Federation
131 O5 Kovylkino Respublika Mordoviya, W Russian Federation
114 D7 Kowal Włocławek, C Poland
112 J9 Kowalewo Pomorskie Ger. Schönsee. Toruń, N Poland
121 M16 Kowbcha Rus. Kolbcha. Mahilyowskaya Voblasts', E Belarus
Koweit see Kuwait
Kowel see Kovel'
193 F17 Kowhitirangi West Coast, South Island, NZ
167 O15 Kowloon Chin. Jiulong. Hong Kong, S China
165 N7 Kox Kuduk well NW China
142 D16 Köyceğiz Muğla, SW Turkey
129 N6 Koyda Arkhangel'skaya Oblast', NW Russian Federation
152 D10 Koymat Turkm. Goymat. Balkanskiy Velayat, NW Turkmenistan
152 D10 Koymatdag, Gory Turkm. Goymatdag. hill range NW Turkmenistan
161 L15 Koyna Reservoir ◙ W India
171 M11 Koyoshi-gawa ◄ Honshū, C Japan
Koysanjaq see Koi Sanjaq
Koytash see Qŭytosh
41 N9 Koyuk Alaska, USA
41 N9 Koyuk River ◄ Alaska, USA
41 O9 Koyukuk Alaska, USA
41 O9 Koyukuk River ◄ Alaska, USA
142 J13 Kozaklı Nevşehir, C Turkey
170 F13 Kōzan Hiroshima, Honshū, SW Japan
142 M14 Kozan Adana, S Turkey
117 E14 Kozáni Dytikí Makedonía, N Greece
114 F10 Kozara ▲ NW Bosnia and Herzegovina
119 P3 Kozelets' Rus. Kozelets. Chernihivs'ka Oblast', NE Ukraine
119 S6 Kozel'shchyna Poltavs'ka Oblast', C Ukraine
130 J5 Kozel'sk Kaluzhskaya Oblast', W Russian Federation
Kozhikode see Calicut
129 V9 Kozhimiz, Gora ▲ NW Russian Federation
128 L9 Kozhozero, Ozero ◎ NW Russian Federation
129 T7 Kozhva Komi, NW Russian Federation
129 T7 Kozhva ◄ NW Russian Federation
129 U6 Kozhym Respublika Komi, NW Russian Federation
112 N13 Kozienice Radom, C Poland
111 S13 Kozina SW Slovenia
116 H7 Kozloduy Oblast Montana, NW Bulgaria
131 Q3 Kozlovka Chuvashskaya Respublika, W Russian Federation
131 P3 Koz'modem'yansk Respublika Mariy El, W Russian Federation
118 J6 Kozova Ternopil's'ka Oblast', W Ukraine
115 P20 Kožuf ▲ S FYR Macedonia
172 S13 Kōzu-shima island E Japan
119 S6 Kozyatyn Rus. Kazatin. Vinnyts'ka Oblast', C Ukraine
79 Q16 Kpalimé var. Palimé. SW Togo
79 Q16 Kpandu E Ghana
101 F15 Krabbendijke Zeeland, SW Netherlands
178 Hh10 Krabi var. Muang Krabi. Krabi, SW Thailand
178 Gg13 Kra Buri Ranong, SW Thailand
178 Ji13 Krâchéh prev. Kratie. Krâchéh, E Cambodia
79 Q15 Kragero Telemark, S Norway
114 M13 Kragujevac Serbia, C Yugoslavia

114 D12 Krajina cultural region SW Croatia
Krakatau, Pulau see Rakata, Pulau
Krakau see Kraków
113 L16 Kraków Eng. Cracow, Ger. Krakau; anc. Cracovia. Kraków, S Poland
113 K16 Kraków off. Województwo Krakowskie. Eng. Cracow, Ger. Krakau. ◇ province S Poland
102 L9 Krakower See ◎ NE Germany
Krakowskie, Województwo see Kraków
178 Ii12 Krâlănh Siĕmréab, NW Cambodia
47 Q16 Kralendijk Bonaire, E Netherlands Antilles
114 B10 Kraljevica It. Porto Re. Primorje-Gorski Kotar, NW Croatia
114 M13 Kraljevo prev. Rankovićevo. Serbia, C Yugoslavia
Kralup an der Moldau see Kralupy nad Vltavou
113 C16 Kralupy nad Vltavou Ger. Kralup an der Moldau. Středni Čechy, NW Czech Republic
119 W7 Kramators'k Rus. Kramatorsk. Donets'ka Oblast', SE Ukraine
95 H17 Kramfors Västernorrland, C Sweden
117 D15 Kranéa Dytikí Makedonía, N Greece
110 M7 Kranebitten ✈ (Innsbruck) Tirol, W Austria
117 G20 Kranídi Pelopónnisos, S Greece
111 T11 Kranj Ger. Krainburg. NW Slovenia
117 F16 Krannón battleground Thessalía, C Greece
Kranz see Zelenogradsk
114 D7 Krapina Krapina-Zagorje, N Croatia
114 E8 Krapina ◄ N Croatia
114 D8 Krapina-Zagorje off. Krapinsko-Zagorska Županija. ◇ province NW Croatia
116 L7 Krapinets ◄ NE Bulgaria
113 I15 Krapkowice Ger. Krappitz. Opole, SW Poland
Krappitz see Krapkowice
129 O12 Krasavino Vologodskaya Oblast', NW Russian Federation
125 Ff5 Krasino Novaya Zemlya, Arkhangel'skaya Oblast', N Russian Federation
127 N18 Kraskino Primorskiy Kray, SE Russian Federation
120 J11 Kràslava Krāslava, SE Latvia
121 N14 Krasnaluki Rus. Krasnoluki. Vitsyebskaya Voblasts', N Belarus
121 P17 Krasnapollye Rus. Krasnopol'ye. Mahilyowskaya Voblasts', E Belarus
121 J18 Krasnaya Slabada var. Chyrvonaya Slabada, Rus. Krasnaya Sloboda. Minskaya Voblasts', S Belarus
Krasnaya Sloboda see Krasnaya Slabada
121 J15 Krasnaye Rus. Krasnoye. Minskaya Voblasts', C Belarus
113 O14 Kraśnik Rus. Kratznick. Lublin, E Poland
113 O14 Kraśnik Fabryczny Lublin, SE Poland
119 O9 Krasni Okny Odes'ka Oblast', SW Ukraine
151 P7 Krasnoarmeysk Kokshetau, N Kazakhstan
131 P8 Krasnoarmeysk Saratovskaya Oblast', W Russian Federation
Krasnoarmeysk see Krasnoarmiys'k
127 Oo4 Krasnoarmeyskiy Chukotskiy Avtonomnyy Okrug, NE Russian Federation
119 W7 Krasnoarmiys'k Rus. Krasnoarmeysk. Donets'ka Oblast', SE Ukraine
129 P11 Krasnoborsk Arkhangel'skaya Oblast', NW Russian Federation
130 K14 Krasnodar prev. Ekaterinodar, Yekaterinodar. Krasnodarskiy Kray, SW Russian Federation
130 K13 Krasnodarskiy Kray ◇ territory SW Russian Federation
119 Z7 Krasnodon Luhans'ka Oblast', E Ukraine
Krasnogor see Kallaste
131 T2 Krasnogorskoye Latv. Sarkaņi. Udmurtskaya Respublika, NW Russian Federation
Krasnograd see Krasnohrad
Krasnogvardeysk see Bulunghur
130 M9 Krasnogvardeyskoye Stavropol'skiy Kray, SW Russian Federation
Krasnogvardeyskoye see Krasnohvardiys'ke
119 U6 Krasnohrad Rus. Krasnograd. Kharkivs'ka Oblast', E Ukraine
119 S12 Krasnohvardiys'ke Rus. Krasnogvardeyskoye. Respublika Krym, S Ukraine
126 L16 Krasnokamensk Chitinskaya Oblast', S Russian Federation
129 U14 Krasnokamsk Permskaya Oblast', W Russian Federation
131 U8 Krasnokholm Orenburgskaya Oblast', W Russian Federation
119 U5 Krasnokuts'k Rus. Krasnokutsk. Kharkivs'ka Oblast', E Ukraine
130 L7 Krasnolesnyy Voronezhskaya Oblast', W Russian Federation
Krasnoluki see Krasnaluki
Krasnoosel'skoye Vodokhranilishche see Chervonoosil's'ke Vodokhovyshche
119 X6 Krasnoperekops'k Rus. Krasnoperekopsk. Respublika Krym, S Ukraine

119 U4 Krasnopillya Sums'ka Oblast', NE Ukraine
Krasnopol'ye see Krasnapollye
126 H9 Krasnosel'kup Yamalo-Nenetskiy Avtonomnyy Okrug, N Russian Federation
128 L5 Krasnoshchel'ye Murmanskaya Oblast', NW Russian Federation
131 T2 Krasnoslobodsk Respublika Mordoviya, W Russian Federation
131 O5 Krasnoslobodsk Volgogradskaya Oblast', SW Russian Federation
Krasnostav see Krasnystaw
125 F10 Krasnotur'insk Sverdlovskaya Oblast', C Russian Federation
125 E11 Krasnoufimsk Sverdlovskaya Oblast', C Russian Federation
125 Ee10 Krasnoural'sk Sverdlovskaya Oblast', C Russian Federation
131 V5 Krasnousol'skiy Respublika Bashkortostan, W Russian Federation
129 U12 Krasnovishersk Permskaya Oblast', W Russian Federation
152 A10 Krasnovodskiy Zaliv Turkm. Krasnovodsk Aylagy. lake gulf W Turkmenistan
152 B10 Krasnovodsk Plato Turkm. Krasnovodsk Platosy. plateau NW Turkmenistan
Krasnovodsk Aylagy see Krasnovodskiy Zaliv
Krasnovodsk Platosy see Krasnovodsk Plato
126 Hh14 Krasnoyarsk Krasnoyarskiy Kray, S Russian Federation
131 X7 Krasnoyarskiy Orenburgskaya Oblast', W Russian Federation
126 I12 Krasnoyarskiy Kray ◇ territory C Russian Federation
126 I14 Krasnoyarskoye Vodokhranilishche ◙ S Russian Federation
Krasnoye see Krasnaye
152 J15 Krasnoye Znamya Turkm. Gyzylbaydak. Maryyskiy Velayat, S Turkmenistan
129 R11 Krasnozatonskiy Respublika Komi, NW Russian Federation
120 D13 Krasnoznamensk Ger. Lasdehnen, Ger. Haselberg. Kaliningradskaya Oblast', W Russian Federation
119 R11 Krasnoznam"yans'kyy Kanal canal S Ukraine
113 P14 Krasnystaw Rus. Krasnostav. Chełm, SE Poland
130 H4 Krasnyy Smolenskaya Oblast', W Russian Federation
131 P2 Krasnyye Baki Nizhegorodskaya Oblast', W Russian Federation
131 Q13 Krasnyye Barrikady Astrakhanskaya Oblast', SW Russian Federation
128 K15 Krasnyy Kholm Tverskaya Oblast', W Russian Federation
131 Q8 Krasnyy Kut Saratovskaya Oblast', W Russian Federation
Krasnyy Liman see Krasnyy Lyman
119 Y7 Krasnyy Luch prev. Krindachevka. Luhans'ka Oblast', E Ukraine
119 X6 Krasnyy Lyman Rus. Krasnyy Liman. Donets'ka Oblast', SE Ukraine
131 R3 Krasnyy Steklovar Mariy El, W Russian Federation
131 P8 Krasnyy Tekstil'shchik Saratovskaya Oblast', W Russian Federation
131 R13 Krasnyy Yar Astrakhanskaya Oblast', SW Russian Federation
118 L5 Krasyliv Khmel'nyts'ka Oblast', C Ukraine
113 O21 Krasna Rom. Crasna. ◄ Hungary/Romania
194 I13 Kratke Range ▲ C PNG
175 Y11 Kratovo NE FYR Macedonia
113 J15 Kratznick see Kraśnik
176 Ji12 Krau Irian Jaya, E Indonesia
178 Ii13 Krăvanh, Chuŏr Phnum Eng. Cardamom Mountains, Fr. Chaine des Cardamomes. ▲ W Cambodia
Kravasta Lagoon see Karavastasë, Laguna e
79 Q16 Krawang see Karawang
Kraxatau see Rakata, Pulau
131 Q13 Kraynovka Respublika Dagestan, SW Russian Federation
120 D12 Krāžiai Kaunas, C Lithuania
29 P11 Krebs Oklahoma, C USA
103 D15 Krefeld Nordrhein-Westfalen, W Germany
Kreisstadt see Krosno Odrzańskie
117 D17 Kremastón, Technití Límni ◙ C Greece
Kremenchug see Kremenchuk
Kremenchugskoye Vodokhranilishche/Kremenchuk Reservoir see Kremenchuts'ke Vodoskhovyshche
119 S6 Kremenchuk Rus. Kremenchug. Poltavs'ka Oblast', NE Ukraine
119 R6 Kremenchuts'ke Vodoskhovyshche Eng. Kremenchuk Reservoir, Rus. Kremenchugskoye Vodokhranilishche. ◙ C Ukraine
118 K4 Kremenets' Pol. Krzemieniec. Rus. Kremenets. Ternopil's'ka Oblast', W Ukraine
100 I9 Kremmen Noord-Holland, C Netherlands
39 R4 Kremmling Colorado, C USA
111 V3 Krems ◄ NE Austria
111 W3 Krems an der Donau var. Krems. Niederösterreich, N Austria

Kremsier see Kroměříž
111 S4 Kremsmünster Oberösterreich, N Austria
40 M17 Krenitzin Islands island Aleutian Islands, Alaska, USA
Kresena see Kresna
116 G11 Kresna var. Kresena. Sofiyska Oblast', SW Bulgaria
131 T2 Krespoljin Serbia, E Yugoslavia
27 N4 Kress Texas, SW USA
127 Pp4 Kresta, Zaliv bay E Russian Federation
117 D20 Krëstena prev. Selinoûs. Dytikí Ellás, S Greece
128 H14 Krestsy Novgorodskaya Oblast', W Russian Federation
126 Kk11 Krestyakh Respublika Sakha (Yakutiya), NE Russian Federation
122 J11 Kretinga Ger. Krottingen. Kretinga, NW Lithuania
112 E12 Kreuz see Križevci, Croatia
Kreuz see Risti, Estonia
Kreuzburg/Kreuzburg in Oberschlesien see Kluczbork
Kreuzingen see Bol'shakovo
110 H6 Kreuzlingen Thurgau, NE Switzerland
103 K25 Kreuzspitze ▲ S Germany
103 F16 Kreuztal Nordrhein-Westfalen, W Germany
121 I15 Kreva Rus. Krevo. Hrodzyenskaya Voblasts', W Belarus
Krevo see Kreva
115 L20 Krrabë var. Krraba. Tiranë, C Albania
115 L17 Krrabit, Mali i ▲ N Albania
111 W12 Krško Ger. Gurkfeld; prev. Videm-Krško. E Slovenia
85 K19 Kruger National Park national park Northern, N South Africa
83 J21 Krugersdorp Gauteng, NE South Africa
40 D16 Krugloi Point headland Agattu Island, Alaska, USA
Krugloye see Kruhlaye
121 N15 Kruhlaye Rus. Krugloye. Mahilyowskaya Voblasts', E Belarus
174 I13 Krui var. Kroi. Sumatera, SW Indonesia
161 N20 Kruibeke Oost-Vlaanderen, N Belgium
101 G16 Kruidfontein Western Cape, SW South Africa
85 G25 Kruiningen Zeeland, SW Netherlands
101 F15 Kruja see Krujë
115 L19 Krujë var. Kruja, It. Croia. Durrës, C Albania
115 L19 Krujës, Mali i ▲ C Albania
Krulevshchina see Krulewshchyna
120 K13 Krulewshchyna Rus. Krulevshchina. Vitsyebskaya Voblasts', N Belarus
27 T5 Krum Texas, SW USA
103 J23 Krumbach Bayern, S Germany
115 M17 Krumë Kukës, NE Albania
Krummau see Český Krumlov
116 K12 Krumovgrad prev. Koshukavak. Khaskovska Oblast', S Bulgaria
116 K12 Krumovitsa ◄ S Bulgaria
116 L10 Krumovo Burgaska Oblast', SE Bulgaria
178 Hh11 Krung Thep var. Krung Thep Mahanakhon, Eng. Bangkok. ● (Thailand) Bangkok, S Thailand
178 Hh12 Krung Thep, Ao var. Bight of Bangkok. bay S Thailand
Krung Thep Mahanakhon see Krung Thep
121 N15 Krupki Rus. Krupki. Minskaya Voblasts', C Belarus
97 G24 Kruså var. Krusaa. Sonderjylland, SW Denmark
Krusaa see Kruså
115 M15 Kruševac Serbia, C Yugoslavia
115 N19 Kruševo SW FYR Macedonia
113 A15 Krušné Hory var. Krushnii Gori, Eng. Ore Mountains, Ger. Erzgebirge. ▲ Czech Republic/Germany see also Erzgebirge
130 M10 Krivodol Oblast Montana, NW Bulgaria
Krivorozh'ye see Kryvorizhzhya
116 J8 Krivoy Rog see Kryvyy Rih
130 M7 Kromy Orlovskaya Oblast', W Russian Federation
103 J23 Kronach Bayern, E Germany
Krone an der Brahe see Koronowo
178 Jj16 Kr-ong Kaôh Kŏng Kaôh Kŏng, SW Cambodia

127 Pp11 Kronotskiy Zaliv bay E Russian Federation
205 O2 Kronprinsesse Märtha Kyst physical region Antarctica
205 V3 Kronprins Olav Kyst physical region Antarctica
128 G12 Kronshtadt Leningradskaya Oblast', NW Russian Federation
Kronstadt see Braşov
85 I22 Kroonstad Free State, C South Africa
126 Kk13 Kropotkin Irkutskaya Oblast', C Russian Federation
130 L14 Kropotkin Krasnodarskiy Kray, SW Russian Federation
Krośnieńskie, Województwo see Krosno
112 J11 Krośniewice Płock, C Poland
113 N17 Krosno Ger. Krossen. Krosno, SE Poland
113 N17 Krosno off. Województwo Krośnieńskie. ◇ province SE Poland
120 C11 Krosno Odrzańskie Ger. Crossen, Kreisstadt. Zielona Góra, W Poland
Krossen see Krosno
112 H13 Krotoszyn Ger. Krotoschin. Kalisz, C Poland
Krottingen see Kretinga
103 F16 Krousón var. Krousón, Kroussón. Kríti, Greece, E Mediterranean Sea
Kroussón see Krousón
115 L20 Krrabë var. Krraba. Tiranë, C Albania
Kría Vrísi see Krýa Vrýsi
161 K17 Krishna, Mouths of the delta SE India
161 I16 Krishnagiri Tamil Nādu, SE India
101 G16 Krishnanagar West Bengal, N India
161 G20 Krishnarājāsāgara Reservoir ◙ SW India
115 L19 Krujë var. Kruja, It. Croia. Durrës, C Albania
97 I19 Kristdala Kalmar, S Sweden
97 E18 Kristiania see Oslo
97 L22 Kristiansand var. Christiansand. Vest-Agder, S Norway
97 J24 Kristianstad Kristianstad, S Sweden
97 J22 Kristianstad ◊ county S Sweden
96 F8 Kristiansund var. Christiansund. Møre og Romsdal, S Norway
Kristianopel see Kristineberg
95 J17 Kristiinankaupunki see Kristinestad
95 I16 Kristineberg Västerbotten, N Sweden
97 L16 Kristinehamn Värmland, C Sweden
95 J17 Kristinestad Fin. Kristiinankaupunki. Vaasa, W Finland
Kristyor see Crişcior
117 J25 Kríti Eng. Crete. ◊ region Greece, Aegean Sea
117 J24 Kríti Eng. Crete. island Greece, Aegean Sea
117 J23 Kritikó Pélagos var. Kretikon Delagos, Sea of Crete; anc. Mare Creticum. sea Greece, Aegean Sea
Kríulyany see Criuleni
114 I12 Krivaja ◄ NE Bosnia and Herzegovina
Krivaja see Mali Idoš
115 N19 Kriva Palanka Turk. Eğri Palanka. NE FYR Macedonia
Krivichi see Kryvychy
Krivoshin see Kryvoshyn
Krivoy Rog see Kryvyy Rih
114 J14 Križevci Ger. Kreuz, Hung. Kőrös. Varaždin, NE Croatia
114 B10 Krk It. Veglia. Primorje-Gorski Kotar, NW Croatia
114 B10 Krk It. Veglia; anc. Curieta. island NW Croatia
111 U12 Krka ◄ SE Slovenia
111 R11 Krka ◄ S Slovenia
Krka see Gurk
113 H16 Krnov Ger. Jägerndorf. Severní Morava, E Czech Republic
Kroatien see Croatia
103 J23 Kroderen Buskerud, S Norway
97 G14 Kroi see Krui
97 G14 Krokilaĵ see Crocodile
116 G6 Krokom Jämtland, C Sweden
119 S2 Krolevets' Rus. Krolevets. Sums'ka Oblast', NE Ukraine
Królewska Huta see Chorzów
113 H18 Kroměříž Ger. Kremsier. Jižní Morava, E Czech Republic
100 I9 Krommenie Noord-Holland, C Netherlands
119 X6 Kreminna Rus. Kremennaya. Luhans'ka Oblast', E Ukraine

Ksar au Soule see Er-Rachidia
76 J5 Ksar El Boukhari N Algeria
76 G5 Ksar-el-Kebir var. Alcázar, Ksar Kebir, Ksar-el-Kébir, Ar. Al-Kasr al-Kebir, Al-Qsar al-Kbir, Sp. Alcazarquivir. NW Morocco
112 H12 Ksiąź Wielkopolski Ger. Xions. Poznań, W Poland
131 O3 Kstovo Nizhegorodskaya Oblast', W Russian Federation
174 Mm4 Kuala Belait W Brunei
174 M7 Kuala Dungun see Dungun
174 C Kualakerian Borneo, C Indonesia
174 M10 Kualakuayan Borneo, C Indonesia
174 H4 Kuala Lipis Pahang, Peninsular Malaysia
174 H5 Kuala Lumpur ● (Malaysia) Kuala Lumpur, Peninsular Malaysia
Kuala Pelabohan Kelang see Pelabuhan Klang
175 Nn3 Kuala Penyu Sabah, East Malaysia
40 E9 Kualapuu Haw. Kualapu'u. Molokai, Hawaii, USA, C Pacific Ocean
173 G6 Kuala, Sungai ◄ Sumatera, W Indonesia
174 Hh3 Kuala Terengganu var. Kuala Trengganu. Terengganu, Peninsular Malaysia
174 Hh9 Kualatungkal Sumatera, W Indonesia
175 O3 Kuamut, Sungai ◄ East Malaysia
175 Qq7 Kuandang Sulawesi, N Indonesia
175 Qq7 Kuandang, Teluk bay Sulawesi, N Indonesia
169 V12 Kuandian Liaoning, NE China
Kuando-Kubango see Cuando Cubango
Kuang-chou see Guangzhou
Kuang-hsi see Guangxi Zhuangzu Zizhiqu
Kuang-tung see Guangdong
Kuang-yuan see Guangyuan
174 Hh4 Kuantan Pahang, Peninsular Malaysia
Kuantan, Batang see Indragiri, Sungai
Kuanza Norte see Cuanza Norte
Kuanza Sul see Cuanza Sul
125 Aa12 Kuban' var. Hypanis. ◄ SW Russian Federation
Kubango see Cubango/Okavango
147 X8 Kubārah NW Oman
95 H16 Kubbe Västernorrland, C Sweden
82 A11 Kubbum Southern Darfur, W Sudan
128 L13 Kubenskoye, Ozero ◎ NW Russian Federation
170 Ee16 Kubokawa Kōchi, Shikoku, SW Japan
116 L7 Kubrat prev. Balbunar. Razgradska Oblast, NE Bulgaria
175 Oo15 Kubu Sumbawa, S Indonesia
114 O13 Kučajske Planine ▲ E Serbia
172 Pp2 Kuccharo-ko ◎ Hokkaidō, N Japan
114 O11 Kučevo Serbia, NE Yugoslavia
174 L6 Kuchan see Qūchān
174 L7 Kuching var. Sarawak. Sarawak, East Malaysia
174 L7 Kuching ✈ Sarawak, East Malaysia
170 Aa17 Kuchinoerabu-jima island Nansei-shotō, SW Japan
170 C13 Kuchinotsu Nagasaki, Kyūshū, SW Japan
111 Q6 Kuchl Salzburg, NW Austria
154 E9 Küchnay Darweyshān Helmand, S Afghanistan
119 O9 Kuchurgan Rus. Kuchurhan. ◄ NE Ukraine
119 O9 Kuchurhan Rus. Kuchurgan. ◄ NE Ukraine
115 L21 Kuçova var. Kuçova; prev. Qyteti Stalin. Berat, C Albania
142 D11 Küçük Çekmece İstanbul, NW Turkey
170 Dd13 Kudamatsu var. Kudamatu. Yamaguchi, Honshū, SW Japan
Kudamatu see Kudamatsu
175 O1 Kudat Sabah, East Malaysia
Küddow see Gwda
161 G17 Kūdligi Karnātaka, W India
Kudowa see Kudowa-Zdrój
113 F16 Kudowa-Zdrój Ger. Kudowa. Wałbrzych, SW Poland
119 P9 Kudryavtsivka Mykolayivs'ka Oblast', S Ukraine
174 L14 Kudus prev. Koedoes. Jawa, C Indonesia
129 T13 Kudymkar Komi-Permyatskiy Avtonomnyy Okrug, NW Russian Federation
Kudzsir see Cugir
Kuei-chou see Guizhou
Kuei-lin see Guilin
119 T13 Kueie see Guiyang
119 T13 Krymiskiy Hory ▲ S Ukraine
Kuei-yang see Guiyang
K'u-erh-lo see Korla
Kueyang see Guiyang
Kufa see Al Kūfah
142 E14 Küfiçayı ◄ C Turkey
111 O6 Kufstein Tirol, W Austria
151 V14 Kugaly Kaz. Qoghaly. Taldykorgan, SE Kazakhstan
149 Y13 Kühestān Sīstan va Balūchestān, SE Iran
149 N3 Kühbonān Kermān, C Iran
154 I5 Kühestān var. Kohsān. Herāt, W Afghanistan
119 W8 Kühnö see Kihnu

◆ Country   ◇ Dependent Territory   ◉ Administrative Region   ▲ Mountain   ◙ Volcano   ◎ Lake
● Country Capital   ○ Dependent Territory Capital   ✈ International Airport   ▲ Mountain Range   ◄ River   ◙ Reservoir

KŪHPĀYEH – LÄÄNEMAA

149 O8 **Kūhpāyeh** Eşfahān, C Iran
178 H13 **Kui Buri** var. Ban Kui Nua. Prachuap Khiri Khan, SW Thailand
Kuibyshev see Kuybyshevskoye Vodokhranilishche
84 D13 **Kuito** Port. Silva Porto. Bié, C Angola
41 X14 **Kuiu Island** island Alexander Archipelago, Alaska, USA
94 L13 **Kuivaniemi** Oulu, C Finland
79 V14 **Kujama** Kaduna, C Nigeria
172 N10 **Kuji** var. Kuzi. Iwate, Honshū, C Japan
Kujto, Ozero see Kuyto, Ozero
Kujū-renzan see Kujū-san
170 D14 **Kujū-san** var. Kujū-renzan. ▲ Kyūshū, SW Japan
45 N7 **Kukalaya, Rio** var. Rio Cuculaya, Rio Kukulaya. ∾ NE Nicaragua
115 O16 **Kukavica** var. Vlajna. ▲ SE Yugoslavia
152 M10 **Kŭkcha** Rus. Kokcha. Bukhoro Wiloyati, C Uzbekistan
115 M18 **Kukës** var. Kukësi. Kukës, NE Albania
115 L18 **Kukës** ◈ district NE Albania
Kukësi see Kukës
194 J14 **Kukipi** Gulf, S PNG
131 S3 **Kukmor** Respublika Tatarstan, W Russian Federation
Kukong see Shaoguan
41 N6 **Kukpowruk River** ∾ Alaska, USA
40 M6 **Kukpuk River** ∾ Alaska, USA
Kukukhoto see Hohhot
Kukulaya, Rio see Kukalaya, Rio
174 Hh7 **Kukup** Johor, Peninsular Malaysia
201 W12 **Kuku Point** headland NW Wake Island
152 G11 **Kukurtli** Akhalskiy Velayat, C Turkmenistan
Kül see Kül, Rūd-e
116 F7 **Kula** Oblast Montana, NW Bulgaria
142 D14 **Kula** Manisa, W Turkey
114 K9 **Kula** Serbia, NW Yugoslavia
155 S8 **Kulāchi** North-West Frontier Province, NW Pakistan
Kulachi see Kolāchi
150 F11 **Kulagino** Kaz. Külagino. Atyrau, W Kazakhstan
174 Hh6 **Kulai** Johor, Peninsular Malaysia
116 M7 **Kulak** ∾ NE Bulgaria
159 T11 **Kula Kangri** var. Kulhakangri. ▲ Bhutan/China
150 E13 **Kulaly, Ostrov** island SW Kazakhstan
153 V9 **Kulanak** Narynskaya Oblast', C Kyrgyzstan
152 B8 **Kulandag** ▲ W Turkmenistan
159 V14 **Kulaura** Chittagong, NE Bangladesh
120 D9 **Kuldīga** Ger. Goldingen. Kuldīga, W Latvia
Kuldja see Yining
Kul'dzhuktau, Gory see Quljuqtov-Toghi
131 N4 **Kulebaki** Nizhegorodskaya Oblast', W Russian Federation
114 E11 **Kulen Vakuf** NW Bosnia and Herzegovina
189 Q9 **Kulgera Roadhouse** Northern Territory, N Australia
Kulhakangri see Kula Kangri
131 T1 **Kuliga** Udmurtskaya Respublika, NW Russian Federation
Kulkuduk see Kalquduq
120 G4 **Kullamaa** Läänemaa, W Estonia
207 O12 **Kullorsuaq** var. Kuvdlorssuak. C Greenland
31 O6 **Kulm** North Dakota, N USA
Kulm see Chełmno
152 D12 **Kul'mach** Balkanskiy Velayat, W Turkmenistan
103 L18 **Kulmbach** Bayern, SE Germany
Kulmsee see Chełmża
153 Q14 **Kŭlob** Rus. Kulyab. SW Tajikistan
94 M13 **Kuloharju** Lappi, N Finland
129 N7 **Kuloy** Arkhangel'skaya Oblast', NW Russian Federation
129 N7 **Kuloy** ∾ NW Russian Federation
143 Q14 **Kulp** Diyarbakır, SE Turkey
Kulpa see Kolpa
79 P14 **Kulpawn** ∾ N Ghana
149 R13 **Kūl, Rūd-e** var. Kūl. ∾ S Iran
150 G12 **Kul'sary** Kaz. Qulsary. Atyrau, W Kazakhstan
159 R15 **Kulti** West Bengal, NE India
95 G14 **Kultsjön** ⊚ N Sweden
142 I14 **Kulu** Konya, W Turkey
127 Nn10 **Kulu** ∾ E Russian Federation
125 G14 **Kulunda** Altayskiy Kray, S Russian Federation
151 T7 **Kulunda Steppe** Kaz. Qulyndy Zhazyghy, Rus. Kulundinskaya Ravnina. grassland Kazakhstan/Russian Federation
Kulundinskaya Ravnina see Kulunda Steppe
190 M9 **Kulwin** Victoria, SE Australia
Kulyab see Kŭlob
119 Q3 **Kulykivka** Chernihivs'ka Oblast', N Ukraine
Kum see Qom
170 Ee15 **Kuma** Ehime, Shikoku, SW Japan
131 P14 **Kuma** ∾ SW Russian Federation
Kumafa see Kumawa, Pegunungan
171 K15 **Kumagaya** Saitama, Honshū, S Japan
172 N6 **Kumaishi** Hokkaidō, NE Japan
174 Ll11 **Kumai, Teluk** bay Borneo, C Indonesia
131 Y7 **Kumak** Orenburgskaya Oblast', W Russian Federation
176 Y9 **Kumamba, Kepulauan** island group E Indonesia
170 Cc14 **Kumamoto** Kumamoto, Kyūshū, SW Japan
170 C14 **Kumamoto** off. Kumamoto-ken. ◈ prefecture Kyūshū, SW Japan
171 Gg17 **Kumano** Mie, Honshū, SW Japan
Kumanova see Kumanovo
115 O17 **Kumanovo** Turk. Kumanova. N FYR Macedonia
193 G17 **Kumara** West Coast, South Island, NZ
188 J8 **Kumarina Roadhouse** Western Australia
159 T15 **Kumarkhali** Khulna, W Bangladesh
79 P16 **Kumasi** prev. Coomassie. C Ghana
176 Vv11 **Kumawa, Pegunungan** var. Kumafa. ▲ Irian Jaya, E Indonesia
Kumayri see Gyumri
81 D15 **Kumba** Sud-Ouest, W Cameroon
116 N13 **Kumbağ** Tekirdağ, NW Turkey
161 J21 **Kumbakonam** Tamil Nādu, SE India
176 Z16 **Kumbe, Sungai** ∾ Irian Jaya, E Indonesia
Kum-Dag see Gumdag
172 O14 **Kume-jima** island Nansei-shotō, SW Japan
131 V6 **Kumertau** Respublika Bashkortostan, W Russian Federation
125 F11 **Kuminskiy** Khanty-Mansiyskiy Avtonomnyy Okrug, C Russian Federation
37 R4 **Kumiva Peak** ▲ Nevada, W USA
165 N8 **Kum Kuduk** well NW China
165 N7 **Kumkuduk** Xinjiang Uygur Zizhiqu, W China
Kumkurgan see Qumqurghon
97 M16 **Kumla** Örebro, C Sweden
142 E17 **Kumluca** Antalya, SW Turkey
102 N9 **Kummerower See** ⊚ NE Germany
79 X14 **Kumo** Bauchi, E Nigeria
151 O13 **Kumola** ∾ C Kazakhstan
178 H1 **Kumon Range** ▲ N Myanmar
126 K14 **Kumora** Respublika Buryatiya, S Russian Federation
85 F22 **Kums** Karas, SE Namibia
161 E18 **Kumta** Karnātaka, W India
164 I6 **Kümük** Xinjiang Uygur Zizhiqu, W China
40 H12 **Kumukahi, Cape** headland Hawaii, USA, C Pacific Ocean
131 Q17 **Kumukh** Respublika Dagestan, SW Russian Federation
Kumul see Hami
131 N9 **Kumylzhenskaya** Volgogradskaya Oblast', SW Russian Federation
147 W6 **Kumzār** N Oman
155 S4 **Kunar** Per. Konarhā. ◈ province E Afghanistan
Kunashiri see Kunashir, Ostrov
127 P16 **Kunashir, Ostrov** var. Kunashiri. island Kuril'skiye Ostrova, SE Russian Federation
120 I3 **Kunda** Lääne-Virumaa, NE Estonia
158 M13 **Kunda** Uttar Pradesh, N India
161 E19 **Kundāpura** var. Coondapoor. Karnātaka, W India
81 O24 **Kundelungu, Monts** ▲ S Zaire
Kundert see Hernád
194 I12 **Kundiawa** Chimbu, W PNG
Kundla see Sāvarkundla
174 Hh7 **Kundur, Pulau** island W Indonesia
155 Q2 **Kunduz** var. Kondoz, Kundūz, Qondūz, Per. Kondūz. Kunduz, NE Afghanistan
155 Q2 **Kunduz** Per. Kondūz. ◈ province NE Afghanistan
Kuneitra see Al Qunayţirah
85 B18 **Kunene** ◈ district NE Namibia
85 A16 **Kunene** var. Cunene. ∾ Angola/Namibia see also Cunene
Kunes see Xinyuan
164 J5 **Künes He** ∾ NW China
97 J19 **Kungälv** Göteborg och Bohus, S Sweden
153 W7 **Kungei Ala-Tau** Rus. Khrebet Kyungëy Ala-Too, Kir. Küngöy Ala-Too. ▲ Kazakhstan/Kyrgyzstan
Küngöy Ala-Too see Kungei Ala-Tau
Kungrad see Qŭnghirot
97 J19 **Kungsbacka** Halland, S Sweden
97 I18 **Kungshamn** Göteborg och Bohus, S Sweden
97 M16 **Kungsör** Västmanland, C Sweden
81 J16 **Kungu** Equateur, NW Zaire
129 V15 **Kungur** Permskaya Oblast', NW Russian Federation
177 G9 **Kungyangon** Yangon, SW Myanmar
113 M22 **Kunhegyes** Jász-Nagykun-Szolnok, E Hungary
178 H5 **Kunhing** Shan State, E Myanmar
170 Cc15 **Kunimi-dake** ▲ Kyūshū, SW Japan
164 D9 **Kunjirap Daban** var. Khūnjerāb Pass. pass China/Pakistan see also Khūnjerāb Pass
Kunlun Mountains see Kunlun Shan
164 H10 **Kunlun Shan** Eng. Kunlun Mountains. ▲ NW China
165 P11 **Kunlun Shankou** pass C China
166 G13 **Kunming** var. K'un-ming; prev. Yunnan. Yunnan, SW China
172 N6 **Kunnui** Hokkaidō, NE Japan
169 X16 **Kunsan** var. Gunsan, Jap. Gunzan. W South Korea
113 L24 **Kunszentmárton** Jász-Nagykun-Szolnok, E Hungary
113 J23 **Kunszentmiklós** Bács-Kiskun, C Hungary
189 N3 **Kununurra** Western Australia
Kunya-Urgench see Këneurgench
Kunyé see Pins, Île des
174 Mm8 **Kunyi** Borneo, C Indonesia
103 I20 **Künzelsau** Baden-Württemberg, S Germany
167 S10 **Kuocang Shan** ▲ SE China
128 H5 **Kuoloyarvi** var. Luolajarvi. Murmanskaya Oblast', NW Russian Federation
95 N16 **Kuopio** Kuopio, C Finland
95 M16 **Kuopio** ◈ province C Finland
95 K17 **Kuortane** Vaasa, W Finland
95 M18 **Kuortti** Mikkeli, S Finland
Kupa see Kolpa
175 R17 **Kupang** prev. Koepang. Timor, C Indonesia
41 Q5 **Kuparuk River** ∾ Alaska, USA
Kupchino see Cupcina
194 L16 **Kupiano** Central, S PNG
188 M4 **Kupingarri** Western Australia
125 G14 **Kupino** Novosibirskaya Oblast', C Russian Federation
120 H11 **Kupiškis** Kupiškis, NE Lithuania
116 L13 **Küplü** Edirne, NW Turkey
41 X13 **Kupreanof Island** island Alexander Archipelago, Alaska, USA
41 O16 **Kupreanof Point** headland Alaska, USA
114 G13 **Kupres** SW Bosnia and Herzegovina
119 W5 **Kup"yans'k** Rus. Kupyansk. Kharkivs'ka Oblast', E Ukraine
119 W5 **Kup"yans'k-Vuzlovyy** Kharkivs'ka Oblast', E Ukraine
164 I6 **Kuqa** Xinjiang Uygur Zizhiqu, NW China
Kür see Kura
143 W11 **Kura** Az. Kür, Geor. Mtkvari, Turk. Kura Nehri. ∾ SW Asia
57 R8 **Kuracki** NW Guyana
170 Ee13 **Kurahashi-jima** island SW Japan
Kura Kurk see Irbe Strait
153 Q10 **Kurama Range** Rus. Kuraminskiy Khrebet. ▲ Tajikistan/Uzbekistan
Kuraminskiy Khrebet see Kurama Range
Kura Nehri see Kura
176 Ww10 **Kurau, Kepulauan** island group E Indonesia
121 J14 **Kuranyets** Rus. Kurenets. Minskaya Voblasts', C Belarus
170 Ff14 **Kurashiki** var. Kurasiki. Okayama, Honshū, SW Japan
160 L10 **Kurasia** Madhya Pradesh, C India
Kurasiki see Kurashiki
170 G12 **Kurayoshi** var. Kurayosi. Tottori, Honshū, SW Japan
Kurayosi see Kurayoshi
169 X6 **Kurbin He** ∾ NE China
151 X10 **Kurchum** Kaz. Kürshim. Vostochnyy Kazakhstan, E Kazakhstan
151 Y10 **Kurchum** ∾ E Kazakhstan
143 X11 **Kürdämir** Rus. Kyurdamir. C Azerbaijan
Kurdestan see Kordestān
145 S1 **Kurdistan** cultural region SW Asia
Kurd Kui see Kord Küy
161 F15 **Kurduvādi** Mahārāshtra, W India
116 J11 **Kŭrdzhali** var. Kirdzhali. Khaskovska Oblast, S Bulgaria
116 J11 **Kŭrdzhali, Yazovir** ⊠ S Bulgaria
170 Ee13 **Kure** Hiroshima, Honshū, SW Japan
199 J5 **Kure Atoll** var. Ocean Island. atoll Hawaiian Islands, Hawaii, USA, C Pacific Ocean
142 J10 **Küre Dağları** ▲ N Turkey
Kurenets see Kuranyets
120 E6 **Kuressaare** Ger. Arensburg; prev. Kingissepp. Saaremaa, W Estonia
126 I9 **Kureyka** Krasnoyarskiy Kray, N Russian Federation
126 I9 **Kureyka** ∾ N Russian Federation
151 P10 **Kurgal'dzhin, Ozero** ⊚ C Kazakhstan
151 Q10 **Kurgal'dzhinskiy** Kaz. Qorghazhyn. Akmola, C Kazakhstan
125 F12 **Kurgan** Kurganskaya Oblast', C Russian Federation
130 L14 **Kurganinsk** Krasnodarskiy Kray, SW Russian Federation
125 Ee12 **Kurganskaya Oblast'** ◈ province C Russian Federation
Kurgan-Tyube see Qŭrghonteppa
203 O2 **Kuria** prev. Woodle Island. island Tungaru, W Kiribati
Kuria Muria Bay see Ḩalāniyāt, Khalij al
Kuria Muria Islands see Ḩalāniyāt, Juzur al
159 T13 **Kurigram** Rajshahi, N Bangladesh
176 Yy16 **Kurik** Irian Jaya, E Indonesia
95 K17 **Kurikka** Vaasa, W Finland
171 M12 **Kurikoma-yama** ▲ Honshū, C Japan
199 Hh3 **Kurile Basin** undersea feature NW Pacific Ocean
Kurile Islands see Kuril'skiye Ostrova
Kurile-Kamchatka Depression see Kurile Trench
199 Hh3 **Kurile Trench** var. Kurile-Kamchatka Depression. undersea feature NW Pacific Ocean
131 Q9 **Kurilovka** Saratovskaya Oblast', W Russian Federation
127 P15 **Kuril'sk** Kuril'skiye Ostrova, Sakhalinskaya Oblats', SE Russian Federation
127 Pp15 **Kuril'skiye Ostrova** Eng. Kurile Islands. island group SE Russian Federation
44 M9 **Kurinwas, Río** ∾ E Nicaragua
Kurisches Haff see Courland Lagoon
Kurkund see Kilingi-Nõmme
130 M4 **Kurlovskiy** Vladimirskaya Oblast', W Russian Federation
82 G12 **Kurmuk** Blue Nile, SE Sudan
Kurna see Al Qurnah
161 H17 **Kurnool** var. Karnul. Andhra Pradesh, S India
171 J13 **Kurobe** Toyama, Honshū, SW Japan
170 Cc13 **Kurogi** Fukuoka, Kyūshū, SW Japan
171 Mm9 **Kuroishi** var. Kuroisi. Aomori, Honshū, C Japan
Kuroisi see Kuroishi
171 Kk14 **Kuroiso** Tochigi, Honshū, S Japan
172 N5 **Kuromatsunai** Hokkaidō, NE Japan
172 Oo17 **Kuro-shima** island SW Japan
171 H16 **Kuroso-yama** ▲ Honshū, SW Japan
193 F21 **Kurow** Canterbury, South Island, NZ
176 Uu13 **Kur, Pulau** island E Indonesia
131 N15 **Kursavka** Stavropol'skiy Kray, SW Russian Federation
120 E11 **Kuršėnai** Šiauliai, N Lithuania
Kürshim see Kurchum
Kurshskaya Kosa/Kuršių Nerija see Courland Spit
130 J7 **Kursk** Kurskaya Oblast', W Russian Federation
130 I7 **Kurskaya Oblast'** ◈ province W Russian Federation
Kurskiy Zaliv see Courland Lagoon
115 N15 **Kuršumlija** Serbia, S Yugoslavia
143 R15 **Kurtalan** Siirt, SE Turkey
125 Ee12 **Kurtamysh** Kurganskaya Oblast', C Russian Federation
Kurtbunar see Tervel
Kurt-Dere see Vŭlchidol
Kurtitsch/Kürtös see Curtici
151 U15 **Kurtty** ∾ SE Kazakhstan
95 L18 **Kuru** Häme, SW Finland
82 C13 **Kuru** ∾ W Sudan
116 M13 **Kuru Dağı** ▲ NW Turkey
164 L7 **Kuruktag** ▲ NW China
85 G22 **Kuruman** Northern Cape, N South Africa
69 T14 **Kuruman** ∾ W South Africa
170 Cc13 **Kurume** Fukuoka, Kyūshū, SW Japan
126 K15 **Kurumkan** Respublika Buryatiya, S Russian Federation
161 J25 **Kurunegala** North Western Province, C Sri Lanka
57 T10 **Kurupukari** C Guyana
129 U10 **Kur"ya** Respublika Komi, NW Russian Federation
150 E15 **Kuryk** prev. Yeraliyev. Mangistau, SW Kazakhstan
142 B15 **Kuşadası** Aydın, SW Turkey
117 M19 **Kuşadası Körfezi** gulf SW Turkey
170 Aa16 **Kusagaki-guntō** island SW Japan
Kusaie see Kosrae
151 T12 **Kusak** ∾ C Kazakhstan
Kusary see Qusar
178 Hh8 **Ku Sathan, Doi** ▲ NW Thailand
171 H15 **Kusatsu** var. Kusatu. Shiga, Honshū, SW Japan
Kusatu see Kusatsu
144 F11 **Kuseifa** Southern, C Israel
142 C12 **Kuş Gölü** ⊚ NW Turkey
130 L12 **Kushchevskaya** Krasnodarskiy Kray, SW Russian Federation
171 H16 **Kushida-gawa** ∾ Honshū, SW Japan
170 Bb15 **Kushikino** var. Kusikino. Kagoshima, Kyūshū, SW Japan
170 C17 **Kushima** var. Kusima. Miyazaki, Kyūshū, SW Japan
170 G17 **Kushimoto** Wakayama, Honshū, SW Japan
172 Q7 **Kushiro** var. Kusiro. Hokkaidō, NE Japan
154 K4 **Kushk** Herāt, W Afghanistan
152 J17 **Kushka** ∾ S Turkmenistan
Kushka see Gushgy
151 N8 **Kushmurun** Kaz. Qusmuryn. Kustanay, N Kazakhstan
151 N8 **Kushmurun, Ozero** Kaz. Qusmuryn. ⊚ N Kazakhstan
131 U4 **Kushnarenkovo** Respublika Bashkortostan, W Russian Federation
Kushrabat see Qŭshrabot
159 T15 **Kushtia** Khulna, W Bangladesh
125 Ee10 **Kushva** Sverdlovskaya Oblast', C Russian Federation
Kusikino see Kushikino
Kusima see Kushima
Kusiro see Kushiro
40 M13 **Kuskokwim Bay** bay Alaska, USA
41 P11 **Kuskokwim Mountains** ▲ Alaska, USA
41 N12 **Kuskokwim River** ∾ Alaska, USA
110 G7 **Küsnacht** Zürich, N Switzerland
172 Qq6 **Kussharo-ko** var. Kussyaro. ⊚ Hokkaidō, NE Japan
Küssnacht see Küssnacht am Rigi
110 F8 **Küssnacht am Rigi** var. Küssnacht. Schwyz, C Switzerland
Kussyaro see Kussharo-ko
150 M7 **Kustanay** Kaz. Qostanay. Kustanay, N Kazakhstan
150 L8 **Kustanay** off. Kustanayskaya Oblast', Kaz. Qostanay Oblysy. ◈ province N Kazakhstan
Kustanayskaya Oblast' see Kustanay
Küstence/Küstendje see Constanța
102 F11 **Küstenkanal** var. Ems-Hunte Canal. canal NW Germany
Küstrin see Kostrzyn
175 T7 **Kusu** Pulau Halmahera, E Indonesia
175 Nn16 **Kuta** Pulau Lombok, S Indonesia
145 T4 **Kutabān** N Iraq
142 E13 **Kütahya** prev. Kutaia. Kütahya, W Turkey
142 E13 **Kütahya** var. Kutaia. ◈ province W Turkey
Kutai see Mahakam, Sungai
Kutaia see Kütahya
143 R9 **K'ut'aisi** W Georgia
Kūt al 'Amārah see Al Kūt
Kut al Hai/Kūt al Ḩayy see Al Ḩayy
Kut al Imara see Al Kūt
126 M12 **Kutana** Respublika Sakha (Yakutiya), NE Russian Federation
Kutaradja/Kutaraja see Bandaaceh
172 Nn5 **Kutchan** Hokkaidō, NE Japan
Kutch, Gulf of see Kachchh, Gulf of
Kutch, Rann of see Kachchh, Rann of
114 F9 **Kutina** Sisak-Moslavina, NE Croatia
114 H9 **Kutjevo** Požega-Slavonija, NE Croatia
113 E17 **Kutná Hora** Ger. Kuttenberg. Střední Čechy, C Czech Republic
112 K12 **Kutno** Płock, C Poland
Kuttenberg see Kutná Hora
81 I20 **Kutu** Bandundu, W Zaire
159 V17 **Kutubdia Island** island SE Bangladesh
82 B10 **Kutum** Northern Darfur, W Sudan
153 Y7 **Kuturgu** Issyk-Kul'skaya Oblast', E Kyrgyzstan
10 M5 **Kuujjuaq** prev. Fort-Chimo. Québec, E Canada
10 I7 **Kuujjuarapik** Québec, C Canada
152 A10 **Kuuli-Mayak** Turkm. Guwlumayak. Balkanskiy Velayat, NW Turkmenistan
120 I6 **Kuulse magi** ▲ S Estonia
94 N13 **Kuusamo** Oulu, E Finland
95 M19 **Kuusankoski** Kymi, S Finland
131 W7 **Kuvandyk** Orenburgskaya Oblast', W Russian Federation
Kuvango see Cubango
Kuvasay see Quwasoy
Kuvdlorssuak see Kullorsuaq
128 I16 **Kuvshinovo** Tverskaya Oblast', W Russian Federation
147 Q4 **Kuwait** off. State of Kuwait, var. Dawlat al Kuwait, Koweit, Kuweit. ◆ monarchy SW Asia
Kuwait see Al Kuwayt
Kuwait Bay see Kuwayt, Jūn al
Kuwait City see Al Kuwayt
Kuwait, Dawlat al see Kuwait
Kuwajleen see Kwajalein Atoll
171 H15 **Kuwana** Mie, Honshū, SW Japan
176 V9 **Kuwawin** Irian Jaya, E Indonesia
145 X9 **Kuwayt** E Iraq
148 K11 **Kuwayt, Jūn al** var. Kuwait Bay. bay E Kuwait
Kuweit see Kuwait
119 P10 **Kuyal'nyts'kyy Lyman** ⊚ SW Ukraine
125 G13 **Kuybyshev** Novosibirskaya Oblast', C Russian Federation
Kuybyshev see Bolgar, Respublika Tatarstan, Russian Federation
Kuybyshev see Samara
119 W9 **Kuybysheve** Rus. Kuybyshevo. Zaporiz'ka Oblast', SE Ukraine
Kuybyshevo see Kuybysheve
Kuybyshev Reservoir see Kuybyshevskoye Vodokhranilishche
Kuybyshevskaya Oblast' see Samarskaya Oblast'
151 O7 **Kuybyshevskiy** Kokshetau, N Kazakhstan
131 R4 **Kuybyshevskoye Vodokhranilishche** var. Kuibyshev, Eng. Kuybyshev Reservoir. ⊠ W Russian Federation
127 N9 **Kuydusun** Respublika Sakha (Yakutiya), NE Russian Federation
129 U16 **Kuyeda** Permskaya Oblast', NW Russian Federation
Küysanjaq see Koi Sanjaq
128 I7 **Kuyto, Ozero** var. Ozero Kujto. ⊚ NW Russian Federation
164 J4 **Kuytun** Xinjiang Uygur Zizhiqu, NW China
126 J15 **Kuytun** Irkutskaya Oblast', S Russian Federation
126 Ii12 **Kuyumba** Evenkiyskiy Avtonomnyy Okrug, C Russian Federation
57 S12 **Kuyuwini Landing** S Guyana
Kuzi see Kuji
40 M9 **Kuzitrin River** ∾ Alaska, USA
131 P6 **Kuznetsk** Penzenskaya Oblast', W Russian Federation
118 K3 **Kuznetsovs'k** Rivnens'ka Oblast', NW Ukraine
128 K6 **Kuzomen'** Murmanskaya Oblast', NW Russian Federation
172 N10 **Kuzumaki** Iwate, Honshū, C Japan
94 H9 **Kvaløya** island N Norway
94 K8 **Kvalsund** Finnmark, N Norway
96 G11 **Kvam** Oppland, S Norway
131 X7 **Kvarkeno** Orenburgskaya Oblast', W Russian Federation
95 G15 **Kvarnbergsvattnet** var. Frostviken. ⊚ N Sweden
114 A11 **Kvarner** var. Carnaro, It. Quarnero. gulf W Croatia
114 B11 **Kvarnerićka Vrata** channel W Croatia
41 O14 **Kvichak Bay** bay Alaska, USA
94 H12 **Kvikkjokk** Norrbotten, N Sweden
97 D17 **Kvina** ∾ S Norway
94 Q1 **Kvitøya** island NE Svalbard
97 F16 **Kvitseid** Telemark, S Norway
97 H24 **Kværndrup** Fyn, C Denmark
81 H20 **Kwa** ∾ W Zaire
79 Q15 **Kwadwokurom** C Ghana
195 X14 **Kwailibesi** Malaita, N Solomon Islands
201 S6 **Kwajalein Atoll** var. Kuwajleen. atoll Ralik Chain, C Marshall Islands
57 W9 **Kwakoegron** Brokopondo, N Suriname
83 J21 **Kwale** Coast, S Kenya
79 U17 **Kwale** Delta, S Nigeria
81 H20 **Kwamouth** Bandundu, W Zaire
Kwando see Cuando
Kwangchow see Guangzhou
Kwangchu see Kwangju
169 X16 **Kwangju** off. Kwangju-gwangyŏksi, var. Guangju, Kwangchu, Jap. Kōshū. SW South Korea
81 H20 **Kwango** Port. Cuango. ∾ Angola/Zaire see also Cuango
Kwangsi/Kwangsi Chuang Autonomous Region see Guangxi Zhuangzu Zizhiqu
Kwangtung see Guangdong
Kwangyuan see Guangyuan
83 F17 **Kwania, Lake** ⊚ C Uganda
Kwanza see Cuanza
79 S15 **Kwara** ◈ state SW Nigeria
176 Ww11 **Kwatisore** Irian Jaya, E Indonesia
85 K22 **KwaZulu/Natal** off. KwaZulu/Natal Province; prev. Natal. ◈ province E South Africa
Kweichow see Guizhou
Kweichu see Guiyang
Kweilin see Guilin
Kweisui see Hohhot
Kweiyang see Guiyang
85 K17 **Kwekwe** prev. Que Que. Midlands, C Zimbabwe
85 G20 **Kweneng** ◈ district S Botswana
Kwesui see Hohhot
41 N12 **Kwethluk** Alaska, USA
41 N12 **Kwethluk River** ∾ Alaska, USA
112 J8 **Kwidzyń** Ger. Marienwerder. Elbląg, N Poland
40 M13 **Kwigillingok** Alaska, USA
194 K16 **Kwikila** Central, S PNG
81 I20 **Kwilu** ∾ W Zaire
Kwito see Cuito
176 V8 **Kwoka, Gunung** ▲ Irian Jaya, E Indonesia
80 I12 **Kyabé** Moyen-Chari, S Chad
191 O11 **Kyabram** Victoria, SE Australia
178 Gg9 **Kyaikkami** prev. Amherst. Mon State, S Myanmar
177 F9 **Kyaiklat** Irrawaddy, SW Myanmar
177 G8 **Kyaikto** Mon State, S Myanmar
126 Jj16 **Kyakhta** Respublika Buryatiya, S Russian Federation
190 G8 **Kyancutta** South Australia
177 F7 **Kyangin** Irrawaddy, SW Myanmar
178 J8 **Ky Anh** Ha Tinh, N Vietnam
177 F5 **Kyaukpadaung** Mandalay, C Myanmar
177 F6 **Kyaukpyu** Arakan State, W Myanmar
177 G5 **Kyaukse** Mandalay, C Myanmar
177 F8 **Kyaunggon** Irrawaddy, SW Myanmar
121 E14 **Kybartai** Pol. Kibarty. Vilkaviškis, S Lithuania
158 I7 **Kyelang** Himāchal Pradesh, NW India
113 G19 **Kyjov** Ger. Gaya. Jižní Morava, SE Czech Republic
117 J21 **Kykládes** var. Kikládhes, Eng. Cyclades. island group SE Greece
27 S11 **Kyle** Texas, SW USA
98 G9 **Kyle of Lochalsh** N Scotland, UK
103 D18 **Kyll** ∾ W Germany
117 F19 **Kyllíni** var. Killini. ▲ S Greece
117 H18 **Kými** prev. Kími. Évvoia, C Greece
95 N18 **Kymi** Swe. Kymmene. ◈ province SE Finland
95 M19 **Kymijoki** ∾ S Finland
117 H18 **Kýmis, Ákra** headland Évvoia, C Greece
Kymmene see Kymi
129 W14 **Kyn** Permskaya Oblast', NW Russian Federation
191 I12 **Kyneton** Victoria, SE Australia
83 G17 **Kyoga, Lake** var. Lake Kioga. ⊚ C Uganda
171 H13 **Kyōga-misaki** headland Honshū, SW Japan
191 V4 **Kyogle** New South Wales, SE Australia
169 W15 **Kyŏnggi-man** bay NW South Korea
169 Z16 **Kyŏngju** Jap. Keishū. SE South Korea
Kyŏngsŏng see Sŏul
Kyōsai-tō see Kōje-do
83 F19 **Kyotera** S Uganda
171 H15 **Kyōto** Kyōto, Honshū, SW Japan
171 H14 **Kyōto** off. Kyōto-fu, var. Kyōto Hu. ◈ urban prefecture Honshū, SW Japan
Kyōto-fu/Kyōto Hu see Kyōto
117 D21 **Kyparissía** var. Kiparissía. Pelopónnisos, S Greece
117 D20 **Kyparissiakós Kólpos** gulf S Greece
Kyperounda see Kyperoúnta
124 N3 **Kyperoúnta** var. Kyperounda. C Cyprus
Kypros see Cyprus
117 H16 **Kyrá Panagiá** island Vóreioi Sporádes, Greece, Aegean Sea
Kyrenia see Girne
Kyrenia Mountains see Beşparmak Dağları
Kyrgyz Republic see Kyrgyzstan
153 U9 **Kyrgyzstan** off. Kyrgyz Republic, var. Kirghizia; prev. Kirgizskaya SSR, Kirghiz SSR, Republic of Kyrgyzstan. ◆ republic C Asia
102 M11 **Kyritz** Brandenburg, NE Germany
Kyrkslätt see Kirkkonummi
96 G8 **Kyrksæterøra** Sør-Trøndelag, S Norway
129 U8 **Kyrta** Respublika Komi, NW Russian Federation
125 Ee12 **Kyshtym** Chelyabinskaya Oblast', S Russian Federation
113 J18 **Kysucké Nové Mesto** prev. Horné Nové Mesto, Ger. Kisutzaneustadtl, Oberneustadtl, Hung. Kiszucaújhely. Stredné Slovensko, N Slovakia
119 N12 **Kytay, Ozero** ⊚ SW Ukraine
117 F23 **Kýthira** var. Kíthira, It. Cerigo; Lat. Cythera. Kýthira, S Greece
117 F23 **Kýthira** var. Kíthira, It. Cerigo; Lat. Cythera. island S Greece
117 I20 **Kýthnos** Kýthnos, Kykládes, Greece, Aegean Sea
117 I20 **Kýthnos** var. Kíthnos, Thermiá, It. Termia; anc. Cythnos. island Kykládes, Greece, Aegean Sea
117 I20 **Kýthnou, Stenó** strait Kykládes, Greece, Aegean Sea
Kythréa see Değirmenlik
Kyungëy Ala-Too, Khrebet see Kungei Ala-Tau
Kyurdamir see Kürdämir
152 C11 **Kyuren, Gora** ▲ W Turkmenistan
172 C15 **Kyūshū** var. Kyûsyû. island SW Japan
199 Gg6 **Kyushu-Palau Ridge** var. Kyusyu-Palau Ridge. undersea feature W Pacific Ocean
170 Cc15 **Kyūshū-sanchi** ▲ Kyūshū, SW Japan
116 F10 **Kyustendil** anc. Pautalia. Sofiyska Oblast, W Bulgaria
Kyûsyû see Kyūshū
Kyusyu-Palau Ridge see Kyushu-Palau Ridge
126 L7 **Kyusyur** Respublika Sakha (Yakutiya), NE Russian Federation
191 P10 **Kywong** New South Wales, SE Australia
119 P4 **Kyyiv** Eng. Kiev, Rus. Kiyev. ● (Ukraine) Kyyivs'ka Oblast', N Ukraine
Kyyiv see Kyyivs'ka Oblast'
119 O4 **Kyyivs'ka Oblast'** var. Kyyiv, Rus. Kiyevskaya Oblast'. ◈ province N Ukraine
119 P3 **Kyyivs'ke Vodoskhovyshche** Eng. Kiev Reservoir, Rus. Kiyevskoye Vodokhranilishche. ⊠ N Ukraine
95 L16 **Kyyjärvi** Keski-Suomi, C Finland
126 I16 **Kyzyl** Respublika Tyva, C Russian Federation
153 S8 **Kyzyl-Adyr** prev. Kirovskoye. Talasskaya Oblast', NW Kyrgyzstan
151 V14 **Kyzylagash** Taldykorgan, SE Kazakhstan
152 C13 **Kyzylbair** Balkanskiy Velayat, W Turkmenistan
Kyzyl-Dzhiik, Pereval see Uzbel Shankou
151 S7 **Kyzylkak, Ozero** ⊚ NE Kazakhstan
151 X11 **Kyzylkesek** Semipalatinsk, E Kazakhstan
153 S10 **Kyzyl-Kiya** Kir. Kyzyl-Kyya. Oshskaya Oblast', SW Kyrgyzstan
150 L11 **Kyzylkol', Ozero** ⊚ C Kazakhstan
139 L8 **Kyzyl Kum** var. Kizil Kum, Qizil Qum, Uzb. Qizilqum. desert Kazakhstan/Uzbekistan
Kyzyl-Kyya see Kyzyl-Kiya
Kyzylrabat see Qizilrawbe
Kyzylrabot see Qizilrabot
Kyzylsu see Kyzyl-Suu
153 X7 **Kyzyl-Suu** prev. Pokrovka. Issyk-Kul'skaya Oblast', NE Kyrgyzstan
153 S12 **Kyzyl-Suu** var. Kyzylsu. ∾ Kyrgyzstan/Tajikistan
153 X8 **Kyzyl-Tuu** Issyk-Kul'skaya Oblast', E Kyrgyzstan
151 Q12 **Kyzylzhar** Kaz. Qyzylzhar. Zhezkazgan, C Kazakhstan
151 N15 **Kzyl-Orda** var. Qizil Orda, Kaz. Qyzylorda; prev. Perovsk. Kzyl-Orda, S Kazakhstan
150 L14 **Kzyl-Orda** off. Kzyl-Ordinskaya Oblast', Kaz. Qyzylorda Oblysy. ◈ province S Kazakhstan
Kzyl-Ordinskaya Oblast' see Kzyl-Orda
151 R7 **Kzyltu** Kaz. Qyzyltū. Kokshetau, N Kazakhstan

L

111 X2 **Laa an der Thaya** Niederösterreich, NE Austria
65 K15 **La Adela** La Pampa, SE Argentina
Laagen see Numedalslågen
111 S5 **Laakirchen** Oberösterreich, N Austria
Laaland see Lolland
106 I11 **La Albuera** Extremadura, W Spain
107 O7 **La Alcarria** physical region C Spain
106 K14 **La Algaba** Andalucía, S Spain
107 P9 **La Almarcha** Castilla-La Mancha, C Spain
107 R6 **La Almunia de Doña Godina** Aragón, NE Spain
43 N5 **La Amistad, Presa** ⊠ NW Mexico
120 F4 **Läänemaa** off. Lääne Maakond. ◈ province NW Estonia

◆ Country ● Country Capital ◇ Dependent Territory ○ Dependent Territory Capital ◈ Administrative Region ✕ International Airport ▲ Mountain ▲ Mountain Range Ж Volcano ∾ River ⊚ Lake ⊠ Reservoir

LÄÄNE-VIRUMAA – LANDSKRON

120 I3 **Lääne-Virumaa** *off.* Lääne-Viru Maakond. ◈ *province* NE Estonia
64 J9 **La Antigua, Salina** *salt lake* W Argentina
101 E17 **Laarne** Oost-Vlaanderen, NW Belgium
82 O13 **Laas Caanood** Nugaal, N Somalia
43 O9 **La Ascensión** Nuevo León, NE Mexico
82 N12 **Laas Dhaareed** Woqooyi Galbeed, N Somalia
57 O4 **La Asunción** Nueva Esparta, NE Venezuela
Laatokka *see* Ladozhskoye Ozero
102 I13 **Laatzen** Niedersachsen, NW Germany
40 E9 **Laau Point** *headland* Molokai, Hawaii, USA, C Pacific Ocean
44 D6 **La Aurora** ✕ (Ciudad de Guatemala) Guatemala, C Guatemala
76 C9 **Laâyoune** *var.* Aaiún. ○ (Western Sahara) NW Western Sahara
130 L14 **Laba** ≈ SW Russian Federation
42 M6 **La Babia** Coahuila de Zaragoza, NE Mexico
13 R7 **La Baie** Québec, SE Canada
175 R16 **Labala** Pulau Lomblen, S Indonesia
64 K8 **La Banda** Santiago del Estero, N Argentina
La Banda Oriental *see* Uruguay
106 K4 **La Bañeza** Castilla-León, N Spain
42 M13 **La Barca** Jalisco, SW Mexico
42 K14 **La Barra de Navidad** Jalisco, C Mexico
197 J13 **Labasa** *prev.* Lambasa. Vanua Levu, N Fiji
179 Q15 **Labason** Mindanao, S Philippines
104 H8 **la Baule-Escoublac** Loire-Atlantique, NW France
Labe *see* Elbe
78 I13 **Labé** Moyenne-Guinée, NW Guinea
25 X14 **La Belle** Florida, SE USA
13 N11 **Labelle** Québec, SE Canada
8 H7 **Laberge, Lake** ◎ Yukon Territory, W Canada
Labes *see* Łobez
Labiau *see* Polessk
114 A10 **Labin** *It.* Albona. Istra, NW Croatia
130 L14 **Labinsk** Krasnodarskiy Kray, SW Russian Federation
107 X5 **La Bisbal d'Empordà** Cataluña, NE Spain
121 P16 **Labkovichy** *Rus.* Lobkovichi. Mahilyowskaya Voblasts', E Belarus
13 S4 **La Blache, Lac de** ◎ Québec, SE Canada
179 Q11 **Labo** Luzon, N Philippines
Laboehanbadjo *see* Labuhanbajo
Laborca *see* Laborec
113 N18 **Laborec** *Hung.* Laborca. ≈ E Slovakia
110 D11 **La Borgne** ≈ S Switzerland
47 T12 **Laborie** SW Saint Lucia
81 F21 **La Bouenza** ◈ *province* S Congo
104 J14 **Labouheyre** Landes, SW France
64 L12 **Laboulaye** Córdoba, C Argentina
11 Q7 **Labrador** *cultural region* Newfoundland and Labrador, SW Canada
66 I6 **Labrador Basin** *var.* Labrador Sea Basin. *undersea feature* Labrador Sea
11 N9 **Labrador City** Newfoundland and Labrador, E Canada
11 Q5 **Labrador Sea** *sea* NW Atlantic Ocean
Labrador Sea Basin *see* Labrador Basin
Labrang *see* Xiahe
56 G9 **Labranzagrande** Boyacá, C Colombia
47 U15 **La Brea** Trinidad, Trinidad and Tobago
61 D14 **Lábrea** Amazonas, N Brazil
13 S6 **Labrieville** Québec, SE Canada
104 K14 **Labrit** Landes, SW France
110 C9 **La Broye** ≈ SW Switzerland
105 N15 **Labruguière** Tarn, S France
174 I8 **Labu** Pulau Singkep, W Indonesia
175 N3 **Labuan** *var.* Victoria. Labuan, East Malaysia
175 N3 **Labuan** ◈ *federal territory* East Malaysia
Labuan *see* Labuan, Pulau
175 N3 **Labuan, Pulau** *var.* Labuan. *island* East Malaysia
175 Pp16 **Labuhanbajo** *prev.* Laboehanbadjo. Flores, S Indonesia
173 G6 **Labuhanbilik** Sumatera, N Indonesia
173 Ee5 **Labuhanhaji** Sumatera, W Indonesia
Labuk *see* Labuk, Sungai
Labuk Bay *see* Labuk, Teluk
175 O2 **Labuk, Sungai** *var.* Labuk. ≈ East Malaysia
175 Oo2 **Labuk, Teluk** *var.* Labuk Bay, Telukan Labuk. *bay* S Sulu Sea
Labuk, Telukan *see* Labuk, Teluk
177 Ff9 **Labutta** Irrawaddy, SW Myanmar
125 G8 **Labytnangi** Yamalo-Nenetskiy Avtonomnyy Okrug, N Russian Federation
80 F10 **Lac** *off.* Préfecture du Lac. ◈ *prefecture* W Chad
115 K19 **Laç** *var.* Laci. Lezhë, C Albania
59 K19 **Lacajahuira, Rio** ≈ W Bolivia
La Calamine *see* Kelmis
64 G11 **La Calera** Valparaíso, C Chile
11 P11 **Lac-Allard** Québec, E Canada
106 L13 **La Campana** Andalucía, S Spain
104 J12 **Lacanau** Gironde, SW France
44 C2 **Lacandón, Sierra del** ▲▲ Guatemala/Mexico
La Cañiza *see* A Cañiza
43 W16 **Lacantún, Río** ≈ SE Mexico
105 Q3 **la Capelle** Aisne, N France
114 K10 **Laćarak** Serbia, NW Yugoslavia
64 L11 **La Carlota** Córdoba, C Argentina
179 Q13 **La Carlota** Negros, S Philippines
106 L13 **La Carlota** Andalucía, S Spain
107 N12 **La Carolina** Andalucía, S Spain
105 O15 **Lacaune** Tarn, S France
13 P7 **Lac-Bouchette** Québec, SE Canada
Laccadive Islands/Laccadive Minicoy and Amindivi Islands, the *see* Lakshadweep
9 Y16 **Lac du Bonnet** Manitoba, S Canada
32 L4 **Lac du Flambeau** Wisconsin, N USA
13 P8 **Lac-Édouard** Québec, SE Canada
44 I4 **La Ceiba** Atlántida, N Honduras
56 E9 **La Ceja** Antioquia, W Colombia
190 J11 **Lacepede Bay** *bay* South Australia
34 G9 **Lacey** Washington, NW USA
105 P12 **la Chaise-Dieu** Haute-Loire, C France
116 G13 **Lachanás** Kentrikí Makedonía, N Greece
128 L11 **Lacha, Ozero** ◎ NW Russian Federation
105 O8 **la Charité-sur-Loire** Nièvre, C France
105 N9 **la Châtre** Indre, C France
110 C8 **La Chaux-de-Fonds** Neuchâtel, W Switzerland
Lach Dera *see* Dheere Laaq
110 G8 **Lachen** Schwyz, C Switzerland
191 Q8 **Lachlan River** ≈ New South Wales, SE Australia
45 T15 **La Chorrera** Panamá, C Panama
13 V7 **Lac-Humqui** Québec, SE Canada
13 N12 **Lachute** Québec, SE Canada
Lachyn *see* Laçın
Laci *see* Laç
143 W13 **Laçın** *Rus.* Lachyn. SW Azerbaijan
105 S16 **la Ciotat** *anc.* Citharista. Bouches-du-Rhône, SE France
20 D10 **Lackawanna** New York, NE USA
9 Q13 **Lac La Biche** Alberta, SW Canada
15 Hh7 **Lac La Martre** Northwest Territories, W Canada
13 R12 **Lac-Mégantic** *var.* Mégantic. Québec, SE Canada
Lacobriga *see* Lagos
42 G5 **La Colorada** Sonora, NW Mexico
9 Q15 **Lacombe** Alberta, SW Canada
32 L12 **Lacon** Illinois, N USA
45 P16 **La Concepción** *var.* Concepción. Chiriquí, W Panama
56 H5 **La Concepción** Zulia, NW Venezuela
56 H5 **La Concepción** Zulia, NW Venezuela
109 C19 **Laconi** Sardegna, Italy, C Mediterranean Sea
21 O9 **Laconia** New Hampshire, NE USA
63 H19 **La Coronilla** Rocha, E Uruguay
La Coruña *see* A Coruña
106 G2 **La Coruña** ◈ *province* Galicia, NW Spain
105 O11 **la Courtine** Creuse, C France
104 J16 **Lacq** Pyrénées-Atlantiques, SW France
13 P9 **La Croche** Québec, SE Canada
31 X3 **la Croix, Lac** ◎ Canada/USA
28 K5 **La Crosse** Kansas, C USA
23 V7 **La Crosse** Virginia, NE USA
34 L9 **La Crosse** Washington, NW USA
32 J7 **La Crosse** Wisconsin, N USA
56 C13 **La Cruz** Nariño, SW Colombia
44 K12 **La Cruz** Guanacaste, NW Costa Rica
42 I10 **La Cruz** Sinaloa, W Mexico
63 F19 **La Cruz** Florida, S Uruguay
44 M9 **La Cruz de Río Grande** Región Autónoma Atlántico Sur, E Nicaragua
56 J4 **La Cruz de Taratara** Falcón, N Venezuela
13 Q10 **Lac-St-Charles** Québec, SE Canada
42 M6 **La Cuesta** Coahuila de Zaragoza, NE Mexico
59 A17 **La Cumbra, Volcán** ✷ Galapagos Islands, Ecuador, E Pacific Ocean
158 J5 **Ladākh Range** ▲▲ NE India
28 I5 **Ladder Creek** ≈ Kansas, C USA
47 X10 **la Désirade** *atoll* E Guadeloupe
Lādhiqīyah, Muḩāfaẓat al *see* Al Lādhiqīyah
85 F25 **Ladismith** Western Cape, SW South Africa
158 G11 **Lādnūn** Rājasthān, NW India
Ladoga, Lake *see* Ladozhskoye Ozero
117 E19 **Ládon** ≈ S Greece
56 E9 **La Dorada** Caldas, C Colombia
128 H11 **Ladozhskoye Ozero** *Eng.* Lake Ladoga, *Fin.* Laatokka. ◎ NW Russian Federation
39 R12 **Ladron Peak** ▲ New Mexico, SW USA
128 J11 **Ladva-Vetka** Respublika Kareliya, NW Russian Federation
191 Q15 **Lady Barron** Tasmania, SE Australia
12 G9 **Lady Evelyn Lake** ◎ Ontario, S Canada
25 W11 **Lady Lake** Florida, SE USA
8 L17 **Ladysmith** Vancouver Island, British Columbia, SW Canada
85 J22 **Ladysmith** KwaZulu/Natal, E South Africa
32 J5 **Ladysmith** Wisconsin, N USA
151 P9 **Ladyzhenka** Akmola, C Kazakhstan
194 K13 **Lae** Morobe, W PNG
201 R6 **Lae Atoll** *atoll* Ralik Chain, W Marshall Islands
42 C3 **La Encantada, Cerro de** ▲ NW Mexico
96 E12 **Lærdalsøyri** Sogn og Fjordane, S Norway
57 N11 **La Esmeralda** Amazonas, S Venezuela
44 G7 **La Esperanza** Intibucá, SW Honduras
32 K8 **La Farge** Wisconsin, N USA
25 R5 **Lafayette** Alabama, S USA
39 T4 **Lafayette** Colorado, C USA
25 R2 **La Fayette** Georgia, SE USA
33 O13 **Lafayette** Indiana, N USA
24 I9 **Lafayette** Louisiana, S USA
22 K8 **Lafayette** Tennessee, S USA
21 N7 **Lafayette, Mount** ▲ New Hampshire, NE USA
La Fe *see* Santa Fé
105 P3 **la Fère** Aisne, N France
104 L6 **la Ferté-Bernard** Sarthe, NW France
104 K5 **la Ferté-Macé** Orne, N France
105 N7 **la Ferté-St-Aubin** Loiret, C France
105 P5 **la Ferté-sous-Jouarre** Seine-et-Marne, N France
79 V15 **Lafia** Plateau, C Nigeria
79 T15 **Lafiagi** Kwara, W Nigeria
9 T17 **Lafleche** Saskatchewan, S Canada
104 K7 **la Flèche** Sarthe, NW France
111 X7 **Lafnitz** *Hung.* Lapines. ≈ Austria/Hungary
197 I6 **La Foa** Province Sud, S New Caledonia
22 M8 **La Follette** Tennessee, S USA
13 N12 **Lafontaine** Québec, SE Canada
24 K10 **Lafourche, Bayou** ≈ Louisiana, S USA
64 K6 **La Fragua** Santiago del Estero, N Argentina
56 H7 **La Fría** Táchira, NW Venezuela
106 J7 **La Fuente de San Esteban** Castilla-León, N Spain
194 G11 **Lagaip** ≈ W PNG
63 B15 **La Gallareta** Santa Fe, C Argentina
131 Q14 **Lagan'** *prev.* Kaspiyskiy. Respublika Kalmykiya, SW Russian Federation
97 L20 **Lagan** Kronoberg, S Sweden
97 K21 **Lågan** ≈ S Sweden
94 L2 **Lagarfljót** *var.* Lögurinn. ◎ E Iceland
39 R7 **La Garita Mountains** ▲▲ Colorado, C USA
179 P9 **Lagawe** Luzon, N Philippines
80 F13 **Lagdo** Nord, N Cameroon
80 F13 **Lagdo, Lac de** ◎ N Cameroon
102 H13 **Lage** Nordrhein-Westfalen, W Germany
96 H12 **Lågen** ≈ S Norway
63 J14 **Lages** Santa Catarina, S Brazil
155 R4 **Laghmān** ◈ *province* E Afghanistan
76 J6 **Laghouat** N Algeria
107 Q10 **La Gineta** Castilla-La Mancha, C Spain
117 E21 **Lagkáda** *var.* Langada. Pelopónnisos, S Greece
116 G13 **Lagkadás** *var.* Langades, Langadhás. Kentrikí Makedonía, N Greece
117 E20 **Lagkádia** *var.* Langádhia, Langadia. Pelopónnisos, S Greece
56 F6 **La Gloria** Cesar, N Colombia
43 O7 **La Gloria** Nuevo León, NE Mexico
94 N3 **Lågneset** *headland* W Svalbard
106 G14 **Lagoa** Faro, S Portugal
La Goagira *see* La Guajira
63 I14 **Lagoa Vermelha** Rio Grande do Sul, S Brazil
143 V10 **Lagodekhi** SE Georgia
44 C7 **La Gomera** Escuintla, S Guatemala
Lagone *see* Logone
109 M19 **Lagonegro** Basilicata, S Italy
65 G16 **Lago Ranco** Los Lagos, S Chile
79 S16 **Lagos** Lagos, SW Nigeria
106 F14 **Lagos** *anc.* Lacobriga. Faro, S Portugal
79 S16 **Lagos** ◈ *state* SW Nigeria
42 M12 **Lagos de Moreno** Jalisco, SW Mexico
Lagosta *see* Lastovo
76 A12 **Lagouira** SW Western Sahara
94 O1 **Lågøya** *island* N Svalbard
34 L11 **La Grande** Oregon, NW USA
105 Q14 **la Grande-Combe** Gard, S France
10 K9 **La Grande Rivière** *var.* Fort George. ≈ Québec, SE Canada
25 R4 **La Grange** Georgia, SE USA
33 P11 **Lagrange** Indiana, N USA
22 L5 **La Grange** Kentucky, S USA
29 V2 **La Grange** Missouri, C USA
23 V10 **La Grange** North Carolina, SE USA
27 U11 **La Grange** Texas, SW USA
107 N7 **La Granja** Castilla-León, N Spain
57 Q9 **La Gran Sabana** *grassland* E Venezuela
56 H7 **La Grita** Táchira, NW Venezuela
La Grulla *see* Grulla
13 R11 **La Guadeloupe** Québec, SE Canada
66 F12 **La Guaira** Distrito Federal, N Venezuela
56 G4 **La Guajira** *off.* Departamento de La Guajira, *var.* Guajira, La Goagira. ◈ *province* NE Colombia
196 I4 **Lagua Lichan, Punta** *headland* Saipan, S Northern Mariana Islands
20 K14 **La Guardia** ✕ (New York) Long Island, New York, NE USA
La Guardia/Laguardia *see* A Guardia
107 P4 **Laguardia** País Vasco, N Spain
La Gudiña *see* A Gudiña
105 O9 **la Guerche-sur-l'Aubois** Cher, C France
105 O13 **Laguiole** Aveyron, S France
L'Agulhas *see* Agulhas
63 K14 **Laguna** Santa Catarina, S Brazil
39 Q11 **Laguna** New Mexico, SW USA
37 T16 **Laguna Beach** California, W USA
37 Y17 **Laguna Dam** *dam* Arizona/California, W USA
42 L7 **Laguna El Rey** Coahuila de Zaragoza, N Mexico
37 V17 **Laguna Mountains** ▲▲ California, W USA
63 B17 **Laguna Paiva** Santa Fe, C Argentina
64 H3 **Lagunas** Tarapacá, N Chile
58 E9 **Lagunas** Loreto, N Peru
59 M20 **Lagunillas** Santa Cruz, SE Bolivia
56 H6 **Lagunillas** Mérida, NW Venezuela
46 C4 **La Habana** *var.* Havana. ● (Cuba) Ciudad de La Habana, W Cuba
175 Oo3 **Lahad Datu** Sabah, East Malaysia
175 Oo3 **Lahad Datu, Teluk** *var.* Telukan Lahad Datu, Teluk Darvel, Teluk Datu; *prev.* Darvel Bay. *bay* Sabah, East Malaysia
40 F10 **Lahaina** Maui, Hawaii, USA, C Pacific Ocean
174 Hh12 **Lahat** Sumatera, W Indonesia
La Haye *see* 's-Gravenhage
Lahej *see* Laḩij
64 G9 **La Higuera** Coquimbo, N Chile
147 S13 **Lahī, Ḩisā' al** *spring/well* NE Yemen
147 O16 **Laḩij** *var.* Laḩj, *Eng.* Lahej. SW Yemen
148 M3 **Lāhījān** Gīlān, NW Iran
121 I19 **Lahishyn** *Pol.* Lohiszyn, *Rus.* Logishin. Brestskaya Voblasts', SW Belarus
Laḩj *see* Laḩij
103 F18 **Lahn** ≈ W Germany
Lähn *see* Wleń
97 J21 **Laholm** Halland, S Sweden
97 J21 **Laholmsbukten** *bay* S Sweden
37 R6 **Lahontan Reservoir** ⊟ Nevada, W USA
155 W8 **Lahore** Punjab, NE Pakistan
155 W8 **Lahore** ✕ Punjab, E Pakistan
57 Q6 **La Horqueta** Delta Amacuro, NE Venezuela
121 K15 **Lahoysk** *Rus.* Logoysk. Minskaya Voblasts', C Belarus
103 F22 **Lahr** Baden-Württemberg, S Germany
95 M19 **Lahti** *Swe.* Lahtis. Häme, S Finland
Lahtis *see* Lahti
42 M14 **La Huacana** Michoacán de Ocampo, SW Mexico
42 K14 **La Huerta** Jalisco, SW Mexico
80 H12 **Laï** *prev.* Behagle, De Behagle. Tandjilé, S Chad
194 G12 **Laiagam** Enga, W PNG
Laibach *see* Ljubljana
178 Ii5 **Lai Châu** Lai Châu, N Vietnam
40 D9 **Laie** *Haw.* Lā'ie. Oahu, Hawaii, USA, C Pacific Ocean
104 L5 **l'Aigle** Orne, N France
105 Q7 **Laignes** Côte d'Or, C France
95 K17 **Laihia** Vaasa, W Finland
Laila *see* Laylā
85 F25 **Laingsburg** Western Cape, SW South Africa
111 U2 **Lainsitz** *Cz.* Lužnice. ≈ Austria/Czech Republic
98 I7 **Lairg** N Scotland, UK
83 I17 **Laisamis** Eastern, N Kenya
Laisberg *see* Leisi
131 R4 **Laishevo** Respublika Tatarstan, W Russian Federation
Laisholm *see* Jõgeva
94 H13 **Laisvall** Norrbotten, N Sweden
95 K19 **Laitila** Turku-Pori, SW Finland
167 P5 **Laiwu** Shandong, E China
167 R4 **Laixi** *var.* Shuiji. Shandong, E China
167 R4 **Laiyang** Shandong, E China
167 O3 **Laiyuan** Hebei, E China
167 R4 **Laizhou** *var.* Ye Xian. Shandong, E China
167 Q4 **Laizhou Wan** *var.* Laichow Bay. *bay* E China
39 S8 **La Jara** Colorado, C USA
63 I15 **Lajeado** Rio Grande do Sul, S Brazil
114 L12 **Lajkovac** Serbia, C Yugoslavia
113 K23 **Lajosmizse** Bács-Kiskun, C Hungary
Lajta *see* Leitha
42 I6 **La Junta** Chihuahua, N Mexico
39 V7 **La Junta** Colorado, C USA
94 J13 **Lakatrask** Norrbotten, N Sweden
Lak Dera *see* Dheere Laaq
Lakeamu *see* Lakekamu
31 P12 **Lake Andes** South Dakota, N USA
24 H9 **Lake Arthur** Louisiana, S USA
197 L15 **Lakeba** *prev.* Lakemba. *island* Lau Group, E Fiji
197 L14 **Lakeba Passage** *channel* E Fiji
31 S10 **Lake Benton** Minnesota, N USA
25 V9 **Lake Butler** Florida, SE USA
191 P8 **Lake Cargelligo** New South Wales, SE Australia
24 G9 **Lake Charles** Louisiana, S USA
29 X9 **Lake City** Arkansas, C USA
39 Q7 **Lake City** Colorado, C USA
25 V9 **Lake City** Florida, SE USA
31 U13 **Lake City** Iowa, C USA
33 P7 **Lake City** Michigan, N USA
31 W9 **Lake City** Minnesota, N USA
23 T13 **Lake City** South Carolina, SE USA
31 Q7 **Lake City** South Dakota, N USA
22 M8 **Lake City** Tennessee, S USA
194 F12 **Lake Copiago** *var.* Kopiago. Southern Highlands, W PNG
8 L17 **Lake Cowichan** Vancouver Island, British Columbia, SW Canada
31 U10 **Lake Crystal** Minnesota, N USA
27 T6 **Lake Dallas** Texas, SW USA
99 K15 **Lake District** *physical region* NW England, UK
20 D10 **Lake Erie Beach** New York, NE USA
31 T11 **Lakefield** Minnesota, N USA
27 V6 **Lake Fork Reservoir** ◎ Texas, SW USA
32 M9 **Lake Geneva** Wisconsin, N USA
20 L9 **Lake George** New York, NE USA
16 O4 **Lake Harbour** Baffin Island, Northwest Territories, NE Canada
38 I12 **Lake Havasu City** Arizona, SW USA
27 W12 **Lake Jackson** Texas, SW USA
194 J14 **Lakekamu** *var.* Lakeamu. ≈ S PNG
188 K13 **Lake King** Western Australia
194 F12 **Lake Kutubu** ◎ W PNG
25 V12 **Lakeland** Florida, SE USA
25 U7 **Lakeland** Georgia, SE USA
189 W4 **Lakeland Downs** Queensland, NE Australia
9 P16 **Lake Louise** Alberta, SW Canada
Lakemba *see* Lakeba
31 V11 **Lake Mills** Iowa, C USA
41 Q10 **Lake Minchumina** Alaska, USA
Lakemti *see* Nek'emtē
194 E13 **Lake Murray** Western, SW PNG
82 F5 **Nasser, Lake** *var.* Buhayrat Nasir, Buḩayrat Nāşir, Buḩeiret Nâşir. ◎ Egypt/Sudan
33 R9 **Lake Orion** Michigan, N USA
202 B16 **Lakepa** NE Niue
31 T11 **Lake Park** Iowa, C USA
20 K7 **Lake Placid** New York, NE USA
20 K9 **Lake Pleasant** New York, NE USA
36 M6 **Lakeport** California, W USA
31 Q10 **Lake Preston** South Dakota, N USA
24 J5 **Lake Providence** Louisiana, S USA
193 E20 **Lake Pukaki** Canterbury, South Island, NZ
191 Q12 **Lakes Entrance** Victoria, SE Australia
39 N12 **Lakeside** Arizona, SW USA
37 V17 **Lakeside** California, W USA
25 S9 **Lakeside** Florida, SE USA
30 K13 **Lakeside** Nebraska, C USA
34 E13 **Lakeside** Oregon, NW USA
23 W6 **Lakeside** Virginia, NE USA
Lakes State *see* El Buhayrat
Lake State *see* Michigan
193 F20 **Lake Tekapo** Canterbury, South Island, NZ
23 O10 **Lake Toxaway** North Carolina, SE USA
31 T13 **Lake View** Iowa, C USA
34 I16 **Lakeview** Oregon, NW USA
27 O3 **Lakeview** Texas, SW USA
29 W14 **Lake Village** Arkansas, C USA
25 W12 **Lake Wales** Florida, SE USA
39 T4 **Lakewood** Colorado, C USA
20 K15 **Lakewood** New Jersey, NE USA
20 C11 **Lakewood** New York, NE USA
33 T11 **Lakewood** Ohio, N USA
25 Y13 **Lakewood Park** Florida, SE USA
25 Z14 **Lake Worth** Florida, SE USA
158 H4 **Lake Wular** ◎ NE India
128 H11 **Lakhdenpokh'ya** Respublika Kareliya, NW Russian Federation
158 L11 **Lakhīmpur** Uttar Pradesh, N India
160 J11 **Lakhnādon** Madhya Pradesh, C India
Lakhnau *see* Lucknow
160 A9 **Lakhpat** Gujarāt, W India
121 K19 **Lakhva** *Rus.* Lakhva. Brestskaya Voblasts', SW Belarus
28 I6 **Lakin** Kansas, C USA
155 S7 **Lakki Marwat** North-West Frontier Province, NW Pakistan
117 F21 **Lakonía** *historical region* S Greece
117 F22 **Lakonikós Kólpos** *gulf* S Greece
78 M17 **Lakota** S Ivory Coast
31 U11 **Lakota** Iowa, C USA
31 P3 **Lakota** North Dakota, N USA
Lak Sao *see* Ban Lakxao
94 L8 **Laksefjorden** *fjord* N Norway
94 K8 **Lakselv** Finnmark, N Norway
161 B21 **Lakshadweep** *prev.* the Laccadive, Minicoy and Amindivi Islands. ◈ *union territory* India, N Indian Ocean
161 C22 **Lakshadweep** *Eng.* Laccadive Islands. *island group* India, N Indian Ocean
159 S17 **Lakshmikāntapur** West Bengal, NE India
114 G11 **Laktaši** N Bosnia and Herzegovina
155 V7 **Lāla Mūsa** Punjab, NE Pakistan
la Laon *see* Laon
116 M11 **Lalapaşa** Edirne, NW Turkey
85 P14 **Lalaua** Nampula, N Mozambique
107 S10 **L'Alcúdia** *var.* L'Alcudia. País Valenciano, E Spain
81 F20 **La Lékoumou** ◈ *province* SW Congo
44 E8 **La Libertad** La Libertad, SW El Salvador
44 E3 **La Libertad** Petén, N Guatemala
44 H6 **La Libertad** Comayagua, SW Honduras
42 E4 **La Libertad** *var.* Puerto Libertad. Sonora, NW Mexico
44 K10 **La Libertad** Chontales, S Nicaragua
44 A9 **La Libertad** ◈ *department* SW El Salvador
58 B11 **La Libertad** *off.* Departamento de La Libertad. ◈ *department* W Peru
64 G11 **La Ligua** Valparaíso, C Chile
145 U5 **La'lī Khān** E Iraq
81 H16 **La Likouala** ◈ *province* NE Congo
106 H3 **Lalín** Galicia, NW Spain
104 L13 **Lalinde** Dordogne, SW France
106 K16 **La Línea** *var.* La Línea de la Concepción. Andalucía, S Spain
La Línea de la Concepción *see* La Línea
158 J14 **Lalitpur** Uttar Pradesh, N India
159 P11 **Lalitpur** Central, C Nepal
158 K10 **Lālkua** Uttar Pradesh, N India
9 R12 **La Loche** Saskatchewan, C Canada
104 M6 **la Loupe** Eure-et-Loir, C France
101 G20 **La Louvière** Hainaut, S Belgium
L'Altissima *see* Hochwilde
106 L14 **La Luisiana** Andalucía, S Spain
39 S14 **La Luz** New Mexico, SW USA
109 D16 **la Maddalena** Sardegna, Italy, C Mediterranean Sea
64 J7 **La Madrid** Tucumán, N Argentina
Lama-Kara *see* Kara
175 R16 **Lamakera, Selat** *strait* Nusa Tenggara, S Indonesia
13 S8 **La Malbaie** Québec, SE Canada
178 Jj10 **Lamam** Xékong, S Laos
107 P10 **La Mancha** *physical region* C Spain
la Manche *see* English Channel
197 C13 **Lamap** Malekula, C Vanuatu
39 W6 **Lamar** Colorado, C USA
29 S7 **Lamar** Missouri, C USA
23 S12 **Lamar** South Carolina, SE USA
109 C19 **La Marmora, Punta** ▲ Sardegna, Italy, C Mediterranean Sea
15 H7 **La Martre, Lac** ◎ Northwest Territories, NW Canada
58 D10 **Lamas** San Martín, N Peru
44 I5 **La Masica** Atlántida, NW Honduras
105 R12 **Lamastre** Ardèche, E France
La Matepec *see* Santa Ana, Volcán de
46 I7 **La Maya** Santiago de Cuba, E Cuba
111 S5 **Lambach** Oberösterreich, N Austria
173 Ff8 **Lambak** Pulau Pini, W Indonesia
104 H5 **Lamballe** Côtes d'Armor, NW France
81 D18 **Lambaréné** Moyen-Ogooué, W Gabon
Lambasa *see* Labasa
175 Q12 **Lambasina Besar, Pulau** *island* C Indonesia
58 B11 **Lambayeque** Lambayeque, W Peru
58 A10 **Lambayeque** *off.* Departamento de Lambayeque. ◈ *department* NW Peru
99 G17 **Lambay Island** *Ir.* Reachrainn. *island* E Ireland
195 O10 **Lambert, Cape** *headland* New Britain, E PNG
205 W6 **Lambert Glacier** *glacier* Antarctica
31 T10 **Lamberton** Minnesota, N USA
29 X4 **Lambert-Saint Louis** ✕ Missouri, C USA
33 R11 **Lambertville** Michigan, N USA
20 J15 **Lambertville** New Jersey, NE USA
175 Pp9 **Lambogo** Sulawesi, N Indonesia
108 D8 **Lambro** ≈ N Italy
15 H2 **Lambton, Cape** *headland* Banks Island, Northwest Territories, NW Canada
35 W11 **Lame Deer** Montana, NW USA
106 H6 **Lamego** Viseu, N Portugal
197 C13 **Lamen Bay** Épi, C Vanuatu
47 X6 **Lamentin** Basse Terre, N Guadeloupe
Lamentin *see* le Lamentin
190 K10 **Lameroo** South Australia
56 F10 **La Mesa** Cundinamarca, C Colombia
37 U17 **La Mesa** California, W USA
39 R16 **La Mesa** New Mexico, SW USA
27 N6 **Lamesa** Texas, SW USA
109 N21 **Lamezia** Calabria, SE Italy
197 I15 **Lami** Viti Levu, C Fiji
117 F17 **Lamía** Stereá Ellás, C Greece
179 Q17 **Lamitan** Basilan Island, SW Philippines
197 J14 **Lamiti** Gau, C Fiji
176 Uu8 **Lamlam** Irian Jaya, E Indonesia
196 B16 **Lamlam, Mount** ▲ SW Guam
111 Q6 **Lammer** ≈ E Austria
193 E23 **Lammerlaw Range** ▲▲ South Island, NZ
97 L20 **Lammhult** Kronoberg, S Sweden
95 L18 **Lammi** Häme, SW Finland
201 U11 **Lamoil** *island* Chuuk, C Micronesia
37 W3 **Lamoille** Nevada, W USA
20 M7 **Lamoille River** ≈ Vermont, NE USA
32 J13 **La Moine River** ≈ Illinois, N USA
179 Pp10 **Lamon Bay** *bay* Luzon, N Philippines
31 V16 **Lamoni** Iowa, C USA
37 R13 **Lamont** California, W USA
29 N8 **Lamont** Oklahoma, C USA
56 E13 **La Montañita** *var.* Montañita. Caquetá, S Colombia
45 N8 **La Mosquitia** *var.* Miskito Coast, *Eng.* Mosquito Coast. *coastal region* E Nicaragua
104 I9 **la Mothe-Achard** Vendée, NW France
196 L15 **Lamotrek Atoll** *atoll* Caroline Islands, C Micronesia
31 P6 **La Moure** North Dakota, N USA
178 H8 **Lampang** *var.* Muang Lampang. Lampang, NW Thailand
178 Ii9 **Lam Pao Reservoir** ⊟ E Thailand
27 S9 **Lampasas** Texas, SW USA
27 S9 **Lampasas River** ≈ Texas, SW USA
43 N7 **Lampazos** *var.* Lampazos de Naranjo. Nuevo León, NE Mexico
Lampazos de Naranjo *see* Lampazos
117 E19 **Lámpeia** Dytikí Ellás, S Greece
103 G19 **Lampertheim** Hessen, W Germany
99 I20 **Lampeter** SW Wales, UK
178 H7 **Lamphun** *var.* Lampun, Muang Lamphun. Lamphun, NW Thailand
9 X10 **Lamprey** Manitoba, C Canada
Lampun *see* Lamphun
174 I13 **Lampung** *off.* Propinsi Lampung. ◈ *province* SW Indonesia
174 Ii13 **Lampung, Teluk** *bay* Sumatera, SW Indonesia
130 K6 **Lamskoye** Lipetskaya Oblast', W Russian Federation
83 K20 **Lamu** Coast, SE Kenya
45 N14 **La Muerte, Cerro** ▲ C Costa Rica
105 S13 **la Mure** Isère, E France
39 S10 **Lamy** New Mexico, SW USA
121 J18 **Lan'** *Rus.* Lan'. ≈ C Belarus
40 E10 **Lanai** *Haw.* Lāna'i. *island* Hawaii, USA, C Pacific Ocean
40 E10 **Lanai City** Lanai, Hawaii, USA, C Pacific Ocean
101 L18 **Lanaken** Limburg, NE Belgium
179 R15 **Lanao, Lake** *var.* Lake Sultan Alonto. ◎ Mindanao, S Philippines
98 J12 **Lanark** S Scotland, UK
98 I13 **Lanark** *cultural region* C Scotland, UK
106 L9 **La Nava de Ricomalillo** Castilla-La Mancha, C Spain
178 Gg13 **Lanbi Kyun** *prev.* Sullivan Island. *island* Mergui Archipelago, S Myanmar
Lancang Jiang *see* Mekong
99 K17 **Lancashire** *cultural region* NW England, UK
13 N13 **Lancaster** Ontario, SE Canada
99 K16 **Lancaster** NW England, UK
37 T14 **Lancaster** California, W USA
22 M6 **Lancaster** Kentucky, S USA
29 U1 **Lancaster** Missouri, C USA
21 O7 **Lancaster** New Hampshire, NE USA
20 D10 **Lancaster** New York, NE USA
33 T14 **Lancaster** Ohio, N USA
20 H16 **Lancaster** Pennsylvania, NE USA
23 R11 **Lancaster** South Carolina, SE USA
27 U7 **Lancaster** Texas, SW USA
23 X5 **Lancaster** Virginia, NE USA
32 J9 **Lancaster** Wisconsin, N USA
207 N10 **Lancaster Sound** *sound* Northwest Territories, N Canada
Lan-chou/Lan-chow/Lanchow *see* Lanzhou
109 K14 **Lanciano** Abruzzi, C Italy
113 O16 **Łańcut** Rzeszów, SE Poland
174 Kk8 **Landak, Sungai** ≈ Borneo, N Indonesia
Landao *see* Lantau Island
Landau *see* Landau an der Isar, Bayern, Germany
Landau *see* Landau in der Pfalz, Rheinland-Pfalz, Germany
103 N22 **Landau an der Isar** *var.* Landau. Bayern, SE Germany
103 F20 **Landau in der Pfalz** *var.* Landau. Rheinland-Pfalz, SW Germany
Land Burgenland *see* Burgenland
110 K8 **Landeck** Tirol, W Austria
101 J19 **Landen** Vlaams Brabant, C Belgium
35 U15 **Lander** Wyoming, C USA
104 F5 **Landerneau** Finistère, NW France
97 K20 **Landeryd** Halland, S Sweden
104 J15 **Landes** ◈ *department* SW France
Landeshut/Landeshut in Schlesien *see* Kamienna Góra
107 R9 **Landete** Castilla-La Mancha, C Spain
101 M18 **Landgraaf** Limburg, SE Netherlands
104 F5 **Landivisiau** Finistère, NW France
Land of Enchantment *see* New Mexico
Land of Opportunity *see* Arkansas
Land of Steady Habits *see* Connecticut
Land of the Midnight Sun *see* Alaska
110 I8 **Landquart** Graubünden, SE Switzerland
110 J9 **Landquart** ≈ Austria/Switzerland
23 P10 **Landrum** South Carolina, SE USA
Landsberg *see* Górowo Iławeckie, Olsztyn, Poland
Landsberg *see* Gorzów Wielkopolski, Gorzów, Poland
103 K23 **Landsberg am Lech** Bayern, S Germany
Landsberg an der Warthe *see* Gorzów Wielkopolski
99 G25 **Land's End** *headland* SW England, UK
103 M22 **Landshut** Bayern, SE Germany
Landskron *see* Lanškroun

◆ Country
● Country Capital
◇ Dependent Territory
○ Dependent Territory Capital
◈ Administrative Region
✕ International Airport
▲ Mountain
▲▲ Mountain Range
✷ Volcano
≈ River
◎ Lake
⊟ Reservoir

97 J22 **Landskrona** Malmöhus, S Sweden
100 I10 **Landsmeer** Noord-Holland, C Netherlands
97 J19 **Landvetter** ✕ (Göteborg) Göteborg och Bohus, S Sweden
Landwarów *see* Lentvaris
25 R5 **Lanett** Alabama, S USA
110 C8 **La Neuveville** ***var.*** Neuveville, ***Ger.*** Neuenstadt. Neuchâtel, W Switzerland
97 G21 **Langå** ***var.*** Langaa. Århus, C Denmark
Langaa *see* Langå
164 G14 **La'nga Co** ◎ W China
Langada *see* Lagkáda
Langades/Langadhás *see* Lagkadás
Langádhia/Langadia *see* Lagkádia
153 T14 **Langar** ***Rus.*** Lyangar. SE Tajikistan
152 M10 **Langar** ***Rus.*** Lyangar. Nawoiy Wiloyati, C Uzbekistan
148 M3 **Langarūd** Gīlān, NW Iran
9 V16 **Langbank** Saskatchewan, S Canada
31 P2 **Langdon** North Dakota, N USA
105 P12 **Langeac** Haute-Loire, C France
104 L8 **Langeais** Indre-et-Loire, C France
82 I8 **Langeb, Wadi** ≈ NE Sudan
Långed *see* Dals Långed
97 G25 **Langeland** *island* S Denmark
101 B18 **Langemark** West-Vlaanderen, W Belgium
103 G18 **Langen** Hessen, W Germany
103 J22 **Langenau** Baden-Württemberg, S Germany
9 V16 **Langenburg** Saskatchewan, S Canada
103 E16 **Langenfeld** Nordrhein-Westfalen, W Germany
110 L8 **Längenfeld** Tirol, W Austria
102 I12 **Langenhagen** Niedersachsen, N Germany
102 I12 **Langenhagen** ✕ (Hannover) Niedersachsen, NW Germany
111 W3 **Langenlois** Niederösterreich, NE Austria
110 E7 **Langenthal** Bern, NW Switzerland
111 W6 **Langenwang** Steiermark, E Austria
111 X3 **Langenzersdorf** Niederösterreich, E Austria
102 F9 **Langeoog** *island* NW Germany
126 Gg11 **Langepas** Khanty-Mansiyskiy Avtonomnyy Okrug, C Russian Federation
97 H23 **Langeskov** Fyn, C Denmark
97 G16 **Langesund** Telemark, S Norway
97 G17 **Langesundsfjorden** *fjord* S Norway
96 D10 **Langevågen** Møre og Romsdal, S Norway
167 P3 **Langfang** Hebei, E China
96 E9 **Langfjorden** *fjord* S Norway
31 Q8 **Langford** South Dakota, N USA
173 G6 **Langgapayung** Sumatera, W Indonesia
108 E9 **Langhirano** Emilia-Romagna, C Italy
99 K14 **Langholm** S Scotland, UK
94 I3 **Langjökull** *glacier* C Iceland
173 Ff2 **Langkawi, Pulau** *island* Peninsular Malaysia
175 R13 **Langkesi, Kepulauan** *island group* C Indonesia
178 Gg15 **Langkha Tuk, Khao** ▲ SW Thailand
12 L8 **Langlade** Québec, SE Canada
8 M17 **Langley** British Columbia, SW Canada
178 Jj7 **Lang Mô** Thanh Hoa, N Vietnam
Langnau *see* Langnau im Emmental
110 E8 **Langnau im Emmental** ***var.*** Langnau. Bern, W Switzerland
105 Q13 **Langogne** Lozère, S France
164 K16 **Langoi Kangri** ▲ W China
104 K13 **Langon** Gironde, SW France
La Ngounié *see* Ngounié
94 G10 **Langøya** *island* C Norway
164 G14 **Langqên Zangbo** ≈ China/India
105 S7 **Langres** Haute-Marne, N France
105 R8 **Langres, Plateau de** *plateau* C France
173 F4 **Langsa** Sumatera, W Indonesia
95 H16 **Långsele** Västernorrland, C Sweden
168 L12 **Lang Shan** ▲▲ N China
97 M14 **Långshyttan** Kopparberg, C Sweden
178 K5 **Lang Sơn** ***var.*** Langson. Lang Sơn, N Vietnam
178 Gg14 **Lang Suan** Chumphon, SW Thailand
95 J14 **Långträsk** Norrbotten, N Sweden
27 N11 **Langtry** Texas, SW USA
105 P16 **Languedoc** *cultural region* S France
105 P15 **Languedoc-Roussillon** ◐ *region* S France
29 X10 **L'Anguille River** ≈ Arkansas, C USA
95 I16 **Långviksmon** Västernorrland, N Sweden
103 K22 **Langweid** Bayern, S Germany
166 J8 **Langzhong** Sichuan, C China
Lan Hsü *see* Lan Yü
9 U15 **Lanigan** Saskatchewan, S Canada
118 K5 **Lanivtsi** Ternopil's'ka Oblast', W Ukraine
143 Y13 **Länkäran** ***Rus.*** Lenkoran'. S Azerbaijan
104 L16 **Lannemezan** Hautes-Pyrénées, S France
104 G5 **Lannion** Côtes d'Armor, NW France
12 M11 **L'Annonciation** Québec, SE Canada
107 V5 **L'Anoia** ≈ NE Spain
20 I15 **Lansdale** Pennsylvania, NE USA
12 L14 **Lansdowne** Ontario, SE Canada
158 K9 **Lansdowne** Uttar Pradesh, N India
32 M3 **L'Anse** Michigan, N USA
13 S7 **L'Anse-St-Jean** Québec, SE Canada
31 Y11 **Lansing** Iowa, C USA
29 R4 **Lansing** Kansas, C USA
33 Q9 **Lansing** *state capital* Michigan, N USA
94 J12 **Lansjärv** Norrbotten, N Sweden
113 G17 **Lanškroun** ***Ger.*** Landskron. Východní Čechy, E Czech Republic
178 Gg16 **Lanta, Ko** *island* S Thailand
167 O15 **Lantau Island** ***Cant.*** Tai Yue Shan, ***Chin.*** Landao. *island* Hong Kong, S China
Lan-ts'ang Chiang *see* Mekong
175 Q7 **Lanu** Sulawesi, N Indonesia
109 D19 **Lanusei** Sardegna, Italy, C Mediterranean Sea
104 H7 **Lanvaux, Landes de** *physical region* NW France
169 W8 **Lanxi** Heilongjiang, NE China
167 R10 **Lanxi** Zhejiang, SE China
La Nyanga *see* Nyanga
167 T15 **Lan Yü** ***var.*** Huoshao Tao, ***var.*** Hungt'ou, Lan Hsü, Lanyü, ***Eng.*** Orchid Island; ***prev.*** Kotosho, Koto Sho. *island* SE Taiwan
66 P11 **Lanzarote** *island* Islas Canarias, Spain, NE Atlantic Ocean
165 V10 **Lanzhou** ***var.*** Lan-chou, Lanchow, Lan-chow; ***prev.*** Kaolan. Gansu, C China
108 B8 **Lanzo Torinese** Piemonte, NE Italy
179 P8 **Laoag** Luzon, N Philippines
179 R12 **Laoang** Samar, C Philippines
178 J5 **Lao Cai** Lao Cai, N Vietnam
Laodicea/Laodicea ad Mare *see* Al Lādhiqīyah
Laoet *see* Laut, Pulau
169 T11 **Laoha He** ≈ NE China
166 M8 **Laohekou** ***prev.*** Guanghua. Hubei, C China
Laoi, An *see* Lee
99 E19 **Laois** ***prev.*** Leix, Queen's County. *cultural region* C Ireland
Laojunmiao *see* Yumen
169 W12 **Lao Ling** ▲▲ N China
66 Q11 **La Oliva** ***var.*** Oliva. Fuerteventura, Islas Canarias, Spain, NE Atlantic Ocean
Lao, Loch *see* Belfast Lough
Lao Mangnai *see* Mangnai
105 P3 **Laon** ***var.*** la Laon; ***anc.*** Laudunum. Aisne, N France
Lao People's Democratic Republic *see* Laos
56 M3 **La Orchila, Isla** *island* N Venezuela
66 O11 **La Orotava** Tenerife, Islas Canarias, Spain, NE Atlantic Ocean
59 E14 **La Oroya** Junín, C Peru
178 Ii7 **Laos** ***off.*** Lao People's Democratic Republic. ◆ *republic* SE Asia
167 R5 **Laoshan Wan** *bay* E China
169 Y10 **Laoye Ling** ▲▲ NE China
62 J12 **Lapa** Paraná, S Brazil
105 P10 **Lapalisse** Allier, C France
56 F9 **La Palma** Cundinamarca, C Colombia
44 F7 **La Palma** Chalatenango, N El Salvador
45 W16 **La Palma** Darién, SE Panama
66 N11 **La Palma** *island* Islas Canarias, Spain, NE Atlantic Ocean
106 J14 **La Palma del Condado** Andalucía, S Spain
63 F18 **La Paloma** Durazno, C Uruguay
63 G20 **La Paloma** Rocha, E Uruguay
63 A21 **La Pampa** ***off.*** Provincia de La Pampa. ◐ *province* C Argentina
57 P8 **La Paragua** Bolívar, E Venezuela
121 O16 **Lapatsichy** ***Rus.*** Lopatichi. Mahilyowskaya Voblasts', E Belarus
63 C16 **La Paz** Entre Ríos, E Argentina
64 I11 **La Paz** Mendoza, C Argentina
59 J18 **La Paz** ***var.*** La Paz de Ayacucho. ● (Bolivia-legislative and administrative capital) La Paz, W Bolivia
44 H6 **La Paz** La Paz, SW Honduras
42 F9 **La Paz** Baja California Sur, NW Mexico
63 F20 **La Paz** Canelones, S Uruguay
59 J16 **La Paz** ◐ *department* W Bolivia
44 B9 **La Paz** ◐ *department* S El Salvador
44 G7 **La Paz** ◐ *department* SW Honduras
La Paz *see* El Alto, Bolivia
La Paz *see* Robles, Colombia
La Paz *see* La Paz Centro, Nicaragua
42 F9 **La Paz, Bahía de** *bay* W Mexico
44 I10 **La Paz Centro** ***var.*** La Paz. León, W Nicaragua
La Paz de Ayacucho *see* La Paz
56 J15 **La Pedrera** Amazonas, SE Colombia
33 S9 **Lapeer** Michigan, N USA
42 K6 **La Perla** Chihuahua, N Mexico
172 Pp1 **La Perouse Strait** ***Jap.*** Sōya-kaikyō, ***Rus.*** Proliv Laperuza. *strait* Japan/Russian Federation
65 I14 **La Perra, Salitral de** *salt lake* C Argentina
Laperuza, Proliv *see* La Perouse Strait
43 Q10 **La Pesca** Tamaulipas, C Mexico
42 M13 **La Piedad Cavadas** Michoacán de Ocampo, C Mexico
Lapines *see* Lafnitz
95 M16 **Lapinlahti** Kuopio, C Finland
Lápithos *see* Lapta
24 K9 **Laplace** Louisiana, S USA
47 X12 **La Plaine** SE Dominica
181 P16 **la Plaine-des-Palmistes** C Réunion
94 K11 **Lapland** ***Fin.*** Lappi, ***Swe.*** Lappland. *cultural region* N Europe
30 M8 **La Plant** South Dakota, N USA
63 D20 **La Plata** Buenos Aires, E Argentina
56 D12 **La Plata** Huila, SW Colombia
23 W4 **La Plata** Maryland, NE USA
La Plata *see* Sucre
47 U6 **la Plata, Río de** ≈ C Puerto Rico
107 W4 **La Pobla de Lillet** Cataluña, NE Spain
107 U4 **La Pobla de Segur** Cataluña, NE Spain
13 S9 **La Pocatière** Québec, SE Canada
106 L3 **La Pola de Gordón** Castilla-León, N Spain
33 O11 **La Porte** Indiana, N USA
20 H13 **Laporte** Pennsylvania, NE USA
31 X13 **La Porte City** Iowa, C USA
64 J8 **La Posta** Catamarca, C Argentina
42 E8 **La Poza Grande** Baja California Sur, W Mexico
95 K16 **Lappajärvi** Vaasa, W Finland
95 L16 **Lappajärvi** ◎ W Finland
95 N18 **Lappeenranta** ***Swe.*** Villmanstrand. Kymi, SE Finland
95 J17 **Lappfjärd** ***Fin.*** Lapväärtti. Vaasa, W Finland
94 L12 **Lappi** ***Swe.*** Lappland. ◐ *province* N Finland
Lappi *see* Lapland
Lappland *see* Lappi
Lappland *see* Lapland, N Europe
Lappo *see* Lapua
63 C23 **Laprida** Buenos Aires, E Argentina
27 P13 **La Pryor** Texas, SW USA
142 B11 **Lâpseki** Çanakkale, NW Turkey
124 Nn2 **Lapta** ***Gk.*** Lápithos. NW Cyprus
Laptev Sea *see* Laptevykh, More
126 Kk5 **Laptevykh, More** ***Eng.*** Laptev Sea. *sea* Arctic Ocean
95 K16 **Lapua** ***Swe.*** Lappo. Vaasa, W Finland
La Puebla *see* Sa Pobla
107 P3 **La Puebla de Arganzón** País Vasco, N Spain
106 L14 **La Puebla de Cazalla** Andalucía, S Spain
106 M9 **La Puebla de Montalbán** Castilla-La Mancha, C Spain
56 I6 **La Puerta** Trujillo, NW Venezuela
179 Qq13 **Lapu-Lapu** C Philippines
Lapurdum *see* Bayonne
42 E7 **La Purísima** Baja California Sur, W Mexico
Lapväärtti *see* Lappfjärd
112 O10 **Łapy** Białystok, E Poland
82 D6 **Laqiya Arba'in** Northern, NW Sudan
64 J4 **La Quiaca** Jujuy, N Argentina
109 J14 **L'Aquila** ***var.*** Aquila, Aquila degli Abruzzi. Abruzzi, C Italy
149 Q13 **Lār** Fārs, S Iran
56 J5 **Lara** ***off.*** Estado Lara. ◐ *state* NW Venezuela
106 G2 **Laracha** Galicia, NW Spain
76 G5 **Larache** ***var.*** al Araïch, El Araïch, El Araïche, ***anc.*** Lixus. NW Morocco
105 T14 **Laragne-Montéglin** Hautes-Alpes, SE France
106 M13 **La Rambla** Andalucía, S Spain
35 Y17 **Laramie** Wyoming, C USA
35 X15 **Laramie Mountains** ▲▲ Wyoming, C USA
35 Y16 **Laramie River** ≈ Wyoming, C USA
62 H12 **Laranjeiras do Sul** Paraná, S Brazil
Larantoeka *see* Larantuka
175 Qq16 **Larantuka** ***prev.*** Larantoeka. Flores, C Indonesia
176 V15 **Larat** Pulau Larat, E Indonesia
176 V15 **Larat, Pulau** *island* Kepulauan Tanimbar, E Indonesia
97 P19 **Lärbro** Gotland, SE Sweden
108 A9 **Larche, Col de** *pass* France/Italy
12 H8 **Larder Lake** Ontario, S Canada
107 O2 **Laredo** Cantabria, N Spain
27 Q15 **Laredo** Texas, SW USA
42 H9 **La Reforma** Sinaloa, W Mexico
100 N11 **Laren** Gelderland, E Netherlands
100 J11 **Laren** Noord-Holland, C Netherlands
104 K13 **la Réole** Gironde, SW France
La Réunion *see* Réunion
Largeau *see* Faya
105 U13 **l'Argentière-la-Bessée** Hautes-Alpes, SE France
155 O4 **Lar Gerd** ***var.*** Largird. Balkh, N Afghanistan
Largird *see* Lar Gerd
25 V12 **Largo** Florida, SE USA
39 Q9 **Largo, Canon** *valley* New Mexico, SW USA
46 D6 **Largo, Cayo** *island* W Cuba
25 Z17 **Largo, Key** *island* Florida Keys, Florida, SE USA
98 H12 **Largs** W Scotland, UK
104 I16 **la Rhune** ***var.*** Larrún. ▲ France/Spain *see also* Larrún
la Riege *see* Ariège
31 Q4 **Larimore** North Dakota, N USA
109 L15 **Larino** Molise, C Italy
Lario *see* Como, Lago di
64 J9 **La Rioja** La Rioja, NW Argentina
64 I9 **La Rioja** ***off.*** Provincia de La Rioja. ◐ *province* NW Argentina
107 O4 **La Rioja** ◐ *autonomous community* N Spain
117 F16 **Lárisa** ***var.*** Larissa. Thessalía, C Greece
Larissa *see* Lárisa
155 Q13 **Lārkāna** ***var.*** Larkhana. Sind, SE Pakistan
Larkhana *see* Lārkāna
Larnaca *see* Lárnaka
124 Nn3 **Lárnaka** ***var.*** Larnaca, Larnax. SE Cyprus
124 Nn3 **Lárnaka** ✕ SE Cyprus
Larnax *see* Lárnaka
99 G14 **Larne** ***Ir.*** Latharna. E Northern Ireland, UK
28 L5 **Larned** Kansas, C USA
106 L3 **La Robla** Castilla-León, N Spain
106 J10 **La Roca de la Sierra** Extremadura, W Spain
101 K22 **La Roche-en-Ardenne** Luxembourg, SE Belgium
104 L11 **la Rochefoucauld** Charente, W France
104 J10 **la Rochelle** ***anc.*** Rupella. Charente-Maritime, W France
104 I9 **la Roche-sur-Yon** ***prev.*** Bourbon Vendée, Napoléon-Vendée. Vendée, NW France
107 Q10 **La Roda** Castilla-La Mancha, C Spain
106 L14 **La Roda de Andalucía** Andalucía, S Spain
47 P9 **La Romana** E Dominican Republic
9 T13 **La Ronge** Saskatchewan, C Canada
9 U13 **La Ronge, Lac** ◎ Saskatchewan, C Canada
24 K10 **Larose** Louisiana, S USA
44 M7 **La Rosita** Región Autónoma Atlántico Norte, NE Nicaragua
189 Q3 **Larrimah** Northern Territory, N Australia
64 N11 **Larroque** Entre Ríos, E Argentina
107 Q2 **Larrún** ***Fr.*** la Rhune. ▲ France/Spain *see also* la Rhune
205 X6 **Lars Christensen Coast** *physical region* Antarctica
41 Q14 **Larsen Bay** Kodiak Island, Alaska, USA
204 I5 **Larsen Ice Shelf** *ice shelf* Antarctica
15 K3 **Larsen Sound** *sound* Northwest Territories, N Canada
La Rúa *see* A Rúa
104 K16 **Laruns** Pyrénées-Atlantiques, SW France
97 G16 **Larvik** Vestfold, S Norway
126 H11 **Lar'yak** Khanty-Mansiyskiy Avtonomnyy Okrug, C Russian Federation
La-sa *see* Lhasa
175 Tt11 **Lasahata** Pulau Seram, E Indonesia
Lasahau *see* Lasihao
39 O6 **La Sal** Utah, W USA
12 C17 **La Salle** Ontario, S Canada
32 L11 **La Salle** Illinois, N USA
47 O9 **Las Americas** ✕ (Santo Domingo) S Dominican Republic
81 G17 **La Sangha** ◐ *province* N Congo
39 V6 **Las Animas** Colorado, C USA
110 D10 **La Sarine** ***var.*** Sarine. ≈ SW Switzerland
110 B9 **La Sarraz** Vaud, W Switzerland
10 H12 **La Sarre** Québec, SE Canada
56 L3 **Las Aves, Islas** ***var.*** Islas de Aves. *island group* N Venezuela
57 N7 **Las Bonitas** Bolívar, C Venezuela
106 K15 **Las Cabezas de San Juan** Andalucía, S Spain
63 G19 **Lascano** Rocha, E Uruguay
64 I5 **Lascar, Volcán** ▲ N Chile
43 T15 **Las Choapas** ***var.*** Choapas. Veracruz-Llave, SE Mexico
39 R15 **Las Cruces** New Mexico, SW USA
Lasdehnen *see* Krasnoznamensk
107 V4 **La See d'Urgel** ***var.*** La Seu d'Urgell, Seo de Urgel. Cataluña, NE Spain
La Selle *see* Selle, Pic de la
64 G9 **La Serena** Coquimbo, C Chile
106 K11 **La Serena** *physical region* W Spain
La Seu d'Urgell *see* La See d'Urgel
105 T16 **la Seyne-sur-Mer** Var, SE France
63 D21 **Las Flores** Buenos Aires, E Argentina
64 H9 **Las Flores** San Juan, W Argentina
9 S14 **Lashburn** Saskatchewan, S Canada
64 I11 **Las Heras** Mendoza, W Argentina
178 Gg4 **Lashio** Shan State, E Myanmar
154 M8 **Lashkar Gāh** ***var.*** Lash-Kar-Gar'. Helmand, S Afghanistan
Lash-Kar-Gar' *see* Lashkar Gāh
175 Qq13 **Lasihao** ***var.*** Lasahau. Pulau Muna, C Indonesia
109 N21 **La Sila** ▲▲ SW Italy
65 H23 **La Silueta, Cerro** ▲ S Chile
44 L9 **La Sirena** Región Autónoma Atlántico Sur, E Nicaragua
112 J13 **Łask** Sieradz, C Poland
111 V11 **Laško** ***Ger.*** Tüffer. C Slovenia
65 H14 **Las Lajas** Neuquén, W Argentina
65 H15 **Las Lajas, Cerro** ▲ W Argentina
64 M6 **Las Lomitas** Formosa, N Argentina
43 V16 **Las Margaritas** Chiapas, SE Mexico
Las Marismas *see* Guadalquivir, Marismas del
56 M6 **Las Mercedes** Guárico, N Venezuela
44 F6 **Las Minas, Cerro** ▲ W Honduras
107 O11 **La Solana** Castilla-La Mancha, C Spain
47 Q14 **La Soufrière** ▲ Saint Vincent, Saint Vincent and the Grenadines
104 M10 **la Souterraine** Creuse, C France
64 N7 **Las Palmas** Chaco, N Argentina
45 Q16 **Las Palmas** Veraguas, W Panama
66 P12 **Las Palmas** ***var.*** Las Palmas de Gran Canaria. Gran Canaria, Islas Canarias, Spain, NE Atlantic Ocean
66 P12 **Las Palmas** ◐ *province* Islas Canarias, Spain, NE Atlantic Ocean
66 Q12 **Las Palmas** ✕ Gran Canaria, Islas Canarias, Spain, NE Atlantic Ocean
Las Palmas de Gran Canaria *see* Las Palmas
42 D6 **Las Palomas** Baja California Sur, W Mexico
107 P10 **Las Pedroñeras** Castilla-La Mancha, C Spain
108 E10 **La Spezia** Liguria, NW Italy
63 F20 **Las Piedras** Canelones, S Uruguay
65 J18 **Las Plumas** Chubut, S Argentina
63 B18 **Las Rosas** Santa Fe, C Argentina
Lassa *see* Lhasa
37 O4 **Lassen Peak** ▲ California, W USA
204 K6 **Lassiter Coast** *physical region* Antarctica
111 V9 **Lassnitz** ≈ SE Austria
13 O12 **L'Assomption** Québec, SE Canada
13 N11 **L'Assomption** ≈ Québec, SE Canada
45 S17 **Las Tablas** Los Santos, S Panama
Lastarria, Volcán *see* Azufre, Volcán
39 V4 **Last Chance** Colorado, C USA
Last Frontier, The *see* Alaska
9 U16 **Last Mountain Lake** ◎ Saskatchewan, S Canada
64 H9 **Las Tórtolas, Cerro** ▲ W Argentina
63 C14 **Las Toscas** Santa Fe, C Argentina
81 F19 **Lastoursville** Ogooué-Lolo, E Gabon
115 F16 **Lastovo** ***It.*** Lagosta. *island* SW Croatia
115 F16 **Lastovski Kanal** *channel* SW Croatia
42 E6 **Las Tres Vírgenes, Volcán** ⛰ W Mexico
42 F4 **Las Trincheras** Sonora, NW Mexico
57 N8 **Las Trincheras** Bolívar, E Venezuela
46 H7 **Las Tunas** ***var.*** Victoria de las Tunas. Las Tunas, E Cuba
La Suisse *see* Switzerland
42 I5 **Las Varas** Chihuahua, N Mexico
42 J12 **Las Varas** Nayarit, C Mexico
64 L10 **Las Varillas** Córdoba, E Argentina
37 X11 **Las Vegas** Nevada, W USA
39 T10 **Las Vegas** New Mexico, SW USA
195 W8 **Lata** Nendö, Solomon Islands
11 R10 **La Tabatière** Québec, E Canada
58 C6 **Latacunga** Cotopaxi, C Ecuador
204 I7 **Latady Island** *island* Antarctica
56 E14 **La Tagua** Putumayo, S Colombia
Latakia *see* Al Lādhiqīyah
94 J10 **Lätäseno** ≈ NW Finland
12 H9 **Latchford** Ontario, S Canada
12 J13 **Latchford Bridge** Ontario, SE Canada
200 Ss12 **Late** *island* Vava'u Group, N Tonga
159 P15 **Lātehār** Bihār, N India
13 R7 **Laterrière** Québec, SE Canada
104 J13 **la Teste** Gironde, SW France
27 V8 **Latexo** Texas, SW USA
20 L10 **Latham** New York, NE USA
Latharna *see* Larne
110 B9 **La Thielle** ***var.*** Thièle. ≈ W Switzerland
29 R3 **Lathrop** Missouri, C USA
109 I16 **Latina** ***prev.*** Littoria. Lazio, C Italy
43 R14 **La Tinaja** Veracruz-Llave, S Mexico
108 J7 **Latisana** Friuli-Venezia Giulia, NE Italy
Latium *see* Lazio
117 K25 **Lató** *site of ancient city* Kríti, Greece, E Mediterranean Sea
197 J7 **La Tontouta** ✕ (Noumea) Province Sud, S New Caledonia
57 N4 **La Tortuga, Isla** ***var.*** Isla Tortuga. *island* N Venezuela
110 C10 **La Tour-de-Peilz** ***var.*** La Tour de Peilz. Vaud, SW Switzerland
105 S11 **la Tour-du-Pin** Isère, E France
104 J11 **la Tremblade** Charente-Maritime, W France
104 L10 **la Trimouille** Vienne, W France
44 J9 **La Trinidad** Estelí, NW Nicaragua
179 P9 **La Trinidad** Luzon, N Philippines
43 V16 **La Trinitaria** Chiapas, SE Mexico
47 Q11 **la Trinité** E Martinique
13 U7 **La Trinité-des-Monts** Québec, SE Canada
20 C15 **Latrobe** Pennsylvania, NE USA
191 P13 **La Trobe River** ≈ Victoria, SE Australia
Lattakia/Lattaquié *see* Al Lādhiqīyah
175 Tt11 **Latu** Pulau Seram, E Indonesia
13 P9 **La Tuque** Québec, SE Canada
161 G14 **Lātūr** Mahārāshtra, C India
120 G8 **Latvia** ***off.*** Republic of Latvia, ***Ger.*** Lettland, ***Latv.*** Latvija, Latvijas Republika; ***prev.*** Latvian SSR, ***Rus.*** Latviyskaya SSR. ◆ *republic* NE Europe
Latvian SSR/Latvija/LatvijasRepublika/Latviyskaya SSR *see* Latvia
195 O12 **Lau** New Britain, E PNG
183 R9 **Lau Basin** *undersea feature* S Pacific Ocean
103 O15 **Lauchhammer** Brandenburg, E Germany
Laudunum *see* Laon
Laudus *see* St-Lô
Lauenburg/Lauenburg in Pommern *see* Lębork
103 L20 **Lauf an der Pegnitz** Bayern, SE Germany
110 D7 **Laufen** Basel, NW Switzerland
111 P5 **Lauffen** Salzburg, NW Austria
94 I2 **Laugarbakki** Nordhurland Vestra, N Iceland
94 I4 **Laugarvatn** Sudhurland, SW Iceland
33 O3 **Laughing Fish Point** *headland* Michigan, N USA
197 L14 **Lau Group** *island group* E Fiji
Lauis *see* Lugano
95 M17 **Laukaa** Keski-Suomi, C Finland
120 D12 **Laukuva** Šilalė, W Lithuania
Laun *see* Louny
191 P16 **Launceston** Tasmania, SE Australia
99 I24 **Launceston** ***anc.*** Dunheved. SW England, UK
56 L7 **La Unión** Nariño, SW Colombia
44 H8 **La Unión** La Unión, SE El Salvador
44 I6 **La Unión** Olancho, C Honduras
42 M15 **La Unión** Guerrero, S Mexico
43 Y14 **La Unión** Quintana Roo, E Mexico
107 S13 **La Unión** Murcia, SE Spain
56 C13 **La Unión** Barinas, C Venezuela
44 B10 **La Unión** ◐ *department* E El Salvador
40 H11 **Laupahoehoe** ***Haw.*** Laupāhoehoe. Hawaii, USA, C Pacific Ocean
103 I23 **Laupheim** Baden-Württemberg, S Germany
189 W3 **Laura** Queensland, NE Australia
201 X2 **Laura** *atoll* Majuro Atoll, SE Marshall Islands
Laurana *see* Lovran
56 L8 **La Urbana** Bolívar, C Venezuela
23 Y4 **Laurel** Delaware, NE USA
25 V14 **Laurel** Florida, SE USA
23 W3 **Laurel** Maryland, NE USA
24 M6 **Laurel** Mississippi, S USA
35 U11 **Laurel** Montana, NW USA
31 R13 **Laurel** Nebraska, C USA
20 H15 **Laureldale** Pennsylvania, NE USA
20 C16 **Laurel Hill** *ridge* Pennsylvania, NE USA
31 T12 **Laurens** Iowa, C USA
23 P11 **Laurens** South Carolina, SE USA
13 P10 **Laurentian Highlands** ***var.*** Laurentian Mountains, ***Fr.*** Les Laurentides. *plateau* Newfoundland and Labrador/Québec, Canada
LaurentianMountains *see* Laurentian Highlands
13 O12 **Laurentides** Québec, SE Canada
Laurentides, Les *see* Laurentian Highlands
109 M19 **Lauria** Basilicata, S Italy
204 I1 **Laurie Island** *island* Antarctica
23 T11 **Laurinburg** North Carolina, SE USA
32 M2 **Laurium** Michigan, N USA
Lauru *see* Choiseul
110 B9 **Lausanne** ***It.*** Losanna. Vaud, SW Switzerland
103 Q16 **Lausche** ***Cz.*** Luže. ▲ Czech Republic/Germany *see also* Luže
103 Q16 **Lausitzer Bergland** ***var.*** Lausitzer Gebirge, ***Cz.*** Gory Lużyckie, Lužické Hory, ***Eng.*** Lusatian Mountains. ▲▲ E Germany
Lausitzer Gebirge *see* Lausitzer Bergland
Lausitzer Neisse *see* Neisse
105 T12 **Lautaret, Col du** *pass* SE France
65 G15 **Lautaro** Araucanía, C Chile
103 F21 **Lauter** ≈ W Germany
110 I7 **Lauterach** Vorarlberg, NW Austria
103 I17 **Lauterbach** Hessen, C Germany
110 E9 **Lauterbrunnen** Bern, C Switzerland
175 Nn12 **Laut Kecil, Kepulauan** *island group* N Indonesia
197 H14 **Lautoka** Viti Levu, W Fiji
175 Nn11 **Laut, Pulau** ***prev.*** Laoet. *island* Borneo, C Indonesia
174 Jj4 **Laut, Pulau** *island* Kepulauan Natuna, W Indonesia
175 Nn11 **Laut, Selat** *strait* Borneo, C Indonesia
173 F4 **Laut Tawar, Danau** ◎ Sumatera, NW Indonesia
201 V14 **Lauvergne Island** *island* Chuuk, C Micronesia
100 M5 **Lauwers Meer** ◎ N Netherlands
100 M4 **Lauwersoog** Groningen, NE Netherlands
104 M14 **Lauzerte** Tarn-et-Garonne, S France
27 U13 **Lavaca Bay** *bay* Texas, SW USA
27 U12 **Lavaca River** ≈ Texas, SW USA
13 O12 **Laval** Québec, SE Canada
104 J6 **Laval** Mayenne, NW France
13 T6 **Laval** ≈ Québec, SE Canada
63 F19 **Lavalleja** ◐ *department* S Uruguay
13 O12 **Lavaltrie** Québec, SE Canada
195 X17 **Lavanggu** Rennell, S Solomon Islands
149 O14 **Lāvān, Jazīreh-ye** *island* S Iran
111 U8 **Lavant** ≈ S Austria
120 G5 **Lavassaare** ***Ger.*** Lawassaar. Pärnumaa, SW Estonia
106 L3 **La Vecilla de Curueño** Castilla-León, N Spain
47 N8 **La Vega** ***var.*** Concepción de la Vega. C Dominican Republic
La Vela *see* La Vela de Coro
56 J4 **La Vela de Coro** ***var.*** La Vela. Falcón, N Venezuela
105 N17 **Lavelanet** Ariège, S France
109 M17 **Lavello** Basilicata, S Italy
38 J8 **La Verkin** Utah, W USA
28 J8 **Laverne** Oklahoma, C USA
27 S12 **La Vernia** Texas, SW USA
95 K18 **Lavia** Turku-Pori, SW Finland
56 L5 **La Victoria** Aragua, N Venezuela
12 I12 **Lavieille, Lake** ◎ Ontario, SE Canada
96 C12 **Lavik** Sogn og Fjordane, S Norway
La Vila Jojosa *see* Villajoyosa
35 U10 **Lavina** Montana, NW USA
204 H5 **Lavoisier Island** *island* Antarctica
25 U2 **Lavonia** Georgia, SE USA
105 R13 **la Voulte-sur-Rhône** Ardèche, E France
127 Q3 **Lavrentiya** Chukotskiy Avtonomnyy Okrug, NE Russian Federation
117 H20 **Lávrio** ***prev.*** Lávrion. Attikí, C Greece
Lávrion *see* Lávrio
85 L22 **Lavumisa** ***prev.*** Gollel. SE Swaziland
155 T4 **Lawarai Pass** *pass* N Pakistan
Lawassaar *see* Lavassaare
147 P16 **Lawdar** SW Yemen
27 Q7 **Lawn** Texas, SW USA
205 Y4 **Law Promontory** *headland* Antarctica
79 O14 **Lawra** NW Ghana
193 E23 **Lawrence** Otago, South Island, NZ
33 P14 **Lawrence** Indiana, N USA
29 Q4 **Lawrence** Kansas, C USA
21 O10 **Lawrence** Massachusetts, NE USA
22 L5 **Lawrenceburg** Kentucky, S USA
22 I10 **Lawrenceburg** Tennessee, S USA
25 T3 **Lawrenceville** Georgia, SE USA
33 N15 **Lawrenceville** Illinois, N USA
23 V7 **Lawrenceville** Virginia, NE USA
29 S3 **Lawson** Missouri, C USA
28 L12 **Lawton** Oklahoma, C USA
146 I4 **Lawz, Jabal al** ▲ NW Saudi Arabia
97 L16 **Laxå** Örebro, C Sweden
129 T5 **Laya** ≈ NW Russian Federation
59 I19 **La Yarada** Tacna, SW Peru
147 S15 **Layjūn** C Yemen
147 Q9 **Laylā** ***var.*** Laila. Ar Riyāḍ, C Saudi Arabia
25 P4 **Lay Lake** ⊞ Alabama, S USA
47 P14 **Layou** Saint Vincent, Saint Vincent and the Grenadines
La Youne *see* El Ayoun
199 Jj5 **Laysan Island** *island* Hawaiian Islands, Hawaii, USA, C Pacific Ocean
38 L2 **Layton** Utah, W USA
36 L5 **Laytonville** California, N USA
180 H17 **Lazare, Pointe** *headland* Mahé, NE Seychelles
127 O14 **Lazarev** Khabarovskiy Kray, SE Russian Federation
114 L12 **Lazarevac** Serbia, C Yugoslavia
Lazareva, Ostrov *see* Lazerew Oroli
67 N22 **Lazarev Sea** *sea* Antarctica
42 M15 **Lázaro Cárdenas** Michoacán de Ocampo, SW Mexico
121 F15 **Lazdijai** Lazdijai, S Lithuania
152 G5 **Lazerew Oroli** ***Rus.*** Ostrov Lazareva. *island* NW Uzbekistan
109 H15 **Lazio** ***anc.*** Latium. ◐ *region* C Italy
113 A16 **Lázně Kynžvart** ***Ger.*** Bad Königswart. Západní Čechy, W Czech Republic
Lazovsk *see* Sîngerei
178 Ii13 **Leach** Poŭthĭsăt, W Cambodia
29 X9 **Leachville** Arkansas, C USA
30 I9 **Lead** South Dakota, N USA
9 S16 **Leader** Saskatchewan, S Canada
21 S6 **Lead Mountain** ▲ Maine, NE USA
39 R5 **Leadville** Colorado, C USA
9 V12 **Leaf Rapids** Manitoba, C Canada
24 M7 **Leaf River** ≈ Mississippi, S USA
27 W11 **League City** Texas, SW USA
25 N7 **Leakesville** Mississippi, S USA
27 Q11 **Leakey** Texas, SW USA
Leal *see* Lihula
85 G15 **Lealui** Western, W Zambia
Leamhcán *see* Lucan
12 C18 **Leamington** Ontario, S Canada
Leamington/Leamington Spa *see* Royal Leamington Spa
Leammi *see* Lemmenjoki
27 S10 **Leander** Texas, SW USA
62 F13 **Leandro N.Alem** Misiones, NE Argentina
99 A20 **Leane, Lough** ***Ir.*** Loch Léin. ◎ SW Ireland
188 G8 **Learmouth** Western Australia
Leau *see* Zoutleeuw
L'Eau d'Heure *see* Plate Taille, Lac de la
202 D12 **Leava** Île Futuna, S Wallis and Futuna
29 R3 **Leavenworth** Kansas, C USA
34 I8 **Leavenworth** Washington, NW USA
29 R4 **Leawood** Kansas, C USA
112 H6 **Łeba** ***Ger.*** Leba. Słupsk, NW Poland
112 I6 **Łeba** ***Ger.*** Leba. ≈ N Poland
103 D20 **Lebach** Saarland, SW Germany
Łeba, Jezioro *see* Łebsko, Jezioro
179 R17 **Lebak** Mindanao, S Philippines
175 Oo11 **Lebani,Teluk** *bay* Sulawesi, C Indonesia
33 O13 **Lebanon** Indiana, N USA
22 L6 **Lebanon** Kentucky, S USA
29 U6 **Lebanon** Missouri, C USA

◆ Country
● Country Capital
◇ Dependent Territory
○ Dependent Territory Capital
◐ Administrative Region
✕ International Airport
▲ Mountain
▲▲ Mountain Range
⛰ Volcano
≈ River
◎ Lake
⊞ Reservoir

21 N9 **Lebanon** New Hampshire, NE USA
34 G12 **Lebanon** Oregon, NW USA
20 H15 **Lebanon** Pennsylvania, NE USA
22 J8 **Lebanon** Tennessee, S USA
23 P7 **Lebanon** Virginia, NE USA
144 G6 **Lebanon** off. Republic of Lebanon, Ar. Al Lubnān, Fr. Liban. ◆ republic SW Asia
22 K6 **Lebanon Junction** Kentucky, S USA
Lebanon, Mount see Liban, Jebel
152 J10 **Lebap** Lebapskiy Velayat, NE Turkmenistan
152 H11 **Lebapskiy Velayat** Turkm. Lebap Welayaty; prev. Rus. Chardzhevskaya Oblast', Turkm. Chärjew Oblasty. ◆ province E Turkmenistan
Lebap Welayaty see Lebapskiy Velayat
101 F17 **Lebbeke** Oost-Vlaanderen, NW Belgium
37 S14 **Lebec** California, W USA
Lebedin see Lebedyn
126 LI12 **Lebedinyy** Respublika Sakha (Yakutiya), NE Russian Federation
130 L6 **Lebedyan'** Lipetskaya Oblast', W Russian Federation
119 T4 **Lebedyn** Rus. Lebedin. Sums'ka Oblast', NE Ukraine
10 I12 **Lebel-sur-Quévillon** Québec, SE Canada
94 L8 **Le Blanc** Indre, C France
104 M9 **Lebo** Kansas, C USA
29 P5 **Lebo** Kansas, C USA
81 L15 **Lebo** Haut-Zaïre, N Zaire
112 H6 **Lębork** var. Lebòrk, Ger. Lauenburg, Lauenburg in Pommern. Shupsk, NW Poland
105 O17 **le Boulou** Pyrénées-Orientales, S France
110 A9 **Le Brassus** Vaud, W Switzerland
106 JI5 **Lebrija** Andalucía, S Spain
112 G6 **Łebsko, Jezioro** Ger. Lebasee; prev. Jezioro Łeba. ⊚ N Poland
65 F14 **Lebu** Bío Bío, C Chile
151 U8 **Lebyazh'ye** Pavlodar, NE Kazakhstan
106 F6 **Leça da Palmeira** Porto, N Portugal
105 U15 **le Cannet** Alpes-Maritimes, SE France
Le Cap see Cap-Haïtien
105 P2 **le Cateau-Cambrésis** Nord, N France
109 Q18 **Lecce** Puglia, SE Italy
108 D7 **Lecco** Lombardia, N Italy
31 V10 **Le Center** Minnesota, N USA
110 J7 **Lech** Vorarlberg, W Austria
103 K22 **Lech** ⚌ Austria/Germany
117 D19 **Lechainá** var. Lehena, Lekhainá. Dytikí Ellás, S Greece
104 J11 **le Château d'Oléron** Charente-Maritime, W France
105 R3 **le Chesne** Ardennes, N France
105 R13 **le Cheylard** Ardèche, E France
110 K7 **Lechtaler Alpen** ⚌ W Austria
102 H6 **Leck** Schleswig-Holstein, N Germany
12 L9 **Lecointre, Lac** ⊚ Québec, SE Canada
24 H7 **Lecompte** Louisiana, S USA
105 Q9 **le Creusot** Saône-et-Loire, C France
Lecumberri see Lekunberri
112 P13 **Łęczna** Lublin, E Poland
112 J12 **Łęczyca** Ger. Lentschiza, Rus. Lenchitsa. Płock, C Poland
102 F10 **Leda** ⚌ NW Germany
101 F17 **Lede** Oost-Vlaanderen, NW Belgium
106 K6 **Ledesma** Castilla-León, N Spain
47 Q12 **le Diamant** SW Martinique
180 J16 **Le Digue** island Inner Islands, NE Seychelles
105 Q10 **le Donjon** Allier, C France
104 M10 **le Dorat** Haute-Vienne, C France
Ledo Salinarius see Lons-le-Saunier
9 L12 **Leduc** Alberta, SW Canada
127 Pp7 **Ledyanaya, Gora** ▲ E Russian Federation
99 C21 **Lee** Ir. An Laoi. ⚌ SW Ireland
31 U5 **Leech Lake** ⊚ Minnesota, N USA
28 K10 **Leedey** Oklahoma, C USA
99 M17 **Leeds** N England, UK
23 U3 **Leeds** Alabama, S USA
31 O3 **Leeds** North Dakota, N USA
100 N6 **Leek** Groningen, NE Netherlands
101 K15 **Leende** Noord-Brabant, SE Netherlands
102 F10 **Leer** Niedersachsen, NW Germany
100 J13 **Leerdam** Zuid-Holland, C Netherlands
100 K12 **Leersum** Utrecht, C Netherlands
25 W11 **Leesburg** Florida, SE USA
23 V3 **Leesburg** Virginia, NE USA
29 R4 **Lees Summit** Missouri, C USA
24 G7 **Leesville** Louisiana, S USA
27 S12 **Leesville** Texas, SW USA
33 U13 **Leesville Lake** ⊚ Ohio, N USA
Leesville Lake see Smith Mountain Lake
191 P9 **Leeton** New South Wales, SE Australia
100 L6 **Leeuwarden** Fris. Ljouwert. Friesland, N Netherlands
188 I14 **Leeuwin, Cape** headland Western Australia
37 R8 **Lee Vining** California, W USA
47 V8 **Leeward Islands** island group E West Indies
Leeward Islands see Vent, Îles Sous le, W French Polynesia
Leeward Islands see Sotavento, Ilhas de, Cape Verde
81 G20 **Léfini** ⚌ S Congo
Lefka see Lefke

117 C17 **Lefkáda** prev. Levkás. Lefkáda, Iónioi Nísoi, Greece, C Mediterranean Sea
117 B17 **Lefkáda** It. Santa Maura; prev. Levkás, anc. Leucas. island Iónioi Nísoi, Greece, C Mediterranean Sea
117 H25 **Lefká Óri** ⚌ Kríti, Greece, E Mediterranean Sea
124 N3 **Lefke** Gk. Léfka. W Cyprus
117 B16 **Lefkímmi** var. Lefkími. Kérkyra, Iónioi Nísoi, Greece, C Mediterranean Sea
Lefkonico/Lefkónikon see Geçitkale
Lefkoşa/Lefkosía see Nicosia
27 O2 **Lefors** Texas, SW USA
188 L12 **Lefroy, Lake** salt lake Western Australia
Legaceaster see Chester
107 N8 **Legacé** Oost-Vlaanderen, NW Belgium
179 U13 **Legaspi** off. Legaspi City. Luzon, N Philippines
Leghorn see Livorno
112 M11 **Legionowo** Warszawa, C Poland
101 K24 **Léglise** Luxembourg, SE Belgium
108 G8 **Legnano** Lombardia, NE Italy
108 D7 **Legnano** Veneto, NE Italy
113 F14 **Legnica** Ger. Liegnitz. Legnica, W Poland
113 E14 **Legnica** off. Województwo Legnickie, Ger. Liegnitz. ◆ province W Poland
Legnickie, Województwo see Legnica
Legnickie, Województwo see Legnica
37 Q9 **Le Grand** California, W USA
105 Q15 **le Grau-du-Roi** Gard, S France
191 U3 **Legume** New South Wales, SE Australia
104 L4 **le Havre** Eng. Havre; prev. le Havre-de-Grâce. Seine-Maritime, N France
le Havre-de-Grâce see le Havre
Lehena see Lechainá
38 L3 **Lehi** Utah, W USA
20 F14 **Leighton** Pennsylvania, NE USA
31 O6 **Lehr** North Dakota, N USA
40 A8 **Lehua Island** island Hawaiian Islands, Hawaii, USA, C Pacific Ocean
155 S9 **Leiah** Punjab, NE Pakistan
111 W9 **Leibnitz** Steiermark, SE Austria
99 M19 **Leicester** Lat. Batae Coritanorum. C England, UK
99 M19 **Leicestershire** cultural region C England, UK
100 H11 **Leiden** prev. Leyden, anc. Lugdunum Batavorum. Zuid-Holland, W Netherlands
100 H11 **Leiderdorp** Zuid-Holland, W Netherlands
100 G11 **Leidschendam** Zuid-Holland, W Netherlands
101 D18 **Leie** Fr. Lys. ⚌ Belgium/France
Leifear see Lifford
192 L4 **Leigh** Auckland, North Island, NZ
99 K17 **Leigh** NW England, UK
190 I5 **Leigh Creek** South Australia
99 M21 **Leighton Buzzard** E England, UK
Léim an Bhradáin see Leixlip
Léim an Mhadaidh see Limavady
Léime, Ceann see Loop Head, Ireland
Léime, Ceann see Slyne Head, Ireland
103 G20 **Leimen** Baden-Württemberg, SW Germany
102 J13 **Leine** ⚌ NW Germany
103 J15 **Leinefelde** Thüringen, C Germany
Léin, Loch see Leane, Lough
99 D19 **Leinster** Ir. Cúige Laighean. cultural region E Ireland
99 F19 **Leinster, Mount** Ir. Stua Laighean. ▲ SE Ireland
121 F15 **Leipalingis** Lazdijai, S Lithuania
94 J12 **Leipojärvi** Norrbotten, N Sweden
33 R12 **Leipsic** Ohio, N USA
117 M20 **Leipsoí** island Dodekánisos, Greece, Aegean Sea
103 M15 **Leipzig** Pol. Lipsk; hist. Leipsic, anc. Lipsia. Sachsen, E Germany
103 M15 **Leipzig Halle** ✈ Sachsen, E Germany
106 F9 **Leiria** anc. Collipo. Leiria, C Portugal
106 F9 **Leiria** ◆ district C Portugal
97 C15 **Leirvik** Hordaland, S Norway
120 E5 **Leisi** Ger. Laisberg. Saaremaa, W Estonia
118 J3 **Leitariegos, Puerto de** pass NW Spain
22 J6 **Leitchfield** Kentucky, S USA
111 Y5 **Leitha** Hung. Lajta. ⚌ Austria/Hungary
Leitir Ceanainn see Letterkenny
Leitmeritz see Litoměřice
Leitomischl see Litomyšl
99 D16 **Leitrim** Ir. Liatroim. cultural region NW Ireland
117 F18 **Leivádia** prev. Leivádhia. Steréa Ellás, C Greece
Leix see Laois
99 F19 **Leixlip** Eng. Salmon Leap, Ir. Léim an Bhradáin. E Ireland
66 N8 **Leixões** Porto, N Portugal
167 N12 **Leiyang** Hunan, S China
166 L16 **Leizhou** var. Haikang. Guangdong, S China
166 L16 **Leizhou Bandao** var. Luichow Peninsula. peninsula S China
100 H13 **Lek** ⚌ SW Netherlands
118 I16 **Lekánis** ⚌ N Greece
180 L13 **Le Kartala** ▲ Grande Comore, NW Comoros
81 G20 **Léfini** ⚌ S Congo
117 D17 **Léfka** see Lefke

81 G20 **Lékéti, Monts de la** ⚌ S Congo
Lehhainá see Lechainá
116 H8 **Lekhchevo** Oblast Montana, NW Bulgaria
94 G11 **Leknes** Nordland, C Norway
81 E21 **Le Kouilou** ◆ province
96 L13 **Leksand** Kopparberg, C Sweden
128 H8 **Leksozero, Ozero** ⊚ NW Russian Federation
107 Q3 **Lekunberri** var. Lecumberri. Navarra, N Spain
175 T16 **Lelai, Tanjung** headland Pulau Halmahera, N Indonesia
47 Q11 **le Lamentin** Lamentin. C Martinique
47 Q11 **le Lamentin** ✈ (Fort-de-France) C Martinique
33 P6 **Leland** Michigan, N USA
24 J4 **Leland** Mississippi, S USA
97 J16 **Lelång** var. Lelängen. ⊚ S Sweden
Lelång see Lelång
Lel'chitsy see Lyel'chytsy
Le Léman see Geneva, Lake
113 I14 **Lelija** ▲ SE Bosnia and Herzegovina
110 C8 **Le Locle** Neuchâtel, W Switzerland
201 Y14 **Lelu** Kosrae, E Micronesia
Lelu see Lelu Island
201 Y14 **Lelu Island** var. Lelu. island Kosrae, E Micronesia
57 V7 **Lelydorp** Wanica, N Suriname
100 K9 **Lelystad** Flevoland, C Netherlands
65 K25 **Le Maire, Estrecho de** strait S Argentina
174 Hh7 **Lemang** Pulau Rangsang, W Indonesia
195 N16 **Lemankoa** Buka Island, NE PNG
104 L6 **le Mans** Sarthe, NW France
31 S12 **Le Mars** Iowa, C USA
174 I11 **Lematan, Air** ⚌ Sumatera, W Indonesia
111 S3 **Lembach Im Mühlkreis** Oberösterreich, N Austria
103 G23 **Lemberg** ▲ SW Germany
Lemberg see L'viv
Lemdiyya see Médéa
124 Qq12 **Lemesós** var. Limassol. SW Cyprus
102 H13 **Lemgo** Nordrhein-Westfalen, C Germany
35 P13 **Lemhi Range** ▲ Idaho, NW USA
16 Oo2 **Lemieux Islands** island group Northwest Territories, NE Canada
175 Q7 **Lemito** Sulawesi, N Indonesia
94 L10 **Lemmenjoki** Lapp. Leammi. ⚌ NE Finland
100 L7 **Lemmer** Fris. De Lemmer. Friesland, N Netherlands
30 L7 **Lemmon** South Dakota, N USA
38 M15 **Lemmon, Mount** ▲ Arizona, SW USA
Lemnos see Límnos
33 O14 **Lemon, Lake** ⊚ Indiana, N USA
104 J5 **le Mont St-Michel** castle Manche, N France
37 Q11 **Lemoore** California, W USA
201 T13 **Lemotol Bay** bay Chuuk Islands, C Micronesia
47 Y5 **le Moule** var. Moule. Grande Terre, NE Guadeloupe
Lemovices see Limoges
Le Moyen-Ogooué see Moyen-Ogooué
103 G20 **Le Moyne, Lac** ⊚ Québec, E Canada
95 L18 **Lempäälä** Häme, SW Finland
44 E7 **Lempa, Río** ⚌ Central America
44 F7 **Lempira** prev. Gracias. ◆ department SW Honduras
Lemsalu see Limbaži
99 D19 **Lemster, Ceann** see Loop Head, Ireland
109 N17 **Le Murge** ▲ SE Italy
129 V6 **Lemva** ⚌ NW Russian Federation
97 F21 **Lemvig** Ringkøbing, W Denmark
177 F8 **Lemyethna** Irrawaddy, SW Myanmar
32 K10 **Lena** Illinois, N USA
133 V14 **Lena** ⚌ NE Russian Federation
181 N13 **Lena Tablemount** undersea feature S Indian Ocean
Lenchitsa see Łęczyca
61 N17 **Lençóis** Bahia, E Brazil
62 K9 **Lençóis Paulista** São Paulo, S Brazil
178 Mm15 **Len Dao** island S Spratly Islands
119 Y9 **Lendava** Ger. Unterlimbach; prev. Dolnja Lendava. NE Slovenia
85 F20 **Lendepas** Hardap, SE Namibia
128 H9 **Lendery** Respublika Kareliya, NW Russian Federation
111 T4 **Lending** Oberösterreich, N Austria
109 I14 **Leonessa** Lazio, C Italy
109 K24 **Lengau** Oberösterreich, N Austria
151 Q17 **Lenger** Yuzhnyy Kazakhstan, S Kazakhstan
165 O9 **Lenghu** Qinghai, C China
165 T19 **Lenglong Ling** ⚌ N China
110 D7 **Lengnau** Bern, W Switzerland
166 M12 **Lengshuitan** Hunan, S China
97 M20 **Lenhovda** Kronoberg, S Sweden
81 E20 **Le Niari** ◆ province SW Congo
151 R9 **Lenin** see Akdepe, Turkmenistan
151 R7 **Lenin** ⚌ SW Russian Federation, Kazakhstan
Lenin see Akdepe, Turkmenistan
Leninabad see Khüjand
Leninakan see Gyumri
119 V12 **Lenine** Rus. Lenino. Respublika Krym, S Ukraine
Leningor see Leninogorsk
Leningrad see Sankt-Peterburg

130 L13 **Leningradskaya** Krasnodarskiy Kray, SW Russian Federation
205 S16 **Leningradskaya** Russian research station Antarctica
128 H12 **Leningradskaya Oblast'** ◆ province NW Russian Federation
Leningradskiy see Leningrad
Lenino see Lyenina, Belarus
Lenino see Lenine, Ukraine
Leninobod see Khüjand
151 X9 **Leninogorsk** Kaz. Leningor. Vostochnyy Kazakhstan, E Kazakhstan
131 T5 **Leninogorsk** Respublika Tatarstan, W Russian Federation
153 T12 **Lenin Peak** Rus. Pik Lenina, Taj. Qullai Lenin. ▲ Kyrgyzstan/Tajikistan
Leninpol' see Talasskaya Oblast', NW Kyrgyzstan
131 P11 **Leninsk** Volgogradskaya Oblast', SW Russian Federation
Leninsk see Akdepe, Turkmenistan
151 T8 **Leninsk** Asaka, Uzbekistan
151 J24 **Leninskiy** Pavlodar, E Kazakhstan
126 H14 **Leninsk-Kuznetskiy** Kemerovskaya Oblast', S Russian Federation
151 N7 **Leninskoye** Kaz. Lenin. Kustanay, N Kazakhstan
129 Z13 **Leninskoye** Kirovskaya Oblast', NW Russian Federation
Leninsk-Turkmenski see Chardzhev
Leninváros see Tiszaújváros
Lenkoran' see Länkäran
47 R15 **Lenne** ⚌ W Germany
103 G16 **Lennestadt** Nordrhein-Westfalen, W Germany
31 R11 **Lennox** South Dakota, N USA
65 J25 **Lennox, Isla** Eng. Lennox Island. island S Chile
23 Q9 **Lenoir** North Carolina, SE USA
22 M9 **Lenoir City** Tennessee, S USA
110 C7 **Le Noirmont** Jura, NW Switzerland
12 L9 **Lenôtre, Lac** ⊚ Québec, SE Canada
31 U15 **Lenox** Iowa, C USA
105 O2 **Lens** anc. Lendum, Lentium. Pas-de-Calais, N France
126 Kk12 **Lensk** Respublika Sakha (Yakutiya), NE Russian Federation
113 F24 **Lenti** Zala, SW Hungary
Lentia see Linz
109 L25 **Lentiira** Oulu, E Finland
Lentini anc. Leontini. Sicilia, Italy, C Mediterranean Sea
Lentium see Lens
Lentschiza see Łęczyca
95 N15 **Lentua** ⊚ E Finland
121 H14 **Lentvaris** Pol. Landwarów. Trakai, SE Lithuania
110 F7 **Lenzburg** Aargau, N Switzerland
111 R6 **Lenzing** Oberösterreich, N Austria
77 V16 **Léo** SW Burkina
111 V7 **Leoben** Steiermark, C Austria
Leobschütz see Głubczyce
46 L9 **Léogâne** S Haiti
175 Q7 **Leok** Sulawesi, N Indonesia
31 O7 **Leola** South Dakota, N USA
99 K20 **Leominster** W England, UK
21 N11 **Leominster** Massachusetts, NE USA
3 V16 **Leon** Iowa, C USA
42 M12 **León** var. León de los Aldamas. Guanajuato, C Mexico
44 I10 **León** León, W Nicaragua
104 I4 **León** Castilla-León, NW Spain
44 I9 **León** ◆ department W Nicaragua
106 K4 **León** ◆ province Castilla-León, NW Spain
León see Cotopaxi
104 K4 **León, Cerro** ▲ NW Paraguay
León de los Aldamas see León
28 H9 **Leonding** Oberösterreich, N Austria
109 I14 **Leonessa** Lazio, C Italy
109 K24 **Leonforte** Sicilia, Italy, C Mediterranean Sea
191 O13 **Leonora** Western Australia, SE Australia
109 N17 **Leonardo da Vinci** prev. Fiumicino. ✈ (Roma) Lazio, C Italy
27 O12 **Leona River** ⚌ Texas, SW USA
43 Z11 **Leona Vicario** Quintana Roo, SE Mexico
103 F22 **Leonberg** Baden-Württemberg, SW Germany
64 M3 **León, Cerro** ▲ NW Paraguay
27 U5 **Leonard** Texas, SW USA
Leonard Murray Mountains see Murray Range
85 J23 **Lesotho** off. Kingdom of Lesotho; prev. Basutoland. ◆ monarchy S Africa

Lépontiennes, Alpes/Lepontine, Alpi see Lepontine Alps
110 G10 **Lépontiennes, Alpes** Fr. Alpes Lépontiennes. It. Alpi Lepontine. ▲ Italy/Switzerland
81 O16 **Le Pool** ◆ province S Congo
181 O16 **le Port** NW Réunion
25 N1 **le Portel** Pas-de-Calais, N France
95 N17 **Leppävirta** Kuopio, C Finland
47 Q11 **le Prêcheur** NW Martinique
Lepsa see Lepsy
151 V13 **Lepsy** Kaz. Lepsi. Taldykorgan, SE Kazakhstan
151 V13 **Lepsy** Kaz. Lepsi. ⚌ SE Kazakhstan
105 Q12 **le Puy** prev. Le Puy-en-Velay, hist. Anicium, Podium Anicensis. Haute-Loire, C France
Le Puy-en-Velay see le Puy
47 X11 **le Raizet** ✈ (Pointe-à-Pitre) Grande Terre, C Guadeloupe
Le Raizet see le Raizet
109 J24 **Lercara Friddi** Sicilia, Italy, C Mediterranean Sea
80 G12 **Léré** Mayo-Kébbi, SW Chad
Leribe see Hlotse
108 E10 **Lerici** Liguria, NW Italy
56 I14 **Lérida** Vaupés, SE Colombia
107 U5 **Lérida** ◆ province Cataluña, NE Spain
Lérida see Lleida
107 N5 **Lerma** Castilla-León, N Spain
42 M13 **Lerma, Río** ⚌ C Mexico
117 F20 **Lérna** prehistoric site Peloponnísos, S Greece
47 R11 **le Robert** E Martinique
117 M21 **Léros** island Dodekánisos, Greece, Aegean Sea
29 Q6 **Le Roy** Illinois, N USA
29 Q6 **Le Roy** Kansas, C USA
31 W11 **Le Roy** Minnesota, N USA
20 F9 **Le Roy** New York, NE USA
97 J19 **Lerum** Älvsborg, S Sweden
98 M7 **Lerwick** NE Scotland, UK
47 Y6 **les Abymes** var. Abymes. Grande Terre, C Guadeloupe
les Albères see Albères, Chaîne des
104 M4 **les Andelys** Eure, N France
47 Q12 **les Anses-d'Arlets** SW Martinique
107 U6 **Les Borges Blanques** var. Borjas Blancas. Cataluña, NE Spain
105 T12 **les Écrins** ▲ E France
110 C10 **Le Sépey** Vaud, W Switzerland
13 T7 **Les Escoumins** Québec, SE Canada
les Gonaïves see Gonaïves
Lesh/Leshi see Lezhë
110 Dd11 **Les Haudères** Valais, SW Switzerland
104 J9 **les Herbiers** Vendée, NW France
129 O8 **Leshukonskoye** Arkhangel'skaya Oblast', NW Russian Federation
124 P14 **Levantine Basin** undersea feature E Mediterranean Sea
104 D10 **Levanto** Liguria, W Italy
109 H10 **Levanzo, Isola di** island Isole Egadi, S Italy
131 Q17 **Levashi** Respublika Dagestan, SW Russian Federation
26 M5 **Levelland** Texas, SW USA
41 P13 **Levelock** Alaska, USA
103 E16 **Leverkusen** Nordrhein-Westfalen, W Germany
113 J21 **Levice** Ger. Lewenz, Hung. Léva. Západné Slovensko, SW Slovakia
Levico Terme Trentino-Alto Adige, N Italy
35 P14 **Leslie** Idaho, NW USA
33 Q10 **Leslie** Michigan, N USA
Lešna/Lesnaya see Lyasnaya
104 F5 **Lesneven** Finistère, NW France
114 F11 **Lešnica** Serbia, W Yugoslavia
129 S13 **Lesnoy** Kirovskaya Oblast', NW Russian Federation
126 I13 **Lesosibirsk** Krasnoyarskiy Kray, C Russian Federation
85 J23 **Lesotho** off. Kingdom of Lesotho; prev. Basutoland. ◆ monarchy S Africa
127 Nn17 **Lesozavodsk** Primorskiy Kray, SE Russian Federation
2 P6 **Levisa Fork** ⚌ Kentucky/Virginia, S USA
117 L21 **Lévitha** island Kykládes, Greece, Aegean Sea
20 L14 **Levittown** Long Island, New York, NE USA
20 J15 **Levittown** Pennsylvania, NE USA
113 L19 **Levoča** Ger. Leutschau, Hung. Locse. Východné Slovensko, NE Slovakia
47 W11 **les Saintes** var. Îles des Saintes. island group S Guadeloupe
105 L5 **Les Salines** (Annaba) NE Algeria
35 S9 **Lesse** SE Belgium
97 M17 **Lessebo** Kronoberg, S Sweden
104 G4 **les Sept Îles** island group NW France
204 M10 **Lesser Antarctica** var. West Antarctica. physical region Antarctica
47 P15 **Lesser Antilles** island group E West Indies
143 T10 **Lesser Caucasus** Rus. Malyy Kavkaz. ▲ SW Asia
118 M8 **Leva** see Levice
94 L8 **Levanger** Finnmark, N Norway
38 L4 **Levan** Utah, W USA
59 E16 **Levanger** Nord-Trøndelag, C Norway

98 F7 **Lewis, Isle of** island NW Scotland, UK
37 U4 **Lewis, Mount** ▲ Nevada, W USA
193 H16 **Lewis Pass** pass South Island, NZ
35 X7 **Lewis Range** ▲ Montana, NW USA
25 N3 **Lewis Smith Lake** ⊚ Alabama, S USA
34 M10 **Lewiston** Idaho, NW USA
21 P7 **Lewiston** Maine, NE USA
31 X10 **Lewiston** Minnesota, N USA
20 D9 **Lewiston** New York, NE USA
38 L3 **Lewiston** Utah, W USA
32 K13 **Lewistown** Illinois, N USA
35 T14 **Lewistown** Montana, NW USA
20 G9 **Lewistown** Pennsylvania, NE USA
27 T14 **Lewisville** Arkansas, C USA
27 T6 **Lewisville** Texas, SW USA
27 T6 **Lewisville, Lake** ⊚ Texas, SW USA
Le Woleu-Ntem see Woleu-Ntem
25 L3 **Lexington** Georgia, SE USA
22 M5 **Lexington** Kentucky, S USA
24 L4 **Lexington** Mississippi, S USA
29 S13 **Lexington** Missouri, C USA
31 N16 **Lexington** Nebraska, C USA
22 J9 **Lexington** North Carolina, SE USA
29 N11 **Lexington** Oklahoma, C USA
23 G9 **Lexington** South Carolina, SE USA
22 G9 **Lexington** Tennessee, S USA
27 T10 **Lexington** Texas, SW USA
23 T6 **Lexington** Virginia, NE USA
23 X5 **Lexington Park** Maryland, NE USA
104 J14 **Leyre** ⚌ SW France
179 R13 **Leyte** island S Philippines
179 R13 **Leyte Gulf** gulf E Philippines
113 O16 **Leżajsk** Rzeszów, SE Poland
115 K18 **Lezhë** var. Lezha; prev. Lesh, Leshi. Lezhë, NW Albania
115 K18 **Lezhë** ◆ district NW Albania
105 O16 **Lézignan-Corbières** Aude, S France
130 J7 **L'gov** Kurskaya Oblast', W Russian Federation
165 P15 **Lhari** Xizang Zizhiqu, W China
165 N16 **Lhasa** Tib. La-sa, Lassa. Xizang Zizhiqu, W China
165 O15 **Lhasa He** ⚌ W China
164 K16 **Lhazê** Xizang Zizhiqu, W China
164 K14 **Lhazhong** Xizang Zizhiqu, W China
173 F3 **Lhoksukon** Sumatera, W Indonesia
165 Q15 **Lhorong** Xizang Zizhiqu, W China
107 W6 **L'Hospitalet de Llobregat** var. Hospitalet. Cataluña, NE Spain
159 R11 **Lhotse** ▲ China/Nepal
165 N17 **Lhozhag** Xizang Zizhiqu, W China
165 O16 **Lhünzê** Xizang Zizhiqu, W China
165 N15 **Lhünzhub** var. Poindo. Xizang Zizhiqu, W China
178 H8 **Li** Lamphun, NW Thailand
179 Rr14 **Lianga** Mindanao, S Philippines
167 P12 **Liangcheng** Sichuan, C China
166 K9 **Liangping** Sichuan, C China
Liangzhou see Wuwei
167 O9 **Liangzi Hu** ⊚ C China
167 R12 **Lianjiang** Fujian, SE China
166 L15 **Lianjiang** Guangdong, S China
167 O13 **Lianping** Guangdong, S China
Lian Xian see Lianzhou
166 M11 **Lianyuan** prev. Lantian. Hunan, S China
167 Q6 **Lianyungang** var. Xinpu. Jiangsu, E China
166 L15 **Lianzhou** var. Linxian; prev. Lian Xian. Guangdong, S China
167 P5 **Liaocheng** Shandong, E China
169 U13 **Liaodong Bandao** var. Liaotung Peninsula. peninsula NE China
169 T13 **Liaodong Wan** Eng. Gulf of Lantung, Gulf of Liaotung. gulf NE China
169 U11 **Liao He** ⚌ NE China
169 W12 **Liao Ling** ▲ NE China
169 U12 **Liaoning** var. Liao, Liaoning Sheng, Shengking; hist. Fengtien, Shenking. ◆ province NE China
Liaoning Sheng see Liaoning
Liaotung, Gulf of see Liaodong Wan
Liaotung Peninsula see Liaodong Bandao
169 U13 **Liaoyang** var. Liao-yang. Liaoning, NE China
169 V11 **Liaoyuan** var. Dongliao, Shuang-liao, Jap. Chengchiatun. Jilin, NE China
169 U12 **Liaozhong** Liaoning, NE China
Liaqatabad see Piplan
8 M10 **Liard** ⚌ W Canada
Liard see Fort Liard
8 L10 **Liard River** British Columbia, W Canada
155 O15 **Liāri** Baluchistān, SW Pakistan
Liatroim see Leitrim
201 S6 **Lib** var. Ellep. island Ralik Chain, C Marshall Islands
Liban see Lebanon
144 H6 **Liban, Jebel** Ar. Jabal al Gharbī, Jabal Lubnān, Eng. Mount Lebanon. ▲ C Lebanon
Libau see Liepāja
85 N7 **Libby** Montana, NW USA
81 D16 **Libenge** Équateur, NW Zaire
28 K3 **Liberal** Kansas, C USA
29 X4 **Liberal** Missouri, C USA
Liberalitas Julia see Évora
113 D15 **Liberec** Ger. Reichenberg. Severní Čechy, N Czech Republic
44 K12 **Liberia** Guanacaste, NW Costa Rica

◆ COUNTRY ◇ DEPENDENT TERRITORY ● ADMINISTRATIVE REGION ▲ MOUNTAIN ⚐ VOLCANO ⊚ LAKE
● COUNTRY CAPITAL ○ DEPENDENT TERRITORY CAPITAL ✈ INTERNATIONAL AIRPORT ▲ MOUNTAIN RANGE ⚌ RIVER ⊟ RESERVOIR

Liberia – Lob Nor

78 K17 **Liberia** off. Republic of Liberia. ◆ republic W Africa
63 D16 **Libertad** Corrientes, NE Argentina
63 E20 **Libertad** San José, S Uruguay
56 K6 **Libertad** Barinas, NW Venezuela
56 J7 **Libertad** Cojedes, N Venezuela
64 G12 **Libertador** off. Región del Libertador General Bernardo O'Higgins. ◐ region C Chile
Libertador General San Martín see Ciudad de Libertador General San Martín
22 L6 **Liberty** Kentucky, S USA
24 J7 **Liberty** Mississippi, S USA
29 R4 **Liberty** Missouri, C USA
20 J12 **Liberty** New York, NE USA
23 T9 **Liberty** North Carolina, SE USA
Libian Desert see Libyan Desert
101 J23 **Libin** Luxembourg, SE Belgium
166 K13 **Libo** Guizhou, S China
Libohova see Libohovë
115 L23 **Libohovë** var. Libohova. Gjirokastër, S Albania
83 K18 **Liboi** North Eastern, E Kenya
104 K13 **Libourne** Gironde, SW France
101 K23 **Libramont** Luxembourg, SE Belgium
115 M20 **Librazhd** var. Librazhdi. Elbasan, E Albania
Librazhdi see Librazhd
81 C18 **Libreville** ● (Gabon) Estuaire, NW Gabon
179 Rr15 **Libuganon** ∼ Mindanao, S Philippines
77 P10 **Libya** off. Socialist People's Libyan Arab Jamahiriya, Ar. Al Jamāhīrīyah al 'Arabīyah al Lībīyah ash Sha'bīyah al Ishtirākīyah; prev. Libyan Arab Republic. ◆ islamic state N Africa
77 T11 **Libyan Desert** var. Libian Desert, Ar. Aş Şahrā' al Lībīyah. desert N Africa
77 T8 **Libyan Plateau** var. Aḍ Diffah. plateau Egypt/Libya
Lībīyah, Aş Şahrā' al see Libyan Desert
64 G12 **Licantén** Maule, C Chile
109 J25 **Licata** anc. Phintias. Sicilia, Italy, C Mediterranean Sea
143 P14 **Lice** Diyarbakır, SE Turkey
99 L19 **Lichfield** C England, UK
85 N14 **Lichinga** Niassa, N Mozambique
111 V3 **Lichtenau** Niederösterreich, N Austria
85 I21 **Lichtenburg** North-West, N South Africa
103 K18 **Lichtenfels** Bayern, SE Germany
100 O12 **Lichtenvoorde** Gelderland, E Netherlands
Lichtenwald see Sevnica
101 C17 **Lichtervelde** West-Vlaanderen, W Belgium
166 L9 **Lichuan** Hubei, C China
29 V7 **Licking** Missouri, C USA
22 M4 **Licking River** ∼ Kentucky, S USA
114 C11 **Lički Osik** Lika-Senj, C Croatia
Ličko-Senjska Županija see Lika-Senj
109 K19 **Licosa, Punta** headland S Italy
121 H16 **Lida** Rus. Lida. Hrodzyenskaya Voblasts', W Belarus
95 H17 **Liden** Västernorrland, C Sweden
31 R7 **Lidgerwood** North Dakota, N USA
Lidhorikíon see Lidoríki
97 K21 **Lidhult** Kronoberg, S Sweden
97 P16 **Lidingö** Stockholm, C Sweden
97 K17 **Lidköping** Skaraborg, S Sweden
Lido di Iesolo see Lido di Jesolo
108 I8 **Lido di Jesolo** var. Lido di Iesolo. Veneto, NE Italy
109 H15 **Lido di Ostia** Lazio, C Italy
Lidokhorikion see Lidoríki
117 E18 **Lidoríki** prev. Lidhorikíon, Lidokhorikion. Stereá Ellás, C Greece
112 K9 **Lidzbark** Ciechanów, N Poland
112 L7 **Lidzbark Warmiński** Ger. Heilsberg. Olsztyn, N Poland
111 U3 **Liebenau** Oberösterreich, N Austria
189 P7 **Liebig, Mount** ▲ Northern Territory, C Australia
111 V8 **Lieboch** Steiermark, SE Austria
110 I8 **Liechtenstein** off. Principality of Liechtenstein. ◆ principality C Europe
101 F18 **Liedekerke** Vlaams Brabant, C Belgium
101 K19 **Liège** Dut. Luik, Ger. Lüttich. Liège, E Belgium
101 K20 **Liège** Dut. Luik. ◐ province E Belgium
Liegnitz see Legnica
95 O16 **Lieksa** Pohjois-Karjala, E Finland
120 F10 **Lielupe** ∼ Latvia/Lithuania
120 G9 **Lielvārde** Ogre, C Latvia
178 Kk14 **Liên Hương** var. Tuy Phong. Bình Thuân, S Vietnam
Liên Nghia see Đuc Trong
111 P9 **Lienz** Tirol, W Austria
120 B10 **Liepāja** Ger. Libau. Liepāja, W Latvia
101 H17 **Lier** Fr. Lierre. Antwerpen, N Belgium
97 H15 **Lierbyen** Buskerud, S Norway
101 L21 **Lierneux** Liège, E Belgium
Lierre see Lier
103 D18 **Lieser** ∼ W Germany
111 U7 **Liesing** ∼ E Austria
110 E6 **Liestal** Basel-Land, N Switzerland
Lietuva see Lithuania
Lievenhof see Līvāni
105 O2 **Liévin** Pas-de-Calais, N France
12 M9 **Lièvre, Rivière du** ∼ Québec, SE Canada
111 T6 **Liezen** Steiermark, C Austria
99 E14 **Lifford** Ir. Leifear. NW Ireland
197 K5 **Lifou** island Îles Loyauté, E New Caledonia
200 Ss13 **Lifuka** island Ha'apai Group, C Tonga
179 Q11 **Ligao** Luzon, N Philippines
Liger see Loire
44 H2 **Lighthouse Reef** reef E Belize
191 Q4 **Lightning Ridge** New South Wales, SE Australia
105 N9 **Lignières** Cher, C France
105 S5 **Ligny-en-Barrois** Meuse, NE France
85 P15 **Ligonha** ∼ NE Mozambique
33 P11 **Ligonier** Indiana, N USA
83 I25 **Ligunga** Ruvuma, S Tanzania
108 D9 **Ligure, Appennino** Eng. Ligurian Mountains. ▲ NW Italy
Ligure, Mar see Ligurian Sea
108 C9 **Liguria** ◐ region NW Italy
Ligurian Mountains see Ligure, Appennino
123 K6 **Ligurian Sea** Fr. Mer Ligurienne, It. Mar Ligure. sea N Mediterranean Sea
Ligurienne, Mer see Ligurian Sea
195 P9 **Lihir Group** island group NE PNG
195 P9 **Lihir Island** island Lihir Group, N PNG
40 B8 **Lihue** Haw. Lihu'e. Kauai, Hawaii, USA, C Pacific Ocean
120 F5 **Lihula** Ger. Leal. Läänemaa, W Estonia
128 I2 **Liinakhamari** var. Linacmamari. Murmanskaya Oblast', NW Russian Federation
Liivi Laht see Riga, Gulf of
166 F11 **Lijiang** var. Dayan, Lijiang Naxizu Zizhixian. Yunnan, SW China
114 C11 **Lika-Senj** off. Ličko-Senjska Županija. ◐ province W Croatia
81 N25 **Likasi** prev. Jadotville. Shaba, SE Zaire
81 L16 **Likati** Haut-Zaïre, N Zaire
8 M15 **Likely** British Columbia, SW Canada
159 Y11 **Likhapāni** Assam, NE India
128 J16 **Likhoslavl'** Tverskaya Oblast', W Russian Federation
201 U5 **Likiep Atoll** atoll Ratak Chain, C Marshall Islands
97 D18 **Liknes** Vest-Agder, S Norway
81 H18 **Likouala** ∼ N Congo
81 H18 **Likouala aux Herbes** ∼ E Congo
202 B16 **Liku** E Niue
Likupang, Selat see Bangka, Selat
29 Y8 **Lilbourn** Missouri, C USA
104 E1 **l'Île-Rousse** Corse, France, C Mediterranean Sea
111 W5 **Lilienfeld** Niederösterreich, NE Austria
167 N11 **Liling** Hunan, S China
97 J18 **Lilla Edet** Älvsborg, S Sweden
105 P1 **Lille** var. l'Isle, Dut. Rijssel, Flem. Ryssel; prev. Lisle, anc. Insula. Nord, N France
97 G24 **Lillebælt** var. Lille Bælt, Eng. Little Belt. strait S Denmark
104 L3 **Lillebonne** Seine-Maritime, N France
96 H12 **Lillehammer** Oppland, S Norway
105 O1 **Lillers** Pas-de-Calais, N France
97 F18 **Lillesand** Aust-Agder, S Norway
97 I15 **Lillestrøm** Akershus, S Norway
95 F18 **Lillhärdal** Jämtland, C Sweden
23 U10 **Lillington** North Carolina, SE USA
107 O9 **Lillo** Castilla-La Mancha, C Spain
8 M16 **Lillooet** British Columbia, SW Canada
85 M14 **Lilongwe** ● (Malawi) Central, W Malawi
85 M14 **Lilongwe** ✈ Central, W Malawi
85 M14 **Lilongwe** ∼ W Malawi
179 Q15 **Liloy** Mindanao, S Philippines
Lilybaeum see Marsala
190 J7 **Lilydale** South Australia
191 P16 **Lilydale** Tasmania, SE Australia
115 J14 **Lim** ∼ Bosnia and Herzegovina/Yugoslavia
59 D15 **Lima** ● (Peru) Lima, W Peru
96 K13 **Lima** Kopparberg, C Sweden
33 R12 **Lima** Ohio, NE USA
59 D14 **Lima** ◐ department W Peru
Lima see Jorge Chávez International
106 G5 **Lima** ∼ N Portugal
Lima see Limia
113 L17 **Limanowa** Nowy Sącz, S Poland
174 I8 **Limas** Pulau Sebangka, W Indonesia
Limassol see Lemesós
99 F14 **Limavady** Ir. Léim an Mhadaidh. NW Northern Ireland, UK
65 J14 **Limay Mahuida** La Pampa, C Argentina
65 H15 **Limay, Río** ∼ W Argentina
103 N16 **Limbach-Oberfrohna** Sachsen, E Germany
83 F22 **Limba Limba** ∼ C Tanzania
109 C17 **Limbara, Monte** ▲ Sardegna, Italy, C Mediterranean Sea
120 G7 **Limbaži** Est. Lemsalu. Limbaži, N Latvia
46 M8 **Limbé** N Haiti
175 Qq7 **Limboto, Danau** ◎ Sulawesi, N Indonesia
101 L19 **Limbourg** Liège, E Belgium
101 K17 **Limburg** ◐ province NE Belgium
101 L16 **Limburg** ◐ province SE Netherlands
103 F17 **Limburg an der Lahn** Hessen, W Germany
96 K13 **Limedsforsen** Kopparberg, C Sweden
62 L9 **Limeira** São Paulo, S Brazil
99 C19 **Limerick** Ir. Luimneach. SW Ireland
99 C20 **Limerick** Ir. Luimneach. cultural region SW Ireland
21 S2 **Limestone** Maine, NE USA
27 U9 **Limestone, Lake** ◎ Texas, SW USA
41 P12 **Lime Village** Alaska, USA
97 F20 **Limfjorden** fjord N Denmark
97 J23 **Limhamn** Malmöhus, S Sweden
106 H5 **Limia** Port. Lima. ∼ NW Spain
95 L14 **Liminka** Oulu, C Finland
Limín Vathéos see Sámos
117 G17 **Límni** Évvoia, C Greece
117 J15 **Límnos** anc. Lemnos. island E Greece
104 M11 **Limoges** anc. Augustoritum Lemovicensium, Lemovices. Haute-Vienne, C France
39 U5 **Limon** Colorado, C USA
45 O13 **Limón** var. Puerto Limón. Limón, E Costa Rica
44 K4 **Limón** Colón, NE Honduras
45 N13 **Limón** off. Provincia de Limón. ◐ province E Costa Rica
108 A10 **Limone Piemonte** Piemonte, NE Italy
Limones see Valdéz
Limonum see Poitiers
105 N11 **Limousin** ◐ region C France
105 N16 **Limoux** Aude, S France
85 L19 **Limpopo** var. Crocodile. ∼ S Africa
166 K17 **Limu Ling** ▲ S China
115 M20 **Lin** var. Lini. Elbasan, E Albania
Linacmamari see Liinakhamari
179 P13 **Linapacan Island** island W Philippines
64 G13 **Linares** Maule, C Chile
56 C13 **Linares** Nariño, SW Colombia
43 O9 **Linares** Nuevo León, NE Mexico
107 N12 **Linares** Andalucía, S Spain
109 G15 **Linaro, Capo** headland C Italy
108 D8 **Linate** ✈ (Milano) Lombardia, N Italy
166 F13 **Lincang** Yunnan, SW China
167 P11 **Linchuan** var. Fuzhou. Jiangxi, S China
63 B20 **Lincoln** Buenos Aires, E Argentina
193 H19 **Lincoln** Canterbury, South Island, NZ
99 N18 **Lincoln** anc. Lindum, Lindum Colonia. E England, UK
37 O6 **Lincoln** California, W USA
32 L13 **Lincoln** Illinois, N USA
28 M4 **Lincoln** Kansas, C USA
21 S5 **Lincoln** Maine, NE USA
29 T5 **Lincoln** Missouri, C USA
31 R16 **Lincoln** state capital Nebraska, C USA
34 F11 **Lincoln City** Oregon, NW USA
178 M10 **Lincoln Island** island E Paracel Islands
207 Q11 **Lincoln Sea** sea Arctic Ocean
99 N18 **Lincolnshire** cultural region E England, UK
23 R10 **Lincolnton** North Carolina, SE USA
27 V7 **Lindale** Texas, SW USA
103 I25 **Lindau** var. Lindau am Bodensee. Bayern, S Germany
Lindau am Bodensee see Lindau
126 L9 **Linde** ∼ NE Russian Federation
57 T9 **Linden** E Guyana
25 O6 **Linden** Alabama, S USA
22 H9 **Linden** Tennessee, S USA
27 X6 **Linden** Texas, SW USA
20 J16 **Lindenwold** New Jersey, NE USA
97 M15 **Lindesberg** Örebro, C Sweden
97 D18 **Lindesnes** headland S Norway
Líndhos see Líndos
83 K24 **Lindi** Lindi, SE Tanzania
83 J24 **Lindi** ◐ region SE Tanzania
81 N17 **Lindi** ∼ NE Zaire
169 V7 **Lindian** Heilongjiang, NE China
193 E21 **Lindis Pass** pass South Island, NZ
85 J22 **Lindley** Free State, C South Africa
97 J19 **Lindome** Göteborg och Bohus, S Sweden
Lindong see Bairin Zuoqi
117 O23 **Líndos** var. Líndhos. Ródos, Dodekánisos, Greece, Aegean Sea
12 I14 **Lindsay** Ontario, SE Canada
37 R11 **Lindsay** California, W USA
35 X8 **Lindsay** Montana, NW USA
29 N11 **Lindsay** Oklahoma, C USA
25 N5 **Lindsborg** Kansas, C USA
97 N21 **Lindsdal** Kalmar, S Sweden
175 Pp9 **Lindu, Danau** ◎ Sulawesi, N Indonesia
Lindum/Lindum Colonia see Lincoln
203 W3 **Line Islands** island group E Kiribati
Linëvo see Linova
166 M5 **Linfen** var. Lin-fen. Shanxi, C China
161 F18 **Linganamakki Reservoir** ⊟ SW India
166 L17 **Lingao** Hainan, S China
179 Oo9 **Lingayen** Luzon, N Philippines
179 Oo9 **Lingayen Gulf** gulf Luzon, N Philippines
166 M6 **Lingbao** var. Guolüezhen. Henan, C China
96 N12 **Lingbo** Gävleborg, C Sweden
Lingeh see Bandar-e Langeh
102 E12 **Lingen** var. Lingen an der Ems. Niedersachsen, NW Germany
Lingen an der Ems see Lingen
174 I8 **Lingga, Kepulauan** island group W Indonesia
174 I8 **Lingga, Pulau** island Kepulauan Lingga, W Indonesia
12 J14 **Lingham Lake** ◎ Ontario, SE Canada
96 M13 **Linghed** Kopparberg, C Sweden
35 Z15 **Lingle** Wyoming, C USA
20 G15 **Linglestown** Pennsylvania, NE USA
81 K18 **Lingomo II** Equateur, NW Zaire
166 L15 **Lingshan** Guangxi Zhuangzu Zizhiqu, S China
166 L17 **Lingshui** Hainan, S China
161 G16 **Lingsugūr** Karnātaka, C India
109 L23 **Linguaglossa** Sicilia, Italy, C Mediterranean Sea
78 H10 **Linguère** N Senegal
165 W8 **Lingwu** Ningxia, N China
Lingxi see Yongshun
167 O12 **Lingxian** var. Ling Xian. Hunan, S China
169 S12 **Lingyuan** Liaoning, NE China
169 U4 **Linhai** Heilongjiang, NE China
167 S10 **Linhai** var. Taizhou. Zhejiang, SE China
61 O20 **Linhares** Espírito Santo, SE Brazil
168 M13 **Linhe** Nei Mongol Zizhiqu, N China
Lini see Lin
145 S1 **Līnik, Chiyā-ē** ▲ N Iraq
97 M18 **Linköping** Östergötland, S Sweden
169 Y8 **Linkou** Heilongjiang, NE China
120 F11 **Linkuva** Pakruojis, N Lithuania
29 V5 **Linn** Missouri, C USA
27 S16 **Linn** Texas, SW USA
27 T2 **Linneus** Missouri, C USA
98 H10 **Linnhe, Loch** inlet W Scotland, UK
121 G19 **Linova** Rus. Linëvo. Brestskaya Voblasts', SW Belarus
167 O5 **Linqing** Shandong, E China
167 N6 **Linruzhen** Henan, C China
62 K8 **Lins** São Paulo, S Brazil
95 F17 **Linsell** Jämtland, C Sweden
166 J9 **Linshui** Sichuan, C China
46 K12 **Linstead** C Jamaica
165 U11 **Lintan** Gansu, N China
165 V11 **Lintao** Gansu, C China
13 Q12 **Lintère** ∼ Québec, SE Canada
110 H8 **Linth** ∼ NW Switzerland
110 H8 **Linthal** Glarus, NE Switzerland
33 N15 **Linton** Indiana, N USA
31 N6 **Linton** North Dakota, N USA
169 R11 **Linxi** Nei Mongol Zizhiqu, N China
165 U11 **Linxia** var. Linxia Huizu Zizhizhou. Gansu, C China
Linxia Huizu Zizhizhou see Linxia
Linxian see Lianzhou
167 Q6 **Linyi** Shandong, S China
167 P4 **Linyi** Shandong, E China
166 M6 **Linyi** Shanxi, C China
111 T4 **Linz** anc. Lentia. Oberösterreich, N Austria
165 S8 **Linze** var. Shahepu. Gansu, N China
46 J13 **Lionel Town** C Jamaica
105 Q16 **Lion, Golfe du** Eng. Gulf of Lion, Gulf of Lions; anc. Sinus Gallicus. gulf S France
Lion, Gulf of/Lions, Gulf of see Lion, Golfe du
85 K16 **Lions Den** Mashonaland West, N Zimbabwe
12 F13 **Lion's Head** Ontario, S Canada
Lios Ceannúir, Bá see Liscannor Bay
Lios Mór see Lismore
Lios na gCearrbhach see Lisburn
Lios Tuathail see Listowel
81 G17 **Liouesso** La Sangha, N Congo
Liozno see Lyozna
179 P11 **Lipa** off. Lipa City. Luzon, N Philippines
27 S7 **Lipan** Texas, SW USA
Lipari Islands/Lipari, Isole see Eolie, Isole
109 L22 **Lipari, Isola** island Isole Eolie, S Italy
118 L8 **Lipcani** Rus. Lipkany. N Moldova
95 N17 **Liperi** Pohjois-Karjala, SE Finland
130 L7 **Lipetsk** Lipetskaya Oblast', W Russian Federation
130 K6 **Lipetskaya Oblast'** ◐ province W Russian Federation
59 K22 **Lipez, Cordillera de** ▲ SW Bolivia
112 E10 **Lipiany** Ger. Lippehne. Szczecin, W Poland
114 G9 **Lipik** Požega-Slavonija, NE Croatia
128 L12 **Lipin Bor** Vologodskaya Oblast', NW Russian Federation
166 L12 **Liping** Guizhou, S China
Lipkany see Lipcani
121 H15 **Lipnishki** Rus. Lipnishki. Hrodzyenskaya Voblasts', W Belarus
112 J10 **Lipno** Włocławek, C Poland
118 F11 **Lipova** Hung. Lippa. Arad, W Romania
Lipovets see Lypovets'
Lippa see Lipova
103 E14 **Lippe** ∼ W Germany
Lippehne see Lipiany
103 G14 **Lippstadt** Nordrhein-Westfalen, W Germany
27 P1 **Lipscomb** Texas, SW USA
Lipsia/Lipsk see Leipzig
112 P7 **Lipsk** Suwałki, NE Poland
Liptau-Sankt-Nikolaus/Liptószentmiklós see Liptovský Mikuláš
113 K19 **Liptovský Mikuláš** Ger. Liptau-Sankt-Nikolaus, Hung. Liptószentmiklós. Stredné Slovensko, N Slovakia
191 O13 **Liptrap, Cape** headland Victoria, SE Australia
166 L13 **Lipu** Guangxi Zhuangzu Zizhiqu, S China
147 X12 **Liqbi** S Oman
83 G17 **Lira** N Uganda
59 F15 **Lircay** Huancavelica, C Peru
109 J15 **Liri** ∼ C Italy
150 M8 **Lisakovsk** Kustanay, NW Kazakhstan
81 K17 **Lisala** Equateur, N Zaire
106 F11 **Lisboa** Eng. Lisbon; anc. Felicitas Julia, Olisipo. ● (Portugal) Lisboa, W Portugal
106 F10 **Lisboa** ◐ Eng. Lisbon. district C Portugal
21 N7 **Lisbon** New Hampshire, NE USA
31 Q6 **Lisbon** North Dakota, N USA
Lisbon see Lisboa
21 Q8 **Lisbon Falls** Maine, NE USA
99 G15 **Lisburn** Ir. Lios na gCearrbhach. E Northern Ireland, UK
40 L6 **Lisburne, Cape** headland Alaska, USA
99 B19 **Liscannor Bay** Ir. Bá Lios Ceannúir. inlet W Ireland
115 Q18 **Lisec** ▲ E FYR Macedonia
166 F13 **Lishe Jiang** ∼ SW China
166 M4 **Lishi** Shanxi, C China
169 V10 **Lishu** Jilin, NE China
167 R10 **Lishui** Zhejiang, SE China
199 Jj5 **Lisianski Island** island Hawaiian Islands, Hawaii, USA, C Pacific Ocean
Lisichansk see Lysychans'k
104 L4 **Lisieux** anc. Noviomagus. Calvados, N France
130 L8 **Liski** prev. Georgiu-Dezh. Voronezhskaya Oblast', W Russian Federation
Lisle/l'Isle see Lille
105 N4 **l'Isle-Adam** Val-d'Oise, N France
105 R15 **l'Isle-sur-la-Sorgue** Vaucluse, SE France
13 S9 **L'Islet** Québec, SE Canada
190 M12 **Lismore** Victoria, SE Australia
99 D20 **Lismore** Ir. Lios Mór. S Ireland
Lissa see Vis, Croatia
Lissa see Leszno, Poland
100 H11 **Lisse** Zuid-Holland, W Netherlands
97 D18 **Lista** peninsula S Norway
97 D18 **Listafjorden** fjord S Norway
205 R13 **Lister, Mount** ▲ Antarctica
130 M8 **Listopadovka** Voronezhskaya Oblast', W Russian Federation
12 F15 **Listowel** Ontario, S Canada
99 B20 **Listowel** Ir. Lios Tuathail. SW Ireland
166 L14 **Litang** Guangxi Zhuangzu Zizhiqu, S China
166 F9 **Litang** Sichuan, C China
166 F10 **Litang Qu** ∼ C China
57 X12 **Litani** var. Itany. ∼ French Guiana/Suriname
144 G8 **Lītani, Nahr el** var. Nahr al Litant. ∼ C Lebanon
Litant, Nahr al see Lītani, Nahr el
Litauen see Lithuania
32 K14 **Litchfield** Illinois, N USA
31 U8 **Litchfield** Minnesota, N USA
38 K13 **Litchfield Park** Arizona, SW USA
191 S8 **Lithgow** New South Wales, SE Australia
117 I26 **Líthino, Ákra** headland Kríti, Greece, E Mediterranean Sea
120 D12 **Lithuania** off. Republic of Lithuania, Ger. Litauen, Lith. Lietuva, Pol. Litwa, Rus. Litva; prev. Lithuanian SSR, Rus. Litovskaya SSR. ◆ republic NE Europe
Lithuanian SSR see Lithuania
111 U11 **Litija** Ger. Littai. C Slovenia
20 H15 **Lititz** Pennsylvania, NE USA
117 F15 **Litóchoro** var. Litohoro, Litókhoron. Kentrikí Makedonía, N Greece
Litohoro/Litókhoron see Litóchoro
113 C15 **Litoměřice** Ger. Leitmeritz. Severní Čechy, N Czech Republic
113 F17 **Litomyšl** Ger. Leitomischl. Východní Čechy, NE Czech Republic
113 G17 **Litovel** Ger. Littau. Severní Morava, E Czech Republic
127 Nn15 **Litovko** Khabarovskiy Kray, SE Russian Federation
Litovskaya SSR see Lithuania
Littai see Litija
Littau see Litovel
46 G1 **Little Abaco** var. Abaco Island. island N Bahamas
113 I21 **Little Alföld** Ger. Kleines Ungarisches Tiefland, Hung. Kisalföld, Slvk. Podunajská Rovina. plain Hungary/Slovakia
157 Q20 **Little Andaman** island Andaman Islands, India, NE Indian Ocean
28 M5 **Little Arkansas River** ∼ Kansas, C USA
192 L4 **Little Barrier Island** island N NZ
Little Belt see Lillebælt
40 M11 **Little Black River** ∼ Alaska, USA
29 O2 **Little Blue River** ∼ Kansas/Nebraska, C USA
46 D8 **Little Cayman** island E Cayman Islands
9 X11 **Little Churchill** ∼ Manitoba, C Canada
177 Ee10 **Little Coco Island** island SW Myanmar
38 L10 **Little Colorado River** ∼ Arizona, SW USA
12 E11 **Little Current** Manitoulin Island, Ontario, S Canada
10 E11 **Little Current** ∼ Ontario, S Canada
40 L8 **Little Diomede Island** island Alaska, USA
46 I5 **Little Exuma** island C Bahamas
31 U7 **Little Falls** Minnesota, N USA
20 J10 **Little Falls** New York, NE USA
26 M5 **Littlefield** Texas, SW USA
31 V3 **Littlefork** Minnesota, N USA
31 V3 **Little Fork River** ∼ Minnesota, N USA
9 N16 **Little Fort** British Columbia, SW Canada
9 Y14 **Little Grand Rapids** Manitoba, C Canada
99 N23 **Littlehampton** SE England, UK
37 T2 **Little Humboldt River** ∼ Nevada, W USA
46 K6 **Little Inagua** var. Inagua Islands. island S Bahamas
23 Q4 **Little Kanawha River** ∼ West Virginia, NE USA
85 F25 **Little Karoo** plateau S South Africa
41 O16 **Little Koniuji Island** island Shumagin Islands, Alaska, USA
46 H12 **Little London** W Jamaica
11 R10 **Little Mecatina** Fr. Rivière du Petit Mécatina. ∼ Newfoundland and Labrador/Québec, E Canada
98 F8 **Little Minch, The** strait NW Scotland, UK
29 T13 **Little Missouri River** ∼ Arkansas, USA
30 J7 **Little Missouri River** ∼ NW USA
30 J3 **Little Muddy River** ∼ North Dakota, N USA
157 Q22 **Little Nicobar** island Nicobar Islands, India, NE Indian Ocean
29 R6 **Little Osage River** ∼ Missouri, C USA
99 P20 **Little Ouse** ∼ E England, UK
155 V2 **Little Pamir** Pash. Pāmīr-e Khord, Rus. Malyy Pamir. ▲ Afghanistan/Tajikistan
23 U12 **Little Pee Dee River** ∼ North Carolina/South Carolina, SE USA
29 V10 **Little Red River** ∼ Arkansas, C USA
Little Rhody see Rhode Island
193 I19 **Little River** Canterbury, South Island, NZ
23 U12 **Little River** South Carolina, SE USA
29 Y9 **Little River** ∼ Arkansas/Missouri, C USA
29 R13 **Little River** ∼ Arkansas/Oklahoma, USA
25 T7 **Little River** ∼ Georgia, SE USA
24 H6 **Little River** ∼ Louisiana, S USA
27 T10 **Little River** ∼ Texas, SW USA
29 V12 **Little Rock** state capital Arkansas, C USA
33 N8 **Little Sable Point** headland Michigan, N USA
105 U11 **Little Saint Bernard Pass** Fr. Col du Petit St-Bernard, It. Colle di Piccolo San Bernardo. pass France/Italy
38 K7 **Little Salt Lake** ◎ Utah, W USA
188 K8 **Little Sandy Desert** desert Western Australia
31 S13 **Little Sioux River** ∼ Iowa, C USA
40 E17 **Little Sitkin Island** island Aleutian Islands, Alaska, USA
9 O13 **Little Smoky** Alberta, W Canada
9 O14 **Little Smoky** ∼ Alberta, W Canada
39 P3 **Little Snake River** ∼ Colorado, C USA
66 A12 **Little Sound** bay Bermuda, NW Atlantic Ocean
39 T4 **Littleton** Colorado, C USA
21 N7 **Littleton** New Hampshire, NE USA
20 D11 **Little Valley** New York, NE USA
32 M15 **Little Wabash River** ∼ Illinois, N USA
12 D10 **Little White River** ∼ Ontario, S Canada
30 M12 **Little White River** ∼ South Dakota, N USA
27 R5 **Little Wichita River** ∼ Texas, SW USA
148 I4 **Little Zab** Ar. Nahraz Zāb aş Şaghīr, Kurd. Zê-i Kōya, Per. Rūdkhāneh-ye Zāb-e Kūchek. ∼ Iran/Iraq
81 D15 **Littoral** ◐ province W Cameroon
Littoria see Latina
Litva/Litwa see Lithuania
113 B15 **Litvínov** Ger. Leutensdorf. Severní Čechy, NW Czech Republic
118 M6 **Lityn** Vinnyts'ka Oblast', C Ukraine
Liu-chou/Liuchow see Liuzhou
169 W11 **Liuhe** Jilin, NE China
Liukang Tenggaya, Kepulauan see Sabalana, Kepulauan
85 Q15 **Liúpo** Nampula, NE Mozambique
85 G14 **Liuwa Plain** plain W Zambia
166 L13 **Liuzhou** var. Liu-chou, Liuchow. Guangxi Zhuangzu Zizhiqu, S China
118 H8 **Livada** Hung. Sárköz. Satu Mare, NW Romania
117 J20 **Liváda, Ákra** headland Tínos, Kykládes, Greece, Aegean Sea
117 L21 **Livádi** island Kykládes, Greece, Aegean Sea
Livanátai see Livanátes
117 G18 **Livanátes** prev. Livanátai. Stereá Ellás, C Greece
120 I10 **Līvāni** Ger. Lievenhof. Preiļi, SE Latvia
67 E25 **Lively Island** island SE Falkland Islands
67 D25 **Lively Sound** sound SE Falkland Islands
41 R8 **Livengood** Alaska, USA
108 I7 **Livenza** ∼ NE Italy
37 O6 **Live Oak** California, W USA
25 U9 **Live Oak** Florida, SE USA
37 O9 **Livermore** California, W USA
22 I6 **Livermore** Kentucky, S USA
21 Q7 **Livermore Falls** Maine, NE USA
26 J10 **Livermore, Mount** ▲ Texas, SW USA
11 P16 **Liverpool** Nova Scotia, SE Canada
99 K17 **Liverpool** NW England, UK
191 S7 **Liverpool Range** ▲ New South Wales, SE Australia
98 J12 **Livingston** C Scotland, UK
25 N5 **Livingston** Alabama, S USA
37 P9 **Livingston** California, W USA
24 J8 **Livingston** Louisiana, S USA
35 S11 **Livingston** Montana, NW USA
22 L8 **Livingston** Tennessee, S USA
27 W9 **Livingston** Texas, SW USA
44 F4 **Lívingston** Izabal, E Guatemala
85 I16 **Livingstone** var. Maramba. Southern, S Zambia
193 B22 **Livingstone Mountains** ▲ South Island, NZ
82 K13 **Livingstone Mountains** ▲ S Tanzania
84 N12 **Livingstonia** Northern, N Malawi
204 G4 **Livingston Island** island Antarctica
27 W9 **Livingston, Lake** ⊟ Texas, SW USA
114 F13 **Livno** SW Bosnia and Herzegovina
130 K7 **Livny** Orlovskaya Oblast', W Russian Federation
95 M14 **Livojoki** ∼ C Finland
33 R10 **Livonia** Michigan, N USA
108 E11 **Livorno** Eng. Leghorn. Toscana, C Italy
Livramento see Santana do Livramento
147 U8 **Liwā** var. Al Liwā'. oasis region S UAE
83 J24 **Liwale** Lindi, SE Tanzania
165 W9 **Liwangbu** Ningxia, N China
85 N15 **Liwonde** Southern, S Malawi
165 V11 **Li Xian** Gansu, C China
166 H8 **Lixian** var. Li Xian; prev. Zagunao. Sichuan, C China
Lixian Jiang see Black River
117 B18 **Lixoúri** prev. Lixoúrion. Kefallinía, Iónioi Nísoi, Greece, C Mediterranean Sea
Lixoúrion see Lixoúri
Lixus see Larache
35 U15 **Lizard Head Peak** ▲ Wyoming, C USA
99 H25 **Lizard Point** headland SW England, UK
114 L12 **Ljig** Serbia, C Yugoslavia
Ljouwert see Leeuwarden
Ljubelj see Loibl Pass
111 U11 **Ljubljana** Ger. Laibach, It. Lubiana; anc. Aemona, Emona. ● (Slovenia) C Slovenia
111 T11 **Ljubljana** ✈ C Slovenia
115 N17 **Ljuboten** ▲ S Yugoslavia
97 P19 **Ljugarn** Gotland, SE Sweden
86 G7 **Ljungan** ∼ N Sweden
95 F17 **Ljungan** ∼ C Sweden
97 K21 **Ljungby** Kronoberg, S Sweden
97 M17 **Ljungsbro** Östergötland, S Sweden
97 I18 **Ljungskile** Göteborg och Bohus, S Sweden
96 M11 **Ljusdal** Gävleborg, C Sweden
96 M11 **Ljusnan** ∼ C Sweden
96 N12 **Ljusne** Gävleborg, C Sweden
97 P15 **Ljusterö** Stockholm, C Sweden
111 X9 **Ljutomer** Ger. Luttenberg. NE Slovenia
65 G15 **Llaima, Volcán** ▲ S Chile
107 X4 **Llançà** var. Llansá. Cataluña, NE Spain
99 J21 **Llandovery** C Wales, UK
99 J20 **Llandrindod Wells** E Wales, UK
99 J18 **Llandudno** N Wales, UK
99 I21 **Llanelli** prev. Llanelly. SW Wales, UK
Llanelly see Llanelli
106 M2 **Llanes** Asturias, N Spain
99 K19 **Llangollen** NE Wales, UK
27 R10 **Llano** Texas, SW USA
27 Q10 **Llano River** ∼ Texas, SW USA
56 I9 **Llanos** physical region Colombia/Venezuela
65 G16 **Llanquihue, Lago** ◎ S Chile
Llansá see Llançà
107 U5 **Lleida** Cast. Lérida; anc. Ilerda. Cataluña, NE Spain
Llera de Canales see Llera
106 K12 **Llerena** Extremadura, W Spain
107 S9 **Llíria** País Valenciano, E Spain
107 W4 **Llivia** Cataluña, NE Spain
107 O3 **Llodio** País Vasco, N Spain
107 X5 **Lloret de Mar** Cataluña, NE Spain
Llorri see Tossal de l'Orri
8 L11 **Lloyd George, Mount** ▲ British Columbia, W Canada
9 R14 **Lloydminster** Alberta/Saskatchewan, SW Canada
Lluchmayor see Llucmajor
38 L6 **Loa** Utah, W USA
174 Mm4 **Loagan Bunut** ◎ East Malaysia
178 Mm14 **Loaita Island** island W Spratly Islands
40 G12 **Loa, Mauna** ▲ Hawaii, USA, C Pacific Ocean
Loanda see Luanda
81 J22 **Loange** ∼ S Zaire
81 E21 **Loango** Le Kouilou, S Congo
108 B10 **Loano** Liguria, NW Italy
64 H4 **Loa, Río** ∼ N Chile
85 I20 **Lobatse** var. Lobatsi. Kgatleng, SE Botswana
Lobatsi see Lobatse
103 Q15 **Löbau** Sachsen, E Germany
81 H16 **Lobaye** ◐ prefecture SW Central African Republic
81 I16 **Lobaye** ∼ SW Central African Republic
101 G21 **Lobbes** Hainaut, S Belgium
63 D23 **Lobería** Buenos Aires, E Argentina
112 F8 **Łobez** Ger. Labes. Szczecin, NW Poland
84 A13 **Lobito** Benguela, W Angola
Lobkovichi see Labkovichy
Lob Nor see Lop Nur

◆ Country ● Country Capital ◇ Dependent Territory ○ Dependent Territory Capital ◐ Administrative Region ✈ International Airport ▲ Mountain ▲ Mountain Range ▲ Volcano ∼ River ◎ Lake ⊟ Reservoir

LOBO – LUBEMBE

176 *W11* **Lobo** Irian Jaya, E Indonesia
106 *J11* **Lobón** Extremadura, W Spain
63 *D20* **Lobos** Buenos Aires, E Argentina
42 *E4* **Lobos, Cabo** *headland* NW Mexico
42 *F6* **Lobos, Isla** *island* NW Mexico
Lobositz *see* Lovosice
Lobsens *see* Łobżenica
Loburi *see* Lop Buri
112 *H9* **Łobżenica** *Ger.* Lobsens. Koszalin, W Poland
110 *G11* **Locarno** *Ger.* Luggarus. Ticino, S Switzerland
98 *E9* **Lochboisdale** NW Scotland, UK
100 *N11* **Lochem** Gelderland, E Netherlands
104 *M8* **Loches** Indre-et-Loire, C France
Loch Garman *see* Wexford
98 *H12* **Lochgilphead** W Scotland, UK
98 *H7* **Lochinver** N Scotland, UK
98 *F8* **Lochmaddy** NW Scotland, UK
98 *J10* **Lochnagar** ▲ C Scotland, UK
101 *E17* **Lochristi** Oost-Vlaanderen, NW Belgium
98 *H9* **Lochy, Loch** ◎ N Scotland, UK
190 *G8* **Lock** South Australia
99 *J14* **Lockerbie** S Scotland, UK
29 *S13* **Lockesburg** Arkansas, C USA
191 *P10* **Lockhart** New South Wales, SE Australia
27 *S11* **Lockhart** Texas, SW USA
20 *F13* **Lock Haven** Pennsylvania, NE USA
27 *N4* **Lockney** Texas, SW USA
102 *O12* **Löcknitz** ≈ NE Germany
20 *E9* **Lockport** New York, NE USA
178 *Jj13* **Lôc Ninh** Sông Be, S Vietnam
109 *N23* **Locri** Calabria, SW Italy
Locse *see* Levoča
29 *T2* **Locust Creek** ≈ Missouri, C USA
25 *P3* **Locust Fork** ≈ Alabama, S USA
29 *Q9* **Locust Grove** Oklahoma, C USA
96 *E11* **Lodalskåpa** ▲ S Norway
191 *N10* **Loddon River** ≈ Victoria, SE Australia
Lodensee *see* Klooga
105 *P15* **Lodève** *anc.* Luteva. Hérault, S France
128 *I12* **Lodeynoye Pole** Leningradskaya Oblast', NW Russian Federation
35 *V11* **Lodge Grass** Montana, NW USA
30 *J15* **Lodgepole Creek** ≈ Nebraska/Wyoming, C USA
155 *T11* **Lodhrān** Punjab, E Pakistan
108 *D8* **Lodi** Lombardia, NW Italy
37 *O8* **Lodi** California, W USA
33 *T12* **Lodi** Ohio, N USA
94 *H10* **Lødingen** Nordland, C Norway
81 *L20* **Lodja** Kasai Oriental, C Zaire
39 *O3* **Lodore, Canyon of** *canyon* Colorado, C USA
107 *Q4* **Lodosa** Navarra, N Spain
83 *H16* **Lodwar** Rift Valley, NW Kenya
112 *K13* **Łódź** *Rus.* Lodz. Łódź, C Poland
112 *K13* **Łódź** *off.* Województwo Łódzkie, *Rus.* Lodz. ◆ *province* C Poland
Łódzkie, Województwo *see* Łódź
178 *I8* **Loei** *var.* Loey, Muang Loei. Loei, C Thailand
100 *I11* **Loenen** Utrecht, C Netherlands
178 *J9* **Loeng Nok Tha** Yasothon, E Thailand
85 *F24* **Loeriesfontein** Northern Cape, W South Africa
97 *H20* **Læsø** *island* N Denmark
Loewoek *see* Luwuk
Loey *see* Loei
78 *J16* **Lofa** ≈ N Liberia
111 *P6* **Lofer** Salzburg, C Austria
94 *F11* **Lofoten** *var.* Lofoten Islands. *island group* C Norway
Lofoten Islands *see* Lofoten
97 *N18* **Loftahammar** Kalmar, S Sweden
131 *O10* **Log** Volgogradskaya Oblast', SW Russian Federation
79 *S12* **Loga** Dosso, SW Niger
31 *S14* **Logan** Iowa, C USA
28 *K3* **Logan** Kansas, C USA
33 *T14* **Logan** Ohio, N USA
38 *L1* **Logan** Utah, W USA
23 *P6* **Logan** West Virginia, NE USA
37 *Y10* **Logandale** Nevada, W USA
21 *O11* **Logan International** ✈ (Boston) Massachusetts, NE USA
9 *N16* **Logan Lake** British Columbia, SW Canada
25 *Q4* **Logan Martin Lake** ▣ Alabama, S USA
8 *G8* **Logan, Mount** ▲ Yukon Territory, W Canada
34 *I7* **Logan, Mount** ▲ Washington, NW USA
35 *P7* **Logan Pass** *pass* Montana, NW USA
33 *O12* **Logansport** Indiana, N USA
24 *F6* **Logansport** Louisiana, S USA
Logar *see* Lowgar
69 *R11* **Loge** ≈ NW Angola
Logishin *see* Lahishyn
Log na Coille *see* Lugnaquillia Mountain
80 *G11* **Logone** *var.* Lagone. ≈ Cameroon/Chad
80 *G13* **Logone-Occidental** *off.* Préfecture du Logone-Occidental. ◆ *prefecture* SW Chad
80 *H13* **Logone Occidental** ≈ SW Chad
80 *G13* **Logone-Oriental** *off.* Préfecture du Logone-Oriental. ◆ *prefecture* SW Chad
80 *H13* **Logone Oriental** ≈ SW Chad
Logone Oriental *see* Pendé
L'Ogooué-Ivindo *see* Ogooué-Ivindo
L'Ogooué-Lolo *see* Ogooué-Lolo
L'Ogooué-Maritime *see* Ogooué-Maritime
Logoysk *see* Lahoysk
107 *P4* **Logroño** *anc.* Vareia, *Lat.* Juliobriga. La Rioja, N Spain
106 *L10* **Logrosán** Extremadura, W Spain
97 *G20* **Løgstør** Nordjylland, N Denmark
97 *H22* **Løgten** Århus, C Denmark
97 *F24* **Løgumkloster** Sønderjylland, SW Denmark
Lögurinn *see* Lagarfljót
197 *B10* **Loh** *island* Torres Islands, N Vanuatu
159 *P15* **Lohārdaga** Bihār, N India
158 *H10* **Lohāru** Haryāna, N India
103 *D15* **Lohausen** ✈ (Düsseldorf) Nordrhein-Westfalen, W Germany
201 *O14* **Lohd** Pohnpei, E Micronesia
194 *I14* **Lohiki** ≈ S PNG
94 *L12* **Lohiniva** Lappi, N Finland
Lohiszyn *see* Lahishyn
95 *L20* **Lohja** *var.* Lojo. Uusimaa, S Finland
175 *O8* **Lohjanan** Borneo, C Indonesia
27 *Q9* **Lohn** Texas, SW USA
102 *G12* **Lohne** Niedersachsen, NW Germany
Lohr *see* Lohr am Main
103 *I18* **Lohr am Main** *var.* Lohr. Bayern, C Germany
111 *T10* **Loibl Pass** *Ger.* Loiblpass, *Slvn.* Ljubelj. *pass* Austria/Slovenia
178 *Gg6* **Loi-Kaw** Kayah State, C Myanmar
95 *K19* **Loimaa** Turku-Pori, SW Finland
105 *O6* **Loing** ≈ C France
178 *Ii6* **Loi, Phou** ▲ N Laos
104 *L7* **Loir** ≈ C France
105 *Q11* **Loire** ◆ *department* E France
104 *M7* **Loire** *var.* Liger. ≈ C France
104 *I7* **Loire-Atlantique** ◆ *department* NW France
105 *O7* **Loiret** ◆ *department* C France
104 *M8* **Loir-et-Cher** ◆ *department* C France
103 *L24* **Loisach** ≈ SE Germany
58 *B9* **Loja** Loja, S Ecuador
106 *M14* **Loja** Andalucía, S Spain
58 *B9* **Loja** ◆ *province* S Ecuador
Lojo *see* Lohja
118 *J4* **Lokachi** Volyns'ka Oblast', NW Ukraine
81 *M20* **Lokandu** Maniema, C Zaire
94 *M11* **Lokan Tekojärvi** ◎ NE Finland
143 *Z11* **Lökbatan** *Rus.* Lokbatan. E Azerbaijan
101 *F17* **Lokeren** Oost-Vlaanderen, NW Belgium
Lokhvitsa *see* Lokhvytsya
119 *S4* **Lokhvytsya** *Rus.* Lokhvitsa. Poltavs'ka Oblast', NE Ukraine
83 *H17* **Lokichar** Rift Valley, NW Kenya
83 *G16* **Lokichokio** Rift Valley, NW Kenya
83 *H16* **Lokitaung** Rift Valley, NW Kenya
94 *M11* **Lokka** Lappi, N Finland
96 *G8* **Løkken Verk** Sør-Trøndelag, S Norway
128 *G16* **Loknya** Pskovskaya Oblast', W Russian Federation
79 *V15* **Loko** Plateau, S Nigeria
79 *U15* **Lokoja** Kogi, C Nigeria
83 *H17* **Lokori** Rift Valley, W Kenya
79 *R16* **Lokossa** S Benin
120 *I3* **Loksa** *Ger.* Loxa. Harjumaa, NW Estonia
16 *P3* **Loks Land** *island* Northwest Territories, NE Canada
82 *C13* **Lol** ≈ S Sudan
78 *K15* **Lola** Guinée-Forestière, SE Guinea
37 *Q5* **Lola, Mount** ▲ California, W USA
83 *H20* **Loliondo** Arusha, NE Tanzania
97 *H25* **Lolland** *prev.* Laaland. *island* S Denmark
195 *O11* **Lolobau Island** *island* E PNG
175 *T6* **Loloda Utara, Kepulauan** *island group* E Indonesia
81 *E16* **Lolodorf** Sud, SW Cameroon
116 *G7* **Lom** *prev.* Lom-Palanka. Oblast Montana, NW Bulgaria
116 *G7* **Lom** ≈ NW Bulgaria
81 *M19* **Lomami** ≈ C Zaire
59 *F17* **Lomas** Arequipa, SW Peru
65 *I23* **Lomas, Bahía** *bay* S Chile
63 *D20* **Lomas de Zamora** Buenos Aires, E Argentina
63 *D20* **Loma Verde** Buenos Aires, E Argentina
188 *K4* **Lombadina** Western Australia
108 *E6* **Lombardia** *Eng.* Lombardy. ◆ *region* N Italy
Lombardy *see* Lombardia
104 *M15* **Lombez** Gers, S France
175 *R15* **Lomblen, Pulau** *island* Nusa Tenggara, S Indonesia
181 *W7* **Lombok Basin** *undersea feature* E Indian Ocean
175 *Nn16* **Lombok, Pulau** *island* Nusa Tenggara, C Indonesia
175 *Nn16* **Lombok, Selat** *strait* S Indonesia
79 *Q16* **Lomé** ● (Togo) S Togo
79 *Q16* **Lomé** ✈ S Togo
81 *L19* **Lomela** Kasai Oriental, C Zaire
27 *R9* **Lometa** Texas, SW USA
81 *F16* **Lomié** Est, SE Cameroon
32 *M8* **Lomira** Wisconsin, N USA
97 *K23* **Lomma** Malmöhus, S Sweden
101 *J16* **Lommel** Limburg, N Belgium
98 *I11* **Lomond, Loch** ◎ C Scotland, UK
207 *R9* **Lomonosov Ridge** *var.* Harris Ridge, *Rus.* Khrebet Lomonsova. *undersea feature* Arctic Ocean
Lomonsova, Khrebet *see* Lomonosov Ridge
Lom-Palanka *see* Lom
Lomphat *see* Lumphăt
37 *P14* **Lompoc** California, W USA
178 *Hh9* **Lom Sak** *var.* Muang Lom Sak. Phetchabun, C Thailand
112 *N9* **Łomża** *Rus.* Lomzha. Łomża, NE Poland
112 *N9* **Łomża** *off.* Województwo Łomżyńskie, *Rus.* Lomzha. ◆ *province* NE Poland
Lomzha/Łomżyńskie, Województwo *see* Łomża
Lonaula *see* Lonāvale
161 *D14* **Lonāvale** *prev.* Lonaula. Mahārāshtra, W India
65 *G15* **Loncoche** Araucanía, C Chile
65 *H14* **Loncopue** Neuquén, W Argentina
101 *G17* **Londerzeel** Vlaams Brabant, C Belgium
Londinium *see* London
12 *E16* **London** Ontario, S Canada
203 *Y2* **London** Kiritimati, E Kiribati
99 *O22* **London** *anc.* Augusta, *Lat.* Londinium. ● (UK) SE England, UK
23 *N7* **London** Kentucky, S USA
33 *S13* **London** Ohio, NE USA
27 *Q10* **London** Texas, SW USA
99 *O22* **London City** ✈ SE England, UK
99 *E14* **Londonderry** *var.* Derry, *Ir.* Doire. NW Northern Ireland, UK
99 *F14* **Londonderry** *cultural region* NW Northern Ireland, UK
188 *M2* **Londonderry, Cape** *headland* Western Australia
65 *H25* **Londonderry, Isla** *island* S Chile
45 *O7* **Londres, Cayos** *reef* NE Nicaragua
62 *I10* **Londrina** Paraná, S Brazil
29 *N13* **Lone Grove** Oklahoma, C USA
12 *E12* **Lonely Island** *island* Ontario, S Canada
37 *T8* **Lone Mountain** ▲ Nevada, W USA
27 *V6* **Lone Oak** Texas, SW USA
37 *T11* **Lone Pine** California, W USA
Lone Star State *see* Texas
85 *D14* **Longa** Cuando Cubango, C Angola
84 *B12* **Longa** ≈ W Angola
85 *E15* **Longa** ≈ SE Angola
169 *W11* **Longang Shan** ⛰ NE China
207 *S4* **Longa, Proliv** *Eng.* Long Strait. *strait* NE Russian Federation
46 *J13* **Long Bay** *bay* W Jamaica
23 *V13* **Long Bay** *bay* North Carolina/South Carolina, E USA
37 *T16* **Long Beach** California, W USA
24 *M9* **Long Beach** Mississippi, S USA
20 *L14* **Long Beach** Long Island, New York, NE USA
34 *F9* **Long Beach** Washington, NW USA
20 *K16* **Long Beach Island** *island* New Jersey, NE USA
67 *M25* **Longbluff** *headland* SW Tristan da Cunha
25 *U13* **Longboat Key** *island* Florida, SE USA
20 *K15* **Long Branch** New Jersey, NE USA
46 *J5* **Long Cay** *island* SE Bahamas
167 *P14* **Longchuan** *prev.* Laolong. Guangdong, S China
Longchuan Jiang *see* Shweli
34 *K12* **Long Creek** Oregon, NW USA
165 *W10* **Longde** Ningxia, N China
191 *P16* **Longford** Tasmania, SE Australia
99 *D17* **Longford** *Ir.* An Longfort. C Ireland
99 *E17* **Longford** *Ir.* An Longfort. *cultural region* C Ireland
167 *P1* **Longhua** Hebei, E China
175 *Nn8* **Longiram** Borneo, C Indonesia
46 *J4* **Long Island** *island* C Bahamas
10 *H8* **Long Island** *island* Northwest Territories, C Canada
194 *K11* **Long Island** *var.* Arop Island. *island* N PNG
20 *L14* **Long Island** *island* New York, NE USA
Long Island *see* Bermuda
20 *M14* **Long Island Sound** *sound* NE USA
166 *K13* **Long Jiang** ≈ S China
169 *U7* **Longjiang** Heilongjiang, NE China
169 *Y10* **Longjing** *var.* Yanji. Jilin, NE China
167 *R4* **Longkou** Shandong, E China
10 *E11* **Longlac** Ontario, S Canada
21 *S1* **Long Lake** ◎ Maine, NE USA
33 *O6* **Long Lake** ◎ Michigan, N USA
33 *R5* **Long Lake** ◎ Michigan, N USA
31 *N6* **Long Lake** ◎ North Dakota, N USA
32 *J4* **Long Lake** ▣ Wisconsin, N USA
101 *K23* **Longlier** Luxembourg, SE Belgium
166 *I13* **Longlin** *var.* Longlin Gezu Zizhixian. Guangxi Zhuangzu Zizhiqu, S China
39 *T3* **Longmont** Colorado, C USA
31 *N13* **Long Pine** Nebraska, C USA
Longping *see* Luodian
12 *F17* **Long Point** *headland* Ontario, S Canada
12 *K15* **Long Point** *headland* Ontario, SE Canada
192 *P10* **Long Point** *headland* North Island, NZ
32 *L2* **Long Point** *headland* Michigan, N USA
12 *G17* **Long Point Bay** *lake bay* Ontario, S Canada
31 *T7* **Long Prairie** Minnesota, N USA
11 *S11* **Long Range Mountains** *hill range* Newfoundland, Newfoundland and Labrador, E Canada
67 *H25* **Long Range Point** *headland* SE Saint Helena
189 *V8* **Longreach** Queensland, E Australia
166 *H7* **Longriba** Sichuan, C China
166 *L10* **Longshan** Hunan, S China
39 *S3* **Longs Peak** ▲ Colorado, C USA
Long Strait *see* Longa, Proliv
104 *K8* **Longué** Maine-et-Loire, NW France
11 *P11* **Longue-Pointe** Québec, E Canada
105 *S4* **Longuyon** Meurthe-et-Moselle, NE France
27 *W7* **Longview** Texas, SW USA
34 *G10* **Longview** Washington, NW USA
67 *H25* **Longwood** C Saint Helena
27 *P7* **Longworth** Texas, SW USA
105 *S3* **Longwy** Meurthe-et-Moselle, NE France
165 *V11* **Longxi** Gansu, C China
178 *J14* **Long Xuyên** *var.* Longxuyen. An Giang, S Vietnam
167 *Q13* **Longyan** Fujian, SE China
94 *O3* **Longyearbyen** ○ (Svalbard) Spitsbergen, W Svalbard
166 *J15* **Longzhou** Guangxi Zhuangzu Zizhiqu, S China
102 *F12* **Löningen** Niedersachsen, NW Germany
29 *V11* **Lonoke** Arkansas, C USA
97 *L21* **Lönsboda** Kristianstad, S Sweden
105 *S9* **Lons-le-Saunier** *anc.* Ledo Salinarius. Jura, E France
33 *O15* **Loogootee** Indiana, N USA
33 *Q9* **Looking Glass River** ≈ Michigan, N USA
23 *X11* **Lookout, Cape** *headland* North Carolina, SE USA
41 *O6* **Lookout Ridge** *ridge* Alaska, USA
189 *N11* **Loongana** Western Australia
101 *I14* **Loon op Zand** Noord-Brabant, S Netherlands
99 *A19* **Loop Head** *Ir.* Ceann Léime. *headland* W Ireland
111 *V4* **Loosdorf** Niederösterreich, NE Austria
164 *G10* **Lop** Xinjiang Uygur Zizhiqu, NW China
114 *J11* **Lopare** NE Bosnia and Herzegovina
Lopatichi *see* Lapatsichy
131 *Q15* **Lopatin** Respublika Dagestan, SW Russian Federation
131 *P7* **Lopatino** Penzenskaya Oblast', W Russian Federation
178 *Hh10* **Lop Buri** *var.* Loburi. Lop Buri, C Thailand
27 *R16* **Lopeno** Texas, SW USA
Lopevi *see* Ulveah
81 *C18* **Lopez, Cap** *headland* W Gabon
100 *I12* **Lopik** Utrecht, C Netherlands
Lop Nor *see* Lop Nur
164 *M7* **Lop Nur** *var.* Lob Nor, Lop Nor, Lo-pu Po. *seasonal lake* NW China
Lopnur *see* Yuli
81 *K17* **Lopori** ≈ NW Zaire
100 *O5* **Loppersum** Groningen, NE Netherlands
94 *I8* **Lopphavet** *sound* N Norway
Lo-pu Po *see* Lop Nur
Lora *see* Lowrah
190 *F3* **Lora Creek** *seasonal river* South Australia
106 *K13* **Lora del Río** Andalucía, S Spain
154 *M11* **Lora, Hāmūn-i** *wetland* SW Pakistan
33 *T11* **Lorain** Ohio, N USA
27 *O7* **Loraine** Texas, SW USA
33 *R13* **Loramie, Lake** ▣ Ohio, N USA
107 *Q13* **Lorca** *Ar.* Lurka; *anc.* Eliocroca, *Lat.* Illur co. Murcia, S Spain
199 *I12* **Lord Howe Island** *island* E Australia
Lord Howe Island *see* Ontong Java Atoll
183 *O10* **Lord Howe Rise** *undersea feature* SW Pacific Ocean
199 *I12* **Lord Howe Seamounts** *undersea feature* W Pacific Ocean
39 *P15* **Lordsburg** New Mexico, SW USA
194 *K8* **Lorengau** *var.* Lorungau. Manus Island, N PNG
27 *N5* **Lorenzo** Texas, SW USA
148 *K7* **Lorestān** *off.* Ostān-e Lorestān, *var.* Luristan. ◆ *province* W Iran
59 *M17* **Loreto** Beni, N Bolivia
108 *J12* **Loreto** Marche, C Italy
42 *F8* **Loreto** Baja California Sur, W Mexico
42 *M11* **Loreto** Zacatecas, C Mexico
58 *E9* **Loreto** *off.* Departamento de Loreto. ◆ *department* NE Peru
83 *K18* **Lorian Swamp** *swamp* E Kenya
56 *E6* **Lorica** Córdoba, NW Colombia
104 *G7* **Lorient** *prev.* l'Orient. Morbihan, NW France
113 *K22* **Lőrinci** Heves, NE Hungary
12 *G11* **Loring** Ontario, S Canada
35 *V6* **Loring** Montana, NW USA
105 *R13* **Loriol-sur-Drôme** Drôme, E France
23 *U12* **Loris** South Carolina, SE USA
59 *I18* **Loriscota, Laguna** ◎ S Peru
191 *N13* **Lorne** Victoria, SE Australia
98 *G11* **Lorn, Firth of** *inlet* W Scotland, UK
Loro Sae *see* Timor Timur
103 *F24* **Lörrach** Baden-Württemberg, S Germany
105 *T5* **Lorraine** ◆ *region* NE France
Lorungau *see* Lorengau
96 *L11* **Los** Gävleborg, C Sweden
37 *P14* **Los Alamos** California, W USA
39 *S10* **Los Alamos** New Mexico, SW USA
44 *F5* **Los Amates** Izabal, E Guatemala
37 *S15* **Los Angeles** California, W USA
37 *S15* **Los Angeles** ✈ California, W USA
65 *G14* **Los Ángeles** Bío Bío, C Chile
37 *T13* **Los Angeles Aqueduct** *aqueduct* California, W USA
Losanna *see* Lausanne
65 *H20* **Los Antiguos** Santa Cruz, SW Argentina
201 *Q16* **Losap Atoll** *atoll* C Micronesia
37 *P10* **Los Banos** California, W USA
106 *K16* **Los Barrios** Andalucía, S Spain
64 *L5* **Los Blancos** Salta, N Argentina
44 *L12* **Los Chiles** Alajuela, NW Costa Rica
107 *O2* **Los Corrales de Buelna** Cantabria, N Spain
27 *T17* **Los Fresnos** Texas, SW USA
37 *N9* **Los Gatos** California, W USA
112 *O11* **Łosice** Biała Podlaska, E Poland
114 *B11* **Lošinj** *Ger.* Lussin, *It.* Lussino. *island* W Croatia
Los Jardines *see* Ngetik Atoll
65 *G15* **Los Lagos** Los Lagos, C Chile
65 *F17* **Los Lagos** *off.* Región de los Lagos. ◆ *region* C Chile
Loslau *see* Wodzisław Śląski
66 *N11* **Los Llanos** *var.* Los Llanos de Aridane. La Palma, Islas Canarias, Spain, NE Atlantic Ocean
Los Llanos de Aridane *see* Los Llanos
39 *R11* **Los Lunas** New Mexico, SW USA
65 *I16* **Los Menucos** Río Negro, C Argentina
42 *H8* **Los Mochis** Sinaloa, C Mexico
37 *N4* **Los Molinos** California, W USA
106 *M9* **Los Navalmorales** Castilla-La Mancha, C Spain
27 *S15* **Los Olmos Creek** ≈ Texas, SW USA
Losonc/Losontz *see* Lučenec
178 *Jj5* **Lô, Sông** *Chin.* Panlong Jiang. ≈ China/Vietnam
46 *B5* **Los Palacios** Pinar del Río, W Cuba
106 *K14* **Los Palacios y Villafranca** Andalucía, S Spain
175 *Ss16* **Lospalos** Timor, S Indonesia
39 *R12* **Los Pinos Mountains** ⛰ New Mexico, SW USA
39 *R11* **Los Ranchos De Albuquerque** New Mexico, SW USA
42 *M14* **Los Reyes** Michoacán de Ocampo, SW Mexico
58 *B7* **Los Ríos** ◆ *province* C Ecuador
66 *O11* **Los Rodeos** ✈ (Santa Cruz de Ternerife) Tenerife, Islas Canarias, Spain, NE Atlantic Ocean
56 *L4* **Los Roques, Islas** *island group* N Venezuela
45 *S17* **Los Santos** Los Santos, S Panama
45 *S17* **Los Santos** *off.* Provincia de Los Santos. ◆ *province* S Panama
Los Santos *see* Los Santos de Maimona
106 *J12* **Los Santos de Maimona** *var.* Los Santos. Extremadura, W Spain
100 *P10* **Losser** Overijssel, E Netherlands
98 *J8* **Lossiemouth** NE Scotland, UK
63 *B14* **Los Tábanos** Santa Fe, C Argentina
56 *J4* **Los Taques** Falcón, N Venezuela
12 *G11* **Lost Channel** Ontario, S Canada
56 *L5* **Los Teques** Miranda, N Venezuela
37 *Q12* **Lost Hills** California, W USA
38 *I7* **Lost Peak** ▲ Utah, W USA
35 *P11* **Lost Trail Pass** *pass* Montana, NW USA
195 *N15* **Losuia** Kiriwina Island, SE PNG
64 *G10* **Los Vilos** Coquimbo, C Chile
107 *N10* **Los Yébenes** Castilla-La Mancha, C Spain
105 *N13* **Lot** ◆ *department* S France
105 *N13* **Lot** ≈ S France
65 *F14* **Lota** Bío Bío, C Chile
83 *G15* **Lotagipi Swamp** *wetland* Kenya/Sudan
104 *K14* **Lot-et-Garonne** ◆ *department* SW France
85 *K21* **Lothair** Mpumalanga, NE South Africa
35 *R7* **Lothair** Montana, NW USA
81 *L20* **Loto** Kasai Oriental, C Zaire
198 *B8* **Lotofagā** Upolu, SE Western Samoa
110 *E10* **Lötschbergtunnel** *tunnel* Valais, SW Switzerland
27 *T9* **Lott** Texas, SW USA
128 *H3* **Lotta** *var.* Lutto. ≈ Finland/Russian Federation
192 *Q7* **Lottin Point** *headland* North Island, NZ
Lötzen *see* Giżycko
Loualaba *see* Lualaba
178 *I6* **Louangnamtha** *var.* Luong Nam Tha. Louang Namtha, N Laos
178 *I7* **Louangphabang** *var.* Louangphrabang, Luang Prabang. Louangphabang, N Laos
Louangphrabang *see* Louangphabang
204 *H5* **Loubet Coast** *physical region* Antarctica
Loubomo *see* Dolisie
Louch *see* Loukhi
104 *H6* **Loudéac** Côtes d'Armor, NW France
166 *M11* **Loudi** Hunan, S China
81 *F21* **Loudima** La Bouenza, S Congo
22 *M9* **Loudon** Tennessee, S USA
33 *T12* **Loudonville** Ohio, N USA
104 *L8* **Loudun** Vienne, W France
104 *K7* **Loué** Sarthe, NW France
78 *G10* **Louga** NW Senegal
99 *M19* **Loughborough** C England, UK
99 *C18* **Loughrea** *Ir.* Baile Locha Riach. W Ireland
105 *S9* **Louhans** Saône-et-Loire, C France
23 *P5* **Louisa** Kentucky, S USA
23 *V5* **Louisa** Virginia, NE USA
23 *V9* **Louisburg** North Carolina, SE USA
27 *U12* **Louise** Texas, SW USA
13 *P11* **Louiseville** Québec, SE Canada
195 *Q17* **Louisiade Archipelago** *island group* SE PNG
29 *W3* **Louisiana** Missouri, C USA
24 *G8* **Louisiana** *off.* State of Louisiana; also known as Creole State, Pelican State. ◆ *state* S USA
194 *K9* **Lou Island** *island* N PNG
85 *K19* **Louis Trichardt** Northern, NE South Africa
25 *V4* **Louisville** Georgia, SE USA
32 *M15* **Louisville** Illinois, N USA
22 *K5* **Louisville** Kentucky, S USA
24 *M4* **Louisville** Mississippi, S USA
31 *S15* **Louisville** Nebraska, C USA
199 *Jj12* **Louisville Ridge** *undersea feature* S Pacific Ocean
128 *J6* **Loukhi** *var.* Louch. Respublika Kareliya, NW Russian Federation
81 *H19* **Loukoléla** Cuvette, E Congo
106 *G14* **Loulé** Faro, S Portugal
113 *C16* **Louny** *Ger.* Laun. Severní Čechy, NW Czech Republic
31 *O15* **Loup City** Nebraska, C USA
31 *P15* **Loup River** ≈ Nebraska, C USA
13 *S9* **Loup, Rivière du** ≈ Québec, SE Canada
10 *K7* **Loups Marins, Lacs des** *lakes* Québec, NE Canada
104 *K16* **Lourdes** Hautes-Pyrénées, S France
Lourenço Marques *see* Maputo
106 *F11* **Loures** Lisboa, C Portugal
106 *F10* **Lourinhã** Lisboa, C Portugal
117 *C16* **Loúros** ≈ W Greece
106 *G8* **Lousã** Coimbra, N Portugal
166 *M10* **Lou Shui** ≈ C China
191 *O5* **Louth** New South Wales, SE Australia
99 *O18* **Louth** E England, UK
99 *F17* **Louth** *Ir.* Lú. *cultural region* NE Ireland
117 *H15* **Loutrá** Kentrikí Makedonía, N Greece
117 *G19* **Loutráki** Pelopónnisos, S Greece
Louvain *see* Leuven
101 *H19* **Louvain-la Neuve** Walloon Brabant, C Belgium
12 *J8* **Louvicourt** Québec, SE Canada
104 *M4* **Louviers** Eure, N France
32 *K14* **Lou Yaeger, Lake** ▣ Illinois, N USA
95 *J15* **Lövånger** Västerbotten, N Sweden
128 *J14* **Lovat'** ≈ NW Russian Federation
115 *J17* **Lovćen** ▲ S Yugoslavia
116 *I8* **Lovech** Loveshka Oblast, NW Bulgaria
Lovech *see* Loveshka Oblast
27 *V9* **Lovelady** Texas, SW USA
39 *T3* **Loveland** Colorado, C USA
35 *U12* **Lovell** Wyoming, C USA
Lovello, Monte *see* Grosser Löffler
37 *S4* **Lovelock** Nevada, W USA
108 *E7* **Lovere** Lombardia, N Italy
116 *I8* **Loveshka Oblast** *var.* Lovech. ◆ *province* N Bulgaria
32 *L10* **Loves Park** Illinois, N USA
28 *M2* **Lovewell Reservoir** ▣ Kansas, C USA
95 *M19* **Loviisa** *Swe.* Lovisa. Uusimaa, S Finland
39 *V15* **Loving** New Mexico, SW USA
23 *U6* **Lovingston** Virginia, NE USA
39 *V14* **Lovington** New Mexico, SW USA
Lovisa *see* Loviisa
113 *C15* **Lovosice** *Ger.* Lobositz. Severní Čechy, NW Czech Republic
128 *K4* **Lovozero** Murmanskaya Oblast', NW Russian Federation
128 *K4* **Lovozero, Ozero** ◎ NW Russian Federation
114 *B9* **Lovran** *It.* Laurana. Primorje-Gorski Kotar, NW Croatia
118 *E11* **Lovrin** *Ger.* Lowrin. Timiş, W Romania
84 *E10* **Lóvua** Lunda Norte, NE Angola
84 *G12* **Lóvua** Moxico, E Angola
67 *D25* **Low Bay** *bay* East Falkland, Falkland Islands
15 *M6* **Low, Cape** *headland* Northwest Territories, E Canada
35 *N10* **Lowell** Idaho, NW USA
21 *O10* **Lowell** Massachusetts, NE USA
Löwen *see* Leuven
Löwenberg in Schlesien *see* Lwówek Śląski
Lower Austria *see* Niederösterreich
Lower Bann *see* Bann
Lower California *see* Baja California
Lower Danube *see* Niederösterreich
193 *L14* **Lower Hutt** Wellington, North Island, NZ
41 *N11* **Lower Kalskag** Alaska, USA
37 *O1* **Lower Klamath Lake** ◎ California, W USA
37 *Q2* **Lower Lake** ◎ California/Nevada, W USA
99 *E15* **Lower Lough Erne** ◎ SW Northern Ireland, UK
Lower Lusatia *see* Niederlausitz
Lower Normandy *see* Basse-Normandie, France
8 *K9* **Lower Post** British Columbia, W Canada
31 *T4* **Lower Red Lake** ◎ Minnesota, N USA
Lower Rhine *see* Neder Rijn
Lower Saxony *see* Niedersachsen
Lower Tunguska *see* Nizhnyaya Tunguska
99 *Q19* **Lowestoft** E England, UK
155 *Q5* **Lowgar** *var.* Logar. ◆ *province* E Afghanistan
190 *H7* **Low Hill** South Australia
112 *K12* **Łowicz** Skierniewice, C Poland
35 *N13* **Lowman** Idaho, NW USA
155 *P8* **Lowrah** *var.* Lora. ≈ SE Afghanistan
Lowrin *see* Lovrin
191 *N17* **Low Rocky Point** *headland* Tasmania, SE Australia
20 *I8* **Lowville** New York, NE USA
Loxa *see* Loksa
190 *K9* **Loxton** South Australia
83 *G21* **Loya** Tabora, C Tanzania
32 *K6* **Loyal** Wisconsin, N USA
20 *G13* **Loyalsock Creek** ≈ Pennsylvania, NE USA
37 *Q5* **Loyalton** California, W USA
Lo-yang *see* Luoyang
197 *J6* **Loyauté, Îles** *island group* S New Caledonia
Loyev *see* Loyew
121 *O20* **Loyew** *Rus.* Loyev. Homyel'skaya Voblasts', SE Belarus
129 *S13* **Loyno** Kirovskaya Oblast', NW Russian Federation
105 *P13* **Lozère** ◆ *department* S France
105 *Q14* **Lozère, Mont** ▲ S France
114 *J11* **Loznica** Serbia, W Yugoslavia
119 *V7* **Lozova** *Rus.* Lozovaya. Kharkivs'ka Oblast', E Ukraine
Lozovaya *see* Lozova
107 *N7* **Lozoyuela** Madrid, C Spain
Lœvvajok *see* Levajok
Lu *see* Shandong, China
Lú *see* Louth, Ireland
84 *F12* **Luacano** Moxico, E Angola
81 *N21* **Lualaba** *Fr.* Loualaba. ≈ SE Zaire
85 *H14* **Luampa** Western, NW Zambia
85 *H15* **Luampa Kuta** Western, W Zambia
167 *P8* **Lu'an** Anhui, E China
106 *K2* **Luanco** Asturias, N Spain
84 *A11* **Luanda** *var.* Loanda, *Port.* São Paulo de Loanda. ● (Angola) Luanda, NW Angola
84 *A11* **Luanda** ◆ *province* NW Angola
84 *A11* **Luanda** ✈ Luanda, NW Angola
84 *D12* **Luando** ≈ C Angola
Luang *see* Tapi, Mae Nam
85 *G14* **Luanginga** *var.* Luanguinga. ≈ Angola/Zambia
178 *Gg15* **Luang, Khao** ▲ SW Thailand
Luang Prabang *see* Louangphabang
178 *I8* **Luang Prabang Range** *Th.* Thiukhaoluang Phrahang. ⛰ Laos/Thailand
178 *H16* **Luang, Thale** *lagoon* S Thailand
Luangua, Rio *see* Luangwa
84 *E11* **Luangue** ≈ NE Angola
Luanguinga *see* Luanginga
85 *K15* **Luangwa** *var.* Aruângua. Lusaka, C Zambia
85 *K14* **Luangwa** *var.* Aruângua, Rio Luangua. ≈ Mozambique/Zambia
167 *Q2* **Luan He** ≈ E China
202 *G11* **Luaniva, Île** *island* E Wallis and Futuna
167 *P2* **Luanping** *var.* Anjiangying. Hebei, E China
84 *J13* **Luanshya** Copperbelt, C Zambia
64 *K13* **Luan Toro** La Pampa, C Argentina
167 *Q2* **Luanxian** *var.* Luan Xian. Hebei, E China
84 *J12* **Luapula** ◆ *province* N Zambia
81 *O25* **Luapula** ≈ Zaire/Zambia
106 *J2* **Luarca** Asturias, N Spain
174 *Ll7* **Luar, Danau** ◎ Borneo, N Indonesia
81 *L25* **Luashi** Shaba, S Zaire
84 *G12* **Luau** *Port.* Vila Teixeira de Sousa. Moxico, NE Angola
81 *C16* **Luba** *prev.* San Carlos. Isla de Bioco, NW Equatorial Guinea
44 *F4* **Lubaantun** *ruins* Toledo, S Belize
113 *P16* **Lubaczów** *var.* Lúbaczów. Przemyśl, SE Poland
Lubale *see* Lubalo
84 *E11* **Lubalo** Lunda Norte, NE Angola
84 *E11* **Lubalo** *var.* Lubale. ≈ Angola/Zaire
120 *J9* **Lubāna** Madona, E Latvia
Lubānas Ezers *see* Lubāns
179 *P11* **Lubang Island** *island* N Philippines
85 *B15* **Lubango** *Port.* Sá da Bandeira. Huíla, SW Angola
120 *J9* **Lubāns** *var.* Lubānas Ezers. ◎ E Latvia
81 *M21* **Lubao** Kasai Oriental, C Zaire
112 *O13* **Lubartów** *Ger.* Qumälisch. Lublin, E Poland
102 *G13* **Lübbecke** Nordrhein-Westfalen, NW Germany
102 *O13* **Lübben** Brandenburg, E Germany
103 *P14* **Lübbenau** Brandenburg, E Germany
27 *N5* **Lubbock** Texas, SW USA
Lubcz *see* Lyubcha
21 *U6* **Lubec** Maine, NE USA
102 *K9* **Lübeck** Schleswig-Holstein, N Germany
102 *K8* **Lübecker Bucht** *bay* N Germany
81 *M21* **Lubefu** Kasai Oriental, C Zaire
113 *O14* **Lubelska, Wyżyna** *plateau* SE Poland
Lubelskie, Województwo *see* Lublin
Lubembe *see* Luembe

◆ Country
● Country Capital
◇ Dependent Territory
○ Dependent Territory Capital
◆ Administrative Region
✈ International Airport
▲ Mountain
⛰ Mountain Range
Volcano
≈ River
◎ Lake
▣ Reservoir

LÜBEN – MACON

Lüben *see* Lubin
150 *H9* **Lubenka** Zapadnyy Kazakhstan, W Kazakhstan
81 *P18* **Lubero** Nord Kivu, E Zaire
81 *L22* **Lubi** ≈ S Zaire
Lubiana *see* Ljubljana
112 *J11* **Lubień Kujawski** Włocławek, C Poland
69 *T11* **Lubilandji** ≈ S Zaire
112 *F13* **Lubin** *Ger.* Lüben. Legnica, W Poland
113 *O14* **Lublin** ***Rus.*** Lyublin. Lublin, E Poland
112 *O13* **Lublin** ***off.*** Województwo Lubelskie, ***Rus.*** Lyublin. ◐ *province* E Poland
113 *J15* **Lubliniec** Częstochowa, S Poland
Lubnān, Jabal *see* Liban, Jebel
119 *R5* **Lubny** Poltavs'ka Oblast', NE Ukraine
Luboml *see* Lyuboml'
112 *G11* **Luboń** *Ger.* Peterhof. Poznań, W Poland
112 *D12* **Lubsko** *Ger.* Sommerfeld. Zielona Góra, W Poland
81 *N24* **Lubudi** Shaba, SE Zaire
174 *Hh11* **Lubuklinggau** Sumatera, W Indonesia
81 *N25* **Lubumbashi** ***prev.*** Élisabethville. Shaba, SE Zaire
85 *I14* **Lubungu** Central, C Zambia
81 *N18* **Lubutu** Maniema, E Zaire
Luca *see* Lucca
84 *C11* **Lucala** ≈ W Angola
12 *E16* **Lucan** Ontario, S Canada
99 *F18* **Lucan** *Ir.* Leamhcán. E Ireland
Lucanian Mountains *see* Lucano, Appennino
109 *M18* **Lucano, Appennino** ***Eng.*** Lucanian Mountains. ⛰ S Italy
84 *F11* **Lucapa** ***var.*** Lukapa. Lunda Norte, NE Angola
31 *V15* **Lucas** Iowa, C USA
63 *C18* **Lucas González** Entre Ríos, E Argentina
67 *C25* **Lucas Point** *headland* West Falkland, Falkland Islands
33 *S15* **Lucasville** Ohio, N USA
108 *F11* **Lucca** ***anc.*** Luca. Toscana, C Italy
46 *H12* **Lucea** W Jamaica
99 *H15* **Luce Bay** *inlet* SW Scotland, UK
24 *M8* **Lucedale** Mississippi, S USA
179 *Pp11* **Lucena** ***off.*** Lucena City. Luzon, N Philippines
106 *M14* **Lucena** Andalucía, S Spain
107 *S8* **Lucena del Cid** País Valenciano, E Spain
113 *D15* **Lučenec** *Ger.* Losontz, ***Hung.*** Losonc. Stredné Slovensko, S Slovakia
Lucentum *see* Alicante
109 *M16* **Lucera** Puglia, SE Italy
Lucerna/Lucerne *see* Luzern
Lucerne, Lake of *see* Vierwaldstätter See
42 *J4* **Lucero** Chihuahua, N Mexico
127 *Nn17* **Luchegorsk** Primorskiy Kray, SE Russian Federation
107 *Q13* **Luchena** ≈ SE Spain
84 *N13* **Lucheringo** ***var.*** Luchulingo. ≈ N Mozambique
Luchesa *see* Luchosa
Luchin *see* Luchyn
120 *N13* **Luchosa** ***Rus.*** Luchesa. ≈ N Belarus
Luchow *see* Hefei
102 *K11* **Lüchow** Mecklenburg-Vorpommern, N Germany
Luchulingo *see* Lucheringo
121 *N17* **Luchyn** ***Rus.*** Luchin. Homyel'skaya Voblasts', SE Belarus
57 *U11* **Lucie Rivier** ≈ W Suriname
190 *K11* **Lucindale** South Australia
175 *T13* **Lucipara, Kepulauan** *island group* E Indonesia
85 *A14* **Lucira** Namibe, SW Angola
Łuck *see* Luts'k
103 *O14* **Luckau** Brandenburg, E Germany
102 *N13* **Luckenwalde** Brandenburg, E Germany
12 *E15* **Lucknow** Ontario, S Canada
158 *L12* **Lucknow** ***var.*** Lakhnau. Uttar Pradesh, N India
104 *J10* **Luçon** Vendée, NW France
46 *I7* **Lucrecia, Cabo** *headland* E Cuba
84 *F13* **Lucusse** Moxico, E Angola
Lüda *see* Dalian
116 *M9* **Luda Kamchiya** ≈ E Bulgaria
Ludasch *see* Luduş
116 *I10* **Luda Yana** ≈ C Bulgaria
114 *F7* **Ludbreg** Varaždin, N Croatia
31 *P7* **Ludden** North Dakota, N USA
103 *F15* **Lüdenscheid** Nordrhein-Westfalen, W Germany
85 *C21* **Lüderitz** ***prev.*** Angra Pequena. Karas, SW Namibia
158 *H8* **Ludhiāna** Punjab, N India
33 *O7* **Ludington** Michigan, N USA
99 *K20* **Ludlow** W England, UK
37 *W14* **Ludlow** California, W USA
30 *J7* **Ludlow** South Dakota, N USA
20 *M9* **Ludlow** Vermont, NE USA
116 *L7* **Ludogorie** *physical region* NE Bulgaria
25 *W6* **Ludowici** Georgia, SE USA
Ludsan *see* Ludza
118 *I10* **Luduş** *Ger.* Ludasch, ***Hung.*** Marosludas. Mureş, C Romania
97 *M14* **Ludvika** Kopparberg, C Sweden
103 *H21* **Ludwigsburg** Baden-Württemberg, SW Germany
102 *O13* **Lüdwigsfelde** Brandenburg, NE Germany
103 *G20* **Ludwigshafen** ***var.*** Ludwigshafen am Rhein. Rheinland-Pfalz, W Germany
Ludwigshafen am Rhein *see* Ludwigshafen
103 *L20* **Ludwigskanal** *canal* SE Germany
102 *L10* **Ludwigslust** Mecklenburg-Vorpommern, N Germany
120 *K10* **Ludza** *Ger.* Ludsan. Ludza, E Latvia
81 *K21* **Luebo** Kasai Occidental, SW Zaire
27 *Q6* **Lueders** Texas, SW USA
81 *N20* **Lueki** Maniema, C Zaire
84 *F10* **Luembe** ***var.*** Lubembe. ≈ Angola/Zaire
84 *E13* **Luena** ***var.*** Lwena, ***Port.*** Luso. Moxico, E Angola
81 *M24* **Luena** Shaba, SE Zaire
84 *K12* **Luena** Northern, NE Zambia
84 *F13* **Luena** ≈ E Angola
85 *F16* **Luengue** ≈ SE Angola
69 *V13* **Luenha** ≈ W Mozambique
85 *G15* **Lueti** ≈ Angola/Zambia
166 *J7* **Lüeyang** Shaanxi, C China
167 *P14* **Lufeng** Guangdong, S China
81 *N24* **Lufira** ≈ SE Zaire
81 *N25* **Lufira, Lac de Retenue de la** ***var.*** Lac Tshangalele. ◎ SE Zaire
27 *W8* **Lufkin** Texas, SW USA
84 *L11* **Lufubu** ≈ N Zambia
128 *G14* **Luga** Leningradskaya Oblast', NW Russian Federation
128 *G13* **Luga** ≈ NW Russian Federation
Luganer See *see* Lugano, Lago di
110 *H11* **Lugano** *Ger.* Lauis. Ticino, S Switzerland
110 *H12* **Lugano, Lago di** ***var.*** Ceresio, *Ger.* Luganer See. ◎ S Switzerland
Lugansk *see* Luhans'k
197 *B12* **Luganville** Espiritu Santo, C Vanuatu
Lugdunum *see* Lyon
Lugdunum Batavorum *see* Leiden
85 *O15* **Lugela** Zambézia, NE Mozambique
85 *O16* **Lugela** ≈ C Mozambique
84 *P13* **Lugenda, Rio** ≈ N Mozambique
Luggarus *see* Locarno
Lugh Ganana *see* Luuq
99 *G19* **Lugnaquillia Mountain** *Ir.* Log na Coille. ▲ E Ireland
108 *H10* **Lugo** Emilia-Romagna, N Italy
106 *I3* **Lugo** ***anc.*** Lugus Augusti. Galicia, NW Spain
106 *I3* **Lugo** ◐ *province* Galicia, NW Spain
23 *R12* **Lugoff** South Carolina, SE USA
118 *F12* **Lugoj** *Ger.* Lugosch, ***Hung.*** Lugos. Timiş, W Romania
Lugos/Lugosch *see* Lugoj
151 *S16* **Lugovoy** ***var.*** Lugovoye. Zhambyl, S Kazakhstan
Lugovoye *see* Lugovoy
164 *I13* **Lugu** Xizang Zizhiqu, W China
Lugus Augusti *see* Lugo
Luguvallium/Luguvallum *see* Carlisle
119 *Y7* **Luhans'k** ***Rus.*** Lugansk; ***prev.*** Voroshilovgrad. Luhans'ka Oblast', E Ukraine
119 *Y7* **Luhans'k** ✕ Luhans'ka Oblast', E Ukraine
119 *X6* **Luhans'ka Oblast'** ***var.*** Luhans'k; ***prev.*** Voroshilovgrad, ***Rus.*** Voroshilovgradskaya Oblast'. ◐ *province* E Ukraine
167 *Q7* **Luhe** Jiangsu, E China
175 *T11* **Luhu** Pulau Seram, E Indonesia
166 *G8* **Luhuo** ***var.*** Zhaggo. Sichuan, C China
118 *M3* **Luhyny** Zhytomyrs'ka Oblast', N Ukraine
85 *G15* **Lui** ≈ W Zambia
85 *G16* **Luiana** ≈ SE Angola
85 *L15* **Luia, Rio** ***var.*** Ruya. ≈ Mozambique/Zimbabwe
Luichow Peninsula *see* Leizhou Bandao
Luik *see* Liège
84 *C13* **Luimbale** Huambo, C Angola
Luimneach *see* Limerick
108 *D6* **Luino** Lombardia, N Italy
84 *E13* **Luio** ≈ E Angola
94 *L11* **Luiro** ≈ NE Finland
81 *N25* **Luishia** Shaba, SE Zaire
61 *M19* **Luislândia do Oeste** Minas Gerais, SE Brazil
42 *K5* **Luis L.León, Presa** ⊠ N Mexico
Luis Muñoz Marin *see* San Juan
205 *N5* **Luitpold Coast** *physical region* Antarctica
81 *K22* **Luiza** Kasai Occidental, S Zaire
63 *D20* **Luján** Buenos Aires, E Argentina
81 *N24* **Lukafu** Shaba, SE Zaire
Lukapa *see* Lucapa
114 *I11* **Lukavac** NE Bosnia and Herzegovina
81 *I20* **Lukenie** ≈ C Zaire
81 *H19* **Lukolela** Equateur, W Zaire
121 *M14* **Lukoml'skaye, Vozyera** ***Rus.*** Ozero Lukoml'skoye. ◎ N Belarus
Lukoml'skoye, Ozero *see* Lukoml'skaye, Vozyera
116 *I8* **Lukovit** Loveshka Oblast, NW Bulgaria
112 *O12* **Łuków** *Ger.* Bogendorf. Siedlce, E Poland
131 *O4* **Lukoyanov** Nizhegorodskaya Oblast', W Russian Federation
81 *N22* **Lukuga** ≈ SE Zaire
81 *F21* **Lukula** Bas-Zaïre, SW Zaire
85 *G14* **Lukulu** Western, NW Zambia
201 *R17* **Lukunor Atoll** *atoll* Mortlock Islands, C Micronesia
84 *J12* **Lukwesa** Luapula, NE Zambia
95 *K14* **Luleå** Norrbotten, N Sweden
94 *J13* **Luleälven** ≈ N Sweden
142 *C10* **Lüleburgaz** Kırklareli, NW Turkey
166 *M4* **Lüliang Shan** ⛰ C China
81 *O21* **Lulimba** Maniema, E Zaire
24 *K9* **Luling** Louisiana, S USA
27 *T11* **Luling** Texas, SW USA
81 *I18* **Lulonga** ≈ NW Zaire
81 *K22* **Lulua** ≈ S Zaire
Luluabourg *see* Kananga
198 *Dd8* **Luma** Ta'ū, E American Samoa
174 *M16* **Lumajang** Jawa, C Indonesia
164 *G12* **Lumajangdong Co** ◎ W China
84 *G13* **Lumbala Kaquengue** Moxico, E Angola
85 *F14* **Lumbala N'Guimbo** ***var.*** Nguimbo, ***Port.*** Gago Coutinho, Vila Gago Coutinho. Moxico, E Angola
23 *T11* **Lumber River** ≈ North Carolina/South Carolina, SE USA
Lumber State *see* Maine
24 *L8* **Lumberton** Mississippi, S USA
23 *U11* **Lumberton** North Carolina, SE USA
107 *R4* **Lumbier** Navarra, N Spain
85 *Q15* **Lumbo** Nampula, NE Mozambique
128 *M4* **Lumbovka** Murmanskaya Oblast', NW Russian Federation
106 *J7* **Lumbrales** Castilla-León, N Spain
159 *W13* **Lumding** Assam, NE India
84 *F12* **Lumege** ***var.*** Lumeje. Moxico, E Angola
Lumeje *see* Lumege
194 *F10* **Lumi** Sandaun, NW PNG
101 *J17* **Lummen** Limburg, NE Belgium
95 *J20* **Lumparland** Åland, SW Finland
178 *K12* **Lumphăt** ***prev.*** Lomphat. Rôtânôkiri, NE Cambodia
9 *U16* **Lumsden** Saskatchewan, S Canada
193 *C23* **Lumsden** Southland, South Island, NZ
174 *J11* **Lumut, Tanjung** *headland* Sumatera, W Indonesia
163 *P4* **Lün** Töv, C Mongolia
166 *H13* **Lunan** ***var.*** Lunan Yizu Zizhixian. Yunnan, SW China
Lunan Yizu Zizhixian *see* Lunan
118 *I13* **Lunca Corbului** Argeş, S Romania
97 *K23* **Lund** Malmöhus, S Sweden
37 *X6* **Lund** Nevada, W USA
84 *D11* **Lunda Norte** ◐ *province* NE Angola
84 *E12* **Lunda Sul** ◐ *province* NE Angola
84 *M13* **Lundazi** Eastern, NE Zambia
97 *G16* **Lunde** Telemark, S Norway
Lundenburg *see* Břeclav
97 *C17* **Lundevatnet** ◎ S Norway
Lundi *see* Runde
99 *I23* **Lundy** *island* SW England, UK
102 *J10* **Lüneburg** Niedersachsen, N Germany
102 *J11* **Lüneburger Heide** *heathland* NW Germany
105 *Q15* **Lunel** Hérault, S France
103 *F14* **Lünen** Nordrhein-Westfalen, W Germany
11 *P16* **Lunenburg** Nova Scotia, SE Canada
23 *V7* **Lunenburg** Virginia, NE USA
105 *T5* **Lunéville** Meurthe-et-Moselle, NE France
85 *I14* **Lunga** ≈ C Zambia
Lunga, Isola *see* Dugi Otok
164 *H12* **Lungdo** Xizang Zizhiqu, W China
164 *I14* **Lunggar** Xizang Zizhiqu, W China
78 *I15* **Lungi** ✕ (Freetown) W Sierra Leone
Lungkiang *see* Qiqihar
Lungleh *see* Lunglei
159 *W15* **Lunglei** ***prev.*** Lungleh. Mizoram, NE India
164 *L15* **Lungsang** Xizang Zizhiqu, W China
84 *E13* **Lungué-Bungo** ***var.*** Lungwebungu. ≈ Angola/Zambia *see also* Lungwebungu
85 *G14* **Lungwebungu** ***var.*** Lungué-Bungo. ≈ Angola/Zambia *see also* Lungué-Bungo
158 *F12* **Lūni** Rājasthān, N India
158 *F12* **Lūni** ≈ N India
Luninets *see* Luninyets
37 *S7* **Luning** Nevada, W USA
Łuniniec *see* Luninyets
131 *P6* **Lunino** Penzenskaya Oblast', W Russian Federation
121 *J19* **Luninyets** *Pol.* Łuniniec, ***Rus.*** Luninets. Brestskaya Voblasts', SW Belarus
158 *F10* **Lūnkaransar** Rājasthān, NW India
121 *G17* **Lunna** *Pol.* Łunna, ***Rus.*** Lunna. Hrodzyenskaya Voblasts', W Belarus
78 *I15* **Lunsar** W Sierra Leone
85 *K14* **Lunsemfwa** ≈ C Zambia
164 *J6* **Luntai** ***var.*** Bügür. Xinjiang Uygur Zizhiqu, NW China
100 *K11* **Lunteren** Gelderland, C Netherlands
175 *O16* **Lunyuk** Sumbawa, S Indonesia
111 *U5* **Lunz am See** Niederösterreich, C Austria
169 *Y7* **Luobei** ***var.*** Fengxiang. Heilongjiang, NE China
166 *J13* **Luodian** ***var.*** Longping. Guizhou, S China
166 *M15* **Luoding** Guangdong, S China
166 *M6* **Luo He** ≈ C China
166 *L5* **Luo He** ≈ C China
167 *N7* **Luohe** Henan, C China
Luolajarvi *see* Kuoloyarvi
Luong Nam Tha *see* Louangnamtha
166 *L13* **Luoqing Jiang** ≈ S China
167 *O8* **Luoshan** Henan, C China
167 *O12* **Luoxiao Shan** ⛰ S China
167 *N6* **Luoyang** ***var.*** Honan, Lo-yang. Henan, C China
167 *R12* **Luoyuan** Fujian, SE China
81 *F21* **Luozi** Bas-Zaïre, W Zaire
85 *J17* **Lupane** Matabeleland North, W Zimbabwe
166 *I12* **Lupanshui** ***prev.*** Shuicheng. Guizhou, S China
174 *Ll7* **Lupar, Batang** ≈ East Malaysia
Lupatia *see* Altamura
118 *G12* **Lupeni** ***Hung.*** Lupény. Hunedoara, SW Romania
Lupény *see* Lupeni
84 *N13* **Lupiliche** Niassa, N Mozambique
85 *E14* **Lupire** Cuando Cubango, E Angola
179 *Rr16* **Lupon** Mindanao, S Philippines
81 *L22* **Luputa** Kasai Oriental, S Zaire
123 *Jj17* **Luqa** ✕ (Valletta) S Malta
165 *U11* **Luqu** Gansu, C China
47 *U5* **Luquillo, Sierra de** ⛰ E Puerto Rico
28 *L4* **Luray** Kansas, C USA
23 *U4* **Luray** Virginia, NE USA
105 *T7* **Lure** Haute-Saône, E France
84 *D11* **Luremo** Lunda Norte, NE Angola
99 *F15* **Lurgan** *Ir.* An Lorgain. S Northern Ireland, UK
59 *K18* **Luribay** La Paz, W Bolivia
85 *Q14* **Lúrio** Nampula, NE Mozambique
85 *P14* **Lúrio, Rio** ≈ NE Mozambique
Luristan *see* Lorestān
Lurka *see* Lorca
85 *J15* **Lusaka** ● (Zambia) Lusaka, SE Zambia
85 *J15* **Lusaka** ◐ *province* C Zambia
85 *J15* **Lusaka** ✕ Lusaka, C Zambia
81 *L21* **Lusambo** Kasai Oriental, C Zaire
195 *N14* **Lusancay Islands and Reefs** *island group* SE PNG
81 *I21* **Lusanga** Bandundu, SW Zaire
81 *N21* **Lusangi** Maniema, E Zaire
Lusatian Mountains *see* Lausitzer Bergland
Lushnja *see* Lushnjë
115 *K21* **Lushnjë** ***var.*** Lushnja. Fier, C Albania
83 *J21* **Lushoto** Tanga, E Tanzania
104 *L10* **Lusignan** Vienne, W France
35 *Z15* **Lusk** Wyoming, C USA
Luso *see* Luena
104 *L10* **Lussac-les-Châteaux** Vienne, W France
Lussin/Lussino *see* Lošinj
Lussinpiccolo *see* Mali Lošinj
110 *I7* **Lustenau** Vorarlberg, W Austria
167 *T14* **Lü Tao** ***var.*** Huoshao Dao, Lütao, ***Eng.*** Green Island. *island* SE Taiwan
Lūt, Baḩrat/Lut, Bahret *see* Dead Sea
24 *K9* **Lutcher** Louisiana, S USA
149 *T9* **Lūt, Dasht-e** ***var.*** Kavīr-e Lūt. *desert* E Iran
85 *F14* **Lutembo** Moxico, E Angola
Lutetia/Lutetia Parisiorum *see* Paris
Luteva *see* Lodève
12 *G15* **Luther Lake** ◎ Ontario, S Canada
195 *U13* **Luti** Choiseul Island, NW Solomon Islands
Lūt, Kavīr-e *see* Lūt, Dasht-e
99 *N21* **Luton** SE England, UK
99 *N21* **Luton** ✕ (London) SE England, UK
110 *B10* **Lutry** Vaud, SW Switzerland
15 *Ii8* **Łutselk'e** ***prev.*** Snowdrift. Northwest Territories, W Canada
31 *Y4* **Lutsen** Minnesota, N USA
118 *J4* **Luts'k** *Pol.* Łuck, ***Rus.*** Lutsk. Volyns'ka Oblast', NW Ukraine
Luttenberg *see* Ljutomer
Lüttich *see* Liège
85 *G25* **Luttig** Western Cape, SW South Africa
Lutto *see* Lotta
84 *E13* **Lutuai** Moxico, E Angola
119 *Y7* **Lutuhyne** Luhans'ka Oblast', E Ukraine
176 *Ww13* **Lutur, Pulau** *island* Kepulauan Aru, E Indonesia
25 *V12* **Lutz** Florida, SE USA
Lutzow-Holm Bay *see* Lützow Holmbukta
205 *V2* **Lützow Holmbukta** ***var.*** Lutzow-Holm Bay. *bay* Antarctica
83 *L16* **Luuq** *It.* Lugh Ganana. Gedo, SW Somalia
94 *M12* **Luusua** Lappi, NE Finland
25 *Q6* **Luverne** Alabama, S USA
31 *S11* **Luverne** Minnesota, N USA
81 *O22* **Luvua** ≈ SE Zaire
84 *F13* **Luvuei** Moxico, E Angola
83 *H24* **Luwego** ≈ S Tanzania
84 *K12* **Luwingu** Northern, NE Zambia
175 *Qq9* **Luwuk** ***prev.*** Loewoek. Sulawesi, C Indonesia
25 *N3* **Luxapallila Creek** ≈ Alabama/Mississippi, S USA
101 *M25* **Luxembourg** ● (Luxembourg) Luxembourg, S Luxembourg
101 *M25* **Luxembourg** ***off.*** Grand Duchy of Luxembourg, ***var.*** Lëtzebuerg, Luxemburg. ◆ *monarchy* NW Europe
101 *J23* **Luxembourg** ◐ *province* SE Belgium
101 *L24* **Luxembourg** ◐ *district* S Luxembourg
33 *N6* **Luxemburg** Wisconsin, N USA
Luxemburg *see* Luxembourg
105 *U7* **Luxeuil-les-Bains** Haute-Saône, E France
166 *E13* **Luxi** ***prev.*** Mangshi. Yunnan, SW China
84 *E10* **Luxico** ≈ Angola/Zaire
77 *X10* **Luxor** *Ar.* Al Uqşur. E Egypt
77 *X10* **Luxor** ✕ C Egypt
166 *M4* **Luya Shan** ⛰ C China
104 *J15* **Luy de Béarn** ≈ SW France
104 *J15* **Luy de France** ≈ SW France
129 *P12* **Luza** Kirovskaya Oblast', NW Russian Federation
129 *Q12* **Luza** ≈ NW Russian Federation
106 *I16* **Luz, Costa de la** *coastal region* SW Spain
113 *K20* **Lužе** ***var.*** Lausche. ▲ Czech Republic/Germany *see also* Lausche
110 *F8* **Luzern** *Fr.* Lucerne, ***It.*** Lucerna. Luzern, C Switzerland
110 *E8* **Luzern** *Fr.* Lucerne. ◐ *canton* C Switzerland
166 *L13* **Luzhai** Guangxi Zhuangzu Zizhiqu, S China
120 *K12* **Luzhki** ***Rus.*** Luzhki. Vitsyebskaya Voblasts', N Belarus
166 *I10* **Luzhou** Sichuan, C China
Lužická Nisa *see* Neisse
Lužické Hory *see* Lausitzer Bergland
Lužnice *see* Lainsitz
179 *Pp9* **Luzon** *island* N Philippines
179 *Oo6* **Luzon Strait** *strait* Philippines/Taiwan
118 *I5* **L'viv** *Ger.* Lemberg, ***Pol.*** Lwów, ***Rus.*** L'vov. L'vivs'ka Oblast', W Ukraine
L'viv *see* L'vivs'ka Oblast'
118 *I4* **L'vivs'ka Oblast'** ***var.*** L'viv, ***Rus.*** L'vovskaya Oblast'. ◐ *province* NW Ukraine
L'vov *see* L'viv
L'vovskaya Oblast' *see* L'vivs'ka Oblast'
Lwena *see* Luena
Lwów *see* L'viv
112 *F11* **Lwówek** *Ger.* Neustadt bei Pinne. Poznań, W Poland
113 *E14* **Lwówek Śląski** *Ger.* Löwenberg in Schlesien. Jelenia Góra, SW Poland
121 *I18* **Lyakhavichy** ***Rus.*** Lyakhovichi. Brestskaya Voblasts', SW Belarus
Lyakhovichi *see* Lyakhavichy
193 *B22* **Lyall, Mount** ▲ South Island, NZ
Lyallpur *see* Faisalābād
125 *G10* **Lyamin** ≈ C Russian Federation
Lyangar *see* Langar
125 *G10* **Lyantor** Khanty-Mansiyskiy Avtonomnyy Okrug, C Russian Federation
128 *H11* **Lyaskelya** Respublika Kareliya, NW Russian Federation
121 *I18* **Lyasnaya** ***Rus.*** Lesnaya. Brestskaya Voblasts', SW Belarus
121 *F19* **Lyasnaya** *Pol.* Leśna, ***Rus.*** Lesnaya. ≈ SW Belarus
128 *H15* **Lychkovo** Novgorodskaya Oblast', W Russian Federation
Lyck *see* Ełk
95 *I15* **Lycksele** Västerbotten, N Sweden
20 *G13* **Lycoming Creek** ≈ Pennsylvania, NE USA
Lycopolis *see* Asyût
205 *N3* **Lyddan Island** *island* Antarctica
85 *K20* **Lydenburg** Mpumalanga, NE South Africa
121 *L20* **Lyel'chytsy** ***Rus.*** Lel'chitsy. Homyel'skaya Voblasts', SE Belarus
121 *P14* **Lyenina** ***Rus.*** Lenino. Mahilyowskaya Voblasts', E Belarus
120 *L13* **Lyepyel'** ***Rus.*** Lepel'. Vitsyebskaya Voblasts', N Belarus
27 *S17* **Lyford** Texas, SW USA
97 *E17* **Lygna** ≈ S Norway
20 *G14* **Lykens** Pennsylvania, NE USA
117 *E21* **Lykódimo** ▲ S Greece
99 *K24* **Lyme Bay** *bay* S England, UK
99 *K24* **Lyme Regis** S England, UK
112 *L7* **Łyna** *Ger.* Alle. ≈ N Poland
31 *P12* **Lynch** Nebraska, C USA
22 *J10* **Lynchburg** Tennessee, S USA
23 *T6* **Lynchburg** Virginia, NE USA
23 *T12* **Lynches River** ≈ South Carolina, SE USA
34 *H6* **Lynden** Washington, NW USA
190 *I5* **Lyndhurst** South Australia
29 *Q5* **Lyndon** Kansas, C USA
21 *N7* **Lyndonville** Vermont, NE USA
97 *D18* **Lyngdal** Vest-Agder, S Norway
94 *I9* **Lyngen** *inlet* Arctic Ocean
97 *G17* **Lyngør** Aust-Agder, S Norway
94 *I9* **Lyngseidet** Troms, N Norway
21 *P11* **Lynn** Massachusetts, NE USA
Lynn *see* King's Lynn
25 *R9* **Lynn Haven** Florida, SE USA
9 *V11* **Lynn Lake** Manitoba, C Canada
Lynn Regis *see* King's Lynn
120 *I13* **Lyntupy** ***Rus.*** Lyntupy. Vitsyebskaya Voblasts', NW Belarus
105 *R11* **Lyon** ***Eng.*** Lyons; ***anc.*** Lugdunum. Rhône, E France
15 *H3* **Lyon, Cape** *headland* Northwest Territories, NW Canada
20 *K6* **Lyon Mountain** ▲ New York, NE USA
105 *Q11* **Lyonnais, Monts du** ⛰ C France
67 *N25* **Lyon Point** *headland* SE Tristan da Cunha
190 *E5* **Lyons** South Australia
39 *T3* **Lyons** Colorado, C USA
25 *V6* **Lyons** Georgia, SE USA
28 *M5* **Lyons** Kansas, C USA
31 *R14* **Lyons** Nebraska, C USA
20 *G10* **Lyons** New York, NE USA
Lyons *see* Lyon
120 *O13* **Lyozna** ***Rus.*** Liozno. Vitsyebskaya Voblasts', NE Belarus
119 *S4* **Lypova Dolyna** Sums'ka Oblast', NE Ukraine
119 *N6* **Lypovets'** ***Rus.*** Lipovets. Vinnyts'ka Oblast', C Ukraine
Lys *see* Leie
113 *I18* **Lysá Hora** ▲ E Czech Republic
97 *D16* **Lysefjorden** *fjord* S Norway
97 *I18* **Lysekil** Göteborg och Bohus, S Sweden
Lýsi *see* Akdoğan
35 *V14* **Lysite** Wyoming, C USA
131 *P3* **Lyskovo** Nizhegorodskaya Oblast', W Russian Federation
110 *D8* **Lyss** Bern, W Switzerland
97 *H22* **Lystrup** Århus, C Denmark
129 *V14* **Lys'va** Permskaya Oblast', NW Russian Federation
119 *P6* **Lysyanka** Cherkas'ka Oblast', C Ukraine
119 *X6* **Lysychans'k** ***Rus.*** Lisichansk. Luhans'ka Oblast', E Ukraine
99 *K17* **Lytham St Anne's** NW England, UK
193 *I19* **Lyttelton** Canterbury, South Island, NZ
8 *M17* **Lytton** British Columbia, SW Canada
121 *L18* **Lyuban'** ***Rus.*** Lyuban'. Minskaya Voblasts', S Belarus
121 *L18* **Lyubanskaye Vodaskhovishcha** ⊠ C Belarus
118 *M5* **Lyubar** Zhytomyrs'ka Oblast', N Ukraine
Lyubashëvka *see* Lyubashivka
119 *O8* **Lyubashivka** ***Rus.*** Lyubashëvka. Odes'ka Oblast', SW Ukraine
121 *I16* **Lyubcha** *Pol.* Lubcz, ***Rus.*** Lyubcha. Hrodzyenskaya Voblasts', W Belarus
130 *L4* **Lyubertsy** Moskovskaya Oblast', W Russian Federation
118 *K2* **Lyubeshiv** Volyns'ka Oblast', NW Ukraine
128 *M14* **Lyubim** Yaroslavskaya Oblast', NW Russian Federation
116 *K11* **Lyubimets** Khaskovska Oblast, S Bulgaria
Lyublin *see* Lublin
118 *I3* **Lyuboml'** *Pol.* Luboml. Volyns'ka Oblast', NW Ukraine
Lyubotin *see* Lyubotyn
119 *U5* **Lyubotyn** ***Rus.*** Lyubotin. Kharkivs'ka Oblast', E Ukraine
130 *I5* **Lyudinovo** Kaluzhskaya Oblast', W Russian Federation
131 *T2* **Lyuk** Udmurtskaya Respublika, NW Russian Federation
116 *M9* **Lyulyakovo** ***prev.*** Keremitlik. Burgaska Oblast, E Bulgaria
121 *I18* **Lyusina** ***Rus.*** Lyusino. Brestskaya Voblasts', SW Belarus
Lyusino *see* Lyusina

M

144 *G9* **Ma'ād** Irbid, N Jordan
Maalahti *see* Malax
Maale *see* Male'
144 *G13* **Ma'ān** Ma'ān, SW Jordan
144 *H13* **Ma'ān** ***off.*** Muḩāfaẓat Ma'ān, ***var.*** Ma'an, Ma'ān. ◐ *governorate* S Jordan
95 *M16* **Maaninka** Kuopio, C Finland
168 *K7* **Maanīt** Bulgan, C Mongolia
168 *M8* **Maanīt** Töv, C Mongolia
95 *N15* **Maanselkä** Oulu, C Finland
167 *Q8* **Ma'anshan** Anhui, E China
196 *F16* **Maap** *island* Caroline Islands, W Micronesia
120 *H3* **Maardu** *Ger.* Maart. Harjumaa, NW Estonia
Ma'aret-en-Nu'man *see* Ma'arrat an Nu'mān
101 *K16* **Maarheeze** Noord-Brabant, SE Netherlands
Maarianhamina *see* Mariehamn
144 *I4* **Ma'arrat an Nu'mān** ***var.*** Ma'aret-en-Nu'man, *Fr.* Maarret enn Naamâne. Idlib, NW Syria
Maarret enn Naamâne *see* Ma'arrat an Nu'mān
100 *I11* **Maarssen** Utrecht, C Netherlands
Maart *see* Maardu
101 *L17* **Maas** *Fr.* Meuse. ≈ W Europe *see also* Meuse
101 *M15* **Maasbree** Limburg, SE Netherlands
101 *L17* **Maaseik** ***prev.*** Maeseyck. Limburg, NE Belgium
179 *R13* **Maasin** Leyte, C Philippines
101 *L17* **Maasmechelen** Limburg, NE Belgium
100 *G12* **Maassluis** Zuid-Holland, SW Netherlands
101 *L18* **Maastricht** ***var.*** Maestricht; ***anc.*** Traietum ad Mosam, Traiectum Tungorum. Limburg, SE Netherlands
191 *N18* **Maatsuyker Group** *island group* Tasmania, SE Australia
Maba *see* Qujiang
85 *L20* **Mabalane** Gaza, S Mozambique
27 *V7* **Mabank** Texas, SW USA
172 *N10* **Mabechi-gawa** ***var.*** Mabuchi-gawa. ≈ Honshū, C Japan
99 *O18* **Mablethorpe** E England, UK
176 *W9* **Maboi** Irian Jaya, E Indonesia
85 *M19* **Mabote** Inhambane, S Mozambique
34 *J10* **Mabton** Washington, NW USA
Mabuchi-gawa *see* Mabechi-gawa
85 *H20* **Mabutsane** Southern, S Botswana
65 *G19* **Macá, Cerro** ▲ S Chile
62 *Q9* **Macaé** Rio de Janeiro, SE Brazil
84 *N13* **Macaloge** Niassa, N Mozambique
Macan *see* Bonerate, Kepulauan
167 *N15* **Macao** *Chin.* Aomen, ***Port.*** Macau. ◇ *Portugese special territory* E Asia
106 *H9* **Mação** Santarém, C Portugal
60 *J11* **Macapá** *state capital* Amapá, N Brazil
45 *S17* **Macaracas** Los Santos, S Panama
57 *P6* **Macare, Caño** ≈ NE Venezuela
57 *Q6* **Macareo, Caño** ≈ NE Venezuela
Macarsca *see* Makarska
MacArthur *see* Ormoc
190 *L12* **Macarthur** Victoria, SE Australia
58 *C7* **Macas** Morona Santiago, SE Ecuador
Macassar *see* Ujungpandang
61 *Q14* **Macau** Rio Grande do Norte, E Brazil
Macau *see* Macao
Macău *see* Makó, Hungary
67 *E24* **Macbride Head** *headland* East Falkland, Falkland Islands
25 *V9* **Macclenny** Florida, SE USA
99 *L18* **Macclesfield** C England, UK
198 *F6* **Macclesfield Bank** *undersea feature* N South China Sea
MacCluer Gulf *see* Berau, Teluk
189 *N7* **Macdonald, Lake** *salt lake* Western Australia
189 *Q7* **Macdonnell Ranges** ⛰ Northern Territory, C Australia
98 *K8* **Macduff** NE Scotland, UK
106 *I6* **Macedo de Cavaleiros** Bragança, N Portugal
Macedonia Central *see* Kentrikí Makedonía
Macedonia East and Thrace *see* Anatolikí Makedonía kai Thráki
116 *E12* **Macedonia, FYR** ***off.*** the Former Yugoslav Republic of Macedonia, ***var.*** Macedonia, ***Mac.*** Makedonija, ***abbrev.*** FYR Macedonia, FYROM. ◆ *republic* SE Europe
Macedonia West *see* Dytikí Makedonía
61 *Q16* **Maceió** *state capital* Alagoas, E Brazil
78 *K15* **Macenta** Guinée-Forestière, SE Guinea
108 *J12* **Macerata** Marche, C Italy
9 *S11* **MacFarlane** ≈ Saskatchewan, C Canada
190 *H7* **Macfarlane, Lake** ***var.*** Lake Mcfarlane. ◎ South Australia
Macgillicuddy's Reeks Mountains *see* Macgillycuddy's Reeks
99 *B21* **Macgillycuddy's Reeks** ***var.*** Macgillicuddy's Reeks Mountains, *Ir.* Na Cruacha Dubha. ⛰ SW Ireland
9 *X16* **MacGregor** Manitoba, S Canada
155 *O10* **Mach** Baluchistān, SW Pakistan
58 *C6* **Machachi** Pichincha, C Ecuador
85 *M19* **Machaila** Gaza, S Mozambique
Machaire Fíolta *see* Magherafelt
Machaire Rátha *see* Maghera
83 *I19* **Machakos** Eastern, S Kenya
58 *B8* **Machala** El Oro, SW Ecuador
85 *J19* **Machaneng** Central, SE Botswana
85 *M18* **Machanga** Sofala, E Mozambique
82 *G13* **Machar Marshes** *wetland* SE Sudan
104 *I8* **Machecoul** Loire-Atlantique, NW France
167 *O8* **Macheng** Hubei, C China
161 *J16* **Mācherla** Andhra Pradesh, C India
159 *O11* **Machhapuchhre** ▲ C Nepal
21 *T6* **Machias** Maine, NE USA
21 *R3* **Machias River** ≈ Maine, NE USA
21 *T6* **Machias River** ≈ Maine, NE USA
66 *P5* **Machico** Madeira, Portugal, NE Atlantic Ocean
161 *K16* **Machilīpatnam** ***var.*** Bandar Masulipatnam. Andhra Pradesh, E India
56 *G5* **Machiques** Zulia, NW Venezuela
59 *G15* **Machupicchu** Cusco, C Peru
85 *M20* **Macia** ***var.*** Vila de Macia. Gaza, S Mozambique
Macías Nguema Biyogo *see* Bioco, Isla de
118 *M13* **Măcin** Tulcea, SE Romania
191 *T4* **Macintyre River** ≈ New South Wales/Queensland, SE Australia
189 *Y7* **Mackay** Queensland, NE Australia
189 *O7* **Mackay, Lake** *salt lake* Northern Territory/Western Australia
8 *M13* **Mackenzie** British Columbia, W Canada
15 *Gg6* **Mackenzie** ≈ Northwest Territories, NW Canada
205 *Y6* **Mackenzie Bay** *bay* Antarctica
8 *J1* **Mackenzie Bay** *bay* NW Canada
2 *D8* **Mackenzie Delta** *delta* Northwest Territories, NW Canada
207 *P8* **Mackenzie King Island** *island* Queen Elizabeth Islands, Northwest Territories, N Canada
14 *G5* **Mackenzie Mountains** ⛰ Northwest Territories, NW Canada
33 *Q5* **Mackinac, Straits Of** ◎ Michigan, N USA
204 *K5* **Mackintosh, Cape** *headland* Antarctica
9 *R15* **Macklin** Saskatchewan, S Canada
191 *V6* **Macksville** New South Wales, SE Australia
191 *V5* **Maclean** New South Wales, SE Australia
85 *J24* **Maclear** Eastern Cape, SE South Africa
191 *U6* **Macleay River** ≈ New South Wales, SE Australia
MacLeod *see* Fort Macleod
188 *G9* **Macleod, Lake** ◎ Western Australia
8 *I6* **Macmillan** ≈ Yukon Territory, NW Canada
32 *J12* **Macomb** Illinois, N USA
109 *B18* **Macomer** Sardegna, Italy, C Mediterranean Sea
84 *Q13* **Macomia** Cabo Delgado, NE Mozambique
25 *T5* **Macon** Georgia, SE USA
25 *N4* **Macon** Mississippi, S USA
29 *U3* **Macon** Missouri, C USA

◆ Country ● Country Capital ◇ Dependent Territory ○ Dependent Territory Capital ◐ Administrative Region ✕ International Airport ▲ Mountain ⛰ Mountain Range Volcano ≈ River ◎ Lake ⊠ Reservoir

105 R10 **Mâcon** *anc.* Matisco, Matisco Ædourum. Saône-et-Loire, C France

24 J6 **Macon, Bayou** ≈ Arkansas/ Louisiana, S USA

84 G13 **Macondo** Moxico, E Angola

85 M16 **Macossa** Manica, C Mozambique

9 T12 **Macoun Lake** ⊙ Saskatchewan, C Canada

32 K4 **Macoupin Creek** ≈ Illinois, N USA

Macouria *see* Tonate

85 N18 **Macovane** Inhambane, SE Mozambique

191 N17 **Macquarie Harbour** *inlet* Tasmania, SE Australia

199 Ii15 **Macquarie Island** *island* NZ, SW Pacific Ocean

191 T8 **Macquarie, Lake** *lagoon* New South Wales, SE Australia

191 Q6 **Macquarie Marshes** *wetland* New South Wales, SE Australia

183 O13 **Macquarie Ridge** *undersea feature* SW Pacific Ocean

191 Q6 **Macquarie River** ≈ New South Wales, SE Australia

191 P17 **Macquarie River** ≈ Tasmania, SE Australia

205 V5 **Mac. Robertson Land** *physical region* Antarctica

99 C21 **Macroom** *Ir.* Maigh Chromtha. SW Ireland

44 G5 **Macuelizo** Santa Bárbara, NW Honduras

190 G2 **Macumba River** ≈ South Australia

59 I16 **Macusani** Puno, S Peru

58 E8 **Macusari, Río** ≈ N Peru

43 U15 **Macuspana** Tabasco, SE Mexico

144 G10 **Ma'daba** *var.* Mādabā, Madeba; *anc.* Medeba. 'Ammān, NW Jordan

180 G2 **Madagascar** *off.* Democratic Republic of Madagascar, *Malg.* Madagasikara; *prev.* Malagasy Republic. ◆ *republic* W Indian Ocean

180 I5 **Madagascar** ◇ W Indian Ocean

132 L17 **Madagascar Basin** *undersea feature* W Indian Ocean

132 L16 **Madagascar Plain** *undersea feature* W Indian Ocean

69 Y14 **Madagascar Plateau** *var.* Madagascar Ridge, Madagascar Rise, *Rus.* Madagaskarskiy Khrebet. *undersea feature* W Indian Ocean

Madagascar Ridge/ Madagascar Rise *see* Madagascar Plateau

Madagasikara *see* Madagascar

Madagaskarskiy Khrebet *see* Madagascar Plateau

66 N2 **Madalena** Pico, Azores, Portugal, NE Atlantic Ocean

79 Y6 **Madama** Agadez, NE Niger

116 J12 **Madan** Plovdivska Oblast, S Bulgaria

161 I19 **Madanapalle** Andhra Pradesh, E India

194 I11 **Madang** Madang, N PNG

194 I11 **Madang** ◆ *province* N PNG

152 G7 **Madaniyat** *Rus.* Madeniyet. Qoraqalpoghiston Respublikasi, W Uzbekistan

Madanīyin *see* Médenine

79 U11 **Madaoua** Tahoua, SW Niger

Madaras *see* Vťáčnik

159 U15 **Madaripur** Dhaka, C Bangladesh

79 U12 **Madarounfa** Maradi, S Niger

Madarska *see* Hungary

152 B13 **Madau** *Turkm.* Madaw. Balkanskiy Velayat, W Turkmenistan

195 P15 **Madau Island** *island* SE PNG

Madaw *see* Madau

21 S1 **Madawaska** Maine, NE USA

12 J13 **Madawaska River** ≈ Ontario, SE Canada

Madawaska Highlands *see* Haliburton Highlands

177 G4 **Madaya** Mandalay, C Myanmar

109 K17 **Maddaloni** Campania, S Italy

31 O3 **Maddock** North Dakota, N USA

101 I14 **Made** Noord-Brabant, S Netherlands

Madeba *see* Ma'dabā

66 L9 **Madeira** *var.* Ilha de Madeira. Madeira, Portugal, NE Atlantic Ocean

Madeira, Ilha de *see* Madeira

66 O5 **Madeira Islands** *Port.* Região Autónoma da Madeira. ◆ *autonomous region* Madeira, Portugal, NE Atlantic Ocean

66 L9 **Madeira Plain** *undersea feature* E Atlantic Ocean

66 L9 **Madeira Ridge** *undersea feature* E Atlantic Ocean

61 F14 **Madeira, Rio** *Sp.* Río Madera. ≈ Bolivia/Brazil *see also* Madera, Río

103 J25 **Mädelegabel** ▲ Austria/ Germany

13 X6 **Madeleine** ≈ Québec, SE Canada

13 X5 **Madeleine, Cap de la** *headland* Québec, SE Canada

11 Q13 **Madeleine, Îles de la** *Eng.* Magdalen Islands. *island group* Québec, E Canada

31 U10 **Madelia** Minnesota, N USA

35 P3 **Madeline** California, W USA

32 K3 **Madeline Island** *island* Apostle Islands, Wisconsin, N USA

143 O15 **Maden** Elazığ, SE Turkey

151 V12 **Madeniyet** Semipalatinsk, E Kazakhstan

Madeniyet *see* Madaniyat

42 H5 **Madera** Chihuahua, N Mexico

37 Q10 **Madera** California, W USA

58 L13 **Madera, Río** *Port.* Rio Madeira ≈ Bolivia/Brazil *see also* Madeira, Rio

108 D6 **Madesimo** Lombardia, N Italy

---

147 O14 **Madhāb, Wādī** *dry watercourse* NW Yemen

159 V13 **Madhepura** *prev.* Madhipure. Bihār, NE India

Madhipure *see* Madhepura

159 S13 **Madhubani** Bihār, N India

159 Q15 **Madhupur** Bihār, NE India

158 K15 **Madhya Pradesh** *prev.* Central Provinces and Berar. ◆ *state* C India

59 L14 **Madidi, Río** ≈ W Bolivia

161 F20 **Madikeri** *prev.* Mercara. Karnātaka, W India

29 O13 **Madill** Oklahoma, C USA

81 G21 **Madimba** Bas-Zaïre, SW Zaire

144 M4 **Ma'din** Ar Raqqah, C Syria

Madīnah, Minṭaqat al *see* Al Madīnah

78 M4 **Madinani** NW Ivory Coast

147 O17 **Madīnat ash Sha'b** *prev.* Al Ittiḩād. SW Yemen

144 K3 **Madīnat ath Thawrah** *var.* Ath Thawrah. Ar Raqqah, N Syria Asia

181 O6 **Madingley Rise** *undersea feature* W Indian Ocean

81 E21 **Madingo-Kayes** Le Kouilou, S Congo

81 F21 **Madingou** La Bouenza, S Congo

Madioen *see* Madiun

25 U8 **Madison** Florida, SE USA

25 T3 **Madison** Georgia, SE USA

33 P15 **Madison** Indiana, N USA

29 P6 **Madison** Kansas, C USA

21 O4 **Madison** Maine, NE USA

31 S9 **Madison** Minnesota, N USA

24 K5 **Madison** Mississippi, S USA

31 Q14 **Madison** Nebraska, C USA

31 R10 **Madison** South Dakota, N USA

23 U3 **Madison** Virginia, NE USA

23 Q5 **Madison** West Virginia, NE USA

32 L9 **Madison** *state capital* Wisconsin, N USA

23 T6 **Madison Heights** Virginia, NE USA

22 M10 **Madisonville** Kentucky, S USA

23 S9 **Madisonville** Tennessee, S USA

27 V9 **Madisonville** Texas, SW USA

174 Ll15 **Madiun** *prev.* Madioen. Jawa, C Indonesia

Madjene *see* Majene

12 J14 **Madoc** Ontario, SE Canada

83 J18 **Mado Gashi** North Eastern, E Kenya

165 R11 **Madoi** Qinghai, C China

201 O13 **Madolenihmw** Pohnpei, E Micronesia

120 I9 **Madona** *Ger.* Modohn. Madona, E Latvia

109 J23 **Madonie** ▲ Sicilia, Italy, C Mediterranean Sea

147 Y11 **Madrakah, Ra's** *headland* E Oman

161 J19 **Madras** *var.* Chennai. Tamil Nādu, S India

34 U12 **Madras** Oregon, NW USA

161 J19 **Madras** ◇ Tamil Nādu, S India

Madras *see* Tamil Nādu

59 H14 **Madre de Dios** ◇ Departamento de Madre de Dios. ◆ *department* E Peru

65 F22 **Madre de Dios, Isla** *island* S Chile

59 J14 **Madre de Dios, Río** ≈ Bolivia/Peru

27 T6 **Madre, Laguna** ≈ Texas, SW USA

43 Q9 **Madre, Laguna** *lagoon* NE Mexico

39 Q12 **Madre Mount** ▲ New Mexico, SW USA

107 N8 **Madrid** ● (Spain) Madrid, C Spain

31 V14 **Madrid** Iowa, C USA

107 N7 **Madrid** ◆ *autonomous community* C Spain

107 N10 **Madridejos** Castilla-La Mancha, C Spain

106 L7 **Madrigal de las Altas Torres** Castilla-León, N Spain

106 K10 **Madrigalejo** Extremadura, W Spain

36 L3 **Mad River** ≈ California, W USA

44 J8 **Madriz** ◆ *department* NW Nicaragua

106 K10 **Madroñera** Extremadura, W Spain

189 N12 **Madura** Western Australia

Madura *see* Madurai

161 H22 **Madurai** *prev.* Madura, Mathurai. Tamil Nādu, S India

174 M15 **Madura, Pulau** *prev.* Madoera. *island* C Indonesia

Madura, Selat *strait* C Indonesia Mm15

131 Q17 **Madzhalis** Respublika Dagestan, SW Russian Federation

116 K12 **Madzharovo** Khaskovska Oblast, S Bulgaria

85 M14 **Madzimoyo** Eastern, E Zambia

171 K15 **Maebashi** *var.* Maebasi, Mayebashi. Gunma, Honshū, S Japan

Maebasi *see* Maebashi

177 Hh6 **Mae Chan** Chiang Rai, NW Thailand

177 Gg7 **Mae Hong Son** *var.* Maehongson, Muai To. Mae Hong Son, NW Thailand

Mae Nam Khong *see* Mekong

177 Hh7 **Mae Nam Nan** ≈ NW Thailand

178 H10 **Mae Nam Tha Chin** ≈ W Thailand

178 Hh7 **Mae Nam Yom** ≈ W Thailand

39 O3 **Maeser** Utah, W USA

177 Hh6 **Maesteg** S Wales, UK

178 H7 **Mae Sot** *var.* Ban Mae Sot. Tak, W Thailand

177 Ff6 **Mae Suai** *var.* Ban Mae Suai. Chiang Rai, NW Thailand

---

178 H7 **Mae Tho, Doi** ▲ NW Thailand

180 I4 **Maevatanana** Mahajanga, C Madagascar

197 O12 **Maewo** *prev.* Aurora. *island* C Vanuatu

175 T8 **Mafa** Pulau Halmahera, E Indonesia

85 I23 **Mafeteng** W Lesotho

101 J21 **Maffe** Namur, SE Belgium

176 Y10 **Maffin** Irian Jaya, E Indonesia

191 R10 **Maffra** Victoria, SE Australia

83 K23 **Mafia** *island* E Tanzania

83 J23 **Mafia Channel** *sea waterway* E Tanzania

85 I21 **Mafikeng** North-West, N South Africa

62 J12 **Mafra** Santa Catarina, S Brazil

106 F10 **Mafra** Lisboa, C Portugal

149 Q17 **Mafraq/Mafraq, Muḩāfaẓat al** *see* Al Mafraq

127 O14 **Magadan** Magadanskaya Oblast', E Russian Federation

127 N10 **Magadanskaya Oblast'** ◆ *province* E Russian Federation

110 G11 **Magadino** Ticino, S Switzerland

65 G23 **Magallanes** *off.* Región de Magallanes y de la Antártica Chilena. ◇ *region* S Chile

Magallanes *see* Punta Arenas

Magallanes, Estrecho de *see* Magellan, Strait of

12 I14 **Maganasipi, Lac** ⊙ Québec, SE Canada

56 I4 **Magangué** Bolívar, N Colombia

79 V12 **Magaria** Zinder, S Niger

194 M16 **Magarida** Central, SW PNG

179 Pp9 **Magat** ≈ Luzon, N Philippines

29 T11 **Magazine Mountain** ▲ Arkansas, C USA

78 I15 **Magburaka** C Sierra Leone

126 M14 **Magdagachi** Amurskaya Oblast', SE Russian Federation

64 O12 **Magdalena** Buenos Aires, E Argentina

59 M15 **Magdalena** Beni, N Bolivia

42 F4 **Magdalena** Sonora, NW Mexico

39 Q13 **Magdalena** New Mexico, SW USA

56 F5 **Magdalena** *off.* Departamento del Magdalena. ◆ *province* N Colombia

42 E9 **Magdalena, Bahía** *bay* W Mexico

65 G19 **Magdalena, Isla** *island* Archipiélago de los Chonos, S Chile

42 D8 **Magdalena, Isla** *island* W Mexico

49 P6 **Magdalena, Río** ≈ C Colombia

42 F4 **Magdalena, Río** ≈ NW Mexico

Magdalen Islands *see* Madeleine, Îles de la

102 L13 **Magdeburg** Sachsen-Anhalt, C Germany

24 L6 **Magee** Mississippi, S USA

174 Kk15 **Magelang** Jawa, C Indonesia

199 J7 **Magellan Rise** *undersea feature* C Pacific Ocean

65 H24 **Magellan, Strait of** *Sp.* Estrecho de Magallanes. *strait* Argentina/Chile

108 D7 **Magenta** Lombardia, NW Italy

94 K7 **Magerøya** *var.* Mageroy. *island* N Norway

170 B17 **Mage-shima** *island* Nansei-shotō, SW Japan

110 G13 **Maggia** Ticino, S Switzerland

110 G10 **Maggia** ≈ SW Switzerland

108 C6 **Maggiore, Lago** *see* Maggiore, Lake

108 C6 **Maggiore, Lake** *It.* Lago Maggiore. ⊙ Italy/Switzerland

46 J12 **Maggotty** W Jamaica

78 I10 **Maghama** Gorgol, S Mauritania

99 F14 **Maghera** *Ir.* Machaire Rátha. N Northern Ireland, UK

99 F15 **Magherafelt** *Ir.* Machaire Fíolta. C Northern Ireland, UK

196 H5 **Magicienne Bay** *bay* Saipan, S Northern Mariana Islands

107 O13 **Magina** ▲ S Spain

83 H22 **Magingo** Rukwa, S Tanzania

127 Jj14 **Magistral'nyy** Irkutskaya Oblast', S Russian Federation

114 H11 **Maglaj** N Bosnia and Herzegovina

109 Q19 **Maglie** Puglia, SE Italy

38 L2 **Magna** Utah, W USA

Magnesia *see* Manisa

12 G12 **Magnetawan** ≈ Ontario, S Canada

125 Dd12 **Magnitogorsk** Chelyabinskaya Oblast', C Russian Federation

29 T14 **Magnolia** Arkansas, C USA

24 K7 **Magnolia** Mississippi, S USA

27 V10 **Magnolia** Texas, SW USA

Magnolia State *see* Mississippi

97 J15 **Magnor** Hedmark, S Norway

197 K14 **Mago** *prev.* Mango. *island* Lau Group, E Fiji

13 Q13 **Mágoé** Tete, NW Mozambique

13 U13 **Magog** Québec, SE Canada

13 S15 **Magoye** Southern, S Zambia

43 O12 **Magozal** Veracruz-Llave, C Mexico

37 P3 **Magrath** Alberta, SW Canada

107 R10 **Magro** ≈ E Spain

78 I9 **Magta' Lahjar** *var.* Magta Lahjar, Magtá' Lahjar, Magtá Lahjar. Brakna, SW Mauritania

202 J2 **Magude** Maputo, S Mozambique

79 U12 **Magumeri** Borno, NE Nigeria

201 O14 **Magur Islands** *island group* Caroline Islands, C Micronesia

177 Ff6 **Magway** *see* Magwe

177 Ff6 **Magwe** *var.* Magway. Magwe, W Myanmar

177 Ff7 **Magwe** ◆ *division* C Myanmar

---

148 J4 **Mahābād** *var.* Mehabad; *prev.* Säüjbulāgh. Āzarbāyjān-e Bākhtari, NW Iran

180 H5 **Mahabo** Toliara, W Madagascar

Maha Chai *see* Samut Sakhon

161 D14 **Mahād** Mahārāshtra, W India

83 N17 **Mahadday Weyne** Shabeellaha Dhexe, C Somalia

81 Q7 **Mahagi** Haut-Zaïre, NE Zaire

180 I4 **Mahajamba** *seasonal river* NW Madagascar

158 G10 **Mahājan** Rājasthān, NW India

180 I3 **Mahajanga** *var.* Majunga. Mahajanga, NW Madagascar

180 I3 **Mahajanga** ◆ *province* W Madagascar

180 I2 **Mahajanga** ✈ Mahajanga, NW Madagascar

175 N7 **Mahakam, Sungai** *var.* Koetai, Kutai. ≈ Borneo, C Indonesia

85 I19 **Mahalapye** *var.* Mahalatswe. Central, SE Botswana

Mahalatswe *see* Mahalapye

175 Q10 **Mahalona** Sulawesi, C Indonesia

Mahameru *see* Semeru, Gunung

149 S11 **Mahān** Kermān, E Iran

160 N12 **Mahanādi** ≈ E India

180 J5 **Mahanoro** Toamasina, E Madagascar

159 P13 **Mahārājganj** Bihār, N India

160 G13 **Mahārāshtra** ◆ *state* W India

Mahasaragam *see* Maha Sarakham

180 I4 **Mahavavy** *seasonal river* N Madagascar

161 K24 **Mahaweli Ganga** ≈ Sri Lanka

Mahbés *see* El Mahbas

161 I15 **Mahbūbābād** Andhra Pradesh, E India

161 H16 **Mahbūbnagar** Andhra Pradesh, SW India

146 M8 **Mahd adh Dhahab** Al Madīnah, W Saudi Arabia

57 S9 **Mahdia** C Guyana

77 N6 **Mahdia** *var.* Al Mahdīyah, Mehdia. NE Tunisia

161 F20 **Mahe** *Fr.* Mahé; *prev.* Mayyali. Pondicherry, SE India

180 I16 **Mahé** ✈ Mahé, NE Seychelles

180 H16 **Mahé** *island* Inner Islands, NE Seychelles

181 Y17 **Mahebourg** SE Mauritius

158 I11 **Mahendragarh** Haryāna, N India

158 L10 **Mahendranagar** Far Western, W Nepal

83 J23 **Mahenge** Morogoro, SE Tanzania

193 F22 **Maheno** Otago, South Island, NZ

160 I9 **Mahésāna** Gujarāt, W India

160 F11 **Maheshwar** Madhya Pradesh, C India

157 F14 **Mahi** ≈ N India

192 Q10 **Mahia Peninsula** *peninsula* North Island, NZ

121 O16 **Mahilyow** *Rus.* Mogilëv. Mahilyowskaya Voblasts', E Belarus

121 M16 **Mahilyowskaya Voblasts'** *prev. Rus.* Mogilëvskaya Oblast'. ◆ *province* E Belarus

203 P7 **Mahina** Tahiti, W French Polynesia

193 E23 **Mahinerangi, Lake** ⊙ South Island, NZ

85 L22 **Mahlabatini** KwaZulu/Natal, E South Africa

177 G5 **Mahlaing** Mandalay, C Myanmar

111 X8 **Mahldorf** Steiermark, SE Austria

99 C23 **Mahón** *Cat.* Maó, *Eng.* Port Mahon; *anc.* Portus Magonis. Menorca, Spain, W Mediterranean Sea

20 D14 **Mahoning Creek Lake** ⊙ Pennsylvania, NE USA

107 Q10 **Mahora** Castilla-La Mancha, C Spain

171 H14 **Mahoba** Uttar Pradesh, N India

190 I9 **Maitland** South Australia

190 I9 **Maitland** ◇ Ontario, S Canada

191 T8 **Maitland** New South Wales, SE Australia

205 R1 **Maitri** *Indian research station* Antarctica

20 D14 **Maizhokunggar** Xizang Zizhiqu, W China

161 N15 **Maíz, Islas del** *var.* Corn Islands. *island group* SE Nicaragua

45 O10 **Maizuru** Kyōto, Honshū, SW Japan

56 F6 **Majagual** Sucre, N Colombia

43 Z13 **Majahual** Quintana Roo, E Mexico

159 R14 **Majārdah, Wādī** *see* Medjerda, Oued/Mejrda

Majene *prev.* Madjene. Sulawesi, C Indonesia 175 P11

81 K17 **Maj/Majë** *see* Mejit Island

114 M9 **Majevica** ▲ NE Bosnia and Herzegovina

83 M15 **Maji** SW Ethiopia

147 X7 **Majis** NW Oman

116 N11 **Māhwa Dağı** ▲ NW Turkey

107 T6 **Maials** *var.* Mayals. Cataluña, NE Spain

203 O2 **Maiana** *prev.* Hall Island. *atoll* Tungaru, W Kiribati

203 S11 **Maiao** *var.* Tapuaemanu, Tubuai-Manu. *island* Îles du Vent, W French Polynesia

56 H4 **Maicao** La Guajira, N Colombia

Mai Ceu/Mai Chio *see* Maych'ew

99 N22 **Maidenhead** S England, UK

---

9 S15 **Maidstone** Saskatchewan, S Canada

99 P22 **Maidstone** SE England, UK

79 Y13 **Maiduguri** Borno, NE Nigeria

110 I8 **Maienfeld** Sankt Gallen, NE Switzerland

118 J12 **Măieruş** *Hung.* Szászmagyarós. Braşov, C Romania

Maigh Chromtha *see* Macroom

Maigh Eo *see* Mayo

57 N9 **Maigualida, Sierra** ▲ S Venezuela

160 K9 **Maihar** Madhya Pradesh, C India

69 T10 **Maiko** ≈ W Zaire

Mailand *see* Milano

158 L11 **Mailāni** Uttar Pradesh, N India

155 U10 **Maïhlo** Diffa, SE Niger

153 R8 **Maimak** Talasskaya Oblast', NW Kyrgyzstan

Maimāna *see* Meymaneh

Maimansingh *see* Mymensingh

176 Vv11 **Maimuwa** Irian Jaya, E Indonesia

Maimuna *see* Al Maymūnah

103 G18 **Main** ≈ C Germany

117 F22 **Mainburg** Bayern, SE Germany

117 E20 **Maínalo** ▲ S Greece

103 L22 **Mainburg** Bayern, SE Germany

12 E12 **Main Channel** *lake channel* Ontario, S Canada

81 I20 **Mai-Ndombe, Lac** *prev.* Lac Léopold II. ⊙ W Zaire

103 K20 **Main-Donau-Kanal** *canal* SE Germany

21 R6 **Maine** *off.* State of Maine; also known as Lumber State, Pine Tree State. ◆ *state* NE USA

104 K6 **Maine** *cultural region* NW France

104 J7 **Maine-et-Loire** ◆ *department* NW France

21 Q7 **Maine, Gulf of** *gulf* NE USA

79 X12 **Maïné-Soroa** Diffa, SE Niger

178 Gg1 **Maingkwan** *var.* Mungkawn. Kachin State, N Myanmar

Main Island *see* Bermuda

Mainistir Fhear Maí *see* Fermoy

Mainistir na Corann *see* Midleton

Mainistir na Féile *see* Abbeyfeale

98 J5 **Mainland** *island* Orkney, N Scotland, UK

98 L2 **Mainland** *island* Shetland, NE Scotland, UK

165 P16 **Mainling** Xizang Zizhiqu, W China

158 K12 **Mainpuri** Uttar Pradesh, N India

105 N5 **Maintenon** Eure-et-Loir, C France

180 H4 **Maintirano** Mahajanga, W Madagascar

95 M15 **Mainua** Oulu, C Finland

103 D18 **Mainz** *Fr.* Mayence. Rheinland-Pfalz, SW Germany

78 E10 **Maio** *var.* Vila do Maio. Maio, S Cape Verde

78 E10 **Maio** *var.* Mayo. *island* Ilhas de Sotavento, SE Cape Verde

64 G2 **Maipo, Río** ≈ C Chile

64 H2 **Maipo, Volcán** ▲ W Argentina

63 E22 **Maipú** Buenos Aires, E Argentina

64 I11 **Maipú** Mendoza, E Argentina

64 H11 **Maipú** Santiago, C Chile

56 L5 **Maiquetía** Distrito Federal, N Venezuela

110 I10 **Maira** *It.* Mera. ≈ Italy/Switzerland

108 A9 **Maira** ≈ NW Italy

159 U10 **Maïrābāri** Assam, NE India

46 K7 **Maisí** Guantánamo, E Cuba

120 H13 **Maišiagala** Vilnius, SE Lithuania

159 V17 **Maiskhal Island** *island* SE Bangladesh

178 Gg13 **Mai Sombun** Chumphon, SW Thailand

178 H4 **Maitland** South Australia

---

40 B8 **Makahuena Point** *headland* Kauai, Hawaii, USA, C Pacific Ocean

40 D9 **Makakilo City** Oahu, Hawaii, USA, C Pacific Ocean

85 H18 **Makalamabedi** Central, C Botswana

Makale *see* Mek'elē

164 K17 **Makalu Chin.** Makaru Shan. ▲ China/Nepal

95 I14 **Makampi** Mbeya, S Tanzania

151 X12 **Makanchi** *Kaz.* Maqanshy. Semipalatinsk, E Kazakhstan

44 M8 **Makantaka** Región Autónoma Atlántico Norte, NE Nicaragua

202 B16 **Makapu Point** *headland* W Niue

193 C24 **Makarewa** Southland, South Island, NZ

119 O4 **Makariv** Kyyivs'ka Oblast', N Ukraine

193 D20 **Makarora** ≈ South Island, NZ

127 Oo15 **Makarov** Ostrov Sakhalin, Sakhalinskaya Oblast', SE Russian Federation

199 Hh4 **Makarov Basin** *undersea feature* Arctic Ocean

199 Hh4 **Makarov Seamount** *undersea feature* W Pacific Ocean

113 G20 **Makarska** *It.* Macarsca. Split-Dalmacija, SE Croatia

115 F15 **Makarska** *It.* Macarsca. Split-Dalmacija, SE Croatia

129 O15 **Makar'yev** Kostromskaya Oblast', NW Russian Federation

84 L11 **Makasa** Northern, NE Zambia

Makasar, Selat *see* Ujungpandang

Makasar, Selat *see* Makassar Straits

Makassar *see* Ujungpandang

198 Ff8 **Makassar Straits** *Ind.* Selat Makasar. *strait* C Indonesia

150 G12 **Makat** *Kaz.* Maqat. Atyrau, SW Kazakhstan

203 T10 **Makatea** *island* Îles Tuamotu, C French Polynesia

155 U7 **Makātū** E Iraq

180 H6 **Makay** *var.* Massif du Makay. ▲ SW Madagascar

116 J12 **Makaza** *pass* Bulgaria/Greece

176 Uu9 **Makbon** Irian Jaya, E Indonesia

115 M17 **Makedonija** *see* Macedonia, FYR

202 B16 **Makefu** W Niue

78 I15 **Makeni** C Sierra Leone

Makenzen *see* Orlyak

Makeyevka *see* Makiyivka

131 Q16 **Makhachkala** *prev.* Petrovsk-Port. Respublika Dagestan, SW Russian Federation

150 F11 **Makhambet** Atyrau, W Kazakhstan

145 O14 **Makhfar Al Buşayyah** S Iraq

145 R4 **Makhmūr** N Iraq

144 I11 **Makhrūq, Wadi al** *dry watercourse* E Jordan

145 R4 **Makhūl, Jabal** ▲ C Iraq

147 R13 **Makhyah, Wādī** *dry watercourse* N Yemen

176 W11 **Maki** Irian Jaya, E Indonesia

175 Ss8 **Makian, Pulau** *island* Maluku, E Indonesia

193 G21 **Makikihi** Canterbury, South Island, NZ

203 O2 **Makin** *prev.* Pitt Island. *atoll* Tungaru, W Kiribati

83 I20 **Makindu** Eastern, S Kenya

151 Q8 **Makinsk** Akmola, N Kazakhstan

195 Y17 **Makira** *var.* Makira Province. ◆ *province* SE Solomon Islands

Makira *see* San Cristobal

119 X8 **Makiyivka** *Rus.* Makeyevka; *prev.* Dmitriyevsk. Donets'ka Oblast', E Ukraine

146 L10 **Makkah** *Eng.* Mecca. Makkah, W Saudi Arabia

146 M10 **Makkah** *var.* Minṭaqat Makkah. ◆ *province* W Saudi Arabia

11 R7 **Makkovik** Newfoundland and Labrador, NE Canada

100 K6 **Makkum** Friesland, N Netherlands

Mako *see* Makung

113 M25 **Makó** *Rom.* Macău. Csongrád, SE Hungary

12 G9 **Makobe Lake** ⊙ Ontario, S Canada

197 I14 **Makogai** *island* C Fiji

81 F18 **Makokou** Ogooué-Ivindo, NE Gabon

83 G23 **Makongolosi** Mbeya, S Tanzania

83 E19 **Makota** SW Uganda

81 J18 **Makoua** Cuvette, C Congo

112 M10 **Maków Mazowiecki** Ostrołęka, E Poland

113 K17 **Maków Podhalański** Bielsko-Biała, S Poland

179 V14 **Makran** *cultural region* Iran/Pakistan

158 G12 **Makrāna** Rājasthān, N India

149 U15 **Makran Coast** *coastal region* SE Iran

121 F20 **Makrany** *Rus.* Mokrany. Brestskaya Voblasts', SW Belarus

131 R8 **Makrasa** Tahoua, S Niger

45 O10 **Makrinoros** *see* Makrynoros

117 G17 **Makronisos** ▲ C Greece

117 E20 **Makrónisos** *island* Kykládes, Greece, Aegean Sea

117 D17 **Makrynoros** *var.* Makrinoros. ▲ C Greece

117 J15 **Makryplági** ▲ C Greece

161 J15 **Maksatiha** *var.* Maksatikha, Maksaticha. Tverskaya Oblast', W Russian Federation

160 M10 **Maksi** Madhya Pradesh, C India

148 J7 **Mākū** Āzarbāyjān-e Bākhtari, NW Iran

159 T11 **Mākum** Assam, NE India

197 O8 **Makun** *see* Makung

179 R14 **Makung** *var.* Mako, Makun. W Taiwan

170 Bb16 **Makurazaki** Kagoshima, Kyūshū, SW Japan

79 U15 **Makurdi** Benue, C Nigeria

---

125 F12 **Makushino** Kurganskaya Oblast', C Russian Federation

40 L17 **Makushin Volcano** ▲ Unalaska Island, Alaska, USA

85 K16 **Makwiro** Mashonaland West, N Zimbabwe

59 D15 **Mala** Lima, W Peru

Mala *see* Mallow, Ireland

Mala *see* Malaita, Solomon Islands

95 J14 **Mala** Västerbotten, N Sweden

202 G12 **Mala'atoli** Île Uvea, E Wallis and Futuna

179 Qq15 **Malabang** *see* Malabang

161 E21 **Malabar Coast** *coast* SW India

81 C16 **Malabo** *prev.* Santa Isabel. ● (Equatorial Guinea) Isla de Bioco, NW Equatorial Guinea

81 C16 **Malabo** ✈ Isla de Bioco, N Equatorial Guinea

Malaca *see* Málaga

Malacca *see* Melaka

173 G4 **Malacca, Strait of** *Ind.* Selat Malaka. *strait* Indonesia/Malaysia

Malacka *see* Malacky

113 G20 **Malacky** *Hung.* Malacka. Bratislavský Kraj, W Slovakia

35 R16 **Malad City** Idaho, NW USA

119 Q4 **Mala Divytsya** Chernihivs'ka Oblast', N Ukraine

121 J15 **Maladzyechna** *Pol.* Molodeczno, *Rus.* Molodechno. Minskaya Voblasts', C Belarus

202 D12 **Malae** Île Futuna, N Wallis and Futuna

39 V15 **Malaga** New Mexico, USA

56 G8 **Málaga** Santander, C Colombia

106 M15 **Málaga** *anc.* Malaca. Andalucía, S Spain

106 L15 **Málaga** ◆ *province* Andalucía, S Spain

106 M15 **Málaga** ✈ Andalucía, S Spain

Malagasy Republic *see* Madagascar

107 N10 **Malagón** Castilla-La Mancha, C Spain

99 G18 **Malahide** *Ir.* Mullach Íde. E Ireland

195 Y14 **Malaita** *off.* Malaita Province. ◆ *province* N Solomon Islands

195 Y15 **Malaita** *var.* Mala. *island* N Solomon Islands

82 F13 **Malakal** Upper Nile, S Sudan

114 C10 **Mala Kapela** ▲ NW Croatia

27 V7 **Malakoff** Texas, SW USA

155 V7 **Malakula** *see* Malekula

194 J14 **Malalamai** Madang, W PNG

194 J14 **Malalaua** Gulf, S PNG

175 Q11 **Malamala** Sulawesi, C Indonesia

174 M15 **Malang** Jawa, C Indonesia

85 O14 **Malanga** Niassa, N Mozambique

Malange *see* Malanje

94 I9 **Malangen** *sound* N Norway

84 C11 **Malanje** *var.* Malange. Malanje, NW Angola

84 C11 **Malanje** *var.* Malange. ◆ *province* N Angola

154 M16 **Malān, Rās** *headland* SW Pakistan

79 S13 **Malanville** NE Benin

Malapane *see* Ozimek

161 F21 **Malappuram** Kerala, SW India

45 T17 **Mala, Punta** *headland* S Panama

97 N16 **Mälaren** ◇ C Sweden

64 H13 **Malargüe** Mendoza, W Argentina

12 J8 **Malartic** Québec, SE Canada

12 F20 **Malaryta** *Pol.* Maloryta, *Rus.* Malorita. Brestskaya Voblasts', SW Belarus

65 J9 **Malaspina** Chubut, SE Argentina

41 U12 **Malaspina Glacier** *glacier* Alaska, USA

143 N15 **Malatya** *anc.* Melitene. Malatya, SE Turkey

142 M14 **Malatya** ◆ *province* C Turkey

119 Q7 **Mala Vyska** *Rus.* Malaya Viska. Kirovohrads'ka Oblast', S Ukraine

85 M14 **Malawi** *off.* Republic of Malaŵi; *prev.* Nyasaland, Nyasaland Protectorate. ◆ *republic* S Africa

Malawi, Lake *see* Nyasa, Lake

95 I17 **Malax** *Fin.* Maalahti. Vaasa, W Finland

128 M14 **Malaya Vishera** Novgorodskaya Oblast', W Russian Federation

Malaya Viska *see* Mala Vyska

179 R13 **Malaybalay** Mindanao, S Philippines

148 L6 **Malāyer** *prev.* Daulatabad. Hamadān, W Iran

174 Yg3 **Malay Peninsula** *peninsula* Malaysia/Thailand

174 I3 **Malaysia** *var.* Federation of Malaysia; *prev.* the separate territories of Federation of Malaya, Sarawak and Sabah (North Borneo) and Singapore. ◆ *monarchy* SE Asia

143 R8 **Malazgirt** Muş, E Turkey

13 R8 **Malbaie** ⊙ Québec, SE Canada

79 T3 **Malbaza** Tahoua, S Niger

112 J7 **Malbork** *Ger.* Marienburg, Marienburg in Westpreussen. Elbląg, N Poland

102 N9 **Malchin** Mecklenburg-Vorpommern, N Germany

102 M9 **Malchiner See** ⊙ NE Germany

Mälda *see* Māldah

101 D16 **Maldegem** Oost-Vlaanderen, NW Belgium

100 L13 **Malden** Gelderland, SE Netherlands

21 O11 **Malden** Massachusetts, NE USA

29 Y8 **Malden** Missouri, C USA

203 X4 **Malden Island** *prev.* Independence Island. *atoll* E Kiribati

181 Q6 **Maldives** *off.* Maldivian Divehi, Republic of Maldives. ◆ *republic* N Indian Ocean

Maldivian Divehi *see* Maldives

99 P21 **Maldon** E England, UK

◆ COUNTRY ◇ DEPENDENT TERRITORY ✦ ADMINISTRATIVE REGION ▲ MOUNTAIN ⊼ VOLCANO ⊙ LAKE
● COUNTRY CAPITAL ○ DEPENDENT TERRITORY CAPITAL ✈ INTERNATIONAL AIRPORT ▲ MOUNTAIN RANGE ≈ RIVER ⊟ RESERVOIR

63 G20 **Maldonado** Maldonado, S Uruguay

63 G20 **Maldonado** ◆ *department* S Uruguay

43 P17 **Maldonado, Punta** *headland* S Mexico

157 K19 **Male' Div.** Maale ● (Maldives) Male' Atoll, C Maldives

108 G6 **Malè** Trentino-Alto Adige, N Italy

78 K13 **Maléa** *var.* Maléya. Haute-Guinée, E Guinea

117 G22 **Maléas, Ákra** *headland* S Greece

117 L17 **Maléas, Ákra** *headland* Lésvos, E Greece

157 K19 **Male' Atoll** *var.* Kaafu Atoll. *atoll* C Maldives

Malebo, Pool *see* Stanley Pool

160 E12 **Malegaon** Mahārāshtra, W India

83 F15 **Malek** Jonglei, S Sudan

197 B13 **Malekula** *var.* Malakula; *prev.* Mallicolo. *island* W Vanuatu

201 Y15 **Malem** Kosrae, E Micronesia

85 O15 **Malema** Nampula, N Mozambique

81 N23 **Malemba-Nkulu** Shaba, SE Zaire

195 Q10 **Malendok Island** *island* Tanga Islands, NE PNG

128 K9 **Malen'ga** Respublika Kareliya, NW Russian Federation

97 M20 **Målerås** Kalmar, S Sweden

105 O6 **Malesherbes** Loiret, C France

117 G18 **Malesína** Stereá Ellás, E Greece

Maléya *see* Maléa

131 O15 **Malgobek** Chechenskaya Respublika, SW Russian Federation

107 X5 **Malgrat de Mar** Cataluña, NE Spain

82 C9 **Malha** Northern Darfur, W Sudan

145 Q5 **Malḩaţ** C Iraq

34 K14 **Malheur Lake** ◎ Oregon, NW USA

34 L14 **Malheur River** ☞ Oregon, NW USA

78 I13 **Mali** Moyenne-Guinée, NE Guinea

79 O9 **Mali** *off.* Republic of Mali, *Fr.* République du Mali; *prev.* French Sudan, Sudanese Republic. ◆ *republic* W Africa

175 S16 **Maliana** Timor, S Indonesia

178 H1 **Mali Hka** ☞ N Myanmar

Mali Idjoš *see* Mali Idoš

114 K8 **Mali Idoš** *var.* Mali Idjoš, *Hung.* Kishegyes; *prev.* Krivaja. Serbia, N Yugoslavia

114 K9 **Mali Kanal** *canal* N Yugoslavia

175 R8 **Maliku** Sulawesi, N Indonesia

Malik, Wadi al *see* Milk, Wadi el

Mälikwäla *see* Mälewala

178 Gg12 **Mali Kyun** *var.* Tavoy Island. *island* Mergui Archipelago, S Myanmar

97 M19 **Malilla** Kalmar, S Sweden

114 B11 **Mali Lošinj** *It.* Lussinpiccolo. Primorje-Gorski Kotar, W Croatia

Malin *see* Malyn

179 Q15 **Malindang, Mount** ▲ Mindanao, S Philippines

83 K20 **Malindi** Coast, SE Kenya

Malines *see* Mechelen

98 E13 **Malin Head** *Ir.* Cionn Mhálanna. *headland* NW Ireland

175 Pp7 **Malino, Gunung** ▲ Sulawesi, N Indonesia

115 M21 **Maliq** *var.* Maliqi. Korçë, SE Albania

Maliqi *see* Maliq

179 Rr16 **Malita** Mindanao, S Philippines

160 E12 **Malkāpur** Mahārāshtra, C India

142 B10 **Malkara** Tekirdağ, NW Turkey

121 J19 **Mal'kavichy** *Rus.* Mal'kovichi. Brestskaya Voblasts', SW Belarus

Malkiye *see* Al Mālikiyah

116 L11 **Malko Sharkovo, Yazovir** ☐ SE Bulgaria

116 N11 **Malko Tŭrnovo** Burgaska Oblast, SE Bulgaria

Mal'kovichi *see* Mal'kavichy

191 R12 **Mallacoota** Victoria, SE Australia

98 G10 **Mallaig** N Scotland, UK

190 I9 **Mallala** South Australia

77 W9 **Mallawi** C Egypt

107 R5 **Mallén** Aragón, NE Spain

108 F5 **Malles Venosta** Trentino-Alto Adige, N Italy

Mallicolo *see* Malekula

111 Q8 **Mallnitz** Salzburg, S Austria

107 W9 **Mallorca** *Eng.* Majorca; *anc.* Baleares Major. *island* Islas Baleares, Spain, W Mediterranean Sea

99 C20 **Mallow** *Ir.* Mala. SW Ireland

95 F15 **Malm** Nord-Trøndelag, C Norway

97 L19 **Malmbäck** Jönköping, S Sweden

94 J12 **Malmberget** Norrbotten, N Sweden

101 M20 **Malmédy** Liège, E Belgium

85 E25 **Malmesbury** Western Cape, SW South Africa

97 N16 **Malmköping** Södermanland, C Sweden

97 K23 **Malmo** ✈ Malmöhus, S Sweden

97 K23 **Malmö** Malmöhus, S Sweden

97 K23 **Malmöhus** ◆ *county* S Sweden

47 Q16 **Malmok** *headland* Bonaire, S Netherlands Antilles

97 M18 **Malmslätt** Östergötland, S Sweden

129 R16 **Malmyzh** Kirovskaya Oblast', NW Russian Federation

58 A10 **Mal Nombre, Punta** *headland* NW Peru

192 B12 **Malo** *island* W Vanuatu

130 J7 **Maloarkhangel'sk** Orlovskaya Oblast', W Russian Federation

201 V6 **Maloelap** *var.* Maloelap Atoll. *atoll* E Marshall Islands

Maloenda *see* Malunda

110 I10 **Maloja** Graubünden, S Switzerland

84 L12 **Malole** Northern, NE Zambia

197 H13 **Malolo** *island* Mamanuca Group, W Fiji

179 P10 **Malolos** Luzon, N Philippines

20 K5 **Malone** New York, NE USA

81 K25 **Malonga** Shaba, S Zaire

113 L15 **Małopolska** *plateau* S Poland

Malorita/Maloryta *see* Malaryta

128 K9 **Maloshuyka** Arkhangel'skaya Oblast', NW Russian Federation

116 G10 **Mal'ovitsa** ▲ W Bulgaria

151 V15 **Malovodnoye** Almaty, SE Kazakhstan

96 C10 **Måløy** Sogn og Fjordane, S Norway

130 K4 **Maloyaroslavets** Kaluzhskaya Oblast', W Russian Federation

125 F6 **Malozemel'skaya Tundra** *physical region* NW Russian Federation

106 J10 **Malpartida de Cáceres** Extremadura, W Spain

106 K9 **Malpartida de Plasencia** Extremadura, W Spain

108 C7 **Malpensa** ✈ (Milano) Lombardia, N Italy

78 J6 **Malqteïr** *desert* N Mauritania

120 J10 **Malta** Rēzekne, SE Latvia

35 V7 **Malta** Montana, NW USA

123 Jj14 **Malta** ● Republic of Malta. ◆ *republic* C Mediterranean Sea

111 R8 **Malta** *var.* Maltabach. ☞ S Austria

123 L11 **Malta** *island* Malta, C Mediterranean Sea

Maltabach *see* Malta

Malta, Canale di *see* Malta Channel

123 L12 **Malta Channel** *It.* Canale di Malta. *strait* Italy/Malta

85 D20 **Maltahöhe** Hardap, SW Namibia

99 N16 **Malton** N England, UK

175 T11 **Maluku** *off.* Propinsi Maluku, *Dut.* Molukken, *Eng.* Moluccas. ◆ *province* E Indonesia

175 S9 **Maluku** *Dut.* Molukken, *Eng.* Moluccas; *prev.* Spice Islands. *island group* E Indonesia

Maluku, Laut *see* Molucca Sea

79 V13 **Malumfashi** Katsina, N Nigeria

175 P11 **Malunda** *prev.* Maloenda. Sulawesi, C Indonesia

96 K13 **Malung** Kopparberg, C Sweden

96 K13 **Malungsfors** Kopparberg, C Sweden

195 X14 **Maluu** *var.* Malu'u. Malaita, N Solomon Islands

161 D16 **Mālvan** Mahārāshtra, W India

29 X11 **Malvern** Arkansas, C USA

31 S15 **Malvern** Iowa, C USA

46 I13 **Malvern** ▲ W Jamaica

Malvinas, Islas *see* Falkland Islands

119 N4 **Malyn** *Rus.* Malin. Zhytomyrs'ka Oblast', N Ukraine

127 O5 **Malyy Anyuy** ☞ NE Russian Federation

159 U12 **Malyy** *var.* Dangme Chu. ☞ Bhutan/India

131 N3 **Malyye Derbety** Respublika Kalmykiya, SW Russian Federation

Malyy Kavkaz *see* Lesser Caucasus

126 M5 **Malyy Lyakhovskiy, Ostrov** *island* NE Russian Federation

Malyy Pamir *see* Little Pamir

126 Jj4 **Malyy Taymyr, Ostrov** *island* Severnaya Zemlya, N Russian Federation

150 D12 **Malyy Uzen'** *Kaz.* Kishiözen. ☞ Kazakhstan/Russian Federation

126 I16 **Malyy Yenisey** *var.* Ka-Krem. ☞ S Russian Federation

126 K13 **Mama** Irkutskaya Oblast', E Russian Federation

131 S3 **Mamadysh** Respublika Tatarstan, W Russian Federation

119 N10 **Mamaia** Constanţa, E Romania

197 G14 **Mamanuca Group** *island group* Yasawa Group, W Fiji

152 L13 **Mamash** Lebapskiy Velayat, E Turkmenistan

176 W11 **Mamasiware** Irian Jaya, E Indonesia

194 L14 **Mambare** ☞ S PNG

81 O17 **Mambasa** Haut-Zaïre, NE Zaire

176 Xx10 **Mamberamo, Sungai** ☞ Irian Jaya, E Indonesia

81 G15 **Mambéré** ☞ SW Central African Republic

81 G15 **Mambéré-Kadéï** ◆ *prefecture* SW Central African Republic

176 X9 **Mambetaloi** Irian Jaya, E Indonesia

Mambij *see* Manbij

81 N18 **Mambili** ☞ W Congo

85 N18 **Mambone** *var.* Nova Mambone. Inhambane, E Mozambique

179 P11 **Mamburao** Mindoro, N Philippines

180 I16 **Mamelles** *island* Inner Islands, NE Seychelles

101 M23 **Mamer** Luxembourg, SW Luxembourg

104 L6 **Mamers** Sarthe, NW France

80 B14 **Mamfe** Sud-Ouest, W Cameroon

168 I5 **Mamit** Hövsgöl, N Mongolia

168 L7 **Mamit** Töv, C Mongolia

177 X5 **Mamlyutka** Severnyy Kazakhstan, N Kazakhstan

38 M5 **Mammoth** Arizona, SW USA

35 S12 **Mammoth Hot Springs** Wyoming, C USA

Mamoedjoe *see* Mamuju

121 A14 **Mamonovo** *Ger.* Heiligenbeil. Kaliningradskaya Oblast', W Russian Federation

59 N14 **Mamoré, Río** ☞ Bolivia/Brazil

78 I16 **Mamou** Moyenne-Guinée, W Guinea

24 H8 **Mamou** Louisiana, S USA

180 I14 **Mamoudzou** ● (Mayotte) C Mayotte

180 I3 **Mampikony** Mahajanga, N Madagascar

79 P16 **Mampong** C Ghana

112 M7 **Mamry, Jezioro** *Ger.* Mauersee. ◎ NE Poland

175 P10 **Mamuju** *prev.* Mamoedjoe. Sulawesi, S Indonesia

175 O10 **Mamuju, Teluk** *bay* Sulawesi, C Indonesia

85 F19 **Mamuno** Ghanzi, W Botswana

115 K19 **Mamuras** *var.* Mamurras, Mamurrasi. Lezhë, C Albania

Mamurasi/Mamurras *see* Mamuras

78 L16 **Man** W Ivory Coast

57 X9 **Mana** NW French Guiana

58 A6 **Manabí** ◆ *province* W Ecuador

44 G4 **Manabíque, Punta** *var.* Cabo Tres Puntas. *headland* E Guatemala

56 G11 **Manacacías, Río** ☞ C Colombia

60 F13 **Manacapuru** Amazonas, N Brazil

175 Rr6 **Manado** *prev.* Menado. Sulawesi, C Indonesia

196 H5 **Managaha** *island* S Northern Mariana Islands

181 G20 **Manage** Hainaut, S Belgium

44 J10 **Managua** ● (Nicaragua) Managua, W Nicaragua

44 J10 **Managua** ◆ *department* W Nicaragua

44 J10 **Managua** ✈ Managua, C Nicaragua

44 J10 **Managua, Lago de** *var.* Xolotlán. ◎ W Nicaragua

Manaḩ *see* Bilād Manaḩ

20 K16 **Manahawkin** New Jersey, NE USA

192 K11 **Manaia** Taranaki, North Island, NZ

180 J6 **Manakara** Fianarantsoa, SE Madagascar

158 J7 **Manāli** Himāchal Pradesh, NW India

133 U12 **Ma, Nam** *Vtn.* Sông Mã. ☞ Laos/Vietnam

Manama *see* Al Manāmah

194 M10 **Manam Island** *island* N PNG

69 Y13 **Mananara** ☞ SE Madagascar

190 M9 **Manangatang** Victoria, SE Australia

180 J6 **Mananjary** Fianarantsoa, SE Madagascar

78 J12 **Manankoro** Sikasso, SW Mali

79 P12 **Mané** C Burkina

108 E8 **Manerbio** Lombardia, NW Italy

118 K3 **Manevichi** *see* Manevychi

Manevichi *Rus.* Manevichi, *Rus.* Manevichi. Volyns'ka Oblast', NW Ukraine

109 N16 **Manfredonia** Puglia, SE Italy

109 N16 **Manfredonia, Golfo di** *gulf* Adriatic Sea, N Mediterranean Sea

79 P13 **Manga** C Burkina

61 L16 **Mangabeiras, Chapada das** ▲ E Brazil

81 J20 **Mangai** Bandundu, W Zaire

202 L17 **Mangaia** *island group* S Cook Islands

153 R8 **Manas, Gora** ▲ Kyrgyzstan/Uzbekistan

164 H5 **Manas Hu** ◎ NW China

159 P10 **Manaslu** ▲ C Nepal

39 S8 **Manassa** Colorado, C USA

21 W4 **Manassas** Virginia, NE USA

47 S7 **Manatí** C Puerto Rico

194 L14 **Manatuto** Timor, S Indonesia

56 H4 **Manaure** La Guajira, N Colombia

60 F12 **Manaus** *prev.* Manáos. *state capital* Amazonas, NW Brazil

142 E15 **Manavgat** Antalya, SW Turkey

192 M11 **Manawatu** ☞ North Island, NZ

192 L11 **Manawatu-Wanganui** *off.* Manawatu-Wanganui Region. ◆ *region* North Island, NZ

176 Uu12 **Manawoka, Pulau** *island* Kepulauan Gorong, E Indonesia

179 Rr16 **Manay** Mindanao, S Philippines

144 K2 **Manbij** *var.* Mambij, *Fr.* Membidj. Ḩalab, N Syria

176 Vv12 **Manggawitu** Irian Jaya, E Indonesia

152 I13 **Mancha Real** Andalucía, S Spain

104 I4 **Manche** ◆ *department* N France

99 L17 **Manchester** *Lat.* Mancunium. NW England, UK

25 S5 **Manchester** Georgia, SE USA

31 Y13 **Manchester** Iowa, C USA

21 O6 **Manchester** Kentucky, S USA

21 O10 **Manchester** New Hampshire, NE USA

22 K10 **Manchester** Tennessee, S USA

20 M9 **Manchester** Vermont, NE USA

99 L18 **Manchester** ✈ NW England, UK

155 P15 **Manchhar Lake** ◎ SE Pakistan

Man-chou-li *see* Manzhouli

133 X7 **Manchurian Plain** *plain* NE China

Máncio Lima *see* Japiim

Mancunium *see* Manchester

154 J15 **Mand** Baluchistān, SW Pakistan

Mand *see* Mand, Rūd-e

83 H22 **Manda** Iringa, SW Tanzania

180 H6 **Mandabe** Toliara, W Madagascar

168 L5 **Mandal** Hövsgöl, N Mongolia

168 L7 **Mandal** Töv, C Mongolia

95 D17 **Mandal** Vest-Agder, S Norway

177 O5 **Mandal** Mandalay, C Myanmar

177 O5 **Mandalay** ◆ *division* C Myanmar

168 L9 **Mandalgovĭ** Dundgovĭ, C Mongolia

29 N4 **Mandan** North Dakota, N USA

81 O18 **Manguredjipa** Nord Kivu, E Zaire

85 L16 **Mangwendi** Mashonaland East, E Zimbabwe

150 F15 **Mangyshlak, Plato** *plateau* SW Kazakhstan

150 E14 **Mangyshlakskiy Zaliv** *Kaz.* Mangqystaū Shyghanaghy. *gulf* SW Kazakhstan

Mangyshlakskaya *see* Mangistau

168 I5 **Manhan** Hövsgöl, N Mongolia

29 O4 **Manhattan** Kansas, C USA

101 L21 **Manhay** Luxembourg, SE Belgium

85 L21 **Manhiça** *prev.* Vila de Manhiça. Maputo, S Mozambique

85 L21 **Manhoca** Maputo, S Mozambique

61 N20 **Manhuaçu** Minas Gerais, SE Brazil

149 R14 **Māni** Kermān, E Iran

56 H10 **Mani** Casanare, C Colombia

58 A6 **Mani, Bahía de** *bay* W Ecuador

85 M15 **Manica** Manica, NW Mozambique

85 N14 **Manica** *var.* Vila de Manica. Manica, W Mozambique

85 M17 **Manica** *off.* Província de Manica. ◆ *province* W Mozambique

85 L17 **Manicaland** ◆ *province* E Zimbabwe

13 U5 **Manic Deux, Réservoir** ☐ Québec, SE Canada

Manich *see* Manych

11 N11 **Manicoré** Amazonas, N Brazil

11 N11 **Manicouagan** ☞ Québec, SE Canada

13 U6 **Manicouagan, Péninsule de** *peninsula* Québec, SE Canada

11 N11 **Manicouagan, Réservoir** ☐ Québec, E Canada

13 T4 **Manic Trois, Réservoir** ☐ Québec, SE Canada

81 M20 **Maniema** *off.* Région du Maniema. ◆ *region* E Zaire

Maniewicze *see* Manevychi

166 F8 **Maniganggo** Sichuan, C China

9 Y15 **Manigotagan** Manitoba, S Canada

159 R13 **Manihāri** Bihār, N India

203 U9 **Manihi** *island* Îles Tuamotu, C French Polynesia

202 L13 **Manihiki** *atoll* N Cook Islands

183 U8 **Manihiki Plateau** *undersea feature* C Pacific Ocean

206 M14 **Maniitsoq** *var.* Mâniitsoq, *Dan.* Sukkertoppen. S Greenland

159 T15 **Manikganj** Dhaka, C Bangladesh

158 M14 **Mānikpur** Uttar Pradesh, N India

179 P11 **Manila** *off.* City of Manila. ● (Philippines) Luzon, N Philippines

29 Y9 **Manila** Arkansas, C USA

201 N16 **Manila Reef** *reef* W Micronesia

191 T6 **Manilla** New South Wales, SE Australia

200 Qq14 **Maniloa** *island* Tongatapu Group, S Tonga

176 Ww9 **Manim, Pulau** *island* E Indonesia

173 Ff8 **Maninjau, Danau** ◎ Sumatera, W Indonesia

159 W13 **Manipur** ◆ *state* NE India

159 X14 **Manipur Hills** *hill range* E India

142 C13 **Manisa** *var.* Manissa; *anc.* Magnesia. Manisa, W Turkey

142 C13 **Manisa** *var.* Manissa. ◆ *province* W Turkey

Manissa *see* Manisa

33 T12 **Manistee** Michigan, N USA

33 P7 **Manistee River** ☞ Michigan, N USA

33 O4 **Manistique** Michigan, N USA

33 P4 **Manistique Lake** ◎ Michigan, N USA

9 W13 **Manitoba** ◆ *province* S Canada

X16 **Manitoba, Lake** ◎ Manitoba, S Canada

33 N11 **Manitou Island** *island* Michigan, N USA

12 L11 **Manitou Lake** ◎ Ontario, SE Canada

10 E12 **Manitoulin Island** *island* Ontario, S Canada

39 T5 **Manitou Springs** Colorado, C USA

12 G10 **Manitouwabing Lake** ◎ Ontario, S Canada

10 E12 **Manitouwadge** Ontario, S Canada

12 G15 **Manitowaning** Manitoulin Island, Ontario, S Canada

12 B7 **Manitowik Lake** ◎ Ontario, S Canada

33 N11 **Manitowoc** Wisconsin, N USA

12 I5 **Manitsoq** *see* Maniitsoq

145 O7 **Māni', Wādī al** *dry watercourse* W Iraq

10 J12 **Maniwaki** Québec, SE Canada

176 X11 **Maniwori** Irian Jaya, E Indonesia

56 C11 **Manizales** Caldas, W Colombia

114 F12 **Manjača** ▲ N Bosnia and Herzegovina

Manjacaze *see* Mandlakazi

180 H6 **Manja** Toliara, SW Madagascar

175 S10 **Manjeri** Kerala, SW India

111 V7 **Mank** Niederösterreich, C Austria

81 I17 **Mankanza** Equateur, NW Zaire

159 N14 **Mankāpur** Uttar Pradesh, N India

29 S10 **Mankato** Minnesota, N USA

119 O7 **Man'kivka** Cherkas'ka Oblast', C Ukraine

78 M15 **Mankono** Ivory Coast

9 T17 **Mankota** Saskatchewan, S Canada

161 K23 **Mankulam** Northern Province, N Sri Lanka

41 Q9 **Manley Hot Springs** Alaska, USA

20 H10 **Manlius** New York, NE USA

107 W5 **Manlleu** Cataluña, NE Spain

31 S14 **Manly** Iowa, C USA

160 E13 **Mānmād** Mahārāshtra, W India

190 J7 **Mannahill** South Australia

161 J23 **Mannar** *var.* Manar. Northern Province, NW Sri Lanka

161 I24 **Mannar, Gulf of** *gulf* India/Sri Lanka

161 J23 **Mannar Island** *island* N Sri Lanka

Mannersdorf *see* Mannersdorf am Leithagebirge

111 Y5 **Mannersdorf am Leithagebirge** *var.* Mannersdorf. Niederösterreich, E Austria

111 Y6 **Mannersdorf an der Rabnitz** Burgenland, E Austria

103 G20 **Mannheim** Baden-Württemberg, SW Germany

9 O12 **Manning** Alberta, W Canada

31 T14 **Manning** Iowa, C USA

30 K5 **Manning** North Dakota, N USA

23 S13 **Manning** South Carolina, SE USA

203 Y2 **Manning, Cape** *headland* Kiritimati, NE Kiribati

195 V13 **Manning Strait** *strait* NW Solomon Islands

23 S3 **Mannington** West Virginia, NE USA

29 A1 **Mann Ranges** ▲ South Australia

109 C19 **Mannu** ☞ Sardegna, Italy, C Mediterranean Sea

9 R16 **Mannville** Alberta, SW Canada

78 J15 **Mano** ☞ Liberia/Sierra Leone

Mano *see* Mané

41 O13 **Manokotak** Alaska, USA

176 W9 **Manokwari** Irian Jaya, E Indonesia

81 N22 **Manono** Shabo, SE Zaire

27 T10 **Manor** Texas, SW USA

99 D16 **Manorhamilton** *Ir.* Cluainín. NW Ireland

105 S15 **Manosque** Alpes-de-Haute-Provence, SE France

12 L11 **Manouane, Lac** ◎ Québec, SE Canada

169 W12 **Manp'o** *var.* Manp'ojin. NW North Korea

Manp'ojin *see* Manp'o

203 T4 **Manra** *prev.* Sydney Island. *atoll* Phoenix Islands, C Kiribati

107 V5 **Manresa** Cataluña, NE Spain

158 H9 **Mānsa** Punjab, NW India

84 J12 **Mansa** *prev.* Fort Rosebery. Luapula, N Zambia

78 G11 **Mansa Konko** C Gambia

13 Q11 **Manseau** Québec, SE Canada

155 U5 **Mänsehra** North-West Frontier Province, NW Pakistan

15 Mm6 **Mansel Island** *island* Northwest Territories, NE Canada

191 O12 **Mansfield** Victoria, SE Australia

99 M18 **Mansfield** C England, UK

29 S11 **Mansfield** Arkansas, C USA

24 G6 **Mansfield** Louisiana, S USA

21 O12 **Mansfield** Massachusetts, NE USA

33 T12 **Mansfield** Ohio, N USA

18 F12 **Mansfield** Pennsylvania, NE USA

20 M7 **Mansfield, Mount** ▲ Vermont, NE USA

61 M16 **Mansidão** Bahia, E Brazil

104 L11 **Mansle** Charente, W France

78 G12 **Mansôa** C Guinea-Bissau

49 V8 **Manso, Rio** ☞ C Brazil

Mansúra *see* El Manşûra

Mansurabad *see* Mehrān, Rūd-e

33 Q9 **Maple River** ☞ Michigan, N USA

31 P7 **Maple River** ☞ North Dakota/South Dakota, N USA

31 S13 **Mapleton** Iowa, C USA

31 U10 **Mapleton** Minnesota, N USA

31 R5 **Mapleton** North Dakota, N USA

34 F12 **Mapleton** Oregon, NW USA

36 L3 **Mapleton** Utah, W USA

199 I5 **Mapmaker Seamounts** *undersea feature* N Pacific Ocean

194 G10 **Maprik** East Sepik, NW PNG

85 L21 **Maputo** ● (Mozambique) Maputo, S Mozambique

85 L21 **Maputo** ◆ *province* S Mozambique

85 L21 **Maputo** ✈ Maputo, S Mozambique

69 V14 **Maputo** ☞ S Mozambique

Maqanshy *see* Makanchi

Maqat *see* Makat

115 K19 **Maqê** ☞ NW Albania

165 X9 **Maqên** *var.* Dawu. Qinghai, C China

165 S11 **Maqên Gangri** ▲ C China

165 Q11 **Maqu** Gansu, C China

106 M9 **Maqueda** Castilla-La Mancha, C Spain

84 B8 **Maquela do Zombo** Uíge, NW Angola

65 I16 **Maquinchao** Río Negro, C Argentina

31 Z13 **Maquoketa** Iowa, C USA

31 Y13 **Maquoketa River** ☞ Iowa, C USA

11 I3 **Mar** Ontario, S Canada

8 G3 **Mâr** ☞ S Norway

83 E19 **Mara** ◆ *region* N Tanzania

83 G19 **Mara** ☞ N Tanzania

203 P8 **Maraa** Tahiti, W French Polynesia

61 K14 **Marabá** Pará, NE Brazil

65 H5 **Maracaibo** Zulia, NW Venezuela

Maracaibo, Gulf of *see* Venezuela, Golfo de

Bottom legend:

◆ COUNTRY ◇ DEPENDENT TERRITORY ◆ ADMINISTRATIVE REGION ▲ MOUNTAIN ▲ VOLCANO ◎ LAKE
● COUNTRY CAPITAL ◆ DEPENDENT TERRITORY CAPITAL ✈ INTERNATIONAL AIRPORT ▲ MOUNTAIN RANGE ☞ RIVER ☐ RESERVOIR

Maracaibo, Lago de – Mastanli

56 H5 **Maracaibo, Lago de** *var.* Lake Maracaibo. *inlet* NW Venezuela
Maracaibo, Lake *see* Maracaibo, Lago de
60 K10 **Maracá, Ilha de** *island* NE Brazil
61 H20 **Maracaju, Serra de** ▲ S Brazil
60 I11 **Maracanaquará, Planalto** ▲ NE Brazil
56 L5 **Maracay** Aragua, N Venezuela
Marada *see* Marādah
77 R9 **Marādah** *var.* Marada. N Libya
79 U12 **Maradi** Maradi, S Niger
79 U11 **Maradi** ◆ *department* S Niger
83 E21 **Maragarazi** *var.* Muragarazi. ~ Burundi/Tanzania
Maragha *see* Marāgheh
148 J3 **Marāgheh** *var.* Maragha. Āžarbāyjān-e Khāvarī, NW Iran
147 P7 **Marāh** *var.* Marrāt. Ar Riyāḍ, C Saudi Arabia
57 N11 **Marahuaca, Cerro** ▲ S Venezuela
29 R5 **Marais des Cygnes River** ~ Kansas/Missouri, C USA
60 L11 **Marajó, Baía de** *bay* N Brazil
61 K12 **Marajó, Ilha de** *island* N Brazil
203 O2 **Marakei** *atoll* Tungaru, W Kiribati
Marakesh *see* Marrakech
83 I18 **Maralal** Rift Valley, C Kenya
85 G21 **Maralaleng** Kgalagadi, S Botswana
151 U8 **Maraldy, Ozero** ◎ NE Kazakhstan
190 C5 **Maralinga** South Australia
179 R15 **Maramag** Mindanao, S Philippines
Máramarossziget *see* Sighetu Marmației
195 Y16 **Maramasike** *var.* Small Malaita. *island* N Solomon Islands
Maramba *see* Livingstone
204 H3 **Marambio** *Argentinian research station* Antarctica
118 H9 **Maramureș** ◆ *county* NW Romania
38 L15 **Marana** Arizona, SW USA
107 P7 **Maranchón** Castilla-La Mancha, C Spain
148 J2 **Marand** *var.* Merend. Āžarbāyjān-e Khāvarī, NW Iran
Marandellas *see* Marondera
60 L13 **Maranhão** *off.* Estado do Maranhão. ◆ *state* E Brazil
106 H10 **Maranhão, Barragem do** ⊠ C Portugal
155 O11 **Mārān, Koh-i** ▲ SW Pakistan
108 J7 **Marano, Laguna di** *lagoon* NE Italy
58 E9 **Marañón, Río** ~ N Peru
104 J10 **Marans** Charente-Maritime, W France
85 M20 **Marão** Inhambane, S Mozambique
193 B23 **Mararoa** ~ South Island, NZ
Maraș/Marash *see* Kahramanmaraş
109 M19 **Maratea** Basilicata, S Italy
106 G11 **Marateca** Setúbal, S Portugal
117 B20 **Marathiá, Ákra** *headland* Zákynthos, Iónioi Nísoi, Greece, C Mediterranean Sea
10 E12 **Marathon** Ontario, S Canada
25 Y17 **Marathon** Florida Keys, Florida, SE USA
26 L10 **Marathon** Texas, SW USA
Marathón *see* Marathónas
117 H19 **Marathónas** *prev.* Marathón. Attikí, C Greece
175 Oo6 **Maratua, Pulau** *island* N Indonesia
61 O18 **Maraú** Bahia, SE Brazil
149 R3 **Marāveh Tappeh** Māzandarān, N Iran
26 L11 **Maravillas Creek** ~ Texas, SW USA
194 J13 **Marawaka** Eastern Highlands, C PNG
179 R15 **Marawi** Mindanao, S Philippines
Marbat *see* Mirbāṭ
106 L16 **Marbella** Andalucía, S Spain
188 J7 **Marble Bar** Western Australia
38 L9 **Marble Canyon** *canyon* Arizona, SW USA
27 S10 **Marble Falls** Texas, SW USA
29 Y7 **Marble Hill** Missouri, C USA
35 T15 **Marbleton** Wyoming, C USA
Marburg *see* Maribor
Marburg *see* Marburg an der Lahn, Germany
103 H16 **Marburg an der Lahn** *hist.* Marburg. Hessen, W Germany
113 H23 **Marcal** ~ W Hungary
44 G7 **Marcala** La Paz, SW Honduras
113 H24 **Marcali** Somogy, SW Hungary
85 A16 **Marca, Ponta da** *headland* SW Angola
61 I16 **Marcelândia** Mato Grosso, W Brazil
29 T3 **Marceline** Missouri, C USA
62 I13 **Marcelino Ramos** Rio Grande do Sul, S Brazil
57 Y12 **Marcel, Mont** ▲ S French Guiana
99 O19 **March** E England, UK
111 Z3 **March** *var.* Morava. ~ C Europe *see also* Morava
108 I12 **Marche** *Eng.* Marches. ◆ *region* C Italy
105 N11 **Marche** *cultural region* C France
101 J21 **Marche-en-Famenne** Luxembourg, SE Belgium
106 K14 **Marchena** Andalucía, S Spain
59 B17 **Marchena, Isla** *var.* Bindloe Island. *island* Galapagos Islands, Ecuador, E Pacific Ocean
Marches *see* Marche
101 J20 **Marchin** Liège, E Belgium
189 S1 **Marchinbar Island** *island* Wessel Islands, Northern Territory, N Australia
64 L9 **Mar Chiquita, Laguna** ◎ C Argentina
105 Q10 **Marcigny** Saône-et-Loire, C France
25 W16 **Marco** Florida, SE USA
Marcodurum *see* Düren
61 O15 **Marcolândia** Pernambuco, E Brazil
108 I8 **Marco Polo** ✕ (Venezia) Veneto, NE Italy
Marcq *see* Mark
118 M8 **Mărculești** *Rus.* Markuleshty. N Moldova
31 S12 **Marcus** Iowa, C USA
41 S11 **Marcus Baker, Mount** ▲ Alaska, USA
199 Hh5 **Marcus Island** *var.* Minami Tori Shima. *island* E Japan
20 K8 **Marcy, Mount** ▲ New York, NE USA
155 T5 **Mardān** North-West Frontier Province, N Pakistan
65 N14 **Mar del Plata** Buenos Aires, E Argentina
143 Q16 **Mardin** Mardin, SE Turkey
143 Q16 **Mardin** ◆ *province* SE Turkey
143 Q16 **Mardin Dağları** ▲ SE Turkey
168 J9 **Mardzad** Övörhangay, C Mongolia
197 L6 **Maré** *island* Îles Loyauté, E New Caledonia
Marea Neagră *see* Black Sea
107 Z8 **Mare de Déu del Toro** ▲ Menorca, Spain, W Mediterranean Sea
189 W4 **Mareeba** Queensland, NE Australia
98 G8 **Maree, Loch** ◎ N Scotland, UK
Mareeq *see* Mereeg
Marek *see* Dupnitsa
78 J11 **Maréna** Kayes, W Mali
202 I2 **Marenanuka** *atoll* Tungaru, W Kiribati
31 X14 **Marengo** Iowa, C USA
104 J11 **Marennes** Charente-Maritime, W France
109 G23 **Marettimo, Isola** *island* Isole Egadi, S Italy
26 K10 **Marfa** Texas, SW USA
59 P17 **Marfil, Laguna** ◎ E Bolivia
Marganets *see* Marhanets'
27 Q4 **Margaret** Texas, SW USA
188 I14 **Margaret River** Western Australia
194 G12 **Margarima** Southern Highlands, W PNG
57 N4 **Margarita, Isla de** *island* N Venezuela
117 I25 **Margarítes** Kríti, Greece, E Mediterranean Sea
99 Q22 **Margate** *prev.* Mergate. SE England, UK
25 Z15 **Margate** Florida, SE USA
Margelan *see* Marghilon
105 P13 **Margeride, Montagnes de la** ▲ C France
Margherita *see* Jamaame
109 N16 **Margherita di Savoia** Puglia, SE Italy
Margherita, Lake *see* Ābaya Hāyk'
83 E18 **Margherita Peak** *Fr.* Pic Marguerite. ▲ Uganda/Zaire
155 O4 **Marghī** Bāmīān, N Afghanistan
153 S10 **Marghilon** *var.* Margelan, *Rus.* Margilan. Farghona Wiloyati, E Uzbekistan
118 G9 **Marghita** *Hung.* Margitta. Bihor, NW Romania
Margilan *see* Marghilon
118 K8 **Marginea** Suceava, NE Romania
Margitta *see* Marghita
154 K9 **Mārgow, Dasht-e** *desert* SW Afghanistan
101 L18 **Margraten** Limburg, SE Netherlands
8 M15 **Marguerite** British Columbia, SW Canada
204 I6 **Marguerite Bay** *bay* Antarctica
Marguerite, Pic *see* Margherita Peak
119 T9 **Marhanets'** *Rus.* Marganets. Dnipropetrovs'ka Oblast', E Ukraine
194 E15 **Mari** Western, SW PNG
203 R12 **Maria** *island* Îles Australes, SW French Polynesia
203 Y12 **Maria** *atoll* Groupe Actéon, SE French Polynesia
42 I12 **María Cleofas, Isla** *island* C Mexico
64 H4 **María Elena** *var.* Oficina María Elena. Antofagasta, N Chile
97 G21 **Mariager** Århus, C Denmark
63 C22 **María Ignacia** Buenos Aires, E Argentina
191 P17 **Maria Island** *island* Tasmania, SE Australia
42 H12 **María Madre, Isla** *island* C Mexico
42 I12 **María Magdalena, Isla** *island* C Mexico
199 H6 **Mariana Islands** *island group* Guam/Northern Mariana Islands
183 N3 **Mariana Trench** *var.* Challenger Deep. *undersea feature* W Pacific Ocean
159 X12 **Mariāni** Assam, NE India
29 X11 **Marianna** Arkansas, C USA
25 R8 **Marianna** Florida, SE USA
180 J16 **Marianne** *island* Inner Islands, NE Seychelles
97 M19 **Mariannelund** Jönköping, S Sweden
63 D15 **Mariano I.Loza** Corrientes, NE Argentina
Mariano Machado *see* Ganda
113 A16 **Mariánské Lázně** *Ger.* Marienbad. Západní Čechy, W Czech Republic
Máriaradna *see* Radna
35 S7 **Marias River** ~ Montana, NW USA
Maria-Theresiopel *see* Subotica
Máriatölgyes *see* Dubnica nad Váhom
192 H1 **Maria van Diemen, Cape** *headland* North Island, NZ
111 V5 **Mariazell** Steiermark, E Austria
147 P15 **Ma'rib** W Yemen
97 I25 **Maribo** Storstrøm, S Denmark
111 W9 **Maribor** *Ger.* Marburg. NE Slovenia
Marica *see* Maritsa
37 R13 **Maricopa** California, W USA
Maricourt *see* Kangiqsujuaq
83 D15 **Maridi** Western Equatoria, SW Sudan
204 M11 **Marie Byrd Land** *physical region* Antarctica
199 Ll16 **Marie Byrd Seamount** *undersea feature* N Amundsen Sea
47 X11 **Marie-Galante** *var.* Ceyre to the Caribs. *island* SE Guadeloupe
47 Y6 **Marie-Galante, Canal de** *channel* S Guadeloupe
95 J20 **Mariehamn** *Fin.* Maarianhamina. Åland, SW Finland
46 C4 **Mariel** La Habana, W Cuba
101 H22 **Mariembourg** Namur, S Belgium
Marienbad *see* Mariánské Lázně
Marienburg *see* Alūksne, Latvia
Marienburg *see* Malbork, Poland
Marienburg *see* Feldioara, Romania
Marienburg in Westpreussen *see* Malbork
Marienhausen *see* Viļaka
85 D20 **Mariental** Hardap, SW Namibia
20 D13 **Marienville** Pennsylvania, NE USA
Marienwerder *see* Kwidzyń
60 C12 **Marié, Rio** ~ NW Brazil
97 K17 **Mariestad** Skaraborg, S Sweden
25 S3 **Marietta** Georgia, SE USA
33 U14 **Marietta** Ohio, N USA
29 N13 **Marietta** Oklahoma, C USA
83 H18 **Marigat** Rift Valley, W Kenya
105 S16 **Marignane** Bouches-du-Rhône, SE France
Marignano *see* Melegnano
47 O11 **Marigot** NE Dominica
126 Hh14 **Mariinsk** Kemerovskaya Oblast', S Russian Federation
131 Q3 **Mariinskiy Posad** Respublika Mariy El, W Russian Federation
121 E14 **Marijampolė** *prev.* Kapsukas. Marijampolė, S Lithuania
116 G12 **Marikostenovo** Sofiyska Oblast, SW Bulgaria
62 J9 **Marília** São Paulo, S Brazil
84 D11 **Marimba** Malanje, NW Angola
145 T1 **Marī Mīlā** E Iraq
106 G4 **Marín** Galicia, NW Spain
37 N10 **Marina** California, W USA
Marina di Catanzaro *see* Catanzaro Marina
Mar"ina Gorka *see* Mar"ina Horka
121 L17 **Mar"ina Horka** *Rus.* Mar'ina Gorka. Minskaya Voblasts', C Belarus
179 Pp11 **Marinduque** *island* C Philippines
33 S9 **Marine City** Michigan, N USA
33 N6 **Marinette** Wisconsin, N USA
62 I10 **Maringá** Paraná, S Brazil
85 N16 **Maringuè** Sofala, C Mozambique
106 F9 **Marinha Grande** Leiria, C Portugal
109 I15 **Marino** Lazio, C Italy
61 A15 **Mário Lobão** Acre, W Brazil
25 O5 **Marion** Alabama, S USA
29 Y11 **Marion** Arkansas, C USA
32 L17 **Marion** Illinois, N USA
33 P13 **Marion** Indiana, N USA
31 X13 **Marion** Iowa, C USA
29 O5 **Marion** Kansas, C USA
22 H6 **Marion** Kentucky, S USA
23 P9 **Marion** North Carolina, SE USA
33 S12 **Marion** Ohio, N USA
23 T12 **Marion** South Carolina, SE USA
23 Q7 **Marion** Virginia, NE USA
29 O5 **Marion Lake** ⊠ Kansas, C USA
23 S13 **Marion, Lake** ⊠ South Carolina, SE USA
29 S8 **Marionville** Missouri, C USA
57 N7 **Maripa** Bolívar, E Venezuela
57 X11 **Maripasoula** W French Guiana
37 Q9 **Mariposa** California, W USA
63 G19 **Mariscala** Lavalleja, S Uruguay
64 M4 **Mariscal Estigarribia** Boquerón, NW Paraguay
58 C6 **Mariscal Sucre** *var.* Quito. ✕ (Quito) Pichincha, C Ecuador
32 K16 **Marissa** Illinois, N USA
105 U14 **Maritime Alps** *Fr.* Alpes Maritimes, *It.* Alpi Marittime. ▲ France/Italy
Maritimes, Alpes *see* Maritime Alps
Maritime Territory *see* Primorskiy Kray
116 K11 **Maritsa** *var.* Marica, *Gk.* Évros, *Turk.* Meriç; *anc.* Hebrus. ~ SW Europe *see also* Évros/Meriç
Maritsa *see* Simeonovgrad
Marittime, Alpi *see* Maritime Alps
Maritzburg *see* Pietermaritzburg
197 C13 **Marium, Mount** ▲ Ambrym, C Vanuatu
119 X9 **Mariupol'** *prev.* Zhdanov. Donets'ka Oblast', SE Ukraine
57 Q6 **Mariusa, Caño** ~ NE Venezuela
148 J5 **Marīvān** *prev.* Dezh Shāhpūr. Kordestān, W Iran
125 A16 **Mariy El, Respublika** *prev.* Mariyskaya ASSR. ◆ *autonomous republic* W Russian Federation
131 R3 **Mariyets** Respublika Mariy El, W Russian Federation
Mariyskaya ASSR *see* Mariy El, Respublika
120 G4 **Märjamaa** *Ger.* Merjama. Raplamaa, NW Estonia
101 I15 **Mark** *Fr.* Marcq. ~ Belgium/Netherlands
83 N17 **Marka** *var.* Merca. Shabeellaha Hoose, S Somalia
151 Z10 **Markakol', Ozero** *Kaz.* Marqaköl. ◎ E Kazakhstan
78 M12 **Markala** Ségou, W Mali
165 S15 **Markam** *var.* Gartog. Xizang Zizhiqu, W China
97 K21 **Markaryd** Kronoberg, S Sweden
148 L7 **Markazī** *off.* Ostān-e Markazī. ◆ *province* W Iran
12 F14 **Markdale** Ontario, S Canada
29 X10 **Marked Tree** Arkansas, C USA
100 N11 **Markelo** Overijssel, E Netherlands
100 J9 **Markermeer** ◎ C Netherlands
99 N20 **Market Harborough** C England, UK
99 N18 **Market Rasen** E England, UK
126 Kk10 **Markha** ~ NE Russian Federation
10 H16 **Markham** Ontario, S Canada
27 V12 **Markham** Texas, SW USA
194 J13 **Markham** ~ C PNG
205 Q11 **Markham, Mount** ▲ Antarctica
112 M11 **Marki** Warszawa, C Poland
164 F8 **Markit** Xinjiang Uygur Zizhiqu, NW China
119 Y5 **Markivka** *Rus.* Markovka. Luhans'ka Oblast', E Ukraine
37 Q7 **Markleeville** California, W USA
100 L8 **Marknesse** Flevoland, N Netherlands
81 H14 **Markounda** *var.* Marcounda. Ouham, NW Central African Republic
Markovka *see* Markivka
127 P6 **Markovo** Chukotskiy Avtonomnyy Okrug, NE Russian Federation
131 P8 **Marks** Saratovskaya Oblast', W Russian Federation
24 K2 **Marks** Mississippi, S USA
24 I7 **Marksville** Louisiana, S USA
103 I19 **Marktheidenfeld** Bayern, C Germany
103 J24 **Marktoberdorf** Bayern, S Germany
103 M18 **Marktredwitz** Bayern, E Germany
Markt-Übelbach *see* Übelbach
29 V3 **Mark Twain Lake** ⊠ Missouri, C USA
Markuleshty *see* Mărculești
103 E14 **Marl** Nordrhein-Westfalen, W Germany
190 E2 **Marla** South Australia
189 Y8 **Marlborough** Queensland, E Australia
99 M22 **Marlborough** S England, UK
193 I15 **Marlborough** *off.* Marlborough District. ◆ *unitary authority* South Island, NZ
105 P3 **Marle** Aisne, N France
33 S8 **Marlette** Michigan, N USA
27 T9 **Marlin** Texas, SW USA
23 S5 **Marlinton** West Virginia, NE USA
28 M12 **Marlow** Oklahoma, C USA
161 E17 **Marmagao** Goa, W India
Marmanda *see* Marmande
104 L13 **Marmande** *anc.* Marmanda. Lot-et-Garonne, SW France
142 C11 **Marmara** Balıkesir, NW Turkey
142 D11 **Marmara Denizi** *Eng.* Sea of Marmara. *sea* NW Turkey
116 N13 **Marmaraereğlisi** Tekirdağ, NW Turkey
Marmara, Sea of *see* Marmara Denizi
142 C16 **Marmaris** Muğla, SW Turkey
30 J6 **Marmarth** North Dakota, N USA
23 Q5 **Marmet** West Virginia, NE USA
108 H5 **Marmolada, Monte** ▲ N Italy
106 M13 **Marmolejo** Andalucía, S Spain
12 J14 **Marmora** Ontario, SE Canada
41 Q14 **Marmot Bay** *bay* Alaska, USA
105 Q4 **Marne** ◆ *department* N France
105 Q4 **Marne** ~ N France
143 U10 **Marneuli** *prev.* Borchalo, Sarvani. S Georgia
80 I13 **Maro** Moyen-Chari, S Chad
56 L12 **Maroa** Amazonas, S Venezuela
180 J3 **Maroantsetra** Toamasina, NE Madagascar
203 W11 **Marokau** *atoll* Îles Tuamotu, C French Polynesia
180 J5 **Marolambo** Toamasina, E Madagascar
180 J2 **Maromokotro** ▲ N Madagascar
85 L16 **Marondera** *prev.* Marandellas. Mashonaland East, NE Zimbabwe
57 X9 **Maroni** *Dut.* Marowijne. ~ French Guiana/Suriname
191 V2 **Maroochydore-Mooloolaba** Queensland, E Australia
175 P13 **Maros** Sulawesi, C Indonesia
118 H11 **Maros** *var.* Mureș, Mureșul, *Ger.* Marosch, Mieresch. ~ Hungary/Romania *see also* Mureș
Marosch *see* Maros/Mureș
Maroshévíz *see* Toplița
Marosillye *see* Ilia
Marosludas *see* Luduș
Marosújvár/Marosújvárakna *see* Ocna Mureș
Marosvásárhely *see* Târgu Mureș
203 V14 **Marotiri** *var.* Îlots de Bass, Morotiri. *island group* Îles Australes, SW French Polynesia
80 G12 **Maroua** Extrême-Nord, N Cameroon
57 X12 **Marouini Rivier** ~ SE Suriname
180 I3 **Marovoay** Mahajanga, NW Madagascar
57 W9 **Marowijne** ◆ *district* NE Suriname
Marowijne *see* Maroni
Marqaköl *see* Markakol', Ozero
199 M9 **Marquesas Fracture Zone** *tectonic feature* E Pacific Ocean
Marquesas Islands *see* Marquises, Îles
25 W17 **Marquesas Keys** *island group* Florida, SE USA
31 Y12 **Marquette** Iowa, C USA
33 N3 **Marquette** Michigan, N USA
105 N1 **Marquise** Pas-de-Calais, N France
203 X7 **Marquises, Îles** *Eng.* Marquesas Islands. *island group* N French Polynesia
191 Q6 **Marra Creek** ~ New South Wales, SE Australia
82 B10 **Marra Hills** *plateau* W Sudan
82 B11 **Marra, Jebel** ▲ W Sudan
76 E7 **Marrakech** *var.* Marakesh, *Eng.* Marrakesh; *prev.* Morocco. W Morocco
Marrakesh *see* Marrakech
Marrāt *see* Marāh
191 N15 **Marrawah** Tasmania, SE Australia
190 I4 **Marree** South Australia
83 L17 **Marrehan** ▲ SW Somalia
85 N17 **Marromeu** Sofala, C Mozambique
106 J17 **Marroquí, Punta** *headland* SW Spain
191 N8 **Marrowie Creek** *seasonal river* New South Wales, SE Australia
85 O14 **Marrupa** Niassa, N Mozambique
190 D1 **Marryat** South Australia
77 Y10 **Marsa 'Alam** SE Egypt
77 R8 **Marsá al Burayqah** *var.* Al Burayqah. N Libya
83 J17 **Marsabit** Eastern, N Kenya
109 H23 **Marsala** *anc.* Lilybaeum. Sicilia, Italy, C Mediterranean Sea
123 Jj17 **Marsaxlokk Bay** *bay* SE Malta
67 G15 **Mars Bay** *bay* Ascension Island, C Atlantic Ocean
103 H15 **Marsberg** Nordrhein-Westfalen, W Germany
9 R15 **Marsden** Saskatchewan, S Canada
100 H7 **Marsdiep** *strait* NW Netherlands
105 R16 **Marseille** *Eng.* Marseilles; *anc.* Massilia. Bouches-du-Rhône, SE France
Marseille-Marignane *see* Provence
32 M11 **Marseilles** Illinois, N USA
Marseilles *see* Marseille
78 J16 **Marshall** W Liberia
41 N11 **Marshall** Alaska, USA
29 U9 **Marshall** Arkansas, C USA
33 N14 **Marshall** Illinois, N USA
33 Q10 **Marshall** Michigan, N USA
31 S9 **Marshall** Minnesota, N USA
29 T4 **Marshall** Missouri, C USA
23 O9 **Marshall** North Carolina, SE USA
27 X6 **Marshall** Texas, SW USA
201 S4 **Marshall Islands** *off.* Republic of the Marshall Islands. ◆ *republic* W Pacific Ocean
183 Q3 **Marshall Islands** *island group* W Pacific Ocean
199 Ii7 **Marshall Seamounts** *undersea feature* SW Pacific Ocean
31 W13 **Marshalltown** Iowa, C USA
21 P12 **Marshfield** Massachusetts, NE USA
29 T7 **Marshfield** Missouri, C USA
32 K6 **Marshfield** Wisconsin, N USA
46 H1 **Marsh Harbour** Great Abaco, W Bahamas
21 S3 **Mars Hill** Maine, NE USA
23 P9 **Mars Hill** North Carolina, SE USA
24 H10 **Marsh Island** *island* Louisiana, S USA
23 S11 **Marshville** North Carolina, SE USA
13 W5 **Marsoui** Québec, SE Canada
13 R8 **Mars, Rivière à** ~ Québec, SE Canada
97 O15 **Märsta** Stockholm, C Sweden
97 H24 **Marstal** Fyn, C Denmark
97 I19 **Marstrand** Göteborg och Bohus, S Sweden
27 U8 **Mart** Texas, SW USA
178 Gg9 **Martaban** *var.* Moktama. Mon State, S Myanmar
177 G9 **Martaban, Gulf of** *gulf* S Myanmar
109 Q19 **Martano** Puglia, SE Italy
Martapoera *see* Martapura
175 N11 **Martapura** *prev.* Martapoera. Borneo, C Indonesia
101 L23 **Martelange** Luxembourg, SE Belgium
116 L7 **Marten** Razgradska Oblast, NE Bulgaria
12 H10 **Marten River** Ontario, S Canada
9 T15 **Martensville** Saskatchewan, S Canada
Marteskirch *see* Târnăveni
Martes Tolosane *see* Martres-Tolosane
117 K25 **Mártha** Kríti, Greece, E Mediterranean Sea
191 Q6 **Marthaguy Creek** ~ New South Wales, SE Australia
21 P13 **Martha's Vineyard** *island* Massachusetts, NE USA
110 C11 **Martigny** Valais, SW Switzerland
105 R16 **Martigues** Bouches-du-Rhône, SE France
113 J19 **Martin** *Ger.* Sankt Martin, *Hung.* Turócszentmárton; *prev.* Turčianský Svätý Martin. Stredné Slovensko, NW Slovakia
30 L11 **Martin** South Dakota, N USA
22 G8 **Martin** Tennessee, S USA
107 S7 **Martín** ~ E Spain
109 P18 **Martina Franca** Puglia, SE Italy
193 M14 **Martinborough** Wellington, North Island, NZ
27 S11 **Martindale** Texas, SW USA
37 N8 **Martinez** California, W USA
25 V3 **Martinez** Georgia, SE USA
43 Q13 **Martínez de La Torre** Veracruz-Llave, E Mexico
47 Y12 **Martinique** ◇ *French overseas department* E West Indies
1 O15 **Martinique** *island* E West Indies
Martinique Channel *see* Martinique Passage
47 X12 **Martinique Passage** *var.* Dominica Channel, Martinique Channel. *channel* Dominica/Martinique
25 Q5 **Martin Lake** ⊠ Alabama, S USA
117 G18 **Martíno** *prev.* Martínon. Stereá Ellás, C Greece
Martínon *see* Martíno
204 J11 **Martin Peninsula** *peninsula* Antarctica
41 S5 **Martin Point** *headland* Alaska, USA
111 V3 **Martinsberg** Niederösterreich, NE Austria
23 V3 **Martinsburg** West Virginia, NE USA
33 V13 **Martins Ferry** Ohio, N USA
Martinskirch *see* Târnăveni
33 O14 **Martinsville** Indiana, N USA
23 S8 **Martinsville** Virginia, NE USA
67 K16 **Martin Vaz, Ilhas** *island group* E Brazil
Martök *see* Martuk
192 M12 **Marton** Manawatu-Wanganui, North Island, NZ
107 N13 **Martos** Andalucía, S Spain
104 M16 **Martres-Tolosane** *var.* Martes Tolosane. Haute-Garonne, S France
94 M11 **Martti** Lappi, NE Finland
150 J9 **Martuk** *Kaz.* Martök. Aktyubinsk, NW Kazakhstan
143 U12 **Martuni** E Armenia
60 L11 **Marudá** Pará, E Brazil
175 O2 **Marudu, Teluk** *bay* East Malaysia
155 O8 **Ma'rūf** Kandahār, SE Afghanistan
170 F14 **Marugame** Kagawa, Shikoku, SW Japan
193 H16 **Maruia** ~ South Island, NZ
100 M6 **Marum** Groningen, NE Netherlands
81 P23 **Marungu** ▲ SE Zaire
203 Y12 **Marutea** *atoll* Groupe Actéon, C French Polynesia
149 O11 **Marv Dasht** *var.* Mervdasht. Fārs, S Iran
105 P13 **Marvejols** Lozère, S France
29 X12 **Marvell** Arkansas, C USA
38 L6 **Marvine, Mount** ▲ Utah, W USA
145 Q7 **Marwānīyah** C Iraq
158 F13 **Mārwār** *var.* Marwar Junction. Rājasthān, N India
Marwar Junction *see* Mārwār
9 R14 **Marwayne** Alberta, SW Canada
152 I14 **Mary** *prev.* Merv. Maryyskiy Velayat, S Turkmenistan
Mary *see* Maryyskiy Velayat
189 Z9 **Maryborough** Queensland, E Australia
190 M11 **Maryborough** Victoria, SE Australia
Maryborough *see* Port Laoise
85 G23 **Marydale** Northern Cape, W South Africa
119 W8 **Mar"yinka** Donets'ka Oblast', E Ukraine
Mary Island *see* Kanton
23 W4 **Maryland** *off.* State of Maryland; also known as America in Miniature, Cockade State, Free State, Old Line State. ◆ *state* NE USA
27 P7 **Maryneal** Texas, SW USA
99 J15 **Maryport** NW England, UK
11 U13 **Marystown** Newfoundland, Newfoundland and Labrador, SE Canada
38 K6 **Marysvale** Utah, W USA
37 O6 **Marysville** California, W USA
29 O3 **Marysville** Kansas, C USA
33 S13 **Marysville** Michigan, N USA
33 S9 **Marysville** Ohio, NE USA
34 H7 **Marysville** Washington, NW USA
29 R2 **Maryville** Missouri, C USA
23 N9 **Maryville** Tennessee, S USA
Mary Welayaty *see* Maryyskiy Velayat
152 I15 **Maryyskiy Velayat** *var.* Mary, *Turkm.* Mary Welayaty. ◆ *province* S Turkmenistan
Marzūq *see* Murzuq
176 V11 **Mas** Irian Jaya, E Indonesia
44 J11 **Masachapa** *var.* Puerto Masachapa. Managua, W Nicaragua
83 G19 **Masai Mara National Reserve** *reserve* C Kenya
83 I21 **Masai Steppe** *grassland* NW Tanzania
83 F19 **Masaka** SW Uganda
175 N13 **Masalembo Besar, Pulau** *island* S Indonesia
143 Y13 **Masallı** *Rus.* Masally. S Azerbaijan
Masally *see* Masallı
175 Pp10 **Masamba** Sulawesi, C Indonesia
Masampo *see* Masan
169 Y16 **Masan** *prev.* Masampo. S South Korea
Masandam Peninsula *see* Musandam Peninsula
83 J25 **Masasi** Mtwara, SE Tanzania
Masawa *see* Massawa
44 J10 **Masaya** Masaya, W Nicaragua
44 J10 **Masaya** ◆ *department* W Nicaragua
179 Q12 **Masbate** Masbate, N Philippines
179 Qq12 **Masbate** *island* C Philippines
76 I6 **Mascara** *var.* Mouaskar. NW Algeria
181 O7 **Mascarene Basin** *undersea feature* W Indian Ocean
181 O9 **Mascarene Islands** *island group* W Indian Ocean
181 N9 **Mascarene Plain** *undersea feature* W Indian Ocean
181 O7 **Mascarene Plateau** *undersea feature* W Indian Ocean
204 H5 **Mascart, Cape** *headland* Adelaide Island, Antarctica
64 J10 **Mascasín, Salinas de** *salt lake* C Argentina
42 K13 **Mascota** Jalisco, C Mexico
13 O12 **Mascouche** Québec, SE Canada
128 J9 **Masel'gskaya** Respublika Kareliya, NW Russian Federation
85 J23 **Maseru** ● (Lesotho) W Lesotho
85 J23 **Maseru** ✕ W Lesotho
Mashaba *see* Mashava
166 K14 **Mashan** Guangxi Zhuangzu Zizhiqu, S China
85 K17 **Mashava** *prev.* Mashaba. Masvingo, SE Zimbabwe
149 U4 **Mashhad** *var.* Meshed. Khorāsān, NE Iran
172 Oo4 **Mashike** Hokkaidō, NE Japan
Mashiz *see* Bardsīr
155 N14 **Mashkai** ~ SW Pakistan
149 X13 **Māshkel** *var.* Rūd-i Māshkel, Rūd-e Māshkīd. ~ Iran/Pakistan
154 K12 **Māshkel, Hāmūn-i** *salt marsh* SW Pakistan
Māshkel, Rūd-i/Māshkīd, Rūd-e *see* Māshkel
85 K15 **Mashonaland Central** ◆ *province* N Zimbabwe
85 K16 **Mashonaland East** ◆ *province* NE Zimbabwe
85 J16 **Mashonaland West** ◆ *province* NW Zimbabwe
Mashtagi *see* Maştağa
172 Qq6 **Mashū-ko** *var.* Masyû Ko. ◎ Hokkaidō, NE Japan
147 S14 **Masīlah, Wādī al** *dry watercourse* SE Yemen
81 I21 **Masi-Manimba** Bandundu, SW Zaire
83 F17 **Masindi** W Uganda
83 J19 **Masinga Reservoir** ⊠ S Kenya
179 Oo10 **Masinloc** Luzon, N Philippines
Masīra *see* Maşīrah, Jazīrat
Masira, Gulf of *see* Maşīrah, Khalīj
147 Y10 **Maşīrah, Jazīrat** *var.* Masīra. *island* E Oman
147 Y10 **Maşīrah, Khalīj** *var.* Gulf of Masira. *bay* E Oman
Masis *see* Büyükağrı Dağı
81 O19 **Masisi** Nord Kivu, E Zaire
176 U11 **Masiwang** ~ Pulau Seram, E Indonesia
Masjed-e Soleymān *see* Masjed Soleymān
148 L9 **Masjed Soleymān** *var.* Masjed-e Soleymān, Masjid-i Sulaiman. Khūzestān, SW Iran
Masjid-i Sulaiman *see* Masjed Soleymān
Maskat *see* Masqaṭ
145 Q7 **Maskhān** C Iraq
147 X8 **Maskin** *var.* Miskin. NW Oman
99 B17 **Mask, Lough** *Ir.* Loch Measca. ◎ W Ireland
116 N10 **Maslen Nos** *headland* E Bulgaria
180 K3 **Masoala, Tanjona** *headland* NE Madagascar
Masohi *see* Amahai
33 Q9 **Mason** Michigan, N USA
33 R14 **Mason** Ohio, N USA
27 Q10 **Mason** Texas, SW USA
23 P4 **Mason** West Virginia, NE USA
193 B25 **Mason Bay** *bay* Stewart Island, NZ
32 K13 **Mason City** Illinois, N USA
31 V12 **Mason City** Iowa, C USA
Mā, Sông *see* Ma, Nam
20 B16 **Masontown** Pennsylvania, NE USA
147 Y8 **Masqaṭ** *var.* Maskat, *Eng.* Muscat. ● (Oman) NE Oman
108 E10 **Massa** Toscana, C Italy
20 M11 **Massachusetts** *off.* Commonwealth of Massachusetts; also known as Bay State, Old Bay State, Old Colony State. ◆ *state* NE USA
21 P11 **Massachusetts Bay** *bay* Massachusetts, NE USA
37 R2 **Massacre Lake** ◎ Nevada, W USA
109 O18 **Massafra** Puglia, SE Italy
110 G11 **Massagno** Ticino, S Switzerland
80 G11 **Massaguet** Chari-Baguirmi, W Chad
Massakori *see* Massakory
80 G10 **Massakory** *var.* Massakori; *prev.* Dagana. Chari-Baguirmi, W Chad
80 H11 **Massalassef** Chari-Baguirmi, SW Chad
108 F13 **Massa Marittima** Toscana, C Italy
84 B11 **Massangano** Cuanza Norte, NW Angola
85 M18 **Massangena** Gaza, S Mozambique
82 J9 **Massawa** *var.* Masawa, *Amh.* Mits'iwa. E Eritrea
82 K9 **Massawa Channel** *channel* E Eritrea
20 J6 **Massena** New York, NE USA
80 H11 **Massenya** Chari-Baguirmi, SW Chad
8 I13 **Masset** Graham Island, British Columbia, SW Canada
104 L16 **Masseube** Gers, S France
12 E11 **Massey** Ontario, S Canada
105 P12 **Massiac** Cantal, C France
105 P12 **Massif Central** *plateau* C France
Massilia *see* Marseille
33 U12 **Massillon** Ohio, N USA
79 N12 **Massina** Ségou, W Mali
85 N19 **Massinga** Inhambane, SE Mozambique
85 L20 **Massingir** Gaza, SW Mozambique
205 Z10 **Masson Island** *island* Antarctica
Massoukou *see* Franceville
143 Z11 **Maştağa** *Rus.* Mashtagi, Mastaga. E Azerbaijan
Mastanli *see* Momchilgrad

◆ Country ● Country Capital ◇ Dependent Territory ○ Dependent Territory Capital ◆ Administrative Region ✕ International Airport ▲ Mountain ▲ Mountain Range Volcano ~ River ◎ Lake ⊠ Reservoir

MASTERTON – MÊDOG

192 M13 **Masterton** Wellington, North Island, NZ
20 M14 **Mastic** Long Island, New York, NE USA
155 O10 **Mastung** Baluchistān, SW Pakistan
121 J20 **Mastva** *Rus.* Mostva. ≈ SW Belarus
121 G17 **Masty** *Rus.* Mosty. Hrodzyenskaya Voblasts', W Belarus
170 E12 **Masuda** Shimane, Honshū, SW Japan
94 I11 **Masugnsbyn** Norrbotten, N Sweden
Masuku *see* Franceville
85 K17 **Masvingo** *prev.* Fort Victoria, Nyanda, Victoria. Masvingo, SE Zimbabwe
85 K18 **Masvingo** *prev.* Victoria. ◐ *province* SE Zimbabwe
176 W10 **Maswaar, Pulau** *island* East Indies
144 H5 **Maṣyāf** *Fr.* Misiaf. Ḥamāh, C Syria
Masyû Ko *see* Mashū-ko
112 E9 **Maszewo** Szczecin, NW Poland
85 I17 **Matabeleland North** ◐ *province* W Zimbabwe
85 J18 **Matabeleland South** ◐ *province* S Zimbabwe
84 O13 **Mataca** Niassa, N Mozambique
197 G13 **Matacawa Levu** *island* Yasawa Group, NW Fiji
118 G8 **Matachewan** Ontario, S Canada
81 F22 **Matadi** Bas-Zaïre, W Zaire
27 O4 **Matador** Texas, SW USA
44 J9 **Matagalpa** Matagalpa, C Nicaragua
44 K9 **Matagalpa** ◐ *department* W Nicaragua
10 I12 **Matagami** Québec, S Canada
27 U13 **Matagorda** Texas, SW USA
27 U13 **Matagorda Bay** *inlet* Texas, SW USA
27 U14 **Matagorda Island** *island* Texas, SW USA
27 V13 **Matagorda Peninsula** *headland* Texas, SW USA
203 Q8 **Mataiea** Tahiti, W French Polynesia
203 T9 **Mataiva** *atoll* Îles Tuamotu, C French Polynesia
191 O7 **Matakana** New South Wales, SE Australia
192 N7 **Matakana Island** *island* NE NZ
85 C15 **Matala** Huíla, SW Angola
202 G12 **Matala'a Pointe** *headland* Île Uvea, N Wallis and Futuna
161 K25 **Matale** Central Province, C Sri Lanka
202 E12 **Matalesina, Pointe** *headland* Île Alofi, W Wallis and Futuna
78 I10 **Matam** NE Senegal
192 M8 **Matamata** Waikato, North Island, NZ
79 V12 **Matamey** Zinder, S Niger
42 L8 **Matamoros** Coahuila de Zaragoza, NE Mexico
43 P15 **Matamoros** *var.* Izúcar de Matamoros. Puebla, S Mexico
43 Q8 **Matamoros** Tamaulipas, C Mexico
175 Q10 **Matana, Danau** ◎ Sulawesi, C Indonesia
77 S13 **Ma'ṭan as Sārah** SE Libya
84 J12 **Matanda** Luapula, N Zambia
83 J24 **Matandu** ≈ S Tanzania
13 V6 **Matane** Québec, SE Canada
13 V6 **Matane** ≈ Québec, SE Canada
79 S12 **Matankari** Dosso, SW Niger
41 R11 **Matanuska River** ≈ Alaska, USA
56 G7 **Matanza** Santander, N Colombia
46 D4 **Matanzas** Matanzas, NW Cuba
13 V7 **Matapédia** ≈ Québec, SE Canada
13 V6 **Matapédia, Lac** ◎ Québec, SE Canada
202 B17 **Mata Point** *headland* SE Niue
202 D12 **Matapu, Pointe** *headland* Île Futuna, W Wallis and Futuna
64 G12 **Mataquito, Río** ≈ C Chile
161 K26 **Matara** Southern Province, S Sri Lanka
117 D18 **Matarágka** *var.* Mataránga. Dytikí Ellás, C Greece
175 Nn16 **Mataram** Pulau Lombok, C Indonesia
Mataránga *see* Matarágka
189 Q3 **Mataranka** Northern Territory, N Australia
107 W6 **Mataró** *anc.* Illuro. Cataluña, E Spain
192 O8 **Matata** Bay of Plenty, North Island, NZ
198 Cc8 **Matātula, Cape** *headland* Tutuila, W American Samoa
193 D24 **Mataura** Southland, South Island, NZ
193 D24 **Mataura** ≈ South Island, NZ
Mata Uta *see* Matā'utu
202 G11 **Matā'utu** *var.* Mata Uta. ○ (Wallis and Futuna) Île Uvea, Wallis and Futuna
198 B8 **Matāutu** Upolu, C Western Samoa
202 G12 **Matā'utu, Baie de** *bay* Île Uvea, Wallis and Futuna
203 P7 **Mataval, Baie de** *bay* Tahiti, W French Polynesia
202 I16 **Matavera** Rarotonga, S Cook Islands
203 V16 **Mataveri** Easter Island, Chile, E Pacific Ocean
203 V17 **Mataveri** ✕ (Easter Island) Easter Island, Chile, E Pacific Ocean
192 P9 **Matawai** Gisborne, North Island, NZ
13 O10 **Matawin** ≈ Québec, SE Canada
151 V13 **Matay** Taldykorgan, SE Kazakhstan
12 K8 **Matchi-Manitou, Lac** ◎ Québec, SE Canada
43 O10 **Matehuala** San Luis Potosí, C Mexico
47 V13 **Matelot** Trinidad, Trinidad and Tobago
85 M15 **Matenge** Tete, NW Mozambique
109 O18 **Matera** Basilicata, S Italy
113 O21 **Mátészalka** Szabolcs-Szatmár-Bereg, E Hungary
176 Y10 **Matewar** Irian Jaya, E Indonesia
95 H17 **Matfors** Västernorrland, C Sweden
104 K11 **Matha** Charente-Maritime, W France
1 F15 **Mathematicians Seamounts** *undersea feature* E Pacific Ocean
23 X6 **Mathews** Virginia, NE USA
27 S14 **Mathis** Texas, SW USA
158 J11 **Mathura** *prev.* Muttra. Uttar Pradesh, N India
Mathurai *see* Madurai
179 Rr16 **Mati** Mindanao, S Philippines
Matianus *see* Orūmīyeh, Daryācheh-ye
Matiara *see* Matiāri
155 Q15 **Matiāri** *var.* Matiara. Sind, SE Pakistan
43 S16 **Matías Romero** Oaxaca, SE Mexico
45 O13 **Matina** Limón, E Costa Rica
12 D10 **Matinenda Lake** ◎ Ontario, S Canada
21 R8 **Matinicus Island** *island* Maine, NE USA
Matisco/Matisco Ædourum *see* Mâcon
155 Q16 **Mātli** Sind, SE Pakistan
99 M18 **Matlock** C England, UK
61 F18 **Mato Grosso** *prev.* Vila Bela da Santissima Trindade. Mato Grosso, W Brazil
61 G17 **Mato Grosso** *off.* Estado de Mato Grosso; *prev.* Matto Grosso. ◐ *state* W Brazil
62 H8 **Mato Grosso do Sul** *off.* Estado de Mato Grosso do Sul. ◐ *state* S Brazil
61 I18 **Mato Grosso, Planalto de** *plateau* C Brazil
106 G6 **Matosinhos** *prev.* Matozinhos. Porto, NW Portugal
57 Z10 **Matoury** NE French Guiana
Matozinhos *see* Matosinhos
113 L21 **Mátra** ⛰ N Hungary
147 Y8 **Maṭraḥ** *var.* Mutrah. NE Oman
118 L12 **Mătrașești** Vrancea, E Romania
110 M8 **Matrei Am Brenner** Tirol, W Austria
111 P8 **Matrei in Osttirol** Tirol, W Austria
78 I15 **Matru** SW Sierra Leone
77 U7 **Maṭrūḥ** *var.* Mersa Maṭrūḥ; *anc.* Paraetonium. NW Egypt
172 Q13 **Matsubara** *var.* Matubara. Kagoshima, Tokuno-shima, SW Japan
171 K16 **Matsudo** *var.* Matudo. Chiba, Honshū, S Japan
170 F11 **Matsue** *var.* Matsuye, Matue. Shimane, Honshū, SW Japan
171 Mm7 **Matsumae** Hokkaidō, NE Japan
171 J14 **Matsumoto** *var.* Matumoto. Nagano, Honshū, S Japan
171 H16 **Matsusaka** *var.* Matsuzaka, Matusaka. Mie, Honshū, SW Japan
167 S12 **Matsu Tao** *Chin.* Mazu Dao. *island* NW Taiwan
Matsutō *see* Mattō
170 C12 **Matsuura** *var.* Matuura. Nagasaki, Kyūshū, SW Japan
170 Ee14 **Matsuyama** *var.* Matuyama. Ehime, Shikoku, SW Japan
Matsuye *see* Matsue
Matsuzaka *see* Matsusaka
171 J17 **Matsuzaki** Shizuoka, Honshū, S Japan
12 F8 **Mattagami** ≈ Ontario, S Canada
12 F8 **Mattagami Lake** ◎ Ontario, S Canada
64 K12 **Mattaldi** Córdoba, C Argentina
23 Y9 **Mattamuskeet, Lake** ◎ North Carolina, SE USA
23 W6 **Mattaponi River** ≈ Virginia, NE USA
12 I11 **Mattawa** Ontario, SE Canada
12 I11 **Mattawa** ≈ Ontario, SE Canada
21 S5 **Mattawamkeag** Maine, NE USA
21 S4 **Mattawamkeag Lake** ◎ Maine, NE USA
110 D11 **Matterhorn** *It.* Monte Cervino. ▲ Italy/Switzerland *see also* Cervino, Monte
37 W1 **Matterhorn** ▲ Nevada, W USA
34 L12 **Matterhorn** *var.* Sacajawea Peak. ▲ Oregon, NW USA
37 R8 **Matterhorn Peak** ▲ California, W USA
111 Y5 **Mattersburg** Burgenland, E Austria
110 E11 **Matter Vispa** ≈ S Switzerland
57 R7 **Matthews Ridge** N Guyana
46 K7 **Matthew Town** Great Inagua, S Bahamas
111 Q4 **Mattighofen** Oberösterreich, NW Austria
109 N16 **Mattinata** Puglia, SE Italy
147 T9 **Maṭṭī, Sabkhat** *salt flat* Saudi Arabia/UAE
20 M14 **Mattituck** Long Island, New York, NE USA
171 I13 **Mattō** *var.* Matsutō. Ishikawa, Honshū, SW Japan
Matto Grosso *see* Mato Grosso
32 M14 **Mattoon** Illinois, N USA
59 L16 **Mattos, Río** ≈ C Bolivia
Mattu *see* Metu
174 L15 **Matu** Sarawak, East Malaysia
59 E14 **Matucana** Lima, W Peru
Matudo *see* Matsudo
Matue *see* Matsue
197 J16 **Matuku** *island* S Fiji
114 B9 **Matulji** Primorje-Gorski Kotar, NW Croatia
Matumoto *see* Matsumoto
57 P5 **Maturín** Monagas, NE Venezuela
Matusaka *see* Matsusaka
Matuura *see* Matsuura
Matuyama *see* Matsuyama
130 K11 **Matveyev Kurgan** Rostovskaya Oblast', SW Russian Federation
131 O8 **Matyshevo** Volgogradskaya Oblast', SW Russian Federation
159 O13 **Mau** *var.* Maunāth Bhanjan. Uttar Pradesh, N India
85 O14 **Maúa** Niassa, N Mozambique
104 M17 **Maubermé, Pic de** *var.* Tuc de Maubermé, *Sp.* Pico Mauberme; *prev.* Tuc de Maubermé. ▲ France/Spain *see also* Mouberme, Tuc de
Maubermé, Pico *see* Maubermé, Pic de/ Mouberme, Tuc de
Maubermé, Tuc de *see* Maubermé, Pic de/ Mouberme, Tuc de
105 Q2 **Maubeuge** Nord, N France
177 Ff8 **Maubin** Irrawaddy, SW Myanmar
158 L13 **Maudaha** Uttar Pradesh, N India
191 N9 **Maude** New South Wales, SE Australia
205 P3 **Maudheimvidda** *physical region* Antarctica
67 N22 **Maud Rise** *undersea feature* S Atlantic Ocean
111 Q4 **Mauerkirchen** Oberösterreich, NW Austria
Mauersee *see* Mamry, Jezioro
196 K2 **Maug Islands** *island group* N Northern Mariana Islands
105 Q15 **Mauguio** Hérault, S France
199 Kk6 **Maui** *island* Hawaii, USA, C Pacific Ocean
202 M16 **Mauke** *atoll* S Cook Islands
64 G13 **Maule** *off.* Región del Maule. ◐ *region* C Chile
104 J9 **Mauléon** Deux-Sèvres, W France
104 J16 **Mauléon-Licharre** Pyrénées-Atlantiques, SW France
64 G13 **Maule, Río** ≈ C Chile
65 G17 **Maullín** Los Lagos, S Chile
Maulmain *see* Moulmein
33 R11 **Maumee** Ohio, N USA
33 Q12 **Maumee River** ≈ Indiana/Ohio, N USA
29 U11 **Maumelle** Arkansas, C USA
29 T11 **Maumelle, Lake** ⊡ Arkansas, C USA
175 Qq16 **Maumere** *prev.* Maoemere. Flores, S Indonesia
85 G17 **Maun** Ngamiland, C Botswana
Maunāth Bhanjan *see* Mau
Maunawai *see* Waimea
202 H16 **Maungaroa** ▲ Rarotonga, S Cook Islands
192 K3 **Maungatapere** Northland, North Island, NZ
192 K4 **Maungaturoto** Northland, North Island, NZ
203 R10 **Maupiti** *var.* Maurua. *island* Îles Sous le Vent, W French Polynesia
158 K14 **Mau Rānīpur** Uttar Pradesh, N India
24 K9 **Maurepas, Lake** ◎ Louisiana, S USA
105 T16 **Maures** ⛰ SE France
105 O12 **Mauriac** Cantal, C France
Maurice *see* Mauritius
67 J20 **Maurice Ewing Bank** *undersea feature* SW Atlantic Ocean
190 C4 **Maurice, Lake** *salt lake* South Australia
20 I17 **Maurice River** ≈ New Jersey, NE USA
27 Y10 **Mauriceville** Texas, SW USA
100 K12 **Maurik** Gelderland, C Netherlands
78 H8 **Mauritania** *off.* Islamic Republic of Mauritania, *Ar.* Mūrītānīyah. ◆ *republic* W Africa
181 W15 **Mauritius** *off.* Republic of Mauritius, *Fr.* Maurice. ◆ *republic* W Indian Ocean
132 M17 **Mauritius** *island* W Indian Ocean
181 N9 **Mauritius Trench** *undersea feature* W Indian Ocean
104 H6 **Mauron** Morbihan, NW France
105 N13 **Maurs** Cantal, C France
Maurua *see* Maupiti
Maury Mid-Ocean Channel *see* Maury Seachannel
66 L6 **Maury Seachannel** *var.* Maury Mid-Ocean Channel. *undersea feature* N Atlantic Ocean
32 K8 **Mauston** Wisconsin, N USA
111 R8 **Mauterndorf** Salzburg, NW Austria
111 T4 **Mauthausen** Oberösterreich, N Austria
111 Q9 **Mauthen** Kärnten, S Austria
85 F15 **Mavinga** Cuando Cubango, SE Angola
85 M17 **Mavita** Manica, W Mozambique
117 K22 **Mavrópetra, Ákra** *headland* Thíra, Kykládes, Greece, Aegean Sea
117 F16 **Mavrovoúni** ▲ C Greece
192 Q8 **Mawhai Point** *headland* North Island, NZ
177 Ff3 **Mawlaik** Sagaing, C Myanmar
Mawlamyine *see* Moulmein
147 N14 **Mawr, Wādī** *dry watercourse* NW Yemen
205 X5 **Mawson** *Australian research station* Antarctica
205 X5 **Mawson Coast** *physical region* Antarctica
30 M4 **Max** North Dakota, N USA
43 W12 **Maxcanú** Yucatán, SE Mexico
Maxesibebi *see* Mount Ayliff
111 Q5 **Maxglan** ✕ (Salzburg) Salzburg, W Austria
95 K16 **Maxmo** *Fin.* Maksamaa. Vaasa, W Finland
23 T11 **Maxton** North Carolina, SE USA
27 R8 **May** Texas, SW USA
194 E10 **May** ≈ NW PNG
127 N17 **Maya** ≈ E Russian Federation
157 Q19 **Māyābandar** Andaman and Nicobar Islands, India, E Indian Ocean
Mayadin *see* Al Mayādīn
46 L5 **Mayaguana** *island* SE Bahamas
46 L5 **Mayaguana Passage** *passage* SE Bahamas
47 S6 **Mayagüez** W Puerto Rico
47 R6 **Mayagüez, Bahía de** *bay* W Puerto Rico
Mayals *see* Maials
81 G20 **Mayama** Le Pool, SE Congo
39 V8 **Maya, Mesa De** ▲ Colorado, C USA
149 R4 **Mayamey** Semnān, N Iran
44 F3 **Maya Mountains** *Sp.* Montañas Mayas. ⛰ Belize/Guatemala
46 I7 **Mayarí** Holguín, E Cuba
Mayas, Montañas *see* Maya Mountains
20 I17 **May, Cape** *headland* New Jersey, NE USA
82 J11 **Maych'ew** *var.* Mai Chio, *It.* Mai Ceu. N Ethiopia
144 I2 **Maydān Ikbiz** Ḥalab, N Syria
155 Q5 **Maydān Shahr** Wardag, E Afghanistan
82 O12 **Maydh** Sanaag, N Somalia
Maydī *see* Mīdī
Mayebashi *see* Maebashi
Mayence *see* Mainz
104 K6 **Mayenne** Mayenne, NW France
104 J6 **Mayenne** ◐ *department* NW France
104 J7 **Mayenne** ≈ N France
38 K12 **Mayer** Arizona, SW USA
24 J4 **Mayersville** Mississippi, S USA
9 P14 **Mayerthorpe** Alberta, SW Canada
23 S12 **Mayesville** South Carolina, SE USA
193 G19 **Mayfield** Canterbury, South Island, NZ
35 N14 **Mayfield** Idaho, NW USA
22 G7 **Mayfield** Kentucky, S USA
38 L5 **Mayfield** Utah, W USA
168 K9 **Mayhan** Övörhangay, C Mongolia
39 T14 **Mayhill** New Mexico, SW USA
151 T9 **Maykain** *Kaz.* Mayqayyng. Pavlodar, NE Kazakhstan
130 L14 **Maykop** Respublika Adygeya, SW Russian Federation
Maylibash *see* Maylybas
Mayli-Say *see* Mayluu-Suu
153 T9 **Mayluu-Suu** *prev.* Mayli-Say, *Kir.* Mayly-Say. Dzhalal-Abadskaya Oblast', W Kyrgyzstan
150 L14 **Maylybas** *prev.* Maylibash. Kzyl-Orda, S Kazakhstan
Mayly-Say *see* Mayluu-Suu
Maymana *see* Meymaneh
178 Gg5 **Maymyo** Mandalay, C Myanmar
127 P6 **Mayn** ≈ NE Russian Federation
131 Q5 **Mayna** Ul'yanovskaya Oblast', W Russian Federation
23 N8 **Maynardville** Tennessee, S USA
12 J13 **Maynooth** Ontario, SE Canada
8 I6 **Mayo** Yukon Territory, NW Canada
25 U9 **Mayo** Florida, SE USA
99 B16 **Mayo** *Ir.* Maigh Eo. *cultural region* W Ireland
Mayo *see* Maio
80 G12 **Mayo-Kébbi** *off.* Préfecture du Mayo-Kébbi, *var.* Mayo-Kébi. ◐ *prefecture* SW Chad
Mayo-Kébi *see* Mayo-Kébbi
81 F19 **Mayoko** Le Niari, SW Congo
179 Q11 **Mayon Volcano** Ж Luzon, N Philippines
63 A24 **Mayor Buratovich** Buenos Aires, E Argentina
106 L4 **Mayorga** Castilla-León, N Spain
192 N6 **Mayor Island** *island* NE NZ
Mayor Pablo Lagerenza *see* Capitán Pablo Lagerenza
Mayor, Puig *see* Major, Puig
181 I14 **Mayotte** ◇ *French territorial collectivity* E Africa
Mayoumba *see* Mayumba
46 J13 **May Pen** C Jamaica
Mayqayyng *see* Maykain
179 P7 **Mayraira Point** *headland* Luzon, N Philippines
111 N8 **Mayrhofen** Tirol, W Austria
194 F10 **May River** East Sepik, NW PNG
126 Mm15 **Mayskiy** Amurskaya Oblast', SE Russian Federation
131 O15 **Mayskiy** Kabardino-Balkarskaya Respublika, SW Russian Federation
151 U9 **Mayskoye** Pavlodar, NE Kazakhstan
20 J17 **Mays Landing** New Jersey, NE USA
23 N4 **Maysville** Kentucky, S USA
29 R2 **Maysville** Missouri, C USA
176 Y14 **Mayu** *channel* Irian Jaya, E Indonesia
81 D20 **Mayumba** *var.* Mayoumba. Nyanga, S Gabon
175 Ss7 **Mayu, Pulau** *island* Maluku, E Indonesia
33 S8 **Mayville** Michigan, N USA
20 C11 **Mayville** New York, NE USA
31 Q4 **Mayville** North Dakota, N USA
126 M11 **Mayya** Respublika Sakha (Yakutiya), NE Russian Federation
Mayyali *see* Mahe
Mayyit, Al Baḥr al *see* Dead Sea
85 J15 **Mazabuka** Southern, S Zambia
Mazaca *see* Kayseri
Mazagan *see* El-Jadida
34 J7 **Mazama** Washington, NW USA
105 O15 **Mazamet** Tarn, S France
149 O4 **Māzandarān** *off.* Ostān-e Māzandarān. ◐ *province* N Iran
162 F7 **Mazar** Xinjiang Uygur Zizhiqu, NW China
109 H24 **Mazara del Vallo** Sicilia, Italy, C Mediterranean Sea
155 O2 **Mazār-e Sharīf** *var.* Mazār-i Sharif. Balkh, N Afghanistan
Mazār-i Sharif *see* Mazār-e Sharīf
107 R13 **Mazarrón** Murcia, SE Spain
107 R14 **Mazarrón, Golfo de** *gulf* SE Spain
57 S9 **Mazaruni River** ≈ N Guyana
44 B6 **Mazatenango** Suchitepéquez, SW Guatemala
42 I10 **Mazatlán** Sinaloa, C Mexico
38 L12 **Mazatzal Mountains** ⛰ Arizona, SW USA
120 D10 **Mažeikiai** Mažeikiai, NW Lithuania
120 D7 **Mazirbe** Talsi, NW Latvia
42 G5 **Mazocahui** Sonora, NW Mexico
59 I18 **Mazocruz** Puno, S Peru
Mazoe, Rio *see* Mazowe
81 N21 **Mazomeno** Maniema, E Zaire
165 Q6 **Mazong Shan** ▲ N China
85 L16 **Mazowe** *var.* Rio Mazoe. ≈ Mozambique/Zimbabwe
Mazra'a *see* Al Mazra'ah
144 G6 **Mazraat Kfar Debiâne** C Lebanon
120 H7 **Mazsalaca** *Est.* Väike-Salatsi, *Ger.* Salisburg. Valmiera, N Latvia
112 L9 **Mazury** *physical region* NE Poland
121 M20 **Mazyr** *Rus.* Mozyr'. Homyel'skaya Voblasts', SE Belarus
109 K25 **Mazzarino** Sicilia, Italy, C Mediterranean Sea
Mba *see* Ba
85 L21 **Mbabane** ● (Swaziland) NW Swaziland
Mbacké *see* Mbaké
79 N16 **Mbahiakro** E Ivory Coast
81 I16 **Mbaïki** *var.* M'Baiki. Lobaye, SW Central African Republic
81 F14 **Mbakaou, Lac de** ◎ C Cameroon
78 G11 **Mbaké** *var.* Mbacké. W Senegal
84 L11 **Mbala** *prev.* Abercorn. Northern, NE Zambia
85 J18 **Mbalabala** *prev.* Balla Balla. Matabeleland South, SW Zimbabwe
83 G18 **Mbale** E Uganda
81 E16 **Mbalmayo** *var.* M'Balmayo. Centre, S Cameroon
83 H25 **Mbamba Bay** Ruvuma, S Tanzania
81 I18 **Mbandaka** *prev.* Coquilhatville. Equateur, NW Zaire
84 B9 **M'Banza Congo** *var.* Mbanza Congo; *prev.* São Salvador, São Salvador do Congo. Zaire, NW Angola
81 G21 **Mbanza-Ngungu** Bas-Zaïre, W Zaire
69 V11 **Mbarangandu** ≈ E Tanzania
83 E19 **Mbarara** SW Uganda
81 L15 **Mbari** ≈ SE Central African Republic
83 I24 **Mbarika Mountains** ⛰ S Tanzania
Mbatiki *see* Batiki
80 F13 **Mbé** Nord, N Cameroon
83 J24 **Mbemkuru** *var.* Mbwemkuru. ≈ S Tanzania
Mbengga *see* Beqa
180 H13 **Mbéni** Grande Comore, NW Comoros
85 K18 **Mberengwa** Midlands, S Zimbabwe
83 G24 **Mbeya** Mbeya, SW Tanzania
83 G23 **Mbeya** ◐ *region* S Tanzania
81 E19 **Mbigou** Ngounié, C Gabon
Mbilua *see* Vella Lavella
81 F19 **Mbinda** Le Niari, SW Congo
81 D17 **Mbini** W Equatorial Guinea
Mbini *see* Uolo, Río
85 L18 **Mbizi** Masvingo, SE Zimbabwe
83 G23 **Mbogo** Mbeya, W Tanzania
81 N15 **Mboki** Haut-Mbomou, SE Central African Republic
81 G18 **Mbomo** Cuvette, NW Congo
81 L15 **Mbomou** ◐ *prefecture* SE Central African Republic
Mbomou/M'Bomu/Mbomu *see* Bomu
78 F11 **Mbour** W Senegal
78 I10 **Mbout** Gorgol, S Mauritania
81 J14 **Mbrès** *var.* Mbrés. Nana-Grébizi, C Central African Republic
81 L22 **Mbuji-Mayi** *prev.* Bakwanga. Kasai Oriental, S Zaire
194 J9 **M'buke Islands** *island group* N PNG
83 H21 **Mbulu** Arusha, N Tanzania
194 K8 **M'bunai** *var.* Bunai. Manus Island, N PNG
64 N8 **Mburucuyá** Corrientes, NE Argentina
Mbutha *see* Buca
Mbwemkuru *see* Mbemkuru
83 G21 **Mbwikwe** Singida, C Tanzania
11 O15 **McAdam** New Brunswick, SE Canada
27 O5 **McAdoo** Texas, SW USA
37 V2 **McAfee Peak** ▲ Nevada, W USA
29 P11 **McAlester** Oklahoma, C USA
27 S17 **McAllen** Texas, SW USA
23 S11 **McBee** South Carolina, SE USA
9 N14 **McBride** British Columbia, SW Canada
26 M9 **McCamey** Texas, SW USA
35 R15 **McCammon** Idaho, NW USA
37 X11 **McCarran** ✕ (Las Vegas) Nevada, W USA
41 T11 **McCarthy** Alaska, USA
32 M5 **McCaslin Mountain** *hill* Wisconsin, N USA
27 O2 **McClellan Creek** ≈ Texas, SW USA
23 T14 **McClellanville** South Carolina, SE USA
15 Jj2 **McClintock Channel** *channel* Northwest Territories, N Canada
205 R12 **McClintock, Mount** ▲ Antarctica
37 N2 **McCloud** California, W USA
37 N3 **McCloud River** ≈ California, W USA
37 Q9 **McClure, Lake** ⊡ California, W USA
207 O8 **McClure Strait** *strait* Northwest Territories, N Canada
31 N4 **McClusky** North Dakota, N USA
23 T11 **McColl** South Carolina, SE USA
24 K7 **McComb** Mississippi, S USA
20 E16 **McConnellsburg** Pennsylvania, NE USA
33 T14 **McConnelsville** Ohio, N USA
30 M17 **McCook** Nebraska, C USA
23 P13 **McCormick** South Carolina, SE USA
9 W16 **McCreary** Manitoba, S Canada
29 W11 **McCrory** Arkansas, C USA
27 T10 **McDade** Texas, SW USA
25 O8 **McDavid** Florida, SE USA
37 T1 **McDermitt** Nevada, W USA
25 S4 **McDonough** Georgia, SE USA
38 L12 **McDowell Mountains** ⛰ Arizona, SW USA
22 H8 **McEwen** Tennessee, S USA
37 R12 **McFarland** California, W USA
Mcfarlane, Lake *see* Macfarlane, Lake
29 P12 **McGee Creek Lake** ⊡ Oklahoma, C USA
29 W13 **McGehee** Arkansas, C USA
37 X5 **Mcgill** Nevada, W USA
12 K11 **McGillivray, Lac** ◎ Québec, SE Canada
41 P10 **Mcgrath** Alaska, USA
27 T8 **McGregor** Texas, SW USA
35 O12 **McGuire, Mount** ▲ Idaho, NW USA
85 M14 **Mchinji** *prev.* Fort Manning. Central, W Malawi
30 M7 **McIntosh** South Dakota, N USA
16 O3 **McKeand** ≈ Baffin Island, Northwest Territories, NE Canada
203 R4 **McKean Island** *island* Phoenix Islands, C Kiribati
32 J13 **McKee Creek** ≈ Illinois, N USA
20 C15 **Mckeesport** Pennsylvania, NE USA
23 V7 **McKenney** Virginia, NE USA
22 G8 **McKenzie** Tennessee, S USA
193 B20 **McKerrow, Lake** ◎ South Island, NZ
41 Q10 **McKinley, Mount** *var.* Denali. ▲ Alaska, USA
41 R10 **McKinley Park** Alaska, USA
36 K3 **McKinleyville** California, W USA
27 U6 **McKinney** Texas, SW USA
28 I5 **McKinney, Lake** ◎ Kansas, C USA
30 M7 **McLaughlin** South Dakota, N USA
27 O2 **McLean** Texas, SW USA
32 M16 **Mcleansboro** Illinois, N USA
9 O13 **McLennan** Alberta, W Canada
12 L9 **McLennan, Lac** ◎ Québec, SE Canada
8 M13 **McLeod Lake** British Columbia, W Canada
29 N10 **McLoud** Oklahoma, C USA
34 G15 **McLoughlin, Mount** ▲ Oregon, NW USA
39 U15 **McMillan, Lake** ⊡ New Mexico, SW USA
34 G11 **McMinnville** Oregon, NW USA
22 K9 **McMinnville** Tennessee, S USA
205 R13 **McMurdo** *US research station* Antarctica
26 H9 **McNary** Texas, SW USA
39 N13 **Mcnary** Arizona, SW USA
29 N5 **McPherson** Kansas, C USA
McPherson *see* Fort McPherson
25 U6 **McRae** Georgia, SE USA
31 P4 **McVille** North Dakota, N USA
85 J25 **Mdantsane** Eastern Cape, SE South Africa
178 Jj6 **Me** Ninh Binh, N Vietnam
28 J7 **Meade** Kansas, C USA
41 O5 **Meade River** ≈ Alaska, USA
37 Y11 **Mead, Lake** ⊡ Arizona/Nevada, W USA
26 M5 **Meadow** Texas, SW USA
9 S14 **Meadow Lake** Saskatchewan, C Canada
37 Y10 **Meadow Valley Wash** ≈ Nevada, W USA
24 J7 **Meadville** Mississippi, S USA
20 B12 **Meadville** Pennsylvania, NE USA
12 F14 **Meaford** Ontario, S Canada
Meáin, Inis *see* Inishmaan
106 G8 **Mealhada** Aveiro, N Portugal
11 R8 **Mealy Mountains** ⛰ Newfoundland and Labrador, E Canada
9 O10 **Meander River** Alberta, W Canada
34 E11 **Meares, Cape** *headland* Oregon, NW USA
49 V6 **Mearim, Rio** ≈ NE Brazil
Measca, Loch *see* Mask, Lough
99 F17 **Meath** *Ir.* An Mhí. *cultural region* E Ireland
9 T14 **Meath Park** Saskatchewan, S Canada
105 O5 **Meaux** Seine-et-Marne, N France
23 T9 **Mebane** North Carolina, SE USA
176 W9 **Mebo, Gunung** ▲ Irian Jaya, E Indonesia
96 I8 **Mebonden** Sør-Trøndelag, S Norway
84 A10 **Mebridege** ≈ NW Angola
37 W16 **Mecca** California, W USA
Mecca *see* Makkah
31 Y14 **Mechanicsville** Iowa, C USA
20 L10 **Mechanicville** New York, NE USA
101 H17 **Mechelen** *Eng.* Mechlin, *Fr.* Malines. Antwerpen, C Belgium
196 C8 **Mecherchar** *var.* Eil Malk. *island* Palau Islands, Palau
103 D17 **Mechernich** Nordrhein-Westfalen, W Germany
130 L12 **Mechetinskaya** Rostovskaya Oblast', SW Russian Federation
116 J11 **Mechka** ≈ S Bulgaria
Mechlin *see* Mechelen
63 D23 **Mechongué** Buenos Aires, E Argentina
117 L14 **Mecidiye** Edirne, NW Turkey
103 I24 **Meckenbeuren** Baden-Württemberg, S Germany
102 L8 **Mecklenburger Bucht** *bay* N Germany
102 M10 **Mecklenburgische Seenplatte** *wetland* NE Germany
102 L9 **Mecklenburg-Vorpommern** ◐ *state* NE Germany
85 Q15 **Meconta** Nampula, NE Mozambique
113 I25 **Mecsek** ⛰ SW Hungary
85 P14 **Mecubúri** ≈ N Mozambique
85 Q14 **Mecúfi** Cabo Delgado, NE Mozambique
84 O13 **Mecula** Niassa, N Mozambique
173 Ff5 **Medan** Sumatera, E Indonesia
63 A24 **Médanos** *var.* Medanos. Buenos Aires, E Argentina
63 C19 **Médanos** Entre Ríos, E Argentina
161 K24 **Medawachchiya** North Central Province, N Sri Lanka
108 C8 **Mede** Lombardia, N Italy
76 J5 **Médéa** *var.* El Mediyya, Lemdiyya. N Algeria
Medeba *see* Ma'dabā
56 E8 **Medellín** Antioquia, NW Colombia
102 H9 **Medem** ≈ NW Germany
100 J8 **Medemblik** Noord-Holland, NW Netherlands
77 N7 **Médenine** *var.* Madanīyīn. SE Tunisia
78 G9 **Mederdra** Trarza, SW Mauritania
Medeshamstede *see* Peterborough
44 F4 **Medesto Mendez** Izabal, NE Guatemala
21 O11 **Medford** Massachusetts, NE USA
29 N8 **Medford** Oklahoma, C USA
34 G15 **Medford** Oregon, NW USA
32 K6 **Medford** Wisconsin, N USA
41 P10 **Medfra** Alaska, USA
118 M14 **Medgidia** Constanța, SE Romania
Medgyes *see* Mediaș
62 G11 **Medianeira** Paraná, S Brazil
31 Y15 **Mediapolis** Iowa, C USA
118 I11 **Mediaș** *Ger.* Mediasch, *Hung.* Medgyes. Sibiu, C Romania
43 S15 **Medias Aguas** Veracruz-Llave, SE Mexico
Mediasch *see* Mediaș
108 G10 **Medicina** Emilia-Romagna, C Italy
35 X16 **Medicine Bow** Wyoming, C USA
39 S2 **Medicine Bow Mountains** ⛰ Colorado/Wyoming, C USA
35 X16 **Medicine Bow River** ≈ Wyoming, C USA
9 R17 **Medicine Hat** Alberta, SW Canada
28 L7 **Medicine Lodge** Kansas, C USA
28 L7 **Medicine Lodge River** ≈ Kansas/Oklahoma, C USA
114 E7 **Međimurje** *off.* Medimurska Županija. ◐ *province* N Croatia
Medimurska Županija *see* Medimurje
56 G10 **Medina** Cundinamarca, C Colombia
20 E9 **Medina** New York, NE USA
31 O5 **Medina** North Dakota, N USA
33 T11 **Medina** Ohio, N USA
27 Q11 **Medina** Texas, SW USA
Medina *see* Al Madīnah
123 Ll12 **Medina Bank** *undersea feature* C Mediterranean Sea
107 P6 **Medinaceli** Castilla-León, N Spain
106 L6 **Medina del Campo** Castilla-León, N Spain
106 L5 **Medina de Rioseco** Castilla-León, N Spain
Médina Gonassé *see* Médina Gounas
78 H12 **Médina Gounas** *var.* Médina Gonassé. S Senegal
27 S12 **Medina River** ≈ Texas, SW USA
106 K16 **Medina Sidonia** Andalucía, S Spain
Medinat Israel *see* Israel
121 H14 **Medininkai** Vilnius, SE Lithuania
159 R16 **Medinīpur** West Bengal, NE India
Mediolanum *see* Saintes, France
Mediolanum *see* Milano, Italy
Mediomatrica *see* Metz
124 O13 **Mediterranean Ridge** *undersea feature* C Mediterranean Sea
123 L11 **Mediterranean Sea** *Fr.* Mer Méditerranée. *sea* Africa/Asia/Europe
Méditerranée, Mer *see* Mediterranean Sea
81 N17 **Medje** Haut-Zaïre, NE Zaire
123 K11 **Medjerda, Oued** *var.* Mejerda, Wādī Majardah. ≈ Algeria/Tunisia *see also* Mejerda
116 G7 **Medkovets** Oblast Montana, NW Bulgaria
95 J15 **Medle** Västerbotten, N Sweden
131 W7 **Mednogorsk** Orenburgskaya Oblast', W Russian Federation
127 Qq9 **Mednyy, Ostrov** *island* E Russian Federation
104 J12 **Médoc** *cultural region* SW France
165 Q16 **Mêdog** Xizang Zizhiqu, W China

◆ Country ● Country Capital ◇ Dependent Territory ○ Dependent Territory Capital ◐ Administrative Region ✕ International Airport ▲ Mountain ⛰ Mountain Range Ж Volcano ≈ River ◎ Lake ⊡ Reservoir

283

Medora – Miaodao Qundao

30 J5 **Medora** North Dakota, N USA
81 E17 **Médouneu** Woleu-Ntem, N Gabon
108 I7 **Meduna** ~ NE Italy
Medunta *see* Mantes-la-Jolie
Medvedica *see* Medveditsa
128 J16 **Medveditsa** *var.* Medvedica. ~ W Russian Federation
131 O9 **Medveditsa** ~ SW Russian Federation
114 E8 **Medvednica** ▲▲ NE Croatia
129 R15 **Medvedok** Kirovskaya Oblast', NW Russian Federation
127 Nn5 **Medvezh'i, Ostrova** *island group* NE Russian Federation
128 J9 **Medvezh'yegorsk** Respublika Kareliya, NW Russian Federation
111 T11 **Medvode** *Ger.* Zwischenwässern. NW Slovenia
130 J4 **Medyn'** Kaluzhskaya Oblast', W Russian Federation
188 J10 **Meekatharra** Western Australia
39 Q4 **Meeker** Colorado, C USA
11 T12 **Meelpaeg Lake** ◎ Newfoundland, Newfoundland and Labrador, E Canada
Meenen *see* Menen
103 M16 **Meerane** Sachsen, E Germany
103 D15 **Meerbusch** Nordrhein-Westfalen, W Germany
100 I12 **Meerkerk** Zuid-Holland, C Netherlands
101 L18 **Meerssen** *var.* Mersen. Limburg, SE Netherlands
158 J10 **Meerut** Uttar Pradesh, N India
35 U13 **Meeteetse** Wyoming, C USA
101 K17 **Meeuwen** Limburg, NE Belgium
83 J16 **Mēga** S Ethiopia
83 J16 **Mēga Escarpment** *escarpment* S Ethiopia
Megála Kalívia *see* Megála Kalývia
117 E16 **Megála Kalývia** *var.* Megála Kalívia. Thessalía, C Greece
117 H14 **Megáli Panagiá** *var.* Megáli Panayía. Kentrikí Makedonía, N Greece
Megáli Panayía *see* Megáli Panagiá
Megáli Préspa, Límni *see* Prespa, Lake
116 K12 **Megálo Livádi** ▲ Bulgaria/Greece
117 E20 **Megalópoli** *prev.* Megalópolis. Pelopónnisos, S Greece
Megalópolis *see* Megalópoli
176 V9 **Megamo** Irian Jaya, E Indonesia
117 C18 **Meganísi** *island* Iónioi Nísoi, Greece, C Mediterranean Sea
Meganom, Mys *see* Mehanom, Mys
Mégantic *see* Lac-Mégantic
13 R12 **Mégantic, Mont** ▲ Québec, SE Canada
117 G19 **Mégara** Attikí, C Greece
27 R5 **Megargel** Texas, SW USA
100 K13 **Megen** Noord-Brabant, S Netherlands
159 U13 **Meghālaya** ◐ *state* NE India
159 U16 **Meghna** ~ S Bangladesh
143 V14 **Meghri** *Rus.* Megri. SE Armenia
126 Gg11 **Megion** Khanty-Mansiyskiy Avtonomnyy Okrug, C Russian Federation
117 Q23 **Megísti** *var.* Kastellórizon. *island* SE Greece
Megri *see* Meghri
Mehabad *see* Mahābād
118 F13 **Mehadia** *Hung.* Mehádia. Caraş-Severin, SW Romania
94 L7 **Mehamn** Finnmark, N Norway
119 U13 **Mehanom, Mys** *Rus.* Mys Meganom. *headland* S Ukraine
155 P14 **Mehar** Sind, SE Pakistan
188 J8 **Meharry, Mount** ▲ Western Australia
Mehdia *see* Mahdia
118 G14 **Mehedinți** ◐ *county* SW Romania
159 S15 **Meherpur** Khulna, W Bangladesh
23 W8 **Meherrin River** ~ North Carolina/Virginia, SE USA
Meheso *see* Mī'ēso
203 T11 **Mehetia** *island* Îles du Vent, W French Polynesia
120 K6 **Mehikoorma** Tartumaa, E Estonia
Me Hka *see* Nmai Hka
149 N5 **Mehrabad** ✕ (Tehrān) Tehrān, N Iran
148 J7 **Mehrān** Īlām, W Iran
149 Q14 **Mehrān, Rūd-e** *prev.* Mansurabad. ~ W Iran
149 Q9 **Mehrīz** Yazd, C Iran
155 R5 **Mehtarlām** *var.* Mehtar Lām, Meterlam, Methariam, Metharlam. Laghmān, E Afghanistan
105 N8 **Mehun-sur-Yèvre** Cher, C France
81 G14 **Meiganga** Adamaoua, NE Cameroon
166 H10 **Meigu** Sichuan, C China
169 W11 **Meihekou** *var.* Hailong. Jilin, NE China
101 L15 **Meijel** Limburg, SE Netherlands
177 G5 **Meiktila** Mandalay, C Myanmar
Meilbhe, Loch *see* Melvin, Lough
110 G7 **Meilen** Zürich, N Switzerland
Meilu *see* Wuchuan
167 T12 **Meinhua Yu** *island* N Taiwan
103 J17 **Meiningen** Thüringen, C Germany
110 F9 **Meiringen** Bern, S Switzerland
103 O15 **Meissen** *var.* Meißen. Sachsen, E Germany
103 I15 **Meissner** ▲ C Germany
101 K25 **Meix-devant-Virton** Luxembourg, SE Belgium
Mei Xian *see* Meizhou
167 P13 **Meizhou** *var.* Meixian, Mei Xian. Guangdong, S China
69 P2 **Mejerda** *var.* Oued Medjerda, Wādī Majardah. ~ Algeria/Tunisia *see also* Medjerda, Oued
44 F7 **Mejicanos** San Salvador, C El Salvador
Méjico *see* Mexico
64 G5 **Mejillones** Antofagasta, N Chile
201 V5 **Mejit Island** *var.* Mājeej. *island* Ratak Chain, NE Marshall Islands
81 F17 **Mékambo** Ogooué-Ivindo, NE Gabon
82 J10 **Mek'elē** *var.* Makale. N Ethiopia
76 I10 **Mekerrhane, Sebkha** *var.* Sebkha Meqerghane, Sebkra Mekerrhane. *salt flat* C Algeria
Mekerrhane, Sebkra *see* Mekerrhane, Sebkha
78 G10 **Mékhé** NW Senegal
152 G14 **Mekhinli** Ahalskiy Velayat, C Turkmenistan
13 P9 **Mékinac, Lac** ◎ Québec, SE Canada
Meklong *see* Samut Songhram
76 G6 **Meknès** N Morocco
133 U12 **Mekong** *var.* Lan-ts'ang Chiang, *Cam.* Mékôngk, *Chin.* Lancang Jiang, *Lao.* Mènam Khong, *Th.* Mae Nam Khong, *Tib.* Dza Chu, *Vtn.* Sông Tiên Giang. ~ SE Asia
Mekongga, Pegunungan *see* Mengkoka, Pegunungan
Mékôngk *see* Mekong
178 K15 **Mekong, Mouths of the** *delta* S Vietnam
40 L12 **Mekoryuk** Nunivak Island, Alaska, USA
79 R14 **Mékrou** ~ N Benin
174 H6 **Melaka** *var.* Malacca. Melaka, Peninsular Malaysia
174 H6 **Melaka** *var.* Malacca. ◐ *state* Peninsular Malaysia
Melaka, Selat *see* Malacca, Strait of
183 O6 **Melanesia** *island group* W Pacific Ocean
183 P5 **Melanesian Basin** *undersea feature* W Pacific Ocean
175 Ss4 **Melanguane** Pulau Karakelang, N Indonesia
174 L18 **Melawi, Sungai** ~ Borneo, N Indonesia
191 N12 **Melbourne** *state capital* Victoria, SE Australia
29 V9 **Melbourne** Arkansas, C USA
25 Y12 **Melbourne** Florida, SE USA
31 W14 **Melbourne** Iowa, C USA
94 G10 **Melbu** Nordland, C Norway
Melchor de Mencos *see* Ciudad Melchor de Mencos
65 F19 **Melchor, Isla** *island* Archipiélago de los Chonos, S Chile
42 M9 **Melchor Ocampo** Zacatecas, C Mexico
12 C11 **Meldrum Bay** Manitoulin Island, Ontario, S Canada
Meleda *see* Mljet
108 D8 **Melegnano** *prev.* Marignano. Lombardia, N Italy
196 F9 **Melekeok** *var.* Melekeiok. Babeldaob, N Palau
114 L9 **Melenci** *Hung.* Melencze. Serbia, N Yugoslavia
Melencze *see* Melenci
131 N4 **Melenki** Vladimirskaya Oblast', W Russian Federation
131 V6 **Meleuz** Respublika Bashkortostan, W Russian Federation
10 L6 **Mélèzes, Rivière aux** ~ Québec, C Canada
80 I11 **Melfi** Guéra, S Chad
109 M17 **Melfi** Basilicata, S Italy
9 U14 **Melfort** Saskatchewan, S Canada
106 H4 **Melgaço** Viana do Castelo, N Portugal
107 N4 **Melgar de Fernamental** Castilla-León, N Spain
76 L6 **Melghir, Chott** *var.* Chott Melrhir. *salt lake* E Algeria
96 H8 **Melhus** Sør-Trøndelag, S Norway
106 H3 **Melide** Galicia, NW Spain
Meligalá *see* Meligalás
117 E21 **Meligalás** *prev.* Meligalá. Pelopónnisos, S Greece
62 L12 **Mel, Ilha do** *island* S Brazil
122 G11 **Melilla** *anc.* Rusaddir, Russadir. Melilla, Spain, N Africa
73 N1 **Melilla** *enclave* Spain, N Africa
65 G18 **Melimoyu, Monte** ▲ S Chile
175 N8 **Melintang, Danau** ◎ Borneo, N Indonesia
119 U7 **Melioratyvne** Dnipropetrovs'ka Oblast', E Ukraine
65 G11 **Melipilla** Santiago, C Chile
117 I25 **Mélissa, Ákra** *headland* Kríti, Greece, E Mediterranean Sea
15 Kk16 **Melita** Manitoba, S Canada
Melita *see* Mljet
Melitene *see* Malatya
109 M23 **Melito di Porto Salvo** Calabria, SW Italy
119 U10 **Melitopol'** Zaporiz'ka Oblast', SE Ukraine
111 V4 **Melk** Niederösterreich, NE Austria
97 K15 **Mellan-Fryken** ◎ C Sweden
101 E17 **Melle** Oost-Vlaanderen, NW Belgium
102 G13 **Melle** Niedersachsen, NW Germany
Mellersta Finland *see* Keski-Suomi
97 J17 **Mellerud** Älvsborg, S Sweden
104 K10 **Melle-sur-Bretonne** Deux-Sèvres, W France
31 P8 **Mellette** South Dakota, N USA
123 J16 **Mellieha** E Malta
82 B10 **Mellit** Northern Darfur, W Sudan
77 N7 **Mellita** ✕ SE Tunisia
65 G21 **Mellizo Sur, Cerro** ▲ S Chile
102 G9 **Mellum** *island* NW Germany
85 L22 **Melmoth** KwaZulu/Natal, E South Africa
113 D16 **Mělník** *Ger.* Melnik. Střední Čechy, NW Czech Republic
126 H13 **Mel'nikovo** Tomskaya Oblast', C Russian Federation
63 G18 **Melo** Cerro Largo, NE Uruguay
Melodunum *see* Melun
Melrhir, Chott *see* Melghir, Chott
191 P7 **Melrose** New South Wales, SE Australia
190 I7 **Melrose** South Australia
31 T7 **Melrose** Minnesota, N USA
35 Q11 **Melrose** Montana, NW USA
39 V12 **Melrose** New Mexico, SW USA
110 I8 **Mels** Sankt Gallen, NE Switzerland
Melsetter *see* Chimanimani
35 V9 **Melstone** Montana, NW USA
103 I16 **Melsungen** Hessen, C Germany
94 L12 **Meltaus** Lappi, NW Finland
99 N19 **Melton Mowbray** C England, UK
84 Q13 **Meluco** Cabo Delgado, NE Mozambique
105 O5 **Melun** *anc.* Melodunum. Seine-et-Marne, N France
82 F12 **Melut** Upper Nile, SE Sudan
29 P5 **Melvern Lake** ⊡ Kansas, C USA
9 V16 **Melville** Saskatchewan, S Canada
Melville Bay/Melville Bugt *see* Qimusseriarsuaq
47 O11 **Melville Hall** ✕ (Dominica) NE Dominica
189 O1 **Melville Island** *island* Northern Territory, N Australia
207 O8 **Melville Island** *island* Parry Islands, Northwest Territories, NW Canada
16 R7 **Melville, Lake** ◎ Newfoundland and Labrador, E Canada
15 L12 **Melville Peninsula** *peninsula* Northwest Territories, NE Canada
Melville Sound *see* Viscount Melville Sound
27 Q9 **Melvin** Texas, SW USA
99 D15 **Melvin, Lough** *Ir.* Loch Meilbhe. ◎ S Northern Ireland, UK/Ireland
174 M9 **Memala** Borneo, C Indonesia
115 L22 **Memaliaj** Gjirokastër, S Albania
85 Q14 **Memba** Nampula, NE Mozambique
85 Q14 **Memba, Baia de** *inlet* NE Mozambique
Membidj *see* Manbij
Memel *see* Neman, NE Europe
Memel *see* Klaipėda, Lithuania
103 J23 **Memmingen** Bayern, S Germany
29 U1 **Memphis** Missouri, C USA
22 E10 **Memphis** Tennessee, S USA
27 P3 **Memphis** Texas, SW USA
22 E10 **Memphis** ✕ Tennessee, S USA
13 Q13 **Memphrémagog, Lac** *var.* Lake Memphremagog. ◎ Canada/USA *see also* Memphremagog, Lake
21 N6 **Memphremagog, Lake** *var.* Lac Memphrémagog. ◎ Canada/USA *see also* Memphrémagog, Lac
119 Q2 **Mena** Chernihivs'ka Oblast', NE Ukraine
29 S12 **Mena** Arkansas, C USA
Menaam *see* Menaldum
Menado *see* Manado
108 D6 **Menaggio** Lombardia, N Italy
31 T6 **Menahga** Minnesota, N USA
79 R10 **Ménaka** Goa, E Mali
100 K5 **Menaldum** *Fris.* Menaam. Friesland, N Netherlands
Mènam Khong *see* Mekong
76 E7 **Menara** ✕ (Marrakech) C Morocco
27 Q9 **Menard** Texas, SW USA
199 M14 **Menard Fracture Zone** *tectonic feature* E Pacific Ocean
32 M7 **Menasha** Wisconsin, N USA
Mencezi Garagum *see* Tsentral'nyye Nizmennyye Garagumy
200 O10 **Mendaña Fracture Zone** *tectonic feature* E Pacific Ocean
174 M10 **Mendawai, Sungai** ~ Borneo, C Indonesia
105 P13 **Mende** *anc.* Mimatum. Lozère, S France
83 J14 **Mendebo** ▲▲ C Ethiopia
82 J9 **Mendefera** *prev.* Adi Ugri. S Eritrea
207 S7 **Mendeleyev Ridge** *undersea feature* Arctic Ocean
131 T3 **Mendeleyevsk** Respublika Tatarstan, W Russian Federation
103 F15 **Menden** Nordrhein-Westfalen, W Germany
24 L6 **Mendenhall** Mississippi, S USA
40 L13 **Mendenhall, Cape** *headland* Nunivak Island, Alaska, USA
43 P9 **Méndez** *var.* Villa de Méndez. Tamaulipas, C Mexico
82 H13 **Mendī** W Ethiopia
194 G12 **Mendi** Southern Highlands, W PNG
99 K22 **Mendip Hills** *var.* Mendips. *hill range* S England, UK
Mendips *see* Mendip Hills
36 L6 **Mendocino** California, W USA
36 J3 **Mendocino, Cape** *headland* California, W USA
0 B8 **Mendocino Fracture Zone** *tectonic feature* NE Pacific Ocean
37 P10 **Mendota** California, W USA
32 L11 **Mendota** Illinois, N USA
32 K8 **Mendota, Lake** ◎ Wisconsin, N USA
64 I11 **Mendoza** Mendoza, W Argentina
64 I12 **Mendoza** *off.* Provincia de Mendoza. ◐ *province* W Argentina
110 H12 **Mendrisio** Ticino, S Switzerland
174 Hh7 **Mendung** Pulau Mendol, W Indonesia
56 I5 **Mene de Mauroa** Falcón, NW Venezuela
56 I5 **Mene Grande** Zulia, NW Venezuela
142 B14 **Menemen** İzmir, W Turkey
101 C18 **Menen** *var.* Meenen, *Fr.* Menin. West-Vlaanderen, W Belgium
169 Q8 **Menengiyn Tal** *plain* E Mongolia
201 R9 **Meneng Point** *headland* SW Nauru
94 L10 **Menesjärvi** *Lapp.* Menešjávri. Lappi, N Finland
Menešjávri *see* Menesjärvi
109 I24 **Menfi** Sicilia, Italy, C Mediterranean Sea
167 P7 **Mengcheng** Anhui, E China
166 F15 **Menghai** Yunnan, SW China
175 Q11 **Mengkoka, Pegunungan** *var.* Pegunungan Mekongga. ▲▲ Sulawesi, C Indonesia
166 F15 **Mengla** Yunnan, SW China
67 F24 **Menguera Point** *headland* East Falkland, Falkland Islands
166 H13 **Mengzhu Ling** ▲▲ S China
166 H14 **Mengzi** Yunnan, SW China
Menin *see* Menen
190 L7 **Menindee** New South Wales, SE Australia
190 L7 **Menindee Lake** ◎ New South Wales, SE Australia
190 J10 **Meningie** South Australia
105 O5 **Mennecy** Essonne, N France
31 Q12 **Menno** South Dakota, N USA
116 H13 **Menoíkio** ▲▲ NE Greece
33 N5 **Menominee** Michigan, N USA
32 M5 **Menominee River** ~ Michigan/Wisconsin, N USA
32 M8 **Menomonee Falls** Wisconsin, N USA
32 I6 **Menomonie** Wisconsin, N USA
85 D14 **Menongue** *var.* Vila Serpa Pinto, *Port.* Serpa Pinto. Cuando Cubango, C Angola
123 I18 **Menorca** *Eng.* Minorca; *anc.* Balearis Minor. *island* Islas Baleares, Spain, W Mediterranean Sea
107 S13 **Menor, Mar** *lagoon* SE Spain
41 S10 **Mentasta Lake** ◎ Alaska, USA
41 S10 **Mentasta Mountains** ▲▲ Alaska, USA
173 Ff10 **Mentawai, Kepulauan** *island group* W Indonesia
173 G10 **Mentawai, Selat** *strait* W Indonesia
174 Ii10 **Mentok** Pulau Bangka, W Indonesia
105 V15 **Menton** *It.* Mentone. Alpes-Maritimes, SE France
26 K8 **Mentone** Texas, SW USA
Mentone *see* Menton
33 U11 **Mentor** Ohio, N USA
175 Nn7 **Menyapa, Gunung** ▲ Borneo, N Indonesia
165 T9 **Menyuan** *var.* Menyuan Huizu Zizhixian. Qinghai, C China
Menyuan Huizu Zizhixian *see* Menyuan
76 M5 **Menzel Bourguiba** *var.* Manzil Bū Ruqaybah; *prev.* Ferryville. N Tunisia
142 M15 **Menzelet Barajı** ⊡ C Turkey
131 T4 **Menzelinsk** Respublika Tatarstan, W Russian Federation
188 K11 **Menzies** Western Australia
205 V6 **Menzies, Mount** ▲ Antarctica
42 J6 **Meoqui** Chihuahua, N Mexico
85 N14 **Meponda** Niassa, NE Mozambique
100 M8 **Meppel** Drenthe, NE Netherlands
102 E12 **Meppen** Niedersachsen, NW Germany
Meqerghane, Sebkha *see* Mekerrhane, Sebkha
107 T6 **Mequinenza, Embalse de** ⊡ NE Spain
32 M8 **Mequon** Wisconsin, N USA
Mera *see* Maira
190 D3 **Meramangye, Lake** *salt lake* South Australia
29 W5 **Meramec River** ~ Missouri, C USA
Meran *see* Merano
174 H10 **Merangin** ~ Sumatera, W Indonesia
108 G5 **Merano** *Ger.* Meran. Trentino-Alto Adige, N Italy
174 H4 **Merapuh Lama** Pahang, Peninsular Malaysia
108 D7 **Merate** Lombardia, N Italy
175 Nn11 **Meratus, Pegunungan** ▲▲ Borneo, N Indonesia
176 Z16 **Merauke** Irian Jaya, E Indonesia
176 Z16 **Merauke, Sungai** ~ Irian Jaya, E Indonesia
190 L9 **Merbein** Victoria, SE Australia
101 F21 **Merbes-le-Château** Hainaut, S Belgium
Merca *see* Marka
56 C13 **Mercaderes** Cauca, SW Colombia
Mercara *see* Madikeri
37 P9 **Merced** California, W USA
63 C20 **Mercedes** Buenos Aires, E Argentina
63 D15 **Mercedes** Corrientes, NE Argentina
64 J11 **Mercedes** *prev.* Villa Mercedes. San Luis, C Argentina
63 D19 **Mercedes** Soriano, SW Uruguay
27 S17 **Mercedes** Texas, SW USA
37 R9 **Merced Peak** ▲ California, W USA
37 P9 **Merced River** ~ California, W USA
20 B13 **Mercer** Pennsylvania, NE USA
101 G18 **Merchtem** Vlaams Brabant, C Belgium
13 O13 **Mercier** Québec, SE Canada
27 Q9 **Mercury** Texas, SW USA
192 M5 **Mercury Islands** *island group* N NZ
21 O9 **Meredith** New Hampshire, NE USA
67 B25 **Meredith, Cape** *headland* West Falkland, Falkland Islands
39 V6 **Meredith, Lake** ◎ Colorado, C USA
27 N2 **Meredith, Lake** ⊡ Texas, SW USA
83 O16 **Mereeg** *var.* Mareeq, *It.* Meregh. Galguduud, E Somalia
119 V5 **Merefa** Kharkivs'ka Oblast', E Ukraine
Meregh *see* Mereeg
197 C11 **Mere Lava** *island* Banks Islands, N Vanuatu
101 E17 **Merelbeke** Oost-Vlaanderen, NW Belgium
Merend *see* Marand
127 Oo9 **Merenga** Magadanskaya Oblast', E Russian Federation
178 K12 **Mereuch** Môndól Kiri, E Cambodia
Mergate *see* Margate
150 F9 **Mergenevo** Zapadnyy Kazakhstan, NW Kazakhstan
178 Gg12 **Mergui** Tenasserim, S Myanmar
177 G12 **Mergui Archipelago** *island group* S Myanmar
116 L12 **Meriç** Edirne, NW Turkey
116 L12 **Meriç** *Bul.* Maritsa, *Gk.* Évros; *anc.* Hebrus. ~ SE Europe *see also* Évros/Maritsa
43 X12 **Mérida** Yucatán, SW Mexico
106 J11 **Mérida** *anc.* Augusta Emerita. Extremadura, W Spain
56 I6 **Mérida** Mérida, W Venezuela
56 H7 **Mérida** *off.* Estado Mérida. ◐ *state* W Venezuela
20 M13 **Meriden** Connecticut, NE USA
24 M5 **Meridian** Mississippi, S USA
27 S8 **Meridian** Texas, SW USA
104 J13 **Mérignac** Gironde, SW France
104 J13 **Mérignac** ✕ (Bordeaux) Gironde, SW France
95 J18 **Merikarvia** Turku-Pori, SW Finland
191 R12 **Merimbula** New South Wales, SE Australia
190 L9 **Meringur** Victoria, SE Australia
Merín, Laguna *see* Mirim Lagoon
99 I19 **Merioneth** *cultural region* W Wales, UK
196 A11 **Merir** *island* Palau Islands, N Palau
196 B17 **Merizo** SW Guam
Merjama *see* Märjamaa
151 S16 **Merke** Zhambyl, S Kazakhstan
27 P7 **Merkel** Texas, SW USA
121 F15 **Merkinė** Varėna, S Lithuania
101 G16 **Merksem** Antwerpen, N Belgium
101 I15 **Merksplas** Antwerpen, N Belgium
Merkulovichi *see* Myerkulavichy
121 G15 **Merkys** ~ S Lithuania
34 F15 **Merlin** Oregon, NW USA
63 C20 **Merlo** Buenos Aires, E Argentina
144 G8 **Meron, Harē** ▲ N Israel
76 K6 **Merouane, Chott** *salt lake* NE Algeria
82 F7 **Merowe** Northern, N Sudan
188 J12 **Merredin** Western Australia
98 I13 **Merrick** ▲ S Scotland, UK
34 H16 **Merrill** Oregon, NW USA
32 L5 **Merrill** Wisconsin, N USA
33 N11 **Merrillville** Indiana, N USA
21 O10 **Merrimack River** ~ Massachusetts/New Hampshire, NE USA
30 L12 **Merriman** Nebraska, C USA
9 N17 **Merritt** British Columbia, SW Canada
25 Y12 **Merritt Island** Florida, SE USA
25 Y11 **Merritt Island** *island* Florida, SE USA
30 M12 **Merritt Reservoir** ⊡ Nebraska, C USA
191 S7 **Merriwa** New South Wales, SE Australia
191 O8 **Merriwagga** New South Wales, SE Australia
24 G8 **Merryville** Louisiana, S USA
82 K9 **Mersa Fatma** E Eritrea
104 M7 **Mer St-Aubin** Loir-et-Cher, C France
Mersa Maṭrūḥ *see* Maṭrūḥ
101 M24 **Mersch** Luxembourg, C Luxembourg
103 M15 **Merseburg** Sachsen-Anhalt, C Germany
Mersen *see* Meerssen
99 K18 **Mersey** ~ NW England, UK
142 J17 **Mersin** İçel, S Turkey
174 I6 **Mersing** Johor, Peninsular Malaysia
120 E8 **Mērsrags** Talsi, NW Latvia
158 G12 **Merta** *var.* Merta City. Rājasthān, N India
Merta City *see* Merta
158 F12 **Merta Road** Rājasthān, N India
99 J21 **Merthyr Tydfil** S Wales, UK
106 H13 **Mértola** Beja, S Portugal
205 V16 **Mertz Glacier** *glacier* Antarctica
101 M24 **Mertzig** Diekirch, C Luxembourg
27 O9 **Mertzon** Texas, SW USA
83 I18 **Meru** Eastern, C Kenya
105 N4 **Méru** Oise, N France
83 I20 **Meru, Mount** ▲ NE Tanzania
Merv *see* Mary
Mervdasht *see* Marv Dasht
142 K11 **Merzifon** Amasya, N Turkey
103 D20 **Merzig** Saarland, SW Germany
38 L14 **Mesa** Arizona, SW USA
31 V4 **Mesabi Range** ▲▲ Minnesota, N USA
56 H6 **Mesa Bolívar** Mérida, NW Venezuela
109 Q18 **Mesagne** Puglia, SE Italy
41 P12 **Mesa Mountain** ▲ Alaska, USA
117 J25 **Mesará** *lowland* Kríti, Greece, E Mediterranean Sea
39 S14 **Mescalero** New Mexico, SW USA
103 G15 **Meschede** Nordrhein-Westfalen, W Germany
143 Q12 **Mescit Dağları** ▲▲ NE Turkey
201 V13 **Mesegon** *island* Chuuk, C Micronesia
Meseritz *see* Międzyrzecz
56 F11 **Mesetas** Meta, C Colombia
Meshchera Lowland *see* Meshcherskaya Nizina
130 M4 **Meshcherskaya Nizina** *Eng.* Meshchera Lowland. *basin* W Russian Federation
130 J5 **Meshchovsk** Kaluzhskaya Oblast', W Russian Federation
129 R9 **Meshchura** Respublika Komi, NW Russian Federation
Meshed *see* Mashhad
Meshed-i-Sar *see* Bābolsar
82 E13 **Meshra'er Req** Warab, S Sudan
39 R15 **Mesilla** New Mexico, SW USA
110 H10 **Mesocco** *Ger.* Misox. Ticino, S Switzerland
117 D18 **Mesolóngi** *prev.* Mesolóngion. Dytikí Ellás, W Greece
Mesolóngion *see* Mesolóngi
12 E8 **Mesomikenda Lake** ◎ Ontario, S Canada
63 D15 **Mesopotamia** *var.* Mesopotamia Argentina. *physical region* NE Argentina
Mesopotamia Argentina *see* Mesopotamia
37 Y10 **Mesquite** Nevada, W USA
84 Q13 **Messalo, Rio** *var.* Mualo. ~ NE Mozambique
Messana/Messene *see* Messina
101 L25 **Messancy** Luxembourg, SE Belgium
109 M23 **Messina** *var.* Messana, Messene; *anc.* Zancle. Sicilia, Italy, C Mediterranean Sea
85 K19 **Messina** Northern, NE South Africa
Messina, Strait of *see* Messina, Stretto di
109 M23 **Messina, Stretto di** *Eng.* Strait of Messina. *strait* SW Italy
117 E21 **Messíni** Pelopónnisos, S Greece
117 E21 **Messinía** *peninsula* S Greece
117 E22 **Messiniakós Kólpos** *gulf* S Greece
126 H8 **Messoyakha** ~ N Russian Federation
116 H11 **Mesta** *Gk.* Néstos, *Turk.* Kara Su. ~ Bulgaria/Greece *see also* Néstos
Mestghanem *see* Mostaganem
143 R8 **Mestia** *var.* Mestiya. N Georgia
Mestiya *see* Mestia
117 K18 **Mestón, Ákra** *headland* Chíos, E Greece
108 H8 **Mestre** Veneto, NE Italy
61 M16 **Mestre, Espigão** ▲ E Brazil
174 Ii11 **Mesuji** ~ Sumatera, W Indonesia
Mesule *see* Grosser Möseler
8 J10 **Meszah Peak** ▲ British Columbia, W Canada
56 G11 **Meta** *off.* Departamento del Meta. ◐ *province* C Colombia
13 Q8 **Metabetchouane** ~ Québec, SE Canada
16 O4 **Meta Incognita Peninsula** *peninsula* Baffin Island, Northwest Territories, NE Canada
24 K9 **Metairie** Louisiana, S USA
34 M6 **Metaline Falls** Washington, NW USA
64 K6 **Metán** Salta, N Argentina
84 N13 **Metangula** Niassa, N Mozambique
44 E7 **Metapán** Santa Ana, NW El Salvador
56 K9 **Meta, Río** ~ Colombia/Venezuela
108 I11 **Metauro** ~ C Italy
82 H11 **Metema** NW Ethiopia
117 D15 **Metéora** *religious building* Thessalía, C Greece
67 O20 **Meteor Rise** *undersea feature* SW Indian Ocean
195 N9 **Meteran** New Hanover, NE PNG
Meterlam/Methariam/Metharlam *see* Mehtarlām
117 G20 **Methanon** *peninsula* S Greece
34 J6 **Methow River** ~ Washington, NW USA
21 O10 **Methuen** Massachusetts, NE USA
193 G19 **Methven** Canterbury, South Island, NZ
Metis *see* Metz
115 G15 **Metković** Dubrovnik-Neretva, SE Croatia
41 Y14 **Metlakatla** Annette Island, Alaska, USA
111 V13 **Metlika** *Ger.* Möttling. SE Slovenia
111 T8 **Metnitz** Kärnten, S Austria
29 W12 **Meto, Bayou** ~ Arkansas, C USA
174 Ii13 **Metro** Sumatera, W Indonesia
32 M17 **Metropolis** Illinois, N USA
Metropolitan *see* Santiago
37 N8 **Metropolitan Oakland** ✕ California, W USA
117 D15 **Métsovo** *prev.* Métsovon. Ípeiros, C Greece
Métsovon *see* Métsovo
25 V5 **Metter** Georgia, SE USA
101 H21 **Mettet** Namur, S Belgium
103 D20 **Mettlach** Saarland, SW Germany
Mettu *see* Metu
82 H13 **Metu** *var.* Mattu, Mettu. W Ethiopia
175 N7 **Metulang** Borneo, N Indonesia
144 G8 **Metulla** Northern, N Israel
150 G14 **Metvyy Kultuk, Sor** *salt flat* SW Kazakhstan
105 T4 **Metz** *anc.* Divodurum Mediomatricum, Mediomatrica, Metis. Moselle, NE France
103 H22 **Metzingen** Baden-Württemberg, S Germany
173 E4 **Meulaboh** Sumatera, W Indonesia
101 D18 **Meulebeke** West-Vlaanderen, W Belgium
105 U6 **Meurthe** ~ NE France
105 S5 **Meurthe-et-Moselle** ◐ *department* NE France
105 S4 **Meuse** ◐ *department* NE France
86 F10 **Meuse** *Dut.* Maas. ~ W Europe *see also* Maas
195 O11 **Mevelo** ~ New Britain, C Papau New Guinea
Mexcala, Río *see* Balsas, Río
27 U8 **Mexia** Texas, SW USA
60 K11 **Mexiana, Ilha** *island* NE Brazil
42 C1 **Mexicali** Baja California, NW Mexico
28 K8 **Mexico** Missouri, C USA
20 H9 **Mexico** New York, NE USA
27 P15 **Mexico** *off.* United Mexican States, *var.* Méjico, México, *Sp.* Estados Unidos Mexicanos. ◆ *federal republic* N Central America
43 O14 **México** *var.* Ciudad de México, *Eng.* Mexico City. ● (Mexico) México, C Mexico
43 O13 **México** ◐ *state* S Mexico
1 J13 **Mexico Basin** *var.* Sigsbee Deep. *undersea feature* C Gulf of Mexico
Mexico City *see* México
México, Golfo de *see* Mexico, Gulf of
46 B4 **Mexico, Gulf of** *Sp.* Golfo de México. *gulf* W Atlantic Ocean
Meyadine *see* Al Mayādīn
41 Y14 **Meyers Chuck** Etolin Island, Alaska, USA
154 M3 **Meymaneh** *var.* Maimāna, Maymana. Fāryāb, NW Afghanistan
149 N7 **Meymeh** Eṣfahān, C Iran
127 Pp6 **Meynypil'gyno** Chukotskiy Avtonomnyy Okrug, NE Russian Federation
110 A10 **Meyrin** Genève, SW Switzerland
177 F8 **Mezaligon** Irrawaddy, SW Myanmar
43 O15 **Mezcala** Guerrero, S Mexico
116 H8 **Mezdra** Oblast Montana, NW Bulgaria
105 P16 **Mèze** Hérault, S France
129 O6 **Mezen'** Arkhangel'skaya Oblast', NW Russian Federation
129 P8 **Mezen'** ~ NW Russian Federation
Mezen, Bay of *see* Mezenskaya Guba
105 Q13 **Mézenc, Mont** ▲ C France
129 O8 **Mezenskaya Guba** *var.* Bay of Mezen. *bay* NW Russian Federation
125 Bb7 **Mezha** ~ W Russian Federation
Mezha *see* Myazha
126 Hh15 **Mezhdurechensk** Kemerovskaya Oblast', S Russian Federation
125 F4 **Mezhdusharskiy, Ostrov** *island* Novaya Zemlya, N Russian Federation
Mezhëvo *see* Myezhava
Mezhgor'ye *see* Mizhhir"ya
119 V8 **Mezhova** Dnipropetrovs'ka Oblast', E Ukraine
8 J12 **Meziadin Junction** British Columbia, W Canada
113 G16 **Mezileské Sedlo** *var.* Przełęcz Międzyleska. ≍ Czech Republic/Poland
104 L14 **Mézin** Lot-et-Garonne, SW France
113 M24 **Mezőberény** Békés, SE Hungary
113 M25 **Mezőhegyes** Békés, SE Hungary
113 M25 **Mezőkovácsháza** Békés, SE Hungary
113 M21 **Mezőkövesd** Borsod-Abaúj-Zemplén, NE Hungary
Mezőtelegd *see* Tileagd
113 M23 **Mezőtúr** Jász-Nagykun-Szolnok, E Hungary
42 K10 **Mezquital** Durango, C Mexico
108 G6 **Mezzolombardo** Trentino-Alto Adige, N Italy
84 L13 **Mfuwe** Northern, N Zambia
123 J16 **Mġarr** Gozo, N Malta
130 H6 **Mglin** Bryanskaya Oblast', W Russian Federation
Mhálanna, Cionn *see* Malin Head
160 G10 **Mhow** Madhya Pradesh, C India
Miadzioł Nowy *see* Myadzyel
179 Q13 **Miagao** Panay Island, C Philippines
43 R17 **Miahuatlán** *var.* Miahuatlán de Porfirio Díaz. Oaxaca, SE Mexico
Miahuatlán de Porfirio Díaz *see* Miahuatlán
106 K10 **Miajadas** Extremadura, W Spain
Miajlar *see* Myājlār
38 M14 **Miami** Arizona, SW USA
25 Z16 **Miami** Florida, SE USA
29 R8 **Miami** Oklahoma, C USA
27 O2 **Miami** Texas, SW USA
25 Z16 **Miami** ✕ Florida, SE USA
25 Z16 **Miami Beach** Florida, SE USA
25 Y15 **Miami Canal** *canal* Florida, SE USA
33 R14 **Miamisburg** Ohio, N USA
155 U10 **Miān Channūn** Punjab, E Pakistan
148 J4 **Miāndowāb** *var.* Mianduab, Miyāndoāb. Āzarbāyjān-e Bākhtarī, NW Iran
180 H5 **Miandrivazo** Toliara, C Madagascar
Mianduab *see* Miāndowāb
148 K3 **Mīāneh** *var.* Miyāneh. Āzarbāyjān-e Khāvarī, NW Iran
155 O16 **Miāni Hōr** *lagoon* S Pakistan
166 G10 **Mianning** Sichuan, C China
155 T7 **Miānwāli** Punjab, NE Pakistan
166 J7 **Mianxian** *var.* Mian Xian. Shaanxi, C China
166 I8 **Mianyang** Sichuan, C China
Mianyang *see* Xiantao
167 R3 **Miaodao Qundao** *island group* E China

◆ Country ● Country Capital ◇ Dependent Territory ○ Dependent Territory Capital ◐ Administrative Region ✕ International Airport ▲ Mountain ▲▲ Mountain Range Volcano ~ River ◎ Lake ⊡ Reservoir

167 S13 **Miaoli** N Taiwan

125 E12 **Miass** Chelyabinskaya Oblast', C Russian Federation

112 G8 **Miastko** *Ger.* Rummelsburg in Pommern. Słupsk, NW Poland

Miava *see* Myjava

9 O15 **Mica Creek** British Columbia, SW Canada

166 J7 **Micang Shan** ▲ C China

194 I12 **Michael, Mount** ▲ C PNG

Mi Chai *see* Nong Khai

113 O19 **Michalovce** *Ger.* Grossmichel, *Hung.* Nagymihály. Východné Slovensko, E Slovakia

101 M20 **Michel, Baraque** hill E Belgium

41 S5 **Michelson, Mount** ▲ Alaska, USA

47 P9 **Miches** E Dominican Republic

32 M4 **Michigamme, Lake** ⊙ Michigan, N USA

32 M4 **Michigamme Reservoir** ⊠ Michigan, N USA

33 N4 **Michigamme River** ↝ Michigan, N USA

33 O7 **Michigan** ◆ State of Michigan; also known as Great Lakes State, Lake State, Wolverine State. ◆ state N USA

33 O11 **Michigan City** Indiana, N USA

33 O8 **Michigan, Lake** ⊙ N USA

33 P2 **Michipicoten Bay** lake bay Ontario, N Canada

12 A8 **Michipicoten Island** island Ontario, S Canada

12 B7 **Michipicoten River** Ontario, S Canada

Michurin *see* Tsarevo

130 M6 **Michurinsk** Tambovskaya Oblast', W Russian Federation

Mico, Punta/Mico, Punto *see* Monkey Point

44 L10 **Mico, Río** ↝ SE Nicaragua

47 T12 **Micoud** St Saint Lucia

201 N16 **Micronesia** off. Federated States of Micronesia. ◆ federation W Pacific Ocean

183 P4 **Micronesia** island group W Pacific Ocean

174 Jj5 **Midai, Pulau** island Kepulauan Natuna, W Indonesia

Mid-Atlantic Cordillera *see* Mid-Atlantic Ridge

67 M17 **Mid-Atlantic Ridge** var. Mid-Atlantic Cordillera, Mid-Atlantic Rise, Mid-Atlantic Swell. undersea feature Atlantic Ocean

Mid-Atlantic Rise/ Mid-Atlantic Swell *see* Mid-Atlantic Ridge

101 E15 **Middelburg** Zeeland, SW Netherlands

85 H24 **Middelburg** Eastern Cape, S South Africa

85 K21 **Middelburg** Mpumalanga, NE South Africa

97 G23 **Middelfart** Fyn, C Denmark

100 G13 **Middelharnis** Zuid-Holland, SW Netherlands

101 B16 **Middelkerke** West-Vlaanderen, W Belgium

100 I9 **Middenbeemster** Noord-Holland, C Netherlands

100 I8 **Middenmeer** Noord-Holland, NW Netherlands

37 Q2 **Middle Alkali Lake** ⊙ California, W USA

200 Nn6 **Middle America Trench** undersea feature E Pacific Ocean

157 P19 **Middle Andaman** island Andaman Islands, India, NE Indian Ocean

Middle Atlas *see* Moyen Atlas

23 R3 **Middlebourne** West Virginia, NE USA

25 W9 **Middleburg** Florida, SE USA

Middleburg Island *see* 'Eua

Middle Caicos *see* Grand Caicos

27 N8 **Middle Concho River** ↝ Texas, SW USA

Middle Congo *see* Congo

41 R6 **Middle Fork Chandalar River** ↝ Alaska, USA

41 Q7 **Middle Fork Koyukuk River** ↝ Alaska, USA

35 O12 **Middle Fork Salmon River** ↝ Idaho, NW USA

9 T15 **Middle Lake** Saskatchewan, S Canada

30 L13 **Middle Loup River** ↝ Nebraska, C USA

193 E22 **Middlemarch** Otago, South Island, NZ

33 T15 **Middleport** Ohio, N USA

31 U14 **Middle Raccoon River** ↝ Iowa, C USA

31 R3 **Middle River** ↝ Minnesota, N USA

23 N8 **Middlesboro** Kentucky, S USA

99 M15 **Middlesbrough** N England, UK

44 G3 **Middlesex** Stann Creek, C Belize

99 N22 **Middlesex** cultural region SE England, UK

11 P15 **Middleton** Nova Scotia, SE Canada

22 F10 **Middleton** Tennessee, S USA

32 L9 **Middleton** Wisconsin, N USA

41 S13 **Middleton Island** island Alaska, USA

36 M7 **Middletown** California, W USA

23 Y2 **Middletown** Delaware, NE USA

20 D11 **Middletown** New Jersey, NE USA

20 K13 **Middletown** New York, NE USA

33 O15 **Middletown** Ohio, N USA

20 G15 **Middletown** Pennsylvania, NE USA

147 N14 **Midī** var. Maydi. NW Yemen

105 O16 **Midi, Canal du** canal S France

104 K17 **Midi de Bigorre, Pic du** ▲ S France

104 K17 **Midi d'Ossau, Pic du** ▲ SW France

181 R7 **Mid-Indian Basin** undersea feature

181 P7 **Mid-Indian Ridge** var. Central Indian Ridge. undersea feature E Indian Ocean

105 N14 **Midi-Pyrénées** ◆ region S France

27 N8 **Midkiff** Texas, SW USA

12 G13 **Midland** Ontario, S Canada

33 R8 **Midland** Michigan, N USA

25 M10 **Midland** South Dakota, N USA

26 M8 **Midland** Texas, SW USA

85 K17 **Midlands** ◆ province C Zimbabwe

99 D21 **Midleton** *Ir.* Mainistir na Corann. SW Ireland

27 T7 **Midlothian** Texas, SW USA

98 K12 **Midlothian** cultural region S Scotland, UK

180 I7 **Midongy** Fianarantsoa, S Madagascar

104 K15 **Midou** ↝ SW France

199 I6 **Mid-Pacific Mountains** var. Mid-Pacific Seamounts. undersea feature NW Pacific Ocean

Mid-Pacific Seamounts *see* Mid-Pacific Mountains

179 R16 **Midsayap** Mindanao, S Philippines

38 L3 **Midway** Utah, W USA

199 Jj5 **Midway Islands** ◇ US territory C Pacific Ocean

35 X14 **Midwest** Wyoming, C USA

29 N10 **Midwest City** Oklahoma, C USA

158 M10 **Mid Western** ◆ zone W Nepal

100 P5 **Midwolda** Groningen, NE Netherlands

143 Q14 **Midyat** Mardin, SE Turkey

116 F8 **Midzhur** *SCr.* Midžor. ▲ Bulgaria/Yugoslavia see also Midžor

115 Q14 **Midžor** *Bul.* Midzhur. ▲ Bulgaria/Yugoslavia see also Midzhur

171 H16 **Mie** off. Mie-ken. ◆ prefecture Honshū, SW Japan

113 L16 **Miechów** Kielce, S Poland

112 F11 **Międzychód** *Ger.* Mitteldorf. Gorzów, W Poland

Międzyleska, Przełęcz *see* Mezileské Sedlo

112 O12 **Międzyrzec Podlaski** Biała Podlaska, E Poland

112 E11 **Międzyrzecz** *Ger.* Meseritz. Gorzów, W Poland

Mie-ken *see* Mie

104 L16 **Mielan** Gers, S France

112 M15 **Mielec** Rzeszów, SE Poland

97 L21 **Mien** ⊙ S Sweden

43 O8 **Mier** Tamaulipas, C Mexico

118 J11 **Miercurea-Ciuc** *Ger.* Szeklerburg, *Hung.* Csíkszereda. Harghita, C Romania

106 K2 **Mieres** Asturias, NW Spain

Mieresch *see* Maros/Mureş

101 K15 **Mierlo** Noord-Brabant, SE Netherlands

43 O10 **Mier y Noriega** Nuevo León, NE Mexico

Mies *see* Stříbro

82 K13 **Mi'eso** var. Meheso, Miesso. C Ethiopia

Miesso *see* Mi'eso

112 D10 **Mieszkowice** *Ger.* Bärwalde Neumark. Szczecin, W Poland

20 G14 **Mifflinburg** Pennsylvania, NE USA

20 F14 **Mifflintown** Pennsylvania, NE USA

43 R15 **Miguel Alemán, Presa** ⊠ SE Mexico

28 L9 **Miguel Asua** var. Miguel Auza. Zacatecas, C Mexico

Miguel Auza *see* Miguel Asua

45 S15 **Miguel de la Borda** var. Donoso. Colón, C Panama

43 N13 **Miguel Hidalgo** ✈ (Guadalajara) Jalisco, SW Mexico

42 H7 **Miguel Hidalgo, Presa** ⊠ C Mexico

118 J14 **Mihăileşti** Giurgiu, S Romania

118 M14 **Mihail Kogălniceanu** var. Kogălniceanu; prev. Caramurat, Ferdinand. Constanţa, SE Romania

119 N14 **Mihai Viteazu** Constanţa, SE Romania

142 G12 **Mihalıççık** Eskişehir, NW Turkey

170 Ee13 **Mihara** Hiroshima, Honshū, SW Japan

171 Jj17 **Mihara-yama** ☸ Miyako-jima, SW Japan

107 S8 **Mijares** ↝ E Spain

100 J11 **Mijdrecht** Utrecht, C Netherlands

172 Oo5 **Mikasa** Hokkaidō, NE Japan

Mikashevichi *see* Mikashevichy

121 K19 **Mikashevichy** *Pol.* Mikaszewicze, *Rus.* Mikashevichi. Brestskaya Voblasts', SW Belarus

Mikaszewicze *see* Mikashevichy

171 Hh16 **Mikawa-wan** bay S Japan

130 L5 **Mikhaylov** Ryazanskaya Oblast', W Russian Federation

Mikhaylovgrad *see* Montana, Oblast

Mikhaylovgrad *see* Montana/Montana, Oblast

205 Z8 **Mikhaylov Island** island Antarctica

127 T6 **Mikhaylovka** Pavlodar, N Kazakhstan

131 N9 **Mikhaylovka** Volgogradskaya Oblast', SW Russian Federation

Mikhaylovka *see* Mykhaylivka

171 Hh16 **Miki** Hyōgo, Honshū, SW Japan

83 K24 **Mikindani** Mtwara, SE Tanzania

95 N18 **Mikkeli** *Swe.* Sankt Michel. Mikkeli, SE Finland

95 N18 **Mikkeli** *Swe.* Sankt Michel, St.Michel. ◆ province C Finland

112 M13 **Mikołajki** *Ger.* Nikolaiken. Suwałki, NE Poland

121 J7 **Mikonos** *see* Mýkonos

116 I9 **Mikre** Loveshka Oblast, C Bulgaria

116 G12 **Mikrí Préspa, Límni** ⊙ N Greece

129 P4 **Mikulkin, Mys** headland NW Russian Federation

83 J23 **Mikumi** Morogoro, SE Tanzania

129 R10 **Mikun'** Respublika Komi, NW Russian Federation

171 Hh13 **Mikuni** Fukui, Honshū, SW Japan

171 Jj14 **Mikuni-tōge** pass Honshū, C Japan

172 Ss13 **Mikura-jima** island E Japan

31 V7 **Milaca** Minnesota, N USA

64 J10 **Milagro** La Rioja, C Argentina

56 B7 **Milagro** Guayas, SW Ecuador

33 P4 **Milakokia Lake** ⊙ Michigan, N USA

32 J1 **Milan** Illinois, N USA

31 R10 **Milan** Michigan, N USA

29 T2 **Milan** Missouri, C USA

39 Q11 **Milan** New Mexico, SW USA

22 G9 **Milan** Tennessee, S USA

Milan *see* Milano

97 F15 **Milange** ↝ S Norway

85 N15 **Milange** Zambézia, NE Mozambique

108 D8 **Milano** *Eng.* Milan, *Ger.* Mailand; *anc.* Mediolanum. Lombardia, N Italy

27 U10 **Milano** Texas, SW USA

142 C15 **Milas** Muğla, SW Turkey

121 K21 **Milashavichy** *Rus.* Milashevichi. Homyel'skaya Voblasts', SE Belarus

Milashevichi *see* Milashavichy

121 I18 **Milavidy** *Rus.* Milovidy. Brestskaya Voblasts', SW Belarus

109 L23 **Milazzo** *anc.* Mylae. Sicilia, Italy, C Mediterranean Sea

31 R8 **Milbank** South Dakota, N USA

21 T7 **Milbridge** Maine, NE USA

102 L11 **Milde** ↝ C Germany

190 J4 **Mildura** Victoria, SE Australia

143 X12 **Mil Düzü** *Rus.* Mil'skaya Ravnina, Mil'skaya Step'. physical region C Azerbaijan

166 H13 **Mile** Yunnan, SW China

Mile *see* Mili Atoll

189 Y10 **Miles** Queensland, E Australia

27 P8 **Miles** Texas, SW USA

35 X9 **Miles City** Montana, NW USA

9 U11 **Milestone** Saskatchewan, S Canada

109 N22 **Mileto** Calabria, SW Italy

109 K16 **Miletto, Monte** ▲ C Italy

20 M13 **Milford** Connecticut, NE USA

23 Y3 **Milford** var. Milford City. Delaware, NE USA

31 T11 **Milford** Iowa, C USA

21 S6 **Milford** Maine, NE USA

31 R16 **Milford** Nebraska, C USA

21 O10 **Milford** New Hampshire, NE USA

20 J13 **Milford** Pennsylvania, NE USA

27 T7 **Milford** Texas, SW USA

38 K6 **Milford** Utah, W USA

Milford *see* Milford Haven

Milford City *see* Milford

99 H21 **Milford Haven** prev. Milford. SW Wales, UK

29 O4 **Milford Lake** ⊠ Kansas, C USA

193 B21 **Milford Sound** Southland, South Island, NZ

193 B21 **Milford Sound** inlet South Island, NZ

Milhau *see* Millau

170 Dd12 **Milh, Bahr al** *see* Razzāzah, Buhayrat ar

145 T10 **Milḥ, Wādī al** dry watercourse S Iraq

201 W8 **Mili Atoll** var. Mile. atoll Ratak Chain, SE Marshall Islands

112 H13 **Milicz** Wrocław, SW Poland

109 L25 **Militello in Val di Catania** Sicilia, Italy, C Mediterranean Sea

127 Pp11 **Mil'kovo** Kamchatskaya Oblast', E Russian Federation

9 R17 **Milk River** Alberta, SW Canada

46 I13 **Milk River** ↝ C Jamaica

35 W7 **Milk River** ↝ Montana, NW USA

82 D9 **Milk, Wadi el** var. Wadi al Malik. ↝ C Sudan

101 L14 **Mill** Noord-Brabant, SE Netherlands

28 M11 **Minco** Oklahoma, C USA

179 Rr16 **Mindanao** island S Philippines

179 Q14 **Mindanao Sea** *see* Bohol Sea

103 J23 **Mindel** ↝ S Germany

103 J23 **Mindelheim** Bayern, S Germany

Mindelo *see* Mindelo

78 C9 **Mindelo** var. Mindello; prev. Porto Grande. São Vicente, N Cape Verde

12 I13 **Minden** Ontario, S Canada

103 H13 **Minden** var. Minthun. Nordrhein-Westfalen, NW Germany

28 G5 **Minden** Louisiana, S USA

37 Q6 **Minden** Nevada, W USA

190 L8 **Mindona Lake** seasonal lake New South Wales, SE Australia

179 Pp12 **Mindoro** island N Philippines

179 P12 **Mindoro Strait** strait W Philippines

79 I18 **Mine** Gansu, N China

170 Dd12 **Mine** Yamaguchi, Honshū, SW Japan

8 H6 **Mine** Yukon Territory, W Canada

99 E21 **Mine Head** *Ir.* Mionn Ard. headland S Ireland

99 J23 **Minehead** SW England, UK

61 J19 **Mineiros** Goiás, C Brazil

27 V5 **Mineola** Texas, SW USA

27 S13 **Mineral** Texas, SW USA

23 U6 **Mineral** Virginia, NE USA

131 N15 **Mineral'nyye Vody** Stavropol'skiy Kray, SW Russian Federation

32 K9 **Mineral Point** Wisconsin, N USA

22 K9 **Mineral Wells** Texas, SW USA

205 Z11 **Mill Island** island Antarctica

191 T3 **Millmerran** Queensland, E Australia

111 R9 **Millstatt** Kärnten, S Austria

99 B19 **Milltown Malbay** *Ir.* Sráid na Cathrach. W Ireland

20 J17 **Millville** New Jersey, NE USA

29 S13 **Millwood Lake** ⊠ Arkansas, C USA

Milne Bank *see* Milne Seamounts

195 O17 **Milne Bay** ◆ province SE PNG

195 N17 **Milne Bay** bay SE PNG

66 J8 **Milne Seamounts** var. Milne Bank. undersea feature N Atlantic Ocean

31 Q6 **Milnor** North Dakota, N USA

21 R5 **Milo** Maine, NE USA

117 I22 **Mílos** Mílos, Kykládes, Greece, Aegean Sea

117 I22 **Mílos** island Kykládes, Greece, Aegean Sea

Milos *see* Mílos

115 K19 **Milot** var. Miloti. Lezhë, C Albania

Miloti *see* Milot

119 Z5 **Milove** Luhans'ka Oblast', E Ukraine

Milovidy *see* Milavidy

190 L4 **Milparinka** New South Wales, SE Australia

37 N9 **Milpitas** California, W USA

12 G15 **Milton** Ontario, S Canada

193 E24 **Milton** Otago, South Island, NZ

23 V4 **Milton** Delaware, NE USA

25 P8 **Milton** Florida, SE USA

20 G14 **Milton** Pennsylvania, NE USA

20 L7 **Milton** Vermont, NE USA

34 K11 **Milton-Freewater** Oregon, NW USA

99 N21 **Milton Keynes** SE England, UK

29 N3 **Miltonvale** Kansas, C USA

167 N10 **Miluo** Hunan, S China

32 M9 **Milwaukee** Wisconsin, N USA

Milyang *see* Miryang

Mimatum *see* Mende

39 Q15 **Mimbres Mountains** ▲ New Mexico, SW USA

190 D2 **Mimili** South Australia

105 G5 **Mimizan** Landes, SW France

81 E19 **Mimongo** Ngounié, C Gabon

Min *see* Fujian

37 T9 **Mina** Nevada, W USA

149 S14 **Mīnāb** Hormozgān, SE Iran

Mīnā Baranis *see* Berenice

155 R9 **Mina Bāzār** Baluchistān, SW Pakistan

9 V15 **Minnitonas** Manitoba, S Canada

31 U9 **Minius** *see* Miño

167 R12 **Min Jiang** ↝ SE China

166 H10 **Min Jiang** ↝ C China

190 H9 **Minlaton** South Australia

172 N8 **Minmaya** var. Mimmaya. Aomori, Honshū, C Japan

79 U14 **Minna** Niger, C Nigeria

29 N4 **Minneapolis** Kansas, C USA

31 U9 **Minneapolis** Minnesota, N USA

56 K4 **Mirimire** Falcón, N Venezuela

105 T6 **Mirecourt** Vosges, NE France

105 N16 **Mirepoix** Ariège, S France

129 V5 **Mirgorod** *see* Myrhorod

145 W10 **Mīr Ḥājī Khalīl** E Iraq

174 Mm4 **Miri** Sarawak, East Malaysia

79 W2 **Miria** Zinder, S Niger

190 F5 **Mirikata** South Australia

112 F9 **Mirosławiec** Piła, NW Poland

Mirovo *see* Vrattsa

102 N10 **Mirow** Mecklenburg-Vorpommern, N Germany

158 G6 **Mirpur** Jammu and Kashmir, NW India

Mirpur *see* New Mirpur

155 P17 **Mirpur Batoro** Sind, SE Pakistan

155 S9 **Mirpur Khās** Sind, SE Pakistan

155 P17 **Mirpur Sakro** Sind, SE Pakistan

149 T14 **Mīr Shahdād** Hormozgān, S Iran

117 G21 **Mirtóou Pélagos** *Eng.* Mirtoan Sea; *anc.* Myrtoum Mare. sea S Greece

169 Z16 **Miryang** var. Milyang, *Jap.* Mitsuō. SE South Korea

170 Dd14 **Misaki** Ehime, Shikoku, SW Japan

43 Q13 **Misantla** Veracruz-Llave, E Mexico

172 N9 **Misawa** Aomori, Honshū, C Japan

59 Z8 **Mishan** Heilongjiang, NE China

31 O11 **Mishawaka** Indiana, N USA

14 N6 **Misheguk Mountain** ▲ Alaska, USA

171 Jj10 **Mishima** var. Misima. Shizuoka, Honshū, S Japan

170 Dd11 **Mi-shima** island SW Japan

131 V4 **Mishkino** Respublika Bashkortostan, W Russian Federation

159 V10 **Mishmi Hills** hill range NE India

167 Kk11 **Mi Shui** ↝ S China

Misiaf *see* Maşyāf

109 J23 **Misilmeri** Sicilia, Italy, C Mediterranean Sea

Misima *see* Mishima

195 P17 **Misima Island** island SE PNG

Misión de Guana *see* Guana

62 F13 **Misiones** off. Provincia de Misiones. ◆ province NE Argentina

64 P8 **Misiones** off. Departamento de las Misiones. ◆ department S Paraguay

Misión San Fernando *see* San Fernando

Miskin *see* Maskin

Miskito Coast *see* La Mosquitia

45 O7 **Miskitos, Cayos** island group NE Nicaragua

113 M21 **Miskolc** Borsod-Abaúj-Zemplén, NE Hungary

175 T10 **Misoöl, Pulau** island Maluku, E Indonesia

Misox *see* Mesocco

31 Y3 **Misquah Hills** hill range Minnesota, N USA

77 P7 **Mişrātah** var. Misurata. NW Libya

123 Lli5 **Mişrātah, Rās** headland N Libya

13 O1 **Missanabie** Ontario, S Canada

60 E10 **Missão Catrimani** Roraima, N Brazil

12 D6 **Missinaibi** ↝ Ontario, S Canada

12 C7 **Missinaibi Lake** ⊙ Ontario, S Canada

9 T13 **Missinipe** Saskatchewan, C Canada

30 M11 **Mission** South Dakota, N USA

27 S17 **Mission** Texas, SW USA

51 F10 **Missisa Lake** ⊙ Ontario, C Canada

20 M6 **Missisquoi Bay** lake bay Canada/USA

12 G10 **Mississagi** ↝ Ontario, S Canada

12 G15 **Mississauga** Ontario, S Canada

33 P12 **Mississinewa Lake** ⊠ Indiana, N USA

33 P12 **Mississinewa River** ↝ Indiana/Ohio, N USA

24 K4 **Mississippi** off. State of Mississippi; also known as Bayou State, Magnolia State. ◆ state SE USA

12 K3 **Mississippi** ↝ Ontario, SE Canada

10 M10 **Mississippi Delta** delta Louisiana, S USA

12 L13 **Mississippi Lake** ⊙ Ontario, SE Canada

1 **Mississippi River** ↝ C USA

24 M9 **Mississippi Sound** sound Alabama/Mississippi, S USA

35 P9 **Missoula** Montana, NW USA

29 X5 **Missouri** off. State of Missouri; also known as Bullion State, Show Me State. ◆ state C USA

27 V11 **Missouri City** Texas, SW USA

13 Q6 **Missouri River** ↝ C USA

13 Q6 **Mistassibi** ↝ Québec, SE Canada

13 P6 **Mistassini** Québec, SE Canada

13 P6 **Mistassini** ↝ Québec, SE Canada

10 J11 **Mistassini, Lac** ⊙ Québec, SE Canada

111 Y3 **Mistelbach an der Zaya** Niederösterreich, NE Austria

109 L24 **Misterbianco** Sicilia, Italy, C Mediterranean Sea

97 N19 **Misterhult** Kalmar, S Sweden

59 H17 **Misti, Volcán** ☸ S Peru

109 K23 **Mistretta** anc. Amestratus. Sicilia, Italy, C Mediterranean Sea

170 C14 **Misumi** Kumamoto, Kyūshū, SW Japan

170 Ee12 **Misumi** Shimane, Honshū, SW Japan

Misurata *see* Mişrātah

85 S14 **Mitande** Niassa, N Mozambique

42 J13 **Mita, Punta de** headland C Mexico

57 W12 **Mitaraka, Massif du** ▲ NE South America/French Guiana

Mitau *see* Jelgava

189 X9 **Mitchell** Queensland, E Australia

12 E15 **Mitchell** Ontario, S Canada

30 I13 **Mitchell** Nebraska, C USA

34 J12 **Mitchell** Oregon, NW USA

31 P11 **Mitchell** South Dakota, N USA

33 P7 **Mitchell, Lake** ⊠ Michigan, N USA

33 T7 **Mitchell, Lake** ⊠ Alabama, S USA

21 P7 **Mitchell, Mount** ▲ North Carolina, SE USA

189 V3 **Mitchell River** ↝ Queensland, NE Australia

99 D20 **Mitchelstown** *Ir.* Baile Mhistéala. S Ireland

12 M9 **Mitchinamécus, Lac** ⊙ Québec, SE Canada

Mitèmboni *see* Mitemele, Río

81 D17 **Mitemele, Río** ↝ Temboni, Utamboni. SW Equatorial Guinea

155 S12 **Mithánkot** Punjab, E Pakistan

155 T7 **Mithi Tiwāna** Punjab, E Pakistan

155 R17 **Mithi** Sind, SE Pakistan

Mithimna *see* Míthymna

Mí Tho *see* My Tho

117 M18 **Míthymna** var. Míthimna. Lésvos, E Greece

202 L16 **Mitiaro** island S Cook Islands

Mitilíni *see* Mytilíni

13 U7 **Mitis** ↝ Québec, SE Canada

43 S16 **Mitla** Oaxaca, SE Mexico

171 Kk16 **Mito** Ibaraki, Honshū, SW Japan

92 N3 **Mitra, Kapp** headland W Svalbard

192 M13 **Mitre** ▲ North Island, NZ

193 B21 **Mitre Peak** ▲ South Island, NZ

41 O15 **Mitrofania Island** island Alaska, USA

Mitrovica/Mitrowitz *see* Sremska Mitrovica, Serbia, Yugoslavia

Mitrovica/Mitroviçë *see* Kosovska Mitrovica, Serbia, Yugoslavia

110 G11 **Minusio** Ticino, S Switzerland

81 E17 **Minvoul** Woleu-Ntem, N Gabon

147 R13 **Min Xian** var. Minxian. Gansu, C China

165 V13 **Min Xian** *see* El Minya

Minya *see* El Minya

33 R6 **Mio** Michigan, N USA

Mionn Ard *see* Mine Head

81 O25 **Minga** Shaba, SE Zaire

143 W11 **Mingäçevir** *Rus.* Mingechaur, Mingechevir. C Azerbaijan

143 W11 **Mingäçevir Su Anbarı** *Rus.* Mingechaurskoye Vodokhranilishche, Mingechevirskoye Vodokhranilishche. ⊠ NW Azerbaijan

177 G8 **Mingaladon** ✈ (Yangon) Yangon, SW Myanmar

11 P9 **Mingan** Québec, E Canada

155 U5 **Mingāora** var. Mingora, Mongora. North-West Frontier Province, N Pakistan

152 K8 **Mingbuloq** Rus. Mynbulak. Nawoiy Wiloyati, N Uzbekistan

152 K9 **Mingbuloq Botighi** *Rus.* Vpadina Mynbulak. depression N Uzbekistan

Mingechaur *see* Mingäçevir

Mingechaurskoye Vodokhranilishche/Mingech evirskoye *see* Mingäçevir Su Anbarı

177 Ff4 **Mingin** Sagaing, C Myanmar

107 Q10 **Minglanilla** Castilla-La Mancha, C Spain

52 V13 **Mingo Junction** Ohio, N USA

Mingora *see* Mingāora

169 V7 **Mingshui** Heilongjiang, NE China

Mingtcke Daban *see* Mintaka Pass

85 U7 **Minguri** Nampula, NE Mozambique

165 U10 **Minhe** var. Shangchuankou. Qinghai, C China

177 Ff6 **Minhla** Magwe, W Myanmar

178 J15 **Minh Lương** Kiên Giang, S Vietnam

106 G5 **Minho** Sp. Miño. ↝ Portugal/Spain see also Miño

106 G5 **Minho** former province N Portugal

161 C24 **Minicoy Island** island SW India

35 P15 **Minidoka** Idaho, NW USA

120 C11 **Minija** ↝ W Lithuania

188 G9 **Minilya** Western Australia

12 E8 **Minisinakwa Lake** ⊙ Ontario, S Canada

47 T12 **Ministre Point** headland S Saint Lucia

9 V15 **Minitonas** Manitoba, S Canada

44 L12 **Miravalles, Volcán** ☸ NW Costa Rica

147 W13 **Mirbāţ** var. Marbat. S Oman

84 M9 **Mirebalais** C Haiti

31 U9 **Minneapolis** Minnesota, N USA

190 F5 **Mirikata** South Australia

31 X5 **Kk15 Minnedosa** Manitoba, S Canada

28 J7 **Minneola** Kansas, C USA

31 S7 **Minnesota** off. State of Minnesota; also known as Gopher State, New England of the West, North Star State. ◆ state N USA

31 S9 **Minnesota River** ↝ Minnesota/South Dakota, C USA

31 V9 **Minnetonka** Minnesota, N USA

31 O3 **Minnewaukan** North Dakota, N USA

190 F7 **Minnipa** South Australia

106 F7 **Miño** Galicia, NW Spain

106 G5 **Miño** var. Mino, Minius, Port. Minho. ↝ Portugal/Spain see also Minho

171 Ii16 **Minobu** Yamanashi, Honshū, S Japan

171 Ii5 **Minokamo** Gifu, Honshū, SW Japan

32 L12 **Minonk** Illinois, N USA

107 R10 **Minorca** *see* Menorca

30 M3 **Minot** North Dakota, N USA

165 U8 **Minqin** Gansu, N China

121 J16 **Minsk** ● (Belarus) Minskaya Voblasts', C Belarus

121 I16 **Minsk** × Minskaya Voblasts', C Belarus

Minskaya Oblast' *see* Minskaya Voblasts'

121 K16 **Minskaya Voblasts'** prev. Rus. Minskaya Oblast'. ◆ province C Belarus

121 J16 **Minskaya Wzvyshsha** ▲ C Belarus

112 N12 **Mińsk Mazowiecki** var. Nowo-Minsk. Siedlce, E Poland

172 N9 **Misawa** Aomori, Honshū, C Japan

158 I5 **Minster** Ohio, N USA

79 R10 **Minta** Centre, C Cameroon

155 W2 **Mintaka Pass** Pass Chin. Mingtcke Daban. pass China/Pakistan

117 D20 **Mínthi** ▲ S Greece

Minthun *see* Minden

11 O14 **Minto** New Brunswick, SE Canada

8 H6 **Minto** Yukon Territory, W Canada

41 R9 **Minto** Alaska, USA

31 Q3 **Minto** North Dakota, N USA

10 K6 **Minto, Lac** ⊙ Québec, C Canada

205 R16 **Minto, Mount** ▲ Antarctica

9 S13 **Minton** Saskatchewan, S Canada

201 R15 **Minto Reef** atoll Caroline Islands, C Micronesia

39 U6 **Minturn** Colorado, C USA

109 J16 **Minturno** Lazio, C Italy

126 Hh13 **Minusinsk** Krasnoyarskiy Kray, S Russian Federation

---

◆ COUNTRY   ◇ DEPENDENT TERRITORY   ◆ ADMINISTRATIVE REGION   ▲ MOUNTAIN   ☸ VOLCANO   ⊙ LAKE

● COUNTRY CAPITAL   ○ DEPENDENT TERRITORY CAPITAL   ✈ INTERNATIONAL AIRPORT   ▲ MOUNTAIN RANGE   ↝ RIVER   ⊠ RESERVOIR

MITSAMIOULI – MONTEZUMA

180 H12 Mitsamiouli Grande Comore, NW Comoros
180 I3 Mitsinjo Mahajanga, NW Madagascar
Mits'iwa see Massawa
180 H13 Mitsoudjé Grande Comore, NW Comoros
172 Oo7 Mitsuishi Hokkaidō, NE Japan
171 K13 Mitsuke var. Mituke. Niigata, Honshū, C Japan
Mitsuō see Miryang
170 Cc10 Mitsushima Nagasaki, Tsushima, SW Japan
102 G12 Mittelandkanal canal NW Germany
110 J7 Mittelberg Vorarlberg, NW Austria
Mitteldorf see Międzychód
Mittelstadt see Baia Sprie
Mitterburg see Pazin
111 P7 Mittersill Salzburg, NW Austria
103 N16 Mittweida Sachsen, E Germany
56 J13 Mitú Vaupés, SE Colombia
Mituke see Mitsuke
Mitumba, Chaîne des/Mitumba Range see Mitumba, Monts
81 O22 Mitumba, Monts var. Chaîne des Mitumba, Mitumba Range. ▲▲ E Zaire
81 N23 Mitwaba Shaba, SE Zaire
81 E18 Mitzic Woleu-Ntem, N Gabon
84 K11 Miueru Wantipa, Lake ◎ N Zambia
171 Jj17 Miura Kanagawa, Honshū, S Japan
171 M13 Miyagi off. Miyagi-ken. ◈ prefecture Honshū, C Japan
144 M7 Miyāh, Wādī al dry watercourse E Syria
172 Ss13 Miyake Tōkyō, Miyako-jima, SE Japan
172 N11 Miyako Iwate, Honshū, C Japan
172 Q16 Miyako-jima island Sakishima-shotō, SW Japan
170 C16 Miyakonojō var. Miyakonzyô. Miyazaki, Kyūshū, SW Japan
Miyakonzyô see Miyakonojō
172 Pp16 Miyako-shotō island group SW Japan
150 G11 Miyaly Atyrau, W Kazakhstan
Miyāndoāb see Miāndowāb
Miyāneh see Miāneh
170 C15 Miyanojō Kagoshima, Kyūshū, SW Japan
170 Cc16 Miyazaki Miyazaki, Kyūshū, SW Japan
170 C15 Miyazaki off. Miyazaki-ken. ◈ prefecture Kyūshū, SW Japan
171 H13 Miyazu Kyōto, Honshū, SW Japan
Miyory see Myory
170 F13 Miyoshi var. Miyosi. Hiroshima, Honshū, SW Japan
Miyosi see Miyoshi
Miza see Mizë
83 H14 Mīzan Teferī SW Ethiopia
Mizda see Mizdah
77 O8 Mizdah var. Mizda. NW Libya
115 K20 Mizë var. Miza. Fier, W Albania
99 A22 Mizen Head Ir. Carn Uí Néid. headland SW Ireland
118 H7 Mizhhir"ya Rus. Mezhgor'ye. Zakarpats'ka Oblast', W Ukraine
166 L4 Mizhi Shaanxi, C China
118 K13 Mizil Prahova, SE Romania
116 H7 Miziya Oblast Montana, NW Bulgaria
159 W15 Mizo Hills hill range E India
159 W15 Mizoram ◈ state NE India
144 F12 Mizpe Ramon Southern, S Israel
59 L19 Mizque Cochabamba, C Bolivia
59 M19 Mizque, Río ↝ C Bolivia
171 I15 Mizunami Gifu, Honshū, SW Japan
171 Mm12 Mizusawa Iwate, Honshū, C Japan
97 M18 Mjölby Östergötland, S Sweden
97 G15 Mjøndalen Buskerud, S Norway
97 J19 Mjörn ◎ S Sweden
96 I13 Mjøsa var. Mjøsen. ◎ S Norway
Mjøsen see Mjøsa
83 G21 Mkalama Singida, C Tanzania
82 K13 Mkata ↝ C Tanzania
85 K14 Mkushi Central, C Zambia
85 L22 Mkuze KwaZulu/Natal, E South Africa
83 J22 Mkwaja Tanga, E Tanzania
113 D16 Mladá Boleslav Ger. Jungbunzlau. Střední Čechy, N Czech Republic
114 M12 Mladenovac Serbia, C Yugoslavia
116 L11 Mladinovo Khaskovska Oblast, SE Bulgaria
115 O17 Mlado Nagoričane N FYR Macedonia
Mlanje see Mulanje
114 N12 Mlava ↝ E Yugoslavia
112 L9 Mława Ciechanów, C Poland
115 G16 Mljet It. Meleda; anc. Melita. island S Croatia
118 K4 Mlyniv Rivnens'ka Oblast', NW Ukraine
85 I21 Mmabatho North-West, N South Africa
85 I19 Mmashoro Central, E Botswana
46 J7 Moa Holguín, E Cuba
78 J15 Moa ↝ Guinea/Sierra Leone
39 O6 Moab Utah, W USA
189 V1 Moa Island island Queensland, NE Australia
197 J15 Moala island S Fiji
85 L21 Moamba Maputo, SW Mozambique
81 F19 Moanda var. Mouanda. Haut-Ogooué, SE Gabon
175 T16 Moa, Pulau island Kepulauan Leti, E Indonesia
85 M15 Moatize Tete, NW Mozambique
81 P22 Moba Shaba, E Zaire
171 K17 Mobara Chiba, Honshū, S Japan
Mobay see Montego Bay
81 K15 Mobaye Basse-Kotto, S Central African Republic
81 K15 Mobayi-Mbongo Equateur, NW Zaire
27 P2 Mobeetie Texas, SW USA
29 U3 Moberly Missouri, C USA
25 N8 Mobile Alabama, S USA
25 N9 Mobile Bay bay Alabama, S USA
25 N8 Mobile River ↝ Alabama, S USA
31 N8 Mobridge South Dakota, N USA
Mobutu Sese Seko, Lac see Albert, Lake
47 N8 Moca N Dominican Republic
Moçâmedes see Namibe
178 J6 Môc Châu Sơn La, N Vietnam
197 L15 Moce island Lau Group, E Fiji
Mocha see Al Mukhā
200 Oo13 Mocha Fracture Zone tectonic feature SE Pacific Ocean
65 F14 Mocha, Isla island C Chile
58 C12 Moche, Río ↝ W Peru
178 J14 Môc Hoa Long An, S Vietnam
85 I20 Mochudi Kgatleng, SE Botswana
84 Q13 Mocímboa da Praia var. Vila de Mocímboa da Praia. Cabo Delgado, N Mozambique
96 L13 Mockfjärd Kopparberg, C Sweden
23 R9 Mocksville North Carolina, SE USA
34 F8 Moclips Washington, NW USA
84 C13 Môco var. Morro de Môco. ▲ W Angola
56 D13 Mocoa Putumayo, SW Colombia
62 M8 Mococa São Paulo, S Brazil
Môco, Morro de see Môco
42 H8 Mocorito Sinaloa, C Mexico
42 J4 Moctezuma Chihuahua, N Mexico
43 N11 Moctezuma San Luis Potosí, C Mexico
42 G4 Moctezuma Sonora, NW Mexico
43 P12 Moctezuma, Río ↝ C Mexico
Mó, Cuan see Clew Bay
85 O16 Mocuba Zambézia, NE Mozambique
105 U12 Modane Savoie, E France
108 F9 Modena anc. Mutina. Emilia-Romagna, N Italy
38 I7 Modena Utah, W USA
37 O9 Modesto California, W USA
109 L25 Modica anc. Motyca. Sicilia, Italy, C Mediterranean Sea
81 K17 Modjamboli Equateur, N Zaire
111 X4 Mödling Niederösterreich, NE Austria
Modohn see Madona
169 N8 Modot Hentiy, C Mongolia
176 W12 Modowi Irian Jaya, E Indonesia
114 I12 Modračko Jezero ⊞ NE Bosnia and Herzegovina
114 I10 Modriča N Bosnia and Herzegovina
191 O13 Moe Victoria, SE Australia
Moearatewe see Muaratewe
Moei, Mae Nam see Thaungyin
96 H13 Moelv Hedmark, S Norway
94 I10 Moen Troms, N Norway
Moen see Weno, Micronesia
Möen see Møn, Denmark
Moena see Muna, Pulau
38 M10 Moenkopi Wash ↝ Arizona, SW USA
193 F22 Moeraki Point headland South Island, NZ
101 F16 Moerbeke Oost-Vlaanderen, NW Belgium
101 H14 Moerdijk Noord-Brabant, S Netherlands
Moero, Lac see Mweru, Lake
103 D15 Moers var. Mörs. Nordrhein-Westfalen, W Germany
Moesi see Musi, Air
Moeskroen see Mouscron
98 J13 Moffat S Scotland, UK
193 C22 Moffat Peak ▲ South Island, NZ
158 H8 Moga Punjab, N India
81 N19 Moga Sud Kivu, E Zaire
Mogadiscio/Mogadishu see Muqdisho
Mogador see Essaouira
106 J6 Mogadouro Bragança, N Portugal
171 Ll12 Mogami-gawa ↝ Honshū, C Japan
178 Gg2 Mogaung Kachin State, N Myanmar
112 L13 Mogielnica Radom, C Poland
Mogilëv see Mahilyow
Mogilëv-Podol'skiy see Mohyliv-Podil's'kyy
Mogilëvskaya Oblast' see Mahilyowskaya Voblasts'
112 I11 Mogilno Bydgoszcz, C Poland
62 L9 Mogi-Mirim var. Moji-Mirim. São Paulo, S Brazil
85 Q15 Mogincual Nampula, NE Mozambique
116 E13 Moglenítsas ↝ N Greece
108 H8 Mogliano Veneto Veneto, NE Italy
115 M21 Mogliçë Korçë, SE Albania
126 L15 Mogocha Chitinskaya Oblast', S Russian Federation
126 H13 Mogochin Tomskaya Oblast', C Russian Federation
82 F13 Mogogh Jonglei, SE Sudan
176 Vv10 Mogoi Irian Jaya, E Indonesia
178 Gg4 Mogok Mandalay, C Myanmar
39 P14 Mogollon Mountains ▲▲ New Mexico, SW USA
38 M12 Mogollon Rim cliff Arizona, SW USA
63 E23 Mogotes, Punta headland E Argentina
44 J8 Mogotón ▲ NW Nicaragua
106 I14 Moguer Andalucía, S Spain
113 J26 Mohács Baranya, SW Hungary
193 C20 Mohaka ↝ North Island, NZ
30 M2 Mohall North Dakota, N USA
Moḥammadābād see Dargaz
76 F6 Mohammedia prev. Fédala. NW Morocco
76 F6 Mohammed V ✕ (Casablanca) W Morocco
Mohammerah see Khorramshahr
38 H10 Mohave, Lake ⊞ Arizona/Nevada, W USA
38 I12 Mohave Mountains ▲▲ Arizona, SW USA
38 I15 Mohawk Mountains ▲▲ Arizona, SW USA
20 J10 Mohawk River ↝ New York, NE USA
169 T3 Mohe Heilongjiang, NE China
97 L20 Moheda Kronoberg, S Sweden
180 H13 Mohéli var. Mwali, Mohilla, Mohila, Fr. Moili. island S Comoros
40 K12 Mohican, Cape headland Nunivak Island, Alaska, USA
Mohn see Muhu
103 G15 Möhne ↝ W Germany
103 G15 Möhne-Stausee ⊞ W Germany
94 P2 Mohn, Kapp headland NW Svalbard
207 S14 Mohns Ridge undersea feature Greenland Sea/Norwegian Sea
59 I17 Moho Puno, SW Peru
Mohokare see Caledon
97 L17 Moholm Skaraborg, S Sweden
38 J11 Mohon Peak ▲ Arizona, SW USA
83 J23 Mohoro Pwani, E Tanzania
Mohra see Moravice
Mohrungen see Morąg
118 M7 Mohyliv-Podil's'kyy Rus. Mogilev-Podol'skiy. Vinnyts'ka Oblast', C Ukraine
97 D17 Moi Rogaland, S Norway
197 I6 Moindou Province Sud, C New Caledonia
118 K11 Moinești Hung. Mojnest. Bacău, E Romania
Móinteach Mílic see Mountmellick
12 J14 Moira ↝ Ontario, SE Canada
94 G13 Mo i Rana Nordland, C Norway
159 X14 Moirāng Manipur, NE India
117 J25 Moíres Kríti, Greece, E Mediterranean Sea
120 H6 Mõisaküla Ger. Moiseküll. Viljandimaa, S Estonia
Moiseküll see Mõisaküla
13 W4 Moisie Québec, E Canada
13 W3 Moisie ↝ Québec, SE Canada
104 M14 Moissac Tarn-et-Garonne, S France
80 I13 Moïssala Moyen-Chari, S Chad
57 O7 Moitaco Bolívar, E Venezuela
97 P15 Möja Stockholm, C Sweden
107 Q14 Mojácar Andalucía, S Spain
37 T13 Mojave California, W USA
37 V13 Mojave Desert plain California, W USA
37 V13 Mojave River ↝ California, W USA
Moji-Mirim see Mogi-Mirim
115 K15 Mojkovac Montenegro, SW Yugoslavia
Mojnest see Moinești
174 Ll15 Mojokerto prev. Modjokerto. Jawa, C Indonesia
Mōka see Mooka
159 Q13 Mokāma prev. Mokameh, Mukama. Bihār, N India
Mokameh see Mokāma
81 O25 Mokambo Shaba, SE Zaire
40 D9 Mokapu Point headland Oahu, Hawaii, USA, C Pacific Ocean
192 L9 Mokau Waikato, North Island, NZ
192 L9 Mokau ↝ North Island, NZ
37 P7 Mokelumne River ↝ California, W USA
85 J23 Mokhotlong NE Lesotho
Mokil Atoll see Mwokil Atoll
97 N14 Möklinta Västmanland, C Sweden
192 L4 Mokohinau Islands island group N NZ
159 X12 Mokokchūng Nāgāland, NE India
80 F12 Mokolo Extrême-Nord, N Cameroon
193 D24 Mokoreta ↝ South Island, NZ
169 X17 Mokp'o Jap. Moppo. SW South Korea
115 L16 Mokra Gora ▲▲ S Yugoslavia
Mokrany see Makrany
131 O5 Moksha ↝ W Russian Federation
Moktama see Martaban
79 T14 Mokwa Niger, W Nigeria
101 J16 Mol prev. Moll. Antwerpen, N Belgium
109 O17 Mola di Bari Puglia, SE Italy
Molai see Moláoi
43 P13 Molango Hidalgo, C Mexico
117 F22 Moláoi var. Molai. Pelopónnisos, S Greece
43 Z12 Molas del Norte, Punta var. Punta Molas. headland SE Mexico
Molas, Punta see Molas del Norte, Punta
107 R11 Molatón ▲ C Spain
99 K18 Mold NE Wales, UK
Moldau see Moldova
Moldau see Vltava, Czech Republic
Moldavia see Moldova
Moldavian SSR/Moldavskaya SSR see Moldova
96 E9 Molde Møre og Romsdal, S Norway
Moldotau, Khrebet see Moldo-Too, Khrebet
153 V9 Moldo-Too, Khrebet prev. Khrebet Moldotau. ▲▲ C Kyrgyzstan
118 K9 Moldova ↝ N Romania
118 K9 Moldova Eng. Moldavia, Ger. Moldau. former province NE Romania
118 L9 Moldova off. Republic of Moldova, var. Moldavia; prev. Moldavian SSR, Rus. Moldavskaya SSR. ◆ republic SE Europe
118 F13 Moldova Nouă Ger. Neumoldowa, Hung. Újmoldova. Caraş-Severin, SW Romania
118 F13 Moldova Veche Ger. Altmoldowa, Hung. Ómoldova. Caraş-Severin, SW Romania
Moldoveanul see Vârful Moldoveanu
85 I20 Molepolole Kweneng, SE Botswana
46 L8 Môle-St-Nicolas NW Haiti
120 H13 Molėtai Molėtai, E Lithuania
109 O17 Molfetta Puglia, SE Italy
175 R8 Molibagu Sulawesi, N Indonesia
64 G12 Molina Maule, C Chile
107 Q7 Molina de Aragón Castilla-La Mancha, C Spain
107 R13 Molina de Segura Murcia, SE Spain
32 J11 Moline Illinois, N USA
29 P7 Moline Kansas, C USA
81 P23 Moliro Shaba, SE Zaire
109 K16 Molise ◈ region S Italy
97 K15 Molkom Värmland, C Sweden
Moll see Mol
111 Q9 Möll ↝ S Austria
97 J22 Mölle Malmöhus, S Sweden
59 H18 Mollendo Arequipa, SW Peru
107 U5 Mollerussa Cataluña, NE Spain
110 H8 Mollis Glarus, NE Switzerland
97 J19 Mölndal Göteborg och Bohus, S Sweden
97 J19 Mölnlycke Göteborg och Bohus, S Sweden
119 U9 Molochans'k Rus. Molochansk. Zaporiz'ka Oblast', SE Ukraine
119 U10 Molochna Rus. Molochnaya. ↝ S Ukraine
Molochnaya see Molochna
119 U10 Molochnyy Lyman bay N Black Sea
Molodechno/Molodeczno see Maladzyechna
205 V3 Molodezhnaya Russian research station Antarctica
128 J14 Mologa ↝ NW Russian Federation
40 E9 Molokai Haw. Moloka'i. island Hawaii, USA, C Pacific Ocean
183 X3 Molokai Fracture Zone tectonic feature NE Pacific Ocean
128 K15 Molokovo Tverskaya Oblast', W Russian Federation
129 Q14 Moloma ↝ NW Russian Federation
191 R8 Molong New South Wales, SE Australia
85 H21 Molopo seasonal river Botswana/South Africa
117 F17 Mólos Stereá Ellás, C Greece
175 Q7 Molosipat Sulawesi, N Indonesia
Molotov see Severodvinsk, Arkhangel'skaya Oblast', Russian Federation
Molotov see Perm', Permskaya Oblast', Russian Federation
81 G17 Moloundou Est, SE Cameroon
105 U5 Molsheim Bas-Rhin, NE France
15 L12 Molson Lake ◎ Manitoba, C Canada
Moluccas see Maluku
175 Rr8 Molucca Sea Ind. Laut Maluku. sea E Indonesia
Molukken see Maluku
85 O15 Molumbo Zambézia, N Mozambique
176 Uu14 Molu, Pulau island Maluku, E Indonesia
85 P16 Moma Nampula, NE Mozambique
127 N17 Moma ↝ NE Russian Federation
176 Xx13 Momats ↝ Irian Jaya, E Indonesia
44 J11 Mombacho, Volcán ⛰ SW Nicaragua
83 K21 Mombasa Coast, SE Kenya
83 J21 Mombasa ✕ Coast, SE Kenya
Mombetsu see Monbetsu
176 Y16 Mombum Irian Jaya, E Indonesia
116 J12 Momchilgrad prev. Mastanli. Khaskovska Oblast, S Bulgaria
101 F23 Momignies Hainaut, S Belgium
56 E6 Momil Córdoba, NW Colombia
44 I10 Momotombo, Volcán ⛰ W Nicaragua
58 B5 Mompiche, Ensenada de bay NW Ecuador
81 K18 Mompono Equateur, NW Zaire
56 F6 Mompós Bolívar, NW Colombia
97 J24 Møn prev. Möen. island SE Denmark
38 L4 Mona Utah, W USA
Mona, Canal de la see Mona Passage
98 E8 Monach Islands island group NW Scotland, UK
105 V14 Monaco var. Monaco-Ville; anc. Monoecus. ● (Monaco) S Monaco
105 V14 Monaco off. Principality of Monaco. ◆ monarchy W Europe
Monaco see München
Monaco Basin see Canary Basin
Monaco-Ville see Monaco
98 I9 Monadhliath Mountains ▲▲ N Scotland, UK
57 O6 Monagas off. Estado Monagas. ◈ state NE Venezuela
99 F16 Monaghan Ir. Muineachán. N Ireland
99 E16 Monaghan Ir. Muineachán. cultural region N Ireland
45 S16 Monagrillo Herrera, S Panama
26 L8 Monahans Texas, SW USA
47 Q9 Mona, Isla island W Puerto Rico
47 Q9 Mona Passage Sp. Canal de la Mona. channel Dominican Republic/Puerto Rico
45 O14 Mona, Punta headland E Costa Rica
161 K25 Monaragala Uva Province, SE Sri Lanka
35 S9 Monarch Montana, NW USA
14 Ff14 Monarch Mountain ▲ British Columbia, SW Canada
Monasterio see Monesterio
Monasterzyska see Monastyrys'ka
Monastir see Bitola
Monastyriska see Monastyrys'ka
119 O7 Monastyryshche Cherkas'ka Oblast', C Ukraine
118 J6 Monastyrys'ka Pol. Monasterzyska, Rus. Monastyriska. Ternopil's'ka Oblast', W Ukraine
81 E15 Monatélé Centre, SW Cameroon
172 Q4 Monbetsu var. Mombetsu. Hokkaidō, NE Japan
Monbetsu see Monbetsu
108 B8 Moncalieri Piemonte, NW Italy
106 G4 Monção Viana do Castelo, N Portugal
107 Q5 Moncayo ▲ N Spain
107 Q5 Moncayo, Sierra del ▲▲ N Spain
128 J4 Monchegorsk Murmanskaya Oblast', NW Russian Federation
103 D15 Mönchengladbach prev. München-Gladbach. Nordrhein-Westfalen, W Germany
106 F14 Monchique Faro, S Portugal
106 G14 Monchique, Serra de ▲▲ S Portugal
23 S14 Moncks Corner South Carolina, SE USA
43 N7 Monclova Coahuila de Zaragoza, NE Mexico
Moncorvo see Torre de Moncorvo
11 P14 Moncton New Brunswick, SE Canada
106 G8 Mondego ↝ N Portugal
106 F8 Mondego, Cabo headland N Portugal
106 I2 Mondoñedo Galicia, NW Spain
101 N25 Mondorf-les-Bains Grevenmacher, SE Luxembourg
104 M7 Mondoubleau Loir-et-Cher, C France
32 J6 Mondovi Wisconsin, N USA
108 B9 Mondovì Piemonte, NW Italy
107 P3 Mondragón var. Arrasate. País Vasco, N Spain
109 J17 Mondragone Campania, S Italy
111 R5 Mondsee ◎ N Austria
126 J16 Mondy Respublika Buryatiya, S Russian Federation
117 G22 Monemvasía Pelopónnisos, S Greece
20 B15 Monessen Pennsylvania, NE USA
106 J12 Monesterio var. Monasterio. Extremadura, W Spain
12 L8 Monet Québec, SE Canada
29 S8 Monett Missouri, C USA
29 X9 Monette Arkansas, C USA
12 G11 Monetville Ontario, S Canada
108 J7 Monfalcone Friuli-Venezia Giulia, NE Italy
106 H10 Monforte Portalegre, C Portugal
106 I4 Monforte Galicia, NW Spain
83 I24 Monga Lindi, SE Tanzania
81 L16 Monga Haut-Zaïre, N Zaire
83 F15 Mongalla Bahr el Gabel, S Sudan
159 U11 Mongar E Bhutan
178 K6 Mong Cai Quang Ninh, N Vietnam
188 I11 Mongers Lake salt lake Western Australia
195 U14 Mongga Kolombangara Island, NW Solomon Islands
178 Hh6 Möng Hpayak Shan State, E Myanmar
Monghyr see Munger
108 B10 Mongioie ▲ NW Italy
178 Gg5 Möng Küng Shan State, E Myanmar
Mongla see Mungla
196 C15 Mongmong C Guam
178 Gg6 Möng Nai Shan State, E Myanmar
80 I11 Mongo Guéra, C Chad
78 I14 Mongo ↝ N Sierra Leone
169 I8 Mongolia Mong. Mongol Uls. ◆ republic E Asia
133 V8 Mongolia, Plateau of plateau E Mongolia
Mongolküre see Zhaosu
Mongol Uls see Mongolia
81 E17 Mongomo E Equatorial Guinea
79 Y12 Mongonu var. Monguno. Borno, NE Nigeria
Mongora see Mingāora
80 K11 Mongororo Ouaddaï, SE Chad
Mongos, Chaîne des see Bongo, Massif des
81 I16 Mongoumba Lobaye, SW Central African Republic
Mongrove, Punta see Cayacal, Punta
85 G15 Mongu Western, W Zambia
78 I10 Mônguel Gorgol, SW Mauritania
Monguno see Mongonu
178 H4 Möng Yai Shan State, E Myanmar
178 Hh5 Möng Yang Shan State, E Myanmar
178 H3 Möng Yu Shan State, E Myanmar
168 K8 Mönhbulag Övörhangay, C Mongolia
Mönh Sarīdag see Munku-Sardyk, Gora
194 L15 Moni ↝ S Papau New Guinea
117 I15 Moní Megístis Lávras monastery Kentrikí Makedonía, N Greece
117 F18 Moní Osíou Loúkas monastery Stereá Ellás, C Greece
56 F9 Moniquirá Boyacá, C Colombia
105 Q12 Monistrol-sur-Loire Haute-Loire, C France
37 V7 Monitor Range ▲▲ Nevada, W USA
117 I14 Moní Vatopedíou monastery Kentrikí Makedonía, N Greece
179 Rr15 Monkayo Mindanao, S Philippines
Monkchester see Newcastle upon Tyne
85 N14 Monkey Bay Southern, SE Malawi
45 N11 Monkey Point var. Punta Mico, Punte Mono, Punto Mico. headland SE Nicaragua
Monkey River see Monkey River Town
44 G3 Monkey River Town var. Monkey River. Toledo, SE Belize
12 M13 Monkland Ontario, SE Canada
81 J19 Monkoto Equateur, NW Zaire
99 K21 Monmouth Wel. Trefynwy. SE Wales, UK
32 J12 Monmouth Illinois, N USA
34 F12 Monmouth Oregon, NW USA
99 K21 Monmouth cultural region SE Wales, UK
100 I10 Monnickendam Noord-Holland, C Netherlands
79 R15 Mono ↝ C Togo
Monoecus see Monaco
37 R8 Mono Lake ◎ California, W USA
117 O23 Monólithos Ródos, Dodekánisos, Greece, Aegean Sea
21 Q12 Monomoy Island island Massachusetts, NE USA
33 O12 Monon Indiana, N USA
31 Y12 Monona Iowa, C USA
32 L9 Monona Wisconsin, N USA
20 B15 Monongahela Pennsylvania, NE USA
20 B16 Monongahela River ↝ NE USA
109 P17 Monopoli Puglia, SE Italy
Mono, Punte see Monkey Point
113 K23 Monor Pest, C Hungary
Monostor see Beli Manastir
80 K8 Monou Borkou-Ennedi-Tibesti, NE Chad
107 S12 Monóvar País Valenciano, E Spain
107 R7 Monreal del Campo Aragón, NE Spain
109 I23 Monreale Sicilia, Italy, C Mediterranean Sea
25 T3 Monroe Georgia, SE USA
31 W14 Monroe Iowa, C USA
24 I5 Monroe Louisiana, S USA
33 S10 Monroe Michigan, N USA
20 K13 Monroe New York, NE USA
23 S11 Monroe North Carolina, SE USA
38 L6 Monroe Utah, W USA
34 H7 Monroe Washington, NW USA
32 L9 Monroe Wisconsin, N USA
29 V3 Monroe City Missouri, C USA
33 O15 Monroe Lake ⊞ Indiana, N USA
25 O7 Monroeville Alabama, S USA
20 C15 Monroeville Pennsylvania, NE USA
78 J16 Monrovia ● (Liberia) W Liberia
78 J16 Monrovia ✕ W Liberia
107 T7 Monroyo Aragón, NE Spain
101 F20 Mons Dut. Bergen. Hainaut, S Belgium
106 I8 Monsanto Castelo Branco, C Portugal
108 H8 Monselice Veneto, NE Italy
178 Gg9 Mon State ◈ state S Myanmar
100 G12 Monster Zuid-Holland, W Netherlands
97 N20 Mönsterås Kalmar, S Sweden
103 F17 Montabaur Rheinland-Pfalz, W Germany
108 G8 Montagnana Veneto, NE Italy
37 N1 Montague California, W USA
27 S5 Montague Texas, SW USA
191 S11 Montague Island island New South Wales, SE Australia
41 S12 Montague Island island Alaska, USA
41 S13 Montague Strait strait N Gulf of Alaska
104 J8 Montaigu Vendée, NW France
Montaigu see Scherpenheuvel
107 S7 Montalbán Aragón, NE Spain
108 G13 Montalcino Toscana, C Italy
106 H5 Montalegre Vila Real, N Portugal
116 G8 Montana prev. Ferdinand, Mikhaylovgrad. Oblast Montana, NW Bulgaria
110 D10 Montana Valais, SW Switzerland
41 R11 Montana Alaska, USA
35 T9 Montana off. State of Montana; also known as Mountain State, Treasure State. ◈ state NW USA
Montana see Montana, Oblast
116 G8 Montana, Oblast var. Montana; prev. Mikhaylovgrad. ◈ province NW Bulgaria
106 J10 Montánchez Extremadura, W Spain
Montañita see La Montañita
13 Q8 Mont-Apica Québec, SE Canada
106 G10 Montargil Portalegre, C Portugal
106 G10 Montargil, Barragem de ⊞ C Portugal
105 O7 Montargis Loiret, C France
105 O4 Montataire Oise, N France
104 M14 Montauban Tarn-et-Garonne, S France
21 N14 Montauk Long Island, New York, NE USA
21 N14 Montauk Point headland Long Island, New York, NE USA
105 Q7 Montbard Côte d'Or, C France
105 U7 Montbéliard Doubs, E France
27 W11 Mont Belvieu Texas, SW USA
107 U6 Montblanc var. Montblanch. Cataluña, NE Spain
Montblanch see Montblanc
105 Q11 Montbrison Loire, E France
Montcalm, Lake see Dogai Coring
105 Q9 Montceau-les-Mines Saône-et-Loire, C France
105 U12 Mont Cenis, Col du pass E France
104 K15 Mont-de-Marsan Landes, SW France
105 O3 Montdidier Somme, N France
197 J7 Mont-Dore Province Sud, S New Caledonia
22 K10 Monteagle Tennessee, S USA
59 M20 Monteagudo Chuquisaca, S Bolivia
43 R16 Monte Albán ruins Oaxaca, S Mexico
107 R11 Montealegre del Castillo Castilla-La Mancha, C Spain
61 N18 Monte Azul Minas Gerais, SE Brazil
12 M12 Montebello Québec, SE Canada
108 H7 Montebelluna Veneto, NE Italy
62 G13 Montecarlo Misiones, NE Argentina
63 D16 Monte Caseros Corrientes, NE Argentina
62 J13 Monte Castelo Santa Catarina, S Brazil
108 F11 Montecatini Terme Toscana, C Italy
44 H7 Montecillos, Cordillera de ▲▲ W Honduras
64 I12 Monte Comén Mendoza, W Argentina
46 M8 Monte Cristi var. San Fernando de Monte Cristi. NW Dominican Republic
60 C13 Monte Cristo Amazonas, W Brazil
109 E14 Montecristo, Isola di island Archipelago Toscano, C Italy
Monte Croce Carnico, Passo di see Plöcken Pass
60 J12 Monte Dourado Pará, NE Brazil
42 L11 Monte Escobedo Zacatecas, C Mexico
108 I13 Montefalco Umbria, C Italy
109 H14 Montefiascone Lazio, C Italy
107 N14 Montefrío Andalucía, S Spain
46 I11 Montego Bay var. Mobay. W Jamaica
Montego Bay see Sangster
106 J8 Montehermoso Extremadura, W Spain
106 F10 Montejunto, Serra de ▲ C Portugal
Monteleone di Calabria see Vibo Valentia
56 E7 Montelíbano Córdoba, NW Colombia
105 R13 Montélimar anc. Acunum Acusio, Montilium Adhemari. Drôme, E France
106 K15 Montellano Andalucía, S Spain
37 Y2 Montello Nevada, W USA
32 L8 Montello Wisconsin, N USA
65 J18 Montemayor, Meseta de plain SE Argentina
43 O9 Montemorelos Nuevo León, NE Mexico
106 G11 Montemor-o-Novo Évora, S Portugal
106 G8 Montemor-o-Velho var. Montemor-o-Vélho. Coimbra, N Portugal
106 H7 Montemuro, Serra de ▲ N Portugal
104 K12 Montendre Charente-Maritime, W France
63 I15 Montenegro Rio Grande do Sul, S Brazil
115 J16 Montenegro Serb. Crna Gora. ◈ republic SW Yugoslavia
64 G10 Monte Patria Coquimbo, N Chile
47 O9 Monte Plata E Dominican Republic
85 P14 Montepuez Cabo Delgado, N Mozambique
85 P14 Montepuez ↝ N Mozambique
108 G13 Montepulciano Toscana, C Italy
64 L6 Monte Quemado Santiago del Estero, N Argentina
105 O6 Montereau-Faut-Yonne anc. Condate. Seine-St-Denis, N France
37 N11 Monterey California, W USA
22 L9 Monterey Tennessee, S USA
23 T5 Monterey Virginia, NE USA
Monterey see Monterrey
37 N10 Monterey Bay bay California, W USA
56 D6 Montería Córdoba, NW Colombia
59 N18 Montero Santa Cruz, C Bolivia
64 J7 Monteros Tucumán, C Argentina
106 I5 Monterrei Galicia, NW Spain
43 O8 Monterrey var. Monterey. Nuevo León, NE Mexico
34 F9 Montesano Washington, NW USA
109 M19 Montesano sulla Marcellana Campania, S Italy
109 N16 Monte Sant' Angelo Puglia, SE Italy
61 O16 Monte Santo Bahia, E Brazil
109 D18 Monte Santu, Capo di headland Sardegna, Italy, C Mediterranean Sea
61 M19 Montes Claros Minas Gerais, SE Brazil
109 K14 Montesilvano Marina Abruzzi, C Italy
25 P4 Montevallo Alabama, S USA
108 G12 Montevarchi Toscana, C Italy
31 S9 Montevideo Minnesota, N USA
63 F20 Montevideo ● (Uruguay) Montevideo, S Uruguay
39 S7 Monte Vista Colorado, C USA
25 T5 Montezuma Georgia, SE USA
31 W14 Montezuma Iowa, C USA

◆ Country
● Country Capital
◇ Dependent Territory
○ Dependent Territory Capital
◈ Administrative Region
✕ International Airport
▲ Mountain
▲▲ Mountain Range
⛰ Volcano
↝ River
◎ Lake
⊞ Reservoir

MONTEZUMA – MOYIE SPRINGS

28 J6 **Montezuma** Kansas, C USA
105 U12 **Montgenèvre, Col de** pass France/Italy
99 K20 **Montgomery** E Wales, UK
25 Q5 **Montgomery** state capital Alabama, S USA
31 V9 **Montgomery** Minnesota, N USA
20 G13 **Montgomery** Pennsylvania, NE USA
23 Q5 **Montgomery** West Virginia, NE USA
99 K19 **Montgomery** cultural region E Wales, UK
Montgomery see Sāhīwāl
29 V4 **Montgomery City** Missouri, C USA
37 S8 **Montgomery Pass** pass Nevada, W USA
104 K12 **Montguyon** Charente-Maritime, W France
110 C10 **Monthey** Valais, SW Switzerland
29 V13 **Monticello** Arkansas, C USA
25 T4 **Monticello** Florida, SE USA
25 T8 **Monticello** Georgia, SE USA
32 M13 **Monticello** Illinois, N USA
33 O12 **Monticello** Indiana, N USA
31 Y13 **Monticello** Iowa, C USA
22 L7 **Monticello** Kentucky, S USA
31 V8 **Monticello** Minnesota, N USA
24 K7 **Monticello** Mississippi, S USA
29 V2 **Monticello** Missouri, C USA
20 J12 **Monticello** New York, NE USA
39 O7 **Monticello** Utah, W USA
108 F8 **Montichiari** Lombardia, N Italy
104 M12 **Montignac** Dordogne, SW France
101 G21 **Montignies-le-Tilleul** var. Montigny-le-Tilleul. Hainaut, S Belgium
12 J8 **Montigny, Lac de** ◎ Québec, SE Canada
105 S6 **Montigny-le-Roi** Haute-Marne, N France
Montigny-le-Tilleul see Montignies-le-Tilleul
45 R16 **Montijo** Veraguas, S Panama
106 F11 **Montijo** Setúbal, W Portugal
106 J11 **Montijo** Extremadura, W Spain
Montilium Adhemari see Montélimar
106 M13 **Montilla** Andalucía, S Spain
104 L3 **Montivilliers** Seine-Maritime, N France
13 U7 **Mont-Joli** Québec, SE Canada
12 M10 **Mont-Laurier** Québec, SE Canada
13 X5 **Mont-Louis** Québec, SE Canada
105 N17 **Mont-Louis** var. Mont Louis. Pyrénées-Orientales, S France
105 O10 **Montluçon** Allier, C France
13 R10 **Montmagny** Québec, SE Canada
105 S3 **Montmédy** Meuse, NE France
105 P5 **Montmirail** Marne, N France
13 R9 **Montmorency** ≈ Québec, SE Canada
104 M10 **Montmorillon** Vienne, W France
109 J14 **Montorio al Vomano** Abruzzi, C Italy
106 M13 **Montoro** Andalucía, S Spain
35 S16 **Montpelier** Idaho, NW USA
31 P6 **Montpelier** North Dakota, N USA
20 M7 **Montpelier** state capital Vermont, NE USA
105 Q15 **Montpellier** Hérault, S France
104 L12 **Montpon-Ménestérol** Dordogne, SW France
12 G8 **Montreal** ≈ Ontario, S Canada
12 C8 **Montreal** ≈ Ontario, S Canada
Montreal see Mirabel
10 K15 **Montréal** Eng. Montreal. Québec, SE Canada
9 T14 **Montreal Lake** ◎ Saskatchewan, C Canada
12 B9 **Montreal River** Ontario, S Canada
105 N2 **Montreuil** Pas-de-Calais, N France
104 K8 **Montreuil-Bellay** Maine-et-Loire, NW France
110 C10 **Montreux** Vaud, SW Switzerland
110 B9 **Montricher** Vaud, W Switzerland
98 K10 **Montrose** E Scotland, UK
29 W14 **Montrose** Arkansas, C USA
39 Q6 **Montrose** Colorado, C USA
31 Y16 **Montrose** Iowa, C USA
20 H12 **Montrose** Pennsylvania, NE USA
23 X5 **Montross** Virginia, NE USA
13 O12 **Mont-St-Hilaire** Québec, SE Canada
105 S3 **Mont-St-Martin** Meurthe-et-Moselle, NE France
47 V10 **Montserrat** var. Emerald Isle. ◇ UK dependent territory E West Indies
107 V5 **Montserrat** ▲ NE Spain
106 M7 **Montuenga** Castilla-León, N Spain
101 M19 **Montzen** Liège, E Belgium
39 N8 **Monument Valley** valley Arizona/Utah, SW USA
177 G4 **Monywa** Sagaing, C Myanmar
108 D7 **Monza** Lombardia, N Italy
85 J15 **Monze** Southern, S Zambia
107 T5 **Monzón** Aragón, NE Spain
27 T9 **Moody** Texas, SW USA
100 L13 **Mook** Limburg, SE Netherlands
171 Kk15 **Mooka** var. Mōka. Tochigi, Honshū, S Japan
190 K3 **Moomba** South Australia
12 G13 **Moon** ≈ Ontario, S Canada
Moon see Muhu
189 Y10 **Moonie** Queensland, E Australia
198 B10 **Moonless Mountains** undersea feature E Pacific Ocean
190 L13 **Moonlight Head** headland Victoria, SE Australia
Moon-Sund see Väinameri
190 H8 **Moonta** South Australia
Moor see Mór
188 I12 **Moora** Western Australia
100 H12 **Moordrecht** Zuid-Holland, C Netherlands
35 T9 **Moore** Montana, NW USA
29 N11 **Moore** Oklahoma, C USA
27 R12 **Moore** Texas, SW USA
203 S10 **Moorea** island Îles du Vent, W French Polynesia
23 U3 **Moorefield** West Virginia, NE USA
25 X14 **Moore Haven** Florida, SE USA
188 J11 **Moore, Lake** ◎ Western Australia
21 N7 **Moore Reservoir** ⊡ New Hampshire/Vermont, NE USA
46 G1 **Moores Island** island N Bahamas
23 R10 **Mooresville** North Carolina, SE USA
31 R5 **Moorhead** Minnesota, N USA
24 K4 **Moorhead** Mississippi, S USA
176 Ww10 **Moor, Kepulauan** island group E Indonesia
101 F18 **Moorsel** Oost-Vlaanderen, C Belgium
101 C18 **Moorslede** West-Vlaanderen, W Belgium
20 L8 **Moosalamoo, Mount** ▲ Vermont, NE USA
103 M22 **Moosburg** Bayern, SE Germany
35 S14 **Moose** Wyoming, C USA
10 H11 **Moose** ≈ Ontario, S Canada
10 H10 **Moose Factory** Ontario, S Canada
21 Q4 **Moosehead Lake** ◎ Maine, NE USA
9 U16 **Moose Jaw** Saskatchewan, S Canada
9 V14 **Moose Lake** Manitoba, C Canada
31 W6 **Moose Lake** Minnesota, N USA
21 P6 **Mooselookmeguntic Lake** ◎ Maine, NE USA
41 R12 **Moose Pass** Alaska, USA
21 P5 **Moose River** ≈ Maine, NE USA
20 J9 **Moose River** ≈ New York, NE USA
9 V16 **Moosomin** Saskatchewan, S Canada
10 H10 **Moosonee** Ontario, SE Canada
21 N12 **Moosup** Connecticut, NE USA
85 N16 **Mopeia** Zambézia, NE Mozambique
Mopelia see Maupihaa
85 H18 **Mopipi** Central, C Botswana
Moppo see Mokp'o
79 N11 **Mopti** Mopti, C Mali
79 O11 **Mopti** ◈ region S Mali
59 H18 **Moquegua** Moquegua, SE Peru
59 H18 **Moquegua** off. Departamento de Moquegua. ◈ department S Peru
113 I23 **Mór** Ger. Moor. Fejér, C Hungary
80 G11 **Mora** Extrême-Nord, N Cameroon
106 G11 **Mora** Évora, S Portugal
107 N9 **Mora** Castilla-La Mancha, C Spain
96 L12 **Mora** Kopparberg, C Sweden
31 V7 **Mora** Minnesota, N USA
39 T10 **Mora** New Mexico, SW USA
115 J17 **Morača** ≈ SW Yugoslavia
158 K10 **Morādābād** Uttar Pradesh, N India
107 U6 **Móra d'Ebre** var. Mora de Ebro. Cataluña, NE Spain
Mora de Ebro see Móra d'Ebre
107 S8 **Mora de Rubielos** Aragón, NE Spain
180 H4 **Morafenobe** Mahajanga, W Madagascar
112 K8 **Morąg** Ger. Mohrungen. Olsztyn, N Poland
113 L25 **Mórahalom** Csongrád, S Hungary
107 N11 **Moral de Calatrava** Castilla-La Mancha, C Spain
65 G19 **Moraleda, Canal** strait SE Pacific Ocean
56 J3 **Morales** Bolívar, N Colombia
56 D12 **Morales** Cauca, SW Colombia
44 F5 **Morales** Izabal, E Guatemala
180 J5 **Moramanga** Toamasina, E Madagascar
29 Q6 **Moran** Kansas, C USA
27 Q7 **Moran** Texas, SW USA
189 X7 **Moranbah** Queensland, NE Australia
46 L13 **Morant Bay** E Jamaica
98 G10 **Morar, Loch** ◎ N Scotland, UK
Morata see Goodenough Island
107 Q12 **Moratalla** Murcia, SE Spain
110 C8 **Morat, Lac de** Ger. Murtensee. ◎ W Switzerland
86 I11 **Morava** var. March. ≈ C Europe see also March
Morava see Moravia, Czech Republic
Morava see Velika Morava, Yugoslavia
31 W15 **Moravia** Iowa, C USA
113 F18 **Moravia** Cz. Morava, Ger. Mähren. cultural region E Czech Republic
113 H17 **Moravice** Ger. Mohra. ≈ NE Czech Republic
Moravicza see Moravița
113 G17 **Moravská Třebová** Ger. Mährisch-Trübau. Východní Čechy, E Czech Republic
113 E19 **Moravské Budějovice** Ger. Mährisch-Budwitz. Jižní Morava, SE Czech Republic
113 F19 **Moravský Krumlov** Ger. Mährisch-Kromau. Jižní Morava, SE Czech Republic
Morawitza see Moravița
98 J8 **Moray** cultural region N Scotland, UK
98 J8 **Moray Firth** inlet N Scotland, UK
44 B10 **Morazán** ◈ department NE El Salvador
160 C10 **Morbi** Gujarāt, W India
104 G7 **Morbihan** ◈ department NW France
Mörbisch see Mörbisch am See
111 Y5 **Mörbisch am See** var. Mörbisch. Burgenland, E Austria
97 N21 **Mörbylånga** Kalmar, S Sweden
104 J14 **Morcenx** Landes, SW France
Morcheh Khort see Mürcheh Khvort
15 L16 **Morden** Manitoba, S Canada
Mordovia see Mordoviya, Respublika
131 N5 **Mordoviya, Respublika** prev. Mordovskaya ASSR, Eng. Mordovia, Mordvinia. ◈ autonomous republic W Russian Federation
130 M7 **Mordovo** Tambovskaya Oblast', W Russian Federation
Mordovskaya ASSR/Mordvinia see Mordoviya, Respublika
Morea see Pelopónnisos
30 K8 **Moreau River** ≈ South Dakota, N USA
99 K16 **Morecambe** NW England, UK
99 K16 **Morecambe Bay** inlet NW England, UK
191 S4 **Moree** New South Wales, SE Australia
194 E15 **Morehead** Western, SW PNG
23 N5 **Morehead** Kentucky, S USA
194 E15 **Morehead** ≈ SW PNG
23 X11 **Morehead City** North Carolina, SE USA
29 Y8 **Morehouse** Missouri, C USA
110 E10 **Mörel** Valais, SW Switzerland
56 D13 **Morelia** Caquetá, S Colombia
43 N14 **Morelia** Michoacán de Ocampo, S Mexico
107 T7 **Morella** País Valenciano, E Spain
42 I7 **Morelos** Chihuahua, N Mexico
43 O15 **Morelos** ◈ state S Mexico
160 H7 **Morena** Madhya Pradesh, C India
106 L12 **Morena, Sierra** ▲▲ S Spain
39 O14 **Morenci** Arizona, SW USA
33 R11 **Morenci** Michigan, N USA
118 J13 **Moreni** Dâmbovița, S Romania
96 D9 **Møre og Romsdal** ◈ county S Norway
14 Ee12 **Moresby Island** island Queen Charlotte Islands, British Columbia, SW Canada
191 W2 **Moreton Island** island Queensland, E Australia
105 O3 **Moreuil** Somme, N France
37 V7 **Morey Peak** ▲ Nevada, W USA
129 U4 **More-Yu** ≈ NW Russian Federation
105 T9 **Morez** Jura, E France
Mórfou see Güzelyurt
Morfou Bay/Mórfou, Kólpos see Güzelyurt Körfezi
190 J8 **Morgan** South Australia
25 S7 **Morgan** Georgia, SE USA
27 S8 **Morgan** Texas, SW USA
24 J10 **Morgan City** Louisiana, S USA
22 H6 **Morganfield** Kentucky, S USA
37 O10 **Morgan Hill** California, W USA
23 Q9 **Morganton** North Carolina, SE USA
22 J7 **Morgantown** Kentucky, S USA
23 S2 **Morgantown** West Virginia, NE USA
110 B10 **Morges** Vaud, SW Switzerland
Morghāb, Daryā-ye see Murgab
98 I9 **Mor, Glen** var. Glen Albyn, Great Glen. valley N Scotland, UK
105 T5 **Morhange** Moselle, NE France
164 M5 **Mori** var. Mori Kazak Zizhixian. Xinjiang Uygur Zizhiqu, NW China
172 Nn6 **Mori** Hokkaidō, NE Japan
37 Y6 **Moriah, Mount** ▲ Nevada, W USA
39 S11 **Moriarty** New Mexico, SW USA
56 J12 **Morichal** Guainía, E Colombia
194 H14 **Morigio Island** island S PNG
Mori Kazak Zizhixian see Mori
169 U7 **Morin Dawa** var. Morin Dawa Daurzu Zizhiqi. Nei Mongol Zizhiqu, N China
Morin Dawa Daurzu Zizhiqi see Morin Dawa
15 I13 **Morinville** Alberta, SW Canada
171 Mm11 **Morioka** Iwate, Honshū, C Japan
191 T8 **Morisset** New South Wales, SE Australia
171 Mm10 **Moriyoshi-yama** ▲ Honshū, C Japan
94 K13 **Morjärv** Norrbotten, N Sweden
131 R3 **Morki** Respublika Mariy El, W Russian Federation
126 K10 **Morkoka** ≈ NE Russian Federation
104 F5 **Morlaix** Finistère, NW France
97 M20 **Mörlunda** Kalmar, S Sweden
109 N19 **Mormanno** Calabria, SW Italy
38 L11 **Mormon Lake** ◎ Arizona, SW USA
37 Y10 **Mormon Peak** ▲ Nevada, W USA
Mormon State see Utah
47 Y5 **Morne-à-l'Eau** Grande Terre, N Guadeloupe
31 Y15 **Morning Sun** Iowa, C USA
200 O14 **Mornington Abyssal Plain** undersea feature SE Pacific Ocean
65 F22 **Mornington, Isla** island S Chile
189 T4 **Mornington Island** island Wellesley Islands, Queensland, N Australia
117 E18 **Mórnos** ≈ C Greece
155 P14 **Moro** Sind, SE Pakistan
34 I11 **Moro** Oregon, NW USA
194 K14 **Morobe** Morobe, C PNG
194 J14 **Morobe** ◈ province C PNG
33 N12 **Morocco** Indiana, N USA
76 E8 **Morocco** off. Kingdom of Morocco, Ar. Al Mamlakah. ◆ monarchy N Africa
Morocco see Marrakech
83 I22 **Morogoro** Morogoro, E Tanzania
83 H24 **Morogoro** ◈ region SE Tanzania
179 Qq16 **Moro Gulf** gulf S Philippines
43 N13 **Moroleón** Guanajuato, C Mexico
180 H6 **Morombe** Toliara, W Madagascar
46 G5 **Morón** Ciego de Ávila, C Cuba
56 K5 **Morón** Carabobo, N Venezuela
Morón see Morón de la Frontera
169 N8 **Mörön** Hentiy, C Mongolia
168 I6 **Mörön** Hövsgöl, N Mongolia
58 D8 **Morona, Río** ≈ N Peru
58 C8 **Morona Santiago** ◈ province E Ecuador
180 H5 **Morondava** Toliara, W Madagascar
106 K14 **Morón de la Frontera** var. Morón. Andalucía, S Spain
180 G13 **Moroni** ● (Comoros) Grande Comore, NW Comoros
175 Tt6 **Morotai, Pulau** island Maluku, E Indonesia
175 T6 **Morotai, Selat** strait Maluku, E Indonesia
Morotiri see Marotiri
83 H17 **Moroto** NE Uganda
Morozov see Bratan
130 M11 **Morozovsk** Rostovskaya Oblast', SW Russian Federation
99 L14 **Morpeth** N England, UK
Morphou see Güzelyurt
Morphou Bay see Güzelyurt Körfezi
30 I13 **Morrill** Nebraska, C USA
29 U11 **Morrilton** Arkansas, C USA
9 Q16 **Morrin** Alberta, SW Canada
192 M7 **Morrinsville** Waikato, North Island, NZ
9 X16 **Morris** Manitoba, S Canada
32 M11 **Morris** Illinois, N USA
31 S8 **Morris** Minnesota, N USA
12 M13 **Morrisburg** Ontario, SE Canada
207 R11 **Morris Jesup, Kap** headland N Greenland
190 B1 **Morris, Mount** ▲ South Australia
32 K10 **Morrison** Illinois, N USA
38 K13 **Morristown** Arizona, SW USA
20 J14 **Morristown** New Jersey, NE USA
23 O8 **Morristown** Tennessee, S USA
44 L11 **Morrito** Río San Juan, SW Nicaragua
37 P13 **Morro Bay** California, W USA
97 L22 **Mörrum** Blekinge, S Sweden
85 N16 **Morrumbala** Zambézia, NE Mozambique
85 N20 **Morrumbene** Inhambane, SE Mozambique
97 F21 **Mors** island NW Denmark
Mörs see Moers
27 N1 **Morse** Texas, SW USA
131 N6 **Morshansk** Tambovskaya Oblast', W Russian Federation
104 L5 **Mortagne-au-Perche** Orne, N France
104 J8 **Mortagne-sur-Sèvre** Vendée, NW France
106 G8 **Mortágua** Viseu, N Portugal
104 J5 **Mortain** Manche, N France
108 C8 **Mortara** Lombardia, N Italy
61 J17 **Mortes, Rio das** ≈ C Brazil
190 M12 **Mortlake** Victoria, SE Australia
Mortlock Group see Takuu Islands
201 Q17 **Mortlock Islands** prev. Nomoi Islands. island group C Micronesia
31 T9 **Morton** Minnesota, N USA
24 L5 **Morton** Mississippi, S USA
26 M5 **Morton** Texas, SW USA
34 H9 **Morton** Washington, NW USA
1 D7 **Morton Seamount** undersea feature NE Pacific Ocean
47 U15 **Moruga** Trinidad, Trinidad and Tobago
191 P9 **Morundah** New South Wales, SE Australia
Moruroa see Mururoa
191 S11 **Moruya** New South Wales, SE Australia
105 Q8 **Morvan** physical region C France
193 G21 **Morven** Canterbury, South Island, NZ
191 O13 **Morwell** Victoria, SE Australia
129 N6 **Morzhovets, Ostrov** island NW Russian Federation
106 G4 **Mos** Galicia, NW Spain
130 J4 **Mosal'sk** Kaluzhskaya Oblast', W Russian Federation
103 H20 **Mosbach** Baden-Württemberg, SW Germany
97 E18 **Mosby** Vest-Agder, S Norway
35 V9 **Mosby** Montana, NW USA
34 M9 **Moscow** Idaho, NW USA
22 F10 **Moscow** Tennessee, S USA
Moscow see Moskva
103 D19 **Mosel** Fr. Moselle. ≈ W Europe see also Moselle
105 T4 **Moselle** ◈ department NE France
105 T6 **Moselle** Ger. Mosel. ≈ W Europe see also Mosel
34 K9 **Moses Lake** ◎ Washington, NW USA
85 I18 **Mosetse** Central, E Botswana
94 H4 **Mosfellsbær** Sudhurland, SW Iceland
193 F23 **Mosgiel** Otago, South Island, NZ
128 M11 **Mosha** ≈ NW Russian Federation
83 I20 **Moshi** Kilimanjaro, NE Tanzania
112 G12 **Mosina** Poznań, W Poland
32 L6 **Mosinee** Wisconsin, N USA
94 F13 **Mosjøen** Nordland, C Norway
127 Nn13 **Moskal'vo** Ostrov Sakhalin, Sakhalinskaya Oblast', SE Russian Federation
94 I13 **Moskosel** Norrbotten, N Sweden
130 K4 **Moskovskaya Oblast'** ◈ province W Russian Federation
Moskovskiy see Moskva
130 J3 **Moskva** Eng. Moscow. ● (Russian Federation) Gorod Moskva, W Russian Federation
153 Q14 **Moskva** Rus. Moskovskiy; prev. Chubek. SW Tajikistan
130 L4 **Moskva** ≈ W Russian Federation
85 I20 **Mosomane** Kgatleng, SE Botswana
Moson and Magyaróvár see Mosonmagyaróvár
113 H21 **Mosoni-Duna** Ger. Kleine Donau. ≈ NW Hungary
113 H21 **Mosonmagyaróvár** Ger. Wieselburg-Ungarisch-Altenburg; prev. Moson and Magyaróvár, Ger. Wieselburg and Ungarisch-Altenburg. Győr-Moson-Sopron, NW Hungary
Mospino see Mospyne
119 X8 **Mospyne** Rus. Mospino. Donets'ka Oblast', E Ukraine
56 B12 **Mosquera** Nariño, SW Colombia
39 U10 **Mosquero** New Mexico, SW USA
Mosquito Coast see La Mosquitia
33 U11 **Mosquito Creek Lake** ⊡ Ohio, N USA
Mosquito Gulf see Mosquitos, Golfo de los
25 X11 **Mosquito Lagoon** wetland Florida, SE USA
45 N10 **Mosquito, Punta** headland E Nicaragua
45 W14 **Mosquito, Punta** headland NE Panama
45 Q15 **Mosquitos, Golfo de los** Eng. Mosquito Gulf. gulf N Panama
97 H16 **Moss** Østfold, S Norway
Mossâmedes see Namibe
24 G8 **Moss Bluff** Louisiana, S USA
193 C23 **Mossburn** Southland, South Island, NZ
85 G26 **Mosselbaai** var. Mosselbai, Eng. Mossel Bay. Western Cape, SW South Africa
Mosselbai/Mossel Bay see Mosselbaai
81 F20 **Mossendjo** Le Niari, SW Congo
191 N8 **Mossgiel** New South Wales, SE Australia
103 H22 **Mössingen** Baden-Württemberg, S Germany
189 W4 **Mossman** Queensland, NE Australia
61 P14 **Mossoró** Rio Grande do Norte, NE Brazil
25 N9 **Moss Point** Mississippi, S USA
191 S9 **Moss Vale** New South Wales, SE Australia
34 G9 **Mossyrock** Washington, NW USA
113 B15 **Most** Ger. Brüx. Severní Čechy, NW Czech Republic
123 Jj16 **Mosta** var. Musta. C Malta
76 I5 **Mostaganem** var. Mestghanem. NW Algeria
115 H14 **Mostar** S Bosnia and Herzegovina
63 J17 **Mostardas** Rio Grande do Sul, S Brazil
118 K14 **Mostiștea** ≈ S Romania
Mostva see Mastva
Mosty see Masty
118 H5 **Mostys'ka** L'vivs'ka Oblast', W Ukraine
Mosul see Al Mawṣil
97 F15 **Møsvatnet** ◎ S Norway
82 J12 **Mot'a** N Ethiopia
197 C10 **Mota** island Banks Islands, N Vanuatu
81 H16 **Motaba** ≈ N Congo
107 O10 **Mota del Cuervo** Castilla-La Mancha, C Spain
106 L5 **Mota del Marqués** Castilla-León, N Spain
44 F5 **Motagua, Río** ≈ Guatemala/Honduras
121 H19 **Motal'** Brestskaya Voblasts', SW Belarus
97 L17 **Motala** Östergötland, S Sweden
197 C10 **Mota Lava** island Banks Islands, N Vanuatu
203 X7 **Motane** var. Mohotani. island Îles Marquises, NE French Polynesia
158 K13 **Moth** Uttar Pradesh, N India
Mother of Presidents/Mother of States see Virginia
98 I12 **Motherwell** C Scotland, UK
159 P12 **Motīhāri** Bihār, N India
107 Q10 **Motilla del Palancar** Castilla-La Mancha, C Spain
192 N7 **Motiti Island** island NE NZ
67 E25 **Motley Island** island SE Falkland Islands
85 J19 **Motloutse** ≈ E Botswana
43 V17 **Motozintla de Mendoza** Chiapas, SE Mexico
107 N15 **Motril** Andalucía, S Spain
118 G13 **Motru** Gorj, SW Romania
171 Mm5 **Motsuta-misaki** headland Hokkaidō, NE Japan
30 L6 **Mott** North Dakota, N USA
Möttling see Metlika
109 O18 **Mottola** Puglia, SE Italy
192 P8 **Motu** ≈ North Island, NZ
193 I14 **Motueka** Tasman, South Island, NZ
193 I14 **Motueka** ≈ South Island, NZ
Motu Iti see Tupai
43 X12 **Motul** var. Motul de Felipe Carrillo Puerto. Yucatán, SE Mexico
Motul de Felipe Carrillo Puerto see Motul
203 U17 **Motu Nui** island Easter Island, Chile, E Pacific Ocean
203 Q10 **Motu One** var. Bellingshausen. atoll Îles Sous le Vent, W French Polynesia
202 I16 **Motutapu** island E Cook Islands
200 R15 **Motu Tapu** island Tongatapu Group, S Tonga
192 L5 **Motutapu Island** island N NZ
Motyca see Modica
126 I13 **Motygino** Krasnoyarskiy Kray, C Russian Federation
Mouanda see Moanda
Mouaskar see Mascara
107 U3 **Moubermé, Tuc de** Fr. Pic de Maubermé, Sp. Pico Mauberme; prev. Tuc de Maubermé. ▲ France/Spain see also Maubermé, Pic de
47 N7 **Mouchoir Passage** passage SE Turks and Caicos Islands
78 I9 **Moudjéria** Tagant, SW Mauritania
110 C9 **Moudon** Vaud, W Switzerland
Mouhoun see Black Volta
81 E19 **Mouila** Ngounié, C Gabon
81 K14 **Mouka** Haute-Kotto, C Central African Republic
Moukden see Shenyang
191 N10 **Moulamein** New South Wales, SE Australia
Moulamein Creek see Billabong Creek
76 F6 **Moulay-Bousselham** NW Morocco
Moule see le Moule
82 M11 **Moulhoulé** N Djibouti
105 P9 **Moulins** Allier, C France
178 Gg9 **Moulmein** var. Maulmain, Mawlamyine. Mon State, S Myanmar
177 F9 **Moulmeingyun** Irrawaddy, SW Myanmar
76 G6 **Moulouya** var. Mulucha, Muluya, Mulwiya. seasonal river NE Morocco
25 O2 **Moulton** Alabama, S USA
31 W16 **Moulton** Iowa, C USA
27 T11 **Moulton** Texas, SW USA
25 T7 **Moultrie** Georgia, SE USA
23 S14 **Moultrie, Lake** ⊡ South Carolina, SE USA
24 K3 **Mound Bayou** Mississippi, S USA
32 L17 **Mound City** Illinois, N USA
29 R6 **Mound City** Kansas, C USA
29 Q2 **Mound City** Missouri, C USA
31 N7 **Mound City** South Dakota, N USA
80 H13 **Moundou** Logone-Occidental, SW Chad
29 P10 **Mounds** Oklahoma, C USA
23 R2 **Moundsville** West Virginia, NE USA
178 Ii12 **Moŭng Roessei** Bătdâmbâng, W Cambodia
Moun Hou see Black Volta
14 G5 **Mountain** ≈ Northwest Territories, NW Canada
39 S12 **Mountainair** New Mexico, SW USA
37 V1 **Mountain City** Nevada, W USA
23 Q8 **Mountain City** Tennessee, S USA
29 U7 **Mountain Grove** Missouri, C USA
29 U9 **Mountain Home** Arkansas, C USA
35 N15 **Mountain Home** Idaho, NW USA
27 Q11 **Mountain Home** Texas, SW USA
31 W4 **Mountain Iron** Minnesota, N USA
31 T10 **Mountain Lake** Minnesota, N USA
25 S3 **Mountain Park** Georgia, SE USA
37 W12 **Mountain Pass** pass California, W USA
29 T12 **Mountain Pine** Arkansas, C USA
41 Y14 **Mountain Point** Annette Island, Alaska, USA
Mountain State see Montana, USA
Mountain State see West Virginia, USA
29 V7 **Mountain View** Arkansas, C USA
40 H12 **Mountain View** Hawaii, USA, C Pacific Ocean
29 V10 **Mountain View** Missouri, C USA
40 M11 **Mountain Village** Alaska, USA
23 R8 **Mount Airy** North Carolina, SE USA
85 K24 **Mount Ayliff** Xh. Maxesibebi. Eastern Cape, SE South Africa
31 U16 **Mount Ayr** Iowa, C USA
190 J9 **Mount Barker** South Australia
188 J14 **Mount Barker** Western Australia
191 P11 **Mount Beauty** Victoria, SE Australia
12 E16 **Mount Brydges** Ontario, S Canada
33 N16 **Mount Carmel** Illinois, N USA
32 K10 **Mount Carroll** Illinois, N USA
33 S9 **Mount Clemens** Michigan, N USA
193 E19 **Mount Cook** Canterbury, South Island, NZ
85 L16 **Mount Darwin** Mashonaland Central, NE Zimbabwe
21 S7 **Mount Desert Island** island Maine, NE USA
25 W11 **Mount Dora** Florida, SE USA
190 G5 **Mount Eba** South Australia
27 W8 **Mount Enterprise** Texas, SW USA
190 J4 **Mount Fitton** South Australia
85 J24 **Mount Fletcher** Eastern Cape, SE South Africa
12 F15 **Mount Forest** Ontario, S Canada
190 K12 **Mount Gambier** South Australia
189 W5 **Mount Garnet** Queensland, NE Australia
23 P6 **Mount Gay** West Virginia, NE USA
33 S12 **Mount Gilead** Ohio, N USA
194 H12 **Mount Hagen** Western Highlands, C PNG
20 J16 **Mount Holly** New Jersey, NE USA
23 R10 **Mount Holly** North Carolina, SE USA
29 T12 **Mount Ida** Arkansas, C USA
189 T6 **Mount Isa** Queensland, C Australia
23 U4 **Mount Jackson** Virginia, NE USA
20 D12 **Mount Jewett** Pennsylvania, NE USA
20 L13 **Mount Kisco** New York, NE USA
20 B15 **Mount Lebanon** Pennsylvania, NE USA
190 J8 **Mount Lofty Ranges** ▲▲ South Australia
188 J10 **Mount Magnet** Western Australia
192 N7 **Mount Maunganui** Bay of Plenty, North Island, NZ
99 E18 **Mountmellick** Ir. Móinteach Mílic. C Ireland
32 L10 **Mount Morris** Illinois, N USA
33 R9 **Mount Morris** Michigan, N USA
20 F10 **Mount Morris** New York, NE USA
20 B16 **Mount Morris** Pennsylvania, NE USA
32 K15 **Mount Olive** Illinois, N USA
23 V10 **Mount Olive** North Carolina, SE USA
23 N4 **Mount Olivet** Kentucky, S USA
31 Y15 **Mount Pleasant** Iowa, C USA
33 Q8 **Mount Pleasant** Michigan, N USA
20 C15 **Mount Pleasant** Pennsylvania, NE USA
23 T14 **Mount Pleasant** South Carolina, SE USA
22 I9 **Mount Pleasant** Tennessee, S USA
27 W6 **Mount Pleasant** Texas, SW USA
38 L4 **Mount Pleasant** Utah, W USA
65 N23 **Mount Pleasant** ✕ (Stanley) East Falkland, Falkland Islands
99 G25 **Mount's Bay** inlet SW England, UK
37 N2 **Mount Shasta** California, W USA
32 J13 **Mount Sterling** Illinois, N USA
23 N5 **Mount Sterling** Kentucky, S USA
20 E15 **Mount Union** Pennsylvania, NE USA
25 V6 **Mount Vernon** Georgia, SE USA
32 L16 **Mount Vernon** Illinois, N USA
22 M6 **Mount Vernon** Kentucky, S USA
29 S7 **Mount Vernon** Missouri, C USA
33 T13 **Mount Vernon** Ohio, N USA
34 H7 **Mount Vernon** Oregon, NW USA
27 W6 **Mount Vernon** Texas, SW USA
34 K13 **Mount Vernon** Washington, NW USA
22 L5 **Mount Washington** Kentucky, S USA
190 F8 **Mount Wedge** South Australia
32 L14 **Mount Zion** Illinois, N USA
189 Y9 **Moura** Queensland, NE Australia
60 F12 **Moura** Amazonas, NW Brazil
106 H12 **Moura** Beja, S Portugal
106 I12 **Mourão** Évora, S Portugal
78 L11 **Mourdiah** Koulikoro, W Mali
80 K7 **Mourdi, Depression du** desert lowland Chad/Sudan
104 J16 **Mourenx** Pyrénées-Atlantiques, SW France
Mourgana see Mourgkána
117 C15 **Mourgkána** var. Mourgana. ▲ Albania/Greece
99 G16 **Mourne Mountains** Ir. Beanna Boirche. ▲▲ SE Northern Ireland, UK
117 I15 **Moúrtzeflos, Ákra** headland Límnos, E Greece
101 C19 **Mouscron** Dut. Moeskroen. Hainaut, W Belgium
Mouse River see Souris River
80 H10 **Moussoro** Kanem, W Chad
105 T11 **Moûtiers** Savoie, E France
180 J14 **Moutsamoudou** var. Mutsamudu. Anjouan, SE Comoros
76 K11 **Mouydir, Monts de** ▲ S Algeria
81 F20 **Mouyondzi** La Bouenza, S Congo
117 E16 **Mouzáki** prev. Mouzákion. Thessalía, C Greece
Mouzákion see Mouzáki
31 S13 **Moville** Iowa, C USA
84 E13 **Moxico** ◈ province E Angola
180 J14 **Moya** Anjouan, SE Comoros
42 L12 **Moyahua** Zacatecas, C Mexico
83 J16 **Moyalē** S Ethiopia
78 I15 **Moyamba** W Sierra Leone
76 G7 **Moyen Atlas** Eng. Middle Atlas. ▲▲ N Morocco
80 H13 **Moyen-Chari** off. Préfecture du Moyen-Chari. ◈ prefecture S Chad
Moyen-Congo see Congo
85 J24 **Moyeni** var. Quthing. SW Lesotho
78 H13 **Moyenne-Guinée** ◈ state NW Guinea
81 D18 **Moyen-Ogooué** off. Province du Moyen-Ogooué, var. Le Moyen-Ogooué. ◈ province C Gabon
105 S4 **Moyeuvre-Grande** Moselle, NE France
35 N7 **Moyie Springs** Idaho, NW USA

◆ Country ● Country Capital ◇ Dependent Territory ○ Dependent Territory Capital ◈ Administrative Region ✕ International Airport ▲ Mountain ▲▲ Mountain Range Volcano ≈ River ◎ Lake ⊡ Reservoir

287

288

85 K17 **Mvuma** prev. Umvuma. Midlands, C Zimbabwe

84 L13 **Mwanza** Eastern, E Zambia

83 G20 **Mwanza** Mwanza, NW Tanzania

81 N23 **Mwanza** Shaba, SE Zaire

83 F20 **Mwanza** ♦ region N Tanzania

84 M13 **Mwase Lundazi** Eastern, E Zambia

99 B17 **Mweelrea** Ir. Caoc Maol Réidh. ▲ W Ireland

81 K21 **Mweka** Kasai Occidental, C Zaire

84 K12 **Mwenda** Luapula, N Zambia

81 L22 **Mwene-Ditu** Kasai Oriental, S Zaire

85 L18 **Mwenezi** ♣ S Zimbabwe

81 O20 **Mwenga** Sud Kivu, E Zaire

84 K11 **Mweru, Lake** var. Lac Moero. ◎ Zaire/Zambia

84 H13 **Mwinilunga** North Western, NW Zambia

201 V16 **Mwokil Atoll** var. Mokil Atoll. atoll Caroline Islands, E Micronesia

Myadel' see Myadzyel

120 J13 **Myadzyel** Pol. Miadziol Nowy, Rus. Myadel'. Minskaya Voblasts', N Belarus

158 C12 **Myājlār** var. Miajlar. Rājasthān, NW India

127 O9 **Myakit** Magadanskaya Oblast', E Russian Federation

25 W13 **Myakka River** ♣ Florida, SE USA

128 L14 **Myaksa** Vologodskaya Oblast', NW Russian Federation

191 U8 **Myall Lake** ◎ New South Wales, SE Australia

177 Ff7 **Myanaung** Irrawaddy, SW Myanmar

159 Y14 **Myanmar** off. Union of Myanmar, var. Burma. ◆ military dictatorship SE Asia

177 F9 **Myaungmya** Irrawaddy, SW Myanmar

120 N11 **Myazha** Rus. Mezha. Vitsyebskaya Voblasts', NE Belarus

121 O18 **Myerkulavichy** Rus. Merkulovichi. Homyel'skaya Voblasts', SE Belarus

121 N14 **Myezhava** Rus. Mezhëvo. Vitsyebskaya Voblasts', NE Belarus

177 Ff5 **Myingyan** Mandalay, C Myanmar

178 Gg2 **Myitkyina** Kachin State, N Myanmar

177 Ff8 **Myittha** Mandalay, C Myanmar

113 H19 **Myjava** Hung. Miava. Západné Slovensko, W Slovakia

Myjeldino see Myyëldino

119 U9 **Mykhaylivka** Rus. Mikhaylovka. Zaporiz'ka Oblast', SE Ukraine

118 I5 **Mykolayiv** L'vivs'ka Oblast', W Ukraine

119 Q10 **Mykolayiv** Rus. Nikolayev. Mykolayivs'ka Oblast', S Ukraine

119 Q10 **Mykolayiv** × Mykolayivs'ka Oblast', S Ukraine

Mykolayiv see Mykolayivs'ka Oblast'

119 P9 **Mykolayivka** Odes'ka Oblast', SW Ukraine

119 S13 **Mykolayivka** Respublika Krym, S Ukraine

119 P9 **Mykolayivs'ka Oblast'** var. Mykolayiv, Rus. Nikolayevskaya Oblast'. ♦ province S Ukraine

117 J20 **Mýkonos** Mýkonos, Kykládes, Greece, Aegean Sea

117 K20 **Mýkonos** var. Mikonos. island Kykládes, Greece, Aegean Sea

129 R7 **Myla** Respublika Komi, NW Russian Federation

Mylae see Milazzo

95 M19 **Myllykoski** Kymi, S Finland

159 U14 **Mymensingh** var. Maimansingh; prev. Nasīrābād. Dhaka, N Bangladesh

95 K19 **Mynämäki** Turku-Pori, SW Finland

151 S14 **Mynaral** Kaz. Myngaral. Zhambyl, S Kazakhstan

Mynbulak see Mingbuloq

Mynbulak, Vpadina see Mingbuloq Botighi

Myngaral see Mynaral

177 F5 **Myohaung** Arakan State, W Myanmar

169 W13 **Myohyang-sanmaek** ▲ C North Korea

171 Jj13 **Myōkō-san** ▲ Honshū, S Japan

85 J15 **Myooye** Central, C Zambia

120 K12 **Myory** prev. Miory. Vitsyebskaya Voblasts', N Belarus

94 J4 **Mýrdalsjökull** glacier S Iceland

94 G10 **Myre** Nordland, C Norway

119 S5 **Myrhorod** Rus. Mirgorod. Poltavs'ka Oblast', NE Ukraine

117 J15 **Mýrina** var. Mírina. Límnos, SE Greece

119 P5 **Myronivka** Rus. Mironovka. Kyyivs'ka Oblast', N Ukraine

23 V17 **Myrtle Beach** South Carolina, SE USA

34 F14 **Myrtle Creek** Oregon, NW USA

191 P11 **Myrtleford** Victoria, SE Australia

34 E14 **Myrtle Point** Oregon, NW USA

117 K25 **Mýrtos** Kríti, Greece, E Mediterranean Sea

Myrtoum Mare see Mirtóo Pélagos

95 G17 **Myrviken** Jämtland, C Sweden

97 J15 **Mysen** Østfold, S Norway

128 L15 **Myshkin** Yaroslavskaya Oblast', W Russian Federation

113 H17 **Myślenice** Kraków, S Poland

112 D10 **Myślibórz** Gorzów, W Poland

161 G20 **Mysore** var. Maisur. Karnātaka, W India

Mysore see Karnātaka

N

103 M19 **Naab** ♣ SE Germany

100 G12 **Naaldwijk** Zuid-Holland, W Netherlands

40 G12 **Naalehu** var. Nā'ālehu. Hawaii, USA, C Pacific Ocean

95 K19 **Naantali** Swe. Nådendal. Turku-Pori, SW Finland

100 J10 **Naarden** Noord-Holland, C Netherlands

111 U4 **Naarn** ♣ N Austria

99 F18 **Naas** Ir. An Nás, Nás na Ríogh. C Ireland

94 M9 **Näätämöjoki** Lapp. Njávdám. ♣ NE Finland

85 E23 **Nababeep** var. Nababiep. Northern Cape, W South Africa

Nababiep see Nababeep

Nababwip see Navadwip

171 H16 **Nabari** Mie, Honshū, SW Japan

Nabatié/Nabatiyet et Tahta see Nabatîyé

144 G8 **Nabatîyé** var. An Nabatīyah at Taḥtā, Nabatié, Nabatiyet et Tahta. SW Lebanon

Nabatiyet et Tahta see Nabatîyé

197 I13 **Nabavatu** Vanua Levu, N Fiji

202 I2 **Nabeina** island Tungaru, W Kiribati

131 T4 **Naberezhnyye Chelny** prev. Brezhnev. Respublika Tatarstan, W Russian Federation

41 T10 **Nabesna** Alaska, USA

41 T10 **Nabesna River** ♣ Alaska, USA

77 N5 **Nabeul** var. Nābul. NE Tunisia

158 J9 **Nābha** Punjab, NW India

176 Ww11 **Nabire** Irian Jaya, E Indonesia

147 O15 **Nabi Shu'ayb, Jabal an** ▲ W Yemen

197 I13 **Nabiti** Vanua Levu, N Fiji

144 F10 **Nablus** var. Nābulus, Heb. Shekhem; anc. Neapolis, Bibl. Shechem. N West Bank

197 I13 **Nabouwalu** Vanua Levu, N Fiji

Nābul see Nabeul

Nābulus see Nablus

41 W12 **Nabuna** Vanua Levu, N Fiji

179 Rr15 **Nabunturan** Mindanao, S Philippines

85 Q14 **Nacala** Nampula, NE Mozambique

44 H8 **Nacaome** Valle, S Honduras

Na Cealla Beaga see Killybegs

Na-ch'ii see Nagqu

171 Gg17 **Nachikatsuura** var. Nachi-Katsuura. Wakayama, Honshū, SE Japan

83 J24 **Nachingwea** Lindi, SE Tanzania

113 F16 **Náchod** Východní Čechy, NE Czech Republic

Na Clocha Liatha see Greystones

25 Q14 **Naco** Sonora, NW Mexico

27 X8 **Nacogdoches** Texas, SW USA

42 G4 **Nacozari de García** Sonora, NW Mexico

197 H13 **Nacula** prev. Nathula. island Yasawa Group, NW Fiji

79 O14 **Nadawli** NW Ghana

106 I3 **Nadela** Galicia, NW Spain

Nádendal see Naantali

150 M7 **Nadezhdinka** prev. Nadezhdinskiy. Kustanay, N Kazakhstan

Nadezhdinskiy see Nadezhdinka

Nadgan see Nadqān, Qalamat

197 H14 **Nadi** prev. Nandi. Viti Levu, W Fiji

197 H14 **Nadi** prev. Nandi. × Viti Levu, W Fiji

160 D10 **Nadiād** Gujarāt, W India

118 E11 **Nadlac** Ger. Nadlak, Hung. Nagylak. Arad, W Romania

Nadlak see Nadlac

76 H6 **Nador** prev. Villa Nador. NE Morocco

147 S9 **Nadqān, Qalamat** var. Nadgan. well E Saudi Arabia

113 N22 **Nádudvar** Hajdú-Bihar, E Hungary

123 I16 **Nadur** Gozo, N Malta

197 J13 **Naduri** prev. Nanduri. Vanua Levu, N Fiji

118 I7 **Nadvirna** Pol. Nadwórna, Rus. Nadvornaya. Ivano-Frankivs'ka Oblast', W Ukraine

128 J8 **Nadvoitsy** Respublika Kareliya, NW Russian Federation

Nadvornaya/Nadwórna see Nadvirna

126 Gg9 **Nadym** Yamalo-Nenetskiy Avtonomnyy Okrug, N Russian Federation

126 Gg9 **Nadym** ♣ C Russian Federation

194 J13 **Nadzab** Morobe, C PNG

79 X13 **Nafada** Bauchi, E Nigeria

110 H8 **Näfels** Glarus, NE Switzerland

---

117 F21 **Mystrás** var. Mistras. Peloponnísos, S Greece

129 T12 **Mysy** Komi-Permyatskiy Avtonomnyy Okrug, NW Russian Federation

113 K15 **Myszków** Częstochowa, S Poland

178 Jj14 **My Tho** var. Mi Tho. Tiên Giang, S Vietnam

Mytilene see Mytilíni

117 J17 **Mytilíni** var. Mitilíni; anc. Mytilene. Lésvos, E Greece

130 K3 **Mytishchi** Moskovskaya Oblast', W Russian Federation

39 N3 **Myton** Utah, W USA

94 K2 **Mývatn** ◎ C Iceland

129 T11 **Myyëldino** var. Myjeldino. Respublika Komi, NW Russian Federation

84 M13 **Mzimba** Northern, NW Malawi

84 M12 **Mzuzu** Northern, N Malawi

---

117 E18 **Náfpaktos** var. Návpaktos. Dytikí Ellás, C Greece

117 F20 **Náfplio** prev. Návplion. Peloponnísos, S Greece

145 U6 **Naft Khāneh** E Iraq

155 N13 **Näg** Baluchistān, SW Pakistan

179 Q11 **Naga** off. Naga City; prev. Nueva Caceres. Luzon, N Philippines

52 F10 **Nagagami** ♣ Ontario, S Canada

170 E14 **Nagahama** Ehime, Shikoku, SW Japan

171 Hh4 **Nagahama** Shiga, Honshū, SW Japan

159 X12 **Nāga Hills** ▲ NE India

171 Ll13 **Nagai** Yamagata, Honshū, C Japan

Na Gaibhlte see Galty Mountains

41 N16 **Nagai Island** island Shumagin Islands, Alaska, USA

159 X12 **Nāgāland** ♦ state NE India

171 Ji13 **Nagano** Nagano, Honshū, S Japan

171 K13 **Nagano** off. Nagano-ken. ♦ prefecture Honshū, S Japan

159 W12 **Nagaoka** Niigata, Honshū, C Japan

159 W12 **Nagaon** prev. Nowgong. Assam, NE India

161 J21 **Nāgappattinam** var. Negapatam, Negapattinam. Tamil Nādu, SE India

Nagara Nayok see Nakhon Nayok

Nagara Panom see Nakhon Phanom

Nagara Pathom see Nakhon Pathom

Nagara Sridharmaraj see Nakhon Si Thammarat

Nagara Svarga see Nakhon Sawan

161 H16 **Nāgārjuna Sāgar** ◎ E India

44 I10 **Nagarote** León, SW Nicaragua

164 M16 **Nagarzê** var. Nagarzê. Xizang Zizhiqu, W China

170 Bb13 **Nagasaki** Nagasaki, Kyūshū, SW Japan

170 Bb12 **Nagasaki** off. Nagasaki-ken. ♦ prefecture Kyūshū, SW Japan

170 Bb13 **Naga-shima** island SW Japan

170 Dd13 **Naga-shima** island SW Japan

Nagashima see Kii-Nagashima

170 Dd12 **Nagato** Yamaguchi, Honshū, SW Japan

158 F11 **Nāgaur** Rājasthān, NW India

160 I10 **Nāgda** Madhya Pradesh, C India

100 L8 **Nagele** Flevoland, N Netherlands

161 H24 **Nāgercoil** Tamil Nādu, SE India

159 X12 **Nāginimāra** Nāgāland, NE India

172 P14 **Nago** Okinawa, Okinawa, SW Japan

160 K9 **Nāgod** Madhya Pradesh, C India

161 J26 **Nagoda** Southern Province, S Sri Lanka

103 G22 **Nagold** Baden-Württemberg, SW Germany

Nagorno-Karabakhskaya Avtonomnaya Oblast see Nagornyy Karabakh

126 Lll3 **Nagornyy** Respublika Sakha (Yakutiya), NE Russian Federation

143 V12 **Nagornyy Karabakh** var. Nagorno-Karabakhskaya Avtonomnaya Oblast , Arm. Lerrnayin Gharabakh, Az. Dağlıq Qarabağ. former autonomous region SW Azerbaijan

229 R13 **Nagorsk** Kirovskaya Oblast', NW Russian Federation

171 Hh15 **Nagoya** Aichi, Honshū, SW Japan

160 I12 **Nāgpur** Mahārāshtra, C India

162 K10 **Nagqu** Chin. Na-ch'ii; prev. Hei-ho. Xizang Zizhiqu, W China

158 J8 **Nāg Tibba Range** ▲ N India

47 O8 **Nagua** NE Dominican Republic

113 H25 **Nagyatád** Somogy, SW Hungary

Nagybánya see Baia Mare

Nagybecskerek see Zrenjanin

Nagydisznód see Cisnădie

Nagyenyed see Aiud

113 N21 **Nagykálló** Szabolcs-Szatmár-Bereg, E Hungary

113 G25 **Nagykanizsa** Ger. Grosskanizsa. Zala, SW Hungary

Nagykároly see Carei

113 K22 **Nagykáta** Pest, C Hungary

Nagykikinda see Kikinda

113 K23 **Nagykörös** Pest, C Hungary

Nagy-Küküllő see Târnava Mare

Nagylak see Nadlac

Nagymihály see Michalovce

Nagyrőce see Revúca

Nagysomkút see Şomcuta Mare

Nagysurány see Šurany

Nagyszalonta see Salonta

Nagyszeben see Sibiu

Nagyszentmiklós see Sânnicolau Mare

Nagyszöllős see Vynohradiv

Nagyszombat see Trnava

Nagytapolcsány see Topoľčany

Nagyvárad see Oradea

172 Oo15 **Naha** Okinawa, Okinawa, SW Japan

112 H9 **NahACH** Irian Jaya, E Indonesia

Nahang, Rūd-e see Nihing

158 H8 **Nahariya** var. Nahariyya. N Israel

144 F8 **Nahariyya** var. Nahariya. N Israel

148 L6 **Nahāvand** var. Nehavend. Hamadān, W Iran

103 F19 **Nahe** ♣ SW Germany

Na h-Iarmhidhe see Westmeath

201 O13 **Nahnalaud** ▲ Pohnpei, E Micronesia

85 F19 **Nahoi, Cape** see Cumberland, Cape

---

65 H16 **Nahuel Huapi, Lago** ◎ W Argentina

25 W7 **Nahunta** Georgia, SE USA

42 J6 **Naica** Chihuahua, N Mexico

9 U5 **Nain** Saskatchewan, S Canada

169 T11 **Naiman Qi** Nei Mongol Zizhiqu, N China

164 M4 **Naimin Bulak** spring NW China

11 P6 **Nain** Newfoundland and Labrador, NE Canada

149 P8 **Nā'īn** Eşfahān, C Iran

158 K10 **Naini Tāl** Uttar Pradesh, N India

160 J11 **Nainpur** Madhya Pradesh, C India

83 I19 **Nairobi** ● (Kenya) Nairobi Area, S Kenya

83 I19 **Nairobi** × Nairobi Area, S Kenya

84 P13 **Nairoto** Cabo Delgado, NE Mozambique

120 G3 **Naissaar** island N Estonia

Naissus see Niš

197 K13 **Naitaba** var. Naitauba; prev. Naitamba. island Lau Group, E Fiji

197 K13 **Naitamba/Naitauba** see Naitaba

83 I19 **Naivasha** Rift Valley, SW Kenya

83 H19 **Naivasha, Lake** ◎ SW Kenya

149 N8 **Najaf** see An Najaf

149 N8 **Najafābād** var. Nejafabad. Eşfahān, C Iran

147 N7 **Najd** var. Nejd. cultural region C Saudi Arabia

107 O4 **Nájera** La Rioja, N Spain

107 P4 **Najerilla** ♣ N Spain

158 J9 **Najibābād** Uttar Pradesh, N India

Najima see Fukuoka

169 Y11 **Najin** NE North Korea

145 T9 **Najm al Ḥassūn** C Iraq

147 O13 **Najrān** var. Abā as Su'ūd. Najrān, S Saudi Arabia

147 P12 **Najrān** off. Mintaqat an Najrān. ♦ province S Saudi Arabia

85 Q14 **Nakadōri-jima** island Gotō-rettō, SW Japan

85 C21 **Nakagawa** Hokkaidō, NE Japan

40 F9 **Nakalele Pont** headland Maui, Hawaii, USA, C Pacific Ocean

170 D12 **Nakama** Fukuoka, Kyūshū, SW Japan

Nakambé see White Volta

170 E15 **Nakamura** Kōchi, Shikoku, SW Japan

Nakamti see Nek'emtē

171 Jj14 **Nakano** Nagano, Honshū, S Japan

170 Ff11 **Nakano-shima** island Oki-shotō, SW Japan

170 Ff12 **Nakano-umi** var. Naka-umi. ◎ Honshū, SW Japan

171 Mm8 **Nakasato** Aomori, Honshū, C Japan

172 P7 **Nakasatsunai** Hokkaidō, NE Japan

172 Qq7 **Nakashibetsu** Hokkaidō, NE Japan

83 H18 **Nakasongola** C Uganda

172 Pp3 **Nakatonbetsu** Hokkaidō, NE Japan

170 D13 **Nakatsu** var. Nakatu. Ōita, Kyūshū, SW Japan

171 I15 **Nakatsugawa** var. Nakatugawa. Gifu, Honshū, SW Japan

Nakatu see Nakatsu

Nakatugawa see Nakatsugawa

Naka-umi see Naka-umi

172 O5 **Nakayama-tōge** pass Hokkaidō, NE Japan

Nakdong see Naktong-gang

Nakel see Nakło nad Notecią

79 J8 **Nakfa** N Eritrea

Nakhichevan' see Naxçıvan

127 Nn18 **Nakhodka** Primorskiy Kray, SE Russian Federation

126 H8 **Nakhodka** Yamalo-Nenetskiy Avtonomnyy Okrug, N Russian Federation

Nakhon Navok see Nakhon Nayok

178 Hh11 **Nakhon Nayok** var. Nagara Nayok, Nakhon Navok. Nakhon Nayok, C Thailand

178 H11 **Nakhon Pathom** var. Nagara Pathom, Nakhon Pathom. Nakhon Pathom, W Thailand

178 J9 **Nakhon Phanom** var. Nagara Panom. Nakhon Phanom, E Thailand

178 Hh10 **Nakhon Ratchasima** var. Khorat, Korat. Nakhon Ratchasima, E Thailand

178 H10 **Nakhon Sawan** var. Muang Nakhon Sawan, Nagara Svarga. Nakhon Sawan, W Thailand

178 H15 **Nakhon Si Thammarat** var. Nagara Sridharmaraj, Nakhon Sithammarap, Nakhon Si Thammarat, SW Thailand

201 O15 **Nakhon Sithammarap** see Nakhon Si Thammarat

55 Y11 **Nakhrash** SE Iraq

8 I9 **Nakina** British Columbia, W Canada

112 H9 **Nakło nad Notecią** Ger. Nakel. Bydgoszcz, N Poland

158 I6 **Nak Ou** N Laos

34 M14 **Nampa** Idaho, NW USA

78 M11 **Nampala** Ségou, W Mali

169 W14 **Namp'o** SW North Korea

84 M11 **Nampula** Nampula, NE Mozambique

84 P15 **Nampula** off. Provincia de Nampula. ♦ province NE Mozambique

95 E15 **Namsos** Nord-Trøndelag, C Norway

95 F14 **Namsskogan** Nord-Trøndelag, C Norway

---

155 N15 **Nāl** ♣ W Pakistan

168 M7 **Nalayh** Töv, C Mongolia

159 V12 **Nālbāri** Assam, NE India

65 G19 **Nalcayec, Isla** island Archipiélago de los Chonos, S Chile

131 N15 **Nal'chik** Kabardino-Balkarskaya Respublika, SW Russian Federation

161 I16 **Nalgonda** Andhra Pradesh, C India

159 S14 **Nalhāti** West Bengal, NE India

159 U14 **Nalitabari** Dhaka, N Bangladesh

161 I17 **Nallamala Hills** ▲ E India

142 G12 **Nallıhan** Ankara, NW Turkey

106 K2 **Nalón** ♣ NW Spain

178 Gg3 **Nalong** Kachin State, N Myanmar

77 N8 **Nālūt** NW Libya

176 Uu12 **Nama Pulau Manawoka,** E Indonesia

201 O16 **Nama** island C Micronesia

85 O16 **Namacurra** Zambézia, NE Mozambique

196 P9 **Namai Bay** bay Babeldaob, N Palau

31 W2 **Namakan Lake** ◎ Canada/USA

149 O6 **Namak, Daryācheh-ye** marsh N Iran

149 T6 **Namak, Kavīr-e** salt pan NE Iran

178 H6 **Namaklwe** Shan State, E Myanmar

154 I5 **Namaksār, Kowl-e/Namakzār, Daryācheh-ye** see Namakzar

154 I5 **Namakzar Pash.** Daryācheh-ye Namakzār, Kowl-e Namaksār. marsh Afghanistan/Iran

176 W13 **Namalau** Pulau Jursian, E Indonesia

83 I20 **Namanga** Rift Valley, S Kenya

153 S10 **Namangan** Namangan Wiloyati, E Uzbekistan

Namanganskaya Oblast' see Namangan Wiloyati

153 R10 **Namangan Wiloyati** Rus. Namanganskaya Oblast'. ♦ province E Uzbekistan

85 Q14 **Namapa** Nampula, NE Mozambique

85 C21 **Namaqualand** physical region S Namibia

83 G18 **Namasagali** C Uganda

195 P10 **Namatanai** New Ireland, NE PNG

85 I14 **Nambala** Central, C Zambia

83 J23 **Nambanje** Lindi, SE Tanzania

176 Ww9 **Namber** Irian Jaya, E Indonesia

85 G16 **Nambiya** Ngamiland, N Botswana

191 V2 **Nambour** Queensland, E Australia

191 V6 **Nambucca Heads** New South Wales, SE Australia

165 N15 **Nam Co** ◎ W China

178 I15 **Năm Cum** Lai Châu, N Vietnam

178 J6 **Nam Đinh** Nam Ha, N Vietnam

175 Tt11 **Namea, Tanjung** headland Pulau Seram, E Indonesia

101 I20 **Namêche** Namur, SE Belgium

32 J4 **Namekagon Lake** ◎ Wisconsin, N USA

196 F10 **Namekakl Passage** passage Babeldaob, N Palau

Namen see Namur

85 P15 **Nametil** Nampula, NE Mozambique

169 X14 **Nam-gang** ♣ C North Korea

169 Y16 **Nam-gang** ♣ S South Korea

169 Y17 **Namhae-do** Jap. Nankai-tō. island S South Korea

Namhoi see Foshan

85 C19 **Namib Desert** desert W Namibia

85 A15 **Namibe** Port. Moçâmedes, Mossâmedes. Namibe, SW Angola

85 A15 **Namibe** ♦ province SW Angola

85 C18 **Namibia** off. Republic of Namibia, var. South West Africa, Afr. Suidwes-Afrika, Ger. Deutsch-Südwestafrika; prev. German Southwest Africa, South-West Africa. ♦ republic S Africa

67 O17 **Namibia Plain** undersea feature S Atlantic Ocean

171 Ll14 **Namie** Fukushima, Honshū, C Japan

171 Mm8 **Namioka** Aomori, Honshū, C Japan

42 I5 **Namiquipa** Chihuahua, N Mexico

165 P15 **Namjagbarwa Feng** ▲ W China

175 Ss11 **Namlea** Pulau Buru, E Indonesia

164 L16 **Namling** Xizang Zizhiqu, W China

Namnetes see Nantes

178 I8 **Nam Ngum** ♣ C Laos

191 R5 **Namoi River** ♣ New South Wales, SE Australia

201 Q12 **Namoluk Atoll** atoll Mortlock Islands, C Micronesia

201 O15 **Namonuito Atoll** atoll Caroline Islands, C Micronesia

201 T9 **Namorik Atoll** var. Namdik. atoll Ralik Chain, S Marshall Islands

178 I6 **Nam Ou** N Laos

169 V16 **Namp'a** Nampula, NE Mozambique

78 M11 **Nampala** Ségou, W Mali

---

126 M10 **Namsty** Respublika Sakha (Yakutiya), NE Russian Federation

178 H6 **Nam Teng** ♣ E Myanmar

178 I6 **Nam Tha** ♣ N Laos

178 Gg4 **Namtu** Shan State, E Myanmar

8 J15 **Namu** British Columbia, SW Canada

201 T7 **Namu Atoll** var. Namo. atoll Ralik Chain, C Marshall Islands

197 K13 **Namuka-i-lau** island Lau Group, E Fiji

85 O15 **Namuli, Mont** ▲ NE Mozambique

85 P14 **Namuno** Cabo Delgado, N Mozambique

101 I20 **Namur** Dut. Namen. Namur, SE Belgium

101 H21 **Namur** Dut. Namen. ♦ province S Belgium

85 B21 **Namutoni** Kunene, N Namibia

169 Y16 **Namwŏn** Jap. Nangen. S South Korea

178 Mm4 **Namyit Island** island S Spratly Islands

113 H18 **Namysłów** Ger. Namslau. Opole, SW Poland

178 Hh7 **Nan** var. Muang Nan. Nan, NW Thailand

81 G15 **Nana** ♣ W Central African Republic

172 Nn7 **Nanae** Hokkaidō, NE Japan

81 I14 **Nana-Grébizi** ♦ prefecture N Central African Republic

8 L17 **Nanaimo** Vancouver Island, British Columbia, SW Canada

40 C9 **Nanakuli** Haw. Nānākuli. Oahu, Hawaii, USA, C Pacific Ocean

81 G15 **Nana-Mambéré** ♦ prefecture W Central African Republic

167 R13 **Nan'an** Fujian, SE China

191 V2 **Nanango** Queensland, E Australia

171 Ii12 **Nanao** Ishikawa, Honshū, SW Japan

171 Ii11 **Nanatsu-shima** island SW Japan

58 F8 **Nanay, Río** ♣ NE Peru

166 J8 **Nanbu** Heilongjiang, NE China

169 X7 **Nancha** Heilongjiang, NE China

167 P10 **Nanchang** var. Nan-ch'ang, Nanch'ang-hsien. Jiangxi, S China

Nanch'ang-hsien see Nanchang

167 P11 **Nancheng** Jiangxi, S China

166 J9 **Nanchong** Sichuan, C China

166 J10 **Nanchuan** Sichuan, .C China

105 T5 **Nancy** Meurthe-et-Moselle, NE France

193 A22 **Nancy Sound** sound South Island, NZ

158 L9 **Nanda Devi** ▲ NW India

44 I11 **Nandaime** Granada, SW Nicaragua

166 K13 **Nandan** Guangxi Zhuangzu Zizhiqu, S China

161 H14 **Nānded** Mahārāshtra, C India

170 G15 **Nanden** Hyōgo, Awaji-shima, SW Japan

161 I17 **Nandyāl** Andhra Pradesh, E India

167 P11 **Nanfeng** Jiangxi, S China

Nang see Nang Xian

176 Ww11 **Nanganwainami** Irian Jaya, E Indonesia

176 W11 **Napan-Yaur** Irian Jaya, E Indonesia

81 E15 **Nanga Eboko** Centre, C Cameroon

Nangamesi, Teluk see Waingapu, Teluk

155 W4 **Nanga Parbat** ▲ India/Pakistan

174 L8 **Nangapinoh** Borneo, C Indonesia

155 R5 **Nangarhār** ♦ province E Afghanistan

174 M8 **Nangaserawai** var. Nangah Serawai. Borneo, C Indonesia

174 L9 **Nangatayap** Borneo, C Indonesia

Nangen see Namwŏn

105 P5 **Nangis** Seine-et-Marne, N France

169 X13 **Nangnim-sanmaek** ▲ C North Korea

167 O4 **Nangong** Hebei, E China

165 Q4 **Nangqên** Qinghai, C China

178 I11 **Nang Rong** Buri Ram, E Thailand

165 O16 **Nang Xian** var. Nang. Xizang Zizhiqu, W China

167 O12 **Nan Hai** see South China Sea

166 L8 **Nan He** ♣ C China

166 F12 **Nanhua** Yunnan, SW China

Naniwa see Ōsaka

161 G20 **Nanjangūd** Karnātaka, W India

167 Q8 **Nanjing** var. Nan-ching, Nanking; prev. Chiannming, Chian-ning, Kiang-ning. Jiangsu, E China

166 L13 **Nanliu Jiang** ♣ S China

166 L15 **Nan Ling** ▲ S China

201 P13 **Nan Madol** ruins Temwen Island, E Micronesia

166 K15 **Nanning** var. Nan-ning; prev. Yung-ning. Guangxi Zhuangzu Zizhiqu, S China

206 M15 **Nanortalik** S Greenland

201 S8 **Nanpan Jiang** ♣ S China

158 M11 **Nānpāra** Uttar Pradesh, N India

169 W13 **Nansan-ni** North Korea

Namslau see Namysłów

158 Nn4 **Nan-p'ing** prev. Yenping. Fujian, SE China

166 I7 **Nanping** Fujian, SE China

170 Bb12 **Nanri Dao** island SE China

---

172 Q13 **Nansei-shotō** Eng. Ryukyu Islands. island group SW Japan

Nansei Syotō Trench see Ryukyu Trench

207 T10 **Nansen Basin** undersea feature Arctic Ocean

207 T10 **Nansen Cordillera** var. Arctic-Mid Oceanic Ridge, Nansen Ridge. undersea feature Arctic Ocean

Nansen Ridge see Nansen Cordillera

133 T9 **Nan Shan** ▲ C China

179 Nn14 **Nanshan Island** island E Spratly Islands

Nansha Qundao see Spratly Islands

12 G7 **Nantais, Lac** ◎ Québec, NE Canada

105 P5 **Nanterre** Hauts-de-Seine, N France

104 I8 **Nantes** Bret. Naoned; anc. Condivincum, Namnetes. Loire-Atlantique, NW France

20 H3 **Nanticoke** Pennsylvania, NE USA

23 V4 **Nanticoke River** ♣ Delaware/Maryland, NE USA

9 Q17 **Nanton** Alberta, SW Canada

167 S8 **Nantong** Jiangsu, E China

167 S13 **Nant'ou** W Taiwan

105 S10 **Nantua** Ain, E France

21 Q13 **Nantucket** Nantucket Island, Massachusetts, NE USA

21 Q13 **Nantucket Island** island Massachusetts, NE USA

21 Q13 **Nantucket Sound** sound Massachusetts, NE USA

84 P13 **Nantulo** Cabo Delgado, N Mozambique

201 O12 **Nanuh** Pohnpei, E Micronesia

197 K13 **Nanuku Passage** channel NE Fiji

202 D6 **Nanumaga** var. Nanumanga. atoll NW Tuvalu

Nanumanga see Nanumaga

202 D5 **Nanumea Atoll** atoll NW Tuvalu

61 O19 **Nanuque** Minas Gerais, SE Brazil

175 Ss4 **Nanusa, Kepulauan** island group N Indonesia

169 U4 **Nanweng He** ♣ NE China

166 I10 **Nanxi** Sichuan, C China

167 N10 **Nanxian** var. Nan Xian. Hunan, S China

167 N7 **Nanyang** var. Nan-yang. Henan, C China

167 P6 **Nanyang Hu** ◎ E China

171 L13 **Nan'yō** Yamagata, Honshū, C Japan

83 I18 **Nanyuki** Central, C Kenya

166 M8 **Nanzhang** Hubei, C China

107 T11 **Nao, Cabo de La** headland E Spain

10 M9 **Naococane, Lac** ◎ Québec, E Canada

159 S14 **Naogaon** Rajshahi, N Bangladesh

Naokot see Naukot

117 E14 **Náousa** Kentrikí Makedonía, N Greece

37 N8 **Napa** California, W USA

41 O11 **Napaimiut** Alaska, USA

41 N12 **Napakiak** Alaska, USA

126 H7 **Napalkovo** Yamalo-Nenetskiy Avtonomnyy Okrug, N Russian Federation

10 I16 **Napanee** Ontario, SE Canada

176 Ww11 **Napan-Yaur** Irian Jaya, E Indonesia

41 N12 **Napaskiak** Alaska, USA

25 P5 **Napier** Hawke's Bay, North Island, NZ

205 X3 **Napier Mountains** ▲ Antarctica

13 O13 **Napierville** Québec, SE Canada

25 W5 **Naples** Florida, SE USA

27 W5 **Naples** Texas, SW USA

Naples see Napoli

166 I14 **Napo** Guangxi Zhuangzu Zizhiqu, S China

58 D6 **Napo** ♦ province NE Ecuador

31 O6 **Napoleon** Ohio, N USA

33 R11 **Napoleon** Ohio, N USA

Napoléon-Vendée see la Roche-sur-Yon

24 J9 **Napoleonville** Louisiana, S USA

109 K17 **Napoli** Eng. Naples, Ger. Neapel; anc. Neapolis. Campania, S Italy

59 F7 **Napo, Río** ♣ Ecuador/Peru

203 W9 **Napuka** island Îles Tuamotu, C French Polynesia

148 J3 **Naqadeh** var. Āzarbāyjān-e Bākhtarī, NW Iran

145 U6 **Naqneh** E Iraq

Nar see Nera

171 Ha14 **Nara** Nara, Honshū, SW Japan

78 L11 **Nara** Koulikoro, W Mali

171 Gg16 **Nara** off. Nara-ken. ♦ prefecture SW Japan

155 R14 **Nāra Canal** irrigation canal S Pakistan

190 K11 **Naracoorte** South Australia

191 P8 **Naradhan** New South Wales, SE Australia

Naradhivas see Narathiwat

58 B8 **Naranjal** Guayas, W Ecuador

59 Q19 **Naranjos** Santa Cruz, E Bolivia

43 Q12 **Naranjos** Veracruz-Llave, E Mexico

165 Q6 **Naran Sebstein Bulag** spring NW China

149 X12 **Narāqeh** Sīstān va Balūchestān, SE Iran

170 Bb12 **Narao** Nagasaki, Nakadōri-jima, SW Japan

● Country ◇ Dependent Territory ◈ Administrative Region ▲ Mountain ♣ Volcano ◎ Lake
● Country Capital ◇ Dependent Territory Capital ✕ International Airport ▲ Mountain Range ♣ River ▣ Reservoir

289

161 J16 **Narasaraopet** Andhra Pradesh, E India

164 J5 **Narat** Xinjiang Uygur Zizhiqu, W China

178 Hh17 **Narathiwat** *var.* Naradhivas. Narathiwat, SW Thailand

39 V10 **Nara Visa** New Mexico, SW USA

Nārāyani *see* Gandak

Narbada *see* Narmada

Narbo Martius *see* Narbonne

105 P16 **Narbonne** *anc.* Narbo Martius. Aude, S France

Narborough Island *see* Fernandina, Isla

106 J2 **Narcea** ☒ NW Spain

158 J9 **Narendranagar** Uttar Pradesh, N India

66 G11 **Nares Abyssal Plain** *see* Nares Plain

Nares Plain *var.* Nares Abyssal Plain. *undersea feature* NW Atlantic Ocean

207 P10 **Nares Strait** *Dan.* Nares Stræde. *strait* Canada/Greenland

Nares Stræde *see* Nares Strait

112 O9 **Narew** ☒ E Poland

Narew *see* Naraw

161 F17 **Nargund** Karnātaka, W India

85 D20 **Narib** Hardap, S Namibia

Narikrik *see* Knox Atoll

56 B13 **Nariño** *off.* Departamento de Nariño. ◆ *province* SW Colombia

171 Kk17 **Narita** Chiba, Honshū, S Japan

171 Kk17 **Narita ✕** (Tōkyō) Chiba, Honshū, S Japan

Nariya *see* An Nu'ayrīyah

158 J8 **Nārkanda** Himāchal Pradesh, NW India

94 J13 **Narkaus** Lappi, NW Finland

160 H1 **Narmada** *var.* Narbada. ☒ C India

158 H11 **Narnaul** *var.* Nārnaul. Haryāna, N India

109 I14 **Narni** Umbria, C Italy

109 J24 **Naro** Sicilia, Italy, C Mediterranean Sea

Narodichi *see* Narodychi

129 V7 **Narodnaya, Gora** ▲ NW Russian Federation

119 N3 **Narodychi** *Rus.* Narodichi. Zhytomyrs'ka Oblast', N Ukraine

130 J4 **Naro-Fominsk** Moskovskaya Oblast', W Russian Federation

83 H19 **Narok** Rift Valley, SW Kenya

106 H2 **Narón** Galicia, NW Spain

191 S11 **Narooma** New South Wales, SE Australia

Narova *see* Narva

Narovlya *see* Narowlya

155 W8 **Nārowāl** Punjab, E Pakistan

121 N20 **Narowlya** *Rus.* Narovlya. Homyel'skaya Voblasts', SE Belarus

95 J8 **Närpes** *Fin.* Närpiö. Vaasa, W Finland

Närpiö *see* Närpes

191 S5 **Narrabri** New South Wales, SE Australia

191 P9 **Narrandera** New South Wales, SE Australia

191 Q4 **Narran Lake** ☺ New South Wales, SE Australia

191 Q4 **Narran River** ☒ New South Wales/Queensland, SE Australia

188 J13 **Narrogin** Western Australia

191 Q7 **Narromine** New South Wales, SE Australia

23 R6 **Narrows** Virginia, NE USA

206 M15 **Narsarsuaq** ✕ S Greenland

160 I10 **Narsimhapur** Madhya Pradesh, C India

Narsingdi *see* Narsinghdi

159 U15 **Narsinghdi** *var.* Narsingdi. Dhaka, C Bangladesh

160 H9 **Narsinghgarh** Madhya Pradesh, C India

169 Q11 **Nart** Nei Mongol Zizhiqu, N China

Nartēs, Gjol i/Nartēs, Laguna e *see* Nartēs, Liqeni i

115 J22 **Nartēs, Liqeni i** *var.* Gjol i Nartēs, Laguna e Nartēs. ☺ SW Albania

117 F17 **Nartháki** ▲ C Greece

131 O15 **Nartkala** Kabardino-Balkarskaya Respublika, SW Russian Federation

170 FJ15 **Naruto** Tokushima, Shikoku, SW Japan

120 N3 **Narva** *prev.* Narova. Estonia/Russian Federation

120 J3 **Narva Bay** *Est.* Narva Laht, *Ger.* Narwa-Bucht, *Rus.* Narvskiy Zaliv. *bay* Estonia/Russian Federation

Narva Laht *see* Narva Bay

128 F13 **Narva Reservoir** *Est.* Narva Veehoidla, *Rus.* Narvskoye Vodokhranilishche. ☺ Estonia/Russian Federation

Narva Veehoidla *see* Narva Reservoir

94 H10 **Narvik** Nordland, C Norway

158 J9 **Narwāna** Haryāna, NW India

129 R4 **Nar'yan-Mar** *prev.* Beloshchel'ye, Dzerzhinskiy. Nenetskiy Avtonomnyy Okrug, NW Russian Federation

126 H12 **Narym** Tomskaya Oblast', C Russian Federation

151 Y10 **Narymskiy Khrebet** *Kaz.* Naryn Zhotasy. ▲ E Kazakhstan

153 W9 **Naryn** Narynskaya Oblast', C Kyrgyzstan

153 U8 **Naryn** ☒ Kyrgyzstan/Uzbekistan

151 W16 **Narynkol** *Kaz.* Narynqol. Almaty, SE Kazakhstan

Naryn Oblasty *see* Narynskaya Oblast'

Narynqol *see* Narynkol

153 V9 **Narynskaya Oblast'** *Kir.* Naryn Oblasty. ◆ *province* C Kyrgyzstan

Naryn Zhotasy *see* Narymskiy Khrebet

130 J6 **Naryshkino** Orlovskaya Oblast', W Russian Federation

97 L14 **Näs** Kopparberg, C Sweden

94 G13 **Nasa** ▲ C Norway

95 H16 **Näsåker** Västernorrland, C Sweden

197 J14 **Nasau** Koro, C Fiji

118 J9 **Năsăud** *Ger.* Nussdorf, *Hung.* Naszód. Bistrița-Năsăud, N Romania

105 P13 **Nasbinals** Lozère, S France

Na Sceirí *see* Skerries

Nase *see* Naze

193 E22 **Naseby** Otago, South Island, NZ

149 R10 **Nāşerīyeh** Kermān, C Iran

27 X5 **Nash** Texas, SW USA

160 E13 **Nāshik** *prev.* Nāsik. Mahārāshtra, W India

58 E7 **Nashiño, Río** ☒ Ecuador/Peru

31 W12 **Nashua** Iowa, C USA

35 W7 **Nashua** Montana, NW USA

21 O10 **Nashua** New Hampshire, NE USA

29 S13 **Nashville** Arkansas, C USA

25 U7 **Nashville** Georgia, SE USA

32 L16 **Nashville** Illinois, N USA

33 O14 **Nashville** Indiana, N USA

23 V9 **Nashville** North Carolina, SE USA

22 J8 **Nashville** *state capital* Tennessee, S USA

22 J9 **Nashville ✕** Tennessee, S USA

66 H10 **Nashville Seamount** *undersea feature* NW Atlantic Ocean

114 M9 **Našice** Požega-Slavonija, NE Croatia

112 M11 **Nasielsk** Ciechanów, C Poland

95 K18 **Näsijärvi** ☺ SW Finland

Nāsik *see* Nāshik

82 G13 **Nasir** Upper Nile, SE Sudan

155 Q12 **Nasirābād** Baluchistān, SW Pakistan

154 J15 **Nasīrābād** Baluchistān, SW Pakistan

Nasirābād *see* Mymensingh

Nasir, Buhayrat/Nâsir, Buheiret *see* Nasser, Lake

Nāsiri *see* Ahvāz

Nasiriya *see* An Nāşirīyah

109 L23 **Naso** Sicilia, Italy, C Mediterranean Sea

Nasratabad *see* Zābol

8 J11 **Nass** ☒ British Columbia, SW Canada

79 V15 **Nasarawa** Plateau, C Nigeria

46 J1 **Nassau ●** (Bahamas) New Providence, N Bahamas

46 J1 **Nassau ✕** New Providence, C Bahamas

202 J13 **Nassau** *island* N Cook Islands

25 W8 **Nassau Sound** *sound* Florida, SE USA

110 L7 **Nassereith** Tirol, W Austria

97 L19 **Nässjö** Jönköping, S Sweden

101 K22 **Nassogne** Luxembourg, SE Belgium

10 J6 **Nastapoka Islands** *island group* Northwest Territories, C Canada

95 M19 **Nastola** Häme, S Finland

171 L14 **Nasu-dake** ▲ Honshū, S Japan

179 P11 **Nasugbu** Luzon, N Philippines

96 N11 **Näsviken** Gävleborg, C Sweden

Naszód *see* Năsăud

85 J17 **Nata** Central, NE Botswana

56 E11 **Natagaima** Tolima, C Colombia

61 Q14 **Natal** Rio Grande do Norte, E Brazil

173 FJ8 **Natal** Sumatera, N Indonesia

181 L10 **Natal** KwaZulu/Natal, E South Africa

181 L10 **Natal Basin** *var.* Mozambique Basin. *undersea feature* W Indian Ocean

27 R12 **Natalia** Texas, SW USA

69 W15 **Natal Valley** *undersea feature* SW Indian Ocean

Natanya *see* Netanya

149 O7 **Naţanz** Eşfahān, C Iran

11 Q11 **Natashquan** Québec, E Canada

11 Q10 **Natashquan** ☒ Newfoundland and Labrador/Québec, E Canada

24 J2 **Natchez** Mississippi, S USA

24 G6 **Natchitoches** Louisiana, S USA

110 E10 **Naters** Valais, S Switzerland

Nathanya *see* Netanya

94 J3 **Nathorst Land** *physical region* W Svalbard

Nathula *see* Nacula

194 J15 **National Capital District ◆** *province* S PNG

37 U17 **National City** California, W USA

192 M10 **National Park** Manawatu-Wanganui, North Island, NZ

79 N14 **Natitingou** NW Benin

42 B5 **Natividad, Isla** *island* W Mexico

171 M13 **Natori** Miyagi, Honshū, N Japan

20 C14 **Natrona Heights** Pennsylvania, NE USA

83 H20 **Natron, Lake** ☺ Kenya/Tanzania

177 FJ7 **Nattalin** Pegu, C Myanmar

94 J12 **Nattavaara** Norrbotten, N Sweden

111 S3 **Natternbach** Oberösterreich, N Austria

79 P14 **Natwrongo** N Ghana

160 D12 **Navsāri** *var.* Nausari. Gujarāt, W India

197 I15 **Navua** Viti Levu, W Fiji

144 H8 **Nawá** Dar'ā, S Syria

159 S14 **Nawabganj** Rājshāhi, NW Bangladesh

159 N13 **Nawābganj** Uttar Pradesh, N India

155 Q15 **Nawābshāh** *var.* Nawābshah. Sind, SE Pakistan

159 S14 **Nawāda** Bihār, N India

_(center-left continued)

181 V11 **Naturaliste Fracture Zone** *tectonic feature* E Indian Ocean

182 J10 **Naturaliste Plateau** *undersea feature* E Indian Ocean

Nau *see* Nov

105 O14 **Naucelle** Aveyron, S France

85 D20 **Nauchas** Hardap, C Namibia

110 K9 **Nauders** Tirol, W Austria

120 F12 **Naugard** *see* Nowogard

120 F12 **Naujamiestis** Panevėžys, C Lithuania

120 E10 **Naujoji Akmenė** Akmenė, NW Lithuania

155 R16 **Naukot** *var.* Naokot. Sind, SE Pakistan

103 L16 **Naumburg** *var.* Naumburg an der Saale. Sachsen-Anhalt, C Germany

Naumburg am Queis *see* Nowogrodziec

Naumburg an der Saale *see* Naumburg

203 W15 **Naunau** *ancient monument* Easter Island, Chile, E Pacific Ocean

144 G10 **Nā'ūr** 'Ammān, W Jordan

201 Q8 **Nauru** *off.* Republic of Nauru; *prev.* Pleasant Island. ◆ *republic* W Pacific Ocean

183 P5 **Nauru** *island* W Pacific Ocean

201 Q8 **Nauru International ✕** S Nauru

21 Q2 **Nausari** *see* Navsāri

155 P14 **Naushahra Firoz** Sind, SE Pakistan

Naushara *see* Nowshera

197 I14 **Nausori** Viti Levu, W Fiji

58 F9 **Nauta** Loreto, N Peru

159 O12 **Nautanwa** Uttar Pradesh, N India

43 R13 **Nautla** Veracruz-Llave, E Mexico

Nauzad *see* Now Zād

43 N6 **Nava** Coahuila de Zaragoza, NE Mexico

106 L6 **Navabad** *see* Navobod

106 L6 **Nava del Rey** Castilla-León, N Spain

159 S15 **Navadwīp** *prev.* Nabadwip. West Bengal, NE India

197 J14 **Navaga** Koro, W Fiji

106 M9 **Navahermosa** Castilla-La Mancha, C Spain

121 H14 **Navahrudak** *Pol.* Nowogródek, *Rus.* Novogrudok. Hrodzyenskaya Voblasts', W Belarus

121 I16 **Navahrudskaye Wzvyshsha** ▲ W Belarus

38 M8 **Navajo Mount** ▲ Utah, W USA

39 O9 **Navajo Reservoir** ☺ New Mexico, SW USA

179 Qq12 **Naval** Biliran Island, C Philippines

106 K9 **Navalmoral de la Mata** Extremadura, W Spain

106 K10 **Navalvillar de Pelea** Extremadura, W Spain

99 O8 **Navan** *Ir.* An Uaimh. E Ireland

Navanagar *see* Jāmnagar

120 L12 **Navapolatsk** *Rus.* Novopolotsk. Vitsyebskaya Voblasts', N Belarus

155 P6 **Nāwar, Dasht-e-Pash.** Dasht-i-Nawar. *desert* C Afghanistan

127 Q5 **Navarin, Mys** *headland* NE Russian Federation

65 I25 **Navarino, Isla** *island* S Chile

107 Q4 **Navarra** *Eng./Fr.* Navarre. ◆ *autonomous community* N Spain

Navarra *see* Navarra

107 P4 **Navarrete** La Rioja, N Spain

63 C20 **Navarro** Buenos Aires, E Argentina

107 O12 **Navas de San Juan** Andalucía, S Spain

27 V10 **Navasota** Texas, SW USA

27 U9 **Navasota River** ☒ Texas, SW USA

46 I9 **Navassa Island** ◇ *US unincorporated territory* C West Indies

121 L19 **Navasyolki** *Rus.* Novosëlki. Homyel'skaya Voblasts', SE Belarus

121 M17 **Navayel'nya** *Pol.* Nowojelnia, *Rus.* Novoyel'nya. Hrodzyenskaya Voblasts', W Belarus

176 Yy11 **Naver** Irian Jaya, E Indonesia

120 H5 **Navesti** ☒ C Estonia

106 J2 **Navia** Asturias, N Spain

106 J2 **Navia** ☒ NW Spain

61 I21 **Navirai** Mato Grosso do Sul, SW Brazil

94 O3 **Navis** ☒ C Sweden

197 G14 **Naviti** *island* Yasawa Group, NW Fiji

130 I6 **Navlya** Bryanskaya Oblast', W Russian Federation

197 J13 **Navoalevu** Vanua Levu, N Fiji

153 R12 **Navobod** *Rus.* Navabad, Novabad. C Tajikistan

153 P13 **Navobod** *Rus.* Navabad. W Tajikistan

Navoi *see* Nawoiy

42 H9 **Navojoa** Sonora, NW Mexico

42 H9 **Navolat** *var.* Navolato. Sinaloa, C Mexico

Navolato *see* Navolat

197 C12 **Navonda** Ambae, C Vanuatu

Návpaktos *see* Náfpaktos

Návplion *see* Náfplio

79 P14 **Navrongo** N Ghana

_(center-right continued)

158 H11 **Nawalgarh** Rājasthān, N India

Nawāl, Sabkhat an *see* Noual, Sebkhet en

178 Gg4 **Nawnghkio** *var.* Nawngkio. Shan State, C Myanmar

Nawngkio *see* Nawnghkio

152 M11 **Nawoiy** *Rus.* Navoi. Nawoiy Wiloyati, C Uzbekistan

152 K8 **Nawoiy Wiloyati** *Rus.* Navoiyskaya Oblast'. ◆ *province* C Uzbekistan

143 U13 **Naxçıvan** *Rus.* Nakhichevan'. SW Azerbaijan

166 I10 **Naxi** Sichuan, C China

117 R21 **Náxos** *var.* Naxos. Náxos, Kykládes, Greece, Aegean Sea

117 K21 **Náxos** *island* Kykládes, Greece, Aegean Sea

42 I1 **Nayarit** ◆ *state* C Mexico

197 K14 **Nayau** *island* Lau Group, E Fiji

149 S8 **Nāy Band** Khorāsān, E Iran

172 Pp4 **Nayoro** Hokkaidō, NE Japan

26 M4 **Nazaret** Texas, SW USA

Nazareth *see* Nagerat

181 O8 **Nazareth Bank** *undersea feature* W Indian Ocean

126 Hh14 **Nazarovo** Krasnoyarskiy Kray, S Russian Federation

42 K9 **Nazas** Durango, C Mexico

59 F16 **Nazca** Ica, S Peru

1 L17 **Nazca Plate** *tectonic feature*

200 Oo11 **Nazca Ridge** *undersea feature* E Pacific Ocean

172 R13 **Naze** *var.* Nase. Kagoshima, Amami-ōshima, SW Japan

144 G9 **Nazerat** *Ar.* En Nazira, *Eng.* Nazareth. Northern, N Israel

143 R14 **Nazik Gölü** ☺ E Turkey

142 C15 **Nazilli** Aydın, SW Turkey

143 P14 **Nazimiye** Tunceli, E Turkey

126 Gg11 **Nazino** Tomskaya Oblast', C Russian Federation

Nazinon *see* Red Volta

125 FJ13 **Nazyvayevsk** Omskaya Oblast', C Russian Federation

84 J13 **Nchanga** Copperbelt, C Zambia

84 J11 **Nchelenge** Luapula, N Zambia

Ncheu *see* Ntcheu

83 G21 **Ndala** Tabora, C Tanzania

84 B11 **N'Dalatando** *Port.* Salazar, Vila Salazar. Cuanza Norte, NW Angola

82 C16 **Ndali** C Benin

83 E18 **Ndeke** SW Uganda

80 J13 **Ndélé** Bamingui-Bangoran, N Central African Republic

81 E19 **Ndendé** Ngounié, S Gabon

81 E20 **Ndindi** Nyanga, S Gabon

80 G11 **Ndjamena** *var.* N'Djamena; *prev.* Fort-Lamy. ● (Chad) Chari-Baguirmi, W Chad

80 G11 **Ndjamena ✕** Chari-Baguirmi, W Chad

81 D18 **Ndjolé** Moyen-Ogooué, W Gabon

84 J13 **Ndola** Copperbelt, C Zambia

Ndrhamcha, Sebkha de *see* Te-n-Dghâmcha, Sebkhet

81 L15 **Ndu** Haut-Zaïre, N Zaire

83 H21 **Nduguti** Singida, C Tanzania

195 X16 **Nduindui** Guadalcanal, C Solomon Islands

Nduke *see* Kohinggo

117 F19 **Néa Anchíalos** *var.* Nea Anhialos, Néa Ankhíalos. Thessalía, C Greece

Nea Anhialos/Néa Ankhíalos *see* Néa Anchíalos

117 H18 **Néa Artáki** Évvoia, C Greece

99 F15 **Neagh, Lough ☺** E Northern Ireland, UK

34 F7 **Neah Bay** Washington, NW USA

116 K24 **Néa Kaméni** *island* Kykládes, Greece, Aegean Sea

189 O8 **Neale, Lake ☺** Northern Territory, C Australia

190 Q2 **Neales River** *seasonal river* South Australia

65 K15 **Negro, Río** ☒ E Argentina

59 N17 **Negro, Río** ☒ E Bolivia

59 N17 **Negro, Río** ☒ C Paraguay

50 F6 **Negro, Río** ☒ N South America

63 E18 **Negro, Río** ☒ Brazil/Uruguay

Negro, Río *see* Sico Tinto, Río, Honduras

179 O5 **Negros** *island* C Philippines

118 M15 **Negru Vodă** Constanța, SE Romania

11 P13 **Neguac** New Brunswick, SE Canada

12 B7 **Negwazu, Lake ☺** Ontario, S Canada

Négyfalu *see* Săcele

34 F10 **Nehalem** Oregon, NW USA

34 F10 **Nehalem River** ☒ Oregon, NW USA

Nehavend *see* Nahāvand

149 V9 **Nehbandān** Khorāsān, E Iran

169 V6 **Nehe** Heilongjiang, NE China

200 Ss12 **Neiafu** 'Uta Vava'u, N Tonga

47 N9 **Neiba** *var.* Neyba. San Juan, SW Dominican Republic

Néid, Carn Uí *see* Mizen Head

94 M9 **Neiden** Finnmark, N Norway

117 E16 **Néo Monastíri** Thessalía, C Greece

_(center-right continued 2)

158 H11 **Nawalgarh** — see above

30 L14 **Nebraska** *off.* State of Nebraska; also known as Blackwater State, Cornhusker State, Tree Planters State. ◆ *state* C USA

31 S16 **Nebraska City** Nebraska, C USA

109 O24 **Nebrodi, Monti** *var.* Monti Caronie. ▲ Sicilia, Italy, C Mediterranean Sea

8 L14 **Nechako** ☒ British Columbia, SW Canada

31 Q2 **Neche** North Dakota, N USA

27 X6 **Neches** Texas, SW USA

27 W8 **Neches River** ☒ Texas, SW USA

103 H20 **Neckar** ☒ SW Germany

103 H20 **Neckarsulm** Baden-Württemberg, SW Germany

199 K5 **Necker Island** *island* C British Virgin Islands

183 U3 **Necker Ridge** *undersea feature* N Pacific Ocean

63 D17 **Necochea** Buenos Aires, E Argentina

106 H2 **Neda** Galicia, NW Spain

117 E20 **Nédas** ☒ S Greece

27 Y11 **Nederland** Texas, SW USA

Nederland *see* Netherlands

100 K12 **Neder Rijn** *Eng.* Lower Rhine. ☒ C Netherlands

101 L16 **Nederweert** Limburg, SE Netherlands

97 G16 **Nedre Tokke ☺** S Norway

119 S3 **Nedryhayliv** *Rus.* Nedrigaylov. Sums'ka Oblast', NE Ukraine

100 O11 **Neede** Gelderland, E Netherlands

35 T13 **Needle Mountain** ▲ Wyoming, C USA

37 Y14 **Needles** California, W USA

99 M24 **Needles, The** *rocks* Isle of Wight, S England, UK

64 O7 **Neembucú** *off.* Departamento de Neembucú. ◆ *department* SW Paraguay

32 M7 **Neenah** Wisconsin, N USA

9 W16 **Neepawa** Manitoba, S Canada

101 K16 **Neerpelt** Limburg, NE Belgium

76 M6 **Nefta** W Tunisia

127 O16 **Neftegorsk** Krasnodarskiy Kray, SW Russian Federation

131 U3 **Neftekamsk** Respublika Bashkortostan, W Russian Federation

131 O14 **Neftekumsk** Stavropol'skiy Kray, SW Russian Federation

125 G11 **Nefteyugansk** Khanty-Mansiyskiy Avtonomnyy Okrug, C Russian Federation

Neftezavodsk *see* Seydi

84 C10 **Negage** *var.* N'Gage. Uíge, NW Angola

Negapatam/Negapattinam *see* Nāgappattinam

175 N16 **Negara** Bali, Indonesia

175 N10 **Negara** Borneo, C Indonesia

Negara Brunei Darussalam *see* Brunei

33 N4 **Negaunee** Michigan, N USA

83 J15 **Negēlē** *var.* Negelli, *It.* Neghelli. S Ethiopia

81 E19 **Negelli** *see* Negēlē

Negeri Pahang Darul Makmur *see* Pahang

Negeri Selangor Darul Ehsan *see* Selangor

174 H5 **Negeri Sembilan** *var.* Negri Sembilan. ◆ *state* Peninsular Malaysia

86 J9 **Negeri Sembilan** *Mal.* Negeri Sembilan, *Lith.* Nemunas, *Pol.* Niemen, *Rus.* Neman. ☒ NE Europe

Negev *see* HaNegev

Neghelli *see* Negēlē

118 I12 **Negoiu** *var.* Negoiul. ▲ S Romania

Negoiul *see* Negoiu

84 P13 **Negomane** *var.* Negomano. Cabo Delgado, N Mozambique

Negomano *see* Negomane

161 J25 **Negombo** Western Province, SW Sri Lanka

Negoreloye *see* Nyeharelaye

112 N10 **Negotin** Serbia, E Yugoslavia

115 P19 **Negotino** S FYR Macedonia

106 G3 **Negreira** Galicia, NW Spain

118 L10 **Negreşti** Vaslui, E Romania

Negreşti *see* Negreşti-Oaş

118 H8 **Negreşti-Oaş** *Hung.* Avasfelsőfalu; *prev.* Negreşti. Satu Mare, NE Romania

46 H12 **Negril** W Jamaica

_(rightmost column)

29 R8 **Neosho** Missouri, C USA

29 Q7 **Neosho** ✕ SE Kansas, C USA

29 Q7 **Neosho River** ☒ Kansas/Oklahoma, C USA

127 N2 **Nepa** ☒ C Russian Federation

159 N10 **Nepal** *off.* Kingdom of Nepal. ◆ *monarchy* S Asia

158 M11 **Nepalganj** Mid Western, SW Nepal

12 L13 **Nepean** Ontario, SE Canada

38 L4 **Nephi** Utah, W USA

99 B16 **Nephin Ir.** Néifinn. ▲ W Ireland

69 T9 **Nepoko** ☒ N Zaire

20 K15 **Neptune** New Jersey, NE USA

190 Q10 **Neptune Islands** *island group* South Australia

109 I14 **Nera** *anc.* Nar. ☒ C Italy

104 L14 **Nérac** Lot-et-Garonne, SW France

113 Y16 **Neratovice** *Ger.* Neratowitz. Středni Čechy, C Czech Republic

Neratowitz *see* Neratovice

Nerău *see* Nysa

126 L15 **Nercha** ☒ S Russian Federation

126 L15 **Nerchinsk** Chitinskaya Oblast', S Russian Federation

126 L15 **Nerchinskiy Zavod** Chitinskaya Oblast', S Russian Federation

128 M15 **Nerekhta** Kostromskaya Oblast', NW Russian Federation

120 H19 **Nereta** Aizkraukle, S Latvia

108 H13 **Nereto** Abruzzi, C Italy

115 H15 **Neretva** ☒ Bosnia and Herzegovina/Croatia

117 C16 **Nerikós** *ruins* Lefkáda, Iónioi Nísoi, Greece, C Mediterranean Sea

120 B12 **Neringa** *Ger.* Nidden; *prev.* Nida. Neringa, SW Lithuania

85 I15 **Neriquinha** Cuando Cubango, SE Angola

120 I13 **Neris** *Bel.* Viliya, *Pol.* Wilia; *prev. Pol.* Wilja. ☒ Belarus/Lithuania **Neris** *see* Viliya

107 N15 **Nerja** Andalucía, S Spain

124 J13 **Nerl'** ☒ W Russian Federation

106 J13 **Nerva** Andalucía, S Spain

126 Ll13 **Neryungri** Respublika Sakha (Yakutiya), NE Russian Federation

100 I4 **Nes** Friesland, N Netherlands

96 G13 **Nesbyen** Buskerud, S Norway

94 L2 **Neskaupstaður** Austurland, E Iceland

94 H9 **Nesna** Nordland, C Norway

28 K5 **Ness City** Kansas, C USA

110 H7 **Nesslau** Sankt Gallen, NE Switzerland

98 I9 **Ness, Loch ☺** N Scotland, UK

Nesterov *see* Zhovkva

116 I12 **Néstos Bul.** Mesta, *Turk.* Kara Su. ☒ Bulgaria/Greece *see also* Mesta

97 C14 **Nesttun** Hordaland, S Norway

Nesvizh *see* Nyasvizh

144 F11 **Netanya** *var.* Natanya, Nathanya. Central, C Israel

100 I9 **Netherlands** *off.* Kingdom of the Netherlands, *var.* Holland, *Dut.* Koninkrijk der Nederlanden, Nederland. ◆ *monarchy* NW Europe

47 S9 **Netherlands Antilles** *prev.* Dutch West Indies. ◇ *Dutch autonomous region* S Caribbean Sea

Netherlands East Indies *see* Indonesia

Netherlands Guiana *see* Suriname

Netherlands New Guinea *see* Irian Jaya

118 L4 **Netishyn** Khmel'nyts'ka Oblast', W Ukraine

144 E11 **Netivot** Southern, S Israel

109 O21 **Neto** ☒ S Italy

9 O16 **Nettilling Lake ☺** Baffin Island, Northwest Territories, N Canada

31 V3 **Nett Lake ☺** Minnesota, N USA

109 I16 **Nettuno** Lazio, C Italy

43 U16 **Netzahualcóyotl, Presa** ☺ SE Mexico

Netze *see* Noteć

Neu Amerika *see* Puławy

Neubetsche *see* Novi Bečej

Neubistritz *see* Nová Bystřice

103 O7 **Neubrandenburg** Mecklenburg-Vorpommern, NE Germany

103 K22 **Neuburg an der Donau** Bayern, S Germany

110 C8 **Neuchâtel** *Ger.* Neuenburg. Neuchâtel, W Switzerland

110 C8 **Neuchâtel** *Ger.* Neuenburg. ◆ *canton* W Switzerland

110 C8 **Neuchâtel, Lac de** *Ger.* Neuenburger See. ☺ W Switzerland

102 L10 **Neue Elde** *canal* N Germany

Neuenburg *see* Neuchâtel

Neuenburg an der Elbe *see* Nymburk

Neuenburger See *see* Neuchâtel, Lac de

110 F7 **Neuenhof** Aargau, N Switzerland

102 H11 **Neuenland ✕** (Bremen) Bremen, NW Germany

103 C18 **Neuenrade** Rheinland-Pfalz, W Germany

101 K24 **Neufchâteau** Luxembourg, SE Belgium

105 R4 **Neufchâteau** Vosges, NE France

104 M3 **Neufchâtel-en-Bray** Seine-Maritime, N France

111 S3 **Neufelden** Oberösterreich, N Austria

Neugradisk *see* Nova Gradiška

Neuhaus *see* Jindřichův Hradec

Neuhäusel see Nové Zámky
110 G6 Neuhausen var. Neuhausen am Rheinfall. Schaffhausen, N Switzerland
Neuhausen am Rheinfall see Neuhausen
103 I17 Neuhof Hessen, C Germany
Neuhof see Zgierz
Neukuhren see Pionerskiy
Neu-Langenburg see Tukuyu
111 W4 Neulengbach Niederösterreich, NE Austria
115 G15 Neum S Bosnia and Herzegovina
Neumark see Nowy Targ, Nowy Sącz, Poland
Neumark see Nowe Miasto Lubawskie, Toruń, Poland
Neumarkt see Neumarkt im Hausruckkreis, Oberösterreich, Austria
Neumarkt see Neumarkt Am Wallersee, Salzburg, Austria
Neumarkt see Środa Śląska, Wrocław, Poland
Neumarkt see Târgu Secuiesc, Covasna, Romania
Neumarkt see Târgu Mureş, Mureş, Romania
111 Q5 Neumarkt Am Wallersee var. Neumarkt. Salzburg, NW Austria
111 R4 Neumarkt im Hausruckkreis var. Neumarkt. Oberösterreich, N Austria
103 L20 Neumarkt in der Oberpfalz Bayern, SE Germany
Neumarktl see Tržič
Neumoldowa see Moldova Nouă
102 J8 Neumünster Schleswig-Holstein, N Germany
111 X5 Neunkirchen var. Neunkirchen am Steinfeld. Niederösterreich, E Austria
103 E20 Neunkirchen Saarland, SW Germany
Neunkirchen am Steinfeld see Neunkirchen
Neuoderberg see Bohumín
65 I15 Neuquén Neuquén, SE Argentina
65 H14 Neuquén off. Provincia de Neuquén. ◆ province W Argentina
65 H14 Neuquén, Río ✍ W Argentina
Neurode see Nowa Ruda
102 N11 Neuruppin Brandenburg, NE Germany
Neusalz an der Oder see Nowa Sól
Neu Sandec/Neusandez see Nowy Sącz
103 K22 Neusäss Bayern, S Germany
Neusatz see Novi Sad
Neuschliss see Gherla
23 N8 Neuse River ✍ North Carolina, SE USA
111 Z5 Neusiedl am See Burgenland, E Austria
113 G22 Neusiedler See Hung. Fertő. ☺ Austria/Hungary
Neusohl see Banská Bystrica
103 D15 Neuss anc. Novaesium, Novesium. Nordrhein-Westfalen, W Germany
Neuss see Nyon
Neustadt see Neustadt an der Aisch, Bayern, Germany
Neustadt see Neustadt bei Coburg, Bayern, Germany
Neustadt see Prudnik, Opole, Poland
Neustadt see Baia Mare, Maramureş, Romania
102 I12 Neustadt an der Rübenberge Niedersachsen, N Germany
103 J19 Neustadt an der Aisch var. Neustadt. Bayern, C Germany
Neustadt an der Haardt see Neustadt an der Weinstrasse
103 F20 Neustadt an der Weinstrasse prev. Neustadt an der Haardt, hist. Niewenstat, anc. Nova Civitas. Rheinland-Pfalz, SW Germany
103 K18 Neustadt bei Coburg var. Neustadt. Bayern, C Germany
Neustadt bei Pinne see Lwówek
Neustadt in Oberschlesien see Prudnik
Neustadtl see Novo Mesto
Neustadtl in Mähren see Nové Město na Moravě
Neustettin see Szczecinek
110 M8 Neustift im Stubaital var. Stubaital. Tirol, W Austria
102 N10 Neustrelitz Mecklenburg-Vorpommern, NE Germany
Neutitschein see Nový Jičín
Neutra see Nitra
103 J22 Neu-Ulm Bayern, S Germany
Neuveville see La Neuveville
105 N12 Neuvic Corrèze, C France
Neuwarp see Nowe Warpno
102 G9 Neuwerk island NW Germany
103 E17 Neuwied Rheinland-Pfalz, W Germany
Neuzen see Terneuzen
128 H12 Neva ✍ NW Russian Federation
31 V14 Nevada Iowa, C USA
29 R6 Nevada Missouri, C USA
37 R5 Nevada off. State of Nevada; also known as Battle Born State, Sagebrush State, Silver State. ◇ state W USA
37 P6 Nevada City California, W USA
128 G16 Nevel' Pskovskaya Oblast', W Russian Federation
127 Oo16 Nevel'sk Ostrov Sakhalin, Sakhalinskaya Oblast', SE Russian Federation
126 LJ14 Never Amurskaya Oblast', SE Russian Federation
131 Q6 Neverkino Penzenskaya Oblast', W Russian Federation
105 P9 Nevers anc. Noviodunum. Nièvre, C France
20 J12 Neversink River ✍ New York, NE USA

191 Q6 Nevertire New South Wales, SE Australia
115 H15 Nevesinje S Bosnia and Herzegovina
120 G12 Nevėžis ✍ C Lithuania
130 M14 Nevinnomyssk Stavropol'skiy Kray, SW Russian Federation
47 W10 Nevis island Saint Kitts and Nevis
Nevoso, Monte see Snežnik
Nevrokop see Gotse Delchev
142 J14 Nevşehir var. Nevshehr. Nevşehir, C Turkey
142 J14 Nevşehir var. Nevshehr. ◆ province C Turkey
Nevshehr see Nevşehir
125 Ee11 Nev'yansk Sverdlovskaya Oblast', C Russian Federation
83 J25 Newala Mtwara, SE Tanzania
33 P16 New Albany Indiana, N USA
22 M2 New Albany Mississippi, S USA
31 Y11 New Albin Iowa, C USA
57 U8 New Amsterdam E Guyana
191 Q4 New Angledool New South Wales, SE Australia
23 Y2 Newark Delaware, NE USA
20 K13 Newark New Jersey, NE USA
20 G10 Newark New York, NE USA
33 T13 Newark Ohio, N USA
Newark see Newark-on-Trent
37 W5 Newark Lake ☺ Nevada, W USA
99 N18 Newark-on-Trent var. Newark. C England, UK
24 M7 New Augusta Mississippi, S USA
21 P12 New Bedford Massachusetts, NE USA
34 G11 Newberg Oregon, NW USA
23 X10 New Bern North Carolina, SE USA
22 J8 Newbern Tennessee, S USA
33 P4 Newberry Michigan, N USA
23 Q12 Newberry South Carolina, SE USA
20 F15 New Bloomfield Pennsylvania, NE USA
27 X5 New Boston Texas, SW USA
33 S7 New Braunfels Texas, SW USA
33 Q13 New Bremen Ohio, N USA
99 F18 Newbridge Ir. An Droichead Nua. C Ireland
20 B14 New Brighton Pennsylvania, NE USA
20 M12 New Britain Connecticut, NE USA
195 N13 New Britain island E PNG
199 Hh9 New Britain Trench undersea feature W Pacific Ocean
20 J15 New Brunswick New Jersey, NE USA
13 V8 New Brunswick Fr. Nouveau-Brunswick. ◆ province SE Canada
20 K13 Newburgh New York, NE USA
99 M22 Newbury S England, UK
21 P10 Newburyport Massachusetts, NE USA
79 T14 New Bussa Niger, W Nigeria
197 J4 New Caledonia Fr. Nouvelle-Calédonie. ◇ French overseas territory SW Pacific Ocean
197 H5 New Caledonia island SW Pacific Ocean
183 O10 New Caledonia Basin undersea feature W Pacific Ocean
191 T8 Newcastle New South Wales, SE Australia
11 O14 Newcastle New Brunswick, SE Canada
99 C20 Newcastle Ir. An Caisleán Nua. SW Ireland
85 K22 Newcastle KwaZulu/Natal, E South Africa
99 G16 Newcastle Ir. An Caisleán Nua. SE Northern Ireland, UK
32 J14 New Castle Indiana, N USA
22 L5 New Castle Kentucky, S USA
29 N1 New Castle Oklahoma, C USA
20 B13 New Castle Pennsylvania, NE USA
27 R6 Newcastle Texas, SW USA
38 J7 Newcastle Utah, W USA
23 S13 Newcastle Wyoming, C USA
47 W10 Newcastle × Nevis, Saint Kitts and Nevis
99 L14 Newcastle × England, UK
Newcastle see Newcastle upon Tyne
99 L18 Newcastle-under-Lyme C England, UK
99 M14 Newcastle upon Tyne var. Newcastle; hist. Monkchester, Lat. Pons Aelii. NE England, UK
189 Q4 Newcastle Waters Northern Territory, N Australia
Newchwang see Yingkou
20 K13 New City New York, NE USA
33 U13 Newcomerstown Ohio, N USA
20 G15 New Cumberland Pennsylvania, NE USA
23 R3 New Cumberland West Virginia, NE USA
158 I10 New Delhi ● (India) Delhi, N India
9 O17 New Denver British Columbia, SW Canada
30 J9 Newell South Dakota, N USA
23 Q13 New Ellenton South Carolina, SE USA
24 J6 Newellton Louisiana, S USA
30 K6 New England North Dakota, N USA
21 P8 New England cultural region NE USA
New England of the West see Minnesota
191 N10 New England Range ▲ New South Wales, SE Australia
66 O9 New England Seamounts var. Bermuda-New England Seamount Arc. undersea feature W Atlantic Ocean
40 M14 Newenham, Cape headland Alaska, USA

144 F11 Newé Zohar Southern, E Israel
20 D9 Newfane New York, NE USA
99 M23 New Forest physical region S England, UK
16 S8 Newfoundland Fr. Terre-Neuve. island Newfoundland and Labrador, SE Canada
11 R9 Newfoundland and Labrador Fr. Terre Neuve. ◆ province E Canada
67 J8 Newfoundland Basin undersea feature NW Atlantic Ocean
66 I8 Newfoundland Ridge undersea feature NW Atlantic Ocean
66 J8 Newfoundland Seamounts undersea feature N Sargasso Sea
20 G16 New Freedom Pennsylvania, NE USA
195 U14 New Georgia island New Georgia Islands, NW Solomon Islands
195 T15 New Georgia Islands island group NW Solomon Islands
195 U14 New Georgia Sound var. The Slot. sound E Solomon Sea
32 L9 New Glarus Wisconsin, N USA
11 Q15 New Glasgow Nova Scotia, SE Canada
New Goa see Panaji
194 D11 New Guinea Dut. Nieuw Guinea, Ind. Irian. island Indonesia/PNG
199 H9 New Guinea Trench undersea feature SW Pacific Ocean
34 I6 Newhalem Washington, NW USA
31 S14 Newhalen Alaska, USA
31 X13 Newhall Iowa, C USA
12 F16 New Hamburg Ontario, S Canada
21 N9 New Hampshire off. State of New Hampshire; also known as The Granite State. ◇ state NE USA
31 W12 New Hampton Iowa, C USA
32 Z3 New Hanover island NE PNG
20 M13 New Haven Connecticut, NE USA
32 Q12 New Haven Indiana, N USA
29 W5 New Haven Missouri, C USA
99 P23 Newhaven SE England, UK
8 K13 New Hazelton British Columbia, SW Canada
24 I9 New Iberia Louisiana, S USA
183 P9 New Hebrides ▲ C Svalbard
20 H15 New Hebrides Trench undersea feature N Coral Sea
20 H15 New Holland Pennsylvania, NE USA
24 J9 New Iberia Louisiana, S USA
195 N10 New Ireland ◆ province NE PNG
195 N9 New Ireland island NE PNG
67 A24 New Island island W Falkland Islands
20 J15 New Jersey off. State of New Jersey; also known as The Garden State. ◇ state NE USA
20 C14 New Kensington Pennsylvania, NE USA
23 W6 New Kent Virginia, NE USA
29 O8 Newkirk Oklahoma, C USA
23 Q9 Newland North Carolina, SE USA
30 L6 New Leipzig North Dakota, N USA
12 H9 New Liskeard Ontario, S Canada
24 G7 Newllano Louisiana, S USA
21 N13 New London Connecticut, NE USA
31 Y15 New London Iowa, C USA
31 T8 New London Minnesota, N USA
29 V3 New London Missouri, C USA
32 M7 New London Wisconsin, N USA
29 X9 New Madrid Missouri, C USA
188 J8 Newman Western Australia
204 M13 Newman Island island Antarctica
99 P20 Newmarket Ontario, S Canada
99 P20 Newmarket E England, UK
21 P10 Newmarket New Hampshire, NE USA
23 U4 New Market Virginia, NE USA
23 R2 New Martinsville West Virginia, NE USA
34 M12 New Meadows Idaho, NW USA
28 R12 New Mexico off. State of New Mexico; also known as Land of Enchantment, Sunshine State. ◇ state SW USA
25 S4 Newnan Georgia, SE USA
191 P17 New Norfolk Tasmania, SE Australia
24 K9 New Orleans Louisiana, S USA
24 K9 New Orleans × Louisiana, S USA
20 K13 New Paltz New York, NE USA
33 U12 New Philadelphia Ohio, N USA
192 K10 New Plymouth Taranaki, North Island, NZ
192 M6 Ngatea Waikato, North Island, NZ
177 P8 Ngathainggyaung Irrawaddy, SW Myanmar
Ngatik see Ngetik Atoll
Ngau see Gau
174 LI5 Ngawi Jawa, S Indonesia
196 F2 Ngcheangel var. Kayangel Islands. island Palau Islands, N Palau
196 E10 Ngchemiangel Babeldaob, N Palau
196 C8 Ngeaur var. Angaur. island Palau Islands, S Palau
196 F9 Ngerkeai Babeldaob, N Palau
196 F9 Ngermechau Babeldaob, N Palau
196 F9 Ngeruktabel prev. Urukthapel. island Palau Islands, N Palau
201 T17 Ngetik Atoll var. Ngatik; prev. Los Jardines. atoll Caroline Islands, E Micronesia
196 E10 Ngetkip Babeldaob, N Palau

99 I20 New Quay SW Wales, UK
31 V10 New Richland Minnesota, N USA
13 X7 New-Richmond Québec, SE Canada
33 R15 New Richmond Ohio, N USA
32 I5 New Richmond Wisconsin, N USA
44 G1 New River ✍ N Belize
57 T12 New River ✍ SE Guyana
23 R6 New River ✍ West Virginia, NE USA
44 G1 New River Lagoon ◎ N Belize
24 J8 New Roads Louisiana, S USA
20 L14 New Rochelle New York, NE USA
31 O4 New Rockford North Dakota, N USA
99 P23 New Romney SE England, UK
99 F20 New Ross Ir. Ros Mhic Thriúin. SE Ireland
99 F16 Newry Ir. An tIúr. SE Northern Ireland, UK
30 M5 New Salem North Dakota, N USA
New Sarum see Salisbury
31 W14 New Sharon Iowa, C USA
New Siberian Islands see Novosibirskiye Ostrova
25 X10 New Smyrna Beach Florida, SE USA
191 O7 New South Wales ◆ state SE Australia
196 F15 Ngulu Atoll atoll Caroline Islands, W Micronesia
197 C14 Nguna island C Vanuatu
79 W12 N'Gunza var. Sumbe
175 N16 Ngurah Rai × (Bali) Bali, S Indonesia
79 W12 Nguru Yobe, NE Nigeria
79 W12 Ngwaketze se Southern
85 I16 Ngweze ✍ S Zambia
85 M17 Nhamatanda Sofala, C Mozambique
60 G12 Nhamundá, Rio var. Jamundá, Yamundá. ✍ N Brazil
62 J7 Nhandeara São Paulo, S Brazil
84 D12 Nharêa var. N'Harea, Nhareia. Bié, W Angola
N'Harea see Nharêa
Nhareia see Nharêa
178 Kk13 Nha Trang Khanh Hoa, S Vietnam
190 I11 Nhill Victoria, SE Australia
85 L22 Nhlangano prev. Goedgegun. SW Swaziland
189 S1 Nhulunbuy Northern Territory, N Australia
79 N10 Niafounké Tombouctou, W Mali
33 N3 Niagara Wisconsin, N USA
12 H16 Niagara ✍ Ontario, S Canada
12 G15 Niagara Escarpment hill range Ontario, S Canada
12 H16 Niagara Falls Ontario, S Canada
20 D9 Niagara Falls New York, NE USA
16 Pp17 Niagara Falls waterfall Canada/USA
78 K12 Niagassola var. Nyagassola. Haute-Guinée, NE Guinea
79 R2 Niamey ● (Niger) Niamey, SW Niger
79 R2 Niamey × Niamey, SW Niger
79 R14 Niamtougou N Togo
81 O16 Niangara Haut-Zaïre, NE Zaire
79 O10 Niangay, Lac ◎ E Mali
79 N9 Niangoloko SW Burkina
29 U6 Niangua River ✍ Missouri, C USA
81 O19 Nia-Nia Haut-Zaïre, NE Zaire
21 N13 Niantic Connecticut, NE USA
169 U7 Nianzishan Heilongjiang, NE China
173 F7 Nias, Pulau island W Indonesia

195 V15 Nggatokae island New Georgia Islands, NW Solomon Islands
85 C16 N'Giva var. Ondjiva, Port. Vila Pereira de Eça. Cunene, S Angola
81 G20 Ngo Plateaux, SE Congo
178 Jj7 Ngoc Lac Thanh Hoa, N Vietnam
81 Q17 Ngoko ✍ Cameroon/Congo
176 W14 Ngoni, Tanjung headland Maluku, Kepulauan Aru, SE Indonesia
83 H19 Ngorengore Rift Valley, SW Kenya
165 Q11 Ngoring Hu ◎ C China
Ngorolaka see Banifing
83 H20 Ngorongoro Crater crater N Tanzania
81 D19 Ngouni off. Province de la Ngounié. var. La Ngounié. ◆ province S Gabon
81 D19 Ngounié ✍ Congo/Gabon
80 H10 Ngoura var. Ngaoura. Chari-Baguirmi, W Chad
80 G10 Ngouri var. NGouri; prev. Fort-Millot. Lac, W Chad
79 Y10 Ngourti Diffa, E Niger
79 Y11 Nguigmi var. N'Guigmi. Diffa, SE Niger
Nguimbo see Lumbala N'Guimbo
84 D12 Nharêa var. N'Harea, Nhareia. Bié, W Angola
84 O13 Niassa off. Província do Niassa. ◆ province N Mozambique
203 U10 Niau island Îles Tuamotu, C French Polynesia
97 Q20 Nibe Nordjylland, N Denmark
201 Q8 Nibok N Nauru
120 C10 Nīca Liepāja, W Latvia
Nicaea see Nice
44 J9 Nicaragua off. Republic of Nicaragua. ◆ republic Central America
44 K11 Nicaragua, Lago de var. Cocibolca, Gran Lago, Eng. Lake Nicaragua. ◎ S Nicaragua
Nicaragua, Lake see Nicaragua, Lago de
66 D2 Nicaraguan Rise undersea feature NW Caribbean Sea
Nicaria see Ikaría
109 N21 Nicastro Calabria, SW Italy
105 V15 Nice It. Nizza; anc. Nicaea. Alpes-Maritimes, SE France
105 P8 Nièvre ◆ department C France
Nice see Côte d'Azur
Nicephorium see Ar Raqqah
10 M9 Nichicun, Lac ◎ Québec, E Canada
170 C17 Nichinan var. Nitinan. Miyazaki, Kyūshū, SW Japan
46 E4 Nicholas Channel channel N Cuba
Nicholas II Land see Severnaya Zemlya
155 V2 Nicholas Range Pash. Selseleh-ye Kūh-e Vākhān, Taj. Qatorkūhi Vākhon. ▲ Afghanistan/Tajikistan
22 M6 Nicholasville Kentucky, S USA
46 J9 Nicholls Town Andros Island, NW Bahamas
23 U2 Nichols South Carolina, SE USA
57 V9 Nickerie ♦ district NW Suriname
57 V9 Nickerie Rivier ✍ NW Suriname
157 N22 Nicobar Islands island group India, E Indian Ocean
118 I9 Nicolae Bălcescu Botoşani, NE Romania
13 Q11 Nicolet Québec, SE Canada
13 Q12 Nicolet, Lake ◎ Michigan, N USA
13 Q4 Nicolet, Lake ◎ Michigan, N USA

31 U10 Nicollet Minnesota, N USA
63 F19 Nico Pérez Florida, S Uruguay
Nicopolis see Nikopol, Bulgaria
Nicopolis see Nikópoli, Greece
124 R12 Nicosia Gk. Lefkosía, Turk. Lefkoşa. ● (Cyprus) C Cyprus
109 K24 Nicosia Sicilia, Italy, C Mediterranean Sea
109 N22 Nicotera Calabria, SW Italy
44 K13 Nicoya Guanacaste, W Costa Rica
44 L14 Nicoya, Golfo de gulf W Costa Rica
44 L14 Nicoya, Península de peninsula NW Costa Rica
Nictheroy see Niterói
115 L15 Nida ▲ S Poland
Nida see Neringa
110 D8 Nidau Bern, W Switzerland
103 H17 Nidda ✍ W Germany
Nidden see Neringa
97 F17 Nidelva ✍ S Norway
126 J10 Nidym Evenkiyskiy Avtonomnyy Okrug, N Russian Federation
112 L9 Nidzica Ger. Niedenburg. Olsztyn, N Poland
102 H6 Niebüll Schleswig-Holstein, N Germany
Niedenburg see Nidzica
111 N25 Niederanven Luxembourg, C Luxembourg
105 V4 Niederbronn-les-Bains Bas-Rhin, NE France
Niederdonau see Niederösterreich
111 S7 Niedere Tauern ▲ C Austria
103 P14 Niederlausitz Eng. Lower Lusatia. physical region E Germany
111 U5 Niederösterreich off. Land Niederösterreich, Eng. Lower Austria, prev. Niederdonau; prev. Lower Danube. ◇ state NE Austria
102 G12 Niedersachsen Eng. Lower Saxony, Fr. Basse-Saxe. ◇ state N Germany
81 D17 Niefang var. Sevilla de Niefang. NW Equatorial Guinea
85 G23 Niekerkshoop Northern Cape, W South Africa
101 G17 Niel Antwerpen, N Belgium
Niélé see Niéllé
78 M14 Niéllé var. Niélé. N Ivory Coast
81 O22 Niemba Shaba, E Zaire
94 J13 Niemisel Norrbotten, N Sweden
113 H15 Niemodlin Ger. Falkenberg. Opole, SW Poland
102 H12 Nienburg Niedersachsen, N Germany
113 L16 Niepołomice Kraków, S Poland
103 D14 Niers ✍ Germany/Netherlands
103 Q15 Niesky Lus. Nisko. Sachsen, E Germany
Nieśwież see Nyasvizh
Nieuport see Nieuwpoort
100 O8 Nieuw-Amsterdam Drenthe, NE Netherlands
57 W9 Nieuw Amsterdam Commewijne, NE Suriname
101 M14 Nieuw-Bergen Limburg, SE Netherlands
100 O7 Nieuw-Buinen Drenthe, NE Netherlands
100 J12 Nieuwegein Utrecht, C Netherlands
100 P5 Nieuwe Pekela Groningen, NE Netherlands
100 I11 Nieuwkoop Zuid-Holland, C Netherlands
100 M9 Nieuwleusen Overijssel, E Netherlands
100 J11 Nieuw-Loosdrecht Utrecht, C Netherlands
57 U9 Nieuw Nickerie Nickerie, NW Suriname
100 P5 Nieuwolda Groningen, NE Netherlands
101 B17 Nieuwpoort var. Nieuport. West-Vlaanderen, W Belgium
101 G14 Nieuw-Vossemeer Noord-Brabant, S Netherlands
100 N9 Nieuw-Weerdinge Drenthe, NE Netherlands
42 L10 Nieves Zacatecas, C Mexico
66 O11 Nieves, Pico de las ▲ Gran Canaria, Islas Canarias, Spain, NE Atlantic Ocean
105 P8 Nièvre ◆ department C France
Weinstrasse
Niewenstat see Neustadt an der Weinstrasse
142 J15 Niğde Niğde, C Turkey
142 J15 Niğde ◆ province C Turkey
85 J21 Nigel Gauteng, NE South Africa
79 T14 Niger ◆ state C Nigeria
79 T4 Niger off. Republic of Niger. ◆ republic W Africa
79 P8 Niger ✍ W Africa
Niger Cone see Niger Fan
79 T13 Niger Delta delta S Nigeria
69 P9 Niger Fan var. Niger Cone. undersea feature E Atlantic Ocean
79 T13 Nigeria off. Federal Republic of Nigeria. ◆ federal republic W Africa
79 P10 Niger, Mouths of the delta S Nigeria
193 C24 Nightcaps Southland, South Island, NZ
12 F7 Night Hawk Lake ◎ Ontario, S Canada
67 M19 Nightingale Island island S Tristan da Cunha, S Atlantic Ocean
40 M12 Nightmute Alaska, USA
115 F18 Nigríta Kentriki Makedonía, N Greece
154 J15 Nihing Pash. Rūd-e Nahang. ✍ Iran/Pakistan

203 V10 Nihiru atoll Îles Tuamotu, C French Polynesia
Nihommatsu see Nihonmatsu
171 L13 Nihonmatsu var. Nihommatsu, Nihonmatu. Fukushima, Honshū, C Japan
Nihonmatu see Nihonmatsu
64 I12 Nihuil, Embalse del ◎ W Argentina
171 K12 Niigata Niigata, Honshū, C Japan
171 K13 Niigata off. Niigata-ken. ◆ prefecture Honshū, C Japan
170 F15 Niihama Ehime, Shikoku, SW Japan
40 A8 Niihau island Hawaii, USA, C Pacific Ocean
172 Ss13 Nii-jima island E Japan
170 Ff13 Niimi Okayama, Honshū, SW Japan
171 Kk13 Niitsu var. Niitu. Niigata, Honshū, C Japan
Niitu see Niitsu
107 P15 Níjar Andalucía, S Spain
100 K11 Nijkerk Gelderland, C Netherlands
101 H16 Nijlen Antwerpen, N Belgium
100 L13 Nijmegen Ger. Nimwegen; anc. Noviomagus. Gelderland, SE Netherlands
100 N10 Nijverdal Overijssel, E Netherlands
202 G16 Nikao Rarotonga, S Cook Islands
Nikaria see Ikaría
128 I2 Nikel' Murmanskaya Oblast', NW Russian Federation
175 Rr17 Nikiniki Timor, S Indonesia
133 Q15 Nikitin Seamount undersea feature E Indian Ocean
79 S14 Nikki E Benin
171 Kk15 Nikkō var. Nikko. Tochigi, Honshū, S Japan
41 P10 Nikolai Alaska, USA
Nikolaiken see Mikołajki
Nikolainkaupunki see Vaasa
151 U15 Nikolayevka Almaty, SE Kazakhstan
151 O6 Nikolayevka Severnyy Kazakhstan, N Kazakhstan
131 P9 Nikolayevka Volgogradskaya Oblast', SW Russian Federation
Nikolayevsk see Nikolayevsk-na-Amure
127 Nn14 Nikolayevsk-na-Amure Khabarovskiy Kray, SE Russian Federation
131 P6 Nikol'sk Penzenskaya Oblast', W Russian Federation
129 O13 Nikol'sk Vologodskaya Oblast', NW Russian Federation
Nikol'sk see Ussuriysk
40 K17 Nikolski Umnak Island, Alaska, USA
Nikol'skiy see Satpayev
131 V7 Nikol'skoye Orenburgskaya Oblast', W Russian Federation
Nikol'sk-Ussuriyskiy see Ussuriysk
116 J7 Nikopol Nicopolis. Loveshka Oblast, N Bulgaria
119 S9 Nikopol' Dnipropetrovs'ka Oblast', SE Ukraine
117 C17 Nikópoli anc. Nicopolis. site of ancient city Ípeiros, W Greece
142 M12 Niksar Tokat, N Turkey
149 V14 Nikshahr Sīstān va Balūchestān, SE Iran
115 J16 Nikšić Montenegro, SW Yugoslavia
203 R4 Nikumaroro prev. Gardner Island, Kemins Island. atoll Phoenix Islands, C Kiribati
203 P8 Nikunau var. Nukunau; prev. Byron Island. atoll Tungaru, W Kiribati
161 G21 Nilambūr Kerala, SW India
33 X16 Niland California, W USA
69 T3 Nile Ar. Nahr an Nīl. ✍ N Africa
82 G8 Nile former province NW Uganda
77 W7 Nile Delta delta N Egypt
69 T3 Nile Fan undersea feature E Mediterranean Sea
33 O11 Niles Michigan, N USA
33 V11 Niles Ohio, N USA
161 F20 Nileswaram Kerala, SW India
12 K10 Nilgaut, Lac ◎ Québec, SE Canada
164 I5 Nilka Xinjiang Uygur Zizhiqu, NW China
Nil, Nahr an see Nile
95 N16 Nilsiä Kuopio, C Finland
160 F9 Nimach Madhya Pradesh, C India
158 H14 Nimbāhera Rājasthān, N India
78 L15 Nimba, Monts var. Nimba Mountains. ▲ W Africa
Nimba Mountains see Nimba, Monts
Nimburg see Nymburk
105 Q15 Nîmes anc. Nemausus, Nismes. Gard, S France
158 H11 Nimka Ka Thāna Rājasthān, N India
191 R11 Nimmitabel New South Wales, SE Australia
Nimptsch see Niemcza
205 R11 Nimrod Glacier glacier Antarctica
Nimroze see Nīmrūz
154 K8 Nīmrūz var. Nimroze; prev. Chakhānsūr. ◆ province SW Afghanistan
83 F16 Nimule Eastern Equatoria, S Sudan
Nin see Nijmegen
161 C23 Nine Degree Channel channel India/Maldives
20 J6 Ninemile Point headland New York, NE USA
181 S8 Ninetyeast Ridge undersea feature E Indian Ocean
191 P13 Ninety Mile Beach beach Victoria, SE Australia

◆ COUNTRY   ◇ DEPENDENT TERRITORY   ♦ ADMINISTRATIVE REGION   ▲ MOUNTAIN   ⧖ VOLCANO   ◎ LAKE
● COUNTRY CAPITAL   ○ DEPENDENT TERRITORY CAPITAL   × INTERNATIONAL AIRPORT   ▲ MOUNTAIN RANGE   ✍ RIVER   ▨ RESERVOIR

Ninety Mile Beach – North Raccoon River

192 I2 **Ninety Mile Beach** *beach* North Island, NZ
23 P12 **Ninety Six** South Carolina, SE USA
169 Y9 **Ning'an** Heilongjiang, NE China
167 S9 **Ningbo** *var.* Ning-po, Yin-hsien; *prev.* Ninghsien. Zhejiang, SE China
167 U12 **Ningde** Fujian, SE China
167 U12 **Ningdu** Jiangxi, S China
194 E12 **Ningerum** Western, SW PNG
167 R9 **Ningguo** Anhui, E China
167 S9 **Ninghai** Zhejiang, SE China
Ning-hsia *see* Ningxia
Ninghsien *see* Ningbo
166 J15 **Ningming** Guangxi Zhuangzu Zizhiqu, S China
166 H11 **Ningnan** Sichuan, C China
Ning-po *see* Ningbo
Ningsia/Ningsia Hui/Ningsia Hui Autonomous Region *see* Ningxia
166 J5 **Ningxia** *off.* Ningxia Huizu Zizhiqu, *var.* Ning-hsia, Ningsia, *Eng.* Ningsia Hui, Ningsia Hui Autonomous Region. ◈ *autonomous region* N China
165 X10 **Ningxian** Gansu, N China
178 Jj7 **Ninh Binh** Ninh Binh, N Vietnam
178 Kk13 **Ninh Hoa** Khanh Hoa, S Vietnam
194 H7 **Ninigo Group** *island group* N PNG
41 Q12 **Ninilchik** Alaska, USA
29 N7 **Ninnescah River** ≈ Kansas, C USA
205 U16 **Ninnis Glacier** *glacier* Antarctica
172 N10 **Ninohe** Iwate, Honshū, C Japan
101 F18 **Ninove** Oost-Vlaanderen, C Belgium
179 P11 **Ninoy Aquino** ✕ (Manila) Luzon, N Philippines
Nio *see* Íos
31 P12 **Niobrara** Nebraska, C USA
30 M12 **Niobrara River** ≈ Nebraska/Wyoming, C USA
81 I20 **Nioki** Bandundu, W Zaire
78 M11 **Niono** Ségou, C Mali
78 K11 **Nioro** *var.* Nioro du Sahel. Kayes, W Mali
78 G11 **Nioro du Rip** SW Senegal
Nioro du Sahel *see* Nioro
104 K10 **Niort** Deux-Sèvres, W France
180 H14 **Nioumachoua** Mohéli, S Comoros
194 G12 **Nipa** Southern Highlands, W PNG
9 U14 **Nipawin** Saskatchewan, S Canada
10 D12 **Nipigon** Ontario, S Canada
10 D11 **Nipigon, Lake** ⊚ Ontario, S Canada
9 S13 **Nipin** ≈ Saskatchewan, C Canada
12 G11 **Nipissing, Lake** ⊚ Ontario, S Canada
37 P13 **Nipomo** California, W USA
Nippon *see* Japan
144 K6 **Niqniqīyah, Jabal an** ▲ C Syria
64 I9 **Niquivil** San Juan, W Argentina
176 Yy10 **Nirabotong** Irian Jaya, E Indonesia
171 J16 **Nirasaki** Yamanashi, Honshū, S Japan
Niriz *see* Neyrīz
161 I14 **Nirmal** Andhra Pradesh, C India
159 Q13 **Nirmāli** Bihār, NE India
115 O14 **Niš** *Eng.* Nish, *Ger.* Nisch; *anc.* Naissus. Serbia, SE Yugoslavia
106 H9 **Nisa** Portalegre, C Portugal
Nisa *see* Neisse
147 P4 **Nişab** Al Ḩudūd ash Shamālīyah, N Saudi Arabia
147 Q15 **Nişāb** *var.* Anşāb. SW Yemen
115 P14 **Nišava** *Bul.* Nishava. ≈ Bulgaria/Yugoslavia *see also* Nishava
109 K25 **Niscemi** Sicilia, Italy, C Mediterranean Sea
Nisch/Nish *see* Niš
172 Nn5 **Niseko** Hokkaidō, NE Japan
Nishapur *see* Neyshābūr
116 G9 **Nishava** *var.* Nišava. ≈ Bulgaria/Yugoslavia *see also* Nišava
120 L11 **Nishcha** *Rus.* Nishcha. ≈ N Belarus
172 Qq7 **Nishibetsu-gawa** ≈ Hokkaidō, NE Japan
170 E13 **Nishi-gawa** ≈ Honshū, SW Japan
170 Ee13 **Nishi-Nōmi-jima** *var.* Nōmi-jima. *island* SW Japan
170 Bb17 **Nishinoomote** Kagoshima, Tanega-shima, SW Japan
172 Ss16 **Nishino-shima** *Eng.* Rosario. *island* Ogasawara-shotō, SE Japan
171 Hh16 **Nishio** *var.* Nisio. Aichi, Honshū, SW Japan
170 C13 **Nishi-Sonogi-hantō** *peninsula* Kyūshū, SW Japan
171 Gg14 **Nishiwaki** *var.* Nisiwaki. Hyōgo, Honshū, SW Japan
147 U14 **Nishtūn** SE Yemen
Nisiros *see* Nísyros
Nisiwaki *see* Nishiwaki
Niska *see* Niesky
115 O14 **Niška Banja** Serbia, SE Yugoslavia
10 D6 **Niskibi** ≈ Ontario, C Canada
113 O15 **Nisko** Tarnobrzeg, SE Poland
8 H7 **Nisling** ≈ Yukon Territory, W Canada
101 H22 **Nismes** Namur, S Belgium
Nismes *see* Nîmes
118 M10 **Nisporeni** *Rus.* Nisporeny. W Moldova
Nisporeny *see* Nisporeni
97 K20 **Nissan** ≈ S Sweden
195 R11 **Nissan Island** *island* Green Islands, NE PNG
Nissan Islands *see* Green Islands
97 F16 **Nisser** ⊚ S Norway
97 E21 **Nissum Bredning** *inlet* NW Denmark
31 U6 **Nisswa** Minnesota, N USA
Nistru *see* Dniester
117 M22 **Nísyros** *var.* Nisiros. *island* Dodekánisos, Greece, Aegean Sea
120 H8 **Nītaure** Cēsis, C Latvia
62 P10 **Niterói** *prev.* Nictheroy. Rio de Janeiro, SE Brazil
12 F16 **Nith** ≈ Ontario, S Canada
98 J13 **Nith** ≈ S Scotland, UK
Nitinan *see* Nichinan
113 I21 **Nitra** *Ger.* Neutra, *Hung.* Nyitra. Západné Slovensko, SW Slovakia
113 I20 **Nitra** *Ger.* Neutra, *Hung.* Nyitra. ≈ W Slovakia
23 Q5 **Nitro** West Virginia, NE USA
125 F11 **Nitsa** ≈ C Russian Federation
97 H14 **Nittedal** Akershus, S Norway
Niuatobutabu *see* Niuatoputapu
200 S11 **Niuatoputapu** *var.* Niuatobutabu; *prev.* Keppel Island. *island* N Tonga
200 Q15 **Niu'Aunofa** *headland* Tongatapu, S Tonga
Niuchwang *see* Yingkou
202 B16 **Niue** ◇ *self-governing territory in free association with NZ* S Pacific Ocean
202 F10 **Niulakita** *var.* Nurakita. *atoll* S Tuvalu
202 E6 **Niutao** *atoll* NW Tuvalu
95 L15 **Nivala** Oulu, C Finland
104 J15 **Nive** ≈ SW France
101 G19 **Nivelles** Walloon Brabant, C Belgium
105 P8 **Nivernais** *cultural region* C France
13 N8 **Niverville, Lac** ⊚ Québec, SE Canada
29 T7 **Nixa** Missouri, C USA
37 R5 **Nixon** Nevada, W USA
27 S12 **Nixon** Texas, SW USA
Niya *see* Minfeng
152 K12 **Niyazov** Lebapskiy Velayat, NE Turkmenistan
161 H14 **Nizāmābād** Andhra Pradesh, C India
161 H15 **Nizām Sāgar** ⊚ C India
129 N16 **Nizhegorodskaya Oblast'** ◈ *province* W Russian Federation
126 K14 **Nizhneangarsk** Respublika Buryatiya, S Russian Federation
Nizhnegorskiy *see* Nyzhn'ohirs'kyy
131 S4 **Nizhnekamsk** Respublika Tatarstan, W Russian Federation
131 U3 **Nizhnekamskoye Vodokhranilishche** ⊠ W Russian Federation
127 O5 **Nizhnekolymsk** Respublika Sakha (Yakutiya), NE Russian Federation
127 N16 **Nizhne Leninskoye** Yevreyskaya Avtonomnaya Oblast', SE Russian Federation
126 Ii14 **Nizhneudinsk** Irkutskaya Oblast', S Russian Federation
126 Gg11 **Nizhnevartovsk** Khanty-Mansiyskiy Avtonomnyy Okrug, C Russian Federation
126 Ll6 **Nizhneyansk** Respublika Sakha (Yakutiya), NE Russian Federation
131 Q11 **Nizhniy Baskunchak** Astrakhanskaya Oblast', SW Russian Federation
126 M11 **Nizhniy Bestyakh** Respublika Sakha (Yakutiya), NE Russian Federation
131 O6 **Nizhniy Lomov** Penzenskaya Oblast', W Russian Federation
131 P3 **Nizhniy Novgorod** *prev.* Gor'kiy. Nizhegorodskaya Oblast', W Russian Federation
129 T8 **Nizhniy Odes** Respublika Komi, NW Russian Federation
Nizhniy Pyandzh *see* Panji Poyon
125 Ee11 **Nizhniy Tagil** Sverdlovskaya Oblast', C Russian Federation
129 T9 **Nizhnyaya-Omra** Respublika Komi, NW Russian Federation
129 P5 **Nizhnyaya Pesha** Nenetskiy Avtonomnyy Okrug, NW Russian Federation
125 F11 **Nizhnyaya Tavda** Tyumenskaya Oblast', C Russian Federation
126 Jj12 **Nizhnyaya Tunguska** *Eng.* Lower Tunguska. ≈ N Russian Federation
119 Q3 **Nizhyn** *Rus.* Nezhin. Chernihivs'ka Oblast', NE Ukraine
142 M17 **Nizip** Gaziantep, S Turkey
147 X8 **Nizwá** *var.* Nazwāh. NE Oman
Nizza *see* Nice
108 C9 **Nizza Monferrato** Piemonte, NE Italy
Njávdám *see* Näätämöjoki
Njellim *see* Nellim
83 H24 **Njombe** Iringa, S Tanzania
83 G23 **Njombe** ≈ C Tanzania
94 I10 **Njunis** ▲ N Norway
95 H17 **Njurunda** Västernorrland, C Sweden
96 N11 **Njutånger** Gävleborg, C Sweden
81 D14 **Nkambe** Nord-Ouest, NW Cameroon
Nkata Bay *see* Nkhata Bay
81 F21 **Nkayi** *prev.* Jacob. La Bouenza, S Congo
85 J17 **Nkayi** Matabeleland North, W Zimbabwe
84 N13 **Nkhata Bay** *var.* Nkata Bay. Northern, N Malawi
83 E22 **Nkonde** Kigoma, N Tanzania
81 D15 **Nkongsamba** *var.* N'Kongsamba. Littoral, W Cameroon
85 E16 **Nkurenkuru** Okavango, N Namibia
79 Q15 **Nkwanta** E Ghana
178 H1 **Nmai Hka** *var.* Me Hka. ≈ N Myanmar
Noardwâlde *see* Noordwolde
41 N7 **Noatak** Alaska, USA
41 N7 **Noatak River** ≈ Alaska, USA
Nobeji *see* Noheji
170 D15 **Nobeoka** Miyazaki, Kyūshū, SW Japan
29 N11 **Noble** Oklahoma, C USA
33 P13 **Noblesville** Indiana, N USA
172 O6 **Noboribetsu** *var.* Noboribetu. Hokkaidō, NE Japan
Noboribetu *see* Noboribetsu
61 H18 **Nobres** Mato Grosso, W Brazil
109 N21 **Nocera Terinese** Calabria, S Italy
43 Q16 **Nochixtlán** *var.* Asunción Nochixtlán. Oaxaca, SE Mexico
27 S5 **Nocona** Texas, SW USA
65 K21 **Nodales, Bahía de los** *bay* S Argentina
29 Q2 **Nodaway River** ≈ Iowa/Missouri, C USA
29 R8 **Noel** Missouri, C USA
97 C17 **Nærbø** Rogaland, S Norway
97 I24 **Næstved** Storstrøm, SE Denmark
42 H3 **Nogales** Chihuahua, NW Mexico
42 F3 **Nogales** Sonora, NW Mexico
38 M17 **Nogales** Arizona, SW USA
Nogal Valley *see* Dooxo Nugaaleed
104 K15 **Nogaro** Gers, S France
112 J7 **Nogat** ≈ N Poland
170 D12 **Nōgata** Fukuoka, Kyūshū, SW Japan
131 P15 **Nogayskaya Step'** *steppe* SW Russian Federation
104 M6 **Nogent-le-Rotrou** Eure-et-Loir, C France
105 O4 **Nogent-sur-Oise** Oise, N France
105 P6 **Nogent-sur-Seine** Aube, N France
126 I10 **Noginsk** Evenkiyskiy Avtonomnyy Okrug, N Russian Federation
130 L3 **Noginsk** Moskovskaya Oblast', W Russian Federation
127 O14 **Nogliki** Ostrov Sakhalin, Sakhalinskaya Oblast', SE Russian Federation
171 I14 **Nōgōhaku-san** ▲ Honshū, SW Japan
168 D5 **Nogoonnuur** Bayan-Ölgiy, NW Mongolia
63 C18 **Nogoyá** Entre Ríos, E Argentina
113 K21 **Nógrád** *off.* Nógrád Megye. ◈ *county* N Hungary
107 U5 **Noguera Pallaresa** ≈ NE Spain
107 U4 **Noguera Ribagorçana** ≈ NE Spain
172 N9 **Noheji** *var.* Nobeji. Aomori, Honshū, C Japan
103 E19 **Nohfelden** Saarland, SW Germany
40 A8 **Nohili Point** *headland* Kauai, Hawaii, USA, C Pacific Ocean
106 G3 **Noia** Galicia, NW Spain
105 N16 **Noire, Montagne** ▲▲ S France
13 P12 **Noire, Rivière** ≈ Québec, SE Canada
12 J10 **Noire, Rivière** ≈ Québec, SE Canada
Noire, Rivière *see* Black River
104 G6 **Noires, Montagnes** ▲▲ NW France
104 H8 **Noirmoutier-en-l'Île** Vendée, NW France
104 H8 **Noirmoutier, Île de** *island* NW France
171 Jj17 **Nojima-zaki** *headland* Honshū, S Japan
195 W8 **Noka** Nendō, E Solomon Islands
85 G17 **Nokaneng** Ngamiland, NW Botswana
95 L18 **Nokia** Häme, SW Finland
154 K11 **Nok Kundi** Baluchistān, SW Pakistan
32 L14 **Nokomis** Illinois, N USA
32 K5 **Nokomis, Lake** ⊚ Wisconsin, N USA
80 G9 **Nokou** Kanem, W Chad
197 B12 **Nokuku** Espiritu Santo, W Vanuatu
97 J18 **Nol** Älvsborg, S Sweden
81 H16 **Nola** Sangha-Mbaéré, SW Central African Republic
27 P7 **Nolan** Texas, SW USA
129 R15 **Nolinsk** Kirovskaya Oblast', NW Russian Federation
194 F12 **Nomad** Western, SW Papau New Guinea
170 B15 **Noma-zaki** *headland* Kyūshū, SW Japan
42 K10 **Nombre de Dios** Durango, C Mexico
44 J5 **Nombre de Dios, Cordillera** ▲▲ N Honduras
40 M9 **Nome** Alaska, USA
31 Q6 **Nome** North Dakota, N USA
40 M9 **Nome, Cape** *headland* Alaska, USA
Nōmi-jima *see* Nishi-Nōmi-jima
12 M11 **Nominingue, Lac** ⊚ Québec, SE Canada
Nomoi Islands *see* Mortlock Islands
170 Bb13 **Nomo-zaki** *headland* Kyūshū, SW Japan
200 S13 **Nomuka** *island* Nomuka Group, C Tonga
200 S14 **Nomuka Group** *island group* W Tonga
201 Q15 **Nomwin Atoll** *atoll* Hall Islands, C Micronesia
15 I8 **Nonacho Lake** ⊚ Northwest Territories, NW Canada
Nondaburi *see* Nonthaburi
41 P12 **Nondalton** Alaska, USA
169 V10 **Nong'an** Jilin, NE China
178 I10 **Nong Bua Khok** Nakhon Ratchasima, C Thailand
178 I9 **Nong Bua Lamphu** Udon Thani, E Thailand
178 J7 **Nông Hèt** Xiangkhoang, N Laos
Nongkaya *see* Nong Khai
178 I8 **Nong Khai** *var.* Mi Chai, Nongkaya. Nong Khai, E Thailand
178 Gg15 **Nong Met** Surat Thani, SW Thailand
85 L22 **Nongoma** KwaZulu/Natal, E South Africa
178 Hh10 **Nong Phai** Phetchabun, C Thailand
159 U13 **Nongstoin** Meghālaya, NE India
85 C19 **Nonidas** Erongo, N Namibia
Nonni *see* Nen Jiang
42 I7 **Nonoava** Chihuahua, N Mexico
203 O3 **Nonouti** *prev.* Sydenham Island. *atoll* Tungaru, W Kiribati
178 Hh11 **Nonthaburi** *var.* Nondaburi, Nontha Buri. Nonthaburi, C Thailand
104 L11 **Nontron** Dordogne, SW France
189 P1 **Noonamah** Northern Territory, N Australia
30 K2 **Noonan** North Dakota, N USA
101 E14 **Noord-Beveland** *var.* North Beveland. *island* SW Netherlands
101 J14 **Noord-Brabant** *Eng.* North Brabant. ◈ *province* S Netherlands
100 H7 **Noorder Haaks** *spit* NW Netherlands
100 H9 **Noord-Holland** *Eng.* North Holland. ◈ *province* NW Netherlands
Noordhollandsch Kanaal *see* Noordhollands Kanaal
100 H8 **Noordhollands Kanaal** *var.* Noordhollandsch Kanaal. *canal* NW Netherlands
Noord-Kaap *see* Northern Cape
100 L8 **Noordoostpolder** *island* N Netherlands
47 P16 **Noordpunt** *headland* Curaçao, C Netherlands Antilles
100 I8 **Noord-Scharwoude** Noord-Holland, NW Netherlands
Noordwes *see* North-West
100 G11 **Noordwijk aan Zee** Zuid-Holland, W Netherlands
100 H11 **Noordwijkerhout** Zuid-Holland, W Netherlands
100 M7 **Noordwolde** *Fris.* Noardwâlde. Friesland, N Netherlands
Noordzee *see* North Sea
100 H10 **Noordzee-Kanaal** *canal* NW Netherlands
95 K18 **Noormarkku** *Swe.* Norrmark. Turku-Pori, SW Finland
41 N8 **Noorvik** Alaska, USA
8 J17 **Nootka Sound** *inlet* British Columbia, W Canada
84 A9 **Nóqui** Zaire, NW Angola
97 L15 **Nora** Örebro, C Sweden
153 Q13 **Norak** *Rus.* Nurek. W Tajikistan
16 P14 **Noranda** Québec, SE Canada
31 W12 **Nora Springs** Iowa, C USA
97 M14 **Norberg** Västmanland, C Sweden
12 K13 **Norcan Lake** ⊚ Ontario, SE Canada
207 R12 **Nord** N Greenland
80 F13 **Nord** *Eng.* North. ◈ *province* N Cameroon
105 P2 **Nord** ◈ *department* N France
94 P1 **Nordaustlandet** *island* NE Svalbard
97 G24 **Nordborg** *Ger.* Nordburg. Sønderjylland, SW Denmark
Nordburg *see* Nordborg
97 F23 **Nordby** Ribe, W Denmark
9 P15 **Nordegg** Alberta, SW Canada
102 E9 **Norden** Niedersachsen, NW Germany
102 G10 **Nordenham** Niedersachsen, NW Germany
126 Ii4 **Nordenshel'da, Arkhipelag** *island group* N Russian Federation
94 O3 **Nordenskiold Land** *physical region* W Svalbard
102 E9 **Norderney** *island* NW Germany
102 J9 **Norderstedt** Schleswig-Holstein, N Germany
96 C11 **Nordfjord** *physical region* S Norway
96 D11 **Nordfjord** *fjord* S Norway
96 D11 **Nordfjordeid** Sogn og Fjordane, S Norway
94 G11 **Nordfold** Nordland, C Norway
Nordfriesische Inseln *see* North Frisian Islands
102 H7 **Nordfriesland** *cultural region* N Germany
103 K15 **Nordhausen** Thüringen, C Germany
27 T13 **Nordheim** Texas, SW USA
96 C13 **Nordhordland** *physical region* S Norway
102 E12 **Nordhorn** Niedersachsen, NW Germany
94 I1 **Nordhurfjördhur** Vestfirdhir, NW Iceland
94 J1 **Nordhurland Eystra** ◈ *region* N Iceland
94 I2 **Nordhurland Vestra** ◈ *region* N Iceland
180 H16 **Nord, Île du** *island* Inner Islands, NE Seychelles
97 F20 **Nordjylland** *off.* Nordjyllands Amt. ◈ *county* N Denmark
94 K7 **Nordkapp** *Eng.* North Cape. *headland* N Norway
94 O1 **Nordkapp** *headland* N Svalbard
94 L7 **Nordkinn** *headland* N Norway
81 N19 **Nord Kivu** *off.* Région du Nord Kivu. ◈ *region* E Zaire
94 G12 **Nordland** ◈ *county* C Norway
103 J21 **Nördlingen** Bayern, S Germany
95 I16 **Nordmaling** Västerbotten, N Sweden
97 K15 **Nordmark** Värmland, C Sweden
Nord, Mer du *see* North Sea
96 F8 **Nordmøre** *physical region* S Norway
102 I8 **Nord-Ostee-Kanal** *canal* N Germany
1 J3 **Nordostrundingen** *headland* NE Greenland
81 D14 **Nord-Ouest** *Eng.* North-West. ◈ *province* NW Cameroon
Nord-Ouest, Territoires du *see* Northwest Territories
105 N2 **Nord-Pas-de-Calais** ◈ *region* N France
103 F19 **Nordpfälzer Bergland** ▲▲ W Germany
Nord, Pointe *see* Fatua, Pointe
197 H5 **Nord, Province** ◈ *province* C New Caledonia
94 J9 **Nordreisa** Troms, N Norway
103 D14 **Nordrhein-Westfalen** *Eng.* North Rhine-Westphalia, *Fr.* Rhénanie du Nord-Westphalie. ◈ *state* W Germany
Nordsee/Nordsjøen/Nordsøen *see* North Sea
102 H7 **Nordstrand** *island* N Germany
95 E15 **Nord-Trøndelag** ◈ *county* C Norway
99 E19 **Nore** *Ir.* An Fheoir. ≈ S Ireland
31 Q14 **Norfolk** Nebraska, C USA
23 X7 **Norfolk** Virginia, NE USA
99 P19 **Norfolk** *cultural region* E England, UK
199 Ii11 **Norfolk Island** ◇ *Australian external territory* SW Pacific Ocean
183 P9 **Norfolk Ridge** *undersea feature* W Pacific Ocean
29 U8 **Norfork Lake** ⊠ Arkansas/Missouri, C USA
100 N6 **Norg** Drenthe, NE Netherlands
Norge *see* Norway
97 D14 **Norheimsund** Hordaland, S Norway
27 S16 **Norias** Texas, SW USA
171 J14 **Norikura-dake** ▲ Honshū, S Japan
126 I8 **Noril'sk** Taymyrskiy (Dolgano-Nenetskiy) Avtonomnyy Okrug, N Russian Federation
12 I13 **Norland** Ontario, SE Canada
23 V8 **Norlina** North Carolina, SE USA
32 L13 **Normal** Illinois, N USA
29 N11 **Norman** Oklahoma, C USA
Norman *see* Fort Norman
195 O16 **Normanby Island** *island* SE PNG
Normandes, Îles *see* Channel Islands
60 G9 **Normandia** Roraima, N Brazil
104 L5 **Normandie** *Eng.* Normandy. *cultural region* N France
104 J5 **Normandie, Collines de** *hill range* NW France
Normandy *see* Normandie
27 V9 **Normangee** Texas, SW USA
23 Q10 **Norman, Lake** ⊠ North Carolina, SE USA
46 K13 **Norman Manley** ✕ (Kingston) E Jamaica
189 U5 **Norman River** ≈ Queensland, NE Australia
189 U4 **Normanton** Queensland, NE Australia
15 Gg5 **Norman Wells** Northwest Territories, NW Canada
10 H12 **Normétal** Québec, S Canada
9 V15 **Norquay** Saskatchewan, S Canada
96 N11 **Norra Dellen** ⊚ C Sweden
Norra Karelen *see* Pohjois-Karjala
95 G15 **Norråker** Jämtland, C Sweden
96 N12 **Norrala** Gävleborg, C Sweden
Norra Ny *see* Stöllet
94 G13 **Norra Storfjället** ▲ N Sweden
94 I13 **Norrbotten** ◈ *county* N Sweden
Nørre Aaby *see* Nørre Åby
97 G23 **Nørre Åby** *var.* Nørre Aaby. Fyn, C Denmark
97 I24 **Nørre Alslev** Storstrøm, SE Denmark
97 E23 **Nørre Nebel** Ribe, W Denmark
97 G20 **Nørresundby** Nordjylland, N Denmark
23 N8 **Norris Lake** ⊠ Tennessee, S USA
20 I15 **Norristown** Pennsylvania, NE USA
97 N17 **Norrköping** Östergötland, S Sweden
Norrmark *see* Noormarkku
96 N13 **Norrsundet** Gävleborg, C Sweden
97 P15 **Norrtälje** Stockholm, C Sweden
188 L12 **Norseman** Western Australia
95 I14 **Norsjö** Västerbotten, N Sweden
97 G16 **Norsjø** ⊚ S Norway
126 Mm15 **Norsk** Amurskaya Oblast', SE Russian Federation
Norske Havet *see* Norwegian Sea
197 C13 **Norsup** Malekula, C Vanuatu
203 V15 **Norte, Cabo** *headland* Easter Island, Chile, E Pacific Ocean
56 F7 **Norte de Santander** *off.* Departamento de Norte de Santander. ◈ *province* N Colombia
63 E21 **Norte, Punta** *headland* E Argentina
23 R13 **North** South Carolina, SE USA
North *see* Nord
20 L10 **North Adams** Massachusetts, NE USA
115 L17 **North Albanian Alps** *Alb.* Bjeshkët e Namuna, *SCr.* Prokletije. ▲▲ Albania/Yugoslavia
99 M15 **Northallerton** N England, UK
188 J12 **Northam** Western Australia
85 J20 **Northam** Northern, N South Africa
1 **North America** *continent*
1 N12 **North American Basin** *undersea feature* W Sargasso Sea
1 C5 **North American Plate** *tectonic feature*
20 M11 **North Amherst** Massachusetts, NE USA
99 N20 **Northampton** C England, UK
99 M20 **Northamptonshire** *cultural region* C England, UK
157 P18 **North Andaman** *island* Andaman Islands, India, NE Indian Ocean
67 D25 **North Arm** East Falkland, Falkland Islands
23 Q13 **North Augusta** South Carolina, SE USA
181 W8 **North Australian Basin** *Fr.* Bassin Nord de l' Australie. *undersea feature* E Indian Ocean
33 R11 **North Baltimore** Ohio, N USA
9 T15 **North Battleford** Saskatchewan, S Canada
12 H11 **North Bay** Ontario, S Canada
10 H6 **North Belcher Islands** *island group* Belcher Islands, Northwest Territories, C Canada
31 R15 **North Bend** Nebraska, C USA
34 E14 **North Bend** Oregon, NW USA
98 K12 **North Berwick** SE Scotland, UK
North Beveland *see* Noord-Beveland
North Borneo *see* Sabah
191 P5 **North Bourke** New South Wales, SE Australia
North Brabant *see* Noord-Brabant
190 F2 **North Branch Neales** *seasonal river* South Australia
46 M6 **North Caicos** *island* NW Turks and Caicos Islands
28 L10 **North Canadian River** ≈ Oklahoma, C USA
33 U12 **North Canton** Ohio, N USA
11 R13 **North, Cape** *headland* Cape Breton Island, Nova Scotia, SE Canada
192 I1 **North Cape** *headland* North Island, NZ
195 N9 **North Cape** *headland* New Ireland, NE PNG
North Cape *see* Nordkapp
20 J17 **North Cape May** New Jersey, NE USA
10 C9 **North Caribou Lake** ⊚ Ontario, C Canada
23 U10 **North Carolina** *off.* State of North Carolina; *also known as* Old North State, Tar Heel State, Turpentine State. ◈ *state* SE USA
North Celebes *see* Sulawesi Utara
161 J24 **North Central Province** ◈ *province* N Sri Lanka
33 S4 **North Channel** *lake channel* Canada/USA
99 G14 **North Channel** *strait* Northern Ireland/Scotland, UK
23 S14 **North Charleston** South Carolina, SE USA
33 N10 **North Chicago** Illinois, N USA
205 Y10 **Northcliffe Glacier** *glacier* Antarctica
33 Q14 **North College Hill** Ohio, N USA
27 O8 **North Concho River** ≈ Texas, SW USA
21 O8 **North Conway** New Hampshire, NE USA
29 V14 **North Crossett** Arkansas, C USA
30 L4 **North Dakota** *off.* State of North Dakota; *also known as* Flickertail State, Peace Garden State, Sioux State. ◈ *state* N USA
North Devon Island *see* Devon Island
99 O22 **North Downs** *hill range* SE England, UK
20 C11 **North East** Pennsylvania, NE USA
85 I18 **North East** ◈ *district* NE Botswana
67 G15 **North East Bay** *bay* Ascension Island, C Atlantic Ocean
40 L10 **Northeast Cape** *headland* Saint Lawrence Island, Alaska, USA
178 Mm13 **Northeast Cay** *island* NW Spratly Islands
83 J17 **North Eastern** ◈ *province* Kenya
North East Frontier Agency/North East Frontier Agency of Assam *see* Arunāchal Pradesh
67 E25 **North East Island** *island* E Falkland Islands
201 V11 **Northeast Island** *island* Chuuk, C Micronesia
46 L12 **North East Point** *headland* E Jamaica
46 L6 **Northeast Point** *headland* Great Inagua, S Bahamas
46 K5 **Northeast Point** *headland* Acklins Island, SE Bahamas
203 Z2 **Northeast Point** *headland* Kiritimati, E Kiribati
46 H2 **Northeast Providence Channel** *channel* N Bahamas
103 J14 **Northeim** Niedersachsen, C Germany
31 X14 **North English** Iowa, C USA
144 G8 **Northern** ◈ *district* N Israel
84 M12 **Northern** ◈ *region* N Malawi
194 L15 **Northern** ◈ *province* S PNG
85 J20 **Northern** *off.* Northern Province; *prev.* Northern Transvaal. ◈ *province* NE South Africa
82 D7 **Northern** ◈ *state* N Sudan
84 K12 **Northern** ◈ *province* NE Zambia
82 B13 **Northern Bahr el Ghazal** ◈ *state* SW Sudan
Northern Border Region *see* Al Ḩudūd ash Shamālīyah
85 F24 **Northern Cape** *off.* Northern Cape Province, *Afr.* Noord-Kaap. ◈ *province* W South Africa
202 K14 **Northern Cook Islands** *island group* N Cook Islands
82 B8 **Northern Darfur** ◈ *state* NW Sudan
Northern Dvina *see* Severnaya Dvina
99 F14 **Northern Ireland** *var.* The Six Counties. *political division* UK
82 D9 **Northern Kordofan** ◈ *state* C Sudan
197 K14 **Northern Lau Group** *island group* Lau Group, NE Fiji
196 K3 **Northern Mariana Islands** ◇ *US commonwealth territory* W Pacific Ocean
161 J23 **Northern Province** ◈ *province* N Sri Lanka
Northern Rhodesia *see* Zambia
Northern Sporades *see* Vóreioi Sporádes
190 D1 **Northern Territory** ◈ *territory* N Australia
Northern Transvaal *see* Northern
Northern Ural Hills *see* Severnyye Uvaly
86 I9 **North European Plain** *plain* N Europe
29 V2 **North Fabius River** ≈ Missouri, C USA
67 D24 **North Falkland Sound** *sound* N Falkland Islands
31 V9 **Northfield** Minnesota, N USA
21 O9 **Northfield** New Hampshire, NE USA
183 Q8 **North Fiji Basin** *undersea feature* N Coral Sea
99 Q22 **North Foreland** *headland* SE England, UK
37 P6 **North Fork American River** ≈ California, W USA
41 R7 **North Fork Chandalar River** ≈ Alaska, USA
30 K7 **North Fork Grand River** ≈ North Dakota/South Dakota, N USA
23 O6 **North Fork Kentucky River** ≈ Kentucky, S USA
41 Q7 **North Fork Koyukuk River** ≈ Alaska, USA
41 Q10 **North Fork Kuskokwim River** ≈ Alaska, USA
28 K11 **North Fork Red River** ≈ Oklahoma/Texas, SW USA
28 K3 **North Fork Solomon River** ≈ Kansas, C USA
25 W14 **North Fort Myers** Florida, SE USA
33 P5 **North Fox Island** *island* Michigan, N USA
102 G6 **North Frisian Islands** *var.* Nordfriesische Inseln. *island group* N Germany
207 N9 **North Geomagnetic Pole** *pole* Arctic Ocean
20 M13 **North Haven** Connecticut, NE USA
192 J5 **North Head** *headland* North Island, NZ
20 L6 **North Hero** Vermont, NE USA
37 O7 **North Highlands** California, W USA
North Holland *see* Noord-Holland
83 I16 **North Horr** Eastern, N Kenya
157 K21 **North Huvadhu Atoll** *var.* Gaafu Alifu Atoll. *atoll* S Maldives
67 A24 **North Island** *island* W Falkland Islands
192 N9 **North Island** *island* N NZ
23 U14 **North Island** *island* South Carolina, SE USA
33 O11 **North Judson** Indiana, N USA
North Kazakhstan *see* Severnyy Kazakhstan
33 V10 **North Kingsville** Ohio, N USA
169 Y13 **North Korea** *off.* Democratic People's Republic of Korea, *Kor.* Chosŏn-minjujuŭi-inmin-kanghwaguk. ◆ *republic* E Asia
159 X11 **North Lakhimpur** Assam, NE India
192 J3 **Northland** *off.* Northland Region. ◈ *region* North Island, NZ
199 J12 **Northland Plateau** *undersea feature* S Pacific Ocean
37 X11 **North Las Vegas** Nevada, W USA
33 O11 **North Liberty** Indiana, N USA
31 X14 **North Liberty** Iowa, C USA
29 V12 **North Little Rock** Arkansas, C USA
30 M13 **North Loup River** ≈ Nebraska, C USA
157 K18 **North Maalhosmadulu Atoll** *var.* North Malosmadulu Atoll, Raa Atoll. *atoll* N Maldives
33 U10 **North Madison** Ohio, N USA
33 P12 **North Manchester** Indiana, N USA
33 P6 **North Manitou Island** *island* Michigan, N USA
31 U10 **North Mankato** Minnesota, N USA
25 Z15 **North Miami** Florida, SE USA
157 K18 **North Miladummadulu Atoll** *atoll* N Maldives
North Minch *see* Minch, The
25 W15 **North Naples** Florida, SE USA
183 P8 **North New Hebrides Trench** *undersea feature* N Coral Sea
25 Y15 **North New River Canal** ≈ Florida, SE USA
157 K20 **North Nilandhe Atoll** *var.* Faafu Atoll. *atoll* C Maldives
38 L2 **North Ogden** Utah, W USA
North Ossetia *see* Severnaya Osetiya, Respublika
37 S10 **North Palisade** ▲ California, W USA
201 U11 **North Pass** *passage* Chuuk Islands, C Micronesia
30 M15 **North Platte** Nebraska, C USA
35 X17 **North Platte River** ≈ C USA
67 G14 **North Point** *headland* Ascension Island, C Atlantic Ocean
180 I16 **North Point** *headland* Mahé, NE Seychelles
33 S6 **North Point** *headland* Michigan, N USA
33 R5 **North Point** *headland* Michigan, N USA
41 S9 **North Pole** Alaska, USA
207 R9 **North Pole** *pole* Arctic Ocean
25 O4 **Northport** Alabama, S USA
25 W14 **North Port** Florida, SE USA
34 L6 **Northport** Washington, NW USA
34 L12 **North Powder** Oregon, NW USA
31 U13 **North Raccoon River** ≈ Iowa, C USA

◆ Country ● Country Capital ◇ Dependent Territory ○ Dependent Territory Capital ◈ Administrative Region ✕ International Airport ▲ Mountain ▲▲ Mountain Range Volcano ≈ River ⊚ Lake ⊠ Reservoir

NORTH RHINE-WESTPHALIA – NUSHKI

North Rhine-Westphalia *see* Nordrhein-Westfalen
99 M16 **North Riding** *cultural region* N England, UK
98 G5 **North Rona** *island* NW Scotland, UK
98 K4 **North Ronaldsay** *island* NE Scotland, UK
38 L2 **North Salt Lake** Utah, W USA
9 P15 **North Saskatchewan** Alberta/Saskatchewan, S Canada
37 X5 **North Schell Peak** ▲ Nevada, W USA
North Scotia Ridge *see* South Georgia Ridge
88 D10 **North Sea** *Dan.* Nordsøen, *Dut.* Noordzee, *Fr.* Mer du Nord, *Ger.* Nordsee, *Nor.* Nordsjøen; *prev.* German Ocean, *Lat.* Mare Germanicum. *sea* NW Europe
37 T6 **North Shoshone Peak** ▲ Nevada, W USA
North Siberian Lowland/North Siberian Plain *see* Severo-Sibirskaya Nizmennost'
31 R13 **North Sioux City** South Dakota, N USA
98 K4 **North Sound, The** *sound* N Scotland, UK
191 T4 **North Star** New South Wales, SE Australia
North Star State *see* Minnesota
191 V3 **North Stradbroke Island** *island* Queensland, E Australia
North Sulawesi *see* Sulawesi Utara
North Sumatra *see* Sumatera Utara
12 D17 **North Sydenham** Ontario, S Canada
20 H9 **North Syracuse** New York, NE USA
192 K9 **North Taranaki Bight** *gulf* North Island, NZ
202 I2 **North Tarawa** *atoll* Tungaru, W Kiribati
10 H9 **North Twin Island** *island* Northwest Territories, C Canada
98 E8 **North Uist** *island* NW Scotland, UK
99 L14 **Northumberland** *cultural region* N England, UK
189 Y7 **Northumberland Isles** *island group* Queensland, NE Australia
11 Q14 **Northumberland Strait** *strait* SE Canada
34 G14 **North Umpqua River** Oregon, NW USA
47 Q13 **North Union** Saint Vincent, Saint Vincent and the Grenadines
8 L17 **North Vancouver** British Columbia, SW Canada
20 K9 **Northville** New York, NE USA
99 Q19 **North Walsham** E England, UK
41 T10 **Northway** Alaska, USA
85 G21 **North-West** *off.* North-West Province, *Afr.* Noordwes. ◐ *province* N South Africa
North-West *see* Nord-Ouest
66 I6 **Northwest Atlantic Mid-Ocean Canyon** *undersea feature* N Atlantic Ocean
188 G8 **North West Cape** *headland* Western Australia
40 J9 **Northwest Cape** *headland* Saint Lawrence Island, Alaska, USA
84 H13 **North Western** ◐ *province* W Zambia
161 J24 **North Western Province** ◐ *province* W Sri Lanka
155 U4 **North-West Frontier Province** ◐ *province* NW Pakistan
98 H8 **North West Highlands** ▲ N Scotland, UK
199 Hh4 **Northwest Pacific Basin** *undersea feature* NW Pacific Ocean
203 Y2 **Northwest Point** *headland* Kiritimati, E Kiribati
46 G1 **Northwest Providence Channel** *channel* N Bahamas
11 Q8 **North West River** Newfoundland and Labrador, E Canada
15 I15 **Northwest Territories** *Fr.* Territoires du Nord-Ouest. ◐ *territory* NW Canada
99 K18 **Northwich** C England, UK
27 Q5 **North Wichita River** Texas, SW USA
20 J17 **North Wildwood** New Jersey, NE USA
23 R9 **North Wilkesboro** North Carolina, SE USA
21 P8 **North Windham** Maine, NE USA
207 Q6 **Northwind Plain** *undersea feature* Arctic Ocean
31 V11 **Northwood** Iowa, C USA
31 Q4 **Northwood** North Dakota, N USA
99 M15 **North York Moors** *moorland* N England, UK
27 V9 **North Zulch** Texas, SW USA
28 K2 **Norton** Kansas, C USA
33 S13 **Norton** Ohio, N USA
23 P7 **Norton** Virginia, NE USA
41 N9 **Norton Bay** *bay* Alaska, USA
Norton de Matos *see* Balombo
33 O9 **Norton Shores** Michigan, N USA
40 M10 **Norton Sound** *inlet* Alaska, USA
29 Q3 **Nortonville** Kansas, C USA
104 I8 **Nort-sur-Erdre** Loire-Atlantique, NW France
205 N2 **Norvegia, Cape** *headland* Antarctica
20 L13 **Norwalk** Connecticut, NE USA
31 V14 **Norwalk** Iowa, C USA
33 S11 **Norwalk** Ohio, N USA
21 P7 **Norway** Maine, NE USA
33 N5 **Norway** Michigan, N USA
95 E17 **Norway** *off.* Kingdom of Norway, *Nor.* Norge. ◆ *monarchy* N Europe
9 X13 **Norway House** Manitoba, C Canada
207 R16 **Norwegian Basin** *undersea feature* NW Norwegian Sea
86 D6 **Norwegian Sea** *Nor.* Norske Havet. *sea* NE Atlantic Ocean
207 S17 **Norwegian Trench** *undersea feature* NE North Sea
12 F16 **Norwich** Ontario, S Canada
99 Q19 **Norwich** E England, UK
21 N13 **Norwich** Connecticut, NE USA
20 I11 **Norwich** New York, NE USA
31 U9 **Norwood** Minnesota, N USA
33 Q15 **Norwood** Ohio, N USA
12 H11 **Nosbonsing, Lake** ◎ Ontario, S Canada
Nösen *see* Bistriţa
172 P1 **Noshappu-misaki** *headland* Hokkaidō, NE Japan
171 M9 **Noshiro** *var.* Nosiro; *prev.* Noshirominato. Akita, Honshū, C Japan
Noshirominato/Nosiro *see* Noshiro
119 Q3 **Nosivka** *Rus.* Nosovka. Chernihivs'ka Oblast', NE Ukraine
69 T14 **Nosop** *var.* Nossob, Nossop. Botswana/Namibia
129 S4 **Nosovaya** Nenetskiy Avtonomnyy Okrug, NW Russian Federation
Nosovka *see* Nosivka
149 V11 **Noşratābād** Sīstān va Balūchestān, E Iran
97 J18 **Nossebro** Skaraborg, S Sweden
98 K6 **Noss Head** *headland* N Scotland, UK
Nossi-Bé *see* Be, Nosy
85 E20 **Nossob** E Namibia
Nossob/Nossop *see* Nosop
180 J2 **Nosy Be** ✕ Antsiranana, N Madagascar
180 J6 **Nosy Varika** Fianarantsoa, SE Madagascar
12 L10 **Notawassi** Québec, SE Canada
12 M9 **Notawassi, Lac** ◎ Québec, SE Canada
38 J5 **Notch Peak** ▲ Utah, W USA
112 G10 **Noteć** *Ger.* Netze. NW Poland
Nótiες Sporádes *see* Dodekánisos
117 J22 **Nótion Aigaíon** *Eng.* Aegean South. ◐ *region* E Greece
117 H18 **Nótios Evvoïkós Kólpos** *gulf* E Greece
117 B16 **Nótio Stenó Kérkyras** *strait* W Greece
109 L25 **Noto** *anc.* Netum. Sicilia, Italy, C Mediterranean Sea
171 J12 **Noto** Ishikawa, Honshū, SW Japan
97 G15 **Notodden** Telemark, S Norway
109 L25 **Noto, Golfo di** *gulf* Sicilia, Italy, C Mediterranean Sea
171 J12 **Noto-hantō** *peninsula* Honshū, SW Japan
171 J12 **Noto-jima** *island* SW Japan
172 Qq5 **Notoro-ko** ◎ Hokkaidō, NE Japan
11 T11 **Notre Dame Bay** *bay* Newfoundland, Newfoundland and Labrador, E Canada
13 P6 **Notre-Dame-de-Lorette** Québec, SE Canada
12 L11 **Notre-Dame-de-Pontmain** Québec, SE Canada
13 T8 **Notre-Dame-du-Lac** Québec, SE Canada
13 Q6 **Notre-Dame-du-Rosaire** Québec, SE Canada
13 U8 **Notre-Dame, Monts** ▲ Québec, S Canada
79 R16 **Notsé** S Togo
172 R7 **Notsuke-suidō** *strait* Japan/Russian Federation
172 R7 **Notsuke-zaki** *headland* Hokkaidō, NE Japan
12 G14 **Nottawasaga** Ontario, S Canada
12 G14 **Nottawasaga Bay** *lake bay* Ontario, S Canada
10 I11 **Nottaway** Québec, SE Canada
25 S1 **Nottely Lake** ⊡ Georgia, SE USA
97 H16 **Nøtterøy** *island* S Norway
99 M19 **Nottingham** C England, UK
16 N5 **Nottingham Island** *island* Northwest Territories, NE Canada
99 N18 **Nottinghamshire** *cultural region* C England, UK
23 V7 **Nottoway** Virginia, NE USA
23 V7 **Nottoway River** Virginia, NE USA
78 G7 **Nouâdhibou** *prev.* Port-Étienne. Dakhlet Nouâdhibou, W Mauritania
78 G7 **Nouâdhibou** ✕ Dakhlet Nouâdhibou, W Mauritania
78 F7 **Nouâdhibou, Dakhlet** *prev.* Baie du Lévrier. *bay* W Mauritania
78 F7 **Nouâdhibou, Râs** *prev.* Cap Blanc. *headland* NW Mauritania
78 G9 **Nouakchott** ● (Mauritania) Nouakchott District, SW Mauritania
78 G9 **Nouakchott** ✕ Trarza, SW Mauritania
123 K13 **Noual, Sebkhet en** *var.* Sabkhat an Nawāl. *salt flat* C Tunisia
78 G8 **Nouâmghâr** *var.* Nouamrhar. Dakhlet Nouâdhibou, W Mauritania
Nouamrhar *see* Nouâmghâr
Nouă Sulița *see* Novoselytsya
197 I7 **Nouméa** ○ (New Caledonia) Province Sud, S New Caledonia
81 E15 **Noun** C Cameroon
79 N12 **Nouna** W Burkina
85 H24 **Noupoort** Northern Cape, C South Africa
Nouveau-Brunswick *see* New Brunswick
Nouveau-Comptoir *see* Wemindji
13 T4 **Nouvel, Lacs** ◎ Québec, SE Canada
13 W7 **Nouvelle** Québec, SE Canada
13 W7 **Nouvelle** Québec, SE Canada
Nouvelle-Calédonie *see* New Caledonia
Nouvelle Écosse *see* Nova Scotia
105 R3 **Nouzonville** Ardennes, N France
153 Q11 **Nov** *Rus.* Nau. NW Tajikistan
61 I21 **Nova Alvorada** Mato Grosso do Sul, SW Brazil
Novabad *see* Navobod
113 D19 **Nová Bystřice** *Ger.* Neubistritz. Jižní Čechy, S Czech Republic
118 H13 **Novaci** Gorj, SW Romania
Nova Civitas *see* Neustadt an der Weinstrasse
Novaesium *see* Neuss
62 H10 **Nova Esperança** Paraná, S Brazil
108 H11 **Novafeltria** Marche, C Italy
62 Q9 **Nova Friburgo** Rio de Janeiro, SE Brazil
84 D12 **Nova Gaia** *var.* Cambundi-Catembo. Malanje, NE Angola
111 S12 **Nova Gorica** W Slovenia
114 G10 **Nova Gradiška** *Ger.* Neugradisk, *Hung.* Újgradiska. Brod-Posavina, NE Croatia
62 K7 **Nova Granada** São Paulo, S Brazil
62 O10 **Nova Iguaçu** Rio de Janeiro, SE Brazil
119 S10 **Nova Kakhovka** *Rus.* Novaya Kakhovka. Khersons'ka Oblast', SE Ukraine
Nová Karvinná *see* Karviná
Nova Lamego *see* Gabú
Nova Lisboa *see* Huambo
114 C11 **Novalja** Lika-Senj, W Croatia
121 M14 **Novalukoml'** *Rus.* Novolukoml'. Vitsyebskaya Voblasts', N Belarus
Nova Mambone *see* Mambone
85 P16 **Nova Nabúri** Zambézia, NE Mozambique
119 Q9 **Nova Odesa** *var.* Novaya Odessa. Mykolayivs'ka Oblast', S Ukraine
62 H10 **Nova Olímpia** Paraná, S Brazil
63 I15 **Nova Prata** Rio Grande do Sul, S Brazil
12 H12 **Novar** Ontario, S Canada
108 C7 **Novara** *anc.* Novaria. Piemonte, NW Italy
Novaria *see* Novara
119 P7 **Novarkanels'k** Kirovohrads'ka Oblast', C Ukraine
11 P15 **Nova Scotia** *Fr.* Nouvelle Écosse. ◐ *province* SE Canada
1 M9 **Nova Scotia** *physical region* SE Canada
36 M8 **Novato** California, W USA
199 Jj8 **Nova Trough** *undersea feature* W Pacific Ocean
118 L7 **Nova Ushtsya** Khmel'nyts'ka Oblast', W Ukraine
85 M17 **Nova Vanduzi** Manica, C Mozambique
119 U5 **Nova Vodolaha** *Rus.* Novaya Vodolaga. Kharkivs'ka Oblast', E Ukraine
126 L13 **Novaya Chara** Chitinskaya Oblast', S Russian Federation
126 J14 **Novaya Igirma** Irkutskaya Oblast', C Russian Federation
Novaya Kakhovka *see* Nova Kakhovka
150 E10 **Novaya Kazanka** Zapadnyy Kazakhstan, W Kazakhstan
128 I12 **Novaya Ladoga** Leningradskaya Oblast', NW Russian Federation
125 Ee10 **Novaya Lyalya** Sverdlovskaya Oblast, C Russian Federation
131 R5 **Novaya Malykla** Ul'yanovskaya Oblast', W Russian Federation
Novaya Odessa *see* Nova Odesa
126 M4 **Novaya Sibir', Ostrov** *island* Novosibirskiye Ostrova, NE Russian Federation
Novaya Vodolaga *see* Nova Vodolaha
121 P17 **Novaya Yel'nya** *Rus.* Novaya Yel'nya. Mahilyowskaya Voblasts', E Belarus
125 G4 **Novaya Zemlya** *island group* N Russian Federation
Novaya Zemlya Trough *see* East Novaya Zemlya Trough
116 K10 **Nova Zagora** Burgaska Oblast, C Bulgaria
107 S12 **Novelda** País Valenciano, E Spain
113 H19 **Nové Mesto nad Váhom** *Ger.* Waagneustadtl, *Hung.* Vágújhely. Západné Slovensko, W Slovakia
113 F17 **Nové Město na Moravě** *Ger.* Neustadtl in Mähren. Jižní Morava, E Czech Republic
Novesium *see* Neuss
113 I21 **Nové Zámky** *Ger.* Neuhäusel, *Hung.* Érsekújvár. Západné Slovensko, SW Slovakia
125 C6 **Novgorod** Novgorodskaya Oblast', W Russian Federation
Novgorod-Severskiy *see* Novhorod-Sivers'kyy
125 C6 **Novgorodskaya Oblast'** ◐ *province* W Russian Federation
119 R8 **Novhorodka** Kirovohrads'ka Oblast', C Ukraine
119 R2 **Novhorod-Sivers'kyy** *Rus.* Novgorod-Severskiy. Chernihivs'ka Oblast', NE Ukraine
33 R10 **Novi** Michigan, N USA
Novi *see* Novi Vinodolski
114 L9 **Novi Bečej** *prev.* Új-Becse, Vološinovo, *Ger.* Neubetsche, *Hung.* Törökbecse. Serbia, N Yugoslavia
27 Q8 **Novice** Texas, SW USA
114 A9 **Novigrad** Istra, NW Croatia
116 G9 **Novi Iskŭr** Grad Sofiya, W Bulgaria
108 C9 **Novi Ligure** Piemonte, NW Italy
101 L22 **Noville** Luxembourg, SE Belgium
204 I10 **Noville Peninsula** *peninsula* Thurston Island, Antarctica
Noviodunum *see* Soissons, Aisne, France
Noviodunum *see* Nevers, Nièvre, France
Noviodunum *see* Nyon, Vaud, Switzerland
Noviomagus *see* Lisieux, France
Noviomagus *see* Nijmegen, Netherlands
116 M8 **Novi Pazar** Varnenska Oblast, NE Bulgaria
115 M15 **Novi Pazar** *Turk.* Yenipazar. Serbia, S Yugoslavia
114 K10 **Novi Sad** *Ger.* Neusatz, *Hung.* Újvidék. Serbia, N Yugoslavia
119 T6 **Novi Sanzhary** Poltavs'ka Oblast', C Ukraine
114 H12 **Novi Travnik** *prev.* Pučarevo. C Bosnia and Herzegovina
114 B10 **Novi Vinodolski** *var.* Novi. Primorje-Gorski Kotar, NW Croatia
60 F12 **Novo Airão** Amazonas, N Brazil
131 N14 **Novoaleksandrovsk** Stavropol'skiy Kray, SW Russian Federation
150 I10 **Novoalekseyevka** Aktyubinsk, W Kazakhstan
126 H14 **Novoaltaysk** Altayskiy Kray, S Russian Federation
131 N9 **Novoanninskiy** Volgogradskaya Oblast', SW Russian Federation
60 F13 **Novo Aripuanã** Amazonas, N Brazil
119 Y6 **Novoaydar** Luhans'ka Oblast', E Ukraine
119 X9 **Novoazovs'k** *Rus.* Novoazovsk. Donets'ka Oblast', E Ukraine
126 Mm16 **Novobureyskiy** Amurskaya Oblast', SE Russian Federation
131 Q3 **Novocheboksarsk** Chuvashskaya Respublika, W Russian Federation
131 R5 **Novocheremshansk** Ul'yanovskaya Oblast', W Russian Federation
130 L12 **Novocherkassk** Rostovskaya Oblast', SW Russian Federation
131 R6 **Novodevich'ye** Samarskaya Oblast', W Russian Federation
128 M8 **Novodvinsk** Arkhangel'skaya Oblast', NW Russian Federation
Novograd-Volynskiy *see* Novohrad-Volyns'kyy
Novogrudok *see* Navahrudak
63 I15 **Novo Hamburgo** Rio Grande do Sul, S Brazil
61 H16 **Novo Horizonte** Mato Grosso, W Brazil
62 K8 **Novo Horizonte** São Paulo, S Brazil
118 M4 **Novohrad-Volyns'kyy** *Rus.* Novograd-Volynskiy. Zhytomyrs'ka Oblast', N Ukraine
150 L14 **Novokazalinsk** *Kaz.* Zhangaqazaly. Kzyl-Orda, SW Kazakhstan
130 M8 **Novokhopersk** Voronezhskaya Oblast', W Russian Federation
131 R6 **Novokuybyshevsk** Samarskaya Oblast', W Russian Federation
126 H14 **Novokuznetsk** *prev.* Stalinsk. Kemerovskaya Oblast', S Russian Federation
205 R1 **Novolazarevskaya** *Russian research station* Antarctica
Novolukoml' *see* Novalukoml'
111 V12 **Novo Mesto** *Ger.* Rudolfswert; *prev. Ger.* Neustadtl. SE Slovenia
130 K15 **Novomikhaylovskiy** Krasnodarskiy Kray, SW Russian Federation
114 L8 **Novo Miloševo** Serbia, N Yugoslavia
Novomirgorod *see* Novomyrhorod
130 L5 **Novomoskovsk** Tul'skaya Oblast', W Russian Federation
119 U7 **Novomoskovs'k** *Rus.* Novomoskovsk. Dnipropetrovs'ka Oblast', E Ukraine
119 V8 **Novomykolayivka** Zaporiz'ka Oblast', SE Ukraine
119 Q7 **Novomyrhorod** *Rus.* Novomirgorod. Kirovohrads'ka Oblast', S Ukraine
126 I12 **Novonazimovo** Krasnoyarskiy Kray, C Russian Federation
131 N8 **Novonikolayevskiy** Volgogradskaya Oblast', SW Russian Federation
131 P10 **Novonikol'skoye** Volgogradskaya Oblast', SW Russian Federation
131 X7 **Novoorsk** Orenburgskaya Oblast', W Russian Federation
130 M13 **Novopokrovskaya** Krasnodarskiy Kray, SW Russian Federation
Novopolotsk *see* Navapolatsk
119 Y5 **Novopskov** Luhans'ka Oblast', E Ukraine
Novoradomsk *see* Radomsko
Novo Redondo *see* Sumbe
131 R8 **Novorepnoye** Saratovskaya Oblast', W Russian Federation
130 K14 **Novorossiysk** Krasnodarskiy Kray, SW Russian Federation
Novorossiyskiy *see* Novorossiyskoye
150 J10 **Novorossiyskoye** *prev.* Novorossiyskiy. Aktyubinsk, NW Kazakhstan
126 Jj6 **Novorybnaya** Taymyrskiy (Dolgano-Nenetskiy) Avtonomnyy Okrug, N Russian Federation
128 F15 **Novorzhev** Pskovskaya Oblast', W Russian Federation
Novoselitsa *see* Novoselytsya
119 S12 **Novoselivs'ke** Respublika Krym, S Ukraine
Novosëlki *see* Navasyolki
116 G6 **Novo Selo** Oblast Montana, NW Bulgaria
115 M14 **Novo Selo** Serbia, C Yugoslavia
118 K8 **Novoselytsya** *Rom.* Nouă Sulița, *Rus.* Novoselitsa. Chernivets'ka Oblast', W Ukraine
131 U7 **Novosergiyevka** Orenburgskaya Oblast', W Russian Federation
130 L11 **Novoshakhtinsk** Rostovskaya Oblast', SW Russian Federation
126 Gg14 **Novosibirsk** Novosibirskaya Oblast', C Russian Federation
125 G13 **Novosibirskaya Oblast'** ◐ *province* C Russian Federation
126 M4 **Novosibirskiye Ostrova** *Eng.* New Siberian Islands. *island group* N Russian Federation
130 K6 **Novosil'** Orlovskaya Oblast', W Russian Federation
128 G16 **Novosokol'niki** Pskovskaya Oblast', W Russian Federation
131 Q6 **Novospasskoye** Ul'yanovskaya Oblast', W Russian Federation
131 X8 **Novotroitsk** Orenburgskaya Oblast', W Russian Federation
Novotroitskoye *see* Brlik, Kazakhstan
Novotroitskoye *see* Novotroyits'ke, Ukraine
119 T11 **Novotroyits'ke** *Rus.* Novotroitskoye. Khersons'ka Oblast', S Ukraine
Novoukrainka *see* Novoukrayinka
119 Q8 **Novoukrayinka** *Rus.* Novoukrainka. Kirovohrads'ka Oblast', C Ukraine
131 Q5 **Novoul'yanovsk** Ul'yanovskaya Oblast', W Russian Federation
131 W8 **Novouralets** Orenburgskaya Oblast', W Russian Federation
Novo-Urgench *see* Urganch
118 I4 **Novovolyns'k** *Rus.* Novovolynsk. Volyns'ka Oblast', NW Ukraine
119 S9 **Novovorontsovka** Khersons'ka Oblast', S Ukraine
153 Y7 **Novovoznesenovka** Issyk-Kul'skaya Oblast', E Kyrgyzstan
129 R14 **Novovyatsk** Kirovskaya Oblast', NW Russian Federation
Novoyel'nya *see* Navayel'nya
119 O6 **Novozhyvotiv** Vinnyts'ka Oblast', C Ukraine
130 H6 **Novozybkov** Bryanskaya Oblast', W Russian Federation
114 F9 **Novska** Sisak-Moslavina, NE Croatia
Nový Bohumín *see* Bohumín
113 D15 **Nový Bor** *Ger.* Haida; *prev.* Bor u České Lípy, Hajda. Severní Čechy, N Czech Republic
113 E16 **Nový Bydžov** *Ger.* Neubidschow. Východní Čechy, N Czech Republic
121 G18 **Novy Dvor** *Rus.* Novyy Dvor. Hrodzyenskaya Voblasts', W Belarus
113 I17 **Nový Jičín** *Ger.* Neutitschein. Severní Morava, E Czech Republic
120 K12 **Novy Pahost** *Rus.* Novyy Pogost. Vitsyebskaya Voblasts', NW Belarus
Novyy Bug *see* Novyy Buh
119 R9 **Novyy Buh** *Rus.* Novyy Bug. Mykolayivs'ka Oblast', S Ukraine
119 Q4 **Novyy Bykiv** Chernihivs'ka Oblast', N Ukraine
Novyy Dvor *see* Novy Dvor
Novyye Aneny *see* Anenii Noi
131 P7 **Novyye Burasy** Saratovskaya Oblast', W Russian Federation
Novyy Margilan *see* Farghona
130 K8 **Novyy Oskol** Belgorodskaya Oblast', W Russian Federation
Novyy Pogost *see* Novy Pahost
131 R2 **Novyy Tor"yal** Respublika Mariy El, W Russian Federation
126 K14 **Novyy Uoyan** Respublika Buryatiya, S Russian Federation
126 Gg9 **Novyy Urengoy** Yamalo-Nenetskiy Avtonomnyy Okrug, N Russian Federation
127 N15 **Novyy Urgal** Khabarovskiy Kray, E Russian Federation
150 F15 **Novyy Uzen'** *Kaz.* Zhangaözen. Mangistau, W Kazakhstan
125 G12 **Novyy Vasyugan** Tomskaya Oblast', C Russian Federation
113 N16 **Nowa Dęba** Tarnobrzeg, SE Poland
113 G15 **Nowa Ruda** *Ger.* Neurode. Wałbrzych, SW Poland
112 F12 **Nowa Sól** *var.* Nowasól, *Ger.* Neusalz an der Oder. Zielona Góra, W Poland
29 Q8 **Nowata** Oklahoma, C USA
148 M6 **Nowbarān** Markazī, W Iran
112 J8 **Nowe** Bydgoszcz, N Poland
112 K9 **Nowe Miasto Lubawskie** *Ger.* Neumark. Toruń, N Poland
112 L13 **Nowe Miasto nad Pilicą** Radom, C Poland
112 D8 **Nowe Warpno** *Ger.* Neuwarp. Szczecin, NW Poland
Nowgong *see* Nagaon
112 E8 **Nowogard** *var.* Nowógard, *Ger.* Naugard. Szczecin, NW Poland
112 N9 **Nowogród** Łomża, NE Poland
Nowogródek *see* Navahrudak
113 E14 **Nowogrodziec** *Ger.* Naumburg am Queis. Jelenia Góra, SW Poland
Nowojelnia *see* Navayel'nya
Nowo-Mińsk *see* Mińsk Mazowiecki
35 V13 **Nowood River** Wyoming, C USA
Nowosądeckie, Województwo *see* Nowy Sącz
Nowo-Święciany *see* Švenčionėliai
191 S10 **Nowra-Bomaderry** New South Wales, SE Australia
155 T5 **Nowshera** *var.* Naushahra, Naushara. North-West Frontier Province, NE Pakistan
112 J7 **Nowy Dwór Gdański** *Ger.* Tiegenhof. Elbląg, N Poland
112 L11 **Nowy Dwór Mazowiecki** Warszawa, C Poland
113 M17 **Nowy Sącz** *Ger.* Neu Sandec. Nowy Sącz, S Poland
113 L18 **Nowy Sącz** *off.* Województwo Nowosądeckie, *Ger.* Neusandez. ◐ *province* S Poland
113 L18 **Nowy Targ** *Ger.* Neumark. Nowy Sącz, S Poland
112 F11 **Nowy Tomyśl** *var.* Nowy Tomysl. Poznań, W Poland
154 M7 **Now Zād** *var.* Nauzad. Helmand, S Afghanistan
25 N4 **Noxubee River** Alabama/Mississippi, S USA
126 Gg10 **Noyabr'sk** Yamalo-Nenetskiy Avtonomnyy Okrug, N Russian Federation
104 L8 **Noyant** Maine-et-Loire, NW France
41 X14 **Noyes Island** *island* Alexander Archipelago, Alaska, USA
105 O3 **Noyon** Oise, N France
104 I7 **Nozay** Loire-Atlantique, NW France
84 L12 **Nsando** Northern, NE Zambia
85 N16 **Nsanje** Southern, S Malawi
79 Q17 **Nsawam** SE Ghana
84 K12 **Nsombo** Northern, NE Zambia
84 H13 **Ntambu** North Western, NW Zambia
85 N14 **Ntcheu** *var.* Ncheu. Central, S Malawi
81 D17 **Ntem** *prev.* Campo, Kampo. Cameroon/Equatorial Guinea
85 I14 **Ntemwa** North Western, NW Zambia
Ntlenyana, Mount *see* Thabana Ntlenyana
81 I19 **Ntomba, Lac** *var.* Lac Tumba. ◎ NW Zaire
83 E19 **Ntungamo** SW Uganda
83 E18 **Ntusi** SW Uganda
85 H18 **Ntwetwe Pan** *salt lake* NE Botswana
95 M15 **Nuasjärvi** ◎ C Finland
82 F11 **Nuba Mountains** ▲ C Sudan
70 J9 **Nubian Desert** *desert* NE Sudan
118 G10 **Nucet** *Hung.* Diófás. Bihor, W Romania
Nu Chiang *see* Salween
151 U9 **Nuclear Testing Ground** *nuclear site* Pavlodar, E Kazakhstan
58 E9 **Nucuray, Río** N Peru
27 R14 **Nueces River** Texas, SW USA
9 V9 **Nueltin Lake** ◎ Manitoba/Northwest Territories, C Canada
101 K15 **Nuenen** Noord-Brabant, S Netherlands
64 G6 **Nuestra Señora, Bahía** *bay* N Chile
63 D14 **Nuestra Señora Rosario de Caa Catí** Corrientes, NE Argentina
56 J9 **Nueva Antioquia** Vichada, E Colombia
Nueva Caceres *see* Naga
43 O7 **Nueva Ciudad Guerrera** Tamaulipas, C Mexico
57 N4 **Nueva Esparta** *off.* Estado Nueva Esparta. ◐ *state* NE Venezuela
46 C5 **Nueva Gerona** Isla de la Juventud, S Cuba
44 H8 **Nueva Guadalupe** San Miguel, E El Salvador
44 M11 **Nueva Guinea** Región Autónoma Atlántico Sur, SE Nicaragua
63 D19 **Nueva Helvecia** Colonia, SW Uruguay
65 J25 **Nueva, Isla** *island* S Chile
42 M14 **Nueva Italia** Michoacán de Ocampo, SW Mexico
58 D6 **Nueva Loja** *var.* Lago Agrio. Sucumbíos, NE Ecuador
44 F6 **Nueva Ocotepeque** *prev.* Ocotepeque. Ocotepeque, W Honduras
63 D19 **Nueva Palmira** Colonia, SW Uruguay
43 N6 **Nueva Rosita** Coahuila de Zaragoza, NE Mexico
44 E7 **Nueva San Salvador** *prev.* Santa Tecla. La Libertad, SW El Salvador
44 J8 **Nueva Segovia** ◐ *department* NW Nicaragua
Nueva Tabarca *see* Plana, Isla
Nueva Villa de Padilla *see* Nuevo Padilla
63 B21 **Nueve de Julio** Buenos Aires, E Argentina
46 H6 **Nuevitas** Camagüey, E Cuba
63 D18 **Nuevo Berlín** Río Negro, W Uruguay
42 I4 **Nuevo Casas Grandes** Chihuahua, N Mexico
45 T14 **Nuevo Chagres** Colón, C Panama
43 W15 **Nuevo Coahuila** Campeche, E Mexico
65 K17 **Nuevo, Golfo** *gulf* S Argentina
43 O7 **Nuevo Laredo** Tamaulipas, NE Mexico
43 N8 **Nuevo León** ◐ *state* NE Mexico
43 P10 **Nuevo Padilla** *var.* Nueva Villa de Padilla. Tamaulipas, C Mexico
58 E6 **Nuevo Rocafuerte** Napo, E Ecuador
168 G6 **Nuga** Dzavhan, W Mongolia
82 O13 **Nugaal** *off.* Gobolka Nugaal. ◐ *region* N Somalia
193 E24 **Nugget Point** *headland* South Island, NZ
195 R9 **Nuguria Islands** *island group* E PNG
192 P10 **Nuhaka** Hawke's Bay, North Island, NZ
144 M10 **Nuhaydayn, Wādī an** *dry watercourse* W Iraq
202 E7 **Nui Atoll** *atoll* W Tuvalu
Nu Jiang *see* Salween
Nûk *see* Nuuk
190 G7 **Nukey Bluff** *hill* South Australia
Nukha *see* Şäki
127 O9 **Nukh Yablonevyy, Gora** ▲ E Russian Federation
195 T13 **Nukiki** Choiseul Island, NW Solomon Islands
194 F10 **Nuku** Sandaun, NW PNG
200 R15 **Nuku** *island* Tongatapu Group, NE Tonga
200 Qq15 **Nuku'alofa** Tongatapu, S Tonga
200 Qq15 **Nuku'alofa** ● (Tonga) Tongatapu, S Tonga
202 G12 **Nukuatea** *island* N Wallis and Futuna
202 F7 **Nukufetau Atoll** *atoll* C Tuvalu
202 G12 **Nukuhifala** *island* E Wallis and Futuna
203 W7 **Nuku Hiva** *island* Îles Marquises, NE French Polynesia
199 L19 **Nuku Hiva Island** *island* Îles Marquises, N French Polynesia
202 F9 **Nukulaelae Atoll** *var.* Nukulailai. *atoll* E Tuvalu
Nukulailai *see* Nukulaelae Atoll
202 G11 **Nukuloa** *island* N Wallis and Futuna
195 W10 **Nukumanu Islands** *prev.* Tasman Group. *island group* NE PNG
Nukunau *see* Nikunau
202 J9 **Nukunonu Atoll** *island* C Tokelau
202 J9 **Nukunonu Village** Nukunonu Atoll, C Tokelau
201 S18 **Nukuoro Atoll** *atoll* Caroline Islands, S Micronesia
152 H8 **Nukus** Qoraqalpoghiston Respublikasi, W Uzbekistan
202 G11 **Nukutapu** *island* N Wallis and Futuna
41 O9 **Nulato** Alaska, USA
41 O10 **Nulato Hills** ▲ Alaska, USA
107 T9 **Nules** País Valenciano, E Spain
Nuling *see* Sultan Kudarat
190 C6 **Nullarbor** South Australia
188 M11 **Nullarbor Plain** *plateau* South Australia/Western Australia
169 S12 **Nulu'erhu Shan** ▲ N China
79 X14 **Numan** Adamawa, E Nigeria
171 K14 **Numata** Gunma, Honshū, S Japan
172 Oo4 **Numata** Hokkaidō, NE Japan
83 C15 **Numatinna** W Sudan
171 J17 **Numazu** Shizuoka, Honshū, S Japan
97 F14 **Numedalen** *valley* S Norway
97 G14 **Numedalslågen** *var.* Laagen. S Norway
95 L19 **Nummela** Uusimaa, S Finland
125 G9 **Numto** Khanty-Mansiyskiy Avtonomnyy Okrug, N Russian Federation
191 O11 **Numurkah** Victoria, SE Australia
Nunap Isua *see* Uummannarsuaq
56 H9 **Nunchia** Casanare, C Colombia
99 M20 **Nuneaton** C England, UK
159 W14 **Nungba** Manipur, NE India
40 L12 **Nunivak Island** *island* Alaska, USA
158 I5 **Nun Kun** ▲ NW India
100 L10 **Nunspeet** Gelderland, E Netherlands
109 C18 **Nuoro** Sardegna, Italy, C Mediterranean Sea
77 R12 **Nuqayy, Jabal** *hill range* S Libya
56 C9 **Nuquí** Chocó, W Colombia
149 O4 **Nūr** Māzandarān, N Iran
151 Q9 **Nura** N Kazakhstan
149 N11 **Nūrābād** Fārs, C Iran
Nurakita *see* Niulakita
Nurata *see* Nurota
Nuratau, Khrebet *see* Nurota Tizmasi
142 L17 **Nur Dağları** ▲ S Turkey
Nurek *see* Norak
Nuremberg *see* Nürnberg
142 M15 **Nurhak** Kahramanmaraş, S Turkey
190 J9 **Nuriootpa** South Australia
131 S5 **Nurlat** Respublika Tatarstan, W Russian Federation
95 N15 **Nurmes** Pohjois-Karjala, E Finland
103 K20 **Nürnberg** *Eng.* Nuremberg. Bayern, S Germany
103 K20 **Nürnberg** ✕ Bayern, SE Germany
152 M10 **Nurota** *Rus.* Nurata. Nawoiy Wiloyati, C Uzbekistan
153 N10 **Nurota Tizmasi** *Rus.* Khrebet Nuratau. ▲ C Uzbekistan
155 T8 **Nūrpur** Punjab, E Pakistan
191 P6 **Nurri, Mount** *hill* New South Wales, SE Australia
27 T13 **Nursery** Texas, SW USA
175 P16 **Nusa Tenggara** *Eng.* Lesser Sunda Islands. *island group* C Indonesia
175 O15 **Nusa Tenggara Barat** *off.* Propinsi Nusa Tenggara Barat, *Eng.* West Nusa Tenggara. ◐ *province* S Indonesia
175 Q17 **Nusa Tenggara Timur** *off.* Propinsi Nusa Tenggara Timur, *Eng.* East Nusa Tenggara. ◐ *province* S Indonesia
176 Vv12 **Nusawulan** Irian Jaya, E Indonesia
143 Q16 **Nusaybin** *var.* Nisibin. Manisa, SE Turkey
41 O14 **Nushagak Bay** *bay* Alaska, USA
41 O13 **Nushagak Peninsula** *headland* Alaska, USA
41 O13 **Nushagak River** Alaska, USA
166 E11 **Nu Shan** ▲ SW China
155 N11 **Nushki** Baluchistān, SW Pakistan

◆ Country ● Country Capital ◇ Dependent Territory ○ Dependent Territory Capital ◐ Administrative Region ✕ International Airport ▲ Mountain ▲ Mountain Range Volcano River ◎ Lake ⊡ Reservoir

NUSSDORF – ÖLAND

Nussdorf *see* Năsăud
114 *J9* **Nuštar** Vukovar-Srijem, E Croatia
101 *L18* **Nuth** Limburg, SE Netherlands
102 *N13* **Nuthe** ≈ NE Germany
Nutmeg State *see* Connecticut
41 *T10* **Nutzotin Mountains** ▲ Alaska, USA
66 *I5* **Nuuk** *var.* Nûk, *Dan.* Godthaab, Godthåb. ○ (Greenland) SW Greenland
94 *L13* **Nuupas** Lappi, NW Finland
203 *O7* **Nuupere, Pointe** *headland* Moorea, W French Polynesia
203 *O7* **Nuuroa, Pointe** *headland* Tahiti, W French Polynesia
168 *M8* **Nüürst** Töv, C Mongolia
Nuwara *see* Nuwara Eliya
161 *K25* **Nuwara Eliya** *var.* Nuwara. Central Province, S Sri Lanka
190 *E7* **Nuyts Archipelago** *island group* South Australia
85 *F17* **Nxaunxau** Ngamiland, NW Botswana
41 *N12* **Nyac** Alaska, USA
125 *Ff10* **Nyagan'** Khanty-Mansiyskiy Avtonomnyy Okrug, N Russian Federation
Nyagassola *see* Niagassola
83 *I18* **Nyahururu** Central, W Kenya
190 *M10* **Nyah West** Victoria, SE Australia
164 *M15* **Nyainqêntanglha Feng** ▲ W China
165 *N15* **Nyainqêntanglha Shan** ▲ W China
82 *B11* **Nyala** Southern Darfur, W Sudan
85 *M16* **Nyamapanda** Mashonaland East, NE Zimbabwe
83 *H25* **Nyamtumbo** Ruvuma, S Tanzania
Nyanda *see* Masvingo
128 *M11* **Nyandoma** Arkhangel'skaya Oblast', NW Russian Federation
85 *M16* **Nyanga** *prev.* Inyanga. Manicaland, E Zimbabwe
81 *D20* **Nyanga** *off.* Province de la Nyanga, *var.* La Nyanga. ◆ *province* SW Gabon
81 *E20* **Nyanga** ≈ Congo/Gabon
83 *F20* **Nyantakara** Kagera, NW Tanzania
83 *G19* **Nyanza** ◆ *province* W Kenya
83 *E21* **Nyanza-Lac** S Burundi
70 *J14* **Nyasa, Lake** *var.* Lake Malawi; *prev.* Lago Nyassa. ◎ E Africa
Nyasaland/Nyasaland Protectorate *see* Malawi
Nyassa, Lago *see* Nyasa, Lake
121 *J17* **Nyasvizh** *Pol.* Nieśwież, *Rus.* Nesvizh. Minskaya Voblasts', C Belarus
177 *G8* **Nyaunglebin** Pegu, SW Myanmar
177 *G5* **Nyaung-u** Magwe, C Myanmar
97 *H24* **Nyborg** Fyn, C Denmark
97 *N21* **Nybro** Kalmar, S Sweden
121 *J16* **Nyeharelaye** *Rus.* Negoreloye. Minskaya Voblasts', C Belarus
205 *W3* **Nye Mountains** ▲ Antarctica
83 *I19* **Nyeri** Central, C Kenya
120 *M11* **Nyeshcharda, Vozyera** ◎ N Belarus
94 *O2* **Ny-Friesland** *physical region* N Svalbard
97 *L14* **Nyhammar** Kopparberg, C Sweden
167 *F17* **Nyikog Qu** ≈ C China
164 *L14* **Nyima** Xizang Zizhiqu, W China
85 *L14* **Nyimba** Eastern, E Zambia
165 *P16* **Nyingchi** Xizang Zizhiqu, W China
113 *O21* **Nyírbátor** Szabolcs-Szatmár-Bereg, E Hungary
113 *N21* **Nyíregyháza** Szabolcs-Szatmár-Bereg, NE Hungary
Nyiro *see* Ewaso Ng'iro
Nyitra *see* Nitra
Nyitrabánya *see* Handlová
95 *K16* **Nykarleby** *Fin.* Uusikaarlepyy. Vaasa, W Finland
97 *I25* **Nykøbing** Storstrøm, SE Denmark
97 *I22* **Nykøbing** Vestsjælland, C Denmark
97 *F21* **Nykøbing** Viborg, NW Denmark
97 *N17* **Nyköping** Södermanland, S Sweden
97 *L15* **Nykroppa** Värmland, C Sweden
Nyland *see* Uusimaa
85 *J20* **Nylstroom** Northern, NE South Africa
191 *P7* **Nymagee** New South Wales, SE Australia
191 *V5* **Nymboida** New South Wales, SE Australia
191 *U5* **Nymboida River** ≈ New South Wales, SE Australia
113 *D16* **Nymburk** *var.* Neuenburg an der Elbe, *Ger.* Nimburg. Střední Čechy, C Czech Republic
97 *O16* **Nynäshamn** Stockholm, C Sweden
191 *Q6* **Nyngan** New South Wales, SE Australia
Nyoman *see* Neman
110 *A10* **Nyon** *Ger.* Neuss; *anc.* Noviodunum. Vaud, SW Switzerland
81 *D16* **Nyong** ≈ SW Cameroon
105 *S14* **Nyons** Drôme, E France
81 *D14* **Nyos, Lac** *Eng.* Lake Nyos. ◎ NW Cameroon
Nyos, Lake *see* Nyos, Lac
129 *U11* **Nyrob** *var.* Nyrov. Permskaya Oblast', NW Russian Federation
Nyrov *see* Nyrob
113 *H15* **Nysa** *Ger.* Neisse. Opole, SW Poland
Nysa Łużycka *see* Neisse
Nyslott *see* Savonlinna
34 *M13* **Nyssa** Oregon, NW USA
Nystad *see* Uusikaupunki
97 *I25* **Nysted** Storstrøm, SE Denmark
129 *U14* **Nytva** Permskaya Oblast', NW Russian Federation
171 *L19* **Nyūdō-zaki** *headland* Honshū, C Japan
129 *P9* **Nyukhcha** Arkhangel'skaya Oblast', NW Russian Federation
128 *H8* **Nyuk, Ozero** *var.* Ozero Njuk. ◎ NW Russian Federation
129 *O12* **Nyuksenitsa** *var.* Njuksenica. Vologodskaya Oblast', NW Russian Federation
81 *O22* **Nyunzu** Shaba, SE Zaire
126 *Kk11* **Nyurba** Respublika Sakha (Yakutiya), NE Russian Federation
126 *Kk12* **Nyuya** Respublika Sakha (Yakutiya), NE Russian Federation
126 *Kk12* **Nyuya** ≈ NE Russian Federation
119 *T10* **Nyzhni Sirohozy** Khersons'ka Oblast', S Ukraine
119 *U12* **Nyzhn'ohirs'kyy** *Rus.* Nizhnegorskiy. Respublika Krym, S Ukraine
83 *G21* **Nzega** Tabora, C Tanzania
78 *K15* **Nzérékoré** Guinée-Forestière, SE Guinea
84 *A10* **N'Zeto** *prev.* Ambrizete. Zaire, NW Angola
81 *M24* **Nzilo, Lac** *prev.* Lac Delcommune. ◎ SE Zaire

O

31 *O11* **Oacoma** South Dakota, N USA
31 *N9* **Oahe Dam** *dam* South Dakota, N USA
30 *M9* **Oahe, Lake** ⊡ North Dakota/South Dakota, N USA
40 *C9* **O'ahu** *Haw.* O'ahu. *island* Hawaii, USA, C Pacific Ocean
172 *Qq6* **O-Akan-dake** ▲ Hokkaidō, NE Japan
190 *K8* **Oakbank** South Australia
21 *P13* **Oak Bluffs** Martha's Vineyard, New York, NE USA
38 *K4* **Oak City** Utah, W USA
39 *R3* **Oak Creek** Colorado, C USA
37 *P8* **Oakdale** California, W USA
24 *H8* **Oakdale** Louisiana, S USA
31 *P7* **Oakes** North Dakota, N USA
24 *J4* **Oak Grove** Louisiana, S USA
99 *N19* **Oakham** C England, UK
34 *H7* **Oak Harbor** Washington, NW USA
23 *R5* **Oak Hill** West Virginia, NE USA
37 *N8* **Oakland** California, W USA
31 *T15* **Oakland** Iowa, C USA
21 *Q7* **Oakland** Maine, NE USA
23 *T3* **Oakland** Maryland, NE USA
31 *R14* **Oakland** Nebraska, C USA
33 *N11* **Oak Lawn** Illinois, N USA
35 *P16* **Oakley** Idaho, NW USA
28 *I4* **Oakley** Kansas, C USA
33 *N10* **Oak Park** Illinois, N USA
9 *X16* **Oak Point** Manitoba, S Canada
34 *G13* **Oakridge** Oregon, NW USA
22 *M9* **Oak Ridge** Tennessee, S USA
192 *K10* **Oakura** Taranaki, North Island, NZ
24 *L7* **Oak Vale** Mississippi, S USA
12 *G16* **Oakville** Ontario, S Canada
27 *V8* **Oakwood** Texas, SW USA
193 *F22* **Oamaru** Otago, South Island, NZ
98 *F13* **Oa, Mull of** *headland* W Scotland, UK
175 *Q7* **Oan** Sulawesi, N Indonesia
193 *J17* **Oaro** Canterbury, South Island, NZ
37 *X2* **Oasis** Nevada, W USA
205 *S15* **Oates Land** *physical region* Antarctica
191 *P17* **Oatlands** Tasmania, SE Australia
38 *I11* **Oatman** Arizona, SW USA
43 *R16* **Oaxaca** *var.* Oaxaca de Juárez; *prev.* Antequera. Oaxaca, SE Mexico
43 *Q16* **Oaxaca** ◆ *state* SE Mexico
Oaxaca de Juárez *see* Oaxaca
125 *G8* **Ob'** ≈ C Russian Federation
12 *G9* **Obabika Lake** ◎ Ontario, S Canada
Obagan *see* Ubagan
120 *M12* **Obal'** *Rus.* Obol'. Vitsyebskaya Voblasts', N Belarus
81 *E16* **Obala** Centre, SW Cameroon
12 *C6* **Oba Lake** ◎ Ontario, S Canada
171 *H14* **Obama** Fukui, Honshū, SW Japan
98 *H11* **Oban** W Scotland, UK
Oban *see* Halfmoon Bay
171 *L112* **Obanazawa** Yamagata, Honshū, C Japan
Obando *see* Puerto Inírida
106 *I4* **O Barco** *var.* El Barco, El Barco de Valdeorras, O Barco de Valdeorras. Galicia, NW Spain
O Barco de Valdeorras *see* O Barco
Obbia *see* Hobyo
95 *J16* **Obbola** Västerbotten, N Sweden
Obbrovazzo *see* Obrovac
Obchuga *see* Abchuha
Obdorsk *see* Salekhard
Óbecse *see* Bečej
120 *I11* **Obeliai** Rokiškis, NE Lithuania
62 *F13* **Oberá** Misiones, NE Argentina
110 *E8* **Oberburg** Bern, W Switzerland
111 *Q9* **Oberdrauburg** Salzburg, S Austria
Oberglogau *see* Głogówek
111 *W4* **Ober Grafendorf** Niederösterreich, NE Austria
103 *E15* **Oberhausen** Nordrhein-Westfalen, W Germany
Oberhollabrunn *see* Tulln
Oberlaibach *see* Vrhnika
103 *Q15* **Oberlausitz** *physical region* E Germany
28 *J2* **Oberlin** Kansas, C USA
24 *H8* **Oberlin** Louisiana, S USA
33 *T11* **Oberlin** Ohio, N USA
105 *U5* **Obernai** Bas-Rhin, NE France
111 *R4* **Obernberg am Inn** Oberösterreich, N Austria
Oberndorf *see* Oberndorf am Neckar
103 *G23* **Oberndorf am Neckar** *var.* Oberndorf. Baden-Württemberg, SW Germany
111 *Q5* **Oberndorf bei Salzburg** Salzburg, W Austria
Oberneustadtl *see* Kysucké Nové Mesto
191 *S8* **Oberon** New South Wales, SE Australia
111 *Q4* **Oberösterreich** *off.* Land Oberösterreich, *Eng.* Upper Austria. ◆ *state* NW Austria
Oberpahlen *see* Põltsamaa
103 *M19* **Oberpfälzer Wald** ▲ SE Germany
111 *Y6* **Oberpullendorf** Burgenland, E Austria
Oberradkersburg *see* Gornja Radgona
103 *G18* **Oberursel** Hessen, W Germany
111 *Q8* **Obervellach** Salzburg, S Austria
111 *X7* **Oberwart** Burgenland, SE Austria
Oberwischau *see* Vișeu de Sus
111 *T7* **Oberwölz** *var.* Oberwölz-Stadt. Steiermark, SE Austria
Oberwölz-Stadt *see* Oberwölz
33 *S13* **Obetz** Ohio, N USA
Ob', Gulf of *see* Obskaya Guba
56 *G8* **Obia** Santander, C Colombia
60 *H12* **Óbidos** Pará, NE Brazil
106 *F10* **Óbidos** Leiria, C Portugal
Obidovichi *see* Abidavichy
153 *Q13* **Obigarm** W Tajikistan
172 *P7* **Obihiro** Hokkaidō, NE Japan
Obi-Khingou *see* Khingov
153 *P13* **Obikiik** SW Tajikistan
115 *N16* **Obilić** Serbia, S Yugoslavia
131 *O12* **Obil'noye** Respublika Kalmykiya, SW Russian Federation
22 *F8* **Obion** Tennessee, S USA
22 *F8* **Obion River** ≈ Tennessee, S USA
175 *T9* **Obi, Pulau** *island* Maluku, E Indonesia
172 *Oo4* **Obira** Hokkaidō, NE Japan
175 *T9* **Obi, Selat** *strait* Maluku, E Indonesia
131 *N11* **Oblivskaya** Rostovskaya Oblast', SW Russian Federation
127 *N16* **Obluch'ye** Yevreyskaya Avtonomnaya Oblast', SE Russian Federation
130 *K4* **Obninsk** Kaluzhskaya Oblast', W Russian Federation
116 *J8* **Obnova** Loveshka Oblast, N Bulgaria
81 *N15* **Obo** Haut-Mbomou, E Central African Republic
82 *M11* **Obock** E Djibouti
Obol' *see* Obal'
Obolyanka *see* Abalyanka
176 *Vv11* **Obome** Irian Jaya, E Indonesia
112 *G11* **Oborniki** Poznań, W Poland
81 *G19* **Obouya** Cuvette, C Congo
130 *J8* **Oboyan'** Kurskaya Oblast', W Russian Federation
128 *M9* **Obozerskiy** Arkhangel'skaya Oblast', NW Russian Federation
114 *L11* **Obrenovac** Serbia, N Yugoslavia
114 *D12* **Obrovac** *It.* Obbrovazzo. Zadar-Knin, W Croatia
Obrovo *see* Abrova
37 *Q3* **Observation Peak** ▲ California, W USA
126 *H7* **Obskaya Guba** *Eng.* Gulf of Ob'. *gulf* N Russian Federation
181 *N13* **Ob' Tablemount** *undersea feature* S Indian Ocean
181 *T10* **Ob' Trench** *undersea feature* E Indian Ocean
79 *P16* **Obuasi** S Ghana
119 *P5* **Obukhiv** *Rus.* Obukhov. Kyyivs'ka Oblast', N Ukraine
Obukhov *see* Obukhiv
129 *U14* **Obva** ≈ NW Russian Federation
119 *V10* **Obytichna Kosa** *spit* SE Ukraine
119 *V10* **Obytichna Zatoka** *gulf* SE Ukraine
107 *O3* **Oca** ≈ N Spain
25 *W10* **Ocala** Florida, SE USA
42 *M7* **Ocampo** Coahuila de Zaragoza, NE Mexico
56 *G7* **Ocaña** Norte de Santander, N Colombia
107 *N9* **Ocaña** Castilla-La Mancha, C Spain
39 *T9* **Ocate** New Mexico, SW USA
Ocavango *see* Okavango
50 *D6* **Occidental, Cordillera** ▲ Bolivia/Chile
50 *D6* **Occidental, Cordillera** ▲ W Colombia
59 *D14* **Occidental, Cordillera** ▲ W Peru
23 *Q6* **Oceana** West Virginia, NE USA
23 *Z4* **Ocean City** Maryland, NE USA
20 *J17* **Ocean City** New Jersey, NE USA
8 *K15* **Ocean Falls** British Columbia, SW Canada
Ocean Island *see* Kure Atoll
Ocean Island *see* Banaba
66 *J9* **Oceanographer Fracture Zone** *tectonic feature* NW Atlantic Ocean
37 *U17* **Oceanside** California, W USA
24 *M9* **Ocean Springs** Mississippi, S USA
Ocean State *see* Rhode Island
27 *O9* **O C Fisher Lake** ⊡ Texas, SW USA
119 *Q10* **Ochakiv** *Rus.* Ochakov. Mykolayivs'ka Oblast', S Ukraine
Ochakov *see* Ochakiv
Ochamchira *see* Och'amch'ire
143 *Q9* **Och'amch'ire** *Rus.* Ochamchira. W Georgia
Ochansk *see* Okhansk
129 *T15* **Ocher** Permskaya Oblast', NW Russian Federation
117 *I19* **Óchi** ▲ Évvoia, C Greece
172 *R8* **Ochiishi-misaki** *headland* Hokkaidō, NE Japan
25 *S9* **Ochlockonee River** ≈ Florida/Georgia, SE USA
46 *K12* **Ocho Rios** C Jamaica
Ochrida *see* Ohrid
Ochrida, Lake *see* Ohrid, Lake
103 *J19* **Ochsenfurt** Bayern, C Germany
25 *U7* **Ocilla** Georgia, SE USA
96 *N13* **Ockelbo** Gävleborg, C Sweden
Ocker *see* Oker
97 *I19* **Öckerö** Göteborg och Bohus, S Sweden
25 *U6* **Ocmulgee River** ≈ Georgia, SE USA
118 *H11* **Ocna Mureș** *Hung.* Marosújvár; *prev.* Ocna Mureșului; prev. *Hung.* Marosújvárakna. Alba, C Romania
Ocna Mureșului *see* Ocna Mureș
118 *H11* **Ocna Sibiului** *Ger.* Salzburg, *Hung.* Vizakna. Sibiu, C Romania
118 *H13* **Ocnele Mari** *prev.* Vioara. Vâlcea, S Romania
118 *L7* **Ocnița** *Rus.* Oknitsa. N Moldova
25 *U4* **Oconee, Lake** ⊡ Georgia, SE USA
25 *U5* **Oconee River** ≈ Georgia, SE USA
32 *M9* **Oconomowoc** Wisconsin, N USA
32 *M6* **Oconto** Wisconsin, N USA
32 *M6* **Oconto Falls** Wisconsin, N USA
32 *M6* **Oconto River** ≈ Wisconsin, N USA
106 *I3* **O Corgo** Galicia, NW Spain
43 *V16* **Ocosingo** Chiapas, SE Mexico
44 *J8* **Ocotal** Nueva Segovia, NW Nicaragua
44 *F6* **Ocotepeque** ◆ *department* W Honduras
Ocotepeque *see* Nueva Ocotepeque
42 *L13* **Ocotlán** Jalisco, SW Mexico
43 *R16* **Ocotlán** *var.* Ocotlán de Morelos. Oaxaca, SE Mexico
Ocotlán de Morelos *see* Ocotlán
43 *U16* **Ocozocuautla** Chiapas, SE Mexico
23 *Y10* **Ocracoke Island** *island* North Carolina, SE USA
104 *I3* **Octeville** Manche, N France
October Revolution Island *see* Oktyabr'skoy Revolyutsii, Ostrov
45 *R17* **Ocú** Herrera, S Panama
85 *Q14* **Ocua** Cabo Delgado, NE Mozambique
Ocumare *see* Ocumare del Tuy
56 *M5* **Ocumare del Tuy** *var.* Ocumare. Miranda, N Venezuela
79 *P17* **Oda** SE Ghana
170 *F12* **Ōda** *var.* Oda. Shimane, Honshū, SW Japan
94 *K3* **Ódadhahraun** *lava flow* C Iceland
176 *Y14* **Odammun** ≈ Irian Jaya, E Indonesia
171 *Mm9* **Ōdate** Akita, Honshū, C Japan
171 *J16* **Odawara** Kanagawa, Honshū, S Japan
97 *D14* **Odda** Hordaland, S Norway
97 *G22* **Odder** Århus, C Denmark
Oddur *see* Xuddur
31 *T13* **Odebolt** Iowa, C USA
106 *H14* **Odeleite** Faro, S Portugal
27 *Q4* **Odell** Texas, SW USA
27 *T14* **Odem** Texas, SW USA
106 *F13* **Odemira** Beja, S Portugal
142 *C14* **Ödemiş** İzmir, SW Turkey
Ödenburg *see* Sopron
85 *I22* **Odendaalsrus** Free State, C South Africa
Odenpäh *see* Otepää
97 *H23* **Odense** Fyn, C Denmark
103 *H19* **Odenwald** ▲ W Germany
86 *H10* **Oder** *Cz./Pol.* Odra. ≈ C Europe
Oderberg *see* Bohumín
102 *P11* **Oderbruch** *wetland* Germany/Poland
Oderhaff *see* Szczeciński, Zalew
102 *O11* **Oder-Havel-Kanal** *canal* NE Germany
Oderhellen *see* Odorheiu Secuiesc
102 *P13* **Oder-Spree-Kanal** *canal* NE Germany
Odertal *see* Zdzieszowice
108 *I7* **Oderzo** Veneto, NE Italy
124 *Pp4* **Odesa** *Rus.* Odessa. Odes'ka Oblast', SW Ukraine
Odesa *see* Odes'ka Oblast'
97 *L18* **Ödeshög** Östergötland, S Sweden
119 *O9* **Odes'ka Oblast'** *var.* Odesa, *Rus.* Odesskaya Oblast'. ◆ *province* SW Ukraine
26 *M8* **Odessa** Texas, SW USA
34 *K8* **Odessa** Washington, NW USA
Odessa *see* Odesa
Odesskaya Oblast' *see* Odes'ka Oblast'
125 *Ff13* **Odesskoye** Omskaya Oblast', C Russian Federation
Odessus *see* Varna
104 *F6* **Odet** ≈ NW France
106 *I14* **Odiel** ≈ SW Spain
78 *L14* **Odienné** NW Ivory Coast
179 *Pp12* **Odiongan** Tablas Island, C Philippines
118 *L12* **Odobești** Vrancea, E Romania
112 *H13* **Odolanów** *Ger.* Adelnau. Kalisz, SW Poland
178 *J13* **Ŏdôngk** Kâmpóng Spoe, S Cambodia
27 *N6* **O'donnell** Texas, SW USA
100 *O7* **Odoorn** Drenthe, NE Netherlands
Odorhei *see* Odorheiu Secuiesc
118 *J11* **Odorheiu Secuiesc** *Ger.* Oderhellen, *Hung.* Vámosudvarhely; *prev.* Odorhei; *Ger.* Hofmarkt. Harghita, C Romania
Odra *see* Oder
114 *J9* **Odžaci** *Ger.* Hodschag, *Hung.* Hodság. Serbia, NW Yugoslavia
61 *N14* **Oeiras** Piauí, E Brazil
106 *F11* **Oeiras** Lisboa, C Portugal
103 *G14* **Oelde** Nordrhein-Westfalen, W Germany
30 *J11* **Oelrichs** South Dakota, N USA
Oels/Oels in Schlesien *see* Oleśnica
103 *M17* **Oelsnitz** Sachsen, E Germany
31 *X12* **Oelwein** Iowa, C USA
Oeniadae *see* Oiniádes
203 *N17* **Oeno Island** *atoll* Pitcairn Islands, C Pacific Ocean
Oesel *see* Saaremaa
110 *L7* **Oetz** *var.* Ötz. Tirol, W Austria
143 *P11* **Of** Trabzon, NE Turkey
32 *K15* **O'Fallon** Illinois, N USA
29 *W4* **O'Fallon** Missouri, C USA
109 *N16* **Ofanto** ≈ S Italy
99 *D18* **Offaly** *Ir.* Ua Uíbh Fhailí; *prev.* King's County. *cultural region* C Ireland
103 *H18* **Offenbach** *var.* Offenbach am Main. Hessen, W Germany
Offenbach am Main *see* Offenbach
103 *F22* **Offenburg** Baden-Württemberg, SW Germany
190 *C2* **Officer Creek** *seasonal river* South Australia
Oficina María Elena *see* María Elena
Oficina Pedro de Valdivia *see* Pedro de Valdivia
117 *K22* **Ofidoússa** *island* Kykládes, Greece, Aegean Sea
Ofiral *see* Sharm el Sheikh
94 *H10* **Ofotfjorden** *fjord* N Norway
198 *D8* **Ofu** *island* Manua Islands, E American Samoa
171 *Mm12* **Ōfunato** Iwate, Honshū, C Japan
171 *M10* **Oga** Akita, Honshū, C Japan
Ogaadeen *see* Ogadēn
171 *M11* **Ogachi** Akita, Honshū, C Japan
171 *M11* **Ogachi-tōge** *pass* Honshū, C Japan
83 *N14* **Ogadēn** *Som.* Ogaadeen. *plateau* Ethiopia/Somalia
171 *M10* **Oga-hantō** *peninsula* Honshū, C Japan
171 *Hh14* **Ōgaki** Gifu, Honshū, SW Japan
30 *L15* **Ogallala** Nebraska, C USA
174 *I12* **Ogan, Air** ≈ Sumatera, W Indonesia
172 *T16* **Ogasawara-shotō** *Eng.* Bonin Islands. *island group* SE Japan
12 *I9* **Ogascanane, Lac** ◎ Québec, SE Canada
172 *N9* **Ogawara-ko** ◎ Honshū, C Japan
79 *T15* **Ogbomosho** Oyo, W Nigeria
31 *U13* **Ogden** Iowa, C USA
38 *L2* **Ogden** Utah, W USA
20 *I6* **Ogdensburg** New York, NE USA
197 *L16* **Ogea Driki** *island* Lau Group, E Fiji
197 *L16* **Ogea Levu** *island* Lau Group, E Fiji
25 *W5* **Ogeechee River** ≈ Georgia, SE USA
Oger *see* Ogre
152 *F6* **Ogiyon Shŭrkhogi** *wetland* NW Uzbekistan
171 *K12* **Ogi** Niigata, Sado, C Japan
8 *H5* **Ogilvie** Yukon Territory, NW Canada
8 *H4* **Ogilvie** ≈ Yukon Territory, NW Canada
8 *H5* **Ogilvie Mountains** ▲ Yukon Territory, NW Canada
Oginskiy Kanal *see* Ahinski Kanal
152 *B10* **Oglanly** Balkanskiy Velayat, W Turkmenistan
25 *T5* **Oglethorpe** Georgia, SE USA
25 *T2* **Oglethorpe, Mount** ▲ Georgia, SE USA
108 *F7* **Oglio** *anc.* Ollius. ≈ N Italy
105 *T8* **Ognon** ≈ E France
175 *Pp7* **Ogoamas, Pegunungan** ▲ Sulawesi, N Indonesia
127 *N14* **Ogodzha** Amurskaya Oblast', S Russian Federation
79 *W16* **Ogoja** Cross River, S Nigeria
10 *C10* **Ogoki** ≈ Ontario, S Canada
10 *D11* **Ogoki Lake** ◎ Ontario, C Canada
168 *K10* **Ögöömör** Ömnögovĭ, S Mongolia
81 *F19* **Ogooué** ≈ Congo/Gabon
81 *E18* **Ogooué-Ivindo** *off.* Province de l'Ogooué-Ivindo, *var.* L'Ogooué-Ivindo. ◆ *province* N Gabon
81 *E19* **Ogooué-Lolo** *off.* Province de l'Ogooué-Lolo, *var.* L'Ogooué-Lolo. ◆ *province* C Gabon
81 *C19* **Ogooué-Maritime** *off.* Province de l'Ogooué-Maritime, *var.* L'Ogooué-Maritime. ◆ *province* W Gabon
170 *Cc13* **Ogōri** Fukuoka, Kyūshū, SW Japan
170 *Dd13* **Ogōri** Yamaguchi, Honshū, SW Japan
116 *H7* **Ogosta** ≈ NW Bulgaria
114 *Q9* **Ograđen** *Bul.* Ograzhden. ▲ Bulgaria/FYR Macedonia *see also* Ograzhden
116 *G12* **Ograzhden** *Mac.* Ograđen. ▲ Bulgaria/FYR Macedonia *see also* Ograđen
120 *G9* **Ogre** *Ger.* Oger. Ogre, C Latvia
120 *H9* **Ogre** ≈ C Latvia
114 *C10* **Ogulin** Karlovac, NW Croatia
79 *S16* **Ogun** ◆ *state* SW Nigeria
152 *A12* **Ogurdzhaly, Ostrov** *Turkm.* Ogurjaly Adasy. *island* W Turkmenistan
Ogurjaly Adasy *see* Ogurdzhaly, Ostrov
79 *U16* **Ogwashi-Uku** Delta, S Nigeria
193 *B23* **Ohai** Southland, South Island, NZ
153 *Q10* **Ohangaron** *Rus.* Akhangaran. Toshkent Wiloyati, E Uzbekistan
153 *Q10* **Ohangaron** *Rus.* Akhangaran. ≈ E Uzbekistan
85 *C16* **Ohangwena** ◆ *district* N Namibia
171 *K17* **Ōhara** Chiba, Honshū, S Japan
32 *M10* **O'Hare** ✕ (Chicago) Illinois, N USA
172 *Nn8* **Ōhata** Aomori, Honshū, C Japan
192 *L13* **Ohau** Manawatu-Wanganui, North Island, NZ
193 *E20* **Ohau, Lake** ◎ South Island, NZ
Ohcejohka *see* Utsjoki
101 *J20* **Ohey** Namur, SE Belgium
203 *X15* **O'Higgins, Cabo** *headland* Easter Island, Chile, E Pacific Ocean
O'Higgins, Lago *see* San Martín, Lago
33 *S12* **Ohio** *off.* State of Ohio; also known as The Buckeye State. ◆ *state* N USA
1 *L10* **Ohio River** ≈ N USA
Ohlau *see* Oława
103 *H16* **Ohm** ≈ C Germany
200 *R16* **Ohonua** 'Eua, E Tonga
25 *V5* **Ohoopee River** ≈ Georgia, SE USA
102 *L12* **Ohre** *Ger.* Eger. ≈ Czech Republic/Germany
Ohri *see* Ohrid
115 *M20* **Ohrid** *Turk.* Ochrida, Ohri. SW FYR Macedonia
115 *M20* **Ohrid, Lake** *var.* Lake Ochrida, *Alb.* Liqeni i Ohrit, *Mac.* Ohridsko Ezero. ◎ Albania/FYR Macedonia
Ohridsko Ezero/Ohrit, Liqeni i *see* Ohrid, Lake
192 *L9* **Ohura** Manawatu-Wanganui, North Island, NZ
60 *J9* **Oiapoque** Amapá, E Brazil
60 *J10* **Oiapoque, Rio** *var.* Fleuve l'Oyapok, Oyapock. ≈ Brazil/French Guiana *see also* Oyapok, Fleuve l'
13 *O9* **Oies, Île aux** *island* Québec, SE Canada
94 *L13* **Oijärvi** Oulu, C Finland
94 *L12* **Oikarainen** Lappi, N Finland
196 *F10* **Oikuul** Babeldaob, N Palau
20 *C13* **Oil City** Pennsylvania, NE USA
20 *C12* **Oil Creek** ≈ Pennsylvania, NE USA
37 *R13* **Oildale** California, W USA
Oileán Ciarral *see* Castleisland
Oil Islands *see* Chagos Archipelago
117 *D18* **Oiniádes** *anc.* Oeniadae. *site of ancient city* Dytikí Ellás, W Greece
117 *L18* **Oinoússes** *island* E Greece
Oírr, Inis *see* Inisheer
101 *J15* **Oirschot** Noord-Brabant, S Netherlands
105 *N4* **Oise** ◆ *department* N France
105 *P3* **Oise** ≈ N France
101 *J14* **Oisterwijk** Noord-Brabant, S Netherlands
47 *O14* **Oistins** S Barbados
170 *D14* **Ōita** Ōita, Kyūshū, SW Japan
170 *D14* **Ōita** *off.* Ōita-ken. ◆ *prefecture* Kyūshū, SW Japan
117 *E17* **Oíti** ▲ C Greece
172 *O6* **Oiwake** Hokkaidō, NE Japan
37 *R14* **Ojai** California, W USA
96 *K13* **Öje** Kopparberg, C Sweden
95 *J14* **Öjebyn** Norrbotten, N Sweden
170 *Bb12* **Ojika-jima** *island* SW Japan
42 *K5* **Ojinaga** Chihuahua, N Mexico
171 *K13* **Ojiya** *var.* Oziya. Niigata, Honshū, C Japan
42 *M11* **Ojo Caliente** *var.* Ojocaliente. Zacatecas, C Mexico
42 *D6* **Ojo de Liebre, Laguna** *var.* Laguna Scammon, Scammon Lagoon. *lagoon* W Mexico
64 *I7* **Ojos del Salado, Cerro** ▲ W Argentina
107 *R7* **Ojos Negros** Aragón, NE Spain
42 *M12* **Ojuelos de Jalisco** Aguascalientes, C Mexico
131 *N4* **Oka** ≈ W Russian Federation
85 *D19* **Okahandja** Otjozondjupa, C Namibia
192 *L9* **Okahukura** Manawatu-Wanganui, North Island, NZ
192 *J3* **Okaihau** Northland, North Island, NZ
85 *D18* **Okakarara** Otjozondjupa, N Namibia
11 *P5* **Okak Islands** *island group* Newfoundland and Labrador, E Canada
8 *M17* **Okanagan** ≈ British Columbia, SW Canada
9 *N17* **Okanagan Lake** ◎ British Columbia, SW Canada
Ókanizsa *see* Kanjiža
85 *C16* **Okankolo** Otjikoto, N Namibia
34 *K6* **Okanogan River** ≈ Washington, NW USA
194 *I13* **Okapa** Eastern Highlands, C PNG
85 *D18* **Okaputa** Otjozondjupa, N Namibia
155 *V9* **Okāra** Punjab, E Pakistan
28 *M10* **Okarche** Oklahoma, C USA
152 *B13* **Okarem** *Turkm.* Ekerem. Balkanskiy Velayat, W Turkmenistan
201 *X14* **Okat Harbor** *harbor* Kosrae, E Micronesia
24 *M5* **Okatibbee Creek** ≈ Mississippi, S USA
85 *C17* **Okaukuejo** Kunene, N Namibia
Okavanggo *see* Cubango/Okavango
85 *E17* **Okavango** ◆ *district* NW Namibia
85 *G17* **Okavango** *var.* Cubango, Kavango, Kavengo, Kubango, Okavanggo, *Port.* Ocavango. ≈ S Africa *see also* Cubango
85 *G17* **Okavango Delta** *wetland* N Botswana
171 *J15* **Okaya** Nagano, Honshū, S Japan
170 *Ff14* **Okayama** Okayama, Honshū, SW Japan
170 *F13* **Okayama** *off.* Okayama-ken. ◆ *prefecture* Honshū, SW Japan
171 *I16* **Okazaki** Aichi, Honshū, C Japan
112 *M12* **Okęcie** ✕ (Warszawa) Warszawa, C Poland
25 *Y13* **Okeechobee** Florida, SE USA
25 *Y14* **Okeechobee, Lake** ◎ Florida, SE USA
28 *M9* **Okeene** Oklahoma, C USA
25 *V8* **Okefenokee Swamp** *wetland* Georgia, SE USA
99 *J24* **Okehampton** SW England, UK
29 *P10* **Okemah** Oklahoma, C USA
79 *U16* **Okene** Kogi, S Nigeria
102 *K13* **Oker** *var.* Ocker. ≈ NW Germany
103 *J14* **Oker-Stausee** ◎ C Germany
127 *O13* **Okha** Ostrov Sakhalin, Sakhalinskaya Oblast', SE Russian Federation
129 *U15* **Okhansk** *var.* Ochansk. Permskaya Oblast', NW Russian Federation
127 *N10* **Okhota** ≈ E Russian Federation
127 *Nn11* **Okhotsk** Khabarovskiy Kray, E Russian Federation
199 *I2* **Okhotsk, Sea of** *sea* NW Pacific Ocean
119 *T4* **Okhtyrka** *Rus.* Akhtyrka. Sums'ka Oblast', NE Ukraine
199 *Gg6* **Oki-Daitō Ridge** *undersea feature* W Pacific Ocean
85 *E23* **Okiep** Northern Cape, W South Africa
Oki-guntō *see* Oki-shotō
170 *Ff11* **Oki-kaikyō** *strait* SW Japan
172 *P15* **Okinawa** Okinawa, SW Japan
172 *Oo14* **Okinawa** *off.* Okinawa-ken. ◆ *prefecture* Okinawa, SW Japan
172 *Oo14* **Okinawa** *island* SW Japan
172 *Q14* **Okinoerabu-jima** *island* Nansei-shotō, SW Japan
170 *Dd15* **Okino-shima** *island* SW Japan
170 *Ff11* **Oki-shotō** *var.* Oki-guntō. *island group* SW Japan
79 *T16* **Okitipupa** Ondo, SW Nigeria
177 *G8* **Okkan** Pegu, SW Myanmar
29 *N10* **Oklahoma** *off.* State of Oklahoma; also known as The Sooner State. ◆ *state* C USA
29 *N11* **Oklahoma City** *state capital* Oklahoma, C USA
27 *Q4* **Oklaunion** Texas, SW USA
25 *W10* **Oklawaha River** ≈ Florida, SE USA
29 *P10* **Okmulgee** Oklahoma, C USA
Oknitsa *see* Ocnița
24 *M3* **Okolona** Mississippi, S USA
172 *Q4* **Okoppe** Hokkaidō, NE Japan
9 *Q16* **Okotoks** Alberta, SW Canada
82 *H6* **Oko, Wadi** ≈ NE Sudan
81 *G19* **Okoyo** Cuvette, W Congo
79 *S15* **Okpara** ≈ Benin/Nigeria
94 *J8* **Øksfjord** Finnmark, N Norway
176 *Z12* **Oksibil** Irian Jaya, E Indonesia
129 *R4* **Oksino** Nenetskiy Avtonomnyy Okrug, NW Russian Federation
94 *G13* **Oksskolten** ▲ C Norway
Oksu *see* Oqsu
150 *M8* **Oktaybr'skiy** Kustanay, N Kazakhstan
194 *E11* **Ok Tedi** Western, W PNG
Oktemberyan *see* Hoktemberyan
177 *G7* **Oktwin** Pegu, C Myanmar
150 *I10* **Oktyabr'sk** Aktyubinsk, W Kazakhstan
131 *R6* **Oktyabr'sk** Samarskaya Oblast', W Russian Federation
129 *N12* **Oktyabr'skiy** Arkhangel'skaya Oblast', NW Russian Federation
127 *Pp12* **Oktyabr'skiy** Kamchatskaya Oblast', E Russian Federation
131 *T5* **Oktyabr'skiy** Respublika Bashkortostan, W Russian Federation
131 *O11* **Oktyabr'skiy** Volgogradskaya Oblast', SW Russian Federation
Oktyabr'skiy *see* Aktsyabrski
131 *V7* **Oktyabr'skoye** Orenburgskaya Oblast', W Russian Federation
126 *J3* **Oktyabr'skoy Revolyutsii, Ostrov** *Eng.* October Revolution Island. *island* Severnaya Zemlya, N Russian Federation
170 *C15* **Ōkuchi** *var.* Ōkuti. Kagoshima, Kyūshū, SW Japan
Okulovka *see* Uglovka
171 *Mm5* **Okushiri-tō** *var.* Okusiri Tô. *island* NE Japan
Okusiri Tô *see* Okushiri-tō
79 *S15* **Okuta** Kwara, W Nigeria
Ōkuti *see* Ōkuchi
85 *F19* **Okwa** *var.* Chapman's. ≈ Botswana/Namibia
127 *O10* **Ola** Magadanskaya Oblast', E Russian Federation
29 *T11* **Ola** Arkansas, C USA
Ola *see* Ala
37 *T11* **Olacha Peak** ▲ California, W USA
94 *J1* **Ólafsfjördhur** Nordhurland Eystra, N Iceland
94 *H3* **Ólafsvík** Vesturland, W Iceland
Oláhbrettye *see* Bretea-Română
Oláhszentgyörgy *see* Sângeorz-Băi
Oláh-Toplicza *see* Toplița
37 *T11* **Olancha** California, W USA
44 *J5* **Olanchito** Yoro, C Honduras
44 *J6* **Olancho** ◆ *department* E Honduras
97 *O20* **Öland** *island* S Sweden

◆ Country ◇ Dependent Territory ◆ Administrative Region ▲ Mountain ▲ Volcano ◎ Lake
● Country Capital ○ Dependent Territory Capital ✕ International Airport ▲ Mountain Range ≈ River ⊡ Reservoir

Ölands norra udde – Orlovskaya Oblast'

97 O19 **Ölands norra udde** *headland* S Sweden
97 N22 **Ölands södra udde** *headland* S Sweden
190 K7 **Olary** South Australia
29 R4 **Olathe** Kansas, C USA
63 C22 **Olavarría** Buenos Aires, E Argentina
94 O2 **Olav V Land** *physical region* C Svalbard
113 H14 **Oława** *Ger.* Ohlau. Wrocław, SW Poland
109 D17 **Olbia** *prev.* Terranova Pausania. Sardegna, Italy, C Mediterranean Sea
46 G5 **Old Bahama Channel** *channel* Bahamas/Cuba
Old Bay State/Old Colony State *see* Massachusetts
8 H2 **Old Crow** Yukon Territory, NW Canada
Old Dominion *see* Virginia
Oldeberkeap *see* Oldeberkoop
100 M7 **Oldeberkoop** *Fris.* Oldeberkeap. Friesland, N Netherlands
100 L10 **Oldebroek** Gelderland, E Netherlands
100 L8 **Oldemarkt** Overijssel, N Netherlands
96 E11 **Olden** Sogn og Fjordane, C Norway
102 G10 **Oldenburg** Niedersachsen, NW Germany
102 K8 **Oldenburg** Schleswig-Holstein, N Germany
100 P10 **Oldenzaal** Overijssel, E Netherlands
94 I9 **Olderdalen** Troms, N Norway
20 J8 **Old Forge** New York, NE USA
Old Goa *see* Goa
99 L17 **Oldham** NW England, UK
41 Q14 **Old Harbor** Kodiak Island, Alaska, USA
46 J13 **Old Harbour** C Jamaica
99 C22 **Old Head of Kinsale** *Ir.* An Seancheann. *headland* SW Ireland
22 J8 **Old Hickory Lake** ⊠ Tennessee, S USA
Old Line State *see* Maryland
Old North State *see* North Carolina
83 I17 **Ol Doinyo Lengeyo** ▲▲ C Kenya
9 Q16 **Olds** Alberta, SW Canada
21 O7 **Old Speck Mountain** ▲ Maine, NE USA
21 S6 **Old Town** Maine, NE USA
9 T17 **Old Wives Lake** ◎ Saskatchewan, S Canada
168 J7 **Öldziyt** Arhangay, C Mongolia
169 N10 **Öldziyt** Dornogovĭ, SE Mongolia
196 H6 **Oleai** *var.* San Jose. Saipan, S Northern Mariana Islands
21 O11 **Olean** New York, NE USA
112 O7 **Olecko** *Ger.* Treuburg. Suwałki, NE Poland
108 C7 **Oleggio** Piemonte, NE Italy
126 L13 **Olëkma** Amurskaya Oblast', SE Russian Federation
126 L13 **Olëkma** ≈ C Russian Federation
126 L12 **Olëkminsk** Respublika Sakha (Yakutiya), NE Russian Federation
119 W7 **Oleksandrivka** Donets'ka Oblast', E Ukraine
119 R7 **Oleksandrivka** *Rus.* Aleksandrovka. Kirovohrads'ka Oblast', C Ukraine
119 Q9 **Oleksandrivka** Mykolayivs'ka Oblast', S Ukraine
119 S7 **Oleksandriya** *Rus.* Aleksandriya. Kirovohrads'ka Oblast', C Ukraine
95 B20 **Ølen** Hordaland, S Norway
128 J4 **Olenegorsk** Murmanskaya Oblast', NW Russian Federation
126 K8 **Olenëk** Respublika Sakha (Yakutiya), NE Russian Federation
126 Jj9 **Olenëk** ≈ NE Russian Federation
126 Kk6 **Olenëkskiy Zaliv** *bay* N Russian Federation
128 K6 **Olenitsa** Murmanskaya Oblast', NW Russian Federation
104 I11 **Oléron, Île d'** *island* W France
113 H14 **Oleśnica** *Ger.* Oels, Oels in Schlesien. Wrocław, SW Poland
113 I15 **Olesno** *Ger.* Rosenberg. Częstochowa, S Poland
118 M3 **Olevs'k** *Rus.* Olevsk. Zhytomyrs'ka Oblast', N Ukraine
127 Nn18 **Ol'ga** Primorskiy Kray, SE Russian Federation
189 P8 **Olga, Mount** ▲ Northern Territory, C Australia
94 P2 **Olgastretet** *strait* E Svalbard
168 D5 **Ölgiy** Bayan-Ölgiy, W Mongolia
97 F23 **Ølgod** Ribe, W Denmark
106 H14 **Olhão** Faro, S Portugal
95 L14 **Olhava** Oulu, C Finland
114 B12 **Olib** *It.* Ulbo. *island* W Croatia
85 B16 **Olifa** Kunene, NW Namibia
85 E20 **Olifants** *var.* Elephant River. ≈ E Namibia
85 E25 **Olifants** *var.* Elefantes. ≈ SW South Africa
85 G22 **Olifantshoek** Northern Cape, N South Africa
196 L15 **Olimarao Atoll** *atoll* Caroline Islands, C Micronesia
Ólimbos *see* Ólympos
Olimpo *see* Fuerte Olimpo
61 Q15 **Olinda** Pernambuco, E Brazil
Olinthos *see* Ólynthos
85 I20 **Oliphants Drift** Kgatleng, SE Botswana
Olisipo *see* Lisboa
Olita *see* Alytus
107 Q4 **Olite** Navarra, N Spain
64 K10 **Oliva** Córdoba, C Argentina
107 T11 **Oliva** País Valenciano, E Spain
106 I12 **Oliva de la Frontera** Extremadura, W Spain
Olivares *see* Olivares de Júcar
64 H9 **Olivares, Cerro de** ▲ N Chile
107 P9 **Olivares de Júcar** *var.* Olivares. Castilla-La Mancha, C Spain
24 L1 **Olive Branch** Mississippi, S USA
23 O5 **Olive Hill** Kentucky, S USA
37 O6 **Olivehurst** California, W USA
106 G7 **Oliveira de Azeméis** Aveiro, N Portugal
106 I11 **Olivenza** Extremadura, W Spain
9 N17 **Oliver** British Columbia, SW Canada
105 N7 **Olivet** Loiret, C France
31 Q12 **Olivet** South Dakota, N USA
31 T9 **Olivia** Minnesota, N USA
193 C20 **Olivine Range** ▲▲ South Island, NZ
110 H10 **Olivone** Ticino, S Switzerland
Ölkeyek *see* Ul'kayak
131 O9 **Ol'khovka** Volgogradskaya Oblast', SW Russian Federation
113 K16 **Olkusz** Katowice, S Poland
24 I6 **Olla** Louisiana, S USA
64 I4 **Ollagüe, Volcán** *var.* Oyahue, Volcán Oyahue. ▲ N Chile
201 U13 **Ollan** *island* Chuuk, C Micronesia
196 F7 **Ollei** Babeldaob, N Palau
Ollius *see* Oglio
110 C10 **Ollon** Vaud, W Switzerland
153 Q10 **Olmaliq** *Rus.* Almalyk. Toshkent Wiloyati, E Uzbekistan
106 M6 **Olmedo** Castilla-León, N Spain
58 B10 **Olmos** Lambayeque, W Peru
Olmütz *see* Olomouc
32 M15 **Olney** Illinois, N USA
27 R5 **Olney** Texas, SW USA
97 L22 **Olofström** Blekinge, S Sweden
195 Y15 **Olomburi** Malaita, N Solomon Islands
113 H17 **Olomouc** *Ger.* Olmütz, *Pol.* Ołomuniec. Severní Morava, E Czech Republic
Olomuniec *see* Olomouc
125 Cc6 **Olonets** Respublika Kareliya, NW Russian Federation
179 P10 **Olongapo** *off.* Olongapo City. Luzon, N Philippines
104 J16 **Oloron-Ste-Marie** Pyrénées-Atlantiques, SW France
198 Dd8 **Olosega** *island* Manua Islands, E American Samoa
107 W4 **Olot** Cataluña, NE Spain
152 K12 **Olot** *Rus.* Alat. Bukhoro Wiloyati, C Uzbekistan
114 I12 **Olovo** E Bosnia and Herzegovina
126 Kk16 **Olovyannaya** Chitinskaya Oblast', S Russian Federation
127 Oo6 **Oloy** ≈ NE Russian Federation
103 F16 **Olpe** Nordrhein-Westfalen, W Germany
111 N8 **Olperer** ▲ SW Austria
Olshanka *see* Vil'shanka
Ol'shany *see* Al'shany
Olsnitz *see* Murska Sobota
100 M10 **Olst** Overijssel, E Netherlands
112 L8 **Olsztyn** *Ger.* Allenstein. Olsztyn, N Poland
112 L8 **Olsztyn** *off.* Województwo Olsztyńskie. ◐ *province* N Poland
112 L8 **Olsztynek** *Ger.* Hohenstein in Ostpreussen. Olsztyn, N Poland
Olsztyńskie, Województwo *see* Olsztyn
118 I14 **Olt** ◐ *county* SW Romania
118 I14 **Olt** *var.* Oltul, *Ger.* Alt. ≈ S Romania
110 E7 **Olten** Solothurn, NW Switzerland
118 K14 **Oltenița** *prev.* Eng. Oltenitsa, *anc.* Constantiola. Călărași, SE Romania
Oltenitsa *see* Oltenița
118 H14 **Olteț** ≈ S Romania
26 M4 **Olton** Texas, SW USA
143 R12 **Oltu** Erzurum, NE Turkey
Oltul *see* Olt
152 G7 **Oltynkŭl** Qoraqalpoghiston Respublikasi, NW Uzbekistan
167 S15 **Oluan Pi** *Eng.* Cape Olwanpi. *headland* S Taiwan
Ólubló *see* Stará Ľubovňa
143 R11 **Olur** Erzurum, NE Turkey
106 L15 **Olvera** Andalucía, S Spain
Ol'viopol' *see* Pervomays'k
Olwanpi, Cape *see* Oluan Pi
17 G2 **Olympia** *state capital* Washington, NW USA
117 D20 **Olympía** Dytikí Ellás, S Greece
190 H5 **Olympic Dam** South Australia
34 F7 **Olympic Mountains** ▲▲ Washington, NW USA
124 R12 **Ólympos** *var.* Troodos, *Eng.* Mount Olympus. ▲ C Cyprus
117 F15 **Ólympos** *var.* Ólimbos, *Eng.* Mount Olympus. ▲ N Greece
117 L17 **Ólympos** ▲ Lésvos, E Greece
17 G1 **Olympus, Mount** ▲ Washington, NW USA
Olympus, Mount *see* Ólympos
117 G14 **Ólynthos** *var.* Olinthos; *anc.* Olynthus. *site of ancient city* Kentrikí Makedonía, N Greece
Olynthus *see* Ólynthos
119 Q3 **Olyshivka** Chernihivs'ka Oblast', N Ukraine
127 Q7 **Olyutorskiy, Mys** *headland* E Russian Federation
127 Pp8 **Olyutorskiy Zaliv** *bay* E Russian Federation
194 F11 **Om** ≈ W PNG
133 S6 **Om'** ≈ N Russian Federation
164 I13 **Oma** Xizang Zizhiqu, W China
172 N8 **Ōma** Aomori, Honshū, C Japan
129 P6 **Oma** ≈ NW Russian Federation
171 J14 **Ōmachi** *var.* Ōmati. Nagano, Honshū, S Japan
171 Ii17 **Omae-zaki** *headland* Honshū, S Japan
171 M11 **Ōmagari** Akita, Honshū, C Japan
99 E15 **Omagh** *Ir.* An Ómaigh. W Northern Ireland, UK
31 S15 **Omaha** Nebraska, C USA
85 E19 **Omaheke** ◐ *district* W Namibia
147 W10 **Oman** *off.* Sultanate of Oman, *Ar.* Salṭanat 'Umān; *prev.* Muscat and Oman. ◆ *monarchy* SW Asia
133 O10 **Oman Basin** *var.* Bassin d'Oman. *undersea feature* N Indian Ocean
Oman, Bassin d' *see* Oman Basin
133 N10 **Oman, Gulf of** *Ar.* Khalīj 'Umān. *gulf* N Arabian Sea
192 J3 **Omapere** Northland, North Island, NZ
193 E20 **Omarama** Canterbury, South Island, NZ
114 F11 **Omarska** NW Bosnia and Herzegovina
85 C18 **Omaruru** Erongo, NW Namibia
85 C19 **Omaruru** ≈ W Namibia
85 E17 **Omatako** ≈ NE Namibia
Ômati *see* Ômachi
85 E18 **Omawewozonyanda** Omaheke, E Namibia
172 N7 **Ōma-zaki** *headland* Honshū, C Japan
Omba *see* Ambae
Ombai *see* Alor, Pulau
175 Rr16 **Ombai, Selat** *strait* Nusa Tenggara, S Indonesia
85 C16 **Ombalantu** Omusati, N Namibia
81 H15 **Ombella-Mpoko** ◐ *prefecture* S Central African Republic
Ombetsu *see* Onbetsu
85 B17 **Ombombo** Kunene, NW Namibia
81 D19 **Omboué** Ogooué-Maritime, W Gabon
108 G13 **Ombrone** ≈ C Italy
82 F9 **Omdurman** *var.* Umm Durmān. Khartoum, C Sudan
171 Jj16 **Ōme** Tōkyō, Honshū, S Japan
108 C6 **Omegna** Piemonte, NE Italy
191 P12 **Omeo** Victoria, SE Australia
144 F11 **'Omer** Southern, C Israel
43 P16 **Ometepec** Guerrero, S Mexico
44 K11 **Ometepe, Isla de** *island* S Nicaragua
Om Hager *see* Om Hajer
82 I10 **Om Hajer** *var.* Om Hager. SW Eritrea
171 H14 **Ōmi-Hachiman** *var.* Ōmihachiman. Shiga, Honshū, SW Japan
8 L12 **Omineca Mountains** ▲▲ British Columbia, W Canada
115 F14 **Omiš** *It.* Almissa. Split-Dalmacija, S Croatia
114 B10 **Omišalj** Primorje-Gorski Kotar, NW Croatia
170 Dd12 **Ōmi-shima** *island* SW Japan
85 D19 **Omitara** Khomas, C Namibia
43 O16 **Omitlán, Río** ≈ S Mexico
41 X14 **Ommaney, Cape** *headland* Baranof Island, Alaska, USA
100 N9 **Ommen** Overijssel, E Netherlands
168 K11 **Ömnögovĭ** ◐ *province* S Mongolia
203 X7 **Omoa** Fatu Hira, NE French Polynesia
Omo Botego *see* Omo Wenz
Ómoldova *see* Moldova Veche
127 O6 **Omolon** Chukotskiy Avtonomnyy Okrug, NE Russian Federation
127 O7 **Omolon** ≈ NE Russian Federation
126 Ll8 **Omoloy** ≈ NE Russian Federation
171 M10 **Omono-gawa** ≈ Honshū, C Japan
83 I14 **Omo Wenz** *var.* Omo Botego. ≈ Ethiopia/Kenya
125 Ff13 **Omsk** Omskaya Oblast', C Russian Federation
125 Ff12 **Omskaya Oblast'** ◐ *province* C Russian Federation
127 O8 **Omsukchan** Magadanskaya Oblast', E Russian Federation
172 Q4 **Ōmu** Hokkaidō, NE Japan
112 M9 **Omulew** ≈ NE Poland
118 J12 **Omul, Vârful** *prev.* Vîrful Omu. ▲ C Romania
85 D16 **Omundaungilo** Ohangwena, N Namibia
170 C13 **Ōmura** Nagasaki, Kyūshū, SW Japan
85 B17 **Omusati** ◐ *district* N Namibia
170 Cc13 **Ōmuta** Fukuoka, Kyūshū, SW Japan
129 S14 **Omutninsk** Kirovskaya Oblast', NW Russian Federation
Omu, Vîrful *see* Omul, Vârful
31 V7 **Onamia** Minnesota, N USA
23 Y5 **Onancock** Virginia, NE USA
12 E10 **Onaping Lake** ◎ Ontario, S Canada
32 M12 **Onarga** Illinois, N USA
13 R6 **Onatchiway, Lac** ◎ Québec, SE Canada
31 S14 **Onawa** Iowa, C USA
172 Pp7 **Onbetsu** *var.* Ombetsu. Hokkaidō, NE Japan
85 B16 **Oncócua** Cunene, SW Angola
107 S9 **Onda** País Valenciano, E Spain
113 N18 **Ondava** ≈ NE Slovakia
Ondjiva *see* N'Giva
79 T16 **Ondo** Ondo, SW Nigeria
79 T16 **Ondo** ◐ *state* SW Nigeria
169 N8 **Öndörhaan** Hentiy, E Mongolia
85 D18 **Ondundazongonda** Otjozondjupa, N Namibia
157 K21 **One and Half Degree Channel** *channel* S Maldives
197 L15 **Oneata** *island* Lau Group, E Fiji
128 L9 **Onega** Arkhangel'skaya Oblast', NW Russian Federation
125 Dd6 **Onega** ≈ NW Russian Federation
Onega Bay *see* Onezhskaya Guba
Onega, Lake *see* Onezhskoye Ozero
20 I10 **Oneida** New York, NE USA
22 M8 **Oneida** Tennessee, S USA
20 H9 **Oneida Lake** ◎ New York, NE USA
31 P13 **O'Neill** Nebraska, C USA
127 Pp13 **Onekotan, Ostrov** *island* Kuril'skiye Ostrova, SE Russian Federation
25 P3 **Oneonta** Alabama, S USA
20 J11 **Oneonta** New York, NE USA
202 I16 **Oneroa** *island* S Cook Islands
118 K11 **Onești** *Hung.* Onyest; *prev.* Gheorghe Gheorghiu-Dej. Bacău, E Romania
200 Qq15 **Onevai** *island* Tongatapu Group, S Tonga
110 A11 **Onex** Genève, SW Switzerland
128 K8 **Onezhskaya Guba** *Eng.* Onega Bay. *bay* NW Russian Federation
125 D6 **Onezhskoye Ozero** *Eng.* Lake Onega. ◎ NW Russian Federation
85 C16 **Ongandjera** Omusati, N Namibia
192 N12 **Ongaonga** Hawke's Bay, North Island, NZ
168 K9 **Ongi** Dundgovĭ, C Mongolia
168 J8 **Ongi** Övörhangay, C Mongolia
169 W14 **Ongjin** SW North Korea
161 J17 **Ongole** Andhra Pradesh, E India
168 K8 **Ongon** Övörhangay, C Mongolia
Ongtüstik Qazaqstan Oblysy *see* Yuzhnyy Kazakhstan
101 I21 **Onhaye** Namur, S Belgium
177 G8 **Onhne** Pegu, SW Myanmar
143 S9 **Oni** N Georgia
31 N9 **Onida** South Dakota, N USA
170 E15 **Onigajō-yama** ▲ Shikoku, SW Japan
180 H7 **Onilahy** ≈ S Madagascar
79 U16 **Onitsha** Anambra, S Nigeria
171 Gg14 **Ōno** Hyōgo, Honshū, SW Japan
197 I15 **Ono** *island* SW Fiji
171 I14 **Ōno** Fukui, Honshū, SW Japan
170 D12 **Onoda** Yamaguchi, Honshū, SW Japan
197 L17 **Ono-i-lau** *island* SE Fiji
170 Cc13 **Ōnojō** *var.* Ōnozyô. Fukuoka, Kyūshū, SW Japan
126 K16 **Onokhoy** Respublika Buryatiya, S Russian Federation
170 F14 **Onomichi** *var.* Onomiti. Hiroshima, Honshū, SW Japan
Onomiti *see* Onomichi
169 O7 **Onon Gol** ≈ N Mongolia
Ononte *see* Orontes
57 N6 **Onoto** Anzoátegui, NE Venezuela
203 O3 **Onotoa** *prev.* Clerk Island. *atoll* Tungaru, W Kiribati
Ōnozyô *see* Ōnojō
97 I19 **Onsala** Halland, S Sweden
85 E23 **Onseepkans** Northern Cape, W South Africa
106 F4 **Ons, Illa de** *island* NW Spain
188 H7 **Onslow** Western Australia
23 W11 **Onslow Bay** *bay* North Carolina, E USA
100 P6 **Onstwedde** Groningen, NE Netherlands
170 Bb16 **On-take** ▲ Kyūshū, SW Japan
171 Ii15 **Ontake-san** ▲ Honshū, S Japan
37 T15 **Ontario** California, W USA
34 M13 **Ontario** Oregon, NW USA
10 D10 **Ontario** ◐ *province* S Canada
15 Gg2 **Ontario, Lake** ◎ Canada/USA
1 L9 **Ontario Peninsula** *peninsula* Canada/USA
Onteniente *see* Ontinyent
107 S11 **Ontinyent** *var.* Onteniente. País Valenciano, E Spain
95 N15 **Ontojärvi** ◎ E Finland
32 L3 **Ontonagon** Michigan, N USA
32 L3 **Ontonagon River** ≈ Michigan, N USA
195 W11 **Ontong Java Atoll** *prev.* Lord Howe Island. *atoll* N Solomon Islands
183 N5 **Ontong Java Rise** *undersea feature* W Pacific Ocean
Onuba *see* Huelva
57 W9 **Onverwacht** Para, N Suriname
Onyest *see* Onești
190 J7 **Oodla Wirra** South Australia
190 F2 **Oodnadatta** South Australia
190 C5 **Ooldea** South Australia
29 Q8 **Oologah Lake** ⊠ Oklahoma, C USA
Oos-Kaap *see* Eastern Cape
Oos-Londen *see* East London
101 E17 **Oostakker** Oost-Vlaanderen, NW Belgium
101 D15 **Oostburg** Zeeland, SW Netherlands
100 K9 **Oostelijk-Flevoland** *polder* C Netherlands
101 B16 **Oostende** *Eng.* Ostend, *Fr.* Ostende. West-Vlaanderen, NW Belgium
101 B16 **Oostende** ✕ West-Vlaanderen, NW Belgium
100 L12 **Oosterbeek** Gelderland, SE Netherlands
101 I14 **Oosterhout** Noord-Brabant, S Netherlands
100 O6 **Oostermoers Vaart** *var.* Hunze. ≈ NE Netherlands
101 F14 **Oosterschelde** *Eng.* Eastern Scheldt. *inlet* SW Netherlands
101 E14 **Oosterscheldedam** *dam* SW Netherlands
100 M7 **Oosterwolde** *Fris.* Easterwâlde. Friesland, N Netherlands
100 I9 **Oosthuizen** Noord-Holland, NW Netherlands
101 H16 **Oostmalle** Antwerpen, N Belgium
Oos-Transvaal *see* Mpumalanga
101 E15 **Oost-Souburg** Zeeland, SW Netherlands
101 E17 **Oost-Vlaanderen** *Eng.* East Flanders. ◐ *province* NW Belgium
100 J5 **Oost-Vlieland** Friesland, N Netherlands
100 F12 **Oostvoorne** Zuid-Holland, SW Netherlands
Ootacamund *see* Udagamandalam
100 O10 **Ootmarsum** Overijssel, E Netherlands
8 K14 **Ootsa Lake** ⊠ British Columbia, SW Canada
116 L8 **Opaka** Razgradska Oblast, N Bulgaria
81 M18 **Opala** Haut-Zaïre, C Zaire
129 Q13 **Oparino** Kirovskaya Oblast', NW Russian Federation
12 H8 **Opasatica, Lac** ◎ Québec, SE Canada
114 B9 **Opatija** *It.* Abbazia. Primorje-Gorski Kotar, NW Croatia
113 N15 **Opatów** Tarnobrzeg, SE Poland
113 I17 **Opava** *Ger.* Troppau. Severní Morava, E Czech Republic
113 H16 **Opava** *Ger.* Oppa. ≈ NE Czech Republic
Ôpazova *see* Stara Pazova
194 L14 **Ope** ≈ S PNG
Ópécska *see* Pecica
12 E8 **Opeepeesway Lake** ◎ Ontario, S Canada
25 R5 **Opelika** Alabama, S USA
24 I8 **Opelousas** Louisiana, S USA
195 O11 **Open Bay** *bay* New Britain, E PNG
12 I12 **Opeongo Lake** ◎ Ontario, SE Canada
101 K17 **Opglabbeek** Limburg, NE Belgium
35 W6 **Opheim** Montana, NW USA
41 P10 **Ophir** Alaska, USA
Ophiusa *see* Formentera
81 N18 **Opienge** Haut-Zaïre, E Zaire
193 G20 **Opihi** ≈ South Island, NZ
10 J9 **Opinaca** ≈ Québec, C Canada
10 J10 **Opinaca, Réservoir** ⊠ Québec, E Canada
119 T5 **Opishnya** *Rus.* Oposhnya. Poltavs'ka Oblast', NE Ukraine
100 I8 **Opmeer** Noord-Holland, NW Netherlands
79 V17 **Opobo** Akwa Ibom, S Nigeria
128 F16 **Opochka** Pskovskaya Oblast', W Russian Federation
112 L13 **Opoczno** Piotrków, C Poland
113 I15 **Opole** *Ger.* Oppeln. Opole, SW Poland
113 H15 **Opole** *off.* Województwo Opolskie. ◐ *province* SW Poland
Opolskie, Województwo *see* Opole
150 G13 **Opornyy** Mangistau, SW Kazakhstan
Oporto *see* Porto
Oposhnya *see* Opishnya
192 P8 **Opotiki** Bay of Plenty, North Island, NZ
25 Q7 **Opp** Alabama, S USA
Oppa *see* Opava
96 G9 **Oppdal** Sør-Trøndelag, S Norway
Oppeln *see* Opole
109 N23 **Oppido Mamertina** Calabria, SW Italy
Oppidum Ubiorum *see* Köln
96 F12 **Oppland** ◐ *county* S Norway
120 J12 **Opsa** *Rus.* Opsa. Vitsyebskaya Voblasts', NW Belarus
28 I8 **Optima Lake** ⊠ Oklahoma, C USA
192 J11 **Opunake** Taranaki, North Island, NZ
203 N6 **Opunohu, Baie d'** *bay* Moorea, W French Polynesia
85 B17 **Opuwo** Kunene, NW Namibia
152 H6 **Oqqal'a** *var.* Akkala, *Rus.* Karakala. Qoraqalpoghiston Respublikasi, NW Uzbekistan
153 V13 **Oqsu** *Rus.* Oksu. ≈ SE Tajikistan
153 P14 **Oqtogh, Qatorkŭhi** *Rus.* Khrebet Aktau. ▲▲ SW Tajikistan
152 M11 **Oqtosh** *Rus.* Aktash. Samarqand Wiloyati, C Uzbekistan
153 N11 **Oqtow Tizmasi** *Rus.* Khrebet Aktau. ▲▲ C Uzbekistan
32 J12 **Oquawka** Illinois, N USA
150 J10 **Or'** *Kaz.* Or. ≈ Kazakhstan/Russian Federation
38 M15 **Oracle** Arizona, SW USA
118 F9 **Oradea** *prev.* Oradea Mare, *Ger.* Grosswardein, *Hung.* Nagyvárad. Bihor, NW Romania
Oradea Mare *see* Oradea
115 M17 **Orahovac** *Alb.* Rahovec. Serbia, S Yugoslavia
114 H9 **Orahovica** Virovitica-Podravina, NE Croatia
158 K13 **Orai** Uttar Pradesh, N India
94 K12 **Orajärvi** Lappi, NW Finland
Oral *see* Ural'sk
76 I5 **Oran** *var.* Ouahran, Wahran. NW Algeria
191 R8 **Orange** New South Wales, SE Australia
105 R14 **Orange** *anc.* Arausio. Vaucluse, SE France
27 Y10 **Orange** Texas, SW USA
23 V5 **Orange** Virginia, NE USA
23 R13 **Orangeburg** South Carolina, SE USA
60 J9 **Orange, Cabo** *headland* NE Brazil
31 S12 **Orange City** Iowa, C USA
Orange Cone *see* Orange Fan
180 J10 **Orange Fan** *var.* Orange Cone. *undersea feature* SW Indian Ocean
Orange Free State *see* Free State
27 S14 **Orange Grove** Texas, SW USA
20 K13 **Orange Lake** New York, NE USA
25 V10 **Orange Lake** ◎ Florida, SE USA
Orange Mouth/Orangemund *see* Oranjemund
25 W9 **Orange Park** Florida, SE USA194 M17
Orangerie Bay *bay* SE PNG
85 E23 **Orange River** *Afr.* Oranjerivier. ≈ S Africa
12 G15 **Orangeville** Ontario, S Canada
38 M5 **Orangeville** Utah, W USA
44 G1 **Orange Walk** Orange Walk, N Belize
44 F1 **Orange Walk** ◐ *district* NW Belize
102 N11 **Oranienburg** Brandenburg, NE Germany
100 O7 **Oranjekanaal** *canal* NE Netherlands
85 D23 **Oranjemund** *var.* Orangemund; *prev.* Orange Mouth. Karas, SW Namibia
Oranjerivier *see* Orange River
47 N16 **Oranjestad** ○ (Aruba) W Aruba
Oranje Vrystaat *see* Free State
176 W9 **Oransbari** Irian Jaya, E Indonesia
Orany *see* Varėna
85 H18 **Orapa** Central, C Botswana
144 F9 **Or 'Aqiva** Haifa, W Israel
114 I10 **Orašje** N Bosnia and Herzegovina
118 G11 **Orăștie** *Ger.* Broos, *Hung.* Szászváros. Hunedoara, W Romania
Orașul Stalin *see* Brașov
113 K18 **Orava** *Hung.* Árva, *Pol.* Orawa. ≈ N Slovakia
Oravainen *see* Oravais
95 K16 **Oravais** *Fin.* Oravainen. Vaasa, W Finland
Oravicabánya *see* Oravița
118 F13 **Oravița** *Ger.* Orawitza, *Hung.* Oravicabánya. Caraș-Severin, SW Romania
Orawa *see* Orava
193 B24 **Orawia** Southland, South Island, NZ
Orawitza *see* Oravița
105 P16 **Orb** ≈ S France
108 C9 **Orba** ≈ NW Italy
164 H12 **Orba Co** ◎ W China
110 B9 **Orbe** Vaud, W Switzerland
109 G14 **Orbetello** Toscana, C Italy
106 K3 **Orbigo** ≈ NW Spain
191 Q12 **Orbost** Victoria, SE Australia
97 O14 **Örbyhus** Uppsala, C Sweden
204 I1 **Orcadas** *Argentinian research station* South Orkney Island, Antarctica
107 P12 **Orcera** Andalucía, S Spain
35 P9 **Orchard Homes** Montana, NW USA
39 P5 **Orchard Mesa** Colorado, C USA
20 D10 **Orchard Park** New York, NE USA
Orchid Island *see* Lan Yü
117 G18 **Orchómenos** *var.* Orhomenos, Orkhómenos; *prev.* Skripón, *anc.* Orchomenus. Stereá Ellás, C Greece
Orchomenus *see* Orchómenos
108 B7 **Orco** ≈ NW Italy
105 R8 **Or, Côte d'** *physical region* C France
31 O14 **Ord** Nebraska, C USA
Ordat' *see* Ordats'
121 O15 **Ordats'** *Rus.* Ordat'. Mahilyowskaya Voblasts', E Belarus
38 K8 **Orderville** Utah, W USA
106 H2 **Ordes** Galicia, NW Spain
37 V14 **Ord Mountain** ▲ California, W USA
Ordos Desert *see* Mu Us Shamo
196 B16 **Ordot** C Guam
143 N11 **Ordu** *anc.* Cotyora. Ordu, N Turkey
142 M11 **Ordu** ◐ *province* N Turkey
143 V14 **Ordubad** SW Azerbaijan
107 O3 **Orduña** País Vasco, N Spain
39 U6 **Ordway** Colorado, C USA
150 L8 **Ordzhonikidze** Kustanay, N Kazakhstan
119 T9 **Ordzhonikidze** Dnipropetrovs'ka Oblast', E Ukraine
Ordzhonikidze *see* Vladikavkaz, Russian Federation
Ordzhonikidze *see* Yenakiyeve, Ukraine
Ordzhonikidzeabad *see* Kofarnihon
57 U9 **Orealla** E Guyana
115 G15 **Orebić** *It.* Sabbioncello. Dubrovnik-Neretva, S Croatia
97 M16 **Örebro** Örebro, C Sweden
97 L16 **Örebro** ◐ *county* C Sweden
27 W6 **Ore City** Texas, SW USA
32 L10 **Oregon** Illinois, N USA
29 Q2 **Oregon** Missouri, C USA
33 R11 **Oregon** Ohio, N USA
34 H13 **Oregon** *off.* State of Oregon; also known as Beaver State, Sunset State, Valentine State, Webfoot State. ◐ *state* NW USA
34 G11 **Oregon City** Oregon, NW USA
97 P14 **Öregrund** Uppsala, C Sweden
Orekhov *see* Orikhiv
130 L3 **Orekhovo-Zuyevo** Moskovskaya Oblast', W Russian Federation
Orekhovsk *see* Arekhawsk
Orel *see* Oril'
130 J6 **Orël** Orlovskaya Oblast', W Russian Federation
58 E11 **Orellana** Loreto, N Peru
106 L11 **Orellana, Embalse de** ⊠ W Spain
38 L3 **Orem** Utah, W USA
Ore Mountains *see* Erzgebirge/Krušné Hory
131 V7 **Orenburg** *prev.* Chkalov. Orenburgskaya Oblast', W Russian Federation
131 V7 **Orenburg** ✕ Orenburgskaya Oblast', W Russian Federation
131 T7 **Orenburgskaya Oblast'** ◐ *province* W Russian Federation
Orense *see* Ourense
196 E10 **Oreor** *var.* Koror. ● (Palau) Oreor, N Palau
196 E10 **Oreor** *var.* Koror. *island* N Palau
193 B24 **Orepuki** Southland, South Island, NZ
116 L12 **Orestiáda** *prev.* Orestiás. Anatolikí Makedonía kai Thráki, NE Greece
Orestiás *see* Orestiáda
Öresund/Øresund *see* Sound, The
193 C23 **Oreti** ≈ South Island, NZ
192 L5 **Orewa** Auckland, North Island, NZ
176 Y14 **Oreyabo** Irian Jaya, E Indonesia
67 A25 **Orford, Cape** *headland* West Falkland, Falkland Islands
46 B5 **Órganos, Sierra de los** ▲▲ W Cuba
39 R15 **Organ Peak** ▲ New Mexico, SW USA
107 N9 **Orgaz** Castilla-La Mancha, C Spain
Orgeyev *see* Orhei
168 I6 **Orgil** Hövsgöl, C Mongolia
107 O15 **Orgiva** *var.* Orjiva. Andalucía, S Spain
168 I9 **Örgön** Bayanhongor, C Mongolia
119 N9 **Orhei** *var.* Orheiu, *Rus.* Orgeyev. N Moldova
Orheiu *see* Orhei
107 R3 **Orhi** *var.* Orhy, Pico de Orhy, Pic d'Orhy. ▲ France/Spain *see also* Orhy
Orhomenos *see* Orchómenos
168 L6 **Orhon Gol** ≈ N Mongolia
104 J16 **Orhy** *var.* Orhi, Pico de Orhy, Pic d'Orhy. ▲ France/Spain *see also* Orhi
Orhy, Pic d'/Orhy, Pico de *see* Orhi/Orhy
36 L2 **Orick** California, W USA
34 L6 **Orient** Washington, NW USA
50 D6 **Oriental, Cordillera** ▲▲ Bolivia/Peru
50 D6 **Oriental, Cordillera** ▲▲ C Colombia
59 H16 **Oriental, Cordillera** ▲▲ C Peru
65 M15 **Oriente** Buenos Aires, E Argentina
107 R12 **Orihuela** País Valenciano, E Spain
119 V9 **Orikhiv** *Rus.* Orekhov. Zaporiz'ka Oblast', SE Ukraine
115 K22 **Orikum** *var.* Orikumi. Vlorë, SW Albania
Orikumi *see* Orikum
119 V6 **Oril'** *Rus.* Orel. ≈ E Ukraine
12 H14 **Orillia** Ontario, S Canada
95 M19 **Orimattila** Uusimaa, S Finland
35 Y15 **Orin** Wyoming, C USA
49 R4 **Orinoco, Río** ≈ Colombia/Venezuela
194 G15 **Oriomo** Western, SW PNG
32 K11 **Orion** Illinois, N USA
31 Q5 **Oriska** North Dakota, N USA
159 P17 **Orissa** ◐ *state* NE India
Orissaar *see* Orissaare
120 E5 **Orissaare** *Ger.* Orissaar. Saaremaa, W Estonia
109 B19 **Oristano** Sardegna, Italy, C Mediterranean Sea
109 A19 **Oristano, Golfo di** *gulf* Sardegna, Italy, C Mediterranean Sea
56 D13 **Orito** Putumayo, SW Colombia
95 L18 **Orivesi** Häme, SW Finland
95 N17 **Orivesi** ◎ SE Finland
60 H12 **Oriximiná** Pará, NE Brazil
43 Q14 **Orizaba** Veracruz-Llave, E Mexico
43 Q14 **Orizaba, Volcán Pico de** *var.* Citlaltépetl. ▲ S Mexico
97 I16 **Ørje** Østfold, S Norway
115 I16 **Orjen** ▲▲ Bosnia and Herzegovina/Yugoslavia
Orjiva *see* Orgiva
96 G8 **Orkanger** Sør-Trøndelag, S Norway
96 G8 **Orkdalen** *valley* S Norway
97 K22 **Örkelljunga** Kristianstad, S Sweden
Orkhaniye *see* Botevgrad
Orkhómenos *see* Orchómenos
96 H9 **Orkla** ≈ S Norway
Orkney *see* Orkney Islands
67 J22 **Orkney Deep** *undersea feature* Scotia Sea/Weddell Sea
98 J4 **Orkney Islands** *var.* Orkney, Orkneys. *island group* N Scotland, UK
Orkneys *see* Orkney Islands
26 K8 **Orla** Texas, SW USA
37 N5 **Orland** California, W USA
25 X11 **Orlando** Florida, SE USA
25 X12 **Orlando** ✕ Florida, SE USA
109 K23 **Orlando, Capo d'** *headland* Sicilia, Italy, C Mediterranean Sea
Orlau *see* Orlová
105 N6 **Orléanais** *cultural region* C France
36 L2 **Orleans** California, W USA
21 Q12 **Orleans** Massachusetts, NE USA
105 N7 **Orléans** *anc.* Aurelianum. Loiret, C France
13 R10 **Orléans, Île d'** *island* Québec, SE Canada
Orléansville *see* Chlef
113 F16 **Orlice** *Ger.* Adler. ≈ NE Czech Republic
126 Ii15 **Orlik** Respublika Buryatiya, S Russian Federation
129 Q14 **Orlov** *prev.* Khalturin. Kirovskaya Oblast', NW Russian Federation
113 I17 **Orlová** *Ger.* Orlau, *Pol.* Orłowa. Severní Morava, SE Czech Republic
Orlov, Mys *see* Orlovskiy, Mys
130 J6 **Orlovskaya Oblast'** ◐ *province* W Russian Federation

◆ Country
● Country Capital
◇ Dependent Territory
○ Dependent Territory Capital
◐ Administrative Region
✕ International Airport
▲ Mountain
▲▲ Mountain Range
Volcano
≈ River
◎ Lake
⊠ Reservoir

ORLOVSKIY, MYS – OZERNOVSKIY

128 M5 **Orlovskiy, Mys** var. Mys Orlov. headland NW Russian Federation
Orłowa see Orlová
105 O5 **Orly** × (Paris) Essonne, N France
121 G16 **Orlya** Rus. Orlya. Hrodzyenskaya Voblasts', W Belarus
116 M7 **Orlyak** prev. Makenzen, Trubchular, Rom. Trupcilar. Varnenska Oblast, NE Bulgaria
154 L16 **Ormāra** Baluchistān, SW Pakistan
179 Qq13 **Ormoc** off. Ormoc City, var. MacArthur. Leyte, C Philippines
25 X10 **Ormond Beach** Florida, SE USA
111 X10 **Ormož** Ger. Friedau. NE Slovenia
12 J13 **Ormsby** Ontario, SE Canada
99 K17 **Ormskirk** NW England, UK
Ormsö see Vormsi
13 N13 **Ormstown** Québec, SE Canada
Ormuz, Strait of see Hormuz, Strait of
105 T8 **Ornans** Doubs, E France
104 K5 **Orne** ⬖ department N France
104 K5 **Orne** ~ N France
94 G12 **Ørnes** Nordland, C Norway
112 L7 **Orneta** Elbląg, N Poland
97 P16 **Ornö** Stockholm, C Sweden
39 Q3 **Orno Peak** ▲ Colorado, C USA
95 I16 **Örnsköldsvik** Västernorrland, C Sweden
169 X13 **Oro** E North Korea
47 T6 **Orocovis** C Puerto Rico
56 H10 **Orocué** Casanare, E Colombia
79 N13 **Orodara** SW Burkina
107 S4 **Oroel, Peña de** ▲ N Spain
35 N10 **Orofino** Idaho, NW USA
168 I9 **Orog Nuur** ◎ S Mongolia
37 U14 **Oro Grande** California, W USA
39 S15 **Orogrande** New Mexico, SW USA
203 Q7 **Orohena, Mont** ⛰ Tahiti, W French Polynesia
Orolaunum see Arlon
Orol Dengizi see Aral Sea
201 S15 **Oroluk Atoll** atoll Caroline Islands, C Micronesia
11 O15 **Oromocto** New Brunswick, SE Canada
203 S4 **Orona** prev. Hull Island. atoll Phoenix Islands, C Kiribati
203 V17 **Orongo** ancient monument Easter Island, Chile, E Pacific Ocean
144 I3 **Orontes** var. Ononte, Ar. Nahr el Aassi, Nahr al 'Aṣī. ~ SW Asia
106 L9 **Oropesa** Castilla-La Mancha, C Spain
107 T8 **Oropesa** País Valenciano, E Spain
Oropeza see Cochabamba
169 U5 **Oroqen Zizhiqi** Nei Mongol Zizhiqu, N China
179 Qq15 **Oroquieta** var. Oroquieta City. Mindanao, S Philippines
42 J8 **Oro, Río del** ~ C Mexico
61 O14 **Orós, Açude** ⊠ E Brazil
109 D18 **Orosei, Golfo di** gulf Tyrrhenian Sea, C Mediterranean Sea
113 M24 **Orosháza** Békés, SE Hungary
Orosirá Rodhópis see Rhodope Mountains
113 I22 **Oroszlány** Komárom-Esztergom, W Hungary
196 B16 **Orote Peninsula** peninsula W Guam
127 O9 **Orotukan** Magadanskaya Oblast', E Russian Federation
37 O5 **Oroville** California, W USA
34 K6 **Oroville** Washington, NW USA
37 O5 **Oroville, Lake** ⊠ California, W USA
0 G15 **Orozco Fracture Zone** tectonic feature E Pacific Ocean
66 I7 **Orphan Knoll** undersea feature NW Atlantic Ocean
31 V3 **Orr** Minnesota, N USA
97 M21 **Orrefors** Kalmar, S Sweden
190 I7 **Orroroo** South Australia
33 T12 **Orrville** Ohio, N USA
96 L12 **Orsa** Kopparberg, C Sweden
Orschowa see Orşova
Orschütz see Orzyc
121 O14 **Orsha** Rus. Orsha. Vitsyebskaya Voblasts', NE Belarus
131 Q2 **Orshanka** Respublika Mariy El, W Russian Federation
110 C11 **Orsières** Valais, SW Switzerland
125 Dd13 **Orsk** Orenburgskaya Oblast', W Russian Federation
118 F13 **Orşova** Ger. Orschowa, Hung. Orsova. Mehedinţi, SW Romania
96 D10 **Ørsta** Møre og Romsdal, S Norway
97 O15 **Örsundsbro** Uppsala, C Sweden
142 D16 **Ortaca** Muğla, SW Turkey
109 M16 **Orta Nova** Puglia, SE Italy
142 I17 **Orta Toroslar** ▲▲ S Turkey
56 E11 **Ortega** Tolima, W Colombia
106 H1 **Ortegal, Cabo** headland NW Spain
Ortelsburg see Szczytno
104 J15 **Orthez** Pyrénées-Atlantiques, SW France
59 K14 **Orthon, Río** ~ N Bolivia
62 J10 **Ortigueira** Paraná, S Brazil
106 H1 **Ortigueira** Galicia, NW Spain
108 H5 **Ortisei** Ger. Sankt-Ulrich. Trentino-Alto Adige, N Italy
42 F6 **Ortiz** Sonora, NW Mexico
56 L5 **Ortiz** Guárico, N Venezuela
Ortler see Ortles
108 F5 **Ortles** Ger. Ortler. ▲ N Italy
109 K14 **Ortona** Abruzzi, C Italy
31 R8 **Ortonville** Minnesota, N USA
153 W8 **Orto-Tokoy** Issyk-Kul'skaya Oblast', NE Kyrgyzstan
95 I15 **Örträsk** Västerbotten, N Sweden
102 J12 **Örtze** ~ NW Germany
Oruba see Aruba
148 I3 **Orūmīyeh** var. Rizaiyeh, Urmia, Urmiyeh; prev. Reẕā'īyeh. Āẕarbāyjān-e Bākhtarī, NW Iran
148 J3 **Orūmīyeh, Daryācheh-ye** var. Matianus, Sha Hi, Urumi Yeh, Eng. Lake Urmia; prev. Daryācheh-ye Reẕā'īyeh. ◎ NW Iran
59 K19 **Oruro** Oruro, W Bolivia
59 J19 **Oruro** ⬖ department W Bolivia
97 I18 **Orust** island S Sweden
Oruzgān/Orūzgān see Ūrūzgān
108 H13 **Orvieto** anc. Velsuna. Umbria, C Italy
204 K7 **Orville Coast** physical region Antarctica
116 H7 **Oryakhovo** Oblast Montana, NW Bulgaria
Oryokko see Yalu
119 R5 **Orzhytsya** Poltavs'ka Oblast', C Ukraine
112 M9 **Orzyc** Ger. Orschütz. ~ NE Poland
112 N8 **Orzysz** Ger. Arys. Suwałki, NE Poland
96 I10 **Os** Hedmark, S Norway
97 C14 **Os** Hordaland, S Norway
129 U15 **Osa** Permskaya Oblast', NW Russian Federation
31 W11 **Osage** Iowa, C USA
29 U5 **Osage Beach** Missouri, C USA
29 P5 **Osage City** Kansas, C USA
29 U7 **Osage Fork River** ~ Missouri, C USA
29 U5 **Osage River** ~ Missouri, C USA
171 Gg15 **Ōsaka** hist. Naniwa. Ōsaka, Honshū, SW Japan
171 Gg15 **Ōsaka** off. Ōsaka-fu, var. Ōsaka Hu. ⬖ urban prefecture Honshū, SW Japan
Ōsaka-fu/Ōsaka Hu see Ōsaka
151 R10 **Osakarovka** Karaganda, C Kazakhstan
170 G15 **Ōsaka-wan** bay SW Japan
31 T7 **Osakis** Minnesota, N USA
45 N16 **Osa, Península de** peninsula S Costa Rica
62 M10 **Osasco** São Paulo, S Brazil
29 R5 **Osawatomie** Kansas, C USA
28 L3 **Osborne** Kansas, C USA
181 S8 **Osborn Plateau** undersea feature E Indian Ocean
97 L21 **Osby** Kristianstad, S Sweden
Osca see Huesca
94 N2 **Oscar II Land** physical region W Svalbard
29 Y10 **Osceola** Arkansas, C USA
31 V15 **Osceola** Iowa, C USA
29 S6 **Osceola** Missouri, C USA
31 Q15 **Osceola** Nebraska, C USA
103 N15 **Oschatz** Sachsen, E Germany
102 K13 **Oschersleben** Sachsen-Anhalt, C Germany
33 R7 **Oscoda** Michigan, N USA
Ösel see Saaremaa
96 H6 **Osen** Sør-Trøndelag, S Norway
170 Aa12 **Ōse-zaki** headland Fukue-jima, SW Japan
153 T10 **Osh** Oshskaya Oblast', SW Kyrgyzstan
85 C16 **Oshakati** Oshana, N Namibia
172 Nn6 **Oshamambe** Hokkaidō, NE Japan
85 C16 **Oshana** ⬖ district N Namibia
126 Ii12 **Osharovo** Evenkiyskiy Avtonomnyy Okrug, N Russian Federation
12 H15 **Oshawa** Ontario, SE Canada
171 Mm13 **Oshika-hantō** peninsula Honshū, C Japan
85 C16 **Oshikango** Ohangwena, N Namibia
Oshikoto see Otjikoto
170 Cc12 **Ō-shima** island SW Japan
171 M7 **Ō-shima** island NE Japan
171 Jj17 **Ō-shima** island S Japan
170 G17 **Ō-shima** island SW Japan
172 N6 **Oshima-hantō** ▲▲ Hokkaidō, NE Japan
85 D17 **Oshivelo** Otjikoto, N Namibia
30 K14 **Oshkosh** Nebraska, C USA
32 M7 **Oshkosh** Wisconsin, N USA
Oshmyany see Ashmyany
Osh Oblasty see Oshskaya Oblast'
79 T16 **Oshogbo** Osun, W Nigeria
153 S11 **Oshskaya Oblast'** Kir. Osh Oblasty. ⬖ province SW Kyrgyzstan
81 J20 **Oshwe** Bandundu, C Zaire
Osiek see Osijek
114 I9 **Osijek** prev. Osiek, Osjek, Ger. Esseg, Hung. Eszék. Osijek-Baranja, E Croatia
114 I9 **Osijek-Baranja** off. Osječko-Baranjska Županija. ⬖ province E Croatia
108 J12 **Osimo** Marche, C Italy
126 H15 **Osinniki** Kemerovskaya Oblast', S Russian Federation
126 J14 **Osinovka** Irkutskaya Oblast', C Russian Federation
Osintorf see Asintorf
114 N11 **Osipaonica** Serbia, NE Yugoslavia
Osipenko see Berdyans'k
Osipovichi see Asipovichy
Osječko-Baranjska Županija see Osijek-Baranja
Osjek see Osijek
31 W15 **Oskaloosa** Iowa, C USA
29 Q4 **Oskaloosa** Kansas, C USA
97 N20 **Oskarshamn** Kalmar, S Sweden
97 J21 **Oskarström** Halland, S Sweden
12 M8 **Oskélanéo** Québec, SE Canada
Öskemen see Ust'-Kamenogorsk
Oskil see Oskol
119 W5 **Oskol** Ukr. Oskil. ~ Russian Federation/Ukraine
95 D20 **Oslo** prev. Christiania, Kristiania. ● (Norway) Oslo, S Norway
95 D20 **Oslo** ⬖ county S Norway
95 D21 **Oslofjorden** fjord S Norway
161 G15 **Osmānābād** Mahārāshtra, C India
142 J11 **Osmancık** Çorum, N Turkey
142 L16 **Osmaniye** Adana, S Turkey
97 O16 **Ösmo** Stockholm, C Sweden
120 E3 **Osmussaar** island W Estonia
102 G13 **Osnabrück** Niedersachsen, NW Germany
112 D11 **Ośno Lubuskie** Ger. Drossen. Gorzów, W Poland
Osogovske Planine see Osogovski Planina
115 P18 **Osogovski Planina** var. Osogovske Planine, Mac. Osogovski Planini. ▲▲ Bulgaria/FYR Macedonia
Osogovski Planini see Osogovski Planina
172 N8 **Osore-yama** ▲ Honshū, C Japan
Oşorhei see Târgu Mureş
63 J16 **Osório** Rio Grande do Sul, S Brazil
65 G16 **Osorno** Los Lagos, C Chile
106 M4 **Osorno** Castilla-León, N Spain
9 N17 **Osoyoos** British Columbia, SW Canada
56 J6 **Ospino** Portuguesa, N Venezuela
100 K13 **Oss** Noord-Brabant, S Netherlands
106 H11 **Ossa** ▲ S Portugal
117 F15 **Óssa** ▲▲ C Greece
25 X6 **Ossabaw Island** island Georgia, SE USA
25 X6 **Ossabaw Sound** sound Georgia, SE USA
191 O16 **Ossa, Mount** ▲ Tasmania, SE Australia
106 H11 **Ossa, Serra d'** ▲▲ SE Portugal
79 U16 **Osse** ~ S Nigeria
32 J6 **Osseo** Wisconsin, N USA
111 S9 **Ossiacher See** ◎ S Austria
20 K13 **Ossining** New York, NE USA
96 I12 **Ossjøen** ◎ S Norway
127 P9 **Ossora** Koryakskiy Avtonomnyy Okrug, E Russian Federation
128 I15 **Ostashkov** Tverskaya Oblast', W Russian Federation
102 H9 **Oste** ~ NW Germany
Ostee see Baltic Sea
Ostend/Ostende see Oostende
119 P3 **Oster** Chernihivs'ka Oblast', N Ukraine
97 O14 **Österbybruk** Uppsala, C Sweden
97 M19 **Österbymo** Östergotland, S Sweden
96 K12 **Österdalälven** ~ C Sweden
96 I12 **Østerdalen** valley S Norway
97 L18 **Östergötland** ⬖ county S Sweden
102 H10 **Osterholz-Scharmbeck** Niedersachsen, NW Germany
Östermark see Teuva
Östermyra see Seinäjoki
Osterode/Osterode in Ostpreussen see Ostróda
103 J14 **Osterode am Harz** Niedersachsen, C Germany
96 C13 **Osterøy** island S Norway
Österreich see Austria
95 G16 **Östersund** Jämtland, C Sweden
97 N14 **Östervåla** Västmanland, C Sweden
103 H22 **Ostfildern** Baden-Württemberg, SW Germany
97 H16 **Østfold** ⬖ county S Norway
102 E9 **Ostfriesische Inseln** Eng. East Frisian Islands. island group NW Germany
102 F10 **Ostfriesland** historical region NW Germany
97 P14 **Östhammar** Uppsala, C Sweden
Ostia Aterni see Pescara
108 G8 **Ostiglia** Lombardia, N Italy
97 J14 **Östmark** Värmland, C Sweden
97 K22 **Östra Ringsjön** ◎ S Sweden
113 I17 **Ostrava** Severní Morava, E Czech Republic
112 K8 **Ostróda** Ger. Osterode, Osterode in Ostpreussen. Olsztyn, N Poland
Ostrog/Ostróg see Ostroh
130 L8 **Ostrogozhsk** Voronezhskaya Oblast', W Russian Federation
118 L4 **Ostroh** Pol. Ostróg, Rus. Ostrog. Rivnens'ka Oblast', NW Ukraine
Ostrołęckie, Województwo see Ostrołęka
112 N9 **Ostrołęka** Ger. Wiesenhof, Rus. Ostrolenka. Ostrołęka, NE Poland
112 M10 **Ostrołęka** off. Województwo Ostrołęckie, Rus. Ostrolenka. ⬖ province NE Poland
113 A16 **Ostrov** Ger. Schlackenwerth. Západní Čechy, NW Czech Republic
128 F15 **Ostrov** Latv. Austrava. Pskovskaya Oblast', W Russian Federation
Ostrovets see Ostrowiec Świętokrzyski
115 M21 **Ostrovicës, Mali i** ▲ SE Albania
172 T6 **Ostrov Iturup** island NE Russian Federation
116 L7 **Ostrovo** prev. Golema Ada. Razgradska Oblast, NE Bulgaria
129 N15 **Ostrovskoye** Kostromskaya Oblast', NW Russian Federation
Ostrów see Ostrów Wielkopolski
Ostrowiec see Ostrowiec Świętokrzyski
113 M14 **Ostrowiec Świętokrzyski** var. Ostrowiec, Rus. Ostrovets. Kielce, SE Poland
112 P13 **Ostrów Lubelski** Lublin, E Poland
112 N10 **Ostrów Mazowiecka** var. Ostrów Mazowiecki. Ostrołęka, NE Poland
Ostrów Mazowiecki see Ostrów Mazowiecka
Ostrowo see Ostrów Wielkopolski
112 H13 **Ostrów Wielkopolski** var. Ostrów, Ger. Ostrowo. Kalisz, C Poland
Ostryna see Astryna
112 I13 **Ostrzeszów** Kalisz, C Poland
109 P18 **Ostuni** Puglia, SE Italy
Ostyako-Voguls'k see Khanty-Mansiysk
Osum see Osumit, Lumi i
116 I9 **Osŭm** ~ N Bulgaria
170 Bb17 **Ōsumi-hantō** ▲▲ Kyūshū, SW Japan
170 Bb17 **Ōsumi-kaikyō** strait SW Japan
115 L22 **Osumit, Lumi i** var. Osum. ~ SE Albania
79 T16 **Osun** ⬖ state SW Nigeria
106 L14 **Osuna** Andalucía, S Spain
62 J8 **Osvaldo Cruz** São Paulo, S Brazil
Osveya see Asvyeya
20 I7 **Oswegatchie River** ~ New York, NE USA
29 Q7 **Oswego** Kansas, C USA
20 H9 **Oswego** New York, NE USA
99 K19 **Oswestry** W England, UK
113 J16 **Oświęcim** Ger. Auschwitz. Bielsko-Biała, S Poland
171 K15 **Ōta** Gunma, Honshū, S Japan
193 E22 **Otago** off. Otago Region. ⬖ region South Island, NZ
193 F23 **Otago Peninsula** peninsula South Island, NZ
170 E13 **Ōtake** Hiroshima, Honshū, SW Japan
192 L13 **Otaki** Wellington, North Island, NZ
171 L14 **Ōtakine-yama** ▲ Honshū, C Japan
95 M15 **Otanmäki** Oulu, C Finland
151 T15 **Otar** Zhambyl, SE Kazakhstan
172 O5 **Otaru** Hokkaidō, NE Japan
193 C24 **Otatara** Southland, South Island, NZ
193 C24 **Otautau** Southland, South Island, NZ
95 M18 **Otava** Mikkeli, SE Finland
113 B18 **Otava** Ger. Wottawa. ~ SW Czech Republic
58 C6 **Otavalo** Imbabura, N Ecuador
85 D17 **Otavi** Otjozondjupa, N Namibia
171 Kk15 **Ōtawara** Tochigi, Honshū, S Japan
85 B16 **Otchinjau** Cunene, SW Angola
118 F12 **Oţelu Roşu** Ger. Ferdinandsberg, Hung. Nándorhgy. Caras-Severin, SW Romania
193 E21 **Otematata** Canterbury, South Island, NZ
120 I6 **Otepää** Ger. Odenpäh. Valgamaa, SE Estonia
34 K9 **Othello** Washington, NW USA
117 A15 **Othonoí** island Iónioi Nísoi, Greece, C Mediterranean Sea
Othris see Óthrys
117 F17 **Óthrys** var. Othris. ▲▲ C Greece
79 Q14 **Oti** ~ N Togo
42 K10 **Otinapa** Durango, C Mexico
193 G17 **Otira** West Coast, South Island, NZ
39 V3 **Otis** Colorado, C USA
10 L10 **Otish, Monts** ▲▲ Québec, E Canada
85 C17 **Otjikondo** Kunene, N Namibia
85 C17 **Otjikoto** var. Oshikoto. ⬖ district N Namibia
85 E18 **Otjinene** Omaheke, NE Namibia
85 D18 **Otjiwarongo** Otjozondjupa, N Namibia
85 D18 **Otjosondu** var. Otjosundu. Otjozondjupa, C Namibia
Otjosundu see Otjosondu
85 D18 **Otjozondjupa** ⬖ district C Namibia
114 C11 **Otočac** Lika-Senj, W Croatia
172 Pp6 **Otofuke-gawa** ~ Hokkaidō, NE Japan
168 M14 **Otog Qi** Nei Mongol Zizhiqu, N China
172 Pp3 **Otoineppu** Hokkaidō, NE Japan
114 J10 **Otok** Vukovar-Srijem, E Croatia
118 K14 **Otopeni** × (Bucureşti) Bucureşti, S Romania
192 L8 **Otorohanga** Waikato, North Island, NZ
10 D9 **Otoskwin** ~ Ontario, C Canada
170 F15 **Ōtoyo** Kōchi, Shikoku, SW Japan
97 E16 **Otra** ~ S Norway
109 R19 **Otranto** Puglia, SE Italy
Otranto, Canale d' see Otranto, Strait of
109 Q18 **Otranto, Strait of** It. Canale d'Otranto. strait Albania/Italy
113 H18 **Otrokovice** Ger. Otrokowitz. Jižní Morava, SE Czech Republic
Otrokowitz see Otrokovice
33 P10 **Otsego** Michigan, N USA
33 Q6 **Otsego Lake** ◎ Michigan, N USA
20 I11 **Otselic River** ~ New York, NE USA
171 H15 **Ōtsu** var. Ōtu. Shiga, Honshū, SW Japan
171 Jj16 **Ōtsuki** var. Otuki. Yamanashi, Honshū, S Japan
96 G11 **Otta** Oppland, S Norway
201 U13 **Otta** island Chuuk, C Micronesia
96 F11 **Otta** ~ S Norway
201 U13 **Otta Pass** passage Chuuk Islands, C Micronesia
97 J22 **Ottarp** Malmöhus, S Sweden
12 L12 **Ottawa** ● (Canada) Ontario, SE Canada
32 L11 **Ottawa** Illinois, N USA
29 Q5 **Ottawa** Kansas, C USA
33 R12 **Ottawa** Ohio, N USA
12 L12 **Ottawa** var. Uplands. × Ontario, SE Canada
12 M12 **Ottawa** Fr. Outaouais. ~ Ontario/Québec, SE Canada
10 I4 **Ottawa Islands** island group Northwest Territories, C Canada
20 L8 **Otter Creek** ~ Vermont, NE USA
38 L6 **Otter Creek Reservoir** ⊠ Utah, W USA
100 L11 **Otterlo** Gelderland, E Netherlands
96 D9 **Otterøya** island S Norway
31 S6 **Otter Tail Lake** ◎ Minnesota, N USA
31 R7 **Otter Tail River** ~ Minnesota, C USA
97 H23 **Otterup** Fyn, C Denmark
101 H19 **Ottignies** Walloon Brabant, C Belgium
103 L23 **Ottobrunn** Bayern, SE Germany
194 I12 **Otto, Mount** ▲ C PNG
31 X15 **Ottumwa** Iowa, C USA
Ōtu see Ōtsu
85 B16 **Otuazuma** Kunene, NW Namibia
Otuki see Ōtsuki
79 V16 **Oturkpo** Benue, S Nigeria
200 Ss14 **Otu Tolu Group** island group SE Tonga
190 M13 **Otway, Cape** headland Victoria, SE Australia
65 H24 **Otway, Seno** inlet S Chile
Ötz see Oetz
110 L8 **Ötztaler Ache** ~ W Austria
110 L9 **Ötztaler Alpen** It. Alpi Venoste. ▲▲ SW Austria
29 T12 **Ouachita, Lake** ⊠ Arkansas, C USA
29 R11 **Ouachita Mountains** ▲▲ Arkansas/Oklahoma, C USA
29 U13 **Ouachita River** ~ Arkansas/Louisiana, C USA
Ouadaï see Ouaddaï
78 J7 **Ouadâne** var. Ouadane. Adrar, C Mauritania
80 K13 **Ouadda** Haute-Kotto, N Central African Republic
80 J10 **Ouaddaï** off. Préfecture du Ouaddaï, var. Ouadaï, Wadai. ⬖ prefecture SE Chad
79 P13 **Ouagadougou** var. Wagadugu. ● (Burkina) C Burkina
79 P13 **Ouagadougou** × C Burkina
79 O12 **Ouahigouya** NW Burkina
Ouahran see Oran
81 J14 **Ouaka** ⬖ prefecture C Central African Republic
81 J15 **Ouaka** ~ S Central African Republic
Oualam see Ouallam
78 M9 **Oualâta** var. Oualata. Hodh ech Chargui, SE Mauritania
79 R11 **Ouallam** var. Oualam. Tillabéri, W Niger
180 H14 **Ouanani** Mohéli, S Comoros
57 Z10 **Ouanary** E French Guiana
80 L13 **Ouanda Djallé** Vakaga, NE Central African Republic
81 N14 **Ouando** Haut-Mbomou, SE Central African Republic
81 L15 **Ouango** Mbomou, S Central African Republic
79 N14 **Ouangolodougou** var. Wangolodougou. N Ivory Coast
180 I13 **Ouani** Anjouan, SE Comoros
81 M15 **Ouara** ~ E Central African Republic
78 K7 **Ouarâne** desert C Mauritania
13 O11 **Ouareau** ~ Québec, SE Canada
76 K7 **Ouargla** var. Wargla. NE Algeria
76 F8 **Ouarzazate** S Morocco
79 Q11 **Ouatagouna** Gao, E Mali
76 G6 **Ouazzane** var. Ouezzane, Ar. Wazan, Wazzan. N Morocco
Oubangui see Ubangi
Oubangui-Chari see Central African Republic
Oubari, Edeyen d' see Awbārī, Idhān
100 G13 **Oud-Beijerland** Zuid-Holland, SW Netherlands
100 F13 **Ouddorp** Zuid-Holland, SW Netherlands
79 P9 **Oudeïka** oasis C Mali
100 G13 **Oude Maas** ~ SW Netherlands
101 E18 **Oudenaarde** Fr. Audenarde. Oost-Vlaanderen, SW Belgium
101 H14 **Oudenbosch** Noord-Brabant, S Netherlands
100 P6 **Oude Pekela** Groningen, NE Netherlands
Ouderkerk see Ouderkerk aan den Amstel
100 I10 **Ouderkerk aan den Amstel** var. Ouderkerk. Noord-Holland, C Netherlands
100 I6 **Oudeschild** Noord-Holland, NW Netherlands
101 G14 **Oude-Tonge** Zuid-Holland, SW Netherlands
100 I12 **Oudewater** Utrecht, C Netherlands
Oudjda see Oujda
100 L5 **Oudkerk** Friesland, N Netherlands
104 J7 **Oudon** ~ NW France
100 I9 **Oudorp** Noord-Holland, NW Netherlands
85 G25 **Oudtshoorn** Western Cape, SW South Africa
101 I16 **Oud-Turnhout** Antwerpen, N Belgium
76 F7 **Oued-Zem** C Morocco
197 H5 **Ouégoa** Province Nord, C New Caledonia
78 L13 **Ouéléssébougou** var. Ouolossébougou. Koulikoro, SW Mali
79 N16 **Ouellé** E Ivory Coast
79 R16 **Ouémé** ~ C Benin
197 J7 **Ouen, Île** island S New Caledonia
79 O13 **Ouessa** S Burkina
104 D5 **Ouessant, Île d'** Eng. Ushant. island NW France
81 H17 **Ouesso** La Sangha, NW Congo
81 D15 **Ouest** Eng. West. ⬖ province W Cameroon
202 G11 **Ouest, Baie del'** bay Wallis, Wallis and Futuna
13 Y7 **Ouest, Pointe de l'** headland Québec, SE Canada
Ouezzane see Ouazzane
101 K20 **Ouffet** Liège, E Belgium
81 H14 **Ouham** ⬖ prefecture NW Central African Republic
80 I13 **Ouham** ~ Central African Republic/Chad
81 G14 **Ouham-Pendé** ⬖ prefecture W Central African Republic
79 R16 **Ouidah** Eng. Whydah, Wida. S Benin
76 H6 **Oujda** Ar. Oudjda, Ujda. NE Morocco
78 I7 **Oujeft** Adrar, C Mauritania
95 L15 **Oulainen** Oulu, C Finland
Ould Yanja see Ould Yenjé
78 J10 **Ould Yenjé** var. Ould Yanja. Guidimaka, S Mauritania
95 L14 **Oulu** Swe. Uleåborg. Oulu, C Finland
95 M14 **Oulu** Swe. Uleåborg. ⬖ province N Finland
95 L15 **Oulujärvi** Swe. Uleträsk. ◎ C Finland
95 M14 **Oulujoki** Swe. Uleälv. ~ C Finland
95 L14 **Oulunsalo** Oulu, C Finland
108 A8 **Oulx** Piemonte, NE Italy
80 J9 **Oum-Chalouba** Borkou-Ennedi-Tibesti, NE Chad
78 M16 **Oumé** C Ivory Coast
76 F7 **Oum er Rbia** ~ C Morocco
80 J10 **Oum-Hadjer** Batha, E Chad
94 K10 **Ounasjoki** ~ N Finland
80 J7 **Ounianga Kébir** Borkou-Ennedi-Tibesti, N Chad
Ouolossébougou see Ouéléssébougou
Oup see Auob
101 K19 **Oupeye** Liège, E Belgium
101 N21 **Our** ~ NW Europe
39 Q7 **Ouray** Colorado, C USA
105 R7 **Ource** ~ C France
106 G9 **Ourém** Santarém, C Portugal
106 H4 **Ourense** Cast. Orense; Lat. Aurium. Galicia, NW Spain
106 I4 **Ourense** ⬖ province Galicia, NW Spain
61 O15 **Ouricuri** Pernambuco, E Brazil
62 J9 **Ourinhos** São Paulo, S Brazil
106 G13 **Ourique** Beja, S Portugal
61 M20 **Ouro Preto** Minas Gerais, NE Brazil
Ours, Grand Lac de l' see Great Bear Lake
101 K20 **Ourthe** ~ E Belgium
171 Mm11 **Ou-sanmyaku** ▲▲ Honshū, C Japan
99 M17 **Ouse** ~ N England, UK
Ouse see Great Ouse
104 H7 **Oust** ~ NW France
Outaouais see Ottawa
13 T4 **Outardes Quatre, Réservoir** ⊠ Québec, SE Canada
13 T5 **Outardes, Rivière aux** ~ Québec, SE Canada
98 E8 **Outer Hebrides** var. Western Isles. island group NW Scotland, UK
32 K3 **Outer Island** island Apostle Islands, Wisconsin, N USA
37 S16 **Outer Santa Barbara Passage** passage California, SW USA
106 G3 **Outes** Galicia, NW Spain
85 C18 **Outjo** Kunene, N Namibia
9 T16 **Outlook** Saskatchewan, S Canada
95 N16 **Outokumpu** Pohjois-Karjala, SE Finland
98 M2 **Out Skerries** island group NE Scotland, UK
197 J5 **Ouvéa** island Îles Loyauté, NE New Caledonia
105 S14 **Ouvèze** ~ SE France
190 L9 **Ouyen** Victoria, SE Australia
41 Q14 **Ouzinkie** Kodiak Island, Alaska, USA
143 O13 **Ovacık** Tunceli, E Turkey
108 C9 **Ovada** Piemonte, NE Italy
197 I14 **Ovalau** island C Fiji
64 G9 **Ovalle** Coquimbo, N Chile
85 C17 **Ovamboland** physical region N Namibia
56 L10 **Ovana, Cerro** ▲ S Venezuela
106 G7 **Ovar** Aveiro, N Portugal
116 L10 **Ovcharitsa, Yazovir** ⊠ SE Bulgaria
56 E6 **Ovejas** Sucre, NW Colombia
103 E16 **Overath** Nordrhein-Westfalen, W Germany
100 F13 **Overflakkee** island SW Netherlands
95 F15 **Overhalla** Nord-Trøndelag, C Norway
101 H19 **Overijse** Vlaams Brabant, C Belgium
100 N10 **Overijssel** ⬖ province E Netherlands
100 M9 **Overijssels Kanaal** canal E Netherlands
94 K13 **Överkalix** Norrbotten, N Sweden
29 R4 **Overland Park** Kansas, C USA
101 L14 **Overloon** Noord-Brabant, SE Netherlands
101 K16 **Overpelt** Limburg, NE Belgium
37 Y10 **Overton** Nevada, W USA
27 W7 **Overton** Texas, SW USA
94 K13 **Övertorneå** Norrbotten, N Sweden
97 N18 **Överum** Kalmar, S Sweden
94 G13 **Överuman** ◎ N Sweden
168 H6 **Övgödiy** Dzavhan, C Mongolia
119 P11 **Ovidiopol'** Odes'ka Oblast', SW Ukraine
118 M14 **Ovidiu** Constanţa, SE Romania
47 N10 **Oviedo** SW Dominican Republic
106 K2 **Oviedo** anc. Asturias. Asturias, NW Spain
106 K2 **Oviedo** × Asturias, N Spain
Ovilava see Wels
120 D7 **Oviši** Ventspils, W Latvia
169 P10 **Ovoot** Sühbaatar, SE Mongolia
163 O4 **Övörhangay** ⬖ province C Mongolia
96 E12 **Øvre Årdal** Sogn og Fjordane, S Norway
97 J14 **Övre Fryken** ◎ C Sweden
94 J11 **Övre Soppero** Norrbotten, N Sweden
119 N3 **Ovruch** Zhytomyrs'ka Oblast', N Ukraine
168 J8 **Övt** Övörhangay, C Mongolia
193 E24 **Owaka** Otago, South Island, NZ
81 H18 **Owando** prev. Fort-Rousset. Cuvette, C Congo
171 Gg17 **Owase** Mie, Honshū, SW Japan
29 P9 **Owasso** Oklahoma, C USA
31 V10 **Owatonna** Minnesota, N USA
181 O4 **Owen Fracture Zone** tectonic feature W Arabian Sea
193 H15 **Owen, Mount** ▲ South Island, NZ
193 H15 **Owen River** Tasman, South Island, NZ
22 I6 **Owensboro** Kentucky, S USA
37 T11 **Owens Lake** salt flat California, W USA
12 F14 **Owen Sound** Ontario, S Canada
12 F13 **Owen Sound** ◎ Ontario, S Canada
37 T10 **Owens River** ~ California, W USA
194 K15 **Owen Stanley Range** ▲▲ S PNG
29 V5 **Owensville** Missouri, C USA
22 M4 **Owenton** Kentucky, S USA
79 U17 **Owerri** Imo, S Nigeria
192 M10 **Owhango** Manawatu-Wanganui, North Island, NZ
23 N5 **Owingsville** Kentucky, S USA
152 K10 **Owminzatovo-Toshi** Rus. Gory Auminzatau. ▲▲ N Uzbekistan
79 T16 **Owo** Ondo, SW Nigeria
33 R9 **Owosso** Michigan, N USA
37 V1 **Owyhee** Nevada, W USA
34 L14 **Owyhee, Lake** ◎ Oregon, NW USA
34 L15 **Owyhee River** ~ Idaho/Oregon, NW USA
94 K1 **Öxarfjördhur** var. Axarfjördhur. fjord N Iceland
96 K12 **Oxberg** Kopparberg, C Sweden
9 V17 **Oxbow** Saskatchewan, S Canada
97 O17 **Oxelösund** Södermanland, S Sweden
193 H18 **Oxford** Canterbury, South Island, NZ
99 M21 **Oxford** Lat. Oxonia. S England, UK
25 Q3 **Oxford** Alabama, S USA
24 L2 **Oxford** Mississippi, S USA
31 N16 **Oxford** Nebraska, C USA
20 H16 **Oxford** New York, NE USA
23 U8 **Oxford** North Carolina, SE USA
33 Q14 **Oxford** Ohio, N USA
20 I11 **Oxford** Pennsylvania, NE USA
9 X12 **Oxford House** Manitoba, C Canada
31 Y13 **Oxford Junction** Iowa, C USA
9 X12 **Oxford Lake** ◎ Manitoba, C Canada
99 M21 **Oxfordshire** cultural region S England, UK
Oxia see Oxyá
43 X12 **Oxkutzcab** Yucatán, SE Mexico
37 R15 **Oxnard** California, W USA
Oxonia see Oxford
12 I12 **Oxtongue** ~ Ontario, S Canada
Oxus see Amu Darya
117 E15 **Oxyá** var. Oxia. ▲ C Greece
171 H13 **Oyabe** Toyama, Honshū, SW Japan
Oyahue/Oyahue, Volcán see Ollagüe, Volcán
171 K16 **Oyama** Tochigi, Honshū, S Japan
49 U5 **Oyapock** ~ E French Guiana
Oyapock see Oiapoque, Rio
57 Z10 **Oyapok, Baie de L'** bay Brazil/French Guiana
57 Z11 **Oyapok, Fleuve l'** var. Oyapock, Rio Oiapoque. ~ Brazil/French Guiana see also Oiapoque, Rio
81 E17 **Oyem** Woleu-Ntem, N Gabon
9 R16 **Oyen** Alberta, SW Canada
97 I15 **Øyeren** ◎ S Norway
168 G6 **Oygon** Dzavhan, N Mongolia
98 I7 **Oykel** ~ N Scotland, UK
127 N9 **Oymyakon** Respublika Sakha (Yakutiya), NE Russian Federation
81 H19 **Oyo** Cuvette, C Congo
79 S15 **Oyo** Oyo, W Nigeria
79 S15 **Oyo** ⬖ state SW Nigeria
58 D13 **Oyón** Lima, C Peru
105 S10 **Oyonnax** Ain, E France
152 L10 **Oyoqighitma** Rus. Ayakagytma. Bukhoro Wiloyati, C Uzbekistan
152 M9 **Oyoqquduq** Rus. Ayakkuduk. Nawoiy Wiloyati, N Uzbekistan
34 F9 **Oysterville** Washington, NW USA
97 D14 **Øystese** Hordaland, S Norway
153 U10 **Oy-Tal** Oshskaya Oblast', SW Kyrgyzstan
153 T10 **Oy-Tal** ~ SW Kyrgyzstan
151 S16 **Oytal** Zhambyl, S Kazakhstan
Oyyl see Uil
179 Qq15 **Ozamiz** Mindanao, S Philippines
Ozarichi see Azarychy
25 R7 **Ozark** Alabama, S USA
29 S10 **Ozark** Arkansas, C USA
29 T8 **Ozark** Missouri, C USA
29 T8 **Ozark Plateau** plain Arkansas/Missouri, C USA
29 T6 **Ozarks, Lake of the** ⊠ Missouri, C USA
199 Jj11 **Ozbourn Seamount** undersea feature W Pacific Ocean
113 L20 **Ózd** Borsod-Abaúj-Zemplén, NE Hungary
114 D11 **Ozeblin** ▲ C Croatia
127 Pp12 **Ozernovskiy** Kamchatskaya Oblast', E Russian Federation

◆ Country
● Country Capital
◇ Dependent Territory
○ Dependent Territory Capital
⬖ Administrative Region
× International Airport
▲ Mountain
▲▲ Mountain Range
⛰ Volcano
~ River
◎ Lake
⊠ Reservoir

Ozërnoye – Paraguá, Río

150 M7 **Ozërnoye** *var.* Ozërnyy. Kustanay, N Kazakhstan
Ozërnyy *see* Ozërnoye
117 D18 **Ozerós, Límni** ◎ W Greece
121 D14 **Ozersk** *prev.* Darkehnen, *Ger.* Angerapp. Kaliningradskaya Oblast', W Russian Federation
130 L4 **Ozery** Moskovskaya Oblast', W Russian Federation
Özgön *see* Uzgen
109 C17 **Ozieri** Sardegna, Italy, C Mediterranean Sea
113 I15 **Ozimek** *Ger.* Malapane. Opole, SW Poland
131 R8 **Ozinki** Saratovskaya Oblast', W Russian Federation
Oziya *see* Ojiya
27 O10 **Ozona** Texas, SW USA
Ozorkov *see* Ozorków
112 J12 **Ozorków** *Rus.* Ozorkov. Łódź, C Poland
170 E14 **Ōzu** Ehime, Shikoku, SW Japan
143 R10 **Ozurget'i** *prev.* Makharadze. W Georgia

P

101 J17 **Paal** Limburg, NE Belgium
197 C13 **Paama** *island* C Vanuatu
206 M14 **Paamiut** *var.* Pâmiut, *Dan.* Frederikshåb. S Greenland
178 Gg9 **Pa-an** Karen State, S Myanmar
103 L22 **Paar** ≈ SE Germany
85 E26 **Paarl** Western Cape, SW South Africa
95 L15 **Paavola** Oulu, C Finland
98 E8 **Pabbay** *island* NW Scotland, UK
175 P12 **Pabbiring, Kepulauan** *island group* C Indonesia
159 T15 **Pabna** Rajshahi, W Bangladesh
111 U4 **Pabneukirchen** Oberösterreich, N Austria
120 H13 **Pabradė** *Pol.* Podbrodzie. Švenčionys, SE Lithuania
58 L13 **Pacahuaras, Río** ≈ N Bolivia
Pacaraima, Sierra/Pacaraim, Serra *see* Pakaraima Mountains
58 B11 **Pacasmayo** La Libertad, W Peru
44 D6 **Pacaya, Volcán de** Ѫ S Guatemala
117 K23 **Pachía** *island* Kykládes, Greece, Aegean Sea
109 L26 **Pachino** Sicilia, Italy, C Mediterranean Sea
58 F12 **Pachitea, Río** ≈ C Peru
160 I11 **Pachmarhi** Madhya Pradesh, C India
124 N4 **Páchna** *var.* Pakhna. SW Cyprus
117 H25 **Páchnes** ▲ Kríti, Greece, E Mediterranean Sea
56 F9 **Pacho** Cundinamarca, C Colombia
160 F12 **Pāchora** Mahārāshtra, C India
43 P13 **Pachuca** *var.* Pachuca de Soto. Hidalgo, C Mexico
Pachuca de Soto *see* Pachuca
29 W5 **Pacific** Missouri, C USA
199 Jj15 **Pacific-Antarctic Ridge** *undersea feature* S Pacific Ocean
34 F8 **Pacific Beach** Washington, NW USA
37 N10 **Pacific Grove** California, W USA
31 S15 **Pacific Junction** Iowa, C USA
198-200 **Pacific Ocean** *ocean*
133 Z10 **Pacific Plate** *tectonic feature*
115 J15 **Pačir** ▲ SW Yugoslavia
190 L5 **Packsaddle** New South Wales, SE Australia
34 H9 **Packwood** Washington, NW USA
Padalung *see* Phatthalung
175 Q12 **Padamarang, Pulau** *island* C Indonesia
173 G9 **Padang** Sumatera, W Indonesia
174 Hh5 **Padang Endau** Pahang, Peninsular Malaysia
Padangpandjang *see* Padangpanjang
173 G8 **Padangpanjang** *prev.* Padangpandjang. Sumatera, W Indonesia
173 Ff7 **Padangsidempuan** *prev.* Padangsidimpoean. Sumatera, W Indonesia
Padangsidimpoean *see* Padangsidempuan
128 I9 **Padany** Respublika Kareliya, NW Russian Federation
95 M18 **Padasjoki** Häme, SW Finland
59 M22 **Padcaya** Tarija, S Bolivia
103 H14 **Paderborn** Nordrhein-Westfalen, NW Germany
Padeşul/Padeş, Vîrful *see* Padeş, Vârful
118 F12 **Padeş, Vârful** *var.* Padeşul; *prev.* Vîrful Padeş. ▲ W Romania
114 L10 **Padinska Skela** Serbia, N Yugoslavia
Padma *see* Brahmaputra
159 S14 **Padma** *var.* Ganges. ≈ Bangladesh/India *see also* Ganges
108 H8 **Padova** *Eng.* Padua; *anc.* Patavium. Veneto, NE Italy
84 A10 **Padrão, Ponta do** *headland* NW Angola
27 T16 **Padre Island** *island* Texas, SW USA
106 G3 **Padrón** Galicia, NW Spain
120 K13 **Padsvillye** *Rus.* Podsvil'ye. Vitsyebskaya Voblasts', N Belarus
190 K11 **Padthaway** South Australia
Padua *see* Padova
22 G7 **Paducah** Kentucky, S USA
27 P4 **Paducah** Texas, SW USA
107 N15 **Padul** Andalucía, S Spain
203 P8 **Paea** Tahiti, W French Polynesia
193 L14 **Paekakariki** Wellington, North Island, NZ
169 X11 **Paektu-san** *var.* Baitou Shan. ▲ China/North Korea
169 V15 **Paengnyŏng-do** *island* NW South Korea
192 M7 **Paeroa** Waikato, North Island, NZ
56 D12 **Páez** Cauca, SW Colombia
123 Mm4 **Páfos** *var.* Paphos. W Cyprus
123 Mm4 **Páfos** ✕ SW Cyprus
85 L19 **Pafúri** Gaza, SW Mozambique
114 C12 **Pag** *It.* Pago. Lika-Senj, W Croatia
114 B11 **Pag** *It.* Pago. *island* C Croatia
179 Qq16 **Pagadian** Mindanao, S Philippines
173 G11 **Pagai Selatan, Pulau** *island* Kepulauan Mentawai, W Indonesia
173 Ff10 **Pagai Utara, Pulau** *island* Kepulauan Mentawai, W Indonesia
196 K4 **Pagan** *island* C Northern Mariana Islands
117 G16 **Pagasitikós Kólpos** *gulf* E Greece
38 L8 **Page** Arizona, SW USA
31 Q5 **Page** North Dakota, N USA
120 D13 **Pagėgiai** *Ger.* Pogegen. Šilutė, SW Lithuania
23 S11 **Pageland** South Carolina, SE USA
83 G16 **Pager** ≈ NE Uganda
155 Q5 **Paghmān** Kābul, E Afghanistan
Pago *see* Pag
196 C16 **Pago Bay** *bay* E Guam, W Pacific Ocean
117 M20 **Pagóndas** *var.* Pagóndhas. Sámos, Dodekánisos, Greece, Aegean Sea
Pagóndhas *see* Pagóndas
198 C8 **Pago Pago** ○ (American Samoa) Tutuila, W American Samoa
39 R8 **Pagosa Springs** Colorado, C USA
40 H12 **Pahala** *var.* Pāhala. Hawaii, USA, C Pacific Ocean
174 H4 **Pahang** *off.* Negeri Pahang Darul Makmur. ◐ *state* Peninsular Malaysia
Pahang *see* Pahang, Sungai
174 Hh5 **Pahang, Sungai** *var.* Pahang, Sungei Pahang. ≈ Peninsular Malaysia
155 S8 **Pahārpur** North-West Frontier Province, NW Pakistan
193 B24 **Pahia Point** *headland* South Island, NZ
192 M13 **Pahiatua** Manawatu-Wanganui, North Island, NZ
40 H12 **Pahoa** *Haw.* Pāhoa. Hawaii, USA, C Pacific Ocean
25 Y14 **Pahokee** Florida, SE USA
37 X9 **Pahranagat Range** ▲▲ Nevada, W USA
37 W11 **Pahrump** Nevada, W USA
Pahsien *see* Chongqing
37 V9 **Pahute Mesa** ▲▲ Nevada, W USA
178 H7 **Pai** Mae Hong Son, NW Thailand
40 F10 **Paia** *Haw.* Pā'ia. Maui, Hawaii, USA, C Pacific Ocean
Pai-ch'eng *see* Baicheng
120 H4 **Paide** *Ger.* Weissenstein. Järvamaa, N Estonia
99 J24 **Paignton** SW England, UK
192 K3 **Paihia** Northland, North Island, NZ
95 M18 **Päijänne** ◎ S Finland
116 F13 **Páiko** ▲ N Greece
59 M17 **Paila, Río** ≈ C Bolivia
178 I12 **Pailin** Bătdâmbâng, W Cambodia
56 F6 **Pailitas** Cesar, N Colombia
40 F9 **Pailolo Channel** *channel* Hawaii, USA, C Pacific Ocean
95 K19 **Paimio** *Swe.* Pemar. Turku-Pori, SW Finland
172 O17 **Paimi-saki** *var.* Yaeme-saki. *headland* Iriomote-jima, SW Japan
104 G5 **Paimpol** Côtes d'Armor, NW France
174 Gg9 **Painan** Sumatera, W Indonesia
65 G23 **Paine, Cerro** ▲ S Chile
33 U11 **Painesville** Ohio, N USA
33 S14 **Paint Creek** ≈ Ohio, N USA
38 L10 **Painted Desert** *desert* Arizona, SW USA
Paint Hills *see* Wemindji
32 M4 **Paint River** ≈ Michigan, N USA
27 P8 **Paint Rock** Texas, SW USA
23 O6 **Paintsville** Kentucky, S USA
Paisance *see* Piacenza
98 I12 **Paisley** W Scotland, UK
34 I15 **Paisley** Oregon, NW USA
107 R10 **País Valenciano** *var.* Valencia, *Cat.* València; *anc.* Valentia. ◐ *autonomous community* NE Spain
107 O3 **País Vasco** *Basq.* Euskadi, *Eng.* The Basque Country, *Sp.* Provincias Vascongadas. ◐ *autonomous community* N Spain
58 A9 **Paita** Piura, NW Peru
197 J7 **Paita** Province Sud, S New Caledonia
175 O1 **Paitan, Teluk** *bay* Sabah, East Malaysia
106 H7 **Paiva** ≈ N Portugal
94 K12 **Pajala** Norrbotten, N Sweden
106 K3 **Pajares, Puerto de** *pass* NW Spain
56 G9 **Pajarito** Boyacá, C Colombia
56 G4 **Pajaro** La Guajira, S Colombia
Pakanbaru *see* Pekanbaru
57 Q10 **Pakaraima Mountains** *var.* Serra Pacaraim, Sierra Pacaraima. ▲▲ N South America
178 Hh11 **Pak Chong** Nakhon Ratchasima, C Thailand
127 Pp7 **Pakhachi** Koryakskiy Avtonomnyy Okrug, E Russian Federation
Pakhna *see* Páchna
153 O11 **Pakhtakor** Jizzakh Wiloyati, C Uzbekistan
201 U16 **Pakin Atoll** *atoll* Caroline Islands, E Micronesia
155 Q12 **Pakistan** *off.* Islamic Republic of Pakistan, *var.* Islami Jamhuriya e Pakistan. ◆ *republic* S Asia
Pakistan, Islami Jamhuriya e *see* Pakistan
178 I8 **Pak Lay** *var.* Muang Pak Lay. Xaignabouli, C Laos
Paknam *see* Samut Prakan
177 Ff5 **Pakokku** Magwe, C Myanmar
112 I10 **Pakość** *Ger.* Pakosch. Bydgoszcz, C Poland
Pakosch *see* Pakość
155 V10 **Pākpattan** Punjab, E Pakistan
178 H16 **Pak Phanang** *var.* Ban Pak Phanang. Nakhon Si Thammarat, SW Thailand
114 G9 **Pakrac** *Hung.* Pakrácz. Požega-Slavonija, NE Croatia
Pakrácz *see* Pakrac
120 F11 **Pakruojis** Pakruojis, N Lithuania
113 J24 **Paks** Tolna, S Hungary
Pak Sane *see* Pakxan
Paksé *see* Pakxé
178 I11 **Pak Thong Chai** Nakhon Ratchasima, C Thailand
155 R6 **Paktīā** ◐ *province* SE Afghanistan
155 Q7 **Paktīkā** ◐ *province* SE Afghanistan
175 Pp9 **Pakuli** Sulawesi, C Indonesia
83 F17 **Pakwach** NW Uganda
178 I8 **Pakxan** *var.* Muang Pakxan, Pak Sane. Bolikhamxai, C Laos
178 Jj10 **Pakxé** *var.* Paksé. Champasak, S Laos
80 G12 **Pala** Mayo-Kébbi, SW Chad
63 A17 **Palacios** Santa Fe, C Argentina
27 V13 **Palacios** Texas, SW USA
107 X5 **Palafrugell** Cataluña, NE Spain
109 L24 **Palagonia** Sicilia, Italy, C Mediterranean Sea
115 E17 **Palagruža** *It.* Pelagosa. *island* SW Croatia
117 G20 **Palaiá Epídavros** Pelopónnisos, S Greece
124 Nn3 **Palaichóri** *var.* Palekhori. C Cyprus
117 H25 **Palaiochóra** Kríti, Greece, E Mediterranean Sea
117 A15 **Palaiolastritsa** *religious building* Kérkyra, Iónioi Nísoi, Greece, C Mediterranean Sea
117 J19 **Palaiópoli** Ándros, Kykládes, Greece, Aegean Sea
105 N5 **Palaiseau** Essonne, N France
Palakkad *see* Pālghāt
160 N11 **Pāla Laharha** Orissa, E India
85 G19 **Palamakoloi** Ghanzi, C Botswana
117 E16 **Palamás** Thessalía, C Greece
107 X5 **Palamós** Cataluña, NE Spain
120 J5 **Palamuse** *Ger.* Sankt-Bartholomäi. Jõgevamaa, E Estonia
191 Q14 **Palana** Tasmania, SE Australia
127 P9 **Palana** Koryakskiy Avtonomnyy Okrug, E Russian Federation
120 C11 **Palanga** *Ger.* Polangen. Palanga, NW Lithuania
149 V10 **Palangān, Kūh-e** ▲▲ E Iran
Palangkaraja *see* Palangkaraya
174 Mm10 **Palangkaraya** *prev.* Palangkaraja. Borneo, C Indonesia
161 H22 **Palani** Tamil Nādu, SE India
Palanka *see* Bačka Palanka
160 D9 **Pālanpur** Gujarāt, W India
Palantia *see* Palencia
85 I19 **Palapye** Central, SE Botswana
161 J19 **Pālār** ≈ SE India
106 H3 **Palas de Rei** Galicia, NW Spain
127 O10 **Palatka** Magadanskaya Oblast', E Russian Federation
25 W10 **Palatka** Florida, SE USA
196 B9 **Palau** *var.* Belau. ◆ *republic* W Pacific Ocean
133 Y14 **Palau Islands** *var.* Palau. *island group* N Palau
198 Aa8 **Palauli Bay** *bay* Savai'i, Western Samoa, C Pacific Ocean
178 Gg12 **Palaw** Tenasserim, S Myanmar
179 Oo15 **Palawan** *island* W Philippines
179 Oo15 **Palawan Passage** *passage* W Philippines
198 F7 **Palawan Trough** *undersea feature* S South China Sea
179 P10 **Palayan City** Luzon, N Philippines
161 H23 **Pālayankottai** Tamil Nādu, SE India
109 L25 **Palazzola Acreide** *anc.* Acrae. Sicilia, Italy, C Mediterranean Sea
120 G3 **Paldiski** *prev.* Baltiski, *Eng.* Baltic Port, *Ger.* Baltischport. Harjumaa, NW Estonia
114 I13 **Pale** SE Bosnia and Herzegovina
Palekhori *see* Palaichóri
175 Q7 **Paleleh, Pegunungan** ▲▲ Sulawesi, N Indonesia
175 Qq7 **Paleleh, Teluk** *bay* Sulawesi, N Indonesia
174 I11 **Palembang** Sumatera, W Indonesia
65 G18 **Palena** Los Lagos, S Chile
65 G18 **Palena, Río** ≈ S Chile
106 M5 **Palencia** *anc.* Palantia, Pallantia. Castilla-León, NW Spain
106 M3 **Palencia** ◐ *province* Castilla-León, N Spain
37 X15 **Palen Dry Lake** ◎ California, W USA
43 V15 **Palenque** Chiapas, SE Mexico
43 V15 **Palenque** *var.* Ruinas de Palenque. *ruins* Chiapas, SE Mexico
47 O9 **Palenque, Punta** *headland* S Dominican Republic
Palenque, Ruinas de *see* Palenque
Palerme *see* Palermo
109 I23 **Palermo** *Fr.* Palerme; *anc.* Panhormus, Panormus. Sicilia, Italy, C Mediterranean Sea
27 V8 **Palestine** Texas, SW USA
27 V7 **Palestine, Lake** ⊟ Texas, SW USA
109 I15 **Palestrina** Lazio, C Italy
177 F5 **Paletwa** Chin State, W Myanmar
161 G21 **Pālghāt** *var.* Palakkad; *prev.* Pulicat. Kerala, SW India
158 F13 **Pāli** Rājasthān, N India
178 Gg16 **Palian** Trang, SW Thailand
201 O12 **Palikir** ● (Micronesia) Pohnpei, E Micronesia
179 R17 **Palimbang** Mindanao, S Philippines
Palimé *see* Kpalimé
109 L19 **Palinuro, Capo** *headland* S Italy
117 H15 **Palioúri, Ákra** *var.* Akra Kanestron. *headland* N Greece
35 R14 **Palisades Reservoir** ⊟ Idaho, NW USA
101 J23 **Paliseul** Luxembourg, SE Belgium
160 C11 **Pālitāna** Gujarāt, W India
120 F4 **Palivere** Läänemaa, W Estonia
43 V14 **Palizada** Campeche, SE Mexico
95 L18 **Pälkäne** Häme, SW Finland
161 J22 **Palk Strait** *strait* India/Sri Lanka
161 J23 **Pallai** Northern Province, NW Sri Lanka
Pallantia *see* Palencia
108 C6 **Pallanza** Piemonte, NE Italy
131 Q9 **Pallasovka** Volgogradskaya Oblast', SW Russian Federation
Pallene/Pallíni *see* Kassándra
193 L15 **Palliser Bay** *bay* North Island, NZ
193 L15 **Palliser, Cape** *headland* North Island, NZ
203 U9 **Palliser, Îles** *island group* Îles Tuamotu, C French Polynesia
107 X9 **Palma** *var.* Palma de Mallorca. Mallorca, Spain, W Mediterranean Sea
107 X9 **Palma** ✕ Mallorca, Spain, W Mediterranean Sea
84 Q12 **Palma** Cabo Delgado, N Mozambique
107 X10 **Palma, Badia de** *bay* Mallorca, Spain, W Mediterranean Sea
106 L13 **Palma del Río** Andalucía, S Spain
Palma de Mallorca *see* Palma
109 J25 **Palma di Montechiaro** Sicilia, Italy, C Mediterranean Sea
108 J7 **Palmanova** Friuli-Venezia Giulia, NE Italy
56 J7 **Palmarito** Apure, C Venezuela
45 N15 **Palmar Sur** Puntarenas, SE Costa Rica
62 I12 **Palmas** Paraná, S Brazil
61 K16 **Palmas do Tocantins** Tocantins, C Brazil
56 D11 **Palmaseca** ✕ (Cali) Valle del Cauca, SW Colombia
109 B21 **Palmas, Golfo di** *gulf* Sardegna, Italy, C Mediterranean Sea
46 I7 **Palma Soriano** Santiago de Cuba, E Cuba
25 Y12 **Palm Bay** Florida, SE USA
37 T14 **Palmdale** California, W USA
63 H14 **Palmeira das Missões** Rio Grande do Sul, S Brazil
84 A11 **Palmeirinhas, Ponta das** *headland* NW Angola
41 R11 **Palmer** Alaska, USA
21 N11 **Palmer** Massachusetts, NE USA
27 U7 **Palmer** Texas, SW USA
204 H4 **Palmer** *US research station* Antarctica
12 R11 **Palmer** ≈ Québec, SE Canada
39 T5 **Palmer Lake** Colorado, C USA
204 J6 **Palmer Land** *physical region* Antarctica
12 F15 **Palmerston** Ontario, SE Canada
193 F22 **Palmerston** Otago, South Island, NZ
202 K15 **Palmerston** *island* S Cook Islands
Palmerston *see* Darwin
192 M12 **Palmerston North** Manawatu-Wanganui, North Island, NZ
78 L18 **Palmés, Cap des** *headland* SW Ivory Coast
25 V13 **Palmetto** Florida, SE USA
Palmetto State *see* South Carolina
109 M22 **Palmi** Calabria, SW Italy
56 D11 **Palmira** Valle del Cauca, W Colombia
58 F8 **Palmira, Río** ≈ N Peru
63 D19 **Palmitas** Soriano, SW Uruguay
Palmnicken *see* Yantarnyy
37 V15 **Palm Springs** California, W USA
29 V2 **Palmyra** Missouri, C USA
20 G10 **Palmyra** New York, NE USA
20 G15 **Palmyra** Pennsylvania, NE USA
23 V5 **Palmyra** Virginia, NE USA
Palmyra *see* Tudmur
199 K7 **Palmyra Atoll** ◇ *US privately owned unincorporated territory* C Pacific Ocean
160 P12 **Palmyras Point** *headland* E India
37 N9 **Palo Alto** California, W USA
27 O1 **Palo Duro Creek** ≈ Texas, SW USA
Paloe *see* Palu
Paloe *see* Denpasar, Bali, C Indonesia
174 Hh6 **Paloh** Johor, Peninsular Malaysia
82 F12 **Paloich** Upper Nile, SE Sudan
42 I3 **Palomas** Chihuahua, N Mexico
109 I15 **Palombara Sabina** Lazio, C Italy
107 S13 **Palos, Cabo de** *headland* SE Spain
106 I14 **Palos de la Frontera** Andalucía, S Spain
62 G11 **Palotina** Paraná, S Brazil
34 M9 **Palouse** Washington, NW USA
34 L9 **Palouse River** ≈ Washington, NW USA
37 Y16 **Palo Verde** California, W USA
59 E16 **Palpa** Ica, W Peru
97 M16 **Pålsboda** Örebro, C Sweden
95 M15 **Paltamo** Oulu, C Finland
175 Pp9 **Palu** *prev.* Paloe. Sulawesi, C Indonesia
143 P14 **Palu** Elâzığ, E Turkey
175 Q16 **Palu, Pulau** *island* S Indonesia
175 P8 **Palu, Teluk** *bay* Sulawesi, C Indonesia
158 I11 **Palwal** Haryāna, N India
127 Oo4 **Palyavaam** ≈ NE Russian Federation
79 Q13 **Pama** SE Burkina
180 J14 **Pamandzi** ✕ (Mamoudzou) Petite-Terre, E Mayotte
Pamangkat *see* Pemangkat
149 R11 **Pā Mazār** Kermān, C Iran
85 N19 **Pambarra** Inhambane, SE Mozambique
176 Xx10 **Pamdai** Irian Jaya, E Indonesia
176 X10 **Pami** Irian Jaya, E Indonesia
105 N16 **Pamiers** Ariège, S France
153 T14 **Pamir** *var.* Daryā-ye Pāmīr, *Taj.* Dar"yoi Pomir. ≈ Afghanistan/Tajikistan *see also* Pāmīr, Daryā-ye
Pamir/Pāmīr, Daryā-ye *see* Pamirs
155 U1 **Pāmīr, Daryā-ye** *var.* Pamir, *Taj.* Dar"yoi Pomir. ≈ Afghanistan/ nTajikistan *see also* Pamir
Pāmīr-e Khord *see* Little Pamir
133 Q8 **Pamirs** *Pash.* Daryā-ye Pāmīr, *Rus.* Pamir. ▲▲ C Asia
Pâmiut *see* Paamiut
23 X10 **Pamlico River** ≈ North Carolina, SE USA
23 Y10 **Pamlico Sound** *sound* North Carolina, SE USA
27 O2 **Pampa** Texas, SW USA
Pampa Aullagas, Lago *see* Poopó, Lago
63 B21 **Pampa Húmeda** *grassland* E Argentina
58 A10 **Pampa las Salinas** *salt lake* NW Peru
59 F15 **Pampas** Huancavelica, C Peru
64 K13 **Pampas** *plain* C Argentina
57 O4 **Pampatar** Nueva Esparta, NE Venezuela
Pampeluna *see* Pamplona
106 H8 **Pampilhosa da Serra** *var.* Pampilhosa de Serra. Coimbra, N Portugal
181 Y15 **Pamplemousses** N Mauritius
56 G7 **Pamplona** Norte de Santander, N Colombia
107 Q3 **Pamplona** *Basq.* Iruñea; *prev.* Pampeluna, *anc.* Pompaelo. Navarra, N Spain
116 I11 **Pamporovo** *prev.* Vasil Kolarov. Plovdivska Oblast, S Bulgaria
142 D15 **Pamukkale** Denizli, W Turkey
23 W5 **Pamunkey River** ≈ Virginia, NE USA
158 K5 **Pamzal** Jammu and Kashmir, NW India
32 L14 **Pana** Illinois, N USA
43 Y11 **Panabá** Yucatán, SE Mexico
37 Y8 **Panaca** Nevada, W USA
117 E19 **Panachaikó** ▲ S Greece
12 F11 **Panache Lake** ◎ Ontario, S Canada
116 I10 **Panagyurishte** Plovdivska Oblast, W Bulgaria
174 I14 **Panaitan, Pulau** *island* S Indonesia
174 Ii14 **Panaitan, Selat** *strait* Jawa, SW Indonesia
117 D18 **Panaitolikó** ▲ C Greece
161 E17 **Panaji** *var.* Pangim, Panjim, New Goa. Goa, W India
45 T14 **Panama** *off.* Republic of Panama. ◆ *republic* Central America
45 T15 **Panamá** *var.* Ciudad de Panamá, *Eng.* Panama City. ● (Panama) Panamá, C Panama
45 U14 **Panamá** *off.* Provincia de Panamá. ◐ *province* E Panama
45 U15 **Panamá, Bahía de** *bay* N Gulf of Panama
200 Oo8 **Panama Basin** *undersea feature* E Pacific Ocean
45 T15 **Panama Canal** *canal* E Panama
25 R9 **Panama City** Florida, SE USA
45 T14 **Panama City** ✕ Panamá, C Panama
Panama City *see* Panamá
25 Q9 **Panama City Beach** Florida, SE USA
45 T17 **Panamá, Golfo de** *var.* Gulf of Panama. *gulf* S Panama
Panama, Gulf of *see* Panamá, Golfo de
Panama, Isthmus of *see* Panamá, Istmo de
45 T15 **Panamá, Istmo de** *Eng.* Isthmus of Panama; *prev.* Isthmus of Darien. *isthmus* E Panama
37 U11 **Panamint Range** ▲▲ California, W USA
109 L22 **Panarea, Isola** *island* Isole Eolie, S Italy
108 G9 **Panaro** ≈ N Italy
179 Q14 **Panay Gulf** *gulf* C Philippines
179 Pp13 **Panay Island** *island* C Philippines
37 W7 **Pancake Range** ▲▲ Nevada, W USA
114 M11 **Pančevo** *Ger.* Pantschowa, *Hung.* Pancsova. Serbia, N Yugoslavia
115 M15 **Pančićev Vrh** ▲ SW Yugoslavia
118 L12 **Panciu** Vrancea, E Romania
118 F10 **Pâncota** *Hung.* Pankota; *prev.* Pincota. Arad, W Romania
Pancsova *see* Pančevo
85 N20 **Panda** Inhambane, SE Mozambique
176 X9 **Pandaidori, Kepulauan** *island group* E Indonesia
27 N11 **Pandale** Texas, SW USA
174 H7 **Pandang, Pulau** *island* W Indonesia
174 Kk9 **Pandang Tikar, Pulau** *island* N Indonesia
63 F20 **Pan de Azúcar** Maldonado, S Uruguay
120 H11 **Pandėlys** Rokiškis, NE Lithuania
161 F15 **Pandharpur** Mahārāshtra, W India
190 J1 **Pandie Pandie** South Australia
175 Pp9 **Pandiri** Sulawesi, C Indonesia
63 F20 **Pando** Canelones, S Uruguay
59 J14 **Pando** ◐ *department* N Bolivia
199 Ii10 **Pandora Bank** *undersea feature* W Pacific Ocean
97 G20 **Pandrup** Nordjylland, N Denmark
159 V12 **Pandu** Assam, NE India
81 J15 **Pandu** Equateur, NW Zaire
Paneas *see* Bāniyās
61 F15 **Panelas** Mato Grosso, W Brazil
120 G12 **Panevėžys** Panevėžys, C Lithuania
Panfilov *see* Zharkent
131 N9 **Panfilovo** Volgogradskaya Oblast', SW Russian Federation
81 N17 **Panga** Haut-Zaïre, N Zaire
200 Ss13 **Pangai** Lifuka, C Tonga
116 H13 **Pangaío** ▲ N Greece
81 G20 **Pangala** Le Pool, S Congo
83 J22 **Pangani** Tanga, E Tanzania
83 I21 **Pangani** ≈ NE Tanzania
195 U13 **Panggoe** Choiseul Island, NW Solomon Islands
81 N20 **Pangi** Maniema, E Zaire
194 H12 **Pangia** Southern Highlands, W PNG
Pangim *see* Panaji
173 F4 **Pangkalanbrandan** Sumatera, W Indonesia
Pangkalanbun *see* Pangkalanbuun
174 Ll10 **Pangkalanbuun** *var.* Pangkalanbun. Borneo, C Indonesia
174 J10 **Pangkalpinang** Pulau Bangka, W Indonesia
9 U17 **Pangman** Saskatchewan, S Canada
Pang-Nga *see* Phang-Nga
16 Nn2 **Pangnirtung** Baffin Island, Northwest Territories, NE Canada
158 K6 **Pangong Tso** *var.* Bangong Co. ◎ China/India *see also* Bangong Co
38 K7 **Panguitch** Utah, W USA
195 S12 **Panguna** Bougainville Island, NE PNG
179 Pp17 **Pangutaran Group** *island group* Sulu Archipelago, SW Philippines
27 N2 **Panhandle** Texas, SW USA
Panhormus *see* Palermo
176 X12 **Paniai, Danau** ◎ Irian Jaya, E Indonesia
81 L21 **Pania-Mutombo** Kasai Oriental, C Zaire
Panicherevo *see* Dolno Panicherevo
197 H5 **Panié, Mont** ▲ C New Caledonia
158 I10 **Pānīpat** Haryāna, N India
153 Q14 **Panj** *Rus.* Pyandzh; *prev.* Kirovabad. SW Tajikistan
153 P15 **Panj** *Rus.* Pyandzh. ≈ Afghanistan/Tajikistan
155 O5 **Panjāb** Bāmīān, C Afghanistan
153 O12 **Panjakent** *Rus.* Pendzhikent. W Tajikistan
154 L14 **Panjgūr** Baluchistān, SW Pakistan
Panjim *see* Panaji
169 U12 **Panjin** Liaoning, NE China
153 P14 **Panji Poyon** *Rus.* Nizhniy Pyandzh. SW Tajikistan
155 Q4 **Panjshīr** ≈ E Afghanistan
Pankota *see* Pâncota
79 W14 **Pankshin** Plateau, C Nigeria
169 Y10 **Pan Ling** ▲▲ N China
Panlong Jiang *see* Lô, Sông
160 J9 **Panna** Madhya Pradesh, C India
101 M16 **Panningen** Limburg, SE Netherlands
155 R13 **Pāno Āqil** Sind, SE Pakistan
124 Nn3 **Páno Léfkara** S Cyprus
124 N3 **Páno Panagiá** *var.* Pano Panayia. W Cyprus
Pano Panayia *see* Páno Panagiá
Panopolis *see* Akhmîm
31 U14 **Panora** Iowa, C USA
62 I8 **Panorama** São Paulo, S Brazil
117 I24 **Pánormos** Kríti, Greece, E Mediterranean Sea
Panormus *see* Palermo
169 W11 **Panshi** Jilin, NE China
61 H19 **Pantanal** *var.* Pantanalmato-Grossense. *swamp* SW Brazil
Pantanalmato-Grossense *see* Pantanal
63 H16 **Pântano Grande** Rio Grande do Sul, S Brazil
175 R16 **Pantar, Pulau** *island* Kepulauan Alor, S Indonesia
23 X9 **Pantego** North Carolina, SE USA
109 G25 **Pantelleria** *anc.* Cossyra, Cosyra. Sicilia, Italy, C Mediterranean Sea
109 G25 **Pantelleria, Isola di** *island* SW Italy
Pante Macassar/Pante Makassar *see* Pante Makasar
175 Rr17 **Pante Makasar** *var.* Pante Macassar, Pante Makassar. Timor, C Indonesia
158 K10 **Pantnagar** Uttar Pradesh, N India
117 A15 **Pantokrátoras** ▲ Kérkyra, Iónioi Nísoi, Greece, C Mediterranean Sea
Pantschowa *see* Pančevo
179 Rr16 **Pantukan** Mindanao, S Philippines
43 P11 **Pánuco** Veracruz-Llave, E Mexico
43 P11 **Pánuco, Río** ≈ C Mexico
166 I12 **Panxian** Guizhou, S China
173 G7 **Panyabungan** Sumatera, N Indonesia
79 W14 **Panyam** Plateau, C Nigeria
163 N13 **Panzhihua** *prev.* Dukou, Tu-k'ou. Sichuan, C China
81 I22 **Panzi** Bandundu, SW Zaire
44 E5 **Panzós** Alta Verapaz, E Guatemala
Pao-chi/Paoki *see* Baoji
Pao-king *see* Shaoyang
109 N20 **Paola** Calabria, SW Italy
123 Jj17 **Paola** E Malta
29 R5 **Paola** Kansas, C USA
33 O15 **Paoli** Indiana, N USA
197 D14 **Paonangisu** Éfaté, C Vanuatu
175 Tt11 **Paoni** *var.* Pauni. Pulau Seram, E Indonesia
39 Q5 **Paonia** Colorado, C USA
203 O7 **Paopao** Moorea, W French Polynesia
Pao-shan *see* Baoshan
Pao-ting *see* Baoding
Pao-t'ou/Paotow *see* Baotou
81 H14 **Paoua** Ouham-Pendé, W Central African Republic
Pap *see* Pop
113 H23 **Pápa** Veszprém, W Hungary
44 J12 **Papagayo, Golfo de** *gulf* NW Costa Rica
40 H11 **Papaikou** *var.* Pāpa'ikou. Hawaii, USA, C Pacific Ocean
43 R15 **Papaloapan, Río** ≈ S Mexico
192 L6 **Papakura** Auckland, North Island, NZ
43 Q13 **Papantla** *var.* Papantla de Olarte. Veracruz-Llave, E Mexico
Papantla de Olarte *see* Papantla
203 P8 **Papara** Tahiti, W French Polynesia
192 K4 **Paparoa** Northland, North Island, NZ
193 G16 **Paparoa Range** ▲▲ South Island, NZ
117 K20 **Pápas, Ákra** *headland* Ikaría, Dodekánisos, Greece, Aegean Sea
98 L2 **Papa Stour** *island* NE Scotland, UK
192 L6 **Papatoetoe** Auckland, North Island, NZ
193 E25 **Papatowai** Otago, South Island, NZ
98 K4 **Papa Westray** *island* NE Scotland, UK
203 T10 **Papeete** ○ (French Polynesia) Tahiti, W French Polynesia
102 F11 **Papenburg** Niedersachsen, NW Germany
100 H13 **Papendrecht** Zuid-Holland, SW Netherlands
203 Q7 **Papenoo** Tahiti, W French Polynesia
203 Q7 **Papenoo Rivière** ≈ Tahiti, W French Polynesia
203 N7 **Papetoai** Moorea, W French Polynesia
94 L3 **Papey** *island* E Iceland
Paphos *see* Páfos
42 H5 **Papigochic, Río** ≈ NW Mexico
120 E10 **Papilė** Akmenė, NW Lithuania
31 S15 **Papillion** Nebraska, C USA
13 T5 **Papinachois** ≈ Québec, SE Canada
194 I15 **Papua, Gulf of** *gulf* S PNG
194 H13 **Papua New Guinea** *off.* Independent State of Papua New Guinea; *prev.* Territory of Papua and New Guinea, *abbrev.* PNG. ◆ *commonwealth republic* NW Melanesia
199 H10 **Papua Plateau** *undersea feature* N Coral Sea
114 G9 **Papuk** ▲ NE Croatia
177 G8 **Papun** Karen State, S Myanmar
44 L14 **Paquera** Puntarenas, W Costa Rica
57 V9 **Para** ◐ *district* N Suriname
60 I13 **Pará** *off.* Estado do Pará. ◐ *state* NE Brazil
Pará *see* Belém
126 H12 **Parabel'** Tomskaya Oblast', C Russian Federation
188 I8 **Paraburdoo** Western Australia
59 E16 **Paracas, Peninsula de** *peninsula* W Peru
61 L19 **Paracatu** Minas Gerais, NE Brazil
198 F7 **Paracel Islands** ◇ *disputed territory* SE Asia
190 I6 **Parachilna** South Australia
155 R6 **Pārachinār** North-West Frontier Province, NW Pakistan
114 N13 **Paraćin** Serbia, C Yugoslavia
12 K8 **Paradis** Québec, SE Canada
41 N11 **Paradise** *var.* Paradise Hill. Alaska, USA
37 O5 **Paradise** California, W USA
37 X11 **Paradise** Nevada, W USA
Paradise Hill *see* Paradise
39 R11 **Paradise Hills** New Mexico, SW USA
Paradise of the Pacific *see* Hawaii
38 L13 **Paradise Valley** Arizona, SW USA
37 T2 **Paradise Valley** Nevada, W USA
117 O22 **Paradisi** ✕ (Ródos) Ródos, Dodekánisos, Greece, Aegean Sea
176 X10 **Paradoi** Irian Jaya, E Indonesia
160 P12 **Parādwīp** Orissa, E India
Paraetonium *see* Matrūḥ
119 R4 **Parafiyivka** Chernihivs'ka Oblast', N Ukraine
38 K7 **Paragonah** Utah, W USA
29 X9 **Paragould** Arkansas, C USA
49 X8 **Paraguaçu** *var.* Paraguassú. ≈ E Brazil
62 J9 **Paraguaçu Paulista** São Paulo, S Brazil
56 H4 **Paraguaipoa** Zulia, NW Venezuela
64 O6 **Paraguarí** Paraguarí, S Paraguay
64 O7 **Paraguarí** *off.* Departamento de Paraguarí. ◐ *department* S Paraguay
57 O8 **Paragua, Río** ≈ SE Venezuela
59 O16 **Paraguá, Río** ≈ NE Bolivia

◆ Country ● Country Capital ◇ Dependent Territory ○ Dependent Territory Capital ◐ Administrative Region ✕ International Airport ▲ Mountain ▲▲ Mountain Range Ѫ Volcano ≈ River ◎ Lake ⊟ Reservoir

PARAGUASSÚ – PELOTAS, RIO

Paraguassú see Paraguaçu
64 N5 **Paraguay** ◆ republic C South America
49 U10 **Paraguay** var. Río Paraguay. ≈ C South America
Parahiba/Parahyba see Paraíba
61 P15 **Paraíba** off. Estado da Paraíba; prev. Parahiba, Parahyba. ◐ state E Brazil
Paraíba see João Pessoa
62 P9 **Paraíba do Sul, Rio** ≈ SE Brazil
Parainen see Pargas
45 N14 **Paraíso** Cartago, C Costa Rica
43 U14 **Paraíso** Tabasco, SE Mexico
59 O17 **Paraíso, Río** ≈ E Bolivia
Parajd see Praid
79 S14 **Parakou** C Benin
124 O3 **Paralimni** E Cyprus
117 G18 **Paralímni, Límni** ◎ C Greece
194 G15 **Parama Island** island SW PNG
57 W8 **Paramaribo** ● (Suriname) Paramaribo, N Suriname
57 W9 **Paramaribo** ◐ district N Suriname
57 W9 **Paramaribo** ✕ Paramaribo, N Suriname
Paramithiá see Paramythiá
58 C13 **Paramonga** Lima, W Peru
127 Pp13 **Paramushir, Ostrov** island SE Russian Federation
117 C16 **Paramythiá** var. Paramithiá. Ípeiros, W Greece
64 M10 **Paraná** Entre Ríos, E Argentina
62 H11 **Paraná** off. Estado do Paraná. ◐ state S Brazil
49 U11 **Paraná** var. Alto Paraná. ≈ C South America
62 K12 **Paranaguá** Paraná, S Brazil
61 J20 **Paranaíba, Rio** ≈ E Brazil
63 C19 **Paraná Ibicuy, Río** ≈ E Argentina
61 H15 **Paranaíta** Mato Grosso, W Brazil
62 H9 **Paranapanema, Rio** ≈ S Brazil
62 K11 **Paranapiacaba, Serra do** ▲▲ S Brazil
62 H9 **Paranavaí** Paraná, S Brazil
149 N5 **Parandak** Markazī, W Iran
116 I12 **Paranéstio** Anatolikí Makedonía kai Thráki, NE Greece
203 W11 **Paraoa** atoll Îles Tuamotu, C French Polynesia
192 L13 **Paraparaumu** Wellington, North Island, NZ
59 N20 **Parapeti, Río** ≈ SE Bolivia
56 L10 **Paraque, Cerro** ▲ W Venezuela
160 I11 **Parāsia** Madhya Pradesh, C India
117 M23 **Paraspóri, Ákra** headland Kárpathos, SE Greece
62 O10 **Parati** Rio de Janeiro, SE Brazil
61 K14 **Parauapebas** Pará, N Brazil
105 Q10 **Paray-le-Monial** Saône-et-Loire, C France
Parbatsar see Parvatsar
160 G13 **Parbhani** Mahārāshtra, C India
102 L10 **Parchim** Mecklenburg-Vorpommern, N Germany
Parchwitz see Prochowice
112 P13 **Parczew** Biała Podlaska, E Poland
62 L8 **Pardo, Rio** ≈ S Brazil
113 E16 **Pardubice** Ger. Pardubitz. Východní Čechy, C Czech Republic
Pardubitz see Pardubice
121 F16 **Parechcha** Pol. Porzecze, Rus. Porech'ye. Hrodzyenskaya Voblasts', W Belarus
61 F17 **Parecis, Chapada dos** var. Serra dos Parecis. ▲▲ W Brazil
Parecis, Serra dos see Parecis, Chapada dos
106 M4 **Paredes de Nava** Castilla-León, N Spain
201 U12 **Parem** island Chuuk, C Micronesia
201 O12 **Parem Island** island E Micronesia
192 I1 **Parengarenga Harbour** inlet North Island, NZ
13 N8 **Parent** Québec, SE Canada
104 J14 **Parentis-en-Born** Landes, SW France
Parenzo see Poreč
193 G20 **Pareora** Canterbury, South Island, NZ
175 P12 **Parepare** Sulawesi, C Indonesia
117 B16 **Párga** Ípeiros, W Greece
95 K20 **Pargas** Swe. Parainen. Turku-Pori, SW Finland
66 O5 **Pargo, Ponta do** headland Madeira, Portugal, NE Atlantic Ocean
Paria, Golfo de see Paria, Gulf of
57 N6 **Pariaguán** Anzoátegui, NE Venezuela
47 X17 **Paria, Gulf of** var. Golfo de Paria. gulf Trinidad and Tobago/Venezuela
59 I15 **Pariamanu, Río** ≈ E Peru
38 L8 **Paria River** ≈ Utah, W USA
Parichi see Parychy
42 M14 **Paricutín, Volcán** ☼ C Mexico
45 P16 **Parida, Isla** island SW Panama
57 T8 **Parika** NE Guyana
95 O18 **Parikkala** Kymi, SE Finland
60 E10 **Parima, Serra** var. Sierra Parima. ▲▲ Brazil/Venezuela see also Parima, Sierra
57 N11 **Parima, Sierra** var. Serra Parima. ▲▲ Brazil/Venezuela see also Parima, Serra
59 F17 **Parinacochas, Laguna** ◎ SW Peru
49 P8 **Pariñas, Punta** headland NW Peru
60 H12 **Parintins** Amazonas, N Brazil
105 O5 **Paris** anc. Lutetia, Lutetia Parisiorum, Parisii. ● (France) Paris, N France
203 Y2 **Paris** Kiritimati, E Kiribati
29 S11 **Paris** Arkansas, C USA
35 S16 **Paris** Idaho, NW USA
33 N14 **Paris** Illinois, N USA
22 M5 **Paris** Kentucky, S USA
29 V3 **Paris** Missouri, C USA
22 H8 **Paris** Tennessee, S USA
27 V5 **Paris** Texas, SW USA
Parisii see Paris
45 S16 **Parita** Herrera, S Panama
45 S16 **Parita, Bahía de** bay S Panama
Parkan/Párkány see Štúrovo
95 K18 **Parkano** Häme, SW Finland
29 N6 **Park City** Kansas, C USA
38 L3 **Park City** Utah, W USA
38 I12 **Parker** Arizona, SW USA
25 R9 **Parker** Florida, SE USA
31 R11 **Parker** South Dakota, N USA
37 Z14 **Parker Dam** California, W USA
31 W13 **Parkersburg** Iowa, C USA
23 Q3 **Parkersburg** West Virginia, NE USA
31 T7 **Parkers Prairie** Minnesota, N USA
179 R17 **Parker Volcano** ☼ Mindanao, S Philippines
189 W13 **Parkes** New South Wales, SE Australia
32 K4 **Park Falls** Wisconsin, N USA
Parkhar see Farkhor
12 E16 **Parkhill** Ontario, S Canada
31 T5 **Park Rapids** Minnesota, N USA
31 Q3 **Park River** North Dakota, N USA
31 Q11 **Parkston** South Dakota, N USA
8 L17 **Parksville** Vancouver Island, British Columbia, SW Canada
39 S3 **Parkview Mountain** ▲ Colorado, C USA
107 N8 **Parla** Madrid, C Spain
31 S8 **Parle, Lac qui** ⊡ Minnesota, N USA
117 F20 **Parlía Tyroú** Pelopónnisos, S Greece
161 G14 **Parli Vaijnāth** Mahārāshtra, C India
108 F9 **Parma** Emilia-Romagna, N Italy
33 T11 **Parma** Ohio, N USA
Parnahyba see Parnaíba
60 N13 **Parnaíba** var. Parnahyba. Piauí, E Brazil
67 J14 **Parnaíba Ridge** undersea feature C Atlantic Ocean
60 N13 **Parnaíba, Rio** ≈ NE Brazil
117 F18 **Parnassós** ▲▲ C Greece
193 J17 **Parnassus** Canterbury, South Island, NZ
190 H10 **Parndana** South Australia
117 H19 **Párnitha** ▲▲ C Greece
117 F21 **Párnon** ▲▲ S Greece
120 G5 **Pärnu** Ger. Pernau, Latv. Pērnava; prev. Rus. Pernov. Pärnumaa, SW Estonia
120 G6 **Pärnu** var. Parnu Jõgi, Ger. Pernau. ≈ SW Estonia
120 G5 **Pärnu-Jaagupi** Ger. Sankt-Jakobi. Pärnumaa, SW Estonia
Parnu Jõgi see Pärnu
120 G5 **Pärnu Laht** Ger. Pernauer Bucht. bay SW Estonia
120 F5 **Pärnumaa** off. Pärnu Maakond. ◐ province SW Estonia
159 T11 **Paro** W Bhutan
159 T11 **Paro** ✕ (Thimphu) W Bhutan
193 G17 **Paroa** West Coast, South Island, NZ
169 X14 **P'aro-ho** var. Hwach'ŏn-chŏsuji. ⊡ N South Korea
191 N6 **Paroo River** seasonal river New South Wales/Queensland, SE Australia
Paropamisus Range see Sefīdkūh, Selseleh-ye
117 J21 **Páros** Páros, Kykládes, Greece, Aegean Sea
117 J21 **Páros** island Kykládes, Greece, Aegean Sea
38 K7 **Parowan** Utah, W USA
105 U13 **Parpaillon** ▲▲ SE France
110 I9 **Parpan** Graubünden, S Switzerland
64 G13 **Parral** Maule, C Chile
Parral see Hidalgo del Parral
191 T9 **Parramatta** New South Wales, SE Australia
23 Y6 **Parramore Island** island Virginia, NE USA
42 M8 **Parras** var. Parras de la Fuente. Coahuila de Zaragoza, NE Mexico
Parras de la Fuente see Parras
44 M14 **Parrita** Puntarenas, S Costa Rica
12 G13 **Parry Island** island Ontario, S Canada
207 O9 **Parry Islands** island group Northwest Territories, NW Canada
12 G12 **Parry Sound** Ontario, S Canada
112 F7 **Parsęta** Ger. Persante. ≈ NW Poland
30 L3 **Parshall** North Dakota, N USA
29 Q7 **Parsons** Kansas, C USA
22 H9 **Parsons** Tennessee, S USA
23 T3 **Parsons** West Virginia, NE USA
Parsonstown see Birr
102 P11 **Parsteiner See** ◎ NE Germany
109 L24 **Partanna** Sicilia, Italy, C Mediterranean Sea
110 J8 **Partenen** Graubünden, E Switzerland
104 K9 **Parthenay** Deux-Sèvres, W France
97 J19 **Partille** Göteborg och Bohus, S Sweden
109 I23 **Partinico** Sicilia, Italy, C Mediterranean Sea
113 I20 **Partizánske** prev. Šimonovany, Hung. Simony. Západné Slovensko, W Slovakia
60 H11 **Paru de Oeste, Rio** ≈ N Brazil
190 K9 **Paruna** South Australia
60 I11 **Paru, Rio** ≈ N Brazil
Parvān see Parwān
161 M14 **Pārvatipuram** Andhra Pradesh, E India
158 G12 **Parvatsar** prev. Parbatsar. Rājasthān, N India
155 Q5 **Parwān** Per. Parvān. ◐ province E Afghanistan
164 I15 **Paryang** Xizang Zizhiqu, W China
121 M18 **Parychy** Rus. Parichi. Homyel'skaya Voblasts', SE Belarus
85 J21 **Parys** Free State, C South Africa
37 T15 **Pasadena** California, W USA
27 W11 **Pasadena** Texas, SW USA
58 B8 **Pasaje** El Oro, SW Ecuador
143 T9 **P'asanauri** N Georgia
173 G10 **Pasapuat** Pulau Pagai Utara, W Indonesia
178 Gg7 **Pasawng** Kayah State, C Myanmar
116 L13 **Paşayiğit** Edirne, NW Turkey
25 N9 **Pascagoula** Mississippi, S USA
24 M8 **Pascagoula River** ≈ Mississippi, S USA
118 F12 **Paşcani** Hung. Páskán. Iaşi, NE Romania
111 T4 **Pasching** Oberösterreich, N Austria
34 K10 **Pasco** Washington, NW USA
58 E13 **Pasco** off. Departamento de Pasco. ◐ department C Peru
203 N11 **Pascua, Isla de** var. Rapa Nui, Eng. Easter Island. island E Pacific Ocean
65 G21 **Pascua, Río** ≈ S Chile
105 N1 **Pas-de-Calais** ◐ department N France
102 P10 **Pasewalk** Mecklenburg-Vorpommern, NE Germany
9 T10 **Pasfield Lake** ◎ Saskatchewan, C Canada
Pa-shih Hai-hsia see Bashi Channel
Pashkeni see Bolyarovo
Pashmakli see Smolyan
179 P10 **Pasig** Luzon, N Philippines
159 X10 **Pāsighāt** Arunāchal Pradesh, NE India
143 Q12 **Pasinler** Erzurum, NE Turkey
Pasi Oloy, Qatorkŭhi see Zaalayskiy Khrebet
44 E3 **Pasión, Río de la** ≈ N Guatemala
174 Gg10 **Pasirganting** Sumatera, W Indonesia
Pasirpangarayan see Bagansiapiapi
174 H2 **Pasir Puteh** var. Pasir Putih. Kelantan, Peninsular Malaysia
174 L6 **Pasir, Tanjung** headland East Malaysia
97 N20 **Påskallavik** Kalmar, S Sweden
Páskán see Paşcani
112 K7 **Pasłęk** Ger. Preußisch Holland. Elbląg, N Poland
112 K7 **Pasłęka** Ger. Passarge. ≈ N Poland
154 K16 **Pasni** Baluchistān, SW Pakistan
65 I18 **Paso de Indios** Chubut, S Argentina
56 L7 **Paso del Caballo** Guárico, N Venezuela
63 E15 **Paso de los Libres** Corrientes, NE Argentina
63 E18 **Paso de los Toros** Tacuarembó, C Uruguay
37 P12 **Paso Robles** California, W USA
13 Y7 **Paspébiac** Québec, SE Canada
9 U14 **Pasquia Hills** ▲▲ Saskatchewan, S Canada
155 W7 **Pasrūr** Punjab, E Pakistan
32 M1 **Passage Island** island Michigan, N USA
67 B24 **Passage Islands** island group W Falkland Islands
15 I1 **Passage Point** headland Banks Island, Northwest Territories, NW Canada
Passarge see Pasłęka
117 C15 **Passarón** ancient monument Ípeiros, W Greece
Passarowitz see Požarevac
103 O22 **Passau** Bayern, SE Germany
24 M9 **Pass Christian** Mississippi, S USA
109 L26 **Passero, Capo** headland Sicilia, Italy, C Mediterranean Sea
179 Q13 **Passi** Panay Island, C Philippines
63 H14 **Passo Fundo** Rio Grande do Sul, S Brazil
62 H13 **Passo Fundo, Barragem de** ⊡ S Brazil
63 E15 **Passo Real, Barragem de** ⊡ S Brazil
61 L20 **Passos** Minas Gerais, NE Brazil
178 M11 **Passu Keah** island S Paracel Islands
120 J13 **Pastavy** Pol. Postawy, Rus. Postavy. Vitsyebskaya Voblasts', NW Belarus
58 D7 **Pastaza** ◐ province E Ecuador
58 D9 **Pastaza, Río** ≈ Ecuador/Peru
63 A21 **Pasteur** Buenos Aires, E Argentina
13 V3 **Pasteur** ≈ Québec, SE Canada
153 Q12 **Pastigav** Rus. Pastigov. W Tajikistan
Pastigov see Pastigav
56 C13 **Pasto** Nariño, SW Colombia
40 M10 **Pastol Bay** bay Alaska, USA
39 O8 **Pastora Peak** ▲ Arizona, SW USA
107 O8 **Pastrana** Castilla-La Mancha, C Spain
174 M15 **Pasuruan** prev. Pasoeroean. Jawa, C Indonesia
120 F11 **Pasvalys** Pasvalys, N Lithuania
113 K21 **Pásztó** Nógrád, N Hungary
201 U12 **Pata** var. Patta. atoll Chuuk Islands, C Micronesia
38 M16 **Patagonia** Arizona, SW USA
65 H20 **Patagonia** physical region Argentina/Chile
Patalung see Phatthalung
160 D9 **Pātan** Gujarāt, W India
160 J10 **Pātan** Madhya Pradesh, C India
175 T8 **Patani** Pulau Halmahera, E Indonesia
Patani see Pattani
13 V7 **Patapédia Est** ≈ Québec, SE Canada
118 K13 **Pătâriagele** prev. Pătîriagele. Buzău, SE Romania
Patavium see Padova
190 I5 **Patawarta Hill** ▲ South Australia
190 L10 **Patchewollock** Victoria, SE Australia
192 K11 **Patea** Taranaki, North Island, NZ
192 K11 **Patea** ≈ North Island, NZ
79 U15 **Pategi** Kwara, C Nigeria
83 K20 **Pate Island** var. Patta Island. island SE Kenya
107 S10 **Paterna** País Valenciano, E Spain
111 R9 **Paternion** Slvn. Špatrjan. Kärnten, S Austria
109 L24 **Paternò** anc. Hybla, Hybla Major. Sicilia, Italy, C Mediterranean Sea
34 J7 **Pateros** Washington, NW USA
20 J14 **Paterson** New Jersey, NE USA
34 J10 **Paterson** Washington, NW USA
193 C25 **Paterson Inlet** inlet Stewart Island, NZ
100 N6 **Paterswolde** Drenthe, NE Netherlands
158 H7 **Pathānkot** Himāchal Pradesh, N India
Pathein see Bassein
35 W15 **Pathfinder Reservoir** ⊡ Wyoming, C USA
178 Hh11 **Pathum Thani** var. Patumdhani, Prathum Thani. Pathum Thani, C Thailand
174 L14 **Pati** Jawa, C Indonesia
56 C12 **Patía** var. El Bordo. Cauca, SW Colombia
158 I9 **Patiāla** var. Puttiala. Punjab, NW India
56 B12 **Patía, Río** ≈ SW Colombia
175 T8 **Patinti, Selat** strait Maluku, E Indonesia
196 D15 **Pati Point** headland NE Guam
Pătîriagele see Pătâriagele
58 C13 **Pativilca** Lima, W Peru
178 Gg1 **Pātkai Bum** var. Patkai Range. ▲▲ Myanmar/India
Patkai Range see Pātkai Bum
117 L20 **Pátmos** Pátmos, Dodekánisos, Greece, Aegean Sea
117 L20 **Pátmos** island Dodekánisos, Greece, Aegean Sea
159 P13 **Patna** var. Azimabad. Bihār, N India
160 M12 **Patnāgarh** Orissa, E India
179 Pp13 **Patnongon** Panay Island, C Philippines
143 S13 **Patnos** Ağrı, E Turkey
62 H12 **Pato Branco** Paraná, S Brazil
33 O16 **Patoka Lake** ⊡ Indiana, N USA
94 L9 **Patoniva** Lapp. Buoddobohki. Lappi, N Finland
115 K21 **Patos** var. Patosi. Fier, SW Albania
Patos see Patos de Minas
61 K19 **Patos de Minas** var. Patos. Minas Gerais, NE Brazil
Patosi see Patos
63 I17 **Patos, Lagoa dos** lagoon S Brazil
64 J9 **Patquía** La Rioja, C Argentina
117 E19 **Pátra** Eng. Patras; prev. Pátrai. Dytikí Ellás, S Greece
Pátrai/Patras see Pátra
117 D18 **Patraïkós Kólpos** gulf S Greece
94 G2 **Patreksfjördhur** Vestfirdhir, W Iceland
26 M7 **Patricia** Texas, SW USA
65 F21 **Patricio Lynch, Isla** island S Chile
Patta see Pata
Patta Island see Pate Island
178 Hh17 **Pattani** var. Patani. Pattani, SW Thailand
178 Hh12 **Pattaya** Chon Buri, S Thailand
21 S4 **Patten** Maine, NE USA
37 O9 **Patterson** California, W USA
24 J10 **Patterson** Louisiana, S USA
37 R7 **Patterson, Mount** ▲ California, W USA
33 P4 **Patterson, Point** headland Michigan, N USA
109 L23 **Patti** Sicilia, Italy, C Mediterranean Sea
109 L23 **Patti, Golfo di** gulf Sicilia, Italy, C Mediterranean Sea
95 L14 **Pattijoki** Oulu, W Finland
199 Mm5 **Patton Escarpment** undersea feature E Pacific Ocean
29 S2 **Pattonsburg** Missouri, C USA
1 D6 **Patton Seamount** undersea feature NE Pacific Ocean
8 J12 **Pattullo, Mount** ▲ British Columbia, W Canada
Patuakhali see Patukhali
44 M5 **Patuca, Río** ≈ E Honduras
159 U16 **Patukhali** var. Patuakhali. Khulna, S Bangladesh
Patumdhani see Pathum Thani
42 M14 **Pátzcuaro** Michoacán de Ocampo, SW Mexico
44 C6 **Patzicía** Chimaltenango, S Guatemala
104 K16 **Pau** Pyrénées-Atlantiques, SW France
104 J12 **Pauillac** Gironde, SW France
177 F5 **Pauk** Magwe, W Myanmar
15 H3 **Paulatuk** Northwest Territories, NW Canada
44 K5 **Paulayá, Río** ≈ NE Honduras
24 M6 **Paulding** Mississippi, S USA
33 Q12 **Paulding** Ohio, N USA
31 S12 **Paullina** Iowa, C USA
61 P15 **Paulo Afonso** Bahia, E Brazil
40 M16 **Pauloff Harbor** var. Pavlor Harbour. Sanak Island, Alaska, USA
29 N12 **Pauls Valley** Oklahoma, C USA
177 F7 **Paungde** Pegu, C Myanmar
Pauni see Paoni
158 K9 **Pauri** Uttar Pradesh, N India
Pautalia see Kyustendil
176 Z11 **Pauwasi** ≈ Irian Jaya, E Indonesia
148 J5 **Pāveh** Kermānshāhān, NW Iran
130 L5 **Pavelets** Ryazanskaya Oblast', W Russian Federation
108 D8 **Pavia** anc. Ticinum. Lombardia, N Italy
120 C9 **Pāvilosta** Liepāja, W Latvia
129 P14 **Pavino** Kostromskaya Oblast', NW Russian Federation
116 J8 **Pavlikeni** Loveshka Oblast, N Bulgaria
151 T8 **Pavlodar** Pavlodar, NE Kazakhstan
151 S9 **Pavlodar** off. Pavlodarskaya Oblast', Kaz. Pavlodar Oblysy. ◐ province NE Kazakhstan
Pavlodar Oblysy/Pavlodarskaya Oblast' see Pavlodar
Pavlograd see Pavlohrad
119 U7 **Pavlohrad** Rus. Pavlograd. Dnipropetrovs'ka Oblast', E Ukraine
Pavlor Harbour see Pauloff Harbor
151 R9 **Pavlovka** Akmola, C Kazakhstan
131 V4 **Pavlovka** Respublika Bashkortostan, W Russian Federation
131 Q7 **Pavlovka** Ul'yanovskaya Oblast', W Russian Federation
131 N3 **Pavlovo** Nizhegorodskaya Oblast', W Russian Federation
130 L9 **Pavlovsk** Voronezhskaya Oblast', W Russian Federation
130 L13 **Pavlovskaya** Krasnodarskiy Kray, SW Russian Federation
119 S7 **Pavlysh** Kirovohrads'ka Oblast', C Ukraine
108 F10 **Pavullo nel Frignano** Emilia-Romagna, C Italy
29 P8 **Pawhuska** Oklahoma, C USA
23 U13 **Pawleys Island** South Carolina, SE USA
178 Gg6 **Pawn** ≈ C Myanmar
32 K14 **Pawnee** Illinois, N USA
29 O9 **Pawnee** Oklahoma, C USA
39 U2 **Pawnee Buttes** ▲ Colorado, C USA
31 S17 **Pawnee City** Nebraska, C USA
28 K5 **Pawnee River** ≈ Kansas, C USA
33 O10 **Paw Paw** Michigan, N USA
33 O10 **Paw Paw Lake** Michigan, N USA
21 O12 **Pawtucket** Rhode Island, NE USA
Pax Augusta see Badajoz
117 I25 **Paximádia** island SE Greece
Pax Julia see Beja
117 B16 **Paxoí** island Iónioi Nísoi, Greece, C Mediterranean Sea
41 S10 **Paxson** Alaska, USA
32 M13 **Paxton** Illinois, N USA
128 J11 **Pay** Respublika Kareliya, NW Russian Federation
177 G8 **Payagyi** Pegu, SW Myanmar
110 C9 **Payerne** Ger. Peterlingen. Vaud, W Switzerland
34 M13 **Payette** Idaho, NW USA
34 M13 **Payette River** ≈ Idaho, NW USA
129 V2 **Pay-Khoy, Khrebet** ▲▲ NW Russian Federation
10 K4 **Payne, Lac** ◎ Québec, NE Canada
31 T8 **Paynesville** Minnesota, N USA
174 M4 **Payong, Tanjung** headland East Malaysia
Payo Obispo see Chetumal
63 D18 **Paysandú** Paysandú, W Uruguay
63 D17 **Paysandú** ◐ department W Uruguay
104 I7 **Pays de la Loire** ◐ region NW France
38 L12 **Payson** Arizona, SW USA
38 L4 **Payson** Utah, W USA
129 W4 **Payyer, Gora** ▲ NW Russian Federation
Payzawat see Jiashi
143 Q11 **Pazar** Rize, NE Turkey
142 F10 **Pazarbaşı Burnu** headland NW Turkey
142 M16 **Pazarcık** Kahramanmaraş, S Turkey
116 I10 **Pazardzhik** prev. Tatar Pazardzhik. Plovdivska Oblast, SW Bulgaria
56 H9 **Paz de Ariporo** Casanare, E Colombia
114 A10 **Pazin** Ger. Mitterburg, It. Pisino. Istra, NW Croatia
44 D7 **Paz, Río** ≈ El Salvador/Guatemala
115 O18 **Pčinja** ≈ N FYR Macedonia
200 Qq15 **Pea** Tongatapu, S Tonga
29 O6 **Peabody** Kansas, C USA
9 O12 **Peace** ≈ Alberta/British Columbia, W Canada
Peace Garden State see North Dakota
9 Q10 **Peace Point** Alberta, C Canada
9 O12 **Peace River** Alberta, W Canada
25 W13 **Peace River** ≈ Florida, SE USA
9 N17 **Peachland** British Columbia, SW Canada
38 J10 **Peach Springs** Arizona, SW USA
Peach State see Georgia
25 S4 **Peachtree City** Georgia, SE USA
201 Y13 **Peacock Point** point SE Wake Island
99 M18 **Peak District** physical region C England, UK
191 Q7 **Peak Hill** New South Wales, SE Australia
67 G15 **Peak, The** ▲ C Ascension Island
107 O13 **Peal de Becerro** Andalucía, S Spain
201 X11 **Peale Island** island N Wake Island
39 O6 **Peale, Mount** ▲ Utah, W USA
41 O4 **Peard Bay** bay Alaska, USA
25 Q7 **Pea River** ≈ Alabama/Florida, S USA
27 W11 **Pearland** Texas, SW USA
40 D9 **Pearl City** Oahu, Hawaii, USA, C Pacific Ocean
40 D9 **Pearl Harbor** inlet Oahu, Hawaii, USA, C Pacific Ocean
Pearl Islands see Perlas, Archipiélago de las
Pearl Lagoon see Perlas, Laguna de
24 M5 **Pearl River** ≈ Louisiana/Mississippi, S USA
27 Q13 **Pearsall** Texas, SW USA
25 U7 **Pearson** Georgia, SE USA
27 P5 **Pease River** ≈ Texas, SW USA
10 F7 **Peawanuk** Ontario, C Canada
85 P16 **Pebane** Zambézia, NE Mozambique
67 C23 **Pebble Island** island N Falkland Islands
67 C23 **Pebble Island Settlement** Pebble Island, N Falkland Islands
115 L16 **Peć** Alb. Pejë, Turk. Ipek. Serbia, S Yugoslavia
27 R8 **Pecan Bayou** ≈ Texas, SW USA
24 H10 **Pecan Island** Louisiana, S USA
62 L12 **Peças, Ilha das** island S Brazil
32 L10 **Pecatonica River** ≈ Illinois/Wisconsin, N USA
110 G10 **Peccia** Ticino, S Switzerland
Pechenegi see Pechenihy
Pechenezhskoye Vodokhranilishche see Pechenіz'ke Vodoskhovyshche
128 I2 **Pechenga** Fin. Petsamo. Murmanskaya Oblast', NW Russian Federation
119 V5 **Pechenihy** Rus. Pechenegi. Kharkivs'ka Oblast', E Ukraine
119 V5 **Pechenіz'ke Vodoskhovyshche** Rus. Pechenezhskoye Vodokhranilishche. ⊡ E Ukraine
129 U7 **Pechora** Respublika Komi, NW Russian Federation
129 R6 **Pechora** ≈ NW Russian Federation
Pechora Bay see Pechorskaya Guba
Pechora Sea see Pechorskoye More
129 S3 **Pechorskaya Guba** Eng. Pechora Bay. bay NW Russian Federation
125 Ff6 **Pechorskoye More** Eng. Pechora Sea. sea NW Russian Federation
118 E11 **Pecica** Ger. Petschka, Hung. Ópécska. Arad, W Romania
26 K8 **Pecos** Texas, SW USA
27 N11 **Pecos River** ≈ New Mexico/Texas, SW USA
113 I25 **Pécs** Ger. Fünfkirchen; Lat. Sopianae. Baranya, SW Hungary
45 T17 **Pedasí** Los Santos, S Panama
Pedde see Pedja
191 O17 **Pedder, Lake** ◎ Tasmania, SE Australia
46 M10 **Pedernales** SW Dominican Republic
57 Q5 **Pedernales** Delta Amacuro, NE Venezuela
27 R10 **Pedernales River** ≈ Texas, SW USA
64 H6 **Pedernales, Salar de** salt lake N Chile
Pedhoulas see Pedoulás
57 X11 **Pédima** var. Malavate. SW French Guiana
190 F1 **Pedirka** South Australia
175 T7 **Pediwang** Pulau Halmahera, E Indonesia
120 I5 **Pedja** var. Pedja Jõgi, Ger. Pedde. ≈ E Estonia
Pedja Jõgi see Pedja
124 N3 **Pedoulás** var. Pedhoulas. W Cyprus
61 N18 **Pedra Azul** Minas Gerais, NE Brazil
106 I3 **Pedrafita, Porto de** var. Puerto de Piedrafita. pass NW Spain
78 E9 **Pedra Lume** Sal, NE Cape Verde
45 P16 **Pedregal** Chiriquí, W Panama
56 J4 **Pedregal** Falcón, N Venezuela
42 L9 **Pedriceña** Durango, C Mexico
62 L11 **Pedro Barros** São Paulo, S Brazil
41 Q13 **Pedro Bay** Alaska, USA
64 H4 **Pedro de Valdivia** var. Oficina Pedro de Valdivia. Antofagasta, N Chile
64 P4 **Pedro Juan Caballero** Amambay, E Paraguay
65 L15 **Pedro Luro** Buenos Aires, E Argentina
107 O10 **Pedro Muñoz** Castilla-La Mancha, C Spain
161 J22 **Pedro, Point** headland NW Sri Lanka
190 K9 **Peebinga** South Australia
98 J13 **Peebles** SE Scotland, UK
33 S15 **Peebles** Ohio, N USA
98 J12 **Peebles** cultural region SE Scotland, UK
20 K13 **Peekskill** New York, NE USA
99 I16 **Peel** W Isle of Man
14 F4 **Peel** ≈ Northwest Territories/Yukon Territory, NW Canada
15 I1 **Peel Point** headland Victoria Island, Northwest Territories, NW Canada
15 K1 **Peel Sound** passage Northwest Territories, N Canada
102 N9 **Peene** ≈ NE Germany
101 K17 **Peer** Limburg, NE Belgium
12 H14 **Pefferlaw** Ontario, S Canada
193 I18 **Pegasus Bay** bay South Island, NZ
123 Mm3 **Pégeia** var. Peyia. SW Cyprus
111 V7 **Peggau** Steiermark, SE Austria
103 L19 **Pegnitz** Bayern, SE Germany
103 L19 **Pegnitz** ≈ SE Germany
107 T11 **Pego** País Valenciano, E Spain
177 G8 **Pegu** var. Bago. Pegu, SW Myanmar
177 G7 **Pegu** ◐ division S Myanmar
176 W7 **Pegun, Pulau** island Kepulauan Mapia, E Indonesia
201 N13 **Pehleng** Pohnpei, E Micronesia
116 M12 **Pehlivanköy** Kırklareli, NW Turkey
79 R14 **Péhonko** C Benin
63 B21 **Pehuajó** Buenos Aires, E Argentina
Pei-ching see Beijing/Beijing Shi
102 J13 **Peine** Niedersachsen, C Germany
Pei-p'ing see Beijing/Beijing Shi
Peipsi Järv/Peipus-See see Peipus, Lake
120 J5 **Peipus, Lake** Est. Peipsi Järv, Ger. Peipus-See, Rus. Chudskoye Ozero. ◎ Estonia/Russian Federation
117 H19 **Peiraías** prev. Piraiévs, Eng. Piraeus. Attikí, C Greece
Peisern see Pyzdry
62 I8 **Peixe, Rio do** ≈ S Brazil
61 I16 **Peixoto de Azevedo** Mato Grosso, W Brazil
174 J8 **Pejantan, Pulau** island W Indonesia
Pejë see Peć
114 N11 **Pek** ≈ E Yugoslavia
178 I7 **Pèk** var. Xieng Khouang; prev. Xiangkhoang. Xiangkhoang, N Laos
174 Kk14 **Pekalongan** Jawa, C Indonesia
174 Gg7 **Pekanbaru** var. Pakanbaru. Sumatera, W Indonesia
32 L12 **Pekin** Illinois, N USA
Peking see Beijing/Beijing Shi
Pelabohan Kelang/Pelabuhan Kelang see Pelabuhan Klang
173 G5 **Pelabuhan Klang** var. Kuala Pelabohan Kelang, Pelabohan Kelang, Pelabuhan Kelang, Port Klang, Port Swettenham. Selangor, Peninsular Malaysia
174 J15 **Pelabuhan Ratu, Teluk** bay Jawa, SW Indonesia
123 L12 **Pelagie, Isole** island group SW Italy
Pelagosa see Palagruža
24 L5 **Pelahatchie** Mississippi, S USA
175 N11 **Pelaihari** var. Pleihari. Borneo, C Indonesia
105 U14 **Pelat, Mont** ▲ SE France
118 F12 **Peleaga, Vârful** prev. Vîrful Peleaga. ▲ W Romania
Peleaga, Vîrful see Peleaga, Vârful
126 K12 **Peleduy** Respublika Sakha (Yakutiya), NE Russian Federation
12 C18 **Pelee Island** island Ontario, S Canada
47 Q11 **Pelée, Montagne** ▲ N Martinique
12 D18 **Pelee, Point** headland Ontario, S Canada
175 R9 **Pelei** Pulau Peleng, N Indonesia
Peleliu see Beliliou
175 R9 **Peleng, Pulau** island Kepulauan Banggai, N Indonesia
175 Qq9 **Peleng, Selat** strait Sulawesi, C Indonesia
25 T7 **Pelham** Georgia, SE USA
113 E18 **Pelhřimov** Ger. Pilgram. Jižní Čechy, S Czech Republic
41 W13 **Pelican** Chichagof Island, Alaska, USA
203 Z3 **Pelican Lagoon** ◎ Kiritimati, E Kiribati
31 U6 **Pelican Lake** ◎ Minnesota, N USA
31 V3 **Pelican Lake** ◎ Minnesota, N USA
32 L5 **Pelican Lake** ◎ Wisconsin, N USA
46 G1 **Pelican Point** Grand Bahama Island, N Bahamas
85 B19 **Pelican Point** headland W Namibia
31 S6 **Pelican Rapids** Minnesota, N USA
Pelican State see Louisiana
9 U13 **Pelikan Narrows** Saskatchewan, C Canada
117 L18 **Pelinaío** ▲ Chíos, E Greece
Pelinnaeum see Pelinnaío
117 E16 **Pelinnaío** anc. Pelinnaeum. ruins Thessalía, C Greece
115 N20 **Pelister** ▲ SW FYR Macedonia
115 G15 **Pelješac** peninsula S Croatia
94 M12 **Pelkosenniemi** Lappi, NE Finland
31 W15 **Pella** Iowa, C USA
116 F13 **Pélla** site of ancient city Kentrikí Makedonía, N Greece
25 P3 **Pell City** Alabama, S USA
63 A22 **Pellegrini** Buenos Aires, E Argentina
94 K12 **Pello** Lappi, NW Finland
102 G7 **Pellworm** island N Germany
8 H6 **Pelly** ≈ Yukon Territory, NW Canada
15 L3 **Pelly Bay** Northwest Territories, N Canada
8 I8 **Pelly Mountains** ▲▲ Yukon Territory, W Canada
Pélmonostor see Beli Manastir
39 P13 **Pelona Mountain** ▲ New Mexico, SW USA
Peloponnese/Peloponnesus see Pelopónnisos
117 E20 **Pelopónnisos** Eng. Peloponnese. ◐ region S Greece
117 E20 **Pelopónnisos** var. Morea, Eng. Peloponnese; anc. Peloponnesus. peninsula S Greece
109 L23 **Peloritani, Monti** anc. Pelorus and Neptunius. ▲▲ Sicilia, Italy, C Mediterranean Sea
109 M22 **Peloro, Capo** var. Punta del Faro. headland S Italy
Pelorus and Neptunius see Peloritani, Monti
63 H17 **Pelotas** Rio Grande do Sul, S Brazil
63 I14 **Pelotas, Rio** ≈ S Brazil

◆ Country
● Country Capital
◇ Dependent Territory
○ Dependent Territory Capital
◐ Administrative Region
✕ International Airport
▲ Mountain
▲▲ Mountain Range
☼ Volcano
≈ River
◎ Lake
⊡ Reservoir

◆　COUNTRY　　　　◇　DEPENDENT TERRITORY　　　　✕　ADMINISTRATIVE REGION　　　　▲　MOUNTAIN　　　　▲　VOLCANO　　　　⊗　LAKE
●　COUNTRY CAPITAL　　　○　DEPENDENT TERRITORY CAPITAL　　　✕　INTERNATIONAL AIRPORT　　　▲　MOUNTAIN RANGE　　　♣　RIVER　　　☉　RESERVOIR

299

◆ COUNTRY ◆ COUNTRY CAPITAL ◇ DEPENDENT TERRITORY ○ DEPENDENT TERRITORY CAPITAL ◆ ADMINISTRATIVE REGION ✗ INTERNATIONAL AIRPORT ▲ MOUNTAIN ▲ MOUNTAIN RANGE ☼ VOLCANO ✆ RIVER ⊞ LAKE ⊞ RESERVOIR

Poechos, Embalse – Portsmouth

58 A9 **Poechos, Embalse** ◎ NW Peru
57 W10 **Poeketi** Sipaliwini, E Mynamar
102 L8 **Poel** *island* N Germany
85 M20 **Poelela, Lagoa** ◎ S Mozambique
Poerwodadi *see* Purwodadi
Poetovio *see* Ptuj
85 E23 **Pofadder** Northern Cape, W South Africa
108 I9 **Po, Foci del** *var.* Bocche del Po. ≈ NE Italy
118 E12 **Pogăniș** ≈ W Romania
Pogegen *see* Pagėgiai
108 G12 **Poggibonsi** Toscana, C Italy
109 I14 **Poggio Mirteto** Lazio, C Italy
111 V4 **Pöggstall** Niederösterreich, N Austria
118 L13 **Pogoanele** Buzău, SE Romania
Pogónion *see* Delvináki
115 M21 **Pogradec** *var.* Pogradeci. Korçë, SE Albania
Pogradeci *see* Pogradec
127 N18 **Pogranichnyy** Primorskiy Kray, SE Russian Federation
40 M16 **Pogromni Volcano** ▲ Unimak Island, Alaska, USA
169 Z15 **P'ohang** *Jap.* Hokō. E South Korea
13 T9 **Pohénégamook, Lac** ◎ Québec, SE Canada
95 L20 **Pohja** *Swe.* Pojo. Uusimaa, SW Finland
Pohjanlahti *see* Bothnia, Gulf of
95 N16 **Pohjois-Karjala** *Swe.* Norra Karelen. ◈ *province* C Finland
201 U16 **Pohnpei** ◈ *state* E Micronesia
201 O12 **Pohnpei** ✕ Pohnpei, E Micronesia
201 O12 **Pohnpei** *prev.* Ponape Ascension Island. *island* E Micronesia
113 F19 **Pohořelice** *Ger.* Pohrlitz. Jižní Morava, SE Czech Republic
111 V10 **Pohorje** *Ger.* Bacher. ▲ N Slovenia
119 N6 **Pohrebyshche** Vinnyts'ka Oblast', C Ukraine
Pohrlitz *see* Pohořelice
175 Qq9 **Poh, Teluk** *bay* Sulawesi, C Indonesia
167 P9 **Po Hu** ⊞ E China
118 G15 **Poiana Mare** Dolj, S Romania
Poictiers *see* Poitiers
131 N6 **Poim** Penzenskaya Oblast', W Russian Federation
197 I6 **Poindimié** Province Nord, C New Caledonia
Poindo *see* Lhünzhub
205 Y13 **Poinsett, Cape** *headland* Antarctica
31 R9 **Poinsett, Lake** ◎ South Dakota, N USA
24 I10 **Point Au Fer Island** *island* Louisiana, S USA
41 X14 **Point Baker** Prince of Wales Island, Alaska, USA
27 U13 **Point Comfort** Texas, SW USA
Point de Galle *see* Galle
46 K10 **Pointe à Gravois** *headland* SW Haiti
24 L10 **Pointe a la Hache** Louisiana, S USA
47 Y6 **Pointe-à-Pitre** Grande Terre, C Guadeloupe
13 U7 **Pointe-au-Père** Québec, SE Canada
13 V5 **Pointe-aux-Anglais** Québec, SE Canada
47 T10 **Pointe Du Cap** *headland* N Saint Lucia
81 E21 **Pointe-Noire** Le Kouilou, S Congo
47 X6 **Pointe Noire** Basse Terre, W Guadeloupe
81 E21 **Pointe-Noire** ✕ Le Kouilou, S Congo
47 U15 **Point Fortin** Trinidad, Trinidad and Tobago
40 M6 **Point Hope** Alaska, USA
41 N5 **Point Lay** Alaska, USA
20 B16 **Point Marion** Pennsylvania, NE USA
20 K16 **Point Pleasant** New Jersey, NE USA
23 P4 **Point Pleasant** West Virginia, NE USA
47 R14 **Point Salines** ✕ (St.George's) SW Grenada
104 L9 **Poitiers** *prev.* Poictiers, *anc.* Limonum. Vienne, W France
104 K9 **Poitou** *cultural region* W France
104 K10 **Poitou-Charentes** ◈ *region* W France
105 N3 **Poix-de-Picardie** Somme, N France
Pojo *see* Pohja
39 S10 **Pojoaque** New Mexico, SW USA
158 E11 **Pokaran** Rājasthān, NW India
191 R4 **Pokataroo** New South Wales, SE Australia
121 P18 **Pokats'** *Rus.* Pokot'. ≈ SE Belarus
31 V5 **Pokegama Lake** ◎ Minnesota, N USA
192 L6 **Pokeno** Waikato, North Island, NZ
159 O11 **Pokhara** Western, C Nepal
131 T6 **Pokhvistnevo** Samarskaya Oblast', W Russian Federation
57 W10 **Pokigron** Sipaliwini, C Suriname
94 L10 **Pokka** *Lapp.* Bohkká. Lappi, N Finland
81 N16 **Poko** Haut-Zaïre, NE Zaire
Pokot' *see* Pokats'
Po-ko-to Shan *see* Bogda Shan
153 S7 **Pokrovka** Talasskaya Oblast', NW Kyrgyzstan
Pokrovka *see* Kyzyl-Suu
126 M11 **Pokrovsk** Respublika Sakha (Yakutiya), NE Russian Federation
119 V8 **Pokrovs'ke** *Rus.* Pokrovskoye. Dnipropetrovs'ka Oblast', E Ukraine
Pokrovskoye *see* Pokrovs'ke
Pola *see* Pula
39 N10 **Polacca** Arizona, SW USA
106 L2 **Pola de Laviana** Asturias, N Spain
106 K2 **Pola de Lena** Asturias, N Spain
106 L2 **Pola de Siero** Asturias, N Spain
203 Y3 **Poland** Kiritimati, E Kiribati
112 H12 **Poland** *off.* Republic of Poland, *var.* Polish Republic, *Pol.* Polska, Rzeczpospolita Polska; *prev. Pol.* Polska Rzeczpospolita Ludowa, Polish People's Republic. ◆ *republic* C Europe
Polangen *see* Palanga
112 G7 **Połanów** *Ger.* Pollnow. Koszalin, NW Poland
142 H13 **Polatlı** Ankara, C Turkey
120 L12 **Polatsk** *Rus.* Polotsk. Vitsyebskaya Voblasts', N Belarus
112 F8 **Połczyn-Zdrój** *Ger.* Bad Polzin. Koszalin, NW Poland
152 I16 **Polekhatum** *prev.* Pul'-I-Khatum. Akhalskiy Velayat, S Turkmenistan
155 Q3 **Pol-e Khomrī** *var.* Pul-i-Khumri. Baghlān, NE Afghanistan
207 S10 **Pole Plain** *undersea feature* Arctic Ocean
149 P5 **Pol-e Safīd** *var.* Pol-e-Sefid, Pul-i-Sefid. Māzandarān, N Iran
Pol-e-Sefid *see* Pol-e Safīd
120 B13 **Polessk** *Ger.* Labiau. Kaliningradskaya Oblast', W Russian Federation
Polesskoye *see* Polis'ke
175 P11 **Polewali** Sulawesi, C Indonesia
116 G11 **Polezhan** ▲ SW Bulgaria
80 F13 **Poli** Nord, N Cameroon
Poli *see* Pólis
109 M19 **Policastro, Golfo di** *gulf* S Italy
112 D8 **Police** *Ger.* Pölitz. Szczecin, NW Poland
180 I17 **Police, Pointe** *headland* Mahé, NE Seychelles
117 L17 **Polichnítos** *var.* Polihnitos, Polikhnítos. Lésvos, E Greece
Poligiros *see* Polýgyros
109 P17 **Polignano a Mare** Puglia, SE Italy
105 S9 **Poligny** Jura, E France
Polihnitos *see* Polichnítos
Polikastro/Políkastron *see* Polýkastro
Polikhnítos *see* Polichnítos
116 K8 **Polikrayshte** Loveshka Oblast, N Bulgaria
179 Pp10 **Polillo Islands** *island group* N Philippines
111 Q9 **Polinik** ▲ SW Austria
123 Mm3 **Pólis** *var.* Poli. W Cyprus
Polish People's Republic *see* Poland
Polish Republic *see* Poland
119 O3 **Polis'ke** *Rus.* Polesskoye. Kyyivs'ka Oblast', N Ukraine
109 N22 **Polistena** Calabria, SW Italy
Politz *see* Police
Políyiros *see* Polýgyros
31 V14 **Polk City** Iowa, C USA
112 F13 **Polkowice** *Ger.* Heerwegen. Legnica, W Poland
161 G22 **Pollāchi** Tamil Nādu, SE India
111 W7 **Pöllau** Steiermark, SE Austria
201 T13 **Polle** *atoll* Chuuk Islands, C Micronesia
Pollensa *see* Pollença
Pollnow *see* Połanów
31 N7 **Pollock** South Dakota, N USA
94 L8 **Polmak** Finnmark, N Norway
32 L10 **Polo** Illinois, N USA
200 Qq15 **Poloa** *island* Tongatapu Group, N Tonga
44 E5 **Polochic, Río** ≈ C Guatemala
Pologi *see* Polohy
119 V9 **Polohy** *Rus.* Pologi. Zaporiz'ka Oblast', SE Ukraine
12 M10 **Polonais, Lac des** ◎ Québec, SE Canada
63 G20 **Polonio, Cabo** *headland* E Uruguay
161 K24 **Polonnaruwa** North Central Province, C Sri Lanka
118 L5 **Polonne** *Rus.* Polonnoye. Khmel'nyts'ka Oblast', NW Ukraine
Polonnoye *see* Polonne
Polotsk *see* Polatsk
111 T7 **Pöls** *var.* Pölsbach. ≈ E Austria
Pölsbach *see* Pöls
Polska/Polska, Rzeczpospolita/Polska Rzeczpospolita Ludowa *see* Poland
116 L10 **Polski Gradets** Burgaska Oblast, SE Bulgaria
116 K8 **Polsko Kosovo** Loveshka Oblast, N Bulgaria
35 P8 **Polson** Montana, NW USA
119 T6 **Poltava** Poltavs'ka Oblast', NE Ukraine
Poltava *see* Poltavs'ka Oblast'
119 R5 **Poltavs'ka Oblast'** *var.* Poltava, *Rus.* Poltavskaya Oblast'. ◈ *province* NE Ukraine
Poltoratsk *see* Ashgabat
Poltavskaya Oblast' *see* Poltavs'ka Oblast'
120 I5 **Põltsamaa** *Ger.* Oberpahlen. Jõgevamaa, E Estonia
120 I4 **Põltsamaa** *var.* Põltsamaa Jõgi. ≈ C Estonia
Põltsamaa Jõgi *see* Põltsamaa
125 F10 **Polunochnoye** Sverdlovskaya Oblast', C Russian Federation
125 G8 **Poluy** ≈ N Russian Federation
120 J6 **Põlva** *Ger.* Põlwe. Põlvamaa, SE Estonia
95 N16 **Polvijärvi** Pohjois-Karjala, SE Finland
Põlwe *see* Põlva
117 I22 **Polýaigos** *island* Kykládes, Greece, Aegean Sea
117 I22 **Polyaígou Folégandrou, Stenó** *strait* Kykládes, Greece, Aegean Sea
128 J3 **Polyarnyy** Murmanskaya Oblast', NW Russian Federation
129 W5 **Polyarnyy Ural** ▲ NW Russian Federation
117 G14 **Polýgyros** *var.* Poligiros, Políyiros. Kentrikí Makedonía, N Greece
116 F13 **Polýkastro** *var.* Polikastro; *prev.* Políkastron. Kentrikí Makedonía, N Greece
199 Kk9 **Polynesia** *island group* C Pacific Ocean
117 J15 **Polýochni** *site of ancient city* Límnos, E Greece
43 Y13 **Polyuc** Quintana Roo, E Mexico
111 V10 **Polzela** C Slovenia
Polzen *see* Ploučnice
176 Ww9 **Pom** Irian Jaya, E Indonesia
58 D12 **Pomabamba** Ancash, C Peru
193 D23 **Pomahaka** ≈ South Island, NZ
108 F12 **Pomarance** Toscana, C Italy
106 G9 **Pombal** Leiria, C Portugal
78 D9 **Pombas** Santo Antão, NW Cape Verde
85 N19 **Pomene** Inhambane, SE Mozambique
112 G8 **Pomerania** *cultural region* Germany/Poland
112 D7 **Pomeranian Bay** *Ger.* Pommersche Bucht, *Pol.* Zatoka Pomorska. *bay* Germany/Poland
33 T15 **Pomeroy** Ohio, N USA
34 L10 **Pomeroy** Washington, NW USA
119 Q8 **Pomichna** Kirovohrads'ka Oblast', C Ukraine
195 O12 **Pomio** New Britain, E PNG
Pomir, Dar"yoi *see* Pamir/Pāmīr, Daryā-ye
29 T6 **Pomme de Terre Lake** ⊞ Missouri, C USA
31 S8 **Pomme de Terre River** ≈ Minnesota, N USA
Pommersche Bucht *see* Pomeranian Bay
37 T15 **Pomona** California, W USA
116 N9 **Pomorie** Burgaska Oblast, E Bulgaria
Pomorska, Zatoka *see* Pomeranian Bay
129 Q4 **Pomorskiy Proliv** *strait* NW Russian Federation
Pomorze Zachodnie *see* Szczecin
129 T10 **Pomozdino** Respublika Komi, NW Russian Federation
Pompaelo *see* Pamplona
175 Q9 **Pompangeo, Pegunungan** ▲ Sulawesi, C Indonesia
25 Z15 **Pompano Beach** Florida, SE USA
109 K18 **Pompei** Campania, S Italy
35 V10 **Pompeys Pillar** Montana, NW USA
Ponape Ascension Island *see* Pohnpei
31 R13 **Ponca** Nebraska, C USA
29 O8 **Ponca City** Oklahoma, C USA
47 T6 **Ponce** C Puerto Rico
25 X10 **Ponce de Leon Inlet** *inlet* Florida, SE USA
24 K8 **Ponchatoula** Louisiana, S USA
28 M8 **Pond Creek** Oklahoma, C USA
161 J20 **Pondicherry** *var.* Puduchcheri, *Fr.* Pondichéry. Pondicherry, SE India
157 I20 **Pondicherry** *var.* Puduchcheri, *Fr.* Pondichéry. ◈ *union territory* India
Pondichéry *see* Pondicherry
207 N11 **Pond Inlet** Baffin Island, Northwest Territories, NE Canada
197 I6 **Ponérihouen** Province Nord, C New Caledonia
106 J4 **Ponferrada** Castilla-León, NW Spain
192 N13 **Pongaroa** Manawatu-Wanganui, North Island, NZ
178 I12 **Pong Nam Ron** Chantaburi, S Thailand
83 C14 **Pongo** ≈ S Sudan
158 I7 **Pong Reservoir** ⊞ N India
113 N14 **Poniatowa** Lublin, E Poland
178 J13 **Pônley** Kâmpóng Chhnăng, C Cambodia
161 I20 **Ponnaiyār** ≈ SE India
9 Q15 **Ponoka** Alberta, SW Canada
131 U6 **Ponomarevka** Orenburgskaya Oblast', W Russian Federation
174 L15 **Ponorogo** Jawa, C Indonesia
128 M5 **Ponoy** Murmanskaya Oblast', NW Russian Federation
125 E5 **Ponoy** ≈ NW Russian Federation
104 K11 **Pons** Charente-Maritime, W France
Pons *see* Ponts
Pons Aelii *see* Newcastle upon Tyne
Pons Vetus *see* Pontevedra
101 G20 **Pont-à-Celles** Hainaut, S Belgium
104 K16 **Pontacq** Pyrénées-Atlantiques, SW France
66 P3 **Ponta Delgada** São Miguel, Azores, Portugal, NE Atlantic Ocean
66 P3 **Ponta Delgado** ✕ São Miguel, Azores, Portugal, NE Atlantic Ocean
66 N2 **Ponta do Pico** ▲ Pico, Azores, Portugal, NE Atlantic Ocean
62 J11 **Ponta Grossa** Paraná, S Brazil
105 S5 **Pont-à-Mousson** Meurthe-et-Moselle, NE France
105 T9 **Pontarlier** Doubs, E France
108 G11 **Pontassieve** Toscana, C Italy
104 L4 **Pont-Audemer** Eure, N France
24 K9 **Pontchartrain, Lake** ◎ Louisiana, S USA
104 I8 **Pontchâteau** Loire-Atlantique, NW France
105 R10 **Pont-de-Vaux** Ain, E France
106 G4 **Ponteareas** Galicia, NW Spain
108 J6 **Pontebba** Friuli-Venezia Giulia, NE Italy
106 G4 **Ponte Caldelas** Galicia, NW Spain
109 J16 **Pontecorvo** Lazio, C Italy
106 G5 **Ponte da Barca** Viana do Castelo, N Portugal
106 G5 **Ponte de Lima** Viana do Castelo, N Portugal
108 F11 **Pontedera** Toscana, C Italy
106 H10 **Ponte de Sor** Portalegre, C Portugal
106 H2 **Pontedeume** Galicia, NW Spain
108 F6 **Ponte di Legno** Lombardia, N Italy
9 T17 **Ponteix** Saskatchewan, S Canada
61 N20 **Ponte Nova** Minas Gerais, NE Brazil
61 G18 **Pontes e Lacerda** Mato Grosso, W Brazil
106 G4 **Pontevedra** *anc.* Pons Vetus. Galicia, NW Spain
106 G3 **Pontevedra** ◈ *province* Galicia, NW Spain
106 G4 **Pontevedra, Ría de** *estuary* NW Spain
32 M12 **Pontiac** Illinois, N USA
33 R9 **Pontiac** Michigan, N USA
174 Kk8 **Pontianak** Borneo, C Indonesia
109 I16 **Pontino, Agro** *plain* C Italy
Pontisarae *see* Pontoise
104 H6 **Pontivy** Morbihan, NW France
104 F6 **Pont-l'Abbé** Finistère, NW France
105 N4 **Pontoise** *anc.* Briva Isarae, Cergy-Pontoise, Pontisarae. Val-d'Oise, N France
9 W13 **Ponton** Manitoba, C Canada
104 J5 **Pontorson** Manche, N France
24 M2 **Pontotoc** Mississippi, S USA
27 R9 **Pontotoc** Texas, SW USA
108 E10 **Pontremoli** Toscana, C Italy
110 J10 **Pontresina** Graubünden, S Switzerland
107 U5 **Ponts** *var.* Pons. Cataluña, NE Spain
105 R14 **Pont-St-Esprit** Gard, S France
99 K21 **Pontypool** *Wel.* Pontypŵl. SE Wales, UK
99 J22 **Pontypridd** S Wales, UK
Pontypŵl *see* Pontypool
45 R17 **Ponuga** Veraguas, SE Panama
192 L6 **Ponui Island** *island* N NZ
121 K14 **Ponya** *Rus.* Ponya. ≈ N Belarus
109 I17 **Ponziane, Isole** *island* C Italy
190 F7 **Poochera** South Australia
99 L24 **Poole** S England, UK
27 S6 **Poolville** Texas, SW USA
Poona *see* Pune
190 M8 **Pooncarie** New South Wales, SE Australia
191 N6 **Poopelloe Lake** *seasonal lake* New South Wales, SE Australia
59 K19 **Poopó** Oruro, C Bolivia
59 K19 **Poopó, Lago** *var.* Lago Pampa Aullagas. ◎ W Bolivia
192 L3 **Poor Knights Islands** *island* N NZ
41 P10 **Poorman** Alaska, USA
190 E3 **Pootnoura** South Australia
153 R10 **Pop** *Rus.* Pap. Namangan Wiloyati, E Uzbekistan
119 X7 **Popasna** *Rus.* Popasnaya. Luhans'ka Oblast', E Ukraine
Popasnaya *see* Popasna
56 D12 **Popayán** Cauca, SW Colombia
101 B18 **Poperinge** West-Vlaanderen, W Belgium
126 K7 **Popigay** Taymyrskiy (Dolgano-Nenetskiy) Avtonomnyy Okrug, N Russian Federation
126 Jj7 **Popigay** ≈ N Russian Federation
119 O5 **Popil'nya** Zhytomyrs'ka Oblast', N Ukraine
190 K8 **Popiltah Lake** *seasonal lake* New South Wales, SE Australia
35 X7 **Poplar** Montana, NW USA
9 Y14 **Poplar** ≈ Manitoba, C Canada
29 X8 **Poplar Bluff** Missouri, C USA
35 X6 **Poplar River** ≈ Montana, NW USA
43 P14 **Popocatépetl** ▲ S Mexico
174 Ll16 **Popoh** Jawa, S Indonesia
81 H21 **Popokabaka** Bandundu, SW Zaire
109 J15 **Popoli** Abruzzi, C Italy
195 X16 **Popomanaseu, Mount** ▲ Guadalcanal, C Solomon Islands
194 L15 **Popondetta** Northern, S PNG
114 F9 **Popovača** Sisak-Moslavina, NE Croatia
116 J10 **Popovitsa** Loveshka Oblast, C Bulgaria
116 L8 **Popovo** Razgradska Oblast, N Bulgaria
Popovo *see* Iskra
Popper *see* Poprad
32 M5 **Popple River** ≈ Wisconsin, N USA
113 L19 **Poprad** *Ger.* Deutschendorf, *Hung.* Poprád. Východné Slovensko, NE Slovakia
113 L18 **Poprad** *Ger.* Popper, *Hung.* Poprád. ≈ Poland/Slovakia
113 L19 **Poprad-Tatry** ✕ (Poprad) Východné Slovensko, N Slovakia
23 X7 **Poquoson** Virginia, NE USA
155 O15 **Porāli** ≈ SW Pakistan
192 N12 **Porangahau** Hawke's Bay, North Island, NZ
61 K17 **Porangatu** Goiás, C Brazil
121 G18 **Porazava** *Pol.* Porozow, *Rus.* Porozovo. Hrodzyenskaya Voblasts', W Belarus
160 A11 **Porbandar** Gujarāt, W India
8 I13 **Porcher Island** *island* British Columbia, SW Canada
106 M13 **Porcuna** Andalucía, S Spain
12 F7 **Porcupine** Ontario, S Canada
66 M6 **Porcupine Bank** *undersea feature* N Atlantic Ocean
9 V15 **Porcupine Hills** ▲ Manitoba/Saskatchewan, S Canada
32 L3 **Porcupine Mountains** *hill range* Michigan, N USA
66 M7 **Porcupine Plain** *undersea feature* E Atlantic Ocean
14 F4 **Porcupine River** ≈ Canada/USA
108 I7 **Pordenone** *anc.* Portenau. Friuli-Venezia Giulia, NE Italy
56 H9 **Pore** Casanare, E Colombia
114 A9 **Poreč** *It.* Parenzo. Istra, NW Croatia
62 I9 **Porecatu** Paraná, S Brazil
Porech'ye *see* Parechcha
131 P4 **Poretskoye** Chuvashskaya Respublika, W Russian Federation
79 Q13 **Porga** N Benin
194 G12 **Porgera** Enga, W PNG
95 K18 **Pori** *Swe.* Björneborg. Turku-Pori, SW Finland
193 L14 **Porirua** Wellington, North Island, NZ
94 I12 **Porjus** Norrbotten, N Sweden
128 G14 **Porkhov** Pskovskaya Oblast', W Russian Federation
57 O4 **Porlamar** Nueva Esparta, NE Venezuela
104 I8 **Pornic** Loire-Atlantique, NW France
194 G12 **Poroma** Southern Highlands, W PNG
127 Oo15 **Poronaysk** Ostrov Sakhalin, Sakhalinskaya Oblast', SE Russian Federation
117 G20 **Póros** Póros, S Greece
117 C19 **Póros** Kefallinía, Iónioi Nísoi, Greece, C Mediterranean Sea
117 G20 **Póros** *island* S Greece
83 G24 **Poroto Mountains** ▲ SW Tanzania
114 B10 **Porozina** Primorje-Gorski Kotar, NW Croatia
Porozovo/Porozow *see* Porazava
205 X15 **Porpoise Bay** *bay* Antarctica
67 G15 **Porpoise Point** *headland* NE Ascension Island
67 C25 **Porpoise Point** *headland* East Falkland, Falkland Islands
110 C6 **Porrentruy** Jura, NW Switzerland
108 F10 **Porretta Terme** Emilia-Romagna, C Italy
106 G4 **Porriño** Galicia, NW Spain
94 L7 **Porsangen** *fjord* N Norway
94 K8 **Porsangerhalvøya** *peninsula* N Norway
97 G16 **Porsgrunn** Telemark, S Norway
142 E13 **Porsuk Çayı** ≈ C Turkey
Porsy *see* Boldumsaz
59 N18 **Portachuelo** Santa Cruz, C Bolivia
190 I9 **Port Adelaide** South Australia
99 F15 **Portadown** *Ir.* Port An Dúnáin. S Northern Ireland, UK
33 P10 **Portage** Michigan, N USA
20 D15 **Portage** Pennsylvania, NE USA
32 K8 **Portage** Wisconsin, N USA
32 M3 **Portage Lake** ◎ Michigan, N USA
9 X16 **Portage la Prairie** Manitoba, S Canada
33 R11 **Portage River** ≈ Ohio, N USA
29 Y8 **Portageville** Missouri, C USA
30 L2 **Portal** North Dakota, N USA
8 L17 **Port Alberni** Vancouver Island, British Columbia, SW Canada
12 E15 **Port Albert** Ontario, S Canada
106 I10 **Portalegre** *anc.* Ammaia, Amoea. Portalegre, E Portugal
106 H10 **Portalegre** ◈ *district* C Portugal
39 V12 **Portales** New Mexico, SW USA
41 X14 **Port Alexander** Baranof Island, Alaska, USA
85 I25 **Port Alfred** Eastern Cape, S South Africa
8 J16 **Port Alice** Vancouver Island, British Columbia, SW Canada
24 J8 **Port Allen** Louisiana, S USA
Port Amelia *see* Pemba
Port An Dúnáin *see* Portadown
34 G7 **Port Angeles** Washington, NW USA
46 L12 **Port Antonio** NE Jamaica
117 D16 **Pórta Panagiá** *religious building* Thessalía, C Greece
27 T14 **Port Aransas** Texas, SW USA
99 E18 **Portarlington** *Ir.* Cúil an tSúdaire. C Ireland
191 P17 **Port Arthur** Tasmania, SE Australia
18 Mm15 **Port Arthur** Texas, SW USA
98 G12 **Port Askaig** W Scotland, UK
190 I7 **Port Augusta** South Australia
46 M9 **Port-au-Prince** ● (Haiti) C Haiti
46 M9 **Port-au-Prince** ✕ E Haiti
24 I8 **Port Barre** Louisiana, S USA
157 Q19 **Port Blair** Andaman and Nicobar Islands, SE India
27 X12 **Port Bolivar** Texas, SW USA
107 X4 **Portbou** Cataluña, NE Spain
79 N17 **Port Bouet** ✕ (Abidjan) SE Ivory Coast
190 I8 **Port Broughton** South Australia
12 F17 **Port Burwell** Ontario, S Canada
10 G17 **Port Burwell** Québec, NE Canada
190 M13 **Port Campbell** Victoria, SE Australia
13 V4 **Port-Cartier** Québec, SE Canada
193 F23 **Port Chalmers** Otago, South Island, NZ
25 W14 **Port Charlotte** Florida, SE USA
40 L9 **Port Clarence** Alaska, USA
8 I13 **Port Clements** Graham Island, British Columbia, SW Canada
33 S11 **Port Clinton** Ohio, N USA
12 H17 **Port Colborne** Ontario, S Canada
13 Y7 **Port-Daniel** Québec, SE Canada
Port Darwin *see* Darwin
191 O17 **Port Davey** *headland* Tasmania, SE Australia
46 K8 **Port-de-Paix** NW Haiti
189 W4 **Port Douglas** Queensland, NE Australia
8 J13 **Port Edward** British Columbia, SW Canada
85 K24 **Port Edward** KwaZulu/Natal, SE South Africa
60 J12 **Portel** Pará, NE Brazil
106 H12 **Portel** Évora, S Portugal
12 E14 **Port Elgin** Ontario, S Canada
47 Y14 **Port Elizabeth** Bequia, Saint Vincent and the Grenadines
85 I26 **Port Elizabeth** Eastern Cape, S South Africa
98 G13 **Port Ellen** W Scotland, UK
Portenau *see* Pordenone
99 H16 **Port Erin** SW Isle of Man
47 Q13 **Porter Point** *headland* Saint Vincent, Saint Vincent and the Grenadines
193 G18 **Porters Pass** *pass* South Island, NZ
85 E25 **Porterville** Western Cape, SW South Africa
37 R12 **Porterville** California, W USA
Port-Étienne *see* Nouâdhibou
190 L13 **Port Fairy** Victoria, SE Australia
192 M4 **Port Fitzroy** Great Barrier Island, Auckland, NE NZ
Port Florence *see* Kisumu
Port-Francqui *see* Ilebo
81 C18 **Port-Gentil** Ogooué-Maritime, W Gabon
81 C18 **Port-Gentil** ✕ Ogooué-Maritime, W Gabon
190 I7 **Port Germein** South Australia
24 J6 **Port Gibson** Mississippi, S USA
41 Q13 **Port Graham** Alaska, USA
79 U17 **Port Harcourt** Rivers, S Nigeria
8 J16 **Port Hardy** Vancouver Island, British Columbia, SW Canada
Port Harrison *see* Inukjuak
11 R14 **Port Hawkesbury** Cape Breton Island, Nova Scotia, SE Canada
188 I6 **Port Hedland** Western Australia
41 O15 **Port Heiden** Alaska, USA
99 I19 **Porthmadog** *var.* Portmadoc. NW Wales, UK
12 I15 **Port Hope** Ontario, SE Canada
11 S9 **Port Hope Simpson** Newfoundland and Labrador, E Canada
67 C24 **Port Howard Settlement** West Falkland, Falkland Islands
33 T9 **Port Huron** Michigan, N USA
109 K17 **Portici** Campania, S Italy
143 Y13 **Port-Iliç** *Rus.* Port Il'ich. SE Azerbaijan
Port Il'ich *see* Port-Iliç
106 G14 **Portimão** *var.* Vila Nova de Portimão. Faro, S Portugal
27 T17 **Port Isabel** Texas, SW USA
20 J13 **Port Jervis** New York, NE USA
57 S7 **Port Kaituma** NW Guyana
130 K12 **Port Katon** Rostovskaya Oblast', SW Russian Federation
191 S9 **Port Kembla** New South Wales, SE Australia
190 F8 **Port Kenny** South Australia
Port Klang *see* Pelabuhan Klang
Port Láirge *see* Waterford
191 S8 **Portland** New South Wales, SE Australia
190 L13 **Portland** Victoria, SE Australia
192 K4 **Portland** Northland, North Island, NZ
33 Q13 **Portland** Indiana, N USA
21 P8 **Portland** Maine, NE USA
33 Q9 **Portland** Michigan, N USA
31 Q4 **Portland** North Dakota, N USA
34 G11 **Portland** Oregon, NW USA
22 J8 **Portland** Tennessee, S USA
27 T14 **Portland** Texas, SW USA
34 G11 **Portland** ✕ Oregon, NW USA
190 L13 **Portland Bay** *bay* Victoria, SE Australia
46 K13 **Portland Bight** *bay* S Jamaica
99 L24 **Portland Bill** *var.* Bill of Portland. *headland* S England, UK
Portland, Bill of *see* Portland Bill
191 P15 **Portland, Cape** *headland* Tasmania, SE Australia
8 J12 **Portland Inlet** *inlet* British Columbia, W Canada
192 P11 **Portland Island** *island* E NZ
67 F15 **Portland Point** *headland* SW Ascension Island
46 J13 **Portland Point** *headland* C Jamaica
105 P16 **Port-la-Nouvelle** Aude, S France
Portlaoighise *see* Port Laoise
99 E18 **Port Laoise** *var.* Portlaoise, *Ir.* Portlaoighise; *prev.* Maryborough. C Ireland
27 U13 **Port Lavaca** Texas, SW USA
190 G9 **Port Lincoln** South Australia
41 Q14 **Port Lions** Kodiak Island, Alaska, USA
78 I15 **Port Loko** W Sierra Leone
67 E24 **Port Louis** East Falkland, Falkland Islands
47 Y5 **Port-Louis** Grande Terre, N Guadeloupe
181 X16 **Port Louis** ● (Mauritius) NW Mauritius
Port Louis *see* Scarborough
Port-Lyautey *see* Kénitra
190 K12 **Port MacDonnell** South Australia
191 U7 **Port Macquarie** New South Wales, SE Australia
Portmadoc *see* Porthmadog
Port Mahon *see* Mahón
46 K12 **Port Maria** C Jamaica
8 K16 **Port McNeill** Vancouver Island, British Columbia, SW Canada
11 P11 **Port-Menier** Île d'Anticosti , Québec, E Canada
41 N15 **Port Moller** Alaska, USA
46 L13 **Port Morant** E Jamaica
46 K13 **Portmore** C Jamaica
194 I16 **Port Moresby** ● (PNG) Central/National Capital District, SW PNG
Port Natal *see* Durban
27 Y11 **Port Neches** Texas, SW USA
190 G9 **Port Neill** South Australia
13 S6 **Portneuf** ≈ Québec, SE Canada
13 R6 **Portneuf, Lac** ◎ Québec, SE Canada
85 D23 **Port Nolloth** Northern Cape, W South Africa
20 J17 **Port Norris** New Jersey, NE USA
Port-Nouveau-Québec *see* Kangiqsualujjuaq
106 G6 **Porto** *Eng.* Oporto; *anc.* Portus Cale. Porto, NW Portugal
106 G6 **Porto** *var.* Pôrto. ◈ *district* N Portugal
106 G6 **Porto** ✕ Porto, W Portugal
63 I16 **Porto Alegre** *var.* Pôrto Alegre. *state capital* Rio Grande do Sul, S Brazil
Porto Alexandre *see* Tombua
84 B12 **Porto Amboim** Cuanza Sul, NW Angola
Porto Amélia *see* Pemba
Porto Bello *see* Portobelo
45 T14 **Portobelo** *var.* Porto Bello, Puerto Bello. Colón, N Panama
62 G10 **Pôrto Camargo** Paraná, S Brazil
27 U13 **Port O'Connor** Texas, SW USA
Pôrto de Mós *see* Porto de Moz
60 J12 **Porto de Moz** *var.* Pôrto de Mós. Pará, NE Brazil
66 O5 **Porto do Moniz** Madeira, Portugal, NE Atlantic Ocean
61 H16 **Porto dos Gaúchos** Mato Grosso, W Brazil
Porto Edda *see* Sarandë
109 J24 **Porto Empedocle** Sicilia, Italy, C Mediterranean Sea
61 H20 **Porto Esperança** Mato Grosso do Sul, SW Brazil
108 E13 **Portoferraio** Toscana, C Italy
98 G6 **Port of Ness** NW Scotland, UK
47 U14 **Port-of-Spain** ● (Trinidad and Tobago) Trinidad, Trinidad and Tobago
Port of Spain *see* Piarco
104 E2 **Porto, Golfe de** *gulf* Corse, France, C Mediterranean Sea
Porto Grande *see* Mindelo
108 I7 **Portogruaro** Veneto, NE Italy
37 P5 **Portola** California, W USA
197 B12 **Port-Olry** Espiritu Santo, C Vanuatu
95 J17 **Pörtom** *Fin.* Pirttikylä. Vaasa, W Finland
Porto Omna *see* Portumna
61 G21 **Porto Murtinho** Mato Grosso do Sul, SW Brazil
61 K16 **Porto Nacional** Tocantins, C Brazil
79 S16 **Porto-Novo** ● (Benin) S Benin
25 X10 **Port Orange** Florida, SE USA
34 G8 **Port Orchard** Washington, NW USA
Porto Re *see* Kraljevica
34 E15 **Port Orford** Oregon, NW USA
Porto Rico *see* Puerto Rico
108 J13 **Porto San Giorgio** Marche, C Italy
109 F14 **Porto San Stefano** Toscana, C Italy
66 P5 **Porto Santo** *var.* Vila Baleira. Porto Santo, Madeira, Portugal, NE Atlantic Ocean
66 Q5 **Porto Santo** ✕ Porto Santo, Madeira, Portugal, NE Atlantic Ocean
66 P5 **Porto Santo** *var.* Ilha do Porto Santo. *island* Madeira, Portugal, NE Atlantic Ocean
62 H9 **Porto São José** Paraná, S Brazil
61 O19 **Porto Seguro** Bahia, E Brazil
109 B17 **Porto Torres** Sardegna, Italy, C Mediterranean Sea
61 J23 **Porto União** Santa Catarina, S Brazil
104 F3 **Porto-Vecchio** Corse, France, C Mediterranean Sea
61 E15 **Porto Velho** *var.* Velho. *state capital* Rondônia, W Brazil
58 A6 **Portoviejo** *var.* Puertoviejo. Manabí, W Ecuador
193 B26 **Port Pegasus** *bay* Stewart Island, NZ
12 H15 **Port Perry** Ontario, SE Canada
191 N12 **Port Phillip Bay** *harbor* Victoria, SE Australia
190 I8 **Port Pirie** South Australia
98 G9 **Portree** N Scotland, UK
Port Rex *see* East London
Port Rois *see* Portrush
46 K13 **Port Royal** E Jamaica
23 R15 **Port Royal** South Carolina, SE USA
23 R15 **Port Royal Sound** *inlet* South Carolina, SE USA
99 F14 **Portrush** *Ir.* Port Rois. N Northern Ireland, UK
77 W7 **Port Said** *Ar.* Būr Sa'īd. N Egypt
25 R9 **Port Saint Joe** Florida, SE USA
25 Y11 **Port Saint John** Florida, SE USA
85 K24 **Port St.Johns** Eastern Cape, SE South Africa
105 R16 **Port-St-Louis-du-Rhône** Bouches-du-Rhône, SE France
46 K10 **Port Salut** SW Haiti
67 E24 **Port Salvador** *inlet* East Falkland, Falkland Islands
67 D24 **Port San Carlos** East Falkland, Falkland Islands
11 S10 **Port Saunders** Newfoundland, Newfoundland and Labrador, SE Canada
85 K24 **Port Shepstone** KwaZulu/Natal, E South Africa
47 O11 **Portsmouth** *var.* Grand-Anse. NW Dominica
99 N24 **Portsmouth** S England, UK
21 P10 **Portsmouth** New Hampshire, NE USA

◆ Country ● Country Capital ◇ Dependent Territory ○ Dependent Territory Capital ◈ Administrative Region ✕ International Airport ▲ Mountain ▲ Mountain Range ▲ Volcano ≈ River ◎ Lake ⊞ Reservoir

PORTSMOUTH – PUERTA, ACOSTA

33 S15 **Portsmouth** Ohio, N USA
23 X7 **Portsmouth** Virginia, NE USA
12 E17 **Port Stanley** Ontario, S Canada
67 B25 **Port Stephens** inlet West Falkland, Falkland Islands
67 B25 **Port Stephens Settlement** West Falkland, Falkland Islands
99 F14 **Portstewart** Ir. Port Stíobhaird. N Northern Ireland, UK
Port Stíobhaird see Portstewart
82 I7 **Port Sudan** Red Sea, NE Sudan
24 L10 **Port Sulphur** Louisiana, S USA
Port Swettenham see Klang/Pelabuhan Klang
99 J22 **Port Talbot** S Wales, UK
94 L11 **Porttipahdan Tekojärvi** ◎ N Finland
34 G7 **Port Townsend** Washington, NW USA
106 H9 **Portugal** off. Republic of Portugal. ◆ republic SW Europe
107 O2 **Portugalete** País Vasco, N Spain
56 J6 **Portuguesa** off. Estado Portuguesa. ◈ state N Venezuela
Portuguese East Africa see Mozambique
Portuguese Guinea see Guinea-Bissau
Portuguese Timor see Timor Timur
Portuguese West Africa see Angola
99 D18 **Portumna** Ir. Port Omna. W Ireland
Portus Cale see Porto
Portus Magnus see Almería
Portus Magonis see Mahón
105 P17 **Port-Vendres** var. Port Vendres. Pyrénées-Orientales, S France
190 H9 **Port Victoria** South Australia
197 C14 **Port-Vila** var. Vila. ● (Vanuatu) Éfaté, C Vanuatu
190 I9 **Port Wakefield** South Australia
33 N8 **Port Washington** Wisconsin, N USA
59 J14 **Porvenir** Pando, NW Bolivia
65 I24 **Porvenir** Magallanes, S Chile
63 D18 **Porvenir** Paysandú, W Uruguay
95 M19 **Porvoo** Swe. Borgå. Uusimaa, S Finland
Porzecze see Parechcha
106 M10 **Porzuna** Castilla-La Mancha, C Spain
63 E14 **Posadas** Misiones, NE Argentina
106 L13 **Posadas** Andalucía, S Spain
Poschega see Slavonska Požega
110 J11 **Poschiavino** ~ Italy/Switzerland
110 J10 **Poschiavo** Ger. Puschlav. Graubünden, S Switzerland
114 D12 **Posedarje** Zadar-Knin, W Croatia
Posen see Poznań
128 L14 **Poshekhon'ye** Yaroslavskaya Oblast', W Russian Federation
94 M13 **Posio** Lappi, NE Finland
Poskam see Zepu
Posnania see Poznań
175 Pp9 **Poso** Sulawesi, C Indonesia
61 P15 **Poço da Cruz, Açude** ▣ E Brazil
175 Pp10 **Poso, Danau** ◎ Sulawesi, C Indonesia
143 R10 **Posof** Kars, NE Turkey
175 Pp9 **Poso, Sungai** ~ Sulawesi, C Indonesia
27 R6 **Possum Kingdom Lake** ▣ Texas, SW USA
27 N6 **Post** Texas, SW USA
Postavy/Postawy see Pastavy
10 I7 **Poste-de-la-Baleine** Québec, NE Canada
101 M17 **Posterholt** Limburg, SE Netherlands
85 G22 **Postmasburg** Northern Cape, N South Africa
Pôsto Diuarum see Campo de Diauarum
61 I16 **Pôsto Jacaré** Mato Grosso, W Brazil
111 T12 **Postojna** Ger. Adelsberg, It. Postumia. SW Slovenia
Postumia see Postojna
31 X12 **Postville** Iowa, C USA
Pöstyén see Piešťany
115 G14 **Posušje** SW Bosnia and Herzegovina
175 Pp16 **Pota** Flores, C Indonesia
117 G23 **Potamós** Antikýthira, S Greece
57 S9 **Potaru River** ~ C Guyana
85 I21 **Potchefstroom** North-West, N South Africa
29 R11 **Poteau** Oklahoma, C USA
27 R12 **Poteet** Texas, SW USA
117 G14 **Poteídaia** site of ancient city Kentrikí Makedonía, N Greece
Potentia see Potenza
109 M18 **Potenza** anc. Potentia. Basilicata, S Italy
193 A24 **Poteriteri, Lake** ◎ South Island, NZ
106 M2 **Potes** Cantabria, N Spain
85 J20 **Potgietersrus** Northern, NE South Africa
27 S12 **Poth** Texas, SW USA
34 J9 **Potholes Reservoir** ▣ Washington, NW USA
143 Q9 **P'ot'i** W Georgia
79 X13 **Potiskum** Yobe, NE Nigeria
34 M9 **Potlatch** Idaho, NW USA
35 N9 **Pot Mountain** ▲ Idaho, NW USA
115 H14 **Potoci** S Bosnia and Herzegovina
23 V3 **Potomac River** ~ NE USA
29 W6 **Potosi** Missouri, C USA
59 L20 **Potosí** Potosí, S Bolivia
44 H9 **Potosí** Chinandega, NW Nicaragua
59 K21 **Potosí** ◈ department SW Bolivia
64 H7 **Potrerillos** Atacama, N Chile
44 H5 **Potrerillos** Cortés, NW Honduras
64 H8 **Potro, Cerro del** ▲ N Chile
102 N12 **Potsdam** Brandenburg, NE Germany
20 J7 **Potsdam** New York, NE USA
111 X5 **Pottendorf** Niederösterreich, E Austria
111 X5 **Pottenstein** Niederösterreich, E Austria
197 G4 **Pott, Île** island Îles Belep, W New Caledonia
20 I15 **Pottstown** Pennsylvania, NE USA
20 H14 **Pottsville** Pennsylvania, NE USA
161 L25 **Pottuvil** Eastern Province, SE Sri Lanka
155 U6 **Potwar Plateau** plateau NE Pakistan
104 J7 **Pouancé** Maine-et-Loire, W France
197 H5 **Pouébo** Province Nord, C New Caledonia
197 H6 **Pouembout** Province Nord, W New Caledonia
13 R6 **Poulin de Courval, Lac** ◎ Québec, SE Canada
20 L9 **Poultney** Vermont, NE USA
197 H5 **Poum** Province Nord, W New Caledonia
61 L21 **Pouso Alegre** Minas Gerais, NE Brazil
198 Bb8 **Poutasi** Upolu, SE Western Samoa
178 Ii12 **Poŭthĭsăt** prev. Pursat. Poŭthĭsăt, W Cambodia
178 Ii13 **Poŭthĭsăt, Stœng** prev. Pursat. ~ W Cambodia
104 J9 **Pouzauges** Vendée, NW France
Po, Valle del see Po Valley
108 F8 **Po Valley** It. Valle del Po. valley N Italy
113 I19 **Považská Bystrica** Ger. Waagbistritz, Hung. Vágbeszterce. Stredné Slovensko, NW Slovakia
128 J10 **Povenets** Respublika Kareliya, NW Russian Federation
192 Q9 **Poverty Bay** inlet North Island, NZ
114 K12 **Povlen** ▲▲ W Yugoslavia
106 G6 **Póvoa de Varzim** Porto, NW Portugal
131 N8 **Povorino** Voronezhskaya Oblast', W Russian Federation
Povungnituk see Puvirnituq
10 J3 **Povungnituk, Rivière de** ~ Québec, NE Canada
12 H11 **Powassan** Ontario, S Canada
37 U17 **Poway** California, W USA
35 W14 **Powder River** Wyoming, C USA
35 Y10 **Powder River** ~ Montana/Wyoming, NW USA
34 L12 **Powder River** ~ Oregon, NW USA
35 W13 **Powder River Pass** pass Wyoming, C USA
35 U12 **Powell** Wyoming, C USA
67 I22 **Powell Basin** undersea feature NW Weddell Sea
38 M8 **Powell, Lake** ◎ Utah, W USA
39 R4 **Powell, Mount** ▲ Colorado, C USA
8 L17 **Powell River** British Columbia, SW Canada
33 N5 **Powers** Michigan, N USA
30 K2 **Powers Lake** North Dakota, N USA
23 V6 **Powhatan** Virginia, NE USA
33 V13 **Powhatan Point** Ohio, N USA
99 J20 **Powys** cultural region E Wales, UK
197 I6 **Poya** Province Nord, C New Caledonia
167 P10 **Poyang Hu** ◎ S China
126 Mm16 **Poyarkovo** Amurskaya Oblast', SE Russian Federation
32 L7 **Poygan, Lake** ◎ Wisconsin, N USA
111 Y2 **Poysdorf** Niederösterreich, NE Austria
114 N11 **Požarevac** Ger. Passarowitz. Serbia, NE Yugoslavia
43 Q13 **Poza Rica** var. Poza Rica de Hidalgo. Veracruz-Llave, E Mexico
Poza Rica de Hidalgo see Poza Rica
114 L13 **Požega** Serbia, W Yugoslavia
Požega see Slavonska Požega
114 H9 **Požega-Slavonija** off. Požeško-Slavonska Županija. ◈ province NE Croatia
129 U13 **Pozhva** Komi-Permyatskiy Avtonomnyy Okrug, NW Russian Federation
112 G11 **Poznań** Ger. Posen, Posnania. Poznań, W Poland
112 G11 **Poznań** off. Województwo Poznańskie, Ger. Posen, Posnania. ◈ province W Poland
Poznańskie, Województwo see Poznań
107 O13 **Pozo Alcón** Andalucía, S Spain
64 H3 **Pozo Almonte** Tarapacá, N Chile
106 L12 **Pozoblanco** Andalucía, S Spain
107 Q11 **Pozo Cañada** Castilla-La Mancha, C Spain
64 N5 **Pozo Colorado** Presidente Hayes, C Paraguay
65 J20 **Pozos, Punta** headland S Argentina
Pozsega see Slavonska Požega
Pozsony see Bratislava
57 N5 **Pozuelos** Anzoátegui, NE Venezuela
109 L26 **Pozzallo** Sicilia, Italy, C Mediterranean Sea
109 K17 **Pozzuoli** anc. Puteoli. Campania, S Italy
79 P17 **Pra** ~ S Ghana
Prabumulih see Perabumulih
113 C19 **Prachatice** Ger. Prachatitz. Jižní Čechy, SW Czech Republic
Prachatitz see Prachatice
178 Hh11 **Prachin Buri** var. Prachinburi. Prachin Buri, C Thailand
Prachuab Girikhand see Prachuap Khiri Khan
178 H13 **Prachuap Khiri Khan** var. Prachuab Girikhand. Prachuap Khiri Khan, SW Thailand
113 H16 **Praděd** Ger. Altvater. ▲ NE Czech Republic
56 D11 **Pradera** Valle del Cauca, SW Colombia
105 O17 **Prades** Pyrénées-Orientales, S France
61 O19 **Prado** Bahia, SE Brazil
56 E11 **Prado** Tolima, C Colombia
Prae see Phrae
Prag/Praga/Prague see Praha
29 O10 **Prague** Oklahoma, C USA
113 D16 **Praha** Eng. Prague, Ger. Prag, Pol. Praga. ● (Czech Republic) Střední Čechy, NW Czech Republic
118 J13 **Prahova** ◈ county SE Romania
118 J13 **Prahova** ~ S Romania
78 E10 **Praia** ● (Cape Verde) Santiago, S Cape Verde
85 M21 **Praia do Bilene** Gaza, S Mozambique
85 M20 **Praia do Xai-Xai** Gaza, S Mozambique
118 J10 **Praid** Hung. Parajd. Harghita, C Romania
28 I3 **Prairie Dog Creek** ~ Kansas/Nebraska, C USA
32 J9 **Prairie du Chien** Wisconsin, N USA
29 S9 **Prairie Grove** Arkansas, C USA
33 P10 **Prairie River** ~ Michigan, N USA
Prairie State see Illinois
27 V11 **Prairie View** Texas, SW USA
178 Ii11 **Prakhon Chai** Buri Ram, E Thailand
111 R4 **Pram** ~ N Austria
111 S4 **Prambachkirchen** Oberösterreich, N Austria
120 H2 **Prangli** island N Estonia
160 J13 **Prānhita** ~ C India
180 I15 **Praslin** island Inner Islands, NE Seychelles
117 O23 **Prasonísi, Ákra** headland Ródos, Dodekánisos, Greece, Aegean Sea
113 I14 **Praszka** Częstochowa, S Poland
121 M18 **Pratasy** Rus. Protasy. Homyel'skaya Voblasts', SE Belarus
178 I10 **Prathai** Nakhon Ratchasima, E Thailand
Prathet Thai see Thailand
Prathum Thani see Pathum Thani
65 F21 **Prat, Isla** island S Chile
108 G11 **Prato** Toscana, C Italy
105 O17 **Prats-de-Mollo-la-Preste** Pyrénées-Orientales, S France
28 L6 **Pratt** Kansas, C USA
110 E6 **Pratteln** Basel-Land, NW Switzerland
199 L2 **Pratt Seamount** undersea feature N Pacific Ocean
25 P5 **Prattville** Alabama, S USA
Praust see Pruszcz Gdański
116 M7 **Pravda** prev. Dogrular. Razgradska Oblast, NE Bulgaria
121 B14 **Pravdinsk** Ger. Friedland. Kaliningradskaya Oblast', W Russian Federation
106 K2 **Pravia** Asturias, N Spain
120 L12 **Prazaroki** Rus. Prozoroki. Vitsyebskaya Voblasts', N Belarus
Prázsmár see Prejmer
178 J11 **Preăh Vihéar** Preăh Vihéar, N Cambodia
118 J12 **Predeal** Hung. Predeál. Braşov, C Romania
111 S8 **Predlitz** Steiermark, SE Austria
9 V15 **Preeceville** Saskatchewan, S Canada
Preenkuln see Priekule
104 K6 **Pré-en-Pail** Mayenne, NW France
111 T4 **Pregarten** Oberösterreich, N Austria
56 H7 **Pregonero** Táchira, NW Venezuela
120 J10 **Preiļi** Ger. Preli. Preiļi, SE Latvia
118 J12 **Prejmer** Ger. Tartlau, Hung. Prázsmár. Braşov, S Romania
115 J16 **Prekornica** ▲▲ SW Yugoslavia
Preli see Preiļi
Prëmet see Përmet
102 M12 **Premnitz** Brandenburg, NE Germany
27 S15 **Premont** Texas, SW USA
115 H14 **Prenj** ▲▲ S Bosnia and Herzegovina
Prenjas/Prenjasi see Përrenjas
24 L7 **Prentiss** Mississippi, S USA
Preny see Prienai
102 O10 **Prenzlau** Brandenburg, NE Germany
126 Jj12 **Preobrazhenka** Irkutskaya Oblast', C Russian Federation
177 Ee9 **Preparis Island** island SW Myanmar
Prerau see Přerov
113 H18 **Přerov** Ger. Prerau. Severní Morava, E Czech Republic
Preschau see Prešov
12 K14 **Prescott** Ontario, SE Canada
38 K12 **Prescott** Arizona, SW USA
29 T13 **Prescott** Arkansas, C USA
34 L10 **Prescott** Washington, NW USA
32 H6 **Prescott** Wisconsin, N USA
193 A24 **Preservation Inlet** inlet South Island, NZ
114 O7 **Preševo** Serbia, SE Yugoslavia
31 N10 **Presho** South Dakota, N USA
60 M13 **Presidente Dutra** Maranhão, E Brazil
62 I8 **Presidente Epitácio** São Paulo, S Brazil
64 N5 **Presidente Hayes** off. Departamento de Presidente Hayes. ◈ department C Paraguay
62 I9 **Presidente Prudente** São Paulo, S Brazil
Presidente Stroessner see Ciudad del Este
Presidente Vargas see Itabira
62 I8 **Presidente Venceslau** São Paulo, S Brazil
199 L11 **President Thiers Seamount** undersea feature C Pacific Ocean
26 J11 **Presidio** Texas, SW USA
Preslav see Veliki Preslav
113 M19 **Prešov** var. Preschau, Ger. Eperies, Hung. Eperjes. Východné Slovensko, NE Slovakia
115 N20 **Prespa, Lake** Alb. Liqen i Prespës, Gk. Límni Megáli Préspa, Limni Prespa, Mac. Prespansko Ezero, Serb. Prespansko Jezero. ◎ SE Europe
Prespa, Limni/Prespansko Ezero/Prespansko Jezero/Prespës, Liqen i see Prespa, Lake
21 S2 **Presque Isle** Maine, NE USA
20 B11 **Presque Isle** headland Pennsylvania, NE USA
Pressburg see Bratislava
79 P17 **Prestea** SW Ghana
113 B17 **Přeštice** Ger. Pschestitz. Západní Čechy, W Czech Republic
99 K17 **Preston** NW England, UK
25 S6 **Preston** Georgia, SE USA
35 R16 **Preston** Idaho, NW USA
31 Z13 **Preston** Iowa, C USA
31 X11 **Preston** Minnesota, N USA
23 O6 **Prestonsburg** Kentucky, S USA
98 I13 **Prestwick** W Scotland, UK
85 J21 **Pretoria** var. Epitoli, Tshwane. ● (South Africa-administrative capital) Gauteng, NE South Africa
Pretoria-Witwatersrand-Vereeniging see Gauteng
Pretusha see Pretushë
115 M21 **Pretushë** var. Pretusha. Korçë, SE Albania
Preussisch Eylau see Bagrationovsk
Preussisch-Stargard see Starogard Gdański
Preußisch Holland see Pasłęk
117 C17 **Préveza** Ípeiros, W Greece
39 V3 **Prewitt Reservoir** ▣ Colorado, C USA
178 J13 **Prey Vêng** Prey Vêng, S Cambodia
150 M12 **Priaral'skiye Karakumy, Peski** desert SW Kazakhstan
126 L16 **Priargunsk** Chitinskaya Oblast', S Russian Federation
40 K14 **Pribilof Islands** island group Alaska, USA
115 K14 **Priboj** Serbia, W Yugoslavia
113 C17 **Příbram** Ger. Pibrans. Střední Čechy, W Czech Republic
38 M4 **Price** Utah, W USA
39 N5 **Price River** ~ Utah, W USA
25 N8 **Prichard** Alabama, S USA
27 R8 **Priddy** Texas, SW USA
107 P8 **Priego** Castilla-La Mancha, C Spain
106 M14 **Priego de Córdoba** Andalucía, S Spain
120 C10 **Priekule** Ger. Preenkuln. Liepāja, SW Latvia
120 C12 **Priekulė** Ger. Prökuls. Gargždai, W Lithuania
121 F14 **Prienai** Pol. Preny. Prienai, S Lithuania
85 G23 **Prieska** Northern Cape, C South Africa
34 M7 **Priest Lake** ▣ Idaho, NW USA
34 M7 **Priest River** Idaho, NW USA
106 M3 **Prieta, Peña** ▲ N Spain
42 J10 **Prieto, Cerro** ▲ C Mexico
113 J19 **Prievidza** var. Priewitz, Ger. Priwitz, Hung. Privigye. Stredné Slovensko, C Slovakia
Priewitz see Prievidza
114 F10 **Prijedor** NW Bosnia and Herzegovina
115 K14 **Prijepolje** Serbia, W Yugoslavia
Prikaspiyskaya Nizmennost' see Caspian Depression
115 O19 **Prilep** Turk. Perlepe. S FYR Macedonia
110 B9 **Prilly** Vaud, SW Switzerland
Priluki see Pryluky
64 L10 **Primero, Río** ~ C Argentina
31 S12 **Primghar** Iowa, C USA
114 B9 **Primorje-Gorski Kotar** off. Primorsko-Goranska Županija. ◈ province NW Croatia
120 A13 **Primorsk** Ger. Fischhausen. Kaliningradskaya Oblast', W Russian Federation
128 G12 **Primorsk** Fin. Koivisto. Leningradskaya Oblast', NW Russian Federation
Primorsk/Primorskoye see Prymors'k
127 Nn17 **Primorskiy Kray** prev. Eng. Maritime Territory. ◈ territory SE Russian Federation
116 N10 **Primorsko** prev. Keupriya. Burgaska Oblast, SE Bulgaria
130 K13 **Primorsko-Akhtarsk** Krasnodarskiy Kray, SW Russian Federation
119 U13 **Primors'kyy** Respublika Krym, S Ukraine
115 D14 **Primošten** Šibenik, S Croatia
9 R13 **Primrose Lake** ◎ Saskatchewan, C Canada
9 T14 **Prince Albert** Saskatchewan, S Canada
85 G25 **Prince Albert** Western Cape, SW South Africa
15 I1 **Prince Albert Peninsula** peninsula Victoria Island, Northwest Territories, NW Canada
15 I3 **Prince Albert Sound** inlet Northwest Territories, N Canada
15 Mm2 **Prince Charles Island** island Northwest Territories, NE Canada
205 W6 **Prince Charles Mountains** ▲▲ Antarctica
Prince-Édouard, Île-du see Prince Edward Island
180 M13 **Prince Edward Fracture Zone** tectonic feature SW Indian Ocean
11 P14 **Prince Edward Island** Fr. Île-du Prince-Édouard. ◈ province SE Canada
11 Q14 **Prince Edward Island** Fr. Île-du Prince-Édouard. island SE Canada
181 M12 **Prince Edward Islands** island group S South Africa
23 X4 **Prince Frederick** Maryland, NE USA
8 M14 **Prince George** British Columbia, SW Canada
23 W6 **Prince George** Virginia, NE USA
207 O8 **Prince Gustaf Adolf Sea** sea Northwest Territories, N Canada
207 Q3 **Prince of Wales, Cape** headland Alaska, USA
189 V1 **Prince of Wales Island** island Queensland, E Australia
15 Jj1 **Prince of Wales Island** island Queen Elizabeth Islands, Northwest Territories, NW Canada
41 Y14 **Prince of Wales Island** island Alexander Archipelago, Alaska, USA
Prince of Wales Island see Pinang, Pulau
15 I1 **Prince of Wales Strait** strait Northwest Territories, N Canada
207 O8 **Prince Patrick Island** island Parry Islands, Northwest Territories, NW Canada
15 Kk1 **Prince Regent Inlet** channel Northwest Territories, N Canada
8 J13 **Prince Rupert** British Columbia, SW Canada
Prince's Island see Príncipe
23 Y5 **Princess Anne** Maryland, NE USA
205 R1 **Princess Astrid Kyst** physical region Antarctica
189 W2 **Princess Charlotte Bay** bay Queensland, NE Australia
205 W7 **Princess Elizabeth Land** physical region Antarctica
8 J14 **Princess Royal Island** island British Columbia, SW Canada
47 U15 **Princes Town** Trinidad, Trinidad and Tobago
9 N17 **Princeton** British Columbia, SW Canada
32 L11 **Princeton** Illinois, N USA
33 N16 **Princeton** Indiana, N USA
31 Z14 **Princeton** Iowa, C USA
22 H7 **Princeton** Kentucky, S USA
31 V8 **Princeton** Minnesota, N USA
29 S1 **Princeton** Missouri, C USA
20 J15 **Princeton** New Jersey, NE USA
23 R6 **Princeton** West Virginia, NE USA
41 S12 **Prince William Sound** inlet Alaska, USA
69 P9 **Príncipe** var. Príncipe Island, Eng. Prince's Island. island N Sao Tome and Principe
Príncipe Island see Príncipe
34 I13 **Prineville** Oregon, NW USA
30 J11 **Pringle** South Dakota, N USA
27 N1 **Pringle** Texas, SW USA
101 H14 **Prinsenbeek** Noord-Brabant, S Netherlands
100 L6 **Prinses Margriet Kanaal** canal N Netherlands
205 T2 **Prinsesse Ragnhild Kyst** physical region Antarctica
205 U2 **Prins Harald Kyst** physical region Antarctica
94 N2 **Prins Karls Forland** island W Svalbard
45 N8 **Prinzapolka** Región Autónoma Atlántico Norte, NE Nicaragua
44 L8 **Prinzapolka, Río** ~ NE Nicaragua
125 Ff9 **Priob'ye** Khanty-Mansiyskiy Avtonomnyy Okrug, N Russian Federation
106 H1 **Prior, Cabo** headland NW Spain
31 V9 **Prior Lake** Minnesota, N USA
128 H11 **Priozersk** Fin. Käkisalmi. Leningradskaya Oblast', NW Russian Federation
121 J20 **Pripet** Bel. Prypyats', Ukr. Prypyat'. ~ Belarus/Ukraine
121 J20 **Pripet Marshes** wetland Belarus/Ukraine
Prishtinë see Priština
130 J8 **Pristen'** Kurskaya Oblast', W Russian Federation
115 N16 **Priština** Alb. Prishtinë. Serbia, S Yugoslavia
102 M10 **Pritzwalk** Brandenburg, NE Germany
105 R13 **Privas** Ardèche, E France
109 I16 **Priverno** Lazio, C Italy
Privigye see Prievidza
114 C12 **Privlaka** Zadar-Knin, W Croatia
128 M15 **Privolzhsk** Ivanovskaya Oblast', NW Russian Federation
131 P7 **Privolzhskaya Vozvyshennost'** var. Volga Uplands. ▲▲ W Russian Federation
131 P8 **Privolzhskoye** Saratovskaya Oblast', W Russian Federation
Priwitz see Prievidza
131 N13 **Priyutnoye** Respublika Kalmykiya, SW Russian Federation
115 M17 **Prizren** Alb. Prizreni. Serbia, S Yugoslavia
Prizreni see Prizren
109 I24 **Prizzi** Sicilia, Italy, C Mediterranean Sea
115 P19 **Probištip** NE FYR Macedonia
174 M15 **Probolinggo** Jawa, C Indonesia
Probstberg see Wyszków
113 F14 **Prochowice** Ger. Parchwitz. Legnica, SW Poland
31 W5 **Proctor** Minnesota, N USA
27 R8 **Proctor** Texas, SW USA
27 R8 **Proctor Lake** ▣ Texas, SW USA
161 I18 **Proddatūr** Andhra Pradesh, E India
106 H9 **Proença-a-Nova** Castelo Branco, C Portugal
97 I24 **Præstø** Storstrøm, SE Denmark
101 I21 **Profondeville** Namur, SE Belgium
43 W11 **Progreso** Yucatán, SE Mexico
126 Mm16 **Progress** Amurskaya Oblast', SE Russian Federation
131 O15 **Prokhladnyy** Kabardino-Balkarskaya Respublika, SW Russian Federation
Prokletije see North Albanian Alps
126 H14 **Prokop'yevsk** Kemerovskaya Oblast', S Russian Federation
Prökuls see Priekulė
115 O15 **Prokuplje** Serbia, SE Yugoslavia
128 H14 **Proletariy** Novgorodskaya Oblast', W Russian Federation
130 M12 **Proletarsk** Rostovskaya Oblast', SW Russian Federation
130 J8 **Proletarskiy** Belgorodskaya Oblast', W Russian Federation
177 Ff7 **Prome** var. Pyè. Pegu, C Myanmar
62 J8 **Promissão** São Paulo, S Brazil
62 J8 **Promissão, Represa de** ▣ S Brazil
129 V4 **Promyshlennyy** Respublika Komi, NW Russian Federation
121 O16 **Pronya** Rus. Pronya. ~ E Belarus
8 M11 **Prophet River** British Columbia, W Canada
32 K11 **Prophetstown** Illinois, N USA
61 P16 **Propriá** Sergipe, E Brazil
104 E3 **Propriano** Corse, France, C Mediterranean Sea
Prościejów see Prostějov
Proskurov see Khmel 'nyts'kyy
116 H12 **Prosotsáni** Anatolikí Makedonía kai Thráki, NE Greece
179 Rr15 **Prosperidad** Mindanao, S Philippines
34 J10 **Prosser** Washington, NW USA
Prossnitz see Prostějov
113 G18 **Prostějov** Ger. Prossnitz, Pol. Prościejów. Jižní Morava, SE Czech Republic
119 V8 **Prosyana** Dnipropetrovs'ka Oblast', E Ukraine
113 L16 **Proszowice** Kraków, S Poland
Protasy see Pratasy
180 J11 **Protea Seamount** undersea feature SW Indian Ocean
117 D21 **Próti** island S Greece
116 N8 **Provadiya** Varnenska Oblast, NE Bulgaria
105 S15 **Provence** prev. Marseille-Marignane. ✕ (Marseille) Bouches-du-Rhône, SE France
105 T14 **Provence** cultural region SE France
105 T14 **Provence-Alpes-Côte d'Azur** ◈ region SE France
22 H6 **Providence** Kentucky, S USA
21 N12 **Providence** state capital Rhode Island, NE USA
38 L1 **Providence** Utah, W USA
Providence see Fort Providence
69 X10 **Providence Atoll** var. Providence. atoll S Seychelles
12 D12 **Providence Bay** Manitoulin Island, Ontario, S Canada
25 R6 **Providence Canyon** valley Alabama/Georgia, S USA
24 I5 **Providence, Lake** ◎ Louisiana, S USA
37 X13 **Providence Mountains** ▲▲ California, W USA
46 L6 **Providenciales** island W Turks and Caicos Islands
127 Q4 **Provideniya** Chukotskiy Avtonomnyy Okrug, NE Russian Federation
21 Q12 **Provincetown** Massachusetts, NE USA
105 P5 **Provins** Seine-et-Marne, N France
38 L3 **Provo** Utah, W USA
9 R15 **Provost** Alberta, SW Canada
114 G13 **Prozor** SW Bosnia and Herzegovina
Prozoroki see Prazaroki
62 I11 **Prudentópolis** Paraná, S Brazil
41 R5 **Prudhoe Bay** Alaska, USA
41 R4 **Prudhoe Bay** bay Alaska, USA
113 H16 **Prudnik** Ger. Neustadt, Neustadt in Oberschlesien. Opole, SW Poland
121 J16 **Prudy** Rus. Prudy. Minskaya Voblasts', C Belarus
103 D18 **Prüm** Rheinland-Pfalz, W Germany
103 D18 **Prüm** ~ W Germany
Prusa see Bursa
112 J7 **Pruszcz Gdański** Ger. Praust. Gdańsk, N Poland
112 M12 **Pruszków** Ger. Kaltdorf. Warszawa, C Poland
118 K8 **Prut** Ger. Pruth. ~ E Europe
Pruth see Prut
110 L8 **Prutz** Tirol, W Austria
Pružana see Pruzhany
121 G19 **Pruzhany** Pol. Prużana. Brestskaya Voblasts', SW Belarus
128 I11 **Pryazha** Respublika Kareliya, NW Russian Federation
119 U10 **Pryazovs'ke** Zaporiz'ka Oblast', SE Ukraine
Prychornomors'ka Nyzovyna see Black Sea Lowland
Prydniprovs'ka Nyzovyna/Prydnyaprowskaya Nizina see Dnieper Lowland
205 Y7 **Prydz Bay** bay Antarctica
119 R4 **Pryluky** Rus. Priluki. Chernihivs'ka Oblast', NE Ukraine
119 V10 **Prymors'k** Rus. Primorsk; prev. Primorskoye. Zaporiz'ka Oblast', SE Ukraine
29 Q9 **Pryor** Oklahoma, C USA
35 U11 **Pryor Creek** ~ Montana, NW USA
Pryp"yat'/Prypyats' see Pripet
112 M10 **Przasnysz** Ostrołęka, NE Poland
113 K14 **Przedbórz** Piotrków, S Poland
Przemyskie, Województwo see Przemyśl
113 P17 **Przemyśl** Rus. Peremyshl. Przemyśl, SE Poland
113 O16 **Przemyśl** off. Województwo Przemyskie, Rus. Peremyshl. ◈ province SE Poland
113 O16 **Przeworsk** Przemyśl, SE Poland
Przheval'sk see Karakol
112 L13 **Przysucha** Radom, SE Poland
117 H18 **Psachná** var. Psahna, Psakhná. Évvoia, C Greece
Psahna/Psakhná see Psachná
117 K18 **Psará** island E Greece
117 I16 **Psathoúra** island Vóreioi Sporádes, Greece, Aegean Sea
Pschestitz see Přeštice
Psein Lora see Pishin Lora
119 S5 **Psël** ~ Russian Federation/Ukraine
117 M21 **Psérimos** island Dodekánisos, Greece, Aegean Sea
Pseyn Bowr see Pishin Lora
Pskem see Piskom
153 R8 **Pskemskiy Khrebet** Uzb. Piskom Tizmasi. ▲▲ Kyrgyzstan/Uzbekistan
128 F14 **Pskov** Ger. Pleskau, Latv. Pleskava. Pskovskaya Oblast', W Russian Federation
120 K6 **Pskov, Lake** Est. Pihkva Järv, Ger. Pleskauer See, Rus. Pskovskoye Ozero. ◎ Estonia/Russian Federation
128 F15 **Pskovskaya Oblast'** ◈ province W Russian Federation
Pskovskoye Ozero see Pskov, Lake
114 G9 **Psunj** ▲▲ NE Croatia
113 J17 **Pszczyna** Ger. Pless. Katowice, S Poland
Ptačnik/Ptacsnik see Vtáčnik
117 D17 **Ptéri** ▲ C Greece
Ptich' see Ptsich
117 E14 **Ptolemaïda** prev. Ptolemaïs. Dytikí Makedonía, N Greece
Ptolemaïs see Ptolemaïda, Greece
Ptolemaïs see 'Akko, Israel
123 Gg10 **Ptolemy Seamounts** undersea feature C Mediterranean Sea
121 M19 **Ptsich** Rus. Ptich'. Homyel'skaya Voblasts', SE Belarus
121 M18 **Ptsich** Rus. Ptich'. ~ SE Belarus
111 X10 **Ptuj** Ger. Pettau; anc. Poetovio. NE Slovenia
194 E9 **Pua** ~ NW PNG
63 A23 **Puán** Buenos Aires, E Argentina
198 B7 **Pu'apu'a** Savai'i, C Western Samoa
198 A7 **Puava, Cape** headland Savai'i, NW Western Samoa
58 F12 **Pucallpa** Ucayali, C Peru
59 J17 **Pucarani** La Paz, NW Bolivia
Pučarevo see Novi Travnik
163 U12 **Pucheng** Fujian, SE China
166 L6 **Pucheng** Shaanxi, C China
129 N16 **Puchezh** Ivanovskaya Oblast', W Russian Federation
113 I19 **Púchov** Hung. Puhó. Stredné Slovensko, NW Slovakia
118 J13 **Pucioasa** Dâmboviţa, S Romania
112 I6 **Puck** Gdańsk, N Poland
32 L8 **Puckaway Lake** ◎ Wisconsin, N USA
65 G15 **Pucón** Araucanía, S Chile
95 M14 **Pudasjärvi** Oulu, C Finland
154 L8 **Pūdeh Tal, Shelleh-ye** ~ SW Afghanistan
131 S1 **Pudem** Udmurtskaya Respublika, NW Russian Federation
Pudewitz see Pobiedziska
128 K11 **Pudozh** Respublika Kareliya, NW Russian Federation
99 M17 **Pudsey** N England, UK
Puduchcheri see Pondicherry
157 H21 **Pudukkottai** Tamil Nādu, SE India
176 Z10 **Pue** Irian Jaya, E Indonesia
43 P14 **Puebla** var. Puebla de Zaragoza. Puebla, S Mexico
43 P15 **Puebla** ◈ state S Mexico
106 L11 **Puebla de Alcocer** Extremadura, W Spain
Puebla de Don Fabrique see Puebla de Don Fadrique
107 P13 **Puebla de Don Fadrique** var. Puebla de Don Fabrique. Andalucía, S Spain
106 J11 **Puebla de la Calzada** Extremadura, W Spain
106 J5 **Puebla de Sanabria** Castilla-León, N Spain
106 I4 **Puebla de Trives** Galicia, NW Spain
Puebla de Zaragoza see Puebla
39 T6 **Pueblo** Colorado, C USA
39 N10 **Pueblo Colorado Wash** valley Arizona, SW USA
63 C16 **Pueblo Libertador** Corrientes, NE Argentina
42 J10 **Pueblo Nuevo** Durango, C Mexico
44 J8 **Pueblo Nuevo** Estelí, NW Nicaragua
56 J3 **Pueblo Nuevo** Falcón, N Venezuela
44 B6 **Pueblo Nuevo Tiquisate** var. Tiquisate. Escuintla, SW Guatemala
43 Q11 **Pueblo Viejo, Laguna de** lagoon E Mexico
65 J14 **Puelches** La Pampa, C Argentina
106 L14 **Puente-Genil** Andalucía, S Spain
107 Q3 **Puente la Reina** Navarra, N Spain
106 L12 **Puente Nuevo, Embalse de** ▣ S Spain
59 D14 **Puente Piedra** Lima, W Peru
166 F14 **Pu'er** Yunnan, SW China
47 V6 **Puerca, Punta** headland E Puerto Rico
39 R12 **Puerco, Rio** ~ New Mexico, SW USA
59 J17 **Puerto Acosta** La Paz, W Bolivia

◆ Country ● Country Capital ◇ Dependent Territory ○ Dependent Territory Capital ◈ Administrative Region ✕ International Airport ▲ Mountain ▲▲ Mountain Range ⩚ Volcano ~ River ◎ Lake ▣ Reservoir

Puerto Aisén – Qogir Feng

65 G19 Puerto Aisén Aisén, S Chile
43 R17 Puerto Ángel Oaxaca, SE Mexico
43 T17 Puerto Arista Chiapas, SE Mexico
45 O16 Puerto Armuelles Chiriquí, SW Panama
Puerto Arrecife see Arrecife
56 D14 Puerto Asís Putumayo, SW Colombia
56 L9 Puerto Ayacucho Amazonas, SW Venezuela
59 C18 Puerto Ayora Galapagos Islands, Ecuador, E Pacific Ocean
59 C18 Puerto Baquerizo Moreno var. Baquerizo Moreno. Galapagos Islands, Ecuador, E Pacific Ocean
44 G4 Puerto Barrios Izabal, E Guatemala
Puerto Bello see Portobelo
56 F8 Puerto Berrío Antioquia, C Colombia
56 F9 Puerto Boyaca Boyacá, C Colombia
56 K4 Puerto Cabello Carabobo, N Venezuela
45 N7 Puerto Cabezas var. Bilwi. Región Autónoma Atlántico Norte, NE Nicaragua
56 L9 Puerto Carreño Vichada, E Colombia
56 E4 Puerto Colombia Atlántico, N Colombia
44 H4 Puerto Cortés Cortés, NW Honduras
56 J4 Puerto Cumarebo Falcón, N Venezuela
Puerto de Cabras see Puerto del Rosario
57 Q5 Puerto de Hierro Sucre, NE Venezuela
66 O11 Puerto de la Cruz Tenerife, Islas Canarias, Spain, NE Atlantic Ocean
66 Q11 Puerto del Rosario var. Puerto de Cabras. Fuerteventura, Islas Canarias, Spain, NE Atlantic Ocean
65 J20 Puerto Deseado Santa Cruz, SE Argentina
42 F8 Puerto Escondido Baja California Sur, W Mexico
43 R17 Puerto Escondido Oaxaca, SE Mexico
62 G12 Puerto Esperanza Misiones, NE Argentina
58 D6 Puerto Francisco de Orellana var. Coca. Napo, N Ecuador
56 H10 Puerto Gaitán Meta, C Colombia
Puerto Gallegos see Río Gallegos
62 G12 Puerto Iguazú Misiones, NE Argentina
58 F12 Puerto Inca Huánuco, N Peru
56 L11 Puerto Inírida var. Obando. Guainía, E Colombia
44 K13 Puerto Jesús Guanacaste, NW Costa Rica
43 Z11 Puerto Juárez Quintana Roo, SE Mexico
57 N5 Puerto La Cruz Anzoátegui, NE Venezuela
56 E14 Puerto Leguízamo Putumayo, S Colombia
45 N5 Puerto Lempira Gracias a Dios, E Honduras
Puerto Libertad see La Libertad
56 I11 Puerto Limón Meta, E Colombia
56 D13 Puerto Limón Putumayo, SW Colombia
Puerto Limón see Limón
107 N11 Puertollano Castilla-La Mancha, C Spain
65 K17 Puerto Lobos Chubut, SE Argentina
56 I3 Puerto López La Guajira, N Colombia
107 Q14 Puerto Lumbreras Murcia, SE Spain
43 V17 Puerto Madero Chiapas, SE Mexico
65 K17 Puerto Madryn Chubut, S Argentina
Puerto Magdalena see Bahía Magdalena
59 J15 Puerto Maldonado Madre de Dios, E Peru
Puerto Masachapa see Masachapa
Puerto México see Coatzacoalcos
65 G17 Puerto Montt Los Lagos, C Chile
43 Z12 Puerto Morelos Quintana Roo, SE Mexico
56 L10 Puerto Nariño Vichada, E Colombia
65 H23 Puerto Natales Magallanes, S Chile
45 X15 Puerto Obaldía San Blas, NE Panama
46 H6 Puerto Padre Las Tunas, E Cuba
56 L9 Puerto Páez Apure, C Venezuela
42 E3 Puerto Peñasco Sonora, NW Mexico
57 N5 Puerto Píritu Anzoátegui, NE Venezuela
47 N8 Puerto Plata var. San Felipe de Puerto Plata. N Dominican Republic
47 N8 Puerto Plata ✈ N Dominican Republic
Puerto Presidente Stroessner see Ciudad del Este
179 Oo14 Puerto Princesa off. Puerto Princesa City. Palawan, W Philippines
Puerto Princesa City see Puerto Princesa
Puerto Príncipe see Camagüey
Puerto Quellón see Quellón
62 F13 Puerto Rico Misiones, NE Argentina
59 K14 Puerto Rico Pando, N Bolivia
56 E12 Puerto Rico Caquetá, S Colombia
47 U5 Puerto Rico off. Commonwealth of Puerto Rico; prev. Porto Rico. ◇ US commonwealth territory C West Indies
66 F11 Puerto Rico island C West Indies
66 G11 Puerto Rico Trench undersea feature NE Caribbean Sea
56 I8 Puerto Rondón Arauca, E Colombia
Puerto San José see San José
65 J21 Puerto San Julián var. San Julián. Santa Cruz, SE Argentina
65 I22 Puerto Santa Cruz var. Santa Cruz. Santa Cruz, SE Argentina
Puerto Sauce see Juan L.Lacaze
59 Q20 Puerto Suárez Santa Cruz, E Bolivia
56 D13 Puerto Umbría Putumayo, SW Colombia
42 J13 Puerto Vallarta Jalisco, SW Mexico
65 G16 Puerto Varas Los Lagos, C Chile
44 M13 Puerto Viejo Heredia, NE Costa Rica
Puertoviejo see Portoviejo
59 B18 Puerto Villamil var. Villamil. Galapagos Islands, Ecuador, E Pacific Ocean
56 F8 Puerto Wilches Santander, N Colombia
65 H20 Pueyrredón, Lago var. Lago Cochrane. ◎ S Argentina
131 R7 Pugachëv Saratovskaya Oblast', W Russian Federation
131 T3 Pugachëvo Udmurtskaya Respublika, NW Russian Federation
34 H8 Puget Sound sound Washington, NW USA
109 O17 Puglia var. Le Puglie, Eng. Apulia. ◈ region SE Italy
109 N17 Puglia, Canosa di anc. Canusium. Puglia, SE Italy
120 I6 Puhja Ger. Kawelecht. Tartumaa, SE Estonia
Puhó see Púchov
107 V4 Puigcerdà Cataluña, NE Spain
Puigmal see Puigmal d'Err
105 N17 Puigmal d'Err var. Puigmal. ▲ S France
78 I16 Pujehun S Sierra Leone
Puka see Pukë
193 E20 Pukaki, Lake ◎ South Island, NZ
40 F10 Pukalani Maui, Hawaii, USA, C Pacific Ocean
202 J13 Pukapuka atoll N Cook Islands
203 X9 Pukapuka atoll Îles Tuamotu, E French Polynesia
Pukari Neem see Purekkari Neem
203 X11 Pukarua var. Pukaruha. atoll Îles Tuamotu, E French Polynesia
Pukaruha see Pukarua
12 A7 Pukaskwa ∼ Ontario, S Canada
9 V12 Pukatawagan Manitoba, C Canada
203 X16 Pukatikei, Maunga ※ Easter Island, Chile, E Pacific Ocean
190 C1 Pukatja var. Ernabella. South Australia
169 Y12 Pukch'ŏng E North Korea
115 L18 Pukë var. Puka. Shkodër, N Albania
192 L6 Pukekohe Auckland, North Island, NZ
192 L7 Pukemiro Waikato, North Island, NZ
202 D12 Puke, Mont ▲ Île Futuna, W Wallis and Futuna
Puket see Phuket
193 C20 Puketeraki Range ▲▲ South Island, NZ
192 N13 Puketoi Range ▲▲ North Island, NZ
193 F21 Pukeuri Junction Otago, South Island, NZ
121 L16 Pukhavichy Rus. Pukhovichi. Minskaya Voblasts', C Belarus
Pukhovichi see Pukhavichy
128 M10 Puksoozero Arkhangel'skaya Oblast', NW Russian Federation
114 A10 Pula It. Pola; prev. Pulj. Istra, NW Croatia
169 U14 Pulandian var. Xinjin. Liaoning, NE China
169 T14 Pulandian Wan bay NE China
179 Rr15 Pulangi ∼ Mindanao, S Philippines
201 O15 Pulap Atoll atoll Caroline Islands, C Micronesia
20 H9 Pulaski New York, NE USA
22 I10 Pulaski Tennessee, S USA
23 R7 Pulaski Virginia, NE USA
176 Yy13 Pulau, Sungai ∼ Irian Jaya, E Indonesia
112 N13 Puławy Ger. Neu Amerika. Lublin, E Poland
103 E16 Pulheim Nordrhein-Westfalen, W Germany
Pulicat see Pālghāt
161 J19 Pulicat Lake lagoon SE India
194 M12 Pulie ∼ New Britain, C PNG
Pul'-I-Khatum see Polekhatum
Pul-i-Khumri see Pol-e Khomrī
Pul-i-Sefid see Pol-e Safīd
Pulj see Pula
111 W2 Pulkau ∼ NE Austria
95 L15 Pulkkila Oulu, C Finland
125 Gc6 Pul'kovo ✈ (Sankt-Peterburg) Leningradskaya Oblast', NW Russian Federation
34 M9 Pullman Washington, NW USA
110 B10 Pully Vaud, SW Switzerland
42 F7 Púlpita, Punta headland W Mexico
112 M10 Pułtusk Ciechanów, C Poland
164 H10 Pulu Xinjiang Uygur Zizhiqu, W China
143 P13 Pülümür Tunceli, E Turkey
201 N16 Pulusuk island Caroline Islands, C Micronesia
201 N16 Puluwat Atoll atoll Caroline Islands, C Micronesia
27 N11 Pumpville Texas, SW USA
203 P7 Punaauia var. Hakapehi. Tahiti, W French Polynesia
58 B8 Puná, Isla island SW Ecuador
193 G16 Punakaiki West Coast, South Island, NZ
159 T11 Punakha C Bhutan
59 L18 Punata Cochabamba, C Bolivia
161 E14 Pune prev. Poona. Mahārāshtra, W India
85 M17 Pungoè, Rio var. Púnguè, Pungwe. ∼ C Mozambique
23 X10 Pungo River ∼ North Carolina, SE USA
Púnguè/Pungwe see Pungoè, Rio
81 N19 Punia Maniema, E Zaire
64 H8 Punilla, Sierra de la ▲▲ W Argentina
167 P14 Puning Guangdong, S China
64 G10 Punitaqui Coquimbo, C Chile
158 H8 Punjab ◈ state NW India
155 T9 Punjab prev. West Punjab, Western Punjab. ◈ province E Pakistan
133 Q9 Punjab Plains plain N India
95 O17 Punkaharju var. Punkasalmi. Mikkeli, SE Finland
Punkasalmi see Punkaharju
59 I17 Puno Puno, SE Peru
59 H17 Puno off. Departamento de Puno. ◈ department S Peru
63 B24 Punta Alta Buenos Aires, E Argentina
65 H24 Punta Arenas prev. Magallanes. Magallanes, S Chile
47 T6 Punta, Cerro de ▲ C Puerto Rico
45 T15 Punta Chame Panamá, C Panama
59 G17 Punta Colorada Arequipa, SW Peru
42 F9 Punta Coyote Baja California Sur, W Mexico
64 G8 Punta de Díaz Atacama, N Chile
63 G20 Punta del Este Maldonado, S Uruguay
65 K17 Punta Delgada Chubut, SE Argentina
57 O5 Punta de Mata Monagas, NE Venezuela
57 O4 Punta de Piedras Nueva Esparta, NE Venezuela
44 F4 Punta Gorda Toledo, SE Belize
45 N11 Punta Gorda Región Autónoma Atlántico Sur, SE Nicaragua
25 W14 Punta Gorda Florida, SE USA
44 M11 Punta Gorda, Río ∼ SE Nicaragua
64 H6 Punta Negra, Salar de salt lake N Chile
42 D5 Punta Prieta Baja California, NW Mexico
44 L13 Puntarenas Puntarenas, W Costa Rica
44 L13 Puntarenas off. Provincia de Puntarenas. ◈ province W Costa Rica
56 J4 Punto Fijo Falcón, N Venezuela
107 S4 Puntón de Guara ▲ N Spain
20 D14 Punxsutawney Pennsylvania, NE USA
95 M14 Puolanka Oulu, C Finland
59 N19 Pupuya, Nevado ▲ W Bolivia
167 O10 Puqi Hubei, C China
59 F16 Puquio Ayacucho, S Peru
126 H9 Pur ∼ N Russian Federation
194 I13 Purari ∼ S PNG
29 N11 Purcell Oklahoma, C USA
9 O16 Purcell Mountains ▲▲ British Columbia, SW Canada
107 P14 Purchena Andalucía, S Spain
29 S8 Purdy Missouri, C USA
120 I2 Purekkari Neem prev. Pukari Neem. headland N Estonia
39 U7 Purgatoire River ∼ Colorado, C USA
Purgstall see Purgstall an der Erlauf
111 V5 Purgstall an der Erlauf var. Purgstall. Niederösterreich, NE Austria
160 O13 Puri var. Jagannath. Orissa, E India
Puriramya see Buriram
111 X4 Purkersdorf Niederösterreich, NE Austria
100 I9 Purmerend Noord-Holland, C Netherlands
157 G16 Pūrna ∼ C India
Purnea see Pūrnia
159 R13 Pūrnia prev. Purnea. Bihār, NE India
Pursat see Poŭthĭsăt, Poŭthĭsăt, W Cambodia
Pursat see Poŭthĭsăt, Stœng, W Cambodia
Purulia see Puruliya
156 L13 Puruliya prev. Purulia. West Bengal, NE India
49 G7 Purus, Rio Sp. Río Purús. ∼ Brazil/Peru
194 G15 Purutu Island island SW PNG
95 N17 Puruvesi ◎ SE Finland
24 L7 Purvis Mississippi, S USA
116 J11 Pŭrvomay prev. Borisovgrad. Plovdivska Oblast, C Bulgaria
174 J14 Purwakarta prev. Poerwakarta. Jawa, C Indonesia
174 L15 Purwodadi prev. Poerwodadi. Jawa, C Indonesia
174 K15 Purwokerto prev. Poerwokerto. Jawa, C Indonesia
174 Kk15 Purworejo prev. Poerworedjo. Jawa, C Indonesia
22 H8 Puryear Tennessee, S USA
160 H13 Pusad Mahārāshtra, C India
169 Z16 Pusan off. Pusan-gwangyŏksi, var. Busan, Jap. Fusan. SE South Korea
173 Ee4 Pusatgajo, Pegunungan ▲▲ Sumatera, NW Indonesia
Puschlav see Poschiavo
Pushkin see Tsarskoye Selo
131 Q8 Pushkino Saratovskaya Oblast', W Russian Federation
Pushkino see Biläsuvar
113 M22 Püspökladány Hajdú-Bihar, E Hungary
120 J3 Püssi Ger. Isenhof. Ida-Virumaa, NE Estonia
118 I5 Pustomyty L'vivs'ka Oblast', W Ukraine
128 F16 Pustoshka Pskovskaya Oblast', W Russian Federation
Pusztakalán see Călan
178 H1 Putao prev. Fort Hertz. Kachin State, N Myanmar
192 M8 Putaruru Waikato, North Island, NZ
Puteoli see Pozzuoli
167 R12 Putian Fujian, SE China
109 O17 Putignano Puglia, SE Italy
Putivl' see Putyvl'
43 Q16 Putla var. Putla de Guerrero. Oaxaca, SE Mexico
Putla de Guerrero see Putla
21 N12 Putnam Connecticut, NE USA
27 Q7 Putnam Texas, SW USA
20 M10 Putney Vermont, NE USA
113 L20 Putnok Borsod-Abaúj-Zemplén, NE Hungary
Putorana, Gory/Putorana Mountains see Putorana, Plato
126 Ii8 Putorana, Plato var. Gory Putorana, Eng. Putorana Mountains. ▲▲ N Russian Federation
64 H2 Putre Tarapacá, N Chile
161 J24 Puttalam North Western Province, W Sri Lanka
161 J24 Puttalam Lagoon lagoon W Sri Lanka
101 H17 Putte Antwerpen, C Belgium
100 K11 Putten Gelderland, C Netherlands
102 K7 Puttgarden Schleswig-Holstein, N Germany
Puttiala see Patiāla
103 D20 Püttlingen Saarland, SW Germany
56 D14 Putumayo off. Intendencia del Putumayo. ◈ province S Colombia
50 E7 Putumayo, Río var. Rio Içá. ∼ NW South America see also Içá, Rio
174 K8 Putus, Tanjung headland Borneo, N Indonesia
118 J8 Putyla Chernivets'ka Oblast', W Ukraine
119 S3 Putyvl' Rus. Putivl'. Sums'ka Oblast', NE Ukraine
95 M18 Puula ◎ SE Finland
95 N18 Puumala Mikkeli, SE Finland
120 I5 Puurmani Ger. Talkhof. Jõgevamaa, E Estonia
101 G17 Puurs Antwerpen, N Belgium
Pu'uUla'ula see Red Hill
40 A8 Puuwai Niihau, Hawaii, USA, C Pacific Ocean
10 J4 Puvirnituq prev. Povungnituk. Québec, NE Canada
34 H8 Puyallup Washington, NW USA
167 O5 Puyang Henan, C China
167 R9 Puyang Jiang var. Tsien Tang. ∼ SE China
105 O11 Puy-de-Dôme ◈ department C France
105 N15 Puylaurens Tarn, S France
104 M13 Puy-l'Evêque Lot, S France
105 N17 Puymorens, Col de pass S France
58 C7 Puyo Pastaza, C Ecuador
193 A24 Puysegur Point headland South Island, NZ
154 J8 Pūzak, Hāmūn-e Pash. Hāmūn-i-Puzak. ◎ SW Afghanistan
Puzak, Hāmūn-i- see Pūzak, Hāmūn-e
83 J23 Pwani Eng. Coast. ◈ region E Tanzania
81 O23 Pweto Shaba, SE Zaire
99 I19 Pwllheli NW Wales, UK
201 O14 Pwok Pohnpei, E Micronesia
126 Gg10 Pyakupur ∼ N Russian Federation
128 M6 Pyalitsa Murmanskaya Oblast', NW Russian Federation
128 K10 Pyal'ma Respublika Kareliya, NW Russian Federation
Pyandzh see Panj
128 I6 Pyaozero, Ozero ◎ NW Russian Federation
177 Ff9 Pyapon Irrawaddy, SW Myanmar
121 J15 Pyarshai Rus. Pershay. Minskaya Voblasts', C Belarus
126 I6 Pyasina ∼ N Russian Federation
116 I10 Pyasŭchnik, Yazovir ▣ C Bulgaria
125 B13 Pyatigorsk Stavropol'skiy Kray, SW Russian Federation
Pyatikhatki see P"yatykhatky
119 S7 P"yatykhatky Rus. Pyatikhatki. Dnipropetrovs'ka Oblast', E Ukraine
177 G6 Pyawbwe Mandalay, C Myanmar
131 T3 Pychas Udmurtskaya Respublika, NW Russian Federation
Pyè see Prome
177 F6 Pyechin Chin State, W Myanmar
121 G17 Pyeski Rus. Peski. Hrodzyenskaya Voblasts', W Belarus
121 L19 Pyetrykaw Rus. Petrikov. Homyel'skaya Voblasts', SE Belarus
95 M16 Pyhäjärvi ◎ C Finland
95 O17 Pyhäjärvi ◎ SE Finland
95 L15 Pyhäjoki Oulu, W Finland
95 L15 Pyhäjoki ∼ W Finland
95 M15 Pyhäntä Oulu, C Finland
95 M16 Pyhäsalmi Oulu, C Finland
95 O17 Pyhäselkä ◎ SE Finland
95 M19 Pyhtää Swe. Pyttis. Kymi, S Finland
177 G6 Pyinmana Mandalay, C Myanmar
117 N24 Pylés var. Piles. Kárpathos, SE Greece
117 D21 Pýlos var. Pilos. Pelopónnisos, S Greece
20 B12 Pymatuning Reservoir ▣ Ohio/Pennsylvania, NE USA
169 X15 P'yŏngt'aek NW South Korea
169 V14 P'yŏngyang var. P'yŏngyang-si, Eng. Pyongyang. ● (North Korea) SW North Korea
P'yŏngyang-si see P'yŏngyang
37 Q4 Pyramid Lake ◎ Nevada, W USA
39 P15 Pyramid Mountains ▲▲ New Mexico, SW USA
39 R5 Pyramid Peak ▲ Colorado, C USA
117 D17 Pyramíva var. Piramiva. ▲ C Greece
Pyrenaei Montes see Pyrenees
88 B12 Pyrenees Fr. Pyrénées, Sp. Pirineos; anc. Pyrenaei Montes. ▲▲ SW Europe
104 J16 Pyrénées-Atlantiques ◈ department SW France
105 N17 Pyrénées-Orientales ◈ department S France
117 L19 Pyrgí var. Pirgi. Chíos, E Greece
117 D20 Pýrgos var. Pírgos. Dytikí Ellás, S Greece
Pyritz see Pyrzyce
117 E19 Pýrros ∼ S Greece
119 R4 Pyryatyn Rus. Piryatin. Poltavs'ka Oblast', NE Ukraine
112 D9 Pyrzyce Ger. Pyritz. Szczecin, NW Poland
128 F15 Pytalovo Latv. Abrene; prev. Jaunlatgale. Pskovskaya Oblast', W Russian Federation
117 M20 Pythagóreio var. Pithagorio. Sámos, Dodekánisos, Greece, Aegean Sea
12 L11 Pythonga, Lac ◎ Québec, SE Canada
96 E10 Pyttegga ▲ S Norway
Pyttis see Pyhtää
177 G7 Pyu Pegu, C Myanmar
177 G8 Pyuntaza Pegu, SW Myanmar
159 N11 Pyuthan Mid Western, W Nepal
112 H12 Pyzdry Ger. Peisern. Konin, C Poland

Q

144 H13 Qā' al Jafr ◎ S Jordan
207 O11 Qaanaaq var. Qânâq, Dan. Thule. N Greenland
144 G7 Qabb Eliâs E Lebanon
Qabil see Al Qābil
Qabırrı see Iori
Qābis see Gabès
Qābis, Khalīj see Gabès, Golfe de
147 S14 Qabr Hūd C Yemen
Qacentina see Constantine
154 L4 Qādes Bādghīs, NW Afghanistan
145 T11 Qādisīyah S Iraq
Qadmoûs/Qadmūs see Al Qadmūs
149 O4 Qā'emshahr prev. 'Alīābad, Shāhī. Māzandarān, N Iran
149 U7 Qā'en var. Qain, Qāyen. Khorāsān, E Iran
147 U13 Qafa spring/well SW Oman
Qafşah see Gafsa
169 V9 Qagan Nur ◎ NE China
169 Q11 Qagan Nur ◎ N China
Qagan Us see Dulan
164 H13 Qagcaka Xizang Zizhiqu, W China
Qahremānshahr see Bākhtarān
165 Q10 Qaidam He ∼ C China
162 L8 Qaidam Pendi basin C China
Qain see Qā'en
Qala Āhangarān see Chaghcharān
145 U3 Qalā Diza var. Qal 'at Dīzah. NE Iraq
Qal'ah Sālih see Qal'at Şāliḩ
153 R13 Qal'aikhum Rus. Kalaikhum. S Tajikistan
Qala Nau see Qal'eh-ye Now
147 V17 Qalansīyah Suquṭrā, W Yemen
Qala Panja see Qal'eh-ye Panjeh
Qala Shāhar see Qal'eh Shahr
Qalāt see Kalāt
145 W9 Qal'at Aḩmad E Iraq
147 N11 Qal'at Bīshah 'Asīr, SW Saudi Arabia
144 H4 Qal'at Burzay Ḩamāh, W Syria
Qal 'at Dīzah see Qalā Diza
145 W9 Qal'at Ḩusayh E Iraq
145 V10 Qal'at Majnūnah S Iraq
145 X11 Qal'at Şāliḩ var. Qal'ah Sālih. E Iraq
145 V10 Qal'at Sukkar SE Iraq
Qalba Zhotasy see Kalbinskiy Khrebet
149 Q12 Qal'eh Biābān Fārs, S Iran
155 N4 Qal'eh Shahr Pash. Qala Shāhar. Sar-e Pol, N Afghanistan
154 L4 Qal'eh-ye Now var. Qala Nau. Bādghīs, NW Afghanistan
155 T2 Qal'eh-ye Panjeh var. Qala Panja. Badakhshān, NE Afghanistan
Qamar Bay see Qamar, Ghubbat al
147 U14 Qamar, Ghubbat al Eng. Qamar Bay. bay Oman/Yemen
147 V13 Qamar, Jabal al ▲▲ SW Oman
Qambar see Kambar
165 R14 Qamdo Xizang Zizhiqu, W China
197 K13 Qamea prev. Nggamea. island N Fiji
77 R7 Qamīnis NE Libya
Qamishly see Al Qāmishlī
Qânâq see Qaanaaq
Qandahār see Kandahār
82 Q11 Qandala Bari, NE Somalia
144 L2 Qanṭārī Ar Raqqah, N Syria
143 V13 Qapiciğ Dağı Rus. Gora Kapydzhik. ▲ SW Azerbaijan
164 H5 Qapqal var. Qapqal Xibe Zizhixian. Xinjiang Uygur Zizhiqu, NW China
Qapqal Xibe Zizhixian see Qapqal
Qapshagay Böyeni see Kapchagayskoye Vodokhranilishche
206 M15 Qaqortoq Dan. Julianehåb. S Greenland
77 U8 Qâra var. Qārah. NW Egypt
145 T4 Qara Anjīr N Iraq
Qarabāgh see Qarah Bāgh
Qaraböget see Karaboget
Qarabulaq see Karabulak
Qarabutaq see Karabutak
Qaraghandy/Qaraghandy Oblysy see Karaganda
Qaraghayly see Karagayly
145 U4 Qara Gol NE Iraq
Qārah see Qâra
154 J4 Qarah Bāgh var. Qarabāgh. Herāt, NW Afghanistan
144 G7 Qaraoun, Lac de var. Buḩayrat al Qir'awn. ◎ S Lebanon
Qaraoy see Karaoy
Qaraqoyyn see Karakoyyn, Ozero
Qara Qum see Garagumy
Qarasū see Karasu
Qaratal see Karatal
Qarataū see Karatau, Khrebet, Kazakhstan
Qarataū see Karatau, Zhambyl, Kazakhstan
Qaraton see Karaton
82 P13 Qardho var. Kardh, It. Gardo. Bari, N Somalia
148 M6 Qareh Chāy ∼ N Iran
148 K2 Qareh Sū ∼ NW Iran
Qariateïne see Al Qaryatayn
Qarkilik see Ruoqiang
153 O13 Qarluq Rus. Karluk. Surkhondaryo Wiloyati, S Uzbekistan
153 U12 Qarokŭl Rus. Karakul'. E Tajikistan
153 T12 Qarokŭl Rus. Ozero Karakul'. ◎ E Tajikistan
Qarqan see Qiemo
164 K9 Qarqan He ∼ NW China
Qarqannah, Juzur see Kerkenah, Îles de
Qarqaraly see Karkaralinsk
155 O1 Qarqīn Jowzjān, N Afghanistan
Qars see Kars
Qarsaqbay see Karsakpay
152 M12 Qarshi Rus. Karshi; prev. Bek-Budi. Qashqadaryo Wiloyati, S Uzbekistan
152 L12 Qarshi Chŭli Rus. Karshinskaya Step. grassland S Uzbekistan
152 M13 Qarshi Kanali Rus. Karshinskiy Kanal. canal Turkmenistan/Uzbekistan
Qaryatayn see Al Qaryatayn
152 M12 Qashqadaryo Wiloyati Rus. Kashkadar'inskaya Oblast'. ◈ province S Uzbekistan
Qasigianguit see Qasigiannguit
207 N13 Qasigiannguit var. Qasigianguit, Dan. Christianshåb. C Greenland
Qaşim, Mintaqat see Al Qaşim
145 P8 Qaşr 'Amij C Iraq
145 R9 Qaşr Darwīshāh C Iraq
148 J6 Qaşr-e Shīrīn Kermānshāhān, W Iran
77 V10 Qaşr Farâfra W Egypt
Qassim see Al Qaşim
147 O16 Qa'ṭabah SW Yemen
144 H7 Qaṭanā var. Katana. Dimashq, S Syria
149 N15 Qatar off. State of Qatar, Ar. Dawlat Qaṭar. ◆ monarchy SW Asia
Qatrana see Al Qaṭrānah
149 Q12 Qaṭrūyeh Fārs, S Iran
Qattara Depression/Qaṭṭārah, Munkhafaḍ al see Qaṭṭāra, Monkhafad el
77 U8 Qaṭṭâra, Monkhafad el var. Munkhafaḍ al Qaṭṭārah, Eng. Qattara Depression. desert NW Egypt
Qaṭṭīnah, Buḩayrat see Ḩimş, Buḩayrat
Qaydār see Qeydār
Qāyen see Qā'en
153 Q11 Qayroqqum Rus. Kayrakkum. NW Tajikistan
153 Q10 Qayroqqum, Obanbori Rus. Kayrakkumskoye Vodokhranilishche. ▣ NW Tajikistan
145 U7 Qazānīyah var. Dhū Shaykh. E Iraq
Qazaqstan/Qazaqstan Respublikasy see Kazakhstan
143 T9 Qazbegi Rus. Kazbegi. NE Georgia
155 P15 Qāzi Ahmad var. Kazi Ahmad. Sind, SE Pakistan
143 Y12 Qazimämmäd Rus. Kazi Magomed. SE Azerbaijan
Qazris see Cáceres
148 M4 Qazvīn var. Kazvin. Zanjān, NW Iran
197 K12 Qelelevu Lagoon lagoon NE Fiji
77 X10 Qena var. Qinā; anc. Caene, Caenepolis. E Egypt
115 L23 Qeparo Vlorë, S Albania
Qeqertarssuaq see Qeqertarsuaq
207 N13 Qeqertarsuaq var. Qeqertarssuaq, Dan. Godhavn. S Greenland
206 M13 Qeqertarsuaq island W Greenland
207 N13 Qeqertarsuup Tunua Dan. Disko Bugt. inlet W Greenland
Qerveh see Qorveh
149 S14 Qeshm Hormozgān, S Iran
149 R14 Qeshm var. Jazīreh-ye Qeshm, Qeshm Island. island S Iran
Qeshm Island/Qeshm, Jazīreh-ye see Qeshm
148 L4 Qeydār var. Qaydār. Zanjān, NW Iran
148 K5 Qezel Owzan var. Ki Zil Uzen, Qi Zil Uzun. ∼ NW Iran
148 L5 Qezel Owzan, Rūd-e ∼ NW Iran
Qian see Guizhou
Qian Gorlo see Qian Gorlos
169 V9 Qian Gorlos var. Qian Gorlo, Qian Gorlos Mongolzu Zizhixian, Qianguozhen. Jilin, NE China
Qian Gorlos Mongolzu Zizhixian/Qianguozhen see Qian Gorlos
167 N9 Qianjiang Hubei, C China
166 K10 Qianjiang Sichuan, C China
166 L14 Qian Jiang ∼ S China
166 G9 Qianning var. Gartar. Sichuan, C China
169 U13 Qian Shan ▲▲ NE China
166 H10 Qianwei Sichuan, C China
166 J11 Qianxi Guizhou, S China
165 Q7 Qiaowan Gansu, N China
Qibilī see Kebili
164 K9 Qiemo var. Qarqan. Xinjiang Uygur Zizhiqu, NW China
166 J10 Qijiang Sichuan, C China
165 N5 Qijiaojing Xinjiang Uygur Zizhiqu, NW China
155 P9 Qila Saifullāh Baluchistān, SW Pakistan
165 S9 Qilian Qinghai, C China
140 Nn10 Qilian Shan var. Kilien Mountains. ▲▲ N China
207 O11 Qimusseriarsuaq Dan. Melville Bugt, Eng. Melville Bay. bay NW Greenland
Qinā see Qena
165 W11 Qin'an Gansu, C China
Qing see Qinghai
169 W7 Qing'an Heilongjiang, NE China
167 R5 Qingdao var. Ching-Tao, Ch'ing-tao, Tsingtao, Tsintao, Ger. Tsingtau. Shandong, E China
169 V8 Qinggang Heilongjiang, NE China
Qinggil see Qinghe
165 P11 Qinghai var. Chinghai, Koko Nor, Qing, Qinghai Sheng, Tsinghai. ◈ province C China
165 S10 Qinghai Hu var. Ch'ing Hai, Tsing Hai, Mong. Koko Nor. ◎ C China
Qinghai Sheng see Qinghai
164 M3 Qinghe var. Qinggil. Xinjiang Uygur Zizhiqu, NW China
166 L4 Qingjian Shaanxi, C China
166 L9 Qing Jiang ∼ C China
Qingjiang see Huaiyin
Qingkou see Ganyu
166 I12 Qinglong var. Liancheng. Guizhou, S China
167 Q2 Qinglong Hebei, E China
Qingshan see Dedu
165 R12 Qingshuihe Qinghai, C China
Qingyang see Jinjiang
169 V11 Qingyuan Liaoning, NE China
164 L13 Qingzang Gaoyuan var. Xizang Gaoyuan, Eng. Plateau of Tibet. plateau W China
167 Q4 Qingzhou prev. Yidu. Shandong, E China
163 R9 Qin He ∼ C China
167 Q2 Qinhuangdao Hebei, E China
166 K7 Qin Ling ▲▲ C China
Qin Xian see Qinxian
167 N5 Qinxian var. Qin Xian. Shanxi, C China
167 N6 Qinyang Henan, C China
166 K15 Qinzhou Guangxi Zhuangzu Zizhiqu, S China
Qiong see Hainan
166 L17 Qionghai prev. Jiaji. Hainan, S China
166 H9 Qionglai Sichuan, C China
166 H8 Qionglai Shan ▲▲ C China
166 L17 Qiongzhou Haixia var. Hainan Strait. strait S China
169 U7 Qiqihar var. Ch'i-ch'i-ha-erh, Tsitsihar; prev. Lungkiang. Heilongjiang, NE China
149 P12 Qīr Fārs, S Iran
164 H10 Qira Xinjiang Uygur Zizhiqu, NW China
Qir'awn, Buḩayrat al see Qaraoun, Lac de
144 F11 Qiryat Gat Southern, C Israel
144 G8 Qiryat Shemona Northern, N Israel
Qishlaq see Garmsār
147 U14 Qishn SE Yemen
144 G9 Qishon, Naḩal ∼ N Israel
Qita Ghazzah see Gaza Strip
162 K5 Qitai Xinjiang Uygur Zizhiqu, NW China
169 Y8 Qitaihe Heilongjiang, NE China
147 W12 Qitbīt, Wādī dry watercourse S Oman
167 O5 Qixian var. Qi Xian, Zhaoge. Henan, C China
Qizān see Jīzān
Qizil Orda see Kzyl-Orda
Qizil Qum/Qizilqum see Kyzyl Kum
153 V14 Qizilrabot Rus. Kyzylrabot. SE Tajikistan
152 J10 Qizilrawbe Rus. Kyzylrabat. Bukhoro Wiloyati, C Uzbekistan
Qi Zil Uzun see Qezel Owzan
145 S4 Qizil Yār N Iraq
152 G7 Qizqetkan Rus. Kazanketken. Qoraqalpoghiston Respublikasi, W Uzbekistan
Qoghaly see Kugaly
Qogir Feng see K2

◆ Country ● Country Capital ◇ Dependent Territory ○ Dependent Territory Capital ◈ Administrative Region ✈ International Airport ▲ Mountain ▲▲ Mountain Range ※ Volcano ∼ River ◎ Lake ▣ Reservoir

◆ COUNTRY ● COUNTRY CAPITAL ◇ DEPENDENT TERRITORY ○ DEPENDENT TERRITORY CAPITAL ◆ ADMINISTRATIVE REGION ✈ INTERNATIONAL AIRPORT ▲ MOUNTAIN ▲ MOUNTAIN RANGE ∕ RIVER ⊚ LAKE ⊡ RESERVOIR ☈ VOLCANO

RARAKA – RIBNITZ-DAMGARTEN

203 V10 **Raraka** atoll Îles Tuamotu, C French Polynesia
203 V10 **Raroia** atoll Îles Tuamotu, C French Polynesia
202 H15 **Rarotonga** ✕ Rarotonga, S Cook Islands, C Pacific Ocean
202 H16 **Rarotonga** island S Cook Islands, C Pacific Ocean
153 P12 **Rarz** W Tajikistan
Ras al 'Ain see Ra's al 'Ayn
145 N2 **Ra's al 'Ayn** var. Ras al 'Ain. Al Ḥasakah, N Syria
144 H3 **Ra's al Basīṭ** Al Lādhiqīyah, W Syria
Ra's al-Hafgi see Ra's al Khafjī
147 R5 **Ra's al Khafjī** var. Ra's al-Hafgi. Ash Sharqīyah, NE Saudi Arabia
Ras al-Khaimah/Ras al Khaimah see Ra's al Khaymah
149 R15 **Ra's al Khaymah** var. Ras al Khaimah. Ra's al Khaymah, NE UAE
149 R15 **Ra's al Khaymah** var. Ras al-Khaimah. ✕ Ra's al Khaymah, NE UAE
144 G13 **Ra's an Naqb** Ma'ān, S Jordan
63 B26 **Rasa, Punta** headland E Argentina
176 W10 **Rasawi** Irian Jaya, E Indonesia
Râşcani see Rîşcani
82 J10 **Ras Dashen Terara** ▲ N Ethiopia
157 K19 **Rasdu Atoll** atoll C Maldives
120 E12 **Raseiniai** Raseiniai, C Lithuania
77 X8 **Râs Ghârib** E Egypt
168 D6 **Rashaant** Bayan-Ölgiy, W Mongolia
168 L10 **Rashaant** Dundgovĭ, C Mongolia
168 J6 **Rashaant** Hövsgöl, N Mongolia
145 Y11 **Rashīd** E Iraq
77 V7 **Rashîd** Eng. Rosetta. N Egypt
148 M3 **Rasht** var. Resht. Gīlān, NW Iran
145 S2 **Rashwān** N Iraq
Rasik see Raasiku
115 M15 **Raška** Serbia, C Yugoslavia
121 P15 **Rasna** Rus. Ryasna. Mahilyowskaya Voblasts', E Belarus
118 J12 **Râşnov** prev. Rîşno, Rozsnyó, Hung. Barcarozsnyó. Braşov, C Romania
120 L11 **Rasony** Rus. Rossony. Vitsyebskaya Voblasts', N Belarus
Ra's Shamrah see Ugarit
131 N7 **Rasskazovo** Tambovskaya Oblast', W Russian Federation
121 O16 **Rasta** ≈ E Belarus
Rastadt see Rastatt
Rastâne see Ar Rastān
147 S6 **Ra's Tannūrah** Eng. Ras Tanura. Ash Sharqīyah, NE Saudi Arabia
Ras Tanura see Ra's Tannūrah
103 G21 **Rastatt** var. Rastadt. Baden-Württemberg, SW Germany
Rastenburg see Kętrzyn
155 V7 **Rasūlnagar** Punjab, E Pakistan
201 U6 **Ratak Chain** island group Ratak Chain, E Marshall Islands
121 K15 **Ratamka** Rus. Ratomka. Minskaya Voblasts', C Belarus
95 G17 **Ratan** Jämtland, C Sweden
158 G11 **Ratangarh** Rājasthān, NW India
Rat Buri see Ratchaburi
178 H11 **Ratchaburi** var. Rat Buri. Ratchaburi, W Thailand
31 W15 **Rathbun Lake** ⊠ Iowa, C USA
Ráth Caola see Rathkeale
177 F5 **Rathedaung** Arakan State, W Mynamar
102 M12 **Rathenow** Brandenburg, NE Germany
99 C19 **Rathkeale** Ir. Ráth Caola. SW Ireland
98 F13 **Rathlin Island** Ir. Reachlainn. island N Northern Ireland, UK
99 C20 **Ráthluirc** Ir. An Ráth. SW Ireland
Ratibor see Racibórz
Ratisbon/Ratisbona/Ratisbonne see Regensburg
Rätische Alpen see Rhaetian Alps
40 E17 **Rat Island** island Aleutian Islands, Alaska, USA
40 E17 **Rat Islands** island group Aleutian Islands, Alaska, USA
160 F10 **Ratlām** prev. Rutlam. Madhya Pradesh, C India
161 D15 **Ratnāgiri** Mahārāshtra, W India
161 K26 **Ratnapura** Sabaragamuwa Province, S Sri Lanka
118 J2 **Ratne** Rus. Ratno. Volyns'ka Oblast', NW Ukraine
Ratno see Ratne
Ratomka see Ratamka
39 U8 **Raton** New Mexico, SW USA
145 O7 **Ratqah, Wādī ar** dry watercourse W Iraq
Ratschach see Radeče
178 H17 **Rattaphum** Songkhla, SW Thailand
28 L6 **Rattlesnake Creek** ≈ Kansas, C USA
96 L13 **Rättvik** Kopparberg, C Sweden
102 K9 **Ratzeburg** Mecklenburg-Vorpommern, N Germany
102 K9 **Ratzeburger See** ⊙ N Germany
8 J10 **Ratz, Mount** ▲ British Columbia, SW Canada
63 D22 **Rauch** Buenos Aires, E Argentina
43 U16 **Raudales** Chiapas, SE Mexico
Raudhatain see Ar Rawḍatayn
Raudnitz an der Elbe see Roudnice nad Labem
94 K1 **Raufarhöfn** Nordhurland Eystra, NE Iceland
96 H13 **Raufoss** Oppland, S Norway
Raukawa see Cook Strait
192 Q8 **Raukumara** ▲ North Island, NZ
199 J12 **Raukumara Plain** undersea feature N Coral Sea
192 P8 **Raukumara Range** ▲ North Island, NZ
97 F15 **Rauland** Telemark, S Norway
95 J19 **Rauma** Swe. Raumo. Turku-Pori, SW Finland
96 F10 **Rauma** ≈ S Norway
Raumo see Rauma
120 H8 **Rauna** Cēsis, C Latvia
174 Mm16 **Raung, Gunung** ▲ Jawa, S Indonesia
160 N11 **Raurkela** prev. Rourkela. Orissa, E India
97 J22 **Raus** Malmöhus, S Sweden
172 R6 **Rausu** Hokkaidō, NE Japan
172 R6 **Rausu-dake** ▲ Hokkaidō, NE Japan
95 M17 **Rautalampi** Kuopio, C Finland
95 N16 **Rautavaara** Kuopio, C Finland
118 M9 **Raŭtel** ≈ C Moldova
95 O18 **Rautjärvi** Kymi, SE Finland
Rautu see Sosnovo
203 V11 **Ravahere** atoll Îles Tuamotu, C French Polynesia
109 J25 **Ravanusa** Sicilia, Italy, C Mediterranean Sea
149 S9 **Rāvar** Kermān, C Iran
153 Q11 **Ravat** Oshskaya Oblast', SW Kyrgyzstan
20 K11 **Ravenna** New York, NE USA
108 H10 **Ravenna** Emilia-Romagna, N Italy
31 O15 **Ravenna** Nebraska, C USA
33 U11 **Ravenna** Ohio, N USA
103 I24 **Ravensburg** Baden-Württemberg, S Germany
189 W4 **Ravenshoe** Queensland, NE Australia
188 K13 **Ravensthorpe** Western Australia
23 Q4 **Ravenswood** West Virginia, NE USA
155 U9 **Rāvi** ≈ India/Pakistan
114 C9 **Ravna Gora** Primorje-Gorski Kotar, NW Croatia
111 U10 **Ravne na Koroškem** Ger. Gutenstein. N Slovenia
145 P6 **Rāwah** W Iraq
203 T4 **Rawaki** prev. Phoenix Island. atoll Phoenix Islands, C Kiribati
155 U6 **Rāwalpindi** Punjab, NE Pakistan
112 L13 **Rawa Mazowiecka** Skierniewice, C Poland
145 T2 **Rawāndiz** var. Rawandoz, Rawāndūz. N Iraq
Rawandoz/Rawāndūz see Rawāndiz
176 Vv9 **Rawarra** ≈ Irian Jaya, E Indonesia
176 V9 **Rawas** Irian Jaya, E Indonesia
145 O4 **Rawḍah** ⊙ E Syria
112 G13 **Rawicz** Ger. Rawitsch. Leszno, W Poland
Rawitsch see Rawicz
188 M11 **Rawlinna** Western Australia
35 W16 **Rawlins** Wyoming, C USA
65 K17 **Rawson** Chubut, SE Argentina
165 R16 **Rawu** Xizang Zizhiqu, W China
159 P12 **Raxaul** Bihār, N India
30 K3 **Ray** North Dakota, N USA
174 M9 **Raya, Bukit** ▲ Borneo, C Indonesia
161 I18 **Rāyachoti** Andhra Pradesh, E India
Rāyadrug see Rāyagarha
161 M14 **Rāyagarha** prev. Rāyadrug. Orissa, E India
144 H7 **Rayak** var. Rayaq, Riyāq. E Lebanon
Rayaq see Rayak
145 T2 **Rāyat** E Iraq
174 J10 **Raya, Tanjung** headland Pulau Bangka, W Indonesia
11 R13 **Ray, Cape** headland Newfoundland, Newfoundland and Labrador, E Canada
126 Mm16 **Raychikhinsk** Amurskaya Oblast', SE Russian Federation
131 U5 **Rayevskiy** Respublika Bashkortostan, W Russian Federation
9 Q17 **Raymond** Alberta, SW Canada
24 K6 **Raymond** Mississippi, S USA
34 F9 **Raymond** Washington, NW USA
191 T8 **Raymond Terrace** New South Wales, SE Australia
27 T17 **Raymondville** Texas, SW USA
9 U16 **Raymore** Saskatchewan, S Canada
41 Q8 **Ray Mountains** ▲ Alaska, USA
24 H9 **Rayne** Louisiana, S USA
43 O12 **Rayón** San Luis Potosí, C Mexico
42 G4 **Rayón** Sonora, NW Mexico
178 Hh12 **Rayong** Rayong, S Thailand
27 T5 **Ray Roberts, Lake** ⊠ Texas, SW USA
20 E15 **Raystown Lake** ⊠ Pennsylvania, NE USA
147 V13 **Raysūt** SW Oman
29 R4 **Raytown** Missouri, C USA
24 I5 **Rayville** Louisiana, S USA
148 L5 **Razan** Hamadān, W Iran
145 S9 **Razāzah, Buḥayrat ar** var. Baḥr al Milḥ. ⊙ C Iraq
116 L9 **Razboyna** ▲ E Bulgaria
Razdan see Hrazdan
Razdolnoye see Rozdol'ne
Razelm, Lacul see Razim, Lacul
145 U2 **Razga** E Iraq
116 L8 **Razgrad** Razgradska Oblast, NE Bulgaria
Razgrad see Razgradska Oblast
116 K7 **Razgradska Oblast** var. Razgrad. ◐ province NE Bulgaria
119 N13 **Razim, Lacul** prev. Lacul Razelm. lagoon NW Black Sea
116 G11 **Razlog** Sofiyska Oblast, SW Bulgaria
120 K10 **Rāznas Ezers** ⊙ SE Latvia
104 E6 **Raz, Pointe du** headland NW France
Reachlainn see Rathlin Island
Reachrainn see Lambay Island
99 N22 **Reading** S England, UK
20 H15 **Reading** Pennsylvania, NE USA
50 C7 **Real, Cordillera** ▲ C Ecuador
64 K12 **Realicó** La Pampa, C Argentina
27 R15 **Realitos** Texas, SW USA
110 G9 **Realp** Uri, C Switzerland
178 Ii12 **Reăng Kesei** Bătdâmbâng, W Cambodia
203 Y11 **Reao** atoll Îles Tuamotu, French Polynesia
Reate see Rieti
188 L11 **Rebecca, Lake** ⊙ Western Australia
Rebiana Sand Sea see Rabyānah, Ramlat
128 H8 **Reboly** Respublika Kareliya, NW Russian Federation
172 P1 **Rebun** Rebun-tō, NE Japan
172 P1 **Rebun-suidō** strait E Sea of Japan
172 P1 **Rebun-tō** island NE Japan
108 J12 **Recanati** Marche, C Italy
Rechitsa see Rechytsa
111 Y7 **Rechnitz** Burgenland, SE Austria
121 J20 **Rechytsa** Rus. Rechitsa. Brestskaya Voblasts', SW Belarus
121 O19 **Rechytsa** Rus. Rechitsa. Homyel'skaya Voblasts', SE Belarus
61 Q15 **Recife** prev. Pernambuco. state capital Pernambuco, E Brazil
85 I26 **Recife, Cape** Afr. Kaap Recife. headland S South Africa
Recife, Kaap see Recife, Cape
180 I16 **Récifs, Îles aux** island Inner Islands, NE Seychelles
103 E14 **Recklinghausen** Nordrhein-Westfalen, W Germany
102 M8 **Recknitz** ≈ NE Germany
101 K23 **Recogne** Luxembourg, SE Belgium
63 C15 **Reconquista** Santa Fe, C Argentina
205 O6 **Recovery Glacier** glacier Antarctica
61 G15 **Recreio** Mato Grosso, W Brazil
29 X9 **Rector** Arkansas, C USA
112 E9 **Recz** Ger. Reetz Neumark. Gorzów, NW Poland
101 L24 **Redange** var. Redange-sur-Attert. Diekirch, W Luxembourg
Redange-sur-Attert see Redange
20 C13 **Redbank Creek** ≈ Pennsylvania, NE USA
11 S9 **Red Bay** Québec, E Canada
25 N2 **Red Bay** Alabama, S USA
37 N4 **Red Bluff** California, W USA
26 J8 **Red Bluff Reservoir** ⊠ New Mexico/Texas, SW USA
32 K16 **Red Bud** Illinois, N USA
32 J5 **Red Cedar River** ≈ Wisconsin, N USA
9 R17 **Redcliff** Alberta, SW Canada
85 K17 **Redcliff** Midlands, C Zimbabwe
190 L9 **Red Cliffs** Victoria, SE Australia
31 P17 **Red Cloud** Nebraska, C USA
24 L8 **Red Creek** ≈ Mississippi, S USA
9 P15 **Red Deer** Alberta, SW Canada
9 Q16 **Red Deer** ≈ Alberta, SW Canada
41 O11 **Red Devil** Alaska, USA
37 N3 **Redding** California, W USA
99 L20 **Redditch** W England, UK
31 P9 **Redfield** South Dakota, N USA
26 J12 **Redford** Texas, SW USA
47 V13 **Redhead** Trinidad, Trinidad and Tobago
190 I8 **Red Hill** South Australia
40 F10 **Red Hill** Haw. Pu'u'ula'ula. ▲ Maui, Hawaii, USA, C Pacific Ocean
28 K7 **Red Hills** hill range Kansas, C USA
11 T12 **Red Indian Lake** ⊙ Newfoundland, Newfoundland and Labrador, E Canada
128 J16 **Redkino** Tverskaya Oblast', W Russian Federation
10 A10 **Red Lake** Ontario, C Canada
38 I10 **Red Lake** salt flat Arizona, SW USA
31 S4 **Red Lake Falls** Minnesota, N USA
31 R4 **Red Lake River** ≈ Minnesota, N USA
37 U15 **Redlands** California, W USA
20 G16 **Red Lion** Pennsylvania, NE USA
35 U11 **Red Lodge** Montana, NW USA
34 H13 **Redmond** Oregon, NW USA
38 L5 **Redmond** Utah, W USA
34 H8 **Redmond** Washington, NW USA
Rednitz see Regnitz
31 T15 **Red Oak** Iowa, C USA
20 K12 **Red Oaks Mill** New York, NE USA
104 I7 **Redon** Ille-et-Vilaine, NW France
47 W10 **Redonda** island SW Antigua and Barbuda
106 G4 **Redondela** Galicia, NW Spain
106 H11 **Redondo** Évora, S Portugal
41 Q12 **Redoubt Volcano** ⛰ Alaska, USA
9 Y16 **Red River** ≈ Canada/USA
133 U12 **Red River** var. Yuan, Chin. Yuan Jiang, Vtn. Sông Hông Hà. ≈ China/Vietnam
27 W4 **Red River** ≈ S USA
24 H7 **Red River** ≈ Louisiana, S USA
32 M6 **Red River** ≈ Wisconsin, N USA
Red Rock, Lake see Red Rock Reservoir
31 W14 **Red Rock Reservoir** var. Lake Red Rock. ⊠ Iowa, C USA
194 J5 **Redscar Bay** bay S PNG
82 H7 **Red Sea** ◐ state NE Sudan
77 Y9 **Red Sea** anc. Sinus Arabicus. sea Africa/Asia
23 T11 **Red Springs** North Carolina, SE USA
15 Gg6 **Redstone** ≈ Northwest Territories, NW Canada
9 V17 **Redvers** Saskatchewan, S Canada
79 P13 **Red Volta** var. Nazinon, Fr. Volta Rouge. ≈ Burkina/Ghana
9 Q14 **Redwater** Alberta, SW Canada
30 M16 **Red Willow Creek** ≈ Nebraska, C USA
31 W9 **Red Wing** Minnesota, N USA
37 N9 **Redwood City** California, W USA
31 T9 **Redwood Falls** Minnesota, N USA
198 Ff7 **Reed Bank** undersea feature C South China Sea
33 P7 **Reed City** Michigan, N USA
30 K6 **Reeder** North Dakota, N USA
37 R11 **Reedley** California, W USA
35 T11 **Reedpoint** Montana, NW USA
32 K8 **Reedsburg** Wisconsin, N USA
34 E13 **Reedsport** Oregon, NW USA
195 X8 **Reef Islands** island group Santa Cruz Islands, E Solomon Islands
193 H16 **Reefton** West Coast, South Island, NZ
22 F8 **Reelfoot Lake** ⊙ Tennessee, S USA
99 D17 **Ree, Lough** Ir. Loch Rí. ⊙ C Ireland
Reengus see Rīngas
37 U4 **Reese River** ≈ Nevada, W USA
100 M8 **Reest** ≈ E Netherlands
Reetz Neumark see Recz
143 N13 **Refahiye** Erzincan, C Turkey
25 N4 **Reform** Alabama, S USA
97 K20 **Reftele** Jönköping, S Sweden
27 T14 **Refugio** Texas, SW USA
112 E8 **Rega** ≈ NW Poland
Regar see Tursunzoda
103 O21 **Regen** Bayern, SE Germany
103 M20 **Regen** ≈ SE Germany
103 M21 **Regensburg** Eng. Ratisbon, Fr. Ratisbonne; hist. Ratisbona, anc. Castra Regina, Reginum. Bayern, SE Germany
103 M21 **Regenstauf** Bayern, SE Germany
76 I10 **Reggane** C Algeria
100 N9 **Regge** ≈ E Netherlands
Reggio see Reggio nell' Emilia
Reggio Calabria see Reggio di Calabria
109 M23 **Reggio di Calabria** var. Reggio Calabria, Gk. Rhegion; anc. Regium, Rhegium. Calabria, SW Italy
Reggio Emilia see Reggio nell' Emilia
108 F9 **Reggio nell' Emilia** var. Reggio Emilia, abbrev. Reggio; anc. Regium Lepidum. Emilia-Romagna, N Italy
118 I10 **Reghin** Ger. Sächsisch-Reen, Hung. Szászrégen; prev. Reghinul Săsesc, Ger. Sächsisch-Regen. Mureș, C Romania
Reghinul Săsesc see Reghin
9 U16 **Regina** Saskatchewan, S Canada
9 U16 **Regina** ✕ Saskatchewan, S Canada
57 Z10 **Régina** E French Guiana
9 U16 **Regina Beach** Saskatchewan, S Canada
Reginum see Regensburg
Registan see Rīgestān
62 L11 **Registro** São Paulo, S Brazil
Regium see Reggio di Calabria
Regium Lepidum see Reggio nell' Emilia
103 K19 **Regnitz** var. Rednitz. ≈ SE Germany
42 K10 **Regocijo** Durango, W Mexico
106 H12 **Reguengos de Monsaraz** Évora, S Portugal
103 M18 **Rehau** Bayern, E Germany
85 D19 **Rehoboth** Hardap, C Namibia
Rehoboth/Rehovoth see Reḥovot
23 Z4 **Rehoboth Beach** Delaware, NE USA
144 F10 **Reḥovot** var. Rehoboth, Rehovoth. Central, C Israel
83 J20 **Rei** spring/well S Kenya
Reichenau see Rychnov nad Kněžnou, Czech Republic
Reichenau see Bogatynia, Poland
103 M17 **Reichenbach** var. Reichenbach im Vogtland. Sachsen, E Germany
Reichenbach see Dzierżoniów
Reichenbach im Vogtland see Reichenbach
Reichenberg see Liberec
189 O11 **Reid** Western Australia
25 V6 **Reidsville** Georgia, SE USA
23 T8 **Reidsville** North Carolina, SE USA
Reifnitz see Ribnica
99 O22 **Reigate** SE England, UK
Reikjavik see Reykjavík
104 I10 **Ré, Île de** island W France
39 N15 **Reiley Peak** ▲ Arizona, SW USA
105 Q4 **Reims** Eng. Rheims; anc. Durocortorum, Remi. Marne, N France
65 G23 **Reina Adelaida, Archipiélago** island group S Chile
47 O16 **Reina Beatrix** ✕ (Oranjestad) C Aruba
110 F7 **Reinach** Aargau, W Switzerland
110 E6 **Reinach** Basel-Land, NW Switzerland
66 O11 **Reina Sofía** ✕ (Tenerife) Tenerife, Islas Canarias, Spain, NE Atlantic Ocean
31 W13 **Reinbeck** Iowa, C USA
102 J10 **Reinbek** Schleswig-Holstein, N Germany
9 U12 **Reindeer** ≈ Saskatchewan, C Canada
9 U11 **Reindeer Lake** ⊙ Manitoba/Saskatchewan, C Canada
Reine-Charlotte, Îles de la see Queen Charlotte Islands
Reine-Élisabeth, Îles de la see Queen Elizabeth Islands
96 F13 **Reineskarvet** ▲ S Norway
192 H1 **Reinga, Cape** headland North Island, NZ
107 N3 **Reinosa** Cantabria, N Spain
111 R8 **Reisseck** ▲ S Austria
23 W3 **Reisterstown** Maryland, NE USA
Reisui see Yŏsu
100 N5 **Reitdiep** ≈ NE Netherlands
203 V10 **Reitoru** atoll Îles Tuamotu, C French Polynesia
97 M17 **Rejmyre** Östergötland, S Sweden
Reka see Rijeka
Reka Ili see Ili
97 N16 **Rekarne** Västmanland, C Sweden
15 Ii7 **Reliance** Northwest Territories, C Canada
35 U16 **Reliance** Wyoming, C USA
76 I5 **Relizane** var. Ghelizâne, Ghilizane. NW Algeria
190 I7 **Remarkable, Mount** ▲ South Australia
56 E8 **Remedios** Antioquia, N Colombia
45 Q16 **Remedios** Veraguas, W Panama
44 D8 **Remedios, Punta** headland SW El Salvador
Remi see Reims
101 N25 **Remich** Grevenmacher, SE Luxembourg
101 J19 **Remicourt** Liège, E Belgium
12 H8 **Rémigny, Lac** ⊙ Québec, SE Canada
57 Z10 **Rémire** NE French Guiana
131 N13 **Remontnoye** Rostovskaya Oblast', SW Russian Federation
176 V13 **Remoon** Pulau Kur, E Indonesia
101 L20 **Remouchamps** Liège, E Belgium
105 R15 **Remoulins** Gard, S France
181 X16 **Rempart, Mont du** var. Mount Rempart. hill W Mauritius
103 E15 **Remscheid** Nordrhein-Westfalen, W Germany
31 S12 **Remsen** Iowa, C USA
96 I12 **Rena** Hedmark, S Norway
96 I11 **Rena** ≈ S Norway
Renaix see Ronse
120 H7 **Renceni** Valmiera, N Latvia
120 D9 **Renda** Kuldīga, W Latvia
109 N20 **Rende** Calabria, SW Italy
101 K21 **Rendeux** Luxembourg, SE Belgium
Rendina see Rentína
32 L16 **Rend Lake** ⊠ Illinois, N USA
195 U15 **Rendova** island New Georgia Islands, NW Solomon Islands
102 I8 **Rendsburg** Schleswig-Holstein, N Germany
110 B9 **Renens** Vaud, SW Switzerland
12 K12 **Renfrew** Ontario, SE Canada
98 I12 **Renfrew** cultural region SW Scotland, UK
174 H8 **Rengat** Sumatera, W Indonesia
159 W12 **Rengma Hills** ▲ NE India
64 H12 **Rengo** Libertador, C Chile
118 M12 **Reni** Odes'ka Oblast', SW Ukraine
82 F11 **Renk** Upper Nile, E Sudan
95 L19 **Renko** Häme, SW Finland
100 L12 **Renkum** Gelderland, SE Netherlands
190 K9 **Renmark** South Australia
195 W17 **Rennell** var. Mu Nggava. island S Solomon Islands
189 Q4 **Renner Springs Roadhouse** Northern Territory, N Australia
104 I6 **Rennes** Bret. Roazon; anc. Condate. Ille-et-Vilaine, NW France
205 S16 **Rennick Glacier** glacier Antarctica
9 Y16 **Rennie** Manitoba, S Canada
37 Q5 **Reno** Nevada, W USA
108 H10 **Reno** ≈ N Italy
37 Q5 **Reno-Cannon** ✕ Nevada, W USA
85 F24 **Renoster** ≈ SW South Africa
13 T5 **Renouard, Lac** ⊙ Québec, SE Canada
20 F13 **Renovo** Pennsylvania, NE USA
167 O3 **Renqiu** Hebei, E China
166 I9 **Renshou** Sichuan, C China
33 N12 **Rensselaer** Indiana, N USA
20 L11 **Rensselaer** New York, NE USA
107 Q2 **Rentería** Basq. Errenteria. País Vasco, N Spain
117 E17 **Rentína** var. Rendina. Thessalía, C Greece
31 T9 **Renville** Minnesota, N USA
79 O13 **Réo** W Burkina
13 O12 **Repentigny** Québec, SE Canada
152 K13 **Repetek** Lebapskiy Velayat, E Turkmenistan
95 J16 **Replot** Fin. Raippaluoto. island W Finland
Reppen see Rzepin
Reps see Rupea
29 T7 **Republic** Missouri, C USA
34 K7 **Republic** Washington, NW USA
29 N3 **Republican River** ≈ Kansas/Nebraska, C USA
15 Ll4 **Repulse Bay** Northwest Territories, N Canada
58 F9 **Requena** Loreto, NE Peru
107 R10 **Requena** País Valenciano, E Spain
105 O14 **Réquista** Aveyron, S France
142 M12 **Reşadiye** Tokat, N Turkey
Reschenpass see Resia, Passo di
Reschitza see Reşiţa
115 N20 **Resen** Turk. Resne. SW FYR Macedonia
62 J11 **Reserva** Paraná, S Brazil
9 V15 **Reserve** Saskatchewan, S Canada
39 P13 **Reserve** New Mexico, SW USA
Reshetilovka see Reshetylivka
119 S6 **Reshetylivka** Rus. Reshetilovka. Poltavs'ka Oblast', NE Ukraine
Resht see Rasht
108 F5 **Resia, Passo di** Ger. Reschenpass. pass Austria/Italy
Resicabánya see Reşiţa
64 N7 **Resistencia** Chaco, NE Argentina
118 F12 **Reşiţa** Ger. Reschitza, Hung. Resicabánya. Caraş-Severin, W Romania
Resne see Resen
207 N9 **Resolute** Cornwallis Island, Northwest Territories, N Canada
Resolution see Fort Resolution
16 P4 **Resolution Island** island Northwest Territories, NE Canada
193 A23 **Resolution Island** island SW NZ
13 W7 **Restigouche** Québec, SE Canada
9 W17 **Reston** Manitoba, S Canada
12 H11 **Restoule Lake** ⊙ Ontario, S Canada
56 F10 **Restrepo** Meta, C Colombia
44 B6 **Retalhuleu** Retalhuleu, SW Guatemala
44 A1 **Retalhuleu** off. Departamento de Retalhuleu. ◐ department SW Guatemala
99 N18 **Retford** C England, UK
105 Q3 **Rethel** Ardennes, N France
Rethimno/Réthimnon see Réthymno
117 I25 **Réthymno** var. Rethimno; prev. Réthimnon. Kríti, Greece, E Mediterranean Sea
Retiche, Alpi see Rhaetian Alps
101 J16 **Retie** Antwerpen, N Belgium
113 J21 **Rétság** Nógrád, N Hungary
111 W2 **Retz** Niederösterreich, NE Austria
181 N15 **Réunion** off. La Réunion. ◇ French overseas department W Indian Ocean
132 L17 **Réunion** island W Indian Ocean
107 U6 **Reus** Cataluña, E Spain
101 J15 **Reusel** Noord-Brabant, S Netherlands
110 F7 **Reuss** ≈ NW Switzerland
Reuṭel see Ciuhuru
103 H22 **Reutlingen** Baden-Württemberg, S Germany
110 L7 **Reutte** Tirol, W Austria
101 M16 **Reuver** Limburg, SE Netherlands
30 K7 **Reva** South Dakota, N USA
Reval/Revel' see Tallinn
128 J4 **Revda** Murmanskaya Oblast', NW Russian Federation
125 Ee11 **Revda** Sverdlovskaya Oblast', C Russian Federation
105 N16 **Revel** Haute-Garonne, S France
9 O16 **Revelstoke** British Columbia, SW Canada
45 N13 **Reventazón, Río** ≈ E Costa Rica
108 G9 **Revere** Lombardia, N Italy
41 Y14 **Revillagigedo Island** island Alexander Archipelago, Alaska, USA
105 R3 **Revin** Ardennes, N France
94 O3 **Revnosa** headland C Svalbard
Revolyutsii, Pik see Revolyutsiya, Qullai
153 T13 **Revolyutsiya, Qullai** Rus. Pik Revolyutsii. ▲ SE Tajikistan
113 L19 **Revúca** Ger. Grossrauschenbach, Hung. Nagyrőce. Východné Slovensko, E Slovakia
160 K9 **Rewa** Madhya Pradesh, C India
158 I11 **Rewāri** Haryāna, N India
35 R14 **Rexburg** Idaho, NW USA
80 G13 **Rey Bouba** Nord, NE Cameroon
94 L3 **Reydharfjördhur** Austurland, E Iceland
59 K16 **Reyes** Beni, NW Bolivia
36 L8 **Reyes, Point** headland California, W USA
56 B12 **Reyes, Punta** headland SW Colombia
142 L17 **Reyhanlı** Hatay, S Turkey
45 U16 **Rey, Isla del** island Archipiélago de las Perlas, SE Panama
94 H2 **Reykhólar** Vestfirdhir, W Iceland
94 K2 **Reykjahlídh** Nordhurland Eystra, NE Iceland
94 I4 **Reykjanes** ◐ region SW Iceland
207 O16 **Reykjanes Basin** var. Irminger Basin. undersea feature N Atlantic Ocean
207 N17 **Reykjanes Ridge** undersea feature N Atlantic Ocean
94 H4 **Reykjavík** var. Reikjavik. ● (Iceland) Höfudhborgarsvaedhi, W Iceland
20 D13 **Reynoldsville** Pennsylvania, NE USA
43 P8 **Reynosa** Tamaulipas, C Mexico
Reẓā'īyeh see Orūmīyeh
Reẓā'īyeh, Daryācheh-ye see Orūmīyeh, Daryācheh-ye
104 I8 **Rezé** Loire-Atlantique, NW France
120 K10 **Rēzekne** Ger. Rositten; prev. Rus. Rezhitsa. Rēzekne, SE Latvia
Rezhitsa see Rēzekne
119 N9 **Rezina** NE Moldova
116 N11 **Rezovo** Turk. Rezve. Burgaska Oblast, SE Bulgaria
116 N11 **Rezovska Reka** Turk. Rezve Deresi. ≈ Bulgaria/Turkey see also Rezve Deresi
Rezve see Rezovo
116 N11 **Rezve Deresi** Bul. Rezovska Reka. ≈ Bulgaria/Turkey see also Rezovska Reka
Rhadames see Ghadāmis
Rhaedestus see Tekirdağ
110 J10 **Rhaetian Alps** Fr. Alpes Rhétiques, Ger. Rätische Alpen, It. Alpi Retiche. ▲ C Europe
110 I8 **Rhätikon** ▲ C Europe
103 G14 **Rheda-Wiedenbrück** Nordrhein-Westfalen, W Germany
100 M12 **Rheden** Gelderland, E Netherlands
Rhegion/Rhegium see Reggio di Calabria
Rheims see Reims
Rhein see Rhine
103 E17 **Rheinbach** Nordrhein-Westfalen, W Germany
102 F13 **Rheine** var. Rheine in Westfalen. Nordrhein-Westfalen, NW Germany
Rheine in Westfalen see Rheine
Rheinfeld see Rheinfelden
103 F24 **Rheinfelden** Baden-Württemberg, S Germany
110 E6 **Rheinfelden** var. Rheinfeld. Aargau, N Switzerland
103 E17 **Rheinisches Schiefergebirge** var. Rhine State Uplands, Eng. Rhenish Slate Mountains. ▲ W Germany
103 D18 **Rheinland-Pfalz** Eng. Rhineland-Palatinate, Fr. Rhénanie-Palatinat. ◐ state W Germany
103 G18 **Rhein/Main** ✕ (Frankfurt am Main) Hessen, W Germany
Rhénanie du Nord-Westphalie see Nordrhein-Westfalen
Rhénanie-Palatinat see Rheinland-Pfalz
100 K12 **Rhenen** Utrecht, C Netherlands
Rhenish Slate Mountains see Rheinisches Schiefergebirge
Rhétiques, Alpes see Rhaetian Alps
102 N10 **Rhin** ≈ NE Germany
Rhin see Rhine
86 F10 **Rhine** Dut. Rijn, Fr. Rhin, Ger. Rhein. ≈ W Europe
32 L5 **Rhinelander** Wisconsin, N USA
Rhineland-Palatinate see Rheinland-Pfalz
Rhine State Uplands see Rheinisches Schiefergebirge
102 N11 **Rhinkanal** canal NE Germany
83 F17 **Rhino Camp** NW Uganda
76 D7 **Rhir, Cap** headland W Morocco
108 D7 **Rho** Lombardia, N Italy
21 N12 **Rhode Island** off. State of Rhode Island and Providence Plantations; also known as Little Rhody, Ocean State. ◐ state NE USA
21 O13 **Rhode Island** island Rhode Island, NE USA
21 O13 **Rhode Island Sound** sound Maine/Rhode Island, NE USA
Rhodes see Ródos
Rhode-Saint-Genèse see Sint-Genesius-Rode
86 L14 **Rhodes Basin** undersea feature E Mediterranean Sea
Rhodesia see Zimbabwe
116 I12 **Rhodope Mountains** var. Rodhópi Óri, Bul. Rhodope Planina, Rodopi, Gk. Orosirá Rodhópis, Turk. Dospad Dagh. ▲ Bulgaria/Greece
Rhodope Planina see Rhodope Mountains
Rhodos see Ródos
103 I18 **Rhön** ▲ C Germany
99 J21 **Rhondda** S Wales, UK
105 Q10 **Rhône** ◐ department E France
88 C12 **Rhône** ≈ France/Switzerland
105 R12 **Rhône-Alpes** ◐ region E France
123 J6 **Rhône Fan** undersea feature W Mediterranean Sea
100 G13 **Rhoon** Zuid-Holland, SW Netherlands
98 G9 **Rhum** var. Rum. island W Scotland, UK
Rhuthun see Ruthin
99 J18 **Rhyl** NE Wales, UK
61 K18 **Rialma** Goiás, S Brazil
106 L3 **Riaño** Castilla-León, N Spain
107 O9 **Riansáres** ≈ C Spain
158 H6 **Riāsi** Jammu and Kashmir, NW India
174 Gg7 **Riau** off. Propinsi Riau. ◐ province W Indonesia
Riau Archipelago see Riau, Kepulauan
174 I8 **Riau, Kepulauan** var. Riau Archipelago, Dut. Riouw-Archipel. island group W Indonesia
107 O6 **Riaza** Castilla-León, N Spain
107 N6 **Riaza** ≈ N Spain
83 K17 **Riba** spring/well NE Kenya
106 H4 **Ribadavia** Galicia, NW Spain
106 J2 **Ribadeo** Galicia, NW Spain
106 L2 **Ribadesella** Asturias, N Spain
106 G10 **Ribatejo** former province C Portugal
149 Q8 **Ribāṭ-e Rizāb** Yazd, C Iran
85 P15 **Ribáuè** Nampula, N Mozambique
99 K17 **Ribble** ≈ NW England, UK
97 F23 **Ribe** Ribe, W Denmark
97 F23 **Ribe** off. Ribe Amt, var. Ripen. ◐ county W Denmark
106 G3 **Ribeira** Galicia, NW Spain
66 O5 **Ribeira Brava** Madeira, Portugal, NE Atlantic Ocean
66 P3 **Ribeira Grande** São Miguel, Azores, Portugal, NE Atlantic Ocean
62 L8 **Ribeirão Preto** São Paulo, S Brazil
62 L11 **Ribeira, Rio** ≈ S Brazil
109 I24 **Ribera** Sicilia, Italy, C Mediterranean Sea
59 L14 **Riberalta** Beni, N Bolivia
107 W4 **Ribes de Freser** Cataluña, NE Spain
32 L6 **Rib Mountain** ▲ Wisconsin, N USA
111 U12 **Ribnica** Ger. Reifnitz. S Slovenia
119 N9 **Ribniţa** var. Râbniţa, Rus. Rybnitsa. NE Moldova
102 M8 **Ribnitz-Damgarten** Mecklenburg-Vorpommern, NE Germany

◆ Country ● Country Capital ◇ Dependent Territory ○ Dependent Territory Capital ◐ Administrative Region ✕ International Airport ▲ Mountain ▲ Mountain Range ⛰ Volcano ≈ River ⊙ Lake ⊠ Reservoir

Říčany – Rømø

113 D16 **Říčany** *Ger.* Ritschan. Střední Čechy, W Czech Republic
31 U7 **Rice** Minnesota, N USA
32 J5 **Rice Lake** Wisconsin, N USA
12 I15 **Rice Lake** ◎ Ontario, SE Canada
12 E8 **Rice Lake** ◎ Ontario, S Canada
25 V3 **Richard B.Russell Lake** ▣ Georgia, SE USA
27 U6 **Richardson** Texas, SW USA
9 R11 **Richardson** 〰 Alberta, C Canada
8 I3 **Richardson Mountains** ▲▲ Yukon Territory, NW Canada
193 C21 **Richardson Mountains** ▲▲ South Island, NZ
44 F3 **Richardson Peak** ▲ SE Belize
78 G10 **Richard Toll** N Senegal
30 L5 **Richardton** North Dakota, N USA
12 F13 **Rich, Cape** *headland* Ontario, S Canada
104 L8 **Richelieu** Indre-et-Loire, C France
35 P15 **Richfield** Idaho, NW USA
38 K5 **Richfield** Utah, W USA
20 J10 **Richfield Springs** New York, NE USA
20 M6 **Richford** Vermont, NE USA
29 R6 **Rich Hill** Missouri, C USA
11 P14 **Richibucto** New Brunswick, SE Canada
110 G8 **Richisau** Glarus, NE Switzerland
25 S6 **Richland** Georgia, SE USA
29 U6 **Richland** Missouri, C USA
27 U8 **Richland** Texas, SW USA
34 K10 **Richland** Washington, NW USA
32 K8 **Richland Center** Wisconsin, N USA
23 W11 **Richlands** North Carolina, SE USA
23 Q7 **Richlands** Virginia, NE USA
27 R9 **Richland Springs** Texas, SW USA
191 S8 **Richmond** New South Wales, SE Australia
8 L17 **Richmond** British Columbia, SW Canada
12 L13 **Richmond** Ontario, SE Canada
13 Q12 **Richmond** Québec, SE Canada
193 I14 **Richmond** Tasman, South Island, NZ
37 N8 **Richmond** California, W USA
33 Q14 **Richmond** Indiana, N USA
22 M6 **Richmond** Kentucky, S USA
29 S4 **Richmond** Missouri, C USA
27 V11 **Richmond** Texas, SW USA
38 L1 **Richmond** Utah, W USA
23 W6 **Richmond** *state capital* Virginia, NE USA
12 H15 **Richmond Hill** Ontario, S Canada
193 J15 **Richmond Range** ▲▲ South Island, NZ
29 S12 **Rich Mountain** ▲ Arkansas, C USA
33 S13 **Richwood** Ohio, N USA
23 R5 **Richwood** West Virginia, NE USA
106 K5 **Ricobayo, Embalse de** ▣ NW Spain
Ricomagus *see* Riom
Ridā' *see* Radā'
100 H13 **Ridderkerk** Zuid-Holland, SW Netherlands
35 N16 **Riddle** Idaho, NW USA
34 F14 **Riddle** Oregon, NW USA
12 L13 **Rideau** 〰 Ontario, SE Canada
37 T12 **Ridgecrest** California, W USA
20 L13 **Ridgefield** Connecticut, NE USA
24 K5 **Ridgeland** Mississippi, S USA
23 R15 **Ridgeland** South Carolina, SE USA
22 F8 **Ridgely** Tennessee, S USA
12 D17 **Ridgetown** Ontario, S Canada
Ridgeway *see* Ridgway
23 R12 **Ridgeway** South Carolina, SE USA
20 D13 **Ridgway** *var.* Ridgeway. Pennsylvania, NE USA
9 W16 **Riding Mountain** ▲▲ Manitoba, S Canada
Ried *see* Ried im Innkreis
111 R4 **Ried im Innkreis** *var.* Ried. Oberösterreich, NW Austria
111 X8 **Riegersburg** Steiermark, SE Austria
110 E6 **Riehen** Basel-Stadt, NW Switzerland
101 K18 **Riemst** Limburg, NE Belgium
94 J9 **Rieppe** ▲ N Norway
103 O15 **Riesa** Sachsen, E Germany
65 H24 **Riesco, Isla** *island* S Chile
109 K25 **Riesi** Sicilia, Italy, C Mediterranean Sea
85 F25 **Riet** 〰 SW South Africa
85 I23 **Riet** 〰 SW South Africa
120 D11 **Rietavas** Plungė, W Lithuania
85 F19 **Rietfontein** Omaheke, E Namibia
109 I14 **Rieti** *anc.* Reate. Lazio, C Italy
86 D14 **Rif** *var.* Er Rif, Er Riff, Riff. ▲▲ N Morocco
Riff *see* Rif
39 Q4 **Rifle** Colorado, C USA
33 R7 **Rifle River** 〰 Michigan, N USA
83 H18 **Rift Valley** ◈ *province* Kenya
Rift Valley *see* Great Rift Valley
120 F9 **Rīga** *Eng.* Riga. ● (Latvia) Rīga, C Latvia
Rigaer Bucht *see* Riga, Gulf of
120 F6 **Riga, Gulf of** *Est.* Liivi Laht, *Ger.* Rigaer Bucht, *Latv.* Rīgas Jūras Līcis, *Rus.* Rizhskiy Zaliv; prev. *Est.* Riia Laht. *gulf* Estonia/Latvia
149 U12 **Rīgān** Kermān, SE Iran
Rīgas Jūras Līcis *see* Riga, Gulf of
13 N12 **Rigaud** 〰 Ontario/Québec, SE Canada
35 R14 **Rigby** Idaho, NW USA
154 M10 **Rīgestān** *var.* Registan. *desert region* S Afghanistan
34 M11 **Riggins** Idaho, NW USA
11 R8 **Rigolet** Newfoundland and Labrador, NE Canada
80 G9 **Rig-Rig** Kanem, W Chad
120 F4 **Riguldi** Läänemaa, W Estonia
Riia Laht *see* Riga, Gulf of
95 L19 **Riihimäki** Häme, S Finland
205 O2 **Riiser-Larsen Ice Shelf** *ice shelf* Antarctica
205 U2 **Riiser-Larsen Peninsula** *peninsula* Antarctica
67 P22 **Riiser-Larsen Sea** *sea* Antarctica
42 D2 **Riíto** Sonora, NW Mexico
114 B9 **Rijeka** *Ger.* Sankt Veit am Flaum, *It.* Fiume, *Slvn.* Reka; *anc.* Tarsatica. Primorje-Gorski Kotar, NW Croatia
101 I14 **Rijen** Noord-Brabant, S Netherlands
101 H15 **Rijkevorsel** Antwerpen, N Belgium
Rijn *see* Rhine
100 G11 **Rijnsburg** Zuid-Holland, W Netherlands
Rijssel *see* Lille
100 N10 **Rijssen** Overijssel, E Netherlands
100 G12 **Rijswijk** *Eng.* Ryswick. Zuid-Holland, W Netherlands
94 I10 **Riksgränsen** Norrbotten, N Sweden
172 Q6 **Rikubetsu** Hokkaidō, NE Japan
171 Mm12 **Rikuzen-Takata** Iwate, Honshū, C Japan
29 O4 **Riley** Kansas, C USA
101 I17 **Rillaar** Vlaams Brabant, C Belgium
Rí, Loch *see* Ree, Lough
116 G11 **Rilska Reka** 〰 W Bulgaria
79 T12 **Rima** 〰 N Nigeria
147 N7 **Rimah, Wādī ar** *var.* Wādī ar Rummah. *dry watercourse* C Saudi Arabia
Rimaszombat *see* Rimavská Sobota
203 R12 **Rimatara** *island* Îles Australes, SW French Polynesia
113 L20 **Rimavská Sobota** *Ger.* Gross-Steffelsdorf, *Hung.* Rimaszombat. Stredné Slovensko, SE Slovakia
9 Q15 **Rimbey** Alberta, SW Canada
97 P15 **Rimbo** Stockholm, C Sweden
97 M18 **Rimforsa** Östergötland, S Sweden
108 I11 **Rimini** *anc.* Ariminum. Emilia-Romagna, N Italy
Rîmnicu-Sărat *see* Râmnicu Sărat
Rîmnicu Vîlcea *see* Râmnicu Vâlcea
155 Y3 **Rimo Muztāgh** ▲▲ India/Pakistan
13 U7 **Rimouski** Québec, SE Canada
164 M16 **Rinbung** Xizang Zizhiqu, W China
168 I5 **Rinchinlhümbe** Hövsgöl, N Mongolia
64 I5 **Rincón, Cerro** ▲ N Chile
106 M15 **Rincón de la Victoria** Andalucía, S Spain
Rincón del Bonete, Lago Artificial de *see* Río Negro, Embalse del
107 Q4 **Rincón de Soto** La Rioja, N Spain
96 G8 **Rindal** Møre og Romsdal, S Norway
117 J20 **Ríneia** *island* Kykládes, Greece, Aegean Sea
158 H11 **Rīngas** *prev.* Reengus, Rīngus. Rājasthān, N India
97 H24 **Ringe** Fyn, C Denmark
96 H11 **Ringebu** Oppland, S Norway
Ringen *see* Rõngu
195 U14 **Ringgi** Kolombangara Island, NW Solomon Islands
25 R1 **Ringgold** Georgia, SE USA
24 G5 **Ringgold** Louisiana, S USA
27 S5 **Ringgold** Texas, SW USA
97 E22 **Ringkøbing** Ringkøbing, W Denmark
97 E21 **Ringkøbing** *off.* Ringkøbing Amt. ◈ *county* W Denmark
97 E22 **Ringkøbing Fjord** *fjord* W Denmark
35 S10 **Ringling** Montana, NW USA
29 N13 **Ringling** Oklahoma, C USA
96 H13 **Ringsaker** Hedmark, S Norway
97 I23 **Ringsted** Vestsjælland, E Denmark
Rīngus *see* Rīngas
94 I9 **Ringvassøy** *island* N Norway
20 K13 **Ringwood** New Jersey, NE USA
Rinn Duáin *see* Hook Head
102 H13 **Rinteln** Niedersachsen, NW Germany
Rio *see* Rio de Janeiro
117 E18 **Río** Dytikí Ellás, S Greece
58 C7 **Riobamba** Chimborazo, C Ecuador
62 P9 **Rio Bonito** Rio de Janeiro, SE Brazil
61 C16 **Rio Branco** *state capital* Acre, W Brazil
63 H18 **Río Branco** Cerro Largo, NE Uruguay
Rio Branco, Território de *see* Roraima
43 P8 **Río Bravo** Tamaulipas, C Mexico
65 G16 **Río Bueno** Los Lagos, C Chile
57 P5 **Río Caribe** Sucre, NE Venezuela
56 M5 **Río Chico** Miranda, N Venezuela
65 H18 **Río Cisnes** Aisén, S Chile
62 L9 **Rio Claro** São Paulo, S Brazil
47 V14 **Rio Claro** Trinidad, Trinidad and Tobago
56 J5 **Río Claro** Lara, N Venezuela
65 K15 **Rio Colorado** Río Negro, E Argentina
64 K11 **Río Cuarto** Córdoba, C Argentina
62 P10 **Rio de Janeiro** *var.* Rio. *state capital* Rio de Janeiro, SE Brazil
62 P9 **Rio de Janeiro** *off.* Estado do Rio de Janeiro. ◈ *state* SE Brazil
45 R17 **Río de Jesús** Veraguas, S Panama
36 K3 **Rio Dell** California, W USA
62 K13 **Rio do Sul** Santa Catarina, S Brazil
65 I23 **Río Gallegos** *var.* Gallegos, Puerto Gallegos. Santa Cruz, S Argentina
63 I18 **Rio Grande** *var.* São Pedro do Rio Grande do Sul. Rio Grande do Sul, S Brazil
26 I9 **Rio Grande** 〰 Texas, SW USA
65 J24 **Río Grande** Tierra del Fuego, S Argentina
42 L10 **Río Grande** Zacatecas, C Mexico
44 J9 **Río Grande** León, NW Nicaragua
47 V5 **Río Grande** E Puerto Rico
27 R17 **Rio Grande City** Texas, SW USA
61 P14 **Rio Grande do Norte** *off.* Estado do Rio Grande do Norte. ◈ *state* E Brazil
63 G15 **Rio Grande do Sul** *off.* Estado do Rio Grande do Sul. ◈ *state* S Brazil
67 M17 **Rio Grande Fracture Zone** *tectonic feature* C Atlantic Ocean
67 J18 **Rio Grande Gap** *undersea feature* S Atlantic Ocean
Rio Grande Plateau *see* Rio Grande Rise
67 J18 **Rio Grande Rise** *var.* Rio Grande Plateau. *undersea feature* SW Atlantic Ocean
56 G4 **Ríohacha** La Guajira, N Colombia
45 S16 **Río Hato** Coclé, C Panama
27 T17 **Rio Hondo** Texas, SW USA
58 D10 **Rioja** San Martín, N Peru
43 Y11 **Río Lagartos** Yucatán, SE Mexico
105 P11 **Riom** *anc.* Ricomagus. Puy-de-Dôme, C France
106 F10 **Rio Maior** Santarém, C Portugal
105 O12 **Riom-ès-Montagnes** Cantal, C France
62 J12 **Rio Negro** Paraná, S Brazil
65 I15 **Río Negro** *off.* Provincia de Río Negro. ◈ *province* C Argentina
63 D18 **Río Negro** ◈ *department* W Uruguay
49 V12 **Río Negro, Embalse del** *var.* Lago Artificial de Rincón del Bonete. ▣ C Uruguay
109 M17 **Rionero in Vulture** Basilicata, S Italy
143 S9 **Rioni** 〰 W Georgia
107 P12 **Riópar** Castilla-La Mancha, C Spain
63 H16 **Rio Pardo** Rio Grande do Sul, S Brazil
39 R11 **Rio Rancho Estates** New Mexico, SW USA
44 L11 **Río San Juan** ◈ *department* S Nicaragua
56 E9 **Ríosucio** Caldas, W Colombia
56 C7 **Ríosucio** Chocó, NW Colombia
64 K10 **Río Tercero** Córdoba, C Argentina
56 J5 **Río Tocuyo** Lara, N Venezuela
Riouw-Archipel *see* Riau, Kepulauan
61 J19 **Rio Verde** Goiás, C Brazil
43 O12 **Río Verde** *var.* Rioverde. San Luis Potosí, C Mexico
37 O8 **Rio Vista** California, W USA
114 M11 **Ripanj** Serbia, N Yugoslavia
108 J13 **Ripatransone** Marche, C Italy
Ripen *see* Ribe
24 M2 **Ripley** Mississippi, S USA
33 R15 **Ripley** Ohio, N USA
22 F9 **Ripley** Tennessee, S USA
23 Q4 **Ripley** West Virginia, NE USA
107 W4 **Ripoll** Cataluña, NE Spain
99 M16 **Ripon** N England, UK
32 M7 **Ripon** Wisconsin, N USA
109 L24 **Riposto** Sicilia, Italy, C Mediterranean Sea
101 L14 **Rips** Noord-Brabant, SE Netherlands
56 D9 **Risaralda** *off.* Departamento de Risaralda. ◈ *province* C Colombia
118 L8 **Rîşcani** *var.* Râşcani, *Rus.* Ryshkany. NW Moldova
158 J9 **Rishikesh** Uttar Pradesh, N India
172 P2 **Rishiri-suidō** *strait* E Sea of Japan
172 Oo2 **Rishiri-tō** *var.* Risiri Tô. *island* NE Japan
172 P2 **Rishiri-yama** ⛰ Rishiri-tō, NE Japan
27 R7 **Rising Star** Texas, SW USA
33 Q15 **Rising Sun** Indiana, N USA
Risiri Tô *see* Rishiri-tō
104 L4 **Risle** 〰 N France
Rîşno *see* Râşnov
29 V13 **Rison** Arkansas, C USA
97 G17 **Risør** Aust-Agder, S Norway
94 H10 **Risøyhamn** Nordland, C Norway
103 I23 **Riss** 〰 S Germany
120 G4 **Risti** *Ger.* Kreuz. Läänemaa, W Estonia
13 V8 **Ristigouche** 〰 Québec, SE Canada
95 N18 **Ristiina** Mikkeli, SE Finland
95 N14 **Ristijärvi** Oulu, C Finland
196 C14 **Ritidian Point** *headland* N Guam
Ritschan *see* Říčany
37 R9 **Ritter, Mount** ▲ California, W USA
33 T12 **Rittman** Ohio, N USA
34 L9 **Ritzville** Washington, NW USA
108 F7 **Riva** *var.* Riva del Garda. Trentino-Alto Adige, N Italy
63 A21 **Rivadavia** Buenos Aires, E Argentina
Riva del Garda *see* Riva
108 B8 **Rivarolo Canavese** Piemonte, W Italy
44 K11 **Rivas** Rivas, SW Nicaragua
44 J11 **Rivas** ◈ *department* SW Nicaragua
105 R11 **Rive-de-Gier** Loire, E France
63 A22 **Rivera** Buenos Aires, E Argentina
63 F16 **Rivera** Rivera, NE Uruguay
63 F17 **Rivera** ◈ *department* NE Uruguay
37 P9 **Riverbank** California, W USA
78 K17 **River Cess** SW Liberia
30 M4 **Riverdale** North Dakota, N USA
32 I6 **River Falls** Wisconsin, N USA
9 T16 **Riverhurst** Saskatchewan, S Canada
191 O10 **Riverina** *physical region* New South Wales, SE Australia
82 G8 **River Nile** ◈ *state* NE Sudan
65 F19 **Rivero, Isla** *island* Archipiélago de los Chonos, S Chile
9 W16 **Rivers** Manitoba, S Canada
79 U17 **Rivers** ◈ *state* S Nigeria
193 D23 **Riversdale** Southland, South Island, NZ
85 F26 **Riversdale** Western Cape, SW South Africa
37 U15 **Riverside** California, W USA
27 W9 **Riverside** Texas, SW USA
39 U3 **Riverside Reservoir** ▣ Colorado, C USA
8 K15 **Rivers Inlet** British Columbia, SW Canada
8 K15 **Rivers Inlet** *inlet* British Columbia, SW Canada
9 X15 **Riverton** Manitoba, S Canada
193 C24 **Riverton** Southland, South Island, NZ
32 L13 **Riverton** Illinois, N USA
38 L3 **Riverton** Utah, W USA
35 V15 **Riverton** Wyoming, C USA
12 G10 **River Valley** Ontario, S Canada
11 P14 **Riverview** New Brunswick, SE Canada
105 O17 **Rivesaltes** Pyrénées-Orientales, S France
38 H11 **Riviera** Arizona, SW USA
27 S15 **Riviera** Texas, SW USA
25 Z14 **Riviera Beach** Florida, SE USA
13 Q10 **Rivière-à-Pierre** Québec, SE Canada
13 T9 **Rivière-Bleue** Québec, SE Canada
13 T8 **Rivière-du-Loup** Québec, SE Canada
181 Y15 **Rivière du Rempart** NE Mauritius
47 R12 **Rivière-Pilote** S Martinique
181 O17 **Rivière St-Etienne, Point de la** *headland* SW Réunion
11 S10 **Rivière-St-Paul** Québec, E Canada
Rivière Sèche *see* Bel Air
118 K4 **Rivne** *Pol.* Równe, *Rus.* Rovno. Rivnens'ka Oblast', NW Ukraine
Rivne *see* Rivnens'ka Oblast'
118 K3 **Rivnens'ka Oblast'** *var.* Rivne, *Rus.* Rovenskaya Oblast'. ◈ *province* NW Ukraine
108 B8 **Rivoli** Piemonte, NW Italy
165 Q14 **Riwoqê** Xizang Zizhiqu, W China
101 H19 **Rixensart** Walloon Brabant, C Belgium
Riyadh/Riyāḍ, Minṭaqat ar *see* Ar Riyāḍ
Riyāq *see* Rayak
Rizaiyeh *see* Orūmīyeh
143 P11 **Rize** Rize, NE Turkey
143 P11 **Rize** *prev.* Çoruh. ◈ *province* NE Turkey
167 R5 **Rizhao** Shandong, E China
Rizhskiy Zaliv *see* Riga, Gulf of
Rizokarpaso/Rizokárpason *see* Dipkarpaz
109 O21 **Rizzuto, Capo** *headland* S Italy
97 F15 **Rjukan** Telemark, S Norway
97 D16 **Rjuven** ▲▲ S Norway
78 H9 **Rkîz** Trarza, W Mauritania
97 H14 **Roa** Oppland, S Norway
107 N5 **Roa** Castilla-León, N Spain
47 T9 **Road Town** ○ (British Virgin Islands) Tortola, C British Virgin Islands
98 F6 **Roag, Loch** *inlet* NW Scotland, UK
39 O5 **Roan Cliffs** *cliff* Colorado/Utah, W USA
23 P9 **Roan High Knob** *var.* Roan Mountain. ▲ North Carolina/Tennessee, SE USA
Roan Mountain *see* Roan High Knob
105 Q10 **Roanne** *anc.* Rodunma. Loire, E France
25 R4 **Roanoke** Alabama, S USA
23 S7 **Roanoke** Virginia, NE USA
23 Z9 **Roanoke Island** *island* North Carolina, SE USA
23 W8 **Roanoke Rapids** North Carolina, SE USA
23 X9 **Roanoke River** 〰 North Carolina/Virginia, SE USA
39 O4 **Roan Plateau** *plain* Utah, W USA
39 R5 **Roaring Fork River** 〰 Colorado, C USA
27 O5 **Roaring Springs** Texas, SW USA
44 J4 **Roatán** *var.* Coxen Hole, Coxin Hole. Islas de la Bahía, N Honduras
44 I4 **Roatán, Isla de** *island* Islas de la Bahía, N Honduras
Roat Kampuchea *see* Cambodia
Roazon *see* Rennes
149 T7 **Robāṭ-e Chāh Gonbad** Khorāsān, E Iran
149 R7 **Robāṭ-e Khān** Khorāsān, C Iran
149 T7 **Robāṭ-e Khvosh Āb** Khorāsān, E Iran
149 R8 **Robāṭ-e Posht-e Bādām** Khorāsān, NE Iran
183 S8 **Robbie Ridge** *undersea feature* W Pacific Ocean
23 T10 **Robbins** North Carolina, SE USA
191 N15 **Robbins Island** *island* Tasmania, SE Australia
23 N10 **Robbinsville** North Carolina, SE USA
190 J12 **Robe** South Australia
23 W9 **Robersonville** North Carolina, SE USA
27 P8 **Robert Lee** Texas, SW USA
37 V5 **Roberts Creek Mountain** ▲ Nevada, W USA
95 J15 **Robertsfors** Västerbotten, N Sweden
29 R11 **Robert S.Kerr Reservoir** ▣ Oklahoma, C USA
40 L12 **Roberts Mountain** ▲ Nunivak Island, Alaska, USA
85 F26 **Robertson** Western Cape, SW South Africa
204 H4 **Robertson Island** *island* Antarctica
78 J16 **Robertsport** W Liberia
190 J8 **Robertstown** South Australia
Robert Williams *see* Caála
13 P7 **Roberval** Québec, SE Canada
33 N15 **Robinson** Illinois, N USA
200 Oo12 **Róbinson Crusoe, Isla** *island* Islas Juan Fernández, Chile, E Pacific Ocean
188 J9 **Robinson Range** ▲▲ Western Australia
194 L16 **Robinson River** Central, S PNG
190 M9 **Robinvale** Victoria, SE Australia
107 P11 **Robledo** Castilla-La Mancha, C Spain
56 G5 **Robles** *var.* La Paz, Robles La Paz. Cesar, N Colombia
Robles La Paz *see* Robles
9 V15 **Roblin** Manitoba, S Canada
195 U13 **Rob Roy** *island* NW Solomon Islands
9 S17 **Robsart** Saskatchewan, S Canada
9 N15 **Robson, Mount** ▲ British Columbia, SW Canada
27 T14 **Robstown** Texas, SW USA
27 P6 **Roby** Texas, SW USA
106 E11 **Roca, Cabo da** *headland* C Portugal
Rocadas *see* Xangongo
43 S14 **Roca Partida, Punta** *headland* C Mexico
49 X6 **Rocas, Atol das** *island* E Brazil
109 L18 **Roccadaspide** *var.* Rocca d'Aspide. Campania, S Italy
109 K15 **Roccaraso** Abruzzi, C Italy
108 H10 **Rocca San Casciano** Emilia-Romagna, C Italy
108 G13 **Roccastrada** Toscana, C Italy
63 G20 **Rocha** Rocha, E Uruguay
63 G19 **Rocha** ◈ *department* E Uruguay
99 L17 **Rochdale** NW England, UK
104 L11 **Rochechouart** Haute-Vienne, C France
101 J22 **Rochefort** Namur, SE Belgium
104 J11 **Rochefort** *var.* Rochefort sur Mer. Charente-Maritime, W France
Rochefort sur Mer *see* Rochefort
129 N10 **Rochegda** Arkhangel'skaya Oblast', NW Russian Federation
32 L10 **Rochelle** Illinois, N USA
27 Q9 **Rochelle** Texas, SW USA
11 P13 **Rocher Percé** *island* Rocher Percé, Québec, E Canada
13 V3 **Rochers Ouest, Rivière aux** 〰 Québec, SE Canada
99 O22 **Rochester** *anc.* Durobrivae. SE England, UK
33 O12 **Rochester** Indiana, N USA
31 W10 **Rochester** Minnesota, N USA
21 O9 **Rochester** New Hampshire, NE USA
20 F9 **Rochester** New York, NE USA
27 P5 **Rochester** Texas, SW USA
33 S9 **Rochester Hills** Michigan, N USA
Rocheuses, Montagnes/Rockies *see* Rocky Mountains
66 M6 **Rockall** *island* UK, N Atlantic Ocean
66 L6 **Rockall Bank** *undersea feature* N Atlantic Ocean
86 B8 **Rockall Rise** *undersea feature* N Atlantic Ocean
86 C9 **Rockall Trough** *undersea feature* N Atlantic Ocean
37 U2 **Rock Creek** 〰 Nevada, W USA
27 T10 **Rockdale** Texas, SW USA
205 N12 **Rockefeller Plateau** *plateau* Antarctica
32 K11 **Rock Falls** Illinois, N USA
25 Q5 **Rockford** Alabama, S USA
32 L10 **Rockford** Illinois, N USA
13 Q12 **Rock Forest** Québec, SE Canada
9 T17 **Rockglen** Saskatchewan, S Canada
189 Y8 **Rockhampton** Queensland, E Australia
23 R11 **Rock Hill** South Carolina, SE USA
188 I13 **Rockingham** Western Australia
23 T11 **Rockingham** North Carolina, SE USA
32 J11 **Rock Island** Illinois, N USA
27 U12 **Rock Island** Texas, SW USA
12 C10 **Rock Lake** Ontario, S Canada
31 O2 **Rock Lake** North Dakota, N USA
12 I12 **Rock Lake** ◎ Ontario, SE Canada
12 M12 **Rockland** Ontario, SE Canada
21 R7 **Rockland** Maine, NE USA
190 L11 **Rocklands Reservoir** ▣ Victoria, SE Australia
37 O7 **Rocklin** California, W USA
25 R3 **Rockmart** Georgia, SE USA
33 N16 **Rockport** Indiana, N USA
29 Q1 **Rock Port** Missouri, C USA
27 T14 **Rockport** Texas, SW USA
34 I7 **Rockport** Washington, NW USA
31 S11 **Rock Rapids** Iowa, C USA
32 K11 **Rock River** 〰 Illinois/Wisconsin, N USA
46 I3 **Rock Sound** Eleuthera Island, C Bahamas
35 U17 **Rock Springs** Wyoming, C USA
27 P11 **Rocksprings** Texas, SW USA
57 T9 **Rockstone** C Guyana
31 S12 **Rock Valley** Iowa, C USA
33 N14 **Rockville** Indiana, N USA
23 W3 **Rockville** Maryland, NE USA
27 U6 **Rockwall** Texas, SW USA
31 U13 **Rockwell City** Iowa, C USA
33 S10 **Rockwood** Michigan, N USA
22 M9 **Rockwood** Tennessee, S USA
27 Q8 **Rockwood** Texas, SW USA
39 U6 **Rocky Ford** Colorado, C USA
12 D9 **Rocky Island Lake** ◎ Ontario, S Canada
23 V9 **Rocky Mount** North Carolina, SE USA
23 S7 **Rocky Mount** Virginia, NE USA
35 Q8 **Rocky Mountain** ▲ Montana, NW USA
9 P15 **Rocky Mountain House** Alberta, SW Canada
39 T3 **Rocky Mountain National Park** *national park* Colorado, C USA
2 E12 **Rocky Mountains** *var.* Rockies, *Fr.* Montagnes Rocheuses. ▲▲ Canada/USA
44 H1 **Rocky Point** *headland* NE Belize
85 A17 **Rocky Point** *headland* NW Namibia
97 F14 **Rødberg** Buskerud, S Norway
97 I25 **Rødby** Storstrøm, SE Denmark
97 I25 **Rødbyhavn** Storstrøm, SE Denmark
11 T10 **Roddickton** Newfoundland, Newfoundland and Labrador, SE Canada
97 F23 **Rødding** Sønderjylland, SW Denmark
97 M22 **Rödeby** Blekinge, S Sweden
100 N6 **Roden** Drenthe, NE Netherlands
64 H9 **Rodeo** San Juan, W Argentina
105 O14 **Rodez** *anc.* Segodunum. Aveyron, S France
Rodholívos *see* Rodolívos
Rodhópi Óri *see* Rhodope Mountains
Ródhos/Rodi *see* Ródos
109 N15 **Rodi Gargancio** Puglia, SE Italy
103 N20 **Roding** Bayern, SE Germany
115 J19 **Rodinit, Kepi i** *headland* W Albania
118 I9 **Rodnei, Munţii** ▲▲ N Romania
192 L4 **Rodney, Cape** *headland* North Island, NZ
40 L9 **Rodney, Cape** *headland* Alaska, USA
128 M16 **Rodniki** Ivanovskaya Oblast', W Russian Federation
121 Q16 **Rodnya** *Rus.* Rodnya. Mahilyowskaya Voblasts', E Belarus
Rodó *see* José Enrique Rodó
116 H13 **Rodolívos** *var.* Rodholívos. Kentrikí Makedonía, NE Greece
Rodopi *see* Rhodope Mountains
117 O22 **Ródos** *var.* Ródhos, *Eng.* Rhodes, *It.* Rodi. Ródos, Dodekánisos, Greece, Aegean Sea
117 O22 **Ródos** *var.* Ródhos, *Eng.* Rhodes, *It.* Rodi; *anc.* Rhodos. *island* Dodekánisos, Greece, Aegean Sea
Rodosto *see* Tekirdağ
61 A14 **Rodrigues** Amazonas, W Brazil
181 P8 **Rodrigues** *var.* Rodriquez. *island* E Mauritius
Rodriquez *see* Rodrigues
Rodunma *see* Roanne
188 I7 **Roebourne** Western Australia
85 J20 **Roedtan** Northern, NE South Africa
100 H11 **Roelofarendsveen** Zuid-Holland, W Netherlands
Roepat *see* Rupat, Pulau
Roer *see* Rur
101 M16 **Roermond** Limburg, SE Netherlands
101 C18 **Roeselare** *Fr.* Roulers; *prev.* Rousselaere. West-Vlaanderen, W Belgium
15 Ll5 **Roes Welcome Sound** *strait* Northwest Territories, N Canada
Roeteng *see* Ruteng
Rofreit *see* Rovereto
Rogachëv *see* Rahachow
59 L15 **Rogagua, Laguna** ◎ NW Bolivia
97 C16 **Rogaland** ◈ *county* S Norway
27 Y9 **Roganville** Texas, SW USA
111 W11 **Rogaška Slatina** *Ger.* Rohitsch-Sauerbrunn; *prev.* Rogatec-Slatina. E Slovenia
Rogatec-Slatina *see* Rogaška Slatina
114 J13 **Rogatica** SE Bosnia and Herzegovina
Rogatin *see* Rohatyn
95 F17 **Rogen** ◎ C Sweden
29 S9 **Rogers** Arkansas, C USA
31 P5 **Rogers** North Dakota, N USA
27 T9 **Rogers** Texas, SW USA
33 R5 **Rogers City** Michigan, N USA
Roger Simpson Island *see* Abemama
37 T14 **Rogers Lake** *salt flat* California, W USA
23 Q8 **Rogers, Mount** ▲ Virginia, NE USA
35 O16 **Rogerson** Idaho, NW USA
9 O16 **Rogers Pass** *pass* British Columbia, SW Canada
23 O8 **Rogersville** Tennessee, S USA
101 L16 **Roggel** Limburg, SE Netherlands
Roggeveen *see* Roggewein, Cabo
200 Nn12 **Roggeveen Basin** *undersea feature* E Pacific Ocean
203 X16 **Roggewein, Cabo** *var.* Roggeveen. *headland* Easter Island, Chile, E Pacific Ocean
104 F1 **Rogliano** Corse, France, C Mediterranean Sea
109 N21 **Rogliano** Calabria, SW Italy
94 G12 **Rognan** Nordland, C Norway
102 K10 **Rögnitz** 〰 N Germany
Rogozhina/Rogozhinë *see* Rrogozhinë
112 G10 **Rogoźno** Piła, NW Poland
34 E15 **Rogue River** 〰 Oregon, NW USA
118 I6 **Rohatyn** *Rus.* Rogatin. Ivano-Frankivs'ka Oblast', W Ukraine
201 O14 **Rohi** Pohnpei, E Micronesia
Rohitsch-Sauerbrunn *see* Rogaška Slatina
155 Q13 **Rohri** Sind, SE Pakistan
158 I10 **Rohtak** Haryāna, N India
Roi Ed *see* Roi Et
178 Ii10 **Roi Et** *var.* Muang Roi Et, Roi Ed. Roi Et, E Thailand
203 U9 **Roi Georges, Îles du** *island group* Îles Tuamotu, C French Polynesia
159 Y10 **Roing** Arunāchal Pradesh, NE India
120 E7 **Roja** Talsi, NW Latvia
63 B20 **Rojas** Buenos Aires, E Argentina
155 R12 **Rojhān** Punjab, E Pakistan
43 Q12 **Rojo, Cabo** *headland* C Mexico
47 Q10 **Rojo, Cabo** *headland* W Puerto Rico
173 G7 **Rokan Kanan, Sungai** 〰 Sumatera, W Indonesia
173 G7 **Rokan Kiri, Sungai** 〰 Sumatera, W Indonesia
Rokha *see* Rokhah
155 R4 **Rokhah** *var.* Rokha. Kāpīsā, E Afghanistan
120 I11 **Rokiškis** Rokiškis, NE Lithuania
172 Nn9 **Rokkasho** Aomori, Honshū, C Japan
113 B17 **Rokycany** *Ger.* Rokytzan. Západní Čechy, W Czech Republic
119 P6 **Rokytne** Kyyivs'ka Oblast', N Ukraine
118 L3 **Rokytne** Rivnens'ka Oblast', NW Ukraine
Rokytzan *see* Rokycany
164 L11 **Rola Co** ◎ W China
31 V13 **Roland** Iowa, C USA
97 D15 **Røldal** Hordaland, S Norway
100 O7 **Rolde** Drenthe, NE Netherlands
31 O2 **Rolette** North Dakota, N USA
29 V6 **Rolla** Missouri, C USA
31 O2 **Rolla** North Dakota, N USA
110 A10 **Rolle** Vaud, W Switzerland
189 X8 **Rolleston** Queensland, E Australia
193 H19 **Rolleston** Canterbury, South Island, NZ
193 G18 **Rolleston Range** ▲▲ South Island, NZ
12 H8 **Rollet** Québec, SE Canada
24 J4 **Rolling Fork** Mississippi, S USA
22 L6 **Rolling Fork** 〰 Kentucky, S USA
12 J11 **Rolphton** Ontario, SE Canada
Röm *see* Rømø
189 X10 **Roma** Queensland, E Australia
109 I15 **Roma** *Eng.* Rome. ● (Italy) Lazio, C Italy
97 P19 **Roma** Gotland, SE Sweden
23 T14 **Romain, Cape** *headland* South Carolina, SE USA
11 P11 **Romaine** 〰 Newfoundland and Labrador/Québec, E Canada
27 R17 **Roma Los Saenz** Texas, SW USA
116 H8 **Roman** Oblast Montana, NW Bulgaria
118 L10 **Roman** *Hung.* Románvásár. Neamţ, NE Romania
66 M13 **Romanche Fracture Zone** *tectonic feature* E Atlantic Ocean
63 C15 **Romang** Santa Fe, C Argentina
175 T15 **Romang, Pulau** *var.* Pulau Roma. *island* Kepulauan Damar, E Indonesia
175 Ss15 **Romang, Selat** *strait* Nusa Tenggara, S Indonesia
113 O24 **Romania** *Bul.* Rumŭniya, *Ger.* Rumänien, *Hung.* Románia, *Rom.* România, *SCr.* Rumunjska, *Ukr.* Rumuniya; *prev.* Republica Socialistă România, Roumania, Rumania, Socialist Republic of Romania, *Rom.* Romînia. ◆ *republic* SE Europe
119 T14 **Roman-Kash** ▲ S Ukraine
25 W16 **Romano, Cape** *headland* Florida, SE USA
46 G5 **Romano, Cayo** *island* C Cuba
126 Kk15 **Romanovka** Respublika Buryatiya, S Russian Federation
131 N8 **Romanovka** Saratovskaya Oblast', W Russian Federation
110 I6 **Romanshorn** Thurgau, NE Switzerland
105 R12 **Romans-sur-Isère** Drôme, E France
201 U12 **Romanum** *island* Chuuk, C Micronesia
Románvásár *see* Roman
41 S5 **Romanzof Mountains** ▲▲ Alaska, USA
Roma, Pulau *see* Romang, Pulau
105 S4 **Rombas** Moselle, NE France
176 Xx10 **Rombebai, Danau** ◎ Irian Jaya, E Indonesia
25 R2 **Rome** Georgia, SE USA
20 I9 **Rome** New York, NE USA
Rome *see* Roma
33 S9 **Romeo** Michigan, N USA
Römerstadt *see* Rýmařov
Rometan *see* Romitan
105 P5 **Romilly-sur-Seine** Aube, N France
Romînia *see* Romania
152 L11 **Romitan** *Rus.* Rometan. Bukhoro Wiloyati, C Uzbekistan
23 U3 **Romney** West Virginia, NE USA
119 S4 **Romny** Sums'ka Oblast', NE Ukraine
97 E24 **Rømø** *Ger.* Röm. *island* SW Denmark

◆ Country
● Country Capital
◇ Dependent Territory
○ Dependent Territory Capital
◈ Administrative Region
✕ International Airport
▲ Mountain
▲▲ Mountain Range
⛰ Volcano
〰 River
◎ Lake
▣ Reservoir

Romodan – Rybinsk Reservoir

119 *S5* **Romodan** Poltavs'ka Oblast', NE Ukraine
131 *P5* **Romodanovo** Respublika Mordoviya, W Russian Federation
Romorantin *see* Romorantin-Lanthenay
105 *N8* **Romorantin-Lanthenay** *var.* Romorantin. Loir-et-Cher, C France
174 *Hh5* **Rompin, Sungai** ~ Peninsular Malaysia
96 *F9* **Romsdal** *physical region* S Norway
96 *F10* **Romsdalen** *valley* S Norway
96 *E9* **Romsdalsfjorden** *fjord* S Norway
35 *P8* **Ronan** Montana, NW USA
61 *M14* **Roncador** Maranhão, E Brazil
195 *W12* **Roncador Reef** *reef* N Solomon Islands
61 *J17* **Roncador, Serra do** ⛰ C Brazil
23 *S6* **Ronceverte** West Virginia, NE USA
109 *H14* **Ronciglione** Lazio, C Italy
106 *L15* **Ronda** Andalucía, S Spain
96 *G11* **Rondane** ⛰ S Norway
106 *L15* **Ronda, Serranía de** ⛰ S Spain
97 *H22* **Rønde** Århus, C Denmark
Rōņdik *see* Rongrik Atoll
61 *E16* **Rondônia** *off.* Estado de Rondônia; *prev.* Território de Rondônia. ◐ *state* W Brazil
61 *I18* **Rondonópolis** Mato Grosso, W Brazil
96 *G11* **Rondslottet** ▲ S Norway
97 *P20* **Ronehamn** Gotland, SE Sweden
166 *L13* **Rong'an** *var.* Chang'an, Rongan. Guangxi Zhuangzu Zizhiqu, S China
201 *R4* **Rongelap Atoll** *var.* Rōņļap. *atoll* Ralik Chain, NW Marshall Islands
Rongerik *see* Rongrik Atoll
166 *L13* **Rong Jiang** ~ S China
166 *K12* **Rongjiang** *prev.* Guzhou. Guizhou, S China
Rong, Kas *see* Rŭng, Kaôh
178 *Hh8* **Rong Kwang** Phrae, NW Thailand
201 *T4* **Rongrik Atoll** *var.* Rōņdik, Rongerik. *atoll* Ralik Chain, N Marshall Islands
201 *X2* **Rongrong** *island* SE Marshall Islands
166 *L13* **Rongshui** *var.* Rongshui Miaozu Zizhixian. Guangxi Zhuangzu Zizhiqu, S China
Rongshui Miaozu Zizhixian *see* Rongshui
120 *I6* **Rõngu** *Ger.* Ringen. Tartumaa, SE Estonia
166 *L15* **Rongxian** *var.* Rong Xian. Guangxi Zhuangzu Zizhiqu, S China
Roniu *see* Ronui, Mont
201 *N13* **Ronkiti** Pohnpei, E Micronesia
Rōņļap *see* Rongelap Atoll
97 *L24* **Rønne** Bornholm, E Denmark
97 *M22* **Ronneby** Blekinge, S Sweden
204 *J7* **Ronne Entrance** *inlet* Antarctica
204 *L6* **Ronne Ice Shelf** *ice shelf* Antarctica
101 *E19* **Ronse** *Fr.* Renaix. Oost-Vlaanderen, SW Belgium
203 *R8* **Ronui, Mont** *var.* Roniu. ♨ Tahiti, W French Polynesia
32 *K14* **Roodhouse** Illinois, N USA
85 *C19* **Rooibank** Erongo, W Namibia
Rooke Island *see* Umboi Island
67 *N24* **Rookery Point** *headland* NE Tristan da Cunha
176 *W10* **Roon, Pulau** *island* E Indonesia
181 *V7* **Roo Rise** *undersea feature* E Indian Ocean
158 *J9* **Roorkee** Uttar Pradesh, N India
101 *H15* **Roosendaal** Noord-Brabant, S Netherlands
27 *P10* **Roosevelt** Texas, SW USA
39 *N3* **Roosevelt** Utah, W USA
49 *T8* **Roosevelt** ~ W Brazil
205 *O13* **Roosevelt Island** *island* Antarctica
8 *L10* **Roosevelt, Mount** ▲ British Columbia, W Canada
9 *P17* **Roosville** British Columbia, SW Canada
31 *X10* **Root River** ~ Minnesota, N USA
113 *N16* **Ropczyce** Rzeszów, SE Poland
189 *Q3* **Roper Bar** Northern Territory, N Australia
26 *M5* **Ropesville** Texas, SW USA
104 *K14* **Roquefort** Landes, SW France
63 *C21* **Roque Pérez** Buenos Aires, E Argentina
60 *E10* **Roraima** *off.* Estado de Roraima; *prev.* Território de Rio Branco, Território de Roraima. ◐ *state* N Brazil
60 *F9* **Roraima, Mount** ▲ N South America
176 *X10* **Rori** Irian Jaya, E Indonesia
Ro Ro Reef *see* Malolo Barrier Reef
96 *I9* **Røros** Sør-Trøndelag, S Norway
110 *I7* **Rorschach** Sankt Gallen, NE Switzerland
95 *E14* **Rørvik** Nord-Trøndelag, C Norway
121 *G17* **Ros'** *Rus.* Ross'. Hrodzyenskaya Voblasts', W Belarus
121 *G17* **Ros'** *Rus.* Ross'. ~ W Belarus
119 *O6* **Ros'** ~ N Ukraine
46 *K7* **Rosa, Lake** ◎ Great Inagua, S Bahamas
34 *M9* **Rosalia** Washington, NW USA
203 *W15* **Rosalia, Punta** *headland* Easter Island, Chile, E Pacific Ocean
47 *P12* **Rosalie** E Dominica
37 *T14* **Rosamond** California, W USA
37 *S14* **Rosamond Lake** *salt flat* California, W USA
63 *B18* **Rosario** Santa Fe, C Argentina
42 *J11* **Rosario** Sinaloa, C Mexico
42 *G6* **Rosario** Sonora, NW Mexico
64 *O6* **Rosario** San Pedro, C Paraguay
63 *E20* **Rosario** Colonia, SW Uruguay
56 *H5* **Rosario** Zulia, NW Venezuela
Rosario *see* Rosarito
42 *B4* **Rosario, Bahía del** *bay* NW Mexico
64 *K6* **Rosario de la Frontera** Salta, N Argentina
63 *C18* **Rosario del Tala** Entre Ríos, E Argentina
63 *F16* **Rosário do Sul** Rio Grande do Sul, S Brazil
61 *H18* **Rosário Oeste** Mato Grosso, W Brazil
42 *E7* **Rosarito** Baja California, NW Mexico
42 *B1* **Rosarito** *var.* Rosario. Baja California, NW Mexico
42 *E7* **Rosarito** Baja California Sur, W Mexico
106 *L9* **Rosarito, Embalse del** ⊡ W Spain
109 *N22* **Rosarno** Calabria, SW Italy
58 *B5* **Rosa Zárate** *var.* Quinindé. Esmeraldas, SW Ecuador
Roscianum *see* Rossano
31 *O8* **Roscoe** South Dakota, N USA
27 *P7* **Roscoe** Texas, SW USA
104 *F5* **Roscoff** Finistère, NW France
Ros Comáin *see* Roscommon
99 *C17* **Roscommon** *Ir.* Ros Comáin. C Ireland
33 *Q7* **Roscommon** Michigan, N USA
99 *C17* **Roscommon** *Ir.* Ros Comáin. *cultural region* C Ireland
Ros. Cré *see* Roscrea
99 *D19* **Roscrea** *Ir.* Ros. Cré. C Ireland
47 *X12* **Roseau** *prev.* Charlotte Town. ● (Dominica) SW Dominica
31 *S2* **Roseau** Minnesota, N USA
181 *Y16* **Rose Belle** SE Mauritius
191 *O16* **Rosebery** Tasmania, SE Australia
23 *U11* **Roseboro** North Carolina, SE USA
27 *T9* **Rosebud** Texas, SW USA
35 *W10* **Rosebud Creek** ~ Montana, NW USA
34 *F14* **Roseburg** Oregon, NW USA
24 *J3* **Rosedale** Mississippi, S USA
101 *H21* **Rosée** Namur, S Belgium
57 *U8* **Rose Hall** E Guyana
181 *X16* **Rose Hill** W Mauritius
82 *H12* **Roseires, Reservoir** *var.* Lake Rusayris. ⊡ E Sudan
Rosenau *see* Rožnov pod Radhoštěm, Czech Republic
Rosenau *see* Rožňava, Slovakia
27 *V11* **Rosenberg** Texas, SW USA
Rosenberg *see* Olesno, Poland
Rosenberg *see* Ružomberok, Slovakia
102 *I10* **Rosengarten** Niedersachsen, N Germany
103 *M24* **Rosenheim** Bayern, S Germany
Rosenhof *see* Zilupe
107 *X4* **Roses** Cataluña, NE Spain
107 *X4* **Roses, Golf de** *gulf* NE Spain
109 *K14* **Roseto degli Abruzzi** Abruzzi, C Italy
9 *S16* **Rosetown** Saskatchewan, S Canada
Rosetta *see* Rashîd
37 *O7* **Roseville** California, W USA
32 *J12* **Roseville** Illinois, N USA
31 *V8* **Roseville** Minnesota, N USA
31 *R7* **Rosholt** South Dakota, N USA
108 *F12* **Rosignano Marittimo** Toscana, C Italy
118 *I14* **Roşiori de Vede** Teleorman, S Romania
116 *K8* **Rositsa** ~ N Bulgaria
Rositten *see* Rēzekne
97 *J23* **Roskilde** Roskilde, E Denmark
97 *I23* **Roskilde** *off.* Roskilde Amt. ◐ *county* E Denmark
Ros Láir *see* Rosslare
130 *H5* **Roslavl'** Smolenskaya Oblast', W Russian Federation
34 *I8* **Roslyn** Washington, NW USA
101 *K14* **Rosmalen** Noord-Brabant, S Netherlands
Ros Mhic Thriúin *see* New Ross
115 *P19* **Rosoman** C FYR Macedonia
104 *F6* **Rosporden** Finistère, NW France
193 *F17* **Ross** West Coast, South Island, NZ
8 *J7* **Ross** ~ Yukon Territory, W Canada
Ross' *see* Ros'
98 *H8* **Ross and Cromarty** *cultural region* N Scotland, UK
109 *O20* **Rossano** *anc.* Roscianum. Calabria, SW Italy
24 *L5* **Ross Barnett Reservoir** ⊡ Mississippi, S USA
9 *W16* **Rossburn** Manitoba, S Canada
12 *H13* **Rosseau** Ontario, S Canada
12 *H13* **Rosseau, Lake** ◎ Ontario, S Canada
195 *R17* **Rossel Island** *prev.* Yela Island. *island* SE PNG
205 *P12* **Ross Ice Shelf** *ice shelf* Antarctica
11 *P16* **Rossignol, Lake** ◎ Nova Scotia, SE Canada
85 *C19* **Rössing** Erongo, W Namibia
205 *Q14* **Ross Island** *island* Antarctica
Rossitten *see* Rybachiy
Rossiyskaya Federatsiya *see* Russian Federation
9 *N17* **Rossland** British Columbia, SW Canada
99 *F20* **Rosslare** *Ir.* Ros Láir. SE Ireland
99 *F20* **Rosslare Harbour** Wexford, SE Ireland
103 *M14* **Rosslau** Sachsen-Anhalt, E Germany
78 *G10* **Rosso** Trarza, SW Mauritania
104 *X14* **Rosso, Cap** *headland* Corse, France, C Mediterranean Sea
95 *H16* **Rosson** Jämtland, C Sweden
99 *K21* **Ross-on-Wye** W England, UK
Rossony *see* Rasony
130 *L9* **Rossosh'** Voronezhskaya Oblast', W Russian Federation
189 *Q7* **Ross River** Northern Territory, N Australia
8 *J7* **Ross River** Yukon Territory, W Canada
205 *O15* **Ross Sea** *sea* Antarctica
25 *R1* **Rossville** Georgia, SE USA
Rostak *see* Ar Rustāq
149 *P14* **Rostāq** Hormozgān, S Iran
119 *N5* **Rostavytsya** ~ N Ukraine
9 *T15* **Rosthern** Saskatchewan, S Canada
102 *M8* **Rostock** Mecklenburg-Vorpommern, NE Germany
128 *L16* **Rostov** Yaroslavskaya Oblast', W Russian Federation
Rostov *see* Rostov-na-Donu
130 *L12* **Rostov-na-Donu** *var.* Rostov, *Eng.* Rostov-on-Don. Rostovskaya Oblast', SW Russian Federation
Rostov-on-Don *see* Rostov-na-Donu
130 *L10* **Rostovskaya Oblast'** ◐ *province* SW Russian Federation
94 *G13* **Røsvatnet** ◎ C Norway
95 *J14* **Rosvik** Norrbotten, N Sweden
25 *S3* **Roswell** Georgia, SE USA
39 *U14* **Roswell** New Mexico, SW USA
96 *K12* **Rot** Kopparberg, C Sweden
103 *I23* **Rot** ~ S Germany
106 *J15* **Rota** Andalucía, S Spain
196 *K9* **Rota** *island* S Northern Mariana Islands
27 *P6* **Rotan** Texas, SW USA
Rotcher Island *see* Tamana
102 *I11* **Rotenburg** Niedersachsen, NW Germany
Rotenburg *see* Rotenburg an der Fulda
103 *I16* **Rotenburg an der Fulda** *var.* Rotenburg. Thüringen, C Germany
103 *L18* **Roter Main** ~ E Germany
103 *K20* **Roth** Bayern, SE Germany
103 *G16* **Rothaargebirge** ⛰ W Germany
Rothenburg *see* Rothenburg ob der Tauber
103 *J20* **Rothenburg ob der Tauber** *var.* Rothenburg. Bayern, S Germany
204 *H6* **Rothera** *UK research station* Antarctica
193 *I17* **Rotherham** Canterbury, South Island, NZ
99 *M17* **Rotherham** N England, UK
98 *H12* **Rothesay** W Scotland, UK
110 *E7* **Rothrist** Aargau, N Switzerland
204 *H6* **Rothschild Island** *island* Antarctica
175 *Qq18* **Roti, Pulau** *island* S Indonesia
Roti, Pulau *see* Rote, Pulau
175 *R18* **Roti, Selat** *strait* Nusa Tenggara, S Indonesia
191 *O8* **Roto** New South Wales, SE Australia
192 *N8* **Rotoiti, Lake** ◎ North Island, NZ
Rotomagus *see* Rouen
109 *N19* **Rotondella** Basilicata, S Italy
104 *E2* **Rotondo, Monte** ▲ Corse, France, C Mediterranean Sea
193 *I15* **Rotoroa, Lake** ◎ South Island, NZ
192 *N8* **Rotorua** Bay of Plenty, North Island, NZ
192 *N8* **Rotorua, Lake** ◎ North Island, NZ
103 *N22* **Rott** ~ SE Germany
110 *F10* **Rotten** ~ S Switzerland
111 *T6* **Rottenmann** Steiermark, E Austria
100 *H12* **Rotterdam** Zuid-Holland, SW Netherlands
20 *K10* **Rotterdam** New York, NE USA
97 *M21* **Rottnen** ◎ S Sweden
100 *N4* **Rottumeroog** *island* Waddeneilanden, NE Netherlands
100 *N4* **Rottumerplaat** *island* Waddeneilanden, NE Netherlands
103 *G23* **Rottweil** Baden-Württemberg, S Germany
203 *O7* **Rotui, Mont** ♨ Moorea, W French Polynesia
105 *P1* **Roubaix** Nord, N France
113 *C15* **Roudnice nad Labem** *Ger.* Raudnitz an der Elbe. Severní Čechy, N Czech Republic
104 *M4* **Rouen** *anc.* Rotomagus. Seine-Maritime, N France
176 *Y11* **Rouffaer Reserves** *reserve* Irian Jaya, E Indonesia
Rouffaer-Rivier *see* Tariku, Sungai
13 *N10* **Rouge, Rivière** ~ Québec, SE Canada
22 *J6* **Rough River** ~ Kentucky, S USA
22 *J6* **Rough River Lake** ⊡ Kentucky, S USA
Rouhaïbé *see* Ar Ruḩaybah
104 *K11* **Rouillac** Charente, W France
Roulers *see* Roeselare
Roumania *see* Romania
181 *Y15* **Round Island** *var.* Île Ronde. *island* NE Mauritius
12 *J12* **Round Lake** ◎ Ontario, SE Canada
37 *U7* **Round Mountain** Nevada, W USA
27 *R10* **Round Mountain** Texas, SW USA
191 *U5* **Round Mountain** ▲ New South Wales, SE Australia
27 *S10* **Round Rock** Texas, SW USA
35 *U10* **Roundup** Montana, NW USA
57 *Y10* **Roura** NE French Guiana
Rourkela *see* Raurkela
98 *J4* **Rousay** *island* N Scotland, UK
Rousselaere *see* Roeselare
105 *O17* **Roussillon** *cultural region* S France
13 *V7* **Routhierville** Québec, SE Canada
101 *K25* **Rouvroy** Luxembourg, SE Belgium
12 *I7* **Rouyn-Noranda** Québec, SE Canada
Rouyuanchengzi *see* Huachi
94 *L12* **Rovaniemi** Lappi, N Finland
108 *E7* **Rovato** Lombardia, N Italy
129 *N11* **Rovdino** Arkhangel'skaya Oblast', NW Russian Federation
Roven'ki *see* Roven'ky
119 *Y8* **Roven'ky** *var.* Roven'ki. Luhans'ka Oblast', E Ukraine
Rovenskaya Oblast' *see* Rivnens'ka Oblast'
Rovenskaya Sloboda *see* Rovyenskaya Slabada
108 *G7* **Rovereto** *Ger.* Rofreit. Trentino-Alto Adige, N Italy
178 *J12* **Rôviĕng Tbong** Preăh Vihéar, N Cambodia
Rovigno *see* Rovinj
108 *H8* **Rovigo** Veneto, NE Italy
114 *A10* **Rovinj** *It.* Rovigno. Istra, NW Croatia
56 *E10* **Rovira** Tolima, C Colombia
Rovno *see* Rivne
131 *P9* **Rovnoye** Saratovskaya Oblast', W Russian Federation
84 *Q12* **Rovuma, Rio** *var.* Ruvuma. ~ Mozambique/Tanzania *see also* Ruvuma
121 *O19* **Rovyenskaya Slabada** *Rus.* Rovenskaya Sloboda. Homyel'skaya Voblasts', SE Belarus
191 *R5* **Rowena** New South Wales, SE Australia
23 *T11* **Rowland** North Carolina, SE USA
15 *M1* **Rowley** ~ Baffin Island, Northwest Territories, NE Canada
15 *M2* **Rowley Island** *island* Northwest Territories, NE Canada
181 *W8* **Rowley Shoals** *reef* NW Australia
179 *Pp12* **Roxas** Mindoro, N Philippines
179 *Q13* **Roxas City** Panay Island, C Philippines
23 *U8* **Roxboro** North Carolina, SE USA
193 *D23* **Roxburgh** Otago, South Island, NZ
98 *K13* **Roxburgh** *cultural region* SE Scotland, UK
190 *H5* **Roxby Downs** South Australia
97 *M17* **Roxen** ◎ S Sweden
27 *V5* **Roxton** Texas, SW USA
13 *P12* **Roxton-Sud** Québec, SE Canada
35 *U8* **Roy** Montana, NW USA
39 *U10* **Roy** New Mexico, SW USA
99 *E17* **Royal Canal** *Ir.* An Chanáil Ríoga. *canal* C Ireland
32 *L1* **Royale, Isle** *island* Michigan, N USA
39 *S6* **Royal Gorge** *valley* Colorado, C USA
99 *M20* **Royal Leamington Spa** *var.* Leamington, Leamington Spa. C England, UK
99 *O23* **Royal Tunbridge Wells** *var.* Tunbridge Wells. SE England, UK
26 *L9* **Royalty** Texas, SW USA
104 *J11* **Royan** Charente-Maritime, W France
67 *B24* **Roy Cove Settlement** West Falkland, Falkland Islands
105 *O3* **Roye** Somme, N France
97 *H15* **Røyken** Buskerud, S Norway
95 *F14* **Røyrvik** Nord-Trøndelag, C Norway
27 *U6* **Royse City** Texas, SW USA
99 *O21* **Royston** E England, UK
25 *U2* **Royston** Georgia, SE USA
116 *L10* **Roza** *prev.* Gyulovo. Burgaska Oblast, E Bulgaria
115 *L16* **Rožaje** Montenegro, SW Yugoslavia
112 *M10* **Różan** Ostrołęka, E Poland
119 *O10* **Rozdil'na** Odes'ka Oblast', SW Ukraine
119 *S12* **Rozdol'ne** *Rus.* Razdolnoye. Respublika Krym, S Ukraine
151 *Q9* **Rozhdestvenka** Akmola, C Kazakhstan
118 *I6* **Rozhnyativ** Ivano-Frankivs'ka Oblast', W Ukraine
118 *J3* **Rozhyshche** Volyns'ka Oblast', NW Ukraine
Roznau am Radhost *see* Rožnov pod Radhoštěm
113 *L19* **Rožňava** *Ger.* Rosenau, *Hung.* Rozsnyó. Východné Slovensko, E Slovakia
118 *K10* **Roznov** Neamţ, NE Romania
113 *I18* **Rožnov pod Radhoštěm** *Ger.* Rosenau, Roznau am Radhost. Severní Morava, E Czech Republic
Rózsahegy *see* Ružomberok
Rozsnyó *see* Râşnov, Romania
Rozsnyó *see* Rožňava, Slovakia
115 *K18* **Rranxë** Shkodër, NW Albania
115 *L18* **Rrëshen** *var.* Rresheni, Rrshen. Lezhë, C Albania
Rresheni *see* Rrëshen
Rrogozhina *see* Rrogozhinë
115 *K20* **Rrogozhinë** *var.* Rogozhina, Rogozhinë, Rrogozhina. Tiranë, W Albania
Rrshen *see* Rrëshen
114 *O13* **Rtanj** ▲ E Yugoslavia
131 *O7* **Rtishchevo** Saratovskaya Oblast', W Russian Federation
192 *N12* **Ruahine Range** *var.* Ruarine. ⛰ North Island, NZ
193 *L14* **Ruamahanga** ~ North Island, NZ
Ruanda *see* Rwanda
192 *M10* **Ruapehu, Mount** ▲ North Island, NZ
193 *C25* **Ruapuke Island** *island* SW NZ
Ruarine *see* Ruahine Range
192 *O9* **Ruatahuna** Bay of Plenty, North Island, NZ
192 *Q8* **Ruatoria** Gisborne, North Island, NZ
192 *K4* **Ruawai** Northland, North Island, NZ
13 *N8* **Ruban** ~ Québec, SE Canada
83 *I22* **Rubeho Mountains** ⛰ C Tanzania
172 *Q5* **Rubeshibe** Hokkaidō, NE Japan
Rubezhnoye *see* Rubizhne
115 *L18* **Rubik** Lezhë, C Albania
56 *H7* **Rubio** Táchira, W Venezuela
119 *X6* **Rubizhne** *Rus.* Rubezhnoye. Luhans'ka Oblast', E Ukraine
83 *F20* **Rubondo Island** *island* N Tanzania
126 *Gg15* **Rubtsovsk** Altayskiy Kray, S Russian Federation
41 *P9* **Ruby** Alaska, USA
37 *W3* **Ruby Dome** ▲ Nevada, W USA
37 *W4* **Ruby Lake** ◎ Nevada, W USA
37 *W4* **Ruby Mountains** ⛰ Nevada, W USA
35 *Q12* **Ruby Range** ⛰ Montana, NW USA
120 *C10* **Rucava** Liepāja, SW Latvia
Rūdān *see* Dehbārez
Rudelstadt *see* Ciechanowiec
Rudensk *see* Rudzyensk
121 *G14* **Rūdiškės** Trakai, S Lithuania
97 *H24* **Rudkøbing** Fyn, C Denmark
127 *Nn17* **Rudnaya Pristan'** Primorskiy Kray, SE Russian Federation
151 *V14* **Rudnichnyy** *Kaz.* Rūdnīchnyy. Taldykorgan, SE Kazakhstan
129 *S13* **Rudnichnyy** Kirovskaya Oblast', NW Russian Federation
116 *N9* **Rudnik** Varnenska Oblast, E Bulgaria
Rudny *see* Rudnyy
130 *H4* **Rudnya** Smolenskaya Oblast', W Russian Federation
131 *O8* **Rudnya** Volgogradskaya Oblast', SW Russian Federation
150 *M7* **Rudnyy** *var.* Rudny. Kustanay, N Kazakhstan
126 *Hh1* **Rudol'fa, Ostrov** *island* Zemlya Frantsa-Iosifa, NW Russian Federation
83 *H16* **Rudolf, Lake** *var.* Lake Turkana. ◎ N Kenya
Rudolfswert *see* Novo Mesto
103 *L17* **Rudolstadt** Thüringen, C Germany
33 *Q4* **Rudyard** Michigan, N USA
35 *S7* **Rudyard** Montana, NW USA
121 *K16* **Rudzyensk** *Rus.* Rudensk. Minskaya Voblasts', C Belarus
106 *L6* **Rueda** Castilla-León, N Spain
116 *F10* **Ruen** ▲ Bulgaria/FYR Macedonia
82 *G10* **Rufa'a** Gezira, C Sudan
104 *L10* **Ruffec** Charente, W France
23 *R14* **Ruffin** South Carolina, SE USA
83 *J23* **Rufiji** ~ E Tanzania
63 *A20* **Rufino** Santa Fe, C Argentina
78 *F11* **Rufisque** W Senegal
85 *K14* **Rufunsa** Lusaka, C Zambia
120 *J9* **Rugāji** Balvi, E Latvia
167 *R7* **Rugao** Jiangsu, E China
99 *M20* **Rugby** C England, UK
31 *N3* **Rugby** North Dakota, N USA
102 *N7* **Rügen** *headland* NE Germany
Ruhaybeh *see* Ar Ruḩaybah
167 *N7* **Ru He** ~ C China
83 *E19* **Ruhengeri** NW Rwanda
Ruhja *see* Rūjiena
102 *M10* **Ruhner Berg** *hill* N Germany
120 *F7* **Ruhnu** *var.* Ruhnu Saar, *Swe.* Runö. *island* SW Estonia
Ruhnu Saar *see* Ruhnu
103 *G15* **Ruhr** ~ W Germany
93 *V6* **Ruhr Valley** *industrial region* W Germany
167 *S11* **Rui'an** *var.* Rui an. Zhejiang, SE China
167 *P10* **Ruichang** Jiangxi, S China
26 *J11* **Ruidosa** Texas, SW USA
39 *S14* **Ruidoso** New Mexico, SW USA
167 *P12* **Ruijin** Jiangxi, S China
166 *D13* **Ruili** Yunnan, SW China
100 *N8* **Ruinen** Drenthe, NE Netherlands
101 *D17* **Ruiselede** West-Vlaanderen, W Belgium
66 *P5* **Ruivo de Santana, Pico** ▲ Madeira, Portugal, NE Atlantic Ocean
42 *J12* **Ruiz** Nayarit, SW Mexico
56 *E10* **Ruiz, Nevado del** ♨ W Colombia
144 *J9* **Rujaylah, Ḩarrat ar** *salt lake* N Jordan
Rujen *see* Rūjiena
120 *H7* **Rūjiena** *Est.* Ruhja, *Ger.* Rujen. Valmiera, N Latvia
81 *I18* **Ruki** ~ W Zaire
83 *E22* **Rukwa** ◐ *region* SW Tanzania
83 *F23* **Rukwa, Lake** ◎ SE Tanzania
27 *P6* **Rule** Texas, SW USA
24 *K3* **Ruleville** Mississippi, S USA
Rum *see* Rhum
114 *K10* **Ruma** Serbia, N Yugoslavia
Rumadiya *see* Ar Ramādī
147 *Q7* **Rumāḩ** Ar Riyāḑ, C Saudi Arabia
Rumaitha *see* Ar Rumaythah
Rumania/Rumänien *see* Romania
Rumänisch-Sankt-Georgen *see* Sângeorz-Băi
145 *Y13* **Rumaylah** SE Iraq
145 *P2* **Rumaylah, Wādī** *dry watercourse* NE Syria
176 *V10* **Rumbati** Irian Jaya, E Indonesia
83 *E14* **Rumbek** El Buhayrat, S Sudan
176 *W10* **Rumberpon, Pulau** *island* E Indonesia
Rumburg *see* Rumburk
113 *D14* **Rumburk** *Ger.* Rumburg. Severní Čechy, N Czech Republic
46 *J4* **Rum Cay** *island* C Bahamas
101 *M26* **Rumelange** Luxembourg, S Luxembourg
101 *D20* **Rumes** Hainaut, SW Belgium
21 *P7* **Rumford** Maine, NE USA
112 *I6* **Rumia** Gdańsk, N Poland
115 *J17* **Rumija** ⛰ SW Yugoslavia
105 *T11* **Rumilly** Haute-Savoie, E France
145 *O6* **Rūmiyah** W Iraq
Rummah, Wādī ar *see* Rimah, Wādī ar
Rummelsburg in Pommern *see* Miastko
172 *Oo4* **Rumoi** Hokkaidō, NE Japan
84 *M12* **Rumphi** *var.* Rumpi. Northern, N Malawi
Rumpi *see* Rumphi
31 *V7* **Rum River** ~ Minnesota, N USA
196 *F16* **Rumung** *island* Caroline Islands, W Micronesia
Rumuniya/Rumŭniya/ Rumunjska *see* Romania
193 *G16* **Runanga** West Coast, South Island, NZ
192 *P7* **Runaway, Cape** *headland* North Island, NZ
99 *K18* **Runcorn** C England, UK
120 *K10* **Rundāni** Ludza, E Latvia
85 *L18* **Runde** *var.* Lundi. ~ SE Zimbabwe
85 *E16* **Rundu** *var.* Runtu. Okavango, NE Namibia
95 *I16* **Rundvik** Västerbotten, N Sweden
83 *G20* **Runere** Mwanza, N Tanzania
27 *S13* **Runge** Texas, SW USA
178 *I14* **Rŭng, Kaôh** *prev.* Kas Rong. *island* SW Cambodia
81 *O16* **Rungu** Haut-Zaïre, NE Zaire
83 *F23* **Rungwa** Rukwa, W Tanzania
83 *G22* **Rungwa** Singida, C Tanzania
96 *M13* **Runn** ◎ C Sweden
26 *M4* **Running Water Draw** *valley* New Mexico/Texas, SW USA
Runö *see* Ruhnu
Runtu *see* Rundu
201 *V12* **Ruo** *island* Caroline Islands, C Micronesia
164 *L9* **Ruoqiang** *var.* Jo-ch'iang, *Uigh.* Charkhlik, Charkhliq, Qarkilik. Xinjiang Uygur Zizhiqu, NW China
165 *S7* **Ruo Shui** ~ N China
95 *L18* **Ruovesi** Häme, SW Finland
114 *B9* **Rupa** Primorje-Gorski Kotar, NW Croatia
190 *M11* **Rupanyup** Victoria, SE Australia
174 *H6* **Rupat, Pulau** *prev.* Roepat. *island* W Indonesia
174 *Gg6* **Rupat, Selat** *strait* Sumatera, W Indonesia
118 *J11* **Rupea** *Ger.* Reps, *Hung.* Kőhalom; *prev.* Cohalm. Braşov, C Romania
101 *G17* **Rupel** ~ N Belgium
Rupella *see* la Rochelle
35 *P15* **Rupert** Idaho, NW USA
23 *R5* **Rupert** West Virginia, NE USA
Rupert House *see* Fort Rupert
10 *J10* **Rupert, Rivière de** ~ Québec, C Canada
204 *M13* **Ruppert Coast** *physical region* Antarctica
102 *N11* **Ruppiner Kanal** *canal* NE Germany
57 *S11* **Rupununi River** ~ S Guyana
103 *D16* **Rur** *Dut.* Roer. ~ Germany/Netherlands
60 *H13* **Rurópolis Presidente Medici** Pará, N Brazil
203 *S12* **Rurutu** *island* Îles Australes, SW French Polynesia
Rusaddir *see* Melilla
85 *L17* **Rusape** Manicaland, E Zimbabwe
Rusayris, Lake *see* Roseires, Reservoir
Ruschuk/Rusçuk *see* Ruse
116 *K7* **Ruse** *var.* Ruschuk, Rustchuk, *Turk.* Rusçuk. Razgradska Oblast, N Bulgaria
111 *W10* **Ruše** NE Slovenia
116 *K7* **Rusenski Lom** ~ N Bulgaria
99 *G17* **Rush** *Ir.* An Ros. E Ireland
167 *S4* **Rushan** *var.* Xiacun. Shandong, E China
Rushan *see* Rŭshon
Rushanskiy Khrebet *see* Rushon, Qatorkŭhi
31 *V7* **Rush City** Minnesota, N USA
39 *V5* **Rush Creek** ~ Colorado, C USA
31 *X10* **Rushford** Minnesota, N USA
160 *N13* **Rushikulya** ~ E India
12 *D8* **Rush Lake** ◎ Ontario, S Canada
32 *M7* **Rush Lake** ◎ Wisconsin, N USA
30 *J10* **Rushmore, Mount** ▲ South Dakota, N USA
153 *S13* **Rŭshon** *Rus.* Rushan. S Tajikistan
153 *S14* **Rushon, Qatorkŭhi** *Rus.* Rushanskiy Khrebet. ⛰ SE Tajikistan
28 *M12* **Rush Springs** Oklahoma, C USA
47 *V15* **Rushville** Trinidad, Trinidad and Tobago
32 *J13* **Rushville** Illinois, N USA
30 *K12* **Rushville** Nebraska, C USA
191 *O11* **Rushworth** Victoria, SE Australia
27 *W8* **Rusk** Texas, SW USA
95 *I14* **Rusksele** Västerbotten, N Sweden
120 *C12* **Rusnė** Šilutė, W Lithuania
116 *M10* **Rusokastrenska Reka** ~ E Bulgaria
Russadir *see* Melilla
111 *X3* **Russbach** ~ NE Austria
9 *V16* **Russell** Manitoba, S Canada
192 *K2* **Russell** Northland, North Island, NZ
28 *L4* **Russell** Kansas, C USA
23 *O4* **Russell** Kentucky, S USA
195 *W15* **Russell Islands** *island group* C Solomon Islands
22 *L7* **Russell Springs** Kentucky, S USA
25 *O2* **Russellville** Alabama, S USA
29 *T11* **Russellville** Arkansas, C USA
22 *J7* **Russellville** Kentucky, S USA
103 *G18* **Rüsselsheim** Hessen, W Germany
94 *K8* **Russenes** Finnmark, N Norway
Russia *see* Russian Federation
Russian America *see* Alaska
127 *N17* **Russian Federation** *off.* Russian Federation, *var.* Russia, *Latv.* Krievija, *Rus.* Rossiyskaya Federatsiya. ◆ *republic* Asia/Europe
41 *N11* **Russian Mission** Alaska, USA
36 *M7* **Russian River** ~ California, W USA
204 *L13* **Russkaya** *Russian research station* Antarctica
126 *H3* **Russkaya Gavan'** Novaya Zemlya, Arkhangel'skaya Oblast', N Russian Federation
126 *J4* **Russkiy, Ostrov** *island* N Russian Federation
111 *Y5* **Rust** Burgenland, E Austria
Rustaq *see* Ar Rustāq
143 *U10* **Rust'avi** SE Georgia
23 *T7* **Rustburg** Virginia, NE USA
Rustchuk *see* Ruse
94 *L8* **Rustefjelbma** Finnmark, N Norway
85 *I21* **Rustenburg** North-West, N South Africa
24 *H5* **Ruston** Louisiana, S USA
83 *E21* **Rutana** SE Burundi
64 *I4* **Rutana, Volcán** ▲ N Chile
Rutanzige, Lake *see* Edward, Lake
Rutba *see* Ar Ruṭbah
106 *M14* **Rute** Andalucía, S Spain
175 *Pp16* **Ruteng** *prev.* Roeteng. Flores, C Indonesia
204 *L8* **Rutford Ice Stream** *ice feature* Antarctica
37 *X6* **Ruth** Nevada, W USA
103 *G15* **Rüthen** Nordrhein-Westfalen, W Germany
12 *D17* **Rutherford** Ontario, S Canada
23 *Q10* **Rutherfordton** North Carolina, SE USA
99 *J18* **Ruthin** *Wel.* Rhuthun. NE Wales, UK
110 *G7* **Rüti** Zürich, N Switzerland
Rutlam *see* Ratlām
20 *M9* **Rutland** Vermont, NE USA
99 *N19* **Rutland** *cultural region* C England, UK
23 *N8* **Rutledge** Tennessee, S USA
164 *G12* **Rutog** *var.* Rutok. Xizang Zizhiqu, W China
Rutok *see* Rutog
81 *P19* **Rutshuru** Nord Kivu, E Zaire
100 *L8* **Rutten** Flevoland, N Netherlands
131 *Q17* **Rutul** Respublika Dagestan, SW Russian Federation
95 *L14* **Ruukki** Oulu, C Finland
100 *N11* **Ruurlo** Gelderland, E Netherlands
149 *S15* **Ru'ūs al Jibāl** *headland* Oman/UAE
144 *I7* **Ru'ūs aţ Ţiwāl, Jabal** ⛰ W Syria
83 *H23* **Ruvuma** ◐ *region* SE Tanzania
83 *I25* **Ruvuma** *var.* Rio Rovuma. ~ Mozambique/Tanzania *see also* Rovuma, Rio
Ruwais *see* Ar Ruways
144 *L9* **Ruwayshid, Wadi ar** *dry watercourse* NE Jordan
147 *Z10* **Ruways, Ra's ar** *headland* E Oman
81 *P18* **Ruwenzori** ⛰ Uganda/Zaire
147 *Y8* **Ruwī** NE Oman
116 *F9* **Ruy** ▲ Bulgaria/Yugoslavia
Ruya *see* Luia, Rio
83 *E20* **Ruyigi** E Burundi
131 *P5* **Ruzayevka** Respublika Mordoviya, W Russian Federation
121 *G18* **Ruzhany** *Rus.* Ruzhany. Brestskaya Voblasts', SW Belarus
116 *I10* **Rŭzhevo Konare** *var.* Rŭzhevo Konare. Plovdivska Oblast, C Bulgaria
Ruzhin *see* Ruzhyn
116 *G7* **Ruzhintsi** Oblast Montana, NW Bulgaria
119 *N5* **Ruzhyn** *Rus.* Ruzhin. Zhytomyrs'ka Oblast', N Ukraine
113 *K19* **Ružomberok** *Ger.* Rosenberg, *Hung.* Rózsahegy. Stredné Slovensko, N Slovakia
113 *C16* **Ruzyně** ✈ (Praha) Praha, C Czech Republic
83 *D19* **Rwanda** *off.* Rwandese Republic; *prev.* Ruanda. ◆ *republic* C Africa
Rwandese Republic *see* Rwanda
97 *G22* **Ry** Århus, C Denmark
Ryasna *see* Rasna
130 *L5* **Ryazan'** Ryazanskaya Oblast', W Russian Federation
130 *L5* **Ryazanskaya Oblast'** ◐ *province* W Russian Federation
130 *M6* **Ryazhsk** Ryazanskaya Oblast', W Russian Federation
120 *B13* **Rybachiy** *Ger.* Rossitten. Kaliningradskaya Oblast', W Russian Federation
128 *J2* **Rybachiy, Poluostrov** *peninsula* NW Russian Federation
Rybach'ye *see* Balykchy
128 *L15* **Rybinsk** *prev.* Andropov. Yaroslavskaya Oblast', W Russian Federation
128 *K14* **Rybinskoye Vodokhranilishche** *Eng.* Rybinsk Reservoir, Rybinsk Sea. ⊡ W Russian Federation
Rybinsk Reservoir/ Rybinsk Sea *see* Rybinskoye Vodokhranilishche

◆ Country
● Country Capital
◇ Dependent Territory
○ Dependent Territory Capital
◐ Administrative Region
✈ International Airport
▲ Mountain
⛰ Mountain Range
♨ Volcano
~ River
◎ Lake
⊡ Reservoir

RYBNIK – ST.MARY, MOUNT

113 *I16* **Rybnik** Katowice, S Poland
Rybnitsa *see* Rîbniţa
113 *F16* **Rychnov nad Kněžnou** *Ger.* Reichenau. Východní Čechy, NE Czech Republic
112 *I12* **Rychwał** Konin, C Poland
9 *O13* **Rycroft** Alberta, W Canada
97 *L21* **Ryd** Kronoberg, S Sweden
97 *L20* **Rydaholm** Jönköping, S Sweden
204 *I8* **Rydberg Peninsula** *peninsula* Antarctica
99 *P23* **Rye** SE England, UK
35 *T10* **Ryegate** Montana, NW USA
37 *S3* **Rye Patch Reservoir** ⊠ Nevada, W USA
97 *D15* **Ryfylke** *physical region* S Norway
97 *H16* **Rygge** Østfold, S Norway
112 *N13* **Ryki** Lublin, E Poland
Rykovo *see* Yenakiyeve
130 *I7* **Ryl'sk** Kurskaya Oblast', W Russian Federation
191 *S8* **Rylstone** New South Wales, SE Australia
113 *H17* **Rýmařov** *Ger.* Römerstadt. Severní Morava, E Czech Republic
150 *E11* **Ryn-Peski** *desert* W Kazakhstan
171 *K12* **Ryōtsu** *var.* Ryôtu. Niigata, Sado, C Japan
Ryôtu *see* Ryōtsu
112 *K10* **Rypin** Włocławek, C Poland
Ryshkany *see* Rîşcani
Ryssel *see* Lille
Ryswick *see* Rijswijk
97 *M24* **Rytterknægten** *hill* E Denmark
171 *Kk16* **Ryūgasaki** Ibaraki, Honshū, S Japan
198 *G5* **Ryukyu Trench** *var.* Nansei Syotō Trench. *undersea feature* S East China Sea
112 *D11* **Rzepin** *Ger.* Reppen. Gorzów, W Poland
113 *N16* **Rzeszów** Rzeszów, SE Poland
113 *N16* **Rzeszów** *off.* Województwo Rzeszowskie. ◈ *province* SE Poland
Rzeszowskie, Województwo *see* Rzeszów
128 *I16* **Rzhev** Tverskaya Oblast', W Russian Federation
Rzhishchev *see* Rzhyshchiv
119 *P5* **Rzhyshchiv** *Rus.* Rzhishchev. Kyyivs'ka Oblast', N Ukraine

S

144 *E11* **Sa'ad** Southern, W Israel
111 *P7* **Saalach** ≈ W Austria
103 *L14* **Saale** ≈ C Germany
103 *L17* **Saalfeld** *var.* Saalfeld an der Saale. Thüringen, C Germany
Saalfeld *see* Zalewo
Saalfeld an der Saale *see* Saalfeld
110 *C8* **Saane** ≈ W Switzerland
103 *D19* **Saar** *Fr.* Sarre. ≈ France/Germany
103 *E20* **Saarbrücken** *Fr.* Sarrebruck. Saarland, SW Germany
Saarburg *see* Sarrebourg
Saare *see* Saaremaa
120 *D6* **Sääre** *var.* Sjar. Saaremaa, W Estonia
120 *D5* **Saaremaa** *off.* Saare Maakond. ◈ *province* W Estonia
120 *E6* **Saaremaa** *Ger.* Oesel, Ösel; *prev.* Saare. *island* W Estonia
94 *L12* **Saarenkylä** Lappi, N Finland
Saargemund *see* Sarreguemines
95 *L17* **Saarijärvi** Keski-Suomi, C Finland
Saar in Mähren *see* Žďár nad Sázavou
94 *M10* **Saariselkä** *Lapp.* Suoločielgi. Lappi, N Finland
94 *L10* **Saariselkä** *hill range* NE Finland
103 *D20* **Saarland** *Fr.* Sarre. ◈ *state* SW Germany
Saarlautern *see* Saarlouis
103 *D20* **Saarlouis** *prev.* Saarlautern. Saarland, SW Germany
110 *E11* **Saaser Vispa** ≈ S Switzerland
143 *X12* **Saatlı** *Rus.* Saatly. C Azerbaijan
Saatly *see* Saatlı
Saaz *see* Žatec
176 *X9* **Saba** Irian Jaya, E Indonesia
47 *V9* **Saba** *island* N Netherlands Antilles
144 *J7* **Sab' Ābār** *var.* Sab'a Biyar, Sa'b Bi'ār. Ḩimş, C Syria
Sab'a Biyar *see* Sab' Ābār
114 *K11* **Šabac** Serbia, W Yugoslavia
107 *W5* **Sabadell** Cataluña, E Spain
171 *Hh13* **Sabae** Fukui, Honshū, SW Japan
175 *O3* **Sabah** *prev.* British North Borneo, North Borneo. ◈ *state* East Malaysia
174 *Gg4* **Sabak** *var.* Sabak Bernam. Selangor, Peninsular Malaysia
Sabak Bernam *see* Sabak
40 *D16* **Sabak, Cape** *headland* Agattu Island, Alaska, USA
83 *J20* **Sabaki** ≈ S Kenya
175 *P14* **Sabalana, Kepulauan** *var.* Kepulauan Liukang Tenggaya. *island group* C Indonesia
148 *L2* **Sabalān, Kuhhā-ye** ▲ NW Iran
160 *H7* **Sabalgarh** Madhya Pradesh, C India
46 *E4* **Sabana, Archipiélago de** *island group* C Cuba
44 *H7* **Sabanagrande** *var.* Sabana Grande. Francisco Morazán, S Honduras
56 *E5* **Sabanalarga** Atlántico, N Colombia
43 *W14* **Sabancuy** Campeche, SE Mexico
47 *N8* **Sabaneta** NW Dominican Republic
56 *J4* **Sabaneta** Falcón, N Venezuela
196 *H4* **Sabaneta, Puntan** *prev.* Ushi Point. *headland* Saipan, S Northern Mariana Islands
176 *Y12* **Sabang** Irian Jaya, E Indonesia
118 *L10* **Săbăoani** Neamţ, NE Romania
161 *J26* **Sabaragamuwa Province** ◈ *province* C Sri Lanka
Sabaria *see* Szombathely
160 *D10* **Sābarmati** ≈ NW India
175 *T6* **Sabatai** Pulau Morotai, E Indonesia
147 *Q15* **Sab'atayn, Ramlat as** *desert* C Yemen
109 *I16* **Sabaudia** Lazio, C Italy
59 *J19* **Sabaya** Oruro, S Bolivia
Sa'b Bi'ār *see* Sab' Ābār
Sabbioncello *see* Orebić
154 *I8* **Şāberī, Hāmūn-e** *var.* Daryācheh-ye Hāmūn, Daryācheh-ye Sīstān. ◎ Afghanistan/Iran *see also* Sīstān, Daryācheh-ye
29 *P2* **Sabetha** Kansas, C USA
77 *P10* **Sabhā** C Libya
69 *V13* **Sabi** *var.* Rio Save. ≈ Mozambique/Zimbabwe *see also* Save, Rio
120 *E8* **Sabile** *Ger.* Zabeln. Talsi, NW Latvia
33 *R14* **Sabina** Ohio, N USA
42 *I3* **Sabinal** Chihuahua, N Mexico
27 *Q12* **Sabinal** Texas, SW USA
27 *Q11* **Sabinal River** ≈ Texas, SW USA
107 *S4* **Sabiñánigo** Aragón, NE Spain
43 *N6* **Sabinas** Coahuila de Zaragoza, NE Mexico
43 *O8* **Sabinas Hidalgo** Nuevo León, NE Mexico
43 *N6* **Sabinas, Río** ≈ NE Mexico
24 *F9* **Sabine Lake** ◎ Louisiana/Texas, S USA
94 *O3* **Sabine Land** *physical region* C Svalbard
27 *W7* **Sabine River** ≈ Louisiana/Texas, SW USA
143 *X12* **Sabirabad** C Azerbaijan
Sabkha *see* As Sabkhah
179 *P12* **Sablayan** Mindoro, N Philippines
11 *P16* **Sable, Cape** *headland* Newfoundland and Labrador, SE Canada
25 *X17* **Sable, Cape** *headland* Florida, SE USA
11 *R16* **Sable Island** *island* Nova Scotia, SE Canada
12 *L11* **Sables, Lac des** ◎ Québec, SE Canada
12 *E10* **Sables, Rivière aux** ≈ Ontario, S Canada
104 *K7* **Sable-sur-Sarthe** Sarthe, NW France
129 *U7* **Sablya, Gora** ▲ NW Russian Federation
79 *U14* **Sabon Birnin Gwari** Kaduna, C Nigeria
79 *V11* **Sabon Kafi** Zinder, C Niger
106 *I6* **Sabor, Rio** ≈ N Portugal
12 *J8* **Sabourin, Lac** ◎ Québec, SE Canada
104 *J14* **Sabres** Landes, SW France
205 *X13* **Sabrina Coast** *physical region* Antarctica
146 *M11* **Sabt al Ulayā** 'Asīr, SW Saudi Arabia
106 *I8* **Sabugal** Guarda, N Portugal
31 *Z13* **Sabula** Iowa, C USA
147 *N13* **Şabyā** Jīzān, SW Saudi Arabia
Sabzawar *see* Sabzevār
Sabzawaran *see* Sabzvārān
149 *S4* **Sabzevār** *var.* Sabzawar. Khorāsān, NE Iran
149 *T12* **Sabzvārān** *var.* Sabzawaran; *prev.* Jiroft. Kermān, SE Iran
Sacajawea Peak *see* Matterhorn
84 *C9* **Sacandica** Uíge, NW Angola
44 *A2* **Sacatepéquez** *off.* Departamento de Sacatepéquez. ◈ *department* S Guatemala
106 *F11* **Sacavém** Lisboa, W Portugal
31 *T13* **Sac City** Iowa, C USA
107 *P8* **Sacedón** Castilla-La Mancha, C Spain
118 *J12* **Săcele** *Ger.* Vierdörfer, *Hung.* Négyfalu; prev. *Ger.* Sieben Dörfer, *Hung.* Hétfalu. Braşov, C Romania
10 *C8* **Sachigo** Ontario, C Canada
10 *C7* **Sachigo** ≈ Ontario, C Canada
10 *C8* **Sachigo Lake** ◎ Ontario, C Canada
169 *Y16* **Sach'ŏn** *Jap.* Sansenhō; *prev.* Samch'ŏnpŏ. S South Korea
103 *O15* **Sachsen** *Eng.* Saxony, *Fr.* Saxe. ◈ *state* E Germany
103 *K14* **Sachsen-Anhalt** *Eng.* Saxony-Anhalt. ◈ *state* C Germany
111 *R9* **Sachsenburg** Salzburg, S Austria
Sachsenfeld *see* Žalec
15 *H1* **Sachs Harbour** Banks Island, Northwest Territories, N Canada
Sächsisch-Reen/Sächsisch-Regen *see* Reghin
20 *H8* **Sackets Harbor** New York, NE USA
11 *P14* **Sackville** New Brunswick, SE Canada
21 *P9* **Saco** Maine, NE USA
21 *P8* **Saco River** ≈ Maine/New Hampshire, NE USA
37 *O7* **Sacramento** *state capital* California, W USA
39 *T14* **Sacramento Mountains** ⛰ New Mexico, SW USA
37 *N6* **Sacramento River** ≈ California, W USA
37 *N5* **Sacramento Valley** *valley* California, W USA
38 *I10* **Sacramento Wash** *valley* Arizona, SW USA
107 *N15* **Sacratif, Cabo** *headland* S Spain
118 *F9* **Săcueni** *prev.* Săcuieni, *Hung.* Székelyhíd. Bihor, W Romania
Săcuieni *see* Săcueni
107 *R4* **Sádaba** Aragón, NE Spain
Sá da Bandeira *see* Lubango
144 *I6* **Şadad** Ḩimş, W Syria
147 *O13* **Şa'dah** NW Yemen
170 *Dd14* **Sadamisaki-hinto** *peninsula* Shikoku, SW Japan
175 *P12* **Sadang, Sungai** ≈ Sulawesi, C Indonesia
178 *H17* **Sadao** Songkhla, SW Thailand
148 *L8* **Sadd-e Dez, Daryācheh-ye** ◎ W Iran
21 *S3* **Saddleback Mountain** *hill* Maine, NE USA
21 *P6* **Saddleback Mountain** ▲ Maine, NE USA
178 *J114* **Sa Đec** Đông Thap, S Vietnam
147 *W13* **Sadḩ** S Oman
78 *J11* **Sadiola** Kayes, W Mali
155 *R12* **Sādiqābād** Punjab, E Pakistan
159 *Y10* **Sadiya** Assam, NE India
145 *W9* **Sa'dīyah, Hawr as** ◎ E Iraq
171 *K12* **Sado** *var.* Sadoga-shima. *island* C Japan
Sadoga-shima *see* Sado
106 *F12* **Sado, Rio** ≈ S Portugal
116 *I8* **Sadovets** Loveshka Oblast, N Bulgaria
131 *O11* **Sadovoye** Respublika Kalmykiya, SW Russian Federation
107 *W9* **Sa Dragonera** *var.* Isla Dragonera. *island* Islas Baleares, Spain, W Mediterranean Sea
97 *H20* **Sæby** Nordjylland, N Denmark
107 *P9* **Saelices** Castilla-La Mancha, C Spain
Saena Julia *see* Siena
Saetabicula *see* Alzira
116 *O12* **Safaalan** Tekirdağ, NW Turkey
Safad *see* Ẕefat
Şafāqis *see* Sfax
198 *B8* **Safata Bay** *bay* Upolu, Western Samoa, C Pacific Ocean
Safed *see* Ẕefat
Safed, Āb-i- *see* Sefīd, Darya-ye
145 *X11* **Şaffāf, Ḩawr aş** *wetland* S Iraq
97 *J16* **Säffle** Värmland, C Sweden
39 *N15* **Safford** Arizona, SW USA
76 *E7* **Safi** W Morocco
149 *V9* **Safīdābeh** Khorāsān, E Iran
148 *M4* **Safīd, Rūd-e** ≈ NW Iran
130 *I4* **Safonovo** Smolenskaya Oblast', W Russian Federation
142 *H11* **Safranbolu** Zonguldak, N Turkey
145 *Y13* **Safwān** SE Iraq
164 *J16* **Saga** *var.* Gya'gya. Xizang Zizhiqu, W China
170 *Cc13* **Saga** Saga, Kyūshū, SW Japan
170 *Cc13* **Saga** *off.* Saga-ken. ◈ *prefecture* Kyūshū, SW Japan
171 *Ll12* **Sagae** Yamagata, Honshū, C Japan
177 *G5* **Sagaing** Sagaing, C Mynamar
177 *G3* **Sagaing** ◈ *division* N Mynamar
171 *Jj16* **Sagamihara** Kanagawa, Honshū, S Japan
171 *Jj17* **Sagami-nada** *inlet* SW Japan
171 *Jj17* **Sagami-wan** *bay* SW Japan
Sagan *see* Żagań
31 *Y3* **Saganaga Lake** ◎ Minnesota, N USA
161 *F18* **Sāgar** Karnātaka, W India
160 *I9* **Sāgar** *prev.* Saugor. Madhya Pradesh, C India
13 *S8* **Sagard** Québec, SE Canada
Sagarmatha *see* Everest, Mount
179 *Qq13* **Sagay** Negros, C Philippines
Sagebrush State *see* Nevada
149 *V11* **Sāghand** Yazd, C Iran
21 *N14* **Sag Harbor** Long Island, New York, NE USA
Saghez *see* Saqqez
33 *R8* **Saginaw** Michigan, N USA
33 *R8* **Saginaw Bay** *lake bay* Michigan, N USA
150 *H11* **Sagiz** Atyrau, W Kazakhstan
66 *H6* **Saglek Bank** *undersea feature* W Labrador Sea
11 *P5* **Saglek Bay** *bay* SW Labrador Sea
Saglouc/Sagluk *see* Salluit
104 *E2* **Sagonne, Golfe de** *gulf* Corse, France, C Mediterranean Sea
107 *P13* **Sagra** ▲ S Spain
106 *F14* **Sagres** Faro, S Portugal
39 *S7* **Saguache** Colorado, C USA
46 *J7* **Sagua de Tánamo** Holguín, E Cuba
46 *E5* **Sagua la Grande** Villa Clara, C Cuba
13 *R7* **Saguenay** ≈ Québec, SE Canada
76 *C9* **Saguia al Hamra** *var.* As Saqia al Hamra. ≈ N Western Sahara
Sagunt/Saguntum *see* Sagunto
107 *S9* **Sagunto** *var.* Sagunt, *Ar.* Murviedro; *anc.* Saguntum. País Valenciano, E Spain
144 *H10* **Saḩāb** 'Ammān, NW Jordan
56 *E6* **Sahagún** Córdoba, NW Colombia
106 *L4* **Sahagún** Castilla-León, N Spain
147 *X8* **Saḩam** N Oman
70 *F9* **Sahara** *desert* Libya/Algeria
77 *U9* **Sahara el Gharbîya** *var.* Aş Şaḩrā' al Gharbīyah, *Eng.* Western Desert. *desert* C Egypt
77 *X9* **Sahara el Sharqîya** *var.* Aş Şaḩrā' ash Sharqīyah, *Eng.* Arabian Desert, Eastern Desert. *desert* E Egypt
Saharan Atlas *see* Atlas Saharien
158 *J9* **Sahāranpur** Uttar Pradesh, N India
66 *L10* **Saharan Seamounts** *var.* Saharian Seamounts. *undersea feature* E Atlantic Ocean
159 *Q13* **Saharsa** Bihār, NE India
69 *O7* **Sahel** *physical region* C Africa
159 *R14* **Sāhibganj** Bihār, NE India
145 *Q7* **Sahīlīyah** C Iraq
144 *H4* **Sāḩilīyah, Jibāl as** ⛰ NW Syria
116 *M13* **Şahin** Tekirdağ, NW Turkey
155 *U8* **Sāhīwāl** Punjab, E Pakistan
155 *U9* **Sāhīwāl** *prev.* Montgomery. Punjab, E Pakistan
147 *W11* **Saḩmah, Ramlat as** *desert* C Oman
145 *T13* **Şaḩrā' al Ḩijārah** *desert* S Iraq
42 *H5* **Sahuaripa** Sonora, NW Mexico
38 *M16* **Sahuarita** Arizona, SW USA
42 *L13* **Sahuayo** *var.* Sahuayo de José Mariá Morelos; *prev.* Sahuayo de Díaz, Sahuayo de Porfirio Díaz. Michoacán de Ocampo, SW Mexico
Sahuayo de Díaz/Sahuayo de José Mariá Morelos/Sahuayo de Porfirio Díaz *see* Sahuayo
181 *W8* **Sahul Shelf** *undersea feature* N Timor Sea
178 *Hh17* **Sai Buri** Pattani, SW Thailand
76 *I6* **Saïda** NW Algeria
144 *G7* **Saïda** *var.* Şaydā, Sayida; *anc.* Sidon. W Lebanon
Sa'īdābād *see* Sīrjān
82 *B13* **Sa'id Bundas** Western Bahr el Ghazaĺ, SW Sudan
194 *J12* **Saidor** Madang, N PNG
159 *S13* **Saidpur** *var.* Syedpur. Rajshahi, NW Bangladesh
110 *C7* **Saignelégier** Jura, NW Switzerland
170 *G11* **Saigō** Shimane, Dōgo, SW Japan
Saigon *see* Hô Chi Minh
168 *I12* **Saihan Toroi** Nei Mongol Zizhiqu, N China
Saihon Tal *see* Sonid Youqi
Sai Hun *see* Syr Darya
94 *M11* **Saija** Lappi, NE Finland
170 *Ee14* **Saijō** Ehime, Shikoku, SW Japan
170 *Dd15* **Saiki** Ōita, Kyūshū, SW Japan
176 *Uu9* **Saileen** Irian Jaya, E Indonesia
95 *N18* **Saimaa** ◎ SE Finland
95 *N18* **Saimaa Canal** *Fin.* Saimaan Kanava, *Rus.* Saymenskiy Kanal. *canal* Finland/Russian Federation
Saimaan Kanava *see* Saimaa Canal
42 *L10* **Saín Alto** Zacatecas, C Mexico
98 *L12* **St Abb's Head** *headland* SE Scotland, UK
9 *Y16* **St.Adolphe** Manitoba, S Canada
105 *O15* **St-Affrique** Aveyron, S France
13 *Q10* **St-Agapit** Québec, SE Canada
99 *O21* **St Albans** *anc.* Verulamium. E England, UK
20 *L6* **Saint Albans** Vermont, NE USA
23 *Q5* **Saint Albans** West Virginia, NE USA
99 *M24* **St Alban's Head** *var.* St.Aldhelm's Head. *headland* S England, UK
9 *Q14* **St.Albert** Alberta, SW Canada
St. Aldhelm's Head *see* St Alban's Head
13 *S8* **St-Alexandre** Québec, SE Canada
13 *O11* **St-Alexis-des-Monts** Québec, SE Canada
105 *P2* **St-Amand-les-Eaux** Nord, N France
105 *O9* **St-Amand-Montrond** *var.* St-Amand-Mont-Rond. Cher, C France
13 *Q7* **St-Ambroise** Québec, SE Canada
181 *P16* **St-André** NE Réunion
12 *M12* **St-André-Avellin** Québec, SE Canada
104 *K12* **St-André-de-Cubzac** Gironde, SW France
98 *K11* **St Andrews** E Scotland, UK
25 *Q9* **Saint Andrews Bay** *bay* Florida, SE USA
25 *W7* **Saint Andrew Sound** *sound* Georgia, SE USA
Saint Anna Trough *see* Svyataya Anna Trough
46 *J11* **St.Ann's Bay** C Jamaica
11 *T10* **St.Anthony** Newfoundland, Newfoundland and Labrador, SE Canada
35 *R13* **Saint Anthony** Idaho, NW USA
190 *M11* **Saint Arnaud** Victoria, SE Australia
193 *I15* **St.Arnaud Range** ⛰ South Island, NZ
13 *T8* **St-Arsène** Québec, SE Canada
11 *R10* **St-Augustin** Québec, E Canada
25 *X9* **Saint Augustine** Florida, SE USA
99 *H24* **St Austell** SW England, UK
105 *T4* **St-Avold** Moselle, NE France
105 *N17* **St-Barthélemy** ⛰ S France
104 *L17* **St-Béat** Haute-Garonne, S France
99 *I15* **St Bees Head** *headland* NW England, UK
181 *P16* **St-Benoit** E Réunion
105 *T13* **St-Bonnet** Hautes-Alpes, SE France
St.Botolph's Town *see* Boston
99 *G21* **St Brides Bay** *inlet* SW Wales, UK
104 *H5* **St-Brieuc** Côtes d'Armor, NW France
104 *H5* **St-Brieuc, Baie de** *bay* NW France
104 *L7* **St-Calais** Sarthe, NW France
13 *Q10* **St-Casimir** Québec, SE Canada
12 *H16* **St.Catharines** Ontario, S Canada
47 *S14* **St.Catherine, Mount** ▲ N Grenada
66 *C11* **St Catherine Point** *headland* E Bermuda
25 *X6* **Saint Catherines Island** *island* Georgia, SE USA
99 *M24* **St Catherine's Point** *headland* S England, UK
105 *N13* **St-Céré** Lot, S France
110 *A10* **St.Cergue** Vaud, W Switzerland
105 *R11* **St-Chamond** Loire, E France
35 *S16* **Saint Charles** Idaho, NW USA
29 *X4* **Saint Charles** Missouri, C USA
105 *P13* **St-Chély-d'Apcher** Lozère, S France
Saint Christopher-Nevis *see* Saint Kitts and Nevis
33 *S9* **Saint Clair** Michigan, N USA
12 *D17* **St.Clair** ≈ Canada/USA
191 *O17* **St.Clair, Lake** ◎ Tasmania, SE Australia
12 *C17* **St.Clair, Lake** *var.* Lac à L'eau Claire. ◎ Canada/USA
33 *S10* **Saint Clair Shores** Michigan, N USA
105 *S10* **St-Claude** *anc.* Condate. Jura, E France
47 *X6* **St-Claude** Basse Terre, SW Guadeloupe
25 *X12* **Saint Cloud** Florida, SE USA
31 *U8* **Saint Cloud** Minnesota, N USA
47 *T9* **Saint Croix** *island* S Virgin Islands (US)
32 *J4* **Saint Croix Flowage** ⊠ Wisconsin, N USA
21 *T5* **Saint Croix River** ≈ Canada/USA
31 *W7* **Saint Croix River** ≈ Minnesota/Wisconsin, N USA
47 *S14* **St.David's** SE Grenada
99 *H21* **St David's** SW Wales, UK
99 *G21* **St David's Head** *headland* SW Wales, UK
66 *C12* **St David's Island** *island* E Bermuda
181 *O16* **St-Denis** ○ (Réunion) NW Réunion
105 *U6* **St-Dié** Vosges, NE France
105 *R5* **St-Dizier** *anc.* Desiderii Fanum. Haute-Marne, N France
13 *N11* **St-Donat** Québec, SE Canada
13 *N11* **Ste-Adèle** Québec, SE Canada
13 *N11* **Ste-Agathe-des-Monts** Québec, SE Canada
9 *Y16* **Ste.Anne** Manitoba, S Canada
47 *R12* **Ste-Anne** Grande Terre, E Guadeloupe
47 *Y6* **Ste-Anne** SE Martinique
180 *I16* **Sainte Anne** *island* Inner Islands, NE Seychelles
13 *Q10* **Ste-Anne** ≈ Québec, SE Canada
13 *W6* **Ste-Anne-des-Monts** Québec, SE Canada
12 *M10* **Ste-Anne-du-Lac** Québec, SE Canada
13 *U4* **Ste-Anne, Lac** ◎ Québec, SE Canada
13 *S10* **Ste-Apolline** Québec, SE Canada
13 *U7* **Ste-Blandine** Québec, SE Canada
13 *R10* **Ste-Claire** Québec, SE Canada
13 *Q10* **Ste-Croix** Québec, SE Canada
110 *B8* **Ste.Croix** Vaud, SW Switzerland
105 *P14* **Ste-Énimie** Lozère, S France
29 *Y6* **Sainte Genevieve** Missouri, C USA
105 *S12* **St-Egrève** Isère, E France
41 *T12* **Saint Elias, Cape** *headland* Kayak Island, Alaska, USA
41 *U11* **Saint Elias, Mount** ▲ Alaska, USA
8 *G8* **Saint Elias Mountains** ⛰ Canada/USA
57 *Y10* **St-Élie** N French Guiana
105 *O10* **St-Eloy-les-Mines** Puy-de-Dôme, C France
13 *S7* **Ste-Maguerite Nord-Est** ≈ Québec, SE Canada
13 *R7* **Ste-Marguerite** ≈ Québec, SE Canada
13 *V4* **Ste-Marguerite, Pointe** *headland* Québec, SE Canada
13 *V3* **Ste-Marguesite** ≈ Québec, SE Canada
13 *R10* **Ste-Marie** Québec, SE Canada
47 *Q11* **Ste-Marie** NE Martinique
181 *P16* **Ste-Marie** NE Réunion
105 *U6* **Ste-Marie-aux-Mines** Haut-Rhin, NE France
10 *J14* **Ste-Marie, Lac** ⊠ Québec, S Canada
180 *K4* **Sainte Marie, Nosy** *island* E Madagascar
104 *L8* **Ste-Maure-de-Touraine** Indre-et-Loire, C France
105 *R4* **Ste-Menehould** Marne, NE France
Ste-Perpétue *see* Ste-Perpétue-de-l'Islet
13 *S9* **Ste-Perpétue-de-l'Islet** *var.* Ste-Perpétue. Québec, SE Canada
47 *X11* **Ste-Rose** Basse Terre, N Guadeloupe
181 *P16* **Ste-Rose** E Réunion
9 *W15* **Ste.Rose du Lac** Manitoba, S Canada
104 *J11* **Saintes** *anc.* Mediolanum. Charente-Maritime, W France
47 *X7* **Saintes, Canal des** *channel* SW Guadeloupe
Saintes, Îles des *see* les Saintes
181 *P16* **Ste-Suzanne** N Réunion
13 *P10* **Ste-Thècle** Québec, SE Canada
105 *Q12* **St-Étienne** Loire, E France
104 *M4* **St-Étienne-du-Rouvray** Seine-Maritime, N France
Saint Eustatius *see* Sint Eustatius
12 *M11* **Ste-Véronique** Québec, SE Canada
13 *T7* **St-Fabien** Québec, SE Canada
13 *P7* **St-Félicien** Québec, SE Canada
13 *O11* **St-Félix-de-Valois** Québec, SE Canada
104 *F1* **St-Florent** Corse, France, C Mediterranean Sea
104 *F1* **St-Florent, Golfe de** *gulf* Corse, France, C Mediterranean Sea
105 *P6* **St-Florentin** Yonne, C France
105 *N9* **St-Florent-sur-Cher** Cher, C France
105 *P12* **St-Flour** Cantal, C France
28 *H2* **Saint Francis** Kansas, C USA
85 *H26* **St.Francis, Cape** *headland* S South Africa
29 *X10* **Saint Francis River** ≈ Arkansas/Missouri, C USA
24 *J8* **Saint Francisville** Louisiana, S USA
13 *Q12* **St-François** ≈ Québec, SE Canada
47 *Y6* **St-François** Grande Terre, E Guadeloupe
13 *R11* **St-François, Lac** ◎ Québec, SE Canada
29 *X7* **Saint Francois Mountains** ⛰ Missouri, C USA
St-Gall/Saint Gall/St.Gallen *see* Sankt Gallen
104 *L16* **St-Gaudens** Haute-Garonne, S France
13 *R12* **St-Gédéon** Québec, SE Canada
189 *X10* **Saint George** Queensland, E Australia
66 *B12* **St George** N Bermuda
40 *K15* **Saint George** Saint George Island, Alaska, USA
23 *S14* **Saint George** South Carolina, SE USA
38 *J8* **Saint George** Utah, W USA
11 *R12* **St.George, Cape** *headland* Newfoundland, Newfoundland and Labrador, E Canada
195 *P11* **St.George, Cape** *headland* New Ireland,
40 *J15* **Saint George Island** *island* Pribilof Islands, Alaska, US
40 *J15* **Saint George Island** *island* Pribilof Islands, Alaska, USA
25 *S10* **Saint George Island** *island* Florida, SE USA
101 *J19* **Saint-Georges** Liège, E Belgium
13 *R11* **St-Georges** Québec, SE Canada
57 *Z11* **St-Georges** E French Guiana
47 *R14* **St.George's** ● (Grenada) SW Grenada
11 *R12* **St.George's Bay** *inlet* Newfoundland, Newfoundland and Labrador, E Canada
99 *G21* **Saint George's Channel** *channel* Ireland/Wales, UK
195 *P10* **St.George's Channel** *channel* NE PNG
66 *B11* **St George's Island** *island* E Bermuda
101 *I21* **Saint-Gérard** Namur, S Belgium
St-Germain *see* St-Germain-en-Laye
13 *P12* **St-Germain-de-Grantham** Québec, SE Canada
105 *N5* **St-Germain-en-Laye** *var.* St-Germain. Yvelines, N France
104 *H8* **St-Gildas, Pointe du** *headland* NW France
105 *R15* **St-Gilles** Gard, S France
104 *I9* **St-Gilles-Croix-de-Vie** Vendée, NW France
181 *O16* **St-Gilles-les-Bains** W Réunion
104 *M16* **St-Girons** Ariège, S France
Saint Gotthard *see* Szentgotthárd
110 *G9* **St.Gotthard Tunnel** *tunnel* Ticino, S Switzerland
99 *H22* **St Govan's Head** *headland* SW Wales, UK
36 *M7* **Saint Helena** California, W USA
67 *F24* **Saint Helena** ◇ *UK dependent territory* C Atlantic Ocean
69 *O12* **Saint Helena** *island* C Atlantic Ocean
85 *E25* **St.Helena Bay** *bay* SW South Africa
67 *M16* **Saint Helena Fracture Zone** *tectonic feature* C Atlantic Ocean
36 *M7* **Saint Helena, Mount** ▲ California, W USA
23 *S15* **Saint Helena Sound** *inlet* South Carolina, SE USA
33 *Q7* **Saint Helen, Lake** ◎ Michigan, N USA
191 *Q16* **Saint Helens** Tasmania, SE Australia
99 *K18* **St Helens** NW England, UK
34 *G10* **Saint Helens** Oregon, NW USA
34 *H10* **Saint Helens, Mount** 🌋 Washington, NW USA
99 *L26* **St Helier** ○ (Jersey) S Jersey, Channel Islands
13 *S9* **St-Hilarion** Québec, SE Canada
101 *K22* **Saint-Hubert** Luxembourg, SE Belgium
13 *T8* **St-Hubert** Québec, SE Canada
13 *P12* **St-Hyacinthe** Québec, SE Canada
St.Iago de la Vega *see* Spanish Town
33 *Q4* **Saint Ignace** Michigan, N USA
13 *O10* **St-Ignace-du-Lac** Québec, SE Canada
10 *D12* **St.Ignace Island** *island* Ontario, S Canada
110 *C7* **St.Imier** Bern, W Switzerland
99 *G25* **St Ives** SW England, UK
31 *U10* **Saint James** Minnesota, N USA
8 *I15* **St.James, Cape** *headland* Graham Island, British Columbia, SW Canada
13 *O13* **St-Jean** *var.* St-Jean-sur-Richelieu. Québec, SE Canada
57 *X9* **St-Jean** NW French Guiana
13 *R8* **St-Jean** ≈ Québec, SE Canada
Saint-Jean-d'Acre *see* 'Akko
104 *K11* **St-Jean-d'Angély** Charente-Maritime, W France
105 *N7* **St-Jean-de-Braye** Loiret, C France
104 *I16* **St-Jean-de-Luz** Pyrénées-Atlantiques, SW France
105 *T12* **St-Jean-de-Maurienne** Savoie, E France
104 *I9* **St-Jean-de-Monts** Vendée, NW France
105 *Q14* **St-Jean-du-Gard** Gard, S France
13 *Q7* **St-Jean, Lac** ◎ Québec, SE Canada
104 *I16* **St-Jean-Pied-de-Port** Pyrénées-Atlantiques, SW France
13 *S9* **St-Jean-Port-Joli** Québec, SE Canada
St-Jean-sur-Richelieu *see* St-Jean
13 *N12* **St-Jérôme** Québec, SE Canada
27 *T5* **Saint Jo** Texas, SW USA
11 *O15* **St.John** New Brunswick, SE Canada
28 *L6* **Saint John** Kansas, C USA
78 *K16* **Saint John** ≈ C Liberia
47 *T9* **Saint John** *island* C Virgin Islands (US)
24 *I6* **Saint John, Lake** ◎ Louisiana, S USA
21 *Q2* **Saint John** *Fr.* Saint-John. ≈ Canada/USA
47 *W10* **St John's** ● (Antigua and Barbuda) Antigua, Antigua and Barbuda
11 *V12* **St.John's** Newfoundland, Newfoundland and Labrador, E Canada
39 *O12* **Saint Johns** Arizona, SW USA
33 *Q9* **Saint Johns** Michigan, N USA
11 *V12* **St.John's** ✕ Newfoundland, Newfoundland and Labrador, E Canada
25 *X11* **Saint Johns River** ≈ Florida, SE USA
47 *N12* **St.Joseph** W Dominica
181 *P17* **St-Joseph** S Réunion
24 *J6* **Saint Joseph** Louisiana, S USA
33 *O10* **Saint Joseph** Michigan, N USA
29 *R3* **Saint Joseph** Missouri, C USA
22 *I10* **Saint Joseph** Tennessee, S USA
24 *R9* **Saint Joseph Bay** *bay* Florida, SE USA
13 *R11* **St-Joseph-de-Beauce** Québec, SE Canada
10 *C10* **St.Joseph, Lake** ◎ Ontario, C Canada
33 *Q11* **Saint Joseph River** ≈ N USA
12 *C11* **Saint Joseph's Island** *island* Ontario, S Canada
13 *N11* **St-Jovite** Québec, SE Canada
123 *Jj16* **St Julian's** N Malta
St-Julien *see* St-Julien-en-Genevois
105 *T10* **St-Julien-en-Genevois** *var.* St-Julien. Haute-Savoie, E France
104 *M11* **St-Junien** Haute-Vienne, C France
105 *Q11* **St-Just-St-Rambert** Loire, E France
98 *D8* **St Kilda** *island* NW Scotland, UK
47 *V10* **Saint Kitts** *island* Saint Kitts and Nevis
47 *U10* **Saint Kitts and Nevis** *off.* Federation of Saint Christopher and Nevis, *var.* Saint Christopher-Nevis. ◆ *commonwealth republic* E West Indies
9 *X16* **St.Laurent** Manitoba, S Canada
St-Laurent *see* St-Laurent-du-Maroni
57 *X9* **St-Laurent-du-Maroni** *var.* St-Laurent. NW French Guiana
St-Laurent, Fleuve *see* St.Lawrence
104 *J12* **St-Laurent-Médoc** Gironde, SW France
11 *N12* **St.Lawrence** *Fr.* Fleuve St-Laurent. ≈ Canada/USA
11 *Q12* **St.Lawrence, Gulf of** *gulf* NW Atlantic Ocean
40 *K10* **Saint Lawrence Island** *island* Alaska, USA
12 *M14* **Saint Lawrence River** ≈ Canada/USA
101 *L25* **Saint-Léger** Luxembourg, SE Belgium
11 *N14* **St.Léonard** New Brunswick, SE Canada
13 *P11* **St-Léonard** Québec, SE Canada
181 *O17* **St-Leu** W Réunion
104 *J4* **St-Lô** *anc.* Briovera, Laudus. Manche, N France
9 *T15* **St.Louis** Saskatchewan, S Canada
105 *V7* **St-Louis** Haut-Rhin, NE France
181 *O17* **St-Louis** S Réunion
78 *G10* **Saint Louis** NW Senegal
29 *X4* **Saint Louis** Missouri, C USA
31 *W5* **Saint Louis River** ≈ Minnesota, N USA
105 *T7* **St-Loup-sur-Semouse** Haute-Saône, E France
13 *O12* **St-Luc** Québec, SE Canada
47 *X13* **Saint Lucia** ◆ *commonwealth republic* SE West Indies
49 *S3* **Saint Lucia** *island* SE West Indies
85 *L22* **St.Lucia, Cape** *headland* E South Africa
47 *Y13* **Saint Lucia Channel** *channel* Martinique/Saint Lucia
85 *L22* **St.Lucia Estuary** KwaZulu/Natal, E South Africa
25 *Y14* **Saint Lucie Canal** *canal* Florida, SE USA
25 *Z13* **Saint Lucie Inlet** *inlet* Florida, SE USA
98 *L2* **St Magnus Bay** *bay* N Scotland, UK
104 *K10* **St-Maixent-l'École** Deux-Sèvres, W France
9 *Y16* **St.Malo** Manitoba, S Canada
104 *I5* **St-Malo** Ille-et-Vilaine, NW France
104 *H4* **St-Malo, Golfe de** *gulf* NW France
46 *L9* **St-Marc** C Haiti
46 *L9* **St-Marc, Canal de** *channel* W Haiti
105 *S12* **St-Marcellin-le-Mollard** Isère, E France
98 *K5* **St Margaret's Hope** NE Scotland, UK
34 *M9* **Saint Maries** Idaho, NW USA
25 *T9* **Saint Marks** Florida, SE USA
110 *D11* **St.Martin** Valais, SW Switzerland
Saint Martin *see* Sint Maarten
33 *O5* **Saint Martin Island** *island* Michigan, N USA
24 *I9* **Saint Martinville** Louisiana, S USA
193 *E20* **St.Mary, Mount** ▲ South Island, NZ

◆ Country ● Country Capital ◇ Dependent Territory ○ Dependent Territory Capital ◈ Administrative Region ✕ International Airport ▲ Mountain ⛰ Mountain Range 🌋 Volcano ≈ River ◎ Lake ⊠ Reservoir

San Antonio de Caparo – Sânnicolaul-Mare

56 H7 **San Antonio de Caparo** Táchira, W Venezuela
64 J5 **San Antonio de los Cobres** Salta, NE Argentina
56 H7 **San Antonio del Táchira** *var.* San Antonio. Táchira, W Venezuela
37 T15 **San Antonio, Mount** ▲ California, W USA
65 K16 **San Antonio Oeste** Río Negro, E Argentina
27 T13 **San Antonio River** ~ Texas, SW USA
56 J5 **Sanare** Lara, N Venezuela
105 T16 **Sanary-sur-Mer** Var, SE France
27 X8 **San Augustine** Texas, SW USA
147 T13 **Sanāw** *var.* Sanaw. NE Yemen
43 O11 **San Bartolo** San Luis Potosí, C Mexico
109 L16 **San Bartolomeo in Galdo** Campania, S Italy
108 K13 **San Benedetto del Tronto** Marche, C Italy
44 E3 **San Benito** Petén, N Guatemala
27 T17 **San Benito** Texas, SW USA
56 E6 **San Benito Abad** Sucre, N Colombia
37 P11 **San Benito Mountain** ▲ California, W USA
37 O10 **San Benito River** ~ California, W USA
110 H10 **San Bernardino** Graubünden, S Switzerland
37 U15 **San Bernardino** California, W USA
110 H10 **San Bernardino, Passo del** *pass* SE Switzerland
64 H11 **San Bernardo** Santiago, C Chile
42 J8 **San Bernardo** Durango, C Mexico
170 F12 **Sanbe-san** ▲ Kyūshū, SW Japan
42 J12 **San Blas** Nayarit, C Mexico
42 H8 **San Blas** Sinaloa, C Mexico
45 V14 **San Blas** *off.* Comarca de San Blas. ◆ *special territory* NE Panama
45 U14 **San Blas, Archipiélago de** *island group* NE Panama
25 Q10 **San Blas, Cape** *headland* Florida, SE USA
45 V14 **San Blas, Cordillera de** ▲ NE Panama
64 J8 **San Blas de los Sauces** Catamarca, NW Argentina
108 G8 **San Bonifacio** Veneto, NE Italy
31 S12 **Sanborn** Iowa, C USA
42 M7 **San Buenaventura** Coahuila de Zaragoza, NE Mexico
107 S5 **San Caprasio** ▲ N Spain
61 L21 **San Carlos** São Paulo, SE Brazil
64 G13 **San Carlos** Bío Bío, C Chile
42 E9 **San Carlos** Baja California Sur, W Mexico
43 N5 **San Carlos** Coahuila de Zaragoza, NE Mexico
43 P9 **San Carlos** Tamaulipas, C Mexico
44 L12 **San Carlos** Río San Juan, S Nicaragua
45 T16 **San Carlos** Panamá, C Panama
179 P9 **San Carlos** *off.* San Carlos City. Luzon, N Philippines
38 M14 **San Carlos** Arizona, SW USA
63 G20 **San Carlos** Maldonado, S Uruguay
56 K5 **San Carlos** Cojedes, N Venezuela
San Carlos *see* Quesada, Costa Rica
San Carlos *see* Luba, Equatorial Guinea
63 B17 **San Carlos Centro** Santa Fe, C Argentina
179 Q13 **San Carlos City** Negros, C Philippines
San Carlos de Ancud *see* Ancud
65 H16 **San Carlos de Bariloche** Río Negro, SW Argentina
63 B21 **San Carlos de Bolívar** Buenos Aires, E Argentina
56 H6 **San Carlos del Zulia** Zulia, W Venezuela
56 L12 **San Carlos de Río Negro** Amazonas, S Venezuela
San Carlos, Estrecho de *see* Falkland Sound
38 M14 **San Carlos Reservoir** ⊡ Arizona, SW USA
44 M12 **San Carlos, Río** ~ N Costa Rica
67 D24 **San Carlos Settlement** East Falkland, Falkland Islands
63 C23 **San Cayetano** Buenos Aires, E Argentina
105 O8 **Sancerre** Cher, C France
164 G7 **Sanchakou** Xinjiang Uygur Zizhiqu, NW China
Sanchoku *see* Samch'ŏk
43 O12 **San Ciro** San Luis Potosí, C Mexico
107 P10 **San Clemente** Castilla-La Mancha, C Spain
37 T16 **San Clemente** California, W USA
63 E21 **San Clemente del Tuyú** Buenos Aires, E Argentina
37 S17 **San Clemente Island** *island* Channel Islands, California, W USA
105 O9 **Sancoins** Cher, C France
195 Z17 **San Cristobal** *var.* Makira. *island* SE Solomon Islands
63 B16 **San Cristóbal** Santa Fe, C Argentina
46 B4 **San Cristóbal** Pinar del Río, W Cuba
47 O9 **San Cristóbal** *var.* Benemérita de San Cristóbal. S Dominican Republic
56 H7 **San Cristóbal** Táchira, W Venezuela
San Cristóbal *see* San Cristóbal de Las Casas
43 U16 **San Cristóbal de Las Casas** *var.* San Cristóbal. Chiapas, SE Mexico
200 Oo8 **San Cristóbal, Isla** *var.* Chatham Island. *island* Galapagos Islands, Ecuador, E Pacific Ocean
44 D5 **San Cristóbal Verapaz** Alta Verapaz, C Guatemala
46 F6 **Sancti Spíritus** Sancti Spíritus, C Cuba
105 O11 **Sancy, Puy de** ▲ C France
97 D15 **Sand** Rogaland, S Norway
175 Oo2 **Sandakan** Sabah, East Malaysia
190 K9 **Sandalwood** South Australia
Sandalwood Island *see* Sumba, Pulau
96 D11 **Sandane** Sogn og Fjordane, S Norway
116 G12 **Sandanski** *prev.* Sveti Vrach. Sofiyska Oblast, SW Bulgaria
78 J11 **Sandaré** Kayes, W Mali
97 J19 **Sandared** Älvsborg, S Sweden
96 N12 **Sandarne** Gävleborg, C Sweden
194 E10 **Sandaun** *prev.* West Sepik. ◈ *province* NW PNG
98 K4 **Sanday** *island* NE Scotland, UK
179 N14 **Sand Cay** *island* W Spratly Islands
33 P15 **Sand Creek** ~ Indiana, N USA
97 H15 **Sande** Vestfold, S Norway
97 H16 **Sandefjord** Vestfold, S Norway
79 O15 **Sandégué** E Ivory Coast
79 P14 **Sandema** N Ghana
39 O11 **Sanders** Arizona, SW USA
26 M11 **Sanderson** Texas, SW USA
25 U4 **Sandersville** Georgia, SE USA
94 H4 **Sandgerdhi** Sudhurland, SW Iceland
30 K14 **Sand Hills** ▲ Nebraska, C USA
27 S14 **Sandia** Texas, SW USA
37 T17 **San Diego** California, W USA
27 S14 **San Diego** Texas, SW USA
142 F14 **Sandıklı** Afyon, W Turkey
158 L12 **Sandila** Uttar Pradesh, N India
123 J15 **San Dimitri, Ras** *var.* San Dimitri Point. *headland* Gozo, NW Malta
174 Gg11 **Sanding, Selat** *strait* W Indonesia
32 J3 **Sand Island** *island* Apostle Islands, Wisconsin, N USA
97 C16 **Sandnes** Rogaland, S Norway
94 F13 **Sandnessjøen** Nordland, C Norway
81 L24 **Sandoa** Shaba, S Zaire
113 N15 **Sandomierz** *Rus.* Sandomir. Tarnobrzeg, SE Poland
Sandomir *see* Sandomierz
56 C13 **Sandoná** Nariño, SW Colombia
108 I7 **San Donà di Piave** Veneto, NE Italy
128 K14 **Sandovo** Tverskaya Oblast', W Russian Federation
177 Ff7 **Sandoway** Arakan State, W Burma
99 M24 **Sandown** S England, UK
41 N16 **Sand Point** Popof Island, Alaska, USA
67 N24 **Sand Point** *headland* E Tristan da Cunha
33 R7 **Sand Point** *headland* Michigan, N USA
34 M7 **Sandpoint** Idaho, NW USA
95 H14 **Sandsele** Västerbotten, N Sweden
8 I14 **Sandspit** Moresby Island, British Columbia, SW Canada
29 P9 **Sand Springs** Oklahoma, C USA
31 W7 **Sandstone** Minnesota, N USA
38 K15 **Sand Tank Mountains** ▲ Arizona, SW USA
33 S8 **Sandusky** Michigan, N USA
33 S11 **Sandusky** Ohio, N USA
33 S12 **Sandusky River** ~ Ohio, N USA
85 D22 **Sandverhaar** Karas, S Namibia
97 L24 **Sandvig** Bornholm, E Denmark
97 H15 **Sandvika** Akershus, S Norway
96 N13 **Sandviken** Gävleborg, C Sweden
32 M11 **Sandwich** Illinois, N USA
Sandwich Island *see* Éfaté
Sandwich Islands *see* Hawaiian Islands
159 V16 **Sandwip Island** *island* SE Bangladesh
9 U12 **Sandy Bay** Saskatchewan, C Canada
191 N16 **Sandy Cape** *headland* Tasmania, SE Australia
178 Mm14 **Sandy Cay** *island* NW Spratly Islands
38 L3 **Sandy City** Utah, W USA
33 U12 **Sandy Creek** ~ Ohio, N USA
23 O5 **Sandy Hook** Kentucky, S USA
20 K15 **Sandy Hook** *headland* New Jersey, NE USA
152 J15 **Sandykachi** *Turkm.* Sandykgachy. Maryyskiy Velayat, S Turkmenistan
Sandykgachy *see* Sandykachi
152 L13 **Sandykly, Peski** *desert* E Turkmenistan
9 Q13 **Sandy Lake** Alberta, W Canada
10 B8 **Sandy Lake** Ontario, C Canada
10 B8 **Sandy Lake** ◎ Ontario, C Canada
25 S3 **Sandy Springs** Georgia, SE USA
26 H8 **San Elizario** Texas, SW USA
101 L25 **Sanem** Luxembourg, SW Luxembourg
44 K5 **San Esteban** Olancho, C Honduras
107 O6 **San Esteban de Gormaz** Castilla-León, N Spain
42 E5 **San Esteban, Isla** *island* NW Mexico
San Eugenio/San Eugenio del Cuareim *see* Artigas
64 H11 **San Felipe** *var.* San Felipe de Aconcagua. Valparaíso, C Chile
42 D3 **San Felipe** Baja California, NW Mexico
42 N12 **San Felipe** Guanajuato, C Mexico
56 K5 **San Felipe** Yaracuy, NW Venezuela
46 B5 **San Felipe, Cayos de** *island group* W Cuba
San Felipe de Aconcagua *see* San Felipe
San Felipe de Puerto Plata *see* Puerto Plata
39 R11 **San Felipe Pueblo** New Mexico, SW USA
San Feliú de Guixols *see* Sant Feliu de Guíxols
200 Oo11 **San Félix, Isla** *Eng.* San Felix Island. *island* W Chile
San Felix Island *see* San Félix, Isla
56 L11 **San Fernando de Atabapo** Amazonas, S Venezuela
42 C4 **San Fernando** *var.* Misión San Fernando. Baja California, NW Mexico
43 P9 **San Fernando** Tamaulipas, C Mexico
179 P9 **San Fernando** Luzon, N Philippines
179 P10 **San Fernando** Luzon, N Philippines
106 J16 **San Fernando** *prev.* Isla de León. Andalucía, S Spain
47 U14 **San Fernando** Trinidad, Trinidad and Tobago
37 S15 **San Fernando** California, W USA
56 L7 **San Fernando** *var.* San Fernando de Apure. Apure, C Venezuela
San Fernando de Apure *see* San Fernando
64 L8 **San Fernando del Valle de Catamarca** *var.* Catamarca. Catamarca, NW Argentina
San Fernando de Monte Cristi *see* Monte Cristi
43 P9 **San Fernando, Río** ~ C Mexico
25 X11 **Sanford** Florida, SE USA
21 P9 **Sanford** Maine, NE USA
23 T10 **Sanford** North Carolina, SE USA
27 N2 **Sanford** Texas, SW USA
41 T10 **Sanford, Mount** ▲ Alaska, USA
44 G8 **San Francisco** *var.* Gotera, San Francisco Gotera. Morazán, E El Salvador
45 R16 **San Francisco** Veraguas, C Panama
179 Pp11 **San Francisco** *var.* Aurora. Luzon, N Philippines
37 L8 **San Francisco** California, W USA
56 H5 **San Francisco** Zulia, NW Venezuela
36 M8 **San Francisco** ✕ California, W USA
37 N9 **San Francisco Bay** *bay* California, W USA
63 C24 **San Francisco de Bellocq** Buenos Aires, E Argentina
42 I6 **San Francisco de Borja** Chihuahua, N Mexico
44 J6 **San Francisco de la Paz** Olancho, C Honduras
42 J7 **San Francisco del Oro** Chihuahua, N Mexico
42 M12 **San Francisco del Rincón** Jalisco, SW Mexico
47 O8 **San Francisco de Macorís** C Dominican Republic
San Francisco de Satipo *see* Satipo
San Francisco Gotera *see* San Francisco
San Francisco Telixtlahuaca *see* Telixtlahuaca
109 K23 **San Fratello** Sicilia, Italy, C Mediterranean Sea
San Fructuoso *see* Tacuarembó
84 C12 **Sanga** Cuanza Sul, NW Angola
58 C5 **San Gabriel** Carchi, N Ecuador
165 S15 **Sa'ngain** Xizang Zizhiqu, W China
160 E13 **Sangamner** Mahārāshtra, W India
158 H12 **Sāngāner** Rājasthān, N India
Sangan, Koh-i- *see* Sangān, Kūh-e
155 N6 **Sangān, Kūh-e** *Pash.* Koh-i-Sangan. ▲ C Afghanistan
126 Ll10 **Sangar** Respublika Sakha (Yakutiya), NE Russian Federation
175 O8 **Sangasanga** Borneo, C Indonesia
105 N1 **Sangatte** Pas-de-Calais, N France
109 B19 **San Gavino Monreale** Sardegna, Italy, C Mediterranean Sea
59 D16 **Sangayan, Isla** *island* W Peru
32 L14 **Sangchris Lake** ◎ Illinois, N USA
175 P15 **Sangeang, Pulau** *island* S Indonesia
118 I10 **Sângeorgiu de Pădure** *prev.* Erdăt-Sângeorz, Singeorgiu de Pădure, *Hung.* Erdőszentgyörgy. Mureş, C Romania
118 I9 **Sângeorz-Băi** *var.* Singeroz Băi, *Ger.* Rumänisch-Sankt-Georgen, *Hung.* Oláhszentgyőrgy; *prev.* Singeorz-Băi. Bistriţa-Năsăud, N Romania
37 R10 **Sanger** California, W USA
27 T5 **Sanger** Texas, SW USA
Sângerei *see* Singerei
103 L15 **Sangerhausen** Sachsen-Anhalt, C Germany
47 S6 **San Germán** W Puerto Rico
San Germano *see* Cassino
167 N2 **Sanggan He** ~ E China
175 Oo16 **Sanggar, Teluk** *bay* Nusa Tenggara, S Indonesia
174 L8 **Sanggau** Borneo, C Indonesia
81 H16 **Sangha** ◈ Central African Republic/Congo
81 G16 **Sangha-Mbaéré** ◈ *prefecture* SW Central African Republic
155 Q15 **Sānghar** Sind, SE Pakistan
117 F22 **Sangiás** ▲ S Greece
Sangihe, Kepulauan *see* Sangir, Kepulauan
175 S4 **Sangihe, Pulau** *var.* Sangir. *island* N Indonesia
56 G8 **San Gil** Santander, C Colombia
108 F12 **San Gimignano** Toscana, C Italy
154 M8 **Sangīn** *var.* Sangin. Helmand, S Afghanistan
109 O21 **San Giovanni in Fiore** Calabria, SW Italy
109 M16 **San Giovanni Rotondo** Puglia, SE Italy
108 G12 **San Giovanni Valdarno** Toscana, C Italy
Sangir *see* Sangihe, Pulau
175 Rr6 **Sangir, Kepulauan** *var.* Kepulauan Sangihe. *island group* N Indonesia
168 K9 **Sangiyn Dalay** Dundgovĭ, C Mongolia
168 H9 **Sangiyn Dalay** Govĭ-Altay, C Mongolia
168 K11 **Sangiyn Dalay** Ömnögovĭ, S Mongolia
168 K8 **Sangiyn Dalay** Övörhangay, C Mongolia
169 Y15 **Sangju** *Jap.* Shōshū. C South Korea
178 Ii11 **Sangkha** Surin, E Thailand
175 Oo7 **Sangkulirang** Borneo, N Indonesia
175 Oo7 **Sangkulirang, Teluk** *bay* Borneo, N Indonesia
161 E16 **Sāngli** Mahārāshtra, W India
81 E16 **Sangmélima** Sud, S Cameroon
37 V15 **San Gorgonio Mountain** ▲ California, W USA
39 T8 **Sangre de Cristo Mountains** ▲ Colorado/New Mexico, C USA
63 A20 **San Gregorio** Santa Fe, C Argentina
63 F18 **San Gregorio de Polanco** Tacuarembó, C Uruguay
47 V14 **Sangre Grande** Trinidad, Trinidad and Tobago
165 N16 **Sangri** Xizang Zizhiqu, W China
158 H9 **Sangrūr** Punjab, NW India
46 I11 **Sangster** *off.* Sir Donald Sangster International Airport, *var.* Montego Bay. ✕ (Montego Bay) W Jamaica
61 G17 **Sangue, Rio do** ~ W Brazil
107 R4 **Sangüesa** Navarra, N Spain
63 C16 **San Gustavo** Entre Ríos, E Argentina
Sangyuan *see* Wuqiao
42 C6 **San Hipólito, Punta** *headland* W Mexico
25 W15 **Sanibel** Sanibel Island, Florida, SE USA
25 V15 **Sanibel Island** *island* Florida, SE USA
62 F13 **San Ignacio** Misiones, NE Argentina
44 F2 **San Ignacio** *prev.* Cayo, El Cayo. Cayo, W Belize
59 L16 **San Ignacio** Beni, N Bolivia
59 O18 **San Ignacio** Santa Cruz, E Bolivia
44 M14 **San Ignacio** *var.* San Ignacio de Acosta. San José, W Costa Rica
42 E6 **San Ignacio** Baja California Sur, W Mexico
42 J10 **San Ignacio** Sinaloa, W Mexico
58 B9 **San Ignacio** Cajamarca, N Peru
San Ignacio de Acosta *see* San Ignacio
42 D7 **San Ignacio, Laguna** *lagoon* W Mexico
10 I6 **Sanikiluaq** Belcher Islands, Northwest Territories, C Canada
179 Pp9 **San Ildefonso Peninsula** *peninsula* Luzon, N Philippines
Saniquillie *see* Sanniquellie
63 D20 **San Isidro** Buenos Aires, E Argentina
45 N14 **San Isidro** *var.* San Isidro de El General. San José, SE Costa Rica
San Isidro de El General *see* San Isidro
56 E5 **San Jacinto** Bolívar, N Colombia
37 U16 **San Jacinto** California, W USA
37 V15 **San Jacinto Peak** ▲ California, W USA
63 F14 **San Javier** Misiones, NE Argentina
63 C16 **San Javier** Santa Fe, C Argentina
107 S13 **San Javier** Murcia, SE Spain
63 D18 **San Javier** Río Negro, W Uruguay
63 C16 **San Javier, Río** ~ C Argentina
166 L12 **Sanjiang** *var.* Guyi, Sanjiang Dongzu Zizhixian. Guangxi Zhuangzu Zizhiqu, S China
Sanjiang Dongzu Zizhixian *see* Sanjiang
171 Kk13 **Sanjō** *var.* Sanzyô. Niigata, Honshū, C Japan
59 M15 **San Joaquín** Beni, N Bolivia
57 O6 **San Joaquín** Anzoátegui, NE Venezuela
37 O9 **San Joaquin River** ~ California, W USA
37 P10 **San Joaquin Valley** *valley* California, W USA
63 A18 **San Jorge** Santa Fe, C Argentina
195 W15 **San Jorge** *island* N Solomon Islands
42 D3 **San Jorge, Bahía de** *bay* NW Mexico
65 J19 **San Jorge, Golfo** *var.* Gulf of San Jorge. *gulf* S Argentina
San Jorge, Gulf of *see* San Jorge, Golfo
196 K8 **San Jose** Tinian, S Northern Mariana Islands
179 Pp12 **San Jose** Mindoro, N Philippines
37 N9 **San Jose** California, W USA
63 F14 **San José** Misiones, NE Argentina
59 P19 **San José** *var.* San José de Chiquitos. Santa Cruz, E Bolivia
44 M14 **San José** ● (Costa Rica) San José, C Costa Rica
44 C7 **San José** *var.* Puerto San José. Escuintla, S Guatemala
42 G6 **San José** Sonora, NW Mexico
107 U11 **San José** Eivissa, Spain, W Mediterranean Sea
56 H5 **San José** Zulia, NW Venezuela
44 M14 **San José** *off.* Provincia de San José. ◈ *province* W Costa Rica
63 E19 **San José** ◈ *department* S Uruguay
44 M13 **San José** ✕ Alajuela, C Costa Rica
San José *see* San José del Guaviare, Colombia
San José *see* San José de Mayo, S Uruguay
179 P9 **San Jose City** Luzon, N Philippines
179 Pp13 **San Jose de Buenavista** Panay Island, C Philippines
San José de Cúcuta *see* Cúcuta
63 D16 **San José de Feliciano** Entre Ríos, E Argentina
57 O6 **San José de Guanipa** *var.* El Tigrito. Anzoátegui, NE Venezuela
64 I9 **San José de Jáchal** San Juan, W Argentina
42 G10 **San José del Cabo** Baja California Sur, W Mexico
56 G12 **San José del Guaviare** *var.* San José. Guaviare, S Colombia
63 E20 **San José de Mayo** *var.* San José. San José, S Uruguay
56 I10 **San José de Ocuné** Vichada, E Colombia
43 O9 **San José de Raíces** Nuevo León, NE Mexico
65 K17 **San José, Golfo** *gulf* E Argentina
42 F9 **San José, Isla** *island* W Mexico
45 U16 **San José, Isla** *island* SE Panama
27 U14 **San Jose Island** *island* Texas, SW USA
64 I10 **San Juan** San Juan, W Argentina
47 N9 **San Juan** *var.* San Juan de la Maguana. C Dominican Republic
59 E17 **San Juan** Ica, S Peru
47 U5 **San Juan** ○ (Puerto Rico) NE Puerto Rico
64 H10 **San Juan** *off.* Provincia de San Juan. ◈ *province* W Argentina
47 U5 **San Juan** *var.* Luis Muñoz Marin. ✕ NE Puerto Rico
San Juan *see* San Juan de los Morros
64 O7 **San Juan Bautista** Misiones, S Paraguay
37 O10 **San Juan Bautista** California, W USA
San Juan Bautista *see* Villahermosa
San Juan Bautista Cuicatlán *see* Cuicatlán
San Juan Bautista Tuxtepec *see* Tuxtepec
81 C17 **San Juan, Cabo** *headland* S Equatorial Guinea
107 S12 **San Juan de Alicante** País Valenciano, E Spain
56 H7 **San Juan de Colón** Táchira, NW Venezuela
42 L9 **San Juan de Guadalupe** Durango, C Mexico
San Juan de la Maguana *see* San Juan
56 G4 **San Juan del Cesar** La Guajira, N Colombia
42 L15 **San Juan de Lima, Punta** *headland* SW Mexico
44 I8 **San Juan de Limay** Estelí, NW Nicaragua
45 N12 **San Juan del Norte** *var.* Greytown. Río San Juan, SE Nicaragua
56 K4 **San Juan de los Cayos** Falcón, N Venezuela
42 M12 **San Juan de los Lagos** Jalisco, C Mexico
56 L5 **San Juan de los Morros** *var.* San Juan. Guárico, N Venezuela
42 K9 **San Juan del Río** Durango, C Mexico
43 O13 **San Juan del Río** Querétaro de Arteaga, C Mexico
44 J11 **San Juan del Sur** Rivas, SW Nicaragua
56 M9 **San Juan de Manapiare** Amazonas, S Venezuela
42 E7 **San Juanico** Baja California Sur, W Mexico
42 D7 **San Juanico, Punta** *headland* W Mexico
34 G6 **San Juan Islands** *island group* Washington, NW USA
42 I6 **San Juanito** Chihuahua, N Mexico
42 I12 **San Juanito, Isla** *island* C Mexico
39 R8 **San Juan Mountains** ▲ Colorado, C USA
56 E5 **San Juan Nepomuceno** Bolívar, NW Colombia
46 E5 **San Juan, Pico** ▲ C Cuba
203 W15 **San Juan, Punta** *headland* Easter Island, Chile, E Pacific Ocean
44 M12 **San Juan, Río** ~ Costa Rica/Nicaragua
43 S15 **San Juan, Río** ~ SE Mexico
39 O8 **San Juan River** ~ Colorado/Utah, W USA
San Julián *see* Puerto San Julián
63 B17 **San Justo** Santa Fe, C Argentina
111 W5 **Sankt Aegyd am Neuwalde** Niederösterreich, E Austria
111 U9 **Sankt Andrä** *Slvn.* Šent Andraž. Kärnten, S Austria
Sankt Andrä *see* Szentendre
Sankt Anna *see* Sântana
110 K8 **Sankt Anton am Arlberg** Vorarlberg, W Austria
103 E16 **Sankt Augustin** Nordrhein-Westfalen, W Germany
Sankt-Bartholomäi *see* Palamuse
103 F24 **Sankt Blasien** Baden-Württemberg, SW Germany
111 R3 **Sankt Florian am Inn** Oberösterreich, N Austria
110 I7 **Sankt Gallen** *var.* St.Gallen, *Eng.* Saint Gall, *Fr.* St-Gall. Sankt Gallen, NE Switzerland
110 H8 **Sankt Gallen** *var.* St.Gallen, Eng. Saint Gall, *Fr.* St-Gall. ◈ *canton* NE Switzerland
110 J8 **Sankt Gallenkirch** Vorarlberg, W Austria
111 Q5 **Sankt Georgen** Salzburg, N Austria
Sankt Georgen *see* Đurđevac, Croatia
Sankt-Georgen *see* Sfântu Gheorghe, Romania
111 R6 **Sankt Gilgen** Salzburg, NW Austria
Sankt Gotthard *see* Szentgotthárd
103 E20 **Sankt Ingbert** Saarland, SW Germany
Sankt-Jakobi *see* Viru-Jaagupi, Lääne-Virumaa, Estonia
Sankt-Jakobi *see* Pärnu-Jaagupi, Pärnumaa, Estonia
Sankt Johann *see* Sankt Johann in Tirol
111 T7 **Sankt Johann am Tauern** Steiermark, E Austria
111 Q7 **Sankt Johann im Pongau** Salzburg, NW Austria
111 P6 **Sankt Johann in Tirol** *var.* Sankt Johann. Tirol, W Austria
Sankt-Johannis *see* Järva-Jaani
110 L8 **Sankt Leonhard** Tirol, W Austria
Sankt Margarethen *see* Sankt Margarethen im Burgenland
111 Y5 **Sankt Margarethen im Burgenland** *var.* Sankt Margarethen. Burgenland, E Austria
Sankt Martin *see* Martin
111 X8 **Sankt Martin an der Raab** Burgenland, SE Austria
111 U7 **Sankt Michael in Obersteiermark** Steiermark, SE Austria
Sankt Michel *see* Mikkeli
Sankt Moritz *see* St.Moritz
110 E11 **Sankt Niklaus** Valais, S Switzerland
111 S7 **Sankt Nikolai** *var.* Sankt Nikolai im Sölktal. Steiermark, SE Austria
Sankt Nikolai im Sölktal *see* Sankt Nikolai
111 U9 **Sankt Paul** *var.* Sankt Paul im Lavanttal. Kärnten, S Austria
Sankt Paul im Lavanttal *see* Sankt Paul
Sankt Peter *see* Pivka
111 W9 **Sankt Peter am Ottersbach** Steiermark, SE Austria
128 J13 **Sankt-Peterburg** *prev.* Leningrad, Petrograd, *Eng.* Saint Petersburg, *Fin.* Pietari. Leningradskaya Oblast', NW Russian Federation
102 H8 **Sankt Peter-Ording** Schleswig-Holstein, N Germany
111 V4 **Sankt Pölten** Niederösterreich, N Austria
111 W7 **Sankt Ruprecht** *var.* Sankt Ruprecht an der Raab. Steiermark, SE Austria
Sankt Ruprecht an der Raab *see* Sankt Ruprecht
Sankt-Ulrich *see* Ortisei
111 T4 **Sankt Valentin** Niederösterreich, C Austria
Sankt Veit am Flaum *see* Rijeka
111 T9 **Sankt Veit an der Glan** *Slvn.* Šent Vid. Kärnten, S Austria
101 M21 **Sankt-Vith** *var.* Saint-Vith. Liège, E Belgium
103 E20 **Sankt Wendel** Saarland, SW Germany
111 R6 **Sankt Wolfgang** Salzburg, NW Austria
81 K21 **Sankuru** ~ C Zaire
42 D8 **San Lázaro, Cabo** *headland* W Mexico
143 O16 **Şanlıurfa** *prev.* Sanli Urfa, Urfa, *anc.* Edessa. Şanlıurfa, S Turkey
143 O16 **Şanlıurfa** *prev.* Urfa. ◈ *province* SE Turkey
143 O16 **Şanlıurfa Yaylası** *plateau* SE Turkey
63 B18 **San Lorenzo** Santa Fe, C Argentina
59 M21 **San Lorenzo** Tarija, S Bolivia
58 C5 **San Lorenzo** Esmeraldas, N Ecuador
44 H8 **San Lorenzo** Valle, S Honduras
107 N8 **San Lorenzo de El Escorial** *var.* El Escorial. Madrid, C Spain
42 E5 **San Lorenzo, Isla** *island* NW Mexico
59 C14 **San Lorenzo, Isla** *island* W Peru
65 G20 **San Lorenzo, Monte** ▲ S Argentina
42 I9 **San Lorenzo, Río** ~ C Mexico
106 J15 **Sanlúcar de Barrameda** Andalucía, S Spain
106 J14 **Sanlúcar la Mayor** Andalucía, S Spain
42 F11 **San Lucas** Baja California Sur, NW Mexico
42 E6 **San Lucas** *var.* Cabo San Lucas. Baja California Sur, W Mexico
42 G11 **San Lucas, Cabo** *var.* San Lucas Cape. *headland* W Mexico
San Lucas Cape *see* San Lucas, Cabo
64 J11 **San Luis** San Luis, C Argentina
44 E4 **San Luis** Petén, NE Guatemala
42 D2 **San Luis** *var.* San Luis Río Colorado. Sonora, NW Mexico
44 M7 **San Luis** Región Autónoma Atlántico Norte, NE Nicaragua
38 H15 **San Luis** Arizona, SW USA
39 T8 **San Luis** Colorado, C USA
56 J4 **San Luis** Falcón, N Venezuela
64 J11 **San Luis** *off.* Provincia de San Luis. ◈ *province* C Argentina
43 N12 **San Luis de la Paz** Guanajuato, C Mexico
42 K8 **San Luis del Cordero** Durango, C Mexico
42 D4 **San Luis, Isla** *island* NW Mexico
44 E6 **San Luis Jilotepeque** Jalapa, SE Guatemala
59 M16 **San Luis, Laguna de** ◎ NW Bolivia
37 P13 **San Luis Obispo** California, W USA
39 R7 **San Luis Peak** ▲ Colorado, C USA
43 N11 **San Luis Potosí** San Luis Potosí, C Mexico
43 N11 **San Luis Potosí** ◈ *state* C Mexico
37 O10 **San Luis Reservoir** ⊡ California, W USA
San Luis Río Colorado *see* San Luis
39 S8 **San Luis Valley** *basin* Colorado, C USA
109 C19 **Sanluri** Sardegna, Italy, C Mediterranean Sea
63 D23 **San Manuel** Buenos Aires, E Argentina
38 M15 **San Manuel** Arizona, SW USA
108 F11 **San Marcello Pistoiese** Toscana, C Italy
109 N20 **San Marco Argentano** Calabria, SW Italy
56 E6 **San Marcos** Sucre, N Colombia
44 M14 **San Marcos** San José, C Costa Rica
44 B5 **San Marcos** San Marcos, W Guatemala
44 F6 **San Marcos** Ocotepeque, SW Honduras
43 O16 **San Marcos** Guerrero, S Mexico
27 S11 **San Marcos** Texas, SW USA
44 A5 **San Marcos** *off.* Departamento de San Marcos. ◈ *department* W Guatemala
San Marcos de Arica *see* Arica
42 E6 **San Marcos, Isla** *island* W Mexico
108 H11 **San Marino** ● (San Marino) C San Marino
108 I11 **San Marino** *off.* Republic of San Marino. ◆ *republic* S Europe
64 I11 **San Martín** Mendoza, C Argentina
56 F11 **San Martín** Meta, C Colombia
58 D11 **San Martín** *off.* Departamento de San Martín. ◈ *department* C Peru
204 I5 **San Martín** *Argentinian research station* Antarctica
65 H16 **San Martín de los Andes** Neuquén, W Argentina
106 M8 **San Martín de Valdeiglesias** Madrid, C Spain
65 G21 **San Martín, Lago** *var.* Lago O'Higgins. ◎ S Argentina
108 H6 **San Martino di Castrozza** Trentino-Alto Adige, N Italy
59 N16 **San Martín, Río** ~ N Bolivia
San Martín Texmelucan *see* Texmelucan
37 N9 **San Mateo** California, W USA
57 O6 **San Mateo** Anzoátegui, NE Venezuela
44 B4 **San Mateo Ixtatán** Huehuetenango, W Guatemala
59 Q18 **San Matías** Santa Cruz, E Bolivia
65 K16 **San Matías, Golfo** *var.* Gulf of San Matías. *gulf* E Argentina
San Matías, Gulf of *see* San Matías
13 O8 **Sanmaur** Québec, SE Canada
167 T10 **Sanmen Wan** *bay* E China
166 M6 **Sanmenxia** *var.* Shan Xian. Henan, C China
Sânmiclăuş Mare *see* Sânnicolau Mare
63 D14 **San Miguel** Corrientes, NE Argentina
59 L16 **San Miguel** Beni, N Bolivia
44 G8 **San Miguel** San Miguel, SE El Salvador
42 L6 **San Miguel** Coahuila de Zaragoza, N Mexico
42 J9 **San Miguel** *var.* San Miguel de Cruces. Durango, C Mexico
45 U16 **San Miguel** Panamá, SE Panama
37 P12 **San Miguel** California, W USA
44 B9 **San Miguel** ◈ *department* E El Salvador
43 N13 **San Miguel de Allende** Guanajuato, C Mexico
San Miguel de Cruces *see* San Miguel
San Miguel de Ibarra *see* Ibarra
63 D21 **San Miguel del Monte** Buenos Aires, E Argentina
64 J7 **San Miguel de Tucumán** *var.* Tucumán. Tucumán, N Argentina
45 V16 **San Miguel, Golfo de** *gulf* S Panama
37 P15 **San Miguel Island** *island* California, W USA
44 L11 **San Miguelito** Río San Juan, S Nicaragua
45 T15 **San Miguelito** Panamá, C Panama
59 N18 **San Miguel, Río** ~ E Bolivia
58 D6 **San Miguel, Río** ~ Colombia/Ecuador
42 I7 **San Miguel, Río** ~ N Mexico
44 G8 **San Miguel, Volcán de** ⁂ SE El Salvador
167 Q12 **Sanming** Fujian, SE China
108 F11 **San Miniato** Toscana, C Italy
San Murezzan *see* St.Moritz
Sannār *see* Sennar
109 M15 **Sannicandro Garganico** Puglia, SE Italy
42 H6 **San Nicolás** Sonora, NW Mexico
63 C19 **San Nicolás de los Arroyos** Buenos Aires, E Argentina
37 R16 **San Nicolas Island** *island* Channel Islands, California, W USA
Sânnicolaul-Mare *see* Sânnicolau Mare

◆ Country ● Country Capital ◇ Dependent Territory ○ Dependent Territory Capital ◈ Administrative Region ✕ International Airport ▲ Mountain ▲ Mountain Range ⁂ Volcano ~ River ◎ Lake ⊡ Reservoir

Sarandi – Scott Island

63 *H14* **Sarandi** Rio Grande do Sul, S Brazil
63 *F19* **Sarandí del Yí** Durazno, C Uruguay
63 *F19* **Sarandí Grande** Florida, S Uruguay
179 *Rr17* **Sarangani Islands** *island group* S Philippines
131 *P5* **Saransk** Respublika Mordoviya, W Russian Federation
117 *C14* **Sarantáporos** 〜 N Greece
116 *H9* **Sarantsi** Sofiyska Oblast, W Bulgaria
131 *T3* **Sarapul** Udmurtskaya Respublika, NW Russian Federation
Sarâqeb *see* Sarāqib
144 *I3* **Sarāqib** ***Fr.*** Sarâqeb. Idlib, N Syria
56 *J5* **Sarare** Lara, N Venezuela
57 *O10* **Sarariña** Amazonas, S Venezuela
149 *S10* **Sar Ashk** Kermān, C Iran
25 *V13* **Sarasota** Florida, SE USA
119 *O11* **Sarata** Odes'ka Oblast', SW Ukraine
118 *I10* **Sărăţel** ***Hung.*** Szeretfalva. Bistriţa-Năsăud, N Romania
27 *X10* **Saratoga** Texas, SW USA
20 *K10* **Saratoga Springs** New York, NE USA
131 *P8* **Saratov** Saratovskaya Oblast', W Russian Federation
131 *P8* **Saratovskaya Oblast'** ◈ *province* W Russian Federation
131 *Q7* **Saratovskoye Vodokhranilishche** ⊟ W Russian Federation
Saravan/Saravane *see* Salavan
194 *K12* **Sarawaget Range** ***var.*** Saruwaged Range. ▲▲ C PNG
174 *M5* **Sarawak** ◈ *state* East Malaysia
Sarawak *see* Kuching
145 *U6* **Sarāy** ***var.*** Sarāi. E Iraq
142 *D10* **Saray** Tekirdağ, NW Turkey
78 *J12* **Saraya** SE Senegal
149 *W14* **Sarbāz** Sīstān va Balūchestān, SE Iran
149 *U8* **Sarbīsheh** Khorāsān, E Iran
113 *J24* **Sárbogárd** Fejér, C Hungary
Şărcad *see* Sarkad
29 *S7* **Sarcoxie** Missouri, C USA
158 *L11* **Sārda** ***Nep.*** Kali. 〜 India/Nepal
158 *G10* **Sardārshahr** Rājasthān, NW India
109 *C18* **Sardegna** ***Eng.*** Sardinia. ◈ *region* Italy, C Mediterranean Sea
109 *A18* **Sardegna** ***Eng.*** Sardinia. *island* Italy, C Mediterranean Sea
44 *K13* **Sardinal** Guanacaste, NW Costa Rica
56 *G7* **Sardinata** Norte de Santander, N Colombia
Sardinia *see* Sardegna
123 *K8* **Sardinia-Corsica Trough** *undersea feature* Tyrrhenian Sea, C Mediterranean Sea
24 *L2* **Sardis** Mississippi, S USA
24 *L2* **Sardis Lake** ⊟ Mississippi, S USA
29 *P12* **Sardis Lake** ⊟ Oklahoma, C USA
94 *H12* **Sarek** ▲▲ N Sweden
155 *N3* **Sar-e Pol** ***var.*** Sar-i-Pul. Sar-e Pol, N Afghanistan
155 *O3* **Sar-e Pol** ◈ *province* N Afghanistan
Sar-e Pol *see* Sar-e Pol-e Żahāb
148 *J6* **Sar-e Pol-e Żahāb** ***var.*** Sar-e Pol, Sar-i Pul. Kermānshāhān, W Iran
176 *Ww10* **Sarera, Teluk** ***var.*** Teluk Irian. *bay* W Pacific Ocean
153 *T13* **Sarez, Kŭli** ***Rus.*** Sarezskoye Ozero. ◎ SE Tajikistan
Sarezskoye Ozero *see* Sarez, Kŭli
66 *G10* **Sargasso Sea** *sea* W Atlantic Ocean
155 *U8* **Sargodha** Punjab, NE Pakistan
80 *I13* **Sarh** ***prev.*** Fort-Archambault. Moyen-Chari, S Chad
149 *P4* **Sārī** ***var.*** Sari, Sāri. Māzandarān, N Iran
117 *N23* **Saría** *island* SE Greece
Sariasiya *see* Sariosiyo
42 *F3* **Saric** Sonora, NW Mexico
196 *K6* **Sarigan** *island* C Northern Mariana Islands
142 *D14* **Sarıgöl** Manisa, SW Turkey
145 *T6* **Sārihah** E Iraq
143 *R12* **Sarıkamış** Kars, NE Turkey
174 *L6* **Sarikei** Sarawak, East Malaysia
153 *U12* **Sarikol Range** ***Rus.*** Sarykol'skiy Khrebet. ▲▲ China/Tajikistan
189 *Y7* **Sarina** Queensland, NE Australia
Sarine *see* La Sarine
107 *S5* **Sariñena** Aragón, NE Spain
153 *O13* **Sariosiyo** ***Rus.*** Sariasiya. Surkhondaryo Wiloyati, S Uzbekistan
Sar-i-Pul *see* Sar-e Pol, Afghanistan
Sar-i Pul *see* Sar-e Pol-e Żahāb, Iran
Sariqamish Kŭli *see* Sarykamyshkoye Ozero
155 *V1* **Sarī Qūl** ***Rus.*** Ozero Zurkul', ***Taj.*** Zŭrkŭl. ◎ Afghanistan/Tajikistan *see also* Zŭrkŭl
77 *Q12* **Sarīr Tībistī** ***var.*** Serir Tibesti. *desert* S Libya
27 *S15* **Sarita** Texas, SW USA
169 *W14* **Sariwŏn** SW North Korea
116 *P12* **Sarıyer** İstanbul, NW Turkey
99 *L26* **Sark** ***Fr.*** Sercq. *island* Channel Islands
113 *N24* **Sarkad** ***Rom.*** Şărcad. Békés, SE Hungary
151 *W14* **Sarkand** Taldykorgan, SW Kazakhstan
Sarkaņi *see* Krasnogorskoye
158 *D11* **Sarkāri Tala** Rājasthān, NW India
142 *G15* **Şarkîkaraağaç** ***var.*** Şarki Karaağaç. Isparta, SW Turkey
142 *L13* **Şarkışla** Sivas, C Turkey
142 *C11* **Şarköy** Tekirdağ, NW Turkey
Sárköz *see* Livada
Sarlat *see* Sarlat-la-Canéda
104 *M13* **Sarlat-la-Canéda** ***var.*** Sarlat. Dordogne, SW France
111 *S3* **Sarleinsbach** Oberösterreich, N Austria
176 *Y10* **Sarmi** Irian Jaya, E Indonesia
65 *I19* **Sarmiento** Chubut, S Argentina
65 *H25* **Sarmiento, Monte** ▲ S Chile
96 *J11* **Särna** Kopparberg, C Sweden
110 *F8* **Sarnen** Obwalden, C Switzerland
110 *F9* **Sarner See** ◎ C Switzerland
12 *D16* **Sarnia** Ontario, S Canada
118 *L3* **Sarny** Rivnens'ka Oblast', NW Ukraine
175 *Q10* **Saroako** Sulawesi, C Indonesia
120 *L13* **Sarochyna** ***Rus.*** Sorochino. Vitsyebskaya Voblasts', N Belarus
174 *Hh10* **Sarolangun** Sumatera, W Indonesia
172 *Q5* **Saroma** Hokkaidō, NE Japan
172 *Q5* **Saroma-ko** ◎ Hokkaidō, NE Japan
Saronic Gulf *see* Saronikós Kólpos
117 *H20* **Saronikós Kólpos** ***Eng.*** Saronic Gulf. *gulf* S Greece
108 *D7* **Saronno** Lombardia, N Italy
142 *B11* **Saros Körfezi** *gulf* NW Turkey
113 *N20* **Sárospatak** Borsod-Abaúj-Zemplén, NE Hungary
131 *P12* **Sarpa** Respublika Kalmykiya, SW Russian Federation
131 *P12* **Sarpa, Ozero** ◎ SW Russian Federation
115 *M18* **Šar Planina** ▲▲ FYR Macedonia/Yugoslavia
97 *I16* **Sarpsborg** Østfold, S Norway
145 *U5* **Sarqalā** N Iraq
105 *U4* **Sarralbe** Moselle, NE France
Sarre *see* Saar, France/Germany
Sarre *see* Saarland, Germany
105 *U5* **Sarrebourg** ***Ger.*** Saarburg. Moselle, NE France
Sarrebruck *see* Saarbrücken
105 *U4* **Sarreguemines** ***prev.*** Saargemund. Moselle, NE France
106 *I3* **Sarria** Galicia, NW Spain
107 *S8* **Sarrión** Aragón, NE Spain
44 *F4* **Sarstoon** ***Sp.*** Río Sarstún. 〜 Belize/Guatemala
Sarstún, Río *see* Sarstoon
126 *M9* **Sartang** 〜 NE Russian Federation
104 *E3* **Sartène** Corse, France, C Mediterranean Sea
104 *K7* **Sarthe** ◈ *department* NW France
104 *K7* **Sarthe** 〜 N France
117 *H15* **Sárti** Kentrikí Makedonía, N Greece
172 *Pp2* **Sarufutsu** Hokkaidō, NE Japan
172 *Oo7* **Saru-gawa** 〜 Hokkaidō, NE Japan
Saruhan *see* Manisa
158 *G9* **Sarūpsar** Rājasthān, NW India
143 *U13* **Şărur** ***prev.*** Il'ichevsk. SW Azerbaijan
Saruwaged Range *see* Sarawaget Range
Sarvani *see* Marneuli
113 *G23* **Sárvár** Vas, W Hungary
149 *P11* **Sarvestān** Fārs, S Iran
176 *X9* **Sarwon** Irian Jaya, E Indonesia
151 *P17* **Saryagach** ***Kaz.*** Saryaghash. Yuzhnyy Kazakhstan, S Kazakhstan
Saryaghash *see* Saryagach
Saryarqa *see* Kazakhskiy Melkosopochnik
153 *W8* **Sary-Bulak** Narynskaya Oblast', C Kyrgyzstan
153 *U10* **Sary-Bulak** Oshskaya Oblast', SW Kyrgyzstan
119 *S14* **Sarych, Mys** *headland* S Ukraine
153 *Z7* **Sary-Dzhaz** ***var.*** Aksu He. 〜 China/Kyrgyzstan *see also* Aksu He
151 *T14* **Saryesik-Atyrau, Peski** *desert* E Kazakhstan
150 *G13* **Sarykamys** ***Kaz.*** Saryqamys. Mangistau, SW Kazakhstan
152 *F8* **Sarykamyshkoye Ozero** ***Uzb.*** Sariqamish Kŭli. *salt lake* Kazakhstan/Uzbekistan
Sarykol'skiy Khrebet *see* Sarikol Range
150 *M10* **Sarykopa, Ozero** ◎ C Kazakhstan
151 *V15* **Saryozek** ***Kaz.*** Saryözek. Taldykorgan, SE Kazakhstan
Saryqamys *see* Sarykamys
151 *S13* **Saryshagan** ***Kaz.*** Saryshahan. Zhezkazgan, SE Kazakhstan
Saryshahan *see* Saryshagan
151 *O13* **Sarysu** 〜 S Kazakhstan
153 *T11* **Sary-Tash** Oshskaya Oblast', SW Kyrgyzstan
152 *J15* **Saryyazynskoye Vodokhranilishche** ⊟ S Turkmenistan
108 *E10* **Sarzana** Liguria, NW Italy
42 *F3* **Sásabe** ***var.*** Aduana del Sásabe. Sonora, NW Mexico
196 *B17* **Sasalaguan, Mount** ▲ S Guam
159 *O14* **Sasarām** Bihār, N India
195 *W14* **Sasari, Mount** ▲ Santa Isabel, N Solomon Islands
170 *C12* **Sasebo** Nagasaki, Kyūshū, SW Japan
12 *I9* **Saseginaga, Lac** ◎ Québec, SE Canada
Saseno *see* Sazan
9 *R13* **Saskatchewan** ◈ *province* SW Canada
9 *U14* **Saskatchewan** 〜 Manitoba/Saskatchewan, C Canada
9 *T15* **Saskatoon** Saskatchewan, S Canada
9 *T15* **Saskatoon** ✕ Saskatchewan, S Canada
126 *K7* **Saskylakh** Respublika Sakha (Yakutiya), NE Russian Federation
44 *L7* **Saslaya, Cerro** ▲ N Nicaragua
40 *G17* **Sasmik, Cape** *headland* Tanaga Island, Alaska, USA
121 *N19* **Sasnovy Bor** ***Rus.*** Sosnovyy Bor. Homyel'skaya Voblasts', SE Belarus
131 *N5* **Sasovo** Ryazanskaya Oblast', W Russian Federation
27 *S12* **Saspamco** Texas, SW USA
111 *W9* **Sass** ***var.*** Sassbach. 〜 SE Austria
78 *M17* **Sassandra** S Ivory Coast
78 *M17* **Sassandra** ***var.*** Ibo, Sassandra Fleuve. 〜 S Ivory Coast
Sassandra Fleuve *see* Sassandra
109 *B17* **Sassari** Sardegna, Italy, C Mediterranean Sea
Sassbach *see* Sass
100 *H11* **Sassenheim** Zuid-Holland, W Netherlands
Sassmacken *see* Valdemārpils
102 *O7* **Sassnitz** Mecklenburg-Vorpommern, NE Germany
101 *E16* **Sas van Gent** Zeeland, SW Netherlands
151 *W12* **Sasykkol', Ozero** ◎ E Kazakhstan
119 *O12* **Sasyk Kunduk, Ozero** ◎ SW Ukraine
78 *J12* **Satadougou** Kayes, SW Mali
107 *V11* **Sa Talaiassa** ▲ Eivissa, Spain, W Mediterranean Sea
170 *B17* **Sata-misaki** *headland* Kyūshū, SW Japan
28 *I7* **Satanta** Kansas, C USA
161 *E15* **Sātāra** Mahārāshtra, W India
198 *Aa7* **Sātaua** Savai'i, NW Western Samoa
196 *M16* **Satawal** *island* Caroline Islands, C Micronesia
201 *R17* **Satawan Atoll** *atoll* Mortlock Islands, C Micronesia
25 *Y12* **Satellite Beach** Florida, SE USA
97 *M14* **Säter** Kopparberg, C Sweden
Sathmar *see* Satu Mare
25 *V7* **Satilla River** 〜 Georgia, SE USA
59 *F14* **Satipo** ***var.*** San Francisco de Satipo. Junín, C Peru
125 *E11* **Satka** Chelyabinskaya Oblast', C Russian Federation
159 *T16* **Satkhira** Khulna, SW Bangladesh
160 *K9* **Satna** ***prev.*** Sutna. Madhya Pradesh, C India
105 *R11* **Satolas** ✕ (Lyon) Rhône, E France
113 *N20* **Sátoraljaújhely** Borsod-Abaúj-Zemplén, NE Hungary
151 *O12* **Satpayev** ***prev.*** Nikol'skiy. Zhezkazgan, C Kazakhstan
160 *G11* **Sātpura Range** ▲▲ C India
170 *Bb16* **Satsuma-hantō** *peninsula* Kyūshū, SW Japan
178 *Hh12* **Sattahip** ***var.*** Ban Sattahip, Ban Sattahipp. Chon Buri, S Thailand
94 *L11* **Sattanen** Lappi, NE Finland
Satul *see* Satun
118 *H9* **Satulung** ***Hung.*** Kővárhosszúfalu. Maramureş, N Romania
Satul-Vechi *see* Staro Selo
118 *G8* **Satu Mare** ***Ger.*** Sathmar, ***Hung.*** Szatmárrnémeti. Satu Mare, NW Romania
118 *G8* **Satu Mare** ◈ *county* NW Romania
178 *H17* **Satun** ***var.*** Satul, Setul. Satun, SW Thailand
198 *Aa8* **Satupaiteau** Savai'i, W Western Samoa
Sau *see* Sava
12 *F14* **Sauble** 〜 Ontario, S Canada
12 *F13* **Sauble Beach** Ontario, S Canada
63 *C16* **Sauce** Corrientes, NE Argentina
Sauce *see* Juan L.Lacaze
38 *K15* **Sauceda Mountains** ▲▲ Arizona, SW USA
63 *C17* **Sauce de Luna** Entre Ríos, E Argentina
65 *L15* **Sauce Grande, Río** 〜 E Argentina
42 *K6* **Saucillo** Chihuahua, N Mexico
97 *D15* **Sauda** Rogaland, S Norway
94 *J2* **Saudhárkrókur** Nordhurland Vestra, N Iceland
147 *P9* **Saudi Arabia** ***off.*** Kingdom of Saudi Arabia, ***Ar.*** Al 'Arabīyah as Su'ūdīyah, Al Mamlakah al 'Arabīyah as Su'ūdīyah. ◆ *monarchy* SW Asia
103 *D19* **Sauer** ***var.*** Sûre. 〜 NW Europe *see also* Sûre
103 *F15* **Sauerland** *forest* W Germany
12 *F14* **Saugeen** 〜 Ontario, S Canada
20 *K12* **Saugerties** New York, NE USA
Saugor *see* Sāgar
8 *K15* **Saugstad, Mount** ▲ British Columbia, SW Canada
Sāūjbulāgh *see* Mahābād
104 *J11* **Saujon** Charente-Maritime, W France
31 *T7* **Sauk Centre** Minnesota, N USA
32 *L8* **Sauk City** Wisconsin, N USA
176 *Vv8* **Sau Korem** Irian Jaya, E Indonesia
31 *U7* **Sauk Rapids** Minnesota, N USA
57 *Y11* **Saül** C French Guiana
105 *O7* **Sauldre** 〜 C France
103 *I23* **Saulgau** Baden-Württemberg, SW Germany
105 *Q8* **Saulieu** Côte d'Or, C France
120 *G8* **Saulkrasti** Rīga, C Latvia
13 *S6* **Sault-aux-Cochons, Rivière du** 〜 Québec, SE Canada
33 *Q4* **Sault Sainte Marie** Michigan, N USA
10 *F14* **Sault Ste.Marie** Ontario, S Canada
202 *E13* **Sauma, Pointe** *headland* Île Alofi, W Wallis and Futuna
176 *Uu15* **Saumlaki** ***var.*** Saumlakki. Pulau Yamdena, E Indonesia
Saumlakki *see* Saumlaki
13 *R12* **Saumon, Rivière au** 〜 Québec, SE Canada
104 *K8* **Saumur** Maine-et-Loire, NW France
193 *F23* **Saunders, Cape** *headland* South Island, NZ
205 *N13* **Saunders Coast** *physical region* Antarctica
67 *B23* **Saunders Island** *island* NW Falkland Islands
67 *C24* **Saunders Island Settlement** Saunders Island, NW Falkland Islands
84 *F11* **Saurimo** ***Port.*** Henrique de Carvalho, Vila Henrique de Carvalho. Lunda Sul, NE Angola
57 *S11* **Sauriwaunawa** S Guyana
176 *V8* **Sausapor** Irian Jaya, E Indonesia
84 *D12* **Sautar** Malanje, NW Angola
47 *S13* **Sauteurs** N Grenada
104 *K13* **Sauveterre-de-Guyenne** Gironde, SW France
121 *O14* **Sava** ***Rus.*** Sava. Mahilyowskaya Voblasts', E Belarus
86 *H11* **Sava** ***Eng.*** Save, ***Ger.*** Sau, ***Hung.*** Száva. 〜 SE Europe
44 *J5* **Savá** Colón, N Honduras
35 *Y8* **Savage** Montana, NW USA
191 *N16* **Savage River** Tasmania, SE Australia
198 *Aa7* **Savai'i** *island* NW Western Samoa
79 *R15* **Savalou** S Benin
32 *K10* **Savanna** Illinois, N USA
25 *X6* **Savannah** Georgia, SE USA
29 *R2* **Savannah** Missouri, C USA
22 *H10* **Savannah** Tennessee, S USA
23 *O12* **Savannah River** 〜 Georgia/South Carolina, SE USA
Savannakhét *see* Khanthabouli
46 *H12* **Savanna-La-Mar** W Jamaica
10 *B10* **Savant Lake** ◎ Ontario, S Canada
161 *F17* **Savanūr** Karnātaka, W India
95 *J16* **Sävar** Västerbotten, N Sweden
Savaria *see* Szombathely
160 *C11* **Sāvarkundla** ***var.*** Kundla. Gujarāt, W India
118 *F11* **Săvârşin** ***Hung.*** Soborsin; ***prev.*** Săvîrşin. Arad, W Romania
142 *C13* **Savaştepe** Balıkesir, W Turkey
Savat *see* Sawot
85 *N18* **Save** Inhambane, E Mozambique
104 *L16* **Save** 〜 S France
85 *L17* **Save** ***var.*** Sabi. 〜 Mozambique/Zimbabwe *see also* Sabi
Save *see* Sava
79 *R15* **Savè** SE Benin
148 *M6* **Sāveh** Markazī, W Iran
118 *L8* **Săveni** Botoşani, NE Romania
105 *N16* **Saverdun** Ariège, S France
105 *U5* **Saverne** ***var.*** Zabern; ***anc.*** Tres Tabernae. Bas-Rhin, NE France
Savichi *see* Savichy
121 *O21* **Savichy** ***Rus.*** Savichi. Homyel'skaya Voblasts', SE Belarus
108 *B9* **Savigliano** Piemonte, NW Italy
Savigsivik *see* Savissivik
Savinichi *see* Savinichy
121 *Q16* **Savinichy** ***Rus.*** Savinichi. Mahilyowskaya Voblasts', E Belarus
111 *T10* **Savinjske Alpe** ***var.*** Kamniške Alpe, Sanntaler Alpen, ***Ger.*** Steiner Alpen. ▲▲ N Slovenia
Savinski *see* Savinskiy
125 *Dd6* **Savinskiy** ***var.*** Savinski. Arkhangel'skaya Oblast', NW Russian Federation
108 *H11* **Savio** 〜 C Italy
Săvîrşin *see* Săvârşin
207 *O11* **Savissivik** ***var.*** Savigsivik. N Greenland
95 *N18* **Savitaipale** Kymi, SE Finland
115 *J15* **Šavnik** Montenegro, SW Yugoslavia
195 *W15* **Savo** *island* C Solomon Islands
110 *I9* **Savognin** Graubünden, S Switzerland
105 *T12* **Savoie** ◈ *department* E France
108 *C10* **Savona** Liguria, NW Italy
95 *N17* **Savonlinna** ***Swe.*** Nyslott. Mikkeli, SE Finland
95 *N17* **Savonranta** Mikkeli, SE Finland
40 *K10* **Savoonga** Saint Lawrence Island, Alaska, USA
32 *M13* **Savoy** Illinois, N USA
119 *O8* **Savran'** Odes'ka Oblast', SW Ukraine
143 *R11* **Şavşat** Artvin, NE Turkey
97 *L19* **Sävsjö** Jönköping, S Sweden
Savu, Kepulauan *see* Sawu, Kepulauan
94 *M11* **Savukoski** Lappi, NE Finland
Savu, Pulau *see* Sawu, Pulau
197 *J13* **Savusavu** Vanua Levu, N Fiji
175 *Q17* **Savu Sea** ***Ind.*** Laut Sawu. *sea* S Indonesia
85 *H17* **Savute** Chobe, N Botswana
145 *N7* **Şawāb, 'Uqlat** *well* W Iraq
144 *M7* **Sawāb, Wādī as** *dry watercourse* W Iraq
158 *H13* **Sawāi Mādhopur** Rājasthān, N India
175 *Tt10* **Sawai, Teluk** *bay* Pulau Seram, E Indonesia
Sawakin *see* Suakin
178 *Ii9* **Sawang Daen Din** Sakon Nakhon, E Thailand
178 *H8* **Sawankhalok** ***var.*** Swankalok. Sukhothai, NW Thailand
171 *Kk17* **Sawara** Chiba, Honshū, S Japan
171 *Jj12* **Sawasaki-bana** *headland* Sado, C Japan
39 *R5* **Sawatch Range** ▲▲ Colorado, C USA
147 *N12* **Sawdā', Jabal** ▲ SW Saudi Arabia
77 *P9* **Sawdā', Jabal as** ▲▲ C Libya
Sawdirī *see* Sodiri
176 *W9* **Saweba, Tanjung** *headland* Irian Jaya, E Indonesia
99 *F14* **Sawel** ▲ C Northern Ireland, UK
Sawhāj *see* Sohâg
79 *O15* **Sawla** N Ghana
153 *P11* **Sawot** ***Rus.*** Savat. Sirdaryo Wiloyati, E Uzbekistan
147 *X12* **Şawqirah** ***var.*** Suqrah. S Oman
147 *X12* **Şawqirah, Dawḩat** ***var.*** Ghubbat Sawqirah, Sukra Bay, Suqrah Bay. *bay* S Oman
Sawqirah, Ghubbat *see* Şawqirah, Dawḩat
191 *V5* **Sawtell** New South Wales, SE Australia
144 *K7* **Şawt, Wādī aş** *dry watercourse* S Syria
175 *Q18* **Sawu, Kepulauan** ***var.*** Kepulauan Savu. *island group* S Indonesia
Sawu, Laut *see* Savu Sea
175 *Qq18* **Sawu, Pulau** ***var.*** Pulau Savu. *island* Kepulauan Sawu, S Indonesia
107 *S12* **Sax** País Valenciano, E Spain
Saxe *see* Sachsen
110 *C11* **Saxon** Valais, SW Switzerland
Saxony *see* Sachsen
Saxony-Anhalt *see* Sachsen-Anhalt
79 *R12* **Say** Niamey, SW Niger
13 *V7* **Sayabec** Québec, SE Canada
Sayaboury *see* Xaignabouli
151 *U12* **Sayak** ***Kaz.*** Sayaq. Zhezkazgan, E Kazakhstan
59 *D14* **Sayán** Lima, W Peru
126 *Hh15* **Sayanogorsk** Respublika Khakasiya, S Russian Federation
126 *J15* **Sayansk** Irkutskaya Oblast', S Russian Federation
133 *T6* **Sayanskiy Khrebet** ▲▲ S Russian Federation
Sayaq *see* Sayak
152 *K13* **Sayat** Lebapskiy Velayat, E Turkmenistan
44 *D3* **Sayaxché** Petén, N Guatemala
Şaydā/Sayida *see* Saïda
147 *T15* **Sayḩūt** E Yemen
31 *U14* **Saylorville Lake** ⊟ Iowa, C USA
Saymenskiy Kanal *see* Saimaa Canal
169 *N10* **Saynshand** Dornogovĭ, SE Mongolia
168 *J11* **Saynshand** Ömnögovĭ, S Mongolia
168 *F7* **Sayn-Ust** Govĭ-Altay, W Mongolia
Say-Ötesh *see* Say-Utës
144 *J7* **Şayqal, Baḩr** ◎ S Syria
Sayrab *see* Sayrob
164 *H4* **Sayram Hu** ◎ NW China
28 *K11* **Sayre** Oklahoma, C USA
20 *H12* **Sayre** Pennsylvania, NE USA
20 *K15* **Sayreville** New Jersey, NE USA
153 *N13* **Sayrob** ***Rus.*** Sayrab. Surkhondaryo Wiloyati, S Uzbekistan
42 *L13* **Sayula** Jalisco, SW Mexico
147 *R14* **Say 'ūn** ***var.*** Saywūn. C Yemen
150 *G14* **Say-Utës** ***Kaz.*** Say-Ötesh. Mangistau, SW Kazakhstan
8 *K16* **Sayward** Vancouver Island, British Columbia, SW Canada
Saywūn *see* Say 'ūn
Sayyāl *see* As Sayyāl
145 *U8* **Sayyid 'Abīd** ***var.*** Saiyid Abid. E Iraq
115 *J22* **Sazan** ***var.*** Ishulli i Sazanit, ***It.*** Saseno. *island* SW Albania
Sazanit, Ishulli i *see* Sazan
Sazau/Sazawa *see* Sázava
113 *E17* **Sázava** ***var.*** Sazau, ***Ger.*** Sazawa. 〜 C Czech Republic
128 *J14* **Sazonovo** Vologodskaya Oblast', NW Russian Federation
104 *G6* **Scaër** Finistère, NW France
99 *J15* **Scafell Pike** ▲ NW England, UK
Scalabis *see* Santarém
98 *M2* **Scalloway** N Scotland, UK
40 *M11* **Scammon Bay** Alaska, USA
Scammon Lagoon/ Scammon, Laguna *see* Ojo de Liebre, Laguna
86 *F7* **Scandinavia** *geophysical region* NW Europe
Scania *see* Skåne
98 *K5* **Scapa Flow** *sea basin* N Scotland, UK
109 *K26* **Scaramia, Capo** *headland* Sicilia, Italy, C Mediterranean Sea
12 *H15* **Scarborough** Ontario, SE Canada
47 *Z16* **Scarborough** ***prev.*** Port Louis. Tobago, Trinidad and Tobago
99 *N16* **Scarborough** N England, UK
193 *I17* **Scargill** Canterbury, South Island, NZ
98 *E7* **Scarp** *island* NW Scotland, UK
Scarpanto *see* Kárpathos
Scarpanto Strait *see* Karpathou, Stenó
109 *G25* **Scauri** Sicilia, Italy, C Mediterranean Sea
Scealg, Bá na *see* Ballinskelligs Bay
Scebeli *see* Shebeli
102 *K10* **Schaale** 〜 N Germany
102 *K9* **Schaalsee** ◎ N Germany
101 *G18* **Schaerbeek** Brussels, C Belgium
110 *G6* **Schaffhausen** ***Fr.*** Schaffhouse. Schaffhausen, N Switzerland
110 *G6* **Schaffhausen** ***Fr.*** Schaffhouse. ◈ *canton* N Switzerland
Schaffhouse *see* Schaffhausen
100 *I8* **Schagen** Noord-Holland, NW Netherlands
Schaken *see* Šakiai
100 *M10* **Schalkhaar** Overijssel, E Netherlands
111 *R3* **Schärding** Oberösterreich, N Austria
102 *G9* **Scharhörn** *island* NW Germany
Schässburg *see* Sighişoara
Schaulen *see* Šiauliai
32 *M10* **Schaumburg** Illinois, N USA
Schebschi Mountains *see* Shebshi Mountains
100 *P6* **Scheemda** Groningen, NE Netherlands
102 *I10* **Scheessel** Niedersachsen, NW Germany
11 *N8* **Schefferville** Québec, E Canada
Schelde *see* Scheldt
101 *D18* **Scheldt** ***Dut.*** Schelde, ***Fr.*** Escaut. 〜 W Europe
37 *X5* **Schell Creek Range** ▲▲ Nevada, W USA
20 *K10* **Schenectady** New York, NE USA
101 *I17* **Scherpenheuvel** ***Fr.*** Montaigu. Vlaams Brabant, C Belgium
100 *K11* **Scherpenzeel** Gelderland, C Netherlands
27 *S12* **Schertz** Texas, SW USA
100 *G11* **Scheveningen** Zuid-Holland, W Netherlands
100 *G12* **Schiedam** Zuid-Holland, SW Netherlands
101 *M24* **Schieren** Diekirch, NE Luxembourg
100 *M4* **Schiermonnikoog** ***Fris.*** Skiermûntseach. Friesland, N Netherlands
100 *M4* **Schiermonnikoog** ***Fris.*** Skiermûntseach. *island* Waddeneilanden, N Netherlands
101 *K14* **Schijndel** Noord-Brabant, S Netherlands
Schil *see* Jiu
101 *H16* **Schilde** Antwerpen, N Belgium
Schillen *see* Zhilino
105 *V5* **Schiltigheim** Bas-Rhin, NE France
108 *G7* **Schio** Veneto, NE Italy
100 *H10* **Schiphol** ✕ (Amsterdam) Noord-Holland, C Netherlands
Schippenbeil *see* Sępopol
Schiria *see* Şiria
Schivelbein *see* Świdwin
117 *D22* **Schíza** *island* S Greece
183 *U3* **Schjetman Reef** *reef* Antarctica
Schlackenwerth *see* Ostrov
111 *R7* **Schladming** Steiermark, SE Austria
Schlan *see* Slaný
Schlanders *see* Silandro
102 *I7* **Schlei** *inlet* N Germany
103 *D17* **Schleiden** Nordrhein-Westfalen, W Germany
195 *P9* **Schleinitz Range** ▲▲ New Ireland, N PNG
Schlelau *see* Szydłowiec
102 *I7* **Schleswig** Schleswig-Holstein, N Germany
31 *T13* **Schleswig** Iowa, C USA
102 *H8* **Schleswig-Holstein** ◈ *state* N Germany
Schlettstadt *see* Sélestat
110 *F7* **Schlieren** Zürich, N Switzerland
Schlochau *see* Człuchów
Schloppe *see* Człopa
103 *I18* **Schlüchtern** Hessen, C Germany
103 *J17* **Schmalkalden** Thüringen, C Germany
111 *W2* **Schmida** 〜 NE Austria
67 *P19* **Schmidt-Ott Seamount** ***var.*** Schmitt-Ott Seamount, Schmitt-Ott Tablemount. *undersea feature* SW Indian Ocean
Schmiegel *see* Śmigiel
Schmitt-Ott Seamount/ Schmitt-Ott Tablemount *see* Schmidt-Ott Seamount
13 *V3* **Schmon** 〜 Québec, SE Canada
103 *M18* **Schneeberg** ▲ W Germany
Schneeberg *see* Snežnik
Schnee-Eifel *see* Schneifel
Schneekoppe *see* Sněžka
Schneidemühl *see* Piła
103 *D18* **Schneifel** ***var.*** Schnee-Eifel. *plateau* W Germany
Schnelle Körös/Schnelle Kreisch *see* Crişul Repede
102 *I11* **Schneverdingen** ***var.*** Schneverdingen (Wümme). Niedersachsen, NW Germany
Schneverdingen (Wümme) *see* Schneverdingen
Schoden *see* Skuodas
20 *K10* **Schoharie** New York, NE USA
20 *K11* **Schoharie Creek** 〜 New York, NE USA
117 *J21* **Schoinoússa** *island* Kykládes, Greece, Aegean Sea
102 *L13* **Schönebeck** Sachsen-Anhalt, C Germany
Schöneck *see* Skarszewy
102 *O12* **Schönefeld** ✕ (Berlin) Berlin, NE Germany
103 *K24* **Schongau** Bayern, S Germany
102 *K13* **Schöningen** Niedersachsen, C Germany
Schönlanke *see* Trzcianka
Schönsee *see* Kowalewo Pomorskie
33 *P10* **Schoolcraft** Michigan, N USA
100 *O8* **Schoonebeek** Drenthe, NE Netherlands
100 *I12* **Schoonhoven** Zuid-Holland, C Netherlands
100 *H8* **Schoorl** Noord-Holland, NW Netherlands
Schooten *see* Schoten
103 *F24* **Schopfheim** Baden-Württemberg, SW Germany
103 *I21* **Schorndorf** Baden-Württemberg, S Germany
102 *F10* **Schortens** Niedersachsen, NW Germany
101 *H16* **Schoten** ***var.*** Schooten. Antwerpen, N Belgium
191 *Q17* **Schouten Island** *island* Tasmania, SE Australia
194 *H9* **Schouten Islands** *island group* NW PNG
100 *E13* **Schouwen** *island* SW Netherlands
47 *Q12* **Schœlcher** W Martinique
Schreiberhau *see* Szklarska Poręba
111 *U2* **Schrems** Niederösterreich, E Austria
103 *L22* **Schrobenhausen** Bayern, SE Germany
20 *L8* **Schroon Lake** ◎ New York, NE USA
110 *J8* **Schruns** Vorarlberg, W Austria
Schubin *see* Szubin
27 *U11* **Schulenburg** Texas, SW USA
Schuls *see* Scuol
110 *E8* **Schüpfheim** Luzern, C Switzerland
37 *S6* **Schurz** Nevada, W USA
103 *I24* **Schussen** 〜 S Germany
Schüttenhofen *see* Sušice
31 *R15* **Schuyler** Nebraska, C USA
20 *L10* **Schuylerville** New York, NE USA
103 *K20* **Schwabach** Bayern, SE Germany
Schwabenalb *see* Schwäbische Alb
103 *I23* **Schwäbische Alb** ***var.*** Schwabenalb, ***Eng.*** Swabian Jura. ▲▲ S Germany
103 *I22* **Schwäbisch Gmünd** ***var.*** Gmünd. Baden-Württemberg, SW Germany
103 *I21* **Schwäbisch Hall** ***var.*** Hall. Baden-Württemberg, SW Germany
103 *H16* **Schwalm** 〜 C Germany
111 *V9* **Schwanberg** Steiermark, SE Austria
110 *H8* **Schwanden** Glarus, E Switzerland
103 *M20* **Schwandorf** Bayern, SE Germany
111 *S5* **Schwanenstadt** Oberösterreich, NW Austria
174 *M9* **Schwaner, Pegunungan** ▲▲ Borneo, N Indonesia
111 *W5* **Schwarza** 〜 E Austria
111 *P9* **Schwarzach** 〜 S Austria
103 *M20* **Schwarzach** ***Cz.*** Černice. 〜 Czech Republic/Germany
Schwarzach *see* Schwarzach im Pongau, Austria
Schwarzach *see* Svratka, Czech Republic
111 *Q7* **Schwarzach im Pongau** ***var.*** Schwarzach. Salzburg, NW Austria
Schwarzawa *see* Svratka
103 *N14* **Schwarze Elster** 〜 E Germany
Schwarze Körös *see* Crişul Negru
110 *D9* **Schwarzenburg** Bern, W Switzerland
85 *D21* **Schwarzrand** ▲▲ S Namibia
103 *G23* **Schwarzwald** ***Eng.*** Black Forest. ▲▲ SW Germany
Schwarzwasser *see* Wda
41 *P7* **Schwatka Mountains** ▲▲ Alaska, USA
111 *N7* **Schwaz** Tirol, W Austria
111 *Y4* **Schwechat** Niederösterreich, NE Austria
111 *Y4* **Schwechat** ✕ (Wien) Wien, E Austria
102 *P11* **Schwedt** Brandenburg, NE Germany
103 *D19* **Schweich** Rheinland-Pfalz, SW Germany
Schweidnitz *see* Świdnica
103 *J18* **Schweinfurt** Bayern, SE Germany
Schweiz *see* Switzerland
102 *L9* **Schwerin** Mecklenburg-Vorpommern, N Germany
Schwerin *see* Skwierzyna
102 *L9* **Schweriner See** ◎ N Germany
Schwertberg *see* Świecie
103 *F15* **Schwerte** Nordrhein-Westfalen, W Germany
Schwiebus *see* Świebodzin
102 *P13* **Schwielochsee** ◎ NE Germany
Schwihau *see* Švihov
Schwiz *see* Schwyz
110 *G8* **Schwyz** ***var.*** Schwiz. Schwyz, C Switzerland
110 *G8* **Schwyz** ***var.*** Schwiz. ◈ *canton* C Switzerland
12 *J11* **Schyan** 〜 Québec, SE Canada
Schyl *see* Jiu
109 *I24* **Sciacca** Sicilia, Italy, C Mediterranean Sea
Sciasciamana *see* Shashemenē
109 *L26* **Scicli** Sicilia, Italy, C Mediterranean Sea
99 *F25* **Scilly, Isles of** *island group* SW England, UK
113 *H17* **Ścinawa** ***Ger.*** Steinau an der Elbe. Legnica, SW Poland
Scio *see* Chíos
33 *S14* **Scioto River** 〜 Ohio, N USA
38 *L5* **Scipio** Utah, W USA
35 *X6* **Scobey** Montana, NW USA
191 *T7* **Scone** New South Wales, SE Australia
Scoresby Sound/ Scoresbysund *see* Ittoqqortoormiit
Scoresby Sund *see* Kangertittivaq
Scorno, Punta dello *see* Caprara, Punta
36 *K3* **Scotia** California, W USA
49 *Y14* **Scotia Plate** *tectonic feature*
49 *V15* **Scotia Ridge** *undersea feature* S Atlantic Ocean
204 *H2* **Scotia Sea** *sea* SW Atlantic Ocean
31 *Q12* **Scotland** South Dakota, N USA
27 *R5* **Scotland** Texas, SW USA
98 *H11* **Scotland** *national region* UK
23 *W8* **Scotland Neck** North Carolina, SE USA
205 *R13* **Scott Base** *NZ research station* Antarctica
8 *J16* **Scott, Cape** *headland* Vancouver Island, British Columbia, SW Canada
28 *I5* **Scott City** Kansas, C USA
29 *Y7* **Scott City** Missouri, C USA
205 *R14* **Scott Coast** *physical region* Antarctica
20 *C15* **Scottdale** Pennsylvania, NE USA
205 *Y11* **Scott Glacier** *glacier* Antarctica
205 *Q17* **Scott Island** *island* Antarctica

◆ Country ● Country Capital ◇ Dependent Territory ○ Dependent Territory Capital ◈ Administrative Region ✕ International Airport ▲ Mountain ▲▲ Mountain Range Volcano 〜 River ◎ Lake ⊟ Reservoir

Scott Mount – Sfaktiría

28 L11 **Scott, Mount** ▲ Oklahoma, USA
34 G15 **Scott, Mount** ▲ Oregon, NW USA
36 M1 **Scott River** ∾ California, W USA
30 I13 **Scottsbluff** Nebraska, C USA
25 Q2 **Scottsboro** Alabama, S USA
33 P15 **Scottsburg** Indiana, N USA
191 P16 **Scottsdale** Tasmania, SE Australia
38 L13 **Scottsdale** Arizona, SW USA
47 O12 **Scotts Head Village** *var.* Cachacrou. S Dominica
199 Jj17 **Scott Shoal** *undersea feature* S Pacific Ocean
22 K7 **Scottsville** Kentucky, S USA
31 U14 **Scranton** Iowa, C USA
20 I13 **Scranton** Pennsylvania, NE USA
194 G10 **Screw** ∾ NW PNG
31 R14 **Scribner** Nebraska, C USA
Scrobesbyrig' *see* Shrewsbury
12 I14 **Scugog** ∾ Ontario, SE Canada
12 I14 **Scugog, Lake** ◎ Ontario, SE Canada
99 N17 **Scunthorpe** E England, UK
110 K9 **Scuol** *Ger.* Schuls. Graubünden, E Switzerland
Scupi *see* Skopje
Scutari *see* Shkodër
115 K17 **Scutari, Lake** *Alb.* Liqeni i Shkodrës, *SCr.* Skadarsko Jezero. ◎ Albania/Yugoslavia
Scyros *see* Skýros
Scythopolis *see* Bet She'an
27 U13 **Seadrift** Texas, SW USA
23 Y4 **Seaford** *var.* Seaford City. Delaware, NE USA
Seaford City *see* Seaford
12 E15 **Seaforth** Ontario, S Canada
26 M6 **Seagraves** Texas, SW USA
9 X9 **Seal** ∾ Manitoba, C Canada
190 M10 **Sea Lake** Victoria, SE Australia
85 G26 **Seal, Cape** *headland* S South Africa
67 D26 **Sea Lion Islands** *island group* SE Falkland Islands
21 S8 **Seal Island** *island* Maine, NE USA
27 V11 **Sealy** Texas, SW USA
37 X12 **Searchlight** Nevada, W USA
29 V11 **Searcy** Arkansas, C USA
21 R7 **Searsport** Maine, NE USA
37 N10 **Seaside** California, W USA
34 F10 **Seaside** Oregon, NW USA
20 K16 **Seaside Heights** New Jersey, NE USA
34 H8 **Seattle** Washington, NW USA
34 H9 **Seattle-Tacoma** ✈ Washington, NW USA
193 J16 **Seaward Kaikoura Range** ▲▲ South Island, NZ
44 J9 **Sébaco** Matagalpa, W Nicaragua
21 P8 **Sebago Lake** ◎ Maine, NE USA
176 V11 **Sebakor, Teluk** *bay* Irian Jaya, E Indonesia
Sebangan, Sungai *see* Sebangau Besar, Sungai
174 M11 **Sebangan, Teluk** *bay* Borneo, C Indonesia
174 Mm11 **Sebanganu, Teluk** *bay* Borneo, C Indonesia
174 Mm11 **Sebangau Besar, Sungai** *var.* Sungai Sebangan. ∾ Borneo, N Indonesia
174 I8 **Sebanglea, Pulau** *island* W Indonesia
Sebaste/Sebastia *see* Sivas
25 Y12 **Sebastian** Florida, SE USA
42 C5 **Sebastián Vizcaíno, Bahía** *bay* NW Mexico
21 R6 **Sebasticook Lake** ◎ Maine, NE USA
36 M7 **Sebastopol** California, W USA
Sebastopol *see* Sevastopol'
175 Oo4 **Sebatik, Pulau** *island* N Indonesia
21 R5 **Sebec Lake** ◎ Maine, NE USA
78 K12 **Sébékoro** Kayes, W Mali
Sebenico *see* Šibenik
42 G6 **Seberi, Cerro** ▲ NW Mexico
118 H11 **Sebeş** *Ger.* Mühlbach, *Hung.* Szászsebes; *prev.* Sebeşu Săsesc. Alba, W Romania
Sebes-Körös *see* Crişul Repede
Sebeşu Săsesc *see* Sebeş
33 R8 **Sebewaing** Michigan, N USA
128 F16 **Sebezh** Pskovskaya Oblast', W Russian Federation
143 N12 **Şebinkarahisar** Giresun, N Turkey
118 F11 **Sebiş** *Hung.* Borossebes. Arad, W Romania
Sebkra Azz el Matti *see* Azzel Matti, Sebkha
21 Q4 **Seboomook Lake** ◎ Maine, NE USA
76 G6 **Sebou** *var.* Sebu. ∾ N Morocco
22 I6 **Sebree** Kentucky, S USA
25 X13 **Sebring** Florida, SE USA
Sebta *see* Ceuta
Sebu *see* Sebou
175 Nn11 **Sebuku, Pulau** *island* N Indonesia
175 Oo4 **Sebuku, Teluk** *bay* Borneo, N Indonesia
176 Vv10 **Sebyar** ∾ Irian Jaya, E Indonesia
108 F10 **Secchia** ∾ N Italy
8 L17 **Sechelt** British Columbia, SW Canada
58 C12 **Sechin, Río** ∾ W Peru
58 A10 **Sechura, Bahía de** *bay* NW Peru
193 A22 **Secretary Island** *island* SW NZ
161 I15 **Secunderābād** *var.* Sikandarabad. Andhra Pradesh, C India
59 L17 **Sécure, Río** ∾ C Bolivia
120 D10 **Seda** Mažeikiai, NW Lithuania
29 T5 **Sedalia** Missouri, C USA
105 R3 **Sedan** Ardennes, N France
29 P7 **Sedan** Kansas, C USA
107 N3 **Sedano** Castilla-León, N Spain
106 H10 **Seda, Ribeira de** *stream* C Portugal
193 K15 **Seddon** Marlborough, South Island, NZ
193 H15 **Seddonville** West Coast, South Island, NZ
149 U7 **Sedeh** Khorāsān, E Iran
144 E11 **Sederot** Southern, S Israel
67 B23 **Sedge Island** *island* NW Falkland Islands
78 G12 **Sédhiou** SW Senegal
9 U16 **Sedley** Saskatchewan, S Canada
Sedlez *see* Siedlce
125 G12 **Sedel'nikovo** Omskaya Oblast', C Russian Federation
119 Q2 **Sedniv** Chernihivs'ka Oblast', N Ukraine
38 L11 **Sedona** Arizona, SW USA
Sedunum *see* Sion
120 F12 **Šeduva** Radviliškis, N Lithuania
147 Y8 **Seeb** *var.* Muscat Sīb Airport. ✈ (Masqaṭ) NE Oman
Seeb *see* As Sīb
110 M7 **Seefeld in Tirol** Tirol, W Austria
85 E22 **Seeheim Noord** Karas, S Namibia
Seeland *see* Sjælland
205 N9 **Seelig, Mount** ▲ Antarctica
Seeonee *see* Seoni
168 E6 **Seer** Hovd, W Mongolia
104 L5 **Sées** Orne, N France
103 J14 **Seesen** Niedersachsen, C Germany
Seesker Höhe *see* Szeskie Wzgórza
102 J10 **Seevetal** Niedersachsen, N Germany
111 V6 **Seewiesen** Steiermark, E Austria
142 J13 **Şefaatli** *var.* Kızılkoca. Yozgat, C Turkey
155 N3 **Sefīd, Darya-ye** *Pash.* Āb-i-Safed. ∾ N Afghanistan
154 K5 **Sefīdkūh, Selseleh-ye** *Eng.* Paropamisus Range. ▲▲ W Afghanistan
76 G6 **Sefrou** N Morocco
193 E19 **Sefton, Mount** ▲ South Island, NZ
176 U10 **Segaf, Kepulauan** *island group* E Indonesia
175 Oo3 **Segama, Sungai** ∾ East Malaysia
174 Hh6 **Segamat** Johor, Peninsular Malaysia
79 S13 **Ségbana** NE Benin
Segestica *see* Sisak
Segesvár *see* Sighişoara
176 Uu9 **Seget** Irian Jaya, E Indonesia
Segewold *see* Sigulda
128 J9 **Segezha** Respublika Kareliya, NW Russian Federation
Seghedin *see* Szeged
Segna *see* Senj
109 I16 **Segni** Lazio, C Italy
Segodunum *see* Rodez
107 S9 **Segorbe** País Valenciano, E Spain
78 M12 **Ségou** *var.* Segu. Ségou, C Mali
78 M12 **Ségou** ◐ *region* SW Mali
56 E8 **Segovia** Antioquia, N Colombia
107 N7 **Segovia** Castilla-León, C Spain
106 M6 **Segovia** ◐ *province* Castilla-León, N Spain
Segoviao Wangkí *see* Coco, Río
128 J9 **Segozero, Ozero** ◎ NW Russian Federation
107 U5 **Segre** ∾ NE Spain
104 J7 **Segré** Maine-et-Loire, NW France
Segu *see* Ségou
40 I17 **Seguam Island** *island* Aleutian Islands, Alaska, USA
40 I17 **Seguam Pass** *strait* Aleutian Islands, Alaska, USA
79 Y7 **Séguédine** Agadez, NE Niger
78 M15 **Séguéla** W Ivory Coast
27 S11 **Seguin** Texas, SW USA
40 E17 **Segula Island** *island* Aleutian Islands, Alaska, USA
64 K10 **Segundo, Río** ∾ C Argentina
107 Q12 **Segura** ∾ S Spain
85 G18 **Sehithwa** Ngamiland, N Botswana
160 H10 **Sehore** Madhya Pradesh, C India
195 O16 **Sehulea** Normanby Island, S PNG
155 P15 **Sehwān** Sind, SE Pakistan
111 V8 **Seiersberg** Steiermark, SE Austria
28 L9 **Seiling** Oklahoma, C USA
105 S9 **Seille** ∾ E France
101 J20 **Seilles** Namur, SE Belgium
95 K17 **Seinäjoki** *Swe.* Östermyra. Vaasa, W Finland
10 B12 **Seine** ∾ Ontario, S Canada
104 M4 **Seine** ∾ N France
104 K4 **Seine, Baie de la** *bay* N France
Seine, Banc de la *see* Seine Seamount
105 O5 **Seine-et-Marne** ◐ *department* N France
104 L3 **Seine-Maritime** ◐ *department* N France
86 B14 **Seine Plain** *undersea feature* E Atlantic Ocean
86 B15 **Seine Seamount** *var.* Banc de la Seine. *undersea feature* E Atlantic Ocean
104 E6 **Sein, Île de** *island* NW France
176 Y12 **Seinma** Irian Jaya, E Indonesia
Seisbierrum *see* Sexbierum
111 U5 **Seitenstetten Markt** Niederösterreich, C Austria
Seiyu *see* Chŏnju
97 H22 **Sejerø** *island* E Denmark
112 P7 **Sejny** Suwałki, NE Poland
174 Ii13 **Sekampung, Way** ∾ Sumatera, SW Indonesia
83 G20 **Seke** Shinyanga, N Tanzania
171 I15 **Seki** Gifu, Honshū, SW Japan
167 U12 **Sekibi-sho** *island* China/Japan/Taiwan
172 Pp5 **Sekihoku-tōge** *pass* Hokkaidō, NE Japan
Sekondi *see* Sekondi-Takoradi
79 P17 **Sekondi-Takoradi** *var.* Sekondi. S Ghana
82 J11 **Sek'ot'a** N Ethiopia
Sekseüil *see* Saksaul'skoye
34 J9 **Selah** Washington, NW USA
174 Gg5 **Selangor** *var.* Negeri Selangor Darul Ehsan. ◐ *state* Peninsular Malaysia
Selânik *see* Thessaloníki
174 Hh7 **Selapanjang** Pulau Rantau, W Indonesia
178 Ii10 **Selaphum** Roi Et, E Thailand
176 Uu16 **Selaru, Pulau** *island* Kepulauan Tanimbar, E Indonesia
176 Vv11 **Selassi** Irian Jaya, E Indonesia
173 G3 **Selatan, Selat** *strait* Peninsular Malaysia
41 N8 **Selawik** Alaska, USA
41 N8 **Selawik Lake** ◎ Alaska, USA
175 Pp13 **Selayar, Selat** *strait* Sulawesi, C Indonesia
97 C14 **Selbjørnsfjorden** *fjord* S Norway
96 H8 **Selbusjøen** ◎ S Norway
99 M17 **Selby** N England, UK
31 N8 **Selby** South Dakota, N USA
23 Z4 **Selbyville** Delaware, NE USA
142 B15 **Selçuk** *var.* Akıncılar. İzmir, SW Turkey
41 Q13 **Seldovia** Alaska, USA
109 M18 **Sele** *anc.* Silarius. ∾ S Italy
44 B5 **Selegua, Río** ∾ W Guatemala
133 X7 **Selemdzha** ∾ SE Russian Federation
133 U7 **Selenga** *Mong.* Selenge Mörön. ∾ Mongolia/Russian Federation
168 K6 **Selenge** Bulgan, N Mongolia
168 J6 **Selenge** Hövsgöl, N Mongolia
81 I19 **Selenge** Bandundu, W Zaire
168 L6 **Selenge** ◐ *province* N Mongolia
Selenge Mörön *see* Selenga
126 Jj16 **Selenginsk** Respublika Buryatiya, S Russian Federation
Selenica *see* Selenicë
115 K22 **Selenicë** *var.* Selenica. Vlorë, SW Albania
126 M7 **Selennyakh** ∾ NE Russian Federation
102 J8 **Selenter See** ◎ N Germany
Sele Sound *see* Soela Väin
105 U6 **Sélestat** *Ger.* Schlettstadt. Bas-Rhin, NE France
Selety *see* Sileti
Seleucia *see* Silifke
94 I4 **Selfoss** Sudhurland, SW Iceland
30 M7 **Selfridge** North Dakota, N USA
78 I15 **Seli** ∾ N Sierra Leone
78 I11 **Sélibabi** *var.* Sélibaby. Guidimaka, S Mauritania
Sélibaby *see* Sélibabi
Selidovka/Selidovo *see* Selydove
128 I15 **Seliger, Ozero** ◎ W Russian Federation
38 J11 **Seligman** Arizona, SW USA
29 S8 **Seligman** Missouri, C USA
82 E6 **Selima Oasis** *oasis* N Sudan
78 L13 **Sélingué, Lac de** ⊡ S Mali
Selinoús *see* Kréstena
20 G14 **Selinsgrove** Pennsylvania, NE USA
Selishche *see* Syelishcha
128 I16 **Selizharovo** Tverskaya Oblast', W Russian Federation
96 C10 **Selje** Sogn og Fjordane, S Norway
9 X16 **Selkirk** Manitoba, S Canada
98 K13 **Selkirk** SE Scotland, UK
98 K13 **Selkirk** *cultural region* SE Scotland, UK
9 O16 **Selkirk Mountains** ▲▲ British Columbia, SW Canada
200 Oo12 **Selkirk Rise** *undersea feature* SE Pacific Ocean
117 F21 **Sellasía** Pelopónnisos, S Greece
46 M9 **Selle, Pic de la** *var.* La Selle. ▲ SE Haiti
104 M8 **Selles-sur-Cher** Loir-et-Cher, C France
38 K16 **Sells** Arizona, SW USA
Sellye *see* Sal'a
25 P5 **Selma** Alabama, S USA
37 Q11 **Selma** California, W USA
22 G10 **Selmer** Tennessee, S USA
181 N17 **Sel, Pointe au** *headland* W Réunion
Selseleh-ye Kūh-e Vākhān *see* Nicholas Range
131 S2 **Selty** Udmurtskaya Respublika, NW Russian Federation
Selukwe *see* Shurugwi
64 L9 **Selva** Santiago del Estero, N Argentina
9 T9 **Selwyn Lake** ◎ Northwest Territories/Saskatchewan, C Canada
15 Gg2 **Selwyn Mountains** ▲▲ Yukon Territory, NW Canada
189 T6 **Selwyn Range** ▲▲ Queensland, C Australia
119 W8 **Selydove** *var.* Selidovka, *Rus.* Selidovo. Donets'ka Oblast', SE Ukraine
Selzaete *see* Zelzate
Seman *see* Semanit, Lumi i
174 Ii13 **Semangka, Teluk** *bay* Sumatera, SW Indonesia
174 I13 **Semangka, Way** ∾ Sumatera, SW Indonesia
115 D22 **Semanit, Lumi i** *var.* Seman. ∾ W Albania
174 Kk14 **Semarang** *var.* Samarang. Jawa, C Indonesia
174 Kk6 **Sematan** Sarawak, East Malaysia
175 Qq17 **Semau, Pulau** *island* S Indonesia
175 Nn8 **Semayang, Danau** ◎ Borneo, N Indonesia
175 O4 **Sembakung, Sungai** ∾ Borneo, N Indonesia
81 G17 **Sembé** La Sangha, NW Congo
Semberong *see* Semberong, Sungai
174 Hh6 **Semberong, Sungai** *var.* Semberong. ∾ Peninsular Malaysia
174 M10 **Sembulu, Danau** ◎ Borneo, N Indonesia
Semendria *see* Smederevo
119 R1 **Semenivka** Chernihivs'ka Oblast', N Ukraine
119 S6 **Semenivka** *Rus.* Semenovka. Poltavs'ka Oblast', NE Ukraine
131 O3 **Semenov** Nizhegorodskaya Oblast', W Russian Federation
Semenovka *see* Semenivka
174 M16 **Semeru, Gunung** *var.* Mahameru. ▲ Jawa, S Indonesia
Semey/Semey Oblysy *see* Semipalatinsk
Semezhevo *see* Syemyezhava
130 L7 **Semiluki** Voronezhskaya Oblast', W Russian Federation
35 W16 **Seminoe Reservoir** ⊡ Wyoming, C USA
29 O11 **Seminole** Oklahoma, C USA
26 M6 **Seminole** Texas, SW USA
25 S8 **Seminole, Lake** ⊡ Florida/Georgia, SE USA
150 M8 **Semiozernoye** Kustanay, N Kazakhstan
151 V9 **Semipalatinsk** *Kaz.* Semey. Semipalatinsk, E Kazakhstan
151 V11 **Semipalatinsk** *off.* Semipalatinskaya Oblast', *Kaz.* Semey Oblysy. ◐ *province* E Kazakhstan
149 O9 **Semīrom** *var.* Samirum. Eşfahān, C Iran
40 F17 **Semisopochnoi Island** *island* Aleutian Islands, Alaska, USA
174 Ll7 **Semitau** Borneo, C Indonesia
83 E18 **Semliki** ∾ Uganda/Zaire
149 P5 **Semnān** *var.* Samnān. Semnān, N Iran
149 Q5 **Semnān** *off.* Ostān-e Semnān. ◐ *province* N Iran
101 K24 **Semois** ∾ SE Belgium
110 E8 **Sempacher See** ◎ C Switzerland
Sena *see* Vila de Sena
32 L12 **Senachwine Lake** ◎ Illinois, N USA
61 O14 **Senador Pompeu** Ceará, E Brazil
Sena Gallica *see* Senigallia
61 C15 **Sena Madureira** Acre, W Brazil
161 L25 **Senanayake Samudra** ◎ E Sri Lanka
85 G15 **Senanga** Western, SW Zambia
29 Y9 **Senath** Missouri, C USA
22 L2 **Senatobia** Mississippi, S USA
170 C15 **Sendai** Kagoshima, Kyūshū, SW Japan
171 M13 **Sendai** Miyagi, Honshū, C Japan
170 Bb15 **Sendai-gawa** ∾ Kyūshū, SW Japan
171 M14 **Sendai-wan** *bay* E Japan
103 J23 **Senden** Bayern, S Germany
160 F11 **Sendhwa** Madhya Pradesh, C India
113 H21 **Senec** *Ger.* Wartberg, *Hung.* Szenc; *prev.* Szempcz. Západné Slovensko, W Slovakia
29 P3 **Seneca** Kansas, C USA
29 R8 **Seneca** Missouri, C USA
34 K13 **Seneca** Oregon, NW USA
23 O11 **Seneca** South Carolina, SE USA
20 G11 **Seneca Lake** ◎ New York, NE USA
33 U13 **Senecaville Lake** ◎ Ohio, N USA
78 G11 **Senegal** *off.* Republic of Senegal, *Fr.* Sénégal. ◆ *republic* W Africa
78 H9 **Senegal** *Fr.* Sénégal. ∾ W Africa
33 O4 **Seney Marsh** *wetland* Michigan, N USA
103 P14 **Senftenberg** Brandenburg, E Germany
84 L11 **Senga Hill** Northern, NE Zambia
164 G13 **Sênggê Zangbo** ∾ W China
176 Z11 **Senggi** Irian Jaya, E Indonesia
131 R5 **Sengiley** Ul'yanovskaya Oblast', W Russian Federation
65 I19 **Senguerr, Río** ∾ S Argentina
85 J16 **Sengwa** ∾ C Zimbabwe
Senia *see* Senj
113 H19 **Senica** *Ger.* Senitz, *Hung.* Szenice. Západné Slovensko, W Slovakia
Seniça *see* Sjenica
108 J11 **Senigallia** *anc.* Sena Gallica. Marche, C Italy
142 F15 **Senirkent** Isparta, SW Turkey
Senitz *see* Senica
114 C10 **Senj** *Ger.* Zengg, *It.* Segna; *anc.* Senia. Lika-Senj, NW Croatia
169 O10 **Senj** Dornogovĭ, SE Mongolia
94 H9 **Senja** *prev.* Senjen. *island* N Norway
Senjen *see* Senja
167 U12 **Senkaku-shotō** *island group* SW Japan
143 R12 **Şenkaya** Erzurum, NE Turkey
85 I16 **Senkobo** Southern, S Zambia
105 O4 **Senlis** Oise, N France
178 K13 **Senmonorom** Môndól Kiri, E Cambodia
82 G10 **Sennar** *var.* Sannār. Sinnar, C Sudan
Senno *see* Syanno
Senones *see* Sens
111 W11 **Senovo** E Slovenia
105 P6 **Sens** *anc.* Agendicum, Senones. Yonne, C France
Sensburg *see* Mrągowo
178 J12 **Sên, Stœng** ∾ C Cambodia
44 F7 **Sensuntepeque** Cabañas, NE El Salvador
114 L8 **Senta** *Hung.* Zenta. Serbia, N Yugoslavia
Šent Andraž *see* Sankt Andrä
176 Z10 **Sentani, Danau** ◎ Irian Jaya, E Indonesia
30 J5 **Sentinel Butte** ▲ North Dakota, N USA
8 M13 **Sentinel Peak** ▲ British Columbia, W Canada
61 N16 **Sento Sé** Bahia, E Brazil
Šent Peter *see* Pivka
Šent Vid *see* Sankt Veit an der Glan
194 E10 **Senu** ∾ NW PNG
Seo de Urgel *see* La See d'Urgel
160 I7 **Seondha** Madhya Pradesh, C India
160 J11 **Seoni** *prev.* Seeonee. Madhya Pradesh, C India
Seoul *see* Sŏul
192 I13 **Separation Point** *headland* South Island, NZ
175 O7 **Sepasu** Borneo, N Indonesia
194 F10 **Sepik** ∾ Indonesia/PNG
Sepone *see* Muang Xépôn
112 M7 **Sępopol** *Ger.* Schippenbeil. Olsztyn, N Poland
118 F10 **Şepreuş** *Hung.* Seprős. Arad, W Romania
Seprős *see* Şepreuş
Şepşi-Sângeorz/Sepsiszentgyőrgy *see* Sfântu Gheorghe
13 W4 **Sept-Îles** Québec, SE Canada
107 N6 **Sepúlveda** Castilla-León, N Spain
174 Ii12 **Seputih, Way** ∾ Sumatera, SW Indonesia
106 K8 **Sequeros** Castilla-León, N Spain
106 L5 **Sequillo** ∾ NW Spain
34 G7 **Sequim** Washington, NW USA
37 S11 **Sequoia National Park** *national park* California, W USA
143 Q14 **Şerafettin Dağları** ▲▲ E Turkey
131 N10 **Serafimovich** Volgogradskaya Oblast', SW Russian Federation
175 Rr6 **Serai** Sulawesi, N Indonesia
101 K19 **Seraing** Liège, E Belgium
Sêraitang *see* Baima
Serajgonj *see* Shirajganj Ghat
152 I15 **Serakhs** *var.* Saragt. Akhalskiy Velayat, S Turkmenistan
176 X10 **Serami** Irian Jaya, E Indonesia
Seram, Laut *see* Ceram Sea
Serampore/Serampur *see* Shrīrāmpur
175 Tt11 **Seram, Pulau** *var.* Serang, *Eng.* Ceram. *island* Maluku, E Indonesia
174 J14 **Serang** Jawa, C Indonesia
Serang *see* Seram, Pulau
174 Kk6 **Serasan, Pulau** *island* Kepulauan Natuna, W Indonesia
174 Kk6 **Serasan, Selat** *strait* Indonesia/Malaysia
114 M12 **Serbia** *Ger.* Serbien, *Serb.* Srbija. ◐ *republic* Yugoslavia
Serbien *see* Serbia
Sercq *see* Sark
Serdica *see* Sofiya
131 O7 **Serdobsk** Penzenskaya Oblast', W Russian Federation
151 X9 **Serebryansk** Vostochnyy Kazakhstan, E Kazakhstan
126 Ll13 **Serebryanyy Bor** Respublika Sakha (Yakutiya), NE Russian Federation
113 H20 **Sered'** *Hung.* Szered. Západné Slovensko, SW Slovakia
119 S1 **Seredyna-Buda** Sums'ka Oblast', NE Ukraine
120 E13 **Seredžius** Jurbarkas, C Lithuania
142 I14 **Şereflikoçhisar** Ankara, C Turkey
108 D7 **Seregno** Lombardia, N Italy
105 P7 **Serein** ∾ C France
174 H5 **Seremban** Negeri Sembilan, Peninsular Malaysia
83 H20 **Serengeti Plain** *plain* N Tanzania
84 K13 **Serenje** Central, E Zambia
Seres *see* Sérres
118 J5 **Seret** ∾ W Ukraine
Seret/Sereth *see* Siret
117 I21 **Serfopoúla** *island* Kykládes, Greece, Aegean Sea
131 P4 **Sergach** Nizhegorodskaya Oblast', W Russian Federation
31 S13 **Sergeant Bluff** Iowa, C USA
169 P7 **Sergelen** Dornod, NE Mongolia
169 O9 **Sergelen** Sühbaatar, E Mongolia
173 F4 **Sergeulangit, Pegunungan** ▲▲ Sumatera, NW Indonesia
126 I4 **Sergeya Kirova, Ostrova** *island* N Russian Federation
Sergeyevichi *see* Syarhyeyevichy
151 O7 **Sergeyevka** Severnyy Kazakhstan, N Kazakhstan
Sergiopol *see* Ayaguz
61 P16 **Sergipe** *off.* Estado de Sergipe. ◐ *state* E Brazil
130 L3 **Sergiyev Posad** Moskovskaya Oblast', W Russian Federation
128 K5 **Sergozero, Ozero** ◎ NW Russian Federation
174 L7 **Serian** Sarawak, East Malaysia
174 J13 **Seribu, Kepulauan** *island group* S Indonesia
117 I21 **Sérifos** *anc.* Seriphos. *island* Kykládes, Greece, Aegean Sea
117 I21 **Sérifou, Stenó** *strait* SE Greece
142 F16 **Serik** Antalya, SW Turkey
108 E7 **Serio** ∾ N Italy
Seriphos *see* Sérifos
Serir Tibesti *see* Sarir Tibisti
131 S5 **Sernovodsk** Samarskaya Oblast', W Russian Federation
131 R2 **Sernur** Respublika Mariy El, W Russian Federation
112 M11 **Serock** Warszawa, C Poland
63 B18 **Serodino** Santa Fe, C Argentina
Seroei *see* Serui
107 P14 **Serón** Andalucía, S Spain
101 E14 **Serooskerke** Zeeland, SW Netherlands
107 T6 **Seròs** Cataluña, NE Spain
125 F10 **Serov** Sverdlovskaya Oblast', C Russian Federation
85 I19 **Serowe** Central, SE Botswana
106 H13 **Serpa** Beja, S Portugal
Serpa Pinto *see* Menongue
190 A4 **Serpentine Lakes** *salt lake* South Australia
47 T15 **Serpent's Mouth, The** *Sp.* Boca de la Serpiente. *strait* Trinidad and Tobago/Venezuela
Serpiente, Boca de la *see* Serpent's Mouth, The
130 K4 **Serpukhov** Moskovskaya Oblast', W Russian Federation
62 K13 **Serra do Mar** ▲▲ S Brazil
Sérrai *see* Sérres
109 N22 **Serra San Bruno** Calabria, SW Italy
105 S14 **Serres** Hautes-Alpes, SE France
116 H13 **Sérres** *var.* Seres; *prev.* Sérrai. Kentrikí Makedonía, NE Greece
64 J9 **Serrezuela** Córdoba, C Argentina
61 O16 **Serrinha** Bahia, E Brazil
61 M19 **Serro** *var.* Sêrro. Minas Gerais, NE Brazil
Sêrro *see* Serro
Sert *see* Siirt
Sertá *see* Sertã
106 H9 **Sertã** *var.* Sertá. Castelo Branco, C Portugal
62 L8 **Sertãozinho** São Paulo, S Brazil
166 F7 **Sêrtar** Sichuan, C China
176 X10 **Serui** *prev.* Seroei. Irian Jaya, E Indonesia
85 J19 **Serule** Central, E Botswana
174 Ll10 **Seruyan, Sungai** *var.* Sungai Pembuang. ∾ Borneo, N Indonesia
117 E14 **Sérvia** Dytikí Makedonía, N Greece
166 E7 **Sêrxü** Sichuan, C China
126 Mm15 **Seryshevo** Amurskaya Oblast', SE Russian Federation
Sé San *see* San, Tônle
Sesana *see* Sežana
175 Nn5 **Sesayap, Sungai** ∾ Borneo, N Indonesia
Sesdlets *see* Siedlce
81 N17 **Sese** Haut-Zaïre, N Zaire
83 F18 **Sese Islands** *island group* S Uganda
175 T9 **Sesepe** Pulau Obi, E Indonesia
85 H16 **Sesheke** *var.* Sesheko. Western, SE Zambia
Sesheko *see* Sesheke
108 C8 **Sesia** *anc.* Sessites. ∾ NW Italy
106 F11 **Sesimbra** Setúbal, S Portugal
117 N22 **Sesklió** *island* Dodekánisos, Greece, Aegean Sea
32 L16 **Sesser** Illinois, N USA
Sessites *see* Sesia
108 G11 **Sesto Fiorentino** Toscana, C Italy
108 E7 **Sesto San Giovanni** Lombardia, N Italy
108 A8 **Sestriere** Piemonte, NE Italy
108 D10 **Sestri Levante** Liguria, NW Italy
109 C20 **Sestu** Sardegna, Italy, C Mediterranean Sea
114 E8 **Sesvete** Grad Zagreb, N Croatia
120 G12 **Šeta** Kėdainiai, C Lithuania
Setabis *see* Xàtiva
172 N5 **Setana** Hokkaidō, NE Japan
105 Q16 **Sète** *prev.* Cette. Hérault, S France
60 J11 **Sete Ilhas** Amapá, NE Brazil
61 L20 **Sete Lagoas** Minas Gerais, NE Brazil
62 G10 **Sete Quedas, Ilha das** *island* S Brazil
94 I10 **Setermoen** Troms, N Norway
97 E17 **Setesdal** *valley* S Norway
45 W16 **Setetule, Cerro** ▲ SE Panama
23 Q5 **Seth** West Virginia, NE USA
Setia *see* Sezze
76 K5 **Sétif** *var.* Stif. N Algeria
171 I15 **Seto** Aichi, Honshū, SW Japan
170 F14 **Seto-naikai** *Eng.* Inland Sea. *sea* S Japan
172 Qq13 **Setouchi** *var.* Setoushi. Kagoshima, Amami-Ō-shima, SW Japan
76 F6 **Settat** W Morocco
81 D20 **Setté Cama** Ogooué-Maritime, SW Gabon
9 W13 **Setting Lake** ◎ Manitoba, C Canada
99 L16 **Settle** N England, UK
201 Y12 **Settlement** E Wake Island
106 F11 **Setúbal** *Eng.* Saint Ubes, Saint Yves. Setúbal, W Portugal
106 F11 **Setúbal** ◐ *district* S Portugal
106 F12 **Setúbal, Baía de** *bay* W Portugal
Setul *see* Satun
10 B10 **Seul, Lac** ◎ Ontario, S Canada
105 R8 **Seurre** Côte d'Or, C France
143 U11 **Sevan** C Armenia
143 V12 **Sevana Lich** *Eng.* Lake Sevan, *Rus.* Ozero Sevan. ◎ E Armenia
Sevan, Lake/Sevan, Ozero *see* Sevana Lich
79 N11 **Sévaré** Mopti, C Mali
119 S14 **Sevastopol'** *Eng.* Sebastopol. Respublika Krym, S Ukraine
27 R14 **Seven Sisters** Texas, SW USA
8 K13 **Seven Sisters Peaks** ▲ British Columbia, SW Canada
101 M15 **Sevenum** Limburg, SE Netherlands
105 P14 **Séverac-le-Château** Aveyron, S France
12 H13 **Severn** ∾ Ontario, S Canada
99 L21 **Severn** *Wel.* Hafren. ∾ England/Wales, UK
129 O11 **Severnaya Dvina** *var.* Northern Dvina. ∾ NW Russian Federation
131 N16 **Severnaya Osetiya, Respublika** *Eng.* North Ossetia; *prev.* Severo-Osetinskaya SSR. ◐ *autonomous republic* SW Russian Federation
125 F9 **Severnaya Sos'va** ∾ N Russian Federation
127 N17 **Severnaya Zemlya** *var.* Nicholas II Land. *island group* N Russian Federation
113 C15 **Severní Čechy** *off.* Severočeský Kraj. ◐ *region* NW Czech Republic
113 H17 **Severní Morava** *off.* Severomoravský Kraj. ◐ *region* E Czech Republic
131 T5 **Severnoye** Orenburgskaya Oblast', W Russian Federation
37 S3 **Severn Troughs Range** ▲▲ Nevada, W USA
129 W3 **Severnyy** Respublika Komi, NW Russian Federation
150 I13 **Severnyy Chink Ustyurta** ▲▲ W Kazakhstan
129 Q13 **Severnyye Uvaly** *var.* Northern Ural Hills. *hill range* NW Russian Federation
151 O6 **Severnyy Kazakhstan** *off.* Severo-Kazakhstanskaya Oblast', *var.* North Kazakhstan, *Kaz.* Soltüstik Qazaqstan Oblysy. ◐ *province* N Kazakhstan
129 V9 **Severnyy Ural** ▲▲ NW Russian Federation
Severo-Alichurskiy Khrebet *see* Alichuri Shimolí, Qatorkŭhi
126 K14 **Severobaykal'sk** Respublika Buryatiya, S Russian Federation
Severočeský Kraj *see* Severní Čechy
Severodonetsk *see* Syeverodonets'k
128 M8 **Severodvinsk** *prev.* Molotov, Sudostroy. Arkhangel'skaya Oblast', NW Russian Federation
Severo-Kazakhstanskaya Oblast' *see* Severnyy Kazakhstan
127 Pp13 **Severo-Kuril'sk** Sakhalinskaya Oblast', SE Russian Federation
Severomoravský Kraj *see* Severní Morava
128 J3 **Severomorsk** Murmanskaya Oblast', NW Russian Federation
Severo-Osetinskaya SSR *see* Severnaya Osetiya, Respublika
126 J6 **Severo-Sibirskaya Nizmennost'** *var.* North Siberian Plain, *Eng.* North Siberian Lowland. *lowlands* N Russian Federation
125 Ee10 **Severoural'sk** Sverdlovskaya Oblast', C Russian Federation
126 I12 **Severo-Yeniseyskiy** Krasnoyarskiy Kray, C Russian Federation
130 M11 **Severskiy Donets** *Ukr.* Sivers'kyy Donets'. ∾ Russian Federation/Ukraine *see also* Sivers'kyy Donets'
94 M9 **Sevettijärvi** Lappi, N Finland
38 M5 **Sevier Bridge Reservoir** ⊡ Utah, W USA
38 J4 **Sevier Desert** *plain* Utah, W USA
38 J5 **Sevier Lake** ◎ Utah, W USA
23 N9 **Sevierville** Tennessee, S USA
106 J14 **Sevilla** *Eng.* Seville; *anc.* Hispalis. Andalucía, SW Spain
106 J13 **Sevilla** ◐ *province* Andalucía, SW Spain
Sevilla de Niefang *see* Niefang
45 O16 **Sevilla, Isla** *island* SW Panama
Seville *see* Sevilla
116 J9 **Sevlievo** Loveshka Oblast, C Bulgaria
Sevluš/Sevlyush *see* Vynohradiv
111 V11 **Sevnica** *Ger.* Lichtenwald. E Slovenia
130 I7 **Sevsk** Bryanskaya Oblast', W Russian Federation
78 J15 **Sewa** ∾ E Sierra Leone
41 R12 **Seward** Alaska, USA
31 R15 **Seward** Nebraska, C USA
8 G8 **Seward Glacier** *glacier* Yukon Territory, W Canada
207 Q3 **Seward Peninsula** *peninsula* Alaska, USA
Seward's Folly *see* Alaska
64 H12 **Sewell** Libertador, C Chile
100 K5 **Sexbierum** *Fris.* Seisbierrum. Friesland, N Netherlands
9 O13 **Sexsmith** Alberta, W Canada
43 W13 **Seybaplaya** Campeche, SE Mexico
181 N6 **Seychelles** *off.* Republic of Seychelles. ◆ *republic* W Indian Ocean
69 Z9 **Seychelles** *island group* NE Seychelles
181 N6 **Seychelles Bank** *var.* Le Banc des Seychelles. *undersea feature* W Indian Ocean
Seychelles, Le Banc des *see* Seychelles Bank
180 H17 **Seychellois, Morne** ▲ Mahé, NE Seychelles
94 L2 **Seydhisfjördhur** Austurland, E Iceland
152 J12 **Seydi** *prev.* Neftezavodsk. Lebapskiy Velayat, E Turkmenistan
142 G16 **Seydişehir** Konya, SW Turkey
142 J13 **Seyfe Gölü** ◎ C Turkey
Seyhan *see* Adana
142 K16 **Seyhan Barajı** ⊡ S Turkey
142 K17 **Seyhan Nehri** ∾ S Turkey
142 F13 **Seyitgazi** Eskişehir, W Turkey
130 J7 **Seym** ∾ W Russian Federation
119 S3 **Seym** ∾ N Ukraine
127 O9 **Seymchan** Magadanskaya Oblast', E Russian Federation
116 N12 **Seymen** Tekirdağ, NW Turkey
191 O11 **Seymour** Victoria, SE Australia
85 I25 **Seymour** Eastern Cape, S South Africa
31 W16 **Seymour** Iowa, C USA
29 U7 **Seymour** Missouri, C USA
27 Q5 **Seymour** Texas, SW USA
116 M12 **Şeytan Deresi** ∾ NW Turkey
111 S12 **Sežana** *It.* Sesana. SW Slovenia
105 P5 **Sézanne** Marne, N France
109 I16 **Sezze** *anc.* Setia. Lazio, C Italy
117 H25 **Sfákia** Kríti, Greece, E Mediterranean Sea
117 D21 **Sfaktiría** *island* S Greece

◆ Country ● Country Capital ◇ Dependent Territory ○ Dependent Territory Capital ◐ Administrative Region ✈ International Airport ▲ Mountain ▲▲ Mountain Range ⛰ Volcano ∾ River ◎ Lake ⊡ Reservoir

SFÂNTU GHEORGHE – SHOLDANESHTY

118 J11 **Sfântu Gheorghe** *Ger.* Sankt-Georgen, *Hung.* Sepsiszentgyőrgy; *prev.* Şepşi-Sângeorz, Sfîntu Gheorghe. Covasna, C Romania
119 N13 **Sfântu Gheorghe, Braţul** *var.* Gheorghe Braţul. ≈ E Romania
77 N6 **Sfax** *Ar.* Şafāqis. E Tunisia
77 N6 **Sfax** ✕ E Tunisia
Sfîntu Gheorghe *see* Sfântu Gheorghe
100 H13 **'s-Gravendeel** Zuid-Holland, SW Netherlands
100 F11 **'s-Gravenhage** *var.* Den Haag, *Eng.* The Hague, *Fr.* La Haye. ● (Netherlands-seat of government) Zuid-Holland, W Netherlands
100 G12 **'s-Gravenzande** Zuid-Holland, W Netherlands
Shaan/Shaanxi Sheng *see* Shaanxi
165 X11 **Shaanxi** *var.* Shaan, Shaanxi Sheng, Shan-hsi, Shenshi, Shensi. ◈ *province* C China
Shaartuz *see* Shahrtuz
81 L24 **Shaba** *off.* Région du Shaba. ◈ *region* SE Zaire
Shabani *see* Zvishavane
83 N17 **Shabeellaha Dhexe** *off.* Gobolka Shabeellaha Dhexe. ◈ *region* E Somalia
83 L17 **Shabeellaha Hoose** *off.* Gobolka Shabeellaha Hoose. ◈ *region* S Somalia
Shabeelle, Webi *see* Shebeli
116 O7 **Shabla** Varnenska Oblast, NE Bulgaria
116 O7 **Shabla, Nos** *headland* NE Bulgaria
11 N9 **Shabogama Lake** ◎ Newfoundland and Labrador, E Canada
81 N20 **Shabunda** Sud Kivu, E Zaire
147 Q15 **Shabwah** C Yemen
164 F8 **Shache** *var.* Yarkant. Xinjiang Uygur Zizhiqu, NW China
Shacheng *see* Huailai
205 R12 **Shackleton Coast** *physical region* Antarctica
205 Z10 **Shackleton Ice Shelf** *ice shelf* Antarctica
Shaddādī *see* Ash Shadādah
30 K7 **Shadehill Reservoir** ▣ South Dakota, N USA
125 Ee12 **Shadrinsk** Kurganskaya Oblast', C Russian Federation
33 O12 **Shafer, Lake** ▣ Indiana, N USA
37 R13 **Shafter** California, W USA
26 J11 **Shafter** Texas, SW USA
99 L23 **Shaftesbury** S England, UK
193 F22 **Shag** ≈ South Island, NZ
151 V9 **Shagan** ≈ E Kazakhstan
41 O11 **Shageluk** Alaska, USA
126 I16 **Shagonar** Respublika Tyva, S Russian Federation
193 F22 **Shag Point** *headland* South Island, NZ
150 J12 **Shagyray, Plato** *plain* SW Kazakhstan
Shāhābād *see* Eslāmābād
174 H5 **Shah Alam** Selangor, Peninsular Malaysia
119 O12 **Shahany, Ozero** ◎ SW Ukraine
144 H9 **Shahbā'** *anc.* Philippopolis. As Suwaydā', S Syria
Shahbān *see* Ad Dayr
155 P17 **Shāhbandar** Sind, SE Pakistan
155 P13 **Shāhdādkot** Sind, SW Pakistan
149 T10 **Shahdād, Namakzār-e** *salt pan* E Iran
155 Q15 **Shāhdādpur** Sind, SE Pakistan
160 K10 **Shahdol** Madhya Pradesh, C India
167 N7 **Sha He** ≈ C China
Shahepu *see* Linze
159 N13 **Shāhganj** Uttar Pradesh, N India
158 C11 **Shāhgarh** Rājasthān, NW India
Sha Hi *see* Orūmīyeh, Daryācheh-ye, Iran
Shāhī *see* Qā'emshahr, Māzandarān, Iran
145 Q6 **Shāhimah** *var.* Shahma. C Iraq
Shahjahanabad *see* Delhi
158 L11 **Shāhjahānpur** Uttar Pradesh, N India
Shahma *see* Shāhimah
155 U7 **Shāhpur** Punjab, E Pakistan
Shāhpur *see* Shāhpur Chākar
158 G13 **Shāhpura** Rājasthān, N India
155 Q15 **Shāhpur Chākar** *var.* Shāhpur. Sind, SE Pakistan
154 M5 **Shahrak** Ghowr, C Afghanistan
149 Q11 **Shahr-e Bābak** Kermān, C Iran
149 N8 **Shahr-e Kord** *var.* Shahr Kord. Chahār Maḩall va Bakhtīārī, C Iran
149 O9 **Shahreẕā** *var.* Qomisheh, Qumisheh, Shahriza; *prev.* Qomsheh. Eşfahān, C Iran
153 S10 **Shahrikhon** *Rus.* Shakhrikhan. Andijon Wiloyati, E Uzbekistan
153 N12 **Shahrisabz** *Rus.* Shakhrisabz. Qashqadaryo Wiloyati, S Uzbekistan
153 P11 **Shahriston** *Rus.* Shakhristan. NW Tajikistan
Shahriza *see* Shahreẕā
Shahr-i-Zabul *see* Zābol
Shahr Kord *see* Shahr-e Kord
153 P14 **Shahrtuz** *Rus.* Shaartuz. SW Tajikistan
149 Q4 **Shāhrūd** *prev.* Emāmrūd, Emāmshahr. Semnān, N Iran
Shahsavār/Shahsawar *see* Tonekābon
Shaidara *see* Step' Nardara
Shaikh Ābid *see* Shaykh 'Ābid
Shaikh Fāris *see* Shaykh Fāris
Shaikh Najm *see* Shaykh Najm
144 K5 **Shā'īr, Jabal** ▲ C Syria
160 G10 **Shājāpur** Madhya Pradesh, C India
82 J8 **Shakal, Ras** *headland* NE Sudan
Shakhdarinskiy Khrebet *see* Shokhdara, Qatorkŭhi
Shakhrikhan *see* Shahrikhon
Shakhrisabz *see* Shahrisabz
Shakhristan *see* Shahriston
119 X8 **Shakhtars'k** *Rus.* Shakhtërsk. Donets'ka Oblast', SE Ukraine
127 O15 **Shakhtersk** Ostrov Sakhalin, Sakhalinskaya Oblast', SE Russian Federation
Shakhtërsk *see* Shakhtars'k
151 R10 **Shakhtinsk** Karaganda, C Kazakhstan
130 L11 **Shakhty** Rostovskaya Oblast', SW Russian Federation
131 P2 **Shakhun'ya** Nizhegorodskaya Oblast', W Russian Federation
79 S15 **Shaki** Oyo, W Nigeria
83 J15 **Shakīso** S Ethiopia
119 X8 **Shakmars'k** Donets'ka Oblast', E Ukraine
31 V9 **Shakopee** Minnesota, N USA
172 Nn5 **Shakotan-hantō** *peninsula* Hokkaidō, NE Japan
172 O4 **Shakotan-misaki** *headland* Hokkaidō, NE Japan
41 N9 **Shaktoolik** Alaska, USA
83 J14 **Shala Hāyk'** ◎ C Ethiopia
128 M10 **Shalakusha** Arkhangel'skaya Oblast', NW Russian Federation
151 U8 **Shalday** Pavlodar, NE Kazakhstan
131 P16 **Shali** Chechenskaya Respublika, SW Russian Federation
147 W12 **Shalīm** *var.* Shelim. S Oman
Shaliuhe *see* Gangca
150 F9 **Shalkar, Ozero** *prev.* Chelkar, Ozero. ◎ W Kazakhstan
23 V12 **Shallotte** North Carolina, SE USA
27 N5 **Shallowater** Texas, SW USA
128 K11 **Shal'skiy** Respublika Kareliya, NW Russian Federation
166 F9 **Shaluli Shan** ⛰ C China
83 F22 **Shama** ≈ C Tanzania
9 Z11 **Shamattawa** Manitoba, C Canada
10 F8 **Shamattawa** ≈ Ontario, C Canada
Shām, Bādiyat ash *see* Syrian Desert
Shamiya *see* Ash Shāmīyah
147 X8 **Shām, Jabal ash** *var.* Jebel Sham. ▲ NW Oman
Sham, Jebel *see* Shām, Jabal ash
Shamkhor *see* Şämkir
20 G14 **Shamokin** Pennsylvania, NE USA
27 P2 **Shamrock** Texas, SW USA
Sha'nabī, Jabal ash *see* Chambi, Jebel
145 Y12 **Shanāwah** E Iraq
165 T8 **Shandan** Gansu, N China
Shandī *see* Shendi
167 Q5 **Shandong** *var.* Lu, Shandong Sheng, Shantung. ◈ *province* E China
167 R4 **Shandong Bandao** *var.* Shantung Peninsula. *peninsula* E China
Shandong Peninsula *see* Shandong Bandao
Shandong Sheng *see* Shandong
145 U8 **Shandrūkh** E Iraq
85 J17 **Shangani** ≈ W Zimbabwe
167 O15 **Shangchuan Dao** *island* S China
Shangchuankou *see* Minhe
169 P12 **Shangdu** Nei Mongol Zizhiqu, N China
167 O11 **Shanggao** Jiangxi, S China
167 S8 **Shanghai** *var.* Shang-hai. Shanghai Shi, E China
Shanghai *see* Shanghai Shi
167 S8 **Shanghai Shi** *var.* Hu, Shanghai. ◈ *municipality* E China
167 P13 **Shanghang** Fujian, SE China
166 K14 **Shanglin** Guangxi Zhuangzu Zizhiqu, S China
85 G15 **Shangombo** Western, W Zambia
167 O6 **Shangqiu** *var.* Zhuji. Henan, C China
167 Q10 **Shangrao** Jiangxi, S China
167 S9 **Shangyu** *var.* Baiguan. Zhejiang, SE China
169 X9 **Shangzhi** Heilongjiang, NE China
166 L7 **Shangzhou** *var.* Shang Xian. Shaanxi, C China
169 W9 **Shanhetun** Heilongjiang, NE China
Shan-hsi *see* Shaanxi, China
Shan-hsi *see* Shanxi, China
165 O6 **Shankou** Xinjiang Uygur Zizhiqu, W China
192 M13 **Shannon** Manawatu-Wanganui, North Island, NZ
99 B19 **Shannon** ✕ W Ireland
99 C17 **Shannon** *Ir.* An tSionainn. ≈ W Ireland
178 H6 **Shan Plateau** *plateau* E Myanmar
164 M6 **Shanshan** *var.* Piqan. Xinjiang Uygur Zizhiqu, NW China
Shansi *see* Shanxi
178 Gg5 **Shan State** ◈ *state* E Myanmar
Shantar Islands *see* Shantarskiye Ostrova
127 N13 **Shantarskiye Ostrova** *Eng.* Shantar Islands. *island group* E Russian Federation
167 Q14 **Shantou** *var.* Shan-t'ou, Swatow. Guangdong, S China
Shantung *see* Shandong
Shantung Peninsula *see* Shandong Bandao
169 O14 **Shanxi** *var.* Jin, Shan-hsi, Shansi, Shanxi Sheng. ◈ *province* C China
Shan Xian *see* Sanmenxia
167 P6 **Shanxian** *var.* Shan Xian. Shandong, E China
Shanxi Sheng *see* Shanxi
166 L7 **Shanyang** Shaanxi, C China
167 O13 **Shaoguan** *var.* Shao-kuan, *Cant.* Kukong; *prev.* Ch'u-chiang. Guangdong, S China
Shao-kuan *see* Shaoguan
167 Q11 **Shaowu** Fujian, SE China
167 S9 **Shaoxing** Zhejiang, SE China
166 M12 **Shaoyang** *prev.* Tangdukou. Hunan, S China
166 M11 **Shaoyang** *var.* Baoqing, Shao-yang; *prev.* Pao-king. Hunan, S China
98 K5 **Shapinsay** *island* NE Scotland, UK
129 S4 **Shapkina** ≈ NW Russian Federation
Shāpūr *see* Salmās
164 M4 **Shaqiuhe** Xinjiang Uygur Zizhiqu, W China
145 T2 **Shaqlāwa** *var.* Shaqlāwah. E Iraq
Shaqlāwah *see* Shaqlāwa
144 I8 **Shaqqā** As Suwaydā', S Syria
147 P7 **Shaqrā'** Ar Riyāḑ, C Saudi Arabia
Shaqrā *see* Shuqrah
155 O6 **Sharan** Urūzgān, SE Afghanistan
Sharaqpur *see* Sharqpur
Sharbaqty *see* Shcherbakty
147 X12 **Sharbatāt** S Oman
147 X12 **Sharbithāt, Ras** *var.* Ra's Sharbatāt. *headland* S Oman
12 K14 **Sharbot Lake** Ontario, SE Canada
Shardara Dalasy *see* Step' Nardara
168 H6 **Sharga** Govĭ-Altay, W Mongolia
168 F8 **Sharga** Hövsgöl, N Mongolia
118 M7 **Sharhorod** Vinnyts'ka Oblast', C Ukraine
168 K10 **Sharhulsan** Ömnogövĭ, S Mongolia
172 Qq6 **Shari** Hokkaidō, NE Japan
Shari *see* Chari
145 T6 **Shārī, Buḩayrat** ◎ C Iraq
Sharjah *see* Ash Shāriqah
120 K12 **Sharkawshchyna** *var.* Sharkowshchyna, *Pol.* Szarkowszczyzna, *Rus.* Sharkovshchina. Vitsyebskaya Voblasts', NW Belarus
188 G9 **Shark Bay** *bay* Western Australia
147 Y9 **Sharkh** E Oman
Sharkovshchina/Sharkowshchyna *see* Sharkawshchyna
131 U6 **Sharlyk** Orenburgskaya Oblast', W Russian Federation
Sharm ash Shaykh *see* Sharm el Sheikh
77 Y9 **Sharm el Sheikh** *var.* Ofiral, Sharm ash Shaykh. E Egypt
20 B13 **Sharon** Pennsylvania, NE USA
28 H4 **Sharon Springs** Kansas, C USA
33 Q14 **Sharonville** Ohio, N USA
Sharourah *see* Sharūrah
31 O10 **Sharpe, Lake** ▣ South Dakota, N USA
Sharqī, Al Jabal ash/Sharqi, Jebel esh *see* Anti-Lebanon
Sharqīyah, Al Minţaqah ash *see* Ash Sharqīyah
144 I6 **Sharqīyat an Nabk, Jabal** ⛰ W Syria
155 W8 **Sharqpur** *var.* Sharaqpur. Punjab, E Pakistan
147 Q13 **Sharūrah** *var.* Sharourah. Najrān, S Saudi Arabia
129 O14 **Shar'ya** Kostromskaya Oblast', NW Russian Federation
151 V15 **Sharyn** *var.* Charyn. ≈ SE Kazakhstan
Sharyn *see* Charyn
85 J18 **Shashe** Central, NE Botswana
85 J18 **Shashe** *var.* Shashi. ≈ Botswana/Zimbabwe
83 J14 **Shashemenē** *var.* Shashemenne, Shashhamana, *It.* Sciasciamana. S Ethiopia
Shashemenne/Shashhamana *see* Shashemenē
166 M9 **Shashi** *var.* Sha-shih, Shasi. Hubei, C China
Shashi *see* Shashe
Sha-shih/Shasi *see* Shashi
37 N3 **Shasta Lake** ▣ California, W USA
37 N2 **Shasta, Mount** ▲ California, W USA
131 O4 **Shatki** Nizhegorodskaya Oblast', W Russian Federation
152 J13 **Shatlyk** Maryyskiy Velayat, C Turkmenistan
Shatra *see* Ash Shaţrah
121 K17 **Shatsk** *Rus.* Shatsk. Minskaya Voblasts', C Belarus
131 N5 **Shatsk** Ryazanskaya Oblast', W Russian Federation
28 J9 **Shattuck** Oklahoma, C USA
151 P16 **Shaul'der** Yuzhnyy Kazakhstan, S Kazakhstan
9 S17 **Shaunavon** Saskatchewan, S Canada
Shavat *see* Showot
164 K4 **Shawan** Xinjiang Uygur Zizhiqu, NW China
12 G12 **Shawanaga** Ontario, S Canada
32 M6 **Shawano** Wisconsin, N USA
32 M6 **Shawano Lake** ◎ Wisconsin, N USA
13 P10 **Shawinigan** *prev.* Shawinigan Falls. Québec, SE Canada
Shawinigan Falls *see* Shawinigan
13 P10 **Shawinigan-Sud** Québec, SE Canada
144 J5 **Shawmarīyah, Jabal ash** ⛰ C Syria
29 O11 **Shawnee** Oklahoma, C USA
12 K12 **Shawville** Québec, SE Canada
Shaykh *see* Ash Shakk
145 W9 **Shaykh 'Ābid** *var.* Shaikh Ābid. E Iraq
145 Y10 **Shaykh Fāris** *var.* Shaikh Fāris. E Iraq
145 T7 **Shaykh Ḩātim** E Iraq
Shaykh, Jabal ash *see* Hermon, Mount
145 X10 **Shaykh Najm** *var.* Shaikh Najm. E Iraq
145 W9 **Shaykh Sa'd** E Iraq
153 T14 **Shazud** SE Tajikistan
121 N18 **Shchadryn** *Rus.* Shchedrin. Homyel'skaya Voblasts', SE Belarus
121 H18 **Shchara** ≈ SW Belarus
Shchedrin *see* Shchadryn
Shcheglovsk *see* Kemerovo
130 K5 **Shchëkino** Tul'skaya Oblast', W Russian Federation
129 S7 **Shchel'yayur** Respublika Komi, NW Russian Federation
151 U8 **Shcherbakty** *Kaz.* Sharbaqty. Pavlodar, E Kazakhstan
130 K7 **Shchigry** Kurskaya Oblast', W Russian Federation
Shchitkovichi *see* Shchytkavichy
119 Q2 **Shchors** Chernihivs'ka Oblast', N Ukraine
119 T8 **Shchors'k** Dnipropetrovs'ka Oblast', E Ukraine
Shchuchin *see* Shchuchyn
151 Q7 **Shchuchinsk** *prev.* Shchuchye. Kokshetau, N Kazakhstan
Shchuchye *see* Shchuchinsk
121 G16 **Shchuchyn** *Pol.* Szczuczyn Nowogródzki, *Rus.* Shchuchin. Hrodzyenskaya Voblasts', W Belarus
121 K17 **Shchytkavichy** *Rus.* Shchitkovichi. Minskaya Voblasts', C Belarus
126 H15 **Shebalino** Respublika Altay, S Russian Federation
130 J9 **Shebekino** Belgorodskaya Oblast', W Russian Federation
Shebelē Wenz, Wabē *see* Shebeli
83 L14 **Shebeli** *Amh.* Wabē Shebelē Wenz, *It.* Scebeli, *Som.* Webi Shabeelle. ≈ Ethiopia/Somalia
115 M20 **Shebenikut, Maja e** ▲ E Albania
155 N2 **Sheberghān** *var.* Shibarghān, Shiberghan, Shiberghān. Jowzjān, N Afghanistan
150 F14 **Shebir** Mangistau, SW Kazakhstan
33 N8 **Sheboygan** Wisconsin, N USA
79 X15 **Shebshi Mountains** *var.* Schebschi Mountains. ⛰ E Nigeria
Shechem *see* Nablus
Shedadi *see* Ash Shadādah
11 P14 **Shediac** New Brunswick, SE Canada
130 L15 **Shedok** Krasnodarskiy Kray, SW Russian Federation
82 N12 **Sheekh** Woqooyi Galbeed, N Somalia
40 M11 **Sheenjek River** ≈ Alaska, USA
98 D13 **Sheep Haven** *Ir.* Cuan na gCaorach. *inlet* N Ireland
37 X10 **Sheep Range** ⛰ Nevada, W USA
100 M13 **'s-Heerenberg** Gelderland, E Netherlands
99 P22 **Sheerness** SE England, UK
11 Q15 **Sheet Harbour** Nova Scotia, SE Canada
193 H18 **Sheffield** Canterbury, South Island, NZ
99 M18 **Sheffield** N England, UK
25 O2 **Sheffield** Alabama, S USA
31 V12 **Sheffield** Iowa, C USA
27 N10 **Sheffield** Texas, SW USA
65 H22 **Shehuen, Río** ≈ S Argentina
Shekhem *see* Nablus
155 V8 **Shekhūpura** Punjab, NE Pakistan
Sheki *see* Şäki
128 L14 **Sheksna** Vologodskaya Oblast', NW Russian Federation
127 O4 **Shelagskiy, Mys** *headland* NE Russian Federation
29 V3 **Shelbina** Missouri, C USA
11 P16 **Shelburne** Nova Scotia, SE Canada
12 G14 **Shelburne** Ontario, S Canada
35 R7 **Shelby** Montana, NW USA
23 Q10 **Shelby** North Carolina, SE USA
33 S12 **Shelby** Ohio, N USA
32 L14 **Shelbyville** Illinois, N USA
33 P14 **Shelbyville** Indiana, N USA
22 L5 **Shelbyville** Kentucky, S USA
29 V2 **Shelbyville** Missouri, C USA
22 J10 **Shelbyville** Tennessee, S USA
27 X8 **Shelbyville** Texas, SW USA
32 L14 **Shelbyville, Lake** ▣ Illinois, N USA
31 S12 **Sheldon** Iowa, C USA
40 M11 **Sheldons Point** Alaska, USA
126 J16 **Shelekhov** Irkutskaya Oblast', C Russian Federation
Shelekhov Gulf *see* Shelikhova, Zaliv
127 Oo9 **Shelikhova, Zaliv** *Eng.* Shelekhov Gulf. *gulf* E Russian Federation
41 P14 **Shelikof Strait** *strait* Alaska, USA
Shelim *see* Shalīm
9 T14 **Shellbrook** Saskatchewan, S Canada
30 L3 **Shell Creek** ≈ North Dakota, N USA
Shellif *see* Chelif, Oued
24 I10 **Shell Keys** *island group* Louisiana, S USA
32 I4 **Shell Lake** Wisconsin, N USA
31 W12 **Shell Rock** Iowa, C USA
193 C26 **Shelter Point** *headland* Stewart Island, NZ
20 L13 **Shelton** Connecticut, NE USA
34 G8 **Shelton** Washington, NW USA
Shemakha *see* Şamaxı
151 W9 **Shemonaikha** Vostochnyy Kazakhstan, E Kazakhstan
131 Q4 **Shemursha** Chuvashskaya Respublika, W Russian Federation
40 D16 **Shemya Island** *island* Aleutian Islands, Alaska, USA
31 T16 **Shenandoah** Iowa, C USA
23 U4 **Shenandoah** Virginia, NE USA
23 U4 **Shenandoah Mountains** *ridge* West Virginia, NE USA
23 V3 **Shenandoah River** ≈ West Virginia, NE USA
79 W15 **Shendam** Plateau, C Nigeria
82 G8 **Shendi** *var.* Shandī. River Nile, NE Sudan
78 I15 **Shenge** SW Sierra Leone
151 U15 **Shengel'dy** Almaty, SE Kazakhstan
115 K18 **Shëngjin** *var.* Shëngjini. Lezhë, NW Albania
Shëngjini *see* Shëngjin
Shengking *see* Liaoning
Sheng Xian/Shengxian *see* Shengzhou
167 S9 **Shengzhou** *var.* Shengxian, Sheng Xian. Zhejiang, SE China
Shenking *see* Liaoning
129 N11 **Shenkursk** Arkhangel'skaya Oblast', NW Russian Federation
166 L3 **Shenmu** Shaanxi, C China
115 L19 **Shën Noj i Madh** ▲ C Albania
Shenshi/Shensi *see* Shaanxi
169 V12 **Shenyang** *Chin.* Shen-yang, *Eng.* Moukden, Mukden; *prev.* Fengtien. Liaoning, NE China
167 O15 **Shenzhen** Guangdong, S China
160 G8 **Sheopur** Madhya Pradesh, C India
118 L5 **Shepetivka** *Rus.* Shepetovka. Khmel'nyts'ka Oblast', NW Ukraine
Shepetovka *see* Shepetivka
27 W10 **Shepherd** Texas, SW USA
197 D14 **Shepherd Islands** *island group* C Vanuatu
22 K5 **Shepherdsville** Kentucky, S USA
191 O11 **Shepparton** Victoria, SE Australia
99 P22 **Sheppey, Isle of** *island* SE England, UK
Sherabad *see* Sherobod
99 L23 **Sherborne** S England, UK
78 H16 **Sherbro Island** *island* SW Sierra Leone
13 Q12 **Sherbrooke** Québec, SE Canada
31 T11 **Sherburn** Minnesota, N USA
80 H6 **Sherda** Borkou-Ennedi-Tibesti, N Chad
82 G7 **Shereik** River Nile, N Sudan
130 K3 **Sheremet'yevo** ✕ (Moskva) Moskovskaya Oblast', W Russian Federation
159 P14 **Shergāti** Bihār, N India
29 U12 **Sheridan** Arkansas, C USA
35 W12 **Sheridan** Wyoming, C USA
190 G8 **Sheringa** South Australia
126 L16 **Sherlovaya Gora** Chitinskaya Oblast', S Russian Federation
27 U5 **Sherman** Texas, SW USA
204 J10 **Sherman Island** *island* Antarctica
21 S4 **Sherman Mills** Maine, NE USA
31 O15 **Sherman Reservoir** ▣ Nebraska, C USA
153 N14 **Sherobod** *Rus.* Sherabad. Surkhondaryo Wiloyati, S Uzbekistan
153 O13 **Sherobod** *Rus.* Sherabad. ≈ S Uzbekistan
159 T14 **Sherpur** Dhaka, N Bangladesh
39 T4 **Sherrelwood** Colorado, C USA
101 J14 **'s-Hertogenbosch** *Fr.* Bois-le-Duc, *Ger.* Herzogenbusch. Noord-Brabant, S Netherlands
30 M2 **Sherwood** North Dakota, N USA
9 Q14 **Sherwood Park** Alberta, SW Canada
58 F13 **Sheshea, Río** ≈ E Peru
149 T5 **Sheshtamad** Khorāsān, NE Iran
31 S10 **Shetek, Lake** ◎ Minnesota, N USA
98 M2 **Shetland Islands** *island group* NE Scotland, UK
150 F14 **Shetpe** Mangistau, SW Kazakhstan
160 C11 **Shetrunji** ≈ W India
Shevchenko *see* Aktau
119 W5 **Shevchenkove** Kharkivs'ka Oblast', E Ukraine
83 H14 **Shewa Gīmīra** SW Ethiopia
167 Q9 **Shexian** *var.* Huicheng, She Xian. Anhui, E China
167 R6 **Sheyang** *prev.* Hede. Jiangsu, E China
31 O4 **Sheyenne** North Dakota, N USA
31 P4 **Sheyenne River** ≈ North Dakota, N USA
98 G7 **Shiant Islands** *island group* NW Scotland, UK
127 Pp14 **Shiashkotan, Ostrov** *island* Kuril'skiye Ostrova, SE Russian Federation
33 R9 **Shiawassee River** ≈ Michigan, N USA
147 R14 **Shibām** C Yemen
Shibarghān *see* Sheberghān
171 Kk12 **Shibata** *var.* Sibata. Niigata, Honshū, C Japan
172 Qq7 **Shibecha** Hokkaidō, NE Japan
Shiberghan/Shiberghān *see* Sheberghān
172 Qq6 **Shibetsu** Hokkaidō, N Japan
172 Pp4 **Shibetsu** *var.* Sibetu. Hokkaidō, NE Japan
172 P5 **Shibetsu** *var.* Sibetu. Hokkaidō, NE Japan
Shibh Jazīrat Sīnā' *see* Sinai
Shibīn al Kawm *see* Shibîn el Kôm
77 W8 **Shibîn el Kôm** *var.* Shibīn al Kawm. N Egypt
149 O13 **Shīb, Kūh-e** ⛰ S Iran
10 D8 **Shibogama Lake** ◎ Ontario, C Canada
Shibotsu-jima *see* Zelënyy, Ostrov
171 K14 **Shibukawa** *var.* Sibukawa. Gunma, Honshū, S Japan
170 Bb16 **Shibushi** Kagoshima, Kyūshū, SW Japan
170 C17 **Shibushi-wan** *bay* SW Japan
172 N9 **Shichinohe** Aomori, Honshū, C Japan
201 U13 **Shichiyo Islands** *island group* Chuuk, C Micronesia
Shickshock Mountains *see* Chic-Chocs, Monts
151 S9 **Shiderti** ≈ N Kazakhstan
151 S8 **Shiderty** Pavlodar, NE Kazakhstan
98 G10 **Shiel, Loch** ◎ N Scotland, UK
171 H15 **Shiga** *off.* Shiga-ken, *var.* Siga. ◈ *prefecture* Honshū, SW Japan
Shigatse *see* Xigazê
147 U13 **Shiḩan** *oasis* NE Yemen
Shih-chia-chuang *see* Shijiazhuang
164 K4 **Shihezi** Xinjiang Uygur Zizhiqu, NW China
Shihmen *see* Shijiazhuang
Shiichi *see* Shyichy
115 K19 **Shijak** *var.* Shijaku. Durrës, W Albania
Shijaku *see* Shijak
167 O4 **Shijiazhuang** *var.* Shih-chia-chuang; *prev.* Shihmen. Hebei, E China
172 Nn7 **Shikabe** Hokkaidō, NE Japan
155 Q13 **Shikārpur** Sind, S Pakistan
201 V12 **Shiki Islands** *island group* Chuuk, C Micronesia
170 Ee15 **Shikoku** *var.* Sikoku. *island* SW Japan
199 Gg6 **Shikoku Basin** *var.* Sikoku Basin. *undersea feature* N Philippine Sea
170 Ee15 **Shikoku-sanchi** ⛰ Shikoku, SW Japan
172 S7 **Shikotan, Ostrov** *Jap.* Shikotan-tō. *island* NE Russian Federation
Shikotan-tō *see* Shikotan, Ostrov
172 O6 **Shikotsu-ko** *var.* Sikotu Ko. ◎ Hokkaidō, NE Japan
83 N15 **Shilabo** SE Ethiopia
131 X7 **Shil'da** Orenburgskaya Oblast', W Russian Federation
145 V3 **Shilēr, Āw-e** ≈ E Iraq
159 S12 **Shiliguri** *prev.* Siliguri. West Bengal, NE India
126 Kk16 **Shilka** Chitinskaya Oblast', S Russian Federation
133 V7 **Shilka** ≈ S Russian Federation
20 H15 **Shillington** Pennsylvania, NE USA
159 V13 **Shillong** Meghālaya, NE India
130 M5 **Shilovo** Ryazanskaya Oblast', W Russian Federation
170 C14 **Shimabara** *var.* Simabara. Nagasaki, Kyūshū, SW Japan
170 C14 **Shimabara-wan** *bay* SW Japan
171 Ii17 **Shimada** *var.* Simada. Shizuoka, Honshū, S Japan
170 Ee12 **Shimane** *off.* Shimane-ken, *var.* Simane. ◈ *prefecture* Honshū, SW Japan
170 F11 **Shimane-hantō** *peninsula* Honshū, SW Japan
126 M15 **Shimanovsk** Amurskaya Oblast', SE Russian Federation
Shimbir Berris *see* Shimbiris
82 O12 **Shimbiris** *var.* Shimbir Berris. ▲ N Somalia
172 P6 **Shimizu** Hokkaidō, NE Japan
171 Ii16 **Shimizu** *var.* Simizu. Shizuoka, Honshū, S Japan
158 I8 **Shimla** *prev.* Simla. Himāchal Pradesh, N India
Shimminato *see* Shinminato
171 J18 **Shimoda** *var.* Simoda. Shizuoka, Honshū, S Japan
171 Kk16 **Shimodate** *var.* Simodate. Ibaraki, Honshū, S Japan
161 F18 **Shimoga** Karnātaka, W India
170 Bb14 **Shimo-jima** *island* SW Japan
170 B15 **Shimo-Koshiki-jima** *island* SW Japan
83 J21 **Shimoni** Coast, S Kenya
170 D12 **Shimonoseki** *var.* Simonoseki; *hist.* Akamagaseki, Bakan. Yamaguchi, Honshū, SW Japan
171 Kk16 **Shimotsuma** *var.* Simotuma. Ibaraki, Honshū, S Japan
128 G14 **Shimsk** Novgorodskaya Oblast', NW Russian Federation
171 Jj14 **Shinano-gawa** *var.* Sinano Gawa. ≈ Honshū, C Japan
147 W7 **Shināş** N Oman
154 J6 **Shīndand** Farāh, W Afghanistan
Shinei *see* Hsinying
27 T12 **Shiner** Texas, SW USA
178 Gg1 **Shingbwiyang** Kachin State, N Myanmar
151 W11 **Shingozha** Semipalatinsk, E Kazakhstan
171 Gg17 **Shingū** *var.* Singû. Wakayama, Honshū, SW Japan
12 F8 **Shining Tree** Ontario, S Canada
170 F12 **Shinji-ko** *var.* Sinzi-ko. ◎ Honshū, SW Japan
171 Ll12 **Shinjō** *var.* Sinzyô. Yamagata, Honshū, C Japan
98 I7 **Shin, Loch** ◎ N Scotland, UK
171 Ii13 **Shinminato** *var.* Shimminato, Sinminato. Toyama, Honshū, SW Japan
170 Dd12 **Shinnanyō** *var.* Shin-Nan'yō, Sinn'anyô. Yamaguchi, Honshū, SW Japan
23 S3 **Shinnston** West Virginia, NE USA
144 I6 **Shinshār** *Fr.* Chinnchâr. Ḩimş, W Syria
171 I16 **Shinshiro** *var.* Sinsiro. Aichi, Honshū, SW Japan
Shinshū *see* Chinju
172 P6 **Shintoku** Hokkaidō, NE Japan
83 G20 **Shinyanga** Shinyanga, NW Tanzania
83 G20 **Shinyanga** ◈ *region* N Tanzania
171 M13 **Shiogama** *var.* Siogama. Miyagi, Honshū, C Japan
171 J15 **Shiojiri** *var.* Sioziri. Nagano, Honshū, S Japan
170 G17 **Shiono-misaki** *headland* Honshū, SW Japan
171 Ll15 **Shioya-zaki** *headland* Honshū, C Japan
116 J9 **Shipchenski Prokhod** *pass* C Bulgaria
166 G14 **Shiping** Yunnan, SW China
11 P13 **Shippagan** *var.* Shippegan. New Brunswick, SE Canada
Shippegan *see* Shippagan
20 F15 **Shippensburg** Pennsylvania, NE USA
39 O9 **Ship Rock** ▲ New Mexico, SW USA
39 P9 **Shiprock** New Mexico, SW USA
13 R6 **Shipshaw** ≈ Québec, SE Canada
127 Pp11 **Shipunskiy, Mys** *headland* E Russian Federation
166 K7 **Shiquan** Shaanxi, C China
126 Hh14 **Shira** Respublika Khakasiya, S Russian Federation
170 G16 **Shirahama** Wakayama, Honshū, SW Japan
159 T14 **Shirajganj Ghat** *var.* Serajgonj, Sirajganj. Rajshahi, C Bangladesh
171 Mm7 **Shirakami-misaki** *headland* Hokkaidō, NE Japan
171 L14 **Shirakawa** *var.* Sirakawa. Fukushima, Honshū, C Japan
171 Ii13 **Shirakawa** Gifu, Honshū, SW Japan
171 K14 **Shirane-san** ▲ Honshū, S Japan
171 J16 **Shirane-san** ▲ Honshū, S Japan
172 Pp7 **Shiranuka** Hokkaidō, NE Japan
172 O6 **Shiraoi** Hokkaidō, NE Japan
205 N12 **Shirase Coast** *physical region* Antarctica
172 Pp5 **Shirataki** Hokkaidō, NE Japan
149 O11 **Shirāz** *var.* Shīrāz. Fārs, S Iran
85 N15 **Shire** *var.* Chire. ≈ Malawi/Mozambique
168 G7 **Shiree** Dzavhan, W Mongolia
169 O9 **Shireet** Sühbaatar, SE Mongolia
172 R6 **Shiretoko-hantō** *headland* Hokkaidō, NE Japan
172 R5 **Shiretoko-misaki** *headland* Hokkaidō, NE Japan
131 N5 **Shiringushi** Respublika Mordoviya, W Russian Federation
154 M3 **Shīrīn Tagāb** Fāryāb, N Afghanistan
155 N2 **Shīrīn Tagāb** ≈ N Afghanistan
172 Nn8 **Shiriya-zaki** *headland* Honshū, C Japan
150 I12 **Shirkala, Gryada** *plain* W Kazakhstan
171 Ll13 **Shiroishi** *var.* Siroisi. Miyagi, Honshū, C Japan
Shirokoye *see* Shyroke
171 K12 **Shirone** *var.* Sirone. Niigata, Honshū, C Japan
171 I14 **Shirotori** Gifu, Honshū, SW Japan
171 J13 **Shirouma-dake** ▲ Honshū, S Japan
207 T1 **Shirshov Ridge** *undersea feature* W Bering Sea
Shirshütür *see* Shirshyutyur, Peski
152 K12 **Shirshyutyur, Peski** *Turkm.* Shirshütür. *desert* E Turkmenistan
149 T3 **Shīrvān** *var.* Shirwān. Khorāsān, NE Iran
Shirwa, Lake *see* Chilwa, Lake
Shirwān *see* Shīrvān
165 N5 **Shisanjianfang** Xinjiang Uygur Zizhiqu, W China
40 M16 **Shishaldin Volcano** ▲ Unimak Island, Alaska, USA
Shishchitsy *see* Shyshchytsy
40 M8 **Shishmaref** Alaska, USA
Shisur *see* Ash Shişar
171 I16 **Shitara** Aichi, Honshū, SW Japan
158 D12 **Shiv** Rājasthān, NW India
160 H8 **Shivpuri** Madhya Pradesh, C India
38 J9 **Shivwits Plateau** *plain* Arizona, SW USA
Shiwālik Range *see* Siwalik Range
166 M8 **Shiyan** Hubei, C China
166 H13 **Shizong** Yunnan, SW China
171 Mm13 **Shizugawa** Miyagi, Honshū, NE Japan
165 W8 **Shizuishan** *var.* Dawukou. Ningxia, N China
172 Oo7 **Shizunai** Hokkaidō, NE Japan
171 Ii16 **Shizuoka** *var.* Sizuoka. Shizuoka, Honshū, S Japan
171 Ii16 **Shizuoka** *off.* Shizuoka-ken, *var.* Sizuoka. ◈ *prefecture* Honshū, S Japan
Shklov *see* Shklow
121 N15 **Shklow** *Rus.* Shklov. Mahilyowskaya Voblasts', E Belarus
115 K18 **Shkodër** *var.* Shkodra, *It.* Scutari, *SCr.* Skadar. Shkodër, NW Albania
115 K17 **Shkodër** ◈ *district* NW Albania
Shkodra *see* Shkodër
Shkodrës, Liqeni i *see* Scutari, Lake
Shkumbî/Shkumbin *see* Shkumbinit, Lumi i
115 L20 **Shkumbinit, Lumi i** *var.* Shkumbî, Shkumbin. ≈ C Albania
Shligigh, Cuan *see* Sligo Bay
126 Ii2 **Shmidta, Ostrov** *island* Severnaya Zemlya, N Russian Federation
191 S10 **Shoalhaven River** ≈ New South Wales, SE Australia
9 W16 **Shoal Lake** Manitoba, S Canada
33 O15 **Shoals** Indiana, N USA
170 F13 **Shōbara** *var.* Syôbara. Hiroshima, Honshū, SW Japan
170 Ff14 **Shōdo-shima** *island* SW Japan
171 Ii13 **Shō-gawa** ≈ Honshū, SW Japan
Shōka *see* Changhua
126 J3 **Shokal'skogo, Proliv** *strait* N Russian Federation
172 Oo4 **Shokanbetsu-dake** ⋀ Hokkaidō, NE Japan
153 T14 **Shokhdara, Qatorkŭhi** *Rus.* Shakhdarinskiy Khrebet. ⛰ SE Tajikistan
151 N9 **Sholaksay** Kustanay, N Kazakhstan
Sholāpur *see* Solāpur
Sholdaneshty *see* Şoldăneşti

◆ Country
● Country Capital
◇ Dependent Territory
○ Dependent Territory Capital
◈ Administrative Region
✕ International Airport
▲ Mountain
⛰ Mountain Range
⋀ Volcano
≈ River
◎ Lake
▣ Reservoir

◆ COUNTRY ◇ DEPENDENT TERRITORY ◆ ADMINISTRATIVE REGION ▲ MOUNTAIN ✶ VOLCANO ◎ LAKE
● COUNTRY CAPITAL ○ DEPENDENT TERRITORY CAPITAL ✕ INTERNATIONAL AIRPORT ▲ MOUNTAIN RANGE ♒ RIVER ◎ RESERVOIR

SIPIWESK – SŌFU-GAN

9 X12 **Sipiwesk** Manitoba, C Canada
9 W13 **Sipiwesk Lake** ◎ Manitoba, C Canada
205 O11 **Siple Coast** *physical region* Antarctica
204 K12 **Siple Island** *island* Antarctica
204 K13 **Siple, Mount** ▲ Siple Island, Antarctica
Sipoo *see* Sibbo
114 G12 **Šipovo** W Bosnia and Herzegovina
25 O4 **Sipsey River** ⚡ Alabama, S USA
173 Ff10 **Sipura, Pulau** *island* W Indonesia
0 G16 **Siqueiros Fracture Zone** *tectonic feature* E Pacific Ocean
44 L10 **Siquia, Río** ⚡ SE Nicaragua
179 Qq14 **Siquijor Island** *island* C Philippines
45 N13 **Siquirres** Limón, E Costa Rica
56 J5 **Siquisique** Lara, N Venezuela
161 G19 **Sīra** Karnātaka, W India
97 D16 **Sira** ⚡ S Norway
178 Hh12 **Siracha** *var.* Ban Si Racha, Si Racha. Chon Buri, S Thailand
109 L25 **Siracusa** *Eng.* Syracuse. Sicilia, Italy, C Mediterranean Sea
Sirajganj *see* Shirajganj Ghat
Sirakawa *see* Shirakawa
9 N14 **Sir Alexander, Mount** ▲ British Columbia, W Canada
143 O12 **Şiran** Gümüşhane, NE Turkey
79 Q12 **Sirba** ⚡ E Burkina
149 O17 **Şīr Banī Yās** *island* W UAE
97 D17 **Sirdalsvatnet** ◎ S Norway
Sir Darya/Sirdaryo *see* Syr Darya
153 O11 **Sirdaryo Wiloyati** *Rus.* Syrdar'inskaya Oblast'. ◆ *province* E Uzbekistan
Sir Donald Sangster International Airport *see* Sangster
194 H13 **Sirebi** ⚡ S PNG
189 S3 **Sir Edward Pellew Group** *island group* Northern Territory, NE Australia
118 K8 **Siret** *Ger.* Sereth, *Hung.* Szeret. Suceava, N Romania
118 K8 **Siret** *var.* Siretul, *Ger.* Sereth, *Rus.* Seret, *Ukr.* Siret. ⚡ Romania/Ukraine
Siretul *see* Siret
146 K3 **Sirḥān, Wādī as** *dry watercourse* Jordan/Saudi Arabia
158 I8 **Sirhind** Punjab, N India
118 F11 **Şiria** *Ger.* Schiria. Arad, W Romania
Siria *see* Syria
149 S14 **Sīrīk** Hormozgān, SE Iran
178 Hh8 **Sirikit Reservoir** ◎ N Thailand
60 K12 **Siriituba, Ilha** *island* NE Brazil
176 Ww11 **Siriwo** ⚡ Irian Jaya, E Indonesia
149 R11 **Sīrjān** *prev.* Sa'īdābād. Kermān, S Iran
190 H9 **Sir Joseph Banks Group** *island group* South Australia
94 K11 **Sirkka** Lappi, N Finland
Sirna *see* Sýrna
143 R16 **Şırnak** Şırnak, SE Turkey
143 S16 **Şırnak** ◆ *province* SE Turkey
Siroisi *see* Shiroishi
161 J14 **Sironcha** Mahārāshtra, C India
Sirone *see* Shirone
Síros *see* Sýros
Sirotino *see* Sirotsina
120 M12 **Sirotsina** *Rus.* Sirotino. Vitsyebskaya Voblasts', N Belarus
158 H9 **Sirsa** Haryāna, NW India
181 Y17 **Sir Seewoosagur Ramgoolam** ✕ (Port Louis) SE Mauritius
161 E18 **Sirsi** Karnātaka, W India
Sirte *see* Surt
190 A2 **Sir Thomas, Mount** ▲ South Australia
Sirti, Gulf of *see* Surt, Khalīj
148 J5 **Sīrvān, Rūdkhāneh-ye** *var.* Nahr Diyālá, Sirwan. ⚡ Iran/Iraq *see also* Diyālá, Nahr
120 H13 **Širvintos** Širvintos, SE Lithuania
Sirwan *see* Diyālá, Nahr/Sīrvān, Rūdkhāneh-ye
9 N15 **Sir Wilfrid Laurier, Mount** ▲ British Columbia, SW Canada
12 M10 **Sir-Wilfrid, Mont** ▲ Québec, SE Canada
Sisačko-Moslavačka Županija *see* Sisak-Moslavina
114 E9 **Sisak** *var.* Siscia, *Ger.* Sissek, *Hung.* Sziszek; *anc.* Segestica. Sisak-Moslavina, C Croatia
178 J10 **Si Sa Ket** *var.* Sisaket, Sri Saket. Si Sa Ket, E Thailand
114 E9 **Sisak-Moslavina** *off.* Sisačko-Moslavačka Županija. ◆ *province* C Croatia
178 H8 **Si Satchanala** Sukhothai, NW Thailand
Siscia *see* Sisak
176 W10 **Sisember** Irian Jaya, E Indonesia
85 G22 **Sishen** Northern Cape, NW South Africa
143 V13 **Sisian** SE Armenia
207 N13 **Sisimiut** *var.* Holsteinborg, Holsteinsborg, Holsterborg, Holstensborg. S Greenland
32 M1 **Siskiwit Bay** *lake bay* Michigan, N USA
36 L1 **Siskiyou Mountains** ▲ California/Oregon, W USA
178 I12 **Sisŏphŏn** Bătdâmbâng, NW Cambodia
110 E7 **Sissach** Basel-Land, NW Switzerland
194 F9 **Sissano** Sandaun, NW PNG
Sissek *see* Sisak
31 R7 **Sisseton** South Dakota, N USA
149 W9 **Sīstān, Daryācheh-ye** *var.* Daryācheh-ye Hāmūn, Hāmūn-e Şāberī. ◎ Afghanistan/Iran *see also* Şāberī, Hāmūn-e
149 V12 **Sīstān va Balūchestān** *off.* Ostān-e Sīstān va Balūchestān, *var.* Balūchestān va Sīstān. ◆ *province* SE Iran
105 T14 **Sisteron** Alpes-de-Haute-Provence, SE France
34 H13 **Sisters** Oregon, NW USA
67 G15 **Sisters Peak** ▲ N Ascension Island
23 R3 **Sistersville** West Virginia, NE USA
Sistova *see* Svishtov
Sitakund *see* Sitakunda
159 V16 **Sitakunda** *var.* Sitakund. Chittagong, SE Bangladesh
159 P12 **Sītāmarhi** Bihār, N India
158 L11 **Sītāpur** Uttar Pradesh, N India
Sitaş Cristuru *see* Cristuru Secuiesc
117 L25 **Siteía** *var.* Sitía. Kríti, Greece, E Mediterranean Sea
107 V6 **Sitges** Cataluña, NE Spain
117 H15 **Sithoniá** *peninsula* NE Greece
Sitía *see* Siteía
56 F4 **Sitionuevo** Magdalena, N Colombia
41 X13 **Sitka** Baranof Island, Alaska, USA
41 Q15 **Sitkinak Island** *island* Trinity Islands, Alaska, USA
177 G7 **Sittang** *var.* Sittoung. ⚡ S Myanmar
101 L17 **Sittard** Limburg, SE Netherlands
Sitten *see* Sion
110 H7 **Sitter** ⚡ NW Switzerland
111 U10 **Sittersdorf** Kärnten, S Austria
Sittoung *see* Sittang
177 F6 **Sittwe** *var.* Akyab. Arakan State, W Myanmar
174 Mm15 **Situbondo** *prev.* Sitoebondo. Jawa, C Indonesia
44 L8 **Siuna** Región Autónoma Atlántico Norte, NE Nicaragua
159 R15 **Siuri** West Bengal, NE India
Siut *see* Asyūt
126 M15 **Sivaki** Amurskaya Oblast', SE Russian Federation
142 M13 **Sivas** *anc.* Sebastia, Sebaste. Sivas, C Turkey
142 M13 **Sivas** ◆ *province* C Turkey
143 O15 **Siverek** Şanlıurfa, S Turkey
119 X6 **Sivers'k** Donets'ka Oblast', E Ukraine
128 G13 **Siverskiy** Leningradskaya Oblast', NW Russian Federation
119 X6 **Sivers'kyy Donets'** *Rus.* Severskiy Donets. ⚡ Russian Federation/Ukraine *see also* Severskiy Donets
129 W5 **Sivomaskinskiy** Respublika Komi, NW Russian Federation
142 G13 **Sivrihisar** Eskişehir, W Turkey
101 F22 **Sivry** Hainaut, S Belgium
127 Pp9 **Sivuchiy, Mys** *headland* E Russian Federation
77 U9 **Sīwa** *var.* Sīwah. NW Egypt
Sīwah *see* Sīwa
158 J9 **Siwalik Range** *var.* Shiwālik Range. ▲ India/Nepal
159 O13 **Siwān** Bihār, N India
45 O14 **Sixaola, Río** ⚡ Costa Rica/Panama
Six Counties, The *see* Northern Ireland
105 T16 **Six-Fours-les-Plages** Var, SE France
167 Q7 **Sixian** *var.* Si Xian. Anhui, E China
24 J9 **Six Mile Lake** ◎ Louisiana, S USA
145 V3 **Siyāh Gūz** E Iraq
161 L25 **Siyambalanduwa** Uva Province, SE Sri Lanka
143 Y10 **Siyäzän** *Rus.* Siazan'. NE Azerbaijan
Sizebolu *see* Sozopol
Sizuoka *see* Shizuoka
Sjar *see* Sääre
115 L15 **Sjenica** *Turk.* Seniça. Serbia, SW Yugoslavia
96 G11 **Sjoa** ⚡ S Norway
97 K23 **Sjöbo** Malmöhus, S Sweden
97 I24 **Sjælland** *Eng.* Zealand, *Ger.* Seeland. *island* E Denmark
96 E9 **Sjøholt** Møre og Romsdal, S Norway
94 O1 **Sjuøyane** *island group* N Svalbard
Skadar *see* Shkodër
Skadarsko Jezero *see* Scutari, Lake
119 R11 **Skadovs'k** Khersons'ka Oblast', S Ukraine
94 I2 **Skagaströnd** *prev.* Höfdhakaupstadhur. Nordhurland Vestra, N Iceland
97 H19 **Skagen** Nordjylland, N Denmark
Skagerak *see* Skagerrak
97 L16 **Skagern** ◎ C Sweden
207 T17 **Skagerrak** *var.* Skagerak. *channel* N Europe
96 G12 **Skaget** ▲ S Norway
34 H7 **Skagit River** ⚡ Washington, NW USA
41 W12 **Skagway** Alaska, USA
94 K8 **Skaidi** Finnmark, N Norway
117 F21 **Skála** Pelopónnisos, S Greece
118 K6 **Skalat** *Pol.* Skałat. Ternopil's'ka Oblast', W Ukraine
97 J22 **Skälderviken** *inlet* Denmark/Sweden
94 I12 **Skalka** ◎ N Sweden
116 I12 **Skalotí** Anatolikí Makedonía kai Thráki, NE Greece
97 G22 **Skanderborg** Århus, C Denmark
97 K22 **Skåne** *prev. Eng.* Scania. *cultural region* S Sweden
77 N6 **Skanès** ✕ (Sousse) E Tunisia
97 C15 **Skånevik** Hordaland, S Norway
97 M18 **Skänninge** Östergötland, S Sweden
97 J23 **Skanör** Malmöhus, S Sweden
117 H17 **Skantzoúra** *island* Vóreioi Sporádes, Greece, Aegean Sea
97 K18 **Skara** Skaraborg, S Sweden
97 J18 **Skaraborg** ◆ *county* S Sweden
97 M17 **Skärblacka** Östergötland, S Sweden
97 I18 **Skärhamn** Göteborg och Bohus, S Sweden
97 I14 **Skarnes** Hedmark, S Norway
121 M21 **Skarodnaye** *Rus.* Skorodnoye. Homyel'skaya Voblasts', SE Belarus
112 I8 **Skarszewy** *Ger.* Schöneck. Gdańsk, NW Poland
113 M14 **Skarżysko-Kamienna** Kielce, SE Poland
97 K16 **Skattkärr** Värmland, C Sweden
120 D12 **Skaudvilė** Tauragė, SW Lithuania
94 J12 **Skaulo** Norrbotten, N Sweden
113 K17 **Skawina** Kraków, S Poland
8 K12 **Skeena** ⚡ British Columbia, SW Canada
8 J11 **Skeena Mountains** ▲ British Columbia, W Canada
99 O18 **Skegness** E England, UK
94 J4 **Skeidharársandur** *coast* S Iceland
95 J15 **Skellefteå** Västerbotten, N Sweden
95 I14 **Skelleftealven** ⚡ N Sweden
95 J15 **Skelleftehamn** Västerbotten, N Sweden
27 O2 **Skellytown** Texas, SW USA
97 J19 **Skene** Älvsborg, S Sweden
99 G17 **Skerries** *Ir.* Na Sceirí. E Ireland
97 H15 **Ski** Akershus, S Norway
117 G17 **Skíathos** Skíathos, Vóreioi Sporádes, Greece, Aegean Sea
117 G17 **Skíathos** *island* Vóreioi Sporádes, Greece, Aegean Sea
29 P9 **Skiatook** Oklahoma, C USA
29 P9 **Skiatook Lake** ◎ Oklahoma, C USA
99 B22 **Skibbereen** *Ir.* An Sciobairín. SW Ireland
94 I9 **Skibotn** Troms, N Norway
121 F16 **Skidal'** *Rus.* Skidel'. Hrodzyenskaya Voblasts', W Belarus
99 K15 **Skiddaw** ▲ NW England, UK
Skidel' *see* Skidal'
27 T14 **Skidmore** Texas, SW USA
97 G16 **Skien** Telemark, S Norway
Skiermûntseach *see* Schiermonnikoog
112 L12 **Skierniewice** Skierniewice, C Poland
112 K12 **Skierniewice** *off.* Województwo Skierniewickie. ◆ *province* C Poland
Skierniewickie, Województwo *see* Skierniewice
76 L5 **Skikda** *prev.* Philippeville. NE Algeria
32 M16 **Skillet Fork** ⚡ Illinois, N USA
97 L19 **Skillingaryd** Jönköping, S Sweden
117 B19 **Skinári, Ákra** *headland* Zákynthos, Iónioi Nísoi, Greece, C Mediterranean Sea
97 M15 **Skinnskatteberg** Västmanland, C Sweden
190 M12 **Skipton** Victoria, SE Australia
99 L16 **Skipton** N England, UK
Skiropoula *see* Skyropoúla
Skíros *see* Skýros
97 F21 **Skive** Viborg, NW Denmark
96 F11 **Skjåk** Oppland, S Norway
94 K2 **Skjálfandafljót** ⚡ C Iceland
97 F22 **Skjern** Ringkøbing, W Denmark
97 F22 **Skjern Å** *var.* Skjern Aa. ⚡ W Denmark
Skjern Aa *see* Skjern Å
94 G12 **Skjerstad** Nordland, C Norway
94 I8 **Skjervøy** Troms, N Norway
94 I10 **Skjold** Troms, N Norway
113 I17 **Skoczów** Bielsko-Biała, S Poland
97 I24 **Skælskør** Vestsjælland, E Denmark
111 T11 **Škofja Loka** *Ger.* Bischoflack. NW Slovenia
96 N12 **Skog** Gävleborg, C Sweden
97 K16 **Skoghall** Värmland, C Sweden
33 N10 **Skokie** Illinois, N USA
118 H6 **Skole** L'vivs'ka Oblast', W Ukraine
117 D19 **Skóllis** ▲ S Greece
178 I13 **Skon** Kâmpóng Cham, C Cambodia
117 H17 **Skópelos** Skópelos, Vóreioi Sporádes, Greece, Aegean Sea
117 H17 **Skópelos** *island* Vóreioi Sporádes, Greece, Aegean Sea
130 L5 **Skopin** Ryazanskaya Oblast', W Russian Federation
115 N18 **Skopje** *var.* Úsküb, *Turk.* Üsküp; *prev.* Skoplje, *anc.* Scupi. ● (FYR Macedonia) N FYR Macedonia
115 O18 **Skopje** ✕ N FYR Macedonia
Skoplje *see* Skopje
112 I8 **Skórcz** *Ger.* Skurz. Gdańsk, N Poland
Skorodnoye *see* Skarodnaye
95 H16 **Skorped** Västernorrland, C Sweden
97 G21 **Skørping** Nordjylland, N Denmark
97 K18 **Skövde** Skaraborg, S Sweden
126 Ll14 **Skovorodino** Amurskaya Oblast', SE Russian Federation
21 Q6 **Skowhegan** Maine, NE USA
9 W15 **Skownan** Manitoba, S Canada
96 H13 **Skreia** Oppland, S Norway
Skripón *see* Orchómenos
120 H9 **Skrīveri** Aizkraukle, S Latvia
120 J11 **Skrudaliena** Daugavpils, SE Latvia
120 D9 **Skrunda** Kuldīga, W Latvia
97 C16 **Skudeneshavn** Rogaland, S Norway
85 L20 **Skukuza** Mpumalanga, NE South Africa
99 B22 **Skull** *Ir.* An Scoil. SW Ireland
24 L3 **Skuna River** ⚡ Mississippi, S USA
31 X15 **Skunk River** ⚡ Iowa, C USA
120 C10 **Skuodas** *Ger.* Schoden, *Pol.* Szkudy. Skuodas, NW Lithuania
97 K23 **Skurup** Malmöhus, S Sweden
116 H8 **Skŭt** ⚡ NW Bulgaria
96 O13 **Skutskär** Uppsala, C Sweden
Skvira *see* Skvyra
119 O5 **Skvyra** *Rus.* Skvira. Kyyivs'ka Oblast', N Ukraine
41 Q11 **Skwentna** Alaska, USA
112 E11 **Skwierzyna** *Ger.* Schwerin. Gorzów, W Poland
98 G9 **Skye, Isle of** *island* NW Scotland, UK
34 I8 **Skykomish** Washington, NW USA
Skylge *see* Terschelling
65 F19 **Skyring, Peninsula** *peninsula* S Chile
65 H24 **Skyring, Seno** *inlet* S Chile
117 H17 **Skyropoúla** *var.* Skiropoula. *island* Vóreioi Sporádes, Greece, Aegean Sea
117 I17 **Skýros** *var.* Skíros. Skýros, Vóreioi Sporádes, Greece, Aegean Sea
117 I17 **Skýros** *var.* Skíros; *anc.* Scyros. *island* Vóreioi Sporádes, Greece, Aegean Sea
120 J12 **Slabodka** *Rus.* Slobodka. Vitsyebskaya Voblasts', NW Belarus
97 I23 **Slagelse** Vestsjælland, E Denmark
95 I14 **Slagnäs** Norrbotten, N Sweden
174 Kk15 **Slamet, Gunung** ▲ Jawa, S Indonesia
41 T10 **Slana** Alaska, USA
99 F20 **Slaney** *Ir.* An tSláine. ⚡ SE Ireland
118 J13 **Slănic** Prahova, SE Romania
118 K11 **Slănic Moldova** Bacău, E Romania
115 H16 **Slano** Dubrovnik-Neretva, SE Croatia
128 F13 **Slantsy** Leningradskaya Oblast', NW Russian Federation
113 C16 **Slaný** *Ger.* Schlan. Střední Čechy, NW Czech Republic
10 C10 **Slate Falls** Ontario, S Canada
29 T4 **Slater** Missouri, C USA
118 I14 **Slatina** Olt, S Romania
Slatina *see* Podravska Slatina
27 N5 **Slaton** Texas, SW USA
97 H14 **Slattum** Akershus, S Norway
9 R10 **Slave** ⚡ Alberta/Northwest Territories, C Canada
70 E12 **Slave Coast** *coastal region* W Africa
9 P13 **Slave Lake** Alberta, SW Canada
125 G14 **Slavgorod** Altayskiy Kray, S Russian Federation
Slavgorod *see* Slawharad
Slavonia *see* Slavonija
114 G9 **Slavonija** *Eng.* Slavonia, *Ger.* Slawonien, *Hung.* Szlavonia, Szlavonország. *cultural region* NE Croatia
114 H9 **Slavonska Požega** *prev.* Požega, *Ger.* Poschega, *Hung.* Pozsega. Požega-Slavonija, NE Croatia
114 H10 **Slavonski Brod** *Ger.* Brod, *Hung.* Bród; *prev.* Brod, Brod na Savi. Brod-Posavina, NE Croatia
118 L4 **Slavuta** Khmel'nyts'ka Oblast', NW Ukraine
119 P2 **Slavutych** Chernihivs'ka Oblast', N Ukraine
127 N18 **Slavyanka** Primorskiy Kray, SE Russian Federation
116 J8 **Slavyanovo** Lovechka Oblast, N Bulgaria
Slavyansk *see* Slov"yans'k
130 K14 **Slavyansk-na-Kubani** Krasnodarskiy Kray, SW Russian Federation
121 N20 **Slavyechna** *Rus.* Slovechna. ⚡ Belarus/Ukraine
121 O16 **Slawharad** *Rus.* Slavgorod. Mahilyowskaya Voblasts', E Belarus
112 G7 **Sławno** Słupsk, NW Poland
Slawonien *see* Slavonija
31 S10 **Slayton** Minnesota, N USA
99 N18 **Sleaford** E England, UK
99 A20 **Slea Head** *Ir.* Ceann Sléibhe. *headland* SW Ireland
98 G9 **Sleat, Sound of** *strait* NW Scotland, UK
Sledyuki *see* Slyedzyuki
10 I5 **Sleeper Islands** *island group* Northwest Territories, C Canada
33 O6 **Sleeping Bear Point** *headland* Michigan, N USA
31 T10 **Sleepy Eye** Minnesota, N USA
41 O11 **Sleetmute** Alaska, USA
Sléibhte, Ceann *see* Slea Head
Slēmānī *see* As Sulaymānīyah
205 O5 **Slessor Glacier** *glacier* Antarctica
24 L9 **Slidell** Louisiana, S USA
20 K12 **Slide Mountain** ▲ New York, NE USA
100 I13 **Sliedrecht** Zuid-Holland, C Netherlands
123 Jj16 **Sliema** N Malta
99 G16 **Slieve Donard** ▲ SE Northern Ireland, UK
Sligeach *see* Sligo
99 D16 **Sligo** *Ir.* Sligeach. NW Ireland
99 C16 **Sligo** *Ir.* Sligeach. *cultural region* NW Ireland
99 C15 **Sligo Bay** *Ir.* Cuan Shligigh. *inlet* NW Ireland
20 B13 **Slippery Rock** Pennsylvania, NE USA
97 P19 **Slite** Gotland, SE Sweden
116 L9 **Sliven** *var.* Slivno. Burgaska Oblast, E Bulgaria
116 G9 **Slivnitsa** Sofiyska Oblast, W Bulgaria
Slivno *see* Sliven
116 L7 **Slivo Pole** Razgradska Oblast, NE Bulgaria
31 S13 **Sloan** Iowa, C USA
37 X12 **Sloan** Nevada, W USA
Slobodka *see* Slabodka
129 R14 **Slobodskoy** Kirovskaya Oblast', NW Russian Federation
Slobodzeya *see* Slobozia
119 O10 **Slobozia** *Rus.* Slobodzeya. E Moldova
118 L14 **Slobozia** Ialomiţa, SE Romania
100 O5 **Slochteren** Groningen, NE Netherlands
121 H17 **Slonim** *Pol.* Słonim, *Rus.* Slonim. Hrodzyenskaya Voblasts', W Belarus
100 K7 **Sloter Meer** ◎ N Netherlands
Slot, The *see* New Georgia Sound
99 N22 **Slough** S England, UK
113 J20 **Slovakia** *off.* Slovenská Republika, *Ger.* Slowakei, *Hung.* Szlovákia, *Slvk.* Slovensko. ◆ *republic* C Europe
Slovak Ore Mountains *see* Slovenské Rudohorie
Slovechna *see* Slavyechna
111 S12 **Slovenia** *off.* Republic of Slovenia, *Ger.* Slowenien, *Slvn.* Slovenija. ◆ *republic* SE Europe
Slovenija *see* Slovenia
111 V10 **Slovenj Gradec** *Ger.* Windischgraz. N Slovenia
111 W10 **Slovenska Bistrica** *Ger.* Windischfeistritz. NE Slovenia
111 W10 **Slovenska Konjice** E Slovenia
Slovenská Republika *see* Slovakia
113 K20 **Slovenské Rudohorie** *Eng.* Slovak Ore Mountains, *Ger.* Slowakisches Erzgebirge, Ungarisches Erzgebirge. ▲ C Slovakia
Slovensko *see* Slovakia
119 Y7 **Slov"yanoserbs'k** Luhans'ka Oblast', E Ukraine
119 W6 **Slov"yans'k** *Rus.* Slavyansk. Donets'ka Oblast', E Ukraine
Slowakei *see* Slovakia
Slowakisches Erzgebirge *see* Slovenské Rudohorie
Slowenien *see* Slovenia
112 D11 **Słubice** *Ger.* Frankfurt. Gorzów, W Poland
121 K19 **Sluch** *Rus.* Sluch'. ⚡ C Belarus
118 L4 **Sluch** ⚡ NW Ukraine
101 D16 **Sluis** Zeeland, SW Netherlands
114 D10 **Slunj** *Hung.* Szluin. Karlovac, C Croatia
112 I11 **Słupca** Konin, C Poland
112 G6 **Słupia** *Ger.* Stolpe. ⚡ NW Poland
112 G6 **Słupsk** *Ger.* Stolp. Słupsk, NW Poland
112 G7 **Słupsk** *off.* Województwo Słupskie, *Ger.* Stolp. ◆ *province* NW Poland
Słupskie, Województwo *see* Słupsk
121 K18 **Slutsk** *Rus.* Slutsk. Minskaya Voblasts', S Belarus
121 O16 **Slyedzyuki** *Rus.* Sledyuki. Mahilyowskaya Voblasts', E Belarus
99 A17 **Slyne Head** *Ir.* Ceann Léime. *headland* W Ireland
126 J16 **Slyudyanka** Irkutskaya Oblast', S Russian Federation
29 U14 **Smackover** Arkansas, C USA
97 L20 **Småland** *cultural region* S Sweden
97 K20 **Smålandsstenar** Jönköping, S Sweden
Small Malaita *see* Maramasike
11 O8 **Smallwood Reservoir** ◎ Newfoundland and Labrador, S Canada
121 N14 **Smalyany** *Rus.* Smolyany. Vitsyebskaya Voblasts', NE Belarus
121 L15 **Smalyavichy** *Rus.* Smolevichi. Minskaya Voblasts', C Belarus
76 C9 **Smara** *var.* Es Semara. N Western Sahara
121 I14 **Smarhon'** *Pol.* Smorgonie, *Rus.* Smorgon'. Hrodzyenskaya Voblasts', W Belarus
114 M11 **Smederevo** *Ger.* Semendria. Serbia, N Yugoslavia
114 M12 **Smederevska Palanka** Serbia, C Yugoslavia
97 M14 **Smedjebacken** Kopparberg, C Sweden
118 L13 **Smeeni** Buzău, SE Romania
Smela *see* Smila
109 D16 **Smeralda, Costa** *cultural region* Sardegna, Italy, C Mediterranean Sea
113 J22 **Śmigiel** *Ger.* Schmiegel. Leszno, W Poland
119 Q6 **Smila** *Rus.* Smela. Cherkas'ka Oblast', C Ukraine
100 N7 **Smilde** Drenthe, NE Netherlands
9 S16 **Smiley** Saskatchewan, S Canada
27 T12 **Smiley** Texas, SW USA
Smilten *see* Smiltene
120 I8 **Smiltene** *Ger.* Smilten. Valka, N Latvia
127 O14 **Smirnykh** Ostrov Sakhalin, Sakhalinskaya Oblast', SE Russian Federation
9 Q13 **Smith** Alberta, W Canada
41 P4 **Smith Bay** *bay* Alaska, USA
10 I3 **Smith, Cape** *headland* Québec, NE Canada
28 L3 **Smith Center** Kansas, C USA
8 K13 **Smithers** British Columbia, SW Canada
23 V10 **Smithfield** North Carolina, SE USA
38 L1 **Smithfield** Utah, W USA
23 X7 **Smithfield** Virginia, NE USA
10 I3 **Smith Island** *island* Northwest Territories, C Canada
Smith Island *see* Sumisu-jima
22 H7 **Smithland** Kentucky, S USA
23 T7 **Smith Mountain Lake** *var.* Leesville Lake. ◎ Virginia, NE USA
36 L1 **Smith River** California, W USA
35 R9 **Smith River** ⚡ Montana, NW USA
12 L13 **Smiths Falls** Ontario, SE Canada
35 N13 **Smiths Ferry** Idaho, NW USA
22 K7 **Smiths Grove** Kentucky, S USA
191 N15 **Smithton** Tasmania, SE Australia
20 L14 **Smithtown** Long Island, New York, NE USA
22 K9 **Smithville** Tennessee, S USA
27 T11 **Smithville** Texas, SW USA
Smohor *see* Hermagor
37 Q4 **Smoke Creek Desert** *desert* Nevada, W USA
9 O14 **Smoky** ⚡ Alberta, W Canada
190 F7 **Smoky Bay** South Australia
191 V6 **Smoky Cape** *headland* New South Wales, SE Australia
28 L4 **Smoky Hill River** ⚡ Kansas, C USA
28 L4 **Smoky Hills** *hill range* Kansas, C USA
9 Q14 **Smoky Lake** Alberta, SW Canada
96 E8 **Smøla** *island* W Norway
130 H4 **Smolensk** Smolenskaya Oblast', W Russian Federation
130 H4 **Smolenskaya Oblast'** ◆ *province* W Russian Federation
Smolensk-Moscow Upland *see* Smolensko-Moskovskaya Vozvyshennost'
130 J3 **Smolensko-Moskovskaya Vozvyshennost'** *var.* Smolensk-Moscow Upland. ▲ W Russian Federation
Smolevichi *see* Smalyavichy
117 C15 **Smolikás** ▲ W Greece
116 I12 **Smolyan** *prev.* Pashmakli. Plovdivska Oblast, S Bulgaria
Smolyany *see* Smalyany
35 S15 **Smoot** Wyoming, C USA
10 G12 **Smooth Rock Falls** Ontario, S Canada
Smorgon'/Smorgonie *see* Smarhon'
97 K23 **Smygehamn** Malmöhus, S Sweden
204 I7 **Smyley Island** *island* Antarctica
23 Y3 **Smyrna** Delaware, NE USA
25 S3 **Smyrna** Georgia, SE USA
22 J9 **Smyrna** Tennessee, S USA
Smyrna *see* İzmir
176 W10 **Snabai** Irian Jaya, E Indonesia
99 I16 **Snaefell** ▲ C Isle of Man
94 H3 **Snaefellsjökull** ▲ W Iceland
8 J4 **Snake** ⚡ Yukon Territory, NW Canada
31 O8 **Snake Creek** ⚡ South Dakota, N USA
191 P13 **Snake Island** *island* Victoria, SE Australia
37 Y6 **Snake Range** ▲ Nevada, W USA
34 K10 **Snake River** ⚡ NW USA
31 V6 **Snake River** ⚡ Minnesota, N USA
30 L12 **Snake River** ⚡ Nebraska, C USA
35 Q14 **Snake River Plain** *plain* Idaho, NW USA
15 I7 **Snare** ⚡ Northwest Territories, NW Canada
95 F15 **Snåsa** Nord-Trøndelag, C Norway
23 O8 **Sneedville** Tennessee, S USA
100 K6 **Sneek** Friesland, N Netherlands
Sneeuw-gebergte *see* Maoke, Pegunungan
97 F22 **Snejbjerg** Ringkøbing, C Denmark
126 I8 **Snezhnogorsk** Taymyrskiy (Dolgano-Nenetskiy) Avtonomnyy Okrug, N Russian Federation
Snezhnoye *see* Snizhne
113 G15 **Sněžka** *Ger.* Schneekoppe. ▲ N Czech Republic
111 T13 **Snežnik** *Ger.* Schneeberg, *It.* Monte Nevoso. ▲ SW Slovenia
112 N8 **Śniardwy, Jezioro** *Ger.* Spirdingsee. ◎ NE Poland
Sniečkus *see* Visaginas
119 R10 **Snihurivka** Mykolayivs'ka Oblast', S Ukraine
118 I5 **Snilow** ✕ (L'viv) L'vivs'ka Oblast', W Ukraine
113 O19 **Snina** *Hung.* Szinna. Východné Slovensko, E Slovakia
119 Y8 **Snizhne** *Rus.* Snezhnoye. Donets'ka Oblast', SE Ukraine
94 J3 **Snækollur** ▲ C Iceland
96 G10 **Snøhetta** *var.* Snohetta. ▲ S Norway
94 G12 **Snøtinden** ▲ C Norway
99 I18 **Snowdon** ▲ NW Wales, UK
99 I18 **Snowdonia** ▲ NW Wales, UK
15 I8 **Snowdrift** ⚡ Northwest Territories, NW Canada
Snowdrift *see* Łutselk'e
39 N12 **Snowflake** Arizona, SW USA
23 Y5 **Snow Hill** Maryland, NE USA
23 W10 **Snow Hill** North Carolina, SE USA
204 H3 **Snowhill Island** *island* Antarctica
9 V13 **Snow Lake** Manitoba, C Canada
39 R5 **Snowmass Mountain** ▲ Colorado, C USA
20 M10 **Snow, Mount** ▲ Vermont, NE USA
36 M5 **Snow Mountain** ▲ California, W USA
Snow Mountains *see* Maoke, Pegunungan
35 N7 **Snowshoe Peak** ▲ Montana, NW USA
190 I8 **Snowtown** South Australia
38 K1 **Snowville** Utah, W USA
37 X3 **Snow Water Lake** ◎ Nevada, W USA
191 Q11 **Snowy Mountains** ▲ New South Wales/Victoria, SE Australia
191 Q12 **Snowy River** ⚡ New South Wales/Victoria, SE Australia
46 K5 **Snug Corner** Acklins Island, SE Bahamas
178 Jj13 **Snuŏl** Krâchéh, E Cambodia
118 J7 **Snyatyn** *Rus.* Snyatyn. Ivano-Frankivs'ka Oblast', W Ukraine
28 L12 **Snyder** Oklahoma, C USA
27 O6 **Snyder** Texas, SW USA
180 H3 **Soalala** Mahajanga, W Madagascar
180 J4 **Soanierana-Ivongo** Toamasina, E Madagascar
175 Ss7 **Soasiu** *var.* Tidore. Pulau Tidore, E Indonesia
56 G8 **Soatá** Boyacá, C Colombia
180 I5 **Soavinandriana** Antananarivo, C Madagascar
176 Yy12 **Soba** Irian Jaya, E Indonesia
79 V13 **Soba** Kaduna, C Nigeria
169 Y16 **Sobaek-sanmaek** ▲ S South Korea
82 F13 **Sobat** ⚡ E Sudan
176 Z12 **Sobger, Sungai** ⚡ Irian Jaya, E Indonesia
176 W10 **Sobiei** Irian Jaya, E Indonesia
130 M3 **Sobinka** Vladimirskaya Oblast', W Russian Federation
131 S7 **Sobolevo** Orenburgskaya Oblast', W Russian Federation
Soborsin *see* Săvârşin
170 D15 **Sobo-san** ▲ Kyūshū, SW Japan
113 G14 **Sobótka** Wrocław, SW Poland
61 O15 **Sobradinho** Bahia, E Brazil
Sobradinho, Barragem de *see* Sobradinho, Represa de
61 O16 **Sobradinho, Represa de** *var.* Barragem de Sobradinho. ◎ E Brazil
60 O13 **Sobral** Ceará, E Brazil
107 T4 **Sobrarbe** *physical region* NE Spain
111 R10 **Soča** *It.* Isonzo. ⚡ Italy/Slovenia
112 L11 **Sochaczew** Skierniewice, C Poland
130 L15 **Sochi** Krasnodarskiy Kray, SW Russian Federation
116 G13 **Sochós** *var.* Sohos, Sokhós. Kentrikí Makedonía, N Greece
203 R11 **Société, Archipel de la** *var.* Archipel de Tahiti, Îles de la Société, *Eng.* Society Islands. *island group* W French Polynesia
Société, Îles de la/Society Islands *see* Société, Archipel de la
23 T11 **Society Hill** South Carolina, SE USA
183 W9 **Society Ridge** *undersea feature* C Pacific Ocean
64 I5 **Socompa, Volcán** ▲ N Chile
Soconusco, Sierra de *see* Sierra Madre
56 G8 **Socorro** Santander, C Colombia
39 R13 **Socorro** New Mexico, SW USA
Socotra *see* Suquṭrā
178 Jj15 **Soc Trăng** *var.* Khanh *Hung.* Soc Trăng, S Vietnam
107 P10 **Socuéllamos** Castilla-La Mancha, C Spain
37 W13 **Soda Lake** *salt flat* California, W USA
94 L11 **Sodankylä** Lappi, N Finland
Sodari *see* Sodiri
35 R15 **Soda Springs** Idaho, NW USA
Soddo/Soddu *see* Sodo
22 L10 **Soddy Daisy** Tennessee, S USA
97 N14 **Söderfors** Uppsala, C Sweden
96 N12 **Söderhamn** Gävleborg, C Sweden
97 N17 **Söderköping** Östergötland, S Sweden
97 N17 **Södermanland** ◆ *county* C Sweden
97 O16 **Södertälje** Stockholm, C Sweden
82 D10 **Sodiri** *var.* Sawdirī, Sodari. Northern Kordofan, C Sudan
83 I14 **Sodo** *var.* Soddo, Soddu. SW Ethiopia
96 N11 **Södra Dellen** ◎ C Sweden
97 M19 **Södra Vi** Kalmar, S Sweden
20 G9 **Sodus Point** *headland* New York, NE USA
175 Rr17 **Soe** *prev.* Soë. Timor, C Indonesia
174 J14 **Soekarno-Hatta** ✕ (Jakarta) Jawa, S Indonesia
Soëla-Sund *see* Soela Väin
120 E5 **Soela Väin** *prev. Eng.* Sele Sound, *Ger.* Dagden-Sund, Soëla-Sund. *strait* W Estonia
Soemba *see* Sumba, Pulau
Soembawa *see* Sumbawa
Soemenep *see* Sumenep
Soengaipenoeh *see* Sungaipenuh
Soerabaja *see* Surabaya
103 G14 **Soest** Nordrhein-Westfalen, W Germany
100 J11 **Soest** Utrecht, C Netherlands
102 F11 **Soeste** ⚡ NW Germany
100 J11 **Soesterberg** Utrecht, C Netherlands
117 E16 **Sofádes** *var.* Sofádhes. Thessalía, C Greece
Sofádhes *see* Sofádes
85 N18 **Sofala** Sofala, C Mozambique
85 N17 **Sofala** ◆ *province* C Mozambique
85 N18 **Sofala, Baia de** *bay* E Mozambique
180 J3 **Sofia** *seasonal river* NW Madagascar
Sofia *see* Sofiya
117 G19 **Sofikó** Pelopónnisos, S Greece
Sofi-Kurgan *see* Sopu-Korgon
116 G10 **Sofiya** *var.* Sophia, *Eng.* Sofia; *Lat.* Serdica. ● (Bulgaria) Grad Sofiya, W Bulgaria
116 G9 **Sofiya** ✕ Grad Sofiya, W Bulgaria
Sofiya *see* Sofiyska Oblast
116 G9 **Sofiya, Grad** ◆ *municipality* W Bulgaria
Sofiyevka *see* Sofiyivka
119 S8 **Sofiyivka** *Rus.* Sofiyevka. Dnipropetrovs'ka Oblast', E Ukraine
127 Nn14 **Sofiysk** Khabarovskiy Kray, SE Russian Federation
127 N14 **Sofiysk** Khabarovskiy Kray, SE Russian Federation
116 F10 **Sofiyska Oblast** *var.* Sofiya. ◆ *province* W Bulgaria
128 I6 **Sofporog** Respublika Kareliya, NW Russian Federation
172 Ss15 **Sōfu-gan** *island* Izu-shotō, SE Japan

◆ Country ● Country Capital ◇ Dependent Territory ○ Dependent Territory Capital ◆ Administrative Region ✕ International Airport ▲ Mountain ▲ Mountain Range ⚡ Volcano ⚡ River ◎ Lake ◎ Reservoir

Sovetskoye – Stołeczne Warszawskie, Województwo

Sovetskoye see Ketchenery
152 I15 Sovet"yab prev. Sovet"yap. Akhalskiy Velayat, S Turkmenistan
Sovet"yap see Sovet"yab
119 U12 Sovyets'kyy Respublika Krym, S Ukraine
85 I18 Sowa var. Sua. Central, NE Botswana
85 I18 Sowa Pan salt lake NE Botswana
176 Ww9 Sowek Irian Jaya, E Indonesia
85 J21 Soweto Gauteng, NE South Africa
Sōya-kaikyō see La Perouse Strait
172 Pp1 Sōya-misaki headland Hokkaidō, NE Japan
129 N7 Soyana ≈ NW Russian Federation
152 A8 Soye, Mys var. Mys Suz. headland NW Turkmenistan
84 A10 Soyo Zaire, NW Angola
82 J10 Soyra ▲ C Eritrea
Sozaq see Suzak
121 P16 Sozh Rus. Sozh. ≈ NE Europe
116 N10 Sozopol prev. Sizebolu, anc. Apollonia. Burgaska Oblast, SE Bulgaria
180 J15 Sœurs, Les island group Inner Islands, W Seychelles
101 L20 Spa Liège, E Belgium
204 I7 Spaatz Island island Antarctica
150 M14 Space Launching Centre space station Kzyl-Orda, S Kazakhstan
107 O7 Spain off. Kingdom of Spain, Sp. España; anc. Hispania, Iberia, Lat. Hispana. ◆ monarchy SW Europe
Spalato see Split
99 O19 Spalding E England, UK
12 D11 Spalding Ontario, S Canada
38 L3 Spanish Fork Utah, W USA
66 B12 Spanish Point headland C Bermuda
12 E9 Spanish River ≈ Ontario, S Canada
46 K13 Spanish Town hist. St.Iago de la Vega. C Jamaica
117 H24 Spánta, Ákra headland Kríti, Greece, E Mediterranean Sea
37 Q5 Sparks Nevada, W USA
Sparnacum see Épernay
97 N16 Sparreholm Södermanland, C Sweden
25 U4 Sparta Georgia, SE USA
32 J7 Sparta Illinois, N USA
33 P9 Sparta Michigan, N USA
23 R8 Sparta North Carolina, SE USA
22 L9 Sparta Tennessee, S USA
32 K16 Sparta Wisconsin, N USA
Sparta see Spárti
23 Q11 Spartanburg South Carolina, SE USA
122 F10 Spartel, Cap headland N Morocco
117 F21 Spárti Eng. Sparta. Pelopónnisos, S Greece
109 B21 Spartivento, Capo headland Sardegna, Italy, C Mediterranean Sea
9 P17 Sparwood British Columbia, SW Canada
130 I4 Spas-Demensk Kaluzhskaya Oblast', W Russian Federation
130 M4 Spas-Klepiki Ryazanskaya Oblast', W Russian Federation
127 N17 Spassk-Dal'niy Primorskiy Kray, SE Russian Federation
130 M5 Spassk-Ryazanskiy Ryazanskaya Oblast', W Russian Federation
117 H19 Spáta Attikí, C Greece
124 O12 Spátha, Ákra headland Kríti, Greece, E Mediterranean Sea
Špatrjan see Paternion
30 I9 Spearfish South Dakota, N USA
27 O1 Spearman Texas, SW USA
67 C25 Speedwell Island island S Falkland Islands
67 C25 Speedwell Island Settlement S Falkland Islands
67 G25 Speery Island island S Saint Helena
47 N14 Speightstown NW Barbados
108 I13 Spello Umbria, C Italy
41 R12 Spenard Alaska, USA
Spence Bay see Taloyoak
33 O14 Spencer Indiana, N USA
31 T12 Spencer Iowa, C USA
31 P12 Spencer Nebraska, C USA
23 S9 Spencer North Carolina, SE USA
22 L9 Spencer Tennessee, S USA
23 Q4 Spencer West Virginia, NE USA
32 K6 Spencer Wisconsin, N USA
190 G10 Spencer, Cape headland South Australia
41 V13 Spencer, Cape headland Alaska, USA
190 H9 Spencer Gulf gulf South Australia
20 F9 Spencerport New York, NE USA
33 Q12 Spencerville Ohio, N USA
117 E17 Spercheiáda var. Sperhiada, Sperkhiás. Stereá Ellás, C Greece
117 E17 Spercheiós ≈ C Greece
Sperhiada see Spercheiáda
97 G14 Sperillen ◎ S Norway
Sperkhiás see Spercheiáda
103 I18 Spessart hill range C Germany
Spétsai see Spétses
117 G21 Spétses prev. Spétsai. Spétses, S Greece
117 G21 Spétses island S Greece
98 J8 Spey ≈ NE Scotland, UK
103 G20 Speyer Eng. Spires; anc. Civitas Nemetum, Spira. Rheinland-Pfalz, SW Germany
103 G20 Speyerbach ≈ W Germany
109 N20 Spezzano Albanese Calabria, SW Italy
Spice Islands see Maluku
102 F9 Spiekeroog island NW Germany
111 W9 Spielfeld Steiermark, SE Austria
67 N21 Spiess Seamount undersea feature S Atlantic Ocean
110 E9 Spiez Bern, W Switzerland
100 G13 Spijkenisse Zuid-Holland, SW Netherlands
41 T6 Spike Mountain ▲ Alaska, USA
117 I25 Spíli Kríti, Greece, E Mediterranean Sea
110 D10 Spillgerten ▲ W Switzerland
120 F9 Spilva ✕ (Rīga) Rīga, C Latvia
109 N17 Spinazzola Puglia, SE Italy
155 O9 Spīn Būldak Kandahār, S Afghanistan
Spira see Speyer
Spirdingsee see Śniardwy, Jezioro
Spires see Speyer
31 T11 Spirit Lake Iowa, C USA
31 T11 Spirit Lake ◎ Iowa, C USA
9 N13 Spirit River Alberta, W Canada
9 S14 Spiritwood Saskatchewan, S Canada
29 R11 Spiro Oklahoma, C USA
113 L19 Spišská Nová Ves Ger. Neudorf, Zipser Neudorf, Hung. Igló. Východné Slovensko, E Slovakia
143 T11 Spitak NW Armenia
94 O2 Spitsbergen island NW Svalbard
Spittal see Spittal an der Drau
111 R9 Spittal an der Drau var. Spittal. Kärnten, S Austria
111 V3 Spitz Niederösterreich, NE Austria
96 D9 Spjelkavik Møre og Romsdal, S Norway
27 W10 Splendora Texas, SW USA
115 E14 Split It. Spalato. Split-Dalmacija, S Croatia
115 E14 Split ✕ Split-Dalmacija, S Croatia
115 E14 Split-Dalmacija off. Splitsko-Dalmatinska Županija. ◆ province S Croatia
9 X12 Split Lake ◎ Manitoba, C Canada
Splitsko-Dalmatinska Županija see Split-Dalmacija
110 H10 Splügen Graubünden, S Switzerland
Spodnji Dravograd see Dravograd
27 P12 Spofford Texas, SW USA
120 J11 Špoģi Daugvapils, SE Latvia
34 L8 Spokane Washington, NW USA
34 L8 Spokane River ≈ Washington, NW USA
108 I13 Spoleto Umbria, C Italy
32 I4 Spooner Wisconsin, N USA
32 K12 Spoon River ≈ Illinois, N USA
23 W5 Spotsylvania Virginia, NE USA
34 L8 Sprague Washington, NW USA
178 Ll16 Spratly Island island SW Spratly Islands
198 Ff7 Spratly Islands Chin. Nansha Qundao. ◇ disputed territory SE Asia
34 J12 Spray Oregon, NW USA
114 I11 Spreča ≈ N Bosnia and Herzegovina
102 P13 Spree ≈ E Germany
102 P13 Spreewald wetland NE Germany
103 P14 Spremberg Brandenburg, E Germany
27 W11 Spring Texas, SW USA
33 Q10 Spring Arbor Michigan, N USA
85 E23 Springbok Northern Cape, W South Africa
20 I15 Spring City Pennsylvania, NE USA
22 L9 Spring City Tennessee, S USA
38 L4 Spring City Utah, W USA
37 W3 Spring Creek Nevada, W USA
29 S9 Springdale Arkansas, C USA
33 Q14 Springdale Ohio, N USA
102 I13 Springe Niedersachsen, N Germany
39 U9 Springer New Mexico, SW USA
39 W7 Springfield Colorado, C USA
25 W5 Springfield Georgia, SE USA
32 K14 Springfield state capital Illinois, N USA
22 L6 Springfield Kentucky, S USA
20 M12 Springfield Massachusetts, NE USA
31 T10 Springfield Minnesota, N USA
29 T7 Springfield Missouri, C USA
33 R13 Springfield Ohio, N USA
34 G13 Springfield Oregon, NW USA
31 Q12 Springfield South Dakota, N USA
22 J8 Springfield Tennessee, S USA
20 M9 Springfield Vermont, NE USA
32 K14 Springfield, Lake ⊡ Illinois, N USA
57 T8 Spring Garden NE Guyana
32 K8 Spring Green Wisconsin, N USA
31 X11 Spring Grove Minnesota, N USA
11 P15 Springhill Nova Scotia, SE Canada
25 V12 Spring Hill Florida, SE USA
29 R4 Spring Hill Kansas, C USA
24 G4 Springhill Louisiana, S USA
22 I9 Spring Hill Tennessee, S USA
23 U10 Spring Lake North Carolina, SE USA
26 M4 Springlake Texas, SW USA
37 W11 Spring Mountains ▲▲ Nevada, W USA
67 B24 Spring Point West Falkland, Falkland Islands
29 W9 Spring River ≈ Arkansas/Missouri, C USA
29 S7 Spring River ≈ Missouri/Oklahoma, C USA
85 J21 Springs Gauteng, NE South Africa
193 H16 Springs Junction West Coast, South Island, NZ
189 X8 Springsure Queensland, E Australia
31 W11 Spring Valley Minnesota, N USA
20 K13 Spring Valley New York, NE USA
31 N12 Springview Nebraska, C USA
20 D11 Springville New York, NE USA
38 L3 Springville Utah, W USA
Sprottau see Szprotawa
13 V4 Sproule, Pointe headland Québec, SE Canada
9 Q14 Spruce Grove Alberta, SW Canada
23 T4 Spruce Knob ▲ West Virginia, NE USA
37 X3 Spruce Mountain ▲ Nevada, W USA
23 P9 Spruce Pine North Carolina, SE USA
100 G13 Spui ≈ SW Netherlands
109 O19 Spulico, Capo headland S Italy
27 O5 Spur Texas, SW USA
99 O17 Spurn Head headland E England, UK
101 H20 Spy Namur, S Belgium
97 I15 Spydeberg Østfold, S Norway
193 J17 Spy Glass Point headland South Island, NZ
8 L17 Squamish British Columbia, SW Canada
21 O8 Squam Lake ◎ New Hampshire, NE USA
21 S2 Squa Pan Mountain ▲ Maine, NE USA
41 N16 Squaw Harbor Unga Island, Alaska, USA
12 E11 Squaw Island island Ontario, S Canada
109 O22 Squillace, Golfo di gulf S Italy
109 Q18 Squinzano Puglia, SE Italy
174 L15 Sragen Jawa, C Indonesia
Sráid na Cathrach see Milltown Malbay
178 Jj11 Srâlau Stœng Trêng, N Cambodia
Srath an Urláir see Stranorlar
114 G10 Srbac N Bosnia and Herzegovina
Srbija see Serbia
114 K9 Srbobran var. Bácsszenttamás, Hung. Szenttamás. Serbia, N Yugoslavia
178 Ii14 Srê Âmběl Kaôh Kông, SW Cambodia
114 K13 Srebrenica E Bosnia and Herzegovina
114 I11 Srebrenik NE Bosnia and Herzegovina
116 M10 Sredets prev. Grudovo. Burgaska Oblast, SE Bulgaria
116 K10 Sredets prev. Syulemeshlii. Khaskovska Oblast, C Bulgaria
116 M10 Sredetska Reka ≈ SE Bulgaria
127 P9 Sredinnyy Khrebet ▲▲ E Russian Federation
116 N7 Sredishte Rom. Beibunar; prev. Knyazhevo. Varnenska Oblast, NE Bulgaria
116 I10 Sredna Gora ▲▲ C Bulgaria
127 N7 Srednekolymsk Respublika Sakha (Yakutiya), NE Russian Federation
130 K7 Srednerusskaya Vozvyshennost' Eng. Central Russian Upland. ▲▲ W Russian Federation
126 I9 Srednesibirskoye Ploskogor'ye var. Central Siberian Uplands, Eng. Central Siberian Plateau. ▲▲ N Russian Federation
129 V13 Sredniy Ural ▲▲ NW Russian Federation
178 Jj13 Srê Khtŭm Môndól Kiri, E Cambodia
113 G17 Śrem Poznań, W Poland
114 K10 Sremska Mitrovica prev. Mitrovica, Ger. Mitrowitz. Serbia, NW Yugoslavia
178 Ii11 Srêng, Stœng ≈ NW Cambodia
178 Ii11 Srê Noy Siĕmréab, NW Cambodia
Srepok, Sông see Srêpôk, Tônle
178 K12 Srêpôk, Tônle var. Sông Srepok. ≈ Cambodia/Vietnam
126 L15 Sretensk Chitinskaya Oblast', S Russian Federation
174 Ll7 Sri Aman Sarawak, East Malaysia
119 R4 Sribne Chernihivs'ka Oblast', N Ukraine
161 I25 Sri Jayawardanapura var. Sri Jayawardenepura; prev. Kotte. Western Province, W Sri Lanka
161 M14 Srikākulam Andhra Pradesh, E India
161 I25 Sri Lanka off. Democratic Socialist Republic of Sri Lanka; prev. Ceylon. ◆ republic S Asia
139 Mm15 Sri Lanka island S Asia
159 V14 Srimangal Chittagong, E Bangladesh
Sri Mohangorh see Shri Mohangarh
158 H5 Srinagar Jammu and Kashmir, N India
178 H10 Srinagarind Reservoir ◎ W Thailand
161 F19 Sringeri Karnātaka, W India
161 K25 Sri Pada Eng. Adam's Peak. ▲ S Sri Lanka
Sri Saket see Si Sa Ket
113 G14 Środa Śląska Ger. Neumarkt. Wrocław, SW Poland
112 H12 Środa Wielkopolska Poznań, W Poland
Ssu-ch'uan see Sichuan
Ssu-p'ing/Ssu-p'ing-chieh see Siping
Stablo see Stavelot
101 G15 Stabroek Antwerpen, N Belgium
Stackeln see Strenči
98 I5 Stack Skerry island N Scotland, UK
96 C10 Stad peninsula S Norway
102 I9 Stade Niedersachsen, NW Germany
111 R5 Stadl-Paura Oberösterreich, NW Austria
121 L20 Stadolichy Rus. Stodolichi. Homyel'skaya Voblasts', SE Belarus
100 P7 Stadskanaal Groningen, NE Netherlands
103 H16 Stadtallendorf Hessen, C Germany
103 K23 Stadtbergen Bayern, S Germany
110 G7 Stäfa Zürich, NE Switzerland
97 K23 Staffanstorp Malmöhus, S Sweden
103 K18 Staffelstein Bayern, C Germany
99 L19 Stafford C England, UK
28 L6 Stafford Kansas, C USA
23 W4 Stafford Virginia, NE USA
99 L19 Staffordshire cultural region C England, UK
21 N12 Stafford Springs Connecticut, NE USA
117 H14 Stágira Kentrikí Makedonía, N Greece
120 G7 Staicele Limbaži, N Latvia
Ştaierdorf-Anina see Anina
111 V8 Stainz Steiermark, SE Austria
Stájerlakanina see Anina
119 Y7 Stakhanov Luhans'ka Oblast', E Ukraine
110 E11 Stalden Valais, SW Switzerland
Stalin see Varna
Stalinabad see Dushanbe
Stalingrad see Volgograd
Staliniri see Ts'khinvali
Stalino see Donets'k
Stalinobod see Dushanbe
Stalinov Štít see Gerlachovský štít
Stalinsk see Novokuznetsk
Stalinskaya Oblast' see Donets'ka Oblast'
Stalinski Zaliv see Varnenski Zaliv
Stalin, Yazovir see Iskŭr, Yazovir
113 N15 Stalowa Wola Tarnobrzeg, SE Poland
116 I11 Stamboliyski Plovdivska Oblast, C Bulgaria
116 J8 Stamboliyski, Yazovir ⊡ N Bulgaria
99 N19 Stamford E England, UK
20 L14 Stamford Connecticut, NE USA
27 Q6 Stamford Texas, SW USA
27 Q6 Stamford, Lake ⊡ Texas, SW USA
110 I10 Stampa Graubünden, SE Switzerland
Stampalia see Astypálaia
29 T14 Stamps Arkansas, C USA
94 G11 Stamsund Nordland, C Norway
29 R2 Stanberry Missouri, C USA
205 O3 Stancomb-Wills Glacier glacier Antarctica
85 K21 Standerton Mpumalanga, E South Africa
33 R7 Standish Michigan, N USA
22 M6 Stanford Kentucky, S USA
35 S9 Stanford Montana, NW USA
97 P19 Stånga Gotland, SE Sweden
96 I13 Stange Hedmark, S Norway
85 L23 Stanger KwaZulu/Natal, E South Africa
Stanimaka see Asenovgrad
Stanislau see Ivano-Frankivs'k
37 P8 Stanislaus River ≈ California, W USA
Stanislav see Ivano-Frankivs'k
Stanislavskaya Oblast' see Ivano-Frankivs'ka Oblast'
Stanisławów see Ivano-Frankivs'k
Stanke Dimitrov see Dupnitsa
191 O15 Stanley Tasmania, SE Australia
67 E24 Stanley var. Port Stanley. ○ (Falkland Islands) East Falkland, Falkland Islands
35 O13 Stanley Idaho, NW USA
30 L3 Stanley North Dakota, N USA
23 U4 Stanley Virginia, NE USA
32 J6 Stanley Wisconsin, N USA
81 G21 Stanley Pool var. Pool Malebo. ◎ Congo/Zaire
161 H20 Stanley Reservoir ⊡ S India
Stanleyville see Kisangani
44 G3 Stann Creek ◆ district SE Belize
Stann Creek see Dangriga
127 N17 Stanovoy Khrebet ▲▲ SE Russian Federation
110 F8 Stans Unterwalden, C Switzerland
99 O21 Stansted ✕ (London) Essex, E England, UK
191 U4 Stanthorpe Queensland, E Australia
23 N6 Stanton Kentucky, S USA
33 Q8 Stanton Michigan, N USA
31 Q14 Stanton Nebraska, C USA
30 L5 Stanton North Dakota, N USA
27 N7 Stanton Texas, SW USA
34 H7 Stanwood Washington, NW USA
119 Y7 Stanychno-Luhans'ke Luhans'ka Oblast', E Ukraine
110 K7 Stanzach Tirol, W Austria
100 M9 Staphorst Overijssel, E Netherlands
12 D18 Staples Ontario, S Canada
31 T6 Staples Minnesota, N USA
30 M14 Stapleton Nebraska, C USA
27 S8 Star Texas, SW USA
113 M14 Starachowice Kielce, SE Poland
Stara Kanjiža see Kanjiža
113 M18 Stará Ľubovňa Ger. Altlublau, Hung. Ólubló. Východné Slovensko, E Slovakia
114 L10 Stara Pazova Ger. Altpasua, Hung. Ópazova. Serbia, N Yugoslavia
Stara Planina see Balkan Mountains
116 L9 Stara Reka ≈ C Bulgaria
118 M5 Stara Synyava Khmel'nyts'ka Oblast', W Ukraine
118 I2 Stara Vyzhivka Volyns'ka Oblast', NW Ukraine
Staraya Belitsa see Staraya Byelitsa
121 M14 Staraya Byelitsa Rus. Staraya Belitsa. Vitsyebskaya Voblasts', NE Belarus
131 R5 Staraya Mayna Ul'yanovskaya Oblast', W Russian Federation
121 O18 Staraya Rudnya Rus. Staraya Rudnya. Homyel'skaya Voblasts', SE Belarus
128 H14 Staraya Russa Novgorodskaya Oblast', W Russian Federation
116 K10 Stara Zagora Lat. Augusta Trajana. Khaskovska Oblast, C Bulgaria
31 S8 Starbuck Minnesota, N USA
203 W4 Starbuck Island prev. Volunteer Island. island E Kiribati
29 V13 Star City Arkansas, C USA
114 F13 Staretina ▲▲ W Bosnia and Herzegovina
Stargard in Pommern see Stargard Szczeciński
112 E9 Stargard Szczeciński Ger. Stargard in Pommern. Szczecin, NW Poland
195 Z17 Star Harbour harbor San Cristobal, SE Solomon Islands
Stari Bečej see Bečej
115 F15 Starigrad It. Cittavecchia. Split-Dalmacija, S Croatia
175 Qq12 Staring, Teluk var. Teluk Wawosungu. bay Sulawesi, C Indonesia
128 J16 Staritsa Tverskaya Oblast', W Russian Federation
25 V9 Starke Florida, SE USA
24 M4 Starkville Mississippi, S USA
194 E11 Star Mountains Ind. Pegunungan Sterren. ▲▲ Indonesia/PNG
103 L23 Starnberg Bayern, SE Germany
103 L24 Starnberger See ◎ SE Germany
Starobel'sk see Starobil's'k
119 X8 Starobesheve Donets'ka Oblast', E Ukraine
119 Y6 Starobil's'k Rus. Starobel'sk. Luhans'ka Oblast', E Ukraine
Starobin see Starobyn
121 K18 Starobyn Rus. Starobin. Minskaya Voblasts', S Belarus
130 H6 Starodub Bryanskaya Oblast', W Russian Federation
112 I8 Starogard Gdański Ger. Preussisch-Stargard. Gdańsk, N Poland
151 P16 Staroikan Yuzhnyy Kazakhstan, S Kazakhstan
Starokonstantinov see Starokostyantyniv
118 L5 Starokostyantyniv Rus. Starokonstantinov. Khmel'nyts'ka Oblast', NW Ukraine
130 K12 Starominskaya Krasnodarskiy Kray, SW Russian Federation
116 L7 Staro Selo Rom. Satul-Vechi; prev. Star-Smil. Razgradska Oblast, NE Bulgaria
130 K12 Staroshcherbinovskaya Krasnodarskiy Kray, SW Russian Federation
131 V6 Starosubkhangulovo Respublika Bashkortostan, W Russian Federation
37 S4 Star Peak ▲ Nevada, W USA
Star-Smil see Staro Selo
99 J25 Start Point headland SW England, UK
Startsy see Kirawsk
Starum see Stavoren
121 L18 Staryya Darohi Rus. Staryye Dorogi. Minskaya Voblasts', S Belarus
Staryye Dorogi see Staryya Darohi
131 T2 Staryye Zyatsy Udmurtskaya Respublika, NW Russian Federation
119 U13 Staryy Krym Respublika Krym, S Ukraine
130 K8 Staryy Oskol Belgorodskaya Oblast', W Russian Federation
118 H6 Staryy Sambir L'vivs'ka Oblast', W Ukraine
103 L14 Stassfurt var. Staßfurt. Sachsen-Anhalt, C Germany
113 M15 Staszów Tarnobrzeg, SE Poland
31 W13 State Center Iowa, C USA
20 E14 State College Pennsylvania, NE USA
20 K15 Staten Island island New York, NE USA
Staten Island see Estados, Isla de los
25 U8 Statenville Georgia, SE USA
25 W5 Statesboro Georgia, SE USA
States, The see United States of America
23 R9 Statesville North Carolina, SE USA
97 G16 Stathelle Telemark, S Norway
32 K15 Staunton Illinois, N USA
23 T5 Staunton Virginia, NE USA
97 C16 Stavanger Rogaland, S Norway
101 L21 Stavelot Dut. Stablo. Liège, E Belgium
97 G16 Stavern Vestfold, S Norway
Stavers Island see Vostok Island
100 J7 Stavoren Fris. Starum. Friesland, N Netherlands
130 M14 Stavropol' prev. Voroshilovsk. Stavropol'skiy Kray, SW Russian Federation
Stavropol' see Tol'yatti
130 M14 Stavropol'skaya Vozvyshennost' ▲▲ SW Russian Federation
130 M14 Stavropol'skiy Kray ◆ territory SW Russian Federation
117 H14 Stavrós Kentrikí Makedonía, N Greece
117 J24 Stavrós, Ákra headland Kríti, Greece, E Mediterranean Sea
117 K21 Stavrós, Ákra headland Náxos, Kykládes, Greece, Aegean Sea
116 I12 Stavroúpoli prev. Stavroúpolis. Anatolikí Makedonía kai Thráki, NE Greece
Stavroúpolis see Stavroúpoli
119 O6 Stavyshche Kyyivs'ka Oblast', N Ukraine
190 M11 Stawell Victoria, SE Australia
112 N9 Stawiski Łomża, NE Poland
12 G14 Stayner Ontario, S Canada
39 R3 Steamboat Springs Colorado, C USA
22 M8 Stearns Kentucky, S USA
41 N10 Stebbins Alaska, USA
110 K7 Steeg Tirol, W Austria
29 Y9 Steele Missouri, C USA
31 N5 Steele North Dakota, N USA
204 J5 Steele Island island Antarctica
32 K16 Steeleville Illinois, N USA
29 W6 Steelville Missouri, C USA
101 G14 Steenbergen Noord-Brabant, S Netherlands
Steenkool see Bintuni
9 O10 Steen River Alberta, W Canada
100 M8 Steenwijk Overijssel, N Netherlands
67 A23 Steeple Jason island Jason Islands, NW Falkland Islands
182 J8 Steep Point headland Western Australia
118 L9 Ştefăneşti Botoşani, NE Romania
Stefanie, Lake see Ch'ew Bahir
15 J1 Stefansson Island island Northwest Territories, N Canada
119 O10 Ştefan Vodă Rus. Suvorovo. SE Moldova
65 H18 Steffen, Cerro ▲ S Chile
110 D9 Steffisburg Bern, C Switzerland
97 J24 Stege Storstrøm, SE Denmark
118 G10 Ştei Hung. Vaskohsziklás. Bihor, W Romania
Steier see Steyr
Steierdorf/Steierdorf-Anina see Anina
111 T7 Steiermark off. Land Steiermark, Eng. Styria. ◆ state C Austria
103 J19 Steigerwald hill range C Germany
101 L17 Stein Limburg, SE Netherlands
Stein see Stein an der Donau, Austria
Stein see Kamnik, Slovenia
110 M8 Steinach Tirol, W Austria
Steinamanger see Szombathely
111 W3 Stein an der Donau var. Stein. Niederösterreich, NE Austria
Steinau an der Elbe see Ścinawa
9 Y16 Steinbach Manitoba, S Canada
Steiner Alpen see Savinjske Alpe
101 L24 Steinfort Luxembourg, W Luxembourg
102 H12 Steinhuder Meer ◎ NW Germany
95 E15 Steinkjer Nord-Trøndelag, C Norway
Stejarul see Karapelit
101 F16 Stekene Oost-Vlaanderen, NW Belgium
85 E26 Stellenbosch Western Cape, SW South Africa
100 F13 Stellendam Zuid-Holland, SW Netherlands
41 T12 Steller, Mount ▲ Alaska, USA
104 F1 Stello, Monte ▲ Corse, France, C Mediterranean Sea
108 F5 Stelvio, Passo dello pass Italy/Switzerland
105 R3 Stenay Meuse, NE France
102 L12 Stendal Sachsen-Anhalt, C Germany
120 E8 Stende Talsi, NW Latvia
190 H10 Stenhouse Bay South Australia
97 J23 Stenløse Frederiksborg, E Denmark
97 L19 Stensjön Jönköping, S Sweden
97 K18 Stenstorp Skaraborg, S Sweden
97 I18 Stenungsund Göteborg och Bohus, S Sweden
Stepanakert see Xankändi
143 T11 Step'anavan N Armenia
102 K9 Stepenitz ≈ N Germany
31 O10 Stephan South Dakota, N USA
31 R3 Stephen Minnesota, N USA
29 T14 Stephens Arkansas, C USA
192 J13 Stephens, Cape headland D'Urville Island, Marlborough, SW NZ
23 V3 Stephens City Virginia, NE USA
190 L6 Stephens Creek New South Wales, SE Australia
192 K13 Stephens Island island C NZ
33 N5 Stephenson Michigan, N USA
11 S12 Stephenville Newfoundland, Newfoundland and Labrador, SE Canada
27 S7 Stephenville Texas, SW USA
151 P17 Step' Nardara Kaz. Shardara Dalasy; prev. Shaidara. grassland S Kazakhstan
131 O15 Stepnoye Stavropol'skiy Kray, SW Russian Federation
151 Q8 Stepnyak Kokshetau, N Kazakhstan
198 C9 Steps Point headland Tutuila, W American Samoa
117 F17 Stereá Ellás Eng. Greece Central. ◆ region C Greece
85 J24 Sterkspruit Eastern Cape, SE South Africa
131 U6 Sterlibashevo Respublika Bashkortostan, W Russian Federation
41 R12 Sterling Alaska, USA
39 V3 Sterling Colorado, C USA
32 K11 Sterling Illinois, N USA
28 M5 Sterling Kansas, C USA
27 O8 Sterling City Texas, SW USA
33 S9 Sterling Heights Michigan, N USA
23 W3 Sterling Park Virginia, NE USA
39 V2 Sterling Reservoir ⊡ Colorado, C USA
24 I5 Sterlington Louisiana, S USA
131 U6 Sterlitamak Respublika Bashkortostan, W Russian Federation
Sternberg see Šternberk
113 H17 Šternberk Ger. Sternberg. Severní Morava, E Czech Republic
147 V17 Stēroh Suquṭrā, S Yemen
112 G11 Stęszew Poznań, W Poland
Stettin see Szczecin
Stettiner Haff see Szczeciński, Zalew
9 Q15 Stettler Alberta, SW Canada
33 V13 Steubenville Ohio, N USA
99 O21 Stevenage E England, UK
25 Q1 Stevenson Alabama, S USA
34 H11 Stevenson Washington, NW USA
190 E1 Stevenson Creek seasonal river South Australia
41 Q13 Stevenson Entrance strait Alaska, USA
32 L6 Stevens Point Wisconsin, N USA
41 R8 Stevens Village Alaska, USA
35 P10 Stevensville Montana, NW USA
95 E25 Stevns Klint headland E Denmark
8 J12 Stewart British Columbia, W Canada
8 J6 Stewart ≈ Yukon Territory, NW Canada
8 I6 Stewart Crossing Yukon Territory, NW Canada
65 H25 Stewart, Isla island S Chile
193 B25 Stewart Island island S NZ
189 W6 Stewart, Mount ▲ Queensland, E Australia
8 H6 Stewart River Yukon Territory, NW Canada
29 R3 Stewartsville Missouri, C USA
9 S16 Stewart Valley Saskatchewan, S Canada
31 W10 Stewartville Minnesota, N USA
Steyerlak-Anina see Anina
111 T5 Steyr var. Steier. Oberösterreich, N Austria
111 T5 Steyr ≈ NW Austria
31 P11 Stickney South Dakota, N USA
100 L5 Stiens Friesland, N Netherlands
Stif see Sétif
29 Q11 Stigler Oklahoma, C USA
109 N18 Stigliano Basilicata, S Italy
97 N17 Stigtomta Södermanland, C Sweden
8 I11 Stikine ≈ British Columbia, W Canada
Stilida/Stilís see Stylída
97 G22 Stilling Århus, C Denmark
31 W8 Stillwater Minnesota, N USA
29 O9 Stillwater Oklahoma, C USA
37 S5 Stillwater Range ▲▲ Nevada, W USA
20 I8 Stillwater Reservoir ⊡ New York, NE USA
109 O22 Stilo, Punta headland S Italy
29 R10 Stilwell Oklahoma, C USA
115 N17 Štimlje Serbia, S Yugoslavia
27 N1 Stinnett Texas, SW USA
115 P18 Štip E FYR Macedonia
Stira see Stýra
98 J12 Stirling C Scotland, UK
98 I12 Stirling cultural region C Scotland, UK
188 J14 Stirling Range ▲▲ Western Australia
95 E16 Stjørdal Nord-Trøndelag, C Norway
Stochód see Stokhid
103 H24 Stockach Baden-Württemberg, S Germany
27 S12 Stockdale Texas, SW USA
111 X3 Stockerau Niederösterreich, NE Austria
95 H20 Stockholm ● (Sweden) Stockholm, C Sweden
97 O15 Stockholm ◆ county C Sweden
Stockmannshof see Pļaviņas
99 L18 Stockport NW England, UK
67 K15 Stocks Seamount undersea feature C Atlantic Ocean
37 O8 Stockton California, W USA
28 L3 Stockton Kansas, C USA
29 S6 Stockton Missouri, C USA
32 K3 Stockton Island island Apostle Islands, Wisconsin, N USA
29 S7 Stockton Lake ⊡ Missouri, C USA
99 M15 Stockton-on-Tees var. Stockton on Tees. N England, UK
26 M10 Stockton Plateau plain Texas, SW USA
30 M16 Stockville Nebraska, C USA
95 H17 Stöde Västernorrland, C Sweden
Stodolichi see Stadolichy
178 Jj12 Stœng Trêng prev. Stung Treng. Stœng Trêng, NE Cambodia
115 M19 Stogovo Karaorman ▲▲ W FYR Macedonia
Stoke see Stoke-on-Trent
99 L19 Stoke-on-Trent var. Stoke. C England, UK
190 M15 Stokes Point headland Tasmania, SE Australia
118 J2 Stokhid Pol. Stochód, Rus. Stokhod. ≈ NW Ukraine
Stokhod see Stokhid
94 I4 Stokkseyri Sudhurland, SW Iceland
94 G10 Stokmarknes Nordland, C Norway
Stol see Veliki Krš
115 H15 Stolac S Bosnia and Herzegovina
Stolbce see Stowbtsy
103 D16 Stolberg var. Stolberg im Rheinland. Nordrhein-Westfalen, W Germany
Stolberg im Rheinland see Stolberg
126 L5 Stolbovoy, Ostrov island NE Russian Federation
Stolbtsy see Stowbtsy
Stołeczne Warszawskie, Województwo see Warszawa

◆ Country ● Country Capital ◇ Dependent Territory ○ Dependent Territory Capital ◆ Administrative Region ✕ International Airport ▲ Mountain ▲▲ Mountain Range Volcano ≈ River ◎ Lake ⊡ Reservoir

Stolin – Sunray

121 J20 **Stolin** *Rus.* Stolin. Brestskaya Voblasts', SW Belarus
97 K14 **Stöllet** *var.* Norra Ny. Värmland, C Sweden
Stolp *see* Słupsk
Stolpe *see* Słupia
Stolpmünde *see* Ustka
117 F15 **Stómio** Thessalía, C Greece
12 J11 **Stonecliffe** Ontario, SE Canada
98 L10 **Stonehaven** NE Scotland, UK
99 M23 **Stonehenge** *ancient monument* Wiltshire, S England, UK
25 T3 **Stone Mountain** ▲ Georgia, SE USA
9 X16 **Stonewall** Manitoba, S Canada
23 S3 **Stonewood** West Virginia, NE USA
12 D17 **Stoney Point** Ontario, S Canada
94 H10 **Stonglandseidet** Troms, N Norway
67 N25 **Stonybeach Bay** *bay* Tristan da Cunha, SE Atlantic Ocean
37 N5 **Stony Creek** ≈ California, W USA
67 N25 **Stonyhill Point** *headland* S Tristan da Cunha
12 I14 **Stony Lake** ◎ Ontario, SE Canada
9 Q14 **Stony Plain** Alberta, SW Canada
23 R9 **Stony Point** North Carolina, SE USA
20 G8 **Stony Point** *headland* New York, NE USA
9 T10 **Stony Rapids** Saskatchewan, C Canada
41 P11 **Stony River** Alaska, USA
Stony Tunguska *see* Podkamennaya Tunguska
10 G10 **Stooping** ≈ Ontario, C Canada
102 I9 **Stör** ≈ N Germany
97 M15 **Storå** Örebro, S Sweden
97 J16 **Stora Gla** ◎ C Sweden
97 I16 **Stora Le** *Nor.* Store Le. ◎ Norway/Sweden
94 I12 **Stora Lulevatten** ◎ N Sweden
94 H13 **Storavan** ◎ N Sweden
95 I20 **Storby** Åland, SW Finland
96 E10 **Stordalen** Møre og Romsdal, S Norway
Storebelt *see* Storebælt
97 H23 **Storebælt** *var.* Store Bælt, *Eng.* Great Belt, Storebelt. *channel* Baltic Sea/Kattegat
97 M19 **Storebro** Kalmar, S Sweden
97 J24 **Store Heddinge** Storstrøm, SE Denmark
Store Le *see* Stora Le
95 E16 **Støren** Sør-Trøndelag, S Norway
97 B14 **Store Sotra** *island* S Norway
94 O4 **Storfjorden** *fjord* S Norway
97 L15 **Storfors** Värmland, C Sweden
94 G13 **Storforshei** Nordland, C Norway
Storhammer *see* Hamar
102 L10 **Störkanal** *canal* N Germany
95 F16 **Storlien** Jämtland, C Sweden
191 P17 **Storm Bay** *inlet* Tasmania, SE Australia
31 T12 **Storm Lake** Iowa, C USA
31 S13 **Storm Lake** ◎ Iowa, C USA
98 G7 **Stornoway** NW Scotland, UK
Storojineț *see* Storozhynets'
94 P1 **Storøya** *island* NE Svalbard
129 S10 **Storozhevsk** Respublika Komi, NW Russian Federation
Storozhinets *see* Storozhynets'
118 K8 **Storozhynets'** *Ger.* Storozynetz, *Rom.* Storojineț, *Rus.* Storozhinets. Chernivets'ka Oblast', W Ukraine
Storozynetz *see* Storozhynets'
94 H11 **Storriten** ▲ C Norway
21 N12 **Storrs** Connecticut, NE USA
96 I11 **Storsjøen** ◎ S Norway
96 N13 **Storsjön** ◎ C Sweden
95 F16 **Storsjön** ◎ C Sweden
94 I9 **Storsteinnes** Troms, N Norway
97 I24 **Storstrøm** *off.* Storstrøms Amt. ◐ *county* SE Denmark
95 J14 **Storsund** Norrbotten, N Sweden
95 F16 **Storsylen** ▲ S Norway
94 H11 **Stortoppen** ▲ N Sweden
95 H14 **Storuman** Västerbotten, N Sweden
95 H14 **Storuman** ◎ N Sweden
96 N13 **Storvik** Gävleborg, C Sweden
97 O14 **Storvreta** Uppsala, C Sweden
31 V13 **Story City** Iowa, C USA
9 V17 **Stoughton** Saskatchewan, S Canada
21 O11 **Stoughton** Massachusetts, NE USA
32 L9 **Stoughton** Wisconsin, N USA
99 L23 **Stour** ≈ E England, UK
99 P21 **Stour** ≈ S England, UK
29 T5 **Stover** Missouri, C USA
97 G21 **Støvring** Nordjylland, N Denmark
121 J17 **Stowbtsy** *Pol.* Stolbce, *Rus.* Stolbtsy. Minskaya Voblasts', C Belarus
27 X11 **Stowell** Texas, SW USA
99 P20 **Stowmarket** E England, UK
116 N8 **Stozher** Varnenska Oblast, NE Bulgaria
99 E14 **Strabane** *Ir.* An Srath Bán. W Northern Ireland, UK
123 Gg10 **Strabo Trench** *undersea feature* C Mediterranean Sea
29 T7 **Strafford** Missouri, C USA
191 N17 **Strahan** Tasmania, SE Australia
113 C18 **Strakonice** *Ger.* Strakonitz. Jižní Čechy, SW Czech Republic
Strakonitz *see* Strakonice
102 N8 **Stralsund** Mecklenburg-Vorpommern, NE Germany
101 L16 **Stramproy** Limburg, SE Netherlands
85 E26 **Strand** Western Cape, SW South Africa
96 E10 **Stranda** Møre og Romsdal, S Norway
99 G15 **Strangford Lough** *Ir.* Loch Cuan. *inlet* E Northern Ireland, UK
97 N16 **Strängnäs** Södermanland, C Sweden
99 E14 **Stranorlar** *Ir.* Srath an Urláir. NW Ireland
99 H14 **Stranraer** S Scotland, UK
9 U16 **Strasbourg** Saskatchewan, S Canada
105 V5 **Strasbourg** *Ger.* Strassburg; *anc.* Argentoratum. Bas-Rhin, NE France
39 U4 **Strasburg** Colorado, C USA
31 N7 **Strasburg** North Dakota, N USA
33 U12 **Strasburg** Ohio, N USA
23 U3 **Strasburg** Virginia, NE USA
119 N10 **Strășeni** *var.* Strasheny. C Moldova
Strasheny *see* Strășeni
111 T8 **Strassburg** Kärnten, S Austria
Strassburg *see* Strasbourg, France
Strassburg *see* Aiud, Romania
101 M25 **Strassen** Luxembourg, S Luxembourg
111 R5 **Strasswalchen** Salzburg, C Austria
12 F16 **Stratford** Ontario, S Canada
192 K10 **Stratford** Taranaki, North Island, NZ
37 Q11 **Stratford** California, W USA
31 V13 **Stratford** Iowa, C USA
29 O12 **Stratford** Oklahoma, C USA
27 N1 **Stratford** Texas, SW USA
32 K6 **Stratford** Wisconsin, N USA
Stratford *see* Stratford-upon-Avon
99 M20 **Stratford-upon-Avon** *var.* Stratford. C England, UK
191 O17 **Strathgordon** Tasmania, SE Australia
9 Q16 **Strathmore** Alberta, SW Canada
37 R11 **Strathmore** California, W USA
12 E16 **Strathroy** Ontario, S Canada
98 I6 **Strathy Point** *headland* N Scotland, UK
39 W4 **Stratton** Colorado, C USA
21 P6 **Stratton** Maine, NE USA
20 M10 **Stratton Mountain** ▲ Vermont, NE USA
103 N21 **Straubing** Bayern, SE Germany
94 G12 **Straumen** Nordland, C Norway
102 O12 **Strausberg** Brandenburg, E Germany
34 K13 **Strawberry Mountain** ▲ Oregon, NW USA
31 X12 **Strawberry Point** Iowa, C USA
38 M3 **Strawberry Reservoir** ⊡ Utah, W USA
38 M4 **Strawberry River** ≈ Utah, W USA
27 R7 **Strawn** Texas, SW USA
115 P17 **Straža** ▲ Bulgaria/FYR Macedonia
113 I19 **Strážov** *Hung.* Sztrazsó. ▲ NW Slovakia
190 F7 **Streaky Bay** South Australia
190 E7 **Streaky Bay** *bay* South Australia
32 L12 **Streator** Illinois, N USA
Streckenbach *see* Świdnik
113 J19 **Stredné Slovensko** ◐ *region* C Slovakia
113 C17 **Střední Čechy** *off.* Středočeský Kraj. ◐ *region* W Czech Republic
Strednogorie *see* Pirdop
31 O6 **Streeter** North Dakota, N USA
27 U8 **Streetman** Texas, SW USA
118 G13 **Strehaia** Mehedinți, SW Romania
Strehlen *see* Strzelin
116 I10 **Strelcha** Plovdivska Oblast, C Bulgaria
126 I13 **Strelka** Krasnoyarskiy Kray, C Russian Federation
128 L6 **Strel'na** ≈ NW Russian Federation
120 H7 **Strenči** *Ger.* Stackeln. Valka, N Latvia
110 K8 **Strengen** Tirol, W Austria
108 C6 **Stresa** Piemonte, NE Italy
Streshin *see* Streshyn
121 N18 **Streshyn** *Rus.* Streshin. Homyel'skaya Voblasts', SE Belarus
126 Gg11 **Strezhevoy** Tomskaya Oblast', C Russian Federation
97 G23 **Strib** Fyn, C Denmark
113 A17 **Stříbro** *Ger.* Mies. Západní Čechy, W Czech Republic
194 E13 **Strickland** ≈ SW PNG
Striegau *see* Strzegom
Strigonium *see* Esztergom
100 H13 **Strijen** Zuid-Holland, SW Netherlands
65 H21 **Strobel, Lago** ◎ S Argentina
63 B25 **Stroeder** Buenos Aires, E Argentina
117 C20 **Strofádes** *island* Iónioi Nísoi, Greece, C Mediterranean Sea
Strofilia *see* Strofyliá
117 G17 **Strofyliá** *var.* Strofilia. Évvoia, C Greece
102 O10 **Strom** ≈ NE Germany
109 L22 **Stromboli** ⛰ Isola Stromboli, SW Italy
109 L22 **Stromboli, Isola** *island* Isole Eolie, S Italy
98 H9 **Stromeferry** N Scotland, UK
98 J5 **Stromness** N Scotland, UK
96 N11 **Strömsbruk** Gävleborg, C Sweden
31 Q15 **Stromsburg** Nebraska, C USA
97 K21 **Strömsnäsbruk** Kronoberg, S Sweden
97 I17 **Strömstad** Göteborg och Bohus, S Sweden
95 G16 **Strömsund** Jämtland, C Sweden
95 G15 **Ströms Vattudal** *valley* N Sweden
29 V14 **Strong** Arkansas, C USA
Strongilí *see* Strongylí
109 O21 **Strongoli** Calabria, SW Italy
33 T11 **Strongsville** Ohio, N USA
117 Q23 **Strongylí** *var.* Strongilí. *island* SE Greece
98 K5 **Stronsay** *island* NE Scotland, UK
99 L21 **Stroud** C England, UK
29 O10 **Stroud** Oklahoma, C USA
20 I14 **Stroudsburg** Pennsylvania, NE USA
97 F21 **Struer** Ringkøbing, W Denmark
115 M20 **Struga** SW FYR Macedonia
Strugi-Kranyse *see* Strugi-Krasnyye
128 G14 **Strugi-Krasnyye** *var.* Strugi-Kranyse. Pskovskaya Oblast', W Russian Federation
116 G11 **Struma** *Gk.* Strymónas. ≈ Bulgaria/ Greece *see also* Strymónas
99 G21 **Strumble Head** *headland* SW Wales, UK
115 Q19 **Strumeshnitsa** *Mac.* Strumica. ≈ Bulgaria/FYR Macedonia
115 Q19 **Strumica** E FYR Macedonia
Strumica *see* Strumeshnitsa
116 G11 **Strumyani** Sofiyska Oblast, SW Bulgaria
33 V12 **Struthers** Ohio, N USA
116 I10 **Stryama** ≈ C Bulgaria
116 G13 **Strymónas** *Bul.* Struma. ≈ Bulgaria/Greece *see also* Struma
117 H14 **Strymonikós Kólpos** *gulf* N Greece
118 I6 **Stryy** L'vivs'ka Oblast', NW Ukraine
118 H6 **Stryy** ≈ W Ukraine
113 F14 **Strzegom** *Ger.* Striegau. Wałbrzych, SW Poland
112 E10 **Strzelce Krajeńskie** *Ger.* Friedeberg Neumark. Gorzów, W Poland
113 I15 **Strzelce Opolskie** *Ger.* Gross Strehlitz. Opole, SW Poland
190 K3 **Strzelecki Creek** *seasonal river* South Australia
190 J3 **Strzelecki Desert** *desert* South Australia
113 G15 **Strzelin** *Ger.* Strehlen. Wrocław, SW Poland
112 I11 **Strzelno** Bydgoszcz, C Poland
113 N17 **Strzyżów** Rzeszów, SE Poland
Stua Laighean *see* Leinster, Mount
25 Y13 **Stuart** Florida, SE USA
31 U14 **Stuart** Iowa, C USA
31 O13 **Stuart** Nebraska, C USA
23 S8 **Stuart** Virginia, NE USA
8 L13 **Stuart** ≈ British Columbia, SW Canada
41 N10 **Stuart Island** *island* Alaska, USA
8 L13 **Stuart Lake** ◎ British Columbia, SW Canada
193 B22 **Stuart Mountains** ▲▲ South Island, NZ
190 F3 **Stuart Range** *hill range* South Australia
Stubaital *see* Neustift im Stubaital
97 I24 **Stubbekøbing** Storstrøm, SE Denmark
47 P14 **Stubbs** Saint Vincent, Saint Vincent and the Grenadines
111 V6 **Stübming** ≈ E Austria
116 J11 **Studen Kladenets, Yazovir** ⊡ S Bulgaria
193 G21 **Studholme** Canterbury, South Island, NZ
Stuhlweissenberg *see* Székesfehérvár
Stuhm *see* Sztum
10 C7 **Stull Lake** ◎ Ontario, C Canada
Stung Treng *see* Stœng Trêng
130 L4 **Stupino** Moskovskaya Oblast', W Russian Federation
29 U4 **Sturgeon** Missouri, C USA
12 G10 **Sturgeon** ≈ Ontario, S Canada
33 N6 **Sturgeon Bay** Wisconsin, N USA
12 G11 **Sturgeon Falls** Ontario, S Canada
10 C11 **Sturgeon Lake** ◎ Ontario, S Canada
32 M3 **Sturgeon River** ≈ Michigan, N USA
22 H6 **Sturgis** Kentucky, S USA
33 P11 **Sturgis** Michigan, N USA
30 J9 **Sturgis** South Dakota, N USA
114 D10 **Šturlić** NW Bosnia and Herzegovina
113 J22 **Štúrovo** *Hung.* Párkány; *prev.* Parkan. Západné Slovensko, S Slovakia
190 L4 **Sturt, Mount** *hill* New South Wales, SE Australia
189 P4 **Sturt Plain** *plain* Northern Territory, N Australia
189 T9 **Sturt Stony Desert** *desert* South Australia
85 J25 **Stutterheim** Eastern Cape, S South Africa
103 H21 **Stuttgart** Baden-Württemberg, SW Germany
29 W12 **Stuttgart** Arkansas, C USA
94 H2 **Stykkishólmur** Vesturland, W Iceland
117 F17 **Stylída** *var.* Stilida, Stilís. Stereá Ellás, C Greece
118 K2 **Styr** *Rus.* Styr'. ≈ Belarus/Ukraine
117 I19 **Stýra** *var.* Stira. Évvoia, C Greece
Styria *see* Steiermark
Su *see* Jiangsu
Sua *see* Sowa
175 S17 **Suai** Timor, C Indonesia
56 G9 **Suaita** Santander, C Colombia
82 I7 **Suakin** *var.* Sawakin. Red Sea, NE Sudan
167 T13 **Suao** *Jap.* Suō. N Taiwan
Suao *see* Suau
42 G6 **Suaqui Grande** Sonora, NW Mexico
63 A16 **Suardi** Santa Fe, C Argentina
56 D11 **Suárez** Cauca, SW Colombia
195 N17 **Suau** *var.* Suao. Suaul Island, SE PNG
120 G12 **Subačius** Kupiškis, NE Lithuania
174 Jj14 **Subang** *prev.* Soebang. Jawa, C Indonesia
174 Gg5 **Subang** ✕ (Kuala Lumpur) Pahang, Peninsular Malaysia
133 S10 **Subansiri** ≈ NE India
120 I11 **Subate** Daugvapils, SE Latvia
145 N5 **Subaykhān** Dayr az Zawr, E Syria
165 P8 **Subei** *var.* Dangchengwan, Subei Mongolzu Zizhixian. Gansu, N China
Subei Mongolzu Zizhixian *see* Subei
174 K5 **Subi Besar, Pulau** *island* Kepulauan Natuna, W Indonesia
Subiyah *see* Aş Şubayḩīyah
28 I7 **Sublette** Kansas, C USA
114 K8 **Subotica** *Ger.* Maria-Theresiopel, *Hung.* Szabadka. Serbia, N Yugoslavia
118 K9 **Suceava** *Ger.* Suczawa, *Hung.* Szucsava. Suceava, NE Romania
118 J9 **Suceava** ◐ *county* NE Romania
118 K9 **Suceava** *Ger.* Suczawa. ≈ N Romania
114 E12 **Sučevići** Zadar-Knin, C Croatia
113 K17 **Sucha Beskidzka** Bielsko-Biała, S Poland
113 M14 **Suchedniów** Kielce, SE Poland
44 A2 **Suchitepéquez** *off.* Departamento de Suchitepéquez. ◐ *department* SW Guatemala
Su-chou *see* Suzhou
Suchow *see* Suzhou, Jiangsu, China
Suchow *see* Xuzhou, Jiangsu, China
99 D17 **Suck** ≈ C Ireland
Sucker State *see* Illinois
194 M16 **Suckling, Mount** ▲ S PNG
59 L19 **Sucre** *hist.* Chuquisaca, La Plata. ● (Bolivia-legal capital) Chuquisaca, S Bolivia
56 E6 **Sucre** Santander, N Colombia
58 A7 **Sucre** Manabí, W Ecuador
56 E6 **Sucre** *off.* Departamento de Sucre. ◐ *province* N Colombia
57 O5 **Sucre** *off.* Estado Sucre. ◐ *state* NE Venezuela
58 D6 **Sucumbíos** ◐ *province* NE Ecuador
115 G15 **Sućuraj** Split-Dalmacija, S Croatia
60 K10 **Sucuriju** Amapá, NE Brazil
Suczawa *see* Suceava
81 E16 **Sud** *Eng.* South. ◐ *province* S Cameroon
128 K13 **Suda** ≈ NW Russian Federation
Suda *see* Soúda
119 U13 **Sudak** Respublika Krym, S Ukraine
26 M4 **Sudan** Texas, SW USA
82 C10 **Sudan** *off.* Republic of Sudan, *Ar.* Jumhuriyat as-Sudan; *prev.* Anglo-Egyptian Sudan. ◆ *republic* N Africa
Sudanese Republic *see* Mali
Sudan, Jumhuriyat as- *see* Sudan
12 F10 **Sudbury** Ontario, S Canada
99 P20 **Sudbury** E England, UK
Sud, Canal de *see* Gonâve, Canal de la
82 E13 **Sudd** *swamp region* S Sudan
102 K10 **Sude** ≈ N Germany
Sudest Island *see* Tagula Island
113 E15 **Sudeten** *var.* Sudetes, Sudetic Mountains, Cz./Pol. Sudety. ▲▲ Czech Republic/Poland
Sudetes/Sudetic Mountains/ Sudety *see* Sudeten
94 G1 **Sudhureyri** Vestfirdhir, NW Iceland
94 J4 **Sudhurland** ◐ *region* S Iceland
176 Xx12 **Sudirman, Pegunungan** ▲▲ Irian Jaya, E Indonesia
128 M15 **Sudislavl'** Kostromskaya Oblast', NW Russian Federation
Südkarpaten *see* Carpații Meridionali
81 N20 **Sud Kivu** *off.* Région Sud Kivu. ◐ *region* E Zaire
Südliche Morava *see* Južna Morava
102 E12 **Süd-Nord-Kanal** *canal* NW Germany
130 M3 **Sudogda** Vladimirskaya Oblast', W Russian Federation
Sudostroy *see* Severodvinsk
81 C15 **Sud-Ouest** *Eng.* South-West. ◐ *province* W Cameroon
181 X17 **Sud Ouest, Pointe** *headland* SW Mauritius
197 J7 **Sud, Province** ◐ *province* S New Caledonia
130 J8 **Sudzha** Kurskaya Oblast', W Russian Federation
83 D15 **Sue** ≈ S Sudan
107 S10 **Sueca** País Valenciano, E Spain
116 I10 **Sŭedinenie** Plovdivska Oblast, C Bulgaria
Suero *see* Alzira
77 X8 **Suez** *Ar.* As Suways, El Suweis. NE Egypt
77 W7 **Suez Canal** *Ar.* Qanāt as Suways. *canal* NE Egypt
77 X8 **Suez, Gulf of** *Ar.* Khalīj as Suways. *gulf* NE Egypt
9 R17 **Suffield** Alberta, SW Canada
23 X7 **Suffolk** Virginia, NE USA
99 P20 **Suffolk** *cultural region* E England, UK
148 J2 **Şūfīān** Āžarbāyjān-e Khāvarī, N Iran
33 N12 **Sugar Creek** ≈ Illinois, N USA
32 L13 **Sugar Creek** ≈ Illinois, N USA
33 R3 **Sugar Island** *island* Michigan, N USA
27 V11 **Sugar Land** Texas, SW USA
21 P6 **Sugarloaf Mountain** ▲ Maine, NE USA
67 G24 **Sugar Loaf Point** *headland* N Saint Helena
142 G16 **Suğla Gölü** ◎ SW Turkey
127 O8 **Sugoy** ≈ E Russian Federation
153 U11 **Sugum, Gora** ▲ SW Kyrgyzstan
164 F7 **Sugun** Xinjiang Uygur Zizhiqu, W China
175 O2 **Sugut, Sungai** ≈ East Malaysia
165 O9 **Suhai Hu** ◎ C China
168 K14 **Suhait** Nei Mongol Zizhiqu, N China
147 X7 **Şuḩār** *var.* Sohar. N Oman
168 L6 **Sühbaatar** Selenge, N Mongolia
169 P9 **Sühbaatar** ◐ *province* E Mongolia
103 K17 **Suhl** Thüringen, C Germany
110 F7 **Suhr** Aargau, N Switzerland
167 O12 **Suichuan** Jiangxi, S China
Suid-Afrika *see* South Africa
166 L4 **Suide** Shaanxi, C China
Suidwes-Afrika *see* Namibia
169 Y9 **Suifenhe** Heilongjiang, NE China
Suigen *see* Suwŏn
169 W8 **Suihua** Heilongjiang, NE China
Súilí, Loch *see* Swilly, Lough
167 Q6 **Suining** Jiangsu, E China
166 I9 **Suining** Sichuan, C China
105 Q4 **Suippes** Marne, N France
99 E20 **Suir** *Ir.* An tSiúir. ≈ S Ireland
171 Gg15 **Suita** Ōsaka, Honshū, SW Japan
166 L16 **Suixi** Guangdong, S China
Sui Xian *see* Suizhou
169 T13 **Suizhong** Liaoning, NE China
167 N8 **Suizhou** *prev.* Sui Xian. Hubei, C China
155 P17 **Sujāwal** Sind, SE Pakistan
174 Jj14 **Sukabumi** *prev.* Soekaboemi. Jawa, C Indonesia
174 Kk9 **Sukadana, Teluk** *bay* Borneo, W Indonesia
171 Ll14 **Sukagawa** Fukushima, Honshū, C Japan
Sukarnapura *see* Jayapura
Sukarno, Puntjak *see* Jaya, Puncak
153 R11 **Sŭkh** *Rus.* Sokh. Farghona Wiloyati, E Uzbekistan
Sŭkh *see* Sokh
116 N8 **Sukha Reka** ≈ NE Bulgaria
130 J5 **Sukhinichi** Kaluzhskaya Oblast', W Russian Federation
Sukhne *see* As Sukhnah
133 Q4 **Sukhona** *var.* Tot'ma. ≈ NW Russian Federation
178 H9 **Sukhothai** *var.* Sukotai. Sukhothai, W Thailand
Sukhumi *see* Sokhumi
Sukkertoppen *see* Maniitsoq
155 Q13 **Sukkur** Sind, SE Pakistan
Sukotai *see* Sukhothai
Sukra Bay *see* Şawqirah, Dawḩat
129 V15 **Suksun** Permskaya Oblast', NW Russian Federation
170 E16 **Sukumo** Kōchi, Shikoku, SW Japan
96 B12 **Sula** *island* S Norway
129 Q5 **Sula** ≈ NW Russian Federation
119 R5 **Sula** ≈ N Ukraine
44 H6 **Sulaco, Río** ≈ NW Honduras
Sulaimaniya *see* As Sulaymānīyah
155 S10 **Sulaimān Range** ▲▲ C Pakistan
131 Q16 **Sulak** Respublika Dagestan, SW Russian Federation
131 Q16 **Sulak** ≈ SW Russian Federation
175 Rr10 **Sula, Kepulauan** *island group* C Indonesia
142 I12 **Sulakyurt** *var.* Konur. Kırıkkale, N Turkey
175 R17 **Sulamu** Timor, S Indonesia
98 F5 **Sula Sgeir** *island* NW Scotland, UK
175 Pp10 **Sulawesi** *Eng.* Celebes. *island* C Indonesia
Sulawesi, Laut *see* Celebes Sea
175 P11 **Sulawesi Selatan** *off.* Propinsi Sulawesi Selatan, *Eng.* South Celebes, South Sulawesi. ◐ *province* C Indonesia
175 Q9 **Sulawesi Tengah** *off.* Propinsi Sulawesi Tengah, *Eng.* Central Celebes, Central Sulawesi. ◐ *province* N Indonesia
175 Q11 **Sulawesi Tenggara** *off.* Propinsi Sulawesi Tenggara, *Eng.* South-East Celebes, South-East Sulawesi. ◐ *province* C Indonesia
175 Qq7 **Sulawesi Utara** *off.* Propinsi Sulawesi Utara, *Eng.* North Celebes, North Sulawesi. ◐ *province* N Indonesia
145 T5 **Sulaymān Beg** N Iraq
97 D15 **Suldalsvatnet** ◎ S Norway
112 E12 **Sulechów** *Ger.* Züllichau. Zielona Góra, W Poland
112 E11 **Sulęcin** Gorzów, W Poland
79 U14 **Suleja** Niger, C Nigeria
113 K14 **Sulejów** Piotrków, S Poland
98 I5 **Sule Skerry** *island* N Scotland, UK
Suliag *see* Sohâg
78 J16 **Sulima** S Sierra Leone
119 O13 **Sulina** Tulcea, SE Romania
119 N13 **Sulina Brațul** ≈ SE Romania
102 H12 **Sulingen** Niedersachsen, NW Germany
94 H12 **Suliskongen** ▲ C Norway
94 H12 **Sulitjelma** Nordland, C Norway
58 A9 **Sullana** Piura, NW Peru
25 N3 **Sulligent** Alabama, S USA
32 M14 **Sullivan** Illinois, N USA
33 N15 **Sullivan** Indiana, N USA
29 W5 **Sullivan** Missouri, C USA
Sullivan Island *see* Lanbi Kyun
98 M1 **Sullom Voe** NE Scotland, UK
105 O7 **Sully-sur-Loire** Loiret, C France
Sulmo *see* Sulmona
109 K15 **Sulmona** *anc.* Sulmo. Abruzzi, C Italy
Sulo *see* Shule He
116 M11 **Süloğlu** Edirne, NW Turkey
24 G9 **Sulphur** Louisiana, S USA
29 O12 **Sulphur** Oklahoma, C USA
30 K9 **Sulphur Creek** ≈ South Dakota, N USA
26 M5 **Sulphur Draw** ≈ Texas, SW USA
27 W5 **Sulphur River** ≈ Arkansas/Texas, SW USA
27 V6 **Sulphur Springs** Texas, SW USA
26 M6 **Sulphur Springs Draw** ≈ Texas, SW USA
12 D8 **Sultan** Ontario, S Canada
Sultānābād *see* Arāk
Sultan Alonto, Lake *see* Lanao, Lake
142 G15 **Sultan Dağları** ▲▲ C Turkey
116 N13 **Sultanköy** Tekirdağ, NW Turkey
179 R16 **Sultan Kudarat** *var.* Nuling. Mindanao, S Philippines
158 M13 **Sultānpur** Uttar Pradesh, N India
179 Pp17 **Sulu Archipelago** *island group* SW Philippines
198 Ff7 **Sulu Basin** *undersea feature* SE South China Sea
Sülüktü *see* Sulyukta
Sulu, Laut *see* Sulu Sea
175 Pp1 **Sulu Sea** *Ind.* Laut Sulu. *sea* SW Philippines
151 O15 **Sulutobe** *Kaz.* Sulūtöbe. Kzyl-Orda, S Kazakhstan
153 Q11 **Sulyukta** *Kir.* Sülüktü. Oshskaya Oblast', SW Kyrgyzstan
Sulz *see* Sulz am Neckar
103 G22 **Sulz am Neckar** *var.* Sulz. Baden-Württemberg, SW Germany
103 L20 **Sulzbach-Rosenberg** Bayern, SE Germany
205 N13 **Sulzberger Bay** *bay* Antarctica
Sumail *see* Summēl
115 F15 **Sumartin** Split-Dalmacija, S Croatia
34 H6 **Sumas** Washington, NW USA
174 Gg7 **Sumatera** *Eng.* Sumatra. *island* W Indonesia
173 G9 **Sumatera Barat** *off.* Propinsi Sumatera Barat, *Eng.* West Sumatra. ◐ *province* W Indonesia
174 Hh11 **Sumatera Selatan** *off.* Propinsi Sumatera Selatan, *Eng.* South Sumatra. ◐ *province* W Indonesia
173 Ff6 **Sumatera Utara** *off.* Propinsi Sumatera Utara, *Eng.* North Sumatra. ◐ *province* W Indonesia
Sumatra *see* Sumatera
Šumava *see* Bohemian Forest
Sumayl *see* Summēl
145 U7 **Sumayr al Muḩammad** E Iraq
175 P17 **Sumba, Pulau** *Eng.* Sandalwood Island; *prev.* Soemba. *island* Nusa Tenggara, C Indonesia
152 D12 **Sumbar** ≈ W Turkmenistan
175 P16 **Sumba, Selat** *strait* Nusa Tenggara, S Indonesia
175 Oo16 **Sumbawa** *prev.* Soembawa. *island* Nusa Tenggara, C Indonesia
175 O16 **Sumbawabesar** Sumbawa, S Indonesia
83 F23 **Sumbawanga** Rukwa, W Tanzania
84 B12 **Sumbe** *prev.* N'Gunza, *Port.* Novo Redondo. Cuanza Sul, W Angola
98 M3 **Sumburgh Head** *headland* NE Scotland, UK
113 H23 **Sümeg** Veszprém, W Hungary
82 C12 **Sumeih** Southern Darfur, S Sudan
174 Mm14 **Sumenep** *prev.* Soemenep. Pulau Madura, C Indonesia
Sumgait *see* Sumqayıt, Azerbaijan
Sumgait *see* Sumqayıtçay, Azerbaijan
172 Ss14 **Sumisu-jima** *Eng.* Smith Island. *island* SE Japan
145 Q2 **Summēl** *var.* Sumail, Sumayl. N Iraq
33 O5 **Summer Island** *island* Michigan, N USA
34 H15 **Summer Lake** ◎ Oregon, NW USA
9 N17 **Summerland** British Columbia, SW Canada
11 P14 **Summerside** Prince Edward Island, SE Canada
23 R5 **Summersville** West Virginia, NE USA
23 R5 **Summersville Lake** ⊡ West Virginia, NE USA
23 S13 **Summerton** South Carolina, SE USA
25 R2 **Summerville** Georgia, SE USA
23 S14 **Summerville** South Carolina, SE USA
41 R10 **Summit** Alaska, USA
37 V6 **Summit Mountain** ▲ Nevada, W USA
39 R8 **Summit Peak** ▲ Colorado, C USA
Summus Portus *see* Somport, Col du
31 X12 **Sumner** Iowa, C USA
24 K3 **Sumner** Mississippi, S USA
193 H17 **Sumner, Lake** ◎ South Island, NZ
39 U12 **Sumner, Lake** ⊡ New Mexico, SW USA
171 Kk13 **Sumon-dake** ▲ Honshū, C Japan
170 G15 **Sumoto** Hyōgo, Awaji-shima, SW Japan
113 G17 **Šumperk** *Ger.* Mährisch-Schönberg. Severní Morava, E Czech Republic
44 F7 **Sumpul, Río** ≈ El Salvador/Honduras
143 Z11 **Sumqayıt** *Rus.* Sumgait. E Azerbaijan
143 Y11 **Sumqayıtçay** *Rus.* Sumgait. ≈ E Azerbaijan
153 R9 **Sumsar** Dzhalal-Abadskaya Oblast', W Kyrgyzstan
119 S3 **Sums'ka Oblast'** *var.* Sumy, *Rus.* Sumskaya Oblast'. ◐ *province* NE Ukraine
Sumskaya Oblast' *see* Sums'ka Oblast'
128 J8 **Sumskiy Posad** Respublika Kareliya, NW Russian Federation
23 S12 **Sumter** South Carolina, SE USA
119 T3 **Sumy** Sums'ka Oblast', NE Ukraine
Sumy *see* Sums'ka Oblast'
165 Q15 **Sumzom** Xizang Zizhiqu, W China
129 R15 **Suna** Kirovskaya Oblast', NW Russian Federation
128 I10 **Suna** ≈ NW Russian Federation
172 Oo5 **Sunagawa** Hokkaidō, NE Japan
159 V13 **Sunamganj** Chittagong, NE Bangladesh
165 S8 **Sunan** *var.* Hongwan, Sunan Yugurzu Zizhixian. Gansu, N China
169 W14 **Sunan** ✕ (P'yŏngyang) SW North Korea
Sunan Yugurzu Zizhixian *see* Sunan
21 N9 **Sunapee Lake** ◎ New Hampshire, NE USA
145 P4 **Sunaysilah** *salt marsh* N Iraq
22 M8 **Sunbright** Tennessee, S USA
35 R6 **Sunburst** Montana, NW USA
191 N12 **Sunbury** Victoria, SE Australia
23 X8 **Sunbury** North Carolina, SE USA
20 G14 **Sunbury** Pennsylvania, NE USA
63 A17 **Sunchales** Santa Fe, C Argentina
169 W13 **Sunch'ŏn** SW North Korea
169 Y16 **Sunch'ŏn** *Jap.* Junten. S South Korea
38 K13 **Sun City** Arizona, SW USA
21 O9 **Suncook** New Hampshire, NE USA
Sunda Islands *see* Greater Sunda Islands
35 Z12 **Sundance** Wyoming, C USA
160 M11 **Sundargarh** Orissa, E India
174 Ii14 **Sunda, Selat** *strait* Jawa/Sumatera, SW Indonesia
133 U15 **Sunda Shelf** *undersea feature* S South China Sea
Sunda Trench *see* Java Trench
133 U17 **Sunda Trough** *undersea feature* E Indian Ocean
97 O16 **Sundbyberg** Stockholm, C Sweden
99 M14 **Sunderland** *var.* Wearmouth. NE England, UK
103 F15 **Sundern** Nordrhein-Westfalen, W Germany
142 F12 **Sündiken Dağları** ▲▲ C Turkey
26 M5 **Sundown** Texas, SW USA
9 P16 **Sundre** Alberta, SW Canada
12 H12 **Sundridge** Ontario, S Canada
95 H17 **Sundsvall** Västernorrland, C Sweden
28 H4 **Sunflower, Mount** ▲ Kansas, C USA
Sunflower State *see* Kansas
174 Gg4 **Sungai Bernam** ≈ Peninsular Malaysia
174 Ii12 **Sungaibuntu** Sumatera, SW Indonesia
174 Gg9 **Sungaidareh** Sumatera, W Indonesia
178 Hh17 **Sungai Kolok** *var.* Sungai Ko-Lok. Narathiwat, SW Thailand
174 Gg10 **Sungaipenuh** *prev.* Soengaipenoeh. Sumatera, W Indonesia
174 Kk8 **Sungaipinyuh** Borneo, C Indonesia
Sungari *see* Songhua Jiang
Sungaria *see* Dzungaria
Sungei Pahang *see* Pahang, Sungai
178 Hh8 **Sung Men** Phrae, NW Thailand
85 M15 **Sungo** Tete, NW Mozambique
174 Ii10 **Sungsang** Sumatera, W Indonesia
116 M9 **Sungurlare** Burgaska Oblast, E Bulgaria
142 J12 **Sungurlu** Çorum, N Turkey
114 F9 **Sunja** Sisak-Moslavina, C Croatia
159 Q12 **Sun Koshi** ≈ E Nepal
96 F9 **Sunndalen** *valley* S Norway
96 F9 **Sunndalsøra** Møre og Romsdal, S Norway
97 K15 **Sunne** Värmland, C Sweden
97 O15 **Sunnersta** Uppsala, C Sweden
96 C11 **Sunnfjord** *physical region* S Norway
97 C15 **Sunnhordland** *physical region* S Norway
96 D10 **Sunnmøre** *physical region* S Norway
39 N4 **Sunnyside** Utah, W USA
34 J10 **Sunnyside** Washington, NW USA
37 N9 **Sunnyvale** California, W USA
32 L8 **Sun Prairie** Wisconsin, N USA
Sunqur *see* Sonqor
27 N1 **Sunray** Texas, SW USA

◆ Country
● Country Capital
◇ Dependent Territory
○ Dependent Territory Capital
◐ Administrative Region
✕ International Airport
▲ Mountain
▲▲ Mountain Range
⛰ Volcano
≈ River
◎ Lake
⊡ Reservoir

24 I8 **Sunset** Louisiana, S USA
27 S5 **Sunset** Texas, SW USA
Sunset State see Oregon
189 Z10 **Sunshine Coast** cultural region Queensland, E Australia
Sunshine State see Florida, USA
Sunshine State see New Mexico, USA
Sunshine State see South Dakota, USA
126 Kk1 **Suntar** Respublika Sakha (Yakutiya), NE Russian Federation
41 R10 **Suntrana** Alaska, USA
154 J15 **Suntsar** Baluchistān, SW Pakistan
169 W15 **Sunwi-do** island SW North Korea
169 W6 **Sunwu** Heilongjiang, NE China
79 O16 **Sunyani** W Ghana
Suo see Suao
95 M17 **Suolahti** Keski-Suomi, C Finland
Suoločielgi see Saariselkä
Suomenlahti see Finland, Gulf of
Suomen Tasavalta/ Suomi see Finland
95 N14 **Suomussalmi** Oulu, E Finland
170 D13 **Suō-nada** sea SW Japan
95 M17 **Suonenjoki** Kuopio, C Finland
178 Jj13 **Suông** Kâmpóng Cham, C Cambodia
128 I10 **Suoyarvi** Respublika Kareliya, NW Russian Federation
Supanburi see Suphan Buri
59 D14 **Supe** Lima, W Peru
13 V7 **Supérieur, Lac** ⊚ Québec, SE Canada
Supérieur, Lac see Superior, Lake
38 M14 **Superior** Arizona, SW USA
35 O9 **Superior** Montana, NW USA
31 P17 **Superior** Nebraska, C USA
32 I3 **Superior** Wisconsin, N USA
43 S17 **Superior, Laguna** lagoon S Mexico
33 N2 **Superior, Lake** Fr. Lac Supérieur. ⊚ Canada/USA
38 L13 **Superstition Mountains** ▲ Arizona, SW USA
115 F14 **Supetar** It. San Pietro. Split-Dalmacija, S Croatia
178 H11 **Suphan Buri** var. Supanburi. Suphan Buri, W Thailand
176 W9 **Supiori, Pulau** island E Indonesia
196 K2 **Supply Reef** reef N Northern Mariana Islands
205 O7 **Support Force Glacier** glacier Antarctica
143 R10 **Sup'sa** var. Supsa. ≈ W Georgia
145 W12 **Sūq ash Shuyūkh** SE Iraq
144 H4 **Suqaylibīyah** Ḩamāh, W Syria
167 Q6 **Suqian** Jiangsu, E China
Suqrah see Şawqirah
Suqrah Bay see Şawqirah, Dawḩat
147 V16 **Suquţrā** var. Sokotra, Eng. Socotra. island SE Yemen
147 Z8 **Şūr** NE Oman
Şūr see Soûr
131 P5 **Sura** Penzenskaya Oblast', W Russian Federation
131 P4 **Sura** ≈ W Russian Federation
155 N12 **Sūrāb** Baluchistān, SW Pakistan
Surabaja see Surabaya
174 M15 **Surabaya** prev. Soerabaja. Surabaja. Jawa, C Indonesia
97 N15 **Surahammar** Västmanland, C Sweden
174 L15 **Surakarta** Eng. Solo; prev. Soerakarta. Jawa, S Indonesia
Surakhany see Suraxanı
179 R17 **Surallah** Mindanao, S Philippines
143 S10 **Suram** C Georgia
149 X13 **Sūrān** Sīstān va Balūchestān, SE Iran
113 I21 **Šurany** Hung. Nagysurány. Západné Slovensko, SW Slovakia
160 D12 **Sūrat** Gujarāt, W India
158 G9 **Sūratgarh** Rājasthān, NW India
178 Gg15 **Surat Thani** var. Suratdhani. Surat Thani, SW Thailand
121 Q16 **Suraw** Rus. Surov. ≈ E Belarus
143 Z11 **Suraxanı** Rus. Surakhany. E Azerbaijan
147 Y11 **Surayr** E Oman
144 K2 **Suraysāt** Ḩalab, N Syria
120 O12 **Surazh** Rus. Surazh. Vitsyebskaya Voblasts', NE Belarus
130 K6 **Surazh** Bryanskaya Oblast', W Russian Federation
203 V17 **Sur, Cabo** headland Easter Island, Chile, E Pacific Ocean
114 L11 **Surčin** Serbia, N Yugoslavia
118 H9 **Surduc** Hung. Szurduk. Sălaj, NW Romania
115 P16 **Surdulica** Serbia, SE Yugoslavia
101 L24 **Sûre** var. Sauer. ≈ W Europe see also Sauer
160 C10 **Surendranagar** Gujarāt, W India
20 K16 **Surf City** New Jersey, NE USA
191 V13 **Surfers Paradise** Queensland, E Australia
23 U13 **Surfside Beach** South Carolina, SE USA
104 I10 **Surgères** Charente-Maritime, W France
125 G11 **Surgut** Khanty-Mansiyskiy Avtonomnyy Okrug, C Russian Federation
113 Hh10 **Surgutina** Krasnoyarskiy Kray, C Russian Federation
100 M6 **Surhuisterveen** Friesland, N Netherlands

107 V5 **Súria** Cataluña, NE Spain
149 P10 **Sūriān** Fārs, S Iran
161 J15 **Sūriāpet** Andhra Pradesh, C India
179 R14 **Surigao** Mindanao, S Philippines
178 Ii11 **Surin** Surin, E Thailand
57 U11 **Surinam** off. Republic of Surinam, var. Surinam; prev. Dutch Guiana, Netherlands Guiana. ◆ republic N South America
Sūriya/Sūriyah, Al-Jumhūrīyah al-'Arabīyah as- see Syria
Surkhab, Darya-i- see Kahmard, Daryā-ye
Surkhandar'inskaya Oblast' see Surkhondaryo Wiloyati
Surkhandar'ya see Surkhondaryo
Surkhet see Birendranagar
153 R12 **Surkhob** ≈ C Tajikistan
153 P13 **Surkhondaryo** Rus. Surkhandar'ya. ≈ Tajikistan/Uzbekistan
153 N13 **Surkhondaryo Wiloyati** Rus. Surkhandar'inskaya Oblast'. ◆ province S Uzbekistan
143 P11 **Sürmene** Trabzon, NE Turkey
131 N11 **Surovikino** Volgogradskaya Oblast', SW Russian Federation
126 Jj14 **Surovo** Irkutskaya Oblast', S Russian Federation
37 N11 **Sur, Point** headland California, W USA
197 F3 **Surprise, Île** island N New Caledonia
63 E22 **Sur, Punta** headland E Argentina
Surrentum see Sorrento
30 M3 **Surrey** North Dakota, N USA
99 O22 **Surrey** cultural region SE England, UK
23 X7 **Surry** Virginia, NE USA
110 F8 **Sursee** Luzern, W Switzerland
131 P6 **Sursk** Penzenskaya Oblast', W Russian Federation
131 P5 **Surskoye** Ul'yanovskaya Oblast', W Russian Federation
77 P8 **Surt** var. Sidra, Sirte. N Libya
97 I19 **Surte** Götaland och Bohus, S Sweden
77 Q8 **Surt, Khalīj** Eng. Gulf of Sidra, Gulf of Sirti, Sidra. gulf N Libya
94 I5 **Surtsey** island S Iceland
143 N17 **Suruç** Şanlıurfa, S Turkey
171 Ii17 **Suruga-wan** bay SE Japan
174 Hh10 **Surulangun** Sumatera, W Indonesia
Süs see Susch
108 A8 **Susa** Piemonte, NE Italy
170 E12 **Susa** Yamaguchi, Honshū, SW Japan
Susa see Shūsh
115 E16 **Sušac** It. Cazza. island SW Croatia
170 Ee15 **Susaki** Kōchi, Shikoku, SW Japan
170 G17 **Susami** Wakayama, Honshū, SW Japan
148 K9 **Susangird** var. Susangird. Khūzestān, SW Iran
Susangird see Süsangerd
37 P4 **Susanville** California, W USA
110 J9 **Susch** var. Süs. Graubünden, SE Switzerland
143 N12 **Suşehri** Sivas, N Turkey
Susiana see Khūzestān
113 B18 **Sušice** Ger. Schüttenhofen. Západní Čechy, SW Czech Republic
41 S11 **Susitna** Alaska, USA
41 R11 **Susitna River** ≈ Alaska, USA
131 Q3 **Suslonger** Respublika Mariy El, W Russian Federation
107 N14 **Suspiro del Moro, Puerto del** pass S Spain
20 H16 **Susquehanna River** ≈ New York/Pennsylvania, NE USA
11 O15 **Sussex** New Brunswick, SE Canada
20 J13 **Sussex** New Jersey, NE USA
23 W7 **Sussex** Virginia, NE USA
99 O23 **Sussex** cultural region S England, UK
191 S10 **Sussex Inlet** New South Wales, SE Australia
101 I14 **Susteren** Limburg, SE Netherlands
8 K12 **Sustut Peak** ▲ British Columbia, W Canada
127 Nn9 **Susuman** Magadanskaya Oblast', E Russian Federation
196 H6 **Susupe** Saipan, S Northern Mariana Islands
142 D13 **Susurluk** Balıkesir, NW Turkey
116 M13 **Susuzmüsellim** Tekirdağ, NW Turkey
142 F15 **Sütçüler** Isparta, SW Turkey
118 L13 **Suteşti** Brăila, SE Romania
85 F25 **Sutherland** Western Cape, SW South Africa
30 L15 **Sutherland** Nebraska, C USA
98 I7 **Sutherland** cultural region N Scotland, UK
193 B21 **Sutherland Falls** waterfall South Island, NZ
37 P4 **Sutter Creek** California, W USA
41 S11 **Sutton** Alaska, USA
31 Q16 **Sutton** Nebraska, C USA
23 R4 **Sutton** West Virginia, NE USA
10 F8 **Sutton** Ontario, C Canada
99 M19 **Sutton Coldfield** C England, UK
23 R4 **Sutton Lake** ⊠ West Virginia, NE USA

13 P13 **Sutton, Monts** hill range Québec, SE Canada
10 F8 **Sutton Ridges** ▲ Ontario, C Canada
172 Nn5 **Suttsu** Hokkaidō, NE Japan
41 P15 **Sutwik Island** island Alaska, USA
168 K7 **Süüj** Bulgan, C Mongolia
120 H5 **Suure-Jaani** Ger. Gross-Sankt-Johannis. Viljandimaa, S Estonia
120 J7 **Suur Munamägi** var. Munamägi, Ger. Eier-Berg. ▲ SE Estonia
120 F5 **Suur Väin** Ger. Grosser Sund. strait W Estonia
153 U8 **Suusamyr** Chuyskaya Oblast', C Kyrgyzstan
197 I13 **Suva** ● (Fiji) Viti Levu, W Fiji
197 I13 **Suva** × Viti Levu, W Fiji
115 N18 **Suva Gora** ▲ W FYR Macedonia
120 H11 **Suvainiškis** Rokiškis, NE Lithuania
115 P15 **Suva Planina** ▲ SE Yugoslavia
115 M17 **Suva Reka** Serbia, S Yugoslavia
130 K5 **Suvorov** Tul'skaya Oblast', W Russian Federation
131 N12 **Suvorove** Odes'ka Oblast', SW Ukraine
Suvorovo see Ştefan Vodă
171 J15 **Suwa** Nagano, Honshū, S Japan
149 R14 **Suwaik** see As Suwayq
Suwaira see Aş Şuwayrah
112 O7 **Suwałki** Lith. Suvalkai, Rus. Suvalki. Suwałki, NE Poland
112 N8 **Suwałki** off. Województwo Suwalskie, Lith. Suvalkai, Rus. Suvalki. ◆ province NE Poland
Suwalskie, Województwo see Suwałki
178 Ii10 **Suwannaphum** Roi Et, E Thailand
25 V8 **Suwannee River** ≈ Florida/Georgia, SE USA
Şuwār see Aş Şuwār
202 K14 **Suwarrow** atoll N Cook Islands
Suwayda/Suwaydā', Muḩāfaẓat as see As Suwaydā'
149 R16 **Suwayqiyah var.** Sweiham. Abū Ẓaby, E UAE
Suwayqiyah, Hawr as see Shuwayjah, Hawr ash
77 Q8 **Suways, Khalīj** Eng. Gulf of Suez, Gulf of Suez. gulf N Libya
77 Q8 **Suways, Qanāt as** see Suez Canal
Suweida see As Suwaydā'
Suweon see Suwŏn
169 X15 **Suwŏn** var. Suweon, Jap. Suigen. NW South Korea
Su Xian see Suzhou
149 R14 **Süzä** Hormozgān, S Iran
151 P15 **Suzak** Kaz. Sozaq. Yuzhnyy Kazakhstan, S Kazakhstan
Suzaka see Suzuka
130 M3 **Suzdal'** Vladimirskaya Oblast', W Russian Federation
167 R8 **Suzhou** var. Su Xian. Anhui, E China
167 P7 **Suzhou** var. Soochow, Su-chou, Suchow; prev. Wuhsien. Jiangsu, E China
171 Ji2 **Suzu** Ishikawa, Honshū, SW Japan
171 Hh16 **Suzuka** Mie, Honshū, SW Japan
171 Ji14 **Suzuka** var. Suzaka. Nagano, Honshū, S Japan
171 Ji2 **Suzu-misaki** headland Honshū, SW Japan
96 M10 **Svågan** var. Svågälv. ≈ C Sweden
Svalava/Svaljava see Svalyava
94 K3 **Svalbard** ◇ Norwegian dependency Arctic Ocean
94 J2 **Svalbardhs** Nordhurland Eystra, N Iceland
97 K17 **Svalöv** Malmöhus, S Sweden
118 H7 **Svalyava** Cz. Svalava, Svaljava, Hung. Szolyva. Zakarpats'ka Oblast', W Ukraine
94 G2 **Svanbergfjellet** ▲ C Svalbard
97 M24 **Svaneke** Bornholm, E Denmark
97 L22 **Svängsta** Blekinge, S Sweden
97 J16 **Svanskog** Värmland, C Sweden
97 L16 **Svartå** Örebro, C Sweden
97 L15 **Svartá** var. Svartälv. ≈ C Sweden
94 G12 **Svartisen** glacier C Norway
119 X6 **Svatove** Rus. Svatovo. Luhans'ka Oblast', E Ukraine
Svatovo see Svatove
Svätý Kríž nad Hronom see Žiar nad Hronom
178 Ii12 **Svay Chék, Stœng** ≈ Cambodia/Thailand
178 Jj14 **Svay Riĕng** Svay Riĕng, S Cambodia
94 J0 **Sveagruva** Spitsbergen, W Svalbard
97 K23 **Svedala** Malmöhus, S Sweden
95 G18 **Sveg** Jämtland, C Sweden
120 C12 **Šveikšna** Šilutė, W Lithuania
96 C11 **Svelgen** Sogn og Fjordane, C Norway
97 H15 **Svelvik** Vestfold, S Norway
120 I13 **Švenčionėliai** Pol. Nowo-Święciany. Švenčionys, SE Lithuania
120 I13 **Švenčionys** Pol. Święciany. Švenčionys, SE Lithuania
31 R11 **Swanson** Ohio, N USA
112 G11 **Swarzędz** Poznań, W Poland
97 K19 **Svenljunga** Älvsborg, S Sweden
94 P2 **Svenskøya** island E Svalbard
97 G20 **Svenstrup** Nordjylland, N Denmark
120 I13 **Šventoji** ≈ C Lithuania

119 Z8 **Sverdlovs'k** Rus. Sverdlovsk; prev. Imeni Sverdlova Rudnik. Luhans'ka Oblast', E Ukraine
Sverdlovsk see Yekaterinburg
131 W2 **Sverdlovskaya Oblast'** ◆ province C Russian Federation
126 Hh5 **Sverdrup, Ostrov** island N Russian Federation
Sverige see Sweden
115 O15 **Svetac** prev. Sveti Andrea. It. Sant'Andrea. island SW Croatia
Sveti Andrea see Svetac
Sveti Nikola see Sveti Nikole
115 O18 **Sveti Nikole** prev. Sveti Nikola. C FYR Macedonia
Sveti Vrach see Sandanski
127 O16 **Svetlaya** Primorskiy Kray, SE Russian Federation
130 B2 **Svetlogorsk** Kaliningradskaya Oblast', W Russian Federation
126 J9 **Svetlogorsk** Krasnoyarskiy Kray, N Russian Federation
131 N14 **Svetlograd** Stavropol'skiy Kray, SW Russian Federation
Svetlovodsk see Svitlovods'k
121 A14 **Svetlyy** Ger. Zimmerbude. Kaliningradskaya Oblast', W Russian Federation
131 Y8 **Svetlyy** Orenburgskaya Oblast', W Russian Federation
128 G11 **Svetogorsk** Fin. Enso. Leningradskaya Oblast', NW Russian Federation
Svetozarevo see Jagodina
113 B18 **Švihov** Ger. Schwihau. Západní Čechy, W Czech Republic
114 E13 **Svilaja** ▲ SE Croatia
114 N12 **Svilajnac** Serbia, C Yugoslavia
116 L11 **Svilengrad** prev. Mustafa-Pasha. Khaskovska Oblast, SE Bulgaria
Svinecea Mare, Munte see Svinecea Mare, Vârful
118 F13 **Svinecea Mare, Vârful** var. Munte Svinecea Mare. ▲ SW Romania
153 N14 **Svintsovyy Rudnik** Turkm. Svintsowyy Rudnik. Lebapskiy Velayat, E Turkmenistan
120 I13 **Svir** Rus. Svir'. Minskaya Voblasts', NW Belarus
128 I12 **Svir'** canal NW Russian Federation
Svir', Ozero see Svir, Vozyera
121 I14 **Svir, Vozyera** Rus. Ozero Svir'. ⊚ C Belarus
116 J7 **Svishtov** prev. Sistova. Loveshka Oblast, N Bulgaria
121 F18 **Svislach** Pol. Świsłocz, Rus. Svisloch'. Hrodzyenskaya Voblasts', W Belarus
121 M17 **Svislach** Rus. Svisloch'. Mahilyowskaya Voblasts', E Belarus
121 L17 **Svislach** Rus. Svisloch'. ≈ C Belarus
Svisloch' see Svislach
113 F17 **Svitavy** Ger. Zwittau. Východní Čechy, E Czech Republic
119 S6 **Svitlovods'k** Rus. Svetlovodsk. Kirovohrads'ka Oblast', C Ukraine
Svizzera see Switzerland
126 Mm15 **Svobodnyy** Amurskaya Oblast', SE Russian Federation
116 G9 **Svoge** Sofiyska Oblast, W Bulgaria
94 G11 **Svolvær** Nordland, C Norway
113 F18 **Svratka** Ger. Schwarzach, Schwarzawa. ≈ SE Czech Republic
115 P14 **Srvljig** Serbia, E Yugoslavia
207 U10 **Svyataya Anna Trough** var. Saint Anna Trough. undersea feature N Kara Sea
128 M4 **Svyatoy Nos, Mys** headland NW Russian Federation
126 M5 **Svyatoy Nos, Mys** headland NE Russian Federation
121 X6 **Svyetlahorsk** Rus. Svetlogorsk. Homyel'skaya Voblasts', SE Belarus
167 T7 **Sÿiao Shan** island SE China
102 H11 **Syke** Niedersachsen, NW Germany
96 D10 **Sykkylven** Møre og Romsdal, S Norway
117 F15 **Sykoúri** var. Sikouri; prev. Sikoúrion. Thessalía, C Greece
129 N11 **Syktyvkar** prev. Ust'-Sysol'sk. Respublika Komi, NW Russian Federation
25 Q4 **Sylacauga** Alabama, S USA
96 J9 **Sylene** Swe. Sylarna. ▲ Norway/Sweden
Sylarna see Sylene
159 V14 **Sylhet** Chittagong, NE Bangladesh
102 G6 **Sylt** island NW Germany
23 O10 **Sylva** North Carolina, SE USA
129 V15 **Sylva** ≈ NW Russian Federation
25 W5 **Sylvania** Georgia, SE USA
31 R13 **Sylvania** Ohio, N USA
9 Q15 **Sylvan Lake** Alberta, SW Canada
35 T13 **Sylvan Pass** pass Wyoming, C USA
25 P6 **Sylvester** Georgia, SE USA
27 P6 **Sylvester** Texas, SW USA
8 L11 **Sylvia, Mount** ▲ British Columbia, W Canada
126 Hh12 **Sym** ≈ C Russian Federation
117 N22 **Sými** var. Simi. island Dodekánisos, Greece, Aegean Sea
119 U8 **Synel'nykove** Dnipropetrovs'ka Oblast', E Ukraine
129 U6 **Synya** Respublika Komi, NW Russian Federation
119 P7 **Synyukha** Rus. Sinyukha. S Ukraine
28 H6 **Syracuse** Kansas, C USA
31 S16 **Syracuse** Nebraska, C USA

27 V12 **Sweeny** Texas, SW USA
35 R6 **Sweetgrass** Montana, NW USA
34 G2 **Sweet Home** Oregon, NW USA
27 T12 **Sweet Home** Oregon, NW USA
29 T4 **Sweet Springs** Missouri, C USA
22 M10 **Sweetwater** Tennessee, S USA
27 P7 **Sweetwater** Texas, SW USA
35 V15 **Sweetwater River** ≈ Wyoming, C USA
Sweiham see Suwayqiyah
85 F26 **Swellendam** Western Cape, SW South Africa
113 G15 **Świdnica** Ger. Schweidnitz. Wałbrzych, SW Poland
113 O14 **Świdnik** Ger. Streckenbach. Lublin, E Poland
112 J8 **Świdwin** Ger. Schivelbein. Koszalin, NW Poland
113 F15 **Świebodzice** Ger. Freiburg in Schlesien, Swiebodzice. Wałbrzych, SW Poland
112 E11 **Świebodzin** Ger. Schwiebus. Zielona Góra, W Poland
112 I9 **Świecie** Ger. Schwertberg. Bydgoszcz, N Poland
Święciany see Švenčionys
112 I9 **Świecie** Ger. Schwertberg. Bydgoszcz, N Poland
9 I17 **Swift Current** Saskatchewan, S Canada
100 K9 **Swifterbant** Flevoland, C Netherlands
191 Q12 **Swift's Creek** Victoria, SE Australia
98 E13 **Swilly, Lough Ir.** Loch Súilí. inlet N Ireland
99 M22 **Swindon** S England, UK
Swinemünde see Świnoujście
112 D8 **Świnoujście** Ger. Swinemünde. Szczecin, NW Poland
110 E9 **Switzerland** off. Swiss Confederation, Fr. La Suisse, Ger. Schweiz, It. Svizzera; anc. Helvetia. ◆ federal republic C Europe
99 F17 **Swords Ir.** Sord, Sórd Choluim Chille. E Ireland
20 H13 **Swoyersville** Pennsylvania, NE USA
128 I10 **Syamozera, Ozero** ⊚ NW Russian Federation
128 M13 **Syamzha** Vologodskaya Oblast', NW Russian Federation
120 N13 **Syanno** Rus. Senno. Vitsyebskaya Voblasts', NE Belarus
121 K16 **Syarhyeyevichy** Rus. Sergeyevichi. Minskaya Voblasts', C Belarus
128 I12 **Syas'stroy** Leningradskaya Oblast', NW Russian Federation
Sycaminum see Hefa
32 M10 **Sycamore** Illinois, N USA
130 J3 **Sychëvka** Smolenskaya Oblast', W Russian Federation
113 H14 **Syców** Ger. Gross Wartenberg. Kalisz, SW Poland
12 E17 **Sydenham** ◆ Ontario, S Canada
Sydenham Island see Nonouti
191 T9 **Sydney** state capital New South Wales, SE Australia
11 R14 **Sydney** Cape Breton Island, Nova Scotia, SE Canada
11 R14 **Sydney** see Manra
11 R14 **Sydney Mines** Cape Breton Island, Nova Scotia, SE Canada
Syedlets see Siedlce
Syedpur see Saidpur
121 K18 **Syelishche** Minskaya Voblasts', C Belarus
121 J18 **Syemyezhava** Rus. Semezhevo. Minskaya Voblasts', C Belarus
Syene see Aswān
119 X6 **Syeverodonets'k Rus.** Severodonetsk. Luhans'ka Oblast', E Ukraine
167 T6 **Sÿiao Shan** island SE China
102 H11 **Syke** Niedersachsen, NW Germany

20 H10 **Syracuse** New York, NE USA
Syracuse see Siracusa
131 S2 **Syrdar'inskaya Oblast'** ◆ province C Russian Federation
Syrdar'inskaya Oblast' see Sirdaryo Wiloyati
Syrdariya see Syr Darya
150 L14 **Syr Darya** var. Sai Hun, Sir Darya, Syrdarya, Kaz. Syrdariya, Rus. Syrdar'ya, Uzb. Sirdaryo; anc. Jaxartes. ≈ C Asia
153 P10 **Syrdar'ya** Sirdaryo Wiloyati, E Uzbekistan
144 J6 **Syria** off. Syrian Arab Republic, var. Siria, Syrie, Ar. Al-Jumhūrīyah al-'Arabīyah as-Sūrīyah, Sūrīya. ◆ republic SW Asia
144 L9 **Syrian Desert** Ar. Al Hamad, Bādiyat ash Shām. desert SW Asia
Syrie see Syria
117 L22 **Sýrna** var. Sirna. island Kykládes, Greece, Aegean Sea
117 I20 **Sýros** var. Síros. island Kykládes, Greece, Aegean Sea
95 M18 **Sysmä** Mikkeli, S Finland
129 R12 **Sysola** ≈ NW Russian Federation
Syulemeshlii see Sredets
131 S2 **Syumsi** Udmurtskaya Respublika, NW Russian Federation
116 K10 **Syuyutliyka** ≈ C Bulgaria
194 M7 **Syvash, Zaliv** see Syvash, Zatoka
119 U12 **Syvash, Zatoka** Rus. Zaliv Syvash. inlet S Ukraine
131 Q6 **Syzran'** Samarskaya Oblast', W Russian Federation
113 N21 **Szabolcs-Szatmár-Bereg** off. Szabolcs-Szatmár-Bereg Megye. ◆ county E Hungary
112 G10 **Szamocin** Ger. Samotschin. Piła, N Poland
118 H8 **Szamos** var. Someş, Someşul, Ger. Samosch, Somesch. ≈ Hungary/Romania
Szamosújvár see Gherla
112 G11 **Szamotuły** Poznań, W Poland
Szarkowszczyzna see Sharkawshchyna
113 M24 **Szarvas** Békés, SE Hungary
Szászmagyarós see Măieruş
Szászrégen see Reghin
Szászsebes see Sebeş
Szászváros see Orăştie
113 P15 **Szczebrzeszyn** Zamość, SE Poland
112 D9 **Szczecin** Eng./Ger. Stettin. Szczecin, NW Poland
112 D9 **Szczecin** off. Województwo Szczecińskie; prev. Pomorze Zachodnie. ◆ province NW Poland
112 G8 **Szczecinek** Ger. Neustettin. Koszalin, NW Poland
Szczecińskie, Zalew var. Stettiner Haff, Ger. Oderhaff. bay Germany/Poland
113 K15 **Szczekociny** Częstochowa, S Poland
112 N8 **Szczuczyn** Łomża, NE Poland
Szczuczyn Nowogródzki see Shchuchyn
112 M8 **Szczytno** Ger. Ortelsburg. Olsztyn, NE Poland
Szechuan/Szechwan see Sichuan
113 K21 **Szécsény** Nógrád, N Hungary
113 L25 **Szeged** Ger. Szegedin, Rom. Seghedin, Csongrád, SE Hungary
Szegedin see Szeged
113 L25 **Szeghalom** Békés, SE Hungary
113 N23 **Szekelyhid** see Săcueni
Székelykeresztúr see Cristuru Secuiesc
113 I23 **Székesfehérvár** Ger. Stuhlweissenberg; anc. Alba Regia. Fejér, W Hungary
Szeklerburg see Miercurea-Ciuc
Szekler Neumarkt see Târgu Secuiesc
113 J25 **Szekszárd** Tolna, S Hungary
Szempcz/Szenc see Senec
113 J22 **Szendehro** Ger. Sankt Andrä. Pest, N Hungary
113 L24 **Szentes** Csongrád, SE Hungary
Szentágota see Agnita
113 F23 **Szentgotthárd** Eng. Saint Gotthard, Ger. Sankt Gotthard. Vas, W Hungary
Szentgyörgy see Đurđevac
Szenttamás see Srbobran
Széphely see Jebel
Szeping see Siping
Szered/Szerednye see Sered'
113 N21 **Szerencs** Borsod-Abaúj-Zemplén, NE Hungary
Szeret see Siret
Szeretfalva see Sărăţel
Szilágysomlyó see Şimleu Silvaniei
Szinna see Snina
Sziszek see Sisak
Szitás-Keresztúr see Cristuru Secuiesc
113 H25 **Szigetvár** Baranya, SW Hungary
Szkudy see Skuodas
Szlatina see Podravska Slatina
Szlavónia/Szlavonország see Slavonija
Szluin see Slunj
113 L23 **Szolnok** Jász-Nagykun-Szolnok, C Hungary

113 Ğ23 **Szombathely** Ger. Steinamanger; anc. Sabaria, Savaria. Vas, W Hungary
Szond/Szonta see Sonta
Szováta see Sovata
112 F13 **Szprotawa** Ger. Sprottau, Zielona Góra, W Poland
Sztálinváros see Dunaújváros
112 J8 **Sztum** Ger. Stuhm. Elbląg, N Poland
112 H10 **Szubin** Ger. Schubin. Bydgoszcz, W Poland
Szucsava see Suceava
Szurduk see Surduc
113 M14 **Szydłowiec** Ger. Schlelau. Radom, C Poland

T

179 P11 **Taal, Lake** ⊚ Luzon, NW Philippines
Taastrup see Tåstrup
113 I24 **Tab** Somogy, W Hungary
179 I24 **Tabaco** Luzon, N Philippines
194 M7 **Tabalo** Mussau Island, NE PNG
106 K5 **Tábara** Castilla-León, N Spain
195 P9 **Tabar Island** island Tabar Islands, N PNG
195 P9 **Tabar Islands** island group NE PNG
149 S7 **Tabas** var. Golshan. Khorāsān, C Iran
45 P15 **Tabasará, Serranía de** ▲ W Panama
43 U15 **Tabasco** ◆ state SE Mexico
43 U15 **Tabasco** see Grijalva, Río
131 Q2 **Tabashino** Respublika Mariy El, W Russian Federation
60 B13 **Tabatinga** Amazonas, N Brazil
76 G9 **Tabelbala** N Algeria
9 R15 **Taber** Alberta, SW Canada
176 W14 **Taberfane** Pulau Trangan, E Indonesia
97 L19 **Taberg** Jönköping, S Sweden
194 H12 **Tabibuga** var. Tabibug. Western Highlands, C PNG
203 O3 **Tabiteuea** prev. Drummond Island. atoll Tungaru, W Kiribati
179 Q12 **Tablas Island** island C Philippines
179 Pp12 **Tablas Strait** strait C Philippines
195 P10 **Table Bay** bay SE PNG
192 Q10 **Table Cape** headland North Island, NZ
11 S13 **Table Mountain** ▲ Newfoundland, Newfoundland and Labrador, E Canada
181 P17 **Table, Pointe de la** headland S Réunion
29 S8 **Table Rock Lake** ⊠ Arkansas/Missouri, C USA
38 K14 **Table Top** ▲ Arizona, SW USA
194 J13 **Tabletop, Mount** ▲ C PNG
126 Mm5 **Tabor** Respublika Sakha (Yakutiya), NE Russian Federation
31 S15 **Tabor** Iowa, C USA
113 D18 **Tábor** Jižní Čechy, SW Czech Republic
83 F21 **Tabora** Tabora, W Tanzania
83 F21 **Tabora** ◆ region C Tanzania
23 U12 **Tabor City** North Carolina, SE USA
153 Q10 **Taboshar** NW Tajikistan
78 I14 **Tabou** var. Tabu. S Ivory Coast
148 J2 **Tabrīz** var. Tebriz; anc. Tauris. Āzarbāyjān-e Khāvarī, NW Iran
Tabu see Tabou
203 W1 **Tabuaeran** prev. Fanning Island. atoll Line Islands, E Kiribati
194 E11 **Tabubil** Western, NW PNG
179 P8 **Tabuk** Luzon, N Philippines
146 J4 **Tabūk** Tabūk, NW Saudi Arabia
146 J5 **Tabūk** off. Minţaqat Tabūk. ◆ province NW Saudi Arabia
197 B12 **Tabwemasana, Mount** ▲ Espíritu Santo, W Vanuatu
97 O15 **Täby** Stockholm, C Sweden
43 N14 **Tacámbaro** Michoacán de Ocampo, SW Mexico
44 A5 **Tacaná, Volcan** ▲ Guatemala/Mexico
45 X16 **Tacarcuna, Cerro** ▲ SE Panama
Tachau see Tachov
164 J3 **Tacheng** var. Qoqek. Xinjiang Uygur Zizhiqu, NW China
56 H7 **Táchira** off. Estado Táchira. ◆ state W Venezuela
167 T13 **Tachoshui** N Taiwan
113 A17 **Tachov** Ger. Tachau. Západní Čechy, W Czech Republic
179 R13 **Tacloban** off. Tacloban City. Leyte, C Philippines
59 I19 **Tacna** Tacna, SE Peru
59 H18 **Tacna** off. Departamento de Tacna. ◆ department S Peru
34 G8 **Tacoma** Washington, NW USA
30 L11 **Taconic Range** ≈ NE USA
64 L6 **Taco Pozo** Formosa, N Argentina
59 M20 **Tacsara, Cordillera de** ▲ S Bolivia
63 E18 **Tacuarembó** prev. San Fructuoso. Tacuarembó, C Uruguay
63 E18 **Tacuarembó** ◆ department C Uruguay
63 F17 **Tacuarembó, Río** ≈ C Uruguay
85 I14 **Taculi** North Western, N Zambia
179 R16 **Tacurong** Mindanao, S Philippines

TADAMU-GAWA – TAPOA

171 Kk13 **Tadamu-gawa** ≈ Honshū, C Japan
79 V8 **Tadek** ≈ NW Niger
76 J9 **Tademaït, Plateau du** plateau C Algeria
197 K6 **Tadine** Province des Îles Loyauté, E New Caledonia
82 L11 **Tadjoura** E Djibouti
82 M11 **Tadjoura, Golfe de** Eng. Gulf of Tajura. inlet E Djibouti
Tadmor/Tadmur see Tudmur
9 W10 **Tadoule Lake** ◎ Manitoba, C Canada
13 S8 **Tadoussac** Québec, SE Canada
161 H18 **Tādpatri** Andhra Pradesh, E India
Tadzhikabad see Tojikobod
Tadzhikistan see Tajikistan
169 Y14 **T'aebaek-sanmaek** ▲▲ E South Korea
169 V15 **Taechŏng-do** island NW South Korea
169 X13 **Taedong-gang** ≈ C North Korea
169 Y16 **Taegu** off. Taegu-gwangyŏksi, var. Daegu, Jap. Taikyū. SE South Korea
Taehan-haehyŏp see Korea Strait
Taehan Min'guk see South Korea
169 Y15 **Taejŏn** off. Taejŏn-gwangyŏksi, Jap. Taiden. C South Korea
200 T11 **Tafahi** island N Tonga
107 Q4 **Tafalla** Navarra, N Spain
77 M12 **Tafassâsset, Oued** ≈ SE Algeria
79 W7 **Tafassâsset, Ténéré du** desert N Niger
57 U11 **Tafelberg** ▲ S Suriname
99 J21 **Taff** ≈ SE Wales, UK
Tafila/Ṭafīlah, Muḥāfaẓat aṭ see Aṭ Ṭafīlah
79 N15 **Tafiré** N Ivory Coast
148 M6 **Tafresh** Markazī, W Iran
149 Q9 **Taft** Yazd, C Iran
37 R13 **Taft** California, W USA
27 T14 **Taft** Texas, SW USA
149 W12 **Taftān, Kūh-e** ▲ SE Iran
37 R13 **Taft Heights** California, W USA
201 Y14 **Tafunsak** Kosrae, E Micronesia
198 Aa8 **Tāga** Savai'i, SW Western Samoa
155 O6 **Tagāb** Kāpīsā, E Afghanistan
41 O8 **Tagagawik River** ≈ Alaska, USA
171 M13 **Tagajō** var. Tagazyô. Miyagi, Honshū, C Japan
130 K12 **Taganrog** Rostovskaya Oblast', SW Russian Federation
130 K12 **Taganrog, Gulf of** Rus. Taganrogskiy Zaliv, Ukr. Tahanroz'ka Zatoka. gulf Russian Federation/Ukraine
Taganrogskiy Zaliv see Taganrog, Gulf of
78 J8 **Tagant** ◐ region C Mauritania
154 M14 **Tagas** Baluchistān, SW Pakistan
170 D13 **Tagawa** Fukuoka, Kyūshū, SW Japan
179 P11 **Tagaytay** Luzon, N Philippines
Tagazyô see Tagajō
179 Qq14 **Tagbilaran** var. Tagbilaran City. Bohol, C Philippines
108 B10 **Taggia** Liguria, NW Italy
79 V9 **Taghouaji, Massif de** ▲ C Niger
109 J15 **Tagliacozzo** Lazio, C Italy
108 J7 **Tagliamento** ≈ NE Italy
179 R15 **Tagoloan** Mindanao, S Philippines
155 N3 **Tagow Bāy** var. Bai. Sar-e Pol, N Afghanistan
Tagtabazar see Takhtabazar
61 L17 **Taguatinga** Tocantins, C Brazil
195 Q17 **Tagula** Tagula Island, SE PNG
195 P17 **Tagula Island** prev. Southeast Island, Sudest Island. island SE PNG
179 Rr15 **Tagum** Mindanao, S Philippines
56 C7 **Tagún, Cerro** elevation Colombia/Panama
107 P7 **Tagus** Port. Rio Tejo, Sp. Río Tajo. ≈ Portugal/Spain
66 M9 **Tagus Plain** undersea feature E Atlantic Ocean
203 S10 **Tahaa** island Îles Sous le Vent, W French Polynesia
203 U10 **Tahanea** atoll Îles Tuamotu, C French Polynesia
Tahanroz'ka Zatoka see Taganrog, Gulf of
171 I16 **Tahara** Aichi, Honshū, SW Japan
76 K12 **Tahat** ▲ SE Algeria
169 U5 **Ta He** ≈ NE China
169 U4 **Tahe** Heilongjiang, NE China
168 G9 **Tahilt** Govĭ-Altay, W Mongolia
203 T10 **Tahiti** island Îles du Vent, W French Polynesia
Tahiti, Archipel de see Société, Archipel de la
120 E4 **Tahkuna nina** headland W Estonia
154 K12 **Tāhlāb** ≈ W Pakistan
154 K12 **Tāhlāb, Dasht-i** desert SW Pakistan
29 R10 **Tahlequah** Oklahoma, C USA
37 Q6 **Tahoe City** California, W USA
37 P6 **Tahoe, Lake** ◎ California/Nevada, W USA
Tahoena see Tahuna
27 N6 **Tahoka** Texas, SW USA
34 F8 **Taholah** Washington, NW USA
79 T11 **Tahoua** Tahoua, W Niger
79 T11 **Tahoua** ◐ department W Niger
33 P3 **Tahquamenon Falls** waterfall Michigan, N USA
33 P4 **Tahquamenon River** ≈ Michigan, N USA
145 V10 **Ṭahrīr** S Iraq
8 K17 **Tahsis** Vancouver Island, British Columbia, SW Canada
Tahta see Takhta
77 W9 **Tahta** C Egypt
142 L15 **Tahtalı Dağları** ▲▲ C Turkey
59 I14 **Tahuamanu, Río** ≈ Bolivia/Peru
58 F13 **Tahuanía, Río** ≈ E Peru
203 X7 **Tahuata** island Îles Marquises, NE French Polynesia
175 S6 **Tahulandang, Pulau** island N Indonesia
175 S5 **Tahuna** prev. Tahoena. Pulau Sangihe, N Indonesia
176 Yy10 **Tahun, Danau** see Tahun, Danau
78 L17 **Taï** SW Ivory Coast
167 P5 **Tai'an** Shandong, E China
203 R8 **Taiarapu, Presqu'île de** peninsula Tahiti, W French Polynesia
Taibad see Tāybād
166 K7 **Taibai Shan** ▲ C China
107 Q12 **Taibilla, Sierra de** ▲▲ S Spain
169 Q12 **Taibus Qi** var. Baochang. Nei Mongol Zizhiqu, N China
Taichū see T'aichung
167 S13 **T'aichung** Jap. Taichū; prev. Taiwan. C Taiwan
Taiden see Taejŏn
193 E23 **Taieri** ≈ South Island, NZ
117 E21 **Taígetos** ▲▲ S Greece
167 N4 **Taihang Shan** ▲▲ C China
192 M11 **Taihape** Manawatu-Wanganui, North Island, NZ
167 O7 **Taihe** Anhui, E China
167 O12 **Taihe** Jiangxi, S China
Taihoku see T'aipei
167 R8 **Tai Hu** ◎ E China
167 P9 **Taihu** Anhui, E China
167 O6 **Taikang** Henan, C China
172 P7 **Taiki** Hokkaidō, NE Japan
177 Ff8 **Taikkyi** Yangon, SW Myanmar
Taikyū see Taegu
169 U8 **Tailai** Heilongjiang, NE China
173 Ff10 **Taileleo** Pulau Siberut, W Indonesia
190 J10 **Tailem Bend** South Australia
98 I8 **Tain** N Scotland, UK
167 S14 **T'ainan** Jap. Tainan; prev. Dainan. S Taiwan
117 E22 **Taínaro, Ákra** headland S Greece
167 Q11 **Taining** Fujian, SE China
203 W7 **Taiohae** prev. Madisonville. Nuku Hiva, NE French Polynesia
167 T13 **T'aipei** Jap. Taihoku; prev. Daihoku. ● (Taiwan) N Taiwan
174 Gg3 **Taiping** Perak, Peninsular Malaysia
169 S8 **Taiping Ling** ▲ NE China
172 N6 **Taisei** Hokkaidō, NE Japan
170 F12 **Taisha** Shimane, Honshū, SW Japan
111 R4 **Taiskirchen** Oberösterreich, NW Austria
65 F20 **Taitao, Peninsula de** peninsula S Chile
Taitō see T'aitung
167 T14 **T'aitung** Jap. Taitō. S Taiwan
94 M13 **Taivalkoski** Oulu, E Finland
95 K19 **Taivassalo** Turku-Pori, SW Finland
167 T14 **Taiwan** off. Republic of China, var. Formosa, Formo'sa. ◆ republic E Asia
140 Q11 **Taiwan** var. Formosa. island E Asia
Taiwan see T'aichung
T'aiwan Haihsia/Taiwan Haixia see Taiwan Strait
Taiwan Shan see Chungyang Shanmo
167 R13 **Taiwan Strait** var. Formosa Strait, Chin. T'aiwan Haihsia, Taiwan Haixia. strait China/Taiwan
167 N4 **Taiyuan** prev. T'ai-yuan, T'ai-yüan, Yangku. Shanxi, C China
167 R7 **Taizhou** Jiangsu, E China
Taizhou see Linhai
147 O16 **Ta'izz** SW Yemen
147 O16 **Ta'izz** ✕ SW Yemen
77 P12 **Tajarhī** SW Libya
153 P13 **Tajikistan** off. Republic of Tajikistan, Rus. Tadzhikistan, Taj. Jumhurii Tojikiston; prev. Tajik S.S.R. ◆ republic C Asia
Tajik S.S.R see Tajikistan
171 Kk14 **Tajima** Fukushima, Honshū, C Japan
Tajoe see Tayu
Tajo, Río see Tagus
44 B5 **Tajumulco, Volcán** ▲ W Guatemala
107 P7 **Tajuña** ≈ C Spain
Tajura, Gulf of see Tadjoura, Golfe de
178 H9 **Tak** var. Rahaeng. Tak, W Thailand
201 U4 **Taka Atoll** var. Tōke. atoll Ratak Chain, N Marshall Islands
171 L16 **Takahagi** Ibaraki, Honshū, S Japan
170 Ff13 **Takahashi** var. Takahasi. Okayama, Honshū, SW Japan
170 F13 **Takahashi-gawa** ≈ Honshū, SW Japan
Takahasi see Takahashi
201 P12 **Takaieu Island** island E Micronesia
192 I13 **Takaka** Tasman, South Island, NZ
175 P13 **Takalar** Sulawesi, C Indonesia
170 Ff14 **Takamatsu** var. Takamatu. Kagawa, Shikoku, SW Japan
Takamatu see Takamatsu
170 Cc14 **Takamori** Kumamoto, Kyūshū, SW Japan
170 Cc16 **Takanabe** Miyazaki, Kyūshū, SW Japan
175 O16 **Takan, Gunung** ▲ Pulau Sumba, S Indonesia
171 M9 **Takanosu** Akita, Honshū, C Japan
Takao see Kaohsiung
171 Ii13 **Takaoka** Toyama, Honshū, SW Japan
192 N12 **Takapau** Hawke's Bay, North Island, NZ
203 U9 **Takapoto** atoll Îles Tuamotu, C French Polynesia
192 L5 **Takapuna** Auckland, North Island, NZ
171 Gg14 **Takarazuka** Hyōgo, Honshū, SW Japan
203 U9 **Takaroa** atoll Îles Tuamotu, C French Polynesia
171 Jj15 **Takasaki** Gunma, Honshū, S Japan
171 Gg15 **Takatsuki** var. Takatuki. Ōsaka, Honshū, SW Japan
Takatuki see Takatsuki
171 Ii14 **Takayama** Gifu, Honshū, SW Japan
171 Hh13 **Takefu** var. Takehu. Fukui, Honshū, SW Japan
170 F14 **Takehara** Hiroshima, Honshū, SW Japan
Takehu see Takefu
170 C13 **Takeo** Saga, Kyūshū, SW Japan
Takeo see Takêv
170 B17 **Take-shima** island Nansei-shotō, SW Japan
148 M5 **Tākestān** var. Takistan; prev. Siadehan. Zanjān, W Iran
170 D14 **Taketa** Ōita, Kyūshū, SW Japan
178 J14 **Takêv** prev. Takeo. Takêv, S Cambodia
178 Hh10 **Tak Fah** Nakhon Sawan, C Thailand
145 T13 **Takhādīd** well S Iraq
155 R3 **Takhār** ◐ province NE Afghanistan
Takhiatash see Takhiatosh
152 H8 **Takhiatosh** Rus. Takhiatash. Qoraqalpoghiston Respublikasi, W Uzbekistan
178 J13 **Ta Khmau** Kândal, S Cambodia
152 H9 **Takhta** Turkm. Tahta. Dashkhovuzskiy Velayat, N Turkmenistan
152 J16 **Takhtabazar** var. Tagtabazar. Maryyskiy Velayat, S Turkmenistan
151 O8 **Takhtabrod** Kokshetau, N Kazakhstan
152 H7 **Takhtakŭpir** Rus. Takhtakupyr. Qoraqalpoghiston Respublikasi, NW Uzbekistan
Takhtakupyr see Takhtakŭpir
148 M8 **Takht-e Shāh, Kūh-e** ▲ C Iran
79 V12 **Takiéta** Zinder, S Niger
15 I5 **Takijuq Lake** ◎ Northwest Territories, NW Canada
172 P4 **Takikawa** Hokkaidō, NE Japan
172 Pp4 **Takinoue** Hokkaidō, NE Japan
Takistan see Tākestān
193 B23 **Takitimu Mountains** ▲▲ South Island, NZ
Takkaze see Tekezē
172 N10 **Takko** Aomori, Honshū, C Japan
8 L13 **Takla Lake** ◎ British Columbia, SW Canada
Takla Makan Desert see Taklimakan Shamo
164 H9 **Taklimakan Shamo** Eng. Takla Makan Desert. desert NW China
178 Jj12 **Takôk** Môndól Kiri, E Cambodia
175 P9 **Takolekaju, Pegunungan** ▲▲ Sulawesi, N Indonesia
41 P10 **Takotna** Alaska, USA
Takow see Kaohsiung
126 Kk14 **Taksimo** Respublika Buryatiya, S Russian Federation
170 Cc13 **Taku** Saga, Kyūshū, SW Japan
8 I10 **Taku** ≈ British Columbia, W Canada
177 G15 **Takua Pa** var. Ban Takua Pa. Phangnga, SW Thailand
79 W16 **Takum** Taraba, E Nigeria
203 V10 **Takume** atoll Îles Tuamotu, C French Polynesia
202 L16 **Takutea** island S Cook Islands
195 U11 **Takuu Islands** prev. Mortlock Group. island group NE PNG
121 L18 **Tal'** Rus. Tal'. Minskaya Voblasts', S Belarus
42 L13 **Tala** Jalisco, C Mexico
63 F19 **Tala** Canelones, S Uruguay
Talabriga see Aveiro, Portugal
Talabriga see Talavera de la Reina, Spain
121 N14 **Talachyn** Rus. Tolochin. Vitsyebskaya Voblasts', NE Belarus
155 U7 **Talagang** Punjab, E Pakistan
161 J23 **Talaimannar** Northern Province, NW Sri Lanka
119 R3 **Talalayivka** Chernihivs'ka Oblast', N Ukraine
45 O15 **Talamanca, Cordillera de** ▲▲ S Costa Rica
58 A9 **Talara** Piura, NW Peru
106 L11 **Talarrubias** Extremadura, W Spain
153 S8 **Talas** Talasskaya Oblast', NW Kyrgyzstan
153 S8 **Talas** ≈ NW Kyrgyzstan
195 N11 **Talasea** New Britain, E PNG
Talas Oblasty see Talasskaya Oblast'
153 S8 **Talasskaya Oblast'** Kir. Talas Oblasty. ◐ province NW Kyrgyzstan
153 S8 **Talasskiy Alatau, Khrebet** ▲▲ Kazakhstan/Kyrgyzstan
Talat see Maha Sarakham
79 U12 **Talata Mafara** Sokoto, N Nigeria
175 Ss4 **Talaud, Kepulauan** island group E Indonesia
106 M9 **Talavera de la Reina** anc. Caesarobriga, Talabriga. Castilla-La Mancha, C Spain
106 J11 **Talavera la Real** Extremadura, W Spain
194 L12 **Talawe, Mount** ▲ New Britain, C PNG
25 S5 **Talbotton** Georgia, SE USA
191 R7 **Talbragar River** ≈ New South Wales, SE Australia
64 G13 **Talca** Maule, C Chile
64 F13 **Talcahuano** Bío Bío, C Chile
160 N12 **Tālcher** Orissa, E India
27 W5 **Talco** Texas, SW USA
151 V14 **Taldykorgan** Kaz. Taldyqorghan; prev. Taldy-Kurgan. Taldykorgan, SE Kazakhstan
151 U13 **Taldykorgan** off. Taldykorganskaya Oblast'; prev. Taldy-Kurganskaya Oblast'. ◐ province SE Kazakhstan
Taldykorganskaya Oblast'/Taldy-Kurgan/Taldy-Kurganskaya Oblast'/Taldyqorghan see Taldykorgan
153 Y7 **Taldy-Suu** Issyk-Kul'skaya Oblast', E Kyrgyzstan
153 U10 **Taldy-Suu** Oshskaya Oblast', SW Kyrgyzstan
Tal-e Khosravī see Yāsūj
200 Ss14 **Taleki Tonga** island Otu Tolu Group, C Tonga
200 Ss13 **Taleki Vavu'u** island Otu Tolu Group, C Tonga
104 J13 **Talence** Gironde, SW France
151 U16 **Talgar** Kaz. Talghar. Almaty, SE Kazakhstan
Talghar see Talgar
175 Rr10 **Taliabu, Pulau** island Kepulauan Sula, C Indonesia
117 L22 **Taliarós, Ákra** headland Astypálaia, Kykládes, Greece, Aegean Sea
Ta-lien see Dalian
29 Q12 **Talihina** Oklahoma, C USA
Talimardzhan see Tollimarjon
Talin see T'alin
143 T12 **T'alin** Rus. Talin; prev. Verin T'alin. W Armenia
83 E15 **Tali Post** Bahr el Gabel, S Sudan
Taliq-an see Tāloqān
Talış Dağları see Talish Mountains
148 L2 **Talish Mountains** Az. Talış Dağları, Per. Kūhhā-ye Ṭavālesh, Rus. Talyshskiye Gory. ▲▲ Azerbaijan/Iran
125 F11 **Talitsa** Sverdlovskaya Oblast', C Russian Federation
175 O16 **Taliwang** Sumbawa, C Indonesia
121 L17 **Tal'ka** Rus. Tal'ka. Minskaya Voblasts', C Belarus
Talkang see Dorbod
41 R11 **Talkeetna** Alaska, USA
41 R11 **Talkeetna Mountains** ▲▲ Alaska, USA
Talkhof see Puurmani
94 H2 **Tálknafjördhur** Vestfirdhir, W Iceland
145 Q3 **Tall 'Abṭah** N Iraq
144 M2 **Tall Abyaḍ** var. Tell Abiad. Ar Raqqah, N Syria
25 Q4 **Talladega** Alabama, S USA
145 Q2 **Tall 'Afar** N Iraq
25 S8 **Tallahassee** prev. Muskogean. state capital Florida, SE USA
24 L2 **Tallahatchie River** ≈ Mississippi, S USA
Tall al Abyaḍ see Tall Abyaḍ
145 W12 **Tall al Laḥm** S Iraq
191 N12 **Tallangatta** Victoria, SE Australia
25 R4 **Tallapoosa River** ≈ Alabama/Georgia, S USA
105 T13 **Tallard** Hautes-Alpes, SE France
145 Q3 **Tall ash Sha'īr** N Iraq
25 Q5 **Tallassee** Alabama, S USA
145 R4 **Tall 'Azbah** NW Iraq
144 I5 **Tall Bīsah** Ḥimṣ, W Syria
145 R3 **Tall Ḥassūnah** N Iraq
145 Q2 **Tall Ḥuqnah** var. Tell Huqnah. N Iraq
Tallin see Tallinn
120 G3 **Tallinn** Ger. Reval, Rus. Tallin; prev. Revel. ● (Estonia) Harjumaa, NW Estonia
120 H3 **Tallinn** ✕ Harjumaa, NW Estonia
144 H5 **Tall Kalakh** var. Tell Kalakh. Ḥimṣ, C Syria
145 R2 **Tall Kayf** NW Iraq
Tall Kūchak see Tall Kūshik
145 P2 **Tall Kūshik** var. Tall Kūchak. Al Ḥasakah, E Syria
33 U12 **Tallmadge** Ohio, N USA
24 J5 **Tallulah** Louisiana, S USA
145 Q2 **Tall 'Uwaynāt** NW Iraq
145 Q2 **Tall Ẓāhir** N Iraq
126 H14 **Tal'menka** Altayskiy Kray, S Russian Federation
126 I8 **Talnakh** Taymyrskiy (Dolgano-Nenetskiy) Avtonomnyy Okrug, N Russian Federation
119 P7 **Tal'ne** Rus. Tal'noye. Cherkas'ka Oblast', C Ukraine
Tal'noye see Tal'ne
82 E12 **Talodi** Southern Kordofan, C Sudan
196 B16 **Talofofo** SE Guam
196 B16 **Talofofo Bay** bay SE Guam
28 L9 **Taloga** Oklahoma, C USA
127 O10 **Talon** Magadanskaya Oblast', E Russian Federation
12 H11 **Talon, Lake** ◎ Ontario, S Canada
155 R2 **Tāloqān** var. Taliq-an. Takhār, NE Afghanistan
130 M8 **Talovaya** Voronezhskaya Oblast', W Russian Federation
175 Qq10 **Talowa, Teluk** bay Sulawesi, C Indonesia
15 Kk3 **Taloyoak** prev. Spence Bay. Northwest Territories, N Canada
27 Q8 **Talpa** Texas, SW USA
42 K13 **Talpa de Allende** Jalisco, C Mexico
25 S9 **Talquin, Lake** ▣ Florida, SE USA
Talsen see Talsi
168 H9 **Talshand** Govĭ-Altay, C Mongolia
120 E8 **Talsi** Ger. Talsen. Talsi, NW Latvia
149 V11 **Tal Sīāh** Sīstān va Balūchestān, SE Iran
64 G6 **Taltal** Antofagasta, N Chile
15 I18 **Taltson** ≈ Northwest Territories, NW Canada
174 H8 **Taluk** Sumatera, W Indonesia
94 J8 **Talvik** Finnmark, N Norway
190 M7 **Talyawalka Creek** ≈ New South Wales, SE Australia
Talyshskiye Gory see Talish Mountains
31 W14 **Tama** Iowa, C USA
Tama Abu, Banjaran see Penambo, Banjaran
175 N5 **Tamabo, Banjaran** ▲▲ East Malaysia
202 B16 **Tamakautoga** SW Niue
131 N7 **Tamala** Penzenskaya Oblast', W Russian Federation
79 P15 **Tamale** C Ghana
170 Cc13 **Tamana** Kumamoto, Kyūshū, SW Japan
203 P3 **Tamana** prev. Rotcher Island. atoll Tungaru, W Kiribati
170 Ff14 **Tamano** Okayama, Honshū, SW Japan
76 K12 **Tamanrasset** var. Tamenghest. S Algeria
76 J13 **Tamanrasset** wadi Algeria/ Mali
177 G2 **Tamanthi** Sagaing, N Myanmar
99 I24 **Tamar** ≈ SW England, UK
Tamar see Tudmur
56 H9 **Támara** Casanare, C Colombia
56 F7 **Tamar, Alto de** ▲ C Colombia
181 X16 **Tamarin** E Mauritius
107 T5 **Tamarite de Litera** var. Tararite de Llitera. Aragón, NE Spain
113 I24 **Tamási** Tolna, S Hungary
Tamatave see Toamasina
43 O9 **Tamaulipas** ◐ state C Mexico
43 P10 **Tamaulipas, Sierra de** ▲▲ C Mexico
58 F12 **Tamaya, Río** ≈ E Peru
42 I9 **Tamazula** Durango, C Mexico
42 L14 **Tamazula** Jalisco, C Mexico
Tamazulápam see Tamazulapán
43 Q15 **Tamazulapán** var. Tamazulápam. Oaxaca, SE Mexico
43 P12 **Tamazunchale** San Luis Potosí, C Mexico
78 H11 **Tambacounda** SE Senegal
85 M16 **Tambara** Manica, C Mozambique
175 Pp9 **Tambarana** Sulawesi, N Indonesia
79 T13 **Tambawel** Sokoto, NW Nigeria
195 W15 **Tambea** Guadalcanal, C Solomon Islands
174 Jj7 **Tambelan, Kepulauan** island group W Indonesia
59 E15 **Tambo de Mora** Ica, W Peru
63 E17 **Tambores** Paysandú, W Uruguay
59 F14 **Tambo, Río** ≈ C Peru
58 F7 **Tamboryacu, Río** ≈ N Peru
130 M7 **Tambov** Tambovskaya Oblast', W Russian Federation
130 L6 **Tambovskaya Oblast'** ◐ province W Russian Federation
106 H3 **Tambre** ≈ NW Spain
175 Nn3 **Tambunan** Sabah, East Malaysia
83 C15 **Tambura** Western Equatoria, SW Sudan
175 P8 **Tambu, Teluk** bay Sulawesi, C Indonesia
Tamchaket see Tâmchekket
78 J9 **Tâmchekket** var. Tamchaket. Hodh el Gharbi, S Mauritania
178 Jj7 **Tam Điệp** Ninh Bình, N Vietnam
Tamdybulak see Tomdibuloq
56 H8 **Tame** Arauca, C Colombia
106 H6 **Tâmega, Rio** Sp. Río Támega. ≈ Portugal/Spain
117 H20 **Tamélos, Ákra** headland Kéa, Kykládes, Greece, Aegean Sea
Tamenghest see Tamanrasset
79 V8 **Tamgak, Adrar** ▲ C Niger
78 I13 **Tamgue** ▲ NW Guinea
43 Q12 **Tamiahua** Veracruz-Llave, E Mexico
43 Q12 **Tamiahua, Laguna de** lagoon E Mexico
25 Y16 **Tamiami Canal** canal Florida, SE USA
196 F17 **Tamil Harbor** harbor Yap, W Micronesia
161 H21 **Tamil Nādu** prev. Madras. ◐ state SE India
101 H20 **Tamines** Namur, S Belgium
118 E12 **Tamiš** Ger. Temesch, Hung. Temes, SCr. Tamiš. ≈ Romania/Yugoslavia
178 Kk10 **Tam Ky** Quang Nam-Đa Nẵng, C Vietnam
Tammerfors see Tampere
Tammisaari see Ekenäs
97 N14 **Tämnaren** ◎ C Sweden
203 Q7 **Tamotoe, Passe** passage Tahiti, W French Polynesia
25 V12 **Tampa** Florida, SE USA
25 V12 **Tampa** ✕ Florida, SE USA
25 V13 **Tampa Bay** bay Florida, SE USA
95 L18 **Tampere** Swe. Tammerfors. Häme, SW Finland
43 Q11 **Tampico** Tamaulipas, C Mexico
175 Qq12 **Tampo** Pulau Muna, C Indonesia
178 Kk11 **Tam Quan** Bình Định, C Vietnam
176 V9 **Tamrau, Pegunungan** ▲▲ Irian Jaya, E Indonesia
168 J13 **Tamsag Muchang** Nei Mongol Zizhiqu, N China
Tamsal see Tamsalu
120 I4 **Tamsalu** Ger. Tamsal. Lääne-Virumaa, NE Estonia
111 S8 **Tamsweg** Salzburg, SW Austria
177 Ff3 **Tamu** Sagaing, N Myanmar
43 P12 **Tamuín** San Luis Potosí, C Mexico
196 C15 **Tamuning** NW Guam
191 T6 **Tamworth** New South Wales, SE Australia
99 M19 **Tamworth** C England, UK
94 L8 **Tana** Finnmark, N Norway
94 M8 **Tana** var. Tenojoki, Fin. Teno, Lapp. Deatnu. ≈ Finland/Norway see also Teno
83 K19 **Tana** ≈ SE Kenya
170 G17 **Tanabe** Wakayama, Honshū, SW Japan
41 T10 **Tanacross** Alaska, USA
94 L7 **Tanafjorden** fjord N Norway
40 G17 **Tanaga Island** island Aleutian Islands, Alaska, USA
40 G17 **Tanaga Volcano** ▲ Tanaga Island, Alaska, USA
109 M18 **Tanagro** ≈ S Italy
82 H11 **T'ana Häyk'** Eng. Lake Tana. ◎ NW Ethiopia
173 F8 **Tanahbela, Pulau** island Kepulauan Batu, W Indonesia
175 Pp15 **Tanahjampea, Pulau** island W Indonesia
173 Ff8 **Tanahmasa, Pulau** island Kepulauan Batu, W Indonesia
Tanais see Don
158 L10 **Tanakpur** Uttar Pradesh, N India
Tana, Lake see T'ana Häyk'
189 P5 **Tanami Desert** desert Northern Territory, N Australia
178 Jj14 **Tân An** Long An, S Vietnam
41 Q9 **Tanana** Alaska, USA
Tananarive see Antananarivo
41 Q9 **Tanana River** ≈ Alaska, USA
97 C16 **Tananger** Rogaland, S Norway
196 H5 **Tanapag** Saipan, S Northern Mariana Islands
196 H5 **Tanapag, Puetton** bay Saipan, S Northern Mariana Islands
108 C9 **Tanaro** ≈ N Italy
169 Y12 **Tanch'ŏn** E North Korea
42 M14 **Tancítaro, Cerro** ▲ C Mexico
159 N12 **Tānda** Uttar Pradesh, N India
79 O15 **Tanda** E Ivory Coast
179 Rr14 **Tandag** Mindanao, S Philippines
118 L14 **Țăndărei** Ialomița, SE Romania
65 N14 **Tandil** Buenos Aires, E Argentina
80 H12 **Tandjilé** off. Préfecture du Tandjilé. ◐ prefecture SW Chad
Tandjoeng see Tanjung
Tandjoengpandan see Tanjungpandan
Tandjoengpinang see Tanjungpinang
Tandjoengredeb see Tanjungredeb
155 Q16 **Tando Allāhyār** Sind, SE Pakistan
155 Q17 **Tando Bāgo** Sind, SE Pakistan
155 Q16 **Tando Muhammad Khān** Sind, SE Pakistan
190 L7 **Tandou Lake** seasonal lake New South Wales, SE Australia
96 L11 **Tandsjöborg** Gävleborg, C Sweden
161 H15 **Tāndūr** Andhra Pradesh, C India
170 Bb17 **Tanega-shima** island Nansei-shotō, SW Japan
172 N10 **Taneichi** Iwate, Honshū, C Japan
Tanen Taunggyi see Tane Range
178 H8 **Tane Range** Bur. Tanen Taunggyi. ▲▲ W Thailand
113 P15 **Tanew** ≈ SE Poland
23 W2 **Taneytown** Maryland, NE USA
76 H12 **Tanezrouft** desert Algeria/Mali
144 L7 **Ṭanf, Jabal aṭ** ▲ SE Syria
83 J21 **Tanga** Tanga, E Tanzania
83 I22 **Tanga** ◐ region E Tanzania
159 T14 **Tangail** Dhaka, C Bangladesh
195 Q9 **Tanga Islands** island group NE PNG
161 K26 **Tangalla** Southern Province, S Sri Lanka
Tanganyika and Zanzibar see Tanzania
70 J13 **Tanganyika, Lake** ◎ E Africa
58 E7 **Tangarana, Río** ≈ N Peru
195 W16 **Tangarare** Guadalcanal, C Solomon Islands
203 V16 **Tangaroa, Maunga** ▲ Easter Island, Chile, E Pacific Ocean
76 G5 **Tanger** var. Tangiers, Tangier, Fr./Ger. Tangerk, Sp. Tánger; anc. Tingis. NW Morocco
174 J14 **Tangerang** Jawa, C Indonesia
Tangerk see Tanger
102 M12 **Tangermünde** Sachsen-Anhalt, C Germany
162 K10 **Tanggula Shan** var. Dangla, Tangla Range. ▲▲ W China
165 N13 **Tanggula Shan** ▲ W China
Tanggulashan see Tuotuoheyan
162 K10 **Tanggula Shankou** pass W China
167 N7 **Tanghe** Henan, C China
155 T5 **Tangi** North-West Frontier Province, NW Pakistan
Tangier see Tanger
23 Y5 **Tangier Island** island Virginia, NE USA
Tangiers see Tanger
24 K8 **Tangipahoa River** ≈ Louisiana, S USA
Tangla Range see Tanggula Shan
171 H13 **Tango-hantō** peninsula Honshū, SW Japan
162 I10 **Tangra Yumco** var. Tangro Tso. ◎ W China
Tangro Tso see Tangra Yumco
163 T7 **Tangshan** var. T'ang-shan. Hebei, E China
179 Qq15 **Tangub** var. Tangub City. Mindanao, S Philippines
79 R14 **Tanguiéta** NW Benin
169 X7 **Tangwang He** ≈ NE China
169 X7 **Tangyuan** Heilongjiang, NE China
94 M11 **Tanhua** Lappi, N Finland
176 Uu16 **Tanimbar, Kepulauan** island group Maluku, E Indonesia
Tanintharyi see Tenasserim
145 U4 **Tānjarō** ≈ E Iraq
133 T15 **Tanjong Piai** headland Peninsular Malaysia
Tanjore see Thanjāvūr
175 N10 **Tanjung** prev. Tandjoeng. Borneo, C Indonesia
175 Oo6 **Tanjungbatu** Borneo, N Indonesia
Tanjungkarang see Bandarlampung
174 J11 **Tanjunglabu** Pulau Lepar, W Indonesia
174 J10 **Tanjungpandan** prev. Tandjoengpandan. Pulau Belitung, W Indonesia
174 I7 **Tanjungpinang** prev. Tandjoengpinang. Pulau Bintan, W Indonesia
175 O6 **Tanjungredeb** var. Tanjungredep; prev. Tandjoengredeb. Borneo, C Indonesia
Tanjungredep see Tanjungredeb
155 S8 **Tank** North-West Frontier Province, NW Pakistan
197 D16 **Tanna** island S Vanuatu
95 F17 **Tännäs** Jämtland, C Sweden
Tannenhof see Krynica
110 K7 **Tannheim** Tirol, W Austria
Tannu-Tuva see Tyva, Respublika
175 Rr10 **Tano** Pulau Taliabu, E Indonesia
79 O17 **Tano** ≈ S Ghana
158 D10 **Tanot** Rājasthān, NW India
79 V11 **Tanout** Zinder, C Niger
43 P12 **Tanquián** San Luis Potosí, C Mexico
79 R13 **Tansarga** E Burkina
178 Jj14 **Tan Son Nhat** ✕ (Hô Chi Minh) Tây Ninh, S Vietnam
77 V8 **Tanta** var. Tantā, Tantâ. N Egypt
76 D9 **Tan-Tan** SW Morocco
43 P12 **Tantoyuca** Veracruz-Llave, E Mexico
158 J12 **Tāntpur** Uttar Pradesh, N India
Tan-tung see Dandong
40 M12 **Tanunak** Alaska, USA
177 Ff5 **Ta-nyaung** Magwe, W Myanmar
178 J5 **Tân Yên** Tuyên Quang, N Vietnam
83 F22 **Tanzania** off. United Republic of Tanzania, Swa. Jamhuri ya Muungano wa Tanzania; prev. German East Africa, Tanganyika and Zanzibar. ◆ republic E Africa
Tanzania, Jamhuri ya Muungano wa see Tanzania
169 U9 **Tao'an** var. Taoan, Taonan. Jilin, NE China
169 T8 **Tao'er He** ≈ NE China
165 U11 **Tao He** ≈ C China
T'aon-an see Baicheng
Taongi see Bokaak Atoll
109 M23 **Taormina** anc. Tauromenium. Sicilia, Italy, C Mediterranean Sea
39 S9 **Taos** New Mexico, SW USA
Taoudenit see Taoudenni
79 O6 **Taoudenni** var. Taoudenit. Tombouctou, N Mali
76 G6 **Taounate** N Morocco
167 S13 **T'aoyüan** Jap. Tōen. N Taiwan
120 I3 **Tapa** Ger. Taps. Lääne-Virumaa, NE Estonia
43 V17 **Tapachula** Chiapas, SE Mexico
Tapaiu see Gvardeysk
61 H14 **Tapajós, Rio** var. Tapajóz. ≈ NW Brazil
Tapajóz see Tapajós, Rio
63 C21 **Tapalqué** var. Tapalquén. Buenos Aires, E Argentina
Tapalquén see Tapalqué
Tapanahoni see Tapanahony Rivier
57 W11 **Tapanahony Rivier** var. Tapanahoni. ≈ E Suriname
43 T16 **Tapanatepec** var. San Pedro Tapanatepec. Oaxaca, SE Mexico
193 D23 **Tapanui** Otago, South Island, NZ
Tapanuli, Teluk see Sibolga, Teluk
61 E14 **Tapauá** Amazonas, N Brazil
49 R7 **Tapauá, Rio** ≈ W Brazil
193 I14 **Tapawera** Tasman, South Island, NZ
63 I16 **Tapes** Rio Grande do Sul, S Brazil
78 K16 **Tapeta** C Liberia
160 H11 **Tāpi** prev. Tāpti. ≈ W India
106 J2 **Tapia de Casariego** Asturias, N Spain
58 F10 **Tapiche, Río** ≈ N Peru
178 Gg15 **Tapi, Mae Nam** var. Luang. ≈ SW Thailand
194 K14 **Tapini** Central, S PNG
Tapirapecó, Serra see Tapirapecó, Sierra
57 N13 **Tapirapecó, Sierra** Port. Serra Tapirapecó. ▲▲ Brazil/Venezuela
79 R13 **Tapoa** ≈ Benin/Niger

◆ Country ◆ Country ● Country Capital ● Country Capital ◇ Dependent Territory ○ Dependent Territory Capital ◐ Administrative Region ✕ International Airport ▲ Mountain ▲▲ Mountain Range Volcano ≈ River ◎ Lake ▣ Reservoir

Telč – Thoreau

113 E18 **Telč** *Ger.* Teltsch. Jižní Morava, S Czech Republic
194 E11 **Telefomin** Sandaun, NW PNG
8 J10 **Telegraph Creek** British Columbia, W Canada
202 B10 **Telele** *island* Funafuti Atoll, C Tuvalu
62 J11 **Telêmaco Borba** Paraná, S Brazil
97 E15 **Telemark** ◐ *county* S Norway
64 J13 **Telén** La Pampa, C Argentina
Teleneshty *see* Telenești
118 M9 **Telenești** *Rus.* Teleneshty. C Moldova
106 J4 **Teleno, El** ▲ NW Spain
175 O8 **Telen, Sungai** ≈ Borneo, C Indonesia
118 I15 **Teleorman** ◐ *county* S Romania
118 I14 **Teleorman** ≈ S Romania
27 V5 **Telephone** Texas, SW USA
37 U11 **Telescope Peak** ▲ California, W USA
Teles Pirés *see* São Manuel, Rio
99 L19 **Telford** C England, UK
110 L7 **Telfs** Tirol, W Austria
44 I9 **Telica** León, NW Nicaragua
44 J6 **Telica, Río** ≈ C Honduras
78 I13 **Télimélé** Guinée-Maritime, W Guinea
45 O14 **Telire, Río** ≈ Costa Rica/ Panama
116 I8 **Telish** *prev.* Azizie. Loveshka Oblast, NW Bulgaria
43 R16 **Telixtlahuaca** *var.* San Francisco Telixtlahuaca. Oaxaca, SE Mexico
8 K13 **Telkwa** British Columbia, SW Canada
27 P4 **Tell** Texas, SW USA
Tell Abiad *see* Tall Abyaḍ
Tell Abiad/Tell Abyad *see* At Tall al Abyaḍ
Tell 'Annz *see* Al 'Anz
Tell Bâz *see* Tall Bāz
Tell Brâk *see* Tall Birāk
33 O16 **Tell City** Indiana, N USA
40 M9 **Teller** Alaska, USA
Tell Huqnah *see* Tall Ḥuqnah
161 F20 **Tellicherry** *var.* Thalassery. Kerala, SW India
22 M10 **Tellico Plains** Tennessee, S USA
Tell Kalakh *see* Tall Kalakh
Tell Mardīkh *see* Ebla
56 E11 **Tello** Huila, C Colombia
Tell Shagher Bazar *see* Jāghir Bāzār
Tell Shedadi *see* Ash Shadādah
Tell Tamr *see* Tall Tamir
39 Q7 **Telluride** Colorado, C USA
Tel'man/Tel'mansk *see* Gubadag
119 X9 **Tel'manove** Donets'ka Oblast', E Ukraine
168 H6 **Telmen Nuur** ◎ NW Mongolia
Teloekbetoeng *see* Bandarlampung
43 O15 **Teloloapán** Guerrero, S Mexico
Telo Martius *see* Toulon
129 V8 **Telposiz, Gora** ▲ NW Russian Federation
Telschen *see* Telšiai
65 J17 **Telsen** Chubut, S Argentina
120 D11 **Telšiai** *Ger.* Telschen. Telšiai, NW Lithuania
Teltsch *see* Telč
Telukbetung *see* Bandarlampung
173 F7 **Telukdalam** Pulau Nias, W Indonesia
12 H9 **Temagami** Ontario, S Canada
12 G9 **Temagami, Lake** ◎ Ontario, S Canada
202 H16 **Te Manga** ▲ Rarotonga, S Cook Islands
Temanggoeng *see* Temanggung
174 Kk15 **Temanggung** *prev.* Temanggoeng. Jawa, S Indonesia
203 W12 **Tematangi** *atoll* Îles Tuamotu, S French Polynesia
43 X11 **Temax** Yucatán, SE Mexico
176 X12 **Tembagapura** Irian Jaya, E Indonesia
133 U5 **Tembenchi** ≈ N Russian Federation
174 Hh10 **Tembesi, Sungai** ≈ Sumatera, W Indonesia
57 P6 **Temblador** Monagas, NE Venezuela
107 N9 **Tembleque** Castilla-La Mancha, C Spain
Temboni *see* Mitemele, Río
37 U16 **Temecula** California, W USA
174 Gg3 **Temengor, Tasik** ◎ Peninsular Malaysia
114 L9 **Temerin** Serbia, N Yugoslavia
Temes/Temesch *see* Tamiš
Temeschburg/Temeschwar *see* Timișoara
Temes-Kubin *see* Kovin
Temesmóra *see* Moravița
Temesvár/Temeswar *see* Timișoara
Teminaboean *see* Teminabuan
176 V9 **Teminabuan** *prev.* Teminaboean. Irian Jaya, E Indonesia
151 P17 **Temirlanovka** Yuzhnyy Kazakhstan, S Kazakhstan
151 R10 **Temirtau** *prev.* Samarkandski, Samarkandskoye. Karaganda, C Kazakhstan
12 H10 **Témiscaming** Québec, SE Canada
Témiscamingue, Lac *see* Timiskaming, Lake
13 T8 **Témiscouata, Lac** ◎ Québec, SE Canada
131 N5 **Temnikov** Respublika Mordoviya, W Russian Federation
203 Y13 **Temoe** *island* Îles Gambier, E French Polynesia
191 Q9 **Temora** New South Wales, SE Australia
42 H7 **Témoris** Chihuahua, W Mexico
42 I5 **Temósachic** Chihuahua, N Mexico
195 W8 **Temotu** *off.* Temotu Province. ◐ *province* E Solomon Islands
38 L14 **Tempe** Arizona, SW USA
175 P12 **Tempe, Danau** ◎ Sulawesi, C Indonesia
Tempelburg *see* Czaplinek
109 C17 **Tempio Pausania** Sardegna, Italy, C Mediterranean Sea
44 K12 **Tempisque, Río** ≈ NW Costa Rica
27 T9 **Temple** Texas, SW USA
102 O12 **Templehof** ✕ (Berlin) Berlin, NE Germany
99 D19 **Templemore** *Ir.* An Teampall Mór. C Ireland
102 O11 **Templin** Brandenburg, NE Germany
43 P12 **Tempoal** *var.* Tempoal de Sánchez. Veracruz-Llave, E Mexico
Tempoal de Sánchez *see* Tempoal
43 P13 **Tempoal, Río** ≈ C Mexico
85 E14 **Tempué** Moxico, C Angola
130 J14 **Temryuk** Krasnodarskiy Kray, SW Russian Federation
101 G17 **Temse** Oost-Vlaanderen, N Belgium
65 F15 **Temuco** Araucanía, C Chile
193 G20 **Temuka** Canterbury, South Island, NZ
201 P13 **Temwen Island** *island* E Micronesia
58 C6 **Tena** Napo, C Ecuador
43 W13 **Tenabo** Campeche, E Mexico
Tenaghau *see* Aola
27 X7 **Tenaha** Texas, SW USA
41 X13 **Tenake** Chichagof Island, Alaska, USA
161 K16 **Tenāli** Andhra Pradesh, E India
Tenan *see* Ch'ŏnan
43 O14 **Tenancingo** *var.* Tenencingo de Degollado. México, S Mexico
203 X12 **Tenararo** *island* Groupe Actéon, SE French Polynesia
178 Gg12 **Tenasserim** Tenasserim, S Myanmar
178 H11 **Tenasserim** *var.* Tanintharyi. ◐ *division* S Myanmar
100 O5 **Ten Boer** Groningen, NE Netherlands
99 I21 **Tenby** SW Wales, UK
82 K11 **Tendaho** NE Ethiopia
105 V14 **Tende** Alpes Maritimes, SE France
157 Q20 **Ten Degree Channel** *strait* Andaman and Nicobar Islands, India, E Indian Ocean
82 F11 **Tendelti** White Nile, E Sudan
78 G8 **Te-n-Dghâmcha, Sebkhet** *var.* Sebkha de Ndrhamcha, Sebkra de Ndaghamcha. *salt lake* W Mauritania
171 Ll12 **Tendō** Yamagata, Honshū, C Japan
76 H7 **Tendrara** NE Morocco
119 Q11 **Tendrivs'ka Kosa** *spit* S Ukraine
119 Q11 **Tendrivs'ka Zatoka** *gulf* S Ukraine
Tenencingo de Degollado *see* Tenancingo
79 N11 **Ténenkou** Mopti, C Mali
79 W9 **Ténéré** *physical region* C Niger
79 W9 **Ténére, Erg du** *desert* C Niger
66 O11 **Tenerife** *island* Islas Canarias, Spain, NE Atlantic Ocean
76 J5 **Ténès** NW Algeria
175 Oo15 **Tengah, Kepulauan** *island group* C Indonesia
175 O8 **Tenggarong** Borneo, C Indonesia
168 J15 **Tengger Shamo** *desert* N China
174 I4 **Tenggul, Pulau** *island* Peninsular Malaysia
Tengiz Köl *see* Tengiz, Ozero
151 P9 **Tengiz, Ozero** *Kaz.* Tengiz Köl. *salt lake* C Kazakhstan
78 M14 **Tengréla** *var.* Tingréla. N Ivory Coast
166 M14 **Tengxian** *var.* Teng Xian. Guangxi Zhuangzu Zizhiqu, S China
204 H2 **Teniente Rodolfo Marsh** *Chilean research station* South Shetland Islands, Antarctica
34 G9 **Tenino** Washington, NW USA
114 I9 **Tenja** Osijek-Baranja, E Croatia
196 B16 **Tenjo, Mount** ▲ W Guam
161 H23 **Tenkāsi** Tamil Nādu, SE India
81 N24 **Tenke** Shaba, SE Zaire
Tenke *see* Tinca
126 M7 **Tenkeli** Respublika Sakha (Yakutiya), NE Russian Federation
29 R10 **Tenkiller Ferry Lake** ⊡ Oklahoma, C USA
79 Q13 **Tenkodogo** S Burkina
189 Q5 **Tennant Creek** Northern Territory, C Australia
22 G9 **Tennessee** *off.* State of Tennessee; also known as The Volunteer State. ◐ *state* SE USA
39 R5 **Tennessee Pass** *pass* Colorado, C USA
22 H10 **Tennessee River** ≈ S USA
25 N2 **Tennessee Tombigbee Waterway** *canal* Alabama/Mississippi, S USA
101 K22 **Tenneville** Luxembourg, SE Belgium
94 M11 **Tenniöjoki** ≈ NE Finland
94 L9 **Teno** *var.* Tenojoki, *Lapp.* Dealnu, *Nor.* Tana. ≈ Finland/Norway *see also* Tana
Tenojoki *see* Tana/Teno
175 Nn3 **Tenom** Sabah, East Malaysia
Tenos *see* Tínos
43 V15 **Tenosique** *var.* Tenosique de Pino Suárez. Tabasco, SE Mexico
Tenosique de Pino Suárez *see* Tenosique
171 H15 **Tenri** Nara, Honshū, SW Japan
171 I16 **Tenryū** Shizuoka, Honshū, SW Japan
172 ii15 **Tenryū-gawa** ≈ Honshū, C Japan
24 I6 **Tensas River** ≈ Louisiana, S USA
25 O8 **Tensaw River** ≈ Alabama, S USA
76 E7 **Tensift** *seasonal river* W Morocco
175 Pp10 **Tentena** *var.* Tenteno. Sulawesi, C Indonesia
Tenteno *see* Tentena
191 U4 **Tenterfield** New South Wales, SE Australia
25 X16 **Ten Thousand Islands** *island group* Florida, SE USA
62 H9 **Teodoro Sampaio** São Paulo, S Brazil
61 N19 **Teófilo Otoni** *var.* Theophilo Ottoni. Minas Gerais, NE Brazil
118 K5 **Teofipol'** Khmel'nyts'ka Oblast', W Ukraine
203 Q8 **Teohatu** Tahiti, W French Polynesia
43 P14 **Teotihuacán** *ruins* México, S Mexico
Teotilán *see* Teotitlán del Camino
43 Q15 **Teotitlán del Camino** *var.* Teotilán. Oaxaca, S Mexico
202 G12 **Tepa** Île Uvea, E Wallis and Futuna
203 P8 **Tepaee, Récif** *reef* Tahiti, W French Polynesia
42 L14 **Tepalcatepec** Michoacán de Ocampo, SW Mexico
202 A16 **Tepa Point** *headland* SW Niue
42 L13 **Tepatitlán** *var.* Tepatitlán de Morelos. Jalisco, SW Mexico
Tepatitlán de Morelos *see* Tepatitlán
42 J9 **Tepehuanes** *var.* Santa Catarina de Tepehuanes. Durango, C Mexico
Tepelena *see* Tepelenë
115 L22 **Tepelenë** *var.* Tepelena, *It.* Tepeleni. Gjirokastër, S Albania
Tepeleni *see* Tepelenë
42 K12 **Tepic** Nayarit, C Mexico
113 C15 **Teplice** *Ger.* Teplitz; *prev.* Teplice-Šanov, Teplitz-Schönau. Severní Čechy, NW Czech Republic
Teplice-Šanov/Teplitz/Teplitz-Schönau *see* Teplice
119 O7 **Teplyk** Vinnyts'ka Oblast', C Ukraine
126 Mm10 **Teplyy Klyuch** Respublika Sakha (Yakutiya), NE Russian Federation
42 E5 **Tepoca, Cabo** *headland* NW Mexico
203 W9 **Tepoto** *island* Îles du Désappointement, C French Polynesia
94 L11 **Tepsa** Lappi, N Finland
202 B8 **Tepuka** *atoll* Funafuti Atoll, C Tuvalu
192 N7 **Te Puke** Bay of Plenty, North Island, NZ
42 L13 **Tequila** Jalisco, SW Mexico
43 O13 **Tequisquiapan** Querétaro de Arteaga, C Mexico
106 J5 **Tera** ≈ NW Spain
79 Q12 **Téra** Tillabéri, W Niger
203 V1 **Teraina** *prev.* Washington Island. *atoll* Line Islands, E Kiribati
83 F15 **Terakeka** Bahr el Gabel, S Sudan
109 J14 **Teramo** *anc.* Interamna. Abruzzi, C Italy
100 P7 **Ter Apel** Groningen, NE Netherlands
106 H11 **Tera, Ribeira de** ≈ S Portugal
193 K14 **Terawhiti, Cape** *headland* North Island, NZ
100 N12 **Terborg** Gelderland, E Netherlands
143 P13 **Tercan** Erzincan, NE Turkey
66 O2 **Terceira** ✕ Terceira, Azores, Portugal, NE Atlantic Ocean
66 O2 **Terceira** *var.* Ilha Terceira. *island* Azores, Portugal, NE Atlantic Ocean
Terceira, Ilha *see* Terceira
118 K6 **Terebovlya** Ternopil's'ka Oblast', W Ukraine
131 O15 **Terek** ≈ SW Russian Federation
Terekhovka *see* Tsyerakhowka
153 R9 **Terek-Say** Dzhalal-Abadskaya Oblast', W Kyrgyzstan
174 Hh3 **Terengganu** *var.* Trengganu. ◐ *state* Peninsular Malaysia
131 X7 **Terensay** Orenburgskaya Oblast', W Russian Federation
60 N13 **Teresina** *var.* Therezina. *state capital* Piauí, NE Brazil
62 P9 **Teresópolis** Rio de Janeiro, SE Brazil
112 P12 **Terespol** Biała Podlaska, E Poland
203 V16 **Terevaka, Maunga** 🌋 Easter Island, Chile, E Pacific Ocean
105 P3 **Tergnier** Aisne, N France
45 O14 **Teribe, Río** ≈ NW Panama
128 K3 **Teriberka** Murmanskaya Oblast', NW Russian Federation
Terijoki *see* Zelenogorsk
Terinkot *see* Tarīn Kowt
Terisaqqan *see* Tersakkan
26 K12 **Terlingua** Texas, SW USA
26 K11 **Terlingua Creek** ≈ Texas, SW USA
64 K7 **Termas de Río Hondo** Santiago del Estero, N Argentina
142 M11 **Terme** Samsun, N Turkey
Termez *see* Termiz
Termia *see* Kýthnos
109 J23 **Termini Imerese** *anc.* Thermae Himerenses. Sicilia, Italy, C Mediterranean Sea
43 V14 **Términos, Laguna de** *lagoon* SE Mexico
79 X10 **Termit-Kaoboul** Zinder, C Niger
153 O14 **Termiz** *Rus.* Termez. Surkhondaryo Wiloyati, S Uzbekistan
109 L15 **Termoli** Molise, C Italy
Termonde *see* Dendermonde
100 P5 **Termunten** Groningen, NE Netherlands
175 T7 **Ternate** Pulau Ternate, E Indonesia
175 Ss7 **Ternate, Pulau** *island* E Indonesia
111 T5 **Ternberg** Oberösterreich, N Austria
101 E15 **Terneuzen** *var.* Neuzen. Zeeland, SW Netherlands
127 O17 **Terney** Primorskiy Kray, SE Russian Federation
109 I14 **Terni** *anc.* Interamna Nahars. Umbria, C Italy
111 X6 **Ternitz** Niederösterreich, E Austria
119 V7 **Ternivka** Dnipropetrovs'ka Oblast', E Ukraine
118 K6 **Ternopil'** *Pol.* Tarnopol, *Rus.* Ternopol'. Ternopil's'ka Oblast', W Ukraine
Ternopil' *see* Ternopil's'ka Oblast'
118 I6 **Ternopil's'ka Oblast'** *var.* Ternopil', *Rus.* Ternopol'skaya Oblast'. ◐ *province* NW Ukraine
Ternopol' *see* Ternopil'
Ternopol'skaya Oblast' *see* Ternopil's'ka Oblast'
127 Oo15 **Terpeniya, Mys** *headland* Ostrov Sakhalin, SE Russian Federation
127 Oo15 **Terpeniya, Zaliv** *inlet* Ostrov Sakhalin, SE Russian Federation
Térraba, Río *see* Grande de Térraba, Río
8 J13 **Terrace** British Columbia, W Canada
10 D12 **Terrace Bay** Ontario, S Canada
109 I16 **Terracina** Lazio, C Italy
95 F14 **Terråk** Troms, N Norway
28 M13 **Terral** Oklahoma, C USA
109 B19 **Terralba** Sardegna, Italy, C Mediterranean Sea
Terranova di Sicilia *see* Gela
Terranova Pausania *see* Olbia
107 W5 **Terrassa** *Cast.* Tarrasa. Cataluña, E Spain
13 O12 **Terrebonne** Québec, SE Canada
24 J11 **Terrebonne Bay** *bay* Louisiana, SE USA
33 N14 **Terre Haute** Indiana, N USA
27 U6 **Terrell** Texas, SW USA
Terre-Neuve *see* Newfoundland
Terre Neuve *see* Newfoundland and Labrador
35 Q14 **Terreton** Idaho, NW USA
105 T7 **Territoire-de-Belfort** ◐ *department* E France
35 X9 **Terry** Montana, NW USA
30 I9 **Terry Peak** ▲ South Dakota, N USA
142 H14 **Tersakan Gölü** ◎ C Turkey
151 O10 **Tersakkan** *Kaz.* Terisaqqan. ≈ C Kazakhstan
100 J4 **Terschelling** *Fris.* Skylge. *island* Waddeneilanden, N Netherlands
80 H10 **Tersef** Chari-Baguirmi, C Chad
153 X8 **Terskey Ala-Too, Khrebet** ⛰ Kazakhstan/Kyrgyzstan
Terter *see* Tärtär
107 R8 **Teruel** *anc.* Turba. Aragón, E Spain
107 R7 **Teruel** ◐ *province* Aragón, E Spain
116 M7 **Tervel** *prev.* Kurtbunar, *Rom.* Curtbunar. Varnenska Oblast, NE Bulgaria
95 M16 **Tervo** Kuopio, C Finland
94 L13 **Tervola** Lappi, NW Finland
Tervueren *see* Tervuren
101 H18 **Tervuren** *var.* Tervueren. Vlaams Brabant, C Belgium
114 H11 **Tešanj** N Bosnia and Herzegovina
Teschen *see* Cieszyn
85 M19 **Tesenane** Inhambane, S Mozambique
82 I9 **Teseney** *var.* Tessenei. W Eritrea
41 P5 **Teshekpuk Lake** ◎ Alaska, USA
168 K6 **Teshig** Bulgan, N Mongolia
172 Q6 **Teshikaga** Hokkaidō, NE Japan
172 P2 **Teshio** Hokkaidō, NE Japan
172 P2 **Teshio-gawa** *var.* Tesio Gawa. ≈ Hokkaidō, NE Japan
172 P3 **Teshio-sanchi** ⛰ Hokkaidō, NE Japan
Těšín *see* Cieszyn
Tesio Gawa *see* Teshio-gawa
168 F5 **Tesiyn Gol** *var.* Tes-Khem. ≈ Mongolia/Russian Federation *see also* Tes-Khem
133 T7 **Tes-Khem** *var.* Tesiyn Gol. ≈ Mongolia/Russian Federation *see also* Tesiyn Gol
114 H11 **Teslić** N Bosnia and Herzegovina
8 I9 **Teslin** Yukon Territory, W Canada
8 I8 **Teslin** ≈ British Columbia/Yukon Territory, W Canada
79 Q8 **Tessalit** Kidal, NE Mali
79 V12 **Tessaoua** Maradi, S Niger
101 J17 **Tessenderlo** Limburg, NE Belgium
Tessenei *see* Teseney
12 L7 **Tessier, Lac** ◎ Québec, SE Canada
Tessin *see* Ticino
99 M23 **Test** ≈ S England, UK
Testama *see* Tõstamaa
57 P4 **Testigos, Islas los** *island group* N Venezuela
39 S10 **Tesuque** New Mexico, SW USA
105 O17 **Têt** *var.* Tet. ≈ S France
56 G5 **Tetas, Cerro de las** ▲ NW Venezuela
85 M15 **Tete** Tete, NW Mozambique
85 M15 **Tete** *off.* Província de Tete. ◐ *province* NW Mozambique
9 N15 **Tête Jaune Cache** British Columbia, SW Canada
192 O8 **Te Teko** Bay of Plenty, North Island, NZ
195 U15 **Tetepare** *island* New Georgia Islands, NW Solomon Islands
Teterev *see* Teteriv
118 M5 **Teteriv** *Rus.* Teterev. ≈ N Ukraine
102 M9 **Teterow** Mecklenburg-Vorpommern, NE Germany
116 I9 **Teteven** Loveshka Oblast, W Bulgaria
203 T10 **Tetiaroa** *atoll* Îles du Vent, W French Polynesia
107 P14 **Tetica de Bacares** ▲ S Spain
Tetiyev *see* Tetiyiv
119 O6 **Tetiyiv** *Rus.* Tetiyev. Kyyivs'ka Oblast', N Ukraine
41 T10 **Tetlin** Alaska, USA
35 R8 **Teton River** ≈ Montana, NW USA
76 G5 **Tétouan** *var.* Tetouan, Tetuán. N Morocco
Tetova/Tetovë *see* Tetovo
116 L7 **Tetovo** Razgradska Oblast, NE Bulgaria
115 N18 **Tetovo** *Alb.* Tetova, Tetovë, *Turk.* Kalkandelen. NW FYR Macedonia
117 E20 **Tetrázio** ⛰ S Greece
Tetschen *see* Děčín
Tetuán *see* Tétouan
203 Q8 **Tetufera, Mont** ▲ Tahiti, W French Polynesia
131 R4 **Tetyushi** Respublika Tatarstan, W Russian Federation
110 I7 **Teufen** Sankt Gallen, NE Switzerland
42 L12 **Teul** *var.* Teul de Gonzáles Ortega. Zacatecas, C Mexico
109 B21 **Teulada** Sardegna, Italy, C Mediterranean Sea
Teul de Gonzáles Ortega *see* Teul
9 X16 **Teulon** Manitoba, S Canada
44 I7 **Teupasenti** El Paraíso, S Honduras
172 Oo3 **Teuri-tō** *island* NE Japan
102 G13 **Teutoburger Wald** *Eng.* Teutoburg Forest. *hill range* NW Germany
Teutoburg Forest *see* Teutoburger Wald
95 K17 **Teuva** *Swe.* Östermark. Vaasa, W Finland
109 H15 **Tevere** *Eng.* Tiber. ≈ C Italy
144 G9 **Teverya** *var.* Tiberias. Northern, N Israel
98 K13 **Teviot** ≈ SE Scotland, UK
Tevli *see* Tewli
125 Ff12 **Tevriz** Omskaya Oblast', C Russian Federation
193 B24 **Te Waewae Bay** *bay* South Island, NZ
99 L21 **Tewkesbury** C England, UK
121 F19 **Tewli** *Rus.* Tevli. Brestskaya Voblasts', SW Belarus
165 U12 **Têwo** *var.* Dêngkagoin. Gansu, C China
27 U12 **Texana, Lake** ◎ Texas, SW USA
29 S14 **Texarkana** Arkansas, C USA
27 X5 **Texarkana** Texas, SW USA
27 N9 **Texas** *off.* State of Texas; also known as The Lone Star State. ◐ *state* S USA
27 W12 **Texas City** Texas, SW USA
43 P14 **Texcoco** México, C Mexico
100 I6 **Texel** *island* Waddeneilanden, NW Netherlands
28 H8 **Texhoma** Oklahoma, C USA
27 N1 **Texhoma** Texas, SW USA
39 W12 **Texico** New Mexico, SW USA
26 L1 **Texline** Texas, SW USA
43 P14 **Texmelucan** *var.* San Martín Texmelucan. Puebla, S Mexico
29 O13 **Texoma, Lake** ⊡ Oklahoma/Texas, C USA
27 N9 **Texon** Texas, SW USA
126 I12 **Teya** Krasnoyarskiy Kray, C Russian Federation
85 J23 **Teyateyaneng** NW Lesotho
128 M16 **Teykovo** Ivanovskaya Oblast', W Russian Federation
128 M16 **Teza** ≈ W Russian Federation
43 Q13 **Teziutlán** Puebla, S Mexico
159 W12 **Tezpur** Assam, NE India
15 L8 **Tha-Anne** ≈ Northwest Territories, NE Canada
85 K23 **Thabana Ntlenyana** *var.* Thabantshonyana, Mount Ntlenyana. ▲ E Lesotho
Thabantshonyana *see* Thabana Ntlenyana
85 J23 **Thaba Putsoa** ▲ C Lesotho
178 I8 **Tha Bo** Nong Khai, E Thailand
105 T12 **Thabor, Pic du** ▲ E France
Tha Chin *see* Samut Sakhon
177 G7 **Thagaya** Pegu, C Myanmar
Thai, Ao *see* Thailand, Gulf of
178 Jj6 **Thai Binh** Thai Binh, N Vietnam
178 Jj7 **Thai Hoa** Nghê An, N Vietnam
178 Hh10 **Thailand** *off.* Kingdom of Thailand, *Th.* Prathet Thai; *prev.* Siam. ◆ *monarchy* SE Asia
178 Hh13 **Thailand, Gulf of** *var.* Gulf of Siam, *Th.* Ao Thai, *Vtn.* Vinh Thai Lan. *gulf* SE Asia
Thai Lan, Vinh *see* Thailand, Gulf of
178 Jj6 **Thai Nguyên** Băc Thai, N Vietnam
178 J9 **Thakhèk** *prev.* Muang Khammouan. Khammouan, C Laos
159 S13 **Thakurgaon** Rajshahi, NW Bangladesh
155 S6 **Thal** North-West Frontier Province, NW Pakistan
177 G16 **Thalang** Phuket, SW Thailand
Thalassery *see* Tellicherry
178 I10 **Thalat Khae** Nakhon Ratchasima, C Thailand
111 Q5 **Thalgau** Salzburg, NW Austria
110 G7 **Thalwil** Zürich, NW Switzerland
85 I20 **Thamaga** Kweneng, SE Botswana
Thamarīd *see* Thamarīt
147 V13 **Thamarīt** *var.* Thamarīd, Thumrayt. SW Oman
147 P16 **Thamar, Jabal** ▲ SW Yemen
192 M6 **Thames** Waikato, North Island, NZ
12 D17 **Thames** ≈ Ontario, S Canada
99 O22 **Thames** ≈ S England, UK
192 M6 **Thames, Firth of** *gulf* North Island, NZ
12 D17 **Thamesville** Ontario, S Canada
147 S13 **Thamūd** N Yemen
178 Gg9 **Thanbyuzayat** Mon State, S Myanmar
158 I9 **Thānesar** Haryāna, NW India
178 Jj7 **Thanh Hoa** Thanh Hoa, N Vietnam
Thanintari Taungdan *see* Bilauktaung Range
161 I21 **Thanjāvūr** *prev.* Tanjore. Tamil Nādu, SE India
Thanlwin *see* Salween
105 U7 **Thann** Haut-Rhin, NE France
178 H16 **Tha Nong Phrom** Phatthalung, SW Thailand
178 H13 **Thap Sakae** *var.* Thap Sakau. Prachuap Khiri Khan, SW Thailand
Thap Sakau *see* Thap Sakae
100 L10 **'t Harde** Gelderland, E Netherlands
158 D11 **Thar Desert** *var.* Great Indian Desert, Indian Desert. *desert* India/Pakistan
189 V10 **Thargomindah** Queensland, C Australia
156 D11 **Thar Pārkar** *desert* SE Pakistan
145 S7 **Tharthār al Furāt, Qanāt ath** *canal* C Iraq
145 R7 **Tharthār, Buḥayrat ath** ◎ C Iraq
145 R5 **Tharthār, Wādī ath** *dry watercourse* N Iraq
178 Gg14 **Tha Sae** Chumphon, SW Thailand
178 H15 **Tha Sala** Nakhon Si Thammarat, SW Thailand
116 I13 **Thásos** Thásos, E Greece
117 I14 **Thásos** *island* E Greece
39 N14 **Thatcher** Arizona, SW USA
178 Jj5 **Thât Khê** *var.* Trâng Dinh. Lang Sơn, N Vietnam
178 Gg9 **Thaton** Mon State, S Myanmar
178 J9 **That Phanom** Nakhon Phanom, E Thailand
178 Ii10 **Tha Tum** Surin, E Thailand
105 P16 **Thau, Bassin de** *var.* Étang de Thau. ◎ S France
Thau, Étang de *see* Thau, Bassin de
177 G3 **Thaungdut** Sagaing, N Myanmar
178 Gg8 **Thaungyin** *Th.* Mae Nam Moei. ≈ Myanmar/Thailand
178 J9 **Tha Uthen** Nakhon Phanom, E Thailand
111 W2 **Thaya** *var.* Dyje. ≈ Austria/Czech Republic *see also* Dyje
29 V8 **Thayer** Missouri, C USA
177 Ff7 **Thayetmyo** Magwe, C Myanmar
35 S15 **Thayne** Wyoming, C USA
177 G6 **Thazi** Mandalay, C Myanmar
Thebes *see* Thíva
46 L5 **The Carlton** *var.* Abraham Bay. Mayaguana, SE Bahamas
47 O14 **The Crane** *var.* Crane. S Barbados
34 I11 **The Dalles** Oregon, NW USA
30 M14 **Thedford** Nebraska, C USA
The Hague *see* 's-Gravenhage
Theiss *see* Tisa/Tisza
15 Jj6 **Thelon** ≈ Northwest Territories, N Canada
9 V15 **Theodore** Saskatchewan, S Canada
25 N8 **Theodore** Alabama, S USA
38 L13 **Theodore Roosevelt Lake** ⊡ Arizona, SW USA
Theodosia *see* Feodosiya
Theophilo Ottoni *see* Teófilo Otoni
15 K13 **The Pas** Manitoba, C Canada
33 T14 **The Plains** Ohio, N USA
Thera *see* Thíra
180 H17 **Thérèse, Île** *island* Inner Islands, NE Seychelles
Therezina *see* Teresina
117 L20 **Thérma** Ikaría, Dodekánisos, Greece, Aegean Sea
Thermae Himerenses *see* Termini Imerese
Thermae Pannonicae *see* Baden
Thermaic Gulf/Thermaicus Sinus *see* Thermaïkós Kólpos
123 Gg10 **Thermaïkós Kólpos** *Eng.* Thermaic Gulf; *anc.* Thermaicus Sinus. *gulf* N Greece
Thermiá *see* Kýthnos
117 L17 **Thermís** Lésvos, E Greece
117 E18 **Thérmo** Dytikí Ellás, C Greece
35 V14 **Thermopolis** Wyoming, C USA
191 P10 **The Rock** New South Wales, SE Australia
205 O5 **Theron Mountains** ⛰ Antarctica
117 G18 **Thespiés** Stereá Ellás, C Greece
117 E16 **Thessalía** *Eng.* Thessaly. ◐ *region* C Greece
12 C10 **Thessalon** Ontario, S Canada
117 G14 **Thessaloníki** *Eng.* Salonica, Salonika, *SCr.* Solun, *Turk.* Selânik. Kentrikí Makedonía, N Greece
117 G14 **Thessaloníki** ✕ Kentrikí Makedonía, N Greece
Thessaly *see* Thessalía
86 B12 **Theta Gap** *undersea feature* E Atlantic Ocean
99 P20 **Thetford** E England, UK
13 R11 **Thetford-Mines** Québec, SE Canada
115 K17 **Theth** *var.* Thethi. Shkodër, N Albania
Thethi *see* Theth
101 L20 **Theux** Liège, E Belgium
47 V9 **The Valley** ○ (Anguilla) E Anguilla
29 N10 **The Village** Oklahoma, C USA
27 W10 **The Woodlands** Texas, SW USA
Thiamis *see* Thýamis
Thian Shan *see* Tien Shan
24 J9 **Thibodaux** Louisiana, S USA
31 S3 **Thief Lake** ◎ Minnesota, N USA
31 S3 **Thief River** ≈ Minnesota, C USA
31 S3 **Thief River Falls** Minnesota, N USA
Thièle *see* La Thielle
34 G14 **Thielsen, Mount** ▲ Oregon, NW USA
Thielt *see* Tielt
108 G7 **Thiene** Veneto, NE Italy
Thienen *see* Tienen
105 P11 **Thiers** Puy-de-Dôme, C France
78 F11 **Thiès** W Senegal
83 I19 **Thika** Central, S Kenya
Thikombia *see* Cikobia
157 K18 **Thiladhunmathi Atoll** *var.* Tiladummati Atoll. *atoll* N Maldives
Thimbu *see* Thimphu
159 T11 **Thimphu** *var.* Thimbu; *prev.* Tashi Chho Dzong. ● (Bhutan) W Bhutan
94 H2 **Thingeyri** Vestfirdhir, NW Iceland
94 I3 **Thingvellir** Sudhurland, SW Iceland
197 J6 **Thio** Province Sud, C New Caledonia
105 T4 **Thionville** *Ger.* Diedenhofen. Moselle, NE France
117 K22 **Thíra** Thíra, Kykládes, Greece, Aegean Sea
117 K22 **Thíra** *prev.* Santorin, Santoríni, *anc.* Thera. *island* Kykládes, Greece, Aegean Sea
117 J22 **Thirasía** *island* Kykládes, Greece, Aegean Sea
99 M16 **Thirsk** N England, UK
12 F12 **Thirty Thousand Islands** *island group* Ontario, S Canada
Thiruvanathapuram *see* Trivandrum
97 F20 **Thisted** Viborg, NW Denmark
Thistil Fjord *see* Thistilfjördhur
94 L1 **Thistilfjördhur** *var.* Thistil Fjord. *fjord* NE Iceland
190 G9 **Thistle Island** *island* South Australia
Thithia *see* Cicia
179 N14 **Thitu Island** *island* NW Spratly Islands
Thiukhaoluang Phrahang *see* Luang Prabang Range
117 G18 **Thíva** *Eng.* Thebes; *prev.* Thívai. Stereá Ellás, C Greece
Thívai *see* Thíva
104 M12 **Thiviers** Dordogne, SW France
94 J4 **Thjórsá** ≈ C Iceland
15 L9 **Thlewiaza** ≈ Northwest Territories, NE Canada
15 J9 **Thoa** ≈ Northwest Territories, NW Canada
101 G14 **Tholen** Zeeland, SW Netherlands
101 F14 **Tholen** *island* SW Netherlands
28 L10 **Thomas** Oklahoma, C USA
23 T3 **Thomas** West Virginia, NE USA
29 U3 **Thomas Hill Reservoir** ⊡ Missouri, C USA
25 S5 **Thomaston** Georgia, SE USA
21 R7 **Thomaston** Maine, NE USA
27 T12 **Thomaston** Texas, SW USA
25 O6 **Thomasville** Alabama, S USA
25 T8 **Thomasville** Georgia, SE USA
23 S9 **Thomasville** North Carolina, SE USA
37 N5 **Thomes Creek** ≈ California, W USA
9 W12 **Thompson** Manitoba, C Canada
31 R4 **Thompson** North Dakota, N USA
0 F8 **Thompson** ≈ Alberta/British Columbia, SW Canada
35 O8 **Thompson Falls** Montana, NW USA
31 Q10 **Thompson, Lake** ◎ South Dakota, N USA
36 M3 **Thompson Peak** ▲ California, W USA
29 S2 **Thompson River** ≈ Missouri, C USA
193 A22 **Thompson Sound** *sound* South Island, NZ
15 Hh1 **Thomsen** ≈ Banks Island, Northwest Territories, NW Canada
25 V4 **Thomson** Georgia, SE USA
105 T10 **Thonon-les-Bains** Haute-Savoie, E France
105 O15 **Thoré** *var.* Thore. ≈ S France
39 P11 **Thoreau** New Mexico, SW USA

◆ Country
● Country Capital
◇ Dependent Territory
○ Dependent Territory Capital
◐ Administrative Region
✕ International Airport
▲ Mountain
⛰ Mountain Range
🌋 Volcano
≈ River
◎ Lake
⊡ Reservoir

THORENBURG – TOKACHI-DAKE

Thorenburg see Turda
94 J3 Thórisvatn ◎ C Iceland
94 P4 Thor, Kapp headland S Svalbard
94 I4 Thorlákshöfn Sudhurland, SW Iceland
Thorn see Toruń
27 T10 Thorndale Texas, SW USA
12 H10 Thorne Ontario, S Canada
99 J14 Thornhill S Scotland, UK
27 U8 Thornton Texas, SW USA
Thornton Island see Caroline Island
12 H16 Thorold Ontario, S Canada
34 I9 Thorp Washington, NW USA
205 S3 Thorshavnheiane physical region Antarctica
94 L1 Thórshöfn Nordhurland Eystra, NE Iceland
Thospitis see Van Gölü
178 J14 Thôt Nốt Cân Thơ, S Vietnam
104 K8 Thouars Deux-Sèvres, W France
159 X14 Thoubal Manipur, NE India
104 K9 Thouet ≈ W France
Thoune see Thun
20 H7 Thousand Islands island Canada/USA
37 S15 Thousand Oaks California, W USA
116 J13 Thracian Sea Gk. Thrakikó Pélagos; anc. Thracium Mare. sea Greece/Turkey
Thracium Mare/Thrakikó Pélagos see Thracian Sea
Thrá Lí, Bá see Tralee Bay
35 R11 Three Forks Montana, NW USA
9 Q16 Three Hills Alberta, SW Canada
191 N15 Three Hummock Island island Tasmania, SE Australia
192 H1 Three Kings Islands island group N NZ
183 P10 Three Kings Rise undersea feature W Pacific Ocean
79 O18 Three Points, Cape headland S Ghana
33 P10 Three Rivers Michigan, N USA
27 S13 Three Rivers Texas, SW USA
85 G24 Three Sisters Northern Cape, SW South Africa
34 H13 Three Sisters ▲ Oregon, NW USA
195 Z16 Three Sisters Islands island group SE Solomon Islands
Thrissur see Trichūr
27 Q6 Throckmorton Texas, SW USA
188 M10 Throssell, Lake salt lake Western Australia
117 K25 Thrýptis ▲ Kríti, Greece, E Mediterranean Sea
178 Jj14 Thu Dâu Môt var. Phu Cương. Sông Be, S Vietnam
178 Jj6 Thu Do ✕ (Ha Nôi) Ha Nôi, N Vietnam
101 G21 Thuin Hainaut, S Belgium
155 Q12 Thul Sind, SE Pakistan
Thule see Qaanaaq
85 J18 Thuli var. Tuli. ≈ S Zimbabwe
Thumrayt see Thamarīt
110 D9 Thun Fr. Thoune. Bern, W Switzerland
10 C12 Thunder Bay Ontario, S Canada
32 M1 Thunder Bay lake bay S Canada
33 R6 Thunder Bay lake bay Michigan, N USA
33 R6 Thunder Bay River ≈ Michigan, N USA
29 N11 Thunderbird, Lake ⊠ Oklahoma, C USA
30 L8 Thunder Butte Creek ≈ South Dakota, N USA
110 E9 Thuner See ◎ C Switzerland
178 H16 Thung Song var. Cha Mai. Nakhon Si Thammarat, SW Thailand
110 H7 Thur ≈ N Switzerland
110 G6 Thurgau Fr. Thurgovie. ◈ canton NE Switzerland
Thurgovie see Thurgau
Thuringe see Thüringen
110 J7 Thüringen Vorarlberg, W Austria
103 J17 Thüringen Eng. Thuringia, Fr. Thuringe. ◈ state C Germany
103 J17 Thüringer Wald Eng. Thuringian Forest. ⛰ C Germany
Thuringia see Thüringen
Thuringian Forest see Thüringer Wald
99 D19 Thurles Ir. Durlas. S Ireland
23 W2 Thurmont Maryland, NE USA
Thurø see Thurø By
97 H24 Thurø By var. Thurø. Fyn, C Denmark
12 M12 Thurso Québec, SE Canada
98 J6 Thurso N Scotland, UK
204 I10 Thurston Island island Antarctica
110 I9 Thusis Graubünden, S Switzerland
117 C15 Thýamis var. Thiamis. ≈ W Greece
97 E21 Thyborøn var. Tyborøn. Ringkøbing, W Denmark
205 U3 Thyer Glacier glacier Antarctica
117 L20 Thýmaina island Dodekánisos, Greece, Aegean Sea
85 N15 Thyolo var. Cholo. Southern, S Malawi
191 U6 Tia New South Wales, SE Australia
56 H5 Tía Juana Zulia, NW Venezuela
166 J14 Tiandong var. Pingma. Guangxi Zhuangzu Zizhiqu, S China
167 O3 Tianjin var. Tientsin. Tianjin Shi, E China
Tianjin see Tianjin Shi
167 P3 Tianjin Shi var. Jin, Tianjin, T'ien-ching, Tientsin. ◈ municipality E China
165 S10 Tianjun var. Xinyuan. Qinghai, C China
166 J13 Tianlin prev. Leli. Guangxi Zhuangzu Zizhiqu, S China
Tian Shan see Tien Shan
165 W11 Tianshui Gansu, C China
156 I7 Tianshuihai Xinjiang Uygur Zizhiqu, W China
167 S10 Tiantai Zhejiang, SE China
166 J14 Tianyang Guangxi Zhuangzu Zizhiqu, S China
165 U9 Tianzhu var. Tianzhu Zangzu Zizhixian. Gansu, C China
Tianzhu Zangzu Zizhixian see Tianzhu
203 Q7 Tiarei Tahiti, W French Polynesia
76 J6 Tiaret var. Tihert. NW Algeria
Tiâs see Tiyās
79 N17 Tiassalé S Ivory Coast
198 Bb8 Ti'avea Upolu, SE Western Samoa
Tiba see Chiba
62 J11 Tibagi var. Tibají. Paraná, S Brazil
62 J10 Tibagi, Rio var. Rio Tibají. ≈ S Brazil
Tibaji see Tibagi
Tibají, Rio see Tibagi, Rio
145 Q9 Tibal, Wādī dry watercourse S Iraq
56 G9 Tibaná Boyacá, C Colombia
81 F14 Tibati Adamaoua, N Cameroon
78 K15 Tibé, Pic de ▲ SE Guinea
Tiber see Tevere, Italy
Tiber see Tivoli, Italy
Tiberias see Teverya
144 G8 Tiberias, Lake var. Chinnereth, Sea of Bahr Tabariya, Sea of Galilee, Ar. Bahrat Tabariya, Heb. Yam Kinneret. ◎ N Israel
69 Q5 Tibesti var. Tibesti Massif, Ar. Tibistī. ⛰ N Africa
Tibesti Massif see Tibesti
Tibetan Autonomous Region see Xizang Zizhiqu
Tibet, Plateau of see Qingzang Gaoyuan
Tibistī see Tibesti
12 K7 Tiblemont, Lac ◎ Québec, SE Canada
145 X9 Ţīb, Nahr aţ ≈ S Iraq
Tibni see At Tibni
190 L4 Tibooburra New South Wales, SE Australia
97 L18 Tibro Skaraborg, S Sweden
42 E5 Tiburón, Isla var. Isla del Tiburón. island NW Mexico
Tiburón, Isla del see Tiburón, Isla
25 W14 Tice Florida, SE USA
Tichau see Tychy
116 L8 Ticha, Yazovir ◎ NE Bulgaria
78 K9 Tichît var. Tichitt. Tagant, C Mauritania
Tichitt see Tichît
110 G11 Ticino Fr./Ger. Tessin. ◈ canton S Switzerland
108 D8 Ticino ≈ Italy/Switzerland
110 H11 Ticino Ger. Tessin. ≈ SW Switzerland
Ticinum see Pavia
43 X12 Ticul Yucatán, SE Mexico
97 K18 Tidaholm Skaraborg, S Sweden
Tidjikdja see Tidjikja
78 J8 Tidjikja var. Tidjikdja; prev. Fort-Cappolani. Tagant, C Mauritania
Tidore see Soasiu
175 Ss7 Tidore, Pulau island E Indonesia
Tidra, Ile see Et Tîdra
79 N16 Tiébissou var. Tiebissou. C Ivory Coast
169 V11 Tiefa Liaoning, NE China
110 I9 Tiefencastel Graubünden, S Switzerland
Tiegenhof see Nowy Dwór Gdański
T'ieh-ling see Tieling
100 K13 Tiel Gelderland, C Netherlands
169 W7 Tieli Heilongjiang, NE China
169 V11 Tieling var. T'ieh-ling. Liaoning, NE China
158 L4 Tielongtan China/India
101 D17 Tielt var. Thielt. West-Vlaanderen, W Belgium
T'ien-ching see Tianjin Shi
101 I18 Tienen var. Thienen, Fr. Tirlemont. Vlaams Brabant, C Belgium
Tiên Giang, Sông see Mekong
153 X9 Tien Shan Chin. Thian Shan, Tian Shan, T'ien Shan, Rus. Tyan'-Shan'. ⛰ C Asia
Tientsin see Tianjin
Tientsin see Tianjin Shi
178 K6 Tiên Yên Quang Ninh, N Vietnam
97 O14 Tierp Uppsala, C Sweden
64 H7 Tierra Amarilla Atacama, N Chile
39 R9 Tierra Amarilla New Mexico, SW USA
43 R15 Tierra Blanca Veracruz-Llave, E Mexico
43 O16 Tierra Colorada Guerrero, S Mexico
65 J17 Tierra Colorada, Bajo de la basin SE Argentina
65 I25 Tierra del Fuego off. Provincia de la Tierra del Fuego. ◈ province S Argentina
65 J24 Tierra del Fuego island Argentina/Chile
56 D7 Tierralta Córdoba, NW Colombia
106 K9 Tiétar ≈ W Spain
62 L10 Tietê São Paulo, S Brazil
62 J8 Tietê, Rio ≈ S Brazil
34 I9 Tieton Washington, NW USA
34 J6 Tiffany Mountain ▲ Washington, NW USA
33 S12 Tiffin Ohio, N USA
33 Q11 Tiffin River ≈ Ohio, N USA
Tiflis see T'bilisi
25 U7 Tifton Georgia, SE USA
175 Ss11 Tifu Pulau Buru, E Indonesia
197 K6 Tiga, Île island Îles Loyauté, W New Caledonia
40 L17 Tigalda Island island Aleutian Islands, Alaska, USA
117 I15 Tigáni, Ákra headland Límnos, E Greece
175 O1 Tiga Tarok Sabah, East Malaysia
119 O10 Tighina Rus. Bendery; prev. Bender. E Moldova
127 P10 Tigil' Koryakskiy Avtonomnyy Okrug, E Russian Federation
151 X9 Tigiretskiy Khrebet ⛰ E Kazakhstan
81 F14 Tignère Adamaoua, N Cameroon
11 P14 Tignish Prince Edward Island, SE Canada
Tigranocerta see Siirt
43 O11 Tigre, Cerro del ▲ C Mexico
58 F8 Tigre, Río ≈ N Peru
145 X10 Tigris Ar. Dijlah, Turk. Dicle. ≈ Iraq/Turkey
78 G9 Tiguent Trarza, SW Mauritania
76 M10 Tiguentourine E Algeria
79 V10 Tiguidit, Falaise de ridge C Niger
147 N13 Tihāmah var. Tehama. plain Saudi Arabia/Yemen
Tihert see Tiaret
Ti-hua/Tihwa see Ürümqi
43 Q13 Tihuatlán Veracruz-Llave, E Mexico
42 B1 Tijuana Baja California, NW Mexico
44 E2 Tikal Petén, N Guatemala
160 I9 Tīkamgarh prev. Tehri. Madhya Pradesh, C India
164 L7 Tikanlik Xinjiang Uygur Zizhiqu, NW China
79 P12 Tikaré N Burkina
41 O12 Tikchik Lakes lakes Alaska, USA
203 T9 Tikehau atoll Îles Tuamotu, C French Polynesia
203 V9 Tikei island Îles Tuamotu, C French Polynesia
125 B12 Tikhoretsk Krasnodarskiy Kray, SW Russian Federation
128 I13 Tikhvin Leningradskaya Oblast', NW Russian Federation
199 I10 Tiki Basin undersea feature S Pacific Ocean
78 K13 Tikinsso ≈ NE Guinea
192 Q8 Tikitiki Gisborne, North Island, NZ
81 D16 Tiko Sud-Ouest, SW Cameroon
145 S6 Tikrīt var. Tekrit. N Iraq
128 I8 Tiksha Respublika Kareliya, NW Russian Federation
128 I6 Tikshozero, Ozero ◎ NW Russian Federation
126 L7 Tiksi Respublika Sakha (Yakutiya), NE Russian Federation
173 G8 Tiku Sumatera, W Indonesia
44 A6 Tilapa San Marcos, SW Guatemala
44 L13 Tilarán Guanacaste, NW Costa Rica
101 J14 Tilburg Noord-Brabant, S Netherlands
12 D17 Tilbury Ontario, S Canada
190 K4 Tilcha South Australia
Tilcha Creek see Callabonna Creek
31 Q14 Tilden Nebraska, C USA
27 R13 Tilden Texas, SW USA
12 H10 Tilden Lake Ontario, S Canada
118 G9 Tileagd Hung. Mezőtelegd. Bihor, W Romania
79 Q8 Tilemsi, Vallée de ≈ C Mali
127 Pp8 Tilichiki Koryakskiy Avtonomnyy Okrug, E Russian Federation
Tiligul see Tilihul
Tiligul'skiy Liman see Tilihul's'kyy Lyman
119 P9 Tilihul Rus. Tiligul. ≈ SW Ukraine
119 P10 Tilihul's'kyy Lyman Rus. Tiligul'skiy Liman. ◎ S Ukraine
Tilimsen see Tlemcen
Tilio Martius see Toulon
79 R11 Tillabéri var. Tillabéry. Tillabéri, W Niger
79 R11 Tillabéri ◈ department SW Niger
Tillabéry see Tillabéri
34 F11 Tillamook Oregon, NW USA
34 E11 Tillamook Bay inlet Oregon, NW USA
157 Q22 Tillanchāng Dwip island Nicobar Islands, India, NE Indian Ocean
97 N15 Tillberga Västmanland, C Sweden
Tillenberg see Dyleň
23 S10 Tillery, Lake ⊠ North Carolina, SE USA
79 T10 Tillia Tahoua, W Niger
25 N8 Tillmans Corner Alabama, S USA
12 F17 Tillsonburg Ontario, S Canada
117 N22 Tílos island Dodekánisos, Greece, Aegean Sea
191 N5 Tilpa New South Wales, SE Australia
Tilsit see Sovetsk
33 N13 Tilton Illinois, N USA
130 K7 Tim Kurskaya Oblast', W Russian Federation
56 D12 Timaná Huila, S Colombia
Timan Ridge see Timanskiy Kryazh
129 Q6 Timanskiy Kryazh Eng. Timan Ridge. ridge NW Russian Federation
193 G20 Timaru Canterbury, South Island, NZ
131 S6 Timashevo Samarskaya Oblast', W Russian Federation
130 K13 Timashevsk Krasnodarskiy Kray, SW Russian Federation
Timbaki/Timbákion see Tympáki
24 K10 Timbalier Bay bay Louisiana, S USA
24 K11 Timbalier Island island Louisiana, S USA
194 K12 Timbe ≈ C Papau New Guinea
78 L10 Timbedgha var. Timbédra. Hodh ech Chargui, SE Mauritania
Timbédra see Timbedgha
34 G10 Timber Oregon, NW USA
189 O3 Timber Creek Northern Territory, N Australia
30 M8 Timber Lake South Dakota, N USA
56 D12 Timbío Cauca, SW Colombia
56 C12 Timbiquí Cauca, SW Colombia
85 O17 Timbue, Ponta headland C Mozambique
Timbuktu see Tombouctou
176 Vv10 Timbuni, Sungai ≈ Irian Jaya, E Indonesia
175 Oo4 Timbun Mata, Pulau island E Malaysia
79 P8 Timétrine var. Ti-n-Kâr. oasis C Mali
Timfi see Týmfi
Timfristos see Tymfristós
79 V9 Timia Agadez, C Niger
176 X12 Timika Irian Jaya, E Indonesia
76 I9 Timimoun C Algeria
Timiris, Cap see Timirist, Râs
78 F8 Timirist, Râs var. Cap Timiris. headland NW Mauritania
151 O7 Timiryazevo Severnyy Kazakhstan, N Kazakhstan
118 E11 Timiş ◈ county SW Romania
12 H9 Timiskaming, Lake Fr. Lac Témiscamingue. ◎ Ontario/Québec, SE Canada
118 E11 Timi Soara ✕ Timiş, SW Romania
118 E11 Timişoara Ger. Temeschwar, Temeswar, Hung. Temesvár; prev. Temeschburg. Timiş, W Romania
Timkovichi see Tsimkavichy
79 U8 Ti-m-Meghsoï ≈ NW Niger
102 K8 Timmerdorfer Strand Schleswig-Holstein, N Germany
12 F7 Timmins Ontario, S Canada
23 S12 Timmonsville South Carolina, SE USA
32 K5 Timms Hill ▲ Wisconsin, N USA
176 Vv9 Timoforo ≈ Irian Jaya, E Indonesia
114 P12 Timok ≈ E Yugoslavia
60 N13 Timon Maranhão, E Brazil
175 Rr17 Timor island Nusa Tenggara, C Indonesia
175 S17 Timor Sea sea E Indian Ocean
175 S16 Timor Timur off. Propinsi Timor Timur, var. Loro Sae, Eng. East Timor; prev. Portuguese Timor. ◈ province S Indonesia
Timor Trench see Timor Trough
198 G9 Timor Trough var. Timor Trench. undersea feature NE Timor Sea
63 A21 Timote Buenos Aires, E Argentina
56 I6 Timotes Mérida, NW Venezuela
27 X8 Timpson Texas, SW USA
126 Ll13 Timpton ≈ NE Russian Federation
95 H17 Timrå Västernorrland, C Sweden
22 J10 Tims Ford Lake ⊠ Tennessee, S USA
174 Hh7 Timun Pulau Kundur, C Indonesia
174 H3 Timur, Banjaran ⛰ Peninsular Malaysia
179 R17 Tinaca Point headland Mindanao, S Philippines
56 K5 Tinaco Cojedes, N Venezuela
66 Q11 Tinajo Lanzarote, Islas Canarias, Spain, NE Atlantic Ocean
195 W8 Tinakula island Santa Cruz Islands, E Solomon Islands
56 K5 Tinaquillo Cojedes, N Venezuela
118 F10 Tinca Hung. Tenke. Bihor, W Romania
161 J20 Tindivanam Tamil Nādu, SE India
76 E9 Tindouf W Algeria
76 E9 Tindouf, Sebkha de salt lake W Algeria
106 J2 Tineo Asturias, N Spain
79 R9 Ti-n-Essako Kidal, E Mali
191 T5 Tingha New South Wales, SE Australia
Tingis see Tanger
Tinglett see Tinglev
97 F24 Tinglev Ger. Tinglett. Sønderjylland, SW Denmark
58 E12 Tingo María Huánuco, C Peru
Tingréla see Tengréla
164 K16 Tingri var. Xêgar. Xizang Zizhiqu, W China
97 M21 Tingsryd Kronoberg, S Sweden
97 P19 Tingstäde Gotland, SE Sweden
64 H12 Tinguiririca, Volcán ℛ C Chile
96 F9 Tingvoll Møre og Romsdal, S Norway
194 M9 Tingwon Island island N PNG
196 K8 Tinian island S Northern Mariana Islands
Ti-n-Kâr see Timétrine
Tinnevelly see Tirunelveli
97 G15 Tinnoset Telemark, S Norway
97 F15 Tinnsjø ◎ S Norway
Tino see Chino
117 J20 Tínos Tínos, Kykládes, Greece, Aegean Sea
117 J20 Tínos anc. Tenos. island Kykládes, Greece, Aegean Sea
159 R14 Tinpahar Bihār, NE India
124 O14 Tin, Ra's al headland N Libya
159 X11 Tinsukia Assam, NE India
78 K10 Tintâne Hodh el Gharbi, S Mauritania
64 L7 Tintina Santiago del Estero, N Argentina
190 K10 Tintinara South Australia
106 I14 Tinto ≈ SW Spain
79 S8 Ti-n-Zaouâtene Kidal, NE Mali
Tiobraid Árann see Tipperary
30 K3 Tioga North Dakota, N USA
20 G12 Tioga Pennsylvania, NE USA
27 T5 Tioga Texas, SW USA
37 Q8 Tioga Pass pass California, W USA
20 G12 Tioga River ≈ New York/Pennsylvania, NE USA
176 Y11 Tiom Irian Jaya, E Indonesia
Tioman Island see Tioman, Pulau
174 I5 Tioman, Pulau var. Tioman Island. island Peninsular Malaysia
20 C12 Tionesta Pennsylvania, NE USA
20 D12 Tionesta Creek ≈ Pennsylvania, NE USA
173 G11 Tiop Pulau Pagai Selatan, W Indonesia
175 Qq12 Tioro, Selat var. Tiworo. strait Sulawesi, C Indonesia
79 O12 Tiou NW Burkina
20 H11 Tioughnioga River ≈ New York, NE USA
176 U10 Tip Irian Jaya, E Indonesia
76 J5 Tipasa var. Tipaza. N Algeria
Tipaza see Tipasa
44 J10 Tipitapa Managua, W Nicaragua
33 R13 Tipp City Ohio, N USA
33 O12 Tippecanoe River ≈ Indiana, N USA
99 D20 Tipperary Ir. Tiobraid Árann. S Ireland
99 D19 Tipperary Ir. Tiobraid Árann. cultural region S Ireland
37 R12 Tipton California, W USA
33 P13 Tipton Indiana, N USA
31 Y14 Tipton Iowa, C USA
29 U5 Tipton Missouri, C USA
38 I10 Tipton, Mount ▲ Arizona, SW USA
22 F8 Tiptonville Tennessee, S USA
10 E12 Tip Top Mountain ▲ Ontario, S Canada
161 G19 Tiptūr Karnātaka, W India
Tiquisate see Pueblo Nuevo Tiquisate
60 L13 Tiracambu, Serra do ⛰ E Brazil
Tirana see Tiranë
115 K19 Tirana Rinas ✕ Durrës, W Albania
115 L20 Tiranë var. Tirana. ● (Albania) Tiranë, C Albania
115 K20 Tiranë ◈ district W Albania
146 I5 Tīrān, Jazīrat island Egypt/Saudi Arabia
108 F6 Tirano Lombardia, N Italy
190 I2 Tirari Desert desert South Australia
119 O10 Tiraspol Rus. Tiraspol'. E Moldova
192 M8 Tirau Waikato, North Island, NZ
142 C14 Tire İzmir, SW Turkey
143 O11 Tirebolu Giresun, N Turkey
98 F11 Tiree island W Scotland, UK
Tîrgovişte see Târgovişte
Tirgu see Târgu Cărbuneşti
Tîrgu Bujor see Târgu Bujor
Tîrgu Frumos see Târgu Frumos
Tîrgu Jiu see Târgu Jiu
Tîrgu Lăpuş see Târgu Lăpuş
Tîrgu Mures see Târgu Mureş
Tîrgu-Neamţ see Târgu-Neamţ
Tîrgu Ocna see Târgu Ocna
Tîrgu Secuiesc see Târgu Secuiesc
155 T3 Tirich Mīr ▲ NW Pakistan
78 J5 Tiris Zemmour ◈ region N Mauritania
Tirlemont see Tienen
131 W5 Tirlyanskiy Respublika Bashkortostan, W Russian Federation
Tîrnava Mare see Târnava Mare
Tîrnava Mică see Târnava Mică
Tîrnăveni see Târnăveni
Tírnavos see Týrnavos
Tirnovo see Veliko Tŭrnovo
160 J11 Tirodi Madhya Pradesh, C India
110 K8 Tirol off. Land Tirol, var. Tyrol, It. Tirolo. ◈ state W Austria
Tirolo see Tirol
Tirreno, Mare see Tyrrhenian Sea
109 B19 Tirso ≈ Sardegna, Italy, C Mediterranean Sea
97 H22 Tirstrup ✕ (Århus) Århus, C Denmark
161 I21 Tiruchchirāppalli prev. Trichinopoly. Tamil Nādu, SE India
161 H23 Tirunelveli var. Tinnevelly. Tamil Nādu, SE India
161 J19 Tirupati Andhra Pradesh, E India
161 I20 Tiruppattūr Tamil Nādu, SE India
161 H21 Tiruppur Tamil Nādu, SW India
161 I20 Tiruvannāmalai Tamil Nādu, SE India
114 L10 Tisa Ger. Theiss, Hung. Tisza, Rus. Tissa, Ukr. Tysa. ≈ SE Europe see also Tisza
Tischnowitz see Tišnov
9 U14 Tisdale Saskatchewan, S Canada
29 O13 Tishomingo Oklahoma, C USA
97 M17 Tisnaren ◎ S Sweden
113 F18 Tišnov Ger. Tischnowitz. Jižní Morava, SE Czech Republic
Tissa see Tisa/Tisza
76 J6 Tissemsilt N Algeria
159 S12 Tista ≈ NE India
114 L8 Tisza Ger. Theiss, Rom./Slvn./SCr. Tisa, Rus. Tissa, Ukr. Tysa. ≈ SE Europe see also Tisa
113 L23 Tiszaföldvár Jász-Nagykun-Szolnok, E Hungary
113 M22 Tiszafüred Jász-Nagykun-Szolnok, E Hungary
113 L23 Tiszakécske Bács-Kiskun, C Hungary
113 M21 Tiszaújváros prev. Leninváros. Borsod-Abaúj-Zemplén, NE Hungary
113 N21 Tiszavasvári Szabolcs-Szatmár-Bereg, NE Hungary
Titibu see Chichibu
59 I17 Titicaca, Lake ◎ Bolivia/Peru
202 H17 Titikaveka Rarotonga, S Cook Islands
160 M13 Titilāgarh Orissa, E India
174 Gg4 Titiwangsa, Banjaran ⛰ Peninsular Malaysia
Titograd see Podgorica
Titose see Chitose
Titova Mitrovica see Kosovska Mitrovica
Titovo Užice see Užice
115 M18 Titov Vrv ▲ NW FYR Macedonia
96 F7 Titran Sør-Trøndelag, S Norway
33 Q8 Tittabawassee River ≈ Michigan, N USA
118 J13 Titu Dâmboviţa, S Romania
81 M16 Titule Haut-Zaïre, N Zaire
25 X11 Titusville Florida, SE USA
20 C12 Titusville Pennsylvania, NE USA
78 G11 Tivaouane W Senegal
115 I17 Tivat Montenegro, SW Yugoslavia
12 E14 Tiverton Ontario, S Canada
99 J23 Tiverton SW England, UK
21 O12 Tiverton Rhode Island, NE USA
109 I15 Tivoli anc. Tiber. Lazio, C Italy
27 U13 Tivoli Texas, SW USA
176 W11 Tiwarra Irian Jaya, E Indonesia
147 Z8 Ţīwī NE Oman
Tiworo see Tioro, Selat
176 Ww12 Tiyo, Pegunungan ⛰ Irian Jaya, E Indonesia
43 Y11 Tizimín Yucatán, SE Mexico
76 K5 Tizi Ouzou var. Tizi-Ouzou. N Algeria
76 D8 Tiznit SW Morocco
115 I14 Tjentište SE Bosnia and Herzegovina
Tjepoe/Tjepu see Cepu
100 L7 Tjeukemeer ◎ N Netherlands
Tjiamis see Ciamis
Tjiandjoer see Cianjur
Tjilatjap see Cilacap
Tjiledoeg see Ciledug
97 F23 Tjæreborg Ribe, W Denmark
97 I18 Tjörn island S Sweden
94 O3 Tjuvfjorden fjord S Svalbard
Tkvarcheli see Tqvarch'eli
42 L8 Tlahualillo Durango, N Mexico
43 P14 Tlalnepantla México, C Mexico
43 Q13 Tlapacoyán Veracruz-Llave, E Mexico
43 P16 Tlapa de Comonfort Guerrero, S Mexico
42 L13 Tlaquepaque Jalisco, C Mexico
Tlascala see Tlaxcala
43 P14 Tlaxcala var. Tlascala, Tlaxcala de Xicohténcatl. Tlaxcala, C Mexico
43 P14 Tlaxcala ◈ state S Mexico
Tlaxcala de Xicohténcatl see Tlaxcala
43 P14 Tlaxco var. Tlaxco de Morelos. Tlaxcala, S Mexico
Tlaxco de Morelos see Tlaxco
43 Q16 Tlaxiaco var. Santa María Asunción Tlaxiaco. Oaxaca, S Mexico
76 I6 Tlemcen var. Tilimsen, Tlemsen. NW Algeria
Tlemsen see Tlemcen
144 L4 Tlété Ouâte Rharbi, Jebel ▲ N Syria
118 J7 Tlumach Ivano-Frankivs'ka Oblast', W Ukraine
131 P17 Tlyarata Respublika Dagestan, SW Russian Federation
118 K10 Toaca, Vârful prev. Vîrful Toaca. ▲ NE Romania
Toaca, Vîrful see Toaca, Vârful
197 C13 Toak Ambrym, C Vanuatu
180 J4 Toamasina var. Tamatave. Toamasina, E Madagascar
180 J4 Toamasina ◈ province E Madagascar
180 J4 Toamasina ✕ Toamasina, E Madagascar
23 X6 Toano Virginia, NE USA
203 U10 Toau atoll Îles Tuamotu, C French Polynesia
47 T6 Toa Vaca, Embalse ⊠ C Puerto Rico
64 K13 Toay La Pampa, C Argentina
165 R14 Toba Xizang Zizhiqu, W China
171 Hh16 Toba Mie, Honshū, SW Japan
173 Ff5 Toba, Danau ◎ Sumatera, W Indonesia
47 Y16 Tobago island NE Trinidad and Tobago
155 Q9 Toba Kākar Range ⛰ NW Pakistan
175 T10 Tobalai, Selat strait Maluku, E Indonesia
175 Q9 Tobamawu Sulawesi, N Indonesia
107 Q12 Tobarra Castilla-La Mancha, C Spain
155 U9 Toba Tek Singh Punjab, E Pakistan
175 T6 Tobelo Pulau Halmahera, E Indonesia
12 E12 Tobermory Ontario, S Canada
98 G10 Tobermory W Scotland, UK
172 Oo5 Tōbetsu Hokkaidō, NE Japan
188 M6 Tobin Lake ◎ Western Australia
9 U14 Tobin Lake ◎ Saskatchewan, C Canada
37 T4 Tobin, Mount ▲ Nevada, W USA
171 L10 Tobi-shima island C Japan
174 J11 Toboali Pulau Bangka, W Indonesia
150 M8 Tobol Kaz. Tobyl. Kustanay, N Kazakhstan
150 L8 Tobol Kaz. Tobyl. ≈ Kazakhstan/Russian Federation
125 F11 Tobol'sk Tyumenskaya Oblast', C Russian Federation
Tobruch/Tobruk see Ţubruq
129 R3 Tobseda Nenetskiy Avtonomnyy Okrug, NW Russian Federation
Tobyl see Tobol
129 Q6 Tobysh ≈ NW Russian Federation
56 F10 Tocaima Cundinamarca, C Colombia
61 K16 Tocantins off. Estado do Tocantins. ◈ state C Brazil
61 K15 Tocantins, Rio ≈ N Brazil
25 T2 Toccoa Georgia, SE USA
171 K15 Tochigi var. Totigi. Tochigi, Honshū, S Japan
171 Kk15 Tochigi off. Tochigi-ken, var. Totigi. ◈ prefecture Honshū, S Japan
171 K13 Tochio var. Totio. Niigata, Honshū, C Japan
97 I15 Töcksfors Värmland, C Sweden
44 J5 Tocoa Colón, N Honduras
64 H4 Tocopilla Antofagasta, N Chile
64 I4 Tocorpuri, Cerro de ▲ Bolivia/Chile
191 O10 Tocumwal New South Wales, SE Australia
56 K4 Tocuyo de La Costa Falcón, NW Venezuela
158 H13 Toda Rāisingh Rājasthān, N India
108 H13 Todi Umbria, C Italy
110 G9 Tödi ▲ NE Switzerland
176 Uu9 Todlo Irian Jaya, E Indonesia
172 N12 Todoga-saki headland Honshū, C Japan
61 P17 Todos os Santos, Baía de bay E Brazil
42 F10 Todos Santos Baja California Sur, W Mexico
42 B2 Todos Santos, Bahía de bay NW Mexico
Toeal see Tual
Toeban see Tuban
Toekang Besi Eilanden see Tukangbesi, Kepulauan
Töen see T'aoyüan
193 D25 Toetoes Bay bay South Island, NZ
9 Q14 Tofield Alberta, SW Canada
8 K17 Tofino Vancouver Island, British Columbia, SW Canada
201 X17 Tofol Kosrae, E Micronesia
97 J20 Tofta Halland, S Sweden
97 H15 Tofte Buskerud, S Norway
97 F24 Toftlund Sønderjylland, SW Denmark
200 S13 Tofua island Ha'apai Group, C Tonga
197 B10 Toga island Torres Islands, N Vanuatu
171 Kk17 Tōgane Chiba, Honshū, S Japan
82 N13 Togdheer off. Gobolka Togdheer. ◈ region NW Somalia
Toghyzaq see Toguzak
171 Ii12 Togi Ishikawa, Honshū, SW Japan
41 N13 Togiak Alaska, USA
175 Qq8 Togian, Kepulauan island group C Indonesia
79 Q15 Togo off. Togolese Republic; prev. French Togoland. ◆ republic W Africa
168 F8 Tögrög Govĭ-Altay, SW Mongolia
168 E7 Tögrög Hovd, W Mongolia
Togton-heyan see Tuotuoheyan
150 L7 Toguzak Kaz. Toghyzaq. ≈ Kazakhstan/Russian Federation
39 P10 Tohatchi New Mexico, SW USA
203 O7 Tohiea, Mont ▲ Moorea, W French Polynesia
95 O17 Tohmajärvi Pohjois-Karjala, SE Finland
143 N14 Tohma Çayı ≈ C Turkey
95 L16 Toholampi Vaasa, W Finland
168 M10 Töhöm Dornogovĭ, SE Mongolia
25 X12 Tohopekaliga, Lake ◎ Florida, SE USA
171 J17 Toi Shizuoka, Honshū, S Japan
202 B15 Toi N Niue
95 L19 Toijala Häme, SW Finland
175 Qq9 Toima Sulawesi, N Indonesia
170 C17 Toi-misaki headland Kyūshū, SW Japan
175 Rr17 Toineke Timor, S Indonesia
Toirc, Inis see Inishturk
37 U6 Toiyabe Range ⛰ Nevada, W USA
Tojikiston, Jumhurii see Tajikistan
153 R12 Tojikobod Rus. Tadzhikabad. C Tajikistan
170 F13 Tōjō Hiroshima, Honshū, SW Japan
41 T10 Tok Alaska, USA
172 P5 Tokachi-dake ▲ Hokkaidō, NE Japan

◆ Country ● Country Capital ◇ Dependent Territory ○ Dependent Territory Capital ◈ Administrative Region ✕ International Airport ▲ Mountain ⛰ Mountain Range ℛ Volcano ≈ River ◎ Lake ⊠ Reservoir

172 Pp7 **Tokachi-gawa** var. Tokati Gawa.
☆ Hokkaidō, NE Japan

171 Hh16 **Tōkai** Aichi, Honshū, SW Japan

113 N21 **Tokaj** Borsod-Abaúj-Zemplén,
NE Hungary

171 Jj13 **Tōkamachi** Niigata, Honshū,
C Japan

193 D25 **Tokanui** Southland,
South Island, NZ

82 I7 **Tokar** var. Ţawkar. Red Sea,
NE Sudan

142 L12 **Tokat** Tokat, N Turkey

142 L12 **Tokat** ◆ province N Turkey

169 X15 **Tŏkchŏk-gundo** island group
NW South Korea

Tōke see Taka Atoll

202 J9 **Tokelau** ◇ NZ overseas territory
W Polynesia

Tőketerebes see Trebišov

Tokhtamyshbek see
Tūkhtamish

26 M6 **Tokio** Texas, SW USA

Tokio see Tōkyō

201 W11 **Toki Point** point
NW Wake Island

Tokkuztara see Gongliu

153 V7 **Tokmak** Kir. Tokmok.
Chuyskaya Oblast', N Kyrgyzstan

119 V9 **Tokmak** var. Velykyy Tokmak.
Zaporiz'ka Oblast', SE Ukraine

Tokmok see Tokmak

192 Q8 **Tokomaru Bay** Gisborne,
North Island, NZ

171 Hh16 **Tokoname** Aichi, Honshū,
SW Japan

172 Qq5 **Tokoro** Hokkaidō, NE Japan

192 M8 **Tokoroa** Waikato,
North Island, NZ

172 Q6 **Tokoro-gawa** ☆ Hokkaidō,
NE Japan

78 K14 **Tokounou** Haute-Guinée,
C Guinea

40 M12 **Toksook Bay** Alaska, USA

Toksu see Xinhe

Toksum see Toksun

164 L6 **Toksun** var. Toksum. Xinjiang
Uygur Zizhiqu, NW China

153 T8 **Toktogul** Talasskaya Oblast',
NW Kyrgyzstan

153 T9 **Toktogul'skoye
Vodokhranilishche**
☆ W Kyrgyzstan

Toktomush see Tūkhtamish

200 S12 **Toku** island Vava'u Group,
N Tonga

172 Qq14 **Tokunoshima** Kagoshima,
Tokuno-shima, SW Japan

172 Q14 **Tokuno-shima** island Nansei-
shotō, SW Japan

170 Ff15 **Tokushima** var. Tokusima.
Tokushima, Shikoku, SW Japan

170 F15 **Tokushima off.** Tokushima-ken,
var. Tokusima. ◆ prefecture
Shikoku, SW Japan

Tokusima see Tokushima

170 E13 **Tokuyama** Yamaguchi, Honshū,
SW Japan

171 Jj16 **Tōkyō** var. Tokio. ● (Japan)
Tōkyō, Honshū, S Japan

171 Jj15 **Tōkyō off.** Tōkyō-to. ◆ capital
district Honshū, S Japan

171 K17 **Tōkyō-wan** bay S Japan

151 T12 **Tokyrau** ☆ C Kazakhstan

155 O3 **Tokzār** Pash. Tukzār. Sar-e Pol,
N Afghanistan

201 U12 **Tol** atoll Chuuk Islands,
C Micronesia

192 Q9 **Tolaga Bay** Gisborne, North
Island, NZ

180 I7 **Tôlañaro** prev. Faradofay, Fort-
Dauphin. Toliara, SE Madagascar

168 D6 **Tolbo** Bayan-Ölgiy, W Mongolia

Tolbukhin see Dobrich

62 G11 **Toledo** Paraná, S Brazil

56 G8 **Toledo** Norte de Santander,
N Colombia

179 Qq13 **Toledo off.** Toledo City. Cebu,
C Philippines

107 N9 **Toledo** anc. Toletum.
Castilla-La Mancha, C Spain

32 M14 **Toledo** Illinois, N USA

31 W13 **Toledo** Iowa, C USA

33 R11 **Toledo** Ohio, N USA

34 F12 **Toledo** Oregon, NW USA

34 G9 **Toledo** Washington, NW USA

44 F3 **Toledo** ◇ district S Belize

106 M9 **Toledo** ◆ province
Castilla-La Mancha, C Spain

27 Y7 **Toledo Bend Reservoir**
☆ Louisiana/Texas, SW USA

106 M10 **Toledo, Montes de** ▲ C Spain

108 J12 **Tolentino** Marche, C Italy

Toletum see Toledo

96 H10 **Tolga** Hedmark, S Norway

164 J3 **Toli** Xinjiang Uygur Zizhiqu,
NW China

180 H7 **Toliara** var. Toliary; prev. Tuléar.
Toliara, SW Madagascar

180 H7 **Toliara** ◆ province
SW Madagascar

Toliary see Toliara

56 D11 **Tolima off.** Departamento del
Tolima. ◆ province C Colombia

175 Pp7 **Tolitoli** Sulawesi, C Indonesia

97 K22 **Tollarp** Kristianstad, S Sweden

102 N9 **Tollense** ☆ NE Germany

102 N10 **Tollensesee** ◎ NE Germany

38 K13 **Tolleson** Arizona, SW USA

152 M13 **Tollimarjon** Rus. Talimardzhan.
Qashqadaryo Wiloyati,
S Uzbekistan

Tolmein see Tolmin

111 S11 **Tolmezzo** Friuli-Venezia Giulia,
NE Italy

111 S11 **Tolmin** Ger. Tolmein, It.
Tolmino. W Slovenia

Tolmino see Tolmin

113 I25 **Tolna** Ger. Tolnau. Tolna,
S Hungary

113 I24 **Tolna off.** Tolna Megye.
◆ county SW Hungary

Tolnau see Tolna

81 I20 **Tolo** Bandundu, W Zaire

Tolochin see Talachyn

202 D12 **Toloke** Île Futuna,
W Wallis and Futuna

32 M13 **Tolono** Illinois, N USA

107 Q3 **Tolosa** País Vasco, N Spain

Tolosa see Toulouse

175 Qq10 **Tolo, Teluk** bay Sulawesi,
C Indonesia

41 R9 **Tolovana River** ☆
Alaska, USA

127 Oo10 **Tolstoy, Mys** headland
E Russian Federation

65 G15 **Toltén** Araucanía, C Chile

65 G15 **Toltén, Río** ☆ S Chile

56 H10 **Tolú** Sucre, NW Colombia

43 O14 **Toluca** var. Toluca de Lerdo.
México, S Mexico

Toluca de Lerdo see Toluca

43 O14 **Toluca, Nevado de** ▲ C Mexico

131 R6 **Tol'yatti** prev. Stavropol'.
Samarskaya Oblast', W Russian
Federation

126 H14 **Tom'** ☆ S Russian Federation

79 O12 **Toma** NW Burkina

32 K7 **Tomah** Wisconsin, N USA

32 L5 **Tomahawk** Wisconsin, N USA

119 T8 **Tomakivka** Dnipropetrovs'ka
Oblast', E Ukraine

172 O6 **Tomakomai** Hokkaidō,
NE Japan

172 P3 **Tomamae** Hokkaidō, NE Japan

106 G9 **Tomar** Santarém, W Portugal

127 O15 **Tomari** Ostrov Sakhalin,
Sakhalinskaya Oblast', SE Russian
Federation

117 C16 **Tómaros** ▲ W Greece

Tomaschow see Tomaszów
Lubelski, Poland

Tomaschow see Tomaszów
Mazowiecki, Poland

63 E16 **Tomás Gomensoro** Artigas,
N Uruguay

119 N7 **Tomashpil'** Vinnyts'ka Oblast',
C Ukraine

Tomaszów see Tomaszów
Mazowiecki

113 P15 **Tomaszów Lubelski** Ger.
Tomaschow. Zamość, SE Poland

Tomaszów Mazowiecka see
Tomaszów Mazowiecki

112 L13 **Tomaszów Mazowiecki** var.
Tomaszów Mazowiecka; prev.
Tomaszów, Ger. Tomaschow.
Piotrków, C Poland

42 L13 **Tomatlán** Jalisco, C Mexico

170 F12 **Tombara** Shimane, Honshū,
SW Japan

83 I18 **Tombe** Jonglei, S Sudan

25 N4 **Tombigbee River**
☆ Alabama/Mississippi, S USA

84 A10 **Tomboco** Zaire, NW Angola

79 O10 **Tombouctou** Eng. Timbuktu.
Tombouctou, N Mali

79 N9 **Tombouctou** ◆ region W Mali

39 N16 **Tombstone** Arizona, SW USA

85 A15 **Tombua** Port. Porto Alexandre.
Namibe, SW Angola

85 J19 **Tom Burke** Northern,
NE South Africa

152 L9 **Tomdibuloq** Rus. Tamdybulak.
Nawoiy Wiloyati, N Uzbekistan

152 K9 **Tomditow-Toghi**
▲ N Uzbekistan

64 G13 **Tomé** Bío Bío, C Chile

60 L12 **Tomé-Açu** Pará, NE Brazil

97 L23 **Tomelilla** Kristianstad,
S Sweden

107 O10 **Tomelloso** Castilla-La Mancha,
C Spain

12 H10 **Tomiko Lake** ◎ Ontario,
S Canada

79 N12 **Tominian** Ségou, C Mali

175 Pp8 **Tomini, Gulf of** var. Teluk
Tomini; prev. Teluk Gorontalo.
bay Sulawesi, C Indonesia

175 Pp7 **Tomini, Teluk** see Tomini,
Gulf of

172 Ii15 **Tomioka** Fukushima, Honshū,
C Japan

172 Jj15 **Tomioka** Gunma, Honshū,
S Japan

115 G14 **Tomislavgrad** SW Bosnia
and Herzegovina

189 O9 **Tomkinson Ranges** ▲ South
Australia/Western Australia

126 Lll2 **Tommot** Respublika Sakha
(Yakutiya), NE Russian
Federation

175 Rr7 **Tomohon** Sulawesi, N Indonesia

56 K9 **Tomo, Río** ☆ E Colombia

115 L21 **Tomorrit, Mali i a** ▲ S Albania

9 S17 **Tompkins** Saskatchewan,
S Canada

22 K8 **Tompkinsville** Kentucky,
S USA

93 Tompo Tompo

126 H13 **Tomsk** Tomskaya Oblast',
C Russian Federation

126 Gg12 **Tomskaya Oblast'** ◆ province
C Russian Federation

20 L8 **Toms River** New Jersey,
NE USA

191 O5 **Tom Steed Lake** see Tom Steed
Reservoir

28 L12 **Tom Steed Reservoir** var. Tom
Steed Lake. ◎ Oklahoma, C USA

174 N9 **Tomu** Irian Jaya, E Indonesia

194 F13 **Tomu** ☆ W PNG

164 H6 **Tomur Feng** var. Pik Pobedy.
Pobeda Peak.
▲ China/Kyrgyzstan see also
Pobedy, Pik

201 N13 **Tomworoahlang** Pohnpei,
E Micronesia

43 O17 **Tonalá** Chiapas, SE Mexico

108 F6 **Tonale, Passo del** pass N Italy

171 Ii13 **Tonami** Toyama, Honshū,
SW Japan

60 C12 **Tonantins** Amazonas, W Brazil

34 K6 **Tonasket** Washington, NW USA

57 Y9 **Tonate** var. Macouria.
N French Guiana

32 D10 **Tonawanda** New York, NE USA

175 Rr7 **Tondano** Sulawesi, C Indonesia

175 Rr7 **Tondano, Danau** ◎ Sulawesi,
N Indonesia

106 H7 **Tôndela** Viseu, N Portugal

97 F24 **Tønder** Ger. Tondern.
Sønderjylland, SW Denmark

Tondern see Tønder

171 K16 **Tone-gawa** ☆ Honshū, S Japan

149 N4 **Tonekābon** var. Shahsawar,
Tonkābon; prev. Shahsavār.
Māzandarān, N Iran

34 J10 **Toppenish** Washington,
NW USA

189 N4 **Tonga** off. Kingdom of Tonga,
var. Friendly Islands. ◆ monarchy
SW Pacific Ocean

183 R9 **Tonga** island group
SW Pacific Ocean

85 K23 **Tongaat** KwaZulu/Natal,
E South Africa

167 Q13 **Tong'an** var. Tong an. Fujian,
SE China

29 Q4 **Tonganoxie** Kansas, C USA

41 Y13 **Tongass National Forest**
reserve Alaska, USA

200 Qq16 **Tongatapu** × Tongatapu,
S Tonga

200 R15 **Tongatapu** island Tongatapu
Group, S Tonga

200 S14 **Tongatapu Group** island group
S Tonga

183 S9 **Tonga Trench** undersea feature
S Pacific Ocean

167 N8 **Tongbai Shan** ▲ C China

167 P8 **Tongcheng** Anhui, E China

166 L12 **Tongchuan** Shaanxi, C China

166 L12 **Tongdao** var. Tongdao Dongzu
Zizhixian; prev. Shuangjiang.
Hunan, C China

165 T11 **Tongde** Qinghai, C China

101 K19 **Tongeren** Fr. Tongres. Limburg,
NE Belgium

Tonggou see Tongyu

169 U10 **Tonghae** NE South Korea

166 G13 **Tonghai** Yunnan, SW China

169 W11 **Tonghe** Heilongjiang, NE China

169 X11 **Tonghua** Jilin, NE China

194 L18 **Tongi** Island var. Tong Island N PNG

169 Z6 **Tongjiang** Heilongjiang,
NE China

169 Y13 **Tongjosŏn-man** prev.
Broughton Bay. bay E North Korea

169 V7 **Tongking, Gulf of** ☆ NE China

178 K7 **Tongking, Gulf of** Chin. Beibu
Wan, Vtn. Vinh Bắc Bô. gulf
China/Vietnam

169 U10 **Tongliao** Nei Mongol Zizhiqu,
N China

167 Q9 **Tongling** Anhui, E China

167 R9 **Tonglu** Zhejiang, SE China

197 D14 **Tongoa** island Shepherd Islands,
S Vanuatu

64 G9 **Tongoy** Coquimbo, C Chile

166 L11 **Tongren** Guizhou, S China

165 T11 **Tongren** Qinghai, C China

Tongres see Tongeren

159 U11 **Tongsa** var. Tongsa Dzong.
C Bhutan

Tongsa Dzong see Tongsa

Tongshan see Xuzhou

165 P12 **Tongtian He** ☆ C China

98 I6 **Tongue** N Scotland, UK

46 H3 **Tongue of the Ocean** strait
C Bahamas

35 X10 **Tongue River** ☆ Montana,
NW USA

35 W10 **Tongue River Resevoir**
◎ Montana, NW USA

165 V11 **Tongwei** Gansu, C China

165 W9 **Tongxin** Ningxia, N China

169 U9 **Tongyu** var. Tonggou. Jilin,
NE China

166 J11 **Tongzi** Guizhou, S China

42 G5 **Tónichi** Sonora, NW Mexico

33 V12 **Tonica** Ohio, N USA

158 H13 **Tonj** Warab, SW Sudan

160 H12 **Tonk** Rājasthān, N India

29 Q10 **Tonkawa** Oklahoma, C USA

178 Ii12 **Tônlé Sap** Eng. Great Lake.
◎ W Cambodia

104 L14 **Tonneins** Lot-et-Garonne,
SW France

105 Q7 **Tonnerre** Yonne, C France

37 U8 **Tonopah** Nevada, W USA

170 Ff14 **Tonoshō** Okayama, Shōdo-
shima, SW Japan

45 Q17 **Tonosí** Los Santos, S Panama

97 H16 **Tønsberg** Vestfold, S Norway

11 T11 **Tonsina** Alaska, USA

97 D17 **Tonstad** Vest-Agder, S Norway

200 S14 **Tonumea** island Nomuka Group,
S Tonga

143 O11 **Tonya** Trabzon, NE Turkey

121 K20 **Tonyezh** Rus. Tonezh.
Homyel'skaya Voblasts',
SE Belarus

38 L3 **Tooele** Utah, W USA

126 Ii15 **Toora-Khem** Respublika Tyva,
S Russian Federation

191 O5 **Toorale East** New South Wales,
SE Australia

85 D13 **Toorberg** ▲ S South Africa

191 U3 **Toowoomba** Queensland,
E Australia

29 Q4 **Topeka** state capital Kansas,
C USA

113 M18 **Topľa** Hung. Toplya.
☆ NE Slovakia

126 H14 **Topki** Kemerovskaya Oblast',
C Russian Federation

118 J10 **Topliţa** Ger. Töplitz, Hung.
Maroshévíz; prev. Topliţa
Română, Hung. Oláh-Toplicza,
Toplicza. Harghita, C Romania

**Topliţa Română/
Töplitz** see Topliţa

Toplya see Topľa

113 I20 **Topolčany** Hung.
Nagytapolcsány. Západné
Slovensko, W Slovakia

42 G8 **Topolobampo** Sinaloa,
C Mexico

118 I13 **Topoloveni** Argeş, S Romania

116 L11 **Topolovgrad** prev. Kavakli.
Burgaska Oblast', SE Bulgaria

Topolya see Bačka Topola

128 I6 **Topozero, Ozero**
◎ NW Russian Federation

190 I6 **Torrens, Lake** salt lake
South Australia

104 M3 **Tôtes** Seine-Maritime, N France

Torrent/Torrent de l'Horta
see Torrente

107 S10 **Torrente** var. Torrent, Torrent de
l'Horta. País Valenciano, E Spain

42 L8 **Torreón** Coahuila de Zaragoza,
NE Mexico

107 R13 **Torre Pacheco** Murcia,
SE Spain

108 A8 **Torre Pellice** Piemonte, NE Italy

107 O13 **Torreperogil** Andalucía,
S Spain

63 J15 **Torres** Rio Grande do Sul,
S Brazil

Torres, Îles see Torres Islands

197 B10 **Torres Islands** Fr. Îles Torrès.
island group N Vanuatu

106 G9 **Torres Novas** Santarém,
C Portugal

189 V1 **Torres Strait** strait
Australia/PNG

106 F10 **Torres Vedras** Lisboa,
C Portugal

107 S13 **Torrevieja** País Valenciano,
E Spain

194 F9 **Torricelli Mountains**
▲ NW PNG

98 G8 **Torridon, Loch** inlet
NW Scotland, UK

108 D9 **Torriglia** Liguria, NW Italy

106 M9 **Torrijos** Castilla-La Mancha,
C Spain

20 L12 **Torrington** Connecticut,
NE USA

35 Z15 **Torrington** Wyoming, C USA

95 F16 **Torröjen** var. Torrön.
◎ C Sweden

94 K13 **Töre** Norrbotten, N Sweden

97 L17 **Töreboda** Skaraborg, S Sweden

97 J21 **Torekov** Kristianstad, S Sweden

94 O3 **Torell Land** physical region
SW Svalbard

119 T8 **Torez** Donets'ka Oblast',
SE Ukraine

47 N16 **Torhamn** Blekinge, S Sweden

101 C17 **Torhout** West-Vlaanderen,
W Belgium

108 B8 **Torino** Eng. Turin. Piemonte,
NW Italy

172 Q13 **Tori-shima** island Izu-shotō,
SE Japan

83 F14 **Torit** Eastern Equatoria, S Sudan

195 O11 **Toriu** New Britain, E PNG

154 M4 **Torkestān, Selseleh-ye Band-e**
var. Bandi-i Turkistan.
▲ NW Afghanistan

106 L7 **Tormes** ☆ W Spain

94 K13 **Torneälven** var.Tornejoki, Fin.
Torniojoki. ☆ Finland/Sweden

94 I11 **Torneträsk** ◎ N Sweden

11 O4 **Torngat Mountains**
▲ Newfoundland and Labrador,
NE Canada

26 H8 **Tornillo** Texas, SW USA

94 K13 **Tornio** Swe. Torneå. Lappi,
NW Finland

Tornjoki/Torniojoki see
Torneälven

63 B23 **Tornquist** Buenos Aires,
E Argentina

106 L6 **Toro** Castilla-León, N Spain

64 H9 **Toro, Cerro del** ▲ N Chile

79 R12 **Torodi** Tillabéri, SW Niger

Törökbecse see Novi Bečej

113 L23 **Törökszentmiklós** Jász-
Nagykun-Szolnok, E Hungary

44 G9 **Torola, Río**
☆ El Salvador/Honduras

Toronaíos, Kólpos see
Kassándras, Kólpos

12 H11 **Toronto** Ontario, S Canada

33 V12 **Toronto** Ohio, N USA

Toronto see Lester B.Pearson

33 V10 **Toronto Lake** ◎ Kansas,
C USA

37 V16 **Toro Peak** ▲ California, W USA

128 H16 **Toropets** Tverskaya Oblast',
W Russian Federation

83 F18 **Tororo** E Uganda

142 H16 **Toros Dağları** Eng. Taurus
Mountains. ▲ S Turkey

191 N13 **Torquay** Victoria, SE Australia

99 K24 **Torquay** Eng. Torquay. SW
England, UK

106 M5 **Torquemada** Castilla-León,
N Spain

37 S16 **Torrance** California, W USA

106 G12 **Torrão** Setúbal, S Portugal

109 K18 **Torre, Alto da** ▲ C Portugal

109 K18 **Torre Annunziata** Campania,
S Italy

107 T8 **Torreblanca** País Valenciano,
E Spain

107 P4 **Torrecilla en Cameros** La
Rioja, N Spain

107 Q13 **Torrecilla** ▲ S Spain

107 O4 **Torredelcampo** Andalucía,
S Spain

107 Q13 **Torre del Greco** Campania,
S Italy

106 J6 **Torre de Moncorvo** var.
Moncorvo, Tôrre de Moncorvo.
Bragança, N Portugal

107 U4 **Torrejoncillo** Extremadura,
W Spain

107 N7 **Torrejón de Ardoz** Madrid,
C Spain

107 N7 **Torrelaguna** Madrid, C Spain

106 M2 **Torrelavega** Cantabria, N Spain

142 J11 **Torre Maggiore** Puglia, SE Italy

107 R13 **Torremolinos** Andalucía,
S Spain

96 H13 **Toten** physical region N Norway

85 G18 **Toteng** Ngamiland, C Botswana

104 M3 **Tôtes** Seine-Maritime, N France

110 J15 **Totigi** see Tochigi

Totio see Tochio

Totis see Tata

201 U13 **Totiw** island Chuuk,
C Micronesia

29 N13 **Tot'ma** var. Totma.
Vologodskaya Oblast',
NW Russian Federation

Tot'ma see Sukhona

107 O13 **Totness** Coronie, N Suriname

44 C5 **Totonicapán** Totonicapán,
W Guatemala

44 A2 **Totonicapán off.** Departamento
de Totonicapán. ◆ department
W Guatemala

63 B18 **Totoras** Santa Fe, C Argentina

191 J13 **Totoya** island S Fiji

191 Q7 **Tottenham** New South Wales,
SE Australia

171 G13 **Tottori** Tottori, Honshū,
SW Japan

170 Ff13 **Tottori off.** Tottori-ken.
◆ prefecture Honshū, SW Japan

78 I6 **Touajïl** Tiris Zemmour,
N Mauritania

78 L6 **Touba** W Ivory Coast

78 G11 **Touba** W Senegal

76 E7 **Toubkal, Jbel** ▲ W Morocco

77 N4 **Touchet** Washington, NW USA

105 P7 **Toucy** Yonne, C France

79 O12 **Tougan** W Burkina

76 L7 **Touggourt** NE Algeria

79 N11 **Tougouri** N Burkina

78 J13 **Tougué** Moyenne-Guinée,
NW Guinea

78 K12 **Toukoto** Kayes, W Mali

105 S5 **Toul** Meurthe-et-Moselle,
NE France

78 L16 **Toulépleu** var. Touïobli.
W Ivory Coast

167 T3 **Touliu** C Taiwan

13 D **Toulnustouc** ☆ Québec,
SE Canada

Toulobli see Toulépleu

105 T16 **Toulon** anc. Telo Martius, Tilio
Martius. Var, SE France

32 K12 **Toulon** Illinois, N USA

104 M15 **Toulouse** anc. Tolosa. Haute-
Garonne, S France

104 M15 **Toulouse** × Haute-Garonne,
S France

79 N6 **Toumodi** C Ivory Coast

76 G9 **Tounassine, Hamada** hill range
W Algeria

177 G7 **Toungoo** Pegu, C Myanmar

104 L8 **Touraine** cultural region C France

79 O12 **Tourcoing** Nord, N France

106 F2 **Touriñán, Cabo** headland
NW Spain

78 J6 **Tourine** Tiris Zemmour,
N Mauritania

104 J3 **Tourlaville** Manche, N France

101 D19 **Tournai** var. Tournay, Dut.
Doornik; anc. Tornacum.
Hainaut, SW Belgium

104 L16 **Tournay** Hautes-Pyrénées,
S France

105 R12 **Tournon** Ardèche, E France

105 R9 **Tournus** Saône-et-Loire,
C France

61 Q14 **Touros** Rio Grande do Norte,
E Brazil

104 L8 **Tours** anc. Caesarodunum,
Turoni. Indre-et-Loire, C France

191 Q7 **Tourville, Cape** headland
Tasmania, SE Australia

168 L8 **Tous** ◆ province C Mongolia

56 H7 **Tovar** Mérida, NW Venezuela

130 L5 **Tovarkovskiy** Tul'skaya Oblast',
W Russian Federation

Tovil'-Dora see Tavildara

Tóvis see Teius

143 U9 **Tovuz** Rus. Tauz. ▲ W Azerbaijan

172 N9 **Towada** Aomori, Honshū,
C Japan

172 N9 **Towada-ko** var. Towada Ko.
◎ Honshū, C Japan

192 K3 **Towai** Northland,
North Island, NZ

20 J10 **Towanda** Pennsylvania, NE USA

31 W **Tower** Minnesota, N USA

175 Pp8 **Towera** Sulawesi, N Indonesia

188 M13 **Tower Peak** ▲ Western Australia

37 U11 **Towne Pass** California,
W USA

31 N3 **Towner** North Dakota, N USA

35 R10 **Townsend** Montana, NW USA

189 X6 **Townsville** Queensland,
NE Australia

21 U9 **Towson** Maryland, NE USA

175 Q10 **Towori, Teluk** bay Sulawesi,
C Indonesia

154 K4 **Towraghoudi** Herāt,
NW Afghanistan

23 X3 **Towson** Maryland, NE USA

175 Q11 **Towuti, Danau** Dut. Towti
Meer. ◎ Sulawesi, C Indonesia

Toxkan He see Ak-say

165 Q10 **Toson Hu** ◎ C China

168 H6 **Tosontsengel** Dzavhan,
NW Mongolia

172 Nn6 **Tôya-ko** ◎ Hokkaidō, NE Japan

171 I13 **Toyama** Toyama, Honshū,
SW Japan

171 Ii13 **Toyama off.** Toyama-ken.
◆ prefecture Honshū, SW Japan

171 I13 **Toyama-wan** bay W Japan

171 Ee16 **Tōyō** Kōchi, Shikoku, SW Japan

170 Ee14 **Tōyō** Kōchi, Shikoku, SW Japan

Toyohara see Yuzhno-Sakhalinsk

171 Hh16 **Toyohashi** var. Toyohasi. Aichi,
Honshū, SW Japan

Toyohasi see Toyohashi

171 I10 **Toyokawa** Aichi, Honshū,
SW Japan

171 Gg13 **Tōyooka** Hyōgo, Honshū,
SW Japan

171 Kk12 **Toyosaka** Niigata, Honshū,
C Japan

171 I16 **Toyota** Aichi, Honshū, SW Japan

172 Pp2 **Toyotomi** Hokkaidō, NE Japan

170 Dd12 **Toyoura** Yamaguchi, Honshū,
SW Japan

76 M6 **Tozeur** var. Tawzar. W Tunisia

41 Q8 **Tozi, Mount** ▲ Alaska, USA

143 Q9 **Tqvarch'eli** Rus. Tkvarcheli.
NW Georgia

143 O11 **Trabzon** Eng. Trebizond; anc.
Trapezus. Trabzon, NE Turkey

143 O11 **Trabzon** Eng. Trebizond.
◆ province NE Turkey

11 P13 **Tracadie** New Brunswick,
SE Canada

13 S15 **Tracy** Québec, SE Canada

37 O8 **Tracy** California, W USA

31 S10 **Tracy** Minnesota, N USA

22 K10 **Tracy City** Tennessee, S USA

108 D7 **Tradate** Lombardia, N Italy

86 F6 **Traena Bank** undersea feature
E Norwegian Sea

34 W13 **Traer** Iowa, C USA

106 J16 **Trafalgar, Cabo de** headland
SW Spain

8 B11 **Trail** British Columbia,
SW Canada

60 B17 **Traíra, Serra do** ▲ NW Brazil

111 V5 **Traisen** Niederösterreich,
NE Austria

111 W4 **Traisen** ☆ NE Austria

111 X4 **Traiskirchen** Niederösterreich,
NE Austria

Trajani Portus see Civitavecchia

**Trajectum ad Mosam/
Traiectum Tungorum** see
Maastricht

Trajectum ad Rhenum see
Utrecht

121 H14 **Trakai** Ger. Traken. Pol. Troki.
Trakai, SE Lithuania

Traken see Trakai

99 B20 **Tralee** Ir. Trá Lí. SW Ireland

99 A20 **Tralee Bay** Ir. Bá Thrá Lí. bay
SW Ireland

Trá Lí see Tralee

Trälleborg see Trelleborg

Tralles see Aydın

63 J16 **Tramandaí** Rio Grande do Sul,
S Brazil

110 D7 **Tramelan** Bern, W Switzerland

Trá Mhór see Tramore

99 E20 **Tramore** Ir. Tráigh Mhór,
Trá Mhór. S Ireland

57 L18 **Tranås** Jönköping, S Sweden

64 I7 **Trancas** Tucumán, N Argentina

106 I7 **Trancoso** Guarda, N Portugal

97 J19 **Tranebjerg** Århus, C Denmark

97 K19 **Tranemo** Älvsborg, S Sweden

178 Gg16 **Trang** Trang, S Thailand

176 W14 **Trangan, Pulau** island
Kepulauan Aru, E Indonesia

Tràng Định see Thất Khê

191 Q7 **Trangie** New South Wales,
SE Australia

96 K12 **Trängslet** Kopparberg,
S Sweden

109 N16 **Trani** Puglia, SE Italy

63 F17 **Tranqueras** Rivera, NE Uruguay

41 V6 **Trans-Alaska pipeline** oil
pipeline Alaska, USA

205 O10 **Transantarctic Mountains**
▲ Antarctica

Transcarpathian Oblast see
Zakarpats'ka Oblast'

Transilvania see Transylvania

Transilvaniei, Alpi see Carpaţii
Meridionali

Transjordan see Jordan

180 L11 **Transkei Basin** undersea feature
SW Indian Ocean

127 N17 **Trans-Siberian Railway**
railroad Russian Federation

**Transsylvanische
Alpen/Transylvanian Alps** see
Carpaţii Meridionali

96 K12 **Transtrand** Kopparberg,
C Sweden

118 G10 **Transylvania** Eng. Ardeal,
Transilvania, Ger. Siebenbürgen,
Hung. Erdély. cultural region
NW Romania

178 Ji15 **Tra Ôn** Vĩnh Long, S Vietnam

109 H23 **Trapani** anc. Drepanum. Sicilia,
Italy, C Mediterranean Sea

178 J12 **Trapeăng Vêng** Kâmpóng
Thum, C Cambodia

Trapezus see Trabzon

116 L9 **Trapoklovo** Burgaska Oblast',
E Bulgaria

191 P13 **Traralgon** Victoria, SE Australia

78 H9 **Trarza** ◆ region SW Mauritania

Trasimeno, Lago see
Trasimeno, Lago

108 H12 **Trasimeno, Lago Eng.** Lake of
Perugia, anc. Trasimennus.
◎ C Italy

97 J20 **Träslövsläge** Halland, S Sweden

106 I6 **Trás-os-Montes e Alto Douro**
former province N Portugal

178 I13 **Trat** var. Bang Phra. Trat,
S Thailand

Trá Tholl, Inis see Inishtrahull

Traú see Trogir

111 N4 **Traun** Oberösterreich, N Austria

111 S5 **Traun** ☆ N Austria

Traun, Lake see Traunsee

103 N23 **Traunreut** Bayern, SE Germany

111 N5 **Traunsee** var. Gmundner See,
Eng. Lake Traun. ◎ N Austria

Trautenau see Trutnov

Travelers Rest – Tumen

23 P11 Travelers Rest South Carolina, SE USA
190 L8 Travellers Lake seasonal lake New South Wales, SE Australia
33 P6 Traverse City Michigan, N USA
31 R7 Traverse, Lake ◎ Minnesota/South Dakota, N USA
193 I16 Travers, Mount ▲ South Island, NZ
9 P17 Travers Reservoir ⊡ Alberta, SW Canada
178 Jj15 Tra Vinh var. Phu Vinh. Tra Vinh, S Vietnam
27 S10 Travis, Lake ⊡ Texas, SW USA
114 H12 Travnik C Bosnia and Herzegovina
111 V11 Trbovlje Ger. Trifail. C Slovenia
25 V13 Treasure Island Florida, SE USA
Treasure State see Montana
195 S14 Treasury Islands island group NW Solomon Islands
108 D9 Trebbia anc. Trebia. ≈ NW Italy
102 N8 Trebel ≈ NE Germany
105 O16 Trèbes Aude, S France
Trebia see Trebbia
113 F18 Třebíč Ger. Trebitsch. Jižní Morava, S Czech Republic
115 I16 Trebinje S Bosnia and Herzegovina
Trebišnica see Trebišnjica
115 H16 Trebišnjica var. Trebišnica. ≈ S Bosnia and Herzegovina
113 N20 Trebišov Hung. Tőketerebes. Východné Slovensko, E Slovakia
Trebitsch see Třebíč
Trebizond see Trabzon
Trebnitz see Trzebnica
111 V12 Trebnje SE Slovenia
113 D19 Třeboň Ger. Wittingau. Jižní Čechy, S Czech Republic
106 J15 Trebujena Andalucía, S Spain
102 I7 Treene ≈ N Germany
Tree Planters State see Nebraska
111 S9 Treffen Kärnten, S Austria
Trefynwy see Monmouth
104 G5 Tréguier Côtes d'Armor, NW France
63 G18 Treinta y Tres Treinta y Tres, E Uruguay
63 F18 Treinta y Tres ◐ department E Uruguay
116 F9 Treklyanska Reka ≈ W Bulgaria
175 R10 Treko, Kepulauan island group N Indonesia
104 K8 Trélazé Maine-et-Loire, NW France
65 K17 Trelew Chubut, SE Argentina
97 K23 Trelleborg var. Trälleborg. Malmöhus, S Sweden
115 P15 Trem ▲ SE Yugoslavia
13 N11 Tremblant, Mont ▲ Québec, SE Canada
101 H17 Tremelo Vlaams Brabant, C Belgium
109 M15 Tremiti, Isole island group SE Italy
32 K12 Tremont Illinois, N USA
38 L1 Tremonton Utah, W USA
107 U4 Tremp Cataluña, NE Spain
32 J7 Trempealeau Wisconsin, N USA
13 P8 Trenche ≈ Québec, SE Canada
13 O7 Trenche, Lac ◎ Québec, SE Canada
113 I19 Trenčín Ger. Trentschin, Hung. Trencsén. Západné Slovensko, W Slovakia
Trencsén see Trenčín
Trengganu see Terengganu
63 A21 Trenque Lauquen Buenos Aires, E Argentina
12 J14 Trent ≈ Ontario, SE Canada
99 N18 Trent ≈ C England, UK
Trent see Trento
108 F5 Trentino-Alto Adige prev. Venezia Tridentina. ◐ region N Italy
108 G6 Trento Eng. Trent, Ger. Trient; anc. Tridentum. Trentino-Alto Adige, N Italy
12 J15 Trenton Ontario, SE Canada
25 V10 Trenton Florida, SE USA
25 R1 Trenton Georgia, SE USA
33 S10 Trenton Michigan, N USA
29 S2 Trenton Missouri, C USA
30 M17 Trenton Nebraska, C USA
20 J15 Trenton state capital New Jersey, NE USA
23 W10 Trenton North Carolina, SE USA
22 G9 Trenton Tennessee, S USA
38 L1 Trenton Utah, W USA
Trentschin see Trenčín
Treptow an der Rega see Trzebiatów
63 C23 Tres Arroyos Buenos Aires, E Argentina
63 J15 Três Cachoeiras Rio Grande do Sul, S Brazil
108 E7 Trescore Balneario Lombardia, N Italy
43 V17 Tres Cruces, Cerro ▲ SE Mexico
59 K18 Tres Cruces, Cordillera ▲▲ W Bolivia
115 N18 Treska ≈ NW FYR Macedonia
115 I14 Treskavica ▲▲ SE Bosnia and Herzegovina
61 J20 Três Lagoas Mato Grosso do Sul, SW Brazil
42 H12 Tres Marías, Islas island group C Mexico
61 M19 Três Marias, Represa ⊡ SE Brazil
65 F20 Tres Montes, Península headland S Chile
107 O3 Trespaderne Castilla-León, N Spain
62 G13 Três Passos Rio Grande do Sul, S Brazil
63 A23 Tres Picos, Cerro ▲ E Argentina
65 G17 Tres Picos, Cerro ▲ SW Argentina
62 I12 Três Pinheiros Paraná, S Brazil
61 M21 Três Pontas Minas Gerais, SE Brazil
Tres Puntas, Cabo see Manabique, Punta
62 P9 Três Rios Rio de Janeiro, SE Brazil
Tres Tabernae see Saverne
Trestenberg/Trestendorf see Tășnad
43 R15 Tres Valles Veracruz-Llave, SE Mexico
96 H12 Tretten Oppland, S Norway
Treuburg see Olecko
103 K21 Treuchtlingen Bayern, S Germany
102 N13 Treuenbrietzen Brandenburg, E Germany
97 F16 Treungen Telemark, S Norway
65 H17 Trevelín Chubut, SW Argentina
Treves/Trèves see Trier
108 I13 Trevi Umbria, C Italy
108 E7 Treviglio Lombardia, N Italy
106 J4 Trevinca, Peña ▲ NW Spain
107 P3 Treviño Castilla-León, N Spain
108 I7 Treviso anc. Tarvisium. Veneto, NE Italy
99 G24 Trevose Head headland SW England, UK
Trg see Feldkirchen in Kärnten
191 P17 Triabunna Tasmania, SE Australia
23 W4 Triangle Virginia, NE USA
85 L18 Triangle Masvingo, SE Zimbabwe
117 L23 Tría Nisía island Kykládes, Greece, Aegean Sea
Triberg see Triberg im Schwarzwald
103 G23 Triberg im Schwarzwald var. Triberg. Baden-Württemberg, SW Germany
159 P11 Tribhuvan ✕ (Kathmandu) Central, C Nepal
56 C9 Tribugá, Golfo de gulf W Colombia
189 W4 Tribulation, Cape headland Queensland, NE Australia
110 M8 Tribulaun ▲ SW Austria
9 U17 Tribune Saskatchewan, S Canada
28 H5 Tribune Kansas, C USA
109 N18 Tricarico Basilicata, S Italy
109 Q19 Tricase Puglia, SE Italy
Trichinopoly see Tiruchchirāppalli
117 D18 Trichonída, Límni ◎ C Greece
161 G22 Trichūr var. Thrissur. Kerala, SW India
Tricorno see Triglav
191 O8 Trida New South Wales, SE Australia
37 S1 Trident Peak ▲ Nevada, W USA
Tridentum/Trient see Trento
111 T6 Trieben Steiermark, SE Austria
103 D19 Trier Eng. Treves, Fr. Trèves; anc. Augusta Treverorum. Rheinland-Pfalz, SW Germany
108 K7 Trieste Slvn. Trst. Friuli-Venezia Giulia, NE Italy
Trieste, Golfo di/Triest, Golf von see Trieste, Gulf of
108 J8 Trieste, Gulf of Cro. Tršćanski Zaljev, Ger. Golf von Triest, It. Golfo di Trieste, Slvn. Tržaški Zaliv. gulf S Europe
111 W4 Triesting ≈ W Austria
Trifail see Trbovlje
118 L9 Trifești Iași, NE Romania
111 S10 Triglav It. Tricorno. ▲ NW Slovenia
106 I14 Trigueros Andalucía, S Spain
117 E16 Tríkala prev. Trikkala. Thessalía, C Greece
117 E17 Trikeriótis ≈ C Greece
Trikkala see Tríkala
Trikomo/Tríkomon see İskele
99 F17 Trim Ir. Baile Átha Troim. E Ireland
110 E7 Trimbach Solothurn, NW Switzerland
111 Q5 Trimmelkam Oberösterreich, N Austria
31 U11 Trimont Minnesota, N USA
Trimontium see Plovdiv
Trinacria see Sicilia
161 K24 Trincomalee var. Trinkomali. Eastern Province, NE Sri Lanka
67 K16 Trindade, Ilha da island Brazil, W Atlantic Ocean
49 Y9 Trindade Spur undersea feature SW Atlantic Ocean
113 J17 Třinec Ger. Trzynietz. Severní Morava, E Czech Republic
59 M16 Trinidad Beni, N Bolivia
56 H9 Trinidad Casanare, E Colombia
46 E6 Trinidad Sancti Spíritus, C Cuba
39 U8 Trinidad Colorado, C USA
63 E19 Trinidad Flores, S Uruguay
47 Y17 Trinidad island C Trinidad and Tobago
Trinidad see Jose Abad Santos
47 Y16 Trinidad and Tobago off. Republic of Trinidad and Tobago. ◆ republic SE West Indies
65 F22 Trinidad, Golfo gulf S Chile
63 B24 Trinidad, Isla island E Argentina
109 N16 Trinitapoli Puglia, SE Italy
57 X10 Trinité, Montagnes de la ▲▲ C French Guiana
27 W9 Trinity Texas, SW USA
11 U12 Trinity Bay inlet Newfoundland, Newfoundland and Labrador, E Canada
41 P15 Trinity Islands island group Alaska, USA
37 N2 Trinity Mountains ▲▲ California, W USA
37 S4 Trinity Peak ▲ Nevada, W USA
37 S5 Trinity Range ▲▲ Nevada, W USA
37 N2 Trinity River ≈ California, W USA
27 V8 Trinity River ≈ Texas, SW USA
Trinkomali see Trincomalee
181 Y15 Triolet NW Mauritius
109 O20 Trionto, Capo headland S Italy
173 Ee4 Tripa, Krueng ≈ Sumatera, NW Indonesia
117 J16 Tripití, Ákra headland Ágios Efstrátios, E Greece
144 G6 Tripoli var. Tarābulus, Ţarābulus ash Shām, Trāblous; anc. Tripolis. N Lebanon
31 X12 Tripoli Iowa, C USA
Tripoli see Ţarābulus
117 F20 Trípoli prev. Trípolis. Pelopónnisos, S Greece
Tripolis see Tripoli, Lebanon
Trípolis see Trípoli, Greece
31 Q12 Tripp South Dakota, N USA
159 V15 Tripura var. Hill Tippera. ◐ state NE India
110 K8 Trisanna ≈ W Austria
102 H8 Trischen island NW Germany
67 M24 Tristan da Cunha ◇ dependency of Saint Helena SE Atlantic Ocean
69 P15 Tristan da Cunha island SE Atlantic Ocean
67 L18 Tristan da Cunha Fracture Zone tectonic feature S Atlantic Ocean
178 J14 Tri Tôn An Giang, S Vietnam
178 Ll11 Triton Island island S Paracel Islands
161 G24 Trivandrum var. Thiruvanathapuram. Kerala, SW India
113 H20 Trnava Ger. Tyrnau, Hung. Nagyszombat. Západné Slovensko, W Slovakia
Trnovo see Veliko Tŭrnovo
Trobriand Island see Kiriwina Island
Trobriand Islands see Kiriwina Islands
9 Q16 Trochu Alberta, SW Canada
111 U7 Trofaiach Steiermark, SE Austria
95 F14 Trofors Troms, N Norway
115 E14 Trogir It. Traù. Split-Dalmacija, S Croatia
114 F13 Troglav ▲ Bosnia and Herzegovina/Croatia
109 M16 Troia Puglia, SE Italy
109 K24 Troina Sicilia, Italy, C Mediterranean Sea
181 O16 Trois-Bassins W Réunion
103 E17 Troisdorf Nordrhein-Westfalen, W Germany
76 H5 Trois Fourches, Cap des headland NE Morocco
13 T8 Trois-Pistoles Québec, SE Canada
101 L21 Trois-Ponts Liège, E Belgium
13 P11 Trois-Rivières Québec, SE Canada
57 Y12 Trois Sauts S French Guiana
101 M22 Troisvierges Diekirch, N Luxembourg
125 Ee12 Troitsk Chelyabinskaya Oblast', S Russian Federation
129 T9 Troitsko-Pechorsk Respublika Komi, NW Russian Federation
131 V7 Troitskoye Orenburgskaya Oblast', W Russian Federation
Troki see Trakai
96 F9 Trolla ▲ S Norway
97 J18 Trollhättan Älvsborg, S Sweden
96 E9 Trollheimen ▲▲ S Norway
96 E9 Trolltindane ▲ S Norway
60 H11 Trombetas, Rio ≈ NE Brazil
132 L16 Tromelin, Île island N Réunion
94 I9 Troms ◐ county N Norway
94 I9 Tromsø Fin. Tromssa. Troms, N Norway
86 F5 Tromsøflaket undersea feature W Barents Sea
Tromssa see Tromsø
96 H10 Tron ▲ S Norway
37 U12 Trona California, W USA
65 G16 Tronador, Cerro ▲ S Chile
96 H8 Trondheim Ger. Drontheim; prev. Nidaros, Trondhjem. Sør-Trøndelag, S Norway
96 H7 Trondheimsfjorden fjord S Norway
Trondhjem see Trondheim
109 J14 Tronto ≈ C Italy
Troodos see Ólympos
124 N3 Troödos var. Troodos Mountains. ▲▲ C Cyprus
Troodos Mountains see Troödos
98 I13 Troon W Scotland, UK
109 M22 Tropea Calabria, SW Italy
38 L7 Tropic Utah, W USA
66 L10 Tropic Seamount var. Banc du Tropique. undersea feature E Atlantic Ocean
Tropique, Banc du see Tropic Seamount
Tropoja see Tropojë
115 L17 Tropojë var. Tropoja. Kukës, N Albania
Troppau see Opava
97 O16 Trosa Södermanland, C Sweden
120 H12 Troškūnai Anykščiai, E Lithuania
103 G23 Trossingen Baden-Württemberg, SW Germany
119 T4 Trostyanets' Rus. Trostyanets. Sums'ka Oblast', NE Ukraine
119 N7 Trostyanets' Rus. Trostyanets. Vinnyts'ka Oblast', C Ukraine
118 L11 Trotuș ≈ E Romania
46 M8 Trou-du-Nord N Haiti
27 W7 Troup Texas, SW USA
15 H8 Trout ≈ Northwest Territories, NW Canada
35 N8 Trout Creek Montana, NW USA
34 H10 Trout Lake Washington, NW USA
10 B9 Trout Lake ◎ Ontario, S Canada
35 T12 Trout Peak ▲ Wyoming, C USA
104 L4 Trouville Calvados, N France
99 L22 Trowbridge S England, UK
25 Q6 Troy Alabama, S USA
29 Q3 Troy Kansas, C USA
29 W4 Troy Missouri, C USA
20 L10 Troy New York, NE USA
23 S10 Troy North Carolina, SE USA
33 R13 Troy Ohio, N USA
27 T9 Troy Texas, SW USA
116 I9 Troyan Loveshka Oblast, C Bulgaria
116 I9 Troyanski Prokhod pass N Bulgaria
151 N6 Troyebratskiy Severnyy Kazakhstan, N Kazakhstan
105 Q6 Troyes anc. Augustobona Tricassium. Aube, N France
119 X5 Troyits'ke Luhans'ka Oblast', E Ukraine
37 W7 Troy Peak ▲ Nevada, W USA
115 G15 Trpanj Dubrovnik-Neretva, S Croatia
Tršćanski Zaljev see Trieste, Gulf of
Trst see Trieste
115 N14 Trstenik Serbia, C Yugoslavia
130 I6 Trubchevsk Bryanskaya Oblast', W Russian Federation
Trubchular see Orlyak
Truc Giang see Bên Tre
39 S10 Truchas Peak ▲ New Mexico, SW USA
149 P16 Trucial Coast physical region C UAE
Trucial States see United Arab Emirates
37 Q6 Truckee California, W USA
37 R5 Truckee River ≈ Nevada, W USA
131 Q13 Trudfront Astrakhanskaya Oblast', SW Russian Federation
12 I9 Truite, Lac à la ◎ Québec, SE Canada
44 K4 Trujillo Colón, NE Honduras
58 C12 Trujillo La Libertad, NW Peru
106 K10 Trujillo Extremadura, W Spain
56 I6 Trujillo Trujillo, NW Venezuela
56 I6 Trujillo off. Estado Trujillo. ◐ state W Venezuela
Truk see Chuuk
Truk Islands see Chuuk Islands
31 U10 Truman Minnesota, N USA
29 X10 Truman Arkansas, C USA
38 J9 Trumbull, Mount ▲ Arizona, SW USA
116 F9 Trŭn Sofiyska Oblast, W Bulgaria
191 Q8 Trundle New South Wales, SE Australia
133 U13 Trung Phân physical region S Vietnam
Trupcilar see Orlyak
13 Q15 Truro Nova Scotia, SE Canada
99 H25 Truro SW England, UK
27 P5 Truscott Texas, SW USA
118 K9 Trușești Botoșani, NE Romania
118 H6 Truskavets' L'vivs'ka Oblast', W Ukraine
97 H22 Trustrup Århus, C Denmark
8 M11 Trutch British Columbia, W Canada
39 Q14 Truth Or Consequences New Mexico, SW USA
113 F15 Trutnov Ger. Trautenau. Východní Čechy, NE Czech Republic
105 P13 Truyère ≈ C France
116 K9 Tryavna Loveshka Oblast, C Bulgaria
30 M14 Tryon Nebraska, C USA
96 J12 Trysil Hedmark, S Norway
96 I11 Trysilelva ≈ S Norway
114 D10 Tržac NW Bosnia and Herzegovina
Tržaški Zaliv see Trieste, Gulf of
112 G10 Trzcianka Ger. Schönlanke. Piła, NW Poland
112 E7 Trzebiatów Ger. Treptow an der Rega. Szczecin, NW Poland
113 G14 Trzebnica Ger. Trebnitz. Wrocław, SW Poland
111 T10 Tržič Ger. Neumarktl. NW Slovenia
Trzynietz see Třinec
Tsabong see Tshabong
168 G7 Tsagaanchuluut Dzavhan, C Mongolia
169 P7 Tsagaanders Dornod, NE Mongolia
169 S8 Tsagaannuur Dornod, E Mongolia
168 G8 Tsagaan-Olom Govĭ-Altay, C Mongolia
168 J8 Tsagaan-Ovoo Övörhangay, C Mongolia
168 D5 Tsagaantüngi Bayan-Ölgiy, NW Mongolia
131 P12 Tsagan Aman Respublika Kalmykiya, SW Russian Federation
25 V11 Tsala Apopka Lake ◎ Florida, SE USA
Tsamkong see Zhanjiang
Tsangpo see Brahmaputra
168 L9 Tsant Dundgovĭ, C Mongolia
85 G17 Tsao Ngamiland, NW Botswana
180 I4 Tsaratanana Mahajanga, C Madagascar
116 N10 Tsarevo prev. Michurin. Burgaska Oblast, SE Bulgaria
Tsarigrad see İstanbul
Tsaritsyn see Volgograd
128 G13 Tsarskoye Selo prev. Pushkin. Leningradskaya Oblast', NW Russian Federation
119 T7 Tsarychanka Dnipropetrovs'ka Oblast', E Ukraine
85 H21 Tsatsu Southern, S Botswana
83 J20 Tsavo Coast, S Kenya
85 E21 Tsawisis Karas, S Namibia
Tschakathurn see Čakovec
Tschaslau see Čáslav
Tschenstochau see Częstochowa
Tschernembl see Črnomelj
30 K6 Tschida, Lake ⊡ North Dakota, N USA
Tschorna see Mustvee
85 I17 Tsebanana Central, NE Botswana
168 G8 Tseel Govĭ-Altay, SW Mongolia
130 M13 Tselina Rostovskaya Oblast', SW Russian Federation
Tselinograd/Tselinogradskaya Oblast see Akmola
168 J6 Tsengel Hövsgöl, N Mongolia
168 E7 Tsenher Hovd, W Mongolia
152 E12 Tsentral'nyye Nizmennyye Garagumy Turkm. Merkezi Garagum. desert C Turkmenistan
85 E21 Tses Karas, S Namibia
Tseshevlya see Tsyeshawlya
168 E7 Tsetsegnuur Hovd, W Mongolia
168 J7 Tsetserleg Arhangay, C Mongolia
79 R16 Tsévié S Togo
85 G21 Tshabong var. Tsabong. Kgalagadi, SW Botswana
85 G20 Tshane Kgalagadi, SW Botswana
Tshangalele, Lac see Lufira, Lac de Retenue de la
85 H17 Tshauxaba Central, C Botswana
81 F21 Tshela Bas-Zaïre, W Zaire
81 K22 Tshibala Kasai Occidental, S Zaire
81 J22 Tshikapa Kasai Occidental, SW Zaire
81 L22 Tshilenge Kasai Oriental, S Zaire
81 L24 Tshimbalanga Shaba, S Zaire
81 L22 Tshimbulu Kasai Occidental, S Zaire
Tshiumbe see Chiumbe
81 M21 Tshofa Kasai Oriental, C Zaire
81 K18 Tshuapa ≈ C Zaire
Tshwane see Pretoria
116 G7 Tsibritsa ≈ NW Bulgaria
Tsien Tang see Puyang Jiang
116 I12 Tsigansko Gradishte ▲ Bulgaria/Greece
14 G3 Tsiigehtchic prev. Arctic Red River. Northwest Territories, NW Canada
129 Q7 Tsil'ma ≈ NW Russian Federation
121 J17 Tsimkavichy Rus. Timkovichi. Minskaya Voblasts', C Belarus
130 M11 Tsimlyansk Rostovskaya Oblast', SW Russian Federation
131 N11 Tsimlyanskoye Vodokhranilishche var. Tsimlyansk Vodoskhovshche, Eng. Tsimlyansk Reservoir ⊡ SW Russian Federation
Tsimlyansk Reservoir see Tsimlyanskoye Vodokhranilishche
Tsimlyansk Vodoskhovshche see Tsimlyanskoye Vodokhranilishche
Tsinan see Jinan
Tsing Hai see Qinghai Hu, China
Tsinghai see Qinghai, China
Tsingtao/Tsingtau see Qingdao
Tsingyuan see Baoding
Tsinkiang see Quanzhou
Tsintao see Qingdao
85 D17 Tsintsabis Otjikoto, N Namibia
180 H8 Tsiombe var. Tsihombe. Toliara, S Madagascar
126 Kk14 Tsipa ≈ S Russian Federation
180 H5 Tsiribihina ≈ W Madagascar
180 I5 Tsiroanomandidy Antananarivo, C Madagascar
201 U13 Tsis island Chuuk, C Micronesia
Tsitsihar see Qiqihar
131 Q3 Tsivil'sk Chuvashskaya Respublika, W Russian Federation
143 T9 Ts'khinvali prev. Staliniri. C Georgia
121 J19 Tsna ≈ SW Belarus
128 I15 Tsna var. Zna. ≈ W Russian Federation
168 K11 Tsoohor Ömnögovĭ, S Mongolia
171 H16 Tsu var. Tu. Mie, Honshū, SW Japan
171 K13 Tsubame var. Tubame. Niigata, Honshū, C Japan
171 Ii13 Tsubata Ishikawa, Honshū, SW Japan
172 Q6 Tsubetsu Hokkaidō, NE Japan
171 Kk16 Tsuchiura var. Tutiura. Ibaraki, Honshū, S Japan
172 N7 Tsugaru-kaikyō strait N Japan
171 Kk13 Tsugawa Niigata, Honshū, C Japan
172 Oo5 Tsukigata Hokkaidō, NE Japan
170 Dd15 Tsukumi var. Tukumi. Ōita, Kyūshū, SW Japan
168 E5 Tsul-Ulaan Bayan-Ölgiy, W Mongolia
85 D17 Tsumeb Otjikoto, N Namibia
85 F17 Tsumkwe Otjozondjupa, NE Namibia
170 Cc16 Tsuno Miyazaki, Kyūshū, SW Japan
170 D11 Tsuno-shima island SW Japan
171 H14 Tsuruga var. Turuga. Fukui, Honshū, SW Japan
170 F15 Tsurugi-san ▲ Shikoku, SW Japan
170 Dd15 Tsurumi-zaki headland Kyūshū, SW Japan
171 L11 Tsuruoka var. Turuoka. Yamagata, Honshū, C Japan
171 Hh15 Tsushima var. Tusima. Aichi, Honshū, SW Japan
170 C10 Tsushima var. Tsushima-tō, Tusima. island group SW Japan
Tsushima-tō see Tsushima
170 E12 Tsuwano Shimane, Honshū, SW Japan
170 Ff13 Tsuyama var. Tuyama. Okayama, Honshū, SW Japan
85 G19 Tswaane Ghanzi, W Botswana
121 N16 Tsyakhtsin Rus. Tekhtin. Mahilyowskaya Voblasts', E Belarus
121 P19 Tsyerakhowka Rus. Terekhovka. Homyel'skaya Voblasts', SE Belarus
121 I17 Tsyeshawlya Rus. Cheshevlya, Tseshevlya. Brestskaya Voblasts', SW Belarus
Tsyurupinsk see Tsyurupyns'k
119 R10 Tsyurupyns'k Rus. Tsyurupinsk. Khersons'ka Oblast', S Ukraine
Tu see Tsu
194 H13 Tua ≈ C PNG
Tuaim see Tuam
192 L6 Tuakau Waikato, North Island, NZ
99 C17 Tuam Ir. Tuaim. W Ireland
193 K14 Tuamarina Marlborough, South Island, NZ
Tuamotu, Archipel des see Tuamotu, Îles
199 M10 Tuamotu Fracture Zone tectonic feature E Pacific Ocean
203 W9 Tuamotu, Îles var. Archipel des Tuamotu, Dangerous Archipelago, Tuamotu Islands. island group N French Polynesia
Tuamotu Islands see Tuamotu, Îles
183 X10 Tuamotu Ridge undersea feature C Pacific Ocean
178 I5 Tuân Giao Lai Châu, N Vietnam
179 P8 Tuao Luzon, N Philippines
202 B15 Tuapa NW Niue
45 N7 Tuapí Región Autónoma Atlántico Norte, NE Nicaragua
130 K15 Tuapse Krasnodarskiy Kray, SW Russian Federation
175 Nn2 Tuaran Sabah, East Malaysia
106 I6 Tua, Rio ≈ N Portugal
198 B7 Tuasivi Savai'i, C Western Samoa
193 B24 Tuatapere Southland, South Island, NZ
38 M9 Tuba City Arizona, SW USA
144 H11 Ţūbah, Qaşr aţ castle Ma'ān, C Jordan
Tubame see Tsubame
174 Ll14 Tuban prev. Toeban. Jawa, C Indonesia
147 O16 Tuban, Wādī dry watercourse SW Yemen
63 K14 Tubarão Santa Catarina, S Brazil
100 O10 Tubbergen Overijssel, E Netherlands
Tubeke see Tubize
103 H22 Tübingen var. Tuebingen. Baden-Württemberg, SW Germany
131 W6 Tubinskiy Respublika Bashkortostan, W Russian Federation
101 G19 Tubize Dut. Tubeke. Walloon Brabant, C Belgium
78 J16 Tubmanburg NW Liberia
179 Qq15 Tubod Mindanao, S Philippines
77 T7 Ţubruq Eng. Tobruk, It. Tobruch. NE Libya
203 T13 Tubuai island Îles Australes, SW French Polynesia
Tubuai, Îles/Tubuai Islands see Australes, Îles
42 F3 Tubutama Sonora, NW Mexico
56 K4 Tucacas Falcón, N Venezuela
61 P16 Tucano Bahia, E Brazil
59 P19 Tucavaca, Río ≈ E Bolivia
112 H8 Tuchola Bydgoszcz, NW Poland
113 M17 Tuchów Tarnów, SE Poland
25 S3 Tucker Georgia, SE USA
29 W10 Tuckerman Arkansas, C USA
66 B12 Tucker's Town E Bermuda
Tuckum see Tukums
38 M15 Tucson Arizona, SW USA
64 J7 Tucumán off. Provincia de Tucumán. ◐ province N Argentina
Tucumán see San Miguel de Tucumán
39 V11 Tucumcari New Mexico, SW USA
60 H13 Tucunaré Pará, N Brazil
57 Q6 Tucupita Delta Amacuro, NE Venezuela
60 K13 Tucuruí, Represa de ⊡ NE Brazil
112 F9 Tuczno Piła, NW Poland
Tuddo see Tudu
107 Q5 Tudela Basq. Tutera; anc. Tutela. Navarra, N Spain
106 M6 Tudela de Duero Castilla-León, N Spain
144 K6 Tudmur var. Tadmur, Tamar, Gk. Palmyra; Bibl. Tadmor. Ḥimș, C Syria
120 J4 Tudu Ger. Tuddo. Lääne-Virumaa, NE Estonia
Tuebingen see Tübingen
126 H16 Tuekta Respublika Altay, S Russian Federation
106 I5 Tuela, Rio ≈ N Portugal
159 X12 Tuensang Nāgāland, NE India
142 L15 Tufanbeyli Adana, C Turkey
Tüffer see Laško
194 M15 Tufi Northern, S PNG
199 L3 Tufts Plain undersea feature N Pacific Ocean
Tugalan see Kolkhozobod
69 V14 Tugela ≈ SE South Africa
23 P6 Tug Fork ≈ S USA
41 P15 Tugidak Island island Trinity Islands, Alaska, USA
179 P8 Tuguegarao Luzon, N Philippines
127 N13 Tugur Khabarovskiy Kray, SE Russian Federation
167 P4 Tuhai He ≈ E China
106 G4 Tui Galicia, NW Spain
79 O13 Tui var. Grand Balé. ≈ W Burkina
59 J16 Tuichi, Río ≈ W Bolivia
66 Q11 Tuineje Fuerteventura, Islas Canarias, Spain, NE Atlantic Ocean
45 X16 Tuira, Río ≈ SE Panama
Tuisarkan see Tūysarkān
Tujiabu see Yongxiu
131 W5 Tukan Respublika Bashkortostan, W Russian Federation
175 R13 Tukangbesi, Kepulauan Dut. Toekang Besi Eilanden. island group C Indonesia
153 V13 Tŭkhtamish Rus. Toktomush, prev. Tokhtamyshbek. SE Tajikistan
192 O12 Tukituki ≈ North Island, NZ
Tu-k'ou see Panzhihua
124 N15 Tūkrah NE Libya
14 G2 Tuktoyaktuk Northwest Territories, NW Canada
173 Ff6 Tuktuk Pulau Samosir, W Indonesia
Tukumi see Tsukumi
120 E9 Tukums Ger. Tuckum. Tukums, W Latvia
83 G24 Tukuyu prev. Neu-Langenburg. Mbeya, S Tanzania
Tukzār see Tokzār
43 O13 Tula var. Tula de Allende. Hidalgo, C Mexico
43 O11 Tula Tamaulipas, C Mexico
130 K5 Tula Tul'skaya Oblast', W Russian Federation
Tulach Mhór see Tullamore
Tula de Allende see Tula
165 N10 Tulage Ar Gol ≈ W China
195 X15 Tulaghi var. Tulagi. Florida Islands, C Solomon Islands
Tulagi see Tulaghi
43 P13 Tulancingo Hidalgo, C Mexico
37 R11 Tulare California, W USA
31 P9 Tulare South Dakota, N USA
37 Q12 Tulare Lake Bed salt flat California, W USA
39 S14 Tularosa New Mexico, SW USA
39 P13 Tularosa Mountains ▲▲ New Mexico, SW USA
39 S15 Tularosa Valley basin New Mexico, SW USA
85 E25 Tulbagh Western Cape, SW South Africa
58 C5 Tulcán Carchi, N Ecuador
119 N13 Tulcea Tulcea, E Romania
119 N13 Tulcea ◐ county SE Romania
Tul'chin see Tul'chyn
119 N7 Tul'chyn Rus. Tul'chin. Vinnyts'ka Oblast', C Ukraine
Tuléar see Toliara
37 O1 Tulelake California, W USA
118 J10 Tulgheș Hung. Gyergyótölgyes. Harghita, C Romania
Tul'govichi see Tul'havichy
121 N20 Tul'havichy Rus. Tul'govichi. Homyel'skaya Voblasts', SE Belarus
Tuli see Thuli
27 N4 Tulia Texas, SW USA
22 J10 Tullahoma Tennessee, S USA
191 N12 Tullamarine ✕ (Melbourne) Victoria, SE Australia
191 Q7 Tullamore New South Wales, SE Australia
99 E18 Tullamore Ir. Tulach Mhór. C Ireland
105 N12 Tulle anc. Tutela. Corrèze, C France
111 X3 Tulln var. Oberhollabrunn. Niederösterreich, NE Austria
111 W4 Tulln ≈ NE Austria
24 H6 Tullos Louisiana, S USA
99 F19 Tullow Ir. An Tullach. SE Ireland
189 W5 Tully Queensland, NE Australia
128 J3 Tuloma ≈ NW Russian Federation
116 K10 Tulovo Khaskovska Oblast, C Bulgaria
29 P9 Tulsa Oklahoma, C USA
159 N11 Tulsipur Mid Western, W Nepal
130 K6 Tul'skaya Oblast' ◐ province W Russian Federation
130 L14 Tul'skiy Respublika Adygeya, SW Russian Federation
194 K8 Tulu Manus Island, N PNG
56 D10 Tuluá Valle del Cauca, W Colombia
118 M12 Tulucești Galați, E Romania
41 N12 Tuluksak Alaska, USA
43 Z12 Tulum, Ruinas de ruins Quintana Roo, SE Mexico
126 I15 Tulun Irkutskaya Oblast', S Russian Federation
174 Ll15 Tulungagung prev. Toeloengagoeng. Jawa, C Indonesia
195 S11 Tulun Islands var. Kilinailau Islands; prev. Carteret Islands. island group NE PNG
130 M4 Tuma Ryazanskaya Oblast', W Russian Federation
56 B12 Tumaco Nariño, SW Colombia
56 B12 Tumaco, Bahía de bay SW Colombia
Tuman-gang see Tumen
44 L8 Tuma, Río ≈ N Nicaragua
97 O16 Tumba Stockholm, C Sweden
Tumba, Lac see Ntomba, Lac
174 M9 Tumbangsenamang Borneo, C Indonesia
191 Q10 Tumbarumba New South Wales, SE Australia
58 A8 Tumbes Tumbes, NW Peru
58 A9 Tumbes off. Departamento de Tumbes. ◐ department NW Peru
21 P5 Tumbledown Mountain ▲ Maine, NE USA
9 N13 Tumbler Ridge British Columbia, W Canada
178 I12 Tumbŏt, Phnum ▲ W Cambodia
190 G9 Tumby Bay South Australia
169 Y10 Tumen Jilin, NE China

◆ Country
● Country Capital
◇ Dependent Territory
○ Dependent Territory Capital
◐ Administrative Region
✕ International Airport
▲ Mountain
▲▲ Mountain Range
Volcano
≈ River
◎ Lake
⊡ Reservoir

◆ COUNTRY ◇ DEPENDENT TERRITORY ▲ MOUNTAIN ▲ VOLCANO ◇ LAKE
● COUNTRY CAPITAL ○ DEPENDENT TERRITORY CAPITAL ◆ ADMINISTRATIVE REGION ✕ INTERNATIONAL AIRPORT ▲ MOUNTAIN RANGE ◆ RIVER ◇ RESERVOIR

327

ULAANGOM – UYUNI, SALAR DE

168 E5 **Ulaangom** Uvs, NW Mongolia
168 E7 **Ulaantolgoy** Hovd, W Mongolia
168 I8 **Ulaan-Uul** Bayanhongor, C Mongolia
169 O10 **Ulaan-Uul** Dornogovĭ, SE Mongolia
165 R10 **Ulan** Qinghai, C China
Ulan Bator *see* Ulaanbaatar
168 L13 **Ulan Buh Shamo** *desert* N China
Ulanhad *see* Chifeng
169 T8 **Ulanhot** Nei Mongol Zizhiqu, N China
131 Q14 **Ulan Khol** Respublika Kalmykiya, SW Russian Federation
168 M13 **Ulansuhai Nur** ◎ N China
126 Jj16 **Ulan-Ude** *prev.* Verkhneudinsk. Respublika Buryatiya, S Russian Federation
165 N12 **Ulan Ul Hu** ◎ C China
195 Z16 **Ulawa Island** *island* SE Solomon Islands
144 J7 **'Ulayyānīyah, Bi'r al** *var.* Al Hilbeh. *well* S Syria
127 Nn13 **Ul'banskiy Zaliv** *strait* E Russian Federation
Ulbo *see* Olib
115 J18 **Ulcinj** Montenegro, SW Yugoslavia
169 O7 **Uldz** Hentiy, NE Mongolia
Uleåborg *see* Oulu
Uleälv *see* Oulujoki
97 G16 **Ulefoss** Telemark, S Norway
Uleträsk *see* Oulujärvi
115 L19 **Ulëz** *var.* Ulëza. Dibër, C Albania
Ulëza *see* Ulëz
97 F22 **Ulfborg** Ringkøbing, W Denmark
100 N13 **Ulft** Gelderland, E Netherlands
168 G7 **Uliastay** Dzavhan, W Mongolia
196 F8 **Ulimang** Babeldaob, N Palau
69 T10 **Ulindi** ≈ W Zaire
196 H14 **Ulithi Atoll** *atoll* Caroline Islands, W Micronesia
114 N10 **Uljma** Serbia, NE Yugoslavia
150 L11 **Ul'kayak** *Kaz.* Ölkeyek. ≈ C Kazakhstan
151 Q7 **Ul'ken-Karoy, Ozero** ◎ N Kazakhstan
Ülkenözen *see* Bol'shoy Uzen'
Ülkenqobda *see* Bol'shaya Khobda
106 G3 **Ulla** ≈ NW Spain
Ulla *see* Ula
191 S10 **Ulladulla** New South Wales, SE Australia
159 T14 **Ullapara** Rajshahi, W Bangladesh
98 H7 **Ullapool** N Scotland, UK
97 J20 **Ullared** Halland, S Sweden
107 T7 **Ulldecona** Cataluña, NE Spain
94 I9 **Ullsfjorden** *fjord* N Norway
99 K15 **Ullswater** ◎ NW England, UK
103 I22 **Ulm** Baden-Württemberg, S Germany
35 R8 **Ulm** Montana, NW USA
191 V5 **Ulmarra** New South Wales, SE Australia
118 K13 **Ulmeni** Buzău, C Romania
118 K14 **Ulmeni** Călărași, S Romania
44 L7 **Ulmukhuás** Región Autónoma Atlántico Norte, NE Nicaragua
196 C8 **Ulong** *var.* Aulong. *island* Palau Islands, N Palau
85 N14 **Ulonguè** *var.* Ulongwé. Tete, NW Mozambique
Ulongwé *see* Ulonguè
97 K19 **Ulricehamn** Älvsborg, S Sweden
100 N5 **Ulrum** Groningen, NE Netherlands
169 Z16 **Ulsan** *Jap.* Urusan. SE South Korea
96 D10 **Ulsteinvik** Møre og Romsdal, S Norway
99 D15 **Ulster** ◈ *province* Northern Ireland, UK/Ireland
175 S5 **Ulu** Pulau Siau, N Indonesia
126 Ll12 **Ulu** Respublika Sakha (Yakutiya), NE Russian Federation
44 H5 **Ulúa, Río** ≈ NW Honduras
142 D12 **Ulubat Gölü** ◎ NW Turkey
142 E12 **Uludağ** ▲ NW Turkey
Ulugh Muztag *see* Muztag Feng
164 D7 **Ulugqat** Xinjiang Uygur Zizhiqu, W China
142 J16 **Ulukışla** Niğde, S Turkey
201 O15 **Ulul** *island* Caroline Islands, C Micronesia
85 L22 **Ulundi** KwaZulu/Natal, E South Africa
164 M3 **Ulungur He** ≈ NW China
164 K2 **Ulungur Hu** ◎ NW China
189 P8 **Uluru** *var.* Ayers Rock. *rocky outcrop* Northern Territory, C Australia
197 D13 **Ulveah** *var.* Lopevi. *island* C Vanuatu
99 K16 **Ulverston** NW England, UK
191 O16 **Ulverstone** Tasmania, SE Australia
96 D13 **Ulvik** Hordaland, S Norway
95 J18 **Ulvila** Turku-Pori, SW Finland
119 O8 **Ulyanivka** *Rus.* Ul'yanovka. Kirovohrads'ka Oblast', C Ukraine
Ul'yanovka *see* Ulyanivka
131 Q5 **Ul'yanovsk** *prev.* Simbirsk. Ul'yanovskaya Oblast', W Russian Federation
131 Q5 **Ul'yanovskaya Oblast'** ◈ *province* W Russian Federation
151 S10 **Ul'yanovskiy** Karaganda, C Kazakhstan
Ul'yanovskiy Kanal *see* Ul'yanow Kanali
152 M13 **Ul'yanow Kanali** *Rus.* Ul'yanovskiy Kanal. *canal* Turkmenistan/Uzbekistan
Ulyshylanshyq *see* Uly-Zhylanshyk
28 H6 **Ulysses** Kansas, C USA
151 O12 **Ulytau, Gory** ▲▲ C Kazakhstan
126 K14 **Ulyunkhan** Respublika Buryatiya, S Russian Federation
151 N11 **Uly-Zhylanshyk** *Kaz.* Ulyshylanshyq. ≈ C Kazakhstan
114 A9 **Umag** *It.* Umago. Istra, NW Croatia
Umago *see* Umag
201 V13 **Uman** *atoll* Chuuk Islands, C Micronesia
119 O7 **Uman'** *Rus.* Uman. Cherkas'ka Oblast', C Ukraine
43 W12 **Umán** Yucatán, SE Mexico
Umanak/Umanaq *see* Uummannaq
'Umān, Khalīj *see* Oman, Gulf of
'Umān, Salṭanat *see* Oman
176 Ww12 **Umari** Irian Jaya, E Indonesia
160 K10 **Umaria** Madhya Pradesh, C India
155 R16 **Umarkot** Sind, SE Pakistan
196 B17 **Umatac** SW Guam
196 A17 **Umatac Bay** *bay* SW Guam
145 S6 **Umayqah** C Iraq
128 J5 **Umba** Murmanskaya Oblast', NW Russian Federation
144 I8 **Umbāshī, Khirbat al** *ruins* As Suwaydā', S Syria
82 A12 **Umbelasha** ≈ W Sudan
108 H12 **Umbertide** Umbria, C Italy
63 B17 **Umberto** *var.* Humberto. Santa Fe, C Argentina
194 K11 **Umboi Island** *var.* Rooke Island. *island* C PNG
128 J4 **Umbozero, Ozero** ◎ NW Russian Federation
108 H13 **Umbria** ◈ *region* C Italy
Umbrian-Machigian Mountains *see* Umbro-Marchigiano, Appennino
108 I12 **Umbro-Marchigiano, Appennino** *Eng.* Umbrian-Machigian Mountains. ▲▲ C Italy
95 J16 **Umeå** Västerbotten, N Sweden
95 H14 **Umeälven** ≈ N Sweden
41 Q5 **Umiat** Alaska, USA
85 K23 **Umlazi** KwaZulu/Natal, E South Africa
145 X10 **Umm al Baqar, Hawr** *var.* Birkat ad Dawaymah. *spring* S Iraq
147 U12 **Umm al Ḥayt, Wādī** *var.* Wādī Amilḥayt. *seasonal river* SW Oman
Umm al Qaiwain *see* Umm al Qaywayn
149 R15 **Umm al Qaywayn** *var.* Umm al Qaiwain. Umm al Qaywayn, NE UAE
145 Q5 **Umm al Tūz** C Iraq
144 J3 **Umm 'Āmūd** Ḥalab, N Syria
147 Y10 **Umm ar Ruṣāṣ** *var.* Umm Ruṣayṣ. W Oman
147 X9 **Ummas Samīn** *salt flat* C Oman
147 V9 **Umm az Zumūl** *oasis* E Saudi Arabia
82 A9 **Umm Buru** Western Darfur, W Sudan
82 A12 **Umm Dafag** Southern Darfur, W Sudan
Umm Durmān *see* Omdurman
144 F9 **Umm el Fahm** Haifa, N Israel
82 F9 **Umm Inderab** Northern Kordofan, C Sudan
82 C10 **Umm Keddada** Northern Darfur, W Sudan
146 J7 **Umm Lajj** Tabūk, W Saudi Arabia
144 L10 **Umm Maḥfur** ≈ N Jordan
145 Y13 **Umm Qaṣr** SE Iraq
Umm Ruṣayṣ *see* Umm ar Ruṣāṣ
82 F11 **Umm Ruwaba** *var.* Umm Ruwābah, Um Ruwāba. Northern Kordofan, C Sudan
Umm Ruwābah *see* Umm Ruwaba
149 N16 **Umm Sa'īd** *var.* Musay'īd. S Qatar
144 K10 **Umm Ṭuways, Wādī** *dry watercourse* N Jordan
40 J17 **Umnak Island** *island* Aleutian Islands, Alaska, USA
34 F13 **Umpqua River** ≈ Oregon, NW USA
84 D13 **Umpulo** Bié, C Angola
160 I12 **Umred** Mahārāshtra, C India
145 Y10 **Umr Sawān, Hawr** ◎ S Iraq
Um Ruwāba *see* Umm Ruwaba
Umtali *see* Mutare
85 J24 **Umtata** Eastern Cape, SE South Africa
79 V17 **Umuahia** Abia, SW Nigeria
62 H10 **Umuarama** Paraná, S Brazil
Umvuma *see* Mvuma
85 K18 **Umzingwani** ≈ S Zimbabwe
114 D11 **Una** ≈ Bosnia and Herzegovina/Croatia
114 E12 **Unac** ≈ W Bosnia and Herzegovina
25 T6 **Unadilla** Georgia, SE USA
20 I10 **Unadilla River** ≈ New York, NE USA
61 L18 **Unaí** Minas Gerais, SE Brazil
41 N10 **Unalakleet** Alaska, USA
40 K17 **Unalaska Island** *island* Aleutian Islands, Alaska, USA
193 I16 **Una, Mount** ▲ South Island, NZ
84 N13 **Unango** Niassa, N Mozambique
Unao *see* Unnão
94 L12 **Unari** Lappi, N Finland
147 O6 **'Unayzah** *var.* Anaiza. Al Qaṣīm, C Saudi Arabia
144 L10 **'Unayzah, Jabal** ▲ Jordan/Saudi Arabia
Unci *see* Almería
59 K19 **Uncía** Potosí, C Bolivia
39 Q7 **Uncompahgre Peak** ▲ Colorado, C USA
39 P6 **Uncompahgre Plateau** *plain* Colorado, C USA
97 L17 **Unden** ◎ S Sweden
30 M4 **Underwood** North Dakota, N USA
176 Uu11 **Undur** Pulau Seram, E Indonesia
194 M11 **Unea Island** *island* C PNG
130 H6 **Unecha** Bryanskaya Oblast', W Russian Federation
41 N16 **Unga** Unga Island, Alaska, USA
Ungaria *see* Hungary
191 P8 **Ungarie** New South Wales, SE Australia
Ungarisch-Brod *see* Uherský Brod
Ungarisches Erzgebirge *see* Slovenské Rudohorie
Ungarisch-Hradisch *see* Uherské Hradiště
Ungarn *see* Hungary
10 M4 **Ungava Bay** *bay* Québec, E Canada
10 J2 **Ungava, Péninsule d'** *peninsula* Québec, SE Canada
Ungeny *see* Ungheni
118 M9 **Ungheni** *Rus.* Ungeny. W Moldova
Unguja *see* Zanzibar
Üngüz Angyrsyndaky Garagum *see* Zaunguzskiye Garagumy
152 H11 **Unguz, Solonchakovyye Vpadiny** *salt marsh* C Turkmenistan
Ungvár *see* Uzhhorod
62 I12 **União da Vitória** Paraná, S Brazil
113 G17 **Uničov** *Ger.* Mährisch-Neustadt. Severní Morava, E Czech Republic
112 J12 **Uniejów** Konin, C Poland
114 A11 **Unije** *island* W Croatia
40 L16 **Unimak Island** *island* Aleutian Islands, Alaska, USA
40 L16 **Unimak Pass** *strait* Aleutian Islands, Alaska, USA
29 W5 **Union** Missouri, C USA
34 L12 **Union** Oregon, NW USA
23 Q11 **Union** South Carolina, SE USA
23 R6 **Union** West Virginia, NE USA
64 J12 **Unión** San Luis, C Argentina
63 B25 **Unión, Bahía** *bay* E Argentina
33 Q13 **Union City** Indiana, N USA
33 Q10 **Union City** Michigan, N USA
20 C12 **Union City** Pennsylvania, NE USA
22 G8 **Union City** Tennessee, S USA
34 G14 **Union Creek** Oregon, NW USA
85 G25 **Uniondale** Western Cape, SW South Africa
42 K13 **Unión de Tula** Jalisco, SW Mexico
32 M9 **Union Grove** Wisconsin, N USA
47 Y15 **Union Island** *island* S Saint Vincent and the Grenadines
48 K5 **Union Reefs** *reef* SW Mexico
0 D7 **Union Seamount** *undersea feature* NE Pacific Ocean
25 Q6 **Union Springs** Alabama, S USA
22 H6 **Uniontown** Kentucky, S USA
20 C16 **Uniontown** Pennsylvania, NE USA
29 T1 **Unionville** Missouri, C USA
147 V8 **United Arab Emirates** *Ar.* Al Imārāt al 'Arabīyah al Muttaḥidah, *abbrev.* UAE; *prev.* Trucial States. ◆ *federation* SW Asia
United Arab Republic *see* Egypt
99 H14 **United Kingdom** *off.* UK of Great Britain and Northern Ireland, *abbrev.* UK. ◆ *monarchy* NW Europe
United Mexican States *see* Mexico
United Provinces *see* Uttar Pradesh
18 L9 **United States of America** *off.* United States of America, *var.* America, The States, *abbrev.* U.S., USA. ◆ *federal republic*
128 J10 **Unitsa** Respublika Kareliya, NW Russian Federation
9 S15 **Unity** Saskatchewan, S Canada
Unity State *see* Wahda
107 Q8 **Universales, Montes** ▲▲ C Spain
29 X4 **University City** Missouri, C USA
197 B13 **Unmet** Malekula, C Vanuatu
103 F15 **Unna** Nordrhein-Westfalen, W Germany
158 L12 **Unnão** *prev.* Unao. Uttar Pradesh, N India
197 D15 **Unpongkor** Erromango, S Vauautu
Unruhstadt *see* Kargowa
98 M1 **Unst** *island* NE Scotland, UK
103 K16 **Unstrut** ≈ C Germany
Unterdrauburg *see* Dravograd
Unterlimbach *see* Lendava
103 L23 **Unterschleissheim** Bayern, SE Germany
103 H24 **Untersee** ◎ Germany/Switzerland
102 O10 **Unterueckersee** ◎ NE Germany
110 F9 **Unterwalden** ◈ *canton* C Switzerland
57 N12 **Unturán, Sierra de** ▲▲ Brazil/Venezuela
165 N11 **Unuli Horog** Qinghai, W China
142 M11 **Ünye** Ordu, W Turkey
Unza *see* Unzha
129 O14 **Unzha** *var.* Unza. ≈ NW Russian Federation
81 E17 **Uolo, Río** *var.* Eyo (lower course), Mbini, Uele (upper course), Woleu; *prev.* Benito. ≈ Equatorial Guinea/Gabon
57 Q10 **Uonán** Bolívar, SE Venezuela
167 T12 **Uotsuri-shima** *island* China/Japan/Taiwan
171 J13 **Uozu** Toyama, Honshū, SW Japan
44 L12 **Upala** Alajuela, NW Costa Rica
57 P7 **Upata** Bolívar, E Venezuela
81 M23 **Upemba, Lac** ◎ SE Zaire
207 O12 **Upernavik** *var.* Upernivik. C Greenland
Upernivik *see* Upernavik
85 F22 **Upington** Northern Cape, W South Africa
Uplands *see* Ottawa
198 Bb8 **Upolu** *island* SE Western Samoa
40 G11 **Upolu Point** *headland* Hawaii, USA, C Pacific Ocean
Upper Austria *see* Oberösterreich
Upper Bann *see* Bann
12 M13 **Upper Canada Village** *tourist site* Ontario, SE Canada
20 I16 **Upper Darby** Pennsylvania, NE USA
30 L2 **Upper Des Lacs Lake** ⊟ North Dakota, N USA
193 L14 **Upper Hutt** Wellington, North Island, NZ
31 X11 **Upper Iowa River** ≈ Iowa, C USA
34 H15 **Upper Klamath Lake** ◎ Oregon, NW USA
36 M6 **Upper Lake** California, W USA
37 Q1 **Upper Lake** ◎ California, W USA
8 K9 **Upper Liard** Yukon Territory, W Canada
99 E16 **Upper Lough Erne** ◎ SW Northern Ireland, UK
82 F12 **Upper Nile** ◈ *state* E Sudan
31 T3 **Upper Red Lake** ◎ Minnesota, N USA
33 S12 **Upper Sandusky** Ohio, N USA
Upper Volta *see* Burkina
97 O15 **Upplandsväsby** *var.* Upplands Väsby. Stockholm, C Sweden
97 O15 **Uppsala** Uppsala, C Sweden
97 O14 **Uppsala** ◈ *county* C Sweden
40 J12 **Upright Cape** *headland* Saint Matthew Island, Alaska, USA
22 K6 **Upton** Kentucky, S USA
35 Y13 **Upton** Wyoming, C USA
147 N7 **'Uqlat aş Şuqūr** Al Qaşīm, W Saudi Arabia
Uqturpan *see* Wushi
56 C7 **Urabá, Golfo de** *gulf* NW Colombia
Uracas *see* Farallon de Pajaros
Uradar'ya *see* Ŭradaryo
153 N13 **Ŭradaryo** *Rus.* Uradar'ya. ≈ S Uzbekistan
168 M13 **Urad Qianqi** *var.* Xishanzui. Nei Mongol Zizhiqu, N China
171 Jj17 **Uraga-suidō** *strait* S Japan
172 Pp7 **Urahoro** Hokkaidō, NE Japan
172 Oo8 **Urakawa** Hokkaidō, NE Japan
131 X6 **Ural** *Kaz.* Zayyq. ≈ Kazakhstan/Russian Federation
191 T6 **Uralla** New South Wales, SE Australia
Ural Mountains *see* Ural'skiye Gory
150 F8 **Ural'sk** *Kaz.* Oral. Zapadnyy Kazakhstan, NW Kazakhstan
Ural'skaya Oblast' *see* Zapadnyy Kazakhstan
131 W5 **Ural'skiye Gory** *var.* Ural'skiy Khrebet, *Eng.* Ural Mountains. ▲▲ Kazakhstan/Russian Federation
Ural'skiy Khrebet *see* Ural'skiye Gory
144 I3 **Urām aş Şughrá** Ḥalab, N Syria
191 P10 **Urana** New South Wales, SE Australia
191 V6 **Uranga** New South Wales, SE Australia
9 S10 **Uranium City** Saskatchewan, C Canada
60 F10 **Uraricoera** Roraima, N Brazil
49 S5 **Uraricoera, Rio** ≈ N Brazil
Ura-Tyube *see* Ŭroteppa
171 K16 **Urawa** Saitama, Honshū, S Japan
125 F10 **Uray** Khanty-Mansiyskiy Avtonomnyy Okrug, C Russian Federation
147 R7 **'Uray'irah** Ash Sharqīyah, E Saudi Arabia
32 M13 **Urbana** Illinois, N USA
33 R13 **Urbana** Ohio, N USA
31 V14 **Urbandale** Iowa, C USA
108 I11 **Urbania** Marche, C Italy
176 Uu8 **Urbinasopon** Irian Jaya, E Indonesia
108 I11 **Urbino** Marche, C Italy
59 H16 **Urcos** Cusco, S Peru
150 D10 **Urda** Zapadnyy Kazakhstan, W Kazakhstan
107 N10 **Urda** Castilla-La Mancha, C Spain
168 E7 **Urdgol** Hovd, W Mongolia
Urdunn *see* Jordan
151 X12 **Urdzhar** *Kaz.* Ürzhar. Semipalatinsk, E Kazakhstan
99 L16 **Ure** ≈ N England, UK
121 K18 **Urechcha** *Rus.* Urech'ye. Minskaya Voblasts', S Belarus
Urech'ye *see* Urechcha
131 P2 **Uren'** Nizhegorodskaya Oblast', W Russian Federation
126 H9 **Urengoy** Yamalo-Nenetskiy Avtonomnyy Okrug, N Russian Federation
192 K10 **Urenui** Taranaki, North Island, NZ
197 B10 **Ureparapara** *island* Banks Islands, N Vanuatu
42 G5 **Ures** Sonora, NW Mexico
Urfa *see* Şanlıurfa
152 H9 **Urganch** *Rus.* Urgench; *prev.* Novo-Urgench. Khorazm Wiloyati, W Uzbekistan
Urgench *see* Urganch
142 J14 **Ürgüp** Nevşehir, C Turkey
153 O12 **Urgut** Samarqand Wiloyati, C Uzbekistan
164 K3 **Urho** Xinjiang Uygur Zizhiqu, W China
158 G5 **Uri** Jammu and Kashmir, NW India
110 G9 **Uri** ◈ *canton* C Switzerland
56 F11 **Uribe** Meta, C Colombia
56 H4 **Uribia** La Guajira, N Colombia
118 G12 **Uricani** *Hung.* Hobicaurikány. Hunedoara, SW Romania
59 M21 **Uriondo** Tarija, S Bolivia
42 I7 **Urique** Chihuahua, N Mexico
42 I7 **Urique, Río** ≈ N Mexico
58 E9 **Uritiyacu, Río** ≈ N Peru
151 N7 **Uritskiy** Kustanay, N Kazakhstan
100 K8 **Urk** Flevoland, N Netherlands
142 B14 **Urla** İzmir, W Turkey
118 K13 **Urlaţi** Prahova, SE Romania
131 V4 **Urman** Respublika Bashkortostan, W Russian Federation
153 P12 **Urmetan** W Tajikistan
Urmia *see* Orūmīyeh
Urmia, Lake *see* Orūmīyeh, Daryācheh-ye
Urmiyeh *see* Orūmīyeh
115 N17 **Uroševac** *Alb.* Ferizaj. Serbia, S Yugoslavia
153 P11 **Ŭroteppa** *Rus.* Ura-Tyube. NW Tajikistan
56 D8 **Urrao** Antioquia, W Colombia
Ursat'yevskaya *see* Khowos
168 I11 **Urt** Ömnogövĭ, S Mongolia
131 X7 **Urtazym** Orenburgskaya Oblast', W Russian Federation
61 K18 **Uruaçu** Goiás, C Brazil
42 M14 **Uruapan** *var.* Uruapan del Progreso. Michoacán de Ocampo, SW Mexico
Uruapan del Progreso *see* Uruapan
59 G15 **Urubamba, Cordillera** ▲▲ C Peru
59 G14 **Urubamba, Río** ≈ C Peru
60 G12 **Urucará** Amazonas, N Brazil
63 E16 **Uruguaiana** Rio Grande do Sul, S Brazil
Uruguai, Rio *see* Uruguay
63 E18 **Uruguay** *off.* Oriental Republic of Uruguay; *prev.* La Banda Oriental. ◆ *republic* E South America
63 E15 **Uruguay** *var.* Rio Uruguai, Río Uruguay. ≈ E South America
Uruguay, Río *see* Uruguay
Uruk *see* Erech
Urumchi *see* Ürümqi
164 L5 **Ürümqi** *var.* Tihwa, Urumchi, Urumqi, Urumtsi, Wu-lu-k'o-mu-shi, Wu-lu-mu-ch'i; *prev.* Ti-hua. *autonomous region capital* Xinjiang Uygur Zizhiqu, NW China
Urumtsi *see* Ürümqi
Urundi *see* Burundi
196 C15 **Uruno Point** *headland* NW Guam
127 P15 **Urup, Ostrov** *island* Kuril'skiye Ostrova, SE Russian Federation
147 P11 **'Uruq al Mawārid** *desert* S Saudi Arabia
Urusan *see* Ulsan
131 T5 **Urussu** Respublika Tatarstan, W Russian Federation
192 K10 **Uruti** Taranaki, North Island, NZ
59 K19 **Uru Uru, Lago** ◎ W Bolivia
57 P9 **Uruyén** Bolívar, SE Venezuela
155 O7 **Ūrūzgān** *var.* Oruzgān, Orūzgān. Urūzgān, C Afghanistan
155 N6 **Urūzgān** *Per.* Orūzgān. ◈ *province* C Afghanistan
172 P6 **Uryū-gawa** ≈ Hokkaidō, NE Japan
172 P4 **Uryū-ko** ◎ Hokkaidō, NE Japan
131 N8 **Uryupinsk** Volgogradskaya Oblast', SW Russian Federation
Ürzhar *see* Urdzhar
129 R16 **Urzhum** Kirovskaya Oblast', NW Russian Federation
118 K13 **Urziceni** Ialomiţa, SE Romania
U.S./USA *see* United States of America
170 D13 **Usa** Ōita, Kyūshū, SW Japan
121 L16 **Usa** *Rus.* Usa. ≈ C Belarus
129 T6 **Usa** ≈ NW Russian Federation
142 E14 **Uşak** *prev.* Ushak. Uşak, W Turkey
142 D14 **Uşak** *var.* Ushak. ◈ *province* W Turkey
85 C19 **Usakos** Erongo, W Namibia
83 J21 **Usambara Mountains** ▲▲ NE Tanzania
83 G23 **Usangu Flats** *wetland* SW Tanzania
67 D24 **Usborne, Mount** ▲ East Falkland, Falkland Islands
102 O8 **Usedom** *island* NE Germany
101 M24 **Useldange** Diekirch, C Luxembourg
120 L12 **Ushacha** *Rus.* Ushacha. Vitsyebskaya Voblasts', N Belarus
Ushachi *see* Ushachy
120 L13 **Ushachy** *Rus.* Ushachi. Vitsyebskaya Voblasts', N Belarus
Ushak *see* Uşak
126 I2 **Ushakova, Ostrov** *island* Severnaya Zemlya, N Russian Federation
Ushant *see* Ouessant, Île d'
Üsharal *see* Ucharal
170 Bb14 **Ushibuka** *var.* Usibuka. Kumamoto, Shimo-jima, SW Japan
Ushi Point *see* Sabaneta, Puntan
151 V14 **Ushtobe** *Kaz.* Üshtöbe. Taldykorgan, SE Kazakhstan
65 I25 **Ushuaia** Tierra del Fuego, S Argentina
41 R10 **Usibelli** Alaska, USA
Usibuka *see* Ushibuka
194 I12 **Usino** Madang, N PNG
129 U6 **Usinsk** Respublika Komi, NW Russian Federation
99 K22 **Usk** *Wel.* Wysg. ≈ SE Wales, UK
Uskočke Planine/Uskokengebirge *see* Žumberačka Gora
Üsküb *see* Skopje
116 M11 **Üsküpdere** Kırklareli, NW Turkey
130 L7 **Usman'** Lipetskaya Oblast', W Russian Federation
120 D8 **Usmas Ezers** ◎ NW Latvia
129 U13 **Usol'ye** Permskaya Oblast', NW Russian Federation
126 J15 **Usol'ye-Sibirskoye** Irkutskaya Oblast', C Russian Federation
43 T16 **Uspanapa, Río** ≈ SE Mexico
151 R11 **Uspenskiy** Zhezkazgan, C Kazakhstan
105 O11 **Ussel** Corrèze, C France
169 Z6 **Ussuri** *var.* Usuri, Wusuri, *Chin.* Wusuli Jiang. ≈ China/Russian Federation
127 Nn18 **Ussuriysk** *prev.* Nikol'sk, Nikol'sk-Ussuriyskiy, Voroshilov. Primorskiy Kray, SE Russian Federation
142 J10 **Usta Burnu** *headland* N Turkey
155 P13 **Usta Muhammad** Baluchistān, SW Pakistan
126 K15 **Ust'-Barguzin** Respublika Buryatiya, S Russian Federation
127 P12 **Ust'-Bol'sheretsk** Kamchatskaya Oblast', E Russian Federation
131 N9 **Ust'-Buzulukskaya** Volgogradskaya Oblast', SW Russian Federation
110 G7 **Uster** Zürich, NE Switzerland
109 I22 **Ustica, Isola d'** *island* S Italy
126 J13 **Ust'-Ilimsk** Irkutskaya Oblast', C Russian Federation
113 C15 **Ústí nad Labem** *Ger.* Aussig. Severní Čechy, N Czech Republic
113 F17 **Ústí nad Orlicí** *Ger.* Wildenschwert. Východní Čechy, E Czech Republic
Ustinov *see* Izhevsk
115 J14 **Ustiprača** SE Bosnia and Herzegovina
125 Ff12 **Ust'-Ishim** Omskaya Oblast', C Russian Federation
112 G6 **Ustka** *Ger.* Stolpmünde. Słupsk, NW Poland
127 Pp10 **Ust'-Kamchatsk** Kamchatskaya Oblast', E Russian Federation
151 X9 **Ust'-Kamenogorsk** *Kaz.* Öskemen. Vostochnyy Kazakhstan, E Kazakhstan
127 Oo10 **Ust'-Khayryuzovo** Koryakskiy Avtonomnyy Okrug, E Russian Federation
126 H16 **Ust'-Koksa** Respublika Altay, S Russian Federation
129 S11 **Ust'-Kulom** Respublika Komi, NW Russian Federation
126 Jj14 **Ust'-Kut** Irkutskaya Oblast', C Russian Federation
126 M7 **Ust'-Kuyga** Respublika Sakha (Yakutiya), NE Russian Federation
130 L14 **Ust'-Labinsk** Krasnodarskiy Kray, SW Russian Federation
126 Mm11 **Ust'-Maya** Respublika Sakha (Yakutiya), NE Russian Federation
127 N9 **Ust'-Nera** Respublika Sakha (Yakutiya), NE Russian Federation
126 Ll13 **Ust'-Nyukzha** Amurskaya Oblast', S Russian Federation
126 Kk6 **Ust'-Olenëk** Respublika Sakha (Yakutiya), NE Russian Federation
127 O10 **Ust'-Omchug** Magadanskaya Oblast', E Russian Federation
126 Jj15 **Ust'-Ordynskiy** Ust'-Ordynskiy Buryatskiy Avtonomnyy Okrug, S Russian Federation
126 J15 **Ust'-Ordynskiy Buryatskiy Avtonomnyy Okrug** ◈ *autonomous district* S Russian Federation
129 N8 **Ust'-Pinega** Arkhangel'skaya Oblast', NW Russian Federation
126 Hh8 **Ust'-Port** Taymyrskiy (Dolgano-Nenetskiy) Avtonomnyy Okrug, N Russian Federation
116 L11 **Ustrem** *prev.* Vakav. Burgaska Oblast, SE Bulgaria
113 O18 **Ustrzyki Dolne** Krosno, SE Poland
Ust'-Sysol'sk *see* Syktyvkar
129 R7 **Ust'-Tsil'ma** Respublika Komi, NW Russian Federation
Ust Urt *see* Ustyurt Plateau
129 O11 **Ust'ya** ≈ NW Russian Federation
119 R8 **Ustynivka** Kirovohrads'ka Oblast', C Ukraine
150 H15 **Ustyurt Plateau** *var.* Ust Urt, *Uzb.* Ustyurt Platosi. *plateau* Kazakhstan/Uzbekistan
Ustyurt Platosi *see* Ustyurt Plateau
128 K14 **Ustyuzhna** Vologodskaya Oblast', NW Russian Federation
164 J4 **Usu** Xinjiang Uygur Zizhiqu, NW China
175 Q10 **Usu** Sulawesi, C Indonesia
170 Dd14 **Usuki** Ōita, Kyūshū, SW Japan
44 G8 **Usulután** Usulután, SE El Salvador
44 B9 **Usulután** ◈ *department* SE El Salvador
43 W16 **Usumacinta, Río** ≈ Guatemala/Mexico
Usumbura *see* Bujumbura
Usuri *see* Ussuri
176 X12 **Uta** Irian Jaya, E Indonesia
38 K5 **Utah** *off.* State of Utah; also known as Beehive State, Mormon State. ◈ *state* W USA
38 L3 **Utah Lake** ◎ Utah, W USA
Utaidhani *see* Uthai Thani
95 M14 **Utajärvi** Oulu, C Finland
Utamboni *see* Mitemele, Río
Utaradit *see* Uttaradit
173 G3 **Utara, Selat** *strait* Peninsular Malaysia
172 P5 **Utashinai** *var.* Utasinai. Hokkaidō, NE Japan
Utasinai *see* Utashinai
176 X12 **Uta, Sungai** ≈ Irian Jaya, E Indonesia
200 Ss12 **'Uta Vava'u** *island* Vava'u Group, N Tonga
39 V9 **Ute Creek** ≈ New Mexico, SW USA
120 H12 **Utena** Utena, E Lithuania
39 V10 **Ute Reservoir** ⊟ New Mexico, SW USA
178 H10 **Uthai Thani** *var.* Muang Uthai Thani, Udayadhani, Utaidhani. Uthai Thani, W Thailand
155 O15 **Uthal** Baluchistān, SW Pakistan
20 I10 **Utica** New York, NE USA
107 R10 **Utiel** País Valenciano, E Spain
9 O13 **Utikuma Lake** ◎ Alberta, W Canada
44 I4 **Utila, Isla de** *island* Islas de la Bahía, N Honduras
Utina *see* Udine
61 O17 **Utinga** Bahia, E Brazil
Utirik *see* Utrik Atoll
97 M22 **Utlängan** *island* S Sweden
119 U11 **Utlyuts'kyy Lyman** *bay* S Ukraine
170 Cc14 **Uto** Kumamoto, Kyūshū, SW Japan
97 P16 **Utö** Stockholm, C Sweden
27 Q12 **Utopia** Texas, SW USA
100 J11 **Utrecht** *Lat.* Trajectum ad Rhenum. Utrecht, C Netherlands
85 K22 **Utrecht** KwaZulu/Natal, E South Africa
100 I11 **Utrecht** ◈ *province* C Netherlands
106 K14 **Utrera** Andalucía, S Spain
201 V4 **Utrik Atoll** *var.* Utirik, Utrōk, Utrōnk. *atoll* Ratak Chain, N Marshall Islands
Utrōk/Utrōnk *see* Utrik Atoll
97 B16 **Utsira** *island* SW Norway
94 L8 **Utsjoki** *var.* Ohcejohka. Lappi, N Finland
171 Kk15 **Utsunomiya** *var.* Utunomiya. Tochigi, Honshū, S Japan
131 P13 **Utta** Respublika Kalmykiya, SW Russian Federation
178 Hh8 **Uttaradit** *var.* Utaradit. Uttaradit, N Thailand
158 J8 **Uttarkāshi** Uttar Pradesh, N India
158 K11 **Uttar Pradesh** *prev.* United Provinces, United Provinces of Agra and Oudh. ◈ *state* N India
47 T5 **Utuado** C Puerto Rico
164 K3 **Utubulak** Xinjiang Uygur Zizhiqu, W China
41 N5 **Utukok River** ≈ Alaska, USA
Utunomiya *see* Utsunomiya
195 X9 **Utupua** *island* Santa Cruz Islands, E Soloman Islands
150 G9 **Utva** ≈ NW Kazakhstan
201 Y15 **Utwe** Kosrae, E Micronesia
201 X15 **Utwe Harbor** *harbor* Kosrae, E Micronesia
168 J7 **Uubulan** Arhangay, C Mongolia
120 G6 **Uulu** Pärnumaa, SW Estonia
207 N13 **Uummannaq** *var.* Umanak, Umanaq. C Greenland
206 L16 **Uummannarsuaq** *var.* Nunap Isua, *Dan.* Kap Farvel, *Eng.* Cape Farewell. *headland* S Greenland
168 E4 **Üüreg Nuur** ◎ NW Mongolia
Uusikaarlepyy *see* Nykarleby
95 J19 **Uusikaupunki** *Swe.* Nystad. Turku-Pori, SW Finland
95 L19 **Uusimaa** *Swe.* Nyland. ◈ *province* S Finland
131 S2 **Uva** Udmurtskaya Respublika, NW Russian Federation
115 L14 **Uvac** ≈ W Yugoslavia
27 Q12 **Uvalde** Texas, SW USA
161 K25 **Uva Province** ◈ *province* SE Sri Lanka
121 O18 **Uvaravichy** *Rus.* Uvarovichi. Homyel'skaya Voblasts', SE Belarus
56 J11 **Uvá, Río** ≈ E Colombia
Uvarovichi *see* Uvaravichy
131 N7 **Uvarovo** Tambovskaya Oblast', W Russian Federation
125 Ff11 **Uvat** Tyumenskaya Oblast', C Russian Federation
202 G12 **Uvea, Île** *island* N Wallis and Futuna
83 E21 **Uvinza** Kigoma, W Tanzania
81 O20 **Uvira** Sud Kivu, E Zaire
168 E5 **Uvs** ◈ *province* NW Mongolia
168 F5 **Uvs Nuur** *var.* Ozero Ubsu-Nur. ◎ Mongolia/Russian Federation
170 E15 **Uwa** Ehime, Shikoku, SW Japan
170 E15 **Uwajima** *var.* Uwazima. Ehime, Shikoku, SW Japan
82 B5 **'Uwaynāt, Jabal al** *var.* Jebel Uweinat. ▲ Libya/Sudan
Uwazima *see* Uwajima
Uweinat, Jebel *see* 'Uwaynāt, Jabal al
176 Z14 **Uwimmerah, Sungai** ≈ Irian Jaya, E Indonesia
12 H14 **Uxbridge** Ontario, S Canada
Uxellodunum *see* Issoudun
168 M15 **Uxin Qi** Nei Mongol Zizhiqu, N China
43 X12 **Uxmal, Ruinas** *ruins* Yucatán, SE Mexico
133 Q5 **Uy** ≈ Kazakhstan/Russian Federation
150 K15 **Uyaly** Kzyl-Orda, S Kazakhstan
126 Mm7 **Uyandina** ≈ NE Russian Federation
126 I14 **Uyar** Krasnoyarskiy Kray, S Russian Federation
168 L10 **Üydzen** Ömnogövĭ, S Mongolia
Uyeda *see* Ueda
126 Hh3 **Uyedineniya, Ostrov** *island* N Russian Federation
79 V17 **Uyo** Akwa Ibom, S Nigeria
168 D8 **Üyönch** Hovd, W Mongolia
151 Q15 **Uyuk** Zhambyl, S Kazakhstan
147 V13 **'Uyūn** SW Oman
59 K20 **Uyuni** Potosí, W Bolivia
59 J20 **Uyuni, Salar de** *wetland* SW Bolivia

◆ Country
● Country Capital
◇ Dependent Territory
○ Dependent Territory Capital
◈ Administrative Region
✈ International Airport
▲ Mountain
▲▲ Mountain Range
⛰ Volcano
≈ River
◎ Lake
⊟ Reservoir